March 4–7, 2015
Kansas City, MO, USA

Association for
Computing Machinery

Advancing Computing as a Science & Profession

SIGCSE'15

Proceedings of the 46th ACM Technical Symposium on Computer Science Education

Sponsored by:

ACM SIGCSE

Editors:

Adrienne Decker, Rochester Institute of Technology
Kurt Eiselt, University of British Columbia
Jodi Tims, Baldwin Wallace University
Carl Alphonce, University of Buffalo

Association for
Computing Machinery

Advancing Computing as a Science & Profession

The Association for Computing Machinery
2 Penn Plaza, Suite 701
New York, New York 10121-0701

Notice to Past Authors of ACM-Published Articles

ACM intends to create a complete electronic archive of all articles and/or other material previously published by ACM. If you have written a work that has been previously published by ACM in any journal or conference proceedings prior to 1978, or any SIG Newsletter at any time, and you do NOT want this work to appear in the ACM Digital Library, please inform permissions@acm.org, stating the title of the work, the author(s), and where and when published.

ISBN: 978-1-4503-2966-8 (Digital)

ISBN: 978-1-4503-3512-6 (Print)

Additional copies may be ordered prepaid from:

ACM Order Department
PO Box 30777
New York, NY 10087-0777, USA

Phone: 1-800-342-6626 (USA and Canada)
+1-212-626-0500 (Global)
Fax: +1-212-944-1318
E-mail: acmhelp@acm.org
Hours of Operation: 8:30 am – 4:30 pm ET

Printed in the USA

Welcome from the SIGCSE Chair

Welcome to the *46th SIGCSE Technical Symposium on Computer Science Education* (*SIGCSE 2015*) - the premiere technical conference for computer science educators. *SIGCSE 2015* is sponsored by the ACM Special Interest Group on Computer Science Education (the SIGCSE organization).

SIGCSE is an organization of about 2600 members interested in computer science education. Many of these members volunteer for SIGCSE's numerous activities and events held throughout the year. The largest such event is SIGCSE 2015. I want to give a large thanks to two very special volunteers for organizing this conference, Co-Chairs Adrienne Decker and Kurt Eiselt. Adrienne and Kurt have spent countless hours in planning this event, and in leading a large committee of over fifty volunteers to help make this SIGCSE Symposium a special event to the attendees. They have figured out the logistics of housing and feeding about 1300 attendees, while at the same time creating an exciting and engaging program. On behalf of the SIGCSE Organization, I thank Adrienne and Kurt for their contributions towards the organization and management of this conference.

This conference is a great chance for you to make new connections and to learn about exciting innovations and new pedagogies related to computer science education. I always find great ideas that I am eager to try out in my courses. This conference is also a chance for us to honor two special people who have made significant contributions to our community. The annual SIGCSE award for Outstanding Contribution to Computer Science Education will be awarded to Mark Allen Weiss. Many of us have used one of his data structures textbooks in either C, C++ or Java. The annual SIGCSE award for Lifetime Service will be awarded to Frank Young for his substantial contributions to SIGCSE for over twenty years, from organizing a SIGCSE conference to more recently monitoring the SIGCSE listserv as a SIGCSE Co-Information Director. Join me in congratulating both of them with these honors.

This conference is a chance for you to give the SIGCSE Board feedback on issues in computer science education that you would like us to address. Please look for us at the conference and let us know if you are interested in volunteering for SIGCSE. We encourage you to sign up to volunteer using our online form on the sigcse.org site. The other SIGCSE Board members are Vice Chair Paul Tymann, Secretary Judy Sheard, Treasurer Amber Settle, At-Large Board Members Tiffany Barnes, Sue Fitzgerald, and Alison Clear, and Past Chair Renée McCauley.

Finally, I encourage you to attend the SIGCSE Business meeting on Friday, from 5:10pm to 5:55pm in room 2505A to meet the SIGCSE Board. At this annual meeting we will discuss the overall structure of the SIGCSE organization and describe projects SIGCSE members are currently working on. We hope this will be a first step in getting you more involved with SIGCSE that may lead to many rewarding years working with colleagues on sharing ideas about computer science education.

Enjoy the conference, meet new colleagues and find something interesting to take back with you!

Susan H. Rodger
SIGCSE Chair, 2013-2016

Message from the Symposium and Program Chairs 2015

Welcome to SIGCSE 2015, the 46th ACM Technical Symposium on Computer Science Education. This year's symposium presents the latest advances in computer science education in a variety of formats: papers, posters, panels, special sessions, workshops, birds of a feather meetings and, new this year, demonstrations and lightning talks. This year's symposium theme is "Keep Connected. Keep Committed. Keep Computing." We are asking our attendees to consider how they can use the conference to keep connected to each other and the field, to keep committed to the cause of computing education, and most fundamentally, to keep computing and to demonstrate to all our students how exciting this field truly is.

We are delighted to have Jessica Hodgins of Carnegie Mellon University and Disney Research giving SIGCSE 2015's opening plenary address on Thursday. Her work at Carnegie Mellon and Disney Research will demonstrate what new and exciting things will keep us computing in the coming years. Keith Hampton of Rutgers University is speaking at our Saturday luncheon. His work in social media demonstrates how keeping us connected is an important part of building strong relationships. Finally, it is our pleasure to announce the recipients of the two annual SIGCSE awards, the recipients of which demonstrate keeping committed to the field of computing education and to the SIGCSE organization and community. Frank Young of Rose-Hulman Institute of Technology will receive the SIGCSE Award for Lifetime Service to the Computer Science Education Community, and will speak at our First Timer's Lunch on Thursday. (SIGCSE First Timers will receive their lunch for free. SIGCSE Old Timers are encouraged to purchase a ticket, join us for lunch, meet some First Timers, and recognize Frank's contributions.) Mark Allen Weiss of Florida International University is the recipient of the SIGCSE Award for Outstanding Contributions to Computer Science Education. Mark will give the plenary address on Friday.

As noted above, we are very excited to be introducing two new tracks for SIGCSE 2015. A Demos track will be presented in the exhibit hall during breaks, and a session dedicated to Lightning Talks will take place on Friday afternoon at 3:45pm.

Symposium statistics are presented in the following table. This year's program includes the usual wide selection of events, including the Evening Reception on Thursday and the ACM SIGCSE Student Research Competition, as well as another puzzle challenge. Our exhibit hall features a number of exhibitors showcasing the latest in hardware, software tools, textbooks and educational programs and research.

Proposal type	*Accepted*	*Received*	*Acceptance Rate*
Paper	105	289	36%
Panel	10	18	56%
Special Session	13	25	52%
Workshop	30	71	42%
Poster	51	117	44%
Birds of a Feather	38	55	69%
Demos	10	32	31%
Lightning Talks	11	26	42%

We encourage you to participate in our SIGCSE 2015 Pre-symposium Events. As of the publication deadline for this overview, meetings on the following topics will occur on Wednesday: ACM SIGCAS Symposium on Computing for the Social Good: Educational Practices, CSTeachingTips.org: Tip-A-Thon, GENI in your Classroom, Git and GitHub: Foundations for Educators, LittleFe Build-Out, Managing the Academic Career for Women Faculty in Undergraduate Computing Programs, SIGCSE 2015 Department Chairs Roundtable, and Teaching to Diversity in Computer Science.

Our sincere thanks go out to the people who have made this Symposium extraordinary. First, our Program Committee: Paul Carter, Steve Cooper, Tom Cortina, Michelle Craig, Pam Cutter, R.J. Dake, Lynn Degler, Paul Denny, Peter DePasquale, John Dooley, Brian Dorn, Ria Galanos, Brian Hare, Sarah Heckman, Mike Helmick, Matt Jadud, Cary Laxer, Sara Melnick, Larry Merkle, Alvaro Monge, Briana Morrison, David Musicant, Cheryl Seals, Ann Sobel, Valerie Henderson Summet, Paul Tymann, Henry Walker, and Jian Zhang. Additional thanks go to our Associate Program Chairs who provided meta-reviews for papers: Eric Aaron, Ruth Anderson, Don Blaheta, Alistair Campbell, Stephen Edwards, Mary Anne Egan, Dave Levine, Sam Rebelsky, Brad Richards, Tammy Vandegrift, Ellen Walker, and Steve Wolfman. We would also like to thank our International Liaison Committee (Reyyan Ayfer, Karen Bradshaw, Orit Hazzan, Fredrik Heintz, Jeisson Hidalgo-Céspedes, Meriel Huggard, Ville Isomottonen, Sridhar Iyer, Janet Lin, Chris McDonald, Ian Sanders, Clarisse Sieckenius de Souza, Claudia Szabo, Gary Wong, Mark Zarb, and

Ming Zhang) for helping ensure that SIGCSE 2015 is welcoming to attendees from around the world. Last, but certainly not least, we would like to thank all our student volunteers who help us with all the small details, and of course the authors and reviewers, without whom there would be no program at all.

In addition to our committee, there are others who have given to the symposium in a volunteer capacity and we need to acknowledge their contributions as well. They have added to the experience of the attendees in various ways: Zack Butler from the Rochester Institute of Technology gave his time to challenge us with our Puzzle Challenge, and Tracy Camp and her CONNECT team kept us connected throughout our time at the conference. And it is hard to imagine this conference without a visual identity. Andy Phelps, Director of the MAGIC Center at Rochester Institute of Technology, gave his time and artistic talent to create our conference logo and all of its variations, and who listened to all of our requests for tweaks and changes and actually gave them to us.

We wish to thank all our supporters, vendors, exhibitors and in-kind donors whose participation does more than make the Symposium possible; your participation enhances the collaboration and learning experiences all week. A special thank you to the following supporters: Google (Platinum), Microsoft (Platinum), ABET (Gold), Oracle Academy (Gold), GitHub (Silver), Gradescope (Silver), Piazza (Silver), Teradata University Network (Silver), Zyante (Silver), and Turingscraft (Bronze). Special thanks to Dorothea Heck and her team at D. Lawrence Planners for coordinating an outstanding exhibition and their creative efforts with conference planning and logistics.

We are grateful for the support and guidance given to us by SIGCSE President Susan Rodger and the entire Board, as well as the contributions of the SIGCSE Symposium Site Coordinators Bob Beck and Scott Grissom. ACM provides the infrastructure for conferences and the help of April Mosqus, Ann Lane, Irene Frawley, and Donna Cappo from ACM has been extremely valuable. Sheridan Printing Company brings all the materials for the proceedings together and we thank Lisa Tolles and Adrienne Griscti for all their support through this process. We have truly fallen in love with Kansas City and the people we have met and worked with there. We thank Dennis Cross and all of the staff at the Kansas City Convention Center, as well as Leticia Hickman and Jeremy Sanders and their staff at the Kansas City Marriott Downtown for making our events at both venues just wonderful. Nate Lawrence and his staff at PB & J Catering have done a remarkable job giving us a delectable taste of what Kansas City has to offer from the culinary perspective, and we are grateful for their culinary artistry. Every time we set foot in the city, Jenny Wilson from Visit KC has always shown us the best KC has to offer and has been a wonderful ally in our quest to find the best restaurants and attractions to share with all of you as attendees. Without Jenny, our time in KC would certainly have been less enjoyable.

Special thanks to our home institutions for providing needed resources: Baldwin Wallace University, the Rochester Institute of Technology, the University at Buffalo, and the University of British Columbia. We hope you enjoy the Symposium. Keep connected, keep committed, and keep computing.

Symposium Chairs

Adrienne Decker

Rochester Institute of Technology

Kurt Eiselt

University of British Columbia

Program Chairs

Jodi Tims

Baldwin Wallace University

Carl Alphonce

University at Buffalo

Table of Contents

Special Session

Session Chair: Owen Astrachan *(Duke University)*

Demonstration Session

Session Chair: Stephen Edwards *(Virginia Tech)*

Paper Session: Block Languages

Session Chair: Sen Zhang *(SUNY Oneonta)*

Paper Session: Gender & Diversity

Session Chair: Lina Battestilli *(NCSU)*

Paper Session: Student Engagement: Flipped Classroom

Session Chair: Madeleine Schep *(Columbia College)*

Paper Session: Student Engagement: Self Explanation

Session Chair: Maria Jump *(King's College)*

Paper Session: Focus on K-12: Professional Development

Session Chair: Charles Hardnett *(Gwinnett Technical College)*

Paper Session: Soft Skills: Teamwork & Communication

Session Chair: Sanethia Thomas *(University of Florida)*

Paper Session: Beyond CS2: Cloud Computing

Session Chair: Don Goelman *(Villanova University)*

Special Session

Session Chair: Joel C. Adams *(Calvin College)*

Panel Session

Session Chair: Meimei Gao *(Mercer County Community College)*

Panel Session

Session Chair: Cameron L. Fadjo *(Google, Inc.)*

Paper Session: CS Education Research

Session Chair: Bo Brinkman *(Miami University)*

Paper Session: Focus on K-12: Professional Development

Session Chair: Martha Kosa *(Tennessee Technological University)*

Paper Session: Student Engagement: Active Learning

Session Chair: Susan Hammond *(Faulkner University)*

Paper Session: Testing: Improving Quality of Student Testing

Session Chair: Ahmad Noor *(Northern Virginia Community College)*

Paper Session: Focus on K-12: Engaging Students

Session Chair: Ravi Gandham *(Seattle Colleges)*

Paper Session: Testing: Tools & Techniques

Session Chair: Joan Lucas *(SUNY Brockport)*

Paper Session: Soft Skills: Teamwork

Session Chair: Ruth Anderson *(University of Washington)*

Lightning Talk Session

Session Chair: Stephen Edwards *(Virginia Tech)*

Paper Session: Non-majors/Interdisciplinary

Session Chair: Evan Barba *(Georgetown University)*

Paper Session: Focus on K-12: Outreach/Summer Camps

Session Chair: Christine Moore *(College of Charleston)*

Special Session

Session Chair: Orit Hazzan *(Technion – Israel Institute of Technology)*

Special Session

Session Chair: Owen Astrachan *(Duke University)*

Panel Session

Session Chair: Janet Burge *(Wesleyan University)*

Panel Session

Session Chair: Daniel D. Garcia *(University of California, Berkeley)*

Demonstration Session

Session Chair: Michael E. Caspersen *(Aarhus University)*

Paper Session: Teaching Practices

Session Chair: John Cigas *(Park University)*

Paper Session: Focus on K-12: Miscellaneous Topics

Session Chair: Adrian German *(Indiana University Bloomington)*

Paper Session: Computers & Society

Session Chair: Rachelle Hippler *(Bowling Green State University)*

Paper Session: Beyond CS2: Networking/Security

Session Chair: Faisal Kaleem *(Metropolitan State University)*

Special Session

Session Chair: Nafeesa Dewji *(University of British Columbia)*

Panel Session

Session Chair: Katie Apone *(Code.org)*

Special Session

Session Chair: Nick Parlante *(Stanford University)*

Poster Session I

Poster Session II

Birds of a Feather: Flock I

Birds of a Feather: Flock II

Wednesday Workshops

Friday Workshops

Saturday Workshops

Undergraduate Abstracts

Graduate Abstracts

SIGCSE 2015 Symposium Committee

Symposium Chairs
Adrienne Decker, *Rochester Institute of Technology*
Kurt Eiselt, *University of British Columbia*

Program Chairs
Carl Alphonce, *University at Buffalo*
Jodi Tims, *Baldwin Wallace University*

Panels and Special Sessions
Peter DePasquale, *The College of New Jersey*

Workshops
Paul Carter, *University of British Columbia*
Alvaro Monge, *California State University, Long Beach*

Publications
Jian Zhang, *Texas Woman's University*

Database Administrators
John Dooley, *Knox College*
Henry Walker, *Grinnell College*

Registration
Lynn Degler, *Rose-Hulman Institute of Technology*
Cary Laxer, *Rose-Hulman Institute of Technology*
Larry Merkle, *Computational Optimization Services*

Posters
Michelle Craig, *University of Toronto*

Birds of a Feather
Ria Galanos, *Thomas Jefferson High School for Science and Technology*

Lightning Talks and Demos
Mike Helmick, *Google Inc.*

Student Volunteers and Activities
Pam Cutter, *Kalamazoo College*
Sarah Heckman, *North Carolina State University*
Sara Melnick, *Bronx Academy for Software Engineering*

Treasurer
Paul Tymann, *Rochester Institute of Technology*

Evaluations
Steve Cooper, *Stanford University*

Kids Camp
Cheryl Seals, *Auburn University*
Valerie Henderson Summet, *Emory University*

Publicity / Social Media
Briana Morrison, *Southern Polytechnic State University*

Webmaster
Matt Jadud, *Berea College*

Support / Exhibitor Liaison
Tom Cortina, *Carnegie Mellon University*
Dave Musicant, *Carleton College*

Pre-Conference Events & Affiliated Events Liaison
Brian Dorn, *University of Nebraska Omaha*

K-12 Liaison
RJ Dake, *Kansas State Department of Education*

Local Arrangements
Brian Hare, *University of Missouri – Kansas City*

Student Research Competition
Ann Sobel, *Miami University (Ohio)*

International Liaison
Paul Denny, *University of Auckland, New Zealand*

International Committee
Paul Denny (Chair), *University of Auckland, New Zealand*
Reyyan Ayfer, *Bilkent University, Turkey*
Karen Bradshaw, *Rhodes University, South Africa*
Orit Hazzan, *Technion - IIT, Israel*
Fredrik Heintz, *Linköping University, Sweden*
Jeisson Hidalgo-Céspedes, *University of Costa Rica*
Meriel Huggard, *Trinity College Dublin, Ireland*
Ville Isomottonen, *University of Jyvaskyla, Finland*
Sridhar Iyer, *Indian Inst. of Technology Bombay, India*
Janet Lin, *National Taiwan Normal University, Taiwan*
Chris McDonald, *University of Western Australia*
Ian Sanders, *University of South Africa*
Clarisse Sieckenius de Souza, *PUC-Rio, Brazil*
Claudia Szabo, *The University of Adelaide, Australia*
Gary K. W. Wong, *The Hong Kong Institute of Education*
Mark Zarb, *University of Dundee, Scotland*
Ming Zhang, *Peking University, China*

Associate Program Chairs
Eric Aaron, *Vassar College*
Ruth E. Anderson, *University of Washington*
Don Blaheta, *Longwood University*
Alistair Campbell, *Hamilton College*
Stephen Edwards, *Virginia Tech*
Mary Anne Egan, *Siena College*
Dave Levine, *St. Bonaventure University*
Sam Rebelsky, *Grinnell College*
Brad Richards, *University of Puget Sound*
Tammy Vandegrift, *University of Portland*
Ellen Walker, *Hiram College*
Steve Wolfman, *University of British Columbia*

SIGCSE 2015 Reviewers

Eric Aaron, *Vassar College*
Donald Acton, *University of British Columbia*
Raman Adaikkalavan, *Indiana University South Bend*
Elizabeth S. Adams, *James Madison University*
Robert Adams, *Grand Valley State University*
Paul Addison, *Ivy Tech Community College*
Rajeev Agrawal, *North Carolina A & T State University*
Shakil Akhtar, *Clayton State University*
Farha Ali, *Lander University*
Meghan Allen, *University of British Columbia*
Jamal Alsabbagh, *Grand Valley State University*
Christine Alvarado, *University of California San Diego*
Ashish Amresh, *Arizona State University*
Ruth Anderson, *University of Washington*
Peter Andrews, *Eastern Illinois University*
Steven K. Andrianoff, *St. Bonaventure University*
Marvin Andujar, *University of Florida*
Karen Anewalt, *University of Mary Washington*
Barbara Anthony, *Southwestern University*
Gabriella Anton, *Northwestern University*
Florence Appel, *Saint Xavier University*
Antonio Araujo, *Faculdade de Engenharia da Universidade do Porto*
Michal Armoni, *Weizmann Institute of Science*
David Arnow, *Brooklyn College*
Mansoor Arshad, *SZABIST*
Charles Ashbacher, *Charles Ashbacher Technologies*
Owen Astrachan, *Duke University*
Stephanie E. August, *Loyola Marymount University*
Isabel Azevedo, *ISEP*
Chunyan Bai, *Roger Williams University*
Laura Baker, *St. Edward's University*
Doug Baldwin, *SUNY Geneseo*
Catherine Bareiss, *Olivet Nazarene University*
Ian Barland, *Radford University*
David Barnes, *University of Kent*
Lewis Barnett, *University of Richmond*
N. Dwight Barnette, *Virginia Tech*
Martin Barrett, *East Tennessee State University*
Joao Barros, *Instituto Politecnico de Beja - ESTIG*
Phillip Barry, *University of Minnesota*
Lina Battestilli, *North Carolina State Universit*
Michael Bauer, *University of Hawaii - Leeward Community College*
Robert Beck, *Villanova University*
Andrew Begel, *Microsoft Research*
Tim Bell, *University of Canterbury*
Scott Bell, *Northwest Missouri State University*
Jens Bennedsen, *Aarhus School of Engineering*
Audrey Bennett, *Rensselaer Polytechnic Institute*
Mikael Berndtsson, *School of Humanities and Informatics University of Skovde*
Andrew Berns, *University of Wisconsin-La Crosse*
Gian Mario Besana, *DePaul University*
Bradley Beth, *The University of Texas at Austin*
Ivona Bezakova, *Rochester Institute of Technology*
Marie Bienkowski, *SRI International*
William Birmingham, *Grove City College*
Judith Bishop, *Microsoft Research*
Don Blaheta, *Longwood University*
Adam Blank, *University of Washington*
Stephen Bloch, *Adelphi University*
Cory Boatright, *Grove City College*
Steven Bogaerts, *DePauw University*
William Booth, *Baylor University*
Durell Bouchard, *Roanoke College*
Dennis Bouvier, *Southern Illinois University Edwardsville*
Robert Bowden, *Harvard University*
Kristy Boyer, *North Carolina State University*
James Braman, *Community College of Baltimore County*
Evelyn Brannock, *Georgia Gwinnett College*
Anna Bretscher, *University of Toronto at Scarborough*
Bo Brinkman, *Miami University*
Neil Brown, *University of Kent*
Robert Bryant, *Gonzaga University*
Dennis Brylow, *Marquette University*
Duane Buck, *Otterbein University*
Gregory Bucks, *University of Cincinnati*
Kevin Buell, *Garmin*
Kevin Buffardi, *California State University Chico*
David Bunde, *Knox College*
Barry Burd, *Drew University*
Kevin Burger, *Arizona State University*
Richard Burns, *West Chester University*
Vicky Bush, *University of Gloucestershire*
Candido Cabo, *New York City College of Technology/CUNY*
Andre Paul Calitz, *Nelson Mandela Metropolitan University*
Johan Calu, *KULAB*
Jennifer Campbell, *University of Toronto*
Daniel Canas, *Wake Forest University*
James Caristi, *Valparaiso University*
Martin Carlisle, *US Air Force Academy*
Lori Carter, *Point Loma Nazarene University*
Steven Case, *University of West Florida*
Lillian N. Cassel, *Villanova University*
Sheila Castaneda, *Clarke University*
Tim Chamillard, *University of Colorado at Colorado Springs*
Albert Chan, *Fayetteville State University*
Maiga Chang, *Athabasca University*
Bruce Char, *Drexel University Dept of Computer Science*
Mahesh Chaudhari, *Arizona State University*
Ranjan Chaudhuri, *Eastern Michigan University*
Jimmy Chen, *Salt Lake Community College*

Alessio Gaspar, *University of South Florida*
Dick Gayler, *Kennesaw State University*
Rick Gee, *Okanagan College*
Joe Geigel, *Rochester Institute of Technology*
Adrian German, *Indiana University School of Informatics and Computing*
Paul Gestwicki, *Ball State University*
Lila Ghemri, *Texas Southern University*
Michail Giannakos, *Norwegian University of Science and Technology - NTNU*
J Paul Gibson, *Telecom Sud Paris*
Gurman Gill, *University of Iowa*
Don Goelman, *Villanova University*
Michael Goldweber, *Xavier University*
Mercedes Gomez-Albarran, *Dep. Ingenieria del Software e Inteligencia Artificial*
Pedro Pablo Gomez-Martin, *Universidad Complutense*
Kinnis Gosha, *Morehouse College*
Jean Goulet, *Universite de Sherbrooke*
Michael Gousie, *Wheaton College (MA)*
Becky Grasser, *Lakeland Community College*
Joshua Gross, *Northeastern University*
Andrew Grover, *Thiel College*
Joshua Guerin, *University of Tennessee at Martin*
Carlos Guerrero, *University of the Balearic Islands*
Mandlenkosi Victor Gwetu, *UKZN*
Steven Hadfield, *United States Air Force Academy*
Ranette Halverson, *Midwestern State University*
Nadeem Hamid, *Berry College*
Brian Hanks, *BFH Educational Consulting*
Arthur Hanna, *St. Mary's University*
Stuart Hansen, *University of Wisconsin - Parkside*
Jessen Havill, *Denison University*
Scott Hawker, *Rochester Institute of Technology*
Orit Hazzan, *Technion -- Israel Institute of Technology*
Phillip Heeler, *Northwest Missouri State University*
Cecily Heiner, *Southern Utah University*
James Heliotis, *Rochester Institute of Technology*
Keith Hellman, *Colorado School of Mines*
Michael Helmick, *University of Cincinnati*
David Hemmendinger, *Union College*
Tyson Henry, *California State University Chico*
Katherine Herbert, *Montclair State University*
Matthew Hertz, *Canisius College*
Jose R. Hilera, *University of Alcala*
Rachelle Kristof Hippler, *Bowling Green State University*
Jason Hirschhorn, *CS50 Harvard College*
William Hochstettler, *Franklin*
Mark A. Holliday, *Western Carolina University*
William Hooper, *Belmont University*
Charles Hoot, *Oklahoma City University*
Cay Horstmann, *San Jose State University*
Thomas Horton, *Dept. of Computer Science Univ. of Virginia*
Hoda Hosny, *The American University in Cairo*
Shahadat Hossain, *University of Lethbridge*
Mahmood Hossain, *Fairmont State University*
Dwight House, *Fayetteville State University*
David Hovemeyer, *York College of Pennsylvania*
Brian Howard, *DePauw University*
Trudy Howles, *Rochester Institute of Technology*
Wen-Jung Hsin, *Park University*
Helen Hu, *Westminster College*
Chenglie Hu, *Carroll University*
Meriel Huggard, *Trinity College Dublin*
James Huggins, *Kettering University*
Janet Hughes, *University of Dundee*
Chris Hundhausen, *Washington State University*
Joshua Hursey, *University of Wisconsin-La Crosse*
Steven Huss-Lederman, *Beloit College*
Deborah Hwang, *University of Evansville*
Jorge Eduardo Ibarra-Esquer, *Universidad Autonoma de Baja California*
Petri Ihantola, *Aalto University*
Lubomir Ivanov, *Iona College Computer Science Department*
Sridhar Iyer, *Indian Institute of Technology Bombay*
Clemente Izurieta, *Montana State University*
Jana Jackova, *Matej Bel University in Banska Bystrica*
Matt Jadud, *Berea College*
Mark Jaeger, *Baker College*
Giti Javidi, *Virginia State University*
Lianen Ji, *China University of Petroleum Michigan Technological University*
Yerika Jimenez, *University of Florida*
Osvaldo Jimenez, *University of the Pacific*
Mike Jipping, *Hope College*
William Joel, *Western Connecticut State University*
David John, *Wake Forest University*
Mark Johnson, *Central College*
Colin Johnson, *University of Kent at Canterbury*
Chris Johnson, *University of Wisconsin Eau Claire*
Julie Johnson, *Vanderbilt University*
Michael Jonas, *University of New Hampshire at Manchester*
Anthony Joseph, *Pace University*
Mike Joy, *University of Warwick*
Daniel Joyce, *Villanova University*
Maria Jump, *King's College*
Ilker Kalender, *Bilkent University*
Alan Kaminsky, *Rochester Institute of Technology*
Pankaj Kamthan, *Concordia University*
Elizabeth Katz, *Millersville University*
David Kauchak, *Pomona College*
David G. Kay, *University of California Irvine*
Fereydoun Kazemian, *Rochester Institute of Technology*
Petros Kefalas, *University of Sheffield*
Tom Kelliher, *Goucher College*
Mark Kerstetter, *Western Michigan University*
David Kerven, *Georgia Gwinnett College*

Arshia Khan, *The College of St. Scholastica*
Jeff Kinne, *Indiana State University*
Nancy Kinnersley, *University of Kansas*
Jim Kiper, *Miami University*
Michael Kirkpatrick, *James Madison University*
Carsten Kleiner, *University of Applied Sciences & Arts Hannover*
Jane Kochanov, *Pennsylvania State University - Capital College*
James Kolasa, *Bluegrass Community and Technical College*
Yana Kortsarts, *Widener University Chester*
David Kosbie, *Carnegie Mellon University*
Janet Kourik, *Webster University*
Douglas Kranch, *North Central State College*
Joan Krone, *Denison University*
Jan Kruger, *Unisa School for Business Leadership*
Amruth Kumar, *Ramapo College of New Jersey*
Benjamin Kuperman, *Oberlin College*
Stan Kurkovsky, *Central Connecticut State University*
Zachary Kurmas, *Grand Valley State University*
Clif Kussmaul, *Muhlenberg College*
Brian Ladd, *SUNY Potsdam*
Matthew Lang, *Google Inc.*
Joan Langdon, *Bowie State University*
Yedidyah Langsam, *CIS Department Brooklyn College of CUNY*
Mick Lantis, *Purdue University North Central*
David Largent, *Ball State University*
Brian Larkins, *Coastal Carolina University*
Edurne Larraza-Mendiluze, *University of the Basque Country*
Eric Larson, *Seattle University*
Mary Last, *self-employed*
Robert Law, *Glasgow Caledonian University*
Christopher League, *Long Island University*
Cathie LeBlanc, *Plymouth State College*
Gilliean Lee, *Lander University*
En-Shiun Lee, *University of Waterloo*
Cornell Lee, *Minnesota State University*
Arthur Lee, *Claremont McKenna College*
Cynthia Lee, *Stanford*
Byong Lee, *Bennett College*
Choong-Soo Lee, *St. Lawrence University*
Chi Un Lei, *The University of Hong Kong*
Terry Letsche, *Wartburg College*
David Levine, *St. Bonaventure University*
Anany Levitin, *Villanova University*
Gary Lewandowski, *Xavier University*
John Lewis, *Virginia Tech*
Hai-Ning Liang, *Xi'an Jiaotong-Liverpool University*
Weidong Liao, *Shepherd University*
Panos Linos, *Butler University*
Jigang Liu, *Metropolitan State University*
Yue Liu, *National University of Defense Technology*
Peter Liu, *Seneca College*
William S. Lloyd, *University of West Georgia*
Sergio F. Lopes, *University of Minho*
Salvador Lopez, *Universidad Nacional Autonoma de Mexico*
Joan Lucas, *The College at Brockport State University of New York*
Stephanie Ludi, *Rochester Institute of Techology*
Andrew Luxton-Reilly, *The University of Auckland*
William Lyle, *Murray State University*
Bonnie MacKellar, *St John's University*
Peter Macpherson, *Rogers State University*
Joaquim Madeira, *University of Aveiro*
Manoj Maharaj, *University of KwaZulu-Natal*
James Maher, *Colorado School of Mines*
Davad Malan, *Harvard University*
Bill Manaris, *College of Charleston*
Mercedes Marques, *University Jaume I*
Maíra Marques Samary, *Universidad de Chile*
Hélène Martin, *University of Washington*
Kenneth Martin, *University of North Florida*
Fred Martin, *University of Massachusetts Lowell*
Manuel Martins Barata, *ISEL - Instituto Superior de Engenharia de Lisboa*
Dave Mason, *Ryerson University*
Julian Mason, *Google Robotics*
Suzanne Matthews, *United States Military Academy*
Bruce R. Maxim, *University of Michigan-Dearborn*
Bruce Maxwell, *Colby College*
Chris Mayfield, *James Madison University*
Lester McCann, *The University of Arizona*
Renee McCauley, *College of Charleston*
Robert McCloskey, *University of Scranton*
O. William McClung, *Nebraska Wesleyan University*
Jeffrey McConnell, *Canisius College*
Frank McCown, *Harding University*
Sean McCulloch, *Ohio Wesleyan University*
Chris McDonald, *The University of Western Australia*
Charlie McDowell, *UC Santa Cruz*
Monica McGill, *Bradley University*
James McGuffee, *Northern Kentucky University*
Tim McGuire, *Sam Houston State University*
Hugh McGuire, *Grand Valley State University*
Bonita McVey, *St. Norbert College*
Pedro Medeiros, *Universidade Nova de Lisboa*
Antonio Jose Mendes, *University of Coimbra*
Susan Mengel, *Texas Tech University*
Rachel Menzies, *University of Dundee*
Joseph Mertz, *Carnegie Mellon University*
Jose Carlos Metrolho, *Polytechnic Institute of Castelo Branco*
Timothy Meyer, *Edinboro University of Pennsylvania*
Mark Meysenburg, *Doane College*
Razvan Mezei, *Lenoir-Rhyne University*
Lisa Michaud, *Merrimack College*
Gail Miles, *Lenoir-Rhyne University*
Afsaneh Minaie, *Utah Valley University*

Joe Miro, *Universitat de les Illes Balears*
Selvarajah Mohanarajah, *Claflin University*
Adrian Moise, *Petroleum-Gas University of Ploiesti*
Dagmar Monett Diaz, *CS Department Berlin School of Economics and Law*
Michael Moorman, *Saint Leo University*
Sara Miner More, *Johns Hopkins University*
Nelma Moreira, *University of Porto*
Patricia Morreale, *Kean University*
Srikanth Mudigonda, *Saint Louis University*
Christian Murphy, *University of Pennsylvania*
Michael Murphy, *Concordia University Texas*
Adity Mutsuddi, *University of Cincinnatti – Blue Ash*
Kristine Nagel, *Georgia Gwinnett College*
Mario Nakazawa, *Berea College*
Nannette Napier, *Georgia Gwinnett College*
Krish Narayanan, *Eastern Michigan University*
Pavol Navrat, *Slovak University of Technology*
Rance Necaise, *Randolph-Macon College*
Robert Noonan, *College of William and Mary*
Victor Norman, *Calvin College*
Cindy Norris, *Appalachian State University*
Linda Null, *Penn State University*
Amanda Ochsner, *University of Wisconsin-Madison*
Chris Okasaki, *USMA*
Edward Okie, *Radford University*
Amos Olagunju, *St. Cloud State University*
Joseph Oldham
Nina Onesti, *Indiana University*
Lawrence Osborne, *Lamar University*
Peter-Michael Osera, *University of Pennsylvania*
Barbara Owens, *Southwestern University*
Christopher Painter-Wakefield, *Colorado School of Mines*
Iraklis Paraskakis, *City College Intern. Faculty of the University of Sheffield*
Young Park, *Bradley University*
Jeff Parker, *Harvard Extension*
David Parker, *Salisbury University*
James Paterson, *Glasgow Caledonian University*
Elizabeth Patitsas, *University of Toronto*
Laurie Patterson, *University of North Carolina Wilmington*
Brian Patterson, *Oglethorpe University*
Arnold Pears, *Uppsala University*
Charlie Peck, *Earlham College*
Eileen Peluso, *Lycoming College*
Bin Peng, *Park University*
Manuel A. Perez-Quinones, *Virginia Tech*
Teresa Peterman, *Grand Valley State University*
Andrew Petersen, *University of Toronto Mississauga*
John Peterson, *Western State College*
Chrisila C. Pettey, *Middle Tennessee State University*
Vreda Pieterse, *University of Pretoria*
Nelishia Pillay, *University of KwaZulu-Natal*
Johanna Pirker, *Graz University of Technology*
Francois Pitt, *University of Toronto*
Paul Piwowarski, *University of Kentucky*
Chris Plaue, *The University of Georgia*
Irene Polycarpou, *UCLan Cyprus*
Shana Ponelis, *University of Wisconsin-Milwaukee*
Leo Porter, *Skidmore College*
Lori Postner, *Nassau Community College*
Barbara Price, *Georgia Southern University*
Rhys Price Jones, *Wellesley College*
Roger Priebe, *Texas State University - San Marcos*
David Pritchard, *University of Southern California*
Viera Proulx, *Northeastern University*
Sarah Monisha Pulimood, *The College of New Jersey*
Farzana Rahman, *James Madison University*
Rajendra Raj, *Rochester Institute of Technology*
Muthu Ramachandran, *Leeds Metropolitan University*
Lakshmi Ramachandran, *Pearson Knowledge Technologies*
Raghuram Ramanujan, *Davidson College*
Praveen Rao, *University of Missouri-Kansas City*
Saquib Razak, *Carnegie Mellon University*
Eliseo Reategui, *Universidade Federal do Rio Grande do Sul*
Samuel Rebelsky, *Grinnell College*
Michael Redmond, *La Salle University*
David Reed, *Creighton University*
Donna Reese, *Mississippi State University*
Susan Reiser, *UNC Asheville*
Dan Resler, *Virginia Commonwealth University*
Eugene K. Ressler, *United States Military Academy*
Loren Rhodes, *Juniata College*
Catherine Ricardo, *Iona College*
Brad Richards, *University of Puget Sound*
Detlef Rick, *UniversitÃ¤t Hamburg*
Charles Riedesel, *University of Nebraska - Lincoln*
Kelly Rivers, *Carnegie Mellon University*
Suzanne Rivoire, *Sonoma State University*
Steven Robbins, *University of Texas at San Antonio*
Christian Roberson, *Plymouth State University*
Eric Roberts, *Stanford University*
Stefan Robila, *Montclair State University*
Susan H. Rodger, *Duke University*
Guido Roessling, *Technische Universitaet Darmstadt*
Joel Ross, *University of Puget Sound*
John Ross, *Indiana University Kokomo*
Jerry Roth, *Vanderbilt University*
Krishnendu Roy, *Valdosta State University*
Marc Rubin, *Colorado School of Mines*
Anthony Ruocco, *Roger Williams University*
Amalia Rusu, *Fairfield University*
Adrian Rusu, *Rowan University*
Rebecca Rutherfoord, *Southern Polytechnic State University*

Roberta Evans Sabin, *Loyola College*
Shazia Sadiq, *The University of Queensland*
Waquas Saeed, *TPS Pakistan Pvt. Ltd.*
Mehran Sahami, *Stanford University*
Samuel Sambasivam, *Azusa Pacific University*
Ian Sanders, *University of South Africa*
William Sanders, *University of Hartford*
Vijayalakshmi Saravanan, *Ryerson University Canada & VIT University*
Allison Sauppé, *University of Wisconsin-Madison*
Walter Schilling, *Milwaukee School of Engineering*
Karl Schmitt, *Valparaiso University*
Michael Scott, *Brunel University*
Otto Seppälä, *Aalto University*
Amber Settle, *DePaul University*
Behrooz Seyed-Abbassi, *University of North Florida*
Cliff Shaffer, *Virginia Tech*
Hossain Shahriar, *Kennesaw State University*
Christine Shannon, *Centre College*
Bonita Sharif, *Youngstown State University*
Ching-Kuang Shene, *Michigan Technological University*
Mark Sherriff, *University of Virginia*
Yasuto Shirai, *Shizuoka University*
Scott Sigman, *Drury University*
Gavin Sim, *University of Central Lancashire*
Beth Simon, *University of California San Diego*
Jarmila Skrinarova, *Matej Bel University*
William Slough, *Eastern Illinois University*
Joslyn Smith, *Florida International University*
Peter Smith, *California State University - Channel Islands*
Robert Snapp, *University of Vermont*
Takako Soma, *Illinois College*
Joel Sommers, *Colgate University*
Raja Sooriamurthi, *Carnegie Mellon University*
Jaime Spacco, *Knox College*
Christian Spannagel, *PH Heidelberg*
Greg Speegle, *Baylor University*
Carol Spradling, *Northwest Missouri State University*
Nathan Sprague, *James Madison University*
Alistair Stead, *University of Cambridge*
Michael Stein, *Metropolitan State University*
Theresa Steinbach, *DePaul University*
Stu Steiner, *Eastern Washington University*
Josh Steinhurst, *Intel Corporation*
Ben Stephenson, *University of Calgary*
Tom Stokke, *University of North Dakota*
Christopher Stone, *Harvey Mudd College*
Jeffrey Stone, *Pennsylvania State University*
Fred Strickland, *South University*
Kristina Striegnitz, *Union College*
Catherine Stringfellow, *Midwestern State University*
David Stucki, *Otterbein University*
Deborah Sturm, *College of Staten Island CUNY*
Kalpathi Subramanian, *The Univ. of North Carolina at Charlotte*
John R. Sullins, *Youngstown State University*
Fred Sullivan, *Wilkes University*
Wayne Summers, *Columbus State University*
Weiqing Sun, *University of Toledo*
Ken Surendran, *Southeast Missouri State University*
Rajendran Swamidurai, *Alabama State University*
Robert Tairas, *Vanderbilt University*
Paul Talaga, *University of Cincinnati*
Cara Tang, *Portland Community College*
Rahman Tashakkori, *Appalachian State University*
Michael Tashbook, *Stony Brook University*
Cynthia Taylor, *Oberlin College*
James Teresco, *The College of Saint Rose*
William Thacker, *Winthrop University*
Lynda Thomas, *Aberystwyth University*
Stan Thomas, *Wake Forest University*
Megan Thomas, *California State University Stanislaus*
Rebecca Thomas, *Bard College*
Mariamma Thomas, *Carnegie Mellon University*
Fergus Toolan, *University College Dublin*
Christian Trefftz, *Grand Valley State University*
Deborah Trytten, *University of Oklahoma*
Shengru Tu, *University of New Orleans*
Nicoleta Liviana Tudor, *Petroleum-Gas University of Ploiesti*
William Turkett, *Wake Forest University*
William Turner, *Wabash College*
Hakan Tuzun, *Hacettepe University*
Susan D. Urban, *Texas Tech University*
Timothy Urness, *Drake University*
Jaime Urquiza-Fuentes, *Rey Juan Carlos University/Lecturer*
Ian Utting, *University of Kent at Canterbury*
Jan Vahrenhold, *WWU Münster*
Ignatios Vakalis, *California Polytechnic and State University*
David Valentine, *Slippery Rock University*
James Vallino, *Rochester Institute of Technology*
Robert Van Camp, *Marietta College*
Tammy VanDeGrift, *University of Portland*
James Vanderhyde, *Benedictine College*
Jorge Vasconcelos, *National Autonomous University of Mexico*
Troy Vasiga, *University of Waterloo*
Kam Vat, *University of Macau*
Steven Vegdahl, *University of Portland*
Nanette Veilleux, *Simmons College*
J. Angel Velazquez-Iturbide, *Universidad Rey Juan Carlos*
Giovanni Vincenti, *University of Baltimore*
Ken Vollmar, *Missouri State University*
David Voorhees, *Le Moyne College*
Rosita Wachenchauzer, *Universidad de Buenos Aires*
Paul Wagner, *University of Wisconsin - Eau Claire*
Amber Wagner, *University of Alabama*
Sally Wahba, *Clemson University*
Gursimran Walia, *North Dakota State University*
Ellen Walker, *Hiram College*
Xueyi Wang, *Microsoft*
Xinli Wang, *Michigan Technological University*

Karen Ward, *University of Portland*
Stan Warford, *Pepperdine University*
Richard Wasniowski, *California State University Channel Islands*
Andrew Watkins, *Dept. of Math and Computer Science Baldwin Wallace University*
Thomas Way, *Villanova University*
Amali Weerasinghe, *University of Adelaide*
Stephen Weiss, *University of North Carolina at Chapel Hill*
Scott Weiss, *Mt. St. Mary's University*
Richard Weiss, *The Evergreen State College*
Emily Wenk, *Penn State York*
Linda Werner, *University of California Santa Cruz*
Roger West, *University of Illinois at Springfield*
Elizabeth White, *George Mason University*
Michael Whitney, *University of North Carolina Charlotte*
Howard Whitston, *University of South Alabama*
Judith Williams, *William Penn University*
Craig Wills, *Worcester Polytechnic Institute*
Michael Wirth, *University of Guelph*
Marty Wolf, *Bemidji State University*
David Wolff, *Pacific Lutheran University*
Greg Wolffe, *Grand Valley State University*
Steven Wolfman, *University of British Columbia*
Ursula Wolz, *Riversound Solutions LLC*
Ka Wai Gary Wong, *The Hong Kong Institute of Education*
Yan Wu, *Bowling Green State University*
Karl Wurst, *Worcester State University*
Stelios Xinogalos, *Department of Applied Informatics University of Macedonia*
Arthur Yanushka, *Christian Brothers University*
Juang Yih-Ruey, *Jinwen University of Science & Technology*
Duane Yoder, *University of West Georgia*
Kwok-Bun Yue, *University of Houston-Clear Lake*
Timothy Yuen, *UTSA*
Carol Zander, *University of Washington Bothell*
Mark Zarb, *Robert Gordon University*
Alan Zaring, *Ohio Wesleyan University*
Jinghua Zhang, *Winston-Salem State University*
Lynn Ziegler, *College of St. Benedict/St. John's University*
Stephen Zilora, *Rochester Institute of Technology*
Jill Zimmerman, *Goucher College*
Guy Zimmerman, *Bowling Green State University*
Daniel Zingaro, *University of Toronto*

CALL FOR PARTICIPATION

SIGCSE 2016

Engage, Energize, Empower!

The 47th ACM Technical Symposium on Computer Science Education

March 2 – 5, 2016, Memphis, Tennessee, USA

http://www.sigcse2016.sigcse.org

SIGCSE 2016 welcomes colleagues from around the world to present demos, lightning talks, papers, panels, posters, special sessions, and workshops, and to discuss computer science education in birds-of-a-feather sessions and informal settings. The SIGCSE Technical Symposium addresses problems common among educators working to develop, implement and/or evaluate computing programs, curricula, and courses. The symposium provides a forum for sharing new ideas for syllabi, laboratories, and other elements of teaching and pedagogy, at all levels of instruction.

Submissions are welcomed that are in line with the conference theme, **Engage, Energize, Empower!** The theme encourages all of us to adopt engaging curricula and pedagogy that will energize our students and empower them to become lifelong learners able to adapt in the ever-changing field of Computer Science. We are particularly interested in keeping our community connected with interesting educational efforts in upper level courses, open-source software, outreach, and education research. We are continuing to keep our commitment to the inclusion of a wide-variety of submissions in the program that span the spectrum of experience reports to scientifically rigorous educational studies. We are excited for you to be a part of showing our community why we all need to keep computing.

PAPERS

Papers describe an educational research project, classroom experience, teaching technique, curricular initiative, or pedagogical tool. Submitted papers for review will be anonymous. Papers will undergo a blind reviewing process and must not exceed six pages. Accepted papers will need to submit a non-anonymous version for publication in the proceedings after acceptance. Authors will have 25 minutes for their presentations, including questions and answers.

PANELS

Panels present multiple perspectives on a specific topic. To allow each panelist sufficient time to present his or her perspective and still enable audience participation, a panel will normally have at most four panelists, including one moderator. Panel submissions should include a list of the panelists, their affiliations, and a description of the topic, with brief position statements from panelists. Proposals with more than four panelists must provide a statement connecting the extra panelist to the effectiveness of the panel and must convincingly show that each panelist will be able to speak, and the audience able to respond, within the session time. Panel abstracts must not exceed two pages. A panel session is 75 minutes.

SPECIAL SESSIONS

Special sessions are your opportunity to customize and experiment with the SIGCSE conference format. Possible special sessions include a seminar on a new topic, a committee report, or a forum on curriculum issues. More generally, they must be 75 minutes in length, held in standard conference spaces, and justifiably be distinct from the panel, paper, and poster tracks. Within those constraints, the form is yours to design. Special session abstracts must not exceed two pages.

WORKSHOPS

Workshops offer participants opportunities to learn new techniques and technologies designed to foster education, scholarship, and collaborations. A workshop proposal (including abstract) must not exceed two pages. Proposals must specify equipment needs (e.g., participant-supplied laptops, room configurations, and A/V equipment) and any limitation on the number of participants. Workshops are scheduled for a three-hour session and do not conflict with the technical sessions.

BIRDS OF A FEATHER SESSIONS

Birds of a Feather (BoF) sessions provide an environment for colleagues with similar interests to meet for informal discussions. A maximum one-page description (including abstract) is requested to describe the informal discussion topic. A/V equipment will not be provided for these sessions. Each BoF topic is allocated 45 minutes.

POSTERS

Posters describe computer science education materials or research, particularly works in progress. Proposals (including abstract) are limited to two pages. Poster demonstrations are scheduled to permit one-on-one discussion with conference attendees, typically during session breaks. Prepared handouts are encouraged in order to share your work.

LIGHTNING TALKS

Lightning talks describe works in progress, new and untested ideas, or opportunities for collaborative work. The purpose of a lightning talk can be to start a discussion, find collaborators, or receive input and critique about an idea. Proposals are limited to 500 words and will be anonymously reviewed for acceptance. Lightning talk presentations will be 5 minutes each and given without media/slide support.

Association for Computing Machinery

Advancing Computing as a Science & Profession

SIGCSE ACM Special Interest Group on Computer Science Education

DEMOS

Demos provide a way to showcase an educational tool or project in a live setting. Not designed to be sales pitches, demonstrations are a way for the community to see the relevance, potential and innovation of the tool and allow time for discussion with its creator. Proposals (including abstract) are limited to two pages and will be anonymously reviewed for acceptance. Proposals must specify any equipment needs (e.g., power, A/V equipment, space needs). Demos will be 30 minutes in length and will occur during break periods at a designated space in the exhibition hall.

STUDENT RESEARCH COMPETITION

Research from all areas of computer science is considered for awards in two categories of competition: graduate and undergraduate. All submissions must represent a student's individual research contribution and a student must be an ACM student member to qualify for awards and travel grants. Entry due date is Monday, September 28, 2015.

PROCEEDINGS AVAILABILITY

The proceedings will be publicly available from the ACM Digital Library 14 days before the start of the conference. Therefore, the official publication date for the proceedings will be February 17, 2015.

IMPORTANT DUE DATES

Friday, August 28, 2015: *Paper, Panel, Special Session, and Workshop submissions*
Monday, September 28, 2015: *Student Research Competition submissions*
Friday, October 23, 2015: *Birds of a Feather, Demos, Lightning Talks, and Poster submissions*

PROGRAM COMMITTEE

Symposium Chairs
Carl Alphonce
University at Buffalo
alphonce@buffalo.edu

Jodi Tims
Baldwin Wallace University
jltims@bw.edu

Program Chairs
Michael E. Caspersen
Aarhus University
mec@cse.au.dk

Stephen Edwards
Virginia Tech
edwards@cs.vt.edu

Panels and Special Sessions
Ruth Anderson
University of Washington
rea@cs.washington.edu

Workshops
Alvaro Monge
California State University, Long Beach
alvaro.monge@csulb.edu

Bo Brinkman
Miami University
Bo.Brinkman@MiamiOH.edu

Publications
Peter DePasquale
The College of New Jersey
depasqua@tcnj.edu

Webmaster
Matt Jadud
Berea College
matt_jadud@berea.edu

Registration
Lynn Degler
Rose-Hulman Institute of Technology
degler@rose-hulman.edu

Cary Laxer
Rose-Hulman Institute of Technology
laxer@rose-hulman.edu

Larry Merkle
Computational Optimization Services
l.merkle@ieee.org

Posters
Don Goelman
Villanova University
don.goelman@villanova.edu

Birds Of A Feather
Samuel A. Rebelsky
Grinnell College
rebelsky@grinnell.edu

Student Volunteers and Student Activities
Sarah Heckman
North Carolina State University
sarah_heckman@ncsu.edu

S. Monisha Pulimood
The College of New Jersey
pulimood@tcnj.edu

Treasurer
Scott McElfresh
Longwood University
profscottmcelfresh@gmail.com

Evaluations
Christopher Painter-Wakefield
Colorado School of Mines
cpainter@mines.edu

Student Research Competition
Ann Sobel
Miami University (Ohio)
sobelae@miamioh.edu

Kids' Camp
Valerie Henderson Summet
Emory University
valerie@mathcs.emory.edu

Charles R. Hardnett
Gwinnett Technical College
chardnett@gwinnetttech.edu

Support/Exhibitor Liaisons
Tom Cortina
Carnegie Mellon University
tcortina@cs.cmu.edu

Dave Musicant
Carleton College
dmusican@carleton.edu

Pre-Conference Events & Affiliated Events Liaison
Rachelle Kristof Hippler
Bowling Green University - Firelands
rkristo@bgsu.edu

K-12 Liaison
Jill Pala
Girls Preparatory School, Chattanooga
jpala@gps.edu

Local Arrangements
Laine Agee
White Station High School, Memphis
laineagee@gmail.com

International Liaison
Daryl Hepting
University of Regina, Saskatchewan, Canada
hepting@cs.uregina.ca

Association for Computing Machinery
Advancing Computing as a Science & Profession

SIGCSE
ACM Special Interest Group on Computer Science Education

Recipients of the SIGCSE Award for Outstanding Contributions to Computer Science Education

1981 **William F. Atchison**, *University of Maryland*

1982 **Alan Perlis**, *Yale University*

1983 **Karl V. Karlstrom**, *Prentice-Hall*

1985 **Elliot I. Organick**, *University of Utah*

1986 **Donald Knuth**, *Stanford University*

1987 **Niklaus Wirth**, *ETH, Zurich*

1988 **Grace Murray Hopper**, *Rear Admiral, USN, Digital Equipment Corp.*

1989 **Edsger W. Dijkstra**, *The University of Texas at Austin*

1990 **Curriculum '68 Committee**:
William F. Atchison, Samuel D. Conte, John Hamblen, Thomas E. Hull, Thomas A. Keenan, William B. Kehl, Edward J. McClusey, Silvio O. Navarro, Werner Rheinboldt, Earl J. Schweppe, William Viavant, David M. Young, Jr.

1991 **David Gries**, *Cornell University*

1992 **Daniel D. McCracken**, *City College, City University of New York*

1993 **Alan C. Kay**, *Apple Computer*

1994 **Norman E. Gibbs**, *Software Engineering Institute*

1995 **Robert M. Aiken**, *Temple University*

1996 **Nell B. Dale**, *The University of Texas at Austin*

1997 **Andrew Tannenbaum**, *Vrije University*

1998 **William A. Wulf**, *University of Virginia and National Academy of Engineering*

1999 **Peter J. Denning**, *George Mason University*

2000 **Andries Van Dam**, *Brown University*

2001 **Allen B. Tucker**, *Bowdoin College*

2002 **Elliot Soloway**, *University of Michigan*

2003 **Eric Roberts**, *Stanford University*

2004 **Mordechai Ben-Ari**, *Weizmann Institute of Science*

2005 **Kim Bruce**, *Williams College*

2006 **Richard Pattis**, *Carnegie Mellon University*

2007 **Judith Gal-Ezer,** *Open University of Israel* and **John Hughes**, *University of Technology, Sydney*

2008 **Randy Pausch,** *Carnegie Mellon University*

2009 **Elliot B. Koffman,** *Temple University*

2010 **Sally Fincher,** *University of Kent, Canterbury*

2011 **Matthias Felleisen,** *Northeastern University*

2012 **Harold (Hal) Abelson,** *Massachusetts Institute of Technology*

2013 **Michael Kölling**, *University of Kent, Canterbury*

2014 **Robert M. Panoff,** *The Shodor Education Foundation, Inc.*

2015 **Mark Allen Weiss,** *Florida International University*

Recipients of the SIGCSE Lifetime Service Award

1997 **Richard Austing**, *University of Maryland*
1998 **Della Bonnette**, *University of Southwestern Louisiana*
1999 **Robert Aiken**, *Temple University*
2000 **James E. Miller**, *University of Southern Mississippi*
2001 **Lillian N. (Boots) Cassel**, *Villanova University*
2002 **Joe Turner**, *Clemson University and Zayed University*
2003 **Harriet Taylor**, *National Science Foundation and Louisiana State University*
2004 **Bruce Klein**, *Grand Valley State University*
2005 **Andrew McGettrick**, *University of Strathclyde*
2006 **Joyce Currie Little**, *Towson State University*
2007 **John Impagliazzo**, *Hofstra University*
2008 **Dennis Frailey**, *Raytheon Corporation*
2009 **Michael J. Clancy**, *University of California, Berkeley*
2010 **Peter Denning**, *Naval Postgraduate School*
2011 **Gordon Davies**, *Open University*
2012 **Jane Prey**, *Microsoft Research*
2013 **Henry Walker**, *Grinnell College*
2014 **Andrea Lawrence**, *Spelman College*
2015 **Frank H. Young**, *Rose-Hulman Institute of Technology*

Educating for Both Art and Technology

Jessica Hodgins
Carnegie Mellon University
Disney Research
jkh@cs.cmu.edu

ABSTRACT

Universities have traditionally drawn firm lines between classes in art and those in technology based fields such as computer science, placing them in separate departments, schools, and colleges. Human resources departments of companies have drawn similar lines between their "creative" and their "tech" employees, recruiting from different universities and creating different job titles and pay structures. In this talk, I will argue that the leaders of the next generation are going to be "hybrids" who each contribute to both sides of the art and tech divide and find it natural to interact and collaborate with co-workers with varied and mixed educational and work backgrounds. As an example of this style of education, I will report on an interdisciplinary course entitled Animation Art and Technology, which I have co-taught with Professor James Duesing in the School of Art for the past ten years at Carnegie Mellon University. The students are an interdisciplinary mix drawn from the traditional majors of art, computer science as well as a computer science and art bachelors degree program. The class produces four or five animations each semester, most of which have a substantive technical component, and the students are challenged to consider content innovation as equal to the technical aspects of their projects. Building on this style of education, Carnegie Mellon has recently created a program called IDeATE (Integrative Design, Arts and Technology Network) that offers a variety of minors and concentrations to students interested in blending art and technology in a variety of ways. 120 students enrolled in the first year indicating that the students recognize the need for these "hybrid" skill sets. As an example of the success of these efforts in industry, I will report on several research projects completed at Disney Research that would not have been possible without the highly collaborative efforts of teams of creative and techies.

Categories and Subject Descriptors
K.3.0 [**Computers and Education**]: General

Keywords
Animation, education

SIGCSE '15, Mar 04-07 2015, Kansas City, MO, USA
ACM978-1-4503-2966-8/15/03.
http://dx.doi.org/10.1145/2676723.2694804

BIOGRAPHY

Jessica Hodgins is a Professor in the Robotics Institute and Computer Science Department at Carnegie Mellon University. She is also VP of Research, Disney Research, running research labs in Pittsburgh, Los Angeles and Boston.

Prior to moving to Carnegie Mellon in 2000, she was an Associate Professor and Assistant Dean in the College of Computing at Georgia Institute of Technology. She received her Ph.D. in Computer Science from Carnegie Mellon University in 1989. Her research focuses on computer graphics, animation, and robotics with an emphasis on generating and analyzing human motion. She has received a NSF Young Investigator Award, a Packard Fellowship, and a Sloan Fellowship. She was editor-in-chief of ACM Transactions on Graphics from 2000-2002 and ACM SIGGRAPH Papers Chair in 2003. In 2010, she was awarded the ACM SIGGRAPH Computer Graphics Achievement Award.

Paying Back and Paying Forward

Frank H. Young
Professor Emeritus, Rose-Hulman Institute of Technology
125 Villa Lane
Terre Haute, IN 47802
+1 (812) 242-4965
young@rose-hulman.edu

ABSTRACT

This talk will discuss the value and benefits of volunteering - to one's career, to one's profession, and to one's life.

Categories and Subject Descriptors

A.1 [**General Literature**]: Introductory and Survey
K.3.0 [**Computers and Education**]: General

General Terms

Human Factors.

Keywords

Volunteering

1. SUMMARY

As professionals we need to *pay back* for the many opportunities we have been given, for the benefits we have received, for the sacrifices others have made so that we could thrive, and for support from society and industry. We have been nurtured in many ways and we have an obligation to pay back for this nurturing.

As educators we have an obligation to *pay forward* to ensure that there are replacements for us, to ensure that the computing professions contribute to the welfare of society, to ensure that those being educated for the future have the ability and opportunity to thrive, and to ensure that the computing professions set an example in providing opportunities for all who have the ability to contribute.

Volunteering helps foster a sense of community. Volunteering is absolutely necessary for SIGCSE. The SIGCSE community needs, welcomes, and rewards volunteers. Volunteering also rewards the individual volunteer in many ways.

SIGCSE '15, Mar 04-07 2015, Kansas City, MO, USA
ACM978-1-4503-2966-8/15/03.
http://dx.doi.org/10.1145/2676723.2694802

2. ACKNOWLEDGMENTS

I would like to thank the many colleagues who have encouraged me to volunteer and have supported my volunteer activities. I would also like to thank the many colleagues who worked with me in volunteer activities. They have enriched our profession and also enriched my life.

3. BIOGRAPHY

Frank Young received his B.A. in Mathematics from Haverford College and his Ph.D. in Mathematics from the University of Pennsylvania. He taught mathematics and computer science at Knox College in Illinois for 19 years. During this time he had a visiting appointment in computer science at the University of Iowa, a Fulbright Lectureship at the University of Lagos in Nigeria, and did graduate work in computer science at the University of Illinois at Urbana-Champaign. In 1987 he became Head of the Department of Computer Science at Rose-Hulman Institute of Technology, retiring after 15 years in that position. He has also taught at Haverford College, Temple University, Tougaloo College, and the University of Hawaii at Hilo.

Frank has been on more than 40 accreditation visits to institutions as a program evaluator or team chair. He served on the ad hoc committee that harmonized the ABET accreditation criteria for the four different ABET commissions. He was one of the original software engineering program evaluators. He has just completed a five year term on the Engineering Technology Accreditation Commission of ABET. This July he will begin a term as a member of the Executive Committee of ETAC. In 2012 he was made a Fellow of CSAB.

Frank has served SIGCSE as Symposium Program Co-Chair and Symposium Co-Chair, as Co-Chair of SIGCSE Registration, as Registrar and Treasurer for two ITiCSE Conferences, and as SIGCSE Information Co-Director for the last ten years. He was a regular columnist (with Judith Gersting) for the SIGCSE Bulletin from 1997 to 2003.

Data Structures Courses: Past, Present, and Future

Mark Allen Weiss
Florida International University
Miami, FL 33199
weiss@cs.fiu.edu

ABSTRACT
The "Data Structures" course is arguably one of the most important for computer science majors. In this talk, I will discuss how this course has evolved over the last three decades, and discuss some topics we might want to start thinking about in the next decade.

Categories and Subject Descriptors
K.3.2 [**Computers and Education**]: Computer and Information Science Education – *Computer science education; Information systems education; Curriculum*

Keywords
Programming, Data Structures, Algorithms

BIOGRAPHY

Mark Allen Weiss is an Eminent Scholar Chaired Professor and Associate Director in the School of Computing and Information Sciences at Florida International University in Miami Florida. He is the author of data structures textbooks that have been used by a generation of computer science majors.

Dr. Weiss served on the College Board's Advanced Placement Development Committee for seven years and as chair of the committee for four years. Since 2009, he has served as Associate Director in the School of Computing and Information Sciences, and has been instrumental in securing roughly ten million dollars of state funding in support of FIU's Information Technology related majors. Professor Weiss received his B.E. in Electrical Engineering from The Cooper Union, and his Ph.D. in Computer Science from Princeton University. He is an ACM Distinguished Educator and an AAAS Fellow.

SIGCSE '15, Mar 04-07 2015, Kansas City, MO, USA
ACM 978-1-4503-2966-8/15/03.
http://dx.doi.org/10.1145/2676723.2694801

Connected, Committed and Social? The Consequences of Computing for Relationships

Keith N. Hampton
Rutgers University
4 Huntington Street
New Brunswick, NJ 08901
keith.hampton@rutgers.edu

ABSTRACT

Digital technologies are increasingly an ubiquitous part of everyday communication. These technologies offer contact with friends and family that is both persistent and pervasive. Social ties that at one time would have gone dormant, or vanished entirely, are now made persistent through social media. As we transition through different jobs, neighborhoods, schools, and communities our social ties remain. Contact is no longer reliant on the occasional phone call and holiday card, but has a persistent presence on our screens and through our mobile devices. What are the benefits and the consequences of being connected? Are our relationships more committed? What impact will these emerging developments in computing have for society? It has been said that these technologies offer new opportunities for democratic participation, that they support collective action, and give marginalized individuals a voice. Social capital, once lost through the dormancy of ties, hidden as a result of infrequent contact, can be made visible through the persistent and pervasive nature of these new media. Yet, the practice of social media may not live up to its hype; they may contribute to social isolation, stress, and disengagement. Based on a series of large-scale studies of where people connect, who they connect with, and what they discuss, this presentation explores contradictory evidence of how digital technologies are related to social capital, democratic engagement, and the fear and joy that we may all be missing out.

Categories and Subject Descriptors

H.1.2 User/Machine Systems: Human factors

Keywords

Social capital, social support, deliberation, stress, cost of caring

BIOGRAPHY

Keith Hampton's research focuses on the social aspects of digital communication technologies. His work addresses, and often refutes, common assumptions about the role that digital

SIGCSE '15, Mar 04-07 2015, Kansas City, MO, USA
ACM 978-1-4503-2966-8/15/03.
http://dx.doi.org/10.1145/2676723.2694803

technologies play in everyday life. He is interested in how new forms of communication are used in different social contexts and their potential role in large-scale, social change. His work often takes a social network approach. He has been involved in a series of innovative, large-scale, empirical studies of community involvement, civic and civil engagement, social capital, digital inequality, health and wellness, and the use of public spaces.

Hampton explores the conditions under which people tend to be more or less isolated as a result of their use of new communication technologies, and how the use of these technologies relates to participation in neighborhoods, public spaces, and networks of relationships that provide for social support, deliberation, and political participation.

Hampton's work has been recognized through a number of awards, including the International Communication Association's Outstanding Article Award (2012), the top paper award from the Section on Communication and Information Technologies of the American Sociological Association (2011), and the Walter Benjamin Award for Outstanding Article from the Media Ecology Association (2011).

Hampton is an Associate Professor in the Department of Communication, School of Communication and Information, and an affiliate member of the Graduate Faculty in Sociology at Rutgers University. He is Chair of the Social Media & Society Cluster in the School of Communication and Information. He received his Ph.D. and M.A. from the University of Toronto in sociology, and a B.A. in sociology from the University of Calgary. Before joining the faculty at Rutgers, he was an assistant professor at the Annenberg School for Communication at the University of Pennsylvania, and Assistant Professor and Class of 43 Chair in the Dept of Urban Studies and Planning at the Massachusetts Institute of Technology.

DEMONSTRATION SESSION

EarSketch: A Web-based Environment for Teaching Introductory Computer Science Through Music Remixing

Jason Freeman, *Georgia Institute of Technology*
Brian Magerko, *Georgia Institute of Technology*
Regis Verdin, *Georgia Institute of Technology*
Contact: jason.freeman@gatech.edu

EarSketch (http://earsketch.gatech.edu) is a free integrated curriculum, software toolset, audio loop library, and social sharing site that teaches computing principles through digital music composition and remixing. EarSketch students write code in either Python or JavaScript to make music, with a focus on popular genres such as hip hop and dubstep, while learning computing concepts such as variables, iteration, conditionals, strings, lists, functions, and recursion. Attendees to this demonstration session will be introduced to a new web-based version of EarSketch that integrates a code editor, digital audio workstation (DAW) music production interface, curriculum browser, and sharing service into a single integrated browser-based learning environment. This demo is of interest to secondary and early post-secondary CS educators and to computing education researchers interested in STEAM and/or broadening participation. No prior musical knowledge or experience is expected and no prior programming experience with Python or JavaScript is required.

ACM Categories & Descriptors: J.5 [Arts and Humanities], K.3.2 [Computer Education]: Computers and Information Science Education – *computer science education, curriculum.*

Keywords: Remixing; music composition; broadening participation; education; computer science principles; music production; STEAM.

DOI: http://dx.doi.org/10.1145/2676723.2691869

Blockly Language Creation and Applications: Visual Programming for Media Computation and Bluetooth Robotics Control

Jake Trower, *University of Alabama*
Jeff Gray, *University of Alabama*
Contact: gray@cs.ua.edu

Over the past decade, an increased interest has emerged in block-based languages that have been used to support initial exposure of programming concepts to new learners (children or adult). Such languages can shield initial-learners from some of the frustrations of learning the syntax of a programming language, and allow them to focus on the core computational idea being taught. Blockly is a type of visual block language development kit that allows the rapid construction of new block-based visual programming languages to address a specific pedagogical or content focus. This demo provides a brief tutorial on the steps used to create a new Blockly environment, along with two case studies demonstrating the power of Blockly. The two environments introduced have two different contexts: the manipulation of images via operations on pixels (Pixly), and programmatic control of a Sphero robot (Spherly). Pixly and Spherly serve as a context for introducing how new Blockly languages are created, as well as showcasing the opportunity to use these languages as new educational environments in the context of media computation and robotics. More information can be found at http://outreach.cs.ua.edu/pixly/ and http://outreach.cs.ua.edu/spherly/. This work is supported by an NSF CE21 project and a Google CS4HS award.

ACM Categories & Descriptors: D.3.2 [**Language Classifications**]: Very high-level languages

Keywords: Blockly; Media Computation; Robotics Programming

DOI: http://dx.doi.org/10.1145/2676723.2691916

SIGCSE'15, March 4–7, 2015, Kansas City, MO, USA.
ACM 978-1-4503-2966-8/15/03.

Student Response to Teaching of Memory Cues and Resumption Strategies in Computer Science Classes

Noah John
Colorado State University
njohn@rams.colostate.edu

Jaime Ruiz
Colorado State University
jgruiz@cs.colostate.edu

ABSTRACT

Programming is a creative process that requires the ability to concentrate and juggle multiple concepts simultaneously in one's mind. Existing research shows there is a tangible cost when a programmer is interrupted as the programmer must recover the context of his work and refocus on the task at hand. However, CS students are rarely taught about interruptions and how to manage them. Instead, teaching tends to focus only on technical concepts. In addition, there is little research on interruptions with respect to CS students. Therefore, our research examines what happens when CS students are taught about interruptions and how to cope with them.

The objective of this paper is to determine if CS students are affected by interruptions, what knowledge CS students possess regarding memory cues and resumption strategies, and what their opinion is of this material. We conducted a study with approximately two-hundred undergraduate CS students to answer these questions. Our study was comprised of an initial questionnaire, a seminar on memory cues and resumption strategies, and a follow-up questionnaire. Our results demonstrate that CS students are affected by interruptions, but 73% of students report not knowing methods to mitigate them. After learning about memory cues and resumption strategies, students report that the material was useful and that they want to study it. Their most significant feedback is that they have a strong desire to include these techniques in CS curriculums, reporting a mean score of 7.78 out of 10, where 0 signifies strong disagreement and 10 signifies strong agreement.

Categories and Subject Descriptors

K.3.2 [**Computer and Information Science Education**]: Computer science education; K.3.2 [**Computer and Information Science Education**]: Curriculum; H.1.2 [**User/Machine Systems**]: Human Factors

General Terms

Human Factors

SIGCSE '15 March 04 - 07 2015, Kansas City, MO, USA

ACM 978-1-4503-2966-8/15/03 ...$15.00.
http://dx.doi.org/10.1145/2676723.2677234.

Keywords

interruptions; task resumption; cues; students; teaching

1. INTRODUCTION

Computer science students are taught a myriad of topics over the course of their education. In an undergraduate curriculum, it is common to see classes on programming languages, programming paradigms, data structures, algorithms analysis, and operating systems. As a student, it is important to learn the fundamental concepts taught in these classes to become a knowledgeable software engineer. Furthermore, a large portion of the work CS students do is programming-related. Whether the language is Java, C++, Scheme, or assembly, programming represents a majority of a CS student's homework and is the primary benchmark for a student's performance. And while the technical details and concepts, such as object hierarchy or C++ pointer syntax, are conveyed to students in class, significantly less is conveyed about the art of programming. At its core, programming requires strong logical reasoning, the knack for solving problems, and smart design skills. However, it is also a creative process that requires the ability to concentrate and juggle multiple concepts simultaneously. Additionally, there is a tangible cost when a programmer is interrupted as the programmer must recover the context of his work and refocus on the task at hand. On average, industry software engineers need fifteen minutes to recover from an interruption and return to a focused and productive state [28]. While there has been extensive research on the topic of interruptions, their effects, and methods for minimizing their impact [20], very little has reached CS curriculums.

In contrast, consider an English curriculum. One of its goals is to produce proficient and eloquent writers capable of composing various types of prose. Writing is recognized as a creative process that requires concentration and the managing of multiple ideas at the same time. English students, along with a majority of the general public, are familiar with the term "writer's block", which refers to a condition when an author is unable to produce new material. Furthermore, writing teachers dedicate some of their time to discussing this barrier and how to overcome it. Informal discussion of techniques and experiences has been deemed useful by the writing community and writer's block is one of the concepts covered in an English curriculum. While writer's block is not analogous to a programmer being interrupted and then having to resume a task, there are parallels. In both cases, the person is unproductive for a period of time and must find a way to overcome this state. Additionally, as a writer must remember his train of thought, a programmer must recover his context and his intended next step. We discuss these topics with English students. But how would CS students react if they were taught about interruptions and how to cope with them?

The objective of this paper is to determine if CS students are affected by interruptions, what knowledge students possess regarding memory cues and resumption strategies, and what their opinion is of learning this material.

Our method consisted of conducting a study with approximately two-hundred undergraduate CS students. First, we surveyed their programming habits, their work, and their previous knowledge on memory cues and resumption strategies. Next, we gave a seminar on interruptions, memory cues, and resumption strategies to these same students. Finally, six weeks later, we conducted a follow-up survey to gather their opinions on the seminar and examine if it had any perceived effect on their work.

Our results demonstrate that CS students are affected by interruptions and that they report the same resumption lag as industry engineers. We also see that 73% of students report not knowing about memory cues and resumption strategies. Finally, we find that students believe the material is useful and have a strong desire to learn these techniques.

2. BACKGROUND

There has been extensive research examining the effects of interruptions on productivity. A critical and foundational paper was published by McFarlane and Latorella [22] which thoroughly reviewed existing literature to argue its fundamental place in HCI research and how vitally important it is to understand interruptions and their effects as technology continues to evolve. They began by analyzing three application domains to show the necessity for considering interruptions in informed design decisions. They continued by summarizing their respective research that formalized and categorized interruptions with respect to tasks and summarizing their respective research into managing interruptions. They ultimately concluded with a discussion of existing strategies for mitigating the cost of interruptions and proposed that UI design was the most promising strategy, hence the importance of interruption research in HCI. Generally, research falls into four areas: interruption cost and effects, reasons for interruptions, interruption recovery, and coordinating interruptions. These four areas are summarized below.

2.1 Interuption cost and effects

One area of research has centered on the cost and effects of interrupting a person performing a task. Adamczyk and Bailey [1] conducted a user study to determine which are the least costly moments to interrupt someone's task. Hodgetts and Jones [12] [11] studied the effect of interruptions during different points in a problem-solving process. One objective is to leverage these findings to inform the design of an attention manager system [1]. Robertson *et al.* [26] studied the effects of *immediate-style* interruptions and *negotiated-style* interruptions on users debugging spreadsheet errors. Immediate-style interruptions are interruptions that require user action. Conversely, negotiated-style interruptions were defined in McFarlane's classification of interruptions [21] as interruptions that inform the user of a pending message but do not force them to acknowledge it immediately. Comparing the two styles, Robertson *et al.* found that negotiated-style were more effective.

Iqbal and Bailey [13] identified concepts from cognitive psychology that could be used to estimate the Cost of Interruption (COI) and Salvucci *et al.* [27] proposed a theoretical framework for defining the states of a multitasking continuum which included the states of interruption and resumption. Marulanda-Carter and Jackson [19] studied e-mail usage in a large international car rental company, measuring how e-mail interruptions affected productivity and the prevalence of e-mail addiction.

2.2 Reasons for interruptions

Some researchers have studied the reason for interruptions by observing the behaviors of people in an office and noting interruptions and their motivations. Czerwinski *et al.* [4] conducted a diary study of eleven experienced office software users and found that "returned-to" tasks were most difficult to switch to, required the most time to complete, and experienced the most interruptions (due to the task length). Szóstek and Markopoulos [28] observed the behaviors of people in an office and noted interruptions and their motivations. The study focused on face-to-face communication and highlighted factors such as urgency, employee hierarchy, and perceived availability.

Harr and Kaptelinin [8] thoroughly summarized existing research of interruptions and underlined the lack of attention paid to the social component of interruptions and the various dynamics that are in play. The paper identified four variables that affected the likelihood of an interruption occurring and proposed four related "ripple effects" that add additional cost to an individual interruption. In follow-up work, Harr and Kaptelinin [9] verified the effect of social context in a person's decision to interrupt someone else.

Jett and George [15] defined four types of interruption: intrusion, break, distraction, and discrepancy and detailed the positive and negative consequences for the interrupted person. Jin and Dabbish [16] defined a typology for self-interruptions. They ultimately identified seven types of self-interruption: adjustment, break, inquiry, recollection, routine, trigger, and wait. For each type, he observed their effects and duration.

2.3 Interruption recovery

Another area of research has been how one recovers from an interruption. Altmann and Trafton [2] studied the recovery process of users that were interrupted during the course of playing a computer strategy game and Jackson *et al.* [14] looked at the recovery time for e-mail interruptions of users of Microsoft Outlook in a software company.

There have been GUI prototypes that attempted to intelligently alert and interrupt the user (where the software itself has to interrupt the user) while assisting the user in quickly resuming his previous task after dealing with the interruption [6] and a prototype program that helps users organize related items on the Windows taskbar [4].

Parnin and DeLine [24] conducted a survey of software engineers to compile a list of cues that programmers use to resume a task that had been interrupted and then tested the usefulness of three memory cues: note-taking, a content timeline, and a degree-of-interest (DOI) treeview. In follow-up research, Parnin and Rugaber [25] looked at the techniques and strategies programmers use to resume an interrupted task.

2.4 Coordinating interruptions

The notion of coordinating interruptions is rooted to research done by Latorella [17] and McFarlane [20] where "coordinating interruption" was defined as the method one takes in interrupting someone's task. McFarlane [20] empirically evaluated four methods (immediate, negotiated, mediated, and scheduled) for coordinating interruptions and its results suggested that a method's effectiveness depended on the nature of the task being interrupted. He then built on this paper to evaluate four UI design solutions for coordinating interruptions [21].

Gievska *et al.* [7] looked at computer-mediated coordination and conducted an experiment that compared the performance of users that were interrupted randomly to that of users that were interrupted strategically using an interruption mediator. This paper established that workers were less distracted, were less annoyed, and found their work more manageable with mediated interruptions. Also, Kern *et al.* [18] had their study participants rank the personal and social disturbance level of various interruptions in differing environments. He then experimented with sensors to evaluate a person's personal and social interruptability and achieved a 98.1% recognition score for social interruptability. Palanque *et al.* [23] analyzed interruptions using model-based analytical techniques that could be used in designing interruption-tolerant systems.

2.5 Specialized interruption research

In parallel to the topics already mentioned, in should be noted that a significant portion of research into interruptions focuses on two disciplines: software engineering [3] [24] [25] [26] [29] and e-mail usage [14] [19].

We were unable to find research that investigated the resumption lag of CS students or the effect of teaching them about interruptions. This formed the basis of our motivation to pursue this study.

3. METHOD

Our research goal was to examine the effects on college students of presenting them instruction on interruptions, memory cues, and resumption strategies. More specifically, our objective was to support the following hypotheses:

H1 College students are affected by interruptions and have the same resumption lag as industry software engineers.

H2 College students' knowledge of memory cues and resumption strategies is limited.

H3 College students react favorably to being taught memory cues and resumption strategies in CS courses and believe they should be included in a college curriculum.

- **H3a** The student's age will affect the student's response to being taught these topics.
- **H3b** The student's programming experience will affect the student's response to being taught these topics.
- **H3c** The student's years in college will affect the student's response to being taught these topics.
- **H3d** The student's previous knowledge of memory cues and resumption strategies will affect the student's response to being taught these topics.
- **H3e** College students will report that learning memory cues and resumption strategies benefited them outside of CS courses.

To accomplish this, the study had three components: an initial survey, a seminar on memory cues and resumption strategies, and a follow-up survey. The study involved 198 undergraduate CS students attending a public university. Their ages ranged from 18 to 39, their experience in programming ranged from a few months to ten years, and their college experience ranged from one semester to eight years. They were not compensated for participating.

The surveys and seminar were given to five different computer courses: one freshman-level course, one sophomore-level course, one junior-level course, and two senior-level courses. The first survey and seminar were given in the middle of the semester. The follow-up survey was given at the end of the semester, roughly six weeks later.

3.1 The initial questionnaire

The first questionnaire was given in the middle of the semester and consisted of 18 questions. Students completed the survey in 5 to 10 minutes. The survey gathered three types of data: background information on the student, how they worked on their assignments, and their prior knowledge of memory cues and resumption strategies. Once the questionnaires were completed, the seminar started.

3.2 The seminar on memory cues and resumption strategies

There was a seminar held during the lecture period of five different classes. The format was lecture-based, students were encouraged to interrupt with questions, and a white board was heavily used by the instructor. All seminars covered the same material and lasted 25 to 30 minutes depending on the number of student questions. The material was presented in the following order: Effects of Interruptions, Memory Cues and Resumption Strategies, Notion of a Brain Dump, Resisting to Coordinate Interruptions Immediately [20], Note Taking, Code Commenting, Window Arrangement, Roadblock Cues [25], Selective Suspension [10], and Concept Maps.[1]

3.3 The follow-up questionnaire

The second survey was given six weeks after the seminar. The survey consisted of two parts. Part one was comprised of six continuous rating scale questions. The first three questions had "highly not useful" on the left and "highly useful" on the right. The final three questions had "strongly disagree" on the left and "strongly agree" to the right. Participants were asked to mark a vertical line through a horizontal line scale to indicate their opinion for each of the six statements. We codified their answers by measurement, which gave us real numbers on the continuous interval $[0, 10]$. Figure 1 shows one of the questions. The statements centered on the seminar's effect on students. More details can be found in the subsequent section. The second part of the questionnaire asked for details about the effect of the seminar. It also contained two questions which were identical to questions from the initial questionnaire and asked students about their start and resumption lag times. Space was also provided to allow participants to leave additional comments.

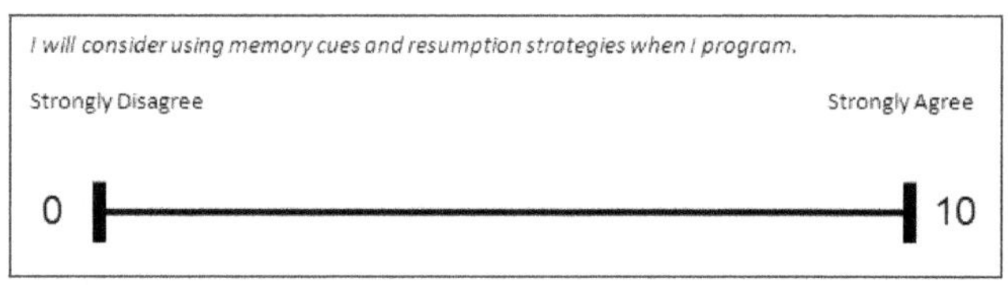

Figure 1: Example of continuous rating scale question from follow-up questionnaire.

4. RESULTS

The goal of this section is to support or reject the hypotheses defined in section 3 by presenting the results of the two questionnaires.

4.1 H1 - College students are affected by interruptions and have the same resumption lag as industry software engineers.

Students reported a mean resumption lag of 15.12 minutes (SD: 12.72). This is consistent with the fifteen minutes cited by industry software engineers in studies by DeMarco and Lister [5] and Solingen *et al.* [29]. Students were also asked what caused a session of work to be productive or unproductive. Table 1 shows a coalesced summary of student responses.

[1]Full description of seminar: http://noahjohn.us/research/memcues.html

Student Response	%
distractions	25%
understanding/clear requirements	24%
state of mind/mood	10%
focus	9%
time	6%
fatigue	5%

Table 1: Top contributors to productive/unproductive work for CS students.

The two most mentioned factors that affected productivity were distractions (25%) and understanding/clear requirements (24%). Distractions were primarily related to environment, which included noise, other people, and non-work technology. These factors were described by students in their feedback.

P76 *"Productive: no distraction from classmates/social media."*
P85 *"[affected by] distractions/loud talking in the computer lab."*
P119 *"If I don't have interruptions, I will be productive."*

We were encouraged by the comments on distractions because in many of the examples cited, the distraction was synonymous with a type of interruption and the seminar would directly deal with this topic. This provided evidence that CS students are affected by interruptions while doing their assignments. While this was expected, we felt it was important to have supporting feedback from students.

4.2 H2 - College students' knowledge of memory cues and resumption strategies is limited.

Nearly three-fourths (73%) of students reported not knowing memory cues or resumption strategies. Of the 27% that heard of these techniques, 42% said they learned about them in a psychology class and 14% did not remember where they learned about them. No student cited a CS class as a source for learning memory cues.

We also asked if they did anything prior to stepping away from an assignment that helped them refocus more quickly when they returned to work, which could indicate if they implicitly used memory cues and resumption strategies. The most common response (48%) was "no". The second most common response (27%) was that they left comments for themselves.

4.3 H3 - College students react favorably to being taught memory cues and resumption strategies in CS courses and believe they should be included in a college curriculum.

Part one of the follow-up questionnaire contained six continuous rating scale questions. For the first three questions (FQ1-3), 0 implied "highly not useful" and 10 implied "highly useful", and for the last three (FQ4-6), 0 implied "strongly disagree" and 10 implied "strongly agree". Table 2 contains a summary of student answers and Figure 2 displays a boxplot for their answers.

Students found the seminar useful (M: 6.24 SD: 2.04) and applicable to their programming assignments (M: 6.27 SD: 2.24). Students elaborated on these positions with their comments:

P17 *"I sometimes leave an assignment without finishing it, so it is helpful to create ways to jumpstart the work when I return."*
P18 *"[The techniques I learned] helped me reduce the time it took to get back into working after a break or interruption."*

Statement	Mean	Median	SD
I found the information in the memory cues seminar to be... (FQ1)	6.24	6.50	2.04
For my programming assignments, I found the information in the memory cues seminar to be... (FQ2)	6.27	6.5	2.24
For my non-CS assignments, I found the information in the memory cues seminar to be... (FQ3)	4.86	5.00	2.28
I will consider using memory cues and resumption strategies when I program. (FQ4)	7.41	7.75	2.02
I think memory cues and resumption strategies should be presented to CS students at some point of their curriculum. (FQ5)	7.78	8.00	1.93
I am interested in learning more about memory cues, resumption strategies, or similar topics. (FQ6)	6.34	6.53	2.40

Table 2: Summary of answers to part one of the follow-up questionnaire.

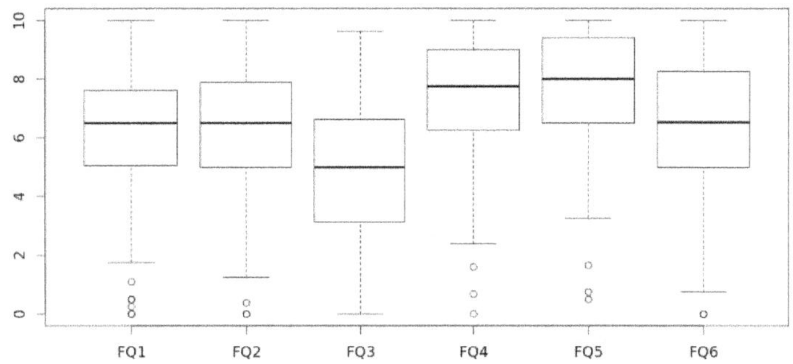

Figure 2: Blox plot of follow-up answers

More strongly, students said they would consider using the techniques (M: 7.41, SD: 2.02) and were highly in favor of teaching memory cues (M: 7.78, SD: 1.93). As one student articulated in his feedback:

P163 *"Seriously, try to get this stuff embedded in the CS courses. It is very important to be aware of this stuff."*

Also, they wanted to learn more about the subject (M: 6.34, SD: 2.40). For example, one student wrote:

P176 *"I'd like to know more about this topic; [I] wish it was covered in some CS course."*

Part two of the follow-up questionnaire focused on the seminar's effect and its answers are summarized in Table 3.

Question	Yes	No
Did the seminar change the way you think about programming?	57%	43%
Did you do anything differently during recent programming assignments?	43%	57%

Table 3: Summary of answers to part two of the follow-up questionnaire.

The 57% of students that cited a difference in thinking were asked to elaborate and provide an example. Here is a sample of what the students said:

P126 *"I always write a note to myself in my program now when I find a stopping place. This helps me resume my original thought process and helps the way I think about programming."*

P95 *"[The seminar] made me aware of the pitfalls of memory and productivity."*

While 57% of students stated they did nothing differently in their recent assignments, 5% of students mentioned their assignments were too short and/or easy to warrant using the cues and recognized their usefulness in the future with more complex assignments. As one student reported:

P66 *"It's [the seminar's topics] good stuff but I didn't use it this semester because the assignments weren't that hard. I'm sure I will next semester."*

Exploring the sub-hypotheses (H3a-H3e), Welch Two Sample t-tests were conducted on the six continuous rating scale questions (FQ1-FQ6) to determine if there was a difference between students that reported prior knowledge of memory cues and resumption strategies and students that did not report prior knowledge. Tests on FQ1 ($p < 0.05$), FQ2 ($p < 0.01$), and FQ4 ($p < 0.10$) showed statistically significant differences, which provided some support to H3d.

However, not all hypotheses were supported. Students did not report a noticable benefit to the seminar outside of CS courses (H3e) (M: 4.86, SD: 2.28). Analysis of variance was conducted to examine the effect of age (H3a), years in college (H3c), and programming experience (H3b) on FQ1-FQ6. Results showed no significant difference among different values of the dependent variable ($p > 0.10$). The only exception was an effect of programming experience on FQ5 ($p < 0.05$). However, post-hoc analysis with Tukey's HSD correction showed no distinguishable differences among different values of the dependent variable. Hence, our study did not demonstrate results that supported H3a, H3b, H3c, or H3e.

5. DISCUSSION

By showing that college students are affected by interruptions in similar ways to industry software engineers (H1), we were able to extend findings of previous research [5][29]. Students' average resumption lag was 15.12 minutes, which is consistent with the fifteen minutes industry software engineers reported.

In addition, we believe the feedback from the 198 students was meaningful and consistent. Respondents generally provided fair amounts of information on the questionnaires as evidenced by their feedback. Consistency was demonstrated by their answers. For example, in the initial survey, we included two questions that were intended to ask the same thing and only differ in wording. In one question, we asked what was the average length of time of a productive sitting for the student. In the other, we asked how long the student was able to "stay in the zone". We performed a Welch Two Sample t-test on the results of the former (M: 2.40, SD: 1.34) and the latter (M: 2.60, SD: 3.43) and found they were indistinguishable ($p > 0.50$).

Students of all ages and experiences are of the strong opinion (M: 7.78, SD: 1.93) that this material should be part of their undergraduate CS curriculum. Furthermore, 57% changed the way they thought about programming as a result of the seminar and 43% did things differently. Additionally, a few more mentioned they would have done something new if their assignments were more challenging. These results tell us that college students react favorably to being taught memory cues and resumption strategies in CS courses and believe they should be included in a college curriculum (H3).

We expected the student's age, years in college, and programming experience to affect the student's response to being taught memory cues and resumption strategies (H3a, H3b, H3c). However, none of these factors affected students' responses significantly. The significant difference was between students with and without prior knowledge of memory cues and resumption strategies (H3d), where the quarter of students with prior knowledge finding the seminar less useful, yet they agreed that the material should be taught.

We also thought students would report a benefit to learning about memory cues and resumption strategies that extended to non-CS courses (H3e). However, our results showed that students were neutral, at best, to that statement.

While other disciplines, namely Psychology, touch on memory cues and resumption strategies, CS teachers in universities cannot rely on students being exposed to these subjects, as shown by the results to H2. Therefore, there is a clear knowledge gap that many CS students have. And, according to their feedback (H3), they desire to fill this gap and learn more.

Finally, we believe another takeaway is that while roughly half of students already intuitively utilized memory cues to some degree, typically in the form of code comments, the seminar reinforced those habits and encouraged students to take more steps to help reduce their resumption lag. As one student wrote:

P181 *"I've been doing something similar [to what was taught in the seminar], but this made it more concrete. I'd like to learn more."*

5.1 Limitations

In this section, we remark on limitations and possible counterarguments to our work.

First, we have not established to what extent memory cues and resumption strategies should be taught, only that students believed that they should be taught. Readers can use the description of the seminar in the method section to see what material was covered, but this is not intended to be a definitive guide of what CS teachers should adopt. Again, our objective was to show that teaching students about interruptions, memory cues, and resumption strategies is welcomed by students, not how it should be done in the classroom.

Secondly, our participants came from the same university. However, our institution is similar to other public state universities. While we believe there was sufficient diversity among our participants, we intend to conduct a second study across multiple education institutions.

Thirdly, students might have been biased to provide positive feedback because they interpreted positive feedback as being helpful. This occurred to the authors at the outset of the study, and clear verbal instructions were emphasized to the participants to be honest and that there were no right answers. Additionally, the course instructors reiterated to their classes that no favoritism or reward would be given to those who participated in the study.

6. FUTURE WORK

A natural progression of this research would be to establish what topics are the most valuable to cover with respect to interruptions, memory cues, and resumption strategies. While our seminar was well-received by students, we have no way of knowing if the seminar could be improved and to what extent material should be covered. Hence, we envision a new study to determine which topics are most valuable to share with students would be a logical next step.

We also believe there is a vast potential for research into "programming as a craft" that could take existing knowledge and research of the creative process and cognitive psychology and apply it to programming. We believe knowledge from these areas that is introduced into CS can only enhance the field and improve the education of its students.

7. CONCLUSION

In this paper we examined if students are affected by interruptions, what knowledge students possess regarding memory cues and resumption strategies, and what their opinion is of learning this material. We found that students were affected by interruptions, but nearly three-fourths of students reported not knowing about methods to mitigate them. After learning about memory cues and resumption strategies, students reported that the material was useful and that they wanted to learn about them. Their most significant feedback was that they had a strong desire to include these techniques in CS curriculums. Furthermore, their feedback, including their interest in learning more and their opinion that it is a worthwhile topic to be covered in class, was independent of their age, college experience, and work experience. Based on our findings, we hope this paper will open the door to more research into teaching students about the creative process, so that like English students, their knowledge extends beyond the technical details of their craft.

8. REFERENCES

[1] P. D. Adamczyk and B. P. Bailey. If not now, when?: The effects of interruption at different moments within task execution. In *Proceedings of the SIGCHI Conference on Human Factors in Computing Systems*, CHI '04, pages 271–278, New York, NY, USA, 2004. ACM.

[2] E. M. Altmann and J. G. Trafton. Timecourse of recovery from task interruption: Data and a model. *Psychonomic Bulletin & Review*, 14(6):1079–1084, 2007.

[3] J. Chong and R. Siino. Interruptions on software teams: A comparison of paired and solo programmers. In *Proceedings of the 2006 20th Anniversary Conference on Computer Supported Cooperative Work*, CSCW '06, pages 29–38, New York, NY, USA, 2006. ACM.

[4] M. Czerwinski, E. Horvitz, and S. Wilhite. A diary study of task switching and interruptions. In *Proceedings of the SIGCHI '04*, pages 175–182. ACM, 2004.

[5] T. DeMarco and T. Lister. Peopleware: Productive projects and teams dorset house. *New York*, 1999.

[6] J. L. Franke, J. J. Daniels, and D. C. McFarlane. Recovering context after interruption. In *Proceedings 24th Annual Meeting of the Cognitive Science Society (CogSci 2002)*, pages 310–315, 2002.

[7] S. Gievska, R. Lindeman, and J. Sibert. Examining the qualitative gains of mediating human interruptions during hci. In *Proceedings 11th International Conference on Human-Computer Interaction, Las Vegas, Nevada*, 2005.

[8] R. Harr and V. Kaptelinin. Unpacking the social dimension of external interruptions. In *Proceedings of the 2007 International ACM Conference on Supporting Group Work*, GROUP '07, pages 399–408, New York, NY, USA, 2007. ACM.

[9] R. Harr and V. Kaptelinin. Interrupting or not: Exploring the effect of social context on interrupters' decision making. In *Proceedings of the 7th Nordic Conference on Human-Computer Interaction: Making Sense Through Design*, NordiCHI '12, pages 707–710, New York, NY, USA, 2012. ACM.

[10] E. Hemingway, G. Seldes, T. Dreiser, L. Hughes, and A. D. Ficke. *Monologue to the maestro: A high seas letter*. Esquire, 1935.

[11] H. M. Hodgetts and D. M. Jones. Resuming an interrupted task: Activation and decay in goal memory. In *Proceedings of the 28th Annual Conference of the Cognitive Science Society (CogSci 2006)*, page 2506, 2006.

[12] H. M. Hodgetts and D. M. Jones. Reminders, alerts and pop-ups: The cost of computer-initiated interruptions. In *Proceedings of the 12th International Conference on Human-computer Interaction: Interaction Design and Usability*, HCI'07, pages 818–826, Berlin, Heidelberg, 2007. Springer-Verlag.

[13] S. T. Iqbal and B. P. Bailey. Leveraging characteristics of task structure to predict the cost of interruption. In *Proceedings of the SIGCHI Conference on Human Factors in Computing Systems*, CHI '06, pages 741–750, New York, NY, USA, 2006. ACM.

[14] T. Jackson, R. Dawson, and D. Wilson. Reducing the effect of email interruptions on employees. *Int. J. Inf. Manag.*, 23(1):55–65, Feb. 2003.

[15] Q. R. Jett and J. M. George. Work interrupted: A closer look at the role of interruptions in organizational life. *Academy of Management Review*, 28(3):494–507, 2003.

[16] J. Jin and L. A. Dabbish. Self-interruption on the computer: a typology of discretionary task interleaving. In *Proceedings of the SIGCHI '09*, pages 1799–1808. ACM, 2009.

[17] L. Kara A. Effects of modality on interrupted flight deck performance: Implications for data link. Technical report, 1998.

[18] N. Kern, S. Antifakos, B. Schiele, and A. Schwaninger. A model for human interruptability: Experimental evaluation and automatic estimation from wearable sensors. In *Proceedings of the Eighth International Symposium on Wearable Computers*, ISWC '04, pages 158–165, Washington, DC, USA, 2004. IEEE Computer Society.

[19] L. Marulanda-Carter and T. W. Jackson. Effects of e-mail addiction and interruptions on employees. *Journal of Systems and Information Technology*, 14(1):82–94, 2012.

[20] D. McFarlane. Coordinating the interruption of people in human-computer interaction. In A. Sasse and C. Johnson, editors, *Human-computer interaction, INTERACT*, volume 99, page 295, 1999.

[21] D. McFarlane. Comparison of four primary methods for coordinating the interruption of people in human-computer interaction. *Hum.-Comput. Interact.*, 17(1):63–139, Mar. 2002.

[22] D. C. McFarlane and K. A. Latorella. The scope and importance of human interruption in human-computer interaction design. *Hum.-Comput. Interact.*, 17(1):1–61, Mar. 2002.

[23] P. Palanque, M. Winckler, J.-F. Ladry, M. H. ter Beek, G. Faconti, and M. Massink. A formal approach supporting the comparative predictive assessment of the interruption-tolerance of interactive systems. In *Proceedings of the 1st ACM SIGCHI Symposium on Engineering Interactive Computing Systems*, EICS '09, pages 211–220, New York, NY, USA, 2009. ACM.

[24] C. Parnin and R. DeLine. Evaluating cues for resuming interrupted programming tasks. In *Proceedings of the SIGCHI Conference on Human Factors in Computing Systems*, CHI '10, pages 93–102, New York, NY, USA, 2010. ACM.

[25] C. Parnin and S. Rugaber. Resumption strategies for interrupted programming tasks. *Software Quality Control*, 19(1):5–34, Mar. 2011.

[26] T. J. Robertson, S. Prabhakararao, M. Burnett, C. Cook, J. R. Ruthruff, L. Beckwith, and A. Phalgune. Impact of interruption style on end-user debugging. In *Proceedings of the SIGCHI Conference on Human Factors in Computing Systems*, CHI '04, pages 287–294, New York, NY, USA, 2004. ACM.

[27] D. D. Salvucci, N. A. Taatgen, and J. P. Borst. Toward a unified theory of the multitasking continuum: From concurrent performance to task switching, interruption, and resumption. In *Proceedings of the SIGCHI Conference on Human Factors in Computing Systems*, CHI '09, pages 1819–1828, New York, NY, USA, 2009. ACM.

[28] A. M. Szóstek and P. Markopoulos. Factors defining face-to-face interruptions in the office environment. In *CHI '06 Extended Abstracts on Human Factors in Computing Systems*, CHI EA '06, pages 1379–1384, New York, NY, USA, 2006. ACM.

[29] R. van Solingen, E. Berghout, and F. van Latum. Interrupts: Just a minute never is. *IEEE Softw.*, 15(5):97–103, Sept. 1998.

Closing The Cyberlearning Loop: Enabling Teachers to Formatively Assess Student Programming Projects

Ashok Basawapatna
AgentSheets Inc.
6560 Gunpark Dr., Suite D
Boulder, CO. 80301
720-838-5838
basawapa@colorado.edu

Alexander Repenning
AgentSheets Inc.
6560 Gunpark Dr., Suite D
Boulder, CO. 80301
303-530-1773
alex@agentsheets.com

Kyu Han Koh
University of Colorado Boulder
Department of Computer Science
Boulder CO. 80303
303-492-1349
kohkh@colorado.edu

ABSTRACT

Teachers are increasingly integrating game design and simulation creation projects as part of their classroom curricula. These projects have many benefits including motivating students in STEM activities and exposing students to computational thinking—a key part of upcoming science standards. However, barriers still exist to project-based computer science in a lab environment. One major issue is that, as students are creating their projects, it is extremely difficult for teachers to know how every student is progressing through a given activity and how to keep every student engaged. This paper introduces a Cyberlearning system entitled REACT (***R****eal-Time* ***E****valuation and* ***A****ssessment of* ***C****omputational* ***T****hinking*) that is an initial step towards giving teachers quickly discernible real-time data corresponding to each student project. REACT provides teachers with a sortable dashboard, consisting of data from each student, that shows the characters students created and used to populate their game or simulation world as well as the semantic meaning behind what students have programmed. A feasibility test with four middle school classrooms shows that REACT helps teachers formatively assess students and provide targeted instruction to struggling individuals. Furthermore, teachers showed excitement at the summative and student self-assessment capabilities of REACT, and every teacher independently stated they would use the REACT system in subsequent end-user programming units.

Categories and Subject Descriptors

K.3.2 Computer and Information Science Education

General Terms: Design, Experimentation, Human Factors

Keywords: K-12 Computer Science Education; Cyberlearning, End-User Game and Simulation Design; Formative Assessment; Summative Assessment; Computational Thinking; Assessment Tools

1. INTRODUCTION

Educational end-user programming tools allow students with little prior programming experience to quickly create games and simulations. Tools such as AgentSheets, Scratch, Starlogo, and Alice have shown to be both motivational and expose novice students to computational thinking [1,2,3]. Furthermore, the adoption of upcoming science standards that stress simulation and modeling activities, such as the Common Core and Next Generation Science Standards, incentivize middle and high school teachers to employ innovative ways of integrating proven end-user programming activities in their classrooms [4,5]. Given this emerging curricular pressure, one can expect teachers' use of game and simulation design programming units to increase.

In our research, we explore K-12 computer programming instruction as part of the Scalable Game Design (SGD) project at the University of Colorado Boulder. The Scalable Game Design project has the ambitious goal of revolutionizing computer science education in public schools through a combination of game design and science, technology engineering, and math (STEM) simulations integrated into the middle-school curriculum. More than 10,000 students from inner-city remote rural, and Native American schools have participated in SGD creating their first 2D and 3D games and simulations [6,7].

Over the past 8 years in the Scalable Game Design Project, our efforts have focused on developing and evaluating a working strategy to bring computer science education into the classroom. Recently, one of the main challenges has been looking at how to systematically scale up this effort and allow the most teachers, with varying computer science expertise, the necessary support to implement game and simulation design units in their classroom. We have found one part of the answer lies in better curriculum materials, school district support, and effective teacher professional development [7]. After observing many teachers around the US, we now believe that the other part of the answer is to employ *assessment-based cyberlearning tools* supporting instructor's quick real-time formative assessment of students [8].

Multiple factors can make programming project-based classroom learning difficult for teachers. Imagine you are a science teacher with limited prior programming and computer instruction experience. To meet the computational thinking requirements in the Next Generation Science Standards, you introduce a game or simulation design project in your classroom. As students start programming their game or simulation, they rapidly differentiate themselves in progress and ability. During class, there is no easy way to monitor how the classroom or individual students are progressing through the assignment. Looking over students' shoulders may not give you a clear indication of student progress. Some engaged students raise their hand when they need help, but other students, such as second language learners, individual lesson plan learners and/or students who may experience learning challenges, often remain silent [9,10]. With no direct way to

SIGCSE '15, March 4 – 7 2015, Kansas City, MO, USA.

http://dx.doi.org/10.1145/2676723.2677269

identify these students, you (the teacher) fail to intervene, these students fall further behind, feel helpless, and quickly lose interest. The barriers described in this scenario can be so significant that teachers may actively avoid in-class technology based project learning in general [11].

An essential part of meeting the upcoming science standards is to provide all teachers with the necessary tools to keep every student engaged. Giving teachers the ability to see what students are accomplishing could help close the learning feedback loop empowering teachers in their project-based programming activity instruction. This paper describes an initial investigation into a cloud-based cyberlearning assessment tool, entitled REACT (***R***eal-time ***E***valuation and ***A***ssessment of ***C***omputational ***T***hinking), aimed at end-user game and simulation design, which gives teachers up to the second information on every student project as it is being created. Teachers can use this data to inform in-class instructional decisions and identify students who are in need of intervention. REACT is an attempt to close the learning feedback loop between students and teachers. The remainder of this paper will describe the REACT system in the context of the Scalable Game Design project, including our working theory of keeping students engaged, then present and discuss data from an initial study with middle school teachers using REACT.

2. Real-Time Evaluation and Assessment of Computational Thinking

The Scalable Game Design project has instructed over 10,000 students in programming their first games and simulations [6,7]. In the Scalable Game Design project, students primarily use the agent-based end-user programming tool AgentSheets, or its 3D version AgentCubes, to rapidly create games and simulations [12]. Recently, Scalable Game Design instructors have also had the option of using a completely browser based version of AgentCubes called AgentCubes Online [13]. Figure 1 shows a screenshot (modified to save space) of a student Frogger game, a classic arcade game from the 1980's, many SGD instructors use as an initial assignment, programmed with AgentCubes online.

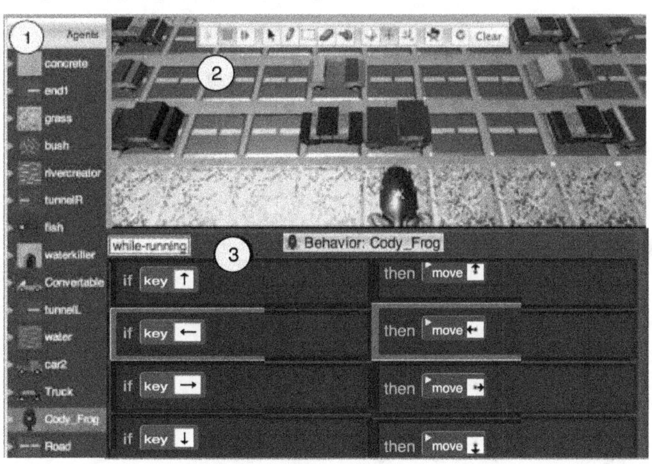

Figure 1: Student Frogger game created in AgentCubes online with labels: 1) Agents Created 2) The World 3) Programmed Behaviors

Label 1 in Figure 1 is the 3D "agents" or in-game characters (listed vertically) that the student created for this game. Label 2 in Figure 1 is the "world" or level wherein agents are placed and game action occurs. Label 3 in Figure 1 is where agent "behaviors" are placed. Behaviors are the programming rules that dictate how agents act. In AgentCubes, behaviors consist of rules and every rule consists of an if/then conditionality statement. AgentCubes programming is graphical—users drag "condition" blocks into the "if" portion of the rule and "action" blocks into the "then" portion of the rule. In Figure 1 label 3, four rules of the frog agent behavior are depicted. The top rule states that when the "key up" condition is met, the "move up" action is executed. Taken together, these four rules dictate that the frog moves up, left, right, and down when the up, left, right, and down arrow keys are pressed respectively.

2.1 Keeping Students Engaged In Computational Thinking

One of the Scalable Game Design project goals is to keep students engaged as they program increasingly more complex games and simulations. As students create a game and/or simulation, they build upon previously learned skills to meet a given challenge. Figure 2 depicts our working theory of engagement entitled "Zones of Proximal Flow" [14], which combines Csíkszentmihályi's concept of *Flow* [15] with Vygotsky's concept of the *Zone of Proximal Development* [16], in the context of the Scalable Game Design project [12, 14].

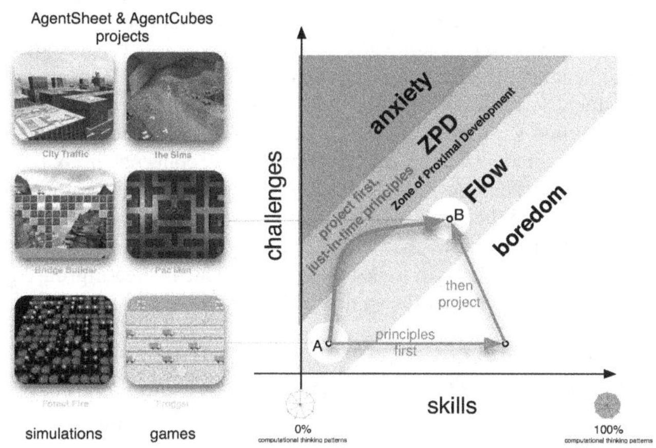

Figure 2: Zones of Proximal Flow combining the concepts of Flow and the Zones of Proximal Development. The y-axis consists of challenges (games and simulations) and the x-axis consists of computational thinking skills

Space limitations prevent a more in-depth description of these concepts, but briefly, Vygotsky states that the Zone of Proximal Development is the domain of what a student can learn with outside help. Csíkszentmihályi states that a person is in the Flow when a given challenge matches that person's skill level. If the person's skill far exceeds the challenge, that person is placed in a state of boredom. Conversely, if the challenge exceeds the person's skill, that person is placed in a state of anxiety. The Scalable Game Design project employs a "project-first just-in-time principles" strategy. Teachers give students increasingly harder challenges in terms of games and simulations that match or slightly exceed their given skill level. However, before the student gets into a state of anxiety, the project attempts to give students appropriate external scaffolding, matching their Zone of Proximal Development region, to guide them back into the Flow. This includes tutorials, instructor help supported by professional development, and cyberlearning tools. The y-axis of Figure 2 shows examples of increasingly harder games and simulations students can create.

However, the question still remains how do we measure what skills a student has mastered on the x-axis? One measure of skill that we have developed is high-level patterns of agent interactions students program as they create games and simulations. These interactions are called Computational Thinking Patterns [17]. Example Computational Thinking Patterns include one agent creating or absorbing another agent or one agent chasing another agent. For example, in the classic arcade game Pacman, a student might implement the Ghost agents chasing the Pacman agent and absorbing the Pacman agent upon Pacman being caught. Similarly, in a Predator/Prey simulation a student might implement a Predator agent chasing a Prey agent when hungry and absorbing the Prey agent when they come in contact. A more exhaustive list of Computational Thinking Patterns can be found in [17]. The x-axis (skills axis) of Figure 2 measures Computational Thinking Patterns through a validated measure called Computational Thinking Pattern Analysis, the details of which can be found in [18], which analyzes programs to decipher which patterns are present in a given student's game. The challenges presented to students combined with a method to measure the skills students have garnered start to make the theoretical Zones of Proximal Flow framework, outlined in Figure 2, actionable.

Currently, the Zones of Proximal Flow framework is useful for summative assessment. Specifically, it gives teachers and curriculum developers a way to pick subsequent game and simulation creation assignments based on previously programmed assignments/skills mastered [6]. Though important, summative assessment is only part of the equation for instructors. During the programming assignment, it would be helpful for teachers to know what skills students have mastered and what concepts individual students or the classroom as a whole are struggling with. Is there a way to leverage the Zones of Proximal Flow framework in real-time to support formative assessment of students in the classroom? To put another way, can we look at what a student is creating during class to indicate whether the student is lost and needs assistance?

2.2 The REACT system: attempting real-time indications of student skills

AgentCubes online is a cloud-based end-user programming tool wherein student games are created in a browser and updated, as well as saved, on a server. This affords the unique opportunity to have the central server analyze student games in real time. A cyberlearning tool residing on the server can analyze games and give teachers an early indication of when students are struggling. REACT is an initial attempt at this tool.

The REACT system was iteratively created using feedback from middle-school teacher consultations. REACT provides teachers with a dashboard, which can be displayed on a computer screen or a tablet, depicting real-time information on each student's project. Figure 3 shows the elements of the REACT system. Figure 3 Label 1 is an early prototype of the REACT dashboard. This displays information on each student project including Number of Worlds, Number of Agents, Number of Shapes (each agent can have multiple shapes such as "Red Ghost" and "Pink Ghost" in a Pacman Ghost agent), Number of Methods in the agent behaviors, Number of Rules, Number of Instructions and the Number of Agents in World currently placed. Student data is color-coded based on amounts, with red being the least amount for a certain category relative to the whole class and green being the most. Furthermore, teachers can sort the class by each column by clicking on that specific column. Therefore, if a teacher wants to see which students are lagging behind in agent creation, the teacher can organize the class in ascending order in terms of Number of Agents created by clicking on the Agents column in Figure 3 Label 1.

If a teacher clicks a specific student in the REACT dashboard, REACT displays a Computational Thinking Pattern Analysis (CTPA) diagram (Figure 3, Label 2) and a REACT Critique System analysis (Figure 3, Label 3) of the student game. The CTPA diagram outlines the relative patterns implemented in a given game in blue as overlaid on the tutorial CTPA diagram in light green [17]. In this way, a teacher can quickly compare how closely the student game aligns with the tutorial game and what specific patterns a student has implemented thus far in their game development. The REACT Critique system consists of a table that lists the state of all the agent interactions that should be present in a given game (in this case the minimal interactions necessary for Frogger). The Critique System parses agent behaviors looking for the presence of specific

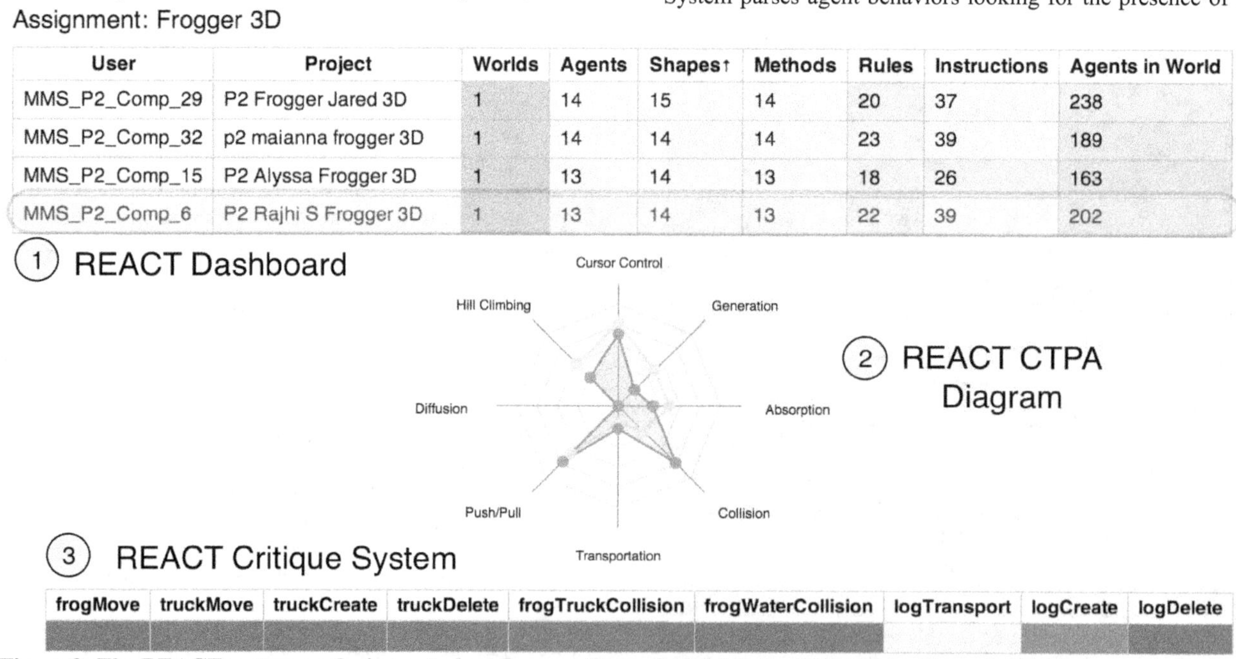
Assignment: Frogger 3D

User	Project	Worlds	Agents	Shapes↑	Methods	Rules	Instructions	Agents in World
MMS_P2_Comp_29	P2 Frogger Jared 3D	1	14	15	14	20	37	238
MMS_P2_Comp_32	p2 maianna frogger 3D	1	14	14	14	23	39	189
MMS_P2_Comp_15	P2 Alyssa Frogger 3D	1	13	14	13	18	26	163
MMS_P2_Comp_6	P2 Rajhi S Frogger 3D	1	13	14	13	22	39	202

Figure 3: The REACT system analyzing a student Frogger Game. Label 1 is the REACT dashboard. Clicking on a student on the dashboard displays a CTPA Diagram (Label 2) and the Critique System (Label 3).

combinations of conditions, actions, and rules necessary to create a given agent interaction. Interactions that are green are programmed correctly, interactions that are yellow are programmed mostly correct, and interactions that are red have not been programmed correctly. The interactions from left to right in the Critique System (Figure 3 Label 3) is the general order students usually implement each interaction, giving teachers a quick way to inspect where a student is in programming progress. In Figure 3, almost every Frogger interaction is programmed correctly with the exception of the Log agent transporting the Frog agent, which needs minor adjustments, and Log agent creation, which is programmed incorrectly.

2.3 Closing the learning loop using REACT

Combining all the elements of a Scalable Game Design classroom, Figure 4 shows how the REACT system supports game and simulation design instruction.

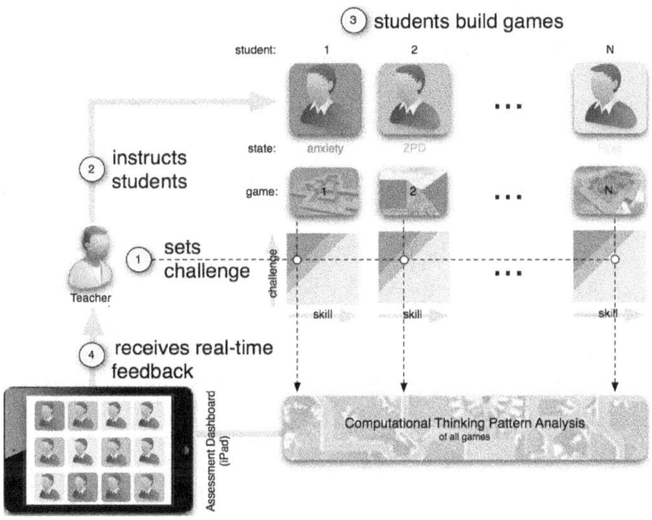

Figure 4: How the REACT system fits into the context of a classroom

The instructor sets a challenge (Figure 4, Label 1), students attempt to program their game/simulation projects (Figure 4, Label 2) putting them in a state of Flow, anxiety or boredom, the REACT system analyzes each student project to determine the up-to-the-second state of each student (Figure 4, Label 3), and finally, the teacher receives (Figure 4, Label 4) and quickly analyzes the REACT data to see if an individual student or the class as a whole need help understanding a certain concept. Hopefully, the teacher can use this information to adjust instruction accordingly or provide one on one help. REACT potentially allows for a teacher to help a student before that student even realizes she/he has a problem. Furthermore, if a student raises her hand, a glance at the REACT system can give the teacher insight into where that student is and what that student might need help with before the teacher goes over to give that student help. In this way, REACT has the potential to help instructors with their programming project based instruction. The remainder of this paper will describe the results of an initial study conducted to determine to what extent this actually occurred and discuss what aspects of REACT were helpful and not so helpful in terms of teacher instruction.

3. INITIAL CLASSROOM FEASIBILITY STUDY USING REACT

The central aim of the REACT study was to establish the feasibility of the REACT system and begin to answer fundamental questions about the most effective way to integrate REACT into the classroom. REACT testing took place over four weeks with four teachers teaching Frogger in AgentCubes online. The study consisted of four different schools, six classes, 23 hours of class time, and 134 student projects. All students were 6th graders with little to no prior programming experience. Table 1 depicts the REACT study details. All teachers had previously taught the Frogger unit, but no teacher had prior REACT experience.

Table 1: The REACT classroom study details

Teacher	Location	#Participants	Contact hours
A	Boulder, CO.	9	2
B	Nederland, CO.	25	5
C	Aurora, CO.	52	6
D	Boulder, CO.	48	10

Teachers used a computer screen and a tablet they would carry around the classroom displaying the REACT data. An instrumentation system was integrated into the REACT system for classroom trials. Anytime a teacher helped a student using the REACT system, the teacher could optionally annotate which student they helped and for what reason.

Teachers all teach the Frogger unit a little differently, but they usually start by introducing AgentCubes online, having students create initial agents (i.e. Frog, Road, Tunnels), place agents in the world and then introduce the programming of agents. All of this happens the first day (first hour) of class and the full unit takes students with little prior programming experience around five hours to complete.

3.1 RESULTS

Teachers annotated 73 instances of helping students. Figure 5 is a pie-chart categorical breakdown of these teacher annotations.

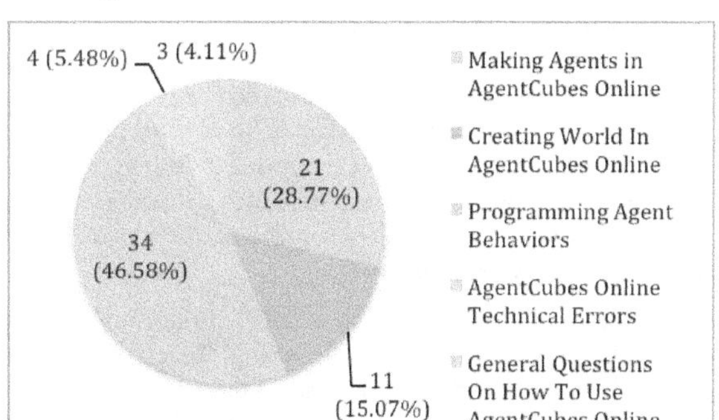

Figure 5: Category breakdown of REACT teacher self-annotation data. Teachers used REACT to help students with programming challenges as well as creating agents and adding agents to the world (Nteachers=4, Nstudents=134)

The amount of these optional annotations made in Figure 5 begins to show the feasibility of REACT in a classroom environment. In general, teachers were able to use REACT often and through all stages in student game development. These stages of game development included students initially creating agents, placing agents in the world, and programming agent behavior challenges.

After the classroom unit was completed, each teacher gave a brief interview explaining how the REACT system effected their instruction. The summary of these consensus results is recorded in Table 2.

Table 2: Summary of Teacher interview Results

- Teachers accomplished more (got further in the lesson) in less time and taught more ambitiously with REACT
- REACT helped support teachers in their classroom instructional decisions
- REACT helped teachers identify problems with and help challenged learners more effectively

Teachers indicated that with REACT they were more comfortable with being ambitious in their instruction. For example, Teacher A compared the REACT class with a non-REACT class coincidentally doing the same instruction earlier in the day. Teacher A stated the following.

"We got more done in this (REACT) class and we asked them to do more. We approached it the same way. In the other (non-REACT) class I couldn't tell where they were I had to rely on the helpers. With REACT, I was able to say 'that person is not up to speed' and send someone over there... I'm a lot more positive about it now than I was just looking at it from before. I see the power in it, and I see very useful things particularly for a beginning class." (Teacher A, 2/4/14, Response 1)

REACT also helped teachers know when to continue moving forward with instruction and detect problems. Teacher C stated the following.

"I really kept track of student progress with the number of agents they were putting in the world-- that was a key indicator that they were progressing and moving along or they forgot to save the world." (Teacher C, 4/1/14, Response 2)

Teacher D further stated that checking REACT and the Critique System (Figure 3 Label 3) before class helped inform that day's instruction.

"For me, the most useful was coming in the next day and be able to check and see where I need to start, depending on where all the kids left off, because you could see some kids didn't get as far as others. I loved that (Critique System) because I could quickly click down through the class and say 'wow everyone's frog is moving,' and then, the next day, we could see where we are and we could have kids jump ahead i.e. having kids program the logs and the turtles." (Teacher D, 3/30/14, Response 3)

As mentioned above, in a computer lab it is not always apparent when or why a given student is struggling. Teachers are forced to rely on students raising their hand, and, if they do not ask for help, it is hard to know that a student is having a problem. Teacher interviews indicate REACT also allowed teachers to focus on struggling and challenged learners in general. Teacher B stated.

"So <student name> didn't have a lot of agents. . . turns out that student had also been logged off the wifi. They were behind so by not having a lot of agents, it was apparent." (Teacher B, 2/8/14, Response 4)

Teacher A stated that REACT helped identify a sick student who was later sent home.

"One student was having a problem -- he was sick, physically.. it showed up as he wasn't getting his stuff done. I definitely saw a benefit. They could see I was paying attention to them and I think a lot of students feel good about that." (Teacher A, 2/4/14, Response 5)

REACT enabled teachers to help all students, but especially challenged learners, as indicated in the following Teacher C quote.

"As everybody was starting the game I feel they benefitted because I could see how they were starting. As they were progressing, I would say it was more attributable to those students who were struggling—not beginners but I would call them challenged learners—my low-end learners who are struggling...I feel like it's better to give those students intervention." (Teacher C, 4/1/14 Response 6)

Most importantly, ***all four teachers independently stated that they would continue using REACT in their classrooms***. Though a small sample size, this highly indicates the effectiveness of this cyberlearning tool to support teachers in their programming project based instruction.

3.2 Discussion

During the interviews teachers, brought up changes and extensions they would like to see in REACT. Table 3 outlines the issues teachers presented in their interviews.

Table 3: Summary of modifications teachers want to the REACT system

- Teachers want the REACT dashboard to be simplified
- Teachers want the Critique System to be part of the REACT Dashboard.
- Teachers were excited at the prospect of using REACT for summative and student self-assessment and asked that REACT be extended to accommodate these.

The initial REACT dashboard (Figure 3 Label 1) tried to include all possible information teachers thought might be helpful. After the study, many teachers pointed out that they used the Number of Agents created and Agents in World columns the most and asked that the table be simplified by eliminating or de-emphasizing lesser-used columns. Furthermore teachers thought that the Critique System (Figure 3 Label 3) was more helpful than the Number of Rules, Number of Instructions and Number of Methods columns. Every teacher stated they would rather not have to click on a student to see the Critique System and requested that in subsequent versions of REACT, the Critique System be integrated into the REACT dashboard.

In addition to formative assessment, teachers were excited at the prospect of using REACT for summative assessment and student self-assessment. For example, Teacher C stated the following.

"If I'm tracking how a kid is doing and taking notes I can take a screenshot of the (Critique System) and add it in there. We use Evernote. If someone needed evidence of how I was doing things, I could paste it into Evernote and share it with my evaluator or principal. So it would be a good tool for me in my teacher evaluation process to show how kids are doing." (Teacher C, 4/1/14, Response 7)

Teacher C went on to state how the system could automatically print out a report for each student and could be used as evidence that the classroom is meeting upcoming science standards. Teacher D, who, in a previous class, had students grade their fellow classmates' assignments, half in jest stated the following while using the REACT Critique System to look through those submissions.

"I can't believe my students lied to me... this is great. It's so easy to see what works and what doesn't!" (Teacher D, 3/30/14, Response 8)

Finally, teachers thought that the information in REACT should also be available to their students. For example, students creating a project in AgentCubes Online should also have the ability to view their Critique System and dashboard statistics to better understand where they might be having issues. Teacher A and Teacher D actually went so far as to excitedly project the REACT dashboard in-class to show the students the REACT information, allowing students to assess and regulate themselves. A few teachers thought that tutorial scaffolding should be added to REACT such that students could click on a Critique System interaction and see an example of how to program that interaction. Finally, teachers were excited at the prospect of REACT being extended to work with other introduction game and simulation activities. Teacher A is already using the REACT CTPA and Dashboard data in non-Frogger projects.

4. CONCLUSION

The REACT system is an embedded assessment cyberlearning tool that leverages a cloud-based 3D end-user programming environment, aimed at novice programmers, to enable formative student assessment and inform teacher instruction and intervention strategies in the computer lab. The initial study presented, highly indicates that the REACT system is useful for empowering teachers to ensure that every student reaches their potential in game and simulation design projects. Future research will focus on a more large-scale study using an updated REACT system incorporating the changes that teachers requested in terms of the dashboard, summative assessment, and student self assessment capabilities. The ultimate goal of this research is to eventually lower the barriers to programming project-based education in the classroom enabling every classroom to complete game and simulation design projects and meet upcoming science standards while equipping students with the computational thinking skills necessary to be successful in the 21st century.

5. ACKNOWLEDGEMENTS

This material is covered by the University of Colorado IRB number 13-0508. This work is supported by the National Science Foundation under Grant Numbers DLR-0833612, IIP-1345523, and IIP-0848962. Any opinions, findings, and conclusions or recommendations expressed in this material are those of the authors and do not necessarily reflect the views of the National Science Foundation. A special thanks to Fred Gluck, Mark Savignano, Maureen McDaniel, and Mark Shouldice and all of the REACT students for their invaluable help. Alexander Repenning is the founder of AgentSheets Inc.

6. REFERENCES

[1] Squire, K. D. (2003). Video games in education. Int. J. Intell. Games & Simulation, 2(1), 49-62.

[2] Kelleher, C., & Pausch, R. (2005). Lowering the barriers to programming: A taxonomy of programming environments and languages for novice programmers. *ACM Computing Surveys (CSUR)* 37.2 (2005): 83-137.

[3] Sengupta, P. et al. (2013). "Integrating computational thinking with K-12 science education using agent-based computation: A theoretical framework." *Education and Information Technologies* 18.2: 351-380.

[4] NGSS Lead States. (2013). Next Generation Science Standards: For States, By States. behalf of the twenty-six states and partners that collaborated on the NGSS.

[5] Common Core State Standards. (2010). National Governors Association Center for Best Practices, Council of Chief State School Officers, Washington, DC.

[6] Koh, K.H., Repenning, A, Nickerson, H., Endo, Y., & Motter, P. (2013). Will it stick?: exploring the sustainability of computational thinking education through game design. In Proc. of SIGCSE '13, ACM.

[7] Repenning, A., Webb, D., & Ioannidou, A. (2010). Scalable game design and the development of a checklist for getting computational thinking into public schools. In Proc. of SIGCSE '10, ACM.

[8] Cyberlearning, N. T. F. O. Fostering Learning in the Networked World: The Cyberlearning Opportunity and Challenge. A 21st Century Agenda for the National Science Foundation. (2008). National Science Foundation.

[9] Tsui, A. (1996). "Reticence and anxiety in second language learning." *Voices from the language classroom*: 145-167.

[10] Karabenick, S.A., and Richard N.S., eds. (2013). "Help seeking in academic settings: Goals, groups, and contexts." Routledge.

[11] Park, S.H., and Peggy E.A. (2008) "Examining barriers in technology enhanced problem based learning: Using a performance support systems approach." British Journal of Educational Technology 39.4: 631-643.

[12] Ioannidou, A., Repenning, A. and Webb, D. (2009). AgentCubes: Incremental 3D End-User Development. Journal of Visual Language and Computing, 20.4, 236-251.

[13] Repenning, A., Basawapatna A., and Klymkowsky, M. (2013). "Making educational games that work in the classroom: A new approach for integrating STEM simulations." In Proc. of IGIC '13, IEEE.

[14] Basawapatna, A., Repenning, A., Koh, K. H., Nickerson, H. (2013). The Zones of Proximal Flow: Guiding Students through a Space of Computational Thinking Skills and Challenges, In Proc. of ICER '13, ACM.

[15] Csikszentmihalyi, M., & Csikszentmihalyi, I. (1975). Beyond boredom and anxiety: The experience of play in work and games. San Francisco: Jossey-Bass.

[16] Vygotsky, L. (1987). Zone of proximal development. Mind in society: The development of higher psychological processes, 52-91, Cambridge, MA, Harvard University Press

[17] Basawapatna, A., Koh, K.H., Repenning, A. Webb, D.C., Marshall, K.S. (2011). Recognizing Computational Thinking Patterns. In Proc. of SIGCSE '11, ACM.

[18] Koh, K.H., Basawapatna, A., Nickerson, H., Repenning, A. (2014). Real Time Assessment of Computational Thinking. In Proc. of VL/HCC '14, IEEE

Analyzing Student Work Patterns Using Programming Exercise Data

Jaime Spacco
Knox College
jspacco@knox.edu

Paul Denny
University of Auckland
paul@cs.auckland.ac.nz

Brad Richards
University of Puget Sound
brichards@pugetsound.edu

David Babcock
David Hovemeyer
James Moscola
York College of Pennsylvania
{dbabcock,dhovemey, jmoscola}@ycp.edu

Robert Duvall
Duke University
rcd@cs.duke.edu

ABSTRACT

Web-based programming exercises are a useful way for students to practice and master essential concepts and techniques presented in introductory programming courses. Although these systems are used fairly widely, we have a limited understanding of how students use these systems, and what can be learned from the data collected by these systems.

In this paper, we perform a preliminary exploratory analysis of data collected by the CloudCoder programming exercise system from five introductory courses taught in two programming languages across three colleges and universities. We explore a number of interesting correlations in the data that confirm existing hypotheses. Finally, and perhaps most importantly, we demonstrate the effectiveness and future potential of systems like CloudCoder to help us study novice programmers.

Categories and Subject Descriptors

K.3.2 [**Computer and Information Science Education**]: Computer science education

General Terms

Measurement

Keywords

programming exercises; student work patterns; outcomes

1. INTRODUCTION

Many students struggle in introductory computer science courses [4]. Web-based programming exercise systems, such as CodingBat [16] and CloudCoder [10], can be a useful way for instructors to provide students with additional opportunities to practice basic concepts and techniques with the ultimate goal being (hopefully) to help students achieve better outcomes.

In these systems, an exercise requires the student to write a small amount of code (perhaps 5–15 lines) to perform a specified computation. The correctness of the student's code is judged automatically by running the code against a set of tests. If all of the tests pass, the student's code is judged to be correct. Because these systems are web-based and the assessments are automatic, students can work wherever and whenever is convenient for them, and receive immediate feedback. This combination of features allows students to receive more feedback for a greater number of homework exercises than would be possible with manually graded assignments.

In addition to the pedagogical benefits of using programming exercises, the data collected by programming exercise systems offers a detailed window into the students' habits. In this paper, we examine data collected using the CloudCoder programming exercise system in five introductory programming courses taught at three different institutions.

This paper makes the following contributions:

- We demonstrate the research potential of collecting and analyzing data from short programming exercise systems such as CodingBat and CloudCoder.
- We find a positive and consistent, although weak, correlation between a student's effort and success on CloudCoder exercises and the student's final exam score.
- We find that more difficult exercises (as measured by the average score achieved by students) require more time and effort to complete, but are not more likely to result in compilation failures.
- We explore possible indications of student struggling (*flailing*), and find that the amount of time spent on an exercise, as well as the frequency of submissions, are weakly inverse-correlated with the chance the code compiles. However, time spent and the frequency of

SIGCSE'15, March 4–7, 2015, Kansas City, MO, USA.

http://dx.doi.org/10.1145/2676723.2677297 .

submissions are *not* consistently correlated with overall success on an exercise.

- We find, unsurprisingly, that over the course of the term, the assigned exercises become more difficult, and the students become more adept at writing syntactically correct programs.

2. RELATED WORK

Numerous hurdles confront students learning to program. Many novice programmers struggle to interpret cryptic compiler error messages and fail to overcome syntax errors [12]. Logic errors generally present an even greater challenge for novices [9], and it is known that poor debugging skills can lead to the introduction of new errors, frustration, and ultimately failure in a course [3, 13].

A wide variety of tools have been developed by computing education researchers to help novice programmers. These tools can also assist researchers, as they can be used to collect data on student behavior, shedding light on the kinds of problems that students encounter and revealing strategies that prove effective. Collecting such data over an extended period of time for research purposes is one of the explicitly stated goals of the Blackbox project outlined by Brown et. al. Blackbox collects information about submissions made by students in the BlueJ environment into a central repository [5]. Given the wide adoption of BlueJ in introductory programming courses around the world, Blackbox data could potentially form the basis for vast cross-institutional studies.

Even at more modest scales, the BlueJ environment has been a rich source of data on novice programmer behavior. Jadud monitored student compilation events within individual BlueJ work sessions with a particular focus on syntax errors [11]. Certain kinds of errors occurred frequently, directing future work efforts toward helping students break out of repetitive error cycles. More fine-grained data, including basic project and file management within BlueJ, was collected by Norris et. al. using their ClockIt data logger [14]. Analysis of this data revealed that students who started work on assignment tasks earlier tended to obtain superior results, echoing the advice of many an instructor.

Automated grading tools have been another source of data used by researchers to explore student work habits. Edwards et. al. analyzed data from Web-CAT, an online tool where students iteratively submit both their source code and the set of tests used to verify their work [8]. Although student behavior was inconsistent over the course of a semester, they found that in general, better outcomes were achieved when students started working on assignments early. A similar result, showing that students who started work earlier tended to earn higher scores, was reported by Spacco et. al. from an analysis of student data collected by the Marmoset automated grading system [17].

Previous work has also examined novice behavior when solving short programming exercises, similar to those found in CodingBat [16] and CloudCoder. An example is the work of Denny et. al. with the CodeWrite tool where students create, as well as solve, the exercises [7]. Their analysis revealed that certain syntax errors consume a great deal of student time and cause significant trouble, prompting a new tool design displaying simplified error messages and associated examples [6]. In this paper, to better understand student work habits when solving short programming exercises, we explore activity data collected by the CloudCoder tool.

3. CloudCoder

CloudCoder [1, 15] is an open source, web-based programming exercise system inspired by CodingBat. It supports exercises in several programming languages, including (at the time of writing) C/C++, Java, Python, and Ruby. The system utilizes a repository of freely-redistributable exercises [2] contributed by users.

One of the goals of the CloudCoder project is to provide a platform for collecting data on how students learn to program. In support of this goal, CloudCoder collects a rich stream of data related to the process students undertake when working on programming exercises. The specific data we analyze in this paper are as follows.

Submissions When working on an exercise, students can click the Submit button to have their code compiled and tested on the server. For each submission event, CloudCoder records the full text of the submission and the result of compiling the submission. Students may submit as many times as they wish without penalty with the system using the best submission as their final score. We compute the best submission as simply the percentage of test cases the student code passes (i.e., 8 test cases passed out of 10 total test cases is 80%).

Test results If a submission compiles successfully, it is executed against each of the exercise's tests and records the test results. Possible results from executing a test are **passed** if the code's result matches the expected result, **failed** if the code's result does not match the expected result, or **exception** if the code misbehaves such as encountering a fatal runtime error or exceeding allowed CPU time.

Code edits As students edit code within CloudCoder, the underlying code editor produces a stream of insertion and deletion events which are captured and recorded. The events are fairly fine-grained: for example, as students type, the insertion events record individual characters.

All of the data described above are recorded with millisecond resolution timestamps, allowing detailed time-based analyses to be performed.

4. ANALYZED DATA SETS

We analyzed data sets collected from five courses taught at three institutions in 2013–2014. An overview of the data used in our research is available in Table 1.

4.1 CS 101 at York College

The two CS 101 course offerings at York College were CS 1 courses taught using C. CloudCoder exercises were made available to accompany the reading assignments, for exam review, and as in-class quizzes and labs. In both semesters, most of the exercises were optional, although the instructors strongly encouraged students to do them. The extent to which different students attempted to complete the exercises varied considerably.

The format of the courses differed somewhat in the two semesters. In both semesters, a substantial chunk of each class meeting was spent on in-class lab activities. In Spring 2013 each class began with a traditional lecture. In Spring

School	Term	Course	Language	# stud.	total # exercises	avg. # started	avg. # finished
York	Spring 2013	CS 1	C	133	62	37	33.9
York	Spring 2014	CS 1	C	86	53	30.2	27.4
Auckland	Fall 2013	Programming for engineers	C	740	12	11.7	11.6
Duke	Fall 2013	CS 1	Python	233	62	44.2	38.2
Duke	Spring 2014	CS 1	Python	194	55	45.2	42.2

Table 1: Overall breakdown of CloudCoder data for the three institutions and five courses.

		Auckland	York 2013	York 2014	Duke 2013	Duke 2014
num. completed vs. final exam	p-value	< 0.001*	0.083	0.004*	< 0.001*	< 0.001*
	R^2	0.089	0.030	0.119	0.231	0.386
num. attempted vs. final exam	p-value	< 0.001*	0.370	0.006*	< 0.001*	< 0.001*
	R^2	0.073	0.008	0.106	0.194	0.382
pct. completed vs. final exam	p-value	< 0.001*	< 0.001*	0.041*	< 0.001*	< 0.001*
	R^2	0.082	0.138	0.06	0.149	0.295

Table 2: Results from linear regressions. All regressions try to predict the final exam score, and all significant results show the score on the final to increase with additional work on CloudCoder. Statistically significant results are marked with a star (*).

2014 we used a fully flipped-classroom approach, with each class meeting starting with a peer instruction quiz. The students in CS 101 consisted of Computer Science, Electrical and Computer Engineering, and (in Spring 2013) Mechanical Engineering majors, along with a small number of Mathematics majors. There were also a small number of students from other majors. The decrease in class size from Spring 2013 to 2014 is due to the Mechanical Engineering program starting its own programming course in Spring 2014.

The "final" exam scores reported for both semesters of data from York are not the official final exam, but rather the last of four midterm exams. The last midterm exam took place during the last week of classes, contained only programming questions where students were asked to write code, and was cumulative; however, some of the questions emphasized topics from later in the course, such as struct types, and so may not necessarily be representative of a traditional final exam. The final exam at York is optional for students who have already achieved their desired grade, and so we have chosen not to include it.

4.2 ENGGEN 131 at University of Auckland

Over 700 students took Engineering 131 at the University of Auckland in the Fall 2013 semester. The course, required of engineering majors, taught two programming languages, C and Matlab. CloudCoder was used for one assignment, containing 12 exercises and worth about 2% of the marks for the course, during the portion of the course taught in C. CloudCoder does not support Matlab, so there were no CloudCoder exercises for that portion of the course. The final exam contained both multiple-choice and code-writing questions covering both C and Matlab. Unfortunately, we do not have the breakdown of which exam questions covered which language.

4.3 CompSci 101 at Duke University

Computer Science 101, Duke's CS 1 course, is taught using Python. Both semesters of the course included in our dataset regularly assigned CloudCoder exercises, worth about 10% of the semester grade. The final exams were traditional written exams containing about half multiple-choice and half code-writing questions; however, we only have the aggregate scores.

5. DATA ANALYSIS

The obvious question is whether CloudCoder exercises help students learn to program. Thus far, we have not been able to perform a large-scale controlled study to address this question directly. Instead, we have performed a post-hoc, exploratory analysis of the data collected by CloudCoder.

5.1 CloudCoder Exercises and Exams

To explore the relationship between CloudCoder exercises and final exam scores, we performed linear regressions of the number of CloudCoder exercises attempted and completed, as well as the percentage of exercises attempted that were completed, against the final exam score for each course in our dataset. We also compare the percent of submissions that compile for each user against their final exam score. Table 2 shows the p-value, and the coefficients of determination (R^2) for these linear regressions.

CloudCoder exercises show the strongest predictive power for the final exam at Duke, and the weakest predictive power at Auckland. This makes sense, as University of Auckland students only completed one 12-exercise CloudCoder assignment, and the final exam covered Matlab (for which there were no online exercises) as well as C; students at Duke University, on the other hand, completed regular CloudCoder assignments, and the final exam asked programming questions that were similar to these exercises.

The data from York College is mixed; it is unclear why the number of exercises attempted and answered was statistically correlated with the exam scores in 2014 but not 2013. One possible explanation is that the CloudCoder exercises were not as well integrated into the course in 2013, given that it was the first full-scale effort to include them. Another possibility was that the student population changed signif-

		Auckland	York 2013	York 2014	Duke 2013	Duke 2014
avg. num. sessions vs. avg. best score	p-value	< 0.001*	< 0.001*	< 0.001*	< 0.001*	< 0.001*
	R^2	0.702	0.770	0.593	0.218	0.654
pct. compilable subs. vs avg. best score	p-value	0.525	0.120	0.109	0.197	0.180
	R^2	0.042	0.040	0.050	0.028	0.034

Table 3: Results from linear regressions against average best score achieved by all users who attempted each exercise. Statistically significant results are marked with a star (*). Work sessions are computed by clustering keystrokes less than 10 minutes apart into work sessions.

		Auckland	York 2013	York 2014	Duke 2013	Duke 2014
total time in mins. vs. pct. compilable subs.	p-value	< 0.001*	< 0.001*	< 0.001*	< 0.001*	< 0.001*
	R^2	0.090	0.007	0.008	0.009	0.019
avg. # subs./min. vs. % compilable subs.	p-value	< 0.001*	< 0.001*	< 0.001*	< 0.001*	< 0.001*
	R^2	0.195	0.026	0.020	0.024	0.020
total time in mins. vs. best score	p-value	0.002*	< 0.001*	< 0.001*	0.034*	0.417
	R^2	0.001	0.004	0.015	< 0.001	< 0.001
avg. # subs./min. vs. best score	p-value	0.507	0.072	0.405	0.017*	0.435
	R^2	< 0.001	< 0.001	< 0.001	< 0.001	< 0.001

Table 4: Results from linear regressions of the total time spent on each exercise, and the average number of submissions per minute for each exercise, against the percent of submissions that compile, and the best score achieved on each exercise. Each data point represents all combined work sessions for a student on a particular problem. Statistically significant results are marked with a star (*). Work sessions are computed by clustering keystrokes less than 10 minutes apart into work sessions. The best score is the maximum score achieved by the student on any submission.

icantly in 2014, with Mechanical Engineering students departing. Finally, there was a significant pedagogical change in 2014, with the course being fully "flipped". In any case, the discrepancy highlights the difficulty of post-hoc analysis.

With the exception of the Spring 2013 York data, all of the relationships indicated in Table 2 are significant, although relatively weak (R^2 at most 0.38). Overall, this suggests a positive relationship between a student's engagement with CloudCoder exercises and their final exam score.

However; we must urge caution when interpreting these results. We do not know what would have happened had these courses been taught *without* CloudCoder, and so we cannot conclude that it was CloudCoder that helped, as opposed to doing homework in general. We hypothesize that CloudCoder's automation enables instructors to assign more practice exercises, which leads to more students learning, but we do not have the data to support this claim.

5.2 Evaluating CloudCoder Exercises

Table 3 explores, over each exercise, predictors of the average best score achieved by each user who attempted the exercise. We compute *average best score* by summing each student's best score on the exercise, and then dividing by the number of students. As might be expected, more difficult exercises (as evidenced by lower average best scores) strongly correlate with more effort by students, as measured by additional work sessions: i.e., students were unable to complete the exercise in a single sitting. We report regression results for the average number of work sessions for each exercise; however, we should note that many other ways of measuring effort, such as average number of minutes per user per problem, average number of keystrokes, etc., also show similar results.

We also note that there is no statistically significant relationship for any of our datasets between the percentage of submissions that compile and the average best score achieved. In other words, for the more difficult exercises, it is not more difficult for students to submit syntactically valid code.

5.3 Students Struggling in CloudCoder

One intriguing use of systems such as CloudCoder would be to detect "flailing" [9] students early enough in the term that the instructor might intervene. However, this begs the obvious question: What does *flailing* look like (i.e., students who are working unproductively, and are unlikely to make progress), and what does *learning* look like (i.e., students who are working productively)? Two common assumptions that all of the authors of this paper have heard from colleagues are 1) sometimes a student is unlikely to complete an exercise, even if given an infinite amount of time, and 2) small changes made in rapid succession with little thought are unlikely to represent productive work. We chose two metrics to represent these concepts: total amount of time spent on an exercise, and average number of submissions per minute of work.

Note that both of these metrics rely on total work time, which we compute by clustering all keystrokes within 10 minutes into the same work session. We acknowledge that this sort of clustering is course-grained, and that the 10-minute cut-off is subjective. Determining an accurate cut-off time by observing students as they work remains future work.

We present our analysis of student struggles in Table 4. Both the total amount of time spent on an exercise, and the number of submissions per minute of work, are inversely correlated with the chances that a submission would compile. In other words, the more time a student works on an exercise, or the more times they submit per minute, the less likely those submissions are to compile. However, other than at Auckland, the R^2 values are quite low, which implies that many other factors contribute to the compilability of a student's submissions.

Our potential measurements of flailing are less effective at predicting a student's best score. Three of five datasets show a statistically significant inverse relationship between minutes of work and the best score, but the relationship is weak; Duke 2013 actually shows a significant, extremely weak, *positive* relationship between minutes and best score, while Duke 2014 shows no statistical relationship. Given these results, it is hard to infer a relationship between time spent working on an exercise, and the best score achieved on that exercise. We also see essentially no relationship between the number of submissions per minute, and the best score achieved, as our only significant result is extremely weak.

One possible interpretation of the data is that short, quick code changes mean something different when the code compiles than when it does not. This data could occur because the immediate feedback from CloudCoder allows students to diagnose and fix problems quickly; however, the data could also happen because a guess-and-check style of coding is, in fact, an effective strategy for short exercise systems. Similarly, additional minutes of work may mean something different when the code compiles than when it does not, presumably because students are working on *semantics* rather than *syntax*.

These interpretations are exploratory and highly speculative, and we must stress that we cannot draw any strong conclusions without more data and a much more nuanced analysis of the data.

5.4 Improvement Over Time

Another question is whether students improve during the semester. To shed light on this question, for each student, we number the exercises in the order in which each student attempted them. The ordering is relative to each student, which means that exercise #1 may not be the same exercise for all students, because students may choose to do the exercises for an assignment in any order, may skip exercises, and may work on multiple exercises at the same time. However, even given these complications, the results in Figure 2 show a striking pattern. We can see very clearly that the exercises assigned at York College and Duke University become progressively more difficult, as evidenced by the lower average best scores achieved on later exercises (the Auckland data was a single assignment, so it is not surprising that the order in which students did the exercises mattered less than at other schools). At the same time, we clearly see that, other than the York 2013 data, the more exercises a student attempts, the *higher* the chance that future exercises will compile, which seems to show clear improvement in compilations. We are unsure why the data from York 2013 suggests that *more* practice somehow makes students worse at compiling their code. One possibility is that stronger students became less likely to do the exercises over time.

Interestingly, the data from Figure 2 suggests that students improve at compiling with practice, and that the improvement happens rapidly for C as well as Python. However, Figure 1 still reveals differences in the overall likelihood that a submission compiles between the datasets, with code written in C less likely to compile than code written in

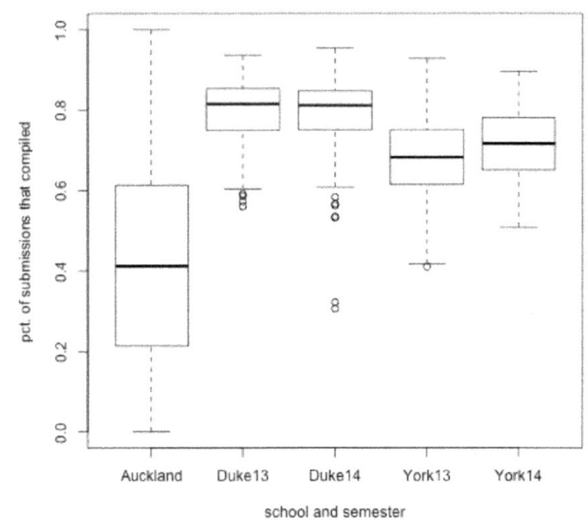

Figure 1: Boxplot of compilation percent for the five datasets. The box depicts and first and third quartiles, while the whiskers are 1.5 × IQR (interquartile range). Outliers are plotted as points.

Python. Given that many schools have switched to Python for the first programming language, at least in part due to its "easier syntax", an open question is whether the choice of language shows a measurable effect on the rate at which students learn to fix syntax errors. This is an extremely difficult question to address, as many things vary between courses taught at different institutions. A very careful and detailed analysis would be required even to begin to answer this question.

6. DISCUSSION AND FUTURE WORK

In this work, we have explored a number of interesting correlations and relationships in data collected from hundreds of novices learning to program in two different programming languages, at three different institutions.

This work represents a first look at the rich dataset we have amassed, and only scratches the surface of possible research angles. We hope to address a number of interesting questions in future work. For example, our current work only includes students who eventually took the final exam. Are there measurable differences in behaviors or outcomes, especially in the first three or four weeks of the term, between students drop the course and those who do not? Coding style is another interesting angle of study: Does code that better follows stylistic guidelines or conventions, perhaps as evaluated with a static style checker, correlate with better outcomes, and does style matter as much for shorter CloudCoder exercises as it does for longer, "nifty" assignments? Finally, there is still much to be learned about compilation and syntax errors for novices.

7. ACKNOWLEDGMENTS

This work was supported by a SIGCSE Special Projects Grant. Cloud-hosting was supported by an Amazon Web

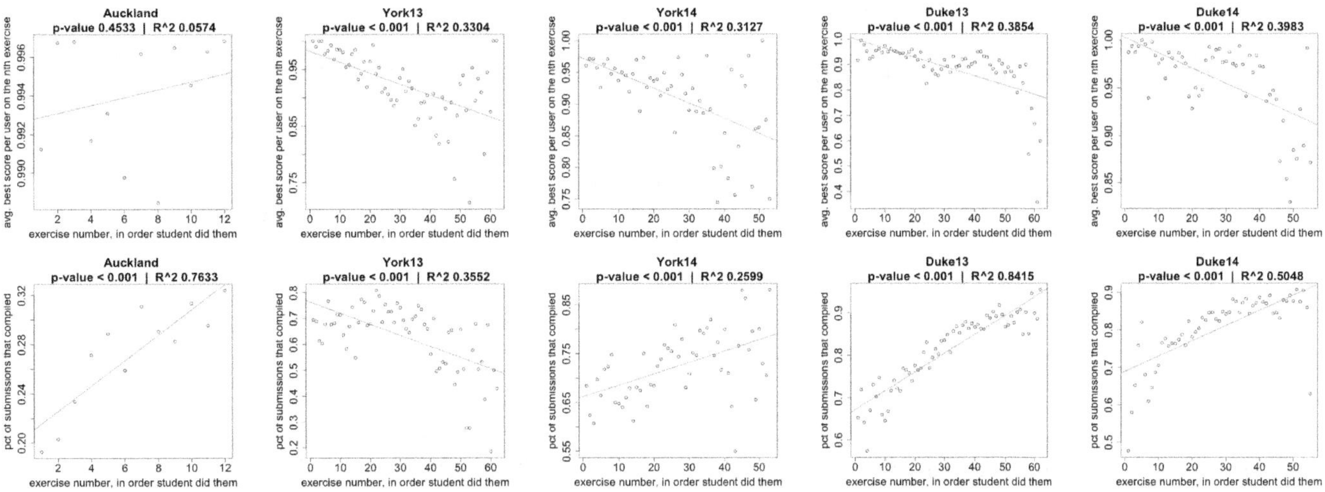

Figure 2: Results from linear regressions. The x-axis is the exercise number from the perspective of each student, i.e., 1 is the first exercise the student started working on, 2 is the second exercise, and so on. Regressions try to predict the average of the best scores achieved by each student, or the percentage of compilable submissions, for each exercise.

Services (AWS) in Education Grant. Thanks to Kevin Hastings for help with statistics.

8. REFERENCES

[1] Cloudcoder - welcome to cloudcoder! http://cloudcoder.org, June 2014.

[2] Cloudcoder exercise repository. https://cloudcoder.org/repo, June 2014.

[3] M. Ahmadzadeh, D. Elliman, and C. Higgins. An Analysis of Patterns of Debugging Among Novice Computer Science Students. *SIGCSE Bull.*, 37(3):84–88, June 2005.

[4] J. Bennedsen and M. E. Caspersen. Failure rates in introductory programming. *SIGCSE Bull.*, 39(2):32–36, June 2007.

[5] N. C. C. Brown, M. Kölling, D. McCall, and I. Utting. Blackbox: A large scale repository of novice programmers' activity. In *Proc. SIGCSE '14*, SIGCSE '14, pages 223–228, New York, NY, USA, 2014. ACM.

[6] P. Denny, A. Luxton-Reilly, and D. Carpenter. Enhancing syntax error messages appears ineffectual. In *Proc. ITiCSE '14*, ITiCSE '14, pages 273–278, New York, NY, USA, 2014. ACM.

[7] P. Denny, A. Luxton-Reilly, and E. Tempero. All syntax errors are not equal. In *Proc. ITiCSE '12*, ITiCSE '12, pages 75–80, New York, NY, USA, 2012. ACM.

[8] S. H. Edwards, J. Snyder, M. A. Pérez-Quiñones, A. Allevato, D. Kim, and B. Tretola. Comparing effective and ineffective behaviors of student programmers. In *Proc. ICER '09*, ICER '09, pages 3–14, New York, NY, USA, 2009. ACM.

[9] S. Fitzgerald, G. Lewandowski, R. McCauley, L. Murphy, B. Simon, L. Thomas, and C. Zander. Debugging: Finding, Fixing and Flailing, a Multi-institutional Study of Novice Debuggers. *Computer Science Education*, 18(2):93–116, 2008.

[10] D. Hovemeyer, M. Hertz, P. Denny, J. Spacco, A. Papancea, J. Stamper, and K. Rivers. Cloudcoder: building a community for creating, assigning, evaluating and sharing programming exercises (abstract only). In *Proc. SIGCSE '13*, SIGCSE '13, pages 742–742, New York, NY, USA, 2013. ACM.

[11] M. C. Jadud. Methods and tools for exploring novice compilation behaviour. In *Proc. ICER '06*, ICER '06, pages 73–84, New York, NY, USA, 2006. ACM.

[12] S. K. Kummerfeld and J. Kay. The Neglected Battle Fields of Syntax Errors. In *Proc. ACE '03*, ACE '03, pages 105–111, Darlinghurst, Australia, Australia, 2003. Australian Computer Society, Inc.

[13] L. Murphy, G. Lewandowski, R. McCauley, B. Simon, L. Thomas, and C. Zander. Debugging: The Good, the Bad, and the Quirky – a Qualitative Analysis of Novices' Strategies. *SIGCSE Bull.*, 40(1):163–167, Mar. 2008.

[14] C. Norris, F. Barry, J. B. Fenwick Jr., K. Reid, and J. Rountree. Clockit: collecting quantitative data on how beginning software developers really work. In *Proc. ITiCSE '08*, ITiCSE '08, pages 37–41, New York, NY, USA, 2008. ACM.

[15] A. Papancea, J. Spacco, and D. Hovemeyer. An open platform for managing short programming exercises. In *Proc. ICER '13*, ICER '13, pages 47–52. ACM.

[16] N. Parlante. Nifty Reflections. *SIGCSE Bull.*, 39(2):25–26, June 2007.

[17] J. Spacco, D. Fossati, J. Stamper, and K. Rivers. Towards improving programming habits to create better computer science course outcomes. In *Proc. ITiCSE '13*, ITiCSE '13, pages 243–248, 2013. ACM.

Teaching Computing as Science in a Research Experience

Jerod Weinman
Dept. of Computer Science
Grinnell College
jerod@acm.org

David Jensen
School of Computer Science
Univ. Massachusetts Amherst
jensen@cs.umass.edu

David Lopatto
Dept. of Psychology
Grinnell College
lopatto@grinnell.edu

ABSTRACT

Many instructors and institutions offer research experiences and training in computing research methods. However, in a national survey, we find that undergraduate students rate their computing research experiences lower than students in other STEM fields. To address this learning gap, we have offered summer undergraduate research experiences in computing that include not only instruction in the important mechanics of research but also grounding in a philosophy of computing science that emphasizes generalized explanation of behavior as a means for control and prediction. After five years, survey results indicate the experience helps close the gap between CS and other STEM fields in benefits gained.

Categories and Subject Descriptors

K.3.2 [**Computers and Education**]: Computer and Information Science Education—*Computer science education*

General Terms

Experimentation

Keywords

Undergraduate research; survey of undergraduate research experiences (SURE); *ergalics*; research methods; situated learning

1. INTRODUCTION

Training computing students in research often involves two core elements: explicit instruction in formal research *methods* and a mentored research *experience*. Over the past few decades, teachers and researchers have proposed many curricula for teaching computing research methods, published numerous experience reports, and held a striking array of conference panels offering advice. This work presents a curriculum for an apprenticed undergraduate research experience that integrates research methods training with an emphasis on computing as a science.

Many authors stress the need for some explicit instruction in formal research *methods*. Holz et al. [16] developed a helpful framework of core and specific skills for reasoning about computing research methods. Some instructors and institutions teach these skills in stand-alone courses offering instruction on various combinations of assessing literature, formulating research questions, preparing formal proposals, designing experiments, analyzing statistics, and communicating results [37, 11, 35, 28, 32, 15, 19].

While methods are important, the undergraduate research *experience* also provides positive benefits. Using the survey of undergraduate research experiences (SURE), Lopatto [22] showed that such experiences in the sciences generally do enhance students' educational experiences, attract students to research careers, and help retain minority students. In computing, several research experience models exist: an integrated curriculum [29, 14], a universal capstone course [30, 34, 19], or the traditional apprenticeship model [4, 36, 18, 27, 7]. Despite these efforts, this work shows that a significant learning gap persists between undergraduate research experiences in computing and the other STEM fields.

Barker [2] found that outcomes of undergraduate computing research experiences depend heavily on the mentor, emphasizing the importance of project structure. However, a recent survey of computer science instructors by Matzen and Alrifai [23] found mixed agreement over the research experience structure. Faculty strongly agreed (over 90%) that "undergraduate research" required some literature search and presentation to peers and faculty. Yet there was hardly consensus about whether student work must "use the scientific method" (62%) or some other "formal process" (67%).

This lack of consensus likely reflects the variety of views and practices in the computing field: engineering, theoretical, and empirical [10]. The latter view is now particularly important, as Denning argues that computing is more than Simon's "science of the artificial"; computing is a natural science [9]. Snodgrass labels this computing research philosophy *ergalics*, stressing the search for predictive, causal models of computation and computational tools [33] with a process applicable across the computing spectrum, including systems [8], algorithm theory [20], and AI [25].

In this paper, we present the results of a national survey gathered over five years that indicate computer science students consistently report lesser benefits from their research experiences than students in other STEM fields (Section 2). To help remedy this issue, we have offered an apprenticeship-based summer research experience that emphasizes not only scientific methodology, but also the philosophy of computing as a science (Section 3). We find that our student cohort reports benefits that more closely match those of the broader STEM student population (Section 4).

2. RESEARCH EXPERIENCE SURVEY

The survey of undergraduate research experiences (SURE) was designed by Lopatto to measure the benefits to students at a broad

SIGCSE'15, March 4–7, 2015, Kansas City, MO, USA.

http://dx.doi.org/10.1145/2676723.2677231.

array of institutions and determine whether research experiences were attracting and retaining students to careers in scientific research.[1] The principal conclusions of the original study were that research enhanced students' educational experiences and sustained or increased their interest in pursuing further education [22].

These findings continue to hold in ten years' of survey data. In this paper, we report on surveys collected from 2009-2013, restricting our analysis to STEM fields (i.e., excluding humanities and social sciences); see Figure 1. Students report on experiences at a variety of institution types. Over 70% of CS students' surveys come from experiences at baccalaureate colleges (compared to 46% for other STEM fields). Due to our institutional context (cf. Section 3.1), we compare to baccalaureate colleges only, though trends are the same for other institution types.

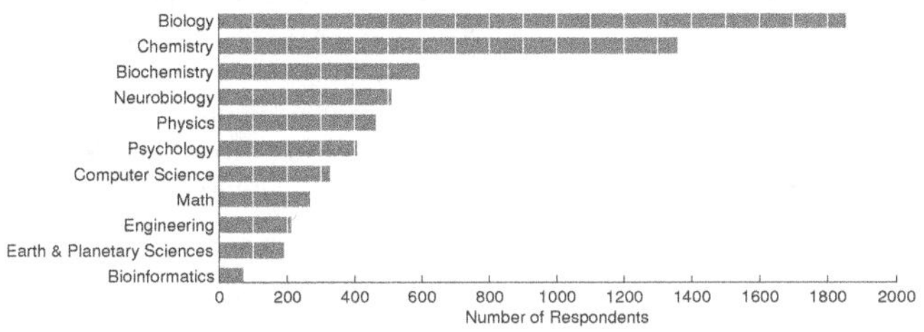

Figure 1: Survey respondents' field of research.

Surveys from computing students ($n \leq 326$) differ significantly from other STEM fields' ($n \leq 6155$) in several ways.

Before their experience, computing students report plans for some form of graduate education at a lower rate: 62% CS vs. 91% STEM. Strong job markets for baccalaureate computing graduates likely contribute to this gap. Few computing students lose a prior interest in graduate school after their experience. However, among those initially not interested, relatively few gain interest after their experience: 29% CS ($n = 103$) versus 57% STEM ($n = 492$). This gap suggests an opportunity for computing faculty to do more to introduce students to a "culture of research" [2].

Table 1: Influence of research experience on interest in graduate education.

	n	Gained Interest	Sustained Interest	No Plans/ Interest	Lost Interest
STEM	5771.	4.9 %	90.3 %	3.7 %	1.1 %
CS	274.	10.9 %	60.2 %	26.6 %	2.2 %

Computing students also consistently report lower gains on a variety of benefits from the experience (see Section 4.1 and Figure 4). We examined other correlates to identify possible explanations for these differences. Computing students work with other undergraduates on a single project much more often than other STEM students (43% vs. 19%), though rates for working on similar but independent projects are more comparable (35% for CS vs. 49%), as are individual projects (20% for CS vs. 17%). However, both populations responded positively (80%) to working with other students. Regarding their research mentors, CS students do not rate them as highly ($p < 10^{-4}$; $\hat{P}_{\text{STEM}>\text{CS}} = 0.565$).[2] They also give inferior evaluations of comparisons to their expectations ($p < .005$; $\hat{P}_{\text{STEM}>\text{CS}} = 0.548$) and the overall experience ($p < .0005$; $\hat{P}_{\text{STEM}>\text{CS}} = 0.552$). See Figure 2.

[1] `http://www.grinnell.edu/academics/areas/psychology/assessnebts/sure-iii-survey`

[2] As ordinal data, all findings of significance are established by a two-tailed Mann-Whitney U test. The common language effect size $\hat{P}_{A>B} = U/mn$ is the probability that a random instance from population A ranks higher than one from population B [13].

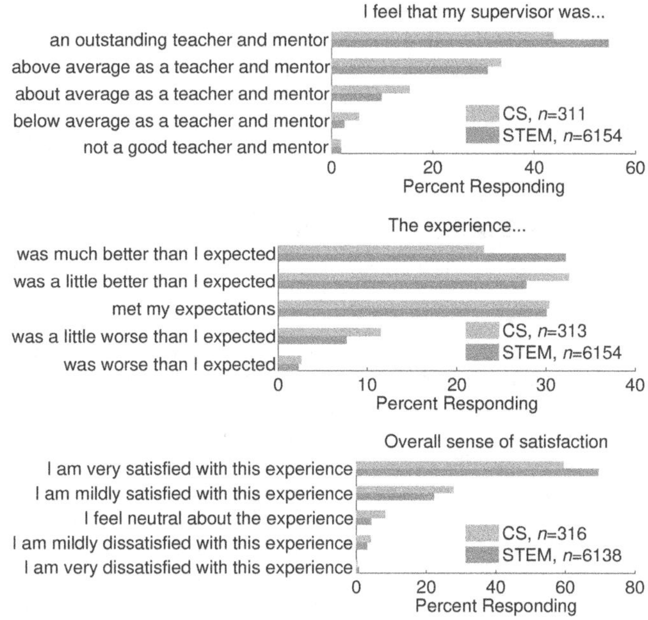

Figure 2: Responses regarding overall experience.

3. TEACHING COMPUTING RESEARCH

In this section we first briefly highlight the motivating philosophy of our approach to narrowing the gap in learning gains. We then describe the institutional context for the undergraduate apprenticeship and the program's essential elements.

Undergraduate research training in computing ranges from laboratory exercises emphasizing empirical measurement, to research skills courses, to independent study/capstone projects or apprenticeship experiences. Many research methods courses teach important *research mechanics* (e.g., proposal, review, presentation). We also emphasize an underlying *empirical philosophy* sometimes neglected by students and practitioners promoting theoretical and problem-solving views of the discipline. In particular, as Snodgrass points out, "Science seeks general, predictive theories that describe and explain observed phenomena" [33, p. 3]. We repeatedly impress this notion upon our students, often through Cohen's comparison of computational behavior to psychology: "Whether your subject is a rat or a computer program, the task of science is the same," [6, p. 3] namely to understand how the system, task, and environment interact to influence behavior (Figure 3).

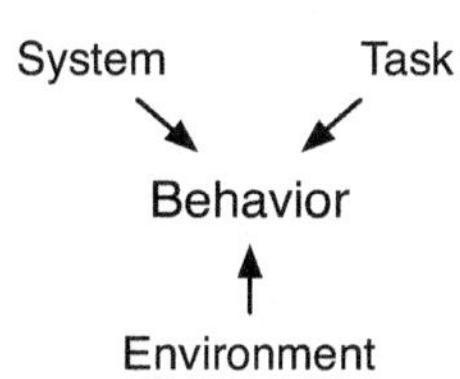

Figure 3: Behavioral influences (after Cohen [6, p. 3], © MIT).

This undergraduate program grew out of a graduate research methods course taught since 2005 by Jensen at UMass Amherst, a comprehensive doctoral program with very high research productivity. (Weinman was a student in the 2005 course.) While the substance of the lectures and writing assignments are nearly identical, many of the graduate course's discussions feature additional *career coaching* and more *statistical methods*. The undergraduate program emphasizes the philosophy of empirical methods for knowledge discovery.

3.1 Institutional context

Grinnell College is a private, highly selective liberal arts college of about 1600 students. For summer research, faculty secure funding for student stipends from the College or (less frequently) external grants. Grinnell's students apply to work on a faculty members' projects or (in rarer cases) may propose their own, and faculty use their own varying criteria in selecting students. A ten-week, full-time summer research project bears four credits, equivalent to a typical course. To ensure College-wide standards, an Associate Dean must review and grant advance approval to a project proposal prepared by the student, usually under close faculty supervision.

The full-time summer research experience uses *legitimate peripheral participation* (LPP) [3]. In LPP, learners are invited to participate in a community of practice (in this case, both the institutional and global computing research community) with an ever-increasing participatory scope. Contextualized learning allows us to emphasize the scientific process and philosophy underlying students' efforts on a real problem.

Although we report institutional context for completeness, we believe the practices outlined below may be applied to any research experience in any institutional context, whether or not the experience is during the academic year or summer, paid or credit-bearing, and regardless of whether the project is primarily the faculty or student's choice. While an apprenticed summer context increases the odds for success, the guiding philosophy and many structural elements have broad application beyond that context.

We use a mixture of implicit and explicit teaching. Whereas undergraduates can easily become overwhelmed by the field's vastness, we prefer often to focus on broad principles and highlight specifics (e.g., statistical tests) as needs arise.

The remainder of this section describes the "curriculum" of the embedded course on research methods and a philosophy of computing science, regular tangible deliverables, and other meetings and activities that structure the work. For additional details, examples, and writing prompts, see the accompanying archived materials.[3]

3.2 Lecture and discussion

We dedicate at least one hour per week to a lecture and discussion (a one-to-few studio model [16]) covering the typical elements of a research skills class while also stressing how the generalities of the scientific method apply to computing:

Computing as science Causal explanations, preferred to descriptions or context, require a careful experimental approach.

Reproducible research Version control and data management.

Selecting projects Framing and assessing research questions.

Scientific activities Question, conjecture, generalize, etc.

Research literature Why and how to read, write, and publish.

Challenges of science Intrinsic, individual, and social.

Exploratory analysis Prioritizing raw data and behavior visualization over model imposition and statistics.

Causality and inference Association, direction, and common cause elimination; deduction, induction, and abduction.

Hypotheses and falsifiability Types and degrees, respectively.

Experiments Designs, validity, and threats.

We integrate many stories from the history and biography of science. For example, the first lecture uses the Wright brothers as a case study demonstrating how focused scientific investigation can underpin rapid technological development. Many topics have "proximal" aims to increase the likelihood of the particular students' success on their project, but many others have only "ultimate" aims to help students become better researchers in graduate training and beyond. Some topics serve both aims. *Reproducible research* introduces students to the project source code version control system and our lab-specific means of recording and replicating experiments;[4] Weinman and prior students have written significant content in both source code and experimental data repositories, which motivates clear documentation either by its helpful presence or conspicuous absence. To develop students' taste in problems, *selecting projects* discusses both Cohen's tripartite framework for research problems (Figure 3) and the "Medawar zone" [21], a conceptual tool for considering the inherent tradeoff between payoff and probability of success. We then exhort students to think broadly so that they undertake a wide range of *scientific activities* in their search for understanding. Keshav [17] and Fong [12] give helpful advice for reading *research literature*. Amid the *challenges of science*, we stress that incomplete knowledge makes science intrinsically hard, individual scientists may have biases or flaws (cf. Bacon's "Idols of the Mind"), and the research community as a human endeavor can suffer from fads, outdated traditions, hobbling disagreements, and outsized personalities. *Exploratory analysis* [26] catalyzes research questions by investigating (often visually) how changes to the system, task, and/or environment influence behavior [6]; Anscombe's quartet (radically different data with nine identical statistics) provides a cautionary tale [1]. In *causality and inference* we stress that explanation is more complete than predictions provided by correlation, and the concomitant control allows us to design effective systems more efficiently. We introduce an ontology of *hypotheses* (existential, compositional, correlational, and causal) and relate Popper's *falsifiability* criteria. *Experimental design* discusses standard methods topics, such as validity (i.e., statistical, internal, external, and construct) and its attentive threats (e.g., range effects, selection, novelty) [31]. In sum, we hope to nurture students' search for general explanations and encourage them to think broadly and critically about hypotheses.

3.3 Writing assignments

These weekly discussions link closely with concrete writing assignments due every 1-2 weeks, the primary course deliverables:

Research description Catalog system, task, environment, and behavior entities and relations, defining the research ontology.

Assessment of current knowledge Critically review papers.

Exploration Visualize behavior and task/environment interactions.

Proposal Identify a research question and hypotheses, sketch methodology, and assess validity.

Experimental design Describe variables, protocol, and analysis.

Experimental results Organize outcomes and draw conclusions.

The *research description* should allow someone to design (rather than implement) the system in question and describe key resources

[3]Lecture slides: `http://dx.doi.org/11084/10002`
Syllabus and assignments: `http://dx.doi.org/11084/10000`

[4]Data repository: `http://dx.doi.org/11084/10001`

(e.g., benchmarks, simulation environments, etc.), noting how well these cover the range of key variables. A deadline at the end of week two allows sufficient time to both learn and write about the system. By week three, students propose at least four papers to review in their *assessment of current knowledge*, allowing the instructor to give essential early feedback on relevance and quality. The review itself, due in week four, asks students to explain others' findings, describe their relevance to their own investigations, and identify gaps in the literature with a synthesis that goes beyond recounting methods. The behavioral and data *exploration* (week five) helps establish directions for research questions by identifying cases of unexpected behavior or unexplored variations in the system, task, and/or environment. This report also introduces considerations for visual communication. Ideally, the proposal required by the College in advance of the apprenticeship would integrate elements of these first three reports. However, learning the requisite background skills and producing a viable proposal for a clearly defined research project both take significant effort [35]. Thus, we have much higher expectations for the highly specific *research proposal* due at the end of week six. Students must position their research question at the knowledge frontier (using their prior assessment), identify falsifiable hypotheses (noting the type, preferably causal), explain how both are motivated by their exploration, and state what the community gains by establishing or rejecting the hypotheses. To guide critical thinking, we ask students to sketch experimental protocols and assess their validity, stringency (avoiding false acceptance), and reliability (avoiding false rejection). Due the following week, the *experimental design* must describe the variables to be measured and categorize them with respect to data type (ordinal, etc.) and status (dependent, randomized, etc.). The protocol for obtaining measurements should be included along with the method of analysis. The *experimental results* of week nine ask for a comparison to expectations and discussion of substantive significance. Reproducibility is expected from proper management of all data and code, which are also submitted. A *final report* integrates content and feedback on each of the milestone reports in the format of a conference or journal paper.

Along the way, students learn document preparation tools (e.g., LaTeX), use version control for supporting software, and document their empirical work in a formal data management system. While reports are informally peer reviewed, experimental code and documentation undergo a formal peer review before submission to the instructor for evaluation.

3.4 Other regular activities

Several other meetings and activities enhance and reinforce the twin objectives of learning and practicing scientific research. Using e-mail as a lightweight mechanism, students and faculty send a *today message* to the entire group [5]. The bulleted activity diary provides semi-public accountability, a searchable record, and opportunities for regular feedback. For medium-range planning, the group meets for *Monday morning milestones*. Each team orally presents their week's plans to the group in a miniature research proposal, noting the explicit motivation, process, and desired outcome or assessment metric for each goal on a whiteboard. All are invited to ask questions and provide feedback. In contrast to the Today message's activity diary, on Friday individuals (rather than teams) *review their week* with an oral presentation of accomplishments or new conclusions. We also ask them to provide metacognitive reflections on their learning, giving students who do not have concrete results something to present and enhancing all participants' awareness of their budding research skills. Because the experience is ultimately graded, students rate their partner's ongoing effort (rather than ability) as well as their own on a simple rubric.

All computing faculty and students (not just the authors' group) also gather midweek to give brief (twenty minute) progress presentations to one another in a *scholarly community*. These semi-informal sessions allow students to practice communicating about their work to a larger audience, solicit wider feedback on their plans or current roadblocks, and conversely provide peer review as audience participants. The instructor evaluates the presentation content for motivation, clarity, preparation, visual materials, and oral skills,[5] giving prompt verbal feedback and often asking peers what they thought was well done or needed improvement.

4. PROGRAM EVALUATION

We concur with Walker [24] and others [2, 19] regarding the need for a structured process with deliverables. However, we view the paper-writing process as secondary to the scientific process our written milestones are designed to engage. We believe the evaluations below reflect this emphasis.

4.1 Survey results

Adapting Jensen's efforts to an undergraduate context, from summers 2009-2014 (except 2012), Weinman has involved one or two pairs of students in his research on computer vision and machine learning, a cohort of 16 students in total. Each summer, an average of 13 ($\hat{\sigma} = 5.4$) students participated in department activities over the same time period.

Figure 4 illustrates the responses of three non-overlapping populations to questions about "a variety of possible benefits you may have gained from your research experience." Possible ordinal responses measure benefits gained: no gain/very small, small, moderate, large, or very large gain. For visualization, Figure 4 (left) graphs the mean response ranks (treated as interval data) of each population. For comparative analysis, Figure 4 (right) graphs effect size $\hat{P}_{A>B}$, the probability that a random member of population A reports a greater benefit than a random member of population B.

As noted earlier, computing students ($213 \leq n \leq 306$; $\bar{n} = 281$) report significantly lower gains on these learning outcomes than do students from other STEM fields ($5727 \leq n \leq 6154$; $\bar{n} = 6031$). Conversely, responses of our cohort ($9 \leq n \leq 12$; $\bar{n} = 12$; $N = 16$) show no significant difference from the broader STEM population, save one: Skill in science writing ($p < 0.035$; $\hat{P}_{JW>STEM} = 0.67$). In addition, eleven of the twenty-one self-reported learning gains of our cohort are significantly higher than those of the broader CS population. The marginal benefits (i.e., total counts over all 21 survey items) show a significant and substantive difference between our cohort and the broader CS population ($p < 10^{-14}$, $\hat{P}_{JW>CS} = 0.639$), but no difference compared to the other STEM fields.

While prior experience could explain the substantial differences in *gain*, CS students report *no* prior research experience over 50% more often than STEM students. However, nearly all (92%) of our respondents began with no prior experience.

4.2 Discussion

Triangulating these self-evaluations, we note that two pairs of our students later co-authored peer reviewed articles with another in preparation, three pairs of students have contributed technical reports for public experimental benchmark data, and half of the students who have graduated (six are still undergraduates) have indeed gone on to some graduate education.

[5]These criteria align (in compressed format) with the *Competent Speaker Speech Evaluation Form* developed by the National Communication Association, as noted by Havill and Ludwig [15].

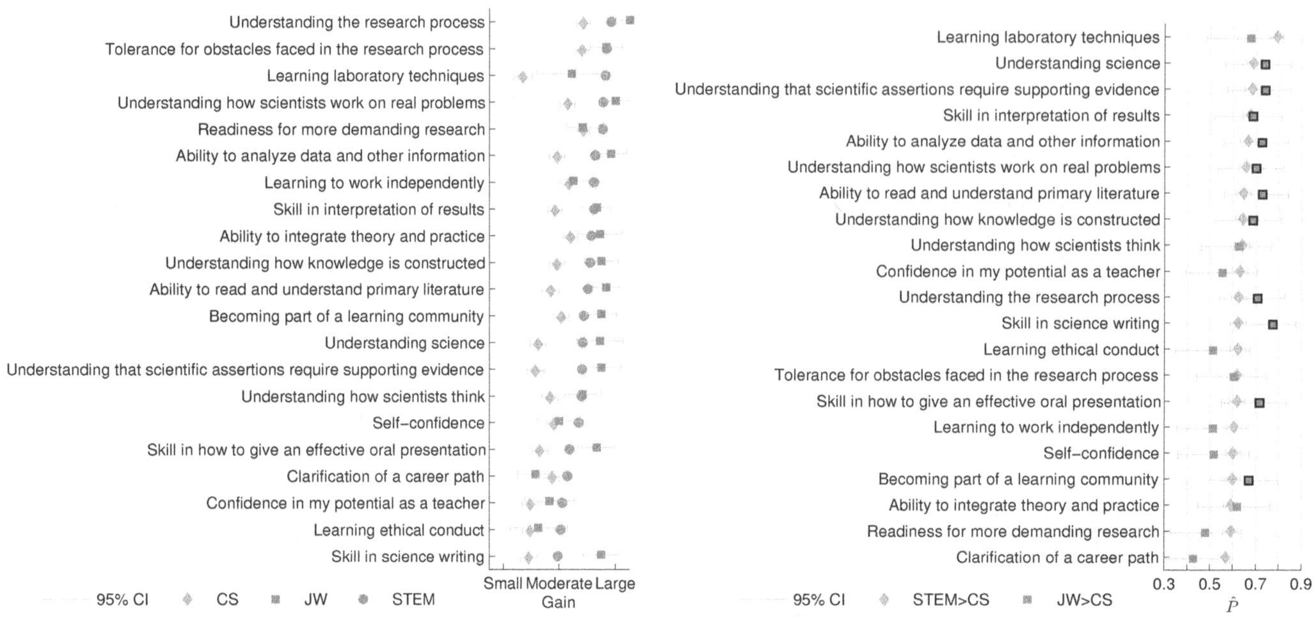

Figure 4: Respondents' learning gains. Left: Response rank means ("Very Small" and "Very Large" options not plotted). Right: Rank effect sizes (see text). All $\hat{P}_{\text{STEM>CS}}$ significant ($p < 10^{-4}$) but only one $\hat{P}_{\text{STEM>JW}}$; significant $\hat{P}_{\text{JW>CS}}$ ($p < 0.05$) in bold outline.

Our written milestones effectively require that students accomplish something, even if those results are narrow with respect to the larger project. We do note several objectively successful experiences: PI's conjectures falsified, important research system software developed, benchmark and model data curated, and contributions to top-ranking performances on international benchmarks.

Students' metacognitive reflections are often the most revealing part of the experience, ranging from variants of "I wish I knew then what I know now" to frequent comments about learning how to communicate better, think more clearly, and work productively.

This evaluation certainly is not a controlled study; such an attempt would be implausible and perhaps unethical [22, p. 130]. Disentangling the effect of the individual mentor is difficult, yet it seems linked to other outcomes (cf. Section 2). We find no significant differences between our students' evaluations of their supervisor and those of the STEM or broader CS populations. As an alternative control, when we compare our undergraduate cohort to other summer computing research programs at the same institution, we find the same (even better) improvements in benefits. Those programs have emphasized advanced project apprenticeship (often software development) over scientific research, suggesting the emphasis of the summer experience matters.

4.3 Related findings

Our survey results corroborate Barker's analysis of NSF-supported undergraduate research opportunities, which (as of 2006) found computing students "were less likely to participate in the 'culture of research' than students of several other STEM majors" [2, p. 5:5].

Several authors report the advantages of many practices similar to ours. Nearly all cited above mention similar content on literature reviews, experimental designs, and statistical methods. Regarding peer mentoring and review, Walker and Slotterbeck [34] note that students working on their second independent research project can help mentor others. While Weinman has not yet had repeat students in the lab (many either graduate or opt for diversity with a subsequent off-campus summer research experience in a different area or a traditional industry internship), we do find that students with more experience in particular areas (regardless of class year) serve effectively as informal mentors, as reflected in peer effort surveys. Although Havill and Ludwig [15] use formal peer review of oral presentations, our informal practice of verbal debriefing as a group seems effective, satisfactory, and less time consuming. Koppelman et al. [19] use formal peer review for proposals and the final research product. In our experience, formative reviews and feedback from peers and mentors, whether informal or formal, seem to be helpful for students in *all* milestones and activities. We believe these to be important elements of the program.

The benefits of community arise repeatedly. Baldwin, Kumar, and Musicant all independently emphasize the importance of group meetings and research teams [24]; Dahlberg et al. [7] also mention the social cohort, which is the primary mechanism of Bernat et al. [4]. Our scholarly community and complementary plans/progress presentations help instantiate these in a concrete way.

5. CONCLUSIONS

Barker's study [2] underscores the importance of structure in an undergraduate research experience and reminds mentors not to assume students know what it means to do research. Although the plethora of panels, publications, and courses on the subject suggest we know this well, computing research experiences rate below those in other STEM fields. Fortunately, few students are dissuaded from pursuing graduate education, though surveys indicate the discipline could do more to attract students to research careers.

Our program attempts to improve the outcomes of students' research experiences, and evidence suggests we have been successful. Surveys do not explain why students seem to benefit less from research experiences in computing than those in other STEM fields, but our interventions indicate a real effect on student learning, particularly with respect to analysis, communication, and many aspects of scientific and research methods.

While Dante suggests we must sometimes be "content with the *quia*" (the "what" rather than the "why"),[6] Virgil offers a potential explanation our students may have found: *Felix, qui potuit rerum cognoscere causas* (happy is the one who has been able to know the causes of things).[7]

Acknowledgments

We thank our students who have enriched these experiences. Weinman and Lopatto thank Grinnell College and HHMI for support of the SURE survey and several summer research students.

6. REFERENCES

[1] F. J. Anscombe. Graphs in statistical analysis. *The American Statistician*, 27(1):17–21, Feb. 1973.

[2] L. Barker. Student and faculty perceptions of undergraduate research experiences in computing. *Trans. Comput. Educ.*, 9(1):5:1–5:28, Mar. 2009.

[3] M. Ben-Ari. Situated learning in computer science education. *Computer Science Education*, 14(2):85–100, 2004.

[4] A. Bernat, P. J. Teller, A. Gates, and N. Delgado. Structuring the student research experience. In *Proc. ITiCSE*, pages 17–20, 2000.

[5] A. B. Brush and A. Borning. 'Today' messages: Lightweight support for small group awareness via email. In *Proc. Hawaii Int. Conf. System Sciences*, page 16a. IEEE, 2005.

[6] P. R. Cohen. *Empirical methods for artificial intelligence*. MIT Press, 1995.

[7] T. Dahlberg, T. Barnes, A. Rorrer, E. Powell, and L. Cairco. Improving retention and graduate recruitment through immersive research experiences for undergraduates. In *Proc. SIGCSE*, pages 466–470, 2008.

[8] P. J. Denning. The locality principle. *Commun. ACM*, 48(7):19–24, July 2005.

[9] P. J. Denning. Computing is a natural science. *Commun. ACM*, 50(7):13–18, July 2007.

[10] P. J. Denning, D. E. Comer, D. Gries, M. C. Mulder, A. Tucker, A. J. Turner, and P. R. Young. Computing as a discipline. *Commun. ACM*, 32(1):9–23, Jan. 1989.

[11] A. Fekete. Preparation for research: Instruction in interpreting and evaluating research. In *Proc. SIGCSE*, pages 93–97, 1996.

[12] P. W. Fong. Reading a computer science research paper. *SIGCSE Bulletin*, 41(2):138–140, 2009.

[13] R. J. Grissom. Probability of the superior outcome of one treatment over another. *J. Applied Psych.*, 79(2):314–316, 1994.

[14] S. Hadfield and D. Schweitzer. Building an undergraduate computer science research experience. In *Proc. IEEE Intl. Conf. Frontiers in Education*, pages 1193–1198, 2009.

[15] J. T. Havill and L. D. Ludwig. Technically speaking: Fostering the communication skills of computer science and mathematics students. In *Proc. SIGCSE*, pages 185–189, 2007.

[16] H. J. Holz, A. Applin, B. Haberman, D. Joyce, H. Purchase, and C. Reed. Research methods in computing: What are they, and how should we teach them? In *Working Group Reports on ITiCSE*, pages 96–114, 2006.

[6] Dante Alighieri, *Purgatory*, Canto III

[7] Virgil, *Georgic* (II, v. 490)

[17] S. Keshav. How to read a paper. *SIGCOMM Computer Communication Review*, 37(3):83–84, 2007.

[18] A. Koeller. Experiences with student research at a primarily undergraduate institution. *J. Comput. Sci. Coll.*, 20(3):181–187, Feb. 2005.

[19] H. Koppelman, B. van Dijk, and G. van der Hoeven. Undergraduate research: A case study. In *Proc. ITiCSE*, pages 288–292, 2011.

[20] K. Leyton-Brown, H. H. Hoos, F. Hutter, and L. Xu. Understanding the empirical hardness of NP-complete problems. *Commun. ACM*, 57(5):98–107, May 2014.

[21] C. Loehle. A guide to increased creativity in research: Inspiration or perspiration? *Bioscience*, 40(2):123–129, Feb. 1990.

[22] D. Lopatto. Exploring the benefits of undergraduate research: The SURE survey. In *Creating Effective Undergraduate Research Programs in Science*, pages 112–132. Teacher's College Press, NY, 2008.

[23] R. Matzen and R. Alrifai. Defining undergraduate research in computer science: A survey of computer science faculty. *J. Comput. Sci. Coll.*, 27(3):31–37, Jan. 2012.

[24] D. Musicant, A. Kumar, D. Baldwin, and E. Walker. Mechanics of undergraduate research at liberal arts colleges: Lessons learned. In *Proc. SIGCSE*, pages 65–66, 2007.

[25] A. Newell and H. A. Simon. Computer science as empirical inquiry: Symbols and search. *Commun. ACM*, 19(3):113–126, Mar. 1976.

[26] NIST/SEMATECH. *e-Handbook of Statistical Methods*, chapter Exploratory Data Analysis. 2012. `http://www.itl.nist.gov/div898/handbook/eda/eda.htm`.

[27] J. Peckham, P. Stephenson, J.-Y. Hervé, R. Hutt, and M. Encarnação. Increasing student retention in computer science through research programs for undergraduates. In *Proc. SIGCSE*, pages 124–128, 2007.

[28] A. M. Quade. Promoting undergraduate research: A classroom model. In *Proc. ITiCSE*, pages 235–235, 2004.

[29] D. Reed, C. Miller, and G. Braught. Empirical investigation throughout the CS curriculum. In *Proc. SIGCSE*, pages 202–206, 2000.

[30] G. M. Schneider. A new model for a required senior research experience. *SIGCSE Bull.*, 34(4):48–51, Dec. 2002.

[31] W. R. Shadish, T. D. Cook, and D. T. Campbell. *Experimental and quasi-experimental designs for generalized causal inference*. Houghton Mifflin, 2002.

[32] C. A. Shaffer. Experiences teaching a graduate research methods course. *SIGCSE Bull.*, 38(2):97–101, June 2006.

[33] R. T. Snodgrass. *Ergalics*: A natural science of computation. `http://www.cs.arizona.edu/projects/focal/ergalics/files/ergalics.pdf`.

[34] E. L. Walker and O. A. Slotterbeck. Integrated research components: A practical and effective alternative to senior projects. *J. Comput. Sci. Coll.*, 22(1):72–83, Oct. 2006.

[35] K. Ward. The fifty-four day thesis proposal: First experiences with a research course. *J. Comput. Sci. Coll.*, 20(2):94–109, Dec. 2004.

[36] E. Wenderholm. Challenges and the elements of success in undergraduate research. *SIGCSE Bull.*, 36(4):73–75, June 2004.

[37] I. H. Witten and T. C. Bell. Getting research students started: A tale of two courses. In *Proc. SIGCSE*, pages 165–169, 1993.

Backward Design: An Integrated Approach to a Systems Curriculum

Michael S. Kirkpatrick, Mohamed Aboutabl, David Bernstein, Sharon Simmons
Department of Computer Science
James Madison University
{kirkpams,aboutams,bernstdh,simmonsj}@jmu.edu

Categories and Subject Descriptors

K.3.2 [**Computing Milieux**]: Computer and Information Science Education—*Computer science education*

General Terms

Human Factors

Keywords

ACM curriculum; systems fundamentals; backward design

ABSTRACT

This paper summarizes our experiences restructuring a core portion of our required courses for majors. Internal and external reviews of our program highlighted areas of concern in our "systems core," including inconsistent student outcomes, missing required material, and inadequate opportunities for programmatic assessment. To fix these problems, we initiated a curricular review to redesign these courses. Our novel approach employed a process known as *backward course design* that starts with desired student outcomes and works backward toward defining content coverage. By extending this design approach to our curriculum as a whole, we have defined a new systems core structure that has tightly integrated curriculum assessment opportunities. The result is a new systems core that changes almost 1/3 of the required courses for the major. This new structure provides increased student control over their learning goals while defining a consistent foundation of systems fundamentals; it also has tightly integrated program objectives and assessments. Applying the backward design philosophy to the curriculum, rather than to a single, pre-defined course, is both a rewarding and challenging experience. In this paper, we describe this approach, summarize the results of the process, and map the outcomes to the ACM 2013 curriculum. We also provide advice and lessons learned for others who may consider such an undertaking.

SIGCSE'15, March 4–7, 2015, Kansas City, MO, USA.

ACM 978-1-4503-2966-8/15/03 ...$15.00.
http://dx.doi.org/10.1145/2676723.2677264.

1. INTRODUCTION

Each program at James Madison University (JMU) is required to complete an internal assessment every year and an external review every five years. Additionally, we work with an external advisory group (EAG) to identify strengths and weaknesses of our program on an annual basis. In recent years, these reviews have highlighted certain aspects of our "systems core" courses (CS 350: Computer Organization, CS 450: Operating Systems, and CS 460: TCP/IP Networks) as areas of concern. Problems included overly broad specifications that led to different student experiences and insufficient programming experiences. Furthermore, our curriculum provided inadequate exposure to newer areas, such as parallel and distributed computing.

Over several years, we attempted a number of modest, incremental changes to address these problems. However, we found these changes failed to achieve all of our desired goals and a more extensive re-evaluation of our curriculum was necessary. Initial discussions of what topics should be covered revealed that we had different views on this matter, and we found that simply enumerating the desired topics by choosing pre-defined objectives from the ACM 2013 Knowledge Areas [1] failed to address our concerns.

Instead, we adopted a *backward design process* similar to an approach for course re-design [3]. In this approach, an instructor begins by identifying desired (or required) student learning outcomes and situational factors that influence the success of achieving these goals. From the outcomes, the instructor defines summative assessment strategies that provide evidence that the outcomes are achieved. Finally, the instructor creates activities and formative assessments that are designed to help students reach desired goals. Thus, assessment and content specifications are tightly integrated to ensure the course activities are aligned with desired outcomes. While our approach is based on Fink's work [3], backward design has been used by others in the education literature [10, 6].

Our work was also motivated by a desire to support learner-centered teaching [9] more explicitly. In this view, the instructor's responsibility changes from dictating the material that students must learn to guiding students through the learning process. In addition, the focus changes from learning the content for its own sake to *using and applying* it. Consequently, learner-centered teaching approaches emphasize active learning techniques [4, 8, 5]. The backward design process, in which content is specified to be deliberately aligned with student learning outcomes, is well-suited for supporting learner-centered teaching and active learning.

The contribution of this work is to describe our experiences with adapting the backward design process to a large-scale curriculum initiative. That is, the backward design process is normally applied to a single course with pre-defined learning outcomes. However, we applied this process to a significant portion of our major curriculum as a whole with no pre-defined learning outcomes that must be achieved. While the ACM 2013 curriculum recommendations provide general guidance for what should be covered, our goals were to re-design a core portion of our major requirements to be well-aligned with our students' backgrounds and career aspirations. Additionally, the backward design process explicitly creates a set of summative assessments that can be used as embedded assessments for systematic program evaluation.

In this paper, we provide background information on the courses that we targeted and how they fit into the major. We then describe our adaptation of the backward design process and our new systems core structure. We also provide advice for others who wish to use our approach to re-examine their curriculum. Overall, we find that the backward design process was a rewarding yet challenging experience, and we feel more confident in the structure of our curriculum and our ability to assess its efficacy. However, we also feel that certain aspects of the Fink model are rather awkward for CS outcomes, and other approaches based on the work of Wiggins & McTighe or Hansen could be more easily applied.

2. CURRICULUM BACKGROUND

CS 350 (Computer Organization) was criticized for inconsistent student experiences. A major contributing factor in this regard was our acceptance of transfer credit from different community colleges in the state. We observed that incoming transfer students were being offered vastly different experiences in the equivalent version of CS 350, particularly in regard to the amount and rigor of programming experiences. Some versions employed extensive C and assembly language assignments, while others had only Java programming or no programming at all. A lack of clear standards regarding the expectations of this course (and acceptable equivalents) was a primary cause.

Recent changes to CS 450 (OS) exacerbated the problems that arose from the CS 350 inconsistencies. While CS 450 traditionally operated as an introduction to systems programming (*e.g.,* developing command-line systems utilities and shells), some recent offerings focused on implementing advanced kernel code. Students who completed CS 350 without gaining exposure to C found themselves unprepared for the added rigor of these newer sections of CS 450.

The criticisms of CS 460 (TCP/IP Networks) arose from the unique history of the course. In the early 2000s, this course became cross-listed with another department, due to decreased enrollments in both, and an agreement was put in place that it would involve no programming component and would focus exclusively on the definition, modeling, and use of protocols. Over time, our faculty found this policy undesirable, as we consider network-based programming to be a fundamental skill for our graduates. Some students got exposure to that material in elective courses, but most students did not.

A common criticism of all three courses was the lack of clear specifications, thus making systematic program assessment challenging. While all faculty were adhering to the official course description, we had no explicitly defined objectives to assess student outcomes and to ensure consistent offerings. Anecdotal evidence from student exit interviews indicated that students perceived significant differences depending on the instructor.

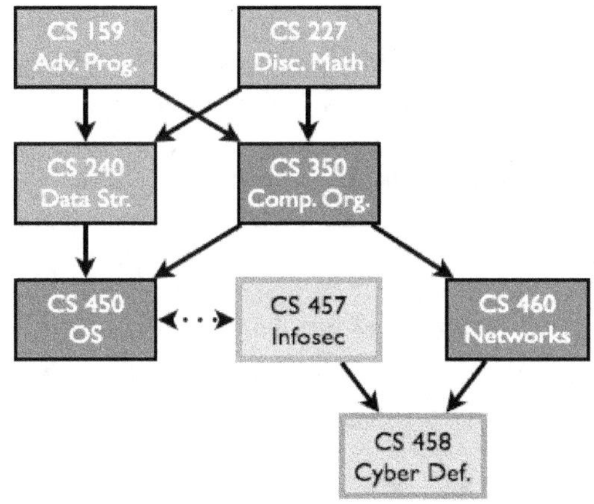

Figure 1: Existing systems core prerequisites

The timing of our courses also presented scheduling challenges for students. CS 350 was only offered in spring semesters, and was a required prerequisite for both CS 450 and CS 460, both offered in the fall. As a result, CS 350 acted as a bottleneck within our curriculum. Students who switched into the major after their freshmen year had difficulty graduating on time. Similarly, students who struggled with CS 350 (which was significantly more difficult than its prerequisite CS 159 – Advanced Programming) had to wait a year to retake the course. Thus, our new structure needs to avoid such a scheduling bottleneck.

Lastly, we felt that our existing course structure was inadequate for the rapidly evolving state of the field. Many concepts, such as principles of locality and communication, are common to several types of systems. In our view, the siloed approach (OS in one course, networking in another) obscured these common themes. Consequently, we desired a course structure that reflected the common foundations and themes of systems. We note that this view is aligned with that of the ACM, which introduced the Systems Fundamentals (SF) Knowledge Area in the 2013 curriculum [1].

3. BACKWARD DESIGN PROCESS

In this section, we will outline the major phases of the backward design process and highlight relevant observations of our experiences.

3.1 Situational Factors

A fundamental preliminary step in the backward design process is identification of situational factors that influence what can and cannot be achieved. We had two factors that restricted our options. First, our department maintains a "three-section, two-prep" teaching policy, where each faculty member teaches three 3-credit-hour sections per semester, with two sections being from the same course. Deviating from this policy would not be considered acceptable by the department.

The second restriction resulted from our relationship with the Virginia Community College System (VCCS). Through a combination of state and institutional policies, we must provide a feasible path for VCCS transfer students to com-

Foundational

1. What key information should our students understand and remember in the future?
2. What key ideas or themes are important for students to comprehend and describe?

Application

3. What kinds of thinking (critical, creative, practical) are important for our students to learn?
4. What software development skills do students need to gain?
5. What skills do our students need to learn about managing complex projects?

Integration

6. What connections should students recognize and make within the curriculum or to professional life?

Human dimension

7. What should students learn about themselves as software developers, users of technology, or as students?
8. What should students learn about understanding others and how they interact with others (including through developed software)?

Caring

9. What changes and values should students adopt in regard to interests or ideas?

Learning how to learn

10. What should students learn about how to work with computer systems?
11. What should students learn about becoming a self-directed learner?

Table 1: Guiding questions for defining learning outcomes

plete a degree in a timely manner. In our current structure, the *prerequisite depth* (*i.e.,* the minimum number of semesters from the first required course to the last required course) was 5, which is at the high end to offer a feasible path for timely completion. Thus, if our final proposal increased this depth, we would need to have a strong rationale and institutional acceptance of the curriculum would be unlikely. Figure 1 shows the relevant prerequisite structure (which is a subset of our overall curriculum) for our systems core. The courses in green are offered every semester, those in blue are spring only, and those in brown are fall only. The two courses in grey are electives, with CS 457 as a corequisite with CS 450.

Another situational factor arose from one of our department's strengths: As one of the seven original National Centers of Academic Excellence in Information Assurance Education (CAE/IAE), our department has a long history of offering multiple courses in information security and cyber defense. These courses require completing the systems core as prerequisites. Lengthening the duration of the core could make it more difficult for students to enroll in these courses, thus reducing the impact of a central departmental priority.

Lastly, the career aspirations of our students created another significant factor. Like many other institutions, our students overwhelmingly go into industry positions rather than graduate programs, though some opt for the latter. Furthermore, given JMU's proximity to Washington, D.C., and our emphasis on information security, many of our graduates go into positions with the federal government. This bias toward industry and government is reflected in our overall curriculum, which emphasizes applied software engineering experience. Thus, our goal for the systems core was to create a foundation of systems knowledge for all students while providing ample opportunities for exploring certain systems in greater detail, particularly for students with an interest in post-graduate work.

3.2 Systems Curriculum Goals

As a starting point for our curriculum re-design, we applied the Fink taxonomy [3] of learning goals to enumerate *all desired outcomes without consideration of feasibility.* That is, we began by asking what we felt all of our students needed to achieve without regard to how much time would be needed to achieve these goals. At this stage, we did not consider how our goals would impact the prerequisite depth issues for VCCS students or our security courses.

To define our desired learning outcomes, we adopted the Fink taxonomy [3]. This model defines 6 areas of learning outcomes as shown in Table 1. In Fink's model, 3 areas (Foundational, Application, Integration) roughly correspond to the cognitive domain concerns underlying Bloom's taxonomy [2]. Fink's model incorporates 3 additional areas that emphasize affective and metacognitive questions that have no direct mapping to counterparts in Bloom's taxonomy. We found defining learning goals for the cognitive areas to be a rather straightforward endeavor, as it is common practice to define cognitive outcomes. Through casual discussions, we had developed an informal understanding of our goals and values. However, enumerating them allowed us to identify mismatches in expectations and assumptions, thus making it possible to come to a consensus on these issues.

The affective and metacognitive questions led to considerably more discussion. Most members of the group were new to this process and unfamiliar with Fink's work; consequently, we found it necessary to spend time coming to an agreement on how to interpret terminology (*e.g.,* what it means to be a "self-directed learner" in computing, what constitutes "caring," what role should a CS department have in addressing the human dimension). In fact, disagreements in later discussions could often be traced back to different views about these questions. Furthermore, standard curriculum descriptions provide considerably less guidance in defining such objectives. For instance, the ACM 2013 has a short chapter describing "Characteristics of Graduates" at a broad level, but does not define specific measurable objectives similar to those defined in the Knowledge Areas. As a result, we found ourselves spending a significant amount of time grappling with this discussion, and others considering this process should be prepared for potential conflicts arising from these questions.

3.3 Guiding Principles and Themes

After enumerating our goals for the systems curriculum[1], we re-examined the list to define a set of higher-level principles. In this regard, we distinguished between goals that were specific to the systems curriculum (our focus) and those that were more universal to all upper-level CS courses. Principles in the former regard focused on the need to develop a system-level perspective and on how platform specifications can impact performance and other requirements.

The primary value of this stage of the process was to identify and prioritize our major goals and themes. In later stages, we would map assessments and modules to these themes to ensure alignment of course definitions with our overall goals. This mapping became particularly valuable when considering the number of hours allocated to topics. In some cases, we found that our initial assignment devoted significant amounts of time to some topics that provided insufficient support for our major goals and themes; our theme list then served as an indispensible tool for resolving these conflicts.

3.4 Assessment Strategies

To ensure a consistent set of experiences for students, we defined a list of modules and specified summative assessments for each. For instance, summative assessment of binary representation of information would consist of writing a program that read in a binary file and displayed the data in a variety of formats. Assessment of information exchange would consist of writing programs that use sockets, IPC, or shared memory.

It is important to emphasize one subtle aspect of this phase of the backward design process: *The modules themselves had not yet been defined.* That is, we were only concerned with specifying how students could demonstrate mastery of the goals and themes we had previously outlined. We had not yet discussed what specific topics needed to be introduced for each module. For instance, in the information exchange module, we had not mentioned any specific protocols, such as TCP/IP. This is the heart of backward design: **Student learning outcomes and assessments must be defined *before* there is any mention of topics to be covered.** The focus of the discussion is on what the students should *do*, rather than what they should *know*.

3.5 Module Definitions

Upon completion of the assessment strategies, we could then begin to define the modules in greater detail. Specifically, our goal at this stage was to construct a sequence of required courses that provided a strong systems foundation for all students, while also providing an opportunity for more detailed study of specific types of systems as desired or needed. That is, our approach was similar to the distinction between Core Tier-1 and Core Tier-2 in the ACM 2013 curriculum.

The module definitions started with the assessments specified previously, then we added the specific instructional objectives that must be met in order to support students' attempts at these assessments. In addition, the module definitions specified what material would be considered prerequisite, what themes were addressed by the module, and how much time was needed. Our initial attempt would have required slightly more than two 3-credit hour courses, so we had to perform multiple iterations of this process. *The previously stated guiding principles were important tools for prioritizing modules in this phase.*

[1]Due to space constraints, we cannot list our goals, principles, themes, strategies, and module definitions here. These will be made available online and can be found by contacting the lead author.

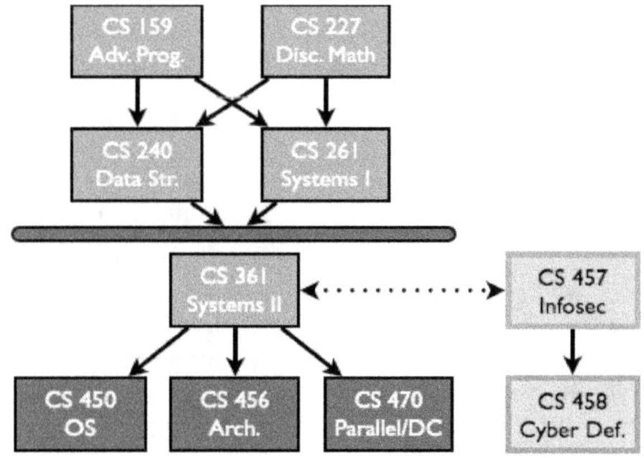

Figure 2: New systems core prerequisites

4. RESULTS

The end result of our work is a new systems core structure as shown in Figure 2. The modules defined as part of the backward design process were assembled into a two-semester Computer Systems I-II sequence. The purple courses denote new "advanced systems courses," that we will be introducing to complement the systems core. CS 240 and CS 261 are both required as prerequisites for CS 361 and CS 456, as denoted by the purple bar.

4.1 Computer Systems I-II

Table 2 shows the modules specified during the backward design process. For each module, we have specified summative assessments, hours of class time (approximate), skills expected, and assumed prerequisites. As shown in the mapping, these courses provide 100% coverage of Core Tier-1 topics in the Systems Fundamentals (SF), Architecture and Organization (AR), Networking and Communication (NC), Operating Systems (OS), Parallel and Distributed Computing (PD), and Computational Science (CN) Knowledge Areas. These courses also provide a foundation of several Core Tier-2 topics that we consider vital for all of our graduates.

Overall, the central themes of CS 261 (Computer Systems I) are the basics of instruction execution and concurrency. These are topics that generally correspond to traditional material in the AR and OS Knowledge Areas. CS 361 (Computer Systems II) focuses more on architectural design questions and communication between parallel software components, thus corresponding to the NC and PD Knowledge Areas.

4.2 Advanced Systems Courses

While our Computer Systems I-II courses provide a solid foundation in the area of systems fundamentals, this sequence alone is insufficient for our desired goals and student learning outcomes. Specifically, these courses provide a breadth of themes and concepts, but do not explore specific systems in detail. As such, we have also introduced three new courses in the areas of Architecture (CS 456), OS (CS

CS 261: Computer Systems I

Module name	*2013 mapping*	*Hours*	*Description*
C basics	n/a	6	Memory model and pointers, transition for students with Java experience
Compiler and debugger use	n/a	3	Introduction to GNU tools
CPU/memory organization	AR-Memory system (T2), PD-Architecture (T1/T2)	3	Registers and cache, principles of locality
Binary representation of data	AR-Machine level (T2)	4.5	Two's complement, IEEE 754, arithmetic instructions
von Neumann cycle	AR-Assembly level (T2)	3	Role of CPU and memory, load/store instructions
Basic circuits and datapath	AR-Interfacing (T2), SF-Paradigms (T1)	6	Logic gates, adders, ALU, control signals
Threads vs. processes	OS-Overview (T1), PD-Fundamentals (T1)	6	Fork vs. thread creation, memory space
Interrupts and OS principles	OS-Principles (T1), AR-Interfacing (T2)	4.5	Interrupts, system calls, kernel- vs. user-mode
System software design and evaluation	SF-Evaluation (T1)	4.5	Benchmarks, complexity, static vs. dynamic analysis

CS 361: Computer Systems II

Module name	*2013 mapping*	*Hours*	*Description*
Architecture analysis, design evaluation	SF-Reliability (T2), SF-Paradigms (T1)	3	Peer-to-peer, client-server, layered architectures
State models	SF-State machines (T1), OS-Concurrency (T2)	4.5	Notion of state, UML, FSM
Mathematical modeling	CN-Modeling (T1), DS-Probability (T1/T2)	3	Basic systems theory
Informaion exchange	PD-Communication (T1/T2), SF-Communication (T1), OS-Concurrency (T2)	6	Communication basics, IPC, sockets
Synchronization primitives	OS-Concurrency (T2)	6	Locks vs. semaphores, concurrency problems, deadlock
Parallel decomposition	PD-Decomposition (T1/T2), SF-Parallelism (T1)	3	Data vs. task, Amdahl's law, fork-join pattern, libraries
Protocol analysis, evaluation, and design	NC-Introduction (T1), SF-Cross layer communication (T1), PL-Reactive programming (T2), PD-Communication (T2)	9	Protocols and services, timing and statecharts, push/pull, flow control, reliability, handshaking, metrics
The Internet	NC-Applications (T2), NC-Reliable data delivery (T2), NC-Routing (T2), NC-LAN (T2), NC-Mobility (T2)	6	HTTP, DNS, DHCP, TCP, UDP IP, 802.3, 802.11, ARP

Table 2: Course definitions for new Computer Systems I-II courses

450), and Parallel and Distributed Computing (CS 470). CS 456 and the new CS 450 include a number of advanced topics that we previously covered in CS 350 and the old CS 450, but are not in the new Systems I-II sequence. These topics are identified as Core Tier-2 material in the ACM 2013 report. CS 470 is an entirely new course.

The key feature that distinguishes the advanced systems courses is the requirement of programming-in-the-large projects, particularly ones that require students to read and comprehend an existing code base. One example would be the Pintos OS projects [7]. Instructors will integrate the fundamental concepts from the Computer Systems I-II sequence throughout the systems core.

4.3 Course Offerings

This new structure offers a number of advantages over our previous curriculum. Whereas CS 350, CS 450, and CS 460 were offered only once per year (thus making CS 350 a bottleneck), CS 261 and CS 361 will both be offered every semester. Consequently, struggling in one or both of these courses will have significantly less impact on students' ability to progress in the major. This new structure also leaves the prerequisite depth at 5, and does not add any time to the security courses. In fact, by eliminating the bottleneck of CS 350, this new structure makes it easier for students to progress on time.

As a major requirement, students must complete one of the advanced systems courses[2], though students will be encouraged and advised to complete more than that. Pro-

[2]Achieving the ACM 2013 recommendation of 80% coverage of Core Tier-2 material would require completing at least three of the advanced systems courses. We consider such a goal infeasible given certain constraints of our curriculum. We note, though, that our previous curriculum also fell short

viding students with these options supports the learner-centered aim of granting students more control over their educational goals. These courses offer scheduling flexibility, with three sections (typically from two different courses) each semester. Furthermore, CS 456 may be taken concurrently with CS 361 for students on a compressed schedule.

5. DISCUSSION

Overall, we are pleased with the process and the end result of this curriculum initiative. Having explicitly defined summative assessments that can be used as embedded questions provides opportunities for systematic program assessment, thus allowing us to ensure consistent student experiences. The new curriculum structure provides greater student choice and avoids scheduling bottlenecks. This structure also maintains a feasible path for VCCS transfer students to complete the curriculum in a timely manner and places no additional barriers to the security courses. The Computer Systems I-II courses provide a breadth-first foundation in systems fundamentals, complemented by a number of courses to explore individual types of systems in depth. This new curriculum is much better aligned with our departmental goals and priorities.

While we strongly encourage backward design as a process for curriculum re-design, we feel less strongly about the details of the Fink taxonomy. In particular, we found the "human dimension" and "caring" areas to be challenging to work with and interpret. Wiggins & McTighe [10] use the terms "perspective" and "empathy" instead, and we find these terms more suitable for CS curricula, particularly for systems courses. That is, we find considerable overlap between these dimensions of both the Fink and the Wiggins & McTighe taxonomies, and our preference is for the latter. For instance, we find it easier to answer questions relating to the perspective of users vs. the perspective of developers, rather than questions of "learning about oneself," which we found to be more difficult to use for crafting measurable objectives. Alternatively, Hansen [6] refers to Big Ideas and Enduring Understandings, rather than a multidimensional taxonomy. While Hansen's model is more intuitive, it (like Bloom's) provides inadequate emphasis on metacognitive and affective goals. It is our view that these non-cognitive domains are critical and often overlooked. Perhaps the best approach would be to use the Wiggins & McTighe model to enumerate objectives, then use Hansen to define themes to unite modules.

Finally, it is important to note that adhering to this process requires significant time and effort. We performed this work over the course of an academic year, generally meeting twice a month. The process was initially slow-moving, as most members of the committee had no experience with the backward design process. As such, we spent considerable time discussing the process and whether or not a more streamlined approach would yield acceptable results. Ultimately, we found that the backward design process, while time-consuming and challenging, was worth the effort and our end result is superior to what would have been achieved by selecting pre-defined objectives. Thus, we would advise others who are re-examining their curriculum to consider the backward design process as an approach. The process facilitates discussions about departmental priorities, program assessments strategies, and instructional techniques, and has several beneficial side effects beyond just the curriculum changes.

of this 80% goal, and our new version is significantly improved in this regard.

6. CONCLUSION AND FUTURE WORK

In this work, we described our experiences using the backward design process to re-design a significant portion of our major requirements. This approach, which integrates assessment and content specifications, provides a framework for creating a learner-centered curriculum that ensures course instructional objectives are aligned with departmental goals and situational factors. We summarized our existing curriculum and how we applied the process to our re-design. We summarized our new course structure and provided advice for others considering this approach.

The current status of our work is that we have received preliminary approval from our department and we are working toward institutional approval. Our intent is to put this curriculum in place beginning with the 2016–17 academic year (with 2015–16 as a transitional step). In the mean time, we will be collecting baseline assessment data from students who complete the existing curriculum. In future work, we will compare these results with assessment data from the new curriculum.

7. REFERENCES

[1] ACM. Computer science curricula recommendations. `http://www.acm.org/education/curricula-recommendations`, 2013. [Online; accessed June 29, 2014].

[2] B. S. Bloom, J. D. Engelhart, E. J. Furst, W. H. Hill, and D. R. Krathwohl. *Taxonomy of Educational Objectives: The Classification of Educational Goals, Handbook I: Cognitive Domain.* David McKay, New York, 1956.

[3] L. D. Fink. *Creating Significant Learning Experiences.* Jossey-Bass, San Francisco, 2003.

[4] S. Freeman, S. L. Eddy, M. McDonough, M. K. Smith, N. Okoroafor, H. Jordt, and M. P. Wenderoth. Active learning increases student performance in science, engineering, and mathematics. *Proceedings of the National Academy of Sciences*, 2014.

[5] R. R. Hake. Interactive-engagement vs. traditional methods: A six-thousand-student survey of mechanics test data for introductory physics courses. *American Journal of Physics*, 66(1):64–74, 1998.

[6] E. Hansen. *Idea-Based Design: A Course Design Process to Promote Conceptual Understanding.* Stylus Publishing, Sterling, VA, 2011.

[7] B. Pfaff, A. Romano, and G. Back. The pintos instructional operating system kernel. In *Proceedings of the 40th ACM Technical Symposium on Computer Science Education*, SIGCSE '09, pages 453–457, New York, NY, USA, 2009. ACM.

[8] M. Prince. Does active learning work? a review of the research. *Journal of Engineering Education*, 93(3), July 2004.

[9] M. Weimer. *Learner-Centered Teaching.* Jossey-Bass, San Francisco, 2002.

[10] G. Wiggins and J. McTighe. *Understanding by Design.* Pearson, Upper Saddle River, NJ, 2005.

A Module-based Approach to Adopting the 2013 ACM Curricular Recommendations on Parallel Computing

Martin Burtscher
Texas State University
burtscher@txstate.edu

Wuxu Peng
Texas State University
wuxu@txstate.edu

Apan Qasem
Texas State University
apan@txstate.edu

Hongchi Shi
Texas State University
hs15@txstate.edu

Dan Tamir
Texas State University
dt19@txstate.edu

Heather Thiry
University of Colorado
heather.smith@colorado.edu

ABSTRACT

The widespread deployment of multicore systems over the last decade has brought about major changes in the software and hardware landscape. The resulting importance of parallel computing is reflected in the 2013 Curriculum Guidelines developed by the joint ACM/IEEE taskforce. The document recommends increased coverage of parallel computing and describes a new Knowledge Area on this topic. These recommendations have already been adopted by several universities in the form of new parallel-programming courses. Implementing the recommendations in a complete curriculum, however, poses many challenges, including deciding on existing material to be removed, complying with administrative and ABET requirements, and maintaining caps on graduation credit hours. This paper describes an alternative approach for adopting the 2013 curricular recommendations on parallel computing. Specifically, we use a module-based approach that introduces parallel computing concepts and re-iterates them through a series of short, self-contained modules taught across several lower-division courses. Most of these concepts are then combined into a new senior-level capstone course on parallel programming. Each module covers parallelism aspects in the context of a conventional computer science topic, thus enabling us to include parallel computing without a major overhaul of the curriculum. Evaluations conducted during the first year show encouraging results for this early-and-often approach in terms of learning outcomes, student interest, and confidence gains.

Categories and Subject Descriptors

K.3.2 [**Computer and Information Science Education**]: Curriculum

Keywords

parallel computing, module-based instruction, pedagogy

SIGCSE'15 March 04-07 2015, Kansas City, MO, USA.

ACM 978-1-4503-2966-8/15/03 ...$15.00.
http://dx.doi.org/10.1145/2676723.2677270.

1. INTRODUCTION

The broad adoption of multicore-based computer systems over the last decade has introduced unprecedented challenges to programmers, who, for the first time, have to find ways to take advantage of multiple threads. Because almost all legacy software was developed to run on a single thread, most programmers lack the skills, knowledge, and experience needed to safely and effectively exploit parallelism. Thus, it is paramount that the next generation of software developers be trained in parallel programming.

In response to this shift in industry, the computer science education community has made efforts to increase the amount of parallel and distributed computing (PDC) concepts in the curriculum. New classes in parallel and distributed programming have been added and existing courses have been bolstered with PDC content. Recently and most notably, the ACM/IEEE joint taskforce on computing curricula has published its guidelines for undergraduate degree programs (henceforth referred to as ACM2013) [3]. This document puts special emphasis on PDC, which has been designated as a new Knowledge Area. Unlike all previous versions, ACM2013 now mandates the inclusion of several core hours of PDC in every CS curriculum.

There are many challenges to implementing the ACM2013 recommendations on parallel computing. Creating a new course or offering an existing course on PDC more frequently gives students the option to be exposed to these concepts. However, making such a course a required part of the curriculum is often problematic because of the cap on the number of credit hours. For instance, in Texas this cap is 120 hours for undergraduates, and at Texas State University more than half of those hours come from non-major areas. These constraints imply that another course covering some fundamental aspects of computer science would need to be eliminated before a new course can be made a requirement. Furthermore, the Knowledge Units in PDC are such that they are better covered in multiple courses for pedagogical reasons, as recommended in ACM2013.

Distributing the PDC concepts over multiple courses raises several pedagogical, curricular, and administrative challenges.

- *Identifying courses for inclusion:* The merit of teaching sequential programming as a *special case* of parallel programming is still under debate, which is why it is not advocated in ACM2013. Hence, the current direction dictates that PDC be introduced in lower-level courses within the paradigm of sequential pro-

gramming. Identifying courses where PDC material can be taught without disrupting the flow of content while satisfying the pre-requisite structure is difficult.
- *Adjusting existing content:* Introducing new material, particularly in lower-division courses, implies that some existing content needs to be eliminated or condensed. It is not readily apparent what this content should be, making it difficult to insert new topics. An even less desirable approach is to concentrate all material in a core upper-level course (e.g., Programming Languages or Operating Systems) where there is some flexibility in organizing the material. Several of the example curricula presented in ACM2013 take this approach. However, by their own admission, this does not provide the coverage of many of the Tier 2 core topics [3].
- *Faculty training:* Faculty teaching introductory courses may not have sufficient experience teaching PDC topics. In many institutions, introductory courses are staffed by a rotating pool of adjunct faculty. This makes it difficult to provide adequate training or maintain consistency across sections of lower-level courses, further complicating the adoption of PDC material.
- *Administrative issues:* At many universities, curriculum revisions require a rather involved process, moving through departmental, college, and university curriculum committees. Changes may be further restricted to satisfy the timeline for *curriculum cycles.*

This paper describes our method to adopting the ACM2013 curricular recommendations on parallel computing that addresses the above issues. In our early-and-often approach, parallel computing concepts are introduced and reiterated through a series of short, self-contained modules across several lower-division courses. Most of these concepts are later combined in a newly designed senior-level capstone course on parallel programming. The development and deployment of the modules are based on three key principles (described in Section 3) that provide pedagogical advantages and facilitate a gradual migration to a PDC-enhanced curriculum.

2. BACKGROUND

Although parallel computing has been an important area within computer science for decades, it did not find its way into mainstream undergraduate CS curricula until recently. Efforts at integrating parallelism can be divided into two periods, delineated by the advent of multicore processors.

2.1 Pre-multicore era integration efforts

Early efforts at integration mostly involved developing an upper-level elective covering various aspects of parallel computing [10] or an elective that focused solely on a specific parallel programming paradigm [6, 9]. These courses were primarily offered at universities that had faculty with research interests in parallel and high-performance computing. The cost of parallel computers further limited the offering of such courses to larger research-oriented universities [6]. A survey of CS undergraduate curricula at 40 universities of varied orientation (e.g., liberal arts, masters, R1 research) conducted by the authors in 2009 revealed a similar trend[1]. Prior to the multicore shift, there had been only a few efforts at a more holistic integration of parallel computing into the curriculum [12]. Most of these efforts either did not sustain or were not adopted beyond the originating college.

[1]The survey was conducted as part of a proposal to NSF and was not published independently.

2.2 Multicore era integration efforts

The industry-wide shift to multicore processors provided strong impetus for integrating PDC into the undergraduate curriculum. Many more parallel computing courses are now being offered with greater regularity. Curricular revisions are also under way to include more parallelism. The Georgia Institute of Technology has adopted a *rolling introduction* to parallel computing concepts in both its CS and ECE curricula [7]. The wide availability of multicore systems has made parallel computers much more affordable. This has allowed smaller liberal arts colleges to incorporate parallelism in their courses. In fact, many of the recent integration efforts have been initiated at such colleges [5, 8].

There are also endeavors at building communities to encourage and aid the adoption of PDC topics across universities, notably the CSinParallel project, whose aim it is to insert parallel computing concepts into various CS courses in multiple curricular contexts [2]. The formation of the TCPP Curriculum committee on PDC by the IEEE and the National Science Foundation is another notable endeavor in the same direction. This multi-institutional committee organizes many activities to encourage adoption of PDC at universities both nationally and internationally [4]. The success of this committee has led to the formation of the CDER Center, a larger body with similar goals [1].

2.3 PDC in ACM2013

ACM2013 underlines the need for integrating Parallel and Distributed Computing into undergraduate CS curricula and includes PDC as a new Knowledge Area. The topics within the PDC area are broken down into nine Knowledge Units. Furthermore, parallelism-related concepts also appear in the System Fundamentals Knowledge Area. Five Core Tier 1 hours on PDC are now recommended, compared to zero in the previous version of the guidelines. An extra 10 hours of Core Tier 2 is also recommended. ACM2013 clearly states the need for spreading PDC topics across many courses in addition to offering a dedicated course on parallelism. It includes four example curricula, all of which demonstrate increased emphasis on parallel computing.

3. OUR APPROACH

For bringing the ACM2013 recommendations to our university (and similar institutions), we employ the early-and-often approach originally proposed by Brown et al. [2]. This strategy introduces PDC concepts through a series of modules dispersed across several courses. In our implementation, we put special emphasis on the coverage of topics in each module individually *and* as a sequence. We also pay attention to *when* they are taught. As depicted in Fig. 1, the key idea is to provide sufficient intersection with PDC topics on every major path through the curriculum. This ensures that students attain a broad perspective on parallel and distributed computing, irrespective of their choice of electives. The development and deployment of the modules is based on three key principles that provide certain pedagogical advantages and facilitate a gradual migration to a PDC-enhanced curriculum. We discuss these principles next.

(1) Introduce concepts at the right level of abstraction: To gain mastery in parallel programming (and se-

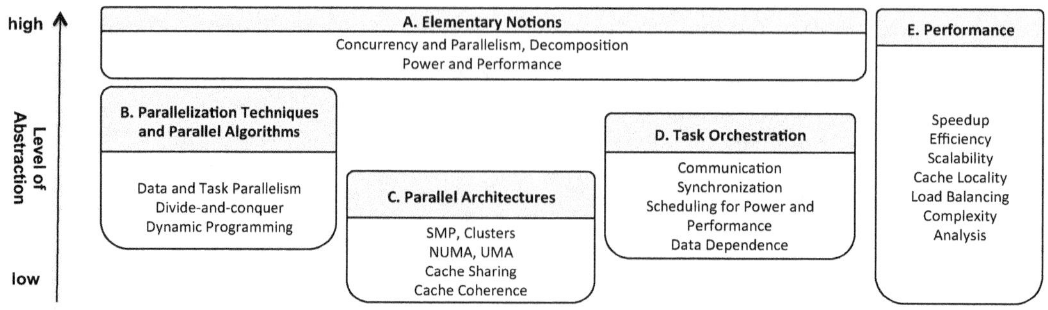

Figure 2: Module classification based on level of abstraction

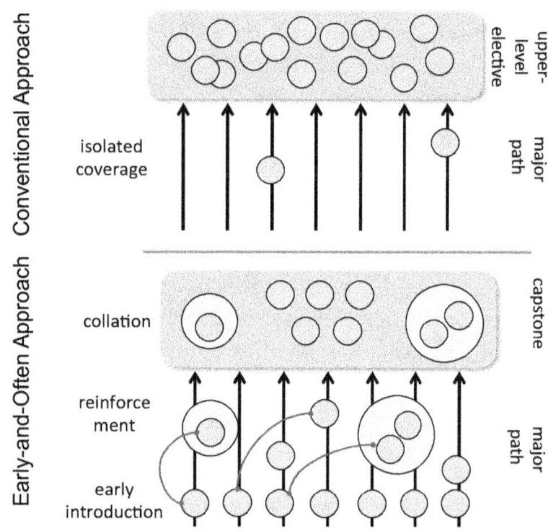

Figure 1: The one-elective (top) and our early-and-often (bottom) approach of introducing PDC

quential programming, for that matter), students need to learn how to think about problems at different levels of abstraction and acquire the ability to switch between levels. Nevertheless, it is important to determine the right level of abstraction for introducing different aspects of parallel problem solving as exposing students to multiple levels all at once can create confusion. We advocate an approach that starts with the most abstract forms of concurrency and progressively reveals lower-level mechanisms. For example, students can learn about Amdahl's law for parallel programs without being able to write parallel programs; therefore, this topic can already be introduced in a CS I module. Fig. 2 shows a classification of module topics based on the level of abstraction. Higher-level concepts are introduced first and reinforced in subsequent years as students are gradually exposed to lower-level ideas. Some topics, such as performance of parallel programs, span multiple levels of abstraction and are covered in several modules.

(2) Provide "parallel context" to key topics in the existing curriculum: Many theories and concepts covered throughout the CS curriculum can enhance a student's comprehension of parallel computing principles. However, such topics are often not taught in a parallel context. For example, almost all data structures courses introduce recursion, and, in many cases, a divide-and-conquer algorithm is used as a primary example. Yet, the fact that divide-and-conquer algorithms naturally lend themselves to parallelism is rarely emphasized. Our approach incorporates parallel context in key topics such as divide-and-conquer algorithms. Since the modules are dispersed over several courses and do not introduce completely new concepts but rather extend topics that are already being covered, they can be introduced with minimal disruption of the original course schedule and content.

(3) Encourage adoption: For our approach to be successful, the modules need to be easy to adopt such that even an instructor with no prior experience in teaching parallel computing can seamlessly plug them into her course. With this goal in mind, the modules are designed to be short (1-3 hours) and self-contained. They include lecture notes, assignments, exercises, exam questions, solutions, and pedagogical notes. Although the modules follow a textbook treatment of the material, they are not tied to any specific textbook and are designed to be mostly programming language independent. Examples and assignments are created for multiple languages, APIs, and platforms, enabling straightforward adoption at other institutions.

4. IMPLEMENTATION

We began implementing the early-and-often approach at Texas State in Fall 2012. In this section, we describe our implementation efforts over the past two years.

4.1 Curriculum Overview

Our university offers both a Bachelor of Arts (BA) and a Bachelor of Science (BS) degree in computer science. The difference between the two programs in terms of major courses is minimal, and the described strategy applies equally to both programs. Thus, we only discuss the BS curriculum, an overview of which is shown in Fig. 3. Not all electives are listed and only Discrete Math is included among the required math courses. The students have to take an additional 46 credit hours of General Education Core, which is not shown in Fig. 3. The CS introductory sequence has a hardware and a software track. In the hardware track, the students progress through CS I, Assembly, Digital Logic, and Computer Architecture. In the software sequence, the students move through CS I, CS II, and Data Structures[2]. Software Engineering and Object Oriented Design and Implementation (OODI) serve as two required capstone courses. Embedded Systems and Human Factors are two of the three project courses that our students are required to take. Hence, most of them will take one of these courses while pursuing their undergraduate degree.

[2]This course doubles as an Algorithms course.

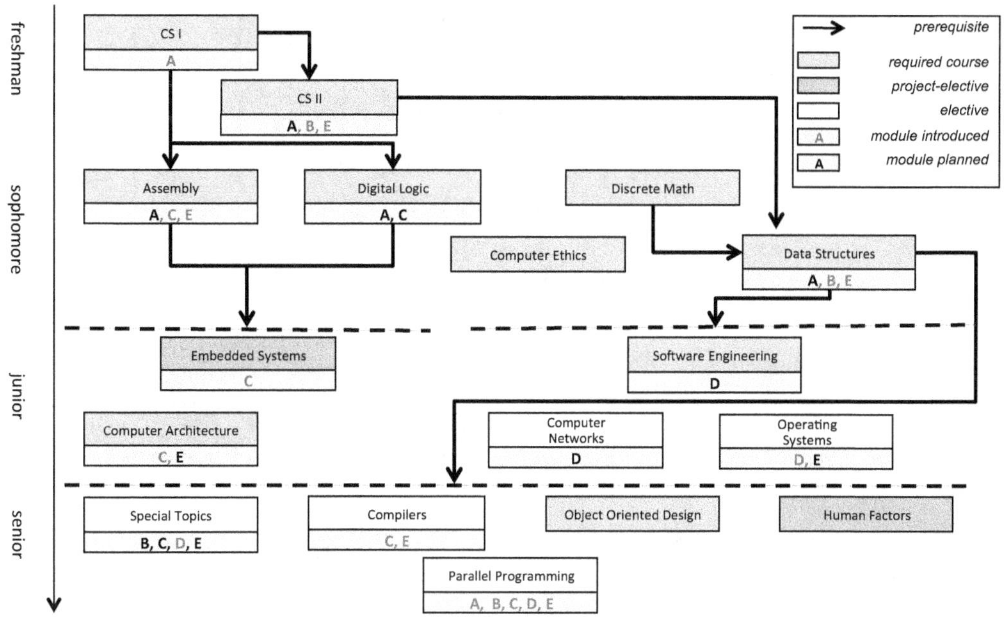

Figure 3: Computer science curriculum and mapping of PDC modules to major courses

Module Category	ACM2013 PDC Knowledge Unit
A. Elementary Notions	Parallelism Fundamentals (PF)
B. Parallel Algorithms	Parallel Decomposition (PD) Parallel Algorithms (PA)
C. Parallel Architecture	Parallel Architecture (PR)
D. Task Orchestration	Communication & Coordination (CC)
E. Parallel Performance	Parallel Performance (PP)

Table 1: Module categories and their correspondence to ACM2013 Knowledge Units

4.2 Coverage of ACM2013 Knowledge Units

To date, we have developed seven modules covering various aspects of parallel computing. These modules are divided into five categories indexed A through E. The module categories and the ACM2013 Knowledge Units (KU) they correspond to are shown in Table 1. The planning and development of the modules began prior to the publication of ACM2013. For this reason, our classification differs slightly from the ACM2013 mandated KUs. This difference is only nominal, however. As shown in Table 2, our module topics map closely to the topics of the corresponding KUs in ACM2013. For instance, module A in Elementary Notions covers all four topics (and corresponding learning outcomes) of the Parallelism Fundamentals KU. Combined, the seven modules provide coverage of all Tier 1 Core topics and most Tier 2 Core topics in the Parallel Algorithms and Parallel Performance KUs.

4.3 Module Placement

Because of the 120-hour cap on graduation hours and many of our students' dependence on financial aid, most CS majors only end up taking about four or five upper-level electives before graduating. This makes careful planning of module integration vital to the success of our strategy.

Before implementing our strategy, we first performed a detailed review and analysis of the material covered in each of our introductory sequence courses and several upper-level electives. In reviewing the existing content, we had two goals: (i) to find *context* for introducing parallel topics and (ii) to identify content that has been removed or de-emphasized in ACM2013. Based on this analysis, we constructed a mapping of our modules to various courses in the curriculum. This mapping is illustrated in Fig. 3. We found opportunities for introducing modules in four introductory courses, both in the hardware and the software track. We also discovered opportunities in four upper-level required courses. Computer Ethics is the only required course where we could not place a module. We identified several electives as good candidates for module integration as shown in Fig. 3.

	ACM2013 PDC Knowledge Unit					
Courses	PF	PD	CC	PR	PA	PP
CS I	0.75					0.25
CS II	0.5	0.5	0.25			0.25
Computer Ethics						
Assembly	0.5			0.5		
Digital Logic	0.5			0.5		
Data Structures	0.25	0.5	0.5		0.5	
Computer Architecture	0.25			1		0.5
OODI					1	0.5
Software Engineering			1			
Embedded Systems				1		
Operating Systems		1			0.5	
Other Elective						
Total	2.75	2	1.75	3	2	1.5

Table 3: PDC coverage in CS major path (grey cells refer to Tier 2 topics)

Most of these opportunities have already been exploited (shown in green text in Fig. 3). We plan to introduce more modules in future years. However, as the data in Table 3 show, our current implementation already provides excellent coverage of ACM2013 PDC topics. A typical major will encounter 8.5 Tier 1 hours and 4.5 Tier 2 and elective hours even without taking the Parallel Programming capstone course. It should be noted, though, that several concepts are reiterated throughout the modules. Hence, the

Module	Topics in ACM2013 PDC Knowledge Units																					
	1a	1b	1c	1d	2a	2b	3a	3b	4a	4b	4c	4d	5a	5b	5c	5d	6a	6b	6c	6d	6e	6f
A	x	x	x	x	x	x	x		x						x					x		
B	x	x	x	x	x	x	x		x						x					x		
C1	x	x									x	x					x	x				x
C2	x	x							x	x							x	x				x
D1	x	x		x	x	x	x	x														
D2	x	x							x	x							x	x	x			x
E	x	x			x	x											x	x		x		x

Table 2: Coverage of ACM2013 topics in PDC modules. Topics are numbered sequentially starting with first Knowledge Unit (i.e., 1a denotes the first topic in KU Parallelism Fundamentals)

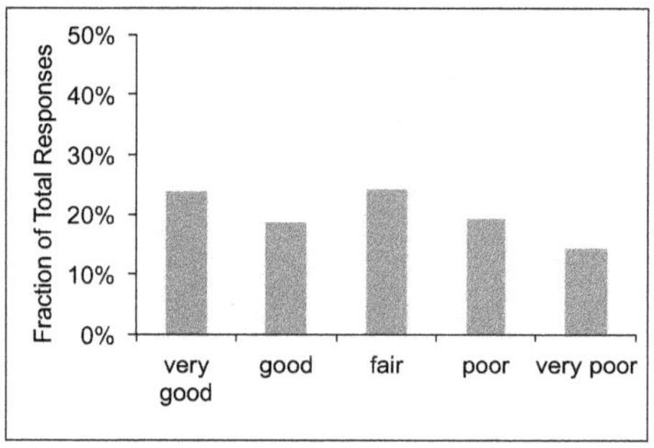

Figure 4: Student performance on PDC topics in all courses where a module was introduced (2013-14)

9.5 cumulative hours in Tier 1 do not quite represent 9.5 hours of coverage of *distinct* PDC topics.

5. EVALUATION

We instated two forms of evaluation during the first year. The assessment plan for the student learning outcomes was designed by the involved faculty whereas the teaching effectiveness and student engagement was evaluated through an independent external evaluator. Additionally, we began collecting and compiling data for a longitudinal study in which we evaluate student performance in the capstone Parallel Programming course in relation to the number of modules the students have encountered as they progressed through the program. At this time, we do not have sufficient longitudinal data to present because only a few students have completed the capstone course who have also taken a class with a PDC module. We hope to publish these results by the end of 2015.

The modules were implemented in 13 sections of six different courses over three semesters. The combined enrollment in these sections was 323. Seven instructors were involved in teaching the modules in the various sections.

5.1 Learning Outcome

For each section in which a module was introduced, a final exam question was prepared to assess student comprehension of the material covered. Although programming assignments and homeworks were associated with most modules, for consistency, we only considered student performance on final exam questions to evaluate the learning outcome. Aside from numeric scoring (which was different for different sections), a rubric was created for each question that graded the student responses on a scale of very poor, poor, fair, good, and very good. Fair or better was considered a passing grade.

Fig. 4 shows the resulting student performance on the final exam questions in all courses where a module was implemented. We observe a satisfactory learning outcome for students who were introduced to new PDC concepts. Overall, 67% of the students received a passing grade on the exam questions. This rate is slightly higher than all majors who score a C or better in these courses.

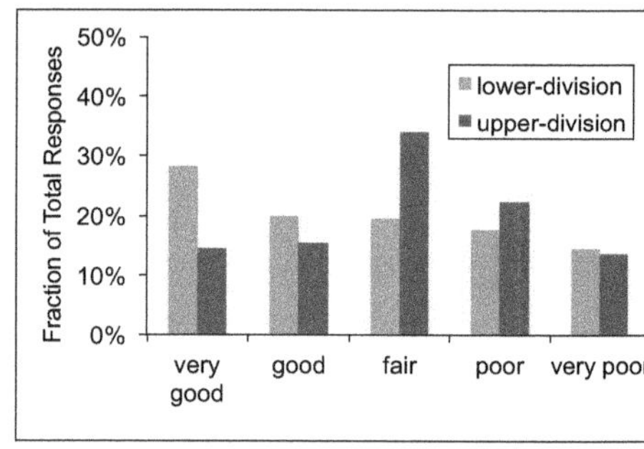

Figure 5: Comparison of student performance in lower- and upper-division courses

Fig. 5 compares the student performance in lower- and upper-division courses. We were apprehensive that the students may perform poorly in some of the lower-division courses because the topics appear to be too advanced to them. Yet, somewhat surprisingly, the passing rate was higher (about 3%) in the lower-division courses, attesting to the suitability of module placement.

After implementing a module for the first time, we obtained feedback both from the instructor and the students on the content and pedagogy. Then we revised and improved the modules based on this feedback. Fig. 6 compares the student performance in courses where a module was introduced for the first time to courses where a revised module was introduced. As we can see, there is almost a 17% increase in the passing rate when a revised module is taught, either by the same instructor or by a different instructor. These results suggest the need for iterative improvement and adjustment of each module.

5.2 Student Interest and Learning Experience

We conducted an independent external evaluation to assess changes in student confidence and interest in computer science as well as the students' perceptions of their classroom learning experiences. To obtain these measurements, the Student Assessment of Learning Gains (SALG) survey [11] was administered electronically at the end of the semester to the students enrolled in courses where a module was introduced.

The strongest reported gains were in confidence and interest in computer science in general and parallel computing in particular. The students also thought that the learning

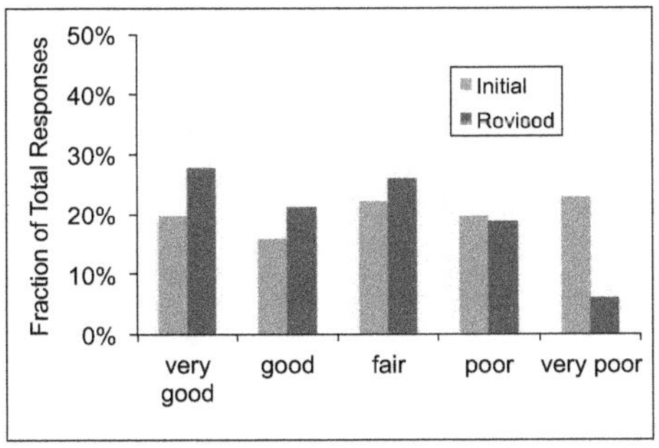

Figure 6: Comparison of student performance during first and second installment of same module

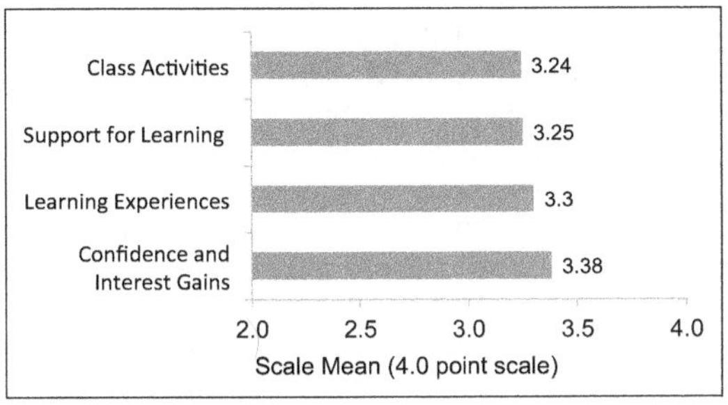

Figure 7: External evaluation summary

experiences and instructional environment in the classroom helped their learning. They rated their interactions with peers and instructors positively and reported that specific class activities, such as lectures, examples, and asking questions, were helpful. The students were slightly positive that course assignments, projects, and tests helped their learning. Fig. 7 summarizes the scale means of the total sample of students from the four SALG survey scales. Next, we highlight specific aspects of this assessment.

Fig. 8 provides a course-wise breakdown of student responses with respect to their learning experience, and confidence and interest gains. The students rated the learning environment in their course positively. Fig. 8 shows the course means for the "learning experiences scale", which measures the efficacy of the general instructional approach and curriculum in the course. The learning environment in each course was rated between "somewhat helpful" (3.0) and "very helpful" (4.0). The mean over all courses was 3.3. The differences among the courses are not statistically significant. Thus, the students were generally satisfied with the teaching strategies in all courses. For instance, 89% of the students found the "instructional approach taken in this class" to be "somewhat" or "very" helpful. Similarly, 88% of students felt that their learning was enhanced by the way that the class sessions, activities, and assignments fit together. Overall, 75% of the students reported that the course had increased their "enthusiasm for this subject" a moderate or great amount. 92% of the students reported that the course had increased their interest in taking more CS courses.

6. CONCLUSIONS

In this paper, we present a strategy for adopting the ACM2013 recommendations that does not require a major overhaul of the curriculum. Our approach addresses several challenges commonly faced when incorporating a substantial amount of new material into an existing curriculum. We have implemented this strategy at our university and so far achieved reasonable success in terms of student learning outcome, engagement, and interest.

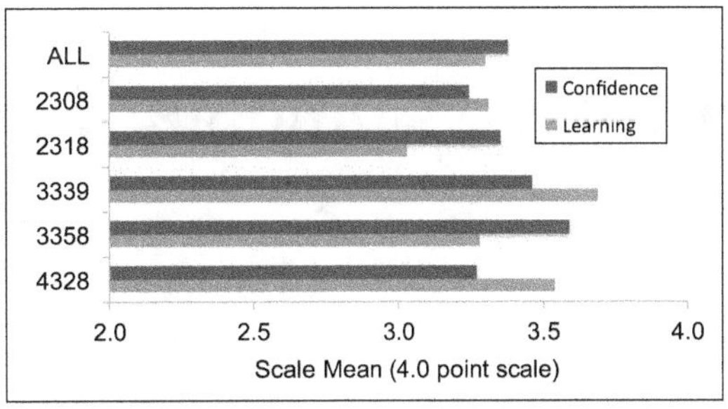

Figure 8: Student learning experience, confidence and interest gains

Acknowledgements

This work was funded by the National Science Foundation under grants DUE-1141022 and CNS-1253292.

7. REFERENCES

[1] Center for parallel and distributed computing curriculum development and educational resources (CDER). `http://www.cs.gsu.edu/~tcpp`.

[2] CSinParallel Project. `http://csinparallel.org/`.

[3] ACM IEEE Joint Task Force on Computing Curricula, Computer Science Curricula Recommendation and Guidelines 2013, 2013.

[4] NSF/IEEE-TCPP Curriculum Initiative on Parallel and Distributed Computing. `http://www.cs.gsu.edu/~tcpp/curriculum`, 2013.

[5] D. J. Ernst and D. E. Stevenson. Concurrent cs: Preparing students for a multicore world. *SIGCSE Bull.*, 40(3):230–234, June 2008.

[6] A. L. Fisher and T. Gross. Teaching the programming of parallel computers. In *Proceedings of the Twenty-second SIGCSE Technical Symposium on Computer Science Education*, SIGCSE '91, pages 102–107, New York, NY, USA, 1991. ACM.

[7] Y. S. Gavrilovska H. H., Schwan L. K. and W. M. Multi-core curriculum development at georgia tech: Experience and future steps. In *UCRC Workshop on Experimental Research in Computer Systems*, 2006.

[8] J. R. Graham. Integrating parallel programming techniques into traditional computer science curricula. *SIGCSE Bull.*, 39(4):75–78, Dec. 2007.

[9] J. Hartman and D. Sanders. Teaching a course in parallel processing with limited resources. *SIGCSE Bull.*, 23(1):97–101, Mar. 1991.

[10] D. G. Hyde. A parallel processing course for undergraduates. *SIGCSE Bull.*, 21(1), 1989.

[11] E. Seymour, D. Wiese, A. Hunter, and S. M. Daffinrud. Creating a better mousetrap: On-line student assessment of their learning gains. In *National Meeting of the American Chemical Society*, 2000.

[12] W. E. Toll. Decision points in the introduction of parallel processing into the undergraduate curriculum. *SIGCSE Bull.*, 27(1):136–140, Mar. 1995.

Creating a Computer Simulator as a CS1 Student Project

Kian L. Pokorny
Division of Computing
McKendree University
Lebanon, IL 62254
618-537-6440
klpokorny@mckendree.edu

ABSTRACT

This paper presents experiences with creating a computer simulator as a student project in a CS1 course. Each student writes the simulator using C++ during the last ten weeks of the course. The project consists of a simulated memory, and simple CPU simulator including a machine language. Additionally, students implement an assembly language and a simple high-level language with associated compiler. The course has no programming prerequisite and can be taken to fulfill a general education requirement or as the first course for students majoring in computer science or information systems.

Integrating such a project in an entry level course has a number of benefits as well as challenges. The project acts as a vehicle that engages students in a breadth of computer science topics, leading into discussions of theoretical considerations, languages, and computing devices. The project components provide an active learning environment. Students are introduced to numbering systems, number conversions, and numeric representations. The computer architecture components include introductions to main memory, CPU, and memory access techniques. The transition from and motivations for, the utilization of machine languages, assembly languages and high-level languages are demonstrated with the implementation of the project. Beginning students are given opportunity to practice programming and problem solving on a project of significant complexity. The biggest challenge is organization. Management of such a project requires a well-defined plan.

Categories and Subject Descriptors

K.3.0 [**Computers and Education**]: General; K.3.2 [**Computers and Education**]: Computer and Information Science Education—computer science education

General Terms

Design, Theory

Keywords

CS1; Computer Simulator; Architecture; Compiler; Active Learning

SIGCSE '15, March 4–7, 2015, Kansas City, MO, USA

http://dx.doi.org/10.1145/2676723.2677210

1. INTRODUCTION

Courses in computer architecture and language translation are often included in the computer science curriculum at the sophomore or higher levels. Usually these courses have as prerequisites a sequence of computer programming courses. ACM's CS2013 curriculum recommendation [3] contains a knowledge area (KA) called System Fundamentals in which a "unified systems perspective and common conceptual foundation for other KAs" is encouraged. This KA considers "what a programmer needs to understand about the underlying system." In the current paper, we consider a CS1 project which provides students insight into the underlying computing and computational systems relative to high-level language programming.

The use of computer simulators and emulators are common in computer organization courses. Some instructors use them in entry level programing courses to explain the instruction process at the machine level. Stone [9] discusses the use of a computer architecture and machine language simulator in CS1 to help improve the understanding of conditional selection and iteration for beginning students. Stanley et. al. [8] found that using a computer emulator in an introductory programming course is very helpful in demonstrating that computers use only binary data. Others have students design and build computer simulators in computer organization courses [7]. Phillips [4] describes building a CPU simulator in a computer organization course. Here he uses MultiMedia Logic software that provides logic gates in a graphical form to design the simulator.

In CS2013 [3], it states that a programming focus for introductory courses can give students, "a too-narrow (and misleading) view of the place of programming in the field. … which may limit the appeal of computer science to some students." ACM's 2001[2] suggests two alternative implementations for a breadth-first introduction. In one of the alternatives, a three semester sequence ($CS101_B$, $CS102_B$, $CS103_B$) that integrates topics in discrete mathematics, theoretical computer science, hardware fundamentals, algorithms and programming, is intended to provide a more holistic view of the discipline [2]. This approach stemming from Denning 1988 is an attempt to integrate mathematics and computing theory into the introductory curriculum and not set it apart as separate courses [1].

In this paper we present experiences with creating a computer simulator using C++ as a student project in CS1. The simulator project which includes a memory, simple architecture, machine language, assembly language, and high-level language with associated compiler helps to provide a "unified systems perspective" in the CS1 course. At our university, students majoring in computer science take subsequent courses in computer programming, discrete mathematics, computer architecture, and compiler construction which expand on topics introduced in this first course.

Our CS1 course has been taught using a breadth-first approach in computing for several years [5]. An update to the course includes a computer simulator project to engage students in the various topics. Powers [6] discusses the importance of introducing topics early and revisiting repeatedly in the curriculum. She delves into the importance of the educational theories of constructivism, spiraling and spacing. In this context, introducing topics early in the curriculum and then reviewing and expanding on the topics allows the student to build a strong understanding of the concepts. Our simulator project integrates topics from discrete mathematics, computer architecture and compiler implementation into problem solving and introductory computer programming. This approach has several goals. First, is to provide a focus for the course. It is a goal that is visualized with a concise overview in the first week of class which is built upon in the remainder of the course. Second, is to provide a vehicle for introducing concepts in programming, problem solving, discrete mathematics, computer architecture and compilers giving students a more holistic view of the discipline. Third, is to allow for a spiraling and spacing approach with the more difficult topics, which are revisited with more detail during the course and given full coverage in later courses.

The remainder of this paper is organized as follows. Section 2 provides a time line of the course including specific weeks for which the project phases are implemented. Section 3 provides a detailed description of the project which is divided into ten smaller project assignments. Section 4 is a discussion of the experiences using the project in several offerings of the course. This includes discussions of both the benefits and challenges with such a project.

2. COURSE TIMELINE

In the first week of the course an overview of computers and computing is given that starts with an intuitive view of a computer which requires memory, processing and input/output mechanisms. Continuing with the overview it is recognized that implementing computing on a machine requires programming and problem solving. At this point, students are given the perspective of a computer as a two state machine, "a bunch of electronic circuits with switches that can be turned on and off." This motivates the need for binary and hexadecimal numbering systems. Continuing, at an overview level, the focus turns to controlling the circuits with computer languages. Machine language represented with binary numbers is presented first, and then assembly language and high-level languages are presented. In the second week of class, an introduction to the C++ programming is given. Working with a spiral pedagogical philosophy, the project requires students to delve deeper into and expands on each of these topics.

During weeks two, three, and four, many of the concepts that form the basis for problem solving and programming are presented. Problem solving and algorithm development is presented in detail during the second week. With this discussion the three basic structures and flowcharting are presented as well as an introduction to C++. Continuing with problem solving in week three and four, C++ loops and conditionals are covered along with examples at the algorithmic level including sequential search and selection sort.

Phases of the project are introduced as the appropriate material is covered throughout the courses. Much care must be taken to properly align course material with project phases. However, a benefit of this approach is that as the course lectures advance through each topic, students are actively engaged in the material while working through various phases of the project. Table 1 provides a chronological list showing the alignment of computing, and programing topics for the course.

Week	Computer Topics	C++ Topics
1	Basic Computing Device. Processor, Memory and I/O Binary, Hexadecimal and Decimal	Program that does nothing
2	Control Structures, flowcharts	I/O, data types, arithmetic and assignment operators.
3	Problem Solving and Algorithms	if-else and while loops
4	Searching and sorting. Code tracing, Boolean expressions	
5	Data Storage and memory types	Arrays and for loops
6	Data representation – character, sign magnitude, Two's complement and floating point.	Manipulating Multi-dimensional arrays
7	Computer Architecture, machine cycle	
8	Instruction Set Architecture, Memory access techniques	
9	Assembly language	strings
10	Formal Languages	structs
11	Regular Expressions, Finite State Machines, Transition graphs	External files
12	Context Free Grammars and Languages, Backus-Naur form	functions
13	Compilers – scanner, symbol table	reference parameters and static variables
14	Parser, code generator	
15	Integration of compiler and CPU simulator	

Table 1: Order of Topics

At weeks five and six, students have some experience with problem solving and programming strategies. At this time an in-depth discussion of data starting with bits and bytes, going through data types, arrays in C++ and working up through the data hierarchy into databases and data centers is given. Additionally, computer representations of characters, integers and floating point values are considered. When the students have more experience with *if-else*-statements, *for*-loops, *while*-loops and arrays, simple searching and sorting algorithms are implemented in C++. At this time the first two phases of the project culminate in a simulated memory.

For weeks seven through nine the focus is on computer architecture and assembly language. Basic concepts from computer architecture are introduced which include a simple processor architecture, instruction set formats, memory access techniques, and an assembly language. Students complete a number of written exercises that allow them to gain experience with these topics. Additionally, students write programs of increasing complexity that require the incorporation of everything studied to this point in the course. The programing projects culminate in a CPU simulator.

Following the computer architecture component, weeks ten and eleven focus on formal languages. This includes presentations of regular expressions, finite state machines, transition graphs and context free grammars. The work product for this phase is a transition graph that represents the scanner and a Backus-Naur form of the context-free grammar for a simple high-level language.

The next two weeks are dedicated to writing a complier for the simple high-level language defined in weeks ten and eleven. The final week is then used to wrap up loose ends and integrating the memory, CPU and compiler programs into one large program. The average length of the final program totals about 650 lines code.

3. PROJECT DESCRIPTION

The project is divided into three distinct parts: memory simulator, CPU simulator, and compiler. These are subdivided into smaller assignments that are manageable for students at the appropriate knowledge level. The assignments are then combined into the computer simulator.

During week 5, memory is studied including external storage, main memory, cache and registers. These are introduced at the level of bits, words, data and instructions. Concurrently, the C++ array is introduced. As a project, students write programs that convert between decimal and binary numbers, with the binary representation being stored as an individual "bit" in a separate element of an *int* array. This engages students in manipulating single dimensional arrays, performing number conversions, and conceptualizing the storage of bits. To accomplish this, students revisit number conversion and binary numbers that were presented in the first week by teaching the processes to a computer in the form of an algorithm. A second project requires students to perform the binary operations of addition, AND, and OR on the binary numbers stored in the arrays. Again, engaging students in the topics and providing practice with loops, decisions and array manipulations.

In week 7, the third project has students create a program that simulates a main memory with an *int* array of size 8X256, representing a memory of 256, 8-bit words. Each word can hold an instruction that is formatted as a 3-bit opcode followed by a 5-bit operand, or a word can store an 8-bit address. This is an extension of the number conversion program. Thus, students are instructed to write a program that can read a decimal value for an opcode (0-7), a decimal value for an operand (0-31), a decimal value for an address (0-255) then convert the value into binary and appropriately store in the memory array. Alternatively, an eight bit instruction can be entered as a "binary" number and stored in memory. That is, one can enter into an *int,* a combination of eight 0s and 1s which are separated and stored in individual array elements. Students have a basic understanding of machine code from discussions in week one allowing them to make the connection to this project. However, at this time there is no discussion of the specifics of the implementation of opcodes.

In weeks 7 and 8 a simple processor architecture is considered (Figure 1) along with instruction set formats. Students expand on the memory simulator to create a CPU simulator of this model. Each register is represented with appropriate sized arrays.

- ACC - 5 bits
- MQ - 5 bits
- IR - 8 bits
- PC – decimal (index on the memory array)
- MDR – 8 bits
- MAR - 8 bits

Opcodes and operands are read in from the keyboard as decimal integers, converted to binary, and stored in the memory simulator. After a program written in this code is completed, it can be executed. The execution process reads instructions from the memory into the CPU simulator where they are executed. Through this process the instruction set (Figure 2) is studied and various instruction types are identified. The instruction set architecture (ISA) implemented with this project has single operand instructions. Students implement jump, add and compare instructions. Also immediate, direct and indirect memory access instructions are implemented. Because it is specified, data can only move along the paths provided in Figure 1. Each instruction implementation requires the student to carefully consider the execution process in a step-by-step manner.

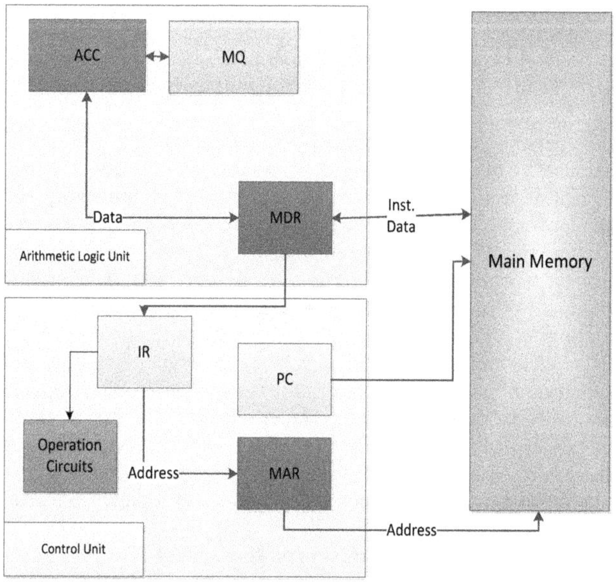

Figure 1: A simple Processor with Memory

For example, to execute the LDID (load indirect) instruction, the instruction is read from memory and stored in the MDR register (array). From there it is copied into the IR array. The first three bits are decoded by converting them to decimal. It is then determined to be 3, the LDID instruction. Then the last 5 bits of the instruction are converted to decimal to get the address of the address of the operand. The address found in the row of the memory array indicated by the last five bits of the instruction, is then loaded into the MAR. This address is converted to decimal, determining the address (array element) of the operand. The operand is then read into the MDR and copied to the ACC array. This tedious process provides significant practice in array manipulation, the use of decision and loop structures, as well as an understanding of the machine cycle required to implement an instruction.

Hex	Binary	Assembly	Action
0	000	HALT	stops execution
1	001	LDIM	Load Immediate
2	010	STORE	Store Direct
3	011	LDID	Load Indirect
4	100	STID	Store Indirect
5	101	ADD	Addition
6	110	CMPE	Equality
7	111	JMPNE	jump not equal

Figure 2: Instruction Set

Because this is an entry level course, students are not expected to derive all of the instructions. Code for the STORE, LDID, and ADD instructions are provided. Students use these examples as a basis to implement the remaining five instructions. Consideration of instruction size and format on memory, bus size, processor design and instruction set size are all demonstrated.

The CPU simulator is the largest phase of the project and considered the most difficult by students both during the course and in hindsight after completing the course. The next project phase extends the CPU simulator project and includes a study of assembly language (Figure 2), which corresponds to studying the C++ string variable type.

With the assembly language project phase, students write a program that allows the instructions for the CPU simulator to be entered as assembly language like mnemonics rather than binary coded machine instructions. These assembly language instructions are then translated into the machine instructions by converting them to the corresponding decimal values and then they are stored in the memory as described previously. These instructions are then executed by the CPU simulator. This phase is, by far, much simpler than the CPU simulator, consisting of about 25 lines of additional code. The hiatus from the laborious coding of the CPU project is appreciated by students at this point and allows time for the instructor to work with students who may be struggling with the CPU simulator project.

At this stage, students have created a program that simulates a memory and CPU which executes the machine level instructions they have implemented. They write programs using assembly instructions that are executed on their simulator. This naturally progresses to the study of high level languages including an introduction to formal languages and translation systems, namely compliers. In weeks 10 and 11, students investigate regular expressions, finite automatons and state transition graphs. They are given a simple high-level language called SCRAP (Figure 3). The projects include creating a transition graph to scan characters of the SCRAP language producing tokens that represent lexemes in the language. With an introduction to context-free grammars and the Backus-Naur Form notation (BNF) students create a BNF for the SCRAP language. The SCRAP language is designed with properties that significantly reduce the complexity of a compiler, making it accessible for students at this level. Specifically, it is noted that expressions can only be in the form of either **constant** *<operator>* **constant** or **variable** *<operator>* **constant**. This eliminates the need for any recursion or complex loop structures in the compiler.

In weeks 12 and 13, from the transition graph students write a scanner program for the SCRAP language, and from the BNF they program a parser. Along with the scanner project a symbol table is coded and with the parser project a code generator that produces the assembly language given in Figure 2. Again, students are provided with code snippets to help them get started writing the compiler. The final result is a compiler for the SCRAP language that produces assembly language code which can be executed by their CPU simulator program.

Source code, written in the SCRAP language, is saved to a file which is subsequently read by the compiler. The compiler then writes target code in the form of the assembly language given in Figure 2 to another file. The CPU simulator project is then modified to read the assembly language program from the file. This requires external file manipulation, which is studied at this time. The final result is the computer simulator. Students can then write programs in the high-level SCRAP language which are compiled and executed on their simulators.

Language Definition

- All programs begin with the keyword ***start*** and end with ***stop***. The only variable type is an integer and the keyword ***integer*** is used to declare variables. Only one variable can be declared in a declaration. Variable names consist of uppercase alphabetic letters.
- = assigns of the value on the RHS to the variable on the LHS. The RHS can be a single number or single expression with a + operator.
- There are 4 operators in the language. & performs a logical AND. | performs a logical OR. The equality operator uses the == to determine equality. + performs addition. Each of the operators can have operands in the form of either **constant** *<operator>* **constant** or **variable** *<operator>* **constant.**
  - Every statement ends with a . (period).
  - There is a selection construct in the form:
    if (equality expression ***)***
    Single statement
  - Every program ends with a # on the line after the **stop** statement.

Figure 3: High-Level Language

4. DISCUSSION

The course, formatted with three lecture hours and two lab hours, provides a breadth-first introduction to computing. Students majoring in Computer Science, Computer Information Systems, and Computational Science are required to take the course as part of the major. In addition, students may enroll in the course to fulfill a general education requirement. Specifically, the goals are to provide:

- a historical perspective of computers and current computer use,
- an introduction to computer hardware components and how they interact,
- algorithmic design concepts,
- structured programming techniques,
- basic constructs of the C++ programming language
- various career fields in computing, and
- foundational concepts of computing and computation.

The course with this project has been well received by most students. The broader view of the system helps to hold the interest of students majoring in computing and with a programming background. Those without a programming background and non-majors have commented that they are fascinated by, "how all these devices work and how they are actually the same at the core."

Here, a constructivist pedagogical approach and relies heavily on spacing and spiraling is utilized. This pedagogical approach extends to the rest of the program from this first course. Difficult topics are introduced early, revisited repeatedly, and built upon throughout the course. The topics of the course are then revisited in later courses. The project acts as a vehicle that provides the foundation on which to build.

The implementation of a CS1 course with a project as significant as creating a computer simulator can be challenging. However, this project focuses students on computing, providing appropriate examples that help students understand computing. The time devoted to providing a background for the computer simulator supplants time previously used to explain other programming projects for the course. The project engages the student in the subject of computing and coding becomes a tool to solve the problem at hand. This allows more focus on the computing topics and helps the student gain a depth of understanding. For example, after students have implemented the machine instructions as 3-bit opcodes followed by a 5-bit operand, a discussion of the ramifications of instruction size on the system is quickly and thoroughly understood.

Another technique that has helped to optimize the material is the flipped classroom approach. A number of videos were created for the class and the flipped classroom approach allows for more material to be covered more effectively. Much of the standard lecture is provided with readings and video. Then when students come to class the focus is on working problems or starting a project phase. As an example, material is provided explaining the machine cycle then, in class, students work on the phase of the project to implement this. This usually entails creating a flowchart and understanding the logic to write the program. Then, in lab the students write the program.

Inevitably, some students do not complete some phases of the project on time. This is handled in several ways. First, the project is structured such that the most challenging phases are followed by less demanding phases. Most students are able to take advantage of the lull in the project to catch up. Second, if a student gets too far behind, the instructor solution is provided as a starting point to continue the project. The second alternative has never been used by a student. Two students offered this solution thought it easier to correct and complete their own code than to interpret the instructor's code.

5. CONCLUSIONS

Creating a computer simulator as a CS1 class project has a number of benefits. It provides, as CS2013 [3] suggests, a "unified systems perspective and common conceptual foundation" that goes beyond a perspective of computer science as programming. Additionally, it provides an introduction to "what a programmer needs to understand about the underlying system."

The project acts as a vehicle that engages students in a breadth of computer science topics. It leads into a natural discussion of underlying theoretical considerations, languages and computing devices. These project components provide an active learning environment that introduces binary and hexadecimal numbering systems, number conversions, and numeric representations of data. The computer architecture components provide a basic understanding of main memory, the CPU, memory access techniques and the trade-off between word size and complexity. The transition from and motivations for, the utilization of machine languages, assembly languages and High-level languages are demonstrated through the implementation of the project.

Additionally, students are given the opportunity to practice programming and problem solving on a project of significant complexity. They are motivated to learn the various aspects of C++ through different goals in creating the Computer simulator. Numerous times in the teaching of the course, students ask, at the appropriate time, "How can we do that in C++?"

A number of challenges presented themselves in teaching the CS1 material with this approach. The most important is organization. Running such a project requires a well-defined plan. The material is interwoven with mathematical, computer, programming and problem solving concepts. Additionally, sequencing material in each of these concepts over the semester must be given careful consideration. Another challenge is adjusting the course from a lecture based course with a lab to a more active learning environment where student interaction dictated much of the normal lecture time. This is needed to allow class time for students to work through the required problem solving in order to complete each of the phases of the project.

Anecdotal evidence from student feedback indicates that most students appreciated the project. One student stated that "the way the projects build on each other and produce an end product is very impressive." Another student enrolled in a computer architecture course stated, "I'm glad I had the course last semester. Now in computer architecture we are delving deeper into the topics and I understand more than the students that did not do the project."

Future work includes continued data collection as students that experience the project and complete the upper level courses in discrete mathematics, computer architecture, and compilers are evaluated.

6. REFERENCES

[1] Peter Denning, Douglas E. Comer, David Gries, Michael C. Mulder, Allen B. Tucker, A. Joe Turner, and Paul R. Young. 1988. Computing as a discipline: preliminary report of the ACM task force on the core of computer science. *SIGCSE Bull.* 20, 1, 41-41, 1988.

[2] IEEE & ACM Joint Task Force on Computing Curricula, Computing Curricula 2001 Computer Science, December 15, 2001, http://acm.org/education/curric_vols/cc2001.pdf, retrieved June 4, 2014.

[3] IEEE Computer Society and Association for Computing Machinery Joint Task Force on Computing Curricula "Computer Science Curricula 2013 " http://www.acm.org/education/CS2013-final-report.pdf retrieved May 26, 2014.

[4] John Phillips. 2007. Simulation of a simple CPU design and its use as an instructional tool in a computer organization course. *J. Comput. Sci. Coll.* 22, 6 (June 2007), 140-146.

[5] Kian L. Pokorny, Introduction to computing: a fresh breadth of disciplines. *J. Comput. Small Coll.* 24, 5, 166-172, 2009. classes. J. Comput. Sci. Coll. 29, 2 (December 2013), 60-66.

[6] Kris D. Powers. 2004. Teaching computer architecture in introductory computing: why? And how?. In *Proceedings of the Sixth Australasian Conference on Computing Education - Volume 30*(ACE '04), Raymond Lister and Alison Young (Eds.), Vol. 30. Australian Computer Society, Inc., Darlinghurst, Australia, Australia, 255-260.

[7] Stanley, Prigmore, Mikolyski, Embrey, Fife, (2007 June) "Pedagogic Value in Understanding Computer Architecture of Implementing the Marie Computer from Null and Lobur in the Logic Emulation Software, Multimedia Logic", Proceedings of the Workshop on Computer Architecture Education, 34th International Symposium on Computer Architecture, p 66-71.

[8] Timothy D. Stanley, Dennis Fairclough, Roger deBry, and Reza Kamali-Sarvestani. 2013. Using a simple emulated computer to facilitate understanding in introductory computer programming and computer organization/architecture classes. *J. Comput. Sci. Coll.* 29, 2 (December 2013), 60-66.

[9] Jeffrey A. Stone. 2006. Using a machine language simulator to teach CS1 concepts. *SIGCSE Bull.* 38, 4 (June 2006), 43-45.

Program Decomposition and Complexity in CS1

Aaron Keen
Computer Science Department
California Polytechnic State University
1 Grand Avenue
San Luis Obispo, CA 93407 USA
akeen@calpoly.edu

Kurt Mammen
Computer Science Department
California Polytechnic State University
1 Grand Avenue
San Luis Obispo, CA 93407 USA
kmammen@calpoly.edu

ABSTRACT

Inexperienced and novice programmers in CS 1 are often faced with the expectation that they will be able to decompose a problem into subproblems, solve these subproblems independently, and then recompose these solutions. As with programming in general, decomposition is a skill that benefits from explicit instruction and that must be practiced to see improvement. This paper introduces a term-long project approach to CS 1 that emphasizes program decomposition. Existing software quality metrics are used to assess student decomposition progression through the project and to compare the decomposition skills of students in courses using the term-long project approach against those in courses using a more typical "stand-alone" project approach.

Categories and Subject Descriptors

K.3.2 [**Computers and Education**]: Computer and Information Science Education—*computer science education*; D.2.3 [**Software Engineering**]: Coding Tools and Techniques—*top-down programming*; D.2.8 [**Software Engineering**]: Metrics—*complexity measures*

General Terms

Design, Measurement

Keywords

Introductory programming; program decomposition; complexity; software quality

1. INTRODUCTION

Introductory computer science courses with a programming focus introduce students to a set of concepts that provide a foundation for further study. This introduction typically includes primitive and structured data, sequential data, conditional reasoning, repetition, and some exposure to decomposition. Many textbooks support introductory courses through a syntactic emphasis on "how" to apply each concept, but often lack a thorough discussion of "why". In particular, we believe that decomposition (specifically, the analysis of a problem and its division into smaller subproblems) receives inadequate treatment: programming examples are generally presented as finished solutions and, unfortunately, many examples do not decompose a problem into subproblems (e.g., consider a traditional presentation of selection sort using nested loops).

SIGCSE'15, March 04–07, 2015, Kansas City, MO, USA.

ACM 978-1-4503-2966-8/15/03 ...$15.00.
http://dx.doi.org/10.1145/2676723.2677219.

As is common, our department's CS 1 makes no explicit assumption of prior programming experience. Even so, we believe that there is an implicit assumption that students know how to think like computer scientists. More specifically, we believe there is a common (i.e., not isolated to our institution) implicit belief that an introductory student will be able to decompose a "large" (for CS 1) problem into subproblems, to solve these subproblems independently, and to recompose these solutions into a solution for the original problem. This is evidenced by the stand-alone style of programming assignments common to CS 1 (i.e., where each assignment presents a new problem unrelated to the previous). These programming assignments either prescribe a specific decomposition (to aid the student) or, more commonly, leave the student to consider their own decomposition (if any). Students without prior programming experience often have a difficult time beginning such assignments because they are unable to determine the smaller steps that make up the "large" solution (i.e., they are unable to decompose the problem into simpler subproblems). Even with some prescribed decomposition, the lack of continuity between such stand-alone assignments does little to motivate students to complete unfinished assignments or to address issues after the due date.

We believe that decomposition is a fundamental skill that demands emphasis in CS 1. Decomposition should be explicitly taught to those new to the discipline and honed by all in preparation for later coursework. In this paper we present a term-long project tailored to introduce and practice decomposition. Our goals for the term-long project are to teach programming skills in the context of an interesting "real world" problem, to foster these skills constructively from data definition to project completion, to provide a contextualized software development process experience, and, primarily, to impress upon students the value of decomposition as an aid in development, in testing, and in debugging.

The rest of this paper is organized as follows. Section 2 discusses work related to our pedagogical approach and provides background context for our analysis. Section 3 elaborates the goals of the term-long project and Section 4 gives details of the project milestones. In Section 5 we compare the complexity of student solutions over the course of the project and on a stand-alone "final" project. Section 6 discusses future work and Section 7 concludes.

2. BACKGROUND AND RELATED WORK

Static analysis of code quality ranges from simple measures (e.g., lines of code in a function), such as those reported by Berry and Meekings[2], to more sophisticated measures that attempt to predict complexity, such as those developed by McCabe[5]. The desire to automatically assess code quality indicates the importance that expert programmers place on the quality of written code. Software maintenance suffers when the code itself is of low quality. As such, we believe code quality should be addressed early in the computing curriculum.

In addition to a simple lines-of-code metric, our analysis, presented in Section 5, uses McCabe's cyclomatic complexity[5] to compare student submissions across cohorts. Cyclomatic complexity relates the number of edges, the number of nodes, and the number of connected components in the control flow graph for a function. Intuitively, this measure correlates to the number of "paths" through a function, so each additional decision point (e.g., as introduced by a conditional or iteration statement) increases the complexity. Though cyclomatic complexity is not strictly a measure of decomposition quality, high complexity correlates with opportunities for further decomposition, as suggested by McCabe.

Patton and McGill[8] propose the use of automated software quality metrics on student portfolios to enable quantitative evaluation of progress through a course of study. Of particular significance to our work is their critique of existing software quality metrics as pedagogical aids. They state that existing metrics do not distinguish the use of advanced language features, few metrics directly address object-oriented issues, and the results of many metrics can be skewed by program length. The development of pedagogically tailored metrics is suggested and specific categories of analysis are proposed, but no specific metric is presented. We agree that existing metrics are not ideal as pedagogical aids; we do not use them as such in this work.

In [10], Truong, et. al., present a framework that uses existing metrics to guide students toward improved code quality. This differs from our work presented here; our students were not exposed to any existing quality metrics, so the student code that we analyze is not influenced by any explicit measurement. Even so, we do appreciate the value of using existing metrics to guide students.

Static quality of student written Java programs is analyzed by Breuker, et. al., in [3]. Student submissions are analyzed for 22 code properties. The majority of these properties are simple counting metrics (e.g., the number of classes in a package and the number of lines of code in a class), but properties requiring greater analysis, such as cyclomatic complexity and code duplicates, are also included. The analysis of these more sophisticated properties is most related to our work, but whereas Breuker, et. al., use these measurements to compare first-year and second-year students, our analysis is aimed at measuring improvements within a single course as the result of a term-long project.

3. TERM PROJECT GOALS

As previously stated, our department's CS 1 makes no explicit assumption about prior programming experience, but the authors believe that there is a common implicit assumption that CS 1 students understand how to decompose problems and recompose solutions. Our goals for the term project are to teach programming skills in the context of an interesting "real-world" problem, to foster these skills constructively from data definition to project completion, to provide a contextualized software development process experience, and, primarily, to impress upon students the value of decomposition as an aid in development, in testing, and in debugging. These goals are addressed in the following ways.

First, the project is structured such that the early milestones (the first two) are very prescriptive; the students are given explicit directions on the code that needs to be written and the required decomposition. These early milestones aid the inexperienced student that is often unsure of how to begin. The later milestones specify the required functionality and a progressively smaller number of explicitly required functions coupled with progressively less direction in terms of decomposition. The students are told that they are expected to decompose their implementations to aid in coding, testing, and debugging as demonstrated in the earlier milestones but the details of this decomposition are left to the student.

Second, no solutions are provided after milestone submissions (though the instructor test cases for the third milestone are made available after the due date). Instead, each student receives detailed feedback on their submission and is required to address incorrect functionality before proceeding to the next milestone. This "maintenance" aspect of the project forces students to address misunderstandings in a (now) familiar context. Requiring students to "live with their code" reinforces the value of decomposition and testing since each milestone directly depends on the prior milestones.

Third, testing (specifically, unit testing at the function level) is emphasized throughout the project[1]. Each student is required to submit (for grading) a minimum of two test cases for each function specified for the milestone. Testing is not a major required component of our department's CS 1, but has been emphasized in our development of this project to motivate the value of decomposition and to impress upon the students the benefits of programmatic testing. The fourth milestone is the first to require (console) output and the fifth milestone is the first to require (file) input (and file output). As such, the students are encouraged (and instructed) to consider testability via unit tests when decomposing the required functionality.

4. TERM PROJECT DESCRIPTION

To address the shortcomings of a traditional stand-alone assignments approach to CS 1, we developed a term-long project split over multiple milestones (the assignments during the first 8.5 weeks of a 10-week quarter are devoted to

[1]It should be noted that while students are encouraged to write tests early, they are not explicitly practicing test-driven development. Experience indicates that the majority of students in these courses, not surprisingly, write their test cases after their best attempt at implementing the solution.

Figure 1: Sample image generated by term-long ray casting project.

this project). The milestones for this project direct students through many facets of the software development process (including testing, implementation, and maintenance).

Over the course of the project, the students implement a ray casting program that will generate an image (in PPM P3 format[6]) consisting of spheres in a three-dimensional virtual world. Ray casting[1] can be viewed as the primitive operation in a ray tracing implementation. The project does not support reflection or refraction, which are typically found in a ray tracer, due to time limitations (a 10-week quarter) and because recursion is not covered in our department's CS 1. Figure 1 shows an image generated by the completed project.

To be clear, though our term-long project shares some characteristics with projects presented in a course practicing project-based learning, the courses in which this project was used did not practice project-based learning. In particular, in our courses, the problem to be solved is predefined, the problem is presented to the students in pieces as they progress through the course, the students work individually to solve the problem, and the majority of what students need to know to solve the problem is presented to them (with the exception, to some degree, of the details of vector mathematics).

The project milestones are discussed in the following subsections. Sufficient details are given to provide context for the discussion of complexity in Section 5.

4.1 Data Representation

The first milestone introduces compound data and testing. Students must define data representations for the mathematical concepts of a point, a vector, a sphere, and a ray. Since our CS 1 implementation language is C, the first milestone also requires the implementation of "creation functions"[2] as a means to prevent common mistakes with the initialization of fields in a `struct` and to introduce testing of very simple functions (using `assert`-like testing macros). This milestone completely specifies the required data and functions; there is no opportunity for further decomposition.

[2]These functions simply initialize the fields of a structure; they can be viewed as analogous to a constructor in an object-oriented language.

4.2 Primitive Operations on Data

The second milestone introduces simple mathematical functions without conditional logic or repetition. Students must define operations to work with the data defined in the first milestone; more specifically, this milestone defines operations on point and vector data. These operations include translating points, scaling and normalizing vectors, and computing the difference between points and between vectors. This milestone completely specifies the required functions; there is no opportunity for further decomposition.

4.3 Ray-Sphere Collision

The third milestone introduces conditional logic and one instance of iteration over an array. Students must define a function that determines if a ray will intersect a sphere and, if it does, compute the point of intersection. This function amounts to solving the quadratic equation and checking which root (if any) determines a valid intersection. This is the first opportunity for students to decompose functionality into additional functions, though they are not explicitly directed or required to do so.

This milestone also requires the implementation of a function that collects the intersection points between a ray and each sphere in an array. This specific function conforms to a coding pattern (a filter) introduced in lecture, leading to little variance in solution.

4.4 Cast Rays

The fourth milestone produces an image[3]. Students are required to implement a function (`cast_ray`) to determine the color of a pixel based on collisions between a corresponding ray and the spheres in the virtual world.

The color for a pixel is determined by the Phong reflection model[9]; the color computation is presented over different parts of the milestone to determine the ambient, diffuse, and specular contributions. Since the computation is split into these separate contributions the `cast_ray` function lends itself to further decomposition. As will be seen in Section 5, not every student decomposes this function further which leads to instructive discussions in lecture after the assignment has been submitted.

Each step in the implementation of the reflection model requires updates to the original data representation of a sphere to store the sphere's color and the ambient, diffuse, and specular components of the sphere's finish. Addressing these modifications provides a brief experience in software maintenance (extending functionality, in this specific case) for all students.

4.5 Program Generalization/Usability

The final milestone increases the usability of the program in two ways. First, the spheres in the world are read from a file (they were previously defined in a test case) and the generated image is written to a file. Second, the image characteristics can be modified by command-line arguments to, for instance, change the position of the "eye" (or camera) viewing the scene, the dimensions of the image, and the position of the light source.

The students are given a description of the input file format and of the command-line arguments that must be supported. Each student is then responsible for decomposing

[3]The image encoding is printed to the console and redirected to a file.

Table 1: Cyclomatic Complexity Progression for Project Cohorts

	Milestone 3			Milestone 4			Milestone 5		
	max	ave	ave σ	max	ave	ave σ	max	ave	ave σ
Cohort 1	9.1	3.79	1.28	6.90	4.24	2.14	8.14	3.72	1.57
Cohort 2	10.38	4.17	1.41	8.57	4.90	2.62	6.89	3.06	1.09
Overall	9.5	3.91	1.33	7.44	4.45	2.32	7.73	3.50	1.46
Cohort 1 (Normalized)	3.03	1.90	n/a	1.73	2.22	n/a	1.63	1.64	n/a
Cohort 2 (Normalized)	3.46	2.09	n/a	2.14	2.57	n/a	1.38	1.35	n/a
Overall (Normalized)	3.17	1.96	n/a	1.86	2.33	n/a	1.55	1.54	n/a
Instructor	3.0	2.0	n/a	4.0	1.91	n/a	5.0	2.27	n/a

the problem and defining appropriate functions to implement the required behavior.

5. ANALYSIS

Our primary goal for the term-long project is to teach and illustrate the value of decomposition. While there is a tendency for introductory students to "write everything in `main`", our goal of improved decomposition does not stem from a desire to combat this issue. Instead, our motivation for emphasizing decomposition stems from a desire to better prepare students for future coursework and to illustrate the advantages as relate to testing and debugging (practices that can contribute to greater success in programming courses).

In this section we analyze decomposition by comparing cyclomatic complexity[5] and lines of code (LOC)[4]. Though these are not ideal measures of decomposition[8], they do exhibit correlation with opportunities for decomposition.

We use the Resource Standard Metrics (RSM) [4] program to measure the cyclomatic complexity, effective lines of code, and number of functions. These measurements were taken for each student submission that compiled (the RSM tool reasonably requires proper syntax in order to analyze a function). Since the analysis begins with the third assignment and only the student's code is considered (i.e., there are no interface issues), these compilation issues are relatively rare.

5.1 Cyclomatic Complexity Progression

To demonstrate consistency in the cyclomatic complexity progression through the project we compare two cohorts that have completed the term-long project described in Section 4: Cohort 1 (70 students) was enrolled during Winter 2013, Cohort 2 (32 students) was enrolled during Winter 2014. These cohorts were selected based on the timing of the course offerings and the composition of the cohorts; specifically, these cohorts consist primarily of computing majors taking CS 1 "on-track" with the same instructor.

Table 1 summarizes the cyclomatic complexity of the milestone submissions. For each student in a cohort, we compute the maximum cyclomatic complexity of any function in their submission and the average cyclomatic complexity over all functions in their submission. These two values are then averaged over all members of a cohort for each of the final three milestones of the project (the expected cyclomatic complexity for each function in the first two milestones is one). The standard deviation of the average cyclomatic complexity over all functions is also given. Since cyclomatic complexity correlates to the number of "paths" through a function, a lower score suggests a less complex function whereas a higher score correlates with opportunities for further decomposition.

Since the cyclomatic complexity between milestones cannot be directly compared, Table 1 also presents results normalized to an instructor solution[5]. Though the absolute average cyclomatic complexity does not significantly decrease between Milestone 3 and Milestone 5, the normalized complexity does. In addition, while the standard deviation increases between Milestone 3 and Milestone 4, for Milestone 5 it returns to a level in-line with that of Milestone 3. These results do suggest improved decomposition over the course of the project.

Of note, the fourth milestone requires selection of the nearest intersection point for a ray cast against multiple spheres. This selection is arguably the most obvious opportunity for a separate function (the same computation is also used to detect shadows), but many students do not write a separate function for this computation. Factoring this selection into another function noticeably reduces the cyclomatic complexity. In addition, the description for the fourth milestone is presented in parts which some students take as a hint at a possible decomposition (the presentation is actually structured to simplify the discussion of the mathematics). Recognition of this potential for decomposition is a promising improvement over the third milestone. These specific opportunities for decomposition are addressed in lecture (after the milestone has been submitted) to aid in thinking about decomposition for Milestone 5.

5.2 Non-Project vs. Project Cohorts

As an opportunity to assess decomposition skills, once the ray casting project is finished, the students must complete a final assignment that consists of three small programs to manipulate image files: Puzzle (from the Nifty Programming Assignments[7]) requires decoding an image hidden in pixels that appear randomly colored, Fade requires fading (darkening) pixels in an image outside of a user-specified circle, and Blur requires computing a pixel's color based on the average color of neighboring pixels. Figure 2 shows an example of an image generated by the Fade program and of an image generated by the Blur program.

[4]Note that these metrics were not presented to the students. Student code was analyzed only after it had been submitted. Moreover, the students were not given any per function LOC target/limit during the course.

[5]The instructor solution was written using only the material/language features introduced to the students and was *not* written with the intent to "game" cyclomatic complexity, so this comparison is not entirely unfair.

Table 2: Non-Project vs. Project Cyclomatic Complexity Comparison

	Puzzle			Fade			Blur		
	max	ave	ave σ	max	ave	ave σ	max	ave	ave σ
Non-Project Cohort	4.6	3.31	1.69	5.22	2.97	1.36	10.41	7.43	4.43
Project Cohort 1	3.25	2.08	0.46	4.48	2.12	0.57	8.80	3.24	1.16
Project Cohort 2	3.36	2.19	0.87	4.29	2.21	1.38	8.14	2.98	0.71
Project Overall	3.28	2.12	0.62	4.42	2.15	0.91	8.59	3.16	1.04
Normalized to Instructor									
Non-Project Cohort	1.53	1.98	n/a	1.74	1.92	n/a	2.08	3.22	n/a
Project Cohort 1	1.08	1.25	n/a	1.49	1.37	n/a	1.76	1.40	n/a
Project Cohort 2	1.12	1.31	n/a	1.43	1.43	n/a	1.63	1.29	n/a
Project Overall	1.09	1.27	n/a	1.47	1.39	n/a	1.72	1.37	n/a
Instructor Solution	3.00	1.67	n/a	3.00	1.55	n/a	5.00	2.31	n/a

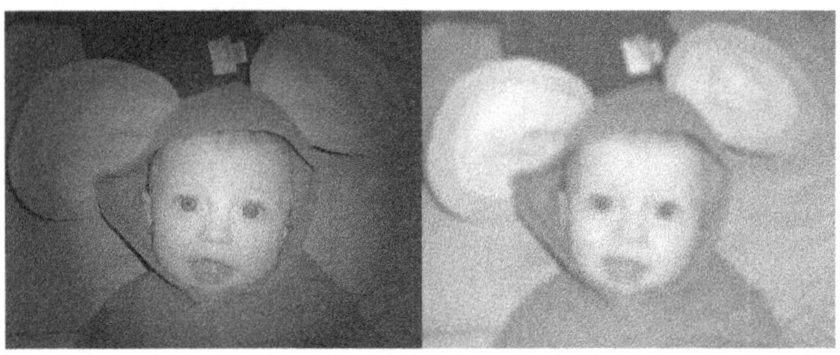

Figure 2: Fade (left) and Blur (right) images generated by final assignment.

This final assignment was given to both Cohort 1 and Cohort 2. Fortunately, this assignment was also used in a more traditional Non-Project CS 1 course[6] (Winter 2012; 113 students, primarily computing majors "on-track" with the same instructor as the project cohorts) wherein each assignment "stood alone" (i.e., there was no continuity between assignments). This provides an opportunity to compare the decomposition of these programs by those that implemented the ray casting term-long project against those that did not.

Table 2 gives the cyclomatic complexity for the maximally complex function (max) and for the average (ave) over all functions in a submission (the standard deviation for the average (ave σ) is also given) for each of the three programs for the Non-Project Cohort and for both Project Cohorts. The results are also normalized to an instructor solution to allow for some comparison between programs. There is a noticeable reduction in cyclomatic complexity among the Project Cohorts in both the maximally complex function and in the average over all functions. This suggests that these students, as a whole, are writing more "simple" functions instead of fewer "complex" functions. The standard deviation for the average complexity over all functions in a submission supports this hypothesis and provides further evidence that the "norm" for the Project Cohorts is functions with lower cyclomatic complexity. This hypothesis is further considered below.

Table 3 further examines the decomposition of these programs by comparing the average number of lines of code in `main`, the average number of lines of code in the longest function (*max*) in each student submission, and the number of functions in each student submission. The submissions for the Non-Project Cohort contained significantly longer `main` functions than those for the Project Cohorts. We believe this is partly attributable to the testing emphasis for the Project Cohorts; Milestones 1 – 4 contained very short `main` functions that served only to initiate unit tests.

It is not uncommon for CS 1 students, when instructed to not "write everything in `main`", to move the vast majority of the functionality into another function that is then invoked by `main` (effectively "renaming" `main`). The average number of lines in the longest function (*max*) for the Project Cohorts (about 60%–70% that of the Non-Project Cohorts) suggests that these students are not simply "renaming" `main`. Moreover, the average number of functions in each submission is significantly higher for the Project Cohorts (from 2 to 2.85 times as many functions) confirming that these students wrote more "simple" functions than their Non-Project counterparts.

5.3 Repeatability

In addition to the cohorts presented above, this approach to CS 1 has been used in "non-major" sections of CS 1 (by the same instructor as the cohorts above) and in parallel sections (during the same terms as those above) offered by a second instructor. Analysis of these other student submissions gives results in-line with those already presented. Our experiences with this term-project approach indicate that the improvement in decomposition skills is repeatable across instructors and across majors.

6. FUTURE WORK

The analysis of decomposition skills presented here is isolated to a single course. By the end of term, the instructor's expectations regarding decomposition are clear and many students have adapted to these expectations and to the course requirements. One point in emphasizing decomposition is preparation for later coursework. As such, we are designing a longitudinal study to track the decomposition skills of these cohorts as they progress through the remainder of the common introductory courses. We hope

[6]It must be noted that this was the penultimate assignment for the Non-Project cohort. In addition, the Blur program for the Project cohorts required processing a number of neighbors as determined by the user whereas the Non-Project cohort needed only analyze a fixed number of neighbors. The variability was allowed as extra credit, but we only analyze the non-extra credit implementations.

Table 3: **Average Number of Lines in `main`/Longest Function, Average Number of Functions**

	Puzzle			Fade			Blur		
	`main`	max	# funcs	`main`	max	# funcs	`main`	max	# funcs
Non-Project Cohort	21.1	25.5	2.6	29.0	33.8	3.8	31.9	40.2	3.4
Project Cohort 1	6.8	15.9	5.2	10.3	23.7	8.0	9.9	28.7	9.4
Project Cohort 2	8.0	15.3	5.4	11.1	22.3	9.1	12.6	26.8	10.2
Project Overall	7.2	15.7	5.3	10.6	23.2	8.4	10.8	28.1	9.7
Project Overall / Non-Project	0.34	0.62	2.03	0.37	0.69	2.21	0.34	0.70	2.85

to determine if these students continue to show improved decomposition (compared to their non-project colleagues) when instructor expectations are less explicit, to determine if these students continue to improve their decomposition skills, or if these students regress to the mean.

Our cyclomatic complexity analysis of student code was only done after the student's final submission of the milestone. The students were never introduced to the complexity metric, so it is incredibly unlikely that any student made an effort to "game" the analysis. As previously stated, we agree with [8] that cyclomatic complexity is lacking as a pedagogical aid to drive decomposition because a student can easily reduce average complexity without meaningfully decomposing the problem. We are considering how we might introduce a metric or tool to provide students with a guide to reducing complexity without driving students toward or rewarding nonsensical decompositions.

7. CONCLUSIONS

After multiple experiences offering CS 1 courses with this term-long project the outcomes have been extremely encouraging. The data presented in Section 5 demonstrates improved decomposition skills among students that work on a constructive term-long project compared to those that experience traditional stand-alone assignments. Anecdotally, many students have remarked positively on the project with some stating that the experience has convinced them that they are sure they want to continue studying computer science.

This term-long project has met our goals of introducing and emphasizing decomposition, of making completion of each assignment a meaningful objective, and of providing a context in which testing is clearly valuable. The structure of this project provides a scaffold to foster decomposition skills. Beginning with prescribed decompositions supports those without prior programming experience, reinforcing decomposition through required testing ascribes specific value to decomposition, and slowly weaning students off of prescribed decompositions gives students the opportunity to apply the decomposition skills they have been practicing. Though each offering to this point has used the same ray casting project, we are working to develop additional projects that support the same approach.

8. REFERENCES

[1] A. Appel. Some techniques for shading machine renderings of solids. In *Proceedings of the April 30–May 2, 1968, Spring Joint Computer Conference*, AFIPS '68 (Spring), pages 37–45, New York, NY, USA, 1968. ACM.

[2] R. E. Berry and B. A. Meekings. A style analysis of c programs. *Commun. ACM*, 28(1):80–88, Jan. 1985.

[3] D. M. Breuker, J. Derriks, and J. Brunekreef. Measuring static quality of student code. In *Proceedings of the 16th Annual Joint Conference on Innovation and Technology in Computer Science Education*, ITiCSE '11, pages 13–17, New York, NY, USA, 2011. ACM.

[4] M Squared Technologies. Resource Standard Metrics (RSM). Retrieved August 26, 2014 from http://msquaredtechnologies.com/Resource-Standard-Metrics.html, 2014.

[5] T. J. McCabe. A complexity measure. *IEEE Transactions on Software Engineering*, 2(4):308–320, July 1976.

[6] Netpbm. Ppm format specification. Retrieved August 26, 2014 from http://netpbm.sourceforge.net/doc/ppm.html, 2013.

[7] N. Parlante, J. Zelenski, K. Schwarz, D. Feinberg, M. Craig, S. Hansen, M. Scott, and D. J. Malan. Nifty assignments. In *Proceedings of the 42Nd ACM Technical Symposium on Computer Science Education*, SIGCSE '11, pages 491–492, New York, NY, USA, 2011. ACM.

[8] A. L. Patton and M. McGill. Student portfolios and software quality metrics in computer science education. *Journal of Computing Sciences in Colleges*, 21(4):42–48, Apr. 2006.

[9] B. T. Phong. *Illumination for Computer-generated Images*. PhD thesis, The University of Utah, 1973. AAI7402100.

[10] N. Truong, P. Roe, and P. Bancroft. Static analysis of students' java programs. In *Proceedings of the Sixth Australasian Conference on Computing Education - Volume 30*, ACE '04, pages 317–325, Darlinghurst, Australia, Australia, 2004. Australian Computer Society, Inc.

Supporting Creativity and User Interaction in CS 1 Homework Assignments

Tammy VanDeGrift
University of Portland
5000 N Willamette Blvd.
Portland, OR 97203
503-943-7256
vandegri@up.edu

ABSTRACT

In this paper, we describe CS 1 programming assignments that encourage design creativity and that utilize user testing. All course assignments allowed for some student-defined specifications; some assignments required user tests to encourage interaction with other people. The open-ended nature of the assignments supported students' creativity and motivation to learn. The user tests provided a platform for students to share their creations and knowledge about computing with others. Both the creative aspect and sharing aspect of the assignments led to students taking ownership of their work. Overall, 41 of 44 (93.2%) students enjoyed the open-ended nature of the assignments and sharing programs with users also enhanced their understanding of their programs and computing concepts.

Categories and Subject Descriptors

K.3.2 [**Computer and Information Science Education**]: Computer Science Education

General Terms

Documentation, Human Factors

Keywords

Novice programmers; motivation; user interaction; creativity

1. INTRODUCTION

"I hear and I forget. I see and I remember. I do and I understand." *Confucius*. Like most university computing courses, our CS 1 students understand the most about computing and programming when constructing their own programs, generally outside of formal instructional time. Like most universities, our students are expected to spend two hours on coursework outside of class for every hour inside class [1]. This poses an interesting challenge for computing faculty: out-of-class time is where the learning unfolds and develops, so homework assignments should be intentionally designed to engage students in the learning process.

SIGCSE'15, March 4–7, 2015, Kansas City, MO, USA.

http://dx.doi.org/10.1145/2676723.2677250

There are several models for designing programming assignments for introductory computing students. Each model has advantages and disadvantages for learning and assessment. For example, one homework model uses precise program specifications, so grading can be automated through test case comparisons between the model solution and the student's solution [10, 13]. This model may be necessary to assess large sets of programming assignments. Another example model uses lab-like problems where students complete functions and methods either from scratch or by extending existing code. This has the advantage that students can get automatic and immediate feedback on a shorter piece of the solution, but may not showcase the creative and design aspects of software development [5, 6].

In our approach, we used three design principles in developing the programming assignments: 1) every assignment includes open-ended elements to encourage students to decide how to define part of the specification and provide latitude for students to be creative in their design and implementation, 2) over half of the assignments have a required user interaction session to encourage the idea that programs are written for other users, and 3) a written summary accompanies each assignment; some written summaries ask students to write a user manual, other summaries ask students to supply their test cases, and other summaries ask students to supply class diagrams. The purpose of the summaries is to challenge students to describe their programs in English and reflect on the design, implementation, and testing process, while scaffolding good documentation habits.

The media computation approach for CS 1 has been successful in providing context and outlets for creativity for students [4]. One of the assignments used in our CS 1 course has elements of media computation (image transformations). Like [4], there were several motivating factors in developing assignments with elements of creativity: provide an opportunity for students to take ownership and pride in their work and to support learning. Another approach described in [8] is to use creative thinking exercises to encourage students to learn about computation; these exercises were not part of the programming itself but focused more on novelty, challenging existing patterns, broadening knowledge and using new environments for stimuli.

The learning theory supporting this programming assignment approach is constructivism [3, 9]. Constructivism is the idea that students build their own interpretations of the material based on their own models and experiences. It also relates to Vygotsky's zones on proximal development [14]. Challenging students to exercise their creativity allows each student to explore at a level that is closest to their zone of proximal development. Also, explaining their code and program to a potential user scaffolds the expansion of their zone of proximal development.

Another consideration in the development of this homework assignment approach is the target audience. Students who were born in the early 1980's to the late 1990's comprise the millennial generation [2]. While it is dangerous practice to stereotype an entire generation, some general trends describe this population of students. Traits of Generation Y include *customization* (students want to personalize their things and experiences), *creativity* (students are more right-brained than left-brained), *authority* (students want to have ownership and authority), and *connected* (students are tightly connected to peers and family). The design of the homework assignments in our CS 1 course takes these generational qualities into consideration. By allowing students to *customize* their solutions, they can exercise *creativity* and take *authority* over the design and development of their programs. Secondly, students can exercise their *connectedness* with others through the user interaction and user tests of their solutions. Note that *connected* is part of the SIGCSE 2015 conference theme.

2. STUDY

This study expands on the work in [12] that describes the injection of creativity in CS 1 programming assignments. The study reported here seeks to examine if the use of creativity-supported assignments motivates students to learn and the impact on learning when students share their programs with users. The hypotheses for this study are two-fold: 1) allowing students to exercise creative freedom motivates students to learn and complete homework, 2) asking students to share their programs with non-programmers engages their learning.

In general, we sought to understand what motivates students to complete programming assignments. Second, will students be motivated to go beyond what is asked in the basic homework requirements? These questions relate to studies regarding student motivation (intrinsic versus extrinsic) and grades. Lin, McKeachie and Kim found that college students with medium extrinsic and high intrinsic motivation have higher course grades than students with low or high extrinsic motivation [7]. Students may be better served when emphasis is on learning and reflection on learning instead of exam and homework grades.

2.1 Context

The University of Portland is a comprehensive, private Catholic university serving ~3700 undergraduate students. The course is CS 203, Introduction to Computer Science, taught in two sections in spring 2012 by the same professor. The two sections had common assignments, lectures, exams, and in-class activities. Java is used to emphasize problem-solving and computer science concepts. In total, 44 students gave consent to be in this study.

The course is required for Computer Science, Electrical Engineering, Math, and Physics majors. Other students can take CS 203 to fulfill elective credits. Of the 44 students, 31 (70.5%) were male and 13 (29.5%) were female. Most students were majoring in computer science, but there was some diversity among the majors: 19 CS, 8 EE, 4 Math, 4 General Engineering, 2 Biology, 2 Mechanical Engineering, 1 Sociology, 1 Psychology, 1 Economics, 1 Education, and 1 Undeclared.

2.2 Homework Assignments

The course included ten assignments. Eight were one-week assignments and two were two-week assignments, split into two parts. In general, students submitted an assignment or part of an assignment every week of the semester. As mentioned previously, every homework assignment had a creative entity and most encouraged students to extend the program beyond the basic requirements. HW 2, 3, 4, 5, 8, and 9 required user interaction and a summary of the user test in the written report. Table 1 briefly describes each homework assignment. See https://sites.up.edu/sigcse2015/ for the full text of each assignment.

Table 1: Descriptions of homework assignments

Assignment	Objective	Creative Bit	Primary CS Concepts Addressed
1: Fortune Teller	Get first Java program written/compiled; use of variables, input and output	Students chose their own fortunes to present to the user, along with the calculation for their 'lucky number'.	Variables I/O Compilation and Execution
2: Madlib	Create a Madlib story, replacing user-input into story with some user input modified using String methods.	Students chose their own Madlib story and missing words. The assignment required that they perform certain operations, such as capitalize just the first letter of the word, switch the order of a two-word phrase, etc., but students chose where to place these operations in their stories.	I/O String manipulation and Java-defined String methods
3: Graphical Greeting Card	Create a graphical greeting card	Students designed the graphics, wrote the code to generate the image, and processed user input (such as the card recipient's name, the sender's name, the desired color, etc) for the custom card.	I/O with dialog boxes Java Graphics (JApplet, Graphics class) Selection statements
4: Golf Simulation	Create a 2D golf landscape and draw a ball flying through the air, given the user's launch angle and velocity.	Students chose how the background of the golf hole was graphically designed. They could include wind direction and speed (optional input).	Java Graphics Selection statements Loops (to draw the ball path)
5: Wheel of Fortune	Create a textual Wheel of Fortune game. Users guess a letter and the locations of the guessed letters are presented to the user.	Students chose the list of potential phrases that could be used as the puzzle. Students could also enhance the game with 'spinning the wheel', earning money, vowels costing money, and supporting multiple players.	Random numbers Selection statements Loops Arrays Methods

6: Library Design	Create UML diagrams for two different classes that would be included in the software to support library users, borrowing books, and/or searching the library's collection. (The University Library was going through a physical renovation at the time, so this system was relevant to the students.)	Students chose the two classes they designed.	UML Class design Methods Instance variables Types
7: Game Player class implementation	Create and implement a Java class to represent a game character for a game of their choice. For example, the class could represent a player in a car racing game, a board game, etc.	Students chose what game they wanted to model for the player in that game.	Class implementation Instance variables Methods Constructors
8: Image Transformations	Implement six different image filters, such as convert color to grayscale, shift right, create a border, create high contrast, brighten, etc.	Students chose their own filters to implement. Some did edge detection, blurring, brightening, pixilation, sepia, etc.	Arrays of objects (the picture was a 2D array of Pixel objects) Java Interfaces Nested loops
9: Inheritance (Choose your own project)	Design and create a program of the student's choice, as long as the program includes inheritance. The inheritance relationship should make sense and not be contrived to satisfy the assignment.	The entire assignment.	Inheritance (class extension) Class relationships Polymorphism
10: Palindromes and Files	Create a program to search for palindromes in the English language (provided as a text document)	Students had to choose some other property to search for (such as words containing the substring 'cs', the number of English words longer than 15 characters).	Recursive methods File I/O Exceptions

2.3 Data Collection and Analysis

The primary data for this study were responses to an IRB-approved end-of-semester paper survey. The survey was administered on paper to encourage a high response rate and to distinguish this survey as separate from the regular on-line course evaluation survey. See Appendix 1 for the full list of survey questions; note that the actual survey instrument spanned multiple pages. This paper focuses on the questions related to creativity in assignments, student motivation, and connectedness regarding the user tests. The open-ended survey responses were coded using content analysis with emergent categories [11]. An individual response may be coded into more than one theme. For example, one student wrote in response to what they liked best about the homework assignments: "They helped me learn the material and gave me practice coding. Also, the room to be creative with assignments was nice." This response was coded into the categories "skill-development" and "creativity". The researcher then went back and re-coded all responses to confirm that the emergent themes were complete and consistent.

3. RESULTS

Results related to creativity, student motivation, user interaction, and overall impact are reported in the subsections below.

3.1 Impact of Creativity

The feature of assignments having creative, open-ended, and flexible components came up as the most popular answer to what students liked best about the homework assignments. Note that students were not told the reasons for this study and this question came before any mention of creativity in the survey questions. Figure 1 shows the top five answers for what students liked best about the homework assignments. 38.6% of students responded that the flexibility, creativity, and open-endedness is what they liked best.

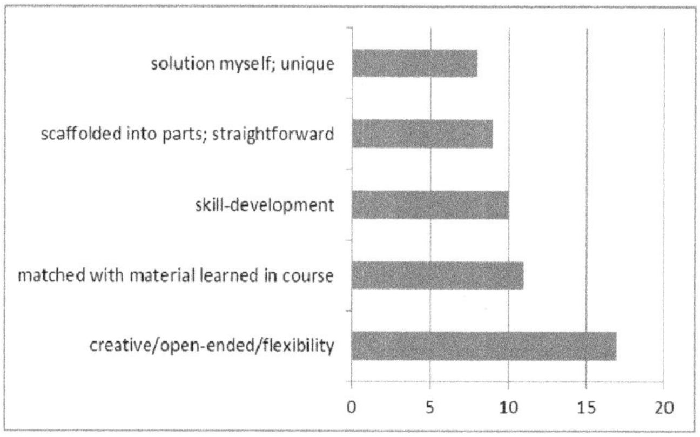

Figure 1: Top 5 Answers: What students liked best about homework assignments

Other reasons that one to two students gave included: wanted to see what CS is like, feeling of accomplishment, additional enrichment in the assignments, they are fun, they have user tests, instructor gives good feedback, can get partial credit, they are challenging, and not too hard.

When asked at the end of the survey if they liked the open-ended nature of the assignments, 41 of the 44 (93.2%) responded that they enjoyed it.

3.2 Impact of Student Motivation

Students were asked via an open-ended question what factors led them to complete homework assignments. Not surprisingly, grades and impact to final grade was the most popular answer. 33 of 44 students said they wanted to get a good grade or the homework scores impacted the final grade. However, only 10 students reported just grades as the only motivator to complete assignments. Other reasons included: interested in how computers work and interest in material (11), wanted to learn concepts (9), wanted to practice programming and improve skills (9), they were fun and satisfying (9), they related to my career (3), and I was capable in completing them (1). In summary, 34 of 44 (77.3%) students had motivations other than grades or in addition to good grades for completing the homework. Students saw value in the task itself (intrinsic) beyond just earning points (extrinsic).

3.3 Impact of User Interaction

User tests were required for HW 2, 3, 4, 5, 8, and 9. Summaries of the user tests were part of the written documentation that accompanied the code submission for each student. Students reported the number of different people with whom they shared their programs over the entire semester. The average number of unique people per student was 3.4, with a minimum of 1 to a maximum of 10. Of those with whom they shared programs, 1.81 people showed an interest in computing. Of the 44 respondents, most shared the programs with friends. The data is as follows: 43 shared with friends, 13 shared with parents, 1 shared with another professor, 10 shared with siblings, and 5 shared with others (girlfriends, housemates, resident assistant, family friend). When they shared their programs, many computing concepts came up during the user tests. Figure 2 shows the self-reported topics (listed in reverse order of presentation in lecture) and number of students who explained that topic when sharing their code.

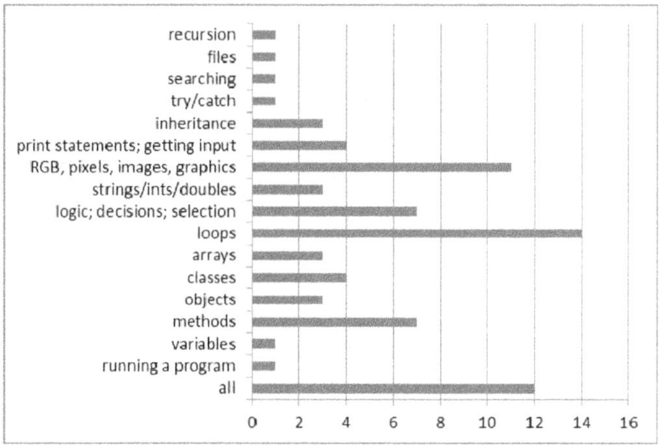

Figure 2: Summary of topics and number of students who described the topics during user tests

Students were also asked if the requirement of sharing a program with a user altered when they started the assignment. The instructor's hypothesis was that students would start assignments that required user tests earlier than assignments that did not require user tests. 34 of 44 (77.3%) responded that sharing the program with another person had no impact on when they started the assignment. Nine (20.5%) responded that they started sooner for those that had user tests and one (2.3%) responded that they started later for those that had user tests. In addition to impact of start time, students were asked if showing their program to another person influenced their effort. 27 of 44 (61.4%) students said it did not influence their effort.

Finally, the students were asked what surprised them when they showed their programs to users. Figure 3 shows the summary of what surprised the CS 1 students during user tests. In some cases, the user helped the CS 1 student make improvements to the program. One student stated, "They seemed to care about things I didn't think they would or they always had suggestions most of which I used." This statement was coded as "improvements". Overall, having users run their programs showcased that people try to input invalid data, people do not read instructions, and testing with other people helped the programmer find bugs.

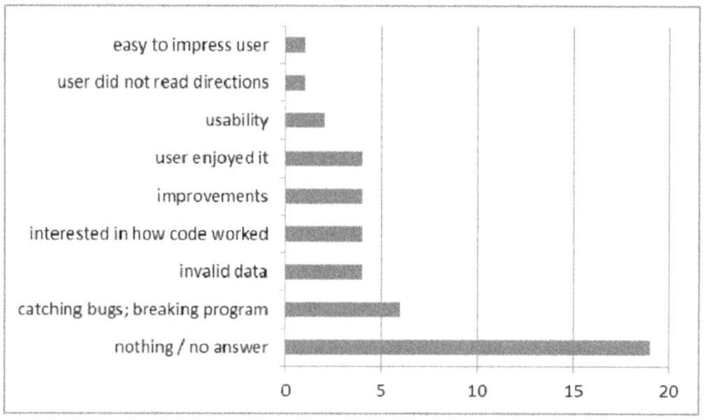

Figure 3: Surprising user test experiences

3.4 Overall Impact in the Course

Overall, students were satisfied with the homework assignments in the course. When asked what could be improved, 15 (34.1%) respondents said nothing – they were already well-designed. No other category of responses had more than four respondents.

Students' favorite assignments were HW 8 (12 respondents), HW 4 (11 respondents), and HW 9 (10 respondents). Creativity in the form of graphical art seems motivating for students. The least favorite assignment was more scattered in terms of responses, but the assignment getting the most votes was HW 6 (11 respondents). HW 6 was a class design-only assignment, and students likely missed the chance to program on this assignment.

In order to assess if students went beyond the explicit homework requirements, students were asked if they completed additional enrichment (optional extensions for no formal credit) during the semester and if they wrote programs that were not assigned as part of the class. 27 (61.3%) completed additional enrichment and 15 (34.1%) wrote programs that were not part of the course (examples include games, sorting numbers, animations, poker game, puzzles, vector experiments, calculators, image transformations, an audio player, and printing random messages.)

Finally, the turn-in rate for homework was high, indicating that students took the course and the assignments seriously. Of 510 possible homework submissions (51 students x 10 assignments), 505 assignments were submitted for grading. The average grades per assignment ranged from 87.2% (HW 10) to 96.0% (HW 1). Even though each homework assignment had open-ended parts, each specification included a grading rubric: 7 points code completion, 7 points code design, and 6 points reflection paper.

4. DISCUSSION

Bias and threats to validity: As with most studies, this study had potential biases in the results. In total, 51 students took CS 203 in spring 2012 and 44 of the 51 gave consent to use their data in the study. It could be that the 44 were not the most representative sample of the students taking the course. Students may have responded more positively in the survey since the instructor had access to the survey responses; however, students were assured that the surveys would be sealed in an envelope until after final grades were submitted. Also, the instructor left the classroom while students completed the survey.

The results regarding creativity indicate that this millennial generation of students may be inspired by the chance to customize and personalize. Over 25% of students stated, without prompting, that the creativity/open-ended nature of the assignments was one of the features they liked best about the homework in the course. Sharing the programs through user tests gave students the opportunity to have share and get feedback about their programs. While the construct of authority or ownership was not explicitly studied or measured, it appears as "I get to do the solution myself and get to do something unique" as the reason eight students offered as to what they liked best about homework.

Although this study presents many of the strengths in giving creative, open-ended programming assignments, this practice does pose challenges. Using creative, open-ended assignments in large classes reduces the amount of automation one can use when grading. At University of Portland, the CS 203 course section size is generally 35 or fewer students, so individual execution of student programs for grading is feasible. If an instructor wants to use automation, perhaps the basic set of features could be graded automatically with scripts and the unique features graded by hand. If done modularly, this approach could work. Another potential drawback of giving students creative freedom is that later in the curriculum, students design and implement software systems to a given specification. However, we decided that getting CS 1 students excited about programming by letting them be creative outweighs the risk of students not conforming to set requirements in later courses. More than half of CS 203 students are not CS majors, so giving them practice in defining programs they want to create and then creating them will serve them well as they use computing as a tool in their careers.

5. CONCLUSION

This paper describes the design aspects of homework assignments and study for a CS 1 course. The design elements include: 1) required and open-ended program specifications, 2) user tests for more than half the assignments, and 3) written documentation that accompanies the code. The results indicate that, not surprisingly, this millennial generation is motivated to complete work for a grade; but, more than that, they appreciate the opportunity to *connect* with users and *connect* their creativity with coding.

6. ACKNOWLEDGMENTS

We thank the introductory computer science students who participated in this study and the course. The author is appreciative of Dr. Karen Eifler, Professor of Education, for fruitful discussions about this work.

7. REFERENCES

[1] Berrett, Dan. 2012. Carnegie, the Founder of the Credit-Hour, Seeks Its Makeover. *The Chronicle of Higher Education.* December 5, 2012.

[2] Elmore, T. 2010. *Generation iY: Our Last Chance to Save Their Future.* Poet Gardener Publishing.

[3] Gonzalez, G. 2004. Constructivism in an introduction to programming course. *Journal of Computing Sciences in Colleges.* 19(4). 299 – 305.

[4] Guzdial, M. 2013. Exploring Hypotheses about Media Computation. In Proceedings of the *International Computing Education Research Conference (ICER).* 19 – 26.

[5] Hovemeyer, D. *et al.* 2014. Using and sharing programming exercises to improve introductory courses. In *Proceedings of the 45th ACM Technical Symposium on Computer Science Education.* 737.

[6] Kumar, A. Problets – The Home Page. URL: http://problets.org. Last accessed September 4, 2014.

[7] Lin, Y., McKeachie, W., and Kim, Y. 2003. College student intrinsic and/or extrinsic motivation and learning. *Learning and Individual Differences.* 13. 251–258.

[8] Miller, L.D. *et al.* 2014. Integrating Computational and Creative Thinking to Improve Learning and Performance in CS1. In Proceedings of *ACM Special Interest Group for Computer Science Education.* 475 – 480.

[9] Piaget, J. 1950. *The Psychology of Intelligence.* New York: Routledge.

[10] Sherman, M., Bassil, S., Lipman, D., Tuck, N., and Martin, F. 2013. Impact of auto-grading on an introductory computing course. *Journal of Computing Sciences in College.* 28(6). 69 – 75.

[11] Stemler, S. 2001. An Overview of Content Analysis. *Practical Assessment, Research & Evaluation.* 7(17). http://pareonline.net/getvn.asp?v=7&n=17 Last accessed September 4, 2014.

[12] VanDeGrift, T. 2007. Encouraging creativity in introductory computer science programming assignments. In *Proceedings of the American Society for Engineering Education Conference (ASEE).*

[13] Vander Zanden, B., and Berry, M. 2013. Improving automatic code assessment. *Journal of Computing Sciences in College.* 29(2). 162 – 168.

[14] Vygotsky, L. S. 1978. *Mind in society: The development of higher psychological processes.* Cambridge: Harvard University Press. 79 – 91.

Appendix 1: Survey Questions

Overall Feedback

1. Overall, what did you like best about CS203 homework assignments?
2. Overall, what would you suggest to improve the CS203 homework assignments?
3. Here is a list of assignments that you completed for CS203. Put an "F" next to the assignment that was your favorite. Put an "L" next to the assignment that was your least favorite. Include any comments/feedback about your choices below.

Assignment	Topics
Homework 1: Fortune Generator	input, output, arithmetic
Homework 2: Madlib	Strings
Homework 3: Greeting Card	Graphics, conditionals
Homework 4: Golf Simulation	Graphics, loops, conditionals
Homework 5: Wheel of Fortune	Arrays, loops, conditionals
Homework 6: Library Design	Class design
Homework 7: GamePlayer	Class implementation (instance variables, methods, constructors)
Homework 8: Image Transformations	2D Arrays, arrays of objects
Homework 9: Choose Your Own	Inheritance
Homework 10: Palindromes	File I/O, recursion

Comments on choices (if any):

4. What factors motivated you to complete the CS203 assignments?

User Tests

5. Several homework assignments asked you to have a friend execute your program and to solicit his/her feedback.

a. With how many *different* people did you share one of your homework programs? ______________

b. Of those with whom you shared your programs, how many showed an interest in computer science or programming? ________________

c. For each person below, check the box if you shared at least one of your homework programs with them:

□ a friend (peer), □ a parent/guardian, □ a professor, □ a sibling, □ other ___________________________

d. Did you explain any computer science or programming concepts when you shared your programs with other users? No/Yes
If so, which concept(s) did you explain?

e. Recall that some homework assignments required you to share your program with a friend and some did not. Select the statement that best fits your experience by checking the box.

□ In general, I finished the programs that I shared with a friend earlier (with respect to the due date) than those that I did not share with a friend.

□ In general, I finished the programs that I shared with a friend later (with respect to the due date) than those that I did not share with a friend.

□ Having a friend run my program had no influence on how early I finished my programs with respect to the due dates.

f. Did having a friend run your programs influence your effort or affect the quality of your programs? Explain why or why not.

g. Describe any results from your user tests (friends running your programs) that surprised you.

Open-Ended Assignments

6. Most of the CS203 assignments had an open-ended component that you got to choose to implement. For example, in the image processing homework (HW 8), you designed and implemented an image filter of your choice. In the greeting card homework (HW 3), you designed the greeting card picture and text. In the madlib homework (HW 2), you designed your own story.

a. Did you enjoy the open-ended parts of the homework assignments? No/Yes/Not applicable

b. Why or why not?

c. Most of the assignments had additional enrichment opportunities (not graded for points) to further your knowledge. Did you complete at least one additional enrichment feature during the semester? No/Yes

7. Did you write any Java programs for your own use (not for graded HW in CS203) during the semester? No/Yes
If so, what did the program(s) do?

8. Do you have any other comments about the homework assignments in CS203? If so, put them here:

Embedding Secure Coding Instruction into the IDE: A Field Study in an Advanced CS Course

Michael Whitney, Heather Lipford Richter, Bill Chu, and Jun Zhu
College of Computing and Informatics
University of North Carolina Charlotte
9201 University City Blvd, Charlotte, NC 28223
[mwhitne6, Heather.Lipford, billchu, jzhu16]@uncc.edu

ABSTRACT

Many of the security vulnerabilities common in today's software can be prevented with standard secure coding practices. Computer science students who will become the developers of that software need to learn about those practices so they can prevent such vulnerabilities. Many computing programs are addressing this need through additional lectures, elective courses, or more holistic approaches to integrate security across curriculums. We are exploring a complementary approach, integrating secure coding education into the IDE to provide a learning opportunity in the context of writing code. In this paper, we report on two field studies using an IDE tool in an advanced Web programming course. Our results indicate that the tool can increase students' awareness and knowledge of secure programming, but to be most effective, instructors may need to incentivize its use through in-class methods and careful timing of its introduction.

Categories and Subject Descriptors

K.3.2 [**Computers and Education**]: Computer and Information Science Education—*computer science education, information systems education*; D.2.6 [**Software Engineering**]: Programming Environments—*Integrated environments*

General Terms

Security; Human Factors; Experimentation

Keywords

Secure Programming; Security Education; IDE

1. INTRODUCTION

The safety and security of today's software is in large part dependent on those who develop and maintain that software. Given this critical importance, "the ability to write secure code should be as fundamental to a university computer science undergraduate as basic literacy" [2, p. 56]. Yet, security vulnerabilities that are fairly easy to prevent are still widespread [9].

Academia's response has been to incorporate security instruction into its curriculums in both classic and innovative ways. Faculty have modified and created new courses, developed programs, implemented security tracks, and integrated thread-based approaches in an attempt to address security education [4, 5, 13]. However, these approaches still fall short in exposing all computing students to the breadth and depth of secure programming instruction [10].

We are exploring a complementary approach through tool support in the IDE. ESIDE (Educational Support in the IDE) monitors a student's workspace and provides instructional guidance and educational materials about secure coding in a contextually based real-time manner as students are writing code. Its purpose is to build upon classroom lessons to deepen the student's knowledge base as they work on assignments and class projects outside of the classroom. Such a resource could theoretically provide continuous secure programming instruction throughout the learning process and across the curriculum.

We had previously evaluated ESIDE in a single, 3-hour laboratory study with students in an advanced computing course [15]. Results indicated the potential for the tool to raise awareness of secure coding, as well as increase students' secure coding behaviors. In this paper we extend these results with two field studies – one for the period of one assignment and the second for an entire semester, in the same advanced computing course. Our results demonstrate that ESIDE does raise security awareness, but that the timing of the tool's introduction, and the support of instructors for tool use may be critical for motivating students to learn and practice secure coding skills.

2. RELATED WORK

There are a variety of ways to add secure coding instruction into curriculums. Adding lectures to existing courses and providing elective courses is a common approach to teaching secure coding. However, this may lead to the unintended effect that security is perceived as a secondary topic – requiring only minimal attention for most or as an elective topic for those who are most interested.

Security tracks (e.g., certificates / minors) and developed programs in security (e.g., baccalaureate degrees) are commendable examples [6] of academia's approaches to holistic instruction, as they develop principles and practices throughout the educational experience [1]. A downside of these approaches is they only attract a small portion of the students

SIGCSE'15, March 4–7, 2015, Kansas City, MO, USA.

ACM 978-1-4503-2966-8/15/03 ...$15.00.
http://dx.doi.org/10.1145/2676723.2677280.

enrolled in computing degree programs and may still not provide a broad range of future developers with sufficient secure coding knowledge.

The threaded model acknowledges the need to incorporate security principles and practices at the earliest point possible in the student's education. The intent of this approach is to develop a holistic security mindset by threading security throughout the curriculum [4]. However, there has been limited research in incorporating security principles across a standard computing curriculum. Towson University has been successfully accomplishing this task through security injections – checklists and accompanying exercises tailored to the content of a variety of programming courses [11, 12].

Our approach complements these holistic approaches by exploring tool support outside of the classroom for providing and reinforcing secure coding skills while students are programming, throughout their curriculum.

3. ESIDE

ESIDE is a Java Eclipse plug-in built upon the original framework known as ASIDE [14], a tool for providing in-situ security vulnerability warnings and mitigations for developers. The approach draws from integrative learning theory which describes how the blending and synthesization of multiple perspectives helps students make connections across curricula [3]. By doing so, the outcome is greater that the some of its parts [7]. ESIDE facilitates the connection between classroom lessons and secure coding practices. The connection is accomplished by providing an instructional intervention the moment a student writes insecure code. In this manner, the learning experience is enhanced because students can directly apply the complementing materials. We are expanding ESIDE's types of warnings, explanations, and the code generated to fit both early and advanced programming courses. This paper focuses on an evaluation we performed with computing students, in an advanced Web development course. Consequently, our examples here focus on the kinds of warnings and knowledge for those students.

ESIDE functions by monitoring student's code for predefined vulnerable code patterns. When found, ESIDE initiates an educational intervention by placing a warning icon in the left margin of the code editor. Hovering over the icon reveals an inviting message to further explore the issues (Figure 1) and a single click reveals a short list of available options based on the code written. Each item on the list is accompanied with an explanative popup and made available upon selection (Figure 2). If a more in-depth explanation is needed, students can follow a link to an informative page which provides background information on the vulnerability discovered, why the issue should be mitigated, and examples on how to remediate the issue.

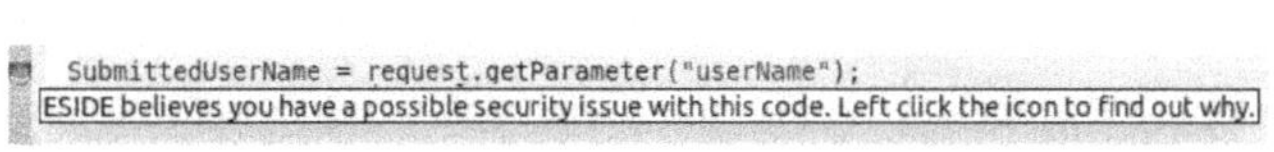

Figure 1: Hovered Icon Message

This advanced version of ESIDE also has the ability to auto-generate remediation code for some types of vulnerabilities. When ESIDE provides the popup list of educational support, some of the list items (Figure 2 e.g., 02 – Filter String Input) can be double clicked to insert auto-generated remediation code (Figure 3) . Upon activation, ESIDE im-

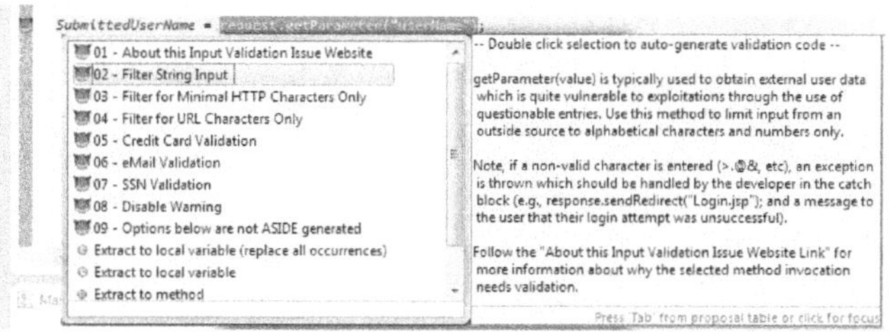

Figure 2: Remediation Options

```
SubmittedUserName = ESAPI.validator().getValidInput("replace with context",
                    request.getParameter("userName"), "SafeString", 200, false);
```

Figure 3: Generated Code

plements the standard validation and encoding routines as available from the open source secure application library, ESAPI [8].

Java has many code-related vulnerabilities and remedies that are beyond the scope of the computing student's developmental needs. Therefore, it was necessary to reduce the list down to the areas that would be most beneficial to the advanced student. Based upon faculty consultation and professional recommendations [9], the list includes the types of vulnerabilities that are caused by lack of input validation, output encoding, and SQL injection. In this advanced class, these code patterns cause real and common vulnerabilities such as cross-site scripting and SQL injection if left unresolved. The following are three examples of lines of code that would initiate ESIDE interaction:

- request.getParameter("userName");
- out.println("<p>You indicated:" + foo + "</p>");
- ResultSet results = query.executeQuery();

We had previously performed a laboratory evaluation of ESIDE with students in the same advanced Web development course at our university [15]. Eighteen participants worked on their own assignment code on a computer with ESIDE for a 3 hour session. Participants regularly interacted with ESIDE (e.g., 70% of warnings clicked) and spent several minutes reading the available content. We found a significant improvement in secure coding post-test scores. ESIDE did influence students to improve the security of their code through both automated code generation and manual implementation of ESIDE's suggested resolutions – 47% of ESIDE's warnings were resolved [15].

However, this evaluation found that students were confused with the various remediation options available to them, and requested simpler explanations on the vulnerabilities [15]. To this end, we simplified the remedy selection popup menu (both presentation and content) for a quicker reference that directly tied into the advanced learning points of interacting with users and stored data. We also developed instructional pages in a layered fashion where messages were simplistic, contextual and straightforward. Examples were written to complement the code used by these students as well as having specific points highlighted. In addition, examples became available only after the student expanded the example option. In this manner, students can explore information that is relevant to them and not be overwhelmed with too much information at first glance.

4. METHODOLOGY

We had previously evaluated ESIDE in a controlled environment for a limited amount of time [15]. Students were aware they were evaluating ESIDE, which may have influenced their attention and interest in the tool. In contrast, the studies we are reporting on here examined ESIDE as deployed in the students' work environment over the period of a single assignment and a whole semester. Student participants were drawn from two sections of our university's Network Based Application Development (NBAD) advanced programming course which has computing students (senior undergraduates and Master's students) incrementally develop a Java based Web application over the period of the semester. Students have likely taken an intro to security course but this does not include secure programming.

We utilized multiple data gathering techniques to obtain feedback about ESIDE's potential to influence the student's secure coding mindset, knowledge base and coding practices as well as to improve the tool for future implementations. Specific goals included:

- How will students interact with ESIDE over time?
- What are the students' impressions of ESIDE?
- How does ESIDE influence the students' awareness and mindset of security?
- Can ESIDE help students advance their secure coding knowledge?
- Will use of ESIDE influence students to integrate secure coding practices into their assignments?

Two instructors from both sections of our university's NBAD course allowed us to invite their students to participate in the single assignment study (fall 2012) and the full semester study (spring 2013). Instructors of this upper level Java-based web application course have their students use Java Servlet technology to develop applications such as an online stock trading application or a flight reservation application or a banking application. Throughout the semester, the NBAD students are minimally exposed to secure coding discussions, presentations or examples (e.g., a few slides).

The structure and data gathering techniques for these studies were similar. ESIDE was available in the college's computer lab and personal PC installation instructions were available through the class Moodle site. For both studies, we provided students with a brief overview of the functionality of ESIDE and then asked them to interact as little or as much as they chose throughout the study. Students from both studies also completed a pre and post-test on secure coding, provided assignments for code reviews, allowed ESIDE to submit interaction logs, and participated in semi-structured and informal interviews. The semester long study also included a focus group.

Interviews consisted of informal interactions throughout deployment and a semi-structured interview at the end of the assignment study. The topics of ESIDE use, impression, and suggestions were explored with this group. Students were also provided with the opportunity to talk about the importance of secure coding. Interview times ranged from a few minutes to 40 minutes. Participation was voluntary, and students were not compensated for participating in either study, although pizza was provided for the focus group.

4.1 Study One: 14 Day Assignment

Eight students from two sections (different instructors) of our university's Fall 2012 Network Based Application Development (NBAD) course participated in the 14-day assignment-based study. Both section instructors followed the same syllabus. We deployed the study on the fourth assignment when students were required to integrate a higher level of user interaction into their application. They had previously developed static pages for the purpose of login, logout, registration and were then required to implement functionality on top of those artifacts. This functionality included the ability to add accounts, display stock details, buy/sell stock and display stock history. Seven students participated in an interview once their assignment was submitted.

4.2 Study Two: Semester Long Deployment

Two sections of NBAD students (different instructors) participated in the Spring 2013 semester long study. In total, 64 students consented to participate in one form or another. Specific numbers for data gathered will be discussed in their respective sections.

Section 1 completed four assignments. The first three progressively developed a stock trading Servlet application. The class started with static HTML as a framework for subsequent assignments that became more dynamic. The final assignment incorporated AJAX to develop a banking Servlet application.

Section 2 had four assignments to complete. These assignments progressively developed interaction with an MVC-based online airline reservation application and, eventually, a banking application. The third assignment incorporated AJAX for communication between the applications and the fourth assignment built further on the communication with the incorporation of XML and SOAP.

A focus group was held halfway through the semester and was used to ascertain ESIDE usage and interaction. We displayed code on an overhead projector and walked through various forms of interaction the students were exposed to while working on code. Doing so helped facilitate a discussion about their impressions and suggestions about the available interaction (e.g., icons, menus, code gen, etc.) as well as how well the available content supported them. We also discussed their perspectives on secure coding and if ESIDE influenced any change in their behavior.

4.3 Pre/Post-Tests and Survey

Participants from both studies completed a pre-test and demographic survey (either online or on paper) at the beginning of their respective study. After they finished their assignment or at the end of the semester, they completed the post-test. Content reflected the concepts and principles represented by ESIDE.

For both studies, we designed two pre/post-test versions with similar questions which we counterbalanced between the two class sections. Study 1 pre/post-tests consisted of 17 yes/no – true/false questions that ranged from general questions about input validation and output encoding to the identification of code statements that required input validation and output encoding. For Study 2, we shortened the pre/post-tests to 12 questions by removing 5 questions that had a high correct response rate (e.g., easily guessed). The following is an example of two survey questions.

1. True / False My application is only used within the company, therefore input from users and other company computers can be trusted.

2. Yes / No Is the following vulnerable to an injection attack, an output encoding attack or both?

```
String homeState = request.getParameter(state);
out.println("<a href=\"http://map.com?state="
+ homeState + "\">Link your home state</a>");
```

In addition to the secure coding test questions, we also included qualitative survey questions on the post-test which asked about ESIDE impressions and recommendations.

5. RESULTS

In total, there were 72 (8/64) students in the two studies. For those who reported, 53 (8/45) were male, 13 (0/13) were female, 29 (3/26) were graduate students, and 29 (5/24) were undergraduates. ESIDE submitted 57 (7/50) individual interaction logs.

5.1 Logged Usage, Interaction and Behavior

We utilized a logging feature to track when ESIDE was running, what vulnerabilities it found and how much the students interacted with the available resources. For Study 1, ESIDE submitted logs for 7 individuals. These students had ESIDE running and available for an average of 3.57 days (1-7 day range) and initiated interaction (hovered or clicked the code warning icon) 513 times. This averaged to 7.3 interactions per active student per day over the span of 10 days. No anomalous usage spikes (e.g., everyone accessing the day the assignment is due) were found over the period of the study.

Study 2 ran for 95 days. Logging activity began in the third week as that is when students start writing targeted code. From that point, ESIDE submitted logs for 50 individuals. These students had ESIDE running an average of 5.56 days (1-34 day range) and 32 students initiated 352 interactions (hovered or clicked the code warning icon). This averaged to less than one interaction per student per day from the time ESIDE started logging until the last assignment was due. ESIDE saw the greatest amount of use and interaction in the beginning of the study when targeted code was first written. Usage then clustered around due dates in a decreasing fashion.

When comparing the logs of the two studies, Study 1 (assignment based) students ran and interacted with ESIDE at a greater rate than Study 2 students. A major contributor to this difference is the timing of the deployments. Study 1 was timed to present ESIDE support at the same time that students were building functionality into their applications that had security implications and likely security vulnerabilities. In doing so, there existed a direct connection between concepts and practices.

Students in Study 2 started receiving ESIDE support three weeks into the semester when they began writing placeholder code (e.g., Login page without functionality). This caused an issue with the support in that students had not yet learned how to make their code functional, yet ESIDE wanted to help them learn how to secure it. Thus, when students later added that functionality, and introduced actual vulnerabilities, they had already viewed and dismissed ESIDE as not particularly helpful.

During both studies, ESIDE provided students the option to auto-generate secure code. Five students in Study 1 opted to use this option but only one student decided to include the generated secure code with their assignment. Four students in Study 2 had ESIDE auto-generate secure code yet none allowed the modification to remain in the final product. One student reported that after reviewing the auto-generated code, he was inspired to create his own remediation methods.

Our interaction log review also revealed that some of the students decided to utilize ESIDE for projects outside of NBAD assignments. This interaction ranged from vulnerability identification to content exploration to code generation. Code was not available to review possible changes but the discovery does reveal that students were interested in using ESIDE across the curriculum.

5.2 Student Perceptions

Overall, students from both studies appreciated the available ESIDE support and felt as if it had a lot of potential as an educational resource. They reported that ESIDE's icon, menus and content were unobtrusive, easily accessible, simple to navigate, and explained topics in an understandable nature. When asked if ESIDE influenced them to write more secure code, they reported that while they did learn about secure coding, their primary focus was on the completion of a functional project as evident with the following comments:

- "great tool" would "play around with it more" if "I was not so tied up with and concentrating on finishing an assignment" (p14).
- "I have not had a chance to work with ESIDE because my main focus was getting [the] project done with full functionality before the due date" (p16).
- "was always concerned about getting the project done and not necessarily the quality (in regards to security) of the finished project" (p50).

Interviews revealed a shift in students' mindset and a better understanding of their insecure code writing behavior. They reported that ESIDE's vulnerable code icon helped them understand that an issue existed but they didn't always spend the time to find out why. The icon started to serve as an important educator itself as it raised their awareness of behaviors – "*I started to be able to predict when the icon would flag my code before I even wrote it*" (p9). Students reported that they were starting to think about their own coding practices and how those practices influence the security of their overall application.

Students also shared why they were hesitant to allow ESIDE to modify their functional code. When students acquired code functionality, they felt as if they accomplished something and wanted to move on to the next task. They felt that any alteration would slow them down by breaking functionality or requiring them to learn how to properly utilize the modification. This is understandable considering they were so focused on a finished product.

5.3 Pre/Post-Test Analysis

Students in Study 1 (assignment) experienced an average pre/post-test increase of 5.0%. Students who had ESIDE running 4 or more days (n=4) experienced a 15.5% gain while those who ran ESIDE less than 4 days (n=4) saw reduced scores (-4.63%).

We collected a total of 18 matching pre/post-tests for Study 2 (semester long). This number is less than expected as, unfortunately, one of the instructors ran too long on the final day of class when we were going to administer the post-test. After dropping two non-related questions, we evaluated both versions of our pre-tests for goodness of fit and found that no significant difference existed between the two using a chi square test χ^2 (9, N=40)=11.03, p=.27. Pre/post-tests that were less than 75% completed were not used in the evaluation. The overall pre/post average increase for all students was 8.3%. Students who had ESIDE running more than five days performed significantly better on the post-test (t(8)=2.48, p=0.03) with a 15.5% increase vs. those who ran ESIDE less than five days only increased by 1.1%.

Average scores for Study 2 were approximately 30% lower than those in Study 1. This was expected as questions with a high correct response rate (easily guessable) were removed from Study 2's pre/post tests.

Table 1: Summary of mean test scores (%)

	pre (SD)	post (SD)	change
Study 1 (n8)	60.4 (16.8)	65.4 (13.5)	5.0
ran ≥4 days (n4)	54.4 (19.2)	69.1 (18.3)	14.7*
ran <4 days (n4)	66.4 (13.9)	61.8 (7.4)	-4.63
Study 2 (n18)	30.6 (25.1)	38.9 (23.5)	8.3
ran >5 days (n9)	27.8 (26.8)	43.3 (30.0)	15.5*
ran <5 days (n9)	33.3 (24.5)	34.4 (15.1)	1.1
*Significant. Note – small sample size.			

5.4 Limitations

The components of these studies were summative in nature as we collected data concerning student interaction with ESIDE in their own work environment. Understandably, limitations will exist. All participants were enrolled in an advanced Java class and interaction with ESIDE might be different with intermediate or early students over the same time periods. Knowledge of participation in the study and exposure to a new application might have influenced interaction. However, interaction was optional and any initial influence would most likely have leveled out over time. It is also possible that minimal guidance into ESIDE use might have decreased interaction and results but this was intentional as we were interested in how ESIDE could autonomously support the student.

6. DISCUSSION

The most significant result of our two studies is that ESIDE led to an increase in students' awareness that their code has security implications. Students reported being able to predict when the warnings would occur, and frequently used some of the language from ESIDE's explanations as we talked with them. Students also reported an appreciation of ESIDE's support and explanations. We believe ESIDE is demonstrating effectiveness in one of our goals – increasing the security mindset of students.

We also found a significant, but small, increase in secure coding knowledge based on the pre- and post-tests. Students who chose to have ESIDE running as little as 4 different days in the short study and 5 different days in the semester study experienced test score gains while the other group saw no noticeable gain. This is encouraging that ESIDE has the potential to serve as an effective means to complement classroom lessons and increase the learning of secure coding practices and principles. However, our sample size is small, as is the gain. In these studies there was no change to the course content or assignments. Thus, the students who saw gain had no incentives for learning and retaining secure coding information beyond self interest. If ESIDE is used to complement and reinforce instruction, rather than solely on its own, we would expect to see additional gains.

Where we did not see any notable effectiveness was in modifying the students' behaviors – to incorporate secure coding practices into their assignments. These two studies revealed two significant lessons that we did not encounter in our initial laboratory study [15].

6.1 Functionality first

Not surprisingly, students in both studies exhibited a task completion mindset that was focused on the core functionality of their code. They were most concerned with just getting things to work. This was related to the goals and content of the course, and rewarded in assignment and exam scores. Thus, once students discovered ESIDE did not help them complete their assignment tasks, their active interaction diminished. As previously mentioned, we did not wish to change the course in any way for these field evaluations. Thus, student participation was completely voluntary with little external incentive beyond helping out the researchers.

Students also reported a fear of breaking their working functionality if they followed ESIDE's guidance and improved the security of their code. Once they got their code working, they were then unwilling to risk doing anything extra that might change that functionality. Thus, even while students interacted with ESIDE and became cognizant of their insecure coding practices, they were unwilling to fix them and potentially hurt their assignment.

In the previous laboratory study, while these fears were present, they did not impede behavior as much [15]. The participants in the lab study were still concerned with breaking their functionality, but many still tried out adding secure coding to their assignments (and then removed it later if desired). However, students were working in a lab, and getting compensated for their time. They may have been willing to spend a little more time experimenting with ESIDE. They may have experienced more trust in ESIDE or felt more pressure to change behavior with researchers in the room.

As with other programming concepts, the skills of secure coding are important to both be aware of, but also to actually practice and employ. These issues around functionality concerns point to a need for some support and integration of ESIDE's goals more directly into the course. Much like the real world, if security is not valued and rewarded at least in some way, those writing code will spend their limited time and efforts on the aspects that are. We need to do additional research to understand the incentives that will influence and increase such behavior change, while still balancing the primary needs of learning and practicing course content.

6.2 Timing

Students in the assignment study used and explored ESIDE at a much greater rate than the semester-long study.

This finding is critical as it is related to the importance of timing the use of a tool such as ESIDE. During the assignment study, students were exposed to ESIDE's warnings and educational materials for the first time as they implemented real functionality with real vulnerabilities into their code. This created a direct connection between their practice and ESIDE's available resources. The semester long group first received warnings on placeholder code, which created a situation where the student was not ready to implement ESIDE's support. This might have caused a desensitization which led to diminished interaction. Consequently, when ESIDE flagged new coding issues (e.g., SQL code introduced later in the semester) the desensitized students were unaware of these new materials because they viewed the icon as a means to reveal content that they had previously explored. Students may not have realized when they were ready and capable of implementing ESIDE's recommendations, as the warnings did not change throughout the semester.

We originally envisioned a tool such as ESIDE being always available as students write code throughout their curriculum. Yet, these results demonstrate that students may not return again and again to ESIDE's warnings if they were not able to make use of earlier warnings. This leads to two design lessons. One is to further investigate what is the proper time for the tool to provide warnings and interaction with students. The second is to provide more controls for instructors to customize how and when different aspects of ESIDE be introduced as students progress through their coursework. We will also need to investigate how to motivate repeated interactions across multiple courses, as the types of security explanations and code patterns will change as students move from early introductory courses through to advanced courses.

7. CONCLUSION AND FUTURE WORK

Computer science curriculums need to provide future software developers with secure programming knowledge and skills. We believe our approach can help to fulfill this need by complementing in-class materials with tool support during students' code construction. In doing so, students at all levels will have the opportunity to expand and reinforce their secure programming knowledge. Our evaluations provide evidence that such an approach can be an effective means for providing instructional support in the IDE over longer periods of time. However, deploying ESIDE also revealed needs for additional investigation of how to best incorporate ESIDE into coursework through incentives and timing of the instructional support.

In the long-term, our goal is to explore if ESIDE can enhance secure coding education at all levels across the curriculum. We are modifying ESIDE to meet the needs of instructors and students from introductory to advanced level classes. Overall, the educational support process will be similar – targeted code is identified, an educational opportunity is made available, and a possible code generation function can be implemented. We are exploring and evaluating methods of tailoring ESIDE support to the students' level and providing additional customization for instructors.

8. ACKNOWLEDGMENTS

Thanks to all faculty, students, and participants for their time. This work is funded in part by NSF-DUE #1044745.

9. REFERENCES

[1] S. Azadegan, M. Lavine, M. O'Leary, A. Wijesinha, and M. Zimand. An undergraduate track in computer security. In *Proceedings of the 8th annual conference on Innovation and technology in computer science education*, ITiCSE '03, pages 207–210, 2003.

[2] M. Bishop and D. Frincke. Teaching secure programming. *IEEE Security Privacy*, 3(5):54–56, 2005.

[3] B. J. Brown Leonard. *Integrative learning as a developmental process: A grounded theory of college students' experiences in integrative studies.* ProQuest, 2007.

[4] D. L. Burley and M. Bishop. Summit on education in secure software: Final report. Technical Report CSE-2011-15, Department of Computer Science, University of California at Davis, Davis, June 2011.

[5] J. Davis and M. Dark. Teaching students to design secure systems. *Security & Privacy, IEEE*, 1(2):56–58, 2003.

[6] National Security Agency (NSA) Central Security Service (CSS). Centers of academic excellence institutions. `http://www.nsa.gov/ia/academic_outreach/nat_cae/institutions.shtml`, 2013.

[7] W. H. Newell. Professionalizing interdisciplinarity: Literature review and research agenda. *Interdisciplinarity: Essays from the literature*, pages 529–563, 1998.

[8] OWASP Foundation. OWASP enterprise security api. `https://www.owasp.org/index.php/Category:OWASP_Enterprise_Security_API`, 2013.

[9] OWASP Foundation. Top ten project. `https://www.owasp.org/index.php/Category:OWASP_Top_Ten_Project`, Jun 2013.

[10] L. F. Perrone, M. Aburdene, and X. Meng. Approaches to undergraduate instruction in computer security. In *Proceedings of the American Society for Engineering Education Annual Conference and Exhibition, ASEE*, 2005.

[11] B. Taylor and S. Azadegan. Using security checklists and scorecards in cs curriculum. In *National Colloquium for Information Systems Security Education*, pages 4–9. Citeseer, 2007.

[12] B. Taylor and S. Azadegan. Moving beyond security tracks: Integrating security in cs0 and cs1. *SIGCSE Bull.*, 40(1):320–324, Mar 2008.

[13] R. B. Vaughn Jr. Application of security to the computing science classroom. In *ACM SIGCSE Bulletin*, volume 32, pages 90–94. ACM, 2000.

[14] J. Xie, B. Chu, H. R. Lipford, and J. T. Melton. ASIDE: IDE support for web application security. In *Proceedings of the 27th Annual Computer Security Applications Conference*, ACSAC '11, pages 267–276, New York, NY, USA, 2011. ACM.

[15] J. Zhu, H. R. Lipford, and B. Chu. Interactive support for secure programming education. In *Proceeding of the 44th ACM technical symposium on Computer science education*, SIGCSE '13, pages 687–692, 2013.

Augmenting Undergraduate Computer Science Education With Programmable Smartwatches

Andrey Esakia, Shuo Niu, D. Scott McCrickard
Department of Computer Science
Virginia Tech
Blacksburg VA 24060-0904
{esakia,shuoniu,mccricks}@vt.edu

ABSTRACT
Smartwatches are emerging as wrist-based computers capable of complex calculation and communication, and the computer science curriculum should reflect the challenges and opportunities that they provide in the education domain. This paper puts forth an experience report focused on efforts to incorporate smartwatches in an upper-level undergraduate mobile application development class during two academic terms. Lectures, in-class activities, homeworks, and projects were tailored toward providing rich design and implementation experiences for the students that engaged them in developing for the smartwatch and a paired mobile device. Our experiences highlighted how incorporating smartwatches into a mobile app development class adds a valuable dimension in terms of design and implementation challenges and allowed students to exercise some of the fundamental computer science topics.

Categories and Subject Descriptors
K.3.2 [Computer and Information Science Education]

General Terms
Design, Human Factors

Keywords
Smartwatch; Pebble; Mobile; Android; Multi-platform

1. INTRODUCTION
A *smartwatch* is a wrist-based computing device with primary functionality as a watch but with added functionality made possible by the inclusion of a capable processor, graphical display, sensors, and wireless communication capabilities. Following many years of speculation and prototypes, major technology companies like Google, Samsung, LG, and Motorola are engaged in smartwatch development and support, and startups like Pebble are attracting record funding. Many of the smartwatch platforms provide open distribution channels for smartwatch applications (apps), providing opportunities to get apps in users' hands quickly and easily. As such, it is important to consider how smartwatches can fit into the computer science (CS) curriculum, toward identifying the most appropriate lessons to be learned from smartwatches and providing opportunities for students to design apps with broad availability.

Key in designing for smartwatches is consideration for their unique form factor. To ensure broad appeal and utility, smartwatches are intended to be attractive and compact, to be resilient to various environmental conditions, and to have a long battery life—supporting constant wear and close integration with daily tasks. Smartwatch manufacturers seek to balance features like screen size and sensor integration with appearance and durability, and while there is not yet consensus on essential features, most smartphones include a screen no larger than 2.5 inches on the diagonal, some sort of accelerometer or motion detector, and a means to communicate wirelessly like Bluetooth or Wi-Fi. Other features in select smartwatches include a camera, thermometer, GPS, touch screen, speaker, heart rate monitor, and external storage. The common features provide a baseline for designing educational activities, while the growing and changing feature set offers opportunities for innovation.

Increased miniaturization of computing and sensor technologies means that smartwatches can act as standalone devices, with significant computing power and capabilities (e.g., Samsung's Tizen smartwatches). But the greatest emerging opportunities seem to reside in coordinated use of smartwatches with other mobile and wearable technologies, seeking to leverage the strengths of each. This model is core in smartwatches such as Pebble, NikeFuel, and Samsung Galaxy Gear. As such, when teaching students to design for smartwatches, it is important to emphasize the multi-device coordination aspects that are essential to maximize utility.

Ironically, the popularization of the new technology brings to the forefront issues from the past that are often covered minimally in many CS education classes—most notably memory management, processing speed, power issues, and small screen design. The need to create a technology that is small and power-efficient leads to devices that lag in performance and capability compared to larger devices (i.e., desktops, laptops, and even tablets and mobile phones). With increased market presence of smartwatches and other very small technologies emerging, it is important that students understand how to design and program for hardware limitations.

In summary, this paper explores four fundamental CS topics that can be exercised through developing for smartwatches in an upper level mobile app development class:

- Considering a unique form factor
- Designing and programming for sensors
- Addressing multi-device coordination
- Handling hardware limitations

The novelty and popularity of smartwatches translates to enthusiasm among CS students, which offers a good building point. This paper puts forth an experience report for integration

SIGCSE '15, March 4–7, 2015, Kansas City, MO, USA.

http://dx.doi.org/10.1145/2676723.2677285

of smartwatches into the computer science curriculum. Specifically, we focused on a junior-senior level mobile design class that students take after completing CS2, and we chose the Pebble smartwatch as our design platform.

This paper first explores key elements of smartwatches that are important to cover in the upper level computer science curriculum. It then examines work related to mobile and wearable sensor-based platforms similar to smartwatches. The remainder of the paper describes two class sections for which smartwatches were an integral part of lectures, in-class activities, assignments, and projects—culminating in lessons learned and challenges for the future.

2. SMARTWATCHES AND EDUCATION

To appropriately integrate a novel device into a CS class curriculum it is important to analyze and understand the characteristics, features, and general nature of the device. We believe that a smartwatch is capable of adding additional dimensions to the educational experience that students get in an advanced (junior-senior) CS class—building on lessons learned in early courses such as C and Java programming, data structures, and algorithms. Additionally, smartwatches have the capacity to provide an exciting platform for key later topics.

This section explores smartwatch characteristics with regard to important aspects of CS education. Each discussion category highlights general features of smartwatches, both with regard to development as well as specific to education, with a focus on the junior-senior undergraduate level for which we have direct experience. We seek to frame the lessons in terms general to all smartwatches, though our experiences were with the Pebble.

Pebble seeks to create an inexpensive smartwatch with long battery life through judicious selection of features. Pebble hardware characteristics reflect a very power efficient embedded class device. Pebble smartwatches have a Cortex M3 CPU with a maximum frequency of 80mhz, 4MB of internal storage, 128kb of RAM (96kb allocated for the OS). In addition to conservative computational capabilities, it has a low resolution monochrome screen with 139 pixels per inch and total resolution of 144x168. For other interactions the Pebble has no touchscreen and no sound—though it can provide haptic feedback through a vibrating motor. Interaction is via four hardware buttons that are located on Pebble's edges. Pebble runs a proprietary operating system that must be programmed in C (limited features can be programmed in JavaScript). Pebble is intended to be paired with another device (e.g., a mobile phone) via Bluetooth, allowing it to serve as an extension to the device and to leverage its more extensive hardware capabilities.

Form factor. Smartwatches are designed to worn as watches—on the wrist at all times. Thus, the smartwatch utilization paradigm is different from the one that is with smartphones and other mobile devices. The dimensions of the smartwatch impose certain limitations on the types of interactions that are possible. For example, the watch-like appearance limits possible display and interactions due to fewer pixels, fewer buttons, and more limited finger input sets. Techniques like voice commands, gestures, and accelerometer inputs are promising, and deserve thorough exploration. These form factor features of smartwatches can present additional challenges to students designing smartwatch apps. Solving such usability problems will allow students to learn to better utilize the unique hardware resources. Lessons learned from such design processes will apply to other devices as well.

Sensors. Smartwatches contain various sensors and devices, that have included accelerometer, magnetometer, microphone, speaker, thermometer, barometer, GPS, touch screen, heart rate monitor, light sensor, and camera. While these sensors may not be new to students with smartphone experience, the limited form factor of the smartwatch often results in unique combinations of sensors, often of lower quality. In addition, having sensors on the wrist tends to have great appeal for students, creating new challenges for the design and implementation of apps.

Multi-device coordination. While it is possible to create standalone smartwatch applications, the most engaging applications for the majority of smartwatch platforms tend to leverage data from one or more companion devices (e.g., via an external internet connection, a larger memory store, or additional sensors). Since Pebble and a companion device run on completely different platforms the communication and its representation in code varies dramatically between the devices. Thus, implementing communication mechanisms on both platforms allows students to gain deeper knowledge about the concepts of device-to-device communication as they implement similar communication functionalities on different platforms.

Limited resources. Smartwatch form factor suggests that the quality of resources available will always lag behind larger devices (e.g., desktops, laptops, and even tablets and mobile phones). As such, programmers will need to address limitations in memory and processing speed when developing for this platform. For example, Pebble hardware runs on a very power efficient embedded class hardware with limited memory, and as such does not support memory allocation using traditional C commands like malloc and sprintf. Thus, limited resources of Pebble give students experience developing for low performance hardware—lessons that will serve them well for smaller devices.

3. RELATED WORK

Smartwatches have been included in CS courses, but generally as an option for projects and not as a major focus point for engaging core CS concepts. However, the four CS topics defined in the previous section certainly have been addressed elsewhere within CS education, particularly in relation to mobile and wearable computing. This section provides a few examples for each topic with mention of their relevance.

Form factor has proven useful and appealing in courses that address issues of mobile and wearable computing throughout different stages of CS education. For example, the Android platform and App Inventor has been used to motivate K-12 students to get involved in computer science [4]. The authors provided students with projects and exercises that covered capabilities such as sensors and networking to teach Java programming and Android SDK development. The Sofia system provided a programming interface to simplify Android programming for early undergraduate CS classes [5]. The Android platform has been used in upper-level courses as well, such as an agile software engineering focus on socially relevant problems like disabilities [9] and in courses focused on operating systems [1] and databases [8] due to the unique dimensions provided or enhanced by the small form factor. The smartwatch takes these challenges to another level, providing fewer pixels and inputs but an even more ubiquitous presence.

Sensors have grown in popularity as an educational topic with the rise of mobile and wearable computing. A working group on mobile computing courses noted that mobile devices provide opportunities for learning about sensors. Mobile and wearable sensors have been the key platform for teaching many sensor-driven application development undergraduate classes (e.g., [4,6,10]). From this prior work, it is clear the importance of sensor issues related to the reliability, lag, threading, and more, and as smartwatches become more sensor-rich, we expect they will be platforms to explore these issues.

Multi-device communication and networking issues are important in mobile phones. Burd and his colleagues note that programming for multiple platforms can put students in a better position to think critically about each platform [2]. Communication between platforms forces students to consider the growing concerns regarding Android OS security threats, toward understanding fundamental security concepts such as cryptography, network security, and security policy [7]. Since smartwatches (particularly the lower-priced ones like Pebble) rely on communication with another device for the bulk of their operations, communication and networking issues will be of even greater importance.

In addressing hardware limitations we can draw from the lessons from years past, when issues like memory and processor speed were important even for relatively small data sets. As noted by the Burd working group [2], issues like these provide the opportunity to introduce classic CS topics like responsiveness, memory allocation, algorithm complexity, and limited graphics and animation. We certainly found this to be true in teaching Pebble, which has extremely limited memory and a slow processor relative to student expectations.

Each of these topics are important on their own, but the issues become more interesting when considered together. Section 3 examines these topics in detail, balancing general facets of them with aspects specific to the Pebble smartphone and our target course. The subsequent sections provide details about smartphone integration into the course, focusing on these topics.

4. SMARTWATCH IN THE CLASSROOM

We taught two consecutive mobile app development courses aimed at junior/senior level CS major students—one in Spring 2014 and another in Summer 2014. Input about the first class was taken into account for the second iteration of the class. Course materials are at http://research.cs.vt.edu/ns/smartwatch

We were able to provide a Pebble smartwatch for over half the members of the first class, and for all of the members of the second class, thanks to a gift from Pebble. The smartwatches were handed out to students at least a week before the instruction about Pebbles to encourage students to use them and better understand potential utility of a smartwatch prior to designing and implementing any applications for it.

4.1 Spring course

The spring semester mobile app development course was our first effort to teach mobile software development on Android as a CS3 level course aimed at juniors and seniors of our university's computer science department. We divided the course into two-week modules, where every module covered fundamental aspects of mobile development with Android OS. One module focused primarily on smartwatches.

Our spring course had a relatively large enrollment of 63 students (56 males). Class met twice a week for 75 minutes per session over a 15-week semester. All students had or were given an Android mobile device for their use during the semester, and over half the students were loaned a Pebble. Pebble assignments were done in pairs, and students were given the option to include a smartwatch in experience reports and a group project.

All of the students had had multiple years of Java experience. Many of the students had CS2 mobile app development class taken that uses Sofia package as the teaching platform for Android development [5], and most others had Android experience gained through their own initiative or other opportunities. Almost all indicated familiarity with the C programing language to a level in which they felt comfortable with pointers, memory allocation, and other relevant features.

4.1.1 Lectures

Two class periods were dedicated to teaching introductory aspects of smartwatches and two class periods specifically focused on teaching Pebble development. We sought to balance a historical view of the evolution of wearables and smartwatches as well as overview of the core features, while focusing also on Pebble specific development. We discussed at a high level the hardware aspects of Pebble; we mentioned hardware limitations such as low memory with slow bandwidth and the resulting restrictions from developer's perspective in C environment. Although the majority of the class was familiar with C, we decided to go over the more challenging parts of C such as pointers, structs and function pointers.

The Pebble API overview and instruction covered core concepts of form factor, multi-device connectivity, sensors, and hardware limitations. We spent significant time on multi-device connectivity, covering the Android side of the development on how to create a companion app on Android and how to exchange information with Pebble. We concluded by informing students about the ways in which the interactive development platforms can be set up for Pebble and how to use them.

One class was a lab-style session in which students practiced app and companion app development for Pebble. Students brought their Pebbles to class and worked individually on the lab, sharing Pebbles as needed to complete our tutorial. The tutorial consisted of series of steps necessary implement a shopping list app that allowed creating a shopping list on the phone and passing the list to the Pebble. Students were given a skeleton code that, when completed, resulted in a shopping list created on a mobile device that could be checked off with the Pebble. With this lab students were exposed to two key smartwatch topics: advantages gained from different form factors and multi-device coordination.

4.1.2 Assignments

Students were required to do the homework for Pebble that we designed for the class. As all students had completed a highly-structured lab, the homework was very open-ended. We asked students to utilize two core smartwatch functionalities: device-to-device communication (as in the lab) and integration of sensors (accelerometer, magnetometer, or light sensor).

4.2 Summer course

We taught the same mobile app development course as a summer course. The course met 5 days per week for 75 minutes per class session over 7.5 weeks. The class underwent changes based on difference in format and on feedback received from the previous course. The background and demographics of this class were similar to the spring offering, though this class had a enrollment of only 14 students (12 males). Due to the smaller size of the class we were able to hand out Pebble smartwatches to every student and make all assignments individual.

4.2.1 Lectures

Most lectures were the same as in the spring, but we added a session in response to feedback received from the spring class (see results section) to provide students with more practical examples and more hands-on experience. Thus, prior to the lab session, we conducted a hands-on lecture for which students were asked to bring their laptops installed with the Pebble development environments. During the lecture we walked students through a development of an example app and asked them to follow along and implement the example app on their laptops. The example app was a synchronized counter that allowed incrementing and decrementing a counter on the Pebble as well as on the companion device (see Figure 1).

It should be noted that the process of displaying a number on the Pebble's screen was not trivial, as memory limitations of the smartwatch had to be addressed (string conversion without sprintf). This example app served as the basis for the homework assignment and it helped students with three core smartwatch lessons: leveraging various form factors, overcoming hardware limitations, and multi-device coordination.

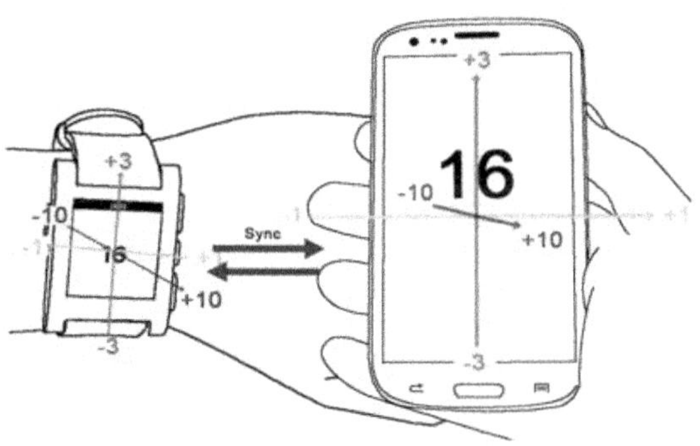

Figure 1. Pebble activity/assignment in which students leverage accelerometers to increment, decrement, and synchronize counters on both devices.

4.2.2 Assignments

For the summer class we decided to establish more control on the learning experience from the homework assignment. As one step, we assigned very specific homework that asked students to build on the counter app from the class activity and enhance it. The app from the activity needed one major improvement: it had no means of verifying successful and failed information deliveries between the Pebble and the companion device. With the app it was very common to see communication interruptions between the Pebble and the companion device, resulting in asynchronous numbers displayed on both devices. We asked the students to fix this problem by utilizing failed and successful message delivery handlers provided by Pebble SDK, thus synchronizing the counter on both Pebble and the companion device (and, of course, broadening the students' understanding of multi-device coordination). We also wanted students to practice accelerometer sensors programing, so we asked them to implement a simple linear gesture detection that would increment and decrement the counter by a number determined by the direction and the axis of the linear gesture. Students were supposed to implement this on both the Pebble and the companion device. This assignment helped students practice cross-platform communication and synchronization as well as accelerometer gesture detection and noise handling—both core concerns for this experience.

5. EXPERIENCE REFLECTIONS

Although our spring and summer classes varied dramatically in terms of enrollment and duration, our results indicate that incorporating Pebble development component into a junior-senior level mobile app development class, did encourage students to explore CS topics in a novel way.

5.1 Spring course experiences

Due to high enrollment in our spring course, students worked on the Pebble homework in pairs. We were able to allocate a full course module (two weeks) for the Pebble homework. Thus, students were given adequate time not only to innovate in terms of app design but also to implement quality apps.

A total of 33 submissions were made for the Pebble homework. Upon analyzing the functionality of the applications submitted we observed a significant diversity in terms of both, design and implementation. The following six applications caught our attention as the most prominent ones that addressed the core lessons we sought to communicate.

(1) **Camera trigger**: A Pebble app that triggers taking a picture from a companion device equipped with a camera.

(2) **Speedometer:** A Pebble app that receives information about the changing location of a companion device, measured by GPS, and calculates and displays the speed on its screen. The app warns the user if certain speed is exceeded.

(3) **Navigator:** A Pebble app that periodically receives navigational directions from a companion device and displays them on its screen.

(4) **Pacekeeper:** This Pebble app allows for a recording of a tapping pattern on the companion device, uploading the pattern to the Pebble and then recreating it via Pebble's vibration feature.

(5) **MLB score updater:** This Pebble app receives latest Major League Baseball scores from the web, through a companion device, and displays the scores on its screen.

(6) **Realtime Twitter:** For this Pebble app, user enters a search term into a companion device and then receives realtime updates, for that term, onto the Pebble's screen.

These example apps serve to demonstrate of how an integration of smartwatch device development into a mobile app development class can add extra dimensions to design and implementation aspects as well as revisit some of the core computer science problems in novel setting. Camera trigger app, for instance, was built as an addition to one of the earlier Android image capture homework apps, adding support for taking pictures remotely from the companion device directly or via a timer. Several of the apps required students to overcome transfer limitations of Pebble to support the intended functionality, in which Pebble does not receive information in chunks bigger than 128 bytes—students divided up the information into 128 byte chunks on the companion device, then sent one chunk at a time and merge upon receipt of all chunks.

We asked all of the students to describe the Pebble homework experience and to identify some of the challenges identified. Upon analyzing the responses we discovered three most prominent issues related to the Pebble development. One on the issues being the lack of proper documentation and consistence across different versions of SDK e.g.,

"*One of the big limitations was the documentation. It seems that there are several built-in functions that do not work from version to version.*"

And

"*In comparison to most other devices and languages, there was hardly any documentation on developing for the Pebble. Even simple things, like reading in data from the accelerometer, were difficult to find. The methods themselves were there, but examples were rare and in some cases, nonexistent.*"

Another obstacle was the lack of support of standard C libraries due to the limited memory resources of the Pebble. Many students were unpleasantly surprised to discover that Pebble does not support conversion from numbers to strings using **sprintf()** function, e.g.,

"*Pebble's current API does not currently support some standard C programming functions. We encountered this problem when attempting to convert a "long" type variable to a "char *" type using C's standard library function "snprtinf". As a workaround, we were able to find an open source adaptation a Pebble user developed to overcome this limitation, but it was surprising to realize Pebble did not support such calls*"

Additionally, a lot of students complained about the lack of a dedicated Pebble SDK for Windows. Currently the only supported operating systems are Linux and Mac OS. Pebble does offer a cloud based IDE, but it lacks debugging support.

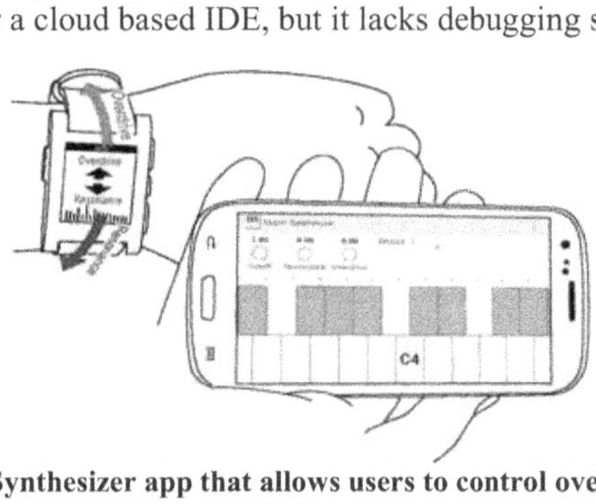

Figure 2. Synthesizer app that allows users to control overdrive and reverberation using Pebble's accelerometer.

5.2 Summer course experiences

In contrast to the spring course, the summer class had far fewer students (14). The duration of the session was half as long, which meant half the time per assignment—only one. With this in mind, and with consideration that all coding assignments were individual, we provided more design details and specific requirements for the assignments. Thus, the Pebble homework did not allow design creativity as much so as in the spring. However, we encouraged students to incorporate Pebble components into their semester project by offering them bonus points and the opportunity to skip the Pebble homework without penalty. As a result, six mobile app term projects incorporated Pebble, with three example term project apps that incorporate Pebble functionality listed here (see Figure 3 for screenshots).

(1) **Facebook page monitor:** An app that aggregates information from the Facebook page into a single screen and notifies its user of updates (see Figure 3). Update notifications (for example, "page like") are pushed both to the mobile device and Pebble within a user specified period, or the Pebble select button can be used to request an update.

(2) **Synthesizer:** An app that simulates a synthesizer keyboard with various sound effects on the mobile device. Pebble acts as an additional interaction device, by pivoting the Pebble against x, y or z axes the synthesizer changes its sound characteristics; e.g., reservation, echo (see Figure 2 & 3).

(3) **Temperature monitor:** An app that allows temperature and humidity monitoring of a remote room. Temperature and humidity sensors are placed in a room and the readings are being sent to a web server. The mobile app retrieves the data from the server and then allows Pebble to request the data from the phone. Pressing the select button on Pebble, downloads temperature and humidity information from the mobile device, and displays it on its screen (see Figure 3)

The Facebook page monitor app was originally conceived as a standalone mobile app, without any wearable components. However, after hearing about the Pebble, the student decided to incorporate its functionality into the term project that had already been designed and partially implemented. Incorporating the Pebble functionality prompted the student to reconsider her design for the app and add the notification functionality, thus naturally simulating a design evolution experience caused by external factors.

Similarly, the student behind the synthesizer app had not planned for Pebble inclusion originally. His original plan was to use mobile device's touchscreen the way rotate virtual knobs that changed synthesizer sound characteristics. After getting accustomed with Pebble and learning about the sensor capabilities through the lecture and homework, he decided to augment the sound altering controls for the accelerometer. The student discovered how to address accelerometer sensitivity issues by processing the accelerometer values prior sending them to the synthesizer app.

Since summer Pebble assignments were individual, all students undertook both design and implementation for Pebble. However, issues that the students experienced were similar to the previous class. Students complained about poor online documentation and lack of important programming supports. We received no complaints about the lack of Windows SDK as we provided students with the instructions that allowed them to install Ubuntu virtual machine that allowed them to use the full Pebble SDK with debugging tools.

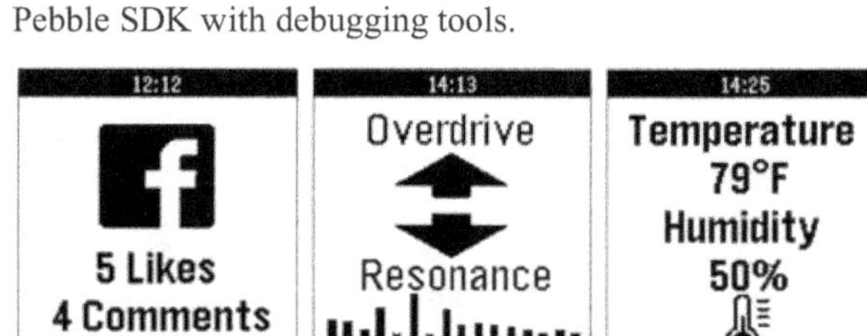

Figure 3. Pebble screenshots from three of the summer apps, highlighting the look and feel of Pebble apps.

5.3 Discussion

By incorporating a novel and "cool" device into a mobile development class, we leveraged student enthusiasm for smartwatches, and wearables in general. Tasks of designing and implementing apps for a smartwatch, helped students think about design and implementation in terms of two devices and helped them think of interactions of users with two devices.

The limitations of our device of choice, Pebble smartwatch, played an important educational role. The limitations often forced the students to devise workarounds in the form of algorithms, in order to implement their ideas. The manifestation of limitations was natural and physical, in a form a smartwatch device. Thus, students solved limitation-induced problems in a natural way—with an actual device with limited capabilities.

From an instructor's perspective, the benefits that stem from the usage of a novel device like a smartwatch come at a price, especially when such device comes from small vendor. Just like our results indicate, the novelty of a device is usually synonymous with limited online documentation and code example availability. This could result in extra workload on teaching staff as the students inevitably will resort to the most available help—instructors and teaching assistants.

6. CONCLUSIONS AND FUTURE WORK

This paper seeks to highlight the potential of smartwatches in enhancing computer science education by incorporating a Pebble smartwatch development into our upper level undergraduate mobile application design class. We taught this class during two semesters and used the experience to evolve our teaching model. Through the smartwatch lectures and assignments the students not only gained knowledge about specific design and development techniques for the unique form factor and integrated sensors, but also tackled some of the fundamental computer science problems that arise due to resource limitations and multi-device communication issues.

At the start of this experience, we identified four key areas relevant to that we felt were most interesting and relevant to smartwatches. We revisit them here, capturing key lessons and challenges for each that seem important for future consideration in incorporating smartwatches into CS courses.

- Consider unique form factor. By repurposing the watch, the smartwatch is restricted to small size—but high accessibility in daily use, even more so than a mobile phone. It is vital to ask students to design for usability, but these lessons must be balanced with opportunities to explore new smartwatch uses.
- Design and program for sensors. The teaching of sensors has been explored and discussed, but the high visibility, small form factor, and decreasing cost of smartwatches positions them as a learning tool throughout the curriculum—from an early-course initial experience with sensor programming to one of many devices in an upper-level course focusing on advanced topics like distributed computing and networking.
- Address multi-device coordination. The vast majority of smartwatches require device pairing through Bluetooth, Wi-Fi, or another communication mechanism to generate broad and interesting apps. Designing for a multi-device situation will be unfamiliar to most students, requiring careful consideration by teachers to provide early experiences addressing it while allowing students to explore possibilities that maximize the capabilities of all coordinated devices.
- Handle hardware limitations. Even though hardware will continually improve, it seems likely that there will continue to be a performance gap between the smaller smartwatch and the larger desktop, laptop, and even tablet and mobile phone (just as [2] noted a gap between mobiles and desktops). This limitation can be viewed as an opportunity—providing the chance for students to broaden their skill set and revisit (or rediscover) design and programming techniques.

This paper puts forth initial areas for consideration in integrating smartwatches into the CS curriculum. Google's Android Wear and Apple's Apple Watch have recently joined the smartwatch market, suggesting that this emerging technology has promise. The computer science education community must be poised to help students design and implement for smartwatches armed with appropriate knowledge and insight. Future plans will leverage the unique hardware, rich interaction capabilities, and seamless developmental experience to exercise human computer interaction aspects associated with the form factor and the information affordance offered such smartwatches.

7. REFERENCES

[1] J. Andrus and J. Nieh, "Teaching operating systems using android. in *Proceedings of the 43rd ACM Technical Symposium on Computer Science Education*, 2012, pp. 613-618.

[2] B. Burd, J. P. Barros, C. Johnson, S. Kurkovsky, A. Rosenbloom, and N. Tillman, "Educating for mobile computing: addressing the new challenges," in *Proceedings of the Final Reports on Innovation and Technology in Computer Science Education 2012 Working Groups*, 2012, pp. 51-63.

[3] H. Chen and K. Damevski, "A teaching model for development of sensor-driven mobile applications," in *Proceedings of the 2014 Conference on Innovation & Technology in Computer Science Education*, 2014, pp. 147-152.

[4] M. H. Dabney, B. C. Dean, and T. Rogers, "No sensor left behind: enriching computing education with mobile devices," in *Proceedings of the 44th ACM Technical Symposium on Computer Science Education*, 2013, pp. 627-632.

[5] S. H. Edwards and A. Allevato, "Sofia: the simple open framework for inventive android applications," in *Proceedings of the 18th ACM Conference on Innovation and Technology in Computer Science Education*, 2013, p. 321.

[6] A. Forster and M. Jazayeri, "Hands-on approach to teaching wireless sensor networks at the undergraduate level," in *Proceedings of the 15th ACM Conference on Innovation and Technology in Computer Science Education*, 2010, pp. 284-288.

[7] M. Guo, P. Bhattacharya, M. Yang, K. Qian, and L. Yang, "Learning mobile security with android security labware," in *Proceedings of the 44th ACM Technical Symposium on Computer Science Education*, 2013, pp. 675-680.

[8] Q. H. Mahmoud, S. Zanin, and T. Ngo, "Integrating mobile storage into database systems courses," in *Proceedings of the 13th Annual Conference on Information Technology Education*, 2012, pp. 165-170.

[9] V. P. Pauca and R. T. Guy, "Mobile apps for the greater good: a socially relevant approach to software engineering," in *Proceedings of the 43rd ACM Technical Symposium on Computer Science Education*, 2012, pp. 535-540.

[10] S. Rollins, "Introducing networking and distributed systems concepts in an undergraduate-accessible wireless sensor networks course," in *Proceedings of the 42nd ACM Technical Symposium on Computer Science Education*, 2011, pp. 405-410.

Simulating IBM Watson in the Classroom

Wlodek Zadrozny, Sean Gallagher, Walid Shalaby, and Adarsh Avadhani
Dept. of Computer Science, University of North Carolina at Charlotte
Charlotte, North Carolina, USA
wzadrozn@uncc.edu, sgalla19@uncc.edu, wshalaby@uncc.edu, amanjuna@uncc.edu

ABSTRACT

IBM Watson exemplifies multiple innovations in natural language processing and question answering. In addition, Watson uses most of the known techniques in these two domains as well as many methods from related domains. Hence, there is pedagogical value in a rigorous understanding of its function. The paper provides the description of a text analytics course focused on building a simulator of IBM Watson, conducted in Spring 2014 at UNC Charlotte. We believe this is the first time a simulation containing *all* the major Watson components was created in a university classroom. The system achieved a respectable (close to) 20% accuracy on *Jeopardy!* questions, and there remain many known and new avenues of improving performance that can be explored in the future. The code and documentation are available on GitHub. The paper is a joint effort of the teacher and some of the students who were leading teams implementing component technologies, and therefore deeply involved in making the class successful.

Categories and Subject Descriptors

K.3.2 [**Computers and Education**]: Computer and Information Science Education,Curriculum

General Terms

Experimentation

Keywords

IBM Watson; Student Research; Question Answering; QA;

1. INTRODUCTION: WATSON CLASS OBJECTIVES AND RESULTS

IBM Watson was a question answering machine which in 2011 won a *Jeopardy!* match against former winners Brad Rutter and Ken Jennings. *Jeopardy!* is a television game show in which participants are tested on general knowledge.

SIGCSE'15, March 04 - 07 2015, Kansas City, MO, USA.
ACM 978-1-4503-2966-8/15/03...$15.00
http://dx.doi.org/10.1145/2676723.2677287.

The 2011 match demonstrated the feasibility of real time question answering in open domains, and was hailed by some as an arrival of a new era of "cognitive computing" [22]. This new era starts with Watson as a machine that can "reprogram" itself using machine learning and knowledge it acquires during a competition.

Most of the *Jeopardy!* questions are "factoid" questions, but there are also others asking for quotations and various kinds of puzzles. Here are some examples of the questions, or clues (with their answers):

- `Factoid:` The Pekingese, Chihuahua, & Tonka's "Pound Puppies" fall under this classification of dogs: *toys.*
- `Factoid:` Don't be intimidated by the skewers; I'll use them on the marinated lamb to make this: *shish kabob.*
- `Quote:` When Ryan O'Neal apologizes to Barbra Streisand in "What's Up, Doc?" she quotes this line from "Love Story": *"Love means never having to say you're sorry"*
- `Fill in the Blank:` Lemon___ Rain___ Cough___: *drop.*

From the educational perspective IBM Watson exemplifies multiple innovations in natural language processing and question answering. These include title-oriented organization of background knowledge and various ways of corpus processing and expansion [9] [28], massive parallelism of semantic evaluation [10], lack of explicit translation from natural language into a "language of meaning" for the purpose of finding an answer to a clue [14], the use of search for candidate answer generation [12], and others [14].

In addition, Watson uses most of the known techniques in these two and in related domains [14][23][26][30]. In particular Watson uses two search engines, and various query transformation techniques, a parser (which also produces a logical form), machine learning, semi-structured databases (such as DBpedia), multiple matching techniques such as "skip bi-grams", and many others.

Therefore there is a pedagogical value in in-depth understanding of how IBM Watson works. That is, a Watson class can be used to teach both about advances in text analytics, as well as about standard methods of text understanding. For example, the use of both Indri [15] and Lucene [25] search engines, raises a natural question about their relative strengths and weaknesses. This question was answered by discussing in class the paper comparing them [29].

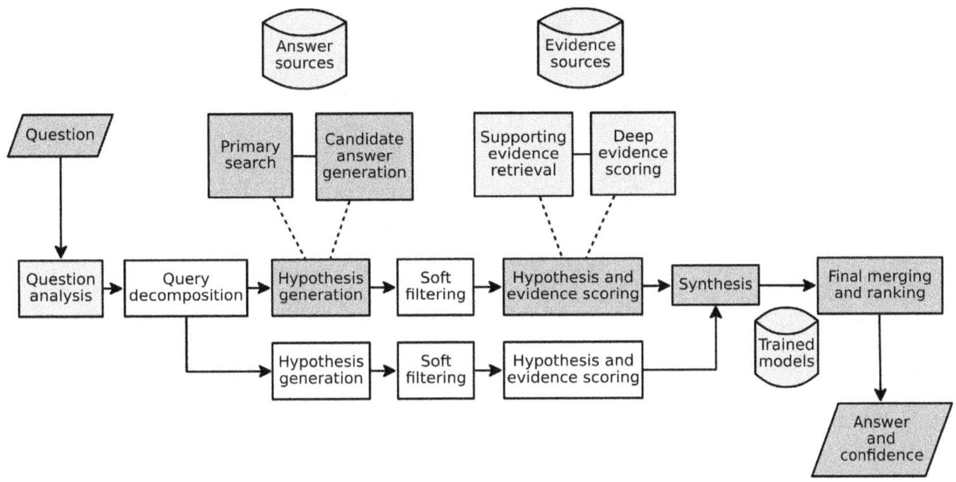

Figure 1: Our Watson simulator reproduced most of the original IBM Watson architecture. Light blue: elements with very similar functionality as IBM Watson, for example primary search. Partly blue are the elements only partly reconstructed, for example we had only 20 evidence scorers compared to over 400 in the IBM system. Original image courtesy of Wikipedia: http://commons.wikimedia.org/wiki/File:DeepQA.svg

Hands-on experience is perhaps the best way for students to gain real understanding of how such a complex system works, and what it takes to make an accurate question answering system. Furthermore, building a Watson simulator requires learning the component technologies including data preparation, search, information extraction, part of speech tagging, parsing, machine learning, among others. This paper provides the description of a text analytics class focused on building a simulator of IBM Watson.

Discussing computer education, Patterson [27] remarked: "The challenge is preventing the large code base from overwhelming the students, interfering with learning the conceptual material of the course" . We believe our class met this challenge.

Brief description of the class

IBM Watson remains proprietary, and therefore cannot be downloaded or used in the class directly. However, it has been described by IBM researchers in collections of papers [14][23][26][30] and patents [7][11]. In addition, *Jeopardy!* questions are freely available from `j-archive.com`.

Therefore, it is possible in principle for anyone to build a Watson simulator, or any question answering system containing components of Watson architecture. (Although commercial uses might be protected by IBM patents).

Yet it is not the case that many systems are replicating the results of the Watson project. This comes as a surprise, given that around the time of Deep Blue many computer chess programs were challenging human chess champions [1][8]. Four years after the Watson – *Jeopardy!* game, no question answering programs seems to approach Watson's performance. This comes in spite of all the technical and scientific innovation embodied in Watson.

While we do not boast equivalent performance, we simulated all the major components and experimented with some additions in the course. We also added the feature of internet search.

Challenges of building a classroom Watson simulator

Obviously, the bar for question answering performance set by IBM Watson is difficult to meet; all time *Jeopardy!* champions are excellently accurate.

However, the level of required expertise was perhaps our biggest challenge. Watson was built by about 20 PhDs and a few experienced software engineers in 5 years, and started with an existing competitive question answering system. Members of the Watson team had at least several years of experience building NLP applications. In contrast, our class had one PhD student with some experience in machine learning, 8 Master's students, and 12 undergraduates with some exposure to artificial intelligence or symbolic programming. For almost all of them this was the first encounter with text analytics.

Moreover, Watson is a very large software system. IBM researcher Gary Booch reports Watson has over 1 million lines of code (mostly in Java) [5]. It operates as an ensemble of integrated subsystems and pipelines rather than any singular, central component. Implementing and testing so many components takes time and labor.

What made the class possible

Three major factors made this class possible. As mentioned above, IBM researchers have cataloged detailed descriptions of how Watson works. IBM also permitted us to use their presentations from a class taught at Columbia University a year earlier. Last but not least, the professor had a history with the Watson team.

Accomplishments of the class

We created a simulation that contains all of the major elements of Watson (shown in Fig.1). By the end of the semester, the performance of our simulator on *Jeopardy!* questions was approximately 20% accuracy, compared with Watson's 70% accuracy [14]. Obviously, the objective of the class wasn't to achieve Watson's performance, but rather to see what can be accomplished in one semester. We hope that our experience, and resources we are releasing will in-

Name	Question class.	Query translatiion	...	Machine learning	`git` commit count	Integration	Passage retrieval	Data Preparation	Indri	Lucene	Bing
student1					✓	✓	★	✓	✓	✓	
student2											✓
student3	✓	✓		✓	✓	✓	✓		★	✓	✓
student4	✓			✓	✓	✓		✓	✓	✓	✓
student5											
student6		✓			✓	✓	✓	✓	✓	✓	
student7	✓	✓			✓	✓		✓	✓	✓	
student8	✓				✓	✓	✓	★	✓	✓	
student9		✓		✓	✓	✓	✓	✓	✓	✓	
student10	✓									✓	
...											
studentx				★	✓	✓	✓	✓ 50%	✓	✓	✓
studentx+1		✓			✓		✓		✓	✓	
studentx+2	✓				✓	✓		✓	✓?	✓	✓

Table 1: The gradesheet at the end of the semester (★ indicates a team lead)

spire others to do better. We note though that the accuracy is higher than the baseline QA system the Watson team started with. [14]

In the months since the class completed, several changes have been made, including several new scorers and other features not available in the simulator at the end of the semester.

Our code and documentation are available on GitHub, and is freely available to anyone wanting to experiment with it.

In the course of creating the software, the students learned about engineering a relatively complex system. They all acquired semantic knowledge in combination with hands-on experience in local and internet search, NLP, and various aspects of text analytics. For many of them, it was a first encounter with version control (specifically `git` and GitHub). Some were also afforded career opportunities: one MS student was hired by the IBM Watson team, and another has an offer pending.

Comparison with prior work

The authors are aware of only two other examples of a Watson-focused class: one at Columbia University, as reported by Gliozzo in 2013 [18], and another at Rensselear Polytechnic (RPI) as reported by Hendler in 2013 [20] and in 2014 [21]. The Columbia class focused on building Watson-inspired tools that could be used for other tasks. The two sets of Hendler's slides discuss the RPI system which recreated portions of the Watson data pipeline. However, no accuracy results are reported.

Our work differs from these two by attempting to completely recreate the original Watson pipeline, and measure the correctness of the resulting system. In addition, we see the opportunity to add additional components, and further improve the question answering accuracy.

We experimented with two local search engines (Lucene and Indri), and two Internet search interfaces (Google and Bing). There were two objectives behind these experiments: Firstly, a large part of the class focused on information retrieval and included comparisons between query languages, corpus content and models for each of the engines. Secondly, adding web search to the system was an easy way of introducing additional scorers and experimenting with machine learning. The use of Internet search as primary search was reported by Hendler in 2013 [20], and again in 2014 [21].

In contrast with Gliozzo et al. [18], we introduced the Apache Unstructured Information Management Architecture (UIMA) [13] late, and the system we built is not UIMA-based. By skipping UIMA we gained 2-3 weeks of developments time. However, we did use one of the student teams to create a UIMA version of our system, and report on it in class. This provided a minimal exposure to UIMA for all students.

Recently, Wollowski reported using in class Watson training data (for machine learning models) [31]. However this effort was an exercise in data mining and did not attempt to recreate any elements of the Watson architecture.

Based on this discussion, we believe we have created a unique methodology for teaching a Watson-focused text processing class. Artefacts are also available for others to use and improve.

2. ORGANIZATION OF THE CLASS

The class time was approximately evenly divided between lectures and system building. The lectures used a collection of slides provided by IBM, which were previously used at Columbia University. The system building was done in teams and sub-teams: data preparation, search, machine learning, scoring, and the integration of the components. Team membership changed throughout the class, although two teams (integration and machine learning) had more stability than others (such as data preparation). Almost all homework was about creating software or data components.

IBM slides were supplemented by additional material from the IBM Journal of Research and Development [3] necessary for understanding of question classification or question preprocessing. The students had access to the whole collection, and some used it to gain deeper understanding of the material.

Throughout the semester the students gave short presentations intended to (a) show the progress of their teams and (b) teach others how to use the technologies. For example, a student could present the basics of `git` version control and the use of GitHub. Afterwords other students were able to contribute to the project directly through GitHub. Teaching material was also presented for maximal impact on the practicum. We started with an introduction to Watson, and proceeded lecturing on information retrieval. When system building was progressing more slowly, short lectures addressed other aspects of Watson, such as its existing and potential applications.

Using Weka [19] allowed a relatively simple way to replace one machine learning algorithm with another. In these experiments logistic regression was indicated to be the best choice. Naive Bayes classifiers performed very poorly. Our later results showed that Weka's default implementation of the multilayer perceptron was marginally more accurate.

The students were graded according to their mastery of the majority of component technologies. We tabulated this according to a matrix of checkmarks relating students to their mastered technologies, as shown in Figure 2. For example, mastery of 80% of the subject technologies translated into a "B" grade. An "A" required substantial contribution throughout the course. A monitoring process was established early in the class. The project leads were monitoring the progress of students in their teams, and discussing it with the professor during office hours. Extensive tutoring, mostly by other students, was available and took place throughout the course. Even the exam time was used for additional testing and integration.

Overall, the class discussed in detail most of the major elements of the Watson architecture. It was unfeasible to cover all of Watson in details. In particular, deeper natural language processing using frameworks similar to OpenNLP wasn't given enough attention. In a future class, we plan to give more time to NLP, at the expense of one of the search engines. We will consider UIMA or other text processing framework (e.g. GATE [16]) in the future. Student opinions were divided on whether we should have based the development on UIMA.

3. TECHNICAL APPROACH

The team clearly did not have the time or expertise to replicate the work of the original Watson team in one semester. The general model of development was to begin with a minimal working subset, only the functionality necessary to answer a question. To complete that, a data source, an index and a search engine were necessary. The structure of the framework was basically to query the engine. The goal was to complete as much of the known architecture of the Watson project as quickly as possible and have a measurable setup at the end. This included passage retrieval, scoring based on evidence, and specialized pipelines based on question types.

Below we describe selected, perhaps most interesting, elements of the technical approach. The details can be found in [17]. We discuss data resources, and how they were used; query generation; supporting evidence scoring. In the next section we briefly discuss performance evaluation.

Data sources

Data collection is a major part of the question answering process, and occupied a large fraction of effort expended by the team. The greatest focus was on retrieving, cleaning, processing and indexing Wikipedia materials. These included the full texts of all Wikipedia articles, page view statistics for 100 days of Wikipedia traffic, the full text of Wikiquotes, and the works of Shakespeare.

Unlike IBM Watson, the course project was not limited to offline data sources. As a result, we also used web search engines such as Google and Bing. We encountered some problems, most notably query quotas, which made mass searches of the magnitude necessary for passage retrieval impractical. Coordinating dozens of students to get a sample of queries on a regular basis is mostly unproductive. The situation with Bing was less restrictive than Google, and therefore Bing was used in measuring performance.

Clue Analysis and Search Query Generation

In our system there are three major question analysis pipelines covering the factoid questions, fill in the blank questions, and quotations. The selection of which pipeline a question would follow was made according to its category (factoid, quotations, common bonds, ...), of which there were a small predefined set; Lally et al. [23] list twelve of them, and then add a few more in a discussion. The majority of the questions were factoids, so we focused on them. Note that question categories or classes as discussed here and in [23] are not the same as *Jeopardy!* categories or topics, which are unlimited.

Evidence Scoring

Supporting passages receive a number of scores, which are intended to be indications of how much evidence the passage gives toward the correctness of the answer for which it was retrieved. Some scores are taken from the original search engines; this is the case for both offline search engines, Lucene and Indri. Lucene bases its score on Term Frequency-Inverse Document Frequency (TF-IDF) and the Vector Space Model, whereas Indri scores are based on Bayesian inference networks [15][25].

Passages are also subjected to a number of n-gram comparisons. This suite of related scorers provided the strongest boost to ranking found in the project.

One additional scorer takes an approach similar to the n-gram models, but in place of n-grams, it searches for the number of common phrase subtrees taken from the OpenNLP dependency parser. Notably, this scorer applies to any length phrase, and common phrases have weight approximately relative to the square of their length on the account that each common smaller phrase will also receive another count.

4. PERFORMANCE EVALUATION AND STUDENT RESEARCH

We viewed frequent evaluation of system performance as a necessary step to see what works and what doesn't. As shown in Fig 2. our progress wasn't smooth. In many cases, usually because of integration errors, the system did not work at all. As mentioned early, the final version achieved the accuracy of slightly less than 20% (which is higher than the Watson's baseline system in 2007). Our MRR (explained

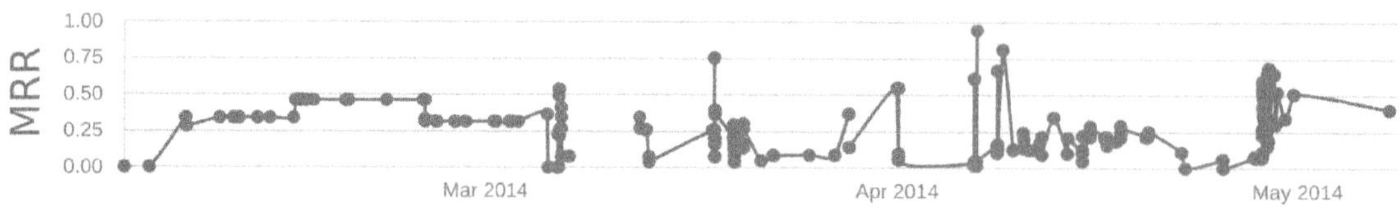

Figure 2: During the class we ran multiple experiments and measured the results. This figure shows the changes in the Mean Reciprocal Rank for different configurations, collections of data sources, and sets of questions. The final MRR from May 2014 was measured on a representative sample of 1000 Jeopardy! questions. As expected, most of them were factoid questions.

Table 2: Results using all sources except Google

Recall of Rank 1	187 (18.70%)
Recall in Top 3	278 (27.80%)
Recall in Full Candidate Answer Set	497 (49.70%)
MRR	0.5072
Total Questions	1000
Total Candidate Answers	46881
Total Runtime (seconds)	23562.1203

below) was 0.5, which means that on average correct answer was in the second position among the final list of scored candidate answers (if a correct answer existed in a list of 70 candidates).

We did not have access to the comprehensive suite of testing tools employed by the Watson team [6]. And given the amount of effort that would be required we made no attempt to recreate it. Instead, the performance tests for the Watson simulator were created using a JUnit test that takes a set of Jeopardy! questions with known correct answers, and collects statistics on the resulting ranked candidate answer lists. These data were tabulated and uploaded online. The results of our final runs are in Table 2. The final tests used Bing search. Since our candidate answers normalization and merging capabilities were limited (see Fig.1), we did not require a perfect match with the answers from J-archive.com. Candidate answers were marked as correct or incorrect based on whether the candidate and known correct answers both contained the same unordered set of words after filtering using the Lucene `EnglishAnalyzer`. Obviously, this mostly did not matter when candidate answers were taken from Wikipedia titles (as in IBM Watson), but possibly made a difference in some other situations.

In addition to assessing performance of the whole system, we evaluated performance of various sets of scoring programs. The data in Fig.2 cover the Spring 2014 semester and one additional experiment at the end of May. In these the Mean Reciprocal Rank was used to indicate scorer quality. For every question for which there was at least one correct answer, the reciprocal rank of the first correct answer was recorded. Then the mean was taken of this list of reciprocals.

Student research: The class provided opportunities for student research, including finding answers to interesting open questions. Clearly, building a Watson simulator was novel. But there were other specific questions answered in experiments. For example, we investigated the value of the Internet search relative to the local search: When trained and used on only the local dataset, the top candidate answer was correct for 12% of questions, and the second or third candidate answers were correct for an additional 2% questions. When the same system was retrained and used with the Bing Internet search engine, we obtained 18.7% accuracy for the first candidate answer, with correct answers in the second or third ranks in an additional 10% of questions. Thus Internet search improved both scores of correct answers, and contributed to better recall.

5. CONCLUSION AND NEXT STEPS

We demonstrated the feasibility of creating a class focused on a very advanced project, and meeting the Patterson's [27] challenge of avoiding "the large code base (...) interfering with learning the conceptual material of the course". The results of the class – in terms e.g. of produced code, the final accuracy, and job prospects of the students – seem to prove this point.

We believe there is value in students attempting large and ambitious projects. It removes a lot of mystery from big accomplishments of computer science, and it is a great learning experience that also allows the students to gain confidence and ambition. Obviously its too early to tell whether this change of attitudes will persist throughout their careers.

As in every project, a course focused on a single project has positive and negative aspects. Combining the output of groups of students makes it possible to achieve a much larger goal; no group of two or three students could have made this project in this timeline. However, when teams can depend on each other's work, it is possible for some students to stall. Elastic group membership was conducive to mitigating this problem. In our case, membership changes were enforced by the grading system represented in Table 1.

We believe, based on students opinions, that to maximize the quality of the resulting project, development should start as early as possible. This is one reason why it is not clear that UIMA is a significant advantage. A steeper learning curve may cost more than a lack of scalability. On the other hand, should someone try to build a more accurate system based on our software, making UIMA part of the class should be considered.

We also see an opportunity to continue this project for example as part of an intelligent system class where other text analytic methods could be introduced (as scoring modules), and various knowledge representation and logical methods could be added as well. This would also produce an opportunity to create research projects for graduate students, and explore some of the avenues that the IBM Watson project did not. To give some examples, available projects which would complement text analytics projects such as ours could include JoBimText since it has a unique distributional semantic approach to knowledge management [4] or Word2Vec (to assist for measuring relationships between phrases) [24], or textual entailment modules such as Excitement Open Platform [2]. These only scratch the surface, and many would not be very difficult to integrate.

6. ACKNOWLEDGMENTS

We would acknowledge IBM for their contribution of lecture material and slides, as well was the substantial contribution to our project by the following students: Chris Gibson, Dhaval Patel, Elliot Mersch, Jagan Vujjini, Jonathan Shuman, Ken Overholt, Phani Rahul,and Varsha Devadas. We also thank the SIGCSE referees for their comments and suggestions. Several of the suggested changes will be incorporated in an expanded version of this paper.

7. REFERENCES

[1] Deep blue (chess computer). http://en.wikipedia.org/wiki/Deep_Blue_(chess_computer).

[2] Excitement Open Platform. http://hltfbk.github.io/Excitement-Open-Platform/.

[3] "IBM J. RES. and DEV" 56 (3.4). 2012.

[4] C. Biemann et al. Jobimtext project. Retrieved September 03 2014 from http://sourceforge.net/projects/jobimtext/, 2014.

[5] G. Booch. Watson under the hood: Booch Describes Jeopardy Champ's System's Architecture. Retrieved September 03 2014 from http://searchsoa.techtarget.com/news/2240038723/Watson-under-the-hood-Booch-describes-Jeopardy-champs-systems-architecture.

[6] E. Brown, E. Epstein, J. W. Murdock, and T.-H. Fin. Tools and methods for building Watson. *IBM Research Report RC 25356.*

[7] E. Brown, D. Ferrucci, A. Lally, and W. W. Zadrozny. System and method for providing answers to questions, September 2012. US Patent 8,275,803.

[8] M. Campbell, A. J. Hoane Jr, and F. Hsu. Deep Blue. *Artificial intelligence*, 134(1):57–83, 2002.

[9] J. Chu-Carroll, J. Fan, N. Schlaefer, and W. Zadrozny. Textual resource acquisition and engineering. *IBM Journal of Research and Development*, 56(3.4):4:1–4:11, May 2012.

[10] E. A. Epstein, M. I. Schor, B. S. Iyer, A. Lally, E. Brown, and J. Cwiklik. Making Watson fast. *IBM Journal of Research and Development*, 56(3.4):15:1–15:12, May 2012.

[11] J. Fan, D. Ferrucci, D. C. Gondek, and W. W. Zadrozny. System and method for providing questions and answers with deferred type evaluation, December 2012. US Patent 8,332,394.

[12] D. Ferrucci et al. Building Watson: An overview of the DeepQA project. *AI Magazine*, 31(3), 2010.

[13] D. Ferrucci and A. Lally. UIMA: an architectural approach to unstructured information processing in the corporate research environment. *Natural Language Engineering*, 10(3-4):327–348, 2004.

[14] D. A. Ferrucci et al. Introduction to "This is Watson". *IBM J. RES. and DEV*, 56(3), 2012.

[15] D. Fisher. Indri retrieval model. Retrieved September 03 2014 from http://sourceforge.net/p/lemur/wiki/Indri Retrieval Model/, 2012.

[16] R. Gaizauskas, H. Cunningham, Y. Wilks, P. Rodgers, and K. Humphreys. GATE: an environment to support research and development in natural language engineering. In *Tools with Artificial Intelligence, 1996., Proceedings Eighth IEEE International Conference on*, pages 58–66. IEEE, 1996.

[17] S. Gallagher, W. Zadrozny, W. Shalaby, and A. Avadhani. Watsonsim: Overview of a question answering engine. *arxiv.org*, 2014.

[18] A. Gliozzo, O. Biran, S. Patwardhan, and K. McKeown. Semantic technologies in IBM Watson. *ACL 2013, http://www.aclweb.org/anthology/W13-3413*, page 85, 2013.

[19] M. Hall, E. Frank, G. Holmes, B. Pfahringer, P. Reutemann, and I. H. Witten. The WEKA data mining software: an update. *ACM SIGKDD explorations newsletter*, 11(1):10–18, 2009.

[20] J. Hendler. Watson at RPI. Retrieved September 03 2014 from http://www.slideshare.net/jahendler/watson-summer-review82013final.

[21] J. Hendler and S. Ells. Retrieved September 03 2014 from http://www.slideshare.net/jahendler/why-watson-won-a-cognitive-perspective?next_slideshow=1.

[22] IBM. IBM Research: Cognitive Computing. Retrieved September 03 2014 from http://www.research.ibm.com/cognitive-computing/.

[23] A. Lally et al. Question analysis: How Watson reads a clue. *IBM J. RES. and DEV*, 56(3/4), 2012.

[24] T. Mikolav et al. Word2Vec project. Retrieved September 03 2014 from http://code.google.com/p/word2vec/, 2014.

[25] R. Muir et al. Lucene `Similarity` class reference. Retrieved September 03 2014 from http://lucene.apache.org/core/4_9_0/core/org/apache/lucene/search/similarities/TFIDFSimilarity.html, 2014.

[26] J. W. Murdock et al. Textual evidence gathering and analysis. *IBM J. RES. and DEV*, 56(3.4), 2012.

[27] D. A. Patterson. Computer science education in the 21st century. *Commun. ACM*, 49(3):27–30, Mar. 2006.

[28] N. Schlaefer, J. Chu-Carroll, E. Nyberg, J. Fan, W. Zadrozny, and D. Ferrucci. Statistical source expansion for question answering. In *Proceedings of the 20th ACM International Conference on Information and Knowledge Management*, CIKM '11, pages 345–354, New York, NY, USA, 2011. ACM.

[29] A. Trotman, C. L. Clarke, I. Ounis, S. Culpepper, M.-A. Cartright, and S. Geva. Open Source Information Retrieval: A Report on the SIGIR 2012 Workshop. *SIGIR Forum*, 46(2):95–101, 2012.

[30] C. Wang et al. Relation extraction and scoring in DeepQA. *IBM J. RES. and DEV*, 56(3/4), 2012.

[31] M. Wollowski. Teaching with Watson. *Fifth AAAI Symposium on Educational Advances in Artificial Intelligence, http://www.aaai.org/ocs/index.php/EAAI/EAAI14/paper/view/8584/8677*, 2014.

Tutorial: Concurrency with Alice 3 and Java

Wanda Dann
Department of Computer Science
Carnegie Mellon University
Pittsburgh, PA 15213
1-412-268-9959
wpdann@cs.cmu.edu

Dennis Cosgrove
Department of Computer Science
Carnegie Mellon University
Pittsburgh, PA 15213
1-412-268-9959
dennisc@cs.cmu.edu

Don Slater
Department of Computer Science
Carnegie Mellon University
Pittsburgh, PA 15213
1- 412-268-9959
dslater@cs.cmu.edu

ABSTRACT

In this special session, attendees will learn about techniques for teaching concepts of concurrency with Alice 3's latest release of a Java IDE plugin. The new plugin makes use of Java 8's lambda expression to provide a *Do together* control structure with simpler syntax. Using this technique and Java 8 plugin, students in early-level programming courses can make use of Alice's *Do together* control structure to create concurrent threads in their Java code.

Categories and Subject Descriptors

K.3.2 [**Computer and Information Science Education**]: Computer science education.

General Terms

Human Factors.

Keywords

Concurrency, Programming, Alice.

1. OBJECTIVE

The ACM/IEEE-CS 2013 model curriculum [1] identifies essential concepts of concurrency and parallelism in programming models and algorithms. CS 2013 dedicates an entire new Knowledge Area to parallel and distributed computing topic as part of the core topics. Our hypothesis is that introducing concurrency in early CS coursework will help to lay the groundwork for success in upper division CS courses on parallelism.

The primary objective of this special session is to provide a tutorial that will enable teachers and students to engage in the study and use of concurrency in early CS courses with a commonly used programming language, Java. The tutorial session will make use of Alice 3and an Alice plugin for a Java 8 IDE. The plugin makes use of the lambda expression introduced in the latest release of Java.

SIGCSE'15, March 4–7, 2015, Kansas City, MO, USA.
ACM 978-1-4503-2966-8/15/03.
http://dx.doi.org/10.1145/2676723.2677316

2. OUTLINE OF SESSION

Dann and Slater will be presenters of the pedagogy and team project framework. Cosgrove (lead software engineer who developed the features to support concurrency using lambda expressions in Java 8) will engage in an interactive session with attendees to answer any questions with regard to feature capability and functionality.

The following list outlines the time allocated to the topic/activities proposed for the special session:

- Introduction the special session [5 minutes]
- Presentation of the concurrency construct in Alice 3 [10 minutes]
- Demonstration of the Alice plugin for a Java 8 IDE.
  - Transfer of code [5 minutes]
  - Do Together in Code Palette [10 minutes]
  - Lambda expression and use [15 minutes]
- Sample Code [10 minutes]
- Question and Answer. [15 minutes]

  Attendees will have an opportunity to interact with presenters and developers to discuss adaptations of the presented code and the features of Alice 3 that support concurrency.

3. EXPECTATIONS

This special session is intended for high school and college-level instructors who want to provide students an opportunity to experience working with concurrency in early CS courses.

This special session will present the use of lambda expressions in Java 8 to allow for simpler syntax in creating concurrent threads in Java code. We expect to provide ideas and stimulate interaction between the attendees, presenters, and software developers to enable communication and facilitate sharing of ideas.

The software system that will be used in this tutorial is Alice3, in its 2014 release. [2] Alice 3 is one of two versions (Alice 2 and Alice 3) available in a suite of Alice tools. The pedagogy and effectiveness of the use of Alice has been reported in formal studies supported by grants from the National Science Foundation and published in SIGCSE proceedings, e.g. [3, 6] and CACM. [5]

Feedback from the attendees will take the form of a Question and Answer session.

4. ACKNOWLEDGMENTS

Our thanks to the sponsors of the Alice Project, who include and have included Oracle, Sun Microsystems, Electronic Arts, Google, Disney, the Hearst Foundations, the Heinz Endowments, and Hyperion.

.

5. REFERENCES

[1] ACM/IEEE-CS Joint Task Force. 2013. Computer Science Curricula 2013. http://ai.stanford.edu/users/sahami/CS2013/ Referenced 8/29/14.

[2] Alice 3. Available online at www.alice.org. Referenced on 8/29/2014.

[3] B. Moskal, D. Lurie, and S. Cooper. Evaluating the Effectiveness of a New Instructional Approach in Proceedings of the ACM SIGCSE 2004 Conference, 2004, pp. 75-79.

[4] Common Core State Standards Initiative. Online at http://www.corestandards.org/resources/myths-vs-facts. Referenced on 9/3/2013.

[5] Dann, W. and Cooper, S. (2009). Alice3: Concrete to abstract. *Communications of the ACM*, 52(8), 27-29.

[6] Dann, W., Cosgrove, D., Slater, D., Culyba, D., and Cooper, S. 2012. Mediated transfer: Alice 3 to Java. In *Proceedings of the 43rd ACM technical symposium on Computer Science Education (SIGCSE '12)*. ACM, New York, NY, USA, 141-146.

Booming Enrollments – Good Times?

Tracy Camp
(Moderator)
Dept. of EECS
Colorado School of Mines
Golden, CO 80401 USA
+1 303-384-2184
tcamp@mines.edu

Stu Zweben
Dept. of CSE
The Ohio State University
2015 Neil Avenue
Columbus, OH 43210 USA
+1 614-292-9526
zweben.1@osu.edu

Ellen Walker
CS Dept.
Hiram College
11715 Garfield Road
Hiram, OH 44234
+1 330-569-5250
walkerel@hiram.edu

Lecia Barker
School of Information
University of Texas at Austin
1616 Guadalupe St.
Austin, TX 78701 USA
+1 512-232-8364
lecia@ischool.utexas.edu

ABSTRACT

This panel will discuss the enrollment boom, as well as potential effective practice strategies to respond to the increasing demand for computing education. Does the current enrollment "boom" represent the "third bubble", or is it here to stay? Is there a difference in what's happening at universities that offer Ph.D. degrees or what's happening at 4-year universities and colleges? What 'best practice' strategies exist (if any) to handle the demand? And, importantly, will this "boom" have a positive or negative effect on underrepresented students? Join us for a lively discussion on the recent student interest in computing education at our universities and colleges.

Categories and Subject Descriptors

K.3.2 Computer and Information Science Education

General Terms

Human Factors

Keywords

Enrollment

1. STATUS: UNIVERSITIES WITH PH.D. DEGREES (STU ZWEBEN)

Our field has faced booming enrollments twice in the past: in the mid-1980s, and in the late 1990s. The current "boom" (e.g., the total undergraduate enrollment in computing majors among U.S. computer science departments rose 13.4% over the past year [1]) shows signs of dramatically exceeding these previous ones, and there is a general sense that this boom is substantially different this time around. For example, in addition to a tremendous increase in majors, we are seeing a large increase in non-major enrollments, and non-majors taking more advanced CS courses. To illustrate these trends, we will review recent data gathered from several U.S. universities that offer Ph.D. degrees in computing during this panel. While our data is from a relatively small number of schools, we believe most U.S. universities that offer Ph.D. degrees in computing are witnessing similar trends.

While booming enrollments is certainly better than the alternative (i.e., plummeting enrollments), the swift increase in students within our departments presents several challenges. We will, therefore, discuss different strategies to respond to the demand for our introductory computer science courses, for our computing major, and for our upper division and graduate courses by non-majors. These strategies, which we believe are the most effective practices currently available, have been gleaned from a number of discussions and community sessions at venues such as the 2014 Snowbird conference [2] and the NCWIT 10th Anniversary Summit [3]. We welcome you to come join the discussion, which will be led by Dr. Zweben, a Professor Emeritus of Computer Science and Engineering at The Ohio State University. He previously served as chair of the department and as Associate Dean of the College of Engineering at OSU.

SIGCSE '15, March 4-7, 2015, Kansas City, MO, USA.
ACM 978-1-4503-2966-8/15/03.
http://dx.doi.org/10.1145/2676723.2677333

2. STATUS: 4-YEAR UNIVERSITIES AND COLLEGES (ELLEN WALKER)

The increases in enrollments and interest in computing programs are also being seen in non-PhD-granting programs in computing. In 2012-13, ACM conducted a comprehensive survey of these programs for the first time [4], thanks to the Non Doctoral Computing (NDC) efforts. The survey indicated an anticipated 13.9% increase in bachelor degree production from 2012 to 2013 from the 77 institutions and 160 degree programs included in the study. Additionally, enrollment in computing programs over all types of institutions grew 11% in one year (from 2012 to 2013). This double-digit enrollment increase in computing programs contrasts with the fact that overall undergraduate degree enrollment for all majors has been nearly flat since 2010 [5]. For example, at Hiram College, the demand for introductory computer science is the highest it has been in the last five years, even though the incoming class size is at its lowest in the same time frame.

These trends leave 4-year universities and colleges in a stressful situation. Without graduate assistants, simply adding sections of popular courses requires faculty overloads, new faculty, or adjuncts. Administrators are extremely conservative in hiring new tenure-track faculty, particularly as many remember the "second bubble" and its subsequent burst. Also, 4-year universities and colleges find themselves competing against doctoral universities for the limited pool of available qualified teaching talent, even for non-tenure-track and adjunct positions.

Meanwhile, our institutions are increasingly feeling pressure from parents to prepare their students for employment, and our current graduates are getting jobs in their field right out of college.

Our response to the current boom will likely shape our departments for years to come. Will we be creative in finding the resources needed to meet the demand? Or will we have to turn away eager students? Ellen Walker, Associate Dean of Academic Affairs and Professor of Computer Science at Hiram College, a small liberal arts college in Ohio, will lead this discussion.

3. IMPACT ON DIVERSITY (LECIA BARKER)

While we enjoy the opportunities and challenges that exist from our current enrollment "boom", many of us in computing have valid concerns over what the "boom" may (or may not) mean for diversity. Thus, in this panel, Lecia Barker, an Associate Professor in the School of Information at the University of Texas at Austin and a Senior Research Scientist for the National Center for Women & Information Technology (NCWIT), will lead a discussion on the boom's potential impact on diversity.

Enrollment caps. Each department is limited by its capacity to enroll students in courses in terms of instructor-student ratios, teaching assistants, and classroom size. Many departments are capping enrollment in classes and in majors. If policies are based purely in randomization, then all students who apply to a major or attempt to enroll in a class will have an equal chance to be admitted. However, policies may go beyond first-come, first-served or randomization. For example, in one university, students are enrolled in the introductory course based on a first-come, first-served approach, unless the student has already declared the CS major, then he or she goes to the top of the list. Students who take computer science in high school are more likely to declare the computer science major, especially those who take Advanced Placement Computer Science [6]. Students who take computer science in high school are more likely to be male, white, or Asian. Many students are not exposed to CS until they are in college, so enrollment policies shaped by pre-college exposure will limit access by underrepresented students.

Differential tuition. Differential tuition is when students in different fields are charged different rates of tuition to allow departments to cover costs of human and other resources (e.g., faculty to teach courses, lab assistants and tutors, teaching assistants, lab expenses, etc.) [7]. Differential tuition may negatively impact the diversity of students in CS. A recent economic study suggests that higher tuition more negatively impacts women and underrepresented minority students than students who are male and white [8].

Class size and weedout. Large-lecture teaching approaches can contribute to students' inability to gauge their progress, unless faculty intervene (e.g., [9]). When one is a minority in a majority setting, it is harder to develop the important ties to study groups and other student-student support mechanisms. Women in particular leave CS at higher rates than men, despite often having better grades than the men who stay [10], partly because they don't understand their standing relative to peers. Increasing enrollments are also likely to lead to faculty desire to cull unqualified students (aka weedout courses). While the intention will be to serve the "most qualified" students, in introductory courses in CS, "most qualified" is likely to be confounded with "students with most programming experience" (i.e., white males). Students with prior programming experience have been shown to be more successful in introductory courses [11], likely because they are reviewing the basic concepts, not learning them for the first time. Experience may be interpreted as talent, while inexperience may be interpreted as inability, translating to poor grades and students leaving for other majors.

How can CS departments manage the enrollment boom, while still maintaining their commitment to diversity?

4. REFERENCES

[1] S. Zweben and B. Bizot, B. 2014. 2013 Taulbee Survey: Second consecutive year of record doctoral degree production; Continued strong undergraduate CS enrollment. *Computing Research News*, 26, 5 (2014).

[2] J. Kurose and E. Lazowska. 2014. The Growing Enrollments in Computing Courses. *2014 CRA Conf. at Snowbird.* http://cra.org/events/snowbird-2014/.

[3] E. Roberts and E. Lazowska. 2014. Tsunami or Sea Change? Responding to the Explosion of Student Interest in Computer Science. *2014 NCWIT Summit on Women and IT.*

[4] J.C. Prey, Y. Timanovsky, J.L. Tims, and S. Zweben. 2013. ACM NDC study: a new annual study of non-doctoral-granting departments in computing. *ACM Inroads.* 4, 3 (2013), 4-14.

[5] Institute of Educational Sciences, Table 303.10. Total fall enrollment in degree-granting postsecondary institutions, by attendance status, sex of student, and control of institution: Selected years, 1947 through 2012, *Digest of Education Statistics* (2014) http://nces.ed.gov/programs/digest/d13/tables/dt13_303.10.asp

[6] K.D. Mattern, et al. 2011. *Advanced Placement Exam Participation: Is AP Exam Participation and Performance Related to Choice of College Major?* Technical Report #2011-6. College Board.

[7] S. Jascik. 2012. The Rise of Differential Tuition. *Inside Higher Ed.*

[8] K.M. Stange. 2013. *Differential Pricing in Undergraduate Education: Effects on Degree Production by Field.* Technical Report #19183. National Bureau of Economic Research.

[9] L. Porter and B. Simon. 2013. Retaining Nearly One-third More Majors with a Trio of Instructional Best Practices in CS1. *Proceeding of the 44th ACM Technical Symposium on Computer Science Education* (New York, NY, USA, 2013), 165–170.

[10] J. Cohoon and W. Aspray. 2006. A critical review of the research on women's participation in postsecondary computing education. *Women and Information Technology: Research on Underrepresentation.* MIT Press. 137–180.

[11] B.C. Wilson and S. Shrock. 2001. Contributing to success in an introductory computer science course: a study of twelve factors. *ACM SIGCSE Bulletin.* 33, 1 (2001), 184–188.

Integrating Live Projects Into Computing Curriculum

J. D. Chase, Prem Uppuluri, Tracy Lewis, Ian Barland, Jeff Pittges
Radford University
Box 6933
Radford VA 24142
540-831-5997
jchase@radford.edu

1. SUMMARY

It is well understood and has been well documented that there is much to gain by using live projects in the computer science classroom [1-13]. Live projects include those that serve a real client with a real problem as well as those those that integrate live datasets. However, the use of live projects has always come with a variety of challenges including supporting the project once it is complete, providing secure and safe access to large data sets, adjusting live client expectations, and limiting the scope of a project to the context of a single term and within the learning outcomes. The purpose of this special session is to provide attendees an introduction to and examples of the way that live projects have been integrated throughout the computing curriculum at Radford University.

2. OVERALL OBJECTIVE

Using live projects in a computer science course provides a variety of benefits for the students including:

- Experience with realistic situations, strict deadlines, teamwork, written and oral communications skills [11, 12]
- Easing the transition from school to work [9]
- Experience with unstable client requirements [7]
- The challenge of working with a large, complex project with uncertain requirements [5]
- Experience with pair and/or team programming working with real clients and real timelines [8]
- Increased motivation from knowing their work will actually be used [4] to having fun with live projects [13]
- Experience with having work critiqued by actual clients [10]
- An integration experience applying concepts learned to live projects [6]

This session will explain how and why live projects have been integrated into the computing curriculum at Radford University, and to help the audience understand how it is possible to overcome the challenges associated with live projects. These challenges include:

- Increased time, organizational and pedagogical demands on the instructor [1] – includes issues such as pre-semester analysis and design and post-project maintenance
- Constraining the scope of a project to meet the academic calendar [6]
- Access to appropriate, secure data sets free of identifying personal information
- Solicitation of clients for one or two term projects
- Management of consistency and synergy when large projects are broken down into one semester chunks

SIGCSE '15, March 4-7, 2015, Kansas City, MO, USA.
ACM 978-1-4503-2966-8/15/03.
http://dx.doi.org/10.1145/2676723.2677320

3. SESSION OUTLINE

This special session is divided into six blocks:

• Introduction	(10 minutes)
• History of Live Projects at RU – the SPSC	(10 minutes)
• Live Data in CS 2	(10 minutes)
• Live Client Projects in Web Development	(10 minutes)
• Live Malicious Data in Security	(10 minutes)
• Live Projects in Software Engineering	(10 minutes)
• Questions and Answers	(15 minutes)

This informal, interactive session will welcome questions and audience participation throughout. Joe Chase will begin the session by introducing the concept of live projects, discussing the benefits and challenges, and presenting several approaches to including live experiences for students (e.g. live clients, live data, historical live projects, historical data sets).

3.1 Live Projects at RU – The SPSC

Jeff Pittges will share experiences gained from the Small Project Support Center (SPSC), a student staffed clearinghouse for live projects. The SPSC would solicit, vet, and evaluate project proposals, liaison with instructors, act as a client proxy, prepare for deployment, test, productize, deploy, and support applications. Pittges will discuss challenges, lessons learned, and recommendations.

3.2 Live Data in CS 2

The session will continue with a discussion, led by Joe Chase, of live data projects in CS 2. At the CS 2 level, students may not yet be ready to work with live clients but they are able to work with live data. At RU, the CS 2 class includes an introduction to JSON formatted data (as described by Depasquale [2]), web services, and the concept of a web crawler. These live, online data sources provide a rich area for CS 2 level projects and in-class discussions. Several example projects will be discussed.

3.3 Live Client Projects in Web Development

Ian Barland will then lead a discussion of the introduction of live projects in Web Development. In Web Development 2, students learn about server-side processing and interacting with a back-end database. Working in teams of 3-5, students develop a project: either one of their own choosing, or one for a live 'external' customer (a local business or charity, or another university unit), or a real-world live project supervised by a faculty member within the department. Several specific projects will be discussed, along with some teaching challenges associated with live projects: helping teams with professionalism and client communication, handling evolving specs, and managing client expectations, as well as having evaluation criteria flexible enough to accommodate disparate projects.

3.4 Live Malicious Data in Security

Prem Uppuluri will discuss the use of live data in Security courses. The word *malicious data* clearly would send shivers through the system administrators of any campus network. Access to live malicious data is therefore not easily available. Through a Radford University internal grant we are able to experiment with a computer network separate from Radford University's networks. The security of this network is completely in the control of the students and the faculty member in charge. Hence, projects such as honeypots and perimeter security are conducted in a live environment. The setup of the network, the costs involved and example projects will be discussed.

3.5 Live Projects in Software Engineering

Tracy Lewis will discuss the integration of live projects in Software Engineering. Using agile software development techniques, software engineering students gather requirements (user stories), prioritize them, write unit tests, and develop fully functional iterations of systems. Completed iterations are presented to the client for acceptance testing. Agile software development is ideal for these projects because most requirements are initially ill-defined, but clients are actively involved to offer guidance and feedback through the 4-week iteration development cycles. We have been able to partner with multi-national corporations, local for-profit and non-profit organizations, as well as departments and offices within Radford University. Projects ranging from components of the RU Mobile app to secure medical inventory systems will be discussed.

4. SESSION EXPECTATIONS

This session will disseminate the live project experiences from Radford University enabling faculty at other institutions to provide similar experiences for their students. The expected audience is computing faculty with a desire to incorporate live projects into their classes and curriculum.

The session covers multiple subjects and multiple levels from CS 2 to senior classes. Each topic will present specific challenges and describe example projects. Attendees will take away enough information to experiment with live projects in their classroom.

5. SUITABILITY

This informal, interactive session will share experiences with live projects at Radford University and engage the audience in the discussion. The short blocks will present challenges, benefits, and examples associated with live projects at different levels and in different disciplines within computer science. The audience will be encouraged to ask questions and participate.

6. REFERENCES

[1] Bickerstaff, D. D. 1985. The evolution of a project oriented course in software development. In *Proceedings of the Sixteenth SIGCSE Technical Symposium on Computer Science Education* (New Orleans, Louisiana, United States, March 14 - 15, 1985). J. E. Miller, Ed. SIGCSE '85. ACM Press, New York, NY, 13-22.

[2] Depasquale, P. 2006. Exploiting on-line data sources as the basis of programming projects. In *Proceedings of the Thirty-Seventh SIGCSE Technical Symposium on Computer Science Education* (Houston, Texas, United States, March 1 - 4, 2006). D. Baldwin, P. Tymann, S. Haller, and I. Russell, Eds. SIGCSE '06. ACM Press, New York, NY, 283-287.

[3] Farkas, D. 1988. Choosing group projects for advanced systems courses. In *Proceedings of the Nineteenth SIGCSE Technical Symposium on Computer Science Education* (Atlanta, Georgia, United States, February 25 - 26, 1988). H. L. Dershem, Ed. SIGCSE '88. ACM Press, New York, NY, 109-115.

[4] Gabbert, P. and Treu, K. 2001. Reality check: working with meaningful projects in and out of the classroom. *J. Comput. Small Coll.* 17, 2 (Dec. 2001), 191-198.

[5] Grisham, P. S., Krasner, H., and Perry, D. E. 2006. Data Engineering education with real-world projects. *SIGCSE Bull.* 38, 2 (Jun. 2006), 64-68.

[6] Joel, W. J. 1987. Realistic student projects. In *Proceedings of the Eighteenth SIGCSE Technical Symposium on Computer Science Education* (St. Louis, Missouri, United States, February 19 - 20, 1987). A. K. Rigler and D. C. St. Clair, Eds. SIGCSE '87. ACM Press, New York, NY, 244-247.

[7] Poger, S. and Bailie, F. 2006. Student perspectives on a real world project. *J. Comput. Small Coll.* 21, 6 (Jun. 2006), 69-75.

[8] Simpson, M., Burmeister, J., Boykiw, A., and Zhu, J. 2003. Successful studio-based real-world projects in IT education. In *Proceedings of the Fifth Australasian Conference on Computing Education - Volume 20* (Adelaide, Australia). T. Greening and R. Lister, Eds. ACM International Conference Proceeding Series, vol. 140. Australian Computer Society, Darlinghurst, Australia, 41-51.

[9] Song, K. 1996. Teaching software engineering through real-life projects to bridge school and industry. *SIGCSE Bull.* 28, 4 (Dec. 1996), 59-64.

[10] Tadayon, N. 2004. Software engineering based on the team software process with a real world project. *J. Comput. Small Coll.* 19, 4 (Apr. 2004), 133-142.

[11] Tan, J. and Phillips, J. 2003. Challenges of real-world projects in team-based courses. *J. Comput. Small Coll.* 19, 2 (Dec. 2003), 265-277.

[12] Tan, J. and Phillips, J. 2005. Real-world project management in the academic environment. *J. Comput. Small Coll.* 20, 5 (May. 2005), 200-213.

[13] Villarreal, E. E. and Butler, D. 1998. Giving computer science students real-world experience. In *Proceedings of the Twenty-Ninth SIGCSE Technical Symposium on Computer Science Education* (Atlanta, Georgia, United States, February 26 - March 01, 1998). D. Joyce and J. Impagliazzo, Eds. SIGCSE '98. ACM Press, New York, NY, 40-44

WebWolf: Towards a Simple Framework for Automated Assessment of Webpage Assignments in an Introductory Web Programming Class

Antonio C. Siochi
Christopher Newport University
One University Place
Newport News, VA 23606, USA
+1(757) 594-7569
siochi@cnu.edu

William R. Hardy
Christopher Newport University
One University Place
Newport News, VA 23606
william.hardy.07@cnu.edu

ABSTRACT

Grading student submissions of webpage assignments is difficult and time-consuming because it involves reading and evaluating source code for compliance with assignment specifications. In addition, the pages must be examined in a browser to check for required functionality such as working links. As a result fewer assignments tend to be given, or instructors spend significant time grading at the expense of working with students or other necessary activities. There is thus a need for automated assessment of webpage assignments. This paper describes WebWolf, a simple framework for automated assessment of assignments in an introductory web programming class. A WebWolf program can load web pages, find and inspect elements, click links and make assertions about expected results. WebWolf was evaluated with assignments from three different classes and on a set of assignment submissions with injected errors. WebWolf correctly identified errors in the submissions. Manual grading of a four page assignment took an average of 17 minutes, while the WebWolf program took 35 seconds.

Categories and Subject Descriptors

K.3.2 [**Computer and Information Science Education**]: Computer Science Education

General Terms

Design, Languages.

Keywords

Automated Assessment; Computer Science Education; Web Programming.

1. INTRODUCTION

In an introductory web programming class it is important to assess students' understanding of the basic structure of a web page and their ability to work with page elements such as paragraphs, headings, images and links. As with Java programming, assessment can't be limited to validation of HTML because neither IDEs nor validators can check if assignment-required elements are missing or if links go to wrong pages. Similarly, just viewing browser-rendered pages may not reveal inconsistencies with assignment specifications. For example, if an assignment requires CSS rather than tables for page layout, the code must be examined.

Reading html code for every assignment submission in a large class is time consuming and prone to inconsistent grading (e.g., failing to see that an element was present). This is a recognized problem [10] and is the same problem found in manual grading of programming assignments. A common approach to this problem is automated assessment.

Carter [5], in a paper reflecting on the results of an international survey on automated assessment, summarizes the issue: "If assessments are graded manually, educators must either set fewer assessment tasks or resign themselves to a greatly increased marking load. In order to cope with increasing student numbers automated assessment is becoming increasingly important in many courses."

Furthermore, Brandle [2] notes that one consequence of an increased load is that students do not receive feedback quickly enough for it to be helpful before their next assignment. He also states that more often than not this feedback is not very detailed.

The goal of this research, therefore, is to produce an assessment framework suitable for grading assignments in an introductory web programming class.

The rest of this paper presents a review of the literature, a description of the framework developed in this research, and illustrations of using that framework. This is followed by a discussion of a basic evaluation of the framework and a conclusion.

2. LITERATURE REVIEW

Traditional development tools, such as online validators, check the HTML syntax of web pages to verify that they meet W3C standards (http://www.w3.org/QA/Tools). While validators verify compliance, they do not check content or functionality of that website. That testing traditionally involves manually assessing rendered pages and underlying code.

In trying to develop a framework that supports such assessments, it is helpful to consider the history of similar efforts for computer programming. Douce [7] outlines that history, which dates back to the 1960's, and describes numerous automated assessment systems. More recent systems include

SIGCSE '15, March 04 - 07 2015, Kansas City, MO, USA
Copyright 2015 ACM 978-1-4503-2966-8/15/03…$15.00
http://dx.doi.org/10.1145/2676723.2677217

QuizPACK [3] and Web-CAT [8]. Some systems have separate mechanisms for handling the testing and the logistics of assignment turn-in and grade reporting. Web-CAT, for example, uses a plug-in architecture for test runners. This provides a way to add testing programs in other languages (e.g., HTML). Because such logistics frameworks are available, this research focused only on the testing framework.

2.1 Testing Frameworks

JUnit [15] and TestNG [1] are two common testing frameworks. While TestNG extends JUnit's capabilities, both provide a mechanism for setting up and running tests. Testers are not required to write drivers that call the test methods or record test results. The tester marks a method with the @Test annotation, and within that test method calls assert methods that evaluate the actual outcomes. If an outcome was not what was expected, JUnit and TestNG will throw an exception, record that the test failed, then run the next test. If the outcome is what was expected, this fact is recorded and the next test is run. This enables testers to write only test cases instead of developing an entire testing system.

2.2 Programmatic Browser Control

2.2.1 Watir

Watir (Web Application Testing In Ruby) [9] is an open source set of Ruby libraries for writing Ruby gems that can control web browsers. Watir works only on Internet Explorer, but there is a version called Watir/WebDriver (i.e., Selenium 2) that works on other browsers. Watir is essentially a Ruby front end for Internet Explorer, and Watir/WebDriver is a Ruby front end for Selenium.

2.2.2 IeUnit

IeUnit (http://sourceforge.net/projects/ieunit/) is a unit testing tool for Web applications. It is based on the xUnit framework. It tests directly with a real browser and javascript engine. It is written in javascript but is dependent on Internet Explorer's services, DHTML model and COM technologies.

2.2.3 HtmlUnit

HtmlUnit (http://htmlunit.sourceforge.net) is a framework for simulating a browser under program control. It is capable of simulating Internet Explorer and Firefox. It also has a built in javascript interpreter. According to its developers it is not a testing framework. It can, however, be used by frameworks such as JUnit (htmlunit.sourceforge.net) to develop web-testing systems. Writing code for HtmlUnit can be complicated. It also simulates a browser rather than controlling an actual browser.

2.2.4 Selenium

Selenium (http://docs.seleniumhq.org) [4] is similar to HtmlUnit in that it provides programmatic control of a browser, not testing methods per se. For example, Selenium provides methods that allow clicking on html elements and links. Unlike HtmlUnit, Selenium does not simulate a browser but makes calls to browsers via its WebDriver. As with HtmlUnit, controlling the browser can require several Selenium method calls.

2.3 Website Assessment Tools

Website assessment automation involves combining testing frameworks such as JUnit with programmatic browser controllers like Selenium. Coffman [6], for example, used TestNG and Selenium to automate the testing of student websites in a course on website security. He used TestNG because it supported different test types (e.g., unit, functional, integration) and because it supported test dependencies. Several generalized systems have been developed using this same approach.

2.3.1 WebTest

WebTest [11] is a Java-based open source web application-testing tool. Test scripts are written as Ant scripts in XML. WebTest uses Ant to drive the scripts, and uses HtmlUnit to run the tested web applications.

2.3.2 Cucumber

Cucumber [13] is a tool that facilitates writing system specifications as scenarios then automating them as functional tests. A scenario describes what should happen between a user and the webpage for a given goal. For example,

```
Scenario: Trying to go to the home page
  When I click the home button
Then I should see the home page
```

Cucumber generates a test by mapping steps in the scenario to Watir code using regular expressions:

```
When /^I click the home button$/ do
  @browser.button(:value => 'Home').click
end
```

Cucumber requires the tester to know Ruby and Watir as well as regular expressions.

2.3.3 APOGEE

APOGEE is a system designed to use Ruby and Watir to automatically evaluate web pages. A prototype, ProtoAPOGEE, was developed using Ruby, Watir, and WatiN (Web Application Testing in .Net, http://watin.org). This tool concentrates on advanced Web computing classes involving "issues such as atomicity of database access, thread safety, reliability, robustness, and security" [10].

2.3.4 AWAT

AWAT [14] is an automated specification based grading system for web applications. Its testing system is similar to Cucumber in that it is specification-based. However, the specifications consist of a table of inputs and expected outputs. It is very simple in that one only has to create spreadsheets with the test tables. Column names are labeled with inputs and results, and each row represents a test case. The labels are mapped to html elements using their name attributes. AWAT's strength is the simplicity of its specification scheme. Unlike Cucumber, AWAT seems applicable only to testing input-output values. AWAT is also dependent on Internet Explorer.

2.3.5 PARSI

PARSI [12] is an environment that allows instructors to specify requirements for word-processing, presentation, spreadsheets, email, and webpages using XML. PARSI uses these requirements to generate assignments and assess the submissions of students. HTML is validated with a separate program. Although the paper does not describe how that program worked, the authors stated that it was similar to validators but also checked other items.

3. RATIONALE

An assessment framework intended for introductory web programming should be simple yet still provide access to full programmatic browser control. Simplicity is needed because introductory assignments are not very complex, and it is important not to overwhelm instructors and introductory students with a large number of concepts or skills. Access to full browser control is needed so that what can be assessed is not restricted.

The framework should leverage technologies familiar to instructors of these courses. Familiarity, along with simplicity, may reduce the psychological hurdles to accepting and using automated assessment. The perceived cost of developing and using tests must be seen as low enough, and the benefit of automated assessment as high enough, for instructors of introductory classes to adopt automated assessment. Since APOGEE, Cucumber, Watir, WebTest require knowledge of another language, and since PARSI is broad in scope, they were not considered for this research.

In addition, because students get confused, frustrated or discouraged if their code "works" with their browser but fails the assessment, it is important that the tool use the actual browser on which students develop, test and deploy, rather than a simulated browser. This eliminates problems due to browser incompatibilities. Since WebTest and HtmlUnit simulate browsers, they were not considered for this research.

Finally, to be broadly usable the tool should be browser agnostic. Since AWAT and IeUnit are browser-dependent, they were not considered for this research.

Because Selenium does not simulate a browser but instead controls actual browsers, and since Selenium can drive different browsers, it is used in the WebWolf framework for programmatic browser control. Because JUnit is familiar to instructors who use unit testing, WebWolf's testing mechanism and API are modeled on those of JUnit.

4. WEBWOLF

4.1 Description

The WebWolf framework allows instructors to write JUnit-like Java programs to test websites typically developed in an introductory web-programming course. WebWolf functions very much like JUnit: test methods are written that simulate user actions on the webpage under test, and assertions are made about what results are expected. When a test program is run, WebWolf calls Selenium methods to interact with the web pages. Like JUnit, WebWolf uses Reflections to determine which methods in the test program are test methods. Unlike JUnit, WebWolf provides a means of specifying the order in which tests are executed. Points can also be assigned in a test method to provide partial credit. WebWolf also provides a simple GUI to configure and monitor the execution of test programs. When all tests are completed, their results are reported.

Although it is possible to use Selenium methods and the WebWolf test runner to develop web tests, this requires good knowledge of Selenium. In addition, several lines of code have to be written to test a web application. For example, a testing program must first call several methods to configure and set up a browser. Tasks such as switching window focus can require calling multiple Selenium methods (see Figure 1). WebWolf contributes an API that does not require a lot of Selenium knowledge. This abstraction also reduces the amount of code that has to be written.

```
WebDriver driver;
// driver configuration is done here
String titleOfWindow = "Rice";
String currentWindow = driver.getWindowHandle();
for (String handle : driver.getWindowHandles()) {
  driver.switchTo().window(handle);
  String title = "";
  try {
    title = driver.getTitle();
  }
  catch (WebDriverException W) {
    title = "Couldn't Get Title";
  }
  if (title.contains(titleOfWindow)) {
    driver.switchTo().window(handle);
    return true;
  }
}
driver.switchTo().window(currentWindow);
```

Figure 1. Selenium code to switch window focus.

A list of 15 commonly used WebWolf methods is provided in Table 1. WebWolf also provides a public field, `driver`, which can be used to invoke Selenium methods.

Table 1. Commonly used WebWolf methods.

Return Type	Method and Parameters
void	defaultURL()
List <WebElement>	findElements(String tagName, String... attributes)
void	assertAtLeast(int minimum, int actual)
void	assertEquals(int expected, int actual)
void	assertEquals(String expected, String actual)
void	assertIDMatches(String expectedIDs, WebElement element)
void	assertTrue(boolean condition)
void	assertPageLoaded(WebElement elt)
void	click(WebElement element)
String	getID(WebElement element)
String	getValueOfAttribute(WebElement e, String attribute)
String	getDefaultURL()
boolean	takeScreenShot(String fileName)
void	toDo(String message, boolean done)
void	goBack()

Other WebWolf methods include support for hovering, right-clicking, selecting web elements, selecting drop-down items, switching frames or windows, executing javascript, detecting alerts, getting browser and URL information, managing the default URL, and waiting for specific elements to load.

Figure 2 shows the simplest WebWolf test program that can be written. It is similar to a JUnit program except that a main method is required to start the test runner. The `@Before` annotated method is used to make the browser load the default

URL before each test, thus guaranteeing the same initial condition for every test.

```
public class SimplestTest {

   public static WebWolf WW;

   public static void main(String args[]) {
     new WebWolf("Recipe.config");
   }

   @Before
   public void goToSite() {
     WW.defaultURL();
   }

   @Test
   public void aTestName() {
     // do something on the page
     // assert something expected about the result
   }
}
```

Figure 2. Minimal WebWolf test program.

4.2 Writing WebWolf Tests

In order to give a sense of how WebWolf works, a brief example is presented here. In what follows below, `WW` is the WebWolf object that was instantiated in Figure 2, and WebElement is a Selenium class.

4.2.1 Finding Elements

One check instructors make for student web pages is to determine whether the required number of a specified element is present on the page. For example, if the assignment specifies that at least three images must be present, the test would find images then assert that at least three are present:

```
List<WebElement> elts = WW.findElements("img");
WW.assertAtLeast(3, elts.size());
```

The `findElements()` method actually has a variable number of arguments where the first argument is the tag name and the other arguments are the attributes. Thus to find a link with an id attribute:

```
elts = WW.findElements("a", "href", "id");
```

4.2.2 Using id Attribute to Check Semantics

When an assignment requires elements to have specific semantics, finding elements using only the tag name may not be sufficient. In a fashion similar to CSS id selectors, assignments should require such elements to have id attributes. Suppose an assignment requires a table of ingredients in a recipe web page. The assignment should require the table to have a specific id since students might put more than one table. For example, if the required `id` is `ingredients`, then the following can be written:

```
elts = WW.findElements("table", "id");
WW.assertIDMatches("ingredients", elts);
```

4.2.3 Following Links

The use of `ids` as semantic markers also allows automated testing of links: did the link load the correct page? Assignments should therefore require a page's `html` tag and every link element to have `id` attributes. The web test would first find the link, check its id, load a page then assert that the loaded page has the expected `id`.

Suppose an assignment requires one link on a page and that the link `id` and the `id` of the loaded page's `html` element must be `recipe1`. Loading a page first involves finding the link on a page and then loading it:

```
elts = WW.findElements("a", "href", "id");
WW.assertIDMatches("recipe1", elts);
WW.assertPageLoaded(elts.get(0));
```

The `assertIDMatches()` method checks that the `id` of the link element matches the `id` required by the assignment specification (`recipe1`). The `assertPageLoaded()` method attempts to load the page whose `url` is contained in the found element `elts.get(0)`. If the load succeeds the browser will be on the loaded page. If it fails, an exception is thrown showing the `url` that did not load, along with any browser error messages (e.g., 404 File not found). This mechanism allows WebWolf tests to detect a common error in student web pages: `urls` with absolute filenames that work on the student's machine but not on the server.

The next step is to check that the correct page loaded. Assuming that the page loaded, the browser is now on the loaded page. This is verified as follows:

```
List<WebElement> h = WW.findElements("html", "id");
WW.assertIDMatches("recipe1", h);
```

This assertIDMatches() checks that the `id` of the new page's `html` tag is the correct `id`. If the `html` tag's `id` is missing or is not `recipe1`, an exception will be thrown, otherwise the test passes.

Figure 3 shows a WebWolf test where these techniques are combined to assess a webpage with multiple links. It also shows how to test for a requirement that the link `id` must match the `html` `id` of the loaded page, rather than a specified `id` as in the code above (i.e., `recipe1`).

```
public void doHomePageLinkIDsMatchRecipePageIDs() {
    int min = 2;
    List<WebElement> links;
    links = WW.findElements("a", "href", "id");
    int numLinks = links.size();
    WW.assertAtLeast(min, numLinks);

    String[] ids = new String[numLinks];
    for (int i = 0; i < numLinks; i++) {
      ids[i] = WW.getID(links.get(i));
    }

    List<WebElement> pg;
    for (int i = 0; i < numLinks; i++) {
      WW.assertPageLoaded(links.get(i));
      pg = WW.findElements("html", "id");
      WW.assertIDMatches(ids[i], pg.get(0));
      WW.goBack();
      links = WW.findElements("a", "href", "id");
    }
}
```

Figure 3. Testing for correctly linked pages.

After checking for the minimum number of required links, the test in Figure 3 creates an array (ids) that holds the ids of each of the links on that page. In the `for` loop that follows, the test loads the linked page, checks that its `id` matches, then goes back to the previous page so that the next link can be tested. The `findElements()` call in this loop is required to avoid what Selenium calls a "stale page" error.[1].

[1] It is possible that the previous page may have changed while the browser was on the linked page.

Figure 4 shows the html code of the home page and the recipe page. The second link in the home page has `recipe2` as its id whereas the id of the html element of the recipe page has `recipe2Page` as its id.

```
<html id="home">
  <head><title>HOME</title></head>
  <body>
    <a href="recipe1.html" id="pork">Pork Adobo</a>
    <a href="recipe2.html" id="recipe2">Rice</a>
  </body>
</html>

<html id="recipe2Page">
  <head><title>Rice</title></head>
  <body>
  ...
  </body>
</html>
```

Figure 4. Html code for home and recipe pages.

Figure 5 shows the WebWolf output for the test of Figure 3 for the home and recipe pages that fail the matching id requirement for links and html tags.

Line Number	Assert Message	File	Result
236		RecipeTests.java	Success
245		RecipeTests.java	Success
247		RecipeTests.java	Success
245		RecipeTests.java	Success
247	(expected id is <recipe2> but got <recipe2Page>)	RecipeTests.java	Failure

Figure 5. Output for test of multiple links.

4.3 Discussion

4.3.1 Initial Evaluation

WebWolf was initially evaluated by using it to develop test suites for two web assignments: one from an introductory web programming course, the other from a programming languages course. The purpose of this exercise was to determine whether the WebWolf API would allow testing of the assignment specifications. Each assignment also had archived student submissions that were used during the testing. The assignments were taken from classes that were no longer in session.

Specifications were extracted from the first assignment and a WebWolf test was developed for each specification. During this process it became clear that the original assignment was loosely specified and contained ambiguous, and hence untestable, specifications such as "Headings must be properly used." Since this assignment did not specify the use of ids, it was added to the specifications and tests written for those specifications. Unsurprisingly when student pages were tested, many cases failed. However, the results helped to identify sections in student code that needed to be edited. In other instances the problems were traced to the tests themselves. The edited code was retested and the next round of test failures used to make the next round of edits. In fact, WebWolf was used exactly as a student or instructor would have used it in a test-driven-development methodology. Interestingly, the process was exactly the same as that used in developing JUnit tests for java programming assignments. This assessment was repeated with the assignment from the Programming Languages class, which confirmed the experience of the first assignment's assessment.

Two issues emerged from this initial evaluation. First, the original API was not self-sufficient, requiring several calls to native Selenium code. Second, Selenium provided no mechanism to detect when a page failed to load, a very common student error at this level. The first problem was addressed by abstracting the repetitive code into WebWolf methods. One example of this is the `findElements()` method. The second problem was solved, ironically, by using HtmlUnit because Selenium's developers would not provide the ability to detect load failures. The developers explained that it was out of project scope (http://code.google.com/p/selenium/issues/detail?id=141). The `assertPageLoaded()` method was written to address this problem.

When the revised API was used to rewrite the tests for the first assignment there was no need to make any calls to native Selenium code. It was also now possible to write tests that checked for page load failures and produced specific error messages indicating such failures (See Figure 6).

Line Number	Assert Message	File	Result
236		RecipeTests.java	Success
245	(FAILED LOAD<file:///Users/StudentX/fingerfood.html> HTTP STATUS=404)	RecipeTests.java	Failure

Figure 6. Output for failed page load.

4.3.2 Evaluation in an In-session Class

This current version of WebWolf was used to write the test suite for one assignment in an HTML programming class. The assignment was written with testable specifications, and students were instructed on the use of the id attribute. A testing jig was developed that collected submitted assignments and ran the test suite on each. Results for each student were saved as separate files, and a grade file was produced summarizing the grades for each student. Students were able to review the results (similar to those shown in Figure 5) and use these to revise their submissions.

WebWolf graded the 24 four-page assignments in less than 16 minutes, or less than 10 seconds per page.

4.3.3 Comparison to Manual Grading

A simplified version of the assignment was developed for a manual grading comparison. One of the student assignments with a perfect score was modified to comply with the simplified assignment and to embed five errors. Seven faculty members and one graduate student, all with expertise in HTML, graded the modified student assignment. They were given a table of assignment specifications and asked to record their start and end times. Only the time spent in actual grading was recorded. They were asked to list the errors they found, and which specification was involved. They took 17 minutes, on average, to grade the four-page assignment, with times ranging from 9 to 24 minutes. For each error, the number of participants who correctly identified that error ranged from 63% to 100%.

The manual grading time reported here could be considered longer than what would be expected since with each succeeding submission two things tend to happen: the human grader becomes more familiar with the types of errors occurring, and he/she internalizes the assignment specifications thus reducing time spent going back and forth between the assignment specifications and the submission. However, there would still be a minimum time spent reading the submission (about 3 minutes for this submission).

In comparison, WebWolf graded the submission in less than 35 seconds, or less than 10 seconds per page. It identified all embedded errors. Of note, the three faculty who teach courses involving HTML asked about using WebWolf in their classes.

4.3.4 The id Question

One might argue that checking for id attributes does not really evaluate the content of a page. Consider the following link:

```
<a href="recipe.html" id="adobo">Adobo</a>
```

Even if the `html` tag of recipe.html had the id `adobo`, how does one know that `recipe.html` really contains the recipe for adobo without looking at that page? However, the same question can be asked of CSS where id attributes are used to select elements. If the id is placed on the wrong element, or the selector is incorrect, the element will not be formatted as desired. Even if the ids match, how can the formatting of that element be checked? The only way to determine this would be by visual inspection. This is similar to the issue with specifications such as "Proper use of headings." The approach WebWolf provides for these types of issues is its `takeScreenShot()` method which saves the screen, and its `toDo()` method which records a comment in the report about what needs to be checked. By scanning the report for `toDo()` comments the instructor can review the page screen shots instead of having to manually load each student's page, find, and click on each element that needs to be inspected.

5. CONCLUSIONS

It was possible to use WebWolf to grade student submissions for simple HTML assignments using the 15 methods listed in Table 1. Although knowledge of Selenium's WebElement class is also required, this is a simple class with a few methods.

WebWolf enabled a greatly reduced grading time as compared to manual grading. As is the case with any automation, it takes significant time to develop the test suite for each assignment. WebWolf's small API and similarity to JUnit should help to reduce this time. In addition, assignments and test suites could be developed before the semester, or by other people,

For assignments to be testable, they must be unambiguously specified and may require the use of id attributes for certain elements. Where this is not possible or desirable, the screenshot mechanism can be used to assist with grading.

While only a basic evaluation was performed, WebWolf shows promise as an assessment framework for grading assignments in an introductory web programming class.

Future work includes the release of a public version[2], a wider and more formal evaluation, and incorporation into systems such as Web-CAT to manage the collection, grading and return of student assignments.

6. REFERENCES

[1] Beust, C. and Suleiman, H., 2008. *Next Generation Java Testing: TestNG and Advanced Concepts*. Pearson Education, Inc., Boston, MA.

[2] Brandle, S., 2009. Automated grading of student programming assignments. *J. Comput. Small Coll. 25*, 1 (October 2009), 83-84.

[3] Brusilovsky, P. and Sosnovsky, S., 2005. Individualized exercises for self-assessment of programming knowledge: An evaluation of QuizPACK. *J. Educ. Resour. Comput. 5*, 3, 6.

[4] Burns, D., 2012. *Selenium 2 Testing Tools Beginner's Guide*. Packt Publishing, Birmingham, UK.

[5] Carter, J., Ala-Mutka, K., Fuller, U., Dick, M., English, J., Fone, W., and Sheard, J., 2003. How shall we assess this? *SIGCSE Bull. 35*, 4, 107-123.

[6] Coffman, J. and Weaver, A.C., 2010. Electronic commerce virtual laboratory. In *Proceedings of the 41st ACM Technical Symposium on Computer Science Education* (Milwaukee, Wisconsin, USA, 2010), ACM, 1734295, 92-96.

[7] Douce, C., Livingstone, D., and Orwell, J., 2005. Automatic test-based assessment of programming: A review. *J. Educ. Resour. Comput. 5*, 3, 4.

[8] Edwards, S.H. and Perez-Quiñones, M.A., 2008. Web-CAT: automatically grading programming assignments. In *Proceedings of the 13th annual conference on Innovation and technology in computer science education (ITiCSE '08)* ACM, New York, NY, USA, 328-328.

[9] Filipin, Ž., 2014. Web Application Testing in Ruby with Selenium and Friends, version 2014-03-08. Retrieved November 17, 2014 from http://leanpub.com/watirbook.

[10] Fu, X., Peltsverger, B., Qian, K., Tao, L., and Liu, J., 2008. APOGEE: automated project grading and instant feedback system for web based computing. *SIGCSE Bull. 40*, 1, 77-81.

[11] Guillemot, M. and König, D., 2006. Web testing made easy. In *Proceedings of the Companion to the 21st ACM SIGPLAN Symposium on Object-Oriented Programming Systems, Languages, and Applications* (Portland, Oregon, USA, 2006), ACM, 1176677, 692-693.

[12] Lahtonen, T. and Isomöttönen, V., 2012. PARSI: a tool for automatic assessment of office documents and basic IT skills. In *Proceedings of the 12th Koli Calling International Conference on Computing Education Research* (Koli, Finland, 2012), ACM, 2401824, 174-180.

[13] Morgan, J., 2013. *Cucumber & Cheese: a Tester's Workshop, version 2013-07-09*. Retrieved July 16, 2013 from http://leanpub.com/cucumber_and_cheese.

[14] Sztipanovits, M., Qian, K., and Fu, X., 2008. The automated web application testing (AWAT) system. In *Proceedings of the 46th Annual Southeast Regional Conference* (Auburn, Alabama, 2008), ACM, 1593128, 88-93.

[15] Tahchiev, P., Leme, F., Massol, V., and Gregory, G., 2011. *JUnit in Action*. Manning Publications Co., Stamford, CT.

[2] See http://www.pcs.cnu.edu/~siochi/webwolf for the current release.

The Role of Automation in Undergraduate Computer Science Education

Chris Wilcox
Computer Science
Colorado State University
1873 Campus Delivery
Fort Collins, Colorado 80523
wilcox@cs.colostate.edu

ABSTRACT

Increasing enrollments in undergraduate computer science courses are overloading faculty, teaching assistants, labs, and other resources. To cope with resource problems, many universities have automated key processes such as program grading. Before replacing a manual process with an automated tool, we believe that two questions should be answered. First and most importantly, does the proposed automation contribute to or detract from student learning? Second, do the benefits outweigh the costs of the automation? In this paper we present results from an introductory programming course in which we have incorporated high levels of automation. We find that carefully designed and managed automation can improve student performance while realizing a significant savings of scarce teaching resources.

Categories and Subject Descriptors

K.3.2 [**Computers and Education**]: Computer and Information Science Education; K.3.1 [**Computer Uses in Education**]: Computer-assisted instruction

Keywords

automated assessment; automated grading; peer instruction

1. INTRODUCTION

The number of students choosing a computer science major is growing rapidly, boosting enrollments at colleges and universities throughout North America. A report from the Computing Research Association shows that from 2009 to 2014 the number of bachelors degrees (combined computer science and computer engineering) awarded increased from fewer than 9,000 to more than 16,000 [1]. Figure 1 shows the enrollment in our introductory programming course, which mirrors this trend with 55% growth in students (157 to 243) that are majoring or taking the course over approximately the same period. The number of high school students completing an advanced placement course in CS is also growing quickly, further increasing the number of students that are expected to enter into the CS major [1]. Unfortunately, higher enrollments do not always translate promptly to the growth of instructional resources. Faculty that teach introductory courses must therefore search for innovative solutions to handle the higher workloads.

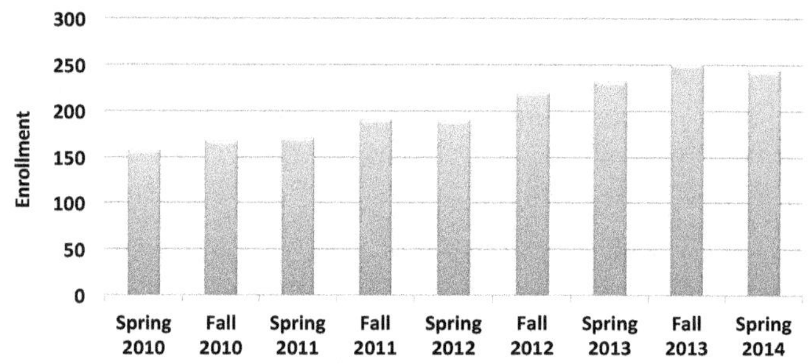

Figure 1: Introductory Enrollment (2010-2014).

The use of automated tools is a common solution to the problem of limited resources, especially for institutions with large class size. Automated grading has been discussed and generally accepted as beneficial [6] and tools such as Web-CAT [2] are used widely. At our institution, we use a variety of tools in our introductory programming course to automate grading and give feedback to students. In this paper we evaluate the effectiveness of these tools, which include a web-based system for automated grading, peer instruction quizzes, and an online programming tutorial. The key questions for this research are as follows:

1. How do automated tools negatively or positively influence student learning?
2. Do the benefits of automation, such as resource savings, outweigh the costs?

To answer these questions we performed a study over the semesters from Fall 2012 to Spring 2014. The author had primary responsibility for our introductory course during this period, thus allowing tight control over course content and processes. To assess the impact on learning we monitored student performance by examining diverse metrics that include exam scores, total points, withdrawal rates, assignment submission frequency and timeliness, and lecture attendance. Resource savings were estimated by comparing the time spent on grading tasks with and without automation. No significant changes to the curriculum were made during the study.

SIGCSE'15, March 4–7, 2015, Kansas City, MO, USA.

http://dx.doi.org/10.1145/2676723.2677226.

During the study we introduced several pedagogic changes that are supported by automated tools. In Spring 2013 we incorporated an online tutorial associated with our textbook. In Fall 2012 we began weekly quizzes that were subsequently turned into peer instruction sessions in Fall 2013. Also in Fall 2013 we revised how student programs were evaluated by introducing a web-based automated grading system that provides 24/7 feedback on their student submissions. A minor modification to the course format accompanied these changes. Until Spring 2012 the course had three lectures, no peer instruction, and a 100-minute lab. The current format consists of two lectures, a peer instruction session, and two 50-minute labs. We have continued the new practices until present, with the exception of the tutorial which we dropped after Fall 2013 and are presently re-evaluating.

A body of related work exists that evaluates the pedagogic techniques discussed in this paper [8], including automated testing [2, 4, 6, 11], peer instruction [3, 7], and online tutorials [5]. In this paper we focus on the use and efficacy of automation to replace time-consuming, manual tasks. Section 4.6 discusses some benefits and drawbacks of automation. However, in this paper we present evidence that the effects are generally positive, as shown by an improvement in academic performance over the study period.

Section 4 shows the study results, which are summarized here. Average scores on our final exam improved from 66.1% in Spring 2013 to 70.3% in Fall 2013, the semester in which we began automated grading and peer instruction. Scores on the final exam continued to improve through Spring 2014 to 73.9%, despite an almost identical exam. Figure 2 presents the withdrawal rate from 2010 to 2014, showing that withdrawals decreased during the same period that exam scores increased. Before Fall 2012 the rate averaged 10.4% and was never less than 8.1%. Since then the rate has averaged 4.9% and has not exceeded 5.3%. Other results include an improvement in the quantity and timeliness of program submissions (Section 4.2), which we attribute to automated grading, and better overall performance (Section 4.4) for students that were assigned an online tutorial. Over the same period we have achieved considerable resource savings from automation (Section 4.5).

2. AUTOMATED TOOLS

In this section we describe tools and processes, including automated grading, peer instruction, and online tutorials. We forgo a discussion of the Blackboard system we use for some additional grading automation, because we consider the underlying grade repository to be unimportant. We also omit a discussion of our use of MediaComp assignments [10], which has been unchanged through the study period.

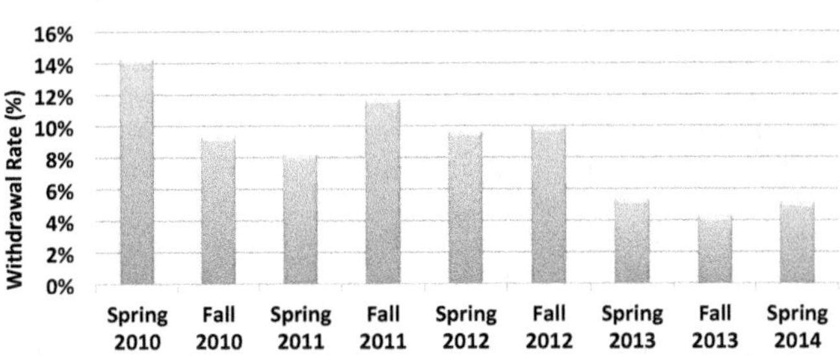

Figure 2: Withdrawal Rate (2010-2014).

2.1 Automated Grading

In an ideal world, instructors carefully review and grade all program submissions to provide feedback to students and identify coding problems. However, the real world requires us to grade large numbers of student programs. Even assignments that can be manually graded in 5-10 minutes are resource intensive. With our current class sizes of 250 or more, such assignments can easily consume 20 hours of manual grading weekly. Allowing multiple submissions per assignment to encourage students to fix defects and improve their code further increases this workload. To meet these requirements within our resource limitations we have adopted automated grading. An informal poll by the author at a BOF session on automated grading at SIGCSE 2013 revealed that a large number of other departments do the same.

A complete description of our grading framework is beyond the scope of this paper; instead we summarize the important features here. The back-end consists of shell scripts that run student programs (individually or batched) through test suites supplied by the instructor. Test suites are defined by configuration files that specify command line and grading parameters for each test. Instructors supply test code, input data, and a solution that is used to generate master output against which student output is compared.

Our framework is very flexible, allowing us to implement a wide variety of test strategies as well as testing programs in different languages. For Java programs, strategies range from simply executing the student program and filtering the output with shell commands, to running sophisticated test programs that control input and output streams. We have long since moved beyond simple comparison of student program output to the use of advanced language features such as Java reflection that allow us to systematically verify the definition and function of student classes, member variables, and methods. We can also verify code structure and style, and testing produced by the students themselves.

In Fall 2013 we added a front-end web interface and test server that support online submission of programs with on-demand grading. The user interface is a web page that lists the name of each assignment and an icon showing completion status. The web page shows the posting date, due date, late deadline, and most recent submission date. Students can examine the code they have submitted at any time. The test server waits for submissions and launches a grading script that posts the results to the web page immediately. Students can therefore receive feedback on their programs 24/7. Our strategy is to create a set of preliminary tests that run interactively and a further set of final tests that are run in batch mode after the due date. We currently use automated grading for programming assignments and quizzes, the latter of which we administer real-time during labs. Figure 3 shows a student view of automated grading.

2.2 Peer Instruction

Peer instruction is a pedagogic technique that promotes student engagement to improve academic performance [3]. Our approach to peer instruction is to replace one lecture each week with an automated quiz on which students collaborate. For the quizzes we assign groups of 3-4 students to work together throughout the semester using iClicker [13] hardware and software adopted by our university in Spring 2007. The technology provides efficient automated grading and timely feedback to students. The peer instruction ses-

Figure 3: Automated Program Grading Interface.

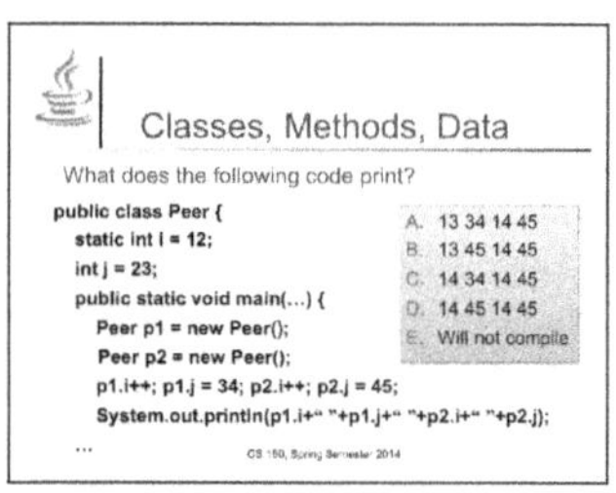

Figure 4: Peer Instruction Example Question.

sions replace quizzes given during lectures in which students answered questions individually. Besides the group format, the newer quizzes differ in difficulty. Previously we asked simple questions that related to reading assignments, now we incorporate questions that require more detailed knowledge of the material. Newer quizzes account for the same 5% of the course grade as the older quizzes. Figure 4 shows a sample question from our of our peer instruction quizzes.

2.3 Online Tutorials

In addition to automated grading and peer instruction, we have recently evaluated the use of an online tutorial. Such tutorials give students a chance to practice programming outside the classroom. They are completely automated, so the instructor only has to select questions, setup dates, and download grades when the submission period is complete. During Spring and Fall 2013 we assigned 137 questions from MyProgrammingLab [9], an online tutorial associated with the textbook we use. In both semesters we gave the same questions from the six chapters covered in the course. In Spring 2013 we assigned the tutorial questions to all students. In Fall 2013 we assigned the tutorial questions to half of the students based on a random selection of lab sections. The purpose of the split was to allow a comparative study of the effectiveness of MyProgrammingLab.

3. EVALUATION METHODOLOGY

Evaluating tools and processes in the context of an ongoing course is challenging, yet we strongly support the need for formal validation in CS education [12]. Ideally, we would introduce new pedagogic techniques one at a time to allow us to isolate and quantify the associated impacts, but in practice this constrains the pace of adopting teaching improvements. We have chosen instead to concurrently evaluate the practices described in Section 2, thereby making it difficult to quantify the effectiveness of each practice individually. However, we believe that in some cases we are justified in linking performance improvements to specific practices because of obvious causal links. For example, we attribute the changes in the number and timeliness of submissions to automated grading.

Our evaluation methodology measures academic performance before and after new processes are introduced, then analyzes the observed differences to see if they are statistically significant. We have chosen a a broad range of measures that include student attendance, withdrawal rates, assignment submission behavior, and the usual academic performance measures such as exam scores and overall grades. In statistical terms, the independent variables are teaching practices and the dependent variables are measures of academic performance. The validity of our work therefore depends on our ability to minimize extraneous variables. More details on threats to validity are presented in Section 5. The list below shows the alternative hypotheses we propose for our study:

1. $\mathbf{H}_{A1}$: The combined adoption of new pedagogic techniques improves the average final exam scores.
2. $\mathbf{H}_{A2}$: The combined adoption of new pedagogic techniques decreases the student withdrawal rate.
3. $\mathbf{H}_{A3}$: The adoption of automated grading increases the number of submissions per student on assignments.
4. $\mathbf{H}_{A4}$: The adoption of automated grading increases the timeliness of student submissions on assignments.
5. $\mathbf{H}_{A5}$: The introduction of a weekly peer instruction quiz improves student attendance.
6. $\mathbf{H}_{A6}$: The adoption of an online programming tutorial improves academic performance in the course.

The null hypothesis corresponding to each alternative hypothesis listed above is that the application of the pedagogic technique in question has no effect on academic performance. We assign to these the labels $\mathbf{H}_{O1}$ through $\mathbf{H}_{O6}$. Our statistical analysis uses the two-tailed Student's t-test to compare the means of performance statistics between semesters or Pearson's chi-squared test for binomial variables. We use a p-value of 0.05 for all tests in accordance with the accepted standard.

We use the same statistical analysis for the online tutorial evaluation, but the comparison of scores differs in that the students being compared were enrolled in the course in the same semester. During Fall 2013 we ran an experiment on the effectiveness of the online tutorial. For the experiment we divided students in the course into two groups based on a random selection of labs. Within each lab all students were either assigned the tutorial, or they were not. Both groups had identical labs except for a single training session on how to use the tutorial, and the course content and grading was identical in every other way. Participants in the study filled out consent forms approved by the compliance office at our institution.

Semester	Zeros Included	Mean	Median	Sample Size	Stddev	Variance	Increase	Statistical Significance
Spring 2013	Yes	66.1	71.0	234	20.3	410.4	+0.0%	base semester
Spring 2013	No	68.5	71.0	234	16.2	264.0	+0.0%	base semester
Fall 2013	Yes	70.3	76.3	252	24.1	582.7	+6.4%	t = 2.07 p = 0.0388
Fall 2013	No	75.7	79.0	252	14.7	216.3	+10.6%	t = 5.04 p < 0.0001
Spring 2014	Yes	73.9	78.0	232	20.5	422.3	+11.8%	t = 4.11 p < 0.0001
Spring 2014	No	77.6	78.0	232	12.5	156.8	+13.3%	t = 6.63 p < 0.0001

Figure 5: Analysis of Exam Scores.

Semester	Enrollment	Completion	Withdrawal	Withdrawal Rate	Statistical Significance
Spring 2011	185	170	15	8.1%	precedes study
Fall 2011	215	190	25	11.6%	precedes study
Spring 2012	209	189	20	9.6%	precedes study
Fall 2012	243	219	24	9.9%	base semester
Spring 2013	245	232	13	5.3%	χ2 = 3.64 p = 0.0565
Fall 2013	261	250	11	4.2%	χ2 = 6.24 p = 0.0125
Spring 2014	256	243	13	5.1%	χ2 = 4.18 p = 0.0409

Figure 6: Analysis of Withdrawal Rates.

Semester	Statistic	Average
Spring 2013	Submissions	231
	Per Student	1.11
Fall 2013	Submissions	677
	Per Student	2.95
Spring 2014	Submissions	856
	Per Student	4.11

Figure 7: Comparison of Submission Rates.

4. RESULTS

4.1 Performance Evaluation

We controlled the content of the final exam from Spring 2013 through Spring 2014 to allow semester-to-semester comparison of student performance. Figure 5 shows final exam statistics over the period. The leftmost columns report the mean, median, sample size, deviation, and variance of scores. The next column shows the percentage improvement in scores from the base semester, which is Spring 2013. The computations are performed with and without zero scores because the scores without zeros are very close to normally distributed, a condition of the Student's t-test. However, we observe the same outcome in both cases. We find an increase in average scores of 6.4% from Spring 2013 to Fall 2013 or 10.6% without zero scores. The scores increase by 11.8% from Spring 2013 to Spring 2014 or 13.3% without zero scores. The differences are statistically significant, as shown by the Student's t-test result in the rightmost column. Based on these results we reject the H_{O1} null hypothesis.

Next we examine the withdrawal rate over the study period to show that under-performing students did not withdraw at higher rates, thereby biasing exam scores. The withdrawal rate is calculated by comparing the census two weeks into the semester to the list of students that complete the course and receive a final grade. Figure 6 shows the number of students enrolled, completion and withdrawal numbers, and the withdrawal percentage for each semester. We include data from several semesters before the study to show the trend. Note that the drop in withdrawal rates precedes the introduction of two of the treatments by one semester, possibly indicating an extraneous factor. For this reason we put the baseline at Fall 2012. We compare later semesters using Pearson's chi-squared test for statistical significance. The comparison to Spring 2013 narrowly misses statistical significance, with a p-value of 0.0565. The comparison to Fall 2013 is significant, as is Spring 2014, with p-values of 0.0125 and 0.0409 successively. Despite the early start, the lower withdrawal rate is stable through the study period, confirming that the higher exam scores are not caused by an increase in withdrawals. Based on this result we reject the H_{O2} null hypothesis.

4.2 Assignment Submissions

Here, we evaluate the effects of automated grading on the behavior of students with respect to programming assignment submission. Our on-demand testing allows students to work on their programs and get feedback anytime. Before automation, assignments were posted at the start of the week and due one week later. Because students lacked an incentive to submit earlier, almost all submissions were near to the deadline and the average number of submissions was very close to one per student. Final grading was posted a few days later and represented the first feedback received by the student. With automated grading, submissions are more timely, and we receive more submissions per student because an incentive now exists for the student to keep working on their program until tests pass. With the current system, preliminary grading feedback is immediate, and final grading is usually completed within 24 hours of the late deadline.

Figure 7 shows the average submissions per assignment and student. The latter statistic includes only the students that submitted at least once. In Spring 2013, before automated testing, the average number of submissions per student for all assignments was 1.11. In Fall 2013, when automated grading was introduced, the average submissions per student increased to 2.95, and this number jumped to 4.11 in Spring 2014. We believe this result reflects mastery of the automated testing system by teaching staff (and students), and the new motivation that automated grading provides to continue working on an assignment until all tests pass. We omit a statistical evaluation because the disparity in the number of submissions is clearly significant and expected because of the difference in the reward structure, and we reject the H_{O3} null hypothesis. Our underlying assumption is that the number of submissions is coupled to student effort.

Figure 8 shows the number of submissions for each day of the week in which the assignment is posted. The percentages are averages for all assignments within each semester. The last two semesters are from the automated grading system and the first semester from our grading repository. As with the number of submissions, we omit a statistical evaluation because the disparity is both obvious and expected, so we reject the H_{O4} null hypothesis. Without automated grading, students predominantly submit on the due date or during the late period, so the chart shows 90% of submissions for

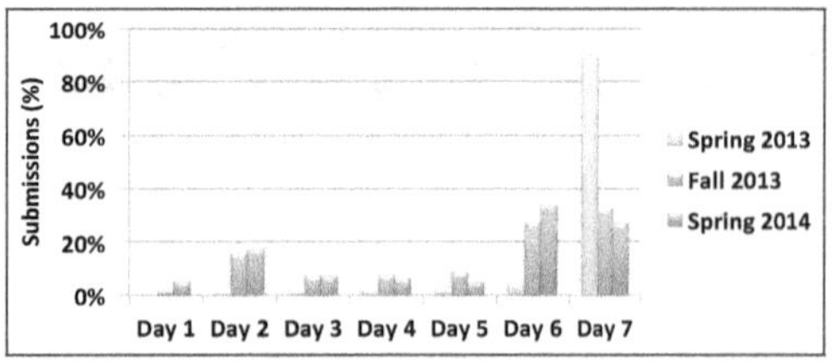

Figure 8: Comparison of Submission Timeliness.

Semester	Sample Size	Average Score	Attendance (Absolute)	Attendance (Percentage)	Statistical Significance
Spring 2013	234	91.36%	191	81.62%	base semester
Fall 2013	252	91.48%	214	84.92%	$\chi 2 = 0.96$ $p = 0.327$
Spring 2014	232	90.39%	196	84.05%	$\chi 2 = 0.25$ $p = 0.619$

Figure 9: Comparison of Attendance Rates.

Spring 2013 on the last day. With automated grading, submissions for Fall 2013 and Spring 2014 are more spread out. Thus 24/7 automated grading has ameliorated at least one of the problems associated with last minute submissions – lab overcrowding, and this has been confirmed by our lab staff. A benefit of this research is that we now have a baseline for comparison of future submission statistics.

4.3 Peer Instruction

We have observed that peer instruction has both improved attendance and allowed us to give more difficult quizzes. Figure 9 displays the average student scores and attendance. In Spring 2013 we gave quizzes that were taken individually; by Fall 2013 we had converted to full peer instruction sessions. Both kinds of quizzes were administered with iClickers and graded automatically. The peer instruction quizzes were much harder, and we received some complaints from students as a result. Despite this, attendance increased from 81.62% in Spring 2013 to 84.92% in Fall 2013, falling back slightly to 84.05% in Spring 2014. However, the differences are not statistically significant as shown by the Pearson's chi-squared test results in the rightmost column, so we cannot reject the H_{O5} null hypothesis.

There is also no statistically significant difference in the scores between the older and newer quizzes, an interesting result given that the peer instruction quizzes are much harder. We attribute the similarity in performance to the collaboration inherent in peer instruction, and our view is bolstered by the large delta in scores that we observe when we first present questions individually and subsequently allow groups to answer them. We find percentage gains of 30-40% in the number of correct answers in this case, and other researchers report similar results [3].

4.4 Online Tutorial

A total of 252 students completed the course in Fall 2013, during which we ran a comparative study on online tutorials. Out of these, we required a treatment group of 110 (44%) to use MyProgrammingLab, and left the remaining 121 (48%) as a control group. Of these students, we dropped 21 (8%) from the study for not completing a consent, not writing their names legibly on the form, or because of withdrawals

Semester	Category	Sample Size	Class Percentage	Average Total	Statistical Significance
Fall 2013	Everyone	252	100%	78.02%	
Fall 2013	Control	121	48%	76.60%	base population
Fall 2013	Treatment	110	44%	80.09%	$t = 1.73$ $p = 0.0421$
Fall 2013	Self Unassigned	8	3%	68.20%	$t = 2.34$ $p = 0.0212$

Figure 10: Online Tutorial Comparative Study.

from the course. The assignment of students was random, based on the lab in which they participated. Only 8 (3%) students did not complete the tutorial that they were assigned. The curriculum was otherwise identical for both groups, except for one lab in which we helped the treatment group learn how to use the online tool.

Figure 10 shows the average points received by students in each category. We use total points to measure overall performance, since it includes all coursework and is used to assign letter grades. The entire class averaged 78.0%, whereas the control group averaged 76.6%, and the treatment group averaged 80.1%. Unsurprisingly, the group that failed to complete the tutorial averaged only 68.2% total points. Both differences are statistically significant, as shown in the rightmost column. The treatment group received 5% of the total points through the tutorial, and the control group received the same points by scaling the remaining grades from 95% to 100%. The average for the treatment group on the tutorial was 70%, so it is unlikely that the difference is caused by the tutorial being easier than other work. Based on the results shown, we reject the H_{O6} null hypothesis.

We find that online resources are increasingly comprehensive and inexpensive, yet require very little management on the part of the instructor. For this reason, we expect that many instructors are (or will be shortly) using them to complement traditional classroom activities.

4.5 Resource Savings

We now compare the time for manual versus automated tasks. Grading time varies with complexity, at the introductory level assignments can often be graded in 5-10 minutes. For class sizes of 250 this still means 20 hours or more of grading. With automation we can write and configure tests and run grading scripts in a total of 3 hours or less. The savings in teaching resource is therefore at least 17 hours per week, or 204 hours per semester based on 12 assignments. We disregard assignment prep time, which is the same with or without automation. Quiz grading is less costly, but paper handling makes it difficult to spend less than a couple of minutes per student. For classes of 250 this is 500 minutes or more than 8 hours weekly. Automated grading of quizzes requires less than an hour per week of instructor time. Thus the savings is 7 hours per week, or 84 hours per semester based on 12 quizzes. We forgo an analysis of resource savings for online tutorials, which are inexpensive to manage and have no equivalent manual process.

From the monetary standpoint, a TA at our institution earns around \$20 an hour, so the savings per semester per class is at least \$4000 for program grading and \$1600 for quiz grading. However, we find that the main benefit of automation is not monetary savings, but the decrease in resource that can now be applied to teaching. Prior to the introduction of automation, the majority of TA time in introductory classes was spent grading. Now the instructor handles grading and assistants spend more time with students. We are also able to give weekly quizzes and tutorials that would be impractical without automation. The development costs of automation are significant, but can be amortized over many classes and semesters.

4.6 Analysis

As stated above, the primary benefit of automation is resource savings. However, we have identified other benefits. For example, the high availability of the grading system reduces lab overcrowding and improves student access. The repository component of the grading system is similarly convenient for students since it allows them to transfer code between lab and personal systems. Our most important finding is that automation does not impair and can actually benefit academic performance and increase student interest in our major, as measured by exit surveys and instructor evaluations. Based on verbal and written feedback, automated grading is also overwhelmingly popular among students.

However, there are drawbacks to automation. One is the difficulty of replicating code reviews, which we believe are especially valuable to novice programmers. Automated grading has an unforgiving nature, and some students find it excessively strict. We also observe that some students work on assignments only until they pass preliminary tests, thereby missing some of the requirements. This raises the concern that students throw submissions at automated grading instead of learning to debug or test their code themselves.

5. THREATS TO VALIDITY

Threats to validity are inherent in empirical studies performed on students in a university setting. Internal validity reflects the strength of evidence of a causal relationship between the independent and dependent variables. In this paper we show that improved academic performance coincides with the introduction of new pedagogic techniques. Threats to internal validity therefore consist primarily of extraneous factors that could account for these observed differences. Examples include semester-to-semester variation in student abilities, staff turnover, and changes in course content. However, we have tried to minimize these threats by keeping the same instructor and course format, and by maintaining consistency on curriculum, lecture and lab materials, programming assignments, and exams.

External validity concerns the applicability of our results outside of our university. While there is no guarantee of identical results, we argue that the conditions at our university are substantially similar to those at other public institutions. Thus we argue that the techniques presented can be reasonably expected to improve academic performance if applied similarly, and many related research papers (as cited in the introduction) have shown success with the application of these techniques at other universities. Due to space limitations the description of our automated grading system is not complete in this paper, but we plan to publish more detail on our testing methodology in the near future.

6. CONCLUSIONS

We conclude that automation of key processes such as program grading can save a significant amount of scarce resources in introductory courses without negatively impacting academic performance. The benefits of automation are both tangible, such as higher exam scores, and intangible, such as increased student engagement and interest. We find this very encouraging, since expanding enrollments will inevitably provide incentive for even more automation.

7. ACKNOWLEDGMENTS

The author would like to acknowledge Fritz Sieker for creating the automated grading framework, Debbie Bartlett and Russ Wakefield for mentoring me as an instructor, and Beth Simon for introducing me to peer instruction and other modern pedagogic practices

8. REFERENCES

[1] 2013 Taulbee Survey. *Computing Research News*, 26(5):10–55, May 2014.

[2] A. Allowatt and S. H. Edwards. IDE Support for Test-driven Development and Automated Grading in Both Java and C++. In *Proc. of the 2005 OOPSLA Workshop on Eclipse Technology eXchange*, Eclipse '05, pages 100–104, New York, NY, USA, 2005. ACM.

[3] C. G. Catherine H. Crouch and E. Mazur. Peer Instruction: Ten years of experience and results. *American Journal of Physics*, 69:970–977, 2001.

[4] C. Douce, D. Livingstone, and J. Orwell. Automatic Test-based Assessment of Programming. *Journal Educational Resources Computing*, 5(3), Sept. 2005.

[5] A. Edgcomb and F. Vahid. Effectiveness of Online Textbooks vs. Interactive Web-Native Content. In *Proc. of 2001 ASEE Annual Conf. and Exposition*, 2014.

[6] S. Edwards. Using Test-Driven Development in the Classroom: Providing Students with Automatic, Concrete Feedback on Performance. In *Proc. International Conf. on Education and Information Systems: Technologies and Applications (EISTA 03)*, pages 421–426, 2003.

[7] L. Porter, C. Bailey Lee, B. Simon, Q. Cutts, and D. Zingaro. Experience report: A multi-classroom report on the value of peer instruction. In *Proc. of the 16th Annual Joint Conf. on Innovation and Technology in Computer Science Education*, ITiCSE '11, pages 138–142, New York, NY, USA, 2011. ACM.

[8] L. Porter and B. Simon. Retaining Nearly One-third More Majors with a Trio of Instructional Best Practices in CS1. In *Proc. of the 44th ACM Technical Symposium on Computer Science Education*, SIGCSE '13, pages 165–170, New York, NY, USA, 2013. ACM.

[9] W. Savitch. *MyProgrammingLab with Pearson eText for Java: Intro to Problem Solving and Programming.* Addison-Wesley Publishing, USA, 6th edition, 2011.

[10] B. Simon, P. Kinnunen, L. Porter, and D. Zazkis. Experience Report: CS1 for Majors with Media Computation. In *Proc. of the Fifteenth Annual Conf. on Innovation and Technology in Computer Science Education*, ITiCSE '10, pages 214–218, New York, NY, USA, 2010. ACM.

[11] J. Spacco, D. Hovemeyer, W. Pugh, F. Emad, J. K. Hollingsworth, and N. Padua-Perez. Experiences with Marmoset: Designing and Using an Advanced Submission and Testing System for Programming Courses, 2006.

[12] A. E. Tew and B. Dorn. The Case for Validated Tools in Computer Science Education Research. *Computer*, 46(9):60–66, 2013.

[13] C. Whitehead and L. Ray. Using the iClicker Classroom Response System to Enhance Student Involvement and Learning. *Journal of Education, Informatics and Cybernetics*, 2(1):18–23, 2010.

Mechanical TA: Partially Automated High-Stakes Peer Grading

James R. Wright
Dept. of Computer Science
University of British Columbia
Vancouver, B.C., Canada
jrwright@cs.ubc.ca

Chris Thornton
Dept. of Computer Science
University of British Columbia
Vancouver, B.C., Canada
cwthornt@cs.ubc.ca

Kevin Leyton-Brown
Dept. of Computer Science
University of British Columbia
Vancouver, B.C., Canada
kevinlb@cs.ubc.ca

ABSTRACT

We describe Mechanical TA, an automated peer review system, and report on our experience using it over three years. Mechanical TA differs from many other peer review systems by involving human teaching assistants (TAs) as a way to assure review quality. Human TAs both evaluate the peer reviews of students who have not yet demonstrated reviewing proficiency and spot check the reviews of students who have. Mechanical TA also features "calibration" reviews, allowing students to quickly gain experience with the peer-review process. We used Mechanical TA for weekly essay assignments in a class of about 70 students, a course design that would have been impossible if every assignment had had to be graded by a TA. We show evidence that it helped to support student learning, leading us to believe that the system may also be useful to others.

Categories and Subject Descriptors

K.3.1 [**Computers and Education**]: Computer Uses in Education—*Collaborative learning*

Keywords

Computer Science Education; Peer Grading; Peer Review; Calibration; Scalability

1. INTRODUCTION

This paper describes our experience with software-supported, anonymous peer grading in a fourth year undergraduate course ("Computers and Society"). The course focuses on reasoning critically about the importance and social implications of computational advances. In earlier offerings of the course, students had to write three essays: on the midterm, final, and for a term project. However, shorter and more frequent essay writing assignments are both a more effective way to teach writing skills [12], as well as providing more opportunities to evaluate and improve writing skills and critical reasoning skills. Our past three offerings (2011, 2012, and 2013) thus shifted to a assigning students a total of 14 essays of about 300 words (11 weekly assignments, plus one essay on the midterm exam and two essays on the final exam). Manually marking essays is very expensive in terms of teaching assistant (TA) time. Furthermore, it can be difficult for students to learn to write such essays well. Peer grading offers a solution to both problems.

Peer grading is far from a new idea. However, students are often concerned that the quality and fairness of the evaluation that they receive from peer grading is lower than it would be from TAs [11, 8, 13]. Most systems (surveyed at the end of this article) attempt to address these concerns by evaluating the quality of the peer reviews in an automated way, whether by reweighting reviews based on some criterion [1, 5], by "review the reviewer" schemes in which students rate the feedback they have received [8, 3, 4, 2], by evaluating how close a review is to the combined "consensus" grade for an assignment [3, 5], or by some combination of these ideas.

We wanted to use peer grading to make more efficient use of TAs, not to replace them entirely. We thus designed a new system, dubbed "Mechanical TA."[1] Our system leverages (human) TAs in three ways. First, students start out in a "supervised" state, in which all of their reviews are marked by a TA. They are only promoted to an "independent" state when they demonstrate that they understand the grading rubric and are able to apply it competently. Second, students may use the system to appeal any peer grade that they consider unfair. (We reduce abuse of this feature by requiring a 100 word explanation of why a student believes that a review was unfair.) Finally, every independent review is eligible to be randomly spot checked by a TA, who can retroactively mark a reviewer's past reviews if they uncover a poor review. We found that students had surprisingly few concerns about fairness in Mechanical TA, and believe that the visible involvement of human TAs in marking assignments—especially in the early part of the class, when most students are supervised—was a major reason why.

Our system of random spot checks and appeals allows students to be persistently promoted. That is, once a student has been promoted, they can remain independent for the remainder of the class (i.e., if they are not demoted again due to a spot check or an appeal). This contrasts with systems such as Calibrated Peer Review (CPR) [1], in which students' review skills are retested at the beginning of each assignment. The time required to complete such calibration was a source of complaints in one study of CPR [13].

[1]Mechanical TA is freely available by contacting the authors.

SIGCSE'15, March 04–07, 2015, Kansas City, MO, USA.

ACM 978-1-4503-2966-8/15/03 ...$15.00.
http://dx.doi.org/10.1145/2676723.2677278.

Our implementation of calibration has a strong element of automated practice rather than just evaluation.[2] To our knowledge, this is a unique feature of our system of calibration. Students receive immediate feedback about their performance on calibration essays, and may optionally choose to perform many more than the required number of calibrations. In Section 4.2, we present our finding that calibration practice significantly improved students' review performance. In Section 3.3 we present evidence that it also improved students' writing performance, as measured by exam scores.

We begin by describing our particular peer review model in detail in Section 2. We survey our three years of experience with this model in Section 3, and compare some outcomes between different offerings of the course, paying particular attention to the differences between the most recent offering—which included automated calibration—and the previous two offerings. In Section 4 we analyze the data from our most recent offering. In addition to showing that calibration practice improved students' review skills, we also demonstrate that the persistent division of students into independent reviewers and supervised reviewers was an effective strategy. After reviewing some related work in Section 5, we conclude in Section 6.

2. PEER EVALUATION MODEL

In brief, our peer review system works as follows. Students submit their essays as free-form text in the Mechanical TA system.[3] After the essay submission deadline, each student is assigned three essays for double-blind peer review. After the deadline for submitting reviews, each essay is assigned the median peer-review mark. Students can register a request for a TA to regrade their essay if they believe that they received an unfair grade. The use of medians to compute grades means that an appeal is only worthwhile if the student believes they received two unfair reviews.

A review consists of a configurable set of text fields and multiple-choice questions. In our "Computers and Society" class, students were asked to rate each essay on a scale of 0–5 along four dimensions—following a detailed rubric that described what an essay would look like to justify each score in each dimension—and provide a textual justification of their scores. The grade assigned to an essay by a review is the sum of the scores in each dimension.[4]

Mechanical TA automatically assigns a selection of essays to the TAs for "spot checking", in which the TA reads the essay and evaluates its reviews. Every essay has a chance of being randomly selected, and *every* essay whose mark is above a configurable threshold is selected. This addresses a potential incentive problem, where a student could avoid the work of properly reviewing essays by simply giving every essay a high grade.

2.1 Supervised and Independent Reviewers

As mentioned above, we classify students as either *supervised* or *independent* reviewers. Every student begins as a supervised reviewer. Every essay that they review is also reviewed by a TA, and peer reviews are disregarded in this case for the purpose of grading: supervised essays are assigned grades from TA reviews. Furthermore, supervised students' reviews are also marked by TAs. Students are promoted from supervised to independent when their average review marks crosses a configurable threshold. Once promoted to independent status, a student automatically receives 100% on each of their reviews unless it is subsequently checked by a TA as described earlier, in which case it is graded.

Supervised reviewers are assigned only the essays of other supervised reviewers; similarly, independent students are only matched with each other. This is important in terms of TA workload: indeed, it minimizes the number of essays that must be read by the TAs who evaluate the supervised reviewers' reviews. If independent and supervised students could review each others' essays, then potentially *every* submitted essay would have at least one supervised reviewer and would hence need to be read. Conversely (and for the same reason), our scheme maximizes the number of essays that are fully peer graded.

2.2 Calibration

In addition to giving them the opportunity to learn by reviewing the work of their peers, Mechanical TA also allows students to practice reviewing via *calibration essays*. A calibration essay is an essay from a past offering of the course[5] which was carefully evaluated by multiple TAs to establish a "gold standard" review. At any time during the course, a student can request a calibration essay from Mechanical TA. The student then enters a review in the usual way. However, immediately after the review is submitted, Mechanical TA shows the student the gold standard review, and highlights the dimensions in which the student's review differed from the gold standard. If the student's review is within a configurable distance of the gold standard review, the student is given a "review point". After the student has collected enough review points over a configurable (potentially decaying) time window, they are promoted to independent status. This makes it possible for students to become independent before a TA has evaluated any of their reviews.

3. EVOLUTION OF OUR DESIGN

Our design of the Mechanical TA system evolved over time. Analyzing data from three consecutive offerings of Computers and Society allows us to argue that our current design helps to achieve better student outcomes. We have described the most recent version of the peer review process in Section 2. In the initial 2011 offering, each essay was reviewed by only two students; its mark was the average of the two reviews. In 2012, we switched to using the median of three reviews. In the most recent 2013 offering, we added the calibration process.

One of the major differences that calibration required was an extensively reworked rubric for reviewers. In the 2011 and 2012 offerings, reviewers were asked to rate each essay along 4 dimensions (Argument, Subject, Evidence, English) on a scale from 0 to 2. We offered minimal guidance about what separated 2/2 on a given dimension from 1/2. We found

[2]Indeed, our evaluation suggests that this aspect was the main benefit offered by calibration in our most recent course offering.

[3]This makes it easy for us to check all essays for plagiarism using TurnItIn, which we do.

[4]The full text of the rubric we used is available at `http://www.cs.ubc.ca/~jrwright/sigcse15/rubric.pdf`.

[5]Mechanical TA allows students to flag whether or not submissions may be used anonymously; we chose essays whose authors had permitted anonymous reuse.

that students were extremely reluctant to give 1/2 marks in this scheme, and received many comments that students did not want to deduct half the possible marks for a dimension. In the 2013 offering, we reworked the rubric in two ways. First, we expanded each dimension's scale to run from 0 to 5. Second, students were given explicit descriptions about what sort of essay deserved each score for each dimension.

In the remainder of this section, we first describe the process of setting up to offer calibration essays for the first time. Offering calibration reviews made a substantial impact, both on students' achievement, and on the workload for the TAs. In the final two subsections we compare 2013 to the earlier offerings by when students were promoted to independent reviewer, and by exam performance.

3.1 Calibration Setup

Constructing a library of calibration essays was a time-intensive process. We started by considering every essay from the previous offering that students had flagged as available for anonymous reuse. We then hand-selected 27 candidate essays. Each of these essays was reviewed by the same four TAs. The review marks were reconciled during in-person meetings, and every essay where the TAs reached consensus was selected as a calibration essay, whereas the other essays were discarded.

One extremely valuable (and unintended) benefit of the process of creating calibration essays was calibrating the TAs themselves. With the exception of the lead TA, our course is run by a new contingent of TAs every year, most or all of whom have no particular past experience in evaluating essays. The meetings and discussions to determine marks for the calibration essays constituted an opportunity to give the TAs extensive extra training.

A one-time benefit of the initial process of creating calibration essays was that it pointed out opportunities to improve our rubric. The rubric went through multiple iterations during the process of calibrating the TAs, as they discovered various ambiguities.

3.2 Independent Reviewers

One bottleneck in our original Mechanical TA design was that all students begin in the supervised pool, requiring extensive TA work at the beginning of term. One of our main motivations for introducing an automated calibration process to reduce this TA workload by encouraging students to be promoted to the independent pool before the first assignment was marked. We were unsuccessful in achieving this goal in our 2013 course offering: no students were promoted to independent before the first assignment, and hence TAs needed to mark every student's essay.[6] However, the opportunity to practice reviewing that the calibration essays provided appears to have had a large effect on students' review skills. More students were promoted to independent early in the 2013 offering than in either of the earlier offerings, and a larger overall proportion of the class (100%!) became independent during the term.

Figure 1 shows how many students reviewed independently over the course of the term in each of our past three offerings. The criteria for becoming independent in 2011 were much

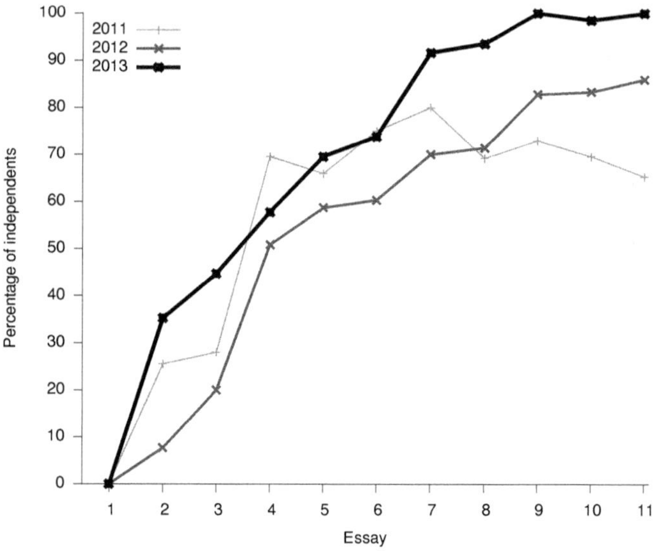

Figure 1: Proportion of independent reviewers at the beginning of each assignment.

more lenient than in 2012, leading to a large number of students becoming independent fairly quickly. However, this lenience seems to have resulted in the promotion of many unreliable reviewers, and so many of these students were later moved back to the supervised pool as a result of spot checks and appeals. In contrast, all but one of the many students who became independent in 2013 stayed in the independent pool throughout the class. Nearly a third of the students became independent after just one assignment; by the end of the course, *every* student was reviewing independently. The criteria for becoming independent based on review quality were identical in 2012 and 2013; the only differences between the two years were the introduction of our calibration system and the improvements we made to the review rubric to support calibration.

3.3 Exam Performance

It would be nice to compare assignment marks between years; however, this is difficult because we made dramatic changes to the rubric. In 2011 and 2012, we marked essays out of 8, and an "acceptable" essay received 8/8. In 2013, we marked essays out of 20, and gave an "acceptable" essay 16/20. Thus, we do not present an analysis of how assignment marks varied from one year to the next.

In contrast to assignments, we marked essays on the midterm and final exams in a very similar way across all three offerings, and indeed offered very similar exams. This makes exams a more suitable target for analysis. Figure 2 gives the cumulative distributions of marks on the midterm and final exams across the three years. We observe that the mark distributions for both exams were strikingly higher in 2013 than in the prior years.[7] We thus conclude that one or both of the improvements associated with our calibration system had a positive impact on student performance.

[6] We've since tweaked our calibration threshold and the number of calibration essays required of students, and believe that this will yield a vastly different outcome in our current, 2014 offering.

[7] A Mann-Whitney rank test confirms this. Both the midterm and final exam distributions for 2013 are significantly higher than the corresponding distribution for both 2011 and 2012 ($p < 0.001$).

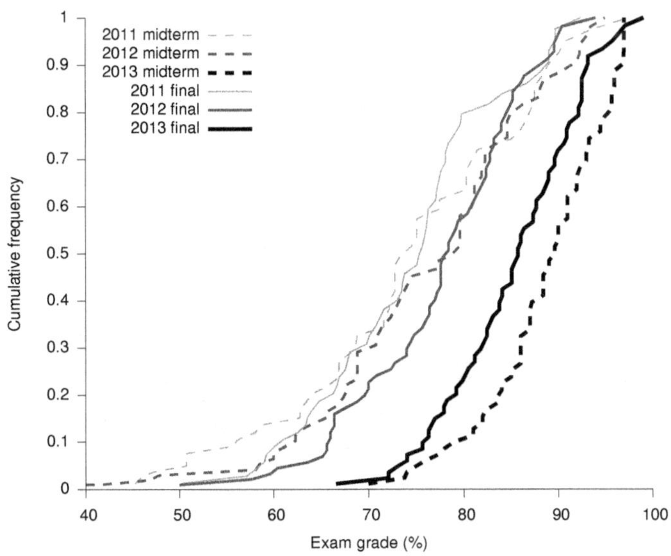

Figure 2: Cumulative distributions of final exam and midterm exam marks.

4. ANALYSIS OF OUR CURRENT DESIGN

We now turn to a deeper analysis of data from the latest offering of Computers and Society. We first confirm that the division of supervised and independent reviewers meaningfully reflects differences in review quality. We then consider the effect of reviewing practice on calibration performance.

4.1 Review Quality

Mechanical TA is designed on the premise that independent reviewers can be trusted to reliably review peer work without oversight, whereas supervised reviewers cannot. An important question is therefore whether the two pools really do differ in terms of review quality. To answer this question, we followed the basic strategy of estimating the average review quality of supervised reviews and the average quality of independent reviews, and checking whether these averages differed significantly. The quality of supervised reviews is easy to estimate, since all of them get marked by a TA. For independent reviews, we had access to TA marks of reviews that were randomly spot checked or appealed, unfortunately without a label indicating which criterion had led to their selection. The spot check selection criterion adds a complication, however: all essays that receive a grade of 80% or higher get spot checked automatically; all other essays are spot checked at random. If the quality of an essay is independent of the quality of its reviews, then this does no harm. However, if high-quality essays are easier to grade, then this selection criterion could add an upward bias to the estimate of the independent reviews' quality, since our sample of independent reviews would contain disproportionately many easily graded essays. We address this by subdividing the independent and supervised reviews into those that were associated with essays that got a mark over 80% and those that did not, giving a total of four groups of observations. This allows us to detect the situation where the supervised reviews have significantly different quality from the independent reviews of high-mark essays, but not significantly different quality from the independent reviews as a whole. Another possible source of bias is appeals, as low-quality reviews may be appealed more frequently than average. We do not attempt to correct for this bias, for two reasons. First, the bias is downward for independent reviews; if we find a statistical difference between the two pools in the presence of this bias, correcting for it will not change our finding. Second, we cannot distinguish retroactive spot checks that were triggered by random spot checks from those that were triggered by appeals.

For each of our four groups of reviews, we estimated a Bayesian joint posterior distribution over the following model:

$$\mu_g \sim \text{Uniform}[0, 10]$$
$$\sigma_g \sim \text{Uniform}[0.0001, 10]$$
$$q_{g,r} \sim \text{N}(\mu_g, \sigma_g) \quad \text{truncated to } [0, 1],$$

where $q_{g,r}$ is the quality of review r in group g. We normalized all marks to lie within $[0, 1]$. The quality of each review in group g is assumed to be drawn from the same Normal distribution, truncated at 0 and 1. We estimated the posterior distributions over the parameters μ_g, σ_g for each group using a Metropolis-Hastings sampler [10] to simulate 12,000 samples after a burn-in period of 4000 samples.[8]

Figure 3 gives the cumulative posterior distribution over the average review quality for each group.[9] The 95% central credible interval for each distribution is shown as a bar on the x-axis.[10]

We observe that there is no overlap between the credible intervals of either independent group with either supervised group. This answers our question: we have strong evidence that independent reviewers perform higher quality reviews.

We are also able to examine whether high-quality essays are easier to review well. In both the independent and supervised groups, the quality of the reviews of essays that received grades of at least 80% did indeed appear to be higher, although not substantially (nor significantly; note that the credible intervals for the above- and below-80% groups intersect). The effect was more pronounced in the supervised group than in the independent group, although again not statistically significant.

4.2 Calibration Performance

We have described two benefits offered by calibration: assessing students' review quality without TA intervention, and providing an opportunity for students to practice reviewing with immediate feedback. In this section, we evaluate whether students benefit from such practice by asking whether students' calibration marks improved as they completed more calibration reviews.

We begin by plotting the performance of each calibration that was completed. We index calibrations by the time of promotion to the independent pool; that is, the last calibration review performed before a student was promoted is calibration number 0, the calibration review completed just before that is calibration number -1, etc. We then perform a Bayesian linear regression by estimating the joint posterior

[8]We used version 2.3 of the PyMC package to implement the sampler; see http://pymc-devs.github.io/pymc/, retrieved September 4, 2014.

[9]Due to the truncation of the Gaussian distributions to the interval $[0, 1]$, this is not identical to the posterior distribution of the μ_g parameter.

[10]A central credible interval is a Bayesian counterpart to a confidence interval. The true value of a parameter lies within its 95% central credible interval with probability 0.95.

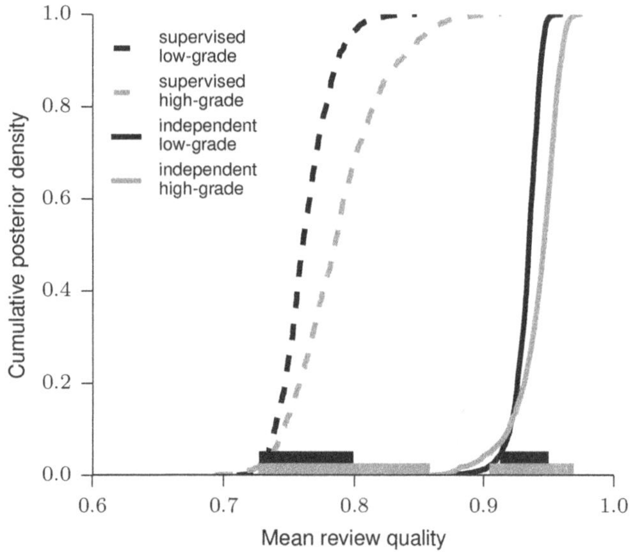

Figure 3: Cumulative posterior distributions for the mean review quality of supervised reviews of low-marked essays, supervised reviews of high-marked essays, independent reviews of low-marked essays, and independent reviews of high-marked essays. 95% central credible intervals for each of the distributions are shown as bars on the x-axis.

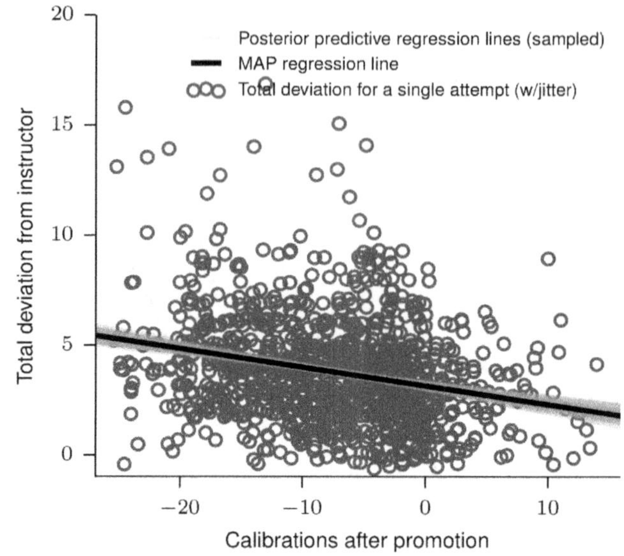

Figure 4: Total deviations from gold standard review on calibration reviews, versus number of calibrations after promotion. The bold line is the maximum a posteriori linear fit with Normal error. The gray lines are samples from the posterior predictive distribution of linear fits.

distribution of the following model:

$$b \sim \mathrm{N}(0,5) \qquad \sigma \sim \mathrm{Uniform}[0,10]$$
$$m \sim \mathrm{N}(0,2) \qquad y_i \sim \mathrm{N}(mx_i + b, \sigma),$$

where m and b are the slope of the regression line, x_i and y_i are the number and performance for each calibration review, and each datapoint (x_i, y_i) has zero-mean Gaussian noise with variance σ. Performance is measured as sum of absolute differences (i.e., the L_1 distance) from the instructor review; smaller performance values thus represent better performance. We again used Metropolis-Hastings sampling to estimate the posterior.

Figure 4 shows a plot of the number and performance for each calibration (with a small amount of jitter). The maximum a posteriori regression line is plotted as a bold line; this is the line whose slope and offset have the highest posterior probability. To illustrate the range of possible fits, we also plot the lines corresponding to 100 samples from the posterior distribution.

The MAP estimate of the slope is -0.085, with a 95% central credible interval of $[-0.104, -0.066]$. The credible interval does not contain 0, so we conclude that students showed a significant improvement in their calibration performance as they practiced. Our rubric grades essays out of 20, so a slope of -0.085 represents an average improvement of approximately 4% with each calibration.

5. RELATED WORK

Now that we have described Mechanical TA in detail, we give a more thorough survey of related work and describe how our own system differs. By far the most widely used online peer review system is Calibrated Peer Review (CPR) [1, 11]. After submitting their own essays, students evaluate three instructor-provided calibration essays of varying known quality. They then anonymously review the essays of other students. Each review is weighted according to the reviewer's performance on the calibration task. Reviewers who do not pass the calibration task on the first two tries "flunk out" of the assignment and are not permitted to review at all. Review quality is further assessed by students' reviewing other students' reviews. The initial calibration essays are entirely for the purpose of evaluating students' reviewing skill, and form a portion of the students' grade. This contrasts with our calibration essays, which do not directly impact a student's grade, and which allow students to practice reviewing in addition to demonstrating reviewing competence.

Kulkarni et AL. [6] combine algorithmic assessment of written answers with peer review in a large online course. A learning algorithm first estimates both the assessment and its confidence in the assessment. These estimates are used to determine how many peer reviews are required for a given item. Other students then assess the peer reviews' accuracy.

Mechanical TA focuses on evaluating the final version of an assignment. SWoRD [2], PRAZE [7], and CaptainTeach [9] allow students to incorporate feedback from peer reviews during the course of an assignment.

CrowdGrader [3] dynamically assigns reviews to reviewers in an online fashion, in an attempt to provide an approximately equal number of reviews to each submission. Similarly to CPR, the quality of each review is assessed by comparing it to the "consensus" (trimmed average) review of the assignment; reviews that are further from the consensus are penalized. The Aropa system [5] combines consistency scoring and weighting by reweighting reviews until a fixed point of weights and consistency with the weighted average is reached. Both systems thus assess review quality "automatically", whereas Mechanical TA assesses review quality directly via TAs. Many other systems use a "review the reviewer" system to evaluate review quality, in which students rate the quality of the reviews they have received [4, 2, 7, 8].

6. CONCLUSIONS

Mechanical TA is a system designed to support a novel model of high-stakes peer grading, in which marks from trusted "independent" reviewers are binding (but can be appealed), but marks from untrusted "supervised" reviewers are replaced by grades from a TA. Students are promoted to independent status based on the quality of their reviews, and after promotion they typically remain independent for the duration of the term. We have successfully used this system to set weekly essay assignments in a class of approximately 70 students. This would not be possible if every assignment had to be graded by a TA, as essays are very time consuming to grade. We have focused here on grading essays, but our system is easily applicable to other domains such as coding assignments or code review.

A major bottleneck in our peer review approach is that the first assignment *does* require that TAs mark every submission along with all of the peer reviews. While we have found that TAs are willing to work hard at the beginning of term given assurances that they will subsequently have a much-reduced workload, this bottleneck nevertheless limits the scalability of our system. We thus introduced calibration reviews in the most recent offering, in which students review carefully chosen assignments with known "correct" gold standard reviews constructed by the instructor and TAs. Each student receives automated feedback comparing their review to the gold standard review, and if they match the gold standard closely enough on enough repetitions, they are automatically promoted to independent status. This calibration mechanism has multiple goals. First, it aims to allow students to become independent before the first assignment, without TA intervention, thereby reducing TA workload on the first assignment. Second, it allows students to practice the reviewing process, with immediate feedback about how well they did. We did not achieve the first goal in our most recent course offering. Nevertheless, offering students practice reviewing had a striking effect. Students in the 2013 offering were promoted sooner and received higher grades on roughly comparable exams than those in the 2011 and 2012 offerings. Students' average review performance improved by approximately 4% per attempted calibration essay.

One additional benefit of a calibration system is that it allows the systematic training of TAs in how to mark according to "subjective" rubrics. (We described how our TAs benefited from constructing calibration questions; we've asked our 2014 TAs to do the existing calibration exercises before the class starts.) We believe that this leads to higher quality marking by TAs and more consistency between TAs.

Calibrating reviewers before the first assignment is a key requirement for increasing the scalability of Mechanical TA's peer review model. In the next offering of the class, we will modify the system in several ways. First, we will modify the calibration promotion threshold, choosing a more appropriate value based on data from the latest offering. Second, we plan to experiment with including calibration essays in independent students' assigned reviews, without indicating which essays are from students in the course, and which are calibration essays; this will enable us to monitor the quality of independent reviews more closely. In particular, it will enable us to validate the calibration system by comparing the review quality of students who are promoted by automatic calibration to the review quality of students who are promoted by TA evaluations.

Acknowledgements

We thank Jessica Dawson for pointers to related literature.

7. REFERENCES

[1] O. L. Chapman. Calibrated Peer Review™, 2001.

[2] K. Cho and C. D. Schunn. Scaffolded writing and rewriting in the discipline: A web-based reciprocal peer review system. *Computers & Education*, 48(3):409–426, 2007.

[3] L. de Alfaro and M. Shavlovsky. CrowdGrader: A tool for crowdsourcing the evaluation of homework assignments. In *Proceedings of the 45th ACM Technical Symposium on Computer Science Education*, SIGCSE '14, pages 415–420, New York, NY, USA, 2014. ACM.

[4] E. F. Gehringer. Electronic peer review and peer grading in computer-science courses. *ACM SIGCSE Bulletin*, 33(1):139–143, 2001.

[5] J. Hamer, K. T. K. Ma, and H. H. F. Kwong. A method of automatic grade calibration in peer assessment. In *Proceedings of the 7th Australasian Conference on Computing Education - Volume 42*, ACE '05, pages 67–72, Darlinghurst, Australia, Australia, 2005. Australian Computer Society, Inc.

[6] C. E. Kulkarni, R. Socher, M. S. Bernstein, and S. R. Klemmer. Scaling short-answer grading by combining peer assessment with algorithmic scoring. In *Proceedings of the First ACM Conference on Learning @ Scale Conference*, L@S '14, pages 99–108, New York, NY, USA, 2014. ACM.

[7] R. A. Mulder and J. M. Pearce. PRAZE: Innovating teaching through online peer review. In *ICT: Providing choices for learners and learning. Proceedings ascilite Singapore*, 2007.

[8] D. E. Paré and S. Joordens. Peering into large lectures: examining peer and expert mark agreement using peerScholar, an online peer assessment tool. *Journal of Computer Assisted Learning*, 24(6):526–540, 2008.

[9] J. G. Politz, D. Patterson, S. Krishnamurthi, and K. Fisler. CaptainTeach: Multi-stage, in-flow peer review for programming assignments. In *ACM SIGCSE Conference on Innovation and Technology in Computer Science Education*, 2014.

[10] C. P. Robert and G. Casella. *Monte Carlo statistical methods.* Springer Verlag, 2004.

[11] R. Robinson. Calibrated Peer Review™ an application to increase student reading & writing skills. *The American Biology Teacher*, 63(7):pp. 474–476+478–480, 2001.

[12] R. Seabrook, G. D. Brown, and J. Solity. Distributed and massed practice: from laboratory to classroom. *Applied Cognitive Psychology*, 19(1):107–122, 2005.

[13] M. E. Walvoord, M. H. Hoefnagels, D. D. Gaffin, M. M. Chumchal, and D. A. Long. An analysis of Calibrated Peer Review (CPR) in a science lecture classroom. *Journal of College Science Teaching*, 37(4):66, 2008.

Are Females Disinclined to Tinker in Computer Science?

Samantha Krieger
Department of Computer Science
University of British Columbia
sfkrieger@gmail.com

Meghan Allen
Department of Computer Science
University of British Columbia
meghana@cs.ubc.ca

Catherine Rawn
Department of Psychology
University of British Columbia
cdrawn@psych.ubc.ca

ABSTRACT
Our study explores the use of tinkering strategies across genders in undergraduate students of Computer Science. We present a definition and a framework for tinkering as it applies to this context, and use these to investigate how students across genders tinker with hardware and software. Our goal is to examine gender-based differences in tinkering behaviour and to discuss the meaning and implications of these differences on teaching and learning in Computer Science. We gathered data via interviews and a questionnaire and used both qualitative and quantitative methods for analysis. Our work is preliminary and suggests further areas of research in this domain.

Categories and Subject Descriptors
K.3.2 [Computer and Information Science Education]: Computer Science Education; K.4.2 [Computer and Society]: Social issues

General Terms
Human Factors

Keywords
computer science education; tinkering; gender; programming

1. INTRODUCTION
Educators and technologists alike have noted the value of tinkering and exploratory play in learning and innovation [9, 13, 14]. However, cross-disciplinary data suggest that 'exploratory learning styles' or 'tinkering behaviours' are expressed more predominantly in males than females across a variety of populations [2, 12, 16]. In Computer Science (CS) literature this gendered tendency has been surmised of CS students [8, 10, 21], but never studied directly as it has in other fields.

As computers, like automobiles, lend themselves to being tinkered with, certain aspects of Computer Science may maintain a culture of tinkering as a dominant method of learning and instruction, both in the field at large and in programming specifically. This may exclude females unaccustomed or inexperienced in this style of learning, from both within and outside the discipline. However, it is plausible that the prevailing culture of CS may cause learners of both genders who enjoy tinkering to self-select and study Computer Science, reducing gender differences in tinkering within undergraduate CS populations.

Recent literature points to a lack of research on gender differences in programming and suggests it merits attention [20]. It is therefore important to investigate gender differences in tinkering behaviour so as to inform educational practices, and to explore whether it is a factor contributing to the gender gap in CS.

The focus of this study is to examine tinkering behaviours between genders on programming assignments and tasks in undergraduate students of Computer Science. Using interviews with CS professors and a questionnaire administered to undergraduate CS students, we attempt to gain a basic understanding of what tinkering may mean in this field. In particular, we seek to explore whether there are indeed gender-based differences in students' definitions of tinkering and in their use of tinkering behaviours in Computer Science.

Our contributions are: (1) a review of the current literature on tinkering behaviour across a variety of disciplines, (2) a preliminary definition and description of tinkering in Computer Science, (3) a test of the hypothesis that female Computer Science students are relatively less likely to exhibit tinkering behaviours than their male peers, as is suggested in [8, 10, 21], and (4) suggestions and implications for academia.

2. BACKGROUND
It is well established that Computer Science is a male dominated field with declining female enrolment and high rates of attrition among women. Despite rising female participation in Computer Science during the 1970s, females' enrolment in the major took a sharp decline in the late 1980s and has generally decreased since then [6]. A trend first documented in Camp's "The Incredible Shrinking Pipeline" [5], this pattern of enrolment has garnered a great deal of attention and has been aggressively studied since.

In his viewpoint article published in 2000, De Palma attributes the drastic rise and fall of female participation in the late 1970s and 1980s to the introduction of the microcomputer [8]. He argues that gender-based tinkering tendencies proliferated with the arrival of the microcomputer, were largely responsible for the shrinking pipeline of the 1980s and 1990s, and continue to contribute to the ongoing gender gap in Computer Science. De Palma appeals for a return to the logic and formal characteristics of Computer Science in an effort to remove the hardware (and software) 'noise' that he alleges may be distracting for both genders, but particularly women. De Palma's argument contains a compelling explanation for the original shrinking pipeline phenomenon of the 1980s and 1990s but carries a significant assumption of the tinkering behaviour of females, one that we will explore.

There is growing interest in the role and importance of microcontrollers and tinkering in technology. The 21st century saw the emergence and commercialization of single-board computers and microcontrollers such as the Raspberry Pi and

SIGCSE '15, March 4–7, 2015, Kansas City, MO, USA
Copyright © 2015 ACM 978-1-4503-2966-8/15/03…$15.00
http://dx.doi.org/10.1145/2676723.2677296

Arduino, tools initially designed as learning aids in the Computer Science classroom [19]. The presence of these tools also facilitated a culture of 'making' and semi-formal tinkering. In 2005 the concretization of this trend became clear in the establishment of "Make Magazine" and the "The Maker Movement" [9], a movement of self-proclaimed hobbyists and tinkerers focused on hardware and technology-based Do-It-Yourself (DIY) projects.

Appeals can now be heard to bridge at-home tinkering with in-school practices [14]. In fact, at the time of writing, Coursera has released its first course on tinkering called "Tinkering Fundamentals: A Constructionist Approach to STEM Learning", which attempts to " ... help educators and enthusiasts develop a practice of tinkering and making" [18]. Ultimately, tinkering and the use of gadgetry like the single-board computer appear to be on the rise and have popularized the notion of tinkering in both formal and informal realms.

In light of this, it seems particularly worthwhile to investigate tinkering behaviour of females and ask: (1) What is tinkering in Computer Science? (2) Are there gender-based differences in tinkering behaviours among students of CS? It is important to note that we are not attempting to make a judgment on whether tinkering tactics are beneficial when learning Computer Science. Our focus is on investigating if their application varies across genders. Although much of the related work describes tinkering as a useful problem solving technique, we contend its utility is context and application specific.

3. RELATED WORK

If there are gender-based differences in tinkering tendencies among Computer Science undergraduates, research in K-12 Science Education suggests that these practices are present from a young age. In a study on tool usage in the elementary school science classroom, Jones et al. report a difference in the way young girls follow instructions as they exhibit less play with instruments involved in science activities than boys [13]. Boys were more competitive, displayed less adherence to rules and directions, and used and manipulated tools in exploratory and inventive ways [13]. These findings are corroborated in a meta-study on major themes in gender in Science Education, which highlights related research on gender differences in exploratory behaviours and manipulation of science equipment [3].

In a study examining tinkering behaviours in the elementary Science classroom, Parsons uses both qualitative and quantitative approaches to investigate the intuitive methods students use and apply in learning physical science concepts [16, 17]. Parsons develops a model of tinkering behaviours providing a number of characteristics pertaining to different types of tinkering that can be observed. Ultimately, she argues that tinkering in most respects can be seen as a method more consistent with common male 'ways of knowing' over females.

Many of these results have been echoed in the field of Human Computer Interaction (HCI). A study on middle-school-aged students' reactions to and perceptions of information and communication technology shows girls exhibiting more goal-oriented behaviour with respect to their use and interest in technological devices, whereas boys tend to be interested in the construction and function of the devices [12].

Beckwith et al. investigated how gender differences interact with end-users' use of software features and end-user programming environments, such as spreadsheet software [1, 2, 24]. Their early findings demonstrated differences in the frequency and degree to which males and females explore new features [2], while their later work examined the strategies adopted by males and females when testing and debugging in more detail [2, 4]. Throughout their research Beckwith et al. discovered gender differences in exploratory behaviours, causing them to investigate the meaning of tinkering and its gendered application across environments.

In an effort to design interfaces that encourage females' exploratory behaviour, Beckwith et al. discovered meaningful differences in how males and females employed tinkering methods in both testing and debugging spreadsheets [2]. They defined tinkering as turning a feature rapidly on and off. In analyzing these patterns they measured tinkering frequency, number of tinkering episodes, and tinkering rate within episodes.

Across multiple studies the group found males tinkered more than females [2, 4]. However, males' tinkering was often found to be counter-productive to effective debugging, particularly in some specific sub-experiments [2]. By contrast, although females were found to tinker less, their approach appeared to be more effective in facilitating a better understanding of the features and led to more productive and successful testing and debugging. Beckwith et al. concluded that pausing and reflecting lay at the crux of effective tinkering for both genders and that this was important in successfully mastering new features of interfaces [2].

What much of this research shows is that there is indeed a female 'lack of proclivity' to tinker within a variety of settings. However, the literature on tinkering is young and diverse and how tinkering is conceptualized and studied across domains is context specific. For Beckwith et al., the term tinkering is used to describe users' actions and practices with interfaces, whereas the tinkering behaviours studied by Parsons in the elementary school classroom were undoubtedly different. In order to examine tinkering behaviours in Computer Science, we first consider the definition of the term in our field.

4. DEFINITION OF TINKERING

There are strong unifying conceptual similarities in how the term tinkering is used across disciplines. To develop a working definition for tinkering in Computer Science, we consider its overall conceptual meaning and a description of how tinkering is practiced in the Computer Science classroom. Our primary goal is to enumerate a number of tinkering-type behaviours that characterize tinkerers and non-tinkerers in order to test tinkering expression among students. We interviewed three Computer Science professors from the University of British Columbia and reviewed academic literature to establish these basic behaviours, in particular looking at tinkering as a method of *problem solving* in Computer Science.

Tinkering appears to be inextricably linked to exploration and exploratory behaviour. It is generally considered an informal practice, often with a purpose of improvement, and is commonly associated with experimentation, or 'trial and error' methods. As a problem solving technique and learning strategy it is often in contrast to formal, established, or prescribed methods.

One important distinction is that the term tinkering can apply to problem solving with both hardware and software. Arguably, the stereotypical view of tinkering in Computer Science is of tinkering with hardware. This vision of tinkering, employed by De Palma, often includes behaviours such as taking apart and building computers or computing equipment, and the use of microcontrollers. In investigating De Palma's assumptions we will start by assessing the integrity of these claims and investigating differences of 'hardware tinkering' across genders. However, we argue that to define tinkering solely with respect to hardware is of limited use in our discipline, and that tinkering is pervasive in software engineering as well.

Tinkering in Computer Science generally involves:

(1) Exploratory behaviours (e.g. examining parts of a code base that students are not required to modify or understand, addition of unrequired extra features on projects).

(2) Deviation from instructions (e.g. deviating from suggested methods of completion on labs and assignments).

(3) Lack of reliance on formal methods of learning and instruction (e.g. using Q&A websites and forums rather than suggested reference material or instructor's office hours).

(4) Use of trial and error techniques (e.g. heavy use of debuggers, using and testing code samples found online).

Taken collectively, we argue that the concert of these practices offers an initial description of tinkering in CS. The list is not meant to be complete. Rather, it should be considered an initial attempt at a categorization of tinkering behaviours.

4.1 Interest and Tinkering

The relationship of interest to tinkering is an important consideration. One might develop a practice of tinkering born from interest in the subject, or one could employ it as a pragmatic approach. Although the motivation causing students to adopt tinkering strategies is not our primary concern, accounting for gender-based differences in computer-related interests is an important part of this exploratory work.

5. THE STUDY

We used an online questionnaire asking students to self-report on a variety of tinkering behaviours. It also included two open-ended questions requesting that students provide a definition of tinkering in CS, and then self-classify as tinkerers or non-tinkerers.

5.1 Questionnaire

The questionnaire included 34 closed-ended questions across four categories.

(1) *General information* - academic and personal information such as students' age, major, gender, and courses completed. (7 items)

(2) *Interest and Experience* - types and extent of computer-related interests pursued, including extra-curricular time spent on a variety of computer-related activities such as programming and reading technology blogs or books. (9 items)

(3) *Tinkering in Hardware* - (de)construction of computing equipment and use of microcontrollers. (3 items)

(4) *Tinkering in Programming* - programming and problem solving practices in labs and assignments. At the University of British Columbia, labs are completed in an on-campus location, and are generally completed in the presence of teaching assistants. Assignments do not have the same venue association, are often less structured, and have a longer time frame for completion. This section includes questions such as frequency and use of the debugger, reliance on different types of reference material, and use of instructor or university provided resources. (15 items)

5.2 Participants

Students attending summer Computer Science courses at the University of British Columbia were recruited to participate in this study using in-class announcements. The study was also advertised in the weekly departmental undergraduate emails. Of the 107 students who completed the questionnaire, data from 93 respondents with a declared major in Computer Science or Computer Engineering were included for analysis. Thirty-three participants were female (35.5%), and 60 participants were male (64.5%). Incomplete responses and responses with no declared gender were not included in the analysis.

Participants ranged in year level with 29% in the first two years of the degree, 40.8% in third, and the remaining 30.2% in fourth or further. Participant age ranged from 17 to 32, with a mean age of 23 (*SD* 3.58). On average, participants had completed five of the eight required Computer Science courses.

6. RESULTS

The following is a summary of the results collected from the survey. The open-ended responses were analyzed using qualitative and quantitative methods.

6.1 Computer Interest and Experience

Females were more likely than males to report no programming experience before university (60% of females, 25% of males, $X^2(1) = 10.341, p = .001$). Males more frequently reported having already learned a programing language (26% of males, 10% of females, $X^2(1) = 3.876, p = .049$), and having played around with or read about computers before university (44% of males, 12% of females, $X^2(1) = 9.640$, p = .002). Males were no more likely to have participated in high school computer science classes or to have reported learning HTML/CSS before university.

On questions concerning computer usage and experience, males reported higher frequency and time spent on computer-related tasks or interests across all relevant questions. Males reported greater average frequency in programming on their own time ($t(85) = -4.67$, $p < 0.001$, $d = 0.98$), reading tech blogs or magazines or reading about technology for pleasure ($t(83) = -4.45$, $p < 0.001$, $d = 2.84$), and playing computer games ($t(66) = -2.38$, $p = 0.021$, $d = 0.52$).

These results are consistent with other studies that have reported a large discrepancy between programming and computer-related interest levels and experiences of male and female Computer Science students [e.g. 10,15]. This suggests our population is similar to those at other universities nationwide and globally.

6.2 Tinkering in Hardware

There were significant differences between male and female practices for both questions related to tinkering with hardware. 79% of male respondents have built or taken apart a computer or piece of computing hardware out of interest, in comparison with 30% of females ($t(60) = -5.15$, $p = <.001$). Additionally, 25% of males and 6% of females own or have made use of single-board computers or microcontrollers (such as the Arduino or Raspberry Pi) for non-academic purposes ($t(88) = -2.59$, $p = .011$).

6.3 Programming Practices

Students answered 15 questions about their problem solving practices in projects, labs, and assignments. The response options were presented in the form of a Likert-type scale with 4 options, ranging from 0 (*Never*) to 3 (*Always*). When asked about both labs and assignments, two items revealed significant differences between males and females. Males were more likely to change the code that is given (outside of what is required) ($t(77) = -3.23$, $p = 0.003$, $d = 0.70$). Females were more likely to ask for help from a TA or instructor during lab ($t(82) = 2.63$, $p = 0.010$, $d = 0.60$). We found no significant differences in exploring extra features to add, attempting the bonus question, using debuggers, using manuals or tutorials on related topics, looking for similar examples and trying to figure out how they work, looking for code snippets and trying to run them, or deviating from instructions.

When asked specifically about assignments, we found that females were again more likely to ask for help from a TA or instructor during their office hours ($t(83) = 3.23$, $p = 0.002$, $d = 0.71$). We found no statistically significant differences between genders for examining parts of the given code that you are not required to understand or change, following the suggested method in the assignment description, posting to the course discussion forum, or posting to external forums.

6.4 Student Definitions of Tinkering

Males' and females' responses to the questions "What does it mean to tinker with computers?" and "How would you define tinkering?" differed in content and style. Females generally used terms and concepts relating to the motivation or intangible purpose for tinkering, while males' responses often involved more details and descriptors of what tinkering with computers specifically entails.

50 out of 60 males (83%), and 26 out of 33 females (78%) completed responses to these questions. We devised a list of 17 concepts that appeared frequently in the responses. We masked gender and classified each response by assigning it to one or more categories, as appropriate. We then consulted with an external rater, and conducted a test for Inter-rater Reliability. A quarter of the responses (25%) were discussed collectively, the remaining 75% were scored by each rater individually, with an error between raters of < 5%. We then established a consensus for the categories that applied to each response.

In their descriptions, both males and females considered tinkering to involve 'playing around', 'experimenting', 'testing', and 'modifying' to see some sort of output, for a purpose of 'improvement'. Both groups describe a process of 'exploring', 'taking apart and building' with a purpose for 'understanding'. These words (or close synonyms) were the most commonly used, and were employed by both groups with each one appearing in at least 10% of valid responses from each gender.

Words and concepts more prevalent in females' responses were 'improvement' (in 23% of females' responses, 12% of males' responses), 'understanding', (30% F, 16% M), 'playing around' (35% F, 18% M), and 'exploration' (31% F, 22% M). This reflects a trend showing females tending toward descriptions centered on the conceptual purpose and motivation behind tinkering. When asked to define tinkering, two typical female examples were "to play with the computer and experiment with it", and "Trying things out for fun and to learn how something works".

Males tended to be more descriptive in their definitions of tinkering in *Computer Science*. Terms or concepts appearing more frequently in males' responses include 'modification' (28% male, 15% female), 'taking apart/building' (26% M, 15% F), 'customization' (12% M, 4% F), and 'deviation from intended purpose' (14% M, 4% F). Males often focused on the nature and substance of tinkering behaviours rather than giving a rationale for the behaviour. Males' responses were often very technical; multiple responses mentioned overclocking, and making setting/BIOS changes. None of these technical details were present in females' responses.

Furthermore, a large number of males explicitly made a point of including both software *and* hardware in their responses. Often males included separate descriptions of tinkering in hardware and software and provided examples of both (42% M, 19% F).

One notable example from the males' responses is the following:

> "To me, "tinkering" with a computer can be broadly defined as making it into something it was not at first. This could be interpreted in a physical sense ("tinkering" with the hardware to upgrade a computer, or assemble one "from scratch" using individual components, case-modding, etc.) or a software one (installing a new OS, programming new capabilities into it, modding and customizing an OS, setting up programs to work together for some purpose, etc.)."

As this response exemplifies, males often included examples of how tinkering is a process that allows the individual to 'customize' their experience and use the computer to 'cater to their needs'. Unlike females' responses, which more often tended to describe tinkering as 'exploratory', males' responses often suggested that tinkering is a goal-oriented behaviour. This behaviour might be initiated out of interest or curiosity, but facilitates the construction of something desirable (e.g. customized experience or improved performance).

It is important to underline that a number of terms or concepts appeared with similar frequencies between males and females, such as 'experiment' (11% female, 12% male), 'testing to see an output' (15% F, 12% M), and 'performance' (8% F, 8% M).

These findings are preliminary and require more investigation for verification. However, the responses do indicate that there may be a gendered understanding of the term 'tinkering' in CS.

There were several limitations in the data analysis. The number of responses from females was fewer by virtue of the number of questionnaire respondents of each gender. This likely had an effect on the breadth of the responses collected from females. Furthermore, we believe that participants' level of interest affected the nature and extent of their descriptions and interpretations of tinkering. As was mentioned previously, interest is a confounding variable that may affect not only tinkering behaviours but also students' descriptions of what tinkering means in CS. This should be considered in future studies on tinkering.

6.5 Student Self-Classifications

With empty responses removed, 35 out of 50 males (70%) said 'yes' or provided positive confirmation (e.g. 'sure', 'of course') to the question "Do you consider yourself a tinkerer?". Thirteen said 'no' or 'not really' (26%) and 2 (4%) had wavering responses (e.g. 'somewhat' or 'sometimes'). Among the 33 females, with 7 empty responses removed, 4 self-classified as tinkerers (15.4%), 12 did not (46%), and 10 (38.4%) provided wavering responses.

7. DISCUSSION

Our data show that males and females report some different tinkering behaviours, self-classify as tinkerers at different rates, and may have different perceptions of the tinkering process. The results demonstrate that in certain ways females as a group tend to tinker less, and do not consider themselves tinkerers. These findings support the theories of De Palma and corroborate behaviours suggested by other authors [8, 10, 21].

Our purpose was not to examine gender differences in interests in computing, or frequency at which males and females utilize computer hardware. Our goal was to explore more generally the presence or absence of gender differences in the application of particular problem solving skills both within and outside the Computer Science classroom. Collectively, we recognized these behaviours as tinkering. In pursuing and investigating 'tinkering type' behaviours we have observed certain problem solving practices that vary along gender lines.

Our assumption is that tinkering is a pursuit that applies to both software and hardware. Furthermore, we contend that if an individual develops a practice of tinkering in one area, this methodology likely pervades their practices in the other. In other words, the methodologies learned from tinkering when solving hardware problems might have implications in how students problem solve, complete assignments, and appeal for help when programming at work, at home, or in the classroom.

Risk taking and confidence are fundamental to the act of tinkering, but are found to be different across genders. We speculate that these factors may contribute to the results we have seen thus far. Moreover, previous research has found gender differences in students' goals in the pursuit of a CS degree [15]. We argue that these differences in perspective on the purpose and utility of a CS major may be reflected in students' perception of the tinkering process as well.

7.1 Risk Taking

Burnett et al. found that tinkering involves aspects of risk taking both with things that are tangible (e.g. expensive equipment) and intangible (e.g. time). In Computer Science, tinkering with a computer could mean the risk of breaking physical or software components, rendering them unusable, or the risk of lost time spent on non-fortuitous computer-related pursuits. Copious amounts of research in the fields of Psychology and HCI have shown large differences in perception of risk and in risk taking behaviours between genders [e.g. 4, 11].

Although a number of males specifically mentioned 'breaking things' in their descriptions of tinkering, females only mentioned this when classifying themselves as non-tinkerers. A female's telling response to the question, "Do you tinker with computers?" was "No, only because I've almost broke [sic] something previously. I am afraid of actually doing something that I cannot reverse." This sentiment was echoed in other females' responses. It is one of many potential reasons for females' inexperience in the construction or deconstruction of computer-related equipment.

Although risk-taking behaviour was not mentioned by our participants in relation to software, we extrapolate that differences in risk taking may be present in programming practices. As four (8%) male students pointed out, tinkering with software also requires 'breaking' code. Although the effects are generally felt differently than with hardware, the tendency to 'break' working source code or aggressively approach programming may not be a tendency that females employ to the same degree as males. An openness to break things may prove to be an efficient strategy on some programming tasks. Thus, aversion to risk could pose a problem for females saddled with a number of different programming or computer-related assignments, all with poor or limited reference material that merely require a little 'playing around'. To males employing or experienced in tinkering practices this exploratory mode may be a more trivial endeavor.

7.2 Confidence in Applied Problem Solving

Research in mathematics shows females performing more poorly when given application-oriented problems, but shows good performance on the theoretical correlates of the same problems [22]. Males do not exhibit this same discrepancy. Vermeer et al. argue that skills needed to solve applied problems go beyond cognitive skills, and that affective variables such as low confidence in females may inhibit problem solving behaviours in these applied mathematical problems [22]. We speculate that this is an issue in Computer Science, and in the utilization of applied problem solving techniques, such as tinkering as well.

Gender-based discrepancies in confidence may have inescapable effects on a number of different behaviours in learning Computer Science. This might leave females struggling with applied problems or applied problem-solving strategies like tinkering. Explicit instruction in applied work through the practice of 'formal' tinkering may help increase females' confidence or acquaint them with alternative applied avenues for learning.

7.3 Goal Orientation

In their seminal work on the gender gap in Computer Science, Fischer, Margolis, and Miller outline the difference in female and male narratives of motivation for and pursuit of a CS degree [10].

> "When the first-year females talk about their personal history with computers, their narratives are not filled with long and detailed accounts... They contextualize their interest in computer science, instead, within a larger purpose: what *they can do in the world.* " [10]

Although this is in reference to reasons for selecting and pursuing a CS major, the description relates to our results of males' and females' definitions of tinkering in CS.

Analogous to the findings of Fischer et al. our results showed a difference between genders in the style and nature of the definitions of tinkering. Female students appeared generally more concerned with the purposes and goals of tinkering (namely in how it facilitates understanding), its general purpose for improvement, and focusing on tinkering as an exploratory pursuit. This was in contrast to the males' responses that showed more emphasis on the details of tinkering and greater preoccupation with what tinkering entails.

As females appear to see tinkering more as an open-ended pursuit, devoid of a tangible purpose, they may be less apt to tinker. On the other hand, since males may tend to recognize its concrete, less general purposes (such as improved performance or customization), they may be more equipped and inclined to tinker at home. Ultimately, if females viewed tinkering as having tangible, meaningful effects, with specific ideas of what it entailed, they may be more inclined to tinker.

8. SUGGESTIONS AND IMPLICATIONS

The implications of these results are potentially far reaching. Here we highlight some key issues and present preliminary suggestions to benefit both tinkering and non-tinkering learners.

8.1 Distribution of Course Resources

As our results show, females are more likely than males to report asking for help from TAs and instructors both in labs and during office hours. Moreover, the use and reliance on more formal methods of instruction in Computer Science has been documented in other related research on gender differences in CS [7]. This research reports females dominating extra tutorial sessions offered by the department, even when computer experience and programming performance are controlled for [7].

In courses where resources are limited, a scarcity of office hours could be a problem for females preferring this mode of learning and assistance. Ensuring the presence of accessible course staff members may be important to both females and non-tinkering males alike.

8.2 Design of Class Materials

The design of assignments and reference material may also affect males and females differently. Our results show a discrepancy between genders in the exploration of supplied assignment code that students are not required to modify. When exploratory behaviour is deemed useful on an assignment or lab, the inclusion of instructions outlining exploratory techniques could benefit those unaccustomed to tinkering. This modification may provide the potential educational benefit of tinkering to both non-tinkering males and females alike.

Ultimately, redesigning course materials for tinkering and non-tinkering types may mean providing stepping-stones to teach tinkering for non-tinkerers. To do so effectively we need to first determine whether tinkering behaviours are useful for students and, if they are, how to encourage these behaviours.

9. FUTURE WORK

Further research is needed to investigate the complexities of these findings and to explore the implications of gender-based differences in tinkering. Although the current maker movement encourages tinkering as a problem solving technique, it is important to consider how, when, and if tinkering is appropriate. We need to consider types of tinkering techniques and strategies, situations in which these techniques and strategies are expressed, and when they may or may not be useful. We can then study the effect of different types of tinkering strategies on academic performance, confidence, and comprehension.

10. CONCLUSION

Our study confirms some of the conjectures on the tinkering behaviours of females with respect to male Computer Science students. Indeed, female Computer Science students do tinker less with hardware, and may show disinclinations to tinker with software as well.

In this exploratory work we have highlighted a number of gender-based tendencies in tinkering behaviours across a variety of computing practices. We investigated gender-based tinkering behaviours in Computer Science not simply as they relate to hardware, but as a pragmatic approach to problem solving in Computer Science overall.

11. ACKNOWLEDGMENTS

We would like to thank the following people for helping us with this project: Patrice Belleville, Paul Carter, Anne Condon, Maria Klawe, Dena Krieger, Alisa Lipson, Kyle Melnick, Gail Murphy, Michele Ng, and Steve Wolfman. We would also like to thank the UBC Computer Science Department for its support, the anonymous reviewers for their helpful suggestions, and the Maria Klawe Endowment fund for funding Samantha's travel to SIGCSE.

12. REFERENCES

[1] Beckwith, L. and Burnett, M. 2004. Gender: An Important Factor in End-User Programming Environments? In *2004 IEEE Symposium on Visual Languages and Human Centric Computing*, 107–114.

[2] Beckwith, L., Kissinger, C., Burnett, M., Wiedenbeck, S., Lawrance, J., Blackwell, A., and Cook, C. 2006. Tinkering and Gender in End-user Programmers' Debugging. In *Proceedings of the SIGCHI Conference on Human Factors in Computing Systems*. ACM. New York, NY, 231–240.

[3] Brotman, J. S. and Moore, F. M. 2008. Girls and science: A review of four themes in the science education literature. In *J. Res. Sci. Teach.* 45 (Nov. 2008), 971–1002.

[4] Burnett, M., Wiedenbeck, S., Grigoreanu, V., Subrahmaniyan, N., Beckwith, L., and Kissinger, C. 2008. Gender in End-user Software Engineering. In *Proceedings of the 4th International Workshop on End-user Software Engineering*. ACM. New York, NY, 21–24.

[5] Camp, T. 1997. The Incredible Shrinking Pipeline. In *CACM.* 40, 10 (Oct. 1997), 103–110.

[6] Camp, T. 2002. The Incredible Shrinking Pipeline. In *SIGCSE Bull.* 34, 2 (Jun. 2002), 129–134.

[7] Carter, J. and Jenkins, T. 1999. Gender and Programming: What's Going on? In *Proceedings of the 4th Annual SIGCSE/SIGCUE ITiCSE Conference on Innovation and Technology in Computer Science Education.* ACM. New York, NY. 1–4.

[8] De Palma, P. 2001. Viewpoint: Why Women Avoid Computer Science. In *CACM.* 44, 6 (Jun 2001), 27–30.

[9] Dougherty, D. 2012. The Maker Movement. In *Innov. Technol. Gov. Glob.* 7, 3, 11–14.

[10] Fisher, A., Margolis, J., and Miller, F. 1997. Undergraduate Women in Computer Science: Experience, Motivation and Culture. In *Proceedings of the Twenty-eighth SIGCSE Technical Symposium on Computer Science Education.* ACM. New York, NY, 106–110.

[11] Gustafson, P. E. 1998. Gender Differences in Risk Perception: Theoretical and Methodological Perspectives. In *Risk Anal.* 18, 6 (Dec. 1998), 805–811.

[12] Hou, W., Kaur, M., Komlodi, A., Lutters, W. G., Boot, L., cotton, S. R., Morrell, C., Ozok, A. A., and Tufekci, Z. 2006. 'Girls Don't Waste Time': Pre-adolescent Attitudes Toward ICT," in *CHI '06 Extended Abstracts on Human Factors in Computing Systems*. ACM. New York, NY, 875–880.

[13] Jones, M. G., Brader-Araje, L., Carboni, L. W., Carter, G., Rua, M. J., Banilower, E., and Hatch, H. 2000. Tool time: Gender and students' use of tools, control, and authority. *J. Res. Sci. Teach.* 37, 8 (Oct. 2000), 760–783.

[14] Lamers, M. H., Verbeek, F. J., and van der Putten, P. W. H. 2013. Tinkering in Scientific Education. In *Advances in Computer Entertainment,* D. Reidsma, H. Katayose, and A. Nijholt, Eds. Springer International Publishing, 568–571.

[15] National Center for Women & Information Technology. 2012. Girls in IT. *The Facts. National Center for Women & Information Technology.* Retrieved August 7, 2014 from http://www.ncwit.org/resources/girls-it-facts.

[16] Parsons, D. S. 1995. Making sense of students' science: The construction of a model of tinkering. *Res. Sci. Educ.* 25, 2 (Jun 1995), 203–219.

[17] Parsons, S. 1990. *The development of a model of tinkering□: a study of children's science*. Doctoral Thesis. University of British Columbia.

[18] Petrich, M., Wilkinson, K., and Anzivino, L. 2014. Tinkering Fundamentals: A Constructionist Approach to STEM Learning. *Coursera.* Retrieved August 1, 2014 from www.coursera.org/course/tinkering.

[19] *Raspberry Pi.* Retrieved August 26, 2014 from http://www.raspberrypi.org/about/.

[20] Sheard, T., Simon, S., Hamilton, M., and Lönnberg, J. 2009. Analysis of Research into the Teaching and Learning of Programming. In *Proceedings of the Fifth International Workshop on Computing Education Research Workshop.* ACM New York, NY, 93–104.

[21] Tillberg, H. K. and Cohoon, J. M. 2005. Attaching Women to the CS Major. *Front. J. Women Stud.* 26, 1, 126–140.

[22] Vermeer, H. J., Boekaerts, M. and Seegers, G. 2000. Motivational and gender differences: Sixth-grade students' mathematical problem-solving behaviour. In *J. Educ. Psychol.* 92, 2, 308.

The Emerging Role of Self-Perception in Student Intentions

Jennifer Dempsey
Dept. of Computer Science
University of Arizona
jendempsey@cs.arizona.edu

Richard T. Snodgrass
Dept. of Computer Science
University of Arizona
rts@cs.arizona.edu

Isabel Kishi
Dept. of Computer Science
University of Arizona
ihkishi@cs.arizona.edu

Allison Titcomb
Biosphere II
University of Arizona
atitcomb@email.arizona.edu

ABSTRACT

Recruitment and retention of women has been a persistent problem in the field of computer science. With a growing number of jobs that require a computer science degree, this problem does not only affect computer science departments with low enrollment, but also impacts industry. There is still no universally accepted explanation for the underrepresentation of women in the computing field. Various solutions have been implemented in an attempt to resolve this problem and yet gender imbalance in fields related to computer science persists.

In this paper we study how perceptions held by students influence their intention to pursue computer science. Through a descriptive study, using a survey given out to first semester students in a computer science class, we measure perceptions, attitudes, self-efficacy, and identity, then we study the correlations between them and students' intentions to further pursue computer science. Our goal is to understand how determinative these constructs are to having students continue in the major.

Interestingly, self-perception, in terms of self-efficacy (does the student feel they are able to use computer science techniques to solve a problem) and identity (does the student see themselves as a computer scientist), emerged as the primary driver for differences in intention. Many other aspects turned out not to exhibit statistically significant gender differences. Understanding at a detailed level what factors influence students to pursue computer science is critical in devising effective interventions that may increase participation in computer science.

Categories and Subject Descriptors

K.3.0 [**Computers and Education**]: General

General Terms

Measurement

SIGCSE'15, March 4–7, 2015, Kansas City, MO, USA.

http://dx.doi.org/10.1145/2676723.2677305.

Keywords

Gender Differences; Perceptions; Student Intentions

1. INTRODUCTION

A commonly-stated concern in the field of computer science (CS) education is the low percentage of women entering the computing field. Shortages in the workforce would be greatly reduced if more women majored in CS [2, 6, 13]. Increasing the percentage of women would also provide a more diverse workforce in computing fields, which is critical in order to meet the challenges of the information age, as technology benefits all members of society [3, 4]. For these reasons, among others, there has been a large effort over a decade to increase the enrollment of women in CS.

To devise a means of closing the gender gap, it is important to understand the underlying causes. Many potential causes have been studied. Among the contributing factors, the limited availability of CS courses before the undergraduate level is frequently mentioned [9]. This dearth of K-12 courses leads to large knowledge gaps among students enrolled in introductory CS courses at the undergraduate level, as only a select group of incoming students enters such courses with a solid background in the field. This knowledge gap is also claimed to differ between genders [9]. Ultimately, it can discourage women from entering a computing-based field.

Numerous new programs, recruitment techniques, and workshops have been implemented in hopes of addressing the potential causes of the gender gap in CS. However, the problem persists: few women choose to pursue a degree or a career in computer science.

In this paper, we consider the extent that various perceptions may contribute to the small percentages of women in the field. Rather than starting from a proposed intervention, we instead analyze the perceptions of students concerning CS. Through administering a survey to introductory students we can identify more precisely the discrepancies in perceptions of CS between genders.

2. RELATED WORK

Previous work that identifies perceptions as a cause of the gender gap typically focuses on a few different types of perception. Perceptions related to CS include students' beliefs as to what CS is, who computer scientists are, and if the student has the abilities that computer scientists possess.

Many students do not comprehend the breadth of the CS field. Unlike other scientific fields, students are not typically exposed to CS until they reach the undergraduate level [9]. Hence, a student may enter an introduction to programming class as an undergraduate with incorrect or incomplete notions about CS, computer scientists, or their own abilities to succeed in computing. Often, incoming student's believe that CS is mainly focused on programming and that the skills taught in these classes cannot be used to solve real world problems. For example, a study by Carter [7] examined why students who would statistically flourish in the CS field, instead continued in another. This study determined that a primary contributing factor is that these students do not have a complete understanding of what topics are covered in a computer science degree. In addition, a study undertaken at Georgia Institute of Technology showed that a belief that CS does not have many real-world applications is among the top reasons women end up leaving the field, whereas this idea does not seem to affect men's choice of major [5].

Another deterrent to students entering the field of CS is that they often associate the field with certain stereotypes [1]. Often individuals with an interest in computing are described as being male, and of either Caucasian or Asian descent. In fact, several of the individuals interviewed for the "Stuck in the Shallow End" book gave reasons for not attempting AP CS that included the notion that it was a class for white and Asian males [12]. Also students with limited knowledge of the CS field negatively described it as a very solitary, repetitive activity, discouraging them from enrolling in a class [7]. This narrow image of the CS field and of the individuals involved is often portrayed in the media, making it increasingly difficult to recruit individuals that lie outside this stereotype into the field.

It has also been shown that a student's intention to pursue computer science is correlated with self-efficacy in computer science. Miura found that men rank themselves higher in self-efficacy in comparison to women [14]. Additionally, this survey found that there was a positive relationship between an intention to take a CS class and self-efficacy in CS. In this study we expand the idea of intentions in CS to consider a wider variety of granularities. This includes if a student intends to learn more about CS on their own, as well as if a student plans to pursue a career in CS.

Finally, it has been shown that females are less likely to be confident that they have the skills needed to pursue CS [9]. It has been observed that girls at a young age are more motivated to work with computers than their male counterparts. However, as individuals age, the confidence gap between men and women reverses and then grows, even as all students have access to computers and CS classes.

Many of the above factors may contribute to the lack of women in CS. However, it is unlikely that the lack of women in CS can be attributed to one single cause. Most likely the gender gap is created by a combination of factors [8].

3. UNDERSTANDING PERCEPTIONS

To address the problem of low enrollment in CS through effective interventions, it is important that we understand the underlying causes for this low enrollment. We present a descriptive study in which we measure various aspects of each student's perceptions, then examine correlations between those and intention to further pursue CS. We focus on students, primarily freshmen, at the University of Arizona taking the introductory CS course. Our goal is to understand how determinative these other constructs are to having students continue in the major.

We devised six psychological constructs that we feel may play a role in a seventh construct: a student's intention to continue in CS. Those six contributing constructs are (a) perceptions of CS, (b) attitudes about science in general, (c) attitudes about CS specifically, (d) science self-efficacy, (e) CS self-efficacy, and (f) CS identity. We measured these constructs at the very beginning of the course, to ensure that experience in that course is not a factor.

The survey consists of 36 items, each a statement that we asked each student to rank on a seven-point Likert scale of Strongly Disagree, Disagree, Somewhat Disagree, Neither Agree nor Disagree, Somewhat Agree, Agree, and Strongly Agree. This scale allows us to decipher smaller amounts of change between groups than with a coarser scale system. Note, we also included questions that are reverse coded, that is, statements where a student's response should typically be opposite of the rest of the questions within the construct. This allows us to tell when a student is not reading the statements carefully. Where possible, we utilized existing, validated instruments, in some cases modified to apply to computer science, as we describe in the following.

Items were presented in one of three orders to students, with about a half dozen items per page, to reduce the effect of interactions between statements.

Additionally, the survey collects some basic demographic information. This including the student's major, prior classes that the student took, and, most relevant to this analysis, gender.

The entire survey was presented to each student in an electronic form that could be completed at a location and time of the student's choosing. The entire survey took about five minutes.

We studied the following perceptions, each of which may influence a student's decision to continue on in the field of computer science.

- Perception of CS (methodologies it includes),
- Attitude towards science in general (feelings about science),
- Attitude towards CS,
- Self-efficacy in doing science (do they have skill in doing science),
- Self-efficacy in doing CS, and
- Self-concept of the individual (do they see themselves as a computer scientist).

We now examine each of these subjects, addressed by the survey, in turn, briefly summarizing the statements that appear for each topic. The survey attempts to be thorough while presenting a small number of questions. The full survey is available at `www.cs.arizona.edu/projects/focal/ergalics/fieldguide/survey2013.pdf`

3.1 Perception of Computer Science

Often perceptions of the CS field are limited to just programming; however, the field of CS contains many more aspects beyond this narrow view. The survey attempts to investigate if students believe CS is solely based on programming and to what extent their perceptions a limited to only certain areas of the field. To do this, the survey uses a series of statements where each statement described a particular aspect CS.

The statements which appear in the survey were adapted from an AWE (Assessing Women and Men in Engineering) assessment. AWE provides these assessment tools for use in educational settings[1]. We altered some of the statements about scientists (e.g., work on things that help the world, analyze experimental data, gather and analyze data to answer questions) and applied them to computer scientists as well (seven items in all).

The survey asks each student how much they agree or disagree that computer scientists partake in the presented activities. For example, one of the statements used reads "Computer scientists analyze experimental data". Stereotypes of computer scientist do not support this statement because it implies that CS is more than just programming, but many computer scientists do gather or analyze data similar to other related fields.

3.2 Attitudes About Science and CS

Attitudes (i.e., how the student feels about science or about CS, such as do they like it, do they think it's important) may also factor into whether a student plans to pursue CS. Formally, attitudes are defined as "evaluations of objects, of events, or of ideas" [10]. The survey considers attitude in terms of attitudes towards science and more specifically, attitudes towards CS. We measured science attitude with a set of statements which assess whether a student's attitude towards science is generally positive or negative. Statements in this section include the following themes: does a student believes science is important, does the student enjoys science, and does a student enjoys taking science-based classes. We considered attitudes towards CS in a similar manner: we simply substituted the term "computer science" for any instance of "science" in each statement. From the previous research discussed above we expect that attitudes towards CS differ between men and women. With such statements we can discern if a student has a negative or positive attitude toward science and toward CS. Our survey contains three statements pertaining to science and six pertaining to CS.

It is important to note that CS is the only science that we consider separately. In general any one particular science may influence a students responses to questions about general science. For example, girls take biology at the same rate as boys and go on to become physicians at similar rates as boys [15], though that is not the case for physics and physicists. One of the goals of this survey is to be able to observe the differences between a student's perceptions of computer science and general science in a reasonable number of questions. To account for the fact that a student may have varying attitudes towards biology compared to physics, our survey could be expanded to include multiple versions of these questions to include many specific branches of science. That would have significantly increased the length of the survey and increase the likelihood that students would skim through the survey and not read through the questions carefully.

[1]This assessment was developed by researchers at the Pennsylvania State University and University of Missouri, `http://www.engr.psu.edu/awe/misc/about.aspx`, retrieved September 5, 2014.

3.3 Self-Efficacy, in Science and CS

Self-efficacy is "a person's belief that he of she is capable of the specific behavior required to produce a desired outcome in a given situation" [11]. As before, the survey measures both science self-efficacy (e.g., does the student feel he or she is able to use the scientific method) and CS self-efficacy (e.g., does the student feel that he or she is able to use CS terms to share their results).

The statements that are used to measure self-efficacy in science include the beliefs that each student can effectively communicate a scientific procedure to others, can use models to explain my results, and could become scientists. To generate statements that measure self-efficacy in CS, similar statements were used except any reference to science was replaced with one to CS and the phrasing was adjusted to encourage the student to read each statement carefully. These statements are designed to measure self-efficacy for a student in general science classes and CS classes outside of the typical misconception that CS is only programming.

The statements used to measure both CS and science self-efficacy were based on a Science Process Skills Inventory[2], which was intended to measure skills needed to process information, rather than content knowledge of science. Mary Arnold, one of the authors of that inventory, gave us permission to adapt the statements and the response scale to fit our needs. We chose a subset of the statements from the initial inventory, to maintain a reasonable total length; for self-efficacy pertaining to computer science we replaced "science" with "computer science". We ended up with six questions pertaining to self-efficacy in science and seven concerning self-efficacy in CS.

3.4 Self-Concept

Finally, we consider CS identity, specifically self-concept: does a student see themselves as a computer scientist. Self-concept is defined to be "the sum total of an individual's beliefs about his or her own personal attributes" [11]. To measure a student's self-concept as a computer scientist, the survey includes three items. These statements are designed to measure the importance of CS as part of who they are: "majoring in CS is important to me." Other statements consider different granularities of this concept, such as, being a computer scientist and being able to use CS to solve problems.

The initial questions, "Do you think you could become a scientist?" and "Do you think you could become a computer scientist?" were originally from a survey measuring attitudes towards STEM [16]. The original questions also asked students to explain their answers. Rather than requiring this explanation, we applied the seven-point scale to the items. The explanations may prove useful in future studies, but for our purposes we just wanted to be able to gauge if a student could identify with being a computer scientist or scientist.

3.5 Intention to Continue in CS

A central objective of the survey is to is gauge a student's intention to continue on in the CS field. This intention is considered at the following granularities: enroll in another course, major in CS, pursue a CS career, and plan to learn

[2]My Science Skills (©2010 Oregon State University, Bourdeau, V.D. & Arnold, M.E. (2010) *The Science Process Skills Inventory. Corvalils, OR: 4-H Youth Development Education, Oregon State University.*

more about CS on their own (four items). Our hypothesis is that such CS intentions may be affected by the above listed perceptions, that is, by what a subject understands or feels.

4. SUBJECT POOL

As outlined above, our approach is a descriptive study, in that we measure perceptions, attitudes, self-efficacy, and identity, then look at correlations between those and intentions to further pursue computer science, to understand how determinative these other constructs are retention rates in computer science.

We gave this survey electronically to students in CS 127A for the Fall 2013 and Spring 2014 semesters after receiving permission from the University of Arizona's Institutional Review Board. After following standard practice to obtain consent, a total of 219 students agreed for their answers to be included in this study, though not all answered every question. Approximately one-quarter of the students were female. Note, this class is an introductory class in the CS major, but it also required for several related fields including, but not limited to, mathematics and engineering. Using this type of subject pool could alter our findings as participants have already decided to take a college level course in computer science. The results are still pertinent as problems concerning retention rates in the field of computer science is just as important as issue with recruitment.

5. ANALYSIS OF SURVEY RESULTS

The goal of this investigation is to gauge (a) whether our specific measures of each of the constructs (described in sections 3.5–3.4) sufficiently hold together (in a statistical sense) to indicate that the construct itself is captured, (b) whether there is a significant difference between genders, and (c) to what extent do the other constructs correlate with CS intentions. We now examine each question in turn.

5.1 Construct Reliability

As discussed above, for each construct we used several items, with the goal that these items "hang together" well, measure the same concept, that is, exhibit construct reliability. A conventional indication of this is Cronbach's Alpha (α), where a value of 0.7–0.8 is considered good.

We consider a construct's answers to be reliable if a student's answers in a single category all fall in the same general area of the seven-point scale, with the exception of questions that are reverse coded, which should have answers on the opposite end of this scale.

Most of the constructs held together quite well: perceptions of CS ($\alpha = 0.837$), science attitudes ($\alpha = 0.779$), CS attitudes ($\alpha = 0.822$), science self-efficacy ($\alpha = 0.855$), CS self-efficacy ($\alpha = 0.837$), and CS identity ($\alpha = 0.814$).

The one construct that did not hold together as well was computer science intentions, with $\alpha = 0.664$. This implies that the individual items are not all testing the same concept, that there are multiple, perhaps overlapping, concepts being tested.

5.2 Gender Differences

We were surprised that for most of the constructs, there were no statistically significant differences (using the t-test) between men and women. In particular, there were no gender differences concerning (a) perceptions of computer science, (b) attitudes of science, (c) attitudes of computer science, or (d) science self-efficacy.

These results have broad implications. As discussed above in Section 2, some of the past research has predicated informally that women perceive CS differently, or that women do not feel that they are good in science. Our results imply that for those we surveyed, those are not significant gender-specific attitudes or perceptions.

There were statistically significant ($p < 0.01$) gender differences in just three constructs: CS self-efficacy (mean $M_f = 4.44$; $M_m = 5.09$) and CS identity ($M_f = 4.44$; $M_m = 5.05$), as well as CS intention ($M_f = 5.00$; $M_m = 5.44$). Note that in all three, females rated themselves lower than males.

These results lead to the initial conclusion that even though CS has "science" in its name and is considered a STEM discipline, computer science seems to be viewed differently than other sciences. It seems that the difference can be attributed broadly to (a) whether the student perceives that he or she can excel in CS (self-efficacy) and (b) whether the student see themselves as a computer scientist (identity). Women to a lesser extent see themselves are being able to *do* computer science and as *being* computer scientists. We again emphasize that here was no difference between men and women on *science* self-efficacy.

Concerning CS intentions, there were significant gender differences on two of the items: "I would like to take another computer science class" ($M_f = 5.16; M_m = 5.63$) and "I plan to major in computer science" ($M_f = 3.82; M_m = 4.68$). For the other two questions ("I would consider a career in computer science" and "I would like to know more about computer science") there were no statistically significant differences. It seems that the distinction in these questions is that women are different than men on *inwardly-oriented* questions but not on the *outwardly-oriented* questions. This also relates to the fact that this construct does not hold together. Interestingly, Cronbach's alpha is higher ($\alpha = .701$) for men if the item "I wouldn't consider a career in computer science" is removed, meaning the construct reliability improves when this item is removed. For women, Cronbach's alpha improves ($\alpha = .731$), if the statement "I would like to know more about computer science," is removed, meaning the other three have a higher construct reliability.

We conclude that it is *not* what women think about CS, but rather how they think about *themselves* within this discipline. The critical challenge is with *identity* and only within CS, not with science in general, which is perhaps why other some sciences are not experiencing problems with participation of women.

5.3 Correlations with Intention

A separate question is, which constructs correlate with CS intentions? We should generally be concerned only with those that do so correlate.

We found that neither science attitudes nor science self-efficacy correlate with CS intentions. This result emphasizes that students do not see computer science as a science.

CS intentions correlate at statistically significant levels with CS perceptions (Pearson's $r = 0.243$), CS self-efficacy (0.256), CS attitudes (0.407), and CS identity (0.646). Unfortunately, in terms of the overarching problem being considered, the strongest correlation, CS identity, exhibits the most gender imbalance. CS self-efficacy seems to also be a factor, but a lesser one.

Table 1: Survey results for men in computer science; 1 is strongly disagree and 7 is strongly agree.

Construct	Number of Participants	Mean	Standard Deviation
Intentions in CS	158	**5.4351**	1.01234
Perceptions of CS	150	5.5124	.81960
Attitudes towards CS	153	5.8420	.69716
Attitudes towards Science	148	5.7523	.91359
Self-efficacy in CS	148	**5.2181**	.86399
Self-efficacy in Science	146	5.5297	.80817
Self-Concept as Computer Scientist	149	**5.0582**	1.18849

Table 2: Survey results for women in computer science; 1 is strongly disagree and 7 is strongly agree.

Construct	Number of Participants	Mean	Standard Deviation
Intentions in CS	61	**4.9918**	1.09541
Perceptions of CS	55	5.6909	.62437
Attitudes towards CS	57	5.7105	.81742
Attitudes towards Science	57	5.5205	1.20023
Self-efficacy in CS	55	**4.6104**	1.19094
Self-efficacy in Science	55	5.3455	.89515
Self-Concept as Computer Scientist	58	**4.4425**	1.20023

(We emphasize that correlation is not causality. We hypothesize that it is the gender differences in CS identity and self-efficacy that are causing the differences observed in CS intensions, but cannot rule out that the causality doesn't go the other way.)

5.4 Summary of Analysis

The final results from the survey are listed in Tables 1 and 2 for men and women, respectively. For most of the constructs listed in these tables there are no statistically significant differences between genders. However, significant gender differences (shown in **bold**) can be observed for both self-efficacy in CS and self-concept as a computer scientist. Additionally, significant differences between men and women were observed concerning intentions to pursue computer science.

6. CONCLUSIONS

Females report having lower computer science self-efficacy and computer science identity. Note, females and males did not differ in science self-efficacy, indicating that this is specific to computer science. In addition, another interesting finding is that women and men did not significantly differ in attitudes of either CS nor science nor perceptions of CS. Lastly, the strongest correlation occurs between intentions to pursue CS and identity as a computer scientist. Identity also happens to be the construct that has the greatest discrepancy between men and women. These results suggest that computer science self-efficacy and computer science identity might play a role in the underrepresentation of women in computer science careers.

From these findings we can conclude that solutions to close the gender gap in CS might be more effective if they also focus on changing women's perceptions of themselves in the computer science field.

7. FUTURE WORK

Our study leaves two distinct areas for future work in terms of determining the role of perceptions on students' intentions to pursue CS. First altering the subject pool for this survey or distributing the survey to the same subject pool multiple times may provide us with more generalizable information. Secondly, the constructs that were created for this survey could be polished to increase construct reliability and to better capture the most important aspects.

7.1 Broadening the Subject Pool

The finding described about leave several opportunities for future work. Among these is to determine if student's perceptions alter after completing an introductory course in CS. Many introductory courses focus on teaching basic programming constructs and could even support common misconceptions about the computer science field. In the introductory course at the University of Arizona, we will be attempting to expose students to a different method of framing CS lessons in a similar manner to other science classes, in addition to the material that emphasizes programming. This approach might allow students to perceive CS as being more closely related to other science courses. The survey data presented in this paper suggests that being able to convince women that CS is a science could positively influence their intentions to pursue computer science. Ultimately, we could observe this change through a survey given at different times throughout the offering of the introductory course.

Additionally, this survey could be applied to students taking a more general CS course that is not part of the major. This would open up our survey to individuals that had not initially intended to pursue a computer science degree. In the Spring of 2015 the University of Arizona is offering another CS course (CSc 170) as a general elective that will focus more on the theories behind CS, rather than just on basic programming concepts. Students in this type of class will typically be interested in learning more about CS but who do not necessarily intend to pursue a degree or career in the field.

Another area of future research could involve tracking how a student's perceptions change as they continue on while pursuing an undergraduate degree in CS. Administering our survey multiple times throughout the career of undergraduate students could give us an opportunity to observe how changes in perceptions can factor in to the retention rates in CS departments.

Lastly, we have made our survey available with the hope of collecting data from other universities in a wider variety of fields and potentially from students at the high school level.

7.2 Changes to the Survey

Our survey could be refined based on the results reported here to better capture differences in perceptions between genders. To begin with, it would be helpful to separate intentions in CS into two separate constructs, one considering intention to pursue a career or other long term goals in the field and the other to gauge intention to pursue CS as an interest or as a tool to support a career in a related field. We believe that this approach may produce two constructs with better construct reliability than our original construct for CS intentions.

Also our survey treats all other sciences in a single general category. In order to get a more accurate comparison between CS and other sciences, the survey could be altered to specify a specific science, such as biology or physics, rather than using general science questions.

Additionally, we did not observe any effects of the common perception that CS mainly involves coding. To better determine if the perception of CS as programming impacts intentions toward CS, it would be useful to create another construct for perception of the CS field that focuses on computer programming. We feel that this is important to study due to the sheer amount of prior research that speculates that this perception is a part of the reason why enrollment in CS courses is low. This new construct would measure student beliefs about the amount of coding ability and creativity needed to be a computer scientist. This construct may also bear light on why some women do not see themselves as computer scientist, while having high self-efficacy in science.

7.3 Potential Interventions

The data from this survey implies that interventions should not focus primarily on perceptions or attitudes of CS. Rather, the problem appears to lie primarily in self-perception and only with reference to CS, not with reference generally to science, and within that, how women think about themselves (inwardly-facing) within their discipline.

Interventions that change self-perception vis-a-vis CS, specifically identity, may be effective. However, the simple fact that there are few women in CS is a daunting situation.

Another potential approach would be to do a better job in framing CS as a science. As noted above, there are not significant gender differences in attitudes or self-efficacy concerning science. If women see CS as more similar to other sciences rather than just programming (CS perceptions), their CS self-efficacy may improve, so as to eliminate this gender difference. This may then contribute to resolving the gender differences in CS identity. Our data also provides support for efforts that moderate the effects of certain stereotypes that may be a cause of gender differences in science self-efficacy.

Acknowledgments

We thank Jaimie Sauls who constructed the original version of our survey and Melanie Brucks for her contributions in developing the constructs and questions used in the final version of the survey and her help with the statistical analysis. Partial support was provided by NSF grants CNS-0938948 and IIS-1016205.

8. REFERENCES

[1] M. Adya and K. Kaiser. Early determinants of women in the IT workforce: a model of girls' career choices. *Information Technology & People*, 18(3):230–259, 2005.

[2] D. E. Agosto, S. Gasson, and M. Atwood. Changing Mental Models of the IT Professions : A Theoretical Framework. *Journal of Information Technology Education*, 7:205–221, 2008.

[3] A. M. Balcita, D. L. Carver, and M. L. Soffa. Shortchanging the future of information technology: the untapped resource. *ACM SIGCSE Bulletin*, 34(2):32–35, 2002.

[4] S. Beyer, K. Rynes, and S. Haller. Deterrents to Women taking computer science courses. *Technology and Society Magazine, IEEE*, 23(1):21–28, 2004.

[5] M. Biggers, A. Brauer, and T. Yilmaz. Student perceptions of computer science: a retention study comparing graduating seniors with CS leavers. *ACM SIGCSE Bulletin*, 40(1):402–406, 2008.

[6] T. Camp. The incredible shrinking pipeline. *Communications of the ACM*, 34(2):129, June 1997.

[7] L. Carter. Why students with an apparent aptitude for computer science don't choose to major in computer science. *ACM SIGCSE Bulletin*, 38(1):27–31, 2006.

[8] S. J. Ceci, D. K. Ginther, S. Kahn, and W. M. Williams. Women in academic science: A changing landscape. *Psychological Science in the Public Interest*, 15(3):75–141, 2014.

[9] J. Cohoon, McGrath, and W. Aspray. *Women and Information Technology: Research on Underrepresentation*, volume 1. The MIT Press, 2006.

[10] M. Gazzaniga, T. Heatherton, and D. Halpern. *Psychological Science*. W. W. Norton & Company, New York, 3 edition, 2010.

[11] S. Kassin, S. Fein, and H. Markus. *Social Psychology*. Wadsworth Cengage Learning, Mason, OH, 8 edition, 2008.

[12] J. Margolis. *Stuck in the shallow end: Education, race, and computing*. MIT Press, 2008.

[13] C. McCullough. Attracting under-represented groups to engineering and computer science. *Population*, 20:1–11, 2002.

[14] I. T. Miura. The relationship of computer self-efficacy expectations to computer interest and course enrollment in college. *Sex Roles*, 16(5-6):303–311, 1987.

[15] R. T. Snodgrass. Broadening cs enrollments: An interview with Jan Cuny. *Ubiquity*, 2013(February):1:1–1:8, Feb. 2013.

[16] S. H. Wingenbach, G. J. Degenhart, K. E. Lindner, J. R. Dooley, D. L. Mowen, and L. Johnson. Middle school students' attitudes toward pursuing careers in science, technology, engineering, and math. *NACTA Journal*, 51(1):52–59, 2007.

StitchFest: Diversifying a College Hackathon to Broaden Participation and Perceptions in Computing

Gabriela T. Richard
University of Pennsylvania
3700 Walnut St
Philadelphia, PA, USA
gric@upenn.edu

Yasmin B. Kafai
University of Pennsylvania
3700 Walnut St
Philadelphia, PA, USA
kafai@upenn.edu

Barrie Adleberg
E-Line Media
363 Seventh Ave
New York, NY, USA
badleberg@elinemedia.com

Orkan Telhan
University of Pennsylvania
200 S. 36th St
Philadelphia, PA, USA
otelhan@upenn.edu

ABSTRACT
While coding competitions and hackathons have steadily increased in number, few women participate. Because these public events present viable opportunities to broaden participation in computing, we designed the theme to focus on "Wear & Care" and collaborative arrangements in a hardware hackathon, called StitchFest, in which 33 undergraduate and graduate students used the LilyPad Arduino to design wearables. Our analysis focused on the interviews conducted with eight female and seven male college participants to understand how targeted recruitment, thematic framing, space arrangements, kinds of materials and material distribution impacted participation and perception. We discuss what we learned about setting a thematic focus and fostering collaborative learning in coding competitions for broadening participation in computing.

Categories and Subject Descriptors
K.3 [COMPUTERS AND EDUCATION]: Computer and Information Science Education – *computer science education, literacy.*

General Terms
Human Factors.

Keywords
Coding competitions; hackathons; wearable computing; broadening participation; gender

1. INTRODUCTION
One of the most pressing issues in computer science education has been to broaden participation of women and minorities. Many efforts on the college level have focused on purposeful recruitment by reaching out to students, providing stronger mentoring opportunities and redesigning curriculum to speak to socially diverse interests opening the potential for personal application [e.g., 2, 10, 15, 21, 25]. Many of these efforts have resulted not only in bringing in more diverse students but also broadening perceptions around computing participation and potential. There is a growing recognition that not one intervention alone but a network of activities is needed for broader success that reaches far beyond the computer science classrooms.

SIGCSE '15, March 04 - 07 2015, Kansas City, MO, USA

http://dx.doi.org/10.1145/2676723.2677310

One activity that has received little attention so far is the increasing popularity of coding competitions or hackathons. Described as "marathon coding competitions" [17], hackathons present both social and professional opportunities to young developers, who are tasked with making a functional prototype to pitch to investors for a prize, working on it for 24 or 48 hours. Hosted within corporate, academic, or community-based settings, by 2011 over 200 hackathons were estimated in the United States alone [17]. Many of these hackathons are organized spontaneously, attracting a hundred or so volunteer participants whereas others, such as the student-organized hackathon, PennApps, which is now in its tenth iteration, attract thousands of college students from all over the world. Leckart [17] argued that "hackathons, with their come-one-come-all ethos, have emerged as the new forum for networking, learning, and beta-testing new apps and ventures." While these hackathons are theoretically open to all, they have been found lacking in diversity unless they are designed as women-only events such as The International Women's Hackathon.

In this paper, we describe the design and implementation of a hardware hackathon, called StitchFest, with the explicit goal to broaden participation by recruiting within affinity networks, promoting new designs with computation, developing new models for collaborative hacking, and impacting perceptions of computing participation. StitchFest took place in February 2014 as part of PennApps, a larger collegiate hackathon. All participants were provided with electronic textiles and computational construction kits to design an application around a theme of "Wear & Care," and 33 participants submitted projects for judging. Analyzing interviews from 15 consenting female and male participants, we addressed the following questions: (1) What motivated participants to join StitchFest? (2) In which ways did coding wearables interest participants? (3) How did the coding space impact involvement and collaboration? and (4) How did perceptions towards computation and hack spaces shift after participating in StitchFest? In the discussion, we address what we learned about the designs of hackathons for broadening participation, projects, and perceptions.

2. BACKGROUND
College CS programs have largely been critiqued for alienating women from participating in computing [18]. Since the early 1980s, there has been a steady decline in the amount of computer science degrees awarded to women [20, 27], and female representation in computer-related careers has significantly declined since the 1990s, according to a census-related report [16]. Research has found that women and girls are less likely than men and boys to be STEM majors at onset or persist in these

majors throughout their college experience, which is highly influenced by learning environment factors [10]. While most of the efforts have focused on formal CS classes, informal learning opportunities such as small and large-scale coding competitions play a significant role in broadening participation in computing. These coding competitions with names like *Coding Wars*, *CodeChef* and *TopCoder,* to name but a few, have increasingly become popular events to highlight international leaderboards and coding accomplishments. Despite their open nature, female participation in major coding competitions has historically been lacking [e.g., 5, 6, 8, 23], though exact numbers are difficult to come by. It is clear that coding competitions have become popular events and their lack of inclusion limits access to learning and career opportunities, as the technology industry increasingly uses these kinds of competitions to source new recruits and innovative concepts.

The sudden relevance of coding competitions for recruitment and skill building has led the National Center for Women and Information Technology (NCWIT) [19] to release a set of recommendations to address the lack of participation of women and minorities. Among their major recommendations are (1) including promotional materials that feature females and a range of students, (2) actively recruit females, (3) provide ongoing encouragement, (4) allow participants to create projects that appeal to them, (5) encourage mixed teams with experienced and inexperienced members, (6) host a tutorial or how-to event, (7) focus on learning and different ways to win, (8) include female mentors, educators and judges, (9) make sure the space is accessible to all, and (10) educate others involved. These different dimensions highlight the complexities involved in designing coding competitions that are inviting and open to participants of diverse backgrounds.

With StitchFest, we designed a hackathon responsive to these needs. We situated it within PennApps, one of the largest and premier college hackathons in the nation. PennApps, which occurs twice a year, has been successful in bringing together thousands of accomplished college hackers from all over the world. In Spring 2014, over 1,200 undergraduates alone participated in the ninth PennApps. But women only made up only 14.8% of the participants, very much in contrast to the first event in 2009, which attracted 35% women participants. Incidentally, the first PennApps was organized and co-sponsored by Penn's Women in Computer Science (WICS) organization. Since then, the percentage of female participants has been hovering around 15% (based on available attendance records from the last five years). Perhaps not surprisingly, the number of winners is even lower: only 9 of the 93 historical PennApps winners were women.

For the design of StitchFest, we drew on research that suggests materials, themes, and spaces of computing cultures strongly influence participation and retention, as well as changes in perceptions [10]. As a first step, we selected the LilyPad Arduino, a microcontroller that facilitates the integration of engineering and computing with crafting and sewing [3] as our coding platform. This electronic textile construction kit includes a range of electrical components such as microcontrollers, sensors, and actuators that can be stitched together with conductive thread to make circuits that can be attached onto fabric and wearable media. By leveraging material affordances and aesthetics, Buechley and colleagues saw the LilyPad as integrating art and engineering in ways that could productively increase diversity in both the composition of the CS and engineering field and the designs and projects produced. The LilyPad is one effort in increasing female and underrepresented participation in STEM, beyond curriculum changes and mentors:

> ...Our work suggests an approach to complement these efforts. In addition to asking 'how can we get girls and women to participate in traditional computer science and support them once they are there?', we should ask: 'how can we integrate computer science with activities and communities that girls and women are already engaged in?' [3]

Second, we developed a design challenge called "Wear & Care" to provide the makers with a common topic that can be addressed differently based on individual interests. The idea here was to frame the open ended experimentations with a function, so that the design would aim to create meaningful experiences in people's lives. What the makers care about obviously varied from entertainment to healthcare and social activism, and the theme also allowed us to observe which topics are more popular among different students that differ in gender, educational background, and so on.

Finally, we paid careful attention to the meeting space (including arrangement of materials), encouraged participants to interact across teams, and tried to engage diverse interests and creativity; research has shown these are instrumental, along with mentors, in getting disadvantaged female youth to design complex electronic textiles [15]. We also focused recruitment through affinity spaces and targeted female undergraduate organizations, which studies show is one key for successfully inclusive programs [25].

The focus of our investigations was to broaden not only participation in computing by reaching larger numbers of female participants but also perceptions of computing through the event composition and theme. Previous research has shown that many college students perceive of computing as too difficult, uninspired, and reserved for smart students [4, 26]. Perceptions are also often gendered, as females are more likely to feel that careers in computing don't apply to their interests and skills [4]. Thus changing perceptions of computing is "a core concern in broadening CS participation... [and] focuses on learners' perceptions of computing, where they see applications for computing, and how they see themselves within the field and future careers" [12].

3. SETTING AND DATA COLLECTION

StitchFest took place in February 2014 as part of PennApps Spring 2014, a larger hackathon,with over 1,200 attendees. We used a design-based approach [24] to investigate the following design features and their relationship to broaden participation, projects and perceptions of computing: (1) intentional recruitment of participants within affinity networks, (2) focus on a theme of "Wear & Care" eliciting a reference to wearables, (3) provision of free hack boxes of computational materials with the same primary components but different sensors and actuators to encourage exchange and interaction amongst teams, and (4) creation of a communal space that situated participants together to encourage collaboration rather than designing in isolation.

3.1 Participants

While 44 students picked up hack boxes, only a total of 33 students (22 men and 11 women) made up 11 final competing teams with two to four members each. Participants ranged in age from 19-26, with 29 undergraduates and four graduate students from universities in the United States and Canada, and with majors from engineering, computer science, art, and industrial design. For all further analysis, we refer to 15 participants (8 men, 7 women) from ten of the eleven final teams who provided consent for research. Three judges, all women, were recruited for the event. One was an experienced industrial designer specialized in fashion and technology, another was an artist with years of experimental fabric and wearable design expertise, and one (Richard) was an educator with a background in physical computing and tangible design with Arduino.

3.2 Design and Materials

The design of the *StitchFest* theme "Wear & Care" was inspired by quilting circles and promoted collaboration between participants by sharing resources. Teams worked with the *LilyPad Arduino*, and a set of components including a wireless module, MP3 player, various sensors and actuators ready to interface with the kit (see Figure 1). Other materials, such as conductive thread and fabric, along with sewing machines, were provided free at workstations (Figure 2).

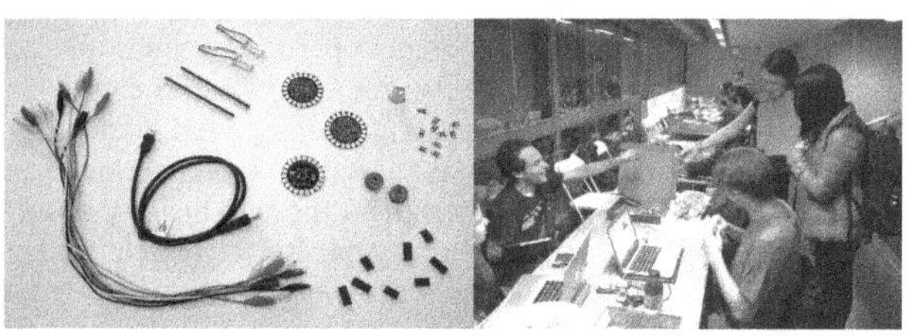

Figure 1: Electronic components (left); Team sharing (right)

Figure 2: Material station (left); Mentor assisting a participant at a material station (right).

3.3 Data Collection and Analysis

Our main data sources were photo documentation of projects designed for the StitchFest judging and debriefing interviews with 15 participants (8 men, 7 women) from ten of the eleven final teams. Interviews were conducted over the phone a few weeks after the event. Questions targeted four principal areas: (1) background and interests, (2) hardware, software, and hackathon experience, (3) StitchFest knowledge, and (4) StitchFest experience. Some questions asked included: Why did you choose to participate in Stitchfest? Did you have previous experience with Arduino / Lilypad Arduino / coding / design? How did you decide on your design? Did you interact with other teams? These interviews were recorded and then transcribed. Two members of the research team coded the interviews using grounded theory [8], with open coding, axial coding and selective coding [23], to identify the themes that are presented in Findings sections in more detail.

4. FINDINGS

StitchFest proved to be a successful event and a productive hackathon experience for our participants. The most visible outcome was that the percentage of female participants in StitchFest was more than double than that in the larger hackathon: while PennApps had 14.8% women among its 1,200 participants, StitchFest counted 33% women among its 33 participants. What did we find out about participants' prior experiences and choices, their final projects, and changes in perceptions?

4.1 Background and Motivations for Joining

In general, female participants were significantly less likely to have hackathon experience than the males we interviewed. Only two women cited being involved in hackathons before, with one having participated PennApps, a software hackathon, and the other stating she had helped organize "small hackathons," which she liked because they were "more hands on." The five females with no previous hackathon experience expressed enjoyment. As one stated, "This is actually my first hackathon ever, and I loved it." In contrast, all of the male participants indicated they had had some form of hackathon experience, whether it be a software-based hackathon or a 48-hour design challenge around "events and spaces rather than programming or hacking." Participants with prior hackathon experience who joined StitchFest expressed: the desire to get "an edge on the competition… [with] a hardware hack"; having a team made up of "programmers and designers"; being able to leverage a hackathon's potential "to learn about [something] in a very accelerated way with a bunch of your friends.."; "...being able to use hardware, which usually has a very steep learning curve…[and is] reserved for electrical engineers"; and being "forced...to be a bit more creative when working with wearables."

Almost all StitchFest participants described having some level of coding experience (2 women expressed limited experience), and most (5 women, 6 men) also had hardware experience (though 2 women and 3 men described their experience as limited). Only one female stated having neither, though described having a design background. She explained that she "thought [StitchFest] was interesting because it could be somewhere a person can be creative, especially since [she] came from a design background." Overall, 6 men and 6 women indicated they had some design experience, though 2 of those men and 2 of those women described their prior experience as limited.

4.2 Diversity in Projects

The final Stitchfest designs included wearable music players, sensory reactive clothing for babies servicing as a parenting aid, responsive purses, wearable games, Twitter pins with changing social justice messages, and a participatory messenger/delivery service to address the needs of students and community-based package delivery (see Figure 3).

The interviews revealed that two particular design dimensions of StitchFest appealed to participants: (1) the design of wearables and (2) thematic focus on "Wear & Care." Wearables emerged as a salient motivation for many participants, but in different ways. Interest in "designing wearables" was cited exclusively by female participants whereas male participants saw them more as a source of novelty. Many female participants remarked on a variety of reasons for StitchFest's appeal, including "creativity," "combining technology, engineering and design," and "more flexibility and opportunities [than] just doing a pure software hack." Participants with prior hackathon experience (8 men, 2 women) expressed: the desire to get "an edge on the competition… [with] a hardware hack"; having a team made up of "programmers and designers"; being able to leverage a hackathon's potential "to learn about [something] in a very accelerated way with a bunch of your friends.."; "...being able to use hardware, which usually has a very steep learning curve…[and is] reserved for electrical engineers"; and being "forced...to be a bit more creative when working with wearables."

Figure 3: Examples of Final StitchFest designs.

Beyond novelty, social responsibility was a driving force for many designs, as well as a perceived need to the bridge between one's virtual context on social media and face-to-face interaction. One creator explained that her design of the Twitter pin served to "bring your online persona into real life so that you can make connections with people who you otherwise...maybe see on everyday basis but wouldn't know you have these things in common [with] or just a way to create conversation...on the street...and not just online." The creator of a responsive system for baby monitoring explained, "The idea was to create a set of electronics using the LilyPad or Arduino as the mother or the central hub. And then, to connect that to a ... thermal sensor and then have that all be sewable into clothing so that if, presumably your child was experiencing deviations in body temperature, then the LilyPad would be able to … send an SMS and an email to you."

4.3 Space for Collaboration within Competition

Participants also reflected on the design of StitchFest event, in particular the setup of the communal space, the sharing of hardware components and collaboration. Those with prior PennApps experience (3 males, 1 female) noted how the communal space at StitchFest created a greater sense of camaraderie and collaboration than usually found at PennApps. A hackathon-experienced male participant, comparing the two, commented on the diversity of the participants and the differences in the experiences:

> I think it kind of goes back to the camaraderie that you saw with a lot of the different groups because it was not so much a competitive thing even though there were prizes to be won… It was really more about seeing everybody succeed at making... and really having a sense of pride and ownership… I enjoyed interacting with other people a lot. It's a different background than you usually get at PennApps. It's a different type of people it attracts, which is cool.

Another male participant noted how the space and novel materials promoted team collaboration: "We got to see everybody else's projects, and see as they were progressing, especially since a lot of us were having some of the same issues at the same time…[and] figuring out how all the hardware worked… having to do a lot of the same fixes." Working with hardware materials and textiles also prompted a greater sense of division of labor within the team. An experienced female participant explained, "Everyone on my team... were pure computer science… and it was just very appealing to... have access to technology that we wouldn't otherwise have." She went on to discuss how StitchFest differed from software hacks she participated in:

> So previous events, we would just focus on software. It was a lot of fun. But there was really no reason to have... our whole group at the hackathon or to be coding... 24 hours... But doing a hardware hack, It ... made a lot more sense for us all to be there… And... we were able to greatly expand what we could build and what we could work on, to make something a lot cooler.

4.4 Diversifying Perceptions

Most novice and experienced computing and hackathon participants (5 women, 6 men) reflected on how StitchFest broadened their perceptions, with the exception of two individuals who already had experience with "wearables" (1 woman, 1 man), one woman with some hardware design experience, and one male participant who described only having a software background and found that working with hardware was not "beginner friendly." Overall, a common theme most participants shared was how using hardware and electronic textiles provided new ways to think about coding and computation. Crafting and making became skill sets that were necessary and instrumental to the process.

Novices, in particular, reflected on the uniqueness of StitchFest as an entry point and as a way to think about technology and computer science differently. A female participant with the least amount tech experience, reflected on how StitchFest was a good entry point to both the hackathon space and informal computer science learning:

> For me because it was… my first big hackathon experience… I felt like it was a nice entry point. I don't know if I would have participated in PennApps

> if it would have been much different, but StitchFest felt more... like a smaller community-based thing within this huge science event.

Another female participant, who had no prior hackathon experience, but some experience with crafting and technology, provided insights on why she decided to participate in StitchFest:

> ... Because it was something new that I haven't seen before, like competitions doing electronic textile type of stuff in person. I've seen online things, but nothing like that... I know how to do all the crafting part, but I'm not really strong on the coding part.

Despite her lack of coding experience, the appeal of combining her interests in crafting and coding influenced her perceptions of how the experience might be accessible to her skillset:

> ... the last half hour when we actually did the crafting part...because that's really my strong suit... connecting the components... I enjoyed that. I enjoyed talking with [another participant] ...and asking him for help and stuff... I enjoyed... networking with other people, meeting people.

While she did discuss having difficulty with coding and working with some of the more difficult components, she felt her skills were valuable to building the final project, and was able to seek and obtain help from fellow participants, with whom she was able to have positive networking experiences.

For most participants with coding or hackathon experience, working with electronic textiles provided new perspectives on computing. An experienced male participant expressed newfound affordances and application working with the LilyPad and textiles:

> I think that...working with some novel technology... was really interesting... It's fun in a way to struggle adapting to the new stuff and getting your hands dirty with the LilyPad and how it works and getting the connections right and actually sewing together the conductive thread to make something happen. It's really interesting especially for a computer programmer... or even people who've only worked with pins and wire hardware. There's really a lot you can do that previously a lot of the computer science people, speaking for myself, didn't think that that would have that much application, the application space would be that wide.

5. DISCUSSION

Results from Spring 2014 event observations, wearable designs and participant reflections indicate that *StitchFest* was successful in diversifying participation and perceptions. Participants stated they would recommend StitchFest to a range of different kinds of students, from art and design majors, to computer science and engineering majors, commenting on how StitchFest and its activities were applicable to a range of skill sets and interests. In reviewing the StitchFest theme, space and activities we found that the recommendations issued by NCWIT [19] captured the different dimensions of how hackathons can be redesigned to diversify participation and perceptions. However, we learned the the hard way when setting up StitchFest Fall 2014 that a list of recommendations alone is no guarantee for success. While the second iteration of StitchFest benefitted from our experiences in setting up the Spring 2014, having available examples of winning designs, we found that this was not sufficient to bring in larger number of female participants as we did in the Fall. We further discuss design dimensions of StitchFest that led participants to this productive experience, which include the hackathon theme and designing for collaboration within competitions.

In an effort to attract participants to StitchFest, we decided to provide a new, but related thematic focus. In Spring 2014, the theme was "Wear & Care" while in Fall 2014 the theme became "Stitch & Assist". Based on recommendations by the PennApps organizer that previous hackathons with focused themes were not well received, we tried to keep the theme broad enough to appeal to a wide range of interest while still pointing to wearables as an outcome. The diversity of projects designed by participants in either StitchFest provides a case in point that such broad themes can provide a good framing for the hackathon experience. But we also note that there are other hackathons that explicitly focus on an overall theme such as coding for a social good and thus bringing participants together that are motivated to contribute to a cause. What we learned is that providing themes can work in both directions—as a tool for recruitment and as a diversion—because themes can compete with current trends. For instance, in Fall 2014, we found that suddenly designing hacks for drones had become popular theme in light of Amazon's proposal to deliver goods with them, while wearables were definitely the hot trend in the Spring 2014 PennApps, with the arrival of the Pebble and wearable phone devices. Despite the addition of a different health-based subhackathon in Fall 2014 in addition to our own assistive theme, the trend of assistive hacks didn't materialize.

A second factor in the design of StitchFest was the focus on designing a space that fostered collaboration within a competition. While this design feature seems counterintuitive at first, we found that the reasons for participating in a hackathon has multiple attractions, winning only being one of them. The social interactions are in fact a key reason that many decide to spend a full weekend of non-stop hanging out together. Beyond the benefits of socializing, we also wanted to foster interaction and collaboration on a design level by not including some hardware components in all hackboxes. We let them know upfront when they picked up their materials that they could find these sensors or actuators in other team boxes and should ask for them. We realize that this request was possible because, unlike in other subhackathons, we were able to provide all materials free of charge thanks to an industry sponsor. We often observed how this particular request got members from different teams talking with each other and also exchange what they knew about the material component. Equally crucial in this context was the presence of mentors, provided by PennApps or through project members, in helping StitchFest members figure out thorny technical details.

Overall, the goal with StitchFest design was to open up coding competitions to other materials, topics, and participants. We found that this intense and short design experience lived up to its potential by bringing in newcomers and engaging them in designing compelling yet complex applications of electronic texiles in a competitive environment, as well as changing general perceptions, across experience levels, around valuable designs in a hackathon space.

6. ACKNOWLEDGMENTS

The research presented in this paper was made possible by a grant from NSF (#1238172). Materials and prizes for StitchFest were sponsored by IBM and Samsung. Any opinions, findings, conclusions and recommendations expressed in this paper are those of the authors and do not necessarily reflect the views of the funders or the University of Pennsylvania.

7. REFERENCES

[1] T.V. Abernathy and R.N. Vineyard. 2001. Academic competitions in science: What are the rewards for children? *The Clearing House, 74*(5), 269-276.

[2] C. Alvarado and E. Judson. 2014. Using targeted conferences to recruit women into computer science. *Communications of the ACM, 57*(3), 70-77.

[3] L. Buechley, M. Eisenberg, J. Catchen and A. Crockett. 2008. The LilyPad Arduino: using computational textiles to investigate engagement, aesthetics, and diversity in computer science education. In *Proceedings of the SIGCHI conference on Human factors in computing systems* (pp. 423-432). ACM.

[4] J. Dimond and M. Guzdial. 2008. More than paradoxes to offer: Exploring motivations to attract women to computing. Georgia Institute of Technology Technical Report. Retrieved July 14, 2014 from http://gacomputes.cc.gatech.edu/Members/jpdimond/dimond Paradoxes.pdf

[5] D. Dougherty. 2013. The maker mindset. In M. Honey & D.E. Kanter (Eds.), *Design, make, play: Growing the next generation of STEM innovators* (pp. 7-11). NY: Routledge.

[6] FIRST LEGO League. 2008. *More than robots: An evaluation of the FIRST Robotics competitions participant and institutional impacts.* Center for Youth and Communities Heller School for Social Policy and Management. Boston, MA: Brandeis University. Retrieved on December 7, 2011 from http://www.usfirst.org/uploadedFiles/Who/ Impact/Brandeis_Studies/FRC_eval_finalrpt.pdf

[7] J.H. Forrester. 2010. Competitive Science Events: Gender, Interest, Science Self-Efficacy, and Academic Major Choice. Unpublished Dissertation. NC: North Carolina University.

[8] B. Glaser and A. Strauss. 1967. *The discovery grounded theory: strategies for qualitative inquiry.* Aldin, Chicago.

[9] T.A. Greenfield. 1995. An exploration of gender participation patterns in science competitions. Journal of Research in Science Teaching, *32* (7), 735-748.

[10] A.L. Griffith. 2010. Persistence of Women and Minorities in STEM Field Majors: Is It the School That Matters? *Economics of Education Review 29*(6): 911–922.

[11] Y.B. Kafai, Q. Burke and C. Mote. 2012. What makes competitions fun to participate?: the role of audience for middle school game designers. In *Proceedings of the 11th International Conference on Interaction Design and Children* (pp. 284-287). ACM.

[12] Y.B. Kafai, E. Lee, K. Searle, D. Fields, E. Kaplan and D. Lui. 2014. A crafts-oriented approach to computing in high school: Introducing computational concepts, practices, and perspectives with electronic textiles. *ACM Transactions on Computing Education (TOCE), 14*(1), 1-20.

[13] Y.B. Kafai, N. Rusk, Q. Burke, C. Mote, K. Peppler, D. Fields, R. Roque, O. Telhan and K. Elinich (2014). Motivating and Broadening Participation: Competitions, Contests, Challenges, and Circles for Supporting STEM Learning. In J.L. Polman, E.A. Kyza, D.K. O'Neill, I. Tabak, W.R. Penuel, A.S. Jurow, K. O'Connor, T. Lee, & L. D'Amico (Eds.) *Proceedings of the 11th International Conference of the Learning Sciences: Learning and Becoming in Practice* (pp. 1219-1227).

[14] I. B. Kearse and C.R. Hardnett. 2008. Computer science olympiad: exploring computer science through competition. *ACM SIGCSE Bulletin, 40*(1), 92-96.

[15] S. Kuznetsov, L.C. Trutoiu, C. Kute, I. Howley, E. Paulos and D. Siewiorek. 2011. Breaking boundaries: strategies for mentoring through textile computing workshops. In *Proceedings of the SIGCHI Conference on Human Factors in Computing Systems* (pp. 2957-2966). ACM.

[16] L.C. Landivar. 2013. Disparities in STEM Employment by Sex, Race, and Hispanic Origin. *American Community Survey Reports, ACS-24,* U.S. Census Bureau, Wash, DC.

[17] S. Leckart. 2012. The Hackathon Is On: Pitching and Programming the Next Killer App. *Wired.* (Feb 17 2012) Retrieved June 10, 2014 from : http://www.wired.com/2012/02/ff_hackathons/

[18] J. Margolis, R. Estrella, J. Goode, J.J. Holme and K. Nao. 2008. *Stuck in the Shallow End.* Cambridge, MA: MIT Press.

[19] National Center for Women and Information Technology. 2013. *Top 10 Ways to Increase Girls' Participation in Computing Competitions* (Dec 2013). Retrieved July 23, 2014 from http://www.ncwit.org/resources/top-10-ways-increase-girls-participation-computing-competitions/top-10-ways-increase-girls

[20] National Science Foundation, National Center for Science and Engineering Statistics. 2013. *Women, Minorities, and Persons with Disabilities in Science and Engineering: 2013.* Special Report NSF 13-304. Arlington, VA. Available at http://www.nsf.gov/statistics/wmpd/.

[21] L. Rich, H. Perry and M. Guzdial. 2004. A CS1 course designed to address interests of women. *SIGCSE Bulletin 36* (1), 190–194.

[22] R. Roque, Y.B. Kafai and D. Fields. 2012. From tools to communities: Designs to support online creative collaboration in Scratch. In *Proceedings of the 11th International Conference on Interaction Design and Children* (pp. 220-223). ACM.

[23] A. Strauss and J.M. Corbin. 1990. *Basics of qualitative research: Grounded theory procedures and techniques.* Sage.

[24] The Design-Based Research Collective. 2003. Design-based research: An emerging paradigm for educational inquiry. *Educational Researcher, 31* (1): 5-8.

[25] L. Tsui. 2009. Recruiting Females into Male Dominated Programs: Effective Strategies and Approaches. *Journal of College Admission, 8* (13), 9-13.

[26] S. Yardi and A. Bruckman. 2007. What is computing? Bridging the gap between teenagers' perceptions and graduate students' experiences. In *Proceedings of the 3rd International Workshop on Computing Education Research.* ACM, Atlanta, GA, 39-50.

[27] S. Zweben. 2012. Computing Degree and Enrollment Trends from the 2010-2011 CRA Taulbee Survey: Computing Research Association. Retrieved June 30 2014 from: http://cra.org/govaffairs/blog/2012/04/undergrad-computerscience-enrollments-rise-for-fourth-straight-year-cra-taulbeereport/

Computer Scientists at the Biology Lab Bench

Andrea Tartaro
Furman University Computer Science Department
3300 Poinsett Hwy.
Greenville, SC 29613
00+1+864-294-2932
andrea.tartaro@furman.edu

Renee J. Chosed
Furman University Biology Department
3300 Poinsett Hwy.
Greenville, SC 29613
00+1+864-294-3248
renee.chosed@furman.edu

ABSTRACT
We present the development, implementation and evaluation of a new team-taught introductory computer science course focused on the topic of bioinformatics. Our course is unique when compared to other bioinformatics and interdisciplinary (biology and computer science) courses taught to undergraduates. Instead of analyzing data provided to them, students collect their own data at the biology lab bench and then analyze their data utilizing various bioinformatics tools in the computer lab. In addition, while other bioinformatics classes focus on programming, our course introduces other computer science topics relevant to the biological problems under investigation such as artificial intelligence, networks and databases. Our approach resulted in students acquiring an appreciation for how biology and computer science function synergistically.

Categories and Subject Descriptors
K.3.2 [**Computers and Education**]: Computer Science Education
J.3 [**Life and Medical Sciences**] Biology and genetics;

General Terms
Measurement, Design, Human Factors

Keywords
Bioinformatics; Genetics

1. INTRODUCTION
Why are students in an Introduction to Computer Science class extracting DNA from samples collected from their dogs in the biology lab? In this paper, we describe Introduction to Computer Science through Bioinformatics, an introductory computer science class where students work in the biology lab and the computer lab to understand the connections between the disciplines. Bioinformatics is typically introduced as an upper-level class with both computer science and biology prerequisites. We argue bioinformatics can be used to introduce students without experience in biology or computer science to various topics in computer science while they *generate* and *analyze* data to solve biological problems. This approach is in response to the call from various organizations to demonstrate how interdisciplinary science is practiced in a professional context [1-3].

SIGCSE '15, March 4-7, 2015, Kansas City, MO, USA

http://dx.doi.org/10.1145/2676723.2677246

In what follows, we provide the motivation for using biological problems and a survey-based approach in introductory computer science, and discuss how our course draws on, and is different from, similar approaches, such as Harvey Mudd's "BioCS1", Wellesley's computational biology and Tuskegee's bioinformatics [4-6]. We then describe how we introduced biological problems and computer science approaches to solving those problems, and summarize student experiences obtained from survey data. We conclude with plans for future offerings of the course based on this feedback.

2. BACKGROUND AND MOTIVATION
2.1 Interdisciplinary Motivation
Science magazine recently described an "explosion" of bioinformatics careers and the need for professionals trained in both the biological and computational sciences [7]. Organizations in both computer science and biological science disciplines also stress the need for undergraduate courses to reflect how science is practiced in professional contexts. Outside of undergraduate institutions distinctions between science disciplines are increasingly blurred. For example, molecular biologists routinely use computer science tools to analyze whole genome sequences to identify single nucleotide polymorphisms (SNPs; alterations to the DNA code) associated with specific disease phenotypes. By creating divisions between science disciplines when teaching undergraduates we are shielding our students from opportunities to see how these disciplines actually function synergistically. Our course challenges students in their first computer science course to blur some of these lines.

Computer science education literature is increasingly contextualizing computing in topic-based or themed introductory courses, including multimedia computing [8], artificial intelligence and games [9]. The IEEE/ACM joint task force on computing curriculum encourages this practice in their new Curriculum 2013 document as a way of illustrating the application of computer science to areas beyond traditional jobs, diversifying the appeal of computer science and attracting new majors [3]. Initial evidence suggests this approach increases enrollment in introductory courses, increases the number of students from other majors who take introductory computer science and increases enrollment of women in CS1 and CS2 classes [9].

Similarly, the American Association for the Advancement of Science (AAAS) urges the intersection of biology with other disciplines, specifically computer science, in undergraduate courses [1]. Their 2011 report states that "all students should have experience applying concepts and subdisciplinary knowledge from within and outside of biology in order to interpret biological phenomena" [1]. The *BIO2010* report from the National Research Council echoed these sentiments and advises demonstrating connections between the science disciplines "so that interdisciplinary thinking and work become second nature" [2].

Our introductory interdisciplinary course aims to address these needs by weaving biological topics into a computer science course and demonstrating the interdependency of the disciplines.

2.2 Survey- and problem- based introductory computer science course

In our previous work, we argue that, in addition to contextualizing computing in an interdisciplinary problem, introductory computer science should use a survey-based approach to introduce the discipline to both majors and non-majors [10]. While there are a number of approaches to computer science curriculum, the traditional sequence of core classes delays introducing students to the breadth of computer science until they take upper-level electives. Our approach introduces programming as one topic, but allows professors to discuss other areas of computer science as they relate to the focus of their course. In this article, we focus on bioinformatics; for additional examples, see [10].

2.3 Where this course fits in the curriculum

Introduction to Computer Science through Bioinformatics is one section of a series of Introduction to Computer Science classes that follow a survey- and problem- based approach. Each section has its own focus problem, and instructors choose computer science topics appropriate to their focus. This course serves as both the first course for CS majors and as a general education requirement or elective for non-majors. Biology students did not receive credit towards the Biology major. We do not consider this course a "CS0" course, because CS0 classes are typically intended for non-majors only. It is also not a "CS1" class, which typically emphasizes programming. Students continuing into a major in computer science will take a traditional CS1 course following this course, or they have the option to take CS1 concurrently.

2.4 Related Courses

Several universities offer introductory and upper level interdisciplinary bioinformatics courses taught within biology and computer science departments [4-6, 11, 12]. Many courses are directed at a specific student audience such as biology majors whereby the biology content is emphasized [6, 11]. The introductory BioCS1 course at Harvey Mudd contains sufficient content to fulfill the introductory requirement for both biology and computer science majors [4]. The computational biology course at Wellesley was designed for computer science students who had taken programming and biology students who had taken molecular genetics [5]. Our course is housed within the computer science department and is the first course in the computer science major.

A unique aspect of our course is the experience our students gain in the biology lab. We feel it was crucial for students to be exposed to biology in the lecture as well as is in the laboratory. Experience generating their own data at the biology lab bench not only allows students to learn how data is collected, but also provides a sense of ownership of the data and subsequently excitement to have the opportunity to analyze it. Similar courses at Harvey Mudd, Wellesley and Tuskegee University involved computer lab experiences but offered no biology wet labs [4-6].

3. COURSE CURRICULUM

Our course incorporated biological concepts as examples for various computer science topics (Figure 1). The course was co-taught: a computer science instructor taught the CS topics and a biology instructor taught the biology topics (Table 1). Our curriculum focused on integrating these topics through all aspects of the course including lecture, labs, homework and exams.

Table 1. Topics covered in the course.

Course Topic (which instructor led topic in parentheses)	Number of lectures (1 ¼ hours)	Number of lab days (2 hours)
Programming (CS)	6	3
Databases (CS)	2	
Algorithms (tree construction) (CS)	1	
Artificial Intelligence (CS)	1.5	
Networks and the Internet (CS)	1.5	
Human Computation (CS)	1	1
Architecture (CS)	1	
Ethics (CS and BIO)	1	
Systems (CS)	1	
Genetics (BIO)	5	
Sequence analysis (BIO)	1	4
Phylogenetic tree construction (BIO)		2
Protein folding and structure (BIO)	3	
Molecular biology wet lab (BIO)	1	4

3.1 Lecture framework

In lectures, we directed students from a basic biological concept, through a biological problem, and then to a computer science solution. For example, introduction of the Central Dogma of molecular biology in lecture paved the way for students to learn Python in order to transcribe and translate a given DNA sequence to its corresponding RNA and amino acid sequence. We taught the students how it is essential to know the amino acid sequence of a protein corresponding to each gene so researchers can determine the corresponding 3D protein structure. To demonstrate the importance of solving protein structure, we described the mechanism of the anti-cancer drug Gleevec and its interactions with amino acids within a specific protein. The problem of solving how proteins "fold" to form these 3D structures has been addressed using a variety of computer science techniques. The various solutions include Rosetta, algorithms for predicting protein structures executed using high-performance computing systems [13], Rosetta@Home, a system that enables users to donate processing power to solve protein structures [14], genetic algorithms for protein predictions (e.g., [15]) and Fold-it, an online game where users interact with 3D models to fold protein structures [16]. These diverse approaches motivated discussions on search trees, artificial intelligence, networks, distributed computing, human computation/crowd-sourcing and human-computer interaction.

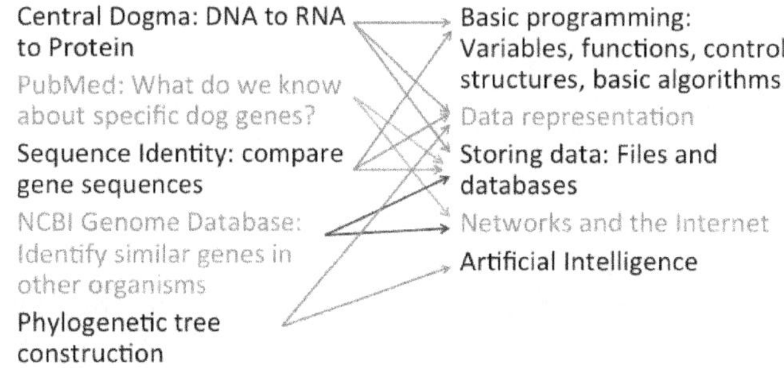

Figure 1. Examples of Computer Science topics (right) with associated Bioinformatics connections (left) employed in this course.

3.2 Laboratory Work – where the biology and computer science complemented one another

Student-generated data in an inquiry-based lab course is essential to demonstrate the inherent connections between biology "at the bench" and data analysis on the computer. In this authentic lab experience, students "experience the success and failure of lab research" which others have shown influences students' perception towards science research [17]. They have the opportunity "actually explore data" that they collected which has proven beneficial to students taking statistics courses [18].

We developed a semester-long series of lab activities that incorporated data collection at the biology lab bench and data analysis in the computer lab. The overall goal of the lab was for students to identify dog breeds and their placement on a phylogenic tree through gene sequence comparisons. The lab was based on an inquiry-based lab developed at Williams College called "Comparison of a Highly Polymorphic Olfactory Receptor Gene Subfamily in Genetically Diverse Dog Breeds" [19]. We gave students cheek cell samples from various dogs obtained from colleagues and students at the university. Students isolated Genomic DNA and used Polymerase Chain Reactions (PCR) to amplify specific olfactory genes. We selected genes based on a study by Tacher *et al.* that identifies various single nucleotide polymorphisms (SNPs) in specific olfactory genes for certain dog breeds [20]. To amplify the genes, students designed primers in the computer lab based on various criteria (i.e. melting temperature, primer length, etc.). Upon successful amplification of the genes, they analyzed and purified the products using gel electrophoresis, and we subsequently sent the products for DNA sequencing. Students performed all of these molecular techniques in the biology lab with guided instructions. The materials required for the wet labs cost approximately $1000. The cost was covered by university lab fees. The biology instructor provided all preparation and supervision for the wet labs so no additional staff were utilized. These biology lab experiences alternated with work in the computer lab. Students were provided with raw DNA sequence files (from their amplified olfactory genes) directly from the sequencing facility. They utilized several programs [21-25] to edit their sequences, translate their sequences, perform multiple sequence alignments, identify SNPs and generate phylogenetic trees to demonstrate relatedness among the dog breeds studied in the course, the Boxer reference sequence and an outlier species. Students presented their findings in the format of a scientific journal article.

In addition to using online tools, students also wrote algorithms or programs using Python for several of these tasks. For example, students wrote a program in the computer lab to calculate the percent sequence identity between two DNA sequences, wrote a program for homework to generate an amino acid sequences from

Table 2. Example of student homework

```
Function header comments, getCodonAt, writeSequenceToFile and transcription removed for brevity.
def codonToAminoAcid(codon):
    # Compares the input String with the possible codon String possibilities. If they are the same,
    # then it will output the String abbreviation of that Amino Acid or Stop if it is a stop codon.
    if codon=="UUU" or codon=="UUC":
        return "Phe"
    elif codon=="UUA" or codon=="UUG":
        return "Leu"
    [additional elifs for other codons removed for brevity]
    # For all cases in which the inputed String does not match any of the above String (codon)
    # possibilities, print out the indicated informative error message and output the string Error"
    else:
        print("A codon consists of a 3 nucleotide unit of mRNA.")
        print("This is not a valid codon.")
        return "Error"
def getSequenceFromFile():
    # Asks the user to get a filename and saves it to a variable
    file = input("Enter the filename that holds your sequence: ")
    # Opens the file and reads it, saving the text to a variable
    rFile = open(file, "r")
    text = rFile.read()
    # Closes the file
    rFile.close()
    # Outputs the sequence as a String
    return text
def translation():
    # Asks the user for the mRNA file sequence
    rnaSeq = getSequenceFromFile()
    # Initializes the String as empty
    aaString = ""
    # Determines the number of codons by dividing the sequence length by three, and saves it to a
    # variable
    numCodons = len(rnaSeq)/3
    # Loops through the sequence in groups of three nucleotides then converts those nucleotides into
    # an Anino Acids and saves that amino acid to a variabe. It then concatenates that amino acid onto
    # the variable designating for the full amino acid string
    for position in range(0,int(numCodons)):
        currentCodon = getCodonAt(rnaSeq,position)
        aaString = aaString+codonToAminoAcid(currentCodon)
    # writes the new amino acid sequence to a file
    writeSequenceToFile(aaString)
```

a given DNA sequences (Table 2), and wrote an algorithm for an exam to calculate the melting temperature for a given sequence (an important step in designing a primer). The exam question then required students to demonstrate their understanding of how to design a primer through additional questions (Table 3).

This process of students accumulating their own data and then analyzing it emphasizes how the biology and computer science disciplines go hand in hand. If students were just provided sequence files from a database to manipulate and generate phylogenies, they would not have gained an appreciation and understanding of where and how those sequence files were obtained. The process of manipulating raw sequence data, utilizing online programs to process the data and writing Python programs that could accomplish some of the steps in this process gave the students an understanding of the complexity of the programming involved in creating those online utilities. These activities demonstrate how biology and computer science disciplines intersect in the area of bioinformatics.

4. STUDENT EXPERIENCES

We conducted an evaluation via pre- and post- surveys to explore why students took the course, what benefits they gained from the course, and how it affected their interest in computing and bioinformatics. Twenty-two students completed the pre-survey and eleven students completed the post survey.

Table 3. Exam questions with selected student responses

Problem 1. Recall from the Primer Design Lab that the formula for calculating the melting temperature for a primer sequence of DNA is: $T_m = 2\ (As + Ts) + 4\ (Gs + Cs)$

Where A is the number of Adenine nucleotides in the sequence,

T is the number of Thymine nucleotides in the sequence,

G is the number of Guanine nucleotides in the sequence, and

C is the number of Cytosine nucleotides in the sequence.

Part 1: Write an algorithm for a program that calculates the melting temperature for a given sequence of DNA.

Part 2: Why is it necessary to calculate the T_m for primers used in a PCR reaction?

Student Responses:

Part 1. *1) Ask the user to input a sequence and save to a variable*

2) Declare and initialize four variable at zero, representing the number of As, Ts, Gs, and Cs

3) Loop through all the letters in the sequence.

A. If the current letter is A, redefine your number of As variable as number of As +1

B. Or if the current letter is T, redefine your number of Ts variable as number of T's +1

C. Or if the current letter is G, redefine your number of Gs variable as number of G's +1

D. Or if the current letter is C, redefine your number of Cs variable as number of C's +1

E. Otherwise, print "Error" and return "Error"

4) Calculate melting temperature using number of As/Ts/Gs/Cs variables and save to a variable

5) Return melting temperature

Part 2. *"PCR requires a specific temperature for primers to anneal to the template."*

4.1 Who took the course

Enrollment in the bioinformatics course included fourteen women and nine men (Table 4). 41% of students specified Computer Science while 27% specified Biology as their intended major on the pre-survey. 32% of the students listed "Other/None" as their intended major (other majors listed instead of or in addition to Computer Science or Biology include: Accounting, Business, Chemistry, Math, Neuroscience, Philosophy, Physics, Pre-health, Sociology and Spanish). According to the pre-survey, five students had computer programming experience prior to the course.

Table 4. Course enrollment data

	Freshman	Sophomore	Junior	Senior	Total
Female	9	4	1	0	14
Male	2	1	1	5	9
Total	11	5	2	5	23

4.2 Why students took the course

Both the pre- and post- surveys used an open-ended question to ask students why they are/were interested in taking the class. Students provided a variety of answers from a general "It sounded interesting" to specific interest in the topic of the course. One student on the pre-survey specifically cited the theme of the course as a reason, and five students on the pre-survey and four students on the post survey mentioned both biology and computer science, or an integration of the two fields, in their reason. Nine students on the pre-survey and three students on the post survey listed the course as a requirement for their major, or recommended for pre-health, and one student said it applied to his or her intended career. Other students took the course because they felt it was important to know about computers and learn about computers in general (4 pre, 3 post; Table 5).

Table 5. Student pre- and post- survey responses to the question: "Why are/were you interested in taking the class."

Reasons mentioned in their written response:	Pre	Post
Required/recommended/first course for major/pre-health	9	3
Interested in CS as a potential major.	2	0
Important to know about computers; To learn about computers in general	4	3
Interested in computational biology, medical field; include both biology and cs topics in their answer	6	4
The theme of the course	1	0
Applicable to their career	1	0
General education credit	1	0
"it sounded interesting"	1	1
Other	1	0

4.3 Benefits of the class

A key motivation for our course is prescriptions from the ACM and IEEE, the National Research Council, and AAAS for courses with interdisciplinary connections in general, and biology and computer science specifically. Did students gain an appreciation for the interdisciplinary nature of computer science and important connections between biology and computer science? The post survey asked, "Which of the following benefits, if any, do you feel like you've gained by taking this course? Select all that apply." Table 6 lists the options and how many respondents selected each response. Notably, nine out of ten respondents selected "A better understanding of how computer science applies to other fields," as a benefit of the course.

Table 6. Student post-survey responses to the question: "Which of the following benefits, if any, do you feel like you've gained by taking this course."

Options	Number of selections
A better understanding of how Computer Science applies to other fields.	9
A greater understanding of algorithmic thinking.	7
Specific abilities I did not previously possess.	3
Other	0
None of the above	1

The survey also asked an open-ended question, "What did you learn in this course?" Six out of ten responses mentioned integration of computer science and biology, or use of algorithms for analyzing biological data. For example, one respondent said, "[I learned] A LOT. I got to see a little bit of how the technology side interacts with the biology side" (emphasis theirs). Note those six responses focused on integration of computer science or algorithms and biology, and did not simply list biology and computer science topics without mention of a relationship between the two disciplines, for example, "How to program using python and the basics of genetics."

Taken together, these results suggest students valued learning computer science in an interdisciplinary context and gained an integrated understanding of bioinformatics.

4.4 Interest in Computing and Bioinformatics

The pre- and post- surveys included several questions to gauge student interest in computing and bioinformatics, including "In general, how interested are you in computer science or applications of computing?" (pre and post); "How interested are you in biology and bioinformatics?" (post only); "How, if at all, did your interest in computer science or applications of computing changed since taking [the course]?" (post only); "How if at all, did your interest in biology and bioinformatics change since taking [the course]?" (post only); "Are you interested in or planning to take [introduction to computer programming, the next course in the major]?" (pre and post); "Would you be interested in a follow-on course to this class on this, or a related, topic?" (pre and post); and "Do you expect to take any other course(s) in the Computer Science Department?" (pre and post). Student responses were mixed and did not change appreciably between the pre- and post- surveys.

5. DISCUSSION

Our distinct approach to teaching an interdisciplinary introductory course required immense "buy-in" from students. It necessitated exposure to diverse content, including computer programming, artificial intelligence, human computation tools, databases, networks and the Internet, as well as genetics, basic biochemistry and molecular genetics lab techniques. Students took the course for assorted reasons (Tables 4 and 5), and their expectations varied. For example, computer science students may have anticipated a course with programming as the main focus. However, this course contained only three weeks of programming. Biology majors enrolled were generally eager to learn direct applications to the biological concepts from previous biology courses. In contrast, students taking the course for mathematical reasoning credit (required as part of our university's general education requirement) could be overwhelmed by the prospect of having to learn two different science disciplines in a single course. In our minds, the course covered bioinformatics as a discipline. Yet students perceived the course as some balance of computer science and biology, and this balance was often not what they were anticipating or preferred. As described below, future offerings of the course will have to address this perception issue.

6. FUTURE PLANS

This course will be taught for a second time in the upcoming academic school year. Based on student survey results from the first offering of this course we gained valuable feedback for future offerings. Student surveys demonstrated mixed feelings of interest in the bioinformatics discipline. We made use of bioinformatics tools when analyzing canine gene sequence data, yet based on student surveys, this was not enough to highlight the utility of the discipline. In the next offering, we plan to take the students to a cancer center affiliated with a local hospital where they will meet researchers utilizing tumor genome sequencing technology to aid in personalized medical care. Students may need to see bioinformatics in action and how tools guide physicians in developing individualized cancer treatment plans.

Another goal is to incorporate the online statistics software program R into the course. This free program uses command line programming, which will be familiar to students due to their experience using Python. Students can use R to model datasets (potentially breast cancer incidence rates). They can then ask biologically relevant questions based on the models [26]. This type of activity clearly links computer science and biology, which may aid in improving students' perception of the bioinformatics discipline, and is useful for biology students who may encounter R in other courses.

The biology lab portion of the course will be modified to include analysis of genes related to visual characteristics of dogs in place of olfactory genes. SNPs in specific dog genes link to variation in coat phenotype (length or curl state) [27], and a single SNP in the *IGF1* gene links to dog height (short versus tall breeds) [28]. Using these genes would allow students to compare photographs of the dogs to their genetic data and consider their results in relation to characteristics they can observe.

Overall, the course resulted in a unique pairing of biology at the bench with specific computer science topics that helped students understand the relationship between the fields.

7. ACKNOWLEDGMENTS

Our thanks to Michele Johnson at Trinity University for sharing her evolution lab experience and teaching materials with us, the Integrative STEM Learning: Pedagogy and Partners Conference hosted by the Trinity University HHMI Program (October, 2012), Kevin Treu, Dennis Haney and Sam Hill.

8. REFERENCES

[1] American Association for the Advancement of Science (AAAS). 2011. Vision and Change In Undergraduate Biology Education: A Call To Action. http://visionandchange.org/files/2013/11/aaas-VISchange-web1113.pdf.

[2] National Research Council (US) Committee on Undergraduate Biology Education to Prepare Research Scientists for the 21st Century. 2003. *BIO2010: Transforming*

Undergraduate Education for Future Research Biologists. Washington, DC.

[3] The Joint Task Force on Computing Curricula Association for Computing Machinery IEEE Computer Society, Curricula 2013: Curriculum Guidelines for Undergraduate Degree Programs in Computer Science. 2013. http://www.acm.org/education/CS2013-final-report.pdf.

[4] Dodds, Z., Libeskind-Hadas, R., and Bush, E. 2012. Biol as CS1: Evaluating a crossdisciplinary CS context. In *Proceedings of the 17th ACM Annual Conference on Innovation and Technology in Computer Science Education*. ACM, 268-272.

[5] Tjaden, B. 2007. A multidisciplinary course in computational biology. *J. Comput. Sci. Coll.* 22, 6, 80-87.

[6] Qin, H. 2009. Teaching computational thinking through bioinformatics to biology students. *SIGCSE Bull.* ACM, 41, 1, 188-191.

[7] Levine, A.G. 2014. An explosion of bioinformatics careers. *Science.* 344, 6189, 1303-1306.

[8] Guzdial, M. 2003. A media computation course for non-majors. *SIGSCE Bull.* ACM, 35, 3, 104-108.

[9] Barr, V. 2012. Creating Two, Three, Many Courses: An Experiment in Contextualized Introductory Computer Science. *Proceedings of CCSC Northeastern Conference*. 19-25.

[10] Tartaro, A., Cottingham, H. in press. A Problem-based, Survey Introduction to Computer Ccience for Majors and Non-Majors. *Journal of Computing Sciences in Colleges.*

[11] Dymond, J.S., Scheifele, L.Z., Richardson, S., Lee, P., Chandrasegaran, S., Bader, J.S., and Boeke, J.D. 2009. Teaching synthetic biology, bioinformatics and engineering to undergraduates: the interdisciplinary build-a-genome course. *Genetics.* 181, 1, 13-21.

[12] Maloney, M., Parker, J., LeBlanc, M., Woodard, C.T., Glackin, M., and Hanrahan, M. 2010. Bioinformatics and the undergraduate curriculum. *CBE-Life Sciences Education.* 9, 3, 172-174.

[13] Raman, S., Qian, B., Baker, D., and Walker, R.C. 2008. Advances in Rosetta protein structure prediction on massively parallel systems. *IBM Journal of Research and Development.* 52, 1.2, 7-17.

[14] Das, R., Qian, B., Raman, S., Vernon, R., Thompson, J., Bradley, P., Khare, S., Tyka, M.D., Bhat, D., and Chivian, D.: 2007. Structure prediction for CASP7 targets using extensive all-atom refinement with Rosetta@home. *Proteins: Structure, Function, and Bioinformatics.* 69, S8, 118-128.

[15] Pedersen, J.T., and Moult, J. 1996. Genetic algorithms for protein structure prediction. *Current Opinion in Structural Biology.* 6, 2, 227-231.

[16] Cooper, S., Khatib, F., Treuille, A., Barbero, J., Lee, J., Beenen, M., Leaver-Fay, A., Baker, D., and Popović, Z. 2010. Predicting protein structures with a multiplayer online game. *Nature.* 466, 7307, 756-760.

[17] Bownell, S.E., Kloser, M.J., Fukami, T., and Shavelson, R. 2012. Undergraduate Biology Lab Courses: Comparing the Impact of Traditionally Based "Cookbook" and Authentic Research-Based Courses on Student Lab Experiences. *J. of Coll. Sci. Teach.* 41, 18-27.

[18] Moore, D.S. 1997. New Pedagogy and New Content: The Case of Statistics. *International Statistical Review.* 65, 2, 123-165.

[19] Banta, L.M., Crespi, E.J., Nehm, R.H., Schwarz, J.A., Singer, S., Manduca, C.A., Bush, E.C., Collins, E., Constance, C.M., and Dean, D. 2012. Integrating genomics research throughout the undergraduate curriculum: a collection of inquiry-based genomics lab modules. *CBE-Life Sciences Education.* 11, 3, 203-208.

[20] Tacher, S., Quignon, P., Rimbault, M., Dreano, S., Andre, C., and Galibert, F. 2005. Olfactory receptor sequence polymorphism within and between breeds of dogs. *The Journal of heredity.* 96, 7, 812-816.

[21] Integrated DNA Technologies (IDT). 2012. PrimerQuest program. http://www.idtdna.com/Scitools.

[22] SerialCloner 2-6-1. 2013. http://serialbasics.free.fr/Serial_Cloner.html.

[23] Galtier, N., Gouy, M., and Gautier, C. 1996. SEAVIEW and PHYLO_WIN: two graphic tools for sequence alignment and molecular phylogeny. *Computer applications in the biosciences: CABIOS.* 12, 6, 543-548.

[24] Gouy, M., Guindon, S., and Gascuel, O. 2010. SeaView version 4: a multiplatform graphical user interface for sequence alignment and phylogenetic tree building. *Molecular biology and evolution.* 27, 2, 221-224.

[25] Larkin, M.A., Blackshields, G., Brown, N., Chenna, R., McGettigan, P.A., McWilliam, H., Valentin, F., Wallace, I.M., Wilm, A., and Lopez, R. 2007. Clustal W and Clustal X version 2.0. *Bioinformatics.* 23, 21, 2947-2948.

[26] R Development Core Team. 2008. R: A Language and Environment for Statistical Computing. http://www.R-project.org.

[27] Cadieu, E., Neff, M.W., Quignon, P., Walsh, K., Chase, K., Parker, H.G., VonHoldt, B.M., Rhue, A., Boyko, A., and Byers, A. 2009. Coat variation in the domestic dog is governed by variants in three genes. *Science.* 326, 5949, 150-153.

[28] Sutter, N.B., Bustamante, C.D., Chase, K., Gray, M.M., Zhao, K., Zhu, L., Padhukasahasram, B., Karlins, E., Davis, S., and Jones, P.G. 2007. A single IGF1 allele is a major determinant of small size in dogs. *Science.* 316, 5821, 112-115.

Data Journalism: Lessons Learned While Designing an Interdisciplinary Service Course

Christopher Plaue
The University of Georgia
Athens, GA
plaue@uga.edu

Lindsey R. Cook
U.S. News & World Report
Washington, DC
lcook@usnews.com

ABSTRACT

We present the design and implementation of an interdisciplinary service course on data journalism, a first-ever collaboration between the computer science department and college of journalism at our institution. The course covered the basics of dataset acquisition, cleaning, and analysis, and taught key programming and web development concepts. Students created an online portfolio of exercises, culminating in a news story and data visualization. The course was well received by students coming from a variety of backgrounds. We provide recommendations for future iterations of this course.

Categories and Subject Descriptors

K.3.2 [Computers and Information Science Education]: Computer Science Education – Curriculum - Literacy.

General Terms

Design, Experimentation.

Keywords

Data journalism; non-majors; curriculum; visualization.

1. INTRODUCTION

The computer science education community has long researched the merits of interdisciplinary coursework. Much of this research involves combining STEM fields, such as biology, physics, or mathematics, with computer science concepts. In addition, the education community is active in researching the design of data-centric courses, such as data mining, database design, and data science. Many of the courses focused on data organization and processing target upper-level undergraduate computer science majors.

In this article, we describe the design, implementation, and evaluation of an experimental service course on data-driven journalism (referred to as data journalism) [9]. This one-semester course introduces core computing and data processing concepts to graduate-level journalism students who have had minimal exposure to advanced mathematical and computer science concepts. Over a 15-week semester, the data journalism course covered four broad topics: data acquisition, data cleaning, programming fundamentals (variables, control structures, functions), web development (HTML/CSS), and data presentation (UX design, JavaScript, HTML, CSS, and tools for making interactives such as TileMill). Class time consisted of a mix of lecture, interactive activities, self-paced lab exercises, and guest speakers. Throughout the semester, students worked on selecting a news story on a health topic. Students produced a final news package with a written article and accompanying data visualization using acquired data sets.

We conducted quizzes at the beginning and end of the semester to gauge student performance. In addition, 55% of the class was interviewed at the end of the semester to gain course feedback beyond traditional course evaluations. Overall, all students indicated that skills obtained in this course allowed them to become more competitive in their fields and knowledgeable talking with peers. We present lessons learned and suggestions for course revisions for future course sections.

SIGCSE '15, March 4–7, 2015, Kansas City, MO, USA
Copyright 2015 ACM 978-1-4503-2966-8/15/03...$15.00
http://dx.doi.org/10.1145/2676723.2677263

2. RELATED WORK

Data journalism is defined as a workflow that consists of:

- obtaining datasets via scraping or Freedom of Information Act Requests
- cleaning (i.e. correcting errors and structuring data) and manipulating large datasets (i.e. using similar fields to combine relevant datasets)
- producing original data analysis using statistical concepts,
- designing graphics, visualizations, or multimedia accompaniments
- using statistics to tell stories and illustrate concepts in an easy-to-understand way
- creating media that has value for readers [9]

Thus, data journalism is inherently interdisciplinary and involves aspects of computation as well as large data sets and processing. In this section, we frame data journalism as a natural extension to the existing body of literature on interdisciplinary computing work, designing curricula involving data, barriers to enrollment, and the importance of guest speakers.

Role and Nature of Interdisciplinary Work: Computer science is increasingly becoming interdisciplinary, and the research community has long discussed and explored the benefits of including interdisciplinary courses within curriculums. Formally, Cassell defines interdisciplinary within computing fields as "collaborative efforts involving at least two fields, with at least one of them being computing" [4]. Several benefits are noted for both majors and non-majors, where the former gain context for how their technical skills can be applied in real world settings, and the latter find the acquisition of new technical skills to extend their craft [3]. Additionally, researchers note a correlation between interdisciplinary computing courses and the recruitment of more women to computing—an underrepresented population [7]. Furthermore, interdisciplinary courses are attractive to high caliber students [13].

We note that many of the interdisciplinary courses discussed in the CS education community focus on combining computing fundamentals with STEM fields, such as mathematics, physics, biology, or chemistry. Additional work combines computing concepts with the arts, humanities, and social sciences [e.g. 12]. Our work extends computing interdisciplinary courses by focusing on journalism, which does not appear to have been heavily explored in the computing education community.

Data Processing and Science Courses: The explosion and availability of data has sparked much academic research on designing computing tools and workflows to manage and process data. Subsequently, much work in the education community aims on designing and implementing courses involving data management, processing, and visualization. For instance, Sullivan describes an introductory course designed to teach non-majors several methods for processing large data collections [14]. Other research outlines strategies to incorporate large data sets into introductory-level computer science courses to provide real-world applications [2] or simply the application of data processing to specific domains such as healthcare, business, and security [16].

Additionally, entire curriculums are focusing on data science, a term by Cleveland to describe an interdisciplinary expansion of statistics involving data analysis collaborations in multiple subject areas [5]. In their paper describing their data science degree program, Anderson *et al* note that at least 19 academic programs of study exist pertaining to data science [1].

Data journalism is a natural extension to explore for interdisciplinary course design, since it stresses the investigation of large data sets, emphasizing communication and story telling.

Practical Knowledge in the Classroom. Interdisciplinary courses provide "real-world" applications for concepts learned in class. However, we note that many other disciplines offer some sort formalized practical experience as part of the curriculum. For instance, pharmacy students are required to perform clinical rotations and primary education majors are required to student teach. Many computing curriculums do not have formal mechanisms for bridging the gap between the curriculum and professional practice, but rely on (optional) uses of guest speakers, adjunct faculty, mentors, internships, and class projects to bridge the gap between theory and practice [8].

In journalism education, Columbia University Dean Nicholas Lemann suggested a "teaching hospital" model in 2009, sparking much discussion in that community [11]. In this model, student work in a newsroom setting during class producing stories or projects as they would in a real newsroom. These stories are published for real audiences. The journalism curriculum at our institution implemented this model of education both for its broadcast journalism majors, but also in the graduate Health and Medical Journalism program, where students submit class assignments to be published in journalism outlets.

As the students in our course were in a program leveraging the teaching hospital model, we were expected to incorporate aspects of this model in the data journalism class. In particular, by using some flipped-classroom strategies, we used class time for students to work on their news stories and visualizations and collaborate with each other. We encouraged, but did not require, students to submit their stories to publication venues. We frequently had a faculty member with extensive journalism experience sit in on class to provide context to the real-world applications.

Barriers to Enrollment: The Stigma of Computer Science: A challenge faced when designing interdisciplinary courses is attracting non-majors. As Davis *et al* note, the stigma and stereotypes of computer science courses may deter participation or enrollment in these courses [6], particularly amongst underrepresented populations. At our institution, for instance, the Bachelor of Science in Computer Science major consists of approximately 84% males, while the Bachelor of Arts in Journalism major is about 72% female. We encountered some barriers to enrollment that we speak more about in Section 3.2.

Journalism: Past and Future. As a discipline, journalism presents several obstacles in designing interdisciplinary courses that are not as prevalent in STEM fields, including minimal exposure to mathematics and computer science classes. In a survey of the journalism curriculum of five highly regarded institutions (Northwestern, Missouri, Arizona State, University of North Carolina, and University of Georgia), we note that all disciplines do not require mathematics courses beyond the core requirements of each institution. Furthermore, none of these curricula require any computer science or general computing courses taught through a computer science department. Within the journalism curriculum of these schools, students are, not surprisingly, heavily exposed to communication and story-telling concepts. In contrast, many computer science programs, especially ABET-accredited, only have students take one or two classes to allow students to develop communication skills.

However, Northwestern does recommend (but does not require) introductory level computer programming courses, an introductory data management and information processing, and human-computer interaction course for journalism students interested in computational journalism [15]. Our proposed service course presents key concepts of introductory programming, data management, and human-computer interaction concepts.

We note evidence indicating a sharp increase in the level of interest of data journalism skills. The National Institute for Computer-Assisted Reporting (NICAR), a top conference on data journalism, has seen attendance nearly triple from 335 to 997 over 2004 to 2014. Also, NICAR has seen an increase in the number of women coders. Major news organizations, including The Washington Post, The New York Times, and Gannett, are expanding desks for interactive graphics, which require the expertise of journalists with coding skills. As the Nieman Foundation at Harvard notes, the number of data journalists having reporting and coding skills is quite low, leading them to be dubbed "journalism unicorns" [10].

3. COURSE DESIGN

3.1 History and Inception

The Health and Medical Journalism (HMJ) graduate program at The University of Georgia is at two-year, non-thesis Master of Arts degree that emphasizes professional training, multimedia skills, and research. Students in the HMJ program have access to interdisciplinary collaborations, namely through the College of Public Health and the Georgia Regents University Medical Partnership. In 2012, Patricia Thomas, the director of the HMJ program, took note at a conference that reporters who manipulated data sets, code, and tell stories through interactive graphics were well-received by symposium attendees. As a result, she reached

Figure 1. Classroom setup for JOUR 7800.

out to the computer science department to start the first-ever collaboration between the College of Journalism and the Department of Computer Science, housed in the College of Arts and Sciences.

JOUR 7800 was designed in collaboration between a computer science faculty member with expertise in information visualization and human-computer interaction, a journalism faculty member with extensive professional experience, and a senior-undergraduate journalism major who was also minoring in computer science. This undergraduate student had substantial reporting experience and had interned with The Washington Post's interactivity team.

3.2 Course Goals

JOUR 7800 was proposed to expose students to the process of acquiring, cleaning, and analyzing large data sets, as well as learning the essentials of user-centered design in order to create effective visualizations for news stories. As a survey course, the initial learning outcomes included:

- using Microsoft Excel to import, clean up, and perform initial analyses of data
- learning the essentials of programming (via JavaScript) and web development (via HTML, and CSS)
- applying the Wehrend and Lewis analytical framework to explore relationships in data
- using investigative tools such as Google Refine
- applying the principles of user-centered design in order to create effective visualizations to tell a story
- searching through government databases effectively
- designing and executing a Freedom of Information Act (FOIA)
- creating an effective, interactive visualization
- creating an interactive map

The head of the Health and Medical Journalism program at UGA recruited students for the class via word of mouth. Since students expressed hesitation at taking a computing concepts course, JOUR 7800 was marketed as an experimental course, and as such, would be a pass-fail elective at the 7000 level. The course was designed assuming no prior programming experience. Nine graduate students enrolled in the pilot class.

3.3 Class Structure

3.3.1 Facility

JOUR 7800 met for a three-hour session one day each week over Spring 2014 semester. This format was required due to scheduling availability of the hybrid discussion-computer laboratory facility (Figure 1). This classroom houses 15 workstations based along the periphery of the classroom and supports students working individually, or be seated in a discussion-friendly format around a large center table. The classroom was equipped with a projector.

3.3.2 Student Information

The course population was predominately female (2 male) and approximately split between first and second year graduate students. The majority of students had earned an undergraduate degree in liberal arts (English, journalism or history). Three students had science backgrounds and earned their undergraduate degrees in biology, biochemisty and neurobiology.

At the beginning of the semester, the class completed a questionnaire to self-rate themselves for various scenarios of using technology (Table 1a). In large, students were strong users of technology; most (7 of 9) had taken a general computing class as undergraduates. No one in the class had taken a programming class and the class was split on attitudes towards mathematics.

The second part of the questionnaire included pop-quiz questions regarding coding concepts and Excel formulas (Table 1b). In large, students knew basic Microsoft Excel and descriptive statistical measures (e.g. when to use a median, mean, and standard deviations), but largely did not understand the more technical concepts related to HTML and while loops.

3.3.3 Class Format

The three-hour block was divided between lecture, presentations, guest speakers, and hands-on laboratories. Students would present their homework results at the beginning of the next class period.

3.3.4 Guest Speakers

To incorporate practical knowledge within the classroom, four guest speakers were invited to give one-hour talks. The invited guest speakers included:

Table 1: Student Demographic Information

Part A: Self-Ratings	No. Positive Responses
I am confident in my abilities to use a search information to find information	9 (100.0%)
I have experience using photo editing software to remove red eye from a digital picture	8 (88.9%)
I have set up a home wireless network	5 (55.6%)
Part B: Code and Formula Questions	
Able to correctly identify a line of code as being HTML	6 (66.7%)
Able to identify how many times a while-loop repeats	1 (11.1%)
Able to correctly identify which Excel formula sums up 10 cells	7 (87.5%)
Able to correctly identify a relative column, absolute cell reference in Excel	4 (50.0%)
Able to correctly identify the hexadecimal representation for the color blue	1 (11.1%)

Table 2: Course Activities and Associated Content

Unit	Course Activities	Associated Content
Data Acquisition ~2 weeks	• Search through government databases for relevant data sets • Prepare a public information request (e.g. FOIA) • Discuss the challenges associated with public information requests	• Guest speaker with extensive experience as a journalist submitting FOIA requests • Guest speaker with extensive experience receiving and providing data requested
Data Cleaning ~ 2 weeks	• Use Microsoft Excel and Google Refine to spot errors and reformat data sets • Know characteristics of suspicious data	• Lab on advanced formulas and pivot table usage in Microsoft Excel • Guest speaker with domain knowledge of data security and integrity
Programming & Web Fundamentals ~ 5 weeks	• Create a web page using HTML and CSS • Use Scalar Vector Graphics • Write a method using JavaScript to accomplish a goal, using selection statements, loops, output, etc.	• Code Academy units on HTML, CSS, and JavaScript • Lecture notes on computational thinking and introducing JavaScript
Data Presentation ~ 5 Weeks	• Create a barchart and map using Google Fusion Tables and embed the HTML code in a Web Page • Create an interactive map using TileMill and Moustache • Create wireframes of Websites and data visualizations • Create a bar chart using D3 and JavaScript • Use the Wehrend and Lewis analytical framework to explore and report relationships in data • Describe proper visualization techniques to effectively convey data, including multi-variate and time-series data.	• Weinschenk, S. *100 Things Every Designer Needs to* Know About People. ISBN: 978-03217675350 • Murray, S. *Interactive Data Visualizations for the Web.* ISBN: 978-1449339739 • Wehrend and Lewis. "A Problem-Oriented Classification of Visualization Techniques", Proc. Vis 90, pp 139-143. • Amar, et al. "Low Level Components of Analytic Activity in Information Visualization," Proc. *Vis 05*, pp 111-117. • Tufte, E. "Visual and Statistical Thinking: Displays of Evidence for Making Decisions", from *Visual Explanations*.

- an expert on designing and executing Freedom of Information Act requests
- the Open Records Manager for the University of Georgia, who is responsible for responding to requests for information from the University under the State of Georgia's Open Records Act
- a computer science faculty member specializing in information and data security, discussing issues impacting the trust of data provided
- a data journalist from the Washington Post discussing her background and the set-up and skill variations on interactive graphics teams in major newsrooms

3.4 Software Packages

One goal for the class was to minimize purchases of additional software. Thus, software packages used in the course were either freely available or were provided through the university. In particular, JOUR 7800 used Microsoft Excel, GitHub, TileMill, Google Refine, Google Fusion Tables, QGIS, and Data-Driven Documents (D3).

To the best of our knowledge, there is no one textbook that covers all of the topics of this course. In particular, general computing textbooks cover a substantial amount of additional material that is not covered in the class. The two required texts for the class were Murray's *Interactive Data Visualization for the Web* and Weinschenk's *100 Things Every Designer Needs to Know About People*, supplemented with selected Fair Use book chapters or conference papers.

3.5 Course Content

The general breakdown of content with associated resources is provided in (Table 2).

3.5.1 Data Acquisition

The unit on data acquisition focused on locating, examining and searching through government data sets. In-class exercises primarily used datasets obtained from HealthData.gov and FDA.gov. To provide practical knowledge about gaining data through public information requests, we had two guest speakers provide their expertise from drastically different viewpoints: the journalist submitting requests and the administrator at our institution who receives requests.

3.5.2 Data Cleaning

Data sets are often "dirty" where it may be formatted incorrectly or inconvenient for data processing. In addition, data sets may contain erroneous data. Our data-cleaning unit focused on using Google Refine and advanced features of Microsoft Excel to spot questionable data and reformat data. Specific topics included:

- using conditional rules to highlight data that exceeds the expected range
- using advanced Excel formulas including VLOOKUP, RIGHT, LEFT, SEARCH to combine and format data
- using Excel formulas to change contents of a cell into more useful formats (e.g. convert a date in the format of 2/13/2014 into 4 columns with a weekday, day, month, and year)
- identifying characteristics of suspicious and/or misleading data.
- using Google Refine to correct spelling mistakes in hand-entered data

3.5.3 Programming Concepts

This unit first taught students the essentials of web development by exposing HTML and CSS via assigned lecture notes and self-paced tutorials. For the tutorials, we selected Codeacademy's interactive lessons on HTML and CSS, available free-of-charge at http://www.codeacademy.com. The Codeacademy tutorials taught essentials of HTML design and how to use CSS selectors and positioning while providing guided feedback to students. In this aspect, we "flipped" the classroom, where individual learning occurred at home and class time was used for interactive group activities and for "connecting the dots" between the two disciplines. Likewise, we introduced essential programming concepts through a mix of assigned lecture notes and Codeacademy's interactive lessons on JavaScript, using class time for group activities and providing hands-on time for students to seek assistance with concepts that they found challenging.

The following is a summary of topics covered in this unit:

- *programming essentials*: expressions, statements, and variables; assignments; for-loops, while-loops, basic I/O, functions

  flow control: if statements, switch statements, Boolean expressions
- *objects:* object-oriented thinking
- *HTML:* structure, tags, tables
- *CSS:* selectors, layout, styles, and rules

3.5.4 Data Reporting and Visualization Techniques

This unit was taught over a period of about 5 weeks and included readings based on Edward Tufte and Susan Weinschenck, both of which feature design principles and recommendations. These design principles were used in an in-class activity critiquing visualizations that the students found. In addition, the instructor taught user-centered design methods. As part of a motivation for the course, Martin Wattenberg's Baby Name Wizard was used as an example of an interactive visualization of a large, public data set. Students critiqued the Name Wizard along dimensions of usability, interaction design, and journalistic value.

In addition to the basic chart capabilities in Microsoft Excel, the following methods of data reporting were presented:

- *Microsoft Excel Pivot Tables*, for large data set summaries
- *Google Fusion Tables* to create basic charts and maps of data, providing HTML code that can be embedded into Web pages
- *TileMill*, an online resource that allows users to design aesthetically pleasing interactive maps using a CSS-like class structure, complete with libraries for geographical landmarks, roads, political boundaries, etc.
- *Data-Driven Documents (D3),* a JavaScript library for creating interactive (and often strikingly beautiful) visualizations.

3.6 Portfolios

For the second half of the semester, students worked on creating online portfolios, applying their HTML and CSS skills learned during lab and homework. Students hosted their portfolios as Web pages on GitHub, which provides free web hosting. During the HTML and CSS labs, we walked students through creating a basic web page. As students completed additional activities, they added references to the web page. Students also were taught how to use Git for version control purposes.

The final project in the course consisted of each student picking a story that he or she wished to focus on, conducting background research, acquiring and clean data, interviewing multiple sources, conducting analysis, and turning in completed visualization with companion story and methods. Many of these students were investigating stories for other health and medical journalism classes and were allowed to continue investigating the stories of interest provided they found new data and created original content for this class.

4. EVALUATION

We administered an electronic pop quiz towards the end of the semester, consisting of JavaScript, HTML, CSS code questions and concepts, and practical knowledge inventory (e.g. URLs and resources). The class scored an average score of 75.1 on the exam (high 92, low of 56), and we provide a summary of performance on code-specific questions in Table 2.

To gain more insight into students' experiences in the course, we offered an extra credit opportunity of having students be interviewed by the teaching assistant. Interviews consisted of a series of open-ended questions regarding their backgrounds, experiences in the course, any plans for using the skills gained in the course, and recommendations for improvement of the course. Interviews lasted for approximately 20-30 minutes. Several themes emerged through comments.

Theme 1: Recognition of the importance for technical skills

Most students said they thought the skills learned in the course would help them gain employment. Two students who had been looking for work after graduation said they had already referenced the class in interviews and were received with great enthusiasm from potential employers._One student remarked, "... *I even mentioned this when I was applying for this job. The fact that I'm in this class that's all about taking numbers and turning it into meaningful stories. I think that's always useful, being able to take raw data and turn it into something people can connect with.* " Another student remarked that, ".... *Because it is a different way of thinking to sit down and figure out the best way to tell your story, and to know that there are those options available, and how can you go about that and either do it yourself or talk to somebody else about how you want to do this.*"

One student noted the growth of interest in data journalism: "*When [the program director] was first telling us about it [the data journalism class] I was just smiling, because I know that this is what everybody is talking about right now in journalism.*" Another student remarked on the potential professional benefits of the skills obtained in the data journalism class: *"[Building data visualizations] will be useful even if they don't use it on a site and I write about something and I just quickly put together something on say Google Fusion, [employers] would appreciate that I think even if they don't use it. Like, 'Wow they put something together, maybe we could come up with something even cooler than Fusion graph table'*"

Theme 2: Increasingly comfortable, but still reserved, with coding principles

One student indicated her increase in being comfortable with coding: *"Yeah, I think I would feel more comfortable now. Really, just going to this class even though I don't know that I would tell*

Table 2: Qualitative Assessment Results

	No. Positive Responses
Able to identify a line of correct HTML code	7 (77.8%)
Able to correctly identify an application of absolute vs. relative Excel statement	6 (66.7%)
Able to correctly identify critical HML tags	7 (77.8%%) 8 (88.9%) 9 (100%)
Able to correctly identify loop output	5 (55.6%)
Able to correctly identify correct JavaScript relational tests	7 (77.8%)

people I can build you any visualization you want. I would at least feel comfortable looking at a [CS] class description and kind of having an idea of 'OK. What is this class going to teach me?' Or talking to a professor and getting an idea of whether a class is even within my range of accessibility. I think that definitely after this class I would feel more comfortable looking at different classes and being confident enough to enter something."

Of the five students interviewed, four said they now felt comfortable enough to take a computer science class from the computer science department. While students expressed that they initially felt comfortable in taking JOUR 7800 because it was offered in the journalism building ("home field advantage"), they also indicate that the class gave them the confidence and skills necessary in order to continue studying computer science. We note that interdisciplinary courses with journalism fields may represent a way to draw interest in computing from women, since most journalism programs are predominately female.

5. CONCLUSIONS

Overall, JOUR 7800 was well received by students. From the perspective of the computer science instructor, who has a strong background in information visualization, it was challenge to teach a class where students did not have strong technical skills, but had exemplarily communication and story-telling skills.

We offer recommendations for future iterations of this course including those targeting undergraduates, as well as similarly designed courses:

- The class should be taught using an A-F grading scheme. Since each lesson built upon the skills acquired each week, an A-F grading scheme would likely encourage students to complete their homework assignments in a timely fashion, using graded homework deliverables. The students who scored weakest on the assessment quiz were often behind on their assignments while meeting other deadlines.
- The JOUR 7800 class should change to a traditional lecture + a lab. The three-hour meeting time was draining for students and was not robust to unexpected weather closings or changes in the curriculum. We often had to make adjustments to the curriculum to adjust to students needs.
- JOUR 7800 should become a joint JOUR/CSCI prefixed course. A mix of journalism and computer science students has the potential to help both populations hone their analytical and communication skills.
- The final project should have more milestones to help students see progress more clearly.
- An introductory level textbook for programming concepts that includes interactive feedback would be beneficial. While Codeacademy is a free resource, we ran into numerous issues in the JavaScript modules with the interactive feedback engine. Students often exhibited frustration while completing these modules. One suggestion would be to use a Pearson textbook that includes MyProgrammingLab where the instructor can assign homework or lab assignments that provide helpful feedback. In addition, the instructor would have instant access to students' performance and be better able to gauge which subject areas students are mastering or struggling in.

6. ACKNOWLEDGEMENTS

We especially thank Patricia Thomas and the Knight Foundation for their exceptional and enthusiastic support of the development of this course. We also thank the following for their contributions: Dean Charles N. Davis, Darla Cameron, Mitch Clayton, Barry Hollander, Kang Li, Cletus Stripling, and the ONA/AP-Google Scholarship. Lastly, we are most appreciative for the additional support provided by the UGA President's Venture Fund.

7. REFERENCES

[1] Anderson, P., Bowring, J., McCauley, R., Pothering, G., Starr, C. An undergraduate degree in data science: curriculum and a decade of implementation experience. In Proceedings of *SIGCSE '14*, Atlanta, GA, pp. 145-150.

[2] Bart, A., Tilevich, E., Hal, S., Allevato, T., Shaffer, C. Transforming introductory computer science projects via real-time web data. In Proceedings of *SIGCSE '14*, Atlanta, GA., pp. 289-294.

[3] Carter, L. Ideas for adding soft skills education to service learning an capstone courses for computer science students. In Proceedings of *SIGCSE '11*, Dallas, TX, pp. 517-522.

[4] Cassel, L. Interdisciplinary computing is the answer: now, what was the question. *ACM Inroads*, 2, 1, pp. 4-6, 2011.

[5] Cleveland, W. Data science: an action plan for expanding the technical areas of the field of statistics. *ISI Review*, 69, pp. 21-26, 2001.

[6] Davis, D., Yuen, T., Berland, M. Multiple case study of nerd identity in a CS1 class. In Proceedings of *SIGCSE '14*, pp. 325-330.

[7] Fisher, A, and Margolis, J. Unlocking the clubhouse: the Carnegie Mellon experience. *SIGCSE Bulletin*, 34(2), pp. 79-83, 2002.

[8] Gibbons, T. Course guides: a model for bringing professionals into the classroom. In Proceedings of *SIGCSE '12*, Raleigh, NC, pp. 105-109.

[9] Gray, J., Chambers, L., Bounegru, L. The data journalism handbook:. O'Reilly Media, 2012.

[10] LaFrance, A. Columbia is launching a new post-bac program to breed journalism unicorns. Nieman Journalism Lab. Retrieved August 1, 2014, from: http://www.niemanlab.org/2013/08/columbia-is-launching-a-new-post-bac-program-to-breed-journalism-unicorns/

[11] Lemann, M. Journalism schools can push coverage beyond breaking news. *Chronicle Review, Chronicle of Higher Education.* November 15, 2009.

[12] Manaris, B., McCauley, R., Mazzone, M., Bares, W. Computing in the arts: a model curriculum. In Proceedings of *SIGCSE '14*, Atlanta, GA, pp. 451-456.

[13] Raicu, D. and Furst, J. Enhancing undergraduate education: a REU model for interdisciplinary research. In Proceedings of *SIGCSE '09*, Chattanooga, TN, pp. 468-472.

[14] Sullivan, D. A data-centric introduction to computer science for non-majors. In Proceedings of *SIGCSE '13*, Denver, CO, pp. 71-76.

[15] Undergraduate Handbook, Medill School of Journalism. Retrieved on August 1, 2014 from http://www.medill.northwestern.edu/_pdf/MedillUGRDHandbook1213FINAL.pdf

[16] Zheng, G., Zhang, C., Li, L. Bringing business intelligence to healthcare informatics curriculum. In Proceedings of *SIGCSE '14*, pp. 205-210.

Introducing Computing Concepts to Non-Majors: A Case Study in Gothic Novels

Heather Bort
Marquette University
MSCS Department – Cudahy Hall
1313 W. Wisconsin Ave.
Milwaukee, WI 5233
heather.bort@marquette.edu

Mimi Czarnik
Alverno College
Department of English
3401 S. 39th Street
Milwaukee, WI 53234
marian.czarnik@alverno.edu

Dennis Brylow
Marquette University
MSCS Department – Cudahy Hall
1313 W. Wisconsin Ave.
Milwaukee, WI 5233
dennis.brylow@marquette.edu

ABSTRACT
This paper presents an approach to integrating computer science and quantitative literacy concepts in an undergraduate English Literature course. We show how students with no prior background in computer science can engage in computing activities directly related to their topic of interest and gain a deeper understanding of their topic as well as a better appreciation and understanding of computer science and quantitative literacy in the process. Students work in an interdisciplinary learning environment focusing on literary analysis and quantitative literacy with computing concepts acting as the bridge between the two areas.

Categories and Subject Descriptors
K.3.2 [**Computer and Info Science Education**]: Computer Science Education

General Terms
Human Factors

Keywords
Computer Science Education; Network Analysis

1. INTRODUCTION
Computing based technology has never been more pervasive, accessible, or consumable. Computer science has altered the way we live, work, and learn. While the technology continues to advance rapidly, advancements in computer science education have been comparatively slow, creating a situation rife with significant social inequality. Foundational computer science concepts and the skills to create and innovate rather than solely consume computing technology are increasingly becoming "privileged knowledge", students are attempting to enter the workforce and institutes of higher education without an understanding of the most influential discipline in science, academia, and the economy today [30].

Many believe that computer science should be elevated to a core subject in our schools. By relegating this relevant and engaging discipline to a superfluous filler status, we do a disservice to the students who will be the innovators of tomorrow [30, 8]. In order for computer science to earn a place amongst the other core academic subjects in our schools, we must show the subject to be independent and academically rigorous while at the same time proving the value of integrating its concepts across the curriculum.

SIGCSE'15, March 04–07 2015, Kansas City, MO, USA.

http://dx.doi.org/10.1145/2676723.2677308

This paper presents and evaluates an approach to integrating computer science and quantitative literacy concepts into an undergraduate English Literature course. The results of this approach are a set of cross-curricular activities that:

1. Deepen understanding of both computer science and English literature, without unnecessarily diluting the content of either, and
2. Inform students of the myriad opportunities available to them with interdisciplinary scholarship in computer science.

The concepts incorporated are used as a tool – a tool that facilitates a deeper level of self-reflection and analysis, which translates to an ability to better understand and present material in the subject to which the tool is applied.

2. PRIOR WORK
There is a great interest in increasing access to computer science education for all students, especially those from underrepresented populations. One of the first steps in an attempt to broaden participation should be to look at the factors that are contributing to the unbalance in representation. A major barrier to increased enrollment in computer science has been identified as student misperception of the discipline. This misperception takes the form of a general lack of understanding and familiarity with the subject [14, 31, 22, 20, 5, 16]. Add to that the pervasive cultural stereotypes that depict computer science as overwhelmingly for white males with innate ability and we have illustrated a large obstacle; not only to increasing participation, but also to effecting positive attitudes toward computer science. One of the goals of our project is to tackle this obstacle, so we directly explore the misperception and stereotypes, with the aim of altering our students understanding of computer science as an interesting and relatable subject.

Once the barrier has been identified, there are many ways in which we can work to overcome it. Some initiatives have focused on changing the way students view computer science outside of the classroom, using a widely popular approach to expose both children [11] and adults [7] to programming by gaming activities. While we applaud the success that these initiatives, and the many like them, have had; we have focused our development on students that would not be interested in the gaming aspect of computing.

Others have had success by redesigning their introductory computer science courses to be more attractive to a diverse student body [23, 1, 2]. One of the better known examples of this method, [1] uses an approach that focuses on three areas of improvement, updating the programming course to be attractive to a broader student population, building community among students in the computer science program starting in the first year of study, and providing research experiences for their students. While our approach does focus on building community through social computing experiences and providing students with opportunities to engage in research; this project differs from these types of initiatives in that it is not a computer science course, and we are not attempting to increase the number of students graduating with a degree in computer science. The goal of our research is instead to introduce students to the ways in which computer science applications and concepts can enhance their work in other fields of study.

Another group of initiatives take advantage of the interdisciplinary nature of computer science and computational thinking by offering undergraduate computer science courses on the general education tract to appeal to non-majors [9, 29, 28, 10, 17]. The case for computing as a general education course as explained by [9], shows how having computer science courses outside of the computing major improves equity of access to learning computer science. Some of the programs use computational thinking concepts in disciplines other than computer science to improve students analytical and problem solving skills [28], expose students to concepts that they may have been previously unaware of in a variety of high interest freshman level courses [10], or in a single course designed to expose a broader pool of students in a transdisciplinary environment [29]. There are even courses that focus on improving a non-major students programming abilities as a way to meet other university requirements [17]. Much of the research in using an inter- or multi-disciplinary approach in computing and general STEM areas has have very positive results [6, 19] and is well recommended even at a K-12 level [26]. Our approach is interdisciplinary, we use computing and quantitative thinking concepts to expose students to computer science outside of a traditional computing course; however, we differ from similar work in that we are not focusing on students in STEM fields and we are not attempting to introduce computer science to students before they have clearly defined ideas about their major. We have based our work in upper level humanities courses so that students can have experiences working with computer science as it applies directly to their major.

3. SETTING

Since the early 1970s, the second author's school has developed and implemented an ability-based curriculum, based on certain assumptions about student learning. These include: education goes beyond knowing to being able to do what one knows; and, educators are responsible for making learning more available by creating and publishing outcomes for student learning in the majors. In order to graduate, students must demonstrate development levels of eight college-wide abilities, as well as advanced outcomes in their disciplinary majors. The college-wide abilities are: communication (which includes quantitative literacy), analysis, problem-solving, social interaction, valuing in decision-making, effective citizenship, developing a global perspective, and aesthetic engagement [21].

In 1999, this institution received an NSF grant to explore and implement assessment of quantitative literacy across the curriculum, and at all levels of instruction. As a part of the project, one of the co-authors of this paper developed an assessment in a course entitled, "The 19th Century British Novel," surrounding the monetary worth of characters in Great Expectations. Using a conversion formula from The Victorian Web [18], which translates 19th-century Victorian pounds into 20th-century American dollars, students calculated each character's wealth, compared the monetary possessions of two characters, and wrote an essay exploring what this exercise revealed about characters and character relationships in the novel. This example of quantitative literacy in the humanities differs from those described in the rest of this paper in that it was a single, free-standing assessment; while the students gleaned new knowledge and new strategies for engaging with Victorian novels, the assessment did not appear to lead to any longer-term changes in the ways the students approached literary analysis.

In the 2014 course offering, we integrated quantitative literacy and computing concepts throughout the course, in ways that supported the course outcomes, and built upon existing student knowledge and abilities in literary analysis. We were able to develop meaningful and useful activities by transposing current scholarly knowledge from its "original habitat" to school by working to rebuild the knowledge in a teachable environment [4]. Information Processing Theory states that meaningfulness improves learning and retention by helping the learner in the process of encoding the information and storing it in long term memory [25].

Since the student population we were working with had no prior background in computing or quantitative literacy, we were careful to engineer the activities so that we stayed within the Zone of Proximal Development (ZPD). Vygotsky's Sociocultural theory explains that the ZPD is not only the level of potential development the learner can achieve through the guidance of a teacher, it is also the interaction between the learner and society where new forms of awareness can occur if the teacher provides the proper scaffolding [25]. As with the information processing theory, it is better to make new information by integrating it with known information, this is the reasoning behind bringing the new computer science and quantitative literacy learning into a context that the learner will already be familiar with.

4. COURSE STRUCTURE & MOTIVATION

Mary Shelley believed readers of the Gothic novel- and she counted herself as one- derived pleasure from the genre because it spoke to the "mysterious fears of our Nature." Almost one hundred years later, Virginia Woolf described the Gothic as the "genre which fulfills the strange human craving for feeling afraid." At its birth in late eighteenth-century Britain, in part as a reaction to the Age of Reason, the Gothic novel reflected the crisis of identity of a nation moving into a new century. And today, in the 21st Century, the literary form still exerts a profound influence on Western popular culture.

This is a course that explores the evolution of the Gothic novel throughout the 19th century. With readings consisting of a classic Gothic novella, an early spoof of Gothic novels, and Victorian fiction which incorporated Gothic elements. The course also examines ways that Gothic elements still appear in popular fiction, movies, and television.

Unit 1: History of the Novel and Introduction to Gothic Themes
Major Texts: *The Vampyre*, by John Polidori (1816), and *Northanger Abbey*, by Jane Austen (1817). Major Framework: Formalist
Unit 2: Madness and Marriage
Major Texts: *Jane Eyre*, by Charlotte Brontë (1847). Major Framework: Feminist
Unit 3: Victorian Childhood
Major Texts: *Great Expectations*, by Charles Dickens (1861). Major Framework: Historical
Unit 4: Fin de Siècle Worldviews
Major Texts: *A Picture of Dorian Gray*, by Oscar Wilde (1890). Major Framework: Psychoanalytical
Unit 5: The Gothic in the 21st Century
Major Texts: Student Choice Major Framework: Review of all

Figure 1: The Five Units of the Course

Organizing questions of the course include:

- What is it about the Gothic that has made it so seductive to readers past and present?
- And what can we learn about our cultures and ourselves at this moment in human history through reading and exploring this genre?

4.1 Course Outcomes

4.1.1 Traditional Outcomes

The course outcomes for this senior-level class, incorporate the school's college-wide ability outcomes [22] of analysis and aesthetic engagement, and English major outcomes.

- To refine reading skills necessary for thorough and timely critical analyses of extended pieces of literary fiction. This includes the use of appropriate literary frameworks to analyze, evaluate, and place in context the novels we will read this semester,
- To analyze and evaluate professional literary criticism with an awareness of the main ideas, assumptions, literary concerns, and historical moment of the essay,
- To identify and describe relationships between the British novel and the culture out of which it grew,
- To formulate theories which explain changes in the form, content, and reputation of the novel, and
- To demonstrate engagement with literature through creative responses.

In addition to abilities that are integral to literary studies, such as analysis and aesthetic engagement, this course validates students in intermediate problem-solving. The student:

- Performs all phases or steps within a disciplinary problem solving process, including evaluation and real or simulated implementation,
- Independently analyzes, selects, uses, and evaluates various approaches to develop solutions, and
- Integrates quantitative abilities to effectively communicate information and respond to problems within a discipline-related context.

4.1.2 New Outcomes

Added to the course's abilities, for the purposes of this project, were school-wide intermediate quantitative literacy criteria, which are:

- Shows evidence of a reflective, deliberate choice to use quantitative information in a discipline related context,
- Considers use of and, as appropriate, effectively uses calculators, and spreadsheet, graphing, or discipline specific software to communicate quantitative information,
- Organizes, appropriately uses, and clearly communicates quantitative information,
- Shows a refined sense of effective ways to present quantitative information for a specific audience, and
- Evaluates her own use of quantitative information and argument and the implications of her choices.

4.2 Course Units

The course is broken up into 5 units, as shown in Figure 1, each focusing on a particular text and critical framework [3]. All of the texts are in the public domain, and available from sites such as Project Gutenburg [15].

5. METHODS

For this study we used two different methods of collecting data. We had the students take a pre-course, free response survey. The survey asked about students' experience with computer science courses and computer programming, their opinions on computer science and mathematics as alternatives to their current major, and their perception of careers in computer science. This survey was taken again after completing the computing activities developed for the course to gain an understanding how the students perception of computer science and their confidence in computing and quantitative tasks was effected by the activities over the semester.

In addition to the survey, we looked at student work over the semester to gauge their understanding of the concepts being presented. The work done during class was collected and evaluated to ensure that students were correctly using the new methods presented to them. In addition to class work, students were asked to give written response to research articles employing the methods explained in class to current and relevant research in literary analysis.

5.1 Survey Demographics

The students in the course all identified themselves as female and English majors in the survey, none of the students indicated that they have taken any computer science or programming courses as undergraduates and many of them did not understand what was meant by the question: *What programming languages do you use?* Some of the representative answers to this question were:

- "What does that even mean?"
- "I am not sure I understand this question enough to answer this."
- "Apparently gibberish, because I'm afraid I'm not certain what this means."

5.2 Course Development

Due to the student demographic we needed to develop activities that would introduce computer science concepts without requiring much background knowledge but would also be involved enough to accurately represent usefulness of computer science to the field of Literary Analysis. We were also careful to leave the original course structure intact, our aim was not to force two courses together and only get half of each. Rather, we sought to find activities that enhanced the learning outcomes and course goals that were already in place, while providing an alternate method of analysis for the students to experience. Each activity was developed to build upon the previous activities in such a way that would provide students with an opportunity to develop their quantitative literacy skills over the course of the semester instead of have a single activity that was disconnected from the other parts of the course.

6. WORD FREQUENCY & TEXT MINING

In unit one the students focused on applying a Formalist framework of literary analysis to *The Vampyre* and *Northanger Abbey*. The first course activity reviews the formalist practice of close-reading applied to a passage from *The Vampyre*, where students analyze a text at the diction level, they look for patterns and vocabulary as well as symbol and metaphor among other literary elements. This is a very common activity in literature courses and lends itself well to computational tools. As an introductory computing activity in class, the students used the online word cloud tool, Wordle [13], to visualize word choice in the assigned passage. Following the prompt: *What does the Wordle tell you about the passage? What do you think about the use of word counts for literary analysis?*

Students engaged in a discussion of word count as literary analysis. They were given an article to read [27] which relayed findings of a recent research endeavor using text mining for literary analysis and were required to write a response to the article. These are responses that are representative of the class:

- "I find it very interesting that diction and syntax can be analyzed with a technological tool and in turn, can give us quantitative data about literature according to different categories."
- "It is extremely fascinating what these computational methods can discover."

The goal of this first exercise was to get the students thinking about how computer science could be used in literary analysis. We used this activity to introduce the students to scholarly research that joined their own discipline to computer science and quantitative literacy.

7. NETWORK ANALYSIS

In literary analysis, using an Historical (Marxist) framework [3], the reader is interested in how socioeconomic status shapes the experiences of the characters. In previous offerings of this course, the students create a character map to show relationships and status of characters from the novel *Great Expectations*. A character map can look very much like a graph, with the characters as nodes and the relationships as edges.

Since *Great Expectations* has an extensive list of characters with complicated relationships, we chose to begin working on graphing with students at the beginning of the semester; the network analysis activity has been a part of every unit in the course. We began with *Northanger Abbey*, asking the students to make a character relationship map for the novel. This is a process that they are familiar with as it is a common assignment in literature courses.

The maps that the students produced in small groups were all very unique, there was no class definition for relationship and therefore each group interpreted it differently, the students used different shapes and colors to represent various types of character relationships. However, all of the maps were similar in that each character was a represented by a point and some form of line connecting the points represented the relationship between characters.

Using this similarity we introduced the concept of graph and showed how this was a construction they were already familiar with through their character relationship maps. After the students had practice constructing graphs from their character maps, we introduced the adjacency matrix and measures of centrality.

In other literature courses, the students have had extensive practice creating character relationship maps for character analysis; the question students use this map to answer is always "*what do the relationships between the characters look like?*" For this activity we wanted the students to see that by learning about graphs they were able to ask many other questions about the character relationships in the novel. The prompt they were given was: *Write a question about characters relationships in Northanger Abbey that you could explore using a graphing technique.* Responses that were representative of the class:

- Can the character relationships in *Northanger Abbey* be compared to those in *The Mysteries of Udolpho*?
- Do the relationships in *Northanger Abbey* strengthen over time in Bath, or lessen during the time in Northanger Abbey?

It is interesting to note that instead of looking at character relationships as a static concept the students are now able to think in terms of time and how the characters develop. We can also compare the social structures of different novels once we have a standardized way of representing character relationships. Students were given a research article where graphing had been used to analyze social networks in literary pieces [24] so that they could see the in class activity in relation to its use in research.

For each novel throughout the course of the semester, students worked on building graphs of character relationships and considering which measures of centrality would be most helpful in answering questions they had about the novel. Each novel in the semester gave them progressively more complicated graphs to construct; when they got to *Great Expectations* they were working with 20 different characters and were getting frustrated having to organize the graphs by hand. At this point we introduced them to an open source graph visualization software, Graph Viz [13]. We decided to use Graph Viz instead of some of the more user-friendly programs available because we wanted to give the students the experience of playing with the code. The students had to abstract the data from their graphs to a structure specified for Graph Viz and then write a syntactically correct statement to represent that data. At this point, we observed many of the English majors experimenting on their own with compile-time and code annotation options to explore more advanced settings of the tool. Some examples of the students' graphs can be seen in figure 2.

The social network analysis activity gave the students experience in constructing graphs, analyzing data, using the same data to answer different questions, and using technology to help with data representation.

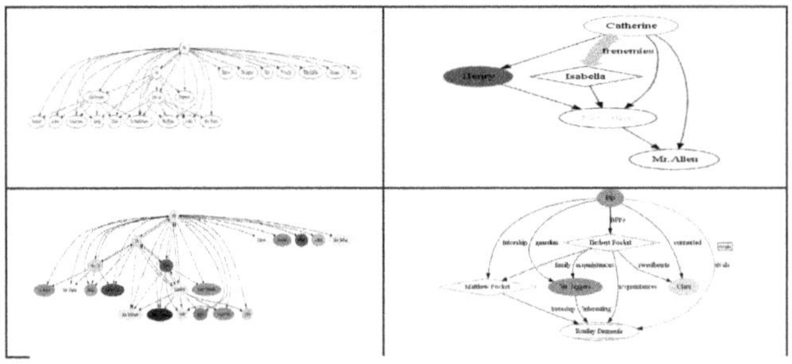

Figure 2: Graphs created by students using GraphViz

One of the survey questions asked why they enjoyed their major; a majority of the students responded that they enjoyed English as a major because it allowed them to be creative. We also asked the students whether they considered computer science to be a creative field. As is clear in figure 3, many of the students did not think computer science would allow them to be creative. After the activities in this course their response to this question changed, showing a majority of students considering computer science to be a creative discipline.

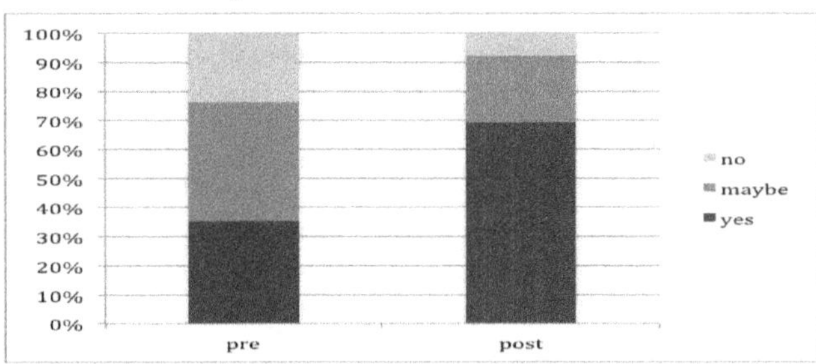

Figure 3: Pre- and Post-Survey Results: Does Computer Science Allow for Creativity?

8. DISCUSSION

When we began to introduce computational strategies in this course, students' first experiences reinforced already-known and practiced approaches in literary analysis. For example, these upper-level students had mastered close-reading annotations, i.e., analyzing literature at the level of diction, looking for patterns, such as repetition, contrast, and development. When the students first employed on-line word-count tools with the 19th century novella, they noted the visual depiction of patterns in imagery that they had already identified through pen-and-paper annotations. They were able to reflect on some of the limitations of word counts, in that straight word counts couldn't reveal multiple meanings of words, group words with similar meanings, or take into account words in their 19th-century literary contexts.

When students began work with graphing, they were exposed to a tool that improved upon their existing literary strategies. We frequently ask students to graph character relationships, as a way to analyze social class and connections in Victorian novels. Having a standard way to visualize character analysis data allowed students to quickly and accurately identify two new aspects of character and character relationships: 1) degree centrality, which character was most connected to other characters in the novel; and 2) the betweenness, how characters have access to other characters in the world of the novel. This technique led to some new insights beyond what we had been able to do with simple maps of characters. For example, students and instructor were surprised to find that John Thorpe was the most ``central'' character of *Northanger Abbey*, a discovery that led to an interesting discussion of "influence." Thorpe is not the main character, nor the best-connected, nor the most appealing. However, our graphs revealed that he had a wide sphere of influence, mostly because of his ability to insinuate himself into the lives of other characters at every social class. As students began to compare graphs at different points of novels, and over time, they discovered that the plot of a Victorian novel became more democratic as the story progressed, and that Victorian novels overall became more democratic as the century progressed.

During the second half of the course, we observed students drawing upon these strategies without prompting; they were applying knowledge and skills from previous units to new texts. For example, when students read *The Vampyre*, they were asked to calculate the distances Aubrey travelled with his mysterious companion from European capital to European capital. Drawing upon knowledge of early 19th-century travel, they discovered that Aubrey's journey, while depicted in only a few pages of the novella, would have taken months, perhaps a year. Students reflected on the mileage in the context of Aubrey's character and relationship: such an arduous, prolonged journey might help to explain Aubrey's lack of awareness of his companion's identity. Later, when reading *Northanger Abbey*, several students noted what a trying journey it must have been for Catherine, a teenager, to travel alone from the Tilney's abbey to her own home. When students began reading Great Expectations, they were aware of a difference in Dickens' treatment of cross-country travel. What was highly emphasized and even tracked in early Victorian novels was glossed over by the mid-century: Pip's move from the country to London is barely mentioned.

Finally, some literature students began imagining themselves studying computers and math in the future; these were the same students who began the semester rolling their eyes or expressing fear at anything related to math. One student approached the co-author about her desire to add a math minor to her degree program and another enrolled in a computer science course.

9. CONCLUSIONS

In this paper we presented our approach to integrating computer science and quantitative literacy concepts in an undergraduate English Literature course. The activities that we incorporated in the course gave students an opportunity to explore computer science applied to literary analysis. We believe that, by engaging with students in a discipline that they were already passionate about, introducing computing concepts applicable to their current interests was integral to the success of this project.

We were able to add computing activities that were of interest to the theme of the course without taking away from any of the learning outcomes present in previous iterations of the course. The original course was kept intact and additional learning outcomes were added that focused on computing as a means to engage students in quantitative skills directly applicable to their interests. Exposure to computing concepts in this course, as applied to literary analysis, gave students a new perspective on and deeper understanding of the nature of the nineteenth century Gothic novel. By focusing on developing activities that relied on the critical frameworks and in fact show the overlap and relationship between those frameworks, we reinforced the idea that computer science can work well to create interdisciplinary learning environments and engage students in new methods for continuing their work of interest. We have seen students' analytical and problem-solving abilities develop through these computational approaches. We have also observed a growing awareness of the importance and usefulness of analyzing literature as data, as well as data in literature.

10. REFERENCES

[1] C.Alvarado and Z.Dodds. Women in CS: An evaluation of three promising practices. In *Proceedings of SIGCSE'10,* pages 57-61, Milwaukee, WI, USA, 2010. ACM.

[2] V.Barr. Create two, three, many courses: An experiment in contextualized introductory computer science. J. *Comput. Sci. Coll.,* 27(6):19-25, June 2012.

[3] C. Barrowman et al. *Critical Theory as Critical Thinking: A Book of Classroom Practice in Literary Criticism.* Alverno College, Milwaukee, WI, USA, 2010.

[4] M. Bosch. Mathematics and Science: The relationships and disconnects between research and education. In *Compendium for Math and Science.,* eds C.Winslow, M.Achiam, Copenhagen:Department of Science Education, 2014.

[5] L. Carter. Why students with an apparent aptitude for computer science don't choose to major in computer science. In *Proceedings of SIGCSE'06,* pages 27-31, Houston, TX, USA, 2006. ACM.

[6] L. Carter. Interdisciplinary computing classes: Worth the effort. In *Proceedings of SIGCSE'14.* Pages 445-450, Atlanta, GA, USA, 2014. ACM.

[7] P. Charters, M.J.Lee, A.J.Ko, and D.Loksa. Challenging stereotypes and changing attitudes: The effect of a brief programming encounter on adults' attitudes toward programming. In *Proceedings of SIGCSE'14,* pages 653-658, Atlanta, GA, USA, 2014. ACM.

[8] CSTA Standards Task Force. CSTA K-12 computer science standards. Association for Computing Machinery, 2011. http://www.acm.org/education/curricula-recommendation.

[9] Q. Cutts, S. Esper, and B. Simon. Computing as the 4th 'R': A general education approach to computing education. In *Proceedings of ICER'11,* pages 133-138, Providence, RI, USA, 2011. ACM.

[10] C. Dierbach, B.Taylor, H.Zhou, and I.Zimand. Experiences with a cs0 course targeted for cs1 success. In *Proceedings of SIGCSE'05,* pages 317-320, St. Louis,MO,USA,2005. ACM.

[11] S. Esper, S.R.Foster, and W.G.Griswold. On the nature of fires and how to spark them when you're not there. In *Proceedings of SIGCSE'13,* pages 305-310, Denver,CO, USA, 2013. ACM.

[12] J. Feinberg. Wordle—beautiful word clouds. http://www.wordle.net.

[13] E.R.Gansner and S.C.North. An open graph visualization system and its applications to software engineering. *Software Practice and Experience,* 30(11):1203, 2000. www.graphviz.org

[14] S. Grover, R.Pea, and S.Cooper. Remedying misperceptions of computer science among middle school students. In *Proceedings of SIGCSE'14,* pages 343-348, Atlanta, GA, USA, 2014. ACM.

[15] Project Gutenburg Archive. http://www.gutenberg.org/.

[16] M. Hewner. Undergraduate conceptinos of the field of computer science. In *Proceedings of ICER'13,* pages 107-114, San Diego, CA, USA, 2013. ACM.

[17] W.L.Honig. Teaching and assessing programming fundamentals for non majors with visual programming. In *Proceedings of ITiCSE'13,* pages 40-45, Canterbury, England, UK, 2013.ACM.

[18] G.P.Landow. Vicorian web. http://www.victorianweb.org/.

[19] B.Lawson, D.Szajda, and L.Barnett. Introducing computer science in an integrated science course. In *Proceedings of SIGCSE'13,* pages 341-346, Denver, CO, USA, 2013.ACM.

[20] C.D.Martin. Draw a computer scientist. In *Working Group Reports from ITiCSE'04*, pages11-12,Leeds,UK, 2004.ACM.

[21] M.Mentkowski. *Leaerning That Lasts: Integrating Learning, Development, And Performance In College And Beyond.* Jossey-Bass, 1999.

[22] A.Mitchell, H.C.Purchase, and J.Hamer. Computing science: What do pupils think? In *Proceedings of ITiCSE'09,* pages 353-353, Paris, France, 2009. ACM.

[23] T.Newhall, L.Meeden, A.Daner, A.Soni, F.Ruiz, and R.Wicentowski. A support program for introductory CS courses that improves student performance and retains students from underrepresented groups. In *Proceedings of SICSES'14,*pages 433-438, Atlanta, GA, USA, 2014. ACM.

[24] Gyeong-Mi Park, Sung-Hwan Kim, Hye-Ryeon Hwang, and Hwan-Gue Cho. Complex System Analysis of Social Networks Extracted from Literary Fictions. *International Journal of Machine Learning and Computing,* 3(1)107-111,2013.

[25] D.Schunk. *Learning Theories: An educational perspective.* Pearson Education Inc, Boston, MA, 2012.

[26] E.K.Stage, H.Asturias, T.Cheuk, P.A.Daro, and S.B.Hampton. Opportunities and challenges in next generation standards. *Science,*340(6130):276-277, 2013.

[27] T.Underwook, M.L.Black, L.Auvil, and B.Capitanu. Mapping mutable genres in structurally complex volumes. In *Proceedings of BigData'13,*pages 95-103. IEEE,2013.

[28] M.VanDyne and J.Braun. Effectiveness of a computational thinking (cs0) course on student analytical skills. In *Proceedings of SIGCSE'14,* pages 133-138, Atlants, GA, USA, 2014. ACM.

[29] J.Walden, M.Doyle, R.Garns, and Z.Hart. An informatics perspective on computational thinking. In *Proceedings of ITiCSE'13,* pages 4-9, Canterbury, England, UK,2013.ACM.

[30] C.Wilson, L.A.Sudol, C.Stephenson, and M.Stehlik. Running on empty: The failure to teach K-12 computer science in the digital age. ACM,2010. http://www.acm.org/Runningonempty/.

[31] S.Yardi and A.Bruckman. What is computing?: Bridging the gap between teenagers' perceptions and graduate students' experiences. In *Proceedings of ICER'07,* pages 39-50, Atlanta, GA, USA, 2007. ACM.

Statistics-infused Introduction to Computer Science

Olaf A. Hall-Holt[a]
olaf@stolaf.edu

Kevin R. Sanft[a,b]
kevin@kevinsanft.com

[a]Department of Mathematics, Statistics, and Computer Science
[b]Center for Interdisciplinary Research
St. Olaf College
Northfield, MN 55057, USA

ABSTRACT

The ability to use computational tools to collect, organize, visualize, and analyze data is a valuable skill both inside and outside of computer science. In this paper we describe the design and implementation of a statistics-infused introduction to computer science, developed in collaboration with statistics faculty, at St. Olaf College. We propose that there exists a growing demographic of 'data-centric' students who expect to write small amounts of code in the context of work in other fields, and who are eager to take a CS course adapted to their needs. This particular data-centric CS1 course has been a catalyst for collaboration between faculty in multiple fields and multiple institutions.

Categories and Subject Descriptors

K.3.2 [**Computer and Information Science Education**]: computer science education, curriculum

General Terms

Design, Human Factors

Keywords

CS1; Computer Science education; data science; statistics

1. INTRODUCTION

CS1 students have sometimes been grouped in two categories: first, potential majors, and second, those who are curious or just fulfilling an academic requirement. A growing third category consists of students who are interested in neither software development nor the frontiers of computing, yet they expect to frequently write small bits of code as part of their work in another field. These students are intrinsically motivated to study computing, yet their needs and aspirations are different from typical CS majors. In this paper, we will call these students *data-centric* students, since their motivation is often related to the increasing importance and availability of data in myriad contexts.

SIGCSE'15, March 4–7, 2015, Kansas City, MO, USA.

ACM 978-1-4503-2966-8/15/03 ...$15.00.
http://dx.doi.org/10.1145/2676723.2677218

In 'A Data-Centric Introduction to Computer Science for Non-Majors', David Sullivan [8] describes a growing audience of students whose primary motivation is "information and skills that could be used in the future– either in their field of study or their career." Sullivan's students rarely wanted to learn about computer science per se. A related group of students may be enrolling in the new 'data science' courses at many universities including Columbia, University of San Francisco, New York University, Stanford, Northwestern, George Mason, Syracuse, University of California at Irvine and Indiana University [5]. The needs of this group are appreciated by statisticians who urge their colleagues to teach specifically about computation as part of a statistical education [6]. This group of students is also represented in other departments, where they receive informal training from scholars who increasingly make use of computational tools [3].

While data-centric students can of course learn a great deal from a traditional computer science curriculum, we propose that addressing the needs of these students directly has numerous benefits. Data-centric students are almost by definition more diverse than traditional CS majors, since they are drawn from a wide variety of disciplines across campus. Building a course to address their needs has enabled us to begin meaningful collaborations across multiple department boundaries. Data-centric students are poised to make contributions in many areas of our society right away, even if they take only one course in computer science. Finally, the number of data-centric students is growing, possibly even more rapidly than the number of traditional CS majors.

Thanks to a strong collaboration with statisticians, we have been able to develop a CS1 course that focuses directly on data-centric students. In section two, we describe this audience in general, argue that the number of data-centric students will grow, and provide details about the students who chose to take our CS1 course. In section three, we describe the approach we followed for developing a CS1 course adapted to this audience. In section four, we describe the content of our course in more detail, noting that other choices are certainly possible. Section five provides some evaluation of this experience, both in terms of student reactions and observations about the course development process. Section six concludes.

2. AUDIENCE AND ENROLLMENT

Data-centric students expect to frequently write small bits of code as part of their work in another field. The code they write may be used only once, and then discarded. These students may be responsible for communicating the results of their work with non-technical audiences, perhaps with an emphasis on visual communication. Data-centric students don't want to spend a lot of time learning to build a piece of software: they view themselves as users of software, rather than builders.

This group of students is part of a broad movement where people in many sectors are making greater use of more types of computation and data [5]. In scientific fields, some of the most compelling problems are extremely complex (like combatting cancer), requiring cross-functional teams working with large amounts of data. On college campuses, an increasing number of colleagues in other fields are computationally savvy, and encourage their students to cultivate similar skills. Outside of academia, many companies are collecting unprecedented amounts of market data, and seeking to use it for competitive advantage. The explosion in mobile technologies is bringing opportunities related to computation and data to a large fraction of the global population. Whether we are talking about 'data science' or 'big data' or emerging computational fields, we believe these trends in addressing difficult problems using both computation and data will continue for a long time, and will involve a larger and more diverse group of students than we have seen before.

The increase in the number of data-centric students is having effects outside of computer science. Statisticians, in particular, are discussing the need for computational expertise among those who focus on data. In a recent column, the president of the American Statistical Association favorably quoted a statistician who said "statistics students should develop deep proficiency in programming." [1] Courses have been developed in statistics departments specifically to teach about computation. An outstanding example is the Statistics Department at U C Berkeley, where all statistics majors are required to take their course in 'Computing with Data'. This course is extremely popular, and is considered one of the reasons for the growth in the number of majors in that department. Other kinds of faculty are also involved in addressing this audience of students, including those who have created new 'data science' master's degree programs.

Our experience so far in focusing on data-centric students is exciting. In the new CS1 course, we administered an anonymous survey with the first homework, designed to assess the students' backgrounds and preparedness for the course. Table 1 shows some basic demographic information. St. Olaf has an unusually high number of Mathematics majors for a small college. The total number of majors/concentrations in the table exceeds the total number of students due to students with multiple majors/concentrations. We had unexpectedly high enrollment, and at the beginning of the course, less than 5% of the students were planning to major in computer science.

We asked several questions designed to assess the students' previous experience and confidence level at the beginning of the course. These responses are shown in Table 2. The large number of students with previous R language experience is due primarily to Statistics concentrators. We expect the number of Statistics concentrators and seniors will stabilize at a lower number for future offerings of the course. The majority of students had some trepidation about launching into a programming course, but did not feel overwhelmed.

In the initial survey, five students listed "pre-calculus" as their most recent math class. The others reported "calculus" (either high-school (6) or college (9)), or "beyond calculus" (30). We later discovered that this range was too broad. Eighteen students listed "no prior background" in statistics. Before introducing loops, we asked students if they had seen loops prior to this course. Of the 43 responses, 17 reported never seeing or using loops before.

Table 1: Initial Class Survey: Demographics (N=50)

Class Year	
First-year	11
Sophomore	11
Junior	14
Senior	14
Major	
Mathematics	27
Statistics (Concentration)	17
Biology	7
Chemistry	7
Computer Science	2
Undecided	5
Other (specified, unspecified)	9, 18

Table 2: Initial Class Survey: Preparation and Confidence (N=50)

Computer Level	
Beginner	12
Moderate (low)	26
Moderate (high)	10
Advanced	2
Confidence in Learning to Program	
Low (it sounds scary)	10
Moderate (like other learning)	28
High	11
N/A (already know how to program)	1
I have already learned about:	
Spreadsheets (like Excel)	45
Creating a web page	9
Using Python	8
Using R	23

Table 3 shows a summary of some of the responses to an open-ended question regarding students' reasons for taking the course.

The students were largely taking the course because they thought it would provide useful skills. This sentiment was supported by a survey at the end of the semester, where we asked students how the course fit into their academic program. Of the 39 responses to that survey, 15 reported that it was a Major/Concentration requirement or elective, 21 reported the course was an elective course (not in a major or concentration), and 2 reported that the class fulfilled a General Education requirement (1 responded "Unsure"). The interest in this course was not limited to students. We were grateful to have three professors (2 statisticians, 1 mathematician) regularly attend the course.

Table 3: Initial Class Survey: Reason for taking the course (summary of open-ended responses) (N=48)

Will be useful in the future	28
Valuable for workplace after graduation	8
Useful for other courses/undergrad research	7
Useful for graduate school	4
Want to learn how to program	7
Interested in Computer Science	9
Interesting	6
Satisfies general education requirement	3

3. COURSE DEVELOPMENT PROCESS

Effectively addressing the needs of data-centric students has required us to re-examine many of our assumptions about CS1 courses. For example, which topics in computer science are most beneficial to this group of students? We have tried before to create compelling applications in CS1 courses that would draw the interest of students in other domains, but this time we decided to start by involving faculty from other fields in the course development process.

The first step was a tentative agreement with Paul Roback, the director of the statistics program, to develop a course that would address needs of both statistics concentrators and computer science majors. We agreed that the new course would be taught by a computer science professor, and that the development process would include weekly meetings with statistics faculty. We received an internal grant to support our collaboration, and began a multi-faceted discussion that grew to include almost all the computer science faculty as well as some colleagues in mathematics, biology, and psychology.

As part of this discussion, one statistician and one computer scientist visited the Berkeley campus to learn about their 'Computing with Data' course. Prof. Deb Nolan graciously arranged for us to sit in on the course and to learn from current and former students, current and former TAs, and current and former instructors. This immersion in a successful existing course provided the basic framework for our new CS1 course, and continued to challenge our assumptions about how this kind of course should work.

A second step in the course development process occurred when we agreed on the sequence of topics. Reaching this agreement required weeks of discussion, but once we had the sequence, the professors who were to teach the course dove into preparation. The two authors decided to team teach the course, and to split responsibilities for developing various sections of the course. We also hired some talented students, some with backgrounds in statistics and some in computer science, to help develop assignments and projects for the course.

The final stage of development happened as the course was underway. The two professors alternated responsibility for leading the class from one day to the next, and thus continued to collaborate closely on many aspects of last-minute development. We were grateful to the larger group of interested students and faculty who continued to provide feedback as the course progressed.

4. COURSE CONTENT

To understand the particular needs of data-centric students, we sought advice from statisticians, applied mathematicians, biologists, psychologists, and many others. We now believe that there is no specific toolset that is clearly most appropriate for this audience. Rather, data-centric students need to be able to quickly pick up new tools as they encounter new problems, after the course is done. Here is how Deb Nolan describes it:

"The goal ... is to remove obstacles to engagement with a problem. If students gain a basic familiarity with various technologies, they can carry these skills with them and build on them to address new problems. In this way, they are more autonomous, more 'can do', and less dependent on others to define the problem and present them with the data."

This view fits with Kaplan's [3] claim that one of the most important skills is to know how to learn to use a new library or package.

4.1 Two languages

One of the most important course development decisions was the choice to use two languages, Python and R. The computer science faculty were initially inclined to teach only one language (Python and R were both candidates), and focus on becoming as proficient as possible in that language. We were surprised at the strong support from statisticians at the suggestion of using two languages. In fact, all four professors in the statistics program at St. Olaf were strongly in favor of using two languages. Part of this support was motivated by a desire to show the students that many of the computing concepts that they were seeing briefly in their statistics courses are not restricted to R. That is, computational and algorithmic thinking is a more general problem solving strategy. Also, by learning two languages, it was hoped that students would have a more diverse toolbox at their disposal and that they would be more confident in their ability to discover and apply new tools in the future.

We chose to use R because it is one of the dominant programming languages in use by statisticians. R is open source, and it features an extensive list of well documented packages for use in a broad variety of data-analysis activities. R is used in most of the statistics courses at St. Olaf.

Python is also widely used among data scientists, who may use Python or Perl or other tools for their initial data collection and formatting, even if they plan to use R in later stages of analysis. Python has a plethora of associated teaching materials for introductory CS students, including a well-written Python book for a general audience by Charles Severance [7] and an excellent beginners code visualization tool by Philip Guo [2].

We chose to start the course with Python. Access to Guo's online environment visualizer motivated this decision. We then switched to R, and returned to Python at the end of the term. The two languages share numerous features, and provide opportunities for fruitful comparison.

4.2 Class structure

The authors team-taught two sections of the course. In a typical class period, we first answered questions on the assigned reading, and then went into group activities that could include writing diagrams to explain some puzzling code or programming exercises. Homework assignments were given three times a week. Five team projects challenged the students to make use of their new skills with real data over a longer period of time. The final project was open-ended, with students choosing their own datasets and whatever type of analysis they deemed appropriate.

4.3 Topics covered and materials

The Python sections of the course were probably quite similar to many other CS1 courses, although a bit truncated. Our intent was to provide enough Python background to allow a student to take some messy data, such as human written records of payments, and write their own Python code to clean it up. We thus introduced the most basic Python data structures and control features, but only briefly considered objects. We also introduced BeautifulSoup and SQLite, for web scraping and basic database manipulation, respectively.

The R section of the course focused on the basic data structures of R: vectors, matrices, lists, data frames, factors and tables, as described in Norm Matloff's text [4]. Many of the team projects involved figuring out how to make use of data stored in one of these structures. We touched on linear modeling in R, and spent a week each on visualization (with the ggplot2 package) and classification (using random decision trees/forests). We did not attempt to teach about statistical modeling, as this is the subject of several complementary statistics courses. Rather, we emphasized informal approaches to exploring data and looking for patterns.

Outside of Python and R, we also touched briefly on basic probability concepts and HTML. The content of the course was thus aimed at providing tools that would allow a student to obtain data from many sources, and then be aware of a wide range of tools that could be used to transform, organize, and analyze the data.

4.4 Avoiding loops

We delayed introduction of loops until about two-thirds of the way through the course! We did so following the advice of those who taught the 'Computing with Data' course at Berkeley. R is a functional language underneath, where many operations are naturally expressed with apply and similar higher order functions. However, students who are told about loops early in a course may be drawn to using loops all the time, in a way that is both non-idiomatic and often inefficient in R. By avoiding loops, we were able to give students practice with functional tools for a couple weeks before introducing iteration. We think this approach was largely effective, but it was not free: for one example early in the course, we were forced to introduce a non-Pythonic example of recursion.

5. DISCUSSION

We utilized several sources of data to assess the effectiveness of the course. These included an anonymous informal survey near the middle of the term, an anonymous course evaluation survey at the end of the term, and two focus groups who met with statistics faculty after the term. We also frequently included requests for feedback as part of the daily homework assignments.

5.1 Evaluation

In the mid-term survey, two trends stood out in the data. First, the students reported enjoying learning two languages. We interpreted this as a sign that students felt both R and Python would be useful in the future and that they were happy to sacrifice depth in one language in exchange for exposure to another language. Second, the students liked having two professors. Team-teaching this course was an experiment made possible by a fortuitous alignment of faculty interest and available resources. It made the course stronger and we were pleased that that students responded favorably.

Our primary goals for the course were that the students would find the material useful and we wanted them to have confidence in their ability to use computation to solve problems they encounter in the future. In the end of the term course evaluation survey, the students responded favorably to questions about achieving these goals. Tables 4 through 7 show the students' responses on some key questions in the course evaluation survey. We were pleased with their responses for the questions about acquiring data from many sources, common data tasks, visualizations, and developing R code. The question about writing Python programs to transform data suggests an area for improvement, which we address in the next section.

Table 4: Course Evaluation Survey: Amount Learned (N=39)

Compared to other courses, the amount you learned was:	
Much more	8
Somewhat more	18
About the same	8
Somewhat less	4
Much less	1

Table 5: Course Evaluation Survey: Course Goals (N=39)

	1	2	3	4	5
How much did you learn about acquiring data from many sources, and about transforming data to make the data usable in applications?	0	0	11	16	12
How much did you practice using R and Python for visualization, classification, and other common data tasks?	1	0	7	9	22

Key:
1=Very little
2=Little
3=Average
4=More
5=A lot

We are perhaps most proud of the extent to which the students found the material to be immediately applicable. In a homework assignment near the end of the term, we asked the students if they had used anything from this course for other classes or projects. More than half the class (24 out of 44 students) reported that they had done so! Many students had used R to write functions or create ggplot2 graphics in mathematics or statistics classes. Others reported using R or Python for research projects, or even just for fun. Several

Table 6: Course Evaluation Survey: Confidence (N=39)

How confident are you that:	1	2	3	4
you could build your own ggplot2 visualizations?	0	0	12	27
you could develop your own R code to analyze new data?	0	5	8	26
you could develop your own Python program to transform data?	2	15	10	11

Key:
1=unlikely
2=possible
3=likely
4=surely

Table 7: Course Evaluation Survey: Overall (N=39)

	NA	1	2	3	4	5
How would you rate this course overall?	1	2	7	10	14	4

Key:
NA=Don't Know or N/A
1=Poor
2=Fair
3=Good
4=Very Good
5=Excellent

students used the final project in our course as an opportunity to improve processes in their research or jobs. For example, one student automated a workflow that previously required manually manipulating data in a spreadsheet for a research project in the Psychology Department. Another student analyzed product offerings and sales patterns at the student-run cafe on campus. Her analysis has helped guide product orders and has literally changed the way the cafe does business.

Our focus groups largely confirmed the messages from our surveys. One focus group was comprised of first-year students, while the other was comprised of seniors. This allowed a diverse range of perspectives. The first-year students believed the material from the course would be useful eventually, but that the course was very time consuming. Many of the senior students reported wishing that the course had been available earlier in their student careers because it would have helped them in other courses. We made no effort to recruit students into the CS major, yet several students mentioned that they would have majored in computer science if they had taken this course earlier.

In the final course evaluation survey, 33 out of 39 students said that they would recommend this course to other students. In the future, we plan to offer both a traditional CS1 course and this statistics-infused CS1. Demand for both courses has been strong, but the demand for the stats-infused version in particular is far greater than our current capacity.

5.2 Challenges and Planned Changes

The course was extremely successful, but it was not without challenges. In this section we discuss further some of the challenges we faced in developing this course, as well as planned changes for the next offering.

5.2.1 *Collaboration, Languages, Topics, and Materials*

Close collaboration with statisticians led to a choice of topics that were not familiar to the CS faculty. We had to learn R, and we are still learning R, since it is a language with a long history and many interesting innovations. We discovered that the materials available for some of our topics are not particularly well suited to an audience of beginning CS students. For example, we had trouble finding an appropriate introduction to classification, since most of the material we found presumed prior knowledge of either computer science or statistics. As usual, a new course also required the development of a substantial number of new homework exercises, exams, and projects. The homework exercises and projects are publicly available on our CS teaching wiki.

It turns out that using R has worked very well at our institution. Our strong statistics program ensures that students will have the opportunity to leverage their expertise in other courses. Macalester College has recently developed a course in R that is to be taken by all science majors, and we are hoping to incorporate some aspects of their course into CS1. Other languages might work well at institutions where R is less well known. For example, collaboration with computationally savvy colleagues in physics or biology might determine that a similar course should utilize Matlab or Excel and perhaps feature more simulation than our course. We believe the particular tools are not as important as exposure to computational thinking and building the students' confidence to discover new tools to attack challenging problems.

Team-teaching worked very well for us and the students enjoyed it, but it is not always feasible and it comes with challenges. One consideration is that team-teaching introduces significant overhead when trying to truly collaborate on developing a course schedule, homework problems and in-class exercises. Two professors does not equal half the work! Rather than split coverage of the course by modules, we generally split the coverage by alternating days. This increased our workload, but ensured that we both had a stake in all the material and encouraged us to find effective compromises. Team-teaching forced us to be more organized, provided an additional level of accountability, and the course benefited from having more than one perspective.

5.2.2 *Reducing Student Workload*

Students felt that the workload was heavy at various points in the course. We consider this a legitimate criticism. In response, we are working to streamline the homework and projects. Several project groups spent a disproportionate amount of their time on trying to figure out how to access data sets from the Linux filesystem from their personal computers. In other projects where the data was hosted on webpages, this process was much smoother. Therefore, we plan to make all the project data sets available on the web. We believe this simple change will significantly reduce the workload and, more importantly, will reduce frustration, and will allow the students to focus more on the important concepts. We are also planning to revise the Python exercises near the end of the term that were devoted to transforming messy data. We had a series of exercises devoted to cleaning up human-recorded data that featured intentional typographic and formatting errors. The exercises built on each other. Unfortunately, some students fell behind in the early exercises and struggled to complete the subsequent ones. In future offerings of the course, we are planning to provide and review successful approaches at each step, so that all students are well prepared to begin each new exercise in the sequence.

In the project feedback questions, some students reported that they disliked having to write repetitive code when the project asked them to perform similar tasks across several different data sets. This subset of students was not fully utilizing the power of writing their own functions! We plan to revise the wording in the early projects to emphasize the proper use of functions, and we will spend more time discussing successful implementations after the students have had the chance to work through the problems.

Finally, we seek to find a better balance between guiding the students toward the solution and asking them to find relevant tools on the Internet themselves. For example, in a project that asked the students to generate an animation of sea ice data, we asked them to use resources on the web to find an R package to accomplish the task. An appropriate web search would lead to a suitable package and example code. However, some students who did not find this package spent a lot of time writing their own detailed code that was more difficult than we intended. We plan to insert intermediate checkpoints into the project to guide the students toward more effective web searches. Learning how to utilize resources on the Internet to address their own problems may be the most important skill students attain in a course like this.

5.2.3 Course Structure Changes

One significant change in the classroom for future offerings of this course will be the use of projectors to display students' code as they type it. We devoted much of our class time to writing diagrams of puzzling code in small groups. This was done on dry-erase-painted walls so that the groups could see what the other groups were doing. We also had success with having students develop code in small groups to solve real problems in class. Our plan is to combine these two activities. We have installed 7 new projectors in the classroom. This will allow students to develop code in small groups and allow other students (and the professor) to see their code in real time.

Another change is the introduction of Calculus 1 as a prerequisite. We found some under-prepared students without a strong quantitative background struggled in the course. We believe these students would have been better served by taking our other introductory computer science course, which also moves at a more moderate pace.

The next offering of this course will not be team-taught. However, we would like to return to the team-teaching format in the future. In the course evaluation, a student suggested having one CS professor and one statistics professor instead of two CS professors. We are not planning to implement this suggestion, but we are inviting a statistician to give a small number of focused lectures on some of the more statistics-oriented course topics. Collaboration with statisticians will continue to be important as we refine the course for future offerings.

6. CONCLUSIONS

We have developed a statistics-infused introduction to computer science that focuses on handling data. The homework and projects for the course are available on the publicly accessible course website. We were pleased by the number of students who reported using techniques from the course in other classes or projects. We believe the course provides a solid foundation in computer science principles and computational thinking that will be useful in future classes and beyond.

More broadly, we believe there exists a significant demographic of data-centric students who may be eager to take a CS1 course designed for them. Other colleges are developing similar courses, sometimes focused on students in the sciences. As computation and data become more necessary in a variety of contexts, CS faculty have an opportunity to support a growing and diverse body of non-majors, while still providing potential majors a valuable start.

7. ACKNOWLEDGMENTS

We are grateful to many who have been contributed toward this work, including Paul Roback, Jill Dietz, Stephen Lee, Roland Brown, Josh Jacobson, Jim Farrell, Deb Nolan, and Norman Matloff. K.S. was supported by NSF grant DMS-1045015.

8. REFERENCES

[1] M. Davidian. Aren't we data science?, July 2013. Retrieved August 18, 2014 from `http://magazine.amstat.org/blog/2013/07/01/datascience/`.

[2] P. Guo, 2014. Retrieved August 18, 2014 from `http://pythontutor.com/`.

[3] D. T. Kaplan. Teaching computation to undergraduate scientists. In *Proceedings of the 35th SIGCSE Technical Symposium on Computer Science Education (SIGCSE '04)*, pages 358–362, 2004.

[4] N. Matloff. *The Art of R Programming: A Tour of Statistical Software Design.* No Starch Press, 2011.

[5] C. C. Miller. Data science: The numbers of our lives, Apr. 2013. Retrieved August 18, 2014 from `http://www.nytimes.com/2013/04/14/education/edlife/universities-offer-courses-in-a-hot-new-field-data-science.html`.

[6] D. Nolan and D. Temple Lang. Computing in the statistics curricula. *The American Statistician*, 64(2):97–107, 2010.

[7] C. Severance. Python for informatics: Exploring information v. 0.0.8, 2013. Retrieved August 18, 2014 from `http://www.py4inf.com/book.php`.

[8] D. G. Sullivan. A data-centric introduction to computer science for non-majors. In *Proceedings of the 44th SIGCSE Technical Symposium on Computer Science Education (SIGCSE '13)*, pages 71–76, 2013.

Building Worlds: Bridging Imperative-First and Object-Oriented Programming in CS1–CS2

Zoë Wood
Computer Science Department
California Polytechnic State University
1 Grand Avenue
San Luis Obispo, CA 93407 USA
zwood@calpoly.edu

Aaron Keen
Computer Science Department
California Polytechnic State University
1 Grand Avenue
San Luis Obispo, CA 93407 USA
akeen@calpoly.edu

ABSTRACT

When teaching introductory computing courses, we are often guilty of writing rudimentary programming assignments – those meant to illustrate one simple language feature, comprised mostly of code that will never be used beyond the assignment. Admittedly, first-year computing students must navigate a myriad of challenges, sometimes learning both imperative and object-oriented programming, in addition to mastering syntax, logic, debugging, and testing. To tackle the difficulties of developing CS 1 and CS 2 courses that engage students in learning while addressing the numerous course objectives, we chose to challenge students to create virtual worlds in one large comprehensive two-quarter long programming project. Students were granted creative freedom within a framework that gradually introduced many programming skills and that required the mastery of object-oriented programming and some engaging algorithms. We present the curriculum, performance comparisons, and observations. Overall, we consider the experimental courses a success that will have an impact on our department's future curricular offerings.

Categories and Subject Descriptors

K.3.2 [**Computers and Education**]: Computer and Information Science Education—*computer science education*

General Terms

Experimentation

Keywords

Introductory programming; object-oriented programming

1. INTRODUCTION

Creating meaningful learning experiences for students in introductory computing courses is a challenge. Many students find themselves overwhelmed with simultaneously learning syntax, logic, program design, decomposition, debugging, algorithms, testing, and object-oriented design (all of which may be required in a first year assignment). In order to address this overwhelming problem space, faculty often rely on small programming assignments to introduce discrete language or programming concepts one at a time. These rudimentary assignments are problematic as they are often decoupled from real-world programming and real-world problems, lessening student engagement and leading to confusion about the true use of these language/design features. This is especially true for object-oriented programming where the design goals (and language features supporting these goals) run almost directly orthogonal to the context of a small, rudimentary program. In short, language support for programming large systems is often unappreciated and poorly motivated in small programs.

Beginning in 2010 our department tackled some of the challenges of introducing students to computing via the use of project-based contextualized learning in CS 0 [11]. Students are introduced to computing via topics such as mobile computing, video games, music, computational art, robotics, and security. The success of these CS 0 offerings inspired us to consider some of the core challenges we face in the subsequent first-year courses (CS 1 and CS 2). Specifically, we set out to design courses with high student engagement that expose students to large "real-world" problems, that require working on a larger-than-typical code base where each assignment's code is dependent on a prior assignment, and that require the creation of a project that truly illustrates the benefits of object-oriented programming. We present details of these courses in Section 3.

Our envisioned CS 1 and CS 2 courses (referenced from here on as CS 1_{ex} and CS 2_{ex} to avoid confusion with the prior CS 1 and CS 2) differ significantly from the existing courses in our department. Details of existing courses are provided here for context.

Our department's CS 1 could be said to implement what the Computing Curricula 2001 [1] terms an "imperative-first" approach. Specifically, CS 1 focuses on programming skills using primitive and structured data, expressions, conditionals, loops, arrays, and (non-recursive) functions. Our department's CS 1 uses `C` as the implementation language, but without any required instruction on pointers (aside from incidental uses inherent in `C`). Our department's CS 2 covers objects and object-oriented programming in Java including classes, interfaces, polymorphism, and inheritance. CS 2 is

SIGCSE'15, March 04–07, 2015, Kansas City, MO, USA.

ACM 978-1-4503-2966-8/15/03 ...$15.00.
http://dx.doi.org/10.1145/2676723.2677249.

also tasked with introducing recursion, searching, sorting, and linked lists. A typical instance of this course requires that students implement very prescriptive assignments with an emphasis on "how" the object-oriented language features work in Java.

Though our department's CS 1 builds a sufficiently solid imperative foundation that supports learning to program in Java, many students at the end of CS 2 are left unsure of the need for or value of object-oriented features. In particular, when early CS 2 assignments require the use of interfaces, it is a challenge to properly motivate the reasons for their use. When early CS 2 assignments *do not* require the use of interfaces, it can be a challenge to motivate their introduction later. Some students have questioned the value of object-oriented programming as a whole since they feel they could implement the assignment more directly in `C`; this is typically due to limited additional complexity in the prescriptive assignments that focus on introducing object-oriented features.

We sought to address these shortcomings by bridging the transition from CS 1 to CS 2 with a single project that spans these two courses. We offered one section of an experimental CS 1 (CS 1_{ex}) during the Winter quarter 2014 and one section of an experimental CS 2 (CS 2_{ex}) course during the Spring quarter 2014, each with approximately 35 students. These sections were co-taught by the authors during both quarters. The course-spanning project required students to create their own virtual worlds with interacting entities/characters. Students were allowed a great deal of creativity in designing the theme, the environment, and the behavior of their worlds and their worlds' inhabitants. The instructors provided high-level requirements that drove the development of a larger program while gradually introducing object-oriented features.

During this project, the students had to contend with code dependencies between assignments, rewrite portions of their program to address shortcomings in design decisions (and, ultimately, to switch languages), test modules before integrating them into the larger program, and implement context-based graph searching algorithms (an extension in scope beyond the searching of sequential structures required in our department's CS 1 and CS 2). These experiences pushed student learning beyond the development of small throw-away programs and contextualized the value and need for more advanced language features and design methodologies.

2. RELATED WORK

There is a large body of work addressing the multitude of challenges (including failure rates [5]) in introductory computer science curricula, including context-based computing, small courses and the use of labs early, making use of pair programming, etc. [10, 8, 13, 7, 6]. Our department has a strong commitment to introductory computing: the introductory courses are kept relatively small with about 35 students per section, each section includes equal lab and lecture time, and the department runs a free tutoring center. Though these academic structures are beneficial, students in introductory courses continue to fail at higher than acceptable rates and there is a perceived mismatch between the skills students gain in introductory courses and the skills desired by upper-division instructors.

In order to address issues related to student failure rates, dwindling enthusiasm, language battles, and upper-division skill mismatch, we proposed the experimental course structure described in this paper. The work presented here is strongly founded in the success of using context-based computing in introductory computing courses [10, 8, 11] and our belief in the use of project-based learning [4], especially when considering teaching the utility of object-oriented language features. Additionally, we were inspired to allow students to work in pairs for all major programming assignments, using a casual implementation of pair-programming [13]. Finally, our explorations into using Python as a first programming language were influenced by various sources suggesting Python as a positive starting language [14, 9].

Though our proposed context of a two-dimensional virtual world to motivate learning object-oriented language features may appear reminiscent of GridWorld [12], our work was inspired independently. Moreover, our project requires students to create their own worlds and to write all associated code from scratch. This structure provides a means for students to experience the ramifications of non-ideal design decisions and to appreciate the value of improved design in addressing the shortcomings of earlier decisions.

3. OUR SOLUTION

To address the challenge of developing a CS 1 and CS 2 course sequence that engages students in learning while allowing them to apply their learning to one large comprehensive programming project, we designed a two-quarter sequence focused on the construction of a virtual world[1]. Students were granted creative freedom within the framework of the required technology specifications.

Initially, the students were asked to design worlds that met the following requirements:

- The world is confined to two dimensions.
- The world must contain multiple characters with different behavior. In particular, the first specification of the world required the definition of:
    - a **gatherer(s)** that would move through the world seeking a resource.
    - a **generator(s)** that would generate a resource (in a location relative to the generator).
- The world must include consumable resources that are *generated* and *gathered*.

Later extensions to the project required:

- Obstacles in the world that prevented or restricted movement.
- Character transformations based on interactions with the world, with a resource, or with another character.
- A world changing event affecting all elements of the world within a given (geometric) range.

[1]Those interested can find materials for this curriculum at `http://users.csc.calpoly.edu/~akeen/courses/csc101x`.

Although it was not necessary, we opted to require that each world be displayed in 2D in order to give the students improved visual feedback on the state of their world and to allow for creative visual expression to enhance engagement.

In order to address the diverse curricular needs of CS 1_{ex} and CS 2_{ex}, each quarter had a slightly divergent emphasis and development environment.

- CS 1_{ex}: The first course focused on programming skills using primitive and structured data (via classes and objects), expressions, conditionals, loops, lists, and functions. This course used Python as the implementation language with worlds displayed using pygame [3].
- CS 2_{ex}: The second course focused on object-oriented programming with increased exposure to classes and objects and an introduction to interfaces, polymorphism, and inheritance. This course also covered recursion, searching, sorting, and the implementation of linked lists. Due to our department's requirement that students entering CS 3 must know how to program in Java, this course included a transition from Python and pygame to Java with Processing [2].

Lecture material covered introductory programming and project-relevant topics with students completing short related lab assignments each week and with the virtual world project split into multiple major homework assignments. Students were allowed to choose between working on these major assignments in pairs or as individuals. Over the two quarters of this experiment, the composition of pairs and individual projects varied but at the end of CS 2_{ex} eleven projects were completed by pairs and eight were completed by individuals. Key assignments were as follows:

- CS 1_{ex}, HW 1: Provide a description of the theme, environment, and characters in the virtual world. Define data representations for some of the characters in the virtual world.

  This assignment introduced the entire virtual world project by requiring students to describe the world they intended to build. This assignment also introduced students to programming and Python through the implementation and testing of simple classes and objects to represent characters in the world (as defined by properties such as the x- and y-location, the number of resources gathered, and the frequency at which a resource is generated). These two extremes provided a creative context (the grand vision) in which to project the introductory minutiae of defining simple data (the characters).

- CS 1_{ex}, HW 2: Build the basic structure to visualize the world in 2D. Populate the world with characters and implement movement for a subset of them.

  This assignment required that a gatherer move toward a resource and stop once the resource is reached. In this context, the students were introduced to decision-making, conditional logic, and looping. This assignment also served to introduce pygame for displaying the world.

- CS 1_{ex}, HW 3: Increase the complexity of interactions in the world, increase the visual complexity of the world, and visualize reactions to interactions.

  This assignment required support for primitive user-interaction via pygame events (both mouse and keyboard) including a visual response to selection of resources and movement of a gatherer to the nearest or farthest resource (by choice). In addition, the visual theme of the virtual world was improved through the selection or creation of sprites.

- CS 1_{ex}, HW 4: Build a program to allow a user to "create" a specific instance of a world by placing entities and background sprites using the mouse and keyboard (including functionality to save and load worlds).

  This assignment required the management of multiple characters (objects) of varying types through the use of lists and the 2D grid. This included the presentation of characters that could be placed over different types of background tiles necessitating managing multiple objects in the same 2D world "cell". This assignment also emphasized data conversion in the form of save files (conversion of an object to/from a string) and movement of a "view window" in the world (conversion of window coordinates to/from world coordinates).

- CS 1_{ex}, HW 5: Bring the world to life by implementing clock-based movement and animation. Some characters must transform (with a corresponding animation) based on actions taken.

  This assignment completed the first phase of the two-quarter virtual world project with a "live" world in which characters move through the world to take actions (e.g., gather or deposit resources). This required triggering actions based on a timer, preventing movement of characters through obstacles (with some naive effort to bypass obstacles), and changing the state of the world (creating and/or removing entities) during execution.

Though it was infeasible to force students completing CS 1_{ex} to continue with CS 2_{ex}, of the eleven students in CS 1_{ex} that did not continue on to CS 2_{ex}, none continued on to any CS 2. The majority of these students were "non-majors" that are not required to take CS 1 or CS 2.

While we did have control over registration priority for CS 2_{ex}, enrollment demands necessitated adding ten students to CS 2_{ex} that had not taken CS 1_{ex}. These ten students had completed traditional non-objects CS 1 courses (using `C`). To support these new students and to aid any continuing CS 1_{ex} students that did not complete their assignments perfectly, we offered the opportunity to start fresh with an instructor provided world implementation (approximately 1700 lines of code). Five projects were continued from the students' own original code, eleven projects used the instructor provided code, and three projects started with the instructor code but modified it to fit their own world. Major assignments in CS 2_{ex} included:

- CS 2_{ex}, HW 1: Refactor the code to group functionality for each character/class into methods. Justify this factoring in a written design document.

  This assignment required moving the reasonable associated behavior for each character (and other class) from stand-alone functions (as used in CS 1_{ex}) to methods. Through this assignment students were introduced to objects with behavior, extending their notion of a data-holding object from CS 1_{ex}.

- CS 2_{ex}, HW 2: Improve character movement within the world.

  This assignment required improving character movement by replacing the naive search from CS 1_{ex} with the A* (A-star) search algorithm. The implementation of A* for this assignment required students to consider the representation of the search space in order to select neighbors, the representation and manipulation of open and closed sets, and how to reinitiate a search (the world remains active, so a character will move again). This assignment also introduced recursion for reconstructing the shortest path.

- CS 2_{ex}, HW 3: Refactor the world code to use inheritance for the world entities.

  In many cases, the movement of stand-alone functions to methods in HW 1 involved duplication of code. In some cases, the duplicated code contained an "instance of" check to determine the action to take. This assignment introduced the concept of inheritance and required that students refactor duplicate code into a parent class while specializing behavior in subclasses.

- CS 2_{ex}, HW 4: Convert the world project from Python with pygame to Java with Processing.

  This assignment introduced Java through a code rewrite. The Python (with pygame) implementation had to be converted to Java (with Processing). Of particular note, this rewrite required that students contend with type annotations, access modifiers, interfaces, checked exceptions, generics, and support for lists in Java's API.

- CS 2_{ex}, HW 5: Integrate a 'world changing' event into the world.

  This assignment required the implementation of a triggered event that starts at a specified location and that has some local extent. Furthermore, the assignment required that the event be visualized by changing the images of the associated grid elements and that the event affect different characters differently (creating both a change in the physical appearance of the characters along with a change in the behavior of one of the character types).

In addition to submitting these assignments, students were required (twice each quarter) to demonstrate their world and code in front of the instructors and their classmates. These class code reviews provided an excellent opportunity for students to share their solutions and discuss their design decisions.

An important note about this experimental course is that it was a break from the traditional CS 1 and CS 2 for our department in many ways. We used different programming languages, different assignments, and a different lecturing style. Both authors worked collaboratively on all aspects of the course: co-designing lab and homework assignments, co-writing exams (lab and lecture), and sharing lecturing (trading-off approximately weekly or by topic). Each instructor attended every lecture and genuinely co-taught the course.

Table 1: CS 1 Traditional vs Experimental scores

	CS 1 30 Overall 28 Computing*		CS 1_{ex} 31 Overall 23 Computing*	
	mean	std. dev.	mean	std. dev.
Midterms				
Exam 1				
Overall	80.9%	14.6	82.5%	13.4
Computing*	80.4%	14.8	87.2%	9.0
Exam 2				
Overall	76.9%	15.5	75.1%	23.3
Computing*	76.5%	16.0	83.2%	16.4
Lab Exam				
Overall	82.0%	17.7	82.1%	23.3
Computing*	81.3%	18.0	86.2%	22.2
Final Exam				
Overall	79.7%	14.2	77.4%	17.4
Computing*	79.1%	14.4	82.9%	12.7

4. PERFORMANCE COMPARISONS

In measuring the success of our experimental CS 1_{ex} and CS 2_{ex} courses we consider both student outcomes and the participating faculty's perspectives.

For student outcomes, we compare student success in the experimental section versus the traditional CS 1 and CS 2 courses taught during the same quarters. At this time we do not have statistics on the long-term contribution to student success (in subsequent courses), but can report positive outcomes for each comparative section.

We compare the performance in the CS 1_{ex} course against a traditional CS 1 course taught by one of the authors during the same quarter. The same midterms, lab exams, and final exam were used in each course, but with each adapted to the appropriate syntax for the course (`C` in CS 1 and Python in CS 1_{ex}). Table 1 lists each section's scores for students that took the final exam, broken down into the 'Overall' class and the 'Computing*' students, which includes computer science, software engineering, computer engineering, and 'liberal arts and engineering studies' (LAES) majors (these are the majors that typically continue on to CS 2). When comparing all students ('Overall') in each course, the CS 1_{ex} students performed slightly better or just barely below their their traditional CS 1 counterparts in all assessments.

It is worth noting that the experimental section student population included an uncommonly high number of non-computing majors. The creative theme attracted ten non-computing and non-engineering majors (including students from art, business, political science, and agriculture) out of a total student population of 36 students, while in the traditional class the vast majority of students were computing or engineering majors. When comparing computing and engineering majors between the two sections(designated 'Computing*' in Table 1), *the students in the experimental section did better in all categories.*

For student outcomes in CS 2_{ex}, we can only compare the experimental section against traditional sections taught by faculty members *other* than the authors. In addition, due to the more divergent material in the experimental CS 2_{ex} course (with its heavy emphasis on path-finding algorithms and object-oriented design/refactoring from an existing large code base), the material between the CS 2 variants was more diverse. However, the same final exam was used across experimental and traditional sections with the exception of two questions out of twelve (20 points out the the 95 total points). For the experimental section the average on the final exam was 80.8%, while three other traditional section final exam averages were 79.6%, 83%, and 68.9%. Comparing the total number of students enrolled in the CS 2 sections (experimental versus traditional), 82% of the students in the experimental section received a passing grade, while in the three traditional sections 86% (of two sections) and 77% of another section of the students received passing grades.

In total, the performance comparisons indicate that the students in the experimental section performed on par with their counterparts in the traditional sections. We feel students in the experimental sections had additional gains documented below.

5. OBSERVATIONS AND IMPRESSIONS

When reflecting on the CS 1_{ex} and CS 2_{ex} experiment, the participating faculty perceived some very clear positive outcomes. Perhaps the clearest outcome for both faculty was an increased appreciation for the use of Python as an introductory programming language. Using Python in CS 1_{ex} drastically reduced the amount of lab and office hour time that instructors spent explaining strange and obscure program errors so common with `C` in an introductory course. We will not repeat all of the advantages here, as many are well-documented [14, 9], but, for example, beginning with Python instills some simple good programming practices from the outset, such as initializing variables before use.

Moreover, the transition from Python to Java in CS 2_{ex} provided a means to bootstrap object-oriented concepts in a manner that is not easily replicated when transitioning from `C` to Java. In particular, since CS 1_{ex} introduced objects as aggregates of data, we could begin CS 2_{ex} with a discussion of adding behavior to objects (still in Python) without any concern for the syntactic and semantic overhead of access modifiers and `static` data/methods. Continuing in Python, the introduction of inheritance was simplified by the omission of access modifiers and their interaction with inheritance and by the omission of the distinctions (in Java) between extending a class and implementing interfaces. In addition, each modification (e.g., the refactoring of a function into methods or joining a set of classes at a parent through inheritance) could be made and tested iteratively since the function-based aspects of the code continue to work in Python. After this experience, students found these concepts (objects with behavior, inheritance, polymorphism) more readily understandable in Java and showed greater appreciation for the use and value of interfaces.

Another aspect of the experimental offering that we found to be very effective was the use of a large, cohesive project in CS 2_{ex}. The large virtual world programming project requiring complex interacting objects with some shared and divergent behavior (benefiting from polymorphism and inheritance), made the introduction of many of the object-oriented topics more natural and immediately useful to students. The 2D world context provided a great stage for students to apply searching/pathing algorithms; the introduction of these algorithms improved student engagement leading to many in-class discussions and outside research into and coding of variants of the pathing algorithms. Even students that struggled with this topic continued to be engaged and to work hard on these projects in order to accomplish their goal of moving their gatherer to a resource along a "good" path. For some, this led to continued work on tuning their pathing during later assignments when the emphasis was no longer on pathing.

Some of the general observations we came away from this experience with are as follows. In the experimental sections, it was a positive experience for faculty and students:

- to include project appropriate pathing algorithms in CS 2_{ex} (specifically depth first search and A*).
- to have assignments that built on prior assignments (students were more accountable for their code and had to "stick with it" to get their program to work).
- to rewrite a large Python code base in Java. This activity required a level of precision and code understanding that previously used rudimentary assignments did not require.
- to use object-oriented language features in the context of a relatively large code base to implement the virtual world.

In addition, we strongly suspect that the students in our experimental section have a better understanding of the need for and value of object-oriented language features and object-oriented programming in Java than they would have after completing our traditional CS 2 (though our CS 2_{ex} students were not exposed to as much of the Java API). We intend to do longitudinal tracking for these students in CS 3 to evaluate their performance compared to students in traditional sections.

The aspect of the experimental section that was most challenging for students (reflected in their verbal comments on the class) was requiring two different programming languages in one quarter (during CS 2_{ex}). However, each student had a diverse reaction to the two very different languages they needed to use throughout this two-quarter long project. At the end of CS 2_{ex} we asked students to express their preference for Python or Java (including the option of saying they liked both). Twelve students commented that they enjoyed Java while eighteen said that they did not like Java or that they preferred Python. Student comments about the languages included opinions such as: "I hate shoving everything into classes", "I don't like types", "I like the freedom of Python", "Java had a great IDE", and "I liked the constraints and structure in Java". This varied opinion of the two languages is a positive indicator that exposing introductory students to various languages allows them to find the programming tools that best match either the specific problem they are solving or, when given a choice, that best match their own computational thinking style.

The one aspect of the experimental sections that did not go as well as predicted was the very open-ended nature of the projects at the beginning of CS 1_{ex}. We found that during the first few weeks of CS 1_{ex}, when students were designing their worlds but had fairly limited programming experience, they struggled a bit with understanding what they needed to do and what they *could* accomplish. For future offerings of this sequence, we strongly feel that providing more structured assignments while introducing world designing and building would be beneficial in CS 1.

Figure 1: Example world visualizations developed during CS 1_{ex} and CS 2_{ex}: base world provided post-CS 1_{ex}(left); a world with knights gathering diamonds (middle); a world featuring witches gathering potion ingredients (right).

Similarly, the one aspect of the experimental sections that was disappointing for the participating faculty was the fact that allowing students the creative freedom to design their own worlds was less important to the students than expected. Gauging student interest based on those who continued with some version of their own world in CS 2_{ex}, only 42% of the students were committed to designing their own individualized creative world. This commitment to an individualized world did vary by student ranging from those that clearly made little effort to find a set of visually cohesive sprites to those that took the time to create their own set of sprites. Some examples of virtuals worlds are shown in Figure 1. These examples include a world where knights seek diamonds and a world where witches gather potions. A particularly notable student-designed world modeled molecules joining together to create more complex structures.

6. CONCLUSIONS

Overall, we consider the experimental courses a success that will have an impact on our department's future curricular offerings. Very few aspects did not work as well as predicted while other aspects like language and context-based object-oriented projects were very strong wins. One strong outcome from this experiment is the department voting to change the programming language used in CS 1 from `C` to Python in all sections. Longer term curricular outcomes include examining the use of a quarter-long project-based curriculum in CS 2 and an examination of the topics and sequence of topics in CS 2 and CS 3.

The experience, in and of itself, of co-teaching this course is worth commenting on. The process was very rewarding but not without its challenges in terms of the overhead in communication and variation in teaching style. As university professors we so often are alone in our classrooms and do not need to share the stage. The process of seeing another faculty member teach a co-designed lesson is incredibly rewarding – providing insight into methodology for explaining certain concepts and insight into general classroom and lecturing style. This experience encouraged one of the instructors, with a typically reserved teaching style, to experiment with different forms of in-lecture interaction.

7. REFERENCES

[1] Computing curricula 2001. *J. Educ. Resour. Comput.*, 1(3es), Sept. 2001.

[2] Processing– http:\\www.processing.org, 2014.

[3] pygame– http:\\www.pygame.org, 2014.

[4] M. Barg, A. Fekete, T. Greening, O. Holl, J. Kay, H. Kingston, and K. Crawford. Problem-based learning for foundation computer science courses. *Computer Science Education*, 10:109–128, 2000.

[5] J. Bennedsen and M. E. Caspersen. Failure rates in introductory programming. *SIGCSE Bull. 39*, pages 32–36, 2007.

[6] K. E. Boyer, R. S. Dwight, C. S. Miller, C. D. Raubenheimer, M. F. Stallmann, and M. A. Vouk. A case for smaller class size with integrated lab for introductory computer science. In *Proceedings of the 38th SIGCSE Technical Symposium on Computer Science Education*, SIGCSE '07, pages 341–345, New York, NY, USA, 2007. ACM.

[7] J. P. Cohoon and L. A. Tychonievich. Analysis of a CS1 approach for attracting diverse and inexperienced students to computing majors. In *Proceedings of the 42Nd ACM Technical Symposium on Computer Science Education*, SIGCSE '11, pages 165–170, New York, NY, USA, 2011. ACM.

[8] Z. Dodds, R. Libeskind-Hadas, C. Alvarado, and G. Kuenning. Evaluating a breadth-first CS 1 for scientists. In *ACM SIGCSE Bulletin*, volume 40, pages 266–270. ACM, 2008.

[9] M. H. Goldwasser and D. Letscher. Teaching an object-oriented CS1 – with python. *SIGCSE Bull.*, 40(3):42–46, June 2008.

[10] M. Guzdial. Does contextualized computing education help? *ACM Inroads*, 1(4):4–6, Dec. 2010.

[11] M. Haungs, C. Clark, J. Clements, and D. Janzen. Improving first-year success and retention through interest-based CS0 courses. In *Proceedings of the ACM Technical Symposium on Computer Science Education*, 2012.

[12] C. Horstmann. Gridworld– http:\\horstmann.com\gridworld, 2008.

[13] N. Nagappan, L. Williams, M. Ferzli, E. Wiebe, K. Yang, C. Miller, and S. Balik. Improving the CS1 experience with pair programming. *SIGCSE Bull.*, 35(1):359–362, Jan. 2003.

[14] A. Radenski. "Python first": A lab-based digital introduction to computer science. *SIGCSE Bull.*, 38(3):197–201, June 2006.

A Data Programming CS1 Course

Ruth E. Anderson, Michael D. Ernst
University of Washington
Seattle, WA
{rea, mernst}@cse.uw.edu

Robert Ordóñez
Southern Adventist University
Collegedale, TN
rordonez@southern.edu

Paul Pham
The Evergreen State College
Olympia, WA
phamp@evergreen.edu

Ben Tribelhorn
Seattle University
Seattle, WA
tribelhb@seattleu.edu

ABSTRACT

This paper reports on our experience teaching introductory programming by means of real-world data analysis. We have found that students can be motivated to learn programming and computer science concepts in order to analyze DNA, predict the outcome of elections, detect fraudulent data, suggest friends in a social network, determine the authorship of documents, and more. The approach is more than just a collection of "nifty assignments"; rather, it affects the choice of topics and pedagogy.

This paper describes how our approach has been used at four diverse colleges and universities to teach CS majors and non-majors alike. It outlines the types of assignments, which are based on problems from science, engineering, business, and the humanities. Finally, it offers advice for anyone trying to integrate the approach into their own institution.

Categories and Subject Descriptors

K.3.2 [**Computers and Education**]: Computer and Information Science Education—Computer science education

General Terms

Design, Experimentation, Human Factors.

Keywords

CS1; introductory computing; data programming; data processing.

1. INTRODUCTION

Traditional introductory programming courses often take their examples and assignments from the domains of puzzles, games, and abstract mathematics. For instance, students might be shown how to reverse a list or assigned to compute the Fibonacci sequence. This approach works well for some students, but others may fail to see how the concepts being taught can be applied to the world beyond computing. This lack of connection to the real world can have a negative impact on students' motivation and interest in CS.

Recently there has been an explosion in the number of datasets available from every conceivable field, and "Big Data" is in the news everywhere [16]. Graduate students find they need to take programming courses to solve problems in domains such as biology, physics, economics, and the social sciences [e.g. 27].

We have developed a CS1 course with a "data programming" orientation that teaches students introductory programming and computing concepts by means of real-world data analysis problems. The course is intended for undergraduate students with no prior programming experience. The materials were originally developed at the University of Washington where the course has been taught three times, and they have been adapted and used at multiple other institutions. This paper reports on our experience at a diverse set of four of these schools.

The key idea of our approach is that assignments use an existing dataset to answer a question that is relevant to science, engineering, business, or the humanities. Neither the questions nor the datasets are artificial. We have successfully used this approach to

- motivate and excite students about computation,
- teach computer programming & computer science concepts,
- enable students to process data to solve real problems of interest to them, and
- serve both CS and non-CS majors.

Although the approach is not necessarily tied to any one language, the offerings we report on have been in the Python programming language. Our goal in this paper is not to formally evaluate these offerings but rather to describe the courses, show the variety of settings where the approach has been applied, and enable other instructors to reuse the ideas and/or materials in new settings.

2. RELATED WORK

Many educators have suggested alternatives to the puzzles-and-games approach to CS1. Several have noted the benefits of placing CS concepts in contexts students find motivating [5]. Well-known examples include media computation [20, 26], robotics [15], and animation [6]. Stevenson's real-world programming assignments [23, 24] are a web crawler, spam evaluator, and steganography. De-Pasquale [7] presents three data sources: stock quotes and the APIs from Google and Slashdot. These domains are mostly connected to entertainment and computers, whereas our approach shows computation applied to science, engineering, business, and the humanities.

Other educators have sought to show students how the skills they are learning can have impact on the world beyond computing. The ITiCSE working group [12] offers 14 projects related to "social good" that motivate students and provide them with skills to solve complex problems; Erkan et al. [11] do the same for a data structures course. By contrast, we weave the theme of solving problems with real-world impact throughout the course. Some courses that address realistic problems and data focus on visualization [21], statistics [3], or databases [25]. Ours is a CS1 course that teaches computational thinking and programming.

Others have sought to create CS1 courses that demonstrate the applicability of CS to STEM fields [2, 29]. Many, though not all [18], of these courses use the Python language as we do. Dodds et

SIGCSE'15, March 4–7, 2015, Kansas City, MO, USA.

http://dx.doi.org/10.1145/2676723.2677309

al. created a breadth-first CS1 course for scientists [8]. Hambrusch et al. used problems from scientific domains to teach computational thinking [14]. Our course teaches practical programming skills, and our strong focus on real datasets has an impact on our pedagogy, course topics, and assignment structure.

3. OUR INSTITUTIONS

We have successfully implemented this approach in four different courses taught by five different instructors at our four institutions.

3.1 University of Washington (UW)

UW is a public, R1 university with approximately 40,000 students. UW has a thriving two-quarter CS1 and CS2 sequence in Java that is a prerequisite for admission to the CS major. Entrance to the major is competitive and while there is no CS minor at UW, there are eight non-majors CS courses available on topics ranging from web programming to artificial intelligence.

The goal of the data programming course at UW is to offer an alternative to students who are not attracted to the CS major or to the Java CS1 offering. CSE 160 Data Programming has been offered three times (Summer 2012, Winter 2013, Winter 2014) by two different instructors to classes of approximately 50 students. UW is on a ten-week quarter system, and students in CSE 160 attended three 50-minute lectures and one 50-minute recitation section per week.

CS majors are not permitted to register for CSE 160. Students from a variety of other majors have taken the course, and some have gone on to double-major in CS as well as their original field (e.g. Bioengineering, Oceanography). Students have multiple times ranked the course among the 10 best in the College of Engineering, and it always has a waiting list.

3.2 Pacific Union College (PUC)

Pacific Union College is a private, liberal arts parochial four-year college with approximately 1,700 students.

The data programming approach was used in CPTR 115 Introduction to Computer Programming during two consecutive quarters (Fall 2012 and Winter 2013). This course is a prerequisite for a "breadth-first CS1" [4] course for computer science majors (usually taught in C) that assumes prior programming knowledge. It is also a cognate (requirement outside the major department) and usually the only programming course for mathematics, biomathematics, engineering, and physics majors, as well as an option in the Practical and Applied Arts area of the general education requirements at PUC. Thus it is a course required of CS majors and taken by students from several other majors simultaneously. It met for three 50-minute lectures and one 3-hour lab period per week during a ten-week quarter.

The two offerings of CPTR 115 were taught by the same instructor to 16 and 8 students, respectively. Roughly half of those students were declared CS majors. A handful were high school students in a dual-enrollment program, two of whom went on to become CS majors the following year. Focusing on real-world data sets in a variety of fields made this course far more engaging for its broad audience, compared to previous offerings. Starting this focus from the very beginning of the term enabled students to tackle a sizable open-ended data analysis project within the confines of a 10-week quarter. Anecdotal feedback from students indicated a higher-than-usual level of enthusiasm for the kinds of problems tackled and a sense of accomplishment at doing real data analysis — even for those who had previously done a bit of game programming.

3.3 The Evergreen State College

The Evergreen State College is a public, liberal arts teaching college with approximately 4,400 students. Evergreen is known for its unique interdisciplinary approach. The demographic of Evergreen students includes a higher percentage of non-traditional students than those at an R1 university: older adult students, working and single parents, and veterans.

Data programming was first offered at Evergreen in Fall 2013. This course was the first (CS1) of a three-quarter sequence in introductory computer programming. The remaining two programming courses in the sequence were taught in Java and did not use a data programming approach. This sequence is combined with two other three-quarter sequences (in computer architecture and discrete mathematics) to form a lower-division CS curriculum (called a program), which is a prerequisite for an analogous three-quarter upper-division CS program. Although Evergreen does not have official majors and departments, students who take these two programs self-identify as CS majors. Evergreen is on a ten-week quarter system, and for this course students attended two 2-hour lectures and one 2-hour lab per week.

The 68 students in the CS1 course consisted of both majors (who intend to continue onto the upper-division CS program) and non-majors (students for whom this course will be their only exposure to CS). The CS1 course received positive reviews from students, students were highly engaged in the class, and the turnover rate to the follow-on Java CS2 course was low.

3.4 Seattle University (SU)

Seattle University is a private, masters-level university with about 7,300 students, mostly undergraduates.

CPSC 192 Data Driven Programming is a new course designed for non-CS majors and CS minors. It serves as the first course in the CS minor and as the CS requirement for the Environmental Science major as well as some tracks of other science majors (i.e. Math). Students majoring in CS at SU take a two-quarter sequence in C++. All CS courses except the data programming course are closed to non-majors, so demand for this course is expected to remain high as entry into the CS major is difficult for existing students. CPSC 192 was first offered in Spring 2014. The course is limited to around 20 students. SU is on a ten-week quarter system, and for this course students attended three 75-minute "lectures" (held in a lab) each week.

The 18 students taking the course in Spring 2014 were a diverse group of non-major students, predominantly science and engineering majors, and was a roughly even composition of freshmen through seniors. In the course evaluations, the lab time and direct instructor interaction was well reviewed. About half of the students felt that they might use Python for a future project in their discipline. An in-class informal evaluation showed a large variance in students' view of the "fun-factor" of the assignments, validating the variety of topics included.

4. A DATA PROGRAMMING CS1 COURSE

This section discusses course topics and pedagogy, then describes some of the programming assignments used in the course. While our experience is with teaching an entire CS1 course oriented towards data programming, we expect some instructors may be interested in adopting only parts of our approach or individual assignments.

4.1 Effect on Course Topics and Pedagogy

Supporting students' experience with realistic datasets requires a few changes to the topics, order, and presentation of traditional CS1 material. Students learn similar concepts to those in any other CS1 course, but a slightly different toolset. Our choice of topics is also motivated by viewing our course not just as CS1 but also as CS-Omega: it should give a solid foundation for subsequent practical and theoretical work, but should also be useful even if the student never takes another CS course.

The overall focus in our course is on providing students with the tools necessary to process data provided as files. This focus on processing data provided in files guides the choice and ordering of topics. For example, we introduce the foreach loop but not the for loop with an explicit index. We use file I/O extensively, with only limited use of console I/O. We do not create GUIs nor any other user interface. Students use complex data structures such as dictionaries and graphs, but they do not re-implement basic data structures like linked lists nor algorithms like sorting. We introduce recursion at the end of the term, as an enrichment topic, but it is not used in assignments. We introduce a few concepts that are often missing from CS1 courses but are desirable for data analysis, such as basic statistics and how to plot a graph.

Most assignments gave students some supporting code or libraries. Early in the course, students are given examples of documented, modular code that they may explore at their own pace but are not required to understand until later assignments. We have found it useful to provide a first assignment consisting of a few short programming exercises that does not do any real-world data analysis while students are becoming familiar with an IDE or command line editor and the basics of Python syntax.

We use the Python language, because it is easy to use and is widely adopted in the sciences. Because Python has a significant and usable procedural subset, we do not discuss object orientation. Python's rich set of libraries provides the opportunity to give students valuable experience reading the documentation for a real library and successfully using it. We have used the Python networkX graph library, matplotlib, numpy, scipy, and urllib. However, the overall approach is not tied to Python, and similar assignments could be done with Java, MATLAB, Mathematica, or other programming languages.

At UW, readings were drawn from *Introduction to Computation and Programming Using Python* by Guttag [13], as well as free online resources like *Think Python* by Downey [9] and the Python Tutorial [19]. We also prepared documents on topics such as Python evaluation rules, using the command line, interacting with files, using csv.DictReader, and debugging. At SU, *Python Programming in Context* by Miller and Ranum [17] was the recommended text.

4.2 Sample Programming Assignments

Below we describe several of the assignments used in the courses at our institutions. We list them in the approximate order they were given to students and indicate which assignments were used at which schools. In addition to these assignments, most schools also used a first assignment consisting of a few short exercises that did not do any data analysis. Other assignments used included Twitter sentiment analysis, image analysis, processing stock market data, and linguistic analysis [30].

DNA Analysis (UW, PUC, Evergreen, SU)

DNA can be described as a string over the alphabet of base pairs: {A, C, G, T}. The GC content (the fraction of nucleotides that are either G's or C's) is biologically important. For example, GC content can identify types of genes and can be used in determining classification of species.

In the DNA Analysis assignment, students are given files from a DNA sequencer and are asked to use loops and if statements to count nucleotides, categorize organisms, and compute other statistics about the files they are given. This is students' first look at reading files, although the code for reading files is given to them for this assignment. This is also students' first look at the notion of data cleaning (some DNA sequences contain "junk" base pairs) — an important idea for students to be exposed to in preparation for examining their own data files. Students and instructors have commented that this assignment is a bit simpler than the following ones. While this allows students to succeed early in the course, it could also lull them into thinking future assignments will be as simple.

Oceanographic Data Integration (UW, PUC)

In the Oceanographic Data Integration assignment, students work with real measurements of physical and biological variables from the Puget Sound. The research question they are addressing is "Which environmental variables correlate with the abundance of Ammonia-Oxidizing Archaea (AOA)?" The dataset students are using comes from an NSF-funded project, "Significance of nitrification in shaping planktonic biodiversity in the ocean".

Students are faced with the common task of having to integrate data spread across several CSV files into one file. The provided Python code reads CSV files and computes Pearson correlations, but is missing the bodies of functions to compute mean and standard deviation functions needed by the Pearson code. This assignment introduces students to the common situation where the format of collected data is not always convenient for analysis, and the idea that by reading the data into a program it can be transformed to other formats. Students gain practice with Python lists, functions, loops, and file I/O.

Social Networking (UW, Evergreen)

We are not the first to notice that students are motivated by projects related to social networking [22]. In this assignment, students address the research question, "Which of two collaborative-filtering approaches is better for recommending friends?" The dataset is the Facebook New Orleans social network.

Students are introduced to the idea of a graph as a data structure and use the networkX library both to create a simple graph by hand and to read data from a file into a data structure. We provide scaffolding in the form of function signatures that students need to fill in, as well as a series of assert statements that show the expected output of the functions. Students make use of previous knowledge about file I/O, functions, loops, and conditionals. Learning objectives include using graphs to solve a problem, as well as gaining experience using sets, dictionaries, and sorting. Discussion of various sorting approaches is optional; students only need to know how to use Python's built-in sorting methods.

Election Prediction (UW, Evergreen, SU)

The 2012 US presidential election was a watershed in the fight between pundits and statisticians to accurately predict the outcome of political campaigns. The rivalry became front-page news, with many pundits loudly proclaiming that the statisticians would be humiliated on November 6. In fact, the opposite happened: statistician Nate Silver (of the website FiveThirtyEight.com) correctly predicted the outcome in every state, whereas pundits' predictions varied significantly. In this assignment, students replicate Nate Silver's results by using polling data to predict the outcome of the 2012 US presidential election. Students solve a complex problem using lists, sets and dictionaries and are thus able to appreciate the benefits of good problem decomposition, data structure choice, and testing practices. Most students found this assignment to be quite challenging due to the use of nested data structures. At UW we found providing a preliminary quiz forcing students to examine the data structures closely helped significantly in this respect.

Fraud Detection (UW, PUC, SU)

In the fraud detection assignment, students look for fraud in datasets using two different approaches, broken into two separate assignments. First, students examine the least significant digits of the vote totals in election returns from the disputed 2009 Iranian presidential election. We would expect the digits in the ones and tens place to be uniformly distributed in a valid dataset but students examine the Iranian results themselves and explore issues such as the impact of sample size. In addition to the Iranian data, other election results (e.g. 2008 U.S. presidential election, 2012 Egyptian presidential election) can also be brought in for comparison. In the second part of the assignment, students use Benford's law to evaluate the validity of two datasets: 1) US Census data showing the population of US cities and 2) populations of fictional places from literature and pop culture.

In both parts of the assignment students are guided through an approach to statistics and hypothesis testing through simulation. The basic question posed in this assignment and that students are likely to wrestle with in their own work is "I have observed something. Was it unusual? How unusual?" Our approach to answering this question is to have students write code to generate many possible datasets, then measure the thing of interest in those datasets to produce p-values. Students also plot their results using matplotlib.pyplot. For this assignment students are not given any supporting code thus are asked to write a Python program in good style without a provided template. They make use of loops and lists, as well as string and numerical manipulation.

Estimating Avogadro's Number (SU)

Estimating Avogadro's number using microscopy data and the concept of Brownian motion was a student favorite at SU. In this assignment students were given a sequence of images of polystyrene beads in water and are asked to track the beads to estimate self-diffusion. This was adapted from a Nifty assignment [28] to act as a final project with exposure to post CS1 topics. The objective was threefold: to give students the enthusiasm to try their own future projects, to see some cool science, and to think about data structures. Students were required to conform to complex third party data structures (both B/W & color images), and to create their own data structures (tracking blobs/beads). The introduction of data structures that are open-ended, e.g., "What data do you need to track a bead?", encourages students to stretch their minds around design and data management. As a bonus, a discussion of algorithmic efficiency from too many nested loops can be addressed with more advanced students. Students enjoyed seeing the science in action and the freedom to create and manipulate data in their own way.

Open-ended Final Project (UW, PUC)

At UW and PUC, the final assignment was a multi-week open-ended project addressing a research question of each student's choice. Students could work together in groups of two students. Completion of this project demonstrated a key goal of the course — enabling students to process data to solve real problems of interest to them. At the beginning of the course, we told students about the project and showed example topics addressed by students in previous iterations of the course. This served to motivate students to acquire the tools necessary to accomplish this task throughout the quarter, and it got them thinking about project ideas from day one. Topics addressed by students included the decay mechanisms of the Higgs Boson, the correlation between firearm ownership and violent crimes, school district performance vs. financing, the home court advantage in sports, music classification via note analysis, and forecasting company health from financial statements.

One of the biggest hurdles to picking a research question is finding an appropriate dataset. We required students to use publicly available datasets to enable the course staff to evaluate their work. We provided students with links to quite a few possible datasets to get them started.

We have found it useful to break the project into multiple phases to prevent students from waiting until the last minute and to allow for re-direction of project ideas that are too simple or too ambitious. The first checkpoint requires students to locate a dataset and propose a research question. Later checkpoints ask them to provide background and motivation, flesh out their technique and evaluation method, and finally to present and discuss their results. We have used the final exam period in the course for project presentations. This session became a celebration of the students' accomplishments. Allowing students to see what their peers have accomplished in this manner serves to support the notion that what they have learned in the course can be applied to answer questions from a wide variety of domains.

5. ADAPTING TO YOUR CONTEXT

The first version of the course was piloted at UW in Summer 2012. Since then it has been offered at multiple other institutions. Assignments and course structure were adapted by each instructor to their unique context. Below we discuss issues of interest to instructors wishing to adopt our approach at their institution.

5.1 CS1 with Minimal Infrastructure

At most schools CS1 is one of the largest CS courses offered. Students new to programming are often aided by armies of TAs who have previously taken the course themselves. There may be a dedicated lab that is manned with course staff many hours of the day or there may be hands-on lab sessions scheduled for credit hours. When offering a new or alternative CS1 course, your first few offerings may need to survive without these amenities.

At SU, the course format of "lab in every lecture" offered supervised coding practice in every period. In a 75-minute period, lecture was limited to 45 minutes, and labs were assigned typically at the end of lecture. Overall there were approximately 20 coding exercises used, graded on an effort-only basis. This approach addressed several issues. Given the diversity of backgrounds of these non-major students in terms of major, class standing, and coding experience, it was imperative to require extra coding practice. Additionally, as the tutors at SU know mostly C++ or C#, they were not ideal for helping with the course. This in-class lab time allowed the instructor to fill the tutoring gap for students. Finally, since many students at SU work, they are not able to attend tutoring or office hours regularly, so for some this was the only time to get in-person assistance. Most students appreciated having this time, as it helped reinforce the lecture topics. This mandated extra practice also improved students' coding confidence. This seemed to be especially true for some female students that were initially hesitant to get started for fear of writing "wrong" code on their first attempt. Ultimately, holding lecture in a lab room every period allowed for the flexibility to adapt the time spent on labs to the needs of an individual group of students, and the extra mandated coding was a boon particularly to the weakest students.

Other strategies used at UW and Evergreen to support students new to programming without requiring significant infrastructure included pointing students to online Python resources such as Codecademy.com and CodingBat.com to provide more hands-on practice and immediate feedback. The courses at PUC and UW also used pythontutor.com to help students visualize the structure of data and the effect of control constructs. Overall this is an area to pay attention to as students are likely to be aware of the resources provided to students in your "main" CS1 course and may feel they are being asked to get by with less support.

5.2 Adjusting Assignments to Your Students

As described in Section 4.2, the authors have successfully adapted many of the original assignments from UW for use at their institutions. Here we discuss some of the adjustments made.

In all offerings of the course, students were provided considerable starter code at the beginning of the term, then less and less starter code as the term progressed. (No code was provided for the fraud detection assignment, nor for the final project.) The goal was to make students read well-structured and well-documented code, and to reduce their workload.

However, some students were frustrated when the provided code did not make intuitive sense to them. These students found the assignments' provision of a problem approach and starter code restrictive rather than helpful. At SU, we improved their completion rate by increasing the flexibility of assignments: providing less code, shortening the assignment write-ups, and, in the later part of the course, allowing students to add/remove/rename functions and function parameters.

This introduced students more rapidly to the experiences of problem analysis and program organization, including choosing how to store and manipulate data. It also forced students to better comprehend the assignment goals, specifically to begin by addressing the structure of the data as pre and post conditions. This flexibility made the starter code smaller and more approachable. On the other hand, these sparser specifications required more in-class time be spent on explanations, they reduced the utility of staff test suites, and they required more effort to grade.

In all offerings, we found the "wishful thinking" approach to problem decomposition effective: when faced with an unsolved part of the problem, the students could name and specify a routine that would solve it, use that hypothetical routine, and come back later to implement it [1]. A live coding lecture demonstrating "wishful thinking" was effective in encouraging students to write additional functions. We grounded this method in practices that are common to students, such as outlining a paper before writing.

At Evergreen, the difficulty of the material was challenging to students, some of whom worked multiple jobs or had to support families. These students could not devote their full attention to learning as much as younger students at traditional universities. To adapt the original data programming course, we only selected four of the assignments and subdivided each of those in half to create eight mini-assignments. Turn-in dates were flexible, and students were allowed to time-box their efforts (for example, 11 hours of outside time per week) to attempt as many problems as possible within that time. The extent to which students were able to complete assignments provided valuable data to adjust the difficulty of assignments for this demographic in the future.

None of our offerings have used all of the assignments we have collected. Thus, expanding the course from a quarter to a semester can be easily accomplished by adding assignments, expanding the final project, or reducing the pace. One could also add enrichment topics, such as an introduction to object orientation — so long as the focus is on how it is useful for real-world data analysis.

5.3 Non-majors and Non-traditional Students

The course delivery at SU was specifically focused on catering to non-majors, which presented the additional challenge of motivating students who view the course as only secondarily important. The style of this course, which focuses on practicality for students taking only one CS course, was helpful in that respect. However, many students were surprised by how much time it took to master data programming. Interesting assignments were key to motivating students outside of class. Interactive in-class activities were the solution of choice to keep students alert and attentive during lecture. Methods that were successful and minimally interruptive at SU included code something very small and report before continuing lecture (using the interpreter), have everyone stand and then vote by sitting, using a suit of cards to define a sorting algorithm, and writing algorithms on paper.

At Evergreen, the data programming approach was especially appealing to both non-majors (who were initially interested in applying CS to other sciences such as biochemistry) and non-traditional students. Older adult students appreciated the real-life applications, which seemed less contrived or condescending than "hello world" examples or toy problems. Subdividing assignments into smaller pieces and keeping due dates flexible were important for keeping this group of students motivated and engaged.

5.4 Articulation into (a non-Python) CS2

While designed to serve students well as both the first and last programming course they may take, we have found the course has also worked well for students pursuing more CS courses, usually offered in a language other than Python. Several institutions use Python in their CS1 courses and some have reported on their experience with students articulating into a non-Python CS2 [10].

At UW, where the course has now been taught three times, we have seen a number of students from the class go on to major in CS (and serve as TAs for the course). During the first offering of the course, we held a parallel one-credit Java basics course with the goal of helping prepare students to take CS2 in Java. At UW we also offer a one-quarter combined CS1/CS2 course in Java that is an ideal follow-on course for students interested in majoring in CS after taking our course, since they already have most of the conceptual background provided by the CS1 course but are not familiar with the Java terminology and toolset.

At Evergreen, where the data programming course served as the first course for both CS majors and non-majors alike, the change from Python in the fall quarter to Java in the winter quarter required several adjustments. One difference is that our data programming assignments provided more supporting code than is typical for a CS1 or CS2 course. When moving to the next course, Evergreen students had to adjust to implement more from scratch.

At SU, CS majors take CS1 and CS2 courses offered in C++ (the primary language used in the major). SU plans to offer an alternative CS2 to follow the data programming course which will include an introduction to C++. The goal is to serve CS minors and non-majors who have to take additional CS courses. This will mean that people wanting to switch to the CS major after taking data programming can do so without having "wasted" a course. This alternate path is garnering significant interest from previous and prospective students of the data programming course.

At PUC, the next course students take after the data programming course is a "breadth-first CS1" [4] that assumes prior programming experience. This second course expects that students do not come in knowing the language required for the course and includes a transition to another language, usually C.

6. CONCLUSION

Students in CS1 can do real-world data analysis. We have described how multiple diverse schools have successfully implemented the data programming approach. We welcome other instructors to join in the fun! Course syllabi, assignments, and other resources can be found at our instructor resources site [30].

7. REFERENCES

[1] H. Abelson, G. J. Sussman, J. Sussman. *Structure and Interpretation of Computer Programs.* MIT Press, 1996.

[2] J.C. Adams and R.J. Pruim. Computing for STEM majors: enhancing non CS majors' computing skills. In *SIGCSE 2012*, 457-462.

[3] R. Catrambone and M. Guzdial. Computational freakonomics. http://swiki.cc.gatech.edu/compfreak, 2012.

[4] D. E. Comer, D. Gries, M. C. Mulder, A. Tucker, A. Joe Turner, P. R. Young. Computing as a discipline. *Commun. ACM 32*, 1 (January 1989), 9-23.

[5] S. Cooper and S. Cunningham. Teaching computer science in context. *ACM Inroads* 1, 1 (March 2010), 5-8.

[6] W.P. Dann, S. Cooper, and R. Pausch. *Learning to Program with Alice* (2 ed.). Prentice Hall Press, 2008.

[7] P. DePasquale. Exploiting on-line data sources as the basis of programming projects. In *SIGCSE 2006*, 283-287.

[8] Z. Dodds, R. Libeskind-Hadas, C. Alvarado, and G. Kuenning. Evaluating a breadth-first cs 1 for scientists. In *SIGCSE 2008*, 266-270.

[9] A. B. Downey. Think Python, http://www.greenteapress.com/thinkpython/, 2012.

[10] R.J. Enbody, W.F. Punch, and M. McCullen. Python CS1 as preparation for C++ CS2. In *SIGCSE 2009*, 116-120.

[11] A. Erkan, T. Pfaff, J. Hamilton, and M. Rogers. Sustainability themed problem solving in data structures and algorithms. In *SIGCSE 2012*, 9-14.

[12] M. Goldweber, J. Barr, T. Clear, R. Davoli, S. Mann, E. Patitsas, and S. Portnoff. A framework for enhancing the social good in computing education: a values approach. *ACM Inroads* 4, 1 (March 2013), 58-79.

[13] J. V. Guttag. *Introduction to Computation and Programming Using Python.* MIT Press, 2013.

[14] S. Hambrusch, C. Hoffmann, J.T. Korb, M. Haugan, and A.L. Hosking. A multidisciplinary approach towards computational thinking for science majors. *SIGCSE 2009*, 183-187.

[15] P.B. Lawhead, M.E. Duncan, C.G. Bland, M. Goldweber, M. Schep, D.J. Barnes, and R.G. Hollingsworth. A road map for teaching introductory programming using LEGO© Mindstorms robots. *SIGCSE Bull.* 35, 2(June 2002),191-201.

[16] S. Lohr. The age of big data. *New York Times*, Feb 2012.

[17] B. N. Miller and D. L. Ranum. *Python Programming In Context.* Jones & Bartlett, 2013.

[18] Princeton Univeristy, Computer Science 126: General Computer Science, http://www.cs.princeton.edu/~cos126

[19] The Python Tutorial. https://docs.python.org/2/tutorial/

[20] L. Rich, H. Perry, and M. Guzdial. A CS1 course designed to address interests of women. In *SIGCSE 2004*, 190-194.

[21] K. A. Robbins, D. M. Senseman, and P. E. Pate. Teaching biologists to compute using data visualization. In *SIGCSE 2011*, 335-340.

[22] M. Sahami, FacePamphlet: Implementing a Simple Social Network, Retrieved Dec 1, 2014 http://nifty.stanford.edu/2009/sahami-face-pamphlet/

[23] D. E. Stevenson and P. J. Wagner. Developing real-world programming assignments for CS1. In *ITICSE '06*, 158-162.

[24] D. E. Stevenson, M. R. Wick, and S. J. Ratering. Steganography and cartography: interesting assignments that reinforce machine representation, bit manipulation, and discrete structures concepts. In *SIGCSE 2005*, 277-281.

[25] D. G. Sullivan. A data-centric introduction to computer science for non-majors. In *SIGCSE 2013*, 71-76.

[26] S. L. Tanimoto. *An Interdisciplinary Introduction to Image Processing: Pixels, Numbers, and Programs.* MIT Press, 2012.

[27] Teaching Lab Skills for Scientific Computing, Retrieved Dec. 1, 2014 http://software-carpentry.org/

[28] K. Wayne, Estimating Avogadro's Number, Retrieved Dec. 1, 2014 http://nifty.stanford.edu/2013/wayne-avogadro.html

[29] G. Wilson, C. Alvarado, J. Campbell, R. Landau, and R. Sedgewick. CS-1 for scientists. In *SIGCSE 2008*, 36-37.

[30] Data Programming Instructor Resources, http://tinyurl.com/dataprogramming/instructor-resources

A Descent into the Maelstrom: Teaching Legacy Programming and Re-engineering

Michael Wirth
School of Computer Science
University of Guelph
Guelph, Ontario, Canada N1G2W1
mwirth@uoguelph.ca

ABSTRACT

Computer science is a discipline which has swiftly evolved since its inception in the 1950s. This has invariably meant that new courses introduced into a curriculum are often of the bleeding-edge sort: genetic algorithms, parallel processing, mobile-based applications. Programming languages too have changed as progress ensues. Yet little is discussed of the darker side of computer science - the huge repositories of what some term *legacy* software running our financial, scientific and engineering systems. This paper looks at the introduction of a course which teaches legacy languages and the process of re-engineering with the aim to instill a reverence for the role legacy software plays in the modern world.

Categories and Subject Descriptors

D.2.7 [**Software Engineering**]: Distribution, Maintenance and Enhancement—*restructuring, reverse engineering, reengineering*; D.3.3 [**Programming Languages**]: Language Constructs and Features; K.3.2 [**Computers and Education**]: Computer and Information Science Education

General Terms

Languages

Keywords

legacy software, reengineering, Ada, Fortran, Cobol

1. INTRODUCTION

The concept of modern programming evolved from the introduction of the Fortran programming language in 1955. Although not the first programming language (there were various machine-specific assembly languages), it was the first foray into a general purpose, English-syntax based language. In the intervening six decades, languages have come and gone, often made redundant by a newer language with more newfangled features. Yet even though many of the languages which first appeared in the 1950s are still with us, there almost seems to be a feeling of pandemonium associated with creating programs using them, or even mentioning the idea. Many students go to university with the perception that computer science revolves around programming in Java or C#, because they are the languages of industry. But are they? They yearn for the latest bleeding-edge courses in quantum computing, the design of mobile-based applications, or big data. Yet in the global village of software, modern mainframes run 64-bit Linux and Java alongside vintage code built using languages such as Cobol. There are approximately 200 billion lines of active Cobol code processing 75% of the world's business data, and 90% of financial transactions. In addition several billion lines of new Cobol are added every year [7]. IBM estimates that more than 30 billion transactions occur within Cobol programs every day [10]. To put this into perspective, Google averages about 6 billion searches a day, and it is estimated that 65% of all software is written in Cobol, representing a vast investment in infrastructure. Cobol runs the computational core of many banking institutions - for example, the Bank of New York Mellon, operates in the range of 112,500 Cobol programs representing 343 million lines of code [11]. According to Microfocus, the average American interacts with a Cobol program 13 times a day [10].

In 1972, Jean Sammet wrote a paper on the history and future of programming languages [13]. Discussing the earliest years, 1952-1956, he remarked, *"Of all the languages developed in this time period, only FORTRAN and APT have lasted till today, and both have undergone numerous revisions"*. By then Fortran had lasted nearly 20 years. In future developments, he stated *"It seems likely that FORTRAN and COBOL will be with us for at least five, and probably ten more years"*. Yet in reality, both languages have last nearly four decades more, and may last another three to four decades. Ironically, even APT, a language used to generate instructions for numerically controlled machine tools, developed in the late 1950s is *still* a standard internationally and used by companies to program CNC machines. In reality there is nothing inherently wrong with these languages, they too have evolved over the intervening decades. So why has academe forsaken them? Part of the reason is the need to integrate new material into the curriculum, often by displacing older material. The other reason? - legacy languages are often perceived as being "uncool" and "outdated". The University of Limerick in Ireland is one of the few universities teaching Cobol, with the course concentrating only on Cobol programming. Ryerson University (Canada) of-

SIGCSE'15, March 4–7, 2015, Kansas City, MO, USA.
Copyright © ACM 978-1-4503-2966-8/15/03 ...$15.00.
http://dx.doi.org/10.1145/2676723.2677213.

fers a similarly flavoured course in the guise of mainframe application programming. This paper describes our experiences offering a course focused on the task of designing and re-engineering software in legacy computing systems. The demand for this area of computing is increasing as support infrastructure for legacy systems intensifies.

2. LEGACY SYSTEMS AND SOFTWARE

Legacy software often runs on legacy systems, but what does this mean? Definitions abound in the literature, but it generally can be reduced to the notion of "large software systems that we don't know how to cope with but that are vital to our organization" [1], or similarly "programs which have been developed with an outdated technology make-up for the vast majority of programs in many user application environments" [15]. Legacy systems can be composed of vintage hardware (e.g. mainframes), and/or software constructed using old programming language (e.g. Cobol, Fortran, PL/1). Legacy systems can be difficult to maintain, largely due to a scarcity of experts, lack of up-to-date documentation, obsolete hardware, and ad-hoc modifications made over the lifetime of the system. The systems may also be monolithic, with a rigid architecture, making them hard to integrate into more contemporary infrastructures.

In many respects, most software is legacy software. Even apps for mobile devices have legacy-like tendencies especially when a new version of an operating system is released. A program to calculate compound interest written in Cobol in 1970 functions in the same way when executed in 2011, however users probably won't use a command-line driven program - they expect a visually based application which is transparent with respect to its inner workings - or there is another layer hiding the Cobol code. The way the code was constructed in 1970 differs, although the algorithm remains the same. Changes to a piece of software are usually made incrementally by individuals who may not understand the underlying design concepts of the software. As updates continue over time, knowledge on how the software functions diminishes, often exacerbated by a failure to update documentation. The result is a system which runs, but whose underlying infrastructure becomes less maintainable over time. This eventually causes the quality of such systems to decay, leading to software *aging* [12]. This is a concept which can be hard to imagine, because software is often thought of as a quasi-mathematical entity - if it runs today, it will run tomorrow and 100 years from now. Decay has many facets including increased software complexity due to systems modifications, decreasing reliability, increasing compatibility problems, and a decrease in user satisfaction [17].

So why are legacy systems still maintained? There are a multitude of reasons. Foremost, there is nothing inherently wrong with much of underlying legacy code. It functions just as efficiently as contemporary software, often with the benefit of being easier to understand. A recent article in Computerworld UK, cites Cobol as having better security, and faster performance than similar code written in Java [5]. Some of the reasons for keeping legacy software include:

- The system works satisfactorily and there is no reason for changing it.
- The costs of redesigning the system are prohibitive because it is large, monolithic, or highly complex.
- Retraining on a new system can be costly.
- The system is mission critical and requires close to 100% availability. Good examples include air traffic control, nuclear power plants, military installations.
- The system itself is legacy. For example, GE has nuclear-power plant robots being controlled by assembler on a PDP-11 that are expected to run until at least 2050.
- Very little is known about the system's structure.

Naturally, legacy software can't just be left in a closed room to continue running forever. Sneed poses a number of choices when dealing with legacy software (Sneed, 1998):

1. Continue to maintain the existing program as is.
2. Redevelop the program from scratch, thereby not having to deal with the legacy code at all.
3. Wrap the existing programs in another language, thereby maintaining the legacy code.
4. Re-engineer the program.

At the heart of all these options lies an in-depth understanding of the programs underlying infrastructure. Legacy software generally has a large economic value to companies, and there may be a substantial risk involved in replacing such systems. Risks may include a loss in performance, roll-out delays, system instability, or residual errors. There are also underlying issues with the process of re-engineering, which may manifest as increases in the size of the code base [16], or a decrease in efficiency [6].

3. RATIONALE FOR A COURSE ON LEGACY PROGRAMMING

Fourteen years on from ground-zero year 2000, Y2K is but a distant memory - a US$300 billion memory. In the early 1970s when commercial software became more widespread, storage space was limited and expensive. Storing a year using 2 digits instead of 4 was a 50% savings. As the roll-over of the millennium approached, the savings became a liability - an inability to distinguish between the years 2000 and 1900 - and to a lesser extent issues with the calculation of leap years [19]. The greater misconception may have been that the software systems written in the 1970s and 80s would eventually be re-written - over sixty years of Cobol have taught us otherwise. Students often become embroiled in designing complex apps for mobile applications, but have little or no knowledge of simple systems with limited resources.

The lack of understanding the intricacies of legacy systems stems largely from a students limited exposure during their studies. It is often not until they undertake a co-op work-term that the realization sinks in that they have no understanding of these systems. For example, a student undertakes a work-term in a power-plant and is tasked with updating a piece of software - which has been in operation for 20+ years on a mainframe system. The student likely has little knowledge of the languages used to program the system, let alone the underlying hardware infrastructure. While courses on designing *apps* for mobile devices are in vogue, it is important to remember that the industries underlying software infrastructure is largely dependent on these legacy software in one form or another.

A course on legacy software has two primary roles: (i) to expose students to various legacy programming languages, and (ii) to foster an understanding of the process of software re-engineering legacy programs. Most contemporary programming languages, Java, C++, C#, Objective C, have C lineage. Students are therefore only exposed to one family of programming languages from a syntactic viewpoint. They learn pointers in C, and object-oriented concepts in Java, yet they miss out on some of the more interesting language structures. They often believe that one language can solve all problems, and it isn't until they undertake work-terms that they realize that language selection is associated with relevant tasks-at-hand. Structures such as *goto* can not be fully appreciated unless seen in the context of unstructured code. The use of goto in C seems like a convenience, the use of *goto* in Fortran, under the guise of arithmetic *if* or otherwise is another matter all together.

By introducing students to the notion of software reengineering, they experience a side of software rarely encountered in academia - existing software. There are many industries which require legacy programs to be (i) ported to a new machine; (ii) migrated to a new language, (iii) converted to a newer dialect of the same language (e.g. removing obsolete structures), or (iv) have additions made to the existing code. Writing a system from scratch is a much different skill to renovating an existing one.

3.1 Course structure

The course is offered in a distance mode, in part to allow it to be taken by interested students globally, but also due in part to the prevalence of syntax, which makes for less than exciting lecture material. The course is offered in the third year of our curriculum, after students have gained some work-experience, although motivated students can take it earlier. It focuses on three languages - Fortran, Ada and Cobol, both their basic syntactic structures, and how their legacy forms can be re-engineered. Students are provided with extensive notes on basic language syntax - largely because many of the textbooks still available in libraries are ancient. There are also numerous examples by way of pracniques to illustrate various language concepts, and re-engineering case studies. They can practice concepts using weekly exercises. Assessment is by means of four projects: one from each language, playing on the strengths and weaknesses of each language, and one which allows students to use the knowledge gained to solve a more complex problem, or undertake a multi-language comparison. The assignments relating to Fortran and Cobol are presented in the manner of re-engineering projects.

4. CHOICE OF LEGACY LANGUAGES

In the 1950's a number of core families of programming languages emerged: Fortran (1954), Cobol (1959), Algol (1958) and Lisp (1958). A second tier of families appeared in the 1960s: APL (1960), Forth (1969), and Snobol (1962). Fortran forms one of the first family of languages, so it effectively has no direct ancestors, and whilst it has been influenced by other languages, it has maintained its innate structure. Ada stems from the Algol family of languages, and while early renditions of C were influenced by Algol 60, Algol 68 influenced the design of Pascal, which in turn influenced the design of Ada. Cobol too formed one of the core families of languages, however it has not really spawned any descendants. While it is easy to translate syntactical knowledge within a family of languages, it is more difficult across language families.

We have chosen to concentrate on three legacy languages: Fortran, Ada, and Cobol. From a historical perspective, these three languages have long been maligned by the computer science community, even thought they have been extensively used commercially. None more so than Cobol. Cobol was developed by industry, and due to its focus on commercial file processing, was of little importance to computer scientists who were more focused on engineering problems, and systems programming [14]. This prejudice likely stems from the wordy, non-scientific form of Cobol. The negative stance towards Cobol reached a peak by the early 1980s, with Dijkstra stating that *"with respect to Cobol you can really do only one of two things: fight the disease or pretend that it does not exist"* [4], and that *"the use of Cobol cripples the mind"*. Fortran suffered a little better, although it was relegated more to the task of numerical analysis. Dijkstra's view on Fortran - *"the infantile disorder"* being too clumsy and too risky to use. Ada too was designed by industry, and so was never adopted by academe, and very few texts were ever written which extolled the virtues of the language - most are mere reference guides. Ironically Dijkstra was one of the reviewers of language specifications which lead to Ada - his comment on the proposal which was chosen - *"Technical incompetence, probably enhanced by dishonesty"* [3]. In reality all of these languages have lasted longer than their creators, or detractors, ever imagined.

4.1 Fortran

Fortran was designed by John W. Backus in 1953 at IBM, as an alternative to using assembly language on the IBM 704 mainframe. Nearly 60 years later, Fortran is still extensivey used in scientific computing: from numerical weather prediction, computational fluid dynamics, and computational physics, to high performance computing. It has remained a viable language largely because of its ability to produce optimized machine code, and its backwards compatibility. For example array addressing is achieved via array indices in Fortran, but via pointers in C making code analysis more complicated in C. There are also extensive numerical libraries (e.g. NAG) which have been created over the years. Fortran is introduced as the first legacy language. For many students it is somewhat of a shock after the experience of programming in a C-structured language. Whilst modern dialects of Fortran seem pleasant enough, just introducing those would be negligent. Students are introduced to Fortran proper by having to re-engineer legacy programs in Fortran IV/77 to modern dialects. When concepts such as goto are covered in an introductory programming course and students are warned to avoid their use, they often don't fully understand the rationale. After a few weeks with legacy Fortran programs they begin to understand the notion of structured programming.

4.2 Ada

Released in 1980, Ada was originally designed by Jean Ichbiah of CII Honeywell Bull, under contract to the United States Department of Defense (DoD). It was designed to replace the hundreds of programming languages used by the DoD at the time. From 1983 to 1996, the number of programming languages fell from 450 to 37. Ada is considered legacy, even though by rights, C at an age of 40+ years makes it a legacy language as well. Ada is often used in mission critical and real-time applications. Ricky Sward of MITRE Corporation recently said of Ada: *"The original goals of Ada still apply to systems where a loss of life may occur, i.e. safety critical, high integrity systems"* [18]. So far from being a language whose time is over, there seems to be a renaissance of Ada. Ada provides students with an introduction to a real-time language, which provides feedback in a way that C-based languages do not. Ada also encourages good programming practices by incorporating software principles with strong typing, modularity, reusability, readability, portability, and exception handling. It also allows for less complex code. For example the French national railroad, SNCF designed a system to provide location, speed, distance, switch, operations, and safety information about each train. The initial prototype was 300,000 lines of code (LOC) of C, but was difficult to maintain and suffered reliability problems. The system was re-engineered in Ada using only 22,000 LOC.

4.3 Cobol

One of the oldest programming languages, COBOL first appeared in 1959 after a six month period of development by the Conference on Data Systems Languages (CODASYL). This committee was a formed by a joint effort of industry, major universities, and the United States Government. Its ancestry included FLOWMATIC developed by Grace Murray Hopper, and the first English-like data processing language. Cobol was designed primarily as a data processing language for business, and applications between 10-30 years old are not uncommon. Cobol has a number of distinct features which make it one of the most challenging languages for students to comprehend, due to their lack of exposure to similar languages. Despite the fact that the language is simple, the feature most often cited by students as being problematic is its verbose, English-like syntax. It has no pointers, user defined types or functions, however it does require the input to be specified accurately. Conversely file I/O is easy to incorporate and COBOL is self documenting. Students also learn to program differently in the face new programming languages. The use of Cobol forces them to make decisions about situations they have never encountered before. For example, Cobol has no functions in the same way C-based languages do, functions must be external subroutines. It is also weakly typed, meaning that automatic datatype conversions are often problematic. It has an enforced structure, and extensive data handling features.

5. PROGRAM RE-ENGINEERING

Legacy programming is not only about learning the syntax and structures of old programming languages. It is just as much about the process of dealing with the legacy software. For legacy systems, the goal is often to augment the system, re-engineer, or replace it - without disrupting service. Whilst it is possible for smaller organizations to replace legacy systems with more modern languages, for example a conversion from Cobol to Java, for larger institutions, migrating large-scale systems is just too costly and too risky. Companies will invest in software that creates new revenue streams - replacing existing legacy software most often does not.

The process of *re-engineering* which is not something that can be taught in a theoretical sense - it has to be experienced. Not everyone will go and work in companies designing mobile apps. Some will work in companies that have to deal with legacy software, so they have to understand the process of re-engineering. This is no different to a structural engineer who has to integrate the structure of an old building into a new building. One can't always just demolish old structures. In the scope of re-engineering, there are three core ideas:

- translation - programs are translated from legacy language to contemporary one.
- migration - programs are converted from a legacy language to a newer dialect.
- porting - programs are modified to work on a new platform.

The course focuses on the processes of translation and migration. Migration involves transforming a legacy program to a contemporary vernacular of the same language. For example migrating from Cobol 74 to Cobol 85, or Fortran 77 to Fortran 90/95. Translation, alternatively involves converting a legacy program to a different language, e.g. Cobol to Java, PL/I to Ada or Basic to Fortran. There is no definitive re-engineering process per se, each program is handled in its own unique manner. Any re-engineering process first requires comprehending the code and deciding what it does. Part of the learning curve in re-engineering involves deciding how to tackle the code. It is not just a process of writing new code. The code must be converted in portions, and testing must occur along the way to ensure that integrity is maintained.

6. EXERCISES AND PROJECT WORK

In the course we have designed reengineering in the form of vintage Fortran and Cobol programs which must be converted to a more modern dialect.

6.1 Fortran re-engineering

Fortran is a mystifying language to many students, not because of the large scale use of go to like jump statements in legacy code, but rather its varied nomenclature. The Fortran project normally exists of a piece of legacy code, either Fortran 77 or earlier which must be migrated to a contemporary dialect. One such project is a Fortran program to calculate the National Fire Danger Rating Index first introduced in the U.S. in 1964 [9]. This program contains a number of structures which need to be modified, or removed, to make the program more maintainable: computed GO TO, arithmetic IF, Hollerith characters. Another project consists of migrating a F77 version of the game of Hangman to F95. The challenge here? - The 145 line program contains 34 GO TO instructions. The goal of this project is to reduce the prevalence of unstructured code, whilst streamlining the program, and introducing some form of modularization.

6.2 Cobol re-engineering

Re-engineering Cobol may be one of the most challenging tasks students encounter. One would think that Cobol's english-like syntax would be a positive characteristic, however for students who are use to languages such as C, the opposite is true. One of the projects involves converting a Cobol program for calculating Easter Sunday published by Donald Knuth in 1962 [8]. He notes that *"There are many indications that the sole important application of arithmetic in Europe during the Middle Ages was the calculation of Easter date"*. In the paper he provides two programs, one in Algol and the other in Cobol. The Cobol program prepares a printed table of Easter from 500 to 4999 A.D. The initial code is 110 lines in length, and the process of re-engineering the code to a modern dialect of Cobol seems easy. Re-engineering the program into a modern dialect of Cobol is challenging. Firstly the code does not compile because of the presence of obsolete structures. Once these are fixed, the code has to be analyzed to determine the program's flow. This analysis can then be used to remove the unstructured jumps within the code, re-configure the control-flow structures, and compacting the code by reducing verbosity (replacing words with symbols). Another project involves an archaic Cobol program used to perform statistical analysis of text. The caveat with this program is that it does not produce correct results. Students first have to decipher the reason for the incorrect results, and then re-engineer the program.

6.3 Problem solving in Ada

Whilst it is possible to find small vintage programs for Fortran and Cobol, Ada is more challenging. For this task we usually set a more complex problem to be implemented in Ada. One example we use is solving the 8-Queens problem using two approaches: (i) a non-recursive algorithm which uses an ADT such as a stack (using an Ada package), and (ii) the recursive algorithm of Wirth [20], originally given in Pascal, but converted to Fortran. The exercise requires writing all 92 solutions to file in text-graphic format. The two approaches are compared with respect to easy of implementation/translation and efficiency. The recursive algorithm is trivial, it is the non-recursive algorithm that provides the challenge. An adaptation compares the recursive algorithm in Ada to one written in C. The conversion from Pascal to Ada is trivial, due to the similarities in data structures - i.e. the ability to use arbitrary array index ranges in Ada. The algorithm posed by Wirth uses a series of arrays which contain negative indices, making it more of a challenging task to use zero-based indices such as those found in C. Other projects have included a non-recursive maze traversal and Sudoku solver using data structures represented using packages.

6.4 Language Translation

A study of legacy languages is not complete unless they are put into the proper context. This can be achieved by having the students compare an algorithm coded in a legacy language to (i) other legacy languages, and (ii) contemporary languages such as C and Python. As one of the final assignment projects, students may choose from a number of different translation projects. For example, implementing *"The Sieve"* (Sieve of Eratosthenes) in five languages - the three legacy languages taught in the course, and two of their own choosing. The idea is to design the programs and test them for efficiency by calculating the primes in the first 1,000,000 numbers. What seems like a simple task in C, and okay in Ada becomes inherently more complicated in Fortran as students attempt to create dynamic arrays - and find out it's actually easy. When they hit Cobol it becomes another story all together. There are no real dynamic structures in Cobol, and a limit to the size of arrays that can be created.

7. OBSERVATIONS

The course has been offered twice so far. What have we learned? Enrollment increased 50% from the first to the second offering of the course, with over 60 students. Most students genuinely enjoy the challenge of learning new languages they have never experienced before. Learning three new languages in the span of twelve weeks may seem like a daunting task, however few students have ever complained - and it may be on par with some of the rigors faced in industry. What do students learn in a class on legacy software? They obtain a greater appreciation of the world of software. Their understanding of software systems is often limited to the C-family of languages and some exposure to scripting languages such as Python. While there is nothing inherently wrong with this, it does not provide a comprehensive perspective of software as it relates to industry.

Programming in modern Fortran is not an issue. If anything Fortran requires students to re-think aspects of algorithm design such as array indexing, which without the 0-based limitation of C, actually makes deriving some algorithms easier. Things become more complicated when legacy Fortran programs have to be re-engineered. Here students must come to terms with unstructured programming using the many varied forms of jump instruction. Even in a small program this can be challenging - and it really requires an ability to comprehend what is happening in the program. Sometimes there is no documentation except a flow-chart, so students must analyze the program to obtain an understanding of what it does. Some of the challenges cited by students include the lack of structure in the legacy code, and problems comprehending it, and variable name readability. It is easy to loose context with goto statements that jump around the program.

Students seem to take the task of programming in Ada in stride - the similarity to Fortran certainly helps this. Some students were discouraged by the increase in verbosity (e.g. use of begin-end, if-then-end if), whilst others appreciated Ada's strong typing, reduced errors, and OO-flavour (packages). Cobol, of all three languages, seems to be the least liked by students. Part of this stems from the extreme verbosity of the language, something many students have never experienced. A case in point is the use of the COMPUTE statement in implementing simple arithmetic statements. Although it was believed that the "English-like" statements would make programs easier to read, the opposite is true for students who are use to languages which are more precise, and concise - it is almost counter intuitive. Cobol is considered *"too wordy and somehow unscientific"* [14]. Cobol was found by some students to be too "syntactically challenging", maybe in part due to the lack of real modularity.

Overall, students obtain a greater appreciation of concepts such as jump instructions (go to), global variables, and modularization. They also learn that different languages have different ways of doing things, and syntactic structure isn't necessarily universal. A case in point is the use of strings.

Whilst a string, X, of length 20 can to be created in any language - each will handle it differently.

- C allows any size string from 1 to 19 characters in length to be stored in X.
- Ada is less flexible, requiring exactly 20 characters to be stored. This is because a string in Ada is an array of characters of a fixed length. To circumvent this restriction, Ada provides unbounded strings, which are allocated using heap memory.
- Fortran provides both strings and character arrays - which are not the same thing.
- Cobol provides a rich infrastructure for string handling.

There are inevitably some issues with knowledge transfer, such as assignment statements - students use to = are flummoxed by the use of := in Ada, although it might be the better construct given the confusion novice programmers have over = and == in C. Students gain an understanding of the process of re-engineering, and an appreciation of language structures. A side-effect of the course is that students gain experience with program *comprehension*. By reading and deciphering legacy programs it is possible to learn more about the structure, function and stylistic aspects of the code. The ability to read and understand programs allows a program to be re-engineered whilst retaining its logical, functional, and stylistic integrity [2].

8. CONCLUSIONS

Society is sitting on a Eyjafjallajökull of legacy software. Most of it will happily chug along for decades to come if left to its own devices, yet it must be dealt with either through maintenance, or re-engineering. Cobol is uncool - that message is quite clear. However applications built on Cobol are unlikely to disappear in the near future, nor will they all be ported to languages such as Java. Were the systems running Cobol to suddenly fail, systems such as ATMs, retail/POS, credit card would all become in-operational, rendering modern society at a standstill. Fortran is still extensive used in the broader scientific community, and Ada provides high reliability for embedded applications. There is nothing inherently wrong with legacy code. The problem lies not with the legacy code per-say, but with the lack of people qualified to maintain it. The loss of institutional level knowledge and shortage of programmers proficient in legacy languages such as Cobol will likely result in future challenges to societies software infrastructure. From this point alone it is important to offer students some form of exposure to legacy software. It is hoped in the future that a module on language interaction can be added to the course, whereby students obtain a better understanding of how legacy languages can be integrated with scripting languages. Ideally this course should be supplemented by a project course which deals with the task of re-engineering a reasonably large system (10,000 LOC), or integrating a legacy system with a contemporary system. Software will continue to age, and we must endeavour to instill an appreciation for the role legacy software plays in the modern world, and an awareness of how it can be kept in check.

9. REFERENCES

[1] K. Bennett. Legacy systems: coping with stress. *IEEE Software*, 12(1):19–23, 1995.

[2] L. Deimel and J. Naveda. Reading computer programs: Instructors guide and exercises. `http://repository.cmu.edu/sei/245/`, 1990. Accessed: 2014-01-07.

[3] E. Dijkstra. On the green language submitted to the dod. *ACM SIGPLAN Notices*, 13(10):16–21, 1978.

[4] E. Dijkstra. How do we tell truths that might hurt? *ACM SIGPLAN Notices*, 17(5):13–15, 1982.

[5] D. du Preez. Banks will stick with cobol because java has performance issues, claims quality guru bill curtis. `http://www.computerworlduk.com/news/applications/3452537/banks-will-stick-with-cobol-because-java-has-performance-issues-claims-quality-guru-bill-curtis/`, 2013. Accessed: 2014-02-01.

[6] J. Howe, S. Baden, T. Grimmett, and K. Nomura. Modernization of legacy application software. In *4th Int. Workshop on Applied Parallel Computing*, pages 255–262, 1998.

[7] R. Kizior, D. Carr, and P. Halpern. Does cobol have a future? In *Proc. of the Information Systems Education Conference*, page 126, 2000.

[8] D. Knuth. The calculation of easter. *Communications of the ACM*, 5(4):209–210, 1962.

[9] W. Main. Computer calculation of fire danger. `http://nrs.fs.fed.us/pubs/rn/rn_nc079.pdf`, 1969. Accessed: 2012-07-01.

[10] Microfocus. Cobol infographic. `http://www.microfocus.com/assets/cobol-infographic_tcm6-206787.pdf`. Accessed: 2013-10-12.

[11] R. Mitchell. Brain drain: Where cobol systems go from here? `http://www.computerworld.com/s/article/9227263/The_Cobol_Brain_Drain`, 2012. Accessed: 2014-02-01.

[12] D. L. Parnas. Software aging. In *IEEE Int. Conf. on Software Engineering*, pages 279–287, 1994.

[13] J. Sammet. Programming languages: History and future. *Communications of the ACM*, 15(7):601–610, 1972.

[14] B. Schneiderman. The relationship between cobol and computer science. *Annals of the History of Computing*, 7(4):348–352, 1985.

[15] H. Sneed. Wrapping legacy software for reuse in a soa. *Multikonferenz Wirtschaftsinformatik*, 2:345–360, 2006.

[16] H. Sneed. Migrating from cobol to java. In *IEEE Conf. on Software Maintenance*, pages 1–7, 2010.

[17] H. Sneed and E. Nya'ry. Salvaging an ancient legacy system at the german foreign office. In *IEEE Conf. on Software Maintenance*, pages 434–436, 1999.

[18] R. Sward. The rise, fall and persistence of ada. In *SIGAda 2010*, pages 71–74, 2010.

[19] A. van Deursen. The leap year problem. *The Year 2000 Journal*, 2(4):65–70, 1998.

[20] N. Wirth. *Algorithms + Data Structures = Programs.* Prentice Hall, EnglewoodCliffs, N.J., 1975.

A Framework for Teaching Programming Languages

Kent D. Lee
Luther College
700 College Drive
Decorah, IA 52101 USA
kentdlee@luther.edu

ABSTRACT

This paper provides a description of a framework for programming language implementation that is accessible to students in a one semester course focused on programming languages. Rather than concentrating solely on language features, this paper describes a framework where imperative, functional, and logic programming languages are all used to develop a compiler for a non-trivial subset of a functional programming language. Provided by the framework are a virtual machine, a disassember of Python programs, a partial implementation of a Standard ML compiler with suggested tests, and a partial implementation of a type inference system implemented using Prolog, again with suggested tests.

Classroom experience gained while using this framework is also shared. A suggested fourteen week sequence is provided. Real reactions from students and reflections on coverage of the ACM 2013 Curricula guildelines conclude the paper.

Categories and Subject Descriptors

K.3.2 [**Computers and Education**]: Computer and Information Science Education—*Computer science education*

General Terms

Languages,Theory

Keywords

Programming Languages, Compilers, Virtual Machines, Type Inference, Type Checking

1. INTRODUCTION

Doing is better than seeing. This has been said many times before by many Computer Science professors and professionals. The premise holds for learning about programming languages as well. Using a programming language to implement something of substance, more than just a few lines of code, helps students form a better understanding of a language and how it can best be used. Some texts on programming languages are primarily surveys of programming languages where important aspects of languages are described, mostly with short examples. For instance, type systems are very important, but students have a hard time getting invested in learning about type checking and type inference without a real goal in mind. Recently, several texts on programming languages have abandoned this survey approach to teaching programming languages in favor of using programming languages to implement programming languages[2, 1, 3, 4], giving students more purpose in their language exploration.

SIGCSE'15, March 4–7, 2015, Kansas City, MO, USA.

ACM 978-1-4503-2966-8/15/03 ...$15.00.
http://dx.doi.org/10.1145/2676723.2677245

Doing is more complicated than seeing. Of course, the tradeoff is added complexity versus time. There is only so much time in a semester and language implementation is a generally complex problem. It is critical that this approach be accessible while still having substance. This paper presents a successfully taught framework for the implementation of programming languages. In particular, a compiler is developed from the bottom-up for a substantial subset of Standard ML including portable code generation for a virtual machine, support for higher-order functions and closures, and type infererence.

The paper begins by introducing CoCo, a virtual machine based on the Python virtual machine. The Python virtual machine is an excellent choice since the language supports higher-order functions and closures. The framework includes a disassembler for Python programs. This makes it possible for students to write Python programs and discover the necessary virtual machine instructions. This disassembly and discovery makes learning the machine language and code generation relatively fast so other facets of programming languages and their implementation may be explored.

The paper goes on to demonstrate compiling a non-trivial Standard ML program and all that entails. Language implementation issues are explored including the CoCo virtual machine, currying, mutually recursive functions, and type inference. The paper concludes with a proposed fourteen week course outline based on past teaching experience. Finally, reflections on that experience from both teachers and students is provided. And perhaps best of all, the resources for this framework are freely available on-line.

2. THE FRAMEWORK

The language implementation framework can be divided into three pieces. From the bottom up they are a virtual machine and Python disassembler, a partial implementation of a Standard ML compiler written in Standard ML, and a partial implementation of a type inference system for Standard ML written in Prolog. The virtual machine, called CoCo, is written in C++ and is a faithful implementation of a subset of the Python virtual machine. The Python virtual machine was chosen because Python has some functional features and supports nested functions, higher-order functions, and static scope.

The next sections cover each of these three parts of the framework while compiling a simple, but non-trivial Standard ML program. Consider the Standard ML program in figure 1. *println* is a polymorphic function that prints its value to the screen and returns *unit*, or the unit equivalent of *None* from the Python virtual machine.

```
let fun f 0 y = y
      | f x y = g x (x*y)
    and g x y = f (x-1) y
in
   println (f 10 1)
end
```

Figure 1: A Standard ML Program

The program features two function definitions using pattern matching. The two functions are mutually recursive, essentially counting down to zero while multiplying the values together, in the end computing and printing 10!. The next sections use this program as an example, taking it through the same process, much abbreviated for this paper, that students work through using this framework in a semester long course.

```
import disassembler

def f(x,y):
    if x==0:
        return y
    return g(x,x*y)
def g(x,y):
     return f(x-1,y)
def main():
    print(f(10,1))

disassembler.disassemble(f)
disassembler.disassemble(g)
disassembler.disassemble(main)
```

Figure 2: A Python Program

2.1 The Disassembler and VM

The CoCo VM (Virtual Machine) is based on Python 3.2. The framework includes a disassembler that outputs CoCo VM programs. The CoCo disassembler uses the Python disassembler, which is supplied with the Python distribution. Python does not guarantee backwards compatibility of its virtual machine, so Python 3.2 is required to run the disassembler. Consider the Standard ML program in figure 1. The Python program in figure 2 is in many ways similar to the Standard ML program. Calling the *main* function of this program has the same result. In this case the disassembler module was imported and the three functions were disassembled. The output from the disassembler is CoCo VM assembly language as shown in figure 3. The instructions are taken from the Python 3.2 VM specification with just a few minor differences to support the CoCo VM.

```
Function: f/2
Constants: None, 0
Locals: x, y
Globals: g
BEGIN
              LOAD_FAST              0
              LOAD_CONST             1
              COMPARE_OP             2
              POP_JUMP_IF_FALSE label00
              LOAD_FAST              1
              RETURN_VALUE
label00:      LOAD_GLOBAL            0
              LOAD_FAST              0
              LOAD_FAST              0
              LOAD_FAST              1
              BINARY_MULTIPLY
              CALL_FUNCTION          2
              RETURN_VALUE
END
Function: g/2
Constants: None, 1
Locals: x, y
Globals: f
BEGIN
              LOAD_GLOBAL            0
              LOAD_FAST              0
              LOAD_CONST             1
              BINARY_SUBTRACT
              LOAD_FAST              1
              CALL_FUNCTION          2
              RETURN_VALUE
END
Function: main/0
Constants: None, 10, 1
Globals: print, f
BEGIN
              LOAD_GLOBAL            0
              LOAD_GLOBAL            1
              LOAD_CONST             1
              LOAD_CONST             2
              CALL_FUNCTION          2
              CALL_FUNCTION          1
              POP_TOP
              LOAD_CONST             0
              RETURN_VALUE
END
```

Figure 3: A CoCo VM Program

Each function is defined separately in the CoCo language. All constant values used in a function are defined in the *Constants* list. The *Locals* includes all locally initialized variables including function arguments. *Globals* include identifiers defined outside the current function definition, including built-in functions. Labels are used in the common assembly language format as the targets of jumps and branches. The */2* that appears in the *Function: f/2* definition indicates that *f* is a function of two arguments.

CoCo is a stack-based VM, like the Python and Java virtual machines. Operands are pushed onto the stack before the instruction that operates on them. Calling a function is accomplished by pushing the function and the arguments onto the stack and then executing the *CALL_FUNCTION* instruction as shown on line 37-42 of figure 3. The 1 or 2 that appears as the operand for the call function instructions indicates the number of arguments. The arguments appear on top of the function to be called on the operand stack of the VM.

Much can be gleaned from exercises like this. The correlation between VM instructions and Python code helps to inform the student of each instruction's meaning. That, together with available documentation means a shorter learning curve to writing CoCo assembly directly from similar examples.

The function in figure 1 is a curried function. The Python program in figure 2 is not written in curried form. Python does not support writing functions in curried form. But, currying can be thought of as syntactic sugar. Any curried function can be rewritten as a series of one argument functions. The Python program in figure 4 provides one possible uncurry transformation applied to the program in figure 2. The transformed program now contains two higher-order functions as shown. The function *f* takes one argument and returns another function, *f3* that also takes one argument. In this sense, the function f is now curried, taking its arguments one at a time. The same transformation applies to *g*.

```
def f(v0):
  def f3(v1):
    def f2(x,y):
      if x==0:
        return y
      return g(x)(x*y)
    return f2(v0,v1)
  return f3
def g(v4):
  def g7(v5):
    def g6(x,y):
      return f(x-1)(y)
    return g6(v4,v5)
  return g7
def main():
    print(f(10)(1))
if __name__=="__main__":
  main()
```

Figure 4: A Curried Python Program

Again, the disassembler can be used to see how the two higher-order functions in figure 4 are implemented in the VM. Disassembling the function *f* automatically disassembles any nested functions, in this case *f3* and *f2*. The disassembled code for function *f* appears in figure 5.

The CoCo VM supports nested functions. In figure 5 the second line begins the nested function *f3* inside the *f* function. The variable *v0* is used in the function *f3* and is the argument to the function *f*. Since *v0* is referenced from the enclosing scope of *f3* it is a free variable in *f3* as shown on line 25 of the CoCo VM code. The usefulness of the disassembler is evident in understanding how to properly generate code for non-trivial programs like the code in figure 4.

```
1  Function: f/1
2    Function: f3/1
3      Function: f2/2
4      Constants: None, 0
5      Locals: x, y
6      Globals: g
7      BEGIN
8                LOAD_FAST                 0
9                LOAD_CONST                1
10               COMPARE_OP                2
11               POP_JUMP_IF_FALSE   label00
12               LOAD_FAST                 1
13               RETURN_VALUE
14 label00:      LOAD_GLOBAL               0
15               LOAD_FAST                 0
16               CALL_FUNCTION             1
17               LOAD_FAST                 0
18               LOAD_FAST                 1
19               BINARY_MULTIPLY
20               CALL_FUNCTION             1
21               RETURN_VALUE
22     END
23   Constants: None, code(f2)
24   Locals: v1, f2
25   FreeVars: v0
26   BEGIN
27             LOAD_CONST                  1
28             MAKE_FUNCTION               0
29             STORE_FAST                  1
30             LOAD_FAST                   1
31             LOAD_DEREF                  0
32             LOAD_FAST                   0
33             CALL_FUNCTION               2
34             RETURN_VALUE
35   END
36 Constants: None, code(f3)
37 Locals: v0, f3
38 CellVars: v0
39 BEGIN
40           LOAD_CLOSURE                  0
41           BUILD_TUPLE                   1
42           LOAD_CONST                    1
43           MAKE_CLOSURE                  0
44           STORE_FAST                    1
45           LOAD_FAST                     1
46           RETURN_VALUE
47 END
```

Figure 5: A Higher-order Function Definition

Encountering the *MAKE_CLOSURE* instruction on line 43, students are naturally curious as to what the instruction does. As mentioned earlier in the paper, the CoCo VM is implemented in C++, making it possible to investigate the meaning of an instruction by looking at its implementation.

The implementation of the make closure instruction is provided in figure 6. Consulting both the code in figure 6 and the example CoCo program in figure 5 helps in determining that a closure is made up of code and environment. Lines 40-41 of figure 5 build a tuple containing the variable *v0* from the enclosing environment. Line 42 loads the code for *f3* onto the operand stack. Line 43 builds the closure of the code and environment. Line 44 stores that closure in the local variable *f3* so it can be returned by *f*.

```
case MAKE_CLOSURE:
    u = safetyPop();
    v = safetyPop();
    w = new PyFunction(*((PyCode*) u),
          globals, v);
    opStack->push(w);
    break;
```

Figure 6: The MAKE_CLOSURE Implementation

From the C++ code in figure 6 and the example of its use in figure 5 the closure of a function is found to be the environment (i.e. the variable from the enclosing scope) along with the code. A closure is environment and function together. The closure provides the static scoping of the language. Rather than just tell students about closures, how nice it is to show them its significance in a program by examining the CoCo VM and a sample program that needs the closure.

Writing and disassembling Python programs, consulting the disassembled code, and examining the C++ implementation of CoCo all work together toward providing a means for the understanding of code generation for a non-trivial language. A next step towards further understanding is to implement a compiler for a completely different language, like Standard ML.

2.2 A Standard ML Compiler

The investigative techniques discussed in the previous section are put to use to develop a compiler for a subset of SML (Standard ML) that includes datatypes like int, real, bool, lists, and tuples. Pattern-matching is supported. Function definition and invocation is implemented including higher-order and mutually recursive functions like the example that appears in figure 1.

As we saw earlier, curried functions can be transformed into higher-order functions of one argument. A transformation like that employed in figure 4 is provided to students and is used during the parsing of curried functions. The consequence of this syntactic transformation appears in figure 7 where the abstract syntax of SML programs only includes functions of one argument. Any curried function will have already been transformed into a series of one argument functions before it is represented in SML abstract syntax. Any uncurried function of more than one argument is actually a function of one argument, a tuple.

Compiling the program from figure 1 builds the AST shown in figure 8. The currying transformation generated the extra functions named **anon@**x. The Python program in figure 4 is a very literal translation of the AST in figure 8 into Python code. In figure 4 the *anon@3* is called *f3* and *anon@2* is called *f2*. In the function *g* the *anon@7* is named *g7* in figure 4 and *anon@6* is named *g6*.

```
structure MLAS = struct
datatype
exp = int of string
     | ch of string
     | str of string
     | boolval of string
     | id of string
     | listcon of exp list
     | tuplecon of exp list
     | apply of exp * exp
     | infixexp of string * exp * exp
     | expsequence of exp list
     | letdec of dec * (exp list)
     | raisexp of exp
     | handlexp of exp * match list
     | ifthen of exp * exp * exp
     | whiledo of exp * exp
     | func of int * match list
and
match = match of pat * exp
and
pat = intpat of string
     | chpat of string
     | strpat of string
     | boolpat of string
     | idpat of string
     | wildcardpat
     | infixpat of string * pat * pat
     | tuplepat of pat list
     | listpat of pat list
     | aspat of string * pat
and
dec = bindval of pat * exp
     | bindvalrec of pat * exp
     | funmatch of string * match list
     | funmatches of
         (string * match list) list
end;
```

Figure 7: SML Abstract Syntax

The SML compiler's responsibility is to translate an AST like the one that appears in figure 8 into a CoCo VM program, like the partial program that appears in figure 5. The target language has some requirements. First, function definitions must appear before they are called in the CoCo language. However, anonymous functions denoted by a *func* descriptor in the SML abstract syntax, may appear anywhere an expression can appear. In addition, every function definition must contain lists of the constants, locals, globals, free variables, and cell variables used by the function. These requirements dictate how code is generated from SML ASTs like the one that appears in figure 8. Several passes over the AST are required to generate the target program with the correct ordering of parts.

Consider generating the list of constants used by a function. Building this list entails traversing the patterns used by a function definition. Consider figure 1. In the patterns used in the definition of f a 0 appears. Constants may also appear in the body of a function. The body is called *exp* in the code below. Constants in the body of a function include 1 and 10 in figure 1. The code below traverses the definition of patterns and expressions in a function definition looking for all constants that were used in its definition. The constants *None*, *'Match Not Found'* and 0 are added for all function definitions. *removeDups* removes duplicate values from the list.

```
val consts = (removeDups ("None"::
    "'Match Not Found'"::"0"::
     (List.foldr (fn (match(pat,exp),y) =>
        (patConsts pat)@(constants exp)@y)
        [] expList)))
```

Building the list of constants is one of the simpler tasks. Teaching compiler generation for such a language would be a daunting task to undertake in a semester course without the proper approach. Extending the compiler to compile a set of test programs provides the proper organization to make learning compiler generation in a semester manageable.

```
letdec(
 funmatches([
 funmatch('f',[
  match(idpat('v0'),func('anon@3',[
     match(idpat('v1'),
        apply(func('anon@2',[
        match(tuplepat([intpat(0),
           idpat('y')]),id('y')),
        match(tuplepat([idpat('x'),
           idpat('y')]),
              apply(apply(id('g'),
           id('x')),apply(id('*'),
        tuple([id('x'),id('y')]))))
     ]),tuple([id('v0'),id('v1')])))
  ]))])
 ,funmatch('g',[
  match(idpat('v4'),func('anon@7',[
     match(idpat('v5'),
        apply(func('anon@6',[
        match(tuplepat([idpat('x'),
        idpat('y')]),apply(apply(id('f'),
        apply(id('-'),tuple([id('x'),
        int('1')]))),id('y')))
     ]),tuple([id('v4'),id('v5')])))
  ]))])
])
;
[
apply(id('println'),
   apply(apply(id('f'),int('10')),int('1')))
])
```

Figure 8: SML Program AST

For example, attempting to compile the program in figure 9 results in an error. The compiler code initially given to students will not compile this code. Attempting to run the compiler produces the following output.

```
Attempt to get constants for expression not
currently supported!
Expression was: ifthen
An error occurred while compiling!
```

The *if-then-else* expression was not supported by the *constants* function. Students look for this error message within the compiler, look at other surrounding code, and fix the problem once they understand how the problem occurred. Then, they try to compile again, potentially finding the next problem. Eventually, they get to the point where code must be generated for the *if-then-else* expression. A little bit of guidance may be needed here, but that can be provided by the Python disassembler!

```
let val x = Int.fromString(
        input("Please enter an integer: "))
    val y = Int.fromString(
        input("Please enter an integer: "))
in
  print "The maximum is ";
  println (if x > y then x else y)
end
```

Figure 9: SML Compiler test4.sml

Code generation is the last step to getting executable code for correct SML programs. Once the *if-then-else* code generation is added, code is generated for programs like the one in figure 9 which can be run on the CoCo VM. But, one important aspect of the compiler is still missing. Type inference is one of the unique features of the Standard ML language. Teaching type inference is covered in the next section.

2.3 Standard ML Type Inference

Type inference is the perfect kind of program to implement in Prolog and the framework presented in this paper includes a partially implemented type inference system. Like the code generation part of the compiler, the type inference system needs to be extended to correctly type check some of the test programs.

Implementing type inference is much easier when type inference rules are supplied. The framework provides a complete set of type inference rules for the supported subset of Standard ML. Consider the program in figure 1 which contains two functions that are mutually recursive. In a language other than Prolog handling mutual recursion would be difficult since it requires unification to properly infer the type of the mutually recursive functions. The type inference rule for mutually recursive functions appears in figure 10.

$$\frac{\forall i\ 1 \leq i \leq n, \forall j\ 1 < j \leq n, \quad n \geq 1, \quad [id_1 \mapsto \alpha_1 \to \beta_1 \ \{,\ id_j \mapsto \alpha_j \to \beta_j\}] \oplus \varepsilon \vdash id_i\ matches_i : \alpha_i \to \beta_i}{\varepsilon \vdash fun\ id_1\ matches_1\ \{and\ id_j\ matches_j\} \Rightarrow [id_1 \mapsto close(\alpha_1 \to \beta_1)\ \{,\ id_j \mapsto close(\alpha_j \to \beta_j)\}]}$$

Figure 10: The FunDecs Type Inference Rule

The type inference rule reads as follows: A set of functions separated by *and* keywords are correctly typed if each function has a function type that is consistent across all the matches. A match is a pattern and expression used in a function definition. For a function type to be consistent in a mutually recursive definition requires both its definition and application be consistently typed. The use of *close* freezes the definition of these function types so the types may be used in subsequent applications of these functions. Closing types is necessary when types may be polymorphic which Standard ML supports.

```
gatherFuns([],[]).
gatherFuns([funmatch(FName,_)|Tail],
  [(FName,fn(_,_))|FEnv]) :-
  gatherFuns(Tail,FEnv).
typecheckDec(Env,funmatches(L),NewEnv):-
  gatherFuns(L,NewEnv),
  append(NewEnv,Env,FunEnv),
  typecheckFuns(FunEnv,L),
  closeFunTypes(NewEnv).
```

Figure 11: FunDecs in Prolog

The type inference rule in figure 10 is implemented by the Prolog predicates appearing in figure 11. The *gatherFuns* predicate creates function types for each mutually recursive function. These types, through unification, instantiate to the (possibly polymorphic) types of the functions. The *closeFunTypes* predicate closes the function types for polymorphic types. The program in figure 1, using this type inference rule among others, passes the typechecker and prints the following output.

```
val g = fn : int -> int -> int
val f = fn : int -> int -> int
val it : unit
The program passed the typechecker.
```

Students build on this type inference system in the same manner as the compiler. Test programs that currently are not supported are introduced and students work to enhance the type inference system to support these test programs.

3. CONCLUSIONS

This paper has presented a very abbreviated look at a framework for teaching programming languages. A more thorough treatment of the framework is covered in a textbook[2] that, like this paper, builds from the bottom-up covering assembly language on a stack-based virtual machine, virtual machine implementation in C++, compiler implementation for a subset of Standard ML written in Standard ML, and type inference written in Prolog. Students are guided in their investigation of programming languages by extending the framework to compile and infer the types of test programs.

The CoCo VM, Standard ML compiler, and type inference system are all freely available at http://github.com/kentdlee. Two versions exist. A publicly available version is available to students to download. A private, but still free, version containing the full source code for CoCo, the Standard ML Compiler, and for inferring types is available for instructors upon request.

The framework has been used in a Programming Languages course for two years with excellent results. A fourteen week semester is divided up as follows. About one week is devoted to learning about context free grammars, derivations, and abstract syntax trees. One week is spent learning the CoCo VM and writing a few CoCo programs. C++ and the implementation of the CoCo VM is studied for approximately two weeks. Two weeks is spent learning functional programming and in particular Standard ML. This is separate from the compiler project. Two weeks is spent compiling the subset of Standard ML presented in this framework. Two weeks is spent learning how to program in the Prolog programming language. Finally, two weeks is spent studying and implementing type inference. This leaves a couple of weeks to include administering exams and some flexibility in the topics being covered.

The framework's coverage of the ACM Computer Science Curricula 2013 guidelines is thorough, covering all but one area of the tier 1 and 2 guidelines and several elective guidelines as well. Functional and OOP programming paradigms are covered. These two programming paradigms, type systems, program representation, language translation and execution are all tier 1 and 2 (i.e. mandatory) topics of the guidelines. Elective guidelines covered by this framework include syntax analysis, compiler semantics, code generation, runtime systems, static analysis, advanced programming constructs, and logic programming. Of the tier 1 and 2 requirements, absent is only event-driven and reactive programming which is often covered in other courses.

Students feel a sense of real accomplishment in getting their test cases to compile, typecheck, and run correctly. With a clearly defined purpose, programming languages can be an exciting and interesting course. Class evaluations were anonymous and students were allowed to comment on the strengths of the course. Here are a couple anonymous comments about the course and using this framework.

> *This course is designed to make you learn about programming languages and their implementation. I think the goal was achieved very well.*
>
> *Programming Languages has been a fantastic course. I feel as though I have gained quite an understanding of how many languages work and behave. It has been really fun and interesting figuring this out in a classroom setting. Definitely the most fun computer science class I have taken so far.*

While the language implementation is non-trivial there is much that can still be done with it including garbage collection in the VM, extending the VM for threaded computation, support for object-oriented languages within the VM, implementation of a richer subset of Standard ML, or compiler development for a completely different language. These projects can serve well as undergraduate research topics. In practice, after students have gotten familiar with the framework and what can be achieved using it, several have expressed interest in further extending the framework through independent study.

4. REFERENCES

[1] S. Krishnamurthi. *Programming Languages: Application and Interpretation.* Shriram Krishnamurthi, 2012.

[2] K. D. Lee. *Foundations of Programming Languages.* Springer, 2015.

[3] M. L. Scott. *Programming Language Pragmatics.* Morgan Kaufmann, 2009.

[4] P. Sestoft. *Programming Language Concepts.* Springer, 2012.

The Interpreter In An Undergraduate Compilers Course

John H. E. Lasseter
Hobart & William Smith Colleges
Geneva, NY USA
lasseter@hws.edu

ABSTRACT

An undergraduate compilers course poses significant challenges to students, in both the conceptual richness of the major components and in the programming effort necessary to implement them. In this paper, I argue that a related architecture, the *interpreter*, serves as an effective conceptual framework in which to teach some of the later stages of the compiler pipeline. This framework can serve both to unify some of the major concepts that are taught in a typical undergraduate course and to structure the implementation of a semester-long compiler project.

Categories and Subject Descriptors

K.3.2 [**Computer and Information Science Education**]: computer science education; D.2.11 [**Software Architectures**]: patterns; D.3.4 [**Processors**]: compilers,interpreters,

General Terms

Design,Languages

Keywords

compilers education; design patterns; partial evaluation; abstract interpretation

1. INTRODUCTION

> "Interpreters are the second-class citizens of the compiler construction world: everybody employs them, but hardly any author pays serious attention to them."—Grune *et al.*, *Modern Compiler Design*, p. 49

The undergraduate compiler construction course at our school is a one-semester, upper-division elective, offered every other year. The class is a mix of software engineering concerns and conceptual material from a traditional core (lexing, parsing, semantic analysis, and code generation), and at its heart is the construction by each student of a working compiler, completed over the 15-week semester. For its balance of simplicity and realistic features, we focus on the Tiger programming language, originally developed by Andrew Appel for his project-based "Modern Compiler Implementation" suite of C, ML, and Java textbooks [1, 3]. Our projects differ from his work in that we do not tackle some of the more advanced back-end problems such as register allocation and liveness analysis, concentrating instead on the simpler task of code generation for a virtual machine. In order to facilitate modularity between the assignments (and prevent early difficulties from having a cumulative effect on later work), the students build their work from a skeleton Java source code distribution, consisting of some utility code, a set of AST classes, and interfaces for traversal of the AST. Following the lead of more recent texts ([4, 6, 14], for example), this traversal is done according to the well-known *visitor pattern* [8], in both the semantic analysis and code generation phases.

Through several versions of this course, an unfortunate trend in student performance has emerged. Students do well with the material on lexing and parsing, but too many of them begin to struggle during implementation of the semantic analysis phase. They find overwhelming both the conceptual material underlying type checking, the details of the visitor pattern in traversing an AST, and the interplay of this traversal technique with the complexities of a realistic semantic analysis implementation. It is not uncommon for students to fall behind badly at this point, with the result that their final effort—AST- based code generation—is less successful than it should be, even with the relative modularity of the accompanying assignments. The reappearance of AST traversal in the code generation phase does serve to deepen the understanding of the semantic analysis phase, but often this benefit comes only at or near the end of the semester.

In meetings with individual students, I have often used the basic structure of a language's *interpreter* as a touchstone for explanation of these two phases. Though it was not a scheduled topic in the class, this approach was one that proved almost uniformly effective among the students with whom I discussed it, so much so that I began to reorganize the classroom lectures introducing both compiler phases to include this structure as a reference point.

This paper proposes to teach this connection explicitly, through a version of the undergraduate compilers course that treats the interpreter as a first class citizen. In this approach, the semester-long compiler construction project

SIGCSE'15, March 4–7, 2015, Kansas City, MO, USA.

http://dx.doi.org/10.1145/2676723.2677314.

includes an interpreter for the source language, which is organized in a way that makes plain the congruence between this interpreter's basic structure and that of the semantic analyzer and the code generator. With some changes to the semester's topic schedule, a module on interpreters and their implementation is presented early in the semester, after construction of the parser, as the first substantial example of the AST traversal technique. After a few days' study of the structure of this interpreter, the more traditional type-checking material is introduced, followed by intermediate-form translation. Despite the apparent impracticality and distraction from "core" material, student learning of this topic can offer several practical and conceptual benefits.

The key point here is not the observation that all three tasks involve a similar recursive descent of the AST. Rather, it is an explicit emphasis on teaching both compiler stages as forms of interpretation. This approach has the immediate practical advantage of providing a tool—the interpreter—which gives a lightweight implementation of the language's reference semantics for later testing of the completed compiler. Moreover, it establishes an early code base that supports both reuse and the comprehension of new design and algorithmic patterns in the subsequent semantic analysis and code generation implementations. Most importantly, it provides a lucid, unified framework in which key ideas in both type checking and code generation can be explained as forms of explicit-control evaluation over different forms of abstract value domain.

In the remainder of this paper, we develop a model curriculum for this approach. Section 2 positions this work within the relevant literature. The development proper begins in Section 3 with an overview of the standard distribution for the course's semester-long project. Section 4 introduces the primary innovation of this paper, in its presentation of an *interpreter* for the semester project's target language, along with a discussion of the interpreter's place in the semester schedule. Sections 5 and 6 discuss the semantic analysis and code generation phases, the teaching of which is the principal motivation for the development *a priori* of an interpreter. There are frequent references throughout to the source code of a model semester-long project. This code is freely available by request from the author.

2. RELATED WORK

From a theoretical perspective, it is well known that both semantic analysis and code generation are closely related to a language's *interpreter*, the former a simulation of program execution on abstract value domains [5] and the latter a specialization of the interpreter with respect to a program's source code [10]. It is therefore unsurprising that the implementation of an interpreter shares many structural characteristics with the implementation of both the semantic analysis and code generation phases. However, the details of these correspondences are likely inaccessible to the typical undergraduate student, and moreover, they are a distraction. An undergraduate course in compiler construction generally focuses on a narrow range of language features, emphasizing instead many real-world concerns such as efficient symbol table construction, separation of front and back ends through an intermediate representation, call stack frames, and (time permitting) various code-improving transformation techniques. As a consequence, interpreters, if they are included at all, generally serve as a foil for the superior performance of compiled code [12, 16], or else as material for a more breadth-based course on general language implementation [14, 15].

On the other hand, the construction of interpreters plays a prominent role in many courses on programming language design. The simplicity of an interpreter's core structure and the close correspondence to a language's semantics makes this a natural teaching tool, both for conceptual organization and for prototypical implementation of various language features [7, 11]. Abelson and Sussman's classic CS1 text [2] even uses this structure to introduce the structure of a simple compiler, though the correspondence between the two is quickly buried in the details of code generation, and their compiler lacks many real-world features such as a semantic analysis phase.

Several undergraduate-level texts on programming language theory make the formal connection between a language's type system and its concrete semantics explicit (for example, Harper [9]). The correspondence between an interpreter and a type-checker is an easy consequence of this.

Pagan proposes the inclusion of material on partial evaluation to derive a code generator from a language's interpreter [13]. However, his work in that paper is more focused on the specialization of an interpreter for a program with respect to a file of known input values, and the way in which this can be used to generate a more efficient intermediate representation (Pascal source code). He does not address the correspondence between interpretation and semantic analysis.

3. A SEMESTER COMPILER PROJECT

Tiger was introduced by Andrew Appel as a simple yet realistic teaching language for compiler construction [3]. It is an imperative language, with a feature set drawn from a simplification of Pascal. It offers a standard assortment of imperative control flow constructs, procedure definition and call, nested variable declaration scopes, and nested procedure definitions, and there is a rudimentary standard library to support string-related operations and user interaction. Data types are limited to integers, strings, arrays, and programmer-defined records. There is no support for either object-oriented or functional programming features.

Following Appel's lead, students in our course implement a compiler for Tiger from a skeleton distribution, consisting of some utility classes, a collection of classes representing the possible types, and interfaces for important components of code generation, such as stack frames, abstractions of frame access, labels, and so on. There is a complete set of AST classes, corresponding to the concrete grammar illustrated in Figure 1.

Finally, the distribution includes a pair of interfaces to support traversal of according to the *visitor pattern*. Behaviors that are defined by traversal of an AST implement the appropriate *visit()* methods:

```
public interface IAbsynVisitor {
    void visit(ExpInt e);
    void visit(ExpIfElse e);
    void visit(ExpLet e);
    void visit(ExpWhile e);

          ... (etc.)
}
```

```
e     :=  ⟨int⟩ | ⟨str⟩ | nil | var            (constants, vars)
          | var := e                          (assignment)
          | ( exp-seq_opt )                   (sequence)
          | e op e | -e                       (operators)
          | id ( exp-list_opt )               (procedure calls)
          | id { field-list_opt }             (record allocation)
          | id [ e ] of e                     (array allocation)
          | if e then e
          | if e then e else e
          | while e do e
          | for id := e to e do e
          | break
          | let decl+ in exp-seq end          (declarations)

decl  :=  type id = type
          | var id := e | var id:id := e
          | function id ( exp-list_opt ) = e
          | function id ( exp-list_opt ) :  id = e

type  :=  id                                  (type aliases)
          | { type field list }               (record types)
          | array of id                       (array types)
```

Figure 1: Tiger language syntax (abbreviated)

In turn, each of the AST node classes includes an *accept()* method

```
public interface IVisitable {
    void accept(IAbsynVisitor v);
}
```

with each *accept()* implementation dispatching the appropriate behavior (*i.e.*, *visit()* call) for an object's type. For example,

```
public class ExpLet implements IVisitable {
        ...
    public void accept(IAbsynVisitor v) {
        v.visit(this);
    }
        ...
}
```

A common motivation behind the use of this pattern is the need to defer the definition of one or more operations on a collection of data without having to later modify the definitions of those classes themselves, and at the same time providing some compile-time assurance that the behavior definition is exhaustive on the collection of class definitions. This need to separate future behavioral commitments from a fixed set of data types is particularly acute in the case of a student compiler project, as students must learn the AST hierarchy weeks before they encounter the last stages of the compiler.

The disadvantage is any implementation of a visitor pattern is, at best, complicated, and the first encounter with this pattern and its multiple redirection of control often proves confusing. To ameliorate this confusion, students first encounter AST traversal through the visitor pattern as they finish learning basic parsing and syntax-directed translation. At this point, they have each built a working grammar specification file with production rules whose associated actions result in the construction of an AST from the concrete source code. Among the tools in the standard distribution is a fully implemented pretty-print visitor, which is used to test the generated parsers. The final day in which we study syntax-directed translation is actually dedicated to the study of this pretty-printer, and through this, students are given an introduction to the visitor pattern.

4. INTERPRETER COMPONENTS

Once parsing is finished, it seems to be customary to move immediately into the next stage of the compiler pipeline, semantic analysis. This is the approach given in project-based texts such as Fischer/LeBlanc/Cytron [6] and Appel [4], for example, and it is the one we have until recently used in our course.

At this point in the class, however, it is possible to add a few days of material on interpretation and the structure of an interpreter's implementation. While challenging in its own way, a basic interpreter is considerably simpler to understand than a compiler for the same language, particularly if real-world concerns of performance are ignored. Aside from the AST itself, the critical components of interpretation are a domain of runtime values produced by programs, an understanding of the traversal algorithm underlying interpretation, and an *environment i.e.*, a record of the bindings of current names to their values.

The environment is necessary to support the declaration and subsequent use of identifiers, whether they refer to variables, procedures, or type aliases. In a compiler, this is the *symbol table*, and efficient construction of these can involve some complicated data structures. In its essence, however, it has a very simple interface, needing only the ability to retrieve the value associated with an identifier, add new identifier/value bindings, and record the entry to and exit from a scope:

```
public class Table<T> {
    public T get(Symbol key) { ... }
    public void put(Symbol key, T value) { ... }

    public void beginScope() { ... }
    public void endScope() { ... }
}
```

Our distribution includes a "semant" package that provides students with a complete implementation of this class, along with a "wrapper" class, Env, which adds on a few utility methods.

```
public abstract class Env<T> {
    public final Table<T> env;

    protected static Symbol sym(String s) {
        return Symbol.symbol(s);
    }
       ... (etc.)
}
```

Typically, a compilers text will cover the problem of symbol table data structures in some detail, though many courses (including ours) elide this. The project distribution used in our class realizes a fairly efficient implementation using hashtables and "binding" objects that support fast addition and disposal of scopes. However, if one wanted students to gain experience implementing such tables on their own, a more straightforward, stack-based prototype could be provided at this point instead.

The declaration of the Env class as both generic and abstract reflects the broader theme of this project: each of the "interpreter-like" stages of the compiler, semantic analysis, and code generation, will have its own version of an environment. Yet where the interpreter uses the environment to store symbol/value bindings, the abstract forms of interpretation will store bindings of symbols to *value abstractions*. In our work, this is reflected in the fact that the interpreter, semantic analyzer, and code generator all define a comparable hierarchy of Entry classes, reflecting the differences across the three uses of the environment. Following Appel [3], we use an abstract Entry superclass and two child entries, VarEntry and FunEntry:

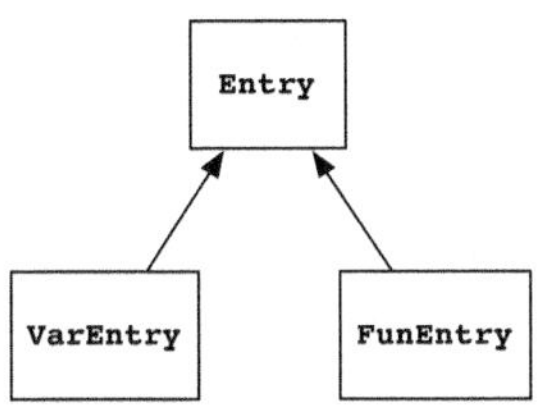

The difference is that we have a separate version of this hierarchy for each of the interpretation, semantic analysis, and code generation components. Although each of these stages needs to distinguish bindings of procedure names from ordinary value bindings, the difference in their respective levels of abstraction means that, for example, a VarEntry (*i.e.*, name/value binding) for an interpreter means something different from the corresponding VarEntry during code generation.

It is these Entry families that parameterize Env declarations, in the concrete environment designed for a stage. For example, our interpreter uses a representation of "value" (for Tiger, this means integers, strings, records, or arrays) to define the notion of a VarEntry and FunEntry, which leads in turn to

```
public class EnvInt extends
     tigerc.semant.Env<tigerc.semant.interp.Entry> {
     ...
}
```

Finally, there is the interpreter itself. The version developed for this paper is a single class, which includes a value environment (EnvInt), a utility error message handler, and which implements the AST visitor (*IAbsynVisitor*), with the result field storing the 'return" value of each visit() call:

```
public class InterpV implements IAbsynVisitor {
    private IValue result = null;
    private EnvInt env;
        ...
    public void visit(ExpInt e) {
        result = new ValInt(e.value);
    }
    public void visit(ExpOp e) {
        e.left.accept(this);
        IValue v1 = this.result;
        e.right.accept(this);
        IValue v2 = this.result;

        switch (e.oper) {
        case PLUS: {
          this.result =
              new ValInt(((ValInt) v1).val
                                   + ((ValInt) v2).val);
          break;
        }
        ...
        }
    }
    public void visit(ExpLet e) {
        env.env.beginScope();
        for (Decl dec : e.decls) {
            dec.accept(this);
        }
        e.body.accept(this);
        env.env.endScope();
    }

    ... (etc.)
}
```

It is worth noting the problem of type safety here. Although Tiger is a statically typed language, students have not yet learned anything about semantic analysis. Two options are possible here. On the one hand, we can simply "cheat" on the language specification and add easy dynamic checks of safety to the visit() bodies (or, worse, we can ignore the problem altogether). Alternately, we can use the problem of unsafe methods in the interpreter to motivate type checking, with students diving in immediately to the implementation of semantic analysis, though applied here to the interpreter. At present, it is unclear, which of these leads to a smoother outcome in learning semantic analysis implementation.

The InterpV class can be given to students as a complete product, with a couple of days devoted to studying its details. Alternately, one might choose a partial distribution, with the expectation that they complete it on their own. However, the purpose of this digression in the course is to provide a richer basis of study and comprehension for the actual later compiler stages, so it is important that students finish this component of the course with a fully functional interpreter to study, whether that is provided *a priori* or *a posteriori*.

5. SEMANTIC ANALYSIS

Semantic analysis is the last "filter" of bad programs before the back end phase(s), and languages of a realistic scale (even one as small as Tiger) include a complicated array of requirements: compatibility of value types with operators, declaration of variables before use (and use only within a given scope), non-assignability of bounded loop counters, enclosing loops for nonstandard jumps such as break, noncircularity of type alias definitions, and so on. At root, however, all of these verification tasks can be understood as the simulation of program execution on a suitable set of abstractions of the possible concrete values. This is not only true as a theoretical statement [5], it is a useful lens for comprehension of the type checking process.

Our implementation of semantic analysis is structured to reflect this view in a simple manner. À la Appel, the semantic analysis package (tigerc.semant.analysis) makes use of a collection of "type" objects, (tigerc.semant.types), instead of the IValue hierarchy of the interpreter. Similarly, it includes the following Entry hierarchy:

```
public interface Entry {}

public class VarEntry implements Entry {
```

```
    public final Type ty;
    public final boolean assignable;
        ...
}

public class FunEntry implements Entry {
    public final List<Pair<Symbol, Type>> formals;
    public final Type result;
        ...
}
```

These value abstractions are used to implement an environment of symbol/type bindings:

```
public class EnvTC extends
  tigerc.semant.Env<tigerc.semant.analysis.Entry> {

    protected final Table<Type> tenv;
    public EnvTC() {
        tenv = new Table<Type>();

        // Bindings for the primitive types.

        tenv.put(sym("int"), PrimTy.INT_T);
        tenv.put(sym("string"), PrimTy.STRING_T);

        makeStdLib();
    }
         ... (etc.)
}
```

This version of the environment specializes its generic parent with its own, abstract notion of Entry. Hidden inside is a second symbol table, to support Tiger's requirement that an identifier can exist as both a variable and a type name definition.

With these abstractions of value (the semant.types classes) and environment, we are ready to implement semantic analysis in a form highly congruent to that of the interpreter:

```
public class SemantV implements IAbsynVisitor {

    private Type ty = null;  // the "return value"
    private EnvTC env;
    private ErrorMsg err;
      ...
    public void visit(ExpInt e) {
        this.ty = new INT();
    }

    public void visit(VarSimple v) {
        Entry en = env.env.get(v.name);
        if (en == null) {
            err.error( ... );
            this.ty = ERROR.instance();
        } else if (en instanceof FunEntry) {
            err.error( ... );
            this.ty = ERROR.instance();
        } else {
            VarEntry var = (VarEntry) en;
            this.ty = var.ty;
        }
    }

    ... (etc.)
}
```

6. CODE GENERATION

In its industrial-strength form, code generation is the most formidable of the stages in a compiler. When a physical architecture is targeted, it is common to translate the AST into an intermediate representation that, although still tree-structured, more closely resembles the assembly language of real machines. Even in the case where the target language is a virtual machine like the JVM, a realistic compiler must perform extensive data flow analysis and code-improving transformations.

At the core, though, is a partial evaluation of the interpreter: literally, a traversal of the AST, for which the result is the machine code that corresponds to the execution steps the interpreter would take. This is true whether our target is virtual machine code or an intermediate tree language.

In this stage, the abstraction of value is not a type but rather a description of the resources that must be laid out for a value, either a register or a stack frame. For our project, that means an abstraction of *frames* and *access* within a frame:

```
public interface IFrame {
    IAccess allocLocal(Type t);

    IAccess popLocal();
    // removes and returns the resource allocated at
    // the end of this frame.

    int frameEnd();
    //offset of the first available word in this frame
}

public interface IAccess {
    int offset();
    Type getType();
}
```

To aid in calculating access properties on some machines, we will need to make use of types here, though we only need record them, rather than checking, since they are all presumed correct at this point. This gives rise to an environment definition abstracted as

```
public class EnvTrans extends
              tigerc.semant.Env<Entry> {
    public final Table<Type> tenv;

    ... (etc.)
}

public class VarEntry implements Entry {
    public final Type ty;
    public final IAccess access;
     ...
}

public class FunEntry implements Entry {

    public final List<Pair<Symbol, Type>> formals;
    public final Type result;

    private Label label;
    private Class<?> extern;
    private IFrame frame;
     ...
}
```

Unfortunately, there are a some practical issues that arise with a straightforward analogy to interpreters here, primarily in the need to distinguish more carefully the use of a variable as an l-value or r-ralue. The code generated for these is often quite different. For example, suppose we are targeting JVM code (as our project does). For simple identifiers, we don't need to put the lefthand-side (LHS) value on the stack. It suffices to compute the righthand side (RHS), then store the value. For array subscripts and record fields, however, we need to do a little more work in computing the LHS. Too, the address on the record/array must be put on the stack, just below the top (which will contain the value of the RHS). Nonetheless, the interpreter/code generation correspondence is very close:

```
public class JVMGeneratorV implements
          tigerc.semant.translate.ICodegen,
            tigerc.syntax.absyn.IAbsynVisitor {


    private IFrame frame = new JVMFrame();
    private EnvTrans env;
    private java.io.PrintWriter tgtOut;
    // Target destination for generated code
    private Type expType;
    // type of the most recently-visited expression

    public void visit(ExpInt e) {
        emitLn(this.code, "ldc " + e.value);
        this.expType = PrimTy.INT_T;
    }

    public void visit(ExpAssign e) {
        if (e.lhs instanceof VarSimple) {
            e.rhs.accept(this);

            this.rvalueMode = false;
            e.lhs.accept(this);
            this.rvalueMode = true;
        } else {
            ...
        }
        this.expType = PrimTy.VOID_T;
    }

    public void visit(VarSimple x) {
        VarEntry v = (VarEntry) env.env.get(x.name);
        String loadstore =
            (this.rvalueMode ? "load" : "store");

        if (v.ty.coerceTo(PrimTy.INT_T)) {
            emitLn(this.code, "i" + loadstore
                      + " " + v.access.offset());
        } else {
            emitLn(this.code, "a" + loadstore
                      + " " + v.access.offset());
        }
        this.expType = v.ty.actual();
    }
        ...
}
```

7. CONCLUSION AND FUTURE WORK

This paper has shown how to use a known set of theoretical connections between a language's interpreter and key stages in the back end of a compiler for that language to structure the last few weeks of a compilers course. It provides both an elegant, reusable body of code and a set of patterns through which students can organize their understanding of these topics.

Future opportunities include the assessment of this approach among a larger population of students, as our own institution is small enough to make substantial data gathering of this kind impractical. Too, there remains the question of other opportunities within the pipeline in which to leverage this analogy. In more advanced courses, for example, is it helpful to bring in some of the original insights from abstract interpretation, in order to explain the task of data flow analysis? Is there a corresponding notion of interpretation of machine code versus abstractions of interpretation on tree-valued intermediate form? The prospect of future investigation in these directions is exciting.

8. REFERENCES

[1] EPITA Tiger compiler project. Available (as of December 4, 2014) at `https://www.lrde.epita.fr/~akim/ccmp/tiger.html`.

[2] H. Abelson, G. J. Sussman, and J. Sussman. *Structure and Interpretation of Computer Programs.* MIT Press, 2nd edition, 1996.

[3] A. Appel. *Modern Compiler Implementation in Java.* Cambridge U. P., 1st edition, 1997.

[4] A. Appel and J. Palsberg. *Modern Compiler Implementation in Java.* Cambridge U. P., 2nd edition, 2002.

[5] P. Cousot. Types as abstract interpretations. In *Proc. 24th Conference on Principles of Programming Languages (POPL '97)*, pages 316–331. ACM Press, 1997.

[6] C. N. Fischer, R. K. Cytron, and R. J. LeBlanc. *Crafting A Compiler.* Addison-Wesley, 3rd edition, 2010.

[7] D. P. Friedman and M. Wand. *Essentials of Programming Languages.* MIT Press, 3rd edition, 2008.

[8] E. Gamma, R. Helm, R. Johnson, and J. Vlissides. *Design Patterns: Elements of Reusable Object-Oriented Software.* Addison-Wesley, 1995.

[9] R. Harper. *Practical Foundation for Programming Languages.* Cambridge U. P., 2013.

[10] N. D. Jones, C. K. Gomard, and P. Sestoft. *Partial Evaluation and Automatic Program Generation.* Prentice Hall, 1993.

[11] S. N. Kamin. *Programming Languages.* Addison-Wesley, 1990.

[12] R. Mak. *Writing Compilers and Interpreters: A Software Engineering Approach.* Wiley, 3rd edition, 2009.

[13] F. G. Pagan. Partial evaluation as a practical aid in the compiler construction course. *SIGCSE Bulletin*, 21(2):2–7, June 1989.

[14] T. Parr. *Language Implementation Patterns.* Pragmatic Bookshelf, 2010.

[15] M. L. Scott. *Programming Language Pragmatics.* Morgan Kaufmann, 3rd edition, 2009.

[16] D. Watt and D. Brown. *Programming Language Processors in Java: Compilers and Interpreters.* Prentice Hall, 2000.

Panel on Flipped Classrooms

Jesse M. Heines (Moderator)
Univ. of Massachusetts Lowell
Dept. of Computer Science
Lowell, MA 01854
1-978-934-3634
heines@cs.uml.edu

Jeffrey L. Popyack
Drexel University
Dept. of Computer Science
Philadelphia, PA 19104
1-215-895-1846
jpopyack@cs.drexel.edu

Briana Morrison
Southern Polytechnic State Univ.
School of Comp. & Software Eng.
Marietta, GA 30060
1-678-915-4295
bmorriso@spsu.edu

Kate Lockwood
University of St. Thomas
Computer & Information Sciences
St. Paul, MN 55116
1-651-962-5374
aklockwood@stthomas.edu

Doug Baldwin
SUNY Geneseo
Dept. of Mathematics
Geneseo, NY 14454
1-585-245-5659
baldwin@geneseo.edu

SUMMARY

Flipped classrooms are a new twist on an old idea: homework. The basic formula is simple: do the prep work before coming to class and come to class ready to discuss that work, do an activity to reinforce what you learned, or even take a quiz on the reading or research that was assigned. But as with all approaches to teaching, the reality is never that simple.

This panel will report the experiences of four "flippers" and explore the pros and cons of those experiences. Educators who are considering flipping all or part of their courses will gain insight into how to do so to their—and, more importantly, their students'—advantage, while those who have used this technique may gain new insights into approaches that might help them be more successful if they faced any issues similar to those of the panelists.

1. JEFFREY L. POPYACK

Drexel University

We changed the format and delivery of our freshman computer science curriculum from three 1-hour lectures per week to one 80-minute lecture plus one 2-hour, team-oriented lab, with an individual, out-of-class, pre-lab exercise each week. The results were so dramatic that we have now been doing this for a dozen years, and the same format has been applied to our entry level courses for non-majors, as well.

We originally began by replacing one lecture per week with a lab experience in which students worked individually. This showed modest improvement, but we felt teamwork would improve learning and scale better. Sacrificing a second lecture took a lot of faith, but we worked any material not covered in lecture into a lab exercise. We also added a pre-lab exercise for each lab. These pre-lab exercises were designed to be doable without supervision, take students about an hour, and provide a common experience to prepare them for the lab exercises. In essence, we replaced two-thirds of our lecture time with hands-on, interactive exercises that engage students more in learning than simply listening to a lecture.

The benefits of this approach are as follows:

(a) Students are actually doing something and remain engaged rather than passively sitting in and listening to (some portion of) a lecture.

(b) The pre-lab and lab exercises involve reading, but it is embedded directly in the exercises with links to relevant material. Thus, students have an immediate use for what they are reading.

(c) By grouping students with a variety of skill levels, we are coercing (or at least making more likely) that some peer-learning and near-peer learning will occur as part of the exercises.

As a consequence, our students are doing more work than they ever did while complaining less about the workload. Even when the material is something they already know (which is nearly always the case for somebody), they still have to put their knowledge to work. Some students complain that the lectures aren't valuable, saying they learn much more in the labs. I view this as a positive.

2. BRIANA MORRISON

Southern Polytechnic State University

My conversion to a flipped classroom occurred as a last resort. We have a graduate level transition course in introductory programming that covers approximately 1.5 semesters of our undergraduate programming sequence. This course was originally offered in a traditional, twice-a-week, 90-minute lecture format, with both face-to-face and online cohorts. The face-to-face lectures were recorded and the online students could attend the lectures virtually or watch the recordings on their own.

In the fall of 2012, the course was scheduled as a hybrid course. That is, it would have only one 90-minute meeting per week and the remaining material would be available online. After two weeks of attempting to collapse two lectures into one, I quickly reached the conclusion that a flipped classroom was the only

SIGCSE '15, Mar 04-07 2015, Kansas City, MO, USA
ACM 978-1-4503-2966-8/15/03.
http://dx.doi.org/10.1145/2676723.2677328

scenario that made sense. The course has been offered in this hybrid, flipped format ever since.

The fall 2012 semester was a scramble to find and post enough resources to allow students to understand the material while trying to determine how best to spend the 90 minutes of lecture time. I learned a great deal that semester about what worked—and what didn't—in a flipped classroom. That initial semester experience will be discussed during my presentation, including the lessons learned (the hard way).

Since that initial semester I have improved both the online resources as well as my approach to the classroom time. The next two semesters went fairly well (from both the instructor's and students' points of view), and I believed that I had mastered the technique. However, the spring 2014 course offering ended up being *less* successful for various reasons. My presentation will discuss my thoughts why, after two successful semesters, my flipped classroom failed. I will present student success rates for the classes along with student feedback. I will relay the instructor experience through both the ups and downs in an attempt to share this valuable knowledge with the community.

3. KATE LOCKWOOD

University of St. Thomas

Over the last three years I have taught several courses in the programming sequence at California State University, Monterey Bay (CSUMB), using the flipped classroom. I taught introductory C++ flipped using all self-created materials and introductory Python flipped using all found materials. My presentation will discuss the pros and cons of self-created vs. found materials as well as student reaction to the different types of work assigned.

In addition to flipping my own courses, a colleague and I ran a faculty co-op for four semesters during which we helped other instructors from across CSUMB to flip portions of their courses. Last spring we surveyed all faculty at our institution about their experiences with flipping their classrooms.

I'll briefly present some of the highlights from both the survey and the co-op that address a few of the most prevalent faculty concerns when flipping courses. These include:

- student reaction,
- department support, and
- effort required to convert an existing course.

I'll also draw from the survey data to share techniques that address some of these concerns and that have been successfully employed by either my colleagues or myself.

4. DOUG BALDWIN

State University of New York Geneseo

I made my first foray into flipping a classroom in the spring 2014 semester via an introductory programming course for non-majors. I wanted to find out how thoroughly I could move one-to-many communication of basic concepts out of the face-to-face classroom and how completely I could use face-to-face time to mentor students' hands-on active learning. I therefore became an aggressive flipper: I planned the course around the idea that class time would be used for laboratory-style exercises, I insisted that students take ownership of their initial learning through the readings and videos I assigned, and I adopted a strict policy of only lecturing for short times and in response to questions that students asked or ran into during exercises.

My students understood intellectually what I was doing and why it would be good for them, but they were still very resistant in practice. Many seemed to get very little from the out-of-class readings and videos, and no one asked questions publicly in class. As a result, I hardly ever lectured. Nonetheless, by the end of the semester the class as a whole had learned all they were supposed to.

I met many surprises as a first-time flipper and experienced both the pleasure and the pain that others considering flipping a class should expect. Following are some of my observations.

- Classical three-hours-per-week lecturing is a colossal waste of time—it was humbling yet refreshing to see my students learning what I wanted without it.
- Conversely, hands-on activity is an amazingly effective way to learn—it, and the private questions and research it motivated, is where my students learned my course content.
- Flipping a class needn't be an all-or-nothing decision—I have asked students to do readings outside of class and used class time for a mixture of discussions, exercises, and lecture based on those readings for years, but only after the more aggressive flip do I recognize that as part of a spectrum of flipped instruction.
- The instructor in a flipped class plays a vital role in picking topics, readings, and videos, sequencing those things, planning exercises to reinforce them, and above all mentoring students through them, but students don't see that—mine widely felt, with justification from their perspective, that "we had to learn everything on our own."
- Lack of appreciation of the instructor's role in a flipped class surely extends to the general public—educators may need to explain the benefits and costs of flipped instruction not just to students, but to parents, employers, political leaders, and similar stakeholders.

5. ACKNOWLEDGMENTS

The organizer and moderator thanks the 30 SIGCSE members who responded to his original post to the ACM SIGCSE listserv entitled "Looking for Participants for a Panel on Flipped Classrooms." There were many responses that shared interesting and thoughtful experiences, as well as strong encouragement to propose this panel. The four educators who were ultimately invited to be members of this panel represent a wide sampling of the experiences of the other 26 respondents.

Prof. Popyack's material is based upon work supported by the National Science Foundation under Grants No. DUE-0089009 and CNS-1301171. Prof. Heines's material is based upon work supported by the National Science Foundation under Grants No. DUE-1118435 and CNS-0722161. Any opinions, findings, and conclusions or recommendations expressed in this material are those of the author(s) and do not necessarily reflect the views of the National Science Foundation.

Computer Science Principles Curricula: On-the-Ground, Adoptable, Adaptable, Approaches to Teaching

Daniel D. Garcia
University of California, Berkeley
ddgarcia@cs.berkeley.edu

Owen Astrachan
Duke University
ola@cs.duke.edu

Bennett Brown
Project Lead The Way
bbrown@pltw.org

Jeff Gray
University of Alabama
gray@cs.ua.edu

Calvin Lin
U. Texas at Austin
lin@cs.utexas.edu

Bradley Beth
U. Texas at Austin
bbeth@cs.utexas.edu

Ralph Morelli
Trinity College
ralph.morelli@trincoll.edu

Marie desJardins
U. Maryland, Baltimore County
mariedj@cs.umbc.edu

Nigamanth Sridhar
Cleveland State University
n.sridhar1@csuohio.edu

Categories and Subject Descriptors

K.3.2 [**Computers and Education**]: Computer and Information Science Education – *computer science education*

General Terms

Measurement, Experimentation, Standardization

Keywords

Computer Science Education; K-12 Curriculum; CS Principles; Professional Development

1. Summary

Previous sessions and presentations at SIGCSE have explained to the community many details about the development, piloting, and exam format of the NSF/College Board Computer Science Principles (CSP) [1-3] project --- a project that is intended and designed to be a rigorous, engaging, and broadly appealing Advanced Placement (AP) course taught in high schools, for which students can earn placement and/or credit for a college course. We are now less than two years from the launch of the course as an official Advanced Placement course in 2016-2017. Hundreds of high schools have offered courses designed around the CSP Framework, but these courses differ in many respects – from choice of programming language, to the degree of emphasis on the Internet, to varying focuses on modeling/simulation, and more.

As schools move to adopt the CSP framework, develop courses, and deliver them, teachers and administrators look to national models for curricula that can be adopted and adapted to suit local needs. In this session, we highlight both NSF-funded projects and private/non-profit-funded projects that have developed, piloted, and made available CSP curricula designed around the same framework [4]. These curricula share the same framework, but differ in important ways. We present a matrix, hosted on the CS10K Community of Practice, that highlights the similarities and differences between the approaches represented here. In the session, each curriculum project will be represented by a very short (five-minute) flash talk describing the curriculum. Brief synopses or elevator pitches of the curricula aimed separately at teachers and administrators will also be included in the session as written documents. The matrix and associated documents will be available online and as resources accessible during the session. There will be ample time to engage the audience in questions about the approaches.

SIGCSE'15, March 4–7, 2015, Kansas City, MO, USA.
ACM 978-1-4503-2966-8/15/03.
http://dx.doi.org/10.1145/2676723.2677323

2. Overview of Approaches (Owen Astrachan)

We provide a brief overview of the CS Principles project: its design, implementation, and direction. We expect general familiarity with the project but include this overview to ensure that those in the audience are aware of recent changes regarding the scope and format of the exam.

Owen Astrachan is the PI of the CS Principles project. He works to help the community of educators working on this and related projects achieve their goals. He helps to coordinate CSP initiatives for the CS10K Community of Practice.

2.1 Project Engage (Calvin Lin/Bradley Beth)

Project Engage is a dual-enrollment program in which high school students have the opportunity to earn computer science credit at the University of Texas at Austin. The accompanying project-based curriculum, *Thriving in Our Digital World,* is aligned with both the C*omputer Science: Principles* framework and the Texas College and Career Readiness Standards. The curriculum and instructional supports are freely available online, for adoption by teachers outside of the Project Engage Community.

2.2 Project Lead the Way (PLTW, Bennett Brown)

Project Lead The Way (PLTW) is a non-profit organization providing K-12 curriculum, professional development, and assessment to over 6,000 U.S. schools in three pathways: engineering, biomedical sciences, and computer science. The computer science pathway includes Computer Science and Software Engineering (CSE), a CS Principles course that is being implemented in more than 200 schools. PLTW courses use a problem-based learning approach. With PLTW professional development occurring at over 50 universities, this implementation of CS Principles is immediately scalable.

2.3 CISS Ohio (Nigamanth Sridhar)

The ComPASS project, developed by a team led by Beth Simon at UC San Diego, is being adopted in Ohio as part of the CISS project. The project uses a hybrid professional development model combining online delivery with face-to-face delivery, and a network model to provide academic year support by way of the Ohio STEM Learning Network. Through this network, the project has reach throughout the state of Ohio.

2.4 Mobile CSP (Ralph Morelli)

The Mobile CSP project engages teachers and schools in Connecticut and more broadly through the development of App Inventor and a CS4HS-funded MOOC for teachers delivered in the summer of 2014. This project includes several pilot schools from the College Board CSP pilot program.

2.5 CS4Alabama (Jeff Gray)

The CS4Alabama project uses a master teacher model and has delivered an online-accessible curriculum using a CS4HS-funded MOOC. The curriculum has been developed through the master teacher model. Several teachers in this project are part of the College Board CS pilot program.

2.6 CS Matters in Maryland (Marie desJardins)

The “CS Matters in Maryland” CS10K-funded project also uses a master teacher model and is piloting a CSP curriculum across Maryland, using resources that are connected to both the College Board CS Principles pilot program and to Code.org.

2.7 Beauty and Joy of Computing (Daniel D. Garcia)

The Beauty and Joy of Computing (BJC) project has been part of the College Board pilot project since that project began. BJC is a programming-heavy curriculum by CSP standards, covering the powerful ideas of recursion and higher-order functions using Snap!, a free, HTML5/Javascript-based reimplementation of Scratch adding first class procedures and first class lists. Readings are taken from current events and from [5]. Hundreds of teachers have participated in BJC professional development. Four 5-week "MOOClets" are under development and will launch in the Fall 2015-Spring 2016 school year as a Small, Private, Online Course (SPOC) as well. During 2015-19 we are partnering with Education Development Center (EDC), a nonprofit curriculum developer, to package all these materials into a teacher-friendly form (with a teachers' manual, scope and sequence, etc.) and to bring this curriculum to 100 New York City public high schools.

3. Intended Audience

This special session is designed for all educators interested in broadening participation in computer science teaching, particularly in high school; however, the lessons of the projects here also extend beyond high school to post-secondary institutions. The varied approaches to a Computer Science Principles curricula have been developed using best practices in educational research, in established pedagogical approaches designed to change how students learn, and in providing professional development opportunities for teachers. The partnerships represented in this special session continue a community-driven collaboration to support adoption by many different groups rapidly and at scale.

4. References

[1] O. Astrachan, J. Cuny, D. Garcia, L. Snyder, and C. Stephenson, “The CS10K Project and CS Principles,” presented at the National Coalition of Women in Technology (NCWIT) Summit on Women in Technology, New York City, 2011.

[2] A. Arpaci-Dusseau, O. Astrachan, D. Barnette, M. Bauer, M. Carrell, R. Dovi, B. Franke, C. Gardner, J. Gray, J. Griffin, R. Kick, A. Kuemmel, R. Morelli, D. Muralidhar, R. B. Osborne, and C. Uche, “Computer Science Principles: Analysis of a Propsed Advanced Placement Course,” in *SIGCSE Technical Symposium on Computer Science Education*, Denver, CO, 2013.

[3] B. Franke, J. Century, M. Lach, C. Wilson, M. Guzdial, G. Chapman, and O. Astrachan, “Expanding Access to K-12 Computer Science Education: Research on the Landscape of Computer Science Professional Development,” in *SIGCSE Technical Symposium on Computer Science Education*, Denver, CO, 2013.

[4] CS Principles framework, from http://csprinciples.org

[5] H. Abelson, K. Ledeen, H. Lewis. *Blown to Bits: Your Life Liberty and Happiness after the Digital Explosion*, Addison-Wesley, 2008

DEMONSTRATION SESSION

A Classroom Tested Accessible Multimedia Resource for Engaging Underrepresented Students in Computing: The University of Maryland Curriculum in a Box

Elissa Redmiles, *University of Maryland*
Mary Allison Abad, *University of Maryland*
Isabella Coronado, *University of Maryland*
Sean Kross, *University of Maryland*
Amelia Malone, *University of Maryland*
Contact: eredmiles@cs.umd.edu

In 2012, women earned 18% of computer science degrees; African American and Hispanic students made up less than 20% of computing degree holders that year. Research shows that relatable role models and engaging curriculum are required to engage underrepresented students in computing. There is a need for engaging and relatable curriculum to be delivered to students at the middle school level, when these students first begin to lose interest in computing. Thus, based on the results of a survey of current and former middle school computing teachers and a comprehensive literature review, we developed the University of Maryland Curriculum In A Box (CIAB). The CIAB includes profiles of relatable computing role models, accessible video and text curriculum and challenge projects for HTML/CSS. To simulate a "real world" programming environment, the CIAB guides students through programming within open source social media frameworks and Github. The CIAB also includes teacher enablement resources such as assessments and a week-by-week implementation guide. The CIAB was successfully implemented with a group of 6th and 7th grade students in Prince Georges (PG) County, a majority minority county in Maryland. Our demo will provide a walk-through of the CIAB assets, accessibility features and design process, as well as implementation advice informed by our CIAB implementation in PG County.

ACM Categories & Descriptors: K.3.2 [Computer and Information Science Education]: Computer Science Education

Keywords: Active learning; web-based; accessible; curriculum; middle school

DOI: http://dx.doi.org/10.1145/2676723.2691870

SIGCSE'15, March 4–7, 2015, Kansas City, MO, USA.
ACM 978-1-4503-2966-8/15/03.

Using BlueJ to Code Java on the Raspberry Pi

Amjad Altadmri, *University of Kent*
Neil C. C. Brown, *University of Kent*
Michael Kölling, *University of Kent*
Contact: nccb@kent.ac.uk

The Raspberry Pi is an affordable and powerful (for its size) credit-card sized computer that has become very popular since its launch two years ago. It functions as a desktop machine but with easy access to peripheral hardware, such as buttons, sensors and LEDs, via its GPIO pins. Using a Java IDE like Eclipse or NetBeans is out of the question as the Pi is not powerful enough to run those. However, the beginners' Java IDE BlueJ is ideal in this situation: lightweight enough to run on the Pi, but well-featured and designed for education. This demo will show how BlueJ's features such as the object bench allow easy exploration and manipulation of the Pi's GPIO pins, and how easy it can be to write some Java to interact with peripherals connected to the Pi. More information on BlueJ and the Raspberry Pi is available at http://bluej.org/raspberrypi/

ACM Categories & Descriptors: K.3.2 [Computers and Education]: Computer science education

Keywords: BlueJ; Raspberry Pi

DOI: http://dx.doi.org/10.1145/2676723.2691872

DBSnap: Learning Database Queries by Snapping Blocks

Yasin N. Silva
Arizona State University
ysilva@asu.edu

Jaime Chon
Arizona State University
jchon@asu.edu

ABSTRACT

A significant amount of recent research in Computer Science Education has focused on studying block-based programming. In this approach, computer programs are created by connecting blocks and the blocks' shapes determine the permitted connections. The focus is on the program's logic instead of its syntax. This paper introduces DB*Snap*, a web-based application to build database queries, particularly relational algebra queries, by snapping blocks. DB*Snap* fully supports the construction of intuitive database query trees, which is one of the most effective approaches to teach database queries. DB*Snap* is also highly dynamic and shows the query results as the query is being built. The user can also inspect, at any time, the intermediate results of any query node. This paper presents DB*Snap*'s design and implementation details, an evaluation of its effectiveness as a learning environment, and a thorough comparison with alternative ways to teach query languages. DB*Snap* is publicly available and aims to have the same transformational effect on database learning as previous block-based systems had on traditional programming learning.

Categories and Subject Descriptors

K.3.2 [**Computers and Education**]: Computer and Information Science Education

General Terms

Design, Experimentation

Keywords

Databases curricula; query languages; relational algebra

1. INTRODUCTION

Learning computer languages is a challenging endeavor that requires students not only to focus on a logical specification of instructions to be executed by a computer but also on a fully correct syntactical representation of the instructions. The latter component frequently frustrates students because a program will not execute, even if it has a correct logic, due to minor syntactical errors. Recently, a significant amount of research in the Computer Science Education community has focused on the design and development of block-based programming environments, e.g., Mindstorm [6], Scratch [7], Blockly [8], Snap! [11], and App Inventor [15]. The key idea is to enable students to create programs by just dragging and connecting blocks and thus, the focus is on the program's logic instead of its syntax. This idea has revolutionized the way instructors can teach computer programming and has also enabled the introduction of programming concepts to younger students.

This paper introduces DB*Snap*, a web-based application to build database queries, particularly relational algebra queries, by snapping blocks. A key feature of DB*Snap* is the representation of queries as trees. This representation has been one of the most effective approaches to teach database queries because it intuitively represents the organization of the query operators and the flow of intermediate results. This feature and the fact that DB*Snap* dynamically shows the intermediate results as the query is being built are two of several differences between DB*Snap* and the work by Gorman et al. that recently introduced a block-based system to build relational algebra expressions [5]. This paper presents the design, implementation details, and evaluation of DB*Snap*. The main contributions of the paper are:

- The introduction of DB*Snap*, a web-based and dynamic application that enables the construction of highly intuitive database query trees.
- A detailed description of DB*Snap*'s design and implementation guidelines. Our goal is to enable other researchers to extend or customize DB*Snap*.
- The evaluation of DB*Snap*'s effectiveness as a learning environment and a detailed comparison with alternative systems and tools to teach database query languages.
- The public availability of DB*Snap* to be used by any instructor or student and a set of query examples. DB*Snap* aims to have a transformational effect on database learning.

The rest of the paper is organized as follows. Section 2 presents the design details of DB*Snap*. Section 3 describes the details of implementing DB*Snap* as a web application.

SIGCSE'15, March 4–7, 2015, Kansas City, MO, USA.

ACM 978-1-4503-2966-8/15/03 ...$15.00.
http://dx.doi.org/10.1145/2676723.2677220.

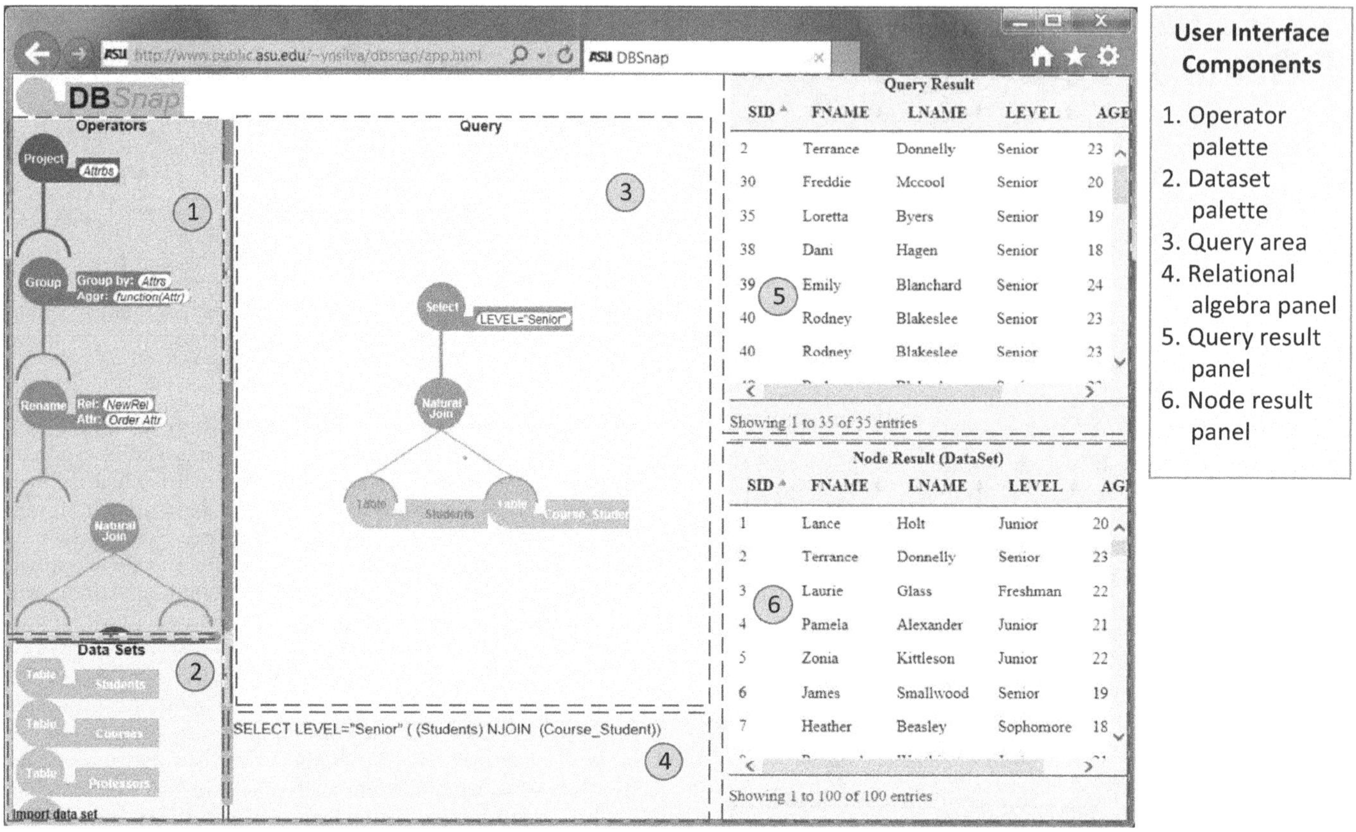

Figure 1: DB*Snap*'s User Interface.

Section 4 presents the comparison of DB*Snap* with other systems and tools to teach relational algebra queries. Section 5 presents a discussion of various facets of integrating DB*Snap* into the Database curricula. Section 6 concludes the paper.

2. DBSnap'S DESIGN

Fig. 1 shows DB*Snap*'s user interface. The main components in the window are: (1) Operator palette, (2) dataset palette, (3) query area, (4) relational algebra panel, (5) query result panel, and (6) node result panel. Building a query tree is highly intuitive and consists of dragging operator and dataset blocks and connecting them in the query area. As the user builds a new query, the query result panel is automatically updated with the current query result and the relational algebra panel with the corresponding relational algebra expression. The user can also inspect the intermediate result produced by any intermediate node by clicking on that node. The intermediate result will appear in the node result panel. The remaining part of this section describes in detail several components of DB*Snap*.

2.1 Dataset Palette

DB*Snap* includes by default a small database (University Database) composed of several relations (datasets or tables). This database has the following schema:

```
Students (SID, LName, FName, Level)    [100]
Courses (CID, CName)                   [20]
Professors (PID, LName, FName)         [20]
Course_Student (CID, SID)              [125]
Course_Professor (CID, PID)            [20]
```

The underlined attributes are the primary keys, i.e., attributes that uniquely identify a record in the dataset. The number included at the end of each dataset represents the number of records in this dataset. The University Dataset has a size and complexity that enables building simple and relatively complex queries while maintaining small query results that can be easily inspected. DB*Snap*'s dataset palette lists all the available dataset blocks and also includes a link to import additional datasets. This last feature enables customizing the tool for specific class assignments or projects. Each dataset block has a distinctive orange color, a left circular handle to connect the dataset with its parent node, and a right text area that shows the relation name. Observe in Fig. 1 that the block shape clearly shows that a dataset is a leaf node, i.e., it does not have a connection link to add a node underneath it.

2.2 Operator Palette

DB*Snap* supports a wide array of relational algebra operators including basic operators (e.g., Selection and Projection), Join operators, and highly useful extensions like the Aggregation operator. Each operator is represented as a block in the operator palette and each operator type has a distinguishing color. Fig. 2 shows a subset of the supported operators. In each sub-figure, the left tree is the query representation in DB*Snap* while the right one is the usual representation in database textbooks, e.g., [4, 12]. Observe that

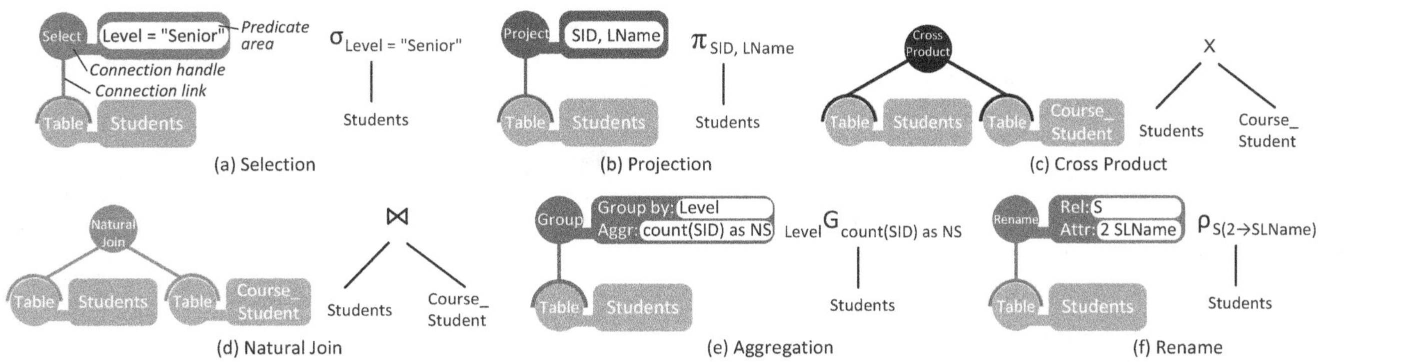

Figure 2: Some DB*Snap* Operators.

DB*Snap* queries closely follow the intuitive tree representations used in textbooks. A key property of DB*Snap* is the use of innovative block shapes aimed to facilitate block manipulation and query tree construction. As shown in Fig. 2.a, a DB*Snap* operator has in general three visual components: (i) top-left: a circular connection handle to connect the operator with a parent node, (ii) top-right: a predicate area to specify required operator information, and (iii) bottom: one or two connection links to connect this operator with its operand(s). The visual shape of operators make it easy to detect operators without required operands or predicates, and do not permit adding more operands than needed. We present next the details of several DB*Snap* operators.

- Selection: $\sigma_\theta(R)$. This operator selects all the records of relation R that satisfy the predicate θ. Fig. 2.a shows the query $\sigma_{Level=\text{“}Senior\text{”}}(Student)$. Observe that the predicate area is used to specify the selection condition ($Level$ = "*Senior*").
- Projection: $\pi_{a_1,...,a_n}(R)$. This operator removes all the attributes of R not contained in $a_1, ..., a_n$. An example of this operator ($\pi_{SID,LName}(Students)$) is shown in Fig. 2.b. The predicate area in this case stores the list of attributes ($SID, LName$).
- Cross Product: $R \times S$. This binary operator pairs each record of R with each record of S. Fig. 2.c shows the graphical representation of *Students* × *Course_Student*.
- Theta-join (θ-join): $R \bowtie_\theta S$. Returns a similar result as the Cross Product but selecting only the rows that satisfy the predicate θ.
- Natural Join: $R \bowtie S$. This operator is similar to the θ-join where the θ predicate is the equality of all the common attributes between R and S. Fig. 2.d represents *Students* ⋈ *Course_Student*. The implicit join predicate is *Student.SID=Course_Student.SID*.
- Aggregation: ${}_{g_1,...,g_m}G_{f_1(a_1),...,f_k(a_k)}(R)$. This operator groups the records of R forming a group for each unique occurring permutation of the grouping attributes $g_1, ..., g_m$. For each group, the operator computes the aggregation functions $f_1(a_1), ..., f_k(a_k)$ where $a_1, ..., a_k$ are attributes of R and the supported functions are *sum*, *count*, *average*, *maximum* and *minimum*. By default, $count(SID)$ counts all the occurrences of *SID* including duplicates. DB*Snap* also supports $distinct{-}count(SID)$ which counts only distinct values. DB*Snap* supports the use of $*$ instead of an attribute name. While $count(SID)$ ignores *null* values, $count(*)$ counts these values too. For convenience, DB*Snap* allows renaming the attribute corresponding to an aggregation function using the keyword "as". Fig. 2.e shows the query ${}_{Level}G_{count(SID)}(Students)$ where the attribute containing the results of the aggregation function *count* has been renamed to *NS*. In this case, the predicate area has two fields: the top one stores the grouping attributes (*Level*) and the bottom one the aggregation functions ($count(SID)$).

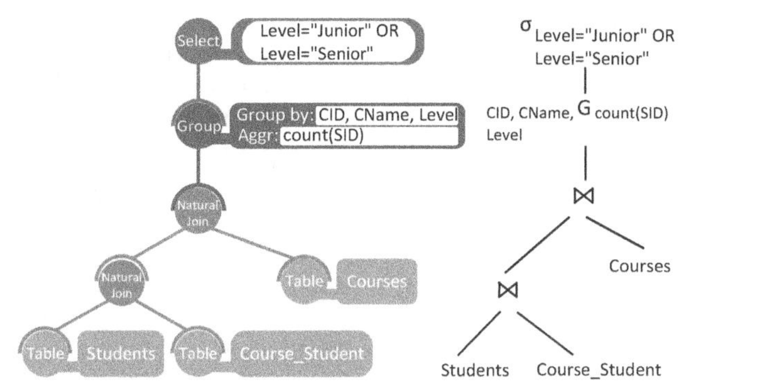

Figure 3: A DB*Snap* Query.

- Other set operations. DB*Snap* also supports common set operations such as Set Union ($R \cup S$), Set Difference ($R - S$) and Set Intersection ($R \cap S$).
- Rename: $\rho_{S(i_1 \to b_1,...,i_k \to b_k)}(R)$. This operator changes the name of relation R to S and the name of the attribute at position i_j to b_j. Fig. 2.f represents the query $\rho_{S(2 \to SLName)}(Student)$. The top predicate field stores the new relation name (S) and the bottom one specifies the position and new attribute name (2 $SLName$).

2.3 Query Area

The query area is where queries are constructed. This area gets dynamically resized as the query grows. Relational algebra queries in DB*Snap* are represented as trees. Representing a query as a tree is a powerful analogy to teach relational algebra and SQL (Structured Query Language) query plans. A query tree clearly shows the structure of a query and how the intermediate data generated by an operator is used as the input of other operators. In many database systems, in fact, a query (e.g., an SQL query) is parsed and converted into a query plan tree by the query processing engine. This plan can also be transformed into more efficient plans by the query optimizer using a set of transformation rules. Since DB*Snap* allows the dynamic manipulation of query trees, it is also an effective tool to teach query optimization.

Fig. 3 shows a query that computes the number of students of each level registered in each course considering only Junior and Senior students. The left tree is the DB*Snap* query while the right one is the equivalent query using the tree representation commonly found in textbooks. The DB*Snap* query structure is very similar to the one of the conventional query tree, and the use of colors further simplifies the quick identification of operations involved in the query. In this example, it is easy to recognize that the query is combining three datasets, grouping the intermediate result and then selecting a subset of the groups. The relational algebra expression of this query is:

$$\sigma_{Level=\text{``}Junior\text{''}\ \mathrm{OR}\ Level=\text{``}Senior\text{''}}$$
$$({}_{CID,CName,Level}G_{count(SID)}$$
$$((Students \bowtie Course\_Student) \bowtie Courses))$$

Even in this small example, the relational algebra expression may be intimidating for many students learning this language. DB*Snap* aims to simplify the understanding of queries by using an intuitive tree-based representation. Anytime the student adds a new block to the query, the system automatically shows the corresponding relational algebra expression. This feature is aimed to help students make the connection between a relational algebra expression and its intuitive tree-based representation.

2.4 Result Panels

As shown in Fig. 1, the query result panel, and the node result panel are located at the right-hand side of DB*Snap*'s user interface. The query result panel shows the results of evaluating the current query and is dynamically updated anytime the user modifies the query. This key feature allows students to see the query results as they build the query and also enables them to quickly explore the effects of query modifications. Many times, specifically while building complex queries, students need to examine the results of intermediate nodes. DB*Snap* supports exploring the results of any query node. When the student clicks on a query node, the intermediate results of this node are shown in the node result panel.

3. IMPLEMENTING DBSnap

One of the core goals while implementing DB*Snap* was to maximize its availability so that any student or instructor can use it without the need to use specialized software or hardware. With this goal in mind, we implemented DB*Snap* as a web application that only uses standard internet browser features (HTML5 and JavaScript). DB*Snap* can be used with most internet browsers (e.g., Internet Explorer, Firefox, Safari, and Chrome) and hardware devices (e.g., desktops, laptops, tablets, and smartphones).

Fig. 4 shows the architecture of DB*Snap*. As shown in this figure, the system has four main components: an HTML web page (DBSnap.html) and three JavaScript libraries (GUI.js, DBBlocks.js, and Morphic.js). DBSnap.html has three container elements: the DB*Snap* Query Canvas (which contains the block palettes and the query area), and the two result panels (which get populated with the query and current node results). DBSnap.html dynamically interacts with GUI.js to calculate the position and size of each HTML container, support the manipulation of blocks, and display query results. GUI.js, in turn, interacts with DBBlocks.js to support the manipulation of queries and query blocks. DBBlocks.js defines the visual representation and behavior of all the graphical elements in the Query Canvas: operator blocks, dataset blocks, palettes, and queries. DBBlocks.js includes the Query Handler module that maintains an internal representation of the current query. This module interacts with the Query Evaluation module to obtain the result of the current query and with the Query to Relational Algebra Translation module to obtain the relational algebra expression of the current query. DBBlocks.js uses Morphic.js, another JavaScript library. Morphic.js provides lower-level classes such as *Morph* which specifies basic behavior of blocks and *WorldMorph* which implements a canvas where other visual shapes (blocks) can be manipulated. Morphic.js was developed by Jens Mönig and is available under GNU license [10]. Morphic.js is also used in Snap! [11], a popular block-based programming application.

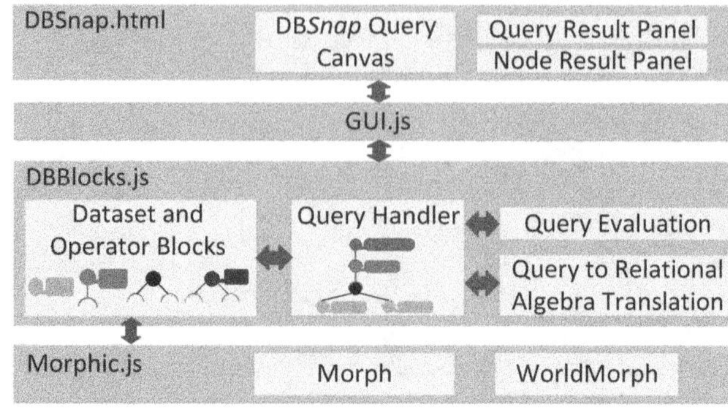

Figure 4: DB*Snap*'s Architecture.

Another DB*Snap* implementation goal was to make it highly extensible. To this end, we have modularized the code and organized the class hierarchy such that it facilitates the addition of new operators.

4. RELATED LEARNING TOOLS

This section describes several related educational tools for database query languages, specifically for relational algebra. We describe the key properties of each tool and highlight important differences between these tools and DB*Snap*. Fig. 5 summarizes the key supported features of the considered tools.

WinRDBI. WinRDBI [3] is a Java-based educational application that allows the specification of queries in relational algebra, relational calculus and SQL. The interface provides a panel to write the query, another one to show the query results, and a database browser to explore the available relations. WinRDBI allows both specifying relations and importing them. The tool allows naming queries such that they can be used as operands in other queries. The key differences in comparison with DB*Snap* are that WinRDBI: (i) is not

Feature	DB*Snap*	WinRDBI	iDFQL	Relational	RALT	Query Visualiser	Bags
Implementation technologies	HTML5, JavaScript	Java	Borland C++	Python	Java Swing	.NET, Mono	HTML5, JavaScript
Publicly available	•	•	•	•	•	•	•
Open source code	•			•		•	•
Block-based query editor	•		•		•		•
Shows RA expression	•	•		•		•	
Web application	•						•
Uses tree-based representation to build queries	•		•		•		
Automatically updates query result	•				•		
Intermediate results	•		•		•	•	•
Side-by-side queries	•	•	•		•	•	•
Can work without DB connection	•	•		•		•	•
Build-in datasets	•	•		•		•	•
Allows importing or connecting to custom data	•	•	•	•	•	•	
Views				•		•	

Figure 5: Comparison of Educational Tools for Relational Algebra Queries.

a block-based tool, (ii) requires the user to write text-based queries, e.g., requires writing a correct relational algebra expression, (iii) does not support the tree-based query representation, and (iv) does not automatically show the query results as the query is being built.

iDFQL. This tool provides a graphical interface to create relational algebra queries [1]. The tool allows creating a query using a set of icons or blocks that form a flow diagram. A key difference with DB*Snap*, is that operator blocks in iDFQL do not include the connection links, these links have to be added separately using a toolbar component. Operators in DB*Snap* already include the expected number of connection links simplifying the creation of a query. Furthermore, the predicates of an operator in iDFQL are represented using additional blocks while in DB*Snap* they are integral part of the operator block. When a query is built, iDFQL does not show the actual relational algebra expression (limiting its usefulness as a tool to learn relational algebra) and does not automatically show the query results. Moreover, the tool requires a connection with an external database, is not currently maintained, and suffers from some software compatibility issues, e.g., did not run in Windows 7 or 8.

Relational. This educational tool implemented in Python provides a workspace to write relational algebra expressions [14]. The tool allows the visualization of results and the exploration of available relations. Queries in Relational are text-based and specified in a single line. Operators are represented as special Unicode symbols that can be inserted using the buttons of a toolbar. Relational is not a block-based tool, does not support tree-based queries, does not dynamically show the query results, and does not allow the exploration of intermediate results.

RALT. This tool allows building relational algebra queries using an extended query tree structure [9]. Like DB*Snap*, RALT represents queries using trees. RALT, however, adds intermediate nodes (tables) to show the results of every operator and uses additional nodes to represent operator predicates. The inclusion of these extra nodes significantly increases the size of the query and it quickly fills the available query space. Constructing queries is simple for very small queries but becomes complex for relatively large queries. RALT requires a connection with an external database and does not show the relational algebra expressions of queries.

Query Visualiser. Query Visualiser (QV) [2] is another tool that allows the specification of written relational algebra expressions. After a query is built, QV generates a hierarchical representation of the query that enables exploring its intermediate results. QV also supports side-by-side query comparison and reports various query evaluation statistical measures. The key difference with DB*Snap* is that QV doesn't use a block-based approach. Instead, QV requires users to specify text-based queries. Another difference is that QV does not automatically show the query results while a query is modified.

Bags. Bags is a block-based tool to build relational algebra queries [5]. Like DB*Snap*, Bags allows the user to build a query by dragging and connecting blocks. The tool allows the visualization of the query results and includes several built-in datasets. A fundamental difference with DB*Snap*, however, is the type of query representation used by the tool. Bags was built extending Snap! [11], a block-based tool designed to teach conventional computer programming. A program in Snap! looks, in fact, very similar to the corresponding code in an imperative programming language. The operators and relation blocks of Bags have exactly the same look and feel as blocks in Snap!. A query in Bags is not a relational algebra expression nor a direct representation of the corresponding query tree. Moreover, the tool does not show the corresponding relational algebra expression of a query. DB*Snap* in contrast uses a tree-based query representation that has been extensively used by database educators and textbooks as an intuitive way to represent a relational algebra query. Additionally, DB*Snap* shows the relational algebra expression of any query specified in the tool. Another difference is that a block in Bags does not prevent the inclusion of a sequence of two or more consecutive blocks as a single operand (which would produce an incorrect query). In the case of DB*Snap* the rounded shape of a connection link allows the inclusion of only one block (or rooted sub-query). Bags allows the exploration of the result of any query node but does not automatically update the overall query result as the user builds the query.

While DB*Snap* is not the first tool to build relational algebra queries, it includes a set of features aimed to make it highly effective to teach relational algebra and database queries in general. Specifically, DB*Snap* differentiates from the rest in that it is the only block-based tool that uses a tree-based query representation that fully matches the highly intuitive query trees used by many educators and textbooks. Furthermore DB*Snap* is a highly interactive tool that automatically shows the query results and the equivalent relational algebra expression while a query is being modified, and allows the inspection of the output of any intermediate node.

5. DISCUSSION

DB*Snap* can be used to teach relational algebra and query optimization in introductory and advanced database courses. DB*Snap* is a publicly available web application [13] that can be used by educators and students on a wide array of devices. DB*Snap*'s extended availability makes it a suitable tool to be used in in-class activities as well as in assignments and projects. In the case of relational algebra, a common learning objective is that students understand the semantics of key operators and are able to build queries to answer specific questions. DB*Snap* can be an important resource to meet this goal. The tool can be used by the instructor to introduce and show the output of each operator and to highlight the relationships between query trees (also used in database textbooks) and the corresponding relational algebra expressions. DB*Snap* can then be used in hands-on class activities where students explore the operators and build several assigned queries. The interactive features of DB*Snap* (automatically showing the query result and corresponding relational algebra expression) make it an environment where students can experiment with different query arrangements, get immediate feedback, and improve their solutions until they find the correct answers. Instructors can also prepare projects or assignments where students use DB*Snap* to build queries that generate specific reports. Since DB*Snap* supports importing datasets, instructors can prepare custom datasets for these assignments. DB*Snap* can also be used to teach database query optimization. Specifically, DB*Snap* can be used to show that multiple query arrangements (generated by query transformation rules) can produce the same result and that some arrangements may be faster than others. The use of query trees (query plans) is in fact one of the most useful representations of a query to teach the effects of transformation rules. DB*Snap* can be used to dynamically transform a query into an equivalent one by re-arranging the query blocks.

To assess the effectiveness of DB*Snap* as a learning tool, the authors used it in a relational algebra class and prepared an end-of-class survey. While this was a small class, the results are promising. The survey results are presented next (1: Agree - 4: Disagree). To the question "*I am able to recognize the key properties of relational algebra operators and build queries to answer specific questions*", 80% of students agree and 20% moderately agree. To the question "*The use of DBSnap helped me to have a clear understanding of relational algebra operators*", 80% of students agree and 20% moderately agree. To the question "*DBSnap significantly helped me to learn how to build relational algebra queries*", 78% of students strongly agree and 22% moderately agree. In the open ended questions, students gave positive comments about DB*Snap*, e.g., "*DBSnap really helps the user follow the query as it is being built*", "*It is very easy to make changes on the query by rearranging blocks and subtrees*", "*It is so simple, user-friendly and I liked all the colors*", and "*The ability to see the result of every node is very helpful*".

6. CONCLUSIONS

A clear understanding of relational algebra operators and the ability to write relational algebra queries are two key learning objectives in database courses. Furthermore, a solid grasp of relational algebra and query plans provides a good foundation to learn the SQL-like query languages that are used in many modern database systems. This paper introduces DB*Snap*, an open-source tool aimed to facilitate the learning of relational algebra and query plans. One of DB*Snap*'s key and differentiating features is that it uses a tree-based query structure that is highly similar to the intuitive query trees used by many textbooks and educators. DB*Snap* is also a highly interactive tool that shows the query result and equivalent relational algebra expression while a query is being built. This paper presents the different design features of DB*Snap*, provides its implementation details, describes guidelines to use it in database courses, and evaluates is effectiveness as an educational tool.

7. REFERENCES

[1] A. P. Appel, E. Q. Silva, C. Traina, and A. J. M. Traina. idfql: A query-based tool to help the teaching process of the relational algebra. In *WCETE*, 2004.

[2] G. Constantinou. Relational algebra and sql query visualisation. Technical report, Dept. of Computing, Imperial College, 2010.

[3] S. W. Dietrich, E. Eckert, and K. Piscator. Winrdbi: A windows-based relational database educational tool. In *ACM SIGCSE*, 1997.

[4] R. A. Elmasri and S. B. Navathe. *Fundamentals of Database Systems*. Addison-Wesley, 6 edition, 2010.

[5] J. Gorman, S. Gsell, and C. Mayfield. Learning relational algebra by snapping blocks. In *ACM SIGCSE*, 2014.

[6] S. H. Kim and J. W. Jeon. Programming lego mindstorms nxt with visual programming. In *ICCAS*, 2007.

[7] J. H. Maloney, K. Peppler, Y. Kafai, M. Resnick, and N. Rusk. Programming by choice: Urban youth learning programming with scratch. In *ACM SIGCSE*, 2008.

[8] A. Marron, G. Weiss, and G. Wiener. A decentralized approach for programming interactive applications with javascript and blockly. In *AGERE!*, 2012.

[9] P. Mitra. Relational algebra learning tool. Technical report, Dept. of Computing, Imperial College, 2009.

[10] J. Mönig. morphic.js - source code. `https://github.com/jmoenig/morphic.js`.

[11] C. North and B. Shneiderman. Snap-together visualization: Can users construct and operate coordinated visualizations? *Int. J. Hum.-Comput. Stud.*, 53(5):715–739, 2000.

[12] A. Silberschatz, H. Korth, and S. Sudarshan. *Database Systems Concepts*. McGraw-Hill, Inc., 6 edition, 2010.

[13] Y. N. Silva and J. Chon. Dbsnap. `http://www.public.asu.edu/~ynsilva/dbsnap`.

[14] S. Tomaselli. Relational - educational tool for relational algebra. `https://github.com/ltworf/relational/`.

[15] D. Wolber. App inventor and real-world motivation. In *ACM SIGCSE*, 2011.

Language Migration in non-CS Introductory Programming through Mutual Language Translation Environment

Yoshiaki Matsuzawa
Graduate School of Informatics,
Shizuoka University
3-5-1 Johoku, Nakaku, Hamamatsu
Shizuoka, Japan
matsuzawa@inf.shizuoka.ac.jp

Takashi Ohata
Graduate School of Informatics,
Shizuoka University
3-5-1 Johoku, Nakaku, Hamamatsu
Shizuoka, Japan
ohata@sakailab.info

Manabu Sugiura
Keio University
5322 Endo, Fujisawa
Kanagawa, Japan
manabu@sfc.keio.ac.jp

Sanshiro Sakai
Graduate School of Informatics,
Shizuoka University
3-5-1 Johoku, Nakaku, Hamamatsu
Shizuoka, Japan
sakai@inf.shizuoka.ac.jp

ABSTRACT

In the past decade, improvements have been made to the environments used for introductory programming education, including by the introduction of visual programming languages such as Squeak and Scratch. However, migration from these languages to text-based programming languages such as C and Java is still a problem. Hence, using the OpenBlocks framework proposed at the Massachusetts Institute of Technology, we developed a system named BlockEditor, which can translate bidirectionally between Block (the block language used here) and Java. We conducted an empirical study of this system in an introductory programming course taken by approximately 100 university students not majoring in computer science. When students were given opportunities to select the language to solve their programming assignments, we traced their selection by tracking working time with BlockEditor or Java for each individual student. The results illustrate the nature of the seamless migration from Block to Java, and show that there is great diversity in the timing and speed of migration to Java by each individual. Additionally, we found that students with low self-evaluation of their skill chose to use Block at a significantly higher rate than did students with high self-evaluation. This suggests that BlockEditor can act as scaffolding for students by promoting mixed programming between Block and Java in their migration phase.

SIGCSE'15, March 4–7, 2015, Kansas City, MO, USA.

http://dx.doi.org/10.1145/2676723.2677230.

Categories and Subject Descriptors

D.1.7 [**Programming Techniques**]: Visual Programming; D.2.2 [**Software Engineering**]: Design Tools and Techniques; K.3.2 [**Computers and Education**]: Computer and Information Science Education

General Terms

Design, Human Factors, Measurement

Keywords

Programming Education; Visual Programming; Language Migration; Scaffolding

1. INTRODUCTION

In the past decade, environments have been developed by researchers for the purpose of supporting introductory programming education. The most popular approach is to use a visual programming language such as Squeak [8] or Scratch [19]. The visual programming approach enables beginning learners to build their program by mouse operations, which eliminates typing and makes grammatical errors impossible. In this paper, we focus on the building-block approach [13], a visual programming approach exemplified by languages such as Squeak Etoys and Scratch (hereinafter, block languages' generally and Block for our specific environment). Using block languages, we can create programs by building with blocks [1] that represent elements of the programming language (e.g., commands, branching, and variable declaration), putting these blocks together in a jigsaw puzzle style [13]. Grammatical errors are prevented while programming in block languages because it is not possible

[1]In the Squeak community, what we called blocks here are called tiles [10]

to connect blocks unless those blocks can connect grammatically.

The main purpose of introductory programming courses is not to develop an understanding of the grammar of particular programming languages but rather to develop the computational problem-solving skills that facilitate so-called "computational thinking" [22]. In 2002, the United Nations Educational, Scientific and Cultural Organization described the task of such courses as "designing a task-oriented algorithm," where programming was defined in the following way.

> Programming at this level is not a technical subject. By and large, it means changing a task you can "do for your yourself" into one which can be "done by others". This means describing a task as a procedure in sufficient and complete detail so that another person or a device can perform it precisely and repetitively [20].

Researchers and developers of visual programming languages believe that the visual programming approach is an effective way to support learners in developing computational thinking during introductory programming courses. In theory, by using a visual approach, learners can focus on their problem-solving tasks and thereby come to understand programming concepts [5] more easily than with text-based programming. However, no clear evidence of the advantages has been shown in literature [11]. Additionally, there have been no reports that learners can successfully transform their visual programming skills into text-based programming skills.

Hence, in this research we propose an environment that supports learners in migrating from a visual language to a text-based language. The environment has two interfaces, one for a visual-block language (Block) and one for a text-based language (Java), as well as a system for bidirectional translation between Block and Java. We based the system on OpenBlocks[18] which was developed at the Massachusetts Institute of Technology (MIT). Learners can choose their language from between the two, and they can freely switch between languages to solve programming tasks. We hypothesized that learners would choose the Block language first; this language would then act as scaffolding [23] during their learning of programming, and students would gradually migrate to Java on their own schedule.

2. RELATED WORK

There have been many reports on using block languages for introductory programming education [12, 15], as well as reports on the development of new block languages [8, 19, 3, 2, 6]. Researchers agree that block languages feel familiar to beginners because they can avoid grammatical errors while programming. However, several researchers have proposed text-based educational programming languages, such as Dolittle [9]. These researchers argue that visual programming approaches have disadvantages for learners, and particularly that students have difficulty in moving to text-based programming after their introductory programming course.

There have been some studies on migration from block-based languages to text-based languages. Pasternak [17] proposed offering the ability to translate a program written in Block to a program written in Java. Google Blockly [6] can be translated into multiple languages (e.g., into Javascript or Python) from its block representation. In 2012, Dann et al. tackled the problem of figuring out how students can transfer their knowledge of Alice3 (a block-based language) to Java programming, and they reported that experience with a block language acted as helpful scaffolding for students learning to program in Java [4]. A key difference between our study and previous studies is that in those studies, the environments offered translation in only one direction: from block to text. We used a bidirectional translation environment. In 2008, Warth et al. proposed a bidirectional translation system, "TileScript," between a block language and JavaScript [21], although that research verified only that the technical requirements could be met to implement the prototype system. They did not propose a block editing system that could be used in actual education, nor did they evaluate the use of such a system.

The present research is an attempt to raise the "ceiling of programming" up to practical programming levels. Harvey et al. [7] proposed a functionality they called BYOB ("Build Your Own Block") in Scratch. This functionality expands the descriptive capabilities of the block language. The purpose of the project is to support a block language suitable for a wide range of users, from beginners to professionals. They stress the importance of structured programming, as discussed in the book *Structure and Interpretation of Computer Programs (SICP)* [1], and the support that block languages offer to structured programming. Although we fundamentally agree with the importance of structured programming, our suggested approach is to implement it by migrating to a language suitable for practical use.

3. TOOL DESIGN

3.1 Basic Function and Interface

We have developed a tool named BlockEditor. This tool was designed as a support for creating programs in the Block language, and it was embedded into the programming environment that we used for an introductory programming course whose target language is Java. The resulting environment has two interfaces, one for the (visual) Block language and one for the textual Java language, as well as a system for bidirectional translation between the two languages. Figure 1 shows the user interface for the environment.

The BlockEditor is shown at the left bottom of Figure 1. Users can build a program by using blocks in the center pane of the BlockEditor. Then, users can take blocks from the right pane of the BlockEditor. When a user presses the button labeled "save as Java," the Block program is translated to Java. The translated program is shown in the Java development window, which can be seen at the right top of the figure. When users edit the Java program that results from translation and then save it, the Java program is automatically translated back into a Block program and shown in the BlockEditor. The developed program can be compiled and run from either window.

3.2 Design of Block and Translation

We based the developed system on OpenBlocks [18], which was developed at MIT. We made some modifications to the original OpenBlocks in order to accommodate the Java translation. Although the translation function does not cover the entire grammar for Java, enough grammar is cov-

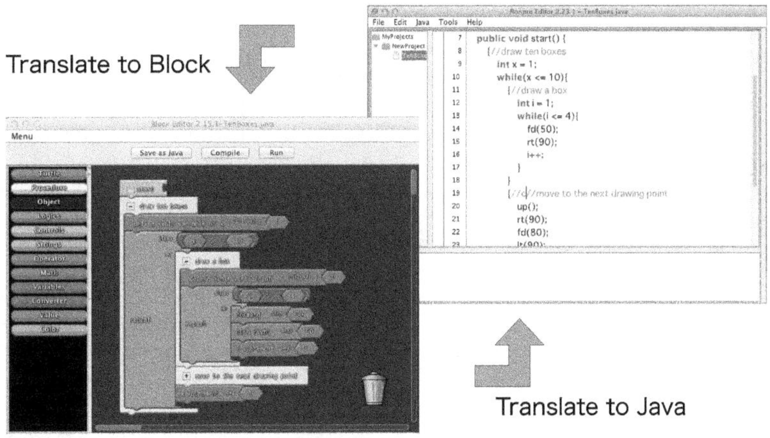

Figure 1: Overview of the proposed environment.

(a) context menu for variable definition

(b) context menu for object variable definition

Figure 2: Context menu interface of BlockEditor

ered for the tasks that are assigned to beginners in introductory programming courses.

Command blocks for Turtle Graphics [16] were designed to mirror those embedded in the sample of OpenBlocks. Because we developed the Turtle Graphics library in Java, the blocks for the Turtle Graphics library can be translated into Java. For example, as shown in Figure 1, the block "forward 100" can be translated into "fd(100);", and the block "turn right 90" can be translated into "rt(90);".

The primitive variable types available for blocks are the same as in Java. It is not typically considered necessary to distinguish between `int` and `double` in block languages, as a result of which only one number type is considered in general block languages such as Scratch and Squeak. However, unifying the numeric types is difficult because of technical considerations such as translation, and the intent is for learners to come to understand Java primitive types. The current version of the system provides the `int`, `double`, `boolean`, and `String` types as primitive types. We created a block type for variable definitions, and users can take obtain blocks for reference to the variable and for assigning values into the variable by using a pull-down menu, as shown in Figure 2(a)

Decision blocks (i.e., conditionals) and repetition blocks are each represented by only one type of block. This means that we convert all repetition structures in Java (e.g., `while` statements, `for` statements, and `foreach` statements) into a single block type, the "repeat" block, and conditional structures are similarly merged to one block type, the "conditional" block. Once the Java program is converted into the block language, information about the original representation is lost. Therefore, for example, if the user writes a program using a `for` statement in Java and this is subsequently translated into a repetition block, then translation back to Java will result in a `while` statement, even though the meaning and effects of the program have not changed.

The blocks to define functions (methods) have the same design as in the original OpenBlocks. Because OpenBlocks does not have blocks for object-oriented programming, we implemented a richer set of blocks to allow defining, creating, and using the objects. We can define variables for the defined types (classes), and we can obtain call-method blocks from a pull-down menu, as is shown in Figure 2(b).

The system has offers bi-directional translation between Block and Java. It is technically implemented through a block description file formatted according to the XML format specified for OpenBlocks. In the case of conversion from Block to Java, the system generates a description file for the blocks by calling a function in OpenBlocks. Then, the system reads the file and converts the result into Java code. In case of a conversion from Java to Block, the system converts the Java source into an abstract syntax tree; the system generates the block description file in the XML format defined for OpenBlocks. BlockEditor shows no blocks when a user tries to convert a Java program that contains syntax errors. Although we could build some of the blocks by ignoring parts of the errors, we thought that this might confuse learners about the errors.

4. EMPIRICAL STUDY METHOD

4.1 Research Question and Hypothesis

We conducted an empirical study in our introductory programming class. The goal of the study was to evaluate the effectiveness of the proposed environment (BlockEditor). The research question was "How do students select their languages when given the opportunity to select the language they use to solve their programming assignments?" Students were given the opportunity to select the language they used to solve their programming assignments, which could be completed in Block or Java. We traced their selection by tracking working time with BlockEditor and with Java for each individual student. We began with two hypotheses:

Hypothesis I Learners will choose to use Block first, which will act as scaffolding [23] for learning programming, and then learners will gradually migrate to Java on their own schedule.

Hypothesis II Students with low self-evaluation of their skills will use Block at a higher relative frequency than students with higher self-evaluation.

4.2 Educational Environment Descriptions

An experimental evaluation of the tool was conducted throughout the introductory programming course at our university. The course was designed for art students, rather than for computer science students. Therefore, the objective of the course is to develop an understanding of task-oriented programming, which is independent from any language. Approximately 100 students participated in this course; two lecturers and six teaching assistants conducted the class.

In this class, all students were assigned 3–5 tasks per week. The given tasks were all to build a program (there were no paper tests, and no tasks such as filling in a missing part of a program). Students were given one of the following sets of instructions for how to solve each task:

- B (Block Task):Students MUST use BlockEditor to build a program.
- J (Java Task):Students MUST use Java to build a program.
- A (ANY):Students can select the language used to build a program, and this choice can be freely changed.

The number of assignment types for all weeks are shown in Table 1. We assigned at least one Block task and one Java task for each of the first 4 weeks in order to give students exposure to both languages; we assigned only ANY tasks in the last part of the course.

4.3 Method of Data Collection

The actual effort time was recorded and provided by PPV [14]. The working time was calculated by summing up the time and excluding periods of longer than 5 min with no user operation. We defined the two calculated times as follows:

Tb Working Time with BlockEditor

Tj Working Time with Java

Then, we calculated the BlockEditing Rate (Rb) by using the following equation.

$$Rb = \frac{Tb}{Tb + Tj} \quad (1)$$

Table 1: Curriculum of the introductory programming course.

Week	Contents	B	J	A
1	Setup & Guidance	-	-	-
2	Introduction of Turtle Graphics	1	1	3
3	Variables, Conditionals	1	2	2
4	Loops, Nested Loops	1	2	4
5	Creating Animation	1	2	2
6	Handling Key and Mouse Input	0	0	2
Middle	Your Own Product	-	-	1
7	Console & Calculation (Expense Sharing)	0	0	3
8	Console & Calculation (BMI Calculation)	0	1	5
9	Method (with Arguments)	0	1	3
10	Method (with Return Value)	0	2	4
11	Method (Recursion)	0	1	3
12	Collection	0	0	2
13	Sorting Algorithm	0	0	2
14	Dictionary	0	0	0
15	Your Own Product (in Teams)	-	-	-

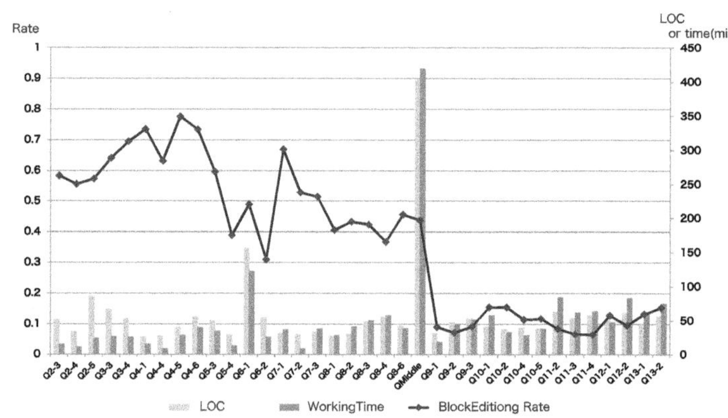

Figure 3: Relative rate of working with BlockEditor, total working time, and the lines of code (LOC) for each assignment.

5. RESULTS

5.1 BlockEditing Rate

The chart in Figure 3 shows the averages of the rate of BlockEditor use (Rb), lines of code (LOC), and the total working time (in minutes), for each task. All the ANY tasks assigned to students are shown in increasing chronological order.

The mean of Rb was 0.6 near the start of the course, 0.4 in the middle of the course, and 0.1 in the latter part of the course. The average rate was gradually decreasing, although the slope was steep down to around assignment Q9-1. This change is likely because QMiddle required a relatively longer program than the other tasks did. Students were asked to create their own game in the QMiddle assignment. As the average LOC reached 400, it became difficult to manage the program in BlockEditor.

We created a grid representation of the rate of BlockEdi-

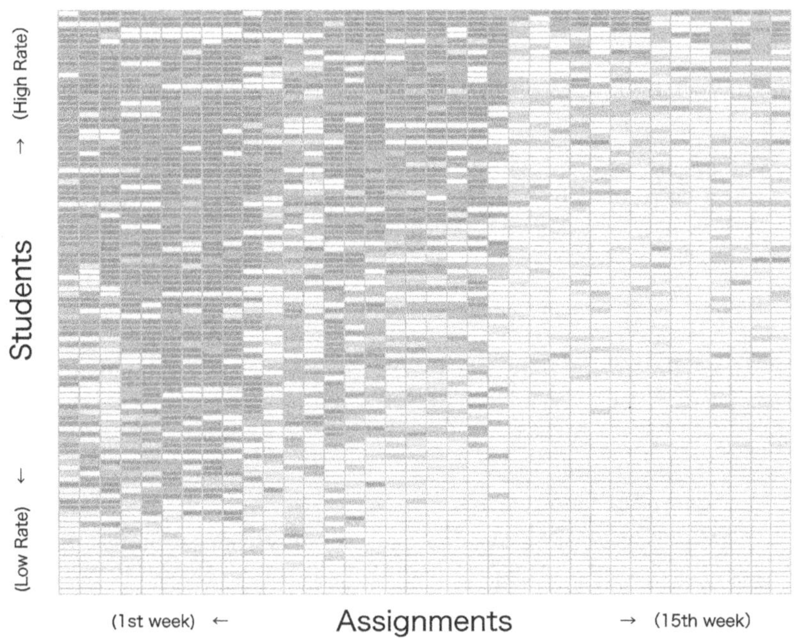

Figure 4: Grid representation of relative rate of working with BlockEditor for each student (color intensity indicates the rate of BlockEditor use).

tor use (*Rb*) to illustrate the nature of the seamless migration from Block to Java. The representation is shown in Figure 4. Each column represents one task assigned to students, arranged in chronological order. Each row represents one student; the rows are sorted by course-average *Rb*, with higher rows indicating higher average use. Each cell thus represents the value of *Rb* for a particular student completing a particular task. High-intensity color indicates a high *Rb*, and white indicates an *Rb* of 0 (i.e., using only Java).

We can observe that the bottom 10% of students (in terms of *Rb*) did not select BlockEditor at all, and the top 10% of students almost always used BlockEditor until the end of the course. The remaining 80% of students gradually migrated from Block to Java. We can observe the seamless migration both overall (by the number of students who used Java in the class) and at the individual level. Low-level rates at the individual level indicate that those students built their programs with both languages, which is noteworthy. The data show wide diversity in the schedule and speed of migration by each individual.

5.2 Self-evaluation and BlockEditor Selection

By questionnaire survey, we asked students to self-evaluate their programming skill level on a four-point scale (VG: very good; G: good; NG: not good; NGA: not good at all). We obtained answers for three levels (G, NG, and NGA); no student marked VG. We compared the three groups on block editing rate. The results are shown in Figure 5.

The descriptive statistics were as follows: G ($n = 11, sd = 0.25, avg = 0.25$), NG ($n = 47, sd = 0.20, avg = 0.41$), NGA ($n = 28, sd = 0.15, avg = 0.44$). Welch's t-test was conducted between groups G and NG and between groups G and NGA. The difference between G and NG was marginally significant ($t(13.29) = 2.04$, $.05 < p < .10$). The difference between G and NGA was significant ($t(13.15) = 2.39$, $p < .05$). These results show that students who evaluated their programming skills as low selected to use BlockEditor more often than did students who rated their skills as high.

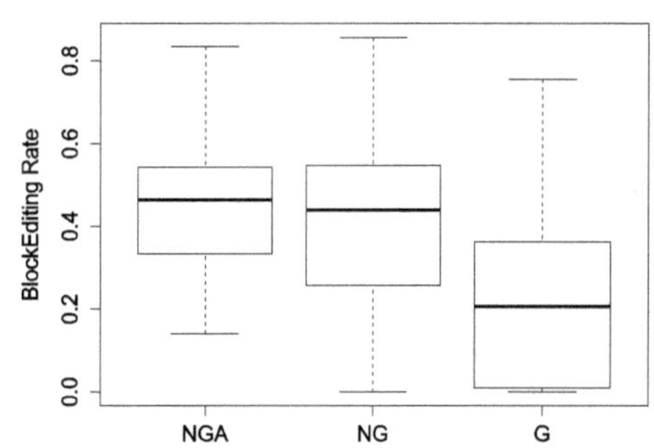

Figure 5: Distributions of rates of working with BlockEditor, by self-evaluated programming skill level.

6. DISCUSSION

The results indicate that the environments succeeded in promoting learners' seamless migration from Block to Java. Additionally, the results of the questionnaire given to students were similar. The illustration of the rate of selecting Block fades along the positive time axis, with the rate of use gradually dropping. These results therefore provide evidence that a block language can successfully act as scaffolding for students learning text-based programming. One of the considerations when verifying this result is to discern whether the students had the meta-cognitive skills necessary to select the language appropriate to their learning. We have assumed that the students did have sufficient knowledge both because they were university students and because we exposed the students to both languages before offering a choice. Many students used Block only partially, although the teacher did not explicitly teach this usage. We consider that is an evidence that the students were aware of their own level of understanding.

The results indicated that there is little relation between the rate of using BlockEditing and length of program, as well as little relation between the use rate and working time. Whereas the factor of the programming experience, and individual differences have a high relationship with the rate of use. Both Hypothesis I (that learners will choose a block language first and then gradually migrate to Java) and Hypothesis II (that the block language will be used relatively more by students with low self-evaluation of their skills) were supported by the results.

A limitation of this research is that we analyzed only the language selection rate. This is not direct evidence that the learners' understanding is being enhanced. However, the same course was taught in the previous year entirely in Java using the same content. In the range of our observations, we confirmed that students' understanding level between the two classes was equivalent (or better understood by the class that used Block). The negative atmosphere in the classroom was dramatically changed into a positive one. We strongly believe that the results will encourage teachers who use a block language in introductory programming education.

7. REFERENCES

[1] H. Abelson, G. J. Sussman, and J. Sussman. *Structure and Interpretation of Computer Programs - 2nd ed.* MIT Press, 1996.

[2] J. C. Cheung, G. Ngai, S. C. Chan, and W. W. Lau. *Filling the gap in programming instruction: a text-enhanced graphical programming environment for junior high students.* SIGCSE' 09 Proceedings of the 40th ACM technical symposium on Computer science education, New York, NY, USA, 2009.

[3] S. Cooper, W. Dann, and R. Pausch. Teaching objects-first in introductory computer science. In *Proceedings of the 34th SIGCSE technical symposium on Computer science education*, SIGCSE '03, pages 191–195, New York, NY, USA, 2003. ACM.

[4] W. Dann, D. Cosgrove, D. Slater, D. Culyba, and S. Cooper. Mediated transfer: Alice 3 to java. In *Proceedings of the 43rd ACM Technical Symposium on Computer Science Education*, SIGCSE '12, pages 141–146, 2012.

[5] M. Fal and N. Cagiltay. How Scratch Programming May Enrich Engineering Education. In *2nd International Engineering Education Conference(IEEC2012)*, pages 107–113, 2012.

[6] Google Inc. Blockly:a visual programming editor. `http://code.google.com/p/blockly/`, referenced at 2013.03.17.

[7] B. Harvey and J. Monig. Bringing " no ceiling " to scratch: Can one language serve kids and computer scientists? *Constructionism 2010, Paris*, 2010.

[8] D. Ingalls, T. Kaehler, J. Maloney, S. Wallace, and A. Kay. Back to the future: The story of squeak, a practical smalltalk writtern in itself. *Proc. of ACM OOPSLA' 97*, page 318, 1997.

[9] S. Kanemune, T. Nakatani, R. Mitarai, S. Fukui, and Y. Kuno. Dolittle - experiences in teaching programming at K12 schools. In *Second International Conference on Creating, Connecting and Collaborating through Computing(C5)*, pages 177–184, 2004.

[10] A. Kay. Squeak Etoys authoring & media. *Viewpoints Research Institute Research Note*, 2005.

[11] C. Lewis. How programming environment shapes perception, learning and goals: logo vs. scratch. In *Proceedings of the 41st ACM technical symposium on Computer science education (SIGCSE '10)*, pages 346–350, 2010.

[12] C. Lewis. What do Students Learn About Programming From Game, Music Video, And Storytelling Projects? In *Proceedings of the 43rd ACM technical symposium on Computer science education (SIGCSE '12)*, pages 643–648, 2012.

[13] J. Maloney, L. Burd, Y. Kafai, N. Rusk, B. Silverman, and M. Resnick. Scratch: a sneak preview. In *Proceedings Second International Conference on Creating Connecting and Collaborating through Computing 2004*, pages 104–109, 2004.

[14] Y. Matsuzawa, K. Okada, and S. Sakai. Programming Process Visualizer: A Proposal of the Tool for Students to Observe Their Programming Process. In *Innovation and Technology in Computer Science Education (ITiCSE '13)*, pages 46–51, 2013.

[15] D. Ozoran, N. Cagiltay, and D. Topalli. Using Scratch In Introduction to Programming Course for Engineering Students. In *2nd International Engineering Education Conference(IEEC2012)*, pages 125–132, 2012.

[16] S. Papert. *Mindstorms: children, computers, and powerful ideas.* Basic Books, Inc., New York, NY, USA, 1980.

[17] E. Pasternak. Visual programming pedagogies and integrating current visual programming language features. Master's thesis, Carnegie Mellon University Robotics Institute Master's Degree, 2009.

[18] R. V. Roque. Openblocks: An extendable framework for graphical block programming systems. *Master thesis at MIT*, 2007.

[19] Scratch Team Lifelong Kindergarten Group MIT Media Lab. Scratch -imagine.program.share- `http://scratch.mit.edu/`.

[20] UNESCO. ICT Curriculum for School / Program of Teacher Development. `http://unesdoc.unesco.org/images/0012/001295/129538e.pdf`, 2002.

[21] A. Warth, T. Yamamiya, Y. Ohshima, and W. Scott. Toward a more scalable end-user scripting language. In *Proceedings Second International Conference on Creating Connecting and Collaborating through Computing 2008*, pages 172–178, 2008.

[22] J. Wing. Computational Thinking. *Communications of the ACM*, 49(3):33–35, 2006.

[23] D. Wood, J. S. Bruner, and G. Ross. The role of tutoring in problem solving. *Journal of child psychology and psychiatry*, 17(2):89–100, 1976.

Scratch: A Way to Logo and Python

Mark Dorling
Computing at School and Network of Excellence
BCS Chartered Institute for IT
Swindon UK
mark.dorling@computingatschool.org.uk

Dave White
Computing at School and Network of Excellence
BCS Chartered Institute for IT
Swindon UK
dave.white@computingatschool.org.uk

ABSTRACT

There is concern amongst teachers about how to support all pupils in making the transition from popular graphical languages like Scratch to text-based languages like Python. In a new subject, not taught widely before at both primary and secondary education in England, there is inevitably a lack of tuned-in pedagogical expertise. In this paper, the authors address the transition process by exploring established pedagogy in Computer Science, and other subjects including Mathematics, Science and Languages, and by sharing and testing their findings with pupils and teachers in the classroom.

Teaching the fundamentals of programming is well served by applying sequential solutions in both graphical and text-based languages. This practitioner action research paper focuses on scaffolding support for pupils when making the transition from graphical to text-based languages. In an approach which uses graphical languages in conjunction with, not in place of, text-based programming languages, the authors discuss ways to tackle the difficulties presented to pupils by text-based languages, and propose a tested strategy for teachers to enable pupils to undertake the transition successfully.

Categories and Subject Descriptors

K.3.2 [**Computers & Education**]: Computer and Information Science education - *Computer Science Education, Curriculum*
D.3.2 [**Language Classifications**]: Scratch 2.0, Logo, Python 3

General Terms

Theory, Experimentation, Human Factors

Keywords

Graphical programming language, text-based programming language, transition process, computational thinking, unplugged activity, Computer Science Education, Scratch, Logo, Python

.

1 BACKGROUND

From September 2014, pupils in English state-maintained schools will be expected to follow the programmes of study set out in the national curriculum document [4]. Computing at School has responded with a targeted resource [2].

SIGCSE'15, March 4–7, 2015, Kansas City, MO, USA.

ACM 978-1-4503-2966-8/15/03…$15.00.
http://dx.doi.org/10.1145/2676723.2677256

The programme of study has high-level aims in terms of the introduction of computer science [4]. The following extracts illustrate learner capabilities at different stages of primary and secondary education.

At Key Stage 2 (age 7-11) pupils should be able to (amongst other things): "… solve problems by decomposing them into smaller parts." and "use sequence, selection, and repetition in programs; work with variables and various forms of input and output." and also "… detect and correct errors in algorithms and programs." ([4], p. 189).

At Key Stage 3 (ages 11-14) pupils should be able to: "… make appropriate use of data structures [for example, lists, tables or arrays]; design and develop modular programs that use procedures or functions." and also "Understand simple Boolean logic [for example, AND, OR and NOT] and some of its uses in circuits and programming…" ([4], p. 190).

For primary educators there is no specification in the programme of study to teach either a graphical or text-based language, instead the emphasis is placed on teaching concepts and principles. In contrast, the programme of study for secondary education, Key Stage 3 makes it explicit:

Pupils should be able to: use two or more programming languages, at least one of which is textual, to solve a variety of computational problems ([4], p. 190)

2 INTRODUCTION

There is a growing range of graphical programming environments available to teachers, such as Scratch [9], Alice [3], Kodu etc. but little research into how effective they are at supporting pupils to make the transition from graphical to text-based languages. Wolz U. et al reported that after initially learning Scratch, the students' transition to Java or C appeared to be easier [15].

After using graphical programming environments, there is a perception amongst non-specialist teachers in both primary and secondary education that text-based programming is hard. And with some reason: "Beginners need to learn to identify the structure of a problem and the core logic of a program to solve it but they are simultaneously forced to deal with technical details of the programming environment that are not related to these and this can be overwhelming and often discouraging for beginning programmers." [5]. Pupil difficulties with text-based language syntax and error messages are identified in [6], [10], [15]. As a result, some are publicly questioning whether programming is a skill for only the more able pupils, and have asked questions about the body of pedagogical research for teaching pupils with Special Educational Needs (SEN) such as Dyslexia, and English as a Second Language (EAL).

With their experience at opposite ends of the learning spectrum the authors met at a Computing at School meeting and found their teaching paths surprisingly convergent both in content and pedagogy. One, in the Digital Schoolhouse conducting action research to teach primary and secondary pupils directly to program in Scratch and Logo, the other delivering CPD Courses in Computing to Primary and Secondary School teachers from different disciplines, mostly without a background in Computing, on how to teach Scratch and Python to pupils; and at the same time to investigate and consider how their own programming skills might enhance the delivery of their own subjects. The authors concentrated on:

1. Identifying the difficulties associated with learning to program in a text-based language available in the research literature, and their own experiences of the difficulties which arise in teaching programming in Scratch and text-based based languages.
2. Investigating the background knowledge necessary for the cross-curricula topic chosen --- geometric shapes and patterns.
3. Utilising existing pedagogy, by consulting and observing colleagues teaching in different disciplines, --- including Computer Science, Mathematics, Science and Languages, in order to make the transition process for pupils and teachers a realistic proposition.

The focus of this practitioner action research was on upper key Stage 2 and key Stage 3 pupils and their teachers.

2.1 Aims and Methodology

The authors, with their ongoing involvement with pupils and teachers, decided to pool their resources and experience: to see if they could build on pupils' and teachers' confidence and familiarity with Scratch to find a realistic pathway through the transition process to text-based languages, navigable by teachers and their pupils.

The authors experimented with a number of ideas -- some tried and tested approaches – other ideas were researched and pursued with pupils and teachers in the classroom. Those adopted are summarized here:

3 TRANSITION STRATEGY

A constructionist approach to learning programming and concepts in Computer Science developed from the many years that Logo has been in existence[8], underpinned by the elements of Computational Thinking [11]: *abstraction, algorithmic thinking, decomposition, evaluation and generalization.*

To use a methodology that all three languages shared, namely, sequential processing with a sprite/turtle and the reward of the instant feedback of sprite/turtle activity on the screen.

To reduce the number of tasks to accomplish at the screen by undertaking learning away from the computer in the form of a number of 'unplugged' activities , which are targeted to cover the background knowledge of an exciting cross-curricular topic, in this case geometric shapes and patterns and undertake some text-based programming learning experience in a relaxed play setting away from the computer, using UPL (Unplugged Programming language) --- essentially a very small subset of Logo, which drives a pet/robot.

To harness the benefits of Scratch 2.0 and its freedom from syntactical errors in developing sequential solutions to problems along a simple pathway through the topic -- this pathway is designed to take account of the other known difficulties in programming generally, of concurrency, initialization, and variables [6].

To address, in a rudimentary way, the fundamental control structures of programming: *sequence, repetition, function, selection and communication,* in the course of the pathway.

After a solution to an exercise is completed successfully in Scratch, to use the structural similarity of a Scratch program to the equivalent program in text-based languages. The program would be mapped into a Logo/Python program, with the focus now solely on attending to the environment and syntax of the text-based language.

To consult colleagues and observe existing pedagogy in the topic as well as pedagogy in other subjects, including Computer Science, Mathematics, Science and Languages. Some of the difficulties associated with learning text-based languages were tackled directly from these resources. Others were delayed until later in the transition process.

4 DISCUSSION

The authors observed and consulted specialist colleagues teaching Mathematics, Science and Languages in local primary and secondary schools to gain a greater understanding of pedagogy in other subjects, and, in the first instance, how it could be applied to computational thinking and programming in the transitional process the authors were undertaking, and further, to Computer Science in general.

They were particularly interested in Mathematics teachers' approaches to geometrical shapes, symmetry and patterns, mental processes in mental arithmetic and progressing to elementary linear algebra and linear transformations.

Science teachers methods of helping pupils to collect and analyse data, to experiment and hypothesize in Science, including key questioning techniques employed to harness enquiry-based learning, and use of scientific language and concepts for variables and constants.

Language teachers' approaches to teaching pupils learning new languages and applying rules of syntax in languages. Literacy: reading precedes writing [12].

5 THE PATHWAY

The authors have outlined the pathway as a sequential journey through a course of 10 sessions. Each session, unplugged [1], or at the computer may consist of a mixture of: a direct teaching component, an activity, a worksheet with graded exercises (*s ranging from 1-5) and individual coaching/tutoring

In the next section 5.2.1, the authors map out, in more detail than in other sections, how the unplugged session on programming takes pupils through the use of the control structures ***sequence, repetition and use of functions,*** preparing the way for interaction with the computer in subsequent sections. Apart from the two further unplugged sessions, sections up to 5.2.8 summarise how these control structures are programmed in Scratch in the first instance, before mapping to a text-based program in Logo/Python.

5.2.1 Unplugged 1

'Action Geometry' in UPL --- LOGO Unplugged

In this session, we get used to programming a pet/robot/sprite/turtle in a text-based format without a computer. In UPL (an unplugged programming language, essentially Logo, but adapted for unplugged use), a pet/robot is defined by 2 characteristics:

- Its position -- where it is standing, if we are 'walking' the talk, or a point on the paper if we are drawing the path. We start at the origin O.
- The direction in which it is facing at any moment. (We assume it is facing right → to start at O).

We consider 3 of the instructions in UP:

`forward 1 step (or 2 or 3),`
`left turn` (through 90 degrees),
`right turn` (through 90 degrees).

We abbreviate the instructions when writing, for example, to

fd2, lt and rt

The program to draw a straight line of length 2, and return to the starting point facing in the original direction would be:

fd2 lt lt fd2 lt lt

Notice that the pet/robot has turned through what we call a SPIN(360) in this program. Pupils can work in pairs using UPL in a number of ways.

1. 'Walk the talk': one pupil 'talks' the instructions, the other 'walks' the figure
2. 'Draw the talk': one pupil 'talks' the instructions, the other 'draws' the figure
3. Use a combination of 1, 2 interactively to construct a program on paper

Sequence: is setting up the instructions in a program in the right order usually set out one after the other, reading left to right and top to bottom.

- Activity: Using the instructions in UPL in combination, how would you <u>program</u> the pet/robot to: trace a capital letter shape like L, I, T, F, E and return to the starting point and starting direction? Starting point and direction for the pet/robot is at O for the letter L.
- Activity: trace a square of side-length 2 paces and return to the starting point and starting direction.
- Activity: Ex 1. Cracking the Code: what does the pet trace out in the following program?

```
fd2 lt fd2 lt fd2 lt fd2 lt    fd2   fd2 lt fd2 lt fd2 lt fd2 lt
fd2   fd2 lt fd2 lt fd2 lt fd2 lt    lt lt fd2 fd2 lt lt
```

Quite often, the idea of repetition is used to exploit the occurrence of pattern in the code, which in turn reflects the pattern in the figure generated by the code.. A solution code for drawing a square might look something like this:

```
fd2 lt    fd2 lt    fd2 lt    fd2 lt
```

With the 'pronounced' spacing it is evident that 2 instructions 'fd2 lt' are repeated 4 times corresponding to the four sides of the square.

Repetition A repeat structure is a way of repeating a set of instructions as many times as specified.We use the UPL instruction repeat as follows:

repeat4 [fd2 lt]

The repeat structure shortens the program appreciably and makes it more easily interpreted. We have another structure, a *function*, that helps to shorten the code and makes it more easily interpreted in a different way. In Ex 1, we saw a longish UPL program, in which it was hard to see the wood for the trees. If you break it down into its components (***decomposition***) it is:

1. repeat the instructions 2, 3(below) sequentially three times
2. draw a square of 2 paces
3. move forward 2 paces
4. to end up with 3 squares in a row
5. then return the pet to the starting point and direction.

Function: use of a function sq to draw a square.

- Activity: we introduce a new instruction 'sq' in UPL. sq2 draws a square of side 2 paces. In the program in Ex1, identify the code that sq2 stands for. Rewrite the program in UPL using sq2 in place of code wherever you can. Rewrite the program in UPL using sq2 and the repeat structure
- ***Activity : We name a function row which stands for and names the three squares in a row, with each square of sidelength 2 paces. Use row and the repeat structure in UPL, to write a program in UPL to draw a 3x3 array of 9 squares made up of three rows of squares touching.

5.2.2 Unplugged 2: A worksheet

An example of 'joining dots' action geometry in Figures 1 and 2 serves to acquaint pupils with the background knowledge of polygons (a) and stars (b), (d), (e), (f).

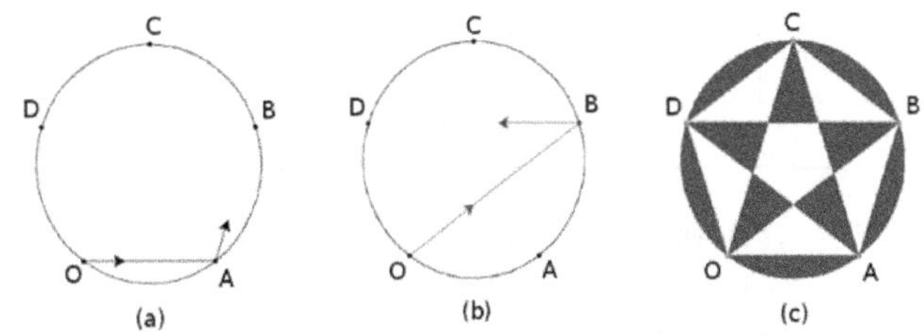

Figure 1. Joining the dots in circles with 5 equally spaced dots at OABCD.

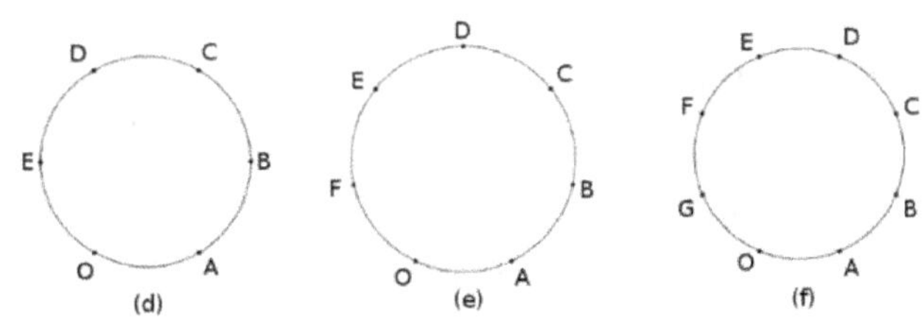

Figure 2. ***action geometry:*** **for the hexagon, heptagon and octagon.**

- Activity

Polygons: (d), (e), (f) Start at O, join dots OA, AB ...
Stars: (e) Start at O, skip a dot, join OB, BD ...
(e) (f) Start at O, skip 2 dots, join OC, CF ...
*** (d) Start at O, skip a dot, Join OB, BD ... What happens? How would you complete a hexagram (star of David)?

5.2.3 Comparison

Scratch, Logo and Python

The similarity between UPL and Logo is obvious in both layout and individual instructions. Logo and Python turtle instructions are closely matched. And the matching structure of a program is reflected in Scratch Logo and Python in Figure 3, where UPL instructions have been entered vertically to facilitate the comparison (similarly for Logo).

Once the pupils had spent time doing unplugged programming and were familiar with programming simple letter shapes and other exercises in UP, the next step was to develop the program to draw a square on screen in the familiar Scratch environment.

Once the program was tested and running, the pupils would attempt to map it onto a Logo/Python program, focusing solely on managing the new environment and getting the specific syntax correct of the text-based language. See Figures 3, 4.

Table 1

Turning Angle	Repeat value	Regular Shape	Shorthand	Length of side
90	4	square	(4, 360/4)	100
45	6, 7 ?			50
60	?			50
?	5	pentagon	(5, 360/5)	75
?	10			?
?	7	heptagon		50
4	90	?		5

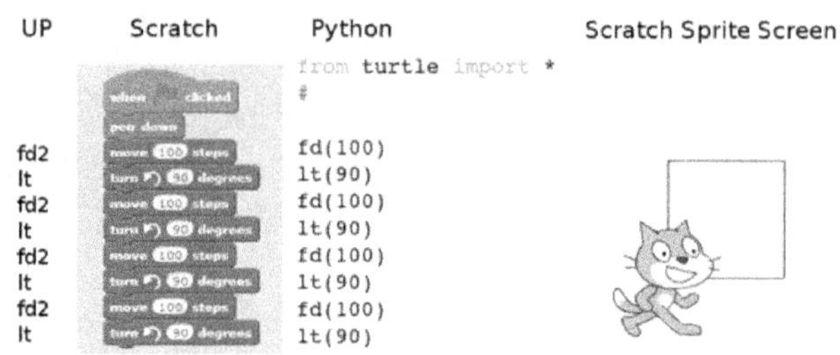

Figure 3. Matching Program structures in UP, Scratch and Python: drawing a square

5.2.4 Repetition

The repetition of the 2 instructions FD 100 LT 90 makes the introduction of the repeat loop welcome, necessary (and useful for experimenting with the values in the loop)

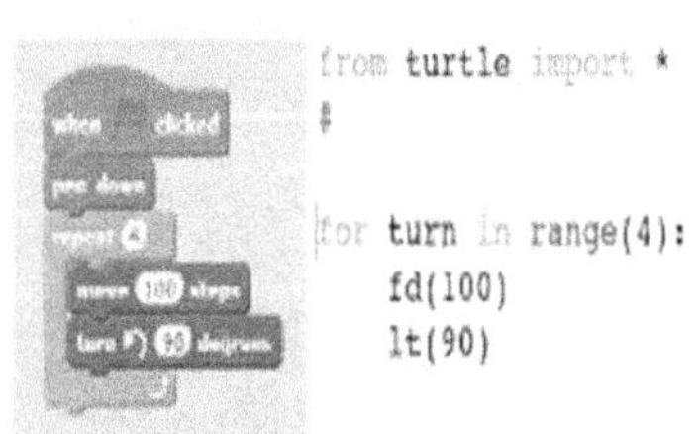

All pupils managed the ordering (sequence) of instructions when designing an algorithm, to draw a square. And having met the repeat structure for drawing a square in UPL, found it straightforward to do the same in Scratch.

Figure 4. The repetition structure in Scratch and Python

5.2.5 Experimentation

As a result of observations and pedagogical consultations, the authors modified their approach to teaching computational thinking [7]. By teasing out *decomposition and generalisation* in 'unplugged' sessions, as well as in coding computing lessons, and extending experimentation to include collection and interpretation of data, the authors introduced a more challenging yet supportive interactive style both oral and written.

When pupils had constructed the repeat loop in Scratch (and Python) see Figure 4, they were then able to experiment with the turning angle (90 degrees) by substituting 45, 30, 60 for 90 degrees in their repeat loop. They were asked to see if they could find another value of the repeat parameter (4) which would result in the turtle 'closing' (returning to the starting point and starting direction) the shape they were drawingSPIN(360). The trial and error process they were engaged in involved *evaluating* the effectiveness of the program they were using albeit with simple changes and was a successful introduction to semantic debugging. Octagons, hexagons, dodecagons (12-sided polygons) readily popped up on their screens, along with some excitement.

The pupils now had accumulated some data as a result of their experimentation in Table 1 below. The authors' dialogue with Science and Mathematics teachers proved invaluable. A period of guessing, hypothesizing and trial and error followed.

- Activity: Complete Table 1: What do you make of the last entry?

Some more able students were able to find the angle for the pentagon. But the heptagon would involve the use of a calculator to record a non-integer value. And the key question to those who found answers was: "Describe how you did it?

(The production of these, and similar unplugged exercise sheets make useful programming projects for pupils (and indeed teachers) when they become more adept programmers. These 'unplugged' worksheets are a good example of how the ability to program can produce learning materials which would otherwise be a difficult chore [14].

5.2.5 Unplugged 3 Enquiry-based learning

Some questions were posed interactively in the classroom --- the questions that follow were set in a CPD worksheet for teachers to adapt for their own classrooms.

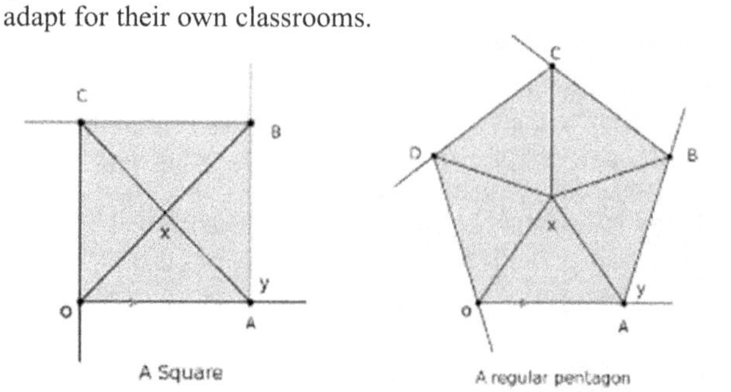

Figure 5. Tracking the square and the pentagon

- Activity: Angles and SPIN(360)

This process could be undertaken as a formal geometry exercise. Here it is introduced calling upon symmetry and 'action geometry' in the computational thinking of *decomposition and generalizing*.

Devise a set of questions to form an enquiry-based exercise to help the reader calculate angles x and y in the square in Figure 5. Afterwards use exactly the same questions but substitute the words 'regular pentagon' wherever you see the word 'square' in your questions. The questions should achieve the same result when applied to the pentagon. Here are a couple of questions to start:

First the Square: (a 4-sided simple, regular, symmetric polygon)

1. What does symmetry mean for a square?
2. Hint: If you turn round completely once and face the same way as you started, how many degrees have you turned through? We will call this a SPIN.

***Generalising* from the known to the unknown**

In the last example with the square, we may have known from our experience what the values of x and y are. In other polygons, we may not be so familiar with angle sizes, hence the importance of *how we work the values of x and y out* with the square. We then have a basis for generalising to the pentagon.

- Activity: More Angles and SPIN(360)

Now the pentagon: (a 5-sided simple, regular, symmetric polygon)

After the unplugged sessions with polygons and stars and plugged-in experimentation, pupils were able to investigate, catalogue and decide which stars could not be drawn straightforwardly. They were then able to test and verify the formal hypothesis (and *generalisation*) for drawing a star: (in shorthand notation)

(n, r * 360/n) where r > 1 and r and n are co-prime, that is, have no common divisor other than 1, and where n is the number of sides of the star, and r runs from 1 to n-1.

In physical terms:

- the r corresponds to starting at O and joining every rth vertex of the star,
- and to r SPINS of the turtle on itself as it traces the star.

For all simple regular polygons r = 1 which generalises this formula to include all regular polygons and stars.

5.2.7 Function

Definition and call, simplifying and (generalizing) with parameters.

The next step, and a crucial one, in extending pupils' interaction with, and learning of, *generalisation* and *abstraction*, is in the creation of their own user functions. In the unplugged programming sessions pupils were able to make use of the user function **'sq2'** for a square with argument 2, without needing to formally define it in a specified format. (Advantage of unplugged! Of course, pupils already make use of system functions like **'fd2'** without seeing a formal definition).

After pupils have practiced *sequence and repetition* using Scratch and transitioned to Logo/Python, they are introduced at this early stage to a function without parameters: 'start-right', which they use at the start of all their Scratch programs. It synchronizes the initialisation of a Scratch Sprite to start from the origin and pointing to the right, with the Python turtle, every time an amended program is re-run. Then they meet the *generalizing* idea of a parameter (sidelength) for a function **'sq'** they have employed in an unplugged setting. See Figures 5 and 6

```
def sq(sidelength):
    #
    for turn in range(4):
        fd(sidelength)
        lt(90)
```

Scratch came of age as a fully-fledged programming language with the arrival of the explicitly defined function facility (custom block), which arrived in Scratch version 2.0 in April 2013.

Figure 5. Function definition of sq(sidelength in Python)

The custom block in Scratch is a good environment in which to learn a difficult concept. It requires careful tuition and practice in both the concept and the process of the definition of a function.

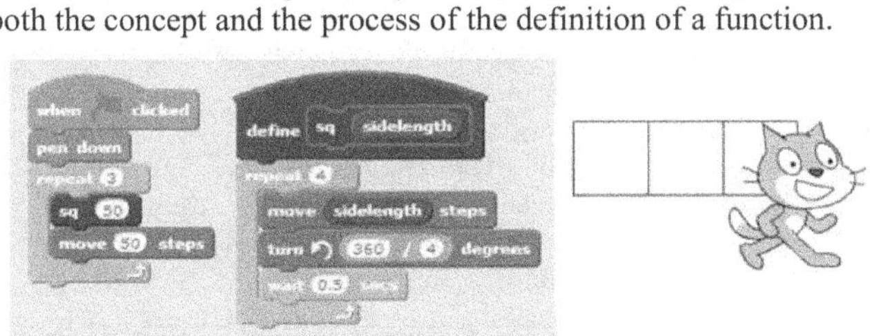

Figure 6. Function definition of sq(sidelength) in Scratch.

Figure 5 encapsulates in the function definition the shorthand form in a repeat loop for a rotation (4, 360/4). In the program the shorthand form, in a repeat loop for a translation of a square through 3 times through 50 steps(pixels), is (3, sq(50), 50). The use of the function, through the shorthand form gives rise to the physical interpretation of translating the square, and replaces the more indecipherable nested loop that would otherwise arise.

The pupils have now learned how to 'hide' the definition of a function (by capping it in a custom block definition and moving it to the side in Scratch 2.0; and by declaring it in a file (module) say 'd.py' and preloading it with 'for d import *' for Python 3. The function can then be inserted as a single instruction in code, thus simplifying the coding on both sides of the transition, (see Figure 7).

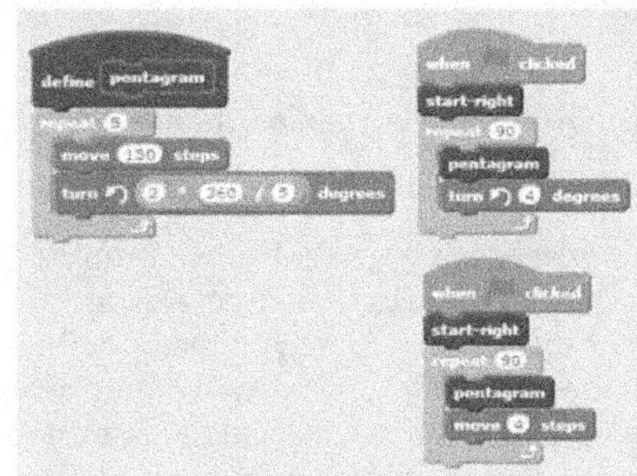

```
from turtle import *
from d import *
#
for turns in range(90):
    pentagram()
    lt(4)
```

```
from turtle import *
from d import *
#
for turns in range(90):
    pentagram()
    fd(4)
```

Figure 7. Function definition for a pentagram (5-star) in Scratch

Pupils are now equipped to devise and program unique patterns and in Python 3 to add colouring-in, which enhances spectacularly their adventures into patterns. The definition of the function pentagram shorthand (5, 2*360/5) illustrates how the shorthand notation and the format of entries in the repeat loop is an aid to *generalizing*. The top program in Figure 7 rotates the pentagram (90, pentagram, lt(4)) and the bottom one translates it (90, pentagram, fd(4)), see Figure 8 and 9 for more examples of rotation and translation.

5.2.8 Patterns

Using functions, rotation and translation. Colouring-in in Python

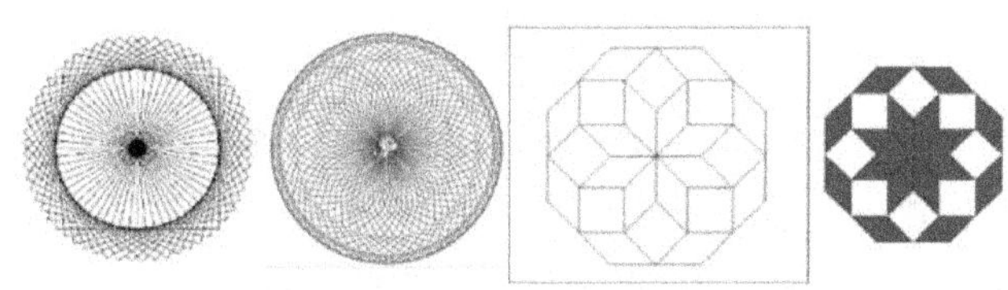

Figure 8. Rotating shapes: square, 11-polygon octagon and octagon coloured (Python)

(a) (b) (c)

Figure 9. A shooting (translating) star, a double spin of a star and translating a circle.

In Figure 9(a), translate a star through 125 pixels, 5 pixels at a time; shorthand form: (125/5, pentagram, fd(5)).

In Figure 9(b), SPIN(2 *360) a pentagram in steps of 2*360/5 degrees; shorthand form:(5, pentagram, 2 * 360/5).

In Figure 9(c) translate a circle through 200 pixels, 4 pixels at a time: shorthand form: (200/4, circle, fd(4))

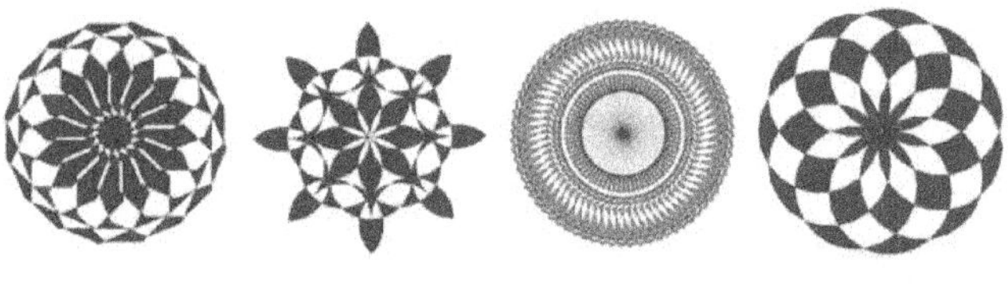

Figure 10. Fancy Rotations of regular shapes

5.2.9 Selection

Drawing a general polygon/star. (algorithmic thinking, decomposition and generalization). Selection structures are best dealt with in a number of scenarios in Scratch directly before a transition takes place to Logo/Python. An activity that arises naturally in the narrative of *generalisation* in patterns is to write an App (function) to draw a polygon/star of any number of sides). And for the drawing to fit in the space available *(selection).*

5.2.10 Communication

Talking to the user; ask and answer in Scratch and print and input in Python. If statements in both. The App above is extended to allow a user to choose the polygon/star to be drawn. In Scratch, a communication with the user may be conducted with the easy-to-use 'ask and wait' block for the program to ask a question, and the reply from the user is entered into the special variable 'answer'. The Python 3 structure can be directly paralleled in the transition.

6 CONCLUSION

The National Curriculum doesn't specify that pupils should learn a graphical language in primary school, only that the pupils should learn two languages in secondary school, one of which should be a text-based language. The National Curriculum is regarded as the minimum expectation of what should be taught to pupils. This paper suggests that a greater focus should be placed by teachers on developing and embedding good pedagogy in computing lessons with teachers paying particular attention to the transition process from their graphical to text-based language. Furthermore, that there is established pedagogy in other subjects that can be effectively used in a Computing lesson. In turn, it was also evident that programming could enhance the delivery of other curricula topics.

Despite the concerns alluded to in the opening of this paper concerning the difficulties for pupils in programming in text-based languages, the anecdotal evidence, that this paper provides, supports the practice of using graphical languages in conjunction with, (in effect using a graphical tool as a form of pseudo coding), not in place of, text-based programming languages, to improve the confidence, independence and resilience of pupils when learning to program using a text-based language, in both primary and secondary education.

Given good pedagogy, expert support for teachers and a strategy (see Section 3) for supporting all pupils with making the transition from graphical to text-based languages, the authors conclude:

- Pupils can learn a text-based programming language whilst at primary school.
- All secondary school pupils are able to master the basics of text-based programming.
- A graphics based language like Scratch would be a good introduction to programming for beginners at both primary and secondary levels.

It is the experience of the first author that this transition process has been a factor in an increased uptake of Computer Science GCSE qualification at Key Stage 4.

7 ACKNOWLEDGMENTS

The first author acknowledges the financial support by the SSAT of the Digital Schoolhouse Trust, and more recently The Digital Schoolhouse London Project funded by the Mayor of London and Department of Education through the London School's Excellence Fund.

8 REFERENCES

[1] Bell, T., Witten, I.H., Fellows, M. 2005. Computer Science Unplugged. http://csunplugged.com/ [last accessed 5 July 2014].

[2] Computer science: A Curriculum for Schools 2012. Available from: http://www.computingatschool.org.uk/data/uploads/ComputingCurric.pdf

[3] Dann, W., Cooper, S. and Pausch, R. 2009. Learning to Program with Alice, Second Edition. Pearson.

[4] Department for Education. 2013. The national curriculum in England, Framework document. Available: www.education.gov.uk/nationalcurriculum [Accessed 13-08-2013].

[5] Kelleher, C. and Pausch, R. 2005. Lowering the barriers to programming: A taxonomy of programming environments and languages for novice programmers. ACM Comput. Survey 37, 2, 83-137.

[6] Meerbaum-Salant, O., Armoni, M. & Ben-Ari, M. (2010) Learning computer science concepts with Scratch. ICER '10 Proceedings of the Sixth international workshop on Computing education research. ACM, 69 – 76

[7] National Research Council. (2011) Report of a workshop of pedagogical aspects of computational thinking, Washington, DC: The National Academies Press

[8] Papert, S. and Harel, I. 1991. Constructionism. Ablex.

[9] Resnick, M., Maloney, J. Monroy-Hernández, A., Rusk, N., Eastmond, E., Brennan, K., Millner, A., Rosenbaum, E., Silver, J., Silverman, B., and Kafai, Y. 2009. Scratch: Programming for all. Commun. ACM, 52, 11, 60-67.

[10] Rizvi, M., Humphries, T., Major, D., Jones, M., and Lauzun, H. (2011). A CS0 course using scratch. J. Comput. Small Coll., 26(3):19-27.

[11] Selby, C. and Woollard, J. (2014) Computational Thinking: The developing definitions. In Proceedings of the 45th ACM Technical Symposium on Computer Science Education, SIGCSE 2014. ACM.

[12] Whalley, J., Lister, R., Thompson, E., Clear, T., Robbins, P., and Prasad, C. 2006. An Australasian study of reading and comprehension skills in novice programmers, using the Bloom and SOLO taxonomies. In Proceedings of the Eighth Australasian Conference Computing Education (Hobart, Australia, January 16-19, 2006), 243-252.

[13] Wing, J. (2006) Computational Thinking. Commun. ACM, 49, 33 – 35

[14] White, D.[no date]. Unplugged: [online]. Available from http://www.ispython.com/unplugged [accessed 5 July 2014]

[15] Wolz, U., Leitner, H. H., Malan, D. J., and Maloney, J. (2009). Starting with scratch in CS 1. SIGCSE Bull. 41, 1, 2-3.

An Effective Alternative to the Grace Hopper Celebration

Gloria Childress Townsend
DePauw University
602 S. College Ave.
Greencastle, IN 46135
(765)658-4726
gct@depauw.edu

Kay Sloan
Rockman et al
3925 E, Hagan St.
Bloomington, IN 47401
(812)333-8883
kay@rockman.com

ABSTRACT
Motivated by the significance and the consequences of women's underrepresentation in computing, researchers evaluated the effectiveness of a project linking ACM-W's (Association for Computing Machinery's Women in Computing) Celebrations of Women in Computing (conferences) with projects sponsored by two additional organizations in the United States, the Anita Borg Institute's Grace Hopper Celebration of Women in Computing (GHC) and the National Center of Women & IT's Annual Summit. The collaborative project, funded by the National Science Foundation and titled, the Grace Hopper Regional Consortium, featured twelve new regional Celebrations of Women in Computing (Celebrations). An external assessment agency surveyed conference organizers and participants. The paper analyzes data derived from the surveying, demonstrating the impact of the conferences on Celebration attendees, and shows for the first time a comparison of identical survey items from separate GHC and Celebrations assessments.

Categories and Subject Descriptors
K.0 [Computing Milieux]: General

General Terms
Human Factors

Keywords
Gender issues, Broadening Participation in Computing, ACM-W

1. INTRODUCTION
The following section presents a statistical portrait of the underrepresentation of women in computing and then turns to implications of the problem. A brief literature review of relevant research concerning promising practices that increase the representation of women follows in Section 3. The selected research studies coincide with goals of the Grace Hopper Regional Consortium (GHRC). Section 4 describes the consortium; and, Section 5, the consortium's conferences. Section 6 describes the assessment design and implementation, aimed at assuring attainment of the consortium goals. A conclusion, acknowledgements, and references form the last three sections of the paper.

SIGCSE'15, March 4–7, 2015, Kansas City, MO, USA.

http://dx.doi.org/10.1145/2676723.2677233

2. BROADENING PARTICIPATION OF WOMEN IN COMPUTING
Classic sources from the literature of gender issues in computing (e.g. [7, 16]) show women's increasing reluctance to pursue computing all along the educational spectrum from high school to undergraduate classes and continuing through graduate school. Data from the National Center for Educational Statistics (USA) [18], which provides annual frequencies of undergraduate computing degrees by gender, reflects the patterns of women's underrepresentation described in the literature for the past twenty years. Figure 1 includes the most current statistics available from NCES and summarizes text from the literature of gender issues in computing in a graphical format.

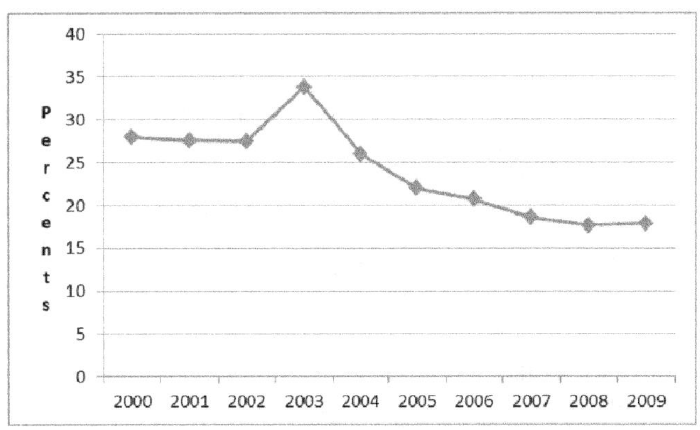

Figure 1: Percent of Bachelor's Degrees Awarded to Women in Computer and Information Sciences and Support Services

3. PROMISING RESEARCH RESULTS
Given the long-term evidence of women's declining engagement in computing, academic organizations' scientists and individual researchers investigate practices designed to reverse the trends indicated by Table 1. Understandably, the complexity of the problem implies that no single practice can provide a solution to the problem, yet sources [9, 16] show that many studies demonstrate localized success with practices that increase women's participation in computing. Section 3 outlines four of the successful practices: intentional role modeling, mentoring, community building, and provision of accurate career information. The organizations (discussed in Section 4) involved in the Grace Hopper Regional Consortium support and

disseminate information about each of the following practices. The consortium's main project – regional Celebrations – also employs the practices; the relationships of each of the practices to the project's goals will be described in Section 5.

3.1 Intentional Role Modeling

Individuals can intentionally convey the values, attitudes, behaviors, and career paths associated with a position, making it possible for observers to imagine themselves in, and aspire to, a similar position [4, 14]. Furthermore, role models can mitigate the negative impact of stereotype threat, which undermines women's confidence and persistence [17]. Both of these positive outcomes from intentional role modeling contribute to women's aspirations and accomplishments in computing.

3.2 Mentoring

Mentoring's positive effects have been documented in numerous settings, including undergraduate programs [6]. Research in undergraduate computer science programs, for example, shows that mentoring motivates greater portions of graduating seniors to proceed directly into graduate school, and to enroll in top-tier programs [8]. Mentoring to improve diversity increases women's retention in computer science [8], and similar amounts of active mentoring for both male and female graduate students improve gender balance in Science/Technology/Engineering/Mathematics (STEM) doctoral programs [11].

3.3 Building Community

Sources indicate that women often leave the computing field due to the sense of isolation felt in being the only woman in a class or one among a very few computer science majors [10, 21]. Social support helps retain women in computing undergraduate and graduate programs [5, 15, 9].

3.4 Providing Accurate Career Information

Women seldom have the same access to accurate and timely career information, especially for technical careers, that informal networks offer men. Formal communication of that information can facilitate women's entry and advancement in occupations where they are underrepresented [11].

Section 5 will demonstrate how each of the preceding four practices affects decisions involving the consortium's conference activities. Section 6 will communicate research project results explicitly tied to regional Celebrations goals.

4. GHRC ORGANIZATIONS

This section describes the partner organizations in the consortium and focuses on the organizations' contributions to and relationships with the regional conferences themselves.

4.1 ACM's Women in Computing

"ACM-W supports, celebrates, and advocates internationally for the full engagement of women in all aspects of the computing field, providing a wide range of programs and services to ACM members and working in the larger community to advance the contributions of technical women [1]." Formed in 1998, ACM-W includes several projects with international influence. Section 5 will describe ACM-W's Celebrations of Women in Computing in detail. The current subsection mentions ACM-W Student Chapters, organizations that recruit, retain, support, and encourage female computing students on campuses around the world. A second example of ACM-W's international mission lies in the forming of ACM-W Councils in Europe and India. The councils promote ACM-W projects from their more localized vantage points.

4.2 Anita Borg Institute (ABI)

While California is the home of ABI [3], students, faculty members, and industry members from many different countries attend the organization's Grace Hopper Celebration of Women in Computing (GHC) [12]. The conference is co-sponsored by ACM and features a large student poster session, opportunities for students to talk about internships and career opportunities with industry leaders, and sessions designed to motivate and encourage students, to offer accurate career and technical information, and to provide intentional role modeling.

4.3 National Center for Women & IT

"NCWIT works to correct the imbalance of gender diversity in technology and computing because gender diversity positively correlates with a larger workforce, better innovation, and increased business performance [19]." A team of social science researchers supports the organization by analyzing research contained in the literature to determine if the work is viable for collection and dissemination, by conducting independent research, and by serving as consultants for research led by members of NCWIT alliances, such as the Academic Alliance (colleges and universities.) NCWIT organizes and conducts an annual summit for its alliances.

5. CELEBRATIONS OF WOMEN IN COMPUTING

Section 4.2 introduced GHC. GHC will celebrate its twentieth anniversary in October, 2014. The inaugural conference, held in June 1994, attracted slightly fewer than five hundred attendees, GHC 2013 attendance exceeded that almost ten-fold, with forty-seven hundred people, from fifty-three countries [12]. GHC provides opportunities for students and faculty members to share their research in poster sessions and in events for large audiences, to connect with mentors and role models, to hear cutting-edge technical presentations, and to learn about career opportunities in academia and industry.

By contrast and by design, the ACM-W model for Celebrations of Women in Computing [22] limits attendance to around seventy-five to one hundred seventy-five attendees. While the smaller Celebrations' program elements mirror GHC events (described below), the conference size allows young women considering computing majors and careers to present their research and exchange ideas in a more intimate, less intimidating setting. An additional difference between GHC and regional Celebrations pertains to the cost of attendance, which is free to minimal, as industry participants provide funding to sponsor the conferences, and the conference sites are purposely chosen to reduce costs and distractions. State park inns provide excellent conference locations. Commuting to the conferences (generally involving a driving radius of two hours or less) is simple and inexpensive; therefore, the time commitment for busy students and professionals is much less than for GHC and does not interfere with school obligations, because the typical time span for a small Celebration is from late Friday afternoon to Saturday mid-afternoon. Finally, the first author's conjecture, based upon organizing or co-organizing six iterations of the Indiana Celebration, conveys the idea that it is more likely that attendees will continue their Celebration connections, after the conclusions of the conferences, and will be more likely to engage in collaborative work with attendees who have shared discussions with them about common research or service projects, simply because they reside in close proximity to each other.

In 2004, ACM-W began sponsoring Celebrations of Women in Computing with a conference held in Indiana. At the time, Australia offered a related technology conference for women. After the initial Indiana Celebration, Ohio, Colorado, Michigan, and Canada developed similar biennial conferences. In 2009, the three organizations described in Section 4 received a National Science Foundation (NSF) grant to create twelve more regional conferences across the United States. The grant also provided funding for selected conference organizers and students to attend GHC and for three Celebration coordinators from each regional conference to attend NCWIT's Annual Summit. The grant expired at the conclusion of 2012, and the conferences returned to the sole supervision of ACM-W, expanding to include several Canada conferences. Europe recently hosted a Celebration at an England site. Puerto Rico, India and Abu Dhabi inaugurated conferences, and Australian Celebrations expanded to New Zealand. Twenty-six conferences have been held or planned for the 2013-14 and 2014-15 academic years, with increasing communication from new regions interested in hosting a Celebration. Section 6 discusses the project's evaluation, conducted by an external assessment agency.

Although no two Celebrations are exactly alike, Section 5 now describes typical features of the conferences, at least some of which each Celebration will adopt. As the small conferences resemble each other, they also resemble GHC, which employs most of the same components listed below. GHC later adopted the Celebration technique (Lightning Talks) listed in Section 5.2 below, so ideas originate in – and then are shared among – both kinds of conferences.

5.1 Multiple Tracks

Typical conference attendees include: undergraduate students, graduate students, faculty members, industry members, and administration individuals. Less frequently, high school girls attend Celebrations. Accordingly, different kinds of sessions must appeal to the diverse population of attendees. Often, conference committees construct a track for undergraduate students interested in pursuing a career in industry, after graduation. A second research track appeals to students in – or expecting to enter – graduate school and to faculty members. A third track (or at least a session or two) follows the interests of faculty members.

A research track allows panels, presentations, workshops, and small discussion groups (Birds-of-a-Feather sessions), where students, industry leaders, and faculty members disseminate research results and introduce new or familiar technical information to conference attendees.

5.2 Keynotes

Conference organizers request that keynote speakers discuss their paths through computing, their research, and struggles that they have overcome, while providing practical hints for success and perseverance in the computing field. The chief goal of the presentations lies in providing intentional role modeling, as described in Section 3.1, so conference organizers carefully prepare speakers regarding their keynote content.

5.3 Building Experience and Confidence

All conferences contain poster sessions, providing students an opportunity to disseminate research results from NSF Research Experiences for Undergraduates (REU) projects or from research sponsored by any university, laboratory, or other organization. In order to increase confidence in all attending students and to provide an opportunity to gain experience with public scientific speaking, conferences allow students to also construct posters concerning curricular, social or ethical issues. The NSF grant offered scholarships for research poster winners in the graduate and undergraduate competitions to attend GHC and to present their work at a larger venue.

Celebrations also contain sessions where students deliver very short talks about research or other computing-related issues. Since the presentations last only five to ten minutes, they are called, lightning talks. As with poster sessions, the goal of these brief talks is to provide a steppingstone model of progress, where students gain experience and confidence in the local conferences, allowing them to present subsequent research at larger conferences.

5.4 Partnership with Industry

At the conclusions of Celebrations, industry sponsors, who provide scholarships for attendees, participate in a Career Fair, talking with young women about their own careers and about opportunities for the students to obtain internships or jobs at their companies. Most conferences also include graduate school information booths along with career/company booths.

5.5 Networking and Community-Building

Section 3.3 describes isolation's toll on women in computing and the contribution of social support to lessen the sense of isolation. Because local Celebrations draw women from institutions that are located in close proximity to each other, there is increased likelihood that women will stay in touch after the conferences and work on shared projects. Simply knowing that the borders among institutions are fluid and that the regional community of women in computing is quite large may decrease the sense of isolation at individual schools, a goal explored and confirmed by evaluation findings shared in the next section of the paper.

Each Celebration hosts events to bring its women together socially and collaboratively. One conference featured a special game incorporating puzzle pieces (for a cooperative puzzle solution) and a scavenger hunt for teams. Another Celebration provided an eTextiles event, where women attached LEDs to their conference bags with conductive thread, switches, and battery packs.

6. ASSESSMENT AND RESULTS

6.1 Introduction

Each of the three years of the GHRC project, Rockman et al [20], a research, evaluation, and consulting company headquartered in San Francisco, provided project assessment and generated a report. Rockman et al worked closely with NSF program leaders to ensure that evaluation coordinated with the goals of the Broadening Participation in Computing (BPC) program within the NSF, which funded the three-year project. This paper reports results from Year 3 (2011-12 academic year), when ten conferences shown in Table 1 occurred.

Table 1: Surveyed Celebrations

Location	Acronym
Indiana Celebration of Women in Computing	INWIC
Carolinas Women in Computing	CWIC
Midwest/Minnesota Celebration of Women in Computing	MINNEWIC
Kentucky Celebration of Women in Computing	KYWIC
Capital Celebration of Women in Computing (Virginia)	CAPWIC
Northwest Regional Celebration of Women in Computing	NWRWIC
Celebration of Women in Computing in Southern California	CWIC-SoCal
Missouri-Iowa-Nebraska-Kansas Celebration of Women in Computing	MINKWIC
Tennessee Celebration of Women in Computing	TNWIC
Louisville and Cincinnati Celebration of Women in Computing	TRIWIC

The project's primary data collection tool was the post-celebration survey, an anonymous, Web-based instrument. Modeled after the GHC survey, the GHRC survey gathers demographic and background information and feedback on the Celebration experience and value of individual sessions. One of the goals of the GHRC evaluation was to explore how the regional Celebrations mirror the make-up and impact of the larger GHC. To that end, the GHRC surveys included a number of the same items as the GHC annual survey, and the discussion here compares regional and national results where appropriate.

Table 2 shows the response rates for the Year 3 post-conference survey, based on actual attendance figures from seven conferences and estimates for the remaining three.

Table 2: Respondents

Number of respondents	Response Rate
542	64%

6.2 The Reach of Celebrations

With the establishment of twelve new conferences, the GHRC project expanded the number of regional Celebrations, and, with new conferences in 2012 in the Washington, DC, and Maryland capital region and in Southern California, spread its geographic reach from coast to coast. Coordinators reported that they easily met their attendance targets, which ranged from 48-183, in some cases having to close registration and turn down interested participants because the designated space could not accommodate them. Feedback and survey data also indicated that Year 3 participants represented at least sixty-five institutions.

In addition to drawing a general profile of the 2011-2012 Celebrations, the discussion below compares the demographics of GHRC to GHC survey respondents, to gauge the extent to which regional Celebrations were microcosms of the national GHC in the audiences they attract and serve, and to highlight any differences in those audiences.

Compared to the GHC faculty sample, the GHRC sample was somewhat less diverse. However, percentages of underrepresented minorities (Latino/a, African-American, and Native American/Alaska native) show that the GHRC student sample included 18% underrepresented minorities, compared to 15% for GHC; for faculty, the breakdown was 7% compared to 11%; for industry, 10% compared to 8%.

As at GHC, students attending the GHRC Celebrations formed the most diverse group of participants. Compared to 92 percent of the faculty participants and 86 of the industry/other respondents, 74 percent (N=268) of the GHRC student post-survey respondents were born in the United States. Those not born in the U.S. represented 31 different countries.

Certain findings suggested that the regional Celebrations reached a population that might not attend a national conference, and may be underserved for reasons associated with support and resources rather than race or ethnicity. Although most of the faculty post-survey respondents had previously attended a technology conference, half of the students had not. Of those who had previously attended conferences, just under a fourth had attended a technical conference in their field of interest; fewer had attended a regional or Grace Hopper Celebration (14% and 15% respectively).

A fifth (20%, N=71) of the student respondent group reported that they were first generation college students, which may also suggest that the Celebrations served students who lacked ready-made support structures for completing degrees and pursuing technical careers.

6.3 Conference Impact

6.3.1 Impact of the Conferences… On Students

Although expectations were high, overall, students felt they were well met by the GHRC Celebrations. Approximately 70 percent of post-survey respondents said their expectations were met "Very" or "Extremely" well; an additional 15 percent reported they were met "Moderately" well. Responses to questions related to commitment, skills and tools, and sense of community all supported the overall ratings and indications that students profited from participation.

6.3.1.1 Commitment to Careers

High percentages of students also indicated that the Celebration had a positive effect on their commitment to degrees and careers:

- Over 70 percent "Agreed" or "Strongly Agreed" that attending the Celebration increased their commitment to complete their degree program, increased their commitment to their technology career, and increased their intention to find a mentor or to mentor women in the field.
- Over 80 percent "Agreed" or "Strongly Agreed" that attending increased their confidence in their ability to pursue a technology career; two-thirds reported that they had also learned about career opportunities at sponsor companies as a result of attendance.
- Over half of the student respondents reported that attending increased their intention to pursue an undergraduate or graduate degree in a technology field and had a positive impact on their professional development.
- And over half of student respondents also reported that attending helped them obtain tools to be successful in their career as a technologist, gain valuable opportunities to be

mentored or to mentor others, and learn about academic program from the university sponsors.

6.3.1.2 Isolation and Sense of Community
Addressing the important issue of community, following the Celebrations:

- About two-thirds of the students "Agreed" or "Strongly Agreed" that they felt less isolated as a woman in technology and that the Celebration had significantly increased their network of technical women.
- Approximately 75 percent "Agreed" or "Strongly Agreed" that they feel part of a larger community of women in technology as a part of attendance.
- Over 85 percent "Agreed" or "Strongly Agreed" that they feel inspired by the role models they saw at the conference.
- Over half intend to stay in touch with people they met at the conference.

6.3.2 Impact ... on Faculty
Similarly high percentages (73%) of post-survey faculty respondents reported that their expectations were met "Very" or "Extremely" well; an additional 12 percent reported they were met "Moderately" well.

6.3.2.1 Commitment to Careers
Although faculty presumably would express high levels of commitment to and knowledge of careers in technology prior to the conference, a high percent still "Agreed" or "Strongly Agreed" that attending the celebration increased their commitment to their technology career (60%), increased their intention to find a mentor or to mentor women in the field (66%), and had a positive impact on their professional development (42%). Close to half "Agreed" or "Strongly Agreed" that attending helped them obtain tools to be successful in their career as a technologist (46%), learn about academic programs from the university sponsors (47%), and learn about career opportunities at sponsor companies (43%).

Other faculty responses related to careers were, not surprisingly, lower. Approximately 22 percent reported that attending the Celebration would help them evaluate the next step in their career, and about a third reported it helped them investigate new research or business collaborations (30%). A much lower percentage reported attending would help them seek a mentor (9%) or find out more about majors and careers in computing or engineering (10%).

6.4 Conference Impact Compared with GHC
Table 3 shows levels of agreement with a series of statements about community and networks of technical women included on all three years of the GHRC post-surveys and on the GHC 2011 survey. Results from Year 3 showed an uptick from previous years in all categories and rates that matched or exceeded the GHC responses. Almost all of the Year 1 and Year 2 Celebrations were first-time conferences. By Year 3, all of the initial Year 1 conferences held their second iterations, so that most of the Year 3 Celebrations were organized by experienced coordinators. Experience certainly could account for improved Celebration ratings, as could the sharing of resources and tips that resulted from collaborative workshops for Celebration coordinators, who attended GHC with GHRC funding.

6. CONCLUSION
Survey results from the GHRC Celebrations (detailed in Section 6.3) are important in themselves, but the Section 6.4 comparisons of the GHRC Celebrations to GHC provide key additional value. This paper contains the first rigorous investigation comparing identical survey items contained in both GHRC Celebrations and GHC assessments. As Section 6.4 and Table 3 indicate, the GHRC Celebrations percentages not only correspond to the GHC percentages; they surpass the larger, more elaborate conference's percentages in two categories. Establishing the comparisons from the survey results is an important first step to a full evaluation of the effectiveness of Celebrations.

The literature already contains many articles about the effectiveness of GHC attendance. The Communications of the ACM (CACM) published one such article in its March 2014 issue [2]. The CACM authors provide several important insights, including: "GHC's influence is strongest on first-year students considering CS [computer science] as a possible major, though many not considering a CS major report attending GHC increased their desire to major in CS" and "Those attending GHC take a second CS course at a significantly higher rate than those who do not attend GHC." Future Celebrations research should focus on studies to replicate the GHC linkages already established in studies (such as the CACM article) that point to the same Celebration relationships between attending a conference or conferences and recruitment and retention of women in computing.

Table 3: Comparison of Celebrations and GHC 2011 Responses [13]

% who agree/strongly agree that...	Year 1 GHRC	Year 2 GHRC	Year 3 GHRC	2011 GHC
the conference increased their commitment to a technology career	73%	62%	82%	82%
attending the Celebration made them to feel part of a community of technical women	73%	69%	88%	77%
they feel less isolated as a technical woman as a result of attending the Celebration	63%	56%	74%	75%
attending the Celebration made them feel more confident/energetic about their career	77%	68%	86%	NA
they felt inspired by the role models they saw at the Celebration	83%	73%	92%	92%
they expanded their network of technical women	58%	55%	70%	66%

The CACM article itself calls for a full evaluation of the effectiveness of Celebrations. "...[B]eyond the main GHC conference, several regional Celebrations of Women in Computing have emerged. Although no studies have yet shown these celebrations provide a similar effect on students' major decisions, the important aspects of community, confidence building, and real-world CS context are still available." Our study certainly does not investigate the impact of Celebrations on first-year students, but it does show that Celebrations build community among attendees, who report that "attending the Celebration made them to feel part of a community of technical women" at a rate of 88% (agree/strongly agree). The identical survey item provided a 77% ratio in the GHC survey.

Celebrations complement GHC: fortunately, because GHCs have space limitations, and registration closes at capacity [13]. The CACM article also cites Celebrations as having "the intention of serving a bigger and more geographically dispersed audience GHC alone could not serve [and as being] "a more comfortable and less-overwhelming venue for students who know nothing about CS." Celebrations serve this purpose and do so much less expensively, involving less travel time for attendees, providing more opportunities for student participation in the program, and maximizing geographic proximity to encourage future collaborations among attendees.

The research results presented in this paper highlight a promising new strategy grounded in practices contained in the literature of gender issues in computing and detailed in Section 3. The results also link to survey-based studies concerning the well-known GHC. Research results from both kinds of celebrations provide important evidence of the effectiveness of women's conference attendance to increasing female representation in computing.

7. ACKNOWLEDGMENTS

The authors recognize the NSF for its support of GHRC, through BPC-A: Collaborative Research proposal 0940595. We thank the grant co-PIs: Telle Whitney, Lucy Sanders, Joanne McGrath Cohoon, and Deanna Kosaraju. We also thank ACM-W and its current chair, Valerie Barr, for oversight and management of Celebrations and invite anyone interested in organizing a Celebration to contact Jodi Tims (jltims@bw.edu). We appreciate Tracy Camp for first recognizing the potential of Celebrations and Elaine Weyuker for funding the inaugural INWIC and its successors, helping us to bring our dream to reality.

8. REFERENCES

[1] ACM-W website. http://women.acm.org. Data downloaded 3/15/14.

[2] Alvarado, C and Judson, E. 2014. Using Targeted Conferences to Recruit Women into Computer Science, *Communications of the ACM*, 57, 3, 70-77.

[3] Anita Borg Institute of Women in Technology website. http://anitaborg.org. Data downloaded 3/16/14.

[4] Barker, L. and Cohoon, J. 2006. Promising practices: intentional role modeling, NCWIT.

[5] Blum, L. and Frieze, C. 2005. The evolving culture of computing: similarity is the difference, *Frontiers*,26, 1, 110-125.

[6] Campbell, T. A. and Campbell, D. E. 1997. Faculty/Student mentor program: effects on academic performance and retention, *Research in Higher Education*, 38, 727-742.

[7] Camp, T. 1997. "The Incredible Shrinking Pipeline". *Communications of the ACM,* 40, 10, 103-110.

[8] Cohoon, J. M., Gonsoulin, M, Layman, J. 2004. Mentoring CS Undergraduates. Human Perspectives in the Internet Society: Culture, Psychology, and Gender. K. Morgan, J. Sanchez, C. A. Brebbia, A. Voiskounsky, Eds., WIT Press, Cadiz, Spain, 199-208.

[9] Cohoon, J. M. 2006. Retaining women in undergraduate computing. In *Women and Information Technology: Research on Under-Representation*, J. M. Cohoon and W. Aspray, Eds., MIT Press, Cambridge, MA, 205-237.

[10] DeClue, T. 1997. Why capable females leave CS1: a qualitative study investigating the causes of attrition. *Journal of Small College Computing*, 12, 4, 290-296.

[11] Fox, M. F. 2001. Women, science, and academia: graduate education and careers. *Gender and Society*. 15, 5, 654-666.

[12] Grace Hopper Celebration of Women in Computing website. http://gracehopper.org. Data downloaded 3/16/14.

[13] Ku, M. C. and Gilmartin, S. Grace Hooper Celebration of Women in Computing 2011 evaluation and impact report, Anita Borg Institute for Women and Technology. http://anitaborginstitute.org/files/GHC_2011_REPORT.pdf. Data downloaded 4/10/2014.

[14] Lockwood, P. 2006. Someone like me can be successful: do college students need same-gender role models? *Psychology of Women Quarterly*.

[15] Lord, H. 2008. Unpublished dissertation. University of Virginia. Charlottesville, VA.

[16] Margolis, J. and Fisher, A. 2002. *Unlocking the Clubhouse: Women in Computing*. The MIT Press. Cambridge, MA.

[17] Marx, D. M. & Roman, J. S. 2002. Female role models: protecting women's math test performance. *Personality and Social Psychology Bulletin*, 28, 9. 1183-1193.

[18] National Center for Education Statistics, Integrated Postsecondary Education Data System, Completions Survey; and National Science Foundation, National Center for Science and Engineering Statistics, Integrated Science and Engineering Resources Data System (WebCASPAR), http://webcaspar.nsf.gov. *Science and Engineering Indicators 2012*. Data downloaded 3/7/2014.

[19] National Center of Women & Information Technology website. http://ncwit.org. Data downloaded 3/16/14.

[20] Rockman et al website. http://rockman.org. Data downloaded 3/23/14.

[21] Seymour, E. and Hewitt, N. 1997. *Talking about Leaving: Why Undergraduates Leave the Sciences*. Westview Press. Boulder, CO.

[22] Townsend, G. C., Barker, L., Cohoon, J. M., Menzel, S. 2008. Grace Hopper in the neighborhood. *Proceedings of the 2008 ACM SIGCSE Technical Symposium*, 40, 1, 513-517.

Improving Undergraduate Student Performance in Computer Science at Historically Black Colleges and Universities (HBCUs) through Industry Partnerships

A. Nicki Washington, Ph.D., Legand Burge, Ph.D., Marlon Mejias, Ketly Jean-Pierre, and Qi'Anne Knox
Howard University
2300 Sixth St. NW Room 2120B
Washington, DC 20059
(202)806-7417
awashington@scs.howard.edu

ABSTRACT

While computer science (CS) continues to permeate every aspect of society, the number of high-school students that are adequately prepared to enroll in university computer science programs is declining. To address the nation's needs it is clear that the retention rates of underrepresented minorities in CS programs across the country must increase, including the instruction and retention of students at Historically Black Colleges and Universities (HBCUs). At the university, a multi-phased program was developed that first partnered the department with Google to develop a unique program that incorporated Google software developers and undergraduate students, as well as course restructuring to better prepare underclassmen in their first three courses of study. First-year results indicated the program was successful in increasing student retention and interest in CS.

Categories and Subject Descriptors

K.3.2 [Computer and Information Science Education]: Computer Science Education

Keywords

Computer science education; Undergraduate; Google; Googler-In-Residence

1. INTRODUCTION

While computer science (CS) continues to permeate every aspect of society, the number of high-school students that are adequately prepared to enroll in university computer science programs is declining. Many high schools do not offer the necessary CS courses to successfully prepare students for CS undergraduate programs [1][17]. In many urban areas, courses such as AP Computer Science are nonexistent. Instead, the lowest-level, introductory computer technology classes teach students basic computer literacy, including how to use applications such as Microsoft Excel and PowerPoint [2]. These courses do not teach computer science fundamentals such as computational thinking and problem solving.

If the U.S. intends to grow its domestic STEM workforce, the focus must not only include what is taught, but before that, who is academically prepared, mentored, and socialized to engineering (and in this case, CS) as a career [26]. To address the nation's needs it is clear that the retention rates of underrepresented minorities in CS programs across the country must increase. This requires placing emphasis on improving undergraduate student instruction and engagement in the first two years of entering university CS programs, particularly at Historically Black Colleges and Universities (HBCUs), where a large pool of the future CS workforce are matriculating.

At the university, a multi-phased program was developed that first partnered the department with Google to develop a unique residency program. This program allows current software developers to serve as full-time faculty members in HBCU CS departments where they teach an introductory CS course and other electives. A peer-led tutoring program was also developed, which allows students to receive additional assistance in the first three courses of study in the major. Freshmen and sophomore students were targeted, as most attrition occurs within the first two years of study. Through activities that provided opportunities for students of all classifications, the program not only increase retention of students within the first two years, but also improved student performance in introductory-level CS programs, in preparation for higher-level CS undergraduate courses.

The remainder of this paper is organized as follows. Section 2 discusses the motivation behind the program. Section 3 presents Phase I of the program. Section 4 presents first-year results of the program. Section 5 concludes the work and discusses Phase II components.

2. MOTIVATION

A review of the literature on computer science education, STEM education, and the attraction, engagement, and retention of K-16 underrepresented students (specifically African-American and Hispanic) in computer science has identified several important points:

1. **There is a lack of diversity in computer science.** According to results of the most recent Taulbee Survey, two-thirds of all bachelor's degrees conferred in computer science were awarded to white, non-

SIGCSE '15, March 4–7, 2015, Kansas City, MO, USA

http://dx.doi.org/10.1145/2676723.2677277

Hispanics, with only 4% awarded to African-Americans [3][11]. Over the next 50 years, it is projected that the minority population will increase at a much faster rate than the non-minority population, with African-Americans and Hispanics increasing from a combined 22% to 40% of the workforce [4] [5].

2. **Students find computer science boring and not applicable to them and their interests**. Engineering suffers from a severe public relations deficit. Researchers found that over half of all college students are not well informed about engineering [20]. This, as well as the negative popular perception of engineers projected by characterizations such as "Dilbert" has depressed interest in STEM [24]. In addition, African-American and Hispanic students do not readily identify computer science as a field that they can successfully pursue. Due to a number of factors, including negative perception of being difficult, lack of understanding about and preparation for computer science courses, and a lack of African-Americans and Hispanics in computer science, many students feel this subject area is not one that includes them or their interests [2] [6][17][19].
3. **Attrition rates for African-Americans and Hispanics are high**. The retention rate of underrepresented minorities in U.S. engineering programs is 40% in comparison to 66% of their counterparts [12][29]. Majority of these students leave the major within the first two years. According to data provided by the College, the department loses close to 50% of its incoming freshman by the end of their sophomore year.

2.1 The Role of HBCUs

The national enrollment and retention rate of African-American students in STEM lags behind that of their white peers. However, Historically Black Colleges and Universities (HBCUs) have traditionally been more successful in attracting, retaining, and graduating African-American STEM students than Predominantly White Institutions (PWIs). African-American students enrolled at HBCUs account for approximately 13% of all African-American students enrolled in college [19]. While they account for only 4% of domestic colleges and universities, HBCUs produce 31% of all African-American STEM majors [12]. They also tend to have lower attrition rates than PWIs. Studies suggest that graduates of HBCU undergraduate institutions in STEM disciplines are more likely to attend graduate school and complete doctoral degrees than African-American graduates from other non-HBCU institutions [27]. This illustrates the critical role that HBCUs play in helping to overcome a nationwide shortage of scientists and engineers who are vital to the nation's future economic growth and competitiveness [10].

3. PROGRAM DESCRIPTION

The goal this project is singular: To increase the retention of African-American CS undergraduates in the first two years of study.

To achieve this goal, the following objectives were outlined:

1. Improve student performance in the first three CS courses in the CS program of study.
2. Improve students' perceptions of CS.
3. Improve department-wide support mechanisms for all classifications.

Phase I of the program included the restructuring of the CS 0 course and creation of the Googler-In-Residence and CS Bootcamp programs.

3.1 CS 0 Course Restructuring

Prior to the 2012-2013 academic year, SCS freshmen were required to take CS 1-Intro to Programming in their first semester and CS 2-Elementary Data Structures in their second semester. These were the two "weed-out" courses that most heavily affected retention rates. Students began taking programming courses, without a proper understanding of what CS was and why C++ programming was an important foundation in the discipline. To circumvent this issue, the department restructured the four-year program of study to require freshmen to complete a new course, CS 0-Introduction to SCS (taken fall-freshmen year), followed by CS 1 (taken spring-freshmen year), and CS 2 (taken fall-sophomore year). The new implementation of CS 0 provided students with a "big picture" of CS, the applications and career paths available, and introduced CS fundamentals such as algorithms, problem-solving, and computational thinking prior to learning programming. The course was designed to help combat the disillusionment cited in the literature, as well as provide students a broad context for future higher-level courses.

Upon completion of the fall 2012 semester, there were numerous issues with the course that were identified by both students and faculty:

1. ***Lack of cohesiveness in course content.*** Faculty presentations varied each week, with no structured format or requirements.
2. ***Course content was too detailed.*** For some tracks, faculty presented material at a level too detailed for freshmen CS students to comprehend.
3. ***Lack of interest/engagement with students.*** Many students expressed that majority of the course content did not engage them and they found the course boring and a waste of time.
4. ***Lack of hands-on activities.*** Most of the lectures were non-interactive. In addition, assignments included reading from a purchased course textbook and writing papers. Students expressed the desire to have more hands-on activities throughout the semester.

3.2 Googler-In-Residence Program

The Googler-in-Residence (GIR) program was piloted in the 2013-2014 academic year. The program was designed to strengthen the relationship between the university and Google, provide direct access to Black Googlers for students, infuse curriculum with real-world context, increase perception of and interest in CS, and increase the number of departmental students apply for and entering Google summer internships and full-time positions.

Through this program, a Google software developer served as a full-time faculty member at the university for the full academic year. The GIR and faculty worked collaboratively infuse CS 0 content with Google's Computer Science Summer Institute (CSSI) curriculum. The CSSI is a three-week summer program implemented in two sessions at Google sites in Mountain View, California and Cambridge, Massachusetts. Approximately 60 incoming freshmen from universities across the country participate in the program, which includes the following goals:

1. To enrich the skills of CS undergraduates early in their academic career, so as to increase the pipeline into CS and retention of students.
2. To provide social and professional networking opportunities for underrepresented students in technology.
3. To empower students, by providing tools, motivation, and confidence to continue pursuing CS as a major.

Students were introduced to CS through introductory lessons and assignments on HTML/CSS, Python, Unix, JavaScript, and AppEngine.

3.3 CS Bootcamp

CS Bootcamp was created to provide additional departmental support for students in their first two years of study. CS Bootcamp is a peer-tutoring program led and conducted by computer science undergraduates. The courses targeted for CS Bootcamp include CS 0, CS 1, and CS 2. Underclassmen can attend Bootcamp four days per week to gain extra practice and assistance with concepts covered in these three classes. This includes practice problems, strategies, reviewing lecture notes, etc.

CS Bootcamp is led by CS upperclassmen (Bootcamp Leaders) who have successfully completed these courses with a grade of 'B' or higher. Leaders are provided course topics and work with students in small groups and individually. Because Bootcamp Leaders are current upperclassmen who have successfully completed these courses, Bootcamp reinforces peer learning.

CS Bootcamp serves two important purposes. First, underclassmen have additional support mechanisms within the department, outside of faculty or teaching assistant office hours. Underclassmen are able to gain assistance from upperclassmen through peer-led tutoring, group discussions, and problem solving. Second, upperclassmen are able to gain experience presenting and teaching CS concepts to groups, and facilitating problem-solving discussions. This ensures that they not only understand, but also can clearly articulate fundamental CS concepts to others, as they prepare for post-graduation job interviews and graduate school.

4. RESULTS

As a result of Phase I (GIR program and CS Bootcamp), course enrollment and performance increased in CS 0 and CS 1 for both SCS majors and non-majors. Table 1 presents the course enrollment for both courses in the 2012-2013 and 2013-2014 academic years. It should be noted that SCS freshmen enrolled in the CS 0 course in the fall semesters and CS 1 in the subsequent spring semester. It should also be noted that CS 0 was only offered in the fall semester of the 2012-2013 academic year. CS 0 experienced an 83% enrollment increase in the fall 2013 semester. In addition, the success of the course resulted in it being offered in the spring 2014 semester. In total, a 297% enrollment increase was experienced. This significant increase was attributed to both increased student transfers to SCS and increased advertising of the course outside of the department and College, in an attempt to attract more non-majors to the course and department.

Table 1. Course Enrollment –CS 0 and CS 1

	Fall 2012	Spring 2013	Fall 2013	Spring 2014
CS 0	25*	N/A	55*	64
CS 1	29	33*	35	48*

**** indicates correct sequence for SCS majors***

Figure 1 presents the course completion rates for CS 0 and CS 1 in the 2012-2013 and 2013-2014 academic years for majors only. Approximately 94% of all SCS students passed CS 0 in the fall 2013 semester, compared to 72% in the fall 2012 semester. For CS 1, approximately 67% of students passed the course in the spring 2014 semester, compared to 59% in the spring 2013 semester. These results indicate that a higher number of students passed the first two CS courses of study in the major than in the year prior to implementation of the new program.

Students also found the CS 1 content easier to understand and apply as a result of first learning Python in CS 0. Upon completion of the semester, students found it more beneficial to have gained basic programming experience using Python than performing other tasks like writing papers. This illustrates that students were not only better prepared for CS 1, but also performed better in the class.

The GIR and CS Bootcamp programs were successful in not only improving the performance of CS underclassmen, but also increasing the interest in computer science for students both within and outside of the department and College. As a result, CS 0 is offered in the fall semester for majors and the spring semester for non-majors. In the fall 2014 semester, approximately 65 SCS students are enrolled. In CS 2 (the first implementation of the course since the program was developed), approximately 35 students are currently enrolled in the fall 2014 semester.

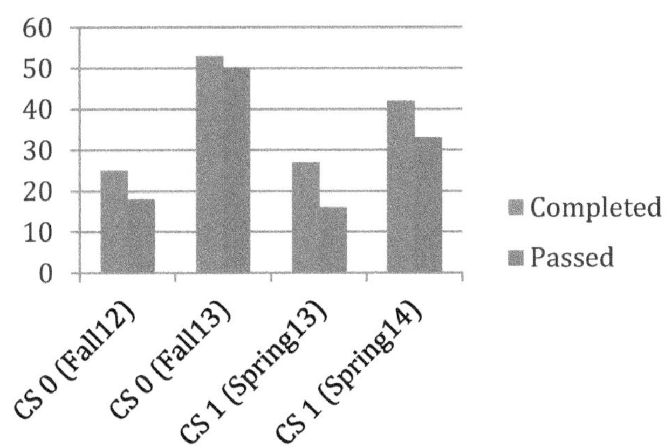

Figure 1. Course Completion and Passing-CS 0 and CS 1

The success of the GIR program has also resulted in the program extending to four additional HBCUs in the 2014-2015 academic year. Each university has a dedicated GIR teaching an Introduction to CS course equivalent as a department faculty member and additional department electives.

5. CONCLUSION

African-American students form an important cohort with respect to the U.S. STEM and CS workforce. This is a large group of students who exit the CS pipeline, due to disillusionment and poor performance. As a result, this is a large population who could fuel the U.S. workforce, if proper intervention, recruitment, and retention ensured that they not only persisted in the discipline, but also excelled. The department's program has been successful in not only instructing and retaining students, but also increasing interest in CS from external departments. Phase 2 of the program includes the implementation of a virtual pre-college program, to be implemented summer 2015.

6. REFERENCES

[1] Fleming, L. et al. 2006. "Why Students Leave Engineering: The Unexpected Bond", Proceeding of the 2006 American Society of Engineering Education Conference and Exposition.

[2] Furr, S. and Elling, T. 2002. "African-American Students in a Predominantly-White University: Factors Associated with Retention." College Student Journal, vol. 36 no. 2.

[3] Gibbons, M. 2006. "Engineering by the Numbers". American Society for Engineering Education.

[4] Goode, J. 2010. "Connecting K-16 Curriculum & Policy: Making Computer Science Engaging, Accessible, & Hospitable for Underrepresented Students." Proceedings of the 40th SIGCSE Technical Symposium on Computer Science Education.

[5] Goode, J. 2008. "Computer Science Segregation: Missed Opportunities." The Voice. 4(2).

[6] Jackson, S.A. "The Quiet Crisis: Falling Short in Producing American Scientific and Technical Talent." Building Engineering and Science Talent.

[7] Margolis, J., Estrella, R., et.al. Stuck in the Shallow End: Education, Race, and Computing.

[8] Margolis, J., Goode, J., Bernier, D. 2011. "The Need for Computer Science." Education Leadership, vol. 68, no.5.

[9] May, G. and Chubin, D. 2003. "A Retrospective on Undergraduate Engineering Success for Underrepresented Minority Students. Journal of Engineering Education.

[10] Members of the 2005 Committee on Science, Engineering, and Public Policy. 2010. Rising Above the Gathering Storm Revisited: Rapidly Approaching Category.

[11] National Academy of Engineers. The Engineer of 2020 Project Prospectus.

[12] National Science Foundation, Division of Science Resources Statistics. 2011. Women, Minorities, and Persons with Disabilities in Science and Engineering.

[13] Taulbee Survey. Computing Degrees and Enrollment Trends.

[14] The President's Council of Advisors on Science and Technology. 2010. Prepare and Inspire: K-12 Education in Science, Technology, Engineering, and Math (STEM) for America's Future.

[15] Toossi, M. 2006. "A New Look at Long-term Labor Force Projections to 2050." Monthly Labor Review.

[16] US Census Bureau. 2004. "US Interim Projections by Age, Sex, Race, and Hispanic Origin."

[17] Yurtseven, H. 2002. "How Does Image of Engineering Affect Recruitment and Retention? A Perspective from the USA". Global Journal of Engineering Education, Vol. 6, No. 1.

A Comparative Study of the Acceptability of Signs for the Brazilian Sign Language Created in Person and Remotely

Francisco C. de M. B. Oliveira
Science Computer Department
State University of Ceará
Fortaleza, Brazil
fran.mb.oliveira@gmail.com

Gerarda N. C. Gomes
Science Computer Department
State University of Ceará
Fortaleza, Brazil
neiva.cardins@gmail.com

Adriano T. de Freitas
Computing Department
Federal Institute of Ceará
Maracanaú, Brazil
adriano.freitas@ifce.edu.br

Anibal C. de Oliveira
Science Computer Department
State University of Ceará
Fortaleza, Brazil
hanibal.ce80@gmail.com

Lidiane C. Silva
Science Computer Department
State University of Ceará
Fortaleza, Brazil
lidcastro@gmail.com

Bruno Queiroz
Distance Education Laboratory for People with Disabilities
Fortaleza, Brazil
bruno@lcaconsulting.com.br

ABSTRACT

Teaching a programming language to a person who is deaf or hearing impaired (DHI) has, along with other challenges, the lack of signs to convey basic concepts in computing. This shortage of signs makes learning even harder for the DHI.

The creation of signs from co-present discussions involving instructors, translators and the DHI can lead to regionalism, which might hinder their acceptance by members of other DHI communities throughout the country. A way to combat regionalism is through the asynchronous collaborative creation of signs, normally supported by web tools.

But are the signs created through web discussions inferior in any way to those created via co-present discussions? This article presents a comparative study on the acceptance of signs created by both methods showing that acceptable and legitimate signs can also be produced using web discussions and the users can not distinguish from which method they come from.

Categories and Subject Descriptors

H.5.3 [**Information Interfaces and Presentation**]: Group and Organization Interfaces—*asynchronous interaction, web-based interaction*; H.1.2 [**Models and Principles**]: User / Machine Systems—*human factors, web-based interaction*; H.4 [**Information Systems Applications**]: Miscellaneous

SIGCSE'15, March 4–7, 2015, Kansas City, MO, USA.

ACM 978-1-4503-2966-8/15/03 ...$15.00.
http://dx.doi.org/10.1145/2676723.2677293.

General Terms

Human Factors

Keywords

Sign Language, Accessibility, Collaborative Web Forum, Deaf

1. INTRODUCTION

The recognition of the Brazilian Sign Language (Libras) by means of Law No. 10,436, of April 24, 2002 [1], allowed its use as a tool of communication and instruction of the Brazilian deaf, guaranteeing them access to education. From this legislation, Libras now can be used not only informally, in everyday life of the deaf, but also formally, in environments such as school and other social institutions. As LIBRAS is a young language, its lexicon is relatively short, notably in specific areas of knowledge such as mathematics, geography and history, etc.

There are some challenges in education for the inclusion of the DHI. One of them is to keep the students motivated, especially when they have several different experiences and distinct communication barriers to be overcome. Regarding computer science education, the summer academy in computing [4] is a 9-week program that starts and contextualizes the academic careers of the DHI, keeping them excited, motivated and engaged.

In Brazil, another major challenge is that there are many terms and concepts that still have no signs in Libras, which makes difficult the access to technical material in the field by the deaf. A natural way to tackle the problem is by creating a bilingual glossary, allowing the creation of missing signs in Libras. The creation of new signs is obviously a collaborative process and should involve deaf, interpreters and IT professionals. Our laboratory has used a classroom process where parties meet and discuss the origin of the concept followed by a presentation and approval of proposals for the new sign. The chosen sign is then cataloged and added to the glossary. Among the disadvantages and risks of this process, there are the timing (the group needs to create a minimum number of signs per session), regionalism (only present at the meeting may opine) and social loafing (only one sub-group among present really helps) [9, 8]. These risks may negatively impact the acceptance of courses produced by the laboratory for part of other members of the deaf community in the country. Using a collaborative web tool for the creation of signs is a manner to attack these disadvantages. However, the classroom method also has virtues, the main one is the fact of the deaf are together for the discussion of proposals. This increases the co-presentiality possibilities of mutual understanding as members have access to the embodied behavior of the others [6]. Thus, for that community, the face-to-face method can be considered the "gold standard", the optimal way to create signals through democratic meetings.

We built a web forum which supports the process of creating signals asynchronous and remotely. A set of ten terms had their signs created by both the classroom method as the web forum tool. Pairs of signs, one coming from meeting and another from the forum, representing the same concept, were presented to a group of deaf from the same community which had to choose which one better represents that concept. A t-Student test shows that there is no clear preference as to which method produces signs better accepted by the community. We also applied a post-experiment questionnaire to collect the participants' perceptions about the two methods. The responses were submitted to the Wilcoxon Signed-Rank Test and again the differences were not significant. Although no difference was found significantly between the two methods, the signs created by the web forum were rated better most of the time.

This article is organized as follows: the Section 2 discusses the importance of the signal in learning, aiming to emphasize how the lack of signals in Libras impairs the acquisition of knowledge by deaf people. Section 3 describes the process of creating classroom signs. The Section 4 provides and discusses some online forums to create signs. In Section 5, we describe a web tool developed by our laboratory and used in our tests. In the Section 6, we explain how we conduct the experiment to compare the two methods. Section 7 presents the results and Section 8, the conclusions and future work.

2. THE IMPORTANCE OF A SIGN

Highlighting the importance of sign language for deaf education, Sacks [11] argues that complex spatial layouts of a sign lead the deaf to place objects and phenomena in a schematic context of connections and specifc locations. Thus, language development and the use of a tongue become critical for cognition.

Vygotsky [12] ensures that the language is not only a factor of communication but also a regulatory function of thought, since it is through language that human thought take form. According to the same author, language development is of greatest importance for abstract thought, given the close link between thought and language. For the author, the individual is developed from interactions with the sociocultural environment. This process occurs by the creation of systems of language that enable sophisticated communication between the individuals.

Language provides the concepts and ways of organization of the real that constitute the mediation between the subject and the object of knowledge. In other words, it is really important the use of signs that translate ideas, feelings and desires of its users accurately.

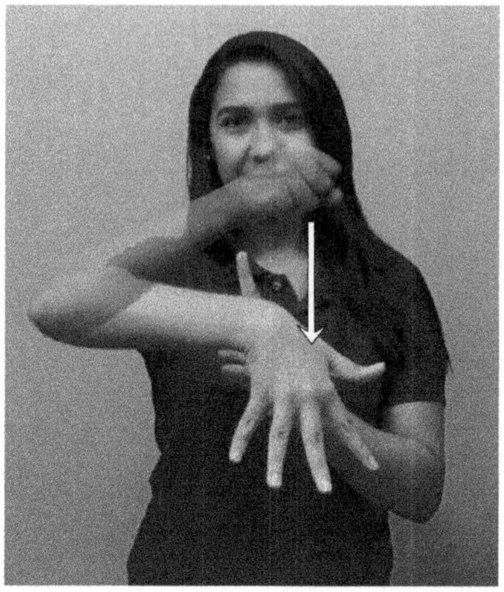

Figure 1: Sign of the term *flowchart*.

3. THE CLASSROOM METHOD

In the classroom meetings for creating signs, it is performed a selection of terminology from the texts produced for a course of Java Programming. After reading this material, the teacher presents the conceptualization of the terms and, thereafter, we investigate the existence of a sign to its representation. When this sign does not exist, a meeting is held among the deaf (who are students of the subject), the Libras interpreter and teacher.

Each definition is explained and discussed. Some signs are suggested for their representation, and then one is chosen by the group. The sign which was chosen and its definitions are reported in Libras through videos and then posted on a virtual learning environment.

The creation of signs, therefore, happens through the analysis of signs considering its meaning and its relationship to the signs already in use by the deaf community.

The Figure 1 illustrates the definition of the sign corresponding to the term flowchart.

4. WEB FORUMS FOR THE CREATION OF SIGNS

Both in Brazil and in other countries, there are many collaborative web tools for the deaf. There are also many bilingual dictionaries and virtual libraries for the translation of terms to the sign language. However, few tools were found providing these two tasks, allowing the creation of a database of translated terms by collaborating users. We now discuss some of them.

The Dicta-Sign Wiki [7] is a research project funded by the European Union and developed in partnership with several universities and research institutes in Europe. Through the sharing of signs, their goal is to make online communication more accessible for the deaf users, They work with the translation of terms in four sign languages: the British Sign Language (BSL), the German Sign Language (DGS), the French (LSF) and the Greek one (GSL). Their difference is in the use of an animated 3D avatar to represent the contributions of users, this way the contributions become anonymous, making it possible to edit the movements of the animated character. For capturing the sign, they use the Microsoft Kinect.

The Claws [10] is a collaborative tool to support interaction of deaf in web pages. It was developed by the Polytechnic School of the University of São Paulo (USP). Installed as a complement to the web browser, it consists of several features that help the deaf user to understand words contained in the web pages. It is a system composed of a dictionary in which each word can be described through images, videos and captions in Libras and Portuguese, it uses an animated 3D avatar. An important feature is the possibility of recording and sharing videos in Libras of untranslated words and terms found during navigation. This sharing is performed by the users of the tool, however, it is possible that interpreters of Libras to interact with signs and explanations of a particular term.

The Deaf Stem Technical Terms [2] is a forum to discuss signs in the areas of math and science. It was developed by Shodor Education Foundation, an american organization of research and education. Apart from videos in American Sign Language (ASL), the terms discussed include a definition written in English, their writing through glossing (a form of sign transcription) and the application of the term in a sentence. Discussions are performed by another system, a paid collaboration service called Voice Thread. For choosing a sign, the users interact and make comments, using written texts and videos recorded by webcam. For interaction between listeners and non-listeners, it is possible to include subtitles on videos. Using a paid monthly service such as Voice Thread makes the Deaf Stem uninviting.

The ASL-Stem forum [3, 5] is a web and collaborative tool for the purpose of disseminating terms and encouraging the growth and use of the American Sign Language (ASL). It was developed by the Department of Computer Science and Engineering at the University of Washington. Its main objective is to standardize and develop a specific vocabulary in the areas of Science, Engineering, Technology and Mathematics. The forum allows its users to add video of signs with no need of having a lot of experience or dedicating much for that. The user just need a personal computer with a webcam.

5. OUR WEB TOOL

We designed a web forum tool in our lab. It uses common components of a personal computer, facilitating and encouraging its use for all kinds of users. Despite its resemblance to the ASL-Stem [3, 5], our tool presents some characteristics which are thought to improve and encourage the participation of the deaf.

A factor that enhances the choice of the signs is the need of a minimum amount of votes so that a proposed sign can be elected as the best choice for a term. Thus, the choice of the signs becomes more careful, since a larger group of users had participated in the process. This feature will serve in the future to combat regionalism, since it will require the participation of diverse communities throughout Brazil.

In the tool, a topic for each term to be translated is created, and each topic has a page where the discussion about the suggested signs occurs. Here, the concept of the term is explained in text format and, by its side, a video with an interpreter translating the text to Libras is also showed. Is the page are videos of proposed signs that users create to represent the term associated with the topic and there are also comments submitted by the community that participates in the application. The suggested videos are sorted in ascending order of notes, and the best rated suggested sign is highlighted in a green panel.

The topics are organized in a tree format for easy viewing. To participate in the tool the user must register informing basic data as name, email, date of birth and password. Once registered, the user can subscribe to a topic, and only when entered, can upload videos of signs and comments and vote for videos uploaded by other users. The application notifies its users by sending emails. Users that subscribe to a topic are informed by e-mail every time a new video with a proposed sign is created or when a comment is posted to subscribed topics. Uploaded videos of proposed signs are made by the webcam of the user. Once a video is posted on the discussion page, it can get votes from other users, the starting score is zero.

Each participant shall vote only in signs proposed by other users and only once, assigning them grades ranging from 1 to 5. A star format was used to represent the notes, and a video that receive 5 stars got actually a grade 5. For each video, the average of all the grades it received is calculated and displayed right below the video.

6. THE EXPERIMENT

In this paper, we study the acceptance of signs created by both methods: the classroom method and the remotely method supported by web tools.

For this, we selected some deaf participants with similar profile, they are all graduate and most of them had finished their graduate courses. The participants are students of the IT area and the majority of them code in Java. They were divided into three groups. The goal was the creation of homogeneous groups regarding the experience in computing to investigate differences in the development processes.

The first group consists of five people aged between 24 and 44 years old, two women and three men. The second group also consists of five people aged between 23 and 35 years old, two female and three male. These two groups, A and B, performed tasks related to the creation of signs. We also defined a third group C which consists of seven people aged between 24 and 39 years, all male. The purpose of this last group was to perform a blind analysis of the signs created by Groups A and B. All the selected participants are Java programmers and students of the area.

The study was divided into two phases: the creation of signs and the blind analysis of the signs. In the first phase, we implement a within-subjects experiment with groups A and B. We selected a set of ten untranslated terms in Libras: boolean, boot, debug, desktop, graphic user interface (GUI), Java ARchive (JAR), javac, javaw, Unix e widgets. The groups participated in the creation of the signs for the terms using the two processes alternately. At the end, for each term, we have two signs: one created using the classroom method and another one created using a web tool developed by our lab. At the end of this phase, we applied a questionnaire among the participants to analyze other aspects of the methods.

In the second phase, the Group C performed a blind review of the signs. The function of the group was to validate the signs created in the different modalities. Without knowing from what process the signs came from, they elected, for each term, the sign that they find more appropriate to the concept.

Table 1: Wilcoxon Signed-Rank Test

Statement	W-Value	Critical Value
My efforts are recognized when creating signs.	15	3 for n=8
I feel comfortable to suggest a new sign.	26.5	8 for n=10
I feel comfortable to discuss and comment about a sign.	7.5	2 for n=7
The participation of all members is effective.	3	2 for n=7
I have more time to think.	-	not defined for n=5
There are people who do not participate or participate little.	13	5 for n=9
I prefer the signs from this method.	10.5	0 for n=6

7. RESULTS AND DISCUSSIONS

Our results can be divided in two parts. The first one is about the experience of the Groups A and B when creating signs using the two methods, this experience was collected through the questionnaire applied. The second one is the analysis of the signs created, the blind-review performed by the Group C.

7.1 Experience of the Participants

The answers of the questionnaire applied in the first phase for the Groups A and B were submitted to the Wilcoxon Signed-Rank Test. For each statement, the participants answered with a score from one (completely disagree) to ten (completely agree). In Table 1, we present the aspects which were considered and the W-values since we are working with a small sample of participants. The critical values are also shown for comparison. We used a significance level of 0.05 and a two-tailed test. The values of n in the last column vary due to the ties.

For the statement *I have more time to think*, we had many ties, so it was not possible to have a critical value with our parameters. For all others aspects the result is considered not significant at $p \leq 0.05$ (W-value is greater than critical value). So this indicates that it is likely that there is no difference between the methods when we analyze the aspects reported in the table, in other words, the chances of obtaining no differences between the classroom method and using the web tool are not small.

7.2 Blind-Review

For each untranslated term, two signs were created: one, using the classroom method, and the other one, using our web tool. Without knowing how the signs were created, we asked Group C to vote which of the two signs they think it is better to represent the term. The results are presented in Table 2.

For the terms *debug*, *GUI* and *boolean*, the signs created using the web tool got almost all the votes. If we analyze the average scores, we notice that the signs produced using the web tool were better evaluated, 4.10 against 2.90 of the signals created by the classroom method. Although most of the signs created using the tool has obtained more votes (7 of 10), there is no significant difference between the acceptability of signs from the two methods. We applied these results to the Student's T-Test with significance level of 0.05, the two-tailed P-value obtained was 0.3009.

Table 2: Voting by Group C

Term	Sign from the Classroom Method	Sign from the web tool
javaw	4	3
debug	1	6
widgets	3	4
GUI	1	6
desktop	5	2
boolean	1	6
boot	2	5
JAR	3	4
javac	6	1
unix	3	4

Thus, we can conclude that the deaf can not distinguish the origin of the signs, and the two processes produce equally acceptable signs by the same community.

7.3 Pros and Cons ot the Methods

We also asked to all the participants to express their opinion on positive and negative aspects of the two processes.

Positive aspects of the classroom method:

- Immediate opinion of the colleagues;
- Immediate clarifications from the teacher;
- Direct Contact with the colleagues;

Negative aspects of the classroom method:

- Some colleagues do not participate in the process;
- It is not possible to search for other sources;
- Limited time for discussions;

Positive aspects of using a web forum:

- The suggestion of a sign is registered and others may have access;
- A greater number of deaf people can participate, including those from other regions;
- It allows everyone to participate equally;
- A greater number of deaf people can vote on suggested signs;

Negative aspects of using a web forum:

- It takes more time to receive a feedback;
- Dependence on factors such as Internet;

8. CONCLUSIONS AND FUTURE WORK

Our lab produces distance courses for training of deaf Java programmers. One of the difficulties encountered in the creation process of these courses lies in the fact that Libras does not have signs to some specifc concepts in the field. We created a web forum tool to support the process of creating signs in a remote, asynchronous and collaborative manner.

We investigated the acceptability of the signs created by the tool, comparing them with the signs created through the classroom method, considered the gold standard. We conclude that although the classroom method is better for mutual understanding due to the direct interaction among its participants, it favors the regionalism, which impairs the reapplication of these courses in Brazil.

With the experiment, we tried to assess whether the method for creation signs would interfere in the quality of these signs. Our conclusion is that we can produce acceptable and legitimate signs using a web forum tool. From the assessment of such signs, the users can not distinguish on which method they were created.

Using a web tool, all Brazilian deaf may play a role in the expansion and enrichment of the technical lexicon in Libras, since it has been proved that it is possible to create legitimate and acceptable signs. Such a tool can be seen as a facilitator for inclusion. As future work, we have the mission to make it available to the representative institutions of the Brazilian deaf community for its democratic use.

9. REFERENCES

[1] About brazilian sign language (libras) and other provisions. Brazilian law No. 10,436 - April,24th 2002 - Diario Oficial da Republica Federativa do Brasil - Brasilia, DF - Brazil.

[2] Deaf stem technical terms website: a forum to discuss signs for commonly used math and science terms. Shodor Education Foundation, Avaiable in http://www.shodor.org/deafstemterms.

[3] J. P. Bigham, D. S. Otero, J. N. DeWitt, A. Cavender, and R. E. Ladner. Asl-stem forum: A bottom-up approach to enabling american sign language to grow in stem fields. In *ICWSM*, 2008.

[4] A. C. Cavender, R. E. Ladner, and R. I. Roth. The summer academy for advancing deaf and hard of hearing in computing. In *ACM SIGCSE Bulletin*, volume 41, pages 514–518. ACM, 2009.

[5] A. C. Cavender, D. S. Otero, J. P. Bigham, and R. E. Ladner. Asl-stem forum: enabling sign language to grow through online collaboration. In *Proceedings of the SIGCHI Conference on Human Factors in Computing Systems*, pages 2075–2078. ACM, 2010.

[6] H. H. Clark. *Arenas of language use.* University of Chicago Press, 1992.

[7] E. Efthimiou, S.-E. Fotinea, T. Hanke, J. Glauert, R. Bowden, A. Braffort, C. Collet, P. Maragos, and F. Lefebvre-Albaret. *The dicta-sign wiki: enabling web communication for the deaf.* Springer, 2012.

[8] T. Gilovich, D. Keltner, and R. Nisbett. *Social Psychology.* W.W. Norton, 2006.

[9] S. J. Karau and K. D. Williams. Social loafing: A meta-analytic review and theoretical integration. *Journal of personality and social psychology*, 65(4):681, 1993.

[10] S. J. O. Martins. *CLAWS: uma ferramenta colaborativa para apoio à interação de surdos com páginas da web.* PhD thesis, Universidade de São Paulo, 2012.

[11] O. Sacks. *Vendo vozes: uma viagem ao mundo dos surdos.* Editora Companhia das Letras, 1998.

[12] L. S. Vygotsy et al. Pensamento e linguagem. *Edição eletrônica: Ed Ridendo Castigat Mores. Disponível em*, 1989.

Beyond the Flipped Classroom: Learning by Doing Through Challenges and Hack-a-thons

Michael Skirpan
Department of Computer Science
University of Colorado at Boulder
michael.skirpan@colorado.edu

Tom Yeh
Department of Computer Science
University of Colorado at Boulder
tom.yeh@colorado.edu

ABSTRACT

Traditionally, the inverted (or flipped) classroom has students complete traditional, passive learning tasks (e.g., watching lectures) while at home and uses class time to actualize what is learned through labs, discussions, and exercises. In this paper, we present an instructional model for teaching computer science (CS) that compounds features of the flipped classroom with components of peer instruction and formative assessment. Outside of class, in lieu of a lecture, students worked collaboratively on *learning challenges* that introduced content through a series of hands-on exercises. During class time, we used *hack-a-thons* to create an active classroom environment to promote peer coding and cultivate the growth of relevant real-world technical skills. Class work was digitally synced to Google Drive in real-time to allow instructors the opportunity to customize on-the-spot feedback. Further, we used journals as a formative assessment measure to synthesize student interests and opinions into our continued design of the class. In this paper, we describe our pedagogical model and discuss the results and lessons learned from the class using mined data from Google Drive and student journal responses.

Categories and Subject Descriptors

K.3.2 [**Computers and Education**]: Computer and Information Science Education – *Computer Science Education, Curriculum.*

Keywords

Flipped classroom; inverted classroom; hack-a-thon; pedagogy; peer instruction; formative assessment

1. INTRODUCTION

In education, there is an age-old tension between traditional and progressive approaches to schooling [12]. The standard division is characterized between classrooms where the teacher is at the center of knowledge construction (e.g., lecturing, delegating required homework, and testing) versus a student-centered approach where student are responsible for building knowledge through their own interests and activities. While this debate has been ongoing, it has recently become central to the discussion of how to best teach STEM content and, central to this paper, computer science (CS).

SIGCSE'15, March 4–7, 2015, Kansas City, MO, USA.

ACM 978-1-4503-2966-8/15/03…$15.00.
http://dx.doi.org/10.1145/2676723.2677224

Figure 1. Weekly hack-a-thons in class where students design, build, and demo a prototype in 150 minutes

Recently, in CS education, attention has been placed on the inverted, or flipped, classroom approach as an alternative to a traditional model [3, 5, 6, 8, 10]. Historically, the philosophy of learning through action derives from experiential educational models suggested by thinkers like John Dewey, William Wirt, and Lev Vygotsky. Contemporary publications primarily draw their model from work done by Eric Mazur in the 1990s. Mazur discussed using computers in the classroom to allow the teacher more time to coach students on specific struggles [9] and later developed a flipped classroom technique involving peer instruction [4]. However innovative, this style has continued to rely on students watching lectures at home while class time is spent taking conceptual quizzes and performing problem-solving exercises in groups. Although this approach takes a step forward to improve the traditional model of instruction, similar issues of engagement and retention are still inherent.

Video lectures often promote limited attention to the instructor because multitasking and personal distractions are in direct competition with the lecture content. Moreover, the overall class content is still centered on what is chosen by the instructor, ceding little ownership to the student in regard to the content learned. Given that student responsibility and "doing over knowing" are two goals of the flipped classroom model [5], there still appears to be room for progress.

Because we believe in the movement toward more progressive approaches to teaching CS yet are cognizant of these issues, we decided to make some further modifications to the flipped classroom model. Namely, we ushered in a formative assessment component to the curriculum to improve student buy-in to class content and scrapped passive lecturing in favor of a fully hands-on approach that emphasizes creating tangible projects.

We explore this modified model and the results from our experience in this paper. It should be noted that, for our first implementation of this model, we chose a full adoption. That is, scheduled class time was 100% hack-a-thon and 0% lecture (see Figure 1). We recognized beforehand that the ideal adoption would likely be less extreme, but we wanted to test the limits of the model and use student feedback to reassess. In sections 2 and 3, we will delineate our model and provide a detailed example of it in action, and in sections 4 and 5, we will share our results and return to the question of ideal adoption.

2. INSTRUCTIONAL MODEL

From a macro-view, we built our model around core of skill building and project delivery. We selected content that was relevant a) to the skills students were most interested in acquiring and b) to the skills applicable to creating professional-quality web applications. Further, all learning was structured around projects; both small projects that would be completed in one or two weeks and a large final project that involved creating a full application that could be incorporated into student portfolios. To accomplish these criteria, we opted to deliver the content in a dynamic manner: Though we created a full syllabus for preparatory reasons, the class content often changed as we learned more about our students and discovered learning struggles that required more time. Despite having dynamic *content*, we adhered to a class model with four major components: learning challenges, journals, in-class hack-a-thons, and a semester project. We used Google Drive as a management tool to track student work and handle submissions, the details of which we will discuss in section 3 on implementation.

2.1 Learning Challenges

Students began each week by going to a link posted on our course website. The link took them to a Google Document (i.e., the learning challenge) where new content would be introduced. These documents guided students through a series of challenges to be completed, usually starting with a simple "hello world" application. A challenge would be highlighted and numbered with a description of a deliverable we expected in their submission document. Each challenge was contextualized with links to helpful pages such as select code documentation and Stack-Overflow answers to common issues. At each of these junctures, students would be asked to reproduce a shown result or implement a solution to a problem given certain constraints. They then submitted a screenshot or code snippet as supporting material to show completion of the challenge.

Challenges would often entail working on different facets of a mini-project being built throughout the homework. Sometimes a challenge could be completed in one screenshot, but often there were a series of sub-challenges that asked them to share smaller parts of their process. For submission, we posted a template in the form of a Google Presentation that would have a single slide for each challenge or sub-challenge deliverable. Completing a submission involved copying the template and placing it in their personal folder having filled in each slide. To leverage the diverse skillsets across the class, we asked students to choose one or two partners each week and provide evidence they worked together by submitting a *selfie* photo of them working together. We imposed this restriction to promote peer instruction, allowing students to help each other.

Though the challenges imposed a strict set of functionality to implement, we opened the door for student creativity by remaining flexible about accepting different approaches to the same solution and allowing students to work on custom content (e.g., personal websites, senior design projects, open source contributions). This was our solution to an inherent tension of wanting to ensure students were pushed to learn new skills while providing them with the opportunity to work on projects within their own range of interests.

Our style of "homework" is one of the most distinguishing features between our implementation of the flipped classroom model and other methods. A common approach in the flipped model is to provide students with online video lectures that pose short-answer and multiple-choice quiz questions along with a few practice exercises along the way [8]. Our model differs primarily in that we drop the lecture component completely and instead scaffold the learning exercises with a narrative (i.e., tutorial) that replaces the didactic content traditionally found in lectures.

2.2 Journals

Every week, the students were given a set of questions to submit with their challenges that encouraged reflection, criticism, and suggestions. Typically, we would survey them with a mixture of quantitative and qualitative questions. We presented both recurring questions, establishing baseline measures on the weekly curricula, and novel questions specific to that week's content.

Common quantitative questions regarded the length of time spent on and the perceived difficulty of the assignment. Qualitatively, we would usually ask students to share resources (i.e., web links) they found useful to complete the homework, explain barriers they hit during the assignment, and what else they would have liked to learn if they were to complete the assignment again. This data would then be used by the instructors to make decisions about what content to include in the weekly hack-a-thon, whom to place in teams for the hack-a-thon, and what topics required more work in the coming weeks. For timing reasons, we did not read all journal entries each week but instead set aside time to glance through them quickly as a way to determine common struggles.

Journals provided a means for us to conduct a formative assessment of the class. Formative assessment is defined as "assessment carried out during the instructional process for the purpose of improving teaching or learning" [11]. In educational research, formative assessment has been cited as one of the most powerful sources to improve student learning and class engagement [7]. Such mechanisms have been implemented in prior CS teaching using a revision cycle for homework questions to improve learning outcomes [2]. However, our focus on formative assessment was designed to improve *teaching*; thus, we used the journal as a direct, private channel for students to inform instructors about what was good or bad, difficult or easy, interesting or boring, regarding each week's assignments and content. All journal responses were submitted in the same Google Presentation document as the challenges. An example is discussed in section 4.3.

2.3 In-Class Hack-a-Thon

Hack-a-thons (also called "sprints") have become a popular method whereby coders come together to produce first versions of projects, create open-source content, share skills and insights in their work, and perform coding work for the public good. Beyond being a norm in the coding community, this spontaneous process is useful for collaboration, generating creative results, and learning to work with deadlines. Thus, to have an active classroom and observe our students' abilities, we used class time to "hack."

The process would start with students either self-selecting or the instructors assigning teams of three to five students. It was known ahead of time that the hack-a-thon would involve an implementation using the materials seen in the previous week's learning challenge, although the specific task would be kept private until students arrived in class. Once students were in their teams, we asked them to go to the course website, where a link had recently been added, directing them to the guidelines for the week. Similar to the learning challenge, the hack-a-thon guidelines were paired with a submission template to fill out.

The hack-a-thon guidelines would offer general design challenges (e.g., make a robot dating website) and list milestones that students needed to accomplish (e.g., take a screenshot of a robot dating profile). Milestones were similar to challenges insofar as they were pieces of functionality that needed to be proven by submitting a screenshot or code snippet. One major difference between the challenge and hack-a-thon is that we enforced a design phase at the beginning of each hack-a-thon that asked the teams to produce an outline of the work to be completed and a declaration of who would be responsible for what parts of the implementation. The design phase would be limited to the first thirty minutes of class and would allow instructors to see each team's goals in real-time by using a similar Google Drive approach from the learning challenges. Using live syncing of the files, we could then observe each team's progress, provide individualized feedback, and offer help to those who struggled.

During the hack-a-thon, the instructors would immerse themselves in discussion and consultation with the teams. The last fifteen minutes of class would be devoted to a short showcase of what each team accomplished because every team often had vastly different strategies for implementation. In the end, the hack-a-thons would be judged by external parties (often friends of the instructors, local coders, or other graduate students) to provide objective feedback on the end products. This allowed students to receive real-world critiques regarding design, usability, and coding patterns that allowed them to improve beyond the requirements of the class. Having external judges allowed the instructors to focus on evaluating student learning fairly and kept subjective judgments out of the grading scheme while still delivering insight to our students on what to expect from authentic users and employers.

The hack-a-thon component of the class is similar to other flipped classrooms in that it generates an active environment during class time. A more common way to achieve this would be to have a series of in-class exercises similar to traditional homework or to present hands-on examples that are traditionally solved by the instructor during lecture [6, 10]. Our model differs slightly in that we use the hack-a-thon to gear class time toward a single project-based learning exercise in which groups work collaboratively toward a result that has no right or wrong answer. Rather than ask students to work toward a predetermined solution, our model attempts to emulate a real-world implementation whereby the creative team is central to the outcome, and failure and iteration are expected parts of the process.

2.4 Semester Project

The culminating component of the class was an in-depth project for which students could use any mixture of the tools we learned about during the semester. Students also had the opportunity to integrate outside skills and interests into their final project. Students were informed of the project at the beginning of the semester and were encouraged to start thinking about what they wanted to create and find a team with which they wanted to work. At the semester midpoint, we asked students to solidify teams and submit a project proposal that outlined the purpose of the project, what functionality they planned to implement, who would be in charge of what aspects of the project, and a GitHub repository where we could find the final project. Once these were submitted, instructors read through them to ensure that they met class expectations and that the work was both reasonable and evenly divided among the team.

As a way to keep a tally on the projects and feel confident in their progress, we asked students to self-impose four milestones (submitted with their weekly learning challenges) that would keep them on track throughout their project. Although milestones were taken into consideration in the final project grades, we primarily used these as motivating factors to ensure that groups stayed on track. For our final class meeting, we held a presentation together with five other CS classes to exhibit the students' work.

Our project takes a similar approach to that described in past hands-on instructional methodologies [1] in that we asked students to develop milestones and report their progress by submitting pieces of code and screenshots. However, we did not place strong structural constraints on the project. The only requirements were based on using some of the tools learned in class and choosing milestones suitable to prove reasonable progress; otherwise, the students were free to implement anything.

3. IMPLEMENTATION: SPRING 2014

We now move on to describe the specific details of the class setting, student population, material taught, and evaluation methodology. The course we chose for this model was "User-Centered Design and Development," a cross-listed undergraduate and graduate course that focused on front-end development skills and creating web servers to host applications. Our class met for 2.5 hours once per week throughout a single 15-week semester, and anticipated a 10-hour weekly work commitment.

3.1 Class Setting and Student Population

Selecting a class setting was important, as we learned on our first day of class when we tried to manage the hack-a-thon in a traditional classroom environment. Not only were the standard single-occupant desks a hindrance for collaboration, but also the lecture-based classroom was too small for instructors to walk readily between groups, neither did it supply enough plugs for every student to code for the entire class time. Thus, we quickly scouted better campus spaces, first trying a lab space (which worked well but presented scheduling issues) and then a lounge space.

As shown in Figure 1, we began hosting the class from a student lounge space that contained large worktables as well as couches and chairs placed around coffee tables. This space proved to be most beneficial for everyone.

The class had 31 students in total: 8 graduate students and 23 undergraduates. Among the 8 graduate students, 7 were master students and 1 was a PhD student. Of the 23 undergraduate students, 22 were computer science majors and 1 was a mechanical engineer. Most of the undergraduates were seniors or juniors (5 and 17, respectively) with the addition of 1 sophomore. Within the total population were 4 female students (2 graduate, 2 undergraduate) and 28 male students. Using student journal data, we found that 94% of the students had previous front-end experience (i.e., HTML, CSS, or JavaScript), but only 32% had experience working with web servers (e.g., Apache).

3.2 Use of Google Drive

To prepare for the semester, we set up Google Drive folders for every student. Permissions were set so that student folders were accessible only by that student and the instructors. This gave students the ability to share documents for collaboration while keeping their journals, project proposal, and feedback private.

For weekly learning challenges and journals, we used a public folder that contained the templates files (Google Presentations with slides for each submission) from which students made personal copies. Submissions for hack-a-thons, on the other hand, were handled within a single, public file. Teams managed their own internal file sharing, but milestone submissions were placed onto a shared Google Presentation, which had preset blocks of slides for different teams to use. The start of the hack-a-thons involved having the instructors post a link on the class website, directing students to the hack-a-thon outline document, and following a further link from there to the submission document where each team laid claim to a block of slides by placing their names at the head slide.

We chose Google Presentations as a primary medium for student submissions because of the extreme flexibility it granted us. Slides could easily be used to add an image, type a journal entry, or work with a mock-up, and the entire document easily turned into a shareable presentation. It also allowed us easy access to an edit history on all student documents.

3.3 Class Content

The content students were required to learn was separated into breadth and depth aspects of the course. The depth content structured the requirements of the semester-long projects. We offered graduate students the option of learning to use the LEAP Motion or the XBOX Kinect. The only depth requirement for undergraduates was that their final project must use the ubiquitous JavaScript library, JQuery.

All weekly assignments were part of the breadth dimension of the class, familiarizing students with a wide range of tools. Core topics included creating website wireframes using Balsamiq and PopApp, website development using Bootstrap, building web-servers with Python Flask and a SQLAlchemy back-end, and application hosting via GitHub and Heroku. During the final weeks of class, when student projects were exhausting more time, we taught "fun" topics based on class interests, which included 3D Modeling in Google Sketchup and OpenSCAD, hardware programming with Picaxe Robots, and tangible interfaces with Makey-Makey. This offered students a full-scope overview of designing a user experience from the backend of a webserver all the way to a physical prototype that can be held by an end-user.

3.4 Course Evaluation

The final grade was weighted as follows: hack-a-thons 25%, learning challenges 30%, journal 15%, and final project 30%. All students kept their own folder on Google Drive, which was shared with the instructors. Learning challenges and journals were due by 11:59 PM the evening before class, and hack-a-thons were due by the end of class.

The weekly learning challenges were graded on three criteria: timeliness, completion, and correctness. Credit was given only to submissions that were handed in before the final deadline, which we tracked via Google Drive. Once we eliminated late submissions, we then credited half a point for turning in any submission for a given challenge and credited the other half point for challenges that were correct. Correctness was a lenient measure, as we were aware that there were always multiple ways to approach a solution thus credit was given as long as the screenshot or code snippet showed a basic competency at completing the task. Journals were graded at the same time as weekly challenges (They were submitted together.), and the only criterion was completion: 1 point for each question answered.

Hack-a-thons were graded on both completion of the basic milestones and effort. We did not take off points for students who had broken pieces of their websites or for unfinished functionality because each week presented a brand new project and punishing

Figure 2. Example of a learning challenge and a journal entry by a student using Google Presentation

students for these shortcomings would likely have promoted less ambitious work. Therefore, although a baseline amount of effort was required to gain credit, the hack-a-thon was primarily about attending and attempting. We encountered almost no issues with students' not working hard in class, possibly due to the Google Drive's syncing and thus causing them to realize that we were aware of their efforts. Due to hack-a-thons, attendance was a major part of each student's grade. Class policy allowed students only one unexcused absence, which could be made up at the end of the semester when we held a makeup hack-a-thon.

Semester projects were graded for completion of milestones and final functionality, both of which were agreed upon in the project proposal.

3.5 One Week Up Close

To solidify how separate working parts of our class model came together in practice, we provide a short tour through a single week. All examples come from week 7 of the semester (March 2–9, 2014) when we taught website hosting using GitHub, Heroku, and Python Flask.

Learning Challenge: This week started by ensuring students knew how to use GitHub. They had the choice of following a GitHub tutorial to which we supplied a link or to demonstrate to us that they already know how to use it by submitting screenshots of a new repository and a fresh commit to the repository. We then linked them to material that introduced Heroku web hosting and set the challenge of using Heroku to host the Python Flask server they had built in previous weeks. Figure 2 (above) provides an example student submission of Heroku server logs. Once students understood the Heroku service, we asked them to take a website mockup from a previous week and generate a static HTML page using Bootstrap (a CSS library taught in a previous week). The page was to be viewable both on a desktop and mobile device. Finally, they were to create a serviceable route to this static page via Python Flask and serve it live on the public web via Heroku.

Journal: Once the learning challenges were complete, we asked students to use our journal template to report on several questions. As mentioned above, some questions were consistent through the weeks, and others were specific to the topic at hand. We then used this content to construct the hack-a-thon and improve on the

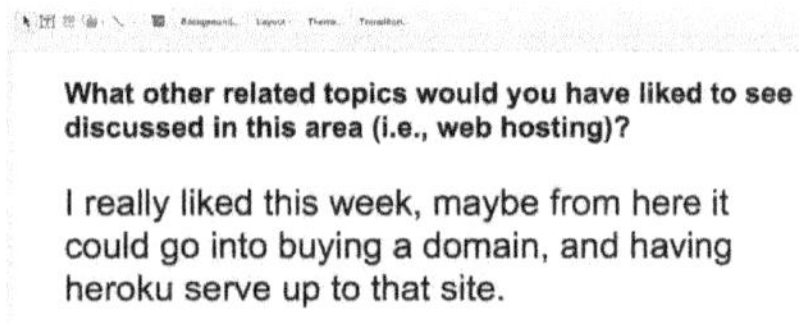

Figure 3. Student's answer to a survey question.

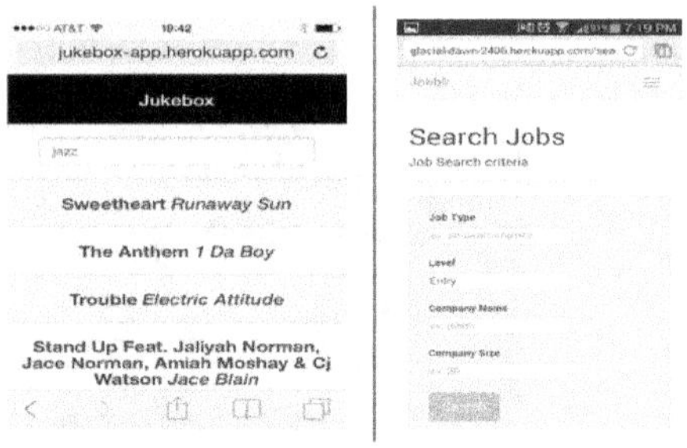

Figure 4. Two prototypes built by hack-a-thon teams

following weeks' challenges. Figure 3 offers a sample suggestion a student offered after completing the web-hosting challenge.

Hack-a-thon: For this week's hack-a-thon, we asked students to create a mobile application similar to what they would pitch for a startup. We asked them to plan, implement, and demo their prototype and submit the planning information, user scenario descriptions, and screenshots. Figure 4 shows two smartphone screenshots of the actual mobile applications submitted by students as a result of the hack-a-thon.

4. RESULTS

Many metrics were collected throughout the semester. We used Google Drive's API and continually read student journals to gather both qualitative and quantitative data about the class.

4.1 Attendance and Completion Rates

Under our model, attendance was a prominent indicator of success in the class. At the beginning of the semester, we expected students to drop the class once they realized that attending and participating in class would be a huge portion of their grade. To the contrary, we maintained a large class size and observed little diminishment of attendance rates. The overall class attendance rate was 92% (excluding excused absences).

Regarding the completion of weekly learning challenges (i.e., homework), we observed high rates of completion. Overall, 89% of challenges were submitted before the deadline and given full credit. The two weeks for which we recorded the lowest scores were when we first asked students to have a fully functional web server (81%) and when they learned OpenSCAD 3D modeling (72%). The first dip was expected, given the incoming experience of the students with web servers, and the second dip in student work may have occurred because it coincided with students' turning in their first project milestone.

Journal completion rates were almost precisely correlated with weekly learning challenges, with an overall average of 89%. This relationship is likely because journals were due at the same time and in the same document as the learning challenges. Thus, if students gave up on completing the homework or chose not to attempt it at all, they were likely not to complete the journal.

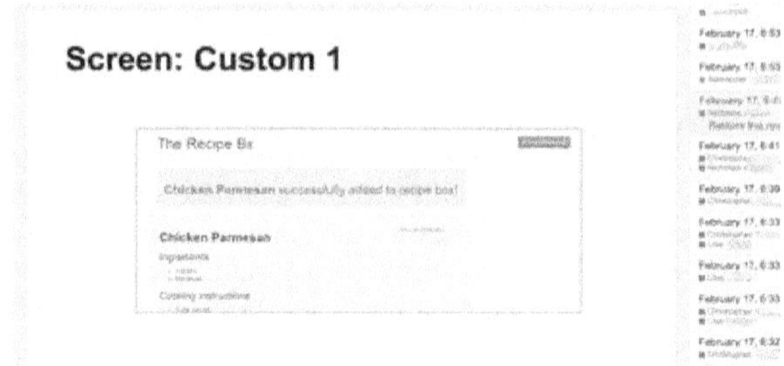

4.2 Student Revisions

One novel affordance of our use of Google Drive was the ability to see fine-grained revision histories on student documents, including the timestamp, username, and restorable revision for each and every edit made to a student document. This is contrasted with a traditional, coarse-grain work history in which student work is seen only upon homework/exam submission. Figure 5 shows what this revision history looks like for hack-a-thon document. This data allowed us to observe how students collaborated. (Each student's activity has a different color.) Also, we could restore old revisions to gain insight into their process.

Further, using the available revision history, we were able to conduct analyses and render graphics that provided instructors with information about student work patterns. These graphics guided us toward improved instructional strategies. Figure 6 is a sample graph from our class data that shows three kinds of student work patterns: those who started and finished early, those who started earlier but finished closer to the deadline, and those who waited until just before the deadline to finish. In light of these patterns, we responded by making a single submission due in the middle of the week to encourage students to start the assignments early because the early workers tended finished more often.

4.3 Student Reporting

Qualitative and quantitative information from the journals were used to determine areas in which the class needed to improve. For instance, in week 7 during the introduction to web servers, we discovered that several students had spent 10+ hours on homework and provided feedback stating they were still very confused about how the routing system worked. In response, we used the next week as a review week and separated the class into "student instructors" and "learners," whereby students who were comfortable with the material helped struggling students.

Another use of student journal reporting was to provide instructors with broad feedback about the class and collect metrics pertinent to the improvement of future iterations of the class. These metrics could be analyzed on their own or in comparison with more objective metrics via the data available from Google Drive. In our reflection section below, many of our suggested improvements for our model are distilled from these student reports. Figure 7 is one such outcome of analyzing student journals. It shows that the time spent on an assignment correlates well with its perceived difficulty. The lines are less correlated in the final weeks when we worked on 3D modeling, a topic students considered easier than coding but more time consuming.

5. REFLECTION & CONCLUSION

5.1 Generalizability

To what extent could our instructional model prove successful for other classes? Our model relies on having instructors willing to devote a large amount of time to the initial course design and to the development of learning challenges and hack-a-thons on a

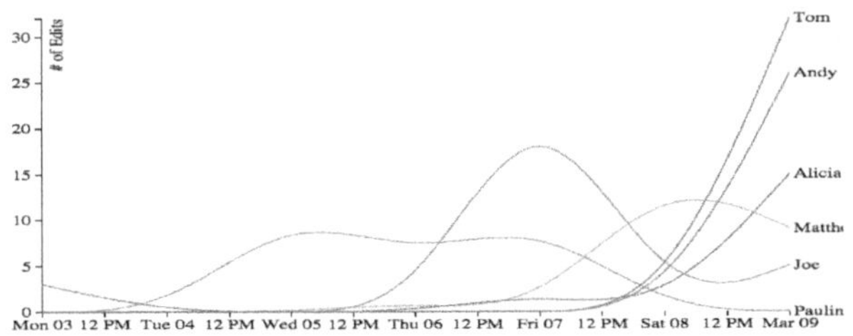

Figure 6. Edit patterns of students' documents for a learning challenge throughout the week it was assigned

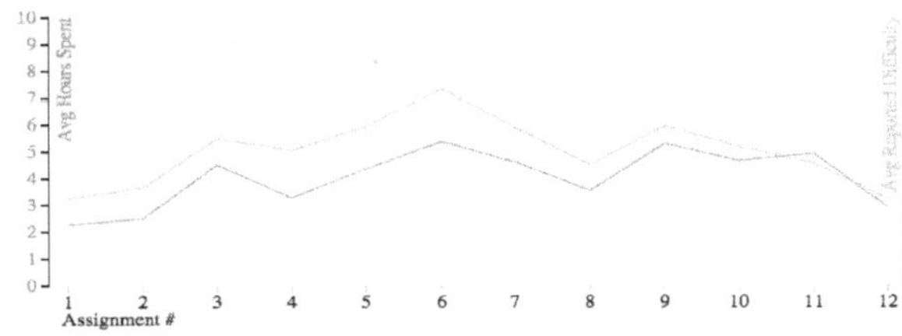

Figure 7. Average hours spent on 12 weekly assignments (blue) compared to reported difficulty (orange)

weekly basis. If full implementation were too difficult, a partial implementation (e.g., using the model every other week) would be possible and useful for most CS classes.

One factor that made our class exceptional was the amount of work that was visual in essence. In contrast, a class that focuses exclusively on code would likely scale down the use of screenshots as submissions and instead require links to GitHub repositories. However, screenshots could still prove useful for showing compilation and runtime errors, and Google Drive syncing could help instructors understand student work patterns. Most importantly, the use of class time for authentic code production seems to be generalizable to almost any coding classroom. In classes teaching large-scale software production (e.g., software engineering), hack-a-thons could build on one another in such a way that a final submission takes many sessions.

Another factor is class time. Our model requires longer class time (2.5 hours) for hack-a-thons to be viable. In CS1 courses, the coding is likely simple enough that 50 minutes would be an effective time, but for advanced courses a short class time would be a severe hindrance to implementing our model.

5.2 Class Discussion

One major change we will make to the class in future iterations is to reserve 20–30 minutes at the beginning of each class for group discussions. Student feedback revealed that, although students loved the hack-a-thon as the fundamental class component, they wished a small amount of time were devoted to overviewing common errors, fielding questions about the week's content, and talking about ideal use cases and competing tools. Using this feedback, we now realize that the ideal class time balance should be closer to 20% discussion/lecture and 80% hack-a-thon.

5.3 Consistency and Structure

Another improvement we will make to the class is on the overall structure of the course and assignments. The students wanted content to build upon itself instead of being asked often to replicate designs to complete work with new tools. This would have taken much more planning but would have improved the number of polished deliverables.

A lack of structure was a trade-off we knowingly made to implement the extreme, no-lecture model of the class. This created a learning curve for students to get comfortable with the weekly class cycle. Although it only took 2–3 weeks for students to settle into the class model, we believe this could be mitigated by having a better class website where all documents, links, and templates are centralized and the submission process is explained.

5.4 Next Implementation

Beginning in fall 2014, we are running a second implementation of this model in a data science class entitled "Big Data." We now provide a 20-minute window at the beginning of class for discussion and 5 minutes at the end of class for students to seek help with the semester-long project. Also, the semester project has become a larger component in the class so that students can use early-semester data collection from their project as content for class hack-a-thons, allowing them to work with data they are interested in and refine their project design. This class will provide further insights into the generalizability of this model.

6. REFERENCES

[1] Balasubramanian, R., York, Z., Doran, M., Biswas, A., Girgin, T., & Sankaralingam, K. Hands-on instroduction to computer science at freshman level. In *SIGCSE '14*. 235-240. DOI= http://doi.acm.org/10.1145/2538862.2538889.

[2] Blaheta, D. Reinventing homework as cooperative, formative assessment. In *SIGCSE '14*. 489-494. DOI= http://doi.acm.org/10.1145/2538862.2538915.

[3] Campbell, J., Horton, D., Craig, M., & Gries, P. Evaluating an inverted CS1. In *SIGCSE '14*. 307-312. DOI= http://doi.acm.org/10.1145/2591708.2591752.

[4] Crouch, C.H. & Mazur, E. Peer instruction: Ten years of experience and results. *American Journal of Physics*, 69(9):970, 2001.

[5] Gannod, G. C., Burge, J. E., & Helmick, M. T. Using the inverted classroom to teach software engineering. In *ICSE '08*. 777-786. DOI= http://doi.acm.org/10.1145/1368088.1368198.

[6] Gehringer, E. F., & Peddycord III, B. W. 2013. The inverted-lecture model: a case study in computer architecture. In *SIGCSE '13*. 489-494. DOI= http://doi.acm.org/10.1145/2445196.2445343.

[7] Hattie, J., & Timperley, H. The power of feedback. *Review of educational research* 77(1), 81-112, 2007.

[8] Horton, D., Craig, M., Campbell, J., Gries, P., & Zingaro, D. Comparing outcomes in inverted and traditional CS1. In *SIGSCE '14*. 261-266. DOI= http://doi.acm.org/10.1145/2591708.2591752.

[9] Mazur, Eric, Feb. 1991, *"Can We Teach Computers to Teach?,"* Retrieved September 1, 2014, from http://mazur.harvard.edu/sentFiles/Mazur_256459.pdf

[10] Rutherfoord, R. H., & Rutherfoord, J. K. Flipping the classroom: is it for you?. In *SIGITE '13*. 19-22. DOI= http://doi.acm.org/10.1145/2512276.2512299.

[11] Shepard, L.A. Formative assessment: caveat emptor. In *The future of assessment: shaping teaching and learning, ETS invitational conference*, New York, 2005.

[12] Tyack, D. B. *The one best system: A history of American urban education.* Harvard University Press, 1974

Flipped Classroom Strategies for CS Education

Mary Lou Maher, Celine Latulipe, Heather Lipford, Audrey Rorrer
Department of Software and Information Systems and Center for Education Innovation
University of North Carolina Charlotte
{m.maher, clatulip, heather.lipford, audrey.rorrer}@uncc.edu

ABSTRACT

The basic principles of a flipped classroom teaching method are to deliver content outside of the class and to move active learning into the classroom. There are many strategies for delivering the content online, such as having instructors prepare online lectures, wrapping the course around a MOOC, and curating online videos from various sources. There are also many strategies for including active learning in the classroom that go beyond providing programming labs, and can include various forms of peer instruction. In this paper we describe our experiences flipping four different computer science classes across multiple semesters over two years. This breadth of experience with classroom flipping has enabled us to compare strategies and approaches and develop an understanding of which approaches appear to work under which circumstances. We discuss how we structured out-of-class preparatory work, how we created or sourced online videos, how we used active learning activities in-class to scaffold skills development and identify students' misconceptions, and how we structured teams for in class activities. This paper contributes a set of flexible strategies to consider for provision of curricular content out-of-class, structuring students' preparatory work, applying active learning of skills and concepts, and leveraging social interaction and peer instruction for CS education. We present the impact of our approaches based upon leading indicators of course evaluations and student surveys. We discuss lessons learned and students' responses to our strategies.

Categories and Subject Descriptors

K.3.2 [Computer Science Education]

General Terms

Education

Author Keywords

Flipped classroom; online video; strategies for active learning

1. INTRODUCTION

The number of alternative teaching methods being explored in Computer Science (CS) education is increasing in an attempt to address both pedagogical and financial challenges, such as creating active learning experiences with increasing financial pressures [8]. Our department is developing strategies for flipped classroom teaching with a goal to change to this model of teaching for a majority of the courses taught in our Bachelors and Masters degree programs. This is part of a university-wide effort to increase retention and reduce the time to graduation by providing learning activities that engage students in the material with more hands-on experiences and more connection with other students.

SIGCSE'15, March 4–7, 2015, Kansas City, MO, USA.

ACM 978-1-4503-2966-8/15/03 ...$15.00.
http://dx.doi.org/10.1145/2676723. 2677252.

A flipped, or inverted, classroom teaching method has two main components: deliver instructional content outside of the classroom (typically online) and move active learning into the classroom[1]. These two components open up four instructional design challenges: how to structure the student's preparatory work; how to deliver the instructional content out-of-class; how to design active learning activities to use in-class to scaffold learning, identify misconceptions and allow students to practice critical skills; and finally, how to structure student interaction to best leverage social learning and peer instruction. In adopting a flipped classroom approach, strategies for these four instructional design components are varied and flexible.

This paper describes how we have dealt with each of these four instructional design challenges in a variety of different ways, always considering the drain on instructional resources associated with major curricular changes. Flipping classrooms can be resource intensive, especially the first time a class is flipped, though this is similar to the resources required to develop any course from scratch. It is our hope that the experiences we report can help computer science educators better understand the options available to them in converting a CS class to the flipped model.

2. BACKGROUND

Since the earliest attempt to use a flipped classroom method to teach an economics course [9], educators have used this teaching method in many courses including Mathematics [10], Biology [12], Business Management [14], Industrial Engineering [16] and Computer Science [5]. The flipped classroom approach has been used in both small and large courses with hundreds of students. In large classrooms however, the students were divided into smaller groups when they were working on class activities [14].

Flipped courses require students to come to the class after completing significant preparatory work, so that they can participate in the class activities. This prep work typically includes learning materials such as lectures and presentations delivered via podcasts or video-on-demand services [14, 16], but may also include narrated or animated PowerPoint presentations, online tutorials, and textbook reading.

---

[1] http://www.knewton.com/flipped-classroom/

Course	Prep Work Required of Students	Video Sourcing	In-Class Activities	Group/Team work uses	Estimated # Hours Sourcing or Creating Videos
ITIS 3150 (Rapid Prototyping and Interface Building)	Read Textbook, Watch Videos, Take Online Quiz	26 videos created by instructor, 8 videos sourced from web	Creating Prototypes, Testing Prototypes, Critiquing Prototypes, Design Pattern Identification	Ad hoc teams/pairs for in class activities	**300 hours** (videos made over course of three semesters, adding more each offering)
ITIS 6400 (HCI)	Watch Videos, Read Assigned Articles	Stanford HCI MOOC, plus a few videos created	Homework quiz, peer grading of quiz, design and evaluation skill practice activiites such as mock interivews, mock surveys, heuristic evaluations, etc.	Course has semester-long team project, so teams generally sat together in class and did activities together	**30 hours** (reviewing MOOC videos to create homework quizzes, plus time to make extra videos to augment curriculum)
ITIS 2300 (Web Applications Development)	Watch Videos, Critique Videos, Read Textbook (also encouraged to enter programs demonstrated in videos)	Sourced from the web (mostly YouTube and thenewboston.com)	Homework Quizzes, Pseudocode problems, coding demonstrations, other short group activities	Ad hoc teams created in class each week	**40-50 hours** sourcing/reviewing videos
ITIS 1212 (Introduction to Media Programming)	Watch videos, Read Textbook, Enter & Submit Textbook Programs, Take Online Quiz	95% sourced from the web, about 5 videos created by instructor	Peer instruction clicker quizzes, pseudocode problems, Parsons' problems, peer critiquing of solutions	Assigned lightweight teams of five students sit together and do all activities together	**70 hours** sourcing/revieiwng and creating videos

Table 1: Flipped classes, their structure elements, and hours spent on video prep by instructors.

Active learning is a central component of the flipped class teaching method [1]. Students spend time in-class working on activities such as solving problems, writing code, design tasks, or discussing concepts with others. This creates a learning environment where students learn by collaborating with their peers. Many studies have shown that working with peers in-class activities improves overall learning, increases student confidence and makes coding fun [5, 7]. Classroom quizzes have also been used as an effective mode of instructor-student interaction and many new technologies including 'Clickers' have successfully been used to foster learning through quizzing [11].

Developing material for flipped classrooms is a challenging task and different instructors have used different approaches. Some institutions and instructors are already recording their lectures for the purpose of online courses, which makes it easy for these instructors to leverage those resources in their flipped classes [4, 5, 16]. However, this tends to mean very long videos are created. Recorded lectures are not liked by all students as many reported that sometimes the lectures were too long and not suited for difficult course materials [4]. Most students suggested that optimal length of video lectures should be 15-30 minutes [5, 16].

The amount of time required to prepare for a flipped class depends on the amount of content to be provided to the students. Some instructors have reported 35 hours of work to create an hour of lecture material [8], while others have reported less [3]. Instructors are also required to develop in-class learning activities and quizzes. The amount of time required for grading also increases as weekly learning activities need to be evaluated regularly [4].

In this paper we add to this literature with a focus on the strategies appropriate for learning both skills and concepts associated with computing courses. Specifically, we have developed and applied our strategies to an introductory programming course, a web application development course, a rapid prototyping and interface building course and a human-computer interaction (HCI) course. In the following section we describe these courses and how they developed into flipped classes. We then compare our various approaches to assigning preparatory work to students, to delivering instructional content online, to development of strategies for in-class activities, and to structuring group work. We discuss preliminary results showing a trend towards a positive attitude from students on the benefits of flipped classrooms.

3. FLIPPED COMPUTING COURSES

We developed our strategies for flipped classrooms for 4 different courses, which have each been taught multiple times. These courses, the terms they were taught and their enrollments are shown in Table 2, ordered by when these classes began to be flipped. We began to formally study our flipped class approaches in 2013, so there is no survey data for earlier semesters.

Course	Semester	Enrollment	Responses	Response Rate
ITIS 3150 (Rapid Prototyping and Interface Building)	Fall 2012	33		
	Spring 2013	30		
	Fall 2013	40	29	73%
ITIS 6400/8400 (Graduate HCI)	Spring 2013	11		
	Spring 2014	50	41	82%
ITIS 2300 (Web Applications Development)	Spring 2013	93		
	Fall 2013	75	61	81%
	Spring 2014	66	36	55%
ITIS 1212 (Introduction to Media Computation)	Fall 2013	87		
	Spring 2014	62	46	74%

Table 2: Flipped classes, enrollments and survey response rates across different semesters.

Rapid Prototyping and Interface Building: This is an upper year course with typically 30-40 students in a class. The topics covered include methods for quickly prototyping a user interface using sketches, paper mock-ups, wireframes, and interactive digital prototypes, as well as how to create coded prototypes using a GUI builder. Students learn a vocabulary of design patterns and learn how to create and critique many alternative designs. This class was originally developed as a traditional lecture class that was augmented by occasional hands-on activities. Over a few years, the instructor slowly migrated the class to a flipped class structure, creating more videos each time the course was offered.

Human Computer Interaction: This is a graduate level course with 10-50 students in the class. The topics covered include need-finding methods, prototyping, design, and evaluation. This class was originally developed as a traditional lecture class, augmented with occasional activities. The instructors were beginning to develop videos to flip this class when Coursera began offering the HCI MOOC course. The isntructors then requested and received permission from Coursera and the Corsera instructor to 'wrap' the HCI course around the MOOC videos.

Web Applications Development: This is a 2000 level course with typically 60-90 students in a class. The topics learned include various web services languages (html, css, javascript, and jquery), as well as design and layout considerations. This class was originally taught in a traditional lecture format, but was fully flipped beginning in 2013. The videos in this class have been curated from various online sources.

Introduction to Media Computation: This is a newly introduced introductory programming course in which students learn Java through a media computation approach [5]. This class has a typical enrollment of 60-100 students. This class was developed over the summer of 2013, and was designed as a flipped class from the start. Thus, no effort was expended creating lectures or slides, rather, significant effort was put into curating introductory programming videos from the web and developing labs, active learning activities and peer instruction quizzes.

4. STRUCTURING THE WORKFLOW

There are many alternatives for structuring the timing for the delivery of learning materials and activities in a flipped classroom. Here we present alternatives for temporal flow of learning and the expectations for students' preparatory work, finishing with some lessons learned.

4.1 Temporal Flow

The temporal structure each week is: students engage with the online instructional content as their preparatory work first and then participate in small group activities during the scheduled class times. In the programming courses a weekly group activity is a programming lab session where they try out the new skills in a structured lab activity with pair programming. In all flipped courses, students engage in group activities such as role playing, design and critique, and problem solving. For the programming courses, the programming lab is scheduled before the problem solving activity so that they can reflect on the skills learned in lab.

4.2 Preparatory Work

While standard classes may have assigned reading for homework, it is often the case that students have no real incentive to complete the reading, since the material will be covered in lecture. Because there is no lecture in flipped classes, the preparatory work is the *only* way for students to get the needed instructional content. Table 1 shows the variety of preparatory work assigned across the four different classes. In all cases there are readings and videos. In the Media Computation and Rapid Prototyping class students were required to complete a Moodle quiz designed to check that they had completed the prep work *before* attending class. In the web application and HCI class, quizzes on the homework were an activity completed in class. Students in the programming courses were required or encouraged to enter the programs from the videos and/or textbook as part of their prep work.

4.3 Lessons Learned

Having students practice skills before diving deeply into discussions of conceptual material allows the discussion of concepts to be contextualized in the activities already completed. This makes class activities and discussion less abstract and much more meaningful. We also found that providing explicit structure is helpful, particularly for freshmen, as there are more course components to track. The Moodle (the UNCC LMS) auto-completion feature was useful to specify the order in which preparatory activities had to be completed, and allowed us to deny access to items like quizzes until other preparatory activities were marked complete.

In early semesters students expressed initial concerns about having graded labs, quizzes, and activities prior to some sort of in-class discussion or instruction by a faculty member. We found that as we improved upon the structure, communicating the purpose and benefits of that structure alleviated many of these concerns.

5. PROVISIONING VIDEO INSTRUCTION

Here we outline three strategies for providing video instruction and our lessons learned.

5.1 Creating videos

The first strategy is to create our own videos, although this is the most time consuming. There were very few online resources available for the Rapid Prototyping course, so the only option was to develop and record customized video lectures. As has been previously noted, video preparation was time consuming because online lectures are shorter than a traditional classroom lecture. Because of the time involved, the instructor took two semesters to convert all lectures into succinct, effective videos. Videos were also created to fill gaps in the out sourced videos for the Media Computation and HCI courses.

5.2 Curating videos

Collecting and curating online videos has many advantages. In the Media Computation and Web Applications courses we curated multiple online videos for each topic covered. We found videos through YouTube and other instructional sites, and included videos from a variety of authors. We also recommended optional videos for additional resources or for more advanced students. Many videos showed a computer screen, with the author typing and narrating a code example. Videos ranged in length from 5 to 35 minutes.

Curating videos became a part of the learning experience for the students. In the Web Applications class students were required to provide critiques of the videos they watched. The students' critiques gave us insight into what aspects of the video instruction they understood, liked and disliked. Through the critique, the students articulated their understanding of the role of the video instruction and how it contributes to their learning. Since this critique was submitted by the students on a weekly basis rather than at the end of the semester, it became part of their learning experience.

5.3 Wrapping a MOOC

In the HCI course, we used the videos from the Coursera HCI course[2], with permission from Coursera and from Scott Klemmer, the instructor of the MOOC. We made the videos available from a link on the UNCC course page or students could visit the Coursera page. The Coursera content matched our needs for lecture-based content, and we added supplemental content for additional topics.

[2] https://www.coursera.org/course/hciucsd

5.4 Lessons Learned

Each instructor gathered or developed videos as best fit their course. The right-most column of Table 1 gives an estimate of instructional time dedicated to creating and/or curating videos across the different courses. Even when videos are curated rather than created, the process of curating videos for a whole course takes a significant amount of time.

We wanted the students to benefit from learning course concepts from more than one perspective. This was particularly important in the Web Applications course, where students had a wide range of expertise from those who had never seen HTML to some who had taken courses in high school or even had some job experience. Providing a range of videos let students find resources that matched their current experience levels and expanded upon what we could cover during the semester.

Students utilized the video resources differently than a lecture, particularly for programming topics. They commented that they were able to follow along with the code on their own, and pause, rewind, and replay as needed. Presenting such examples inside a classroom, with students following along on their own computers, is much more difficult. One student said: *"The good thing about videos is you can pause/play as you please and rewind/fastforward when necessary,..."*

The use of videos from various authors demonstrated the variety of resources that exist on the Internet to help teach and provide examples of code and programming concepts. The diversity in resources promotes self-exploration to students, which they demonstrated later in their homework. Many referred back to the video tutorials while completing their homework, something that is not possible if the lecture is only available live in class. One student posted: *"As I am finishing up my final website, I am going back over the video tutorials for last minute help and ideas. They are much easier to understand at the end of the semester!"*

However, a disadvantage of curated videos was that they did not always present a topic at a conceptual level, nor were they tailored to the common misunderstandings or challenges that students in a particular class have. Students often described situations in which the author of the video didn't present information clearly. *"I thought these videos were very unhelpful. The guy just seems to be putting code on the screen and keeps saying "we will get to that later" and just continues to build his website."*

To alleviate some of these issues, we provided a brief high level conceptual explanation in class the week prior to the topic. However, some students reported this was not sufficient and they would have appreciated more conceptual information within the videos themselves. We are considering the addition of our own short conceptual lecture videos to address this issue.

Another drawback of online instruction is that watching videos is a solitary activity. We are trialing opportunities for students to comment, critique, and reflect on online videos in a more social way, through the Video Collaboratory [14]. The Video Collaboratory is an online system that allows groups of students to privately and asynchronously discuss videos through text and sketch annotations. For example, in our current HCI course, students are required to watch the videos inside the Collaboratory, and annotate them weekly. Members of the group can view each other's annotations and add to the discussion. We plan to extend the use of the Collaboratory to more courses as we gain experience in its use. We believe that the 'shared watching experience' in small groups of 5-10 students creates a more intimate and less intimidating forum for discussion around educational videos.

6. IN-CLASS ACTIVITIES

In addition to creating or collecting online videos, one of the other major challenges for flipped classroom instruction is creating class activities that teach course concepts and skills through active learning. For our programming courses, labs are a critical active learning component. But, the real challenge is to find active learning activities to replace the time that would traditionally be used for lecturing. We have developed two main types of in-class activities: group problem solving and flexible quiz activities.

6.1 Pair Programming Labs

Similar to many programming courses, the Web Applications and Media Computation courses include weekly pair programming lab sessions. Typically, students were asked to edit and extend existing code. In later parts of the course students had to code from scratch. The tasks covered specific skills and language constructs each week. Lab activities were carefully structured to enable completion within the time allocated, assuming the student had prepared. We have tested many strategies for pairing students in the lab, including gender pairing and randomly changing the pair each week or every other week. The purpose of switching partners frequently is to help the students get to know a larger number of students in their class and to make sure that students don't play the same role with the same person each week.

The use of pair programming was successful, and seemed to encourage students to work both with their partner, and over time with other students, to answer questions and learn new techniques. Alternating the pairs was also important, as the skill and knowledge level of students was quite varied.

6.2 Group Problem Solving Activities

For the non-programming courses, and on the non-lab day for the programming-based courses, the problem solving activity is a highly structured activity that is timed. Typically, students work in small groups to encourage conversation and peer instruction. In the HCI and Rapid Prototyping classes, these activities generally involved students practicing design and evaluation skills. For example, in the HCI class, when teaching needfinding, one or two students in a group were asked to develop a persona and role play a typical user, while the others in the group prepared interview questions and conducted an interview. In Rapid Prototyping, student groups utilized different techniques to create prototypes at different levels of fidelity. In Web Applications, activities included finding existing web pages to demonstrate weekly topics, drawing conceptual diagrams and writing pseudo-code. In Media Computation students often solved problems by writing pseudo-code or doing other paper problem solving activities.

In all courses, we emphasize collaboration and critiquing. These activities are then built upon later when students complete their assignments, which test their application of the learned skills without teacher supervision. In the HCI and Rapid Prototyping courses, students can re-use and extend some of their in-class activities as part of their assignments.

6.2 Flexible Quiz Activities

In flipped classrooms, instructors often use quizzes to incentivize students to watch videos and come to class prepared. We also use quizzes as learning activities, especially in the programming courses. This idea is based on the finding that retrieving information from memory improves long term retention [13]. The quiz generally comprised multiple choice questions about textbook and video content, or about code fragments. In contrast to the problem solving activity, the quiz tests and reinforces conceptual knowledge where the problem solving activity provides scaffolding for programming skills or HCI methods.

Throughout the four courses, different techniques were used to make the quiz an activity that encouraged peer learning and the discovery and clarification of misconceptions. We developed several strategies for student interaction around quizzes:

1. Students complete the quiz labeled only with their id number. Quizzes are redistributed to others for peer grading. The instructor directs the peer grading by discussing why particular answers are right or wrong for each question.
2. Students complete the quiz on their own, and then are asked to compare and discuss their answers with the students sitting near them until all students sitting near each other have the same answers. Each student's quiz is graded separately.
3. Students form groups and each group completes a quiz, again, ensuring that the answers are the consensus of the group. All students in a group get the same grade.
4. Students complete the quiz using clickers and can talk to each other before answering. The answers are aggregated on the screen in front of the room, and instructors re-poll as needed. Various game-like methods are used to create competition.
5. Student groups create a quiz based on their annotated videos. Each group takes another group's quiz and the group that created the quiz grades the answers. In this way each group creates a quiz, takes a quiz, and grades a quiz.

In all variations on the way the quiz was administered, the quiz provided the focus for the peer learning and the discovery of misconceptions. When misconceptions were uncovered, the instructors conducted impromptu mini-lectures. Thus, the quiz activities could often take up a significant portion of a class.

6.3 Lessons Learned

All of the in-class activities are designed to be collaborative in some way. We promote peer instruction for the following reasons: the social aspect of peer instruction helps students get to know other students and making friends is important for program retention; when students are socially relaxed they are likely to learn more; some students have an easier time learning from peers than from professors; learning from peers demonstrates that there are many sources of knowledge; learning from peers exposes students to different perspectives on issues; and, teaching peers helps students clarify and solidify their own understanding of course concepts.

In programming labs, we use pair programming with frequent partner switches throughout the semester. In our workshop classes we facilitate student collaborations in a variety of ways. In HCI there is a high-stakes group project and teams typically sit together and work together on in-class activities. In the Web Applications and Rapid Prototyping courses, ad hoc groups or pairs are formed for in-class activities. This works well in upper year classes where students are typically comfortable forming teams and students have friends that they want to work with.

In the Media Computation course, we created lightweight teams consisting of 5 students per team. These teams sit together in assigned seating during the peer instruction workshops each week. These teams are called 'lightweight' because there is no direct link between team activities and an individual's final grade, though the team works together all semester. We find this works well for freshmen courses where students don't know many people.

We found that emphasizing skill development during class activities enabled us to create more open-ended homework assignments that encouraged creativity. For example, in the Web Applications course, students created a website to promote a business or hobby. Many of the websites created were more professional, with greater content, than assignments from prior (non-flipped) years.

7. STUDENT FEEDBACK

The standard student evaluation forms administered at the end of the semester typically start with statements about the instructor. For example "My instructor displays a clear understanding of the course topics." "My instructor has an effective style of presentation." These create an impression that the quality of the course depends on how much the instructor knows rather than on how much the student learned. While it may be appropriate to evaluate the quality of the instructor, flipped classrooms require a survey that primes students to think about the quality of their learning experience. We administered a survey to gather student perceptions about the flipped classroom approach to provide formative evaluation and immediate feedback from students.

Survey Item	Mean	SD
I felt I was more able to learn at my own pace (compared to previous courses).	5.06	1.41
I was more able to recognize when I didn't understand something (compared to previous courses).	5.00	1.34
I looked at extra information beyond the provided material (compared to previous courses).	4.54	1.60
I felt that I learned more during class time (compared to previous courses).	4.89	1.59
I felt that I learned more outside of class time (compared to previous courses).	4.81	1.54
How helpful were the online videos for learning?	5.17	1.48
Learning from other students is just as good as learning from the teacher.	4.76	1.47
Other students helped me to understand the right answers while we were discussing clicker questions.	5.04	1.17
I helped other students to understand the right answers while we were discussing clicker questions.	4.97	1.20
Explaining things to other students helped me to understand them better.	5.35	1.09
How mentally demanding was the course?	4.55	1.24
How successful were you in accomplishing what you were asked to do in this course?	4.35	1.72
How hard did you have to work to accomplish your level of performance in this course?	4.95	1.36

Table 3: Post course student survey average responses.

The post-course survey was conducted across four courses with responses from a total of 213 students. While each survey contained course-specific items, the common part of the survey consisted of 13 Likert-type items with a 7-point rating scale, with

7 being strong agree/very high. There were also three open-ended items inquiring about likes, dislikes and suggestions. The majority of students were pleased with the flipped course approach. The majority of items received positive ratings above 4, with average ratings above 5, and with low standard deviations, an indication of consistency in ratings. Item means are presented in Table 3. Highest average ratings were "explaining things to others," and the online videos. Students also reported moderate to high ratings of feeling successful in the courses.

Themes from the open-ended items indicated that the students were more engaged with the material and with their peers as a result of this approach. The majority of comments were positive and suggest that students liked having hands-on engagement. For example, *"I liked the fact that it was more hands-on than other classes;"* and *"I liked how the lab actually helped me learn in the class and all of the videos were helpful."* Responding to the disliked item, students indicated that they needed more lab time to complete assignments, and a few suggested that having quizzes before lab was undesirable. The majority of students presented constructive feedback, with only a minority complaining about wanting more in-class lecture. While early informal feedback indicated concern about the lack of lectures, most students' perceptions changed by the end of the semester when we had them complete the survey and they had positive responses to learning concepts from online videos. However, a small percentage of students at the end of the semester presented concerns about this approach to teaching: *"We were graded on topics not covered then lectured after;"* and *"time spent outside of the classroom watching videos made me feel like the class was online."* These comments show that even at the end of the semester, a few students had not realized that the content provided in the online instruction and the textbook was part of the learning experience. We are responding to this concern by better communicating our intentions and pedagogical goals.

8. CONCLUSIONS

We have presented our experiences in developing flipped courses: the temporal structure, alternative sources for video instruction and strategies for active learning. Video instruction precedes skills development and concept learning, in-class lab activities scaffold for open ended homework projects and promote peer learning, and in-class quizzes lead to discovery of misconceptions. We have shown how these strategies were implemented across a variety of computing courses and how student perceptions are generally positive about the learning experience. The perception of instructors not spending sufficient time on teaching is important to address, particularly since this method can involve more preparation time (see Table 1) than a traditional class.

Future directions for investigating the impact of this method are analyses of student learning outcomes, including comparisons of grade performance before and after the implementation of the flipped classroom approach, and analyses of subsequent course outcomes as we determine how well this approach prepares students in their academic progression.

9. REFERENCES

[1] Auster, E. R., & Wylie, K. K. (2006). Creating active learning in the classroom: A systematic approach. *Journal of Management Education*, *30*(2), 333-353.

[2] Bruff, D., Fisher, D., McEwen, K. and Smith, B. 2013. Wrapping a MOOC: Student perceptions of an experiment in blended learning. *Journal of Online Learning and Teaching*. 9, 2 (Accepted 2013).

[3] Day, J.A. and Foley, J.D. 2006. Evaluating a Web Lecture Intervention in a Human-Computer Interaction Course. *IEEE Transactions on Education*. 49, 4 (2006), 420–431.

[4] Gannod, G.C., Burge, J.E. and Helmick, M.T. 2008. Using the inverted classroom to teach software engineering. *ACM/IEEE 30th International Conference on Software Engineering, 2008. ICSE '08* (2008), 777–786.

[5] Gehringer, E.F. and Peddycord,III, B.W. 2013. The inverted-lecture model: a case study in computer architecture. *Proceeding of the 44th ACM technical symposium on Computer science education* (New York, NY, USA, 2013), 489–494.

[6] Mark Guzdial. 2013. Exploring hypotheses about media computation. In *Proceedings of the ninth annual international ACM conference on International computing education research* (ICER '13). ACM, New York, NY, USA, 19-26.

[7] Hanks, B. 2006. Student attitudes toward pair programming. *Proceedings of the 11th annual SIGCSE conference on Innovation and technology in computer science education* (New York, NY, USA, 2006), 113–117.

[8] Kaner, C. and Fiedler, R. 2005. Inside Out: A Computer Science Course Gets a Makeover. (2005).

[9] Lage, M.J., Platt, G.J. and Treglia, M. 2000. Inverting the Classroom: A Gateway to Creating an Inclusive Learning Environment. *The Journal of Economic Education*. 31, 1 (Jan. 2000), 30–43.

[10] Lockwood, K. and Esselstein, R. 2013. The inverted classroom and the CS curriculum. *Proceeding of the 44th ACM technical symposium on Computer science education* (New York, NY, USA, 2013), 113–118.

[11] Mayer, R., Stull, A., Almeroth, K., Bimber, B., Chun, D., Bulger, M., Campbell, J., Knight, A. and Zhang, H. *Using Technology-Based Methods to Foster Learning in Large Lecture Classes: Evidence for the Pedagogic Value of Clickers*.

[12] Moravec, M., Williams, A., Aguilar-Roca, N. and O'Dowd, D.K. 2010. Learn before lecture: A strategy that improves learning outcomes in a large introductory biology class. *CBE life sciences education*. 9, 4 (2010), 473–481.

[13] Roediger, H.L. and Karpicke, J.D. 2006. Test-enhanced learning: taking memory tests improves long-term retention. *Psychological science*. 17, 3 (2006), 249–255.

[14] Schullery, N.M., Reck, R.F. and Schullery, S. 202. Toward solving the high enrollment, low engagement dilemma: A case study in introductory business. *International Journal of Business, Humanities and Technology*. 1, 2 (2011), 1–9.

[15] Singh, V., Latulipe, C., Carroll, E., and Lottridge, D. The Choreographers Notebook A video annotation system for dancers and choreographers. In ACM Creativity & Cognition 2011. ACM, 197-206, 2011.

[16] Toto, R. and Nguyen, H. 2009. Flipping the work design in an industrial engineering course. *Proceedings of the 39th IEEE international conference on Frontiers in education conference* (Piscataway, NJ, USA, 2009), 1066–1069.

The Effectiveness of Video Quizzes in a Flipped Class

Lisa L. Lacher
School of Science and Computer Engineering
University of Houston - Clear Lake
2700 Bay Area Blvd.
Houston, TX, USA
Lacher@uhcl.edu

Mark C. Lewis
Department of Computer Science
Trinity University
1 Trinity Place
San Antonio, TX, USA
mlewis@trinity.edu

ABSTRACT

The use of online videos and flipped classrooms is a natural fit for many CS courses, especially in the introductory sequence, and the use of these techniques is growing. However, the benefits of these techniques depend heavily on student preparation before class meetings. This paper presents tests of the effectiveness of basic multiple choice quizzes as gateway checks in a flipped classroom by looking at the impact they have on student grades. Programming aptitude and learning approaches were considered as additional factors. Ignoring aptitude and learning approaches, statistical analysis of the student grades did not support our hypothesis that the gate-check video quizzes would be beneficial. Nor did it support our hypothesis that the benefit of quizzes would be greatest for students who had lower aptitudes entering the class. However, there was some evidence that it might have helped raise the grades of students who have a propensity toward surface learning.

Categories and Subject Descriptors

K.3.2 [**Computer and Information Science Education**]: Computer Science Education

General Terms

Measurement

Keywords

flipped classroom; CS1; video quizzes

1. INTRODUCTION

The concept of a flipped classroom, where students are introduced to material outside of class and class time is used to apply that material, has gained significant momentum in the past several years with the advent of ubiquitous online videos and simple playback. The idea is that students watch the videos, which contain normal lecture material, before coming to class then spend their time in class doing exercises or assignments. This approach has been embraced in Computer Science, as it allows students to spend more of their valuable class time doing hands-on activities instead of sitting passively absorbing information [11, 19, 10, 1]. In the ideal implementation, students figure out in class what things they don't fully understand, and are able to ask the instructor for clarification at that time.

Of course, the effectiveness of this approach depends significantly on students showing up to class prepared. Earlier studies have shown mixed results based on how well students prepare. Students who fail to watch the videos in advance will generally be completely lost during the class time, which one would expect to lead to inferior learning outcomes. If a sufficient fraction of the class fails to prepare, the instructor can be forced to revert to a standard lecture format to make sure that students are getting the most important material. This can be hard to prevent as often both the students and the instructor have a long history with the traditional lecture format, and are comfortable using it.

For this reason, it would be beneficial for instructors who use a flipped classroom approach to find a mechanism that will increase the odds that students will show up to class having done the recommended preparation work. The goal of this study was to see if having an element of the course grade come from online, multiple-choice quizzes over the video material, taken prior to each class meeting, was effective in this regard. Early results of this study, including grades up to the course midterm were presented in [14]. The primary hypothesis in this earlier paper was that pre-class video quizzes (gate-check quizzes) would help students earn better grades, which we assumed would indicated that better grades would correlate with better prepared students. The midterm grade results did not support this hypothesis and we speculated that the quizzes failed because they did not facilitate deep learning. The secondary hypothesis in the earlier paper was that the pre-class video quizzes would help students with lower computer programming aptitudes perform better in the course. We found that the midterm grade results did not support this hypothesis either. In fact, the results indicated that it was the higher aptitude students who benefited most from having the video quizzes. This work adds additional grades to the analysis, and also takes into account student learning approaches, which were not considered previously.

SIGCSE'15, March 4–7, 2015, Kansas City, MO, USA.

http://dx.doi.org/10.1145/2676723.2677302.

2. EXPERIMENTAL DESIGN

These classes were taught using [16]. A full set of video lectures, done as screencasts, have been posted publicly on YouTube [15] for any instructors to use in flipping their classrooms. Students were required to watch these videos in advance of covering each chapter in class. This study was done in the spring of 2014 with three sections of CS1 taught at Trinity University by two different faculty. To determine the effectiveness of the video quizzes, some sections (experimental group) were given quizzes that counted as 10% of their grade in the course whereas other sections did not take the video quizzes and therefore could not be graded on them (control group).

The students were also given three surveys at the beginning of the semester.

- A background information survey to collect data such as their major and their previous background with programming.
- The University of Kent Programming Aptitude Test [18], to measure the students aptitude for programming upon entering the course.
- A learning approaches survey from Royal Free & University College Medical School, London, UK to measure if students had a tendency toward surface, deep, or achievement learning.

We consider eight written assessments given during the course of the semester: six written quizzes, the midterm, and the final exam. Some of the students were required to take gate-check video quizzes. These quizzes were done online before class began and included a mix of multiple choice, true/false, and matching questions that were automatically graded. Students were given multiple attempts at the quizzes. After some experimentation early in the semester, we settled on giving students two attempts to get correct answers for the quizzes.

As the name, gate-check video quiz, implies, these quizzes were created to be simple gate-checks, not assessment of deep learning or skills that the students acquired from watching the videos. The questions were generally simple to answer if students had actually watched the videos. They were also presented in the order that they appeared in the videos. The entire goal of these video quizzes was to provide a strong incentive for students to watch the videos, not to stress items that were important, or to facilitate their learning of the material in the videos.

2.1 Programming Aptitude Test

The programming aptitude test developed at the University of Kent [18] includes twenty six questions that deal with numerical problem solving, logical reasoning, attention to detail, pattern recognition, and the ability to follow complex procedures. It does not involve code/programming topics directly. This makes it appropriate for introductory CS students, as it tests them on skills that are significant for the task of programming without actually testing their knowledge of programming. Students were given forty minutes to complete this test.

2.2 Approaches to Learning and Studying

Students approach studying in different ways, and the way a student approaches a learning task should have an effect on the quality of their learning. One learning theory approach draws a distinction between deep and surface learners [17].

Students who use a deep learning approach intend to look for meaning in study materials. They will sift out general principles and concepts and then relate these concepts to prior knowledge or everyday life by closely examining the material's content. This type of student generally has an interest in the subject; and this interest may be derived from the subject being vocationally relevant, or the student may just want to personally understand the material.

The main desire of students who use a surface learning approach is to only meet a task's requirements such as passing an exam. They want to limit what they have to learn to the bare essentials and they have little real interest in the content. The most common strategy adopted by students using surface learning is rote learning or memorizing the study materials instead of understanding them [17]. Some researchers found that the difference between deep learners and surface learners could be explained by an active or passive attitude to learning [5]. Distinctions between deep and surface learning are also made, where motivation increases deep-level processing and anxiety increases surface-level processing [8]. Surface learners fear failure.

Besides the distinction between the deep and surface approach to learning, further research added a third approach to learning: the achieving (or strategic) approach [4]. This is an achieving orientation, which is about maximizing performance while optimizing efforts to achieve it. The student does this by using whatever technique (deep or surface) that will produce the highest grade, and organizing their time in an effective way to fulfill course requirements [20].

Learning approaches have been reported to have an impact on the outcome of learning; high academic achievement has been positively related to a deep or strategic approach and negatively related to a surface approach [6, 7]. This relationship occurs provided that the assessment requires high levels of understanding from the students [2]. It is generally assumed that the deep learning approach results in higher quality learning outcomes than the surface learning approach [13, 12]. In other words, students who employ more surface learning strategies will not perform as well as students who employ more deep learning strategies. It is also interesting to note, that a deep learning approach has a positive impact on self-directed lifelong learning [2].

2.2.1 Measuring Learning Approaches

The Study Process Questionnaire (SPQ) is a widely used measure of learning approach. Students' scores on the scales of the SPQ are most naturally interpreted as measuring their predispositions to adopt different approaches to learning. The Biggs Study Process Questionnaire (SPQ) is a diagnostic tool to identify the learning approaches of the students. The SPQ, a forty two item questionnaire, provides feedback on the learning approaches in the three dimensions, namely, the surface, deep and achieving dimensions which are further broken down into motives and strategies used. Fox et. al [9] created a shortened eighteen item version of the SPQ and conducted a longitudinal study to measure the stability of the instrument over five to seven years. They concluded that the shortened eighteen item SPQ has proven reliable and stable. Because the eighteen item version was easier to administer to students, we choose to use the shortened SPQ developed by Fox et. al. in our study [9].

2.3 Hypotheses

We had three hypotheses related to requiring the gate-check video quizzes as a means of enforcing that students prepare before coming to class.

1. The students taking the gate-check video quizzes have higher grades on the assessments than those who do not have to take the video quizzes.

2. Students with lower aptitude in programming benefit more from the gate-check video quizzes than those who do not.

3. Students who have a propensity for shallow learning benefit more from the gate-check video quizzes than those who have a propensity for deep learning.

The logic behind the first hypothesis is the reason why we considered making the gate-check video quizzes in the first place. Flipped classrooms only work well when students come to class prepared, and having students participate well in class should improve their grades. The second hypothesis is based on the belief that high aptitude students generally do well and probably would not benefit much from the quizzes, while low aptitude students really need the preparation that the video quizzes provide. The third hypothesis is similar to the second one. Our assumption is that those with a propensity for shallow learning will typically do poorly in CS1 compared to those with a propensity for deep learning. As such, shallow learners have the most to gain. We also believed that the videos, which show live coding and the logic that goes into creating code, would lead students who normally tend toward shallow learning to actually make deeper connections in the material.

2.4 Participants

There were forty seven undergraduate students enrolled in the three sections of Principles of Computer Science I course at Trinity University during the spring semester of 2014. Thirty-two of these students participated in the study and completed quizzes and tests. These sections were taught by two different professors and each section included between fifteen and eighteen students. All students were urged to watch the videos and/or read the book before attending class. Two of the sections, one taught by each instructor, included the gate-check video quizzes as part of their grades.

2.5 Artifacts

The courses used identical written quizzes and tests. The quizzes were graded by a student grader using a rubric developed by the instructors. The exams were graded by the instructors, with each instructor grading all of a particular question, so that each question was graded uniformly across all sections.

Students also completed coding assignments, but those are not included in this study because the results tend to be Boolean in nature. Students who put in the time and effort to complete the assignments get full or nearly full marks, while those who do not get few, if any, points. As we don't have any method of determining how much time and effort students put into the coding assignments, assignment grades to not provide a useful way to analyze the impact of the gate-check video quizzes.

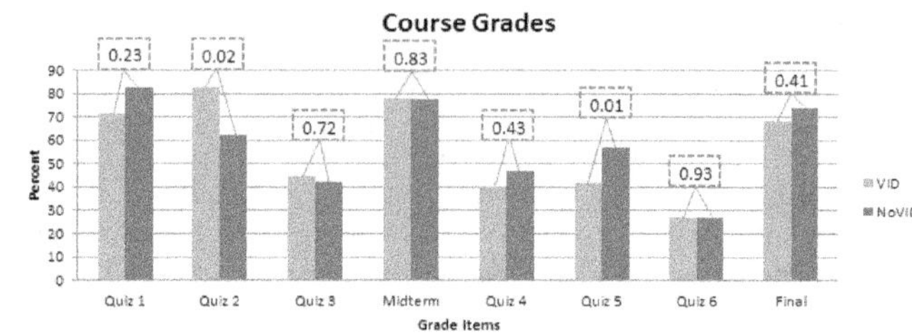

Figure 1: This figure compares the quiz and test grade averages for students who did (VID) and did not (NoVID) have to take the gate-check video quizzes. The differences are generally small. The number above each pair of grades is the t-test p value. Only the p value for quizzes 2 and 5 are below the $\alpha = 0.5$ criteria for significance.

3. ANALYSIS AND RESULTS

To check the first hypothesis, we look at the grades for the different assessments, comparing results from students who had to do the gate-check video quizzes to those who did not. The results of such a comparison are shown in Figure 1. This figure makes it clear that there were not large differences between the two groups. An independent samples t-test was performed on each of these different grades and only quizzes 2 and 5 have a statistically significant difference of $p < \alpha$ for $\alpha = 0.05$. In the case of quiz 2, the students who were taking the gate-check video quizzes scored higher, while the opposite was true for quiz 5.

It is also interesting to note that while the results were very mixed in the first half of the semester, up to the midterm, the group that did not use the gate-check video quizzes had higher grades for all the quizzes after the midterm and the final exam. Granted, the difference was only statistically significant for quiz 5.

These results lead us to conclude that our first hypothesis was incorrect. The gate-check video quizzes did not have a significant positive impact on student grades. Fortunately, they don't have a significant negative impact either.

To test the second hypothesis, we divide the students into three categories, as prescribed by the creators of the programming aptitude test. Students who correctly answered nineteen or more of the twenty-six questions are said to have a high aptitude. Students who correctly answered between thirteen and eighteen questions have an average aptitude. Those who correctly answered fewer than thirteen questions have a low aptitude.

Figure 2 shows a weighted average of the quizzes and tests for each of these aptitude groups for all the students. The average shown is calculated as a weighted average of the student's quiz and exam averages, with the quizzes counting as one third and the exams counting as two thirds. The first thing to note about this is that in both groups, higher aptitudes are correlated with higher grades. It should also be noted that the group that did not take the gate-check video quizzes did not include any low aptitude students. This is the first evidence that our student distribution was not very uniform.

The relative performance of the students in each of the aptitude levels across the VID and NoVID groups is made clearer if we bin the students together by whether they are

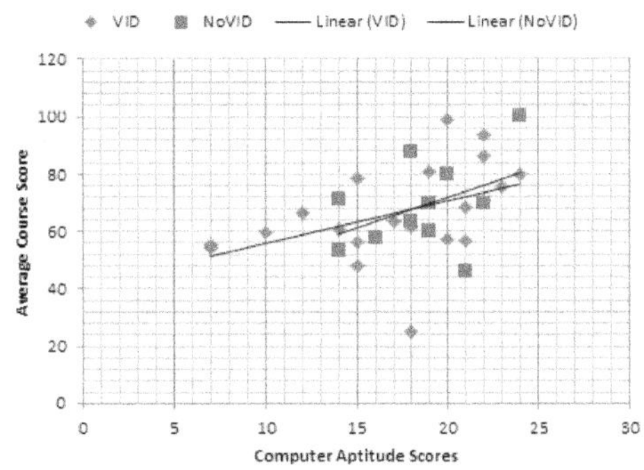

Figure 2: This figure shows weighted course averages as a function of student aptitudes. For both the VID and NoVID groups, there is a positive correlation between aptitude and grades, but there is no clear separation between the VID and NoVID groups.

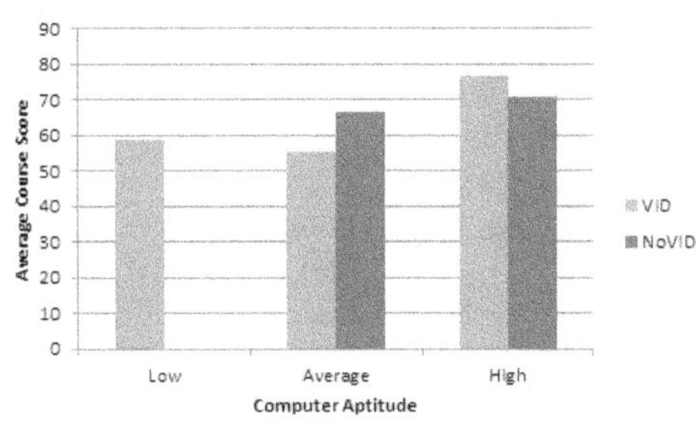

Figure 3: This figure shows weighted course averages binned by student aptitudes. There were no low aptitude students in the NoVID group. The differences in the average and high aptitude groups are not statistically significant according to a t-test.

high, average, or low aptitude. This produces Figure 3. Standard t-tests show that neither the difference in the average aptitude groups, nor the high aptitude groups are statistically significant. For this reason, we have to conclude that our second hypothesis was also false, and that the gate-check quizzes do not have a significant impact on the non-high aptitude students. Unfortunately, the lack of low aptitude students in the NoVID group makes it harder to draw additional conclusions. The average grade of the low aptitude students in the VID group is higher than those in the average aptitude group, but this is largely because of a single outlier in the average group with a very low grade. Reasonable extrapolations for the performance of the NoVID low aptitude students would put them in a range that is consistent with those in the VID group.

To test the third hypothesis, we first looked at the distribution of learning approaches between the students who did and did not take the gate-check video quizzes. This is shown in Figure 4. The p values shown above each style indicate that the differences for the surface and deep approaches are statistically significant, while that for achievement learners is not.

According to [3], students who tend toward deep learning do better in CS1. Based on this, and the skew in our sample,

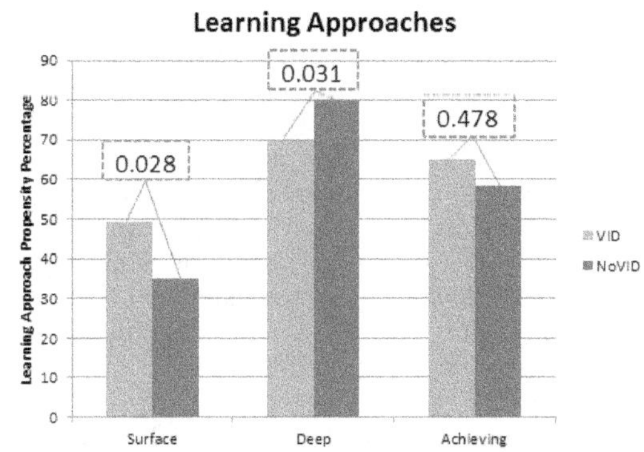

Figure 4: This figure shows how students answered the learning approaches quizzes. For each approach there were several questions which students could answer as tending toward or away from that approach. The vertical axis shows what percentage of the questions were answered in the style of that approach across all students in both the VID and NoVID samples. Our distribution of students was skewed in a statistically significant way such that the NoVID students had a greater average tendency toward deep learning, while the VID students had a greater average tendency toward surface learning.

we would expect that the students who were not taking the gate-check video quizzes should have higher grades on average than those who were taking the video quizzes. However, as was shown in Figure 1, this is not the case. Instead, the two groups had grades that were statistically indistinguishable. This provides some evidence that the third hypothesis might actually be correct, and that the gate-check video quizzes helped to boost the grades of the students who had a propensity for surface learning sufficiently to bring them in line with those who had a propensity for deep learning. Unfortunately, we have not been able to pull apart the effects of the gate-check video quizzes and the learning approaches in our data, so this is weak support for the hypothesis at best.

4. CONCLUSIONS

The most obvious conclusion from this work is that simple, gate-check video quizzes are not sufficient to improve the grades of students in a flipped CS1 classroom. Granted, that conclusion comes with the proviso that we were looking at a small sample size, and the enrollments in the studied class sections had some distinct skew that might have favored the group that was not required to take the video quizzes. However, even with this proviso, it seems reasonable that this is a valid conclusion because of the limited nature of the gate-check video quizzes.

The quiz style that was used for this work was a surface learning tool, not something that really prompted students to think more deeply, make connections, or question their assumptions. It was unlikely that students who had watched the videos only somewhat attentively would find that they couldn't answer the questions and need to go back to re-watch sections, or go to the book for additional assistance.[1] It is quite possible that some form of pre-class assessment could be found that would force students to take these steps, and which might actually produce better results. For that reason, we are looking into using a pre-class assessment that asks students to answer questions that involve filling in gaps in code segments or writing functions to do very simple calculations instead of using quizzes with multiple choice questions. We expect that such an approach would actually facilitate deeper learning by students, and would therefore be more effective at improving their learning.

Another factor to consider is that this work looks only at outcomes in terms of student grades. What we are truly interested in is student learning, and their ability to retain and apply the knowledge from the class. Grades are a convenient numerical proxy for learning, but they are certainly not a perfect metric. Even though the grades did not reflect an improvement due to the gate-check video quizzes here, one of the instructors noted anecdotally that the students were more uniformly prepared when required to take the gate-check video quizzes than they had been in previous semester when they were not.

Over the course of the semester, it is inevitable that students become more or less busy at various times. When their other classes begin to give them a lot of work, things like video watching are often some of the first things to suffer. While these students might be able to cram later to catch up on things for quizzes and tests, the failure to watch videos impacts the flow of the course as there can be days when many students clearly show up unprepared. For one instructor in this study, the gate-check video quizzes did seem to come close to eliminating this behavior. Why that didn't improve grades for students is a separate issue that would be worth exploring.

5. REFERENCES

[1] A. Amresh, A. R. Carberry, and J. Femiani. Evaluating the effectiveness of flipped classrooms for teaching cs1. In *Frontiers in Education Conference, 2013 IEEE*, pages 733–735. IEEE, 2013.

[2] B. Anderson, S. Lee, M. Simpson, and S. Stein. Study orchestrations in distance learning: Identifying dissonance and its implications for distance educators. *The International Review of Research in Open and Distance Learning*, 12(5), 2011.

[3] O. Bälter, M. Cleveland-Innes, K. Pettersson, M. Scheja, and M. Svedin. Student approaches to learning in relation to online course completion. *Canadian Journal of Higher Education*, 43(3):1–18, 2013.

[4] J. B. BIGGS. Dimensions of study behaviour: Another look at ati. *British Journal of Educational Psychology*, 46(1):68–80, 1976.

[5] L. O. Dahlgren and F. Marton. Students' conceptions of subject matter: An aspect of learning and teaching in higher education. *Studies in Higher Education*, 3(1):25–35, 1978.

[1]In a survey of students reported in the earlier paper, students do self-report that a majority of them re-watched parts of the video lectures that were unclear to them. However, we were unable to determine if that was because of the quizzes or their reaction to not understanding the material.

[6] A. Diseth. Personality and approaches to learning as predictors of academic achievement. *European Journal of Personality*, 17(2):143–155, 2003.

[7] A. DISETH and A. MARTINSEN. Approaches to learning, cognitive style, and motives as predictors of academic achievement. *Educational Psychology*, 23(2):195–207, 2003.

[8] N. Entwistle. Strategies of learning and studying: Recent research findings. *British Journal of Educational Studies*, 25(3):225–238, 1977.

[9] R. A. Fox, I. McManus, and B. C. Winder. The shortened study process questionnaire: An investigation of its structure and longitudinal stability using confirmatory factor analysis. *British Journal of Educational Psychology*, 71(4):511–530, 2001.

[10] G. Gannod, J. Burge, and M. Helmick. Using the inverted classroom to teach software engineering. In *Software Engineering, 2008. ICSE '08. ACM/IEEE 30th International Conference on*, pages 777–786, May 2008.

[11] E. F. Gehringer and B. W. Peddycord III. The inverted-lecture model: a case study in computer architecture. In *Proceeding of the 44th ACM technical symposium on Computer science education*, pages 489–494. ACM, 2013.

[12] D. Gijbels, G. Van de Watering, F. Dochy, and P. Van den Bossche. The relationship between students' approaches to learning and the assessment of learning outcomes. *European Journal of Psychology of Education*, 20(4):327–341, 2005.

[13] T. Hau, S. Williams, and P. Hoi. Using the biggs' study process questionnaire (spq) as a diagnostic tool to identify "at-risk" students : A preliminary study, 2004, Retrieved September 5, 2014.

[14] L. L. Lacher and M. C. Lewis. The value of video quizzes in a computer science flipped classroom: An empirical study. In *Proc. Int. Conf. on Frontiers in Education: Computer Science and Computer Engineering (FECS'14)*, pages 94–100, Las Vegas, USA, July 2014. CSREA.

[15] M. C. Lewis. Video playlist: Introduction to the art of programming using scala (part i). `https://www.youtube.com/playlist?list=PL0B0820169DCF0AD2`.

[16] M. C. Lewis. *Introduction to the art of programming using Scala*. CRC Press, 2012.

[17] F. Marton, R. Säljö, et al. Approaches to learning. *The experience of learning*, 2:39–58, 1984.

[18] U. of Kent. Computer programming aptitude test. `https://www.kent.ac.uk/careers/tests/computer-test.htm`, April 2014.

[19] A. Sureka, M. Gupta, D. Sarkar, and V. Chaudhary. A case-study on teaching undergraduate-level software engineering course using inverted-classroom, large-group, real-client and studio-based instruction model. *CoRR*, pages -1–1, 2013.

[20] H. Tait and N. Entwistle. Identifying students at risk through ineffective study strategies. *Higher Education*, 31(1):97–116, 1996.

Reconsidering the Impact of CS1 on Novice Attitudes

Amber Settle, John Lalor, Theresa Steinbach
DePaul University
243 S. Wabash Avenue
Chicago, IL 60604
(312) 362-8381
asettle@cdm.depaul.edu, jlalor@mail.depaul.edu, tsteinbach@cdm.depaul.edu

ABSTRACT

Student success in an introductory programing course is crucial, both because it influences retention and because student attitudes and habits in a first course can have a lasting impact on student success in computer science as a field. In this paper we present results about student attitudes and habits before and after a CS1 class. Statistically significant attitude differences were found in three areas: students were less likely to report they were good at programming, more likely to agree they are challenged by programming problems they can't understand immediately, and are less likely to report that computer science allows them to be creative. Statistically significant differences in female and first-quarter responses were also found.

Categories and Subject Descriptors

K.3.2 [**Computer and Information Science Education**]: Computer science education

Keywords

Attitudes; CS1; confidence; community; engagement; programming; Python

1. INTRODUCTION

For years computing educators have devoted considerable time and energy to improving the student experience in introductory programming courses, typically referred to as CS1 courses. This is energy well spent, as CS1 courses are often the first experience students have in the computer science major. It has been shown that computing experiences affect a student's perception and attitude about the field, which enable or inhibit pathways in the discipline [19]. The efforts at improving CS1 courses have in many cases resulted in lower failure rates, better retention, and in some cases better gender balance [2]. Despite the changes researchers have still found that prior experience and confidence predict male student performance in CS1 courses, and that confidence among peers has almost no effect on students' attitudes or performance [2]. Several STEM researchers have found evidence of a relationship between student perceptions and learning outcomes [11]. Among other findings, students' achievement expectations and self-concept are good predictors of success, students' self-assessment of their ability level impacts their decision to major in computer science, and student beliefs affect how they learn new information [11]. Student attitudes and beliefs about computer science have been previously studied, with researchers finding that student beliefs were more varied in their first than in their last year [16]. Other researchers have examined the impact of CS1 courses on majors vs. non-majors, using various pedagogical and curricular approaches, and examining differences based on course performance [21]. While the classroom experience is often the only thing under the control of educators, student experiences both inside and outside of the classroom can shape their beliefs.

This paper examines student attitudes toward computing and habits in acquiring competency in an introductory programming class, examining if student attitudes and habits regarding computer science change after a single CS1 course. Students who take the CS1 Python course are undergraduates in a major where development is a focus, which during the time of the study included computer science, math/computer science, game development, and information assurance and security engineering. Some non-majors take the course as a part of the requirements for a minor. The Python sequence to which the CS1 course belongs uses several interventions recommended in the literature, including closed labs with collaborative activities, differentiated courses for novice and experienced programmers, and engaged and enthusiastic faculty [3, 6, 10, 17]. The change in attitudes and habits is measured using a survey developed by the authors and based on previous surveys of attitudes toward computer science [7, 15, 22, 23]. The survey was administered pre-quarter and post-quarter in all CS1 Python classes for an entire academic year, and the results analyzed to find statistically significant changes in student responses.

The findings of this research will be used in a larger project being conducted about learning communities. These results will provide a baseline as the initial step in this project. Beginning Fall 2014, a "linked courses" learning community [12] will be created for underrepresented students majoring in one of our development-focused computing degrees that require Python as the introductory language. These students will become a cohort in a content-based course (CS1) and a liberal studies course focused on the Digital Divide [20]. The survey described here will be administered to these students to determine if the learning community has any impact on their attitudes and habits beyond what could be expected from taking the CS1 Python course alone.

2. SURVEY

The survey of student attitudes and habits administered for this work was based on previous surveys of student attitudes, including the Computer Science Attitude Survey [23], the USG Student Computing Survey [22] used in the Georgia Computes! Project [7], and the Science Interest Survey [15]. Because the

SIGCSE'15, March 4–7, 2015, Kansas City, MO, USA.

ACM 978-1-4503-2966-8/15/03…$15.00.
http://dx.doi.org/10.1145/2676723.2677235

survey would be administered in person during sessions of the programming class, brevity was important. Questions were selectively chosen from previous surveys and modified to meet the needs of this study, producing a survey with 33 attitude questions and a single question that asked students to rank resources used to obtain new computing skills. Each of the attitude questions are listed below, and students answered the questions using a five-point Likert scale of 5 = strongly agree, 4 = agree, 3 = neutral, 2 = disagree, and 1 = strongly disagree.

1. I plan to major in a technology-related degree
2. I am sure that I can learn programming
3. I am sure I can do advanced work in computer science
4. I think I could handle more difficult programming problems
5. I can get good grades in computer science
6. I have a lot of self-confidence when it comes to programming
7. I'm not good at programming
8. For some reason even though I work hard at it, programming seems unusually hard for me
9. Computer science has been my worst subject
10. It would make me happy to be recognized as an excellent student in computer science
11. I'd be happy to get top grades in computer science
12. If I got good grades in computer science, I would try to hide it
13. I'll need programming for my future work
14. Knowing programming will help me earn a living
15. I will use programming in many ways throughout my life
16. Taking computer science courses is a waste of time
17. Once I start trying to work on a program, I find it hard to stop
18. I am challenged by programming problems I can't understand immediately
19. I am easily frustrated by difficult programming problems
20. I do as little work in computer science courses as possible
21. I like talking with my friends about programming
22. I like to program in my spare time
23. I belong in the computing field
24. I feel isolated in computer science courses
25. I am part of a community of programmers
26. Computer science offers good financial opportunities after graduation
27. Computer science allows me to be creative
28. Computing offers diverse and broad opportunities
29. I have a lot of support that will help me to succeed in computer science courses
30. Computer science provides opportunities to make a difference in the world
31. I have a lot of friends who are interested in computing
32. My family is happy that I am taking computer science courses
33. I have had good teachers in my computer science courses

There was one additional question that asked students: "Outside of your classroom studies, what are your resources for learning/obtaining new computing skills? Mark all that you use and rank them in order of use. The one you use most should be ranked as 1, the one you use next often as 2, etc." The resources listed were: Friends/peers, Internet/web sites, professional organizations, self study, family members, tutors, faculty, and other (please specify). Students were instructed to leave a resource blank if they did not use it, so that only the resources utilized would be given a ranking.

3. RESULTS

During the academic year 2013-2014, surveys were administered in eleven sections of CSC 241: Introduction to Computer Science I. The students were surveyed once during the first week of the quarter and once either during the last week of the quarter or just prior to the final exam. Following the protocol under which the study was approved, paper copies of the surveys were distributed during the class session by one of the authors, none of whom were instructors for the classes in the study. Students were asked to provide their student ID as a way of matching pre-quarter and post-quarter responses, but no tracking of students during the quarter was done. The responses to the surveys were entered into electronic form and then analyzed, with the student IDs being discarded once pre- and post-quarter responses were verified to both be present. In this section we provide summary statistics for student demographic information and attitude question responses and a statistical analysis of the data.

3.1 Demographics

Both the pre-quarter and post-quarter survey asked students to provide demographic information. While only those students who completed both the pre-quarter and post-quarter surveys are analyzed in depth, a brief summary of the pre-quarter responses is presented prior to the more in-depth analysis.

3.1.1 Pre-quarter responses

There were a total of 259 responses to the pre-quarter survey, with 60 (23%) of them female, 190 (73%) male, and nine (3%) who did not specify gender. While CSC 241 is a first-year course, students sometimes wait several quarters to take it, so students were asked about their current quarter at the university. One hundred fifty (58%) students were in the first quarter, 55 (21%) in their second quarter, 25 (10%) in their third quarter, 18 (7%) in their fourth quarter or beyond, and 11 (4%) did not specify their quarter of study. Students were asked about their GPA, but only the responses from students in the second quarter and beyond are provided, since a GPA for a first-quarter student would not include classes from his/her current institution. Forty-eight (44%) reported a GPA of 3.5 – 4.0, 28 (26%) reported a GPA of 3.0 – 3.49, 13 (12%) reported a GPA of 2.0 – 2.9, and 18 (17%) did not report their GPA. The students were also asked to provide their major. One hundred forty students (54%) reported computer science, 32 (12%) reported game development, 26 (10%) reported mathematics, 21 (8%) reported information assurance and security engineering, nine (3%) reported another major in the College of Computing and Digital Media (CDM), 25 (10%) reported a major outside CDM, and six (2%) were undecided.

3.1.2 Post-quarter responses

There were a total of 197 responses to the post-quarter survey, but only 152 responses from students who had also completed a pre-quarter survey. Only those responses are analyzed here. There were 231 students who completed CSC 241 in the academic year 2013-2014, giving a response rate of 66%.

Of the responses 40 (26%) were female and 112 (74%) male. There were 86 (57%) students in their first quarter, 44 (29%) in their second quarter, 12 (8%) in their third quarter, and 10 (7%) in their fourth quarter or beyond. The reported GPA for the 65 students beyond their first quarter was 33 (51%) with a 3.5 – 4.0, 14 (22%) with a 3.0 – 3.49, and 10 (15%) with a 2.0 – 2.9, and eight (12%) who did not give a GPA. There were 81 (53%) computer science majors, 21 (14%) game development majors, 20 (13%) mathematics majors, 13 (9%) information assurance and security engineering, five (3%) other CDM majors, 10 (7%) other majors, and two (1%) undecided.

3.2 Attitude Questions

The responses to the attitude questions (Q1 – Q33) were analyzed using a one-way ANOVA test to determine if the changes pre-quarter to post-quarter were statistically significant. We performed a test between the pre- and post-survey responses, with a null hypothesis of "Taking the introductory Python class did not affect students' responses regarding ____," with the blank representing each question. Only results significant below $p < .01$ level were considered.

Four of the changes in the overall responses were statistically significant. The results are presented in Table 1.

Table 1. Overall differences pre- or post-quarter

Q	Pre	Post	Result
7	2.539	2.303	$F(1, 151) = 7.97$, $p = .005$
18	3.520	3.783	$F(1, 151) = 10.5$, $p = 0.002$
27	4.132	3.882	$F(1, 151) = 9.17$, $p = 0.003$
33	3.888	4.276	$F(1, 151) = 16.8$, $p = .0007$

We also considered subpopulations of students to determine if there were statistically significant differences in their responses either pre- or post-quarter or if there were statistically significant differences between the pre- and post-quarter responses. The groups we considered were male versus female students and students in particular quarters (first, second, third, and fourth and beyond. The subsections below discuss the results for each subpopulation.

3.2.1 Gender

For male and female students, we first considered whether there were any significant differences in their responses to questions either in the pre-quarter or post-quarter responses. ANOVA analysis revealed 14 questions for which statistically significant results. Only results significant at the $p < .01$ level or lower were considered. Table 2 shows the means and results for each statistically significant question.

We next considered whether male or female responses to any questions had changed in a statistically significant way during the quarter. There were statistically significant results found for two questions, although only at the $p < .05$ level. The results are presented in Table 3.

3.2.2 By Quarter

There were six questions for which statistically significant results were seen when considering students in a given quarter at DePaul. ANOVA analysis indicated that for these six questions, there was a statistically significant difference in the responses by quarter. We performed t-tests as a post-hoc test to identify those quarters where the differences were significant.

Table 4 shows the results of the ANOVA analysis, and Table 5 shows the results of the post-hoc t-tests for the significant results.

Table 2. Gender differences pre- or post-quarter

Q	Pre		Post		Result
	F	M	F	M	
1	3.7	4.446	3.625	4.393	$F(1, 150) = 12.3$, $p = 0.006$
2	4.15	4.634	4.05	4.562	$F(1, 150) = 19.2$, $p = 0.0002$
3	3.575	4.214	3.625	4.223	$F(1, 150) = 12.7$, $p = 0.0005$
4	3.375	3.955	3.45	4.027	$F(1, 150) = 11.5$, $p = 0.0009$
5	4.175	4.348	3.825	4.339	$F(1, 150) = 7.74$, $p = 0.006$
6	3.05	3.75	3.075	3.866	$F(1, 150) = 21.8$, $p = 0.00007$
9	2.275	1.839	2.225	1.679	$F(1, 150) = 10.1$, $p = 0.0018$
13	3.8	4.357	3.725	4.366	$F(1, 150) = 14$, $p = 0.0003$
14	4.0	4.438	3.925	4.446	$F(1, 150) = 10.9$, $p = 0.0012$
15	3.75	4.312	3.575	4.223	$F(1, 150) = 15.5$, $p = 0.00013$
21	2.85	3.411	2.657	3.491	$F(1, 150) = 17.9$, $p = .0004$
22	2.575	3.071	2.625	3.241	$F(1, 150) = 11.1$, $p = 0.0011$
23	3.05	3.902	3.225	3.875	$F(1, 150) = 16.3$, $p = 0.0009$
31	2.95	3.429	2.725	3.357	$F(1, 150) = 8.64$, $p = 0.0038$

Table 3. Gender differences over time

Q	Pre		Post		Result
	F	M	F	M	
5	4.175	4.348	3.825	4.339	$F(1, 150) = 4.85$, $p = 0.029$
19	2.657	2.741	3.125	2.732	$F(1, 150) = 4.88$, $p = 0.029$

Table 4. Quarter differences, ANOVA results

Q	Result
1	$F(3, 145) = 5.41$, $p = 0.0015$
2	$F(3, 145) = 5.34$, $p = 0.0016$
3	$F(3, 145) = 4.91$, $p = 0.0025$
4	$F(3, 145) = 4.41$, $p = 0.0053$
6	$F(3, 145) = 4.55$, $p = 0.0044$
11	$F(3, 145) = 4.44$, $p = 0.0051$

Table 5. Significant differences, by quarter

Q	Mean 1	Mean 2	Result
1	Q1-3.887	Q2-4.587	t(196)=-3.758, p=0.00022
1	Q1-3.887	Q3-4.446	t(187)=-2.824, p=0.0052
3	Q1-3.791	Q2-4.277	t(196)=-3.09, p=0.0023
3	Q1-3.791	Q3-4.284	t(187)=-2.993, p=0.0031
4	Q1-3.617	Q3-4.162	t(187)=-3.456, p=0.0007
6	Q1-3.443	Q3-4.027	t(187)=-3.881, p=0.0001
6	Q2-3.566	Q3-4.027	t(155)=-2.966, p=0.0035
6	Q3-4.027	Q4+-3.375	t(104)=3.618, p=0.0005

3.3 Resource Question

The final question on the survey asked students to rank the use of resources for learning, with 1 assigned to the most frequently used resource. Students were asked to only rank the resources they used. As with the multiple-choice questions we performed a one-way ANOVA test between the pre- and post-survey responses, with a null hypothesis of "Taking the introductory Python class did not affect students' utilization of ____," with the blank representing each resource. There were no significant results at or below the $p < .01$ level for any of the resources when considering the population as a whole.

We also considered subpopulations of students to see if there were any statistically significant differences for certain groups of students after taking the CS1 Python course. The groups we considered were the same as for the attitude questions. There were no significant results for students in particular quarters at or below the $p < .01$ level. The significant results for subpopulations are discussed in the subsections below.

3.3.1 Gender

There was one resource for which statistically significant results were seen when considering female versus male responses pre- or post-quarter. When asked about tutors the female mean was 1.60 pre-quarter and 1.75 post-quarter, and the male mean was 2.83 pre-quarter and 2.688 post-quarter. There was a significant effect at the $p < .01$ level with $F(1, 150) = 10.1$, $p = 0.0018$.

There was also one question on which female versus male responses showed a significant difference from pre- to post-quarter. When asked about friends and peers the female mean was 2.4 pre-quarter and 1.775 post-quarter, and the male mean was 2.304 pre-quarter and 2.589 post-quarter. There was a significant effect at the $p < .05$ level with $F(1, 150) = 4.0$, $p = 0.047$.

4. DISCUSSION

There were four questions for which the overall student population changed their attitudes in a significant way during the course of the quarter. Students were less likely to report they were good at programming (question 7), more likely to agree they are challenged by programming problems they can't understand immediately (question 18), and less likely to report computer science allows them to be creative (question 27). These results appear to show that the CS1 course is diminishing, at least to some degree, both student confidence and student engagement. It does appear, however, that the instructors are not the issue, given that students are more likely to agree they have had good teachers in their computer science courses (question 33). The courses are designed for majors in which application development will be a large part of the focus of the degree, and as such, the material is not easy. While Python is a syntactically simpler language, that also allows instructors to assign more challenging and significant problems, which is a stated purpose of the course. Thus it may be natural that the students' confidence is slightly diminished. The result showing their engagement is diminished is troubling though and suggests that course instructors need to consider how to improve rather than reduce engagement.

4.1 Gender Differences

The majority of statistically significant differences were between male and female responses. The largest number of differences is seen on questions relating to confidence. Female students were less likely to report that they were sure they could learn programming (question 2), that they were sure they could do advanced work in computer science (question 3), that they could handle more difficult programming problems (question 4), that they could get good grades in computer science (question 5), that they have a lot of self-confidence when it comes to programming (question 6), and that they belong in the computing field (question 23). These results are consistent with previous work that has shown women have lower levels of confidence with respect to computer science [5]. Female students were also less likely to agree with the future utility of computer science, indicating lower agreement with the statements "I'll need programming for my future work" (question 13), "knowing programming will help me earn a living" (question 14), and "I will use programming in many ways throughout my life" (question 15). Previous work has shown that an understanding of how computer science can be used in a broader context is more important for women [1], making these results discouraging. The CS1 course was designed to highlight the applicability of programming for computer science, and this result suggests that women are not hearing that message. Female students were more likely to agree that computer science had been their worst subject (question 9) and less likely to agree that they like to program in their spare time (question 22). Perhaps unsurprisingly given that female students are a small minority in the CS1 course, they were less likely to agree that they like to talk with their friends about programming (question 21) and that they have a lot of friends interested in computing (question 31). Social isolation can impact engagement [10], and it may be that instructors for the CS1 course need to do more to connect female students with student organizations and resources to help reduce their isolation [4]. Finally there was one significant difference between male and female students with respect to resource utilization. Female students were less likely to report that they visited tutors, which contradicts a previous study showing that female students were more likely to consult tutors than male students [9].

There were three questions for which male and female responses showed a statistically significant difference over time. Female students' agreement with the statement "I can get good grades in computer science" diminished during the quarter, and female students were more likely to agree with the statement "I am easily frustrated by difficult programming problems" at the conclusion of the quarter. As mentioned earlier, the courses are designed to be challenging, so it may be that extra support of female students would be the most appropriate response to these results. There was also a statistically significant difference between male and female students with respect to their utilization of friends and peers for assistance. Both male and female students were less likely at the conclusion of the quarter to report using friends and peers for help, but the drop in the reported use of that resource was significantly higher for female students. This result can in part be explained by course policies. The courses have closed labs, and during most of these labs students are encouraged to work together. However most, although not all, instructors require that students complete assignments individually, and students are prohibited from discussing the assignments with each other. This policy was developed in response to problems with Academic Integrity violations. Some instructors have begun to develop modified policies that balance the need for adherence to Academic Integrity policies with the benefits gained from students collaborating. Given that previous results show that women are more likely to collaborate on assignments [9] and more likely to respond positively to collaborative activities [13], this could have a positive impact on female students.

4.2 Differences by Quarter

There were statistically significant differences on four questions when considering students in particular quarters. First-quarter students were less likely to indicate that they intended to major in a technology-related degree (question 1) than second- and third-quarter students. They were also less like to indicate agreement with the statement "I am sure I can do advanced work in computer science" (question 3) than second- and third-quarter students. They were less likely to agree that they could handle more difficult programming problems (question 4). The most interesting result is that first-, second-, and third-quarter students were each less likely to agree that they have a lot of self-confidence when it comes to programming (question 6) than more advanced students. This is a valuable extension of earlier work finding differences in attitudes [16] and self-efficacy [18] by time spent in school. It also suggests that the linked-courses learning community will be of value, since its main goal is to improve support for first-quarter female and minority male students in order to bolster their confidence. Improving these aspects of the course would help with persistence and retention [3].

4.3 Limitations

There are some limitations to this study. Some of the questions posed in the survey are sensitive in nature, and participants may have chosen to not complete those portions of the survey causing their data to be discarded in the analysis. Students were asked to provide their student IDs as a part of the survey to enable verification that only those students who completed both parts were included in the analysis, and this may have led students to not participate in the survey. The entire study is based on self-reported values provided by participants, and care must be taken when interpreting the results. Additionally, though care was taken in choosing survey questions and choices that are unambiguous, there is a risk that the participant may have misinterpreted the questions or choices. The study also does not consider the impacts of using the Python language in particular. Because Python is the only first language for development majors at the institution in question, there is no equivalent population with which the results can be compared. Other majors take courses in Ruby on Rails or Java, but the background and preparation of those students is different enough to not allow useful comparisons with the students who take Python.

5. CONCLUSION AND FUTURE WORK

The results presented in this study confirm the previous work of Dorn and Tew [11] in self-assessment of ability when responses are analyzed in totality. However when responses are analyzed by gender, the majority of statistically significant differences were seen on questions relating to confidence, confirming the Beyer et al [5] conclusion that women have lower levels of confidence with respect to computer science. Students in the early stages of their academic career are less likely to agree they have a lot of self-confidence in programming which extends the work of Lewis et al [16] and Ramalingam et al [18]. The studied course was taught using CS1 best practices [1, 3, 6, 10, 17] but did not have an impact on female students learning programming. Female students remained less sure that they would do advanced work in computer science, could handle more difficult programming problems, and would achieve good grades in computer science. Female students also failed to report a sense of belonging in the field which poses difficulties for retention. This work demonstrates that new CS1 approaches alone are not always sufficient for rectifying previous gender-specific classroom issues and that work remains in broadening computer science.

In the bigger picture the authors have plans to compare the baseline results gathered from the Python CS1 course with the data gathered from students recruited for a linked-courses learning community in the Fall 2014. The learning community targets female and minority male students in majors that are required to take the CS1 course. The community provides participating students with two classes in common as well as co-curricular activities such as special lectures, community-service project, visits to technology companies, and extra-curricular activities including peer mentoring, shared meals and gaming events [20]. Learning communities have been shown to be beneficial in enhancing student achievement, reducing attrition rates, and improving interaction between faculty and students [8, 14]. Our hypothesis is that the learning community will enhance student feelings of engagement, self-confidence, and social connection, which given the results here would be a strong benefit for the course.

6. REFERENCES

[1] Alvarado, C. and Dodds, Z.. 2010. Women in CS: an evaluation of three promising practices. In *Proceedings of the 41st ACM Technical Symposium on Computer Science Education* (SIGCSE '10). ACM, New York, NY, USA, 57-61.

[2] Alvarado, C., Lee, C.B., and Gillespie, G. 2014. New CS1 pedagogies and curriculum, the same success factors? In *Proceedings of the 45th ACM Technical Symposium on Computer Science Education* (Atlanta, Georgia, USA, March 2014).

[3] Barker, L.J.,McDowell, C. and Kalahar, K. 2009. Exploring Factors that Influence Computer Science Introductory Course Students to Persist in the Major. *Proceedings of the 40th ACM Technical Symposium on Computer Science Education* (Chattanooga, Tennessee, USA, March 2009).

[4] Besana, G.M. and Dettori, L.. 2004. Together is better: strengthening the confidence of women in computer science via a learning community. *J. Comput. Sci. Coll.* 19, 5 (May 2004), 130-139.

[5] Beyer, S., Rynes, K., Perrault, J., Hay, K., and Haller, S.. 2003. Gender differences in computer science students. In *Proceedings of the 34th SIGCSE Technical Symposium on Computer Science Education* (SIGCSE '03). ACM, New York, NY, USA, 49-53.

[6] Boyer, K.E., Dwight, R. S., Miller, C.S., Raubenheimer, C.D., Stallmann, M.F., and Vouk, M.A. 2007. A Case for Smaller Class Size with Integrated Lab for Introductory Computer Science. In *Proceedings of the 38th ACM Technical Symposium on Computer Science Education* (Covington, Kentucky, USA, March 2007).

[7] Bruckman, A., Biggers, M., Ericson, B., McKlin, T., Dimond, J., DiSalvo, B., Hewner, M., Ni, L., and Yardi, S. 2009. "Georgia computes!": Improving the Computing Education Pipeline. In *Proceedings of the 40th ACM Technical Symposium on Computer Science Education* (Chattanooga, Tennessee, USA, March 2009).

[8] Cargill, K. and Kalikoff, B. 2007. Linked Psychology and Writing Courses Across the Curriculum. *The Journal of General Education*, 56:2, pp. 83-92.

[9] Chinn, D., Sheard, J., Carbone, A., and Laakso, M. 2010. Study habits of CS1 students: what do they do outside the classroom?. In *Proceedings of the Twelfth Australasian Conference on Computing Education* - Volume 103 (ACE '10), Tony Clear and John Hamer (Eds.), Vol. 103. Australian Computer Society, Inc., Darlinghurst, Australia, Australia, 53-62.

[10] Cohoon, J.. 2002. Recruiting and retaining women in undergraduate computing majors. *SIGCSE Bull.* 34, 2 (June 2002), 48-52.

[11] Dorn,B. and Tew, A.E. 2013. Becoming Experts: Measuring Attitude Development in Introductory Computer Science. In *Proceedings of the 44th ACM technical symposium on Computer Science Education.* (Denver, Colorado, USA, March 2013).

[12] Kellogg, K. 1999. Learning Communities. ERIC Digest. Retrieved December 29, 2013 from http://eric.ed.gov/?id=ED430512.

[13] Krause, J., Polycarpou, I., and Hellman, K. 2012. Exploring formal learning groups and their impact on recruitment of women in undergraduate CS. In *Proceedings of the 43rd ACM technical symposium on Computer Science Education* (SIGCSE '12). ACM, New York, NY, USA, 179-184.

[14] Johnson, K.E. 2013. Learning Communities and the Completion Agenda. *Learning Communities Research and Practice*, 1:3.

[15] Lamb, R.L, Annetta, L, Meldrum, J., and Vallett, D. 2012. Measuring Science Interest: Rasch Validation of the Science Interest Survey. *International Journal of Science and Mathematics Education.* 10:3 (June 2012), 643-668.

[16] Lewis, C., Jackson, M.H., and Waite, W.M. 2010. Student and faculty attitudes and beliefs about computer science. *Commun. ACM* 53, 5 (May 2010), 78-85.

[17] Newhall, T., Meeden, L., Danner, A., Soni, A., Ruiz, F., and Wicentowski, R. 2014. A Support Program for Introductory CS Courses that Improves Student Performance and Retains Students from Underrepresented Groups. In *Proceedings of the 45th ACM Technical Symposium on Computer Science Education.* (Atlanta, Georgia, USA, March 2014).

[18] Ramalingam, V. LaBelle, D., and Wiedenbeck S. 2004. Self-efficacy and mental models in learning to program. In *Proceedings of the 9th Annual SIGCSE Conference on Innovation and Technology in Computer Science Education* (ITiCSE '04).

[19] Schulte, C. and Knobelsdorf, M. 2007. Attitudes towards Computer Science-Computing Experiences as a Starting Point and Barrier to Computer Science. In *Proceedings of the Third International Workshop on Computing Education Research* (Atlanta, Georgia, USA, September 2007).

[20] Settle A. and Steinbach, T. 2014 Building a Linked-Courses Learning Community for Introductory Development Majors. In *Proceedings of the International Conference on Frontiers in Education: Computer Science and Computer Engineering* (Las Vegas, Nevada, USA, July 2014).

[21] Simon, B., Hanks, B., McCauley, R., Morrison, B., Murphy, L., and Zander, C.. 2009. For me, programming is .... In *Proceedings of the Fifth International Workshop on Computing Education Research Workshop* (ICER '09). ACM, New York, NY, USA, 105-116.

[22] USG Student Computing Survey, retrieved December 2013 from http://dl.dropboxusercontent.com/u/2635522/USG%20Student%20Survey.pdf.

[23] Wiebe, E.N., Williams, L, Yang, K. and Miller, C. 2003. Computer Science Attitude Survey, Dept. of Computer Science, North Carolina State University, TR-2003-1, http://www4.ncsu.edu/~wiebe/www/articles/prl-tr-2003-1.pdf.

Drop, Fail, Pass, Continue: Persistence in CS1 and Beyond in Traditional and Inverted Delivery

Diane Horton
Department of Computer Science
University of Toronto
dianeh@cs.toronto.edu

Michelle Craig
Department of Computer Science
University of Toronto
mcraig@cs.toronto.edu

ABSTRACT

Much attention has been paid to the failure rate in CS1 and attrition between CS1 and CS2. In our study of 1236 CS1 students, we examine subgroups of students, to find out how characteristics such as prior experience and reason for taking the course influence who drops, fails, or passes, and who continues on to CS2. We also examine whether student characteristics influence outcomes differently in traditional vs inverted offerings of the course. We find that more students in the inverted offering failed the midterm test, but those who failed were much more likely to either drop the course or recover and ultimately pass the course. While we find no difference between the offerings in the overall drop-fail-pass rates or in the percentage and types of students who go on to take CS2, there is a significant, widely felt, boost in exam grades in the inverted offering.

Categories and Subject Descriptors

K.3.2 [**Computers and Education**]: Computer and Information Science Education—*Computer Science Education*

Keywords

inverted classroom; flipped classroom; CS1; novice programming; drop rate; attrition

1. INTRODUCTION

Many studies report that CS1 classes have a high failure rate, both in terms of students who drop out of the course, and those who stay until the end but earn a failing grade [2, 9]. Other studies have examined attrition rates between CS1 and CS2 [7] or explored factors related to persistence through a CS major [1]. It is well known that students arrive in CS1 from a variety of backgrounds and that beginners on average do not do as well as students with a high school programming course [10, 4].

SIGCSE'15, March 4–7, 2015, Kansas City, MO, USA.

http://dx.doi.org/10.1145/2676723.2677273.

In our experience, students' reasons for taking CS1 and their enthusiasm for it can also influence their behaviour and ultimately their success in the course. In this study, we investigate how enthusiasm for the course, reason for taking the course, and prior experience influence who drops, fails, or passes CS1 and who continues into CS2. We hope that by understanding CS1 students better, we will be able to help more students succeed. In addition, by examining whether student characteristics influence outcomes differently in an inverted [6] offering of the course, we hope to discover whether particular groups are advantaged or disadvantaged by the inverted approach.

2. OUR STUDY

This work is part of a larger project examining outcomes in CS1. We studied two offerings of CS1 held in the fall of 2012 and the fall of 2013 at the University of Toronto, involving a total of 1307 participants. The 2012 offering was delivered in a traditional format, while the 2013 offering [3] used an inverted-classroom approach. In an inverted or flipped classroom [6], students learn course material prior to class, perhaps by reading or watching a video, then in the classroom they engage in hands-on activities that apply the material.

In [5] we compared these inverted and traditional offerings[1] of CS1. We found that, while students in the inverted offering did not report increased enjoyment and were no more likely to pass, learning as measured by final exam performance increased significantly. We had hypothesized that inverted teaching would particularly benefit beginners and those not fully fluent in English, but we did not find evidence that this was the case. For example, the pass rate among beginners was no better in the inverted term.

In this paper, we look more closely at what sorts of students progress successfully through CS1, how midterm feedback influences their progress, and who continues on into CS2. We remove from consideration students who did not answer our pre-course survey question about prior programming experience and those who submitted no work in the course, as we have a large number who are only "shopping" for courses very early in the term, and would distort our analyses. The resulting population, which corresponds to

[1]Although they occurred a year apart, a Pearson's Chi-squared test shows no evidence of a significant difference between these traditional and inverted offerings in the proportion of students who have prior programming experience or the proportion who intend to major in CS.

Characteristic	Category	Traditional			Inverted		
		Drop	Fail	Pass	Drop	Fail	Pass
Everyone		50 (9%)	66 (12%)	426 (79%)	71 (10%)	91 (13%)	532 (77%)
Prior Experience	none (beginner)	41 (15%)	43 (16%)	186 (69%)	55 (15%)	71 (19%)	250 (67%)
	high school course	3 (2%)	10 (6%)	162 (93%)	7 (3%)	13 (6%)	200 (91%)
	other experience	6 (6%)	13 (13%)	78 (80%)	9 (9%)	7 (7%)	82 (84%)
English Fluency	fluent	32 (10%)	28 (9%)	260 (81%)	33 (8%)	40 (10%)	321 (82%)
	non-fluent	17 (8%)	38 (18%)	159 (74%)	37 (13%)	47 (16%)	205 (71%)
Initial Enthusiasm	very enthusiastic	15 (7%)	26 (12%)	177 (81%)	17 (6%)	30 (11%)	225 (83%)
	a little enthusiastic	20 (11%)	16 (9%)	148 (80%)	25 (10%)	22 (9%)	193 (80%)
	unenthusiastic	14 (11%)	24 (18%)	94 (71%)	27 (16%)	35 (21%)	108 (64%)
Reason for Taking CS1	intending to major	13 (5%)	26 (9%)	252 (87%)	25 (7%)	38 (10%)	315 (83%)
	for another major	20 (16%)	27 (21%)	80 (63%)	21 (14%)	32 (21%)	101 (66%)
	another reason	17 (14%)	13 (11%)	94 (76%)	25 (15%)	21 (13%)	116 (72%)

Table 1: Student outcomes (drop, fail, or pass) by category of student.

"Pool 2" in [5], consists of 1236 students: 542 in the traditional offering and 694 in the inverted. We divide them into subgroups according to four attributes: prior programming experience, English language fluency, pre-course enthusiasm for the course, and reason for enrolling in it.

Throughout we use an alpha level of .05 when testing for statistical significance. We report exact p-values, unless they are below 0.001.

3. WHO DROPS, FAILS, PASSES?

Table 1 shows the number, and relative percentage, of students who drop, fail, or pass the course in the traditional and inverted offerings. In the first row, we see the results for all students; subsequent rows divide students according to prior programming experience and other relevant attributes. Considering all 1236 students from both offerings, 10% dropped, 13% failed and 77% passed. This pass rate is high compared to rates reported by [2] and [9]. When we compare this overall drop-fail-pass breakdown in the traditional and inverted offerings, a Pearson's Chi-squared test does not show a significant difference between offerings.

Now let's consider the impact of prior programming experience (PE) on these outcomes. Previous work has shown that the effect of PE on student performance varies from one CS course to another and depends on the type of PE. Both Wilson and Shrock [10] and Hagan and Markham [4] found that students with high school programming courses outperformed those without, but Wilson found that PE gained outside of a formal programming course was not a significant predictor of student performance.

In each offering in our study, students with a high school course had the best outcomes. In contrast to [10], even those with experience gained outside a high school programming course had better outcomes than students with no experience.[2] This difference was statistically significant, as was the difference for each offering considered individually (Pearson's Chi-squared test, $p < .001$ in all cases).

Considering the offerings combined, fluent English speakers were more likely to pass the course than non-fluent students, and non-fluent students were more likely to fail and to drop than fluent students. This is statistically significant and perhaps not surprising. More interesting is that the drop rate among non-fluent students was 5 percentage points higher in the inverted offering than in the traditional offering, and that it is an accompanying decrease in the pass rate, not fail rate, that primarily offsets this increase. One possible explanation is that the many inverted-classroom exercises, which involved reading and writing in English, are discouraging to some non-fluent students who then drop the course even though they may well have passed if they had persisted.

Students who begin the course unenthusiastic about it are less likely to pass than those who are a little or very enthusiastic. When considering the students in the inverted term, a 3×3 Pearson's Chi-squared test on enthusiasm level and drop-fail-pass outcomes finds that these variables are dependent ($p < .001$), but when we look at the traditional term the same test fails to meet our alpha cut-off. We conclude that a student's pass-fail-drop outcome is dependent on his or her enthusiasm in the inverted offering but not in the traditional offering.

Subdividing the students based on their reasons for enrolling in the course reveals no significant differences in outcomes between the two offerings. In both offerings, students who take the course because they intend to major in CS have the best outcomes and those who take it as a required course for some other program have the worst.

4. INFLUENCE OF THE MIDTERM

Although improved retention is a common goal, dropping a course is a wise decision for an individual who has fallen behind and is not able or willing to invest the effort necessary to catch up. How does feedback during the term influence a student's decision to stay or drop? We have analyzed students' decisions and their course outcomes (pass or fail), based on whether they passed, failed, or did not write the midterm test (see Figure 1). There are some striking differences between the traditional and inverted offerings.

4.1 More Midterm Failures in Inverted

Because different sections of the course met at different times, there were multiple versions of the midterm in each offering. However instructors worked together and attempted

[2]In our study, students who had exposure to programming from a course outside of high school, including failed or dropped attempts at CS1, were put in the "other experience" category. In [10], similar students may have been counted as having a formal programming course.

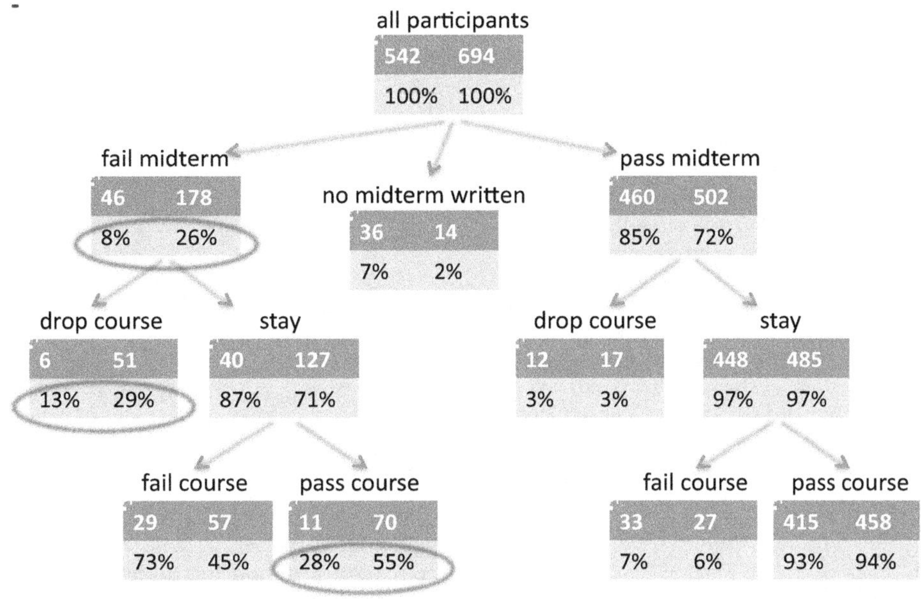

Figure 1: Number of students who drop, fail, and pass in traditional (left column) and inverted (right column) offerings of CS1, organized according to midterm test results. Percentages shown (second row) are of the number in the parent node.

to produce comparable tests, and the one instructor who was common across offerings was responsible for the final tests. In addition, two independent and experienced CS1 instructors conducted a blind assessment of the difficulty of all questions. One rated the midterms in the traditional offering as slightly more difficult; the other rated the midterms in the inverted offering as slightly more difficult. We conclude that they are not significantly different.

The failure rate on the midterm was very high in the inverted offering (26%), much higher than in the traditional offering (8%).

Such a jump in the midterm failure rate, for a test that is of comparable difficulty, would appear to be a failure of the inverted offering. However, as we saw in section 3, when we look at the drop-pass-fail outcomes for the whole course, we find no significant difference. So we ultimately have the same drop-fail-pass outcomes in each offering, but we arrive there differently.

One possible explanation for the difference in midterm failure rates across offerings is that our inverted offering inadvertently allowed some students to engage ineffectively with the work. Students who passively watch the videos and click through the in-video quizzes without much thought may get a false sense of mastery over the material.[3] They may, incorrectly, believe that there is no need to attend class. No marks were associated with attending class in either offering of the course, and attendance was lower in the inverted offering [3]. It is not clear that students possess the judgment to decide whether or not they need to attend, particularly in the fall term, when both of the offerings occurred, and many of the students are experiencing their first term in university. By the time the midterm comes, students who have deluded themselves about their mastery find that out.

Another possible explanation centres on *when* students dropped the course. Figure 2 shows that in the traditional offering, there was a modest but persistent amount of dropping prior to the midterm (held during week seven in both offerings). In the inverted offering, there was virtually none until the midterm, but after the test was returned, there was a huge burst of dropping. The inverted format may have encouraged some students to stick around and give the midterm a try rather than to drop beforehand.

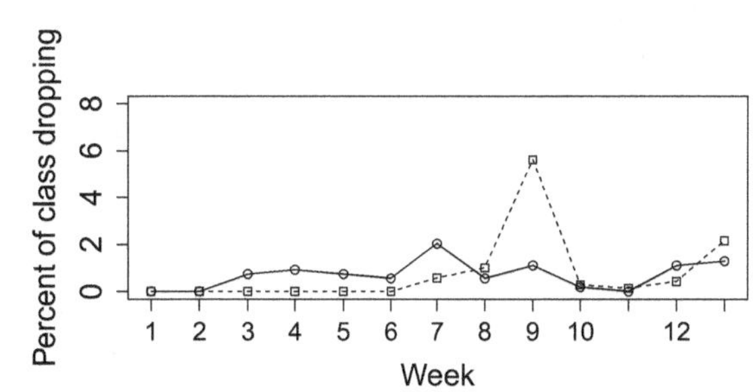

Figure 2: Percentage of the class enrolment that drops each week of term. Percentages are based on enrolment at the start of term.

4.2 Fewer Midterm Failers Persist

Of those who failed the midterm, the percentage who dropped the course was more than twice as high in the inverted offering (29% vs 13%). One would expect the opposite: that among those who failed the midterm, there would be a higher drop rate in the traditional offering where the

[3]The marking scheme gave points for attempting the in-video quiz attempts rather than for correct responses. We know from spot-checking the timing of student responses that at least some students did not watch all the video segments between clicking quiz responses.

midterm average was high at 77%, than in the inverted offering, with a 63% average. Failing a midterm that had a high average is surely a stronger signal that the student is in trouble.

We can only speculate about what caused this behaviour. Perhaps some students in the inverted offering watched the videos and clicked through the in-video quizzes but skipped class and thought incorrectly that this was enough to master the material. Perhaps some were not even keeping up with watching the videos, yet thought that there was still time to catch up, until their midterm result revealed that they were wrong. These students could even have been aware that they were in trouble, but decided to give the midterm a try before making the decision to drop.

4.3 Inverted Classroom Sees More Recovery

In the traditional offering, only 28% of students who fail the midterm go on to pass the course. This result alone will be quite useful when we advise students to avoid "magical thinking" — believing that they can pass the course without having a concrete plan to change their behaviour. The story is very different in the inverted offering, where 55% of those who stayed despite failing the midterm actually recovered well enough to pass the course. These differences are significant (Pearson's Chi-squared test, $p < .001$).

One key characteristic of the inverted delivery that supports student recovery is the availability of the lecture materials throughout the term. Online videos and in-video quizzes, which had been specifically designed for our CS1, were available for students to go back and watch as needed. Contrast this situation with the experience of students in the traditional offering who wanted to renew their efforts in the course after failing the midterm. Such a student who returns to class would have difficulty following the lecture and getting anything out of it. This is particularly the case with CS1, where the material builds continually [8].

5. CS1 EXAM GRADES

We have examined who it is that successfully persists through the course. Another concern is students' level of preparation for CS2. How much did they learn in CS1?

In [5] we report exam-inferred learning gains in the inverted offering compared to the traditional offering, as measured by a significant increase in the average final exam score. The exam average was 7.2 percentage points higher in the inverted offering than in the traditional offering,[4] and the difference in grade distributions was highly significant (t-test, $p < .001$). Although different exams were given in the two offerings, our analysis [5] supports the conclusion that the inverted exam was no easier than the traditional exam. We conclude that students in the inverted offering demonstrated superior understanding.

One explanation for this increase is that students learned more in the inverted offering. If so, we would like to know whether the benefit was evenly spread over subgroups or whether some benefitted more than others. It is even possible that some groups of students benefitted from the inverted offering while it put others at a disadvantage.

[4]In [5], we reported an 8% jump, based on exam averages provided by the course instructors, which included all students. Throughout the present paper, we report on results for only study participants.

	Grades
(Intercept)	40.38 (0.94)**
exp_highschool	10.27 (1.42)**
exp_other	2.50 (0.15)
offering_inverted	4.99 (1.23)**
exp_highschool:offering_inverted	−1.76 (1.89)
exp_other:offering_inverted	6.55 (2.4)*
R^2	0.12
Adj. R^2	0.12
Num. obs.	1069

$^{**}p < 0.001$, $^{*}p < 0.01$

Table 3: Regression model. Baselines for each factor are: experience none, offering traditional, a:b indicates an interaction between predictors a and b.

When we break the grades down according to prior programming experience, fluency in English, enthusiasm for the course, and reason for taking the course, we find that the boost in final exam grades holds up in every category of students (see Table 2), and that the difference in grade distributions between the traditional and inverted offerings is significant for 11 of the 12 categories. In determining significance, we applied a Bonferoni correction; because we broke the data down four ways, we divided our original alpha of 0.05 by four and used 0.0125.

So the grade boost in the inverted offering benefits students across the board. We also see that the size of the boost varies for different groups of students. It may provide insight to consider why.

Regardless of the kind of prior experience with which students enter the course, their exam grades are higher in the inverted offering. The gap is the least for students with a high school programming course. This may be due to a ceiling effect: these students already have the highest exam grades, on average, so their grades have less room to grow. Still, the grade boost is 4.5 percentage points, and is statistically significant. At the other end of the spectrum, students with prior experience gained through other means, such as self-teaching or a university course that involves some programming, had the greatest gain, 16 percentage points. These students may understand what it takes to succeed in programming better than beginners do. They may be less likely to allow themselves to fall behind, or to fool themselves into thinking that they do not need to go to class.

In [5], we used multiple regression to examine the relationships between exam grades, prior experience and offering-type. We found that those with experience outperformed beginners, but found no interaction between the offering and experience. In the present study, we distinguish further between high school experience and other experience, so we re-ran the regression with this three-way split on experience (see Table 3 for the model). The interaction between high school experience and offering is not significant, however, the interaction between other experience and offering is significant — not surprising, given the large difference in grade gaps between these two subgroups. The significant interaction between other experience and offering indicates that students with other experience do significantly better than students with no experience only in the inverted term.

In [5], we reported that, in both the inverted and traditional offerings, those with limited English fluency perform

Characteristic	Category	Traditional		Inverted		Gap	p-value
		n	Exam Avg	n	Exam Avg		
Everyone		473	61.8 %	596	69.0 %	7.2	< .001*
Prior Experience	none (beginner)	217	56.1 %	298	63.0 %	6.9	< .001*
	high school course	168	70.3 %	211	74.8 %	4.5	= .01072*
	other experience	88	59.6 %	87	75.6 %	16.0	< .001*
English Fluency	fluent	280	65.6 %	347	71.7 %	6.1	< .001*
	non-fluent	186	55.9 %	239	65.7 %	9.8	< .001*
Initial Enthusiasm	very enthusiastic	198	62.9 %	245	70.2 %	7.3	< .001*
	a little enthusiastic	156	64.0 %	205	72.3 %	8.3	< .001*
	unenthusiastic	112	56.1 %	136	63.1 %	7.0	= .01028*
Reason for Taking CS1	intending to major	273	64.9 %	343	71.7 %	6.8	< .001*
	for another major	98	51.6 %	124	62.6 %	11.0	< .001*
	another reason	102	63.4 %	129	68.1 %	4.7	= .071

Table 2: Final exam grades by category of student. The Gap column shows the percentage point difference between the exam average in the traditional and in the inverted offering, for a category of student. p-values are for a Welch two-sample t-test and an asterisk indicates statistical significance.

more poorly than fully-fluent students; we did not find evidence, however, that exam grades depend less on English fluency in the inverted offering compared to the traditional offering. Still, we can see here that fluent speakers do better on the exam in the inverted offering and the same holds for non-fluent speakers. As noted above, these differences are statistically significant.

Students who were not enthusiastic about taking the course performed more poorly on the exam, on average, than those who were at least a little enthusiastic. This effect held in both offerings. Regardless of level of enthusiasm for the course, however, the exam average was higher in the inverted offering.

In our experience, students who require CS1 for some major other than CS often struggle with the course. They need the course, but unlike students intending to major, they may not have an interest in the discipline. As one might expect, we can see that in both offerings they had a lower exam average than students who intend to major or who take the course for other reasons such as interest or relevance. However, the exam average was higher in the inverted offering regardless of the reason why students took the course, and this effect was markedly stronger for students who required CS1 for some major other than CS.

Discussion

Perhaps the improvement in exam grades in the inverted offering is not due to better learning but simply due to better mastery of exam-writing skills such as solving problems on paper. If students indeed learned more, one might wonder whether this was because they invested more time in the course, not because of inverted teaching per se. In [5] we found no evidence of this — students did not report a statistically significant difference in time spent on the course — but self-reports may not be reliable. Or perhaps the boost in exam grades occurred because the inverted offering encouraged more of the students who were likely to do poorly in the course to drop the course because the classroom exercises had exposed their inability to solve problems. For example, did the inverted offering cause more beginners to drop? Beginners typically do not perform as well as those with some prior experience [10, 4], and as we saw, our own data support that (see Table 2). But there was no elevation in the drop rate among beginners in the inverted offering. At the same time, we saw above that students who failed the midterm, a strong predictor of a poor grade on the final, were more likely to drop the course in the inverted term.

With the data available, it is impossible to determine how much the increased exam grades are due to differences in who dropped. Perhaps the only way to find out would be to assign students randomly to either a traditional or inverted offering and not allow anyone to drop. Of course, this is not feasible. Still, even if the entire exam grade boost is due to the right students choosing to drop the course and the ones who need to change their approach successfully doing so, this is certainly a very positive outcome.

6. FURTHER STUDIES IN CS

We looked at persistence within the CS program by examining whether a student went on to enrol in CS2 in either of the two subsequent academic terms (Table 4). When we consider each CS1 cohort as a whole, a Pearson's Chi-squared test finds no significant difference between offerings in the number of students who proceed to CS2. We also examined each subcategory of students, applying a Bonferoni correction as before, and found no significant differences.

One minor threat to the validity of this portion of our study is that only two subsequent terms of enrolment information were available for this analysis. Some participants who did not originally intend to major in CS may have been turned on to computer science through CS1, but been unable to fit CS2 into their already-established course schedules within our observation window. We do not expect that these numbers are large enough to significantly change the analysis nor do we expect these students differ between the two offerings on the attributes we have examined, such as prior programming experience.

Looking at the CS1 exam grades of our subjects who went on to take CS2, we find an increase in the average from 69.1% in the traditional to 76.5% in the inverted offering. This gap of 7.4 percentage points is statistically significant (Welch two-sample t-test, $p < .001$). While no greater a proportion of CS1 students go on to take CS2, those who do are arguably better prepared for the course.

Characteristic	Category	Traditional		Inverted	
Everyone		305	56 %	377	54 %
Prior Experience	none (beginner)	104	39 %	142	38 %
	high school course	138	79 %	173	79 %
	other experience	63	65 %	62	63 %
English Fluency	fluent	208	65 %	253	64 %
	non-fluent	94	44 %	119	41 %
Initial Enthusiasm	very enthusiastic	155	71 %	180	66 %
	a little enthusiastic	99	54 %	131	55 %
	unenthusiastic	47	36 %	61	36 %
Reason for Taking CS1	intending to major	243	84 %	285	75 %
	for another major	27	21 %	44	29 %
	another reason	35	28 %	48	30 %

Table 4: Number and percentage of those who started CS1 who go on to take CS2, by category of student.

7. CONCLUSIONS

When we look at the course as a whole, regardless of traditional or inverted delivery, we confirm some known patterns and observe some additional but unsurprising patterns concerning who succeeds in CS1. Students with experience are more likely to complete the course than beginners and they have higher exam marks; experience gained through a high school course is the most beneficial. Fluent speakers of English outperform non-fluent students. Students who intend to major in CS have better outcomes than those who take CS1 as a required course for another major, while those who take it for another reason fall in the middle. Contrary to what others have reported, we find that experience gained other than through a high school course is of benefit in terms of successfully completing the course.

When we compare traditional and inverted delivery, the story becomes more interesting. Many more students failed their midterm in the inverted offering, but those who failed were much more likely to either drop the course, or if they stayed, to recover from their poor midterm result and pass the course. It seems that the inverted offering encourages students to "go big or go home". We consider this to be a very positive effect.

The overall drop-fail-pass rates are not significantly different between the traditional and inverted offerings, and the same percentage and types of students go on to take CS2, but CS1 final exam grades are significantly higher in the inverted offering. When we looked more closely at subgroups with varying characteristics, the improvement in exam grades holds true for each of the 11 subgroups and is statistically significant in all but one. Students with non-traditional prior programming experience, non-fluent students and students forced to take the course to satisfy requirements for a major in something other than CS, benefited the most from this exam grade boost.

It seems that our CS1 students are making wiser decisions about whether to stay in the course, and are recovering more successfully when they get off to a bad start. While the proportion who successfully complete CS1 and the proportion of these who continue into CS2 is no different in the inverted offering, we hope that their significantly higher CS1 exam grades indicate that they are better prepared for their further studies in CS.

8. REFERENCES

[1] L. J. Barker, C. McDowell, and K. Kalahar. Exploring factors that influence computer science introductory course students to persist in the major. *SIGCSE Bull.*, 41(1):153–157, Mar. 2009.

[2] J. Bennedsen and M. E. Caspersen. Failure rates in introductory programming. *SIGCSE Bull.*, 39(2):32–36, June 2007.

[3] J. Campbell, D. Horton, M. Craig, and P. Gries. Evaluating an inverted CS1. In *Proceeding of the 45th ACM Technical Symposium on Computer Science Education*, SIGCSE '14, pages 307–312. ACM, 2014.

[4] D. Hagan and S. Markham. Does it help to have some programming experience before beginning a computing degree program? *SIGCSE Bull.*, 32:25–28, 2000.

[5] D. Horton, M. Craig, J. Campbell, P. Gries, and D. Zingaro. Comparing outcomes in inverted and traditional CS1. In *Proceedings of the 2014 Conference on Innovation and Technology in Computer Science Education*, ITiCSE '14, pages 261–266. ACM, 2014.

[6] M. J. Lage, G. J. Platt, and M. Treglia. Inverting the classroom: A gateway to creating an inclusive learning environment. *The Journal of Economic Education*, 31(1):30–43, Jan. 2000.

[7] L. Porter and B. Simon. Retaining nearly one-third more majors with a trio of instructional best practices in CS1. In *Proceeding of the 44th ACM Technical Symposium on Computer Science Education*, SIGCSE '13, pages 165–170, New York, NY, USA, 2013. ACM.

[8] A. Robins. Learning edge momentum: a new account of outcomes in CS1. *Computer Science Education*, 20(1):37–71, 2010.

[9] C. Watson and F. W. Li. Failure rates in introductory programming revisited. In *Proceedings of the 2014 Conference on Innovation and Technology in Computer Science Education*, ITiCSE '14, pages 39–44, New York, NY, USA, 2014. ACM.

[10] B. C. Wilson and S. Shrock. Contributing to success in an introductory computer science course: a study of twelve factors. *SIGCSE Bull.*, 33(1):184–188, Feb. 2001.

Towards Incremental Separation of Surmountable and Insurmountable Programming Difficulties

Jason Carter
Cisco Systems Inc
Research Triangle Park
NC 27709, USA
01 919 392 4809, USA
jasocart@cisco.com

Prasun Dewan
University of North Carolina
Chapel Hill
NC 27599, USA
01 919 590 6123, USA
dewan@cs.unc.edu

Mauro Pichiliani
Instituto Tecnologico de Aeronautica
50 Praça Marechal Eduardo Gomes
São José do Campos, SP
55113931-6352, Brazil
mauro@pichiliani.com.br

ABSTRACT
In an offering of CS 1, we monitored the amount of help students in a class received through various means. We found that most students wanted help that went beyond office hours and email, and that for the vast majority of them, their grades correlated positively with the amount of help they received. However, increasing help also requires increasing instructional resources unless techniques can be found to separate the surmountable difficulties from the insurmountable ones. We have developed such a technique that looks at individual interaction logs and classifies difficulties incrementally as they occur. The insight behind the technique is that when students face surmountable difficulties, they tend to repeat certain action sequences, which can be detected to distinguish the surmountable difficulties from the insurmountable ones. A lab study shows that the mechanism gives significantly better results than the baselines.

Categories and Subject Descriptors
D.2.6. [**Programming Environments**]: Interactive Environments. K.3.1. **[Computer Uses in Education**]: Collaborative Learning. H.5.3. [**Group and Organization Interfaces**]: Computer-supported cooperative work. H.2.8. [**Database Applications**]: Data Mining

General Terms: Design, Experimentation, Human Factors

Keywords: Help awareness; recommender systems

1. INTRODUCTION
Previous work has monitored student programmers to make several kinds of predictions about their current, past, and future progress. These include whether they were stuck in the past [6], how much time they will take to complete their assignments [5], and whether they are currently frustrated [4]. The anticipated applications of these predictions have been allowing instructors to determine how difficult a milestone is, allowing students to allocate time, and allowing well-wishers to offer encouraging words to frustrated students. In this paper, we consider an environment that allows instructors to provide synchronous help to the more needy students.

SIGCSE'15, March 4–7, 2015, Kansas City, MO, USA.

http://dx.doi.org/10.1145/2676723.2677294

Such an environment raises a host of issues reported in the dissertation of the first author [2]. In this paper, we address a subset of them not reported in our previous publications:

1. Do students feel the need for synchronous help that goes beyond traditional office hours?
2. Is it effective to offer them more help - what is the correlation, if any, between the amount of help students receive and their final grade?
3. Can we incrementally classify difficulties into surmountable and insurmountable ones so that instructors can offer help to the more needy students?

To better understand the goals of our work, we have to define surmountable and insurmountable difficulties. Our definition takes into account the perceptions of both developers and observers. A surmountable difficulty is one in which the developers and observers' perception is that developers are having difficulty, but the developers are later able to overcome the programming barrier without help. They overcome the difficulty by increasing the available resources or reducing the required resources such as looking at documentation or code samples. An insurmountable difficulty is one in which the developers and observers' perception is that developers are having difficulty, but the developers are unable to overcome the difficulty in the time given to them.

The rest of the paper addressed these issues after discussing related work on which we build.

2. PREVIOUS WORK
A variety of research has tried to make inferences about the mental condition of programmers and their progress.

One of the earliest approaches to inferring such state is the LISP Tutor [1] - an intelligent tutoring system (ITS). It uses a rule-based approach to help students who write LISP code to overcome logic errors. It gives students small tasks to solve such as combining two lists into a single list, and checks students' input against a set of rules. There are two types of rules: buggy rules, which represent the logic errors that students may make while solving a problem and correct rules, which represent a correct solution. For example, if the goal is for a student to combine two lists, a correct rule would be: "if the goal is to combine list1 and list2 into a single list, then use the function append", while a buggy rule would be "if the goal is to combine list1 and list2 into a single list, then use the function add, add is the incorrect function name, should use the function append."

One problem with Lisp Tutor was that it constrained students' to follow prescribed rules while programming, which limited their ability to explore and try unanticipated ways of solving a problem. This limitation was overcome to some extent by Piech et al. [6], who allowed students to invoke methods defined by instructors and used statistical models to automatically determine the amount of difficulty students had with their assignments and the milestones they had met. They did so, not by looking at individual assignments, as in LispTutor, but all solutions to an assignment submitted by a class.

Their intuition was that a) incremental submissions of students' programs can be automatically assigned labels such as "the student has just started", b) students transitions from label to label could be graphically modeled to show how students transition through assignments, and c) the amount of difficulty students had on assignments was based on the number of code submissions it took before they moved to the next label. This technique makes bulk predictions based on the code of multiple students.

The notion of using such bulk data to make inferences about programming state was also used by Murphy et al. in Retina [5], which estimated how long students would take on new assignments based on how much time (a) the students took on previous assignments, and (b) similar students in a previous offering of a course took on their assignments.

Our goal was to make task-independent incremental predictions based on the actions of individual students. An important step towards such predictions was taken by Kapoor et al. [4], who inferred when students were frustrated. Their goal was to automatically offer encouraging words to frustrated students so that they did not give up. The intuition behind their work was that frustration correlates with changes in body posture, facial expressions, pressure applied to a mouse, and skin conductance. To create training data, participants clicked on an "I'm frustrated" button. When participants did not click this button, they were labeled as not frustrated. This process gave the researchers data that associated various measured attributes such as pressure on a mouse with the two labels.

A problem with this approach is the overhead of using this non-standard equipment. This limitation was overcome to some extent by Staiano et al. [8], who showed that it was possible to infer frustration by mining features in a video captured by a Webcam. However, while a webcam is standard equipment for some tasks such as a scheduled meeting, it is not standard equipment for the programming task.

This problem can be overcome by analyzing, not attributes of the programmers or programs, but instead the interaction of the programmer with the computer. This was the approach taken by Rodrigo and Baker [7]. Instead of predicting the frustration at a particular point of time, they predicted the fraction of time during a series of labs that a programmer was frustrated. This fraction is called the average frustration level, and provides a summary of the history of programming multiple assignments. Rodrigo and Baker conjectured that the average frustration level could be used to not only automatically offer encouragement but also identify those students who were in danger of quitting computer science so that suitable interventions could be devised

The first author's dissertation [2] showed that frustration and difficulty are related in that some programmers do indeed show physical signs of frustration when facing difficulty. On the other hand, some programmers remain outwardly calm when facing difficulty.

Carter and Dewan [3] showed that it is possible to specifically infer programmer difficulty. They did so, not by monitoring the physical characteristics of the programmers, but their interaction with the programming environment. One of the goals of this work was to increase the amount of help offered in the teaching of software engineering. However, this research did not address if more help was desired by students, what effect it would have on student grades, and how such help would be provided using existing resources. As mentioned earlier, these are the issues addressed by this paper.

3. CS 1 STUDY OF HELP USAGE

As part of his Ph.D. requirement, the first author taught a course on object-oriented programming taken by 35 students. We made use of this opportunity to gather data about the need for help and its effectiveness.

Specifically, we determined the number of times the students in the course were given help. Students were observed during office hours and email for six weeks, and special help sessions for two weeks. Help sessions were different from office hours because students could receive help in a small group (3 people) as opposed to a potentially large group in office hours. These help sessions were offered because a) some students did not feel comfortable asking questions during office hours or class, and b) a few of these students sent the instructor emails asking for one-on-one help. More than half of class (21 out of 35) met the instructor during office hours and asked questions through email (21 out of 35) while a little less than half (17 out of 35) of the class attended help sessions.

During office hours and help sessions, with students' permission, we recorded audio with a voice recorder, and immediately after the office hours and help sessions, transcribed the audio. These recordings, together with email logs, allowed us to get the help data we needed. Through email, help sessions, and office hours 27 students received help a total of 190 times. Help was given only after students attempted to solve problems and failed to solve them. Thus, only insurmountable difficulties were addressed. The first author's dissertation lists all of these difficulties, which included, for instance, importing a class from the wrong package and not being able to create a new type.

To determine the correlation between the amount of help students received and the degree to which they learned the subject, we determined the relationship between the sum of the number of times students received help (in email, office hours, and help sessions) and their letter grade converted to a numerical value in the range 1 to 11 with a uniform step size of 1: A = 11, A- = 10, B+ = 9,..., D = 2, and F = 1.

Figure 1 shows that for the vast majority of students, as the amount of help received increased, the final grade of the student tended to increase. We say "for the vast majority" because this pattern doesn't hold true for 29% of the students (10 out of 35). However, the remaining students performed just as well or better than some who received less help, which is consistent with the intuition that the stellar students would require little help. As the figure shows, several students who received an "A" also received help.

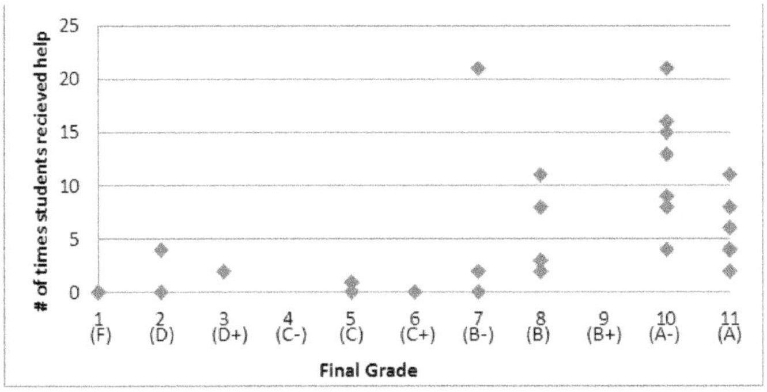

Figure 1. Help vs Grade

As is common in such data, the cause and effect are not separated, and two possible conclusions are: (1) students with higher grades ask for and receive more help, or (2) students who ask for and receive more help get higher grades. Either way, the data show the importance of providing help, even to stellar students. Thus, the data show that for the vast majority of students, receiving help did not have an adverse effect on learning, and may even have had a positive impact if help giving was the cause and the grade was the effect in Figure 1.

Encouraged by these findings we created a collaborative environment that allowed help to be given remotely to distributed students. It provided two ways for the remote helper to learn about student difficulties – the students could ask explicitly for help or the system would infer difficulty using the mechanism of Carter and Dewan described earlier. The first author implemented this environment and used it for the last four of nine assignments.

For the first monitored assignment, students were required to manually ask for help because the instructor was afraid the difficulty detection tool would give false positives. However, only one student pressed the button asking for help. When asked for the reason, students said that they were not sure if the instructor was available to help. Therefore the instructor announced his availability and willingness to help at certain hours. However, this approach resulted in students asking for help with problems they were expected to solve alone. In retrospect, this behavior is not surprising as the second author has found that several students who work outside his office during office hours are quicker to ask for help than those who know help is not immediately available. Therefore, the instructor finally turned on difficulty detection, which proved to be an effective tool.

The instructor was able to offer help 9 times to 8 different students over the last three assignments. There were some days when the tool did not predict that a student had difficulty, but the next day the student came to office hours for help. This result shows the need for explicitly asking for help. But as mentioned above, such requests can lead to over-asking of help. Even automatic detection of difficulties, if turned on for long periods of time, can lead to many true positives. This problem raises the next issue addressed by this research. Is it possible to separate surmountable difficulties from the insurmountable ones so that the instructor can offer help to the more needy students?

4. CLASSIFYING DIFFICULTY LEVEL

Though our work on difficulty classification was motivated by the CS 1 field study, it was carried out after it. Therefore to gather the necessary data, we performed a lab study, involving the development of a GUI. Ten student programmers participated in this study. They were given an hour and a half to complete their tasks. The screens of the students were recorded so that observers could later look at them. In addition, the difficulty detection was turned on, and students could press buttons to correct the predictions and explicitly ask for help. These interactions provided difficulty points, which consisted of a segment of 50 user commands. The size of the segment was defined by the difficulty detection tool.

The first author and an external coder analyzed the difficulty points in the 45 hours of video screen recordings from the GUI study. This analysis occurred in three steps. First, the coders validated participants' perceptions of difficulties using a video observation tool that shows all segments classified as difficult (based on developer status corrections and help requests) and allows coders to agree or not with each classification. Coders agreed on 87% (48/55) of the difficulty points (k=0.70). Second, they went to the moment in the video where participants indicated or confirmed they were having difficulty and scanned backward in the video to find the moment when participants started having difficulty. These moments were identified when participants had an explicit error such as a compiler error or exception, searched the web, executed their programs, or spent a large amount of time outside their programming environment. For example, if developers had incorrect output, they scanned backward to where they first started executing their program to test the behavior they were modifying or implementing in their current task. Third, they scanned forward in the video to find whether participants overcame their difficulty or switched tasks. These moments were identified based on no longer seeing the difficulty or seeing participants implementing a different task. For example, if participants had difficulty with incorrect output, the coders scanned forward in the video until they saw correct output. If participants overcame their difficulties, the coders labeled them as surmountable. If participants could not overcome the difficulties, switched tasks, or the user study ended before participants overcame the difficulty, they labeled these difficulties as insurmountable. Finally, the developers were asked to confirm the difficulties the two coders agreed upon. There were 21 surmountable difficulties and 10 insurmountable difficulties on which both coders and the developers agreed.

Now that we had ground truth, we had to identify appropriate features to classify the difficulties by level. There are at least two ways to do so: create an integrated detection and classification approach or separate them. We chose the latter approach as we envisioned a two-phase prediction approach in which, first certain detection features are used to determine difficulties, and then a new set of classification features is used to classify them as surmountable or insurmountable. The second phase could follow explicit requests for help – it is not tied to difficulty detection.

The challenge now was to identify an appropriate classification scheme. Our scheme is based on the following observations of the logs: developers who had surmountable difficulties tended to cycle through certain command sequences, whereas those with insurmountable difficulties tended to spend a large amount of time between actions and outside the programming environment. The feature set of the difficulty detection tool had been deliberately chosen to ignore wall time so that it did not classify idle phases as difficult ones. We wished to maintain this constraint in difficulty-level classification also. One way to do so was to find the sequences that predict surmountable difficulties, and classify the rest as insurmountable difficulties. This meant we now had to consider the actions that comprised the cyclic sequences and also consider the order/sequence of these actions.

Table 1 gives the commands we found in the cyclic executions. Programming actions marked with an asterisk are new commands, while the others are ones used before in the detection set.

Table 1. Programming actions and their explanations

Programming action	Explanation	Single character representation
ContentAssist*	User invokes intellisense	A
Insertion	User inserts a line of text	B
Deletion	User deletes a line of text	C
Exception*	User has an exception	D
Wait*	User pauses for 1 second between programming actions	E
Run	User executes the program	F
Compilation/Save Code*	User saves the program, which also compiles the program	G
Navigation	User switches from one file to another	H
Gain/Lose Focus	User switches from or to the Eclipse programming environment	I
Break Point	User creates a break point	J
Debug	User invokes the debugger	K
Url Hit*	User goes to a url in the browser	L

To predict whether developers' difficulties are surmountable or insurmountable, we fed the sequences of programming actions into the k-nearest neighbor algorithm. The intuition behind using this algorithm is that it makes predictions using the labels of training sequences (which of course excluded the sequence we are trying to predict) that are closest or more similar to the test sequence. More specifically, given an input sequence and k, the algorithm a) determines the similarity of k sequences to the input sequence and b) classifies the input sequence as the most frequently occurring label in k sequences.

The k-nearest neighbor algorithm needs a real number that reflects the degree to which two sequences are similar. Given that our input is two sequences of programming actions, we need a metric that can measure the similarity of two string values. Two such metrics are the Hamming distance and Levenshtein distance. Hamming distance only works with strings of the same length. The Levenshtein distance can determine the similarity of variable length strings. It is the minimum number of edits needed to change one string into another string. We used this metric.

To compute this metric, we performed two steps. First, we converted each programming activity into a single character, shown in the single character column in Table 1. Second, we divided the log, a sequence of programming actions, into subsequences. We used the top-down insight in Piecah et al [6] of dividing the log in such a way that each subsequence represents a logical unit of work.

We compared two approaches to find these units. One was to split the log by saves, that is, make each segment be the sequence of actions that are saved together by the programmer. The other was to split it by the longest common subsequence between surmountable and insurmountable sequences. Our intuition behind using this approach was that the neighbors found by the k nearest neighbor algorithm would be a subsequence of the longest common subsequence. We implemented an algorithm for finding this sequence and found that it consisted of seven steps: content assist, insertion of text, deletion of text, content assist, content assist, insertion of text, insertion of text. Thus, in this approach, we segmented the log every seven programming actions.

There were 295 surmountable sequences and 121 insurmountable sequences split by save; and 24,142 surmountable sequences and 8,245 insurmountable sequences split by the length of the longest common subsequence. In total, there were 416 surmountable and insurmountable sequences split by save and 32,387 surmountable and insurmountable sequences split by the length of the longest common subsequence. As we see here, split by save makes coarser grained predictions in comparison to split by length of longest subsequence. However, they are finer grained than those made by the difficulty detection module as the number of sequences is much larger than the number of automatically detected difficulty points, with multiple sequences mapping to a single difficulty point. As mentioned earlier, the two prediction schemes are independent and the classification scheme can be used even for explicit help requests.

Now that we have two ways to segment the programming activity logs, we needed to choose a value for k. Choosing this value is still an open research problem. Therefore, we experimented with different values of k to determine their effect on our performance metrics.

We used standard metrics for evaluating a prediction mechanism: The true positive rate identifies how often difficulty classification modules correctly predicted that developers were having surmountable difficulties, the true negative rate identifies how often these modules correctly predicted that developers were having insurmountable difficulties, the false negative rate identifies how often these modules incorrectly predicted that developers were having insurmountable difficulties, and false positive rate indicate how often these modules incorrectly predicted that developers were having surmountable difficulty.

In our evaluations, we used a standard technique, known as k-fold cross validation, which executes k trials of model construction, and splits the logged data so that 90% of the data are used to train the algorithm and 10% of the data are used to test it. We used 10-fold cross validation to compute the performance metrics in different cases.

We needed to choose an odd value for k to avoid ties when determining the most frequently occurring label. We tried all odd values in the range 1 to 50.

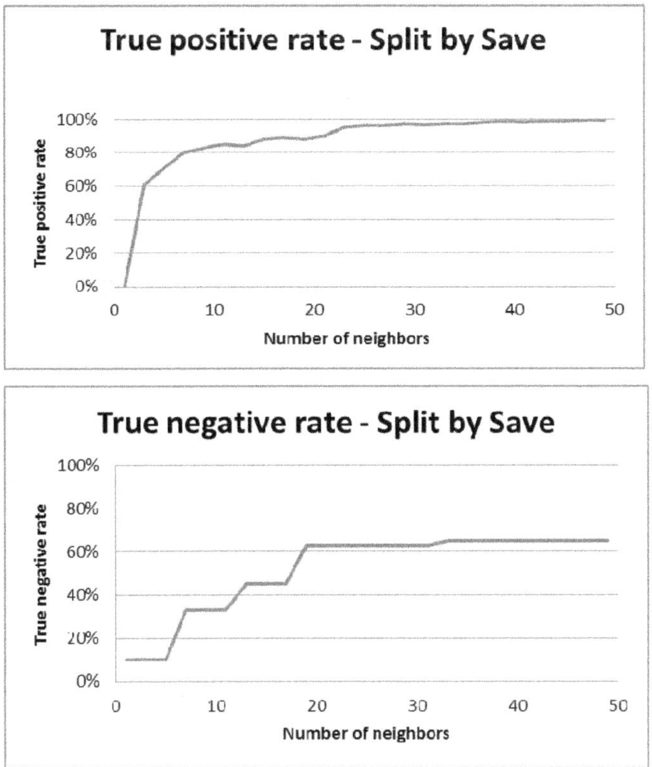

Figure 2. True rates vs. K in split by save.

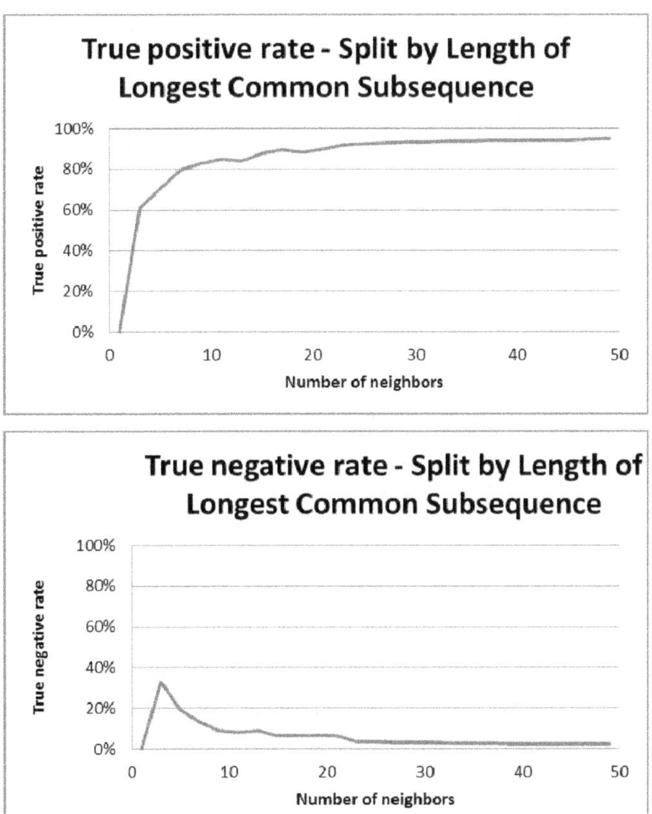

Figure 3. True rates vs. K in Split by longest common subsequence.

Figure 2 and 3 graphs the true positive and negative rates in the split by save and split by length of longest sub-sequence approaches, respectively, as a function of k. In the former approach, the value of each performance metric no longer increases or decreases after k equals 25. Therefore, we chose 25 as the stable value for k. In the latter, this happenes when K is 29; so we chose this value in the second case.

As we know of no previous work that incrementally predicts difficulty levels, we used three standard baselines in our comparisons, all of which make a binary choice between two labels (in this case. surmountable, insurmountable): a) *randomized approach*, which predicts one label 50% of the time and the other label 50% of the time, b) *modal approach*, which always predicts the label that occurs most often, and c) *data distribution approach*, which makes predictions based on the distribution of labels

Tables 2-6 show some of the confusion matrices for various cases we compared. The positive is surmountable and the negative is insurmountable.

Table 2 shows that the K-nearest neighbor split by save prediction algorithm correctly identified 96% of the surmountable difficulties and 63% of the insurmountable difficulties.

Table 3 shows that the K-nearest neighbor split by length of longest common subsequence prediction algorithm does not fare as well. It is heavily biased towards surmountable difficulties: it correctly identified 93% of the surmountable difficulties, but only 3% of the insurmountable difficulties.

As split by save gives better results, we used it in the three baseline algorthms. Table 4 shows that the random baseline correctly identifies 50% of the surmountable barriers and 52% of the insurmountable barriers. We use the binomial test to determine if there is a significant statistical difference between each baseline and the results of our K-nearest neighbor algorithm. The k-nearest neighbor algorithm (with sequences split by save) performs significantly better than the random baseline (TPR=95% vs. TPR=50%, $p < .001$) (TNR=63% vs. TNR=50%, $p < .001$).

Table 5 shows that the modal baseline correctly identifies all of the surmountable barriers, but never identifies the insurmountable barriers. Because of the extreme negative rates, there is no need to use a significance test to compare the modal baseline to our approach.

Table 6 shows that the data distribution baseline identifies 71% of the insurmountable barriers, but only 29% of the surmountable barriers. The true positive rate of the k-nearest neighbor algorithm (with sequences split by save) is significantly better than the data distribution baseline (TPR=95% vs. TPR=29%, $p < .001$). There is not a significant difference between the true negative rate of the k-nearest neighbor algorithm (with sequences split by save) and the data distribution baseline (TNR=63% vs. TNR=71%, $p < .001$).

5. CONCLUSIONS AND FUTURE WORK

The main conclusions of our experiment are that (a) students wanted synchronous help beyond what was provided in face-to-face office hours, (b) in the case of the vast majority of students, those who received more help for insurmountable difficulties (through any of the available means) also got better grades, (c) students often asked for help when they had surmountable difficulties, (d) it was important to automatically distinguish between surmountable and insurmountable difficulties, (e) certain command sequences were repeated during surmountable difficulties, (f) splitting the log by saves gave better predictions than splitting it by length of longest subsequences, (g) the K-nearest neighbor split by save algorithm gave better predictions than the three baselines and the K-nearest split by length of longest subsequence algorithm, and (h) this algorithm was biased towards surmountable difficulties.

Table 2. Confusion matrix for k-nearest neighbor algorithm when k is 25 and segments are split by save

	Predicted Surmountable	Predicted Insurmountable
Actual Surmountable	281 (True positives)	14 (False negatives)
Actual Insurmountable	45 (False positives)	76 (True negatives)

Table 3. Confusion matrix for k-nearest neighbor algorithm when k is 29 and segments are split by the length of the longest common subsequence

	Predicted Surmountable	Predicted Insurmountable
Actual Surmountable	22470 (True positives)	1672 (False negatives)
Actual Insurmountable	7997 (False positives)	248 (True negatives)

Table 4. Confusion matrix for random baseline (split by save)

	Predicted Surmountable	Predicted Insurmountable
Actual Surmountable	148 (True positives)	147 (False negatives)
Actual Insurmountable	60 (False positives)	61 (True negatives)

Table 5. Confusion matrix for modal baseline (split by save)

	Predicted Surmountable	Predicted Insurmountable
Actual Surmountable	295 (True positives)	0 (False negatives)
Actual Insurmountable	121 (False positives)	0 (True negatives)

A practical implication of this bias is that that the tool will often label an insurmountable difficulty as surmountable. However, very few surmountable difficulties will be labelled as insurmountable. Thus, helpers will not waste time with surmountable difficulties but can miss many insurmountable ones. This mechanism, thus, relies on (a) students being persistent in asking for help or (b) an awareness mechanism that allows helpers to monitor workspaces of students whose difficulties were predicted as surmountable after they have addressed those whose difficulties were predicted as insurmountable.

Future work is of course required to improve the predictions, implement them in a robust tool (one that can be used by teachers other than the implementer of the tool), and use the tool in actual classes. One exciting application is an inverted large classroom where the prediction algorithms are used to offer help to the more needy students.

Table 6. Confusion matrix for data distribution baseline (split by save)

	Predicted Surmountable	Predicted Insurmountable
Actual Surmountable	86 (True positives)	209 (False negatives)
Actual Insurmountable	35 (False positives)	86 (True negatives)

6. ACKNOWLEDGMENTS

This research was supported in part by the NSF award IIS 1250702. This work is part of the dissertation of Jason Carter, whose Ph.D. committee, Fred Brooks, Diane Kelley, Dave Stotts, and Wei Wang, helped with the evaluation and presentation of these ideas.

7. REFERENCES

[1] Anderson, J.R. and B.J. Reiser (1985), The LISP tutor: it approaches the effectiveness of a human tutor. Lecture notes in computer science, 1985. 10(4).

[2] Carter, J. (2014), Automatic Difficulty Detection, in Ph.D. Thesis, Department of Computer Science, University of North Carolina (http://youtu.be/HURoaO5f2FA): Chapel Hill.

[3] Carter, J. and P. Dewan (2010) Design, Implementation, and Evaluation of an Approach for Determining When Programmers are Having Difficulty. in Proc. Group 2010. ACM.

[4] Kapoor, A., W. Burlesonc, and R.W. Picard (2007), Automatic Prediction of Frustration. International Journal of Human-Computer Studies, 2007. 65(8).

[5] Murphy, C., G.E. Kaiser, K. Loveland, and S. Hasan (2009) Retina: Helping Students and Instructors Based on Observed Programming Activities. in Proc. ACM SIGCSE.

[6] Piech, C., M. Sahami, D. Koller, S. Cooper, and P. aBlikstein (2012) Modeling how students learn to program. in Proceedings of the 43rd ACM technical symposium on Computer Science Education.

[7] Rodrigo, T. and R. Baker (2009) Coarse-grained detection of student frustration in an introductory programming course. in Proceedings of the fifth computing education research workshop. ACM.

[8] Staiano, J., M. Menéndez, A. Battocchi, A.D. Angeli, and N. Sebe (2012) UX_Mate: from facial expressions to UX evaluation. in Proceedings of the Designing Interactive Systems Conference. ACM.

Illustrating the Interaction of Algorithms and Data Structures Using the Matching Problem

Joan M. Lucas
The College at Brockport, SUNY
350 New Campus Drive
Brockport, NY, 14420, USA
jlucas@brockport.edu

ABSTRACT

A thorough understanding of algorithms and data structures is essential for any student of Computer Science. In this paper we present a sequence of programming projects that elegantly integrate both the study of algorithmic paradigms with an illustration of how the choice of data structure significantly impacts an algorithm. We do this in the context of a single, easily understood problem domain, that of finding a maximum matching in a graph. By focusing on only a single problem, students more fully appreciate the concept that any problem can be solved in a variety of different ways.

Categories and Subject Descriptors

E.1 [Data Structures]: graphs and networks; G.2.2 [Graph Theory]: graph algorithms; K.3.2 [Computer and Information Science Education]

General Terms

Algorithms

Keywords

Algorithm design paradigms, data structures, complexity analysis, matching problem

1. INTRODUCTION

Algorithms and data structures together represent some of the most fundamental concepts in the computing disciplines. These topics have featured prominently in all the main curriculum models published by the ACM, including the recent CS2013 [2]. CS2013 outlines those topics that are considered essential for all computer science majors in what they refer to as Tier 1 of the Core. Of the 165 hours listed in Tier 1, 19 hours are dedicated to topics in the AL (Algorithms and Complexity) Knowledge Area, making this the third highest area with respect to hours among the 18 different areas that comprise the computing field.

Typically algorithms and data structures topics are covered extensively in CS 1 and CS 2 courses, and also in upper-level courses in Algorithm Design and Analysis or Advanced Data Structures. But traditional curriculum offerings frequently separate out these two fundamental topics. Basic algorithms, such as binary search and sorting, are introduced in CS 1, while a survey of the classic data structures (e.g., linked lists, heaps, binary search trees, hash tables, etc.) are given a separate treatment in CS 2. Later students may learn about the fundamental algorithmic paradigms (greedy, divide and conquer, dynamic programming, etc.) in a course on Algorithm Design.

In this paper we present a sequence of programming projects that elegantly integrate both the study of algorithmic paradigms with an illustration of how the choice of data structure significantly impacts an algorithm. We do this in the context of a single, easily understood problem domain. By studying many different algorithms for a single problem, students more fully grasp that any problem can be approached many different ways, and that each solution strategy will have its own advantages and disadvantages. These projects are suitable for courses in either Data Structures or in Algorithm Design and Analysis. Although this paper focuses on "greedy" algorithms, we discuss in the conclusion how this problem domain can also be used to illustrate other algorithmic paradigms.

2. STUDENT LEARNING OUTCOMES AND RELATED WORK

The Student Learning Outcomes associated with these programming projects are the following:

1. Be able to develop and implement different algorithms for a single given problem.
2. Recognize that different heuristic strategies may produce different solutions.
3. Appreciate the inter-dependence of algorithms and data structures, and the impact of the choice of data structures on algorithmic complexity.

The strategy of using a single problem domain as a thread throughout an entire course has also been advocated by Erkan et al. [5] and investigated by Lobo and Baliga [11, 12]. Lobo and Baliga have developed sequences of programming projects for three different problem domains: the Travelling Salesman Problem, Boolean Formula Satisfiability, and Sudoku. These problems are all NP-complete, unlike the domain we consider in this paper. Therefore the projects developed by Lobo and Baliga focus primarily on teaching different algorithmic paradigms associated with intractable problems, such as brute force, heuristic algorithms, approximation, reduction and probabilistic algorithms.

SIGCSE '15, March 04 – 07, 2015, Kansas City, MO, USA.
Copyright 2014 ACM 978-1-4503-2966-8/15/03…$15.00.
http://dx.doi.org/10.1145/2676723.2677212

The projects presented here have a greater emphasis on the data structure issues that arise in the different algorithms, and the impact of the choice of data structure on the complexity analysis of the algorithms.

Coffey [3] also advocates for greater integration within the curriculum for the classic topics in algorithms, data structures and discrete mathematics. He provides a sequence of programming projects to achieve this end, although he outlines a sequence of two courses, and the projects described are drawn from a range of applications, rather than focusing on a single problem domain.

3. PROBLEM DOMAIN

The problem domain we use in this sequence of programming projects is the Matching Problem for graphs. Given a graph G = (V, E) with n nodes and m edges, the problem is to find a set of edges M such that no two edges in M share an endpoint. For example, Figure 1 shows a graph with n = 8 and m = 9. The edges (0,1), (2,5), and (4,3) form a matching in this graph.

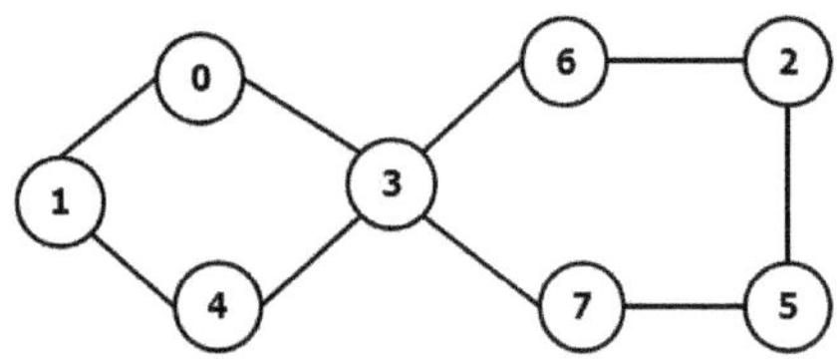

Figure 1. Sample input graph

The Matching Problem can be defined for either weighted or unweighted graphs. If the graph is weighted then we wish to select the set of edges whose sum of edge weights is as large as possible. This is very similar to the Minimum Spanning Tree problem, except we are looking for edges that are disjoint, rather than edges that form a tree. If the input graph is unweighted, then we wish to find the largest possible set of edges, i.e., all edges have unit weight. Note that the set of 3 matched edges given above is not a maximum matching. A better solution is shown in Figure 2. The Matching Problem is presented in a number of standard Algorithms textbooks [4, 7, 9, 10, 17].

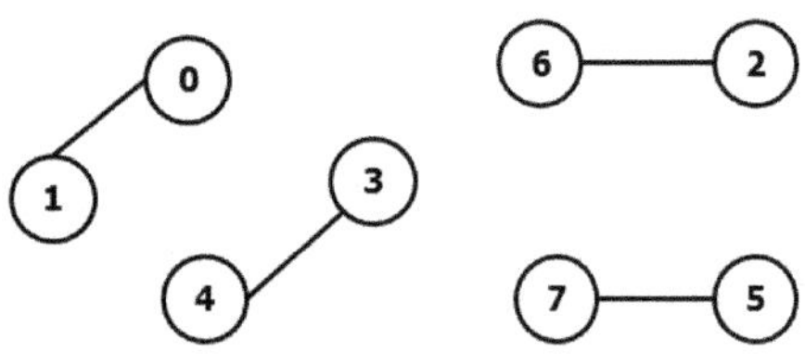

Figure 2. Maximum Matching for the graph in Figure 1

This problem is very easy for students to understand. It also has the advantage that it can be motivated by compelling real-world applications. The Matching Problem arises in a setting that directly impacts peoples' lives. Currently there are tens of thousands of patients in the United States who need a new kidney. Often a patient will have a friend or relative who is willing to donate a healthy kidney. In some cases, the transplant between the two can take place directly. But organ transplant is complicated by the need for a compatible organ; one that will not be rejected by the patient's immune system. Therefore hospitals have started programs of organ swaps, where one pair of patient-and-incompatible-friend is grouped with another pair. For example, the friend of the first patient will donate a kidney to the second patient, and in return the sister of the second patient will donate a kidney to the first patient. When we consider more patient-friend pairs, this situation can be envisioned as a graph. The nodes of the graph are the incompatible-patient-friend pairs and the edges denote those pairs whose compatibility would allow a successful organ-swap. In order to help the greatest number of patients, the problem becomes one of finding a maximum matching in this graph, since each selected edge corresponds to a "kidney swap". Regional centers that facilitate these kidney swaps have been in operation since 2001 [15, 16].

Another interesting application of the Matching Problem is described in [13]. Each year the Association of American Medical Colleges must find a matching between students graduating from medical school and positions in residency-training programs at hospitals. The National Resident Matching Program has existed since 1952, and each year tens of thousands of students participate.

Using the Matching Problem as the basis for these projects has other advantages as well. Both the input and the output of the problem is a graph, which can be easily displayed on the screen. The (x,y) coordinates associated with each vertex in the graph are arbitrary, unlike the case when the graph represents an instance of the Travelling Salesman Problem. Nevertheless, the visual representation is still very helpful to students as they develop and debug their programs. We provide students with all the code necessary to initialize and display graphically both the input graph and the solution set of matched edges, as illustrated in Figures 1 and 2. This allows students to focus their time on implementing the actual matching algorithms. Many authors had advocated the benefits of assignments that have both real-world relevance and also a visual component [14, 19, 20].

There are other benefits to assigning the students a series of projects focused on a single problem. The students have less "conceptual load" that comes from understanding several different problem specifications. But more importantly, the students gain a deep understanding that any given problem can be approached in many different ways, and that some algorithmic strategies yield better solutions that others. The benefits of assigning a sequence of projects based on a single problem domain are also described in Lobo and Baliga [11].

4. PROGRAMMING PROJECTS FOR THE MATHCHING PROBLEM

We now describe the actual programming projects and the algorithmic and data structure issues that arise in each one. One of the goals of these projects is to illustrate the interplay of algorithms and data structures. To allow students to focus on these issues, and not be distracted by tangential programming details, we use the free Java package net-datstructues-5-0.jar developed by Goodrich and Tamassia [8]. This code contains all the classes and methods needed to perform standard graph operations. In our projects we use the AdjacencyListGraph class to create graphs, add vertices and edges, and develop the graph algorithms. We provide the students with the source code of a solution of Prim's greedy algorithm for the Minimum Spanning Tree as an example of using this code to manipulate a graph.

One very useful feature of this graph API is the ability to "decorate" the vertices and edges in the graph with any additional fields that the student wishes to define. Although the Vertex and Edge classes already exist in the library code, this feature allows students to add additional fields (called "decorations") to either the Vertices or the Edges, as needed by their algorithms. For example, the code we provide to the students uses an "identifier" decoration to label each vertex with a unique id number. The students also use "decorations" to label the edges in the graph as either "free edges" or "matched edges". All edges are initially "free", and the goal of the algorithm is to determine which edges should become "matched".

We provide students with all the source code to create the input graph and to display the solution matching visually. Students are only asked to develop the code to implement the matching algorithms. By allowing students to focus on the algorithm and data structures issues in the code, we are able to assign a greater number of different projects during the semester.

Although the Matching Problem can be used to teach several different algorithmic paradigms, we discuss here only those assignments that use the "greedy strategy". Other possible assignments are outlined briefly in the conclusion.

All greedy algorithms follow the same general strategy. Greedy algorithms develop a solution by gradually adding more and more elements to the solution. For the Matching Problem, a greedy algorithm forms the solution set of edges by choosing the edges to be matched using some "greedy heuristic". As is common for all greedy algorithms, once a choice has been made, that decision is never undone, and the edge that was selected to be matched will remain as part of the solution. The interesting algorithmic question concerns what heuristic should be used to make the "greedy choice". The following projects outline several different greedy strategies, each one increasingly more complex.

Project 1 – Simple Greedy with no Heuristic This is the simplest possible algorithm. The students simply write a loop that scans down the list of all of the edges in the graph, and for each edge (x,y), that edge is added to the solution set if-and-only-if neither of the vertices x and y are endpoints of an edge already selected as a matched edge. This assignment is a good warm-up exercise, and allows the students the chance to gain familiarity with the graph API.

Project 2 – Greedy by Vertex Degree This algorithm uses a very simple and intuitive heuristic. Each vertex in the graph has a "degree", which is its number of neighbors in the graph. For example, the degree of vertex 3 in Figure 1 is 4. The algorithm examines the vertices in increasing order by degree, and selects an edge (if possible) from the current vertex x to the neighbor y of x that has the lowest degree among all the free neighbors of x. The intuition is that when an edge (x,y) is selected to be a matched edge, then all of the other edges from x to its neighbors, and from y to y's other neighbors, are no longer eligible to be added to the solution. By choosing x, and then y, with low degree, we are trying to minimize the number of edges that are being "disqualified" from the solution set.

The code for this algorithm is fairly straightforward. The students simply place all the vertices of the graph into a PriorityQueue (i.e., a heap-ordered complete binary tree) based on the vertex degrees at the beginning of the program. The algorithm then repeatedly removes the minimum vertex x from the PriorityQueue and examines all the neighbors of x. The algorithm selects the edge from x to its lowest degree free neighbor y to become a matched edge, if such a vertex y exists.

Note that the objective of these projects is to illustrate the *use* of different data structures (e.g., PriorityQueue), rather than teaching how to *implement* the data structure operations (e.g., removeMin). Students use the PriorityQueue class provided in the java.util library. This philosophy of emphasizing the *application* of data structures, rather than the "under the hood" details has been advocated by several authors [6, 18] since the development of the Java Collections Framework and the Standard Template Library in C++.

We also provide the students with the definition of the Comparator to be used by the PriorityQueue. Since many vertices in the input graph may have the same degree, the output of the algorithm can vary substantially based on the "tie-breaker" rule used by the PriorityQueue. Our Comparator compares vertices based on their degree in the graph, and ties are then broken by ordering the vertices by the value of their identifier decoration. Although the AdjacencyListGraph code provides a method to return the degree of any vertex in the graph, we used a "degree decoration" for each vertex, and it is this decoration that is used by the Comparator of the PriorityQueue. This distinction becomes important in the next programming project.

Students were provided five sample input graphs. The smallest input graph was the one shown in Figure 1. The largest graph contained 225 vertices. For the input graph in Figure 1, this greedy algorithm selects the three edges (0,1), (2,5), and (4,3), in that order, to be the matched edges, since the algorithm breaks ties between vertices with the same degree using the vertex identifiers. It should be noted that all of these greedy algorithms continue to add more edges to the solution set of matched edges, until no more edges can possibly be added. Therefore the solution generated is a "maximal" solution, but is not guaranteed to be "maximum". This simple greedy algorithm does not find the maximum solution for the input graph in Figure 1.

The small size of the input graph in Figure 1 is useful when the students are developing and debugging their code. The larger input graphs are interesting because they let the students see their algorithm in play in a larger setting and also because the solutions generated for the larger input graphs by the different algorithms will vary depending on which heuristic the algorithm uses.

There is an additional benefit in using the Matching Problem as the problem domain. These greedy matching algorithms generate solutions that will be *maximal* sets of edges. It is very simple and efficient to automatically check whether a given set of edges is maximal. This step requires only a single linear time scan of all the edges (x, y) in the graph to check that either x, or y, or both are incident to a matched edge. This algorithm verification step is included in the source code given to the students. The students not only run their algorithms on the given set of five input graphs, but the source code also automatically executes the students' algorithms on 1,000 randomly generated graphs and verifies that the matching generated is indeed maximal.

The students are also asked to analyze the complexity of their algorithm. For this greedy algorithm the analysis is fairly straightforward, and is dominated by the PriorityQueue operations. The overall cost is $O(n \log(n) + m)$, which simplifies to $O(n \log(n))$ for sparse graphs, where m is $O(n)$, and to $O(n^2)$ for dense graphs, where m is $O(n^2)$.

Project 3 – Greedy by Dynamically Updated Vertex Degree This algorithm employs a similar heuristic, i.e., we want to select edges by finding a vertex x with "low degree", and then finding the lowest degree free neighbor y of x. But once an edge (x,y) has been added to the solution set of matched edges, then all the other edges in the graph adjacent to either x or y are no longer eligible to be part of the solution. For example, in Figure 1, when the first edge (0,1) is selected to be matched, then the edges (0,3) and (1,4) are no longer eligible to be matched edges. Therefore those edges can effectively be deleted from the graph. Removing those edges will alter the degrees of the nodes remaining in the graph. For example, vertex 3 should now be considered to have degree 3, and not degree 4. In this project we ask the students to implement this "greedy by degree" algorithm but now the "degree" of each vertex is its number of neighbors in the graph that correspond to edges that are still eligible to be added to the solution set of matched edges. In the previous algorithm, the degree of each vertex was static; it equaled the vertex's degree in the original graph.

This project raises some interesting data structure issues. In this assignment students were given just the basic outline of the greedy strategy described above. Since they had recently completed the "greedy by static degree" algorithm, using a PriorityQueue of vertices, a significant number of students reflexively assumed that the best data structure would again be the PriorityQueue. This led a large fraction of the students to make a number of interesting errors that provided a valuable "teachable moment" in data structures. When an edge (x,y) is added to the solution set of matched edges, the value of the degree of each of the neighbors of x (respectively, of y) must be decreased by one. Using the AdjacencyListGraph class, the algorithm has a direct reference to each of the neighbors of x, via the adjacency list of all the neighbors of x. Many students used this reference to directly decrement the degree decoration/field of each of these neighbor nodes. But this action alters the state of vertices that are currently elements in the PriorityQueue without using any of the methods of the PriorityQueue class, thereby violating the invariant condition of the underlying heap-ordered binary tree representing the PriorityQueue. Performing a removeMin operation on the PriorityQueue is no longer guaranteed to delete the smallest element in the PriorityQueue. So although the students' code would execute and produce a set of matched edges, the code was not in fact implementing the greedy strategy. This scenario provides a nice illustration of how data (i.e., the vertices of the graph) can be elements in more than one data structure at the same time.

Another large group of students avoided this error, but their approach was equally problematic. To decrement the degree of a vertex currently in the PriorityQueue, the students would remove that vertex from the PriorityQueue, update its degree decoration, and then re-insert the vertex back into the PriorityQueue. But the PriorityQueue data structure is not designed to efficiently support the general remove operation. Elements in a PriorityQueue in the Java Collections Framework are stored in a complete heap-ordered binary tree. The smallest element is at the root of the tree, and can be deleted in logarithmic time. But removing an arbitrary vertex from a PriorityQueue requires linear time to first scan the entire heap to simply locate that vertex. So although this solution does correctly implement the greedy strategy, it is extremely inefficient. This issue was discussed in class after the students had completed their projects. This situation provided a good opportunity for students to appreciate that although the code they wrote was simply *using* the PriorityQueue operations (i.e., invoking the remove and removeMin operations), it is still important to understand the underlying *implementation* of classic data structures.

Only about one-third of the students in the class used the following more efficient strategy. This strategy simply maintains the set of free, unmatched vertices in a simple, unordered List. Locating the vertex x with the lowest degree decoration requires a linear time scan of the List, but when (x, y) is selected to become a matched edge, then all of the degree decorations of the neighbors of x and y can be decremented in constant time each.

The students were asked to execute this greedy-by-dynamically-updated-degree algorithm on the same set of five input graphs. For the input graph in Figure 1, this algorithm produces the maximum solution shown in Figure 2. Notice that the identifier for each vertex is carefully selected so that when the Comparator uses the identifiers as the "tie-breaker", the greedy-by-static-degree algorithm finds a solution with 3 edges, in contrast to the greedy-by-dynamic-degree algorithm, which finds a maximum solution of 4 edges. This is the motivation for providing students with the source code definition of the Comparator for vertices.

Again, the students were asked to analyze the algorithm for both sparse and dense graphs. The algorithm that uses a simple Linked List to maintain the set of free vertices has $O(n^2 + m)$ complexity, which is effectively $O(n^2)$ for both sparse and dense graphs. This is less efficient than the greedy-by-static-degree algorithm when the graph is sparse. But this algorithm will usually produce a larger set of matched edges.

Implementing the algorithm correctly using a PriorityQueue instead of a List to store the "free" vertices has complexity $O(n\log(n) + m*n)$, which is never more efficient than using a List. This algorithm illustrates that using a simple data structure (i.e., a List) can sometimes be a better choice than using a sophisticated data structure (i.e., a PriorityQueue). This situation is very similar to the implementation of Dijkstra's shortest path algorithm. In Dijkstra's algorithm it is more efficient to store the vertices in a simple, unordered List, rather than a PriorityQueue, since the decreaseKey operation occurs more frequently in Dijkstra's algorithm than the removeMin operation.

Project 4 – Greedy by Dynamically Updated Vertex Degree using Balanced Trees

This sequence of projects was assigned to the students throughout the course of the semester in a class on Algorithms and Data Structures. The course was organized so that algorithmic paradigms, such as greedy algorithms, divide-and-conquer algorithms, graph algorithms, etc. are studied earlier in the semester, followed by a month focusing on the implementation details of complex data structures (red-black trees, B-trees, etc.). By the time the students had completed the projects above, the class had reached the point of studying balanced binary search tree data structures (e.g., red-black trees). Students were already familiar with simple binary search trees, but had not yet learned about balancing techniques.

At this point we asked the students to re-implement the greedy-by-dynamically-updated-degrees algorithm; only now they were instructed to store the vertices in a balanced binary search tree (i.e., the TreeSet class in the java.util library) instead of a PriorityQueue or a List. Using a TreeSet, students can quickly locate the vertex x with the smallest value (i.e., the lowest degree decoration in the graph). The ability to locate the "minimum key" is the main functionality of a PriorityQueue, but this operation is also efficiently supported in a TreeSet. Bell et al.

[1] also observed that a binary search tree can be used effectively as a PriorityQueue in their study of sorting algorithms.

Beyond locating the smallest value, a TreeSet efficiently implements all of the general operations of search, insert and remove. Therefore it is possible to also update the degree decoration of any neighbor w of the lowest degree vertex x by locating, removing, updating, and then re-inserting that vertex w back into the TreeSet. All of these operations can be carried out by a TreeSet in logarithmic time. Therefore this implementation of the algorithm has complexity O((n+m) log (n)), which is more efficient than using a simple, unordered List when the input graph is sparse.

Although the students could have used a TreeSet in the earlier assignment, fewer than 10% actually did so. These projects can be considered as examples of the constructivist learning model, which emphasizes having students actively engage in their own learning rather than passively receive information. By allowing students to make their own design decisions regarding the choice of data structure, and then seeing how those decisions lead to sub-optimal code, the students gain a deeper appreciation of the interaction between algorithms and data structures.

5. ASSSESSMENT

We have used these projects in a course on Algorithms and Data Structures during 2013-2014. This course is required for all Computer Science majors at Brockport College, which is a mid-sized comprehensive undergraduate institution. At the end of the semester the students were asked to complete a short survey with five questions. The survey used a four-point Likert scale where the responses were: Strongly Agree, Agree, Disagree, and Strong Disagree. Of the 31 students enrolled in the course, 24 (or 77 %) completed the survey. The averages of the student responses are shown in Table 1 below, where 4.0 = Strongly Agree and 1.0 = Strongly Disagree.

Overall the students had a positive attitude towards these projects. Questions 1 and 3, which are most directly related to the learning outcomes of these exercises, received the highest ratings. The students showed only mild agreement with the statement that matching is an interesting problem to study. It must be acknowledged that this problem is not as immediately compelling as other settings, such as games or multi-media. But the tradeoff is that the Matching Problem can be understood immediately. There does exist the drawback that our strategy of using the Matching Problem might give students a narrow view of computing. But we note that our course also covered a variety of other problems in the context of teaching the divide-and-conquer and dynamic programming paradigms, although students were not expected to implement those algorithms.

Students were also asked to provide written feedback on their impressions of this sequence of programming projects. The majority of the comments were positive. A representative sample is provided below:

- It helps you to understand that for a given problem there are multiple ways of solving it. Moreover, the different solutions that we studied in the programming assignments show us how to important are the use of specific data structures.
- Doing the Matching Problem repeatedly to explore different algorithms and data structures helped. It no longer became a problem to understanding how the problem worked, but how to implement the different algorithms.
- This was a well implemented demonstration of the concepts of this class at a level of programming that was reasonable but still appropriately challenging. Both the concepts of algorithm design and the impact of data structures on run-time and design were illustrated and easy to implement.
- I believe the Matching Problem is a great way to explore the topics of the course. The way the instructor requires different strategies and data structures to solve the problem demonstrates how different algorithms can be better than others.
- It worked fine to get the points across but I did not find it that interesting.
- I think having a variety of problems to program solutions to would have given me a wider understanding of Algorithms and Data Structures.

Although these projects were assigned within the context of a single upper-level course on Algorithms and Data Structures, it would be possible to use these ideas across a two-course sequence that includes CS 2. CS 2 usually focuses on the definition and implementations of standard data structures, e.g., linked lists, heaps, binary search trees and hashing. Projects 1-4 could be assigned in CS 2 as applications of the first three of these data structures. Project 4 relies on balanced search trees, which at Brockport is not studied until the junior year. But the concept of balanced trees is intuitive, and can be explained to students without providing details of how the balancing is achieved.

Table 1. Student Feedback on Matching Problem projects

1	I understand that there are several broad strategies/paradigms for developing an algorithm to solve a given problem.	3.79
2	By studying one specific problem (i.e., the Matching Problem), I gained a better understanding of how a problem can have many different algorithms.	3.21
3	I understand that the choice of data structure can have an important impact on the run-time complexity of an algorithm	3.79
4	The Matching Problem is an interesting problem to study.	3.04
5	The programming assignments helped improve my programming skills.	3.00

6. CONCLUSION

This paper has described a sequence of programming projects that elegantly integrate the concept of algorithmic paradigms with the issue of choosing an appropriate data structure. We have described here only the projects that use the "greedy" paradigm and that highlight the choice of data structure. But during the course we also gave students other projects that used other algorithmic paradigms. Many important graph algorithms are based on the fundamental techniques of traversing a graph in linear time using either depth-first-search (DFS) or breadth-first-search (BFS). There are several algorithms for the

Matching Problems that are based on DFS. A DFS traversal of a graph will generate a spanning forest. The matching algorithm can select the matched edges during the DFS traversal in a greedy fashion as the spanning forest is constructed. This can be done in either a top-down manner (i.e. a pre-order strategy), or in a bottom-up fashion (i.e., in the post-order). Once the DFS is completed, a single linear time scan of all the edges in the graph can be performed, to determine if any additional edges can be added to the solution set. This last step insures that the solution is maximal. If the matched edges are selected from the bottom-up, then the solution set is guaranteed to be optimal in the special case where the input graph is acyclic (i.e., is a forest of trees). This is the only case where the greedy algorithms presented here are guaranteed to find the optimal (i.e., maximum) solution.

Another more sophisticated algorithm based on DFS is Edmond's augmenting path algorithm [10]. Unlike the previous algorithms, this strategy is not greedy. It works by repeatedly finding an odd-length path of edges through the graph that alternates between free edges and matched edges, and then toggling every edge on that path from free edge to matched edge, or matched edge to free edge. The algorithm continues until no such augmenting path can be found. Since locating a single augmenting path requires its own DFS traversal of the graph, this assignment is significantly more demanding than the greedy DFS algorithm described above. It is worth noting that this algorithm, unlike the "greedy by degrees" algorithms, is guaranteed to produce a maximum solution when the input graph is bipartite, which is the case in the application of matching doctors to hospitals [13].

Finally, the Matching Problem can also be used to illustrate the technique of "problem reduction" where we can solve an instance of a problem by converting it into an equivalent instance of a different problem. Reduction is the fundamental technique used to prove that a problem is NP-complete. The Vertex Cover problem is NP-complete. But it is possible to generate a 2-approximate solution for an instance of Vertex Cover by reducing it to an instance of the Maximal Matching Problem [4].

In this paper we have shown how the Matching Problem can be used as a domain to illustrate a variety of central issues in the study of algorithms and data structures. The Matching Problem is both conceptually simple to understand, yet also motivated by compelling real-world applications. By developing a variety of algorithms, using several classic algorithm design paradigms, students learn that there are many different ways to solve the same problem, and that the choice of data structure plays a crucial role in the overall complexity of the algorithm. The Java source code that we provide to the students, which initializes the input graph, executes the student's algorithm, and visually displays the solution set of matched edges, together with the project specifications, are available upon request.

7. REFERENCES

[1] Bell, T. and Aspvall, B. *Sorting Algorithms as Special Cases of a Priority Queue Sort,* Proceedings of SIGCSE 2011, pp 123-128. Mar 2011, ACM (2011).

[2] ACM/IEEE-CS Joint Task Force on Computing Curricula. 2013. Computer Science Curricula 2013. ACM Press and IEEE Computer Society Press. DOI: http://dx.doi.org/10.1145/2534860

[3] Coffey, J. *Integrating Theoretical and Empirical Computer Science in a Data Structures Course,* Proceedings of SIGCSE 2013, pp 23-27. Mar 2013, ACM (2013).

[4] Cormen, T. H., Leiserson, C. E., Rivest, R. L., and Stein, C. *Introduction to Algorithms*, 3rd ed.. The MIT Press, Cambridge, MA, 2009.

[5] Erkan, A., Hamilton, J., Pfaff, T., and Rogers, M. *Sustainability Themed Problem Solving in Data Structures and Algorithms,* Proceedings of SIGCSE 2012, pp 9-14. Feb 2012, ACM (2012).

[6] Ernst, D. J., Stevenson, D. E., and Wagner, P. *Hybrid and custom data structures: evolution of the data structures course,* Proceedings of ITiCSE 2009, pp 213-217, July 2009, ACM (2009)

[7] Goodrich, M. T., and Tamassia, R. *Algorithm Design,* John Wiley and Sons, 2002.

[8] Goodrich, M. T., and Tamassia, R., *net-datastructures-5-0.jar*, Retrieved Jan. 20, 2012 from http://net3.datastructures.net/download.html

[9] Kleinberg, J. and Tardos, E. *Algorithm Design,* Pearson Education, 2006.

[10] Levitin, A. *Introduction to the Design and Analysis of Algorithm, 3rd ed.,* Pearson, 2012.

[11] Lobo, A. and Baliga, G. *A Project-based Curriculum for Algorithm Design and Intractability Centered on the Travelling Salesman Problem,* The Journal of Computing Sciences in Colleges, Vol. 29, Number 6, June 2014, p. 108-114.

[12] Lobo, A. and Baliga, G. *NP-completeness for all Computer Science Undergraduates: A Novel Project-Based Curriculum,* The Journal of Computing Sciences in Colleges, Vol. 21, Number 6, June 2006, p. 53-63.

[13] Mangan, K., *In Record-Setting 'Match Day,' 1,100 Medical Students Don't Find Residencies*, The Chronicle of Higher Education, March 15, 2013.

[14] Naps, T., Rossling, G., Almstrum, V. and 9 others, *Exploring the role of visualization and engagement in computer science education,* SIGCSE Bulletin, 35 (issue 2): pp. 131-152, June 2003.

[15] Segev, D., Gentry, S., et al., *Kidney Paired Donation and Optimizing the Use of Live Donor Organs*, JAMA 293(15), April 20, 2005, pp1883-1890.

[16] Segev, D., Gentry, S., et al., 2005. *Optimized Match for Kidney Paired Donation*, Retrieved Jan. 25, 2014 from *www.optimizedmatch.com*

[17] Skiena, S. *The Algorithm Design Manual, 2nd ed.,* Springer-Verlag, 2010.

[18] Tenenberg, J *A Framework Approach to Teaching Data Structures*, Proceedings of SIGCSE 2003, pp 210- 214. Feb 2003, ACM (2003).

[19] Teresco, J. *Highway data and map visualizations for educational use*, Proceedings of SIGCSE 2012, pp 553-558. Mar 2012, ACM (2012).

[20] Yarosh, S. and Guzdial, M. *Narrating Data Structures: the role of context in CS2*, ACM Journal on Educational Resources in Computing, 7(4), pp 1-20, Jan. 2008

Fibonacci in The Curriculum: Not Just a Bad Recurrence *

Saad Mneimneh
Computer Science
Hunter College and the Graduate Center of the
City University of New York (CUNY)
New York, USA
saad@hunter.cuny.edu

ABSTRACT

As an advocate of infusing various algorithmic and mathematical aspects when teaching about programming, I have come to realize that an early such practice is essential for a rounded computer science education. In this paper, I show how this can be done while focusing on one theme: Fibonacci.

Perhaps the most common use of Fibonacci has been to show the power of recurrence in implementing the Fibonacci sequence, which is often accompanied by a caveat that it is not the best implementation (very slow). Nevertheless, the sequence, with its rabbit story and celebrated golden ratio, is a rather exciting "gadget" for many students and it often pays off to introduce it. Therefore, I explore ways to use Fibonacci (the binary word) and the golden ratio for guiding implementation, and to successfully convey an important message of computer science that programming is not just about writing code. This will be done in the context of one dimensional and two dimensional arrays.

1. PART I: SKOLEM GOES DOWN THE RABBIT WHOLE

When teaching about one dimensional arrays, it is often natural to think about sequences. A Skolem sequence, named after its creator Thoralf Skolem in 1957 [5], is a sequence of $2k$ integers $s_1, \ldots, s_{2k}$ such that for every $n \in \{1, \ldots, k\}$ there exist two integers $a_n < b_n$ that satisfy $s_{a_n} = s_{b_n} = b_n - a_n = n$. Interestingly, a closely related formulation was made in parallel by C. Dudley Langford in 1958 after observing his child play with colored cubes [2].

*The theoretical results reported in this paper were obtained by the author during the process of designing homework questions for an introductory course in programming. Although this work lies on the boundary of education and research, the author has determined that this publication is not the proper venue for sharing the mathematical proofs. The proofs are elementary, but they are not strongly relevant for the educational merit of the exposition.

SIGCSE'15, March 4–7, 2015, Kansas City, MO, USA.

http://dx.doi.org/10.1145/2676723.2677215.

Stories like this one make a good introduction and provide some context when talking about abstract problems. That was among several motivations (including the creation of a fresh problem) in considering Skolem sequences. A Skolem sequence for $k = 4$ is shown below:

1 1 3 4 2 3 2 4

Figure 1: A Skolem sequence for $k = 4$: $s_1 = s_2 = 2 - 1 = 1$, $s_5 = s_7 = 7 - 5 = 2$, $s_3 = s_6 = 6 - 3 = 3$, and $s_4 = s_8 = 8 - 4 = 4$.

1.1 The Birth of an Infinite Skolem Squenence

Not every finite k admits a Skolem sequence, and when it does, it is far from trivial to construct one. This lead me to define an infinite Skolem sequence.

DEFINITION 1.1. *(Infinite Skolem Sequence) An infinite Skolem sequence $\{s_i : i \in \mathbb{N}\}$ is such that for every $n \in \mathbb{N}$ there exists exactly one pair of integers $a_n < b_n$ that satisfy $s_{a_n} = s_{b_n} = n$. Furthermore $b_n - a_n = n$.*

As I will illustrate below, constructing an infinite Skolem sequence is much easier.

1.2 The First Lexicographic Infinite Skolem Sequence

It is trivial to construct an infinite Skolem sequence because we can always "fill in the gaps"; for instance, with the smallest unused number (see Figure 2). Furthermore, one could refer to this as the first infinite Skolem sequence in a lexicographic order. Students will appreciate this terminology when they know it is nothing but the dictionary order. In fact, an entertaining exercise would be to prove that the infinite Skolem sequence thus constructed is indeed the first in a lexicographic order. Mathematically, this is equivalent to say $n < m \Leftrightarrow a_n < a_m \Leftrightarrow b_n < b_m$.

In what follows, any reference to the infinite sequence signifies this first lexicographic (thus unique) infinite Skolem sequence. As it turns out, this particular Skolem sequence, given by (a_n, b_n) for every $n \in \mathbb{N}$, exists in the literature under the name Wythoff pairs [6], and has been the subject of study in many publications of the Fibonacci Quarterly. Let us now discover what it looks like!

1.3 Discovering Skolem: A Warm Up

An immediately obvious candidate for a warm up question is to design an algorithm that generates the first, say k,

_	_	_	_	_	_	_	_	_	_	_	_	_	_	_
1	1	_	_	_	_	_	_	_	_	_	_	_	_	_
1	1	2	_	2	_	_	_	_	_	_	_	_	_	_
1	1	2	3	2	_	3	_	_	_	_	_	_	_	_
1	1	2	3	2	4	3	_	_	4	_	_	_	_	_
1	1	2	3	2	4	3	5	_	4	_	_	5	_	_
1	1	2	3	2	4	3	5	6	4	_	_	5	_	6
1	1	2	3	2	4	3	5	6	4	7	_	5	_	6
1	1	2	3	2	4	3	5	6	4	7	8	5	_	6
1	1	2	3	2	4	3	5	6	4	7	8	5	9	6

Figure 2: The leading 15 terms of the first lexicographic infinite Skolem sequence.

integers of this infinite sequence. Why is this an important exercise? Unlike its Fibonacci counterpart, this exercise is not possible without using additional memory (well, at least for now), the kind that only arrays (or more advanced structures) can provide. A typical solution would create an array of the appropriate size k and navigate through it to assign all of its elements. An algorithm is shown in Figure 3 (in pseudocode).

```
for i ← 1...k
  do s[i] ← 0   ▷ gaps
i ← 1
n ← 0
while i ≤ k
   do n ← n + 1   ▷ next number
      s[i] ← n
      if i + n ≤ k   ▷ does it fit?
        then s[i + n] ← n
      while s[i] ≠ 0 ∧ i ≤ k   ▷ find next gap
         do i ← i + 1
```

Figure 3: Algorithm for constructing $s_1, \ldots, s_k$, n will be the largest integer in the sequence.

I list below some aspects that make the implementation tricky and, therefore, worthy of being a non-trivial exercise:

- there is a nested loop
- one needs to keep track of gaps
- the value to be assigned and the array index move at different paces
- one has to use caution when indexing the array, especially when assigning the second value of each pair (which may not fit)

1.4 A Real Programming Challenge

My real interest in the Skolem problem is the following: Given n, find a_n, i.e. the index of the first occurrence of n in the infinite sequence. For example, if $n = 9$, then the answer is 14 (see Figure 2). The reason for my particular interest is to eventually shed some light on an alternative solution for the construction of Figure 3. But more importantly now, to present the student with the typical situation where one must use an array without knowing its size (not even at run time, so this is not about dynamic memory allocation). In Figure 3, when s_i is assigned the value n, $a_n = i$ is automatically revealed. However, it may not be obvious to the student how to choose the size of the array to guarantee $k \geq a_n$ (otherwise, n will not show up). This situation can be avoided with the use of advanced data structures; however, I am excluding this kind of knowledge for beginners. Therefore, the first impression is that this situation cannot be avoided. Consequently, a wishful attempt would be to perform the algorithm of Figure 3 and hope that the desired n will show up (see Figure 4)!

```
Find(n)
  for i ← 1...k
    do s[i] ← 0   ▷ gaps
  i ← 1
  m ← 0
  while i ≤ k
     do m ← m + 1   ▷ next number
        if m = n
          then return i   ▷ this is a_n
        s[i] ← m
        if i + m ≤ k   ▷ does it fit?
          then s[i + m] ← m
        while s[i] ≠ 0 ∧ i ≤ k   ▷ find next gap
           do i ← i + 1
  ▷ now what?!
```

Figure 4: A wishful thinking approach.

The approach illustrated in Figure 4 is not a bad idea for a start. Based on this implementation, one could repeatedly perform the entire process with a larger k until n shows up. This will be correct, but a bit clumsy. A better approach is to guide the students to figure out an upper bound on k. For instance, when $m = n$ in Figure 4, we know that we must have written at most $2(n-1)$ values into the array (m is assigned at most twice to some $s[i]$). Therefore, $a_n \leq 2(n-1)+1 = 2n-1$, and it suffices to make $k = 2n-1$ to guarantee that m will reach n. But we can do better.

1.5 Follow the RabBIT

At this juncture, it is probably a good idea to stop writing code and think. I usually provide the students with some strategy to guide their thoughts and explore the problem. This is what lead me to establish the following interesting theorem about Skolem and the infinite (binary) Fibonacci word [4] (stated without proof, other forms of this theorem are a ready consequence of some classical results about Wythoff pairs and the positions of the nth 1 and the nth 0 in the infinite Fibonacci word): [1]

THEOREM 1.2. *$a_n = n + \sum_{i=1}^{n-1} f(i)$ where $f(n)$ is the nth bit of the infinite Fibonacci word.*

The students are encouraged to explore the problem by studying the behavior of $a_n - a_{n-1}$. This is relevant be-

[1] The infinite Fibonacci word can be constructed by writing 10, then scanning the bits in order starting with the first, and appending the sequence with 110 upon seeing a 1, and 10 upon seeing a 0. The first few bits are as follows: 1011010110...

cause of the following equality:

$$a_n = a_1 + (a_2 - a_1) + (a_3 - a_2) + \ldots + (a_n - a_{n-1})$$

The algorithm of Figure 3 can be easily modified to compute this differential, and upon doing so, one can observe that $a_n - a_{n-1}$ seems to always be either 1 or 2.

$$\begin{aligned} a_2 - a_1 &= 2 \\ a_3 - a_2 &= 1 \\ a_4 - a_3 &= 2 \\ a_5 - a_4 &= 2 \\ a_6 - a_5 &= 1 \\ a_7 - a_6 &= 2 \\ a_8 - a_7 &= 1 \\ a_9 - a_8 &= 2 \\ &\vdots \end{aligned}$$

The good student will hopefully realize that $a_n - a_{n-1}$ is in effect binary (two valued function of n), and that this fact can be expressed in the following way:

$$\begin{aligned} a_2 - a_1 - 1 &= 1 \\ a_3 - a_2 - 1 &= 0 \\ a_4 - a_3 - 1 &= 1 \\ a_5 - a_4 - 1 &= 1 \\ a_6 - a_5 - 1 &= 0 \\ a_7 - a_6 - 1 &= 1 \\ a_8 - a_7 - 1 &= 0 \\ a_9 - a_8 - 1 &= 1 \\ &\vdots \\ a_n - a_{n-1} - 1 &= f(n-1) \end{aligned}$$

Upon making this observation, and with a hint to the infinite Fibonacci word, a student should be able to formulate Theorem 1.2 (without proving it, simply by adding up all the rows and using the fact that $a_1 = 1$). This in turn should provide the idea for a better solution for our challenge because we only require the first $n-1$ bits of infinite Fibonacci word, hence we can work with an array of size $n-1$ (Figure 5).

```
Find(n)
  compute f[1], ..., f[n − 1]   ▷ a nice exercise by itself
  sum ← 0
  for i ← 1 to n − 1
    do sum ← sum + f[i]
  return n + sum
```

Figure 5: Algorithm to find a_n given n.

In fact, the need for an array can be eliminated entirely. A deeper understanding of the infinite Fibonacci word will reveal that:

$$\sum_{i=1}^{n} f_i = \left\lfloor \frac{n+1}{\phi} \right\rfloor$$

where $\lfloor x \rfloor$ is the largest integer $\leq x$, and $\phi = (1+\sqrt{5})/2$ is the golden ratio! Therefore, $a_n = n + \lfloor n/\phi \rfloor = \lfloor n(1+1/\phi) \rfloor = \lfloor n\phi \rfloor$ (and $b_n = n + \lfloor n\phi \rfloor = \lfloor n(1+\phi) \rfloor = \lfloor n\phi^2 \rfloor$), which was proved by Wythoff in [6]. It now becomes interesting to redo the algorithm of Figure 3 without using an array, but I will leave this potential open for imagination.

From the conceptual perspective, this marks the end of the journey to the rabbit hole, but one could offer guidance throughout this journey with various levels of detail. The important points are:

- we start with a warm up question
- we follow it by a challenge
- the challenge could be solved by adapting the warm up solution
- the students are guided to study the problem in a specific way
- they are also either assumed to know about the infinite Fibonacci word or to be told to learn about it
- upon making the connection, the students should be able to come up with a better solution for the challenge

2. PART II: LIVING ON A RANDOM TORUS

We don't see doughnut shapes when we look up in the sky. So it takes a spark of imagination to consider the possibility of living on a planet in the shape of a torus. But when teaching introductory programming to students who have just learned about two-dimensional arrays, all you need is the modulo operator (defined below for $x \in \mathbb{Z}$ and $n \in \mathbb{N}$).

$$x \bmod n = x - n\left\lfloor \frac{x}{n} \right\rfloor$$

The modulo operator is widely recognized as the remainder (an integer) in the division of x by n, ranging from 0 to $n-1$. Surprisingly, in 1970 Larry Niven has explored the possibility of living on a toroidal world in Ringworld [3]. Again, this makes an interesting opening to introduce the students to the problem discussed herein.

2.1 The Birth of a Torus

If we denote the entry at the ith row and the jth column of an $m \times n$ array by $a[i,j]$, where $0 \leq i \leq m-1$ and $0 \leq j \leq n-1$, then $a[i,j-1]$, $a[i,j+1]$, $a[i-1,j]$, and $a[i+1,j]$ represent the *neighbors* of $a[i,j]$. However, even the beginner programmer can immediately tell that a handful of checks are needed before making access to these neighbors, since some of them are non-existent when $a[i,j]$ lies on the array's boundary. This complicates almost every task one could imagine performed on the array; conditional statements must be inserted everywhere.

In such a programming nightmare, the modulo operator can be a blessing: Given an $m \times n$ array, the neighbors of $a[i,j]$ can be safely defined as in Figure 6. The definitions in Figure 6 eliminate boundaries and identify row m with row 0, and column n with column 0. The end result is the folding of the two-dimensional array into a torus, as shown in Figure 7.

The torus is born, and all that remains to be done is adding some life to it! Hence, for an initial programming exercise, let us set every $a[i,j]$ to either a 1 (land) or a 0 (water), and count the islands and pools that form on the torus.

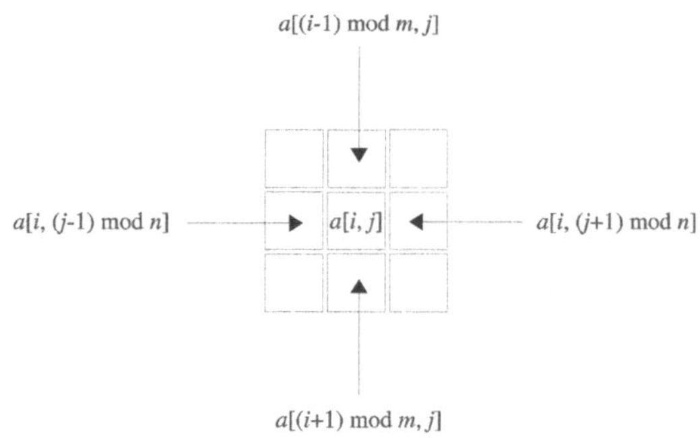

Figure 6: Every $a[i,j]$ has all the neighbors.

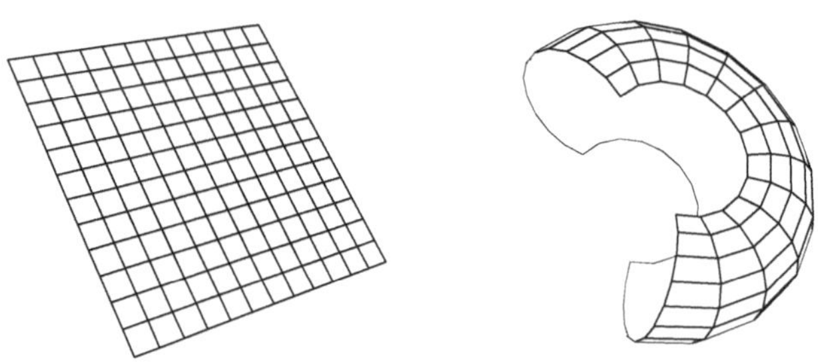

Figure 7: Folding a two-dimensional array into a torus. On the left, the array, and on the right, the folding in action showing a partially folded torus.

2.2 Islands and Pools

Following the ideas in the previous section, our torus is given by an $m \times n$ array in which the entry $a[i,j]$ represents either land ($a[i,j] = 1$) or water ($a[i,j] = 0$), and where neighbors of $a[i,j]$ are as defined in Figure 6.

An island is intuitively understood as a set of neighboring lands (entries with $a[i,j] = 1$), but a precise definition will depend on how we expect to walk on the torus; it will also have implications on the definition of pools, since islands must be separated by water. A walk on the torus consists of moving through neighbors, on land, and without crossing any waters. Moreover, islands cannot overlap, leading to the following definition.

DEFINITION 2.1 (ISLAND). *An island is a maximal set of 1s that are reachable from one another by moving through neighbors and without crossing any 0s.*

A note is in order here. The term "maximal" in the above definition most of the times awakens the attention of the students, as it sounds like "maximum" but is not quite the same word. After explaining what maximal means (not a proper subset of some other set), it is often interesting exercise to ponder on the equivalence of the two flavors: the programmer's perspective (more pragmatic) in which islands do not overlap, and the mathematician's perspective (more of a definition) in which islands are maximal. Oddly enough, it is the second one that gives more insight when it comes to writing a program for counting islands (see following section).

Similarly, neighboring waters must be part of the same pool, and pools cannot overlap. In addition, the definition of an island implies that the diagonally situated $a[i,j] = 0$ and $a[(i \pm 1) \bmod m, (j \pm 1) \bmod n] = 0$ must be in the same pool to justify the inability to cross diagonally from one land to another.

DEFINITION 2.2 (POOL). *A pool is a maximal set of 0s that are reachable from one another by moving through neighbors or diagonally, and without crossing any 1s.*

It is this asymmetry in the formation of islands and pools that will create the interesting behavior discussed in the following sections. Figure 8 shows an example of this formation on a random torus.

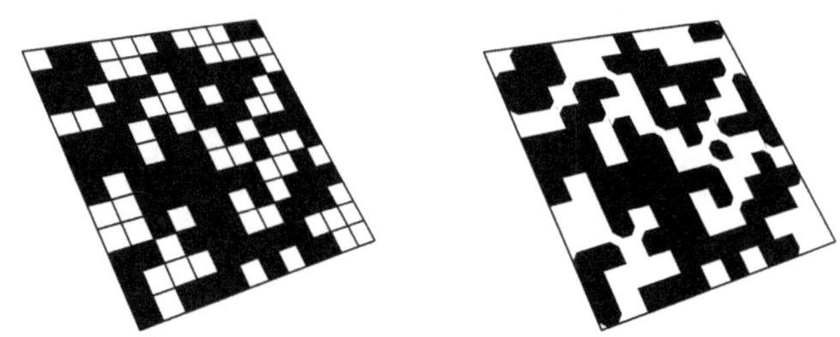

Figure 8: From a two-dimensional array to islands and pools on the torus, showing a total of five islands (black) and two pools (white). Avoid the overcounting of islands and pools when neighbors wrap around in modulo m and/or n.

2.3 Let's Count: A Warm Up

The warm up question here is of course to count islands and pools. This problem is closely related to the flood filling performed by the "bucket" tool of graphics editors, which relies on finding connected components, a standard algorithmic topic. A pseudocode for counting islands and pools on a torus is shown in Figure 9. The code is self explanatory and assumes that students are familiar with recursion. But since recursion is often tricky, this makes it worthy of a nontrivial exercise: Upon seeing a land (water) for the first time, it is marked as visited, the rest of the island (pool) is recursively visited by moving through neighbors (and diagonally). When every branch of the recursion stops, the island (pool) is maximal, and a count is incremented.

Perhaps it is now a good juncture for examining the pseudocode to appreciate how the introduction of the modulo operator freed us from a bundle of conditional statements (not to mention the additional interesting effect of creating the torus). This should help to focus on aspects of the program that are more important than messing with if-then-else.

2.4 A Real Programming Challenge

A question that intrigued me is the following: Consider a random torus where p is the probability of land (and hence $q = 1 - p$ is the probability of water). For what value of p is

```
Visit(i, j, b)  ▷ b is 1 for islands and 0 for pools
  if a[i, j] = b ∧ ¬visited[i, j]
    then visited[i, j] ← TRUE   ▷ mark it as visited
         ▷ recurse through neighbors
         Visit(i, (j − 1) mod n, b)
         Visit(i, (j + 1) mod n, b)
         Visit((i − 1) mod m, j, b)
         Visit((i + 1) mod m, j, b)
         ▷ and diagonally for pools
         if b = 0
           then Visit((i − 1) mod m, (j − 1) mod n, 0)
                Visit((i − 1) mod m, (j + 1) mod n, 0)
                Visit((i + 1) mod m, (j − 1) mod n, 0)
                Visit((i + 1) mod m, (j + 1) mod n, 0)
```

```
Count(b)   ▷ b is 1 for islands and 0 for pools
  for  i ← 0 to m − 1
    for j ← 0 to n − 1
      visited[i, j] ← FALSE
  total ← 0
  for  i ← 0 to m − 1
    for  j ← 0 to n − 1
      if a[i, j] = b ∧ ¬visited[i, j]   ▷ first time seen
        then Visit(i, j, b)   ▷ visit the rest of it
             total ← total + 1   ▷ and increase the count
  return total
```

Figure 9: Pseudocode for counting islands and pools. For correctness, the programming language must return a non-negative integer for the modulo operator. But many don't when $x < 0$ in $x \bmod n$, so a fix can replace $x \bmod n$ with $(x + n) \bmod n$ to avoid a negative x.

the number of islands equal to the number of pools (in the average sense of course)? As in Part I, the solution for the warm up question can be adapted to answer the challenge. A straightforward approach would be to compute for every p the average numbers of islands and pools, and observe when they are approximately equal. A thought experiment is shown in Figure 10 in pseudocode.

```
Try(p)
  avgI ← 0   ▷ average number of islands
  avgP ← 0   ▷ average number of pools
  for i ← 1 to T
    initialize the torus randomly using p
    avgI ← avgI+Count(1)/T
    avgP ← avgP+Count(0)/T
  return avgI − avgP
```

Figure 10: A thought experiment.

My interest in this question, beside it being experimental leading to a result, follows from a simple fact: often a seemingly correct concept can fail to yield the desired result. The thought experiment of Figure 10 is conceptually correct, i.e. repeated use of it with different values of p should reveal the value of p that makes $avgI - avgP \approx 0$. Wrong! And here's why:

- m and n must be large enough to produce the desired effect
- It is not obvious how to try different values for p and what granularity will guarantee to capture the desired value.
- Almost no value of p will make $avgI - avgP$ approximately 0, as a slight discrepancy in the number of islands and pools is magnified by the torus size mn.

Nevertheless, one could still rely on the algorithm of Figure 10 to discover, for instance, when $avgI - avgP$ switches sign. Still, it's a clumsy method and it will only give an approximate range for the desired value of p, which in turn may fail to be identified as any special value. To rectify this problem, the students are encouraged to explore $avgI - avgP$ scaled by the torus size as a function of $p/q = p/(1-p)$ (an alternative is to study $avgI/avgP$ to eliminate the effect of the torus size, but this quantity is unbounded, and it is better to work with a bounded quantity, see below).

2.5 Ringworld*ians* discover the golden ratio!

Humans have always been fascinated by the golden ratio, to the point of abuse [1]. Similarly, the inhabitants of Ringworld will have discovered that divine ratio simply by observing their own world. As it turns out, an attempt to avoid the problems outlined in the previous section leads to the following result (again, stated without proof):

THEOREM 2.3. *Let $avgI$ be the average number of islands and $avgP$ be the average number of pools, then:*

$$\lim_{m,n\to\infty} \frac{avgI - avgP}{mn} = pq(q - p^2)$$

The theorem has several consequences. For large m and n, $avgI - avgP \approx mnpq(q - p^2)$. This also means that $avgI \approx mnpq(q-p^2)$ when p is small, as the number of pools will tend to be small compared to the number of islands. A symmetric argument shows that $avgP \approx mnpq(p^2 - q)$ when p is large. Most importantly, and to quantify what a small or large p would be, the theorem shows that $avgI = avgP$ when $q = p^2$, and since $q = 1 - p$, this means $p/q = \phi$, the golden ratio! Therefore, a small p satisfies $p/q \ll \phi$, and a large p satisfies $p/q \gg \phi$.

COROLLARY 2.4 (GOLDEN TORUS). *For large m and n,*

$$avgI \approx mnpq(q - p^2) \quad p/q \ll \phi$$

$$avgI = avgP \quad p/q = \phi$$

$$avgP \approx mnpq(p^2 - q) \quad p/q \gg \phi$$

where $\phi = (1 + \sqrt{5})/2$ is the golden ratio.

A proper guidance to explore p/q, with a hint to the golden ratio, can improve the attempt of Figure 10 as shown in Figure 11.

It may still be inconvenient to try several values of p, but the range can now be controlled in a pragmatic way through the use of ϵ. Moreover, students can be guided to try

```
Try(p, ϵ)
  avgI ← 0   ▷ average number of islands
  avgP ← 0   ▷ average number of pools
  for i ← 1 to T
    initialize a large m × n torus randomly using p
    avgI ← avgI+Count(1)/T
    avgP ← avgP+Count(0)/T
  if −ϵ < (avgI−avgP)/mn < ϵ
    then return p/(1 − p)
    else return −1
```

Figure 11: An improved experiment.

values of p that are a ratio of consecutive Fibonacci numbers. When m and n are large enough (say $m = n = 100$) and ϵ is small enough, the above program will return a number close to the golden ratio (which is recognizable) or -1 (a failure for the given p). A student can then set $p/q = \phi$, accordingly $p = 1/\phi$, and observe that $\frac{avgI}{mn}$ and $\frac{avgP}{mn}$ are approximately 0.0205. But the 0.0205 is still a mystery to me.

And since silence is also golden, I will stop here by repeating a similar summary for this outer space journey:

- we start with a warm up question
- we follow it by a challenge
- the challenge could be solved by adapting the warm up solution
- the students are guided to study the problem in a specific way
- they are also either assumed to know about the golden ratio or to be told to learn about it
- upon making the connection, the students should be able to come up with a better solution for the challenge

3. A NOTE ON THE TWO PROBLEMS

While it is not hard to believe that $p/q = \phi$ achieves the desired balance of islands and pools on the torus (it can be verified), it takes a leap of faith to believe that $a_n = n + \sum_{i=1}^{n-1} f(i)$ for all $n \in \mathbb{N}$ without a mathematical proof. Given the approach outline herein, however, students might not actually prove any mathematical result, though such a direction can definitely be pursued with the better students. The main goal of this approach remains to be the exposure to mathematical/algorithmic context.

4. CONCLUSION

In this exposition, I showed how to infuse some algorithmic and mathematical aspects to guide the programming experience. The main theme is Fibonacci (and the golden ratio), which is a pleasant topic for many students. The typical paradigm that I support here is to first start with a warm up question (one that is not too trivial), then to follow up on it with a programming challenge that can be solved by adapting the warm up solution, but not to a satisfactory level. The students are then encouraged through hints to explore the problem in a certain way, including the introduction of some mathematical concepts. Finally, upon making the connection between the hints and the original problem, the students are expected to figure out a better solution for the challenge.

5. THE AFTERMATH

Over the years, many of my students end up appreciating the approach outlined above. Students enter the field with the impression that computer science is about the ability to write programs, and that programming is a simple mechanical task. They later hear differently from their peers, those who have had me as their instructor. And while they understand that I will be pulling them out of their comfort zone, students seek to be placed in my sections, as I have managed to create a particular reputation for my teaching. This remains true even for average students who do not actively look for an extra challenge. They opt to pursue this path because they feel that they will be learning something interesting.

It takes a while to understand the philosophy of the kind of challenging, but at the same time guided, assignments. Initially, the students may feel lost in terms of what is being required from them, but they eventually get the hang of it once they become comfortable with my style. They build a level of independence over time, and I have observed that, towards the end of the semester, only a few students will gather at my door.

On a different note, I should say that my approach pays off even when a student is not academically savvy but career oriented. For one thing, many respectful software companies, e.g. Google, follow a similar approach for their interview process. They expect the applicant to first solve a given problem in the most obvious way, with no regards to the efficiency or the elegance of the solution. They then raise the level by guiding the applicant to pursue a certain direction of thought, hopefully leading to a better solution.

Finally, I think we are in great need, more than any time, to rescue the declining mathematical level in computer science education. In my exposition, I illustrated specific examples of how to expose students to contexts that are mathematical and algorithmic in nature. But I hope that I was able to convey the general approach of exploring such a strategy as a guide for writing programs and obtaining solutions.

6. REFERENCES

[1] C. Falbo. The golden ratio: A contrary viewpoint. *The College Mathematics Journal*, 36(2):123–134, 2005.

[2] C. D. Langford. Problem. *Mathematical Gazette*, 42:228, 1958.

[3] L. Niven. Ringworld. *Random House Publishing Group*, 1970.

[4] OEIS. The online encyclopedia of integer sequences. *http://oeis.org/A005614*.

[5] T. Skolem. On certain distributions of integers in pairs with given differences. *Mathematica Scandinavica*, 5:57–58, 1957.

[6] W. A. Wythoff. A modification of the game of nim. *Nieuw Archief voor WisKunde*, 7(2):199–202, 1907.

Randomized Reduction

Brian C. Dean, Raghuveer Mohan, Chad G. Waters
School of Computing, Clemson University
Clemson, SC, USA
{bcdean, rmohan, cgwater}@clemson.edu

ABSTRACT

Despite their power and simplicity, randomized algorithms are often under-emphasized in the classroom (and as a consequence, ultimately in practice) since they can be more challenging to analyze than their deterministic counterparts. In this paper, we describe a simplified framework that streamlines the analysis of dozens of common randomized algorithms and data structures. The key component of this framework, which we call the *randomized reduction lemma*, builds on intuition that is already commonly held by most students based on their experience with deterministic algorithms, and reduces the necessary prerequisites one must know from probability theory to a minimal subset. For example, one can prove that randomized quicksort runs in $O(n \log n)$ time with high probability in two paragraphs, without knowledge of random variables or Chernoff bounds. This paper is intended to be self-contained and written in a sufficiently student-friendly fashion so that it may serve as a classroom handout.

Categories and Subject Descriptors

K.3.2 [**Computer and Information Science Education**]: Computer Science Education

General Terms

Algorithms, Theory

Keywords

Randomized algorithms; Randomization

1. INTRODUCTION

Randomized algorithms and data structures offer many advantages over their deterministic counterparts, including speed, simplicity of implementation, resistance to malicious inputs, and overall elegance. Unfortunately, few would include "ease of analysis" in this list, since the analysis of even simple randomized algorithms can require somewhat intricate formulation, messy calculation, and prior familiarity with many tools from probability theory. The goal of this paper is to help alleviate this problem by introducing a lightweight mathematical framework that simplifies the understanding and analysis of dozens of common randomized algorithms and data structures. It requires minimal prerequisite knowledge of probability theory, and it builds on intuition that is already present in many students from their work with deterministic algorithms.

SIGCSE'15, March 4–7, 2015, Kansas City, MO, USA.

ACM 978-1-4503-2966-8/15/03 ...$15.00.
http://dx.doi.org/10.1145/2676723.2677251.

Let us start with the simple example of binary searching a sorted array $A[1 \ldots n]$ for a value v. We compare v with the value of the middle array element, $A[k]$ (with $k = n/2$), and then recursively search the left side $A[1 \ldots k-1]$ or the right side $A[k+1 \ldots n]$ as appropriate. It is easy to see that this runs in $O(\log n)$ worst-case time, owing to the following simple insight:

LEMMA 1. **(The Reduction Lemma)** *If each iteration of an algorithm reduces the effective size of a problem to at most some constant fraction $q < 1$ of its current size, then the algorithm requires $O(\log n)$ iterations.*

With binary search, each iteration reduces the effective problem size by a factor of $q = 1/2$ (e.g., from n to $n/2$). In our new framework, analysis of many randomized algorithms requires little more than the insight above. We only need to show that each iteration has reasonable likelihood of reducing the effective problem size:

LEMMA 2. **(The Randomized Reduction Lemma)** *If each iteration independently reduces the effective size of a problem to at most some constant fraction $q < 1$ of its current size with at least some constant probability $p > 0$, then we take $O(\log n)$ iterations with high probability.*

The phrase "with high probability" (whp) has come to have a fairly standard meaning in the analysis of randomized algorithms. It means that there is only a $1/n^c$ chance that our algorithm fails to achieve its target of $O(\log n)$ iterations, where c is a constant that can be set arbitrarily high by adjusting the hidden constant in the $O(\log n)$ running time bound. For example, we can take the failure probability to be something as miniscule as $1/n^{100}$ by assuming a sufficiently large constant in the $O(\log n)$ bound. As problem size n increases, a high probability guarantee becomes stronger and stronger, making it nearly certain that our algorithm will run in $O(\log n)$ iterations for large n.

By using the randomized reduction lemma, we can avoid much of the complexity inherent in analyzing randomized

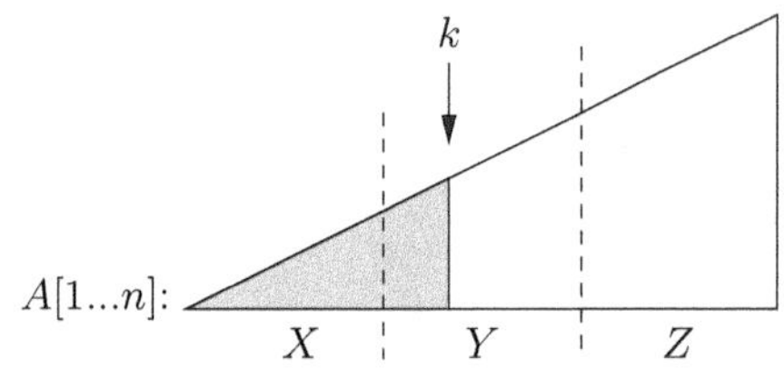

Figure 1: Analysis of randomized binary search. If we are looking for a value $v < A[k]$, then the next subproblem (shaded) will exclude all of region Z.

algorithms, such as random variables and Chernoff bounds (we show in the Appendix how to prove the randomized reduction lemma using these concepts). In some sense, it provides a higher-level interface to the world of probability theory that is specifically designed to simplify the analysis of randomized algorithms. All we need to do to apply the randomized reduction lemma is to provide suitable values for the constants p and q, as in the following example.

1.1 Randomized Binary Search

Suppose we modify binary search so that in each iteration, we compare against an element $A[k]$ with k *randomly* chosen in the range $1 \ldots n$. This may be a more accurate model for, say, a human searching a dictionary, since it is hard to manually open a book to its exact middle page. By mentally picturing the sorted array $A[1 \ldots n]$ divided into three equal-sized regions X, Y, and Z (Figure 1), we see that choice of k from the middle region Y (which happens with probability $1/3$) ensures that the next iteration will involve a subproblem that either excludes all of X or all of Z, and hence will be at most $2/3$ the size of the original problem. Each iteration therefore reduces the effective size of our problem to at most a constant fraction $q = 2/3$ of its original size with at least probability $p = 1/3$. According to the randomized reduction lemma, randomized binary search therefore runs in $O(\log n)$ time whp[1].

1.2 The Union Bound

A simple way we often analyze algorithms is by looking at how much time they spend on each individual input element:

LEMMA 3. *If an algorithm spends $O(f(n))$ time per input element, then it spends $O(nf(n))$ total time.*

For example, an algorithm that invests $O(\log n)$ time processing each of its n input elements takes $O(n \log n)$ total time. The *union bound* (the only other probabilistic tool we need in this paper) allows us to perform the same type of analysis for randomized algorithms:

LEMMA 4. *If an algorithm spends $O(f(n))$ time per input element whp, then it spends $O(nf(n))$ total time whp.*

For example, we will see in a moment that randomized quicksort spends $O(\log n)$ time whp on each single input element (due to the randomized reduction lemma), so it runs in $O(n \log n)$ total time whp.

[1] Many students commonly ask why the simpler choice of $p = q = 1/2$ does not work for this example. We leave this as an exercise for the reader.

To give more mathematical detail, the union bound says that if we have a set of bad events $E_1 \ldots E_n$, the probability at least one of them happens is at most the sum of their probabilities $\sum \mathbf{Pr}[E_i]$. If we let E_i be the event that we spend too much time (e.g., more than $O(\log n)$ time) on input element i, we have $\mathbf{Pr}[E_i] \leq 1/n^c$, so the probability we spend too much time on *any* element of the input is at most $\sum \mathbf{Pr}[E_i] \leq n \times 1/n^c = 1/n^{c-1}$. Since our choice of constant c can be arbitrary, this is still a high probability bound.

1.3 Randomized Quicksort

To sort an array $A[1 \ldots n]$, the popular randomized quicksort algorithm does the following:

1. Choose a random "pivot" value v from the array.
2. Partition the array in $O(n)$ time, rearranging its contents into two pieces $A[1 \ldots k]$ (containing values $\leq v$) and $A[k+1 \ldots n]$ (containing values $\geq v$).
3. Recursively sort the two pieces.

Analysis. Each partition spends $O(1)$ time per element, so the running time spent per element over the entire algorithm is essentially just the number of partitions in which the element takes part. If we can show that each element takes part in $O(\log n)$ partitions whp, the union bound therefore allows us to conclude that randomized quicksort runs in $O(n \log n)$ total time whp.

Why does each element take part in $O(\log n)$ partitions whp? If we look again at Figure 1, suppose we choose a pivot v that would have come from the middle third of our array if it were sorted. In this case, the result of partitioning on v will be two pieces each of size at most $2n/3$. Hence, each time an element takes part in a partition operation, there is at least a $1/3$ probability that the element will afterwards find itself in a subproblem of at most $2/3$ the size of its original enclosing array. The randomized reduction lemma therefore ensures that each element takes part in $O(\log n)$ partitions whp.

2. SIMPLE MATHEMATICAL EXAMPLES

To illustrate some common approaches for applying the randomized reduction lemma, let us show how it simplifies the analysis of several common probabilistic constructions we often encounter in the analysis of algorithms.

2.1 Resetting a Running Minimum

Suppose we maintain a running minimum while scanning through a randomly-ordered array $A[1 \ldots n]$. How many times does the minimum get reset? For simplicity, assume that there is a dummy "$-\infty$" at the end of the array, which becomes the final minimum. As shown in Figure 2(a), imagine following the chain of successive minima uncovered by our scan, only in reverse, starting from the final dummy element. It turns out that the indices we visit (circled in the figure) satisfy the conditions of the randomized reduction lemma with $p = q = 1/2$: if we are at index j, it is equally likely that the preceding minimum lives in $A[1 \ldots j/2]$ versus $A[j/2+1 \ldots j-1]$, owing to the fact that A is randomly ordered. Hence, there is a probability of $1/2$ that our next step takes us into $A[1 \ldots j/2]$ and reduces our current index to at most $1/2$ of its current value. We therefore reset our running minimum $O(\log n)$ times whp.

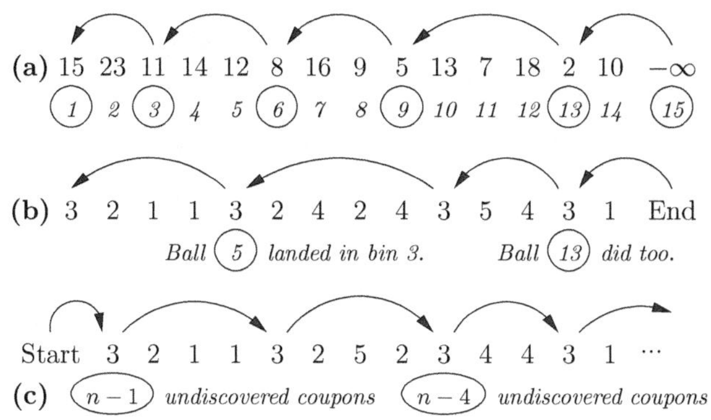

Figure 2: Randomized reduction sequences (circled) obtained from (a) resetting a running minimum while scanning through a randomly-permuted array, (b) random assignment of balls to bins, and (c) coupon collecting.

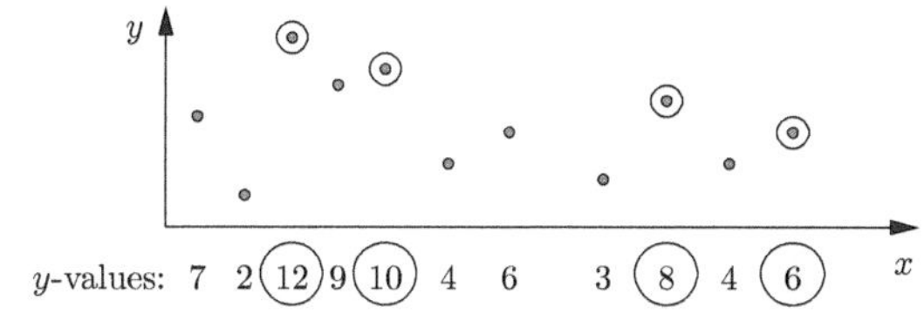

Figure 3: Counting non-dominated points (circled) in the 2D plane.

Applications. The property above leads to several useful algorithmic applications. Chan uses it as the basis for an elegant form of randomized divide and conquer [3], and it leads to a straightforward proof that Dijkstra's shortest path algorithm runs quickly on an n-node, m-edge graph where edge weights are drawn randomly from a common distribution; here, Dijkstra's algorithm makes only $O(n \log n)$ node label updates whp instead of the worst-case possibility of m updates [6]. As another nice example, in a set of points in the 2D plane, a point (x, y) is *non-dominated* if there is no other point (x', y') with $x' \geq x$ and $y' \geq y$. This is an important concept in multi-objective optimization, where a solution for a two-objective problem is generally not worth considering if some other solution dominates it in both objectives. A *random* set of n points has $O(\log n)$ non-dominated points whp. As shown in Figure 3, this follows by scanning the points in decreasing order of x keeping a running maximum in y. A non-dominated point occurs whenever the running maximum is reset.

2.2 Balls in Bins

Suppose we throw n balls randomly into n bins. In Figure 2(b), we have listed the sequence of n bins into which our balls have landed. If we pick a specific bin (bin 3 in the example) and visit in reverse order all the balls that land in it, the sequence of indices we visit (circled in the figure) will satisfy the randomized reduction lemma with $p = 1/4$ and $q = 0$: if we are at index j, the probability that none of the $j - 1$ preceding balls lands in our bin is $(1 - 1/n)^{j-1} \geq (1 - 1/n)^n \geq 1/4$ (for $n \geq 2$). Hence, each bin receives at most $O(\log n)$ balls whp, and by applying a union bound across all the bins, we also conclude that the fullest bin receives $O(\log n)$ balls whp.

Applications. If we need to assign computational tasks to servers, the result above tells us that reasonably good load balancing occurs if we simply assign tasks to servers at random. Another related result is that a random n-node labeled tree has maximum degree $O(\log n)$ whp. There is a one-to-one mapping between an n-node labeled tree and a so-called *Prüfer sequence* [10] of $n - 2$ integers in the range $1 \ldots n$, so the first $n-2$ elements of the length-n balls-in-bins sequence shown in Figure 2(b) codes for a unique random tree. The degree of a node x in the tree is one more than the number of occurrences of x in the Prüfer sequence, so maximum node degree corresponds to the fullest bin.

2.3 Coupon Collecting

Suppose that when we open a box of cereal, we receive (at random) one of n different coupon types. How many boxes of cereal must we plan to open before we expect to receive at least one of each coupon type? Figure 2(c) shows a random sequence of coupon types. Suppose we pick a specific coupon type (3 in this example) and imagine visiting the chain of all its occurrences, writing down at each step the number of yet-undiscovered coupon types (circled in the figure). We claim this sequence satisfies the randomized reduction lemma with $p = q = 1/2$: starting from an occurrence of coupon type c where j undiscovered coupons remain, let us consider the next $j/2$ events that are either of type I (draw a coupon of type c) or type II (draw a coupon type we have never seen before). If the next $j/2$ such events are all of type II, then the next occurrence of coupon c will correspond to a reduction in undiscovered coupon types from j to at most $j/2$, a factor of $q = 1/2$. The probability of this is

$$\left(\frac{j}{j+1}\right)\left(\frac{j-1}{j}\right)\left(\frac{j-2}{j-1}\right)\cdots\left(\frac{j/2+1}{j/2+2}\right) = \frac{j/2+1}{j+1} \geq 1/2.$$

This implies that each coupon type can occur only $O(\log n)$ times in the sequence whp, so we collect all the coupon types after opening $O(n \log n)$ boxes of cereal whp.

Applications. "Coupon collecting" is the fundamental process behind sampling with replacement, and the analysis above tells us that $O(n \log n)$ samples whp are needed to sample each of n different elements at least once. The same process shows up in many algorithmic scenarios. For example, if we perform a random walk in an n-node graph with all edges present (i.e., a complete graph), then we cover all the nodes in the graph in $O(n \log n)$ steps whp.

3. DATA STRUCTURES

Quite a few prominent randomized data structures become much easier to analyze using randomized reduction.

3.1 Randomly-Built Binary Search Trees

Since a binary search tree (BST) can be regarded as the recursion tree resulting from quicksort, there is a well-known "equivalence" between randomized quicksort and the process of building a BST by inserting its n elements in random order. This is illustrated in Figure 4(a), which depicts the tree of recursive subproblems generated by randomized quicksort (i.e., the top row is the array after partitioning on the randomly-chosen pivot 13, the next row shows partitions of the two resulting subproblems, and so on). Pivots

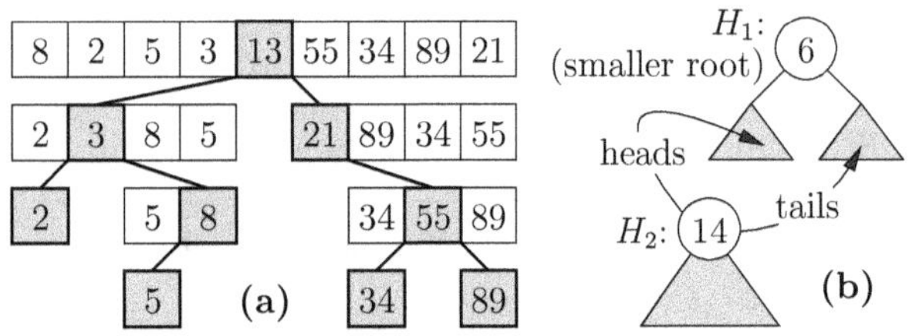

Figure 4: (a) Equivalence of binary search tree construction and quicksort, and (b) Flipping a coin to determine the subtree of heap-ordered tree H_1 into which we should recursively merge heap-ordered tree H_2.

are highlighted, and form a BST – the same tree we would have obtained by inserting elements into an initially-empty BST in the order they were chosen as pivots by randomized quicksort (i.e., random order). The same pairwise comparisons between elements occur during both processes, just in different orders.

Leveraging our previous analysis of randomized quicksort, we can now say many things about randomly-built BSTs. The depth of a node in the BST corresponds to the number of partitions in which it took part, which is $O(\log n)$ whp. Taking a union bound over all nodes, we see that a randomly-built BST has depth $O(\log n)$ whp. This fact leads to several beautiful randomized balancing mechanisms for BSTs, either by making simple random adjustments during the insertion or deletion of elements [8], or by achieving a similar effect by hybridizing a BST and a binary heap to form a so-called "treap" [2]. Both approaches keep the tree always in a state which is as if it had just been built randomly from scratch, so the tree always remains balanced (i.e., $O(\log n)$ depth) whp.

3.2 Randomly-Mergeable Binary Heaps

A binary tree is heap-ordered if the value stored by a parent node is always no larger than its children. Since the minimum resides in an obvious place (the root), such trees are commonly used as priority queues, maintaining a dynamic set of elements from which we can quickly extract the minimum. If we can *merge* two heap-ordered trees into one, then from this we can build all common priority queue operations. For example, we can insert a new element by merging with a single-element tree, and we can extract the minimum (the root) by removing it and merging its two child subtrees together.

Randomization gives a fast and remarkably simple method for merging [5]. Given two heap-ordered trees H_1 and H_2, where H_1 has the smaller root, we recursively merge H_2 with one of the two subtrees of the root of H_1, determined by a coin flip, as shown in Figure 4(b). One of these two subtrees is at most half the size of H_1, so with probability $p = 1/2$, we are left with a merging subproblem where one of our two trees has reduced itself in size by a factor of $q = 1/2$. Merging (and every other fundamental priority queue operation) therefore takes $O(\log n)$ time whp.

3.3 Skip Lists

The skip list [11] was developed as a simpler alternative to the balanced BST with equivalent functionality and speed.

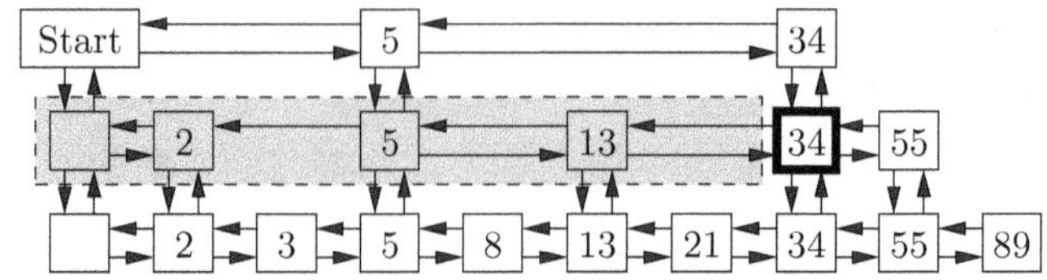

Figure 5: A skip list. The outlined node indicates our current location when traveling back to the start during an "unfind" operation.

As shown in Figure 5, it consists of increasingly-sparser copies of a linked list stacked atop each-other, with corresponding elements linked by "vertical" pointers. Each level contains roughly half the elements from the level beneath it, and this is easy to achieve using a simple randomized approach: each time a new element is inserted (initially into the lowest level), we repeatedly flip a fair coin and continue promoting it to higher levels as long as we flip "heads".

The height of a skip list is $O(\log n)$ whp due to randomized reduction, since each time we move up a level, we reduce the number of elements to at most a $q = 1/2$ fraction of the current level with probability at least $p = 1/2$. This follows directly from the fact that when we flip n fair coins, the probability that we flip at most $n/2$ heads is at least 1/2. We employ several coin-flipping arguments of this form moving forward in this paper, all using the simple fact that after flipping n coins,

$$\mathbf{Pr}[< n/2 \text{ heads}] + \mathbf{Pr}[= n/2 \text{ heads}] + \mathbf{Pr}[> n/2 \text{ heads}] = 1.$$

By symmetry the first and last terms are equal, giving us the analysis above. Later we will deal with coins that are biased, with $\geq 1/2$ probability of landing on heads, tipping the balance between the first and last terms so $\mathbf{Pr}[> n/2 \text{ heads}] \geq \mathbf{Pr}[< n/2 \text{ heads}]$.

It takes $O(\log n)$ time whp to find an element in a skip list by starting in the upper-left corner and repeatedly moving right, only stepping down when our next rightward step would overshoot the element we seek. Insertion and deletion of elements also takes $O(\log n)$ time whp, since finding an element (or in the case of insert, finding the location in which to place a new element) is the bottleneck in both procedures. To analyze the running time for finding an element e, consider instead the equivalent running time for "unfinding" e, where we travel from e back to the start along the reversal of the path find would have taken – stepping up whenever possible, and left otherwise. As we travel, consider the number of elements directly to our left, shown shaded in Figure 5. This number satisfies the conditions of the randomized reduction lemma with $p = 1/4$ and $q = 1/2$: consider event I (our next step moves up, since we flipped heads at the current location during insertion) and II (at most half of the elements to our left flipped heads during insertion and are promoted to the next level). Both I and II are independent and happen with probability at least 1/2 (so $p = 1/4$), and if both happen, then the number of elements to our left reduces to at most 1/2 of the current value on our next step.

There is a straightforward one-to-one mapping between skip lists and BSTs. Using this, the mechanics of the skip list can be "ported" to obtain another simple randomized BST balancing mechanism, whose analysis follows directly from that of skip lists, and therefore also from randomized reduction [4].

Randomized reduction can also be used to show that a skip list occupies $O(n)$ space *whp*, using another useful variation of the randomized reduction lemma:

LEMMA 5. **(Incremental Reduction)** *If an algorithm independently reduces the effective size of a problem in each iteration by 1 with at least some constant probability $p > 0$, then the algorithm takes $O(n)$ iterations whp.*

To show this, we apply the randomized reduction lemma to the quantity 2^n, for which a reduction of 1 in n corresponds to a decrease by a factor of $q = 1/2$. The original randomized reduction lemma therefore implies a bound of $O(\log 2^n) = O(n)$ iterations whp (and in fact the high probability bound here is even stronger, with a failure probability of the form $1/2^{nc}$ instead of $1/n^c$). To apply incremental reduction to skip lists, imagine walking across the skip list from left to right, visiting each column from bottom to top along the way. Each step takes us up with probability 1/2, or to the bottom of the next column otherwise. Letting m denote the number of columns to our right, this quantity satisfies the conditions of the lemma above, so we take $O(n)$ total steps whp.

4. EXAMPLES IN NETWORKING

The domain of networking contains several applications that benefit from randomized reduction analysis.

4.1 Contention Resolution

Suppose n devices are all trying to transmit along a shared communication channel, where in each timestep a device can choose whether or not to attempt transmission, but if multiple devices transmit, they will interfere (and they can detect when this happens). Suppose the devices do not know n, so they do not know how many other devices they are competing against. Here, a reasonable protocol for contention resolution is for each device to flip a coin and attempt transmission if heads. If transmission fails due to a collision, however, all transmitting devices enter a dormant state until the first timestep in which no transmission occurs, then they wake up and resume the same protocol. In the first timestep, roughly half of our devices will attempt transmission and become dormant, followed by roughly a quarter in the next timestep, and so on.

In terms of randomized reduction, a simple coin flip argument tells us that each step reduces the number of active devices by at least a factor of $q = 1/2$ with probability at least $p = 1/2$, so we will have $O(\log n)$ timesteps whp until the end of a "phase", which can be either a successful transmission by one device or a timestep with no transmissions (e.g., if all remaining devices had attempted transmission and gone to sleep). Fortunately, a straightforward argument can show that each phase ends with a successful transmission with probability at least 1/2, giving a reasonable bound on the frequency of successful transmissions.

4.2 Broadcast Along a Random Tree

We already discussed random trees briefly in Section 2.2. Here, we show how randomized reduction helps to analyze a slightly different random tree construction. Suppose we want to broadcast information from node 1 to each of nodes $1 \dots n$ in a network. This is commonly done along a "broadcast tree" emanating outward from node 1 as its root. A simple way to choose such a tree is for each node j to select a random node in $1 \dots j-1$ as its parent. It is easy to show that node n is only $O(\log n)$ steps away from the root whp, and since this is the worst case, the same holds true for every node, so according to a union bound over all nodes, the tree has depth $O(\log n)$ whp. The randomized reduction argument here is almost the same as with our "reset minimum" example: walk from node n back to node 1, observing that each step has a probability of $\geq 1/2$ of moving from node j to a node in the range $1 \dots j/2$, so $p = q = 1/2$.

Another desirable feature of a broadcast tree is that each node should have low degree (or equivalently, not too many children), since otherwise it will be overloaded with outbound communication. Our random construction gives a tree with maximum degree $O(\log n)$ whp also due to randomized reduction. Consider reading off the children of some node x in decreasing order of index (e.g., the children might be nodes 17, 10, 5, and 3). If we are currently at index j, the probability that none of the nodes in the range $2j/3 + 1 \dots j-1$ were joined to x as a parent is

$$\begin{aligned}
\left(1 - \frac{1}{2j/3}\right) \cdots \left(1 - \frac{1}{j-2}\right) &\geq \left(1 - \frac{1}{2j/3}\right)^{j/3-1} \\
&\geq \left[\left(1 - \frac{1}{2j/3}\right)^{2j/3}\right]^{1/2} \\
&\geq [1/4]^{1/2} \quad (\text{for } j \geq 3) \\
&= 1/2,
\end{aligned}$$

so we reduce our index from j by a factor of $q = 2/3$ to a number in $1 \dots 2j/3$ with probability at least $p = 1/2$.

4.3 Gossip Protocols

Suppose a machine wants to transmit a message to n other machines in a distributed network. A simple protocol for doing this is the following: in each timestep, every machine that knows the message transmits it to another machine randomly chosen from $1 \dots n$ (if unlucky, this machine already knows the message, in which case the transmission is wasted). This is a "pushing" variant of a so-called *gossip* protocol; we can similarly conceive of "pulling" variants where machines without the message ask for it from random machines in each timestep.

Randomized reduction gives a nice way to analyze the number of timesteps necessary for a gossip protocol to spread its message to all n machines. In the push variant, for example, let us divide time into two phases: the first phase runs until $\geq n/4$ machines have heard the message, and then the second phase starts. In each timestep of the first phase, suppose we have $k < n/4$ machines with knowledge of the message. Each one pushes to a random machine, and since at least $n/2$ machines don't have the message (even taking into account new machines hearing the message in this timestep), each push succeeds with probability $\geq 1/2$. We can therefore regard this as flipping k coins that are biased to land on heads with probability $\geq 1/2$, so we have $\geq k/2$ heads (successful pushes) with probability $\geq 1/2$. Therefore, we have a probability of at least $p \geq 1/2$ of expanding the number of machines k with the message by a factor of 3/2 (or equivalently, of reducing the quantity n/k by a factor of $q = 2/3$), so the first phase takes $O(\log n)$ timesteps whp.

In the second phase, a direct probability argument suffices. Consider a machine m that doesn't know the message. In each timestep, since $k \geq n/4$, the probability none of our k machines chooses m is $(1-1/n)^k \leq (1-1/n)^{n/4} \leq e^{-1/4}$ (owing to the useful bound $(1-1/n)^n \leq e^{-1}$). If we run for $c \ln n$ timesteps, the probability m doesn't hear the message during any timestep is therefore at most $e^{-c(\ln n)/4} = 1/n^{c/4}$. This gives a high probability bound of success for machine m in $O(\log n)$ timesteps, which after a union bound implies success for all machines in $O(\log n)$ timesteps whp.

5. CONCLUSIONS AND EXTENSIONS

We have shown how the principle of randomized reduction leads to short, simple analyses for a broad number of computational results. For space considerations, there were many more examples we could not mention, including analysis of standard algorithms such as interpolation search [9] and stable in-place randomized quicksort [12], parallel and distributed algorithms (e.g., parallel maximal independent set [1, 7]), algorithms for problems in computational geometry (e.g., convex hull), and methods from other domains as well. We hope this technique helps promote greater adoption of randomized algorithms in computing classes, and ultimately in real-world systems.

Acknowledgements

The first two authors received support from NSF CAREER award CCF-0845593.

6. REFERENCES

[1] N. Alon, L. Babai, and A. Itai. A fast and simple randomized parallel algorithm for the maximal independent set problem. *Journal of Algorithms*, 7(4):567 – 583, 1986.

[2] C.R. Aragon and R. Seidel. Randomized search trees. *Algorithmica*, 16:464–497, 1996.

[3] T.M. Chan. Geometric applications of a randomized optimization technique. In *Proceedings of the Symposium on Computational Geometry*, pages 269–278, 1998.

[4] B.C. Dean and Z.H. Jones. Exploring the duality between skip lists and binary search trees. In *Proceedings of the 45th ACM Southeast Conference (ACMSE)*, pages 395–399, 2007.

[5] A. Gambin and A. Malinowski. Randomized meldable priority queues. In *Conference on Current Trends in Theory and Practice of Informatics*, pages 344–349, 1998.

[6] A.V. Goldberg and R.E. Tarjan. Expected performance of Dijkstra's shortest path algorithm. Technical Report TR-96-063, NEC Research Institute, 1996.

[7] M. Luby. Simple parallel algorithms for the maximal independent set problem. *SIAM Journal on Computing*, 15(4):1036–1053, 1986.

[8] C. Martínez and S. Roura. Randomized binary search trees. *Journal of the ACM*, 45(2):288–323, 1998.

[9] Y. Perl, A. Itai, and H. Avni. Interpolation search — A log log N search. *Communications of the ACM*, 21(7):550–553, 1978.

[10] H. Prüfer. Neuer beweis eines satzes über permutationen. *Archiv für Mathematik und Physik*, 27:142–144, 1918.

[11] W. Pugh. Skip lists: A probabilistic alternative to balanced trees. *Communications of the ACM*, 33(6):668–676, 1990.

[12] R.L. Rivest. A fast stable minimum storage sorting algorithm. Technical Report Rep. 43, Institute de Recherche d'Informatique, Rocquencont, France, 1973.

APPENDIX

For completeness, we now show how to prove the randomized reduction lemma using other tools from probability theory. We also prove that the randomized reduction lemma can give an $O(\log n)$ bound in expectation as well as with high probability, and that it applies also if we can show a reduction in expected problem size during each iteration.

PROOF. Let T be the running time of an algorithm satisfying the conditions of the randomized reduction lemma. If we run just for the first $L = k \ln n$ iterations, let X be the number of these iterations on which we see adequate reduction (by a factor of q). Since reduction in each iteration happens with probability at least p, $\mathbf{E}[X] \geq Lp$. If our algorithm fails to terminate in L units of time, then it must be the case that $X \leq \log_{1/q} n$, since otherwise we would have had enough reducing iterations to go from an initial problem size n down to 1. Hence, $\mathbf{Pr}[T \geq L] \leq \mathbf{Pr}[X \leq \log_{1/q} n]$. Since X has a binomial distribution, we can bound the probability of deviation from its mean using a standard form of the Chernoff bound: for $\alpha \in [0, 1/2]$,

$$\mathbf{Pr}[X \leq \alpha \mathbf{E}[X]] \leq e^{-(1-\alpha)^2 \mathbf{E}[X]/2} \leq e^{-E[X]/8}$$

Setting $\alpha = \frac{1}{k} \log_{1/q} e$ and taking $k \geq 2 \log_{1/q} e$, we have

$$\begin{aligned} \mathbf{Pr}[T \geq L] &\leq \mathbf{Pr}[X \leq \log_{1/q} n] \\ &\leq \mathbf{Pr}[X \leq \alpha \mathbf{E}[X]] \\ &\leq e^{-k(\ln n)/8} \\ &= 1/n^{k/8}, \end{aligned}$$

so we run in $k \ln n = O(\log n)$ iterations whp. □

COROLLARY 6. *If an algorithm satisfies the conditions of the randomized reduction lemma, it runs in $O(\log n)$ expected iterations.*

PROOF. Call a "phase" a set of iterations up to a reducing iteration; we expect each phase to contain $\leq 1/p$ iterations, since each iteration is reducing with probability $\geq p$. After $\log_{1/q} n$ phases the algorithm must have terminated, so by linearity of expectation, the total time on all phases is at most $\frac{1}{p} \log_{1/q} n = O(\log n)$. □

COROLLARY 7. *If each iteration of an algorithm reduces the expected size of our problem to at most a $q < 1$ fraction of its current value with probability at least $p > 0$, then the algorithm satisfies the conditions of the randomized reduction lemma.*

PROOF. Let $q' = (1+q)/2 < 1$, and let X be a random variable indicating the fraction of reduction on a given iteration. According to Markov's inequality, $\mathbf{Pr}[X > q'] \leq \mathbf{E}[X]/q' \leq q/q'$, so $p' = \mathbf{Pr}[X \leq q'] \geq 1 - q/q' = 1/q' - 1 > 0$. We therefore satisfy the randomized reduction lemma with parameters p' and q'. □

Curricular Assessment: Tips and Techniques

Henry M. Walker (Moderator)
Grinnell College
Noyce Science Center
Grinnell, IA 50112
+1 641-269-4208
walker@cs.grinnell.edu

Sue Fitzgerald
Metropolitan State University
700 East Seventh Street
St.Paul, MN 55106
+1 651-793-1473
sue.fitzgerald@metrostate.edu

John F. Dooley
Knox College
2 East South Street
Galesburgh, IL 61401
+1 309-341-7748
jdooley@knox.edu

Categories and Subject Descriptors

K.3.2 [**Computers and Education**]: Computer and Information Science Education – curriculum, self-assessment

General Terms

Management, Measurement, Documentation, Standardization

Keywords

Curriculum; assessment

1. SUMMARY

Assessment of educational programs is an increasingly important topic. Accrediting bodies regularly ask colleges and universities to provide evidence regarding the quality of their educational programs — what are the goals and objectives of each specific major, and how can the institution know that those goals and objectives are achieved [3]? Legislative bodies seek justification for public monies spent on education. And funders such as the National Science Foundation require evaluation of learning outcomes during the merit review process for education-related proposals [1].

In participating in external reviews of other computing departments, and in talking to faculty around the country, the session leaders have observed a remarkable level of activity regarding the assessment of courses and programs. However, in these conversations, three characteristics seem common:

- Faculty often expends very large amounts of time and effort on assessment-related activities.
- Data collection often yields massive amounts of unorganized and unfocused material.
- Once data are collected, faculty and staff often have run out of time or are overwhelmed by the task of connecting the data with possible improvements in a course or program.

Overall, in discussions with faculty around the country, the session leaders have been impressed by both the interest in improving programs and a sense of discouragement in the perception that any meaningful assessment will likely require unreasonable amounts of time and effort. Further, even when faculty is willing to embrace and expand assessment activities, they often do not have a good idea where to start. The subject of assessment may seem overwhelming.

This session seeks to initiate a discussion regarding simple approaches through which faculty can gain meaningful insights into components of their courses and/or programs with only modest expenditures of time and energy.

SIGCSE '15, March 4-7, 2015, Kansas City, MO, USA.
ACM 978-1-4503-2966-8/15/03.
http://dx.doi.org/10.1145/2676723.2677319

2. OVERALL SESSION OBJECTIVE

This session will bring interested faculty together to brainstorm time-effective assessment activities. Since assessment seeks to aid the on-going improvement of programs, discussion will focus upon how faculty can channel their efforts to identify strengths and opportunities within courses and the curriculum and to make refinements. The session will introduce new assessment ideas, and encourage discussion and idea sharing.

3. OUTLINE OF THE SESSION

This session is designed as a collaborative enterprise, in which both leaders and the audience identify the current status of assessment activities at their institutions, describe challenges and opportunities, and share time-effective approaches that may move programs forward — with only modest requirements of faculty time and effort. In order to structure this discussion within the time available, the following 5-part structure is suggested.

Part 1: Preliminaries (5 minutes)

- Introductions
- Session outline

Part 2: Some simple assessment activities (25 minutes)

- Description of several simple activities that can provide meaningful input with relatively few hours of faculty time. Examples will include each of the following:
  - steps to formulate 5-15 learning outcomes for each graduate
  - small data collection to measure student achievement of a learning objective in a course
  - exit interviews of graduating seniors
  - alumni surveys
  - course-specific end-of-course evaluations
  - tapping on-campus resources to help
  - use of ACM/IEEE-CS CS2013 curricular guidelines [2]
  - use of ABET Assessment Planning [3, 4]
- This preliminary discussion is not intended to provide complete information about every aspect of a course or program. However, in each case, leaders have used these

activities, found them to be manageable in implementation, and used the results in meaningful ways.

Part 3: Current Status (10 minutes)

- Audience members will describe the current status of assessment activities at their institutions.
- Audience identification of additional assessment activities that are simple and time effective.

Part 4: Challenges (10 minutes)

- Audience members will outline challenges they experience with assessment.
- Leaders will synthesize and identify 4-5 challenges that reflect a range of issues articulated by the audience.

Part 5: Brainstorming (25 minutes)

- Leaders and audience members will brainstorm approaches to the 4-5 challenges articulated by the audience.
- Depending on the number of session attendees, this part of the session may proceed in 2-3 small groups or as a group of the whole.

4. EXPECTATIONS

For many faculty members, assessment is intimidating, and moving forward can seem overwhelming. This session seeks to help audience participants take a few steps forward from whatever they might be doing for course- or program-level assessment. One session cannot cover the entire subject of assessment, but one session can provide a range of practical ideas and approaches.

Since the session leaders have experience in a wide range of assessment activities — both at their own institutions and during reviews on other campuses, the leaders will present some materials to start discussion and also have additional materials prepared as possible examples and references. The session itself will select those elements that address specific problems identified by attendees. Additional suggestions by other audience members will expand possible ways to address identified problems.

At the end of the session, it is expected that audience members will have identified several practical approaches that might help address current problems regarding assessment at home institutions.

5. SUITABILITY FOR A SPECIAL SESSION

Although the session leaders will begin with examples and approaches that may help seed discussion, this session is designed to be highly interactive and participatory. Leaders will make some short presentations, but the format and intention of the session is to foster sharing, brainstorming, and active problem solving.

6. REFERENCES

[1] National Science Foundation, Merit Review Criteria. *National Science Foundation Board* (Dec. 14, 2011).

[2] ACM/IEEE-CS Task Force, *Computer Science Curricula 2013* ACM and IEEE-CS, December 20, 2013.

[3] ABET Assessment Planning (http://www.abet.org/assessment-planning/), accessed August 26, 2014.

[4] ABET Assessment Planning Resources (http://www.abet.org/assessment-planning-resources/), accessed August 26, 2014.

7. LEADER BIOGRAPHIES

Henry Walker has served as an external reviewer of 35 departments (either computer science or mathematics and computer science) since 1991. He also has been a contributor to the Committee on Consultants of the Mathematical Association of America (MAA) and writer of a LaTeX template for reports of external reviewers for the MAA Report, *Guidelines for Serving as a Consultant in the Mathematical Sciences*, Spring 2009. In addition, he has actively participated in three reviews of his own department, in the 1970s, 1995, and 2007. Currently, he is designated as Professor of Computer Science and Samuel R. and Marie-Louise Rosenthal Professor of Natural Science and Mathematics at Grinnell College.

Sue Fitzgerald, Professor of Computer Science, is the senior faculty member in the Department of Information and Computer Sciences at Metropolitan State University, MN. At present she also serves as Director of Metro State's Center for Faculty Development. She has been employed at Metro State since 1996, serving two terms as department chair from 1996 to 2002. From 2010 to 2012, Dr. Fitzgerald served as a Program Director for the National Science Foundation where she made funding recommendations on grant proposals relating to science education at the undergraduate level.

John Dooley is the William and Marilyn Ingersoll Professor of Computer Science at Knox College, Galesburg, IL. He came to assessment purely by accident and reluctantly. He first encountered assessment when he was in charge of the CS department self-study in 2008-2009. Since then he has been working with the College's Department of Institutional Research and Assessment on assessment surveys, data collection, and analysis. He also worked on a science division-wide council to create learning goals for introductory courses and has served as an external reviewer in several CS program reviews. He headed up the 2013-2014 CS departmental program review at Knox.

Best Practices for IRB Approval: Four Perspectives

Michael S. Kirkpatrick (moderator)
James Madison University
kirkpams@jmu.edu

Janice E. Cuny
National Science Foundation
jcuny@nsf.gov

Mark Guzdial
Georgia Institute of Technology
guzdial@cc.gatech.edu

Amanda Holland-Minkley
Washington & Jefferson College
amh@washjeff.edu

Clifford A. Shaffer
Virginia Tech
shaffer@cs.vt.edu

Categories and Subject Descriptors

K.4.1 [**Computing Milieux**]: Public Policy Issues—*Ethics*; K.3.2 [**Computing Milieux**]: Computer and Information Science Education—*Computer science education*

General Terms

Human Factors

Keywords

human subjects research, irb, ethics

1. SUMMARY

As CS education moves toward a more rigorous approach to pedagogical research, there is a growing push to adhere to standard practices that are used in other social science fields. A critical aspect of this change is a growing awareness that CS education researchers need to follow standard ethical practices and to perform their research with appropriate institutional review board (IRB) oversight. U.S. federal regulations for conducting human subjects research (which includes pedagogical research) can be found in the Code of Federal Regulations, Title 45, Part 46 (45 CFR 46) [1], also known as the "Common Rule." While the Common Rule defines federal policy, interpretation of the policy can vary from one institution to another. For this reason, it is important for researchers to understand both federal requirements and their institution's policies and interpretations.

In this panel session, we will provide an overview of the Common Rule and present four perspectives on best practices for gaining IRB approval. The panel members include an officer from a federal funding agency, an IRB member, and two experienced researchers who can describe both successful and failed attempts to gain IRB approval for a variety of projects. The discussion will focus on best practices for working with IRBs and how to ensure compliance with federal requirements. Panel members will also highlight common problems that can arise and how to address them.

SIGCSE'15, March 4–7, 2015, Kansas City, MO, USA.
ACM 978-1-4503-2966-8/15/03.
http://dx.doi.org/10.1145/2676723.2677330.

2. JANICE E. CUNY

As a National Science Foundation (NSF) Program Officer who handles proposals on education and broadening participation, I often work with principal investigators (PIs) concerning IRB approval. NSF's aim is to ensure the quality of research that we fund, while adhering to the three principles of respect for persons ("individuals should be treated as autonomous agents"), beneficence (researchers must "maximize possible benefit of their work while minimizing possible harm"), and justice ("the burden of risky research" should be equally distributed). To ensure this, NSF (and many other federal agencies) have adopted a set of regulations, called the "Common Rule." Institutions and organizations receiving NSF funds have the responsibility for setting up IRBs to review research protocols and designs, and to ensure compliance with the Common Rule.

Here I discuss many of the issues and pitfalls of IRB approval. The issues include PIs who are not at all familiar with IRB procedures or requirements, extreme time pressure because of the positioning of our solicitations within the funding cycle, the wide variance in how institutional IRBs interpret the regulations, conflicting requirements from multiple institutions involved in a single proposal, difficulties in obtaining consent for subjects under 18, problems with tracking participants over periods of time, requirements for confidentiality of data, failures of PIs to keep IRBs up-to-date, and arbitrating arguments between PIs and IRBs.

3. MARK GUZDIAL

From 2006–2011, I directed an alliance ("Georgia Computes!") funded by the NSF to broaden participation in computing (BPC) across the U.S. state of Georgia at levels from middle school through undergraduate education. Since 2012, I have been one of the leaders of the NSF BPC alliance Expanding Computing Education Pathways (ECEP) which is a service organization to help states make changes to improve and broaden their computing education. Both of these roles have required some complicated IRB protocols that can illustrate some of the difficulties that can arise.

- Example #1: If you have a project across multiple institutions, when can one institution's IRB cover all the activity? We have found that it depends on the institution. For example, if a university has their own human subjects review board, then they will likely want their own protocol at a minimum, with the approval letter from the lead institution's IRB.

- Example #2: IRB will give permission to involve primary and secondary school students who come to your campus (for workshops or summer camps) or an off-site location with caveats like dealing with both assent and consent. However, speaking to students in their schools is amazingly difficult. For three years we tried, and never succeeded. We were able to get approval from our institution. It took us another two years to get permission from the research office of a local school district (after several failures). But then we never found a principal (within a school district that gave us approval) who would allow us to interview within her school.

4. AMANDA HOLLAND-MINKLEY

The federal regulation on the Protection of Human Subjects (45 CFR 46) [1] mandates review processes for research supported by the federal government that involves human subjects. Academic researchers generally encounter these policies in the form of their school's Institutional Review Board. Through serving on an IRB and reviewing projects, as well as participating in writing my institution's IRB Standard Operating Procedure (SOP), I have worked with a number of faculty, staff, and students to help explain the Common Rule and its application to their intended research. As context, it is important to understand that every institution establishes its own SOP, consistent with the Common Rule but customized to be reflective of its own community standards. For this reason, different institutions may treat the same project differently, and researchers should work with their particular IRB to understand their processes and how they apply.

When reviewing a project, there is a detailed list of conditions that an IRB must find hold, but in broad terms review focuses on the proposal's ability to demonstrate that risk to subjects is minimized and reasonable in relation to anticipated benefits, that the obligations of informed consent are met, and that data are adequately protected as they are collected and stored. I have found that the last component is the portion that most frequently requires discussion or revision when looking at education research projects. Review looks at the potential for collected information to cause harm, not just through a risk of criminal or civil liability but also through a risk to the subject's employability or general reputation. Considerations about whether subjects are personally identifiable through the information being collected are another frequent point of focus, as it can dictate the terms of a review. Proposals should consider the set of information collected as a whole and what it reveals about the identity of the subject. It is best for a proposal to be realistic about the potential for reconstructing subject identity, and then balance that risk and the potential harm of the information against the anticipated benefits of the research. Finally, researchers should be attentive to how and where they store their research data and be able to address questions of access as well as duration of storage, particularly if handled through a cloud computing service.

5. CLIFF SHAFFER

I have had a few years of experience with submitting IRB proposals and observing the interactions of colleagues with their IRBs. From this experience I have developed some guidelines for how I think it is best to approach the process. The most important advice is: Don't treat your IRB as the enemy or an obstacle. Doing so won't help you to get done what you need to get done. Instead, keep a positive attitude about the process. If you have any questions about how to do a submission or are not sure how to handle a response from the IRB about your submission, talk to the IRB chair. Get the chair to help you make sure that the submission is acceptable. Expect from the start that you will need to resubmit at least once, as it is common that an IRB submission will generate some requirement for changes.

Whenever possible, sell your study as "standard educational practice." Your IRB might give you exempt status, or at the least approve it easily. This will be easier if you avoid raising red flags (unless you mean to). Some typical red flags include not being clear about how you will maintain privacy in data collection, not using informed consent whenever you reasonably can, and not giving sample documents. At the start, you might not know what your survey or test instrument will look like exactly. That is fine, just submit something reasonable, then amend your submission as needed. The amendment process for updating documents should be easy, and you should just accept such amendments as a standard part of the process. However, if your project requires a non-standard practice to be successful, then don't shy away from standing your ground. For example, I have have successfully gotten protocols approved that do not require informed consent because I discussed it with the chair and made a good case for why informed consent would harm my study.

CS Ed researchers at non-Research 1 schools might have a harder time than those at research schools, because the IRB is less experienced. You might have to help them with interpretation of the rules, and so your positive interaction with the IRB is even more important.

6. REFERENCES

[1] U.S. Department of Health and Human Services. Code of Federal Regulations - Title 45 Public Welfare CFR 46. `http://www.hhs.gov/ohrp/humansubjects/guidance/45cfr46.html`, January 2009. Retrieved September 2, 2014.

Supporting the Computer Science Learning Process

Amy Briggs (Moderator)
Middlebury College
briggs@middlebury.edu

David Bau
Google
davidbau@google.com

Caroline Meeks
Prospect Hill Academy
cmeeks@prospecthillacademy.org

Pat Yongpradit
Code.org
pat@code.org

Categories and Subject Descriptors

K.3.2 [**Computer and Education**]: Computer and Information Science Education – computer science education

General Terms

Measurement, Experimentation, Standardization.

Keywords

Computer Science Education, K-12 Curriculum, CS Principles, Exploring Computer Science, Code.org, Pencil Code, Professional Development.

1. Summary (Amy Briggs)

How do students learn computer science? Successful students climb a ladder of learning and meta-learning. Not only do they learn content, but also they gain proficiency with new processes that aid their learning. Each learner takes her/his own path, of course, but the beginning CS student must clear a number of hurdles that we can identify and help them with. In programming, for example, one might struggle with the leap from visual programming to text programming, or from using well-designed integrated tutorials while learning one language, to the chaos of the Internet when learning another.

Numerous ongoing efforts in computer science education and professional development [5, 6] have contributed to tremendous increases in the numbers of students studying computer science at all levels. These efforts have included academic innovations as well as partnerships with industry, government, and non-profit organizations [7]. Expanded access means that more students have the opportunity to study computer science, but also that the diverse needs of many new learners need to be understood and addressed.

SIGCSE '15, Mar 04-07 2015, Kansas City, MO, USA.
ACM 978-1-4503-2966-8/15/03.
http://dx.doi.org/10.1145/2676723.2677334

Amy Briggs is Professor of Computer Science at Middlebury College in Vermont and co-PI on the NSF/College Board CS Principles project [3]. She is a member of the Liberal Arts Computing Consortium, a group of computer scientists dedicated to undergraduate computer science education and curriculum development. As moderator she will facilitate audience participation, draw connections between the contributions of the panelists, and underscore how curriculum and pedagogy can be enhanced with better understanding of student learning and tools designed to support the learning of new processes and content.

2. A ladder of meta-learning (David Bau)

David Bau is a software engineer for Google and the creator of Pencil Code [4], an open-source educational programming tool. His work focuses on enabling programming students to learn how to learn. Specifically, to learn how to discover, understand, and use new technical tools.

In this panel he will discuss his experience teaching in a variety of different types of programming classrooms, and his point of view that it is important for a programming class to go beyond teaching computational thinking. The meta-learning that comes with grappling with new processes and tools is essential for CS learners. Students go from learning how to navigate tutorials to visual programming, to text programming within constrained sandboxes, to open-ended programming with current technologies popular in the wider community.

Beginning students benefit from explicit guided tutorials that guide them down a single path. Then when using tools like Scratch, students learn how to experiment. The visual palettes provide a safe and constrained way to learn by doing. There is a hurdle when moving from visual programming to text code, but tools with well-organized reference manuals such as the Processing manual give students a predictable sandbox for learning. Eventually, when students are able to use open-ended online information such as material about HTML5 or other popular current technologies, they are able to participate in the wider programming community.

The focus of Bau's work has been to provide tools to help all students climb this ladder. It includes solutions to move students from tutorials to visual coding, from visual coding to sandboxed text coding, and from sandboxed text coding to modern mainstream programming.

3. Supporting the student learning process (Caroline Meeks)

Caroline Meeks is a computer science teacher and technology integration specialist. She teaches at Prospect Hill Academy Charter School, a K-12 urban charter school with approximately 100 students per grade level, located between the campuses of MIT and Harvard. The school population is 85% African American or Hispanic and 70% eligible for free or reduced lunch.

There are two major technology initiatives at the school this year. One is the introduction of a computer science elective for the 9th and 10th grade, focusing on creativity and engagement as well as trying to prepare students to pursue careers with the aspiration that they could get part-time high school or summer jobs. Ms. Meeks is using curriculum from Code.org, CS-First, App Inventor and Pencil Code. The other major initiative is a move from a few computer labs to a 1:1 chromebook environment by 2016, with the associated pedagogical and infrastructural challenges.

Drawing on her experiences in the classroom and in offering professional development to teachers, Meeks will share her insights on what specific challenges students often stumble over when beginning to learn computer science, and what specific supports educators and tool designers can provide.

Meeks is a graduate of MIT and the Technology Innovation and Education program at the Harvard Graduate School of Education. Prior to teaching at Prospect Hill Academy, she volunteered with Sugar Labs working with elementary school students and worked as a product manager for teacher support tools at Amplify Education.

4. Supporting teachers as learners (Pat Yongpradit)

Pat Yongpradit is a former high school computer science teacher who specialized in creating authentic, project-based learning experiences. He has worked as a curriculum consultant for Microsoft, for Pearson, and also as a curriculum team lead for Montgomery County Public Schools. At Code.org he is responsible for creating or curating curriculum and professional development, to provide rich computer science opportunities to every school in the nation.

Code.org [1] is working to support the needs of teachers at all levels. At the elementary school level, Code.org provides modules (featuring videos, puzzles, group activities and game-design) with a curriculum mapped to Common Core standards. At the middle school level they provide computer science and programming activities that integrate into existing math and science courses. And at the high school level they support teachers with introductory computing courses such as Exploring Computer Science [3] and Computer Science Principles [2] through a comprehensive curriculum and professional development model that supports diverse sets of learners.

As an educational non-profit dedicated to growing computer science education, Code.org works with districts around the US and is in a unique position to observe the learning process at all stages. During the panel presentation Yongpradit will share observations and reports from their nationwide work – how are students really learning CS, what are the current and future challenges in helping students move from puzzle solving to independent programming, and how different approaches are working with teachers and students nationwide.

5. Audience and Expectations

This panel is intended for all educators interested in supporting student learning by better understanding how learning happens, and by using the appropriate tools at the right times during the learning process. Panelists will each speak briefly from their different perspectives and backgrounds, and then at least 30 minutes will be dedicated to questions and answers with the audience.

6. REFERENCES

[1] *Code.org*, http://code.org, 2014.

[2] *Computer Science Principles*, http://csprinciples.org, 2014.

[3] *Exploring Computer Science*, http://exploringcs.org, 2014.

[4] *Pencil Code*, http://gym.pencilcode.net, 2014.

[5] O. Astrachan, J. Cuny, C. Stephenson, and C. Wilson, “The CS 10K Project: Mobilizing the Community to Transform High School Computing,” in *SIGCSE Technical Symposium on Computer Science Education,* Dallas, TX, 2011.

[6] B. Franke, J. Century, M. Lach, C. Wilson, M. Guzdial, G. Chapman, and O. Astrachan, "Expanding Access to K-12 Computer Science Education: Research on the Landscape of Computer Science Professional Development," in *SIGCSE Technical Symposium on Computer Science Education*, Denver, CO, 2013.

[7] O. Astrachan, A. Briggs, G. Chapman, Joanna Goode, B. Osborne, P. Yongpradit, “A Public/Private Partnership for Expanding Computer Science in Schools,” in *SIGCSE Technical Symposium on Computer Science Education*, Atlanta, GA, 2014.

DEMONSTRATION SESSION

Looking Glass

Caitlin Kelleher, *Washington University in St. Louis*
Contact: ckelleher@cse.wustl.edu

Looking Glass is the successor to Storytelling Alice designed for middle and high school students. By dragging and dropping, users can construct programs that direct the behavior of characters in a 3D scene. The system consists of a downloadable application and an online community.

Looking Glass is intended to support creative, open-ended programming. To help spark ideas, the Looking Glass community hosts a set of community-created templates and remixes, animations that can be imported into any new world. These templates and remixes can help to inspire a story line. In more formal settings, templates and remixes allow an instructor to provide shared resources for an assignment and for students to collaborate with each other.

Exploring the behavior of existing code examples can be a powerful way to learn new skills. In addition to providing story inspiration, community remixes serve as code examples that students can explore. To support users in learning new skills based on code shared through remixes, Looking Glass includes a play and explore mode in which the environment records an execution history and changes to the 3D scene as a program runs. Users can scroll back in time, see which actions were executing, and replay individual statements.

A free download is available at lookingglass.wustl.edu for Windows, Mac, and Linux.

Acknowledgements: This material is based upon work supported by the National Science Foundation under Grant Nos. 1440996 and 1054587. Any opinions, findings, and conclusions or recommendations expressed in this material are those of the author(s) and do not necessarily reflect the views of the National Science Foundation.

ACM Categories & Descriptors: D.2.6 Programming Environments – Graphical Environments

Keywords: block-based programming; K-12; interactive program visualization; online community

DOI: http://dx.doi.org/10.1145/2676723.2691873

EngageCSEdu: CS1 and CS2 Materials for Engaging and Retaining Undergraduate CS Students

Alvaro Monge, *California State University Long Beach*
Beth A. Quinn, *National Center for Women & Information Technology*
Cameron L. Fadjo, *Google Inc.*
Contact: alvaro.monge@csulb.edu

How do you engage students in the computer science classroom? In this Demo Session we will examine this question within the context of EngageCSEdu (http://www.engage-csedu.org), a web-based collection of instructional materials for introductory CS classes. Developed by computer scientists, social scientists, and learning scientists from California State University, Long Beach, Carnegie Mellon University, University of Pittsburgh, the National Center for Women & Information Technology (NCWIT), and Google, EngageCSEdu is comprised of ~1500 instructional materials (such as assignments, projects, labs, and assessments) and 17 Engagement Practices (strategies and techniques for engaging and retaining students based on CS education and social science research). During this session we will demonstrate key features of EngageCSEdu, discuss how research-based findings on gender diversity and student engagement were used in its development, and invite participants to contribute their ideas for engaging and retaining students. Attendees will explore EngageCSEdu with members of the original development team and discuss how this focused and comprehensive open collection of instructional materials can be effectively used to support instructors. As a product by and for the CS education community, this demo is an opportunity for potential users to provide valuable feedback and input into the on-going development and dissemination of materials on EngageCSEdu. By the end of this demonstration participants will be more familiar with the research-based factors shown to increase engagement among undergraduate students, particularly women and underrepresented minorities, and have an opportunity to play an active role in positioning EngageCSEdu within the CS education community.

ACM Categories & Descriptors: K.3.2 [Computer and Information Science Education]: Computer Science education

Keywords: Student Engagement; Student Retention; Curriculum Issues; Pedagogy; Instruction; CS1; CS2; Gender Diversity; Engagement Practice

DOI: http://dx.doi.org/10.1145/2676723.2691875

SIGCSE'15, March 4–7, 2015, Kansas City, MO, USA.
ACM 978-1-4503-2966-8/15/03.

Expressions of Abstraction: Self-Explanation in Code Production

Leigh Ann Sudol-DeLyser
Computer Science, Psychology
Carnegie Mellon University
Pittsburgh, PA
lsudol@cs.cmu.edu

ABSTRACT

Novices struggle with the implementation of algorithms in code. Assessments asking students to describe algorithms in code have shown that use of abstractions in the descriptions have correlated with students' ability to produce algorithms in code. In this study, 24 introductory computer science students were asked to think out loud while writing code involving simple array algorithms in an online system. Student statements were classified based on the level of abstraction used in the statement. An analysis of the statements revealed that students with greater proficiency at writing code were more likely to use multiple levels of abstraction when describing the code they were writing, and moved between levels with higher frequency than less proficient students. The results align with self explanation research and provide insight into the cognitive mechanisms responsible for the transfer between the skills of reading and writing code.

Categories and Subject Descriptors

K.3.2 [**Computers & Education**]: Computer and Information Sciences Education;Computer Science Education

General Terms

Human Factors

Keywords

Computer Science Education Research; Explain in Plain English; SOLO; novice programmers; Code Comprehension

1. INTRODUCTION

The difficulties faced by novices in introductory CS courses, when writing code to implement algorithms, is well documented [13, 8]. The CS Education research community has begun to identify indicators of student performance that can help identify the stages of proficiency a novice must pass through in their development of expertise. [11, 16] A focus has been on assessing students' ability to read code produced by an instructor, however, little work has been done to document the ability by a student to read and understand code the novice produces for themselves. As novices, students often do not write correct code on their first try.[8] It is during the code writing process that students will need to undergo a series of self explanation steps, first constructing a model of the code behavior as they are writing it and then updating that model as they receive feedback about the actual behavior of the code. This code comprehension process can be an important factor in the relative success students have when practicing the writing of code and has implications for their future learning.[17]

SIGCSE'15, March 04–07, 2015, Kansas City, MO, USA.
Copyright 2015 ACM 978-1-4503-2966-8/15/03. ...$15.00
http://dx.doi.org/10.1145/2676723.2677222

Although experts and novices both report the need to engage in debugging activities, a comparative analysis of experts and novices in code comprehension tasks showed significant differences in the type of self explanation used during debugging.[10] Expertise is not only demonstrated in the accurate communication of domain specific knowledge, but in the sophistication of the mental models for domain content [6]. Practice is an important component of the transition between novice and expert [3]. All practice, however, is not equal and metacognitive factors can play a large role in the effect that practice has on a student's proficiency at a task [5]. In introductory computer science, the practice we assign to students often takes the form of writing code.

This work connects the self explanations students engage in during a code writing task to the code comprehension literature, using the level of abstraction in student statements about their code. The study uses a modified think-aloud protocol while students solved four programming tasks in an online IDE. Student statements are characterized by their level of abstraction, similar to previous work in code comprehension studies. All students made statements about their programs at varying levels of abstraction, however students with a higher proficiency at code writing will make more statements regarding the abstractions in the problem, and transition between levels of abstraction more frequently.

The contributions of this work lie in the collection of student statements during the code production process and analysis of those individual statements. Additionally, the codification of abstraction in individual statements as opposed to a longer response and the transition between the categories of statements is unique in the CS Education literature. A significant discovery of this work is the finding that students with a higher proficiency at code writing will shift between levels of abstraction with greater frequency.

2. SELF EXPLANATIONS IN PRACTICE

Underlying many common instructional and assessment mechanisms in computer science is the need for students to make sense of code that either they or others have written. As students either study examples of code or write and debug their own code, they engage in a process of sense making. This process is characterized by the activation of prior knowledge and the integration of new concepts into the student's conceptual framework for the topic. This sense making process when conducted solely by the student is referred to as self explanation, as the student is explaining to themselves the concepts or examples [4].

Early research in computer science education showed that the acquisition of the skill of programming, is assisted by metacognitive strategies, including self explanation, by the learner [15]. Pirolli and Recker looked at students using worked examples and textbook materials, and also during interactions with the Lisp Tutor [1]. In the protocols subjects were asked to "read and think aloud and, specifically, to explain examples to themselves". Outcomes suggested that acquisition of the skill of programming is "strongly related to the generation of explanations connecting the sample material to the abstract concepts introduced in the text".

Pirolli and others offer cognitive mechanisms to explain correlations between reading and writing code[12], especially when the descriptions of abstract concepts are encoded in the data collected from students' answers. Explain in Plain English questions (EiPE) have been shown to correlate with later performance in introductory computer science classes [14, 18]. More specifically, the ability to use abstractions, as represented either through the SOLO taxonomy[19] or the Block Model [16] correlate with student proficiency at programming tasks. A brief description of the levels of the SOLO Taxonomy [11] is presented in Table 1.

Category	Description
Prestructural	Answer demonstrates a significant misconception or is irrelevant to programming
Unistructural	Answer demonstrates an understanding of some but not all aspects of the problem
Multistructural	Answer demonstrates a correct understanding of the parts of the problem, but there is no evidence of connection between problem parts.
Relational	The parts of the problem are integrated into a coherent structure.

Table 1: SOLO Taxonomy Categories

EiPE questions can be viewed as a structured type of self explanation. I use the term abstraction to describe a language that describes parts of an algorithm together, for example "I looped over the array", instead of the exact code. In the question, the student is asked to describe the code, and researchers evaluate the answer for the level of abstraction, as described in the next section, used in the explanation. The benefits of self explanation offers a mechanism for the alignment between the skills of reading and writing code, as students with the ability to abstract about code they read either in EiPE questions or in their own editor, not only indicates a higher proficiency, but could possibly be a causal factor in the development of proficiency.

This work is unique in that it connects the unprompted abstractions students make in self explanation and the abstraction observed in EiPE type assessments. Other work in CS Education connects course level assessments to high level indicators of a students proficiency with abstractions [2], which is a different granularity of assessment from this paper, and therefore not discussed in detail.

3. COLLECTION OF STATEMENTS

This section describes the participants, setting of the study, problems the students were solving, and data collected. Twenty four participants were recruited from two major universities to participate in think aloud interviews. The participants had either recently completed an introductory programming course, or were in the final month of such a course. Participants were solicited through an email forwarded from their instructor. Although they did not receive any course credit for the study, participants were compensated for their time with $20. The respondents were both graduate and undergraduate students and a mix of genders (M=18, F=6).

3.1 Participant Characteristics

Upon entering the interview participants completed a survey with questions about demographics, prior coursework, expected (or received) grade in the introductory programming class. Of the 24 participants, 15 indicated they received or anticipated receiving a grade of A or A- for the appropriate programming class. Nine (9) participants indicated they would receive a grade less than A, or were unsure of the grade since they were currently enrolled in the class. No participant indicated that they anticipated receiving or had received a failing grade for the class.

3.2 Procedures

After completing the survey, participants were given a description of the task. They were asked to "think out loud and describe any code they were writing or choices they were considering". Participants interacted with a web-based environment on a desktop computer at the researcher's desk. The environment contained an editable text window, a submit button, and a feedback area as seen in Figure ??. When starting a problem the text window contained a partial implementation of the method, a stub. In the stub there is a line of code for the class and a line for the method header, providing participants with the name of any parameters needed to complete the method presented. The code stub also contained a comment that described the method to the student. The submit button was used to compile and test the code entered in the code window. The feedback area presented either the compilation message, the feedback based on test cases or a statement of correctness.

Each participant was asked to write the same algorithms in a set of four problems in the same order. The questions were designed to require the student to loop over an array and return a value. The four algorithms the students were asked to write were a sum of all the values in the array, a search for the maximum number stored in an array, a count of the number of positive values less than a second parameter, and a method to return the index of a value provided in a second parameter. Each algorithm was presented on its own screen and students needed to solve one problem before advancing to the next.

During the interviews the researcher sat in a chair slightly behind the participant. The participants' verbalizations were

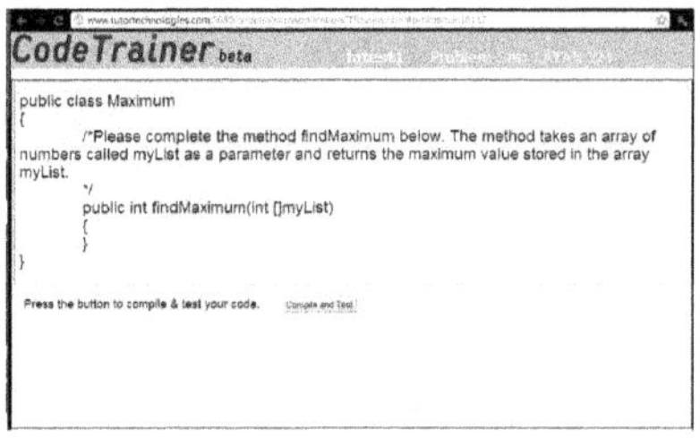

Figure 1: The Online Environment

recorded on a digital recorder, and the online system recorded the code when the participant pressed submit.

3.3 Research Conditions

Participants were assigned to one of four research conditions based on the order they responded to a request to participate in the study. The study was designed to measure the difficulties students had with particular components of the algorithms being implemented, and the understanding of feedback focused on the algorithmic components of a problem. Half of the participants received feedback from an online Java compiler combined with feedback regarding the output of the code when given test input. The other half of the participants received feedback about the algorithmic components in their solution before receiving the compiler and output based feedback. Although there were four research conditions, there were no significant differences in the classification of statements made by students, and therefore the treatments will be ignored by this paper.

3.4 Think Aloud Data

The statements students made while completing the programming tasks were recorded and transcribed. Due to the lack of a formal "answer", the statements made by the students often do not make complete sentences or thoughts. Student statements were divided into individual utterances looking for either a pause in their speech, a clear step to a new idea or topic, or a change in the problem or sub task the student was working on. Overall, 2,950 individual utterances or statements were identified.

Each statement was classified based on the categorization shown in Table 2. The classification was used to determine the relative number of abstract statements made by students, not the degree of abstraction in the entire problem. To reflect the changed goals, the original SOLO Taxonomy was modified to the classification scheme presented in Table 2 and described below. The classification is helpful in indicating if the student was thinking only about the individual code elements and syntax, or if they were attempting to connect the larger program goals to the code they were writing. Also, previous work in self explanation (described in Section 2) indicates that connections to the abstract ideas or larger goals of the problem are important, and the coding scheme is designed to specifically highlight the percentage of time students spend connecting the code statements they are writing to these abstract ideas.

Although SOLO is helpful to connect to prior work of the community, the granularity of analysis is not the same between the student statements and prior uses of SOLO. The SOLO taxonomy applied to novice programmers as described in [11] was used to categorize an entire description of a problem by a student. In this work we are categorizing individual statements during a problem solving task. The individual statements are of a much finer granularity, and therefore I used a coding scheme based on SOLO without replicating it exactly, and consider the modification of the coding scheme and the evaluation of student statements at a different granularity a contribution of this paper.

The NA(No Abstraction) category was used for statements that involved no abstraction beyond an individual line of code. This aligned with the SOLO categories Unistructural and Multistructural. The difference between the two categories in SOLO represent the student understanding of the problem being asked or expressing some misconceptions. The statements made in this study are difficult to judge for accuracy, and the accuracy is less important than the level of abstraction for the analysis presented here. Due to those factors, the two SOLO categories are collapsed into one.

The second category, BL (Block Labeling), was used for statements that move beyond the simple reiteration of the code. Students who engage in Block Labeling often connected pieces of code together in their statements as shown in the examples in Table 2. The BL classification aligns closely with a part of the Relational classification for SOLO.

The MR (Macro Relational) category was used for statements that demonstrated a connection to a macro relationship between elements of the code and the abstract nature of the problem. Statements about the problem itself, without any reference to code were also classified as MR, this often came up at the beginning of each section as the student read the problem aloud. The MR classification encompasses the Extended Abstract SOLO response, however some statements could be classified as relational under SOLO if there is no larger connection to another problem.

The final category, NC, is used to classify statements that are not related to the problem, or its solution. Although SOLO has a Prestructural category that is not represented in the coding used here, the NC category does not require the expression of a misconception, only a statement not directly related to the code of the problem.

In order to verify the classification accuracy of the primary author, an interrater reliability analysis was performed to assess the assignment of categories to student statements. A second expert rater was trained in the classification scheme and used the categories to rate 40 random statements from the data set. Kappa was computed for agreement. The ratings produced by the primary author and second expert generated a kappa of 0.601, a good agreement [9].

4. ANALYSIS OF DATA

Measures of student abstraction are often correlated with student proficiency at writing algorithms in code. There are many ways to indicate student proficiency at writing code. In this work I use the number of submissions the student needed to solve the problem as a rough estimate of proficiency. As we are not ordering students based on their performance an exact measure of proficiency is not needed.

There is a weaknesses in using the number of submissions, as students sometimes struggle with syntax errors which increase the number of submits, but have no effect on the student's understanding of the abstractions involved in the algorithm. The variability introduced by number of submissions is reduced by aggregating students into a high and low category as described in section 4.2.

Table 2: Categorization of Student Statements

Category	Label	Description	Example
No Abstraction	NA	Statements refer specifically to the code. They do not include statements that generalize	"int count =0", "That is myList dot length"
Block Labeling	BL	Statements refer to a block of code with a label as opposed to the character being typed.	"I need to define an int parameter named sum", "So if both of these are true, then we add one to the counter"
Macro Structure or Relations	MR	Statements connect elements together or relate an element to its purpose in the algorithm.	"So after we are doing with the for loop we want to return the counter", "I think I may need to use bubble sort to sort the.."
Feedback Response	FR	Statements refer to the feedback messages or the specific debugging elements in the problem solving process	"Um, I don't know what that means", "So it was looking for a 12 but returned..", "Ok, forgot a semicolon"
Not Code Specific	NC	The statement focused on the student's feelings or progress, not on the code.	"Ok, I want to try it", "I think thats right"

4.1 Initial Data Analysis

The data contains 2950 statements made by 24 subjects across four problems. Table 3 contains the aggregate count of each code broken down by problem the students were solving at the time the statement was made, as well as aggregate totals. The most frequently used code was NA, making up 35% of the statements coded. Surprisingly, 20% of the statements were NC or Not Code Specific, not focused on the code the student was writing for the problem. The particular problem students were working on was not a significant factor in the breakdown or total number of statements made, and therefore the problems are collapsed for analysis in the remainder of the paper.

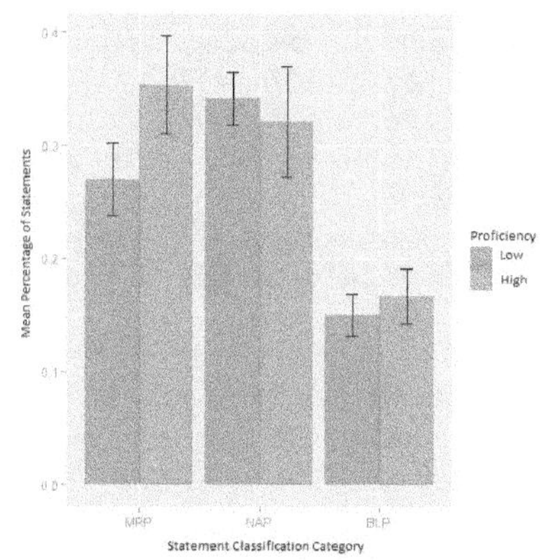

Figure 2: Statements by Proficiency

Table 3: Statement Codes by Problem

Problem	NA	BL	MR	FR	NC
1	305	89	194	61	212
2	310	216	239	40	164
3	243	72	186	35	90
4	166	67	170	26	65
Total	1024	444	789	162	531

During the session students were engaged in the task of writing code which involved the typing of the actual syntax, so it is unsurprising that many of their statements were made about the code itself and were labeled NA. Additionally, students also needed to parse problem descriptions in order to determine the appropriate code to write, and so the high percentage of abstract (MR) statements is also to be expected [7]. In the next section we look at the relationship between the statements of each type (No Abstraction, Block Level, and Macro Relation) to the proficiency of the student.

4.2 Abstractions Correlate with Proficiency

The initial expectation based upon prior work with EiPE questions, was that students with a higher proficiency would use more abstract statements and less non-abstract statements when thinking aloud while programming. There was a correlation between the number of submits and the raw number of statements made in each category (NA, BL, MR), however this is not an accurate metric for determining the difference between students. A student who took more submits to solve the problem often spent more time solving the problem and therefore talked for a longer period of time, making more statements in general. The raw data was transformed to represent the percentage of statements made by the student in each category, and the transformation is used for the remainder of the analysis in this paper.

An Analysis of Variance (ANOVA) showed no significant relationship ($p=.38$) between the raw proficiency of the student (as measured by number of submits) and the percentage of statements made at each level. Although the number of statements made in total was high, the number of students in the study was relatively low and a lack of power may account for the lack of significance. As a discipline we often categorize students into high and low performers, and a similar categorization proved useful for analysis here.

The median number of submits for all students was 15.5. Students were classified as high proficiency (HP), less submits than median, or low proficiency(LP), more submits than median. The median score of the HP students was 8.5, while the median of the LP students was 25.

As shown in Figure 2, there was no significant difference ($p>.1$) between the percentage of NA or BL statements made by HP or LP students. There was, however, a significant difference between the mean percentage of MR statements made by students of HP and LP students ($p < .05$, Means=.27, .35, SD=.12, .14). This would indicate that higher proficiency students are more likely to use abstract statements during the self explanation process.

4.3 Transitions Correlate with Proficiency

There is an additional dimension to the data beyond the percentages of statements students make at various levels of abstraction. The statements were also coded for transitions between classification categories. A transition is defined as a statement that was coded differently from immediately prior statements. For example if a student said *"So after we are done with the for loop, we want to return the counter"* it was coded as a MR. In the next statement the student may have verbalized typing the return statement with *"return c, semicolon"* which would be coded as NA and marked as a transition statement.

Statements coded as NC or FR were not considered transitions. It was common for a student to express a feeling or read feedback as a part of problem solving without changing the level of abstraction in the surrounding statements. For example, a student could be typing a for loop and make the statement *"that is myList dot length"* (NA), and then say *"I remember this from the last class"* (NC), and return to a statement *"i plus plus parenthesis"* (NA). The student inserted a contextual cue, or statement focused on something outside the problem scope, but still continued to act at the same level of abstraction as prior to the statement. To normalize the number of transitions, the percent of statements which were transitions between classification categories in all of the following analysis were used.

Figure 3 shows a comparison box plot between high and low proficiency students and the percentage of statements they made which transitioned between categories. There is a significant($p<.01$) difference between the percentage of transitions in low and high proficiency students. High proficiency students transitioned between categories on average in 38.3% of statements, while low proficiency students transitioned between categories, on average, only 30.2% times.

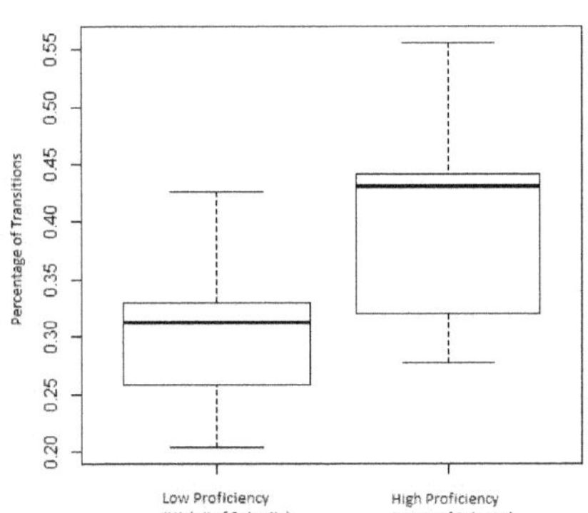

Figure 3: Transitions by Proficiency

The increase in the percentage of transitions indicates that students of higher proficiency move between the concrete code they are writing and the more abstract problem or relationship between an individual line of code and the entire algorithm more often. Examples from the text show indications that students were engaging in self explanation, connecting the specific code to the larger goals of the problem.

For example, a high proficiency student engaged in the a dialog where they were able to transition between the specific code they were writing to the relationship to the larger problem as they progressed. The dialog from the student, along with category classifications is shown in Table 4.

Statement	Category
for int i, so check out the for loop at first	NA
just so I am understanding, this argument passed in, this is the number that each element in the array has to be less than? ok	MR
Ok, I'm pretty sure the loop is right on	NC
myList i is greater than or equal to 0	NA
and less than value	NA
I see it now	NC
I thought it meant to return the sum of all those numbers, it just wanted the total number of all those numbers. I see the difference	MR

Table 4: A High Proficiency Student

Dialog from a low proficiency student at a similar point in the same problem is shown in Table 5.

Statement	Category
0 less than scores.length i plus plus	NA
so if, I'm just checking the condition	NA
if scores dot of I hm, ok.	NA
is less than 0	NA
so that I won't get confused if I use places	NC
and scores of I is greater	NA
and 0 also comes under that	NA
so 0 to greater than or equal to 0	NA
and less than passing grade	NA

Table 5: A Low Proficiency Student

In the same part of the problem, the low proficiency student did not relate the code they were writing verbally back to the larger problem, or the abstract nature of the algorithm they were attempting to write. When looking at the difference in the percent of transitions, 8% may see small. However, when the relative amount of time spent on each problem is considered combined with the higher use of MR statements by the high proficient students, low proficient students will spend a significantly longer amount of time discussing the individual code elements and syntax while engaging in practice.

5. CONCLUSIONS

The data presented in this paper offers a novel view of the levels of abstraction students use when thinking aloud during programming. The classification of individual statements, and subsequent analysis of the transitions between classification categories offers insight into a significant difference between low proficiency and high proficiency students.

5.1 Reading and Writing Code

The reading and writing of code are separate skills, however there is a strong correlation between a student's ability to describe code, including any relevant abstractions and relationships to other contexts, and their ability to write code. The results presented in sections 4.2 and 4.3 demonstrate a significant relationship no only with the number of statements made that focus on the abstract nature of the problem, but also on the transitions between levels of abstraction within a singular code writing session.

The transitions between levels that occur during the code writing process may help to shed light on the cognitive mechanism responsible for the correlation of two skills, reading and writing code. Often, towards the later part of an introductory programming course, students are asked to write code which will not fit in their working memory. A novice's working memory is limited to storing a set of individual tokens, or elements, related to the task they are working on [6]. Once a program extends beyond a few lines of code, each containing several tokens, the novice will not be able to hold the entire program in their working memory.

The implications of this are that students may need to engage in a code comprehension task if they are distracted, move from one part of the code to another, or are engaged in debugging. If a students is constantly self explaining, and connecting the code they are writing with the abstractions in the problem they will be more likely to stay focused on the appropriate task and recall code segments that together will produce a correct algorithm.

6. ACKNOWLEDGMENTS

This work was supported through the Program for Interdisciplinary Education Research (PIER) at Carnegie Mellon University, funded through Grant R305B040063 to Carnegie Mellon University, from the Institute of Education Sciences, US Department of Education. The opinions expressed are those of the author and do not represent the views of the Institute or the US Department of Education. The author would also like to thank the Pittsburgh Science of Learning Center for discussions and Thomas Harris and Tutor Technologies for maintaining the student login platform.

7. REFERENCES

[1] ANDERSON, J., AND REISER, B. The lisp tutor: it approaches the effectiveness of a human tutor. *Lecture 174* (1985).

[2] BENNEDSSEN, J., AND CASPERSEN, M. E. Abstraction ability as an indicator of success for learning computing science? In *ICER '08: The 4th International Workshop on Computing Education Research* (New York, NY, USA, 2008), ACM, pp. 15–26.

[3] CHARNESS, N., KRAMPE, R., AND MAYR, U. *The role of practice and coaching in entrepreneurial skill domains: An International comparison of life-span chess skill acquisition.* Erlbaum, 1996, pp. 51–80.

[4] CHI, M., BASSOK, M., LEWIS, M., REIMANN, P., AND GLASER, R. Self-explanations: How students study and use examples in learning to solve problems. *Cognitive Science 13* (1989), 145–182.

[5] CHI, M. T. H., SLOTTA, J. D., AND DE LEEUW, N. From things to processes: A theory of conceptual change for learning science concepts. *Learning and Instruction 4* (1994), 27–43.

[6] COUNCIL, N. R. *How People Learn: Brain, Mind, Experience and School.* National Academy Press, 2000.

[7] CUTTS, Q., ESPER, S., FECHO, M., FOSTER, S., AND SIMON, B. The abstraction transistion taxonomy: developing desired learning outcomes through the lens of situated cognition. *ICER '12: Proceedings of the ninth annual International conference on Computing Education Research* (2012), 63–70.

[8] JADUD, M. A first look at novice compilation behavior using bluej. *Computer Science Education 15*, 1 (2005).

[9] JR LANDIS, G. K. The measurement of observer agreement for categorical data. *Biometrics 33(1)* (1977), 159–174.

[10] LATOZA, T. D., GARLAN, D., HERBSLEB, J. D., AND MYERS, B. A. Program comprehension as fact finding. In *Proceedings of the the 6th joint meeting of the European software engineering conference and the ACM SIGSOFT symposium on The foundations of software engineering* (New York, NY, USA, 2007), ESEC-FSE '07, ACM, pp. 361–370.

[11] LISTER, R., SIMON, B., THOMPSON, E., WHALLEY, J., AND PRASAD, C. Not seeing the forest for the trees: Novice programmers and the solo taxonomy. *Information Technology in Computer Science Education Conference* (2006).

[12] LOPEZ, M., WHALLEY, J., ROBBINS, P., AND LISTER, R. Relationships between reading, tracing and writing skills in introductory programming. In *ICER '08: The 4th International Workshop on Computing Education Research* (New York, NY, USA, 2008), ACM, pp. 101–112.

[13] MCCRACKEN, M., ALMSTRUM, V., DIAZ, D., GUZDIAL, M., HAGAN, D., KOLIKANT, Y. B.-D., LAXER, C., THOMAS, L., UTTING, I., AND WILUSZ, T. A multi-national, multi-institutional study of assessment of programming skills of first-year cs students. *SIGCSE Bull. 33* (December 2001), 125–180.

[14] MURPHY, L., MCCAULEY, R., AND FITZGERALD, S. 'explain in plain english' questions: Implications for teaching. *Proceedings of the 43rd ACM Special Interest Group on CS Education* (2012).

[15] PIROLLI, P., AND RECKER, M. Learning strategies and transfer in the domain of programming. *Cognition and Instruction 12* (1994), 235–275.

[16] SCHULTE, C. Block model: an educational model of program comprehension as a tool for a scholarly approach to teaching. *Proceedings of the 4th Annual Workshop on CS Education* (2008).

[17] SUDOL-DELYSER, L.A., S. M. C. S. Code comprehension problems as learning events. *Proceedings of the 17th ACM conference on Innovation and Technology in CS Education* (2012).

[18] VENABLES, A., TAN, G., AND LISTER, R. A closer look at tracing, explaining and code writing skills in the novice programmer. In *ICER '09: Proceedings of the fifth international workshop on Computing education research workshop* (New York, NY, USA, 2009), ACM, pp. 117–128.

[19] WHALLEY, J. L., LISTER, R., THOMPSON, E., CLEAR, T., ROBBINS, P., KUMAR, P. K. A., AND PRASAD, C. An australasian study of reading and comprehension skills in novice programmers, using the bloom and solo taxonomies. In *Proceedings of the 8th Austalian Conference on Computing Education - Volume 52* (Darlinghurst, Australia, 2006), Australian Computer Society, Inc., pp. 243–252.

Generating Practice Questions as a Preparation Strategy for Introductory Programming Exams

Paul Denny
Department of Computer Science
The University of Auckland
Auckland, New Zealand
paul@cs.auckland.ac.nz

ABSTRACT

Written exams are a common form of assessment in introductory programming courses. Creating exam questions is normally the responsibility of the course instructor, however the process of authoring such questions may be a useful learning activity in itself. We explored this idea with a randomized controlled experiment ($n > 700$) in which a group of first-year programming students generated practice questions prior to an exam. Even though all questions were available to every student in the course for practice, the group that generated the questions performed significantly better on the exam. The effects were most pronounced when students answered exam questions on topics that were targeted by questions they had generated. We suggest that some existing tools for computer science education may benefit from incorporating related activities.

Categories and Subject Descriptors

K.3.2 [**Computers and Education**]: Computer and Information Science Education—*computer science education*

General Terms

Design, Human Factors

Keywords

multiple-choice; exams; programming; PeerWise; student authored questions

1. INTRODUCTION

Assessment is fundamental to education, and exams form a key component of many assessment strategies at the tertiary level. Exams are typically administered after a period of instruction to ensure that intended learning outcomes have been achieved. Indeed, most university courses conclude with a high-stakes final exam which ultimately determines the success or failure of each student. Students are known to adopt a wide variety of techniques, some more effective than others, when preparing for an exam [5, 8]. Identifying successful study strategies is therefore of great interest. In this work, we evaluate the effectiveness of having students generate their own practice questions as preparation for an exam in an introductory programming course.

SIGCSE'15, March 4–7, 2015, Kansas City, MO, USA.
Copyright © 2015 ACM 978-1-4503-2966-8/15/03 ...$15.00.
http://dx.doi.org/10.1145/2676723.2677253.

2. BACKGROUND

Paper-based, written exams are not the best way to assess many of the practical skills that students develop when learning to program [12, 17]. Writing code on paper, without the support of an editor or a compiler, is a difficult and unnatural task [2]. Nevertheless, high-stakes written exams are commonplace in programming courses and, for certain concepts, can be an effective way of assessing knowledge. For example, a student's ability to comprehend code can be demonstrated by answering written questions that present code fragments to be traced. Not only is code tracing an important debugging skill, but some minimal competence at code tracing must almost certainly be developed before code can be successfully written [20].

Multiple-choice questions are commonly used to examine code comprehension and numerous studies of novice programming exams involve this format [10]. An investigation by Shuhidan et al. into the use of multiple-choice questions in CS1 exams revealed that a majority of programming instructors believed such questions could adequately test understanding of the low level programming concepts required for successful code tracing [18].

The activity we describe in this paper, in which students author their own multiple-choice practice questions, leverages a highly robust effect from the cognitive psychology literature, the *generation effect.* This refers to the finding that individuals tend to remember information better when they take an active role in generating it, rather than being provided with information generated by others [19]. Consider the various ways that students engage with course concepts when authoring their own questions. They must reflect on the material they are learning to identify the topics that are most relevant. They may review related material from their textbook and execute example fragments of code while constructing answers to their questions. As the questions are to be reviewed by their peers, they must be clear and unambiguous, and possible misunderstandings should be considered to create good plausible alternative answers. In this study, we compare the exam performance of students who generate a small number of practice questions with students who simply use these generated questions to practice.

3. RELATED WORK

The impact on learning of having students author content-related questions has been studied in various settings. Early work in this area focused on text comprehension tasks. For example, Frase et al. conducted an experiment in which students were given a biographical passage and informed they would be examined on its content [7]. They found that students who were asked to generate potential test questions while they read performed significantly better when actually tested than students who simply read the text. This result was reinforced by similar experiments carried out independently by Denner et al. and Lehman et al. [3, 9].

However, these studies also revealed a limitation of the approach. The superior performance of students who had authored questions relating to the studied material was limited to certain post-test items. The question-generating students only performed better on post-test items that targeted the same content as the questions they had authored themselves. This suggests that the benefits observed from authoring questions are a direct result of active engagement with the related concepts.

The efficacy and limitations of student-generated questions were further explored in an experiment by Foos et al. where students were provided a 5-page scientific passage to study [6]. Half of the students authored questions and used them to prepare for a post-test, whereas the remaining students did not generate questions but were provided with the questions generated by the first group. There was no performance difference between the student groups on post-test questions that did not target material covered by the generated questions. However, students who generated study questions that were directly related to post-test items performed significantly better on those items than students who simply used the generated questions to study. As a result of this work, Foos et al. conclude that "generating potential test questions while preparing for an examination is a very effective technique".

In computer science, the relationship between exam performance and participation in a question authoring activity was previously explored by Luxton-Reilly et al. [11]. Although in their experiment student participation was self-selected, they reported a positive correlation between the number of practice questions students authored and their final exam scores. Of particular note, the authors concluded their work by encouraging other researchers to push beyond correlational studies when measuring the impact of interventions on student learning.

We present here an investigation of the causal relationship between question authoring and exam performance with a randomized controlled experiment in a large introductory programming course.

4. METHODOLOGY

In this section we provide background on the course in which our experiment was conducted and we outline details of the question authoring task and the exam that followed. We also describe how the student's questions were classified by topic and we list our two primary research questions.

At the University of Auckland, the Bachelor of Engineering degree is a four-year program. In the first year of the degree, all students take a set of compulsory courses before specializing in their second year. One of these courses is a programming course which introduces students to engineering computation in the MATLAB environment. We report here on data collected in 2012 when 729 students were enrolled in the course.

A total of three end-of-module exams were held during the semester at the conclusion of various modules, and a final exam was held at the end of the course. Our experiment concludes with the first end-of-module exam, held on the 9th of August, at the end of the fourth week of instruction. This exam consisted of 10 multiple-choice questions and contributed 5% towards each student's final grade. All students in the course sat the exam at the same time, and had 45 minutes to complete the 10 questions. The topics that had been covered in the course at the time of this exam included logical operators, conditional statements, loops, functions, matrices and matrix operations. We use the results of this exam to answer our first research question:

> **RQ1:** *Do students who generate questions as preparation for an exam perform better on individual questions, and overall, compared with students who simply use the generated questions to study?*

Students were allocated at random to one of two groups. To ensure balanced group sizes, this allocation was performed by generating a random sequence of integers between 1 and 729 inclusive, and using this sequence to partition the class list into two near-equal sized groups. One group, labeled "Authoring", contained 364 students and the other group, labeled "Non-Authoring", contained 365 students.

The task was introduced to students on the 30th of July, 11 days prior to the exam. Students in the "Authoring group" were asked to author *three* multiple-choice questions, along with an explanation of the correct answer, and submit them to an online repository prior to midnight on the 5th of August. This was an unsupervised activity to be completed outside of formal class time. Students in the "Non-Authoring" group were not able to submit questions to this repository, however all students could view and practice answering any of the submitted questions. Answering questions was voluntary, however a small amount of course credit (2%) was awarded to students in the "Authoring" group for completing the task by contributing a minimum of three questions to the repository. For fairness, students in the "Non-Authoring" group were given an equivalent opportunity later in the course, after the completion of our experiment, to earn the same amount of credit.

As a way of motivating students to practice answering the generated questions, the course instructors announced that questions appearing in the repository may "form a basis for questions in the exam". Indeed, once the question authoring deadline had passed, the course instructors reviewed all of the student-authored questions and chose a set of high-quality questions for inclusion on the exam. The researchers were not involved in the selection of these questions. Of the 10 multiple-choice questions that appeared on the exam, 9 were selected from the repository of student-authored questions and just 1 was authored by the course instructors.

Once the exam had been finalized by the course instructors, we examined the 10 questions and identified the main topic they each targeted. We then performed a similar classification of the student-authored questions using the topics identified from the exam questions. For each topic, we could

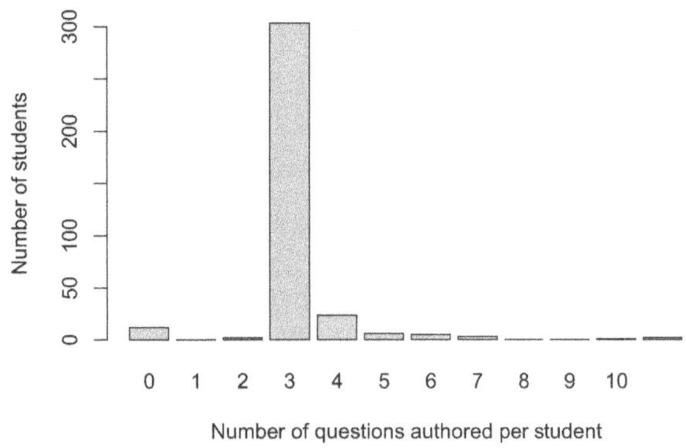

Figure 1: Histogram showing the number of questions authored by students in the "Authoring" group

therefore partition students into three groups — those in the "Authoring" group who had authored at least one question on the topic, those in the "Authoring" group who had not authored any questions on the topic, and the remaining students in the "Non-Authoring" group (who had not authored any questions). We use this partitioning to explore our second research question:

> **RQ2:** *Do students who author questions on particular topics perform better on exam questions that target those topics compared with students who author questions on different topics, and compared with students who do not author questions?*

To support the question authoring activity in our experiment we used a web-based tool called PeerWise, which enables students to enter and format their questions directly in a web browser [4]. PeerWise also allows students to practice answering questions created by their peers and generates feedback after each attempt which includes the answer and explanation as provided by the question author, along with a summary of all previous responses to the question.

5. RESULTS

We begin this section by presenting an overview of student participation with the question authoring task. We also illustrate when questions were authored and answered with respect to the authoring deadline and the day of the exam.

5.1 Summary of authoring activity

A total of 1,133 questions were published by students in the "Authoring" group prior to the exam (6:15pm on the 9th of August). Of the 364 students in the "Authoring" group, 348 (96%) created at least one question. The overwhelming majority of these students published exactly 3 questions which corresponds to the minimum requirements for earning course credit. Figure 1 illustrates just how infrequently this minimum contribution level was surpassed.

Figure 2A shows the number of questions authored per hour over the duration of our experiment. A large spike corresponds to the deadline for earning course credit (midnight, 5th August), and more than 40% of all questions were authored sometime on the 5th of August. Authoring activity drops sharply after the deadline, with only 50 new questions

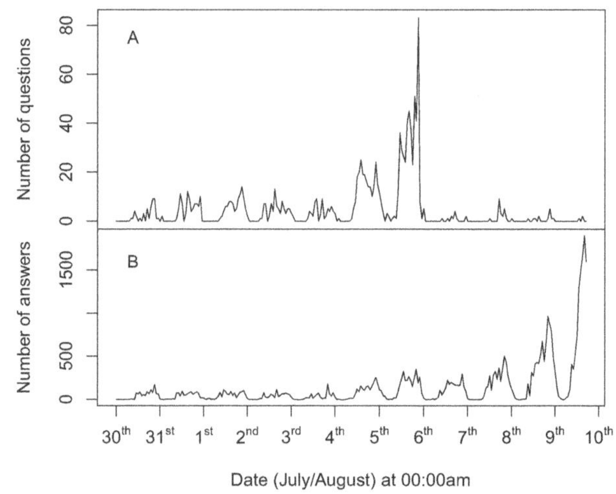

Figure 2: The number of questions authored per hour (A) and the number of answers submitted per hour (B) over the duration of the experiment

added to the repository prior to the exam. Figure 2B shows, over the same period, the number of answers submitted per hour to questions in the repository. Although answering questions was voluntary, this chart exhibits a rapid growth in activity as the exam approaches. A total of 34,602 answers were submitted to the student authored questions.

5.2 Effect of authoring on exam performance

Of the 729 students who were enrolled in the course, 712 sat the exam. Overall, these 712 students performed very well, achieving an average score of 7.65 out of 10 with a standard deviation of 1.63. Only 29 students answered fewer than 5 questions correctly. Assuming a minimum exam score of 50% corresponds to a "pass", the class-wide pass rate for students who sat the exam was extremely high at 95.9%. We note however that this pass rate is consistent with that of the corresponding exam both the year before (97.2%) and the year after (96.2%) our experiment, likely due to the highly competitive nature of the course and the inherent reliability of a 10 question, 5-option, multiple-choice exam.

5.2.1 Total exam score

Our hypothesis was that students in the "Authoring" group would perform better on the exam than students in the "Non-authoring" group, due to the potential learning benefits of the question authoring activity. The exam scores achieved by students in the "Authoring" and "Non-authoring" groups are shown on the histogram in Figure 3. Note that the 17 students who did not sit the exam are recorded with a score of 0. While the distribution of marks between these two groups is similar, there are notable differences when looking at scores greater than or less than the average exam mark. For example, students in the "Non-Authoring" group more frequently scored 5, 6 or 7 (below the average mark), whereas students in "Authoring" group more often scored 8, 9 or 10 (above the average mark) .

Our data exhibits a ceiling effect as a result of the high exam scores and so we compare the two groups with a non-parametric test, the Wilcoxon rank sum test, which con-

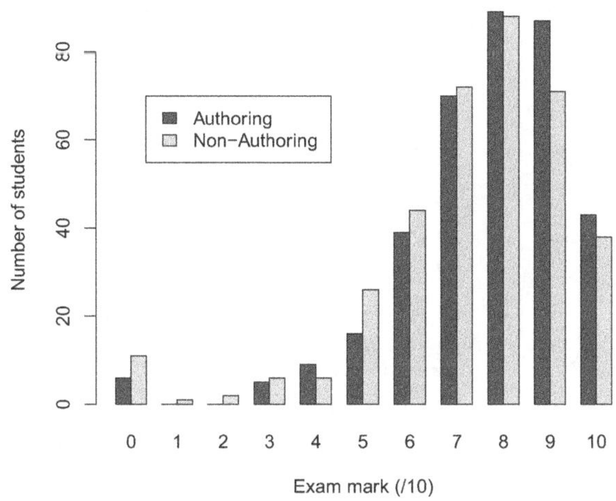

Figure 3: Histogram of exam scores by group ($n = 729$). Scores of 0 correspond to students who did not sit the exam (6 from the "Authoring" group and 11 from the "Non-Authoring" group)

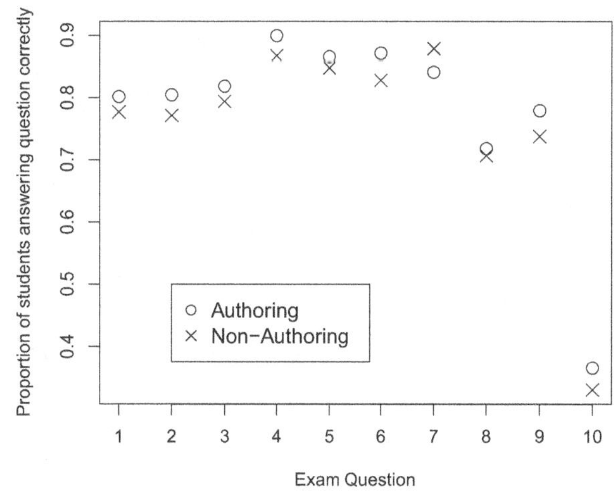

Figure 4: Proportion of students in each group answering each exam question correctly ($n = 712$)

siders only the order in which the observations from the two samples fall. In this case, our alternative hypothesis is that the exam scores achieved by the "Authoring" group are greater than those achieved by the "Non-Authoring" group. Table 1 presents the results of a formal comparison between exam scores of the two groups. Note that two tests have been conducted – one in which all students are included ($n = 729$), and another which excludes the 17 students who did not sit the exam ($n = 712$).

Although the effect sizes are small, for example the average score of students who sat the exam is just 3% higher for "Authoring" students, the distribution of scores differ significantly between the two groups. In other words, students in the "Authoring" group performed better overall than students in the "Non-Authoring" group and our experimental design implies that this difference is a result of the question authoring activity.

Table 1: Comparison of exam performance for students in the "Authoring" and "Non-Authoring" groups. Separate analyses consider all students ($n = 729$) and only those who sat the exam ($n = 712$)

n	Authoring		Non-Authoring		Wilcoxon test
	μ	σ	μ	σ	p-value
729	7.64	1.84	7.31	2.10	0.0197
712	7.77	1.57	7.54	1.68	0.0360

5.2.2 *Accuracy per question*

Analyzing student performance on each of the 10 exam questions individually provides further evidence that students in the "Authoring" group outperformed students in the "Non-Authoring" group. Figure 4 shows the proportion of students in each group that correctly answered each of the 10 exam questions. The "Authoring" group performed better on 9 of the 10 questions. The likelihood of this outcome can be tested formally with a binomial test in which the null hypothesis assumes that the probability of students in the "Authoring" group performing better on a given exam question is 0.5. The results of such a test are statistically significant ($p = 0.0107$), indicating that it is highly likely the question authoring activity had a positive impact on the exam performance of students in the "Authoring" group.

5.3 Exam performance by topic

Although question authoring has been shown to be a useful learning strategy in various disciplines, previous research has highlighted that the benefits are often limited to the specific topics targeted by the authored questions. This may help to explain the small effect sizes seen in our previous analysis. For example, some students in the "Authoring" group may have created perfectly valid questions, but none of those questions directly targeted concepts needed to answer the exam questions. Similarly, certain exam questions may have required the understanding of concepts that were targeted by only a small number of student authored questions. Either scenario may mask some of the benefits of the activity if we consider all "Authoring" students as a group.

In this section we examine groups of exam questions that target a specific topic. We investigate how well these groups of questions were answered by those students who authored questions on the same topic compared with other students who also authored questions, but on different topics.

We begin by presenting our topic-classification of the 10 exam questions. Two of the questions required students to trace through provided while loops, two of the questions involved evaluating boolean expressions consisting of both logical and relational operators, and two of the questions involved tracing through code that operated on matrices using built-in MATLAB operators such as element-wise multiplication and matrix composition. The remaining four exam questions were more complex, compound style questions that targeted multiple topics. For the purposes of this analysis we focus only on the exam questions that targeted a single topic. Table 2 shows the three primary topics we identified, lists the exam questions to which they relate, and gives a brief description of each question.

Table 2: Exam questions targeting a single topic

Topic	Q	Description of exam questions
While loops	2, 7	Tracing through while loops. In one case identifying the correct output; in the other identifying which one of the provided loops would not terminate
Boolean expressions	3, 4	Evaluating boolean expressions involving relational and logical operators. In one case tracing through provided code; in the other determining which of the provided input values would produce the given output
Matrix operations	8, 9	Tracing code that manipulates matrices. In one case transposition and element-wise multiplication of two matrices; in the other the composition of arrays through concatenation

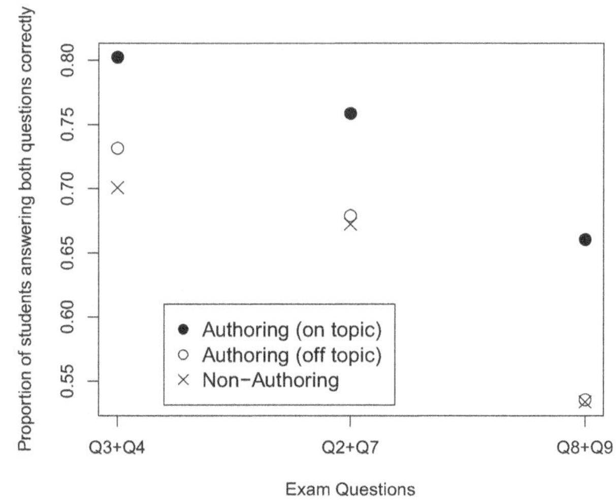

Figure 5: The proportion of students who correctly answered *both* questions on a related topic, based on whether or not they had authored a question on that topic

Students in the "Authoring" group could freely select the topics on which to base their three questions. Of the 1,133 questions generated in total, 99 targeted "While loops", 99 targeted "Boolean expressions" and 124 targeted "Matrix operations" and these were authored, respectively, by 86, 87 and 106 students. Figure 5 shows how well students answered each pair of questions on the exam, based on whether or not they authored questions on the corresponding topic. Students who did not author questions at all performed almost identically to students who authored questions that did not target the exam question topics. Consistent with previous research, it appears that the topic on which questions are authored plays an important role in the effectiveness of the question generation activity.

We use a two-sample test for equality of proportions to test our hypothesis that students in the "Authoring" group who authored at least one question on a related topic performed better on the corresponding pair of exam questions than students who authored questions on different topics. Although the differences are larger than those from our earlier analyses (effect sizes of between 10% and 20% across the question pairs), the differences are statistically significant only for the "Matrix operations" topic, shown as Q8+Q9 on Figure 5 ($p = 0.0197$).

6. DISCUSSION

In our experiment, asking students in an introductory programming course to author three practice questions was sufficient to cause a measurable, but small, improvement in scores on a subsequent exam. Students randomly allocated to the "Authoring" group performed significantly better overall, and on individual questions, than students in the "Non-authoring" group who were able to review the generated questions but did not author any of their own.

We also replicated results from other domains which show that the topics on which students author their questions are important. Students who generated questions on a particular topic were more successful answering related exam questions compared with students who authored questions on different topics. We note that in our experiment topics were self-selected, and so students may have tended to author questions on topics they already understood well. Nonetheless, the act of generating questions does appear to have had a positive effect as the "Authoring" students exhibited superior performance with respect to the control group.

Despite the apparent benefits of question generation, we must acknowledge a potential disparity in the time that students spent preparing for the exam in our experiment. It is difficult to measure this time accurately, as each student adopts their own strategies and these are conducted outside of the classroom. However, at least for activities directly related to our experiment, we can approximately measure the effort and time expended by students in each group.

First, we can examine differences between the two groups with respect to the number of *answers* submitted to questions in the repository. We find that students in the "Authoring" group were more likely to answer questions than students in the "Non-Authoring" group. Of the 664 students who answered at least one question prior to the test, 345 (52%) were from the "Authoring" group and 319 (48%) were from the "Non-Authoring" group. Moreover, the 345 active "Authoring" students submitted 58.2 answers on average compared with just 45.5 answers from the 319 active "Non-Authoring" students, and these answer distributions differ significantly ($p = 0.0023$). A likely explanation for this is that students in the "Authoring" group were essentially required to log in to PeerWise to receive course credit for authoring their questions. Even though they were not required to answer any questions, doing so is relatively simple once the barrier of logging in is overcome.

We can also estimate the actual time spent by each student in the "Authoring" group creating their questions by examining log files maintained by the PeerWise tool. The median time taken to author a single question was 12.8 minutes, indicating that the majority of students in this group would have spent approximately half an hour generating their three questions. Combined with the fact that these students also tended to answer more questions, it could be argued that even once all other study activities are taken into account, the "Authoring" students spent more time preparing for the exam thus explaining their superior performance. We cannot rule this out, and a more careful measure of the efficacy of question authoring would involve having the "Non-

Authoring" students participate with a competing activity for a similar period of time. However, students are known to adopt various strategies for exam preparation, and not all are effective [8]. Our data shows that question authoring can be an effective activity, even when just a few questions are generated taking most students little more than half an hour.

The main focus of this work was to investigate the benefits to students of authoring practice questions prior to an exam. An associated benefit was the rapid creation of a large repository of questions, without any instructor effort, which became a well utilized practice resource. Practice testing is known to be a useful learning strategy, particularly when immediate corrective feedback is produced [16], for which the multiple-choice format is well suited. Recent educational research in various disciplines has shown that student generated questions are of acceptably high quality for such purposes [1, 15]. Specifically in computer science education, various tools have been developed which provide students with banks of instructor-created exercises with which to practice [14, 13]. In light of the benefits associated with generating questions, we encourage designers of such tools to consider approaches that would allow students to develop their own exercises and contribute them to these platforms.

7. CONCLUSIONS

In this work, we investigated the impact of a student-generated question activity on subsequent exam performance in an introductory programming course. Previous work involving similar activities in computer science courses have reported positive correlations between question authoring and exam performance, suggesting a relationship exists, but these studies have not been controlled.

We conducted a large-scale ($n > 700$) randomized controlled experiment, where each student in the experimental group was asked to author three practice questions prior to a summative exam. Students in the control group used these questions to prepare for the exam but did not generate questions of their own. We found that students who authored questions performed better on the exam overall, and on individual questions, and these effects were most pronounced when students answered exam questions on topics that their own questions targeted.

While our work has been limited to multiple-choice questions, we note that numerous tools have been created by the computer science education community which may lend themselves well to similar activities. We encourage designers of such tools to consider approaches that would allow students to contribute their own exercises to these platforms.

8. REFERENCES

[1] S. P. Bates, R. K. Galloway, J. Riise, and D. Homer. Assessing the quality of a student-generated question repository. *Phys. Rev. ST Phys. Educ. Res*, Jul 2014.

[2] J. Bennedsen and M. E. Caspersen. Assessing process and product: a practical lab exam for an introductory programming course. In *Proc. of the 36th Annual ASEE/IEEE Frontiers in Education Conf.*, 2006.

[3] P. R. Denner and J. P. Rickards. A developmental comparison of the effects of provided and generated questions on text recall. *Contemporary Educational Psychology*, 12(2):135 – 146, 1987.

[4] P. Denny, A. Luxton-Reilly, and J. Hamer. The PeerWise system of student contributed assessment questions. In *Proc. 10th Australasian Comp Ed Conf (ACE 2008)*, pp 69–74, Wollongong, Australia, ACS.

[5] J. Dunlosky. Strengthening the student toolbox: Study strategies to boost learning. *American Educator*, 37(3):12–21, September 2013.

[6] P. W. Foos, J. J. Mora, and S. Tkacz. Student study techniques and the generation effect. *Journal of Educational Psychology*, 86(4):567–576, 1994.

[7] L. Frase and B. Schwartz. Effect of question production and answering on prose recall. *Journal of Educational Psychology*, 67(5):628–635, 1975.

[8] R. Gurung. How do students really study (and does it matter)? *Teaching of Psychology*, 32:238–240, 2005.

[9] J. R. Lehman and K. M. Lehman. The relative effects of experimenter and subject generated questions on learning from museum case exhibits. *Journal of Research in Science Teaching*, 21(9):931–935, 1984.

[10] R. Lister, E. S. Adams, S. Fitzgerald, W. Fone, J. Hamer, M. Lindholm, R. McCartney, J. E. Moström, K. Sanders, O. Seppälä, B. Simon, and L. Thomas. A multi-national study of reading and tracing skills in novice programmers. *SIGCSE Bull.*, 36(4):119–150, June 2004.

[11] A. Luxton-Reilly, D. Bertinshaw, P. Denny, B. Plimmer, and R. Sheehan. The impact of question generation activities on performance. In *Proceedings of SIGCSE '12*, pp 391–396, New York, USA, 2012. ACM.

[12] M. D. Medley. On-line Finals for CS1 and CS2. *SIGCSE Bull.*, 30(3):178–180, Aug. 1998.

[13] A. Papancea, J. Spacco, and D. Hovemeyer. An open platform for managing short programming exercises. In *Proceedings of ICER '13*, pp 47–52, New York, USA, 2013. ACM.

[14] N. Parlante. Nifty reflections. *SIGCSE Bull.*, 39(2):25–26, June 2007.

[15] H. Purchase, J. Hamer, P. Denny, and A. Luxton-Reilly. The quality of a PeerWise MCQ repository. In *Proc. 12th Australasian Comp Ed Conf (ACE 2010)*, pp 137–146, Brisbane, Australia, ACS.

[16] H. L. Roediger and A. C. Butler. Retrieval practice (testing) effect. *In H. L. Pashler (Ed.), Encyclopedia of the Mind, Sage Publishing Co.*, pages 660–661, 2013.

[17] J. Sheard, Simon, A. Carbone, D. D'Souza, and M. Hamilton. Assessment of programming: Pedagogical foundations of exams. In *Proceedings of ITiCSE '13*, pp 141–146, New York, USA, 2013. ACM.

[18] S. Shuhidan, M. Hamilton, and D. D'Souza. Instructor perspectives of multiple-choice questions in summative assessment for novice programmers. *Computer Science Education*, 20:229–259, 2010.

[19] N. Slamecka and P. Graf. The generation effect: Delineation of a phenomenon. *Journal of Experimental Psychology*, 4:592–604, 1978.

[20] A. Venables, G. Tan, and R. Lister. A closer look at tracing, explaining and code writing skills in the novice programmer. In *Proceedings of ICER '09*, pp 117–128, New York, USA, 2009. ACM.

Benefits of Self-explanation in Introductory Programming

Arto Vihavainen
University of Helsinki
P.O. Box 68 (Gustaf Hällströmin katu 2b)
Helsinki, Finland
avihavai@cs.helsinki.fi

Craig S. Miller
DePaul University
243 S. Wabash Avenue
Chicago, Illinois 60604
cmiller@cdm.depaul.edu

Amber Settle
DePaul University
243 S. Wabash Avenue
Chicago, Illinois 60604
asettle@cdm.depaul.edu

ABSTRACT

One approach for helping students learn to program is the use of self-explanation assignments. In these assignments, students explain instructional materials using domain knowledge covered in the course. In this work, we describe a randomized experiment where students in an introductory programming course were given two kinds of self-explanation assignments. One randomly selected group worked on self-explanation assignments with supporting questions while the alternate group had the same self-explanation questions but no additional supporting exercises. The combined groups performed better on comparable test questions than students from the previous year, who did not use self-explanation questions. The group with supporting questions performed better than the group with no additional support. Based on our results and previous research on self explanation, we argue that embedding self-explanation questions into programming material is beneficial for students. Moreover, further gains are achieved from supporting questions that help focus their explanations.

Categories and Subject Descriptors

K.3.1 [**Computers and Education**]: Computer Uses in Education—*Computer-assisted instruction (CAI), Distance learning*; K.3.2 [**Computers and Education**]: Computer and Information Science Education—*Computer science education*

Keywords

introductory programming; programming education; cs1; self-explanation; self-explanation questions; scaffolding

1. INTRODUCTION

The main focus of introductory programming courses is teaching students elementary programming skills, which is most commonly achieved by requiring them to write code. However, previous research shows that there is a relationship between the ability of novice programmers to read and explain code and their ability to write code. Research studies have shown strong correlations among the ability to trace programs, explain code in plain English, and write code in pencil-and-paper exams [25] as well as correlations between explanations of code and developing code on a computer in an exam situation [12]. A recent study confirmed the connection between plain English explanations of code and the ability to write code in courses beyond CS1 [8], suggesting that the importance of being able to explain code is relevant for more advanced programming students.

Taking a broader view of the computing curriculum, one of the skills that is often lacking is communication and explanation of relevant concepts. This is not for a lack of emphasis on communication skills in curricular models. In the Computer Science Curricula 2013 [16] written and verbal communications are part of the core in the Social Issues and Professional Practice (SP) Knowledge Area under Professional Communication. As suggested by the CS Curricula 2013 and by the computing education community, the best approach to improving students' communication skills is not necessarily the creation of a separate course on professional communication. Instead these practices should be embedded throughout the curriculum in a meaningful manner [4, 11].

The educational value of student explanations is a topic of great interest for academics outside of computer science. In self-explanation studies, learners are asked to spontaneously explain the meaning of content, typically passages of text or other written material, as they study a targeted domain. Resulting explanations are then coded for quality. The self explanations are finally compared with any learning gains demonstrated by the students. Multiple studies in a variety of fields, but particularly in science and math, have found high-quality self-explanations to be positively correlated with learning gains [21]. Surprisingly, self-explanations have received less attention in the computing education community.

Here, we describe an experiment in which we embedded two types of self-explanation questions into the material of an introductory programming course. In the first type of self-explanation question the students did not receive any guidelines beyond the question, while the second type provided help in the form of a relevant multiple-choice question upon which the student had to further elaborate. The experiment was designed to study whether self-explanation questions that are not assessed improve students' explanations in course exams, and whether the students' performance varies depending on the type of self-explanation question that they are given. In addition, we compare the performance of

SIGCSE'15 March 04 - 07 2015, Kansas City, MO, USA

http://dx.doi.org/10.1145/2676723.2677260.

students from Summer 2013, when no self-explanation questions were given, to students from Summer 2014, who had access to self-explanation questions. This year-to-year comparison provides some indication of how students benefit from answering self-explanation questions.

In the remainder of this paper we discuss related work, including self-explanation results from other disciplines and plain language explanation and multiple-choice question studies in computer science education. We then describe the experiment in which students were asked to complete self-explanation questions as a part of an introductory programming class and discuss the results from course exams. We conclude by connecting this work with the literature and discussing the next steps for the research.

2. RELATED WORK

The impact of self-explanation exercises on students has been widely studied in a variety of fields. Self-explanation is a constructive and active-learning activity intended to engage learners in material in a meaningful way while allowing for monitoring of their understanding [21]. In the research, distinctions are made between high-quality self-explanations and low-quality self-explanations. High-quality self-explanations demonstrate inferences about missing information found in material being explained, integrative statements about the material, and comments that reflect deeper analysis of the resources. Low-quality self-explanations are typically simple paraphrasing of statements found in the material [21]. A majority of the work in self explanations has been done in the areas of math and science, where numerous studies have found high-quality self-explanations to be positively correlated with learning gains [21]. The specific domains studied include physics [5, 7], biology [6], algebra word problems [14], geometry [1], and logic [13].

The purpose, design, and results of the studies vary somewhat. In one study in the domain of physics the subjects proceeded through two phases. A knowledge-acquisition phase involves students studying written material and examples and solving knowledge-based questions. The problem-solving phase involves students answering questions similar to the ones seen in the first phase. An analysis found that students who successful solved problems also produced higher-quality self-explanations [5]. Two other studies, one in the area of physics and the other in a geometry course, focused more heavily on using a tutoring system, requiring students to take a pencil-and-paper pre-test, then to study examples using the system, and finally to take a pencil-and-paper post-test with problems equivalent to those in the pre-test [1, 7]. The geometry study involved high-school students and had one group give explanations while solving problems. This study found that students who explained their steps learned with greater understanding than those who did not explain their steps [1]. The physics study involved university-level students, and had two main results. Rich scaffolding for self-explanation improved students' performance at an early learning stage, and more proficient students can produce better self-explanations with even minimal prompts to assist them [7]. A similar structure was used in the biology study, in which two groups of eighth-graders were asked to read a passage in a biology text. Before reading the text they took a pre-test and after reading they took a post-test. One group simply read the text twice, whereas the other group were prompted after each sentence to explain what the sentence meant. Both groups showed gains in learning from pre-test to post-test, but the prompted group showed larger gains [6]. The algebra study involved six female ninth-grade students and asked the students to solve three problems while thinking aloud. The experimenter probes were limited to short requests for clarification during the session at at the end. Whether the students solved the first two problems or not, they were provided with solutions and asked to study them. The researchers found that certain kinds of self-explanations helped with the transition from the problem representation stage to the equation extraction phase [14].

Several of the studies involved intelligent-tutoring systems [1, 7], including one in the field of history [18]. More recent work has extended research into the learning of second-language grammar [27] and examined elementary-school science texts [2]. Not all self-explanation activities are equally valuable, and some work has focused on conveying successful strategies for designing activities for students, including that the focus should be on self-explanation over instructional explanation and that feedback to provide comprehension monitoring is necessary [20]. It is hypothesized that instructional explanations should be provided on learner demand, kept minimal, designed in a progressive way, and focused on the underlying principles of the domain [20].

There are far fewer studies of self-explanation activities in the area of computing. One notable early study was of students learning Lisp programming [17]. In the study, students without any previous Lisp programming experience were randomly assigned to groups. All of the students worked through a series of lessons on Lisp programming that involved reading a booklet followed by solving exercises on recursion using a Lisp tutor. The experiment showed that subjects performed better overall when the example provided was of the same type as the problem solved. The results of the study suggested that the acquisition of cognitive skills associated with Lisp programming were facilitated by higher metacognition including more self-generated explanation goals and strategies. The researchers also found that explanations focusing on novel concepts and reflections on problem solutions focusing on the abstractions underlying the programs and how programs work were related to improved learning [17]. In a follow-up article, the researchers focused on learning and self-explanation strategies of subjects using a hypertext environment as compared with subjects learning via a more standard, linear instruction model [19].

A recent article considered the ways in which tutors should frame and phrase questions in order to help students in an introductory programming class better understand and learn information [3]. The questions asked by tutors were classified according to the instructional goals for the interaction with the student and the question types. Self-explanations were somewhat tangential to the study, with the authors noting that tutors' natural tendencies are to provide information for students rather than to elicit self-explanations from the students [3].

A pair of recent studies examined why students have difficulty producing good explanations. These studies compared performance on written explanations and multiple-choice questions in examinations [23, 24]. While the studies found that students appear to have difficulty reading and understanding the code, they did not examine the long-term learning benefits of writing explanations.

A significant contribution to the design and development

of multiple-choice questions in computer science is PeerWise. In this system novice programming students create multiple-choice questions and answer questions written by their peers [9]. Initial work suggested that writing and using the questions resulted in learning gains [9]. Follow-up studies were not uniformly able to replicate the work and led to the identification of factors that impact the effectiveness of the system, including instructor engagement and usage requirements [10]. Not all research on multiple-choice questions finds them of equal utility. One study of English classes found that students preparing for multiple-choice exams were more likely to use surface learning approaches [22]. A paper that finds a more balanced approach to multiple-choice questions examined their use in four distinct disciplines [15]. The author found that while multiple-choice questions require the recognition of the correct answer rather than the construction of the correct answer, the questions could be useful in supporting learners' self-regulation. The research suggests that not just the content and format of multiple-choice questions is relevant, but rather that the wider context in which they are used also should be considered [15].

3. RESEARCH QUESTIONS AND METHODOLOGY

In this study, we investigate how the inclusion of self-explanation questions in an introductory programming course material affects students course outcomes. Two types of self-explanation questions are investigated: one that provides students support questions that help students focus their explanation, and another that does not. Our research questions are as follows:

- Does the introduction of self-explanation questions into course material influence students' overall explanation skills, measured by success in course exam explanation questions?
- Do the different types of self-explanation questions influence students' success in the course and course outcomes? If so, how?

The first research question is addressed by comparing the performance of students from the Summer 2013, when the course material did not include self-explanation questions, to students from the Summer 2014, when the course material included self-explanation questions.

During the Summer 2014 all students had self-explanation questions, but the students were divided randomly into two groups. Group one was always shown the self-explanation questions with support, while group two was shown the self-explanation questions without support.

3.1 Participants and Course Content

The participants in the study are students who enrolled in introductory programming courses at the Open University during the Summers 2013 and 2014. The Open University is a branch of the University of Helsinki, where anyone can study university courses, regardless of age, gender, race, or educational background. Enrolling in a single course at the Open University costs a nominal fee (comparable to 50 US dollars) if the student is not enrolled at the University of Helsinki. The courses offered at the Open University are free for University of Helsinki students.

The introductory programming course is organized by instructors from the University of Helsinki. A single course lasts one and a half months and is taught in Java. It provides students basic skills, including knowledge of elementary procedural programming (input, output, conditional statements, loops, methods, and working with lists) and object-oriented programming (class design, object composition, working with objects). The course assessment is based on both course assignments and a final exam, each worth 50% of the course points. The final exam contains one question where the student has to explain various course concepts and program code, and two to three pen-and-paper programming questions, where the student has to create programs that solve specific problems. While the exam questions vary between courses, the exam structure and higher-level course requirements have remained the same for several years. Similarly, during each course, the students have received a note that outlines strategies for studying for the exam, which has also not changed over the years. Students need to receive half of the overall points and half of the exam points to pass the course. The total estimated workload of the course in total is 125 hours.

3.2 Material and Self-explanation Questions

The course material is provided as an online textbook with embedded programming and self-explanation assignments. The course had 20-30 weekly programming exercises and 3 weekly self-explanation exercises that were introduced to the material during the second week of the course. Students authenticate when opening the course material. The authentication is also used for tracking students' progress and their answers to self-explanation questions. The randomization was done based on enrollment order due to no additional student details being available. The programming assignments are completed using an off-the-shelf programming environment. Here students are instructed to write their self-explanations into text areas within the material.

The structure and learning objectives of the self-explanation questions was the same for both groups. They started with motivational text, typically containing a code snippet, and then were asked to explain the content such as to their friends. For the group with supporting questions, additional multiple-choice questions were provided. Students were required to do the self-explanations in addition to answering the multiple choice questions.

The following is an example of a self-explanation question, taken from the second week of the course. Students had previously learned about the use of loops and variables. While the self-explanation questions in the course are typically larger, this question was selected to provide a perspective on the questions while still fitting to the size constraints of the article. The question has been translated into English by the authors.

Self-explanation question: Gift Cards

Your friend was recruited by a hamburger chain to work on an application, which is used to determine whether a new visitor receives a gift card. The functionality of the application should be as follows: (1) after the first thousand visitors, every twenty-fifth visitor should receive a gift card, and in addition, (2) every two thousandth visitor should receive a larger gift card. Others do not get anything, except to buy burgers. The code of your friend's application is currently in the following state.

```
Scanner reader = new Scanner(System.in);

System.out.print("Visitor number: ");
int visitor = Integer.parseInt(reader.nextLine());

if (visitor >= 1000 && visitor % 25 == 0) {
    System.out.println("Receives a gift card!");
} else if (visitor % 2000 == 0) {
    System.out.println("Receives a large gift card!");
} else {
    System.out.println("Receives nothing.");
}
```

Your friend's program isn't working as he hopes. Explain to your friend the issues that are in his code and explain what causes them. Also, propose fixes for him.

[*Available only to the group with support questions*: In addition, what should the value of the variable *visitor* be for the current application to print "Receives a large gift card"? (a) 0, (b) 1000, (c) 1500, (d) 2000, (e) none of the given options.]

[text area for providing the explanation]

The explanations were not limited in length, and the students themselves determined what consisted a good self-explanation answer. It was announced at the start of the course that the self-explanation answers are not explicitly assessed, but students get exercise points for doing their best in answering the questions.

3.3 Analysis Methods

The study is conducted as a between subjects design, where a student in one group never enters the other group. This means that the students are affected only by one question type, and thus, the overall results are comparable. The same instructor was responsible for grading the exam and the grading rubric has remained the same over the courses. Furthermore, the provided exam guidelines have remained the same over the course instances.

The first research question, "*Does the introduction of self-explanation questions into course material influence students' overall explanation skills, measured by success in course exam explanation questions?*", is answered by comparing the students' success in the explanation questions in the Summer 2014 exam to the students' success in explanation questions in the Summer 2013 course exam. The second research question, "*Do the different types of self-explanation questions influence students' success in the course and course outcomes? If so, how?*", is answered by comparing the exam success between the student groups.

The exam questions are selected from a large pool of questions, and have been similar in content and difficulty over years. The explanation questions have e.g. asked students to provide answers to the following questions; "(1) *What is a variable? What is meant by the type of a variable? How do primitive and reference types differ from each others? [Explain and] Provide a few examples of variables that have primitive- and reference types.*", "(2) *What is a method? How and for what are methods used?*", and "(3) *What is an object and what is a class? What is the relationship between an object and a class?*".

4. RESULTS

We present the results organized by the two research questions. As we analyze the results in the light of exam questions, we only investigate students who participated in the course exam (N=51)[1]

4.1 Comparison to Past Results

Each of the three explanation questions was graded from 0 to 2 points, with resulting scores in the overall exam explanation question ranging from 0 to 6. The mean score for the year without self-explanation was 3.7 (SD=1.9, N=67) and the mean score for the year with self-explanation was 4.6 (SD=1.3, N=51). A test on the equality of variances revealed a significant difference between the variances of the two samples, $F' = 2.21$, $p = 0.004$. A two-sample t-test adjusted for unequal variances revealed a significant difference for the means, $t(114.4) = -3.2$, $p = 0.002$.

4.2 Comparison of Self-explanation Groups

Comparing student performance between the two randomly-assigned self-explanation conditions, two of the three problem-oriented questions were selected and scored from the final exam (the last question was not uniformly completed and consequently dropped from the analysis). The sum of these two questions produced scores ranging from 0 to 11. The mean score for the group with supporting multiple choice questions was 8.4 (SD=1.8, N=29) and the mean score for the group without multiple choice questions was 6.7 (SD=3.6, N=22). A test on the equality of variances revealed a significant difference between the variances of the two samples, $F' = 3.27$, $p = 0.004$. A two-sample t-test adjusted for unequal variances revealed a marginally significant difference for the means, $t(30.6) = -2.0$, $p = 0.054$.

Additional analysis considered the inclusion of the first exam question and the last exam question. While these scores produced differences consistent with the second and third questions, their differences were not statistically significant.

5. DISCUSSION

Our results suggest that the addition of self-explanation exercises to the introductory course improved student learning. The results also provide some evidence that incorporating multiple choice questions in support of self-explanation further benefits learning. In this section, we discuss these interpretations and the limitations of the findings.

5.1 Benefit of Self-Explanation

Given previous empirical results and theoretical work showing the benefit of self-explanation in learning, the higher student scores in the year-over-year comparison are arguably due to the addition of self-explanation exercises. Our study replicates the findings of past studies where the inclusion of self-explanation assignments have improved students' explanation skills. However, in many of the previous self-explanation studies, the effect of self-explanation exercises has been studied within a single session [2, 6, 7, 14, 18, 19, 27], or during a short time span [1, 17]. Our results add to the smaller body of knowledge suggesting that learners may benefit from dispersing the practice over a longer period of time [5].

Naturally, this study has limitations and factors that may have contributed to the improved performance. For example,

[1]Initially, some 110 participants enrolled to the course. While this drop-out rate is high, it is typical for the Open University summer courses, where only some 30-50% of participants attend the exam.

the student population and course results across years may not be comparable, and the course instruction and instructors may have improved over the year. However, the first concern is mitigated when we compare the exam results for explanation questions organized at the University of Helsinki by the same instructors, as well as the results of the exams at Open University over the previous years. The past exam results at both institutions are similar to the results from Open University during the previous year with no self-explanation questions; however, we included only one course instance to the comparison due to the instructor responsible for grading the examinations being the same. In the other instances, the instructor who was responsible for grading the examinations varied over time.

The second issue, that course instruction and instructors may have improved over the years, is mitigated by the way the programming courses at the University of Helsinki (and consequently Open University) are organized. The material and exercises as well as the instruction have remained very much the same at the Open University over the last few years. The summer course has a single lecture (of 2 hours), and most of the work is done in guided labs where the students are helped by teaching assistants. The teaching assistants who help with the course are new each year as we seek to provide a teaching experience for all of our students who wants to participate in teaching; see [26] for details.

5.2 Benefit of Supporting Questions

While self-explanations arguably supports learning, effective approaches for introducing self-explanations into computing courses are less clear. Our study compared two approaches for providing students' with self-explanation opportunities, one with additional support in form of multiple-choice questions, and another without the additional support. The addition of multiple choice questions to support self-explanation promotes learning in at least one of the following ways: (1) The questions provide a clear, concrete activity for reflecting on the sample of code, (2) The questions ask the student to focus on the relevant parts of the example, (3) The questions ask the student to compare the different answers and assess each one of them. There is precedent in the literature for including prompting questions in conjunction with self-explanation exercises[18].

Our results indicate a clear difference in student outcomes due to the supporting questions. The difference is most notable with the smaller variance in student scores for the supporting-question condition. This condition also yielded a higher mean score, albeit with a less statistically reliable difference. The difference in variance between the two conditions has possible implications for for how supporting questions affect learning. Without the supporting multiple choice questions, the student performance varied considerably, which suggests that, for the supporting-question condition, the otherwise lower-scoring students mostly benefited from the supporting questions. Of course, it is also possible that all students benefit from the questions, but the perceived benefit was limited by a ceiling effect. That is, the benefit is masked by students who are already capable of obtaining the maximum score. To further explore both possibilities, additional studies should use exam questions that measure a greater range of student learning.

We hypothesize that the multiple choice questions are not adequate by themselves, and argue that self-explanations are critical for connecting the relevant elements in a cohesive narrative, an essential component for deep processing and substantive learning. Our hypothesis is supported, albeit in a different setting, by studies that indicate that the use of multiple choice questions in exam contexts may lead to students' studying with surface learning approaches (see e.g. [22]). This hypothesis could be further tested with an additional study with three conditions: multiple choice only, self-explanation only, and multiple-choice supporting self-explanation.

The random assignment provides a strong guard against any selection bias. One potential concern is that the different dropout rates for the two conditions could skew the results. However, given the reasonable assumption that students having the most difficulty are most likely to drop out of the study, their inclusion in the study would only increase the difference between the two conditions.

6. CONCLUSIONS

In this work, we reported on a study where students in an introductory programming course were assigned into two groups. One group had material with self-explanation questions, while another group had supporting multiple choice questions that were embedded to the self-explanation exercises.

There are several practical contributions of this work. This study brings approaches used by researchers studying self-explanations into the CS1 classroom and contributes to the existing body of research measuring the impact that the process of explaining code has on students' ability to program.

As expected, our results showed that the inclusion of self-explanation questions on course assignments results in better student explanations on exams. In a year-to-year comparison, the students that had used the material with self-explanation questions performed significantly better in explanation-related exam questions than students that had used the material without self-explanation questions.

Furthermore, our work draws connections between the types of self-explanation questions used and the students' learning outcomes. In our study, the students with the supporting multiple choice questions performed better in the studied programming-related exam questions as well. This provides support for the hypothesis that multiple-choice questions aid students in producing more effective self-explanations. More broadly, the work gives additional ways that communication skills can be emphasized in the computing curriculum.

As a part of our future work, we are conducting this experiment in a larger course, in which we are gathering data on the students' backgrounds as well as reasons for dropping from the course. We are also interested in replicating the study at other institutions, to determine if the results can be replicated in a different context.

7. REFERENCES

[1] V. A. Aleven and K. R. Koedinger. An effective metacognitive strategy: learning by doing and explaining with a computer-based cognitive tutor. *Cognitive Science*, 26(2):147 – 179, 2002.

[2] R. Best, Y. Ozuru, and D. S. McNamara. Self-explaining science texts: Strategies, knowledge, and reading skill. In *Proceedings of the 6th International*

Conference on Learning Sciences, ICLS '04, pages 89–96. International Society of the Learning Sciences, 2004.

[3] K. E. Boyer, W. Lahti, R. Phillips, M. D. Wallis, M. A. Vouk, and J. C. Lester. Principles of asking effective questions during student problem solving. In *Proceedings of the 41st ACM Technical Symposium on Computer Science Education*, SIGCSE '10, pages 460–464, New York, NY, USA, 2010. ACM.

[4] J. E. Burge, G. Gannod, M. Carter, A. Howard, B. Schultz, M. Vouk, D. Wright, and P. Anderson. Developing cs/se students' communication abilities through a program-wide framework. In *Proceedings of the 45th ACM Technical Symposium on Computer Science Education*, SIGCSE '14, pages 579–584, New York, NY, USA, 2014. ACM.

[5] M. T. Chi, M. Bassok, M. W. Lewis, P. Reimann, and R. Glaser. Self-explanations: How students study and use examples in learning to solve problems. *Cognitive Science*, 13(2):145–182, 1989.

[6] M. T. Chi, N. De Leeuw, M.-H. Chiu, and C. Lavancher. Eliciting self-explanations improves understanding. *Cognitive Science*, 18(3):439–477, 1994.

[7] C. Conati, K. Vanlehn, et al. Toward computer-based support of meta-cognitive skills: A computational framework to coach self-explanation. *International Journal of Artificial Intelligence in Education (IJAIED)*, 11:389–415, 2000.

[8] M. Corney, S. Fitzgerald, B. Hanks, R. Lister, R. McCauley, and L. Murphy. 'explain in plain english' questions revisited: Data structures problems. In *Proceedings of the 45th ACM Technical Symposium on Computer Science Education*, SIGCSE '14, pages 591–596, New York, NY, USA, 2014. ACM.

[9] P. Denny, J. Hamer, A. Luxton-Reilly, and H. Purchase. Peerwise: Students sharing their multiple choice questions. In *Proceedings of the Fourth International Workshop on Computing Education Research*, ICER '08, pages 51–58, New York, NY, USA, 2008. ACM.

[10] P. Denny, B. Hanks, B. Simon, and S. Bagley. Peerwise: Exploring conflicting efficacy studies. In *Proceedings of the Seventh International Workshop on Computing Education Research*, ICER '11, pages 53–60, New York, NY, USA, 2011. ACM.

[11] P. Gruba and R. Al-Mahmood. Strategies for communication skills development. In *Proceedings of the Sixth Australasian Conference on Computing Education - Volume 30*, ACE '04, pages 101–107, Darlinghurst, Australia, Australia, 2004. Australian Computer Society, Inc.

[12] L. Murphy, S. Fitzgerald, R. Lister, and R. McCauley. Ability to 'explain in plain english' linked to proficiency in computer-based programming. In *Proceedings of the Ninth Annual International Conference on International Computing Education Research*, ICER '12, pages 111–118, New York, NY, USA, 2012. ACM.

[13] Y. Neuman, L. Leibowitz, and B. Schwarz. Patterns of verbal mediation during problem solving: A sequential analysis of self-explanation. *The Journal of Experimental Education*, 68(3):197–213, 2000.

[14] Y. Neuman and B. Schwarz. Substituting one mystery for another: the role of self-explanations in solving algebra word-problems. *Learning and Instruction*, 10(3):203 – 220, 2000.

[15] D. Nicol. E-assessment by design: using multiple-choice tests to good effect. *Journal of Further and Higher Education*, 31(1):53–64, 2007.

[16] A.-C. J. T. F. on Computing Curricula. Computer science curricula 2013. Technical report, ACM Press and IEEE Computer Society Press, December 2013.

[17] P. Pirolli and M. Recker. Learning strategies and transfer in the domain of programming. *Cognition and Instruction*, 12(3):235–275, 1994.

[18] E. Poitras, S. Lajoie, and Y.-J. Hong. Using the metahistoreasoning tool training module to facilitate the acquisition of domain-specific metacognitive strategies. In *Proceedings of the 11th International Conference on Intelligent Tutoring Systems*, ITS'12, pages 511–516, Berlin, Heidelberg, 2012. Springer-Verlag.

[19] M. M. Recker and P. Pirolli. Modeling individual differences in students' learning strategies. *Journal of the Learning Sciences*, 4(1):1–38, 1995.

[20] A. Renkl. Worked-out examples: instructional explanations support learning by self-explanations. *Learning and Instruction*, 12(5):529 – 556, 2002.

[21] M. Roy and M. T. Chi. The self-explanation principle in multimedia learning. *The Cambridge handbook of multimedia learning*, pages 271–286, 2005.

[22] K. Scouller. The influence of assessment method on students' learning approaches: Multiple choice question examination versus assignment essay. *Higher Education*, 35(4):453–472, 1998.

[23] Simon and S. Snowdon. Explaining program code: Giving students the answer helps - but only just. In *Proceedings of the Seventh International Workshop on Computing Education Research*, ICER '11, pages 93–100, New York, NY, USA, 2011. ACM.

[24] Simon and S. Snowdon. Multiple-choice vs free-text code-explaining examination questions. In *Proceedings of the 14th Koli Calling International Conference on Computing Education Research*, Koli Calling '14, pages 91–97, New York, NY, USA, 2014. ACM.

[25] A. Venables, G. Tan, and R. Lister. A closer look at tracing, explaining and code writing skills in the novice programmer. In *Proceedings of the Fifth International Workshop on Computing Education Research Workshop*, ICER '09, pages 117–128, New York, NY, USA, 2009. ACM.

[26] A. Vihavainen, T. Vikberg, M. Luukkainen, and J. Kurhila. Massive increase in eager TAs: Experiences from extreme apprenticeship-based CS1. In *Proceedings of the 18th ACM Conference on Innovation and Technology in Computer Science Education*, ITiCSE '13, pages 123–128, New York, NY, USA, 2013. ACM.

[27] R. Wylie, K. Koedinger, and T. Mitamura. Extending the self-explanation effect to second language grammar learning. In *Proceedings of the 9th International Conference of the Learning Sciences - Volume 1*, ICLS '10, pages 57–64. International Society of the Learning Sciences, 2010.

Growing a K-12 Community of Practice *

Stephen Cooper
Stanford University
Stanford, CA
coopers@cs.stanford.edu

Susan H. Rodger
Duke University
Durham, NC
rodger@cs.duke.edu

Madeleine Schep
Columbia College
Columbia, SC
mschep@columbiasc.edu

RoxAnn H. Stalvey
College of Charleston
Charleston, SC
stalveyr@cofc.edu

Wanda Dann
Carnegie Mellon University
Pittsburgh, PA
wpdann@andrew.cmu.edu

ABSTRACT

In this experience report, we share our experiences in growing a community of practice for middle and high school teachers focused on teaching introductory computing with Alice. We have offered professional development for over four hundred teachers, teachers who each year provide nearly 2,000 students with an introductory computing experience in courses during the school day. We report on several lessons learned in creating, growing, and supporting a community of practice.

Categories and Subject Descriptors

K.3.2 [**Computing Milieux**]: Computers and Education-Computer and Information Science Education

General Terms

Human Factors

Keywords

Alice; K-12 education; middle school; high school; introductory computer science

1. INTRODUCTION

In 2006 we were awarded the first of our two National Science Foundation (NSF) Innovative Technology Experiences for Students and Teachers (ITEST) grants. The track under which we were awarded the grant, teacher professional development, was intended to be used to provide K-12 teachers with exposure to technology-related tools that they could incorporate into their STEM classrooms. In conversations with other ITEST awardees at the annual NSF ITEST principal investigator (PI) meeting, it was clear that the other PIs, most of whom were in the sciences (and a few who were in mathematics), faced a very different task than we faced. For the other PIs, there were already in place existing science departments and established curricula. Their challenge was in helping the teachers to whom they would be offering professional development, strategies to get the teachers' existing science departments to adapt the new technologies being presented.

But for us, the teachers to whom we would be providing professional development had generally no existing computer science department. Our teachers were typically a math or science teacher, though a sizeable number were from other disciplines such as language arts, history, or foreign language. These teachers were tasked with offering CS in addition to their regular teaching load. We also had a sizable number of teachers in business or in a career and technical education (CTE) group, where many of their fellow CTE teachers taught such classes as automotive repair and home economics. On the one hand this was good – they would not need to persuade the rest of their department to adopt the technology they had learned. But on the other hand, the absence of being in a computer science department meant that they faced enormous other challenges. There often were no standards for computer science in their home states or localities. There were no certifications for becoming a CS teacher. (This meant that any other teachers with whom they would be working would likely not have technical content knowledge in computing. Thus trying to persuade fellow teachers to adopt the technology they had learned would be much harder.) There often was no other advocate on behalf of teaching computing in their entire school. And frequently they were the only computing teacher at their school, meaning there was no one else to help them work through the difficulties/challenges they would be facing.

In 2005, the CSTA (which would become a huge advocate on behalf of K-12 computing teachers) was just getting started. We were nearly a decade before code.org, which has helped encourage students, parents, and teachers to push for widespread inclusion of computing within schools. We were nearly a half decade before the creation of the CS 10K community, an NSF-supported US effort to prepare 10,000 highly qualified K-12 CS teachers[10]. And we were nearly a half-decade before the Computer Science Principles project started, revitalizing the teaching of computer science as part of an exciting new AP course. It was clear to us that we

*The work of these authors are supported by the National Science Foundation grant DRL-1031351, DRL-1031029, DRL-1031356 and IBM Faculty Awards

SIGCSE'15, March 4–7, 2015, Kansas City, MO, USA.

http://dx.doi.org/10.1145/2676723.2677255.

would need to do more than simply showing teachers who would be attending our workshops a cool new technology. It would be necessary to build a community of practice with and for our K-12 teachers.

2. RELATED RESEARCH

2.1 CSTA

The Computer Science Teachers Association (CSTA), has produced numerous documents informing the community about the status of CS education, and the needs of K-12 CS teachers. Their documents form a great basis off of which to plan to build a community of practice. In The New Educational Imperative[20], the CSTA covered the needs of high school teachers regarding content knowledge, as well as pedagogic knowledge. That report advocated for the need to provide high-quality in-service (as well as pre-service) teacher professional development to teachers who would be teaching CS in high schools. While the focus of that report is on high school, many of the report's observations are just as applicable to CS teachers of younger students. Another important contribution of that report was in exploring the means to effect change, and that any such process needed to be holistic.

The CSTA K-12 Computer Science Standards[18] identify a set of national standards. This is particularly important as many states do not have standards for computing education in K-12. And, having a set of national standards against which to align a course or curriculum is very important.

CSTA's Core Equity report[19] is an important document addressing the equity issue of under-representation in CS. As this is such a pressing issue, any attempt at building a community of practice needs to address broadening participation, and this document is a key place to start.

2.2 Communities of Practice

The idea of establishing communities of practice dates back a couple of decades to work done by Wenger[22, 23]. He explored organizations as "social learning systems." Lave and Wenger's seminal work on Legitimate Peripheral Participation[12] explored how newcomers join, belong and learn in such communities. This work and related work on the organization of communities, especially knowledge building within communities by Brown and Duguid[5], have lessons and ideas for successfully creating, organizing and growing communities and the shared social knowledge among them.

Within computer science, Fincher and Tenenberg[11, 21] studied how communities of practice could be created and nurtured within higher education. They focus on how best to document and share knowledge within computing classrooms. Ni's doctoral dissertation[15, 16, 13] focused on creating successful communities of practice for high school computing teachers. She has focused on many of the needs of high school computing teachers (many of the needs are similar to what has been reported by the CSTA), and how best to help them. There is a wide collection of good materials available at http://www.disciplinarycommons.org/ . Cooper and Grover[9, 8] describe the history of communities of practice and their connections with growing communities of practice within computer science in greater detail.

Expanding beyond the traditional communities of practice, the American Institutes for Research[3] and the Computing at School working group[2] have been designing web portals to serve as virtual communities of practice. While these virtual communities have much greater promise towards scaling communities of practice, we believe that they have yet to realize their potentials.

3. AN ALICE COMMUNITY OF PRACTICE

The remainder of this paper describes the Alice community of practice we have built with middle and high school teachers. Our project is integrating computing into middle and high schools by initially providing extensive professional development for teachers to teach them programming with the Alice programming environment and working with them to develop discipline specific lesson plans. The teachers then create/modify courses, and deliver their lesson plans during the academic year with their students. We follow up with the teachers and provide them with support during the academic year, and the teachers return the following summer for additional curricular development, to provide us with feedback, and to share their experiences using Alice with their students.

Our current community involves four universities who run professional development, Duke University, Columbia College, the College of Charleston and Stanford University in three states: North Carolina, South Carolina and California. While the original ITEST grant had us creating small regional communities of practice in six states (CA, CO, MS, NC, SC, and VA), our scale-up ITEST grant has focused on growing communities throughout the state in the three states. Our project team includes the PI's from the four Universities and a project manager. We have also worked closely with the Alice team at Carnegie Mellon University, giving them feedback on our teachers' needs and issues. We work with many teachers who have never been exposed to computer programming before, so we want to introduce them in a comfortable environment and provide a lot of practice.

We run approximately three to five professional development workshops each summer mostly for public middle and high school teachers, as well as a few private school teachers. Since fall 2011, our Alice teachers have taught more than 5000 students how to program in Alice. Our Adventures in Alice Programming website[17] contains mostly curriculum materials for integrating computing into a wide range of disciplines for middle and high school teachers and has been visited more than 45,000 times since we started tracking it in September 2012. Our Alice programming curricular materials website[4] with full curriculums for computing courses has been visited more than 50,000 times during that time period.

3.1 Professional Development Workshops

Details of our professional development plans from our first three years have been described elsewhere[7], so we only provide a brief overview here. Our professional development runs two weeks in the summer. Teachers typically live at the corresponding university and immerse themselves in programming for those two weeks. We use Alice as it has been designed for novices, and also its storytelling nature is attractive to students. Teachers return the following summer for another week of practice, to provide feedback and to share with other teachers what they have done with Alice.

The Duke University workshop is organized in the following way. Teachers come to Duke University from all over the state of NC plus a few from out of state, and stay in a nearby hotel. We have had teachers attend our workshops from more than half of the NC counties since 2008. We get about half middle school and half high school teachers. Several are CTE teachers and come from a wide variety of disciplines. Most of our teachers are integrating computing into their specific discipline, by teaching enough computing so students will be able to create projects for their discipline. We have a few teachers who are interested in teaching a full programming course. The first week we focus on walking the teachers through our tutorials, and giving them practice problems to solve. We have several question and answer sessions, we show many sample Alice projects from many disciplines. We get a lot of feedback from teachers on their understanding and get ideas every summer on how to improve the workshop. In the second week we continue with some new instruction, but the focus shifts to working with the teachers to help them develop lesson plans in their discipline. Near the end of the week, the teachers present their lesson plans and receive anonymous feedback from the other teachers. They revise and submit their lesson plans and we place them on our website. Also that week we take the teachers on a tour of a virtual reality cave at Duke University. This gives the teachers a chance to step into a 3-D world so they can take that perspective back to their students who will be creating 3-D worlds.

The SC workshops offer one week of Alice instruction followed by a second three-day period that combines Alice instruction with curricular development. While the workshop offered at Duke University is attended by many middle school teachers from varying disciplines, the SC workshops target high school teachers. Most are business teachers. The South Carolina State Department of Education places computer science under the umbrella of high school business departments. Most teachers attending the South Carolina workshops have little or no formal Computer Science education. This realization has led to a slight change in the way information is presented in the workshops. In earlier offerings of the workshop, teachers were given a more fast paced introduction to Alice with more days devoted to course material development. Now the workshop offers more Alice instruction at a slower pace to ensure teachers are given adequate time to comprehend the programming concepts. Also the SC workshops are offered at two universities. Columbia College is located in the central part of the state and the College of Charleston is located in the lowcountry. This has allowed us to accommodate teachers from throughout the state. To date, we have had teachers attend our workshops from over 65% of South Carolina counties.

The Stanford University workshop is our newest site with its first workshop run in 2014 for teachers from Oakland public schools. The overall process of the workshops was quite similar to the process followed in NC and SC. Differences included the use of presentations rather than teachers working through tutorials. Additionally, rather than bringing the teachers, to Stanford University, we travelled to Oakland to run the workshop at a lab in a school provided by the school district.

3.1.1 Cross-site coordination

A real advantage of running similar professional development at multiple sites is that we can take advantage of each others' experiences. The team has been meeting regularly, with additional meetings prior to professional development workshops at the various sites. Additionally, when unexpected events arise at a given site, we discuss these events. This enables us to more promptly respond to issues, and for the other sites to be made aware of possible situations ahead of time. Thus, a given site has been able to take advantage of issues and solutions to those issues by other sites.

3.2 Curricular Materials

Our project has a main site at[17] which links to our other sites. At this main site we have provided many resources all available for free. Our curriculum materials include over 100 tutorials on Alice and over 200 teacher lesson plans for a variety of disciplines. Our website is tracked by Google Analytics since September 2012 and has over 25,000 users and over 45,000 visits. Our tutorials include getting started tutorials, computer science topic tutorials, animation topic tutorials, project tutorials, and challenges (Alice programs that are mostly built with pieces missing). We also provide helper objects that include code that can be imported into a program and used to get started faster.

We provide many types of resources on our website. Tutorials are provided in pdf and PowerPoint so teachers can modify for their needs. Tutorials provide a finished world and a video of the finished world. Some come with a starter world if there is a lot of setup. Some tutorials are available in video format. Teachers requested video tutorials divided into small 5 minute pieces. We also have many Alice sample worlds, organized by discipline.

3.3 Teacher Developed Materials

The teacher lesson plans are the lesson plans the teachers developed while attending our workshop. Each lesson plan includes an Alice world and a description of how the teacher plans to use the Alice world and the curriculum standards the plan maps to. Our lesson plans are organized by discipline and by age level. We have lesson plans on math, science, foreign language, language arts, ESL, history, art, music, theater, business technology, and computer applications.

3.4 School-year support

We provide support to the teachers during the academic year. Our project manager calls the teachers to see how they are using Alice, and any issues they are having that we can help them with. The Alice team at CMU provides an email listserv that our teachers all sign up for and for which they can get their questions answered. We have found this listserv to be very helpful to the teachers as they can also learn from others asking questions and receiving answers. If the teachers are having a problem with an Alice world, they first try to describe the problem to the listserv and it gets answered that day. Sometimes the answer comes back with an example Alice world to illustrate a better way to solve the problem. If the teacher is still having problems, they can email the Alice world to the listserv manager who then finds the problem, resolves it and sends the world back to the teacher with comments on how it was resolved.

We run outreach events with our community of teachers and their students. We attend teacher conferences and give presentations at conferences such as the NC Career and Technical Education Conference, North Carolina Catholic Schools Education Conference, and the Bridging the Gap Conference: Uniting North Carolina K-16 STEM Education.

Examples of other types of events we have presented at include the Technology Showcase for Durham Public Schools, and the Region 5 School Library Media and Technology Directors/Supervisors for Orange County. We have given presentations at our teachers' schools and have run outreach events at Duke University and recruited students from the teachers close to Duke University.

3.5 Alice Community Communication

Our most successful means of communicating with our community has been through listservs and e-mail lists. Our teachers use the Alice educators listserv when they have a simple content or pedagogic question for which they need a quick response. The leaders check our e-mail on a regular basis, and can generally get responses back to the community in a timely fashion. We have e-mail lists for each local community (loosely organized into groups corresponding to the three states). These e-mail lists provide for discussion for local issues, as well as providing us a means to get evaluation data and reports back from the teachers.

The Alice web site maintains a community forum. However, our teachers have typically not been active participants on this forum. We guess that it is not as easy to search through from an educator's perspective. The teachers typically go to our Alice Adventures in Programming and Alice Programming sites[4, 17] when searching for curricular materials and/or suggestions.

3.6 Alice Symposium

In 2013 we organized a one-day symposium on Alice that was attended by 120 participants, and brought together many of our NC and SC teachers from the past in addition to other teachers, university faculty and community college faculty interested in Alice. The Symposium program included a keynote, paper sessions, a poster session, a panel and an invited talk from an Alice team artist who designs the 3-D models. With the Alice team, we provided six workshops before and after the symposium ranging from two to four days. Two of the workshops were the NC and SC followup workshops, and one was the second week of the SC two-week workshop. The other workshops were beginner workshops on Alice version 2, Alice version 3, and Alice with Media Computation. In particular, for the Alice 2 workshop, the presentations and example materials were focused on developing an understanding of Alice 2 and teaching methods suitable for introducing fundamental programming concepts in middle school modules and early high school introductory courses. The Alice 3 workshop (4 days) targeted high school and college instructors interested in Alice 3 as a tool for teaching pre-AP CS, AP CS, and computing courses for non-majors. This workshop was divided into two components - days 1 and 2 were focused on developing an understanding of Alice 3 and days 3 and 4 were focused on transition from Alice 3 to Java using an Alice 3 plugin for a Java IDE. The last workshop showed how to combine Alice with the Media Computation approach. These workshops were a chance for teachers from our previous workshops to return to learn something new (the later two workshops) and for those who had not been able to participate in one of our previous workshops to learn some Alice. Many of our former teachers participated in the poster session at the Symposium. The Symposium included an Alice programming contest in which teachers could submit their students' Alice programs in advance. Winners were decided in three categories: K-8, high school and college.

3.7 3D Alice model creation

Participants in each ITEST workshop were asked, "What models would you find useful for creating animations for use in your math, science, or computing course?" In particular, we wanted input as to what models would be useful for STEM teachers in creating simulation and animation projects related to traditional curricula topics. We compiled a list of requested models and some specifics in terms of functionality. We prioritized the list in terms of: (1) which models were in greatest demand, and (2) which models would work best in a 3D animation environment.

At the time of this writing, 121 new 3D models have been constructed and added to the Alice 2 gallery, which is an integral part of the software. In addition, about a dozen "broken" models were reconstructed and replaced. This is a major achievement in that the construction of one single 3D model takes about two weeks, on average, from design to completion for the software release. Our two-four student interns received training in 3D modeling and construction techniques needed for creating Disney- and Pixar-like models for the Alice 2 gallery.

Newly added gallery models, where appropriate, are now outfitted with texture maps that are designed to increase diversity in clothing, age, ethnicity, and gender. For example, six new people models are now in the gallery that have varying skin color and are dressed in clothing typical of students in urban settings. With these models, Alice can be used to create film-shorts and games having characters with whom today's students can easily relate.

Some new model sets are particularly aimed at interdisciplinary themes. The Pilgrim set contains models of Native Americans, Pilgrims, a "Mayflower-like" ship, and items for a Thanksgiving celebration (pumpkin, turkey, cornucopia, etc.). The Space and Solar System set now has asteroids, satellite dish, space ship, space station, planets, moons, asteroids, and moon phases. The Science set has lab equipment such as a balance and Bunsen burner as well as a DNA matrix strand, a plant in 4 successive stages of sprouting, and computer components. The Math set has a 6-sided die, a 20-value spinner, and a 6-value spinner, which are useful for demonstration of probability. The Nature and Ocean sets have been dramatically increased with new species. Such models provide new contexts for teaching and learning in traditional STEM courses as well as in other disciplines.

On a pedagogy-related issue, the Alice team received feedback from workshop participants that secondary school students often have difficulty with decomposition – breaking a story down into simple steps to create a storyboard (algorithm). Students struggle with the level of detail in terms of how many steps are needed. The questions asked by students are typically along the line of, "How do you know when the steps are simple enough?" The curriculum specialists in the Alice team decided to investigate the use of comic strips as a tool for illustrating successive frames of the actions in a story. Thanks to the generosity of Paws, Inc., the Alice Project received the rights to build the Garfield comic strip characters as Alice 3D models. These models were used in our summer 2014 workshops with enthusiastic responses from our teachers.

4. LESSONS LEARNED

As part of a project that has been running for close to a decade, we made several mistakes, and have come across many issues. We identify some of the ones we believe to be more salient for the wider computing education community:

Workshop location: Unless the teachers are dedicated in advance, we found that it was much better to have the participants travel to our location, rather than having us travel to them. Our pilot in Virginia Beach[6] that we traveled to went superbly. The teachers from this school district were dedicated to the project, developed their own hierarchy of leaders, and worked together to ensure the project's success. However, traveling to Oakland to run a workshop for a group of teachers from the Oakland Unified School District (OUSD) did not go as well. Teachers were (initially) much less invested in having the project succeed. The fact that all teachers commuted to the workshop meant that they were less willing to separate the rest of their lives from what was occurring in the workshop. At the Duke workshop, where the teachers came from all over the state of NC, the majority of teachers lived at one site during the workshop. They spent their evenings socializing and even programming together. They clearly bonded from spending so much time together.

Multiple teachers from a school or school district: For many teachers, being able to actually teach an Alice course at their school in the school year following their professional development workshop often took much more effort than they had anticipated. Getting a letter of support from their principal to attend the professional development workshop did not mean that the principal would automatically honor, or even remember their commitment. It was often necessary for the teacher to have to navigate bureaucracy, staff changes, and simply inertia to get a programming class into their school. Having multiple teachers fighting this battle together has been much more successful than having a teacher need to "go it alone."

Support of IT Director: To be successful on running Alice at their school, it was essential to have the support of the IT Director. Alice is freely available, but not on the approved list of state approved software. After clearing that hurdle, teachers not having buy-in from their IT Director had problems. Alice runs best installed on a computer but at some schools it needed to run from a server or from a thumbdrive. Would students be able to save files? Would students have access to the global library of 3-D objects? Teachers had other IT issues including not having access to the computer lab, and computer labs being replaced with classrooms.

Team communication: As noted in the cross-site coordination section above, many workshops ran into similar issues – dealing with the tensions between CTE versus traditional teachers, handling state standards and their absence, dealing with the tension between CTE and college-bound courses, etc. We were generally able to converse about these issues among ourselves, and allow a solution identified by one leader/site to be used by the others.

Website support: There are two significant issues here. The first is the importance of curated materials. Keeping the "signal to noise ratio" strong (so that a teacher searching for materials to use is much more likely to find something of high quality) has been absolutely essential to keeping the usability of our sites high, and to keep teachers going back to the sites when they need to find materials. Many teachers have created lesson plans as part of our project, but only the truly excellent ones (as we have identified) have been made readily available to the larger community. The second issue, having a single point for all partners, has not been handled well, as we have two sites and the Alice team has their own site:[1, 4, 17]. Certainly, there have been logistical issues in terms of getting one another 'write' access to each other's sites, but the net result, having three sites where information is kept, has been less than ideal. The CS 10K community[3] site, as a single entry point, does this well, as does the computing at schools[2] site.

School-year interactions with teachers: As noted above, we have found that school-year interactions between the site leaders (who offer the initial summer professional development) and their teachers to be very important. Certainly, the teachers feel much less isolated when they have regular school-year communication with their college partners, and have someone to turn to when they run into issues. We are not logistically able to visit all our schools, but we have visited many and we have run out-reach programs for students and asked regional teachers to send us their students.

Teacher outreach: Several of our teachers have taught Alice camps in addition to integrating Alice into their course at their school. In addition to teachers creating their own camps, we have recommended teachers as programming instructors to several summer camp programs. We could have encouraged more teachers to do this.

Mesh networks: Presently, most communication between teachers is run as a hub and spoke network, where teacher questions are directed to group leaders. While we have had some success in encouraging teachers to respond to one another's questions through the Alice listserv, the reality is that too many of the teachers' questions ultimately get answered by the group leaders or by the Alice team at CMU. We wish we had a better solution to this situation.

Local communities of practice: We have found it important for groups of teachers who are within driving distance of one another to be able to form a sub-community. This way, they can meet during common in-service days to address and resolve issues as a sub-group. This is one of the key successes from the pilot run at Virginia Beach[6].

Partnerships with the Department of Education (DOE): Support of the state DOE has been vital for us, especially in NC and SC. The DOE helps disseminate information, ensures that the teachers have a course supported by the state that can be taught in their school and increases student and teacher participation. They have also been helpful in advertising and recruiting teachers for our workshops.

Follow-up workshops: We found follow-up workshops, run the summer after the initial professional development workshop, to be an ideal way for us to get feedback on how we can help the teachers and to reward those teachers who have successfully integrated Alice into their courses/curricula.

Rewarding successful teachers: For teachers who had successes, such as winning awards (at the school or district or state level), we have shared their successes with the larger group of teachers. We have also invited teachers who have been particularly successful to help us in the running of later workshops. Having K-12 teachers involved in the professional development has been good both for the teacher who is doing the professional development as well as for the teachers receiving it.

Evaluation: Evaluation is important both formatively (to be able to make changes to the project as it is ongoing) as well as summatively (to be able to argue overall for the project's impact). There are two major issues we have faced with regards to evaluation. The first has been data collection with respect to student data. Permission forms from parents have been hard to collect, even when directly appealing to them at events such as back to school nights. Parents are often not used to providing such permissions. Working only with private schools would likely have made student data collection easier, but would have raised other issues.

The second evaluation issue relates to the teachers themselves. We have found it critical to maintain regular contact with the teachers regarding evaluation throughout the school year, encouraging them to complete project evaluation forms. Calling them at the end of their school day has generally worked well for us.

Formal and informal (e.g. after-school and/or weekend student meetings) education: Often, teachers who are not successfully able to navigate their schools to offer computing instruction can still get engaged (as informal education is easier to incorporate, logistically, than formal). And teachers who run after-school programming clubs one year can result in student and parent interest in getting computing into school in subsequent years.

5. CONCLUSIONS AND FUTURE WORK

When we first started on this project some nine years ago, we did not know in detail the situation we would find in K-12 CS education. We simply had an approach, in teaching with Alice, that had been shown to be successful at the college level[14], for which we had anecdotal evidence could be successful in K-12. Our hope is that in documenting our experiences, sharing our successes and failures, we can help inform the larger CS education community in general, and those given the opportunity to create/grow their own communities of practice in particular, about actions to try, and actions that are perhaps not as likely to succeed.

6. REFERENCES

[1] Alice website, 2014. Retrieved September 1, 2014 from http://alice.org.

[2] Computing at school website, 2014. Retrieved September 1, 2014 from http://www.computingatschool.org.uk.

[3] Cs10k community website, 2014. Retrieved September 1, 2014 from http://www.cs10kcommunity.org.

[4] Learning to program with alice, 2014. Retrieved September 1, 2014 from http://aliceprogramming.net.

[5] J. S. Brown and P. Duguid. Organizational learning and communities-of-practice: Toward a unified view of working, learning, and innovation. *Organization Science*, 2(1):40–57, 1991.

[6] S. Cooper, W. Dann, and J. Harrison. A k-12 college partnership. In *Proceedings of the 41st ACM Technical Symposium on Computer Science Education*, SIGCSE '10, pages 320–324, New York, NY, USA, 2010. ACM.

[7] S. Cooper, W. Dann, D. Lewis, P. Lawhead, S. Rodger, M. Schep, and R. Stalvey. A pre-college professional development program. In *Proceedings of the 16th Annual Joint Conference on Innovation and Technology in Computer Science Education*, ITiCSE '11, pages 188–192, New York, NY, USA, 2011. ACM.

[8] S. Cooper, S. Grover, R. Pea, and L. Bookey. *Building a virtual community of practice: A report from a working meeting in support of the cs10k community.* Stanford University, November 7-8, 2013, 2013.

[9] S. Cooper, S. Grover, and B. Simon. Building a virtual community of practice for k-12 cs teachers. *Commun. ACM*, 57(5):39–41, May 2014.

[10] J. Cuny. Finding 10,000 teachers. In *CSTA Voice, 5, 6*, pages 1–2, Jan 2010.

[11] S. Fincher and J. Tenenberg. Warren's question. In *Proceedings of ICER*, pages 51–60. ACM, 2007.

[12] J. Lave and E. Wenger. *Situated learning: Legitimate peripheral participation.* Cambridge university press, 1991.

[13] B. Morrison, L. Ni, and M. Guzdial. Adapting the disciplinary commons model for high school teachers: Improving recruitment, creating community. In *The Ninth Annual International Conference on International Computing Education Research (ICER '12)*, pages 47–54, 2012.

[14] B. Moskal, D. Lurie, and S. Cooper. Evaluating the effectiveness of a new instructional approach. In *Thirty-Fifth SIGCSE Technical Symposium on Computer Science Education*, pages 75–9, 2004.

[15] L. Ni. Building professional identity as computer science teachers: supporting secondary computer science teachers through reflection and community building. In *ICER*, pages 143–144, 2011.

[16] L. Ni, M. Guzdial, A. E. Tew, B. Morrison, and R. R. Galanos. Building a community to support hs cs teachers: The disciplinary commons for computing educators. In *The 42nd ACM Technical Symposium on Computer Science Education (SIGCSE '11)*, pages 553–558, 2011.

[17] S. Rodger. Adventures in alice programming, 2014. Retrieved September 1, 2014 from http://www.cs.duke.edu/csed/alice/aliceInSchools/.

[18] D. Seehorn, S. Carey, B. Fuschetto, I. Lee, D. Moix, D. O'Grady-Cunniff, B. Owens, C. Stephenson, and A. Verno. Csta k-12 computer science standards, revised 2011, 2011.

[19] C. Simard, C. Stephenson, and D. Kosaraju. Addressing core equity issues in k-12 computer science education: Identifying barriers and sharing strategies, 2009.

[20] C. Stephenson, J. Gal-Ezer, B. Haberman, and A. Verno. The new educational imperative: Improving high school computer science education, 2005.

[21] J. Tenenberg and S. Fincher. Opening the door of the computer science classroom: The disciplinary commons. In *The 38th SIGCSE Technical Symposium on Computer Science Education (SIGCSE '07)*, pages 514–518, 2007.

[22] E. Wenger. *Communities of practice: Learning, meaning, and identity.* Cambridge university press, 1998.

[23] E. Wenger, R. McDermott, and W. Snyder. *Cultivating Communities of Practice: A Guide to Managing Knowledge.* Harvard Business School Press, 2002.

Computing on the Silicon Prairie: The State of CS in Nebraska Public Schools

Brian Dorn
University of Nebraska at Omaha
Omaha, NE 68182
bdorn@unomaha.edu

Derek Babb
Omaha North High School
Omaha, NE 68111
derek.babb@ops.org

Dawn M. Nizzi
Westside High School Career Center
Omaha, NE 68144
nizzi.dawn@westside66.net

Cory M. Epler
Nebraska Department of Education
Lincoln, NE 68509
cory.epler@nebraska.gov

ABSTRACT

Access to high quality K-12 computer science education has garnered considerable public attention in the United States in the wake of Code.org's December 2013 Hour of Code. An increasing number of states are now counting CS coursework towards high school graduation requirements, and teacher certification for computing courses is being revisited across the country. In this work, we explore the current state of computer science education in Nebraska public schools using objective enrollment data from the 2013–2014 academic year. We find limited access to introductory programming courses, while basic computer/IT literacy coursework is commonplace. Lack of CS courses is particularly acute in small schools, which make up a majority of Nebraska's public schools. We also present data illustrating limited pursuit of IT teaching endorsement/certification in the state and highlight current issues for teacher training programs that lead to such certification in Nebraska.

Categories and Subject Descriptors

K.3.2 [**Computers and Education**]: Computer and Information Science Education—*computer science education*

Keywords

K-12 computing, teacher certification

1. INTRODUCTION

Calls from academia, industry, and the general community for increased access to formal computing education experiences are by no means new, but they have been amplified by the remarkable success of Code.org's 2013 Hour of Code and ongoing public awareness campaign. The general issues have been well-documented in a series of recent reports: access to introductory computer science (CS) courses in K-12 environments has declined in the last 10 years, and there is a common misconception among stakeholders that computer science education is synonymous with teaching general information technology (IT) literacy [13]; computer science coursework remains elective and cannot be used to satisfy either high school graduation requirements or college admissions requirements in most states [4]; and there is a lack of rigorous teacher preparation and certification in computing and information technology even among those teaching Advanced Placement CS courses [4, 2]. Thankfully, advocacy efforts in several states have begun yielding results over the past 12 months. However, to continue this forward progress across the country, academics, teachers, administrators, and legislators need to understand the unique contextual issues facing each state.

As is the case in many states, Nebraska has few specifically designated K-12 CS teachers, no required training in CS in order to teach computing courses [13, 4], no standardized high school CS curricula, and only a few students taking the AP CS exam. At the same time, Nebraska is experiencing considerable growth in the information technology sector, so much so that a 2012 New York Times article dubbed it part of the "Silicon Prairie" [6]—an area in the central midwest with a burgeoning tech start-up culture. Further, a 2013 study by the Omaha Chamber of Commerce projected considerable IT job growth in the next two years and raised concerns about a shortfall of IT workers despite increasing enrollments in area university programs [12].

Nebraska's relatively large geographic size and predominately rural demographic presents additional challenges with respect to increasing access to K-12 computing education programs. The population density of Nebraska is very sparse as compared to many states, and it is heavily skewed towards the eastern third of the state around the Omaha and Lincoln metropolitan areas. According to the 2012-2013 State of the Schools Report database [10], there are 267 public secondary schools in the state (excluding public alternative schools). Of these, 200 (75%) enroll 250 or fewer total students across grades 9-12, and these small schools are responsible for instruction of 23% of all students statewide. Offering elective courses in subjects like computer science in these small schools presents a logistical challenge for students, teachers, and administrators alike. At the same time, 44 (17%) secondary schools enroll 1000 or more students and account for 57% of all 9-12 grade students enrolled. By looking at these statistics alone, it is clear that a "one-size-

SIGCSE'15, March 4–7, 2015, Kansas City, MO, USA

ACM 978-1-4503-2966-8/15/03 ...$15.00.
http://dx.doi.org/10.1145/2676723.2677261.

fits-all" approach to addressing K-12 computing education concerns in Nebraska is doomed to fail.

In this paper, we seek to explore the state of computer science and information technology-related coursework in public K-12 settings across Nebraska in order to better understand the challenges and opportunities for future outreach, curriculum development, and teacher training efforts. We are particularly interested in the existing level of access to formal course experiences in IT and the current state of disciplinary-specific teacher training and certification.

2. BACKGROUND AND RELATED WORK

Two high profile reports sponsored by the CSTA and the ACM have examined nationwide trends related to K-12 computing and information technology education. "Running on Empty" [13] focuses on coverage of the ACM/CSTA Model Computer Science Standards in the expressed state-level standards for technology, math, and science. Overall, the report concludes that while states have placed significant emphasis on improving "technology literacy," these efforts have largely focused on skills-based activities for how to use a computer to complete other learning tasks, rather than focusing on the fundamental principles and capabilities of computing that would more typically be recognized as learning objectives in computer science. In their analysis, Nebraska's curricular standards incorporated 100% of skills-based objectives and 86% of Level 1 objectives for grades K–8. However, the state's standards addressed 0% of level 2 (grades 9–10), 0% of level 3 (grades 10–11), and only 5% of the conceptual learning objectives across the board. Like many states, they conclude that Nebraska's standards are "very heavily application based" [13, p.60].

Historically, local control delegates considerable authority over educational decision making to local school boards [11], and Nebraska policies reflect a strong commitment to local control. Individual districts are solely responsible for the development of curricula in both elective and core areas, and each school board sets minimum graduation requirements. Thus, state standards and suggested courses act as aids for districts' decisions about curriculum, and the admissions requirements for the state university system play a role in influencing graduation requirements. We recognize that this commitment to local control is a reality and poses challenges for efforts like developing model computing curricula.

The 2013 report "Bugs in the System" [4] examined nationwide trends related to teacher certification in K-12 computer science. They found that the majority of states have no formal teacher certification process and/or do not require any form of specialized certification to teach computer science/IT coursework. Even among those that do have a certification program, the requirements show little consistency in their definition of computer science and where it should be included in the K-12 curriculum. Nebraska is identified as one of the few states offering a form of "computer science certificate," but their analysis included now-outdated information about current endorsement programs in the state.

Concerted efforts to advance K-12 computer science education have been successful in a handful of US states. In particular, Georgia is often highlighted for its systematic, state-wide reforms related to curriculum revision [13], adoption of teacher certification, allowing CS coursework to count towards high school science graduation requirements, and increasing underrepresented student enrollments in AP CS [7]. The "Georgia Computes!" initiative led by Guzdial and Ericson is cited as playing a key role in the policy changes and instructional support that led to these reforms [7]. Building on these successes, other states are pursuing similar efforts—e.g., the Commonwealth Alliance for IT Education in Massachusetts led by the Univ. of Massachusetts, Amherst [1].

A common theme in all of these reports is that a significant obstacle to making progress rests in the high degree of inconsistency and uniqueness of the educational landscape in each state. Thus, a necessary precondition to efforts that aim to affect state-wide change is a deep understanding of the current context of computing education in the particular state in question. For example, desJardins recently conducted a survey study of Maryland teachers to "gather data and evidence that can be used to provide support for systemic changes, and to build a community that can work together to create the conditions that will ultimately enable these changes" [5, p.712]. We echo those objectives in this work where we seek to better characterize computing education in Nebraska in order to inform future education, outreach, policy, and advocacy efforts.

3. DATA AND ANALYSIS METHODS

This paper presents secondary analyses of data originally collected by the Nebraska Department of Education (NDE) as part of annual state-wide reporting practices. The first dataset included course enrollment head counts across all public schools in Nebraska during the 2013-2014 academic year for all courses classified in the state's "Communications and Information Systems" sub-category (ie., career field) within Career and Technical Education. The original data provided was disaggregated by NDE at the district, school, and instructor/section levels. Section 4 of the paper presents summary statistics of this data alongside other relevant observations about the dataset.

The second dataset consisted of annual data reported by approved teacher education programs to NDE over the four year period from 2009 to 2013. This data detailed how many new teaching endorsements of each type were granted by each approved program. We present these data alongside an analysis of other publicly available documents regarding the teacher preparation programs in Section 5 of the paper.

4. CS/IT COURSE OFFERINGS

A key issue in recent calls for K-12 computing is the need to increase student access to formal coursework in schools. Each year NDE publishes a set of approved courses, including course descriptions and their coverage of accompanying standards, for each content area (see [8]). Computing coursework resides alongside other career education programs, and the "Communication and Information Systems" career field outlines 21 pre-defined course codes plus 5 generic "other" courses. Only the courses designated as "other" are recommended for students earlier than 9th grade. Individual schools/districts must map their actual course offerings to these approved course codes when reporting enrollment data to the state. In addition, each course code defines one or more "clearing endorsements" which denote the official qualifications instructors of the course should have.

Table 1 presents enrollment data for 18 of these courses over the 2013–2014 academic year, and the 3 remaining courses in media production (ie., journalism) were dropped from our analysis for lack of relevance here. The vast majority of these courses were offered in secondary/high schools but a small number of middle/junior-high schools offering IT coursework are included in this data as well. For readability,

Table 1: AY2013–2014 Student Enrollments in Communications and IS Courses

Course Name	Qualifying Endorsement IT	Math	Business	Other	Total Enrolled	# Classes	# Schools	Avg Class Size
Computing								
Programming I	*	*			780	50	46	15.6 ($\sigma = 21.4$)
Programming II	*	*			292	31	29	9.4 ($\sigma = 8.5$)
Programming III	*	*			14	6	6	2.3 ($\sigma = 1.0$)
AP CS A	*	*			62	6	6	10.3 ($\sigma = 2.4$)
Network Systems	*				48	10	10	4.8 ($\sigma = 4.3$)
CISCO I: IT Essentials	*				31	5	5	6.2 ($\sigma = 5.3$)
CISCO II: CCNA Discovery	*				12	3	3	4 ($\sigma = 2.6$)
CISCO III: CCNA Exploration	*				4	1	1	4 (n/a)
Applications								
IT Applications I	*		*		10,414	292	202	35.7 ($\sigma = 40.0$)
IT Applications II	*		*		3,998	161	129	24.8 ($\sigma = 31.9$)
IT Fundamentals	*		*		987	30	29	32.9 ($\sigma = 69.2$)
IT Support	*		*		46	6	6	7.7 ($\sigma = 8.1$)
PC Support/Maintenance	*		*		78	10	10	7.8 ($\sigma = 5.4$)
Design								
Digital Media	*		*		2,918	154	126	18.9 ($\sigma = 26.8$)
Web Design	*		*		1,296	98	92	13.2($\sigma = 14.5$)
Intro to Digital Design	*		*	Art	1,276	73	64	17.5 ($\sigma = 22.1$)
Intermediate Digital Design	*		*	Art	329	30	28	11.0 ($\sigma = 9.6$)
Advanced Digital Design	*		*	Art	45	11	11	4.1 ($\sigma = 6.4$)
Comm. & Info Systems Other 1–5	*		*		4783	142	97	33.7 ($\sigma = 48.5$)

Table 2: AY2013–2014 Offerings by School Size

Student Body Size (as of AY'12-'13)	# Schools	Prog 1	Prog 2	IT App 1	IT App 2	Web Design	Digital Media
1–100	120	2.5%	1.7%	58.3%	35.0%	24.2%	32.5%
101–250	80	11.3%	3.8%	76.3%	52.5%	30.0%	45.0%
251–500	23	34.8%	13.0%	87.0%	52.2%	56.5%	60.9%
501–1000	15	40.0%	40.0%	100.0%	66.7%	66.7%	53.3%
1001–	29	69.0%	51.7%	89.7%	69.0%	51.7%	72.4%

we have clustered courses into three thematic groups: computing, applications, and design. These groups are based on the authors' interpretation of course descriptions and qualifying endorsements, and are not part of NDE's classification system. For each course, we show the state-approved teaching endorsement(s) needed, the total number of students who took the course, the number of classes/sections taught, the number of unique schools at which the course was offered, and the average class size along with the standard deviation in parentheses.

As introduced above, there are 267 public secondary/high schools in the state [10]. Thus, students at approximately 17% of these schools had access to a first course in programming, while over 75% of schools provided at least one stand-alone IT applications course. Further, classes in the computing category were considerably smaller than those in any of the other categories.[1] These data reinforce the interpretation that technology education in Nebraska is predominately focused on skills literacy with using computers.

The contrast is even more stark across rural Nebraska. When analyzing the data at a finer level, we found that the 12 unique Omaha metropolitan area schools offering Programming I enrolled 61% of all students in the course statewide. We found that 87% of the remaining schools, which are in predominantly small, rural districts, did not offer a single programming course. However, 74% of them taught at least one section of IT Applications I, and even the majority of the secondary schools enrolling 100 or fewer total students offered this basic computer literacy course. Table 2 explores course availability in secondary/high school for a subset of these courses based on the 2012-2013 school enrollment totals for grades 9–12. One has to look at the largest group (schools enrolling more than 1000 students) to find a first programming course taught by the majority. Even then, 31% of the very largest schools did not provide a programming course to a single student in the 2013–2014 academic year.

The total number of students who enrolled in all programming courses, including AP CS A, was significantly less than the number who took a second course in computer applications, a first course in digital media, or a first course in web design. Overall, these data demonstrate that few students in Nebraska enrolled in computer science coursework at the secondary level, and those that did were in very small classes and seldom had access to more than one course. Given this, it is perhaps no surprise that only 46 total students in Nebraska, just 5 women, and no students of color took the AP Computer Science A exam in 2013 [3].

Beyond the small pipeline into advanced offerings in computing, there are several other observations that can be made about this dataset. First, there were many courses that were offered at fewer than 10 schools to fewer than 10 students. One could argue that these courses—CISCO courses, IT support, PC maintenance—present the most vocational view of the computing profession, and focus on learning objectives which are not widely recognized as important in preparing students for post-secondary study in computer science and other information technology majors. Coupled with the tight budget and staffing demands faced by many districts, it seems appropriate to revisit the need to continue offering such courses. We see this as a clear opportunity for institutions of higher education to work alongside school districts to modernize K-12 course offerings.

[1]However, there were remarkable standard deviations in class sizes across all courses due to Nebraska's mix of large metropolitan and small rural schools.

While many post-secondary CS departments nationwide are eliminating computer applications courses in favor of those, like CS Principles, that integrate deep computational thinking learning objectives, the large number of K-12 student enrollments in the applications category of classes demands greater attention. Certainly fluency with computer applications is an important skill in the modern world, but how might such courses be re-envisioned to also introduce learners to broader notions of computing and careers in information technology? That is, how can we use these courses to instill in students a view of computing as a powerful tool for co-creation and innovation, rather than to simply teach students to use pre-built applications and consume content provided by others? Further, since most of these courses are taught by those with business education backgrounds, what kinds of professional development experiences must be built to increase teachers' depth of knowledge of computer science? These are critically important questions in Nebraska (and other states) where the challenge of staffing in a large number of rural schools may pragmatically preclude any efforts that require the addition of a separate, new course.

Lastly, it appears that the technology standards and current course descriptions outlined by the state need expanding/updating, and districts could benefit from additional guidance in their application. Almost 5,000 students enrolled in a course reported as one of the five "other" courses. If this were a single course it would be the second-most enrolled course. However, the "other" designations provide no information about content and do not allow for understanding new trends in courses developed by schools.

Since individual districts make mapping decisions and those mappings are not always revisited as curriculum evolves, the quality of the data suffers. In particular, we were surprised by the fact that only 6 unique schools offered the AP CS A course according to the data. Upon closer examination, we found that several schools—including that of one of the authors at the time—were reporting a known AP CS A course as either Programming II or Programming III. This misapplication makes it difficult to track trends in access to computing education statewide and, even worse, could dissuade efforts to count computing coursework towards university admissions requirements.

5. TEACHER CERTIFICATION

Twenty-two states (including the District of Columbia) currently offer some form of CS or IT teaching certification [4]. Only two (Arizona and Wisconsin) require it to teach computing courses, another 7 require it to teach AP CS A, and the remaining 13 offer certification but do not require it to teach computing courses. Nebraska falls in the third group and offers a supplemental K-12 endorsement in Information Technology which must be added to a full licensure in any other primary endorsement area (e.g., secondary mathematics, business, language arts). As shown in Table 1, the only courses that exclusively designate the IT Supplemental Endorsement are Network Systems and the CISCO sequence. All other courses, including AP CS A, permit a teacher's primary endorsement in a non-IT field to suffice.

Using additional data provided by NDE, we examined the proportion of active teachers holding the IT supplemental endorsement. We focused this analysis on the 8 courses listed in the Computing category in Table 1 as they either explicitly required only the endorsement and/or most closely resemble a pipeline into post-secondary computer science programs. Of the 58 teachers offering one or more of these courses in the 2013-2014 academic year, only 24 (41.4%) held the current IT supplemental endorsement or an equivalent prior one.[2] Only 2 of the 9 active teachers for these courses in the state's largest school district (Omaha Public Schools) held the IT endorsement. Despite the fact that Nebraska is in the minority of states offering teacher certification in IT, the lack of content-area training remains a major obstacle.

5.1 The IT Supplemental Endorsement

As so few active teachers hold the supplemental IT endorsement and so few US states even offer such a program, we further investigated Nebraska's state requirements for the endorsement and how these requirements are interpreted by various post-secondary teacher training programs in the state. The Nebraska IT supplemental endorsement qualifies a teacher at the PK-12 level and requires 15 credit hours of study in information technology related coursework. As with every endorsement, the state publishes a set of required learning objectives that must be met by approved teacher training programs. The required current learning objectives for the endorsement include knowledge of [9]:

- IT ethics and intellectual property
- Instructional methods and curricula appropriate for teaching Information Technology
- Concepts and application of programming (procedural and object-oriented languages, principles of programming, IDEs, testing/debugging skills)
- Installation and management of IT infrastructure (operating systems, databases, architecture, communication/troubleshooting skills)
- Interactive media (web design, digital media)
- Basic network systems

Each teacher preparation program wishing to offer this endorsement must map these objectives (and their more specific individual sub-goals) to a set of courses covering the minimum of 15 credit hours. As of the 2014-2015 academic year, NDE reported six approved programs of study leading to the IT supplemental endorsement. Table 3 presents information about the course requirements for the five programs for which data was available publicly through university course catalogs and websites. The table lists anonymized institution names and acronyms, indicates whether the program is offered at the undergraduate (U) or graduate (G) level, and gives the number of IT/CS and teacher education course credits required. We have also separately listed IT/CS-specific education courses (denoted CSEd in the table) when possible based on course descriptions; this includes teaching methods courses specifically tied to the teaching and learning of computing.

There is a great deal of variation in how institutions interpret the state's required learning objectives. Only one of the approved programs allows students to finish within the 15 credit hour minimum. With respect to the depth of CS/IT required, most require at least two semesters of introductory computer science (either CS0/1 or CS1/2) taught by the computing faculty. Other programs, like SPU's, require teachers to complete undergraduate operating systems and upper level programming languages courses, while teachers at LSRU take additional courses in instructional technology taught by faculty in the Teacher Education division. MRU has recently shifted the focus of its program

[2]Individuals teaching courses in multiple districts during AY'13-'14 were counted in each district in this analysis.

Table 3: IT Supplemental Endorsement Programs

Institution	Level	IT/CS	Ed	CSEd	Notes
Small Private Univ (SPU)	U	18	0	2	
Regional State College (RSC)	U/G	15	0	0	Requires 40 hour clinical experiences
Regional State Univ (RSU)	G	12/15	0/3	0	Concentration in the MSEd in Instructional Tech
Metropolitan State Research Univ (MRU)	U	15	0	3	Restructured program for 2014-2015
Large State Research Univ (LSRU)	U	7	6	4	Business and Marketing Ed endorsement required

Table 4: IT Supplemental Endorsements Earned

Academic Year	SPC1*	SPC2*	SPC3*	SPU	RSC	RSU	MRU**	LSRU
2009–2010	1				1			
2010–2011	4		1					
2011–2012	1			1		1	1	
2012–2013	2			1				

*Program eliminated effective Fall 2014
**Program restructured effective Fall 2014

from graduate-level instructional technology courses taught by education faculty to five undergraduate content courses taught by disciplinary computing faculty plus a 3-credit methods course. Despite the endorsement's learning objectives about domain-specific teaching methods, there was little consistency among the programs for inclusion of courses centered on CS pedagogical content knowledge.

Table 4 presents historical data about the number of teachers certified by each approved program since 2009. As of time of writing, data for 2013-2014 was not available. We note that the three smallest institutions (SPC1–SPC3) report effective or official elimination of their programs as of Fall 2014 and are no longer accepting new applicants. Generally speaking, all teacher education programs in the state have sporadically produced 1–2 new endorsed IT teachers annually, which makes it difficult for any single program to foster a cohort model or have the teachers in training share and learn from each other. Of course, this could be due in part to the fact the IT endorsement remains largely optional.

5.2 Endorsement Challenges

On the one hand, the great deal of flexibility in interpretation afforded to institutions could be helpful in crafting programs that address unique needs of the prospective teachers. However, it also creates a number of challenges and opportunities going forward:

Depth/Breadth of CS Content: The lack of consistency in the amount and depth of CS content across teacher training programs results is concerning, but is exacerbated by the required learning objectives set by the endorsement and pre-requisite structures in undergraduate CS curricula. For example, the learning objective regarding the "installation and management of IT infrastructure" is worded such that PC maintenance and systems administration are highlighted as primary outcomes. As we alluded to above, such curricular objectives are somewhat outdated, and the secondary courses currently offered enroll very few students. This can leave teacher training programs in a difficult position because the post-secondary courses offered in CS focus on more conceptual, and less vocational, learning objectives.

A related problem arises from the common curricular structure in post-secondary computing programs, where often a three-course sequence culminating in data structures is required prior to enrolling in the broad range of upper level elective courses (e.g., networking, databases, operating systems). As shown in Table 3, this results in some programs requiring considerable additional CS (either explicitly or implicitly through prerequisites) to meet the requirements with existing courses. Other programs instead opt to create more general purpose "instructional technology" courses housed in teacher education programs. Certainly there is a great difference between the level of content knowledge about topics like databases when taught in these two distinct contexts. Ultimately, we need to re-examine the core set of skills and conceptual knowledge necessary for effective PK-12 computing teaching and construct model teacher-training programs that can be more easily instantiated.

Reaching In-service Teachers: Given that so few of the teachers in Nebraska currently hold the IT supplemental endorsement, it was surprising that the teacher training programs in the state seem to focus primarily on traditional, undergraduate pre-service teacher training. If we are serious about increasing the number of certified teachers both in Nebraska and across the US as part of the CS10K effort [2], a concerted effort needs to be made to enable in-service teachers to retrain in the computing field through graduate coursework. Obviously, this presents a challenge when such teachers may not have taken even a first undergraduate course in programming.

6. DISCUSSION AND FUTURE WORK

These results provide the foundations for a number of efforts that could be undertaken in Nebraska to improve the state of K-12 CS education. Here we enumerate a variety of specific efforts in no particular order, recognizing that to affect substantive change a multifaceted approach by multiple stakeholders incorporating several will be necessary.

Follow-up Survey: While the objective data presented here theoretically provides a more complete picture of the current state of IT education than a self-reported survey, there were some instances where more information from individual schools would be welcomed. In particular, we are interested in exploring the 142 different courses classified as "other 1–5." Conducting a follow-up survey with schools to gain additional qualitative data about their current course offerings, their conceptual coverage, student/teacher demographics, and unique challenges faced by rural schools would further clarify the issues that need to be addressed.

Re-imagine IT Applications 1: In the short term, it may be possible to leverage the significant current infrastructure across schools of all sizes for IT Applications and Web Design courses. Collaboratively authoring new content standards for these courses that explicitly integrate computational thinking, programming, and other valuable conceptual content alongside more traditional IT literacy objectives could yield an immediate impact on exposing students to the field. Doing so would need to involve current teachers in order to adequately address the needs of those whose disciplinary expertise lies in non-CS/IT endorsement areas.

Large-Scale Standards Reform: The list of current courses in information technology (and their accompanying learning objectives) needs to be re-evaluated with respect to current industry needs and their coverage of the CSTA K-12 CS Standards, along with further diffusion of CS learning objectives into math, science, and other career education standards. In particular, special attention should be placed on looking beyond grades 9-12 and incorporating increased emphasis of algorithmic and computational thinking across the board. Including local industry partners in the evolution of standards may also better align them with local needs while providing clear incentives for school districts and their teachers to adopt new recommendations.

Raising Awareness about IT Careers: Conflation of CS with basic IT literacy exacerbates problems related to students' awareness of the wide range of career opportunities afforded by the field. Meeting the immediate projected needs within the Nebraska IT workforce will not only require coursework that allows students to engage deeply with computational concepts, but it will also require cultivation of student interest in seeking out such experiences. Developing programs that allow students to discover computing careers at earlier ages is important, as is the need to find scalable solutions that reach students in rural communities where no local IT industry is readily apparent.

Teaching Certification Summit: The inconsistencies in currently-approved IT teacher training programs in the state demand we have a frank conversation about certification. In particular, members of teacher training institutions, post-secondary CS academics, practicing K-12 teachers, and representatives from NDE need to examine current endorsement requirements and programs with respect to the three unique audiences from which teachers are likely to arise:

1. *Pre-service teachers* earning their initial teaching certification, including issues related to whether or not there are sufficient grounds to warrant a primary (full) endorsement in CS/IT
2. *In-service teachers currently holding business, math, or other primary endorsements* that make up the bulk of the current teaching force; here, re-training programs need to take seriously the potential lack of undergraduate exposure to computer science content
3. *Industry professionals* with a formal background in CS seeking a career-switch into teaching; here general pedagogical practice is important, but the need to eventually earn a primary endorsement in a non-CS/IT area may also impose unnecessary barriers

Providing realistic options for each of these audiences would be an important precondition prior to moving towards mandatory teacher certification for instructors teaching computing/IT coursework. However, an incremental approach, where specific CS certification is required for some, but not all, courses (like AP CS A) would also be needed to further encourage in-service teachers and their districts to pursue such endorsements.

Addressing Rural Nebraska: The fact that so many Nebraska schools have small student populations, have constrained teaching resources, and are geographically separated by large distances is unlikely to change anytime soon. The reality is that there are, and will continue to be, isolated individual students who have an interest in taking their knowledge of computing beyond what their school can realistically provide, even if the other reforms mentioned should be successful. To embrace this challenge head on, rather than saving it as a problem to address later, is not only pragmatic, but it would also have a dramatic impact on improving access to computing education statewide. We need to explore opportunities for high-quality distance education models to meet these demands and, in so doing, open up countless career possibilities for students from rural areas. Considering all of the contextual variables outlined here, this, more than all other next steps, will require a uniquely Nebraskan approach to a uniquely Nebraskan problem.

ACKNOWLEDGMENTS

We sincerely thank our colleagues at NDE for their willingness to share data and work together to improve computing education in the state. We also thank Cody Tienken for his assistance with data preparation prior to analysis and Harvey Siy for his helpful feedback on an earlier draft.

References

[1] W. R. Adrion, R. Fall, M. Matos, and A. R. Peterfreund. Integrating evaluation into program development: Benefits of baselining a NSF-BPC alliance. In *Proc. of SIGCSE'10*, pages 27–31, 2010.

[2] O. Astrachan, J. Cuny, C. Stephenson, and C. Wilson. The CS10K project: Mobilizing the community to transform high school computing. In *Proc. of SIGCSE'11*, pages 85–86, 2011.

[3] College Board. AP program participation and performance data 2013. `http://research.collegeboard.org/programs/ap/data/participation/2013`, 2013.

[4] CSTA Certification Committee. *Bugs in the System.* ACM, 2013.

[5] M. desJardins and S. Martin. CE21–Maryland: The state of computer science education in Maryland high schools. In *Proc. of SIGCSE'13*, pages 711–716, 2013.

[6] J. Eligon. Tech start-ups find a home on the prairie. *The New York Times*, Nov 12 2012.

[7] M. Guzdial, B. Ericson, T. Mcklin, and S. Engelman. Georgia Computes! an intervention in a US state, with formal and informal education in a policy context. *Trans. Comput. Educ.*, 14(2):13:1–13:29, June 2014.

[8] Nebraska Dept of Education. Course codes and clearing endorsements. `http://www.education.ne.gov/nssrs/docs/course_codes_clearing_endorsements_20132014.pdf`, May 2013.

[9] Nebraska Dept of Education. Rule 24 matrix - information technology. `http://nde.ne.gov/EducatorPrep/IHE/ProgramApproval/R24Matrices/2014/InfoTech12.docx`, 2014.

[10] State Board of Education. 2012–2013 state of the schools report: A report on nebraska public schools. `http://reportcard.education.ne.gov/`, Sep 2013.

[11] T. Toch. The fallacy of local control. *Phi Delta Kappan*, 93(5):66–67, 2012.

[12] J. Vaslow. Omaha area IT and engineering study. `http://cdn.aimforbrilliance.org/pdf/2013omahaareaitandengineeringtalentstudy.pdf`.

[13] C. Wilson, L. A. Sudol, C. Stephenson, and M. Stehlik. *Running on Empty: the Failure to Teach K-12 Computer Science in the Digital Age.* ACM, 2010.

Supporting CS10K: A New Computer Science Methods Course for Mathematics Education Students

Robin Flatland
Siena College
Loudonville, New York 12211
flatland@siena.edu

Darren Lim
Siena College
Loudonville, New York 12211
dlim@siena.edu

James Matthews
Siena College
Loudonville, New York 12211
matthews@siena.edu

Scott Vandenberg
Siena College
Loudonville, New York 12211
vandenberg@siena.edu

ABSTRACT

We describe a new methods of teaching computer science (CS) course tailored for mathematics education majors but also applicable to others interested in teaching CS. Goals of the course are enhancing their ability and confidence in developing and offering CS courses at high schools and starting CS courses at high schools that do not offer them. The course involves a combination of reading, programming, lesson/unit plan development, code reviews, and discussion of the various paradigms for introducing CS at the secondary level. Results indicate the course enhances the students' confidence, ability, and preparation for teaching CS in high schools.

Categories and Subject Descriptors

K.3.2 [**Computing Milieux**]: Computers and Education-Computer and Information Science Education

General Terms

Design

Keywords

methods course; Advance Placement Computer Science; CS10K; CS Principles; Snap!

1. INTRODUCTION

Despite a growing demand for computing professionals and predictions by the U.S. Bureau of Labor Statistics that by 2020 one of every two STEM jobs will be in computing [10], most U.S. students do not have the opportunity to take a computer science (CS) course in high school [6]. In 2013, only 3,249 schools offered the Advanced Placement Computer Science (AP CS) course, which is less than a quarter of the number of schools that offered AP Calculus AB and less than a third of those that offered AP Biology [1]. One contributing factor to this low participation rate is that fewer than half of states offer a teacher certification (or license) in computer science [11]. Therefore, few schools have a teacher with the CS background necessary to teach a rigorous, concepts-rich CS course, as opposed to the commonly taught technology classes that cover utilitarian skills in keyboarding and use of commercial software packages.

Because the majority of states do not offer CS certification, there is an effort to train existing mathematics, science, and business instructors to teach computer science. The National Science Foundation (NSF) is supporting the ambitious CS10K initiative with the goal of improved CS curricula being taught in 10,000 high schools by 10,000 qualified teachers, by 2016 [3]. Many professional development programs have been and are currently being implemented [12, 3, 5] to train teachers to teach a computer science course such as the APCS course, the proposed AP CS Principles course [2], or the Exploring Computer Science college-preparatory course [8]. The majority of these programs use summer workshops and in-service days to train teachers in the CS content and pedagogy with the goal of having them establish a CS course at their high school.

Although these efforts are valuable, teachers with greater depth and breadth of knowledge, experience, and confidence in a subject area are more effective. Therefore, we instead take the approach of working with future mathematics teachers during the formative years when they are undergraduate mathematics majors in a secondary education program. By targeting them then, we have the opportunity to get them into the CS educator pipeline earlier. This allows us to work with them over a period of years, rather than weeks or days. We are able to develop their content background in CS, their knowledge of CS pedagogy, and their interest and desire to teach CS in high school.

The capstone course in our program and the focus of this paper is a new methods of teaching CS course (CS methods) that we developed and targeted toward mathematics education majors who are completing a strong minor in CS. Our course teaches pedagogical content knowledge through a mix of readings, discussion, classroom observations, guest speakers, reflections, teaching, and hands-on lab activities. It exposes students to techniques, tools, and resources for

SIGCSE'15, March 4–7, 2015, Kansas City, MO, USA.

http://dx.doi.org/10.1145/2676723.2677274.

teaching computational thinking at the secondary level. Pre- and post-assessment survey results show that our course has had a positive impact on the students' confidence and interest in teaching computer science. Student feedback and our experiences during the first offering of the course led us to make some substantial changes that improved the effectiveness of the second offering of the course, as measured by survey results and based on our own observations. In this paper, we share our experiences, the course curriculum, and the survey results. Given the shortage of CS certifications nationwide, and the dearth of CS-trained CS teachers, there is a growing need for CS methods courses, and thus developing, sharing, and evaluating pedagogy and curricula are important. Even as more U.S. states move towards establishing CS certifications, there will continue to be a need to draw from the ranks of mathematics educators (and others) for some time.

2. CONTEXT AND NOYCE GRANT

Our CS methods course was developed at a small liberal arts college in a state with no CS certification opportunities for teachers. Our college also has a robust and successful mathematics education program. The course was created mainly to support an NSF Robert Noyce Teacher Scholarship grant that Siena College received in 2011. This grant program is designed to encourage talented science, technology, engineering, and mathematics majors to become K-12 mathematics and science teachers. Because of this grant and our context, our program targets mathematics majors in the secondary education program. Our scholarship program is unique in that it requires the mathematics majors to take CS courses that prepare them to teach content-rich high school CS courses. Other majors with similar CS background could also participate.

All students who took the CS methods course were mathematics majors in the secondary education program and awardees of a Noyce scholarship; one of the students was also a double major in computer science. As a requirement for the scholarship, the recipients complete a six-course minor in computer science consisting of a breadth-first introduction to CS, an introduction to programming in Java, data structures (also in Java), analysis of algorithms, a CS elective (that covers a topic that might be useful in a high school CS classroom, like web development or robotics), and the CS methods course. This is more rigorous than the minimum requirements for our CS minor which does not require taking higher level CS courses. In addition, they take a discrete mathematics course which fulfills a requirement of their mathematics major. See Table 1 for details regarding the content of these courses. We note that the first two CS courses in Table 1 are required of all mathematics majors, so the students are taking an additional four CS courses beyond what is required for their mathematics degree. The prerequisites for taking the CS methods course consist of the first three courses in Table 1, although approximately half the students had also taken Analysis of Algorithms and all but one had taken Discrete Mathematics. In addition, most of the students had already completed a methods of teaching mathematics course.

CS Teaching Methods courses have been described and offered elsewhere [14, 9], but the novelty of our approach lies in its tailoring to non-CS majors (to take advantage of unfortunate realities) and its breadth (focusing not just on AP CS or Java programming, but exposing the students to the variety of approaches to introducing CS to students with diverse backgrounds and levels of preparation). In addition, we exposed the students to techniques for managing the logistical (and sometimes political) dimensions of initiating CS education in a high school.

3. CS METHODS COURSE

The Noyce scholarship provides funding for the students to live on campus and take a summer course, so we offered the CS methods course during a four week summer session for two consecutive years. Because several faculty were interested in creating/teaching a CS methods course and each offered different expertise, three CS faculty and one faculty with a joint CS/mathematics appointment co-taught the course. The faculty member with the joint appointment is heavily involved in the college's secondary mathematics education program and is also the Principal Investigator (PI) on the Noyce grant. He teaches the mathematics methods course, places and supervises the mathematics students in their student teaching assignments, and teaches the discrete mathematics course. The other three CS faculty specialize in a variety of areas including teaching introductory CS, data structures, algorithms, programming, and the proposed AP CS Principles course. Although the course could be taught by one faculty member, the course discussions and content were greatly enriched by having the perspectives and expertise of multiple faculty members.

The class met for three hours a day, four days a week in a classroom equipped with computers. Therefore, class sessions consisted of a mix of discussion and hands-on computer work, the details of which are described in the following sections.

3.1 Course Goals

There was a significant shift in the emphasis of the course between the first and second offerings. In the first offering, one of our primary goals was getting the students prepared and excited to teach the AP CS course (on programming in Java). This seemed like a natural goal because high schools value and are often recognized for their college-level course offerings, this is currently the only AP CS course available, and our students had completed a two-semester course sequence on Java programming. To this end, we did such things as having the students take practice AP CS exams, develop lesson plans and materials on Java programming topics, and do Java programming exercises to improve their programming skills. There was no final exam.

However, several things convinced us this was not the right approach. With the AP course material focused on programming and on the details of one particular language, we felt our students were getting too narrow a view of teaching CS in high school. In addition, in other science fields an AP course is not normally the first course taken by students nor is it the first taught by a new teacher. Finally, although the methods students had completed two courses on Java programming (Introduction to Programming and Data Structures) and done well in them, they lacked confidence in their Java programming skills. The difficulty of the AP exam and the fact that the students had not had previous coursework on some of the exam's more advanced object oriented concepts did little to increase their confidence.

Table 1: CS and related courses taken by the Noyce mathematics education students

Course Name	Content
Introduction to Computer Science	Breadth-first CS with non-Java programming
Introduction to Programming	Algorithmic problem solving and object-oriented programming in Java.
Data Structures	In Java; includes stacks, queues, lists, trees, hash tables, and graphs.
Analysis of Algorithms	Includes searching, sorting, trees, graphs, optimization, NP-completeness
CS Elective	High school-appropriate topic: web, graphics, robotics, etc.
Methods of Teaching CS	CS pedagogy course, described herein.
Discrete Mathematics	Sets, functions, induction, order notation, counting, probability, recurrence relations, graphs, trees, Boolean logic, and relations.

Therefore, in the second offering of the course we broadened our approach. Instead of focusing on the AP CS Java course, our goal was to expose students to a variety of different high school CS course curricula and models. In addition, we deemphasized the goal of teaching a college-level course, and instead focused on teaching any content-rich high school CS course. We introduced the Snap! programming language into the course, increased the participation of a local high school CS teacher, focused more on the proposed AP CS Principles course as well as other curricula/models such as Exploring Computing Science and CS Unplugged, and linked the CS concepts/skills to the Common Core State Standards for Mathematical Practice. We also added a take-home final exam to the course to give the students an opportunity to reflect in depth on the topics of the course.

Details on these changes are discussed in the sections that follow. With these changes, we observed an increase during the course in the students' confidence and desire to teach CS, and this was verified by pre- and post-survey results detailed in Section 4.

3.2 Course, Unit, and Lesson Plans

Developing an outline of a year-long CS course for high school students was one of the first things we had the students do. Based on their own course experiences, textbooks, and the internet they came up with reasonable (mostly language independent) course outlines. When they presented their individual outlines, there were significant discussions on the benefits and drawbacks of an objects-first approach verses an objects-later approach. The course outline we ended up adopting and using for our assignments could be described as an objects-early one. The students and instructors came to a consensus on the outline which was displayed on a side board in our classroom/lab for the entire course. We referred to the outline throughout the course, and students were required to work in pairs, writing unit plans for some of the units. Each unit plan included lesson plans, quizzes, tests, lab assignments, and programming assignments. To facilitate discussion and to help us emphasize concepts over language details (although there were plenty of language detail discussions throughout the course), some of the unit plans were written for a Java-based course and some for a Snap!-based one. At least one student for each unit planning pair had completed our methods of teaching mathematics course so they were familiar with unit and lesson planning. The writing and presentation of the unit plans were extremely valuable parts of the course experience.

3.3 Readings

Reading assignments for the course included Jeanette Wing's seminal article on Computational Thinking [13], an article on objects-first versus objects-later approaches [7], sections from the CSTA K-12 CS Standards report [4], and web-based information about the CS Principles course [2]. We asked students to come prepared with at least three questions/comments about each reading and we devoted some class time to discussing the readings. The readings exposed the students to ideas about CS and its teaching that they would not typically encounter in other CS course work. In particular they helped provide valuable context for the ongoing multifaceted efforts at broadening introductory CS education.

One topic that came up in multiple discussions, motivated in part by our experience in the first offering of the course, was the extent to which the current AP CS course focuses on Java idiosyncrasies potentially at the expense of fundamental CS concepts. Both the Wing article and the CS Principles readings helped launch interesting discussions on this topic. The CS Principles reading also formed the basis for some questions on the final exam, in which we asked students to reflect on whether they would rather teach the traditional AP CS course or the upcoming CS Principles course. More detailed questions related to the CS Principles reading were also on the exam (e.g., developing specific exercises to match specific "Big Ideas" and learning objectives within the CS Principles framework).

3.4 Coding Exercises and Code Reviews

Both the first and second offerings of the course utilized code exercises taken from problem sets used at our annual local high school programming contest. Typically, the contest consists of seven problems of increasing difficulty:

1. A simple problem involving expressions
2. A problem that involves conditionals
3. An iteration problem that involves nested loops
4. A one-dimensional array problem
5. A two-dimensional array problem
6. A complex data structure / algorithmic problem
7. A recursive problem

We used problems 1-4 from three previous high school contests as coding exercises for our students. These problems were useful in having our students consider the complexity of introducing computer science concepts and programming to high school students. They emphasized algorithmic thinking and illuminated the multiple approaches students can take

Table 2: Pre- and post-survey results on teaching an AP CS course.

	2013 Offering		2014 Offering	
	pre	post	pre	post
1. Rate your interest in teaching a HS AP CS course [10 - extremely interested, 5 - neutral, 0 - extremely uninterested]	4	4.4	5	6.5
2. Suppose you are given the choice of teaching either a HS AP Calculus or HS AP CS course. Rate your preference. [10 - strong preference for CS, 5 - neutral, 0 - strong preference for Calculus]	3	3.2	2.75	5.25
3. Rate how prepared you are to teach a HS AP CS course. [10 - extremely prepared, 7 - well prepared, 4 - somewhat prepared, 0 - not prepared]	2.9	4.2	3	5
4. Rate your Java programming skills. [10 - excellent, 5 adequate, 0 - poor]	3.8	5.8	4	5

Table 3: Post-survey results on teaching an introductory CS course with Java.

	2013 Offering	2014 Offering
1. Rate your interest in teaching an introductory HS CS course with Java [10 - extremely interested, 5 - neutral, 0 - extremely uninterested]	6	7.5
2. Suppose you are given the choice of teaching either a HS algebra or an introductory HS CS course with Java. Rate your preference. [10 - strong preference for CS, 5 - neutral, 0 - strong preference for Calculus]	2.4	4.5
3. Rate how prepared you are to teach an introductory HS CS course with Java [10 - extremely prepared, 7 - well prepared, 4 - somewhat prepared, 0 - not prepared]	5.8	6.25
4. Degree to which methods course improved ability to teach intro. HS CS with Java [10 - greatly improved, 7 - improved, 4 somewhat improved, 0 - did not improve]	5.5	7.25
5. Degree to which methods course increased interest in teaching intro. HS CS with Java [10 - greatly improved, 7 - increased, 4 - no change, 0 - did not improve]	5.5	7.5
6. Degree to which methods course improved knowledge of Java [10 - greatly improved, 7 - improved, 4 - somewhat improved, 0 - did not improve]	5.4	3.25

on programming assignments. In the first offering of the course, students worked individually on these problems, but in the second offering of the course we utilized more team learning and frequently had students work in pairs.

In the second offering, we also introduced a second programming environment, known as Snap!, from the University of California-Berkeley. An offshoot of the successful Scratch programming environment, Snap! is a visual, drag-and-drop programming language with a full set of control structures necessary for developing computational thinking skills. Class time was allotted for groups to become familiar with the Snap! environment. Students implemented solutions to the programming problems in both Snap! and Java and were able to draw parallels and identify differences between the two languages.

For each of the assignments (either in Java or Snap!), a code review was held. Based on feedback from the first course offering in which the students cited the value of the code reviews, we increased our use of them in the second offering. Students presented their code to the class and explained why coding decisions were made. Instructors and other students would comment on various issues such as documentation, correctness, readability, and efficiency (both in terms of code length and algorithmic performance). In this way, they saw the variety of approaches to solving a problem and could compare/contrast the programming decisions made.

3.5 Guest Speaker and High School Visit

A part of the course that was especially well-received by our students was our collaboration with a local CS high school teacher. In the first course offering, the teacher led a two hour session with the students in which she discussed and answered questions about her highly successful CS program. She started a CS program at her high school in 2009 with 20 students, and in five years she had increased this to 88 students, 38% of whom were female. In addition, 74% of her students who took the AP CS exam earned a score of 4 or 5. Her presentation was so informative and popular that in the second offering of the course, we embraced her suggestion of having our students visit her CS classroom and having her lead additional sessions which we describe here.

On our classroom visit, we observed two CS classes near the end of the school year – an AP CS Java programming class and a pilot class for the AP CS Principles course that is being developed. One thing that our students noted and were impressed by was that most of both (80 minute) class periods consisted of the high school students engaged in self-directed project work. In both classes, the students were creating final projects of their own design and implementing them using Greenfoot, Python, or the Lego Mindstorm system. Several of our students had already done observations of high school mathematics classes and commented on how much more engaging the CS class was compared to the mathematics classes they had observed.

The high school teacher also led three sessions with our students (in our classroom at the college) on topics which included how CS helps achieve mathematics educational goals, her two-year CS course sequence that prepares students to take the AP CS exam, the AP CS Principles course, her efforts to start, equip, and maintain a vibrant CS program, and her efforts in the recruitment of CS students, in particular female students. The difficulties of launching CS education in a high school entirely devoid of it (and in a state with no CS-certified teachers) was a valuable discussion for our students: these are some of the curricular and political realities they will face in the workplace if they want to expand the pipeline, and learning from the high school teacher's experience gives them tools to do this.

3.6 Linking CS to Common Core State Standards for Mathematical Practice (CCSSMP)

A major goal of our course was developing teachers who will be savvy enough to design CS courses which will be approved by their schools and to teach them. The high school teacher who assisted with our course described how she has developed a program at her high school which includes introductory Java classes, two sections of AP CS, and a pilot section of the proposed AP CS Principles course. We will share one aspect of her approach which is to convince colleagues and administrators in the mathematics program about how CS enhances the teaching of CCSSMP. The eight practice standards listed below are part of the core curriculum in mathematics for every grade level K-12:

1. Make sense of problems and persevere in solving them.
2. Reason abstractly and quantitatively.
3. Construct viable arguments and critique the reasoning of others.
4. Model with mathematics.
5. Use appropriate tools strategically.
6. Attend to precision.
7. Look for and make use of structure.
8. Look for and express regularity in repeated reasoning.

Our students became convinced that CS was an excellent vehicle for teaching these standards through an exercise that mapped CS topics to these standards. They understood that even students who were less than interested in their mathematics classes might develop these practices in a CS setting.

3.7 AP Exam

In the first iteration of the course, we administered the multiple choice portion of a sample AP exam. We did this first on the second day of class and again at the end of the course. As previously noted, it was clear from the subsequent attitudes and discussions that administering a test on the second day for which they were unprepared did not meet our goal of building confidence in teaching programming. While we still think it is important for the students to be able to teach and appreciate such a course, we eliminated a full administration of the AP exam in the second iteration of the course. In its place, we spread a variety of multiple-choice questions throughout the course to make the future teachers aware of the kinds of questions asked on the AP CS exam regarding that day's topics. We also discussed the questions in more detail: what makes a question useful (or useless) for measuring a student's abilities in a particular area, etc. This approach achieved our goals of learning about the current AP CS exam as just one potential goal of a high school CS education, and did so without discouraging the students early in the course.

4. SURVEY RESULTS AND IMPACT

To help evaluate the effectiveness of the CS methods course, we had our students complete pre- and post-surveys to measure changes in their preferences and perceptions. The survey consisted of four questions to which the students responded on a scale from 0 to 10. The questions asked about the students' levels of interest in teaching an AP CS course, the degree to which they felt prepared to teach AP CS, and their self-assessment of their Java programming skills. Table 2 contains the questions and the mean responses. Although our small sample size (9 students, 5 in 2013 and 4 in 2014) does not allow for calculating statistical significance, the trends in the mean responses are very encouraging.

The survey results show that after both offerings of the course, the students' interest (as measured by questions 1 and 2) and confidence (as measured by question 3) in teaching AP CS increased. With the changes we implemented in the second course offering, we were pleased to see a markedly larger increase from the pre- to the post-survey results on questions 1-3 in 2014 as compared to 2013. For example, question 2 measures the students' preference for teaching AP CS or AP Calculus if given a choice of teaching either. Students responded on a 0-10 scale (0 = strong preference for AP Calculus, 10 = strong preference for AP CS). In 2013, there was only a 6% shift in preference towards AP CS after taking the methods course. In 2014, however, there was a 90% shift in preference towards AP CS. Similarly, question 1 shows their interest in teaching an AP CS course increased by 10% after the first offering and by 30% percent after the second. For question 4, which has the students assess their Java programming skills, it is not surprising to us that this did not increase by as much in the second offering due to our shift in emphasis away from Java programming and the AP CS exam.

We included six additional questions on the post-survey that were not on the pre-survey. These questions were added primarily to measure the students' desire to teach an introductory high school CS course, rather than an AP CS course. The questions and the average responses are shown in Table 3. On questions 1-5, the mean responses show that the students in the 2014 offering of the course had more interest in teaching and felt better prepared to teach an introductory high school CS course as compared to the students in the 2013 offering. The average response to question 6, which asked the degree to which the methods course improved their Java programming skills, was lower in 2014 than it was in 2013, but again we are not surprised given the curriculum changes we made.

Other impacts of our unique Noyce Scholarship grant program have been significant. Despite advisement to do so, in the 12 years previous to our grant, only 4 out of 65 mathematics majors earning secondary teaching certification completed a strong minor in computer science which included courses in data structures and analysis of algorithms. With our Noyce program, 14 out of 20 students in a four year period will have not only completed the strong CS minor but will have also completed our methods of teaching CS course. Significantly, 11 of these 14 students (78%) are females.

5. CONCLUSIONS, FUTURE WORK, AND RECOMMENDATIONS

In this paper, we describe a new CS methods course that is unique in that it targets mathematics education majors having some prior coursework in computer science, with the goal of preparing them and increasing their level of interest in starting/teaching content-rich high school CS courses. Based on our experiences, survey results, and student comments, our second offering of the course was more successful than the first and this improved version of the course furthers the capabilities and confidence of the students to teach CS at the secondary level.

A course similar to ours could be offered at any college or university that has a mathematics education program and CS faculty willing to help address the inadequacy of the current CS education pipeline. We took advantage of the Noyce opportunity to launch the course, but with sufficient student interest and staffing, it could be taught at any time of the year, with or without the Noyce grant to entice students. We have initially taught it as a CS topics course, but it could evolve (here or elsewhere) into a regular course in the curriculum. Our students also benefited from learning and teaching in a room with computers available: much hands-on work was required of them, but some of the activities of the course could certainly be completed in a computer-free facility. Having at least one faculty with mathematics education experience involved in the course is highly recommended. Students who have taken at least data structures would be good candidates for such a course.

We plan to continue offering this course for at least the next two years. Future work also includes tracking the course's alumni to see how many of them actually teach CS, what kinds of course(s) they teach in CS, and their experiences with the teaching.

6. ACKNOWLEDGMENTS

This work was supported by a National Science Foundation Robert Noyce Teacher Scholarship Program grant 1136322. We would like to thank Pauline White for allowing us to observe her HS CS classroom and sharing her experiences and expertise with us.

7. REFERENCES

[1] AP program participation and performance data 2013. Retrieved 2014-08-31 from `http://research.collegeboard.org/programs/ap/data/participation/2013`.

[2] CS Principles. Retrieved 2014-08-31 from `http://apcsprinciples.org/`.

[3] CS10K community. Retrieved 2014-08-31 from `http://cs10kcommunity.org/page/about-cs10k-community`.

[4] CSTA K-12 Computer science standards. Retrieved 2014-09-3 from `http://csta.acm.org/Curriculum/sub/CurrFiles/CSTA_K-12_CSS.pdf`.

[5] A. Bruckman, M. Biggers, B. Ericson, T. McKlin, J. Dimond, B. DiSalvo, M. Hewner, L. Ni, and S. Yardi. Georgia computes!: Improving the computing education pipeline. In *Proceedings of the 40th ACM Technical Symposium on Computer Science Education (SIGCSE)*, pages 86–90. ACM, March 2009.

[6] J. Cuny. Transforming high school computing: A call to action. *ACM Inroads*, 3(2):32–36, 2012.

[7] A. Ehlert and C. Schulte. Empirical comparison of objects-first and objects-later. In *ICER*, pages 15–26. ACM.

[8] J. Goode, G. Chapman, and J. Margolis. Beyond curriculum: The exploring computer science program. *ACM Inroads*, 3(2):47–53, 2012.

[9] O. Hazzan, T. Lapidot, and N. Ragonis. *Guide to Teaching Computer Science: An Activity-Based Approach*. Springer, 2011.

[10] L. Kaczmarczyk and R. Dopplick. 2014. Rebooting the Pathway to Success: Preparing Students for Computing Workforce Needs in the United States. A report by The Association for Computing Machinery. Retrieved 2014-09-1 from `http://pathways.acm.org/ACM_pathways_report.pdf`.

[11] K. Lang, R. Galanos, J. Goode, D. Seehorn, F. Trees, P. Phillips, and C. Stephenson. 2013. Bugs in the System: Computer Science Teacher Certification in the U.S. A report by The Computer Science Teachers Association and The Association for Computing Machinery. Retrieved 2014-08-31 from `http://csta.acm.org/ComputerScienceTeacherCertification/sub/CSTA_BugsInTheSystem.pdf`.

[12] J. Lui, E. Hasson, Z. Barnett, and P. Zhang. A survey on computer science K-12 outreach: Teacher training programs. In *Frontiers in Education Conference (FIE)*, pages T4F-1 – T4F-6. IEEE.

[13] J. M. Wing. Computational thinking. *Comm. ACM*, 49(3):33–35, March 2006.

[14] A. Yadav and J. Kor. Learning to teach computer science: The need for a methods course. *Comm. ACM*, 55(11):31–33, November 2012.

Using a Message Board as a Teaching Tool in an Introductory Cyber-Security Course

Raymond Greenlaw, Christopher Brown, Zachary Dannelly, and Andrew Phillips
United States Naval Academy
Annapolis, Maryland 21402
410-293-6806
greenlaw@usna.edu

Sarah Standard
AVIAN LLC
22111 Three Notch Rd
Lexington Park, MD 20653
301-866-2070 x 156
sarah.standard@avianllc.com

ABSTRACT
In this work we describe how a *message board* can be used to teach a number of important concepts in cyber security in a novel and hands-on manner. The message board is used daily in class and serves the routine functions of disseminating information to students, offering a forum for interactive discussions, allowing a convenient method to copy and paste complex expressions, providing a venue for class interaction, permitting archiving of information, and serving as a general blackboard. We use the message board to illustrate and teach important cyber-security concepts and common attacks such as the following: authentication and cookies, cross-site scripting and injection attacks, man-in-the-middle attack on public-key cryptography, password selection, and password-file management. From the student-learning perspective the tool appears to work very well. We hope that others can make use of the message board in their lessons or incorporate parts of it to improve the educational experience of their students. The message board can be integrated seamlessly into a class to enhance hands-on learning.

Categories and Subject Descriptors
K.3.2 [**Computers and Education**]: Computer and Information Science Education – *curriculum.*

General Terms
Design and Security.

Keywords
Cyber-security, message board, and teaching tool.

1. INTRODUCTION
We teach a required introductory cyber-security [1] course to freshmen [1]. The concepts in cyber-security often appear abstract and difficult to grasp, especially for a non-technical student or for those who are seeing such concepts for the first time. The course's external mirror site is publicly accessible at http://www.usna.edu/cs/si110. In our course we introduced a message board to help illustrate important cyber-security concepts in a hands-on manner. From the very first days of class, our students begin to use and become comfortable with the message board. The message board display is really just a webpage on the school's intranet. So, students can load the message board by visiting a URL that is associated with the instructor and a given class section. The name of a person posting to the message board is shown in boldface before the post. For example,

Instructor Lee: Please read pages 14–32 in your textbook.
Student Wiley: The key to that Caesar Cipher is 12.

Normally, the words "Instructor" and "Student" are not used, but here are shown for context. The instructor has an account on the message board, and the students setup their own accounts on the message board on an as needed basis. They choose a username and password, and this exercise provides the instructor with an opportunity to introduce the concept of authentication and the jargon associated with it. We give students some basic guidance on password selection such as choosing a long password, not one that is used elsewhere, not one that is susceptible to dictionary attacks, not one that will embarrass them if it is displayed in front of the class, and so on. The message board is also useful for providing links for the students to click on and also complex expressions to students that they can cut-and-paste. For example,

Instructor Lee: Enter this command in your shell to generate a public/private key pair: openssl genrsa -out keypair.pem 2048

The students can simply copy and paste the shell command and so do not need to type it in. Additionally, the instructor can prepare material and post it to the message board before class. For example, calculations to compute the number of passwords of a given length meeting standard password requirements can be input to the message board and discussed in class. This preparation can save class time, and it also is a good way to test things out before class. Students can also post responses to questions, as the example shown earlier indicated.

In addition to the routine uses of the message board described, which are beneficial to help the students become familiar and comfortable with the tool, we use the message board for teaching more-advanced, cyber-security concepts. The advantage of this approach is that students see that the message board is a real tool that it is useful, but that it can also be attacked. Once the students have a good grasp of the message board and are familiar with it, the message board helps give context and familiarity to their learning of cyber-security concepts. Our approach shares some things in common with the classic approach of using a capture-the-flag-type exercise to teach concepts in cyber-security [2-4].

2. MESSAGE BOARD ARCHITECTURE
The message board makes use of HTML forms, for example, there is a text box input field and a post-message button. During a 110-minute lab, we describe the architecture of the message board to

[1] Note that in this paper we use the terms *cyber-security* and *information assurance* interchangeably.

SIGCSE'15, March 04–07, 2015, Kansas City, MO, USA.
ACM 978-1-4503-2966-8/15/03…$15.00
http://dx.doi.org/10.1145/2676723.2677221

the students as below, and explain to them that many websites have a similar architecture.

1. The user *smith* goes to: http://www.server.edu/~jones/msg/mb.html and enters "Hello World!" (See box below.)
2. The user presses the post message button; the browser sends a "GET" request with URL for a new page: http://www.server.edu/~jones/msg/mb.cgi?msg=Hello+World!
3. The server executes the script mb.cgi with input *Hello World.* The script modifies the file mb.html by inserting <b>smith</b>: Hello World! into the body of the HTML code. The message is inserted character-by-character prefaced by the user's username (in bold).

mb.html as rendered by browser	**mb.html** HTML code

```
<html>
<body>
<h1>Message Board</h1>
<hr>
  <form action="mb.cgi">
    <input type="text" name="msg">
    <input type="button"
        onclick="submit()" value="post message">
  </form>
</body>
</html>
```

4. The server then sends the browser simple HTML code that redirects it back to mb.html (that is, document.location = http://www.server.edu/~jones/msg/mb.html).
5. The browser displays the new version of mb.html.

mb.html as rendered by browser	**mb.html** HTML code

```
<html>
<body>
<h1>Message Board</h1>
<hr>
<b>smith</b>: Hello World!<br>
  <form action="mb.cgi">
    <input type="text" name="msg">
    <input type="button" onclick="submit()"
        value="post message">
  </form>
</body>
</html>
```

Students learn that clicking a button to submit an HTML form triggers an action on a web server, and a program is run that returns a new webpage. For this specific HTML form, the emphasis is that the message board script redirects the user back to the same message board, which has now been updated to include the user's post.

Armed with this level of understanding of the message board operation and architecture, the instructor uses the remainder of the lab to demonstrate and teach students about authentication, cookies, injection attacks, and cross-site scripting attacks. The instructor also explains methods to protect a website or yourself against these attacks. Students learn about sanitizing user input through escaping special characters and user awareness and responsibility are stressed.

3. AUTHENTICATION & COOKIES

In our introductory cyber-security class students learn the five pillars of Information Assurance (IA): confidentiality, integrity, availability, non-repudiation, and authentication [1]. They learn tools that can help strengthen the IA pillars, and they learn that an attack must defeat the tools and violate the pillars. The importance of password complexity and length are illustrated and reinforced throughout the course, and the message board plays an important role in these lessons. In one of the first lectures the instructor demonstrates the message board as a tool to disseminate information. But it is usually not until the 110-minute lab following prior lessons on HTML, client-side, server-side scripting and HTML forms where students are asked to create an account on the message board.

On the new account creation page, the students are given a text area where they can enter a username – it is another HTML form with a password input field, as well as a create account button. This HTML form however uses a different method to send data to the server, POST. Although the POST method is not specifically taught in the course, a discussion is held regarding the difference between POST and GET and how webserver logs store GET requests, with the URL requested, IP address, and date/time of request. The instructor points out that if the method for sending your password to the server was GET, then your password would be a part of the URL and therefore vulnerable via eavesdropping, as well as someone accessing the server logs. Therefore, the POST method, which does not log the URL in the server logs, helps to strengthen the pillar of authentication. The instructor also explains that since the message board is not using HTTPS, their passwords are part of the HTTP request, and thus still in danger of being seen by eavesdroppers

The students discover, as they create their usernames and passwords, that there is no strict input checking of usernames, and no restrictions on a username, other than that the username has not already been selected. Similarly, there are no requirements for the password. Even introductory students are somewhat surprised by the lack of requirements, as they are used to conforming to multiple rules and having to type in an initial password two times for verification when registering on most websites. The omission of rules that a password must conform to on the message board provides us with a good teaching opportunity to discuss the utility of such password rules: length of password, use of special symbols, uppercase letters, characters different from last password, and so on. We explain that these features of a password, which many web sites require, are enforced by sites to help strengthen the IA pillar of authentication because a password which is long, unique to the site, and uses random characters, will be difficult to guess.

We also use the message board to define and illustrate the use of cookies. Users do not want to have to enter a username and password to the browser each time that they make a request to a web server. So, the browser handles this requirement on behalf of the user by saving and sending the user's credentials in cookies. We show the students how to display their cookies using the browser tools (Figure 1). We explain that servers store information on users' machines in the form of cookies and that some cookies can be used to track the websites that a user visits. It is usually at this point of the lab, after the instructor has displayed, via the projector, their own cookies to the class, that one or more students successfully authenticate to the message board as the instructor demonstrating a weakness in basic authentication methods. The instructor also demonstrates how to delete stored cookies on a computer and how to prevent cookies from being stored, leading to a reminder of a recurring course theme: the tradeoff between security and functionality. The discussion of cookies is a good lead-in to our next topic in the lab of injection and cross-site scripting attacks.

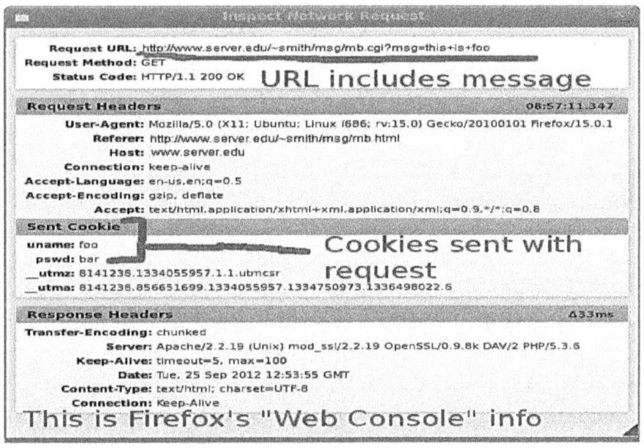

Figure 1: Demonstrating the cookies in the web browser and server communication.

4. INJECTION ATTACKS AND CSS

In step 3 of the architectural process described in section 2 students learn that characters they type into the input field for the form are literally inserted into the message-board file. Thus, they learn and experiment with injecting HTML into the message-board posts to spruce them up. The initial posts by students contain bold or underlined text, followed by color and images or youtube video embeds. Since the instructor's message board is usually displayed on a screen in front of the class, all students can see and build on what other students are doing. Due to the design and coding of the message board, the page can be easily cleared (reset) using a shell on the server and executing the configuration command *./mbconf clear*. This command retains the user accounts, but removes all prior posts from the mb.html file, thus clearing the message board. Instructors issue the clear command anytime the message board is too cluttered or if a successful injection attack has rendered the page unavailable. In this lab, the clear command is invaluable because eventually, someone will enter some JavaScript coded HTML such as:

```
<script type="text/javascript">var i = 0; while (i < 100) { document.write("I'm cool! "); i = i + 1; }</script>
```

This code will result in "I'm cool!" being printed on the message board 100 times. Students sometimes forget the closing tags for HTML, such as the closing script tag, the closing underline, or a closing anchor tag. These errors serve as valuable teaching opportunities as well since humans make these types of mistakes. The result can render the message board inaccessible to posts, or just result in everything being underlined or everything being clickable after the starting tag that was never closed. Either a student figures out, or the instructor demonstrates to the students, how to execute a successful denial-of-service attack by bringing down the message board with an infinite loop, or redirecting the message board to another site. Typing

```
<script type="text/javascript">
document.location="http://www.myserver.edu";</script>
```

redirects the message board to myserver, attacking the IA pillar of availability. After the first successful denial of service attack, the message board is cleared. Injection attacks and message board clearing continue in order to allow each student the opportunity to attack. Then, to demonstrate the concept of reflection, the instructor injects:

```
<script type="text/javascript">alert(document.cookie);</script>
```

This reinforces the point that each browser is storing their cookie for the message board and leads nicely into using the message board to demonstrate the idea of a cross-site scripting attack. In this demo the professor sends an email with an enticing HTML attachment to an unsuspecting student, or to all students in the section. When a student opens the attachment, the student's message-board login credentials are used to post a message to the message board. For example, a message is posted as follows: **Student:** *My professor is a real doofus!*

Since the professor is normally projecting the message board on a screen to the entire class, everyone sees this message or multiple messages if many students opened the attachment. The student who unknowingly posted the message denies having posted such a message. Everyone has a good laugh, and students then see how opening an email from a phishing attack can have undesirable consequences. And, a discussion of more-serious consequences such as stolen personal information, credit-card information, or banking credentials ensues.

A second cross-site scripting attack is conducted where the students are encouraged to enter a message on the message board while the instructor also posts a message. The instructor's post appears to simply be an image; however the image is being served by a simple webserver running on the instructor's computer. The HTML post by the instructor also contains JavaScript:

```
Here's a nice kitten picture:
<script type="text/javascript">document.write('<img
src="http://10.53.21.171/cutekitten.jpg?' + document.cookie +
'" width = "300">');</script>
```

The student sees Figure 2.

Figure 2: Innocent looking cross-site scripting attack.

The instructor then begins announcing the passwords for every student by reading the webserver log for the server running on the instructor computer, demonstrating another weakness in authentication. The instructor also explains how these two attacks could be combined so that instead of posting "My professor is a real doofus" unknowingly to the message board, the student instead posts the kitten image and therefore, without even having access to the site, the attacker can steal the cookies for all users on such a site.

To end the lab, the instructor discusses the importance of sanitizing inputs and how to accomplish this task by escaping the symbols used to denote HTML tags, the < and > symbols. Students are reminded of the importance of sanitizing input at the source of the script (server-side sanitizing for server-side scripts). The instructor then uses the configuration script on the server to impose server-side sanitizing of user input by executing the configuration command *./mbconf escapeall*. The students test to see that the symbols < and > are indeed not treated as HTML tags, but instead are simply characters in their posts.

5. DEMONSTRATION OF MITM ATTACK ON PUBLIC-KEY

The message board is very useful for the encryption lessons taught in the course [1]. Students learn about both symmetric (secret key) and asymmetric (public key) encryption. The message board is used in these lessons to allow students to send each other encrypted messages and as a primary tool for recognizing the limitation of symmetric encryption – sharing a secret key in a public space, such as the message board. After these lessons, the students have a 110-minute lab focused on the public key infrastructure, digital certificates, and the X.509 system. In order to motivate the need for the public key infrastructure system, the lab begins with an instructor led demonstration of a man-in-the-middle attack on public-key encryption algorithms. A man-in-the-middle attack involves three parties: Bob, Alice, and Eve. Bob and Alice are attempting to communicate securely, while a third party Eve is trying to eavesdrop on the conversation.

In the asymmetric encryption lesson, students learned to use an RSA asymmetric-encryption tool. They are able to generate their own public-private key pairs and to send or receive encrypted messages. In a hands-on exercise, students work together in groups of two. Suppose students Mary and Sue are one such group. Each student generates a personal key pair and posts her public key on the message board.

Mary, for example, can then post an encrypted message for Sue and vice versa. Students learn that they can use the public key of someone to send that person an encrypted, confidential message that only the receiver can decrypt with their private key. Similarly, they also learn that they can instead encrypt a message with their own private key, but that anyone could decrypt the message using the sender's public key, and that this would provide some level of certainty that the message came from the sender, the owner of the private key that is paired with the public key shared. Combining the two methods where the sender encrypts first with their own private key, and then encrypts the result with the receiver's public key, provides confidential, authenticated communication.

The receiver of the message can then decrypt the message using their own private key first and then decrypt again using the sender's public-key retrieved from the message board. This exercise helps students to become familiar with key pairs and some basic concepts in public-key encryption, and serves as a warm-up to the more-complex, man-in-the-middle attack. .

In the man-in-the-middle attack demonstration using the message board, the instructor sets up two separate message boards. Both of these message boards are displayed to the class. In this case we will call the two students, Alice and Bob, and the professor, Eve. On message board 1 we have the following exchange between Alice and Eve, who is impersonating Bob:

Alice: here is my public-key
Bob: here is my public-key

On message board 2 a similar exchange takes place between Bob and Eve, who in this case is impersonating Alice. Next Alice sends an encrypted message to Bob via message board 1.

Alice: message encrypted with Alice's private key, and then encrypted again using Bob's public key from message board 1 (which is really Eve's Public Key)

Eve retrieves the message, decrypts the message using first her own Private key, and then using Alice's public-key and is able to read the message. Eve then re-encrypts the message using her private key, and encrypts again using the public key for Bob from message board 2. She then posts the cipher to message board 2 for Bob. Bob then decrypts the cipher using his private key and then again using the public key that he thought he got from Alice, and since he is able to decrypt the message successfully, he assumes that the message came from Alice. He is not aware that Eve has just executed a man-in-the-middle attack. The student, who is playing the role of Bob, then sends a message back to Alice, and again Eve (the professor) is able to perform a successful man-in-the-middle attack. This demonstration shows students in a hands-on fashion how a man-in-the-middle attack works. Students then break into groups of three with one student playing the role of Eve. The exercise helps them to understand public-key encryption and matched-key pairs, as well as the vulnerabilities in distributing keys. The demonstration provides a justification for why a trusted third party, a certificate authority, that both Alice and Bob trust, is needed to certify that a public key really belongs to the identity sharing the public key. Therefore, Eve could not claim to be Bob, or Alice and would not be able to pull off the man-in-the-middle attack.

6. PASSWORD FILE ITEMS

6.1 Introduction

After the students have been introduced to cryptographic hashing, they experiment with generating an md5 hash for strings in the Windows shell. The instructor emphasizes that when you hash a specific string, the resulting hash value will always be the same. Changing just one bit, or one byte, or one character, yields an entirely different hash value. As an introduction to the password activity, instructors explain that hashes allow us to check the integrity of a message, that is, check that the message has not been tampered with, even without a copy of the "original" message. In the setting of passwords, this means that we can check a password without ever storing a copy of the password, which is important for security.

Students are directed to connect to their virtual machines in the course's virtual sandbox for the password activity. The virtual environment is used for this activity due to the password cracking tools that are provided to the students to use during the activity. The information technology department will not support providing the password cracking tools to students on their actual laptops. Within the virtual environment, students see the same version of the message board that is normally used. The instructor issues the command *./mbconf init insecure escapeall*, which will initializes the message board—clearing all settings that were in place, removing file-permission protection on the password file, and escaping the characters "<" and ">" to protect from injection attacks. All of these functionalities are included in the coding of the message board. The students are directed to the virtual environment's message board and to create a new account on that message board, choosing a password not used anywhere else.

6.2 Plaintext Passwords

As soon as all of the students have created an account and posted an innocuous message, the instructor encourages students to view the message board's raw HTML source. The instructor then reviews how the message board uses a server-side script, mb.cgi, and suggests trying to view the script by requesting the file from the server using the browser's address bar. The question is then posed to the students, "Is there a file mentioned within the mb.cgi script that might be of interest?" Invariably, a student will spot the pswd.txt file within the lines of the mb.cgi file:

```
# read & store passwd file
open(PWF,"< pswd.txt");
```

The students then are reminded that pswd.txt is also a file on the server; therefore, they can send a request for that file to the server using the browser's address bar. After all the students have the password file displayed in their browsers, there is usually a lively discussion regarding the passwords that everyone has used for their accounts.

The instructor explains that since the server is poorly configured, in particular file permissions are not protecting access to this important file, an attacker who finds the file will have every user's password. Students are told that password files get stolen all of the time; Adobe, LinkedIn, Yahoo!, dropbox, and more all had password data stolen and posted on the web. Another example is the rockyou.com break in where 40 million user passwords were stored in an accessible plaintext file, such as pswd.txt for the message board. The instructor then displays the top 20 passwords in the rockyou.com dictionary with the count included for how many users were using the password; see Figure 3 for the top 5.

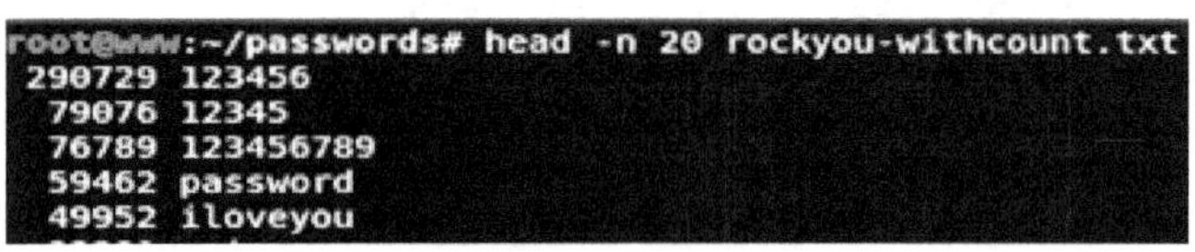

Figure 3: Display of top 5 passwords from rockyou.com site when the password file was stolen: # of occurrences/password.

The instructor points out that a server owner should not risk storing user passwords on the machine because the consequences are catastrophic if someone breaks in, and suggests that we need a way to verify a password without actually storing that password. The instructor explains that if a server stores the password's hash value, instead of the actual password, then if the password file is stolen, the attacker only gets password hashes, and thus hashing passwords enhances the site's security for users. A review of hashing is then performed in the virtual environment, which is Linux. Students learn how to compute the md5 hash of a string in a Linux shell.

Figure 4: Stolen password file showing hashes.

6.3 Hashed Passwords

The instructor then issues the command *./mbconf hash* which clears the message board accounts, the message board itself, and implements computing hashes and storing hashes for passwords in the password file. Again, the hash functionality is included in the coding of the message board. Once again, students are told to create an account on the message board, and post a message. They are then encouraged to steal the password file again. They now see the hashes instead of the plaintext passwords, Figure 4. Students are directed to compute the md5 hash of their password to confirm that the displayed hash value is in fact their password's hash value. If any hash values are identical within the password file, as with student 2 and student 5 in Figure 4, the instructor points out that this indicates the two users probably used the same password!

The instructor poses another question, "what if after I stole this password file, I really wanted to find the password for student 3, what would I have to do?" The class discusses using the list of rockyou.com passwords and going though that list, hashing each password to see if the hash matches student 3's stored hash value. This is defined for the students as a "dictionary attack" where the rockyou.com list is the "dictionary." We explain that we will use a program to more efficiently perform the hashing and comparing process using a file that stores the pre-computed hashes of all of the rockyou.com passwords. The course program on their virtual machines, called dcrackT, performs a dictionary attack using the pre-computed rockyou.com dictionary of hashes, and a hash that the student provides to the program. Students are assigned the user hash above theirs in the password file (the instructor targets the hash of the student on the bottom of the list), and they perform the dictionary attack on that hash value, Figure 5.

Figure 5: Dictionary attack on a hash from the password file.

At this point, many of the students, although they saw the top 20 passwords from the rockyou.com list, still did not create a more-complex password because they did not anticipate the password hashes were going to be cracked. Approximately half or more of the passwords are successfully and quickly cracked using the dictionary attack. The instructor then discusses how an attacker might perform a brute-force attack to try to crack the passwords that were not in the dictionary by trying all-possible passwords, up to the length that the site allows (starting with the minimum that the site requires). The instructor then defines *rainbow tables* for the students, explaining that these are lists of pre-computed hashes for brute-force attacks.

Finally, the instructor describes the basics of the LinkedIn break in where the passwords were hashed, but still a large number were cracked using the rockyou.com dictionary, and many critics were disappointed that LinkedIn did not use another common technique, *salting* passwords. The instructor describes what salt is and how it is different for every user, randomly assigned, and concatenated to the password prior to hashing and explains that the password file stores the username, hash value of the password+salt, and the salt assigned for each user.

6.4 Salted Passwords

The instructor then issues the command *./mbconf salt* that clears the message board accounts, the message board itself, and implements salt in the password file. The salt functionality is included in the coding of the message board. Once again, students are told to create an account on the message board, and post a message. They are then encouraged to steal the password file again. They now see a hash and salt, Figure 6. The instructor points out that now if two users happen to have the same password, no two hashes will be the same since the salt is randomly assigned and is unique for each user. Thus the computed hash of the password+salt will always be different. Students are directed to compute the md5 hash of their password+salt for their username, to confirm that the displayed hash value is in fact a hash of their password+salt.

Figure 6: Password file showing salt and hash of password + salt.

The instructor reminds the students that the dictionary attack with dcrackT will not work at this point because the tool used pre-computed password hashes with no salt. Another program is available to the students, called drack, which will take the hash and the salt values for a specific user and use the plaintext rockyou.com passwords. The program will calculate the hash of the rockyou.com password + the provided salt, and compare the result to the provided hash. Students are again assigned to attack, and the attack takes longer, because the program must first concatenate the salt to each of the rockyou.com passwords before hashing and then compare the result to the given hash value. The instructor explains that using salt slows down the attacker's speed of cracking password hashes. The instructor then summarizes the responsibilities of a website in protecting user passwords: a) Hash passwords, b) Salt passwords, and c) Protect the password file.

6.5 Keylogger Demonstration

The instructor now issues the command *./mbconf init salt secure escapeall* that initializes the message board, clears the message board itself, implements hashing and salt for the password file, sets the file permissions on the password file, and escapes the "<" and ">" characters to protect from injection attacks. Students are told that the instructor has done their part to protect passwords and students now also need to do their part by choosing a strong password. At the start of the lesson, unbeknownst to the students, the instructor has activated key loggers that are running on the student virtual machines to record their key strokes. Now that the students think they are protected from the password file being stolen and understand how to create a strong password, the instructor selects one of the student user names and reads (from the key-logger files) the student's password. A discussion follows about how servers doing their part protecting files, hashing, salting, and users doing their part choosing strong passwords, is only the beginning. The instructor concludes the password activity by defining more techniques or methods: online attacks, offline attacks, password stretching, site-wide salt, throttling, and in particular, multi-factor authentication.

7. STUDENT PERSPECTIVE

As a student in the introductory cyber-security class, I would like to share the student perspective on the use of the message board as a teaching tool for cyber-security concepts. One of the most-difficult challenges in an educational environment is to find methods that allow us to focus on subjects that are hard to relate to in everyday life. Few students, including myself, find much satisfaction in learning about the tendencies for cytosine and guanine to bond, yet most would have an interest in learning about good investment strategies as an application is much easier to identify. When applied to cyber-security, this effect is greatly multiplied. The use of a message board in classroom discussions helps students visualize places to utilize the lessons and in turn elevates their interest in the class as whole.

As students, we engage in discussion more readily when we can draw from personal experience, and in our digital world, message-board usage is an area of expertise. From search engines like Google to Social media like Facebook and Twitter, we are inundated with boxes and fields waiting to be filled. Login screens are so ingrained in our daily operations that we usually see them as a nuisance rather than a security measure. We give little thought to how and why a computer knows that we typed in the correct password with our username, until our instructor shows the class the message board's unsecured password files. Suddenly, a flood of questions and suspicions fill the class discussion. We must now ponder how our instructor so easily accessed what we thought to be impenetrable, and examine if the same vulnerabilities lay within the programs that we trust on a daily basis to hold some of our most-personal information. We are able to engage a much-more meaningful discussion about password validation when we can see it in a context that we understand.

A final point, and I would argue most-powerful function of the message board is the hands-on programming it offers to students. My favorite exercise using the message board is the injection-attack testing. Students, some with little knowledge of computers outside of running Internet browsers, are able to carry out elaborate attacks on the message board to deface it, crash it, or redirect it to other addresses. This thrill of success validates the cliché: "With knowledge comes power—and power is addicting."

8. SUMMARY

We have described many but not all of our hands-on uses of the message board as a teaching tool in our introductory cyber-security class. Our experience is that both instructors and students benefit from the using the message board. We continue to refine our lessons using the message board and hope that others will be able to make use of the message board in their classes.

REFERENCES

1. Brown, C. et al 2012. Anatomy, Dissection, and Mechanics of an Introductory Cyber-Security Class's Curriculum at the United States Naval Academy. *ASEE Computers in Education Journal*, 3(3), (Jul.-Sep. 2012), 63–80.
2. Eagle, C. and Clark, J. 2004. *Capture-The-Flag: Learning Computer Security Under Fire.* Naval Post Graduate School. DOI= http://www.dtic.mil/cgi-bin/GetTRDoc?AD=ADA435319.
3. Werther, J., Zhivich, M, and Leek T. (2011). *Experiences In Cyber Security Education: The MIT Lincoln Laboratory Capture-the-Flag Exercise.* Syracuse University. DOI= http://www.cis.syr.edu/~sueo/papers/ace-wecs.pdf.
4. Radcliffe, J. 2007. *Capture the flag for education and mentoring: A case study on the use of competitive games in computer security training.* SANS Institute. DOI= http://www.sans.org/reading-room/whitepapers/casestudies/capture-flag-education-mentoring-33018

Further Evaluations of Industry-Inspired Pair Programming Communication Guidelines with Undergraduate Students

Mark Zarb
School of Computing Science
Robert Gordon University
Aberdeen, Scotland
+44 (0)1224 262 768
m.zarb@rgu.ac.uk

Janet Hughes
School of Computing
University of Dundee
Dundee, Scotland
+44 (0)1382 385 195
j.z.hughes@dundee.ac.uk

John Richards
IBM T.J. Watson Research Center
Yorktown Heights
New York, USA
+1 914 945 2632
ajtr@us.ibm.com

ABSTRACT

Pair programming has several benefits when it is successfully used by students and experts alike. However, research shows that novice pairs find the necessary pair communication to be one of the main challenges in adopting this process. A set of industry-inspired pair programming guidelines have been derived and evaluated from qualitative examinations of expert pairs, with the aim of helping novice programmers communicate within their pair. This research describes a further evaluation of these guidelines with a number of student pairs, and demonstrates how novice pairs who were exposed to the guidelines became comfortable communicating with their partners.

Categories and Subject Descriptors

K.3.2 [**Computer and Information Science Education**]: Computer science education.

General Terms

Measurement, Performance, Experimentation, Human Factors, Standardization.

Keywords

Pair programming; communication skills; software engineering; collaboration; students; CS education research study.

1. INTRODUCTION

Pair programming is a method that describes two programmers working together, usually sharing a keyboard and a computer. Typically, each member of the pair takes on a different role, swapping roles frequently: the driver creates the code while the navigator reviews it [11]. Pair programming requires pairs to communicate frequently, which leads the pair to experience certain benefits over "solo" programming, such as greater enjoyment, and increased knowledge distribution [2].

SIGCSE '15, March 04 - 07 2015, Kansas City, MO, USA
Copyright 2014 ACM 978-1-4503-2966-8/15/03…$15.00
http://dx.doi.org/10.1145/2676723.2677241

Novices find communication to be a barrier when they are pair programming [9, 11], and industry-inspired guidelines have been presented as a possible solution [17]. These guidelines have been evaluated [16], with initial results showing that pairs who had been exposed to the guidelines reported an improved communication experience whilst debugging existing code.

This research presents a follow-up study that evaluates the guidelines with novice pairs beyond debugging. In the study reported in this paper, pairs were responsible for coding solutions to given problems. Therefore the aim is to find out whether these guidelines can have a positive impact on the communication experience of pairs who are actively creating new code.

2. BACKGROUND

Due to the nature of pair programming, communication - both verbal and non-verbal - occurs nearly continuously. Williams and Kessler [12] write that effective communication is "paramount", and Sharp and Robinson [8] describe pairing as a highly communication-intensive process. Within the classroom, pair programming is seen as being generally valuable [1, 12]. Students working in pairs have been found to be more satisfied with their work output, solve problems faster than non-paired students, and have improved team effectiveness. Paired students are also more likely to complete CS courses when compared to their solo counterparts, gain an improved comprehension of unfamiliar topics, and enjoy increased levels of confidence [3, 4, 9, 13, 14].

Many programmers approach their first pairing experience with scepticism, having doubts about their partner's working habits and programming style, and about the added communication demands that this programming style requires [13]. In a pilot study, approximately 50% of first-time novice pair programmers reported that they perceived communication to be the main problem with the pairing process [7]. Many authors simply state that *communication* is an issue; few studies have investigated which aspects of communication within an agile team are most problematic [8, 10].

2.1 Pair Programming Guidelines

Industry-inspired pair programming guidelines had earlier been created with the aim of delivering concise, industry-derived instructions to novice pairs to improve their understanding of successful pair communication. The creation of these guidelines has been previously reported in [15] and [17], with preliminary qualitative studies suggesting that the guidelines could help improve novice pairs' experienced intra-pair communication. A previous study has shown that when debugging code, pairs who were exposed to these guidelines had a more positive communication experience [16].

Appendix 1 provides a summary of these guidelines.

3. EVALUATION

Results obtained from a previous study [16] suggest that use of the guidelines led to an improved communication experience when pairs were engaged in a debugging task. The study reported here aims to understand whether the guidelines could also help improve the communication experience in a task where pairs are creating new code.

Quantitative data was to be gathered, with the following hypotheses as per the original study:

- Exposure to the pair programming guidelines positively impacts the pair's success rate.
- Exposure to the pair programming guidelines leads to an improvement in the pair's ease of communication.
- Exposure to the pair programming guidelines positively affects the way partners contribute to the pairing session.

3.1 Methodology

3.1.1 Materials

One of the summer school programmes at the University of Dundee's School of Computing uses a custom programming tool that has been developed to teach programming topics: the Abstract Programming Environment (APE)[1]. The APE tool runs on the NetBeans IDE and provides a graphical front-end (Figure 1) which can be manipulated using Java code. This allows students to 'see' what they are programming. Note that the contrast in Figure 1 has been adjusted to make the image suitable for printing.

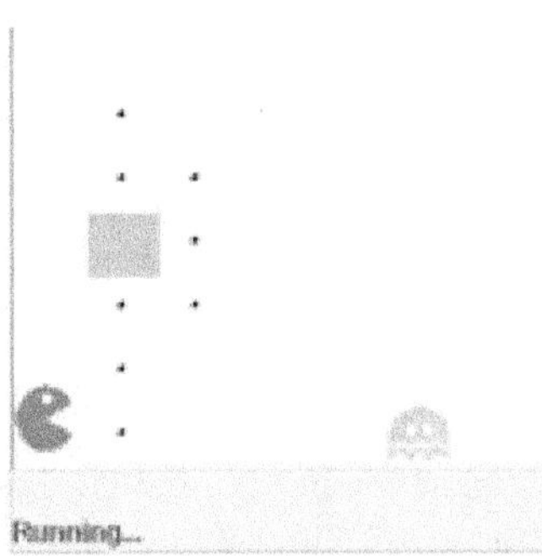

Figure 1: The APE graphical front-end

The APE tool consists of several challenges (or 'maps') in which students need to move the character around, eating a number of dots; students must write this movement using Java code. Once all the dots have been eaten, the 'map' is considered complete, and students can move on to the next one.

[1] The APE tool was created by Heron and Belford (see http://monkeys.imaginary-realities.com) and used with permission.

3.1.2 Participants

Participants were recruited from the School of Computing at the University of Dundee. An e-mail was circulated to all students, asking for their participation in exchange for a small compensation in the form of vouchers. A total of 28 participants were recruited (first-year undergraduates: 10 students; third-year undergraduates: 18 students). All had previously used Java as a programming language as part of their courses.

Pairs were arranged so that each pair consisted of students at the same year of study. Within each year, 50% of the pairs were randomly allocated to a group that would be exposed to the guidelines (n = 7 pairs), leaving the rest of the sample (n = 7 pairs) as a control group.

3.1.2.1 Previous Pairing Experience

Each participant was asked to complete a post-test survey immediately following their participation in the study consisting of questions relating to the individual's experience with solo programming, pair programming, and previous pair programming experience with their session's partner. These results were analysed to understand group tendencies and variance, as reported in Table 1 below and analysed using Mann-Whitney U tests.

Table 1: Students' Programming Experience

	Exposed Group		Non-Exposed Group	
	M	**SD**	**M**	**SD**
Solo Programming Experience (years)	3.7	2.17	2.7	1.86
Pair Programming Experience (years)	0.3	0.59	0.2	0.41

The data show that the groups had somewhat different levels of experience; on average, more individuals in the "exposed" pairs had solo programming experience. This difference may complicate interpreting further results. Few students reported previous experience with pair programming – furthermore, any reported experience was limited to a number of months, or 'since the start of the semester'. Statistical tests were carried out to establish whether the differences between the two groups were significant and whether they might cause the results to be biased:

No significant differences in 'solo' programming experience were found between the experimental and control groups: $U = 125$, $z = 1.266$, $p = 0.227$ ($p > 0.05$).

Similarly, no significant differences in pair programming experience were found between the experimental and control groups: $U = 106.5$, $z = 0.427$, $p = 0.670$ ($p > 0.05$).

While some caution is warranted, these results suggest that further analysis should not be unduly complicated by what appears to be a small difference in prior experience.

3.1.2.2 Perceived Benefits of Pair Programming

Likert scale data from the post-test surveys were analysed to determine whether there were any significant statistical differences reported between the students who were exposed to the guidelines and those who were not.

As each individual completed their own post-test survey, the population consisted of 28 students, 14 of whom were exposed and 14 students who were not.

Shapiro-Wilk tests were carried out to understand whether the data being analysed were normally distributed. *Ease of Communication* scores for both exposed and unexposed groups were not normally distributed ($p < 0.05$). Similarly, scores for *Perceived Partner Contribution* for both groups were not normally distributed ($p < 0.05$). As the data are not normally distributed for both sets of scores, non-parametric tests were used.

Students were asked to rate the statement *'I feel pair programming is more beneficial than solo programming'* on a 5-point Likert scale.

The exposed group (M=4.5, SD=0.52) and the control group (M=4.1, SD=0.62) report similar scores. As observed in previous studies, there was no significant difference in perceived pair programming benefit between exposed students ($Mdn = 4.0$) and unexposed students ($Mdn = 4.5$), $U = 133$, $z = 1.834$, $p = 0.067$.

These results show that following the session, the student perception was that pair programming was more beneficial than solo programming, regardless of whether they were exposed to the guidelines or not.

3.1.3 Procedure

The study was carried out during a 4-week period during the students' second semester of study. Pairs were invited to the test room separately, and on different days. The test room was equipped with one laptop, and consisted of a camera and a voice recorder. Ten APE maps were chosen at random for the students to solve. All pairs were given a maximum time-limit of 45 minutes to solve as many maps as they could in a sequential order. During this time, the recording equipment was switched on, and the researcher left the room.

Pairs were provided with a list of basic instructions to move the character (Table 2), but were free to implement solutions using any programming technique at their disposal (e.g. in this study, students have used *for* loops and *do..while* loops to move the character. Some of the pairs were also observed to write a parser, which allowed for a more domain-specific way of telling the character how to move across the map).

Table 2: Basic instructions for the APE tool

Instruction	What it does
main.move();	Makes the yellow character move one space forward in whatever direction is being faced.
main.turnLeft();	Makes the character turn 90 degrees to the left.
main.turnRight();	Makes the character turn 90 degrees to the right.

Each pair was responsible for the whole programming process: from discussing possible solutions, to attempting to implement the correct code and testing it.

Both the control group and the test group followed the process described above; prior to the task, pairs within the test group were also exposed to the pair programming guidelines by watching a short 3-minute video[2] which showed an experienced pair applying the guidelines in three separate scenarios. This video was supplemented by a printed copy of the guidelines (Appendix 1), which was left with the pair for reference.

Following the test period, the researcher would return, log the number of programs completed by the pair, and distribute the post-test surveys, which were completed individually by the members of the pair. The five-question survey was based on the survey used in [16], and was used to collect data from the individual developers immediately after their debugging session. This data was used to determine if there was any significant difference between the groups that could bias the results. Each survey consisted of Likert-scale questions relating to their experience with communication and partner contribution during the test, as well as questions on the student's experience with programming. These were used to measure central tendencies and variance within the groups, in order to ascertain that there were no significant differences between the groups that would threaten the validity of the work.

3.2 Results

Three measures were taken for each pair, based on the measures taken in [16]: *success* was measured by the number of programs completed successfully (when compared to the number of programs attempted); *ease of communication* and *perceived partner contribution* were measured using the post-test Likert scales as discussed above.

3.2.1 Successfully Completed Programs

Following the test period, the number of tasks attempted was noted by the researcher, and scored at a later date. Each attempt was scored by the researcher, and also compiled, to see if the correct result was produced (i.e. if each map was solved successfully). The total number of successfully completed tasks was then noted for each pair.

An independent-samples t-test was run to determine if there were differences in completion scores between pairs who were exposed to the pair programming guidelines ($n = 7$), and those who were not ($n = 7$). The tasks completed for each level of exposure were normally distributed, as assessed by Shapiro-Wilks test ($p > 0.05$), and there was homogeneity of variances, as assessed by Levene's Test for Equality of Variances ($p = 0.903$).

The exposed pairs completed a slightly greater number of tasks (4.0 ± 1.00) than the unexposed pairs (3.3 ± 0.76). The difference is not statistically significant: $t(12) = -1.508$, $p = 0.158$.

This result shows that exposing pairs to the guidelines does not increase their chances of successfully completing their tasks: exposure does not improve success rate at least for this short programming task.

3.2.2 Ease of Communication

'Ease of Communication' was reported as a Likert scale on the post-test survey in response to the following statement: "*During this session, I found communicating with my partner to be easy*". The scale ranged from 1 (strongly disagree) to 5 (strongly agree). The post-test survey results relating to *ease of communication*

[2] A copy of this video is available at the following URL: http://youtu.be/ONnYCT_LJio. Should this link be broken, please contact the lead author.

were analysed, and descriptive statistics were used to further understand the results (Table 3).

Table 3: Descriptive Statistics for Ease of Communication

	Exposed		Not Exposed	
	M	SD	M	SD
Ease of Communication	4.9	0.27	4.0	0.78

It can be seen that the students who were exposed to the guidelines reported a higher score than students who were not, with a lower variance.

As the data used is extracted from Likert scales, a Mann-Whitney U test was used for its analysis [6]. This test was run to determine any differences in *ease of communication* between the exposed group, and the control group.

There was a statistically significant difference in ease of communication scores between exposed students (Mdn = 5.0) and unexposed students (Mdn = 4.0), U = 169, z = 3.721, p = 0.001.

In this case, $p < 0.05$, therefore the null hypothesis (*the distribution of the pair's ease of communication is equal across the two groups*) was rejected.

3.2.3 Perceived Partner Contribution

'Perceived Partner Contribution' was reported as a Likert scale on the post-test survey in response to the following statement: "*Rate your partner's contribution to today's session*". The scale ranged from 1 (no participation) to 5 (excellent). Descriptive statistics were used to gain an overview of detail (Table 4).

Table 4: Descriptive Statistics for Perceived Partner Contribution

	Exposed		Not Exposed	
	M	SD	M	SD
Perceived Partner Contribution	4.9	0.36	3.9	1.07

It can be seen that typically, students who were exposed to the guidelines rate their partner's contribution to be quite high, with low variance.

A Mann-Whitney U test was run to determine if there were differences in Perceived Partner Contribution between the exposed and unexposed groups. There was a statistically significant difference in perceived partner contribution scores between exposed students (Mdn = 5.0) and unexposed students (Mdn = 4.0), U = 146, z = 2.587, p = 0.027.

In this case, $p < 0.05$, therefore the null hypothesis (*the distribution of the pair's perceived partner contribution is equal across the two groups*) was rejected.

3.3 Driver-Navigator Role Preference

As part of the post-test surveys for this study, students were asked to indicate which role they had experienced for the duration of the session of the study.

Results were as follows:

- 9 students indicated that they were drivers;
- 11 students indicated they were navigators;
- 8 students ticked both boxes, indicating that they experienced both roles during the session.

This data shows that more students indicated they performed as the navigator over the driver role, with an approximate ratio of 45:55.

The data was then explored on a 'pair-by-pair' basis, giving the following results:

- 9 pairs consisted of a driver and a navigator;
- 2 pairs consisted of a navigator and an individual who indicated they had experienced both roles;
- 3 pairs consisted of both members within the pair indicating they experienced both roles.

The first and last responses are consistent with the typical role relationships in pair programming, and with what students are taught: a pair consists of a driver and a navigator, and these roles should be switched often (although switching often in a short 45-minute coding session is not highly likely).

The second statement does not fit this pattern, showing that whilst one member of the pair was a permanent navigator, the second member of the pair found it necessary to switch between the two roles. A review of the audio files was performed. It revealed that in both cases, the driver would sometimes stop typing, and brainstorm possible solutions and next steps with the navigator. Following this, he or she would go back to driving the session. It is possible that during these brainstorming sessions, the driver felt that he or she was also navigating, and thus felt they had experienced both roles during the session. It is unclear as to why the driver felt the need to switch back-and-forth between the roles, or why their navigator did not take over the driver role, but this hints at possible pair programming dynamics that may exist outside of the traditional 'driver-navigator' claim.

3.4 Discussion

The data gathered from this study supports the following hypotheses:

1. The distribution of the pair's ease of communication scores differs with exposure to the guidelines; i.e. pairs who were exposed to the guidelines reported significantly higher scores for ease of communication than the control group.
2. The distribution of the pair's perceived partner contribution scores differs with exposure to the guidelines; i.e. pairs who were exposed to the guidelines reported significantly higher scores for perceived partner contribution than the control group.
3. The mean number of completed tasks for pairs who were exposed to the guidelines and pairs who were not exposed is equal in the population; i.e. there was no significant difference in the number of completed programs between pairs who were exposed to the guidelines, and the control group.

These results show that the guidelines may help improve students' experience of communication within their pair. It is posited that this stronger 'partner contribution' was due to the fact that individual members of the pair were more confident communicating their ideas (possibly due to the additional advice provided by the guidelines) and contributed more successfully as a result.

Furthermore, the use of the guidelines may support students in dealing with issues and barriers that typically arise during pair programming sessions in a structured way. However, whilst these guidelines can be seen to aid the pairs' perceived communication, there is no evidence to suggest that the guidelines have any impact on student success, at least in such a short programming session.

3.5 Limitations and Further Work

These findings are limited by the subject sample (from a single institution), and a relatively small sample group. A sample size of 28 participants gives a margin of error of 18.51% (CI: 95%).

The margin of error could be reduced by running this study with more participants (e.g. with 50 participants, the margin of error drops to 13.84%). Increasing the sample size could give evidence to further support these conclusions, and allow these results to be further generalised beyond the scope of this study.

Finally, data from the post-test surveys on the distribution of driver-navigator roles reported in section 3.3 shows that on some occasions, pairs did not work in pairs consisting of one driver and one navigator, and hints that these roles may be more fluid based on the situation currently being tackled. Similar work can be seen in [5]. A study considering possible pair dynamics outside the traditional driver-navigator roles would allow for further understanding of these pair dynamics, and how certain combinations may impact successful collaboration.

4. CONCLUSION

Previous research indicates that the pair programming guidelines help novice pairs communicate more effectively whilst working on debugging tasks. The research presented in this paper shows that the guidelines contribute to greater communication effectiveness when students are creating new code; significant differences were identified between the students who had been exposed to the guidelines and the control group when considering the individual members' perceptions of (i) their experienced communication and (ii) their partner's contribution to the session.

5. ACKNOWLEDGMENTS

The authors would like to thank all the student pairs who have contributed time, effort and invaluable feedback towards evaluating these guidelines.

6. REFERENCES

[1] Begel, A. and N. Nagappan. *Pair programming: what's in it for me?* in *Proceedings of the Second ACM-IEEE international symposium on Empirical software engineering and measurement*. 2008: ACM.

[2] Bryant, S., P. Romero, and B. du Boulay, *The Collaborative Nature of Pair Programming*, in *Extreme Programming and Agile Processes in Software Engineering*, P. Abrahamsson, M. Marchesi, and G. Succi, Editors. 2006, Springer Berlin/Heidelberg. p. 53-64.

[3] McDowell, C., B. Hanks, and L. Werner, *Experimenting with pair programming in the classroom.* SIGCSE Bull., 2003. **35**(3): p. 60-64.

[4] Nagappan, N., et al. *Improving the CS1 experience with pair programming*. in *ACM SIGCSE Bulletin*. 2003: ACM.

[5] Plonka, L., et al., *Collaboration in pair programming: driving and switching*, in *Agile Processes in Software Engineering and Extreme Programming*. 2011, Springer. p. 43-59.

[6] Ryu, E. and A. Agresti, *Modeling and inference for an ordinal effect size measure.* Statistics in Medicine, 2008. **27**(10): p. 1703-1717.

[7] Sanders, D., *Student Perceptions of the Suitability of Extreme and Pair Programming*, in *Extreme Programming Perspectives*, M. Marchesi, et al., Editors. 2002, Addison-Wesley Professional. p. 168-174.

[8] Sharp, H. and H. Robinson, *Three 'C's of agile practice: collaboration, co-ordination and communication*, in *Agile Software Development*. 2010, Springer. p. 61-85.

[9] Srikanth, H., et al., *On Pair Rotation in the Computer Science Course*, in *Proceedings of the 17th Conference on Software Engineering Education and Training*. 2004, IEEE Computer Society. p. 144-149.

[10] Stapel, K., et al., *Towards Understanding Communication Structure in Pair Programming*, in *Agile Processes in Software Engineering and Extreme Programming*, A. Sillitti, et al., Editors. 2010, Springer Berlin Heidelberg. p. 117-131.

[11] Williams, L. and R. Kessler, *All I really need to know about pair programming I learned in kindergarten.* Communications of the ACM, 2000. **43**(5): p. 108-114.

[12] Williams, L. and R. Kessler, *Pair Programming Illuminated.* 2002: Addison-Wesley Longman Publishing Co., Inc. 288.

[13] Williams, L., et al., *Strengthening the Case for Pair Programming.* IEEE Software, 2000. **17**(4): p. 19-25.

[14] Williams, L., et al., *In Support of Pair Programming in the Introductory Computer Science Course.* Computer Science Education, 2002. **12**(3): p. 197-212.

[15] Zarb, M., *Developing a coding scheme for the analysis of expert pair programming sessions*, in *Proceedings of the 3rd annual conference on Systems, programming, and applications: software for humanity*. 2012, ACM: Tucson, Arizona, USA. p. 237-238.

[16] Zarb, M., J. Hughes, and J. Richards, *Evaluating Industry-Inspired Pair Programming Communication Guidelines with Undergraduate Students* in *Proceedings of the 45th ACM technical symposium on Computer Science Education*. 2014, ACM: Atlanta, GA, USA.

[17] Zarb, M., J. Hughes, and J. Richards, *Industry-inspired guidelines improve students' pair programming communication*, in *Proceedings of the 18th ACM conference on Innovation and technology in computer science education*. 2013, ACM: Canterbury, England, UK. p. 135-140.

Appendix 1: The Pair Programming Guidelines

Restarting Guidelines	If you and your partner are stuck in a silent period and cannot seem to progress, actively break your focus by discussing something completely off-topic and unrelated to the issues at hand. This will allow you to tackle the problem with a fresh outlook.	Following this stage, attempt to: - Look back on your last couple of steps and review your previous work; - Identify a fresh start; - Try to think about your end goal when suggesting next steps in order to make progress.	If your partner is attempting to break focus, do not dismiss this. Breaking one's focus using jokes and private conversations can lead to a fresh perspective, which you and your partner may need.	If you are in disagreement with your partner, you may find it helpful to break for lunch/coffee/etc. – during which you should physically walk away from your desk.	Give your partner space to read the code before suggesting next steps.
Planning Guidelines	Suggestions and reviews are both useful states that will allow you to drive your work forward. When in these states, feel free to communicate about a range of things; a potential cycle could be as follows: - Review previous code - Suggest an improvement - Review methods to be changed - Suggest potential impact	At any stage, do not hesitate to ask your partner for clarification about any suggestions that they make, or actions they are working on that you do not necessarily understand.	Think about what your partner is saying and doing. Offering an interpretation of your own understanding of the current state can help move the work forward.	Learning to say I *don't know* or *I don't understand* is critical. Always explain things immediately – try to avoid replying to a question with *you'll see in a while*, as this will distract your partner.	Make a note of previously discussed suggestions and reviews so that similar discussions are not unnecessarily repeated over and over.
Action Guidelines	*(for the driver):* Whilst you are programming or thinking about how to structure your code, try to be more verbal – for example, by muttering whilst you are typing. This tends to help the navigator to know that you are actively working, and have a clear sense of how you are approaching the task at hand. If you verbalise your thoughts, this will help the navigator make informed suggestions based on your current actions.	*(for the navigator):* Whilst the driver is programming, actively look to make suggestions that contribute to the code.	*(for the navigator):* If the driver is muttering, use this opportunity to make sure your suggestions have been properly understood.	*(for the driver):* When silent, it can look as if you are clicking randomly on the screen, which risks your navigator becoming bored and distracted. Voicing your thoughts can help counter this.	*(for the navigator):* Think ahead, since you'll be driving in a short while: what is the current course of action not covering? Is there anything worth verifying that might have been left out?

Supporting Programming Assignments with Activity Streams: An Empirical Study

Christopher D. Hundhausen*, Adam S. Carter*, and Olusola Adesope[†]
Human-centered Environments for Learning and Programming (HELP) Lab
*School of Electrical Engineering and Computer Science
[†]College of Education
Washington State University
Pullman, WA 99164
+1 509-335-4590
hundhaus@wsu.edu, cartera@wsu.edu, olusola.adesope@wsu.edu

ABSTRACT

Social learning theory emphasizes the importance of providing learners with opportunities to observe their peers, and to participate actively in a community. Unfortunately, early computing courses tend to emphasize individual programming assignments, which discourage learners from observing and working with their peers. In order to explore the possibility that increased opportunities for social awareness and interaction while working on programming assignments might influence learning outcomes in early computing courses, we are studying the design and use of social networking-style activity streams in such courses. In an empirical study of the use of two types of activity streams in a CS 2 course—one that was part of a learning management system, and one integrated directly into students' programming environment—we found that students who used the integrated stream were twice as socially active; however, social participation in both environments was positively correlated with students' grades. Our results suggest that the use of activity streams as an adjunct to individual programming assignments can positively influence learning; computing instructors would do well to find ways to get their students to participate actively in activity streams during the programming process.

Categories and Subject Descriptors

K.3.1 [**Computer Uses in Education**]: *Collaborative learning*; K.3.2 [**Computer and Information Science Education**]: *Computer science education, Curriculum.*

General Terms

Design, Experimentation, Human Factors.

Keywords

Social learning theory, programming assignments, Activity streams, social networking, CS 2

1. INTRODUCTION

An important component of early computing courses has traditionally been the *individual* programming assignment, which emphasizes individual problem solving and programming. In such assignments, students are typically discouraged or forbidden from observing and collaborating with their peers; they are asked to "go it alone," presumably to ensure that they learn the target skills and do not cheat.

There are at least two good reasons to call this traditional approach into question. First, the approach may not adequately prepare students for jobs in the computing profession, which, in addition to technical programming skills, are increasingly requiring so-called "soft" skills, including communication, teamwork, and collaboration (see, e.g., [3]). Second, the approach goes against contemporary social learning theory, which holds both that active participation in a community of peers and experts fosters learning [11], and that students have the best chance of sticking with the discipline if they are afforded opportunities to observe, and assess themselves relative to, their peers [1].

Given the above observations, computing educators would do well to consider ways of making the programming process less isolating and more social—especially in early computing courses, which typically suffer from high attrition rates [2]. Inspired by modern trends in social networking, we have been exploring the use of social networking-style *activity streams* (see Figure 1) to increase students' social awareness and engagement as they work on individual programming assignments. In social media environments such as Facebook, the activity stream enables people to participate in an asynchronous social community by

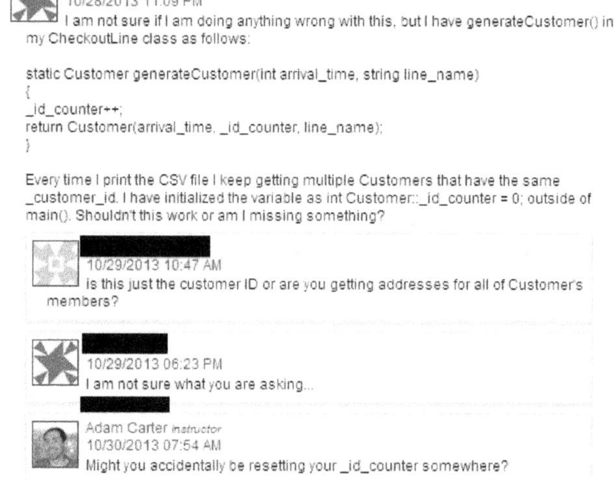

Figure 1. An Activity Stream in a Computing Course

SIGCSE'15, March 4–7, 2015, Kansas City, MO, USA.
Copyright © 2015 ACM 978-1-4503-2966-8/15/03…$15.00.
http://dx.doi.org/10.1145/2676723.2677276

sharing their life activities, as well as posing and answering questions. The idea extends naturally to learning communities of programmers: using an activity stream, learners are able to share their programming activities, and to ask and answer questions about programming, under the watchful eye of course teaching personnel, who can also contribute to the conversation as needed.

We suspect that activity streams are already commonly used by students during the programming process; however, no published research has investigated their instructional design and use in computing courses, or their impact on learning. Indeed, the use of activity streams as an adjunct to traditional individual programming assignments raises several research questions related to their use and educational effectiveness:

RQ1:	*To what extent do students appropriate an activity stream as they engage in computer programming assignments?*

RQ2:	*How is students' use of an activity stream related to their learning outcomes?*

RQ3:	*How does activity stream usage change over time, and what impact do changes have on performance?*

To explore these questions, this paper presents an empirical study of the use of activity streams in a CS 2 course at Washington State University. As an initial step toward exploring the design space of activity streams, we studied students' use of two alternative forms of activity streams during the programming process:

- A "traditional" activity stream that resides in a learning management system.
- An "integrated" activity stream that is embedded directly within the programming environment in which students complete course assignments.

Our results indicate that students were twice as active in the integrated activity stream as they were in the traditional activity stream. However, student participation within the activity stream positively correlated with course grades in both cases. As the first empirical study to consider a potential link between online social activity and programming outcomes, our study contributes to the empirical literature on the design of programming assignments, providing a theoretically-motivated and empirically-grounded basis for designing "social" programming assignments supported by an online activity stream.

2. BACKGROUND AND RELATED WORK

Social learning theory furnishes a compelling theoretical basis for efforts to make the learning of computer programming more social. Bandura's *self-efficacy theory* [1] posits that students develop a positive sense of their own programming abilities (so-called *self-efficacy*) by being able to observe the activities of their peers, and by being able to evaluate themselves relative to their peers. Not surprisingly, positive self-efficacy has been strongly correlated with persistence in the computing discipline [16]. Likewise, *situated learning theory* [11] holds that participation in a community of practice, which involves both the observation of others and actual participation in community activities, is essential to learning. Both of these social theories of learning suggest that learners may have difficulties making progress if they are forced to program in isolation from a broader community, as has traditionally been the case in computing education—especially in the individual programming assignments that are common in early computing courses.

Within the computing education research community, there have been several notable efforts to make computer programming more collaborative and social. One approach, with which this research has much in common, is to create online learning and teaching communities specifically focused on learning and teaching computer programming (see, e.g., [4, 12]). A second approach is to enable programmers to collaborate on programming tasks over a networked environment (e.g, [7, 10]). Indeed, having students collaboratively program solutions, as embodied in the *pair programming* approach (see, e.g., [17]), has been shown to be an effective form of collaborative learning (see, e.g., [15]). However, the approach proves incompatible with the kinds of programming scenarios targeted by this research: those in which students collaborate in the process of designing *their own* solutions to the same problem.

A third approach is to build specialized search tools to help novice programmers locate code written by others that is relevant to their current context (e.g., [6, 8]). In contrast, our research views programming not as a solo activity in which learners search for related examples when they get stuck, but rather as a *community* activity in which learners actively participate in the learning process by asking other community members (including experts) for help, and by offering help to others.

Educational researchers have long been interested in understanding the relationship between learning processes and learning outcomes. In the field of Computer-Supported Collaborative learning (CSCL), researchers have studied online learning discourse, in an attempt to understand the kinds of discourse that might be associated with better learning outcomes (e.g., [5]). In a similar vein, computing educators have been interested in understanding the ways in which programming processes might correlate with programming and course outcomes (e.g., [17]). Within computing education, our research extends this work by exploring relationships between social behavior and learning outcomes.

3. EMPIRICAL STUDY

In order to explore the use and effectiveness of online activity streams in the process of completing programming assignments, we conducted a between subjects, quasi-experimental study with two treatments: *Traditional* and *Integrated.* These treatments corresponded to the fall 2013 and spring 2014 offerings of the CS 2 course at Washington State University. These two course offerings were identical in many important ways. Focusing on the C and C++ programming languages, both had three 50-minute lectures and one 170-minute lab period per week; three exams (two midterms and a final); and seven or eight individual programming assignments due at roughly two week intervals. Both courses were taught by the second author.

The two treatments were defined by the differing ways in which they implemented the use of activity streams as an adjunct to the individual programming assignments. In the *Traditional* treatment, students used an online activity stream that was part of the online learning management environment used for the course. In contrast, in the *Integrated* treatment, students used an activity stream directly integrated into the programming environment in which they completed the programming assignments.

A second difference between the two treatments was whether or not students were *required* to post to the activity stream. In the *Traditional* treatment, they were not, whereas in the *Integrated* treatment, they were required to make at least two posts, and to reply to at least two posts, per programming assignment.

Dependent measures included the number of posts and replies made (collected via transcripts of the activity streams), together with student grades—both the final course grade, and the grades for individual programming assignments and exams.

3.1 Participants

The fall 2013 course (the *Traditional* treatment) enrolled 150 students, of whom 135 completed the course with a grade. The spring 2014 course (the *Integrated* treatment) enrolled 140 students, of whom 129 completed the course with a grade. Students participated in the activity streams as part of their normal course activities. At the end of the semester, students were given the option of signing an informed consent form to release their activity stream posts and grades for research purposes. 102 students in the *Traditional* treatment, and 108 students in the *Integrated* treatment, consented to release their data.

3.2 Materials and Procedure

Students in the *Traditional* treatment used OSBLE [13], a learning management environment developed at Washington State University. In addition to hosting course materials and enabling the electronic submission of student assignments, OSBLE supported an online activity stream in which conversations could go one level deep (posts and replies; see Figure 1). Here, students were invited to engage in an online conversation about topics relevant to the course, although they were not required to participate in the conversation.

In contrast, students in the *Integrated* treatment used OSBIDE [14], a "social" plugin to Microsoft Visual Studio, the IDE in which students completed course assignments (see Figure 2). OSBIDE enabled students both to submit their assignments, and to participate in an online activity stream in which conversations could go one level deep.[1] Students in the *Integrated* treatment were *required* to make at least two posts per programming assignment, and to reply to at least two posts per programming assignment. Whereas students in the *Traditional* treatment completed eight programming assignments, students in the *Integrated* treatment completed only seven. Six of these were identical between the two treatments; a seventh was similar.

To perform the analyses presented in this paper, we extracted transcripts of the activity streams generated in each treatment. These transcripts, together with student grade data obtained from the course instructor, were exported to a database, enabling us to run queries to obtain the data to be analyzed.

[1]OSBIDE supports additional social networking features, including the ability to view other students' programming activities (and their relation to one's own programming activities) in the activity stream, and the ability to highlight a block of code and ask a question about it in the activity stream; however, students' use of these features is not considered in the study presented here.

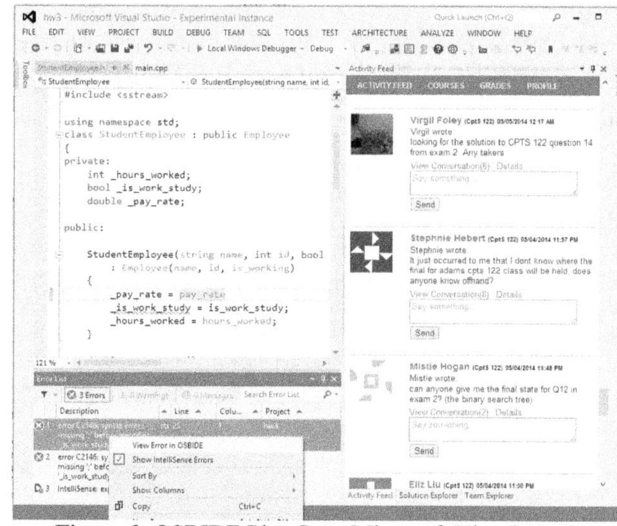

Figure 2. OSBIDE Plug-In to Microsoft Visual Studio

3.3 Results and Discussion

We organize the presentation and discussion of our results around the three research questions we targeted for this study.

3.3.1 *To what extent is the activity stream used?*

Based on social learning theory [11] , which emphasizes the importance of *regular* participation within a learning community, we decided to consider two-week snapshots of student activity within each treatment—approximately the time interval between assignments. Our participation level metric, described in Table 1, ranges from 1 to 4, based on the number of posts and replies made by a student in a given two-week interval. To define the extremes of the metric, we defined level 1 as no participation at all, and level 4 as two or more posts and two or more replies—the requirement for full credit in the *Integrated* treatment. Levels 2 and 3 fall in between these two extremes.

Table 2 presents the mean participation level for each two-week interval, as well as the averages across the entire semester. As the table indicates, students in the *Integrated* treatment participated more actively in the activity stream. Indeed, a non-parametric Kruskal-Wallis ANOVA showed a statistically significant difference in level of participation between the two groups (H = 90.479, $df = 1$, $p < 0.001$), with students in the *Integrated* treatment maintaining a regular participation level that was nearly twice that of the *Traditional* treatment.

These results suggest that students will tend to appropriate an activity stream even if they are not required to do so, as was the case in the *Traditional* treatment. However, the combination of requiring students to participate in the activity stream and integrating the activity stream directly into an IDE appears to lead to a significant increase in students' participation level. Unfortunately, in this study, we were unable to disentangle the individual effect of making participation in the activity stream a requirement from the effect of integrating the activity stream into students' programming environment.

Table 1. Definition of Participation Level Metric

Level	Definition
1	No posts or replies
2	At least one post or reply, but no more than one of either
3	At least two posts and fewer than two replies, or at least two replies and fewer than two posts
4	Two or more posts and two or more replies

Table 2. Participation Level Averages by Two-Week Intervals (Standard Deviations in Parenthesis)

Weeks	Traditional (Fa 13)	Integrated (Sp 14)
1-2	1.20 (0.52)	1.68 (0.98)
3-4	1.46 (0.76)	2.66 (1.27)
5-6	1.31 (0.68)	2.73 (1.22)
7-8	1.39 (0.76)	2.63 (1.26)
9-10	1.24 (0.59)	2.16 (1.20)
11-12	1.41 (0.79)	2.30 (1.26)
13-14	1.26 (0.65)	2.59 (1.28)
15-16	1.39 (0.75)	2.31 (1.32)
Avg.	1.33 (0.70)	2.38 (0.89)

3.3.2 How is activity stream usage related to grades?

In order to determine whether or not regular participation was a reliable predictor of academic success, we considered each student's semester-long participation level average. In the case of the *Integrated* treatment, in which participation was mandatory, we were concerned that participation level might co-vary with prior computing grades: Since there was academic incentive to participate in the discussion, higher-achieving students might be more motivated to participate. Indeed, in the *Integrated* treatment, a correlational analysis between a student's level of participation and prior grade in CS 1 was found to be significant ($r = .468$, $p < 0.001$). However, in the *Traditional* treatment, this was not the case ($r = .12$, $p = 0.26$). Hence, we decided to retain prior CS 1 grade as a covariate in further analyses with the *Integrated* treatment (by using a MANCOVA), whereas we used a MANOVA for the Traditional treatment, while adding prior CS 1 grade as a separate independent variable for comparison purposes.

Tables 3 and 4 present the results of these analyses. As Table 3 shows, CS 1 grade was not a significant predictor of student performance in the *Traditional* treatment. In contrast, in the *Integrated* treatment, students' prior CS 1 grade was a significant predictor of students' exam scores and final grade. The partial eta squared (η^2) values indicate that the strength of the relationship between CS 1 grade and these two items was weak.

Table 4 tells a slightly different story: Participation level predicted student performance with respect to *all* graded items and the final grade in both treatments. Moreover, in all cases, the partial eta squared values indicate that participation level was a stronger predictor of student grades than was prior CS 1 grade, as it accounted for roughly twice the variance.

In order to further explore differences in students' grades vis-à-vis participation level, we partitioned students into quartiles based on their overall average participation level. Table 5 presents the mean final grade (percentage) by quartile. In both treatments, a between-subjects ANOVA detected a statistically-significant difference between the quartiles (*Traditional*: $df = 3$, $F = 5.51$, $p < 0.002$; *Integrated*: $df = 3$, $F = 11.62$, $p < 0.001$). In the traditional treatment, a post-hoc Bonferoni test revealed a significant difference between the lowest and top-most quartile. A post-hoc Bonferoni test in the Integrated treatment revealed differences between the top two quartiles and the lowest quartile ($p < 0.01$) and the 2nd and 4th quartile ($p < 0.045$).

In order to determine the specific impact of participation quartile on student grades, we ran a regression analysis. In the case of the *Traditional* treatment, a change from one quartile to the next corresponded to a grade change of 6%. In the case of the *Integrated* treatment, a one-quartile change corresponded to a grade change of 4%. Thus, in both treatments, a one-quartile change equated to a difference of roughly one-half of a letter grade.

These results suggest that activity stream usage does, in fact, predict student grades in both treatments; students would do well to take a more active role in the activity stream. One possible explanation is that students who make and reply to posts are participating in valuable learning activities; active participation in the activity stream actually enhances learning. This explanation is favored by the social learning theories that form the foundation for this study. Indeed, according to Self-Efficacy Theory [1], while *vicarious* learning experiences in which students observe others without actively participating are valuable, *enactive* learning experiences in which students actively participate are absolutely essential.

Table 3. Extent to Which CS 1 Grade Predicted Course Grades

	Traditional (Fa13)			Integrated (Sp14)		
Graded Item	**F**	**Sig.**	η^2	**F**	**Sig.**	η^2
Assignments	0.26	0.61	0.00	1.39	0.24	0.01
Quizzes	1.86	0.18	0.02	3.81	0.54	0.04
Exams	0.68	0.41	0.01	9.88	**0.01**	0.09
Final Grade	0.04	0.95	0.00	6.67	**0.01**	0.07

Table 4. Extent to Which Participation Level (see Table 1) Predicted Course Grades

	Traditional (Fa 13)			Integrated (Sp 14)		
Graded Item	**F**	**Sig.**	η^2	**F**	**Sig.**	η^2
Assignments	6.74	**0.02**	0.06	10.5	**0.01**	0.10
Quizzes	6.08	**0.02**	0.06	14.9	**0.01**	0.13
Exams	6.33	**0.02**	0.06	9.50	**0.01**	0.09
Final Grade	13.2	**0.01**	0.17	23.2	**0.01**	0.20

Table 5. Final Grades (%) by Participation Level Quartile

	Traditional (Fa 13)			Integrated (Sp 14)		
Quartile	**N**	**M**	**SD**	**N**	**M**	**SD**
1	22	66.0	17.6	20	76.9	13.3
2	9	75.5	19.9	29	84.8	8.1
3	10	75.6	21.5	24	86.2	5.9
4	25	85.3	10.3	36	90.5	5.9

3.3.3 *How does activity stream usage change over time, and what impact do changes have on performance?*

Figures 3 and 4 present, for each treatment, state transition networks depicting the probability that students will transition, from one two-week interval to the next, to each of the four participation levels defined in Table 1. In these networks, edges are labeled with their associated probabilities; thicker and redder edges indicate higher-probability transitions. As can be seen, the most likely transitions are self-transitions to the same level of participation at the two extremes (level 1 and level 4). In other words, high-participating students tended to continue to participate actively, while low-participating students tended to continue not participating.

To explore whether changes in participation levels over time influenced student grades, we first rank-ordered participants based on their participation level by time period; participants whose participation level increased over time were ranked higher. We then performed a multiple regression analysis, with final examination as the dependent variable and participation level quartile and participation ranking as independent variables.

With an adjusted R^2 value of .15, the regression model explained 15% of variance in student grades: 15% of the variability in grades was predicted by participation rank and level. In fact, participation rank was found to be a significant factor in the model in both treatments ($p = .004$): Students who increased their participation over time tended to be associated with higher grades.

This result suggests that students may learn better and obtain higher grades if they engage in *increasingly* active participation in the activity stream. This result is in line with *situated learning theory* [10]—especially the notion that increasingly central participation in a community of practice (which in our study equated to increasingly active participation in the activity stream) constitutes evidence of learning. Indeed, it appears that as the semester progressed, higher-achieving participants in our study were increasingly involved in the practices of the community and were more willing to participate.

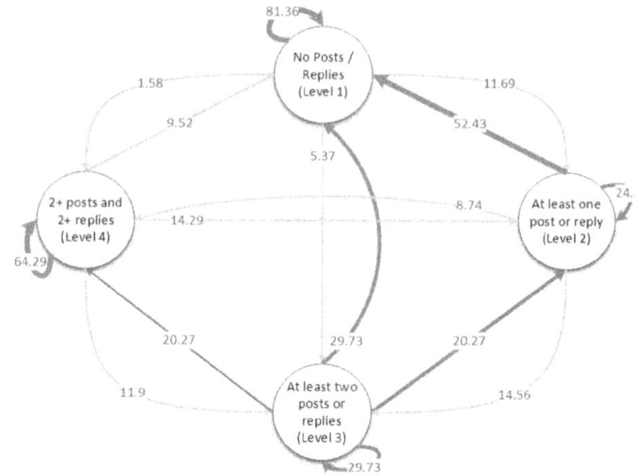

Figure 3. Probabilistic State-Transition Diagram for Traditional Treatment

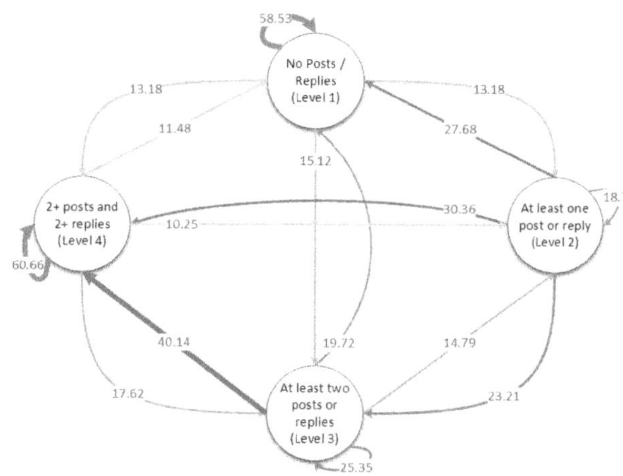

Figure 4. Probabilistic State-Transition Diagram for Integrated Treatment

4. CONCLUSION

In this paper, we have presented a comparative study of two alternative versions of activity streams in an early computing course. Our study sought to explore not only the extent to which students might use the alternative activity streams, but also the relationship between such usage and course performance. We found that students used the integrated activity stream significantly more than the traditional one. However, such increased usage did not appear to lead to any advantages in terms of course performance: in *both treatments,* participation level, as well as an increase in participation level, was positively correlated with course grades—a result that can be explained by social learning theory.

4.1 Limitations

It is important to point out three limitations of our study. First, it considered only the *quantity* of participation in the activity stream, without considering *quality*. Clearly, a more sophisticated analysis would have attempted to code students' activity stream posts based on their content, in order to explore more deeply relationships between the quality and focus of students' posts, and their course performance.

Second, this study considered two different CS 2 courses of moderate to large size at Washington State University taught by the second author of this paper. The fact that the second author—a stakeholder in the particular technology used in the *Integrated* treatment—was involved as a participant in these studies may have influenced his participation. Moreover, although we believe they are representative of typical CS 2 courses at many universities, caution must be exercised in any attempt to generalize this study's results beyond the two CS 2 courses considered in the study.

Third, because students in the *Integrated* treatment were required to post, whereas students in the *Traditional* treatment were not, this study was unable to disentangle the influence of posting as a requirement from the influence of integrating the activity feed into the IDE. Clearly, disentangling these two issues is an important topic for future study.

4.2 Implications for Computing Education

Our results have important implications for the instructional design of individual programming assignments in computing education. Integrating an online activity stream into students' out-of-class programming assignments appears to be a best practice that can yield positive benefits for student course performance. As this study has shown, and as social learning theory predicts, students who participate actively in an activity stream will tend to do better in the course. Instructors who can find ways to get their students to participate more actively in an activity stream can make a real difference in their students' course success.

At the same time, our study results have implications for the design of the activity stream used for course assignments. While an activity stream integrated directly into the IDE used by students will tend to promote more active student participation than a traditional activity stream not integrated into an IDE, such increased participation may not be associated with improved student performance. According to our results, instructors may do just as well to enlist a traditional activity stream supported by a learning management environment or commercial social networking tool.

4.3 Future Work

This preliminary research into the relationship between students' online social activity and their programming success raises intriguing possibilities for future research. In future work, we are interested in pursuing the following two research directions:

Activity stream post quality. As mentioned above, a key limitation of our study was that it focused squarely on the quantity of activity stream posts, without considering what was actually written in the posts. In a preliminary study conducted in a CS ½ and CS 1 course, we have performed a content analysis of activity streams [9]; however, that study made no attempt to correlate post content and quality with student grades. In ongoing work, we are performing a content analysis of the activity streams of the two CS 2 courses considered in this study, so that we can gain further insights into what students discuss in an activity stream and how the content and quality of their discussions relate to course performance.

Integrating students' programming activities into an activity stream. The OSBIDE social plug-in used in the *Integrated* treatment logs all of students' programming activities, including their edits, build errors, debugging events, and run-time exceptions. How can these data about programming activities be integrated into an activity stream, and what educational benefits might the inclusion of such data have? In ongoing work, we are exploring this design space, including the use of a social recommendation system to make students aware of other students who are encountering similar programming issues. The goal is to develop a new breed of *social* programming environments that leverage social learning theory to make introductory computing less isolating and more community-based.

5. ACKNOWLEDGMENTS

This project is funded by the National Science Foundation under grant no IIS-1321045.

6. REFERENCES

[1] Bandura, A. 1997. *Self-efficacy: the exercise of control.* Worth Publishers.

[2] Beaugouef, T. and Mason, J. 2005. Why the high attrition rate for computer science students: Some thoughts and observations. *ACM SIGCSE Bulletin.* 37, 2 (2005), 103–106.

[3] Begel, A. and Simon, B. 2008. Novice software developers, all over again. *Proceeding of the Fourth International Workshop on Computing Education Research.* ACM. 3–14.

[4] Brennan, K. 2009. Scratch-Ed: an online community for scratch educators. *Proceedings of the 9th international conference on Computer supported collaborative learning* (Rhodes, Greece, 2009), 76–78.

[5] Dennen, V.P. 2008. Looking for evidence of learning: Assessment and analysis methods for online discourse. *Computers in Human Behavior.* 24, 2 (2008), 205 – 219.

[6] Goldman, M. and Miller, R.C. 2009. Codetrail: connecting source code and web resources. *Journal of Visual Languages and Computing.* 20, 4 (2009), 223–235.

[7] Goldman, M. and Miller, R.C. 2011. Real-time collaborative coding in a web IDE. *Proceedings of the 24th annual ACM symposium on User interface software and technology* (Santa Barbara, CA, USA, 2011), 155–164.

[8] Hartmann, B. et al. 2010. What would other programmers do: suggesting solutions to error messages. *Proc. 28th Conference on Human Factors in Computing Systems.* ACM. 1019–1028.

[9] Hundhausen, C.D. and Carter, A.S. 2014. Facebook me about your code: an empirical study of the use of activity streams in early computing courses. *J. Comput. Sci. Coll.* (2014).

[10] Jenkins, J. et al. 2012. Perspectives on active learning and collaboration: JavaWIDE in the classroom. *Proceedings of the 43rd ACM technical symposium on Computer Science Education* (Raleigh, NC, USA, 2012), 185–190.

[11] Lave, J. and Wenger, E. 1991. *Situated learning: Legitimate peripheral participation.* Cambridge Univ Pr.

[12] Maloney, J. et al. 2010. The Scratch Programming Language and Environment. *Trans. Comput. Educ.* 10, 4 (2010), 1–15.

[13] Online Studio-Based Learning Environment: 2012. *https://osble.org/.* Accessed: 2012-01-14.

[14] OSBIDE - Home: *http://osbide.codeplex.com/.* Accessed: 2012-10-17.

[15] Radermacher, A. et al. 2012. Assigning student programming pairs based on their mental model consistency: an initial investigation. *Proc. 43rd ACM Technical Symposium on Computer Science Education.* ACM. 325–330.

[16] Rosson, M.B. et al. 2011. Orientation of Undergraduates Toward Careers in the Computer and Information Sciences: Gender, Self-Efficacy and Social Support. *Trans. Comput. Educ.* 11, 3 (2011), 1–23.

[17] Watson, C. et al. 2014. No tests required: comparing traditional and dynmaic predictors of programming success. *Proceedings of the 45th ACM Technical Symposium on Computer Science Education* (2014), 469–474.

[18] Williams, L. and Kessler, R.R. 2001. Experimenting with industry's "pair-programming" model in the computer science classroom. *Computer Science Education.* 11, 1 (2001), 7–20.

Hands-On Network Programming Projects in the Cloud

Weiying Zhu
Metropolitan State University of Denver
Department of Mathematical and Computer Sciences
P.O. Box 173362, Campus Box 38
Denver, Colorado 80217-3362
(303) 352 7278
wzhu1@msudenver.edu

ABSTRACT

Hands-on activities are important for computer science students to achieve their learning objectives. Compared to developing and maintaining on-campus physical or virtual laboratories, using the public cloud to host hands-on activities is a very promising approach because of the scalability, flexibility, security, cost-efficiency, and accessibility of the services offered in the public cloud. This paper presents the design of four cloud-based network programming projects and our experience of using the services and infrastructure in the public cloud for these hands-on projects in our Computer Networks course. Each student was able to use multiple virtual machines in the public cloud together with a local computer to develop and test networking programs. Both the instructor's observation and student surveys demonstrated that our approach has a strong positive impact on the student learning experience. A vast majority of the students favor using the public cloud not only in this course but also in other computer science courses if applicable.

Categories and Subject Descriptors

K.3.2 [**Computers and Education**]: Computer and Information Science Education – *computer science education, information systems education, curriculum.*

General Terms

Design, Experimentation, Languages.

Keywords

Computer Networks; Network Programming; Hands-on Projects; Cloud Computing; Amazon Web Services.

1. INTRODUCTION

Network programing techniques and networking protocols are essential contents of the Computer Networks course of many Computer Science (CS) curricula. Upon completion of our CS3700-Computer Networks, students need to be able to appraise web, email, and other network applications, contrast reliable and unreliable transport layer services, compare routing algorithms, explain link-layer media access control methods, and develop Internet applications using network programming techniques. Hands-on network programming projects are very helpful for students not only to learn how to develop Internet applications, but also to understand protocols and algorithms in different layers.

SIGCSE'15, March 4–7, 2015, Kansas City, MO, USA.

ACM 978-1-4503-2966-8/15/03…$15.00.
http://dx.doi.org/10.1145/2676723.2677257

Large research universities have built on-campus networking laboratories to support their hands-on networking and/or network security projects or courses. Yang et al. built a lab for testing computer and network security principles and practices at the University of Houston [13]. Students physically go to the lab for lab experiments. In [5], Du et al. at Syracuse University present a general lab environment called SEED for security education. SEED includes virtual machines (VMs) and virtual routers that are created on a physical computer to form virtual networks. A student may create the SEED environment on any computer for lab activities. The Virtual Computing Lab (VCL) at North Carolina State University delivers computing resources over the Internet to students and faculty [8, 10]. Sun *et al.* at Stony Brook University-SUNY implemented a platform called V-NetLab for security experiments [11]. Dinita *et al.* developed a local computing cloud for teaching computer networks [4]. Xu *et al.* at Arizona State University developed a cloud-based resource and service sharing platform, called V-Lab, for networking laboratories [12]. The infrastructures of VCL [8, 10], V-NetLab [11], the local computing cloud [4], and V-Lab [12] are similar to each other. Each includes a cluster of Linux servers, network servers, and network equipment. On top of such infrastructure, VMs are run constantly or per user request. Virtual routers and switches are also included in the latter two approaches [4, 12]. Users remotely connect to these virtual labs for lab activities.

Building a physical or virtual networking lab or an on-campus cloud is practical in large research universities; however, it is not feasible or cost-efficient in CS programs like ours. To build and maintain a dedicated networking lab, in addition to general-purpose student computing labs, is too demanding of resources in terms of equipment, technical support, physical space, etc. Moreover, the majority of our students live off campus. Secure remote access to the lab would be a concern even if the lab were virtualized. Hence, previously, most of the time our students ran all client and server programs in a network programming project as different processes on a single computer.

With the fast growth of cloud computing services in recent years, using the public cloud for teaching has attracted educators' attention. Cappos *et al.* at the University of Washington built up a community-driven educational research platform [3] for teaching courses like cloud computing, distributed systems, grid computing, etc. Vendors such as Amazon[1], Microsoft[2], and

[1] https://aws.amazon.com/
[2] https://azure.microsoft.com/

Google[3] offer a variety of cloud computing services. The on-demand virtual computing resources are offered on top of their physical servers and equipment via the Internet. Holden *et al.* have used the public cloud for lab exercises in their database administration course and implemented a cloud-based design model for their database curriculum [6, 7]. In [9], Salah shares their experience of using the public cloud to facilitate the practical cybersecurity experience and training. In [14], Yue *et al.* describe how they use the public cloud as a platform to support the lab exercises of their computer and network security course.

Using the public cloud as the platform for hands-on network projects and/or courses is a very attractive approach not only for CS programs in large research institutions but also for programs like ours. The services offered by the public cloud are on-demand, scalable, flexible, secure, easy for remote management and access, and highly cost-efficient. For example, although our use of the Amazon Web Services (AWS) cloud was free, thanks to an AWS in Education Grant[4], the regular price of each Amazon t2.micro virtual Linux machine is only $0.013 per hour[5] and a VM is not charged when it is stopped. There is no need for on-campus technical support. Students can access the AWS cloud and work on their VMs anywhere as long as ports 443 (HTTPS) and 22 (SSH) are open. Students can conveniently stop and restart their VMs without losing their data and programs as long as they do not terminate the VMs. This paper reports our experience of using the AWS cloud for hands-on network programing projects in CS3700-Computer Networks in Spring 2014, the design of cloud-based programming projects, and the instructor's observation and students' perceptions of the impact on their learning. It is shown that using the public cloud overcomes most of the disadvantages of our previous approach, i.e., running client and server programs on the same computer. The majority of the students appreciated the positive impact not only on their learning in this course, but also on their future careers. The remainder of this paper is organized as follows. Section 2 introduces the features of the AWS cloud that were used in CS3700. Section 3 includes the design of cloud-based network programming projects. Section 4 discusses the benefits and costs of using the public cloud in our course. Finally, we present our conclusions in Section 5.

2. THE PUBLIC CLOUD

In the AWS cloud, Amazon globally deploys high-performance servers that host AWS products and services [1, 2]. As of today, these servers are geographically located not only domestically in north Virginia, Oregon, and north California, but also internationally in Ireland, Singapore, Tokyo, Sydney, and Sao Paulo. These servers host a variety of services for computing and networking, storage and content delivery network (CDN), database, analytics, application, and deployment and management. The users of the AWS cloud remotely access these services through the Internet and use the processing power to run their applications. To run their applications, users start their own VMs. These VMs are simulated by software running on one or multiple physical high-performance servers in the cloud and, hence, are scalable to the needs of a user. A user can easily deploy the applications on servers having different geographic locations.

To support the network programming projects individually assigned to students, we used two AWS services, Identity and Access Management (IAM) and Elastic Compute Cloud (EC2). IAM enables customers to manage users and user permissions in the AWS cloud [1]. EC2 provides re-sizeable computing capacity for customers to build and host their software systems [2].

2.1 Managing Student Users via IAM

I chose to apply the AWS credit from the grant we received to my AWS account instead of having students set up their separate accounts. Using IAM, I created a log-in for each student user and set up permissions that controlled student access to AWS resources. This approach allowed me to centrally manage access for students, limit their use of the AWS cloud only to the services that were needed by our network programming projects, and monitor their usage of the AWS cloud. The only concern of this approach is that each student user has access to the full amount of the grant. If it is not managed properly, the shared credit can be quickly diminished. The strategies that we used to address this concern will be discussed later in this paper.

On the AWS management console, I created a new group for our class. I also created a user login for each student, and added all the student users to the group for our class. A password was created for each user to log onto the AWS management console at a link that was created for CS3700, Spring 2014. Student user log-ins did not work at the link for general AWS accounts.

A policy is a formal statement of group permissions. To create a policy, IAM provides three tools: policy template, policy generator, and custom policy. I attached two group policies to the group for the student users in our class. The first one was attached by selecting the policy template named "Amazon EC2 Read Only Access". It allowed student users to list all the EC2 instances to be created and to display the description of each EC2 instance, but neither to perform any operation on an EC2 instance nor to use any other AWS service. The second policy, shown in Figure 1, was generated by the policy generator. It allowed student users to start and stop an existing EC2 instance, but not to launch or terminate an EC2 instance. This is the first strategy for preventing the shared credit from being wasted for any other AWS service or EC2 resource not needed by our projects.

```
{
  "Version": "2012-10-17",
  "Statement": [
  {
    "Sid": "Stmt1387414602000",
    "Effect": "Allow",
    "Action": [
      "ec2:StartInstances"
    ],
    "Resource": [
      "*"
    ]
  },
  {
    "Sid": "Stmt1387414666000",
    "Effect": "Allow",
    "Action": [
      "ec2:StopInstances"
    ],
    "Resource": [
      "*"
    ]
  }
  ]
}
```

Figure 1. Policy document of the 2nd group policy.

[3] https://cloud.google.com/

[4] http://aws.amazon.com/grants/

[5] http://aws.amazon.com/ec2/pricing/

2.2 Launching EC2 Instances

EC2 instances are VMs that run on the physical servers deployed globally. To launch an EC2 instance, a pre-configured Amazon Machine Image (AMI) needs to be selected or a customized AMI needs to be created. An AMI specifies the details to boot an instance such as operating system, libraries, and applications [2]. Depending on the need, the type of an EC2 instance can be chosen from general purpose instances with a balanced set of resources, compute optimized instances with proportionally more CPU resources (up to 32 virtual CPUs) than memory (up to 60 GB), memory optimized instances that offer large memory sizes up to 244 GB, and storage optimized instances that provide very high disk I/O performance with up to 24 × 2 TB of hard disk drive local instance storage, and very low-cost micro instances offering enough compute power and memory for our projects [2].

At the beginning of the semester, I launched 48 micro EC2 instances, two for each student in our class, one of which is in north Virginia and the other of which is in Sydney. Figure 2 shows a snapshot of some instances in the AWS management console, which were launched on the Amazon server(s) in north Virginia. The AMI of these instances is *ami-8614e3ef*, and the AMI of the ones in Sydney is *ami-c5138eff*. The platforms of both AMIs were Ubuntu. They were all t1.micro instances with 613 MB of memory, 1 virtual CPU, and network-attached EBS (Elastic Block Store) volumes for storage.

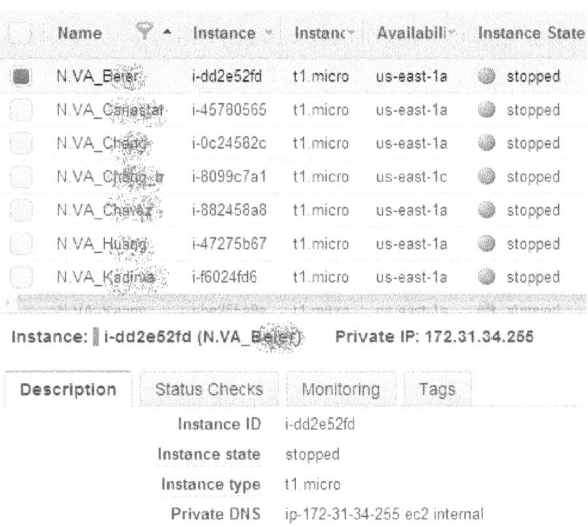

Figure 2. A snapshot of some EC2 instances in N. Virginia.

A security group was created and assigned to each instance. It included a set of firewall rules that allowed incoming and outgoing traffic on all ports. Thus any network port could potentially be used by students' networking programs.

When an EC2 instance was launched, a unique key pair consisting of a public key and a private key was created. AWS stored the public key. I downloaded the private key and shared it only with the student for whom the EC2 instance was created. A student could securely connect into his or her own EC2 instance via either a standalone SSH client or a browser-based Java SSH client using the private key file of this EC2 instance. Whenever an EC2 instance is started, a private IP address and a public IP address are automatically assigned to it. The public IP address is used for connecting to an EC2 instance from a computer outside the Amazon virtual private network. Figure 3 shows a Java SSH client connected to a running EC2 instance. Using such SSH clients, students could work on their networking programs. The SFTP plugin could be used to transfer files between the local computer and this EC2 instance.

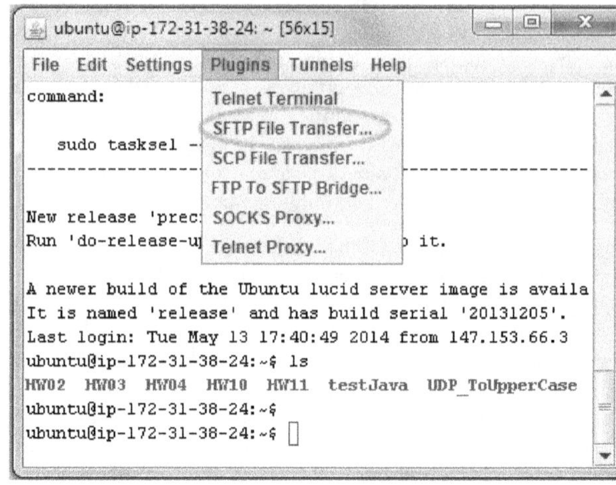

Figure 3. A Java SSH client connected to an EC2 instance.

All the EC2 instances could be listed, started, and stopped by everyone in the class although only the owner, who had the private key file, could connect to an EC2 instance. Reminders were given in the student user guide and homework assignments to request students to stop their EC2 instances when they were not working on them, and not to start or stop other people's instances. This is another strategy for preventing waste of shared credits.

3. PROJECTS IN THE CLOUD

Six network programming projects were assigned to students individually. Before the AWS cloud was used, all of them were designed as single-computer based projects.

3.1 Cloud-based Programming Projects

In accordance with the student learning objectives, four projects were re-designed as cloud-based projects.

1. *Query*: students need to write a Query Client program and a Query Server program using UDP sockets. The Client gets the item ID from the user input, sends query to the Server, and displays the response from the Server. The Server maintains detailed information regarding a list of items, and responds to the query UDP packet.
2. *Simplified HTTP*: Students need to write an HTTP (Hypertext Transfer Protocol) Client program and an HTTP Server program to implement a simplified version of HTTP using TCP sockets. The Client constructs an HTTP request message using the information collected from user inputs, sends the HTTP request message to the Server, receives and displays the HTTP response message, and saves the enclosed data to an .html file if any. The Server constructs the HTTP response message upon receiving the HTTP request message, encloses an .html file if requested, and sends the HTTP response message back.
3. *Simplified SMTP*: Students need to write an SMTP (Simple Mail Transfer Protocol) Client program and an SMTP Server program to implement a simplified version of SMTP using TCP sockets. The Client collects the information regarding an email via user inputs, constructs and sends SMTP commands and the Mail message to the Server, one at a time after receiving the response to the previous command, and displays each response. Following the 3-phase data transfer procedure, the Server responds to each SMTP command. If the incoming SMTP command is invalid or out of order, the Server responds with a

"503 5.5.2" response to ask for the correct command. The Server displays the SMTP commands and the Mail message.

4. *Simulation of CSMA/CD*: Students need to write a Host program and a Channel program to simulate the CSMA/CD (Carrier Sense Multiple Access with Collision Detection) method. The Host gets the information on when a frame is ready for transmission and how long the transmission delay is from user inputs, and simulates how a host senses whether the channel is idle, starts transmission, detects collision, aborts transmission, and backs off for retransmission. The Channel gets the number of hosts and the propagation delay from user inputs, and simulates whether the channel is idle or busy, or there is a collision based on the transmission stages of the hosts. The Host and the Channel communicate with each other using UDP or TCP sockets, where the Host is the client program and the Channel is the server program.

In the first three projects, the logic of both Client and Server programs repeats if the user chooses to continue after one round.

3.2 Testing Programs in the Cloud

The EC2 service provides a great environment for students to run their networking programs on real networked systems that are geographically dispersed, instead of on a single computer or on a few computers that are in the same LAN (Local Area Network).

In each project, every student was able to run his or her programs on at least three computers. A typical running scenario is plotted in Figure 4. The Server program was required to support multiple Client programs. A student could run the Server program on his or her EC2 instance in north Virginia, U.S.A., one Client program on his or her EC2 instance in Sydney, Australia, and the other Client program on a local laptop or lab computer. The student remotely logged into an EC2 instance using a standalone SSH client or a Java SSH client from the browser as shown in Figure 3.

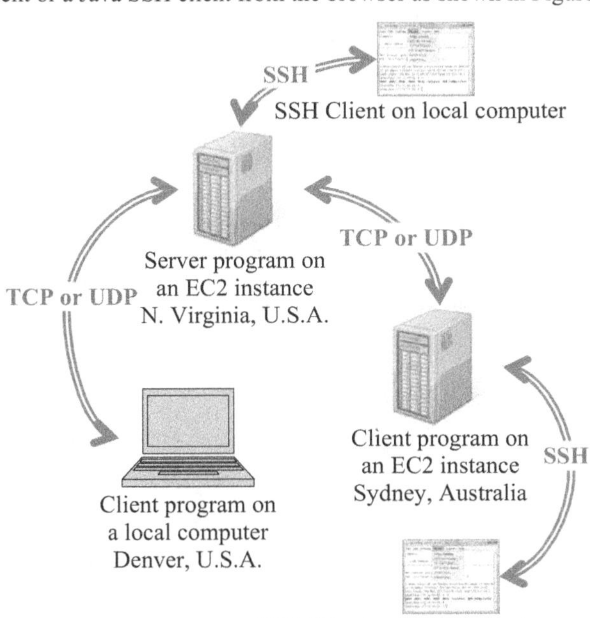

Figure. 4. A typical setup for networking programs.

The public IP address of the EC2 instance in north Virginia, U.S.A. needs to be used by the Client programs for establishing the TCP connection or sending UDP packets and, thus, is required by the Client program as a user input. The Server program gets the public IP address of each Client program from the TCP connection or the UDP packet for sending a response. Since the security rules do not block traffic on any port, a student can choose a port number for the communication on TCP or UDP. The Client program in each cloud-based project is required to measure the round-trip time (RTT), which is the time between the moment when the Client program sends a request or command to the Server program and the moment when the Client program receives the corresponding response from the Server program. In all the projects, the time for the Server program to process and respond to a request is much less than RTT and, therefore, can be ignored. The testing results showed that the RTT from a local computer to an EC2 instance in north Virginia is normally around 70 ms and the RTT from an EC2 instance in Sydney to an EC2 instance in north Virginia is normally around 200 ms.

4. ASSESSMENT

The impact of using the AWS cloud in our course is assessed through both the instructor's observation and student surveys.

4.1 Instructor's Observation

Unlike some other CS courses, the programming for a variety of topics in the Computer Networking course often needs the involvement of multiple computers. In different layers, students need to learn the protocols and scenarios for making multiple parties such as clients and servers, peers, routers, or hosts communicate and work with each other. In real world applications, these parties reside on different computers in the network, which can be far from each other.

The instructor has observed several benefits of using the AWS cloud for our network programming projects. Previously, a student normally ran multiple processes on the same computer with the same IP address to simulate server and client programs on different computers in each project. When the AWS cloud is used, as discussed in Section 3.2, a student can conveniently use at least three different VMs on or off campus. This is very helpful for clarifying concepts regarding client/server mode and the roles of different programs in the network. Several students have told me that they couldn't make programs work in the cloud initially because they used the IP address of the client computer as the server's IP address for TCP or UDP data transmission.

Even if a student may use a laptop for the Client program and a lab computer for the Server program, using the AWS cloud still has advantages over the traditional approach. First of all, for some tasks such as testing the round-trip time, it is desirable that the computers running network programs reside in subnets that are far apart, or at least not in the same LAN. Both the laptop and the lab computer are inside the campus network. When the AWS cloud is used as shown in Figure 4, Client and Server programs run on computers in three subnets that are physically dispersed. Secondly, for network security, most ports are blocked in the local wireless network on our campus except for a few ports reserved for network services such as HTTP, HTTPS, and SSH. Since almost all students' laptops are connected to the Internet using WiFi, students won't be able to use unblocked ports for the TCP connection or UDP packet exchange implemented in the program running on the laptop. However, when the AWS cloud is used, students can remotely work on the EC2 instances using SSH clients (see Figure 4) since the port for SSH is open. Then the Client and Server programs running on EC2 instances can exchange TCP or UDP packets with each other using any port since the security group assigned to all EC2 instances allows incoming and outgoing traffic on all ports. Thirdly, every Server program in our projects is required to simultaneously support multiple Client programs. A certain number of EC2 instances can be easily launched for each student as needed.

Linux and Unix are popularly used as the operating systems of network servers in real-world applications because of their durability and stability. Therefore, all the EC2 instances were launched in Ubuntu, a Linux operating system. This provides an opportunity for students to gain experience working on Linux.

The price for the benefits of using the AWS cloud in our course is that the instructor needs to spend some extra time for preparation and management. At the beginning of the semester, the instructor needs to create a student user account and launch two EC2 instances for each student, create and send students the passwords of their user accounts and their private key files, and write a student user guide on how to use the AWS management console and their EC2 instances. During the semester, the instructor also needs to manage and moderate usage of the AWS cloud.

4.2 Survey Results

Two anonymous surveys were given to the students in CS3700, Spring 2014. Survey I was given in the first week to gain insight into their experience using cloud computing and other relevant skills. Survey II was given in the last week to assess the possible improvement in their skills relevant to cloud computing as well as their perceptions of using the AWS cloud. 24 students were on the roll at the beginning of the semester and 20 of them remained till the end. 19 students responded to Survey I and 18 students responded to Survey II.

The following questions were included in Survey I and the survey result is plotted in Figure 5. We can see that most of the students had heard about cloud computing, however, none of them had taken a course using AWS EC2 before and only a few had used another cloud computing platform in other courses.

Q1. Have you heard about any cloud computing platform?
Q2. Have you taken any course where AWS EC2 was used?
Q3. Have you taken any course where any cloud computing platform other than AWS EC2 was used?

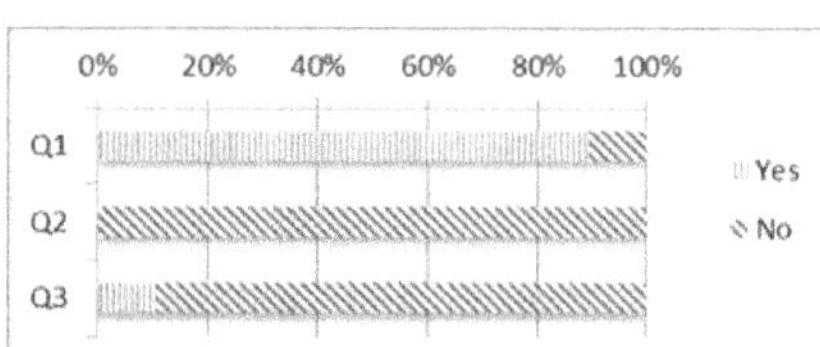

Figure 5. Experience on cloud computing prior to this course.

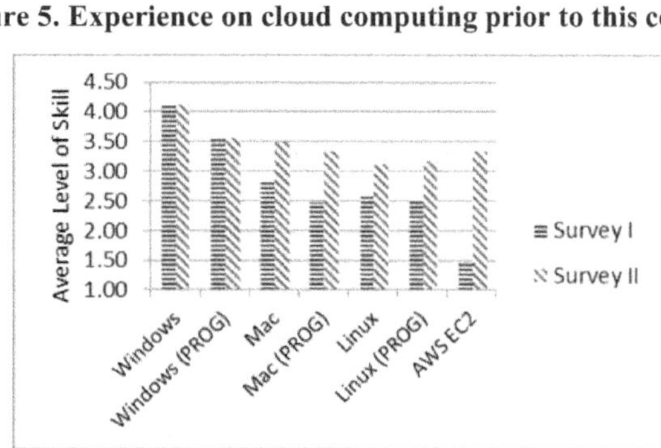

Figure 6. Average self-rated levels of skills (5 – Total Guru, 4 – Advanced, 3 – Intermediate, 2 – Beginner, 1 – Clueless)

In both Surveys I and II, students were asked to rate their skills in using Windows, programming (PROG) on Windows, using MAC, programming on MAC, using Linux, programming on Linux, and using AWS EC2. As shown in Figure 6, students' skills in using AWS EC2 significantly increased from 1.5 (half way between "Clueless" and "Beginner") to 3.3 (higher than "Intermediate"). The platform of students' EC2 instances was Ubuntu. Students used Mac or Windows to write their programs locally, connect to EC2 instances, and work on their programs remotely. Thus, their Mac and Linux skills increased too. Interestingly, being the highest at the beginning, their Windows skills did not change.

The following questions were also included in Survey II.

Q4. It is easy to learn how to use AWS EC2 to accomplish the relevant tasks given in homework assignments.
Q5. Using AWS EC2 to perform the tasks is convenient.
Q6. Using AWS EC2 makes it feasible to test networking programs on two computers when security restrictions are applied to local networks (e.g., most of the ports are blocked on campus WiFi).
Q7. Using AWS EC2 allows me to set up the running environment of my programs and access it anywhere to continue my work.
Q8. Using AWS EC2 allows me to test my client/server programs in the real network, i.e., on at least three different computers instead of on the same computer.
Q9. Using AWS EC2 allows me to run network commands or test my network programs on computers physically residing in different subnets far away from each other.
Q10. Using AWS EC2 in this course is beneficial for me to accomplish learning objectives in this course.
Q11. Using AWS EC2 is helpful for improving my skills in programming and running programs in the cloud.
Q12. Using AWS EC2 is helpful for improving my skills in programming and running programs on Linux.
Q13. Overall, I am in favor of using AWS EC2 in this course.
Q14. I would like to use AWS EC2 or other cloud computing services in other CS courses whenever it is appropriate.
Q15. The experience of using AWS EC2 in this course is helpful for my career development.

Q4 through Q9 were used to get students' opinions on the experience and benefits of using AWS EC2 in our course. The survey result is shown in Figure 7. We can see that all or a vast majority of the class agreed with Q6, Q8, and Q9 and no student disagreed. Most of the class agreed with Q4 and Q7 and only about 10% of the class somewhat disagreed. Interestingly, although more than half of the class agreed with the convenience of using AWS EC2, about 18% of the class somewhat disagreed.

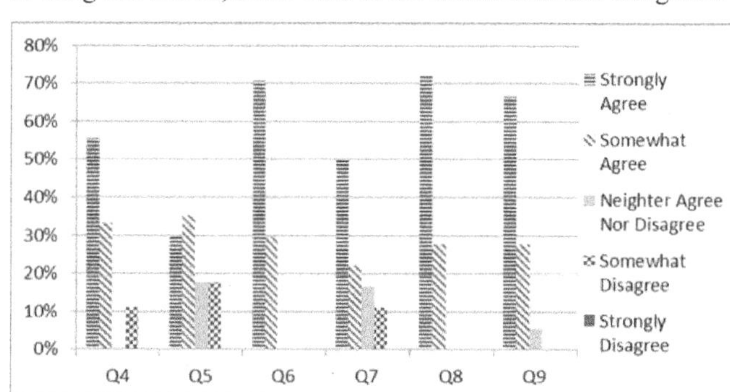

Figure 7. Perceptions of the experience and benefits.

Q10 through Q15 were used to get students' perceptions of the use of AWS EC2 for learning. In Figure 8, we can clearly see that more than 60% of the class strongly agreed and about 20% of the class somewhat agreed that using AWS EC2 had a positive impact on their learning experience and they are in favor of using cloud computing platforms for learning not only in this course but also in other CS courses if it is appropriate. No one disagreed with these statements except that about 10% of the class somewhat disagreed with the help to their Linux skills.

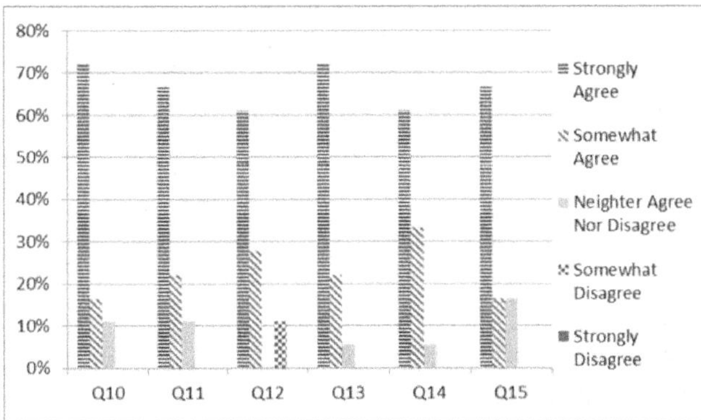

Figure 8. Perceptions of the use of AWS EC2 for learning.

5. CONCLUSION

This paper presents our experience of using two services, IAM and EC2, in the AWS cloud to support hands-on network programming projects in our Computer Networks course. IAM was used to create and manage student user accounts, and control student users' access to the AWS cloud. EC2 instances, i.e., VMs, were launched for students to develop and test their networking programs throughout the semester. The benefits and price of using the AWS cloud in our course were assessed via the instructor's observation and student surveys. Thanks to the AWS cloud, students were able to develop and test their networking programs on real networked systems located on two continents. Students could conveniently access the AWS cloud both on and off campus. The majority of students agreed that using the AWS cloud was helpful for their learning in this course and career development, and were in favor of using the AWS cloud not only in this course but also in other CS courses if applicable.

6. ACKNOWLEDGMENTS

Our thanks to Amazon Web Services for supporting our work via an AWS in Education Coursework Grant.

7. REFERENCES

[1] AWS Identity and Access Management: Using IAM (API Version 2010-05-08). Website= http://docs.aws.amazon.com/IAM/latest/UserGuide/IAM_Introduction.html.

[2] Amazon Elastic Compute Cloud Documentation. Website= http://aws.amazon.com/documentation/ec2/

[3] Cappos, J., Beschastnikh, I., Krishnamurthy, A., Anderson, T. 2009. Seattle: a platform for educational cloud computing. In *Proceedings of the 40th ACM technical symposium on Computer science education* (Chattanooga, TN, March 4 - 7, 2009). SIGCSE '09. ACM, New York, NY, 111-115. DOI=http://dl.acm.org/citation.cfm?id=1508905&bnc=1.

[4] Dinita, R.I., Wilson, G., Winckles, A., Cirstea, M., and Jones, A. 2012. A cloud-based virtual computing laboratory for teaching computer networks. In *Proceedings of 13th International Conference on Optimization of Electrical and Electronic Equipment* (Brasov, Romania, May 24 - 26, 2012). OPTIM 2012. IEEE, 1314-1318.

[5] Du, W. and Wang, R. 2008. SEED: A Suite of Instructional Laboratories for Computer Security Education. *J. Educ. Resour. Comput.* 8, 1 (March 2008), 3:1-3:24. DOI=http://dl.acm.org/citation.cfm?id=1348716.

[6] Holden, E. P., Kang, J. W., Anderson, G. R., Bills, D. P. 2011. Databases in the cloud: a status report. In *Proceedings of the 2011 conference on Information technology education* (West Point, NY, October 19 - 22, 2011). SIGITE '11. ACM, New York, NY, 171-176. DOI=http://dl.acm.org/citation.cfm?id=2047642.

[7] Holden, E. P., Kang, J. W., Bills, D. P., and Ilyassov, M. 2009. Databases in the cloud: a work in progress. In *Proceedings of the 10th ACM conference on SIG-information technology education* (Fairfax, Virginia, October 22 - 24, 2009). SIGITE '09. ACM, New York, NY, 138-143. DOI=http://dl.acm.org/citation.cfm?id=1631765.

[8] Nagappan, M., Peeler, A., and Vouk, M. 2011. Modeling Cloud Failure Data: A Case Study of the Virtual Computing Lab. In *Proceedings of the 2nd International Workshop on Software Engineering for Cloud Computing* (Honolulu, HI, May 22, 2011). SECLOUD '11. ACM, New York, NY, 8-14. DOI=http://dl.acm.org/citation.cfm?id=1985503.

[9] Salah, K. 2014. Harnessing the cloud for teaching cybersecurity. In *Proceedings of the 45th ACM technical symposium on Computer science education* (Atlanta, GA, March 5 - 8, 2014). SIGCSE '14. ACM, New York, NY, 529-534. DOI= http://dl.acm.org/citation.cfm?id=2538880.

[10] Schaffer, H. E., Averitt, S. F., Hoit, M. I., Peeler, A., Sills, E. D., and Vouk, M. A. 2009. NCSU's Virtual Computing Lab: A Cloud Computing Solution. *Computer*, 47, 7 (July 2009), 94-97.

[11] Sun, W., Katta, V., Krishna, K., and Sekar, R. 2008. V-NetLab: an approach for realizing logically isolated networks for security experiments. In *Proceedings of the conference on Cyber security experimentation and test* (San Jose, CA, July 28, 2008). CSET '08. USENIX Association, Berkeley, CA, 5:1-5:6. DOI=http://dl.acm.org/citation.cfm?id=1496667

[12] Xu, L., Huang, D., and Tsai, W.-T. 2012. V-Lab: A Cloud-based Virtual Laboratory Platform for Hands-On Networking Courses. In *Proceedings of the 17th ACM annual conference on Innovation and technology in computer science education* (Haifa, Israel, July 03 - 05, 2012). ITiCSE '12. ACM, New York, NY, 256-261. DOI=http://dl.acm.org/citation.cfm?doid=2325296.2325357.

[13] Yang, T. A. and Nguyen, T. A. 2006. Network security development process: a framework for teaching network security courses. *J. Comput. Small Coll.* 21, 4 (April 2006), 203-209. DOI=http://dl.acm.org/citation.cfm?id=1127428.

[14] Yue, C., Zhu, W., Williams, G. L., Chow, E. 2012. Using Amazon EC2 in Computer and Network Security Lab Exercises: Design, Results, and Analysis. In *Proceedings of 2012 American Society for Engineering Education Annual Conference & Exposition* (San Antonio, TX, June 10 - 13, 2012). ASEE.

Teaching Cybersecurity Analysis Skills in the Cloud [*]

Richard Weiss
The Evergreen State College
Olympia, WA 98505 U.S.A.
weissr@evergreen.edu

Stefan Boesen
Dartmouth College
Hanover, NH U.S.A.
stefan.boesen@gmail.com

James Sullivan
Michael Locasto
The University of Calgary
Alberta, Ontario, CA
locasto@ucalgary.ca
sullivan.james.f@gmail.com

Jens Mache
Erik Nilsen
Lewis & Clark College
Portland, OR U.S.A.
jmache@lclark.edu nilsen@lclark.edu

ABSTRACT

This paper reports on the experience of using the EDURange framework, a cloud-based resource for hosting on-demand interactive cybersecurity scenarios. Our framework is designed especially for the needs of teaching faculty. The scenarios we have implemented each are designed specifically to nurture the development of *analysis skills* in students as a complement to both theoretical security concepts and specific software tools.

Our infrastructure has two features that make it unique compared to other cybersecurity educational frameworks. First, EDURange is scalable because it is hosted on a commercial, large-scale cloud environment. Second, EDURange supplies instructors with the ability to dynamically change the parameters and characteristics of exercises so they can be replayed and adapted to multiple classes. Our framework has been used successfully in classes and workshops for students and faculty. We present our experiences building the system, testing it, and using feedback from surveys to improve the system and boost user interest.

Categories and Subject Descriptors

C.2.0 [**Computer-Communication Networks**]: General—*Security and Protection*; K.6.5 [**Management of Computing and Information Systems**]: Security and Protection—*Hacking*

General Terms

Security, Measurement

*This work was partially supported by NSF grants 1141341 and 1141314

SIGCSE'15, March 04-07, 2015, Kansas City, MO, USA.

ACM 978-1-4503-2966-8/15/03 ...$15.00.
http://dx.doi.org/10.1145/2676723.2677290

Keywords

offensive security; hacker curriculum; analysis skills; EDURange

1. INTRODUCTION

The US faces a major shortage of cybersecurity workers to defend our information infrastructure from attack [11]. In recognition of this need, security has been included as a core topic in the new ACM/IEEE Computer Science 2013 Curricula [16]. Cybersecurity is also mentioned in more than half of the other knowledge areas in this report. At educational conferences such as SIGCSE and regional CCSC conferences, we are also seeing a growing interest in cybersecurity among faculty who do not have expertise in this area. Given the tight constraints of the Computer Science curriculum, many schools do not have the luxury of offering a separate class in cybersecurity. We are seeing a growing concensus articulated in the CS 2013 Curricula and in the ACM report "Toward Curricular Guidelines for Cybersecurity" [14] to integrate cybersecurity into the Computer Science curriculum at multiple levels in multiple courses.

One of our primary goals for EDURange is to create exercises that nurture analysis skills. When speaking of analysis skills, we mean the ability to reason about large, complex, and opaque data and systems. Strong analytical skills enable people to impose structure and meaning on such artifacts, reason about these relationships, and draw meaningful conclusions or inferences. These are precisely the kinds of skills that we believe are useful in many cybersecurity scenarios from security policy design to reverse engineering to vulnerability analysis. Analysis skills work in conjunction with the security mindset, which is the ability to think about how systems can fail, and be made to fail in different ways. Questioning assumptions plays an important role in both defense and attack. In designing our exercises, we focus on the following analysis skills:

1. **Verifying assumptions** by checking network messages, protocols, file formats and other input data constraints to see if layers of abstraction are coherent and correct. Enumerating and checking if failure modes, exceptions, and errors are controlled, caught or anticipated.
2. **Gaining understanding** of program, network, or system behavior and semantics, network topology or organization, or a defense posture. Observing and enumerating how software components or network elements are actually composed.

3. **Extracting Information** from opaque artifacts. For example, analyzing a raw dump of network traffic or intrusion alerts or firewall logs and recognizing true anomalies.
4. **Creating Emergent Resilience** by understanding a system well enough to design and propose enhancements to reliability, fault tolerance, or availability.

One of the major obstacles to integrating the teaching of these skills and the security mindset into the curriculum is the amount of work required to create and set up new hands-on exercises that can be readily adapted to existing courses. There was a gap between what we wanted and what we could access, so we decided to build our own tools and exercises satisfying the following criteria:

1. *Flexibility* to use simple scripts to specify exercises at a high level and create variations. Many of the exercises written by others were good but not exactly what we wanted, and they were not easily modified. A big threat to creating *long-term teaching tools* with those approaches is that exercises become stale and answers become easy to Google.
2. *Ease-of-use for faculty*, which includes providing easy access to exercises, making them easy to create (not requiring configuration of VMs manually), easy to modify, and easy to share.
3. *Educational goals*: we wanted to implement scenarios that would teach analysis skills, the *security mindset,* and address the CS2013 guidelines.

This paper is about the design of our current set of exercises (Section 3.1) and our experience creating the framework and delivering the exercises to a variety of audiences (Section 4). We used surveys to evaluate whether students found the exercises interesting and considered them worthwhile. We also employed surveys and informal discussion to get feedback that we used to improve the exercises and the system. The main lessons learned were about the scaffolding required for the students, the interface required for the faculty, and the level of interaction required for the developers, which are discussed in Section 5. That section also discusses the mapping from exercises to the CS2013 curricula Security Knowledge Area. The next section describes related work and how our exercises and infrastructure extend previous work on hands-on exercises.

2. RELATED WORK

There is a growing pool of curriculum material, instructor/faculty training, and VM-based labs. Yet, it has been observed that most deployed exercises and hosted environments had several shortcomings that made them difficult to leverage in our classrooms [19]. For example, Towson's "Security Injections" [17] mainly focus on several important secure programming patterns, but do not emphasize analysis. The SEED [8] project presents a mature, well-documented set of exercises, which are not typically interactive or dynamic and require significant work to set up and run.

Our philosophy on information security education stems from our understanding and teaching of the hacker curriculum as described by Bratus [1]. This approach is predicated on the utility of understanding failure modes. Rather than teaching students the "success" cases, we attempt to deliver a culture shock that makes them disrespect API boundaries and adopt a cross-layer view of the CS discipline as described by Bratus et al. [3]. We also routinely encourage our students to adopt a dual frame of mind (attacker and defender) when solving problems to prevent artificial abstraction layers from becoming boundaries of competence [20]. The importance of analysis skills as explained by S. Bratus et al. [2] is based on linking expected behavior to actual behavior as seen in network traces, log files, program binaries, rules/policies, system call traces, network topologies, network interactions, unknown protocols, injected backdoor code, etc. All of our exercises are based on these skills. A tool that actually applies this type of analysis is NetCheck [21] which is used to debug network applications. Using a simplified model of normal network behavior, NetCheck collects information about network applications using strace.

Our work follows the tradition of creating cybersecurity games or exercises, which are known to engage students [18, 12]. This includes competitions such as CCDC[1], Plaid[2], notsosecure[3], iCTF[4] [7], CSAW[5] [12], TRACER FIRE[6], Packetwars[7], and many others. From our perspective, one problem with these competitions is that they require a significant amount of infrastructure and preparation by the organizers. For example, it took several grad students six months to create the exercises for iCTF [7]. Some competitions such as CCDC and Packetwars require the installation of physical hardware, and they require that students and their faculty travel to participate. There are also a number of non-technical games with the goal of interesting students with no technical background in cybersecurity. These include Control-Alt-Hack [6], [d0x3d!] [13], Security Cards[8], CyberCIEGE[9] [5] and Werewolves [9]. The last of these introduces players to the concept of covert channels in a non-technical context. Our exercises are intended to create scenarios that are closer technically to real-world situations that a security professional would face.

Cloud-based testbeds, such as DETERlab [15] and The RAVE were designed for large-scale security experiments and have also been used for teaching. However, they were not designed for the bursty demand for VMs produced by large classes. By using Amazon's EC2, our framework has a greater capacity for elasticity, hence scalability in terms of the number and size of classes that can access the testbed simultaneously as well as the total number of VMs. In addition, the former do not provide an easy-to-use framework for intructors to script the creation of exercises. The National Cyber Range is also of note, but its primary use is as a secure testbed for research. The Seattle Testbed[10] is a research environment with several security exercises including one on reference monitors [4]. The PacketWars game was a model for some of the EDURange exercises. It has provided students with access to "live" exercises on a small scale, and the overhead is high in terms of time and money. Table 1 shows the *strengths and weaknesses of existing cybersecurity labs, exercises, and curricula with respect to our goals.*

3. DESIGN OF THE EDURANGE FRAMEWORK

One of the main requirements was the ease of use in terms of accessibility and user interface. We address this accessibility requirement by deploying our framework on Amazon's AWS EC2 cloud. Students and faculty do not need to sign up in advance. The resources are always available, and students can work from

[1] http://nationalccdc.org/
[2] http://www.pwning.net/
[3] http://ctf.notsosecure.com/
[4] http://ictf.cs.ucsb.edu/
[5] https://csaw.isis.poly.edu/
[6] http://csr.lanl.gov/tf/
[7] http://packetwars.com/
[8] http://securitycards.cs.washington.edu/
[9] http://www.cisr.us/cyberciege/
[10] http://seattle.poly.edu/

Table 1: ***A Comparison of our Project and Other Projects.*** **EDURange focuses on developing cybersecurity analysis skills. This table is not a criticism of existing efforts, but rather meant to highlight the ways in which our project differs from the main characteristics of existing projects — note that these projects may have been built with different criteria in mind. Security Knitting Kit was not directly available from the website.**

Project	Primary Weakness	Primary Strength
CyberCIEGE	non-technical analysis	interactivity of training scenarios
SEED	lacks competitive interaction	comprehensive documentation
Security Injections	focus on defensive coding patterns	introductory; clear documentation; CS1, CS2
CCDC	requires travel; limited remote access	interactive and competitive
PacketWars	requires travel; limited availability	engaging, dynamic, competitive scenarios
ITSEED	minimal instructor support, distrib by flash drive	good documentation for students
Google Gruyere	narrow focus (web apps)	cloud-based; well-documented
The RAVE	limited scalability, complex to modify	cloud-based; existing lab manual
Seattle Testbed	limited in scope	easy-to-use; scalable; includes mobile devices
DETERlab	limited scalability	range of exercises
EDURange	limited number of exercises	flexible, easy-to-use, interactive, cloud-based

anywhere. The original interface was an ssh client, and we now have a browser interface. We decided against the alternative of running VMs on a local cluster because that would have been more expensive to create and more work to maintain. Running the Recon 1 exercise for a class of 30 students only costs $0.40 per hour.

An important way in which we achieved flexiblity is through the use of tools such as Chef that script the installation of software. The same Chef script can install packages for a wide range of operating systems. The base VMs on AWS don't change frequently, and the Chef scripts that install software can handle upgrades transparently.

Each EDURange exercise is specified by a YAML file. YAML is similar to XML but more concise. A small number of types of entities recur in all of our scenarios. Based on a Scenario Description Language [10], we chose our primitive types to be: networks, instances (host computers, nodes), software that is directly involved in the exercise, participants (users), groups (teams of users), artifacts (flags), and goals (scoring events). Some exercises clearly involve networks and subnets. For example, Recon 1 and Recon 2 have a subnet for the battlespace and a subnet for each team. The ELF Infection exercise has a simple network topology with a subnet for each team and a subnet for the infected VM. An "instance" is usually a VM with an operating system. The special software for Recon 1 includes nmap and tcpdump. The scoring events in this exercise would include the IP addesses of the instances in the battlespace.

Our scenario description language together with the interpreter provide flexiblity to modify exercises each time they are run. In our pedagogical model, students repeat exercises. For example, with Recon 1, a student may try a set of options for nmap and discover that it takes too long or is not stealthy enough. We want the student to have time to think about trying different options after experiencing the problem. Analysis takes time, which is a limitation of most competitions. They tend to reward speed and don't allow time for in-depth analysis. Repeating exercises is not viable if the network configuration is static. Scripting in EDURange makes network configuration dynamic. For example in Recon 1, instructors can change the IP addresses of hosts in the BattleSpace through the YAML file. In Elf Infection, an instructor with help from us was able to change which binaries were infected.

3.1 Scenarios

An educational goal of each scenario is the development of analysis skills; in other words, the student would come away from the experience with not only an appreciation for the content knowledge involved or a basic understanding of the tools, but also with *insight* and a *logical approach* for understanding the conceptual issues at play. EDURange is a work in progress, and we have a number of exercises under development. Each exercise has multiple levels, and except for Recon, we only describe the first level. Each exercise addresses information assurance and security (IAS) goals in the ACM/IEEE CS2013 Curricula [16], page numbers refer to that document.

- **Recon 1** is about mapping a network and understanding network protocols, such as TCP, UDP, ICMP. The learning outcome being able to diagram a network for security (p. 107)
- **Recon 2** includes intrusion detection and prevention. The student trades off speed with stealth, the attacker must be able to map a network without triggering the defenses. In the attacker/defender mode, background traffic is injected into the network. The defender must distinguish between the attack and background. This addresses network monitoring and intrusion detection (p. 106)
- **ELF Infection** is about forensics and reverse engineering. The student is given a VM, which has an infected utility. They must discover which utility is infected and where the malicious behavior is. This an example of malware (p. 105)
- **ScapyHunt** is a puzzle set in a software defined network. The players must find data on a target host that is behind a gateway by passively examining network traffic and crafting packets to reveal specific information. The style of play is similar to a text adventure game. This is an example of diagraming a network and network monitoring (p. 106).
- **Firewall** is about creating a set of rules to control traffic in and out of a network. More generally, it requires understanding how a complex set of rules implements an access conrol policy. (p. 106)
- **Fuzzing** In the simplest version, the defender is given the grammar for a calculator and must implement an interpreter for that grammar. The attacker tries to fuzz the interpreter to produce incorrect results or get it to reject a valid expression. This is an attacker/defender game. Fuzzing is a Core Tier2 elective (p. 104)
- **Process Records (strace)** involves dynamic analysis of bi-

naries and poses the challenge of understanding what a process is doing based on its system calls. Students learn to filter large amounts of data to distinguish between normal and anomalous behavior indicative of malware. (p. 105)

4. TESTING EXERCISES

4.1 Methodology

For this initial study, we focused on two research questions:

1. Would our framework meet the needs of faculty?
2. Would our exercises be engaging for students?

We administered surveys and interviewed participants at several events, including SISMAT, classes in computer security, the two hackathons, and workshops for faculty at conferences such as SIGCSE and CCSC. *SISMAT is a summer program for college undergraduates* that includes a two-week intensive program in cyber security at Dartmouth College followed by a summer internship. Students do extensive lab work, and Recon 1 is one of the exercises used. A PacketWars competition is held on the last day, set up and run by a Packet Master, who is independent of the SISMAT program. A survey is given at the end of the two weeks to assess the exercises, including PacketWars, and how they affect student interest in security. The survey questions can be found in the Appendix. We also used Recon 1 in four security classes and we gave abbreviated surveys in those classes.

Hackathons lasting two days have been used twice to facilitate the development of exercises and infrastructure. The participants were faculty and students. The activities included design sessions for new scenarios and software architecture, implementation sessions for current scenarios; and testing sessions for implemented scenarios (Recon 1). An independent evaluator attended these hackathons, observed some sessions and interviewed participants.

Several workshops lasting 1.5 – 3.0 hours were offered to faculty. They were given a brief introduction and asked to play the Recon 1 exercise in pairs. The surveys focused on what faculty got from the workshop.

4.2 A Detailed View: The Recon 1 Exercise

The Recon 1 exercise was inspired by a largely similar execise from PacketWars. We chose it as the first exercise to implement because it is simple, we understood it, and it exhibits the characteristics of the types of scenarios we are interesting in deploying and supporting in our framework. This enabled us to concentrate on building the infrastructure without having to worry about specifying the scenario. A diagram of the network topology is shown in Figure 1.

We have now run the Recon 1 exercise with over 120 students in 6 different settings spanning four different institutions as shown in the table below. The first roll out of the Recon 1 exercise was at the SISMAT 2013 program. Recon 1 was one of 6 lab experiences that the students participated in during the 10 day workshop. Student feedback indicated that there were problems. However, student responses on a post-class survey revealed that students felt that the exercise was worthwhile and that it increased their interest in cybersecurity education (one-tailed t-test found ratings well above neutral $p < .01$). This p-value indicates that the likelihood that we would have measured this result if the students had been selected at random from a population that was on average neutral is less than 1%. See Appendix for a list of the survey questions. Further investigation revealed what background information and skills the students needed. For example, a better understanding of network partitioning, TCP and UDP protocols, and more practice with

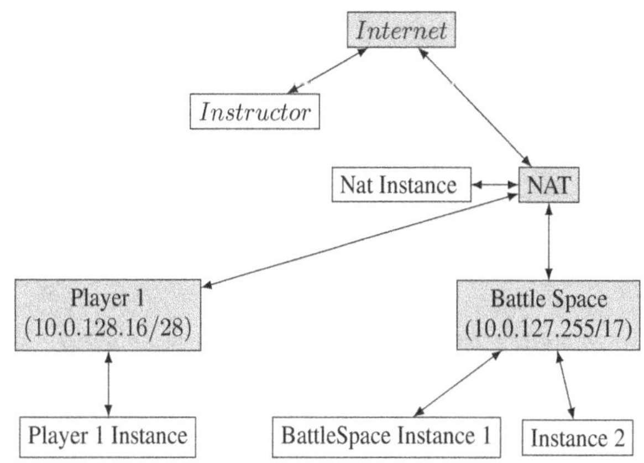

Figure 1: Conceptual diagram of the Recon I game. Note subnets are shaded (blue)

using nmap. An updated version of Recon 1 was given again at SISMAT 2014, and qualitative results show that it was ranked second out of six compared with fourth out of six in 2013. The top-ranked exercise was still PacketWars, which was the only exercise run as a competitive game. The ranking of PacketWars over all other exercises was statistically significant using a Friedman test. Since the content was similar to Recon 1, this supports the claim that live competitions are more exciting than non-competitive exercises. However, we did not assess learning in this trial, and we did not control for instructor.

Eleven College students along with four professors spent two days in August 2013 in an intensive hackathon that included 2 trials of the Recon 1 exercise, once with advanced students with previous computer security coursework and once with students with no prior computer security training. This workshop uncovered several issues with remote configuration and set up of the infrastructure, that were subsequently fixed. We also learned that the prerequisite knowledge needed for students with no prior security training should include the OSI model for network layers.

The Recon 1 exercise has also been piloted with 85 students in four classes at three schools. In one of these courses (CS 495), student surveys conducted at the end of the semester indicate that students found the Recon 1 exercise worthwhile in their learning (M=5.25 on a 7 point likert scale, $p < .005$). **Conclusion: The Recon 1 exercise was engaging for students in a variety of settings.**

Along with testing the Recon 1 exercise with over 120 students, we also held workshops for 29 faculty at three different conferences. As you can see in the table below, we targeted a variety of institutions, including instructors at two year colleges, small liberal arts colleges and research universities. Our workshop attendees also differed widely in experience with respect to teaching Computer Security courses, some had no experience yet while others had taught several different courses at both undergraduate and graduate levels. At each conference, we made adjustments based on feedback and challenges experienced in the how to present the Recon 1 Scenario. We also gave post workshop surveys at each conference. At each conference participants felt that taking the workshop increased their interest in the topic of Cyber Security (all $p < .02$). At our SIGCSE workshop, some felt that Recon 1 was too challenging, while others said it was easy. **Conclusion: Recon 1 did not meet the needs of some faculty in that it was too challenging for them without additional preparation.**

Table 2: Classes and workshops. The cost of each event in terms of cloud usage was less than $20. Each VM costs $0.013 per hour. We ran 30 VMs for 48 hours for the hackathons.

Date	Site	Audience	Attendance	student or faculty
June 2013	Dartmouth	SISMAT	12	student
Aug 2013	Lewis & Clark	Hackathon	11	student
Oct 2013	CCSC-NW	workshop for faculty (Liberal Arts)	8	faculty
Nov 2013	Evergreen	Network Security class	40	student
Jan 2014	MPICT	faculty (2-year Colleges)	7	faculty
Feb 2014	Lewis & Clark	CS 495 Cybersecurity	19	student
Feb 2014	Univ. of Calgary	CPSC 601 Seminar: Security Analysis	4	grad student
March 2014	Univ. of Calgary	CPSC 525 Network Security	25	student
March 2014	SIGCSE	faculty workshop (Broad Scope)	14	faculty
May 2014	Lewis & Clark	Hackathon	15	student & faculty
June 2014	Dartmouth	SISMAT	17	student
Fall 2014	Wellesley	CS342	28	student
Fall 2014	Lewis & Clark	CS393 Networking	20	student
Oct 2014	CCSC-NW	workshop for faculty (Liberal Arts)	14	student & faculty

4.3 A Detailed View: ScapyHunt

ScapyHunt has been tested twice. Once with a small class of graduate students together with Recon 1, and a second time at SISMAT 2014. The exercise provides a login prompt and little else beyond the directive "find the hidden resource in this hidden network topology." Students found it to be significantly harder than Recon 1, and based on this feedback we are designing an introductory level. They also expressed a wish for a simple canned demo or hint to start off with. There is a constant stream of network data that students must analyze, and the software defined network (SDN) has a complex topology with multiple subnets, which students must discover and diagram. This addresses both analysis of complex data and a complex network topology.

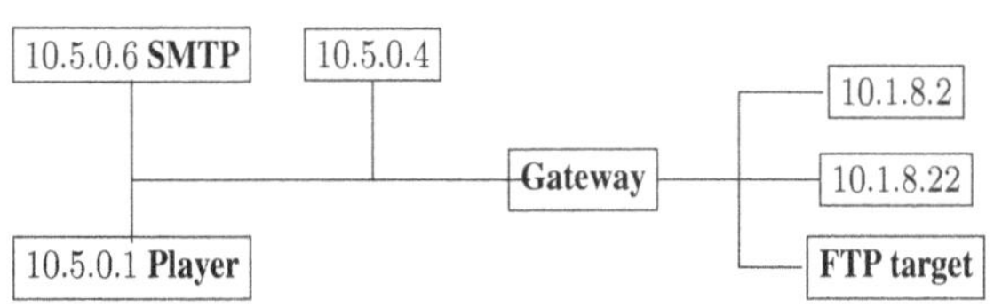

Figure 2: *The ScapyHunt Topology*. Students must discover this topology by crafting packets and observing how the network reacts.

The students required prompting during most of the interaction. For example, the students needed prompting to open a terminal and use standard network command line tools and utilities (e.g., Wireshark) to discover network information. They quickly fixated on nmap, although nmap is ultimately of little utility for this exercise. To us, this confirms that we need an exercise or demo to bridge the gap between Recon 1 and ScapyHunt. We prompted students to both "write" to the network (via ping, nmap, netcat, and some packet-crafting tools) and simultaneously "read" from the network to observe both their own actions and the actions of the entities in the software defined network (SDN). They also did not use any notes, drawings, or scripts. This kind of mistake is unlikely to be repeated when they repeat the exercise because they saw how "big" the task was in terms of the amount of information generated by the tools they eventually used.

5. DISCUSSION AND LESSONS LEARNED

Based on informal feedback from faculty, there is a demand for hands-on cybersecurity exercises, and they want them to be easy to use. This demand seems to come from a wide range of faculty, and they have expressed interest in our exercises.

We learned from surveys, using a 7-point likert scale with 4 as neutral, at CCSC-NW 2013 (CC) and SIGCSE 2014 (SI), that there was significant interest in using these exercises 1) as an introduction to a topic to stimulate further interest and lay the groundwork for class ($p(>4)=.01$ for both); 2) as a tool to use during lecture/instruction to help teach the key concepts ($p(>4)= .02$ CC, $p(>4)= .01$ SI); and 3) to test students' knowledge ($p(>4)= .002$ CC, $p(>4)= .004$ SI). Thus, faculty felt most strongly that EDURange could be used for assessment.

We learned from our classes and SISMAT that hands-on exercises provide a starting point for discussing important topics. For example, Recon 1 can be an opportunity to discuss the OSI model, subnet masking, broadcast addresses, even using the command line. Based on survey results, students were positive that the exercises were worthwhile and contributed to their learning. We conclude from this that they were able to use our exercises for formative self-assessment. Unlike with exams, where students do not want to admit what they don't know, with hands-on exercises such as Recon 1, students were able to reflect on what they didn't know in the context of what they wished they had known when trying the exercise. Since Recon 1 is a very focused exercise, students were able to identify at SISMAT and hackathons the need for more tutorials and canned demos on specific topics, such as TCP, ICMP and subnetworks. With exercises such as Recon 1, there is no way to fake the knowledge needed. On the other hand, we learned that the game must be at the appropriate level for the audience. If students haven't studied networking and don't have experience with the command line, they will have difficulty and may get frustrated. In response, we have started to create some tutorials and "level zero" versions.

6. CONCLUSION AND FUTURE WORK

Our framework provides a scalable infrastructure to an audience of instructors that have few local resources or capacity to set up complex systems. By using a public industry "best of breed" cloud, EDURange is unique and cost effective, and avoids some of the limitations associated with dedicated testbeds. Many of our student and instructor audiences were positive about its potential.

While our framework has significant advantages as a teaching platform over existing infrastructure, it is not intended to replace such environments (The RAVE, DETERlab). Our main focus is on providing dynamic, flexible cybersecurity scenarios that teach analysis skills (rather than toolsets or specific attacks). While the exercises we designed lead to the analysis of large, opaque artifacts, our framework can also incorporate exercises that teach background knowledge. We believe that support for customizing scenarios represents a natural evolution of cybersecurity education infrastructure. We have plans to add a scoring mechanism which will make it possible for the system to give continuous feedback to students and provide summative assessment data to faculty.

7. REFERENCES

[1] BRATUS, S. What hackers learn that the rest of us don't: Notes on hacker curriculum. *IEEE Security and Privacy 5* (2007), 72–75.

[2] BRATUS, S., D'CUNHA, N., SPARKS, E., AND SMITH, S. W. Toctou, traps, and trusted computing. In *Trusted Computing-Challenges and Applications*. Springer, 2008, pp. 14–32.

[3] BRATUS, S., SHUBINA, A., AND LOCASTO, M. E. Teaching the principles of the hacker curriculum to undergraduates. In *Proceedings of the 41st ACM technical symposium on Computer science education* (New York, NY, USA, 2010), SIGCSE '10, ACM, pp. 122–126.

[4] CAPPOS, J., AND WEISS, R. Teaching the security mindset with reference monitors. In *Proceedings of the 45th ACM Technical Symposium on Computer Science Education* (New York, NY, USA, 2014), SIGCSE '14, ACM, pp. 523–528.

[5] CONE, B. D., IRVINE, C. E., THOMPSON, M. F., AND NGUYEN, T. D. A video game for cyber security training and awareness. *Computers & Security 26*, 1 (2007), 63 – 72.

[6] DENNING, T., LERNER, A., SHOSTACK, A., AND KOHNO, T. Control-alt-hack: the design and evaluation of a card game for computer security awareness and education. In *Proceedings of the 2013 ACM SIGSAC conference on Computer & communications security* (2013), ACM, pp. 915–928.

[7] DOUPÉ, A., EGELE, M., CAILLAT, B., STRINGHINI, G., YAKIN, G., ZAND, A., CAVEDON, L., AND VIGNA, G. Hit 'em where it hurts: A live security exercise on cyber situational awareness. In *Proceedings of the 27th Annual Computer Security Applications Conference* (New York, NY, USA, 2011), ACSAC '11, ACM, pp. 51–61.

[8] DU, W., AND WANG, R. Seed: A suite of instructional laboratories for computer security education. *J. Educ. Resour. Comput. 8* (March 2008), 3:1–3:24.

[9] ENSAFI, R., JACOBI, M., AND CRANDALL, J. R. Students Who Don't Understand Information Flow Should Be Eaten: An Experience Paper. In *Proceedings of the 5th USENIX conference on Cyber Security Experimentation and Test (CSET'12)* (2012), pp. 10–10.

[10] FITE, B. Simulating cyber operations: A cyber security training framework, 2014. http://www.sans.org/reading-room/whitepapers/bestprac/simulating-cyber-operations-cyber-security-training-framework-34510.

[11] FRYER-BIGGS, Z. DoD faces cyber expert talent shortage. *Computer 33*, 12 (2000), 52–59.

[12] GAVAS, E., MEMON, N., AND BRITTON, D. Winning cybersecurity one challenge at a time. *Security & Privacy, IEEE 10*, 4 (2012), 75–79.

[13] GONDREE, M., AND PETERSON, Z. N. Valuing security by getting [d0x3d!]: Experiences with a network security board game. In *Presented as part of the 6th Workshop on Cyber Security Experimentation and Test* (Berkeley, CA, 2013), USENIX.

[14] MCGETTRICK, A., CASSEL, L. N., DARK, M., HAWTHORNE, E. K., AND IMPAGLIAZZO, J. Toward curricular guidelines for cybersecurity. In *Proceedings of the 45th ACM Technical Symposium on Computer Science Education* (New York, NY, USA, 2014), SIGCSE '14, ACM, pp. 81–82.

[15] PETERSON, P. A., AND REIHER, P. L. Security exercises for the online classroom with deter. *Proc. of the 3rd USENIX CSET* (2010).

[16] SAHAMI, M., GUZDIAL, M., MCGETTRICK, A., AND ROACH, S. Setting the stage for computing curricula 2013: computer science–report from the acm/ieee-cs joint task force. In *Proceedings of the 42nd ACM technical symposium on Computer science education* (2011), ACM, pp. 161–162.

[17] TURNER, C. F., TAYLOR, B., AND KAZA, S. Security in computer literacy: a model for design, dissemination, and assessment. In *Proceedings of the 42nd ACM technical symposium on Computer science education* (New York, NY, USA, 2011), SIGCSE '11, ACM, pp. 15–20.

[18] VIGNA, G. Teaching Network Security through Live Exercises. In *Proc. 3rd Ann. World Conf. Information Security Education (WISE 03)* (2003), Kluwer Academic, pp. 3–18.

[19] WEISS, R., MACHE, J., AND NILSEN, E. Top 10 hands-on cybersecurity exercises. *Journal of Computing Sciences in Colleges 29*, 1 (2013), 140–147.

[20] WHITE, G., AND NORDSTROM, G. Security across the Curriculum: Using Computer Security to Teach Computer Science Principles. In *Proceedings of the 19th National Information Systems Security Conference* (1996), NIST, pp. 483–488.

[21] ZHUANG, Y., GESSIOU, E., PORTZER, S., FUND, F., MUHAMMAD, M., BESCHASTNIKH, I., AND CAPPOS, J. Netcheck: Network diagnoses from blackbox traces. In *11th USENIX Symposium on Networked Systems Design and Implementation (NSDI'14), USENIX.*

APPENDIX

Survey given to SISMAT students

The following questions were given at the end of the two-week intensive training. A seven-point Likert scale was used, except for question 3 which asks for a ranking.

1. What was your level of interest in each exercise?
2. How many hours did you spend on each exercise?
3. Rank the activities from most interesting to least interesting
4. The time spent on the activity was worthwhile
5. The activity contributed to my overall understanding of the material
6. Preparation (reading, lecture) were sufficient for me to successfully understand the lab
7. What was the level of difficulty?

A Cloud Computing Course: From Systems to Services

M. Suhail Rehman[1], Jason Boles[2], Mohammad Hammoud[2], Majd F. Sakr[1]
suhailr@cs.cmu.edu, jboles@cmu.edu, mhhamoud@cmu.edu, msakr@cs.cmu.edu

[1]School of Computer Science
Carnegie Mellon University
Pittsburgh, PA, USA

[2]Carnegie Mellon University in Qatar,
Education City, P.O Box 24866,
Doha, Qatar

ABSTRACT

We have designed, developed and administered a course on cloud computing that was taught to over 700 students at our institution over two years. The goal of this project-based course is to provide students with foundational systems concepts as well as experience in developing the required skills to design and deploy viable, robust and elastic web-services within performance and budgetary constraints. We present our objectives, learning outcomes, projects, learning model, outcomes and lessons learned. So far, for this demanding course, our student retention rate is above 80% and enrollment is doubling every year.

Categories and Subject Descriptors:

K.3.2 [**Computers and Education**]: Computer and Information Science Education – *computer science education, curriculum*

General Terms: Design

Keywords: Distance Education; Web-Based Techniques; Instructional Technologies; Cloud Computing.

1. INTRODUCTION

Cloud computing offers a paradigm shift in the way organizations procure, use and manage information technology. The cloud offers computing facilities on-demand, served over a network from a shared pool of resources, typically residing in a large data center. Cloud computing offers a new approach to the way applications are written and deployed.

One of the primary benefits of cloud computing is *elasticity*, whereby resources can be automatically expanded during demand spikes, or contracted during demand lulls; thereby improving user experience and system utilization. As the cloud model is rapidly gaining acceptance, industry is scrambling to find experienced people who can effectively leverage, employ and operate the model. In contrast, academia has not responded quickly enough (so far) to offer a satisfactory number of well-trained cloud computing engineers, architects, developers and researchers.

To help fill this critical void, we designed a novel course on cloud computing that was taught to over 700 students across over the last two years. The course methodically covers the building blocks and enabling technologies of cloud computing, including data centers, virtualization, cloud storage, cloud programming models, and analytics engines, among others. We were successful at accomplishing our specified pedagogical goals, and learned a great deal of lessons throughout the process. As a result, the course became popular at our university, and currently enrollment is doubling every year.

In this paper, we report on our experience in offering the course. In particular, we discuss the course content, its design and implementation, outcomes, and the lessons learned. Our objective is to share our experience with instructors who aim at offering similar courses in cloud computing.

SIGCSE '15, March 4–7, 2015, Kansas City, MO, USA
Copyright © 2015 ACM 978-1-4503-2966-8/15/03…$15.00
http://dx.doi.org/10.1145/2676723.2677298

2. MOTIVATION & GOALS

Cloud computing is an emerging technology that affects users, developers and organizations alike. With the fast growth of the cloud, it is very likely that computer science graduates, at various levels, will find themselves evaluating, developing and/or deploying systems, services and applications for the cloud.

A recent report from the Bureau of Labor Statistics (BLS) indicated that hiring in data processing, hosting and related services has been growing steadily in 2013. Over 3600 new jobs were added in July 2013, marking the strongest growth since June 1998[36]. The report also projects that over 671,300 new jobs will be added in this sector by 2020. Alongside, the International Data Corporation (IDC) reported that two-thirds of the industry are either planning, implementing or using cloud computing, with 50 percent of businesses acknowledging that cloud computing is currently a top priority[21].The report also estimates that 1.7 million cloud-related positions remained unfulfilled worldwide due to lack of necessary skills and/or adequate training.

Moreover, students who are planning to pursue research in computer science or other fields will find that cloud computing is increasingly being adopted in a variety of domains, from Big Data management and storage, to analytics, through computational science, to online education; hence, making studying cloud computing crucial.

Our goal is to develop students' foundational knowledge in systems and hands-on skills in cloud services in order to equip them with the skills necessary to meet current and future industry demands as well as to enable them to carry out applied research on the cloud. To achieve this task, we intentionally placed the course content and projects at the intersection between systems concepts and cloud services.

3. DESIGN

3.1 Intended Audience

This course was tailored for junior and senior undergraduate Computer Science and Engineering students as well as graduate students from various technical majors. The course was designed as a 9-unit (i.e., 9 work-hours per week) course for undergraduate students and a 12-unit course for graduate students. The extra 3 units, for graduate students, require them to work on a large team-based project. Students who wish to take the course must have completed an introductory computer systems course as a prerequisite.

3.2 Course Objectives

The course was designed to be an introductory course on cloud computing. It provides an overview of the field, while offering hands-on experience with various cloud computing services and infrastructures. Students gain a broad understanding of the economic and technological factors that led to the emergence of cloud computing. In addition, they attain a considerable comprehension of the main building blocks (e.g., resource sharing, storage and programming models) that compose a cloud system and the ensuing cloud services.

We also struck a balance between theory and practice in the course to provide our students with satisfactory preparation to target either industry or academia. The projects were designed to give practical experience with several cloud enabling services and systems such as Amazon Web Services (AWS), Hadoop[40], and NoSQL systems[37]. In short, we attempted to craft a course that covers the cloud computing field with sufficient depth and breadth. We intended to allow students to easily proceed with, and hopefully excel at, a cloud-related position in industry or academia.

3.3 Learning Outcomes

Given our motivation, goals, intended audience and objectives, we specified the following high-level Learning Outcomes (LOs) for the course. Specifically, after finishing the course, students are expected to: (1) explain the core concepts of the cloud computing paradigm: how and why this paradigm shift came about, and the characteristics, advantages and challenges introduced by the various models and services in cloud computing; (2) apply the fundamental concepts in data centers to understand the tradeoffs in power, efficiency and cost; (3) discuss the virtualization technology and outline its role in enabling cloud computing; (4) illustrate the key concepts of cloud storage such as Amazon S3[3] and HDFS[14], DynamoDB[5], HBASE[27] and; (5) analyze different cloud programming models such as Elastic MapReduce[2]; (6) develop working experience with big-data analysis on public cloud platforms; (7) demonstrate the high-level use of resource management front-ends to develop elastic applications to meet performance constraints; (8) demonstrate proficiency in deploying, and comparing and contrasting new generation cloud-based storage systems; (9) employ MapReduce to solve a real-world data analytics problem; (10) design, assemble, deploy and evaluate an end-to-end web-service solution for a very large data set given performance and cost constraints.

3.4 Bottom-Up Approach

The course organization was motivated by presenting concepts from the bottom-up to facilitate learning, performance and retention. In particular, the sequence of topics started with an introduction, then presented data centers and their design considerations, virtualization technologies, cloud storage solutions and then programming models. The approach was to gradually peel away the layers that comprise any cloud. For each concept, we started by presenting a bird's eye view of the concept prior to delving systematically into the details. By that, we sought for students to easily grasp the material and effectively piece together the various cloud technologies and principles. We further attempted to teach students, not only how a certain system (e.g., MapReduce) works, but also how it can be built so as to enable their creativity in suggesting novel ideas and systems. As an example, in Unit 5, we initially discussed the foundation and the pros and cons of every programming, computational, parallelism and architectural model by which a cloud analytics engine can be constructed, and, subsequently, demonstrated how MapReduce and other frameworks apply such foundations and models.

4. TOPICS COVERED

We now elaborate on the topics that we covered throughout the course. Specifically, we present the main concepts that we studied in each of the five Units, the introduction, data centers, virtualization, cloud storage, and cloud programming models and analytics engines Units, respectively.

4.1 Introduction

As an introduction to the cloud computing field, we discussed in Unit 1 the motivating factors, benefits, challenges, economic and business models, service models (i.e., software-as-a-service, platform-as-a-service and infrastructure-as-a-service), deployment models (i.e., private, public and hybrid clouds), and the main building blocks (i.e., data centers, virtualization, storage, and analytics engines) of cloud computing.

4.2 Data centers

Data centers constitute the infrastructure of every cloud deployment model, being private, public or hybrid. They enable many of the economic and technological benefits of the cloud paradigm. In Unit 2, we described several concepts behind data center design and management. In particular, we provided historical overview of data centers, outlined the major components and architectures of modern data centers, and indicated the design considerations for building cloud infrastructures for various cloud deployment models.

4.3 Resource Sharing and Virtualization

Virtualization is an important layer in cloud computing. Virtual resources are typically constructed from the underlying physical resources and act as proxies to them. In Unit 3, we studied various ingredients of the virtualization technology and the crucial role it plays in enabling cloud computing. Specifically, we first identified major reasons for why virtualization is becoming essential, especially for the cloud. Second, we discussed how multiple hardware and software images can share a single resource while provided with security, resource and failure isolations; all being critical for cloud computing. Third, we examined two virtual machine types, process and system virtual machines. Lastly, we studied how CPU, memory and I/O resources are virtualized, with examples from Xen[12] and VMWare[9]. We concluded with a representative case study, using the Amazon Elastic Compute Cloud[1].

4.4 Cloud Storage

The cloud storage is used as a repository for Big Data. In Unit 4, we described storage concepts for clouds, including problems of Big Data scale, management, distribution, durability, consistency and redundancy. We detailed the three distinct layers of cloud storage; that is, data (i.e., structured vs. unstructured and static vs.

dynamic), abstractions (i.e., file systems, databases and object storage), and physical and virtual block devices. We concluded with multiple case studies, including HDFS[14], PVFS[34], Apache HBase[27], Apache Cassandra[30], and Amazon's S3[3].

4.5 Programming Models and Analytics Engines

Researchers and practitioners have evolved various models that mitigate the challenges for designing and implementing software systems that successfully exploit the capabilities of the cloud. The current generation of these models builds upon *classical* predecessors. In Unit 5, we studied some classical programming (e.g., shared-memory and message-passing), computational (e.g., synchronous and asynchronous), architectural (e.g., master-slave and peer-to-peer), and parallelism (e.g., data-parallel and graph-parallel) models by which cloud programs and analytics engines can be constructed. Afterwards, we present popular cloud analytics engines (such as MapReduce) and designate the programming, computational, architectural and parallelism models that each of them adopts and offers.

5. LEARNING MODEL

Cloud computing has been taught twice at our university as a traditional course with typical in-class lectures and recitations. From spring 2013 semester onwards, the instructors decided to transform this course to an online version so as to enable:

- Students from across the globe to access elite college materials and instructions
- Students to learn at their own pace and time
- Students to choose among a variety of learning styles and explore course material in an interactive fashion.

With these objectives in mind, we designed and offered an introductory undergraduate/graduate online course in cloud computing, which suits the needs of the students across our university's global campuses.

The learning model that we chose to deploy this course on engages students in four different settings (Figure 1). Particularly, students access the course content on the Online Learning Initiative (OLI) Platform[7], ask questions on Piazza[8], complete projects on Amazon Web Services (AWS)[1] and attend, or watch videotaped, weekly recitations.

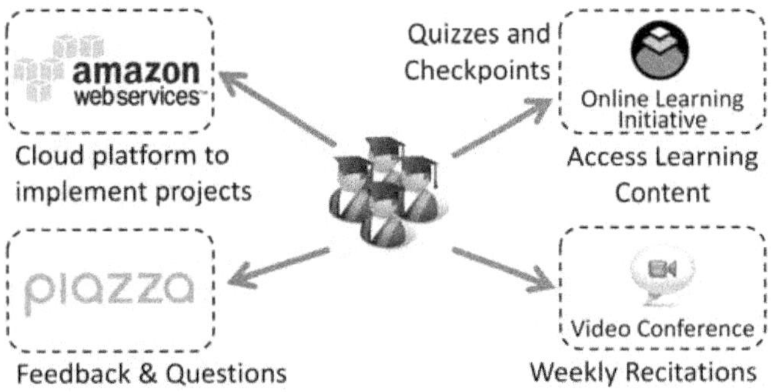

Figure 1. The learning model for this course

5.1 Online Learning Initiative (OLI)

The Open Learning Initiative (OLI) is a grant-funded effort at Carnegie Mellon University. OLI's approach to instructional design is outcome-driven, evidence-based, and technology-assisted. Its infrastructure offers high-quality, scientifically-based, and classroom-tested tools for online course design, development, delivery, and assessment[39].

OLI provides a web-based platform which allows developers to encode course content, including text, images and videos. The content is structured hierarchically as *Units* that contain a sequence of *Modules*. In return, each Module constitutes a sequence of *Pages*. OLI allows developers to embed various types of activities and assessment methods. A crucial aspect of OLI's web platform is the ability to provide hints and specific feedback based on students' responses to different activities. In addition, OLI offers a learning dashboard which provides extended information to educators. For example, instructors can quickly see which topics are mostly confusing students or how individual students are overall performing.

5.2 Amazon Web Services (AWS)

In a course on cloud computing, it is necessary to give students hands-on experience with a public cloud platform. For that sake, we chose Amazon Web Services (AWS), an industry-leader in online cloud computing services. AWS has fairly wide portfolio of cloud services including Compute (i.e., Amazon Elastic Compute Cloud), and Storage (i.e., Amazon Elastic Block Store and Simple Storage Service) services, to mention a few. According to[31], AWS is the most widely-used cloud platform, making many of its services de-facto industry standards. Of course, the cloud computing market is still evolving. As such, we tried to ensure that the basic skills that our students get on AWS are transferrable to other platforms or providers.

Although our university has multiple private clouds, we avoided using any of them in this course. This is because on our private clouds (and typically on similar private clouds), there is always the risk of not having enough resources to satisfy the class demand, especially during peak periods (e.g., at submission deadlines). Such a risk is completely eliminated on AWS.

5.3 Piazza

In addition to OLI and AWS, students in this online course need to clarify doubts and conduct discussions with their peers. We chose Piazza, an online Q&A platform that is designed for university courses. Piazza is easy to use and popular among students. Students and instructors can post notes and queries on Piazza. In return, queries can be answered by instructors, TAs, or other enrolled students.

5.4 Recitations

In order to allow students to obtain some face-time with the instructors, weekly recitation sessions were arranged and videotaped. During these sessions, announcements were made and pressing issues were discussed. When necessary, certain aspects of the programming projects were demoed for the students' benefit.

6. DEVELOPMENT

Course development commences after defining the course objectives, LOs and course outlines. This phase included the development of the individual Units and their content, activities for students to practice what they learn, quizzes to test and assess student learning, and programming projects to develop expertise in cloud systems and services. Although we have offered the course in the traditional format twice before, the course had to be re-designed to better suit the web-based style of OLI, and the material had to be updated and evolved to reflect the latest developments in cloud technologies.

6.1 Student Assessment

As with any course, a good LO assessment plan is important to gauge the progress students have made in retaining and applying the knowledge offered by the course. In this course, student assessment is done in two forms: The end-of-unit quizzes and programming projects. Since the hands-on experience is a main objective of this course, we chose to emphasize the programming projects by making 75% of the final grade assigned to programming projects and 25% to end-of-unit quizzes.

6.1.1 Quizzes

Each of the 5 Units of the course comes with a checkpoint quiz, which the students have to complete within a stipulated deadline. The quizzes consists of 20-50 questions (depending on the Unit), and typically take 2-3 hours to complete. Each question is selected from a pool of questions randomly to limit cheating. The quiz questions are encoded as a checkpoint activity in OLI, which will track the student progress and will automatically grade the students on their work. Students will have one attempt at the quiz before the due date. After the due date, they will receive their scores and feedback for each individual question they have attempted.

6.1.2 Projects

The programming projects in this course were designed to give the students hands-on experience with systems concepts and cloud services that Amazon provides. The projects were designed to be easily transformed to other public cloud platforms. The projects address the hands-on LOs of the course. We designed 5 projects, the details of which are summarized below:

Project 1 was designed to be the introductory project, whereby students can get familiar with AWS and big data. After creating accounts and linking them with the course for payment purposes, they used EC2 instances to explore a data set, and created simple UNIX tools/scripts as well as sequential code to extract information and answer questions based on a small sample of the data set. Afterwards, a much larger version of the data set was provided for students to analyze. It would be impractical to analyze the larger data set on a single machine using their sequential code. Students, hence, get their first taste of a big data analytics problem and then proceed to employ a MapReduce job to carry out their analysis. The scenario employed for Project 1 was to find trending topics given the Wikipedia page views information[10]. The small data set asked them to analyze a single hour's worth of page views, while the larger data set required finding overall trending topics based on the page views of an entire month.

Project 2 dealt with a real world scenario to evaluate scaling methods to meet a web service's performance constraints. Students learned to use the AWS SDK to manage and monitor EC2 instances, and programmatically scale them up and down using Amazon's AutoScale API and Elastic Load Balancer (ELB) to meet the demands of a varying web load generator.

In Project 3, students worked on and evaluated the capabilities and limitations of various cloud storage technologies. Students compared flat files and databases for storing structured information. They also evaluated different storage back-ends on Amazon to compare their performance for an OLTP benchmark[4]. Students then implemented a horizontally scaling database using the Elastic Load Balancer and Amazon AutoScaling. Students worked with Amazon DynamoDB (a NoSQL database) to create an image archive[23] that was reachable from a web interface. Finally, students employed the Yahoo! Cloud Serving Benchmark (YCSB)[18] to compare and contrast two NoSQL systems, DynamoDB[5] and HBase[27].

In the fourth project, students worked on developing an application using the MapReduce programming model. As a final task, students developed an input text predictor, similar to Google Autocomplete, by using a subset of the Gutenberg[28] or Wikipedia [25] text corpora. Students performed a number of NLP tasks, using MapReduce, including generating a list of n-grams from the text corpus and creating a statistical language model. Finally students created a database to access the language model in real-time from a web interface.

In the team-based project for graduate students, the theme was to build an end-to-end cloud service to meet service specifications, performance and cost constraints. The input data set is a large dump of tweets collected using the Twitter streaming API over a period of several months. Student need to build a web service that can respond to specific queries of varying complexity. Students must then choose an appropriate scalable database backend, perform Extract Transform Load (ETL) to ingest the data and design and connect a scalable front end to service the web queries. An automated load generation system was developed and employed to test the students' web services. Students' systems were evaluated based on correctness, performance and the cost, per-hour, to run their web service on the public cloud. In order to encourage competition between teams, a live web-based scoreboard ranks teams on performance and cost so teams can improve their cloud service.

6.1.3 Cheat Checking

All projects were performed on AWS's infrastructure, with each student having an individual account on AWS. All the student accounts were linked to a master paying account owned by the university. This enables us to collect a log of student provisioning, activity and expenditure. The project descriptions and instructions were all encoded on OLI, and students had to complete a project checkpoint activity after they have completed each task within a project. The checkpoint activity asks for a random item or value that can only be obtained after the project is completed successfully. This enables different students to answer questions for different parts of the data set and the system can automatically grade students on their project work. As mentioned above, some projects required an entire testing system to be developed. Since students utilized system images designed by the course staff, all work on these instances was logged to a server for verification. Furthermore, student code submissions were compared to current and past submissions using MOSS[6] which generated a similarity report.

To identify potential cheating cases, we developed an analytics system that ingests data from the multiple end points described above. Our system applies certain pre-determined rules to red-flag students who may have cheated. Examples include, correctly answering the checkpoint quiz without provisioning the necessary resources on AWS. This system is extremely powerful at letting students know that we are collecting information and can, with a little bit of effort, build a lot of evidence to prove a cheating case. Interviews with red-flagged students shed a lot of light on how much collaboration took place and dissuades all students from committing violations of academic integrity.

7. OUTCOMES

7.1 Matriculation, Attrition and Performance

The course has had a very favorable response with students from diverse programs and majors. So far 700 students have enrolled in the course over the last 2 years. About 10% are undergraduate, 1% are PhDs, and the rest are Masters students. Our retention rate hovers between 82% and 83%, which is similar compared to traditional courses at our department (80-85%). Successful completion rates are in the high ninety percent. The student grades follow a similar distribution to other courses offered at our institution.

7.2 Costs

Since we have adopted a public cloud infrastructure for our projects, evaluating cost is an important long-term factor for sustainability and scale. The course was supported by an AWS educational grant [4]. In the first few semesters, our university granted additional funds towards AWS costs for the course. In our first few offerings, we struggled with managing runaway costs by negligent students. During the first three offerings, the course cost approximately $300, on average, per student.

However, with the deployment of near-real-time logging, monitoring and alarm systems, we have significantly reduced abuse. Furthermore, the cost of AWS resources has significantly decreased in the last 12-months. Students who spend more than the pre-set project budget receive an automatic warning email indicating their infraction. Repeat offenders are liable to receive grade penalties. As a result, we have been able to reduce costs down to approximately $150 per student. Another aspect of cost is Teaching Assistant (TA) support. The TAs provide logistical and technical support via Piazza, office hours and the weekly recitation. They are also involved in the developing and testing our projects, load generator, auto-grading and cheat-checking systems. At our institution, every twenty five students allow the hiring of a single TA who can spend up to 20 hours a week supporting the course.

7.3 Student Feedback

At the end of each course offering, we administer an anonymous online survey, which 90% of the students respond to. Overall student feedback on the course has been steadily positive with most respondents saying that they would recommend this course to their friends. This has been reflected in doubling enrollment with each year. Overall, students were very enthusiastic about learning new programming models such as MapReduce and have asked for future versions of the course to spend more time on such topics. Students found the Unit dealing with programming models to be the most useful in the course, followed by cloud storage. Initially, students did not find the Unit on data centers particularly useful. Since then we have revamped the material and its relevance to the course which has improved their views of this unit. The graduate survey responders found Project 5 to be very useful and believed that they learned the most from it. However, these students complained that the project demanded a lot of their time given the open-ended scenario and rigorous evaluation. Students indicated that they enjoyed combining several technologies and services together to create a full-fledged application.

7.4 Lessons Learned

The course development required a large time investment to design and develop content, videos, activities, auto-graded quizzes and partially auto-graded projects. With platforms such as OLI, this has to be completed well in advance before the semester starts. Significant testing is required to remove bugs in activities, quizzes and projects before they are presented to students. Good and timely feedback is critical in enabling student learning. Instructors should maximize the capabilities of their chosen platforms to provide a variety of activities with useful feedback. Our content benefits from properly structured and well-thought activities, quizzes and projects that are aligned with the course objectives and learning outcomes. This enables the systematic evaluation and assessment of the course to enable learning. Such efforts are always a work in progress and require ongoing updates.

From observing the OLI dashboard and AWS activity, it is clear that students are deadline driven and typically do not consume content or work on projects until close to the deadlines. It is best for students to have weekly deliverables on content and projects. We are experimenting with the idea of expiring tokens to encourage students to test their solutions against our load generators prior to the deadline.

Instructors planning to offer similar courses with projects on AWS must pay careful attention to cost. Projects that require expensive resources such as larger instance types or faster storage can drive up costs very quickly. Daily monitoring of student activity and resource usage is important to keep the course within budget. Carelessness on the part of students who forget to terminate resources after they are done can be especially precarious to budgets if left unchecked.

8. SIMILAR COURSES

Border[13] presented his experience in teaching cloud computing at Rochester. He stressed on the necessity to teach the cloud's enabling technologies in order to allow students to effectively apply the cloud computing concepts. Indeed, many universities have already started featuring undergraduate and/or graduate courses on cloud computing. For instance, University of Maryland's course on cloud computing[11] is generally regarded as the first in the field, wherein it focuses mainly on MapReduce [24]. University of California at Berkeley has also a graduate-level seminar course on cloud computing[20] as well as an undergraduate-level one, which focuses on programming the cloud[15]. Cornell teaches two classes on the cloud, one that stresses on resource sharing[17] and another that mainly concentrates on cloud storage[22].

To the contrary of developing a new standalone course dedicated to cloud computing, Radenski[33] at Chapman University suggested integrating cloud computing in a High-Performance Computing course. The course focuses on data-intensive processing with MapReduce as a main, available and easy-to-use parallel programming model for cloud computing. Holden[29] proposed using cloud computing to teach a databases course at Rochester. In particular, the course uses AWS to provide a secure, flexible and adaptable lab environment that is accessible off-campus and meets the course's predefined curricular needs. Likewise, Salah[35] at Khalifa University of Science, Technology and Research, UAE promoted utilizing cloud-based labs in a cybersecurity course. The course aims at leveraging the cloud to provide hands-on experience and training to students as well as remedy the cost, operation, scheduling, and management problems typically associated with classical cybersecurity labs. Lastly, Wang[31] at Michigan Technological University incorporated cloud computing into a computer systems and network administration course through a single high-level class project. Specifically, the project entails building and testing two clouds using Eucalyptus[32] and Xen[12].

To this end, some cloud courses are also being taught online, and seem to be catering primarily to industry professionals. Notable among these are Berkeley's Software-as-a-Service course (CS169.2X) on edX[19], and Stanford's cloud computing course

(CS309A)[16]. We find that most of these online courses focus either too much on a few technologies or offer a very broad overview from an information system's perspective.

As compared to all these cloud-enriched or pure-cloud classical and online courses, our course is uniquely positioned to provide foundational knowledge in systems with practical hands-on experience with designing, building and evaluating real-world solutions using real-world scenarios and data sets. Students develop projects while optimizing for performance and running cost under a strict development budget. This course bridges the gap between academia and industry with respect to preparing the next generation of cloud computing architects, engineers, developers and researchers.

9. FUTURE OFFERINGS

The course is offered every semester for students at our institution. We plan to continue to incorporate many enhancements based on feedback collected and lessons learned. We plan to explore a more diverse set of topics such as streaming programming models, cloud-enabled mobility, security and software defined networks and storage[26,38]. Furthermore, we are exploring the possibility of incorporating our projects on multiple public cloud infrastructures such as Microsoft and Google public clouds. It is our intent that students will get to choose the cloud platform for each project as part of their solution design.

10. REFERENCES

[1] Amazon Elastic Compute Cloud http://aws.amazon.com/ec2/

[2] Amazon Elastic MapReduce http://aws.amazon.com/elasticmapreduce/

[3] Amazon S3 http://aws.amazon.com/s3/

[4] AWS in Education http://aws.amazon.com/education/

[5] DynamoDB http://aws.amazon.com/dynamodb/

[6] MOSS: A System for Detecting Software Plagiarism http://theory.stanford.edu/~aiken/moss/

[7] Online Learning Initiative http://oli.cmu.edu

[8] Piazza Technologies http://www.piazza.com

[9] VMWare http://www.vmware.com

[10] Wikipedia Page Views http://dumps.wikimedia.org/other/pagecounts-raw/

[11] Web-Scale Information Processing Applications http://www.umiacs.umd.edu/~jimmylin/cloud-2008-Spring/index.html

[12] Barham, P., Dragovic, B., Fraser, K., Hand, S., Harris, T., Ho, A., Neugebauer, R., Pratt, I., and Warfield, A., 2003. Xen and the art of virtualization. *ACM SIGOPS Operating Systems Review 37*, 5

[13] Border, C.B., 2013. Cloud computing in the curriculum: fundamental and enabling technologies. In *Proceeding of the 44th ACM technical symposium on Computer science education* ACM, 147-152.

[14] Borthakur, D., 2008. HDFS architecture guide. *Hadoop Apache Project. http://hadoop.apache.org/common /docs/current/hdfs_design.pdf*

[15] CS 194-17: Programming the cloud http://db.cs.berkeley.edu/w/cs-194-17-programming-the-cloud/

[16] CS309: Cloud Computing http://cs309a.stanford.edu/

[17] CS5412: Cloud Computing http://www.cs.cornell.edu/courses/cs5412/2012sp/

[18] Cooper, B.F., Silberstein, A., Tam, E., Ramakrishnan, R., and Sears, R., 2010. Benchmarking cloud serving systems with YCSB. In *Proceedings of the 1st ACM symposium on Cloud computing* ACM, 143-154.

[19] CS169.2x, Software as a Service https://www.edx.org /course/uc-berkeley/cs-169-2x/software-service/1005

[20] CS 294: Cloud computing: systems, networking, and frameworks http://www.cs.berkeley.edu/~istoica/classes/cs294/11/

[21] Cushing, A. and Gantz, J.F., *Climate Change: Cloud's Impact on IT Organizations and Staffing, IDC Whitepaper.* IDC.

[22] CS5320: Big Data http://www.cs.cornell.edu/Courses/cs4320/2012fa/

[23] Caltech-256 Dataset http://www.vision.caltech.edu/Image_Datasets/Caltech256/

[24] Dean, J. and Ghemawat, S., 2008. MapReduce: simplified data processing on large clusters. *Communications of the ACM 51*, 1

[25] Wikimedia Downloads http://dumps.wikimedia.org/

[26] Foundation, O.N., 2012. Software-defined networking: The new norm for networks. *ONF White Paper*

[27] George, L., 2011. *HBase: the definitive guide*. O'Reilly Media, Inc.

[28] Project Gutenberg http://www.gutenberg.org/

[29] Holden, E.P., Kang, J.W., Bills, D.P., and Ilyassov, M., Databases in the cloud: a work in progress. In *Proceedings of the Proceedings of the 10th ACM conference on SIG-information technology education* (Fairfax, Virginia, USA2009)

[30] Lakshman, A. and Malik, P., 2010. Cassandra: a decentralized structured storage system. *ACM SIGOPS Operating Systems Review 44*, 2

[31] Leong, L., Toombs, D., Gill, B., Petri, G., and Haynes, T., 2014. *Magic Quadrant for Cloud Infrastructure as a Service.* Gartner. ID: G00261698

[32] Nurmi, D., Wolski, R., Grzegorczyk, C., Obertelli, G., Soman, S., Youseff, L., and Zagorodnov, D., 2009. The Eucalyptus Open-Source Cloud-Computing System. In *Cluster Computing and the Grid, 2009. CCGRID '09. 9th IEEE/ACM International Symposium on*, 124-131.

[33] Radenski, A., 2012. Integrating data-intensive cloud computing with multicores and clusters in an HPC course. In *Proceedings of the 17th ACM annual conference on Innovation and technology in computer science education* ACM, 69-74.

[34] Ross, R.B. and Thakur, R., 2000. PVFS: A parallel file system for Linux clusters. In *in Proceedings of the 4th Annual Linux Showcase and Conference*, 391-430.

[35] Salah, K., Harnessing the cloud for teaching cybersecurity. In *Proceedings of the Proceedings of the 45th ACM technical symposium on Computer science education* (Atlanta, Georgia, USA2014)

[36] Bureau of Labor Statistics, Employment Situation Summary http://www.bls.gov/news.release/empsit.nr0.htm

[37] Stonebraker, M., 2010. SQL databases v. NoSQL databases. *Communications of the ACM 53*, 4

[38] Thereska, E., Ballani, H., O'shea, G., Karagiannis, T., Rowstron, A., Talpey, T., Black, R., and Zhu, T., IOFlow: a software-defined storage architecture. In *Proceedings of the Proceedings of the Twenty-Fourth ACM Symposium on Operating Systems Principles* (Farminton, Pennsylvania2013)

[39] Thille, C., 2008. Building open learning as a community-based research activity. *Iioshi and Kumar (Eds.). Opening up Education: The Collective Advancement of Education through Open Technology, Open Content, and Open Knowledge*

[40] White, T., 2012. *Hadoop: the definitive guide*. O'Reilly.

Budget Beowulfs:
A Showcase of Inexpensive Clusters for Teaching PDC

Joel C. Adams
(Organizer) Calvin College
adams@calvin.edu

Jacob Caswell
St. Olaf College
caswell@stolaf.edu

Suzanne J. Matthews
U.S. Military Academy
suzanne.matthews@usma.edu

Charles Peck
Earlham College
charliep@cs.earlham.edu

Elizabeth Shoop
Macalester College
shoop@macalester.edu

David Toth
Centre College
david.toth@centre.edu

Categories and Subject Descriptors
C.1.4 [**Processor Architectures**]: Parallel Architectures – *Distributed architectures*
K.3.2 [**Computers and Education**]: Computer and Information Science Education – *Computer Science Education.*

General Terms
Experimentation, Performance

Keywords
Architecture; Beowulf; Clusters; Computing; Distributed; Education; Hardware; Inexpensive; Multicore; Parallel; Processes; Teaching; Threads

1. SUMMARY
In response to the shift to multicore processors, the ACM-IEEE CS2013 curriculum recommendations [1] include parallel and distributed computing (PDC) as a new core knowledge area. Some of the key concepts in PDC are the distinctions between shared-memory, distributed-memory, and heterogeneous system architectures.

Most CS educators would agree that providing students with hands-on experience improves their students' learning. Given the ubiquity of multicore processors, it is quite easy to give today's students hands-on experience developing software on shared-memory architectures. By contrast, providing students with hands-on experience developing software for distributed architectures has typically required access to a Beowulf cluster, the price of which was beyond the reach of many institutions. However, hardware manufacturers have recently begun producing a variety of inexpensive "system on a board" multiprocessors. Creative CS educators are using these multiprocessors to design and build inexpensive Beowulf clusters, and using them to provide students with hands-on experience with shared-memory, distributed-memory, and heterogeneous computing paradigms.

In this special session, several PDC educators will bring, present, and demonstrate their innovative Beowulf clusters; each designed and built using a different inexpensive multiprocessor board.

SIGCSE '15, March 4–7, 2015, Kansas City, MO, USA
ACM 978-1-4503-2966-8/15/03.
http://dx.doi.org/10.1145/2676723.2677317

2. SESSION OBJECTIVE
Most CS educators have heard of the *Raspberry Pi* [9], but many are unaware of more powerful system-on-a-board computers, such as Adaptiva's *Parallella* [3], the *CubieBoard2* [5], the Nvidia *Jetson* [7], or the *ODROID-U3* [6]. In this session, our primary objective is to give CS educators the opportunity to:

1. Learn about these inexpensive multiprocessor boards;
2. See how their peers have used them to build clusters; and
3. Hear how their peers are using those clusters to teach PDC.

A secondary objective is our hope that, by showcasing the innovative work of these CS educators, we can inspire other CS educators to create their own clusters – some undoubtedly using multiprocessors that are not yet invented – and thus unleash a wave of innovation in PDC education.

3. SESSION OUTLINE
Some of these "system on a board" multiprocessors are no bigger than a credit card. Thanks to these diminutive sizes, each presenter will bring his or her entire cluster to the conference. Before the session begins, the presenters will set up their clusters for display and demonstration on tables at the front of the room.

In the first 25 minutes of the session, each presenter will give a 5-minute, 5-slide "lightning talk" on his or her cluster, including its specifications and how they use it to teach PDC.

The middle 25 minutes will be a "Group Q&A" in which audience members can direct questions to the presenters as a group.

The last 25 minutes will be a "Show&Tell" session in which the presenters will move to their clusters and audience members can approach and interact with the presenters individually.

Table 1 presents a concise overview of the session.

What	Who	Duration
Introduction	Joel Adams	3 min.
StudentPi and *StudentParallella*	Suzanne Matthews	5 min.
PIsToGo	Jacob Caswell	2 min.
HSC-1 and *HSC-2*	David Toth	5 min.
Rosie	Elizabeth Shoop	5 min.
LittleFe	Charlie Peck	5 min.
Group Q&A	Audience	25 min.
Show&Tell	Everyone	25 min.

Table 1. Session Overview

This 75-minute session is thus one third presentations, a third all-group Q&A, and a third Show&Tell.

In the remainder of this section, we provide descriptions for each presenter and the cluster he or she will present. For each of these clusters, the total cost includes everything needed to build the system (interconnect, parts, shipping, etc.), except for a monitor, mouse, and keyboard. The presenters' slides and the disk images for their clusters will be archived at *csinparallel.org* [4].

3.1 Joel Adams (Organizer)

Dr. Adams is a professor of computer science at Calvin College. He has designed and built four Beowulf clusters, including Microwulf [2], a portable sub-$2500 system that was the first cluster to break the $100/GFLOP barrier. He will introduce each presenter, and moderate the Q&A and Show&Tell segments.

3.2 Suzanne Matthews

Dr. Matthews is an assistant professor of computer science at the United States Military Academy. She will present two clusters:

- *StudentPi* has 4 Raspberry Pi nodes. Each node has an ARM 1176JSFS (700 MHz) CPU, a videocore 4 GPU, 512MB RAM, and 4GB of microSD storage. The nodes are connected using Gigabit Ethernet. The total cost was $240 ($60/core).
- *StudentParallella* has 4 Parallella nodes. Each node has a Zynq 7000-series dual core ARM A9 (1 GHz) CPU, an Epiphany coprocessor with 16 (800 MHz) cores, 1 GB RAM, and 16GB of microSD storage. The nodes are connected using Gigabit Ethernet. The total cost was $650 (~$10/core).

3.3 Jacob Caswell

Jacob is a sophomore CS and Physics major at St. Olaf College. He will present *PIsToGo*, a complete five-node passively cooled Raspberry Pi cluster-in-a-briefcase that cost $300 (~$60/core).

3.4 David Toth

Dr. Toth is an assistant professor of computer science at Centre College. He will present two "Half-Shoebox Clusters", each of which is about half the size of a shoebox:

- *HSC-1* has two CubieBoard2 nodes. Each node has an ARM Cortex-A7 dual-core (1GHz) CPU, 1 GB RAM, and 4 GB of micro-SD storage. The nodes are connected with 100 Mbps Ethernet. The total cost was $198.27 (~$50/core).
- *HSC-2* has two ODROID-U3 nodes, each with a Samsung Exynos 4412 ARM Cortex-A9 quad-core (1.7GHz) CPU, 2 GB RAM, and 8 GB of micro-SD storage. The nodes are connected with 100 Mbps Ethernet. The total cost was $211.28 (~$26/core).

3.5 Elizabeth Shoop

Dr. Shoop is a professor of computer science at Macalester College. She will present *Rosie*, a cluster with six Nvidia Jetson-TK1 nodes. Each node has an ARM Cortex-A15 quad core (2.2GHz) CPU, a Kepler GPU with 192 (950MHz) CUDA cores, and 2GB RAM. The nodes share a 500GB hard disk and are connected with Gigabit Ethernet. The total cost was $1350 (~$56/ARM core; ~$1.70/ARM+CUDA core).

3.6 Charles Peck

Dr. Peck is a professor of computer science at Earlham College. He will present *LittleFe* [8], the original cluster-in-a-suitcase. LittleFe has six custom-built nodes. Each has an Intel dual-core Atom (1.8GHz) CPU, an Nvidia ION2 GPU with 16 (475 MHz) CUDA cores, and 2 GB RAM. The nodes share a 160GB disk, and are connected with Gigabit Ethernet. The total cost was $2500 (but *LittleFe Buildout* participants get theirs for free!), including a shock- and water-proof carrying case.

4. EXPECTATIONS

We believe that hands-on exercises in which students must apply abstract concepts improve their understanding of those concepts. However, the hardware needed for students to experience some PDC topics (e.g., scalability) has traditionally been expensive.

The clusters featured in this session range in price from $200 to $2500, making them much more affordable than traditional Beowulf clusters. One instructor is using a lab fee to provide each student with his or her own personal cluster! People attending this session will thus learn about a range of clusters at a variety of prices, how CS educators are using those clusters, and will have the opportunity to ask detailed questions to those educators.

As a result, this session will be of interest to anyone who is interested in PDC or is teaching a course that covers PDC topics. Such courses include: *Algorithms*, *Computer Architecture*, *Computer Organization*, *Graphics*, *Operating Systems*, *Parallel Computing, Software Engineering*, *System Fundamentals*, the *Senior Capstone* course, and others. This special session will thus be of interest to instructors from a wide variety of CS courses.

5. SPECIAL SESSION SUITABILITY

The presenters will bring, display, and demonstrate their clusters, making this 75-minute session a "show and tell" style session. During the first third, the audience will receive an overview of all the systems being presented. The middle third's "Group Q&A" will allow the audience to engage with the presenters in a format that lets everyone hear all questions and answers. In the final third's "Show&Tell" session, presenters will concurrently demonstrate their clusters to interested audience members, who can move from cluster to cluster, view the clusters up close, and ask detailed questions. This session's structure will thus be quite different from that of a typical paper or a panel session.

6. REFERENCES

Parts of this work were supported by NSF DUE #1225739.

7. REFERENCES

[1] ACM/IEEE CS Joint Task Force. "Computer Science Curriculum 2013". Online. Accessed 2014-08-01. http://ai.stanford.edu/users/sahami/CS2013/.

[2] J. Adams and T. Brom. "Microwulf: A Beowulf Cluster for Every Desk", *Proc. of the 39th SIGCSE Technical Symposium*, March, 2008, p. 121-125, DOI= 10.1145/1352135.1352178.

[3] Adapteva. "Parallella". Online, accessed 2014-08-01: http://www.adapteva.com/parallella/.

[4] R. Brown, L. Shoop, J. Adams. "CSinParallel: Parallel Computing in the CS Curriculum". Online, accessed 2014-08-01. http://csinparallel.org.

[5] CubieBoard. "CubieBoard2". Online, accessed 2014-08-01: http://cubieboard.org/.

[6] Hardkernel. "ODROID-U3". Online, accessed 2014-08-01: http://hardkernel.com.

[7] Nvidia. "Jetson-Tk1". Online, accessed 2014-08-01: https://developer.nvidia.com/jetson-tk1.

[8] C. Peck, et al. "LittleFe: Parallel and Cluster Computing On The Move". Online, accessed 2014-08-01: http://littlefe.net.

[9] Raspberry Pi Foundation. "Raspberry Pi". Online, accessed 2014-08-01: http://www.raspberrypi.org.

Using App Inventor in Introductory CS Courses

Meimei Gao
Mercer County Community College
Business & Technology Division
1200 Old Trenton Road
West Windsor, NJ 08550
gaom@mccc.edu

Julie Johnson
Vanderbilt University
Elec. Eng. & Comp. Sci. Dept.
2301 Vanderbilt Place
Nashville, TN 37235
Julie.l.johnson@vanderbilt.edu

Dale Reed
University of Illinois at Chicago
Dept. of Computer Science
851 S. Morgan St. (MC 152)
Chicago, IL 60607-7053
reed@uic.edu

Cate Sheller
Kirkwood Community College
Math/Science Dept.
6301 Kirkwood Blvd SW
Cedar Rapids, IA 52402 USA
Cate.Sheller@kirkwood.edu

Franklyn Turbak (Moderator)
Wellesley College
Computer Science Dept.
136 Central St.
Wellesley MA, 02481
fturbak@wellesley.edu

Categories and Subject Descriptors

K.3.2 [**Computers and Education**]: Computer and Information Science Education—*Computer science education*; D.2.6 [**Programming Environments**]: Graphical environments

General Terms

Human Factors, Languages

Keywords

CS0; CS1; mobile application programming; visual programming; blocks programming

1. SUMMARY

MIT App Inventor [3] is a visual programming environment targeted at novices for creating mobile apps for Android devices. It lowers barriers to programming and app development through a browser-based visual blocks language that reduces syntactic errors and encapsulates mobile device features into high-level abstractions that are easy to incorporate into apps. This panel explores how App Inventor can be integrated into undergraduate computer science and engineering courses to introduce computational thinking [5, 6] in the context of building mobile apps.

The moderator will begin with an overview of the NSF TUES *Computational Thinking through Mobile Computing* project [1], which has developed numerous materials to support the teaching of computational thinking with App Inventor and has sponsored several workshops for undergraduate faculty interested in using App Inventor in their courses.

The panelists were participants in a 2.5-day Summer 2013 workshop [4] who are now teaching with App Inventor in their courses. The panelists will describe how they use App Inventor in their courses. The panelists represent many different perspectives, including the type of institution (community college, liberal arts college, university), type of course (CS0, CS1), and level of App Inventor integration in the course (short module, short course, full-semester course).

The presentations by the moderator and the panelists will be limited to 8 minutes each, leaving over 30 minutes for discussion based on questions from the audience. We expect discussion topics to include student diversity, whether students take additional CS courses, and Android devices vs. emulators.

SIGCSE'15, March 4–7, 2015, Kansas City, MO, USA.
ACM 978-1-4503-2966-8/15/03.
http://dx.doi.org/10.1145/2676723.2677335.

2. FRANKLYN TURBAK (MODERATOR)

In addition to teaching a full-semester CS0 course, *Inventing Mobile Apps*, based on App Inventor, I am the lead Principal Investigator of the *Computational Thinking through Mobile Computing* project. This NSF TUES project is a collaboration between Wellesley College, MIT, Trinity College, University of Massachusetts Lowell, and the University of San Francisco.

Making the situated nature of mobile devices (including sensors, location awareness, social networks, and Internet connectivity) accessible to introductory students opens up compelling opportunities for computer science education. Our team has identified big ideas of *mobile computational thinking* that augment traditional problem solving and programming concepts: mobile computing is event-based, leverages device features, emphasizes useful programs embedded in social contexts, takes advantage of a larger informational ecosystem, and involves design, engineering, and entrepreneurship.

We have developed online curricular materials (web-based tutorials, video lectures, screencasts, programming exercises, blocks-based quizzes, and maker/concept cards) that use App Inventor to teach mobile computational thinking. We have also created and are evaluating techniques (including surveys and project rubrics) for assessing students' computational thinking knowledge in the context of our courses and materials. Finally, we have launched an App Inventor educators website [2], where members share resources and discuss how to teach with App Inventor.

3. MEIMEI GAO

I started teaching App Inventor in Fall 2013, soon after I completed the *Computational Thinking Through Mobile Computing* workshop held at University of Massachusetts Lowell that summer. Since then, I have been teaching this CS0 course every semester. The course is called *Introduction to Programming with Mobile App Development.* It is a new course that is designed to help students with little or no programming experience to learn programming concepts; to help students, regardless of their major, to explore the world of computing and new technologies; and to increase students' interest and confidence in programming. App Inventor serves these purposes very well. The graphical drag-and-drop development environment helps students to focus on problem solving and logic thinking without worrying about syntax. Students learn programming concepts and explore computing technologies by building interesting and useful mobile apps.

I teach the course in hybrid format — 50% face-to-face meeting and 50% online activities. Students are asked to follow the online tutorials to create an app before the class. In class, we discuss the problems and learn the concepts from the app and students then continue working on their app by adding more functionality or create a new app using the similar concepts. This course has attracted students from 11 different majors.

4. JULIE JOHNSON

I have just completed my third year of teaching App Inventor to first year engineering students. The class is unique in several ways. It is a 14-lecture module that is offered three times each semester. The students are not necessarily CS majors. Most of them have little to no programming experience and many do not anticipate studying computer science beyond a CS1 course as required by their major. This short-course model necessitates that a lot of information is packed into a course that is meant to be fun and engaging, introducing students to the creativity that CS can spark. A secondary goal is to get students to the point where they can begin completing mobile apps on their own as early as possible in the module. I have seen first hand how quickly students can grasp the basic constructs needed to start building working apps, and how App Inventor facilitates the discussion of complex programming structures at a level that most students can grasp. Using App Inventor, I have been able to engage students of varying interest levels and experience in a single class, providing them with the resources and freedom to create and discover how fun and natural programming can be.

5. DALE REED

I've used App Inventor in my CS0 introductory computer science course for non-majors (CS 100) for the last two years. I struggled trying to use App Inventor briefly during the Spring 2013 semester, but it wasn't until I participated in the Summer 2013 App Inventor workshop that I was equipped to implement it as a significant component of my CS 100 course. App Inventor provides the ease of use of a visual programming environment coupled with the caché of creating software that runs on students' phones.

We use App Inventor to introduce the ideas of variables, assignments, mathematical and relational operators and lists, all within the context of creating games and utilities that run on students' phones. While they have not pursued it, several students each semester create apps that would be attractive to a wider audience. Creating apps with App Inventor has the added bonus of being able to use location and motion sensors, as well as the ability to store shared information such as high scores for games in the Cloud. Students readily see the ability to write programs for their phones as a relevant skill for many different majors.

6. CATE SHELLER

I use App Inventor in my Engineering Problem Solving course as a gentle introduction to programming for engineering majors. This CS1 course covers basic programming concepts (flow of control, procedural abstraction, data handling) in the context of engineering problems (specifically in statics, circuits and engineering economy), and requires that students use C and MATLAB. I have incorporated App Inventor into the first four weeks of the course, enabling students to learn programming concepts without being burdened with syntax, and to think about solving problems in their everyday lives using a device (Android phone) that most of them carry around. My experience thus far has been positive; students like the idea of writing programs they can use and share with others, and they make the transition into C already knowing the basic principles underlying the programs they will write in a less friendly language. Decoupling the conceptual hurdles from the syntax frustration seems to make programming less intimidating for these students, most of whom have no prior programming experience.

I also use App Inventor as the basis for a faculty development workshop I entitled *Programming for Everyone.* I am trying to get my colleagues to start thinking about computer science, or programming at any rate, as a core skill (a p to go with the three r's) that all students (and their teachers) should have some aptitude in. In my 2-hour workshop, I had my colleagues develop a simple app (Magic 8-ball) and brainstorm about how they might introduce programming as a supplementary skill in their own disciplines. I plan to repeat the workshop this November.

7. ACKNOWLEDGMENTS

This work was supported by the National Science Foundation under grants DUE-1225680, DUE-1225719, DUE-1225745, DUE-1225976, and DUE-1226216.

8. REFERENCES

[1] Computational Thinking through Mobile Computing. NSF TUES project website, `http://nsfmobilect.wordpress.com`, accessed Sep. 5, 2014.

[2] MIT App Inventor for Educators website. `http://educators.appinventor.mit.edu`, accessed Sep. 5, 2014.

[3] MIT App Inventor website. `http://appinventor.mit.edu`, accessed Sep. 5, 2014.

[4] Mobile CT Workshop June 2013 website. `https://sites.google.com/site/mobilectworkshopjune2013/`, accessed Sep. 5, 2014.

[5] T. Raja. We can code it: Why computer literacy is key to winning the 21st century. *Mother Jones*, June 2014.

[6] J. Wing. Computational thinking. *CACM*, 49(3), Mar. 2006.

Research, Resources and Communities: Informal Ed as a Partner in Computer Science Education

Cameron L. Fadjo
(Moderator)
Google, Inc.
Mountain View, CA
cameronfadjo@google.com

Betsy DiSalvo
Georgia Institute of Technology
Atlanta, GA
bdisalvo@cc.gatech.edu

Irene Lee
Santa Fe Institute
Santa Fe, New Mexico
lee@santafe.edu

Karen Peterson
National Girls Collaborative Project
Lynnwood, WA
kpeterson@edlabgroup.org

SUMMARY

Informal computer science (CS) education is currently taking shape within the myriad of social and technological solutions available to a wider audience. Increased access to low-cost mobile devices has led to the proliferation of web-based CS education programs accessible by more and more people. Online social networks further bolster the dissemination of information and help establish connections among individuals knowledgeable about the discipline. The disconnection comes when a solution is created but no strategy is devised to support distribution among the general population. In this overview we will outline the scope of this problem within the context of informal CS education by illustrating the range of programs and issues addressed by the panelists. We will highlight how each program contributes to core challenges within informal CS education and situate them within an approach that has the potential to transform how informal CS education programs are supported, developed, and scaled.

Categories and Subject Descriptors

K.3.2 [**Computers and Education**]: Computer and Information Science Education – *Computer science education, Curriculum*

General Terms: Measurement, Design, Human Factors

Keywords: Informal CS education, Search Engine, Custom Search, Access, Out-of-school Program, After School Program

1. INTRODUCTION

Recent interest from the general population in teaching all students to 'code' or learn computer science (CS) has led to a surge in the number of structured, high-quality, web-based CS education programs, such as Code.org, Khan Academy, and Codecademy. While there are a number of programs for increasing access among students from typically underserved populations (Black Girls Code, Made With Code, Girls Who Code), there remains a large segment of the general population for whom access to high-quality materials and information is largely absent or difficult to understand [2]. In this panel, we hear from researchers, developers, and advocates leading innovative programs and initiatives designed to specifically address the general population for whom computer science, computer programming, or 'coding' is not a familiar concept. The session is designed to inform the computer science education community of the challenges associated with identifying who is (and who is not) using informal learning resources, as well as highlight the range of solutions that have the potential to significantly impact and transform access to informal CS education among the general population. Knowledge of some of the limitations with existing informal CS education programs will help researchers, developers, and policy leaders create more effective solutions and programs.

In this session project leaders and directors of various programs will talk briefly about their informal CS education projects and highlight action-oriented strategies that have been implemented to address their specific challenge within the informal CS education space. Contributions collected by each panelist from the informal CS education community will illustrate how theory and practice intersect within their particular project or program. Effective implementation strategies will be shared and the panelists will facilitate a discussion with the audience on next steps within the informal CS education space.

SIGCSE'15, March 4–7, 2015, Kansas City, MO, USA.
ACM 978-1-4503-2966-8/15/03.
http://dx.doi.org/10.1145/2676723.2677329

2. INFORMAL CS EDUCATION ACCESS

(Betsy DiSalvo)

Computer science is a topic that has been on the forefront of informal educational technology. Parents and children can freely access amazing CS educational technology tools such as drag and drop programing languages or instructional sites and programs. However, the evidence suggests that children of well-educated and wealthy parents are disproportionately using these sites [4]. This leaves students from less educated and poor families less likely to form an early interest in CS and further behind if they do enter a CS class.

The issues that impact parents and children's access to information about informal CS education are more than means of access to the Internet. Multiple dimensions of access to information technology, including autonomy of use and social support [1] and issues of credibility [3], demonstrate that design of computer interactions directly impacts access to resources.

This session will present research on common CS education search terms among a low-income population and their results on Google search engine. Findings demonstrate a lack of informal CS learning resources for this population. The goal of the session is to discuss solutions to help address this issue, as a community of CS educators, and to develop and adopt standards of best practices that make our sites and resources more available.

Betsy DiSalvo is an Assistant Professor in the School of Interactive Computing at Georgia Institute of Technology. She focuses on understanding how culture impacts people's practices with technology and designing new learning environment.

3. FINDING MATERIALS (Cameron L. Fadjo)

Searching for the 'right' resource, whether it's a classroom activity for students or an after school program for a child, is very challenging if using discipline-specific words is the primary way to access this information and knowledge of such terms is limited. Research shows that online searches by parents or educators with limited experience or exposure to computer science using generic phrases (such as "kids computer learning") often yields search results that are inefficient or unproductive [2].

Google, in response to these limitations, created a custom search engine for computer science education ('Computer Science Custom Search') to address the issue of finding appropriate resources encountered by users with a limited 'CS vocabulary.' Launched on the CS4HS website (cs4hs.com/resources/cscs.html) in November 2014, CS Custom Search contains over 550 websites, primarily for the K-12 audience, that comprise the breadth of available CS education websites on the Internet.

This session will highlight the key features of the site, including the guidance provided by CS Custom Search to support those with limited 'CS vocabulary' and share findings from the CS community illustrating the benefits of using custom search to support the efforts of informal CS education initiatives.

Cameron L. Fadjo is Project Lead for Computer Science Custom Search at Google, Inc.

4. RECRUITING STUDENTS FOR CS IN AFTERSCHOOL (Irene Lee)

Project GUTS—Growing Up Thinking Scientifically— is an afterschool program that engages middle school students in scientific research with the aim of increasing the number of students prepared for high school science classes and careers in STEM and Computing.

Recruitment of diverse student populations for Project GUTS has been achieved through reaching out to the local community at schools. A two-fold recruitment strategy was used. Family CS Nights were offered at a local elementary school to introduce families from underrepresented groups in CS (primarily Hispanic/Latino and low SES) to computer science through hands-on design and build activities in Scratch and StarLogo, and to raise awareness of CS as a potential career track for students. These evening events also served to prime students to look for Project GUTS clubs upon reaching middle schools throughout the city. At local middle schools, information booths were set up and presentations were made at back-to-school nights and school-wide assemblies. Older near-peer Project GUTS student mentors served as recruiters and middle school teachers were asked to refer students to Project GUTS.

In this presentation affordances of informal CS programs will be shared and discussion of how to bridge from grassroots outreach approaches to incorporate other methods to share information on CS resources with parents and students will ensue.

Irene Lee is the director of the Learning Lab at Santa Fe Institute. She was the principal investigator of Santa Fe Institute's Project GUTS (NSF-AYS #0639637, 01/01/07-12/31/10) and GUTS y Girls (NSF-ITEST #1031421, 09/01/10-08/31/14).

5. BROADER NETWORKS (Karen Peterson)

Launched in 2000, the National Girls Collaborative Project (NGCP) has scaled to serve 39 states and serves more than 15,000 programs. Funded primarily by the National Science Foundation, this network of informal education programs includes CS programs operating in a variety of formats. The NGCP model has been successfully implemented via the Computer Science Collaboration Project, which identified and implemented strategies to increase access for youth with disabilities and Hispanic/Latino(a) youth.

The NGCP implements a tested, comprehensive program that uses collaboration to expand and strengthen computer science opportunities for underserved youth. Regional Collaborative leadership teams use the NGCP model to create a network of professionals, researchers, and practitioners, facilitating collaboration within this network, and delivering high-quality research-based professional development.

This session will highlight the research-based exemplary practices, program models, and products that are designed to strengthen project and program capacity for informal CS educators and learners.

Karen Peterson is the Principal Investigator for the National Girls Collaborative Project (NGCP). Designed by Peterson, the NGCP seeks to maximize access to shared resources for public and private sector organizations interested in expanding girls' participation in science, technology, engineering, and mathematics (STEM).

6. INTENDED AUDIENCE

This panel is designed for all educators and leaders, especially those working in the local or global community to create, support, and/or scale informal CS education programs. This session is intended for educators interested in research- and field-based implementations of community-based programs, leaders interested in best practices for effective scaling strategies of informal CS education programs, and researchers interested in strategies for evaluating and improving equity and access among non-traditional CS learner populations.

7. REFERENCES

[1] DiMaggio, P., Hargittai, E., Celeste, C., and Shafer, S., 2004. Digital Inequality: From Unequal Access to Differentiated Use. *Social inequality*, 355-400.

[2] DiSalvo, B., Reid, C., and Khanipour Roshan, P., 2014. They Can't Find Us: The Search for Informal Cs Education. In *Proceedings of the SIGCSE* (Atlanta, GA2014).

[3] Flanagin, A.J. and Metzger, M.J., 2000. Perceptions of Internet Information Credibility. *Journalism & Mass Communication Quarterly* 77, 3, 515-540.

[4] Reardon, S.F., 2011. The Widening Academic Achievement Gap between the Rich and the Poor: New Evidence and Possible Explanations. *Whither opportunity*, 91-116

Recursion vs. Iteration: An Empirical Study of Comprehension Revisited

Renée McCauley
College of Charleston
Charleston, SC USA
mccauleyr@cofc.edu

Brian Hanks
BFH Educational Consulting
Seattle, WA USA
brianhanks@acm.org

Sue Fitzgerald
Metropolitan State U.
St. Paul, MN
sue.fitzgerald@metrostate.edu

Laurie Murphy
Pacific Lutheran U.
Tacoma, WA USA
lmurphy@plu.edu

ABSTRACT
This study compares differences in students' ability to comprehend recursive and iterative programs by replicating a 1996 study. These studies are interesting for the following reasons: (1) there have been few studies on the comprehension of recursive programs, (2) there have been few studies of recursion that involve the use of data structures, (3) subjects were asked to read and comprehend code that manipulated linked lists recursively. In a 1996 study, subjects found a recursive version of a linked list search function easier to comprehend than an iterative version. The results of this study contradict these earlier findings; subjects in this study were equally likely to correctly describe the purpose of the search algorithm, regardless of iterative or recursive implementation. Consistent with the findings in the 1996 study, subjects in this study were more likely to correctly describe the copy task using the iterative version of this problem rather than the recursive version. Subjects who correctly described the purpose of the copy method wrote abstract summaries. Many of the subjects who did not recognize the purpose of the code, and who answered incorrectly, provided a line-by-line (partial) trace of the code. While revealing some understanding of the execution of the code, these subjects were generally not able to see the forest for the trees.

Categories and Subject Descriptors
K.3.2 [**Computing Milieux**]: Computers and Education - Computer and Information Science Education

General Terms
Experimentation, Human Factors

Keywords
Computer science education research; recursion; iteration; programming; CS2; linked lists

1. INTRODUCTION
There appears to be a (mis)perception among computer science educators; and perhaps students, that recursion is a difficult concept to learn.[1] Since the introduction of recursive programming in ALGOL 60 [6], there have been many publications on the teaching and learning of recursion (see [14] for a partial list). A relatively small subset of these papers presents research findings. Recursion has been studied from the points of view of mental and conceptual models, program comprehension, common misconceptions, and how to teach effectively. A number of studies [1][9][17][18][12] discuss the relative ease of learning iteration and recursion. In a 1996 study involving manipulation of linked lists, Benander, Benander, and Pu [3] found that recursive search and copy routines were no harder to comprehend than iterative ones. In this paper we report on a replication of their study comparing differences in students' ability to comprehend recursive and iterative programs. The study reported here replicates the Benander et al. study and goes one step further by qualitatively analyzing students' incorrect responses in an attempt to explain their understandings.

Related work is discussed in section 2 of this paper. A detailed description of the Benander, Benander, and Pu study is provided in section 3. In section 4 the methodology for this study is described and results are presented in section 5. Implications for teaching are discussed in section 6 and future research ideas are outlined in section 7.

2. BACKGROUND
Recursion has been studied from a wide variety of perspectives. Several researchers have focused on the relationships between learning recursion and iteration. Some have tried to answer questions such as, "Does knowledge of iteration facilitate learning of recursion?" and, "Does knowledge of recursion facilitate learning of iteration?".

In a study of how middle-school students learn recursion, Anzai and Uesato [1] found learning iteration first facilitated the learning of recursion. The subjects in the Anzai and Uesato study did no programming and did not read code; they were presented with a specification on how to compute a solution (iteratively or recursively) for some instance of a problem and asked to calculate the solution to a larger instance.

Kessler and Anderson [9] investigated the relationship between writing recursive code and writing iterative code. The participants in their study were undergraduate students with little or no programming experience. The study was conducted over two sessions in two days, using a language designed specifically for the study. They found positive transfer from writing iterative

SIGCSE '15, March 4–7, 2015, Kansas City, MO, USA

http://dx.doi.org/10.1145/2676723.2677227

[1] Many articles include a statement similar to "it is generally understood that recursion is a difficult concept to learn." See Gal-Ezer and Harel [7] for an example.

functions to writing recursive functions, but not vice versa. They also found subjects had such poor mental models of recursion that learning recursion first hindered students' ability to learn iteration.

Wiedenbeck [17] found subjects were able to transfer experience with iteration to recursion and suggests there are "complex mutual influences" in learning iteration and recursion. However, she was not able to identify those influences. Wiedenbeck's later research [18] contradicted her earlier results by showing prior work with iteration examples did not help with learning recursion and prior work with recursion examples did not help with learning iteration.

Mirolo [12] studied undergraduate programmers in an attempt to determine whether recursion or iteration was easier to learn. This questionnaire-based study required both written answers and coding. The actual questions were not included in their paper and it is not clear how much code participants were asked to write. Mirolo found no evidence students were more successful at solving problems with iteration than with recursion.

3. ORIGINAL EXPERIMENT

Benander et al. [3] investigated whether recursive or iterative code was easier for students to comprehend. Their study is interesting for the following reasons: (1) there have been few studies on the comprehension of recursive programs, (2) there have been few studies of recursion involving the use of data structures, (3) half of the code used in the study manipulated linked lists recursively. Recursive manipulation of lists is recommended by McCracken [11] and Rohl [15] but is not commonly presented in textbooks except for those using functional languages.

The participants in the Benander et al. study were undergraduate students enrolled in a data structures course using Pascal where linked lists were manipulated iteratively and binary search trees were manipulated recursively. Data was collected from two sections of the same 10-week data structures course taught in each of three consecutive years. During the last week of the term, participants were presented with either a recursive or iterative version of an algorithm that sequentially searched a linked list. One section received the recursive version; the other received the iterative version. Instructions given to the participants were:

> *Assume nodeptr is a Pascal pointer type used to define a linked list with records having a data field called item and a pointer field called next. Using only one sentence, what does the following procedure (function) do?* [3]

The code provided to students by Benander et al. is included in Appendix A.

At the following class meeting, participants were presented with an algorithm which made a copy of a linked list. Participants who worked on a recursive algorithm in the first class session received an iterative algorithm in the second session, and vice versa. Again, participants were asked to write a single sentence explaining the purpose of the code.

A total of 275 responses were collected. Answers for both algorithms were marked as correct or incorrect. For the search algorithm, Benander et al. found participants were more likely to answer correctly when the algorithm was implemented recursively rather than iteratively. This result was statistically significant. For the copy algorithm, students were more likely to answer correctly when the algorithm was implemented iteratively. However, this result was not statistically significant.

Benander et al. also compared the mean times required to complete the iterative and recursive comprehension tasks for all correct answers. For both tasks it took less time on average to comprehend the recursive implementation than the iterative version; the difference for the copy task was statistically significant. No discussion of the actual written answers was presented in the Benander paper.

4. REPLICATED EXPERIMENT

In this multi-institution study, we replicated the comprehension task portion of Benander et al. The same programming tasks, implemented in Java, were used. We also examined the students' responses in an effort to gain insight about their understanding of recursion. Times to complete the task were not recorded.

4.1 Participants

Participants were 78 students completing an undergraduate course covering basic data structures. Topics included linked lists manipulated iteratively and binary search trees manipulated recursively. The programming language used was Java. The participants attended three different U.S. universities (22 participants from a large public commuter institution serving primarily adult students – institution A; 38 participants from a residential, public institution serving primarily traditional students – institution B; 18 participants from a small private, liberal arts institution serving traditional students – institution C).

4.2 Comprehension Tasks

The search and copy algorithms from Benander et al. were implemented in Java. (See Appendix B for the Java code used.) These tasks involved the manipulation of recursively defined linked lists. The code presented to participants varied slightly across institutions – at each institution the code was written to reflect what was normal for those participants. For example, at one institution the code was modified slightly to use Java generics with lists containing nodes that stored data of type E rather than int. Also, at two institutions, a picture of a linked list was included on the test instrument.

The test instrument included the Java class definitions for the Node and List classes and the following directions: "*Describe in one sentence, what the following code does:*" and "*Do your scratch work, if any, on this page.*"

4.3 Data Collection and Analysis

The comprehension tasks were included as part of the final exam for the data structures class at each institution. At two institutions, the comprehension tasks were graded as part of the exam; at the third institution the tasks were included as optional bonus questions; despite the fact that the exercise was optional, all students provided responses. The answers were hand-written on the exam paper provided by the instructor at all three institutions.

Four analysts collaboratively read each answer and marked it as correct or incorrect. This was a fairly simple task – there were only a few answers that were so poorly articulated as to require discussion among the analysts. The response distributions of correct and incorrect answers for the three institutions are shown in Tables 1 and 2. Fisher's exact test was used at the $p = .05$ level to determine whether the null hypothesis ("There is no difference in comprehension between the iterative and recursive tasks") could be rejected.

Table 1: Search comprehension task

Institution	Iterative		Recursive		*p*
	Correct	Incorrect	Correct	Incorrect	
A	11	1	10	1	1
B	17	2	18	1	1
C	8	1	7	2	1
All	36	4	35	4	1

Table 2: Copy comprehension task

Institution	Iterative		Recursive		*p*
	Correct	Incorrect	Correct	Incorrect	
A	7	4	5	7	0.414
B	13	6	3	16	0.003
C	6	3	3	6	0 347
All	26	13	11	29	0.001

5. RESULTS

While presentation of the questions varied slightly across institutions, as discussed previously, the differences were designed to benefit the students and likely made the tasks easier. The original study by Benander et al. focused primarily on correct versus incorrect answers. We discuss these results first.

5.1 Correct versus Incorrect Responses

When asked to explain the Java search code in this study, participants in both the iterative and the recursive groups were equally likely to answer the problem correctly (see Table 1) and the null hypothesis cannot be rejected. This result contradicts the findings of Benander et al. whose subjects found the recursive version of the search task easier to comprehend; their result was statistically significant.

For the copy task, participants were more likely to correctly answer the iterative version of this problem, which is consistent with the findings of Benander et al. Unsurprisingly, the eight students who were not able to recognize or comprehend the search problem were also not able to recognize the copy task.

The pattern holds for all three institutions, and is statistically significant for all students as a group and for the students at institution B (see Table 2). Thus, the null hypothesis that there was no difference in comprehension between the iterative and recursive versions of the task can be rejected for the copy problem.

5.2 Discussion of the Search Task

To understand the different results achieved in this study and that of its predecessor, a look at the Pascal and Java code used in the studies may be informative.

The Pascal code for the search used in the Benander et al. study is shown in Appendix A. The iterative routine uses states (x, y and z) to terminate the repeat loop, while the function in their recursive version exits immediately upon determination of the correct result. The intention of the succinct, recursive version appears more obvious. One may only need to recognize the meaning of the code segment

```
else if k = head^.item then
    Boo := true
```

in the recursive version to determine that this routine is searching the list for the value in variable k. The task accomplished in the iterative version, however, is not so obvious, for several reasons. First, the use of states with generic names x, y, and z may obscure the meanings of the state values (state x means *advance to the next node and loop again*; the state y means *the list has been exhausted and exit the loop*, and state z means *the value of k has been found in the list and exit the loop*). The entire loop body, seven lines of code, must be studied in order to identify these three meanings. Second, one must understand the semantics of Pascal's *repeat-until* control structure: the loop body executes at least once and continues to execute until the condition following the `until` keyword is *true*. Finally, the statement that assigns the truth-value to the function name

```
Boo := state = z;
```

may be difficult for some to comprehend. Reges [13] discusses the complexities of comprehending statements such as this one that involve reading and understanding code and having a proper mental model of program execution: the value of the right-hand side of the assignment must be recognized as generating a *true* or *false* value, and the generated value can only be determined if the meaning of the z state variable is correctly understood. Based on a study of answers to an Advanced Placement Computer Science test, Reges found the ability to correctly understand the meaning of the statement b := (b = *false*) was a predictor of success on most of the other questions on the exam and suggests it may be "testing something fundamental about a student's ability to approach computer science problems" [13]. This sort of statement may be harder to discern than a direct assignment of *true* to the function name, as used in the recursive version of the code.

The code in the Benander study is identical to examples presented in *Recursion via Pascal* by Rohl [15] except for changes in module and variable names. Naturally, Benander et al. purposely obfuscated the code by providing no documentation and using meaningless identifiers "so as to give no clue as to its purpose" [3].

Rohl presents two iterative versions of search, one identical to that used by Benander et al., but with state-names *searching*, *notthere*, and *found* instead of x, y and z, respectively (Appendix C, algorithm 1). Rohl's second algorithm (Appendix C, algorithm 2) is described as "the traditional non-recursive version" [15]. This version uses a single boolean to indicate whether the search target has been found.

One wonders if students might not have found this "traditional" version (Appendix C, algorithm 2) easier to comprehend, even though Rohl claims that version 1 (with states) is "a more elegant solution" [15] and that "this function is closely related to the recursive one - indeed it would be hard to separate the two on the score of naturalness" [15].

It should be noted the Pascal language specification did not specify short-circuit evaluation of boolean operations (for example, both sides of an `and` operation were evaluated even when the left side was *false*). Therefore, programmers had to avoid constructs such as

```
while (head <> nil) and (k != head^.item)
```

which would cause a runtime error when `head` was `nil`, because the `item` field of `head` would still be referenced. The use of states was suggested by Atkinson [2] as a way to write code that avoided this problem and was clearer in meaning.

We suspect the code based on states was not obvious to students and may explain why the subjects in the Benander et al. study did poorly on comprehension of the iterative search code.

In the current study, we chose to implement both the iterative and recursive versions of the search routine in ways we thought would be most natural to our students, instead of mimicking the Benander et al. code (see Appendix B). The students were familiar with Java's short-circuit evaluation semantics, and using states may have made the code seem artificial to them.

The Java implementations of the iterative and recursive search routines are more similar to each other than those in Benander et al. in terms of the number of lines of code and the actual statements that detect when a search is successful. The iterative and recursive versions of the code both have conditionals similar to:

```
if (h.getInt() == value)
   return true;
```

We suspect even if a student did not understand recursion, the above conditional gives a strong clue as to what the method accomplishes. This might account for why students in the current study did equally well regardless of whether they were presented with the recursive or the iterative version of the search task.

5.3 Discussion of the Copy Task

For the copy task, participants in both studies were more likely to answer the iterative version correctly.

Upon examination, the recursive version of Benander et al's copy task (see Appendix A) seems simpler than their iterative version; it is shorter and does not require any pointer (^) access. However, it may be the recursive version hides too much information by traversing through the list via changes to parameters in a series of recursive calls rather than through explicit assignment.

The Java copy methods used in this study (see Appendix B) are similar in length, although the iterative version requires two local variables and the recursive version requires two methods. One might consider the recursive version complex since the recursive call is an actual parameter in the invocation of the Node constructor:

```
return new Node (h.getInt(), testProc(h.getNext()));
```

Although the iterative version also contains a fairly dense statement in:

```
c2.setNext(new Node(c.getNext().getInt(),null));
```

However, as discussed in Section 5.1, students found the iterative version easier to comprehend.

5.4 Qualitative results

Many students struggled with the recursive copy task. In an effort to learn what students might have been thinking as they tried to comprehend this recursive code to copy a list, we analyzed their descriptions. Specifically, we considered the 11 correct responses, and 25 (of 29) incorrect responses, considering only those of participants who answered the iterative search task correctly.

Analysis of these responses led to the following questions:

Did the students recognize recursion? Only three of the eleven correct responses included the word *recursion* or *recursive*, as in "Recursive method to...". So, it is unclear if all of the students who answered the problem realized recursion was used. Of the 25 students who answered the problem incorrectly, only six appeared to recognize the method was implemented using recursion; five of these students used the terms *recursive* or *recursion* in their answers and one implied recursion by stating the method was "constantly being called again."

Did the students recognize that a list would be traversed? Of the 25 students who gave incorrect answers, nine gave answers suggesting the code was only operating on a single node rather than traversing the list. Most referred to the "head" or the "front" of the list, and one simply stated "this code returns null." It is possible many of these students only considered the base case. Another nine participants referred to operating on all of the nodes in the list. Examples include "traverse to the end of the list" and "returns all the values in the linked list."

Did students imply looping or understand recursion in terms of loops? Six students who answered incorrectly explicitly mentioned or implied looping, as in "loops through the list" and "while the next data value does not equal null."

Were students able to provide a concise, abstract summary of the code's purpose? All but one of the correct answers provided an abstract summary such as:

> *Returns a deep copy of a linked list*

Close to half (11 of 25) of the students who did not recognize the purpose of the code, and who answered incorrectly, provided a line-by-line (partial) trace of the code. Here are examples of such incorrect traces:

> *This code check[s] to see if there [is] a node after head, if there's a node return the value in the node and set head to that node, if the node after head is null, then return null.*

> *Calls a helper method that gets the value of head and its next and then sets the head of a new list l to that new node and returns the list.*

Overall, many students did not articulate an abstract understanding of recursion. While revealing some understanding of the execution of the code, these subjects were generally not able to see the forest for the trees. This analysis is consistent with the relational and multi-structural categories of the SOLO taxonomy [4].

6. IMPLICATIONS FOR TEACHING

Students in this study had been introduced to both linked lists and recursion in their data structures classes. They had also used recursion in the context of binary search trees, which, like linked lists, are recursively defined data structures. However, they had not specifically studied recursion in the context of linked lists. Most data structures textbooks using Java or other non-functional languages introduce linked lists early and separately from recursion, which may be studied several weeks or even months later in the course. An argument for separating these two topics is that conflating recursion, references/pointers and lists may confuse students. With this approach, recursion is often introduced in the context of simple mathematical functions such as factorial, power or Fibonacci and then later combined with recursive data structures, typically binary trees.

Some educators argue recursion should be introduced in the context of recursively-defined objects, specifically lists that are defined recursively and behave similarly to lists in a functional language [5][16]. They argue this is more natural than using recursion to solve mathematical functions. Additionally, teaching recursion and linked lists together in this fashion can both reinforce object-oriented programming, in that the code may employ abstract classes and inheritance, and it also allows lists to be processed without conditionals and the use of null to detect the end of a list [5]. This avoids typical base cases, which have been shown to be particularly problematic for novices [8].

7. FUTURE WORK

Additional research is needed to investigate whether introducing recursion in the context of recursively-defined objects, such as lists, is more advantageous for learning recursion than the typical approach of introducing recursion in the context of mathematical functions. To understand deeply what students are thinking as they try to comprehend code, it would be beneficial to interview students who incorrectly identified the purpose of recursive code used in this study. Through careful questioning, we might learn what they do and do not understand about recursion.

The iterative search code used by Benander et al. and in this study is quite different, as discussed previously. A future study might compare the comprehensibility of these two algorithms.

Finally, some believe manipulating linked lists recursively is too complicated for data structures students; others believe students will not find the recursive routines any more complicated than the iterative routines. A study could test these beliefs.

8. ACKNOWLEDGMENTS

Our thanks to our non-authoring colleagues who collected data for us: William Bares at College of Charleston and Kenneth Blaha at Pacific Lutheran University.

9. REFERENCES

[1] Anzai, Y. and Uesato, Y. 1982. Learning recursive procedures by middle school children. *Proceedings of the Fourth Cognitive Science Conference* (Ann Arbor, MI, USA, August, 1982). 100-102.

[2] Atkinson, L. 1978. Know the state you are in. *Pascal News* 13 (Dec. 1978), 66-69.

[3] Benander, A., Benander, B. and Pu, H. 1996. Recursion vs. iteration: An empirical study of comprehension. *The Journal of Systems and Software* 32, 1, 73-82.

[4] Biggs, J. and Collis, K. 1982. *Evaluating the Quality of Learning: The SOLO Taxonomy (Structure of the Observed Learning Outcome).* Academic Press, New York, NY.

[5] Bloch, S. 2003. Teaching linked lists and recursion without conditionals or null. *J. Comput. Small Coll.* 18, 5 (May 2003), 96-108.

[6] Daylight, E. G. 2011. Dijkstra's rallying cry for generalization: The advent of the recursive procedure, late 1950s-early 1960s. *The Computer Journal* 54, 11, 1756-1772.

[7] Gal-Ezer, J. and Harel, D. 1998. What (else) should CS educators know? *Communications of the ACM* 41, 9, 77-84.

[8] Haberman, B. and Averbuch, H. 2002. The case of base cases: Why are they so difficult to recognize? Student difficulties with recursion. In *Proceedings of the Seventh Annual Conference on Innovation and Technology in Computer Science Education* (Aarhus, Denmark, June 24-26, 2002). ITiCSE '02. ACM, New York, NY, USA, 84-88.

[9] Kessler, C. and Anderson, J. 1986. Learning flow control: Recursive and iterative procedures. *Human-Computer Interaction* 2, 135-166.

[10] Lewis, C. Exploring Variation in Students' Correct Traces of Linear Recursion (Glasgow, Scotland, Aug. 11-13, 2014). ICER 2014. New York, NY, ACM, 67-74.

[11] McCracken, D. 1987. Ruminations on Computer Science Curricula. *Communications of the ACM* 30, 1, 3-5.

[12] Mirolo, C. 2012. Is iteration really easier to learn than recursion for CS1 students? In *Proceedings of the Ninth Annual International Conference on Computing Education Research* (Auckland, New Zealand, Sept. 10-12, 2012). ICER '12. New York, NY, ACM, 99-104.

[13] Reges, S. 2008. The mystery of "b := (b = false)". In *Proceedings of the 39th SIGCSE Technical Symposium on Computer Science Education* (Portland, OR, USA, March 12-15, 2008). SIGCSE'08. New York, NY, ACM, 21-25.

[14] Rinderknecht, C. 2014. A survey on teaching and learning recursive programming. *Informatics in Education* 13, 1, 87-119.

[15] Rohl, J. 1984. *Recursion via Pascal.* Cambridge University Press, Cambridge, 1984.

[16] Sher, D. B. 2004. Recursive objects - an object oriented presentation of recursion. *Mathematics and Computer Education* 38, 1, 97-109.

[17] Wiedenbeck, S. 1988. Learning recursion as a concept and as a programming technique. In P*roceedings of the Nineteenth International Technical Symposium on Computer Science Education* (Atlanta, Georgia, USA, Feb. 25-26, 1988). SIGCSE'88. New York, NY, ACM, 275–278.

[18] Wiedenbeck, S. 1989. Learning iteration and recursion from examples. *International Journal of Man-Machine Studies* 30, 1, 1–22.

APPENDIX A: Pascal code used in the Benander et al. study

Recursive version of search

```
function boolean Boo(head: nodeptr,
   k: integer):boolean;

begin
   if head = nil then
      Boo := false
   else if k = head^.item then
      Boo := true
   else
      Boo := Boo(head^.next, k)
end;
```

Iterative version of search

```
function boolean Boo(head: nodeptr,
   k: integer):boolean;

type statetype = (x,y,z);
var state : statetype;
begin
   state := x;
   repeat
      if head = nil then
         state := y
      else
         if k == head^.item then
            state :== z;
         else
            head := head^.next
   until state <> x;
   Boo := state = z;
```

```
end;
```

Recursive version of copy

```
procedure Testproc (var head1 : nodeptr;
   head2 : nodeptr);

begin
   if head2 = nil then
      head1 := nil
   else begin
      new(head1);
      head1^.item := head2^.item;
      Testproc(head1^.next, head2^.next)
      end
end;
```

Iterative version of copy

```
procedure Testproc(var head1 : nodeptr;
   head 2 : nodeptr);
var p : nodeptr;
begin
   if head2 = nil then
      head1 := nil
   else begin
      new (head1);
      head1^.item := head2^.item;
      head2 := head2^.next;
      p := head1;
      while head2 <> nil do begin
         new (p^.next);
         p^.next^.item := head2^.item;
         p := p^.next;
         head2 := head2^.next
      end;
      p^.next := nil
   end
end;
```

APPENDIX B: Java code used in this study

Recursive version of search

```
public boolean boo(int value) {
   return boo(head, value);
}
private boolean boo(Node h, int w) {
   if (h==null)
      return false;
   else if (h.getInt() == w)
      return true;
   else
      return boo(h.getNext(), w);
}
```

Iterative version of search

```
public boolean boo(int value) {
   Node h = head;
   while (h != null) {
      if (h.getInt() == value)
         return true;
      else
         h = h.getNext();
   }
   return false;
}
```

Recursive version of copy

```
public List testProc() {
   List l = new List();
   l.head = testProc(head);
   return l;
}

private Node testProc(Node h) {
   if (h != null)
      return new Node(h.getInt(),
                      testProc(h.getNext()));
   else
      return null;
}
```

Iterative version of copy

```
public List testProc() {
   List l = new List();
   if (head != null) {
      l.head = new Node(head.getInt(), null);
      Node c = head;
      Node c2 = l.head;
      while (c.getNext() != null){
         c2.setNext(new Node(c.getNext().getInt(),
                                   null));
         c = c.getNext();
         c2 = c2.getNext();
      }
   }
   return l;
}
```

APPENDIX C: Rohl's (1984) iterative search code (using Benander's module and variable names)

Iterative search – algorithm 1

```
function boolean Boo(head: nodeptr,
   k: integer):boolean;
var state : (searching, noththere, found);
begin
   state := searching;
   repeat
     if head = nil then
        state := notthere
     else
         if k == head^.item then
            state :== found;
         else
            head := head^.next
   until state <> searching;
   Boo := state = found;
end;
```

Iterative search – algorithm 2

```
function boolean Boo(head: nodeptr,
   k: integer):boolean;
var found: boolean;
begin
   found := false;
   while (head <> nil) and not found do
      begin
         found := k = head^.item;
         head := head^.next
      end
   Boo := found;
end;
```

Tracking Student Learning from Class to Exam using Isomorphic Questions

Daniel Zingaro
University of Toronto Mississauga
Mississauga, ON, Canada
daniel.zingaro@utoronto.ca

Leo Porter
University of California, San Diego
La Jolla, CA, USA
leporter@cs.ucsd.edu

ABSTRACT

Recent computer science education research using isomorphic questions in Peer Instruction (PI) classes demonstrates that students learn from talking to their peers and listening to the instructor's follow-up explanation. These results provide evidence of the effectiveness of the PI process but are limited to what happens in a single class session. The present work extends the use of isomorphic questions to investigate how in-class learning translates to success on the final exam. Despite considerable time between in-class questions and the final exam, we find that students who learn in class are shown to retain that learning and to perform better than students who did not learn in class. In addition, compared to students already understanding the material, those who learned the material in class are almost (87%) as likely to correctly answer isomorphic exam questions. Our results have implications for the value of difficult PI questions and the meaning of in-class response graphs.

Categories and Subject Descriptors

K.3.2 [**Computer Science Education**]: Computer and Information Science Education

Keywords

peer instruction; clickers; final exam

1. INTRODUCTION

The last few years have yielded a significant body of research attesting to the effectiveness of Peer Instruction (PI) as a pedagogical approach for teaching CS courses. A typical CS class often includes a significant lecture component, perhaps augmented with live-coding or student exercises. PI foregrounds these student exercises by engaging the class in the discussion and analysis of multiple choice questions [3]. No longer the core of a class meeting, lectures play a supporting role to student discussion and active involvement.

SIGCSE'15, March 4–7, 2015, Kansas City, MO, USA.

http://dx.doi.org/10.1145/2676723.2677239.

Among the various measures of pedagogical effectiveness (including student interest and enjoyment, instructor preparedness, and cost of implementation), what students actually learn is certainly one of the most important. Several PI-based research projects investigate the extent to which students learn from in-class multiple choice questions and the extent to which this learning manifests on a final exam [5, 8, 9, 14, 15]. The general finding is that increases in correctness during class are evidence of learning, not copying from neighbors. Several such projects extend this analysis to directly connect in-class learning to the final exam [7, 8, 15]. In those works, the authors use correlations to examine whether gains in class correspond to gains on the final exam and find statistically significant relationships. However, one criticism of those works is that the final exam may not test the same concepts as do the in-class questions and, more generally, that single in-class questions do not correspond to single final exam questions. The present work seeks to remedy these drawbacks.

In this work, we use isomorphic (same-concept) questions in class to measure what students learn from their peers and the instructor. We then include another isomorphic version of the question on the exam to measure long-term retention of learning. We find that students who learn in class perform very well on the final exam: they perform almost as well as those who understood concepts prior to the classes in which those concepts were taught. Somewhat unsurprisingly, we find that those who fail to learn from the PI process in class perform poorly on the final exam, showing that this group of students was unable to "make-up ground" outside of class. Our results also show that a large proportion of students in the class (25%) both learn from PI in class and demonstrate that learning on the final exam. These findings provide evidence of a strong link between student conceptual learning in class and later demonstration of that learning. Breaking questions down by difficulty shows that difficult questions provide more opportunity for students to learn (echoing [16]): 35% of students demonstrate learning from difficult questions compared to only 10% for easy questions. For the many instructors who are already using PI (and those considering its adoption), these results support the use of challenging questions to incite change in student understanding.

2. BACKGROUND

2.1 Why Pedagogical Change?

Numerous research studies suggest that, for many students, our introductory computing courses are not having the desired effects. A foreboding tone was set in the research literature over 30 years ago, when Soloway presented a seemingly simple problem to his students [12]: "Write a program that repeatedly reads in integers, until it reads the integer 99999. After seeing 99999, it should print out the correct average. That is, it should not count the final 99999". Of those three-quarters of the way through a CS1, only 14% of students gave a satisfactory solution to this question. More recently, Lister and colleagues [4] studied the performance of novice students on code-reading and code-explaining tasks. Unfortunately, performance was again poor, with students scoring on average 60%.

Such student difficulties are reified when examining failure rates. One often-cited study suggests that one-third of students fail a CS1 [2]; a more recent systematic literature review supports this finding using a dataset of 161 courses from a variety of countries [13].

Pedagogical change in CS is thus driven by at least two overlapping factors: the mismatch between what instructors expect and what students learn, and worrying student failure rates. And on both counts, the research shows that PI holds some promise. In terms of student learning, one study compared a PI and a lecture-based CS0, both taught by the same instructor, and found almost a 6% difference on exam scores [9]. A similar comparison of a PI and lecture-based CS1, taught by different instructors, found a near-significant 4.5% exam grade advantage for PI students [14]. Research additionally finds that PI significantly reduces failure rates in a variety of CS courses including CS1 and CS1.5 [6].

2.2 Peer Instruction

Peer Instruction (PI) may be understood as a pedagogical script that scaffolds the discursive processes in which teacher and students engage [10]. The script itself structures students' cognition in ways that facilitate valid reasoning in the discipline. The PI "script", shown in Figure 1a, is as follows:

- The instructor poses a conceptual multiple choice question to the class.
- Students answer the question individually, typically using clickers.
- Students discuss the question with their seatmates for several minutes and vote again.
- The instructor leads a classwide discussion of the important content- and conceptual-based features of the question.

This script is repeated several times per class.

As far as pedagogical scripts go, PI can be considered minimally-structured. It does dictate when students are to work alone, when students are to work in groups, and when the instructor should offer explanation; and it does suggest the amount of time spent on each step. But the instructor continues to make important pedagogical decisions, including which questions to ask, how to structure student discussions, how to form student groups, and when to follow-up with new, just-in-time questions. In fact, in this student-centred pedagogy, some have argued that the instructor's role remains as important as ever [16].

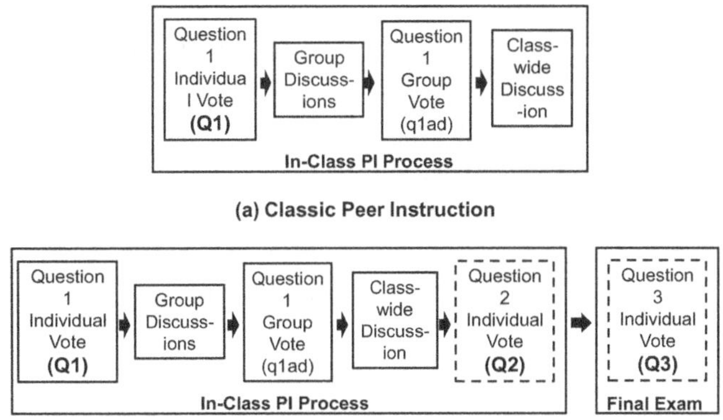

(b) Modified PI Format and Isomorphic Questions for this Experiment

Figure 1: PI process and modifications for this experiment.

2.3 Isomorphic Questions

As students vote twice per question, it is natural for instructors to compare scores between the first and second vote. Increases in correctness might indicate student learning. However, such gains could also indicate active copying or passive agreement with others. Prior research has used isomorphic questions to distinguish these possibilities. Two questions are isomorphic when they test the same concept using different cover stories [11]. In two studies that have used in-class isomorphic PI questions in CS, the common finding is that what students learn on the first question of an isomorphic pair persists in terms of correctness on the second [5, 16]. A third work examines PI questions that are highly predictive of student success on final exam code-writing questions and finds that some of the more predictive votes by students are on isomorphic questions [8]. A fourth study examines whether isomorphic votes explain student outcomes on the final exam, but does so without using isomorphic questions on the exam [15]. While it is found that gains on isomorphic questions are related to increased exam scores, that study design does not allow the tracking of specific conceptual knowledge from in-class isomorphic questions to similar questions on the final exam. The present work addresses this gap in the research.

3. RESEARCH QUESTIONS

- What is the overall relationship between scores on isomorphic questions in class and on the final exam?
- Binned by in-class correctness, how well do student subgroups demonstrate learning on the final exam?
- What percentage of students demonstrates learning from PI, as measured by exam performance?

4. METHOD

4.1 Study Context

In Fall 2013, a PI-based CS1 was offered by the first author of this paper at a large Canadian research university. The original version of the PI course was offered in Fall 2012, and the Fall 2013 course is an incremental improvement of that course with improved questions and response choices based on student feedback. The instructor of the course is

Table 1: **Isomorphic questions given in-class and on the exam. Difficulty is based on Q1 correctness: easy ($\geq 50\%$) or hard($< 50\%$).**

Week	Topic	Concept	Difficulty
2	Function documentation	Detecting inconsistencies between code and documentation	hard
3	Conditionals	Tracing nested if-statements	hard
4	While-loops	Tracing a variable through loop iterations	easy
6	Nested loops	Tracing 2-D ragged list accesses	hard
6	Files	Looping until the end of a file header	hard
9	Object equality	Interpreting equality based on a given `__eq__` method	easy
11	Sorting	Tracing one pass of bubble sort on a list	easy

a lecturer in the computer science department, and has significant PI teaching experience (including the original development of the course in 2012 and refinement in 2013). The material for the Fall 2013 course is available online [1]. In the course, students learn the imperative features of Python, testing and test case development, and introductory sorting and complexity material.

The course consisted of three 50-minute lectures per week, for a total of 12 weeks. A common feature of PI classes is reading quizzes [3], where students complete a small amount of reading and respond to several questions before each lecture. Reading quizzes were used in this course, and were graded based on submission (not correctness). Clickers and multiple choice questions were used for the majority of the in-class portion of the course. Again, responses were based on submission rather than correctness. Each week, students attended one pair-programming lab supported by TAs. Students completed three assignments, a quiz in week 4, a midterm in week 6, and a final exam. 95 students took the final exam and provide the data for this study.

4.2 Isomorphic Question Administration

For the majority of PI questions in the course, the "classic PI" protocol was followed, as shown in Figure 1a. That is, students were given a multiple choice question, responded individually, discussed in a group, responded again, and then participated in classwide discussion. These questions are not the focus of this paper.

In addition to these questions, one question per lecture was chosen by the course instructor to be the first of an isomorphic pair of questions. Each selected question addressed a core concept that the instructor thought particularly important. For example, in a lecture on while-loops, the question selected for an isomorphic pairing focused on tracing variable values as a loop executes. These administrations followed the same protocol as "classic PI", except that an additional question was asked after the classwide discussion. This second question was designed to be isomorphic to the first question, and students were to respond to it individually (with no group discussion). In this way, scores on the second isomorphic question reflect what students individually understand about a topic after having experienced the complete PI cycle for the question. To investigate the relationship between these in-class questions and student outcomes, we randomly selected seven questions for which to pose a third version (isomorphic to the first two) as a multiple choice question on the final exam. These questions are the focus of this work; more information on the questions is provided in Table 1. As shown in Figure 1b, each set of questions provides three datapoints. These datapoints and associated terminology are as follows:

- **Q1**: the individual vote on the first (in-class) question.
- **Q2**: the individual vote on a second (in-class), isomorphic question.
- **Q3**: the response to a third isomorphic question on the final exam.

Note that we ignore the group vote, $Q1_{ad}$, in this work. That vote may not accurately reflect what students individually know [16]. In addition, we focus only on the 7 multiple choice exam questions that are isomorphic to the in-class questions. The exam contained other multiple choice, code-writing, code-explaining, and code-reading questions; analysis of that type of data for a different course is analyzed elsewhere [15]. Students were told that there would be multiple choice questions on the exam, but not that any of them would be explicitly patterned after ones they had studied in class.

Based on our previous work [5, 16], we have found that designing isomorphic questions requires care and multiple perspectives. To that end, the three versions of each set of isomorphic questions were written by the first author, and sent to the second author for validation. The second author is an experienced instructor and researcher of PI courses in CS. Question isomorphs were discussed and negotiated until both authors agreed that the questions were conceptually equivalent and of similar difficulty. As an additional control for matching difficulty, random numbers were used in each case to determine which of the three questions would be Q1, Q2, and Q3.

5. RESULTS

The use of isomorphic questions both in class and on the final exam yields a rich dataset. To correspond with our three research questions given earlier, we analyze the data in three ways. We report overall correctness on each type of vote (Q1, Q2, and Q3), track student response patterns from in-class to the exam, and quantify absolute percentages of students that demonstrate longer-term learning from the PI process.

5.1 Isomorphic Question Correctness

How do students perform overall on Q1, Q2, and Q3? Do they improve on each subsequent isomorphic version of the questions? In previous studies examining in-class isomorphic questions, the general finding is that students improve from the first isomorph to the second [5, 16]. Here, we extend this analysis to include isomorphs on the final exam.

Table 2: Average percentage of students correct per question type.

	Q1	Q2	Q3
Students Correct	49%	74%	70%

Table 2 provides the average percentage correct on each vote (Q1, Q2, and Q3). Corroborating earlier work, there is a substantial gain from Q1 (49% correct) to Q2 (74% correct). This suggests that students are able to learn from their peers and instructor and apply that knowledge to new questions. This is encouraging, but the time lapse between Q1 and Q2 is only a few minutes. Would students demonstrate this learning at a later point? In addition, by virtue of first answering Q1, students are attuned to the type of question being asked and may be able to activate only the particular pieces of knowledge required to correctly answer Q2. Would students be able to answer a question without first being primed by an isomorph? Bringing Q3 into the analysis provides answers to both of these questions: Q3 occurs several weeks (or, for some questions, months) later than any Q1-Q2 pair, and there are no explicit cues on the exam telling students that Q3 is an isomorph of a question that had been studied earlier.

We observe a Q3 correctness of 70%. This is much closer to the Q2 average than the Q1 average, and so we conclude that most of what students learn during the PI cycles is observable on the final exam.

Average correctness is useful for examining the broad changes from Q1 to Q2 to Q3, but such analysis does not indicate the particular subgroups of students that are making these gains. As such, we now turn to a more fine-grained grouping of student paths through the three question votes.

5.2 Tracking Student Response Patterns

Figure 2 traces student response patterns on each of Q1, Q2, and Q3 for the 7 sets of isomorphic questions. To begin, consider the top of the tree, whose two branches correspond to the percentage of students correctly (left branch) or incorrectly (right branch) answering Q1. This yields the previously-described finding that 49% of students correctly answer Q1. The next layer down further distinguishes these two Q1 groups by their performance (correct or incorrect) on Q2. For example, of students who answer Q1 correctly (i.e. those students on the left of the top layer), 79% answer Q2 correctly. However, of students who answer Q1 incorrectly (i.e. those students on the right of the top layer), only 69% answer Q2 correctly.

Finally, consider the third and bottom layer of the tree. This layer further splits the second-layer groupings into those students who correctly or incorrectly answer Q3. As an example, we can interpret the value of 81% (the underlined, far left value) as follows: among students who answer Q1 correctly and then answer Q2 correctly, 81% answer Q3 correctly.

There are two particular groups in Figure 2 that warrant elaboration and comparison. The terminology with which we refer to these groups is from [5].

- **Control Group (CG):** the group of students who correctly answer Q1 and correctly answer Q2. These are the students that likely understood the material before class. (The alternative is that these students made a fortunate guess on Q1, and then learned the relevant concept as part of the PI process in order to correctly answer Q2. We cannot make such a distinction using our PI data.) 81% of the CG correctly answer Q3 (underlined in Figure 2).
- **Potential Learner Group (PLG):** the group of students who incorrectly answer Q1 and then correctly answer Q2. These are students who did not understand the relevant concept at the point that Q1 was asked, but were able to learn and apply the concept to Q2. The PLG reflect the most obvious subgroup of students that may have learned from the PI process. 70% of the PLG correctly answer Q3 (bolded in Figure 2).

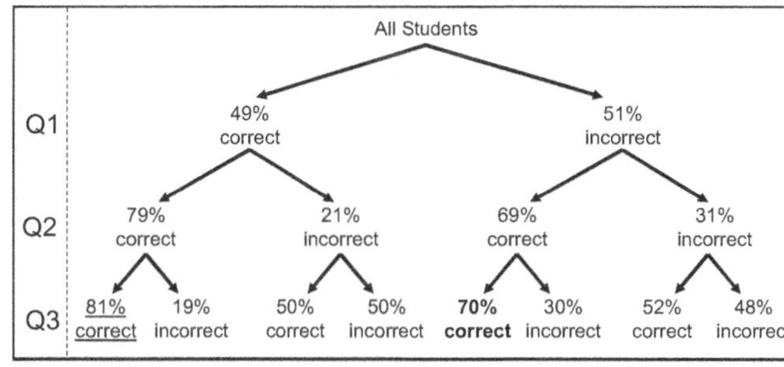

Figure 2: Flowchart of students through responses (correct or incorrect) to questions Q1, Q2, and Q3.

Although both the CG and PLG students fare well on Q3, the CG performs slightly better. Perhaps this is because the CG possesses more stable and generalizable knowledge acquired prior to or during course instruction. While such raw comparisons are useful, we have argued elsewhere [5] for the use of a more meaningful metric referred to as Weighted Learning Gain (WLG). In brief, we should weight our expectation of the PLG by the Q3 correctness of the CG. As such, the WLG metric divides the "new learner" correctness by the "existing knowledge" correctness. In this case, the WLG is 70% divided by 81% which is 87%. This can be interpreted by saying that the PLG is 87% as likely as the CG to correctly answer Q3. Though not quite equal, this does show that the PLG performs much like the CG on the exam questions under study.

As we have now compared the two groups of students that correctly answer Q2, it is interesting to make a further comparison with the students who *incorrectly* answer Q2. There are two groups of students who incorrectly answer Q2: those that correctly answer Q1 and then incorrectly answer Q2, and those that incorrectly answer Q1 and then incorrectly answer Q2. For both of these groups, the correctness on Q3 is effectively 50% (50% in one case, 52% in the other). Therefore, for those students who answer Q2 incorrectly, performance on Q3 is poor irrespective of Q1 performance. It is the response on Q2 (given in light of peer discussion and instructor explanation), not the response on Q1, that "seems to matter" in terms of Q3 scores. In addition, comparing the 50% group to the PLG shows that the PLG scored substantially better on the exam (a 20% difference). This suggests that students who can learn during the PI process are also those students that can demonstrate that learning on the exam; the students that do not learn during the PI process fail to "make up for it" throughout the semester.

5.3 Class Impact

Recall that the values in Figure 2 are relative, in that the correct/incorrect percentage values are relative along each path (e.g., 79% *of the students who answer Q1 correctly* answer Q2 correctly). These percentages are independent of the absolute number of students in each group, and therefore do not indicate the raw proportion of the class that falls into each of the 8 correctness bins. Figure 3 is similar to Figure 2, but uses absolute percentages rather than relative percentages. Figure 3 provides these absolute percentages broken up by question difficulty: "Easy" (Q1 correctness is $\geq 50\%$), "Hard" (Q1 correctness is $< 50\%$), and "All" questions. We begin by examining the tree for "All" questions as this corresponds with the relative data from Figure 2. For example, looking at the bottom tree labelled "All", 31% of students follow the path of answering Q1 correctly, Q2 correctly, and Q3 correctly. (This 31% is represented in Figure 2 as 81% of 79% of 49%.)

The most interesting group for this analysis is again the PLG: these students follow the path of answering Q1 incorrectly and Q2 correctly. Of the PLG, those who answer Q3 correctly account for 25% of the entire class. This is an encouraging result, demonstrating that a large portion of a PI class learns from the PI process and then goes on to succeed on the final exam. In fact, this group is the second-largest group in the class, paled only by those who answer all three questions correctly.

Also evident in these classwide, absolute percentages is the benefit associated with difficult questions. The percentage of the class who answer all three "easy" questions correctly is 51%, with only 10% of the students learning from the PI process during class and then demonstrating that learning on the exam. In contrast, for hard questions, only 18% of students answer all three questions correctly (possibly demonstrating what they already knew), but a considerable 35% of the class learns from the PI process and demonstrates that learning on the exam. Although the small number of questions in each group (3 in easy, 4 in hard) limits the generalizability of these conclusions, as in [16] we find strong support for the value of hard questions in PI classes.

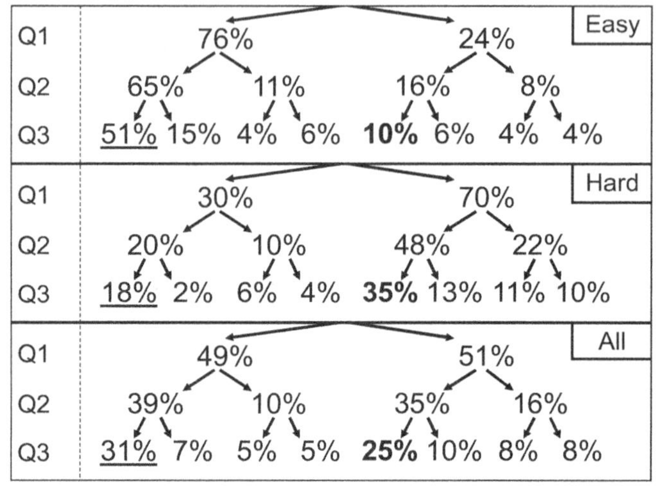

Figure 3: Flowcharts of students for easy questions, hard questions, and all questions. As in Figure 2, left arrows indicate correct and right arrows indicate incorrect. Each value denotes an absolute percentage of the class. The percentage of the CG that answers Q3 correctly is underlined and the percentage of the PLG that answers Q3 correctly is in bold.

6. THREATS TO VALIDITY

Previous work that tracks student performance on isomorphic questions [5, 16] has used only in-class questions. This tightly controls what students can learn from one vote to the next. In the present study, however, several weeks or more pass between the in-class isomorphs and the final exam. This has at least two implications.

First, we have no knowledge of what students do from the time of Q1 and Q2 to the time of Q3. Some students may revisit Q1 and Q2, or may thoroughly study the associated topics, while others may not. Scores on Q3 therefore represent not only what students learned from the PI process, but also what they learn on their own. Despite this limitation, our data suggests that PI itself powerfully predicts Q3 scores. Relative to the PLG, those who respond incorrectly to Q2 perform poorly on Q3. These Q2-incorrect students may have indeed studied the relevant topics again prior to the exam, but this evidently did not make up for failing to learn the material during the PI process. What remains unclear is *why* the Q2-incorrect students failed to learn from PI, and whether this group of students would be larger in the absence of PI.

Second, our in-class isomorphs were spread throughout the semester (from week 2 to week 12), and therefore the time delay between these isomorphs and the final exam varies by question. Our data therefore collapses the effects of early and late PI activity when tracking students from in-class to the exam. The latest questions may involve recency effects, and the earliest questions may be rendered very easy by the time of the exam; it is unclear to what extent these processes are at work. The average on the first four (early) isomorphic questions on the exam is 75%, and the average on the remaining three (late) questions is 57%, so no ceiling effect seems to have been reached.

7. DISCUSSION

Our three research results are complementary and contribute to an overall story of student learning in a PI class. First, scores on Q3 are similar to Q2, suggesting that most of the gain from Q1 to Q2 is retained. Second, the PLG scores much better than Q2-incorrect students on the exam, and in fact are comparable on the exam to the CG. This, again, shows that learning is sustained and demonstrated on the exam. Finally, we see that this type of learning is not restricted to a small portion of the class: we can classify one-quarter of our students as retaining what they learned from peers and the instructor.

One might suspect that Q3 scores would be higher than Q2 scores. After all, Q3 scores represent student knowledge at the end of the course. Surely the students would have made strides from the time of Q2 to the time of the exam? Indeed, we suspect that they have done so, but that the Q2 and Q3 contexts are sufficiently different so that Q3 scores cannot reach Q2 scores, even for students who have learned a great deal in the interim. Exams are conceptually rich, drawing from many weeks of instruction, with no explicit indication of which material is operative at any given time. Therefore, in addition to demonstrating knowledge, students must first select and use the conceptual material that they will demonstrate. Knowing *how* to use a concept, and knowing *when* to use a concept, are distinct and non-trivial tasks. We suggest that Q2 is a reasonable estimate of students' knowledge of a particular concept, but that it is likely a slight overestimation of the extent to which students' could activate that conceptual knowledge in the absence of the Q1 trigger.

We reported earlier that the weighted learning gain (WLG) between the CG and PLG is 87%. This measure bears striking resemblance to the WLG reported in other articles where isomorphic questions are used. For example, the WLGs reported in two upper-division CS courses are 89% and 85% [5]; the WLG reported in a CS1 course is 92% [16]; and the WLG from a genetics course is 86% [11]. In these other articles, the CG and PLG are defined using Q1 and $Q1_{ad}$, and reflect correctness on Q2 (not Q3 as in the present article). That is, those articles show that the PLG is almost as likely to correctly answer Q2 as is the CG. The current article extends this finding, so that we can now say that the PLG is almost as likely as the CG to correctly answer Q3 on the final exam. That is, not only is the PLG "keeping up" with the CG in-class, but they are also keeping up as the semester proceeds and demonstrating comparable abilities on the exam.

8. CONCLUSION

Previous studies of isomorphic PI questions provide evidence that students learn from their peers, learn from the instructor, and demonstrate this knowledge shortly after learning it. Missing from that prior work is an answer to the question: do students retain and demonstrate this learning as measured by isomorphs on the final exam? Our work uses isomorphic questions both in-class and on the final exam to address this very question. We find that those who learn from the PI process are quite likely to correctly answer isomorphic questions given on the final exam. In fact, these students are 87% as likely as students with existing prior knowledge to answer exam isomorphs correctly, and represent a substantial 25% of the overall class. That is, one-quarter of the students not only demonstrate learning in-class, but also demonstrate their learning on the final exam. We also find, somewhat unsurprisingly, that difficult questions impact a larger percentage of students than easy questions. In summary, isomorphic questions provide strong evidence that students learn introductory programming concepts from the in-class PI process and that this learning persists weeks (or months) later on the final exam.

9. ACKNOWLEDGMENTS

This work was supported in part by NSF grant 1140731.

10. REFERENCES

[1] Peer instruction for computer science. `peerinstruction4cs.org`, 2013.

[2] J. Bennedsen and M. E. Caspersen. Failure rates in introductory programming. *SIGCSE Bulletin*, 39:32–36, 2007.

[3] C. H. Crouch, J. Watkins, A. P. Fagen, and E. Mazur. Peer instruction: Engaging students one-on-one, all at once. In E. F. Redish and P. J. Cooney, editors, *Research-Based Reform of University Physics.* American Association of Physics Teachers, College Park, MD, 2007.

[4] R. Lister, E. S. Adams, S. Fitzgerald, W. Fone, J. Hamer, M. Lindholm, R. McCartney, J. E. Moström, K. Sanders, O. Seppälä, et al. A multi-national study of reading and tracing skills in novice programmers. *ACM SIGCSE Bulletin*, 36(4):119–150, 2004.

[5] L. Porter, C. Bailey-Lee, B. Simon, and D. Zingaro. Peer instruction: Do students really learn from peer discussion in computing? In *Proceedings of the Seventh International Conference on Computing Education Research*, pages 45–52, 2011.

[6] L. Porter, C. B. Lee, and B. Simon. Halving fail rates using peer instruction: A study of four computer science courses. In *Proceedings of the 44th ACM technical symposium on Computer science education*, pages 177–182, 2013.

[7] L. Porter and D. Zingaro. Importance of early performance in CS1: Two conflicting assessment stories. In *Proceedings of the 45th ACM technical symposium on Computer Science Education*, pages 295–300, 2014.

[8] L. Porter, D. Zingaro, and R. Lister. Predicting student success using fine grain clicker data. In *Proceedings of the Tenth International Conference on Computing Education Research*, pages 51–58, 2014.

[9] B. Simon, J. Parris, and J. Spacco. How we teach impacts student learning: peer instruction vs. lecture in CS0. In *Proceedings of the 44th ACM technical symposium on Computer science education*, pages 41–46, 2013.

[10] J. D. Slotta. Knowledge community and inquiry: New opportunities for scripting and orchestration. OISE - University of Toronto, 2013.

[11] M. K. Smith, W. B. Wood, W. K. Adams, C. Wieman, J. K. Knight, N. Guild, and T. T. Su. Why peer discussion improves student performance on in-class concept questions. *Science*, 323:122–124, 2009.

[12] E. Soloway, J. Bonar, and K. Ehrlich. Cognitive strategies and looping constructs: An empirical study. *Communications of the ACM*, 26(11):853–860, 1983.

[13] C. Watson and F. W. Li. Failure rates in introductory programming revisited. In *Proceedings of the 19th annual conference on Innovation and technology in computer science education*, pages 39–44, 2014.

[14] D. Zingaro. Peer instruction contributes to self-efficacy in CS1. In *Proceedings of the 45th ACM technical symposium on Computer Science Education*, pages 373–378, 2014.

[15] D. Zingaro and L. Porter. Peer instruction: a link to the exam. In *Proceedings of the 19th annual conference on Innovation and technology in computer science education*, pages 255–260, 2014.

[16] D. Zingaro and L. Porter. Peer instruction in computing: The value of instructor intervention. *Computers & Education*, 71:87–96, 2014.

The Effectiveness of Visualization for Learning Expression Evaluation

Amruth N. Kumar
Ramapo College of New Jersey
505 Ramapo Valley Road
Mahwah, NJ 07430, USA
201 684 7712
amruth@ramapo.edu

ABSTRACT

A controlled study was conducted to evaluate the effectiveness of providing visualization as part of feedback in a problem-solving software tutor on arithmetic expression evaluation. Data was collected over six semesters from multiple institutions. ANOVA analysis of the collected data was conducted in three stages. Statistically significant results include that visualization helped students learn more concepts; visualization did not improve the speed of learning; the benefits of visualization accrued primarily to less-prepared students; and visualization may affect different demographic subgroups differently. Incidental results include that there was no difference among demographic groups (male/female, traditional/underrepresented, Computer Science/non-CS) in the number of concepts learned using the software tutor, although some groups (female, underrepresented) were less-prepared before using the tutor than their counterparts, and some groups learned concepts with fewer practice problems (male, traditionally represented) than their counterparts. Concurrence of the results obtained whether the analysis was conducted based on pre-condition (need) or post-condition (benefit) of using the tutor strengthens the claims made as a result of this study.

Categories and Subject Descriptors

K.3.2 [**Computer and Information Science Education**]: Computer Science Education

General Terms

Measurement, Performance, Experimentation.

Keywords

Visualization; Evaluation.

1. INTRODUCTION

Software visualization includes algorithm visualization and program visualization. Whereas algorithm visualization deals with algorithms at a high level of abstraction, program visualization deals with programs at lower levels of abstraction [1]. The term program visualization is used to mean both static and dynamic visualization, the latter commonly referred to as program animation. Program visualization systems have also been classified as specialized versus generic systems: specialized systems visualize specific programming constructs whereas generic systems deal with entire programming languages [1]. The subject of the current study is static program visualization, specialized for expression evaluation.

Numerous systems have been developed over the years for software visualization. A meta-study of the effectiveness of algorithm visualization [2] found that in roughly half the studies reviewed in the meta-study, no significant difference was found between algorithm visualization and an alternative treatment provided to the students. A systematic review of generic program visualization and animation systems cataloged a mix of systems that were never evaluated, those that did not yield positive results, those whose positive results were not statistically significant and those with significant positive results [1]. Another survey of successful evaluations of visualization systems noted that about half the evaluations were only about usability; and a third of the evaluations were informal, "with little contribution to future improvements" [3].

Few of the specialized visualization systems, i.e., those built for specific programming constructs, have been evaluated. Among those that have been evaluated, one study found that animation was no more effective than text explanation for learning the semantics of C++ pointers [4]. Another study found that graphic visualization with text explanation was better than graphic visualization alone when learning expression evaluation [5]. Clearly, the effort to definitively establish whether and when visualization benefits learning is ongoing.

In this context, a controlled study was conducted to evaluate the effectiveness of providing static visualization as part of feedback in problem-solving software tutors on expression evaluation. The questions addressed in the study included whether and when visualization benefited student learning. This being the study of a specialized program visualization system, while the results may not be directly comparable with those of generic program visualization/animation systems or algorithm visualization systems, they would add to the accumulating evidence on whether and when visualization helps improve learning.

2. METHODOLOGY

2.1 The Software Tutor

For this study, a software tutor on arithmetic expression evaluation was used. The tutor presents expressions to the

SIGCSE '15, March 4–7, 2015, Kansas City, MO, USA
Copyright 2015 ACM 978-1-4503-2966-8/15/03…$15.00
http://dx.doi.org/10.1145/2676723.2677301

student, has the student evaluate each expression one operator at a time, grades the student's answer and provides feedback. The feedback includes whether the student's answer is correct and step-by-step explanation of the correct answer, which has been shown to help students learn [6]. A snapshot of the tutor is shown in Figure 1. In the figure, the student's answer is shown in the left panel. The feedback provided to the student is shown in the right panel.

The tutor covers the following concepts: correct evaluation, precedence, and associativity of five operators (addition, subtraction, multiplication, division and remainder), parentheses, coercion, and errors associated with the operators (e.g., divide-by-zero error).

The tutor is accessible over the web – students can use it anytime, anywhere, and at their own convenience. It is part of a suite of problem-solving tutors available for introductory programming topics, available for free for educational use called problets (problets.org).

2.2 Protocol

The software tutor administers pre-test-practice-post-test protocol as follows:

- **Pretest** – During pretest, the tutor presents one problem per concept. If a student solves a problem correctly, the student is given credit for the corresponding concept. No feedback is provided to the student, and no more problems on the concept are presented to the student. On the other hand, if the student solves a problem incorrectly, feedback is presented to the student immediately after the student submits his/her solution to the problem. Additional problems are presented on the concept during the subsequent stages.
- **Adaptive practice** – During this stage, additional problems are presented to the student on only the concepts on which the student solved problems incorrectly during the pre-test. For each such concept, the student is presented multiple problems until the student masters the concept, i.e., solves at least 60% of the problems correctly. On each problem, the student receives feedback explaining the correct answer.
- **Post-test** - During this stage, the student is presented test problems on the concepts that the student mastered during adaptive practice.
- **Demographics** - Students are provided the option to identify their demographic information, including sex and race. Demographic information is solicited after the pre-test-practice-post-test protocol to avoid the effects of stereotype threat [7].

The pre-test-practice-post-test protocol was limited to 30 minutes and was administered back-to-back, entirely over the web.

A concept is considered to have been learned if the student solves the problem on that concept incorrectly during pre-test, solves enough problems during adaptive practice to master the concept, and solves the post-test problem on the concept correctly. Since the entire pre-test-practice-post-test protocol was limited to 30 minutes, not all the concepts on which a student solves the problem incorrectly during pre-test turn into learned concepts: the student may run out of time and never get to solve practice problems or post-test problem on some concepts.

The study was controlled, i.e., participant schools were divided into control and test groups. The tutoring experience of control and test groups was identical except for the feedback provided to them after they incorrectly solved a problem during pre-test and after every problem during practice. Control group received only text feedback explaining each step in the evaluation of the expression, e.g.,

```
10 / 6 returns 1
Since both the operands are integers,
integer division is performed.
Any fraction in the result is discarded.
```

In addition to text feedback, test group also received graphic feedback in the form of an underbrace spanning the operator (/ in the above example) and operands (10 and 6 above), with the intermediate result (1 above) drawn centered underneath the underbrace. Both forms of feedback are shown in the right-hand panel in Figure 1.

The graphic visualization explains the order of evaluation of operators, but not concepts such as coercion and errors. So, it was provided in addition to rather than instead of text explanation. Such simultaneous presentation of the same information in text and visual forms is recommended by dual coding theory [8], which postulates that visual and verbal information are processed differently, in separate channels, to organize the information and create separate mental representations, either of which can be used later to recall the information.

2.3 Data Collection

Data was collected over six semesters: Fall 2011-Spring 2014. The same version of the tutor was used in all six semesters. The tutor was used by students in introductory programming courses from multiple institutions, mostly baccalaureate institutions, but also some community colleges and high schools.

The pre-test contained 16 problems. Since students could use the tutor as often as they pleased, when a student used the tutor multiple times, only the first attempt when the student solved all 16 pre-test problems was considered. If the student never solved all 16 pre-test problems, the attempt with the most number of pre-test problems solved was considered. In order to eliminate trial or unserious attempts by students, only those records were considered where students solved at least 10 pre-test problems. After this winnowing, 1415 students remained in control group and 1872 students in test group.

2.4 Data Analysis

A typical expression contains one or more operators. Students' answers were graded by the software tutor as the number of operators correctly evaluated by the student, divided by the total number of operators in the expression. Therefore, the score on each problem was normalized to 0 → 1.0 regardless of the number of operators in the expression.

Univariate ANOVA analysis was conducted for the following dependent variables:

- Pre-test mean score per problem, calculated as the total pre-test score divided by the number of pre-test problems solved – this normalized the variation in the number of problems solved by students (10-16);

- Number of concepts learned;
- Number of practice problems solved per learned concept, calculated as the number of practice problems solved, divided by the number of concepts learned, once again, to normalize the variation in the number of concepts learned by students.

The following fixed factors were used for analysis:

- Sex: male or female - participants were asked to identify their sex (biological notion) rather than their gender (social/cultural notion of man/woman) [9].
- Representation – traditionally represented (Caucasians and Asians [10]) versus underrepresented (the other racial groups, viz., Black/African American, Hispanic/Latino, Native American, Native Hawaiian/Pacific Islander and Other races)
- Discipline – Computer Science (CS) versus non-CS (all other majors, including Information Systems, Engineering, Other Sciences, Business, Arts, Social Sciences, Humanities and Other.)

When student records are complete, i.e., sex, race, and major of every student is known, a single multi-factor ANOVA analysis suffices, e.g., ANOVA of a dependent variable (e.g., concepts learned), with treatment, sex, representation, and discipline as multiple fixed factors. Since providing demographic data was optional, not all student records were complete. Carrying out a single multi-factor ANOVA analysis would have reduced the subject pool to only those student records that were complete, eliminating from consideration partial student records that could have contributed to analysis of some, but not all the independent factors (e.g., analysis by sex, but not discipline).

In order to maximize the insight offered by the collected data, ANOVA analysis of each dependent variable was carried out in three stages:

1. With treatment as the sole fixed factor: the entire subject pool was utilized; and only the main effect of treatment was analyzed;
2. With treatment and one demographic factor (e.g., sex): the subset of the subject pool that identified the demographic factor was utilized; and both the main effect of the demographic factor and interaction of the demographic factor with treatment were analyzed;
3. With treatment and *all* the demographic factors: the subset of the subject pool that identified all the demographic factors was utilized; and only interactions among treatment and/or more than one demographic factor were analyzed.

The sample size was the largest in the first stage, varied by the demographic factor in the second stage, and was the smallest in the third and final stage of analysis. If the student records were complete, results of the third stage would have subsumed the results of the first two stages.

Analysis was conducted for two subsets of the subject pool:

- Those who **needed the tutor**, i.e., scored 0.95 or fewer points per pre-test problem, the maximum score per problem being 1.0;
- Those who **benefited from the tutor**, i.e., learned one or more concepts by using the tutor.

While there is overlap between those who needed the tutor and those who benefited from it, those who needed the tutor also included students who ran out of time and did not learn any concept; those who benefited from the tutor also included students who scored over 0.95 but less than 1.0 per problem on the pre-test and went on to learn one or more concepts.

3. RESULTS

3.1 Students who needed the tutor

Treatment only: Analysis of pre-test score per problem with treatment as the fixed factor yielded no significant main effect [$F(1,1813) = 0.095$, $p = 0.758$], i.e., *there was no difference in the prior knowledge of the control and test groups as measured by the pre-test.* So, any subsequent difference between the groups can be attributed to the use of the tutor.

Analysis of the concepts learned yielded a significant main effect for treatment [$F(1,1116) = 3.925$, $p = 0.048$]: control group students without visualization learned significantly fewer concepts (1.596 ± 0.098) than test group students with visualization (1.731 ± 0.090). In other words, *visualization helped students learn more concepts.*(All means are presented at 95% confidence levels.)

Students in both control and test conditions were separated into two groups: those who scored above average (0.8118 points per problem) and those who scored average or below average on the pre-test. Analysis was repeated with both treatment and above average grouping as fixed factors. A marginally significant interaction was observed between treatment and above average grouping as shown in Table 1. The improvement from control to test condition was statistically significant only for the average or below average group [$F(1,536) = 4.23$, $p = 0.04$]: *the benefits of visualization accrued primarily to less-prepared students.*

Table 1. Treatment x Above-Average Grouping on the Concepts Learned

Grouping	Control	Test
Average or below	2.062 (242)	2.302 (295)
Above average	1.173 (266)	1.194 (314)

Analysis of the number of practice problems solved per learned concept yielded no significant main effect for treatment [$F(1,1116) = 0.166$, $p = 0.683$]: *visualization did not improve the speed of learning.*

Treatment and Sex: Analysis of the pre-test score per problem yielded a marginally significant main effect for sex [$F(1,1721) = 3.092$, $p = 0.079$]: female students scored less (0.804 ± 0.013) than male students (0.817 ± 0.008), i.e., *female students were less-prepared before using the tutor than male students.*

Analysis of the concepts learned yielded no significant main effect for sex [$F(1,1066) = 0.067$, $p = 0.795$]: *no significant difference was found in the number of concepts learned by female and male students.*

Analysis of the practice problems per learned concept yielded a marginally significant main effect for sex [$F(1,1066) = 3.228$, $p = 0.073$]: male students learned with significantly fewer problems per concept (3.213 ± 0.173) than female students

(3.524 ± 0.291], i.e., *male students learned faster than female students.*

Treatment and Representation: Analysis of the pretest score per problem yielded a significant main effect for representation [F(1,1423) = 27.479, p < 0.001]: traditionally represented students scored more per problem (0.83 ± 0.008) than underrepresented students (0.785 ± 0.015), i.e., *underrepresented students were less-prepared before using the tutor than traditionally represented students.*

Analysis of the number of concepts learned yielded no significant main effect for representation [F(1,897) = 0.095, p = 0.758]: *no significant difference was found in the number of concepts learned by underrepresented and traditionally represented students.*

Analysis of the practice problems per learned concept yielded a significant main effect for representation [F(1,897) = 5.343, p = 0.021]: traditionally represented students learned with significantly fewer problems per concept (3.218 ± 0.184) than underrepresented students (3.682 ± 0.348], i.e., *traditionally represented students learned faster than underrepresented students.*

Treatment and Discipline: Analysis of the pretest score per problem yielded a significant main effect for discipline [F(1,1417) = 5.883, p = 0.015]: surprisingly, Computer Science majors scored significantly less (0.808 ± 0.013) than non-CS students (0.826 ± 0.009), i.e., *Computer Science majors were less-prepared before using the tutor than non-CS majors.* One explanation for this counter-intuitive result may be that the subject pool contained over 660 Engineering majors, who may have had better Math preparation than Computer Science majors.

Analysis of the number of concepts learned yielded no significant main effect for discipline [F(1,895) = 0.572, p = 0.45]: *no significant difference was found in the number of concepts learned by Computer Science and non-CS students.*

Similarly, analysis of the problems solved per learned concept yielded no significant main effect for discipline [F(1,895) = 0.185, p = 0.667]: *no significant difference was found in the speed of learning of Computer Science and non-CS students.*

Treatment, Sex, Representation and Discipline: Analysis of the number of concepts learned yielded a marginally significant interaction between treatment, sex and discipline [F(1,842) = 2.834, p = 0.093], as shown in Table 2, where mean scores are followed by N in parentheses: whereas male CS students and female non-CS students learned more concepts with visualization than without, the vice-versa was true for female CS students, and no difference was observed between control and test treatments for male non-CS students. In other words, *visualization may affect different demographic subgroups differently.* If so, interactions among demographic groups and subgroups must be considered when evaluating the effectiveness of visualization. Among the differences in Table 2, only the difference for female non-CS students was statistically significant: t(172) = -2.506, p = 0.013. So, *when visualization increased the number of concepts learned by the overall subject pool, it was primarily for non-CS female students.*

Table 2. Treatment x Sex x Discipline Interaction on the Concepts Learned

Sex	Discipline	Control	Test
Male	CS	1.568 (113)	1.649 (112)
	Non-CS	1.729 (165)	1.731 (231)
Female	CS	1.469 (32)	1.333 (20)
	Non-CS	1.457 (84)	2.024 (86)

3.2 Students who benefited from the tutor

Most of the very same results were observed for students who benefited from the tutor as for students who needed the tutor. So, the discussion in this section is abbreviated, except where differences between the results of the two groups were observed. *Concurrence of the results obtained whether the analysis was conducted based on pre-condition (need) or post-condition (benefit) of using the tutor strengthens the claims made as a result of this study.*

Treatment only: *There was no difference in the prior knowledge of the control and test groups* [F(1,1203) = 0.757, p = 0.384].

Students with visualization learned more concepts (1.697 ± 0.085) *than those without* (1.569 ± 0.093) [F(1,1203) = 4.009, p = 0.045].

Even though the size of above-average group increased in both control (295, up from 266) and test conditions (362, up from 314), the improvement from control to test condition was still not statistically significant for the group. In other words, *the benefits of visualization accrued primarily to less-prepared students.*

Visualization did not improve the speed of learning measured as the number of practice problems solved per learned concept [F(1,1203) = 0.093, p = 0.760].

Treatment and Sex: Analysis of the pre-test score per problem yielded a significant main effect for sex [F(1,1147) = 5.141, p = 0.024]: female students scored less (0.789 ± 0.015) than male students (0.810 ± 0.009), i.e., *female students were less-prepared before using the tutor than male students.*

No significant difference was found in the number of concepts learned by female and male students [F(1,1147) = 0.298, p = 0.585].

Male students learned faster than female students (3.133 ± 0.163 versus 3.429 ± 0.274 problems per learned concept), the difference being marginally significant [F(1,1147) = 3.318, p = 0.069].

Treatment and Representation: *Underrepresented students were less-prepared before using the tutor than traditionally represented students* [F(1,964) = 12.415, p < 0.001].

No significant difference was found in the number of concepts learned by underrepresented and traditionally represented students [F(1,964) = 0.2, p = 0.655]..

Traditionally represented students learned faster than underrepresented students (3.137 ± 0.173 versus 3.586 ± 0.33 problems per concept) [F(1,964) = 5.606, p = 0.018].

Treatment and Discipline: Analysis of the pretest score per problem did *not* yield a significant main effect for discipline [F(1,961) = 2.056, p = 0.152].

No significant difference was found in the number of concepts learned by Computer Science and non-CS students [F(1,961) = 0.567, p = 0.451].

No significant difference was found in the speed of learning of Computer Science and non-CS students [F(1,961) = 0.162, p = 0.687].

Treatment, Sex, Representation and Discipline: In analysis of concepts learned, once again, significant interaction was found between treatment, sex and discipline [F(1,904) = 3.821, p = 0.051], as shown in Table 3. *So, the effect of visualization varies with demographic subgroups.* The demographic composition of the subject pool may significantly affect the outcome of visualization studies. As a case in point, the difference between control and test groups was statistically significant only for non-CS female students (t(185) = -2.727, p = 0.007), i.e., *the increase in the number of concepts learned due to visualization applied primarily to non-CS female students.*

Table 3. Treatment x Sex x Discipline Interaction on the Concepts Learned

Sex	Discipline	Control	Test
Male	CS	1.536 (121)	1.607 (121)
	Non-CS	1.716 (180)	1.703 (245)
Female	CS	1.567 (33)	1.321 (22)
	Non-CS	1.427 (90)	1.960 (93)

4. DISCUSSION

Visualization helped students learn significantly more concepts. It primarily benefited less-prepared students. This result favors the inclusion of visualization in software tutors to improve their effectiveness and broaden their appeal.

Visualization was found to affect different demographic groups differently. In this study, it was primarily female non-CS students who benefited from visualization. This suggests that when evaluating visualization, interactions among demographic subgroups should be taken into consideration, as has been recommended in the literature [11]. Barring that, the success of evaluation will depend on the demographic composition of the subject pool.

It was encouraging to find that even though some demographic subgroups were less-prepared than others, there was no difference in the number of concepts learned by the various subgroups using the software tutor. This is a piece of evidence in support of the broadness of appeal of software tutors for learning, technological and social preferences of individual demographic subgroups notwithstanding.

This study was conducted using a software tutor on arithmetic expression evaluation – arguably one of the easier topics covered in introductory programming courses. The introductory nature of the topic was a confounding factor of the study – not as many subjects were expected to benefit from using the software tutor. The visualization used in the study was redundant: it was in addition to rather than instead of text explanation and merely duplicated in graphic form, some, but not all of the information already provided in text form. This redundant nature of visualization was also a confounding factor of the study – it was not apparent that redundant presentation of the same information would lead to increased learning. Finally, the level of engagement of the visualization used in this study is classified as "viewing", which is considered to be one of the lowest levels of engagement of visualization [12]. This was yet another confounding factor of this study. The statistically significant results of this study are especially significant given these confounding factors – *even when the information presented using visualization was redundant and merely for viewing, and the topic was not challenging, visualization was found to help students learn more concepts.*

Future work includes repeating the study with more advanced topics and alternative forms of visualization appropriate for the topic. Questions that will be explored include whether visualization of harder topics will still only benefit less-prepared students; and whether the benefits will still vary by demographic subgroups.

5. ACKNOWLEDGMENTS

Partial support for this work was provided by the National Science Foundation under grants DUE-0817187 and DUE 1432190. Any opinions, findings, and conclusions or recommendations expressed in this material are those of the author(s) and do not necessarily reflect the views of the National Science Foundation.

6. REFERENCES

[1] Sorva, J., V. Karavirta, and L. Malmi, A Review of Generic Program Visualization Systems for Introductory Programming Education. Transactions on Computing Education, 2013. 13(4): p. 1-64.

[2] Hundhausen, C.D., S.A. Douglas, and J.T. Stasko, A meta-study of algorithm visualization effectiveness. Journal of Visual Languages and Computing, 2002. 13(3): p. 259-290.

[3] Urquiza-Fuentes, J. and J.Á. Velázquez-Iturbide, A Survey of Successful Evaluations of Program Visualization and Algorithm Animation Systems. Transactions of Computing Education, 2009. 9(2): p. 1-21.

[4] Kumar, A.N., Data Space Animation for Learning the Semantics of C++ Pointers, in SIGCSE Technical Symposium2009: Chattanooga, TN. p. 499-503.

[5] Kumar, A.N., Results from the Evaluation of the Effectiveness of an Online Tutor on Expression Evaluation, in 36th SIGCSE Technical Symposium2005: St. Louis, MO. p. 216-220.

[6] Kumar, A.N., Explanation of step-by-step execution as feedback for problems on program analysis, and its generation in model-based problem-solving tutors. Technology, Instruction, Cognition and Learning (TICL) Journal, 2006. 4(1).

[7] Kumar, A.N., A Study of Stereotype Threat in Computer Science. Proc. Innovation and Technology in Computer Science Education (ITiCSE 2012)2012, Haifa, Israel. 273-278.

[8] Paivio, A., Mental representations: A dual coding approach1990, New York: Oxford University Press.

[9] Sears, J., Teaching queerly: Some elementary propositions. , in Queering elementary education: Advancing the dialogue about sexualities and Schooling, W.J. Letts and J. Sears, Editors. 1999, Rowman & Littlefield, Inc.: Lanham, MD. p. 97-110.

[10] Kao, G., Asian Americans as model minorities? A look at their academic performance. American Journal of Education, 1995. 103: p. 121-159.

[11] Kumar, A.N., Need to Consider Variations within Demographic Groups When Evaluating Educational Interventions, in Innovation and Technology in Computer Science Education2009: Paris, France. p. 176-180.

[12] Naps, T.L., et al., Exploring the role of visualization and engagement in computer science education, in SIGCSE Bulletin2003. p. 131-152.

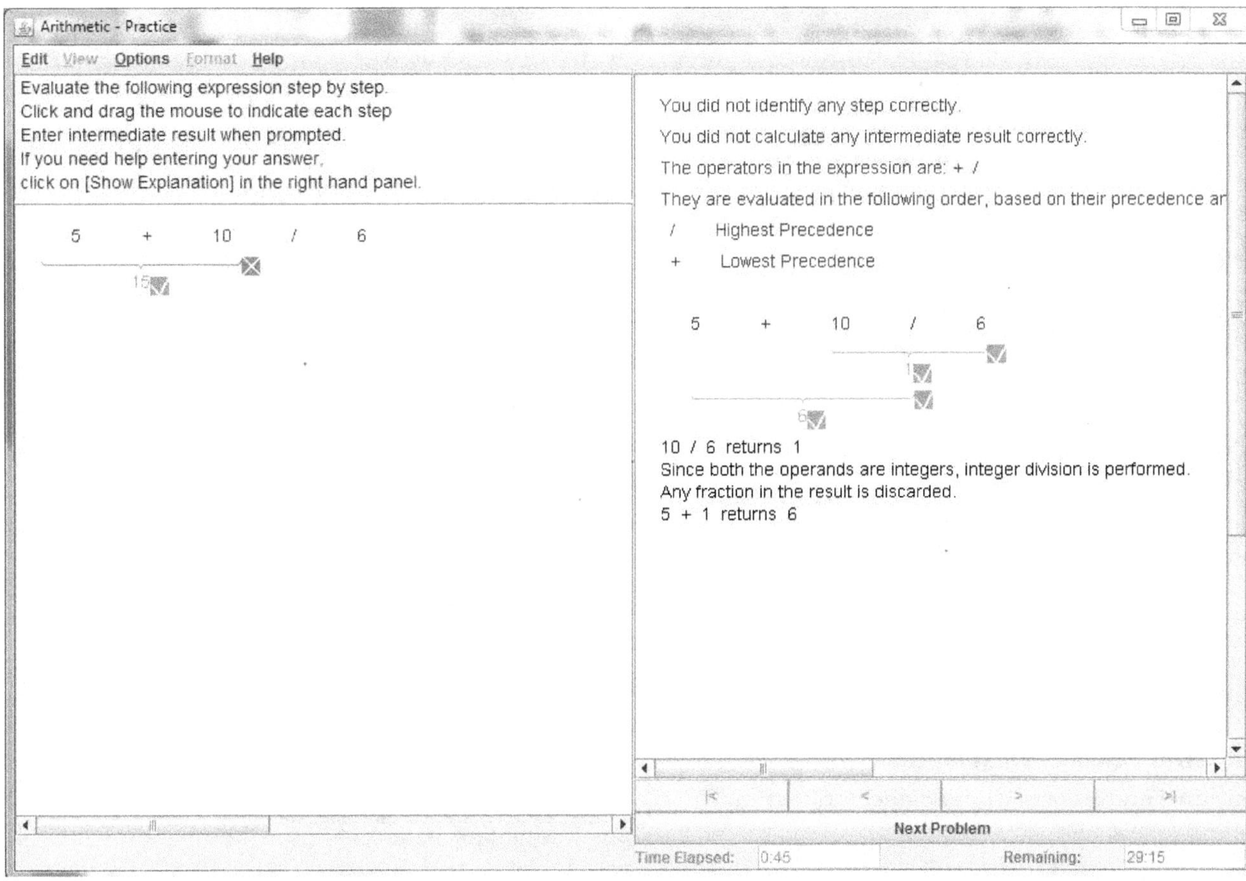

Figure 1. Snapshot of the Arithmetic Expression Evaluation Tutor

Analyzing Year One of a CS Principles PD Project

Ralph Morelli
Computer Science Department
Trinity College
Hartford, CT 06106
ralph.morelli@trincoll.edu

Chinma Uche
Connecticut Computer Science Teachers Assoc.
Greater Hartford Academy of Math and Science
Hartford, CT 06106
cuche@crec.org

Pauline Lake
Computer Science Department
Trinity College
Hartford, CT 06106
pauline.lake@trincoll.edu

Lawrence Baldwin
Baldwin Institutional Research Consulting
2 Everett Street
Sherborn, MA 01770
lawrence.baldwin@verizon.net

ABSTRACT

The Mobile Computer Science Principles (Mobile CSP) project is an NSF-funded CS 10K project. Its goal is to train a new cohort of high school computer science teachers to teach an Advanced Placement (AP) level course based on the emerging Computer Science Principles (CSP) framework. Mobile CSP uses App Inventor, a graphical programming language for Android devices, to engage students in app building as a means to get them interested in computer science. This paper reports on the first year of this effort. In addition to describing the project's Professional Development (PD) course, a 6-week, full-time summer course for teachers, and the Mobile CSP curriculum, the paper provides a preliminary analysis of demographic and performance data obtained from high school students who took the course during the 2013-2014 academic year.

Categories and Subject Descriptors

K.3.2 [**Computer and Information Science Education**]: Computer science education

1. INTRODUCTION

The Mobile Computer Science Principles (Mobile CSP) project is one of several projects funded by the National Science Foundation (NSF) in an effort to address the alarming lack of computer science course offerings at the high school level in the United States. Despite the enormous impact that computing has had on our lives and its growing importance in virtually every field of inquiry, scientific and otherwise, and despite the growing gap between available jobs in computing and high school and college graduates qualified to fill those jobs, U.S. high schools fail to offer rigorous courses in computer science. Connecticut is no exception.

As Table 1 shows, according to the College Board, only 460 CT students took the AP exam in Computer Science in 2013 as opposed to 4229 for AP Calculus AB and 3695 for Biology[5]. Even though Connecticut's numbers in CS have improved in the past two years, they still lag far behind the other STEM fields. This is a direct result of the lack of access to rigorous courses and well-trained CS teachers in Connecticut and elsewhere.

Table 1: Connecticut AP Data since 2011.

Year	2011	2012	2013
AP CS A	298	436	460
AP Calc AB	4046	4208	4229
AP Biology	3470	3331	3695
AP Chemistry	2165	2556	2573

As described in its 2011 solicitation, the goal of the NSF's CS 10K initiative is to increase the effectiveness of computing education in high school

> through the introduction of an entirely new curriculum (based on a proposed, new AP course) concomitant with the preparation of 10,000 high school teachers prepared to teach the new curriculum in 10,000 schools.[7]

The Mobile CSP project was funded in 2012 and addresses the CS 10K initiative through its three primary goals:

- To develop a core group of 30 CS teachers in Connecticut by training them in the Mobile CSP curriculum and supporting their efforts in the classroom.
- To create a complete set of online, openly licensed, curricular and instructional materials that can be disseminated broadly throughout Connecticut and elsewhere.
- To assess the efficacy of the curriculum and its impact on the attitudes and learning outcomes of participating teachers and their students.

SIGCSE'15, March 4–7, 2015, Kansas City, MO, USA.

http://dx.doi.org/10.1145/2676723.2677265.

The project has made good progress in addressing the first two of these goals. In 2013-14, the period covered in this report, 10 Connecticut teachers were provided formal CS training.[1] The training consists of a full-time, six-week summer Professional Development (PD) course.

With respect to the second goal, a complete set of Mobile CSP course materials are currently available online on two parallel *Google Course Builder (GCB)* sites: A teacher-facing site contains lesson plans, grading rubrics, solutions, and other supporting materials and a student-facing site[6] contains the course content.

This report provides an overview of the project, including its PD effort, and focuses primarily on the the efficacy of the Mobile CSP curriculum as measured by demographic and performance data gathered from students who took the course from the 2013 cohort of Mobile CSP teachers.

2. THE CS PRINCIPLES FRAMEWORK

CS Principles is a curricular framework being developed by the College Board for a new language-neutral, breadth-first AP course in computer science that is scheduled for release during 2016-17[1]. The framework is based on seven *big ideas*: 1) Creativity, 2) Abstraction, 3) Data, 4) Algorithms, 5) Programming, 6) The Internet, and 7) Impact.

These are expanded into 23 *enduring understandings*, which are further expanded into 42 specific *learning objectives* (i.e., what students need to be able to do), each of which is further expanded into more than 100 specific *essential knowledge* statements (i.e., what students need to know).

Table 2: Breakdown of a CS Principle

Big Idea	Abstraction
Enduring Understanding	A variety of abstractions built upon binary sequences can be used to represent all digital data.
Learning Objectives	Describe the variety of abstractions used to represent data.
Essential Knowledge	The interpretation of a binary sequence depends on how it is used.

As Table 2 shows, the CS Principles is a *framework*. It *describes* goals for student learning but does not *prescribe* a specific curriculum. This is especially true in the area of programming. Unlike, the CS A course, which requires Java, no programming language is specified for the CS Principles.

The proposed CS Principles course has a unique way of assessing student performance. It supplements the customary AP written exam, with in-course *performance tasks* [1], which count for 50% of the student's grade. Currently, there are two required performance tasks: The *Explore* task requires the student to identify and research a computing innovation that has had a signficant impact on some population and produce written responses to a set of specific prompts as well as a digital artifact (e.g., a video audio, etc.) "to express the effects of your chosen innovation." The *Create* task requires the student to work collaboratively with another student on designing, implementing, and presenting a computer program of the students' choice. These tasks are allotted 8 and 12 hours of class time respectively.

[1]Sixteen additional Connecticut teachers were provided formal training in summer 2014, but data from the 2014 cohort is not included in this report. A final cohort of Connecticut teachers will be trained in summer 2015.

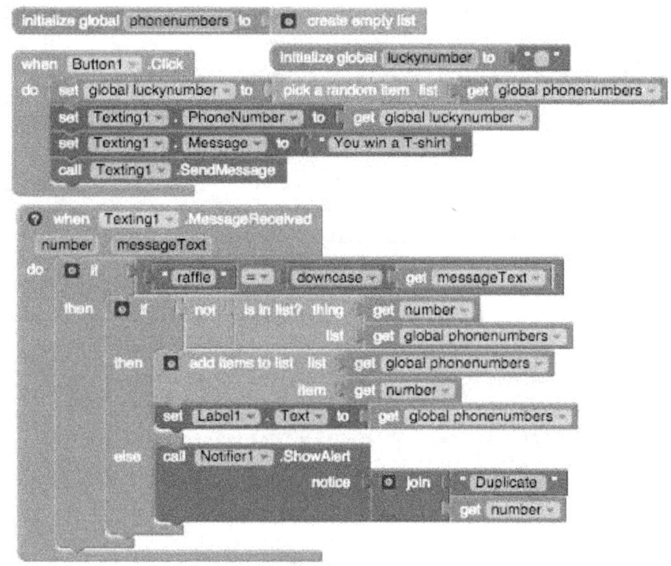

Figure 1: The App Inventor *Raffle* app.

3. APP INVENTOR

The Mobile CSP course uses App Inventor, a blocks-based visual language for programming Android mobile devices[3]. App Inventor is the invention of MIT Professor Hal Abelson and is hosted at the MIT Center for Mobile Learning.

The current version of App Inventor, which was released in September 2013, has more than 700,000 registered users who have created almost 2 million projects. Its usage data indicates that it is growing at a rate of roughly 2,500 new users and 6,500 new projects a day[2].[2] There are almost twice as many active daily users during the schoool year (13,400) as during the summer months (7,600), which suggests that App Inventor is becoming widely used in schools.

What makes App Inventor such an attractive language for introductory CS is its focus on mobile app development and its highly abstracted design. Programs (i.e., apps) are developed in a web browser and downloaded onto Android mobile devices either through a Wifi or USB connection. The download process can occur through *packaging*, in which the entire app is compiled into an Android APK file, or *interactively*, which permits iterative development and testing of the app.

App Inventor is *event-driven* and apps respond to a sequence of events, including User Interface (UI) events, such as button clicks, sensor events, such as orientation and GPS location changes, and communication events, such as phone calls and text messages. The language's blocks are mapped directly to the device's various hardware and software components and to its event hierarchy, making it quite simple for even novice programmers to design and implement sophisticated mobile apps.

App Inventor's powerful abstraction of mobile computing changes the basic formula for teaching introductory programming. Instead of saying "bear with us for a few weeks or months and you will soon be building some cool programs", an App Inventor course starts with building a mobile app on

[2]This growth likely includes users moving from the previous version, which had more than 1.5 million registered users.

the first day, in a matter of minutes. Students can quickly see how to express and implement some of their app ideas. The creative payoff is almost immediate and it is easy to show one's friends.

For example, one app that we have used as a day-one demo is the *Raffle* app. Students text the word "raffle" to the instructor's phone or tablet from any phone that supports SMS and the app registers them for a raffle. Once everyone in class is registered, the instructor presses a button and the app selects a random phone number and sends a "Congratulations, you've won!" message. This app consists of two pieces of code, one to handle the button-click event and one to handle text-message-received events (Figure 1) and can be developed in class in 10-20 minutes.

4. THE MOBILE CSP COURSE

The Mobile CSP course began as a CS0 "Mobile Computing" course at Trinity College in Spring 2011. In the following academic year, it was revised to conform to the CSP curricular framework and it was offered as one of the College Board's Phase 1 Pilot 2 courses, during which it was taught simultaneously at Trinity College and at a local public high school, the Greater Hartford Academy of Math and Science. The current version of the course attempts to conform to the CSP curricular framework layed out by the College Board in its most recent documents[1].

The course is currently organized into seven units and consists of more than 60 lessons, 28 of which are App Inventor lessons[6]. The remaining CSP lessons cover such topics as binary numbers, sorting and searching algorithms, cryptography, and other CS topics. The course includes an extensive collection of interactive *formative assessment exercises* – a collection of questions and exercises that accompany each lesson, including both App Inventor and CSP lessons. The exercises, which come with extensive hints and feedback, are not graded and can be repeated as many times as necessary to get the right answer.

The course takes the approach that creating mobile apps is the motivating factor through which students are introduced to computer science. Programming (app building) is seen as a creative process that requires students to learn some computer science in order to do well.

4.1 Mobile CSP PD

The project's PD consists of an intensive full-time 6-week course offered in the summer. Participants work through the entire Mobile CSP curriculum, from the same perspective that their students will later take. The curriculum includes app-building lessons and there is one lesson in each unit that focuses on readings and discussions of impact topics from *Blown to Bits*[4]. The remaining lessons are on CS topics ranging from the binary number system, to hardware and software abstractions, to algorithm analysis.

PD participants also complete scaled down versions of the CSP performance tasks. In summer 2013, there were three performance tasks, a programming task, a data analysis task, and a research project on the Internet.[3] Because most particants are new to programming – and especially App Inventor programming – we provide additional *creative projects*, which are scaled down versions of the programming performance tasks. Teachers work in pairs on all performance tasks and programming projects and are required to produce a write up and an oral presentation of their work.

Like their students are required to do for the course itself, the teachers maintain Google sites portfolios of their work. These include their personal reflections on the *Blown to Bits* readings, their reflections, as teachers, on the various lessons, and their write ups and documentation of the various performance tasks.

4.2 In-Class Support for Teachers

A very important component of the project's PD is its use of an *itinerant teaching consultant* who conducts regular in-class visits to provide moral support for new teachers and help them with lessons, equipment, and any other issues that come up while teaching the course the first year.[4] In addition to in-class support, teachers also have access to a small online community that reponds quickly to questions on a forum and holds bi-weekly Google hangouts and bimonthly CSTA meetings to talk about the course and any issues that come up.

4.3 The 2013 Mobile CSP Teacher Cohort

In summer 2013, 10 Connecticut teachers participated in the Mobile CSP PD. As a condition for participation both the teacher and their principal signed an agreement that they would teach the Mobile CSP course in their school during the 2013-14 academic year. Teachers received a $6,000 stipend for active participation in the PD, plus another $1,000 stipend if they submitted all of the required data from their students during the year. Of those 10 teachers, 4 were certified in Technology Education, 2 in Social Studies, 2 in Math or Business, 1 in Science and 1 in Art. Three of the teachers had some prior experience teaching programming, one of whom had taught the AP CS A course. Seven of the 10 reported having no prior CS experience.

5. ANALYZING YEAR ONE

5.1 The 2013-14 High School Courses

During the school year, 9 of the 10 teachers taught some variation of the Mobile CSP course. They were joined by several other teachers who did not participate in the PD but who had prior CS experience and asked to participate in the project. A total of 17 sections of the course were taught, with some teachers teaching multiple sections. Seven teachers taught the course as a full-year course, the preferred model. Four taught it as a one-semester course in the fall and two taught it as a one-semester course in both the fall and spring semesters.

Seven of the 10 PD teachers made a good-faith effort to teach the full Mobile CSP course. Three of those succeeded, more or less, in doing so. The other 4 ended up dropping certain lessons or activities for various reasons. Two of the

[3]The College Board has revised the performance tasks. There are currently just two, the data analysis task has been dropped and the Internet task has been broaded to focus on a computing innovation in any area.

[4]The current consultant, author 3, is a 2013 graduate of Trinity College, who double majored in CS and Education and began teaching App Inventor to high school students while still an undergraduate.

PD teachers used only the App Inventor lessons in their courses and one teacher did not teach a course.[5]

5.2 Teacher Confidence and Success

At the end of the school year, 10 teachers completed a survey, 9 of the PD teachers and 1 additional teacher, that consisted of questions about their attitudes towards the course and there preparation for it, as well as their opinions about how each of the lessons went in the classroom.

Of the nine PD teachers surveyed, seven reported that they were very confident (3) or generally confident (4) that the course they were about to teach would go well. Two reported that they were not very confident. At the completion of the school year the 10 teachers who participated in the survey were asked how they liked the course after they had taught it. Five reported that they liked it "very much", four that they liked it "pretty well" and one reported that "it is ok". None reported "not well."

5.3 Analysis of Mobile CSP Lessons

The 2013-2014 version of the Mobile CSP course contained 65 lessons, 27 App Inventor lessons and 38 CSP lessons. The teachers' collective assessment of these lessons are summarized in Table 3.

Table 3: Success with Mobile CSP Lessons

	High	Medium	Low	Unused
Tutorials	72.7%	9.7%	3.2%	14.2%
Mini Projects	88.6%	1.9%	50%	9.6%
Creative Projects	79.3%	0%	0%	20.6%
CSP Lessons	58%	18.9%	0.5%	22%

The 27 App Inventor lessons included 16 *tutorials*, where the student follows a step-by-step lesson that teaches how to build an app, and 11 *mini projects*, where students are given problems and work in pairs to solve them on their own. The problems frequently involve enhancements to the app that was built in the tutorial.

In addition, there were three *creative projects.* These were modeled on the College Board's programming performance task. Students, working in pairs, proposed their own project within certain general constraints – e.g., the app must have a socially useful purpose and must make use of GPS. They then designed and implemented their app, wrote it up on their portfolios, and gave an oral presentation on it to the class.

As Table 3 shows, the App Inventor portion of the course was highly successful in the teachers' opinion. Indeed, if we discount the "Unused" column and count only those opinions among teachers who did the lesson, then the percentage of those saying the lessons were highly successful would be 84.8% for tutorials, 97.8% for mini projects and 100% for creative projects. This is a strong result from the teachers.

The row classified as CSP lessons are all the lessons that did not directly involve App Inventor. As Table 3 shows, the CSP portion of the course did not work as well for teachers as the App Inventor portion, with only 58% percent saying the lessons were highly successful and 18.9% reporting that there were problems in delivering the lessons. Note also that 22% reported "Unused." Indeed, as noted earlier, a couple of teachers seemed to have omitted the CSP portion of the curriculum entirely.

This difference between the App Inventor and non-App Inventor parts of the course was not unexpected and is consistent with the premise that mobile app building would be what attracts teachers and students to the course. As we will see shortly, this same difference arises among student preferences.

5.4 Student Data

The project collected various demographic and performance data from students, including: (1) pre- and post-course surveys of demographic data and attitudes toward CS; (2) mid-term and final examinations that covered both App Inventor and CSP topics through a combination of multiple choice, fill-in and open ended questions; and (3) performance tasks that were graded by teachers using a rubric provided by the project. Of the 354 students who took the Mobile CSP course at 10 schools we were able to collect pre- and post-survey data from 281 students and final exam data from 264 students.

Table 4: Student Demographics, including gender (M/F) and underrepresented (U)

Teacher	UF	F	UM	M	Tot
A	2	9	8	71	90
B	0	0	5	2	7
C	0	14	0	25	39
D	6	5	5	7	23
E	0	1	1	8	10
F	2	4	5	16	27
G	7	0	11	3	21
H	8	2	15	16	41
I	3	1	4	0	8
J	0	0	3	9	12
Totals	28	36	57	160	281
Totals	64		217		

5.5 Demographic Profile of the Students

The pre-course survey asked students for various demographic data, data about their prior experience, and their attitudes toward computing. As shown in Table 4, the male:female breakdown was 77% to 23%. Although the Mobile CSP course is designed for 11th and 12th AP-level, the students came from all grade levels: 9th (24%), 10th (29%), 11th (21%), and 12th (25%).

The racial/ethic breakdown was as follows: Caucasian (58%), African American (15%), Hispanic (14%), Native American, including Hawaiian and Alaskan (4%), Asian (10%), all others (10%).[6] For the purposes of this study an *underrepresented minorty* includes African American, Hispanic, Native American, including native Hawaiian and Alaskan, and girls. There was considerable variation in racial/ethnic backgrond and gender by school, as summarized in Table 4.

The vast majority of the students reported that they were experienced users of various computer applications, including email, Internet searches, social networking, games. But

[5] To try to minimize this type of attrition, we have tightened up our application process and our "contract" with the schools.

[6] Students were allowed to check more than one category so the total exceeds 100%.

Table 5: Change in Confidence

	Less	Same	More
Design something novel and innovative			
All Students	8%	46%	46%
Underrepresented	7%	47%	46%
Solve an unstructured problem			
All students	12%	38%	51%
Underrepresented	15%	43%	42%
Apply an abstract idea to a real problem			
All students	7%	38%	55%
Underrepresented	6%	39%	56%
Identify/fix a problem in a complex process			
All Students	12%	41%	47%
Underrepresented	15%	39%	47%
Work with others in small groups to solve problems			
All students	10%	29%	60%
Underrepresented	14%	28%	58%

relatively few reported prior programming experience; only around 30% of boys and less than 20% for girls. When asked to rate their programming ability at the start of the course, approximately 54% of all students rated themselves as "beginners", and only 11% of girls and 14% of boys described themselves as having "considerable experience" in programming.

5.6 Recruitment and Class Enrollment

Recruitment of students to the Mobile CSP course was a major challenge, especially within the Hartford school district, the primary target demographic. The project directors had little control over whether and how the course was advertised and promoted within the schools and it appears that in some cases it was not widely promoted among students or teachers. In most cases teachers were recruited and selected by the principal. Recruitment and selection of teachers occurred between January and April and in some cases the course was not put into the school's schedule until after students' schedules had been determined.

When asked in the pre-course survey why they took the course, 14% reported that it was recommended by a teacher and 52% said that the course sounded interesting or fun. But 41% also reported that they were assigned to the course.

5.7 Student Problem Solving Ability

Students were asked a number of questions in the pre- and post-course surveys about their confidence along various problem-solving dimensions. As Table 5 summarizes, their confidence as problem solvers seems to have improved overall and there was no significant difference observed for underrepresented minority students.

This is a positive result due, no doubt, to the emphasis and the amount of time spent in the course on designing and development of mobile apps. Moreover, their improved confidence seems to have been justified by the generally good work they did on their mini projects and on the creative performance tasks. For teachers who reported these grades to us, the overall average was 88%.

5.8 Student Attitudes Toward CS

The post-course survey revealed that 65% of students enjoyed the course as opposed to 12% who did not or 23% who were neutral. And 56% said they would probably take another CS course as opposed to 19% who said they would not and 26% who were unsure. Students were evenly divided (37%) on whether or not they might major in CS, with 27% neutral on that question.

Table 6: Attitudes Towards Computer Science

	Disagree	Maybe	Agree
Course improved my understanding of CS			
All students	2%	19%	80%
Underrepresented	1%	17%	22%
Course improved my attitude toward CS			
All students	8%	23%	69%
Underrepresented	2%	21%	77%
Learned I have some programming talent			
All students	5%	25%	69%
Underrepresented	5%	27%	69%
CS is a socially beneficial discipline			
All students	6%	21%	73%
Underrepresented	9%	29%	61%

Table 6 summarizes student responses to some of the questions that probed student attitudes toward various aspects of CS. Their attitudes were generally positive. On the other hand, the survey also revealed that we have more work to do on some of the standard misconceptions about computer science. More than half of the students (51%) agreed with the statement that *computer science is about using application software* and about the same number agreed (31%) and disagreed (29%) with the statement that computer science and programming are the same thing.

5.9 Student Final Exam Performance

The final exam for the course consisted of 40 multiple-choice, short-answer and short-essay questions based largely on the course's formative assessment exercises. Teachers were not given the exam before hand but were told that that students could prepare for the final by reviewing those exercises. We are not sure to what degree the students "studied" for the final. All but two of the teachers factored the final exam scores into the grades they gave their students.

As shown in Table 7 the average score for the 266 students who took the final was 62%, which was also the average for all underrepresented students. Student performance on the final varied considerably from teacher to teacher. There are a number of factors that could explain these differences but the two that stand out the most are (1) the level of the teacher's background and experience in CS and (2) whether the teacher covered all of the topics.

For example, teachers D and E had prior experience teaching CS and both covered the entire Mobile CSP curriculum. Their averages were above 80%. On the other hand teacher I was not experienced but did cover the whole curriculum and gave students time in class to study for the final. Teacher I also reported having received excellent in-class support from the project's itinerant teaching consultant.

By contrast, teachers C and G had prior teaching experience in CS. Teacher G, however, covered almost none of the CSP lessons and teacher C modified the recommended curriculum. Their average scores were in the 60s. On the other hand, teacher A, one of the more inexperienced teachers in the cohort, made a good faith effort to cover the entire curriculum but was unable to do so and was also unable to receive in-class support from the iterant teaching consultant. Student performance was very low (51%) in this case. We will need to take a look at additional data to try understand the reasons.

Table 7: **Student Performance on Final Exam**

Teacher	Score (%)	N-all
A	51	100
B	66	5
C	37	43
D	81	23
E	84	10
F	61	22
G	60	41
H	48	10
I	82	12
Totals	62	266

What do these results say about the PD and the final exam? Clearly, the exam is non-trivial: in classes where the material was not adequately covered, the students did not perform well. At the same time, in most courses where the material was covered, whether by experienced or inexperienced teachers, the students seemed to perform well. In general, student performance on the final seems to suggest that the PD and the in-class support provided by the project do have the potential to deliver AP-level CSP instruction.

6. DISCUSSION

The CS 10K initiative involves three very tough challenges: (1) Recruiting and training teachers with no formal education in CS to teach an AP-level CS course; (2) engaging students with no prior computing background in the study of AP-level computer science; and (3) getting school administrators to add rigorous computer science courses to their curricula in the absence of standards.

Training Teachers. Despite the relatively short training provided to teachers, the Mobile CSP approach seems to have worked at least to some extent. Despite their varied backgrounds, those who participated in the PD came away feeling confident in their ability to teach the course and nearly all who taught it described it as a positive experience.

Looking ahead, most of the 2013 cohort (8 out of 10) are teaching the course for a second year. One area for improvement is to work at making sure that teachers are teaching the full Mobile CSP curriculum.

Student Readiness. While students performed very well over all on the mobile app building projects, their performance on the final exam was not uniformly good. We think this was due to two factors. Some of the students were not ready for an AP-level course – 53% were 9th and 10th graders – and in several cases they were not exposed fully to the entire Mobile CSP curriculum. It is not clear to what degree students had the recommended prerequisites (Algebra I and Geometry) for the course.

This observation raises a broader question about the CS 10K initiative – namely, the goals of trying to offer an AP-level course as an introduction to computer science and also trying to attract an underrepresented demographic may be in tension with each other. This is not to suggest that one or the other of these goals should be dropped. On the contrary, both are worthy and necessary goals. It may suggest that there needs to be a pre-requisite computing course that students can take before taking the AP CSP course.

High School Curricula. We were unable to get 100% participation by the teachers who participated in the PD. One teacher ended up not teaching any course. Some focused mostly on the App Inventor lessons. Recruiting students, especially girls, was a big challenge. Some teachers reported not getting great help from guidance counselors. These challenges were exacerbated by the fact that the course was offered as an "elective," which lessons its attractiveness in the eyes of students and parents.

To address the variation in the "product", we have tightened up the "contract" between the project and the school. This seems to have improved the 2014 teacher cohort – at least in terms that they all agree that they are going to teach the full Mobile CSP curriculum. We also see the need to work with school boards and legislators to get CS accepted as a required course.

7. CONCLUSION

For the most part, the first year of the Mobile CSP PD effort has gone reasonably well.

- The intensive six-week course appears to provide teachers, even those with no prior CS background, with the confidence they need to teach the course.
- The lessons, lesson plans, and other pedagogical moterials seem to be well received by both the teachers and the students.
- The course itself appears to improve student attitudes toward CS and students appear to think that the course has helped improve their problem-solving skills.

These are positive results. Thus, despite the various problems mentioned above, these results do seem to support the project's underlying premise: mobile computing in App Inventor is a suitable and highly attractive means of getting students, including underpresented students, engaged in introductory CS education.

ACKNOWLEDGMENT

This work is supported by NSF Grant CNS-1240841.

8. REFERENCES

[1] Computer Science Principles, `http://csprinciples.org`, accessed Sep 4, 2014.

[2] App Inventor Usage Statistics, `http://ai2.appinventor.mit.edu/stats`, accessed Sep 1, 2014.

[3] The MIT Center for Mobile Learning, `http://appinventor.mit.edu`, accessed Sep 1, 2014.

[4] H. Abelson, K. Ledeen, and H. Lewis. *Blown to Bits: Your Life, Liberty, and Happiness After the Digital Explosion.* Addison-Wesley Professional, 2008.

[5] The College Board. AP Research Data, 2014. `http://research.collegeboard.org/programs/ap/data`, accessed Sep 5, 2014.

[6] The Mobile CSP Project. `http://mobile-csp.org`, accessed Sep 4, 2014.

[7] The National Science Foundation. Computing education for the 21st century, `http://www.nsf.gov/pubs/2010/nsf10619/nsf10619.txt`, accessed Sep 1, 2014.

Field Experiences in Teaching Computer Science: Course Organization and Reflections

Lori Pollock, Chrystalla Mouza, James Atlas, Terry Harvey
University of Delaware
Newark, DE 19716
{pollock, cmouza, jatlas, tharvey}@udel.edu

ABSTRACT

A major challenge for broadening participation in computing within K-12 settings is the lack of trained teachers. While professional development programs provide opportunities for the development of knowledge, skills, and pedagogy in teaching computing, teachers need ongoing support throughout the academic year. In this paper, we describe a course-based model for partnering undergraduates with teachers and students in a field experience model. We describe the model focusing on learning objectives, curriculum, field component and partnership building. We subsequently report on the products that undergraduates were able to create with their partner teachers. Finally, we investigate the impact of the field experience model on undergraduates' content knowledge, pedagogical skills and career development.

Categories and Subject Descriptors

K.3.2 Computer and Information Science Education

General Terms

Design, Human Factors, Languages.

Keywords

CS education, computational thinking, K12, CS principles.

1. INTRODUCTION

Due to efforts from the National Science Foundation, Computer Science Teachers Association, and many other groups advocating for computer science (CS) education in K-12, more states and school districts are recognizing the need for integrating computational thinking into their curricula. To provide all students with the opportunity to develop the fundamental understanding of CS principles, advocates are working on addressing many challenges. One such challenge is the lack of qualified, valued teachers in CS [5].

In the long term, the demand for trained CS teachers could be met by creating teacher preparation programs coupled with certification, robust standards, and curricula [4, 8]. However, the current demand requires multi-faceted professional development helping teachers from across varied disciplines to gain the skills, knowledge, and confidence to become excellent CS teachers [8]. Unfortunately, research shows that one-shot workshops are not sufficient to adequately train and support teachers [12].

SIGCSE '15, March 04-07 2015, Kansas City, MO, USA.
Copyright 2015 ACM 978-1-4503-2966-8/15/03…$15.00.
http://dx.doi.org/10.1145/2676723.2677286

To support the efforts of existing teachers who are working towards integrating CS principles into their classes or establishing a full CS Principles AP course, we have developed a college course-based model that engages undergraduate CS, mathematics education and education majors in field experiences in teaching CS. This model exposes undergraduates to outreach and communication skill-building opportunities that involve their technical skills, while being a part of their curriculum.

In this paper, we first detail the course model in terms of objectives, curriculum, field component and partnership building. We subsequently report on the products that undergraduates are able to create with their partner teachers. Finally, we report on the impact of the field experience model on undergraduates' content knowledge, pedagogical skills and career development. In other related work, we report on the impact of the field experience model on middle school students learning of CS concepts, programming practices, and motivation towards computing [10].

2. RELATED WORK

The Field Experiences in Teaching Computer Science course builds upon earlier efforts to broaden participation in computing such as those of the STARS alliance project [11]. The STARS Alliance is a community of regional partnership among academic, K-12 schools, professional and community groups catalyzed by the STARS Leadership Corps (SLC), a leadership program that engages undergraduates in computing outreach, research, and service to broaden participation in computing [1].

The service learning component builds upon earlier NSF supported efforts to provide university CS students opportunities to develop technical and communication skills by sharing their computing expertise with middle school teachers in the context of game design [3,6]. It also leverages key findings related to the importance of field experience to help undergraduates connect classroom experiences with university coursework, reflect upon their work, and practice their lessons in an environment where the partner teacher is present to create a controlled environment [2]. Finally, the interdisciplinary nature of the model builds upon the efforts of the multi-tiered mentoring model for increasing minority and women participation in computing proposed by the University of Alabama [3,7].

Despite building upon earlier efforts, the Field Experiences model described in this work is unique in two ways: first, it is the first effort to combine and assess all three components identified in the literature in a single model. Second, it engages undergraduates in a course experience that is central to their program and can be counted towards their CS concentration requirement.

3. FIELD EXPERIENCE COURSE MODEL

The field experience course is a 1-3 credits college course open to undergraduates in CS or other STEM (Science-Technology-Engineering-Mathematics) education fields. The course provides an introduction to CS teaching methodology as well as the opportunity to put that knowledge into practice in local schools. Specifically, participants become familiar with the state of CS education in terms of pedagogy, Advanced Placement (AP) exams, and K-12 requirements while also producing written lesson plans, reflective journals, and collaborative projects. The learning objectives are as follows.

In CS education:

- be aware of challenges/strategies for teaching CS
- be knowledgeable of models and approaches to integrating CS at national, state, district, and classroom scale
- be knowledgeable of the role and impact of assessment in education
- appreciate the history of CS in constructive learning approaches

In CS curriculum:

- be aware of existing curricula for teaching CS for K-12 including the AP course on Computer Science Principles (CSP) and the Exploring Computer Science (ESC) course
- be able to explain core ideas in each of the 7 CS principles areas
- have functional skills in using software tools to express/model K-12 CS problem solving skills

In teaching:

- be knowledgeable of education standards such as Common Core State Standards (CCSS) and how CS curriculum ties into these standards
- be confident observing and evaluating teaching of CS lessons
- be confident assisting a classroom teacher in the implementation of CS lesson plans
- be confident developing, planning, and assessing a CS lesson plan
- gain experience leading the implementation of CS lesson plans
- be able to collate a set of lesson plans to form a CS module

In communication:

- collaborate effectively with a team of education specialists
- be able to present the argument for CS education in K-12
- become more reflective on teaching, planning, and educational research
- gain experience in public speaking with multiple audiences

3.1 Field Experience Course Activities

The course combines college classroom meetings with visits in middle or high school classrooms where undergraduate participants co-plan and co-teach computing lessons with a practicing teacher. The 75-minute on-campus class time is devoted to identifying and implementing CS teaching resources targeted toward CS principles, modeling classroom lessons with CS unplugged and other resources, discussing teaching pedagogy, preparing and analyzing lesson plans, and reflecting on the field experiences and teacher partnering experiences.

Table 1. Semester–long Activities in the Field-Experience Course

Week	Computational Activities	Pedagogical Activities	Field-Related Activities
1-3	Learn CS education trends and challenges; Explore online CS resources (e.g., CSTA, CS unplugged and ECS)	Initial self-assessment on confidence in teaching computing; Share experiences in teaching, learning CS and expectations; Discuss giving feedback.	Identify and teach a CS unplugged exercise to peers in preparation for teaching a similar activity to middle/high school students; Give and receive feedback.
4-5	Continue to explore and think about adapting CS resources (e.g., CSTA, CS unplugged and ECS) for middle school students	Discuss effective learning environments; Learn about each school's context and student population; Discuss middle school learning environments; Discuss ways to interact with teachers and students.	Assign field locations; Address transportation issues; Identify appropriate dress code and behaviors within school settings; Conduct a class observation to establish rapport with partner teacher and students.
6-7	Explore Scratch exercises and develop Scratch projects for showcasing to students.	Prepare, discuss, and analyze lesson plan proposals for after-school program.	Observations and co-planning sessions with partner teachers; Discuss field observation experiences, pedagogical strategies used by partner teachers, and anticipated challenges.
8-10	Present Scratch projects to peers; Give/receive feedback; Discuss potential Scratch teaching issues. Discuss technical problems emerging from field lesson plans and propose solutions.	Explore classroom management techniques; Identify a reward system; Discuss what skilled teachers think and do based on field observations; Present lesson plans for after-school program; Give/receive feedback on lesson plans.	Co-plan and co-teach with partner teachers; Weekly updates on participants' experiences in partner schools.
11-13	Create flyers for raising teachers' awareness of CS education to broaden students' and teachers' participation in computing.	Teamwork on generating ideas for the Partner4CS summer professional development workshop based on experience working with partner teachers.	Co-plan/co-teach with partner teachers; Discuss/share what works well and what needs improvement in field teaching; Discuss issues observed in the field (e.g., strategies for responding to students' questions, reinforcing understanding, etc.)
14	Final reflection on overall experiences in teaching and service as well as impacts on future learning and career development; Final self-assessment on confidence in teaching computing.		

The field experiences take place in local middle and high schools where teachers are working on integrating CS principles into their courses and after school programs. Undergraduate participants in the course meet with teachers to discuss their role and plan lessons and activities, lead after school programs, and lead interactive classes and project work during the school's designated class times. Table 1 depicts the course schedule of activities by week, separated into computational, pedagogical, and classroom field-related activities.

3.2 Field Experience Logistics

Partnerships take time to establish. To get the course launched the first semester, we identified two partners, each from different local schools, and each identified through existing relationships with one of the authors who regularly goes into middle schools as part of her educational research projects. A pre-existing relationship helped us to work with teachers who trusted us to prepare the students for the classroom field experience and we knew were anxious to receive support knowing some logistics were not ironed out in the course yet. In following semesters, the partnering teachers had been attendees in our summer CS Principles Professional Development workshop. The week-long workshop experience with undergraduate teaching assistants demonstrates to the teachers the potential support that undergraduate CS and STEM education majors can provide.

After background checks are initiated, pairs or teams of undergraduates are matched with a local teacher for the whole semester based on availability, transportation capacity, and preference. Each participant is expected to go in the field for 1-2 hours per week. Specific schedules as well as CS content focus are identified through initial meetings with the partner teacher.

Throughout the semester, all undergraduate participants maintain a reflective journal on their experiences. Reflection is key to connecting their university experience with their experience in the field, identifying challenges experienced in the field, and thinking about their learning and future actions to improve their partnership connections. A typical reflective entry describes the field activities enacted by each participant during the week, identifies successes and challenges, and presents thoughts for future action (e.g., discuss aspects of the lesson that did not work well with the partner teacher, rethink components of the lesson, rethink approach of providing feedback to students, etc.).

3.3 Student Participation and Assessment

Students can register for 1-3 credits of this course, which determines the amount of field experiences they are required to complete each week. The prerequisites are minimal and include successful completion of at least one prior course in CS. This provides the knowledge needed to prepare lessons at the targeted level, while opening the opportunity to CS minors and other STEM majors that typically only take one course in CS. To encourage education majors to register along with computer science majors, the course is cross-listed as a CS and an Education course. During the three semesters in which the course was offered, however, the majority of the participants were undergraduates in CS. A smaller number of participants came from biomedical engineering and mathematics.

Course grades are based on the quality of a student's contribution in the following areas:

- 30% Journal of student reflection on their learning, readings, and field experiences
- 20% Portfolio related to field work
- 20% In-class participation
- 20% Mock teaching, presentations, and leading activities during the college classroom meetings
- 10% Final Reflective Essay

4. METHODOLOGY

4.1 Research Questions

In this paper, we focus on answering the following research questions with regard to the field experience course model:

1. What kinds of CS activities can undergraduates design and facilitate in their field placements?

2. What is the impact of the field experiences model on undergraduate student participants regarding their content knowledge, pedagogical skills and own career development?

Specifically for this work, we examined what worked well during the three semesters in which the field experience course was offered and what, if anything, should be changed to increase the impacts of the course on undergraduates and their targeted students.

4.2 Data Collection and Analysis

To answer our questions, we collected data using several sources. First, all undergraduate participants were observed during their visits to our partner schools. Each observation included information on the role of the partner teacher, the role of the undergraduate participant, and the lesson itself including introduction, materials, and CS concepts addressed. A short debriefing session with the participants accompanied each field observation to ensure that the observer understood the purpose of the activities. Further, all teaching materials created by undergraduates throughout the duration of the project were collected. These data helped us examine the CS activities designed and implemented by undergraduates in the field.

In addition to course observations, all reflective journals maintained by undergraduates were collected and examined. A total of 200 journal entries were collected throughout the three-semester period. Although the length of each reflective entry varies from week to week and from participant to participant, the average length of each entry was 400 words.

Additionally, at the end of each semester, all undergraduate participants responded to a written questionnaire, which asked them to consider the key benefits of the field experience course for their own learning, their ability to communicate computing concepts to students, and their future career goals.

To answer our two research questions we analyzed the data qualitatively. We first read all classroom observations and reflection entries and summarized the key CS activities designed and implemented by undergraduate participants in their partner schools. We also read participants' reflective entries and identified excerpts in which they discussed the impact of the field experience course on their own learning of content and pedagogy. As analysis for each participant was completed, data were compared to those of other participants to identify similarities and differences as well as emerging themes [9]. Data from written questionnaires as well as course and field observations were used to triangulate findings and accept or dismiss emergent themes.

4.3 Participants

To date, we have offered the field experiences course three times, spring 2013, fall 2013, and spring 2014. The course is being offered each semester to continue the partnerships with the schools throughout their academic year. Table 2 shows participants over time.

Table 2. CS and K-12 Participants

Semester	CS participants	Partner Teachers	G6-12 students reached
Spring 2013	7	2	80
Fall 2013	9	3	30
Spring 2014	8	3	80

5. FINDINGS

5.1. CS Activities Designed and Implemented by Undergraduates

During the three semesters in which the course was offered, students helped plan and lead after school computing programs once a week for two different middle schools: a sub-urban charter school serving approximately 1,350 students in grades K-8 and a local independent school serving approximately 100 students with identified learning, attention, social/emotional, and/or behavioral issues that may impact school success. During those times, undergraduate participants engaged students in a series of programming exercises using Scratch – a programming environment that allows students to design and create interactive programs (or games) using graphical blocks. Table 3 shows the activities designed and implemented by CS undergraduates during the after school programs.

In addition to planning and leading after school programs, undergraduate participants worked collaboratively with classroom teachers to adapt lesson plans and activities from available resources (CSP, ESC, Code.org) and lead classroom sessions in high school engineering classes integrating CS principles into existing STEM curricula. In particular, during fall 2013 and spring 2014, undergraduates worked with a high school teacher to plan and enact three CS modules on (1) website design, (2) human-computer interaction and (3) programming.

During the first unit (fall 2013) on website design, CS undergraduates helped high school students understand what makes a good website following a website evaluation rubric adapted from the ECS curriculum unit on web design. Subsequently, they helped them gain an understanding of the process of website design including storyboarding. In the third week into the unit, they introduced high school students to HTML, guided them through a tutorial and discussed how to create a basic website with HTML.

Table 3. After-school Program Activities Designed and Implemented by CS Undergraduates in Local Schools

	After School Program Activities (Charter School)	After School Program Activities (Independent School)
Week 1	1. Introduction to Scratch. 2. Basic blocks: Motion, Pen Up/Pen Down (Pen) Repeat (Control), Sequence.	1. CS unplugged: Computers do what you tell them to do. Exercise on the importance of specifying *exactly* what computer must do. 2. Introduction to Scratch and basic blocks.
Week 2	1. CS Unplugged (Security and Message Broadcasting): Information hiding: Students calculate their average age without anyone having to reveal to anyone else what their age is. The facilitator announces the average age. 2. Introduction to Broadcasting. 3. Modeling Pair Programming.	1. Introduction to conditionals with daily life examples; "If-then, else" unplugged exercise. Students were asked to raise their hand if they played a sport. If more than half of the people in the room raised their hands, they were supposed to sing, "I'm a little teapot". 2. Intro to Variables (Operators, inputs) with an example of guessing game.
Week 3	1. Broadcasting: Communication with multiple sprites 2. Introduction to Hide/Show blocks 3. Mini Story Project: Creating a short story with 5 slides and 3 sprites that interact with one another	1. Introduction to Loop (forever, repeat…until) and activities. Unplugged exercise: Draw the letter X once on each line of a piece of paper until you run out of lines. 2. Designing a guessing game.
Week 4	1. Reviewing Scratch Concepts: move, turn, broadcast, show/hide, say, play. 2. Intro to Conditionals and Sensing with examples. 3. Work on Mini Story Project: Students worked on their products adding elements related to new CT constructs.	1. CS unplugged for Coding/Pseudo-coding: Peanut butter and Jelly (PB&J) exercise (pseudo-code): Students gave step-by-step instructions on making a PB&J sandwich. Subsequently, each student wrote down steps on papers, made one PB&J sandwich and tried to improve the steps.
Week 5	1. Students continued to work on their projects: Sharing successes and challenges.	1. Designing/programming point-and-click adventure game in a team: Brainstormed game design and created a storyboard.
Week 6	1. Intro to Variables (Operators, inputs) with examples. 2. Guessing game project or calculator project: Students chose one as their second project.	1. Continued to work on programming point-and-click adventure game in a team: Students improved their program flow, storyline and sprites; started making their program using conditionals, loops, algorithms, event handling, logical statements.
Week 7	1. Students continued to work on their second project: College students pseudo-coded the instructions to help them think through the project.	1. Continued to work on programming a point-and-click adventure game in a team: Reinforcing some concepts and introducing applicable blocks; testing and debugging.
Week 8	1. Complete game design & demo day.	1. Complete game design.

They also discussed good practices in HTML coding. As a class, students worked on creating a website that incorporated data and research related to a science project they had just completed in class. Table 4 demonstrates the sequence of this module.

During the second module (spring 2014) on human-computer interaction, CS undergraduates guided high school students through a series of activities spanning a period of 5 weeks, focusing on understanding good interface design. To introduce the topic, CS undergraduates started with a CS unplugged activity (Chocolate factory activity) focusing on interface design practices away from the computer. Subsequently, they discussed forms of human input, such as touch-screens, buttons and the design of modern games including flappy birds, angry birds and fruit ninja. Subsequently, students explored advanced game design techniques by using the programming tool Scratch to create their own versions of flappy birds.

Table 4. Description of HTML Module

Week(s)	Activities
1	What makes a website good: rubric criteria for evaluating websites, examining sample websites
2	Storyboarding: What is it? How do we use it? What should a storyboard for a website contain?
3-4	Introduction to HTML: How to create content for the web, HTML tutorial, CSS tutorial, creating a basic website with HTML and CSS
5	HTML Lessons, good coding practices, Networking concepts, wrap up.

Finally, the third module (spring 2014) on programming was also designed and implemented over a 5-week period and engaged high school students in the design of their own version of flappy birds using Scratch. A unique feature of the game was the use of the webcam and the motion sensor in Scratch which enabled the program to sense motion and respond accordingly.

5.2. Impact of the Field Experiences Course on Undergraduate Participants

Findings from our work indicated that undergraduates became more confident in their CS skills, in their ability to communicate technical information to students and in their pedagogical skills (e.g., moving away from the role of dispenser of information).

Many of the participants, for instance, had not worked with Scratch before, so learning the program's interface was a new skill for them. Even those who had prior experience working with Scratch appreciated the opportunity to learn more. As one participant noted, *teaching the students how to code in Scratch helped me to solidify my knowledge of the basics of programming; so the students were not the only ones learning.*

Besides learning skills specific to Scratch, participants noted various instances in their reflective journals where they improved their content knowledge as a result of their interactions with classroom students. One participant, for example, noted that he was often caught off guard with students' programming solutions because they used approaches different than what he would have implemented. Similarly, another participant noted in one of her entries:

> *One of the students I helped was trying to get a ball to increase speed over time. I knew how to increment speed, but couldn't actually think how to do it based on the amount of time that had passed. Initially, the student had a loop that contained a block with a wait followed by an increment to a time counter. This caused the entire program to wait. I explained what was happening and the student removed the wait block. After that, I explained that the wait time was incremented every time he went through the loop, which was based on the code running rather than external time. I explained how usually, in programming, there was a way to assess how much time had passed while a program was running. That was when the student had the idea of creating a separate script, which started at the same time, and would wait, and then add to his variable. That was a solution that had not occurred to me.*

More importantly, however, participants acquired increased confidence in their content knowledge and often solidified their own understandings as a result of their interactions with teachers and students. One participant, for example, explained that as a result of helping his partner teacher teach the HTML module, he was more prepared for his Advanced Web Technologies course.

Additionally, findings from reflective journals provided ample evidence that close collaboration with experienced teachers created a reciprocal partnership conducive to learning – while undergraduates provided their content expertise, practicing teachers shared their pedagogical expertise. One participant, for example, wrote about feeling proud of offering her content expertise during her school visits, particularly at times when the teacher could not handle students' content questions independently and directed students to her. In their reflections, however, undergraduate participants noted a number of instances where they acquired important pedagogical skills from their partner teachers, particularly related to classroom management and pedagogical interactions with students. One course participant, for example, highlighted how he learned about appropriate times for providing one-on-one assistance versus whole class instruction. He wrote: *If a student has a problem that seems to be trending among the class, the teacher will pause the lesson to address the issue as a whole class. If it is more of an isolated problem, she provides individualized instruction.* Similarly, another undergraduate noticed the way in which his partner teacher provided feedback to her students by writing: *If they were wrong, she would not just tell them they were wrong; she would say something like, good try, but try thinking about it like this...really motivating them to try again and think harder about it.* Many students later adopted pedagogical strategies modeled by their partner teachers in their own efforts.

A key finding was related to participants' ability to explain concepts to students without directly giving out the answers. At the beginning of the semester, this presented a challenge as one participant reflected:

> *I realize how difficult it is to help students formulate their own ideas instead of just telling them what they need to do. I want to be able to help them effectively, but I want them to have the excitement and satisfaction that comes from figuring the problems out for themselves.*

Similarly, other participants also pointed out the need to scaffold student learning without directly giving out answers.

Finally, many participants indicated that participation in the field experiences model directly improved their ability to communicate with diverse audiences, a skill they identified as critical for their own career development. One participant explained:

Often, I needed to answer questions on the spot, which included conceptual questions. This greatly increased my ability to communicate computing ideas. I am much more effective at sharing my projects as a result of the course.

Similarly, another participant explained:

One of the benefits of the course was the interaction with classroom teachers. In my career, I need to be able to work with other people in the context of what they need, and the opportunity to talk to others was really helpful for my ability to speak to people.

6. DISCUSSION AND CONCLUSION

In this work, we discussed the potential of a field experiences model to share undergraduate computing students' knowledge and skills with middle and high school teachers and students. Findings indicate that the experience has positive impacts on undergraduate participants in terms of technical skill confidence, communication skills, and knowledge of good CS teaching pedagogy, which may help with future mentoring opportunities. Further, the final products – lesson plans and activities - created by the undergraduate participants were all used in the field and documented with teacher feedback. The partner teachers continue to seek our support, another indication that the undergraduates are indeed able to create and enact these activities in the field.

In terms of future directions, findings from our work revealed three components that were key to the success of the field experience model but presented room for improvements.

- Trial lessons on teaching CS unplugged: Many students noted that the opportunity to rehearse the teaching of CS unplugged activities early in the semester was a valuable experience. It allowed them to witness firsthand the preparation and planning needed to lead a lesson, the teaching practices of their peers, and how to give and receive feedback in a safe environment. In the words of a student, these experiences helped him transform from a "capable speaker" to "confident classroom leader". Moving forward, it might be important to offer additional opportunities for teaching and modeling within the context of the college meetings.
- Learning theory: At the beginning of the course, we provide an overview of theory related to how people learn and the design of learning environments. Findings indicated that participants appreciated the opportunity to learn theoretical ideas that they could later apply to practice. Participants, however, indicated that they would like additional support in this area and suggested that the course include more opportunities to address issues related to how students learn.
- Lesson development: Participants found the experience of developing and implementing lessons valuable and rewarding. Nevertheless, some participants noted that they were not prepared for the amount of time it required for them to develop or adapt classroom materials for their field placement. As some participants noted, they thought the partner teacher would be taking a more active role in identifying the CS content school students needed. Partner teachers, however, often looked up to the undergraduates making those decisions. In future offerings of the course, we need to provide additional supports as undergraduates take on this leadership role.

In conclusion, our findings indicate that the field experience model holds promise for the successful infusion of CS content in middle and high school classrooms while simultaneously providing numerous benefits to CS undergraduates. Our next challenge is scaling up the model to involve more partners.

7. ACKNOWLEDGEMENTS

This work is supported by a grant from the National Science foundation (Award # 1240905). All opinions are the authors and do not necessarily represent those of the funding agency.

8. REFERENCES

[1] Barnes, T. Dahlberg, T., Buch K., & Bean, K. 2009. The STARS Leadership Corps: An innovative computer science learning community. *Learning Communities Journal*, 1:5–18, 2009.

[2] Blue Ribbon Panel Report on Clinical Preparation and Partnerships for Improved Student Learning. 2010. *Transforming teacher education through clinical practice: A national strategy to prepare effective teachers*. NCATE.

[3] Burns, R., Harvey, T., & Pollock, L. 2012. An Experience Report on Cross-Semester Student Critique and Action in an Integrated Software Engineering, Service Learning Course. In *First International Workshop on Software Engineering Education based on Real-World Experiences (EduRex).*

[4] Century, J., Lach, M., King, H., Rand, S., Heppner, C., Franke, B., & Westrick, J. 2013. Building an Operating System for Computer Science. Chicago, IL: CEMSE, University of Chicago with UEI, University of Chicago. http://outlier.uchicago.edu/computerscience/OS4CS/.

[5] Goode, J., Chapman, G., and Margolis, J. 2012. Beyond Curriculum: The Exploring Computer Science Program. *ACM Inroads, 3*(2), 47-53.

[6] Gray, J., Shaundra, D., MichaelWyss, M., and Cotton, S. 2012. Building a K-12 Computing Pipeline in Alabama that Addresses Participation Diversity. NSF Showcase: SIGCSE.

[7] Johnson, D., MichaelWyss, J., Gray, J., Daily, S., Shih, A., & Abbott, G. 2012. Broadening Participation in Computing: The *Multi-tiered Approach. ACM Southeast Conference.*

[8] Lang, K., Galanos, R., Goode, J., Seehorn, D., Trees, F., Phillips, P., and Stephenson, C. 2013. *Bugs in the System: Computer Science Teacher Certification in the U.S.,* ACM CSTA.

[9] Miles, M. B. and Huberman, A. M. 1994. *Qualitative data analysis: An expanded sourcebook.* Sage.

[10] Mouza, C., Pan, Y., Pollock, L., Atlas, J., & Harvey, T. 2014. Partner4CS: Bringing Computational Thinking to Middle School through Game Design. *FabLearn*, Stanford University, CA. http://fablearn.stanford.edu/2014/wp-content/uploads/fl2014_submission_21.pdf

[11] STARS. STARS Alliance, http://www.starsalliance.org, 2011.

[12] Zepeda, S. 2012. *Professional Development: What Works*, 2nd Ed. Athens, GA: Eye on Education, Inc.

A Mid-Project Report on a Statewide Professional Development Model for CS Principles

Jeff Gray
University of Alabama
Department of Computer Science
Tuscaloosa, AL
gray@cs.ua.edu

Kathy Haynie
Haynie Research and Evaluation
Skillman, NJ
kchaynie@stanfordalumni.org

Sheryl Packman
Haynie Research and Evaluation
Skillman, NJ
sheryl.packman@gmail.com

Mary Boehm
A+ College Ready
Birmingham, AL
marydboehm@bellsouth.net

Carol Crawford
A+ College Ready
Birmingham, AL
carolk.crawford@gmail.com

Deepa Muralidhar
Atlanta Girls School
Atlanta, GA
deepa.muralidhar@gmail.com

ABSTRACT
This paper summarizes our mid-project results in developing and evaluating a CS Principles (CSP) professional development (PD) model for training several cohorts of teachers across an entire state geography. CS4Alabama is an NSF-funded project that has adopted the successful practices of a national AP training program developed by the National Math and Science Initiative (NMSI) in pursuit of scalable deployment and sustainable persistence of new CSP courses across Alabama. We have created a CSP curriculum and PD program based on year-long in-person training and distance learning collaboration, which also was offered as a national MOOC as part of Google CS4HS. A statewide Teacher Leader (TL) model is used, where those who have previously taught rigorous CS courses serve as mentors in training new peer cohorts as they establish CSP courses in their schools. Teachers in these cohorts collaborate together on content and pedagogical learning experiences, fostered by the TLs. This paper reports on assessment results that are uncovering the facets of our model that are most suitable for building a sustainable network of CSP teachers. The paper summarizes our PD model, offers various lessons learned, and details the findings of the project's external evaluation team.

Categories and Subject Descriptors
K.3.2 [**Computer and Information Science Education**]: Computer science education

Keywords
CS Principles; Professional Development

SIGCSE '15, March 4–7, 2015, Kansas City, MO, USA
Copyright 2015 ACM 978-1-4503-2966-8/15/03…$15.00
http://dx.doi.org/10.1145/2676723.2677306

1. INTRODUCTION
As the interest in the new CS Principles (CSP) course grows as it approaches the 2016-2017 inaugural offering by the College Board, an obvious question has emerged: How will we train the mass of teachers needed to offer this course at scale? This paper describes our efforts on a new NSF CE21 proposal that addresses that question from the perspective of a state (Alabama) that has a traditionally low participation level on the current AP CS A exam. The ability to scale and sustain professional development in particular with teachers who have a STEM background but little CS content knowledge, will be vital to growing the CS10k vision.

The three-year participants of our project include: 1) a cohort of 50 high school teachers who will receive year-long professional development training to teach the CSP course; 2) students of those teachers, who will participate in summer camps, weekend study sessions, and statewide competitions; 3) the Alabama State Department of Education; 4) the principal investigators; 5) an evaluation team with extensive experience in evaluating CSP at a national level; 6) a K-12 teacher who has been a national Pilot participant and member of the CSP development committee; and 7) college students from secondary education and computer science majors who will assist with project tasks. The pedagogical approach is centered on inquiry/discovery-based techniques that introduce computer science as a broad set of topics, as defined by the learning objectives contained in the Big Ideas of CSP [5].

The goal of our project is to broaden participation in computing and especially to engage young women and other members of underrepresented minority (URM) groups. All of the efforts were carefully evaluated by an external team (Haynie Research and Evaluation), who provide a detailed view into a computing education intervention across the entire state of Alabama. Our Year 1 data sources include evaluations from over 300 students who completed a CSP course in 2013-2014, 9 secondary school teachers who attended PD sessions and taught the CSP course, and 23 secondary school teachers who began their preparations to teach the new course in 2014-2015. In this paper, we describe our PD model, results for participating instructors, results for implementations of the new CS course, and student course outcomes. We will describe how the first half of this project has broadened participation in Alabama. Several peripheral benefits have emerged as a result of this project, including:

- Alabama became the first state in the US to have CSP officially recognized as a statewide registered course
- a successful collaboration with our State Department of Education to have CSP and CS A count as one of the four math electives needed for high school graduation
- a heightened awareness of the importance of computer science at the highest levels of administration within our state's Department of Education
- the formation of the first CSTA chapter in Alabama

2. TEACHER PD MODEL

The CS4Alabama project aims to impact an entire state by preparing high school teachers to offer CSP courses through a replicable PD model that could be adopted in other states. We have openly made available all of our curriculum materials to anyone interested [1] and also developed online materials as part of a CS4HS MOOC offered throughout 2014 [2]. The specific details of our PD model include the following components:

- conduct year-round PD for a total of 140 hours per year, while training 50 teachers over three years in content knowledge and pedagogy related to CSP, including:
    - summer training (face-to-face and online)
    - bi-weekly meetings throughout the year
    - face-to-face weekend sessions each semester
- utilize the Master Teacher approach that was popularized by UTeach [3] and integrated into the NMSI model
- the Teacher Leader (TL) role allows the project to utilize the existing experience and skills among teachers who are already offering rigorous CS courses

The Logic Model for our project is in Figure 1, which shows a list of the inputs to the project, strategies for project implementation, and the expected short-term and long-term outcomes [4].

3. MID-PROJECT RESULTS

We are at the mid-point of our three-year project. This section describes pertinent evaluation results from the first full year of the project with our TLs, as well as the first half of our second year with a cohort of STEM teachers.

3.1 Year 1: Teacher Leader PD

In Year 1 of the project, ten TLs were recruited from our past contacts with those who we knew were already offering some form of CS at their school. This group of seasoned instructors has an average of 18 years teaching in grades K-12, and 12 years teaching CS at the high school level. All instructors have at least a master's degree, and most had taken at least 30 hours of PD in CS over the last three years. In the first year of the project, these teachers led the creation of teacher-driven lesson plans, pacing guides, and curriculum materials that formed the basis for mentoring of Cohort 2 teachers.

3.1.1 Summer 2013 PD

Summer training for the TLs took place during the last week of June 2013. The entire four-day period was rife with opportunities for developing and refining resources, networking, collaboration, and the building of friendships and team spirit among the teachers. It was evident throughout the PD workshop that a very special and powerful effort was underway to effectively scale up computer science in our state. Another major accomplishment that occurred during the meeting was the formation of a CSTA chapter and the election of officers.

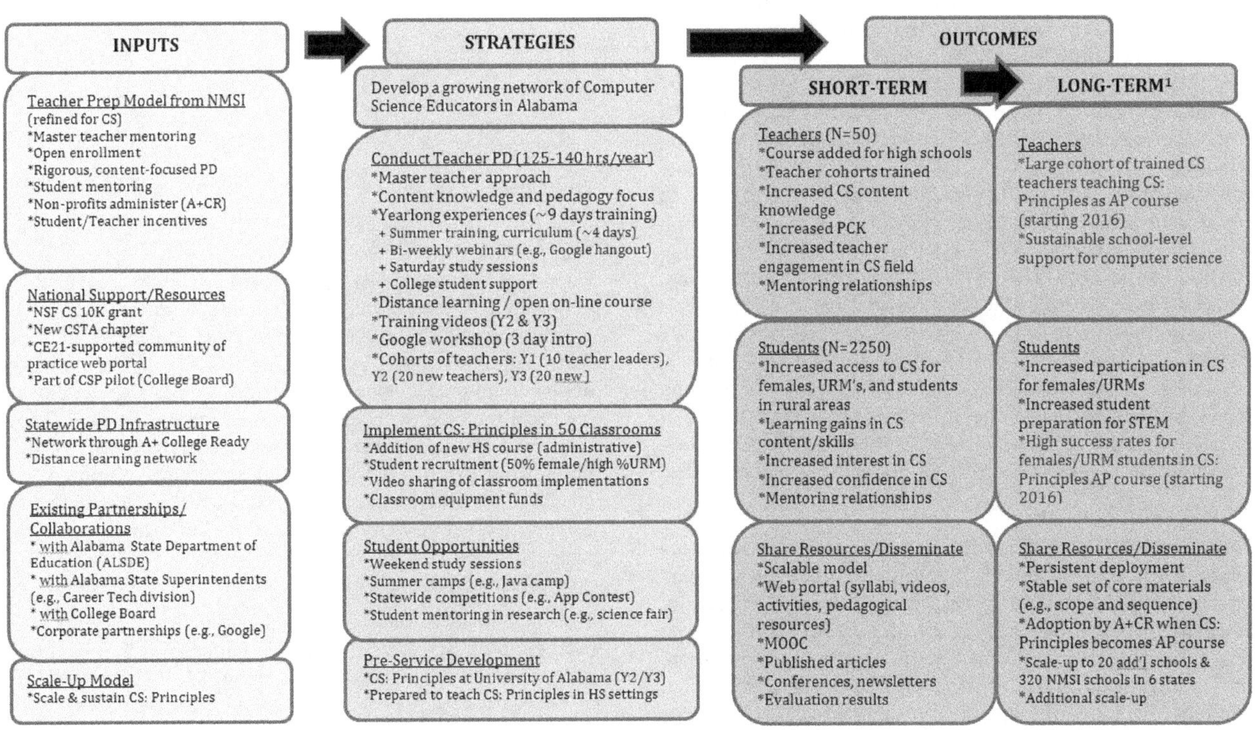

Figure 1: Logic Model for our CS Principles Project

The most critical aspects of the workshop were rated highly by the teacher participants: project overview, requirements of the CSP Performance Tasks, support for syllabus and lesson plan development, discussion of lesson plans, and opportunities for collaboration. High ratings were given to the facilitators' knowledge and effectiveness, the quality and planning of the workshop, the appropriateness of the activities, the enthusiastic and engaging atmosphere, and gaining knowledge and skills/strategies useful for instruction. At the end of the training, instructors wanted more resources and ideas to teach the material, further opportunities for collaboration, and help with technical writing components of required Performance Tasks.

3.1.2 Fall Weekend Session

An all-day PD session took place on October 19, 2013, attended by eight of the TLs. Overall, the session covered several project topics, including pacing guides, common assessment, and topics related to the future of the project. The most focus was given to discussion of the Data Performance Task and the Data Learning Objectives. Overall participant ratings indicated that the workshop was a success in terms of: quality of workshop planning, engagement, pacing, instruction, workshop materials, collaboration, teaching preparation, and learning about Data. Following the one-day session, participants prioritized their next steps as: studying the resources, planning for another section of the course, modifying lesson plans for Big Data, revising the fall pacing guide and implementing what they learned in their classes.

3.1.3 SIGCSE 2014

From March 6-8, 2014, most of the TLs attended the SIGCSE conference, funded by the project. In addition to the poster session presented by our project, the majority of the teachers attended 4-6 sessions, selected on the basis of relevancy and applicability of teaching the CSP course. Our TLs also presented a poster that summarized their first-year experiences, which provided them with a positive experience engaging with questions and conversations, including sharing successes, and helping others who are planning to teach CSP in the future (e.g., teacher recruitment and training). From a post-conference survey, the TLs found their experience at SIGCSE "very good" at developing understandings in content knowledge, tools and applications, curricular materials, and the larger context of CS Education. In addition, teachers mentioned learning about cooperative learning strategies, how to make our CSTA chapter stronger, and engaging girls in computer science. Their SIGCSE experiences helped them gather ideas for mentoring new teachers in Year 2 in terms of: lesson plan ideas and activities; choice of language(s) for CSP; student recruiting ideas; use of sample Performance Task rubrics; pacing guides; virtual trainings; and how to teach the writing aspect of Performance Tasks. The project also sponsored a special CSTA meeting between Alabama and Georgia teachers, providing an opportunity for Alabama teachers to form new collaborations.

3.1.4 Biweekly Meetings

Throughout the 2013-2014 academic year, project participants met every two weeks to discuss needed resources, lesson plan development, implementation successes and concerns (especially implementation of Performance Tasks), collaboration, project logistics, equipment, available tools, project evaluation, preparation for mentoring Cohort 2 teachers, and professional opportunities. These highly productive and amicable meetings focused on areas outlined in teachers' evaluations of PD sessions, as well as issues that arose in day-to-day course implementations. These meetings assisted in assessing the pulse of the project and continuing the collaborations across the TLs.

3.2 Year 2: Teacher Leader and Cohort 2 PD

In Year 2 of the project, twenty-three additional high school instructors were recruited. This group of instructors had an average of 9 years teaching in grades K-12, yet only four of the instructors had experience teaching computer science (1, 2, 2, and 3 years). A majority of instructors had earned masters degrees, with instructors citing degrees and/or certification in the following fields: mathematics education (43%), mathematics (35%), business (35%), engineering (26%), science or science education (22%), and computer science (13% - three of these four teachers all had over a decade of industry experience). Most instructors (74%) had taken 3 or fewer CS courses in college. Only two Cohort 2 teachers came from a school that already offered CS in 2013-2014. Figure 2 shows the geographic distribution of TLs from year one (orange/red) and the new Cohort 2 teachers (blue).

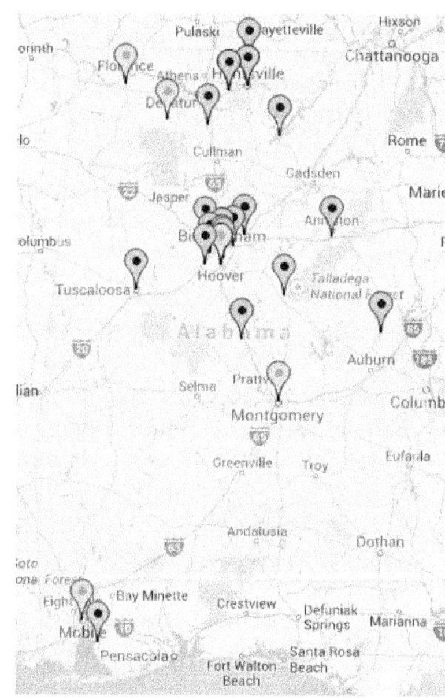

Figure 2: Locations of Teacher Leaders and Cohort 2 Teachers

3.2.1 Summer 2014 PD

Prior to the summer 2014 PD meeting, Cohort 2 teachers had an opportunity to learn the course content online. A MOOC was provided to these teachers, which was expanded to a national focus through support by Google CS4HS [2]. The online portion of the training provided content knowledge that would be built upon via the face-to-face teacher meeting in late June. The online content of the training summarized the CSP Curriculum Framework [5], offered lessons on important Learning Objectives of the CSP Big Ideas, facilitated virtual office hours through Google Hangouts, introduced the Performance Tasks, and engaged the participating teachers with CSP community leaders who offered virtual talks that are archived on YouTube.

The face-to-face summer training for the TLs and Cohort 2 teachers took place from June 23th- June 27th, 2014. A total of 9 TLs attended on June 23 and June 24; twenty-one Cohort 2 teachers attended the training from June 24-June 27. On June 24th,

Table 1: Self-Reported Cohort 2 Gains in Big Ideas and Computational Thinking Practices

	Average Before PD	Average After PD	Diff	ttest
Total for Big Ideas	*17.13*	*21.33*	*4.20*	*p=0.002*
1) Creativity	2.80	3.13	0.33	N.S.
2) Abstraction	2.10	2.87	0.73	p=0.002
3) Data and information	2.27	3.00	0.73	p=0.003
4) Algorithms	2.20	2.87	0.67	p=0.002
5) Programming	2.33	3.00	0.67	p<0.001
6) The Internet	2.67	3.27	0.60	p=0.017
7) Global Impact	2.73	3.20	0.47	N.S.
Total for CT Practices	*15.61*	*17.60*	*1.99*	*p=0.046*
1) Connecting computing	2.53	3.07	0.53	p=0.020
2) Creating computational artifacts	2.08	2.67	0.59	p=0.015
3) Abstracting	2.07	2.67	0.60	p=0.011
4) Analyzing problems & artifacts	2.47	2.93	0.47	p=0.034
5) Communicating	3.20	3.13	-0.07	N.S.
6) Collaborating	3.27	3.13	-0.13	N.S.

*1 = None, 2 = Novice, 3 = Apprentice, 4 = Expert

all teachers from both years were present. On this day, five working groups were formed that matched two TLs with five Cohort 2 teachers. The summer PD was rated very highly by all instructors. Not surprisingly, Cohort 2 instructors' overall ratings as to specific elements of the PD were slightly lower than those of the TLs; however, Cohort 2 instructors also gave themselves higher ratings in terms of gaining skills and knowledge as a result of the PD experience. Cohort 2 instructors rated themselves before and after the PD and the online study on the Big Ideas and Computational Thinking practices. Most of the gains found were significant, some highly significant (Table 1). The 4+point gain for the total Big Ideas score was highly significant, and gains for each of the Big Ideas were also significant, with exception of Creativity (Big Idea 1) and Global Impact (Big Idea 7). The almost 2-point gain for the total of Computational Thinking practices was significant ($p<.05$), as were the gains for four of the six individual Computational Thinking practices. The exceptions to this were communicating and collaborating. It is interesting that the significant gains were found in the most content-intensive areas (the areas we typically think of when considering computer science) and non-significant gains were found for broader or less content-intensive areas (i.e., creativity, global impact, communicating, and collaborating). These areas also had the highest ratings in their categories before PD, so there may have been a ceiling effect for some respondents.

Not surprisingly, after the summer 2014 PD, self-rated levels of preparation for TLs were much higher than those of Cohort 2 instructors. Combining both cohorts, major gains in perceived preparation were found particularly for cultivating students' interest in CS and implementation/classroom instruction. Highest gains (24 percentage points or more) were found for using Performance Tasks in CSP instruction, facilitating self-directed learning and project-based work, developing lesson plans, teaching CS to URM students, facilitating cooperative learning, and integrating principles of social justice into instruction. After the PD, most instructors felt unprepared to differentiate instruction for students with a variety of learning needs (e.g., English-language learners, students with learning disabilities).

Instructors felt that the best aspects of the PD were the flash talks that were offered by the TLs. These flash talks were 15 minute "lessons learned" or content/pedagogy suggestions offered by the TLs to the Cohort 2 teachers (these lessons are also available on our MOOC [2]). The teachers from Cohort 2 reported that the most helpful parts of the PD were the opportunities to work with the TLs, the community building, and the resources and recommendations for implementation. Cohort 2 instructors would improve PD to include more time with content and tools doing hands-on activities such as Snap! (and less time with pedagogy). Follow-up assistance was requested in terms of the regular online meetings, mentoring and direct support for Cohort 2 teachers, and more examples, activities, and lesson plans.

3.3 Attitudes and Self-Rated Understandings

The pre- and post-course student surveys included many identical items to gauge the impact of the course on key constructs related to success in computer science. Only students with matched pre/post data were included in these analyses. To equalize the impact of all TLs, a weighted sample was created with all courses having a sample of 20 students. The weighted sample was 68% male, 59% White, 72% non-URM, and 47% female or URM. In addition, 29% of students were in the 11th grade, 28% in 12th grade, 27% in 9th grade, and 16% in 10th grade.

3.3.1 Students' Attitudes

The pre- and post-course student surveys included 30 items to assess confidence, interest, and motivation for computer science as well as students' beliefs about computer science and its usefulness. All scales had acceptable reliability (0.78 – 0.93),

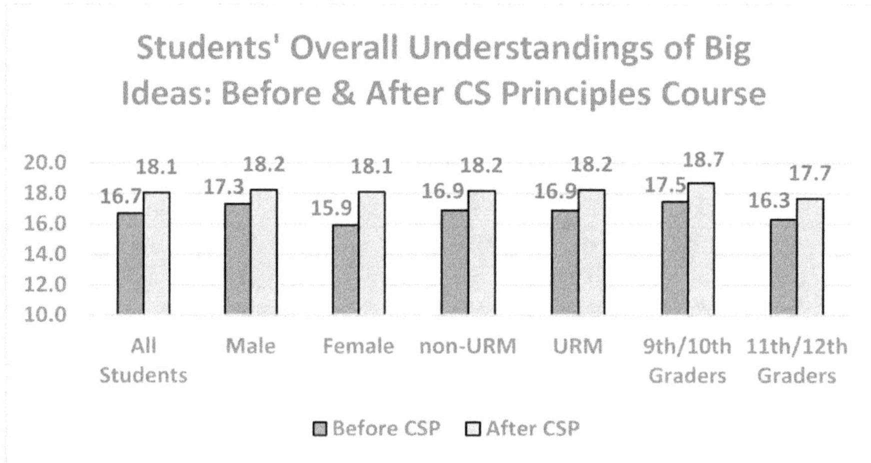

Figure 3: Analysis of Student Responses for Self-Efficacy

except for the beliefs scale. Results from the pre-course and post-course surveys were analyzed to determine if there were changes in confidence, interest, usefulness, motivation, and beliefs from the beginning to the end of the course. The only subscore that was significantly different from pre- to post-course was usefulness, which showed a decline. A repeated measures analysis of variance (ANOVA) was conducted to determine if there were significant mean differences by gender, URM status, and year in school. The only significant differences were found for interest and usefulness by year in school. In both cases, there were significant decreases for juniors and seniors with very small effect sizes.

3.3.2 Students' Understandings of Big Ideas

Students were also asked to rate their understanding of each Big Idea before and after taking the course. Responses were given on a 3-point Likert scale: 1=No Understanding, 2=Some Understanding, 3=Strong Understanding. The highest ratings were for Big Idea 7, Global Impacts of Computing, while the lowest ratings were for Big Idea 2, Abstraction. Scores went up for every Big Idea, with the greatest gains for Big Idea 2 (Abstraction) and Big Idea 4 (Algorithms).

A measure of students' overall understandings of the Big Ideas was the sum of the seven ratings, with a potential range of 0 to 21. A repeated measures ANOVA was conducted to determine if there were any pre/post differences in understandings for all students and for demographic subgroups. Overall understandings increased significantly for all students (p<.01). The only significant difference by subgroup was for gender whereby both males and females showed a significant gain from pre- to post-course, but that gain was greater for females (effect size=.03). In fact, females started the course with a lower overall knowledge of the Big Ideas and ended up almost identical to the males in their post-course ratings, which was an encouraging result.

3.3.3 Students' Self-Efficacy

Students rated their self-efficacy levels before and after the course in five areas directly related to the CSP Curriculum Framework [5]. Responses were entered on a 4-point Likert scale. The highest ratings were for "I am persistent at solving logic problems" and the lowest were for "I can write successful computer programs" Significant gains were found for "I can write successful computer programs," "I can effectively use abstractions and models to achieve goals," and "I can effective analyze the ethical, legal, and social implications of computing."

All self-efficacy items were summed together to create a total self-efficacy score for each respondent (with a potential range of 5 to 20). There was a significant increase in overall self-rated abilities from pre- to post-course (p=.00, effect size=0.12). A repeated measures ANOVA was conducted to determine if there were any differences by subgroup. The only significant finding was for URM status whereby non-URM students had significantly higher gains in self-efficacy (p<.01); however, the effect size was very small (0.04).

3.4 Common Assessment

A Common Assessment was developed by the TLs, who contributed items intended to assess six of the seven Big Ideas in the course: abstraction, algorithms, data, Internet, programming, and impact. Project leaders reviewed all items and selected 20 multiple-choice items - four items were selected for each subscale, except impact. Each instructor administered the common assessment online to their students within the last two weeks of their course.

To control for any teacher effects, each course implementation (N=9) was weighted to the same number of students (N=23) and only the first administration of the assessment was used for teachers with multiple course implementations. The total weighted sample of 207 students was 34% female, 25% URM, and 48% female or URM (a project goal is a sample of at least 50% female or URM students). A majority of students (57%) were in the 11th or 12th grade. The overall internal consistency reliability of the 20 items in the Common Assessment was 0.658; 19 of the 20 items exhibited acceptable item discrimination levels (>0.20).

For the total student sample, the mean total correct was 12.3 of 20 items (SD=3.3). There was a significant difference in performance by gender, whereby females (M=13.1) performed better than males (M=11.9) (p<.02; η^2=.03). There was also a surprisingly significant difference in performance by year in school, whereby 9th and 10th graders (M=13.5) performed better than 11th and 12th graders (M=11.4) (p=00; η^2=.09). There were no differences by racial/ethnic group or URM status.

4. DISCUSSION OF ASSESSMENT

This section discusses several of the most significant results of student learning from the first full year of the project and suggests a reflective approach to updating the project PD needs based on the formative assessment feedback [6].

4.1.1 *Students' Self-Ratings*

What is most promising in these findings is that the gender gap across all Big Ideas disappeared from pre to post. This is certainly a promising finding and suggests that the instructors of the classes with substantial proportions of female students (four classes were over 30% female) were successful in helping female students succeed, perhaps even relative to their male counterparts. Surprising, neither males nor females showed significant gains in confidence, interest, or motivation from pre to post. However, in addition to the learning gains for Big Ideas, students' self-efficacy levels increased in a number of areas including writing successful computer programs, and using abstraction and models. This suggests that students' beliefs in their abilities to do some key course-related activities were impacted more relative to their general perceptions of their confidence in computer science. Curiously, although there was not a significant gain in students' ratings of their knowledge of Big Idea 7, "Computing has Global Impacts," overall self-efficacy ratings significantly increased for the statement, "I can effectively analyze the ethical, legal, and social implications of computing." This suggests that the more specific wording may have elicited greater student recognition.

4.1.2 *Student Performance on Common Assessment*

While the common assessment results are certainly promising, some interpretation of these findings is needed. On the surface, it seems counter-intuitive that the 9th and 10th graders in our sample would significantly outperform the 11th and 12th graders. However, the two highest scoring classes of students were comprised almost entirely of 9th graders; these students also spent considerably more time on the common assessment, compared with the rest of the students. One of these high-scoring classes included one 10th grader and one 11th grader. The second class, from a technology magnet school, was entirely 9th graders. Please notice that the starting baseline (Figure 3) of understanding for these 9th/10th graders was also higher than the starting baseline for the 11th/12th grade participants. In addition, the class from the technology magnet school – by far the highest scoring school in our sample (averaging 1 to 5 more items correct than the other schools) – was 72% female. Further study indicated that this technology magnet school was ranked 8th in the state, out of hundreds of high schools. When this unique school was removed from our analysis, the average difference by grade level disappeared, and the "gender gap" was reduced by 23%.

With only nine participating schools in our Year 1 sample, it is difficult to generalize these student outcomes, since one school can greatly influence the aggregate results. However, considering this sample both without the outstanding magnet school, the females in the sample outperformed the males (the gender difference was largest for the Internet items), the under-represented minority students performed about as well as the non-URM students, and there was little or no difference between students in upper and lower grades.

5. CONCLUSION

We believe that the particular challenges that we face in our project (e.g., geographic displacement of teachers, wide range of teacher preparation and experiences, diversity in student and teacher populations) represent a microcosm of similar challenges that are emerging nationally to scale and sustain a new cohort of computer science teachers. The challenge of geographic displacement of teachers has driven the need for a blended model of professional development that has both online and face-to-face instruction in content preparation and pedagogical strategies. The diversity of teacher background and preparation has led us to the implementation of the TL model, whereby more experienced teachers help to create curriculum resources and lead the mentoring process. One of the aspects of our project that we are most excited about is that the majority of lesson plans associated with our project are all teacher-created, and address the specific needs of peer teachers and their daily challenges faced when introducing a new computer science course. Likewise, for the 2014-2015 school year, all of the online mentoring of biweekly Hangouts is led by pairs of TLs who are assigned groups of Cohort 2 teachers who have similar backgrounds (e.g., career tech teacher group, math instructor group). We believe that the empowerment and growth of the TLs will drive the sustainability of our efforts long after the funding for our project has ended.

There is still much work to do on our project. The mentoring and assessment of our model for Cohort 2 teachers continues throughout the project, and a third cohort of 20-25 teachers will be recruited for participation in initial PD for summer 2015. Although the challenges will continue regarding the lack of computer science content preparation among future teachers, we also believe that the TLs' experience and the growing richness of our curriculum resources will assist in expanding computer science in Alabama both in terms of quantity and quality.

REFERENCES

This project was funded in part by an NSF CE21 award (1240944) and several Google CS4HS awards.

REFERENCES

[1] CS4Alabama, http://cs4alabama.org/

[2] CSP4HS MOOC, https://csp-cs4hs.appspot.com/

[3] UTeach, http://changetheequation.org/featured-programs/uteach

[4] Michael S. Garet, Andrew C. Porter, Laura Desimone, Beatrice F. Birman and KwangSuk Yoon, "What Makes Professional Development Effective? Results from a National Sample of Teachers," American Educational Research Journal, Vol. 38, No. 4 (Winter, 2001), pp. 915-945.

[5] CS Principles Curriculum Framework, http://apcsprinciples.org/cs-principles-documents/

[6] Laura M. Desimone, "Improving Impact Studies of Teachers' Professional Development: Toward Better Conceptualizations and Measures," Educational Research, August 2009, 38. pp. 181-199.

Integrating Role-Playing Games into Computer Science Courses as a Pedagogical Tool

David Toth
Centre College
600 West Walnut St
Danville, KY 40422
+1 (859) 238-5404
david.toth@centre.edu

Mary Kayler
University of Mary Washington
1301 College Avenue
Fredericksburg, VA 22401
+1 (540) 654-1577
mkayler@umw.edu

ABSTRACT

Gaming has been identified as a way to increase student engagement in the classroom. This qualitative study explored 78 undergraduate students' experiences with a role-playing game infused into two computer science courses. Open-ended student surveys served as the primary data source to explore, "In what ways, if any, does role-playing quest based curriculum support student learning and engagement?" Key curricular innovations are described along with assignments and assessments that were integrated. Three broad themes emerged and identified personalized learning, deepened content understandings, and enhanced collaboration skills as three areas that supported student learning and engagement. Many students felt that the infusion of role-playing aspects into the courses supported their learning and engagement, but some students did not.

Categories and Subject Descriptors

K.3.2 [**Computer Science Education**]: Computer and Information Science Education – *Computer science education*

General Terms

Design, Experimentation, Human Factors.

Keywords: Education; games; engagement.

1. INTRODUCTION

Learning is complex and engaging students in the learning process can be challenging. The authors engaged in two scholarly investigations to more deeply explore the ways in which the inclusion of a role-playing (RPG) game layer enhanced or diminished undergraduate students engagement and learning in two computer science courses. To more deeply understand the role-playing process and curricular integration student's perspectives and experiences were instrumental in unpacking the implications of this pedagogical innovation.

SIGCSE '15, March 4–7, 2015, Kansas City, MO, USA

http://dx.doi.org/10.1145/2676723.2677236

In the first author's second semester at our institution, he taught the Network Principles and Applications course where the majority of students did not fully engage with course material regardless of which pedagogical strategy he employed, including techniques that had worked in his previous years of teaching. He decided to explore alternative ways to engage students and attended a game-based learning workshop on ways to incorporate game pedagogy into courses. "A game is a system in which players engage in an abstract challenge, defined by rules, interactivity, and feedback, that results in a quantifiable outcome often eliciting an emotional reaction" [1]. A good game design is also good pedagogy in that it promotes engagement through game elements of goals, conflict, competition, cooperation, rewards, levels, rules, and feedback. These are all opportunities for students to take ownership of their learning and provide multiple opportunities to 'do over' in beating the game. In terms of teaching, this moves the professor and students from 'covering content' to 'interacting with content' and constructing their own understandings.

It was then that the first author decided to try his hand at infusing a role-playing game (RPG) into course curriculum. Drawing upon the first author's past and current experiences with role-playing games and the existence of numerous types of role-playing games on the market (video games, computer games, board games, and classic book and dice versions) that many students seem to enjoy, it seemed a logical next step to create and infuse his own role playing game into his curriculum. Role-playing games fall into a genre that contains a setting, narrative or plot, characters, quests (smaller milestones) and an ultimate goal. In a role-playing game "players assume the role of characters in a fictional setting and players take responsibility for acting these roles out within a narrative, either through literal acting or through a process of structured decision-making to foster character development. Actions taken within the game succeed or fail according to a formal system of rules and guidelines" [2].

For the first author's RPG, each student would control a character over the course of the semester. Students would name and determine which character class they wanted to role-play in a story narrative that was developed and written by the first author. Individual and team quests (connected to course projects) along with on-campus treasure hunts where students needed to solve clues (on campus) were created as ways to immerse students into the RPG genre. As the characters interact with the fictional world, a story unfolds (over the course of the semester).

High Scores

Rank	Level	Class	Character	XP Earned	XP Attempted	XP Available	Current %	Max Possible XP
1	L-6	Rogue	DataLore	19613	19900	8100	99	27713
2	L-6	Warrior	Col. Glasseater	19582	19900	8100	98	27682
3	L-6	Cleric	Dejavu	19031	19900	8100	96	27131
4	L-5	Wizard	Gruntilda	18621	19900	8100	94	26721
5	L-5	Cleric	Ricky Spanish	18569	19900	8100	93	26669
6	L-5	Warrior	Ezekiel Wolf	18525	19900	8100	93	26625
7	L-5	Wizard	Valerius	18154	19900	8100	91	26254
8	L-5	Cleric	Laxrufus	17456	19900	8100	88	25556

Figure 1 - A Portion of the Leaderboard

As the characters go on quests (small milestones or objectives that often build toward the ultimate goal, such as stopping some big monster from destroying the world), they find treasure, earn experience (XP), and when the characters earn enough experience, they become more powerful or "level up." As part of the leveling up process, players may customize their characters by giving them new abilities and purchasing special gear by visiting a Magic Shop. In the course syllabi, the amount of XP the characters needed to 'level up' corresponded to the minimum grade that they would earn for the course. For example, a student had to earn 16,800 XP in one course to earn a D, 20,440 for a C, and so on. The amount of XP that corresponded to the letter grades was a percent of the possible points a student could earn. Thus, to earn an A-, students needed to earn 90% of the possible XP for the course. This value was calculated before the course started and was listed on the syllabus. However, the fact that students needed to earn 90% was not mentioned explicitly; rather, the syllabus stated students needed to earn 25, 200 XP to earn an A-. A syllabus from the one of the courses is posted at (http://web.centre.edu/david.toth/courses/rpg/) for those wishing to see more detail.

As students earned XP, a web page was updated with each student's XP and level so they could easily see how they were doing in the course and to inspire some competition amongst students to try to be on top of the "leaderboard." The XP was posted using each student's character name, rather than their real name in order to preserve confidentiality. The top few entries of the leaderboard from one of the courses are shown in figure 1.

At various points throughout the course, when a student had earned enough XP to level up, she was given a "scroll" with a clue to find a hidden treasure. A sample clue is shown in figure 2. The treasures were hidden in various locations on campus that were places students should visit to get the most out of their education, with the intent that students would take the opportunity of visiting the location to learn about the services offered there. For example, treasures were hidden at the writing center, library, and career services office. The treasures were contained in black pouches and consisted of some plastic coins and gems, the next chapter of the story, and occasionally a "magical item." Students could decide to save their coins and gems for later or visit the "magic shop," which was run by one of the authors. In the magic shop, the students could cash in the gems and coins and purchase items to make their characters more powerful, including potions, wands, rings, magical weapons, and other items. An assortment of treasures from the courses is shown in figure 3. A portion of one chapter of the story is shown in figure 4. The complete set of stories and materials are available at (http://web.centre.edu/david.toth/courses/rpg/).

2. RPG CURRICULUM REVISIONS

2.1 Operating Systems Assignments

In addition to exams and quizzes, which were not customized to include RPG elements but were worth XP, there were three programming projects in the Operating Systems course that were designed to keep within the theme of an RPG while requiring the students to use systems programming concepts.

The first project was a combat simulator. Students had their programs read a list of characters and a list of monsters from a file, spawning a new thread for each character and for each monster. The characters and monsters fought until either all the characters or all the monsters were dead. Students needed to use semaphores to ensure that the health of each character and monster was always calculated correctly.

Wizards find spells on scrolls
but more often in a book.
A tower with thousands of them
might be a good place to look.

The first hunt was easy.
This one not so.
'Fore the treasure is gone
away you must go!

Watch your back now
for traps and gnolls, too.
Lest you wind up
in somebody's stew!

You're on **Adventure**.
I've been leading you.
A **search through the catalog**
is what you should do!

Figure 2 - A Treasure Clue

The second programming project was to create a program that handled the inventory of a potion shop. The inventory of the shop was held in shared memory so that multiple processes could access the inventory at once. Semaphores were used to protect the shared memory when it was written, but not when it was read, to make it a realistic situation and to keep it consistent, ensuring that there could never be negative numbers of potions on the shelves. Processes were created to simulate customers who would look at the inventory and try to purchase potions and processes were created to stock potions.

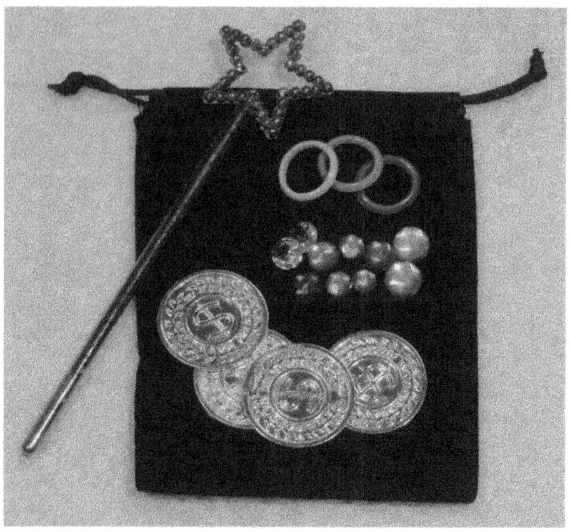

Figure 3 – An Assortment of Treasures from the Courses

For the third project, students wrote a client-server program using TCP sockets to simulate the election of a new head wizard. The server was multithreaded to allow simultaneous connections by the wizards casting their votes.

The programs read in a list of candidates and mutexes were used to protect each candidate's vote count. Signals were used to allow the server to "close the voting" when the election was over. When the server received a SIGINT it caught the signal and handled it, printing out a final tally of the votes and shutting down gracefully.

2.2 Computer Systems and Architecture Assignments

The assessments in the Computer Systems and Architecture course were not customized to include RPG elements and were just standard homework assignments, quizzes, programming projects, and exams. However, the homework assignments were required to be done in groups, which incorporated the "party" theme of RPGs.

In Operating Systems (the first course) students chose a character class and created a 'game name' that was not revealed to anybody other than the professor. Students were encouraged to optionally form groups of 4 to "adventure together" and the instructor wrote individual story lines to move the narrative along. Participation in the RPG aspects of the course was optional due to the instructor's concerns about religious objections. Student survey data indicated that 'optional questing' did not fully engage students, as it was a choice to play or not to play.

In Computer Systems and Architecture (second course), quest-based learning was more fully integrated into the course. All students were required to complete various quests and earn XP. Students were also placed into parties (groups) of four for the semester. Once parties were formed, each was provided a character sheet that described each type of character. Students were able to choose which party member would take which character type. Story narrative is a central element of role playing games and placing students into parties allowed the instructor to create four main stories knowing that each party consisted of a cleric, rogue, warrior, and a wizard.

3. METHODOLOGY

3.1 Participants

The design for this study was qualitative in order to capture 78 undergraduate students' perspectives of their learning and engagement with the revised role-playing curricular changes. All undergraduate students enrolled in Operating Systems and Computer Systems and Architecture participated in this qualitative research study. These courses are required for the computer science major and may be used as electives for the computer science minor. Operating Systems is taken by seniors while Computer Systems and Architecture is taken by sophomores or juniors.

You arrive at the cave before dark and your rogue notices fresh tracks leading into the cave and points them out to the party. "I thought we cleaned this place out you grumble quietly." As you start to head in, the rogue spies a chest off to the side of the entrance. (S)he has just opened it and started pulling out things when the gnolls jump you all from behind. The battle is fast and furious, with spells zinging through the air, people and monsters howling in pain and rage, and blood everywhere. When the dust settles, two things are clear:

1 - You all almost lost (the party is battered and bloody).

2 - They were expecting you.

Along with some gold and gems, the chest contains some interesting objects that appear to be magical. You try to find a place away from the cave to rest for the night and the night passes uneventfully, but none of you sleep well, even with somebody keeping watch. You make a quick unappetizing breakfast of dried rations, and head back to the cave.

Figure 4 - Part of a Story from a Treasure Pouch

3.2 Surveys and Data Analysis

In order to glean students' learning experiences in a role-playing genre and curriculum, an anonymous open-ended survey was used as the primary data source to solicit student feedback. Survey questions are shown in figures 5 and 6. The researchers received IRB approval. 78 students (60 males, 18 females) completed an open-ended survey for each course during the last week of classes with an 87% response rate. The instructor left the room and students completed the survey and placed it in a collection box in the front of the room. The second author collected student surveys and compiled student responses into a database. Once all the student responses were entered, the second author conducted qualitative data analysis to identify emergent themes. Data analysis was inductive and utilized the constant comparison method [3, 4]. This process for analyzing data allowed the researcher to develop themes that characterized students' perspectives and experiences of learning in a role-playing game. A part of the process of using the constant comparison method to analyze data consists of allowing themes to emerge from the data rather than imposing a pre-established set of codes onto the data [5]. The second author read through the data multiple times to write analytic memos and to create codes that categorized the data. Nine descriptive codes were identified; Characters, XP, Fun, Content Connections, Affective, Teaming, Leaderboard, Questing, and Magic Shop. These codes were then combined to create three emergent themes. Survey finding themes were then shared with the instructor and curricular revisions/strengths/areas to improve were identified.

3.3 Findings

The primary research question that guided our inquiry was: In what ways, if any, does the addition of a role-playing game layer support or hinder learning and student engagement? Overall, we found that students had a range of positive experiences related to role-playing game elements that increased their engagement with course content and team collaboration.

3.3.1 Role-Playing Personalized Student Learning

This theme conveys the ways in which the use of characters, character development, and story narrative engaged students. The introduction of a variety of characters and allowing students choice in selecting their characters mattered. Students 'named' their characters and worked to ensure that their character did well in the course and 'leveled up' gaining additional powers, gems, etc. One student shared, "I actually had an extra incentive to try and do well so my character would not die!" Another shared, "LOVED naming my character." Taking on a character's role and developing that character hinged on course content mastery. Students reported on how the 'story" unfolded over the course of the semester added an element of fun. Students wrote that it: "gave the class a story plot" and "the story made it easier for me to learn, I get bored too easily." And another shared, "I looked forward to reading future parts of the story. It gave the course a general feeling of moving forward." Students reported an appreciation and anticipation of receiving the next chapter as "getting the stories about the parties was always amusing." However, a few students felt little engagement with their character or unfolding story. One wrote, "While it put a light-hearted feel on the class, I don't feel like it improved or worsened the class."

1. In what ways, if any, did the RPG aspect of class make learning enjoyable for you? Give an example.

2. In what ways, if any, did the RPG aspect of the course make learning difficult? Give an example (if needed).

3. In what ways, if any, did the RPG aspect of the course add to your motivation to learn? Give an example.

4. In what ways, if any, did the RPG aspect of the course negatively impact to your motivation to learn? Give an example (if needed).

5. In what ways, if any, did the RPG aspect add to your motivation to attend class (no difference, some impact, big impact) more frequently? Why?

6. Would any positive impacts on education that the RPG aspect help with be accomplished with just the XP system and not the RPG aspect?

7. In what ways, if any, do you think the RPG aspect made you think we covered less material? Give example.

8. Did you "go on quests" to find the items hidden on campus? If so, did you enjoy that experience? Why? Give an example. If not, why didn't you go?

9. In what ways, if any, did the 'go on quests' aspect of the course add to your learning of course material?

10. Do you think we should continue the 'go on quests' aspect of the course? If so, what suggestions can you offer for improvement or additional quests?

11. Now that you have had an experience of learning through RPG and you had a choice between an RPG version of a course and a non-RPG version, which would you choose? Why?

12. What other feedback (related to the RPG aspect of the course) would you like to give?

Figure 5 - Survey from the First Course

Students valued the opportunity to earn XP over the course of the semester. Numerous students identified earning XP as an essential element that increased their engagement and course participation. For some students, the role of competition motivated them to earn XP. One shared, "I felt competitive when I saw my rank which drove me to excel." Other students appreciated knowing where they were on the XP ranking. One student wrote, "I only liked the scoring concept because I could constantly 'level up' and check where I am." Another shared, that it "allowed me to easily track my grade and prioritize work." However, some students pointed out that the XP scale was just like a regular grading scale. One shared, "XP was just a thin layer over the same grade system in other classes." Others engaged only with the scoring concept of the genre. The ability to level up through quest completion was appreciated by students and they liked how the workload was spread out over the course of the semester. A student shared that it "gave the class a layer of short term accomplishments. Normal classes and their [there] work load all come down to a final grade while this course offered accomplishments in the present time." Another student wrote, "I liked that I could earn my grade over time."

The inclusion of a leaderboard was another effective element in engaging students in learning course material. Students referenced the role competition played in conjunction with the leaderboard. One student wrote, "It was nice to be able to see our rankings in the class anonymously. It also increased our incentives for doing the work." Another shared, "competing with classmates and knowing I was doing much better than others; it motivated me to try even harder in other classes." And this student wrote, "seeing our progress through the course as gaining levels and skills make it seem cooler; highlighting the fact that knowledge is power and that I could do new things."

It is interesting to note that some students "just wanted to learn the material in class." Some students felt the RPG game layer didn't really add to their learning experiences and one student shared her concern in this way, "additional time taken away from content and traditional instructional methods."

1. Time and money was spent organizing the magic shop. Do you feel that this investment had value? Why or why not?

2. At the beginning of the semester we talked about the importance of teams working together. How did your team develop over the course of the semester?

3. In what ways, if any, did the RPG aspect of class make learning enjoyable for you? Give an example.

In what ways, if any, did the RPG aspect of the course make learning difficult? Give an example (if needed).

4. In what ways, if any, did the RPG aspect of the course add to your motivation to learn? Give an example.

In what ways, if any, did the RPG aspect of the course negatively impact to your motivation to learn? Give an example (if needed).

5. In what ways, if any, did the RPG aspect impact your learning, positively or negatively?

Figure 6 - Survey from the Second Course

3.3.2 RPG's Can Strengthen Content Connections

This second theme captured how the integration of course projects, assignments, and quests promoted a deeper understanding of course content. Students shared several ways the role-playing game layer promoted their engagement and created opportunities to apply course content to role-playing connected assignments. For example, students identified how coding became more meaningful. One student wrote, "writing the code became more enjoyable for me, it cemented the concepts in my mind as in the case of shared memory." And another shared, "The RPG aspect made the class a lot more enjoyable because it integrates with super boring/difficult concepts and make it feel not quite as hard." The assignments and the inclusion of treasure hunts also supported content understanding. Students shared:

> "Treasure hunts and assignments forced me to know them [content] because not knowing meant wasting time and energy finding the treasure chest"

> "really forced me to understand and sometimes relearn material."

> "Decieferring [sic] clues to find the treasure is a good example of how the RPG helped me learn. It provided more chances to practice topics we were learning."

Projects connected to the RPG themes were viewed as an important aspect to the course and added an element of fun to learning. One student wrote: "themes of projects are more fun to be based off players and potions instead of random things." And another felt, "kept the material fresh without making project too easy." And yet another student shared, "a mental break from subject matter that is generally considered dry and technical."

3.3.3 Learning Beyond the Role-Playing Game

This third theme brings to light additional learning experiences students had that went beyond course content mastery. Students were able to identify additional benefits of engaging in a role-playing game. For example, students appreciated how the quest layer promoted a light-hearted feel and promoted collaboration. Students shared how they enjoyed going to parts of campus they normally would not visit. One wrote, "I liked going out and finding things! It was fun going to the different places on campus I never went to before." And another shared, "the quests encouraged us to go to parts of campus we might not normally." Students were able to visit student support services to learn about additional resources that may be helpful to their success at the university. And on a side note, these support services appreciated an opportunity to spend time with students who they might not have met otherwise. Visits to the Magic Shop were mixed. Some students connected to the role of the Magic Shop and character development whereas students who had little previous RPG experiences struggled to make connection and purchases that would strengthen their character and team. For example, "it [Magic Shop] encouraged us to actually find clues so we could use the money with each one. The inclusion of items our team bought in the shop was a great touch. It made us feel like the decisions we made at the shop mattered." Others commented on how the Magic Shop added an element of fun. One student wrote, "It had a fun twist to the class not to mention since you go as a team you get to know your team a bit better." Another shared, "was an interesting idea, however, there needs to be more obvious benefit to buying items.

Students wrote treasure hunts were an opportunity to "interact more with my team" and "created a sense of accomplishment." Students became collaborative problem solvers as they worked together and most enjoyed the process. One shared, "I really enjoyed going on 'treasure hunts' and figuring out where the treasure was hidden." Students experienced and developed their team collaboration skills over the course of the semester. One wrote, it "helped me develop a team approach to learning and completing tasks." And many students shared how their earlier team collaborations needed to change and developed strategies to improve. For example, "we got better over the course of the semester" and "realized that we had to communicate if we wanted to do well so we started to talk more regularly." Others identified skills that they used in terms of organizing, communicating, and planning. And as one student shared, "we learned how important it was to work in teams and rely on our team." Teams also found it difficult to find time as many students are involved in sports, work, or commute to campus. Some teams struggled over the course of the semester and reported that they "developed remarkably poorly." Not surprising, a few students reported that they "like to work alone."

In summary, while students identified clear benefits and engagement in the RPG game layer that supported their learning, added an element of fun, and helped to create a less stressful learning environment, not all students fully embraced the RPG experience citing reasons not all that uncommon in other traditional pedagogical practices.

4. CONCLUSIONS

Integration and alignment of a role-playing game with course content is central to the creation of 'good game design.' When content was closely connected to the RPG story line, students were more likely to fully engage with the RPG elements of the course. Students valued closely aligned projects, assignments, and quests and supported content rigor in a creative and engaging manner; a fun factor.

When planning an RPG game layer be sure to check your assumptions. The author assumed that all students would be familiar with this genre of game and found that a number of students had little experience playing this type of game. Students who had first-hand experience tended to more fully engage with the RPG course aspects and served as a bridge to non-experienced RPG players. If you are planning on using a team aspect to accomplish RPG course assignments, it would be beneficial to place experienced RPG players with non-experienced RPG players. One might also consider holding a brief game play session to get everyone up to speed prior to engaging with course play.

One lesson learned is the importance of having students level up early on and frequently as a way to engage them in the RPG. Providing multiple opportunities for success in the early stages could increase student buy-in. It is also important to acknowledge that game pedagogy is based on active engagement and students will need to be supported in moving from the traditional content coverage methodology they have experienced. There is an importance of learning over time; students need opportunities to stop and reflect on their progress not only in terms of content learning but also on the skills they are developing through the use of an RPG. The role of student ownership over their learning can be an empowering factor as some students thrive in competitive contexts. It is important to remember that not all students thrive in this context so the importance of teamwork should be nurtured as a way to support learning and also skills. Faculty who engage in a leaderboard and/or use XP have to be comfortable with students determining their own grade. Not all students will strive for an A or even a B. Some students are happy with a C. Knowing this be sure to scaffold your curriculum and align your point/percentages so that students will be assured of obtaining the essential knowledge of your course.

It is also helpful to build bridges with others on campus who might want to support a RPG course. Partners bring an authentic element to the game and also can integrate key campus partners that provide student services. While it may seem unnecessary, students did appreciate the 'gems, coins, potions, rings, clues, etc.' As the person who ran the Magic Shop it was fascinating to see teams thoughtfully think through their buying options and be excited by 'the toys they bought.'

For those thinking of creating an RPG game layer, it is important to remember that games are complex systems and learning is complex. Be thoughtful in your course design and infuse a few RPG elements with course content. Be sure to solicit student insights and experiences, as they are the roadmap to level up your own pedagogical powers!

5. FUTURE WORK

We intend to refine this method of teaching further over the upcoming semesters. One enhancement we will work on is to try to create more assignments that fit the RPG theme of the course, similar to the ones used in our operating systems course, but for other courses we teach. Another enhancement is to create more stories so that students taking multiple courses using this theme have different stories so they don't get bored by seeing the same one again. We would like to create a follow-on story that continues where the first one left off, so students taking a course in one semester and then the next one can continue with their character, leveling up further and becoming more powerful, and hopefully becoming even more excited about classes using this method of motivation. We are also considering adding an electronic component to the course in one of two ways. One way would be to create a client-server program that allows the character creation process to be done online and each student to progress through the game online. Another possible method is to create a mobile application that students can use with their smart phones as they hunt for the treasures.

6. ACKNOWLEDGMENTS

This work was supported by the University of Mary Washington's Center for Teaching Excellence and Innovation.

7. REFERENCES

[1] Koster, R (2013). A theory of fun for game design. Sebastopol, CA: O'Reilly Media.

[2] http://en.wikipedia.org/wiki/Role-playing_game

[3] Bogdan, R. & Biklen, S. (2006). Qualitative research in education: An introduction to theories and methods. (Fifth Edition). Upper Saddle Hall, NJ: Prentice Hall, Inc.

[4] Glasser, B. & Strauss, A. (1967). The discovery of grounded theory: Strategies for qualitative research. Chicago, IL:Aldine.

[5] Emmerson, R., Fretz, R. & Shaw, L. (1995). In the field: Participating, observing, and jotting notes. *Writing Ethnographic Fieldnotes* (pp. 17-35). Chicago: University of Chicago Press.

Structuring Flipped Classes with Lightweight Teams and Gamification

Celine Latulipe N. Bruce Long Carlos E. Seminario
Software and Information Systems Department
University of North Carolina at Charlotte
Charlotte, NC 28223 USA
{clatulip, nblong, cseminar}@uncc.edu

ABSTRACT

We present a new approach to help make computer science classes both more social and more effective: "lightweight teams". Lightweight teams are class teams in which the team members have little or no direct impact on each other's final grades, yet where there is a significant component of peer teaching, peer learning and long-term socialization built into the curriculum. We explain how lightweight teams have been used in a CS1 class at our institution, and how this approach, combined with a flipped class approach and gamification, has led to high levels of student engagement, despite the difficulty of the material and the frustration that is common to those first learning to program.

Categories and Subject Descriptors

K.3.2 [**Computer Science Education**]

General Terms

Education

Keywords

lightweight teams, flipped classes, gamification, computing education, cooperative learning, team-based learning, CS1

1. INTRODUCTION

Students who self-select into computing disciplines are often considered to be less socially adept than average, or possibly just more introverted. While this stereotype is not true of all computing students, we do know that first-year students in all areas of study experience social anxiety when they arrive at university [6]. For students entering computing disciplines without a significant computing background (i.e. those without a CS AP course), this social anxiety coincides with the year when they learn the most basic computer science programming and problem solving concepts. Learning how to solve problems through programming is notoriously hard [13], and correlates with a high attrition rate in the first year computer science classes [26].

We have developed an approach to help address this issue of social anxiety paired with the difficulty of learning programming: the use of lightweight teams. In this paper, we define what we mean by lightweight teams and describe how we have used this approach in a new CS1 course, building on the trifecta of best practices (media computation, peer instruction and pair programming) shown by Porter and Simon to have significant impacts on learning in CS1 [21]. We extend beyond this trifecta by using a flipped classroom approach along with lightweight teams and gamification elements. Lightweight teams and gamification provide the structure and motivation for in-class activities required by flipped classrooms. This new CS1 course has been taught twice with an enrollment of 92 and 65 students in the Fall 2013 and Spring 2014 semesters, respectively. We report on our experiences as the teaching team as well as on survey responses from students taking these courses.

1.1 Lightweight Teams Defined

We define lightweight teams as teams of students who work together in a class, but where the work done as a team has minimal direct impact on a student's final grade. Thus, there is no large, high-stakes team project worth a large percentage of the final grade. Similarly, the teams don't complete any assignments or exams together. The team's work effort is focused on low-stakes activities and the team sits together for the whole semester in assigned seating in the classroom. Working on activities together throughout the semester gives the students a chance to get to know each other, become comfortable, and learn from one another.

1.2 Hypotheses

While we have not collected enough long-term data at this point to make any strong claims about the effectiveness of lightweight teams and gamification in combination with a flipped class structure, we do have some hypotheses about this combined approach. In general, we are interested in determining whether this combined approach encourages student learning, increases engagement in course-related activities, and increases feelings of community.

We posit the following hypotheses:

H1. Lightweight teams enhance the student's ability to learn the course material.

H2. Lightweight teams make the course more engaging for students.

SIGCSE'15, March 4–7, 2015, Kansas City, MO, USA.

ACM 978-1-4503-2966-8/15/03 ...$15.00.
http://dx.doi.org/10.1145/2676723.2677240.

H3. Gamification elements (stamps, tokens and the leaderboard) encourage students to work harder.

H4. Gamification elements make the course more engaging for students.

H5. Students become socially integrated with their peers.

2. BACKGROUND

While we don't generally think of college as a lonely place, it can be lonely for freshman who have not yet made friends. Our work draws heavily on the idea of cultivating communities of learners [15], because there is significant evidence that students become more engaged in their activities when they are part of such groups. These ideas are also supported by the work of Rogoff on the cognitive benefits that accrue from an apprenticeship model of learning [22]. Increased engagement is likely to have positive impacts on learning, as engagement is a key factor in helping students increase their self-efficacy and improve their performance [19].

We were also inspired by the practices that have flourished in many classrooms based on Michaelsen's team-based learning approach [18]. In this approach, teams of students are strongly dependent on one another to work together to produce final outcomes that are graded. While this approach makes sense in upper year courses where students have the skills to complete more complex projects, it seems less useful in an introductory computing course. However, belonging to a group or a team can have significant positive benefits both in the current context, and for sustained success in college [1]. We wanted a way to leverage the increased engagement that comes with team social interaction and the cognitive benefits that come from apprenticeship learning. However, we also know that high-stakes group work tends to lead to high amounts of stress for many students. Students commonly complain about group work, typically because one or more team-members are not doing their fair share of the work. *Lightweight teams are designed to leverage the benefits associated with team-based learning and apprenticeship learning, but to remove the stress associated with high-stakes group projects.*

Gamification is the use of game mechanics and elements in non-game settings [16] in order to engage participants and have them perform desired patterns of behavior to reach established goals [9]. Typical gamification elements include point systems, badges, levels and challenges. Gamification has been applied to entire courses in game design [23]. We are beginning to see evidence that gamification contributes to learning in CS1 [3, 20, 8]. McGonigal argues that games promote learning and help people to socialize [17]. While gamification holds promise for increasing motivation and engagement, we are particularly interested in how it combines with lightweight teams, because a course designer can employ both individual and team-based gamification elements.

There has been significant research on the flipped or inverted classroom model [24, 25, 11, 14, 5]. In this model, content delivery occurs outside of the classroom, and in-class time is devoted to active learning activities. This approach means that instructors, through interaction with students in class, can determine where students have developed misconceptions. This is in direct opposition to the traditional 'sage on the stage' model which creates a social barrier between the instructor and the students. Recent research has shown that the flipped model can have a positive impact in CS1 classes [10]. The challenge associated with the flipped class approach is developing in class activities. We believe lightweight teams and gamification provide structure and motivation for in-class activities.

3. FLIPPED MEDIA COMPUTATION

At our institution, we recently created a separate, additional track for introductory programming that runs in parallel to the traditional programming courses and is open to both majors in the CS and IS tracks and to non-majors. The first class in the new track is ITIS 1212: Introduction to Media Computation and meets twice weekly, Wednesday lab and Friday workshop. This course extends the media computation approach (for Java) [7] to a flipped class setting. Thus, students read the textbook, enter textbook programs, watch videos about programming concepts, and take a short online quiz before they come to the programming lab. The Wednesday lab meets in two smaller sections where students work through programming exercises with a same-gender peer, and lab partners change every two weeks. The last weekly activity is a 3-1/2 hour Friday workshop where we use the lightweight teams.

3.1 Lightweight Teams in ITIS 1212

Team Creation and Seating

Prior to the first class of the semester, we use Moodle's auto-grouping function to generate random teams with approximately five students per team. We then make minor adjustments so that female students are on a team with at least one other female. On the first day of class, we ask team members to choose a name for their team.

To encourage teamwork, we believe it is important that students sit together with their team every week, so we create a seating plan based on the classroom layout. While this seems strange to the students, we think that for many students there is anxiety about where to sit in class. Lightweight teams means that students don't have to choose where to sit, who to sit with, or even wonder if anyone will choose to sit next to them. We observed that over the semesters, students came in and began immediately talking with their team-mates and while this chat was often purely social, they sometimes used this time to discuss class work. This is quite unlike traditional large freshmen courses, which, in our experience, tend to be quite quiet before the start of class.

Peer Instruction Clicker Quizzes

We typically open the Friday workshop sessions by asking the students if they have questions about course content, and if they do, we spend 5 or 10 minutes answering questions. We then conduct the clicker quizzes[1], which are multiple choice quizzes run using a modified peer instruction method [2]. We project a question on screen and encourage students to talk with their team-mates *before* answering. Each student has their own clicker and is free to enter the answer they think is correct. We evaluate the responses to each question before continuing; if we feel that not enough people are getting the right answer, we ask students to 'find someone with a different answer and convince them that you are right'. This leads to teams debating with other teams, so the discussion can become quite loud. This means that not only are students talking with and getting to know the

[1]http://www.turningtechnologies.com/higher-education

people on their own team, they are often getting to know the people on other teams as well.

Our clicker quizzes typically contain 15-20 challenging questions and will take 90-120 minutes to complete, depending on how much discussion is generated. Because questions and answers about Java code can be lengthy, we often distribute hardcopies for teams to share, promoting discussion. We also design non-trivial questions that really challenge the students, often requiring them to get out a pen and paper and work through a section of code to predict output or understand how something works. Finally, we use multiple similar questions that repeatedly test a concept, giving students a chance to cement their understanding. Because we have also entered the team rosters and team names into the clicker quiz software, we are able to display live team stats during the clicker quiz, showing which teams have earned the most points so far, generating competition and excitement.

The clicker quizzes are worth a total of 10% of each student's final grade. So, in the end, they are not a significant portion of a student's grade. However, feedback from students indicate that these team-based quizzes are one of the most useful parts of the course in terms of testing and developing their understanding of core programming concepts.

Other Peer Instruction Activities

While the clicker quiz often takes up more than half of the Friday workshop sessions, there is usually about an hour left. Some weeks this hour is devoted to one of the five tests (which are taken individually, not as a team). When we aren't giving tests, students engage with their team on other hands-on activities. These include paper problem solving activities, where students are asked to write pseudocode to solve a problem, or Parson's Problems [4], where they are given lines of pseudocode that need to be put in the correct order to solve a problem. For these activities, we sometimes ask teams to trade solutions and then do peer grading or peer critiquing of the other team's solution.

3.2 Gamification in ITIS 1212

To complement lightweight teams, we employed three simple gamification strategies to motivate and engage students.

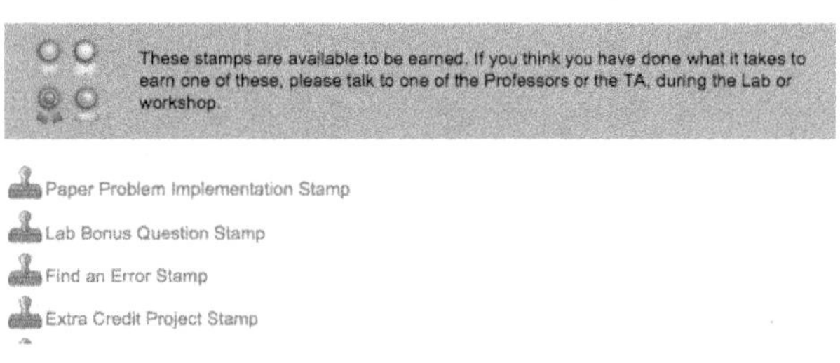

Figure 1: Stamps available to be earned.

Stamps

We used the Moodle stamp collection module to give students stamps for small achievements that indicate extra engagement (Figure 1 shows a subset of the stamps available). The students could collect as many stamps as they wanted, and for every 10 stamps they collected, they would earn a 1% increase in their final grade. Stamps were given for activities such as answering forum questions, completing programming lab bonuses, implementing paper problem solutions from workshop, or completing Problet tutorials [12].

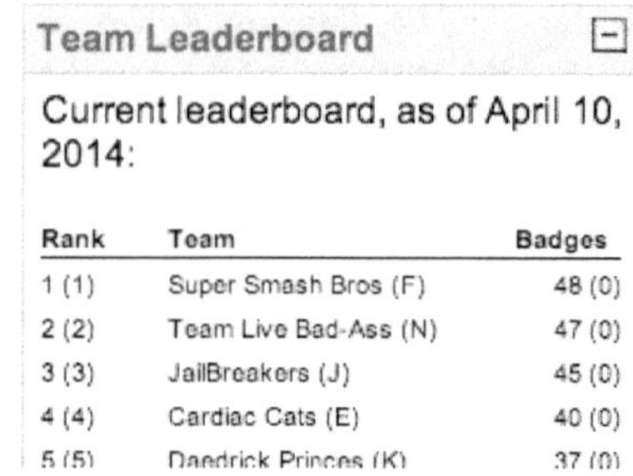

Figure 2: Partial screen-shot of the team leaderboard on Moodle, showing the total stamps earned by members of each team.

Leaderboard

While stamps were collected individually by students, we wanted students to encourage each other to participate more fully. To do this, we implemented a team leaderboard on Moodle which was updated weekly to reflect the number of stamps collectively earned by each of the teams. The board showed changes from previous weeks as well as total stamps earned. The top three teams at the end of the semester were awarded special prizes. Thus, the stamps and the leaderboard turned the course into a tournament.

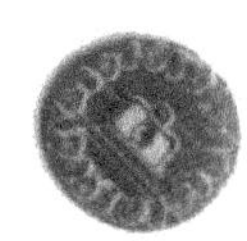

Figure 3: The 3D printed media computation token.

Question Tokens

We designed and 3D-printed special 'media computation' tokens (see Figure 3), that we gave out to students during the labs. Each student got one token per week and their goal was to hold on to their token and turn it in to their team during the Friday workshop. If a five person team could hand in a full set of five tokens, they would all earn stamps. However, if a student wanted to ask a question of a Professor or TA during the lab, they would have to turn their token in if we determined that they should have known the answer from their weekly preparation. This was designed to encourage students to fully prepare for class, to learn to solve programming problems on their own, and to get help from each other and from online sources.

4. RESULTS

We collected anonymous survey information from our ITIS 1212 students in both semesters, to get their perspectives on these pedagogical approaches. The surveys were conducted twice per semester (as "early feedback" and "late feedback") and consisted of 44 and 50 questions, respectively; they were conducted during the Fall 2013 (N=45 and 45, response rates of 52%) and Spring 2014 (N=59 and 44, response rates of 94% and 70%) semesters. Our response rates were higher in Spring because we gave students time to complete the surveys in class. The surveys consisted of agreement statements on a 5-point Likert scale (1= strongly disagree, 3 = neutral, 5 = strongly agree). Table 1 presents the responses

Table 1: Survey Results: Average scores from ITIS 1212, Fall 2013 and Spring 2014 semesters.

ID	Agreement Statement (Scale is 1-5: 1 Strongly Disagree, 3 Neutral, 5 Strongly Agree)	Fall 2013 Early	Fall 2013 Late	Spring 2014 Early	Spring 2014 Late	Average
Flipped	The flipped structure of this class is working well for me (I am learning a lot).	3.17	3.76	3.76	4.05	3.69
Team-1	Working with my team members to answer clicker questions helps me to learn.	4.54	4.38	4.52	4.60	4.51
Team-2	The team aspect of the course makes the course overall more engaging.	4.11	3.96	4.22	4.28	4.14
Team-3	I like being part of a team and sitting with my team each week.	4.28	4.44	4.26	4.48	4.37
Stamp-1	Stamps provide a good incentive to get me to put more effort into this course.	3.26	3.07	4.00	3.75	3.52
Stamp-2	The leaderboard on Moodle showing which team has the most stamps adds to my desire to earn more stamps.	3.47	3.04	3.75	3.37	3.41
Stamp-3	The addition of 1% to my final grade for every 10 stamps earned adds to my desire to earn more stamps.		3.53		3.91	3.72
Token-1	The use of tokens makes me try hard to figure out the lab with my partner.	3.54	3.07	3.72	3.37	3.38
Token-2	The tokens are fun and cool.	2.65	2.80	3.56	3.36	3.02
Token-3	Because of the tokens I am becoming a more self-reliant learner.	2.85	2.86	3.47	3.09	3.03
Token-4	The potential loss of a token has discouraged me from asking for help, even when I really need it.		3.93		3.30	3.72
Overall	Because of this course, I am likely to take another programming course.		3.89		3.95	3.92

related to the flipped class, lightweight teams and gamification elements.

Flipping the media computation curriculum is seen as positive in early feedback, but receives higher scores in later feedback, indicating a change in attitude over the semester. The scores across most questions, including the flipped class, are higher in the Spring offering, likely because of a few refinements made after the initial offering. The results for Team-1, Team-2 and Team-3 show that students think very positively about lightweight teams, not only for enhancing their learning experience and engaging in the workshop, but also for the social/community benefits. In the Overall question, students responded positively regarding their likelihood to take another programming course, a question that was only on the late semester feedback survey.

We compared average scores between representative survey questions (see Table 1) Team-1, Team-2, Stamp-1, Stamp-2, and Token-1, for each of the four surveys and for all respondents. Results for Team-1 are significantly higher than Team-2 ($p<.05$), Stamp-1 and Stamp-2 ($p<.001$), and Token-1 ($p<.001$). Team-2 results are significantly higher than Stamp-1 ($p<.02$)[2], Stamp-2 ($p<.02$), and Token-1 ($p<.02$). The gamification elements such as the stamps, tokens and the leaderboard received positive ratings, but not as positive as the team elements. In general, stamps and leaderboard average scores were higher than scores related to tokens, however, there were no significant differences found in comparisons between Stamp-1, Stamp-2, and Token-1.

We also analyzed differences in average scores due to gender (male, female) and major (computing, other/undeclared) for each of the four surveys and across all survey questions, paying particular attention to questions related to lightweight teams and gamification. In both Fall 2013 surveys, we found one survey question (Stamp-2, $p<.05$) where females scored significantly higher than males; none of these were found to have significant differences in the Spring 2014 surveys. So at least for the Fall 2013 semester, it appeared that female students were more excited about the stamp competition than male students. An interesting hypothesis we could posit in the future would be that while females may not be motivated by individual competition, they may strongly want their team to excel. We were looking for response consistency to assess differences in gender and major across all four surveys, especially across both semesters. We found only one instance of this consistency: the Team-3 question, where the other/undeclared majors scored significantly higher than the computing majors ($p<.05$) in the Fall 2013 and Spring 2014 semesters. In other words, non-computing majors liked being part of a team more than computing majors. Anecdotally, in the early Fall 2013 survey, other/undeclared majors scored significantly higher than the computing majors ($p<.05$) in the Team-1 question which might help explain why other/undeclared majors liked being part of a team, i.e., it helps them to learn. In both Spring 2014 surveys, we found that computing majors scored significantly higher than other/undeclared majors in this question: "I try all the required programming exercises from the book before each Moodle quiz and lab."; this would perhaps indicate that the computing majors learned more on their own than in a team setting.

Students had the opportunity to give us open-ended feedback through the surveys. The vast majority of this feedback was positive, and much of it relates to the lightweight teams. For example, one student commented: "Being able to work with people is the highlight of this course." And yet another simply stated that the best part of the course was "the bond of friends". One student summed up the Friday workshop: "I really enjoyed going to workshop. Going through a clicker quiz with a team made it easier to learn the material." Multiple students made positive comments about taking clicker quizzes as a team and how valuable that was to them. The students were also very positive about the flipped class style, with one student commenting: "This course was excellent. The unconventional style hit the same subject in so many different angles that helped me a lot." Another student noted: "At first, I did not like the flipped classroom idea, but now I find it isn't that bad if you do the work." There were two students who expressed

[2]Team-2 vs Stamp-1 difference was not significant in the Spring 2014 Early survey.

strongly negative opinions about the flipped class structure, one of them advising: "Go back to a traditional class set up. We pay to be taught and this is not what we got."

Post-Course Performance

Of the 92 students who enrolled in our first semester ITIS 1212 class, 56 students went on to take ITCS 1213 in Spring 2014, an object-oriented Java course offered in the CS track within our college. The other 198 students enrolled in this follow-on course took ITCS 1212 as the pre-requisite course. ITCS 1212 has three significant differences from ITIS 1212: it is not flipped, there are no teams or gamification, and the programming language taught is procedural C++. Our ITIS 1212 graduates fared well in ITCS 1213, earning a class GPA of 3.06 (std.dev of 0.9), compared to students from the traditional intro class (ITCS 1212), who earned a class GPA of 2.66 (std.dev. of 1.17). Compared to the other ITCS 1213 students, our ITIS 1212 students had higher percentages of A's and B's and lower percentages of C's, D's, and F's at the end of the semester (see Figure 4). Comparing the average ITCS 1213 final grades, students from ITIS 1212 course scored higher than ITCS 1212 students (84.19, st.dev. of 9.02 vs. 80.28, st.dev. of 12.5, $p < 0.3$). It is unclear which factors (flipped class structure, lightweight teams and gamification, knowledge of Java) led to our students performing better in ITCS 1213. Regardless, the high performance of our students in the follow-on course suggests that the learning outcomes from our ITIS 1212 class are positive.

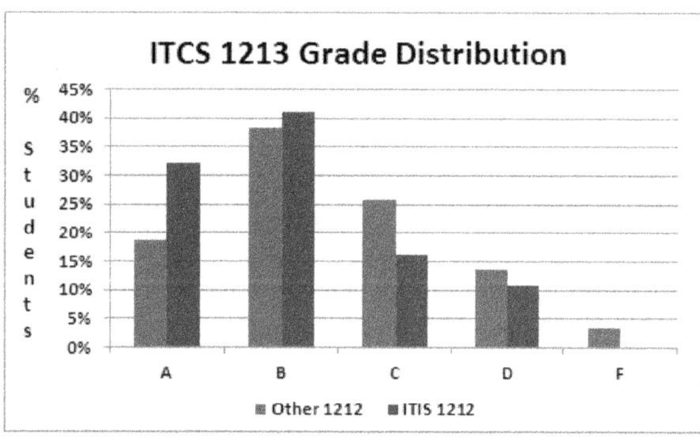

Figure 4: Histogram of performance of our ITIS 1212 students (blue) in the ITCS 1213 course, compared to students from ITCS 1212 (red).

5. DISCUSSION

Based on the results shown in Table 1, and the significant differences between lightweight team and gamification results, hypotheses H1 and H2 related to lightweight teams are accepted; hypotheses H3 and H4 related to gamification scored lower and are considered marginally accepted for this analysis. Based on the number of friends made, we accept H5. Our interpretation of these results are that (1) lightweight teams exert a strong positive influence on students' ability to learn, engage in the course, and establish a sense of community, and (2) gamification elements (stamps, leaderboard, tokens) also exert positive influence on the student's work ethic and self-reliance, however, the use of these elements needs further refinement. In particular, we are concerned with the results of the Token-4 question because we don't want students to withhold their questions when they really need help. On a positive note, the average score for the Token-4 question dropped significantly ($p<.02$) between Fall 2013 and Spring 2014 indicating that students were, in fact, spending the token to get help; our intent is to continue to monitor this concern.

The instructional team observed friendships form over both semesters of this course. We observed sets of these students hanging out outside of class and coming to office hours as a group. Students who started the semester without knowing anyone in the class left at the end of the semester with a set of new friends. We describe the phenomenon of lightweight teams as 'handing freshman students four friends on a platter'. Figure 5 displays one of the most exciting results from this class: 62% of respondents in Fall 2013 and 55% of respondents in Spring 2014 reported making 5 or more new friends as a result of taking ITIS 1212. This suggests that not only did students make friends on their teams but across teams. We believe that these students making so many new friends will have positive impacts on program and institutional retention because we have helped them become connected to their student community.

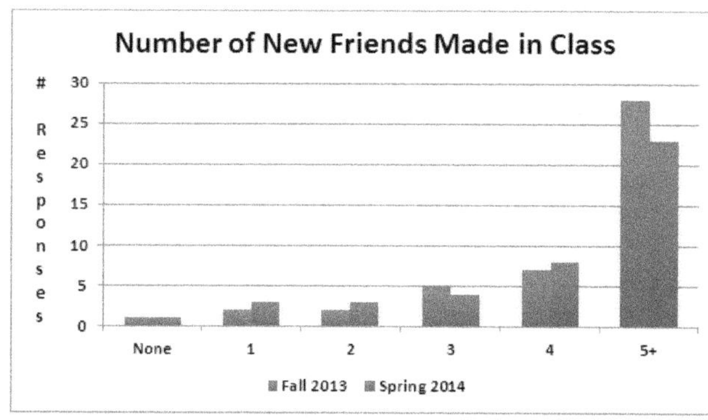

Figure 5: Histogram showing the number of new friends each respondent reported making as a result of taking ITIS 1212 in Fall 2013 or Spring 2014.

We paid considerable attention to gender issues in our pedagogical design because we wanted this first programming class to be a positive and confidence-building experience for our female students. We had gendered pairs for pair programming in the lab because of our experiences seeing 'guys take over' in the lab when they are partnered with a female for programming activities. In survey questions about this practice, the female respondents (n=17 in late Fall 2013) and (n=7 in late Spring 2014) were generally in agreement that gendered pairs was a good policy, although there were a few detractors. We observed that this practice ensured that everyone was able to fully participate in labs.

Our workshop sessions were held in standard lecture halls containing rows of tables with chairs attached. These rooms are definitely not optimally designed for lightweight teams. In designing the seating plan, we did not sit teams along a row, as that would make collaboration difficult. Rather we put two team members in one row and the other three team members directly behind them or in front of them. Because the chairs could swivel, we found that students could turn around and talk to each other as needed. Rooms with round tables for each team would enhance the interaction, but traditional lecture halls can be made to work.

6. CONCLUSIONS AND FUTURE WORK

We have presented our initial experience with using lightweight teams and gamification elements within a flipped class structure to enhance the trifecta of best practices for CS1 [21]. Lightweight teams are designed to address students' social needs without the stress associated with high-stakes team projects and the gamification elements are designed to increase engagement and provide a coalescing goal for teams. Our initial results suggest that this combination of elements provides the needed activity structure for a fully flipped classroom and leads to positive experiences for students and high overall engagement; it would be interesting, in the future, to assess the benefits of each component individually. Our results indicate that students (1) strongly agree with the lightweight teaming aspect of this course, and (2) made numerous friends (5+) in this course as a direct result of lightweight teaming. We will continue to track our students to see how they fare as they progress through our undergraduate programs. It is our expectation that the social aspects of lightweight teams will lead to students feeling more embedded in the College community and will have positive impacts on long-term program retention.

In the future we are interested in investigating how lightweight teams and gamification scale to larger class sizes. In addition, we plan to explore how lightweight teams might enable more social learning experiences in massively open online classes (MOOCs) and other online educational settings where learning can be a lonely experience.

7. REFERENCES

[1] A. W. Astin. What matters in college, 1993.

[2] C. H. Crouch, J. Watkins, A. P. Fagen, and E. Mazur. Peer instruction: Engaging students one-on-one, all at once. *Research-Based Reform of University Physics*, 1(1), 2007.

[3] A. Decker and E. L. Lawley. Life's a game and the game of life: How making a game out of it can change student behavior. In *Proc. of the 44th ACM Technical Symposium on Computer Science Education*, 2013.

[4] P. Denny, A. Luxton-Reilly, and B. Simon. Evaluating a new exam question: Parsons problems. In *Proceedings of the Fourth International Workshop on Computing Education Research*. ACM, 2008.

[5] J. Foertsch, G. Moses, J. Strikwerda, and M. Litzkow. Reversing the lecture/homework paradigm using eteach® web-based streaming video software. *Journal of Engineering Education-Washington*, 91(3), 2002.

[6] L. J. Friedlander, G. J. Reid, N. Shupak, and R. Cribbie. Social support, self-esteem, and stress as predictors of adjustment to university among first-year undergraduates. *Journal of College Student Development*, 48(3), 2007.

[7] M. Guzdial. A media computation course for non-majors. In *Proceedings of the 8th Annual Conference on Innovation and Technology in Computer Science Education*. ACM, 2003.

[8] L. Haaranen, P. Ihantola, L. Hakulinen, and A. Korhonen. How (not) to introduce badges to online exercises. In *Proc. of the 45th ACM Technical Symposium on Computer Science Education*, 2014.

[9] J. Hamari, J. Koivisto, and H. Sarsa. Does gamification work? – A Literature Review of Empirical Studies on Gamification. In *Proceedings of the 47th Hawaii International Conference on System Sciences*. IEEE Computer Society, 2014.

[10] D. Horton, M. Craig, J. Campbell, P. Gries, and D. Zingaro. Comparing outcomes in inverted and traditional CS1. In *Proceedings of the 2014 Conference on Innovation & Technology in Computer Science Education*. ACM, 2014.

[11] B. Kelley, S. Miner, and F. Haggar. Technogogy and faculty development. *Academic Exchange Quarterly*, 16(1), 2012.

[12] A. N. Kumar. Using problets for problem-solving exercises in introductory C++/Java/C# courses. In *Frontiers in Education Conference*. IEEE, 2013.

[13] D. M. Kurland, C. A. Clement, R. Mawby, and R. D. Pea. Mirrors of minds: Patterns of experience in educational computing. Ablex Publishing Corp., 1987.

[14] M. Lage, G. Platt, and M. Treglia. Inverting the classroom: A gateway to creating an inclusive learning environment. *The Journal of Economic Education*, 31(1), 2000.

[15] J. Lave and E. Wenger. *Situated learning: Legitimate peripheral participation*. Cambridge Univ. Press, 1991.

[16] J. J. Lee and J. Hammer. Gamification in education: What, how, why bother? *Academic Exchange Quarterly*, 15(2), 2011.

[17] J. McGonigal. Reality is broken. *Jonathan Cape, London*, 2011.

[18] L. K. Michaelsen, A. B. Knight, and L. D. Fink. *Team-based learning: A transformative use of small groups*. Greenwood Publishing Group, 2002.

[19] P. R. Pintrich and D. H. Schunk. *Motivation in education: Theory, research, and applications*. Merrill, 1996.

[20] J. Pirker, M. Riffnaller-Schiefer, and C. Gütl. Motivational active learning: Engaging university students in computer science education. In *Proceedings of the 2014 Conference on Innovation & Technology in Computer Science Education*. ACM, 2014.

[21] L. Porter and B. Simon. Retaining nearly one-third more majors with a trio of instructional best practices in CS1. In *Proc. of the 44th ACM Technical Symposium on Computer Science Education*, 2013.

[22] B. Rogoff. Developing understanding of the idea of communities of learners. *Mind, culture, and activity*, 1(4), 1994.

[23] L. Sheldon. *The multiplayer classroom: Designing coursework as a game*. Cengage Learning, 2012.

[24] J. Strayer. *The effects of the classroom flip on the learning environment: a comparison of learning activity in a traditional classroom and a flip classroom that used an intelligent tutoring system*. PhD thesis, The Ohio State University, 2007.

[25] J. Thornburg. If you build it, will they come? – Flipping the Classroom. *Mining Key Pedagogical Approaches*, 2012.

[26] C. Watson and F. W. Li. Failure rates in introductory programming revisited. In *Proceedings of the 2014 Conference on Innovation & Technology in Computer Science Education*. ACM, 2014.

Blending Problem- and Project-Based Learning in Internet of Things Education: Case Greenhouse Maintenance

Hanna Mäenpää Sasu Tarkoma Samu Varjonen Arto Vihavainen

Department of Computer Science
University of Helsinki
Helsinki, Finland
<firstname.lastname>@cs.helsinki.fi

ABSTRACT

This article describes an experimental course where students developed Internet of Things device prototypes to improve the upkeep of an urban rooftop greenhouse. With the help of a problem-based learning approach, students were first familiarized with their new learning environment and encouraged to find issues that could be improved as a meaningful personal learning experience. A project-based learning approach was then used to develop innovative solutions while validating their relevance in collaboration with gardeners that were taking care of the greenhouse. As a result, a number of practical applications for monitoring the state of the greenhouse were developed along with new practices for its maintenance. As participants were given the freedom to choose both the topic and technologies to work with, the course provided a learning experience that was tailored to suit personal interests and competences. Having the common background story allowed students to practice teamwork skills and collaborative software engineering in the context of the emerging topic of Internet of Things.

Categories and Subject Descriptors

K.3.2 [**Computers and Education**]: Computer and Information Science Education; D.2.m [**Miscellaneous**]: Rapid prototyping; J.7 [**Computer Applications**]: Computers in Other Systems

Keywords

problem-based learning; project-based learning; internet of things; greenhouse

1. INTRODUCTION

Computing has become more pervasive and embedded systems are becoming a natural part of our lives [11, 14]. While applied computer science provides many tools for other disciplines, software engineers play a central role in solving problems, including environmental challenges [10]. This work is done in teams where experts from various fields come together to share their knowledge.

In this article, we describe an experimental blended problem- and project-based learning course, where students develop solutions to support taking care of a greenhouse. The driving problem was outlined with a professional gardener and a caretaker team. The course started by brainstorming solutions to a problem and transitioned to identifying and outlining projects that the students chose for themselves.

Our motivation was to increase the students' capabilities to work in diverse environments. Therefore, students were allowed to choose their individual projects' hardware and software architecture independently from a selection of very heterogeneous options. While each of their solutions were different, our goal was to make them work together as a holistic system to provide a solution for the initial problem. The ACM 2013 Computer Science Curricula emphasizes that the education offered to students should prepare them for the workforce in a more holistic way than simply conveying technical facts, and highlights the importance of soft skills such as teamwork and problem solving as well as attributes such as sense of social responsibility [16]. We feel that our learning experiment was especially well suited for this purpose.

This article is organized as follows. Section 2 outlines the relevant technological and pedagogical concepts. Section 3 presents the experiment setting, its position in the curriculum, as well as student deliverables, including hardware prototypes, and individual learning goals. Section 4 discusses the lessons learned from the course arrangement and reflects on the knowledge that the course staff, students, and the greenhouse care team gathered during the project, and finally, Section 5 concludes this article.

2. BACKGROUND

2.1 Technologies

Internet of Things (IoT) is an umbrella term that is used to describe a technological paradigm where everyday objects are enclosed with small, uniquely identifiable, internet enabled hardware components [1]. With these so-called "Smart Devices", product developers seek to help people in their daily tasks, and to create new ways for working and communicating. Smart Devices are predicted to shape the technological landscape of the near future in a radical man-

SIGCSE'15 March 04 – 07 2015, Kansas City, MO, USA

http://dx.doi.org/10.1145/2676723.2677262.

ner. A recent study by Ericsson [9] forecasted that by the year 2020 there will be 50 billion objects that are connected to the Internet. It is expected that this movement will provide new business opportunities for hardware manufacturers and ICT companies at an unforeseen scale.

IoT devices typically contain sensors that can provide information about the environment they are located in. Data produced by the devices is disseminated through a wireless Internet connection to cloud-based data storage services that are provided by third party companies or organizations. In addition to storing the data, these services allow their users to analyze the data application programming interfaces (API) that allow creating solutions at ease, allowing very short development cycles.

2.2 Pedagogical Underpinnings

The experiment described in this article builds on the constructivist view of learning that suggests that people actively construct knowledge rather than receive and store it (see e.g. [8, 12, 4]). Constructivists view knowledge as something that cannot be copied from what a teacher said, define it as unique to those who have constructed it, and, as a consequence, promote student-centered, active learning models of instruction. Many of these views stem from the work by Dewey, who wrote that "probably the greatest and commonest mistake that we make is to forget that learning is a necessary incident of dealing with real life situations" [7]. According to Dewey, personal experience can not be substituted by even the most sophisticated learning materials.

Our experiment started with a problem-based set up. In problem-based learning students are sent to solve realistic and substantial problems [15, 3]. The problem creates focus for the project, stimulates the student's thinking, positioning the individual at the epicenter of the learning experience. According to Norman, instructors should provide only limited help in form of guidance in order to allow the students to develop domain-specific knowledge and effective problem-solving skills. While students engage in the problem independently, they are guided to find their own thinking strategies and ways of working which improves their self-directed learning skills [15]. Barrows [3] outlines five guidelines for teachers who want to use this approach in their tuition:

1. The teacher must provide a driving question that students seek answers to, without any predetermined outcome.
2. Learning objectives and goals need to be centered around the problem.
3. Students should approach the problem through constructive investigations.
4. They should work in an autonomous manner.
5. Projects need to be realistic so that students can make connections to authentic situations and draw from their past experiences

The problem-based learning theory is supported by the Inductive learning theory, which is defined by Prince et al. [19] as an experience where students are given a starting point from which they gather observations that drive their further actions. As the insight individuals gain is a highly personal interpretation, their learning pathways become diversified.

The "Exact Greenhouse"-course was carried out as a seven-week project. In project-based learning students have more freedom to choose the task that they will be working on and the domain is at least partially known beforehand [5, 21]. Authors such as Barron et al. [2] have suggested combining problem- and project-based learning in a way that students are provided with a problem that acts as the framework of the project and helps students form initial knowledge, which can be further developed in a project:

> *For example, by beginning with a simulated problem, students develop a level of shared knowledge and skill that prepares them to undertake actual projects. By following the problem with a project, students are likely to develop more flexible levels of skills and understanding.* [2]

2.3 Related Courses in Literature

Even though little work can be found on experiments that combine computer science with horticulture, a body of academic knowledge exist on educational experiments with a cross-disciplinary approach for IoT innovation. The studies underline student empowerment and aim at increasing motivation and self-direction.

A number of studies emphasize the practicality of IoT courses (see e.g. [17, 6]). Another part of related literature describes settings where students' prior knowledge is low and the curriculum of the course is driven by technological motives. Kortuem et al. [13] describe an online course where students were expected to buy a small hardware component and to compose a simple program that uses the Scratch [20] drag-and-drop programming environment. Another educational experiment by Callaghan [6] introduced modular *Buzz-Boards* for students as the sole platform for creating interconnected IoT devices. Learnings from these experiments emphasize creating holistic constructs rather than concentrating on details of the technology [6].

Osipov and Riliskis describe a learning experiment that did not involve hardware. In their example, graduate students worked over a span of three courses that had a common IoT theme [17]. In this example, students developed cloud-based software applications while using a simulator to replace physical hardware components. Student experiences were described as mostly positive and enthusiastic, while some had perceived the workload as high.

When comparing the related research with our experiment, most of the IoT-related courses are organized around an existing set of hardware components or simulators that are provided to the students, and the problems have been typically designed based on technologies. In our experiment the problem came first, and many of the components that were used in the course were ordered during the course based on the individual needs of the students, creating a novel approach for IOT education.

3. THE GREENHOUSE PROJECT

The Exact Greenhouse is a research laboratory that is located on the roof terrace of the Department of Computer Science of the University of Helsinki. It was originally set up for Green ICT research where the goal was to study the possibility of cooling computer servers with unconditioned outside air, while harvesting exhaust heat into a greenhouse during winter time. This setup has previously been described in [18].

3.1 Course Setup and Curriculum

Our seven week project course had a tangible and well framed narrative that was initially presented to the students in the course description. The criteria for student selection was that the students should be MSc students who were at the very end of their studies. A total of thirteen students were selected from 25 enrolled. Limiting the amount of participants was done to ensure meaningful learning experiences and to facilitate studying the course structure and organization.

Two instructors were assigned to team-teach the course. One of the instructors was a PhD student in Software Systems Engineering, and the other a recent PhD graduate with knowledge on networking and relevant IoT technologies. The curriculum of the experiment consisted of a kickoff meeting, three milestones and wrap-up meeting where students presented their project outcomes. The course communication was arranged mainly on a course Facebook page. The majority of the students were present in an internet (IRC) chat room that had originally been created for the greenhouse maintenance team's internal communication. Voluntary weekly meetings were arranged, yet only a few students felt the need for attending them.

3.1.1 Week 1: Discovering the domain

The course narrative was elaborated in full detail to the students on their first meeting on Monday, June 2nd. Participants were taken to visit the greenhouse with one of the gardeners to observe and discuss characteristics of the structure and needs for plant care. Afterwards, they were asked to pick a theme for their projects. Students brainstormed problems in maintaining the greenhouse and sketched solutions for solving them. Numerous project ideas emerged, including topics such as "Smart Flowerpot", "Hydroponics", "Temperature" and "Ventilation" among others.

Next, participants were introduced to their solution domain: a set of microcontroller equipment that had been reserved for the course. They were encouraged to choose any platform, including but not limited to the devices that were available at the moment. After the meeting participants were set off with the hardware and their first task: to get to know the technology and to identify components that were required for their project implementation.

3.1.2 Week 2: Creating project requirements

On their second meeting on Monday 9th, students met a professional gardener who further outlined problems related to greenhouse maintenance and provided feedback on the relevance of the students' plans. The feasibility of some of the project ideas were also discussed with the course staff and, finally, a compromised list of components to order was composed. Orders were placed immediately from manufacturers that were known for fast delivery. The second assignment was to document their full plans to a course blog. This was the first milestone of the course.

3.1.3 Weeks 3-5: Autonomous project work

During the following weeks, students built their hardware prototypes and developed related software. Voluntary weekly meetings were arranged on Mondays and the course staff provided technical help on demand.

3.1.4 Week 6: Ensuring integration

A second milestone was set to ensure that all projects had found a means to make data yielded from their IoT devices available into a human-readable form. The students had to show that their prototypes were connected to the Internet and that data they produced was stored in a cloud service.

3.1.5 Week 7: Wrap-up

A course wrap-up meeting was arranged on July 14th, where the students demonstrated their project deliverables. Having learned about IoT technologies and seeing the solutions of others, the students were able to compare differences of technologies and to contemplate on how choosing an another microcontroller environment could possibly have changed their workflow. As their last milestone, students were expected to document their project outcomes and reflect on their learning in the course blog.

3.2 Learning Objectives and Assessment

As is normal for problem-based learning, the learning objectives of the course were not stated at the start of the course. However, it was determined beforehand by the course instructors that students should learn IoT concepts, learn how their skills can be used in places where one does not typically think about it, and that the students should also be able to design and develop a small solution that helps the greenhouse management at least in some fashion. No restrictions were put on how students approached the problem, outside the rough course schedule that was outlined in the previous section; students were naturally encouraged to collaborate as well as help each other.

The course was graded pass/fail. In order to pass, students had to pass three milestones (weeks 1, 2 and 7), demonstrate their solution that consisted of a working hardware prototype and source code, and provide the sources to their project via a version control system (in our case, GitHub[1]). The assessment approach was chosen due to the variety of different paths that students could take as well as due to the open-ended nature of the project.

3.3 Resources and Budget

While no fixed cost budget was set up for the course, resources were very limited and thus inexpensive microcontroller platforms such as the Arduino[2], Raspberry Pi[3], Electric IMP[4], and Intel Galileo[5] were preferred over out-of-the box, programmable smart greenhouse devices that were available on the market. However this did not limit the students. Even though they could design their hardware architecture quite freely, the total cost of the course was approximately 500 US dollars. For application development and data storage, students used cloud-based service providers that offered free access for small-scale developers[6,7]. Table 1 summarizes the types and cost of components that were used in individual projects.

---

[1]http://github.com

[2]http://www.arduino.cc

[3]http://www.raspberrypi.org

[4]http://www.electricimp.com

[5]http://arduino.cc/en/ArduinoCertified/IntelGalileo

[6]http://www.heroku.com

[7]http://www.firebase.com

Table 1: The overall cost of the projects.

Item	Cost
Project 1: Visualization	
Arduino Duemilanove	$20
DHT-11 temperature humidity Sensor	$5
	$25
Project 2: Humidity A	
Arduino Uno	$25
SeedStudio Grove - Moisture Sensor	$5
Simple photoresistor	$0
Actuators: buzzer, RGB LED	$5
	$35
Project 3: Humidity B	
Electric Imp and breakout board	$45
SeedStudio Grove - Moisture Sensor	$5
SeedStudio Soil Moisture and Temp. Sensor	$40
	$90
Project 4: Temperature	
Intel Galileo	$100
DS18B20 temperature sensors + cables	$55
	$155
Project 5: Air Flow	
Arduino Uno	$25
Computer case fans	$5
Power source 12v	$5
Prototyping breadboards	$10
Misc. electronics(resistors, transistors)	$5
	$50
Project 6: Hydroponics	
Arduino YÚN	$75
Stackable PCB headers	$2
Seedstudio One Wire Temperature Sensors	$12
Seedstudio Grove - UV Sensor	$10
Seedstudio Grove Base Shield	$18
Grove humidity and temperatur pro sensors	$15
Grove air quality sensor	$10
	$143
Project 7: Visitors	
Raspberry Pi with WiFi dongle	$50
Raspberry Pi Board For NFC-Tags	$40
MiFare Classic NFC Keychain Fobs	$13
	$103
Total	$510

3.4 Student projects

In this chapter, we give an overview of the student projects. The examples are expected to provide an authentic and practical representation on both the scale and scope of the experiment.

3.4.1 *Visualization (1)*

To be able to support the work of gardeners, all projects were required to have a human readable user interface. This was first achieved by project 1 in which the student composed a web application that allowed pushing data from any

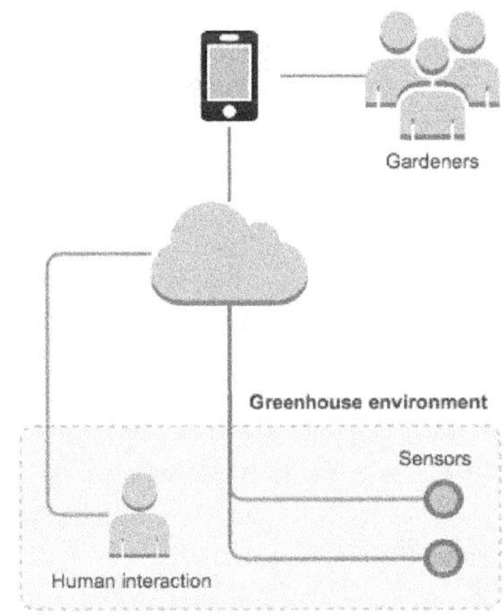

Figure 1: High level architecture of the Greenhouse Care project.

IoT device into a cloud-based storage and provided a chart representation. Other projects utilized this application for either visualizing their own data or yielding data for their own purposes. The few students that did not, created their own user interfaces for displaying their data according to their own plans.

3.4.2 *Humidity (2,3)*

The most recurring greenhouse care task is to check for humidity of soil and add water and fertilizer if needed. Two student projects (2,3) approached facilitating this task by creating independent solutions for sensing humidity inside a planting container. The main emphasis of the first project was on interacting with people and creating alarms to indicate when it was time to add water the soil. The other product focused on product innovation: how a "smart flowerpot" could be transformed into a commercial product.

3.4.3 *Temperature and air (4,5)*

At times a space heater was needed to heat the greenhouse. While the greenhouse was custom-built from inexpensive components, its ventilation was compromised and heat distributed unevenly. The "Temperature" project (4) concentrated on monitoring six different parts of the greenhouse with air temperature sensors and the "Air Flow" project (5) utilized this data to help circulate heat more evenly within the greenhouse.

3.4.4 *Hydroponics (6)*

One of the installments in the greenhouse was a tank where plants were grown in nutrient solution, without using soil. The system was not working correctly, leading to plants dying after a few weeks of their installation. One student aimed at building a measurement device for this small-scale ecosystem. The solution consisted of an imaginative amount of sensors that could be used for measuring both air and water quality.

3.4.5 *Visitors (7)*

The question "Has anybody visited the greenhouse?" was one of the most common phrases in the communication of the caretaker team. Therefore, a status reporting device was created, allowing visitors to the greenhouse to flash Near Communication Field (NFC) enabled keychains to a reader located inside the greenhouse. A requirement for the system was that it should be usable with wet and dirty hands.

4. DISCUSSION

After the initial problem-based learning phase, students were given the freedom to choose their own project topic and scope. In this section we first reflect on how this freedom affected solution architecture design and consequently, the course budget. Finally, we contemplate the expectations and learning outcomes of both students and course personnel.

4.1 Budget Guidance

During the first meeting the instructors suggested microcontroller platforms that could be chosen as a starting point for projects. We did not communicate how much each individual project should cost and emphasized that the options were not limited to the suggested technologies. Participants became inspired by the possibilities. Some envisioned concepts that were impossible to implement within the timeframe and some requested high-cost, professional sensors.

The people who were guided to cut back their plans, naturally, expressed their disappointment. However, the negative emotions subsided after they received the more affordable hardware components we had helped them to choose. We believe that if a finite cost limit would have been given for each student project, it might have helped to mitigate the initial plans. However, having a fixed budget might have led to less inspired plans and at worst, students trying to fill up their budgets with components that they might not have a need in the end.

4.2 Grading the Individual Learning Process

After students had completed their demos, the instructors reviewed the projects and gave students a simple pass or fail grade. In this section, we present the highlights of each student's learning pathways. Table 2 summarizes learning themes the instructors identified each student had touched with while their project work.

Table 2: The learning theme matrix.

	P1	P2	P3	P4	P5	P6	P7
Hardware							
Microcontroller technology				•	•	•	
Sensor technology		•			•	•	
Hardware integration		•			•		
Physical design (3d)		•					
Testing					•		
Software							
Web application development	•		•				•
Microcontroller programming	•	•	•		•	•	•
Software integration	•	•		•	•	•	
Other							
Product development			•				
Group work	•	•			•	•	

4.2.1 *Project 1: Visualization*

Both IoT technologies and web applications were a part of this student's professional career. He was very active and took a central role in the project and offered his work for others to use, too.

4.2.2 *Project 2: Humidity A*

This student had done some microcontroller-based projects before the course. In this project, he struggled with hardware organization and thus learned about physical design. The merit of his work was that the result was strongly connected to human interaction and solving a concrete problem.

4.2.3 *Project 3: Humidity B*

This team consisted of two students who chose a streamlined technology, making their solution almost effortless to compose. The merit of their result was in their ability to see their result as a commercial product for the near future development of which they had a clear plan. They never seemed to leave their comfort zone to learn about the IoT technology itself.

4.2.4 *Project 4: Temperatures*

This student had excellent background knowledge in IoT technologies. His output was not a learning experience, but proof of learning that had happened before the course. He worked very independently, without much communication with others.

4.2.5 *Project 5: Air Flow*

The student was very eager to learn new things and progressed through trial and error. Even though many of his plans were never realized, he retained his enthusiasm and presented a wide array of new knowledge.

4.2.6 *Project 6: Hydroponics*

The student eagerly pulled together a meritious sensor system with many hardware components. However, it remained unclear whether he had understood the purpose of his system, and its relation to its users.

4.2.7 *Project 7: Visitors*

This student had no prior experience with microcontrollers. He was very active in the design stage of his system and showed understanding of the requirements engineering process. When it was time for implementation, he isolated himself and was absent a lot. The resulting system was designed to fulfill a clear purpose and was technologically sound.

4.3 Unexpected learning outcomes

For the whole duration of the course, students were participating in the greenhouse caretaker team's online chat. The encounters encounters led to discussions on what type of knowledge would be useful for facilitating the team's work. They also created new knowledge for the maintenance team on how their inter-person collaboration could be facilitated.

Contrary to our expectations, we quickly observed that prototyping simple ideas using microcontrollers and connecting them to the internet was easy for the participants. As devices were built and left running for a time, we discovered that the microcontrollers used plenty of electricity considering their size and functionality. Even the simplest prototype measuring the level of lighting of a room emptied its batteries in a few days. This led us to discussions on energy efficiency and the carbon footprint of the devices that we use in everyday life. The students explored various optimization strategies such as disconnecting the components from the internet for longer periods and activating components only when needed. While doing so, they also learned to consider issues such as measurement accuracy. These topics were new to both students and the course staff.

At the wrap-up meeting, the students were expected to present their projects. As some students were absent, they were allowed to present their work to a course instructor separately. Those that were not able to attend the get-together, missed a great peer-to-peer discussion while participants compared their solutions that shared a similar purpose, but were built on very different technologies. As one of the students put it:

> *During the demo session, I understood how different the solutions were both from the hardware- and software-perspective. I would not have been able to compare technologies without my own project, as my knowledge was not at a level that I could have talked about it in a meaningful way.*

5. CONCLUSIONS

In this article, we have described an experimental low-cost course where students develop Internet of Things applications for improving the maintenance of a greenhouse. The course was organized in two phases. First, a problem-based learning approach was used to learn about the environment, identify problems and to come up with solutions for improving them. In the second phase, the students worked on projects, where these solution ideas were made real. The outcome of this project contrasted the wide array of possibilities that blending problem- and project-based learning approaches can provide for students and teachers.

None of the course instructors and students had previous experience of maintaining a greenhouse. Overall, the experience did not only teach students about technical aspects that were related to the Internet of Things, but also provided viewpoints on urban sustainability and Green ICT. The project also demonstrated to the department that the organization of such loosely defined projects with little predefined hardware and a relatively small budget can provide both a successful and valuable learning experience. Both the gardeners and the students in the course gained experiences that are likely to benefit their future, many of them praising the course as an eye-opening experience. Due to the success and demand of the course, we are planning to repeat the course in the future, and will especially focus on approaches for introducing the course to students who are at an earlier stage in their studies.

6. REFERENCES

[1] L. Atzori, A. Iera, and G. Morabito. The internet of things: A survey. *Computer networks*, 54(15):2787–2805, 2010.

[2] B. J. Barron, D. L. Schwartz, N. J. Vye, A. Moore, A. Petrosino, L. Zech, and J. D. Bransford. Doing with understanding: Lessons from research on problem-and project-based learning. *Journal of the Learning Sciences*, 7(3-4):271–311, 1998.

[3] H. S. Barrows. Problem-based learning in medicine and beyond: A brief overview. *New Directions for Teaching and Learning*, 1996(68):3–12, 1996.

[4] M. Ben-Ari. Constructivism in computer science education. *Journal of Computers in Mathematics and Science Teaching*, 20(1):45–73, 2001.

[5] P. C. Blumenfeld, E. Soloway, R. W. Marx, J. S. Krajcik, M. Guzdial, and A. Palincsar. Motivating project-based learning: Sustaining the doing, supporting the learning. *Educational psychologist*, 26(3-4):369–398, 1991.

[6] V. Callaghan. Buzz-Boarding; practical support for teaching computing based on the internet-of-things. 2012.

[7] J. Dewey. *The School and the Society: Rev. Ed.* University of Chicago Press, 1967.

[8] R. Driver and B. Bell. Students' thinking and the learning of science: A constructivist view. *School science review*, 67(240):443–56, 1986.

[9] Ericsson. More than 50 Billion Connected Devices - Taking Connected Devices to Mass Market and Profitability. White paper 284 23-3149 Uen, 2011.

[10] K. A. Frenkel. Computer science meets environmental science. *Commun. ACM*, 52(9):23–23, Sept. 2009.

[11] A. Galloway. Intimations of everyday life: Ubiquitous computing and the city. *Cultural Studies*, 18(2-3):384–408, 2004.

[12] T. Greening. Emerging constructivist forces in computer science education: Shaping a new future? In *Computer science education in the 21st century*, pages 47–80. Springer, 2000.

[13] G. Kortuem, A. K. Bandara, N. Smith, M. Richards, and M. Petre. Educating the internet-of-things generation. *Computer*, 46(2):53–61, 2013.

[14] M. Kranz, P. Holleis, and A. Schmidt. Embedded interaction: Interacting with the internet of things. *Internet Computing, IEEE*, 14(2):46–53, 2010.

[15] G. R. Norman and H. G. Schmidt. The psychological basis of problem-based learning: a review of the evidence. *Academic medicine*, 67(9):557–65, 1992.

[16] A.-C. J. T. F. on Computing Curricula. Computer science curricula 2013. Technical report, ACM Press and IEEE Computer Society Press, December 2013.

[17] E. Osipov and L. Riliskis. Educating innovators of future internet of things. In *Frontiers in Education Conference, 2013 IEEE*, pages 1352–1358. IEEE, 2013.

[18] M. Pervilä, L. Remes, and J. Kangasharju. Harvesting heat in an urban greenhouse. In *ACM SIGMETRICS Performance Evaluation Review*, volume 41, pages 95–97, 2013.

[19] M. Prince and R. Felder. Inductive teaching and learning methods: Definitions, comparisons, and research bases. *Journal of engineering education*, 95(2):123–138, 2006.

[20] M. Resnick, J. Maloney, A. Monroy-Hernández, N. Rusk, E. Eastmond, K. Brennan, A. Millner, E. Rosenbaum, J. Silver, B. Silverman, et al. Scratch: programming for all. *Communications of the ACM*, 52(11):60–67, 2009.

[21] J. W. Thomas. A review of research on project-based learning. 2000.

Can the Security Mindset Make Students Better Testers? *

Sara Hooshangi
The George Washington University
Washington, DC 20052 U.S.A.
shoosh@gwu.edu

Richard Weiss
The Evergreen State College
Olympia, WA 98505 U.S.A.
weissr@evergreen.edu

Justin Cappos
New York University
Brooklyn, NY 11201, U.S.A.
jcappos@nyu.edu

ABSTRACT

Writing secure code requires a programmer to think both as a defender and an attacker. One can draw a parallel between this model of thinking and techniques used in test-driven development, where students learn by thinking about how to effectively test their code and anticipate possible bugs. In this study, we analyzed the quality of both attack and defense code that students wrote for an assignment given in an introductory security class of 75 (both graduate and senior undergraduate levels) at NYU. We made several observations regarding students' behaviors and the quality of both their defensive and offensive code. We saw that student defensive programs (i.e., assignments) are highly unique and that their attack programs (i.e., test cases) are also relatively unique. In addition, we examined how student behaviors in writing defense programs correlated with their attack program's effectiveness. We found evidence that students who learn to write good defensive programs can write effective attack programs, but the converse is not true. While further exploration of causality is needed, our results indicate that a greater pedagogical emphasis on defensive security may benefit students more than one that emphasizes offense.

Categories and Subject Descriptors

K.3.2 [**Computer and Information Science Education**]: Computer science education; K.6.5 [**Security and Protection**]: Unauthorized access; D.2.5 [**Software Engineering**]: Testing and Debugging

General Terms

Security, Experimentation, Measurement

*This work was partially supported by NSF grants 1141341, 1223588, 1205415, 1241568 and 1241653.

SIGCSE'15, March 4-7, 2015, Kansas City, MO, USA.

ACM 978-1-4503-2966-8/15/03 ...$15.00.
http://dx.doi.org/10.1145/2676723.2677268

Keywords

Security; Python; Access Control; Testing

1. INTRODUCTION

Testing is an integral part of any real-world software development process. As such, software testing has become an integral part of computer science (CS) curricula in recent years [14, 4]. Researchers have extensively examined students' test-writing skills [16, 19, 7] and the primary focus has been on quantifying the quality of students' test codes, measuring their bug-revealing capabilities, and developing techniques to assess student-written software tests. Secure coding and software security testing, on the other hand, are relatively recent areas of exploration within the pedagogical community. In the wake of an increasing number of security breaches caused by software vulnerabilities, it has become essential that tomorrow's developers acquire crucial skills of writing secure code and developing software packages that can withstand malicious attacks.

In order to write secure code, students must learn how to think about system failure and software vulnerability, by developing what is often called a security mindset. They must learn how to think as an attacker and find ways to circumvent and exploit code flaws. In such a scenario, the program under attack is considered a *defense program* and the test case that is trying to break or exploit the defense program is an *attack program.* Writing programs that can defend against an attacker is at least as difficult as writing reliable programs. Acquiring the mindset to foresee potential vulnerabilities in a program is a valuable skill for students to learn.

We anticipate that including software security testing techniques as part of the typical software testing exercises used in CS classrooms will expand students' programming toolset and make them better equipped to tackle programming tasks. Software tests look for bugs that produce errors despite plausible input, whereas an attack program can trigger bugs with any possible input. A student who is able to write both defensive and attack programs is already thinking about ways to exploit vulnerabilities and ways to protect against possible breaches. Our study suggests that this more holistic approach may enhance students' programming skills and help them become more proficient in finding flaws in their own programs. The recent addition of IAS (Information Assurance and Security) to ACM/IEEE Computer Science Curricula 2013 [3] is a good starting point, but faculty need more examples of how to integrate these topics into their existing curriculum.

To test our hypothesis and to examine the overall effect of employing a security mindset approach in teaching CS, we examined students' abilities in writing both defensive and offensive programs, using a set of publicly available programming assignments [2]. Our study focused on both the quality of students' defense and attack programs, and the correlation between the two, in the context of a security assignment. Thus, we investigated more than traditional test-writing skills and quality of student-written tests. Specifically, students were first asked to write a defense program. After this, they were asked to write attack programs that would find a comprehensive set of bugs (including performance bugs and security related bugs) in the defense programs of all students in the class.

Using common techniques employed by the pedagogical community, such as the 'all-pair method ' [10, 9, 7], we explored students' ability to write resilient defensive programs, effective attack programs, and the relationship between the two skills. We observed the effectiveness of the security mindset approach on the overall performance of our students. Although some of our findings only reinforce what has already been shown by others in the context of students' test-writing skills, some of our results are unique to our experiment. Specifically, we observed the following outcomes using this particular attack-defense assignment, administrated to 75 students in a single class.

- In general, students wrote unique defense and attack programs.
- The number of attacks correlated with the quality of attacks. Thus, students who wrote more attack programs generally had more effective attacks.
- Some skills were indicative of students possessing other skills. For example, knowledge of how to scope variables appropriately correlated with the ability to write relatively bug free programs.
- Students who wrote good defense programs also wrote good attack programs. However writing good attack programs did not correlate with writing good defense programs.
- Students who could subsequently attack their own defense programs had written poor defensive programs.

In Section 2, we explain how our work relates to previous work on the pedagogy of testing. In Section 3, we describe the assignment, the class in which it was used, and how the data were collected. In Section 4, we present an analysis of our data and provide conclusions we draw from that data.

2. RELATED WORK

Over the past two decades, many CS educators have advocated for the integration of software testing into the CS curriculum [18, 11, 15]. Different strategies have been proposed for introducing software testing early on in undergraduate programs [13, 16, 10, 5, 17, 9]. Although introducing students to software testing is now common practice, assessing the quality of student-written tests has been a harder problem to address. The use of automated assessment tools [12, 5, 20, 6] and mutation analysis techniques [1, 19] have been examined as a way to assess the quality of student written tests. Most of these techniques measure 'code coverage ability' of student-written tests, but recent work has shown that such tools might produce an overestimation of student-written test quality [7].

Some have suggested that the quality of a test can be assessed by its ability to detect bugs or faults in a software program rather than by looking at its coverage of execution paths [7]. One technique for measuring the quality of testing is the 'all-pairs' technique proposed by Goldwasser in 2002 [10] and further developed by Edwards et al. [9, 7]. Using this approach, all student tests are run against all student programs.

How well do student written tests find significant bugs? Researchers have reported that students' tests are not high quality and that there is a large degree of similarity among student-written test programs. Moreover, most students are only able to find a small portion of bugs in a given program. Happy path testing–writing tests for typical scenarios–has been targeted as one reason that student-written tests tend to be quite similar [8].

3. PRELIMINARIES

3.1 The Assignment

Our observations in this paper are based on a two-part assignment [2] about access control *defense monitors*. A defense monitor, which runs as a user program, is similar to a reference monitor, which is an abstract machine that mediates all access to objects by subjects. Defense monitors can be used to allow, deny, or change the behavior of any set of calls. One critical aspect in creating a defense monitor is ensuring that it cannot be bypassed. This is one of the central concepts of computer security; successfully creating secure code requires a security mindset.

The assignment was given to students in two separate parts. In Part 1, students were asked to create a defense monitor to stop a user from reading data, writing over existing data, or writing new data to the end of a file if there was no permission to do so. This was more fine-grained than the usual Linux permissions. Students implemented five functions, as described in Table 1.

Function	Description
setread	Enable or disable reading from the file
setwrite	Enable or disable writing to the file
setappend	Enable or disable appending to the file
readat	Read data from the file if read permission is on
writeat	Overwrite existing data if write permission is on

Table 1: Summary of functions used in this assignment

In the assignment scenario, a user might have all, some, or none of the permissions enabled at any given time. By default, these permissions would be disabled. The readat function would allow the user to read data from the file if and only if the user has read permissions. The writeat function would allow the user to overwrite existing data if and only if write permissions are enabled. Similarly, the user could append new data to the file if and only if append permissions were enabled. Attempts to overwrite or append data when the user does not have permissions to do so would result in nothing being written. The assignment provided students with an experience of thinking as a defender and reinforced concepts of how to build a secure system.

Figure 1 shows a code snippet from the [inadequate] defense monitor that was provided to the students.

```
def setread(self,enabled):
    mycontext['read'] = enabled

def readat(self,bytes,offset):
    if not mycontext['read']:
      raise ValueError
    return self.file.readat(bytes,offset)
```

Figure 1: An excerpt from the example (inadequate) defensive program students were given.

Students were asked to adhere to three design criteria when writing their defense monitor programs:

- Precision: The security layer should only stop certain actions from being blocked. All other actions should be allowed even when combined with blocked actions. For example, if a user tries to overwrite data and append new data in the same write, and has permissions to write, but not append, then the write should succeed and the append should fail. Thus, data would be overwritten up to the end of the file, but nothing would be appended.

- Efficiency: The security layer should use a minimum number of resources so that performance is not compromised. The code should also avoid actions such as re-reading a file before each write.

- Security: The attacker should not be able to circumvent the security layer. Hence, if any data can be written without the corresponding permission, security will be compromised.

In Part 2, each student wrote one or more attack programs to circumvent the defense monitors written by others in Part 1. The second part of the assignment was not given until after all students had submitted their defense monitors, which were then made available to the entire class. This allowed students to view security from an attacker's standpoint and to think about how to trigger failures. A complete module write-up for each part, with detailed instructions (and instructor-only solutions), is available publicly online from the assignment creators [2].

3.2 The Population

This assignment has been used in a dozen classes at four different institutions. For this study, we selected the class with the largest number of students. In Fall 2013, 75 students completed the assignment described above for an 'Introduction to Security' course at NYU. This course is a senior/first-year graduate level class designed for Computer Science BS / MS students and also for Cybersecurity MS students. All programs were written in a subset of Python [2]. The students were given one week to complete each part. In order to make the assignments easier to complete, especially for students with no experience with Python, we gave the students a template for a simple defense monitor that inadequately checks for a desired security property. Students submitted their defense monitors to complete Part 1 of the assignment. Each student submitted one monitor and we received a total of 75 monitors. To ensure that student monitors were free of syntax errors, all monitors were run against an instructor-written attack test to check for validity. A total of 61 working, error-free monitors were identified. Students were strongly warned about consequences of cheating and all submitted programs were checked for evidence of cheating by examining code similarity as well as behavioral similarity. We removed student assignments that showed evidence of cheating, but we cannot be certain we caught all instances.

After students completed the defensive assignment (Part 1), they were given a copy of all the students' defensive programs and told to write attack programs that would bypass as many defense programs as possible (constituting Part 2 of the assignment). Students were encouraged to write each attack case as a separate file because any test that produced incorrect results for an instructor-written defense monitor would be discarded entirely. A total of 444 attack test files were submitted. The attack programs were first run against the instructor-written defense monitor to remove incorrect attacks. All of the attack programs that printed that they bypassed the instructor's defense monitor were manually inspected and none were found to be correct. 68 students produced viable attacks and a total of 325 viable attack files were found. The number of attack files submitted by each student varied from 1 to 14, with a median of 5. After careful examination of the attack files, it was determined that 28 files were identical to the sample attack file that the instructor had given the students as a guide.

4. RESULTS AND ANALYSIS

To analyze students' ability to attack and defend, we used an 'all-pairs testing' strategy that has been shown to be effective [10, 19, 9]. Our automated script ran each attack test file against each defense monitor, for a total of 19,825 trials. An attack test was flagged as being successful for a specific instance if the attack test was able to cause an error in the defense monitor or to bypass its defense. The outcome of each instance was recorded in a 2D matrix, which helped us keep track of all attack/defense pairs. Below we describe our findings and data analysis.

4.1 Were Student Submissions Unique?

The first area we explored was whether or not student submissions were primarily unique or similar to others. For example, did many students write defensive programs that had the same flaws? Did submitted attack programs effectively test the same flaws?

Methodology. To examine the variations in students programs, we first looked for uniqueness in individual attack tests. Two tests were considered different if there was at least one defense monitor for which they gave different results.

We observed that there were 150 unique tests; they had an attack that differed from every other attack on at least one monitor. We also looked at individual students' work and observed that 47 students (out of 68) had produced a testing pattern that was different from the rest of the class. These results show that variations exist both in the individual programs and the collected test functionality provided by a student's attack programs. We also analyzed similarities across the defense monitors. Two monitors were considered different if they behaved differently in response to at least one student attack test. In the 61 working monitors submitted, 49 produced unique responses to the student attacks.

Conclusion. *We find that student submissions for defenses have a high degree of uniqueness*, with about 80% being unique. This shows that secure coding is a complex problem and different students find different solutions.

However, we found that just over half (51%) of the attack programs were unique. We think the reason for a lower number of unique test cases was due to two factors. First, students were encouraged to submit individual, separate tests for small cases. Thus, many students may have decided to just submit the same basic test provided by the instructor. (In fact, dozens of students submitted one of the trivial example programs we had provided on the assignment sheet.) Second, there were many more attack programs than defense monitors, with most students (90%) submitting multiple attack programs. Since there were 325 attack programs, there was a higher chance of non-uniqueness. We note that 78% of all students had at least one unique test in their submissions. These factors are evidence that *attack programs submitted by students are also very unique.*

4.2 Do Multiple Attacks Benefit Performance?

Given that most students wrote several unique attack programs, it is natural to ask what we can learn from their submissions. We investigated to see if there was a common pattern that would suggest which students benefitted from multiple attack submissions and which ones did not. We also explored the more specific question of whether the total number of submissions was correlated with attack effectiveness.

Methodology. To examine the possible benefit of writing multiple attack cases, we first measured the quality of student attacks by defining a Student Attack Quality (SAQ score) as a student's overall ability to attack all monitors. For students who submitted more than one attack file, a student's effort was considered a successful attack against a monitor if at least one of her/his attack files was able to break that particular monitor. The overall SAQ score for the student was then calculated as the sum of all successful attacks divided by the total number of monitors. Using this data, we were able to look at whether students who wrote more tests did better. Figure 2 summarizes, in one graph, the results of our analysis. In this graph, students are sorted according to the number of tests that they wrote (secondary y-axis), and within each category students are sorted according to their overall SAQ score (primary y-axis). We can see that there was a wide range in SAQ scores–from 23% to 92%. This shows a wide range in testing skills and strategies. Also, students who wrote between four and six tests had the highest overall SAQ scores. We found that there was a weak correlation between the number of tests and SAQ score (correlation of r = 0.63, data not shown).

We next looked at how individual tests contributed to a student's overall SAQ score. We wanted to know whether students partitioned the attack space into equal parts and wrote an attack for each part or whether they had one attack

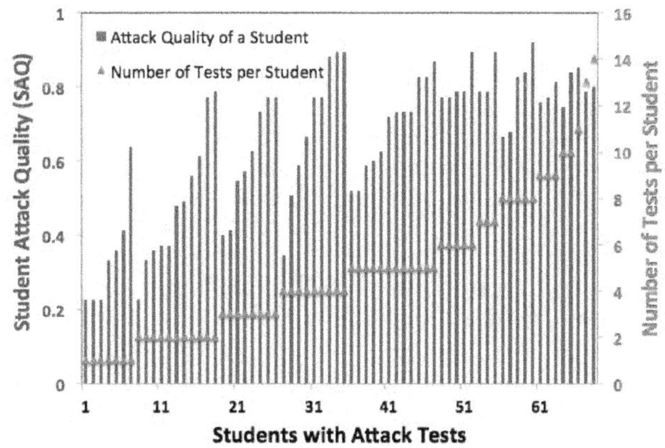

Figure 2: Students' quality of attack versus number of tests submitted. X-axis represents students who submitted at least one attack program. Left y-axis represents the SAQ score for each student and the right y-axis represents the number of tests submitted by each student.

script that accounted for most of their total, but added additional scripts that played only a minor role. This analysis is captured in Figure 3, which compares a student's overall SAQ score with the maximum score for a single script for that particular student.

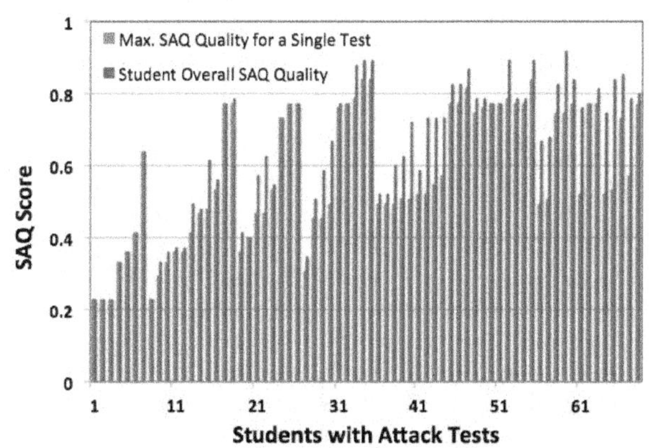

Figure 3: The benefit of having multiple attack tests. The overall SAQ score (blue bar) and max SAQ scores on a single test (red bar) are plotted for all 68 students. Students are sorted on the x-axis by the number of tests per student.

Conclusion. We can see from Figure 3 that the maximum score is usually very close to the overall score, suggesting that students wrote one script that accounted for most of their points. At first glance, this seems to be at odds with the first result that students who wrote more tests did better. However, there are two different types of attacks that students wrote: those that focused on specific types of errors, and those that focused on a particular feature or capability addressed by the monitor. The former turned out to be much more powerful for finding vulnerabilities. For example, if the monitor made the implicit assumption that only one file would be open at a time, it was very likely to have a bug that would be triggered by opening multiple files. Writing an attack script to trigger this bug worked for a large number of monitors. It seems that students who had this realization were also thorough and checked several features of the monitor, e.g., whether it handled read permissions correctly, whether it handled write permissions correctly, etc.

4.3 What Accounts For The Difference Between Max and Overall SAQ?

We explored the source of the differential between maximum (max) and overall SAQ scores in student attacks. We first studied whether the diversity of attack programs might contribute to students' low differential between max and overall SAQ scores before zeroing in on a primary reason.

Methodology. The class instructor looked through the attacks written by the 10 students with the highest difference between their max and overall SAQ scores (and thus benefited the most from additional tests) and the 10 students who had the lowest difference between their max and overall SAQ (who received no benefit from additional tests). Without knowing which were which, the instructor tried to rate the level of diversity in the student attack programs. For example, submitted attack programs that used different calls/permissions patterns were considered diverse because they would be likely to touch different code paths in defense monitors. (The detailed results of this categorization are omitted for space reasons.) 18 of the submissions were rated to have a reasonable degree of diversity (all 10 with the highest differential were in this category.)

Conclusion. Students who did well wrote diverse tests (as one may expect). However, many students who exhibited no benefit from any additional tests also wrote diverse tests. We concluded that *diversity was not sufficient to determine whether additional attacks were useful.*

With further investigation, we identified the main contributing factor to be when a student wrote a multi-file attack program and did not generate other attacks of high quality. In our data set, some students wrote a defense monitor that incorrectly placed information about permissions in the global scope instead of treating them as a per-file property. In our pool of student defenses, those defenses that did correctly scope the permissions data to a file instance also did not contain simple mistakes in the monitor. Thus *the understanding of how to appropriately scope variables was an indicator of student ability to write reasonably error free code for the remainder of the assignment.*

4.4 Are Attack/Defense Abilities Correlated?

Another question to emerge from our work is to what extent attack and defense abilities are correlated. For example, does skill in one indicate skill in the other?

Methodology.

We compared attack ability with student defense ability. We first defined Defense against Attack Quality (DAQ score) as the measure of a defense monitor's resistance against students' attack programs. The DAQ score for a defense monitor was calculated as the ratio of the number of students who were not successful in attacking a particular monitor divided by the total number of students who had viable attack programs (68 in our case). The SAQ scores were then plotted against DAQ scores, as shown in Figure 4. We labeled the student points on this graph based upon whether the student submitted an attack that could bypass their own defense monitor.

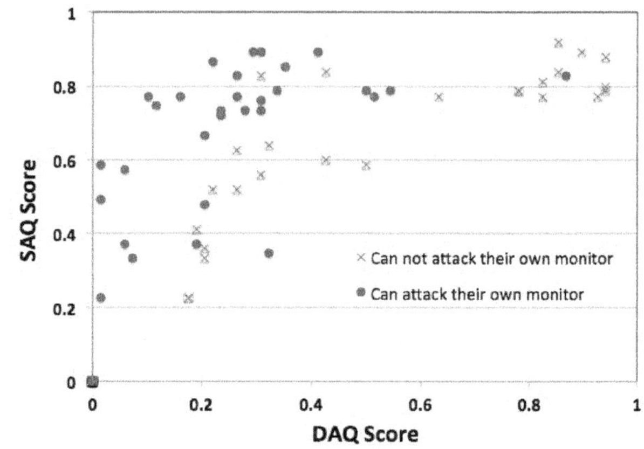

Figure 4: Quality of attack as a function of quality of defense. Blue circles indicate students who are able to break their own monitors and red x's indicate students who are not able to bypass their own monitors.

Conclusion. Our observations here bring us back to the security mindset to reveal something that was not clear at first. The security mindset requires the ability to trigger failure modes, but when it comes to secure coding, it also requires an ability to recognize and reflect on assumptions. There were a number of students who were able to attack other reference monitors, and they seem to have a part of the security mindset, but only some of them were able to draw on that mindset to write secure programs. Moreover, we saw that students who were able to attack their own defense monitors were the least skilled at applying the security mindset in general and that their attacks were also the weakest. A stronger measure of the security mindset is whether one can write secure code.

Our findings show that *students' defensive ability is indicative of their ability to attack.* Having the ability to defend entails being able to consider, and handle, possible attacks. However, *attack ability is not indicative of talent with defense.* Thus, a student may be a capable attacker, yet not be able to write defensive programs. We plan to further investigate this point in future work.

We also found that *students who were able to break their own defensive programs typically wrote very poor defensive programs.* One might be tempted to conclude that a student's ability to self-attack may serve as a meter of their abilities. However, since students are given each other's defensive programs to examine when writing attacks, their observations of other students' defensive programs may bias the findings.

5. CONCLUSIONS AND FUTURE WORK

We have examined the effect of teaching the security mindset by analyzing students' writing of attack and defense monitors. In our study, both students' defense and attack programs showed a high degree of uniqueness. This stands in contrast to observations that students tend to write test codes similar to their classmates when they are testing their own code. However, diversity alone does not guarantee attack test quality. In addition, we found that students who wrote good defense monitors also wrote good attack tests. These results suggest that the defense monitor exercise that we used, and similar strategies, could be useful in improving the quality of tests that students write. However, our experiments do not prove causation. In the future we would like to analyze whether there is a causal relationship. Another question that we would like to test using our quantitative framework is whether students who have written one defense monitor do better when writing another one that has significantly different content.

The assignment we used is not the only way to teach the security mindset, and that opens up the possibility that there may be other exercises that would improve testing and secure coding skills. In future work we intend to explore similar assignments in lower level classes. We also hope to perform a follow up study where we examine how student attack and defense abilities carry over in classes that specialize in these topics.

6. REFERENCES

[1] K. Aaltonen, P. Ihantola, and O. Seppälä. Mutation analysis vs. code coverage in automated assessment of students' testing skills. In *Proceedings of the ACM International Conference Companion on Object Oriented Programming Systems Languages and Applications Companion*, SPLASH '10, pages 153–160, New York, NY, USA, 2010. ACM.

[2] J. Cappos and R. Weiss. Teaching the security mindset with reference monitors. In *Proceedings of the 45th ACM Technical Symposium on Computer Science Education*, SIGCSE '14, pages 523–528, New York, NY, USA, 2014. ACM.

[3] Computer science curricula 2013. `http://www.acm.org/education/CS2013-final-report.pdf/`.

[4] C. Desai, D. S. Janzen, and J. Clements. Implications of integrating test-driven development into CS1/CS2 curricula. *SIGCSE Bull.*, 41(1):148–152, Mar. 2009.

[5] S. H. Edwards. Using software testing to move students from trial-and-error to reflection-in-action. In *Proceedings of the 35th SIGCSE Technical Symposium on Computer Science Education*, SIGCSE '04, pages 26–30, New York, NY, USA, 2004. ACM.

[6] S. H. Edwards and M. A. Pérez-Quiñones. Experiences using test-driven development with an automated grader. *J. Comput. Sci. Coll.*, 22(3):44–50, Jan. 2007.

[7] S. H. Edwards and Z. Shams. Comparing test quality measures for assessing student-written tests. In *Companion Proceedings of the 36th International Conference on Software Engineering*, ICSE Companion 2014, pages 354–363, New York, NY, USA, 2014. ACM.

[8] S. H. Edwards and Z. Shams. Do student programmers all tend to write the same software tests? In *Proceedings of the 2014 Conference on Innovation & Technology in Computer Science Education*, ITiCSE '14, pages 171–176, New York, NY, USA, 2014. ACM.

[9] S. H. Edwards, Z. Shams, M. Cogswell, and R. C. Senkbeil. Running students' software tests against each others' code: New life for an old 'gimmick'. In *Proceedings of the 43rd ACM Technical Symposium on Computer Science Education*, SIGCSE '12, pages 221–226, New York, NY, USA, 2012. ACM.

[10] M. H. Goldwasser. A gimmick to integrate software testing throughout the curriculum. *SIGCSE Bull.*, 34(1):271–275, Feb. 2002.

[11] T. B. Hilburn and M. Townhidnejad. Software quality: A curriculum postscript? *SIGCSE Bull.*, 32(1):167–171, Mar. 2000.

[12] D. Jackson and M. Usher. Grading student programs using assyst. *SIGCSE Bull.*, 29(1):335–339, Mar. 1997.

[13] U. Jackson, B. Z. Manaris, and R. A. McCauley. Strategies for effective integration of software engineering concepts and techniques into the undergraduate computer science curriculum. In *Proceedings of the Twenty-eighth SIGCSE Technical Symposium on Computer Science Education*, SIGCSE '97, pages 360–364, New York, NY, USA, 1997. ACM.

[14] D. S. Janzen and H. Saiedian. Test-driven learning: Intrinsic integration of testing into the CS/SE curriculum. *SIGCSE Bull.*, 38(1):254–258, Mar. 2006.

[15] E. L. Jones. Software testing in the computer science curriculum – a holistic approach. In *Proceedings of the Australasian Conference on Computing Education*, ACSE '00, pages 153–157, New York, NY, USA, 2000. ACM.

[16] E. L. Jones. Integrating testing into the curriculum-arsenic in small doses. *SIGCSE Bull.*, 33(1):337–341, Feb. 2001.

[17] W. Marrero and A. Settle. Testing first: Emphasizing testing in early programming courses. *SIGCSE Bull.*, 37(3):4–8, June 2005.

[18] R. McCauley and U. Jackson. Teaching software engineering early - experiences and results. In *Frontiers in Education Conference, 1998. FIE '98. 28th Annual*, volume 2, pages 800–804, Nov 1998.

[19] Z. Shams and S. H. Edwards. Toward practical mutation analysis for evaluating the quality of student-written software tests. In *Proceedings of the Ninth Annual International ACM Conference on International Computing Education Research*, ICER '13, pages 53–58, New York, NY, USA, 2013. ACM.

[20] J. Spacco and W. Pugh. Helping students appreciate test-driven development (tdd). In *Companion to the 21st ACM SIGPLAN Symposium on Object-oriented Programming Systems, Languages, and Applications*, OOPSLA '06, pages 907–913, New York, NY, USA, 2006. ACM.

An Empirical Study of Iterative Improvement in Programming Assignments

Raymond Pettit, John Homer, Roger Gee, and Adam Starbuck
School of Information Technology and Computing
Abilene Christian University
Abilene, TX, USA
{rsp05b, jdh08a, rpg11a, acs11e}@acu.edu

Susan Mengel
Department of Computer Science
Texas Tech University
Lubbock, TX, USA
susan.mengel@ttu.edu

ABSTRACT

As automated tools for grading programming assignments become more widely used, it is imperative that we better understand how students are utilizing them. Other researchers have provided helpful data on the role automated assessment tools (AATs) have played in the classroom. In order to investigate improved practices in using AATs for student learning, we sought to better understand *how* students iteratively modify their programs toward a solution by analyzing more than 45,000 student submissions over 7 semesters in an introductory (CS1) programming course. The resulting metrics allowed us to study what steps students took toward solutions for programming assignments. This paper considers the incremental changes students make and the correlating score between sequential submissions, measured by metrics including source lines of code, cyclomatic (McCabe) complexity, state space, and the 6 Halstead measures of complexity of the program. We demonstrate the value of throttling and show that generating software metrics for analysis can serve to help instructors better guide student learning.

Categories and Subject Descriptors

K.3.2 [Computers and Education]: Computers and Information Science Education – *computer science education, information systems education, self-assessment.*

General Terms

Experimentation

Keywords

computer science education; computer aided instruction; automated feedback; automated assessment tools

SIGCSE '15, March 4–7, 2015, Kansas City, MO, USA

ACM 978-1-4503-2966-8/15/03…$15.00
http://dx.doi.org/10.1145/2676723.2677279

1. INTRODUCTION

One challenge facing instructors of computer programming is identifying how students learn the material through hands-on practice that takes place beyond the instructor's observation, often outside the classroom.

A better understanding of how students iteratively modify their programs toward a solution can help us improve programming instruction over time. Examining a final submission can determine if a student eventually created a properly working program but does not indicate how efficiently or systematically he or she approached the problem.

This paper examines data collected from more than 45,000 student submissions over 7 semesters in an introductory (CS1) programming course. Each semester, we gave students 75 C++ programming assignments, increasing in difficulty over the course of the semester. Students submitted their work to an online system, Athene (created in-house), which stored, compiled, and ran each submission against a suite of specific test cases and carefully generated random test cases. The Athene system then automatically scored each submission, so students received feedback immediately. Programs that did not pass the entire test suite received either a compile error message or information about one or more failed test cases as feedback. For failed test cases, students received a report of their input, the expected output, and the actual output from their program. Students had the opportunity to modify and resubmit their program in an attempt to improve their grade. A student session consisted of all submissions by one student for a given problem. There was no limit on the number of submissions that a student could attempt until the deadline, although we experimented with "throttling," a technique that limited a student's attempted solutions within a rolling 15-minute time period. This paper also considers the effects of this throttling on submission behavior.

With this approach, we intend to encourage students to complete each assignment, overcoming early errors to eventually reach a final correct solution. Automated scoring is made possible by preprocessing and other source modifications, then compiling and linking with both standard and specialized libraries. The system scores student submissions by direct inspection of required features (such as functions) and validation of program output.

We look more closely at two key moments in each student session in order to see the amount of change and meaningful progress that takes place (1) between a student's first and second submissions and (2) between a student's first and last submissions. In our courses, 83% of student sessions reach a score of 100%.

2. RELATED WORK

Automated assessment tools (AAT) have been in use since 1960 [6]. Ala-Mutka [3], Douce [5], and Ihantola [7] all offer good reviews of the capabilities of tools that have come into existence since. Other relevant tools include ALOHA [1], Style++ [2], JUG [4], BlueJ [8], Autograder [9], ClockIt [10], Fitchfork [11], Mooshak [12], Bottlenose [13], AutoLep [14], and AutogradeMe [15]. We provide a more specific review of selected research below, as comparable examples of automated assessment tools (AATs) provide important context in considering our Athene AAT.

In June 2005, Kirsti M. Ala-Mutka surveyed a range of assessment tools available at that time, reviewing their abilities in dynamic testing to construct a secure running environment and check program functionality, efficiency, and student testing skills; and in static testing to check coding style and programming errors, collect software metrics, and assess design [3]. In September 2005, Christopher Douce, et al., provided a historical overview of the development of AATs and a survey of related research, concluding with a series of useful criteria for evaluating such tools, including whether the system "does what it is supposed to do," whether "it is liked by its users," and whether "it helps students become more proficient at programming" [5]. In 2010, Petri Ihantola, et al., followed up with a review of AAT development between 2006–2010, determining that the most significant differences among programs had to do with "how tests are defined, how resubmissions are handled, and how the security is guaranteed" [7].

Since the publication of these surveys, several key papers have devoted expanded attention to more recent programs. For example, Mark Sherman, et al., looked at the web-based Bottlenose framework and considered how students responded to instant automated feedback in contrast to time-delayed instructor feedback, finding that students made 50% more submissions per assignment when using the AAT. Sherman's article does not discuss final submission quality with or without the AAT, but does note the straightforward effect that with the AAT, students continue to modify and re-submit assignments, presumably in response to the system's feedback—an advantage in a course where they might otherwise submit several assignments before receiving instructor feedback [13]. The article does not go into detail regarding what Bottlenose assesses in providing feedback; for examples of how such programs work, we can look at papers including those from Manuel Rubio-Sánchez, et al. [12] and Tiantian Wang, et al. [14].

Rubio-Sánchez's group reviewed the widely available Mooshak system, using both qualitative and quantitative analysis to evaluate its effectiveness in student learning. Responding to earlier studies that had noted a negative correlation between the introduction of Mooshak and student drop-out rates, Rubio-Sánchez's group observed that those studies had not held other variables constant—in particular, the studies had changed teaching methodology simultaneously with introducing Mooshak. In their study, then, Rubio-Sánchez's group included both test and control groups in the form of courses with near-identical syllabi and teaching methodologies, some of which used Mooshak and some of which did not. Qualitatively, students self-reported appreciating instant feedback but had complaints about Mooshak specifically, because while it is effective in assessing whether a program has succeeded or failed, it does not provide feedback to help students make changes along the way. The Mooshak tool was originally created for use in programming contests and still lacks features present in many tools designed for use in courses. Holding other factors constant, Rubio-Sánchez's group did not find a statistical change in the dropout rate of courses using Mooshak.

In contrast, Wang's group wrote about AutoLEP, an AAT they developed at the Harbin Institute of Technology in Heilongjiang, China, which combines static analysis with dynamic testing to provide students with location-specific feedback on the syntactic, structural, and logical features in their programs. AutoLEP seems more like Bottlenose in allowing for feedback and multiple submissions, but with the apparent advantage of more precision due to its simultaneous static and dynamic feedback.

The issue of whether AATs ought to allow for multiple submissions comes up again in Vrada Pieterse's paper on the use of AATs—in particular, his group's Fitchfork software—in massive open online courses (MOOCs) that teach programming. Pieterse argues that throttling (limiting the number of submissions per assignment) is inappropriate in a MOOC environment in part because the open enrollment format means students are working voluntarily and should have the opportunity to use AATs for repeated revisions as needed to learn the material. A correlative argument, however, is that unlimited submissions carries a risk to the traditional, credit-based classroom where students may be more tempted to "game the system" in an attempt to get a desired grade rather than to master learning the material [11]. Such a conjecture corresponds to an observation by Ihantola's group, who write, "we believe that the very fact that the assessment is automatic is likely to change how some students approach the exercise. Knowingly submitting a weak or even incorrect solution that gets accepted by a machine is quite likely more socially acceptable than trying to cheat a person." Pieterse's paper, then, raises the challenge to AAT developers to consider an appropriate level of throttling for the system's target user environment.

Overall, these articles point to a series of features relevant in developing AATs, including secure running environments (sandboxes), static and dynamic testing, and resubmissions and throttling. In our Athene program, we chose to give students feedback primarily from dynamic testing while running static analysis later for examining its usefulness. We also implemented a throttling rule for several semesters to see how that changed student behavior.

3. METHODOLOGY

3.1 Population Characterization

We collected data from 290 students in a Programming I course over seven semesters. We taught the course using the C++ programming language. Our curriculum is a late objects curriculum and subject matter in the course is typical of a CS1 course, including input/output, basic data types, decision structures, repetition, functions, and arrays.

The course serves primarily as a first programming course required of Computer Science majors, but students also include majors in Engineering, Physics, Mathematics, Information Technology, and other related disciplines.

3.2 Description of Data Collected

Each semester, we give students 75 programming assignments for homework, most of which are completed outside of class. The data included in this paper comes from all 75 unique assignments.

The students receive their assignments through the Athene online automated system.

Figure 1 shows a representative assignment, typically assigned in the third week of a 15-week semester, shortly after introducing decision structures. In this case, students are assigned to write a console-based program that asks the user to enter 3 integers and returns the largest of the 3. The goal of this assignment is to give the students practice in using `if-else` statements. As with all Athene assignments, the student is given a problem description, along with at least 1 test case and the expected output for that test case.

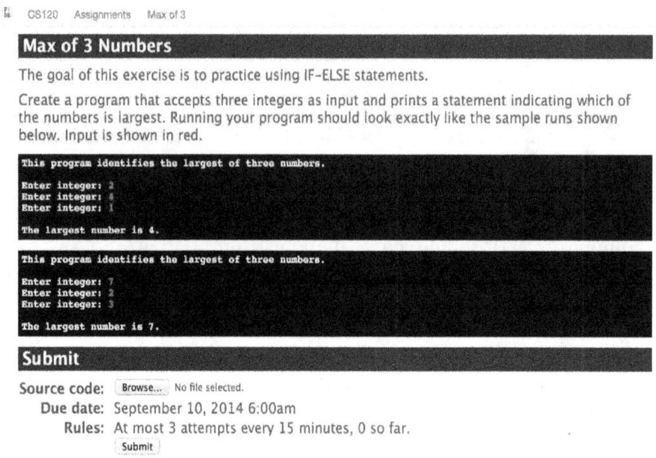

Figure 1. Representative assignment as it appears in the Athene online automated system.

For each assignment, a student writes a program and submits the source code to the Athene system, which checks grading and provides feedback. The student may re-submit a program repeatedly until he or she has successfully written the code.

After the student submits a source code file, the Athene system immediately compiles, runs, and tests the program against established test cases to provide a response. Figures 2 through 5 show a series of representative submissions and their corresponding feedback, all from the same student session in attempting to solve the assignment shown in Figure 1.

Each time a student submits an assignment, the automated system records the following information:

- user id
- filename of the submitted source code
- time/date of the submission
- full source code submitted
- score
- input and expected output for the first failed case
- actual output of the first failed test case

From the data that is stored in the submission database, we can later go back and analyze summary data of student behavior.

Examining the source code of a single submission, we calculate:

- the number of source lines of code (SLOC)
- the state space (number of unique variables)
- the cyclomatic (McCabe) complexity of the program
- the 6 Halstead measures of complexity of the program

We compute SLOC by counting all source lines, then deleting all blank lines and comment lines. We compute the McCabe complexity by adding the total number of branch possibilities (if, for, while, and case statements, adding in short-circuit analysis of boolean conditionals) to the total number of functions defined.

The 6 Halstead complexity measures are: Vocabulary, Length, Computed Length, Volume, Difficulty, and Effort. The Halstead numbers are computed by counting the number of unique and total operators and operands and using them in the appropriate Halstead formulas.

Figure 2 shows feedback given to a particular student after an early attempt at solving the assignment shown in Figure 1. This feedback is displayed almost instantaneously after the student submits a source code file. The top of the Athene page displays the student's ID, submission time, score achieved, course in which he or she was enrolled, and the assignment name. The middle section of the feedback page displays the first expected output line the student's submission failed to produce, followed by the actual output that the student's submission did produce. The bottom section of the feedback page shows the contents of the student's submitted source code file.

If we examine the source code, we can see that the student wrote a program that would perform correctly for both examples given in the problem description shown in Figure 1. But this student didn't consider different types of test cases, such as two of the three input numbers being the same value. So the submitted source file show in Figure 2 passed many of the test cases and was awarded a score of 64 (out of 100), but failed for the first time when the test input was `5 9 9`. The student received the feedback message, "`expected output: The largest number is 9`," and could then review to see that his or her actual output did not contain that statement.

Figure 3 shows the student's next attempt at the assignment. The student added some additional `if` statements to catch the test case he or she had just missed but still did not cover all possible test cases. [Also worth noting, the student should have corrected his or her existing `if` statements, instead of adding more of them. The Athene system did not provide feedback on this point.]

Figure 4 shows the student's third attempt at the assignment. The student once again added some additional `if` statements to catch the missed test case, but still did not cover all possible test cases. Because of the additional test cases passed, the student achieved a score of 88.

Figure 5 shows the student's fourth attempt at the assignment. To catch the test case in which all input numbers are the same value, the student added an additional `if` statement checking specifically for that case. With that addition, all test cases were successfully passed and the student received a score of 100, although the code is overly complex.

Reviewing this assignment and the given student's 4 submissions, we can see that the student eventually turned in a solution that produced the correct output but was not written to be efficient. The metrics for the source code from each of these submissions is shown in Table 1. Looking at metrics, specifically McCabe, can tell an instructor a great deal about the student's solution. For this assignment, the expected McCabe value is 7. The function counts for 1 and each `if` statement counts for 2, given the possibility of short circuit evaluation for each. When an instructor sees a McCabe value of 17 for this assignment, the instructor can recognize that the student has not created the expected solution.

User:
Time: 2013-02-11 22:13:11
Score: 64
Class: 1320_CS12001
Problem: 03-Max_of_3

expected output:

```
The largest number is 9.
```

actual output:

```
This program identifies the largest of three numbers.

Enter integer: 5
Enter integer: 9
Enter integer: 9
```

max3.cpp

```
#include <iostream>
using namespace std;

int main()
{

        int x, y, z;

        cout << "This program identifies the largest of three numbers." << endl << endl;

    cout << "Enter integer: ";
    cin >> x;
    cout << "Enter integer: ";
    cin >> y;
    cout << "Enter integer: ";
    cin >> z;
    cout << endl;

    if (x > y && x > z)
    {
        cout << "The largest number is " << x << ".";
    }
    else if (y > x && y > z)
    {
        cout << "The largest number is " << y << ".";

    }
    else if (z > x && z > y)
    {
        cout << "The largest number is " << z << ".";
    }
}
```

Figure 2. Representative first submission with Athene feedback.

User:
Time: 2013-02-11 22:22:29
Score: 76
Class: 1320_CS12001
Problem: 03-Max_of_3

expected output:

```
The largest number is 13.
```

actual output:

```
This program identifies the largest of three numbers.

Enter integer: 13
Enter integer: 13
Enter integer: 2
```

max3.cpp

```
#include <iostream>
using namespace std;

int main()
{

        int x, y, z;

        cout << "This program identifies the largest of three numbers." << endl << endl;

    cout << "Enter integer: ";
    cin >> x;
    cout << "Enter integer: ";
    cin >> y;
    cout << "Enter integer: ";
    cin >> z;
    cout << endl;

    if (x > y && x > z)
    {
        cout << "The largest number is " << x << ".";
    }
    else if (y > x && y > z)
    {
        cout << "The largest number is " << y << ".";

    }
    else if (z > x && z > y)
    {
        cout << "The largest number is " << z << ".";
    }
    if (x > y && x == z)
    {
        cout << "The largest number is " << x << ".";
    }
    else if (y > x && y == z)
    {
        cout << "The largest number is " << y << ".";

    }
    else if (z > x && z == y)
    {
        cout << "The largest number is " << z << ".";
    }
}
```

Figure 3. Representative second submission with Athene feedback.

User:
Time: 2013-02-11 22:27:00
Score: 88
Class: 1320_CS12001
Problem: 03-Max_of_3

expected output:

```
The largest number is 43.
```

actual output:

```
This program identifies the largest of three numbers.

Enter integer: 43
Enter integer: 43
Enter integer: 43
```

max3.cpp

```
#include <iostream>
using namespace std;

int main()
{

        int x, y, z;

        cout << "This program identifies the largest of three numbers." << endl << endl;

    cout << "Enter integer: ";
    cin >> x;
    cout << "Enter integer: ";
    cin >> y;
    cout << "Enter integer: ";
    cin >> z;
    cout << endl;

    if (x > y && x > z)
    {
        cout << "The largest number is " << x << ".";
    }
    else if (y > x && y > z)
    {
        cout << "The largest number is " << y << ".";

    }
    else if (z > x && z > y)
    {
        cout << "The largest number is " << z << ".";
    }
    if (x > y && x == z)
    {
        cout << "The largest number is " << x << ".";
    }
    else if (y > x && y == z)
    {
        cout << "The largest number is " << y << ".";

    }
    else if (z > x && z == y)
    {
        cout << "The largest number is " << z << ".";
    }
    else if (x > z && x == y)
    {
        cout << "The largest number is " << x << ".";
    }
}
```

Figure 4. Representative third submission with Athene feedback.

User:
Time: 2013-02-11 22:29:42
Score: 100
Class: 1320_CS12001
Problem: 03-Max_of_3

Success.

max3.cpp

```
#include <iostream>
using namespace std;

int main()
{

        int x, y, z;

        cout << "This program identifies the largest of three numbers." << endl << endl;

    cout << "Enter integer: ";
    cin >> x;
    cout << "Enter integer: ";
    cin >> y;
    cout << "Enter integer: ";
    cin >> z;
    cout << endl;

    if (x > y && x > z)
    {
        cout << "The largest number is " << x << ".";
    }
    else if (y > x && y > z)
    {
        cout << "The largest number is " << y << ".";

    }
    else if (z > x && z > y)
    {
        cout << "The largest number is " << z << ".";
    }
    if (x > y && x == z)
    {
        cout << "The largest number is " << x << ".";
    }
    else if (y > x && y == z)
    {
        cout << "The largest number is " << y << ".";

    }
    else if (z > x && z == y)
    {
        cout << "The largest number is " << z << ".";
    }
    else if (x > z && x == y)
    {
        cout << "The largest number is " << x << ".";
    }
    else if (x == y && x == z)
    {
        cout << "The largest number is " << x << ".";
    }
}
```

Figure 5. Representative fourth submission with Athene feedback.

Table 1. Source code metrics for example submissions

	1st Submission (Figure 2.)	2nd Submission (Figure 3.)	3rd Submission (Figure 4.)	4th Submission (Figure 5.)
SLOC	17	23	25	27
State Space	3	3	3	3
McCabe Complexity	7	13	15	17
Halstead Vocabulary	28	35	37	39
Halstead Length	95	145	162	179
Halstead Computed Length	108.28	148.09	160.27	172.66
Halstead Volume	456.1	743.75	843.93	946.09
Halstead Difficulty	16.07	16.27	16.71	17.09
Halstead Effort	7976.46	12101.37	14103.39	16167.95

4. RESULTS

Table 2 describes the overall data that was analyzed in this paper.

Table 2. Overview of data collected.

Total # of Semesters	7
Total # of Students	290
Total # of Submissions	45,128
Total # of Sessions	12,452
Percent of Sessions Completed Successfully	83.2%

In analyzing the data, we gave extra attention to factors that changed when students showed positive progress. Table 3 represents the data from only those submissions that come out of multiple-attempt sessions, and we always ignored the first attempt (as there would not be a previous submission to compare it against). We call these submissions "new maximums." 32.2% of eligible submissions were new maximums.

Table 3. Average changes students made in achieving a new maximum submission.

Change from Last Submission	New Max
Average score increase for a new max	57
Average SLOC increase	0.43
Average State Space increase	0.04
Average McCabe Increase	0.33
Average Halstead Vocabulary increase	0.73

Also of special interest to us is the effect that throttling had on what students changed from submission to submission. For semesters 1–4, we allowed students unlimited submissions in any time period without throttling; for semesters 5–7, we established a throttle that limited students to 3 submissions per 15-minute period. This action corresponded with distinctions in student behavior and data outcomes. This data is shown in Table 4.

5. DISCUSSION

We recognize two primary areas of new knowledge emerging from this study. First, we see that throttling of submissions does indeed have an impact on the quality of student submissions. Table 4 shows that the average score of multiple attempt sessions that eventually scores 100% increased from 11 all the way to 28. Knowing that submissions were throttled made students more careful in making their first submission, hopefully putting more thought into their work and doing independent testing instead of only relying on the grading system.

Second, dynamic testing is important, but instructors and students can also benefit from considering style and content. In January 2004, Ala-Mutka published an executive study on the use of Style++ to promote good style practices in students. The AAT was able to discern and respond to a number of unhealthy programming practices with an appropriate grade and feedback on how the student should improve the efficiency of their program. Ala-Mutka found that "students implement more reliable and understandable programs" after having only been required to submit assignments to Style++ for a year [2]. However, Ala-Mutka's study focused on independent student use of the Style++ tool in advance of submitting final assignments, allowing instructors to "concentrate on giving feedback on the more advanced features of program design and course specific issues."

We argue that the examples in the session shown in Figures 2 through 5 show us that instructors can learn a great deal more about student submission by employing some basic metric analysis of submitted code. By using these other types of analysis, we can identify gaps in understanding, even when a student finishes with a score of 100%. With a focus on style, the student may be more capable of thinking in terms of efficiency and efficacy for each line in their code, which can help prevent situations similar to that in Figures 2-5 wherein the student needlessly increased complexity and length of code rather than rewriting existing code to achieve the desired output.

Overall, we can infer that both an emphasis on technique and use of throttling submissions encourage a reflective perspective of one's work.

6. FUTURE WORK

In the future, we would like to more seamlessly integrate static analysis tools—giving students more feedback (such as reporting to them the actual complexity level of their submitted program and the expected level).

Another interesting project would be to automatically analyze individual problems to identify the most common student problems, so instructors can address these issues more effectively in class.

Table 4. Effect of throttling on submissions.

	All Semesters	No Throttling (Semesters 1-4)	With Throttling (Semesters 5-7)
Total students	290	170	120
Total submissions	45,128	31,753	13,375
Total sessions	12,452	7,949	4,503
Average submissions per session	3.62	3.99	2.97
Average score of first submission for sessions with multiple attempts that eventually scored 100%	19	11	28
Average score change from first to second submission	30	31	30
Average McCabe change from first to last submission	0.69	0.81	0.58
Average Halstead Vocabulary change from first to last submission	2.34	2.81	1.87

7. ACKNOWLEDGMENTS

Special thanks to Heidi Nobles and Kayla Holcomb for their editorial support in preparing this manuscript.

8. REFERENCES

[1] Ahoniemi, T., and Reinikainen, T. ALOHA - a grading tool for semi-automatic assessment of mass programming courses. In *Proceedings of the 6th Baltic Sea Conference on Computing education research* (Baltic Sea, 2006). Koli Calling '06. ACM, New York, NY, 139-140.

[2] Ala-Mutka, K. M., Uimonen, T., and Järvinen, H. Supporting students in C++ programming courses with automatic program style assessment. *Journal of Information Technology Education* 3,1 (2004), 245-262.

[3] Ala-Mutka, K. M. A survey of automated assessment approaches for programming assignments. *Computer Science Education* 15,2 (2005), 83-102.

[4] Brown, C., Pastel, R., Siever, B., and Earnest, J. JUG: a JUnit generation, time complexity analysis and reporting tool to streamline grading. In *Proceedings of the 17th ACM Annual Conference on Innovation and Technology in Computer Science Education* (2012). ITiCSE '12. ACM, New York, NY, 99-104.

[5] Douce, C. Livingstone, D., and Orwell, J. Automatic test-based assessment of programming: A review. *Journal on Educational Resources in Computing* 5,3 (September 2005), Article 4.

[6] Hollingsworth, J. Automatic graders for programming classes. *Communications of the ACM* 3,10 (October 1960), 528-529.

[7] Ihantola, P., Ahoniemi, T., Karavirta, V., and Seppälä, O. Review of recent systems for automatic assessment of programming assignments. In *Proceedings of the 10th Koli Calling International Conference on Computing Education Research* (2010.) Koli Calling '10. ACM, New York, NY, USA, 86-93.

[8] Jadud, M. C. A first look at novice compilation behaviour using BlueJ. *Computer Science Education* 15,1 (2005), 25-40.

[9] Nordquist, P. Providing accurate and timely feedback by automatically grading student programming labs. *Journal of Computer Science Coll.* 23,2 (December 2007), 16-23.

[10] Norris, C., Barry, F., Fenwick, J. B., Jr., Reid, K., and Rountree, J. ClockIt: collecting quantitative data on how beginning software developers really work. *SIGCSE Bull.* 40,3 (June 2008), 37-41.

[11] Pieterse, V. Automated assessment of programming assignments. In *Proceedings of the 3rd Computer Science Education Research Conference on Computer Science Education Research* (2013). CSERC '13. M. van Eekelen, e. Barendsen, P. Sloep, and G. van der Veer, Eds. Open Universiteit, Heerlen, The Netherlands, Article 4.

[12] Rubio-Sánchez, M., Kinnunen, P., Pareja-Flores, C., and Velázquez-Iturbide, Á. Student perception and usage of an automated programming assessment tool. *Computers in Human Beha*vior 31 (February 2014), 453-460.

[13] Sherman, M., Bassil, S., Lipman, D., Tuck, N., and Martin, F. Impact of auto-grading on an introductory computing course. *Journal Computing Sciences in Colleges* 28,6 (June 2013), 69-75.

[14] Wang, T., Su, X., Ma, P., Wang, Y., and Wang, K. Ability-training-oriented automated assessment in introductory programming course. *Computers & Education* 56,1 (January 2011), 220-226.

[15] Zimmerman, D. M., Kiniry, J. R., and Fairmichael, F. Toward instant gradeification. In *Proceedings of the 2011 24th IEEE-CS Conference on Software Engineering Education and Training* (2011). CSEET '11. IEEE Computer Society, Washington, DC, 406-410.

Reconsidering Automated Feedback: A Test-Driven Approach

Kevin Buffardi
California State University, Chico
O'Connell Technology Center 215
Chico, California 95929-0410
+1 530-898-5617
kbuffardi@csuchico.edu

Stephen H. Edwards
Virginia Tech
2202 Kraft Drive
Blacksburg, VA 24060
+1 540-231-5723
edwards@cs.vt.edu

ABSTRACT

Writing meaningful software tests requires students to think critically about a problem and consider a variety of cases that might break the solution code. Consequently, to overcome bugs in their code, it would be beneficial for students to reflect over their work and write robust tests rather than relying on trial-and-error techniques. Automated grading systems provide students with prompt feedback on their programming assignments and may help them identify where their interpretation of requirements do not match the instructor's expectations.

However, when automated grading systems help students identify bugs in their code, the systems may inadvertently discourage students from thinking critically and testing thoroughly and instead encourage dependence on the instructor's tests. In this paper, we explain a framework for identifying whether a student has adequately tested a specific feature of their code that is failing an instructor's tests. Using an implementation of the framework, we analyzed an automated grading system's feedback for programming assignments and found that it often provided hints that may discourage reflective testing.

Categories and Subject Descriptors

K.3.2 [**Computers and Education**]: Computer and Information Science Education; D.1.5 [**Programming Techniques**]: Object oriented Programming; D.2.5 [**Software Engineering**]: Testing and Debugging.

Keywords

Software development process; Test-Driven Development (TDD); Test-first; Unit testing; Automated testing; Web-CAT; Instructional Technology.

1. INTRODUCTION

Current computer science curricula [1][2] emphasize the importance of students gaining proficiency in software testing. Consequently, programming assignments often require students to write unit tests for their programs. Meanwhile, automated grading systems such as Web-CAT [9] and Marmoset [13] have incorporated features to evaluate the quality of students' tests. In addition, these grading systems provide feedback to students to identify shortcomings in both solution correctness and thoroughness of testing. However, concerns arise about whether automated feedback systems empower students with effective software testing practices. In particular, multiple instructors have independently expressed worries that their students rely upon Web-CAT's automated testing feedback to supplant the need for thorough testing and critical thinking.

Since the point of testing is to verify that software behaves as expected, the practice of writing tests should involve reflecting over a variety of different test cases and confirming that each produces the expected outcome. In performing due diligence in testing, a student should consider not only the mainstream cases, but also which unusual cases may cause bugs, or unexpected outcomes. To the contrary, we have found that students write "happy path" tests—only those mainstream cases unlikely to cause unexpected bugs [11].

After students submit their work to Web-CAT, they receive feedback on the correctness of their solutions—as determined by a set of obscured reference tests provided by the instructor—as well as measurements of how much of their own code they have exercised with their own tests. In addition, failed reference test cases generate hints that instructors use to give students general direction in identifying what is malfunctioning without revealing the specific details of the reference test. Web-CAT's correctness score provides students with confirmation of how well their solution performs according to the project specifications. While the hints do not necessarily indicate exactly which test cases are not working, they also provide students with insight into which features they need to fix in their solution code. Both types of feedback may be well intended to help students make progress on their programming assignments; however, they also relieve at least some of the burden of software testing.

Ideally, students would test their own code thoroughly enough that without any feedback from the instructor, they would have strong confidence that their code behaves correctly by its performance against their tests alone. In non-academic settings, software developers do not usually have the benefit of an instructor's thorough checks to make sure their software is sound and robust. Instead, they would have to rely on their own estimates of the code quality to determine if it is ready to deploy. Nevertheless, it may be unrealistic to expect students to know how to test effectively without assistance.

SIGCSE '15, March 4–7, 2015, Kansas City, MO, USA

ACM 978-1-4503-29966-8/15/03…$15.00
http://dx.doi.org/10.1145/2676723.2677313

Consequently, programming courses should find a compromise between alleviating the burden of quality assurance from the students and demanding professional-quality testing proficiency immediately. In this paper, we reconsider students' interaction with automated grading systems. We describe a model for scaffolding feedback in Web-CAT to encouraging students to reflect over their code and concentrate on writing effective software tests to reveal bugs instead of relying on external sources.

2. BACKGROUND

When students submit programming assignments to Web-CAT, test coverage estimates the quality of their tests. Traditionally, Web-CAT evaluates the percentage of methods, lines of code, and conditions within a student's solution code are executed by her unit tests. This combination of method, line, and condition coverage provides a general perspective of the breadth of code exercised by the student's tests. However, even 100% code coverage does not necessarily indicate that tests have thoroughly checked the program's behavior. For example, consider the following code segment:

```
if ( a && (b || c) )
{
    return true;
}
else
{
    return false;
}
```

Figure 1. Example of IF-ELSE Control with a Compound Condition

The above code can achieve full coverage in two test cases: one where the variables `a` `b` and `c` are true (which returns true) and one where they are all false (which returns false). With these two test cases, we have executed each line in the code and have executed both outcomes of the `if` condition (`true` and `false`). However, with these tests, we have not considered other cases with different combinations of values for the variables. While the compound condition has been both true and false, variations of the atomic decisions are not thoroughly tested. For example, if **a** and **b** are true but **c** is false, does the code's outcome (true) match the expected behavior of the program?

There are alternate approaches for estimating test quality beyond traditional coverage measurements. One study compared coverage to two other techniques—mutation testing and all-pairs testing—to determine how well they predict bugs in students' actual code [10]. Mutation testing involves making multiple versions of a student's source code with minor modifications—each called a "mutant"—and identifying whether the student's tests "kill" mutants by producing different outcomes from the test with its original code. Meanwhile, all-pairs testing involves running a student's tests against all other students' implementations of the same assignment and measures how many bugs it identifies. The study found that all-pairs testing was most effective at determining a test suite's ability to identify bugs while mutation testing was no better than coverage at doing so.

However, all-pairs testing has caveats that limit the practicality of using it in automated grading systems like Web-CAT. First, as the number of students in the class (and the number of tests they write) grows the computational expense of running tests against all other students' code increases exponentially. Perhaps more poignantly, Web-CAT allows students to submit their assignment multiple times throughout development so each student's code and all-pairs score will change over time (until submissions are no longer accepted). Consequently, the first students to submit their code would have less comprehensive all-pairs analysis and the results may change as others submit their work.

Modified Condition / Decision Coverage (MC/DC) is another approach for measuring comprehensiveness of software tests [8]. Unlike conventional coverage where a decision only requires an overall true and false evaluation, MC/DC requires showing that each *atomic* condition affects a "decision's outcome by varying just that condition while holding fixed all other possible conditions" [7]. As one form of MC/DC, *masking MC/DC* takes advantage of setting one operand of an operator so that the other operand cannot affect the value of the operator. Reconsidering the example in **Figure 1**, the operand **b** can be masked by holding **c** true so that it will evaluate as true regardless of **b**'s value; likewise, **a** can be masked by holding **(b || c)** false so that the expression will evaluate to false regardless of **a**'s value. Because masking MC/DC examines conditions with more detail, it subsumes Web-CAT's approach of measuring coverage for each method, line, and control decision.

In addition to challenges of measuring the thoroughness of students' tests, automated grading systems need to encourage students to test their code more thoroughly rather than depend on automated feedback to tell them whether their code works. Instead, it should provoke students to reflect, "What other test cases might possibly break my code?" However, our previous studies found that students' responses to Web-CAT's feedback concentrate predominantly on fixing errors in their code to improve their correctness score [3][4]. While students also aim to earn full credit for testing by obtaining 100% coverage, their approach does not reflect the mentality of trying to expose weaknesses in their code. Rather, their testing behaviors more closely demonstrate a desire to extend the least amount of work to obtain 100% coverage, a relatively superficial objective for testing.

Nevertheless, students' responses to Web-CAT's feedback is understandable since they are driven to achieve good grades (which 100% coverage allows), and the feedback already provides some insight into how acceptable their code is without having to test it sufficiently themselves. Our previous attempts with adaptive feedback with overt encouragement to test had no long-term impacts on their testing behaviors [3]. However, the adaptive feedback interventions supplemented other feedback that still gave students insight into the quality of their code, perhaps undermining the efforts to encourage testing. Consequently, we designed a model for scaffolding feedback that still provides students with help on improving their code, but with a strategic approach emphasizing testing.

3. METHOD

3.1 A Framework for Targeting

Previous approaches considered overall coverage of the student's entire programming project. Of course, students' projects usually include many methods and often even multiple classes. Consider a situation where a student submits a project that is not behaving perfectly (according to the instructor's specifications) and has some (but not exhaustive) testing. Web-CAT detects some bugs in the student's code from some of the instructor's tests failing and gathers the hints associated with each failed test. For one feature of the project, the student thoroughly tested her code but the feature was not implemented precisely to the instructor's specifications: the text output in her implementation uses commas to separate values but the instructor expected line breaks instead. The problem with this feature is not one caused by a lack of testing, but rather by a misunderstanding of the requirements. It is unlikely that more testing will expose the problem and without some insight from the hints, it may be frustrating to overcome this relatively superficial bug.

However, in the same submission to Web-CAT, the student may have another feature that is incorrectly implemented but has not discovered the problem because she has not tested that feature as thoroughly. Unlike the previous example, revealing a hint to correct this bug would be inappropriate because the student should first try to reflect over what test cases she neglected in her test suite. Nevertheless, by only considering the coverage of the entire project, the automated grader cannot determine which feature has been thoroughly tested or which hints are appropriate to show.

Consequently, in order to choose appropriate guidance for students, automated feedback must first identify testing quality feature-by-feature. To do so, we developed a custom runner for JaCoCo [12]—an open source coverage tool for Java—that produced a coverage report for each instructor reference test independently. After identifying which reference tests fail against a student's submission, the system then reviews the report for each test and identifies which method(s) within which class(es) of the student's code the test executes. As a result, the system can associate failed tests with particular features within the student's submission. While these features cannot always be localized to a single method, they narrow the scope considerably because unit tests by definition concentrate on small portions of code.

A reference test suite may include many test cases for a single feature and, as a result, create duplicate hints and execute the same methods in the student's code. As Web-CAT traditionally eliminates redundant hints, our system records the number of times a hint occurs for a single submission and considers it one unique hint. After recording the test results, for each unique hint, it determines whether the student has tested the feature associated with that hint enough to warrant revealing the hint. To do so, the system calculates the masking MC/DC of the student's own tests against the method(s) associated with that hint.

If the student has not sufficiently tested the atomic decisions within the methods' control structures, the system will withhold the hint and instead direct the student to the method(s) that need more testing. However, if masking MC/DC is fully satisfied on each of the methods associated with the reference test failure, the system reveals the hint. Accordingly, this framework requires students to reflect over each feature of their work and test it thoroughly before receiving hints. In that manner, students cannot rely upon hints to supplant the burden of testing.

3.2 Evaluation of Existing Technology

The aforementioned framework emphasizes offering hints only on features of the student's code that have been adequately tested. The precision of this feature-by-feature feedback would be demonstrated by a lack of both false positives and false negatives in providing hints. A false positive occurs when a hint is provided to a student when the feature it tests has not been tested well by the student. Meanwhile, a false negative occurs when a student has sufficiently tested a feature but does not receive a hint generated by a reference test that failed the same feature. To compare the framework's approach to hint precision to existing approaches in automated testing, we empirically tested the occurrences of false positives and false negatives using Web-CAT's traditional hint mechanism.

Web-CAT allows instructors to customize how many hints students receive for any given assignment submission. However, its default setting is to show a maximum of three hints, where hints with multiple occurrences (multiple failed reference tests generating the same hint) are given precedence. If additional hints are generated by failed tests, they are obscured until later submissions resolve the bugs responsible for the revealed hints. Consequently, hints shown may include those generated by reference tests that fail on features that the student has not tested (a false positive). Likewise, if a student has tested a feature well but a reference test's hint is not within the top three hints, this represents a false negative. Since traditional automated graders do not follow our feature-by-feature scaffolding framework, we hypothesized that Web-CAT does not discriminate between earned (true positives) and unearned hints (false positives) any better than it discriminates obscuring unearned hints (true negatives) from earned hints (false negatives).

To test our hypothesis, we analyzed existing student submissions to Web-CAT's traditional automated feedback system. Using the procedures described in the previous section, we performed post-hoc analysis of which features each reference test exercised as well as whether the students earned each hint (both revealed and obscured) according to masking MC/DC. The student submissions were from two programming assignments from the Fall 2011 term of a CS2 course. We previously collected consent from students to analyze the results of this assignment. After excluding submissions from students who chose not to consent and removing errant submissions (such as non-compiling code), we analyzed 3,688 submissions from 86 individual students.

Students averaged submitting to Web-CAT approximately 24 times (M=23.94, sd=19.62) per assignment. For each failed test within a submission, we evaluated the masking MC/DC score for the methods that particular test exercised and recorded whether it earned the hint with complete masking MC/DC on corresponding methods. After analyzing each unique hint generated for a submission, we also recorded how many unique methods in the student's code needed improved MC/DC to earn all hints. On average, each submission required additional testing on 2.70 (sd=2.05) unique methods, or 12.55% (sd=13.16%) of its solution methods; **Figure 2** shows the distribution across all submissions.

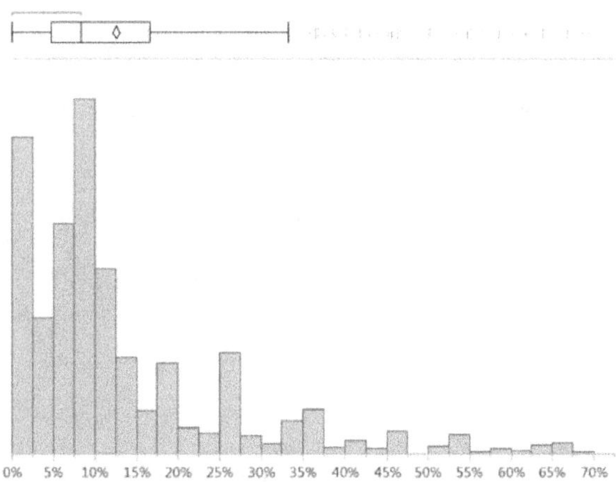

Figure 2. Distribution and Box-plot of Methods Requiring More Testing

Meanwhile, the failed reference tests produced an average of 14.55 (sd=15.38) unique hints per submission. **Figure 3** shows the distribution of earned (full MC/DC for applicable methods) and unearned hints (incomplete MC/DC for applicable methods) that were revealed per submission.

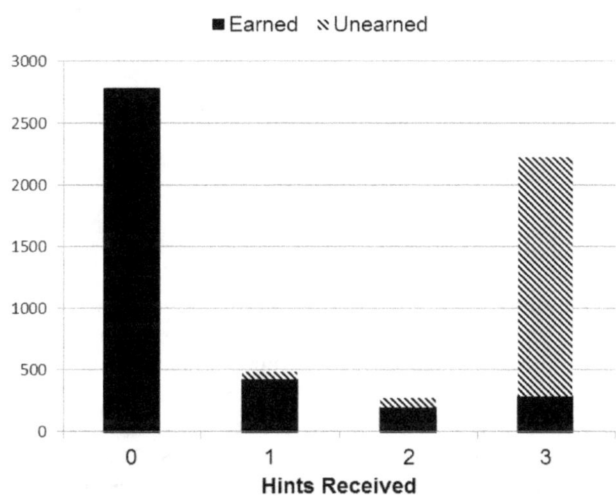

Figure 3. Distribution of Hints Revealed Per Submission, Earned Versus Unearned

As the distribution shows, the vast majority of submission received three hints of which none (0) were earned. This chart reflects only the top three hints that a student could receive on each given submission. The unearned (striped) bars demonstrate instances of false positives: hints that students may depend upon instead of testing the feature robustly. Separately, we also evaluated any remaining hints – those obscured because they were not in the top three – and whether or not they were earned. **Figure 4** shows the distribution of earned and unearned hints among obscured hints.

In this figure, unearned (solid) bars represent true negatives, while earned (dotted) bars greater than zero (0) represent false negatives—hints that were earned but not revealed. False negatives may unnecessarily withhold insight into student's misunderstandings of the assignment specifications.

We used the Shapiro-Wilk test to check for normality of these distributions. The test rejected the null hypothesis (that the data are

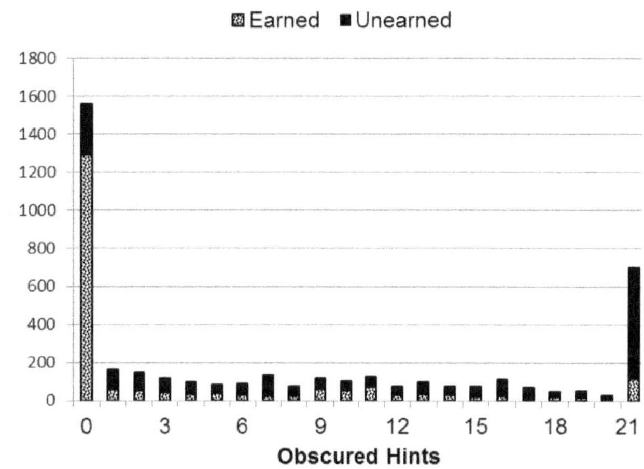

Figure 4. Distribution of Obscured Hints Per Submission, Earned Versus Unearned

normally distributed) for both the unique methods ($p<.01$) and unique hints ($p<.01$). Consequently, to test our hypotheses by comparing the incidents of false positives and true positives for revealed hints to false negatives to true negatives of obscured hints, we used the Friedman's test for within-subject comparisons of non-parametric distributions.

4. RESULTS

To test our hypothesis, we performed a Friedman test comparing the rate of earned-to-unearned hints between those revealed and obscured, when averaged across multiple submissions within-subject. The test found that there was no significant difference ($F(2,1)=0.01$, $p=0.92$) between the rate at which revealed hints were earned (M=0.20, sd=0.36) and obscured hints were earned (M=0.20, sd=0.31). This test rejects the null hypothesis that revealed hints have a higher rate of earned-to-unearned hints than obscured hints.

We also investigated the false positive (revealed but unearned hints) and false negative (obscured but earned hints) rates for each assignment independently. **Table 1** shows the false positive and false negatives of the earlier (minesweeper game) and later (linked and array based queue implementations) projects.

Table 1. False Positive and False Negative Rates, by Project

Project	Submissions	False Positives (M, sd)	False Negatives (M, sd)
Minesweeper	1604	0.72, 0.41	0.19, 0.33
Queues	2084	0.84, 0.32	0.21, 0.30

Note that both projects experienced high false positive rates, showing that regardless of the assignment, most hints revealed were not earned. Moreover, both projects maintained false negative rates, where on average, about one-out-of-five hints that were obscured had actually been earned.

5. DISCUSSION

The post-hoc analysis of hints that Web-CAT natively reveal and obscure supported our hypothesis that the automated feedback often results in both false positives and false negatives. False positives inadvertently relieve some of the burden of testing thoroughly by providing insight into failing tests for features that have not been thoroughly tested. In fact, false positives (revealing unearned hints) were roughly four times more common than true positives (earned hints revealed). Meanwhile, earned hints were no more likely to be revealed than they were to be obscured. With such high false positive and false negative rates, it should not be surprising that the current hint mechanism does not promote students to practice reflective testing before trial-and-error in response to failed hints.

One might consider configuring Web-CAT to remove the limitation to a maximum of three hints per submission. Doing so would eliminate all false negatives. However, the false positive rate would continue to overwhelm the number of earned hints and continue to undermine attempts to encourage students to rely on their own testing instead of using Web-CAT as a crutch. While the interventions described in our previous studies [4][5][6] avoid static restrictions on how many tests Web-CAT reveals, their designs do not account for precision of hints served on a feature-by-feature basis. Consequently, there is no reason to believe that they would have any better success at preventing false positives and false negatives than the default Web-CAT settings did.

To the contrary, our proposed framework offers a unique approach to scaffolding feedback to guide students to revisit their extent of their testing without depending on Web-CAT to determine behavioral acceptability for them. For example, without any test cases, our framework could first indicate only that features in the student's assignment have not been tested—no indication of the program's correctness or results from reference tests. Then, as the student adds test cases and resubmits, the feedback scaffold would give more direction by identifying features that are not working properly and need more thorough testing. Finally, when the student has thoroughly tested a feature but has not resolved its disparity from the project specifications, the framework would provide detailed hints about why the feature fails reference tests.

This framework's approach to scaffolding feedback is modeled after Vygotsky's Zone of Proximal Development [14]. Before a student has written tests, her immediate need in effective software development and problem solving is to reflect over her solution and consider its possible flaws. As she continues to reflect and test thoroughly, she will gradually approach a mastery of the problem where she can use hints to reconcile differences between her implementation and the expected solution.

In addition, it is worth acknowledging that there is no *de facto* standard for measuring test effectiveness. Therefore, while our use of masking MC/DC in our application of the framework should provide more accurate estimations of test thoroughness than conventional coverage, the framework is not explicitly tied to masking MC/DC. As we continue to study methods of evaluating student testing on programming assignments, other measurements could replace masking MC/DC without upsetting the framework's infrastructure. In conclusion, we hope to evaluate how interaction with our framework influences student testing behaviors while continuing to investigate options for assessing test quality.

6. REFERENCES

[1] ABET (2013). "Criteria for Accrediting Computing Programs, 2013-2014." Retrieved November, 2013, from http://www.abet.org/DisplayTemplates/DocsHandbook.aspx?id=3148.

[2] ACM (2014). "Computer Science 2014: Curriculum Guidelines for Undergraduate Programs in Computer Science." Retrieved Nov. 2014, from http://www.acm.org/education/curricula-recommendations.

[3] Buffardi, K. and S.H. Edwards (2014). "A Formative Study of Influences on Student Testing Behaviors." Proc. of Computer Science Education Symposium.

[4] Buffardi, K. and S.H. Edwards (2014). "Responses to Adaptive Feedback for Software Testing." Proceedings of the 19th ACM annual conference on Innovation and technology in computer science education. Uppsala, Sweden

[5] Buffardi, K. and S. H. Edwards (2012). Exploring influences on student adherence to test-driven development. Proceedings of the 17th ACM annual conference on Innovation and technology in computer science education. Haifa, Israel, ACM: 105-110.

[6] Buffardi, K. and S. H. Edwards (2012). "Impacts of Teaching test-driven development to Novice Programmers." International Journal of Information and Computer Science 1(6): 9.

[7] Chilenski, J. J. (2001). "An Investigation of Three Forms of the Modified Condition Decision Coverage (MCDC) Criterion."

[8] Chilenski, J. J. and S. P. Miller (1994). Applicability of modified condition/decision coverage to software testing. Software Engineering Journal 193-200.

[9] Edwards, S. H. "Web-CAT.", from https://web-cat.cs.vt.edu.

[10] Edwards, S. H. and Z. Shams (2014). Comparing test quality measures for assessing student-written tests. Companion Proceedings of the 36th International Conference on Software Engineering. Hyderabad, India, ACM.

[11] Edwards, S. H. and Z. Shams, (2014). Do Student Programmers All Tend to Write the Same Software Tests? Proceedings of the 19th ACM annual conference on Innovation and technology in computer science education. Uppsala, Sweden.

[12] "JaCoCo Java Code Coverage Library." 2014, from http://www.eclemma.org/jacoco/

[13] Spacco, J. "Marmoset." 2013, from http://marmoset.cs.umd.edu/.

[14] Vygotsky, L. S. (1978). Mind in Society: Development of Higher Psychological Processes, Harvard University Press.

MC-Live: A Portable Computing Environment for Computer Science Students

Lee Wittenberg
Maryville College
Maryville, TN, USA
Lee.Wittenberg@maryvillecollege.edu

ABSTRACT

Computer Science departments have special requirements for their computing environments, distinct from the "normal" requirements of most other departments. However, shrinking budgets and other factors make it difficult for many of us to provide an adequate computing environment for our students, above and beyond the generic support provided by our school's computing services division. This paper describes the use of bootable, "live" USB keys to provide students with a standard, portable environment that they can use on their own computers as well as in our labs.

Categories and Subject Descriptors

K.3.2 [**Computers and Education**]: Computer and Information Science Education

General Terms

Management, Standardization

Keywords

Linux, live CD, live USB

1. INTRODUCTION

More and more, college administrators are relying on the fact that students have their own computers in order to reduce funding for on-campus computer labs. This is a particular problem for computer science departments, which need specialized software not normally pre-installed on student computers. This is especially true with regard to introductory programming courses, where students cannot be expected to be skilled enough to install system software on their own machines.

Large universities can still afford to have dedicated labs for computer science; smaller schools less so (and much less so if current trends continue). Many different methods have been used to deal with this problem: public access Unix systems such as SDF [10] and WSUnix [12], "live" Linux systems on CD or DVD-ROMs [1, 2, 4, 5], virtualization [6, 9, 11][1], and "cloud-based" environments accessed via web browser [7, 8, 14] Each of these approaches has its benefits and drawbacks [3].

The author has long been involved with the Greater New York Region of the International Collegiate Programming Contest, where we have been running the contest off of bootable CDs and USBs for many years [13]. Based on this work, we have developed at Maryville a bootable USB key containing a complete Linux computing environment, which can be used throughout a computer science student's college career. Students who bring their laptops to class can boot from their keys for lab exercises; the remaining students can use their keys to boot the lab machines[2]. All students can boot their keys on their machines in the dorm or at home.

The key does not require students to install any software or reconfigure their PCs in any way, nor is it dependent on Internet access. Unlike live CDs, the USB key has a persistent home directory where students can save their work.

2. THE MC-LIVE KEY

We use a 4GB key, divided into four partitions:

1. A FAT[3] partition named SHARE, used for transferring files to and from other machines and operating systems. This must be the first partition, since Windows only recognizes the first partition on a USB key.
2. A Linux partition named HOME, which serves as a persistent home directory for student files.
3. A FAT partition named LIVE, which contains the files necessary for booting and running Linux. Many implementations of UEFI booting require this partition to be FAT.
4. A Linux swap partition. Modern machines generally have enough memory so that this is not necessary, but not having a swap partition when one is needed can cause strange problems. Also, the inclusion of a swap partition allows the key to be used on older hardware with limited memory.

[1]Thomas and Whitener [11] also describe a less-than-successful attempt to provide students with laptops preconfigured to dual-boot Linux and Windows.

[2]Our lab machines automatically re-image themselves every night, so this is not the security problem it might otherwise be.

[3]See appendix for explanations of this and other acronyms.

SIGCSE'15, March 4–7, 2015, Kansas City, MO, USA.

http://dx.doi.org/10.1145/2676723.2677216.

Our environment is based on the Fedora distribution, but other distributions provide similar tools for creating bootable USBs. The image is updated every year so that incoming students will have the latest versions of the included software. However, the differences are not significant, so returning students can use their older keys without problems.

3. EXPERIENCE

The initial version of the MC-Live key used a 32-bit Linux kernel and an MBR partition table, as the "lowest common denominator" intended to work on the greatest variety of hardware. Due to previous failed attempts to make a Mac-bootable USB for contest work, no attempt was made to make the key bootable on a Macintosh.

We bought the keys for between $6 and $7 each. We "sold" them to our student ACM chapter for $5 each, who then sold them to our students for $10 apiece. We thus reduced our cost somewhat, at the same time providing a small income stream for our student chapter. Having students pay even a nominal amount also encourages them to treat the keys with more respect than they might if the keys were free.

We have not yet discovered how best to make the keys available to our students. Initially, one of our lab assistants was responsible for providing the keys and collecting the money. However, he was not easy to find outside of class, so students were not always able to get replacement drives when needed. We then tried having a small number of keys available from our department secretary, which helped somewhat, but was still less than ideal. Currently, the keys are in the charge of the faculty member teaching our introductory programming course. This seems to be a satisfactory solution (students in other classes can easily find him during off-class hours), but we are still searching for an optimal arrangement.

3.1 Fall Semester: Teething Pains

As with any new venture, our initial attempts brought unforeseen problems. The first obstacle arose as soon as we tried booting the keys on student laptops with Windows 8 installed. By default, these machines only allow booting from GPT drives configured for UEFI booting. Although each system permitted "legacy" booting, they all had different methods to allow this. It was also necessary to disable the "secure boot" option on machines with this capability. It took a great deal of time to figure out how to properly configure each student's machine, but this was eventually accomplished. Unfortunately, some systems (the author's laptop included), when configured in "legacy" mode, would no longer boot Windows 8, which necessitated constant changing of boot settings. There was no getting around this more-than-minor irritation.

The second hurdle was a bit more serious, but we were still able to handle it. Our USB supplier was less than first-rate, and many of the keys went bad during the semester for no apparent reason. The drives themselves would also tend to slip out of their casings. A little glue solved the latter problem, while the former was dealt with by allowing students to exchange bad drives for new ones.

However, the news was not all bad. Students with Macs reported that the keys booted on their machines without problems. Additionally, the author found that knowing the structure of student drives made grading in-class lab exercises much easier than they otherwise would have been. He was able to write scripts that could automatically mount a student's SHARE partition, find the required file(s), copy them over to his own home area, unmount the SHARE partition, and check the student's work for errors, after which the drive could be returned to the student.

Since the initial problems were technical, amenable to technical solutions, it seemed reasonable to continue using the keys in the following semester.

3.2 Winter Break: Regrouping

During the winter break we dealt with the technical issues raised in the fall semester. We found a more reliable supplier, and revised the image on the USB. This time we used a 64-bit Linux kernel and a hybrid GPT/MBR partition table in an attempt to make a "universal" key that would be usable on as many different machines as possible. We also made a number of keys with a 32-bit kernel in case any students still had 32-bit machines. This turned out to be unnecessary.

3.3 Spring Semester: Stability

We allowed students to exchange their fall semester (unreliable) keys for the new (reliable) ones. The hybrid keys turned out to work extremely well. They booted on all the machines we tried them on, both Macs and PCs. Secure boot no longer needed to be disabled, nor was it necessary to enable "legacy" booting.

Only two keys went bad during the course of the semester, both due to student mishandling. Another of the new keys even went through the wash (but not the dryer) without going bad! A tremendous improvement over the previous semester.

One problem still remained. Windows 8 refused to recognize the SHARE partition on the hybrid key. Windows 7, Vista and XP had no problem with this, nor did OS X. We discovered that changing from a hybrid to a GPT-only partition table was all that was needed to allow Windows 8 to recognize SHARE.

3.4 Summer: Consolidation

During the summer we re-evaluated the software provided on the key, and expanded the list of packages provided. The key is no longer aimed only at introductory courses, but now has software to support our entire curriculum. We experimented with a GPT-only key, but found that some Windows 7 machines could not boot it (although XP machines could!), so we have decided to continue with a hybrid version, providing a "`win8`" script that will allow students to adjust their keys, if necessary.

4. STUDENT REACTION

Since our primary motivation was to overcome the technical limitations of our lab environment, we have not made any effort to survey student opinions about the key. On the whole, however, student response has been quite favorable. Some students with previous programming experience have reverted to what they were used to, but others have adopted the key as their preferred programming environment.

5. CONCLUSION

The MC-Live key has turned out to be useful in introductory classes, and seems as if it will be equally useful in advanced classes, so we have decided to continue its use for the foreseeable future. It provides an identical environment (with a graphical interface) for all users, yet does not require a student to install any software (unlike a virtual machine); it is not dependent on network access (unlike a server or cloud-based environment); and it has a persistent home area for storing files (unlike a live DVD or CD-ROM). We will be using the next few semesters to adjust the software on the key, adding packages as necessary and removing those that turn out not to be needed.

The MC-Live key also turns out to be quite budget-friendly. A minimal amount of labor is necessary to maintain the keys, once an image has been standardized. An afternoon or so of work is necessary each year to deal with incompatibilities introduced with new Linux distribution releases, and the image must be copied onto the USBs, but all in all, the total costs work out to no more than $10 per key, which can be passed along to the students, if desired (or necessary). This can turn out to be, as it has for us, a nice money-maker for the local student ACM chapter.

Because the key runs Linux, instead of the latest version of Windows or OS X, it runs quite well on older hardware, which somewhat alleviates the cost of maintaining a lab. In fact, it's not even necessary for lab machines to have an operating system (or any software) installed. The keys can run on bare hardware. The total cost of using live USB keys, therefore, compares very favorably with that of a fully equipped, fully maintained computer lab. And, unlike a traditional computer lab, students have complete access to all the software they need wherever they happen to be—in the dorm, at home, or anywhere else—as long as they have their MC-Live key and access to a computer.

6. ACKNOWLEDGMENTS

The author would like to thank Jeff Bay, Robert Lowe, and the Maryville College administration for their support in this work; Adam Florence and John Buck for their work with programming contest USBs; and (of course) the students who actually had to use the USB keys and deal with the "teething" problems described above.

7. REFERENCES

[1] E. Crowley. Live cds and security lab configuration. In *Proceedings of the 2Nd Annual Conference on Information Security Curriculum Development*, InfoSecCD '05, pages 24–26, New York, NY, USA, 2005. ACM.

[2] E. Crowley. Open source centric information security lab development. In *Proceedings of the 6th Conference on Information Technology Education*, SIGITE '05, pages 57–63, New York, NY, USA, 2005. ACM.

[3] M. K. Gardner and W. Feng. Broadening accessibility to computer science for k-12 education. In *Proceedings of the Fifteenth Annual Conference on Innovation and Technology in Computer Science Education*, ITiCSE '10, pages 229–233, New York, NY, USA, 2010. ACM.

[4] T. Hamada and K. committers. Knoppix/math: A live system for enjoying mathematics with computer. *ACM Commun. Comput. Algebra*, 42(3):175–176, Feb. 2009.

[5] D. Johnson. Teaching kernel programming using knoppix. *J. Comput. Sci. Coll.*, 21(3):69–75, Feb. 2006.

[6] D. J. Malan. From cluster to cloud to appliance. In *Proceedings of the 18th ACM Conference on Innovation and Technology in Computer Science Education*, ITiCSE '13, pages 88–92, New York, NY, USA, 2013. ACM.

[7] D. Pritchard and T. Vasiga. Cs circles: An in-browser python course for beginners. In *Proceeding of the 44th ACM Technical Symposium on Computer Science Education*, SIGCSE '13, pages 591–596, New York, NY, USA, 2013. ACM.

[8] K. Salah. Harnessing the cloud for teaching cybersecurity. In *Proceedings of the 45th ACM Technical Symposium on Computer Science Education*, SIGCSE '14, pages 529–534, New York, NY, USA, 2014. ACM.

[9] A. Sayler, D. Grunwald, J. Black, E. White, and M. Monaco. Supporting cs education via virtualization and packages: Tools for successfully accommodating "bring-your-own-device" at scale. In *Proceedings of the 45th ACM Technical Symposium on Computer Science Education*, SIGCSE '14, pages 313–318, New York, NY, USA, 2014. ACM.

[10] Sdf.Org. Sdf public access unix system, 2014. Retrieved August 6, 2014 from http://sdf.org/.

[11] S. J. Thomas and P. M. Whitener. In the zone: Virtual computing on a budget. In *Proceedings of the 41st ACM Technical Symposium on Computer Science Education*, SIGCSE '10, pages 366–370, New York, NY, USA, 2010. ACM.

[12] Washington State University. Public unix system, 2005. Retrieved August 6, 2014 from http://www.wsu.edu/itunix/cluster/wsunix.html.

[13] L. Wittenberg. Pain-free programming contest management, 2011. Retrieved August 8, 2014 from https://ciiwiki.ecs.baylor.edu/index.php/Pain-free_Programming_Contest_Management.

[14] D. Yoo, E. Schanzer, S. Krishnamurthi, and K. Fisler. Wescheme: The browser is your programming environment. In *Proceedings of the 16th Annual Joint Conference on Innovation and Technology in Computer Science Education*, ITiCSE '11, pages 163–167, New York, NY, USA, 2011. ACM.

APPENDIX

Acronyms & Abbreviations

FAT File Allocation Table: a legacy file system, originally designed for floppy disks, supported by almost all modern operating systems.

GPT GUID Partition Table: a new standard for partitioning disks, designed to remove the limitations of the earlier MBR partition tables (see below).

GUID Globally Unique Identifier.

MBR Master Boot Record: an earlier standard for partitioning disks and booting from them, superseded by the GPT (see above) and UEFI (see below) standards.

UEFI Unified Extensible Firmware Interface: a new standard for providing hardware-related booting and runtime services (only the former is relevant here).

Teaching Virtualization by Building a Hypervisor

Abhinand Palicherla
Tintri, Inc.
303 Ravendale Dr.
Mountain View, CA 94043
apalicherla@tintri.com

Tao Zhang
Department of Computer Science
Stony Brook University
Stony Brook, NY 11794
zhtao@cs.stonybrook.edu

Donald E. Porter
Department of Computer Science
Stony Brook University
Stony Brook, NY 11794
porter@cs.stonybrook.edu

ABSTRACT

Virtual machines (VMs) are an increasingly ubiquitous feature of modern computing, yet the interested student or professional has limited resources to learn how VMs work. In particular, there is a lack of "hands-on" exercises in constructing a virtual machine monitor (VMM, or hypervisor), which are both simple enough to understand completely but realistic enough to capture the practical challenges in using this technology. This paper describes a set of assignments to extend a small, pedagogical operating system (OS) to form a hypervisor and host itself. This pedagogical hypervisor, called HOSS, adds roughly 1,000 lines of code to the MIT JOS source, and includes a set of guided exercises. Initial results with HOSS in an upper-level virtualization course indicate that students enjoyed the assignments and were able to apply what they learned to solve different virtualization-related problems. HOSS is publicly available.

Categories and Subject Descriptors

D.4.0 [**Operating Systems**]: General; K.3.2 [**Computers and Education**]: Computer and Information Science Education—*Computer Science Education*

General Terms

Design, Experimentation

Keywords

Operating Systems; Virtual Machines; Instructional Tools

1. INTRODUCTION

Virtual Machines (VMs) are an increasingly important component of modern computing. VMs offer several attractive benefits, including security isolation, the ability to run applications designed for different operating systems (OSes) on the same hardware platform, and the ability to migrate applications from one physical machine to another. As a result, VMs have become the backbone of cloud computing, grown increasingly common on desktops, and are even emerging as a way to separate business and personal applications and numbers on a single mobile phone [4, 14].

Unfortunately, there are very few tools available to help students and instructors learn how virtualization works, especially "hands-on" exercises. A few OS textbooks have added overviews of virtualization [29, 33], but there is very little between these very high-level descriptions and the very low-level details of the ISA programming manual, technical research papers [7, 11] and other references [12, 30]. Although open source hypervisors are widely used, Xen [7] is hundreds of thousands of lines of code, and KVM is scattered across 15 million lines of Linux source code. The interested student lacks a "middle ground" environment that is simple enough to completely understand, but realistic enough to appreciate the real-world challenges of working with this technology.

This paper describes **HOSS**, a simple OS that can host instances of itself as virtual machine guests. In the HOSS exercises, students directly program Intel's hardware virtualization extensions (called VT-x) [34], create extended page tables, handle hypercalls and other traps, as well as implement a paravirtual guest system. To build HOSS, we extended the MIT JOS [20] pedagogical OS. In both JOS and HOSS, boilerplate code is provided, and students implement the interesting components of the system. The provided code is small enough to understand (about 14,000 LoC), but structurally similar to much larger OS codebases, such as Linux. HOSS adds roughly 1,000 LoC to JOS.

Initial experiences with HOSS in the classroom are positive. The HOSS assignment was initially assigned in a new course on virtualization, including a mix of senior undergraduate and graduate students. After completing the HOSS assignments, students were able to complete an open-ended final project that involved modifying a production hypervisor. The HOSS assignments are publicly available at `http://www.cs.stonybrook.edu/~porter/hoss` and solutions are available to instructors upon request. Enhancements and support for HOSS are ongoing (§6).

2. RELATED WORK

To our knowledge, HOSS is the first pedagogical hypervisor. In addition to JOS, a number of pedagogical OSes have been developed and used [6, 10, 13, 19, 24, 27, 32], but these OSes do not include exercises in hypervisor construction. This paper demonstrates that adding a hypervisor to such a pedagogical OS is straightforward—adding roughly

SIGCSE'15, March 4–7, 2015, Kansas City, MO, USA.

ACM 978-1-4503-2966-8/15/03 ...$15.00.
http://dx.doi.org/10.1145/2676723.2677254.

one thousand lines of additional code. Northwestern has a course which involves adding features to a research hypervisor [16], but the coding assignment is an open-ended project, not structured assignments implementing core hypervisor features.

Lguest is perhaps closest to HOSS—a simple, but functionally limited hypervisor for Linux [28]. Lguest is written primarily to document and test Linux-internal interfaces for writing a hosted hypervisor; KVM also uses these internal interfaces. Lguest would be useful in the classroom as a code review assignment, but it would be difficult to create assignments that worked with core virtualization concepts that did not amount to reimplementing existing code.

A number of OS educators have shifted to using real-world OSes, such as Linux, in the classroom [3, 18, 23]. To our knowledge, published experiences and exercises have not introduced virtualization concepts. Andrus and Nieh [5] argue for the use of Android in the OS classroom because it is an increasingly ubiquitous technology with unique characteristics; we believe this argument applies equally to hypervisors.

Finally, we note that several papers have been published on the effectiveness of virtual machine platforms as *classroom infrastructure*—scaling limited hardware to large classrooms, simplifying administrative tasks, and addressing other classroom challenges [15, 21, 22, 25, 31]. HOSS helps students learn how such useful technology works.

3. BACKGROUND

This section summarizes background on the JOS operating systems courseware, as well as concepts unique to virtual machine monitors (VMMs, or hypervisors) compared to a traditional OS kernel.

3.1 JOS

The JOS [20] operating system is written in C and assembly, and runs on 32-bit x86 (PC) hardware. A completed JOS solution is about 14,000 lines of C code and 600 lines of assembly[1]. Over the course of 6 assignments, students complete substantial portions of core system components, including the memory manager, scheduler, file system, shell, and network driver. In particular, JOS requires students to program x86 hardware including configuring the page tables, context switching the CPU, handling interrupts, and writing an e1000 network card driver.

The JOS architecture is best described as an exokernel [17], wherein the OS kernel manages hardware and exports hardware-like interfaces to the application. Unlike a monolithic kernel, most familiar POSIX-style abstractions, such as file descriptors or even `fork` and `exec` are implemented in an application *library OS*. The only exception is the file system, which runs as a shared, microkernel-style daemon.

An essential feature of JOS is that students develop intuitions which apply to much larger OS code bases, such as Linux or FreeBSD. Although JOS supports fewer architectures and features than a production-quality OS, it retains a similar kernel structure and requires students to write core system components. JOS was developed at MIT, and has been used at a number of universities, including Stanford, Texas, UCLA, Washington, Harvard, and Stony Brook.

[1]We note that JOS also includes a 25,000 LoC user-level socket library, but students do not need to understand this code to complete the assignments.

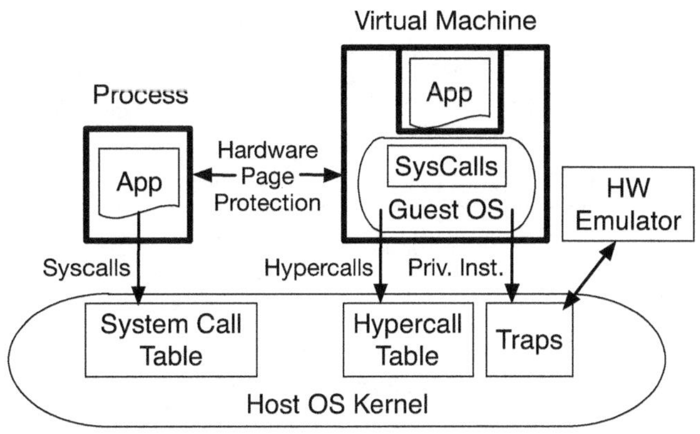

Figure 1: Comparison of an application in a process (left) to a virtual machine (right). Both execute in an isolated address space, implemented with hardware page tables. The primary difference is the ABI—system calls versus hypercalls and emulated hardware. A host OS kernel can execute a mixture of processes and VMs.

3.2 Hypervisor Implementation Techniques

Virtual machines are, in many respects, quite similar to OS processes (illustrated in Figure 1). VMs execute in a hardware-isolated virtual address space, and at a lower privilege level than the host OS kernel. The primary difference is the application binary interface (ABI) exported by the host OS kernel to the guest. The process ABI includes higher-level abstractions, such as file descriptors, signals, and network sockets, whereas a VM manipulates emulated hardware abstractions, such as a virtual disk, CPU interrupts, and a virtual network card. In other words, adding VM support to a legacy OS, such as adding KVM to Linux, requires replacing the system call table with a hypercall table, the ability to trap accesses to privileged hardware, and a PC hardware model, generally running as a separate process. As a result, desktop and server OSes can run both traditional processes and VMs (this is sometimes called a Type 2, or hosted hypervisor); a Type 1 hypervisor, such as VMware ESX server or Xen, runs on bare metal and only executes VMs.

We summarize three essential concepts specific to modern hypervisor implementations, which are not required to understand a traditional OS kernel.

Trap-and-emulate. VMs run a potentially-unmodified guest OS in a lower hardware privilege level (or ring in x86 parlance), yet include privileged instructions that directly access hardware. Hypervisors must be able to trap each of these privileged instructions, emulate its effect, and then advance the CPU's program counter transparently to the guest OS. We note that, before the introduction of Intel's VT extensions [34], the x86 architecture did not trap on all privileged instructions, but failed silently on some, rendering it unvirtualizable. Thus, VMware Workstation and other early hypervisors required binary translation techniques to detect these instructions [11].

Once a privileged instruction is trapped, the instruction's effects must be emulated. For instance, sending a packet on a virtual network card should ultimately result in a packet being sent on the physical network (or to another VM within a virtual network). As a result, most hypervisors also require

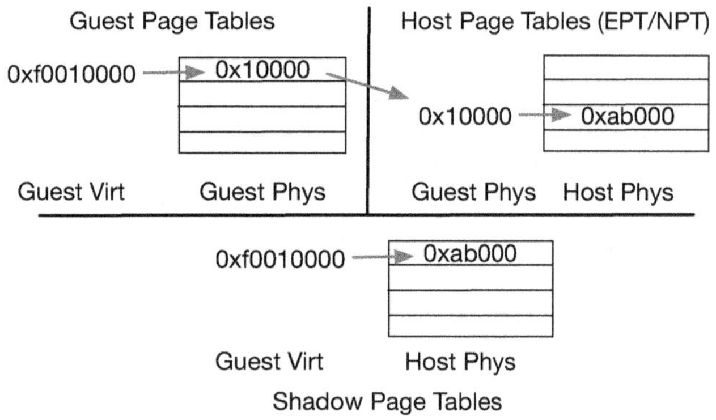

Figure 2: Both a guest and host OS include page tables, which translate virtual to physical addresses, or the guest's view of physical memory to the hosts' view of physical memory. Newer hardware directly traverses both page tables using extended, or nested page tables (EPT/NPT). For older hardware with only one level of paging, the hypervisor must construct a shadow page table (bottom), that directly translates guest virtual to host physical addresses.

models of common PC hardware, such as a widely-supported network card, disk controller, and video device. KVM obtains this from the qemu machine emulator [8], which runs as a process on the host OS. VMware Workstation has a similar process, called `vmx`.

Memory Translation. A VM runs in a virtual address space, similar to a process, but then creates nested virtual address spaces for each application. This creates a problem for CPUs that only export one level of page translation hardware, requiring the hypervisor to combine two levels of page translation into a single *shadow page table* for the hardware to use. Shadow page tables are illustrated in Figure 2, which directly map guest virtual addresses onto host physical addresses. Emulating paging hardware can be particularly expensive and complex because the hypervisor must trap every write to the memory containing the guest OS's page tables, and then update the shadow page tables.

To reduce this complexity and improve performance, recent Intel and AMD CPUs now support two levels of hardware page tables [1], allowing the hypervisor and VM to independently manage their own address translations. We note that, even with two-level paging, running a hypervisor inside of a VM will still require shadow paging (e.g., to map three page tables onto two) [9]. Although conceptually similar, hypervisor-level page tables and CPU control structures are not identical to traditional page tables. Even if a student has written context switching code for an x86 OS, context switching into and out of a VM requires understanding different control structures and a different control flow. For instance, returning from a system call leaves the kernel stack empty, whereas entering a VM leaves frames on the kernel stack.

Paravirtualization and hypercalls. Paravirtualization makes small modifications to a guest OS so that particularly expensive hardware emulation can be replaced with simpler software abstractions, such as replacing an emulated disk controller with a simple software ring buffer [7]. The hypervisor must export these abstractions to the guest using a *hypercall* interface (similar to an OS kernel's system call table), and the guest OS must be modified to invoke these hypercalls rather than using privileged instructions to modify hardware directly.

Intuitively, paravirtualization improves performance by reducing the total number of traps to the hypervisor, as well as reducing the overhead of emulating specific hardware. The changes required of the guest OS are simple, small, and often encapsulated in dynamically loaded device drivers. We observe that modern paravirtual hypervisor designs share many similarities with an exokernel: exporting an interface to applications that either directly accesses hardware features where safe, or using system calls that export low-level, hardware-like abstractions to the process. As a result, the conceptual and implementation gap between supporting an exokernel-style library OS and a paravirtualized guest OS is relatively small.

4. HOSS EXERCISES

Similar to JOS, course staff provided students with HOSS "skeleton code", and students implement the remaining portions of the hypervisor. Students also make changes to the guest code to support paravirtualization. Both the JOS guest and HOSS host share a code base; all guest or host-specific code is delimited with C preprocessor macros (e.g., `#ifdef VMM_GUEST`). In order to increase the virtual address space for the host system, we ported JOS to the 64-bit x86 architecture; we omit the details of the 64-bit port, as these details are orthogonal to the hypervisor.

Students completed the assignments using the bochs PC emulator, which can emulate Intel's VT-x extensions. Using bochs eliminated the need for each student to have access to physical hardware, removing artificial constraints on enrollment. Moreover, bochs allows the student to connect a debugger directly to the running hypervisor or guest OS, facilitating debugging compared to bare metal.

The HOSS exercises reflect essential lessons, including the principles of hypervisor construction summarized in §3.2, which we explain in the rest of this section.

4.1 A VM is (almost) a Process

In HOSS, each process (`struct Env`) includes a flag that indicates whether it is a normal process or a VM. Most of the process-management code works unmodified. The two pieces of VM-specific code students must implement are for memory management and context switching.

Students must write code that creates and manages extended (or nested), hypervisor-level page tables. The processor expects a slightly different layout in these page tables than in a single-level page table; we provide the students with helper functions and pointers to the Intel documentation to manipulate these structures. Moreover, at this point, the students have a small, working implementation of guest-level page tables, so they have a related reference implementation. The kernel data structures to manage allocated and free memory are unchanged. When a virtual page mapping is created for a process, HOSS uses the VM flag to determine whether to call the handler written for extended or single-level page tables.

Students must also write context switching code that uses the `vmlaunch` and `vmresume` instructions. This component introduced the most differences. When an application traps to a traditional OS kernel, an x86 CPU transfers control to a handler specified in the interrupt descriptor table (IDT) and pushes the application's registers onto an address specified by the kernel. By ubiquitous convention, this is an empty stack frame; when the kernel finishes handling an interrupt, the final return (`iret` instruction) pops the registers and returns to the application. In other words, between any two interrupts or system calls, there is no active state on the kernel stack. In contrast, Intel's VT instructions maintain live state on the stack when context switching into a VM. Students had to write code that compensated for this difference by properly switching to a different stack when switching between multiple VMs.

Beyond these complication with context switching, students also had to understand the fields of the VM control structure (VMCS)—a region of physical memory where guest and host registers are saved and restored, as well as a structure that includes flags controlling VM behavior, such as which events cause traps. Students wrote short inline assembly code to detect whether the CPU supports VT and extended page tables, as well as context switching into and out of the VM. As a result, students gained experience working with these hardware abstractions.

4.2 The Guest Kernel is Just a Program

Students are asked to take an ELF loader, for loading application binaries into a process, and convert this to an ELF loader that launches a guest kernel in a VM. Students discover that this requires very few changes, except emulating the behavior of a PC BIOS, such as loading the bootloader at an expected address in memory and communicating the layout of (virtualized) physical memory to the guest kernel.

4.3 Hypercalls, Traps, and Emulation

We export the JOS system call table to the guest kernel as hypercalls in HOSS. Students implement the code that handles traps from the VM and redirects hypercalls to the system call table.

Students also get an introduction to hardware emulation by implementing the `cpuid` instruction. This instruction places information about the CPU's capabilities in several registers, according to a format defined by the CPU vendor. Most OSes use this instruction during boot for runtime configuration. The VMCS in HOSS is configured to trap on a `cpuid` instruction. The students write a trap handler that places appropriate flags in the correct registers and manually advances the program counter before returning control to the VM. In practice, this feature is often used to hide the presence of features such as extended paging from a guest VM when a hardware capability is already in use and software emulation is not available.

4.4 Paravirtualization

Finally, students implement a paravirtual disk. The baseline JOS code has a file system daemon, which issues hardware-level commands directly to an IDE disk controller. In the HOSS lab code, this is placed in a host-only preprocessor macro, and students are asked to instead request blocks of a disk image file from the host. These disk image file requests are issued using host-level IPC, as illustrated in Figure 3. The host-level file system transparently handles requests for the disk image file just like any other file. This design does require the guest-level IPC mechanism to translate guest vir-

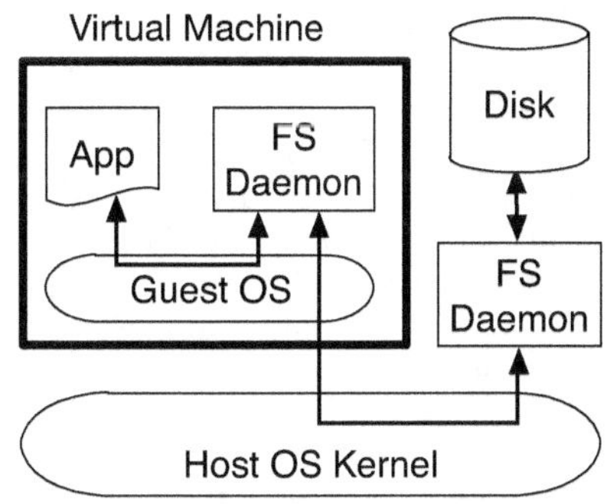

Figure 3: HOSS paravirtualized file system architecture. Both guest and host kernel execute a microkernel-style file system daemon. The guest FS daemon uses a hypercall to issue an IPC to the host daemon to access its disk image. The host FS daemon accesses the disk directly.

tual to guest physical addresses. Representing a hard drive as a disk image file is extremely common, and this gives students a clear understanding that a hard drive can easily be represented as a file.

5. THE VIRTUALIZATION COURSE

HOSS was used as part of a new course on virtualization for senior undergraduates and graduate students. The course included two undergraduates, nineteen M.S. students, and four doctoral students, for a total of 25 students. All students in the course had completed an undergraduate OS course, and some had completed a graduate OS course.

In addition to the HOSS assignments, students read seminal and recent research papers on hypervisor design, virtual I/O, and security. About three quarters of class sessions were discussions about the assigned research papers, and one quarter were in-class programming days to help students work the assignments. Paper discussions spent equal time on understanding the technical details of how a prototype system was constructed (and its relevance to the HOSS assignment), as well as critically assessing the merit of the research idea and its evaluation.

The HOSS assignments were completed about halfway through the semester, and the remainder of the semester was spent on open-ended final projects. The final projects could be research-oriented or development tasks, and could be extensions to HOSS or any other open-source hypervisor. Students were allowed to work the HOSS assignments and final project in self-selected teams of up to three people, although some students chose to work alone.

5.1 Final Projects

One underlying goal of the final project is to evaluate whether students can apply what they have learned to new projects or codebases. This is a somewhat noisy, but mostly positive indicator, and cases that were not clear successes indicate further gaps in the instructional tools available (§6).

Here we list a sample of final projects and outcomes:

- **Adding suspend and resume support to lguest.** Lguest is a simple hypervisor written for a Linux host, using the same kernel-internal interfaces as KVM [28]. The undergraduate students were able to independently read, understand, and extend the lguest source code with suspend and resume support.

- **Virtual Networking.** Several groups added virtual networking support to HOSS, but with different strategies. In general, most successful groups adopted a paravirtual strategy, which exposed a new interface for packet delivery to the guest via ring buffers, and wrote a new guest driver using these paravirtual interfaces.
- **Better VM benchmarks.** Several students felt that virtualization research would benefit from standardized microbenchmarks. These teams successfully added timing and other instrumentation to benchmark KVM.
- **Multi-Processor Support.** One team developed multiprocessor support for HOSS, such that multiple guests can run concurrently on different cores. This team was delayed somewhat by an underlying bug in JOS's support for multiple processors, which they fixed. By the end of the semester, the host kernel supported multiple CPUs, but guests were still single-CPU.
- **AMD Virtualization Hardware.** One student tried to port HOSS from Intel's VT to AMD's SVM equivalent [1]. Intel and AMD expose comparable, but different interfaces and abstractions for virtualization support. Unfortunately, no emulator exposes the AMD instructions, and the student worked directly on bare metal. Without the ability to attach a debugger to the system, and lacking debugging information from the emulator itself, this project proved too ambitious for the time frame.

In general, these results indicate that students understood the architecture of the system, and were able to solve new problems and work with new code bases.

5.2 Student Feedback

At the end of the course, students were given both an anonymous, university-issued survey, as well as the opportunity to give feedback directly to the instructor. Numerically, the course evaluation scores were positive: overall a 4.65 out of 5, compared to a 4.34 university average. However, the qualitative comments from both surveys tended to be more informative. We observe the following trends:

- The course contained a mix of students who had previously completed JOS and those who had not. The students who did not complete JOS previously felt that they needed to complete most of the previous assignments to fully understand the code, even when given a solution.
- Comments about HOSS itself were quite positive. Students repeatedly commented that they learned a lot and found the exercises worthwhile. Students generally requested more HOSS exercises, which we will add in future versions of the course.
- Most students enjoyed learning to read research papers, but a minority prefer a textbook-and-lecture style course. Most found a useful connection between programming assignments and the higher-level performance and functionality analysis of the research papers.

Based on this feedback, HOSS's hands-on approach to learning about virtualization was effective, and students generally wanted more system implementation exercises.

6. FUTURE WORK

HOSS is an ongoing effort, which we will use in future courses. We plan to add the following features to HOSS:

- **More exercises with device emulation in software.** A little device emulation goes a long way, as this task quickly becomes tedious. We envision providing a mostly-complete model of a disk or network card, and then asking students to add missing feature and use the model to implement trap-and-emulate behavior.
- **Execute an unmodified Guest OS.** The current JOS guest requires light modifications, primarily to avoid such emulation. We ultimately want to be able to support an unmodified JOS guest, as well as a mainstream OS, such as Linux or Windows.
- **Add binary translation for systems without virtualization hardware.** For older x86 systems, binary translation was necessary to properly catch and replace certain privileged instructions. We plan to add exercises that program a binary translator, such as the one used internally by qemu.

Most of these tasks require relatively straightforward engineering effort, and exercises using these features can be kept manageable for students. The current HOSS assignments cover the essential concepts, but the ability to boot an unmodified binary kernel within a semester would make the project more attractive for students.

We would also like to provide exercises programming recent IOMMU hardware that allows direct device management from a VM [2] and network cards that can be exported as multiple virtual NICs [26]. Unfortunately, current hardware emulators do not support this feature. In fact, most emulators and simulators do not include virtualization extensions at all. In our experience, students can grasp concepts and solve problems more quickly with familiar debugging tools—tools that are harder to support on bare metal. Thus, an important direction for future work is simply building emulator infrastructure for teaching and debugging.

A substantial limitation of this work is that it is part of an advanced, two-course sequence. An important direction for future education research is to develop a stand-alone variation of the course or to adapt components of this work to exercises in isolation, emulation or performance analysis for a core undergraduate systems course.

7. CONCLUSION

HOSS gives students hands-on experience with hypervisor construction. These exercises target an advanced, two-course OS/virtualization sequence. The exercises are suitable for an advanced undergraduate or graduate student, and yield intuitions that are applicable to new problems and other hypervisors. Our initial experiences with HOSS are positive, although there is room for improvement in the assignments as well as current emulation tools. Our assignment code and exercises are publicly available at `http://www.cs.stonybrook.edu/~porter/hoss` and solutions are available to instructors upon request.

8. ACKNOWLEDGMENTS

We thank the many contributors to JOS for creating a wonderful building block for HOSS. We thank Michael Tashbook and the anonymous reviewers for insightful comments on earlier drafts of this paper. This research was supported in part by NSF grants CNS-1149229, CNS-1161541, CNS-1228839, and the Office of the Vice President for Research at Stony Brook University.

References

[1] AMD. AMD-V Nested Paging. White Paper, AMD: `http://developer.amd.com/assets/NPT-WP-1\%201-final-TM.pdf`, July 2008.

[2] AMD. AMD I/O Virtualization Technology (IOMMU) Specification Revision 1.26. White Paper, AMD: `http://support.amd.com/us/Processor_TechDocs/34434-IOMMU-Rev_1.26_2-11-09.pdf`, Nov 2009.

[3] C. L. Anderson and M. Nguyen. A survey of contemporary instructional operating systems for use in undergraduate courses. *J. Comput. Sci. Coll.*, 21(1):183–190, Oct. 2005.

[4] J. Andrus, C. Dall, A. V. Hof, O. Laadan, and J. Nieh. Cells: A virtual mobile smartphone architecture. In *SOSP*, pages 173–187, 2011.

[5] J. Andrus and J. Nieh. Teaching operating systems using android. In *SIGCSE*, pages 613–618, 2012.

[6] B. Atkin and E. G. Sirer. Portos: An educational operating system for the post-pc environment. In *SIGCSE*, pages 116–120, 2002.

[7] P. Barham, B. Dragovic, K. Fraser, S. Hand, T. Harris, A. Ho, R. Neugebauer, I. Pratt, and A. Warfield. Xen and the art of virtualization. In *SOSP*, pages 164–177, 2003.

[8] F. Bellard. Qemu, a fast and portable dynamic translator. In *USENIX ATC*, pages 41–41, 2005.

[9] M. Ben-Yehuda, M. D. Day, Z. Dubitzky, M. Factor, N. Har'El, A. Gordon, A. Liguori, O. Wasserman, and B.-A. Yassour. The Turtles Project: Design and implementation of nested virtualization. In *OSDI*, 2010.

[10] D. Brylow. An experimental laboratory environment for teaching embedded operating systems. In *SIGCSE*, pages 192–196, 2008.

[11] E. Bugnion, S. Devine, M. Rosenblum, J. Sugerman, and E. Y. Wang. Bringing virtualization to the x86 architecture with the original VMware workstation. *ACM Trans. Comput. Syst.*, 30(4):12:1–12:51, Nov. 2012.

[12] D. Chisnall. *The Definitive Guide to the Xen Hypervisor.* Prentice Hall Press, 1st edition, 2007.

[13] W. A. Christopher, S. J. Procter, and T. E. Anderson. The nachos instructional operating system. In *USENIX Winter Conference*, pages 4–4, 1993.

[14] S. Cooper. Vmware android handset virtualization hands-on. Retrieved Sept. 1, 2014 from `http://www.engadget.com/2011/02/15/vmware-android-handset-virtualization-hands-on/`, 2011.

[15] R. Davoli and M. Goldweber. Virtual square (v2) in computer science education. In *ITiCSE*, pages 301–305, 2005.

[16] P. Dinda. Eecs 441: Resource virtualization, winter 2014. Retrieved Sept. 1, 2014 from `http://pdinda.org/virt-w14/`.

[17] D. R. Engler, M. F. Kaashoek, and J. O'Toole, Jr. Exokernel: An operating system architecture for application-level resource management. In *SOSP*, pages 251–266, 1995.

[18] R. Hess and P. Paulson. Linux kernel projects for an undergraduate operating systems course. In *SIGCSE*, pages 485–489, 2010.

[19] D. A. Holland, A. T. Lim, and M. I. Seltzer. A new instructional operating system. In *SIGCSE*, pages 111–115, 2002.

[20] JOS OS Lab. Retrieved Sept. 1, 2014 from `http://pdos.csail.mit.edu/6.828`.

[21] M. Ketel. A virtualized environment for teaching IT/CS laboratories. In *SE*, pages 92:1–92:2, 2010.

[22] O. Laadan, J. Nieh, and N. Viennot. Teaching operating systems using virtual appliances and distributed version control. In *SIGCSE*, pages 480–484, 2010.

[23] B. Lawson and L. Barnett. Using ipodlinux in an introductory os course. In *SIGCSE*, pages 182–186, 2008.

[24] H. Liu, X. Chen, and Y. Gong. Babyos: A fresh start. In *SIGCSE*, pages 566–570, 2007.

[25] J. Owens. Using virtualization to teach Linux system administration in online courses. In *IBM ICVCI*, 2007.

[26] PCI-SIG. Address translation services 1.1 specification. `http://www.pcisig.com/members/downloads/specifications/iov/ats_r1.1_26Jan09.pdf`.

[27] B. Pfaff, A. Romano, and G. Back. The pintos instructional operating system kernel. In *SIGCSE*, pages 453–457, 2009.

[28] R. Russell. Lguest: The simple x86 hypervisor. Retrieved Sept. 1, 2014 from `http://lguest.ozlabs.org`.

[29] A. Silberschatz, P. B. Galvin, and G. Gagne. *Operating System Concepts.* 9th edition, 2012.

[30] J. Smith and R. Nair. *Virtual Machines: Versatile Platforms for Systems and Processes.* Morgan Kaufmann Publishers Inc., 2005.

[31] W. Sun, V. Katta, K. Krishna, and R. Sekar. V-NetLab: An approach for realizing logically isolated networks for security experiments. In *CSET*, pages 5:1–5:6, 2008.

[32] A. S. Tanenbaum. A unix clone with source code for operating systems courses. *OSR*, 21(1):20–29, Jan. 1987.

[33] A. S. Tanenbaum and H. Bos. *Modern Operating Systems.* 4th edition, 2014.

[34] R. Uhlig, G. Neiger, D. Rodgers, A. L. Santoni, F. C. Martins, A. V. Anderson, S. M. Bennett, lain Kägi, F. H. Leung, and L. Smith. Intel virtualization technology. In *IEEE Computer*, pages 48 – 56, 2005.

MiniOS: An Instructional Platform for Teaching Operating Systems Projects

Rafael Román Otero
Department of Computer Science
University of Northern British Columbia
Prince George, BC, Canada
romanot@unbc.ca

Alex A. Aravind
Department of Computer Science
University of Northern British Columbia
Prince George, BC, Canada
csalex@unbc.ca

ABSTRACT

Operating systems is a central subject in computer science curriculum, and teaching it successfully has been a challenge. Effective learning requires carefully designed programming projects that can facilitate deep thinking and enhance hands-on experience. This paper presents MiniOS, an instructional embedded operating system designed to carry out operating systems projects successfully. We explain MiniOS approach, the rationale behind it, and compare it with other similar approaches.

Categories and Subject Descriptors

D.4.7 [**Operating Systems**]: [Organization and Design]; K.3.2 [**Computers and Education**]: [Computer and Information Science Education]

General Terms

Design

Keywords

MiniOS; operating systems; education; teaching;

1. INTRODUCTION

Operating systems (OS) is a core course in computer science and the understanding of other main subjects in computer science heavily depends on the understanding of OS concepts and functionalities. Due to its role in computing and technological advancements, operating systems have evolved in several dimensions. An operating system is a complete functional system with high dynamics involving variety of concepts, ideas, techniques, and design principles. A good understanding of operating systems requires the knowledge of: (a) the computer architecture; (b) the best software design practices; and (c) functional requirements of operating systems. Therefore, teaching such a complex subject successfully has been, no doubt, a challenge.

SIGCSE'15, March 4–7, 2015, Kansas City, MO, USA.

http://dx.doi.org/10.1145/2676723.2677299.

Several approaches exist for teaching operating systems, from purely theoretical approaches to programming projects based approaches attempting to enforce concepts taught in the classroom. It is our opinion that having hands-on experience is a minimal requirement for proper understanding of the concepts discussed in the classroom — particularly hands on the source code. Nonetheless, providing it as part of an operating system course is challenging. In our experience we have found this is because of: (a) *Inherent concurrency* — students are faced with asynchronous interrupts, shared memory, debugging of data races, and other concurrent programming problems; (b) *Low-level programming* — the OS must deal with the machine at the lowest level, thus requiring precise knowledge of the programming language in use and the machine inner workings; (c) *Complex hardware platform* — computers are quite complex machines, and a semester is not enough time for students to become fluent with the specificities of the platform; (d) *Complexity of the operating system itself* — modifying an existing operating system requires understanding the design and the components being modified. Most of the key components of an operating system are very complex on their own; a file systems, for instance.

Although the complexity of concurrency and low-level programming cannot be avoided fully, several approaches have successfully alleviated the complexity involved in the projects and helped to improve students' understanding. We are interested in pushing this direction of efforts further. Primarily, our approach is motivated from three aspects: simplicity, completeness, and practical use of designing operating system projects.

First of all, we would like to maximize the students' learning experience — maximum learning with minimal effort. Next, the operating system built from the course projects is expected, possibly with a minimal additional effort, to be reasonably functional. Finally, it would be nice if it can be further enhanced and used in practice by many students even after they graduate.

If we ask students how many of them would end up designing a general purpose operating system — whether it is commercial or instructional, the response would be overwhelmingly negative. This is due to the fact that almost all of us use a few operating systems such as Windows, Linux, and OS X. It is likely that this trend in general purpose operating systems will continue in the future. If we ask the question whether it is possible to build a reasonably functional general purpose operating system as a course project, again the answer would be highly negative. Therefore, the projects based on general purpose operating systems seem to mostly have academic value than pragmatic values. On the other hand, automation is steadily increasing in our day-to-day life. Therefore, building an embedded operating system based on micro-controllers appears to be highly appealing.

First of all, it is feasible to design a functional embedded operating system because it will have a limited set of well defined functions specific to the intended application. The experience and the confidence gained in building such an embedded operating system with satisfactory functionality, we believe, will encourage many students to continue and build their own operating systems for embedded systems for specific applications. Even such a possibility and potential could motivate the students to learn the subject and complete the project well. We introduced the MiniOS approach last year in our operating system course, and the students response was hugely positive. In this article, we would like to share the MiniOS approach, our experience, and the lessons we learned.

2. RELATED WORK

It is nearly impossible to describe the approaches to the operating systems projects and assignments. However, they can be broadly classified into five categories: (i) No programming projects (only theory assignments); (ii) Purely simulation based (important components or services are simulated rather than implemented); (iii) Modifying commercial operating systems; (iv) Modifying instructional operating systems; and (v) Building a toy operating system from scratch.

The first approach is typically simple and superficial, and therefore have the potential only for very limited learning experience. Simulation based approaches are attractive for capturing higher level functionality with suitable visual representations, but they can hardly give the experience of real operating system implementations. Modifying commercial operating systems has the advantage of working with a real fully functional operating system. The main disadvantage is the learning curve involved in understanding the huge code. Students can only be able to modify selected components, leaving out several important aspects. This leaves the student with an incomplete understanding, even with a humongous effort. Our approach is more related to the last two approaches and hence we will describe them in more detail next.

- **Modifying an Instructional OS Approach:** In this approach students are given the task of manipulating an instructional OS. Unlike an actual operating system (e.g. GNU/Linux), those with pedagogic purposes tend to be more compact; thus reducing the code, concepts, and technical details students need to know to be able to complete lab projects. Assignments are typically in the form of adding functionality or modifying the existing one. Examples in this category are: Nachos [5], Pintos [11], OS/161 [9], GeekOS [10], among others (a survey of instructional OSes can be found in [1]).

  There are several advantages to this approach: (a) Smaller size makes them easier to deal with than real operating systems; (b) they resemble *real* operating systems; and (c) Students need not interact directly with hardware.

  On the downside, resembling a *real* operating system entails complexity. Albeit simpler in appearance, it is not simple enough to be mastered in a term. The learning curve is still considerably large. Also, though there is no need to directly interact with the hardware, pre-made OS components still do it. Understanding the partly implemented OS components, the concepts and technical details behind the source code, and how all the functional pieces fit together in a semester time is challenging.

- **Building a Toy OS from Scratch:** In this approach students get to build their own toy OS from scratch. Typically a virtual machine (e.g. bochs) is used as development platform, though it is possible, with some assistance, to have students execute their OS in actual hardware. Example of instructional operating systems following this philosophy are the uMPS/Kaya platform [8], and Black's OS described in [3].

  This approach has the advantage that there is no pre-existing operating system to assimilate. Moreover, from previous experiences we know students find it rewarding to build their own operating system from scratch. The disadvantage is that students need to directly deal with complex hardware. Even with assistance and sample code the learning curve is quite steep. Also, given the complexity of writing an OS from scratch, there is virtually no opportunity to cover topics in more than their most rudimentary forms. Writing a basic peripheral driver or switching to protected mode (in the case BIOS is being used to handle I/O) are simply out of scope. The final OS is thus a toy and hence the experience is very limited.

  An intermediate approach that fits in the two previous discussed categories is the one behind XINU [6, 4], which was originally designed for instructional purposes. XINU is peculiar in that a guide (in the form of a book) to its design and implementation is available.

3. THE PROPOSED APPROACH

We propose to design operating systems projects with the objective of developing a minimal embedded operating system from scratch. We refer to it as MiniOS. The idea behind MiniOS is influenced by uMPS/Kaya and Black's OS in that students can build their OS entirely from scratch. MiniOS borrows from these two approaches with a subtle yet significant difference. More specifically, our hardware platform is a low-end embedded hardware platform. Namely, a low-end 32-bit ARM-based board. For this reason, the functionality requirement is minimal and relatively well defined.

Our approach offers the following advantages: (a) Similar to building a Toy OS from scratch, there is no pre-existing operating system to assimilate; (b) embedded hardware platforms are simpler than their desktop counterparts, which lessens the effort of dealing directly with hardware; (c) the final OS is not necessarily a toy, as many low-end embedded applications require very little and specific functionality (hence even a small OS build together from scratch in three months may have enough functionality to serve a purpose, say an OS for a weather station computer); (d) due to its use in industry, the development environment for MiniOS is highly matured and fairly stable; and (d) being

```
...
#define QUEUE_SIZE          MAX_NUM_THREADS          //Thread Queue Size

static Minithread queue[QUEUE_SIZE];                 //Queue of threads
static uint32_t head = 0;
static uint32_t tail = 0;

static void set_next_active_thread(bool first_thread){
        if(!first_thread){
                //enqueue pre-empted thread
                queue[tail] = active_thread;
                tail = (tail + 1) % QUEUE_SIZE;
        }

        //dequeue new thread.
        active_thread = queue[head];
        head = (head + 1) % QUEUE_SIZE;
}

void scheduler_thread_create( void (*initial_pc)(void), uint8_t* name, uint32_t stack_size ){
        ...
        //starts thread (enqueues)
        queue[tail] = threads[num_of_threads];
        tail = (tail + 1) % QUEUE_SIZE;

        num_of_threads++;
}
```

Figure 4.16

As last step we implement a FIFO scheduling policy by keeping a circular queue of threads. When a new thread is to be scheduled the pre-empted thread is place in the back of the queue, and the head of the queue is made the active thread. The corresponding code is in Figure 4.16.

For testing the entire system we implement proper system calls via *thread_create* and *thread_get_current* in minilib, and use it with the example application in Figure 4.17. When executed the interleaving of threads can be clearly appreciated. See Scheduler – Interleaving Demo.

Figure 1: MiniOS Code Excerpt

an embedded platform, sensors and actuators are integrated as peripherals, which, in our experience, appeals to students — especially when a final project component is part of the course.

At the same time, the proposed approach is similar to XINU as MiniOS has a guide to its design and implementation. The main difference, however, between XINU's approach and ours is the size of the project. In terms of effort involved, ours is nearly the same as in the Toy OS from scratch approach (which we believe is reasonable for a semester time), while XINU, given its size, suffers from the same complexity problem instructional OSes do.

3.1 An embedded OS as teaching tool

An embedded OS is much simpler than a desktop OS. Yet we believe the very essence is preserved, and this is enough to supply students the hands-on experience required to enforce the concepts taught in the classroom, while keeping the complexity low. For instance, consider Figure 1, which is an excerpt corresponding to the last page of the scheduler section. The link in the excerpt is a link to a video demonstrating the interleaving of threads as it should occur if implemented adequately.

Our view of moving away from desktop computers roughly complies with the one in [2], where they have used Android as instructional operating system. Nevertheless, we prefer the *from scratch* approach described earlier.

Building the system from the ground up, in our opinion, provides students with an understanding of how everything fits together. In the words of one of the students (gathered through written feedback): "[the] code base is quite small and it is easy to hold [the] entire system in your head". In this sense our technique is similar to the one in [7]. For instance, the solution to the scheduler (not including previous labs) is composed of 300 lines of code.

Building the system from the ground up is already complex enough, and thus prevents getting into sophisticated implementations details. Hence, students can only implement simple inefficient abstractions. Of course some OS courses may have the target outcome of teaching operating systems as designed in reality; case in which MiniOS is a rather poor fit. However for those interested in teach-

Figure 2: Hardware

ing/learning the principles that are common among different operating system, MiniOS is a good fit.

With regards to the processor choice, we have opted for ARM due to their dominance in the mobile and embedded systems industries [12, 13]. Although, sometimes neglected and considered less relevant than desktop computers, embedded computers are by far more pervasive than the latter ones.

3.2 Hardware Platform

The operating system must be tied to an specific platform, and, instead of a tailor-made hardware, a prototyping board from the embedded systems market was selected. This comes with advantages: (a) being a prototyping board there is drivers support from the manufacturer; (b) the board comes with an on-board debugger and a pre-loaded bootloader, which eliminates the need of having an expensive emulator attached to a JTAG port; (c) the board can be purchased by anyone interested in taking or delivering the tutorial; and (d) the board integrates seamlessly with the

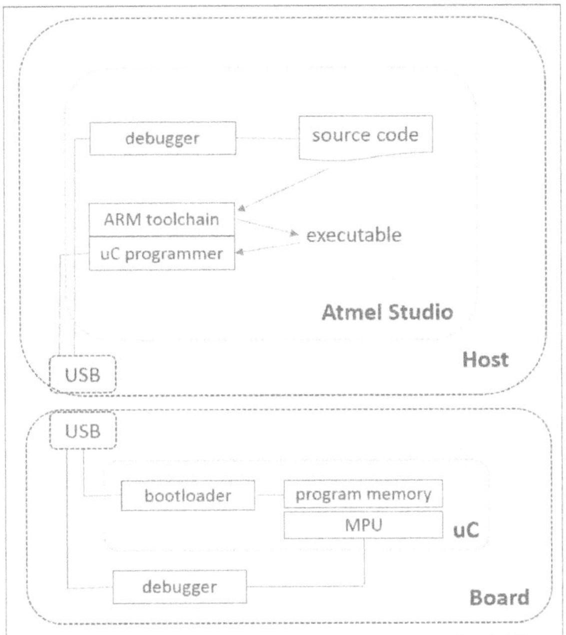

Figure 3: Development Environment

development tools provided by the manufacturer as it is an *official* prototyping/evaluation board.

More specifically, as shown in Figure 2, we have selected the Atmel SAM4S Xplained Pro board together with some of its extension boards.

The selected board is equipped with enough peripherals to make projects interesting. It integrates an OLED screen, four buttons, five LEDs, a light sensor, a temperature sensor, a microSD card slot, a USB port, an on-board 2GB NAND flash, a prototyping board, an LCD display header, and exposed pins for GPIO, USART, ADC, PWM, I2C, SPI, and an IRQ.

3.3 Development Environment

Another circumstantial yet important benefit of working with an embedded platform are the availability of mature debugging facilities. Modifying an instructional desktop OS or building one from scratch relies on open source tools, which are limited in debugging sophistication (not because it is not possible, but simply because tools are not available). ARM processors, on the contrary, come with JTAG capabilities, which integrate seamlessly with vendor chipset and software that allows to debug the micro-controller almost as a regular desktop application program. In particular, Atmel Studio 6 — based on Microsoft Visual Studio — integrates all the necessary tools to *off-the-shelf* develop and debug firmware for the Atmel SAM4S Xplained Pro.

Figure 3 roughly depicts the development environment for MiniOS. The platform comes with an on-board debugger that connects to the micro-controller for debugging firmware, and a pre-loaded boot-loader to update firmware. On the host side (the desktop computer used to write MiniOS), all the required development tools are integrated in Atmel Studio: source code editor, the GNU toolchain for ARM processors, host-side debugger software, and software for reprogramming the micro-controller. The source code is first compiled to an executable, which in turn is flashed to the micro-controller's program memory. When debugging, it is possible to do source-level step debugging of the flashed firmware, while memory, and the CPU and I/O registers are available for inspection.

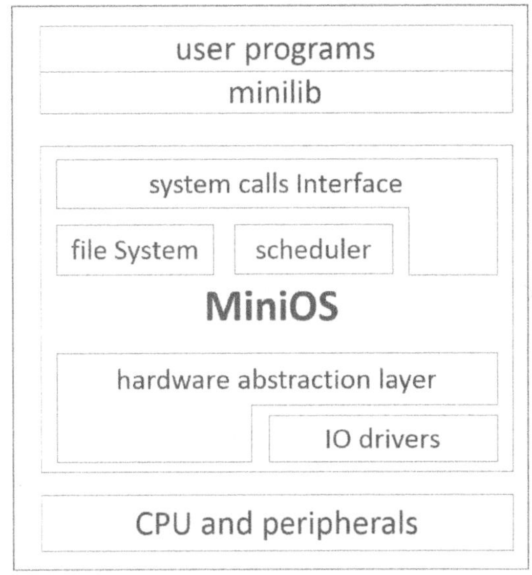

Figure 4: MiniOS Architecture

3.4 Architecture

Striving for simplicity MiniOS has the simplest monolithic kernel possible — although to be fair MiniOS itself is a kernel. As shown in Figure 4, user programs call the functionality defined in *minilib*, while minilib is responsible of invoking MiniOS system calls (system calls dealing with the file system, the scheduler, and the HAL). Some example functions in minilib are thread_create, oled_write, button_start, time_get, thread_yield, among others. Except for the drivers themselves, within MiniOS there is no direct interaction with hardware. Instead a hardware abstraction layer written by students sits in between to simplify access to it. IO drivers, on the contrary, are provided and implement very basic drivers for peripherals. For instance, consider

3.5 Design Principles

Borrowing some of the design principles behind Pintos projects in [11] and adding from our own goals and experience, the design principles for MiniOS are as follows:

- **Maximize creative freedom:** For the most part project assignments do not to prescribe specific implementations. Bonus tasks are suggested for students who go beyond requirements.

- **There is no single correct answer:** In our experience, lab assignments with a single correct answer are less popular among students and tend to be completed less than the rest. Also presents itself easy for plagiarism, as any discussion among students would result in giving away the answer.

- **Test-Driven Labs:** Test cases serve as guidelines for students to write their own solutions as well as for evaluating them. This also clarifies some possible source of ambiguity in lab assignment descriptions.

- **Focus is on the system, not the platform:** When writing an OS, the system and the platform are inseparable. Yet, when possible, emphasis is placed on operating systems concepts, as opposed to the platform. This permits students to concentrate on what really matters. Very technical pieces of code that require a precise understanding of the machine are thus provided (e.g. context switching, changing the processor from kernel to user mode, basic driver functionality, etc.). All these pieces of code, however, are derived. Meaning, every single line given comes with an accompanying explanation as to their origin.

- **Write the system from scratch:**Except for drivers, which are very complex on their own, there is documentation explaining in detail how to derive the code as to make projects truly *from scratch*, and at the same time allows motivated students to make changes to it.

- **Provide students with C programming and debugging tutorials:** For most students operating systems is their first encounter with C. Students consistently reported much of the struggle with assignments came from a poor understanding of the C programming language.

  Concerning Debugging, we have encountered more than a few students, who having always programmed in high-level programming languages, lack the patience and the required debugging skills to complete assignments.

3.6 Lab Projects

Despite the lack of *single right solutions* labs build on each other, therefore, after every lab, solutions are made available. This accounts for students who did not complete assignments, as well as buggy solutions which may fail in the future. Students are encouraged to use their own solutions or incorporate their own to the solutions handed in, however. Every lab is handed out with an example application and a video demonstrating the use of the functionality that has to be implemented.

- **Project 1 (Introduction):** A high-level introduction to micro-controllers, embedded systems, ARM processors, the hardware platform, and development tools is supplied. Use of the development tools is demonstrated with accompanying videos.

- **Project 2 (Hardware Abstraction Layer):** In this section students are asked to implement a basic set of functionalities to access hardware; functionality which is used by upper layers to communicate with the machine. In the particular case of peripheral drivers, given their complexity, they are handed out (with example code and demonstrative videos). Students then use them to build more complex functionality. Functionality accessing the OLED display, the system timer, buttons, LEDs, and light sensor. While for bonus marks, available options are temperature sensor, miniSD Card-related functions, PWM, USART, USB CDC, GPIO, I2C, and ADC. Students willing to go further are free to wire their own peripherals through the prototyping board (perhaps an Xbee communication module) and incorporate them into MiniOS.

- **Project 3 (User Mode and minilib):** Processor modes, the memory protection unit (MPU), and software interrupts are introduced. To lessen the complexity, how make a software interrupts and how to change the processor from kernel to user mode (and vice versa) is included in the lab accompanying text. Students must then use software interrupts to write a library *minilib* and a system call layer in MiniOS as to enable separation of applications running in user mode from the operating system running in kernel mode. For bonus point students may choose from various available tasks: further protection of kernel data and code via the MPU; perform a simple performance study to determine the overhead of implementing system calls as software interrupts; among other tasks.

- **Project 4 (CPU Scheduler):** A basic pre-emptive FIFO scheduler is derived from scratch. All the details of context switching, creation and scheduling of threads is explained in detail. It is student's task to add support for priorities to threads, and add support for cooperative scheduling. For bonus marks students may choose from enhancing CPU utilization by allowing threads to block when waiting for I/O, implementing basic thread signalling functionality (wait, notify, notify all), modifying the scheduler to enable thread termination, implementation of priority inheritance, use Cortex-M4 atomic read/write instructions to implement a semaphore, et cetera.

- **Project 5 (File System):** Students must write a simple file system for the miniSD Card. In particular, creation, deletion, and renaming of files and directories. As bonus points, students are asked to implement a simple USB Shell that will allow them to invoke functionality from the file system remotely (working examples of USB connectivity are provided).

- **Final Project:** At the end of the semester students get to team up in pairs to show off their new acquired skills with a project of their own choice. Some suggestions are: memory management functionality, a microkernel-based MiniOS, an event-scheduler, an interprocess communication layer, a shell, a thread library, a fancy file system, a tailor-made OS for some embedded system, et cetera.

  Some of the notable final projects made by students during the last two years we tried MiniOS were: (i) Implementation and study of different CPU scheduling algorithms; (ii) An OS for a quad-copter (including the quad-copter itself and a semaphore to handle concurrency issues); (iii) An OS for a coffee maker (iv) Linux-like thread signalling; (v) A shell (host-side written in Java); (vi) SimpleOS (a tailor-made embedded OS); and (vii) A Java SD Card interface.

3.7 Lessons learned

A preliminary version of MiniOS with the accompanying tutorial was used in fall 2013 and fall 2014 as the laboratory component in an introductory course to operating systems at the University of Northern BC. At the end of each semester half-day symposium were held where students demonstrated their final projects to the department — educating takes a village. Students were positive of the learning experience and showed themselves motivated and enthusiastic of developing their final projects. While feedback from students was favourable, there were a few things needed to be taken into consideration:

- Many of the difficulties faced during lab assignment came from students' poor C skills. Hence the lab instructor ought to set aside time specifically for C tutorials—this is very important.
- Coming from a Java background, many students do not have the debugging skills or the patience to debug low-level C. Even if the tools are available, they are not used properly. Teaching students to debug and be meticulous is essential to the success of the labs.
- Although the document goes in detail step by step, some students seemed to learn better when the same material was explained in the whiteboard during assigned tutorial times. Hence it is recommended to guide students through the material.
- Dealing with drivers can be very technical and challenging. During the course students had all the code and examples needed. Still for final projects, tutoring students on how to integrate sensors and actuators was necessary.
- Depending on the circumstances it might be necessary to adjust the course. For instance, to give enough time to work on projects, we removed the File System Lab in the middle of the course. To account for those students who needed a file system to work on their projects, we added to MiniOS a pre-existing Fat file system for embedded devices.
- Since students are exploring new territories, in the first lab tutorial, setting up and using the development tools must be demonstrated with the actual hardware platform; including, software installation, re-flashing of new firmware, debugging, and other features of the IDE. This is why we have decided to include demonstrative videos with the tutorial.

4. CONCLUDING REMARKS

This paper presents MiniOS, a minimal instructional embedded operating system that is intended for teaching operating systems projects. We have adopted this approach at our university and we found it successful. We would like to share our experience with SIGCSE audience and make the approach and supporting resources available for others to try out. MiniOS is intended to be used either as part of an undergraduate operating systems course, or followed independently by anyone from home.

The main limitation of our approach is that it may not be suitable for a class which is primarily interested in understanding the mainstream operating system functionalities, irrespective of its practical use. A simpler architecture such as a low-end ARM does not come with many features a desktop processor does (e.g. memory management unit). An embedded OS may be, then, too simple and have little resemblance to an actual fully-featured desktop operating system.

Acknowledgments

This work was partly supported by NSERC Discovery Grant (312162- 2010). The author would like to thank the anonymous reviewers for their constructive comments.

5. REFERENCES

[1] C. L. Anderson and M. Nguyen. A survey of contemporary instructional operating systems for use in undergraduate courses. *J. Comput. Sci. Coll.*, 21(1):183–190, Oct. 2005.

[2] J. Andrus and J. Nieh. Teaching operating systems using android. In *Proceedings of the 43rd ACM Technical Symposium on Computer Science Education*, SIGCSE '12, pages 613–618, New York, NY, USA, 2012. ACM.

[3] M. D. Black. Build an operating system from scratch: A project for an introductory operating systems course. *SIGCSE Bull.*, 41(1):448–452, Mar. 2009.

[4] D. Brylow. An experimental laboratory environment for teaching embedded operating systems. In *Proceedings of the 39th SIGCSE Technical Symposium on Computer Science Education*, SIGCSE '08, pages 192–196, New York, NY, USA, 2008. ACM.

[5] W. A. Christopher, S. J. Procter, and T. E. Anderson. The nachos instructional operating system. In *Proceedings of the USENIX Winter 1993 Conference Proceedings on USENIX Winter 1993 Conference Proceedings*, USENIX'93, pages 4–4, Berkeley, CA, USA, 1993. USENIX Association.

[6] D. Comer. *Operating System Design: The XINU Approach.* Prentice-Hall, Inc., Upper Saddle River, NJ, USA, 1984.

[7] P. J. Desnoyers. Teaching operating systems as how computers work. In *Proceedings of the 42Nd ACM Technical Symposium on Computer Science Education*, SIGCSE '11, pages 281–286, New York, NY, USA, 2011. ACM.

[8] M. Goldweber, R. Davoli, and M. Morsiani. The kaya os project and the umps hardware emulator. *SIGCSE Bull.*, 37(3):49–53, June 2005.

[9] D. A. Holland, A. T. Lim, and M. I. Seltzer. A new instructional operating system. In *Proceedings of the 33rd SIGCSE Technical Symposium on Computer Science Education*, SIGCSE '02, pages 111–115, New York, NY, USA, 2002. ACM.

[10] D. Hovemeyer, J. K. Hollingsworth, and B. Bhattacharjee. Running on the bare metal with geekos. *SIGCSE Bull.*, 36(1):315–319, Mar. 2004.

[11] B. Pfaff, A. Romano, and G. Back. The pintos instructional operating system kernel. In *Proceedings of the 40th ACM Technical Symposium on Computer Science Education*, SIGCSE '09, pages 453–457, New York, NY, USA, 2009. ACM.

[12] D. Travios. Arm holdings and qualcomm: The winners in mobile, February 2013.

[13] A. Vence. The unlikely tail of how arm came to rule the world, February 2014.

Achieving a Shared Goal with AP Computer Science A and AP Computer Science Principles

Paul T. Tymann
Rochester Institute of Technology
Rochester, NY 14623
+1 585-475-7908
paul.tymann@rit.edu

Frances P. Trees
Rutgers,
The State University of New Jersey
Piscataway, NJ 08854
+1 848-445-7299
fran.trees@cs.rutgers.edu

Lester Wainwright
Charlottesville High School
Charlottesville, VA 22901
+1 434-245-2410
Lester.Wainwright
@charlottesvilleschools.org

Richard Kick
Newbury Park High School
Newbury Park, CA 91320
+1 805-498-3676
kickrg@gmail.com

Sandy Czajka
Riverside Brookfield High School
Riverside, IL 60546
+1 708-442-7500
czajkas@rbhs208.net

Andrew Kuemmel
Madison West High School
Madison, WI 53726
+1 608-204-4100
andykuemmel@gmail.com

Lien Diaz (Moderator)
College Board, AP Program
Duluth, GA
770-225-4012
ldiaz@collegeboard.org

Categories and Subject Descriptors: K.3.2 [Computer and Information Science Education]: computer science education, curriculum

General Terms: Algorithms, Design, Experimentation

Keywords: CS0; CS1; case studies; active learning; computing applications

1.SUMMARY

College Board has joined national efforts to improve the state of STEM education, in particular to address the challenge of increasing participation with a diverse population of computer scientists to meet the growing demands of the field of computing. The Advanced Placement (AP) Program is pleased to endeavor in enhancing AP Computer Science offerings by maintaining college level integrity and addressing issues of equity and access for students and teachers. In addition to the established AP Computer Science A course, the AP Program is engaged in the development of a forthcoming AP Computer Science Principles course. The additional option for high school students to study college level computing will provide more students with an opportunity to be introduced to important computer science concepts, gain a broader perspective of the field of study, and have access to a larger pathway into computing.

This session will review information regarding the AP Computer Science A course and will discuss plans for collecting feedback from college faculty regarding course content and approaches to programming techniques and languages. It will then discuss the new Computer Science Principles course and plans for the development and launch of the course and exam. The session will conclude with a Q&A session addressing questions regarding both courses. The session will be moderated by Lien Diaz from the AP Program at the College Board.

SIGCSE'15, March 4–7, 2015, Kansas City, MO, USA.
ACM 978-1-4503-2966-8/15/03.
http://dx.doi.org/10.1145/2676723.2677325

2.SESSION OBJECTIVES

In recent years, the AP CS A course and examination has been the subject of substantial discussion and debate. How should computer science be introduced? What topics should be included? What pedagogy is appropriate? To what extent should programming be involved? This session seeks to clarify the role of the AP CS A course and examine how the new AP CS Principles course will complement the exam offerings of the College Board. This motivation leads to the following session objectives.

- Review information regarding the AP Computer Science A course and learn about how college professors will be engaged to provide feedback on course alignment with in introductory college computer science courses.
- Review information about the AP Computer Science Principles Course and Exam and learn about a new blended assessment model that includes a through-course assessment and an end-of-course exam.
- Examine similarities and differences between the AP Computer Science A and the AP Computer Science Principles course and discuss a shared goal to increase access and participation with more diverse students to study computer science via these AP courses
- Learn how an enhanced AP Computer Science program will help to address national challenges in computer science education.

3.OUTLINE OF THE SESSION

The following outline envisions questions and discussion during the last 45 minutes of the session. Realistically, some questions may arise during the initial presentations, so the question-answer time may be revised as the session progresses.

- The AP CS A course and examination --- 10 minutes, Tymann
  - Purpose: college credit and/or placement
  - Content overview and plans for a college faculty colloquium
  - The AP CS Principles course and examination --- 10 minutes, Trees
    - Purpose and motivation for the Course
    - Assessment components
- AP Computer Science Program – A shared goal of increasing diversity and participation --- 10 minutes, Diaz/Wainwright/Kuemmel
- Questions, audience feedback, discussion --- 45 minutes

4.EXPECTATIONS

This proposed session will serve several audiences:

- Teachers of introductory computer science (at HS and College levels) who are interested in nation-wide trends and practices regarding their courses.
- Educators and administrators who want to better understand the role and goals of AP CS A and CS Principles.
- Guidance counselors and student advisors who want to guide students in the transition from high school CS courses to college courses.
- Department chairs and deans who are monitoring placement and credit policies regarding AP courses.
- AP CS teachers who are interested in having their students receive college credit

With the diversity of practices regarding introductory CS at the college level, the results reported in this session will likely generate considerable discussion and debate. Thus, the session will conclude with a 45-minute question-answer-feedback session involving attendees.

5.SUITABILITY FOR A SPECIAL SESSION

This special session responds to many inquiries over the years regarding the extent to which the AP CS A course and examination relate to introductory CS courses at the college level. Thus, this special session serves as something of a report by the AP CS A Development Committee.

- *The session does not represent a traditional SIGCSE paper:* The material presented discusses the direction the AP CS program is taking. The session is not a presentation of educational research or pedagogy, following the form for usual SIGSE papers.
- *The session does not bring together multiple viewpoints as would be found in a typical SIGCSE panel:* The session leaders represent the AP CS Development Committees, and the session will discuss practices used by the College Board and the AP CS Development Committees over the next few years.

Altogether, the material for this session continues an on-going dialog between the AP CS program and the broad computing community, The nature of the session does not seem to fit well with either a paper or panel format, but the content seems of general interest to the overall community. The special session framework seems best suited for this type of discussion.

6.ACKNOWLEDGMENTS

The Advanced Placement Computer Science A Development Committee thanks the College Board for its efforts in obtaining feedback from community college, college, and university faculty throughout the United States regarding introductory courses at the college level.

7.REFERENCES

[1] College Board, *Advanced Placement Computer Science College Curriculum Study,* June 2011.

[2] College Board, *The Computer Science A Course Description*, 2010. http://apcentral.collegeboard.com/apc/public/repository/ap-computer-science-course-description.pdf

[3] College Board, *The Computer Science A Course Description*, 2014.

[4] College Board, *Computer Science College Comparability Study*, 2012.

[5] College Board, *AP Computer Science Faculty Colloquium Results*, December 10, 2008.

[6] College Board, *AP Computer Science College Curriculum Study Results*, 2008.

[7] College Board, *Draft AP Computer Science Principles Curriculum Framework*, June 2014.

[8] College Board, *Draft AP Computer Science Principles Performance Tasks*, June 2014.

Towards Grand Challenges in Computing Education Across Disciplines: Setting an Agenda for Research and Pedagogy

Lecia Barker (Moderator)
School of Information
University of Texas at Austin
+1 512-232-8364
lecia@ischool.utexas.edu

Stephen Cooper
Computer Science Department
Stanford University
+1 650-723-9798
coopers@stanford.edu

Andrew McGettrick
Computer and Information Sciences
University of Strathclyde
+44 141 552 4400
andrew.mcgettrick@strath.ac.uk

Jason Thatcher
Department of Management
Clemson University
+1 864-656-3751
jason.b.thatcher@gmail.com

Heikki Topi
Computer Information Systems
Bentley University
+1 781-891-2799
htopi@bentley.edu

Categories and Subject Descriptors

K.3.2 Computer and Information Science Education

General Terms

Human Factors

Keywords

Computing education research; Information systems education research; Interdisciplinary; Grand Challenges

1. SUMMARY

PACE, the Partnership for Advancing Computing Education, held a workshop on Computing Education Research in Washington DC on August 21st and 22nd 2014. The goals of this invitation-only workshop were to

- explore the possibilities for developing a forward looking and challenging research agenda for computing education as a whole, one that will extend and enhance the computing education research community;
- enhance the standing of the computing education research community and galvanize it into meaningful and effective action;
- understand the ways in which professional and academic computing societies can best serve the computing education research community; and
- establish a joint understanding and strengthen the sharing of research agendas and directions on computing education across various computing-related sub-disciplines.

One of the many conclusions from the workshop was that the community should consider articulating a set of Grand Challenges for computing education. If this could be achieved in a meaningful manner, it would directly support several of the goals of the workshop. For instance, it could address the research agenda: a true shared understanding of the Grand Challenges of computing education would have the potential to serve as a guiding mechanism for computing education research agenda. Identification of the Grand Challenges would also address the issue of the status and standing of computing education in general and computing education research in specific.

The purpose of this Special Session is to advance the discussion about Grand Challenges for computing education, specifically by including the community in that discussion. In line with the multi-disciplinary nature of the PACE workshop, the intent of this process is to incorporate the perspectives of all major computing (sub)disciplines.

2. TOPICS

Grand Challenges are not new. These have been used over the years within a number of research communities to provide a focus for activity and often funding in science and engineering. See [1], for instance. In the past, the mainstream research community in computing has identified as grand challenges topics such as autonomous vehicles, speech recognition, computer vision, automated reasoning, and natural language understanding. See also [2]. Even within the computing education community there have been earlier attempts to specify Grand Challenges [3].

In order to place the discussion on a sound footing, the Special Session will address fundamental issues such as

- Background on Grand Challenges in computing education, including lessons learned from earlier efforts.
- What should characterize a Grand Challenge in computing education?

SIGCSE '15, March 4-7, 2015, Kansas City, MO, USA.
ACM 978-1-4503-2966-8/15/03.
http://dx.doi.org/10.1145/2676723.2677326

- Why are Grand Challenges important and what role can they play?
- Are Grand Challenges in computing education research and practice similar? How can we construct an environment where research and practice inform each other? Can Grand Challenges of computing education practice truly inform computing education research?
- What broad themes appear across the computing disciplines? Which Grand Challenges are shared across all computing disciplines and which more specific?

The panel members will provide examples of what they regard as Grand Challenges. Discussion of these within the community is, however, the most critical component of the special session. At some level, the community has to be seen to own the challenges so that they will seek to engage with them. Ideally, the challenges may even serve to expand the community, invigorate it, and expand connections between various computing disciplines.

The discussion during this special session is not expected to provide a definitive list of challenges. Instead, it can be seen as an early step in a set of discussions that will identify current core challenges for computing education and through this process, invigorate computing education research.

3. PANELISTS

LECIA BARKER (MODERATOR)

Lecia Barker, as chair of the PACE Board, will act as moderator and chair the session.

JASON THATCHER

Jason Thatcher, will discuss the importance of the concept of a grand challenge and provide information regarding efforts to engage the wider community beyond SIGCSE.

HEIKKI TOPI

Heikki Topi will provide background information and provide a perspective on what constitutes a grand challenge.

ANDREW MCGETTRICK and STEPHEN COOPER

Andrew McGettrick and Stephen Cooper will provide initial ideas for grand challenges.

4. EXPECTATIONS

The session will highlight potential Grand Challenges that surfaced in the PACE workshop, but will include ample time for discussion. In addition to the workshop results, there will be discussion of the relationship between computing education practice and computing education research in framing curriculum guidelines and informing research questions. The participation of the SIGCSE community is highly desired and will contribute to a fuller understanding of the issues involved in defining Grand Challenges in Computing Education.

The results of the session will be incorporated into a NSF-sponsored report on the state of Computing Education Research and shared with the ACM Education Board. A report of the session will be prepared and communicated with the SIGCSE community through Inroads and/or posts to the mailing list, as well as through the Ensemble portal.

5. SUITABILTY FOR A SPECIAL SESSION

SIGCSE Special Sessions were originally designed to provide a forum for connecting SIGCSE participants to results of NSF initiatives and other organizations with a commitment to computing education. This session matches that purpose exactly by fostering a conversation about an important computing education workshop that was conducted with funding from NSF. The topic is one of current interest and the involvement of ACM and NSF provides both resources and expertise to address the issue effectively. This opportunity to bring the results to the SIGCSE community is a natural and important component of the effort.

6. ACKNOWLEDGMENTS

The PACE Computing Education Research Workshop was supported by the National Science Foundation through Grant #1355395.

7. REFERENCES

[1] Office of Science and Technology Policy, Executive Office of the President. A Research and Development Strategy for High Performance Computing. Washington, D.C. November 20, 1987.

[2] Tony Hoare and Robin Milner (editors) *Grand Challenges in Computing: Research*, published by the British Computer Society, London, 2004.

[3] Andrew McGettrick, Roger Boyle, Roland Ibbett, John Lloyd, Gillian Lovegrove and Keith Mander. *Grand Challenges in Computing: Education*, published by the British Computer Society, London, 2004.

DEMONSTRATION SESSION

Exploring Computer Science Topics with Programmable Smartwatches

Shuo Niu, *Virginia Tech*
Andrey Esakia, *Virginia Tech*
D. Scott McCrickard, *Virginia Tech*
Contact: shuoniu@vt.edu

This demo features smartwatch applications created by junior/senior CS students in a mobile development course. The course featured the Pebble smartwatch, with an e-ink display, vibrating motor, and accelerometer. Smartwatches enhance mobile device use by acting as a secondary display and providing immediate notifications, but designing for them has challenges in memory management, sensor programming, networking issues, and display size. Incorporating Pebble smartwatch development in a mobile app development class allowed students to exercise core computer science concepts to overcome Pebble hardware and software limitations and to develop applications that leverage Pebble affordances. Two sections of the class featured Pebble-focused assignments, including an open-ended homework, a focused homework, and a term design project coordinating smartphone-smartwatch use. The two-semester experience yielded apps in all Pebble-defined categories, including tools and utilities, notifications, remotes, health and fitness, and games. Examples of the students' work from each of the categories will be presented in this demo on topics such as music synthesizing, remote camera operation, course management alerts, and server management. The presented apps reflect student understanding of the sensor functionalities, hardware capabilities and limitations, and interactions of the phone-watch pair. This demo will serve as a valuable resource for those who plan to incorporate smartwatch development into their teaching practice. Based on the educational experience gleaned, future opportunities can explore the role of the smartwatch in mobile development and programming education for college and K-12 students.

ACM Categories & Descriptors: K.3.2 [Computer and Information Science Education]

Keywords: Mobile, Smartwatch, Pebble, Development, Application

DOI: http://dx.doi.org/10.1145/2676723.2691874

SIGCSE'15, March 4–7, 2015, Kansas City, MO, USA.
ACM 978-1-4503-2966-8/15/03.

ENGAGE: A Game-based Learning Environment for Middle School Computational Thinking

Kristy Boyer, *North Carolina State University*
Philip Buffum, *North Carolina State University*
Kirby Culbertson, *North Carolina State University*
Megan Frankosky, *North Carolina State University*
James Lester, *North Carolina State University*
Allison Martinez-Arocho, *North Carolina State University*
Wookhee Min, *North Carolina State University*
Bradford Mott, *North Carolina State University*
Fernando Rodriguez, *North Carolina State University*
Eric Wiebe, *North Carolina State University*
Contact: keboyer@ncsu.edu

We present ENGAGE, a game-based learning environment for teaching computational thinking to middle school students. This project has dual aims: introducing computational thinking practices to students at a young age, and improving computational thinking attitudes among underrepresented students. In pursuit of these two goals, the ENGAGE team has mapped the learning objectives of the AP CS Principles course to the middle school level, and then built an immersive game experience upon that foundation. Students choose computer scientist avatars to represent themselves, and then play in pairs as they investigate a data-related mystery in an underwater research station, solving computational thinking challenges along the way. ENGAGE is currently being implemented as part of a quarterly elective in four middle schools in North Carolina. During the elective, students spend a total of ten classroom sessions playing the game, supplemented by "unplugged" activities that reinforce concepts learned in the game environment. We plan to expand to more middle schools in the 2015-2016 school year. In this demo, members of the SIGCSE community will be able to experience the ENGAGE game for themselves and learn more about its development and future directions. We will also discuss our success in recruiting and teaching the ENGAGE curriculum to middle school teachers who had no prior computer science experience, and the success of those middle school teachers in implementing ENGAGE within their classrooms.

ACM Categories & Descriptors: K.3.2 [Computer and Information Sciences Education]: Computer Science Education

Keywords: Game-based learning; Computational thinking; Middle school

Acknowledgment: This work is supported in part by the National Science Foundation through Grant CNS-113897.

DOI: http://dx.doi.org/10.1145/2676723.2691876

Correlation of Topic Model and Student Grades Using Comment Data Mining

Shaymaa E. Sorour
Kafr Elsheikh University, Egypt
Kyushu University, Japan
Motooka,Fukuoka 819-0395
shaymaa@ma.ait.kyushu-u.ac.jp

Kazumasa Goda
Kyushu Institute of Information Science, Japan
Dazaifu, Fukuoka 818-0117
gouda@kiis.ac.jp

Tsunenori Mine
Kyushu University, Japan
Motooka, Fukuoka 819-0395
mine@ait.kyushu-u.ac.jp

ABSTRACT

Assessment of learning progress and learning gain play a pivotal role in education fields. New technologies like comment data mining promote the use of new types of contents; student comments highly reflect student learning attitudes and activities compared to more traditional methods and they can be a powerful source of data for all forms of assessment. A teacher just asks students after every lesson to freely describe and write about their learning situations and behaviors. This paper proposes new methods based on a statistical latent class "Topics" for the task of student grade prediction; our methods convert student comments using latent semantic analysis (LSA) and probabilistic latent semantic analysis (PLSA), and generate prediction models using support vector machine (SVM) and artificial neural network (ANN) to predict student final grades. The experimental results show that our methods can accurately predict student grades based on comment data.

Categories and Subject Descriptors

H.2.8 [**Database Applications**]: Data mining
; K.3.2 [**Computer and Information Science Education**]: Self-assessment.

General Terms

Experimentation, Human factors.

Keywords

Comment Data Mining, Student Grade Prediction, LSA, PLSA.

1. INTRODUCTION

Education is being boosted by new attitudes to improving the learning process, and learning analytics is one of the most promising tools for the purpose. Although there is a debate about the definition of learning analytics, we adopt the definition of the learning analytics term introduced in the call for papers of the 1st LAK conference[1] : "Learning analytics is the measurement, collection, analysis and reporting of data about learners and their contexts, for purposes of understanding and optimizing learning and the environments in which it occurs."

Today, the use of learning analytics is becoming more necessary in assessment fields; teachers cannot take care of so many students in detail in the classroom. They want to estimate their learning situations at an early stage of their class and teach more advanced contents to high achieving students or others whose results are being improved. Average students have to be analyzed so that teachers can figure out problems or difficulties they have. Poor-achieving students or others who are likely to fail in their final examination need much care [4].

Goda et al.[6, 5] proposed the PCN method to estimate learning situations from comments freely written by students. The PCN method categorizes the comments into three items: P (Previous activity), C (Current activity), and N (Next activity). Item P indicates the learning activity before the class time. Item C shows the understanding and achievements of class subjects during the class time, and item N expresses the learning activity plan until the next class. The comments provide data expressing student learning status and their self-observation, self-judgment, and self-reflection.

To further contribute to the understanding of student attitudes and to enhance individualized feedback to them, this paper presents a study that applies text mining techniques to students' comments to predict their grades. In this study, we employ LSA and PLSA models to grasp students' learning attitudes and learning situations. LSA constructs a conceptual vector space in which each comment is represented as a vector in the space. It not only greatly reduces the dimensionality but also uncovers the important associative relationship between comments. PLSA finds some aspects of words known as "topics" that can deeply distinguish comments with different meaning. In this paper we introduce PLSA to improve the results of LSA. Comment data analyzed by PLSA have some benefits for student assessment in education fields such as understanding student behavior and situations, focusing on topics with different meanings, topics

SIGCSE'15, March 4-7, 2015, Kansas City, MO, USA.

http://dx.doi.org/10.1145/2676723.2677259.

[1]https://tekri.athabascau.ca/analytics/
"1st International Conference on Learning Analytics and Knowledge 2011."

which can reflect student learning attitudes, understanding of subjects, difficulties in learning, and student learning activities in each lesson. We create prediction models based on comments analyzed by PLSA and LSA using ANN and SVM methods and compare the accuracy of the models. The experiments are conducted using data from two classes (Class A and Class B) for each lesson, using the data for one class for training and the data for other as test data. Although students learn the same subject in the two classes, there are differences between the comments in the two classes; the difficulty of the subject in the lesson also affects student attitudes to expressing their behavior and sometimes does not give the students leeway to write comments. Therefore this is a challenging problem. The contributions of our work are the following:

- PLSA and LSA models are employed to analyze patterns and relationships between the extracted words and latent concepts contained in unstructured collections of texts (student comments).
- The PLSA model is improved to reflect student attitudes and situations more deeply in each lesson and to achieve higher reliability in predicting student grades.
- ANN and SVM models are employed to predict student grades; they are two popular strategies for supervised machine learning and classification, and it's not clear which method is better for a particular problem.
- The experiments are conducted to validate the proposed methods by calculating the F-measure and accuracy for each lesson in estimating final student grades.

The rest of the paper is organized as follows. Section 2 discuses related work. Section 3 introduces the overview of our research. Section 4 introduces the procedures and methodology of the proposed method. Section 5 discusses some of the highlighted experimental results. Finally, Section 6 concludes the paper and describes our future work.

2. RELATED WORK

The ability to predict student performance is very important in educational environments. Increasing students' success in their learning environment is a long-term goal in all academic institutions. In recent years, there is a growing interest in employing educational data mining techniques (EDM) to conduct the automatic analysis of learner performance and behavioral data in learning environments. Various experiments have been carried out in the EDM area that assess student learning performance, improve the learning process, guide student learning, provide feedback, adapt learning recommendations based on student learning behaviors, and evaluate learning materials and courseware [1, 11, 7]. An emerging trend in EDM is the use of text mining which is an extension of data mining to text data.

Text mining focuses on finding and extracting useful or interesting patterns from unstructured text such as text documents, chat messages and emails. As an automated technique, text mining can be used to efficiently and systematically identify, extract, manage, integrate, and exploit knowledge for research and education [7]. Currently, there are only several studies about how to use comment mining to analyze learning related data.

Goda et al.[6] proposed the PCN method to estimate student learning situations on the basis of freestyle student comments written just after lesson. Goda et al.[5] also conducted another study on using the PCN scores to determining the level of validity of assessment based on student comments and showed there are strong correlations between the PCN scores and the accuracy of predicting final student grades. They employed multiple regression analysis to calculate the PCN scores, and the results indicated that student comments with high PCN scores are considered to appropriately describe the student learning attitude.

For the purpose of predicting student grades from comment data, Sorour et al.[13] proposed a new method based on the C-comment from the PCN method. They applied the LSA technique and K-means clustering method. They conducted their experiments from lesson 7 to 15 by combining comment data from the two classes. To improve the prediction accuracy results, Sorour et al.[15] proposed similarity measuring and overlap methods based on their previous method [13]. Their previous method achieved an average 66.4% prediction accuracy using the k-means clustering method, and the scores were increased to 73.6% and 78.5% by adding the overlap method and the similarity measuring method, respectively. Different from the above studies, Sorour et al.[14] applied another type of machine learning technique: artificial neural network (ANN) and made it learn the relationships between comment data analyzed by LSA and final student grades. They constructed a network model for each lesson. The average prediction accuracy of final student grades was 82.6%.

The goal of our study is to understand individual students more deeply and to recognize their learning status and attitude so as to give feedback to them. In this study we focus on the accuracy of predicting final student grades using P, C and N comments; we try to predict their final grades in each lesson by separately using data in each lesson for two different classes.

3. BACKGROUND

3.1 Subject of the study

Comment data were collected from Goda's courses consisting of 15 lessons. The main subject from lesson 1 to 6 is computer literacy, giving information on how to use some IT tools such as word processors, spread sheets, and presentation tools. Computer literacy education is compulsory throughout senior high schools in Japan, with only a few differences in the details of course contents. From lesson 7 to 15, students begin to learn the basics of programming. The main subject in those lessons is introductory C programming. In the 7th lesson, most students are novices at programming; it's a new subject and not required until they enter university [6]. Table 1. shows examples of PCN comments written by student from lessons 1 to 6 and lessons 7 to 15.

3.2 Overview of the proposed approach

In this paper, two types of framework are proposed for the analysis of learning performance based on free-style comment data in each lesson by comparing the PLSA model with the LSA model. Fig.1 shows the overall procedures of the proposed method consisting of the following four phases: 1)Comment data collection, 2)Data preparation, 3)Training phase, 4)Test phase.

Table 1: Examples of comments written by students

Viewpoint	Comment data from lesson 1 to 6
P	I trained typing, and achieved the speed of 200 strokes per minute.
C	The way of input is quite difficult; I feel that I could hardly follow all the steps.
N	I would like to practice again, because I'm not so good in designing slides.
	Comment data from lesson 7 to 15
P	I read the text of programming for the next lesson, but I didn't understand.
C	I was completely able to understand the subject of this lesson.
N	I recognized that I should do exercise not only in mind but also by hand.

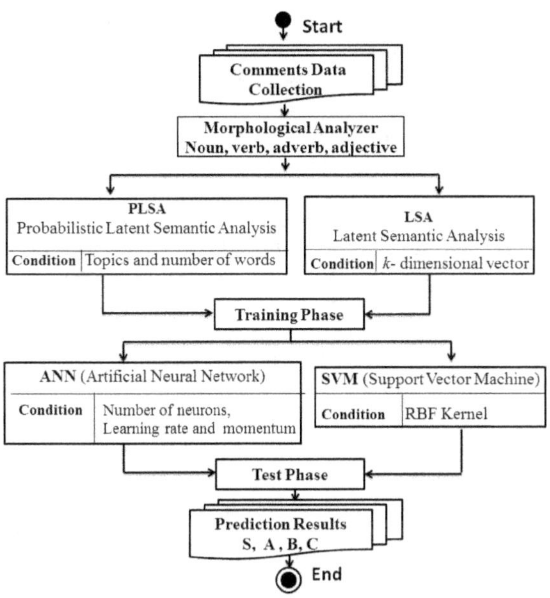

Figure 1: Mechanism of the proposed method.

1. Comment Data Collection: This phase focuses on collecting student comments after each lesson.

2. Data Preparation: The data preparation phase covers all the activities required to construct the data set for the training and test phases from the initial raw data. Our methods analyze P, C and N comment data, extract words and parts of speech (verb, noun, adjective, and adverb) with Mecab program[1], which is a Japanese morphological analyzer, create a word-by-comment matrix with extracted words. This word-by-comment matrix, say A, is comprised of m words $w_1, w_2, ..., w_m$ in n comments $c_1, c_2, ..., c_n$, where the value of each cell a_{ij} indicates the total occurrence frequencies of word w_j in comment c_i. We then employ LSA and PLSA models to analyze patterns and relationships between the extracted words and latent concepts contained in the unstructured collection of texts (student comments).

3. Training Phase: This phase builds prediction models of student grades based on LSA and PLSA results by using ANN and SVM models.

4. Test Phase: This phase evaluates the performance of prediction models by their Accuracy and F-measure.

[1]http://sourceforge.net/projects/mecab/

3.2.1 Comment Data Collection

Comment data were collected from 123 students in two classes: 60 in Class A and 63 in Class B. We considered the prediction of a final student grade from his/her comments. We chose one of five grades: S, A, B, C and D instead of the mark itself as a student result. The assessment of each student was done by considering the average mark of three assigned reports, and his/her attendance rate.

Although we have 123 students, some students didn't submit their comments because they didn't write any comments or were absent, especially for those achieving grades C and D. Fig.2 displays the average real number of C-comments in class A and class B. It can be seen that there is little difference from lesson 1 to 6 between the number of comments of grades C and D in class A and B. The numbers of comments from lesson 7 to 15 with grade A, C and D in class A are smaller than those in class B, e.g. the number of comments with grade D is about 64% smaller. In addition, more than 50% of students with grade D didn't submit comments, whose total number is less than 7. So we combined comment data in grades C and D into one grade C and use 4-grade categories: S, A, B and C.

The number of words appearing in each comment averages 14 words, and the number of words in the comments by each class is about 780 words. In addition, the number of distinct words in each class is over 310 words.

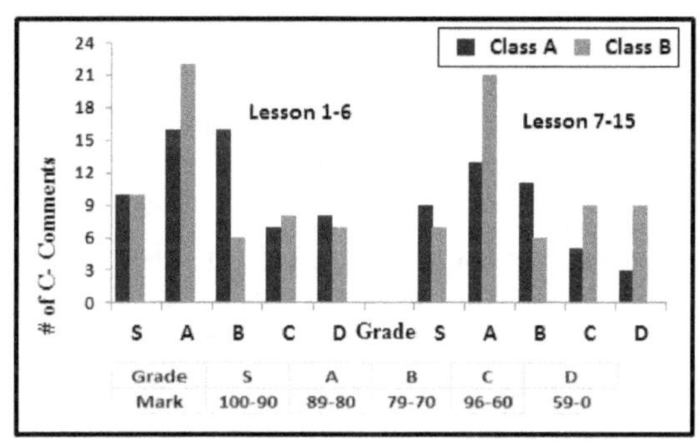

Figure 2: The relation between the number of comments and student grades.

4. METHODOLOGY

This section describes our methodology for predicting student performance from free-style comment data. We applied LSA and PLSA models to the analyzed comments, then employed ANN and SVM techniques to build prediction models of final student grades: S, A, B and C. After testing both methods, results will be compared.

4.1 Latent Semantic Analysis

Latent semantic analysis (LSA) is a well-known representative of semantic approaches. It identifies the hidden meaning of textual information in documents by considering occurrences and co-occurrences of terms. In preparing for LSA, log entropy term weighting was applied to the original word-by-comment matrix to balance the effect of word frequencies in all the comments. To extract semantic patterns from comment data, we use a rank-validation procedure. This procedure enables the identification of a maximal number of semantic patterns where each pattern can be used to represent a specific topic. The rank-validation procedure is successfully evaluated by using LSA with singular value decomposition (SVD), a form of factor analysis [2]. The singular value decomposition of matrix A is defined as

$$A = USV^T \tag{1}$$

where U and V are the matrices of the term vectors and comment vectors. $S = diag(r_1, ..., r_n)$ is the diagonal matrix of singular values. The general claim for using LSA is that similarities between comments or between comments and queries (new comments) can be more reliably estimated in the reduced latent space representation than in the original representation. To reduce the dimensions, we can simply choose the k largest singular values and the corresponding left and right singular vectors[2].

4.2 Probabilistic Latent Semantic Analysis

Probabilistic latent semantic analysis (PLSA) [9] provides a probabilistic formulation to model documents in a text collection. It assumes that the words are generated from a mixture of latent aspects (topics) which can be decomposed from a document. In our experiment, we briefly outline the principle of the PLSA after preparing the comment data and extracting the word-by-comment matrix.

Suppose a collection that contains M comments is denoted by $C = c_1, ..., c_M$, and each comment c_i is represented with the count of its words from a vocabulary $W = w_1, ..., w_N$. The whole collection is summarized by an $N \times M$, where each entry $n(w_j, c_i)$ indicates the count of the word w_j in the comment c_i. In the framework of the PLSA, the observed word W is conditionally independent of the comment C given a latent variable $Z = z_1, ..., z_k$, which is referred to as "latent aspect."

In the context of comment analysis, the joint probability of an observed word w_j and a comment c_i is

$$P(w_j, c_i) = P(c_i)P(w_j|c_i) \tag{2}$$

Assuming that (w_j, c_i) is conditionally independent for a given latent aspect Z, we can marginalize the conditional probability $P(w_j|c_i)$ over the latent aspect z_k

$$P(w_j|c_i) = \sum_{k=1}^{K} P(z_k|c_i)P(w_j|z_k) \tag{3}$$

where $P(z_k|c_i)$ is the probability of aspect z_k occurring in a comment c_i and $P(w_j|z_k)$ is the probability of word w_j occurring in a particular aspect z_k. Substituting Eq.(3) into Eq.(2), we get

$$P(w_j, c_i) = P(c_i)\sum_{k=1}^{K} P(z_k|c_i)P(w_j|z_k) \tag{4}$$

Fitting the model to the observed data can be completed using the well-known Expectation Maximization (EM) algorithm [3]. The EM algorithm maximizes the likelihood of observed data estimating the parameters $P(w_j|z_k)$ and $P(z_k|c_i)$

$$L = \prod_{i=1}^{M}\prod_{j=1}^{N} P(c_i)\sum_{k=1}^{K} P(z_k|c_i)P(w_j|z_k)^{n(w_j,c_i)} \tag{5}$$

Maximizing the log of likelihood L in Eq. (5) with respect to the probabilistic distribution, the iteration equations can be obtained by E**-Step** and M**-Step** of the EM algorithm [9, 8].

The main difficulty in using the general PLSA model is to consider the trade-off between predictive performance on the training data and unseen new data, i.e. the problem of overfitting to the training data. To solve this problem we reduced the number of topics in the training data and examined the number of words w_j in each topic from lesson 1 to 15. Here, the aspects of words (topics) for training data become observable. We called this model PLSA*. After some trials, we chose the optimum number of topics and examined the number of words with high probability for each lesson.

4.3 Model Estimation by ANN

A three-layered perceptron was established in our research to estimate student grades. We constructed a network model for each lesson. Layer 1 of each network, which is the input layer, consists of a k-dimensional vector of LSA results that characterize similarity between words or the PLSA matrix after obtaining the optimum number of topics and the top number of words in each topic. Layer 2 consists of one hidden layer; the number of neurons in the hidden layer is chosen heuristically because they showed the least error during the training of the data set with classes A and B. The number of the neurons established for all lessons by using the LSA method was between 14 and 19 and when using the PLSA and PLSA* model, it was between 8 and 12. Layer 3, the output layer, consists of 4 neurons denoting student grades: S, A, B, and C. The total output produced by the neuron can be summarized by

$$y_k = g'(a_k) \tag{6}$$

where g' is the activation function of output units and a_k is the total weight from the previous layer. The ANN was trained by Back Propagation (BP)[12] which is based on the principle of gradient descent learning. Each network weight will be adjusted according to the presented input and the error to the network as shown in Eq.(8):

$$w_{ij}(n+1) = w_{ij}(n) + \eta.e_i(n)x_j(n) + \alpha(w_{ij}(n) - w_{ij}(n-1)) \tag{7}$$

where η is a learning rate parameter of error e_i that is adjusted with the weight of presented input, w_{ij} is a weight between processing elements (i) and (j) at iteration (n), and $x_j(n)$ is an input value at processing element (j). α is a momentum parameter. For the purpose of training data, we set the weight randomly for all input parameters. The weight values for updating η and α were set from 0.1 to 0.3 for η, and from 0.65 to 0.85 for α for all lessons. Each network was trained with more than 1000 iterations to determine the predictive power.

4.4 Model Estimation by SVM

SVM is a powerful solution to the classification problems. The main advantages of SVM used as a classifier are its extremely powerful learning procedure and the ability that it leads to the global minimum of the defined error function[10]. LibSVM is a library supporting vector machines. Its goal is to promote SVM as a convenient tool. In our research, we used the MATLAB LibSVM tool [2] to predict student grades based on the results obtained by PLSA and LSA models. We employed the SVM method with RBF kernel to generate models from lesson 1 to 15 and predict a student grade as one of four grades: S, A, B and C based on the analyzed comment data.

[2]http://www.csie.ntu.edu.tw/cjlin/libsvm/index.html

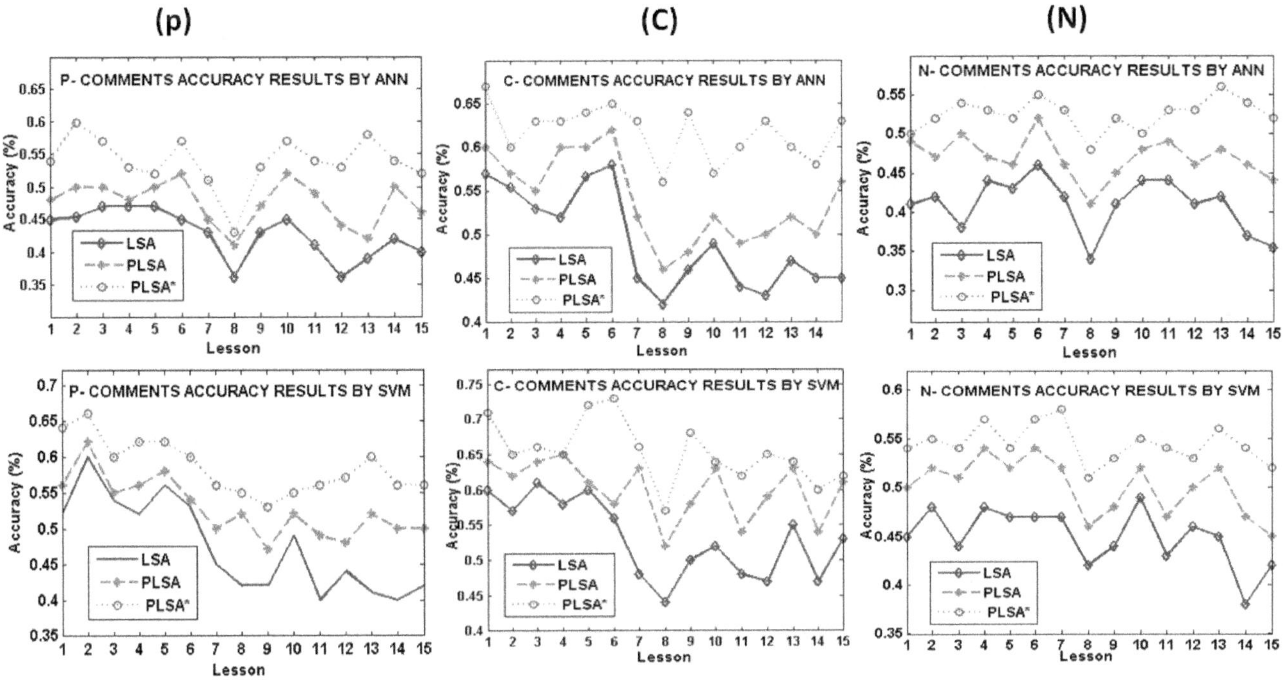

Figure 3: Overall accuracy results for PCN comment.

5. EXPERIMENTAL RESULTS

We evaluated the prediction performance of our proposed models by 2-fold cross validation. We constructed a model from comment data in one class. Then, as a test, we applied the model to the comment data in the other class. We compared the predicted grade with the grade in the corresponding original data. The procedure was repeated in each lesson and the results were averaged. We run evaluation experiments by calculating Accuracy and F-measure as follows: Let G be 4-grade categories (S, A, B and C), and X be a subset of G; let obs (s_i, X) be a function that returns 1 if the grade of student s_i is included in X, 0 otherwise, where $1 \leq i \leq n$, and n is the number of students; $pred(s_i)$ be a function that returns a set of grade categories only including a predicted grade for student s_i; $!pred(s_i)$ returns a complement of $pred(s_i)$.

$TP = \{s_i | obs(s_i, pred(s_i)) = 1\}$, $FP = \{s_i | obs(s_i, pred(s_i)) = 0\}$
$FN = \{s_i | obs(s_i, !pred(s_i)) = 1\}$, $TN = \{s_i | obs(s_i, !pred(s_i)) = 0\}$
$\text{Precision} = \frac{TP}{TP+FP}$
$\text{Recall} = \frac{TP}{TP+FN}$
$F\text{-}measure = 2 * \frac{(Precision * Recall)}{(Precision + Recall)}$
$\text{Accuracy} = \frac{TP+TN}{TP+TN+FP+FN}$

5.1 Overall Prediction Results

Fig.3 displays the average accuracy of overall prediction results obtained using ANN and SVM techniques based on P, C and N comments and analyzed using LSA and PLSA models. To achieve highly accurate prediction results from student comments with LSA method, we examined the different number of k-dimensions with ANN and SVM techniques from lesson 1 to 15, with P, C and N comments. For example, the average accuracy results for C-comments from lesson 1 to 6 using ANN had the higher rate between k =18 and k =22. It scored 50%. The highest rate scored 54% with k =20. From lesson 7 to 15, the higher rate scored from k =3 to k =12. It scored 46%. The highest rate scored 48% with k =10. On the other hand, PLSA automatically determines the number of topics and the number of words in each topic. For example in lesson 7 and after choosing C-comments, 7 topics and 30 words in each topic were obtained using the EM algorithm. We manually chose the number of topics and the number of words in each topic for PLSA*. In this case, we chose 3 topics and 20 words in each topic after some trials. The average accuracy results were 50%, 56% and 63% for LSA, PLSA and PLSA*, respectively.

Table 2: Overall accuracy results

	ANN Model						SVM Model					
	Lesson 1-6			Lesson 7-15			Lesson 1-6			Lesson 7-15		
Method	P	C	N	P	C	N	P	C	N	P	C	N
LSA	0.467	0.554	0.423	0.413	0.454	0.464	0.554	0.597	0.475	0.431	0.498	0.454
PLSA	0.517	0.590	0.485	0.465	0.516	0.464	0.583	**0.643**	0.513	0.501	0.563	0.492
PLSA*	0.563	**0.647**	0.572	0.523	**0.605**	0.553	**0.632**	**0.683**	0.557	0.586	**0.631**	0.554

From Fig.3 and Table 2, we can see that C-comments have higher accuracy results than P and N comments. The performance of PLSA was better than LSA in all lessons using ANN and SVM models. Furthermore, the PLSA* model had the best prediction results with 3 viewpoints: P, C and N items. As can easily be seen from Table 2, the SVM model had the best results. Also, N comments had the lowest results; students didn't describe well their plans concerning the next lesson. In addition, the overall accuracy results from lesson 1 to 6 were higher than those from lessons 7 to 15; this means that the difficulty of the subject in lesson 7 to 15 affected students' ability to accurately describe their experience.

Table 3: Overall prediction results by grade

		P				C				N			
Grade	Method	Precision	Recall	*F*-Measure	Accuracy	Precision	Recall	*F*-Measure	Accuracy	Precision	Recall	*F*-Measure	Accuracy
	LSA	0.550	0.527	0.535	0.562	0.500	0.592	0.541	0.643	0.500	0.533	0.508	0.538
S	PLSA	0.750	0.519	0.600	0.619	0.668	0.707	0.687	0.690	0.583	0.636	0.609	0.571
	PLSA*	0.623	0.650	0.636	0.643	**0.739**	**0.742**	**0.739**	**0.714**	0.577	0.658	0.614	0.643
	LSA	0.557	0.575	0.562	0.549	0.475	0.598	0.528	0.671	0.506	0.499	0.495	0.500
A	PLSA	0.676	0.591	0.631	0.671	0.770	0.673	0.718	0.744	0.575	0.591	0.583	0.598
	PLSA*	0.695	0.700	0.692	0.695	**0.766**	**0.780**	**0.772**	**0.768**	0.592	0.667	0.627	0.622
	LSA	0.455	0.432	0.443	0.478	0.484	0.625	0.541	0.587	0.432	0.409	0.420	0.457
B	PLSA	0.596	0.600	0.596	0.565	0.739	0.642	0.687	0.630	0.522	0.495	0.508	0.500
	PLSA*	0.642	0.668	0.654	0.587	0.826	0.610	0.702	0.652	0.586	0.636	0.606	0.522
	LSA	0.455	0.477	0.465	0.478	0.500	0.458	0.477	0.478	0.348	0.359	0.350	0.435
C	PLSA	0.603	0.492	0.530	0.500	0.583	0.442	0.499	0.522	0.542	0.442	0.478	0.478
	PLSA*	0.611	0.500	0.549	0.522	0.683	0.542	0.604	0.543	0.600	0.542	0.568	0.522

5.2 Correlation of PCN comments and grade prediction performance

Table 3. shows the average prediction results of student grades obtained using the SVM model; we can distinguish higher grades A and S from lower ones B and C. In addition the results for grade A with PLSA and PLSA* were better than those with LSA. Predicting student grades using the PLSA* model had the highest accuracy and *F*-measure. Moreover, the accuracy and *F*-measure results for C-comment are better than for P- and N-comments.

6. CONCLUSIONS

In this paper, we extended the PLSA model to predict student grades based on the bag-of-words representation of student comments. We chose the number of topics and the number of words in each topic from lesson 1 to 15. This approach significantly improved the overall prediction accuracy results compared with the LSA and PLSA models. SVM and ANN techniques were introduced to predict student grades. SVM obtained higher accuracy results than the ANN method.

From the previous results, we can conclude that the difficulty of the subject influences the quality of the written comments; students wrote better comments while they were learning Computer Literacy in lesson 1 to 6 than while learning C programming in lesson 7 to 15. Also, they described their current activities (C-comments) better than previous and next activities (P- and N-comments); this tendency is reflected in the accuracy of their predicted grades.

In the future, we will try to improve our results by automatically detecting the number of topics and the number of words in each topic in order to give feedback to students. We will try to extract some clues from the meaning of the different topics. In addition, student comments evaluation must be continued throughout the semester in order to continue delivering optimum feedback and motivate them to write good comments and improve their tendency and attitudes in each lesson.

7. ACKNOWLEDGMENTS

This work was partially supported by JSPS KAKENHI Grant Numbers 25350311 and 26540183.

8. REFERENCES

[1] R. S. Baker. Data mining for education. *International Encyclopedia of Education (3rd edition). Oxford, UK: Elsevier.*, 2009.

[2] S. Deerwester, S. T. Dumais, G. W. Furnas, T. K. Landauer, and R. Harshman. Indexing by latent semantic analysis. *Journal of the American Society for Information Science*, 41(6):391 – 407, 1990.

[3] A. P. Dempster, N. M. Laird, and D. B. Rubin. Maximum likelihood from incomplete data via the em algorithm. *Journal of the Royal Statistical Society. Series B (Methodological)*, 39(1):1–38, 1977.

[4] K. Goda, S. Hirokawa, and T. Mine. Automated evaluation of student comments on their learning behavior. In *ICWL 2013, LNCS 8167, Springer-Verlag Berlin Heidelberg*, pages 131 – 141, 2013.

[5] K. Goda, S. Hirokawa, and T. Mine. Correlation of grade prediction performance and validity of-self-evaluation comments. In *Proc. of SIGITE '13 conference on Information technology education*, pages 35–42, 2013.

[6] K. Goda and T. Mine. Analysis of students' learning activities through quantifying time-series comments. In *Proc. of KES 2011, Part II, LNAI 6882, Springer-Verlag Berlin Heidelberg*, pages 154–164, 2011.

[7] P. Gorissen, J. van Bruggen, and W. Jochems. Usage reporting on recorded lectures. *International Journal of Learning Technology*, 7(1):23–40, 2012.

[8] T. Hofmann. Probabilistic latent semantic analysis. In *Uncertainity in Artificial Intelligence, UAI'99, Stockholm*, 2001.

[9] T. Hofmann. Unsupervised learning by probabilistic latent semantic analysis. *Machine Learning*, 42:177–196, 2001.

[10] C.-W. Hsu, C.-C. Chang, and C.-J. Lin. A practical guide to support vector classification. *National Taiwan University, Taipei 106, Taiwan*, pages 1–16, 2010.

[11] C. Romero, P. G. Espejo, A. Zfra, J. R. Romero, and S. Ventura. Web usage mining for predicting final marks of students that use moodle courses. *Computer Applications in Engineering Education*, 2010.

[12] D. E. Rumelhart, G. E. Hinton, and R. J. Williams. *Learning internal representations by error propagation*, volume 1, chapter 8, pages 318–361. 1986.

[13] S. E. Sorour, T. Mine, K. Goda, and S. Hirokawa. Efficiency of lsa and k-means in predicting students' academic performance based on their comments data. In *Proc. of CSEDU 2014 conference on Computer Supported Education*, pages 63–74, 2014.

[14] S. E. Sorour, T. Mine, K. Goda, and S. Hirokawa. Predicting students' grades based on free style comments data by artificial neural network. In *Proc. of FIE 2014 conference on IEEE Frontiers in Education*, pages 2475–2483, 2014.

[15] S. E. Sorour, T. Mine, K. Goda, and S. Hirokawa. Prediction of students' grades based on free-style comments data. In *Proc. of ICWL 2014, LNCS 8613, Springer-Verlag Berlin Heidelberg*, pages 142–151, 2014.

Bats, Balls, and Lures: Cognitive Style in CS Education

Barry Wittman
Elizabethtown College
wittmanb@etown.edu

Jean Pretz
Elizabethtown College
pretzj@etown.edu

ABSTRACT

If a bat and a ball cost $1.10 in total and the bat costs $1.00 more than the ball, how much does the ball cost? Many people trained in logical reasoning answer this question incorrectly. Is the kind of logical trap posed by this question similar to the logical traps in computer science? This paper examines the similarity between computer science programming problems with intuitive yet incorrect "lure" answers and logical problems from psychology and economics that share this characteristic. We find that there are fundamental similarities between these kinds of problems and that these problems can even be used as predictors of grades in introductory programming courses. Furthermore, we demonstrate that certain cognitive styles identified in recent psychological literature perform better on such problems.

Categories and Subject Descriptors

K.3.2 [**Computers and Education**]: Computer and Information Science Education—*computer science education*

General Terms

Human Factors

Keywords

cognitive style; intuition; cognitive bias

1. INTRODUCTION

This paper examines a facet of what makes learning to program so hard. Introductory programming courses are notoriously difficult for students, who often fail such courses and achieve low proficiency in the skills being taught [5]. In the computer science education community, this problem has been heavily studied, but no definitive consensus has been reached about how best to help the largest number of students succeed.

Key educational "threshold concepts" are described in [7] and studied in a computer science context in [1]. One of the distinguishing features of threshold concepts is that they are potentially troublesome: conceptually difficult, alien, and counter-intuitive. This counter-intuitive feature is particularly apparent in computer science, where code is executed with inflexible logic at impossible speed in a mysterious, invisible world inside the computer.

SIGCSE'15, March 4–7, 2015, Kansas City, MO, USA.

ACM 978-1-4503-2966-8/15/03 ...$15.00.
http://dx.doi.org/10.1145/2676723.2677291.

Yet counter-intuitive issues have also been studied heavily in psychology. To leverage those results, we compare logical problems studied outside of computer science to problems that can be found in typical introductory programming courses. We focus on problems with attractive, intuitive, and apparently straightforward answers which are nevertheless incorrect. This tendency to jump to incorrect but intuitive solutions to logic problems is sometimes called cognitive bias [4].

The bat-and-ball problem is a part of a test of cognitive style studied in [3]. There, the problem is stated as follows.

> A bat and a ball cost $1.10 in total. The bat costs $1.00 more than the ball. How much does the ball cost?

For a variety of reasons, many people jump to the conclusion that the bat costs $1.00 and the ball costs $0.10, although solving two equations with two unknowns proves that the bat must cost $1.05 and the ball $0.05. Similar logical problems with obvious but incorrect answers must be solved when programming, and choosing the incorrect approach can lead to off-by-one errors, array indexing problems, infinite loops, null pointer dereferences, and a host of other errors that plague new and seasoned programmers alike.

The Wason selection task described in [13] is another test of reasoning. In this test participants must flip over cards to verify the truth of a logical proposition. An example of such a proposition is that all cards showing an even number must be red on their other side. In [13], fewer than 10% of subjects were able to flip over precisely the right cards. However, later work in [2] suggests that people perform better on the test if the proposition being tested is based on familiar, concrete rules of social exchange. Thus, it may be that the abstract nature of the logical problems that arise when programming contributes to their difficulty.

In this paper, we attempt to measure the cognitive styles of students in introductory programming courses and manipulate their cognitive strategies. Ultimately, we are looking for correlations between cognitive styles that avoid these counter-intuitive pitfalls and students who are successful at computer science tasks.

Much work [14] has been devoted to predicting performance in introductory programming courses. We present evidence that cognitive styles which perform well on problems like the ball-and-bat problem also perform well in such courses. However, a deeper contribution of this paper is to provide additional insight about what makes such courses difficult and to construct links to an existing body of work in psychology and economics whose results may further efforts to teach programming.

2. METHODOLOGY

We administered a survey to students in the first two introductory programming courses in our sequence, CS121 and CS122. We wanted to measure cognitive style with the broadest possible array of students, ideally at an early stage in their computer science education. CS121 is the first course for computer science and information systems majors, but it also has a large population of non-majors who are required to take the course. CS122 is a standard CS2 course, with a larger proportion of majors, but minors as well as engineering students are required to take the course as well. Beyond CS122, the population of non-majors drops very low, and even a significant percentage of majors leave the program.

Our survey contained the Cognitive Reflection Test (CRT) described in [3] as a well-studied measure of aptitude for solving logical problems that present an intuitive but incorrect "lure" answer. We then devised five programming problems that exhibit a similar feature. Our survey also contained the Types of Intuition Scale [10] to measure intuition, the Rational Experiential Inventory [9] to measure cognitive style, and a few additional demographic questions. The entire survey was distributed as a single paper document, and students were given 30 minutes to complete the questions.

2.1 Cognitive reflection test

The CRT is made up of three questions. Each question is free-response with a logically correct answer and another incorrect answer that often appeals to the subject's intuition. The first question is the ball-and-bat problem described above. The second and third are given below.

> If it takes 5 machines 5 minutes to make 5 widgets, how long would it take 100 machines to make 100 widgets?

The lure answer is 100 minutes, but 5 machines making 5 widgets in 5 minutes establishes a rate of 1 widget per machine per 5 minutes. Thus, 100 machines can make 100 widgets in 5 minutes.

> In a lake, there is a patch of lily pads. Every day, the patch doubles in size. If it takes 48 days for the patch to cover the entire lake, how long would it take for the patch to cover half the lake?

The lure answer is 24 days, but the lily pads are exhibiting exponential growth by doubling. Thus, the patch will cover at least half the lake after 47 days.

2.2 Computer science lure questions

We developed five computer science questions that were both practical and exhibited lure properties similar to the CRT questions. Because our introductory courses are taught in Java, our questions are formulated in that language. Arrays and lists are a fertile area for counter-intuitive programming problems, so three out of the five questions involve arrays. In order to guarantee that students had a strong enough grasp of arrays to be able to solve the problems even in CS121, we waited to administer the surveys until the 13th and 14th weeks of a 15-week semester. For multiple choice questions, the answers were provided in the order given.

Our first question asks what value `START` should have in order to guarantee that the largest value in the array `list` is printed.

```
int largest = START;
for(int i = 0; i < list.length; ++i)
    if(list[i] > largest)
        largest = list[i];
System.out.println(largest);
```

Unlike the questions in the CRT, multiple choice responses were provided for this question. We gave the values `0`, `1000000`, `Integer.MIN_VALUE`, and `Integer.MAX_VALUE` as responses. We considered the lure value to be `Integer.MAX_VALUE`, since students are often mistakenly attracted to large initial values when trying to find the largest value in an array. The correct answer is `Integer.MIN_VALUE`.

The second question gives the formula for the area of a triangle ($A = \frac{1}{2}bh$) and then asks the student to complete the following code to find the area.

```
Scanner in = new Scanner(System.in);
double b = in.nextDouble();
double h = in.nextDouble();
double A =
```

The lure answer is `A = 1/2*b*h`, which always computes a result of `0.0` because of integer division in Java. The correct answer is `A = .5*b*h` or `A = b*h/2`.

The third question asks the student to find the logical negation of the Boolean expression `raining || temperature < 40`, where `raining` is a `boolean` variable and `temperature` is an `int`. The following are the four multiple choice responses given.

a. `!raining || !(temperature < 40)`

b. `!raining || temperature >= 40`

c. `!raining && temperature > 40`

d. `!raining && temperature >= 40`

Both a. and b. responses were considered lures, since each ignores De Morgan's Law. Response d. is correct.

The fourth question asks the student to consider an array of `int` values that will be used to record the number of times that each temperature in a range of possible values has been seen. The range of possible values is from -60 up to 90. In other words, the first element in the array would record the number of times that the temperature -60 had been seen, and the last element in the array will record the number of times that the temperature 90 has been seen. The student must write down the total number of elements in the array.

The lure answer in this case is 150 since $60 + 90 = 150$. However, this answer ignores the element corresponding to the value 0, making the correct answer 151.

Finally, the fifth question asks the student to consider four methods, each of which is intended to test if an array of `int` values is sorted in ascending order. Space constraints prevent us from listing the incorrect responses, but the correct method is given below.

```
public boolean isSorted(int[] list) {
   for(int i = 0;i < list.length - 1;++i)
      if(list[i] > list[i + 1])
         return false;
   return true;
}
```

One of the lure answers adds an `else` between the two `return` statements, effectively leaving the method after checking the ordering of only the first pair of values. The second lure answer is exactly like the correct answer except that `>` is replaced by `<`, making it test whether the list is sorted in *descending* order. The third incorrect answer combines both errors.

2.3 Experimental intervention

Before administering the tests above, we generated experimental and control versions of the CS questions. The text of the questions and the multiple choice responses (where applicable) are the same in both versions of the survey. However, the experimental survey begins with instructions suggesting that the student should try to think like a computer, identify human assumptions, distrust intuition, and then test his or her answer with random values, remembering the differences between mathematical operations and Java operations.

Furthermore, each experimental CS question contains two additional prompts. The first asks the student to write down his or her assumptions. The second asks the student to describe the strategy used to verify his or her answer.

We distributed equal numbers of experimental and control surveys in each class section at random. Experimental students were not given any additional verbal instructions, and to the best of our knowledge, students were not aware that there was more than one version of the survey being administered.

When developing the survey, we predicted that students whose cognitive style is skeptical, analytical, and reflective will have higher grades in their programming courses and better scores on the CS questions. For that reason, we wanted to test the efficacy of instructing students to adopt such a cognitive style.

3. ANALYSIS

3.1 Connections between CRT and CS performance

The data we collected exhibited a number of interesting patterns. First, there was a positive correlation (0.414) between good performance on the CRT and the CS questions. We coded responses to the CRT and to the CS questions as "correct," "lure," and "incorrect" where "lure" responses are those that fell prey to the intuitive but incorrect answer and "incorrect" responses are incorrect for some other reason. There was also a positive correlation, though somewhat weaker (0.231), between making "lure" responses on the CRT and making "lure" responses on the CS questions.

Moreover, there is a strong correlation (0.611) between performance on our CS questions and the final grade in the course. Thus, our CS questions appear to be good predictors of computer science performance, though they were chosen primarily for structural similarity to CRT questions. This result is reminiscent of work in [12] that demonstrates that a small number of programming questions can accurately predict overall performance on the CS AP exam, which is accepted for credit for a CS1 course in most universities in the United States.

The most predictive question in [12] is (after translation into Java syntax), "If `b` is a `boolean` variable, then the statement `b = (b == false);` has what effect?" The non-intuitive nature of this question is similar to the questions we used. In fact, we considered including this question, but we wanted each question to have a concrete answer and felt that the formulation of the code might look like a syntax error to an inexperienced programmer.

Unsurprisingly, there was a substantial improvement on CS question performance between CS121 and CS122 students. On average, CS121 students scored about 18.6% correct while CS122 students scored about 62.3%. There was also a gap in CRT performance, but it was not as pronounced, with a 54.8% score for CS121 students and a 60.3% score for CS122 students.

It is noted in [12] that the performance predicting questions given there all test the mental model of program execution. It is heartening to believe that an additional semester of programming education is improving our students' understanding of program execution, but the CRT does not depend on any specialized knowledge at all. When comparing CS questions with the CRT, it would be ideal if we could generate logical programming problems that do not depend on knowledge of syntax, but doing so is impossible: Learning to solve problems with a programming language cannot be divorced from learning syntax.

The fact that CS122 students perform somewhat better on the CRT suggests that some capacity for logical reasoning has developed. Admittedly, this improvement may be due to population self-selection or greater intellectual maturity.

3.2 Cognitive styles

A more broad-ranging question is whether or not certain cognitive styles or personalities are more likely to succeed on either the CRT or the CS questions. If this hypothesis is true, students with a particular cognitive style might be encouraged to pursue computer science at an earlier stage in education, though we note the dangers of blindly encouraging only students with particular traits and effectively discouraging others. Furthermore, students struggling in computer science could be encouraged to adopt certain cognitive traits or approaches in order to succeed.

The Myers-Briggs Type Indicator (MBTI) [8] is a common way of classifying personalities in popular culture. Despite its popularity, work in the psychology community [6] is critical of the validity and usefulness of the MBTI. Some research has found that computer science students tend to fall into particular Myers-Briggs types [15], but the types do not seem to be strong predictors of success or failure.

Instead, we included in our survey recently developed tests for measuring cognitive style, the Rational Experiential Inventory (REI) [9] and the Types of Intuition Scale (TIntS) [10, 11].

The REI measures a preference for rationality, thinking logically and analytically, and a preference for experientiality, using feelings and intuition to make decisions. In our survey, there was a positive correlation (.365) between a preference for rationality and CS problem accuracy. Likewise, there was a negative correlation (-.329) between experientiality and CS problem accuracy. Although these results are not unexpected, it is compelling that a self-reported preference for a certain style of thought predicts performance on CS questions.

The TIntS focuses on kinds of intuition used: holistic, inferential, and affective. "Holistic intuitions integrate diverse sources of information in a Gestalt-like, non-analytical manner; inferential intuitions are based on previously analytical processes that have become automatic; and affective intuitions are based on feelings" [11]. Furthermore, holistic intuition can be sub-divided into holistic-big picture, thinking about the problem as a whole, and holistic-abstract, thinking about concrete facts and working from theories.

In this framework, there was a strong positive correlation (.468) between holistic-abstract intuition and CS problem accuracy. What is perhaps more interesting is that there was an almost equally strong negative correlation (-.445) between holistic-abstract intuition and giving the lure responses on the CS questions as well as a weaker negative correlation (-.281) between holistic-abstract and giving the lure responses on the CRT. In other words, this kind of intuition appears to aid students in solving programming problems while simultaneously inoculating them against lures, even when they solve the problem incorrectly.

On the other end of the spectrum, there was a negative correlation (-.351) between affective intuition and CS problem accuracy. Thus, a tendency toward feelings- or emotions-based intuition led students to incorrect answers.

3.3 Intervention

An intervention that could improve students' success rates on the CS questions based purely on manipulating their cognitive styles would be a strong result indeed. Such an intervention could be the seed for a new pedagogical strategy in the computer science classroom. We have not given up hope on this goal, but our intervention fell somewhat short.

When looking at success rates on the CS questions, there was no statistical difference between the experimental and the control groups. In a few subtle areas, the intervention appeared to have some small impacts. For example, the holistic-abstract correlation with CRT accuracy was stronger for the control group (.466) compared to the experimental group (.195). Likewise, inferential intuition had hardly any relationship with falling for CS lure responses in the experimental group (.178), but it was negatively correlated for controls (-.366). Holistic-abstract intuition also had a weaker negative correlation in the experimental group (-.373) than it did among controls (-.507). Another interesting result is that the correlation between course grade and CS accuracy is relatively weak among the control group (.242). However, the same correlation is much stronger in the experimental group (.611).

Although our population was too small ($N = 40$) to put much confidence in these subtle effects, it appears that the intervention helped students work against type. Specifically, the importance of having holistic-abstract intuition was not as pronounced when the students were being told to question their assumptions and give strategies for verifying their work. Likewise, it seems that the better students (as measured by final course grade) were able to shine more brightly when given the same instructions.

Since the intervention largely took the form of additional responses listing the assumptions for each problem and strategies for checking the answer, we can measure student participation in the intervention. 80.5% of these additional responses were completed, suggesting that students were participating at a significant level. All experimental students participated to some degree, but some tended to leave either the list of assumptions or the strategies for verification blank.

It is always difficult to do qualitative analysis, but repeated patterns of answers suggest that some students either did not understand the instructions given by the intervention or had not developed the skills needed to follow it. When asked to state his or her assumptions for question three, which asks for the negation of a Boolean expression, one student responded, "My assumptions are that I need to find the opposite of the above statement." When asked for a strategy to verify the answer, the same student responded, "I would run the program and test it." On the same question, another student responded, "check on a thermometer." Such responses betray a misunderstanding of the prompt for a logical strategy that could be used at that moment to add confidence to the student's answer.

In many other cases, students used the request for their assumptions or their strategy as an opportunity to explain their thought processes but still failed to find the flaw in their logic. For question four, which asks students to count the locations in an array whose indexes correspond to the values between -60 and 90, assumptions were given as, "you just need to add 60 + 90," "it would just be 90 - (-60) which = 150," and variations on the theme.

4. FUTURE WORK

Our findings suggest different avenues through which programming problem solving performance can be predicted, measured, and hopefully improved. However, these avenues have only begun to be explored.

A key step to validating and extending our work is to expand to a larger population size. Because of scheduling problems, sections of CS121 we had planned to include could not participate. As a consequence, our total surveyed population was only 40 students.

It may also be informative to extend this study to upper division computer science students. Because of the self-selection process, such students may exhibit a preference for rationality and holistic-abstract intuition, or they may not. Presumably such students would also have a better knowledge of the syntax and semantics of at least one programming language. Thus, we could more closely compare their responses to computer science problems with lures to similar problems without computer science content. Similarly, it would be valuable to study the improvement from CS121 to CS122. It may be possible to control for self-selection and focus only on the learning that has occurred in CS122.

Although our CS questions exhibited interesting connections both to overall course performance and CRT scores, better questions could be developed. When we coded responses to the CS questions as "lure" or otherwise, it became clear that some questions (particularly question five) had more than one distinct lure, in contrast to the CRT questions which each have a single, easily defined lure. At the very least, the CS questions have syntactical complexity which could be simplified.

Of course, the most important area for future work lies in crafting a better intervention. Our intervention did not have as great of an impact as we could have wished, not least because many students did not understand its instructions. In terms of practical application, an intervention with substantive impact could serve as the basis of new classroom techniques for teaching programming. We plan to examine both psychology and education literature for better ways to manipulate cognitive style.

5. CONCLUSIONS

Learning to program is hard, but computer science is not the only domain filled with difficult logical problems. We show a connection between skill at programming tasks and skill at performing well-studied tasks in logical problem solving. A key similarity we have identified is the role of a lure answer, an intuitive but incorrect answer to a problem whose appeal is so great that many people embrace it in spite of rational evidence to the contrary. By harnessing existing literature in psychology and economics about overcoming such lures, we hope that new techniques can be developed for introductory programming courses and beyond.

Furthermore, we demonstrate that cognitive style plays a role in overcoming traditional lure answers such as those studied in the CRT and ones that we developed for a computer science context. Subjects who prefer rational thinking to intuition based on experiences performed better on CS questions. Although *intuition* is a loaded term, recent research in psychology has produced classifications of intuition that may be valuable in the computer science classroom. In particular, self-reported preference for holistic-abstract intuition predicted better results on CS questions.

These insights into cognitive style could be employed to improve advising for students considering computer science or related disciplines as a career path. Likewise, it may be possible to encourage beneficial cognitive styles such as holistic-abstract intuition among students who naturally tend toward other cognitive styles. Alternatively, educational approaches specifically tailored to other cognitive styles could be developed in order to make computer science a more inclusive field.

6. REFERENCES

[1] J. Boustedt, A. Eckerdal, R. McCartney, J. E. Moström, M. Ratcliffe, K. Sanders, and C. Zander. Threshold concepts in computer science: Do they exist and are they useful? *SIGCSE Bull.*, 39(1):504–508, Mar. 2007.

[2] L. Cosmides and J. Tooby. Cognitive adaptations for social exchange. In J. Barkow, L. Cosmides, and J. Tooby, editors, *The Adapted Mind: Evolutionary Psychology and the Generation of Culture*, chapter 3, pages 163–228. Oxford UP, New York, NY, USA, 1992.

[3] S. Frederick. Cognitive reflection and decision making. *J. of Economic Perspectives*, 19(4):25–42, 2005.

[4] T. Gilovich, D. Griffin, and D. Kahneman, editors. *Heuristics and Biases: The Psychology of Intuitive Judgment.* Cambridge UP, 2002.

[5] M. Guzdial. From science to engineering. *Commun. ACM*, 54(2):37–39, Feb. 2011.

[6] R. R. McCrae and P. T. Costa. Reinterpreting the Myers-Briggs Type Indicator from the perspective of the five-factor model of personality. *J. of Personality*, 57(1):17–40, 1989.

[7] J. H. Meyer and R. Land. Threshold concepts and troublesome knowledge (2): Epistemological considerations and a conceptual framework for teaching and learning. *Higher Education*, 49:373–388, 2005.

[8] I. B. Myers and M. H. McCaulley. *Manual: A Guide to the Development and Use of the Myers-Briggs Type Indicator.* Consulting Psychologists Press, 1985.

[9] R. Pacini and S. Epstein. The relation of rational and experiential information processing styles to personality, basic beliefs, and the ratio-bias phenomenon. *J. of Personality and Social Psychology*, 76(6):972–987, 1999.

[10] J. E. Pretz, J. B. Brookings, L. A. Carlson, T. K. Humber, M. Roy, M. Jones, and D. Memmert. Development and validation of a new measure of intuition: The types of intuition scale. *J. Behav. Dec. Making*, 2014.

[11] J. E. Pretz and K. S. Totz. Measuring individual differences in affective, heuristic, and holistic intuition. *Personality and Individual Differences*, 43(5), 2007.

[12] S. Reges. The mystery of "b := (b = false)". *SIGCSE Bull.*, 40(1):21–25, Mar. 2008.

[13] P. C. Wason. Reasoning. In B. Foss, editor, *New Horizons in Psychology*, pages 131–151. Penguin Books, 1966.

[14] C. Watson, F. W. Li, and J. L. Godwin. No tests required: Comparing traditional and dynamic predictors of programming success. In *Proceedings of the 45th ACM Technical Symposium on Computer Science Education*, SIGCSE '14, pages 469–474, New York, NY, USA, 2014. ACM.

[15] L. H. Werth. Predicting student performance in a beginning computer science class. *SIGCSE Bull.*, 18(1):138–143, Feb. 1986.

SOLO Taxonomy for Assessing Novices' Algorithmic Design

David Ginat*
CS Group, Science Education Department
Tel-Aviv University
ginat@post.tau.ac.il

Eti Menashe
CS Group, Science Education Department
Tel-Aviv University
menashee@post.tau.ac.il

ABSTRACT

We present the utilization of the educational SOLO taxonomy for assessing algorithmic features of introductory programming. The SOLO taxonomy was recently studied by CS research educators, with respect to code reading and code writing. Most of the studies focused on code reading. In this paper we offer a framework of SOLO utilization for assessing basic algorithmic design features of code writing. Our novelty stems from focusing on: selection, flexible manipulation, and composition of basic design patterns, as well as on capitalization on unfolded task characteristics. We specify SOLO levels with respect to algorithmic design, and relate to common errors. We display our findings of applying the suggested framework in an ordered study with CS1 students.

Categories and Subject Descriptors

K.3.2 **[Computers and Education]:** Computer and Information Science Education – Computer science education.

General Terms

Design, Measurement.

Keywords

Taxonomy; Assessment; Algorithmic Design.

1. INTRODUCTION

Consider the following three computational tasks:

1. Given a list of the amounts of rain in the 365 days of the year, output (the index of the) last rainy day.
2. Given a list of N stock values in a period of time, output the number of appearances of the maximum.
3. Given a list of 1000 girls and 1000 boys, ordered arbitrarily, output the maximal size of a group of girls and boys we can select, in which the number of girls equals the number of boys and <u>all</u> the chosen girls appear before <u>all</u> the chosen boys in the list (e.g., for the following list G B B G B G B G the output will be 2, as we may select the first 2 G's and the last 2 B's).

* This study was supported by ISF grant #937/08

SIGCSE '15, March 4–7, 2015, Kansas City, MO, USA
Copyright © 2015 ACM 978-1-4503-2966-8/15/03…$15.00
http://dx.doi.org/10.1145/2676723.2677311

The three computational tasks involve rather basic algorithmics, of different levels, and may be posed to novice programmers in CS1/CS2. In our experience, students offer diverse solutions to these tasks, some of which are erroneous, or inefficient.

The 1st task involves searching. Yet, the required search is not the simplest, *generic* search for a particular value, but for a slightly different element – the last of a given value. This diversion requires some flexibility of the algorithmic design, which is not always trivial for all students (as we will show later).

The 2nd task requires a computation that combines max search and counting. A simple approach involves separate, concatenated computations of the two schemes – first the max search, then the counting. This approach involves two "passes" over the input. We may do better by going only once over the input, while interleaving the two schemes. Some students struggle in designing such an interleaved composition.

The 3rd task requires preliminary analysis. Then, one may offer a solution which involves interleaved counting and max computation – two counters will keep: the amounts of G's read so far and the number of B's not yet read; and the max group size "so far" will be repeatedly updated as the input is read. An insightful analysis yields a simpler and much more elegant solution – the output is exactly the number of G's in the first half of the list (which equals the number of B's in the second half of the list).

The above three tasks represent various facets of algorithmic design. They require the invocation and composition of fundamental computation schemes, such as counting, searching, and max computation. The algorithmic design involves several considerations: 1. *Unfolding* of hidden task characteristics (on which to capitalize); 2. *Recognition* of the relevant generic design schemes to use; 3. *Flexible adaptation* of these schemes to the task at hand; and, 4. *Composition* of these schemes.

In introductory programming, the amount of fundamental design schemes, or design patterns [1,3], from which to compose a solution is rather small. The key principles are *abstraction* and *reuse*. The challenge is in selecting and properly manipulating the appropriate patterns. How can we orderly assess student behaviours in this respect? During the last decade, several studies offered the use of educational taxonomies for assessing novices' programming behaviours (e.g., [4,14]). These studies examined code reading and code writing aspects of comprehension and assembly of programming constructs; but they did not explicitly examine the algorithmic considerations indicated above.

Yet, these considerations are core, essential considerations in programming, already from the very beginning [1,3,5,11]. If we had a framework for "algorithmically" examining and evaluating programming tasks and their solutions, we could utilize it for orderly characterizing and assessing algorithmic features, including difficulties, of our students' designs. The objective of this paper is to offer and illustrate such a framework.

In recent years, a variety of studies examined the application of educational taxonomies for assessing novice programming. Two primary directions involve the Bloom taxonomy and the SOLO taxonomy. Fuller et al. [4] reviewed and examined several taxonomies, discussed their relatedness to computer science, and offered a revised, two-dimensional adaptation of Bloom's taxonomy. They divided Bloom's six levels, or categories, into Producing and Interpreting dimensions, the former including the categories of Apply and Create and the latter involving the categories of Remember, Understand, Analyze, and Evaluate. A later study by Thompson et al. [14] returned to the linear structure, and debated about how to draw the line between the two code-design categories of Apply and Create.

Lister and others (in several studies, including [6,7,10,15]), adapted the SOLO taxonomy to programming. They distinguished between SOLO for code reading and SOLO for code writing. For each of the two perspectives they specified the five (linear) SOLO levels of Prestructural, Unistructural, Multistructural, Relational, and Extended-Abstract. They conducted several code reading studies, including examination of the correlation between their SOLO code reading findings and students' designs [10]. Much less was done with respect to SOLO code writing. An initial, thorough study in this perspective was conducted by Whalley et al. [15], who examined very elementary programming solutions.

A recent, empirical study by Whalley and Kasto [16] examined the use of software metrics for assessing student code writing. Their metrics involved: cyclomatic complexity [9], average nested block depth, number of commands, number of operators, and a few additional metrics measuring quantitative features of programs, not explicitly tied to the program's goal.

The above studies offer diverse measures of novice programming, including code comprehension, language constructs' utilization, and quantitative measures. While these measures are indeed illuminating, they shed indirect, limited light on explicit algorithmic aspects.

In this paper, we take the SOLO perspective of code writing one step further, and offer a SOLO taxonomy for examining and assessing algorithmic design. We developed our approach based on long experience with students' algorithmic designs, in a variety of tasks, of different levels. We applied the offered taxonomy in an ordered study of novice solutions of basic algorithmic tasks.

In the next section we motivate and display our suggested SOLO utilization. In the section that follows we display our experience with its application with novice programmers. In the last section we discuss its characteristics and relevance for CS educators.

2. SOLO Taxonomy for Algorithmic Design

The educational SOLO taxonomy stands for "Structure of Observed Learning Outcomes". It was developed by Biggs and Collis more than three decades ago [2], and is claimed to be applicable to any subject area. It involves five levels of increasing complexity in student's understanding of the subject area. Computer science educators who adapted the taxonomy regard the three lower levels of the taxonomy as more quantitative (with respect to element details), and the two upper levels as more qualitative (with an emphasis on integration and the notion of coherent whole) [7,10,15]. Whalley et al. [15] define the SOLO taxonomy levels of code writing for a specified programming task as follows.

The SOLO taxonomy offered in studies of code writing:

- **Prestructural [P].** Substantially lacks knowledge of programming constructs or is unrelated to the question.
- **Unistructural [U].** Represents a direct translation of the specifications. The code will be in the sequence of the specifications.
- **Multistructural [M].** Represents a translation that is close to a direct translation. The code may have been reordered to make a valid solution.
- **Relational [R].** Provides a valid well-structured program that removes all redundancy and has a clear logical structure. The specifications have been integrated to form a logical whole.
- **Extended Abstract [A].** Used constructs and concepts beyond those required in the exercise to provide an improved solution.

Whalley et al. explicitly refer to the notion of *direct translation of the specifications* and the notion of *redundancy*. Indeed, in the very elementary levels of programming, the specification may be directly translated to code. This is much less the case when the level of programming tasks increases. The notion of redundancy is referred-to in the sense of redundant pieces of code that could be improved (e.g., repeated `if` statements).

Whalley et al. relate taxonomy levels to programming tasks. The level related to a task derives from the characteristics of the task's suitable solution, and the task's phrasing (which may be more oriented or less oriented towards direct translation).

The programming elements looked-at in Whalley et al.'s analyses are primarily the structures of `if` statements, `for` loops, and subroutine calls and their parameters. These elements are indeed essential, yet if one wants to explicitly assess algorithmic features, one should (also) explicitly analyze elements that we mentioned earlier, and present below.

Assessing Algorithmic Design

Taking an algorithmic perspective we embed in our offered SOLO utilization the algorithmic considerations terms of: selection, flexible manipulation, and composition of design patterns, together with the notion of insightful task characteristics.

We also use the term *generic design pattern*, to indicate the simplest, basic scheme that captures the notion of a pattern (as we illustrated with the 1st task of the Introduction). We consider modifications to the basic, generic scheme as flexible manipulations of the pattern. In the next section, we illustrate the latter, with a few basic patterns.

The SOLO taxonomy we offer for algorithmic design

- **Prestructural [P].** Substantial lack of knowledge of selection and implementation of generic design patterns.
- **Unistructural [U].** Direct translation of the specifications into a straightforward implementation of a generic design pattern.
- **Multistructural [M].** A translation of the specifications into flexible manipulation of a generic design pattern; or a simple, elementary composition of more than one generic pattern.
- **Relational [R].** A valid well-structured solution that involves the composition of two or more design patterns, integrated in a non-simple, interleaved manner, to form a logical whole.

- **Extended Abstract [A].** Insightful capitalization on hidden task characteristics; and/or a generalized structure that encapsulates abstraction beyond the required solution.

SOLO levels are related to tasks, and to solutions. A task's level is determined according to the task's features, as we describe below. A suitable solution is considered to be at the level of the task, and an inefficient or erroneous solution may be either (still) at the task's level, or at a lower level.

Unistructual tasks. We regard tasks whose solutions require direct application of a generic pattern, such as a simple counting or a simple max computation, as *Unistructural*.

Multistructural tasks. When a task requires direct application of two (or more) generic patterns, in a simple composition, such as concatenation, we regard the task as *Multistructural*, as it involves more than one element but requires trivial composition of the elements. Such a task is, for example, the task of reversing an input list. This task involves the simple concatenation of the generic patterns of reading a list into an array and then printing the array in reverse.

We also regard as *Multistructural* tasks that require some flexible manipulation of a generic pattern. A simple example of such task is the 1st task of the Introduction, which asks for the computation of the last rainy day. The basic, generic pattern of linear search finds the first element with some specified property. But here, the last element with that property is required. One should flexibly invoke the notion of keeping "the last rainy day so far". Obviously, an experienced programmer, and a novice acquainted with code manipulation, will immediately recognize the required flexible adaptation. But, some novices may struggle with the necessary adaptation (as we will show in the next section).

Relational tasks. When a task requires an interleaved composition of patterns, we regard the task as *Relational*. This is the case with the 2nd task of the Introduction. The suitable solution of the task involves interleaved composition of patterns, which means that different pieces of the patterns are merged and integrated together into a coherent whole. Problem solvers that may offer a simpler solution of concatenating the two patterns of max computation and counting, reflect only a *Multistructural* level, due to the inefficient computation.

Extended Abstract tasks. When a task enables abstract aspects, which reflect generalization into broader cases, we regard it as offering *Extended Abstract* solutions. Such phenomena may occur with parameterization of specified task elements. An additional case of abstraction derives from capitalization on hidden task characteristics. The 3rd task of the Introduction, of grouping girls and boys, exemplifies such a case. The suitable, elegant solution of this task may be obtained only after extracting the relevant, hidden characteristic that: the number of G's in the first half of the input equals the number of B's in the second half. The insight is obtained by abstracting, and ignoring the unimportant details.

Erroneous solutions may be at the same level as the task when the error is "local", or minor, such as inaccuracy in a loop upper limit. A minor error may yield erroneous output in some cases, but the solution may still reflect the desired integration of patterns. However, if the error reflects erroneous selection of patterns, or inappropriate composition of patterns, then the solution is likely to reflect a level lower than the desired one.

Cases of inappropriate, erroneous pattern selection may reflect a *Prestructural* level. Cases of erroneous composition may often occur when the selected patterns are suitable to the task, but their non-simple composition yields the phenomena of: *missing*, *misplaced*, *malformed*, or *spurious* pieces of code [12] (the case of *missing* may appear, for example, with a missing initialization).

Inefficient solutions may also reflect a level lower than the desired one, if they derive from lack of insight of the task characteristics, or from a simplified pattern composition, which yields unnecessary extra time or space of the computation. We illustrate and elaborate further on errors and inefficient solutions in the next section.

In the next section we illustrate the above with a study we conducted with novices who studied CS1.

3. Application of the Taxonomy

Methodology. We applied the above suggested framework, with three groups of 69, 81, and 95 11th grade students, who studied CS1 with Java. Each group was requested to solve in 90 minutes a questionnaire with three or four programming tasks, which focused on diverse utilization of basic generic patterns.

The generic patterns included: linear search, counting, summation, min/max computation, previous-current computation (as with Fibonacci numbers, where the current value in the latest iteration becomes the previous value in the next iteration), and array reading and writing, including the notion of an array of counters (in one of the groups). The students learnt not only straightforward utilizations of these patterns, but also flexible manipulations, diverse compositions, and capitalizations on simple hidden task characteristics.

Findings. In what follows we display and analyze student solutions to some of the tasks that were posed to them. In order to focus on algorithmic considerations, we do not display Java code, but rather simple, schematic pseudo-code.

Unistructural Level.

Grades. Given a list of 30 student grades, output the number of grades that are above 80.

The task requires a straightforward implementation of the generic pattern of (conditional) counting. It was posed to 69 students. All the student answers reflected the *Unistructural* level – 48 students provided the correct desired code, and the solutions of the remaining 21 students included minor errors, such as an extra loop iteration, or a inaccurate comparison such as >= instead of >.

Milk. Given a list of the milk production in each of the 30 days of a month, output the (indices of the) days in which their production was lower than the preceding day.

Here, one had to implement the generic pattern of previous-current, since a comparison between adjacent values is required. Students often avoid the invocation of this pattern, by keeping the input values in an array. We required no use of arrays here. Out of 69 students, 60 provided solutions of the following scheme:

```
read(previous);
for day←2 to 30 do
   read(current);
   if current<previous then write(day);
   previous←current
od
```

Nine other students offered inappropriate solutions that reflected a *Prestructural* level. Five of them computed the minimum of the list and printed the index of each day that caused a change of the global minimum. In a following interview, a student who offered this solution explained that repeated updates of the minimum yield the desired goal. Four additional students provided the following solution:

```
for day←1 to 15 do
   read(previous); read(current);
   if current<previous then write(day)
od
```

Again, a *Prestructral* solution. The processing is conducted on disjoint pairs of elements rather than on all the adjacent pairs of elements. In a following interview, a student who offered this solution explained that this was the best he could, and admitted lack of sufficient knowledge of the previous-current pattern.

Multistructural Level.

Last Rainy Day. Given a list of the amounts of rain in the 365 days of the year, output (the index of the) last rainy day.

This task, which was discussed earlier, requires some flexibility in the implementation of basic linear search. The task was posed to 95 students, of whom 72 provided the following suitable solution, after we let them assume that there is at least one rainy day:

```
for day←1 to 365 do
   read(rain);
   if rain>0 then last←day
od;
write(last)
```

Unfortunately, 23 of the students demonstrated difficulties with either selecting the suitable scheme, or properly manipulating the linear search scheme. A few counted the number of rainy days. Other inappropriate solutions calculated the value of the minimal rain, and some of them tried to calculate the index of the min:

```
read(min); index←1;
for day←1 to 365 do
   read(rain);
   if rain<min then {min←rain; last←day}
od;
write(day)
```

This is an attempt to use min (with erroneous initialization, as the 1st input may be 0). This pattern actually involves the notion of "the last element with the property so far", but those who offered it failed to flexibly adapt it to the task at hand.

One solution calculated the first, rather than the last rainy day. Four solutions implemented the linear search pattern as is, thus printing <u>all</u> the rainy days; and five additional solutions calculated the day before that last non-rainy day of the year:

```
for day←1 to 365 do
   read(rain);
   if rain=0 then last=day-1
od;
write(last)
```

The reader may wonder about some of these awkward solutions, as we did. But, apparently (as we also learnt from interviews with students), some of the students were able to select the relevant pattern, and realized that they should adapt it to the task at hand; yet could not devise the suitable adaptation. We regard these solutions as *Unistructural*, as they still involve proper selection and implementation (possibly with minor errors) of a relevant generic pattern.

Fence. Given a list of N piles of tiles, output a message telling whether the total number of tiles may be used to build a fence whose columns are all equal and are of one of the heights 5..10.

The solution requires a simple concatenation of two basic patterns – the pattern of summation (of tiles) and the pattern of linear search (for checking divisibility by 5,6,...). We posed this task to a group of 81 students, of whom 64 offered the suitable solution:

```
read(N);
sum←0;
for i←1 to N do
   read(pile); sum←sum+pile
od;
possible←false;
for i←5 to 10 do
   if (sum mod i)=0 then possible←true
od;
write(possible)
```

Both patterns involve initialization. Nine of the 64 students provided solutions in which one, or both, of the initializations were *missing*, or *misplaced.* We were debating whether to consider their solutions as lower than *Multistructural*, but after interviewing a couple we decided to still regard their solutions as *Multistructural*, with a remark on their mistakes.

The 17 students not among the above 64 struggled with the second pattern. Some *misplaced* a `break` statement; and others wrote a long nested `if` instead of the second loop. We regarded the solutions that were correct but cumbersome as *low Multistructural*, as they did include the relevant elements, but were structured in an inelegant, or an inaccurate way.

Relational Level.

Min Difference. Given a list of 50 integers, output the minimal absolute difference between adjacent integers.

A suitable solution encapsulates an interleaved composition of the patterns of previous-current and min computation. In addition, one should be careful with the initialization of the min pattern. We posed it to 95 students, of whom 43 offered the following suitable scheme:

```
read(previous); read(current);
min←|current-previous|
for i←3 to 50 do
   previous←current;
   read(current);
   if |current-previous|<min
      then min←|current-previous|
od;
write(min)
```

The challenge here is to integrate the two relevant schemes in a suitable manner. One has to carefully decompose each of the patterns into pieces and recompose the pieces in a correct, interleaved way. Obviously, one may properly conduct the latter only if she/he comprehends each of the patterns and its pieces.

Nineteen of the students offered solutions that process disjoint pairs of elements rather than all the element adjacencies. They did offer a suitable interleaved composition of the min pattern, and a "degenerated" version of the previous-current pattern. Thus, their solutions may be considered *low Relational*, but with a significant remark of no comprehension of one of the patterns.

Most of the rest of the students demonstrated difficulties in interleaved composition. The initialization of one or both of the patterns was *missing* or *misplaced*; some of their updates of the min were erroneous, and some of their progression with the previous-current patterns were *missing*. In addition, some solved the problem of max computation, rather than min, possibly because it was simpler to initialize. All in all, it seemed that most of the solutions suited the *Multistructural* level, as they did include the patterns, but with partial integration. A few, who included only one of the patterns suited the *Unistructural* level.

Elections. Given a list of N votes (N>9999) for five candidates, named 1, 2, 3, 4, 5, output the candidates that received more than 4000 votes.

The solution of this task requires the concatenation of two patterns – the pattern of counting (the votes of each candidate), and the pattern of linear search (for printing). But the key element that "puts" this task here and not in the *Multistructural* level is the relevance of keeping an array of counters. This data structure links between the two stages of the computation and is not straight-forward for everyone. We posed the task to the group of 81 students, of whom 37 offered the suitable solution:

```
read(N);
for i←1 to 5 do A[i]←0;
for i←1 to N do
   read(candidate); A[candidate]++
od
for i←1 to 5 do
   if A[i]>4000 then write(i)
od
```

Some of the students used a counters-array, but updated it in an inelegant way. Their first stage of the solution was:

```
...;
for i←1 to N do
   read(candidate);
   if candidate=1 then A[1]++;
   if candidate=2 then A[2]++;
   ...
od
...
```

This cumbersome solution involves unnecessary redundancy, and shows no abstraction with respect to the utilization of input elements as array indices. However, the utilization of an array did allow them to implement the second stage with a loop. Some other students avoided even that, and wrote five `if` statements in the first loop and five `if` statements instead of the second loop. We considered these solutions as *Multistructural*.

A third type of inelegant solution involved only a single counter, an array of size N, for keeping the input, and a nested loop:

```
for i←1 to N do read(A[i]);
for i←1 to 5 do
   counter←0;
   for j←1 to N do
      if A[j]=i then counter++
   od
   if counter>4000 then write(i)
od
```

This inefficient solution (particularly space-wise) is correct, but involves a simple composition of two patterns, in the form of inclusion – an outer pattern of repetition, and an inner pattern of counting. We regard it as *Multistructural*.

Extended Abstract Level.

It may be possible to regard the latter task as an *Extended Abstract* task due to the required abstraction of using input values as array indices. We illustrated earlier, with the 3rd task of the Introduction, the notion of hidden characteristics. An insightful observation yielded a very elegant solution. We further illustrate this notion with a more common task.

Sequences. Given a list of 5000 0's and 1's, output the lengths of the sub-sequences of equal values.

The abstract element to express here is the insightful observation of the task characteristics on which to capitalize. The point to recognize is that: *a new sub-sequence begins whenever two adjacent elements are of different values*. This observation may be translated into code with an interleaved composition of the patterns of previous-current and counting. 43 out of 95 students offered this solution. We omit it due to lack of space.

Other solutions involved various errors that derived from limited recognition and capitalization on the relevant task characteristics. One such solution involved the following, less insightful solution:

```
read(bit);
for i←2 to 5000 do
   counter←0;
   while bit=1 do {counter++; read(bit)} od
   write(counter);
   counter←0;
   while bit=0 do {counter++; read(bit)} od
   write(counter);
od
```

There are several errors here, including a problematic termination. But the more important element here is the missing insightful characteristics mentioned above. We regard this solution between *Multistructural* and *Unistructural*, as it lacks insight and interleaved composition, and involves a simple, but erroneous concatenation of two instances of the same design pattern (of counting).

4. DISCUSSION

The focus in our utilization of the SOLO taxonomy is on the selection and manipulation of design patterns. The amount of design patterns in CS1 is small. They include counting, summation, linear search, min/max computation, previous-current computation (that we described earlier), a few array utilizations, mathematical calculations (e.g., the decomposition of an integer into its digits), and some additional repetition (`while`) schemes.

The primary principle is in *reusing* patterns. We would like our students to abstract the basic patterns' structures, and conceive them as templates that can be manipulated in diverse ways. Abstraction is enhanced by repeated use of patterns, in various contexts, and reduces cognitive load [3,5,13].

Thus, in teaching our students programming, it may be most beneficial to explicitly teach them and direct them to recognize the patterns relevant for the tasks at hand, and flexibly use and compose them. This practice should be embedded in the teaching of programming language features and modeling of information.

In our application of the presented framework, we extracted the algorithmic elements of the student solutions, analyzed these elements, and indicated to ourselves the taxonomy levels of the solutions. For each solution it was possible to observe the knowledge and competence with selection, flexibility, and composition of patterns; and to characterize the errors.

Flexible manipulations and compositions are central elements of schema utilization [8]. Flexibility may be developed with diverse variations. Composition may be taught gradually. The simplest composition form is *concatenation*. A slightly subtler form is *inclusion*, which usually appears in the form of nested loops. The subtlest form of composition is merging, or *interleaving*.

Interleaving involves decomposition of patterns into pieces and re-composition of these pieces in an interleaved structure. The challenge is in integration into a coherent whole. In the previous section we have shown student difficulties with such integration.

The requirement for subtle integration appears only in the upper, qualitative, fourth and fifth levels of the SOLO taxonomy. In the lower levels of our suggested framework, the focus is on proper selection and flexible manipulation of patterns. In the *Unistructural* level the emphasis is on selection (of a basic pattern); in the *Multistructural* level – on flexibility and simple composition; in the *Relational* level – on interleaving and coherent integration; and in the *Extended Abstract* – on abstraction and the recognition of hidden task characteristics.

Previous studies of SOLO utilization with code writing referred explicitly to the notions of redundancy and direct translation of the task specifications [7,15]. We refer to the latter notion only with respect to basic pattern selection. Our reference to redundancy appears only indirectly, with efficiency considerations of the time and space of the computation.

The notion of efficiency is fundamental in programming and algorithmic design. In our framework, it is relevant in the upper two levels of the taxonomy. In the *Relational* level, interleaved compositions yields more efficient computations, both time-wise and space-wise.

The *Extended Abstract* level encapsulates the notion of *seeing beyond*. This notion appears in the abstraction of program features and components, as well as in unfolding of hidden patterns. The latter is derived from being able to "mask" details of the task at hand, and focus on the desired characteristics. We illustrated this phenomenon in both tasks of this level – the girls and boys task of the Introduction, and the Sequences task in the last section.

Our presented SOLO utilization offers ordered examination of diverse solutions (as shown in the previous section), and includes reference to errors. We regard minor errors as not decreasing the taxonomy level of a solution. Yet, errors that involve lack of conceptual knowledge, or lack of competent integration, reflect a solution of lower levels. We offer that a note about an error, and its kind, may be added to the taxonomy level of the solution.

It is our hope that the presented utilization of the SOLO taxonomy may: enhance tutors' perspectives of algorithmic considerations in introductory programming; deepen and broaden the assessment of student solutions; and assist in pin-pointing novice difficulties in program designs.

Future work in this direction may involve more detailed examination of errors, and more detailed SOLO adaptation for algorithmic evaluation.

5. REFERENCES

[1] Astrachan, O., Berry, G., Cox, L., & Mitchener, G. 1998. Design patterns: an essential component of CS Curricula. *SIGCSE'98*, 153-160.

[2] Biggs, J.B. & Collis, K.F. 1982. *Evaluating the Quality of Learning: The SOLO Taxonomy (Structure of The Observed Learning Outcome)*, Academic Press.

[3] Clancy, M.J. & Linn, M.C. 1999. Patterns and pedagogy, *SIGCSE'99*, ACM Press, 37-42.

[4] Fuller, U., Johnson, C.G., Ahoniemi, T., Cukierman, D., Hernan-Losada, I., Jackova, J., Lahtinen, E., Lewis, T.L., Thompson, D.M., Riedesel, C., & Thompson, E. 2007. Developing a computer science-specific learning taxonomy, *Inroads*, *39*(4), 152-170.

[5] Linn, M.C. 1985. The cognitive consequences of programming instruction in classrooms. *Educational Researcher*, 14-19.

[6] Lister, R., Simon, B., Thompson, E., Whalley, J., & Prasad, C. 2006. Not seeing the forest for the trees: novice programmers and the SOLO taxonomy, *ITiCSE'2006*, 118-122.

[7] Lister, R., Clear, T., Simon, B., Bouvier, D.J., Carter, P., Eckerdal, A., Jackova, J., Lopez, M., McCartney, R., Robbins, P., Seppala, O., & Thompson, E. 2009. Naturally occurring data as research instrument: analyzing examination responses to study the novice programmer, *Inroads*, *41*(4), 156-173.

[8] Marshall, S.P. 1995. *Schemas in Problem Solving*, Cambridge University Press.

[9] McCabe, T. 1976. A software complexity measure. *IEEE Transactions on Software Engineering*, *2*(4), 308-320.

[10] Sheard, J., Carbone, A., Lister, R., Simon, B., Thompson, E., Whalley, J. 2008. Going SOLO to assess novice programmers, *ITiCSE'2008*, 209-213.

[11] Soloway, E. 1986. Learning to program = learning to construct mechanisms and explanations, *Communications of the ACM*, *29*(9), 850-858.

[12] Spohrer, J.C., Soloway, E., & Pope, E. 1985. A Goal/plan analysis of buggy Pascal programs. *Human-Computer Interaction 1*(2), 163-207.

[13] Sweller, J. 1988. Conitive load during problem solving: effects on learning. *Cognitive Science*, 12, 257-285.

[14] Thompson, E., Luxton-Reilly, A., Wahlley, J., Hu, M., and Robinns, P. 2008. Bloom's taxonomy for CS Assessment, *ACE'2008*, 155-161.

[15] Whalley, J., Clear, T., Robbins, P., & Thompson, E. 2011. Salient elements in novice solutions to code writing problems, *ACE'2011*, 37-46.

[16] Whalley, J., & Kasto, N. 2014. How difficult are novice code writing tasks? A software metrics approach, *ACE'2014*, 105-112.

What Does It Take to Do Computer Programming? Surveying the K-12 Students' Conceptions

Antti-Jussi Lakanen, Ville Isomöttönen
Department of Mathematical Information Technology
University of Jyväskylä, Finland
{antti-jussi.lakanen, ville.isomottonen}@jyu.fi

ABSTRACT

Phenomenographic studies in computing education research have previously focused on learning "programming thinking" [3], the act of learning to program [2], and conceptions of learning generally in an engineering context [10]. In the present study we analyze and discuss "what it takes to do computer programming" using phenomenography as research approach. This study is based on a large survey dataset gathered in summer outreach courses for K-12 students. The analysis resulted in 12 qualitatively different categories belonging to five separate, emergent themes: *Syntax and language features*, *nature of programming work generally*, *computational thinking and problem solving*, *prerequisites*, and *auxiliary skills*. We additionally reviewed whether the students' previous experience explains the categories, and observed that a mechanistic view of programming was prevailing among the inexperienced users, while experienced students more often stressed algorithmic thinking and logical reasoning.

This study resembles work done by Eckerdal et al. [3], but gives a K-12 perspective to the question, "what does it takes to do programming?"

Categories and Subject Descriptors

K.3.2. [**Computers and education**]: Computers and Information Science Education—*Computer Science Education*

General Terms

Experimentation, Human Factors

Keywords

phenomenography; K-12; outreach; game programming

1. INTRODUCTION

There has been a growing interest in students' conceptions of programming in the recent years. On one hand, it is important for instructors and scholars to know what are the students' views of programming. This information helps instructors to adapt their teaching accordingly during their introductory programming courses to improve the students' learning outcome. On the other hand, computer science (CS) educators' interest in conceptions of programming can be argued to be topical due to the rise of the "Computing at schools" debate. For instance, in the United Kingdom, computer science has become an acknowledged school subject in schools (see [18]), and in Estonia programming is taught at an elementary school level. In Finland, which is the context of the present study, there is also a related curriculum debate under way, with the current curriculum proposals including references to computer science instead of mere information and communications technology (ICT).

Motivated by the aspects above, this paper describes the variation in the students' answers regarding the general question of what it takes to do computer programming. Our research insights into the young students' experiences with programming originate from our outreach project, in which we organized week-long game programming summer courses for middle and high school students. We have systematically collected both quantitative and qualitative research data, and reported on the quantitative findings (and the qualitative findings for some extent) from several perspectives (e.g. [6, 9]).

The current paper reports specifically on the findings from the qualitative investigation. As a part of the large pre-survey routinely issued to all the summer programming course students on the first day of their event, three open-ended questions were included attempting to disclose students' understanding of what programming requires. We categorized the resulting qualitative data, and considered whether the students' view on their prior experiences in programming would explain any of the responses.

Variation of the conceptions among a study population is typically studied with phenomenography [11, 12]. The research we report here was not initially undertaken according to phenomenography, making it an untypical phenomenographic study. In particular, the planning and data collection were not initially informed by phenomenography, while the analysis phase resembles a phenomenographic study. However, as we later discuss in Section 3.5, we considered the dataset to be appropriate for a phenomenographic analysis.

This study shares many features with an earlier study made by Eckerdal et al. [3], who investigated first-year university students on their understanding of what learning to program means. Instead of university students, our focus

SIGCSE'15, March 4–7, 2015, Kansas City, MO, USA.

ACM 978-1-4503-2966-8/15/03 ...$15.00.
http://dx.doi.org/10.1145/2676723.2677229.

is on K-12 students and voluntary outreach activity. Furthermore, in the study by Eckerdal et al., students were interviewed *after* taking an introductory programming course, while in the present study, the data was requested *before* the course. Thus, the main contribution of this study is providing the categorization for a group not studied before with phenomenography.

2. RELATED WORK

Research on K-12 outreach has previously received attention from the perspective of how to increase student interest in the computing field, including the challenges related to underrepresented groups. Recently, due to the efforts in many countries, debate is transforming into how to introduce computing into schools. Examples are already numerous in the literature. Sentance et al. [18] describe the changes undertaken in the UK, including the challenges in and models for teacher education. Their goal is that "all children from 5–16 study some form of CS." Rogers et al. [15] describe education of middle school teachers regarding how they could integrate computing into their discipline using Alice. Guzdial et al. [5] describe a state-level successful effort for broadening the student participation in computing in Georgia, and in general emphasize the challenge related to decentralized education system. Rolandsson and Skogh [16] provide an interesting exposition on how the past could inform the recent curriculum changes related to computing is provided by. For us, the recent curricular changes and the related literature set the context for and motivate empirical research in the present paper.

As noted, we focus on student conceptions, which are typically addressed with the approach of phenomenography. Research made in this area seem to echo similar findings from different research perspectives. These perspectives include both ones specific to a computing context such as "what programming is," and "how you learn to program," and ones comprising a broader perspective, such as "learning in general in engineering context."

Regarding "what programming is," Thuné and Eckerdal report [21] the following categories: (1) use of language to write program texts, (2) way of thinking that relates instructions to execution of the program, (3) production of computer programs appearing in everyday life, (4) method of reasoning, and (5) a skill usable outside a computer programming context. These categories were extracted from the data collected at the end of an introductory programming course. As for "how to learn to program," Bruce et al. [2] report categories reflecting the stages from a beginner ("following") to a self-directed practitioner ("participating").

Regarding "learning in general," Marshall et al. [10] studied students' conceptions of learning over the one-year foundation course. They report that learning is found to be (1) memorizing definitions, equations, and procedures, (2) applying equations and procedures, (3) making sense of physical concepts and procedures, (4) seeing phenomena in a new way, and (5) a change as a person. These findings are quite similar to the categories reported by Säljö [17] and Marton et al. [13] about students' conceptions of learning across many disciplines.

From the field of psychology of programming, we additionally found a study by Blackwell [1], which provides definitions for programming. Historic definitions traced and presented by Blackwell point to clear definitions that refer to operations and the calculations of the machine, while the broader and more recent definitions he proposes carry the idea that computer users should be seen as programmers, and, in considering what programming is, research should focus on the experiences with activities perceived as programming.

To summarize, the present study is motivated by the topical call for empirical results about how students perceive programming in the sense of what it takes to program. Our work contributes to the body of phenomenographic studies in computing education research considering its novel target group (K-12), large number of study subjects, and the timing of the survey (prior to the course). Further, the results can be contrasted with the study by Marshall et al. [10] and Eckerdal et al. [3]; in the later sections we will shortly discuss about the possible similarities in the categories, although our context and phrasing of the research question is different.

3. THE STUDY

3.1 Research context

The context of this study originates from a week-long summer course, which is a five-day, five-hours-a-day study module targeted at middle and high school students (aged 12–18 years in Finland). Earlier programming experience is not assumed from the students. The course is given several times per summer, with a maximum of 25–30 students in a course. During these events, besides teaching students some basic programming skills, we wanted to emphasize the connection between creating computer games and real-world problems in computer science. Obviously, another goal was to create a positive image of the field and the industry. We also provided a comprehensive toolkit so that students could continue programming independently after the course. We used textual programming envinronment, C# language, and a *Jypeli* programming library built in-house.

The outreach courses have been offered since 2009 and have received a good response. For more information about the courses, see `http://bit.ly/pelikurssi`.

3.2 Research focus

This phenomenographic study focuses on the following question: *What are students' (pre-)conceptions on what it takes to do computer programming?* More precisely, the present study identifies the views on how students *see* the phenomenon of what it takes to do computer programming *before* participating in a week-long game programming course. Here, we put the word "pre" in parentheses because some of the participants do have earlier programming experience. Therefore, the conceptions of these more experienced students are not necessarily preconceptions anymore.

In addition, the study investigates how prior experience in programming appears in the distribution of students' views; that is, are any conceptions more typical to nonprogrammers than those with some earlier exposure to computer science?

3.3 Study subjects

The subjects of this study were a total of 541 students aged 11–18 years who attended a week-long game programming course presented in Section 3.1. The data was collected during the years 2010–2014 from 24 classes. The participants came to the courses voluntarily, which were arranged in the summer outside the school year. Boys dominated the gender distribution: of all the participants, 33 (6 percent) were girls. The mean age was 14.5 years.

The reasons for participating in these outreach events varied. In our earlier study [9] we identified, for instance, *enthusiasts* who already had a "mature" view of the computer science field, and came to the course to learn. On the other hand, some students were urged to participate by their parents, or came because of a friend, and so on. The students also had a varying level of previous programming experience: 36.5 percent had no experience at all, 22.3 percent had tried programming, and 36.5 percent had some prior knowledge.

3.4 Survey

The data for this study originated from a survey. Each student filled out the survey on the first day of each summer class during the first hour. Among other questions related to demographics and background, the survey included one Likert-scale question and three open-ended questions about (pre-)conceptions about programming. The four questions were phrased as follows: *Programming is hard* (scale 1–5), *What makes it hard to do programming?* (open-ended), *What do you think (or assume) is easy in programming?*, and *What do you think (or assume) it takes to do computer programming?* (open-ended).

The survey has changed little over the years, with the questions concerning the topic of the present study have remained identical.

3.5 Phenomenographic analysis

The analysis of this study was made using phenomenography, which aims to investigate and describe the qualitatively different ways in which people experience or think about some phenomenon [12, p. 111]. Via the survey questions mentioned in Section 3.4, we wanted to capture how students express their perceptions of the phenomenon. The result of the analysis is a set of *categories of description*, which form the so-called *outcome space* of the phenomenographic analysis [12, pp. 121–122]. Because the aim of this study was not to generalize but rather to generate the set of conceptions of programming within a particular context, these conceptions and their characterizations are not complete but provide a premise for further discussion and analysis (cf. [10, p. 305]).

In phenomenographic studies, the data is typically collected via interviews with a small, purposive sample of subjects. However, in the present study, the data originated from a survey, primarily because the number of subjects was large ($n = 541$). While carefully contemplating the different aspects of the dataset, we found it to be rich enough to be used as the basis for a phenomenographic analysis.

The analysis was done iteratively and constant interpretation and comparison of the data points were required to find the qualitatively different categories, as discussed earlier. Students' answers were placed onto a spreadsheet, where our findings were located close to the original data. This gave us as researchers a holistic view of the variation due to easy navigation between data incidents and the coding. After the first author made the initial categorical scheme, the second author cross-checked the scheme and pointed out his considerations.

We fully acknowledged the possibility for over-interpretation arising from the fairly short student responses. This concern was mitigated by undertaking intensive cross-checking and discussions between the two authors. For instance, the cross-checking increased the number of categories and yielded re-interpretations of single responses. After several iterations, the agreement of the final categorical scheme was reached.

4. INTERPRETATION OF STUDENTS' CONCEPTIONS

Due to the number of respondents, a large set of views could be discovered. We summarized the underlying focus of the responses into five major, qualitatively different *themes* on "What does it take to do computer programming?":

1. Syntax and language features
2. Nature of programming work generally
3. Computational thinking and problem solving
4. Prerequisites
5. Auxiliary skills

Here, the themes resulted from grouping the more fine-grained categories that emerged from the analysis, as is typical in qualitative data analysis [14]. In each of these themes, a number of *categories* were identified. A total of 12 categories were found; they are shown in Table 1 below the corresponding themes.

These categories indicate different perspectives. A perspective can be detailed (e.g., *Meticulousness*, "A small error can cause many errors") or holistic (e.g., *Perseverance*, "Programming takes commitment"), and it is unique to the theme. The themes represent the categories that relate to each other; yet each category expresses distinct characteristics of the student conceptions. In contrast to most phenomenographic work, we did not find a strict hierarchy among the categories (or themes). By glancing at themes A, B, and C in Table 1, such a hierarchy could seem legitimate. However, deeper investigation of the categories indicate that all of these views were distinct.

The following subsections are arranged so that we introduce the categories within each theme. Along with the category name, we present two or three representative excerpts from the data. Finally, we describe the category in detail and offer our interpretation of the students' view on "what it takes to do computer programming."

4.1 Theme A: Syntax and language features

Category A1: Mechanicality. *"You can just write the code there – if you know how to." "I think you can do it if you are given the exact instructions."* Programming is perceived as writing program code. Further, programming is a mechanical task that requires routine-like operations, like reading and fast typing skills. As such, it is a simple activity; one just needs to write down the program code that satisfies the given (human) instructions. Presumably, the writer has to know the way of writing the code by heart (see Category B1).

Category A2: Meticulousness. *"A small [error] can cause 10+ errors!! >:(" "All the codes should be [written] correctly, and sometimes it's hard to figure out what is wrong." "Advanced software can find the errors for you."* Programming requires a hefty amount of meticulousness. Making the tiniest error in writing the code causes series problems

Theme A: Syntax and language features	Theme B: Nature of programming work generally	Theme C: Computational thinking and problem solving
A1 Mechanicality	**B1** Memorization	**C1** Algorithmic thinking and logical reasoning
A2 Meticulousness	**B2** Perseverance	**C2** Problem solving
	B3 Constant learning	**C3** Imagination, application
Theme D: Prerequisites	**Theme E: Auxiliary skills**	
D1 Fluent computer usage	**E1** Additional skills of software construction	
D2 Notion of the computer	**E2** Group work	

Table 1: Categories of description for each theme

in the product. Meticulousness reflects a state of *fear*, as one can be afraid of writing faulty code. On the other hand, confidence for the automated software (IDEs) to spot the errors can ease the anxiety and do some manual work for the programmer.

4.2 Theme B: Nature of programming work generally

Category B1: Memorization. *"In programming there are a lot of things that are difficult to remember." "It is hard to remember the right places for all the different characters, learn the right commands, and so on."* In programming it is essential to learn things by heart. For instance, a programmer needs to remember vocabulary, syntax, and semantics to make programs.

Category B2: Perseverance. *"[Programming takes] tolerating caffeine overdose and commitment." "My code works, and I don't know why. My code doesn't work, and I don't know why."* In this category, programming is seen to require patience and perseverance, because programming takes time. Programming is not necessarily difficult but takes a lot of practice and effort.

Category B3: Constant learning. *"Starting it is always hard, but when you've learned one language, learning another one is easier."* Programming is strongly affected by the constant and rapid change of computer science as a field. This puts a programmer under the pressure of constantly learning new information.

4.3 Theme C: Computational thinking and problem solving

Category C1: Algorithmic thinking and logical reasoning. *"It makes you think abstract and apply mathematical reasoning." "Logic and making things systematically."* Programming requires systematic and algorithmic thinking. Mathematics plays an important role in programming and helps in abstract and logical reasoning.

Category C2: Problem solving. *"Ability to perceive and solve problems." "[One has] to implement conceptual things onto computer."* Programmers need to have and use problem solving skills and quickly piece together what it is that "you have to do" in each situation.

Category C3: Imagination, application. *"There are many styles to do the same thing." "[One has] to apply the skills he has learned."* Solving a particular problem in programming is possible in multiple ways. A programmer can and must use his or her creativity and imagination in choosing how to solve the problem at hand. Choosing the right way to solve a particular problem requires applying learned skills. Programmers must also take into account the given (and possibly limited) constraints, such as the tool set, schedule, and budget. Therefore, programming also requires making compromises.

4.4 Theme D: Prerequisites

Category D1: Fluent computer usage. *"Good computer usage skills are important." "Programmer needs to be in control of technical devices."* Computers are perceived as technological devices that need to be tamed. Therefore, fluent computer usage skills are needed in programming to do it efficiently. These skills include both software (using program applications the right way) and hardware (understanding computers as technical devices).

Category D2: Notion of the computer. *"Programmer needs to understand how a computer thinks and works."* Programming requires understanding of the "notion of the machine," of how the computer executes the commands written in the program code.

4.5 Theme E: Auxiliary skills

Category E1: Additional skills of software construction. *"I like to do designs – I have a lot of ideas. I also like doing graphics for games." "Making characters and other visual designs."* Programming is related to several auxiliary activities or skills, which contribute to software construction as a whole. These skills include language skills, visual or graphic skills, and mastering different tool sets. The additional skills that students mentioned were often linked to computer games, which was naturally emphasized in the course (marketing) materials.

Category E2: Group work. *"[In programming you would need] group working skills."* In one answer programming was associated with skills needed to work in a group. Despite being the single occurrence, we find the category distinct from other categories.

4.6 Effect of prior experience

In addition to the preceding phenomenographic analysis, we investigated the connection between the 12 categories and the different levels of students' earlier knowledge on programming. In other words, we wanted to examine if some *views* (categories) occurred more often with students with zero background in programming than with students with some prior knowledge.

The question of the effect of prior programming experience is in addition to the actual phenomenographic analysis, but interesting to instructors. We find that descriptive statistical information has been included to add value in phenomenographic studies [7, 19], while studying the background attributes is not as common.

We divided the students based on their answers to the question, "I have earlier programming experience (1: None, ..., 5: Much)" into two groups: the first one contained those who answered 1 or 2, and the other group contained the students who gave 3, 4, or 5. The relative distribution of students into the categories is shown in Figure 1. The division (1 and 2 to one group; 3, 4 and 5 to the other) was based on our observations from the data that many of the students actually answered 2 even if they had not actually programmed before – they may have tried writing web pages with HTML, for instance.[1]

We found that there are some differences in how the "non-programmers" and students with more experience are distributed into the categories. First, students with prior experience were more often identified within the *C1 Algorithmic thinking and logical reasoning* category than students without prior knowledge (44.1 percent vs. 24.3 percent). Second, non-programmers more often stressed the mechanical view (*A1 Mechanicality*) compared to other students. In the other categories, the proportion of students remained roughly the same. We also note that *B1 Memorization* had the largest number of occurrences ($n = 147$), making it the most typical view in the answers. Naturally, there is no right or wrong way of seeing the programming phenomenon. However, compared to earlier research [8, 10, 21], we find it surprising that students with prior knowledge were so often identified within this category.

5. DISCUSSION AND CONCLUSIONS

How novice students perceive computer programming is an important question to instructors and scholars working in the field of computing education. We studied the middle and high school students' (pre-)conceptions of computer programming, specifically the conceptions of "what it takes to do computer programming." Through phenomenographic analysis we identified 12 distinct categories, which we further summarized into five themes. The themes and categories (Table 1) need to be understood in the context of K-12 outreach, and provide insight that can be used by educators running similar programs. In contrast to most phenomenographic work, we did not find a strict hierarchy among the categories (or themes). This suggests that a scale of programming conceptions applies to youngsters who have not

[1]However, we *did* run the crosstabs for the division where only "ones" (no earlier experience at all) were in a separate group, and the rest was placed in the other. The results were not very different to from what we have presented in this section.

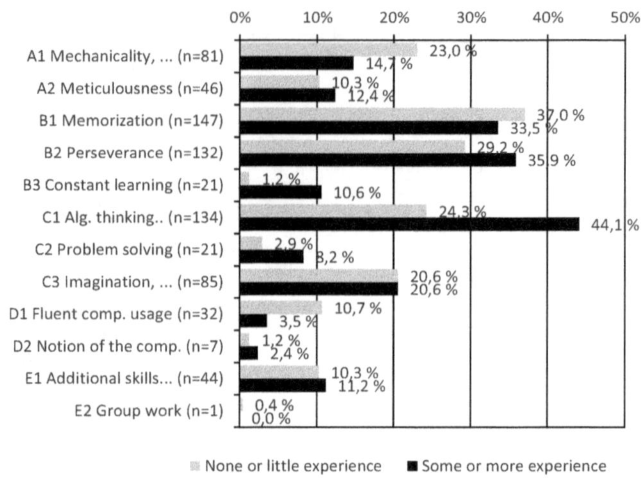

Figure 1: Comparison of the (relative) distribution of non-programmers vs programmers into the categories. For instance, 23.0 percent of *all* students *with* none or little earlier experience were identified within the *A1 Mechanicality* category, whereas 14.7 percent of *all* students *with* some or more experience were identified within the category. Students could appear in multiple categories, not just one. We look at the points where the bars differ the most.

programmed before, and these conceptions can be quite unrelated. Here, we notice that in [3, 2], the questions posed to students were specific to the course. In our study, questions not pointing to a particular context yielded a more diverse set of categories. For instance, we see often-occurring categories relating to the nature of programming work generally (Theme B), which are not reported by Eckerdal et al. [3]. In the following, we will give some examples to suggest how the different themes comprising the categories could be applied in the programming education.

Regarding the *Syntax and language features* (Theme A), emphasizing creativity in the programming assignments can give perspective to the students who perceives programming to be (only) a mechanical task. By creativity we mean that students can add a personal "touch" (for example, a visual) in the implementation of the assignment to enhance the ownership in the end result. Students contemplating the *Meticulousness* of writing program code can benefit from detailed tutorials and guidance.

Taking into account that most of the study subjects, if not all, are still beginners, the prevailing category, *Memorization*, under the *Nature of programming work generally* (Theme B), suggests that students (pre-)conceive of programming as a cognitively challenging task. This accords with cognitive theorists who often refer to high cognitive load present in programming (see [20]). In one sense, the Theme B speaks for the use of beginner environments or languages during introductory courses, and these environment should use intelligent features that help novice programmers in writing the code, thus, reducing the need for sheer *Memorization*. Students that see programming to require *Perseverance* may benefit from tasks that are small-sized, do not require too much working time, and are contextualized to help students understand the usefulness of what they are learning (see, [4]).

Perhaps the more experienced students emphasizing the category *Algorithmic thinking and logical reasoning* under *Computational thinking and problem solving* (Theme C) can identify different notions of the cognitive challenges related to programming, and thus are able to differentiate rote learning from (systematic) algorithmic thinking and reasoning.

The Theme D and Theme E were small but speak for the necessary skills that the students see relating to programming. Another aspect to consider is how design skills (i.e. game design, graphic design) could contribute to or be better integrated in programming education to enhance student motivation. For example, *Additional skills of software construction* category describes that design skills are needed to do programming, but from the educators' point of view, design and programming are often effectively segregated to "keep things simple."

Whether the students consider that their conceptions of programming have changed after attending the course is left for future study. This will contribute to the knowledge on the effects of courses presented in this paper, and gives valuable information for instructors running similar programs.

6. ACKNOWLEDGEMENTS

This study and the programming course presented in this paper were partly funded by the Technology Industries of Finland Centennial Foundation, Google, and Microsoft.

7. REFERENCES

[1] A. F. Blackwell. What is programming? In *14th workshop of the Psychology of Programming Interest Group*, pages 204–218, 2002.

[2] C. Bruce, L. Buckingham, J. Hynd, C. McMahon, M. Roggenkamp, and I. Stoodley. Ways of experiencing the act of learning to program: A phenomenographic study of introductory programming students at university. *Journal of Information Technology Education: Research*, 3(1):145–160, 2004.

[3] A. Eckerdal, M. Thuné, and A. Berglund. What does it take to learn "programming thinking"? In *Proceedings of the First International Workshop on Computing Education Research*, ICER '05, pages 135–142, New York, NY, USA, 2005. ACM.

[4] M. Guzdial. Does Contextualized Computing Education Help? *ACM Inroads*, 1(4):4–6, Dec. 2010.

[5] M. Guzdial, B. Ericson, T. Mcklin, and S. Engelman. Georgia computes! an intervention in a US state, with formal and informal education in a policy context. *Trans. Comput. Educ.*, 14(2), June 2014.

[6] V. Isomöttönen, A.-J. Lakanen, and V. Lappalainen. K-12 game programming course concept using textual programming. In *Proceedings of the 42nd ACM Technical Symposium on Computer Science Education*, SIGCSE '11, pages 459–464, New York, NY, USA, 2011. ACM.

[7] D. Kalvaitis and R. M. Monhardt. The architecture of children's relationships with nature: a phenomenographic investigation seen through drawings and written narratives of elementary students. *Environmental Education Research*, 18(2):209–227, July 2011.

[8] P. Kinnunen, R. McCartney, L. Murphy, and L. Thomas. Through the eyes of instructors: A phenomenographic investigation of student success. In *Proceedings of the Third International Workshop on Computing Education Research*, ICER '07, pages 61–72, New York, NY, USA, 2007. ACM.

[9] A.-J. Lakanen, V. Isomöttönen, and V. Lappalainen. Five Years of Game Programming Outreach: Understanding Student Differences. In *Proceedings of the 45th ACM Technical Symposium on Computer Science Education*, SIGCSE '14, pages 647–652, New York, NY, USA, 2014. ACM.

[10] D. Marshall, M. Summer, and B. Woolnough. Students' conceptions of learning in an engineering context. *Higher Education*, 38(3):291–309, Oct. 1999.

[11] F. Marton. Phenomenography: Describing conceptions of the world around us. *Instructional Science*, 10:177–200, 1981.

[12] F. Marton and S. Booth. *Learning and Awareness.* Lawrence Erlbaum Associates, Mahwah, New Jersey, 1997.

[13] F. Marton, G. Dall'Alba, and E. Beaty. Conceptions of learning. *International Journal of Educational Research*, 19(3):277–299, 1993.

[14] M. B. Miles and A. M. Huberman. *Qualitative data analysis: a sourcebook of new methods.* Sage Library of Social Research. Sage Publications, 1984.

[15] S. H. Rodger, D. Brown, M. Hoyle, D. MacDonald, M. Marion, E. Onstwedder, B. Onwumbiko, and E. Ward. Weaving computing into all middle school disciplines. In *Proceedings of the 2014 Conference on Innovation and Technology in Computer Science Education*, ITiCSE '14, pages 207–212, New York, NY, USA, 2014. ACM.

[16] L. Rolandsson and I.-B. Skogh. Programming in school: Look back to move forward. *Trans. Comput. Educ.*, 14(2):12:1–12:25, June 2014.

[17] R. Säljö. *Learning in the Learner's Perspective. I. Some Common-Sense Conceptions.* Institute of Education, Gothenburg University, Sweden, 1979.

[18] S. Sentance, M. Dorling, and A. McNicol. Computer Science in Secondary Schools in the UK: Ways to Empower Teachers. In I. Diethelm and R. Mittermeir, editors, *Informatics in Schools. Sustainable Informatics Education for Pupils of all Ages*, volume 7780 of *Lecture Notes in Computer Science*, pages 15–30. Springer, Berlin Heidelberg, 2013.

[19] V. Slotte, P. Tynjälä, and T. Hytönen. How do HRD practitioners describe learning at work? *Human Resource Development International*, 7(4):481–499, Dec. 2004.

[20] J. Sweller, J. J. G. van Merrienboer, and F. G. W. C. Paas. Cognitive architecture and instructional design. *Educational Psychology Review*, 10(3):251–296, 1998.

[21] M. Thuné and A. Eckerdal. Variation theory applied to students' conceptions of computer programming. *European Journal of Engineering Education*, 34(4):339–347, 2009.

Engaging High School Students in Modeling and Simulation through Educational Media

David R. Musicant
Carleton College
1 N. College Street
Northfield, MN 55057
dmusican@carleton.edu

S. Selcen Guzey
Purdue University
100 N. University Street
West Lafayette, IN 47907
sguzey@purdue.edu

ABSTRACT

The new AP CS Principles curriculum has a significant component regarding modeling and simulation, and many teachers will need to figure out how to accomplish this in their classroom. We have developed a new publicly available media-enhanced approach for teaching modeling and simulation, designated as *TrafficJam*. The approach consists of two core activities, both of which involve students optimizing traffic signals (also known as traffic lights, or stoplights). TrafficJam is likely best distinguished from other classroom simulation exercises in that these activities are introduced, motivated, and demonstrated in a video created by Twin Cities Public Television (TPT). The video uses an inquiry-driven format to feature four high school students who take on the task of improving signal timing in their own neighborhood. A pilot study of TrafficJam in four schools indicates that students find the video engaging, the activities relevant and interesting, and that they gain understanding of modeling and simulation from the experience.

Categories and Subject Descriptors

K.3.2 [**Computer and Information Science Education**]: Computer science education; I.6.0 [**Simulation and Modeling**]: General

General Terms

Algorithms, Experimentation

Keywords

Modeling; simulation; AP CS Principles; media-enhanced

1. INTRODUCTION

Modeling and simulation are dynamic and interactive approaches that can be quite successful at introducing students to computational thinking [4]. The new Advanced Placement (AP) CS Principles course integrates these approaches directly into the "Abstraction" portion of its curriculum, requiring students to use models and simulations to "represent phenomena," as well as to "formulate, refine, and test hypotheses" [8].

The imminent arrival of AP CS Principles charges a large number of teachers to become fluent with a variety of new ideas in computer science [1]. This may be challenging to accomplish. Many existing AP computer science teachers have been teaching the AP CS A course, whose content focuses on object-oriented programming and algorithm analysis, and they will have to learn considerable additional content if they begin to teach AP CS Principles. Many more teachers may begin teaching AP CS Principles who have never taught computer science at all. There is a considerable need for material for this new course, especially content that can be leveraged en masse.

The need for simulation and modeling in high school curricula, and the challenge in bringing it to large numbers of classrooms quickly, served as our main source of motivation in developing a new publicly available media-enhanced approach designated as *TrafficJam*. The approach consists of two core activities, both of which involve students optimizing traffic signals (also known as traffic lights, or stoplights). The activities involve optimizing timing for a single traffic signal via a spreadsheet model, and using a graphical simulation to reduce traffic delay time for an entire neighborhood.

TrafficJam is likely best distinguished from other classroom simulation exercises in that these activities are introduced, motivated, and demonstrated in a video created by Twin Cities Public Television (TPT), an experienced professional nationally-recognized television production team with experience in communicating complex content in ways that engage youth. The video uses an inquiry-driven format to feature four high school students who take on the task of trying to improve signal timing in their own neighborhood. These students in the video learn about traffic signals, collect data, work with a spreadsheet model, experiment with a graphical simulation, and see their ideas implemented. This video is entertaining for students to watch and helps engage them in the activity, but perhaps more importantly, the students in the video serve as role models and guides for real-world students participating in the activity. Furthermore, the video helps teachers to adopt this activity for their classroom. The video is broken up into segments, designed to be shown in-class over multiple days to accompany the work that the class would actually do.

TrafficJam is targeted at students in grades 9–12 who are in their first semester of an introductory computing

SIGCSE'15, March 4–7, 2015, Kansas City, MO, USA.
ACM 978-1-4503-2966-8/15/03.
http://dx.doi.org/10.1145/2676723.2677237.

course. The AP CS Principles Draft Curriculum Framework includes using models and simulation among its learning objectives. We achieve this specifically in Core Activities 1 and 2, which we describe below. TrafficJam is potentially quite useful, however, beyond AP CS Principles. We believe that TrafficJam would serve well in any introductory level computing course where modeling and simulation is a component to be explored. Furthermore, the video can stand alone without the core activities and could be used as a recruiting or motivational tool in order to draw more students – particularly underserved students — to computer science.

TrafficJam is freely available online.[1] It consists of the following contributions:

- A novel approach for optimizing traffic signals that simplifies it appropriately for high school audiences, yet still reasonably accounts for four-way intersections, turning cars, and data collected at such intersections.
- A sample spreadsheet model intended to be used by a teacher to learn about our approach. It is used for optimizing a traffic signal at a single intersection.
- A graphical simulation built in NetLogo for optimizing a neighborhood of traffic lights, which students use to optimize a collection of traffic signals at once.
- Video segments to accompany the classroom activities that engage and guide the students and the teachers.
- A detailed teacher's guide that explains how to implement the exercises and involve students in data collection.

The remainder of this paper is organized as follows. After discussing related work, we present in detail the modeling and simulation core activities. We then describe the creation of and production details for the associated video. This is followed by a description of a pilot study that we ran, and we discuss quantitative and qualitative results from that study. Finally, we conclude and consider future work.

2. RELATED WORK

Previous efforts have used television programs to teach science, with a specific goal of inspiring and engaging kids. One particular approach features students on screen, pursuing their own investigations as they work to solve problems. This approach has been used in different ways in PBS series such as the classic "3-2-1 Contact," and more recent PBS series including "Fetch," "Design Squad," "DragonflyTV," and "SciGirls." Shows such as these feature kids of approximately the same age as the expected audience. These on-screen characters solve scientific problems in much the same way that the audience would, thereby modeling successful behavior. Research has shown that seeing successful behavior modeled can have an significant effect on one's own self-efficacy, i.e, belief in one's own ability to succeed [5]. Television programs with this particular format may act as a source of *vicarious experience* for viewers [5]. Vicarious experience can be quite effective at boosting self-efficacy [12], especially when the models observed are perceived to be similar to the observer [11]. For TrafficJam, we combine this form of television with classroom projects and assignments appropriate for high school students.

The choice that we made to focus on modeling and simulation was motivated in part by the AP CS Principles Draft Curriculum Framework [8], which addresses these topics within the context of "Big Idea 2: Abstraction." Specifically, the framework indicates that one of the enduring understandings conveyed is that "Models and simulations use abstraction to generate new understanding and knowledge."

The specific projects that we develop place these models and simulations in the context of infrastructure engineering, or more specifically, traffic management. Infrastructure engineering is an activity that students are generally not exposed to in high schools within the United States, despite a lack of attention to infrastructure within the US in recent decades [3, 6]. However, most students are aware of traffic problems, and solving a problem in their local neighborhood makes the corresponding activities relevant and meaningful. Traffic engineering has been done previously in high school and/or computer science contexts, though seemingly not very frequently. An Android game was developed to simulate a single intersection in a fairly realistic manner, with the goal of using crowdsourcing to improve timing [7]. This project contrasts with our approach in that we model a single intersection mathematically via a spreadsheet, using data gathered by the students themselves, and then we use a graphical simulation to handle multiple intersections. Our graphical simulation was built with the simulation environment NetLogo [9]. NetLogo comes with a sample simulation of traffic in a grid of intersections [10], which we used as a starting point for our own simulation project. We extended the capability of this simulation considerably by adding two-way streets and turning cars, but much more importantly, we changed the logic within the simulation engine to incorporate user-entered real-world traffic data.

One of our major challenges in developing this project was in creating a traffic signal optimization procedure that was meaningful and interesting, but not too complex for a high school audience. We based our techniques heavily on procedures which we learned from the infrastructure engineering community. Typically, one begins by optimizing the parameters within a mathematical model for each traffic signal in isolation from the rest, based on traffic data collected on site. This optimization is typically done directly and numerically [2]. However, each traffic signal alters traffic flow in a way that affects the rest of the neighborhood around it, and so once all traffic signals are individually optimized their parameters are used as initial conditions for a traffic simulation. Professional traffic management typically employs commercial software, which traffic engineers experiment with to produce an efficient set of timings. This process, which we simplified appropriately, became the framework for the two core activities for TrafficJam. We describe these in the next two sections.

3. MODELING A SINGLE INTERSECTION

Core Activity 1 engages students by having them build a model in order to optimize timing for a single intersection. Specifically, they implement the following steps:

Data Collection (optional). If students wish, they can collect their own data from an intersection near their home or school, as modeled in the project video. The TrafficJam approach assumes a standard simple four-way intersection, with no turn-lanes; specifically, the traffic signal has a single green, yellow, and red light in each direction. The model requires as input data, for a particular time of day, counts

[1] `http://tpt.pbslearningmedia.org/collection/emacs`

of the number of cars per hour that approach the intersection from each direction and how many of them turn left, turn right, and go straight. This data collection activity can be fun as well as empowering for the students, and can help them experience ownership of the activity. Alternatively, we provide such data for students to use if they or their teacher wish to skip this step.

Model construction. This portion of the task requires the students to build a model that uses as inputs both the data described above, as well as user-entered parameters describing how long the traffic signal should be red, yellow, and green in each direction. (The optimization step, described in the next subsection, allows the students to determine which timing numbers are most desirable.) The students then implement calculations to produce an estimate of average delay time per car, which is defined as the average amount of time a car waits at a red light before it can proceed. Building this model requires some significant effort: it requires students to engage in thinking through how to convert number of cars per hour in a particular direction to time delayed per car, based on the input parameters. The TrafficJam materials describe this process to teachers in considerable detail, and also provide a complete solution for a teacher to use in coming up to speed. We expect that a teacher would spend time with the students in the classroom discussing these ideas before students implement the actual task.

There is much flexibility in what sort of tool a teacher might choose for students to use in implementing this model. It requires students to design a somewhat complex model and implement a variety of calculations, but it does not require programming logic such as conditionals or loops. Our video shows students using a spreadsheet to implement the model, which we chose in part because of its simplicity and visual appeal. That said, the same model could alternatively be done in any textual or visual programming environment.

Model optimization. After students have built a model that outputs average delay time for a particular set of inputs, they determine what traffic signal timings, used as inputs, will result in an optimal average delay time. The materials that we provide explain that while a short delay time is good, making it too short would not give pedestrians time to cross the street. Moreover, this is where the collected data plays a major role; the time for red vs. green lights needs to be appropriately balanced across the different directions.

The approach that the students need to implement is well-known to computer scientists: given a black box model that takes inputs and returns an output, find the set of inputs that produces the optimal output values. Teachers implementing this exercise can make this as simple or as fancy as they like. When shooting our video, we allowed the students to experiment themselves with different input values, and to informally develop their own procedure for doing so. They began with a guess-and-check sort of procedure, but as they continued, they discovered patterns within and eventually followed a hypothesis generation process that hints at something like binary search. We use it as a teaching moment in the video to briefly consider the nature of an algorithm.

At the completion of this task, students have their best estimates of the optimal timing for a single traffic signal. They then use this as an input for the next task, which is a neighborhood simulation.

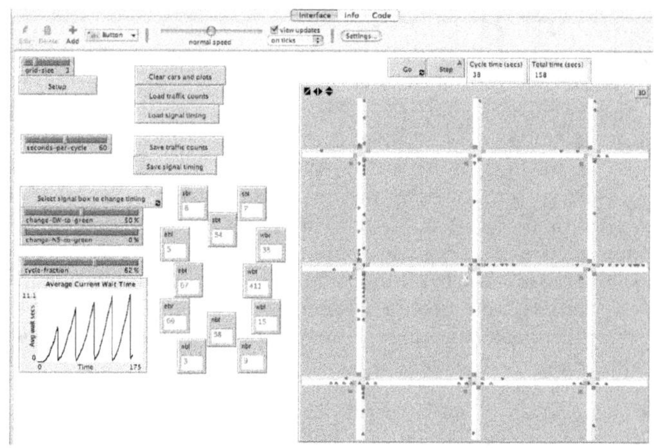

Figure 1: TrafficJam NetLogo simulation: students optimize timing parameters for each traffic signal separately.

4. SIMULATING A NEIGHBORHOOD

Core Activity 2 invites students to find signal timings for an entire neighborhood, which requires a different approach than optimizing each intersection individually. Changing the timing of the traffic signal on one intersection changes the patterns by which vehicles appear at adjacent intersections. Furthermore, the number of parameters that need to be optimized is multiplied by the number of intersections in the neighborhood. Traffic experts agree that this is too complex to solve via a direct model, and so it is typically done via simulation [2]. For TrafficJam, we chose to implement our own neighborhood simulation software. Most existing tools were quite complicated as well as expensive, and so this gave us the opportunity to create a simulation that fit the simplified traffic optimization approach that we constructed. Furthermore, the freely-available simulation environment NetLogo [9] already had a traffic simulation model [10], though we had to modify it considerably to handle car-count data, different timings for different signals, two-directional traffic, and cars turning. We discussed having students implement their own simulation in NetLogo, but concluded that this task is too difficult for the target audience. However, doing NetLogo programming to add capabilities is something that advanced students may wish to pursue, and our teacher's guide lists some possible extensions. For our expected usage, students do not need to know any NetLogo programming.

The simulation that we provide is for a 3 x 3 grid of intersections, resulting in a total of 9 traffic signals to be optimized (Figure 1). Each one of these intersections requires its own set of input data: specifically, the user specifies for each intersection the number of cars that approach it in each direction, and how many turn left, turn right, or proceed forward. This data is perhaps intractable for students to collect from nine real intersections in their city, though they would be welcome to do so. (There is a wonderful opportunity here to have a side-discussion about the value of crowdsourcing.) Many major metropolitan areas have government websites with car-count data, which could potentially be explored. Classes are otherwise welcome to use the sample car-count data which we supply in our downloadable materials, which reflects actual data from our metropolitan area.

Figure 2: Excerpt from TrafficJam video showing the students meeting with a traffic engineer at the city traffic control center.

Figure 3: Excerpt from TrafficJam video showing students collecting data at their intersection.

Our materials describe in detail the task that the students perform. They first use their results from Core Activity 1 as initial conditions for the center traffic signal, then they adjust a variety of timing parameters associated with each traffic signal to influence the location and severity of traffic jams. Data is displayed which shows on average how long every car in the grid waits at a red light. Students strive to reduce that statistic, as well as achieve a general sense of good flow by looking at the graphical simulation.

5. VIDEO PRODUCTION

The TrafficJam video was produced as a collaboration between TPT and academic computing educators. It was decided early on that we would use an inquiry-driven format featuring real high school students solving problems on-screen. (See Section 2 for more details on the benefits of such an approach.) Casting was done by visiting high schools in our metropolitan area and holding auditions. Since there were no AP CS Principles pilot courses being taught in the schools in which we auditioned, we did not recruit students directly from that course. Instead, we cast students who were smart, enthusiastic, had good presence on-screen, and who did not know very much about computer science. One of our goals was to have the students in the video serve as role models for those watching the video, and so we also strove to cast students with varying ethnicities and genders.

The students that we cast were not professional actors, and this was by design. The goal was to show them honestly experiencing on-screen the process of solving problems and the excitement of success. Therefore, most of the video was not scripted word-for-word, as this would never appear natural. Rather, most of the video was outlined by a professional writer, with input from the rest of the team. This outline indicated what activities would happen in each scene, and what concepts were intended to emerge. Most of the actual work that students do in the video is genuine footage of them working to solve problems. To help tie everything together, we did construct a fictional meta-story describing the students as a group of friends who respond to an invitation to work with their city in optimizing timing for a traffic signal close to their home, and end up with their new timing parameters being implemented on that traffic signal. These fictional portions are only outlined as well, and not scripted. For each segment, the general setup was explained to the students with some suggestions that they implemented via role-playing.

The complete 18-minute video that we created consists of the following sections, which are designed to be shown in portions to students as they work on associated activities:

1. "Traffic Jam": This first segment introduces the four students, and shows them responding to an invitation to work with the city to improve timing on a traffic signal near their home. See Figure 2.
2. "Straight to the Source": The students visit their city's traffic management facility, tour the main traffic signal control room, and meet with a traffic engineer who answers some of their questions.
3. "Brainstorm!": The students describe their task to a computer science professor, who works with them to figure out what data they need to collect.
4. "Take the Numbers": The students go to the intersection of interest and collect the data they need. See Figure 3.
5. "Make a Model": The professor from the "Brainstorm!" segment visits with the students again, introducing them to modeling. They experiment with a spreadsheet model in order to optimize the timing for a single traffic signal.
6. "Run a Simulation": The students learn how to use a NetLogo simulation of traffic in an entire neighborhood, optimize timing for 9 traffic signals, and reflect on results.
7. "Mission Accomplished": The new timing for the traffic signal near their home is put in place, and the students celebrate their success on location at the intersection.

Classroom teachers might choose to show these segments in a classroom in differing ways. Our recommendation, which is described in detail in our associated materials, breaks this up into a four day task. On the first day, a class would watch the first four portions of the video, discuss what they see with their teacher, and lay out a plan for data collection. The second day is optional, and involves the class going to an intersection to collect their own data. The third day involves showing the "Make a Model" segment, followed by the class actually building their own models. On the last day, the class watches the "Run a Simulation" segment, experiments themselves with the NetLogo simulation, and then watches the "Mission Accomplished" wrapup. An alternative approach is to use a flipped-classroom arrangement where students watch the videos on their own, either in daily chunks or all at once. And, as mentioned earlier, the video can also be seen as a standalone engagement tool.

Constructing the portion of the video that shows the students working with the spreadsheet model was particularly challenging, and was a learning experience for us. We had originally hoped to show genuine footage of the students building the spreadsheet model from scratch. However, we had chosen the cast members to be students who did not have much computer science experience, as their reactions and behavior would best model students who might be near the beginning of a course such as AP CS Principles. It was always our assumption that in an actual course, once a teacher had chosen a tool for the students to use for modeling (spreadsheet, or other programming environment), the students would have the opportunity to work on more basic assignments to learn how to use that tool. There was no time or funding for us to do all that with our four cast members. In the end, we pointed our students to an online tutorial on spreadsheets before we shot the video, and then had them work on video with a spreadsheet that we had already prepared in advance for them. This approach worked well for us in that our students were still able to experiment with the model we created in order to perform optimization, and there were many valuable discovery moments for the students as part of that process.

6. PILOT STUDY

We chose to apply a quasi-experimental research design to investigate the change on students' engagement in, attitudes towards, and understanding of computer science. We focused our attention on the following research questions:

- Do students find the video engaging?
- Do students find the lesson engaging?
- Does the video increase interest in and confidence in CS-related activities?
- What aspects of the video do students like most/ least?

6.1 Study design

We found four high school teachers that were willing to have their students participate in the study. Two of these teachers agreed to both show our video and spend a number of full class days with their students working through the associated classroom activities. The other two teachers agreed to show the video only, as that was easier and quicker to implement. To make the distinction clear going forward, we refer to the first group as the "whole-project" group, and the second group as the "video-only" group.

Group demographics: The whole-project group consisted of 39 students, and the video-only group included 37 students. A large group of students in the study (whole-project, 57% and video-only 66%) were White/Caucasian. In both groups, approximately half the students were in grades 9–10, with the other half in grades 11–12. All students were enrolled in some sort of computing-related class.

Data collection: The study used a two-group pre-test and post-test non-randomized experimental design. Whole-project students filled out the pre-viewing survey, viewed the video and completed the classroom activities. Afterwards, students were interviewed regarding their opinions about the video and classroom activities. Each focus group interview took about 30 minutes. Video-only group students filled out the pre-viewing survey, viewed the video and then completed the post-viewing survey. Video-only students were also interviewed regarding their opinions about the video.

Survey design: The pre- and post-surveys were not identical. The pre-survey was designed to measure student attitudes towards and interest in computer science and to collect demographic information. The post-survey for the whole-project group was divided into three parts. The first part, designed to measure engagement in the project, asked about how much students liked the video and the classroom activities. The second part, which was intended to measure student attitudes, asked about student interest in computer science in general. Finally, the third part was designed to measure understanding, and tested student learning of targeted computer science concepts. The post-survey for the video-only group was very similar, though it left out all content related to the classroom activities. In addition to these surveys, focus group interviews were conducted mainly for feedback regarding the TrafficJam video.

6.2 Study Results: Quantitative Data

Engagement: Both groups of students rated the video engaging and interesting. One of the main reasons that students were so engaged by the video was its applicability. Over 75% of the whole-project students and over 85% of the video-only students commented that they liked the video because it was a real-world scenario. Students felt that the challenge in the video was personally relevant and engaging. Furthermore, over 50% of both groups indicated that they liked each section of the video by rating it with a 3 or 4 on a scale of 1 (not at all) to 4 (like it a lot), although students tended to like some sections more than others (e.g., they liked the "straight to the source" considerably). Finally, the whole-project students found the classroom activities engaging. They particularly liked working on NetLogo and working in groups. A large number of students wanted to watch more videos like it.

Attitudes: Pre-survey results showed that students in both groups had very a high level of positive attitudes towards and interest in computer science before viewing the video. Due to this high level of initial motivation, the pre-survey and post-survey results for both groups of students showed similar results. Furthermore, no substantial difference was observed between the whole-project students' and video-only students' interest in computer science.

Content Understanding: 83% of the whole-project students indicated via self-reflection that they learned from the TrafficJam video and classroom activities while 72% of the video-only students indicated that they learned from the video. In addition to the self-reflection questions, the post-survey included several multiple choice and true/ false questions about the spreadsheet, model, and simulation in the video. Since whole-project students participated in classroom activities, they were better in particular at questions that were written to measure learning about the spreadsheet and models. The classroom activities that whole-project students participated in helped them better understand certain targeted computer science concepts (such as optimization and graphical simulation).

6.3 Study results: Qualitative Data

As noted earlier, focus group interviews were conducted with both groups of students. Open ended questions gave students the chance to reflect on the video or classroom activities and their learning. The majority of the students expressed that they liked the video, since the challenge within the video is a real-world problem. Students also expressed that it is encouraging to see and learn that they can solve real-world problems. The following are several representative responses by students to the open-ended question "What did you like about the video?" These are direct quotes, and so grammatical errors have not been corrected:

- "I like the fact that it was a real case scenario."
- "The actors were funny and the problem was common."
- "How easy it is to solve daily problems in life and how hardworking the kids were."
- "I like it was in [my own state]."
- "I like how the kids were able to positively affect their neighborhood via simulation."
- "Data collection"
- "It really utilized the structured teamwork and engineering problem-solving to help make the community better!"
- "I like that they actually were able to make a difference with computers."
- "I like how the kids went all the way to the main source to fix the problem that they had."
- "Interesting, informative, direct. Not too wacky or crazy."

While many students liked the video, a few students did not. Those who do not like the video generally thought traffic control was uninteresting. Some of those students also did not like the acting of the students in the video, finding it "cheesy." This was useful feedback; some of the techniques for producing videos such as this one that are successful for general science broadcast programming may be perceived differently for productions to be shown in school, and we would hope to consider this in detail for future work.

In summary, the pilot study gathered data from 76 students in grades 9–12. A majority of the students found the TrafficJam video and classroom activities very engaging. The whole-project students were overwhelmingly positive about the classroom activities associated with the video. While acknowledging some issues such as the acting performance of the students in the video, most agreed that they found the experience very valuable.

7. CONCLUSIONS

The new AP CS Principles curriculum has a significant component regarding modeling and simulation, and many teachers will need to figure out how to accomplish this in their classrooms as the course is adopted by more schools. We have developed a set of materials, which could be used in AP CS Principles or in other contexts, to introduce modeling and simulation. Our work consists of an approach for making this level-appropriate for a high school setting, a set of activities for students to work on, and a set of professionally made videos designed to introduce the ideas and engage the students. A pilot study indicated that students mostly found the activities relevant and interesting, and that they gained a greater understanding of modeling and simulation from the experience.

Looking forward, we hope to evaluate the effectiveness of TrafficJam on student success directly in an actual AP CS Principles course. This will be more easily accomplished as more schools begin to adopt the curriculum. We also plan to develop new media-enhanced projects, using the format of this one, to help improve other aspects of computer science education. We suspect that our approach of having computer science activities accompanied by videos showing inquiry-driven explorations might be particularly effective at engaging and motivating new students into the field, especially those who do not already have a high level of interest. We hope to research this further and produce additional materials aimed at this group of students.

8. ACKNOWLEDGMENTS

This work is supported by NSF CNS grant 1339104. In addition to NSF, we thank many people and organizations who contributed to this project. At TPT, our co-PIs Richard Hudson and Kathleen O'Donnell provided leadership and vision, Marie Domingo and Emily Stevens managed production and logistics, and Angie Prindle handled story design and field production. Traffic engineers Nickolas Van Gunst from the City of Minneapolis and JoNette Kuhnau from Kimley-Horn and Associates provided considerable insight and domain knowledge. Evelyn Beyer of Trafficware provided support on understanding professional traffic management software. Finally, PBS LearningMedia is hosting the website offering EMACS materials for download.

9. REFERENCES

[1] STEM-C Partnerships: Computing education for the 21st century (STEM-CP: CE21). Program Solicitation NSF 14-523. Accessed: 2014-08-25.

[2] *Highway Capacity Manual (HCM)*. TRB Publications, fifth edition, 2010.

[3] Investing in infrastructure: A question of trust. *The Economist*, May 12, 2012.

[4] C. Alvarado. Member Spotlight: Robert Panoff. *ACM SIGCSE Bulletin*, 46(1):6–7, January 2014.

[5] A. Bandura. Self-efficacy. volume 4 of *Encyclopedia of Human Behavior*, pages 71–81, 1994.

[6] E. Lotterman. Campaigns ignore infrastructure, public good. *St. Paul Pioneer Press*, Sept 8, 2012.

[7] D. Riley, G. Nellen, R. Barrera, and J. Quevedo. Crowdsourcing traffic simulation to improve signal timing. *J. Comp. Sci. Coll.*, 29(5):112–118, May 2014.

[8] The College Board. AP Computer Science Principles draft curriculum framework. June 2014.

[9] U. Wilensky. Netlogo. Center for Connected Learning and Computer-Based Modeling, Northwestern University, Evanston, IL, 1999. `http://ccl.northwestern.edu/netlogo/`.

[10] U. Wilensky. Netlogo Traffic Grid model. Center for Connected Learning and Computer-Based Modeling, Northwestern U., Evanston, IL, 2003. `http://ccl.northwestern.edu/netlogo/models/TrafficGrid`.

[11] A. L. Zeldin, S. L. Britner, and F. Pajares. A comparative study of the self-efficacy beliefs of successful men and women in mathematics, science, and technology careers. *Journal of Research in Science Teaching*, 45(9):1036–1058, 2008.

[12] A. L. Zeldin and F. Pajares. Against the odds: Self-efficacy beliefs of women in mathematical, scientific, and technological careers. *American Educational Research Journal*, 37(1):215–246, 2000.

An Analysis of User Engagement in Relation to Computing Workshop Activities

Rachel Menzies
School of Computing
University of Dundee
Dundee
r.menzies@dundee.ac.uk

Michael Crabb
School of Computing
University of Dundee
Dundee
michaelcrabb@acm.com

Daniel Herron
School of Computing
University of Dundee
Dundee
d.herron@dundee.ac.uk

Karen Petrie
School of Computing
University of Dundee
Dundee
k.petrie@dundee.ac.uk

Craig Stewart
School of Computing
University of Dundee
Dundee
c.s.stewart@dundee.ac.uk

Mark Zarb
School of Computing Science
Robert Gordon University
Dundee
m.zarb@rgu.ac.uk

ABSTRACT

Computing is now one of the fastest growing fields of employment, with a large bias placed on developing Science, Technology, Engineering, and Mathematics (STEM) education in schools. However, due to the fast pace of technology development, it is increasingly difficult for schools to keep up with the latest computing methodologies. A possible solution is the use of university outreach programmes, whereby local universities can provide training workshops on areas that can be challenging for schools to implement. This can be problematic, as there is a perceived lack of interest in the methods used to interact with secondary school pupils on a university level.

This paper introduces a week long 'Easter Computing School', comprising of five workshop sessions on different topics. These sessions were analysed in terms of user engagement, to better understand aspects that are important to secondary school pupils. It was found that a combination of theory and interactive workshop sessions can provide the highest levels of engagement and their use is encouraged in future workshop design.

Categories and Subject Descriptors

Computers and Education~General.
Human-centered computing~Usability testing, Human-centered computing~Interface design prototyping, Social and professional topics~Computational science and engineering education.

General Terms

Measurement, Design, Experimentation, and Human Factors.

Keywords: Summer school; user engagement; outreach.

SIGCSE'14, March 4–7, 2015, Kansas City, MO, USA.

http://dx.doi.org/10.1145/2676723.2677272

1. INTRODUCTION

As the development of digital technology increases, there is a growing demand for graduates within the computing sector in Scotland. In order to meet this requirement, higher educational institutions are placing an increasing importance in attracting students to Science, Technology, Engineering, and Mathematics (STEM) subjects in the coming years. However, school-based computing education can be limited due to increasing financial constraints and disparities in teacher knowledge between schools. Initiatives exist that are attempting to overcome this shortfall [5]. The provision of outreach programmes to local schools and communities is becoming more prominent in universities. The aim of these programmes is therefore to develop interest in computing as an educational field and to promote the potential for future employment in this area.

A series of computing workshops was developed and held along with exam revision sessions to engage local school pupils in varying aspects of computing. These were held during Scottish Easter school holidays and marketed to local schools and university applicants as an 'Easter Computing School'. Workshops were a mix of educational and experiential sessions, taking place over a five-day period. Staff, postgraduate and undergraduate students delivered workshops in order to expose participants to a wide range of academic experience. Feedback from these sessions was gathered focusing on individuals' user engagement levels. This was divided into factors relating to user-focussed attention, perceived usability, aesthetics, durability, novelty, and involvement. Analysis was conducted to evaluate the success of the workshops in terms of user engagement, compared to the student's experience of high school computing classes.

2. RELATED WORK

In some cases, there is a lack of interest in computing within schools. This is due to a lack of effective role models, a lack of familiarity with computing fields, and negative perceptions of computing as being "nerdy" [4, 9]. However, there is a clear need for students to become better skilled in computing, with an increasing demand from employers for computing science skills [2]. Across the UK, and particularly in Scotland, there are many more jobs available than university graduates in the field of computing

[15]. However, many school-aged students have a poor understanding of what a career in computing can involve [18].

Outreach activities are often used as a method for universities to encourage a broader participation in computer science higher education [11]. This provides potential students, and the wider community, with valuable exposure to the resources and expertise that the university can offer [7]. The most successful of these allow the community to meet "real world" experts from both academia and industry [19], in order to provide role models.

It is noted that outreach activities that reduce or avoid the need to program provide an effective and scalable way to introduce concepts in computing science [2]. Computer Science Unplugged[1] is an online resource for teaching materials that can be used by teachers and tutors. Alongside activities, suggestions are made of how to integrate them into the school curriculum. This is valuable, as curriculum content can vary greatly between schools, even within one geographical region, due to resources and teacher knowledge. The focus of Computer Science Unplugged activities is to ensure that learning can take place away from computers to increase interaction between participants. Students are engaged in "computational thinking" [17], independently of developing their knowledge of programming languages. Therefore, students with knowledge of different languages can participate in the same session. A similar program, CS Inside [6] also provides lessons for teachers, introducing computing science concepts using everyday technologies as exemplars. This ensures that the lesson is directly applicable to the students, and that they can see the immediate value in the topic. The use of everyday technology also reinforces the relevance of this field of study. The aim of this paper is to report on outreach workshops held at a Scottish university as part of an Easter School.

3. METHODOLOGY

The aim of this work is to examine how the experiences of school age pupils in a variety of workshop sessions compares to their experiences of computing education in a standard computing classroom. Five workshop sessions were organized and pupil experience measured through self-reported questionnaires. This data was collected in order to compare their perceived experiences from a standard computing classroom environment.

3.1 Experimental Variables

Participant user experience (measured through a self-reported questionnaire [12]) was used as a dependent metric. Workshop activity (Arduino, Prototyping, Internet usability, and Mathematics in Games) and standard class engagement was used as independent metrics.

3.2 Participants

A total of 12 participants (10 male, 2 female) participated in this work. Participants were all aged 14-17 and were students of local high schools, studying computing at SQA Higher and Advanced Higher levels [16].

3.3 Materials and Equipment

3.3.1 Workshop Activities

Workshops, and accompanying revision sessions, were promoted as an 'Easter Computing School', which ran for five consecutive days. One workshop and one revision session was held each day with a break for lunch. Posters were sent to local schools in the surrounding areas and were displayed in the computing department or pupil social areas. In addition, emails were sent to all applicants to the university who were studying computing as one of their chosen school subjects. This wider promotion ensured that pupils who would benefit from the revision sessions were individually informed, while offering the workshop activities more broadly within local secondary schools.

The aim of these sessions was to provide local school pupils with additional revision opportunities prior to sitting their SQA exams. The results of these exams, in most cases, will have a direct impact on the individual's course and location of study in higher education. Having a local secondary school teacher run the revision class ensured direct knowledge of the school curriculum. Staff, postgraduate and undergraduate students ran the workshops from the School of Computing, with a wide range of educational and industry experience. The interdisciplinary nature of the workshops meant that little or no computing experience was necessary to complete them.

The remainder of this section introduces the workshop sessions, giving details on the topics covered and the activities undertaken.

Arduino Workshop - Arduino is an open source platform used to create interactive objects and environments. Arduino boards are cheap to purchase (starting at £20 ($30)) and are programmed using open source software. The Arduino board can sense the environment and user interactions by receiving inputs from sensors such as buttons, and can affect the environment by controlling actuators such as LED lights, buzzers and motors. Despite the low cost of each board, multiple purchases are required, as well as knowledge of the topic. As a result, many school pupils are not exposed to microcontrollers in schools.

Participants were invited to explore the world of microcontrollers through a series of activities involving LEDs and potentiometers (a variable resistor, e.g. used as volume control knobs). The tasks included a 'Hello World' program, creating a set of traffic lights and controlling multiple LEDs using a potentiometer. Participants explored the creation of electronic circuits, were encouraged to use modular programming techniques, and to consider future developers by commenting code.

Figure 1 The Final Output of Arduino Workshop - 4 LEDs Controlled by a Potentiometer

Internet Usability Workshop - One key aspect in computing is to develop an understanding into problems that can be faced by the end user when designing digital services. This workshop was intended to examine the importance of Internet Usability guidelines and their implementation in modern websites. This session was split into three separate components: (i) The collection of usability guidelines from online sources, allowing students to understand the large variety of usability issues that exist in designing digital services; (ii) A usability analysis of several live websites, intended to allow

[1] http://www.csunplugged.org

students to examine if the implementation of usability guidelines would either enhance or detract from the user experience of navigating through a live website; (iii) The creation and adaptation of simple websites with a focus on the usability of navigation options.

Figure 2 demonstrates some of the potential adaptations that users could make to websites in order to change the physical appearance of the page, while keeping the content of the page the same.

Figure 2 Website Usability Adaptions

Prototyping Workshop - Prototyping is a powerful tool used in research and industry to conceptualise products in a very visual way. Participants explored the concept of prototyping, learning about the steps involved in creating a prototype, and how prototyping is used in industry today. Students designed, created and presented a prototype wearable technology from scratch. Materials such as clothing, marker pens, and additional paper were provided. Participants were encouraged to keep in mind the reasoning behind all of their decisions; it was not enough to simply state the design of their products, but instead they had to be able to explain how they came to make the decisions that informed these designs. Blue-sky thinking was encouraged throughout the prototyping process, to foster the creation of interesting and novel ideas.

Mathematics in Games Workshop - Both board games and computer games involve mathematics at some level or another; Monopoly, for example, teaches basic concepts such as addition, subtraction, negative numbers, and compound interest. As such, games provide an accessible platform for teaching students about mathematics and programming. In this workshop, participants were introduced to a number of concepts including understanding that theory and mathematics underpin most games. The workshop explores the concept of perfect information (when the behaviour of a player causes the best possible outcome for that player, regardless of an opponent's response) can how this combines with algorithms to create a solved game [13, 1].

Participants completed series of activities, culminating in a task to create an algorithm to play Connect 4 perfectly. In a Connect 4 tournament participants used their algorithms in order to win.

3.3.2 User Experience Questionnaire

A questionnaire measuring participant user experience was used during the workshop sessions. Based on work by O'Brien and Tom [12], questions were adapted to relate to a more generic 'activity' rather than the 'shopping task' used in their work. This work is one of the currently recognised academic sources for measuring user engagement and justifies is use in this case.

The questionnaire consisted of 32 questions, administered on a forced 6-point Likert scale option (*Strongly Disagree, Disagree, Somewhat Disagree, Somewhat Agree, Agree, Strongly Agree, n/a*). This option was used instead of a standard 7-Point scale in order to make participants more likely to give answers on one of the two sides of the scale. Participants were given printed copies of the questionnaire to complete.

Exploratory Principal Component Analysis conducted by O'Brien and Toms concluded that this questionnaire could be split into six separate factors. These, along with a brief explanation into their composition are detailed below:

- *Focused Attention,* 7 questions. This factor is a measure examining users perception of time passing and their ability to recall what was happening out with the current task being created. It is a measure of individuals' ability to concentrate on one single task and not being distracted by any others [10].
- *Perceived Usability,* 8 questions. This factor was used to understand the emotive state of participants throughout a task, with questions examining feelings such as frustration, confusion, and annoyance. In simpler terms, this is described as individuals' perceived effort in completing a seminar workshop.
- *Aesthetics*, 5 questions. This factor is used to measure the visual attractiveness of the task being completed and the overall appearance of any materials used.
- *Endurability,* 5 questions. The endurability factor is used as a measure of workshop success and, to a degree, participants' likelihood to recommend the activity to others. Again, this uses the definition set out by O'Brien and Toms, stating that endurability is "the likelihood to remember things that we have enjoyed and a desire to do again an activity that has been fun" [14].
- *Novelty,* 3 questions. The three questions used in the novelty factor relate to the curiosity felt by participants during a workshop, and also their interest in the task.
- *Involvement,* 4 questions. This factor was used to understand the interest felt by participants throughout the seminar workshop activities. The questions used in this factor focused on the fun, feelings of involvement and the overall interest levels of participants.

3.3.3 Additional Feedback Questionnaire

After the week of workshops was completed, participants were contacted by email and invited to complete an online feedback questionnaire. Participants were invited to comment on which sessions they enjoyed most and least, providing justification for this also.

3.4 Procedure

Workshop activities and revision sessions were organised within the University of Dundee. As part of these workshops, pupils were given *two user experience questionnaires*, the first of these (measuring their standard computer class engagement) was given at the start of the week and the second (measuring their engagement in an individual summer school workshop) was given at the end of each workshop session.

3.5 Analysis

The purpose of analysis is to provide a comparison between pupils' perceived experiences in a standard computing class and that of the four separate education workshop sessions.

Due to the small sample sizes, null hypothesis statistics testing (NHST) is not used due to the low power that would be achieved. Instead, analysis is based on an interpretation in the differences in the six engagement levels across the four workshop activities. This is accomplished through examining the mean and standard deviation levels of baseline and workshop activities. A higher value is indicative of greater engagement. In addition, Cohen's d value acts as a comparative statistic. Cohen's d value is a measure of effect size. Analysis was conducted using R [20].

Quantitative analysis is further explained through an interpretation of qualitative responses gathered from the *Additional Feedback Questionnaire*.

4. RESULTS

Due to the small sample sizes, analysis is based on an interpretation in the differences in the six engagement levels across the workshops by examining the mean and standard deviation levels of baseline and workshop activities.

4.1 Arduino Workshop

The Arduino workshop was organized for the first day of the Easter School and had a total of 4 attendees. Pupils reported that this workshop was more visually attractive than a standard computing class (*aesthetics*) (d=.72). However, they were also less likely to remember aspects of the workshop that were enjoyed (*endurability*) (d=-.96) than if they were participating in a school-based computing class.

Table 1 Arduino Workshop Results

	Baseline		Arduino		
	M	SD	M	SD	d
Focused Attention	4.14	0.48	4.18	1.11	.04
Perceived Usability	5.50	1.04	5.75	0.32	.30
Aesthetics	5.17	0.69	5.67	0.27	.72
Endurability	5.30	0.84	4.60	0.23	-.96
Novelty	5.20	0.99	5.25	0.96	.05
Involvement	4.44	0.36	4.50	0.20	.12

4.2 Internet Usability Workshop

The Internet Usability workshop was organized for the second day of the Easter School and had a total of 6 attendees. Pupils reported that concentrating on a single task during this workshop was more difficult than a standard computing class (d=-1.08). However, they also reported that they felt more involved in this session and had higher levels of overall interest (d=1.85).

4.3 Prototyping Workshop

The Prototyping workshop occurred on the third day of the summer school and had a total of 4 attendees. Again, this workshop was more visually attractive than a standard computing class (d=1.07), as well as having greater endurability of perceived usability. Participants found it more difficult to concentrate on the task (d=-.53).

Table 2 Internet Usability Results

	Baseline		Int. Usability		
	M	SD	M	SD	d
Focused Attention	4.98	1.06	3.76	1.46	-1.08
Perceived Usability	5.94	1.02	5.67	0.88	-.28
Aesthetics	5.67	0.92	5.56	0.82	-.12
Endurability	5.77	0.93	5.87	0.72	.11
Novelty	5.80	0.94	5.80	0.59	-.08
Involvement	4.38	0.67	4.38	0.65	1.85

Table 3 Prototyping Results

	Baseline		Prototyping		
	M	SD	M	SD	d
Focused Attention	4.57	0.80	4.00	1.52	-.53
Perceived Usability	5.58	1.07	6.67	0.32	1.3
Aesthetics	5.33	0.82	6.22	0.57	1.07
Endurability	5.35	0.81	6.27	0.54	1.12
Novelty	5.50	0.93	6.07	0.66	.64
Involvement	4.34	0.39	4.79	0.87	.56

4.4 Mathematics in Games Workshop

The Mathematics workshop was the fourth session and had a total of 6 attendees. All measures showed higher ratings than a standard computing class. Large differences were seen in the aesthetics (d=1.41) and involvement (d=1.61). In addition, the perceived usability (d=.31), endurability (d=.42), and novelty (d=.50) between baseline and workshop sessions all showed a medium effect.

Table 4 Mathematics in Games Results

	Baseline		Maths		
	M	SD	M	SD	d
Focused Attention	4.5	1.44	4.71	1.35	.18
Perceived Usability	5.72	1.00	6.00	0.58	.31
Aesthetics	5.33	1.03	6.5	0.33	1.41
Endurability	5.73	0.97	6.10	0.53	.42
Novelty	5.43	1.08	5.90	0.64	.50
Involvement	4.25	0.60	4.25	0.45	1.64

5. DISCUSSION

This study set out with the aim of assessing the differences that exist in levels of user engagement between a standard computing class environment and four university-based workshops. Prior studies have noted the importance of outreach activities such as this in creating exposure to the expertise that universities have to offer. Analysis therefore focused on six different aspects of user engagement.

5.1 Workshop Discussion

In the first workshop session, the open sourced Arduino platform was introduced to students. This was used to explore several aspects relating to the hardware of computing and focused on the control and manipulation of a simple LED array. The results for this session indicated that pupils experienced higher levels of aesthetic appeal and lower levels of endurability in this workshop compared to their standard computing class. Surprisingly, very little difference was seen in the focused attention and novelty factors reported by pupils when comparing between these two tasks. From this, it is possible to conceive that the use of an emerging technology, such as Arduino, can improve the learning experience of pupils while keeping levels of focused attention and novelty relatively similar. The trade off between task complexity measured by *endurability* and task visual appeal measured by *aesthetics*, while not predicted, is an interesting point to note.

The second workshop session focused on the concept of Internet Usability, allowing students to conduct their own usability analysis of websites before creating their own sites using these principles. It is interesting to note that in this workshop, participants reported involvement was higher than a standard computing class, while user focused attention was lower. All other measures (except perceived usability) had effect sizes lower than 0.2, showing to be lower than Cohen's criterion for a *small* effect. This workshop session placed a significant bias on student self learning, with pupils being firstly asked to research a topic before applying any information that they had found. Due to the complex nature of research skills, it is not surprising that pupils untrained in this area found it difficult to maintain high levels of attention during this task. Higher levels of user involvement is put down to the interactive elements used when pupils were asked to create their own websites at the end of the workshop session.

The third workshop focused on the development of pupils' prototyping skills with an emphasis on wearable technologies. The feedback questionnaires from this session indicated that pupils experienced higher levels of perceived usability, aesthetic appeal and endurability when compared to their standard computing class. Similar to the above workshop, the environment in this workshop was different to that of students' previous experiences. This is likely to have contributed to reduced focused attention levels. This combination of findings provides support for the use of highly interactive session in computing teaching, showing that a combination of academic rigour and blue-sky thinking can improve the engagement of pupils.

The final educational workshop focused on the use of mathematics in gaming, examining how this occurs in both computer and board games. Results from this session showed increases in aesthetic appeal and user involvement, with these both having Cohen's d levels indicating over 68% of non-overlap. All other aspects of user engagement was shown to have increased, with perceived usability, endurability, and novelty all showing to have effect sizes between small and medium according to Cohen's criterion. In general, therefore, it seems that by introducing students to computing principles and then reinforcing this learning through interactive sessions, levels of user engagement can increase across all factors. This has important implications for developing future workshop sessions, with the combination of theory and interactivity showing to have the largest increase in engagement among pupils.

5.2 Overall Discussion

Of the four educational workshops conducted, Mathematics in Games was the only workshop in which differences between the workshop session and a standard computing classroom were all in favour of the workshop session. This workshop also had the highest average effect size calculated across all 6 categories ($d = 0.74$). This increase indicates that the participants were most engaged with this workshop. However, this is in contrast with participant reports that Prototyping was their favourite workshop. While Prototyping had largely positive engagement levels, perceived usability and endurability were the highest scoring. Therefore, student engagement may be defined using a subset of these engagement levels.

The level of focused attention showed only small increases in the Arduino and Mathematics in Games workshops. A medium reduction in focused attention was seen in the Prototyping workshop and a large reduction in the Internet Usability workshop. These reductions are likely due to the environment of the workshops being considerably different to a typical classroom setting. These workshops were student-led, whereby sessions were facilitated by tutors rather than focusing on taught content. In addition, the skills being explored in these workshops required subjective consideration of the subject matter.

The Internet Usability workshop was the only workshop that showed lower levels of perceived usability than the classroom. The complex subjective and research skills needed for Internet Usability may have resulted in this reduction. Participants reported in the post-questionnaire that they found this workshop the most difficult, as concept of usability was not something that they had not previously encountered.

Participants reported higher levels of task visual attractiveness compared to their standard computing class in all workshop sessions apart from Internet Usability. A possible reason for this focuses on the content of this workshop where a focus, in part, was placed on poor design in order to provide a comparison with successful and usable websites. This inclusion of "bad" sites may have impacted on the reported aesthetics level.

Participant feedback for the Arduino workshop rated it as "one of the more fun kinds of computing" but also acknowledged that "it was pretty easy". One participant noted that he was familiar with the workshop, as he had previous experience with the platform.

The novelty level for Prototyping was highest of the workshops. Participant reports that the workshop was "different from usual lessons" are attributed to the practical and interactive content. While this novelty may have contributed to reduced focused attention, it appears to be a key element of engagement.

The involvement ratings reported by pupils in the workshop sessions all had higher levels than that of their standard computing class. Of these, Internet Usability ($d = 1.85$) and Mathematics in Games ($d = 1.64$) were particularly large. While this may be attributable to the small participant numbers, it is encouraging to note that these workshops particularly piqued the curiosity and interest of the participants. Future events might consider the format of these workshops, which comprised combinations of theoretical and practical learning. In addition, regarding the Internet Usability workshop, although the workshop had the lowest level of focused attention, participants showed the highest level of involvement, suggesting that the difficulties were motivating rather than challenging their interest.

5.3 Limitations and Future Work

Results from this study are encouraging, but are limited to the context of this series of workshops. Small participant numbers meant that results could not be widely generalized and NHST could not be conducted. Additionally, different students participated in the four workshops, making it difficult to draw comparisons between each session. Due to the small participant numbers in each workshop session, large changes may be seen due to the reported engagement levels of one participant. Furthermore, there is a greater teacher to pupil ratio than could be expected in schools, which may have contributed to large differences seen.

Future engagement with computing classes in school should be conducted to determine the longer-term effects of the workshops on student engagement.

6. CONCLUSIONS

This paper has reported on a series of workshop activities that were used in conjunction with revision sessions as part of a computing outreach program at the University of Dundee. The purpose of this work was to examine if levels of user engagement for pupils is different across these workshop activities when compared to their previous computing education at school.

The results of this have indicated that the use of interactive workshop sessions can increase the aesthetics, involvement, and endurability experienced by pupils when participating in these sessions. It was also found that in general the focused attention and perceived usability could be increased when focusing on theory-based aspects in this style of workshops. Taken together, these results are aligned with previous work showing that a combination of theoretical principles being reinforced by interactive learning can increase all aspects of user engagement for pupils, may be an area deserving more attention in the future.

The current findings add to a growing body of literature on the use of outreach programs, focusing on the benefits that these can bring to school pupils when participating in computer science higher education. Further investigation into user engagement in relation to classroom and workshop activities would allow for these findings to be validated, generalised, and, moreover, provide further reasoning for the importance of outreach workshops as part of a Universities Agenda.

7. ACKNOWLEDGMENTS

The researchers would like to thank Katie Skinner for providing support during revision sessions. Authors 2 and 5 are supported by RCUK Digital Economy Research Hub EP/G066019/1 – SIDE: Social Inclusion through the Digital Economy.

REFERENCES

[1] Allen J, D., 2010. The Complete Book of Connect 4: History, Strategy, Puzzles. Sterling Publishing Company. ISBN 1402756216.

[2] Bell, T., Alexander, J., Freeman, I. and Grimley, M.. 2009. Computer Science Unplugged: school students doing real computing without computers. The NZ Journal of applied computing and information technology, Volume 13(1), pp 20-29,

[3] Bell, T., Curzon, P., Cutts, Q., Dagiene, V. and Haberman, B.. 2011. Introducing students to computer science with programmes that don't emphasise programming. In Proceedings of the 16th annual joint conference on Innovation and technology in computer science education (ITiCSE '11). ACM, New York, NY, USA, 391-391.

[4] Carter, L. 2006. Why students with an apparent aptitude for computer science don't choose to major in computer science. In Proceedings of the 37th SIGCSE technical symposium on Computer science education (SIGCSE '06). ACM, New York, NY, USA, 27-31.

[5] CASS. (n.d.). About PLAN C. http://www.casscotland.org.uk/plan-c/ Accessed 14/04/2014

[6] Cutts, Q., Brown, M., Kemp, L. and Matheson, C., Enthusing and informing potential computer science students and their teachers, ACM SIGCSE Bulletin, v.39 n.3, September 2007

[7] Fox, R., Newell, G. and Frank, C.. 2004. Experiences hosting high school summer camps to promote university outreach. In Proceedings of Mid-South College Computing Conference. 166-172.

[8] Heersink, D. and Moskal, B. 2010. Measuring high school students' attitudes toward computing. Proceedings of the 41st ACM technical symposium on Computer science education (SIGCSE '10). ACM, New York, NY, USA, 446-450.

[9] Jepson, A. and Teri Perl. 2002. Priming the pipeline. SIGCSE Bull. 34, 2 (June 2002), 36-39.

[10] Matlin, M. 1994. Cognition, 4th ed. Harcourt Press.

[11] Murphy, M., VanDeGrift, T., Richards, B. and Wilson, B. 2005. Models for computer science K-12 outreach activities. J. Comput. Sci. Coll. 21, 1 (October 2005), 274-276.

[12] O'Brien, H. and Toms, E. 2010. The development and evaluation of a survey to measure user engagement. Journal of the American Society for Information Science and Technology, 61(1), 50-69.

[13] Osborne, M. and Rubinstein, A. 1994. "Chapter 6: Extensive Games with Perfect Information". A Course in Game Theory. Cambridge M.A.: The MIT Press.

[14] Read, J., MacFarlane, S. and Casey, C.. 2002. Endurability, engagement and expectations: Measuring children's fun. In Interaction Design and Children (Vol. 2, pp. 1-23). Eindhoven: Shaker Publishing.

[15] ScotlandIS. 2014. Skills Investment Plan for Scotland's ICT and Digital Technologies Sector. http://www.ourskillsforce.co.uk/media/463298/sds_ict_sip.pdf . Accessed 14th April 2014

[16] SQA. (n.d.). Computing. http://www.sqa.org.uk/sqa/2472.html. Accessed 14/04/2014.

[17] Wing, J. 2006. Computational thinking. Communications of the ACM 49(3), 33-35.

[18] Yardi, S. and Bruckman, A. 2007. What is computing?: bridging the gap between teenagers' perceptions and graduate students' experiences. In Proceedings of the third international workshop on Computing education research (ICER '07). ACM, New York, NY, USA, 39-50.

[19] Yehezkel, C. and Haberman, B. 2006. Bridging the gap between school computing and the "real world", Proceedings of the 2006 international conference on Informatics in Secondary Schools - Evolution and Perspectives: the Bridge between Using and Understanding Computers, November 07-11, 2006, Vilnius, Lithuania

[20] R Development Core Team. 2008. R: A language and environment for statistical computing. R Foundation for Statistical Computing, Vienna, Austria.

Unci: a C++-based Unit-testing Framework for Intro Students

Don Blaheta
Longwood University
Farmville, VA, USA
blahetadp@longwood.edu

ABSTRACT

This paper describes Unci, a unit-testing language with a clean and minimal interface suitable for introducing beginning programming students to the ideas of unit testing and test-driven development. We detail why CppUnit, a common C++-based unit-testing framework, is not well-suited for beginners, and present Unci and explain how it addresses the weaknesses of CppUnit. Finally, we present a comparison of CS2 student performance in the two systems, showing that moving from CppUnit to Unci resulted in an approximate doubling in the proportion of students able to write an effective test suite for a lab assignment.

Categories and Subject Descriptors

D.2.5 [**Software engineering**]: Testing and debugging—*Testing tools*; K.3.2 [**Computers and Education**]: Computer and Information Science Education—*Computer science education*

General Terms

Design, Human factors

Keywords

Test-driven development; unit testing; CS1; CS2

1. TEST-DRIVEN DEVELOPMENT IN INTRODUCTORY COURSES

Test-driven development (TDD) is by now a well-established framework for software engineering [1, 5], promoting the idea of developing an application's testing framework before and during, rather than after, the main code development; this is intended to solidify understanding of a project's requirements early in the project and improve communication about those requirements, as well as making the tests themselves less likely to be dependent on particular design choices, hence more likely to be robust. A number of educators have argued that TDD is pedagogically effective, even (or especially) in introductory programming courses [4, 7, 10]. Reasons for this mirror the reasons it is seen as effective as a general software engineering technique: for instance, students can better understand an example if it includes both an interface and an expected result [6], and having a written artifact of the *student's* understanding of the project requirements is helpful if the student needs to ask a question of a TA or professor (who can then quickly verify that the assumptions are correct before trying to answer the question) [11]. From a more cognitive perspective, an intro student—initially overwhelmed by the open-ended task of starting to write code—is well-served by having to first answer the more-constrained question of what a specific function call, with a specific, concrete parameter, should return. In addition, suites of discrete unit tests can be seen as an effective way to perform automatic grading of student work, decreasing grading load for the professor or teaching staff as well as giving the students more rapid feedback on their work [4].

Frameworks to support unit testing and test-driven development have been written for many programming languages. For Java, the original and most widespread is JUnit [8], although others exist to serve various specific niches, including at least one, tester [10], which was designed specifically for intro students. For C++, the unit testing landscape is much more fragmented. CppUnit [2], developed as a port of JUnit, is widespread but a variety of others exist.

At our institution, the introductory CS1/CS2 sequence is taught using C++. When deciding to integrate unit testing into these early courses, we looked at several of the available options, settling on CppUnit: with none of the options apparently targeting the intro programming student, we decided to at least choose one with some wider use.

SIGCSE'15, March 4–7, 2015, Kansas City, MO, USA.

ACM 978-1-4503-2966-8/15/03 ...$15.00.
http://dx.doi.org/10.1145/2676723.2677228.

2. PROBLEMS WITH CPPUNIT

In the Fall 2013 offering of our CS2 course, students were introduced to the concept of unit testing in week 3 (of 14); in their lab section during that week, they were given a template file similar to that shown in Figure 1 to work from, and instructions on how to adapt it to write test cases. Four of the remaining weekly labs contained specific additional instructions on CppUnit syntax or semantics, and two more of the labs did not give additional instructions but included "testing" among their rubric requirements.

We deemed it crucial to give a template for the students to use, not just the first time they were introduced to CppUnit

```
#include <cppunit/TestFixture.h>
#include <cppunit/TextTestRunner.h>
#include <cppunit/extensions/HelperMacros.h>
#include "Xxx.h"

class Xxx_test   : public CppUnit::TestFixture
{
  CPPUNIT_TEST_SUITE( Xxx_test );
  CPPUNIT_TEST( test_somethingMethod );
  CPPUNIT_TEST_SUITE_END();

  private:
    Xxx example1;

  public:
    void setUp()
    {
      example1 = Xxx (arg1, arg2);
    }

    void test_somethingMethod()
    {
      CPPUNIT_ASSERT_EQUAL ( 42, example1.something() );
    }
};

int main( int argc, char **argv)
{
  CppUnit::TextTestRunner runner;
  runner.addTest( Xxx_test::suite() );
  runner.run();
  return 0;
}
```

Figure 1: A minimal CppUnit file

but for the entire rest of the term. A minimal file using CppUnit to implement unit tests—if it is meant to stand alone—must in general contain:

- Three `#include` lines at the top
- A class that inherits from `CppUnit::TestFixture`
- A series of macro calls to build the test suite (where the macro arguments must be the name of the class itself as well as the names of each method designated as a test), and
- A four-line `main` function to bootstrap the test suite runner.

This boilerplate material must be present in addition to the declaration of any fixture variables, and a `setUp` method to give their initial values, and the test methods themselves. It was our hope that by providing a template file, the boilerplate could be abstracted away and the students could focus on the conceptually important part: what do objects of this type look like, and how should they behave?

There was, however, a great deal of friction involved in introducing CppUnit-based unit testing: problems that were not with the core concept of unit testing or with understanding of what the test cases ought to be, but with the framework itself. Some of these were relatively minor, such as misremembering which argument to `CPPUNIT_ASSERT_EQUALS` is the expression to check and which is the expected return value. But many were more major, causing subtle bugs or otherwise delaying or preventing them from addressing the "real" content of the lab.

For instance, a frequent student error was creating a test method and not adding it to the suite. This results in a syntactically valid class that compiles and runs, but doesn't execute that test—meaning the student either assumes a test is passing when it wouldn't, or notices the missing test and loses time trying to figure out what's wrong.

An even larger problem came when students inadvertently made errors in the macros constructing the test suite. Since C++ macros are based purely on text substitution, problems here result in error messages that are utterly incomprehensible to beginners. If a student writes `CPPUNIT_TEST` in place of `CPPUNIT_TEST_SUITE`—an easy mistake for a beginner who doesn't yet understand what these lines are doing—the resulting error message says "`'context' does not name a type`", which is unhelpful at best (although the error does at least indicate the correct line number). The reverse mistake is even worse: it causes the error "`expected '}' at end of input`" and points to the last line of the file. Other mistakes that yield unhelpful or misleading error messages include changing the header of a test method or omitting the inheritance from `TestFixture` in the class header. This sort of misdirection can cost a student hours of fruitless, wasted debugging time, and it prevents them from progressing with the lab.

A further set of problems arose from the fact that fixture values look just like (and technically are) instance variables. In most other circumstances, instance variables would be used for values that are meant to persist across method calls; but in the case of the test suite, this is almost exactly the opposite of what happens, since the variables are reset to their initial values before each test method is run. The reasons behind this are good and fairly interesting, but also subtle and somewhat sophisticated, and this is a source of confusion for students who have just been introducted to object-oriented design.

There are other C++-based unit testing frameworks, of course, but to a greater or lesser extent, they appear to suffer from the same problems in an intro context. For instance, UnitTest++[13] requires its own `#include` and boilerplate `main` function, albeit shorter than those for CppUnit, and works through the preprocessing system to create `SUITE` and `TEST` macros; the fixture, if any, is a user-defined class separate from the test suite (and must be named in the header to every test case). libunittest[9] is similar to UnitTest++ except that it can define its own `main`. Unit++[12] steers clear of the preprocessor but requires individual registration of each test, and uses some fairly exotic syntax (method pointers) and dispreferred techniques (global variables) to get all the pieces to talk to each other; it doesn't appear to support fixtures at all. xUnit++[14] leverages a number of C++11 features to offer extra power to the programmer, but they largely don't help the intro student; it is again macro-based, and fixtures must be built by hand and named at the top of each test case. CxxTest[3] takes the promising step of running as a preprocessor (so it doesn't need a boilerplate `main`) but again uses the C++ preprocessor for the assertions and requires substantial amounts of C++ code to wrap the tests; its fixtures are essentially identical to CppUnit's.

Many of these difficulties are more or less intrinsic to a library-based solution in a language like C++; the limited

```
#include "Xxx.h"

test suite Xxx_test
{
  fixture:
    Xxx example1 = Xxx(arg1, arg2);

  tests:
    test somethingMethod
    {
      check (example1.something()) expect == 42;
    }
}
```

Figure 2: A minimal Unci file

preprocessing capability in C++ itself doesn't let a library writer introduce new syntax or create constructs that would generate substantially reordered or restructured code. As a result, simply trying to fork the CppUnit development (or making a pull request to get changes into CppUnit proper) would not adequately address these issues.

3. A NEW UNIT-TESTING LANGUAGE

To address these concerns, we began developing Unci, a language specifically designed to be a clean interface for writing unit tests. Its syntax would be enough like C++ to feel "comfortable" to students working in that language, but would have the freedom to diverge from C++ when that would yield an improvement in clarity. The main design objectives for this new language were that:

- Users could include a fixture with arbitrary data and arbitrary number of distinct test cases
- Users could include arbitrary C++ code in tests
- It require minimal or no "boilerplate" code that is identical for every file
- Its syntax be accessible to beginners with no unit testing experience and relatively little programming background
- Its test syntax would clearly indicate what is being tested and what outcome is expected
- Any errors in Unci code would be flagged by the Unci compiler, with a helpful error message
- Any errors in embedded C++ code would be passed through to the C++ compiler, to yield the same error message as in other C++ code with the same mistake

The first two of these are present in CppUnit (and other testing libraries had various combinations of the first three), and it was important not to lose those central features in the course of designing the new language. The remainder were in service of our goal of producing a pedagogically appropriate introductory C++-based unit testing framework.

Figure 2 shows an Unci test file with exactly the same semantics as the CppUnit test file in Figure 1. The most obvious change is that all the parts of the CppUnit version that were either always the same or derivable from other parts of the file can be omitted in the Unci source, making it far shorter (and far less susceptible to typo bugs). In what remains, every piece is semantically important; and by using semantically-appropriate labels ("`test suite`" instead of "`class`", "`fixture`" instead of "`private`", etc), the beginner student can see and reinforce the connection to the terminology they're learning to talk about unit testing in general. Indeed, by separating the `fixture` section from the `tests` section and labelling them, we preserve a useful semantic distinction instead of having a fixture that is part `private` and part `public`, or a `public` section that includes both setup code and individual tests.

3.1 Parts of an Unci file

The top portion of an Unci file can contain `#include` directives, `using` directives (such as `using namespace std;`), and comments. Anything else is a syntax error; in particular, we wished to channel students away from declaring global variables in this context.

The remainder of the file is a block headed by `test suite` and given a name. The name is not significant but will be munged into a class name by preceding it with "`Unci_`".

The suite block contains two parts: the `fixture` and the `tests`. Both are optional, but if present they must occur in that order. Since the fixture is optional, it would be possible to write a suite comprised only of independent tests (perhaps in the weeks before fixtures are introduced). The reason the tests are optional is that in a data-first design pedagogy (as in Program By Design [11]) the students are expected to give examples of data first, before any tests are written, and it is useful to be able to compile at this stage.

Within the fixture, every variable must be separately declared in the form

type varname = *value-expr* ;

This is true even if the type in question is a class type and the intended initial value is that provided by the default constructor. Because a class's default constructor is not automatically defined if any other constructor is defined, any code that implicitly requires the default constructor to exist may trigger a compiler error; this error is confusing to students just learning about default constructors (and implicit object construction and constructor overloading), because they don't understand what part of the code they've written is actually calling that constructor. By requiring an *explicit* call to the default constructor here (if that's what is intended), beginner programmers have a better understanding of why the compiler thinks they need to define it in the class definition.

For fixture values that cannot be constructed in a single expression (for instance, container data structures that need to be constructed empty and then have an `add` or `insert` method called), and for fixture data that requires cleanup, the user may define a `setup` block and/or a `teardown` block containing arbitrary C++ code, as shown in Figure 3.

The `tests` section (if present) must contain nothing but test blocks, each preceded by the word `test` and an arbitrary (but distinct) label. Some students were a little frustrated that they couldn't put fixture variable declarations between the test blocks, but this seemed to arise from a misunderstanding of the role of the fixture (that they are available to all tests, and that they reset to initial values before each test). As such, preventing anything but test blocks

```
fixture:
  Set<string>* onlyFoo = new VectorSet<string>();
  Set<int>* twoFive = new VectorSet<int>();

  setup
  {
    onlyFoo->add("foo");
    for (int i = 2; i <= 5; ++i)
      twoFive->add(i);
  }

  teardown
  {
    delete onlyFoo;
    delete twoFive;
  }
```

Figure 3: A sample Unci fixture

in the **tests** section seems to be a useful constraint as the students are developing their understanding of test-driven development.

The test blocks themselves will normally contain some number of check/expect statements, but these can be interspersed with almost completely arbitrary C++ code. The chief restriction is that **check** is a partially-reserved keyword and can't be used as variable or function name in a statement-initial position.

3.2 Check/expect statements

One of the major contributions of Unci is introducing to the C++ unit-testing ecosystem a new, uniform syntax specifically designed for testing: the **check/expect** statement. Regardless of what assertion is being made, these statements take the form

`check (` *expression* `)`

followed by an assertion about what is supposed to happen, headed by the keyword **expect**:

expect == *value*; A basic equality assertion. The given *value* must be of the same type as the *expression* being tested. This makes very explicit that the == operator is what is being used to perform the test.

expect < *value*; By making the == explicit when that is wanted, we reserved a natural place in the syntax for the other comparison operators: <, >, <=, >=, and !=. Any of these can be used to make an assertion about an expected result.

expect true; Most testing libraries (including CppUnit) have a simple ASSERT form that represents an assertion that some expression is true, but it is helpful to make that expectation explicit. Intro students are often not yet comfortable with the idea of first-class boolean values; they find it strange to "assert an expression" but much more comfortable to "assert *that* an expression *is true*".

expect false; Many students at this level have yet to fully come to terms with the use of **not** to negate arbitrary boolean expressions, particularly in an assertion context. They also appreciate the symmetry between **expect true** and **expect false**, and this furthermore makes series of boolean check/expect statements easier to read and edit.

expect about *value* +- *tolerance*; Floating point math is inexact, and test cases involving floating point numbers should properly include a tolerance on either side of the expected value. In this case **about** and **+-** are keywords and reinforce the idea that the testing operation is *not* using == (notwithstanding the fact that the analogous assertion in CppUnit is a three-parameter macro named **CPPUNIT_ASSERT_DOUBLES_EQUAL**, or that JUnit simply uses an **assertEquals** method with a third argument for this purpose).

```
tests:
  test contains
  {
    check (onlyFoo->contains("foo")) expect true;
    check (onlyFoo->contains("bar")) expect false;
    check (twoFive->contains(4)) expect true;
    check (twoFive->contains(7)) expect false;
  }
  test size
  {
    check (onlyFoo->size()) expect == 1;
    check (twoFive->size()) expect == 4;
  }
  test remove
  {
    twoFive->remove(5);
    check (twoFive->contains(2)) expect true;
    check (twoFive->contains(5)) expect false;
    check (twoFive->size()) expect == 3;
  }
  test unrelatedFloat
  {
    double frac = (1.0 / 6.0) * 10000;
    check (frac) expect about 10000.0 / 6 +- 0.00001;
  }
```

Figure 4: Sample Unci tests using fixture from Fig. 3

A sample **tests** section is shown in Figure 4, using the fixture from Figure 3 to test a few standard operations from the Set ADT as well as illustrating the use of the inexact "**expect about**" assertion.

This syntax is the one place we diverged from the most widespread unit-testing terminology, which usually uses some form of the word **assert** here. However, we wanted to be able to syntactically separate the testable expression from the expected outcome, and we wanted to avoid using established keywords with different meanings. (The C++ version of **assert**, while not technically a keyword, is a well-established part of the standard library, available in the **<cassert>** header.) Our usage of **check** and **expect** is inspired by, though not identical to, that seen in the Program By Design curriculum [10].

4. RESULTS

The initial roll-out of Unci was to the Spring 2014 sections of our CS2 course. The overall content of the course was

	N	No handin	Doesn't compile	No real test	Total no testing	Light tests	All one fn	Good tests	Total testing
F13/CppUnit	N=11	2 (18%)	1 (9%)	3 (27%)	55%	1 (9%)	1 (9%)	3 (27%)	45%
S14/Unci	N=27	3 (11%)	4 (15%)	0 (—)	26%	4 (15%)	5 (19%)	11 (41%)	74%

Table 1: Test suite quality on Lab 9

	N	No handin/ no suite	Doesn't compile	Fixture only	Total no testing	Some tests	All tests	Total testing
F13/CppUnit	N=11	2 (18%)	1 (9%)	4 (36%)	64%	0 (—)	4 (36%)	36%
S14/Unci	N=27	3 (11%)	2 (7%)	2 (7%)	25%	5 (19%)	15 (56%)	75%

Table 2: Test suite quality on Lab 11

unchanged from the previous term, and the student body comparable—in both cases coming directly out of a CS1 course the previous term—but all CppUnit-based content was replaced with Unci-based content. There was no longer a need to provide a template file for the students to copy whenever they wanted to create a new test suite, and the students were no longer getting stuck on misleading macro-related error messages.

In the assignment where unit testing was first introduced (the lab during week 3), there were fairly detailed instructions on what to type and how to build the test suite file. Perhaps as a result, both the CppUnit students and the Unci students were generally able to complete this by the end of the allotted week. A more interesting comparison can be seen in two assignments later in the term.

During week 9, the lab assignment was primarily focussed on the Set ADT: specifying what operations it should support, and then writing multiple implementations of it. Part of this process was to write appropriate unit tests for the data structure; but as the students had been practicing writing test cases for several weeks at this point, the lab instructions (during both terms) gave no detail on *how* to write the test suite. Student performance on the test suite portion of this lab diverged substantially between the two terms.

We coded all student submissions on this assignment, from both terms, into six categories (themselves grouped into two larger categories), presented in Table 1. A small number of students did not hand in the assignment at all. Of those who did, some had test suites that did not successfully compile, and others were technically able to make the file compile but couldn't figure out how to put any test cases in it. Students in these three categories clearly were not benefiting from test-driven development on this assignment (although in some cases they were able to successfully implement other parts of the assignment anyway).

The remainder of the students were able to implement at least some testing for their assignment. In some cases the testing was "light", in that there were multiple test functions or `test` blocks, but only with a single assertion—hence not a thorough test. A number of students implemented a series of statements and assertions that was reasonably thorough, but put all of them in a single function or block, thus not operating as a unit test and not taking advantage of the test fixture. Finally, some students were able to write multiple unit tests, covering multiple cases for most or all of the ADT operations. The proportion of students in the latter category went up considerably among the students who wrote their tests using Unci instead of CppUnit: only 27% of the students successfully navigated CppUnit to build a reasonably good test suite, while 41% were able to do so with Unci. The proportion of students who successfully did any testing at all on this assignment rose from 45% to 74%.

Two weeks later, students were given a lab involving binary trees and functions that operate on them, and once again they were expected to write a test suite from scratch with no new instructions on how to do so. Performance on this task is recorded in Table 2, with categories similar to those described above; here the third category refers to those students that successfully built binary trees for the test fixture but wrote no tests for them, and the fourth category covers students that wrote some tests but did not cover all five of the functions required for the lab. As with Lab 9, the best students in the CppUnit section were able to write test cases as requested, but the weak and middle students—who in many ways might benefit most from TDD—were unable to get any test cases written. In the Unci sections, however, most of the students were able to write all the necessary test cases and a wide majority succesfully wrote at least some test cases. The proportion of students able to run automated tests on their code here rose from 36% to 75%. The number of students in each group is low—11 in the CppUnit section, 27 in the Unci sections—but the performance difference is large enough to be persuasive.

5. CONCLUSIONS AND FUTURE WORK

In this paper we have presented Unci, a new unit testing framework for C++ that is more accessible to introductory programmers than the alternatives. It provides a layer of abstraction so that one can write a test suite without understanding the implementation details of the testing engine itself; and the syntax it uses is powerful but constrained enough to steer inexperienced programmers toward good testing practices and (when possible) away from several easy-to-make beginner mistakes. When used in a CS2 programming course, students writing their tests in Unci were much more likely to be able to successfully write example data and test cases that would compile and test their code.

Unci is in many ways still what the entrepreneurs call a "minimum viable product". There are a number of areas where we plan to improve it. There are other assertion types that would be helpful, including array equality and containment, as well as testing that student code correctly throws exceptions. (Indeed, our parser already supports Unci syntax for these `expect` types, but the compiler does not yet produce code for them.) It would be convenient to be able to compile multiple Unci test suites together into a single test executable. Currently, the Unci compiler outputs code that uses the CppUnit macro system, but it will be better to bypass the macros; it would perhaps eventually be good to bypass CppUnit entirely, although continuing to target CppUnit as an intermediate form may be helpful in the short term as we aim for integration with popular C++ IDEs. Finally, there are a few C++11 language features (notably the new curly-bracket-based uniform initialisation syntax) that the Unci parser does not correctly support, which needs to be fixed before those features start making their way into intro textbooks. We continue to use Unci in our CS2 course and consider it to be under active development.

We would also be interested in running larger-scale testing to confirm Unci's helpfulness for students in other C++-based intro curricula.

6. INSTALLATION AND AVAILABILITY

The code and installation instructions are available at our website.[1] The core tool is `unci-translate`, which reads `.u` files and compiles them into C++ code that makes use of the CppUnit library, printed to standard output. The more user-facing compilation tools are `uncic`, a shell script which compiles Unci files directly to object files (which include their own `main` but must be linked against the CppUnit library), and `compile`, which accepts both `.cpp` and `.u` files and dispatches them appropriately, producing an executable file. In our classes, the students are first introduced to the `compile` command as a sort of "one stop shop" for compiling their programs, but once they are introduced to `make` and the idea of a build manager, `uncic` is more appropriate.

The download also includes drop-in configuration files to set up syntax highlighting for Unci files in the Vim text editor.

[1] `http://cs.longwood.edu/~dblaheta/unci`

7. REFERENCES

[1] K. Beck. *Test-driven development: by example.* Addison-Wesley, Boston, 2003.

[2] CppUnit. Retrieved November 30, 2014 from `http://freedesktop.org/wiki/Software/cppunit/`.

[3] CxxTest. Retrieved November 30, 2014 from `http://cxxtest.com`.

[4] S. H. Edwards. Rethinking computer science education from a test-first perspective. In *OOPSLA'03*, Anaheim, 2003.

[5] S. Hammond and D. Umphress. Test driven development: The state of the practice. In *ACMSE'12*, Tuscaloosa, 2012.

[6] D. S. Janzen and H. Saiedian. Test-driven learning: intrinsic integration of testing into the CS/SE curriculum. In *SIGCSE'06*, Houston, 2006.

[7] D. S. Janzen and H. Saiedian. Test-driven learning in early programming courses. In *SIGCSE'08*, Portland, 2008.

[8] JUnit. Retrieved November 30, 2014 from `http://junit.org`.

[9] libunittest. Retrieved November 30, 2014 from `http://libunittest.sourceforge.net`.

[10] V. K. Proulx. Test-driven design for introductory OO programming. In *SIGCSE'09*, Chattanooga, 2009.

[11] V. K. Proulx. Introductory computing: The design discipline. In I. Kalaš and R. Mittermeir, editors, *Informatics in Schools. Contributing to 21st Century Education*, volume 7013 of *Lecture Notes in Computer Science*, pages 177–188. Springer Berlin Heidelberg, 2011.

[12] Unit++. Retrieved November 30, 2014 from `http://unitpp.sourceforge.net/`.

[13] UnitTest++. Retrieved November 30, 2014 from `http://unittest-cpp.sourceforge.net`.

[14] xUnit++. Retrieved November 30, 2014 from `https://bitbucket.org/moswald/xunit`.

Bug Infestation! A Goal-Plan Analysis of CS2 Students' Recursive Binary Tree Solutions

Laurie Murphy
Pacific Lutheran University
Tacoma, WA USA
lmurphy@plu.edu

Sue Fitzgerald
Metropolitan State University
St. Paul, MN
sue.fitzgerald@metrostate.edu

Scott Grissom
Grand Valley State University
Allendale, MI USA
grissom@gvsu.edu

Renée McCauley
College of Charleston
Charleston, SC USA
mccauleyr@cofc.edu

ABSTRACT
A goal-plan analysis was conducted to examine the variety of plans students use in writing a recursive method for an operation on a binary search tree. Students were asked to write a recursive method to count the nodes in a binary search tree with exactly one child. The problem incorporated two goals: traversing the tree and counting nodes with one child. Three traversal plans and four counting plans were observed in student solutions. Over half of the students used the arm's-length recursion plan, which involves testing for the base case before it is actually reached in order to avoid making recursive calls. This strategy creates complex and error prone code. Making students aware of arm's-length recursion may help them avoid introducing bugs into their recursive code. Although nearly all of the 18 participants demonstrated viable plans for solving the problem, their solutions contained a variety of errors: 55 total errors of 15 types. Students had particular difficulty with base cases, misplaced calculations, and missing method calls. Knowledge of these errors can be useful for instructors when developing lecture examples, identifying distractors for peer instruction multiple-choice questions and for designing homework exercises. Instructors can counteract these problems by providing a variety of recursive examples.

Categories and Subject Descriptors
K.3.2 [**Computing Milieux**]: Computers and Education - Computer and Information Science Education.

General Terms
Human Factors.

Keywords
Computer science education research; recursion; data structures; BST; binary search trees; CS2; arm's-length recursion.

SIGCSE'15, March 4–7, 2015, Kansas City, MO, USA.
Copyright © 2015 ACM 978-1-4503-2966-8/15/03…$15.00.
http://dx.doi.org/10.1145/2676723.2677232

1. INTRODUCTION
Computer Science (CS) students typically study recursion and binary search trees (BSTs) early in their CS coursework, often in a second programming course covering simple data structures (CS2). BSTs are intrinsically linked with recursion; they are defined recursively (structural recursion) and students must use recursion to reasonably and succinctly code many BST methods. This is not the case for many introductory problems implemented recursively (e.g., Fibonacci, factorial, string operations, list traversals), which may be more naturally and efficiently written using iteration.

The challenges novice programmers face when learning recursion have been widely studied (see [16]), and BSTs have been identified as a source of common misconceptions for CS students [6][10]. Although previous research has shown that tracing and analyzing recursive BST methods can be difficult for upper-level computer science students [22], an extensive literature review has revealed very little research into the challenges students face when writing recursive BST code.

This paper presents results of a preliminary investigation into the difficulties CS2 students experience while writing recursive BST methods, and addresses the following research questions:

- What plans do CS2 students use when solving recursive BST problems?
- What errors do CS2 students make when writing recursive BST code?
- Are there links between plans and the errors students make?

These questions were explored using students' recursive solutions for counting nodes in a BST with exactly one child. Although the search tree property is not required to solve this problem, we refer to the trees as binary search trees rather than simply binary trees throughout this paper since students were explicitly asked to solve the problem for BSTs.

This paper continues as follows: related work is discussed in section 2, the research methodology is covered in section 3, research findings are presented in section 4, and discussed along with their implications for teaching in section 5. Section 6 suggests directions for future work.

2. RELATED WORK
The basis of the goal-plan analysis discussed here was the work of Spohrer, Soloway and Pope [20] who pioneered the use of goal-plan analysis to identify bugs in novice Pascal programs. Spohrer,

Soloway and Pope categorized errors in code as malformed, misplaced, missing or spurious based on how the errors deviated from correct plans. More recently, Kopec, Yarmish and Cheung [11] and Yarmish and Kopec [24] used the goal-plan analysis technique to evaluate errors made by advanced novice student C programmers on both recursive and non-recursive written exam problems. They found that students often struggled with problems requiring recursion and experienced the most difficulty in correctly expressing base and boundary cases.

In a study of experts, Goldman et al. [7] found that experts ranked "tracing and designing recursive algorithms" to be among the most difficult of thirty-two fundamental programming concepts. Further, experts did not agree on whether "tracing and designing recursive algorithms" was an appropriate topic for a first course. Indeed, students in the current study were not exposed to recursion until their second (CS2) course.

While there has been a good deal of research concerning recursion, very few research studies have been published on the teaching and learning of recursion with data structures. A few studies have investigated students' understanding of recursive algorithms using linked-lists. Benander, Benander and Pu [1] compared comprehension of recursion vs. iteration and found that for a linked-list search algorithm, students did better (with statistical significance) when the algorithm was implemented recursively; but for a copy algorithm, students did better (but not statistically significantly better) when the algorithm was implemented iteratively. In a related debugging study, Benander, Benander and Sang [2] observed that students were more successful finding and fixing bugs in recursive linked-list programs, but that they took about the same time to find and fix bugs in both types of algorithms. Corney et al. [5] found a strong correlation between the ability of data structures students to explain recursive linked-list code at an abstract level and their performance on code writing and code reading test problems.

There has been even less research on recursion in the context of BSTs, despite the fact that BSTs are often more naturally processed recursively than linked-lists. In a study of upper-level CS students, Tenenberg and Murphy [22] found that only half of the 61 study participants were able to correctly answer questions involving tracing and analyzing recursive BST algorithms, even though all of them had completed a data structures course covering these topics.

Concept inventory research has also demonstrated that students have difficulty with BSTs, conflating them with heaps and struggling with duplicate values [6][10], although this work does not specifically address the recursive nature of BSTs or their associated recursive algorithms. Given the difficulty students have with recursion and with BSTs in general it is not surprising that students find recursive BST algorithms challenging.

3. METHODOLOGY

3.1 Participants and Study Context

Study participants included eighteen students enrolled in a second programming course that covers simple data structures (CS2) at a private liberal arts university in the United States. All had successfully completed an introductory (CS1) Java course. Students were asked to write a recursive method to count the number of nodes in a BST with only one child. Solutions were retrieved from written final exams.

The traditional CS2 course topics included object oriented design basics; an introduction to algorithm analysis; basic data structures such as lists, stacks, queues, binary search trees and hash tables; and common sorting algorithms. About 2 ½ weeks in the middle of the term were devoted to introducing recursion and binary search trees. Students were assigned two written homework problem sets from their textbook focusing on recursion and trees. They also completed two programming assignments: one to write a recursive, text-based Boggle™ game, and another to implement numerous BST methods (e.g., size, height, counts of leaves and interior nodes, and pre, post and inorder traversals). The BST assignment also included a 10-question worksheet requiring students to analyze "perfect" binary trees and to generate and plot height and runtime statistics for randomly generated BSTs. Students had additional exposure to recursion while studying sorting algorithms, and to binary trees when learning heaps later in the course.

3.2 Exam Question

The written final exam comprised 25% of the course grade, and the following question was worth 10% of the final exam.

> Write a recursive member method for a BST to determine the number of nodes that have one child. (Hint: countParentsOfOne() will call a private recursive method, that you write, that does all the work). Class BinarySearchTree<E> has a field **root** of type Node<E>, and Node<E> has fields **left**, **right**, and **data**.

```
public int countParentsOfOne()
```

3.3 Goal-Plan Analysis

Based on Spohrer, Soloway and Pope's [20] goal-plan analysis, the researchers identified two goals for this problem: 1) traverse the binary search tree and 2) count nodes with only one child. Each *goal* can be achieved in a variety of ways. Each unique strategy is called a *plan*. Students attempted to achieve the tree traversal and counting goals using several plans. Three researchers classified the unique plans, coming to full consensus (see Table 1).

Table 1. Goal-Plan Categories

Goal: Traverse tree	
Concise plan	Avoids unnecessary statements and recursive calls (Figure 1-a).
Arm's-length recursion plan	Includes unnecessary conditionals to prevent passing leaves to the recursive method (Figure 1-b).
Loop plan (not viable)	Attempts to traverse the tree using loop(s), perhaps in combination with recursive method calls (Figure 2).
Not viable	Exhibits no clear plan or is seemingly unrelated to the problem.
Goal: Count nodes with only one child	
Passive counting plan	Uses return statements to passively count nodes with one child without using a local variable (Figure 1-a & 1-b).
Local variable plan	Uses local variable(s) to count nodes with one child (Figure 3-a).
Non-local variable plan	Uses a non-local variable to count nodes with one child (Figure 3-b).
Parameter plan	Uses an extra formal parameter in the recursive method to count nodes with one child (Figure 3-c).
Not viable	Exhibits no clear plan or is seemingly unrelated to the problem.

Figure 1 shows solutions written by the authors that illustrate viable traversal plans. Solution 1-a shows how the goal could be achieved using a concise traversal plan. This approach minimizes the number of statements and is typical of expert implementations. The traversal goal is accomplished with one base case, one conditional and a pair of recursive calls for nodes with one child (left and right children) and another pair of recursive calls for all remaining conditions. Several students used additional conditional statements to avoid recursive calls, in effect short-circuiting the recursion, as seen in Figure 1-b. This is referred to by some in the CS education community as "arm's-length recursion."[1] Figure 2 shows an example of an incorrect loop plan written by a student.

Both examples in Figure 1 achieve the counting goal by adding 1 to the result of a recursive call. This plan is called passive counting and refers to the absence of any variables to maintain the count. Figure 3 shows segments of several incorrect counting plans using local variables, non-local variables and parameters.

a. concise traversal plan

```
public int parentsOfOne(){
  // call to recursive method
  return count(root);
}
private int count(Node t){
  // base case
  if (t == null)
    return 0;
  // only one child
  if((t.left != null && t.right == null) ||
      (t.left == null && t.right != null))
     return 1 + count(t.left) + count(t.right);
  // otherwise, keep looking
  return count(t.left) + count(t.right);
}
```

b. arm's-length recursion plan

```
public int parentsOfOne(){
  // check for non-empty tree
  if (root != null)
    return count(root);
  else // empty tree
    return 0;
}
private int count(Node t){
  // base case
  if (t == null)
    return 0;
  // leaf node
  else if(t.left == null && t.right == null)
    return 0;
  // only one child (left)
  else if((t.left != null && t.right == null)
     return 1 + count(t.left);
  // only one child (right)
  else if((t.left == null && t.right != null)
     return 1 + count(t.right);
  else // two children
    return count(t.left) + count(t.right);
}
```

Figure 1. Example plans for achieving the travese tree goal

[1] Only one text [14] referring to the phrase arm's-length recursion could be found, although other references appear around the Internet: Wikipedia's recursion page mentions it, there is "What is arm's-length recursion" at quora.com and it appears in Cynthia Lee's CS2 slides at peerinstruction4cs.org. All of these references have connections to Stanford University, where apparently it is widely accepted and has been used by the computer science teaching staff since at least the mid-1980s [12].

3.4 Error Categorization

To establish initial error categories, coding errors were first identified by programming construct or statement type. These include: base case, calculation, conditional, loop, method call, parameter, return value/call/type, and variable. They were then also assigned to one of Spohrer, Soloway and Pope's error types:

attempts to use a loop to traverse tree

```
public int parentsOfOne() {
  while (root != null)
       return count(root);
  return 0;
}
private int count(Node t) {
  int total = 0;
  while(t.left != null) {
    if (t.right == null)
       total++;
    else {
       count(t.left);
       count(t.right);
    }
  }
  return total;
}
```

Figure 2. Example loop traversal plan (not viable)

a. using a local variable to count

```
  int total = 0;
  if(t.left == null && t.right != null)
    total++;
  if(t.left != null && t.right == null)
    total++;
  total += count(t.right)+count(t.left);
    return total;
```

b. using a non-local variable to count

```
  if(t.left == null && t.right != null)
     global_total++;
  if(t.left != null && t.right == null)
     global_total++;
  count(t.right);
  count(t.left);
  return;
```

c. using a parameter to count

```
private int count(Node t, int total){
  if(t.left == null && t.right != null)
     return count(t.left, total + 1);
  return total;
}
```

Figure 3. Code segment examples of poor counting plans

missing, *malformed*, *misplaced* and *spurious* [20]. This yielded a set of 15 distinct error categories (e.g., missing base case, misplaced return statement, malformed method call, etc.). Three researchers then independently identified the errors in students' code and assigned them to one of the 15 categories. The researchers then worked together to come to agreement on categorizations. At least two researchers agreed on 93% of the 55 total errors identified and all agreed on 84% of the errors. Simple syntax errors and unnecessary code that was not erroneous was noted but not considered an error. The error categories are discussed in detail in Section 4.2.

3.5 Threats to Validity

Participants took their final exams using paper and pencil. Use of the computer to compile and test may have altered the results, even given a time-constrained task. However, these solutions are realistic first drafts and as such they provide us insight into where students start and go wrong in their efforts to solve problems such as these.

Because the sample size was small, statistical results are suggestive rather than significant.

4. RESULTS

4.1 Goal-Plan Analysis

A majority of solutions showed signs of being on the right track with reasonable tree traversal plans (see Table 2). Approximately one-quarter of the students provided concise solutions for tree traversal. Over one-half added unnecessary conditionals to avoid calls to the recursive method, the arm's-length recursion shown in Figure 1-b. Two students even attempted to use a loop to traverse the tree as shown in Figure 2. And one solution was too flawed to be viable.

The counting plans were equally varied. Over one-third of the students used the passive counting plan (Figure 1-a & 1-b). About one-fourth used local variables (Figure 3-a) or non-local variables (Figure 3-b) to keep count. Several students attempted to use parameters (Figure 3-c) to maintain the count while three students did not have a viable counting plan.

Table 2. Number of Students Using Each Plan

Goal	Plan	# (%)
Traverse tree	Concise recursion	5 (27%)
	Arm's-length recursion	10 (55%)
	Loop (not viable)	2 (12%)
	Other (not viable)	1 (6%)
Count parent nodes with one child	Passive counting	7 (38%)
	Counting with local vars	4 (22%)
	Counting with non-local vars	1 (6%)
	Counting with parameters	3 (17%)
	Other (not viable)	3 (17%)

4.2 Error Analysis

Students made a surprising number of errors beyond the simple syntax errors common on written exams. Table 3 summarizes those errors by category and type.

Table 3. Error Categorizations

Construct/ Statement Type	Category				Total
	Missing	Malformed	Misplaced	Spurious	
Conditional	5	6		1	12
Method call	10		1		11
Base Case	8	2			10
Calculation			9		9
Return value/call/type	3	3	1		7
Variable		1		2	3
Loop				2	2
Parameter		1			1
Total	26	13	11	5	55

Only four students correctly solved the problem with no errors. Most solutions included multiple errors. The most common errors included missing statements, missing method calls and incorrect base cases. Students routinely failed to account for an empty tree, stopped traversing the tree when the first node with one child was found or otherwise failed to correctly traverse the entire tree. In some cases, conditionals failed to test for nodes with no children or nodes with two children. Less frequently, participants failed to return the count as required.

Situations identified as *missing statements* resulted in failure to consider certain cases such as an empty tree, failure to search an entire tree (some algorithms only searched down the one side of a tree), and failure to make some necessary recursive calls.

Malformed statements included conditionals which attempted to dereference null pointers, conditionals to check if root's data field was null rather than checking for root being null, bad data declarations, and incorrect nesting of conditionals.

Statements for computing counts were sometimes *misplaced* leading to incorrect counts for a variety of reasons. For example, due to misplacement of counting statements some students recognized that a node had a single child only if the child was a leaf node, while others simply counted all nodes or even nodes with two children.

Finally, the few *spurious* errors involved the inclusion of unnecessary code, which sometimes produced incorrect results.

4.3 Plans vs. Errors

Table 4 shows the average number of errors for each of the plans. For example, students who used arm's-length recursion to traverse the tree had an average of 2.5 errors. Students who used passive counting had an average of 1.1 errors.

Table 4. Average Errors per Plan

Goal	Plan	Avg Errors
Traverse tree	Concise recursion	1.6
	Arm's-length recursion	2.5
	Loop (not viable)	6.5
	Other (not viable)	9.0
Count parent nodes with one child	Passive counting	1.1
	Counting with local vars	2.5
	Counting with non-local vars	3.0
	Counting with parameters	3.0
	Other (not viable)	7.0

For the tree traversal goal, the number of errors increases as the plan becomes more complex. The concise plan uses the fewest number of conditional statements and recursive calls and students who used this plan had the fewest number of errors (mean errors = 1.6). On the other end of the spectrum, students without a viable traversal plan had an average of 9.0 errors.

For the counting goal one could argue that passive counting is the simplest solution with complexity growing as local variables, non-local variables and parameters are used for counting. Again, students using the simplest plan exhibited the fewest errors (passive counting, average errors = 1.1) and students with no viable plan had far more errors (average of 7.0).

However, the traversal and counting plans cannot be considered in isolation as both are required for a complete solution. The pairing of traversal plans and counting plans resulted in several combinations (see Table 5). Only two of the combinations were seen more than twice (n=3 or n=4). The combination of concise recursion and passive counting produced 1.5 average errors (n=4), a very good result. But the combination of arm's-length recursion and passive counting produced even fewer errors on average (0.7 average errors, n=3). These results suggest that student comprehension is uneven. Although concise plans are most often correct when considered in isolation, the complexity of combining two plans leads students to find less efficient but more understandable solutions. Of course these results are suggestive rather than statistically significant due to the small sample size but they yield tantalizing glimpses of student thinking.

5. DISCUSSION AND TEACHING IMPLICATIONS

Binary search trees are a natural topic to introduce or reinforce recursion [4][19]. This study highlighted common errors and difficulties students have when writing recursive BST algorithms.

The most common errors for the tree traversal goal were missing and malformed base cases and not accounting for nodes with two children or nodes with no children. Learning to write base cases has been identified as particularly problematic for beginners and deserving of special attention [9]. Guiding students to recognize and distinguish all base case(s) and general case(s) when solving recursive problems may be helpful. Encouraging students to consider a wide variety of tree topologies when testing may also help them to discover missing cases.

That missing and malformed conditionals and base cases were the source of so many errors in this study may support Bloch's argument that linked data structures and recursion should simply be taught without the use of conditionals or null [3].

The plans students used to solve this problem are also pedagogically significant. Students who used the loop traversal plan appear to hold a flawed "looping mental model" of recursion in which recursion is seen as a form of iteration rather than series of instantiations [8]. Tracing exercises incorporating both active and passive flow, which are required by many BST algorithms, may help students develop a correct "copies mental model" of recursion [17].

Both the concise and arm's-length traversal plans are viable, despite the errors observed in many solutions. Chances are, most of these students could eventually correct their faulty initial attempts given additional time and access to a computer. This is also true of students who used unnecessary local variables to achieve the counting goal. Presenting students with alternative solutions that are technically correct yet arguably less elegant offer opportunities to discuss why unnecessary code may lead to errors and decrease readability.

Arm's-length recursion, which was used by over half of the students in this study, is especially interesting because it suggests that students may believe it is desirable to avoid recursion by short-circuiting the base case. For example, they may believe this improves efficiency. Presenting alternative correct traversal solutions, one that is concise and one that uses arm's-length recursion, can facilitate a discussion about why the arm's-length approach should be avoided. It should be emphasized that additional method calls are in fact relatively inexpensive for modern compilers and that avoiding them comes at the cost of additional if statements whose conditions must also be checked repeatedly. Providing students with a specific name by which to identify arm's-length recursion may heighten their awareness of this approach and help them to avoid using arm's-length recursion in the future.

Like local counters, the use of non-local variables and parameters for counting are also viable ways to achieve the counting goal, although none of the students in this study did so correctly. This may be because using these plans successfully requires a nuanced understanding of the language. For example, to successfully use a non-local variable requires remembering to reset the counter to zero in the public method so that it does not retain its previous value in subsequent calls. Using a parameter is also tricky because double counting must be avoided for nodes that have two children. Presenting students with these examples can facilitate a discussion of the subtleties of how non-local variables and parameters behave in the context of recursion.

Providing multiple examples has been shown to be effective when introducing recursion [17][18][23]. The goals, plans and typical solutions provided in this paper can be used to show students concrete examples of correct, concise solutions as well as instances of common mistakes. Common bugs can be used as examples in debugging exercises. The errors noted in this study can also be used as plausible distractors for peer instruction multiple choice questions which have been shown to be an effective teaching strategy [21].

6. FUTURE WORK

It is rare for CS educators to have the opportunity to thoroughly review and systematically analyze a set of responses to a single challenging exam question. There are simply too many exams and too many questions to give a single problem so much attention. Yet the insights gained through analyzing this small dataset illustrate the potential of using naturally occurring exam data in CS education research [13].

Replicating this study on a larger scale or at multiple institutions could confirm persistent misconceptions that should be addressed when introducing BSTs. For example, many students had difficulty traversing the entire BST. Conducting similar research using alternative BST problems such as depth first search, identifying the length of the longest branch or simply counting the

Table 5. Number of Participants and Average Errors by Plan Combination

		Plans for counting parent nodes with one child									
		Passive counting		Counting with local vars		Counting with non-local vars		Counting with parameters		Other (not viable)	
		N	Avg Errors	N	Avg Errors	N	Avg Errors	N	Avg Errors	N	Avg Errors
Traverse tree plans	Concise recursion	4	1.5	1	2						
	Arm's-length recursion	3	0.7	2	2	1	3	2	3	2	5
	Loop			1	4					1	9
	Other (not viable)									1	9

number of nodes may reveal new traversal plans or error types. Observing and interviewing students while they solve recursive BST problems on paper or at a computer would be useful for understanding why they choose particular plans or have difficulties implementing them.

Peer instruction has been shown to reduce failure rates in a variety of CS courses [15]. The value of using the error and plan examples suggested above for debugging exercises or for peer instruction should also be investigated. Such pedagogies could help students avoid bugs, reduce their tendency toward using arm's-length recursion, and improve their ability to write recursive BST code. However, additional data collection and analysis are necessary.

7. ACKNOWLEDGMENTS

We would like to thank Kenneth Blaha for his assistance in collecting data for this study and extend our appreciation to Brian Hanks for his helpful comments and feedback. We also appreciate Cynthia Lee and the other Stanford University teaching staff for their help in tracing the etymology of arm's-length recursion.

8. REFERENCES

[1] Benander, A. C., Benander, B. A., and Pu, H. 1996. Recursion vs. iteration: An empirical study of comprehension. *Journal of Systems and Software* 32, 1, 73-82.

[2] Benander, A. C., Benander, B. A., and Sang, J. 2000. An empirical analysis of debugging performance – differences between iterative and recursive constructs. *Journal of Systems and Software* 54, 1, 17-28.

[3] Bloch, S. 2003. Teaching linked lists and recursion without conditionals or null. *J. Comput. Sci. Coll.* 18, 5, 96–108.

[4] Bruce, K. B., Danyluk, A., and Murtagh, T. 2005. Why structural recursion should be taught before arrays in CS 1. *SIGCSE Bull.* 37, 1, 246-250.

[5] Corney, M., Fitzgerald, S., Hanks, B., Lister, R., McCauley, R., and Murphy, L. 2014. 'Explain in plain English' questions revisited: Data structures problems. In *Proceedings of the 45th ACM Technical Symposium on Computer Science Education* (Atlanta, GA, USA, March 5-8, 2014). SIGCSE '14. ACM, New York, NY, USA, 591-596.

[6] Danielsiek, H., Paul, W., and Vahrenhold, J. 2012. Detecting and understanding students' misconceptions related to algorithms and data structures. In *Proceedings of the 43rd ACM Technical Symposium on Computer Science Education* (Raleigh, NC, USA, Feb. 29-March 3, 2102). SIGCSE '12. ACM, New York, NY, USA, 21-26.

[7] Goldman, K., Gross, P., Heeren, C., Herman, G., Kaczmarczyk, L., Loui, M. C., and Zilles, C. 2008. Identifying important and difficult concepts in introductory computing courses using a Delphi process. *SIGCSE Bull.* 40, 1, 256–260.

[8] Götschi, T., Sanders, I., and Galpin, V. 2003. Mental models of recursion. *SIGCSE Bull.* 35, 1, 346–350.

[9] Haberman, B. and Averbuch, H. 2002. The case of base cases: Why are they so difficult to recognize? Student difficulties with recursion. *SIGCSE Bull.* 34, 3, 84–88.

[10] Karpierz, K. and Wolfman, S. A. 2014. Misconceptions and concept inventory questions for binary search trees and hash tables. In *Proceedings of the 45th ACM Technical Symposium on Computer Science Education* (Atlanta, GA, USA, March 5-8, 2014). SIGCSE '14. ACM, New York, NY, USA, 109–114.

[11] Kopec, D., Yarmish, G., and Cheung, P. 2007. A description and study of intermediate student programmer errors. *SIGCSE Bull.* 39, 2, 146–156.

[12] Lee, C., Roberts, E., Cain, J., Sahami, M., Zelenski, J. and Stuart, R. (personal communication, July 8-12, 2014).

[13] Lister, R., Clear, T., Simon, Bouvier, J., Carter, P., Eckerdal, A., Jacková, J., Lopez, M., McCartney, R., Robbins, P., Seppälä, O. and Thompson, E. 2010. Naturally occurring data as research instrument: analyzing examination responses to study the novice programmer. *SIGCSE Bull.* 41, 4 (January 2010), 156-173.

[14] Mongan, J., Kindler, N., Gigure, E. *Programming Interviews Exposed: Secrets to Landing Your Next Job*, Third Edition. John Wiley & Sons, Inc., Indianapolis, Indiana, 2012.

[15] Porter, L., Lee, C. B., and Simon, B. 2013. Halving fail rates using peer instruction: A study of four computer science courses. In *Proceedings of the 44th ACM Technical Symposium on Computer Science Education* (Denver, CO, USA, March 6-9, 2013). SIGCSE '13. ACM, New York, NY, USA, 177-182.

[16] Rinderknecht, C. 2014. A survey on teaching and learning recursive programming. *Informatics in Education* 13, 1, 87-119.

[17] Sanders, I., Galpin, V. and Götschi, T. 2006. Mental models of recursion revisited. *SIGCSE Bull.* 38, 3 (June 2006), 138-142.

[18] Segal, J. 1995. Empirical Studies of functional programming learners evaluating recursive functions. *Instructional Science* 22, 385-411.

[19] Sher, D. B. 2004. Recursive objects - an object oriented presentation of recursion. Mathematics and Computer Education 38, 1, 97-109.

[20] Spohrer, J. C., Soloway, E., and Pope, E. 1985. A goal/plan analysis of buggy Pascal programs. *Hum.-Comput. Interact.* 1, 2, 163–207.

[21] Sullivan, R. 2009. Principles for constructing good clicker questions: Going beyond rote learning and stimulating active engagement with course content. *Journal of Educational Technology Systems* 37, 3, 335-347.

[22] Tenenberg, J. and Murphy, L. 2005. Knowing what I know: An investigation of undergraduate knowledge and self-knowledge of data structures. *Computer Science Education* 15, 4, 297–315.

[23] Wiedenbeck, S. 1989. Learning iteration and recursion from examples. *International Journal of Man-Machine Studies* 30, 1, 1–22.

[24] Yarmish, G. and Kopec, D. 2007. Revisiting novice programmer errors. *SIGCSE Bull.* 39, 2, 131–137.

Ante Up: A Framework to Strengthen Student-Based Testing of Assignments

Michael K. Bradshaw
Centre College
600 W Walnut St
Danville, KY 40422
michael.bradshaw@centre.edu

ABSTRACT

We introduce the Ante framework to automate the evaluation of student tests in such a way that students will see them as an integral part of the software development process. Our unique approach is to evaluate student testing before students are allowed to submit implementations of the assignment. By evaluating student testing, we can ensure that 1) students understand the assignment before moving on to implementing it and 2) students have a set of tests to aid in implementing their assignment. In this paper we will describe the existing tools and techniques to evaluate student testing, discuss the process of utilizing this framework from both the student and instructor points of view, describe the technical and usability issues in crafting Ante, and report preliminary feedback of student attitudes towards testing in the context of this new paradigm.

Categories and Subject Descriptors

K.3.2 [**Computers and Education**]: Computer and Information Science Education; D.2.5 [**Software Engineering**]: Testing and Debugging
; K.3.1 [**Computers and Education**]: Computer Uses in Education—*Computer-assisted instruction*

General Terms

Languages, Human Factors

Keywords

Testing; LMS; Python; C++; Java; Education; Moodle

1. INTRODUCTION

As students transition from small input-process-output problems to moderately-sized data structure problems, instructors quickly find that the students' previously successful programming approaches are no longer adequate. Left to their own devices, students will utilize the minimalist approach that worked for them before. Debugging is done entirely by staring at the code, hoping something will jump out. Compliance testing is conducted by printing out mystically obscure output. And in too many cases, simply not completing an assignment is seen as an acceptable way to deal with difficult problems. It is the job of educators to demonstrate and enforce efficient approaches to tackle these new programming problems.

One of the popular approaches to developing larger software is the use of test driven development [3]. Instructors face a host of difficulties in introducing and encouraging students to utilize testing as a natural part of their workflow. Formal lectures on the usefulness of unit testing and common approaches are not enough. Students like all human beings are motivated to perform a greedy search to find the solution to any problem. Creating tests takes time and tests are not part of the finished product. Students feel that spending time creating tests is wasteful compared to the time actually solving the "problem". So the question becomes how do instructors evaluate student tests in such a way that students see testing as a useful part of the software development process?

The most common approach is a summative assessment. Instructors collect the unit tests and grade them alongside of implementation code. Students receive feedback on how to create more effective tests and then feedback on why their implementation did not work. Unfortunately, when the next programming assignment is due, many students will provide the same effort and see the same results. Students fail to see a connection between creating good tests and their ultimate performance on the final product. In these situations, many students will commonly create the tests as an afterthought [13]. The students never experience that unit tests help them solve real problems.

The challenge is that students need *feedback* on how they created their tests before they ever touch the implementation. This approach is a formative assessment. Instructors in the humanities understand this and require students to turn in thesis statements or create outlines of their papers before allowing students to complete a full paper. If prep work indicates that the student does not understand the assignment or has a critical fault in their logic, instructors can perform interventions to get students back on the right track. This technique can work for student testing if computer science students only crafted 3 programs a semester. However, weekly, bi-weekly, or even tri-weekly programming assignments are not uncommon. Instructors simply do not have enough time to give feedback on testing in time for students

SIGCSE'15, March 4–7, 2015, Kansas City, MO, USA.

http://dx.doi.org/10.1145/2676723.2677247.

to utilize it in creating implementations. Peer feedback can provide a way to offset instructor workload. However the quality of feedback varies greatly and the workload is instead shifted onto the students.

It is natural for computer science educators to turn to computers to help with pedagogical issues. There are a host of grading tools available to all instructors and several tools specialized for computer science education. Early tools performed simple input and output tests and provided students with a large degree of autonomy on how the program was designed, or tested a common API that students had to adhere to. Over the last decade, education researchers have asked how computers can aid instructors in evaluating student tests and providing instant feedback [2, 6, 8, 11, 13]. These approaches are elegant in that they can provide meaningful feedback on student tests, but fall short of the ideal seen in the humanities. Students are not getting direct feedback on how well their tests find bugs *before* they write their implementations.

We introduce the Ante framework to automate the evaluation of student tests in such a way that students will see them as an integral part of the software development process. Our solution runs within Moodle [1], a popular open source learning management system, which is already present on many campuses and can unify automated grading of student programming assignments as well as quizzes, papers, and attendance. Our unique approach is to evaluate student testing before they may submit implementations of the assignment. By evaluating student testing, we can ensure that 1) students understand the assignment before moving on to implementing it and 2) students have a set of tests to aid in implementing their assignment. In this paper we will describe the existing tools and techniques to evaluate student testing, discuss the process of utilizing this framework from both the student and instructor points of view, describe the technical and usability issues in crafting Ante, and report preliminary feedback of student attitudes towards testing in the context of this new paradigm.

2. RELATED WORK

The use of automated testing to encourage students to create effective tests has been an area of ongoing research over the past decade. The more subtle research areas have been in altering the feedback of automated testing of student implementations. These techniques limit the amount of feedback or the verbosity of feedback [5, 12] to encourage students to write better tests. While there are some small gains from these techniques, they encourage the creation and expansion of tests *after* student implementations have been created.

The bulk of research has revolved around the use of *coverage* as a tool to evaluate student tests [6, 8, 13]. Coverage is a measurement of how many lines of the student implementation is "covered" by the execution of student tests. Coverage is a useful tool in automated testing. First, coverage can be automated without any further input by an instructor and will work without any specified API set by the instructor. Second, a high percentage of coverage is necessary for a successful set of tests. Unfortunately, coverage is not a sufficient evaluation of good student tests. Students can create tests that cover their entire implementation but not make a single `assert` call to determine the correctness of the code that was covered. More alarmingly, coverage is a poor indicator of good student tests. Edwards finds that the use of coverage to evaluate student work leads to students using "happy path testing". Student tests confirmed that code worked but did not go out of its way to detect the presence of bugs [7]. Finally, coverage has an unintended flaw that student tests and implementations are submitted concurrently. There are no mechanisms to enforce that students are writing tests before implementation. Some students only write tests as an afterthought [13].

Mutation has recently been offered as a new technique to evaluate student testing [2]. Mutation takes a good implementation and makes small random changes to the source code which usually produce errors that mimic bugs. A good set of student tests will detect that the changes have created an error. Shams extended the mutation model for classroom settings and evaluated it over existing student data [11]. Interestingly, they demonstrated that evaluation using mutation could be a better measure than coverage for student tests. However, due to the random nature of mutation, many tests are not useful and there is no guarantee that all common bugs would be represented in the resulting evaluation.

Mutation is the only contender for automated evaluation of student tests before students create implementations. While mutation might provide a reasonable measure of how robust a set of student tests are, there are no given mechanisms to provide students feedback on how they could improve their tests.

3. ANTE ALGORITHM

Ante boasts two unique approaches towards student programing that make up the core of the system. First, student tests are evaluated in the absence of student implementations. Second, students are not allowed to submit implementations without earning a perfect score (no defects found) on their student tests. This two pronged approach creates an environment where students can more closely mimic the test driven development approach of creating good tests first and building implementations second than those found in the related works.

The first principle takes advantage of what a student test is. A test is a way of determining if a particular implementation meets all of the specifications. So a perfect test will only *accept* implementations that are correct and *reject* all other incorrect implementations. This is discussed further in Section 3.2.

The second principle is supported by Moodle, a popular Learning Management System. Moodle provides tools to restrict student access to activities until previous activities have been completed in a feature called Conditional Activity. We have extended this functionality to allow for soft deadlines discussed in Section 3.4.

3.1 Ante Architecture

Ante exists as a set of scripts that evaluate and grade student tests. We execute our scripts in Moodle using the Virtual Programming Lab (VPL) [10], a Moodle module for evaluation of programming assignments.

The VPL module collects programming assignments and executes them in a jail server. VPL supports many languages and can provide simple I/O testing and grading with little setup. This provides good support for evaluating simple programs in wide range of languages. However, this base behavior can be bypassed with instructor-provided scripts.

Table 1: Testing configuration file

filename	correct?	error message
correct.py	True	Your test fails the correct one!
accessor.py	False	Did you test all the accessors?
constructor.py	False	Did you test your constructor?

Because VPL can support multiple languages and tools, we can easily add new languages and tool sets to the Ante system. To date we have created 3 sets of scripts to support Python, C++, and Java. These scripts along with example code are available online under a GNU license [4].

3.2 Evaluating Student Tests

Our framework is straightforward. We use the student's testing code to evaluate `N` implementations. One of the implementations is correct and the other `N-1` implementations are incorrect. The framework links the student test to each implementation, compiles if necessary, and requires the student test to exit with signal 0 (normal exit) if the test accepts the implementation and any other signal value(either explicitly, through a failed assert, or by throwing an exception) to reject the implementation.

Instructors must provide `N` implementations and a configuration file to list all of the implementations. Table 1 outlines a configuration file to evaluate student tests. Each line has 3 pieces of information. First the name of the file that contains the implementation to test, second a Boolean value to indicate if the implementation is correct, and finally an error message to display if the student's testing incorrectly accepts or fails to accept an implementation. Instructors are encouraged to provide some form of error message to guide students to create additional testing to find these errors. However, instructors can give very specific hints or, preferably, vague hints to help students build more robust testing.

3.3 Linking Student Tests

Next we must create a link from the student test to each of the implementations. Each of the supported languages has a command to import or include libraries and modules. We require that the student's test import a proxy library called `TEST_LIB`. (i.e. `import TEST_LIB`).

Our script creates a copy of the student's test and replaces the string `TEST_LIB` with the name of the file that contains the first implementation supplied by the instructor. This allows our script to then compile and execute the test and record the response. The script will then repeat this process for each of the other `N-1` implementations.

Because Python and C++ do not require any connection between filenames and class names, files could be named anything and placed in the same directory. However, Java requires that each file have the same name as the class that it contains. This means that the names of all `N` implementations must be identical. We can circumvent this limitation by placing each implementation in its own package (see Figure 1). This solves the Java linking problem and also creates a directory structure to help organize our implementations. Similar techniques can be used for C++ and Python as well. Note that Python requires an empty `__init__.py` file in each directory to indicate that it is a package.

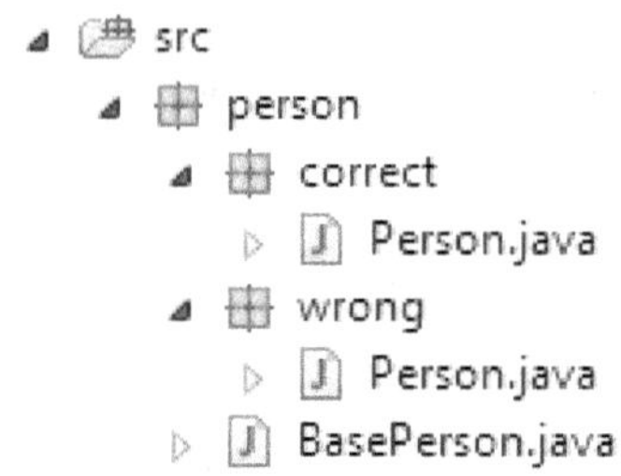

Figure 1: Each Java implementation must be placed in a different package

3.4 Sequencing Assignments

Within a lab, a student must submit a test that correctly categorizes all `N` implementations before attempting to complete the implementation themselves. This means that a lab contains at least two activities. In addition we required that students complete the labs in sequence. For instance, Lab 4 covering pointer-based stacks must be done before students attempt Lab 5 on pointer-based lists.

These requirements cannot be satisfactorily achieved within Moodle and VPL. Moodle has a conditional activity setting that can restrict students from accessing activities before they have completed the prerequisites for that activity. Prerequisites can be the completion of an activity (i.e. any grade was entered) or a particular range of grades. In our case we needed to restrict students from proceeding to the next assignment until they earned a 100 percent on the previous assignment.

At first blush, conditional activities solves the problem. However, a dilemma arises on the topic of deadlines. If we set a deadline on an assignment, and the student does not meet that deadline, they will be locked out from completing that assignment. However, because the rest of the assignments depend on the first assignment, the students cannot complete further assignments. When all labs must be completed in sequence, missing one deadline will keep the student from completing any future assignments.

The other option is to do away with deadlines altogether. Students must complete assignments in order, but there is no penalty to turning in work late. We used this option in an introductory computer science course with disastrous results. Roughly one half of the class was more than 3 weeks behind by the end of the semester. Without some deadline or penalty, the students felt little motivation to keep up and fell hopelessly behind.

To enable both sequencing and deadlines, we created a fork of the VPL software to create soft deadlines. We added two additional fields to setting up a VPL assignment. First we added a checkbox called *Must Complete*. When this field is selected, the VPL module will not record any grades that are less than the maximum credit. The second field we added was a text box called *Drop by Percentage*. For each day that the submission was past the due date, the score would be dropped by that amount. A student that submitted incomplete work would earn no score, and would not be able to continue. A student that submitted work correct 3 days late would earn a 100-20*3=40% grade. That student would then be allowed to attempt the next assignment. A student that successfully completed this assignment 10 days late would receive no credit for the assignment but would be

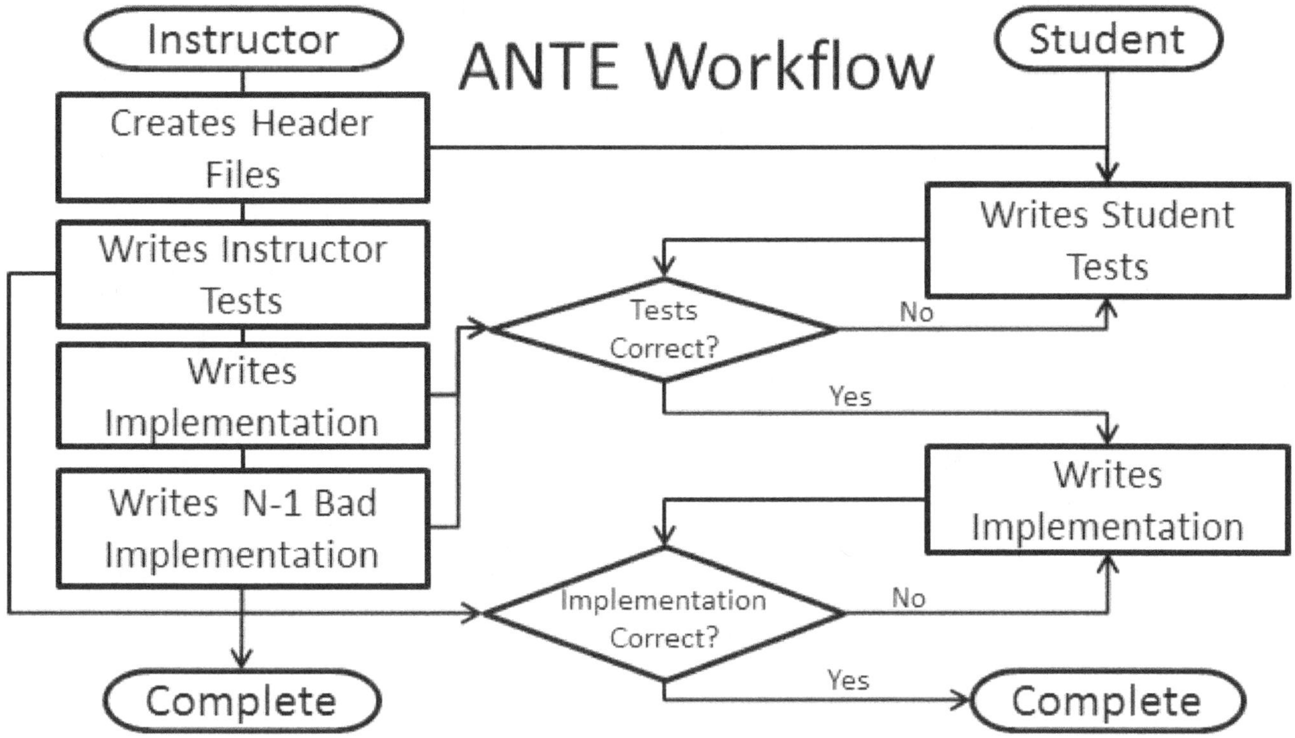

Figure 2: Ante Workflow for instructor and students.

allowed to attempt the next assignment (which might also be late).

Our fork of VPL [4] provided a way to utilize soft deadlines. Students must turn in correct work, and must do so in a timely manner.

4. WORKFLOW

The workflow for using Ante from both the instructor and student views is outlined in Figure 2.

4.1 Instructor Workflow

When the instructor develops an assignment, they must specify the interfaces that will be tested: functions, classes, and methods. If the instructor creates a header file or stub file, they can share this with the students to decrease simple mistakes in interpreting the instructions.

As test driven development indicates, our next step is to write the tests that will be used to verify that the interface works. It is highly appropriate that instructors practice what they preach. This test will be used not only to help the instructor create a correct implementation, but also to test student implementations within the Ante system.

Once the Instructor creates a working implementation, they need to create a set of `N-1` incorrect implementations. Each incorrect implementation should only have one defect present. Introducing more than one mistake per file will make it difficult to communicate which error the student was not able to detect. One can achieve this easily by copying the working implementation and introducing one mistake. This technique is quick, but suffers from one dramatic setback. What if your initial implementation has an undetected error or we wished to add a new interface for testing? All of the implementations will have to be updated in these situations. In object oriented languages, the smarter thing to do is to use inheritance. The correct implementation is the base class and each of the incorrect implementations can be a subclass. Future errors can be quickly corrected in the base class and allows the instructor to add new interfaces more easily.

The number of implementations to create is something of a balancing act. An instructor should create as many implementations as necessary to ensure thorough evaluation of student tests. However, each additional test creates a significant increase in the time necessary to complete the evaluation. For testing a circularly linked list in C++, we used 30 implementations. It took less than a minute to evaluate each student's test and provided students with a robust set of tests to aid them in implementing their solutions.

4.2 Uploading files to Moodle-VPL

Once the instructor creates the `N` implementations and gathers any necessary support libraries, they need to upload them into the VPL module. There are two challenges to this. First, the VPL interface only allows an instructor to upload one file at a time. Second, VPL does not allow users to upload binary files. Luckily, there is a facility to upload an ASCII version of binary files using b64. VPL will decrypt any file with a .b64 extension at evaluation time.

We use an additional script to zip all of the files in a directory and then b64 encrypt the zip file. At evaluation time our script will look for that zip file and uncompress it. This solution removes the drudgery of uploading individual files.

4.3 Student Workflow

The student's workflow mimics much of the instructor's workflow. The only differences are that the student does not (purposefully) create `N-1` incorrect implementations and has the benefit of the Ante system to provide feedback on how well students tests and implementations were constructed.

Each student reads the instructions and downloads the header file supplied by the instructor. The student uses the header file to create a set of tests to evaluate an implementation. Their test should returned 0 from `main()` if the implementation is correct and use simple assert statements to cause the program to fail if it did not. A failed assert would cause the program to return with a non-0 value. Our scripts interpret any non-zero exit value to indicate that the test rejects the implementation.

The student then submits their test to run against the `N` tests created by the instructor. If the student test correctly identifies the correct implementation as well as rejected the `N-1` incorrect implementations, the student earned a perfect score, barring late penalties, and Moodle unlocks the next part of the assignment.

If the student test fails to correctly evaluate any of the `N` implementations, the student receives feedback on what had not been tested properly and are instructed to resubmit their work. Students were not allowed to submit their implementation code until they develop a proven set of tests. This is critical since a good set of tests demonstrates understanding of the problem, but also provides a vital tool in creating the implementation.

Finally, the student writes the implementation. The student should use the tests they developed earlier to evaluate their implementation before submitting it to Ante. Once again if their code is found wanting, Ante will reject the submission and require the student to rework and resubmit their implementation.

4.4 Expanding the Workflow

VPL runs scripts on a jail server with a full Linux distribution. It is possible to fold in the use of additional tools to enhance the effectiveness of the Ante framework. In our class we used Valgrind on all C++ assignments with arrays or memory management. Valgrind is an open source tool which can detect many memory management bugs[9]. This was critical since memory errors cannot be reliably detected with traditional testing. Our Java scripts for Ante use JUnit to provide students and instructors with a richer testing framework.

So far our examples have demonstrated the ability to use tools to augment the evaluation of student tests and implementations. However, Moodle's conditional activity also allows us to add additional steps to the framework described above. For instance, an instructor could add steps using static analysis tools to evaluate coding style or dynamics tools to evaluate code coverage. These additional steps can help students explore refactoring concepts as they will be revisiting working code to improve style and robustness.

5. OBSERVATIONS AND ENHANCEMENTS

We rolled out the new system on the first day of class. There were several surprises with how the students used the framework and what additional feedback they needed in order to complete the assignments.

5.1 The Most Common Bug

When students wrote their tests they jumped in and attempted to cover everything all at once. When there were 10 implementations to test against students would typically get 90%. At first they were delighted until they realized that their tests were rejecting all of the implementations. The students had introduced a logic error either through inattention to detail or a misunderstanding of the assignment.

Students spent most of their lab time correcting this error. Once students corrected the mistake of rejecting all implementations, they were surprised that their scores had dropped. With the primary error fixed, their tests still accepted some incorrect implementations as correct. While the effect was understandable, it led to a loss of morale. Students felt that they had gone backwards when they had obviously improved on their work.

To remedy this, we altered the script to detect if the student test fails to accept the correct implementation. When it fails to accept, the script will stop future evaluations and return a score of 0. This provided two benefits. Students would not (usually) experience a drop in credit as they improved the quality of their tests. Secondly, the script would not waste time processing the other `N-1` implementations. Students could get responses faster and get back to work.

5.2 Feedback

Originally the only feedback provided by Ante when evaluating student tests was the line in the configuration file that hinted what circumstance the student had not accounted for in their testing. Our hypothesis was that the student had overlooked these situations and only needed a nudge in the right direction. However, the students were spending most of their time getting their tests to accept the correct implementation. The message "Your test rejected the correct implementation" does not provide enough direction to help solve the problem. Students had to systematically disable tests to determine which test was incorrectly failing all implementations.

Providing more feedback was a challenge. Simply reporting all of the standard output and error output would overwhelm the student. In most cases there *should* be some form of error message that an assert failed. Instead we stored each of the responses as each of the `N` implementations were tested. If the student's test incorrectly accepted or rejected the test, our script would pass along the output only for those tests that failed. The students overwhelmingly felt that this was the most helpful improvement. They could see which of their tests failed and print out debugging information to aid in diagnosing where they were having problems.

Other than to report that there had been an error, we did *not* give feedback when testing student implementations. In these situations the most common culprit was the lack of local testing. The test already written by the student would have found the error. Students are instructed to run their tests locally on their implementation to find and fix any remaining bugs before submitting their implementation.

6. RESULTS AND CONCLUSIONS

We introduced our framework in a data structures class of 16 students as a second course in sequence for computer science majors during Spring 2014. In addition to the instructor, two other professors audited the class to help evaluate this framework. The instructor gave the students a lab each week to be completed in C++. Students had two hours of in-class time per week to start the lab and were expected to finish the labs outside of scheduled class periods. These assignments were similar to labs given in previous years, students were expected to work a total of 6 hours to complete each lab. During the course of the semester we made additions to Ante to improve student usability. These observations were gathered through informal interviews of students that completed the labs.

- Once feedback on testing was improved (Section 5), students appreciated the test-first paradigm. Testing allowed students to deepen their understanding of the assignments. Many students discovered misconceptions and paid attention to examining boundary conditions as locations to focus testing.
- Students reported that generating the tests was the most time extensive portion of the lab. Once tests were completed, students found the implementations were usually easier to complete than the tests themselves. If there were problems in the implementations, students used their own tests to track down the bugs.
- We had used the labs in the course over the past 4 years. Students averaged 6 hours to complete labs. Testing was always a graded component (submitted at the same time as implementation). Student tests were much more extensive and comprehensive using the Ante systems. Students were not allowed to progress until they had submitted a correct set of tests (Section 3.4). Despite the fact that students were creating more code using the Ante framework than previous cohorts, total time to complete the labs remained flat. Students spent more time writing tests, but less time writing and debugging their implementations.
- We utilized two deadlines throughout the week: One deadline for students to submit their testing code and one deadline for students to submit their implementations. This helped students start sooner and spread their work out over the week. Many students took advantage of the soft deadline mechanism (Section 3.4) and submitted work 1-2 days after the deadlines in order to get help on their assignment, especially since they could not submit incomplete work for grading. Penalties for late work created distributions among student grades.

Because of the small class size and ongoing development, all of these results are promising but preliminary. Expanded formal testing is required to verify these results on a larger scale. More importantly, while we have seen students develop positive attitudes towards testing as part of the programming process, we have no data yet on students' behaviors in subsequent classes. Can the Ante framework instill testing values in students that remain in place even when they are not forced to perform testing? These are all questions for further research.

7. ACKNOWLEDGEMENT

I would like to thank Dr. Barbara Wahl and Professor Jeff Vaughn of Hanover College for auditing my Data Structures class and completing all of the programming assignments along side the students.

8. REFERENCES

[1] The moodle learning management system. `https://moodle.org`. Accessed: 2014-08-20.

[2] K. Aaltonen, P. Ihantola, and O. Seppälä. Mutation analysis vs. code coverage in automated assessment of students' testing skills. In *Proceedings of the ACM International Conference Companion on Object Oriented Programming Systems Languages and Applications Companion*, SPLASH '10, pages 153–160, New York, NY, USA, 2010. ACM.

[3] K. Beck. *Test Driven Development: By Example.* Addison-Wesley Longman Publishing Co., Inc., Boston, MA, USA, 2002.

[4] M. K. Bradshaw. Ante source code. `https://github.com/michaelkbradshaw/AnteUp`.

[5] K. Buffardi and S. H. Edwards. Responses to adaptive feedback for software testing. In *Proceedings of the 2014 Conference on Innovation & Technology in Computer Science Education*, ITiCSE '14, pages 165–170, New York, NY, USA, 2014. ACM.

[6] S. H. Edwards. Improving student performance by evaluating how well students test their own programs. *J. Educ. Resour. Comput.*, 3(3), Sept. 2003.

[7] S. H. Edwards and Z. Shams. Do student programmers all tend to write the same software tests? In *Proceedings of the 2014 Conference on Innovation & Technology in Computer Science Education*, ITiCSE '14, pages 171–176, New York, NY, USA, 2014. ACM.

[8] D. Jackson and M. Usher. Grading student programs using assyst. *SIGCSE Bull.*, 29(1):335–339, Mar. 1997.

[9] N. Nethercote and J. Seward. Valgrind: A framework for heavyweight dynamic binary instrumentation. In *Proceedings of the 2007 ACM SIGPLAN Conference on Programming Language Design and Implementation*, PLDI '07, pages 89–100, New York, NY, USA, 2007. ACM.

[10] J. Rodríguez, E. Rubio Royo, and Z. Hernández. Uses of vpl. In *INTED2011 Proceedings*, 5th International Technology, Education and Development Conference, pages 743–748. IATED, 7-9 March 2011.

[11] Z. Shams and S. H. Edwards. Toward practical mutation analysis for evaluating the quality of student-written software tests. In *Proceedings of the Ninth Annual International ACM Conference on International Computing Education Research*, ICER '13, pages 53–58, New York, NY, USA, 2013. ACM.

[12] J. Spacco, D. Fossati, J. Stamper, and K. Rivers. Towards improving programming habits to create better computer science course outcomes. In *Proceedings of the 18th ACM Conference on Innovation and Technology in Computer Science Education*, ITiCSE '13, pages 243–248, New York, NY, USA, 2013. ACM.

[13] J. Spacco and W. Pugh. Helping students appreciate test-driven development (tdd). In *Companion to the 21st ACM SIGPLAN Symposium on Object-oriented Programming Systems, Languages, and Applications*, OOPSLA '06, pages 907–913, New York, NY, USA, 2006. ACM.

On the Evaluation of Student Team Software Development Projects

Anya Tafliovich
Dept. of Computer and Mathematical Sciences
University of Toronto Scarborough
anya@cs.utoronto.ca

Andrew Petersen
Dept. of Mathematical and Computational Sciences
University of Toronto Mississauga
andrew.petersen@utoronto.ca

Jennifer Campbell
Dept. of Computer Science
University of Toronto
campbell@cs.utoronto.ca

ABSTRACT

Project experience and teamwork have been identified as two of the most important deficiencies of recent graduates, so experiences with team projects are a critical component of computer science and software engineering education. However, evaluating these projects is difficult, as it requires a balance between rewarding the team's effort (and the development of skills that enable the team to work effectively) and recognizing individual contributions. We report on an investigation of the student perspective on evaluation of software development team projects. We find that (a) computer science and software engineering educators hold several misconceptions about students' preferences in teamwork evaluation methods, (b) that students' preferences with regard to evaluation change dramatically as they advance through the program and even in the course of a single term, and (c) that the change in preference occurs early in the term, before they complete any work as a team, with most students shifting their preference towards putting more weight on the team's effort.

Categories and Subject Descriptors

K.3.2 [**Computers and Education**]: Computer and Information Science Education—*Computer Science Education*

General Terms

Human Factors

Keywords

student teamwork; evaluation; students' perspective; motivating students; undergraduate software development project

1. INTRODUCTION

The ability to work effectively in teams is consistently rated highly by employers of Computer Science and Software Engineering graduates. Project experience and teamwork have been identified among the most important knowledge deficiencies of recent graduates, i.e. the most important skills that the prospective employers found were lacking in recent graduates of Computer Science and Software Engineering programs [28, 29]. Unfortunately, the development of teamwork skills is an area poorly understood by the Computer Science and Software Engineering Education community. Educators agree on the importance of having team projects in undergraduate CS and SE courses. However, there is no agreement on best methods of forming and managing student teams and on best policies of evaluating student team projects [26].

Educators agree that an appropriate method of evaluation of team software development projects is essential to ensuring a positive student experience. A method of evaluation that is perceived as unfair can become a significant demotivational factor for students, discouraging team cooperation and communication and hindering the development of a stimulating learning environment.

Anecdotal evidence suggests that educators hold some shared beliefs about the student perspective on evaluating teamwork. For example, the authors encountered the following opinions repeatedly in conversation with colleagues: "Stronger students prefer to be evaluated individually rather than as a team", and even "Most CS students prefer to be evaluated individually rather than as a team". Studying the existing research in the field of Computer Science Education (see Section 2) revealed that very little is known about the students' perspective on teamwork evaluation methods.

In this work, we report on the results of a research study that investigates the student perspective on the evaluation of software development team projects in an undergraduate Computer Science or Software Engineering course setting. We answer the following questions:

1. *What team project evaluation policy do second, third, and fourth year students prefer?*
2. *Which of the factors under consideration, if any, are predictors of a student's initial preference of evaluation policy?*
3. *How do students' preferences change at the end of the term?*
4. *Which of the factors under consideration, if any, are predictors of the change in a student's preference?*
5. *When do the students change their preferences?*

We consider multiple factors as potential predictors of the student's preferences: gender, being in a CS program, English as first language, GPA, expected grade in the course, student's individual performance in the course, the student's

SIGCSE'15, March 4–7, 2015, Kansas City, MO, USA.

ACM 978-1-4503-2966-8/15/03 ...$15.00.
http://dx.doi.org/10.1145/2676723.2677223.

	Team portion (% of the total grade)	Individual portion (% of the total grade)
Option 1	100%	0%
Option 2	80%	20%
Option 3	50%	50%
Option 4	20%	80%
Option 5	0%	100%

Table 1: Survey Question

peer evaluation scores in a recently completed project phase, the student's evaluation of his or her peers in a recently completed project phase, and the grade in this project phase.

The remainder of the paper is organized as follows. Section 2 introduces related studies and work on undergraduate student teamwork. Section 3.1 describes the courses under consideration and the research methodology. Section 4 reports on the results of the study. Section 5 draws conclusions and suggests directions of future research.

2. RELATED WORK

Many groups have looked at team composition and whether attributes of the team members negatively impact the team's overall performance [2, 4, 7, 12, 20, 27, 31]. Faraj et al. found that a team's performance is affected by their communication and coordination styles [10], and Karn and Cowling found that personality issues that lead to disruptions were the most significant factor impacting quality of work [21]. Other groups have found productivity to be linked to trust and to cultural and disciplinary issues between teammates [9] or to social sensitivity [33, 3]. Andreescu et al. reports that successful project teams needed a combination of software development application domain and project management knowledge [1]. A related area of study focuses on tools that support good team formation [6, 23].

Other studies focus on the impact of rewards on teams. Researchers in management cite the need to reward personal achievement to maximize productivity [19]. However, Hoffman et al. argue that a need for cooperation between teammates necessitates more equal sharing of rewards [17]. Similarly, in the classroom, students must balance the need to cooperate with teammates with the urge to demonstrate personal ability (for a better mark). Hazzan's 2003 study asked students to distribute a financial award within a team and observed their behaviour and found that the students tended to divide the majority of the funds equally, reserving a small portion to reward personal achievement [14]. Several groups have worked to teach teamwork skills in the context of software engineering teams and to raise awareness of the tension between collaboration and reward [15, 18, 30].

Self and peer assessments are critical elements in assessment for student team software projects, but some have expressed concerns about the effectiveness of peer assessment [5, 11, 24]. They found evidence of teams colluding to make sure that marks were shared equally – or to punish a single group member [22, 13]. Herbert found that students are both too generous *and* too hard on themselves, suggesting that students' perceptions of effort are not objective [16]. In contrast, Dunsmore et al. notes that peer critiques of contribution were consistent and correlated with perceptions of how much work was completed by team members [8]. Smith and Smarkusky propose a competency based framework for assessment to assist students in making more objective judgements [32].

3. ENVIRONMENT

The study was performed at a large, North American research-intensive university. It included students from four sections of a second-year course, a single-section third year course, and a single-section forth-year course. Each course included a significant team-based software project within a twelve week term.

3.1 Courses

The second-year course (we will call it SE2) introduced students to the programming language Java (the first year is taught in Python), basic Android development, object-oriented analysis and design, simple design patterns, basic version control, and introduction to software modelling. This is the first course in the program that involves significant teamwork, though the students may opt to work with a partner in first year courses. The course project spanned seven weeks (roughly the second half of the term) and consisted of three distinct stages. The end product of the project was a simple Android application. The first stage was the design stage, done in groups of two. The second and third stages involved revisiting the design and developing the application; these were done in groups of four. The teams followed a prescribed, simplified, Scrum-like software development process, closely monitored by the course teaching assistants. Between four sections taught on two campuses, the peak enrolment in the course was 575 students.

The third-year course (SE3) is an introduction to software engineering. In this course the students learn about software processes, with heavy emphasis on Agile software development techniques. The course also covers aspects of software design and software architecture. Since the second year course has not always included a team component in past years, the third year course might also be the first time that a student is involved in a significant team project. The course project spanned 10 weeks of the term and consisted of four distinct stages. The students worked in teams of four or five and developed either a sophisticated Android or web application. The teams followed an extreme programming (XP) software development process under close supervision of the teaching assistants and course instructor. The peak enrolment in the course was 84 students.

The fourth-year course (SE4) is an advanced software engineering course. The students worked on a large (200K+ lines of code) open source project, in teams of six or seven. In the course of the project, the students performed a reverse engineering and analysis of the code base, completed at least two bug fixes, and investigated, designed, and implemented a new feature. The project spanned 10 weeks of the course and consisted of four stages. The teams chose their

Course	Gender		CS major		English First Lang.		GPA				Expected grade			
	Male	Female	Yes	No	Yes	No	< 1.5	1.5-2.5	2.5-3.5	> 3.5	A	B	C	Don't Care
SE2	256	82	291	48	159	176	3	45	71	21	229	95	3	9
SE3	41	4	43	2	24	21	1	16	22	6	27	14	3	1
SE4	38	3	41	0	14	26	0	14	20	6	19	12	3	7

Table 2: Descriptive Statistics

own software development process. The peak enrolment in the course was 63 students.

3.2 Evaluation Preferences

At the beginning of the term, during lecture, the following information was collected: (a) whether the student is majoring in CS, (b) gender, (c) GPA, (d) whether English is the student's first language, and (e) expected grade in the course. At the same time, students were asked to provide informed consent. This information was provided to the investigators at the end of the term. The investigators also received access to all consenting students' term and final grades, as well as peer evaluation data collected during the term. The students were also asked the following question:

> Assume that you are a member of a student team working on a course project that involves developing software. Your project grade will consist of two portions: Team and Individual. In the Team portion of the grade, each team member *receives the same grade*. In the Individual portion of the grade, each team member's grade is allocated *based on his/her individual performance* on the project. The table below outlines five grading options:
> *[See Table 1 for the table in the survey.]*
> Which grading option would you prefer?

In SE2, the students answered the above question three times: (1) before the project teams were formed, (2) after the teams were formed but before they completed a project stage, and (3) at the end of the term. In SE3 and SE4, the students answered the questions twice: (1) at the beginning of the term before teams were formed and (2) at the end of the term.

Each time, the students were informed that their survey responses were made anonymous for the purposes of the study, and that their responses had no impact on the actual method of project evaluation performed in the course.

3.3 Team Formation and Peer Evaluation

In SE2, the students formed teams of two for the first stage of the project. The course instructors then formed teams of four for the second and third stages of the project by merging the pairs from the first stage.

In SE3 and SE4, we allowed students to request a single partner for the team. The course instructors then formed teams and, wherever possible, put the requested partners on the same team.

We used CATME team formation and peer evaluation software to form the teams in all three courses [25]. The team formation criteria included personal schedules (to maximize time available for group meetings), gender (females are not outnumbered in a team) [1], GPA (to group students with dissimilar GPAs), and commitment level (to group students with similar self-reported commitment).

In all three courses we also used CATME to perform peer evaluation, following completion of each stage of the project.

[1]This condition could not be met in SE4, which only had three female students enrolled.

In SE2, the students ranked themselves and their teammates, on a scale of 1 to 5, on (1) contributing to the team's work, and (2) interacting with teammates. In SE3 and SE4, there were additional evaluation criteria: (3) expecting quality and (4) having related knowledge, skills, and abilities. The students were also invited to provide comments to the instructor. Based on these criteria, the CATME software calculates an *adjustment factor* for each student. In SE2, the individual grade for a project stage was calculated as $0.8 \times$ *team grade* $+ 0.2 \times$ *adjustment factor* $\times$ *team grade*, with the adjustment factor capped at 1.05. In SE3 and SE4, the formula was *adjustment factor* $\times$ *team grade*, where the adjustment factor was capped between 0.8 and 1.05.

4. RESULTS

A total of 430 participants provided consent for the study: 342 from SE2 (59.5%), 46 from SE3 (54.8%), and 42 from SE4 (66.7%). Table 2 summarizes the descriptive statistics of the participants' responses to the survey questions (omitting blanks).

4.1 Team Evaluation Preferences: Before

Figure 1 shows the students' team evaluation preferences as reported before the student project teams were formed.

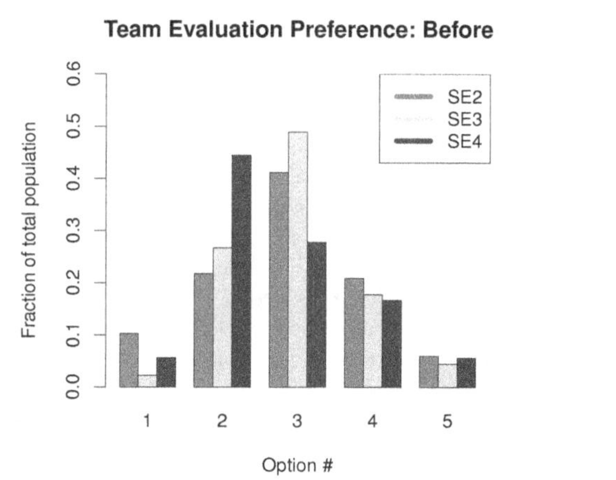

Figure 1: Team Evaluation Preference: Before

Recall that Option #1 is the 0-100 split (0% individual, 100% team) and Option #5 is the 100-0 split (100% individual, 0% team). In the second year course the students' answers form a bell curve around the 50-50 option, but by the fourth year course, the students favour the 20-80 split.

We then asked the question, *"Which of the factors under consideration, if any, are predictors of a student's initial preference of evaluation policy?"*

We used the statistical software package R to run linear regression tests to see whether the following factors are predictors of the student's initial preferred team evaluation

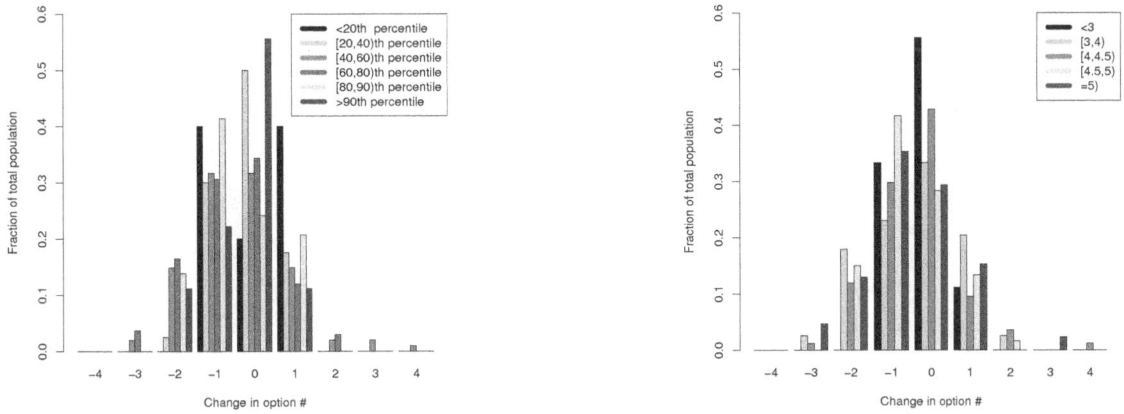

(a) By Individual Grade

(b) By Team Satisfaction Score

Figure 2: No Effect on Preferences: Examples

policy: gender, being in a CS program, English as first language, GPA, and expected grade in the course. We found that none of these factors were predictors.[2]

4.2 Team Evaluation Preferences: After

Figure 3 shows the students' team evaluation preferences as reported at the end of the term.

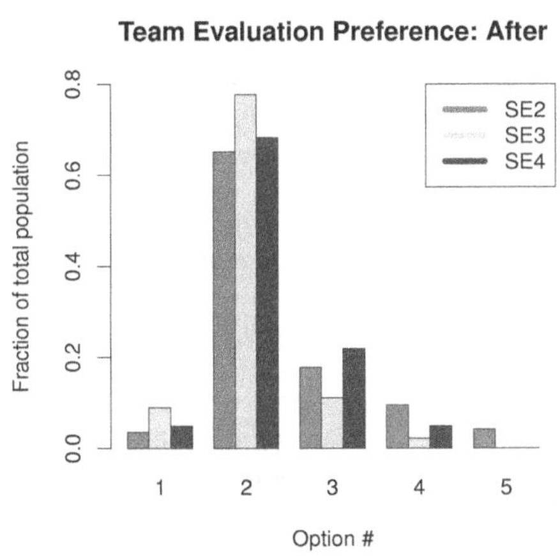

Figure 3: Team Evaluation Preference: After

The students' answers are dramatically different after the course, with the vast majority of students in all three courses preferring the 20-80 split.

Linear regression tests show that, as with the initial preference, gender, being in a CS program, English as first language, GPA, and expected grade in the course are not predictors of the student's preference as recorded at the end of the term.

In addition, we used the same approach to investigate whether the student's individual performance in the course, the student's peer evaluation scores in a recently completed project phase, the student's evaluation of his or her peers in a recently completed project phase, or the grade in this phase are predictors of the team evaluation option. Surprisingly, we found that, in general, these factors were not predictors of the student's preference. In SE4, there was a slight positive correlation between a preference toward higher weight for the individual component and (1) a student's individual grade ($R^2 = 0.19$, $p = 0.007$), (2) the grade in the last project phase ($R^2 = 0.10$, $p = 0.038$), and (3) team satisfaction in a recently completed project phase ($R^2 = 0.17$, $p = 0.005$). However, the smaller sample size in SE4, lack of evidence in the other two courses, and the low values of R^2 suggest that we cannot draw any conclusions from these results.

4.3 Team Evaluation Preferences: Change

The next question we address is, *"How do the students change their preference at the end of the term?"* Figure 4 shows the students' change in team evaluation preferences at the end of the term.

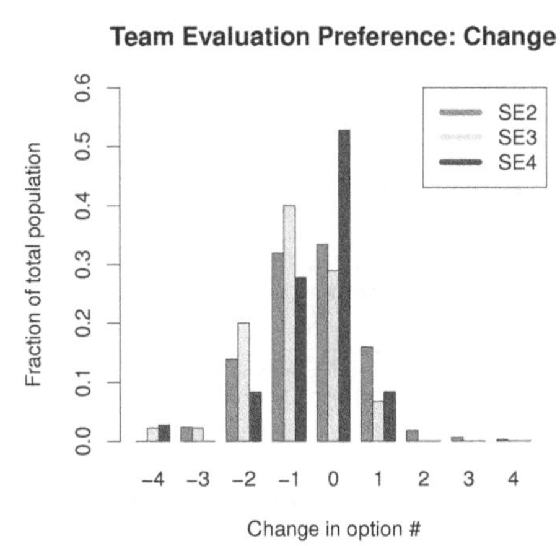

Figure 4: Team Evaluation Preference: Change

We observe that the students in all three courses tend to change their team evaluation preference by increasing the team portion. This effect is more significant in the sec-

[2]The full results of the linear regression analysis are available at `http://www.utsc.utoronto.ca/~atafliovich/`.

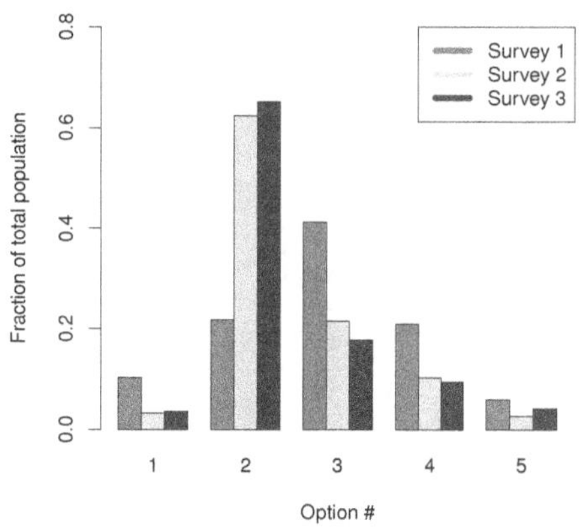

(a) Preferences in SE2: the three surveys

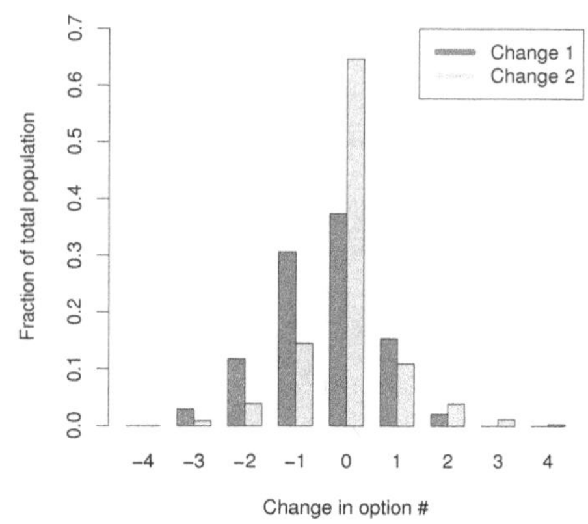

(b) Preferences in SE2: the two changes

Figure 5: Timing of the Change in Preference

ond and third year courses than in the fourth year course (where students were in at least their second significant team project and where there was already a strong preference for a 20-80 split at the beginning of the term).

We then asked the question, *"Which of the factors under consideration, if any, are predictors of the change in students' preferences of the team evaluation policy?"*

Again, linear regression tests show that gender, being in a CS program, English as first language, GPA, expected grade in the course, individual performance in the course, the student's peer evaluation scores in a recently completed project phase, the student's evaluation of his or her peers in a recently completed project phase, or the grade in this project phase are not predictors of the student's change in team evaluation preference at the end of the term.

Anecdotal evidence suggests that educators are frequently surprised that the student's level of satisfaction with his or her teammates' performance is *not* positively correlated with opting for a higher team portion, and neither is it the case that stronger students (students with higher individual grades) prefer an evaluation option with a higher individual portion. Figures 2a and 2b show example distributions of students' change in preferences based on the individual term grade and on the students' ratings of his or her teammates in a recently completed project phase. The distributions for each bin are normally distributed around the mean of the original distribution, confirming that these factors do not affect the student's preference toward evaluation.

Another interesting question is, *"When do the students change their preferences?"* Recall that in SE2 the first answer was recorded before the project teams were formed, the second answer was recorded after the teams were formed but before the students completed a project stage, and the third answer was recorded at the end of the term. Figure 5a provides a histogram of the students' answers in the first, second, and third survey in SE2. We observe that the biggest change occurs between the first and the second surveys, with only a minor further change at the last survey. This tells us that the students' preferences change and settle very soon after they know their teammates, before they had a chance to perform a significant piece of work together or get any feedback on their teamwork. Figure 5b, which shows the distributions of the changes in team evaluation preference that occur between the first and second and the second and third surveys in SE2, confirms this observation.

5. CONCLUSIONS

Our data analysis demonstrates that the student's preference for the method of evaluation in a software development team project depend remarkably on two factors: the student's year of study and the point in the term when the preference is expressed. First, there is a significant difference of opinions between students in their second, third, and fourth year. We found that, when asked in the beginning of the term, in the second year course the students' answers form a bell curve around the 50-50 option (50% for individual contribution and 50% for team grade), but by the fourth year course, the students favour the 20-80 split (20% for individual contribution and 80% for team grade). Second, in all three courses, the students tend to change their preference during the term, to favour a team option more strongly, and this effect is more significant in the second and third year courses than in the fourth year course. Third, we found that the change in the students' preferences occurs very early in the course of the project: before completion of a team project phase, and before receiving any feedback or grade from the TA or instructor.

Additionally, we examined a number of factors that we conjectured may predict the student's initial team evaluation preference or the change in preference during the term. Surprisingly, and contrary to what anecdotal evidence suggests is a commonly shared belief among educators, none of the following factors are predictors: gender, whether the student is majoring in CS, GPA, whether English is the student's first language, expected grade in the course, individual performance in the course, the student's peer evaluation scores in a recently completed project phase, the student's evaluation of his or her peers in a recently completed project phase, or the grade in this project phase.

Our results suggest that the experience of being a member of a development team changes the students' perception of what constitutes fair evaluation of teamwork. Surprisingly, the change is not affected by the team's performance, nor by the individual team members' contributions. Moreover, even a brief exposure to teamwork is enough to cause a significant change in evaluation preference, with students opting to increase the team's portion of the grade.

An important question that our study does not answer is *why* the students change their team evaluation preference. The two possible explanations we consider are decidedly different. It is imaginable that getting to know the team members increases the student's trust in the team, and creates an atmosphere of support and team spirit. On the other hand, one can imagine that students realize the difficulty in assessing the individual contribution, and thus do not trust its results, whether the assessment is performed via peer evaluations or via the TA's or instructor's observations.

As part of future research in this direction, we plan to conduct student interviews with the aim of better understanding the students' reasoning behind the shift in team evaluation preferences. Gaining a better understanding of the students' perspective on peer and supervisor's evaluation will also contribute to this line of research. Since our current results indicate that educators hold several misconceptions about students' preferences in teamwork evaluation, we identify a lack of available research data that would help explain these preferences, and the need for such data.

6. REFERENCES

[1] A. Andreescu, I. Intorsureanu, A. Uta, and R. Mihalca. Team work in software development student projects. In *Proceedings of the 9th International Conference on Computer Systems and Technologies and Workshop for PhD Students in Computing*, pages 80:V.18–80:1, 2008.

[2] M. Barrick, G. Stewart, M. Neubert, and M. Mount. Relating member ability and personality to work-team processes and team effectiveness. *Journal of Applied Psychology*, 83(3):377–391, 1998.

[3] L. Bender, G. Walia, K. Kambhampaty, K. E. Nygard, and T. E. Nygard. Social sensitivity and classroom team projects: An empirical investigation. In *Proceedings of the 43rd ACM Technical Symposium on Computer Science Education*, pages 403–408, 2012.

[4] G. Beranek, W. Zuser, and T. Grechenig. Functional group roles in software engineering teams. *SIGSOFT Softw. Eng. Notes*, 30(4):1–7, 2005.

[5] N. Clark, P. Davies, and R. Skeers. Self and peer assessment in software engineering projects. In *Proceedings of the 7th Australasian Conference on Computing Education - Volume 42*, pages 91–100, 2005.

[6] M. Craig, D. Horton, and F. Pitt. Forming reasonably optimal groups: (frog). In *Proceedings of the 16th ACM International Conference on Supporting Group Work*, pages 141–150, 2010.

[7] Y. Dubinsky and O. Hazzan. Using a role scheme to derive software project metrics. *Journal of Systems Architecture*, 52(11):693–699, 2006.

[8] H. E. Dunsmore, D. P. Moffet, and S. T. Ward. Software engineering team project group member evaluations: Some empirical results. *SIGCSE Bull.*, 21(2):40–45, 1989.

[9] K. Egea, S.-K. Kim, T. Andrews, and K. Behrens. Approaches used by cross-cultural and cross-discipline students in teamwork for a first-year course in web design. In *Proceedings of the Twelfth Australasian Conference on Computing Education - Volume 103*, pages 87–96, 2010.

[10] S. Faraj and L. Sproull. Coordinating expertise in software development teams. *Management Science*, 46(12):1554–1568, 2000.

[11] A. Gates, N. Delgado, and O. Mondragon. A structured approach for managing a practical software engineering course. In *30th Annual Frontiers in Education Conference*, 2000.

[12] N. Gorla and Y. W. Lam. Who should work with whom?: Building effective software project teams. *Commun. ACM*, 47(6):79–82, 2004.

[13] J. H. Hayes, T. C. Lethbridge, and D. Port. Evaluating individual contribution toward group software engineering projects. In *Proceedings of the 25th International Conference on Software Engineering*, pages 622–627, 2003.

[14] O. Hazzan. Computer science students' conception of the relationship between reward (grade) and cooperation. *SIGCSE Bull.*, 35(3):178–182, 2003.

[15] O. Hazzan and Y. Dubinsky. Students' cooperation in teamwork: binding the individual and the team interests. In *Proceedings of the ACM international conference companion on Object oriented programming systems languages and applications companion*, pages 151–152, 2010.

[16] N. Herbert. Quantitative peer assessment: Can students be objective? In *Proceedings of the Ninth Australasian Conference on Computing Education - Volume 66*, pages 63–71, 2007.

[17] J. R. Hoffman and S. G. Rogelberg. A guide to team incentive system. *Team Performance Management: An International Journal*, 4(1):23–32, 1998.

[18] J. M. Hogan and R. Thomas. Developing the software engineering team. In *Proceedings of the 7th Australasian Conference on Computing Education - Volume 42*, pages 203–210, 2005.

[19] D. Ian Brown. TeamâĂŘbased reward plans. *Team Performance Management: An International Journal*, 1(1):23–31, 1995.

[20] M. Ikonen and J. Kurhila. Discovering high-impact success factors in capstone software projects. In *Proceedings of the 10th ACM Conference on SIG-information Technology Education*, pages 235–244, 2009.

[21] J. Karn and T. Cowling. A follow up study of the effect of personality on the performance of software engineering teams. In *Proceedings of the 2006 ACM/IEEE International Symposium on Empirical Software Engineering*, pages 232–241, 2006.

[22] D. Kaufmann, R. Felder, and H. Fuller. Accounting for individual effort in cooperative learning teams. *Journal of Engineering Education*, 89:133–140, 2000.

[23] R. Layton, M. Loughry, M. W. Ohland, and G. D. Ricco. Design and validation of a web-based system for assigning members to teams using instructor-specified criteria. *Advances in Engineering Education*, 2, 2010.

[24] R. Layton and M. Ohland. Peer ratings revisited: Focus on teamwork, not ability. In *Proceedings of American Society for Engineering Education Annual Conference*, 2001.

[25] R. A. Layton, M. L. Loughry, M. W. Ohland, and G. D. Ricco. Design and validation of a web-based system for assigning members to teams using instructor-specified criteria. *Advances in Engineering Education*, 2(1):1–28, 2010.

[26] R. Lingard and E. Berd. Teaching teamwork skills in software engineering based on an understanding of factors affecting group performance. *Frontiers in Education*, 3, 2002.

[27] V. Pieterse, D. G. Kourie, and I. P. Sonnekus. Software engineering team diversity and performance. In *Proceedings of the 2006 Annual Research Conference of the South African Institute of Computer Scientists and Information Technologists on IT Research in Developing Countries*, pages 180–186, 2006.

[28] A. Radermacher and G. Walia. Gaps between industry expectations and the abilities of graduates. In *Proceeding of the 44th ACM Technical Symposium on Computer Science Education*, SIGCSE '13, pages 525–530, 2013.

[29] A. Radermacher, G. Walia, and D. Knudson. Investigating the skill gap between graduating students and industry expectations. In *Companion Proceedings of the 36th International Conference on Software Engineering*, ICSE Companion 2014, pages 291–300, 2014.

[30] A. Radermacher, G. Walia, and D. Knudson. Investigating the skill gap between graduating students and industry expectations. In *Companion Proceedings of the 36th International Conference on Software Engineering*, pages 291–300, 2014.

[31] S.-T. Shen, S. Prior, A. White, and M. Karamanoglu. Using personality type differences to form engineering design teams. *Engineering Education*, 2:54–66, 2007.

[32] H. H. Smith, III and D. L. Smarkusky. Competency matrices for peer assessment of individuals in team projects. In *Proceedings of the 6th Conference on Information Technology Education*, pages 155–162, 2005.

[33] A. Woolley, C. Chabris, A. Pentland, N. Hashmi, and M. Thomas. Evidence for a collective intelligence factor in the performance of human groups. *Science*, 330(6004):686–688, 2010.

An Experience Report at Teaching a Group Based Agile Software Development Project Course

Craig Anslow
Department of Computer Science
University of Calgary
Calgary, Alberta, Canada
craig.anslow@ucalgary.ca

Frank Maurer
Department of Computer Science
University of Calgary
Calgary, Alberta, Canada
frank.maurer@ucalgary.ca

ABSTRACT

Teaching group based Agile software development project courses is difficult. There are many aspects that need to be considered for a project to be successful such as a well defined scope, students working effectively together, and engaging with the customer. In this paper we present an experience report at teaching an Agile software development project course that involved teams developing web applications. The resources developed for the course and discussion about our experience will help inform others who also wish to teach group based software development courses.

Categories and Subject Descriptors

K.3.2 [**Computer and Information Science Education**]: Computer science education

General Terms

Design

Keywords

Agile Software Development; Group Work; Evaluation

1. INTRODUCTION

Agile software development methodologies are now ubiquitous within industry. Some methodologies include Scrum and XP which include a set of practices for developing software in an iterative fashion [3, 31]. Understanding these methodologies and how to apply them are important for students to learn before they enter the software industry.

Teaching group based Agile software development projects at university is difficult. There are many aspects that need to be considered carefully when delivering a group based course such as defining a well scoped project, students working effectively together, and students regularly engaging with the customer. In this paper we describe our experience at teaching a grouped based Agile software development project course using a *learn by doing* approach.

SIGCSE'15, March 4–7, 2015, Kansas City, MO, USA.

ACM 978-1-4503-2966-8/15/03 ...$15.00.
http://dx.doi.org/10.1145/2676723.2677284.

2. RELATED WORK

There are a number of courses at universities around the world who run similar types of group based courses using Agile software development methodologies such as Scrum and XP. Each of these courses have their own intricacies and many of the published findings have found Scrum to be an effective methodology to teachx students about Agile.

Pinto et al. [25] identify the Scrum methodology as suitable for student based group projects. They highlight the benefits of Scrum as increased progress visibility, and increased student focus and motivation.

Rico and Sayani [28] report on the result of the adaptation of final year student courses to Agile methods. They find that proper tutoring and coaching of teams with respect to agile methods is a key factor to the success of a project. They also report on studies of Agile methods used in bachelors and masters-level courses from 2003 to 2008.

Schroeder et al. [30] presented the setup, implementation, and results of two software development labs using Scrum in 2010 and 2011. They found the Scrum methodology to be ideal for introducing software processes. They also found using fun challenges for students helped motivated the students and provided a skeleton and development environment for a quick start to a project.

Devedzic and Milenkovic [6] have been teaching Agile software development courses using Scrum and XP for eight years. They present a number of lessons learned over that time period: eliminate major difficulties early, iterations should be rather short, Agile works with Agile students, mentoring is not always effective sometimes it is best for students to discover things on their own, and teams should be small and self organizing.

Kropp and Meier [16] recently experimented with adopting Agile methods for teaching software development. They found that using these methodologies had a positive effect on students and learning outcomes.

El-Khalili [10] propose teaching Agile software development using problem-based learning. The findings of their case study showed that students developed entrepreneurial skills better than traditional methods based on surveys.

Soria et al. [33] have taught a number of courses that use Scrum and an Agile Coach. They conducted a study using the Capability Maturity Model Integration (CMMI) [14] to compare against the Rational Unified Process (RUP) [17]. The results of their study have shown that a balance among Scrum, the Agile Coach role and CMMI is more appealing to students so that they can obtain a higher coverage of CMMI practices than when using CMMI with RUP.

3. COURSE OUTLINE

The aim of this course was to introduce Agile methodologies (Scrum and XP) to students for software development purposes. This included developing software for a real customer over 13 weeks and involved lectures, group assignments, and lab work. Students leaned Agile practices by doing including continuous deployment, acceptance testing, refactoring, unit testing, incremental design, retrospective analysis, iterative planning, pair programming, progress tracking, and lean engineering management. 14 students enrolled in the course, seven undergraduates and seven graduates which formed two separate teams. We expected each student to work at least 10 hours per week on this course.

3.1 Course Projects

Teams could select a project from a list of projects. The theme of the projects were focused on *big data* and *visual analytics*. All of the projects aimed at producing software that would involve a user interface and a database backend. The selected projects are described as follows.

Petroleum Visual Analytics Explorer: Large amounts of data about petroleum has been accumulated over many years, including well locations, well logs, operational and production data. Some analytical methods have been developed to understand the data. Currently there is no software that integrates analytical and visualization functions for petroleum data. The objective of the project was to develop a web-based GIS application to visualize the petroleum data and the analytical results. The customer was a professor in the Department of Geomatics at our University.

Library Book Analytics: The Library contains a large collection of books and other items which can be loaned out to students and staff. The library does not have effective tools for understanding which resources have been issued, used the most and least, and accessed from what campus. The aim of this project was to build a visualization application that allows librarians to explore what resources have been used the most and least and what the history of these items are. The customer was the IT group in the Library within our University.

3.2 Assignments

The teams had to develop software over four iterations. For each iteration the teams were assessed on a number of facets with respect to Agile practices and artifacts. Iterations 1 and 2 lasted two weeks. Iterations 3 and 4 lasted three weeks. Iterations that were longer were weighted more for assessment. At the end of each iteration the teams gave a 30 minute group presentation to the rest of the class, and each individual completed a reflection report based on their experience in the iteration. The final grade for the undergraduates was weighted 40% for the iteration component, 30% group presentations, and 30% reflection reports. For the graduates the weighting of the iterations was 40% of the final grade which included the group presentations and reflection reports. In addition to these assignments the graduates also had to complete a research paper exploring an Agile concept and give a progress presentation on the research paper. The research paper was weighted 30% and progress research presentation 30%.

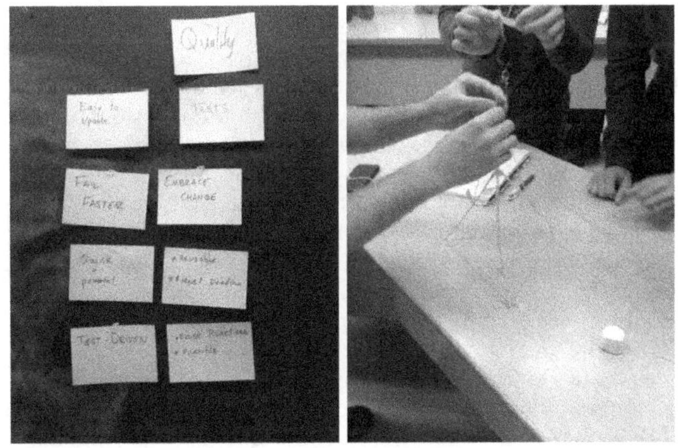

(a) Expectations of the course from students. (b) Marshmallow Challenge: students working in teams.

Figure 1: Course Lectures - interactive exercises.

3.3 Lecture Schedule

There were 25 time slots for lectures. The course involved two lectures and two labs per week. The lectures lasted 75 minutes and the labs 60 minutes. The lectures and labs took place on Tuesday and Thursday each week.

Week one (start of Iteration 0) involved an introduction and welcome to the course. Students were given an overview of the course and what was expected of them. This lecture involved a group exercise where each student wrote down on index cards what they expected to happen during the course and what they hoped to learn from the course. When the students had written their ideas down on the index cards they put them on the black board. Once all the ideas were on the black board students then discussed them and grouped the index cards into categories (see Figure 1(a)).

Week two involved the students participating in the Marshmallow Challenge[1] where they worked in teams to complete an instructive design exercise that encourages teams to experience simple but profound lessons in collaboration, innovation and creativity. The task is eighteen minutes long where teams must build the tallest free-standing structure out of 20 sticks of spaghetti, one yard of tape, one yard of string, and one marshmallow which needs to be on top of the structure (see Figure 1(b)). Another lecture presented an overview of Agile methodologies where the Agile Manifesto was introduced, core strategies of Agile, and an overview of each of the Scrum and XP methods.

Week three introduced release and iteration planning. It was important the students understood what these planning activities were as they are fundamental to Agile. For release planning the emphasis was put on creating user stories, grouping user stories into epics and themes, and prioritizing the stories on an Agile wall with the customer. For iteration planning user stories were described and how they could be broken down into tasks and how they could be estimated.

Week four (start of Iteration 1) introduced progress tracking and knowledge sharing. The purpose for tracking work effort was described and why it is important for all team members to see what is happening on a project. A num-

[1] http://marshmallowchallenge.com/

ber of progress tracking techniques were presented such as Scrum meetings, Agile walls, burn down charts, code coverage tools, and software metrics visualization tools. For knowledge sharing the importance of communication amongst team members and the customer was explained. Various communication techniques were presented such as bug tracking tools and collaborative tools like wikis. To learn about the essence of communication and requirements gathering an exercise was given where students shared messages amongst each other and played three roles. Analysts described the requirements on paper. Messengers carried the requirements on notes from analysts to developers and back, but were not allowed to communicate in any way with other groups. Developers implemented the specification based on the notes.

Week five introduced version and configuration management. Software versioning and configuration management were described, the benefits of continuous integration were highlighted, and some version control tools were presented. The second lecture teams gave the Iteration 1 group presentation and demonstration.

Week six (start of iteration 2) introduced XP practices notably pair programming, test driven development (TDD), and refactoring [2, 11, 34]. Pair programming was described including the benefits for programming in pairs, what roles were involved, how the process works, different options for pairing, and the need for regularly rotating roles. Students performed a pairing exercise[2] where they had a list of a set of simple tasks to complete like writing down information or reading out information. The students performed the task in pairs and switched roles according to their strengths. The aim of the exercise was to convey some of the feeling of what it's like to perform pair programming. For software testing TDD was described and why it is useful for Agile teams, unit testing was described [22], and an empirical study was presented which outlines the benefits of testing [19].

Week seven introduced quality assurance [12] and example driven development. Some techniques such as Framework for Integrated Tests [23] were covered and an empirical study on executable acceptance tests was presented [21]. Students also gave the Iteration 2 group presentation.

Week eight (start of iteration 3) introduced process improvements and Agile retrospectives. Traditional models such as the Capability Maturity Model (CMM) [14] was presented, along with project retrospectives [15], and Agile retrospectives [5]. The importance of retrospectives was explained, what is involved when performing this activity, and how to perform a retrospective was described.

Week nine students worked in teams and performed an Agile retrospective for the previous iteration based on one of the following plans from the retrospective wiki[3]. Figure 2 shows one of the teams performing their retrospective. The other lecture during this week covered a number of papers presenting research about empirical studies on Agile software development. These papers and references included methods for qualitative research [4], the success of Agile methods [35], literature review on agile software development [8], comparative analysis of job satisfaction [20], the role of the customer on Agile teams [18], and self organizing teams [13]. These papers were useful to point the graduate students at to help them with their research papers.

[2]http://xp123.com/articles/pair-practice/

[3]http://retrospectivewiki.org/

Figure 2: A team performing a retrospective with index cards grouped by different categories and a large display screen for additional information.

Week 10 introduced scaling of Agile projects and distributed Agile projects. Ways in which teams could scale projects and how projects could be modified so that they scale for larger teams was presented[4]. The challenges in scaling Agile teams was discussed including coordinating work across teams, integrating work across teams, and maintaining technical integrity of the system. Ways in which teams can be distributed when they work on projects across different buildings, cities, and countries was presented [9]. The challenges with distributed teams were discussed including communication, collaboration, integrating work into one working system, and maintaining successful feedback loops with the customer. Some empirical studies on distributed Agile software development were presented [7, 32]. Students also gave the Iteration 3 group presentation.

Week 11 (start of iteration 4) teams performed an Agile retrospective for iteration 3 and began iteration planning. The second lecture was on Lean Software Development [26, 27]. The principles of Lean were covered and an overview was given on the early history based on processes from Toyota [24]. Students also performed an exercise about creating invitation cards[5]. The exercise taught them that single piece flow is faster than batch and queue process. This exercise led into presenting Lean Software Development and Kanban [1].

Week 12 followed on from the Lean concept and involved watching a video on Lean Startup [29]. The second lecture of this week was the start of the graduate student presentations, where four students presented the progress they had made on their research papers. Each presentation was 15 mins long with up to 5 minutes for questions and change of speaker. The undergraduates were allowed to work on the their projects instead of attending the lecture.

Week 13 involved the remainder of the graduate student research progress presentations and the final group presentations delivered to a larger invited department audience.

[4]http://www.estherderby.com/ and http://www.ambysoft.com/

[5]http://tastycupcakes.org/2009/06/were-having-a-party/

3.4 Labs

Each team had two one hour official labs per week. The teaching assistant (TA) for the course managed the labs and gave technical assistance where required such as use of tools. The labs took place in the computer labs where students were encouraged to pair program and work on tasks from an iteration. The labs were scheduled before the lectures took place. Hence it made a solid couple of hours dedicated to the course. The undergraduate students had their lab two hours before the lecture. During the labs teams had their daily scrum meeting where the TA acted as the Scrum master for the teams. The customer was encouraged to attend these official lab hours to help with the project where needed.

3.5 Assessment

Grading individuals in team based projects is hard. It was important that our assessment criteria was fair on all individuals and that it was clearly understood by all students. We created a rubric based on the content of the lecture material which was used to assess the students for each iteration. Grades were given for each artifact or process. If the students exceeded expectations for that artifact or process they received a 5, if they met expectations they received a 3, and if they did not meet expectations they received a 0. In between grades 2 and 4 were used if students were on the border between the other grades. Each student was given the rubric so they knew what they were being assessed on before the time period. The assessment period for most activities took place in the lab, except for the attendance at lectures, group presentation, and reflection reports. The reflection reports helped complement some of the assessment of the activities.

For lectures we kept track of which students attended. We actively engaged the students during the lectures and encouraged them into dialogs so that they understood the ideas and concepts being presented. We reinforced the ideas by asking students to report their experience at performing some of the processes or to discuss how they were progressing with artifacts. If students attended all lectures and engaged with the rest of the class they exceeded expectations.

During the labs the teams performed Scrum meetings. It was important that all team members were present and followed the rules of a Scrum meeting. We observed these Scrum meetings in action and offered suggestions on how to improve them each week. If the Scrum meetings were running effectively students exceeded expectations.

We monitored how the students engaged with the customers through meetings and online contact. If there were many customer meetings and the customer got involved in the design and coding of the software then the students exceeded expectations.

We regularly checked the code the students produced via commits to the version control system to see that regular commits were happening and that all students were contributing to the project. If there were regular commits and team members were committing then students exceeded expectations. Essentially this assessment component was to make sure that the students were regularly making commits and continuously integrating their software.

We observed the product backlog to make sure that the user stories had been grouped into epics and themes. We expected the product backlog to be a part of the Story Board whether it was physical or digital. We observed how tasks were being tracked on the story board and if enough detail was being added.

For the release plan we wanted to see if the students had thought about the dependencies of the user stories and if they had discussed with the customer prioritization of the stories for each iteration. For the iteration plan we wanted to see if the tasks for the user stories had been described up front and in enough detail, and had estimates for how much time they think it would take to complete a task.

For documentation we checked the students code to ensure they were using established practices and that the team was consistently following the same style. We wanted to see if they had diagrams to explain the architecture of the system to their customers, charts to show the teams progress, and use of any other project reporting tools. We were also looking to see if they did paper prototypes before they developed different aspects of their systems.

For testing we examined the unit tests the students wrote. We did walk throughs of the test and got the students to explain the details of the tests out aloud. We checked to see if they used any code coverage tools and how much of the code was covered by the tests.

For each iteration the students gave a group presentation. Each presentation was graded and we looked to see how clearly and effectively the teams described the key issues of the project, target users, how the customer was involved, release and iteration plans, user stories, tasks, charts to illustrate work effort, pair programming activities, testing of the software, and demonstrating their software in action. In order to give individual grades for this part of the assessment each student on the team was encouraged to present some aspect of the project.

The reflection reports were required to be completed by each team member at the conclusion of each iteration. The purpose of the report was for the students to reflect what they had done in the past iteration and how they could improve the next iteration. In the report we looked to see the contributions made by each student on the project and what all team members did. The report was used as an indicator to confirm that all the students were consistently stating the same activities. The report also gave the opportunity for students to raise any issues about the course.

4. DISCUSSION

There were a number of aspects from this course which we would like to discuss based on our experience and feedback given through student evaluations. Some aspects will help to make a course of this nature be more effective.

Lectures. There were 25 lecture slots for the course which required a lot of material for the students to take in. We used a variety of methods to teach the material such as group exercises, lecture slides, case studies from industry, academic papers on Agile, and videos from the Internet. A number of students found that the material did not necessarily help them with the course assignments and that some of the material was not as engaging. It is hard to accommodate all learning needs, but we tried to use a variety of different methods. Some students had learnt some of the material from previous courses such as testing and version control. Given the course content, the size of the class, and different levels of students (undergraduates and graduates) it is hard to keep all students engaged at once. The students all enjoyed and engaged with the interactive exercises that took place during the lectures. We did not provide the lecture schedule up front at the beginning of the course which some students would have preferred.

To address the amount of lectures we would like to limit the number of lectures per week to one lecture and allow the students more time to work on the assignments so that they can become more productive. The extra hour dedicated to the lecture could be swapped into an hour of official lab time instead. For the lectures that contained no exercises we would do our best to incorporate more learning by doing exercises as required. We would in future provide a detailed lecture schedule up front before the course began.

Customer Involvement. It was difficult at the start of the course to convince both the customer and students of both projects that high customer involvement was needed. This required the lecturer to meet one on one with the customer to explain what Agile methods are and the importance of having weekly meetings and getting involved with the design of the applications. The undergraduate team were slow to adjust at involving the customer. Eventually they scheduled customer requirements meetings with the lead customer and got her graduate students to attend the labs each week to help with the smaller design decisions. The graduates only met the customer once a week but this proved to be sufficient for their team and their customer was happy with the output produced.

To address the lack of customer involvement at the beginning of the course we would invite the customer along to one of the earlier lectures during iteration zero so that the students can get their contact details earlier. We would make it mandatory for customer meetings to happen each week and make sure that the customers attended some of the lab programming times.

Scope Creep. It was hard for students to realize how long user stories and tasks would take to complete due to their lack of experience. Their estimation skills improved but it was still a high learning curve and they fully did not master this activity during the course. Their release planning and iteration planning was not clearly defined at the beginning of each iteration which caused teams to underestimate how long tasks actually took to complete. Quite often at the end of each iteration there were still user stories and tasks not completed by both teams. To help remedy the scope creep we introduced lean management and Kanban at the beginning of Iteration 4. Applying Kanban techniques helped prioritize the tasks and user stories that needed to be completed. By using Kanban the students could see how they could more efficiently use their time rather than spending effort constantly task switching.

To prevent scope creep we would be more stringent at Scrum meetings about what tasks students are working on. We could introduce Lean and Kanban earlier in the lecture schedule so that the students understand completing a task before moving onto the next one is more efficient.

Work Load. There was a lot of material to cover in the course and the projects themselves were quite demanding based on customer requirements. The students had to learn new technologies then learn how to apply them to deliver working software for their customer. We expected students to spend at least 10 hours per week on the course. Due to the students lack of experience at estimating and tracking of tasks this was not as accurate as we expected. Some student's reported working just over 10 hours but were doing more like 20–30 hours for a few weeks. For example the first three iterations students were not tracking all the additional time they spent learning new technologies and setting up their development environments. This caused some frustration for the students and made it hard for the lecturer to understand where some of the issues were attributed to.

To prevent work load issues we would be more stringent at the beginning of the course about tracking time for all tasks students worked on. We would have more emphasis on the tracking of information about tasks, get students to indicate in the Scrum meetings how many hours they had been spending, and look more closely at the reflection reports.

Assessment. For the first two iterations the assessment rubric was not given early enough to the students, hence some of the students were worried about how they were getting assessed. Some of the students did not quite understand the differences between some of the values on the assessment rubric. For example they did not understand what grades 2) and 4) meant. In hindsight it would have been more effective to only have a three point scale and remove grades 2) and 4) for each artifact and process. Given the time it took to review the reflection reports it was not possible to give immediate feedback. This usually took up to a week after the iteration had ended. It would have been more effective to give faster feedback which the students could utilize much earlier in the next iteration.

To accommodate faster feedback we could reduce the size of the reflection reports and not always assess all artifacts and processes for each iteration. We could make it clearer on the course outline more details about the course assessment. We could distribute the information about the assessment rubrics in a more timely manner.

Team Work. The teams were supposed to be self organizing [13]. The graduate team did a good job of organizing themselves early and managed to sort out the tasks amongst themselves evenly. The undergraduates took a little bit more effort as there were some personality conflicts and they were not as open and honest with each other as is required to be successful on Agile teams. Sometimes the undergraduate students failed to turn up to team meetings which showed a lack of commitment. To address the issues with the undergraduates we arranged a special meeting to create a Team Agreement where the students would abide by rules made up to suit their team needs. Applying this technique made the team more coherent and productive for the last two iterations.

To make teams more effective we could potentially put more assessment criteria around mandatory coding sessions so that they turn up. This could, however, be more arduous for the lecturer and TA than required. Ultimately it should be up to the students to make the effort to work together.

Level of Students. The course had both undergraduate and graduate students. This proved challenging with respect to sorting out teams at the beginning of the course and assessing the students during the course based on different grading schemes. Given the even split of students (7 undergraduates and 7 graduates) this subsequently made it easier to group the students into two different project teams.

To address the level of students in the course we would not run a course again with both undergraduates and graduates in the same class. Instead we would make this course only for undergraduates and likely have a reading course on Agile methods and empirical studies for graduates.

5. CONCLUSIONS

Agile software development methodologies (e.g. Scrum and XP) are now ubiquitous within the software development industry. Understanding what these practices and techniques are and how to apply them are important for computer science students to learn before they enter the software development industry.

In this experience report we described our approach at teaching a grouped based Agile software development project course. The students successfully developed visual analytics applications for exploration of petroleum data and online library resources. Based on our experience we found that there was too many lectures, that the customer needed to be involved more, and some teams had scope creep which had to be managed appropriately. Due to the scope creep the work load for some students was unbalanced within the team. The assessment criteria involved too many components and the feedback on the assessment was not fast enough for the students requirements. One team suffered from not being very well organized and had personality conflicts.

In the future we would not have two courses mixed together. By describing our experience at teaching a group based Agile software development project course we hope others can benefit from our efforts for their future courses.

Acknowledgments

Thanks to Tedd Hellmann for being an effective teaching assistant. Thanks to the students for participating in the course. Thanks to Jennifer Ferreira, Angela Martin, Siva Dorairaj, Rashina Hoda, David Pearce, James Noble, and Robert Biddle for advice and feedback. Thanks to Mitacs Elevate program for funding.

6. REFERENCES

[1] D. Anderson. *Kanban: Successful Evolutionary Change for Your Technology Business.* Blue Hole Press, 2010.

[2] K. Beck. *Test Driven Development: By Example.* Addison Wesley, 2002.

[3] K. Beck. *Extreme Programming Explained: Embrace Change.* Addison Wesley, 2004.

[4] J. Creswell. *Research Design: Qualitative, Quantitative, and Mixed Methods Approaches.* SAGE Publications, 2008.

[5] E. Derby and D. Larsen. *Agile Retrospectives – Making Good Teams Great.* The Pragmatic Bookshelf, 2006.

[6] V. Devedzic and S. Milenkovic. Teaching Agile software development: A case study. *IEEE Transactions on Education*, 54(2):273–278, May 2011.

[7] S. Dorairaj and J. Noble. Agile software development with distributed teams: Agility, distribution and trust. In *Proceedings of the International Conference on Agile*, pages 1–10. IEEE, 2013.

[8] T. Dybå and T. Dingsøyr. Empirical studies of Agile software development: A systematic review. *Inf. Softw. Technol.*, 50(9-10):833–859, Aug. 2008.

[9] J. Eckstein. *Agile Software Development with Distributed Teams Perfect.* Dorset House, 2010.

[10] N. El-Khalili. Teaching Agile software engineering using problem-based learning. *Int. J. Inf. Commun. Technol. Educ.*, 9(3):1–12, July 2013.

[11] M. Fowler, K. Beck, J. Brant, W. Opdyke, and D. Roberts. *Refactoring: Improving the Design of Existing Code.* Addison Wesley, 1999.

[12] R. L. Glass. *Facts and Fallacies of Software Engineering.* Addison Wesley, 2002.

[13] R. Hoda, J. Noble, and S. Marshall. Self-organizing roles on Agile software development teams. *IEEE Transactions on Software Engineering*, 39(3):422–444, 2013.

[14] W. Humphrey. *Managing the software process.* Addison Wesley, 1989.

[15] N. Kerth. *Project Retrospectives: A Handbook for Team Reviews.* Dorset House, 2001.

[16] M. Kropp and A. Meier. Teaching Agile software development at university level: Values, management, and craftsmanship. In *Proceedings of the Conference on Software Engineering Education and Training (CSEET)*, pages 179–188. IEEE, May 2013.

[17] P. Kruchten. *The Rational Unified Process: An Introduction.* Addison Wesley, 2003.

[18] A. Martin, R. Biddle, and J. Noble. The XP customer team: A grounded theory. In *Proceedings of the International Conference on Agile*, pages 57–64. IEEE, 2009.

[19] G. Melnik. *Empirical Analysis of Acceptance Test Driven Development.* PhD thesis, Department of Computer Science, University of Calgary, 2007.

[20] G. Melnik and F. Maurer. Comparative analysis of job satisfaction in agile and non-agile software development teams. In *Proceedings of the International Conference on Agile Processes in Software Engineering and Extreme Programming (XP)*, pages 32–42. Springer, 2006.

[21] G. Melnik, F. Maurer, and M. Chiasson. Executable acceptance tests for communicating business requirements: Customer perspective. In *Proceedings of the International Conference on Agile*, pages 35–46. IEEE, 2006.

[22] G. Meszaros. *xUnit Test Patterns: Refactoring Test Code.* Addison Wesley, 2007.

[23] R. Mugridge and W. Cunningham. *Fit for Developing Software: Framework for Integrated Tests.* Prentice Hall, 2005.

[24] T. Ohno. *Toyota Production System: Beyond Large-Scale Production.* Productivity Press, 1988.

[25] L. Pinto, R. Rosa, C. Pacheco, C. Xavier, R. Barreto, V. Lucena, M. Caxias, and C. Figueiredo. On the use of Scrum for the management of practcal projects in graduate courses. In *Proceedings of the Frontiers in Education Conference (FIE)*, pages 1–6. IEEE, 2009.

[26] M. Poppendieck and T. Poppendieck. *Lean Software Development: An Agile Toolkit.* Addison Wesley, 2003.

[27] M. Poppendieck and T. Poppendieck. *Implementing Lean Software Development.* Addison Wesley, 2007.

[28] D. Rico and H. Sayani. Use of Agile methods in software engineering education. In *Proceedings of the International Conference on Agile*, pages 174–179, 2009.

[29] E. Ries. *The Lean Startup: How Today's Entrepreneurs Use Continuous Innovation to Create Radically Successful Businesses.* Crown Business, 2011.

[30] A. Schroeder, A. Klarl, P. Mayer, and C. Kroiss. Teaching Agile software development through lab courses. In *Proceedings of the Global Engineering Education Conference (EDUCON)*, pages 1–10. IEEE, 2012.

[31] K. Schwaber and M. Beedle. *Agile Software Development with Scrum.* Prentice Hall, 2001.

[32] H. Sharp, R. Giuffrida, and G. Melnik. Information flow within a dispersed agile team: A distributed cognition perspective. In *Proceedings of the International Conference on Agile Processes in Software Engineering and Extreme Programming (XP)*, pages 62–76, 2012.

[33] A. Soria, M. Campo, and G. Rodriguez. Improving software engineering teaching by introducing Agile management. In *Proceedings of the Argentine Symposium on Software Engineering (ASSE)*, pages 215–229, 2012.

[34] L. Williams and R. Kessler. *Pair Programming Illuminated.* Addison Wesley, 2002.

[35] C. Zannier, G. Melnik, and F. Maurer. On the success of empirical studies in the international conference on software engineering. In *Proceedings of the International Conference on Software Engineering (ICSE)*, pages 341–350. ACM, 2006.

An Experience Report: Using Mobile Development To Teach Software Design

Jennifer Campbell
Dept. of Computer Science
University of Toronto
campbell@cs.toronto.edu

Anya Tafliovich
Dept. of Computer and Mathematical Sciences
University of Toronto Scarborough
atafliovich@utsc.utoronto.ca

ABSTRACT

We report on our experience with incorporating Android software development in a second-year software design course. Our primary course goals are twofold: (1) teach principles of object-oriented design, and provide students with an opportunity to apply these principles in designing and developing Java programs, and (2) introduce students to the basics of software engineering with a team project that follows a Scrum-like software development process. In this report, we describe a team-based Android application development project that achieves our teaching goals, helps motivate student learning, and increases student satisfaction with the course. We provide an overview of our approach, outcomes, and student feedback. We also describe lessons learnt by the instructors and identify promising directions for improvements.

Categories and Subject Descriptors

K.3.2 [**Computers and Education**]: Computer and Information Science Education—*Computer Science Education*

Keywords

mobile computing; object-oriented software design; motivating students

1. INTRODUCTION

Mobile devices are ubiquitous. According to [9], in 2013 more than one fifth of the world's population owned a smartphone, and a greater proportion of the population owned a smartphone (22%) than a personal computer (20%). Along with the widespread adoption of mobile devices there has also been a surge in mobile software development. The word *app*, an abbreviation for the phrase "software application", was so popular in 2010 that it was named "Word of the Year" by the American Dialect Society [2].

Along with the growth in popularity of mobile devices, there has been an increase in post-secondary courses that teach mobile software development. Some courses focus primarily on mobile development itself, while others use it as a context to teach a variety of other topics [4].

In this paper, we report on our experience with incorporating Android software development in a second-year software design course. Our primary course goals are twofold:

1. teach principles of object-oriented design, and provide students with an opportunity to apply these principles in designing and developing Java programs, and

2. introduce students to the basics of software engineering with a team project that follows a Scrum-like software development process.

Since a priori student interest in the core course topics is not always high, we expected that incorporating mobile development into the course would help motivate student learning and increase the students' satisfaction with the course. In this report we describe a team-based Android application development project that both achieves our teaching goals and increases students' motivation and enjoyment of the course. We provide an overview of our approach, outcomes, and student feedback. We also describe lessons learnt by the instructors and identify promising directions for improvements.

2. RELATED WORK

In recent years, the widespread adoption of mobile devices has prompted more post-secondary institutions to offer courses in mobile computing. Burd et al. [4] point out the tremendous impact that mobile computing has had on students' lives and the opportunity that educators have to take advantage of students' interest in mobile. In their survey of courses that incorporate mobile computing, they found that post-secondary institutions offered courses of two types: standalone courses and courses that use mobile computing as context for teaching other topics. They also found that mobile software development was used for outreach initiatives.

As examples of standalone courses, Sung and Samuel [14] offer two upper-year mobile computing electives, with one focused on the implementation of a mobile application and the other on the design of mobile applications. Fenwick et al. [7] describe upper-year standalone courses that center on Android development.

The course under consideration in this paper falls into the category of courses that use mobile development as the context for teaching other topics. There are a variety of

SIGCSE'15, March 4–7, 2015, Kansas City, MO, USA.

ACM 978-1-4503-2966-8/15/03 ...$15.00.
http://dx.doi.org/10.1145/2676723.2677307.

courses that fall into this category, including CS1 courses [12, 5, 16, 10] and upper-year courses on topics ranging from human computer interaction [11] to games [6] to security [8].

Similarly to our course, Riley [13] employs Android software development in his course as the context for teaching Java as a second programming language and uses a team project to introduce software engineering concepts. The main teaching objective of that course is for students to become competent Java programmers, and three of the 14 weeks of the course are devoted to teaching Android development. Although Riley's course [13] and ours overlap significantly in topics taught, the emphasis differs. Our course focuses more heavily on principles of object-oriented analysis and design, as well as basics of software modelling, while Riley puts more emphasis on teaching a software development process, presentation skills, and on more advanced topics such as multithreading, sensors, networking, databases, and graphics.

3. THE COURSE

The course under consideration is a second-year Computer Science course taught at a large, North American, research-intensive, public university. This course is the third programming course in the standard sequence; CS1 (objects-late) and CS2 (introduction to object-oriented programming and to data structures), both taught in Python, are prerequisites. This course introduces the Java programming language and the overarching theme of the course is software design. Course topics include version control and advanced IDE usage, object-oriented software design, modelling, unit testing, design patterns, and refactoring.

The primary course teaching goals are twofold: (1) teach principles of object-oriented design, and provide students with an opportunity to apply these principles in designing and developing Java programs, and (2) introduce students to the basics of software engineering with a team project that follows a Scrum-like software development process.

Anecdotal evidence suggests that although students do not always immediately value learning abstract concepts, such as object-oriented design principles, many value a practical and popular skill such as mobile development straightaway. In the interest of fulfilling our teaching goals while providing motivation to our students, we introduced mobile development and a team project that involves developing an Android application into the course. We used Android as the context for teaching our main course topics and as a tactic for motivating students.

In Fall 2013, this course was taught on two campuses in a total of four sections. The total peak enrolment was 575. According to a survey of students with 340 respondents, the gender breakdown was 24% female and 76% male. Of the respondents, 85% reported being CS majors.

The course is twelve weeks long, delivered through two 50-minute lecture hours and one 50-minute lab each week.

3.1 Assessments

The majority of coursework was done individually, with the following break-down: labs (5%), three auto-marked exercises (8%), one assignment (8%), a midterm test (10%), and a final exam (40%). One of the essential components of the course is a multi-phase team software development project that was completed in teams of four. The project was worth 29% of the course grade.

3.2 Introduction of Mobile Software Development

To prepare students for the Android development tasks required in the project, mobile software development was introduced as a new course topic. In the middle of the term, an overview of Android software development was presented during one 50-minute lecture hour. The primary content of that lecture was a live demo of the development of a very simple Android application. After lecture, the instructors provided students with a written summary of the steps involved in the development of that application, along with the code.

Approximately two weeks later, the instructors spent another lecture demonstrating the development of a more complex application. The code used for the back-end of this application had previously been developed in lecture, so the students were already familiar with it. In the following lecture, we briefly revisited that example and discussed the pros and cons of the chosen design.

All told, approximately two hours of lecture were spent on Android software development. Because this topic was added to the course without removing any other topics, that was all the time that could be afforded. With only this minimal introduction to Android development, students embarked on the project. Many teams did additional learning on their own and delved much deeper in to the Android API than the instructors had anticipated or expected.

4. THE PROJECT

The team project is a major component of the course. Although students had the option of doing some pair programming in first year, this is the first required team software development project in which students are participating. The department offers several courses that involve team projects. However, the course described here is the only required course in our curriculum that does so; hence, for some students this is the only team project that they will complete in an academic setting.

The project was divided into three phases and spanned seven weeks of the semester. The first phase was completed in self-selected pairs, and the last two phases in teams of four that were formed by the instructors by merging two self-selected pairs.

4.1 Team Formation

Instructors used the CATME SMARTER Teamwork system [1] to collect survey data and form teams of four by merging the self-selected pairs. The survey data included information about gender, availability schedule, willingness to participate in team activities on weekends, the number of hours the student intended to work on the course outside of class, and the grade in the prerequisite course.

The team formation criteria included gender (ensuring that women were not outnumbered on a team), personal schedules (maximizing common unscheduled times), GPA (grouping by dissimilar GPAs), and intended time commitment (grouping by similar commitment levels). Because the pairs were self-selected, the degree to which the team formation criteria could be achieved was constrained, but we ensured that at least the gender criterion was met for all groups.

4.2 Project Phases

The first phase of the project — the design phase — was completed in the self-selected teams of two students and took one week. All teams were provided with the same fictional client request to build a basic Android application for triage in a hospital emergency room. The client request included a feature list that outlined the application's requirements. For this phase of the project, teams completed two main tasks. The first was to prepare a Class Responsibility Collaboration (CRC) Model [3] and the second was to write a design description that described data structures and file formats to be used by the application. Since most students are not yet familiar with database systems, they used flat files to store persistent data.

The second phase of the project lasted three weeks and the students worked in their newly formed teams of four. With each pair having developed their software design in the previous phase, the new teams' first task was to merge their two designs, by adopting the best features of each or choosing the better one. This activity provided an opportunity for the students to evaluate and discuss another team's design, and to appreciate the differences in possible object-oriented design solutions. As a team of four, they prepared a new CRC Model to reflect the updated design. In this phase, students also began implementation of the Android application. The teams were given a subset of the original feature list to implement and that set of features was required to be working by the end of the phase. Teams were evaluated on their CRC model, the functionality and usability of the application, documentation, and coding style. In addition, the teams were evaluated on how well they used the version control system and followed the prescribed software development process that is described in Section 4.3.

The third phase of the project also lasted three weeks and was completed in the same teams of four. The teams were given a set of features to add to their existing application. To begin, the teams revisited their design to incorporate the new features and submitted updated CRC Models. One of the goals of this exercise was for students to see how robust and extensible their original design was and to have a chance to improve it. Each team also refactored and added to the Android application. The evaluation criteria were similar to the previous phase.

4.3 Software Development Process

Although software engineering is not the primary topic in this course, we introduced a simplified, Scrum-like software development process that teams were to follow and on which they were evaluated. Our aim was two-fold:

(1) we used this as an opportunity to foreshadow the third-year software engineering course that involves an agile software development project, and

(2) since most students are novices at working on team software development projects, we provided a structure intended to keep teams on track and guide them to successful project outcomes.

In phases two and three, we required teams to hold two types of meetings (similar to the Scrum model):

- *planning meetings*: held once in the beginning and once mid-way through the project phase. During a planning meeting, the team will (a) decide on a set of tasks the team will accomplish before the next planning meeting, (b) decide who will perform which tasks, and (c) if it is a mid-way meeting, recap on the current state of the project.
- *status meetings*: held at least once a week. During these meetings, each member will report on (a) what (s)he has accomplished since the last meeting, (b) what (s)he plans to accomplish before the next meeting, and (c) if there are any problems or obstacles that prevent him/her from making progress.

Teams were required to submit meeting minutes throughout the project, by committing them to the team's version control repository. As part of the marking scheme, the state of the project described in those minutes was compared to the actual state of the repository at that time. We expected this setup to promote regular use of the version control repository throughout the project phase. It was evaluated by the TAs at the end of each phase and generally served its intended purpose well.

4.4 Peer and Self Evaluations

After each of the three project phases, students completed peer and self evaluations using the CATME system. Using a scale from 1 to 5, each student ranked themselves and their teammates on their (1) contributions to the team's work, and (2) interactions with teammates. Additionally, students could provide comments to their instructor about the project phase or individual members of their team. Based on these criteria, the CATME software calculated an *adjustment factor* for each student. The instructors then used this adjustment factor (capped at 1.05) to calculate the student's individual grade for a project phase as follows:

$$\textit{team grade} \times 0.8 + \textit{adjustment factor} \times \textit{team grade} \times 0.2$$

Investigation into students' preferred breakdown of team project evaluation into team and individual components is explored in [15].

4.5 Role of Teaching Assistants

Starting in phase two, each team was assigned a teaching assistant (TA). The TAs were responsible for providing guidance to their teams during tutorial and on an as-needed basis outside of tutorial, and for marking the team's submission. Having the same TA mark phases two and three of the team's project helped evaluate the evolution of the team's application design. In particular, in the final phase, the TA could check whether design issues identified in the previous phase has been addressed. In addition, it helped promote the mentor-mentee relationship between the team and its TA and help foster the atmosphere of teamwork and collaboration. To ensure consistency in the grading criteria used by the TAs, the instructors provided highly detailed evaluation rubrics for each project phase and held meetings with the TAs to discuss the evaluation.

5. RESULTS

Introducing Android software development into a content-heavy second year course was challenging, but we consider the outcome to be a success. Here we report on project pass rates and give an overview of the student feedback provided through course evaluations.

5.1 Project pass rates

By the end of the project, nearly every team had produced a working mobile application. On Campus A, 96% of students earned a passing grade on the project, and on campus B, the pass rate was 89%. For comparison, the pass rates on the Java programming assignment that was completed individually were 90% and 89%, on the two campuses, respectively. As measured by pass rates, the Android project is as achievable as traditional work in the course.

5.2 Course evaluations

The standard university course evaluations were administered in all sections of the course. Here, we report on the quantitative results of these course evaluations.

A summary of course evaluation scores (with instructor-specific questions omitted) appears in Table 1. Because this is an experience report and no formal evaluation of the course was administered, there is no clear baseline for comparison. To put these scores in context, we compare the scores for our course with the average scores in our departments this semester and with the average scores for the previous three offerings of this course (a total of four sections) on Campus A. Due to privacy restrictions, the scores for previous offerings on Campus B are not available at this time. We acknowledge that the comparison between semesters is not ideal, particularly since the differences between the offerings were not restricted to the introduction of Android development. In particular, on both campuses the course instructors did not teach any of the previous offerings used for comparison.

As shown in the evaluation data in Table 1, students were satisfied with this semester's offering of the course and the course evaluation scores were above the departmental averages. Students from this term were significantly more positive than in the past when asked about whether the coursework improved their understanding of the course material and whether the coursework provided opportunity for them to demonstrate an understanding of the course material. Since the largest part of coursework was the Android project, we view this student feedback as evidence for success of our initiative.

Students also found the workload compared to other courses to be slightly higher this semester than in the past. Promisingly, despite the fact that students from this semester perceived workload to be higher, they responded more positively than in the past when asked whether they would recommend this course to other students and also rated the quality of their learning experience higher.

5.3 Student comments

The standard university course evaluations provide students with an opportunity to comment on the course, and a number of students wrote comments related to Android development and the project. Here we summarize the student feedback from the written sections of the course evaluations.

5.3.1 *Course material was relevant*

One way in which the Android development was positively received was in its perceived relevance by students. Some of the positive student comments on Android mentioned relevance to the "real-world", their future work opportunities, and their personal interests. For example,

- I really enjoyed this course as it gave me the knowledge of programming in java and also preliminary knowledge in android app design. Both of these concepts would probably be used in my future, so it's very applicable to my life.
- The course was interesting, even more to help learning android programming, applying the knowledge to a famous field of nowadays.

Anecdotally, some students also reported continuing to work on the project or developing other Android applications after the course had ended. As well, some students felt confident enough in their skills to list Android development on their resumes.

5.3.2 *Too much independent learning required*

One complaint that students had was that they were required to learn some aspects of Android development on their own. With limited lecture time available, the instructors were only able to provide a minimal introduction to the topic and some students felt that they needed to do too much independent learning:

- Android was thrown into the fray, and was given only 90 minutes of class time, which is not enough.
- We were essentially teaching ourselves how to program Android. There was a lot of material that we needed to know for the project that we did not learn in class.

Interestingly, overcoming the learning curve and producing successful projects gave some students a great sense of pride.

Although we value the students' sense of accomplishment, we did not intend for the students to do quite as much independent learning as they reported doing. As discussed in the next section, we aim to improve the delivery of the material in order to reduce the amount of independent learning required.

6. LESSONS LEARNED

Following the initial offering, the instructors concluded that the addition of Android development was a positive change. To further improve the course, we plan to make several adjustments based on student feedback and on our experiences teaching the course.

6.1 Help students get started

Mobile computing has a steep learning curve. With limited time for teaching Android in lecture, the introduction to mobile software development was fast-paced. As a result, when the teams began to implement their applications in the second phase of the project, some required significant support from the instructor. To reduce this learning curve and to better support students, we will add a 50 minute for-credit laboratory session during which students will work in pairs to develop a very basic Android application. This will move students' first attempt at Android development into a laboratory setting during which they will be supported by TAs. It will replace an optional lab in which team meetings and consultation with the TAs took place, which is a trade-off that the instructors believe to be worthwhile.

Table 1: Course Evaluation Scores

	Scale	Campus A Current term Sec 1 (n=95)	Campus A Current term Sec 2 (n=61)	Campus A Current term Dept avg	Campus A Past 3 terms (n=193)	Campus B Current term Sec 1 (n=56)	Campus B Current term Sec 2 (n=20)	Campus B Current term Dept avg
I found the course intellectually stimulating.	5–A great deal 4–Mostly 3–Moderately 2–Somewhat 1–Not at all	4.0	4.1	3.8	3.45	3.9	4.3	3.7
The course provided me with a deeper understanding of the subject matter.		4.3	4.1	4.0	3.6	4.2	4.2	3.8
Course projects, assignments, tests and/or exams improved my understanding of the course material.		4.1	4.3	4.0	3.725	4.0	4.0	3.9
Course projects, assignments, tests and/or exams provided opportunity for me to demonstrate an understanding of the course material.		4.3	4.2	4.0	3.625	4.2	4.2	3.9
Overall, the quality of my learning experience in this course was...	5–Excellent 4–Very Good 3–Good 2–Fair 1–Poor	3.9	4.0	3.6	3.2	3.9	4.1	3.5
Compared to other courses, the workload for this course was...	5–Very Heavy 4–Heavy 3–Average 2–Light 1–Very Light	3.5	3.6	3.5	3.3	3.7	3.7	3.5
I would recommend this course to other students.	5–Strongly 4–Mostly 3–Moderately 2–Somewhat 1–Not at all	4.2	4.3	3.7	3.45	3.7	3.9	3.4

6.2 Invest in TA training

Since mobile software development is typically not a part of our TAs' post-secondary education, it was a challenge to find qualified TAs for this course. Consequently, some TAs with little or no Android development experience were hired and they were expected to become familiar with Android development through self-study. In addition, the instructors provided (optional) Android development training for those TAs who preferred additional instruction.

This lack of meaningful development experience proved to be problematic, because the TAs lacked confidence and erred on the side of caution, frequently consulting with the course instructors to ensure that they were providing students with correct advice and fair grades throughout the project. Although we appreciated the care that the TAs took to learn Android and guide their teams, this type of consultation proved very time-consuming and is not practical going forward. In future, the instructors will plan a formal training session on Android and will aim to identify TAs who are more expert in this area to become the go-to for this type of consultation.

6.3 Set appropriate expectations

As reported in Section 5.3.2, students felt they needed to do too much learning on their own. The instructors have realized that some of this was due to the disconnect between the students' and the instructors' expectations of the applications they needed to produce. In particular, we have anecdotal evidence that some students devoted a significant effort to learning advanced user interface components, in order to make their applications look as professional as the applications they regularly use on their smartphones. While some of this was due to their enthusiasm and personal interest, we have some anecdotal evidence that it may have been partly due to a misconception of the instructors' expectations for the quality of the user interface. In future course offerings, we plan to be more explicit about expectations for UI and other aspects of the project, so that students do not feel they are required to spend time investigating features of Android that are not relevant to the learning goals of our course.

6.4 Improve the grading process

For phases two and three of the project, the TAs evaluated each of their teams' applications. This involved checking the application out of the version control repository, launching the application using the emulator, pushing necessary files specified in the team's report, and re-launching the application. The marking was done on the department's computing network, because it is a platform on which students can test their work before submitting. This approach to grading proved to be too time consuming, given our limited teaching resources.

Since Android projects involve a large number of directories and files, as well as multiple configuration options, it was common for students to forget to submit a file or to provide an incorrect configuration. This resulted in TAs spending their marking time investigating the cause of the errors, and in the end assigning a low grade as they were not able to successfully launch the application. This situation typically resulted in a remark request from the team, since a very minor fix or an additional file would solve the problem and produce a working application. Because of limited resources, the remarking requests were addressed by the instructors. Using this approach on an ongoing basis is not sustainable.

To address these types of grading issues, we plan to implement the following improvements to the grading process. As part of each project phase, the teams will be required to meet with their TAs, demonstrate their working application (which will include checking it out from the repository, building, pushing necessary files, and launching), and answer TA's questions. Since all parties will be present for the meeting, the minor errors or omissions that hindered the marking process in the past can be resolved quickly. We expect that this process will reduce grading time, improve grading accuracy, and enhance the quality of TA's feedback.

7. SUMMARY AND CONCLUSIONS

We reported on our experience of adding Android software development to a second year computer science course on software design. The goals of this course centre around teaching principles of object-oriented analysis and design and introducing aspects of software engineering through a team project. Our aim was to achieve our teaching goals while appealing to students' desire to learn the latest and most relevant technologies. The instructors' experiences, students' grades, official student course evaluations, and anecdotal evidence all indicate that incorporating Android software development into the course was a success and that our aims were achieved.

We also reported on several pitfalls we have encountered and propose solutions to them that would further improve various aspects of the course, such as lecture content, TA expertise, and assessment methods.

Our experience shows that grafting Android development onto a content heavy course can be done with only a few lecture or lab hours, when combined with the necessary teaching expertise. Students are motivated by and excited to learn Android, and, despite a steep learning curve, are able to produce working Android applications, while obtaining knowledge and practice in core computer science and software engineering concepts.

8. REFERENCES

[1] CATME. `http://www.catme.org`. Accessed 2014-08-27.

[2] "app" voted 2010 word of the year by the american dialect society. `http://www.americandialect.org/woty`, 2010. Accessed 2014-08-25.

[3] K. Beck and W. Cunningham. A laboratory for teaching object oriented thinking. In *Conference Proceedings on Object-oriented Programming Systems, Languages and Applications*, OOPSLA '89, pages 1–6, New York, NY, USA, 1989. ACM.

[4] B. Burd, J. a. P. Barros, C. Johnson, S. Kurkovsky, A. Rosenbloom, and N. Tillman. Educating for mobile computing: Addressing the new challenges. In *Proceedings of the Final Reports on Innovation and Technology in Computer Science Education 2012 Working Groups*, ITiCSE-WGR '12, pages 51–63, New York, NY, USA, 2012. ACM.

[5] D. Defoe, S. Kurkovsky, and E. Graetz. Mobile game development projects for introductory cs courses: Tutorial presentation. *J. Comput. Sci. Coll.*, 26(4):93–94, Apr. 2011.

[6] P. E. Dickson. Experiences building a college video game design course. *J. Comput. Sci. Coll.*, 25(6):104–110, June 2010.

[7] J. B. Fenwick, Jr., B. L. Kurtz, and J. Hollingsworth. Teaching mobile computing and developing software to support computer science education. In *Proceedings of the 42nd ACM Technical Symposium on Computer Science Education*, SIGCSE '11, pages 589–594, New York, NY, USA, 2011. ACM.

[8] M. Guo, P. Bhattacharya, M. Yang, K. Qian, and L. Yang. Learning mobile security with android security labware. In *Proceeding of the 44th ACM Technical Symposium on Computer Science Education*, SIGCSE '13, pages 675–680, New York, NY, USA, 2013. ACM.

[9] J. Heggestuen. One in every 5 people in the world own a smartphone, one in every 17 own a tablet. `http://www.businessinsider.com/smartphone-and-tablet-penetration-2013-10`, 2013. Accessed: 2014-08-25.

[10] I. Ilinkin. Opportunities for android projects in a cs1 course. In *Proceedings of the 45th ACM Technical Symposium on Computer Science Education*, SIGCSE '14, pages 615–620, New York, NY, USA, 2014. ACM.

[11] S. Loveland. Human computer interaction that reaches beyond desktop applications. In *Proceedings of the 42Nd ACM Technical Symposium on Computer Science Education*, SIGCSE '11, pages 595–600, New York, NY, USA, 2011. ACM.

[12] Q. H. Mahmoud and P. Popowicz. A mobile application development approach to teaching introductory programming. In *Proceedings of Frontiers in Education Conference (FIE)*, 2010 IEEE. IEEE, 2010.

[13] D. Riley. Using mobile phone programming to teach java and advanced programming to computer scientists. In *Proceedings of the 43rd ACM Technical Symposium on Computer Science Education*, SIGCSE '12, pages 541–546, New York, NY, USA, 2012. ACM.

[14] K. Sung and A. Samuel. Mobile application development classes for the mobile era. In *Proceedings of the 2014 Conference on Innovation & Technology in Computer Science Education*, ITiCSE '14, pages 141–146, New York, NY, USA, 2014. ACM.

[15] A. Tafliovich, A. Petersen, and J. Campbell. On the evaluation of student team software development projects. In *Proceedings of the 46th ACM Technical Symposium on Computer Science Education*, SIGCSE '15, New York, NY, USA, 2015. ACM. To appear.

[16] J. White, J. Gray, and A. Porter. Smartphones in the curriculum workshop. pages 520–522, 2011.

Lightning Talks

Montessori Methods
+
A Living Textbook
>
Traditional CS Instruction

Nicole Anderson, *Winona State University*
Tim Gegg-Harrison, *Winona State University*
Contact: {nanderson,tgeggharrison}@winona.edu

When it comes to educating children, we may agree that it makes no sense to teach them to write before they have mastered the alphabet. Yet, it is common for CS instructors to forge ahead with the next topic even though some students have failed to gain the necessary understanding of the current topic. The tightly integrated nature of CS topics often makes this "forward progress" turn into no progress at all for those students.

We propose an individualized approach to CS instruction where students progress to more advanced concepts only after they have demonstrated proficiency in prerequisite topics. We use a constructivist model of individualized instruction supported by specialized materials and a support system of instructor and peers: core Montessori components. In our case, the specialized materials are realized in a "living textbook" which incorporates scaffolded lessons delivered to students at the appropriate time based on their individual progress and also integrates a social communication network between students, peers, and the instructor (guide).

Maria Montessori said that "our aim is not only to make the child understand ... but to enthuse them to their innermost core." Our prior work focused on giving our students motivating materials and creating a "Comfort Zone of Proximal Development." Combining this with Montessori methods, we believe we can help all students succeed in Computer Science, some at a slower pace and others exploring more concepts than we previously dreamed possible. We will explore the details of this approach in our (en)lightning talk.

ACM Categories & Descriptors: Active Learning

Keywords: Montessori; Zone of Proximal Development; Scaffolded Instruction; Living Textbook

DOI: http://dx.doi.org/10.1145/2676723.2691879

coaster: Teaching Computer Graphics Incrementally

Robert R. Lewis, *Washington State University*
Contact: bobl@tricity.wsu.edu

coaster is a project that teaches a semester-long introductory computer graphics class by means of ten programming assignments. The assignments are incremental — each one building on the previous ones — and ultimately require implementation of most of the course content in the final one: a first-person rollercoaster simulation. Briefly described, the assignments (and their course contents) are:

1. circles ("warmup", 2D graphics, applying trigonometry),
2. wire track (3D graphics, parametric curves),
3. wire car (meshes),
4. "hedgehog" car (face and vertex normals),
5. shaded car (lighting models and vertex shaders),
6. shaded track (extrusion, model transforms),
7. surfaces (Bézier surfaces, height maps),
8. first person (viewing transforms, animation, splines),
9. dynamics (physics-based modeling), and
10. textures (textures, pixel shaders).

There is also an eleventh project of the student's own (approved) design. Students are provided with template code for the first ten programming assignments. The languages used are C++ on the CPU and GLSL on the GPU. Students are presumed to have access to OpenGL/GLSL 3.3/3.30 and the GLUT and GLEW libraries.

Both undergraduate and graduate students take the class and it has been presented twice at Washington State University, both times with about half of the students on a remote campus receiving it as a live telecourse. Student response has been very positive.

The goal of this lightning talk is to elicit interest from the computer graphics teaching community in making *coaster* systematically available to other universities by providing source code and training to instructors.

ACM Categories & Descriptors: K.3.2 [Computer and Information Science Education]: Computer science education; I.3.7 [Three-Dimensional Graphics and Realism]: *Color, shading, shadowing, and texture*

Keywords: Incremental project-based learning; Programming instruction; OpenGL; GLSL; GPU shaders

DOI: http://dx.doi.org/10.1145/2676723.2691880

Hugging and Bridging: What It Is And Why You Should Be Doing It!

Shuchi Grover, *Stanford University*
Contact: shuchig@cs.stanford.edu

Computational Thinking (CT), now widely recognized as a necessary skill for today's generation of learners, is typically being introduced to students in middle and high school (and even at the college level) in the context of programming in visual, block-based, drag-drop environments such as Scratch, Alice, Blockly, Tynker, Agentsheets and Kodu. How well are these first experiences preparing students to apply their learning successfully to future computational experiences, which are likely to be in the context of higher-order, text-based programming languages? How can we teach so as to facilitate successful 'transfer of learning' to future contexts? The art of teaching for transfer, or *mediating transfer*, has been actively studied for decades in education research. Pedagogies

SIGCSE'15, March 4–7, 2015, Kansas City, MO, USA.
ACM 978-1-4503-2966-8/15/03.

such as ‘bridging’, ‘hugging’, and ‘preparation for future learning’ (PFL) have shown promise in the context of education research in STEM domains at the secondary level. This fun lightning talk will shed light on these very pertinent ideas that CS education will benefit from, and share concrete strategies that can be employed in K-12 and college-level introductory programming classrooms to prepare students for better success with future computational experiences. The broader goal is to get CS educators and researchers thinking about an important aspect of teaching introductory programming and get a conversation started.

ACM Categories & Descriptors: K.3.2 [COMPUTERS AND EDUCATION]: Computer and Information Science Education - *Computer science education*

Keywords: Introductory programming; K-12 Computer Science; Programming languages; Transfer of learning

DOI: http://dx.doi.org/10.1145/2676723.2691881

Making Computer Science a First-Class Object in the K-12 Next Generation Science Standards

Marie Bienkowski, *SRI International*
Contact: marie.bienkowski@sri.com

Researchers, practitioners, and policymakers are (in most states) rallying around the Next Generation Science Standards. First released in 2012, the NGSS address the “mile wide, inch deep” science teaching so prevalent in K-12 and instead emphasize disciplinary core ideas, cross-cutting concepts, and *practices* in science and engineering. The NGSS make a nuanced distinction between science (inquiry) and engineering (design) and include performance standards for engineering design that “literate citizens” are expected to know. Early versions of the NGSS caused kerfluffles in the CS community—“the attention paid to the discipline of computer science does not match its importance in terms of workforce demand.” Ignoring calls from industry and academia to promote computer science, the authors relegated it, like statistics, to a supporting role. Putting CS in a supporting role means that it becomes a second-class object of study—a tool for investigating other disciplines—instead of a first-class object that is investigated in terms of disciplinary core ideas. Part of the problem is the lack of widely accepted core ideas that are easily explained. In the course of our work on building assessments for the Exploring Computer Science course (including drawing from the AP CS Principles framework) we have identified a manageable set of core ideas and mapped them to the NGSS engineering design standards. In this talk, I will point to materials we have developed that the community can use to show how computer science can replace engineering in the NGSS to teach practices and meet standards.

ACM Categories & Descriptors: K.3.2 [COMPUTERS AND EDUCATION]: Computer and Information Science Education - *Computer science education*

SIGCSE'15, March 4–7, 2015, Kansas City, MO, USA.
ACM 978-1-4503-2966-8/15/03.

Keywords: Secondary Computer Science; National Standards; Disciplinary Core Ideas

DOI: http://dx.doi.org/10.1145/2676723.2691882

Launching CROMA: Computational Research On Music & Audio

David Heise, *Lincoln University*
Contact: heised@lincolnu.edu

This lightning talk describes the current effort to create a research group at Lincoln University to conduct Computational Research On Music & Audio (CROMA). A CROMA Team of Interdisciplinary Collaborators (CROMA-TIC) will be assembled to participate in different aspects and applications of computational audio signal processing, drawing from disciplines such as computer science, mathematics, music, psychology, and nursing. This effort is modelled upon the Centre for Interdisciplinary Research in Music Media and Technology (CIRMMT) housed at McGill University, but it will be distinct in its focus on undergraduate research. Further, this research group will be unique among Historically Black Colleges and Universities (HBCUs). A goal of assembling CROMA-TIC and establishing the CROMA-Lab is to inspire participants, especially including minority students, to seek graduate degrees while enriching their undergraduate learning experiences. The initial research aims will focus on sound event separation within musical audio, with the idea that the research conducted by CROMA-TIC will be applicable to a wide array of applications (such as improving the performance of hearing aids in noisy environments or automatic transcription of music recordings, among innumerable possibilities). This effort is just underway; interested faculty and students are invited to attend the presentation and consider participation in CROMA so that it may develop into a truly interdisciplinary, multi-institutional endeavour.

ACM Categories & Descriptors: K.3.2 [Computers and Education]: Computer and Information Science Education - *computer science education*; H.5.5 [Information Interfaces and Presentation]: Sound and Music Computing - *signal analysis, synthesis, and processing*

Keywords: undergraduate research; interdisciplinary research; audio signal processing; music information retrieval; CROMA

DOI: http://dx.doi.org/10.1145/2676723.2691883

Integrating Programming into Physics and Algebra

Eric Freudenthal, *University of Texas at El Paso*
Kien Lim, *University of Texas at El Paso*
Karla Carmona, *University of Texas at El Paso*
Catherine Tabor, *University of Texas at El Paso*
Contact: efreudenthal@utep.edu

We are infusing inquiry-driven programming activities into algebra and physics courses with the objective of strengthening disciplinary understandings and providing all students a meaningful first experience with programming.

The majority of students who complete 9th grade algebra fail to connect its syntactic and graphical representations to concepts related to rate of change. These learning deficits contribute to the well documented failure of high school and college physics courses to effectively convey conceptual understandings of the relationships between force, acceleration, velocity and position.

Our programming activities for algebra and physics classrooms focus student attention towards the principles underlying symbolic and graphical representations of slope. Implementations of these inherently multi-disciplinary activities within math, physics, and even computing classes have previously only been successful when instructors have broad content and pedagogical knowledge. For our most recent implementations within physics lab courses led by inexperienced TAs, instructional modules that introduce and explore the lab course's conventional kinematic experiments were developed.

ACM Categories & Descriptors: K.3.2, J.2

Keywords: Computer Science Education; Mathematics Education; Physics Education; Introductory Programming

DOI: http://dx.doi.org/10.1145/2676723.2691884

HFOSS-Lite in CS2: Incorporating the Ushahidi Crowdmapping Program in a Data Structures and Algorithms Course

Samuel A. Rebelsky, *Grinnell College*
Contact: rebelsky@grinnell.edu

Although undergraduate computer science enrollments are again on the upswing, increased enrollments do not seem to have led to increased diversity – CS, at least in America, remains a field dominated by white males. A variety of evidence shows that many underrepresented groups, such as women and domestic students of color, are often motivated by course work that includes a clear societal benefit. The Humanitarian Free and Open Source Software (HFOSS) approach suggests that working on FOSS projects that have humanitarian benefits provides such motivation.

Unfortunately, adding new themes and topics to courses can be difficult. CS2, in particular, often feels packed enough that it's hard to envision adding something else. And, while HFOSS is attractive, it's sometimes hard for the particular needs of a project to help students develop course-specific knowledge (about data structures and algorithms).

I've recently experimented with an idea that I call "HFOSS-lite". Rather than students contributing directly to an HFOSS project, they use an HFOSS project as a source of data for their data structures and algorithms. The Ushahidi crowdmapping platform has proven especially useful. Students can contribute data to Ushahidi sites and even build their own sites. The data can be used in a variety of exercises, from simple searching to sorting algorithms in which they use different criteria (not just alphabetical or by time, but also by distance from a location and a variety of hybrid approaches) and beyond. And, because they are using the HFOSS software, they think about societal impact.

SIGCSE'15, March 4–7, 2015, Kansas City, MO, USA.
ACM 978-1-4503-2966-8/15/03.

ACM Categories & Descriptors: K.3.2 [Computers and Education]: Computer and Information Science Education–*Computer Science Education*; H.3.5 [Information Storage and Retrieval]: Online Information Services*Web-based services, Data sharing*

Keywords: CSEd4SG; HFOSS; Free and open-source software; CS2; Data Structures and Algorithms

DOI: http://dx.doi.org/10.1145/2676723.2691885

A Peer Tutoring Model for Small Schools with Limited Funding and Resources

Dee A. B. Weikle, *Eastern Mennonite University*
Contact: dee.weikle@emu.edu

Peer tutoring has been used in a variety of contexts and a variety of institutions to both improve learning and retention for the classroom students and to improve the confidence and knowledge base of the peer tutor. Much of the current literature focusses on how to implement peer tutoring with a fairly large program, including at least one graduate TA and multiple undergraduates who have recently taken the course. In addition, these peers were trained outside of the normal classroom hours and/or paid to participate. While useful at larger institutions, or at least those with substantial resources, this model is generally unworkable at a smaller institution without funding to pay students, or a sufficient critical mass of students to enable formal training outside of the classroom. This lightning talk describes a slightly different model that involves the university's academic support center staff for tutoring training, class attendance for technical training, and the giving of credit as opposed to payment for the student. To receive more than one hour of credit the student also works closely with the professor to complete one or more "learning modules" that later become resources for the class and provide an additional learning opportunity for the tutor. This method has been used by the author with over 9 peer tutors across a range of 7 classes, with generally good success.

ACM Categories & Descriptors: K.3.2 [Computer and Information Science Education]: Computer science education

Keywords: Peer-led team learning; communication skill; cooperative learning; peer mentoring.

DOI: http://dx.doi.org/10.1145/2676723.2691886

An Across-Institution Anytime MOOC in Database

Douglas Fisher, *Vanderbilt University*
Contact: douglas.h.fisher@vanderbilt.edu

In Spring 2015, instructors at participating universities and colleges plan to run their Introduction to Database courses using Jennifer Widom's self-paced online course as an optional or required resource. We call the collective of students and instructors who will be moving through Widom's course in relative synchrony, a (loosely) collaborative, distributed open, online course (CDOOC). This way of exploiting a self-paced open online course allows an organized cohort (e.g., a campus course) to move through at the cohort's "own" pace. If the organized cohort's progress through the self-paced course is open to other learners, outside the *a priori* organized cohort (as it will be in our case), then this larger population amounts to a MOOC. Because any instructor can convene such a MOOC at any time, we call it an anytime MOOC.

ACM Categories & Descriptors: K.3.1 Computer Uses in Education - *Collaborative learning; Computer-assisted instruction; Distance learning*; K.3.2 Computer and Information Science Education - *Computer science education*

Keywords: self-paced open online courses; blended learning; anytime MOOC; classroom management; database education; online education; experience report; Web-based technology

DOI: http://dx.doi.org/10.1145/2676723.2691887

The Need for Voices in CS to Address the #GamerGate Controversy

Joseph Kendall-Morwick, *Capital University*
Contact: jkendallmorwick@capital.edu

CS faculty are responsible for educating future software developers and thus have a unique responsibility to combat the problem of sexism within the software development industry. Game development is an important subfield in which to address this problem because of its cultural impact, which extends beyond the developers involved, and its incorporation into pedagogy for the purposes of engagement and retention.

The recent #GamerGate controversy has brought to public attention the issue of sexism within a white male-dominated gaming subculture as it enters the cultural mainstream, particularly due to anonymous threats of violence being made against women who have criticized the #GamerGate movement. This controversy is particularly important for CS because it centers on software developers. In addition to harming the targeted women, such threats create a chilling effect that threatens not only to silence important voices within gaming, but also to undermine progress toward gender equality in CS and the recruitment and retention of female CS students. It is important for CS faculty to evaluate their responsibility to students and to the field in light of these concerns.

This lightning talk will assess the outcome of a round-table to be held with students at Capital University in which this controversy and its broader implications will be discussed. In particular, the talk will focus on outcomes related to CS education and outreach, with the goal that lessons learned through the round-table can inform the efforts of faculty planning to address such issues at their institutions.

ACM Categories & Descriptors: K.3.2 [Computer and Information Science Education]: Computer Science Education

Keywords: Underrepresented students; Retention; Outreach

DOI: http://dx.doi.org/10.1145/2676723.2691888

Learning Computer Networking Through Illustration

Wen-Jung Hsin, *Park University*
Contact: wen.hsin@park.edu

When teaching computer networking courses, over the years, the author has used Java applets and other software tools for illustrating standards, protocols, and networking concepts. Although these Java applets and software tools do perform what they are designed to do, they have their limitations. For example, the Java applets that the author used can only illustrate a fixed set of scenarios, and software tools such as Wireshark need devices to generate traces, posing a problem when the teaching resource is limited. In recent years, our school has joined the Cisco Networking Academy and taught computer networking courses offered through the Academy. Cisco Networking Academy provides a networking software program, Packet Tracer, which allows the users to setup and configure various networks which involve routers, switches, and end devices using various wired and wireless cables and protocols in local area networks or wide area networks. There are several nice features about the Packet Tracer. For example, an instructor can use the Packet Tracer to illustrate networking concepts. A student can use the Packet Tracer to iron out networking design issues by first implementing the network using Packet Tracer before implementing it in a physical lab. Additionally, students can closely examine the header information in each layer of the protocol stack as a packet steps from layer to layer and node to node. In this lightning talk, the author will share the experience of using Packet Trace in teaching computer networking courses.

ACM Categories & Descriptors: K.3.2 [Computers and Education]: Computer and Information Science Education, Computer science education; C.2.0 [Computer-Communication Networks]: General; C.2.6 [Computer-Communication Networks]: Internetworking

Keywords: Computer Networking; Simulator

DOI: http://dx.doi.org/10.1145/2676723.2691889

SIGCSE'15, March 4–7, 2015, Kansas City, MO, USA.
ACM 978-1-4503-2966-8/15/03.

Special Session: Perspectives on Adopting and Facilitating Guided Inquiry Learning

Helen H. Hu
Westminster College
Salt Lake City, UT 84105
hhu@westmincollege.edu

Clifton Kussmaul
Muhlenberg College
Allentown, PA 18104
kussmaul@muhlenberg.edu

Deepa Muralidhar
Atlanta Girls School
Atlanta, GA 30327
deepa.muralidhar@gmail.com

Kristine Nagel
Georgia Gwinnett College
Lawrenceville, GA 30043
knagel@ggc.edu

SUMMARY

POGIL (Process Oriented Guided Inquiry Learning) is based on the principle that students learn more when they construct their own understanding. Instead of attending lecture, student teams work through POGIL activities to discover concepts on their own, while instructors circulate and facilitate learning. Students learn the material better, and this constructivist approach also teaches them important process skills, including critical thinking, team work, and leadership. In this special session, SIGCSE attendees will experience a POGIL activity for themselves, learn about the structure of POGIL activities (through a POGIL meta-activity), and hear perspectives from teachers who recently adopted POGIL activities available at http://cspogil.org. We will share classroom-tested guided inquiry activities and discuss how POGIL can transform CS classes at all levels, from high school to graduate-level classes, from small schools to large universities.

Categories and Subject Descriptors

K.3.2 [Computers and Education] - Computer and Information Science Education - Computer science education, information systems education, literacy, self-assessment

General Terms

Design, Experimentation

Keywords

Active Learning; Cooperative Learning; POGIL; Teams

1. OVERALL SESSION OBJECTIVE

After this session, attendees will be able to describe:

- How POGIL activities are structured and use learning cycles to support knowledge construction.
- How team roles, teacher facilitation, and other scaffolding support learning content and process skills.
- Where they can find field-tested POGIL activities and learn more about facilitating POGIL activities in their own classrooms.

SIGCSE'15, March 4–7, 2015, Kansas City, MO, USA.
ACM 978-1-4503-2966-8/15/03.
http://dx.doi.org/10.1145/2676723.2677324

Process Oriented Guided Inquiry Learning (POGIL), is a research-based instructional strategy that encourages students to cooperatively construct their own understanding of concepts [6]. In POGIL, student teams work together on specifically designed activities that guide students to discover principles on their own. For example, instead of a lecture on numeric type conversion, students might use an interpreter to evaluate a carefully selected set of expressions, and then be guided to articulate the general properties of type conversion. When students discover concepts for themselves, they remember them better.

POGIL has been used successfully since the 1990s in secondary schools, high schools, small colleges, and large universities. Initially developed in chemistry, POGIL has been used in biology, computer science, engineering, math, and other areas. Research shows that students learn content better [5], have higher pass rates [7], and prefer POGIL over traditional lectures [1]. The POGIL Project (www.pogil.org) provides a variety of resources, including workshops to help faculty learn about POGIL practice and theory.

The session leaders have used POGIL in a range of courses, including CSP, CS0, CS1, CS2, data structures and algorithms, and software engineering. One of us (Hu) is the PI on an AAC&U TIDES grant to develop POGIL activities for a CS Principles course to be paired with courses in other departments to broaden the appeal of CS. Another (Kussmaul) is the PI on a NSF TUES grant to develop and disseminate POGIL activities, and we are actively seeking collaborators. The other two leaders (Muralidhar and Nagel) have recently adopted POGIL activities written by others and will speak on their experiences.

2. SESSION OUTLINE

Table 1. Session agenda (75 min total)

#	Time	Speakers	Content
1	5 min	All	Introductions, session overview, form teams.
2	20 min	Hu, Kussmaul	Work through a sample POGIL mini-activity.
3	20 min	Hu, Kussmaul	Work through meta-activity to analyze the POGIL activity structure and facilitation.
4	15 min	Muralidhar, Nagel	Testimonials from recent adopters of POGIL.
5	15 min	All	Q&A and next steps.

This special session will be *experiential* in nature. As summarized in Table 1, the session will start with a brief introduction on POGIL and its effectiveness. Next, we will divide the audience into teams of 3-4 people to work through a POGIL activity and experience POGIL as students would. Third, teams will then work through a meta-activity (an activity about an activity) to better understand how POGIL activities are designed. Fourth, session leaders who have recently adapted POGIL will describe their experiences. We will share links to our POGIL materials with the audience and provide information about upcoming POGIL workshops. The session will conclude with question and answer discussion.

2.1 Presenter Statement - Helen Hu

I have adopted POGIL in multiple CS courses, including my traditional CS1 course in Java for CS majors [2], an introductory CS1 course in Python for science majors [3], and most recently, a CS0 course in AppInventor for non-majors. I have seen increases in student engagement levels as well as in my female students' pass rates [2]. Most of my POGIL activities are available online at http://tinyurl.com/cs1pogil, and I have started creating Instructor's Guides for each activity, with tips on how an instructor should facilitate the activity.

I am encouraged by the increase in publically available POGIL activities at http://cspogil.org. The NCWIT EngageCSEdu collection of inclusive activities for introductory CS courses (http://www.engage-csedu.org/) lists Process Oriented Guided Inquiry Learning (POGIL) as an Engagement Practice, making it easy for instructors to browse and view POGIL activities. CS instructors can now transform their classrooms by adopting one of these POGIL activities, rather than needing to author their own POGIL activities.

2.2 Presenter Statement - Clifton Kussmaul

I first developed and used POGIL activities in a graduate course on soft computing at the University of Kerala, in south India. Since then, I have created and used POGIL activities in CS II, Software Engineering, and other courses [4]. I often use Google Docs for the activities, so teams can edit collaboratively and copy text to and from other tools. Developing activities becomes easier with practice, although it takes effort to refine activities so that other faculty could adopt or adapt them.

As part of the NSF TUES project, I am sharing activities with colleagues, including some high school CS teachers, and we will soon be evaluating the activities more formally. As we pilot and refine activities, we post them to http://cspogil.org.

2.3 Presenter Statement – Deepa Muralidhar

I have been teaching CS at the high school level for the last 14 years. I have taught at various levels - from the introductory courses to the advanced AP classes. I have piloted the soon to become AP CS Principles course for the last three years and am entering the fourth year of piloting the course. This year I am teaching at an all girls independent school where I am beta testing POGIL activities. I have attended a four-day workshop on POGIL and am looking forward to applying POGIL to more CS courses.

2.4 Presenter Statement – Kristine Nagel

I have taught introductory college programming course, using active and contextual learning strategies, including a computational media approach, paired programming, and flipped classroom. Students succeeded in acquiring programming skills, but were not effectively applying those skills to problem solving or to communicate programming process issues, in designing or debugging code. I was interested in POGIL, initially for the guided inquiry approach for the student-centered classroom, but now appreciate the structured teamwork process as well. I attended a summer workshop and have implemented POGIL activities from the first week of programming course. Students have responded positively engaging in programming and with teammates.

3. EXPECTATIONS

This special session should appeal to teachers and instructors interested in incorporating more active learning in their classrooms. Attendees will experience how students discover computer science concepts for themselves while working through POGIL activities. They will learn how POGIL has been used in CS classrooms, how to access POGIL materials at http://cspogil.org, and how to learn more through POGIL workshops and regional meetings hosted by the National POGIL Office (https://pogil.org/events).

4. ACKNOWLEDGMENTS

This material is based upon work supported by the National Science Foundation under Grant No. DUE-1044679, and a grant from the AAC&U TIDES Institute and the Leona M. and Harry B. Helmsley Charitable Trust. We also acknowledge the National POGIL Office (http://pogil.org) for encouragement and support.

5. REFERENCES

[1] D. Hanson and T. Wolfskill. Process workshops - a new model for instruction. J. Chem. Educ., 77:120–130, 2000.

[2] H.H. Hu and T.D. Shepherd. Teaching CS 1 with POGIL activities and roles. . In Proceedings of the SIGCSE Tech. Symp. on CS Education, Atlanta, GA, 2014.

[3] H.H. Hu and T.D. Shepherd. Using POGIL to help students learn to program. Trans. Comput. Educ. 13, 3, Article 13, August 2013.

[4] C. Kussmaul. Process oriented guided inquiry learning (POGIL) for computer science. In Proceedings of the SIGCSE Tech. Symp. on CS Education, Raleigh, NC, 2012.

[5] G. McKnight. Effectiveness of POGIL. Retrieved Sept. 1, 2011 from http://www.pogil.org/about/effectiveness.

[6] R. Moog and J. N. Spencer, eds. Process-Oriented Guided Inquiry Learning. Oxford University Press, 2008.

[7] A. Straumanis and E. Simons. Assessment of student learning in POGIL organic chemistry. In Abstracts of papers of the American Chemical Society, vol 231, March 2006.

Introduction to AccessCS10K and Accessible Tools for Teaching Programming

Andreas Stefik
University of Nevada, Las Vegas
Department of Computer Science
Las Vegas, NV 89154-4019
+1-702-895-3603
stefika@gmail.com

Richard E. Ladner
University of Washington
Department of Computer Science and Engineering
Seattle, WA 98195-2350
+1-206-543-9347
ladner@cs.washington.edu

SUMMARY

This special session is for SIGCSE attendees who are interested in K-12 computing education, especially those who have or are planning to have a NSF CS 10K project. A major goal of CS 10K is broadening participation, which includes providing computing education to students with disabilities. This interactive session will introduce attendees to AccessCS10K, a project to help teachers include students with disabilities in their K-12 computing classes. Furthermore, attendees will have a hands-on experience with the Quorum language, a language designed for youth regardless of disability. It is expected that attendees to the special session will be better prepared to include a student with a disability in their computing classes or to help other teachers do the same.

Categories and Subject Descriptors

K.3.2 [**Computer and Information Science Education**]: Computer Science Education

General Terms

Human Factors

Keywords

Disability; accessibility; usability

1. INTRODUCTION

The objective of the special session is to inform the SIGCSE community, especially those involved in K-12 education, about the new NSF-funded project AccessCS10K. In addition, those who attend will have a hands-on experience learning programming from the perspective of a blind student. Those who attend will be better prepared to include a student with a disability in their computing class or to help other teachers do the same.

1.1 OUTLINE OF THE SESSION

The session will begin with a 20 minute introduction to AccessCS10K and end with a 50 minute hands-on activities writing programs in the Quorum programming language, a language that is universally designed to be learnable by and accessible to young people regardless of their ability to see.

SIGCSE'15, March 4–7, 2015, Kansas City, MO, USA.
ACM 978-1-4503-2966-8/15/03.
http://dx.doi.org/10.1145/2676723.2677321

1.2 EXPECTATIONS

The special session is designed to be interactive. Attendees will learn about the services that AcceessCS10K will provide, but at the same time, the presenters will offer challenges to the attendees that will need their responses. During the hands-on part of the special session, attendees will learn about the Quorum programming language by doing short assignments. They will have the opportunity to write a program with their eyes covered to see what it is like to write a programming by listening and not seeing. Attendees will hopefully experience an attitudinal change to "Yes, I want to have a blind student in my computing class" from "I don't know if I can accommodate a blind student. I'm at a loss of what to do."

1.3 WHY A SPECIAL SESSION

The great thing about a special session is that it is designed to be interactive. Disability is one of those topics that is better for discussion than just being spoken to. Just about everyone knows someone with a disability, so individuals tend to come in with their own personal lens on the topic. Discussion is a great way to see each other's perspectives. In addition, in learning about the language Quorum, attendees will be invited to program without seeing the code. Encouragement and advice will be needed for the attendees to be successful at learning from this experience.

2. ACCESSCS10K

The National Science Foundation (NSF) is supporting efforts to bring computational thinking and programming to K-12 education (CS 10K). This is exemplified by the development and implementation of the new Exploring Computer Science (ECS) and Computer Science Principles (CSP) high school courses throughout the United States. Legislation and educational policies mandate that qualified students with disabilities be fully included in these classes. Approximately 13% of K-12 students are identified as having disabilities and most of them are intellectually capable of learning computational thinking and programming. Importantly, the computing field needs more of the expertise and perspectives of people with disabilities to foster the innovations in the twenty-first century.

The goal of AccessCS10K is to increase the successful participation of students with disabilities in ECS and CSP courses. This goal will be pursued by reaching two objectives:

1. build the capacity of ECS and CSP teachers to serve students with disabilities through professional development training and individual real-time support and,

2. create accessible materials - both tools and curricular units - that ECS and CSP teachers can use in their classrooms.

How will ECS and CSP teachers accommodate a blind student with a curriculum that uses Scratch, Snap, Alice, Processing, or Greenfoot, all with extremely visual user interfaces that are generally inaccessible to blind users? Will these teachers say, "Sorry you cannot take my computing course because you cannot use the tools we are using to teach programming?" Will a guidance counselor recommend to the student that she consider another career choice than the one the student wants to pursue? These scenarios should not happen and AccessCS10K's first objective is intended to make sure that they do not.

The popular programming tools mentioned in the previous paragraph are inherently inaccessible to blind students. Some of the tools that use drag and drop to create programs are difficult to impossible to use for those with mobility related disabilities, such as cerebral palsy. Creating more accessible and usable programming tools and curricula is addressed by AccessCS10K's second objective.

3. QUORUM

The Quorum programming language began as a National Science Foundation project (CNS-0940521) dedicated to teaching blind or visually impaired students computer programming. During this project, Quorum quickly garnered adoption from this group, now with trained teachers at approximately 43% of the schools for the blind in the United States with students on grade level. The tools developed on top of Quorum, like talking debuggers, custom IDE-friendly screen readers, and syntactic choices designed to be easy to "hear," were transformative for the blind community, ultimately moving partner schools from teaching only Microsoft Word or PowerPoint to programs that teach students the fundamentals of inventing their own technology.

3.1 FOUNDATION OF EVIDENCE

As work on Quorum progressed, we were curious whether the types of decisions that were intended for the blind (e.g., syntax like `repeat 10 times` instead of `for(int i = 0; i < 10; i++)`) would be helpful for a wider group. This led to randomized controlled trials on the impact of syntactic choices, finding evidence that syntax can be trivially modified to be more comprehensible. Additionally, evidence from this work suggests that the languages Java and Perl are no easier to use initially than a language designed randomly from the ASCII table – the first known experiment testing a "Placebo" programming language [1].

Given that results with Java or Perl, we became curious as to the standard of evidence used by language designers when making their decisions. Ultimately, this uncovered that, in fact, language designers were often using no evidence at all in regard to the impact on human beings, or at least very little [2]. This has helped lead to a number of research groups running new randomized controlled trials on language design.

For example, while the argument has existed for decades, we now have evidence that static typing is slightly harder for novices to use, but increases human productivity by year 3 of an academic pipeline [3]. We also have evidence that software transactional memory is easier compared to course/fine grained locks [4]. These, and other aspects of language design, are now being uncovered at an increasing pace as language designers, inventors, and users, use stronger evidence in their analysis. In Quorum, which we call an "evidence-oriented" language, all results from the literature that contain rigorously collected evidence are used in making decisions – hence the name.

3.2 HANDS ON ACTIVITIES

As the Quorum programming language projects has progressed, a national workshop has developed to teach teachers how to use the technology, called the Experience Programming in Quorum (EPIQ) workshop, held annually at the Washington State School for the Blind in Vancouver, WA in July. Building on the EPIQ experience, the 50-minute hands on activities in this special session will include a tour of Quorum and its accessibility features in a way that will engage the participants.

As a strategy for learning Quorum, we will also introduce participants to using Quorum online or in an offline IDE, using fun story-driven, screen reader accessible video tutorials. Participants will leave with a broader understanding of how to program using Quorum, where to find materials to learn more, and hands on experience using Quorum like a person with disabilities. Finally, participants will receive a variety of educational materials they can use when teaching or investigating the language.

4. Conclusion

This special session is targeted at K-12 computing teachers and those who are currently involved or plan to be involved in a NSF CS 10K project. This will provide materials on working with students with disabilities, including hands-on training with a commonly used language in the community: Quorum. This session will be especially relevant to any teacher, instructor, or scholar, involved in ECS or CSP curriculum, in addition to those interested in programming languages.

5. ACKNOWLEDGMENTS

This special session is made possible by the support of the National Science Foundation Grant CNS-1042260 and CNS-1440843.

6. REFERENCES

[1] Andreas Stefik and Susanna Siebert. 2013. An Empirical Investigation into Programming Language Syntax. *Trans. Comput. Educ.* 13, 4, Article 19 (November 2013), 40 pages.

[2] Andreas Stefik, Stefan Hanenberg, Mark McKenney, Anneliese Andrews, Srinivas Kalyan Yellanki, and Susanna Siebert. 2014. What is the foundation of evidence of human factors decisions in language design? an empirical study on programming language workshops. In *Proceedings of the 22nd International Conference on Program Comprehension* (ICPC 2014). ACM, New York, NY, USA, 223-231.

[3] Stefan Endrikat, Stefan Hanenberg, Romain Robbes, and Andreas Stefik. 2014. How do API documentation and static typing affect API usability?. In *Proceedings of the 36th International Conference on Software Engineering* (ICSE 2014). ACM, New York, NY, USA, 632-642.

[4] Christopher J. Rossbach, Owen S. Hofmann, and Emmett Witchel. 2010. Is transactional programming actually easier? *SIGPLAN Not.* 45, 5 (January 2010), 47-56.

One-Day Activities for K-12 Face-to-Face Outreach

Daniel D. Garcia (moderator)
University of California, Berkeley
777 Soda Hall
Berkeley, CA 94720
+1 (510) 517-4041
ddgarcia@cs.berkeley.edu

Wei Ding, Joseph Cohen
University of Massachusetts, Boston
100 Morrissey Blvd
Boston, MA 02125
+1 (617) 287-6428
{ding, Joecohen}@cs.umb.edu

Barbara Ericson
Georgia Institute of Technology
801 Atlantic Drive
Atlanta, GA 30332
+1 (404) 385-2107
ericson@cc.gatech.edu

Jeff Gray
University of Alabama
Box 870290
Tuscaloosa, AL 35487-0290
+1 (205) 348-2847
gray@cs.ua.edu

Dale Reed
University of Illinois at Chicago
851 S. Morgan St.
Chicago, IL 60607
+1 (312) 413-9478
reed@uic.edu

Categories and Subject Descriptors
K.3.2 [**Computer and Information Science Education**]: Computer science education

General Terms
Experimentation

Keywords
Computer science education; outreach; K-12

1. SUMMARY

The recent successes of Computer Science Education Week and code.org's *Hour of Code* have meant that more K-12 students than ever are being given an authentic, engaging and eye-opening exposure to the wonders of computer science. There are resources aplenty to help high school and college faculty with outreach. These range from easy-to-learn, open-ended programming environments (Scratch, Alice, Snap!), to online coding challenges (code.org, Lite-bot), to non-computer activities with live performances (CS Unplugged, cs4fn), to having the entire outreach experience delivered "in a box", thanks to NCWIT [1].

We wanted to bring educators together to share experiences with what they've done specifically *with a one-day event*, given these vast resources. Now that there are so many online coding experiences, it is enough to shuttle young students into a computer room, point their browser at one of these experiences, and answer questions as they come up? Is it important to include hands-on *and* hands-off (e.g., nifty demos, inspiring talks) components, and if so, in what order? What do different demographics find the most engaging? Is there any chance that we can do "damage", since these highlight-reel experiences might over-simplify how hard some of the problems are, and that not every important result has a flashy payoff? Do some of the early experiences leave students with the impression that computer science is *only* (say) apps, interactive multimedia programs or solving mazes? Finally, when it's over, what follow-up is appropriate? Participants on the panel will share best practices, common pitfalls, and advice.

SIGCSE'15, March 4–7, 2015, Kansas City, MO, USA.
ACM 978-1-4503-2966-8/15/03.
http://dx.doi.org/10.1145/2676723.2677337

2. DANIEL D. GARCIA

The one-day outreach activities we have been involved with at UC Berkeley come in two flavors. The first, *Cal Day*, is UC Berkeley's open house day for newly accepted freshmen and their families. In addition to the normal tours of the robot lab and maker space and presentations about the CS major, we have a few activities we've run that many find particularly engaging. Younger visitors enjoy our *Scratch drop-in lab*, staffed by friendly undergrads and a faculty mentor. Nearby, we offer a *CS Unplugged* room where undergrads teach our three favorite activities every 30m. Our *Game Theory* and *Teaching Privacy* research groups holds open hands-on labs where visitors can learn about strongly solving board games and privacy in the social media age, respectively. Undergraduates also demonstrate projects that students create in upper-division classes. With close to a thousand visitors circulating through our building before the day is over, we endeavor to have activities that appeal to young and old, and the success is thanks to the many undergrad volunteers.

The second is our CS Education Day, where we bring 500 students from diverse-population local high schools to campus for a highly scripted, staff-intensive day to see the "best of the best" of our department. The students are split into two groups, one has its morning filled with inspiring talks and fun student-led demos, and its afternoon with three hands-on activities (*CS Unplugged*, a *Snap! Hour of Code*, and a Game Theory interactive session) and the other group is reversed. We ask parents to chaperone so that the ratio is 10 kids per adult, and it's an incredibly rewarding experience, also relying on student volunteers to make it run well.

3. WEI DING & JOSEPH COHEN

The annual one-day tech-savvy computing camp has been part of Boston's city-wide initiative since 2010 to increase the interest and participation of intermediate school students in science, technology, and scientific research. The team at the University of Massachusetts Boston aims to create an exciting curriculum for introducing CS in one day, focusing on interactive visual interface design and collaborative teamwork. The outcomes are to educate students on what computer science is, correct any misconceptions they may have, and allow them to have a sense of accomplishment to kick start their computer science career path.

The one-day event is split into algorithm design and software implementation. Computer science algorithms are introduced through group game activities, such as sorting and searching, without involving computers. We isolate algorithms from implementation in order to eliminate the stereotype that computer science entirely involves computers. Software implementation is taught using the *Throw* platform we specially designed for the event. It allows us to promote computer science as a people-oriented major by having collaborative coding where they learn to work on a team. We also have a competition for best creation using the platform by the end of the one-day event.

4. BARBARA ERICSON

The *Institute for Computing Education* at Georgia Tech has offered 3-4 hour workshops for students for years. We have been offering workshops for Girl Scouts since 2005. We also have offered fee-based computing workshops to 4th graders through 8th graders since 2010. We do pre- and post-attitude surveys to measure confidence, enjoyment, perceived usefulness, motivation to succeed, identity and belonging, gender equality, creativity in computing, and intent to persist. We have run workshops on Web Design, Scratch, Alice, LEGO robots (WeDo, NXT, and EV3), App inventor, and EarSketch. Many of these workshops have resulted in statistically significant positive changes in attitudes towards computing, but not all. Some workshops have had negative results where the students found the activities too challenging or boring.

We recommend working with your local Girl Scout council and other youth serving organizations like Black Girls Code in order to reach more girls. We also recommend advertising workshops to local teachers, local schools, and faculty. Hands-on workshops are best with 1 or 2 students per computer. Girls especially enjoy doing something creative and social. Make sure that projects are easy enough for all students to complete and also have challenges for advanced students. Start with partially-completed projects for younger students. We recommend always doing some open-ended project and having the students show off what they have created. Consider including parents in some workshops and give parents brochures from NCWIT or ACM about computing. Try to counter the stereotypes about computing, but don't mention the stereotypes. We found that talking about the stereotypes tended to results in negative changes in attitudes about computing. Connect what the students are doing to careers in computing. Use near-peer helpers to provide role models for the participants. We have shared our successful projects in Alice, Scratch, App Inventor, and LEGO EV3 robots online [2].

5. JEFF GRAY

The goal of our one-day events is to provide initial awareness of opportunities in computer science along with some surface-level example of an exciting topic in computing, often involving a brief programming and/or unplugged activity. When hosted on campus, the visit also provides a tour of different labs that highlight the breadth of computing. The diverse backgrounds of the students who attend our one-day workshops suggest that each workshop should be customized to the particular needs of each student group (either by age, gender, or type and size of their school). After an initial discussion on the opportunities in CS, the remainder of the one-day visit is adjusted based on the interests of the students. They are given the option of several different hands-on activities (e.g., learning how to create an app in App Inventor, programming a robot in a small team) that can be explored during their visit.

We have found that one-day events can be a very fun time for both students and instructors, but need to be carefully planned – for many students, this is their first exposure to true computer science, so there is pressure to deliver a very memorable and informative experience. To facilitate the interaction with students who are visiting for a very short period of time, we have begun to develop a set of Blockly environments that demonstrate topics in computing (e.g., robotics with Spherly and media computation with Pixly) with languages that invite students to explore computer science using an inquiry-focused strategy.

6. DALE REED

UIC has provided CS evangelism in the form of presentations and short hands-on activities to over 10,000 high school students in the Chicago area since 2005. While the majority of these are 50-90 minute classroom visits during the school year, others have been Saturday Open House events using Blockly and LightBot and six-hour Saturday events focusing on Lego Robotics, Scratch with picoBoards or App Inventor. These events typically start with something magical or unexpected to focus the attention of the group, followed by 3-word introductions for everyone in the room (e.g. "I'm Dale Reed from UIC. My 3 words are Computers, Juggling, and Foldup-Bike). A collaborative environment is established as students are asked to work with a partner. When questions inevitably arise, teachers ask students to "ask three before me," as usually there are many more students than teachers/tutors. Activities are hands-on as early as possible.

We recommend that teachers communicate respect for what students already know, connecting the curriculum to it. Even when students don't initially know the technical content, they will quickly come up with interesting applications of the technology that we as teachers might never think of. A more lasting impact can be achieved by choosing some technological tool that students can subsequently continue to explore on their own (e.g. Snap!, Scratch, AppInventor) and which they will be motivated to show to their friends. In our experience, compelling direct-instruction is not as engaging as using guided inquiry with hands-on projects. While acknowledging that each location may be different, we recommend running the activities from 9am–3:30pm, including lunch and breaks. Friendly competition helps motivate interest but should only be used for parts of the event. In our experience the most bang-for-your-buck can be achieved by providing give-away prizes to less than 30% of the attendees. This increases the perceived value of each prize, like stuffed animals at a carnival that are desirable mostly because only a few people have them. It is helpful to end the session with a gallery walk where students can present their work to each other. A guiding philosophy has been to "Leave something in their head and in their hands" so students take away not only stimulating ideas but some concrete reminder of what they have done and learned.

7. REFERENCES

[1] NC-WIT. *Outreach-in-a-Box: Discovering IT*. September, 2014. `www.ncwit.org/resources/outreach-box-discovering-it`

[2] Georgia Tech. *ICE Distance Learning Site*. `http://ice-web.cc.gatech.edu/dl/`

37 Million Compilations: Investigating Novice Programming Mistakes in Large-Scale Student Data

Amjad Altadmri
School of Computing
University of Kent
Canterbury, Kent, UK
aa803@kent.ac.uk

Neil C. C. Brown
School of Computing
University of Kent
Canterbury, Kent, UK
nccb@kent.ac.uk

ABSTRACT

Previous investigations of student errors have typically focused on samples of hundreds of students at individual institutions. This work uses a year's worth of compilation events from over 250,000 students all over the world, taken from the large Blackbox data set. We analyze the frequency, time-to-fix, and spread of errors among users, showing how these factors inter-relate, in addition to their development over the course of the year. These results can inform the design of courses, textbooks and also tools to target the most frequent (or hardest to fix) errors.

Categories and Subject Descriptors

K.3.2 [**Computers And Education**]: Computer and Information Science Education

General Terms

Experimentation

Keywords

Programming Mistakes; Blackbox

1. INTRODUCTION

Knowledge about students' mistakes and the time taken to fix errors is useful for many reasons. For example, Sadler et al [10] suggest that understanding student misconceptions is important to educator efficacy. Knowing which mistakes novices are likely to make or finding challenging informs the writing of instructional materials, such as textbooks, and can help improve the design and impact of beginner's IDEs or other educatoinal programming tools.

Previous studies that have investigated student errors during [Java] programming have focused on cohorts of up to 600 students at a single institution [1, 4, 5, 7, 8, 13]. However, the recently launched Blackbox data collection project [3] affords an opportunity to observe the mistakes of a large number of students across many institutions – for example, in one year of data, the project collected error messages and Java code from around 265,000 users worldwide. A previous study by the authors utilized four months of data from Blackbox to study educators opinions against the frequency of mistakes [2]. The contribution in our proposed paper is to go further, and provide a more detailed investigation into characteristics of the mistakes, trying to answer the following research questions:

- What are the most frequent mistakes in a large-scale multi-institution data set?
- What are the most common errors, and common classes of errors?
- Which errors take the shortest or longest time to fix?
- How do these errors evolve during the academic terms and academic year?

2. RELATED WORK

The concept of monitoring student programming behavior and mistakes has a long history in computing education research. The series of workshops on Empirical Studies of Programming [11] in the 1980s had several papers making use of this technique for Pascal and other languages. More recently, there have been many such studies specifically focused on Java, which is also the topic of this study.

Many of these studies used compiler error messages to classify mistakes. Jadud [8] looked in detail at student mistakes in Java and how students went about solving them. Tabanao et al. [13] looked at the association between errors and student course performance. Denny et al. [4] looked at how long students take to solve different errors. Dy and Rodrigo [5] looked at improving the error messages given to students. Ahmadzadeh et al. [1] looked at student error frequencies and debugging behavior. Jackson et al. [7] identified the most frequent errors among their novice programming students. All six of these studies looked at cohorts of (up to 600) students from a single institution. These studies used compiler error messages to classify errors, while early results from McCall and Kölling [9] suggest that compiler error messages have an imperfect (many-to-many) mapping to student misconceptions.

SIGCSE'15, March 4–7, 2015, Kansas City, MO, USA.

http://dx.doi.org/10.1145/2676723.2677258.

Our study is novel in that it looks at student mistakes from a much larger number of students (over 250,000) from a large number of institutions[1], thus providing more robust data about error frequencies, and error commonality. The Blackbox work was originally presented with a brief list of the most frequent compiler error messages [3], but in this study we do not simply use compiler error messages to classify errors. Instead, we borrow error classifications from Hristova et al. [6], which are based on surveying educators to ask for the most common Java mistakes they saw among their students.

3. METHOD

3.1 Student Mistakes

We use the 18 mistakes from our previous study [2] as a basis for our analysis, which in turn were derived from Hristova et al's [6] twenty student mistakes (derived from interviewing educators). The eighteen mistakes, labeled A through R, are informally categorized as follows:

Misunderstanding (or forgetting) syntax:

- **A**: Confusing the assignment operator (`=`) with the comparison operator (`==`).
  For example: `if (a = b) ...`
- **C**: Unbalanced parentheses, curly or square brackets and quotation marks, or using these different symbols interchangeably.
  For example: `while (a == 0]`
- **D**: Confusing "short-circuit" evaluators (`&&` and `||`) with conventional logical operators (`&` and `|`).
  For example: `if ((a == 0) & (b == 0)) ...`
- **E**: Incorrect semi-colon after an if selection structure before the if statement or after the for or while repetition structure before the respective for or while loop.
  For example:
  ```
  if (a == b);
      return 6;
  ```
- **F**: Wrong separators in for loops (using commas instead of semi-colons)
  For example: `for (int i = 0, i < 6, i++) ...`
- **G**: Inserting the condition of an if statement within curly brackets instead of parentheses.
  For example: `if {a == b} ...`
- **H**: Using keywords as method or variable names.
  For example: `int new;`
- **J**: Forgetting parentheses after a method call.
  For example: `myObject.toString;`
- **K**: Incorrect semicolon at the end of a method header.
  For example:
  ```
  public void foo();
  {
      ...
  }
  ```

[1]We have no way of measuring the number of institutions in the Blackbox data, but simply: the 250,000 students must be split over at least several hundred institutions.

- **L**: Getting greater than or equal/less than or equal wrong, i.e. using `=>` or `=<` instead of `>=` and `<=`.
  For example: `if (a =< b) ...`
- **P**: Including the types of parameters when invoking a method.
  For example: `myObject.foo(int x, String s);`

Type errors:

- **I**: Invoking methods with wrong arguments (e.g. wrong types).
  For example: `list.get("abc")`
- **Q**: Incompatible types between method return and type of variable that the value is assigned to.
  For example: `int x = myObject.toString();`

Other semantic errors:

- **B**: Use of `==` instead of `.equals` to compare strings.
  For example: `if (a == "start") ...`
- **M**: Trying to invoke a non-static method as if it was static.
  For example: `MyClass.toString();`
- **N**: A method that has a non-void return type is called and its return value ignored/discarded.
  For example: `myObject.toString();`
- **O**: Control flow can reach end of non-void method without returning.
  For example:
  ```
  public int foo(int x)
  {
      if (x < 0)
          return 0;
      x += 1;
  }
  ```
- **R**: Class claims to implement an interface, but does not implement all the required methods.
  For example: `class Y implements ActionListener { }`

Note that mistake *N* (ignoring the non-void result of a method) is not always an error (e.g. when you call a remove method that returns the item removed, you may not need to do anything with the return value).

3.2 Student data

Data about student mistakes was taken from the Blackbox data set [3], which collects Java code written by users of BlueJ, the Java beginners' IDE. We used data from the period 1st Sep. 2013 to 31st Aug. 2014 (inclusive), as representing a full year.

We had two methods of detecting mistakes. For four of the student mistakes, *I, M, O, R*, we were able to use the compiler error message directly from Blackbox's compilations to detect the mistake. However, this was not possible for the other errors, as some of them are logical errors that do not cause a compiler error or warning, while in other cases the error messages do not have a one-to-one mapping to our mistakes of interest. Thus for one of the other mistakes (*C*) we performed a post-lexing analysis (matching brackets) and for the final thirteen we used a customized permissive parser to parse the source code and look for the errors. The source code of all the tools used is available for analysis or re-use [2].

We took each source file in the data set, and tracked the file over time. At each compilation we checked the source file for the eighteen mistakes. If the mistake was present, we then looked forward in time to find the next compilation where the mistake was no longer present (or until we had no further data for that source file). When the mistake was no longer found – which could have been because the mistake was corrected or because the offending code was removed or commented out – we counted this as one instance of the mistake. Further occurrences in the same source file were treated as further instances. We calculate the time in seconds between the first appearance of the mistake and the possible fix and cap it at 1000 seconds, for any mistake which takes longer than 1000 seconds to fix, or is never fixed. We also counted the number of distinct users who committed each mistake at least once.

4. RESULTS

Our detector is used to look for the number of instances of mistakes, as described in section 3.2. The data set featured 37,158,094 compilation events, of which 19,476,087 were successful and 17,682,007 were unsuccessful. Each compilation may include multiple source files – the total number of source files input to compilation (i.e. each source file may be counted multiple times) was 46,448,212, of which 24,264,603 were compiled successfully and 22,183,609 were not.

4.1 Mistakes Overview

The Frequencies, number of Distinct Users and Time-to-Fix results of each different mistake are shown in Table 1, along with our informal classification of the error message. It can be seen that although Mistake *C* is the most frequent, the type and semantic errors are generally more frequent than syntax errors. The ranking of frequency is similar to the ranking of the number of distinct users, as shown in Figure 1. This figure confirms that the number of users is related to the frequency of the mistakes. However, each mistake is not made the same number of times by each user that makes it. Figure 2 shows that some mistakes (*F, G, H, L*) are generally made only once by the user – a rare mistake, or one that they easily learn from. In contrast, mistakes such as *C*, *I* and *O* are made repeatedly by students – in the case of *C* (mismatched brackets), a syntax error, this is likely to be an easy accident, but in the case of *I* (wrong types in method call) and *O* (missing return statement) this is more likely to be a lack of understanding or difficulty with the concepts of types and control flow.

It is clear from Table 1 that, as expected, mistakes which don't result in a compiler error tend to take much longer to be fixed, such as Mistakes *N*, *B* and *D*. Mistake *E* gets fixed more quickly; although it does not cause a compile error, it has a more noticeable effect on the program's control flow.

To examine this relation more, Figure 3 shows a scatter plot for the mistake Frequencies against Time-to-Fix. If it was the case that students learned to quickly fix the most frequent errors, we would expect a trend along a diagonal line from top left to bottom right. This is not the case, showing that the time to fix an error is not noticeably related to how often a student will encounter it.

Mistake	Freq.	Distinct Users	Median Time to Fix	Error Type
C	793232	119407	17	Syntax
I	464075	66977	58	Type
O	342891	57129	37	Semantic
A	173938	45082	111	Syntax
N*	121663	27369	$\geq$ 1000	Semantic
B*	121172	29627	$\geq$ 1000	Semantic
M	86625	26527	48	Semantic
R	79462	17521	104	Semantic
P	52862	21904	24	Syntax
E*	49375	18350	401	Syntax
K	38001	19502	51	Syntax
D*	29605	8742	$\geq$ 1000	Syntax
J	18955	10232	34	Syntax
Q	16996	7556	115	Type
L	4214	3317	12	Syntax
F	2719	2244	36	Syntax
H	1097	943	22	Syntax
G	118	112	26	Syntax

Table 1: Statistics for mistakes committed by Blackbox students between 1st Sep. 2013 to 31st Aug. 2014 (inclusive). The results are sorted according to frequency in descending order. Most mistakes will result in a compiler error message being shown to the user – those mistakes which do not cause a compiler error have an asterisk.

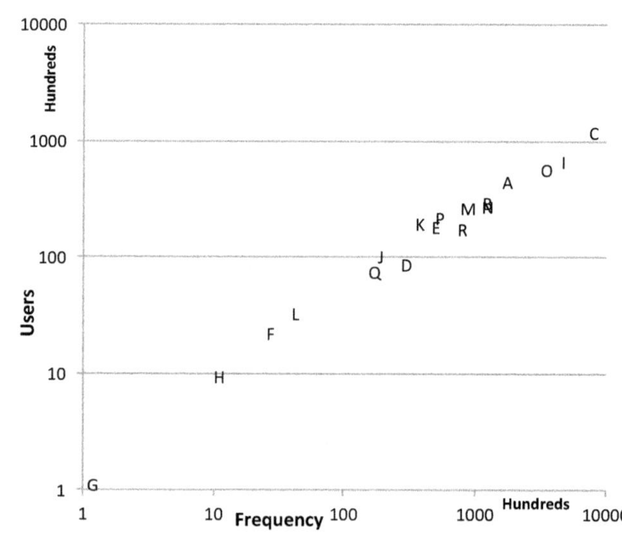

Figure 1: Log-log plot of Frequency vs Distinct users. Mistake *N* overlaps Mistake *B* towards the right.

[2]See: `http://www.cs.kent.ac.uk/~nccb/blackbox/`

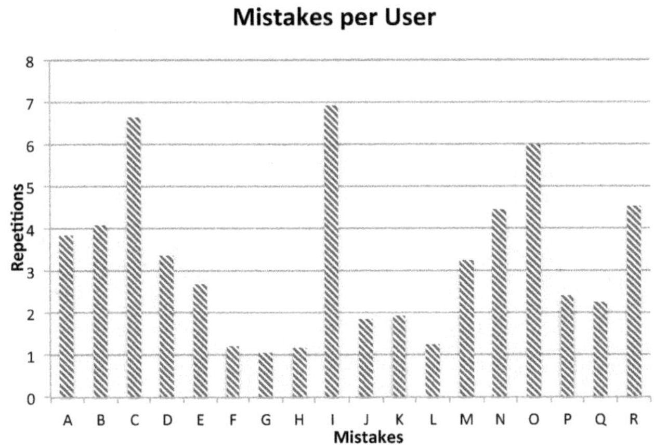

Figure 2: The average of number of times that each user who made a mistake, repeated it. For example, each user who made mistake *G* only made it approximately once, while each user who made mistake *B* made it four times on average.

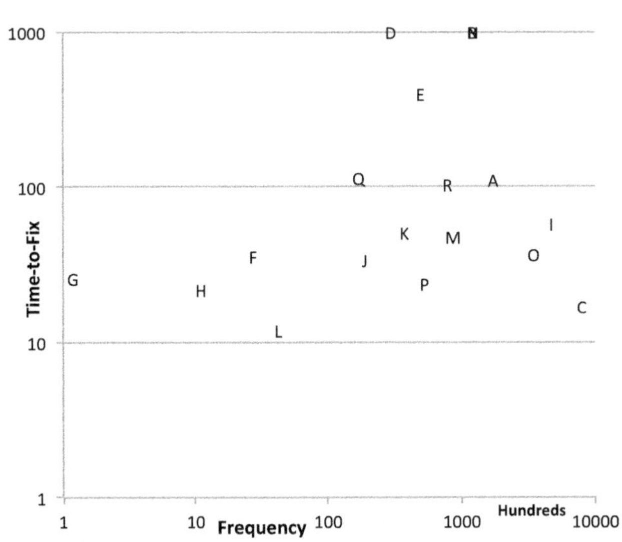

Figure 3: Log-log plot of Frequency vs Time-to-Fix. Mistake *N* overlaps Mistake *B* in the top right. Mistakes *N*, *B* and *D* have a median equal to the cap value of 1000, which means that more than half of the instances appeared took ≥ 1000 seconds to fix or were not fixed at all.

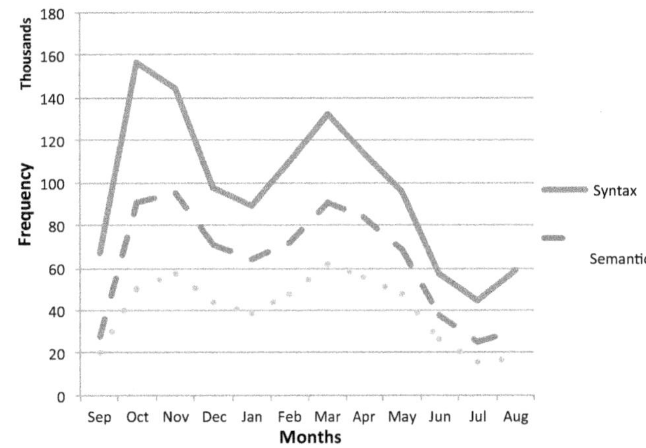

Figure 4: The development of frequency of mistakes categories over months (not normalised). The start of terms is very clear in all of the three categories.

4.2 Mistakes Over Time

To have a deeper look on these factors and to understand the effect of the learning process on these mistakes, we analysed the mistake factors over the course of the year, split into months. Figure 4 outlines the mistake frequencies for the three proposed categories over the course of 12 months, without normalization (i.e. raw figures, which are clearly affected by the number of compilations changing between months). The three curves show clear peaks in the number of errors (and underneath, the number of compilations) in October/November and March.

To allow a better comparison, the data is rendered again in Figure 5 after normalization: we divide the frequencies of the mistakes in each category in each month by the number of total compilations in that month. At the start of the data (and to a smaller degree at the turn of the calendar year), Syntax errors show a small peak at the beginning of the northern hemisphere academic year, but otherwise are fairly flat. In the contrast, the slight peaks for the Semantic and Type categories happen later. We propose that this is due to the order of topics in academic courses: students initially struggle with syntax, but as they master this, they begin to grapple instead with semantic and type errors.

As described in section 4.1, and shown in Table 1, Mistake C is clearly the most frequent mistake – but in general, Semantic mistakes were more frequent than Syntax mistakes. However, Mistake C is also one of the fastest mistakes to fix, and thus could be considered relatively unproblematic. Figure 6 shows the same data as Figure 5, but with mistake C removed. With this adjustment, Syntax errors are much less common, and show less of an early peak, suggesting that students learn, to some extent, to avoid making the C bracket mistakes.

This suggestion that students learn to avoid C is confirmed in figure 7, which shows the normalized number of users making each mistake (not the frequency). Mistake C shows a peak in Aug/Sep at the start of the northern hemisphere academic year, whereas many of the other errors have a fairly flat distribution across the 12 months. This suggests that users are not learning to completely avoid the non-C mistakes over the course of the year.

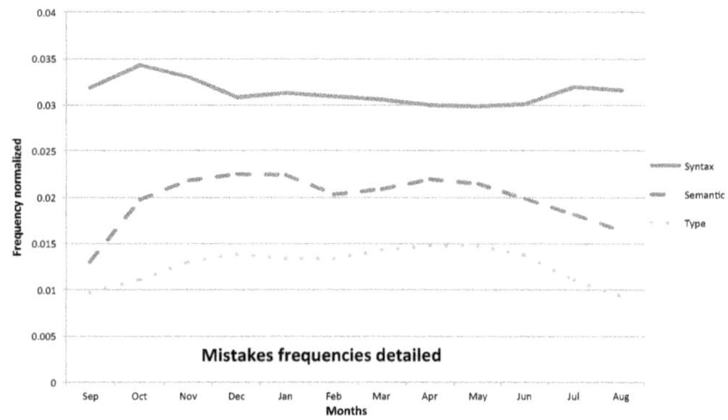

Figure 5: The development of normalized frequency of mistakes categories over months. While the Syntax errors tend to flatten after a while after each term starting, the Semantic and Type ones increase.

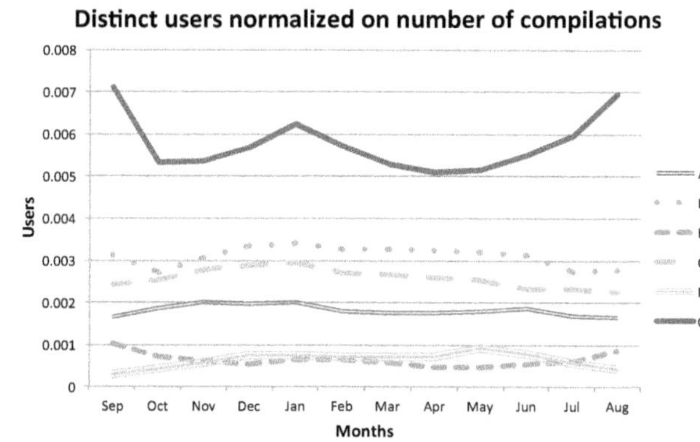

Figure 7: The development of normalized number of distinct users over months, for some selected mistakes. Omitted mistakes have almost the same shape as the ones presented, except C, and been removed for clarity only. The curve representing Mistake C is the most interesting one, showing that around quarter of students learn to avoid it towards the mid of the term.

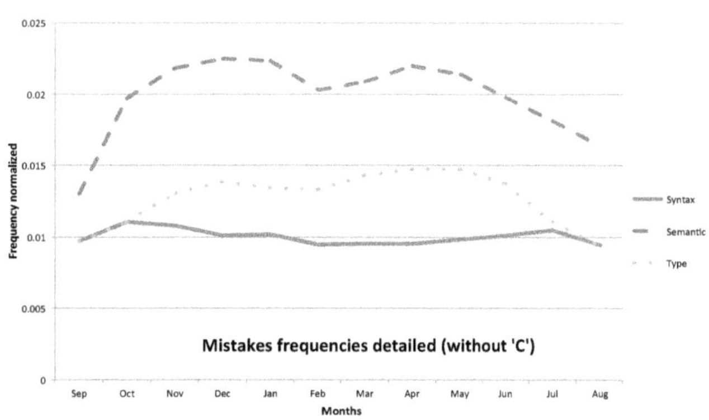

Figure 6: The development of normalized frequency of mistakes categories over months, after omitting Mistake C. The drop of the Syntax errors below the other two categories is very clear, maintaining its shape. This supports the importance of focusing more on the Semantic and Type errors.

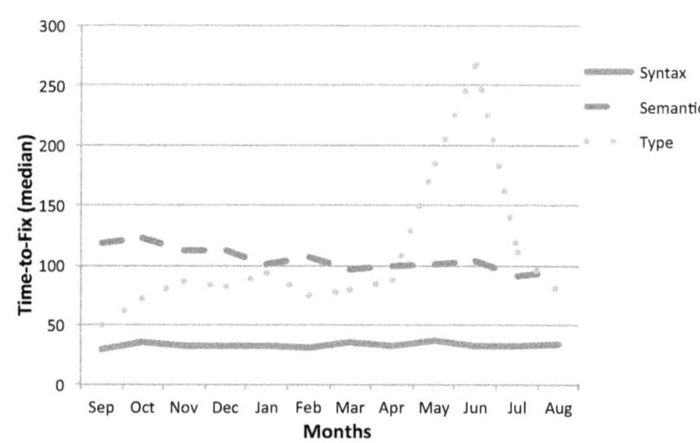

Figure 8: The development of the median of time-to-fix over months for the mistakes' categories. While the Syntax mistakes are almost quick to fix and consistent over time, the Semantic ones need more efforts and this decreases a little over time. The Type curve is interesting as it shows a sudden rise and drop towards the end of the academic year, possibly due to introducing advance types for students.

The time-to-fix statistics are shown in figure 8. Time-to-fix of Syntax mistakes is almost flat, showing that they are quick to fix, but students do not generally get faster at fixing them. In contrast, Semantic mistakes show a decrease of the time needed to fix over the course of the year, Type mistakes show a strange, unexpected shape. The only interpretation we can offer is that with the increase of topics introduced to students, moving from primitive types to generic types and inheritance, students tend to make more mistakes between these 'more difficult' types.

5. CONCLUSIONS

The large sample-size of data from the Blackbox project provides comprehensive information about the frequency, spread of errors among users and time-to-fix of different Java errors, shown in Table 1. Unlike many previous studies, the analysis of errors is decoupled from compiler error messages.

Mismatched brackets and quotations – a syntax error – are the most popular error category among novice programmers, but are also the quickest to be fixed. Other Syntax errors are less frequent than Semantic and Type errors. With the exception of mismatched brackets and quotations, Semantic errors tend to appear higher than the other types. Recent research has suggested that Java has syntax which is not much better than an arbitrary choice of syntax for learning [12], but perhaps the syntax of a language does not matter as much as semantics. It is also clear that some of the mistakes (especially L, F, H and G) are particularly low frequency, in contrast to Hristova et al.'s [6] original aim to find the top 20 errors.

Global starts and finishes of the northern hemisphere's academic terms are detectable, and they have an effect on the frequency of Mistakes and time needed to fix them. The frequency of different classes of mistake changes over time: Semantic mistakes tend to increase in frequency later on in courses, while Syntax mistakes decrease.

We should be careful not to over-interpret this result as it is greatly affected by which mistakes we included in the study, but our results suggest that semantic errors are a more serious challenge than syntax errors.

The mistakes in this study were automatically detected using a set of tools. If these tools were not sufficiently accurate in picking up mistakes, this could have affected our results, and are thus a threat to validity. To this end, the source code is freely available (see section 3.2) in case further investigation is warranted.

6. REFERENCES

[1] M. Ahmadzadeh, D. Elliman, and C. Higgins. An analysis of patterns of debugging among novice computer science students. In *Proceedings of the 10th Annual SIGCSE Conference on Innovation and Technology in Computer Science Education*, ITiCSE '05, pages 84–88, New York, NY, USA, 2005. ACM.

[2] N. C. C. Brown and A. Altadmri. Investigating novice programming mistakes: educator beliefs vs. student data. In *Proceedings of the tenth annual conference on International computing education research*, pages 43–50. ACM, 2014.

[3] N. C. C. Brown, M. Kölling, D. McCall, and I. Utting. Blackbox: A large scale repository of novice programmers' activity. In *Proceedings of the 45th ACM Technical Symposium on Computer Science Education*, SIGCSE '14, pages 223–228, New York, NY, USA, 2014. ACM.

[4] P. Denny, A. Luxton-Reilly, and E. Tempero. All syntax errors are not equal. In *Proceedings of the 17th ACM Annual Conference on Innovation and Technology in Computer Science Education*, ITiCSE '12, pages 75–80, New York, NY, USA, 2012. ACM.

[5] T. Dy and M. M. Rodrigo. A detector for non-literal Java errors. In *Proceedings of the 10th Koli Calling International Conference on Computing Education Research*, Koli Calling '10, pages 118–122, New York, NY, USA, 2010. ACM.

[6] M. Hristova, A. Misra, M. Rutter, and R. Mercuri. Identifying and correcting Java programming errors for introductory computer science students. In *Proceedings of the 34th SIGCSE Technical Symposium on Computer Science Education*, SIGCSE '03, pages 153–156, New York, NY, USA, 2003. ACM.

[7] J. Jackson, M. Cobb, and C. Carver. Identifying top Java errors for novice programmers. In *Frontiers in Education, 2005. FIE '05. Proceedings 35th Annual Conference*, Oct 2005.

[8] M. C. Jadud. Methods and tools for exploring novice compilation behaviour. In *Proceedings of the Second International Workshop on Computing Education Research*, ICER '06, pages 73–84, New York, NY, USA, 2006. ACM.

[9] D. McCall and M. Kölling. Meaningful categorisation of novice programmer errors. In *Frontiers In Education Conference*, pages 2589–2596, 2014.

[10] P. M. Sadler, G. Sonnert, H. P. Coyle, N. Cook-Smith, and J. L. Miller. The influence of teachers' knowledge on student learning in middle school physical science classrooms. *American Educational Research Journal*, 50(5):1020–1049, 2013.

[11] E. Soloway and S. Iyengar, editors. *Empirical Studies of Programmers: Papers Presented at the First Workshop on Empirical Studies of Programmers.* Intellect Books, 1986.

[12] A. Stefik and S. Siebert. An empirical investigation into programming language syntax. *Trans. Comput. Educ.*, 13(4):19:1–19:40, Nov. 2013.

[13] E. S. Tabanao, M. M. T. Rodrigo, and M. C. Jadud. Predicting at-risk novice Java programmers through the analysis of online protocols. In *Proceedings of the Seventh International Workshop on Computing Education Research*, ICER '11, pages 85–92, New York, NY, USA, 2011. ACM.

Looking Glass

A C++ Library for Testing Student Programs through Reflection

Scott Turner
Department of Math and Computer Science
UNC Pembroke
Pembroke, NC
scott.turner@uncp.edu

ABSTRACT

Looking Glass (https://github.com/sturner84/LookingGlass) is a library designed to support the testing of students' C++ code through reflection. Instructors can design tests that compile even if there are mismatches between the instructor's and student's code (like misspelled function names or parameters that do not have the expected types). Using the automatically generated metadata, instructors can search for and call functions or methods in the student code, including the main function, while providing feedback (rather than a compile error) if the required code is not found. Although not suitable for all C++ programs, Looking Glass was designed to support instructors in introductory and intermediate classes and to be transparent to the students.

Categories and Subject Descriptors

D.2.5 [**Software**]: Testing and Debugging – *Testing tools (e.g., data generators, coverage testing).*

General Terms

Languages

Keywords

C++, Reflection, Instructor testing

1. INTRODUCTION

One of the goals for automated graders of computer programs (Web-CAT, autograder, Parikshak, etc.) is to provide immediate and useful feedback to the student [8, 11]. This gives the students an opportunity to learn from their mistakes, correct them, and try again. Generally, this process has the instructors writing unit tests (in a framework like JUnit, CxxTest, or NUnit) with feedback for the student.

When a student submits his or her work, one of three things happens. The first possibility is that the submission compiles, the instructor's tests are run and, if a test fails, the student receives an appropriate hint. The second option is that the student's work fails to compile at all due to errors in the code (incorrect syntax, missing files, etc.). This should be expected since, aside from the case where not all of the required files were uploaded, the error messages should be the same (or nearly the same) as those being provided from the student's compiler.

It is the third case that can cause some unexpected trouble. In this situation, the student's code compiles correctly against itself but fails to compile against the instructor's code. This could be caused by something simple, like a misspelled class name or a method with an extra parameter, but the result may be a cryptic compiler error and no grade at all. Since compiler messages are generally not created with a novice programmer in mind and have a long history of being confusing and opaque, the feedback may be useless and frustrating to the student [2, 9, 10]. It is especially maddening if the error message references the instructor's tests since it is likely that the student has no knowledge of them.

For example, if a student implements a function but swaps the order of the parameters, the error message might be something like what follows:

```
In function 'TableTest::testScaleValue(
double, double)': undefined reference to
'scaleValue(std::basic_istream<char,
std::char_traits<char> >&, double)'
```

To students learning C++, this error may be completely baffling especially since they did not define a function with a parameter of type "*std::basic_istream<char, std::char_traits<char> >&*"; they used "*istream*". The addition of TableTest and testScaleValue is also confusing since they do not exist in the student's code but seem to be the source of the problem. While all of the information that the student needs is contained in the message, it is much harder to parse. An unfortunate side effect is that this error prevents any of the unit tests from being run and curtails any other feedback (or grade) the student might have received.

1.1 Need

How common is this problem? To answer this question, data was collected from three semesters of a CS1 C++ class. The class has 15 programming assignments (nine tiny labs, three slightly bigger labs, and three programming projects). Of those, ten are written entirely in main function and the remaining five require the students to write multiple functions. All of the programs were submitted to an automated grader where they were allowed unlimited submissions.

During the three semesters, 66 students made 2307 submissions and, of those, 389 did not compile. Upon examination, it was determined that almost half (189) of those errors were due to mistakes when declaring the main function or to mismatches

SIGCSE '15, March 04 - 07 2015, Kansas City, MO, USA

ACM 978-1-4503-2966-8/15/03…$15.00
http://dx.doi.org/10.1145/2676723.2677281

between the student's code and what was expected in the instructor's tests (see Table 1).

The data was also divided by the type of assignment (those entirely in main and those with multiple functions) and by assignment to see where the problems were occurring. When looking at the type of assignment, those programs with multiple functions contained the majority of the total errors and of the mismatch errors but used less than half of the submissions (see Table 2).

Table 1: Submission Compile Errors

	Submissions	*Errors*	*Mismatch Errors*
All	2307	389 (16.8%)	189 (8.2%)

When looking at the data by assignment, some fairly predictable patterns were found. The number of errors were very high for the very first programming assignment (L2.1), for the first one using functions (L5.1) and for the projects (especially those with functions – P2 and P3; see Figure 1). Some of the common mismatches included misspelled function names, missing required functions, and incorrectly declared parameters (i.e. not passing them by reference when required by the specifications or putting them in the wrong order). In many cases, the programs with these errors were partially to completely functional when run on their own.

Table 2: Submission by Type of Assignment

	Submissions	*Errors*	*Mismatch Errors*
Main Only	1373 (59.5%)	140 (36.0%)	41 (21.7%)
Multiple Functions	934 (40.5%)	249 (64.0%)	148 (78.3%)

Further analysis showed that while 15 (22.7%) of the students never had this problem, 16 (24.2%) of their classmates *only* had this problem. It should also be noted that 14 (21.2%) of the students submitted an assignment, encountered this problem and then did not submit that assignment again. The data is not detailed enough to provide a reason for why those students did not resubmit but one possibility is that, for at least some of them, they became frustrated and stopped working on the assignment.

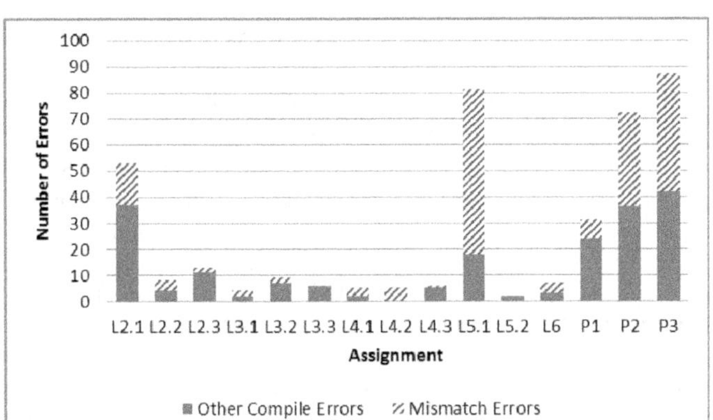

Figure 1: Errors by Assignment

Based on these findings, it appears that a sizable number of students would benefit if this problem was handled better.

1.2 Goals

The overall goal of this project is to handle, gracefully, this mismatch between the student's and instructor's code in C++ programs. This means allowing for useful, clear feedback when the problem occurs while permitting other tests to complete, if possible.

There were two critical requirements that the solution needed to meet:

1. The solution must support the C++ features commonly used in CS1/CS2 classes.

This includes the ability to test variables, functions, operators, classes, and inheritance (i.e. does A inherit from B). It should also be possible to test programs that are entirely or partially located in the main function. These features should be available whether the program is a single file or multiple files.

2. The solution must be completely transparent to the student.

The students should be able to write their code without any knowledge of the tests or how it is being tested. This means no files to include, no "magic" macros to instrument their code, or any other, similar approach.

Secondary goals include:

1. Simplified syntax and use for common tasks (creating objects, calling methods, etc.)
2. Support for common testing features (I/O redirection, tokenization, running the main function, etc.)
3. Streamlined setup for instructors (Eclipse plugin, cross-compiler and cross-OS support)

2. RELATED LIBRARIES/TOOLS

To achieve the goals of this project, the instructor's code would need to determine, at run-time, the structure of the student's code and be able to conditionally create objects, invoke functions and methods and access variables. This requires reflection.

In programming, reflection refers to the ability to determine, at run-time, what classes, methods, variables, etc. exist in a program and to access those values. Many languages, like Java and C# support this kind of functionality directly. For instance, in Java, one can search for the file of a compiled class, load it into memory, instantiate the class, look through its methods and then call one of them. One can determine the number and type of a method's parameters, find out the visibility of a variable, or discover just about anything else that needs to be known about the loaded class without explicitly knowing it at compile time. This meta-programming functionality is needed to decouple the student's and instructor's code.

Since reflection is not natively supported in C or C++ at anything beyond a trivial level, a survey of existing C++ reflection libraries was conducted.

The survey found numerous open source projects that added reflection functionality to C++. These varied greatly in the features they supported and in the maturity of their development. However, most of these libraries required the code being reflected

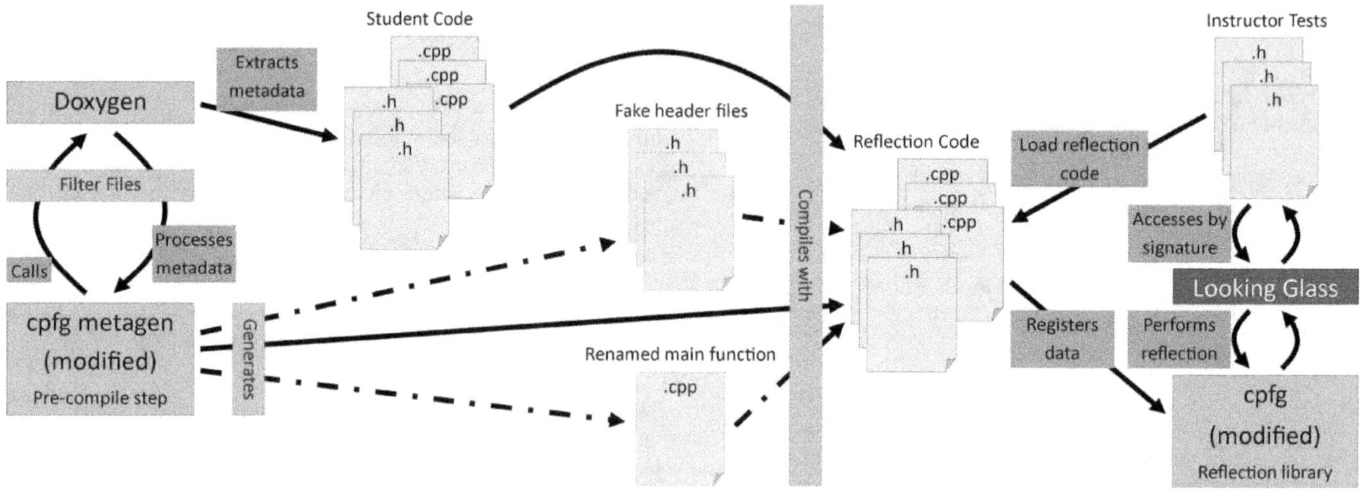

Figure 2: Looking Glass's Reflection Process

to be explicitly registered (by inheriting from certain classes, by using macros, etc.) and, as such, they did not meet the goals of this project. There were a few tools that automatically generated the metadata needed for reflection. These are discussed below.

The XCppRefl library has many of the same general goals as this project and has a simple syntax for accessing the metadata, creating objects, and invoking methods [4]. The authors state that the metadata needed for reflection is created by parsing the code of the reflected files. The paper does not expand on this and an initial examination of the code did not provide much additional information [5]. It would seem that this part of the tool is still in the early stages of development.

Another project, Mirror [3], is being developed with the goal of being included in the Boost libraries [1]. As such, it follows Boost's coding guidelines and it relies very heavily on the use of templates when accessing the reflected code. This makes the code verbose and fairly difficult to read. One of Mirror's sub-projects, MAuReEn, uses Doxygen [6] and xslt to generate the reflection metadata. The documentation does not explicitly state what can be reflected automatically with this tool.

The cpgf library was designed to support reflection and the binding of scripting languages (Lua, Python, etc.) to C++ [13]. The code relies heavily on macros and requires several steps to achieve some common tasks. As a result, the code can be somewhat hard to read and write. The library also includes a Java tool that uses Doxygen to generate metadata. This functions reasonably well but does not include some of the type information that might be desired.

It should be noted that, as far as could be determined, these three libraries do not support the reflection and calling of the main function. Based on the libraries' goals, that is a very reasonable design decision and that functionality would not be needed in any programs that used those libraries. However, that is an important feature when testing code from CS1/CS2 students since some of their programs may be partially or totally contained in main.

One final library to be mentioned is ReflectionSupport [12]. This is a reflection library for Java that aims to streamline common reflection tasks and improve some of the error handling in those processes. The beauty of ReflectionSupport is that it hides most of the complexities of reflection behind its API and reduces each of those common tasks to a single method call that does not require a try-catch. Unless the user wants to handle specific errors, these are handled behind the scenes. This tool is mentioned because it has the kind of simplicity that this project wants to achieve.

3. LOOKING GLASS

At the end of the survey, it was determined that none of the libraries reviewed met the goals of this project either because they did not have the functionality required or they were not transparent to the user. Looking Glass was developed to fill this gap.

Looking Glass was built on top of the cpgf library [13] and uses its metagen tool to generate the reflection metadata. Both have been modified to include more metadata (namespaces, type data, private and protected data, etc.). Looking Glass then adds a layer of abstraction and additional functionality over cpgf to create an interface that supports many of the same features as those found in ReflectionSupport [12].

Looking Glass is open source and can be found at: https://github.com/sturner84/LookingGlass.

3.1 Features

Looking Glass can access and enumerate most of the structures in C++. This includes globally declared items like global variables and constants, functions, enums and structs. Unions are not currently supported. Classes and their fields, methods, operators, enums, inner classes and base classes are also supported. While only public class members are accessible and invokable, private and protected members can be enumerated.

Any of these items can be looked up by its signature or retrieved as a group. Signatures are normalized so that different but equivalent declarations will match (i.e. int const x will match const int x). Filters can be applied to any of the lookups to refine the items returned by visibility, whether they were inherited or not, and by their modifiers. For the modifiers, filters can be used to specify modifiers that are required (i.e. get everything that is const) or modifiers that should be excluded (i.e. get everything that is not mutable) or both. This is useful, for instance, to find all of the variables declared globally that are not constants.

Namespaces can be reflected and enumerated as well. Any item declared in a namespace can be accessed through that namespace.

It should be noted that anonymous namespaces are not currently supported and that, while namespaces can be listed as they were declared, the reflection process effectively ignores namespaces. That means that name collisions (and the compilation errors that result) are possible for items declared in separate namespaces.

Common tasks, such as getting/setting variables, creating objects and calling methods were designed to be as simple as possible and can be done with a single method call. The memory associated with the reflected data is automatically released when it no longer used so there is no need to manually delete the objects created.

Calling the main function is a special case and has some additional support. First, since there are a few different, valid variants for the main function, Looking Glass handles four versions of main: with no parameters or with, optionally, the command line, the environment, or additional OS information (sometimes used on macs). The type of main function implemented can be determined before it is called but that is not required since the library will call main regardless of the parameters given or not given. That is, if it is called without enough parameters, it will supply default values and if it is called with too many, they will be ignored.

Since programs written entirely in main typically use the standard input/output to communicate, cin and cout can be redirected as part of the call to main to streamline the testing. See sections 3.1.1 and 3.2.1.2 for more details about the main function and its use.

3.1.1 Metadata generation

Generating the reflection metadata is done by creating an xml description of data with Doxygen and the processing those files with the metagen tool (see Figure 2). The result is a set of files and a function that, when invoked, registers all of the reflected code with the library. As part of the process, the source files can be filtered. This step generally excludes .cpp files that have .h files of the same name and test files (files that end with Test.h).

Following the filtering, metagen can create header files for any .cpp files that do not already have a matching header file. This allows the instructor to test single file programs without having to teach separate compilation to the students. Global variables and constants are preserved in the creation of the header file so that they can be tested.

Finally, since C++ does not allow the main function to be called directly, a callable version of main can be automatically created. This creates a separate .cpp file with a renamed copy of main.

All of the features mentioned can be modified through metagen's configuration file.

3.1.2 Additional testing features

Looking Glass also provides a number of classes to make testing easier. As mentioned before, I/O redirection is available for cin and cout. There is a class to help with the tokenization of strings and to extract numbers from the string output. Finally, there is support for running tests (or any other methods) in a separate thread. This can be used to check for infinite loops.

3.2 Usage

While Looking Glass is transparent to the student, it does require some extra work from the instructor when creating tests. This includes the one-time tasks of installing and compiling the needed libraries and the per assignment tasks of setting up the compilation environment and the pre-build step for generating the metadata. For detailed information about installing and setting up Looking Glass, visit the wiki on the web site. It also contains additional examples of its use.

3.2.1 Examples of use

The following examples use CxxTest as the unit testing framework. They should be similar in other frameworks.

3.2.1.1 Preparing for reflection

```
bool setUpWorld() {
  //load metadata before first test
  cpptest_meta::
    registerMetaDataToGlobal();
  return true;
}
```

Figure 3: Registering Metadata

Before any reflection can be done, the metadata needs to be registered with the program. Normally, this would be done in a global setup method for the unit tests (see Figure 3), but it is safe to call the registering method multiple times. The name of the method and the namespace it is located in can be modified in metagen's configuration file.

3.2.1.2 Testing main

Since calling and testing the main function is a common task in this context, Looking Glass provides a set of methods to test for its existence and to call it. In this example, the test looks for any valid definition of main before invoking it without parameters. (As noted before, default parameters are supplied as needed if main is defined with parameters.) After the function call, the value returned from main and the text written to cout are compared to the expected output (see Figure 4).

```
void testMain() {
  //check if main was reflected
  LookingGlass::MAIN_TYPE type =
    LookingGlass::doesMainExist();
  //provide a message if not found
  TSM_ASSERT_DIFFERS(
    "No main method could be found!"
    LookingGlass:: NO_MAIN, type);
  std::string out; //store main's output
  //Calls main while redirecting cout
  int val = LookingGlass::invokeMain(
    out);
  //check value returned from main
  TS_ASSERT_EQUALS(val, 0);
  TS_ASSERT_EQUALS("Hello! !olleH\n",
    out); //check output
}
```

Figure 4: Calling the Main Function

3.2.1.3 Creating an object

Most of the functionality in Looking Glass is accessible through the ReflectedData class. It provides the methods for enumerating and accessing the various reflected items. In Figure 5, ReflectedData is used to find a class (testing to see if it exists first). Creating the object requires the constructor's signature and the appropriate parameters.

```
void testCreateObject() {
  //get the reflected data
  ReflectedData* data =
    ReflectedData::getDataInstance();
  //exists?
  TSM_ASSERT("Class Test was not found",
    data->doesClassExist("Test"));
  //get the class
  const ReflectedClass* tClass =
    data->getClass("Test");
  //create the object
  ReflectedObjectPtr tObject =
    tClass->create("Test(int)", 15);
  ETSM_ASSERT("Test object not created",
    tObject);
}
```

Figure 5: Creating an Object

3.2.1.4 Calling a method

Once an object has been created, methods can be called using the invoke and invokeReturn methods (see Figure 6). As with creating an object, both methods use the signature of the method to look it up and call it. The invokeReturn method uses an additional reference parameter to store the result of the method call. Calling functions follows a similar pattern but can be called on the LookingGlass class (like main).

```
void testMethodCall() {
  //get an object and do other setup
  //...
  int result;
  //call a method on tObject
  ETSM_ASSERT("Couldn't call reset",
    tObject->invokeReturn(
      "int reset(bool)", result, true));
  ETSM_ASSERT_EQUALS(
    "reset should return 1", result, 1);
}
```

Figure 6: Calling a Method

3.2.1.5 Modifying a global variable

```
void testModifyVariable() {
  //get an object and do other setup
  //...
  int x;
  TSM_ASSERT("Could not get badVar",
    LookingGlass::getGlobalVariable(x,
     "int badVar");
  x = x + 5; //change value
  //update variable
  TSM_ASSERT("Could not set badVar",
    LookingGlass::setGlobalVariable(x,
      "int badVar");
 }
```

Figure 7: Modifying a Global Variable

Modifying global variables requires that the value be retrieved and then set through the LookingGlass class. Accessing public fields in an object is similar.

3.2.1.6 Enumerating public fields

This example uses a filter to test how well a class is encapsulated. Specifically, the test looks for public fields that are not declared as const by applying a filter to the getFieldNames method (see Figure 8).

```
void testPublicFields() {
  //get an object and do other setup
  //...
  //Filter ignores const fields
  ItemFilter nonConst(Public_Access,
    false, cpgf::metaModifierNone,
    cpgf::metaModifierConst);
  //gets the name of non-const fields
  std::vector<std::string> fNames =
    cppClass->getFieldNames(nonConst);
  //If public fields exist, fail
  if (fNames.size() > 0) {
    std::string fieldStr =
      "The following fields "
      "are public when they should "
      "be declared to be private: ";
    for (std::vector<std::string>
      ::iterator i = fNames.begin();
      i != fNames.end(); i++) {
        fieldStr += *i + " ";
    }
    TS_FAIL(fieldStr);
  }
}
```

Figure 8: Enumerating public fields

3.3 Known Limitations

While Looking Glass handles most of the common reflection tasks well, it does not and cannot reflect everything that can be created in C++. Some of the limitations may be overcome in future versions, but some cannot be.

One limitation that cannot currently be implemented is the reflection of templates. To be able to reflect and instantiate a templated class or invoke a templated function, one would need to be able to compile the template as the reflection code is running. Otherwise, one would already have to know at compile time that the template exists and what data types it can use, which defeats the purpose of reflection. It would be possible to reflect the signatures of these templated structures (like private methods are) but this is not currently supported. Templates that have already been instantiated (like std::string) can be reflected correctly.

Other features not supported include variadic and default parameters, typedefs and #define statement. Supporting these features would add a lot of complexity to the library but not necessarily a lot of benefits and so are not implemented. Partial support may be added later.

4. SUMMARY

Looking Glass was designed as a solution to the problem of students' code not compiling against the instructor's tests. It uses reflection to remove the dependencies between the instructor's tests and the student's code with the goal that, if the student's code compiles, then the instructor's code will compile as well.

This project has met its primary goals of being able to reflect most of the code typical in introductory and intermediate C++ programming classes and to be transparent to the student. Instructors can create code that determines if classes, fields, methods/functions, or other items exist in the student's solution before trying to use them. This lets the instructor provide useful feedback instead of a compile error. It also allows other tests to run despite the errors and to provide information (and a score) for the unaffected parts of the code. The result is a better error message and a more consistent experience for the student.

The use of a tool to generate the reflection metadata hides the process from the students. They can write their code completely in main or as series of source and header files and Looking Glass can appropriately handle either without any special annotations or includes.

Looking Glass also partially met its secondary goals of a simple, streamlined syntax, additional testing support, and a simple setup for instructors. Common tasks can be done with a few lines of code without the need to write a lot of templated code or to deal with the details of the reflection process. Features like I/O redirection and tokenization are provided, as well. What is missing is some of the tool support needed to simplify the setup and use of the library for the instructors. This is discussed briefly in the next section.

5. FUTURE WORK

The next step for Looking Glass is to improve its integration with other tools. This includes developing a plugin for Eclipse to allow instructors to more easily write tests with the library and run them. Integration with Web-CAT [7], an online grader, is also necessary so that instructors can deploy their tests to their students.

Additional work needs to be done to ensure that Looking Glass is usable on multiple platforms and with multiple compilers. The cpgf library has been tested fairly thoroughly in this regard but the modifications and the Looking Glass library, in particular, have not.

Currently, the metadata generation uses Doxygen and regular expressions to pull out the relevant information. While this works, there are likely to be cases that are not covered well. Similarly, the lookup methods that match variable/method signatures to the reflected data may not always find the correct information if two different but equivalent data types are used. Using a typedef, for instance, could cause this problem. One possibility is to use a complier front-end to parse the data as this should alleviate much of the issue. This would require a major reworking of the library and is not currently being pursued.

Finally, the library needs to be continually refined and the support of common tasks improved. Due to the complexity of the C++ language, there are sure to be many edge cases that are not correctly handled. Those need to be identified and corrected if possible.

6. REFERENCES

[1] Boost. *http://www.boost.org/. Accessed 9/2/2014.*

[2] Brown, P.J. 1983. Error messages: the neglected area of the man/machine interface. *Commun. ACM.*

[3] Chochlík, M. *Mirror. http://kifri.fri.uniza.sk/~chochlik/mirror-lib/html/index.html. Accessed 9/1/2014.*

[4] Devadithya, T. et al. 2007. C++ reflection for high performance problem solving environments. *Proceedings of the 2007 spring simulation multiconference - Volume 2* (Norfolk, Virginia, 2007), 435–440.

[5] Devadithya, T. et al. *XCppRefl - C++ Reflection Library. http://www.extreme.indiana.edu/reflcpp/. Accessed 9/1/14.*

[6] Doxygen. *http://www.stack.nl/~dimitri/doxygen/index.html. Accessed 9/2/2014.*

[7] Edwards, S.H. *Web-CAT. http://web-cat.cs.vt.edu/. Accessed 9/1/2014.*

[8] Edwards, S.H. and Perez-Quinones, M.A. 2007. Experiences using test-driven development with an automated grader. *J. Comput. Small Coll.* 22, 3 (2007), 44–50.

[9] Marceau, G. et al. 2011. Mind your language: on novices' interactions with error messages. *Proceedings of the 10th SIGPLAN symposium on New ideas, new paradigms, and reflections on programming and software* (Portland, Oregon, USA, 2011), 3–18.

[10] Nienaltowski, M.-H. et al. 2008. Compiler error messages: what can help novices? *Proceedings of the 39th SIGCSE technical symposium on Computer science education* (Portland, OR, USA, 2008), 168–172.

[11] Nordquist, P. 2007. Providing accurate and timely feedback by automatically grading student programming labs. *J. Comput. Sci. Coll.* 23, 2 (2007), 16–23.

[12] Shams, Z. and Edwards, S.H. 2013. Reflection Support: Java Reflection Made Easy. *The Open Software Engineering Journal*. 7, (2013).

[13] Wang, Q. *cpgf. http://cpgf.org/. Accessed: 9/1/2014.*

Checked Coverage and Object Branch Coverage: New Alternatives for Assessing Student-Written Tests

Zalia Shams and Stephen H. Edwards
Department of Computer Science
Virginia Tech
2202 Kraft Drive
Blacksburg, VA 24060
{zalia18, edwards}@cs.vt.edu

ABSTRACT

Many educators currently use code coverage metrics to assess student-written software tests. While test adequacy criteria such as statement or branch coverage can also be used to measure the thoroughness of a test suite, they have limitations. Coverage metrics assess what percentage of code has been exercised, but do not depend on whether a test suite adequately checks that the expected behavior is achieved. This paper evaluates checked coverage, an alternative measure of test thoroughness aimed at overcoming this limitation, along with object branch coverage, a structure code coverage metric that has received little discussion in educational assessment. Checked coverage works backwards from behavioral assertions in test cases, measuring the dynamic slice of the executed code that actually influences the outcome of each assertion. Object branch coverage (OBC) is a stronger coverage criterion similar to weak variants of modified condition/decision coverage. We experimentally compare checked coverage and OBC against statement coverage, branch coverage, mutation analysis, and all-pairs testing to evaluate which is the best predictor of how likely a test suite is to detect naturally occurring defects. While checked coverage outperformed other coverage measures in our experiment, followed closely by OBC, both were only weakly correlated with a test suite's ability to detect naturally occurring defects produced by students in the final versions of their programs. Still, OBC appears to be an improved and practical alternative to existing statement and branch coverage measures, while achieving nearly the same benefits as checked coverage.

Categories and Subject Descriptors

K.3.2 [**Computers and Education**]: Computer and Information Science Education; D.2.5 [**Software Engineering**]: Testing and Debugging.

General Terms

Experimentation.

Keywords

Software testing; checked coverage; statement coverage; branch coverage; modified condition/decision coverage; mutation testing; automated assessment; automated grading; programming assignments; test coverage; test quality; test metrics.

SIGCSE '15, March 04 - 07 2015, Kansas City, MO, USA

ACM 978-1-4503-2966-8/15/03…$15.00
http://dx.doi.org/10.1145/2676723.2677300.

1. INTRODUCTION

As more educators include software testing activities in their courses, they also seek the best approach to evaluate student-written tests. The most common strategy currently used is to employ a structural code coverage metric, such as statement coverage or branch coverage, in order to measure how much of the code under test is executed by a test suite. Software test adequacy criteria such as these are traditionally viewed as criteria for judging when a test suite is "thorough enough"—as a kind of stopping rule that says when a test suite is sufficiently complete. However, such criteria can also be used in another way: to measure the adequacy or degree of thoroughness of a test suite [13]. When used in this way, they become an indicator of the quality of a test suite. These coverage measures are attractive because tools to measure them are readily available for many programming languages.

Among test adequacy criteria, statement coverage—what proportion of the software's statements are executed by the tests in a test suite—and branch coverage—what proportion of the control flow transfers are executed—are commonly used as adequacy measures because they are widely supported by both commercial and free analysis tools. However, coverage criteria based purely on which parts of the software are executed have limitations. Simply executing a fault in the code does not guarantee that the corresponding test will fail. This can happen, for example, when a test case exercises a code feature but does not completely check all aspects of the expected behavior are achieved.

Checked coverage is a new test quality measure proposed by Schuler and Zeller [10] to address this concern. Checked coverage works backwards from assertions in test cases that check behavioral expectations, measuring the dynamic slice of the executed code that actually influences the outcome of each assertion. As a result, it counts only the subset of code whose execution plays a role in each test case's success or failure outcome, rather than measuring all code that is executed. Schuler and Zeller describe it as a measure of a test suite's "assertion quality", that is, how thoroughly the test suite checks that desired behaviors are achieved, rather than simply executing code. They found checked coverage to be more sensitive to missing assertions in test cases than mutation analysis.

At the same time, we are also investigating stricter code coverage measures that may provide finer-grained information about student test suites. *Object branch coverage* (OBC) is a natural successor to branch coverage, but implemented at a program's object code level instead of its source code level. OBC requires programmers to write more extensive tests when they use compound conditions in their program's logical decisions, and is similar to some weaker forms of modified condition/decision coverage [4], the test adequacy criterion required by the FAA for avionics software [3].

In this paper, we ask the question of whether either checked coverage or object branch coverage is a better indicator of test suite quality than a number of alternative measures—that is, is either a more accurate predictor of a test suite's ability to detect faults? We are interested in assessing test suite quality in an academic context: when training programmers to write software tests, providing a way to assess the quality of their work helps provide more concrete, directed feedback, which hopefully aids to improving their performance.

Based on the experimental results reported here, both checked coverage and OBC do perform marginally better than other coverage criteria, but still do not have a statistically significant correlation with the average likelihood that a test suite will detect a given defect. Before presenting the experiment, Section 2 first summarizes relevant prior work. Section 3 describes the experimental comparison, including the subject pool and the methods used. Results are discussed in Section 4, with conclusions and future work in Section 5.

2. RELATED WORK

Because of the importance of testing, students learning to program should also learn to write software tests along the way. Code coverage is the most common approach used to evaluate student tests, although alternatives such as all-pairs testing [7] and mutation testing [1][11] have also been suggested. In fact, a recent experiment indicated that all-pairs testing was superior to mutation testing, statement coverage, and branch coverage at predicting a test suites ability to find defects [6].

2.1 Code Coverage

Code coverage measures count the percentage of code features (statements, branches, etc.) executed during testing. A test suite cannot possibly detect faults in code that it never executes. *Statement coverage* calculates the percentage of program statements executed by test cases. *Branch coverage* requires that every branch through every control flow statement (if statement, loop, switch statement, etc.) be executed.

2.2 Object Branch Coverage

Object branch coverage (OBC) is similar to branch coverage, but calculated by instrumenting a program's object code instead of its source code. However, for languages that use short-circuit evaluation of logical operators, object code instrumentation will result in much more stringent coverage requirements. As an example, consider this if statement:

```
if (C1 || C2 && C3)
{
    ...
}
```

This if statement contains three simple *conditions* combined with logical operators to form one compound *decision*. With traditional branch coverage, a test suite must ensure that the if statement is executed when the entire decision evaluates to true, and also when the entire decision evaluates to false (a total of two branches). However, when compiled, this compound decision results in a series of object code instructions that contain a separate conditional jump instruction for each simple condition. OBC requires that each conditional jump in the object code be executed when the corresponding condition is true, and also when it is false. In effect, this forces the tester to exercise both sides of each simple condition in every decision. For most decisions containing N simple conditions, there are $N + 1$ separate object code branches that must be exercised to achieve full object branch coverage.

As a result, OBC requires that each simple condition be evaluated to both true and false, and also that each decision as a whole be evaluated to both true and false, making it equivalent to *condition/decision coverage*. However, in languages where Boolean operators use short-circuit evaluation, achieving full OBC implies achieving full *masking MC/DC* (masking modified condition/decision coverage) for compound decisions with certain properties [4], even though OBC is strictly speaking a weaker criterion. An analysis of two industrial applications by Bordin et al. [2] revealed that more than 99% of decisions obey the necessary properties, meaning that in practice, OBC is frequently as strong as masking MC/DC, a criterion considered sufficient for safety-critical systems [4].

For measuring OBC in Java, we used JaCoCo [8], the object code coverage engine underlying the EclEmma plugin for Eclipse. Despite its name, however, OBC is not limited only to bytecode-based languages like Java. It has been used in compiled languages (e.g., the GNAT Ada tool set), and proposed for instrumenting Python programs, among others.

2.3 Checked Coverage

Checked code coverage [10] is an alternative approach for measuring test quality. It uses dynamic slicing to determine which statements actually contribute to test outcomes. The purpose of this approach is to focus on the code features that actually contribute to the behaviors checked by test cases rather than only considering the code features that are executed.

A program slice [12] is the set of statements that may influence the variables used in a given location. The influence can be from a *data dependency* or a *control dependency*. A statement s has a data dependency on statement t when there is a variable, v that is defined (written) in t and used (read) in s without any redefinition of v in between. On the other hand, a statement s is control dependent on a statement t if and only if t is a conditional statement and the execution of t depends on the execution of s. Checked code coverage uses dynamic slices calculated from the variables contained in behavioral assertions inside software tests in order to measure the proportion of code that directly affects the outcome of any test case assertion.

As an example, Figure 1 shows a test (line 8 to 11) that exercises the `dequeue()` method. To compute the checked coverage for this example, the dynamic slice from the call to `assertEquals()` (line 10) is built, and only the statements that are on this slice are considered to be covered. The dynamic backwards data and control dependent statements from the `assertEquals()` method call are shown by solid and dashed arrows. Thus, the dynamic slice consists of the statements on lines 3 and 6, but not lines 4 and 5. A statement coverage measure would include all four lines, however. To cover line 4 using checked coverage, a tester would need to add an assertion to confirm the deque's front element in the test. To cover line 5, the tester would need to check the deque's size as well.

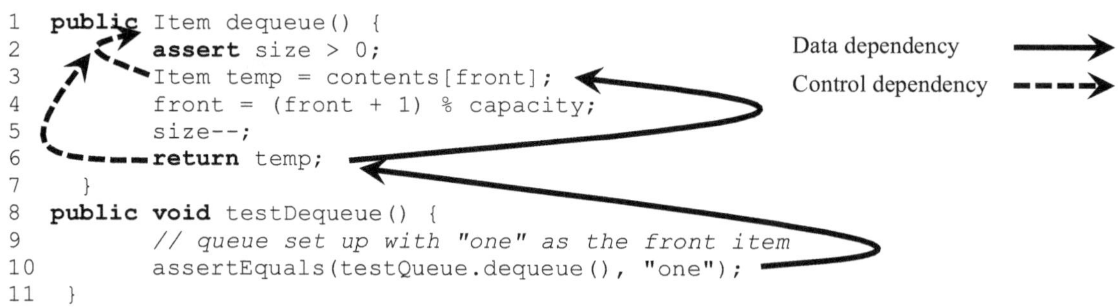

Figure 1: Data and control dependencies in a method call

Checked coverage is a more sensitive measure than statement coverage. It subsumes statement coverage because in order to reach 100% checked coverage every statement has to be on at least dynamic slice generated from some assertion, so it has to be executed at least once. Thus, every test suite that achieves 100% checked coverage also achieves 100% statement coverage. Unfortunately, however, no automated tool is available to measure checked coverage.

3. MEASURING THE ALTERNATIVES

Measuring OBC is straightforward, since tools are readily available. However, theoretically, it is still subject to the same limitations as weaker structural coverage metrics, since it does not reflect how thorough the assertions used in test cases are.

Checked coverage seems more promising for addressing this weakness. However, it is not a mature approach. Schuler and Zeller [10] provided a proof-of-concept evaluation of this metric. They used JavaSlicer [9], a home grown tool in their lab, to calculate dynamic slices from software tests for seven open-source projects. However, JavaSlicer has some limitations and cannot be used directly to measure checked coverage:

1) It creates dynamic slices from code execution traces, but does not directly calculate checked coverage.
2) It creates slices from human-selected source locations, but does not identify behavioral checks inside the test suites (e.g., assert()-style method calls in executable tests). For a small program, manually identifying all such statements may be feasible, but an automatic system must be developed to handle large-scale use of this approach.
3) The slices it creates include code from Java library classes, not just the code under test. As a result, the slices must be filtered in order to measure only the code under test.
4) While JavaSlicer calculates the executed slices, this information by itself is insufficient for measuring checked coverage. One must also measure the portion of the code under test that is not part of any checked slice, so that the checked coverage can be calculated as a percentage of the total (checked and unchecked) code.
5) Finally, JavaSlicer traces each thread separately and cannot reconstruct data dependencies between different threads. Some Junit 4 features such as test case timeouts use threads, preventing data dependencies from being tracked.

In order to evaluate checked coverage, we developed a semi-automated system to evaluate tests using checked coverage. We use a combination of JaCoCo and JavaSlicer in this process:

1) We run the student's tests against his or her own program using JaCoCo to collect coverage data, including how many bytecode instructions are present in each class and method, which is used later in calculating the percentage of code included in checked slices.
2) We identify all executable checks in the test cases. At this stage, all calls to JUnit assert-style methods from a test suite are considered to be checks.
3) JavaSlicer traces each program and generates a combined dynamic slice for all of the identified executable checks.
4) Finally, we use the report from JaCoCo to filter out Java library instructions from slices and to calculate checked coverage scores from the data.

4. COMPARING MEASURES

The goal of including software testing as part of programming assignments is to enable students to test their software better, and thus hopefully produce code with fewer bugs. Further, when students write software tests, they have to articulate their own understanding of what their code is supposed to do, which helps solidify their conceptual understanding.

To evaluate checked coverage and OBC, we conducted an experiment using student-written tests and student solutions produced by students participating in a Java-oriented CS2 course in Spring 2011. This experiment focused on one data structures programming assignment where students were required to write and test two separate implementations of a queue: one using an array-based representation and another using a linked chain of nodes. Students were required to provide full iteration support as well as proper implementations of `hashCode()`, `equals()`, and `toString()` for both representations.

In the semester under consideration, 101 students completed the assignment, writing a total of 2155 individual test cases. All test sets were run against an instructor-provided reference solution. Of the 2155 test cases, 2002 (92.9%) were valid, while 153 test cases (5.8%) were either invalid (failed on the reference implementation, indicating they contained incorrect behavioral expectations), or tested only student-specific design details. The evaluation involved over 200 thousand test case executions.

4.1 Defect-revealing Capability

To evaluate the two proposed measures and compare them to other potential quality measures for student-written tests, we followed the same approach as in prior work [6]. We aimed to compare them with the "true" notion of test quality: the suite's *defect-revealing capability*, or the likelihood that it will discover any given defect. Measuring the actual defect-revealing capability of a test suite is both challenging and expensive, however—

otherwise, practitioners could simply use this measure itself as the (ideal) indicator of test suite quality. To address this issue, we used the actual student programs produced for this assignment as a large (and representative) body of code containing authentically occurring, human-produced errors.

To approximate defect-revealing capability, we constructed a proxy for the set of defects contained in the student programs. We created a large repository of test suites collected from the valid tests written by students plus the instructor provided reference tests. We then ran all students' programs against all test cases. Any two test cases in the repository that have the exact same results (pass or fail) on every program we considered to be behaviorally equivalent. We then reduced the size of the repository by eliminating redundant test cases to form a smaller "master" test suite containing every uniquely distinguishable test from the repository. Each test in the smaller remaining set is represents a unique (hopefully small) equivalence class of defects. Though the test cases of the master suite may overlap, each test case differs from all others in the specific defect(s) that it detects. In other words, the sets of defects detected by any two test cases may overlap, but cannot be identical. This master test suite then serves as a proxy for the set of all defects contained in all of the student-written solutions produced for this assignment. Prior work indicates that test cases in a test suite created in this fashion are strongly correlated with the defects revealed by manual means, justifying the use of this proxy approach [1].

Next, we examined each student-written test suite to see which of the equivalence classes of defects represented in the master test suite this student test suite could detect. At this stage, we already know which of the student programs failed each master suite test case—that is, how many student programs contained a corresponding defect from that equivalence class. We also "weight" each test case in the master suite by the number of programs that fail (the number of programs containing a defect from its equivalence class). By computing a weighted average over all master suite test cases that are subsumed within one student-written test suite, we can compute an approximation of the suite's defect-revealing capability—the probability that for any given defect that occurs in any of the student solutions, this suite will detect that specific defect.

This process produced a master test suite containing just 112 distinct test cases, indicating a very frequent repetition rate among students. All the tests in master suite detected 2468 defects. The average test suite size among all students was 20 test cases (with the smallest containing 6, and the largest containing 23; s.d. = 3.3). There were in fact 10 methods that students were required to implement, and since the queue operations were implemented for both of the two possible implementations, the "typical" student test suite involved a single test for each distinct method written for each of the two queue representations. This is understandable, given the simplistic testing strategy that beginning students first learn, although it does suggest that student test suites were far from comprehensive.

4.2 Calculating Measures

As part of an earlier experiment [6], statement coverage and branch coverage were obtained by using Clover [5]. Since students were scored in class based on their branch coverage, both statement coverage and branch coverage were extremely high. Over three quarters of test suites achieved 100% statement coverage on the corresponding student's solution (mean of 97%). Over half of test suites achieved 100% branch coverage (mean of 96%). As a result, both measures were highly correlated with each other, but neither was a good predictor of test suite performance, since scores were almost uniformly high.

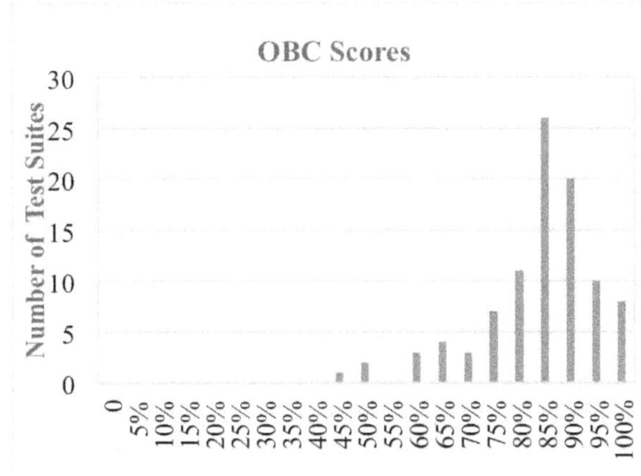

Figure 2: The distribution of OBC scores.

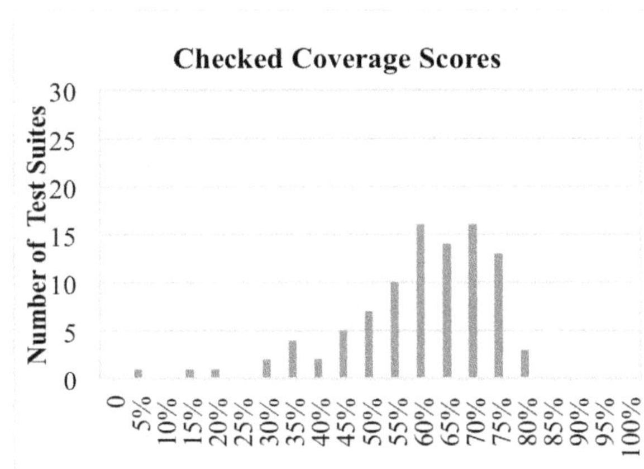

Figure 3: Distribution of checked coverage scores.

Previous experimental results also included mutation analysis scores measured using mutation on a reference solution using Javalanche. The scores were roughly normally distributed, with an average of 70%. No suite achieved a 100% mutation score.

OBC was measured using JaCoCo and is summarized in Figure 2. Although only one test suite in this group achieved 100% OBC coverage, three quarters of the test suites achieved 88% or better (mean of 81%).

Checked coverage scores were then calculated as described in Section 3. As expected, checked coverage scores were lower than other coverage scores, including statement coverage, branch coverage, and OBC. Figure 3 shows the distribution of checked coverage score achieved by student test suites. One half of the suites scored between 50%-68% (mean of 57%).

5. EXPERIMENTAL RESULTS

As part of a previous study [6], we had already compared statement coverage and branch coverage against mutation analysis (detection rate for artificially seeded defects) and all-pairs testing (running each test suite against every student program to measure the proportion of programs where at least one test in the suite fails). By beginning with this prior data as a baseline, we performed a statistical comparison of checked coverage and OBC against all four other measures, as well as against defect-

Table 1: Correlation (Spearman's ρ) between measures (bold entries are statistically significant, * at $\alpha < 0.05$, ** at $\alpha < 0.0001$).

	Statement Coverage	Branch Coverage	OBC	Mutation	Checked Coverage	All-pairs	Defect-revealing Score
Statement Coverage	-	**0.80****	0.00	**0.27***	-0.02	0.01	-0.01
Branch Coverage		-	0.05	0.18	0.03	-0.06	-0.08
OBC			-	**0.32***	**0.60****	0.00	0.12
Mutation				-	0.08	0.03	0.01
Checked Coverage					-	0.06	0.17
All-pairs						-	**0.78****
Defect-revealing Score							-

revealing capability. The results are shown in Table 1. Of the six measures represented here, only the all-pairs score was significantly correlated with a suite's defect-revealing capability. Noticeably, statement coverage, branch coverage, and mutation analysis scores have correlation coefficients approaching zero. While this may not be surprising for statement and branch coverage—since students actively tried to maximize these measures, resulting in minimal variation—it suggests that mutation analysis may not provide much additional information about a suite's ability to detect naturally occurring defects. This is in contrast to the suggestion by Aaltonen *et al.* [1] that mutation analysis would provide better measurement of test quality than simple coverage measures.

Unfortunately, in this experiment neither OBC nor checked coverage was significantly correlated with defect-revealing capability. Both had noticeably higher coefficients than simple coverage measures, however. In fact, both OBC and checked coverage were significantly correlated with each other. Further, OBC was also weakly correlated with mutation score. While all-pairs scores were the only significant predictor of defect-revealing capability (for more details, see [6]), OBC and checked coverage appear to show more promise than mutation analysis as alternatives to simpler coverage measures.

Figure 4 shows the linear relationship between OBC and checked coverage. The majority of test suites lie close to the trend line identified in the plot. However, a small minority of students achieved moderately positive OBC scores (> 80%) but low checked coverage scores (< 40%). This group is visually identifiable in the lower right corner of Figure 4. One plausible explanation is that these test suites exercise the code well, but lack sufficient assertions. Further examination revealed that this group contained only 7 students (7% of the population). As a result, for a large majority of students, OBC and checked coverage scores were approximately linearly related.

Interestingly, while mutation analysis was proposed to address the same limitations of statement and branch coverage, there does not appear to be a direct relation between checked coverage and mutation score. While checked coverage measures the de-

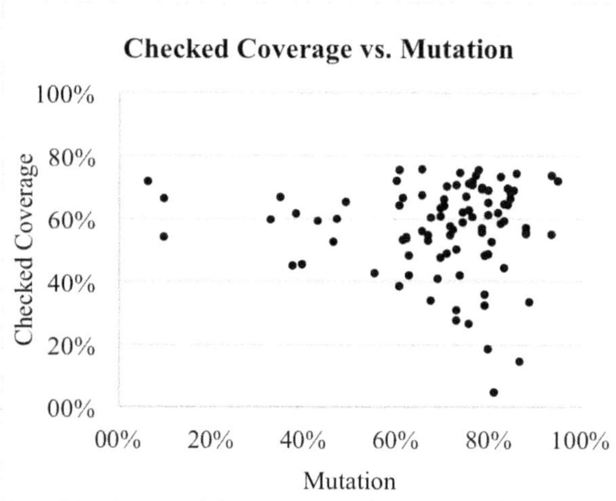

Figure 5: Relationship between checked coverage scores and mutation scores.

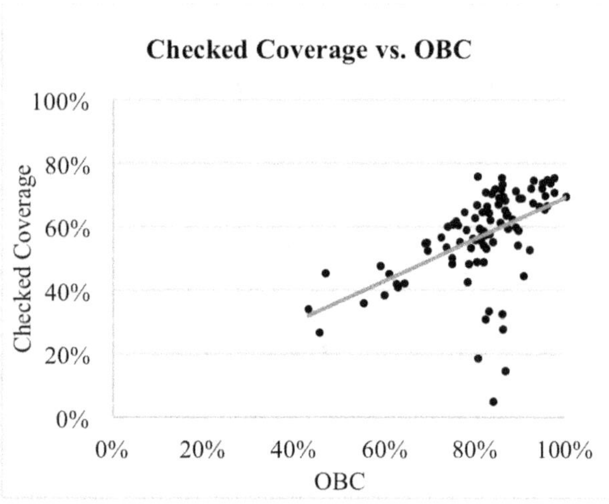

Figure 4: Relationship between checked coverage scores and OBC scores.

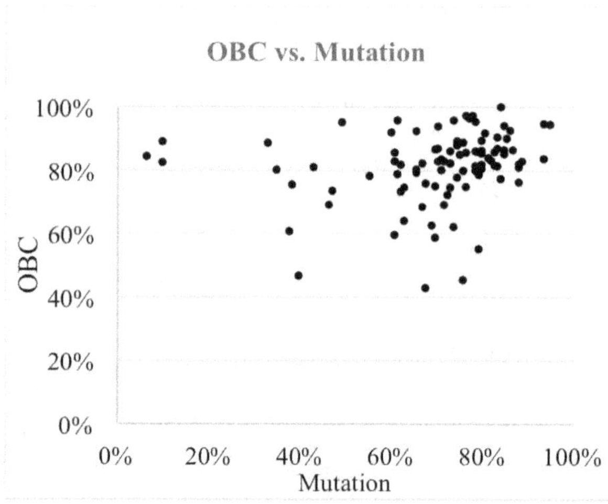

Figure 6: Relationship between OBC scores and mutation scores.

gree to which a suite "covers" the solution with appropriate assertion checks, mutation analysis measures the suite's ability to find artificially injected defects, which presumably also requires appropriate assertion checks. But these two measures were not significantly correlated, as illustrated in Figure 5. From Figure 5, it is clear that some suites with very low mutation detection ability still had average checked coverage scores, while some suites with very low checked coverage scores still had average mutation detection ability. It does not appear that mutation scores or checked coverage scores are measuring the same underlying phenomenon. While OBC has a significant correlation with mutation scores, as shown in Figure 6, the correlation is weak ($\rho = 0.24$).

6. THREATS TO VALIDITY

The experiment reported here gives some insight into how checked coverage and OBC compare to other measures, but it has limitations. First, this experiment was performed using student-written test suites intended for unit-level testing on student-written assignments. While the size of the group is large enough to be representative of many classroom situations, only one assignment was analyzed, sothe results may not be generalizable to other assignments or to students with different levels of experience. Second, because this study was conducted on an academic task, the results cannot be generalized to professional practice. Third, students in this assignment were graded on their testing, as measured by branch coverage. Thus, they naturally improved their test suites to achieve maximum coverage. This begs the question of whether tests developed to meet a different adequacy criterion—such as OBC, or checked coverage—would perform differently. This bias is built into this particular experiment, however, and addressing how removing (or replacing) it would affect the results would require additional investigation. Fourth, the defect-revealing scores are biased towards defects that are less likely to be found, and away from defects that are easier to find (and possibly more common). This raises the question of which defects were present when solutions were in their original, untested, undebugged state? Of course, few (if any) of the students ever had a complete solution in an untested state. Students in this course were taught beforehand to practice TDD and to incrementally develop their tests alongside their code. As a result, it is, impossible in many cases to construct a picture of an individual's code "before testing" to attempt to capture all the defects.

7. CONCLUSIONS

As educators add software testing to more courses, the question of how best to evaluate student-written tests becomes more important. While code coverage tools are readily available and are already seeing use by some educators, code coverage metrics have known limitations as test quality indicators.

This empirical study compared checked coverage and OBC to four previously investigated test quality measures in terms of how well they predicted a test suite's ability to detect actual defects present in students-written programming assignments. To perform this experiment, we developed a semi-automated system to apply checked-coverage to evaluate student-written tests, and used JaCoCo to measure OBC. We compared measures by using a large collection of defects produced by human errors in independently developed solutions to the same problem. The data collected shows that all-pairs testing scores were significantly correlated with a test suite's likelihood of finding any given latent defect. Disappointingly, however, neither checked coverage nor OBC was significantly correlated. At the same time, however, both checked coverage and OBC did appear to perform better than statement coverage, branch coverage, and mutation analysis. Though checked coverage provide more insight about assertion adequacy, there are challenges to implementing checked coverage on a large scale because of lack of tool maturity. In addition, OBC turned out to be equally promising in the sense that there is a linear positive correlation between checked coverage and OBC. It is more feasible to employ on a large scale because of greater tool availability, while being computationally much less demanding.

REFERENCES

[1] K. Aaltonen, P. Ihantola, and O. Seppälä, "Mutation analysis vs. code coverage in automated assessment of students' testing skills," presented at the Proceedings of the ACM international conference companion on Object oriented programming systems languages and applications companion, Reno/Tahoe, Nevada, USA, 2010.

[2] M. Bordin, C. Comar, T. Gingold, J. Guitton, O. Hainque, and T. Quinot. Object and Source Coverage for Critical Applications with the COUVERTURE Open Analysis Framework. In *ERTS (Embedded Real Time Sofware and Systems Conference)*, May 2010.

[3] J. J. Chilenski, "An Investigation of Three Forms of the Modified Condition Decision Coverage (MCDC) Criterion" U.S. Department of Transportation DOT/FAA/AR-01/18, 2001.

[4] C. Comar, J. Guitton, O. Hainque, T. Quinot. Formalization and Comparison of MCDC and Object Branch Coverage Criteria. In ERTS (Embedded Real Time Software and Systems Conference), May 2012.

[5] (9/5/2014). *Clover: Java and Groovy Code Coverage*. Available: https://www.atlassian.com/software/clover/overview

[6] S. H. Edwards and Z. Shams, "Comparing Test Quality Measures for Assessing Student-Written Tests," in *36th International Conference on Software Engineering*, Hyderabad, India, 2014, p. to apprear.

[7] S. H. Edwards, Z. Shams, M. Cogswell, and R. C. Senkbeil, "Running students' software tests against each others' code: new life for an old "gimmick"," presented at the Proceedings of the 43rd ACM technical symposium on Computer Science Education, Raleigh, North Carolina, USA, 2012.

[8] (9/5/2014). *JaCoCo Java Code Coverage Library*. Available: http://www.eclemma.org/jacoco/

[9] (9/5/2014). *JavaSlicer*. Available: http://www.st.cs.uni-saarland.de/javaslicer/

[10] D. Schuler and A. Zeller, "Assessing Oracle Quality with Checked Coverage," presented at the Proceedings of the 2011 Fourth IEEE International Conference on Software Testing, Verification and Validation, 2011.

[11] Z. Shams and S. H. Edwards, "Toward practical mutation analysis for evaluating the quality of student-written software tests," presented at the Proceedings of the ninth annual international ACM conference on International computing education research, San Diego, San California, USA, 2013.

[12] M. D. Weiser, "Program slices: formal, psychological, and practical investigations of an automatic program abstraction method," University of Michigan, 1979.

[13] H. Zhu, P.A.V. Hall, and J.H.R. May, "Software Unit Test Coverage and Adequacy", *ACM Computing Surveys*, 29(4): 366-427, December 1997.

Using SOLO to Classify the Programming Responses of Primary Grade Students

Linda Seiter
John Carroll University
Department of Mathematics and Computer Science
University Heights, OH
lseiter@jcu.edu

ABSTRACT

This paper presents an assessment designed to measure computational thinking skills of fourth grade students. The students in two public schools were given a set of Scratch programming challenges. The SOLO taxonomy was used to classify student programming responses based on the degree of understanding of the problem structure. The majority of fourth grade students from one school demonstrated the ability to synchronize the costume and motion of a single character sprite, as well as synchronize a basic conversation between multiple sprites. However, they struggled to integrate motion and costume changes into a multi-sprite conversation. The majority of fourth grade students from the second school, where reading and math comprehension scores fall below the state minimum requirements for proficiency, were unable to demonstrate a basic understanding of the programming tasks. The results suggest that fourth grade students who read at grade level are capable of understanding the relationships between multiple concerns within a single script, along with synchronizing a single concern across multiple scripts, but are challenged when synchronizing multiple concerns across multiple scripts.

Categories and Subject Descriptors

K.3.2 [Computers and Education]: Computer and Information Science education – Computer Science Education.

General Terms

Measurement, Human Factors

Keywords

Scratch, Assessment, SOLO Taxonomy, Primary Grades.

1. INTRODUCTION

Scratch is a visual programming environment that makes it feasible to introduce children to software programming [12]. The block-style language and drag and drop environment allow children to learn programming concepts while avoiding the syntax hurdles associated with traditional languages. The open source model of project sharing among Scratch users is a powerful mechanism that enables children to explore and learn from one another. While the Scratch environment is child friendly, the underlying programming concepts themselves continue to place challenging cognitive demands on the learner. Children may have fun using Scratch, but what can they actually learn?

This paper presents the results of a new assessment to measure the computational thinking skills of fourth grade students. A set of lessons was developed to guide students in learning how to program. Two of the lessons were goal-oriented activities intended to encourage student learning while also serving as assessment. The first assessment measured the ability to synchronize a sprite's appearance with its motion, while the second assessment involved multi-sprite synchronization. Both assessments were designed as a series of three challenges of increasing complexity. The SOLO (Structure of the Observed Learning Outcome) taxonomy [2] was used to categorize the level of structural complexity demonstrated by each student response.

2. RELATED WORK

Learning taxonomies such as Bloom's [3], Revised Bloom's [1], and SOLO [2] describe the level of understanding exhibited in a response to a problem. Bloom's classifies learning objectives by cognitive complexity, while SOLO classifies learning outcomes according to five levels of increasing structural complexity:

- **Prestructural** - The response contains bits of unconnected information, demonstrating a misconception of the task.
- **Unistructural** - The response focuses on one relevant aspect of the task. Progression to the next level is quantitative.
- **Multistructural** - The response focuses on several aspects, but relationships among aspects and their significance to the whole is missed. Progression to the next level is qualitative.
- **Relational** - Meta-connections are made and the response is holistic, integrating concepts into a coherent whole.
- **Extended abstract**-The response demonstrates conceptualization at a higher level of abstraction, formulating an instance of a general case.

SOLO has been likened to the idiom 'not seeing the forest for the trees'. Does the student see one tree (unistructural), several isolated trees (multistructural) or the forest (relational)? Lister et al use SOLO to compare differences between students and educators in coding exercises [8]. They note that educators demonstrate a holistic view of the problem, while students struggle to see relations between constructs. Sheard et al extend this work to show consistency in SOLO level among a student's

SIGCSE '15, March 4 -7, 2015, Kansas City, MO, USA.
Copyright 2014 ACM 978-1-4503-2966-8/15/03…$15.00
http://dx.doi.org/10.1145/2676723.2677244.

response to multiple coding questions, as well as consistency between code reading and code writing tasks [14].

Meerbaum-Salant et al present a set of tests that combine SOLO and the Revised Bloom's taxonomy [10]. They refute the traditional view that reading code, associated with Bloom's category of applying, is easier than creating code. Abstract concepts such as initialization, variables and concurrency require multistructural and possibly relational ability. Fuller et al also question whether the levels of Bloom's taxonomy are well ordered for assessing a subject such as programming [6]. They propose a new taxonomy that attempts to better reflect the understanding of concepts such as modularity and abstraction. Their taxonomy is a two dimensional adaptation of the Revised Bloom's that separates the ability to understand an existing piece of code from the ability to create a new piece of code.

Lister et al present a refined set of SOLO categories for code explaining and code writing responses [9]. The refined categories are further revised by Whalley et al to define problem-specific levels based on the degree of redundancy, efficiency, generalizability and integration observed in a solution [15]. The revised SOLO categories for code writing are thus:

- **Prestructural** – The code substantially lacks knowledge of programming constructs or is unrelated to the question.
- **Unistructural** – The code represents a direct translation of the specification, it is in the sequence of specifications.
- **Multistructural** – The code represents a translation that is close to direct. The code may have been reordered to make a more integrated, valid solution.
- **Relational** – The code provides a well-structured program that removes all redundancy and has a clear logical structure. The specifications are integrated to form a logical whole.
- **Extended abstract** – The code uses constructs beyond those required in the exercise to provide an improved solution.

To date SOLO has been used to assess computational thinking among middle school, high school and college students. Research on computational thinking in primary grades has primarily been unrelated to learning taxonomies. Lewis compares attitudinal and learning outcomes of sixth grade students programming in Logo or Scratch [7]. Wilson et al analyze proficiency in grades four to seven, showing user interaction, loops and conditionals to be the most commonly used concepts [16]. Dwyer et al studied fourth grade students performing modified CS Unplugged activities, noting their inability to produce precise algorithms that scale [5]. Seiter and Foreman propose the Progression of Early Computational Thinking framework, which synthesizes evidence from student work with Scratch design patterns [13]. Brennan and Resnick recommend assessment through project portfolio analysis, artifact-based interviews, and design scenarios [4].

3. METHODOLOGY

This paper presents the results of using SOLO to evaluate computational thinking among fourth grade students. The author partnered with two public elementary schools to teach a series of weekly Scratch lessons. The lessons were provided at school#1 in two fourth grade classrooms, with the author and teachers present to guide the students. While the teachers had no prior programming experience, they were able to quickly learn the material and contribute valuable support. The lessons at school#2 took place in the computer lab in a combined class containing students from two fourth grade classes. The author and the computer technology teacher were present to instruct.

The weekly lesson material was adapted from curriculum the author had developed while teaching afterschool, weekend and summer outreach programs. Each lesson was provided in both online and paper formats, and was divided into a series of small tasks. The online lesson included a video demonstration of each task. The students worked independently and proceeded at their own pace. A brief description of the weekly lessons follows:

1. Scratch basics.
2. Sprite motion.
3. Sprite monologue.
4. Sprite monologue with costume change (painted costumes).
5. Sprite monologue with costume change (uploaded costumes).
6. Dialogue between two sprites synchronized with wait blocks.
7. **Assessment#1- Synchronizing costume with motion.**
8. Maze Game involving collision detection and key presses.
9. Math Game involving random numbers, variables and input.
10. Continuation of Math Game.
11. Flappy Bird Game.
12. Continuation of Flappy Bird Game.
13. Mad Lib.
14. **Assessment#2- Synchronizing a multi-sprite conversation.**

4. ASSESSMENT#1

The first assessment occurred during the 7th lesson as a goal-oriented activity. The students were given three challenges that involved a sprite roller skating on various backdrops, changing costume as it moved. The first challenge is shown in Figure 1.

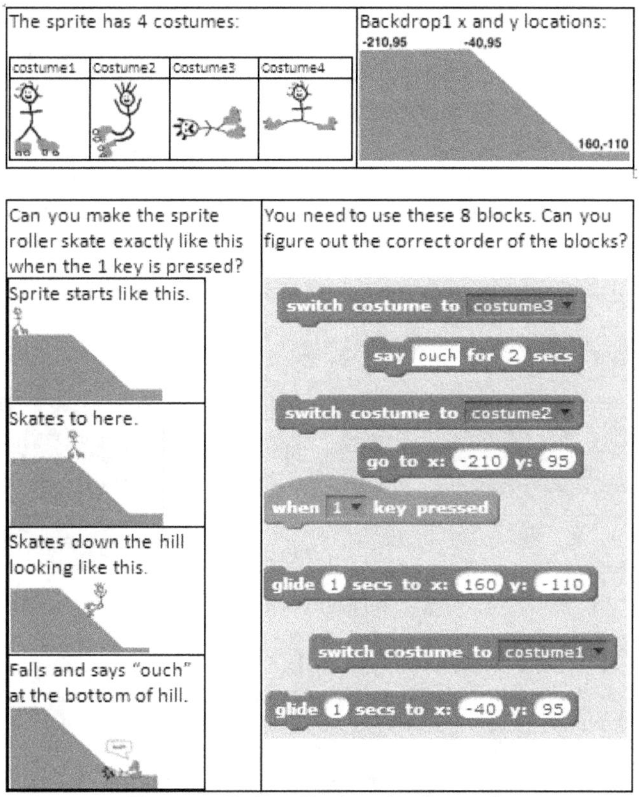

Figure 1: Roller Skating Challenge #1

The students had to synchronize motion (lesson 2) with costume changes (lessons 4 and 5). Lessons 4 and 5 demonstrated how to switch costume prior to a "say" block to alter the sprite appearance while it was speaking. However, the students had yet to learn how to synchronize costume with motion. They remixed a project that contained a stage with three backdrops, scripts for switching the backdrop when 1, 2 or 3 was pressed, and a sprite with four costumes. The online lesson included a video of the animation. The instructions provided the 8 blocks from the solution, as shown in Figure 1. The students were challenged to find the correct sequence of the 8 blocks.

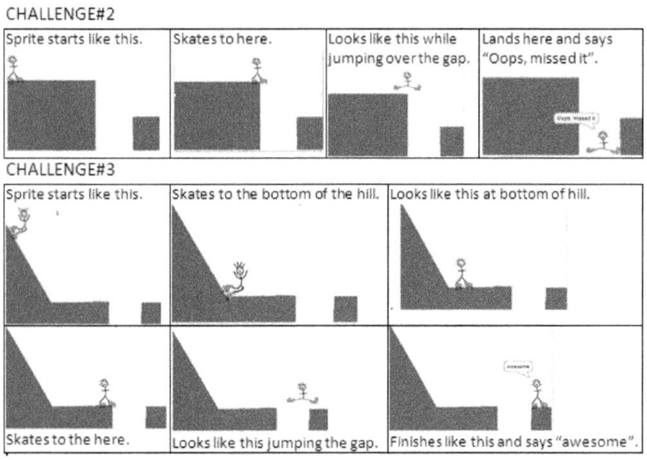

Figure 2: Challenges #2 and #3

Figure 2 lists the animation sequence for the second and third challenges. The instructions showed the motion and costume sequences, which differ among all three challenges, along with relevant backdrop coordinates (not shown in Figure 2). Unlike the first challenge, the students were **not** provided with blocks from the solution. The objective was to determine whether they could recognize and abstract the coding pattern from their first solution to solve the remaining two challenges.

Figure 3 shows the solution scripts. Each script requires the initialization of the sprite location using the "go to" block, along with initialization of the sprite costume using a "switch costume" block. The order of the "go to" and first "switch costume" blocks in each script may be swapped. A "switch costume" block is also required prior to every "glide" and some of the "say" blocks.

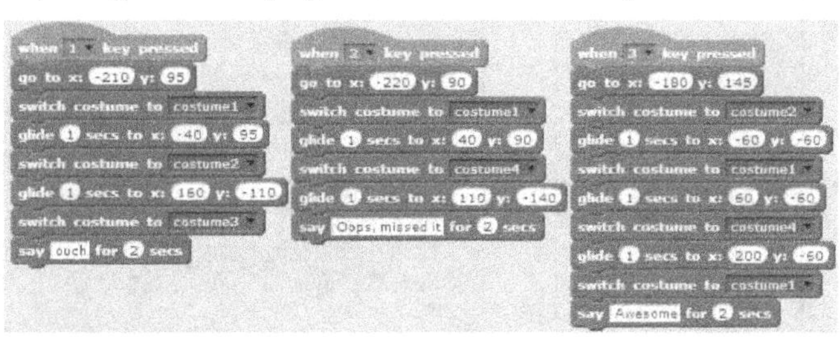

Figure 3: Solution scripts for the roller skating challenges

4.1 Assessment#1 Results

The student programming responses were first scored in terms of functionality, i.e. initialization, synchronization of costume with motion, etc. Points were not deducted if the coordinates differed slightly from the solution. Each program was subsequently assigned a SOLO level. Applying SOLO to code writing problems involves judging the degree of distance between the response and the specification [9, 15]. Not every problem requires a relational response, as the problem specification influences the range of response. If the instructions had been given as "Make the sprite go to -210, 95, then change its costume to costume1, then make it glide to -40, 95, ...", then the first script in Figure 3 would be a unistructural response since it is a direct translation of the specification. However, the instructions contained neither explicit directions for initialization, nor explicit directions to switch costume prior to movement. Instead they state "Sprite starts like this", etc. Students must abstract from the problem the need to initialize and synchronize costume with motion. Each script in Figure 3 thus represents a relational response.

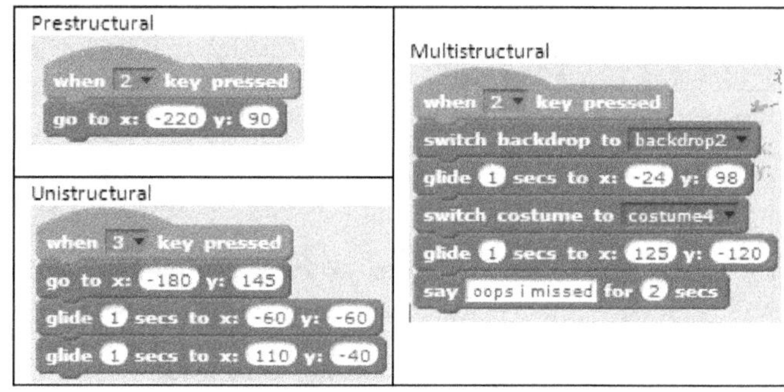

Figure 4: Sample student solutions

In order to illustrate the SOLO levels, Figure 4 contains a sample of actual responses that were given by students:

- **Prestructural** – The script contains a single block. The student does not understand how to animate the sprite.
- **Unistructural** – The script animates motion, but not costume.
- **Multistructural** –The script integrates motion with costume, but does not initialize the costume and location. Initialization errors are common among primary grade students [10, 13].

A perfect score on the first challenge could have been a lucky guess on how to sequence the 8 blocks that had been provided. Correct implementation of the second and third challenges indicates relational thinking. The student understood the significance of the parts, i.e. the individual blocks, with respect to the whole. They abstracted the algorithm of the first challenge and generalized it to solve the remaining two challenges.

	SCHOOL#1 CLASS#1 (18)			SCHOOL#1 CLASS#2 (22)			SCHOOL#2 Class#3 (32)		
Challenge#	1	2	3	1	2	3	1	2	3
Mean Score	93%	81%	65%	98%	93%	80%	30%	9%	0%
Scored 100%	78%	67%	50%	82%	73%	55%	16%	0%	0%
No attempt	0%	6%	22%	0%	5%	14%	9%	85%	100%
Prestructural	0%	11%	0%	0%	0%	0%	44%	3%	0%
Unistructural	6%	0%	6%	0%	0%	6%	9%	0%	0%
Multistructural	11%	16%	22%	14%	18%	13%	22%	12%	0%
Relational	83%	67%	50%	86%	77%	67%	16%	0%	0%

Figure 5: Scores for Assessment #1

Figure 5 lists the results of the 18 students in class#1 and 22 students in class#2 from school #1, along with the 32 students from school#2 who were present for the assessment. The percent of students who did not attempt a particular challenge indicates that it was not a trivial task. However, the majority of students at school#1 gave relational responses to all three challenges, with at least half achieving a perfect score on the third challenge. They understood the relationships between program constructs in the first solution and adapted them to solve the remaining problems.

At school#2, 44% of students provided a prestructural response to the first challenge. Only 16% successfully completed the first challenge and continued on to the second challenge. No one attempted the third challenge. A study by Oliveira et al shows a strong correlation between the ability to compute and student academic performance [11]. The fourth grade reading and math scores for school#2 fall below the minimum state requirements for proficiency. The students struggled each week to read the button labels and menus on the Scratch interface. They could not identify errors in spelling while typing their username or password. Negative numbers and three digit numbers, as found in the Scratch coordinate plane, posed a challenge. The reading and math skills required to understand each individual block in the solution, let alone the computational skills needed to produce the solution, makes the assessment tasks unattainable for children whose reading and math skills are below fourth grade standards.

5. ASSESSMENT#2

The second assessment occurred in the 14th lesson. It consisted of three challenges, each involving a multi-sprite conversation. Figure 6 contains the instructions for the first challenge. The students had previously learned in lesson 6 how to implement a two sprite dialogue using an alternating sequence of say and wait blocks. This challenge required them to adapt the algorithm in order to add a third sprite to a conversation.

Fill in the table with **say** and **wait** blocks. Each scene takes 2 seconds.

Animation	Squirrel	Acorns	Fox

Figure 6: Multi-sprite synchronization challenge #1.

The coding solution in Figure 7 is almost a direct translation of the table in Figure 6. However, the task of filling in the table itself involves multistructural thinking. There are several trees in this forest: each sprite has its own script, each sprite says things, and each sprite waits while the other sprites speak. The students must abstract these details from each scene, and understand that a sprite may need to wait over a sequence of scenes.

Squirrel	Acorn	Fox
when clicked say I eat acorns for 2 secs wait 4 secs say oh rats! for 2 secs	when clicked wait 2 secs say oh nuts! for 2 secs wait 4 secs say FOOD CHAIN! for 2 secs	when clicked wait 4 secs say I eat squirrels for 2 secs

Figure 7: Solution to challenge#1

5.1 Challenge#2: Dog and donut conversation

The second challenge is partially shown in Figure 8 (edited for space), with the solution given in Figure 9. This problem requires a relational response since it involves coordination between two sprites as well as synchronization of motion and appearance with the conversation; each table cell may contain a sequence of blocks. The students remixed a project containing two scripts that implemented the entire solution as shown in Figure 9, except all wait blocks had been removed. They had to fix the code by inserting wait blocks. The objective was to provide a sample conversation involving changes to sprite costume and location in order to prepare the students for the third challenge.

Each scene takes 2 seconds	Dog	Donut
	Go to x:-100 y:-125 Say "I'm hungry" for 2 secs.	Switch costume to "donut". Wait 2 secs.
	Glide 2 secs to x:-15 y:-125	

Figure 8: Multi-sprite synchronization challenge #2

Dog's Script	Donut's Script
when clicked go to x: -100 y: -125 say I'm hungry for 2 secs glide 2 secs to x: -10 y: -125 say Donut! for 2 secs wait 2 secs say Chomp for 2 secs wait 4 secs say Sorry for 2 secs	when clicked switch costume to donut wait 6 secs say Oh no! for 2 secs switch costume to donut2 wait 2 secs say Ouch! for 2 secs say That hurt. for 2 secs

Figure 9: Solution to challenge #2

5.2 Challenge #3 –Frog Prince Fairy Tale

The instructions for the final challenge are shown in Figure 10. The challenge involves a three sprite conversation with costume changes. Students were **not** given a partial solution to debug as in the previous challenge; they needed to determine the code on their own. Each cell in the table in Figure 10 may hold more than just a "say" or "wait" block due to the costume changes. The challenge was to determine the correct sequence of blocks to place within each cell. This requires a relational response in that wait blocks must be used to synchronize the conversation, and costumes must be initialized and synchronized with the conversation across multiple scripts. The solution is given in Figure 11.

Figure 10: Multi-sprite synchronization challenge #3

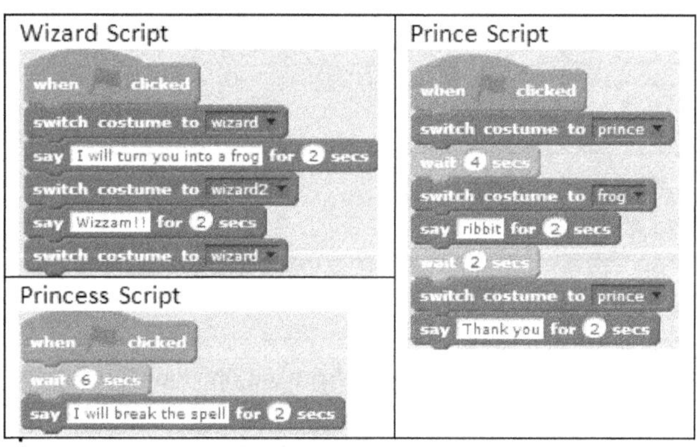

Figure 11: Solution to challenge #3

5.3 Assessment#2 results

The students at school#2 did not perform the second assessment as they were unable to complete the prerequisite lessons. The scores for students at school#1 are given in Figure 12.

5.3.1 Challenge#1 – Food Chain Conversation

Challenge#1 was a basic conversation with no motion or costume changes, designed to elicit a multistructural response. The percent of students in both classes receiving a perfect score (90% and 86%), along with the mean score (96% and 99%), indicate that the students clearly understood how to solve this type of problem. Did students benefit from planning out sprite behavior on paper prior to coding? To answer this question, students in class#1 were required to fill in the tables (Figures 6, 8, 10) prior to writing their programs in Scratch, while students in class#2 were given the handouts but not required to fill them out. Class#2 chose not to fill out the tables, leading to an interesting and unexpected result. The students in class#1 spent much more time on the first challenge than students in class#2, which explains the large "no attempt" percentage for challenge 3. The row in Figure 12 labeled "Correct Table Code" denotes the percent of students who correctly filled in the table, which was only 57% of students in class#1 for the first challenge. After filling in the table, many students wrote the scripts in their entirety before clicking the green flag. The 43% of students who incorrectly filled in the table subsequently had three large scripts to debug. The students in class#2 skipped the tables and jumped directly to coding. They tended to write and test their code incrementally, i.e. one scene of the animation at a time. This allowed them to encounter errors while their scripts were smaller and easier to debug.

	CLASS#1 - (21)			CLASS#2 - (22)		
Challenge#	1	2	3	1	2	3
Correct Table Code	57%	14%	23%	n/a	n/a	n/a
Scored 100%	90%	29%	14%	86%	27%	27%
Mean Score	96%	67%	50%	99%	67%	64%
Attempted Mean	96%	74%	81%	99%	74%	82%
No attempt	0%	9%	43%	0%	9%	23%
Prestructural	5%	0%	0%	0%	5%	0%
Unistructural	0%	5%	0%	0%	5%	0%
Multistructural	95%	62%	43%	100%	45%	50%
Relational	n/a	24%	14%	n/a	36%	27%

Figure 12: Scores for Assessment #2

5.3.2 Challenge#2 – Dog and Donut Conversation

This two-sprite conversation involved motion and costume change. The students were provided with the coding solution of Figure 9, minus the wait blocks. This problem required both code reading and code writing, which turned out to be very difficult. The responses were initially scored on correctness, i.e., was each wait block in the correct place and was it for the correct time. Less than a third of students obtained a perfect score (29% and 27%), while the mean (67% in both classes) was much lower than the previous challenge. Not every student attempted this problem. The row labeled "Attempted Mean" refers to the mean score among those students who made an attempt (74% in both classes).

The programs were subsequently classified with SOLO. One student simply placed a wait block in between every two blocks in the scripts that had been provided, demonstrating a prestructural response. Several students added the correct wait blocks in just one script, demonstrating a unistructural response. The majority of students demonstrated either a multistructural or a relational response. Multistructural responses typically included incorrect wait times that caused an interruption. Note however that it was not necessary to receive a perfect score to demonstrate relational thinking. Several students adapted the animation and did not follow the specification; however their modifications consistently coordinated the sprites and thus were scored as relational. Note also that a perfect score did not necessarily imply relational thinking. While points were not deducted for a sequence of "wait 2 secs" blocks rather than one block summing the wait time, this distinction impacted whether a response was multistructural or relational. A sequence of wait blocks represents a direct translation of the problem in Figure 8, while the single wait block reduces redundancy and shows integrative thinking.

5.3.3 Challenge#3 – Frog Prince Fairy Tale

The final challenge required synchronization of costume with the conversation, and was designed to elicit a relational response.

Many students did not attempt this problem. However, at least half of all students who did attempt the problem produced a multistructural or relational response, with mean scores of 88% and 82%, respectively.

6. CONCLUSION

This paper presents an assessment designed to evaluate computational thinking among fourth grade students. Programming responses were scored both in terms of correctness as well as SOLO. The SOLO score reflects the degree of understanding of the problem structure. Does the student see the forest for the trees? Most of the students in school#1 gave relational responses to all three challenges for the first assessment, demonstrating a holistic view of how to initialize and synchronize sprite properties within a single script. While they excelled at synchronizing a simple conversation, they struggled to synchronize costume changes within a conversation. Perhaps there were too many trees in that forest. The results presented also confirm a previous study linking the ability to compute with student performance in school, with the majority of students at school#2 either not attempting or being unable to demonstrate even a basic understanding of the assessment tasks. This paper demonstrates that in fourteen weeks of instruction, students who read at fourth grade level are capable of learning to synchronize multiple concerns within a single script, along with a single concern (speaking) across multiple scripts, while synchronization of multiple concerns across multiple scripts remained a challenge.

7. ACKNOWLEDGMENTS

The author is very grateful for the valuable collaboration with Chris Dlugosz, Patrick Kelly, Char Shryock, Brian Stern and Michele Evans, all of whom contributed insightful and innovative ideas and practices on the integration of computational thinking within primary grade curriculum.

8. REFERENCES

[1] Lorin W. Anderson, David R. Krathwohl, Peter W. Airasian, Kathleen A., Eds. 2001. A Taxonomy for Learning, Teaching and Assessing. A Revision of Bloom's Taxonomy of Educational Objectives. Addison-Wesley Longman.

[2] John B. Biggs and Kevin F. Collis, 1982. Evaluating the Quality of Learning: The SOLO Taxonomy (Structure of the Observed Learning Outcome). Academic Press.

[3] Benjamin S. Bloom and David R. Krathwohl, 1956. Taxonomy of education objectives: The classification of education goals. Handbook I. Cognitive domain. New York.

[4] Karen Brennan and Mitch Resnick. New frameworks for studying and assessing the development of computational thinking. In *AERA 2012*, 2012.

[5] Hilary Dwyer, Charlotte Hill, Stacey Carpenter, Danielle Harlow, and Diana Franklin. 2014. Identifying elementary students' pre-instructional ability to develop algorithms and step-by-step instructions. In Proceedings of the 45th ACM technical symposium on Computer science education (SIGCSE '14). ACM, New York, NY, USA, 511-516.

[6] Ursula Fuller, Colin G. Johnson, Tuukka Ahoniemi, Diana Cukierman, Isidoro Hernán-Losada, Jana Jackova, Essi Lahtinen, Tracy L. Lewis, Donna McGee Thompson, Charles Riedesel, and Errol Thompson. 2007. Developing a computer science-specific learning taxonomy. *SIGCSE Bull.* 39, 4 (December 2007), 152-170.

[7] Colleen M. Lewis. 2010. How programming environment shapes perception, learning and goals: logo vs. scratch. In *Proceedings of the 41st ACM technical symposium on Computer science education (SIGCSE '10)*. ACM, USA.

[8] Raymond Lister, Beth Simon, Errol Thompson, Jacqueline L. Whalley, and Christine Prasad. 2006. Not seeing the forest for the trees: novice programmers and the SOLO taxonomy. *SIGCSE Bull.* 38, 3 (June 2006), 118-122.

[9] Raymond Lister, Tony Clear, Simon, Dennis J. Bouvier, Paul Carter, Anna Eckerdal, Jana Jacková, Mike Lopez, Robert McCartney, Phil Robbins, Otto Seppälä, and Errol Thompson. 2010. Naturally occurring data as research instrument: analyzing examination responses to study the novice programmer. *SIGCSE Bull.* 41, 4 (January 2010).

[10] Orni Meerbaum-Salant, Michal Armoni, and Mordechai (Moti) Ben-Ari. 2010. Learning computer science concepts with scratch. In *Proceedings of the Sixth international workshop on Computing education research (ICER '10)*. ACM, New York, NY, USA, 69-76.

[11] Osvaldo L. Oliveira, Maria C. Nicoletti, and Luis M. del Val Cura. 2014. Quantitative correlation between ability to compute and student performance in a primary school. In *Proceedings of the 45th ACM technical symposium on Computer science education* (SIGCSE '14). ACM, New York, NY, USA, 505-510.

[12] Mitchel Resnick, John Maloney, Andrés Monroy-Hernández, Natalie Rusk, Evelyn Eastmond, Karen Brennan, Amon Millner, Eric Rosenbaum, Jay Silver, Brian Silverman, and Yasmin Kafai. 2009. Scratch: programming for all. *Commun. ACM* 52, 11 (November 2009), 60-67.

[13] Linda Seiter and Brendan Foreman. 2013. Modeling the learning progressions of computational thinking of primary grade students. In Proceedings of the ninth annual international ACM conference on International computing education research (ICER '13). ACM, New York, USA.

[14] Judy Sheard, Angela Carbone, Raymond Lister, Beth Simon, Errol Thompson, and Jacqueline L. Whalley. 2008. Going SOLO to assess novice programmers. In *Proceedings of the 13th annual conference on Innovation and technology in computer science education* (ITiCSE '08). ACM, New York.

[15] Jacqueline Whalley, Tony Clear, Phil Robbins, and Errol Thompson. 2011. Salient elements in novice solutions to code writing problems. In *Proceedings of the Thirteenth Australasian Computing Education Conference - Volume 114* (ACE '11), John Hamer and Michael de Raadt (Eds.), Vol. 114. Australian Computer Society, Inc.

[16] Amanda Wilson, Thomas Hainey, Thomas Connolly. Evaluation of Computer Games Developed by Primary School Children to Gauge Understanding of Programming Concepts, *6th European Conference on Games-based Learning (ECGBL),* Cork, Ireland, October, 2012.

Floors and Flexibility: Designing a Programming Environment for 4th-6th Grade Classrooms

Charlotte Hill†, Hilary A. Dwyer‡, Tim Martinez†, Danielle Harlow‡, Diana Franklin†

{charlottehill, franklin}@cs.ucsb.edu, {hdwyer, dharlow}@education.ucsb.edu, tmartinez@umail.ucsb.edu

†Computer Science Department
UC Santa Barbara

‡Gevirtz Graduate School of Education
UC Santa Barbara

ABSTRACT

The recent renaissance in early computer science education has provided K-12 teachers with multiple options for introducing children to computer science. However, tools for teaching programming for children with wide-scale adoption have been targeted mostly at pre-readers or middle school and higher grade-levels. This leaves a gap for 4th – 6th grade students, who differ developmentally from older and younger students.

In this paper, we investigate block-based programming languages targeted at elementary and middle school students and demonstrate a gap in existing programming languages appropriate for 4th – 6th grade classrooms. We analyze the benefits of Scratch, ScratchJr, and Blockly for students and curriculum developers. We describe the design principles we created based on our experiences using block-based programming in 4th – 6th grade classrooms, and introduce LaPlaya, a language and development environment designed specifically for children in the gap between grades K-3 and middle school students.

Categories and Subject Descriptors

D.1.7 [**Programming Techniques**]: Visual Programming;
K.3.2 [**Computer and Information Science Education**]: Computer Science Education.

Keywords

Computer science education, elementary school, middle school, graphical programming. novice programming environments

1. INTRODUCTION

In an effort to engage young children in computer science, computer scientists have developed a variety of educational programming platforms, activities [23, 9, 17, 4] and outreach programs [3, 2, 12]. In the past few years, momentum has increased for elementary schools to teach computational thinking in their classrooms. Eighth graders' reported interest in pursuing a career in science and engineering areas is a strong predictor of whether or not they will later pursue a science career [28]. Further, after-school opportunities or summer camps where middle and elementary school students are likely to be introduced to computer science are less available to students from impoverished areas [6]. Adding computational thinking to earlier grade levels and integrating the subject into K-8 schooling will provide students from more backgrounds exposure to computer science at an age when they prepare to make decisions about their future. Moreover, these efforts may increase diversity in computer science fields, combat the dire shortage of computing majors, and create a higher level of the computing literacy that will be necessary for the innovators of the next century.

SIGCSE'15, March 4–7, 2015, Kansas City, MO, USA.

http://dx.doi.org/10.1145/2676723.2677275

In order to gain deeper insight into how 4th – 6th grade students (children ages 9-12) learn computer science, we modified an existing middle-school curriculum from the Animal Tlatoque summer camp to be appropriate for 4th grade [12]. We provided programming activities in a variant of Scratch [23] with starting files that the students manipulated and modified. During the 2013-14 academic year, we revised and refined these activities based on feedback from the classrooms about what students struggled with and excelled in.

Although elementary school students are capable of programming [21, 28], while developing curricula for 4th – 6th grade, we found a gap in the programming languages available for children. Many popular block-based languages are targeted either toward pre-readers or children with math and language skills above 4th – 6th grade. Moreover, these languages are embedded in programming environments with interface features not developmentally appropriate for this age group; they contain features that are too complex, making the floor for entry too high for these students, or they do not provide students appropriate control over their projects. Additionally, existing block-based languages either require curriculum developers to create projects that fit the constraints of the environment, or to have the programming background needed to customize the environment for the project. New tools that are sufficiently flexible and have an entry floor level appropriate level for upper elementary school students are needed to make computer science successful in a regular classroom.

Here we present our design goals for a block-based language targeted towards 4th – 6th grade. Our design goals are influenced by the challenges that students faced during the pilot of our curriculum when using a programming environment not developmentally appropriate for their age. We look at Scratch, ScratchJr, and Blockly, and assess their appropriateness for curriculum development at this age group [23, 13, 10]. Finally, we introduce LaPlaya, the language we designed to fill the gap in development environments for upper elementary school classrooms.

This paper is organized as follows. We provide background on the elementary school classroom setting and a brief summary of related work in Section 2. In Section 3, we look at existing block-based languages (Scratch, ScratchJr, and Blockly). In Section 4 we detail the design principles we used to create a new programming environment, LaPlaya. Finally, Section 5 contains our plans for future work.

2. BACKGROUND & RELATED WORK

Students' academic knowledge and skills increase rapidly as they progress throughout elementary school and into middle school. A development environment for this age group must be flexible and expand as they learn, or the students will outgrow it. Students in upper elementary school differ in important ways from their younger counterparts. In second and third grade, "the mechanical demands of learning to read are so taxing at this point that children have few resources left over to process the content. In fourth through eighth grade, children become increasingly able to obtain new information from print" (p. 333) [26]. In fact, upper elementary school is an important transitional time for children's development. These students are developing linguistic, kinesthetic, and cognitive skills necessary to successfully interact with computers. Further, these students are learning key concepts from other fields, like math and science, needed to successfully program. As examples, key math concepts such as division, negative numbers, and percentages are taught during upper elementary school.

Fourth graders today are commonly described as "digital natives" because they have never known a world without computers or the Internet [5]. Although access to technology varies, particularly depending on students' socioeconomic levels, today's 4th graders have some familiarity with computers and ideas about how to interact with them. Students enter the computer lab already familiar with computers, but as users rather than developers. Kolikant characterizes computer science classes as encounters between intertwined cultures. Students are members of the culture of school, and are already familiar with computers as part of the "user" culture [5], but they are newcomers to the computing culture.

Previous studies have looked at the development environment's influence on students' roles as users or developers. In the creation of ScratchJr, a visual language based on Scratch, the developers removed "instant gratification" buttons, or buttons that produce an immediate effect on the state of the program, so children would spend less time playing with the software's features and more time creating [18]. However, Kazakoff found that kindergarteners using ScratchJr in their classroom still spent a significant time using the environment's paint editor instead of programming [18]. Kerr provided pre-built scenes to students for creating digital stories and found that they used more constructs and methods, and spent twice as long modifying their programs as students who created all the scenes themselves [19]. The development environment itself plays a crucial role in guiding students to be developers rather than users.

Researchers in human computer interaction have identified multiple points to consider when designing software for children, as children interact with computers differently than adults. Bruckman, Bandlow, Dimond, and Forte noted that software designers must attend to the physical and cognitive differences of children such as their limited skills with typing, reading, and manipulating keyboards and mice, as well as their more limited linguistic experiences which prevent them from understanding metaphors common among adults [7]. For example, program designers must attend to children's fine motor control. Compared to adults, children struggle holding down the mouse for extended periods or even double-clicking; therefore, young children tend to perform point-and-click movements more quickly and accurately than drag-and-drop commands [15, 27]. As another example, young children can become easily distracted by complex interfaces, and Halgren et al chose to redesign interface by hiding advanced tools, so children (ages 5-14) would not stumble upon them and get lost in their functionality [16]. These findings influenced our development of LaPlaya, which we describe in Section 5.

Studying children's learning of computer science is additionally complex because the programming environment directly impacts available opportunities for learning. Several programming languages developed for children and novice programmers such as Scratch, Alice, and AgentSheets use graphical programming environments and limit the commands available for students to use [23, 8, 25]. Compared to traditional programming environments, graphical programming lowers the cognitive barriers to programming by removing obstacles such as remembering specific vocabulary and formatting rules of computer languages. Instead of writing out programming commands, users snap commands together to form scripts and see the output of their programs immediately, thereby circumventing most required syntax or specific vocabulary. As a result, these languages offer benefits for novice programmers of all ages. Malan and Leitner advocated using Scratch even at the undergraduate level, as a gateway language to languages like Java [22]. Further, block based languages like Scratch can improve students' attitudes and increase confidence in programming [20].

3. POPULAR BLOCK-BASED ENVIRONMENTS

Block based environments have gained popularity with novice programmers because they reduce the need for typing and get rid of many syntax errors. Unlike textual programming languages, block based languages are closely tied to the development environment in which they are embedded. Many development environments are inspired by Scratch, a block-based language designed for ages 8-16 [23]. Scratch provides blocks of programming commands that users attach together like puzzle pieces to create scripts that control the actions of the sprites, 2D characters on the stage. In this section, we present our findings from using Scratch in 4th – 6th grade classrooms and then look at ScratchJr and Blockly, two other block-based environments, and their appropriateness for this age group [13, 10]. Example scripts from Scratch, ScratchJr, Blockly, and LaPlaya are shown in Figure 1.

3.1 Methods

Our results on Scratch are informed by the pilot of a 4th grade computational thinking curriculum. This curriculum consists of three types of activities: short, pre-populated projects that students can finish within a lab period; off computer activities in the classroom that tie computational thinking concepts back to every day life; and an open-ended design-thinking digital story project. This curriculum was designed specifically for Scratch [12] and introduced multiple concepts necessary for digital storytelling: sequential execution, event-based programming, initialization, message passing, costume changes, and scene changes. The initial version used the original Scratch language in a slightly modified environment; blocks that had not been introduced were hidden in order to support the short, lab-length conceptual learning tasks.

We piloted the curriculum in fifteen 4th – 6th grade classrooms at five schools across California. We refer to these schools as A, B,

C, D and E, with A being the first school trial and E being the last. In schools B and E, we collected only student projects. In schools A, C, and D, we observed instruction and interviewed students. The schools had varying numbers of classrooms, grades participating, start dates, and order of projects.

3.2 Findings

We originally intended our curriculum to use Scratch, but when we piloted it in 4th grade classrooms, we found that students struggled with some math concepts and parts of the interface. For this analysis, we focus on schools A and B, the first to use our pilot materials. For the schools with later start dates (C-E), we used a variant of Scratch and changed the interface to address difficulties students had at schools A and B.

3.2.1 The Interface: Distractions and Difficulties

In our pilot classes, we found aspects of the development environment distracted or allowed students to delete parts of the pre-populated projects without clear ways of recovering lost elements. Some students deleted the scripts or sprites that the file started with, making it difficult or even impossible in some cases to add these back later. In schools A and B (142 students, 516 projects), we found that students deleted provided sprites in at least 4.5% of projects, and deleted provided scripts in at least 9.6% of projects. These numbers might be lower than the actual number of projects where sprites or scripts were deleted. We developed these statistics from final versions of assignments that students submitted, but when students realized they had deleted an element of the project they needed, they frequently restarted with the original version of the provided file.

Additionally, students of this age group are likely to be distracted by "instant gratification" buttons [18]. For example, a "surprise sprite" button adds a new random sprite to the stage every time you click on it. These buttons can be distracting for younger age groups. As an example, one student in our study added 34 sprites to one project. Further, in schools A and B, students added unnecessary sprites in 10.1% of projects. Although it is important to allow students to explore and find different ways of solving the problem, "instant gratification" buttons can switch from being vehicles for exploration to distractions that spread through the computer lab as students observe their peers' computers. Providing the ability to limit such features is important when designing an interface for this age group.

3.2.2 The Language: Math Content

Scripts can move sprites across the screen and change the way they look, from their size to their color. However, many of the blocks needed to change the states of sprites require math concepts above the 4th grade level. Although some of these blocks are appropriate for older groups, Scratch does not provide ways to hide specific blocks when working with younger age groups. In this section, we look at the math concepts used in the Scratch language and when they are introduced in the Common Core Math Standards [24].

Common Core Concept	*Grade*	*Example Scratch Block*
Cartesian coordinates	5	go to x: 0 y: 0
Negative numbers	6	change volume by -10
Percentages	6	set size to 100 %
Decimal numbers	4	wait .1 secs

Table 1. Math Concepts in Scratch and the Common Core

Initializing position and changing values (size, volume, coordinates, variables, time) require mathematical concepts that students have not learned by the start of 4th grade (e,g, x,y coordinates, negative numbers, decimals, and percentages), making the entry floor too high for 4th grade students, our target audience. Table 1 shows each concept, the grade in which this concept appears in the Common Core Math Standards, and an example block that requires this concept [24].

Cartesian Coordinates: Setting a sprite to an absolute location is done with a *go to (sprite or mouse pointer)* block or a *go to x: y: (x and y coordinates)* block. The latter requires an understanding of the Cartesian coordinate system, which is not introduced until 5th grade. Students can use an alternate approach of placing the sprite where they want it to go before selecting the *go to* block, as Scratch auto-populates the proper x and y values. The sequence of moves to memorize would require more repetition than we wanted for our projects, and we do not encourage procedures based on memorizing rather than understanding.

Negative numbers: Negative numbers are used in most motion blocks, and embed in blocks that change the appearance of the sprite (such as the size or color). Scratch's Cartesian plane places the origin, (0,0), in the center of the stage, which means that anything out of the top-right quadrant requires a negative x or y value. Negative numbers are also used by *change (something) by X* blocks to reduce the size, volume, x or y coordinate, and variable value. Negative numbers are not in the Common Core Math Standards until 6th grade, so many students in upper elementary school will not know how to make the value smaller.

Percentages: Size and volume are set with percentages, which are not introduced until 6th grade. Not only must students understand percentage parts of a whole, they also need to understand what 100% means for that variable; for example, the size percentages are of the original picture size, which the students are unlikely to know.

3.3 Other block-based environments

In this section, we look at ScratchJr and Blockly for their appropriateness on 4th – 6th grade classrooms and curriculum. ScratchJr, recently released for the iPad, is aimed toward ages 5-7 [13]. Blockly is used by Code.org in its curriculum and the Hour of Code, a programming initiative that has been massively successful in encouraging students and teachers to try programming [10].

3.3.1 ScratchJr

ScratchJr fixes many of the math and interface issues present when using Scratch with younger age groups. Most the "instant gratification" buttons have been removed to encourage students to focus on programming. The blocks in ScratchJr require less math knowledge, and an optional grid overlay on the stage adds extra support for using x,y coordinates.

Because it is aimed at 5-7 year olds, ScratchJr's ceiling is not as high as is desired for 4th – 6th grades. The programming language uses symbols instead of words and has a smaller block selection than Scratch.

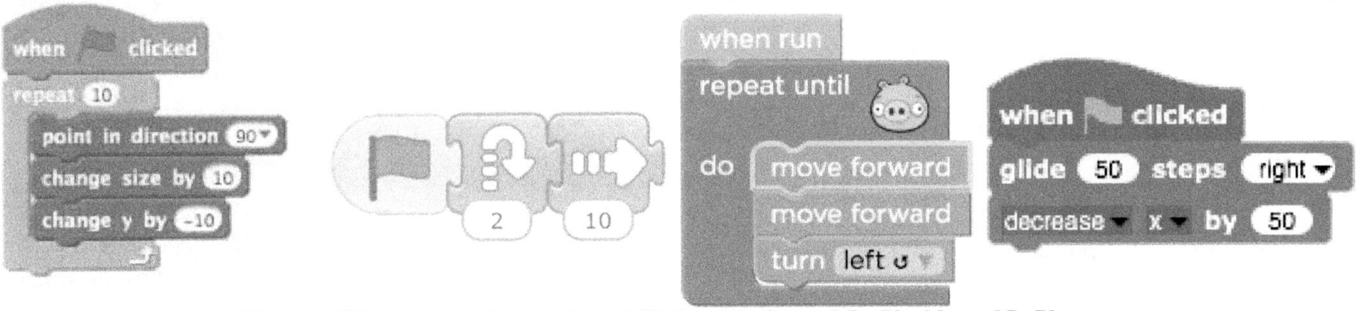

Figure 1. Movement scripts in (from left) Scratch, ScratchJr, Blockly and LaPlaya

It does not have variables, lists, or many of the control structures present in Scratch. Additionally, ScratchJr is more structured than Scratch; users pick scenes for their sprites to act in. ScratchJr lacks the complexity needed to appropriately challenge 4th – 6th graders.

Like Scratch, ScratchJr works best for open-ended projects, but teachers can use pre-populated files for assignments. The danger is that students can see and modify any given sprites and scripts so they may delete sprites and find they need them later on.

3.3.2 Blockly

Blockly is the block-based language used in the popular Hour of Code. Unlike Scratch and ScratchJr, users cannot simply open up Blockly and begin coding; each project is created in Javascript, limiting users to specific projects designed by developers. Projects in Blockly are similar to Scratch and ScratchJr; users create scripts out of blocks to control characters.

Developers create each project in Javascript, which allows them to create unique blocks and interface elements for each project. This added control for developers means that Blockly can be used for any age group, but curriculum developers need to know Javascript to create projects. Additionally, students cannot engage in open-ended, exploratory projects like in Scratch or ScratchJr. Although Blockly can be used to create scaffolded projects for 4th – 6th grade, it lacks the open-ended options present in Scratch and ScratchJr and it has a high overhead for project development. It is unlikely that classroom elementary school teachers will have the background necessary to develop projects using Blockly.

3.4 Bridging the gap with lower floors and greater flexibility

When creating our curriculum, we wanted a language that combined aspects of Scratch, ScratchJr, and Blockly. Scratch gives students low floors, wide walls, and high ceilings, but in some cases (such as the math) the floors are not low enough for our target age group. ScratchJr provides a lower floor and ceiling, but they are too low to be challenging for upper elementary school students. Although Blockly provides more content flexibility, it has too high an overhead for project creation and lacks the open-ended, "playground" environment option present in Scratch and ScratchJr. We wanted a combination of Scratch's "playground" programming environment and low entry point for curriculum developers, ScratchJr's attention to developmental requirements of the target age group, and Blockly's flexibility. We used our experiences with these languages and the feedback from our pilot classrooms to construct a set of design principals that guided our development of a new programming environment, LaPlaya.

4. LAPLAYA

LaPlaya is a block-based language based on Snap!, a development environment inspired by Scratch for supporting higher grade levels [14]. We created a set of design principles for LaPlaya based on existing block-based environments and our experiences in the pilot classrooms. A beta version of LaPlaya was used in some of our pilot classes in the 2013-14 school year, and we plan to use an updated version in the 2014-15 school year.

Our design principles, shown in Table 2, were informed by several criteria. First, we wanted to support different kinds of curricula for 4th – 6th grade, rather than privilege either open-ended or scaffolded projects over each other. Our second criterion was that our interface could support use in formal learning environments with elementary teachers with or without a background in computer science. Practical challenges that teachers face in a traditional classroom create different constraints and opportunities than informal learning environments. Our third criterion was that we wanted the designer interface to support creating student projects and tasks to be accessible to curriculum developers without extensive programming backgrounds. The design principles are informed by existing block-based languages and our own findings during the pilot implementation of our curriculum and while running computer science summer camps for 6th – 8th grade students for three summers [13].

4.1 Support multiple types of tasks.

Our goal was to create an environment that did not limit curriculum designers when developing assignments. This led to the first design principal: support multiple types of tasks. We wanted to support a range of curricular types, from purely open-ended projects that students design and create over long periods of time, to scaffolded curricula with targeted projects of pre-populated sprites and pre-determined goals completed in as little as 10 minutes. The programming environment should offer a wide range of blocks and functionality to support open-ended projects; and developers may want to constrain available blocks and functions to only those necessary to complete the task.

The LaPlaya environment allows developers to create prepopulated projects with options for the scripts and sprites that will be visible to students. Developers can hide sprites or scripts that work in the background; for example, a project with a distinct end goal may include an analysis script that says "Great job!" when the student completes the project. Scripts can be shown as inert examples that do not run but show students how to create the script. Developers can lock scripts or sprites available to students, but that students do not need to manipulate. For example, in Figure 2, students program the car sprite to move to the different cities. Curriculum developers already programmed the other sprites so they are locked. Some

LaPlaya blocks and block categories, such as "Sounds", are hidden since they are not needed for this project. Alternatively, developers may also choose to leave the entire environment visible to students for open-ended projects.

4.2 Require only grade- and age-appropriate content.

The computer science content in the environment should not rely on non-computer science content above grade level. Programming requires both math and literacy skills as programmers must be able to read and understand commands. Some commands require mathematical understandings like addition, which 4th graders do understand, and percentages, which they may not. While we contend that the interface and programming language should support the development of new math and literacy skills, we do not want math and literacy requirements to preclude students from coding. Nor do we want to require teachers to teach content before they would do so in their normal curricular plans.

In LaPlaya, the origin, (0,0), is in the lower left-hand corner of the stage, removing the need for negative numbers in the *go to x: y: (x and y coordinates)* block. All *change (state) by X* blocks were replaced by *increase/decrease (state) by X* blocks so students would not need negative numbers to decrease the value. Finally, LaPlaya has *set size to X* blocks with absolute amounts (small, medium, large) that correspond to absolute sizes on the screen rather than percentages relative to the original picture size. Removing the need for the Cartesian coordinate system is much more challenging and is the subject of ongoing research.

4.3 Include an age-appropriate interface.

The development environment should encourage novice programmers to write code. Those comfortable in the role of "user" might be inclined to avoid coding in favor of activities they are more familiar with, such as manipulating settings or non-programming aspects of the environment, like an image editor. Students today enter the computer lab already familiar with computers as computer users. Using the computer as a developer is a new experience for these students. Kolikant argues that computer science education is a cultural encounter where students have multiple viewpoints; they are newcomers to computer science, students in a classroom, and also computer users [5]. A development environment that introduces students to computer science should encourage students to be developers creating their own programs for an audience rather than users playing with unrelated features of the interface (such as a paint editor).

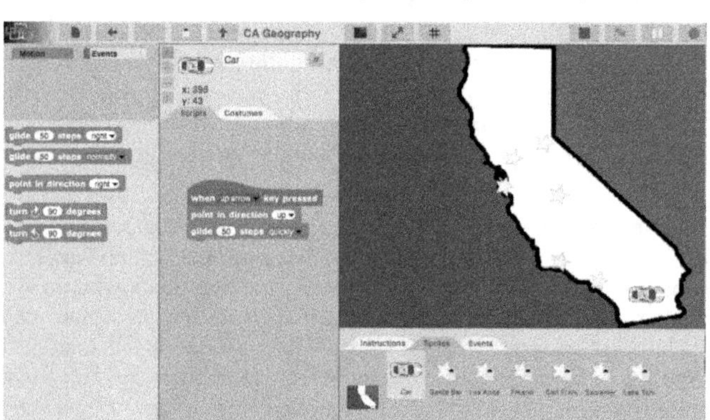

Figure 2. A KELP-CS project in LaPlaya, as seen in student mode

Table 2. Comparison of Scratch, ScratchJr, Blockly and LaPlaya for 4th – 6th grade

Design Principle	*Scratch*	*ScratchJr*	*Blockly*	*LaPlaya*
Support multiple types of tasks				✓
Require only grade- and age-appropriate content			✓	✓
Include an age-appropriate interface			✓	✓
Support project developers	✓	✓		✓

As mentioned earlier, in our pilot classes, we found that "instant gratification" buttons distracted students and led to unrecoverable errors because it was easy to delete sprites and scripts in the pre-populated projects, but hard to get them back. In LaPlaya, developers can hide aspects of the interface that might be distracting for students, such as the "add sprite" button. To encourage students to experiment with the programming blocks (instead of staying in the more familiar role of "user" and playing with non-programming areas), curriculum developers could hide these "non-programming" elements in early projects.

4.4 Support project developers.

Finally, creating a starting file for a project should not require a degree in computer science. Although most computer science teachers at the elementary school level may be more comfortable using existing projects, we believe in lowering the threshold for creating content so someone without a strong computer science background could create new material. In our scenario, any person with facility in Scratch could make a new project in less than a day. As teachers become more comfortable with the environment, they may want to adjust existing material or map projects to their other classroom activities. As such, we contend that the project creation environment (developer mode) should be similar to the environment used by students to finish the projects.

LaPlaya has two modes for viewing and editing a project: a developer mode for project developers and teachers, and a student mode for teachers and students. The developer mode allows developers to manage available content in a project when it is opened in the student version. Developers create projects using the same blocks that could be used in student mode, so creating starting files for assignments does not require more advanced computer science knowledge.

4.5 Summary

Scratch, ScratchJr, and Blockly were not designed to be consistent with our stated design principals, so identifying inconsistencies between the languages and our design principles is not a criticism of these languages, only an indication that they were not ideal for the learning and development context that we are working with.

We found the Scratch interface features and math content were too advanced for 4th – 6th grade. ScratchJr remedied many of these issues but is designed for a younger age group, making it also not developmentally appropriate for 4th – 6th grade. Scratch and ScratchJr can be used with open-ended or scaffolded projects, but their interface designs are problematic when working with pre-populated projects. Blockly provides developers greater control over block options when creating projects and can be used to make grade level-appropriate assignments for 4th – 6th grade. However, experienced programmers must design these projects. Further, Blockly does not have an option for a "playground" environment where students can create their own projects without a starting file. In developing LaPlaya we built on the strengths of each of these interfaces to create a programming environment tailored to 4th – 6th grade students in a classroom setting.

5. FUTURE WORK

We plan to continue studying students' experiences learning computational thinking and how development environments shape their learning. In particular, we will look at the word choice of blocks in visual programming languages, and whether younger students benefit from a language with more blocks that produce visual effects.

In addition, we plan to extend our work to looking at teachers' learning. In our pilot, we found that many teachers did not have prior experience teaching computational thinking. We plan to research how teachers learn computational thinking, and map the terrain of teacher education in science and technology.

6. ACKNOWLEDGMENTS

This work is supported by the National Science Foundation BPC Award CNS-0940491 and CE21 Award CNS-1240985.

7. REFERENCES

[1] Achieve, I. The Next Generation Science Standards. The National Academies Press, 2013.

[2] Alliance, S. The stars alliance: A southeastern partnership for diverse participation in computing. NSF STARS Alliance Proposal. http://www.itstars.org/.

[3] Arroyo, I. et al. Effects of web-based tutoring software on students' math achievement. In AERA, 2004.

[4] Bell, T., Witten, I. H. & Fellows, M. Computer Science Unplugged. 2006.

[5] Ben-David Kolikant, Y. (Some) Grand Challenges of Computer Science Education in the Digital Age: A Socio-Cultural Perspective. In WiPSCE, 2012.

[6] Bradley, R. H., & Corwyn, R. F. (2002, February). Socioeconomic status and child development. Annual Review of Psychology, 53, 371–399.

[7] Bruckman, A., Bandlow, A., & Forte, A. 2012. HCI for kids. In J. A. Jacko (Ed.) *The human-computer interaction handbook: fundamentals, evolving technologies, and emerging applications* (841 – 862). Boca Raton, FL: Taylor & Francis Group, LLC.

[8] Cooper, S., Dann, W., and Pausch, R. 2000. Alice: a 3-D tool for introductory programming concepts. *J. Comput. Sci. Coll.* 15, 5 (April 2000), 107-116.

[9] Dann, W., Cooper, S., & Pausch, R. Making the connection: programming with animated small world. ITiCSE, 2000.

[10] Empson, R. 2 Weeks and 600+ Lines of Code Later, 20M Students Have Learned An "Hour Of Code", TechCrunch. http://techcrunch.com/2013/12/26/code-org-2-weeks-and-600m-lines-of-code-later-20m-students-have-learned-an-hour-of-code/

[11] Flannery, L. P., et al. Designing ScratchJr: Support for Early Childhood Learning Through Computer Programming. In IDC '13.

[12] Franklin, D., Conrad, P., Aldana, G., et. al. Animal Tlatoque: Attracting Middle-School Students to Computing through Culturally-Relevant Themes. In SIGCSE '11.

[13] Franklin, D., Conrad, P., Boe, B., Nilsen, K., Hill, C., Len, M., Dreschler, G., Aldana, G., et al. Assessment of Computer Science Learning in a Scratch-Based Outreach Program. In SIGCSE '13.

[14] Garcia, D., Segars, L. & Paley, J. 2012. Snap! (build your own blocks): tutorial presentation. *J. Comput. Sci. Coll.* 27, 4 (April 2012), 120-121.

[15] Gelderblom, H., & Kotze, P. 2009. Ten design lessons from literature on child development and children's use of technology. In IDC 2009.

[16] Halgren, S., et al. 1995. Amazing Animation™: Movie making for kids design briefing. In SIGCHI '95.

[17] Hood, C. S. & Hood, D. J. Teaching programming and language concepts using legos. In ITiCSE, June 2005.

[18] Kazakoff, E. R. Cats in Space, Pigs that Race: Does self-regulation play a role when kindergartners learn to code? (Unpublished doctoral dissertation). Tufts University, Massachusetts, 2014.

[19] Kerr, J., Kelleher, C., Ellis, R. & Chou, M. 2013. Setting the scene: scaffolding stories to benefit middle school students learning to program. In *IEEE VL/HCC*, 95-98.

[20] Lewis, C. M. 2010. How programming environment shapes perception, learning and goals: Logo vs. scratch. In SIGCSE '10.

[21] Lewis, C. M. 2011. Is pair programming more effective than other forms of collaboration for young students?, Computer Science Education, 22, June 2011, DOI=10.1080/08993408.2011.579805

[22] Malan, D. J. & Leitner, H. Scratch for Budding Computer Scientists. In SIGCSE'07.

[23] Maloney, J., et al. The scratch programming language and environment. Trans. Comput. Educ., 10(4): 1–15, Nov. 2010.

[24] National Governors Association Center for Best Practices, Council of Chief State School Officers. Common Core State Standards (Math), National Governors Association Center for Best Practices, Council of Chief State School Officers, Washington D.C., 2010.

[25] Repenning, A. 1993. Agentsheets: a tool for building domain-oriented visual programming environments. In CHI '93.

[26] Santrock, J. W. *Child Development.* McGraw Hill, Boston, 2004.

[27] Strommen, E. 1994. Children's use of mouse-based interfaces to control virtual travel. In CHI '94.

[28] Tai, R., Liu, C., Maltese, A., & Fan, X. 2006. Planning early for careers in science, Science, 312, 5777, 1143–11.44.

Getting Started in Teaching and Researching Computer Science in the Elementary Classroom

Diana Franklin†, Charlotte Hill†, Hilary Dwyer‡, Ashley Iveland‡, Alexandria Killian‡, Danielle Harlow‡

†Computer Science Department
UC Santa Barbara
{franklin, charlottehill}@cs.ucsb.edu

‡Gevirtz Graduate School of Education
UC Santa Barbara
{hdwyer, aockey, akillian, dharlow}@education.ucsb.edu

ABSTRACT
The recent growth of interest in computer science has created a movement to more readily introduce computer science in K-12 classrooms. However, little research exists on how to successfully bring computer science to lower grade levels. In this paper, we present advice for researchers and curriculum developers who are getting started working with computer science in elementary schools. Specifically, we focus on practical tips for studies of this nature, developed from our experiences piloting a computational thinking curriculum with 4th-6th grade students. We address issues arising in elementary school classrooms such as recruiting and interfacing with teachers and schools, classroom management strategies, student computer literacy and developmental stages, and curriculum life cycles.

Categories and Subject Descriptors
K.3.2 [**Computer and Education**]: Computer Science Education

General Terms
Design; Experimentation; Human Factors

Keywords
K-12; Outreach; Computer Science Education; Curriculum

1. INTRODUCTION
Recent efforts to expand the computer science field have led to a variety of outreach programs and activities, many targeted at underrepresented groups such as girls and students of color (e.g. GirlsWhoCode, BlackGirlsCode, etc.). Since we know that eighth graders' interest in pursuing a career in science and engineering is a strong predictor of whether or not they will later pursue a science career [18], it follows that introducing students to computer science in elementary school can increase the likelihood that they will pursue careers that require computer science in the future. But, bringing computer science to younger grades comes with challenges. Though many K-8 teachers have added computer science to their curriculum [1], they are unlikely to have had formal training in how to teach computer science. In this paper, we provide practical tips for people who are interested in teaching computer science and who are creating material for computer science curricula.

Developing computer science curricula requires knowledge of computer science, understanding of how young children learn, and awareness of how elementary school classrooms function. This requires an interdisciplinary team of experts working together. Computer scientists are needed to identify important computer science content but are unlikely to have experience working with schools, particularly with lower grade levels. Likewise, teachers have extensive knowledge about children, but may be unfamiliar with the content as well as the tools (computers and programming languages). Education researchers bring relevant theory, research methodology, and knowledge about how students learn, but they may not have worked specifically computer science classrooms. To this end, we combined our interdisciplinary experience with research on this age group to compile a set of tips for those seeking to create successful computer science experiences for children.

We narrow our list and discussion to only those ideas most important for getting started. For those familiar with university level computer science teaching, we present nuances of how elementary schools students differ from college students. For those familiar with children and classrooms but not computer science instruction, we present factors that distinguish computer-based instruction from traditional classroom instruction.

The rest of the paper is organized as follows. We provide background on the educational environment of elementary schools in Section 2, followed by a brief summary of related work in Section 3. Section 4 summarizes our classroom experience. Section 5 presents our tips, from preparation through classroom teaching.

2. BACKGROUND
Recent trends in education have made it easier to introduce computer science curricula in elementary school. The amount of technology on school campuses has dramatically increased with the demand of computer assessment practices. With the implementation of Smarter Balanced Assessments, all U.S. students will be required to take national standardized assessments on computers [16]. Thus, many schools now have minimum requirements for Internet bandwidth, operating systems, keyboards, headphones, and screen size.

SIGCSE'15, March 4–7, 2015, Kansas City, MO, USA.
Copyright © 2015 ACM 978-1-4503-2966-8/15/03…$15.00.
http://dx.doi.org/10.1145/2676723.2677288

While the amount of technology present in schools has recently increased, some argue that this does not necessarily indicate meaningful student learning of computational thinking [7]. Students may spend computer lab time rehearsing multiplication facts, playing math games, or playing games to increase the speed and accuracy of their typing, activities that address skills other than computational thinking. However, an increasing national focus on computer programming has left many schools wanting to integrate programming into computer lab time.

Another recent educational movement, the "Hour of Code" has attempted to increase the amount of computer programming present on K-12 school campuses [1]. Since December 2012, over 20,000 teachers from kindergarten to 12th grade have implemented some type of computer programming lesson in their classrooms [14]. This is made possible, in part, by student-friendly programming interfaces such as Alice[8], Scratch[14], ScratchJr (K-3)[9], and LaPlaya[12] that have made programming more accessible to younger populations. The increased attention and accessible avenues for coding have left teachers and administrators eager for more curricula in this developing area.

3. OUR EXPERIENCE

We are developing, piloting, and evaluating a modular Scratch-based computational thinking curriculum for upper elementary school students. The curriculum consists of three types of activities: (1) short, pre-populated projects that students can finish within a lab period, (2) off-computer activities for the classroom rather than a lab designed to relate computational thinking concepts to every day life, and (3) an open-ended design-thinking project. We implemented the first module during the 2013-2014 academic year. On-computer activities were completed in a Scratch variant named LaPlaya [12] with a modified environment that introduced only the concepts necessary for digital storytelling: sequential execution, event-based programming, initialization, message-passing, costume changes, and scene changes. We modified the environment to hide blocks not introduced in our lessons to maximize the short, computer lab times (less than 45 minutes). Further modifications were completed after the pilot study [12].

The curriculum was piloted in fifteen 4th – 6th grade classrooms at five schools across California with over 400 students. We performed a design-based research design study [2] in which we collected data from each school and made changes (to the curriculum, interface, or language) where deemed necessary.

The initial purpose of the data collection was to research students' mental models of the concepts involved in the new curriculum. To this end, we collected three types of data. First, in all classrooms, our software collected snapshots of project data. Second, in classrooms with direct observation, Graduate Student Researchers (GSRs) took field notes as to what issues the students encountered each session and why. Third, as students completed projects, GSRs prompted the elementary school students by asking them to share their work and explain what they did. The elementary school students demonstrated and described their programs in short videos collected on iPhones. Observation and videos were used to identify potential problems, and analysis of snapshots was performed to determine the prevalence of problems (and therefore decide whether to make changes). Details of our research study, data collection, and findings can be found in Hill et al[12]. While our intended purpose was to explore elementary student learning, we found that many of the challenges students faced were due to factors related more to the environment than to the concepts.

Table 1 shows selected demographics of schools that participated in the pilot to demonstrate the different populations. We refer to these schools as A, B, C, D, E, and F, with A being the first school trial and F being the last. In schools B and E, we collected only student project snapshots. In schools A, C, D, and F, we also observed instruction and filmed students explaining their projects. Each school had a varying number of classrooms, grades participating, start dates.

Who was assigned to teach computing varied across schools. In schools A, C, and D, individual classroom teachers taught their own students. In school F, one 4th grade teacher taught computing to all four 4th grade classes. In school B, a technology teacher coordinated the program, but a team of parent volunteers with programming experience taught the curriculum. School E had a programming course taught by a dedicated technology teacher. The schools also differed in the way students accessed the curriculum. In school D, students had their computers on their desks. All other classes went to a dedicated lab for their on-computer activities.

Table 1. Participating school characteristics.

School	% ELL	% Free/ Reduced Lunch	Classes	Grade	Observed
A	23%	35%	2	4th	Yes
B	2%	4%	4	4-5th	No
C	43%	73%	1	4th	Yes
D	82%	92%	2	4th	Yes
E	10%	37%	2	6th	No
F	32%	40%	4	4th	Yes

At the conclusion of the study, we interviewed each participating teacher for suggestions on all aspects of the study, including the curriculum, tools, and interfacing with our team.

The practical tips in this paper are gathered from our observations and data, as well as previous research we used to design our curriculum. The advice in this study can be roughly categorized in three ways: (1) prior research we used when we designed our curriculum that we found to be very successful, (2) advice grounded in prior research that we were unaware of and only discovered as a result of challenges that emerged during our pilot, and (3) advice about situations we were very surprised by, and for which we found no prior research providing solutions or advice.

4. PRACTICAL ADVICE

We start by providing recommendations about early stages of preparation (choosing or developing an interface and language and designing a curriculum), to interfacing with schools and teachers, through delivering content in the classroom.

4.1 Language and environment

When teaching a text-based programming language such as C or Java, choosing the programming environment and language are often two completely separate decisions. For visual block-based languages, a popular choice for elementary school students, the environment and language are often entwined because the environment is necessary to program. Therefore, the decision is typically made together.

Choosing or creating the language and environment requires special attention to the abilities of the target age group, in our case $4^{th} - 6^{th}$ grade. Most upper elementary school students have had experience with computers, but vary widely in the amount and type of computer experiences and comfort levels with the physical tasks required by computing, such as typing or clicking and dragging an object across the screen.

Choose a language that requires only content at or below target grade level
Each school is accountable to state standards for math, literacy, science and social studies. Many states have or are moving towards standards that are aligned with the Common Core State Standards (CCSS)[5,6]. Check the standards for the grade level you are targeting to ensure using the programming language or interface do not require knowledge of math or literacy content above grade level. Math content is especially important: percentages, negative numbers, and fractions are not covered until 3rd-6th grades [6,12].

Use drop-down menus in interfaces whenever possible
Because of the variability in typing skills, drop-down menus should be used in lieu of typing whenever possible. Solomon found spelling and typing difficulties to be common problems for children aged 7-11[17]. Crook found that using the mouse and joystick is much easier than typing for young children [4]. We experienced similar challenges in our classrooms. Often students struggled to type specific strings of characters correctly, leading us to implement drop-down menus as often as possible.

Avoid downloading and uploading files from a shared computer.
Interfaces on browsers and modern operating systems are not well designed for labs configured using identical, parallel file structures for different students on the same computer. Because the parallel file structures differ by only one directory, and this directory may not be obvious in some views, we found this resulted in two common difficulties. First, students sometimes started from a previous student's project rather than their own; and second, they sometimes uploaded the other student's project rather than their own. This is because when opening a file or uploading a file, the browser starts in the most recent location for that application. In both cases, the file will be from the last person who sat on the computer. Because the directories had the same files in them, the students only noticed if he or she looked at the folder name and recognized it as not his or her own student number.

Choose between installation and connectivity-dependence
Most platforms are either installed (requiring downloads of project material) or accessible through the browser (requiring connectivity). This choice depends on the attributes of the target computer environment. If connectivity is reliable and plentiful, then an in-browser platform with files that are easy to locate could be preferred. If connectivity is unreliable, then installing the platform and uploading and downloading the files could be preferred (just be careful about downloading as described above and installation issues as described later).

Further Resources
For more information on the research in languages and interfaces for children, consider looking at conference proceedings from Interaction Design and Children (IDC), Innovation and Technology in Computer Science (ITiCSE), Human Factors in Computing Systems (CHI), and Special Interest Group on Computer Science Education (SIGCSE).

4.2 Teacher and Student Materials

Once you have identified the language and environment, it is time to choose or create a curriculum. If you are designing a curriculum, there are several considerations to keep in mind.

Create an interdisciplinary team of computer scientists, education researchers and teachers.
All three components - computer science researchers, education researchers, and classroom teachers – are critical to designing a curriculum. Computer scientists bring content knowledge, education researchers bring research on how students learn, and classroom teachers bring knowledge on how the curriculum will fit into the current norms and expectations in the classrooms.

Reinforce, but do not depend on, other content knowledge
Our initial projects integrated subjects taught that year (e.g. missions, California geography, physics [13]). We believed that doing so would increase the value of the curriculum and help teachers justify the time dedicated to it because computing is not a required area of elementary school instruction. Our collaborating teachers were also very positive about this idea. Unfortunately, we found two drawbacks. First, teachers choose varying starting times (early or late in school year) and paces (one 40 minute session a week to two one-hour sessions a week). It is challenging for a teacher to time the computer science content to match when they present other material during the year. Second, projects that depend on material from outside subjects make students' success contingent on material not related to computing.

Our solution was to integrate other content areas in ways that reinforced the content, but did not require students to remember any of the other content. For example, instead of providing a planets project with no labels and asking students to fill in the labels and "say bubbles", we provided the planets project with labels and had students fill in the "say bubbles" with those names. That way, students can focus on programming without being distracted or frustrated by their knowledge of outside subjects.

Limit or avoid use of student worksheets in computer lab
Although math and science activities require students to follow written instructions from books or notebooks and write their responses, written materials do not work as well alongside computers. Depending on the lab configuration and students' comfort with computer, it can be difficult to manage worksheets and computer activities in the same space. If the lab is far from the classroom, pencils and paper need to be transported back and forth. Also, there may not be space between computers for students to work on paper. Instead, worksheets can be filled out separately from lab and then brought to lab if they are absolutely necessary.

Tailor writing in workshops to student needs
Students in 4th grade have learned to read, but there is great variation at their comfort and speed when writing. If desired, writing requirements can be limited by providing options to circle words or answers, drawing pictures, or filling in the blank. Other classrooms may want to use the computer time as an opportunity to practice writing and would design more open-ended responses.

Show how your material links to standards in different content areas
Elementary school teachers teach lessons across multiple content areas within the span of a single day. Elementary teachers may

benefit from knowing how curriculum activities from the computer science curriculum reinforce other topics. Consider aligning your materials to content standards to increase available time for computer science. For example, carefully chosen reflection questions that require students to write in specific ways can be designed to address literacy standards.

Provide one-page summary of activity for teacher.
Providing teachers a succinct description of the activity allows teachers to quickly identify the information relevant to the lesson while walking around and working with students at their computers.

Further Resources
If you are interested in using an existing curriculum for this age group, some free choices are CSTA, ScratchJr, ScratchEd, CS Unplugged, KELP CS, and code.org.

4.3 Working with schools

In our project, we worked with a variety of schools, teachers, students, and lab configurations. In this section, we present the lessons we learned across our experiences in schools.

Finding schools partners is easier than you may think
Finding school partners can be daunting for computer scientists without contacts with local schools. Education departments often have existing relationships with local schools. In addition, we found that schools and districts were eager to learn more. We received e-mails from interested teachers and administrators requesting to use our curriculum. Schools were interested in using our computer programming curriculum during their lab time to provide their students with opportunities to learn computer science. Fifteen classrooms participated in the first year, and we anticipate over fifty classrooms will participate in the second year.

Pilot with your own researchers teaching the curriculum
Computing curricula are complex, involving development environments, languages, activities, and students. During the first iteration, members of your team should teach so that you can make rapid changes to any aspect of the environment. Schedule teacher training after this initial pilot so that teachers are trained on the revised material.

Know the context you will be working in
In preparation for teacher training, working with elementary school students, or any other implementation, it is important to figure out how and where the material will be taught. Classroom technology and personnel teaching computer activities vary across schools. In just our study, various combinations of classroom teachers, dedicated technology teachers, and parent volunteers taught computer labs. Moreover, reliable Internet and firewall restrictions varied, as well as the types of devices students used (netbooks, PCs, iPads).

Find out the process for installing and/or using computers
Using software on the web and installing software on the computers may require school level or district permissions. Procedures for granting permission differ across schools and districts.. For web access, you need to learn whether there is a firewall limiting access to websites. Students may not be allowed to access Google or YouTube, so if you have video content, you may need to house it yourself.

Installing software on lab computers has two barriers. The first is obtaining permission for the software to be installed. The second is performing the actual installation. In two of our participating schools, the people responsible for installing software for the schools were located off-site. This meant that there was a considerable delay between the request to install software and the actual installation. Any problems installing can result in additional delays. In the other schools, our staff was responsible for installing the software on every computer. Each change required updating every computer.

4.4 In the classroom

Managing a class of 25-30 students on computers differs from managing students working on paper and pencil tasks. It can be challenging to keep everyone occupied while assisting individual students. The following recommendations are intended to increase student productivity in the classroom or computer lab. In addition, we present different lab configurations we encountered and how we worked with each.

Bookmark web locations for students
As discussed earlier, typing a url is difficult for young students. On the first day, we helped students bookmark important locations for our project.

Use a mouse, not just a laptop touch pad
Younger students may still be developing the manual dexterity required for clicking and dragging objects, especially when using touch pads. There are two separate problems associated with this. The first is that a student who is trying to click may instead trigger a drag of a very short distance. The second is that a student may have difficulty holding down the button while simultaneously dragging.

We identified two solutions. The first is to provide a mouse for every student so they do not depend on the touch pad. If this is not possible, students who have trouble dragging can use two hands. The pointer finger on one hand clicks the button while the pointer finger on the other hand glides across the touch pad.

Create a supportive collaborative environment
Research on college-level pair programming courses found that mixed-gender pairs were the least harmonious, and females had complaints about gender bias [3]. This might be due to a combination of stereotypes and different communication patterns [10]. We observed similar patterns in the elementary classroom: when girls asked a boy for assistance, the boy sometimes took over and fixed it for the girl rather than explaining the concept to the girl. Therefore, we suggest that students be physically next to someone of the same gender or someone with whom they work well. For example, if students are seated linearly, four boys can be seated in a row, then four girls, etc. If students are seated in pairs, students could be paired with a student of the same gender.

Use hands-free visual aid for students to request assistance
When students need help and raise their hands, they are unable to make progress. In order to provide you a clear visual cue and allow students to continue working, you can use visual aids such as red and green paper tents.

Students can create paper tents by placing a green paper on top of a red paper and folding them in half, making a tent with a green paper on the outside and red on the inside. The students keep the green paper on the outside to signal that they are working successfully. When they need help, they place the red on the outside and on top of the monitor, providing a visual cue to the teacher that they request assistance, but leaving their hands free to continue working.

Use sticky notes on monitors to indicate completed students
If students are working on a short, skill-building exercise, then visual cues are also useful to indicate who has completed the exercise. For example, in our curriculum, when students complete the pre-populated projects, they place a sticky note on their monitor and play in "sandbox" area. Placing a sticky note on the monitor allows teachers to easily see who has finished and moved into the "sandbox" or bonus area.

Include bonus options
Students work at different speeds. When students finish the assignment at different times, early finishers may be bored and ready for additional challenges. We found three categories of "bonus" options to be useful. First, the curriculum can provide extra, optional, more challenging tasks for those who finish early. Second, instructors can pose challenges for existing projects such as completing programming tasks with fewer instructions, with a wider variety of instructions, or adding "bells and whistles" to the project. Finally, students can go to a separate, open-ended activity, either within the environment (such as the sandbox in KELP CS) or a separate environment (Scratch project).

Create student experts
Teachers and researchers can use elementary school students as resources for their peers for basic computing issues. In one of our classrooms, the principal had trained small groups of 4th graders in every class to serve as computer ambassadors. These ambassadors learned basic computing and computer knowledge around the school's new netbooks. We found that these student experts helped immensely in managing basic technology concerns such as where to find files, typing websites, and general use of their classrooms computers. As a result, teachers and researcher had time to address more conceptual issues. Moreover, the student ambassadors took pride in being classroom resources, and many of their peers were more comfortable getting help from them than other adults in the room.

Create hands-free attention signal
Elementary school teachers often use a signal to get students' attention, such as having students raise one hand with a peace symbol or repeat a phrase after the teacher. When in a computer lab, use a signal that requires students to use both hands so that students remove their hands from the keyboard. Examples are placing both hands behind the neck, clapping, or wiggling their fingers

Turn off monitors or close laptops during discussions, demonstrations, and directions.
Because computer screens are dynamic and engaging, they compete for students' attention during group activities when students are requested to listen to the teacher or a peer. Turning off the monitor removes this competition.

Have students direct their chairs to the teacher or gather in the middle of the room on the floor during group time.

Even if the computers are closed or screens turned off, students may have difficulty watching demonstrations if their chairs are not turned towards the teacher. Bringing the students together removes them from the computer work, allowing them to focus more on group time..

Analysis and tips for specific configurations
During our pilot study, we encountered three classroom configurations used in the computer labs. Here, we provide discussion of the pros and cons in each of these configurations along with tips to handle any drawbacks.

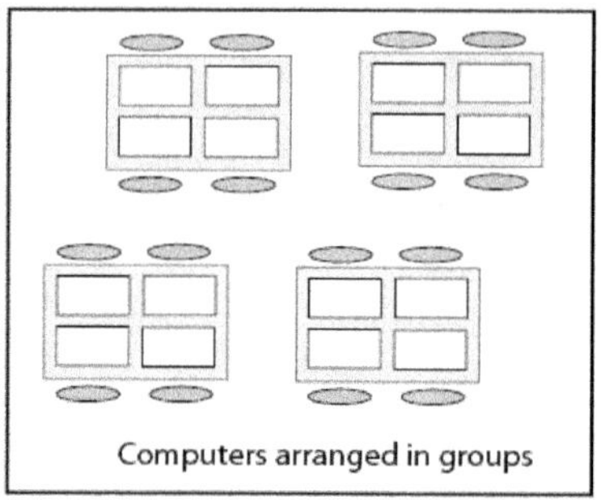

Figure 1: Computers arranged in groups

One arrangement was computers arranged in table groups (Figure 1). This arrangement encouraged students to work together and share ideas. One needs to consider how to group students. Placing students with similar skill levels can help teachers provide targeted support to groups while placing students in mixed ability groupings can facilitate peer support. How well students are comfortable assisting their peers will depend on existing classroom norms. This configuration is challenging for full-class demonstrations, so consider have the "front" of the classroom be to the side of everyone, have students turn their chairs, or assemble students away from the tables for presentations.

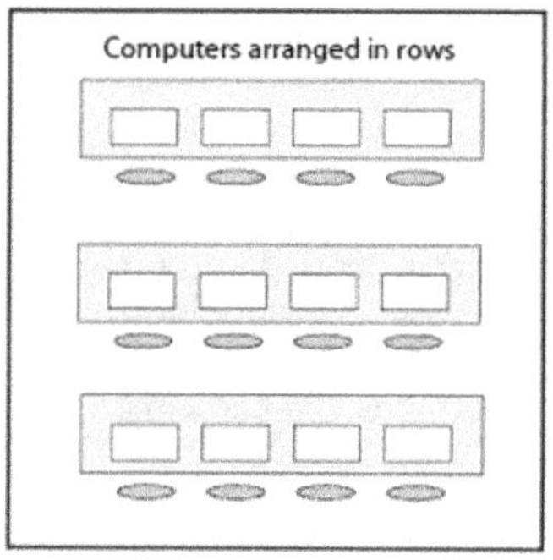

Figure 2: Computers arranged in rows

The second arrangement was computers arranged in rows (Figure 2). This arrangement facilitates students' view of a teacher in the front of the room allows students to work with their neighbors. Because students look over their screens at the board, it is especially important to have them turn off their monitors during group demonstrations.

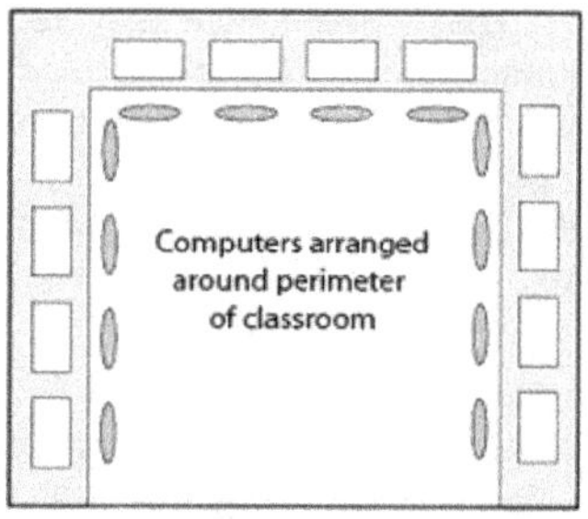

Figure 3: Computers arranged around perimeter

The third arrangement was computers arranged around the perimeter of the classroom (Figure 3). This provides easy access for the instructor to see all of the monitors, but it is very hard for the students to see the instructor. It is imperative that the students turn their chairs for group demonstrations.

4.5 Providing Feedback

Specific and timely feedback has been shown to increase learning and retention [8]. For this age group, the way you determine correctness and the way you express feedback is critical, especially given the variability of comfort with the material. This feedback can be given verbally by in-class instructors or programmed into the programming or project environment (if supported).

Be flexible about your definition of "correct."

Elementary school students are still developing their reading skills, so having very precise instructions to lead students to a single right answer may not be successful. Instead, look at the overarching goals of the project and develop a broad definition of what it means to succeed at these goals.

Be careful about the wording of your feedback.

The majority of elementary school students are new to computing. When they struggle at learning, they may believe this is because they are not good at computing, rather than attribute their difficulties to learning something new. Critical language can reinforce possible preconceived notions that they are not meant for computing. For example, in our feedback we adopted the wording of "You are not finished yet" rather than "The answer is incorrect."

5. CONCLUSIONS

Working in elementary schools is incredibly rewarding: elementary school teachers and students are enthusiastic, and there is the opportunity to make significant contributions through curriculum development or implementation. Working in elementary school classrooms, however, differs from outreach activities – there is more time involved, elementary school teachers may be less comfortable with the material than dedicated outreach providers, and attendance is compulsory rather than voluntary Therefore, it is critical that everyone involved be careful about the languages, development environment, curriculum, and classroom atmosphere. We found that establishing a collaborative team consisting of computer scientists, teachers, and educational researchers facilitated success.

6. ACKNOWLEDGMENTS

This work is supported by the National Science Foundation CE21 Award CNS-1240985.

7. REFERENCES

[1] Alvarado, C. 2014. CS Ed Week 2013: The hour of code. *ACM SIGCSE Bulletin*, *46*(1), 2-4.

[2] Barab, S., & Squire, K., (2004) Design-based research: Putting a stake in the ground, *The Journal of the Learning Sciences*, 13(1) 1-14.

[3] Choi, K. 2013. Evaluating Gender Significance within a Pair Programming Context, *Hawaii International Conference on System Sciences.*

[4] Crook, C. and Bennett, L. 2010. "Does using a computer disturb the organization of children's writing?," *British Journal of Developmental Psychology*, 25, 2, 313–321.

[5] Common Core State Standards Initiative. Common Core Standards for Mathematics. www.commoncorestandards.org/Math

[6] Common Core State Standards Initiative. Common Core Standards for English Language Arts & Literacy in History / Social Studies, Science, and Technical Subjects. www.commoncorestandards.org/ELA-Literacy

[7] Cuban, L., Kirkpatrick, H., and Peck, C. 2001. High access and low use of technologies in high school classrooms: Explaining an apparent paradox. *American Educational Research Journal,* 38, 4, 813-834.

[8] Dann, W., Cooper, S., and Pausch, R.. 2000. Making the connection: programming with animated small world. In *Proceedings of Innovation and Technology in Computer Science Education* (Helsinki, Finland, July 11-13, 2000), . ITiCSE '00. ACM: New York, NY.

[9] Flannery, L., Silverman, S., Kazakoff, E., Umaschi Bers, M., Bontá, P., and Resnick, M. 2013. Designing ScratchJr: support for early childhood learning through computer programming. In *Proceedings of the International Conference on Interaction Design and Children* (New York, NY, June 24-27, 2013). IDC '13. ACM: New York, NY.

[10] Franklin, D. 2013. *Practical Guide to Gender Diversity for CS Faculty*, Morgan-Claypool.

[11] Hattie, J. & Timperley, H. 2007. The Power of Feedback. *Review of Educational Research*, 77, 1, 81-112.

[12] Hill, C., Dwyer, H., Martinez, T., Harlow, D., Franklin, D. 2015. Floors and Flexibility: Designing a programming environment for 4th-6th grade classrooms. *Proceedings of the SIGCSE Technical Symposium.*

[13] Next Generation Science Standards. http://www.nextgenscience.org/next-generation-science-standards

[14] Resnick, M., Maloney, J., Monroy- Hernández, A., Rusk, N., Eastmond, E., Brennan, K., and Kafai, Y. 2009. Scratch: Programming for all. *Communications of the ACM*, 52, 11, 60-67.

[15] Richtel, M. (2014, May 10). Reading, writing, arithmetic, and lately, coding. *The New York Times.*

[16] Smarter Balanced Assessment Consortium. 2014. The smarter balanced technology strategy. Olympia, WA.

[17] P. Solomon. 1993 Children's information retrieval behavior: A case analysis of an opac. *Journal of the American Society for Information Science*, 44, 245–64,.

[18] Tai, R., Liu, C., Maltese, A., & Fan, X. 2006. Planning early for careers in science, *Science*, 312, 5777, 1143–1144.

Improving Non-CS Major Performance in CS1

Victor Norman
Calvin College
1740 Knollcrest Circle SE
Grand Rapids, MI 49506
+1-616-526-7805
vtn2@calvin.edu

Joel Adams
Calvin College
1740 Knollcrest Circle SE
Grand Rapids, MI 49506
+1-616-526-8666
adams@calvin.edu

ABSTRACT

At our comprehensive liberal arts college, we offer a 2-credit hour CS1 course for engineering majors that includes all of the standard learning objectives of a typical 4-credit hour course. To help the students learn the course material in this compressed time frame, we switched our programming language from C++ to Python, and we replaced weekly homework assignments with labs and online problem sets. All other factors in the course were unchanged, including instructor, course and weekly learning objectives, tests, grading criteria, pedagogical style, and even textbook (the textbook came in two versions – a C++ version and a Python version). This transition offered a unique opportunity to observe, compare, and measure student learning outcomes across the two semesters. Our measured results show a moderate but statistically significantly improvement from the semester using C++ and homework assignments to the semester using Python and online problem sets.

Categories and Subject Descriptors

K.3.2 [**Computers and Education**]: Computers and Information Science Education – *computer science education, curriculum*

General Terms

Measurement, Experimentation, Languages

Keywords

CS1; Python; C++; TuringsCraft; CodeLab; Just-in-time teaching.

1. INTRODUCTION

In the U.S., a comprehensive college is a 4-year liberal arts college that includes professional programs such as engineering, accounting, and so on. The authors teach at a comprehensive liberal arts college, where all engineering majors must take a CS1 course to gain basic computer programming skills.

Because of the very full engineering curriculum, the CS1 course for engineers is just 2-credit hours, but still has the same course-level learning objectives as a traditional 4-credit hour CS1 course. Under these time constraints, every efficiency must be used to help the students learn the CS1 programming skills and concepts quickly.

These concepts include algorithmic thinking, problem decomposition, abstraction of functionality, parameterization, control structures, and object-oriented programming topics such as classes, methods, and so on.

SIGCSE '15, March 4–7, 2015, Kansas City, MO, USA

ACM 978-1-4503-2966-8/15/03…$15.00
http://dx.doi.org/10.1145/2676723.2677214

Since the mid-1990s, the authors' college has used C++ as the programming language in this course. In fall 2013, we revised the course by replacing C++ with Python to reduce the amount of syntax students were required to learn. We also replaced weekly programming assignments (using Scribbler robots) with weekly online programming problem sets, using TuringsCraft CodeLab. To the best of the instructor's ability, all other factors in the course were held constant. (See Section 3 below.)

This classroom experience paper details this transition from C++ to Python and out-of-classroom programming assignments to in-class labs and online problem sets, and reports the changes we observed and measured in student learning. In Section 2, we present the work of others that is related to this work. In Section 3, we compare the two versions of our course in detail. In Section 4, we provide some results – both anecdotal and measured – of the differences in the two courses. In Section 5, we present our conclusions.

2. PREVIOUS WORK

Others have documented the results of transitioning an introductory programming course from one language (C++ or Java) to Python. For example, Enbody, Punch, and McCullen [2] studied the effect that changing a CS1 course from C++ to Python had upon the students' performance in CS2, taught in C++. They found that there was no appreciable difference in the performance of the students in CS2 between those that took CS1 using C++ and those that took CS1 using Python. The authors noted that those that took CS1 using Python and CS2 in C++ now had the advantage that they knew two different programming languages.

In [3], Enbody and Punch studied the effect that using Python in CS1 had on student performance in later courses (past CS2). They found no adverse effects, but no positive effects either.

Older studies, such as [6, 8], report anecdotal results from switching to Python in CS1 courses. These results are similar to what the authors have experienced, as reported in Section 4.1 below.

A rigorous study by Stefik and Siebert [9] found that the simpler syntax of Python did in fact assist students in learning their first programming language. This study investigated how well students understood the meaning of keywords in C-like languages (Java and Perl), a language created with random keywords (Randomo), and other languages (Ruby, Python, and Quorum). Their study showed that languages that use more English-like syntax (e.g., **and** instead of the symbols **&&**) helped students overcome the challenge of learning syntax in a first programming language.

Our study differs from these by reporting how a combination of:

1. changing the language from C++ to Python,
2. using TuringsCraft CodeLab exercises for homework, and
3. increasing the number of closed-lab exercises

positively affected student performance within the CS1 course. This is unique in that (i) it demonstrates a positive effect, and (ii) only these three factors between the two course offerings were changed.

3. SIMILARITIES AND DIFFERENCES BETWEEN THE COURSES

Table 1 summarizes the similarities and differences in the courses. We have highlighted the changed elements using boldface.

Table 1. Comparison of the Two Courses

	Fall 2012	Fall 2013
Credit hours	2 (1 hr classroom, 2 hr lab)	2 (1 hr classroom, 2 hr lab)
# of Tests	3	3
# of Students	70 – all 2nd-year engineering majors	90 – all 2nd-year engineering majors
Textbook	How to Think Like a Computer Scientist in C++ (Downey)	How to Think Like a Computer Scientist in Python (Downey)
Instructor	Same	
Labs	Using Scribbler robots	Using Scribbler robots
IDE used	Eclipse	Eclipse
Language used	**C++**	**Python**
Homework	**Programming assignments with robots**	**TuringsCraft online problem sets**

3.1 Similarities

The vast majority of the elements of our CS1 course for engineers did not change when we made the transition from C++ in fall 2012 to Python in fall 2013. Both courses were 2-credit hour courses that met twice each week:

- Tuesday for 1 hour in a traditional classroom, with 25–30 students per section; and
- Thursday or Friday in a computer lab for 2 hours, with 20–24 students per section.

3.1.1 *Tuesday Sessions*

In both courses, Tuesday sessions took place in the same classroom, with seating for 30 students. Both used "Just-in-Time" teaching techniques [1, 7]: students read the assigned chapter over the weekend, and took an online reading quiz before the Tuesday class. One question of the quiz was:

"What questions do you have about the reading, or if you have no questions, what was the most interesting part of the reading?"

From these responses we created a series of "Q and A" slides that comprise the majority of the teaching material for the Tuesday class. We added slides to emphasize and reinforce some of the more difficult learning objectives for the reading. Finally, during Tuesday class, we also had students write short code snippets on 8.5" x 11" personal whiteboards.

3.1.2 *Thursday Sessions*

In both courses, Thursday sessions took place in a computer lab with seating for 24 students. These sessions began by finishing any material that did not get covered on Tuesday, and writing short code snippets on the lab computers to reinforce learning objectives. They ended with prescribed lab exercises.

These prescribed lab exercises focused on learning how to program through controlling Scribbler robots [5], and were designed to emphasize and reinforce the concepts from that week's readings. The labs generally built on one another, and were designed to lead the students through the process of building up a library of functions that generalized and improved the movement capabilities of the Scribbler robots. By the end of the course, the students, using their own library of movement functions, could make the robots optimally go from a prescribed starting point to (x, y) coordinates (measured in centimeters) on whiteboards on the floor, turn a given number of degrees left or right, detect and back away from obstacles, and so on.

3.1.3 *Textbook*

The textbook for the 2012 (C++) course was "How to Think Like a Computer Scientist in C++", by Allen B. Downey [4]. For the 2013 (Python) course we moved to "Think Python: How to Think Like a Computer Scientist in Python", also by Allen B. Downey [10]. The Python version of this textbook is an adaptation of the C++ version, and thus the textbooks are very similar, covering mostly the same concepts in the same chapters.

3.1.4 *Objectives and Course Schedule*

The course-level learning objectives and weekly learning objectives for the courses were nearly identical, modified only by replacing C++-specific objectives with Python-specific objectives, and moving objectives between chapters to align with differences in the textbook. The weekly schedule for the courses is shown in Table 2.

Table 2. Weekly Schedule

Fall 2012: C++	Fall 2013: Python
Introduction	Introduction
Variables and types	Variables, expressions, statements
Functions	Functions
Conditionals	Miscellany, Test 1
Miscellany, Test 1	Conditionals
Fruitful functions	Fruitful functions
Iteration	Iteration
Strings and Things	Strings
Structures, Test 2	Lists, Test 2
Vectors	Lists (continued)
Member Functions	Tuples, Optional Parameters, Files
Classes and Members	Classes and Objects
Classes (continued)	Methods

3.1.5 *Instructor*

The same instructor (Norman) designed and taught both instances of the course.

3.1.6 *Assessment*

Programming assignments were graded similarly in both courses. In addition to functional correctness, the instructor placed heavy emphasis on code "beauty", awarding between 10% and 25% of an assignment's points for program style, including meaningful variable names, good indentation, and thorough, correct, and appropriate documentation in the code.

In both courses, three paper-based tests were given over the course of the semester, during the lab session. The second and third tests were cumulative, with emphasis on the material introduced since the last test. The tests consisted of short-answer questions, some true/false questions, a few multiple-choice questions, and many questions requiring students to write short snippets of code.

3.1.7 *Student Population*

The students were all 2nd-year engineering majors: 70 students took the course in fall 2012 (C++) and 90 in fall 2013 (Python). A very low percentage (less than 5%) of the students had any previous programming experience. The ACT/SAT scores for the two classes, when entering college, were very similar (see section 4.2.6).

3.2 Differences

3.2.1 *Pedagogical*

Two pedagogical changes were made between the two courses:

1. The programming language used was changed from C++ to Python. This change was made primarily because we felt that the high-level thinking skills we wanted our students to learn (e.g., algorithmic thinking, problem decomposition, etc.) were being lost in the burdensome syntax and complexity of C++.
2. The weekly homework programming assignments using Scribbler robots were replaced with in-class labs and weekly online problem sets using TuringsCraft CodeLabs [11]. This change was made for the following reasons:
    a. The instructor felt that, for a 2-credit course, the weekly programming assignments were taking too much time, and that time was not being well-spent. Students were spending many hours fighting the GNU C++ compiler (g++) over syntax errors that they could not understand.
    b. The instructor felt that students would be better served by writing more (simple) code to practice using new structures and syntax to reinforce a given week's learning objectives. In a nutshell, students needed more practice.
    c. The Scribbler robots were being so heavily used by students doing both lab assignments and their homework assignments that more robots were breaking, batteries were too often being discharged and not recharged for others, and in general, the lab facility was not being respectfully maintained by students outside of the Thursday lab sessions.

3.2.2 *Weights*

A change was also made in the weights assigned to the assessments during the courses, as summarized in Table 3.

Table 3. Weights of Assignments

Assessment	Fall 2012: C++	Fall 2013: Python
Reading Quizzes	10%	10%
Labs	**20%**	**35%**
Homeworks	**25%**	**10%**
Test 1	10%	10%
Test 2	15%	15%
Final Exam	20%	20%

In 2013, the instructor increased the labs exercise weights because:

1. With the shift to online problem sets, the lab exercises were the only assessment in which students produced programs that would actually be graded; and
2. The number of lab exercises was increased from five in 2012 to thirteen in 2013, consuming more of a student's time.

The 2013 homework assignments weight was decreased to make up the difference. Also, this was the instructor's first use of the online problem sets. Being unsure of their effectiveness as a pedagogical tool, he did not want to weight them too heavily.

4. RESULTS

In this section, we summarize some of the differences we have discovered in student learning. We begin with some anecdotal observations, and conclude with measured results.

4.1 Anecdotal Observations

4.1.1 *Syntax Errors*

First, while we anticipated that the simpler syntax of Python would significantly benefit students who were learning their first programming language, we found that students still struggled with language syntax. To illustrate, students still:

- struggled with case sensitivity, such as using `true` instead of `True`.
- made the common mistake of confusing = with ==.
- misspelled variable names.
- wrote illegal for loops.
- tried to assign values on the left-hand side of an assignment statement to a variable on the right-hand side.

In other words, switching to Python did not eliminate many of the idiosyncrasies that challenge programming novices. Likewise, many students struggled with understanding the error messages produced by the Python interpreter.

4.1.2 *Semantic Errors*

Semantic errors also seemed consistent across semesters. For example, students would mistakenly place a return statement inside a loop when it should have been placed after the loop. Likewise, many students mixed a function's return mechanism with output, designing functions to print computed values instead of return them.

4.1.3 *Indentation and Formatting Errors*

Unlike C++, Python forces programmers to indent their code consistently. As a result, students in the 2013 (Python) course were frustrated by Python's *IndentationErrors*, in both the lab and the TuringsCraft CodeLab exercises. The students just wanted to get their code to work and did not care about proper indentation. Moreover, some had trouble with the concept of white space and struggled to understand why their indentation was not correct.

In the C++ version of the course, the students also did not indent properly, but for C++, this did not affect code compilation. However, as the course assignments got more difficult, C++ students who indented their code incorrectly had more difficulty solving the programming assignments because they could not easily visualize the flow of execution through their code.

As noted above, in both courses the instructor gave significant points for code "beauty", which included proper indentation. The Python interpreter thus made it harder for students to write "ugly" code, compared to C++. Students in the C++ course were thus more likely to lose points on their assignments due to poor indentation than students in the Python course.

4.1.4 *Assignments*

The online problem sets in the Python course produced similar feedback from students as the weekly Scribbler homework assignments in the C++ course. In both courses, students struggled to understand the problem(s) to be solved, struggled with problem decomposition, struggled with syntax, and other typical CS1 difficulties.

However, students who did the online problem sets did seem to better achieve the weekly learning objectives, as those objectives and the problem sets were closely aligned.

4.2 Measured Results

4.2.1 *Final Exam Scores*

One way we have sought to measure the effects of the changes to the course on the students' learning outcomes is by analyzing the scores on the final exam in the two versions of the course. In both years, the final exam covered all material from the semester, with an emphasis on the material since the second test. Scores on this test should be a good measure of the students' understanding of concepts and mastery of skills from the entire course.

T-tests were applied to the scores on the final exams across the two semesters. Table 4 summarizes our findings.

Table 4. Final Exam Scores

Final Exam	Fall 2012	Fall 2013
Max score	90.7%	100%
Min score	36.4%	34.5%
Mean score	68.4%	72.8% (6.4% improvement)
Standard Deviation	12.8	12.9
T-test: 1-tailed distribution, two-sample, unequal variance	p=0.0159	

The results indicate that the changes made to the course produced a 6.4% improvement in the students' test scores on the final exam, and that this improvement was statistically significant.[1]

Using just these values, we are unable to determine which of the two factors (the change of language or change in weekly homework assignments) contributed more to this improvement in performance. However the results given in Section 4.2.3 provides evidence that changing the language from C++ to Python provided a major boost in student performance.

4.2.2 *Tests 1 and 2*

We also analyzed the students' scores on the other two tests. We were surprised to find that the students in the 2013 (Python) course improved even more on these tests than they did on the final exam, as can be seen in Table 5.

Table 5. Test 1 and Test 2 Scores

	Mean, Fall 2012	Mean, Fall 2013	Percent Improvement	T-test
Test 1	72.6%	78.5%	8.1%	p=0.0071
Test 2	66.0%	72.6%	10%	p=0.0025

4.2.3 *Lab Scores*

Since students in both courses did lab exercises using Scribbler robots, we also analyzed their performance on those lab exercises. Table 6 presents this analysis.

Table 6. Lab Score (Overall Percentage)

	Mean, Fall 2012	Mean, Fall 2013	Percent Improvement	T-test
Lab scores	82.03	91.72	11.8%	p=0.0000006

As can be seen, the students in the 2013 (Python) course did far better on the Scribbler robot lab exercises than the students in the 2012 course. Since the lab exercises involved the same student learning outcomes, this might seem to be directly attributable to changing the language of instruction from C++ to Python.

However, one other difference is that our 2012 (C++) course had just five lab exercises, while the 2013 (Python) course had thirteen exercises. It is thus possible that the 2013 students' better performance on lab exercises was due to the change of language, or the additional exercises, the fact that the labs were done during class time, or a combination of these factors.

4.2.4 *Homework Scores*

Since students in the two courses did markedly different homework assignments (Scribbler programming in 2012 vs online TuringsCraft CodeLab exercises in 2013), we did not feel we could fairly compare the students' performance on homework assignments, so we did not analyze these scores.

4.2.5 *Overall Semester Scores*

We also analyzed the students' overall semester scores, an amalgamation of their scores on lab exercises, homework assignments, quizzes, and tests. Table 7 shows the result.

Table 7. Semester Score

	Mean, Fall 2012	Mean, Fall 2013	Percent Improvement	T-test
Semester scores	79.9%	82.8%	3.6%	p=0.0353

In summary, the students in the 2013 (Python) course did significantly better than those in the 2012 (C++) course, on tests, the lab exercises, the final exam, and the overall semester score.

4.2.6 *Maybe The 2013 Students Were Just Smarter?*

The difference in the scores between the two classes could be explained if the students in the second class were better learners. To explore this possibility, we gathered the ACT (American College Test) and SAT (Scholastic Aptitude Test) scores for the students in the two classes. Table 8 shows these results.

[1] In this paper, we calculate changes by this standard method: (newValue – origValue) / origValue. Thus, a change from 68.4% to 72.8% is not a 4.4% improvement, but a 6.4% improvement.

Table 8. ACT and SAT Scores

	ACT average (max: 36)	SAT average (max: 1600)
Fall 2012	27.6 / 36	1245 / 1600
Fall 2013	28.2 / 36	1264 / 1600
% difference	+2.17%	+1.53%

These scores indicate that the students in the fall 2013 class did enter the course with 2.17% or 1.53% stronger academic abilities, based on their ACT or SAT scores. However, these modest differences in standardized test score averages cannot fully account for the 6.4% improvement we saw in Final Exam scores (see Table 4) or the 8.1% and 10% improvements we saw on tests 1 and 2 (see Table 5). The improvements we saw in student performance were disproportionately larger than the differences in academic or test-taking ability suggested by the students' ACT and SAT scores.

We conclude that the switch from C++ to Python, and from programming homework assignments to online problem sets, is responsible for much of the improvement in the student performance in our course.

5. CONCLUSIONS

From 2012 to 2013, a 2-credit-hour CS1 course for engineering majors was changed in just three ways:

1. The programming language of instruction was changed from C++ to Python.
2. Weekly homework assignments were changed from programming assignments using Scribbler robots to online programming problem sets using TuringsCraft CodeLab.
3. The number of lab exercises using Scribbler robots was expanded from five to thirteen.

Other factors in the course were held constant, including the course instructor, the textbook author and organization, course and weekly learning objectives, pedagogical style, and test style and content.

Anecdotal evidence showed little difference in the two courses. Students learning Python still struggled with syntax errors, understanding cryptic error messages, semantic errors, logic errors, formatting errors, and other longstanding difficulties that make CS1 challenging for students.

However, the 2013 students showed a measurably significant improvement in their performance on the tests (8.1% and 10%, respectively), the final exam (6.4%), the lab exercises (11.8%), and in the semester score (3.6%). Differences in these students' academic abilities and the weighting of lab exercises were not sufficient to account for how much better these students did, compared to their 2012 counterparts.

These results indicate that (i) changing the programming language of instruction from C++ to Python, (ii) changing the homework assignments from Scribbler robot-programming assignments to online TuringsCraft CodeLab exercises, and (iii) increasing the number of Scribber robot-programming lab exercises, were *sufficient* to significantly and measurably improve student performance, especially on tests.

Since this is a classroom experience report and not a controlled experiment, we are unable to quantify the extent to which each change contributed to the improvement in student performance. Put differently, we cannot say that all three of these changes are *necessary* to improve student performance. Exploring this would be an interesting topic for a future study.

6. REFERENCES

[1] Bailey, T. and Forbes, J.,"Just-in-time Teaching for CS0," in *Proceedings of the 36th SIGCSE Technical Symposium on Computer Science Education*, New York, NY, USA, 2005, pp. 366–370.

[2] Enbody, R., Punch, W., and McCullen, M., "Python CS1 As Preparation for C++ CS2," *Proceedings of the 40th ACM Technical Symposium on Computer Science Education*, New York, NY, USA, 2009, pp. 116–120.

[3] Enbody, R. and Punch, W., "Performance of Python CS1 Students in Mid-level Non-python CS Courses," *Proceedings of the 41st ACM Technical Symposium on Computer Science Education*, New York, NY, USA, 2010, pp. 520–523.

[4] "How to Think Like a Computer Scientist." http://greenteapress.com/thinkcpp/. Accessed on 14-Jul-2014.

[5] "Institute for Personal Robots in Education (IPRE)," http://wiki.roboteducation.org/Main_Page. Accessed on 14-Jul-2014.

[6] Necaise, R. D., "Transitioning from Java to Python in CS2," *J Comput Sci Coll*, vol. 24, no. 2, pp. 92–97, Dec. 2008.

[7] Novak, G. M., Gavrin, A., and Wolfgang, C., *Just-in-Time Teaching: Blending Active Learning with Web Technology*, 1st ed. Upper Saddle River, NJ, USA: Prentice Hall PTR, 1999.

[8] Oldham, J. D., "What Happens After Python in CS1?," *J Comput Sci Coll*, vol. 20, no. 6, pp. 7–13, Jun. 2005.

[9] Stefik, A. and Siebert, S., "An Empirical Investigation into Programming Language Syntax," *Trans Comput Educ*, vol. 13, no. 4, pp. 19:1–19:40, Nov. 2013.

[10] "Think Python: How to Think Like a Computer Scientist." http://www.greenteapress.com/thinkpython/. Accessed on 14-Jul-2014.

[11] "Turing's Craft." http://turingscraft.com/. Accessed on 14-Jul-2014.

Can We "Flip" Non-Major Programming Courses Yet?

Douglas Baldwin
Department of Mathematics
SUNY Geneseo
Geneseo, NY 14454
USA
baldwin@geneseo.edu

ABSTRACT

Proponents of "flipped" instruction offer a vision of class meetings devoted to active learning, in exchange for students spending time outside of class acquiring basic knowledge from readings or video lectures. The price paid for this vision is the need to create the readings or videos. However, such materials are becoming available as open educational resources, and if they become widely enough available it may be possible to flip classes without requiring each instructor to develop his or her own materials. In the spring of 2014 I flipped an introductory programming course for non-computing majors in an effort to see if freely available video lectures could support it. This paper reports my findings, notably that open resources can support such a course, but just barely.

Categories and Subject Descriptors

K.3.2 [**Computers and Education**]: Computer and Information Science Education computer science education

General Terms

Design

Keywords

Flipped Classroom; Inverted Classroom; Non-Majors; Introduction

1. INTRODUCTION

In recent years, higher education in general, and my own institution in particular, have been engulfed in a discussion of online educational resources as "disrupters" of traditional college education. While the latest round of discussion is inspired by the emergence of massive open online courses (MOOCs) [21], a wider discussion of technological disruption of higher education has been going on for a long time. Within this discussion, many MOOC developers argue that their courses are resources that make face-to-face instruction more flexible than do traditional lectures [5, 21]. Notable among alternative forms of teaching that become possible is the "flipped" or "inverted" class, in which students use out-of-classroom time to read textbooks or watch prerecorded lectures, and use classroom time for discussion, lab exercises, and similar activities that benefit from group interaction and in-person guidance by an experienced instructor [2]. Nor are MOOCs unique in enabling new forms of teaching: the emergence of open educational resources (OERs) of all sorts should allow instructors to import routine materials into their courses while focusing their own time on the things that make those courses unique. Importing routine parts of a course from elsewhere allows instructors to devote a higher fraction of their time to the most effective and rewarding educational activities, while reducing the time they spend on one-to-many delivery of basic factual content.

This paper describes my exploration of this idea in a non-majors introductory programming course. Specifically, I wanted to determine whether face-to-face lectures for such a course can be replaced with free, publicly available, online material in order to allow a greater portion of student-teacher face time to be devoted to hands-on and active learning. If lectures can be replaced with openly available materials, then any institution can deliver the closer student-teacher interactions of flipped classes without incurring the up-front costs of developing recorded lectures.

1.1 Context

Computer science education at my institution is in flux. The computer science department, which taught several general education computing courses aimed at broad audiences, has been closed, and departments that relied on computer science courses to introduce their students to computing are crafting replacements of their own. In particular, the mathematics department is developing an introduction to programming for mathematics (Math 230) that places a heavy emphasis on active learning. I am part of the team developing this course, and was also offered an opportunity to teach the final offering of the computer science course that it will replace (CSci 120). A large fraction of the student population in CSci 120 is math majors, so this offering was to some extent a transition to the new math course. At the same time, the college administration is highly supportive of "digital learning" efforts of all sorts. These considerations converged to make my offering of CSci 120 an ideal place to explore using external resources to flip a face-to-face course.

Although CSci 120/Math 230 is not a course for computer science majors, and non-majors' motivation for and com-

SIGCSE'15, March 4–7, 2015, Kansas City, MO, USA.
ACM 978-1-4503-2966-8/15/03.
http://dx.doi.org/10.1145/2676723.2677271.

mitment to computer science differs from majors', lessons learned from CSci 120/Math 230 are nonetheless valuable to computer science educators. Introducing non-majors to computation is becoming more and more important to computer science departments, as computational methods gain prominence in other disciplines. Increasing numbers of non-computer-science majors are therefore taking introductory programming courses; those courses then become both services computer science departments provide to their larger institutions, and recruiting grounds for new computer science majors or minors. Furthermore, the core algorithmic thinking developed in introductory programming courses is the same for majors and non-majors, so even if the courses are different (and in many schools they are not), pedagogies used in one can often be adapted to the other. Many of my observations about flipping a non-majors' introduction are thus relevant to instructors considering flipping a majors' CS1 course.

1.2 Related Work

MOOCs seem to be a natural source of lectures with which to flip a course, and their advent triggered several experiments in doing so. For example, Martin [13] taught an artificial intelligence course in which students attended a face-to-face seminar meeting once a week while also taking the highly publicized 2011 Stanford AI MOOC. The face-to-face portion of the course focused on personal attention to students' individual questions, and supported a "directed project," while the MOOC provided supporting lectures and non-programming homework. Fox subsequently coined the term "SPOC," or "Small Private Online Course," to describe such combinations of MOOC technology with face-to-face instruction, emphasizing that the combination allows instructors to concentrate their efforts on "higher-value" one-on-one work with students [5]. Although I did not use a MOOC in CSci 120, I was acting on the beliefs expressed by Martin and Fox that rote one-to-many delivery of information can now be handled by technology, while face-to-face time with students is better devoted to mentoring active learning.

Piccioni et al. delivered CS1 as a SPOC, coupling face-to-face lectures, "exercise sessions," and homework assignments with online short lectures, quizzes, and programming exercises [15]. Horton et al. [9] and Lockwood and Esselstein [12] describe more thoroughly flipped CS1 courses, in which "lecture" time was used for small-group or hands-on exercises with in-person help available from instructional staff. Students watched online videos on the relevant concepts and sometimes solved short preparatory problems prior to these class meetings. More advanced computer science courses have also been flipped, including computer architecture [6] and software engineering [8]. All of these courses, from the introductory ones to the advanced ones, developed their own online materials instead of using open public ones.

Peer instruction [14] is a form of flipped instruction that has received particular attention in computer science. Peer instruction emphasizes students using classroom time to work first as individuals and then in groups to answer short (typically multiple-choice) questions, followed by whole-group discussion of the answers moderated by the instructor. Students typically read about, or sometimes watch recorded lectures on, the ideas exercised in these questions outside of class. Peer instruction has been shown to be effective in improving computer science students' retention, engagement, and learning [17, 16, 18]. It has even been applied to a non-majors introductory programming course similar in many respects to CSci 120/Math 230 [11]. In all of these cases, however, the out-of-class materials used in the peer instruction were custom developed. The literature does not discuss how or if open resources support peer or other flipped instruction.

2. CSCI 120

CSci 120 is a general education introductory programming course whose main goal is to give students an ability to program in a procedural language on a "personal" scale, i.e., do the kinds of programming they may encounter in analyzing data, running an experiment or mathematical model, etc. without primarily being computing professionals. It is required by my institution's mathematics and physics majors, and also satisfies a college general education requirement in "numeric and symbolic reasoning." Different offerings use different programming languages; mine used Matlab. The course traditionally meets for two 1-hour lectures and one 1-hour lab per week.

About 60% of the students in my section were mathematics majors, while 15% were physics majors. The remainder came from other areas of the physical and social sciences, with a handful from business. About half of the students were in their third year of a four-year program, while the rest were roughly evenly distributed between fourth- and second-year students.

To flip CSci 120, I restructured it into two 1-hour labs per week, and expected students to spend about one hour per week reading the textbook and watching short video lectures prior to the labs. The textbook was Attaway's *Matlab: A Practical Introduction to Programming and Problem Solving* [1]. Video lectures came from an online introduction to Matlab from the University of Edinburgh [20], Mathworks (the producer of Matlab) [19], and a variety of ad hoc sources. I discuss the adequacy and sources of the videos in more detail below. Each laboratory lesson asked students to write, debug, and run programs to solve a series of problems based on that lesson's subject. Each lesson typically spanned one to three lab meetings. I and a teaching assistant circulated during the lab sessions to talk to students about their progress and answer questions.

In my effort to see if the available open resources were adequate to support this course, I rigorously avoided lecturing except in response to students' questions. I explained this policy to students, emphasizing that questions were welcome, and consistently soliciting them at the beginning of each meeting. Nonetheless, students very rarely asked any. As a result there were probably only five or six occasions during the entire semester when students received substantial lecture instruction, and then for only five to twenty minutes per "lecture."

I organized students into 3-person study groups for peer support in the labs. I also met weekly with each study group to review their progress on the lab lessons and to give them feedback on their results.

To motivate students to do the readings and watch the videos, I gave quizzes at the beginnings of some labs. Students knew from the course policies that I would sometimes give quizzes, but did not know in advance on what days.

In addition to the lab lessons, I also asked students to complete three out-of-class programming assignments. These assignments let students program in a more open-ended context than the labs provided, and also played a role in evaluating how well the flipped course worked, as explained below. The assignments were...

1. Plot the function $f(x, y) = e^{-\sqrt{x^2+y^2}} \cos(x^2 + y^2)$. This requires a three-dimensional plot, but the main challenge in Matlab is simply to put expressions for manipulating vectors and matrices together with appropriate plotting commands—Matlab's built-in features for plotting and manipulating data are powerful enough that no control structures or advanced graphics functions are needed to solve this problem.
2. Animate some two-dimensional motion. I suggested that a simple object moving in a bounded space, e.g., a ball bouncing in a box, was the appropriate scale for this project, but otherwise left the specific animation up to students. The main programming feature exercised by this project was loops (and conditionals in some animations).
3. Play a game of "Madlibs" (a word game in which players pick words to complete a partial short story; see http://www.madlibs.com/) with the user. I intended this project to involve developing a data structure to represent a Madlib and a function to interpret that structure while interacting with the user. However, an ambiguity in the wording of the assignment allowed many students to interpret it as the much simpler task of merely writing a program with a single Madlib hardwired into it.

3. EVALUATION

The overarching question in this research is "are enough open resources available to support a flipped introductory programming course?" This question has two aspects, each addressed in turn: first, are the resources available, and second, do they in fact support an effective course?

3.1 Resources

The textbook provided adequate readings to support most of my course, so I focused my search for resources on video lectures. Those from Edinburgh and Mathworks cover standard programming constructs in Matlab well. Both cover such things as variables, expressions, conditional and iterative control structures, functions, etc. The two sources complement each other, with Edinburgh providing no-frills lectures on programming in Matlab, while Mathworks slightly favors interactive use of Matlab over programming, and provides occasional interactive quizzes for students. Edinburgh provides a short text document to support their videos, although I did not use it, since my chosen textbook was more complete.

These videos covered individual elements of the core Matlab language, but they did not extend to more advanced Matlab features (e.g., data structures more sophisticated than arrays), and said little about crafting complete programs from individual language elements. For example, the lectures were good at explaining how to write various control structures, but said little about how to recognize when an abstract problem calls for certain control flow, or what to expect when nesting control structures. I relied almost entirely on the textbook to address these issues.

Most of my lab lessons asked students to apply Matlab to mathematical problems. Examples included, among others, Riemann sums for evaluating definite integrals, bisection and Newton's method for finding zeroes, plotting parametric equations, and a pair of lessons that connected the mathematical notion of a relation to relational databases. I needed to provide readings or videos on the mathematics underlying these lessons, but did not find comprehensive sources comparable to the Matlab videos from Edinburgh and Mathworks. However, ad hoc Internet searches found almost everything I needed—YouTube[1] turned out to be my main source, although one that had to be screened carefully for quality, and Khan Academy[2] was occasionally helpful.

There were a couple of topics for which I was completely unable to find open resources. I wanted students to practice the example-driven style of program design and testing advocated by Felleisen et al. [4], but was unable to find prerecorded lectures on it. Somewhat surprisingly, I was also unable to find videos that introduce the abstract definition of the word "algorithm." I made my own videos to introduce both of these ideas. For the lessons on mathematical relations and relational databases I could find no video lecture that reviewed the definition of "relation" without large amounts of extraneous material, so I provided my own written introduction to the subject (time prevented making a video on it).

On balance, publicly available videos were just barely able to support my introductory non-majors' programming course. I was able to find acceptable videos for most of the course content, although apart from the two Matlab-specific collections, I had to filter good-quality and relevant videos out of large pools of less suitable ones. I also had to produce some videos or substitutes myself, and I had to rely more heavily than I would have liked on the textbook for depth and advanced topics.

3.2 Effectiveness

I used two main sources to gauge the effectiveness of the flipped CSci 120. First, I scored anonymous copies of students' out-of-class programming assignments against the course's learning outcomes, assessing which outcomes each project showed achievement of. Second, I invited students to give me their reactions to the flipped class on standard college end-of-semester course opinion surveys.

3.2.1 Assignments

I scored solutions to programming assignments against learning outcomes, while teaching assistants graded the solutions for purposes of students' course grades. Before sending solutions to me for scoring, the TAs replaced students' names with TA-assigned ID numbers so that the solutions were anonymous but I could track which ones came from the same student. Students could choose to participate in the scoring or not. 20 students, out of 48 who started the course, did so.

The scored learning outcomes, as given on the syllabus, were that students would be able to...

- "Write Matlab programs that use input, output, variables, expressions, repetition (both implicit—i.e., via

[1]http://www.youtube.com/

[2]https://www.khanacademy.org/

vectorization[3]—and explicit—i.e., via for and while loops), selection, and sequencing"

- "Write Matlab programs that use numbers, numeric vectors and matrices, strings, and files"
- "Write Matlab programs that produce 2-dimensional plots"
- "Write comments in programs to document how they work"
- "Design and write Matlab programs that use scripts and functions[4]"
- "Devise algorithms for solving simple mathematical problems, and recognize standard algorithms for others; translate algorithms from both sources into Matlab programs"
- "Debug Matlab programs"
- "Select and use test cases to demonstrate that Matlab programs produce correct results, or acceptable approximations to results that cannot be represented exactly by a computer."

The first five of these outcomes deal with using specific programming constructs, and can be evaluated by examining students' code to see if it uses the constructs appropriately. The last three outcomes reflect the process by which students create programs, and are therefore harder to assess from the finished products. As a rough indication, however, I counted the number of solutions that were correct relative to the assigned requirements, in the belief that correct solutions are more likely to reflect an ability to design, test, and debug programs than to reflect other causes. For the Madlibs project, which some students read as being much simpler than intended, I considered solutions to the simplified assignment correct or not based on the simpler requirements, on the grounds that if that is what students thought they were asked to do, that is what they would design their programs for. Programs that addressed the actual intended requirements were assessed relative to them.

Since 20 students participated in this scoring, and there were three assignments, the maximum possible number of correct solutions that could have been turned in was 60. 52 correct solutions were actually turned in, or 87% of what was possible; every participating student turned in at least one correct solution. Of the eight solutions not turned in or not correct, five weren't turned in at all, and three contained incorrect code. Every assignment had two or three missing or incorrect solutions, so the negative results weren't concentrated in any one exercise. Even counting the five missing solutions as incorrect, the course still appears to have been quite effective in developing students' ability to create working programs.

[3]"vectorization" refers to the fact that many Matlab operators map over arrays, so that computations that would be written as explicit loops in other languages can often be written in Matlab as expressions operating on arrays

[4]A "script" in Matlab is a file containing Matlab commands, it executes exactly as if its contents had been typed interactively to the Matlab interpreter; a "function" is like a function in other languages, e.g., it has parameters and a return value, local variables, etc.

To score the construct-related outcomes, I translated them into the list of 18 specific constructs shown in Table 1. For each student, assignment, and construct, I determined whether that student in that assignment had (a) shown an ability to correctly use that construct in a context where it was applicable, (b) either failed to use the construct when it should have been used, or tried to use it but not been able to do so correctly, or (c) had encountered no need for the construct. As when scoring correctness, I judged the need for constructs in the Madlibs project relative to students' understanding of its requirements. While this approach accurately captures what that project shows about students' programming, it does mean that some students were considered to "encounter no need" for programming constructs that were supposed to be exercised by the project.

Table 1: Number and percentage of students able to use Matlab programming constructs, unable to use, and encountering no need

Outcome	Able	Unable	No Need
Input from User	18 (90%)	0	2 (10%)
Output to User	18 (90%)	0	2 (10%)
Variables	20 (100%)	0	0
Expressions	20 (100%)	0	0
Vectorization	20 (100%)	0	0
"For" Loops	10 (50%)	2 (10%)	8 (40%)
"While" Loops	10 (50%)	3 (15%)	7 (35%)
"If" Statements	14 (70%)	0	6 (30%)
Sequencing	20 (100%)	0	0
Numbers	20 (100%)	0	0
Vectors	20 (100%)	0	0
Matrices	19 (95%)	0	1 (5%)
Strings	18 (90%)	0	2 (10%)
Files	3 (15%)	0	17 (85%)
Plots	20 (100%)	0	0
Comments	18 (90%)	2 (10%)	0
Scripts	20 (100%)	0	0
Functions	8 (40%)	0	12 (60%)

The data in Table 1 suggest that students struggled with "for" and "while" loops. Each was used appropriately by only 50% of the students, and some students were demonstrably unable to use each. However, these numbers need to be interpreted carefully: any "for" loop can be written as a "while," and I scored such uses of "while" as correct even if "for" would have been more elegant. Furthermore, the nature of the assignments was such that students had flexibility in what sort of loops they used. For example, solutions to the animation project could either run until some condition was met, (e.g., a ball reaching a wall) with a "while" as the main loop, or run for a fixed number of steps via a "for" loop. Combining the counts for both kinds of loop across all three assignments reveals that 85% of the students (17 individuals) were able to solve all of the iteration problems that they encountered, albeit often by fitting all to a single kind of loop. Three of those 17 students, however, demonstrated appropriate uses of both kinds of loop. Only 1 student showed an inability to use both kinds of loop, and a further 3 students showed inability to use one but not both kinds of loop. While there was thus less mastery of loops than of other constructs, most of the class ended up able to program with them.

The low number of students using "if" statements reflects the facts that many animation projects had no need for it, and students who interpreted the Madlibs project in its simplified form also had no need for it. However, every student who encountered a place where an "if" could reasonably be used was able to do so, and students demonstrated their understanding of the concept elsewhere in the course, e.g., in exams and laboratory lessons.

Finally, none of the assignments absolutely demanded functions, and many students preferred scripts to functions. Few students used files because files ended up being only an extra-credit part of one assignment.

In general, then, almost all students demonstrated an ability to use almost all constructs. Exceptions to this pattern are often artifacts of the measurements I was able to make rather than actual shortcomings in student understanding.

3.2.2 *Student Opinion*

At the end of each semester, my institution gives students an opportunity to offer instructors anonymous feedback on courses. Students rate various aspects of each course they took both numerically and in written comments. I asked my CSci 120 students to use the written part of this survey to give me reactions to flipping the course. 27 students completed the survey, providing a total of 125 distinct comments. While many comments didn't address the flipped class at all, several themes emerged in those that did: liking or disliking learning in a flipped class, being satisfied or dissatisfied with how much was learned, liking or disliking learning in study groups, and liking or disliking weekly study group meetings with me. Table 2 tallies the number of comments expressing various sentiments.

Table 2: Expressions of various feelings towards flipped teaching in end-of-semester student opinion questionnaires

Aspect	Satisfied	Dissatisfied
Learning in flipped class	10	31
Learning with study groups	0	3
Weekly meetings	9	0
Amount learned	9	1

The most striking result in Table 2 is that essentially one quarter of all comments expressed some sort of dissatisfaction with learning in a flipped class. The dissatisfaction was typically that the flipped class abandoned students to learn on their own from the readings and videos. However, a smaller but noticeable group of comments expressed satisfaction with the flipped class, generally saying that the hands-on learning that it enabled helped students master programming. In a related vein, almost all of those comments that addressed the amount learned were positive (i.e., said that the student learned a lot), while only one was negative. Although there were very few comments about study groups, all expressed a sense that the study groups did not help learning, generally mentioning cases in which a study group had suffered from a member who didn't do their share of the work in the lessons. However, the weekly meetings between me and study groups were considered beneficial by everyone who commented on them.

The opinion results thus strongly indicate that students didn't like not having traditional lectures to help them understand course material. Students did, however, like many of the things that not giving and preparing lectures nominally frees instructors to do: hands-on learning during class meetings, and frequent out-of-class meetings between students and instructor. Students' comments about what they learned from the class were infrequent, but those that were made were consistent with the assignment analysis in suggesting that the course provided an effective introduction to programming.

4. DISCUSSION AND CONCLUSIONS

Students in my flipped non-majors' introductory programming course generally achieved the intended learning outcomes. Although I wasn't able to scientifically compare the flipped CSci 120 to a more traditionally taught version, my impression is that student learning in the flipped class was about as complete as it would have been had I used a lecture-plus-laboratory format. I achieved these results while replacing face-to-face lectures with out-of-class readings and videos. However, openly available videos are not yet able to support my full vision for flipping introductory programming. I was able to use open videos for most of the course content, but had to produce my own videos or written substitutes for a few topics, and relied extensively on the textbook for depth. I expected students to learn elementary programming from out-of-class readings and video lectures coupled with in-class programming practice; they did, but many found the experience difficult and unpleasant.

Indeed, one of the biggest surprises in this course was how resistant students were to out-of-class learning. I had expected some resistance, and my policy of not lecturing unless asked was an attempt to force students to try to make enough sense out of the videos and readings to at least formulate questions about them. By and large, however, this just didn't happen. The students did read the assigned textbook sections and watch the assigned videos, but they essentially never asked questions about them, and real understanding came only as students did the laboratory exercises. Isomöttönen et al. report very similar difficulty achieving independent engagement even among masters students in an advanced course, hypothesizing that lack of experience with "self-directed" study may be a core reason [10]. This problem could worsen in an introductory non-majors' course if the material is too foreign to the students for them to engage deeply with on their own, or if those taking the course because it is required by their (non-computing) major rather than out of intrinsic interest are not motivated to persevere with readings and lectures. Whatever the causes though, steps can be taken to improve students' learning from out-of-class material: the peer learning literature suggests that short exercises interleaved with instructor commentary during classes can be effective, and my own experience teaching courses that ask students to do pre-class readings without being fully flipped is that opening class meetings with student summaries of a reading helps students assimilate what they read. Such activities needn't be time-consuming, leaving most class time for the interactions and mentoring enabled by the flipped model.

Like others [3], I found the universe of open educational resources in need of better organization and search methods. However, general-purpose web search engines are able to find good resources, and YouTube is a de facto very large repository of educational videos, although of highly variable quality. Finding two coherent short courses (the University of Edinburgh's and Mathworks's) on my subject also considerably eased locating videos for much of it.

CSci 120 plays a specific role in several majors and my institution's general education program. Thus I could not flip it simply by importing a course or set of lectures wholesale from elsewhere. Rather, I needed individual lectures that I could put in an order appropriate to my goals, that I could combine with lectures from other sources, etc. A large study of how faculty incorporated MOOCs into hybrid courses at the University of Maryland found a similar desire to import course modules rather than whole courses [7].

The need to deliver courses that satisfy local constraints mitigates the frequently expressed concern that mass online education reduces local instructors to mere teaching assistants for remote lecturers [21]. In fact, local instructors are the creative agents who craft courses that meet the needs of specific audiences. My flipped CSci 120 was inspired by curiosity about whether remote lecturers (and other open resources) can absorb some of the costs that local instructors would otherwise bear in developing and delivering such courses. At least in the case of non-majors' introductions to computer science it appears that they can, although not to the full extent that might eventually be possible.

5. ACKNOWLEDGEMENTS

Thanks to Geneseo's provost and subsequently interim president Carol Long for her consistent encouragement of and interest in this project. Samir Farouq and Nick LaVigne were invaluable teaching assistants; the evaluation of this course through the homework projects would have been impossible without their help. And finally, I owe a huge debt of gratitude to the students in CSci 120 for putting up with my exploration of flipped teaching—thank you!

6. REFERENCES

[1] S. Attaway. *Matlab: A Practical Introduction to Programming and Problem Solving.* Butterworth-Heinemann, 3rd edition, 2013.

[2] J. W. Baker. The 'classroom flip': Using web course management tools to become the guide by the side. In *Selected Papers from the* 11th *International Conference on College Teaching and Learning*, pages 9–17. Florida Community College at Jacksonville, 2000.

[3] C. Dichev and D. Dicheva. Open educational resources in computer science teaching. In *Proceedings of the* 43rd *SIGCSE Technical Symposium on Computer Science Education*, pages 619–624. ACM, 2012.

[4] M. Felleisen, R. B. Findler, M. Flatt, and S. Krishnamurthi. *How to Design Programs: An Introduction to Programming and Computing.* MIT Press, 2001.

[5] A. Fox. From MOOCs to SPOCs. *Communications of the ACM*, 56(12):38–40, Dec. 2013.

[6] E. F. Gehringer and B. W. Peddycord. The inverted-lecture model: A case study in computer architecture. In *Proceedings of the* 44th *ACM Technical Symposium on Computer Science Education*, pages 489–494. ACM, Mar. 2013.

[7] R. Griffiths, M. Chingos, C. Mulhern, and R. Spies. Interactive online learning on campus: Testing MOOCs and other platforms in hybrid formats in the university system of Maryland. Technical report, Ithaka S+R, July 2014. http://sr.ithaka.org/research-publications/Interactive-Online-Learning-on-Campus, retrieved July 10, 2104.

[8] M. J. Herold, T. D. Lynch, R. Ramnath, and J. Ramanathan. Student and instructor experiences in the inverted classroom. In *Proceedings of the 2012 IEEE Frontiers in Education Conference*, pages 1–6. IEEE, Oct. 2012.

[9] D. Horton, M. Craig, J. Campbell, P. Gries, and D. Zingaro. Comparing outcomes in inverted and traditional CS1. In *Proceedings of ITiCSE 2014*, pages 261–266. ACM, 2014.

[10] V. Isomöttönen, V. Tirronen, and M. Cochez. Issues with a course that emphasizes self-direction. In *Proceedings of the 2013 ACM Symposium on Innovation and Technology in Computer Science Education (ITiCSE 2013)*, pages 111–116. ACM, July 2013.

[11] C. B. Lee. Experience report: CS1 in MATLAB for non-majors, with media computation and peer instruction. In *Proceedings of the* 44th *ACM Technical Symposium on Computer Science Education*, pages 35–40. ACM, Mar. 2013.

[12] K. Lockwood and R. Esselstein. The inverted classroom and the CS curriculum. In *Proceedings of the* 44th *ACM Technical Symposium on Computer Science Education*, pages 113–118. ACM, Mar. 2013.

[13] F. G. Martin. Will massive open online courses change how we teach? *Communications of the ACM*, 55(8):26–28, Aug. 2012.

[14] E. Mazur. *Peer Instruction: A User's Manual.* Prentice Hall, 1997.

[15] M. Piccioni, C. Estler, and B. Meyer. SPOC-supported introduction to programming. In *Proceedings of ITiCSE 2014*, pages 3–8. ACM, 2014.

[16] L. Porter, C. Bailey-Lee, and B. Simon. Halving fail rates using peer instruction: A study of four computer science courses. In *Proceedings of the* 44th *ACM Technical Symposium on Computer Science Education*, pages 177–182. ACM, Mar. 2013.

[17] L. Porter, C. B. Lee, B. Simon, and D. Zingaro. Peer instruction: Do students really learn from peer discussion in computing. In *Proceedings of the* 7th *International Computing Education Research Workshop (ICER)*, pages 45–52. ACM, Aug. 2011.

[18] B. Simon, S. Esper, L. Porter, and Q. Cutts. Student experience in a student-centered peer instruction classroom. In *Proceedings of the 2013 ACM Conference on International Computing Education Research (ICER)*, pages 129–136. ACM, Aug. 2013.

[19] The Mathworks, Inc. MATLAB tutorials. https://www.mathworks.com/academia/student_center/tutorials/register.html, accessed June 27, 2014.

[20] University of Edinburgh. An interactive introduction to MATLAB. http://www.see.ed.ac.uk/teaching/courses/matlab/getting-started.shtml, accessed June 27, 2014.

[21] J. R. Young. *Beyond the MOOC Hype: A Guide to Higher Education's High-Tech Disruption.* the Chronicle of Higher Education, 2013.

Evaluating Pair-Programming for Non-Computer Science Major Students

Clem O'Donnell, Jim Buckley, Abdulhussain E. Mahdi, John Nelson and Michael English
University of Limerick, Limerick, Ireland
{Clem.ODonnell, Jim.Buckley, Hussain.Mahdi, John.Nelson, Michael.English}@ul.ie

ABSTRACT

The ubiquitous nature of software has resulted in many non-computer-science (NCS) major students taking courses in computer programming. The appeal of learning computer programming for this cohort may be diminished, given that they do not usually have an initial desire to become expert programmers. This, coupled with the difficulty of learning computer programming, means that efforts to heighten their engagement with/learning of, programming skills are required.

Paired programming is an approach that has been hypothesized as increasing computer science students' attendance and performance. The study presented here reports on a controlled study investigating the impact of a pair-programming approach to teaching computer programming to NCS majors. The results indicate that pair programming has a positive impact on student attendance, particularly for weaker students. While a comparison of the paired programming cohort and a traditional lab cohort is not statistically significant with respect to performance, there are definite trends which suggest that pair programming may increase the number of weaker students that succeed in the programming module. These trends are re-enforced by qualitative feedback from the participants.

Categories and Subject Descriptors

K.3 [**Computers & Information Science Educations**]: Computer science education

General Terms

Experimentation, Management, Human Factors

Keywords

Computer Science Education; Pair Programming; Non-Computer Science Students; Collaborative environment; Empirical Study

1. INTRODUCTION

For much of the last 12 years, there has been a marked decline in the number of students opting to study computer science major courses worldwide [2, 13]. Many reasons for this have been suggested including the perception by students that programming is an overly difficult skill, for which they lack the necessary analytical and mathematical abilities [13]. In contrast to this, computing has become increasingly ubiquitous in society over that same period. It is recognised that it now has an influence on every aspect of society [2, 13]. Universities and other third-level institutions have acknowledged this ubiquitous trend by offering new multidisciplinary programmes that overlap with the Information and Communication Technology (ICT) domain [13]. Students on these programmes require programming knowledge and thus teaching these non-Computer Science (NCS) students has become a significant and important function of Computer Science educators.

SIGCSE '15, March 4–7, 2015, Kansas City, MO, USA
Copyright © 2015 ACM 978-1-4503-2966-8/15/03…$15.00
http://dx.doi.org/10.1145/2676723.2677289

It is generally accepted that learning to program is difficult, with high failure rates and low retention rates being reported [3]. This learning difficulty may be exacerbated for students from NCS major courses, who may not have a desire to become expert programmers. This can manifest itself in low attendance levels and high failure rates among these students.

Pair Programming (PP) has been noted as a collaborative learning method that has several positive educational outcomes [10]. These include active learning and increased retention [16], the creation of a more socially inclusive learning environment [19], enhanced assessment outcomes [15] and the development of important generic communication skills that are required in the modern workplace [9].

Interestingly, work by Nagappan et al. [16] and Braught et al. [5, 7] provisionally suggest that the collaborative and social aspects of PP may prove to have even more utility when used to teach programming to the growing population of NCS students. Additionally, Braught et al. suggested that PP may be particularly helpful for weaker students [6, 7].

In this paper we focus on the impact of the adoption of PP as a learning method on both attendance [17] and student performance for all NCS students studying programming and for weaker NCS students in particular. The student performance indicator is the achievement of a grade C or higher in the course [16]. We also investigate students' perceptions of the paired programming approach and the impact that their pairing may have had on these perceptions.

2. RELATED WORK

Research in the use of PP as a collaborative approach to learning programming at 3rd level has focused on best practice experience reports [4, 21], how best to ensure successful student pairs [18, 20], qualitative feedback on the benefits and limitations of PP in pedagogy and quantitative evaluation of students' performance when using the approach.

A core concern is how best to pair students to maximise their learning potential [18] and minimise the occurrence of incompatible pairings [4]. Several studies using random pairing have investigated factors that may affect PP pair compatibility in pedagogy: learning styles, work ethic and time-management skills, programming self-esteem levels, differing personality types, similar perceived skill levels and similar actual skill levels [12]. Overall, the research is inconclusive on how best to form a PP pair [10]. Given that many of these criteria are hard to quantify for entry level programming students [4, 6, 8, 12], several researchers have allowed students to self-select their PP partners with such studies suggesting that self-selection results in few compatibility issues [4, 11, 20].

Qualitative studies such as that by McDowell et al.[14] have provided positive support for the use of pair programming in a 3rd level learning environment with regard to confidence and enjoyment. Carver et al. [8] suggested that the ability to learn from one's partner, the lowering of student frustration and the improving of their communication skills being a definite advantage.

A number of quantitative studies have also been undertaken to investigate the impact of PP. Some studies considered the effect of the use of PP on the quality of programs produced, with both mixed [14], and positive findings [7] suggesting that PP at least does not have a negative impact on program quality. Others looked at course completion and performance (complete with a grade of C or higher) with generally positive results [14, 15].

Nagappan et al. [16], in a post-hoc analysis of a wider PP study, focussed on NCS students only. They found a statistically significant performance improvement for the NCS subjects who adopted PP compared to their (NCS) peers that used the traditional solo method of learning. Braught et al. [5, 7] also found that paired students from a liberal-arts college were more likely to pass the course when adopting PP. While the breakdown of NCS:CS students is a bit unclear in this study, Braught et al. did suggest that the finding was in line with the findings of Nagappan et al. [16], implying a focus on NCS students.

Interestingly, Braught et al. also suggested that the odds of passing the course successfully for students with a lower SAT score in the PP cohort were approximately three times that for NPP students with a similar SAT score. This may suggest that PP is particularly helpful for weaker students. The study conducted in this paper will investigate these findings further to determine if they can be supported.

3. RESEARCH STUDY

This study will examine the impact of PP on entry level NCS students, focusing on the attendance and performance of weaker students. The 4 hypotheses are that:

- Hypothesis 1 (H1): NCS students that participate in computer programming laboratories using the PP approach will have higher attendance levels than their NCS peers who participate in programming laboratories using the traditional solo approach.
- Hypothesis 1a (H1a): Weaker NCS students that participate in computer programming laboratories using the PP approach will have higher attendance levels than their weaker NCS peers who participate in programming laboratories using the traditional solo approach.
- Hypothesis 2 (H2): NCS students designated to use the PP approach in their programming laboratories will have better performance than their NCS peers designated to use the traditional solo approach.
- Hypothesis 2a (H2a): Weaker NCS students designated to use the PP approach in their programming laboratories will have better performance than their weaker peers designated to use the traditional solo approach.

3.1 Study Design

A suitable entry-level programming course was identified of sufficient size that would allow for a PP group and a control (NPP) group. This course had weekly closed labs which could be undertaken in both PP and NPP fashion, and so could be used as an assessment of engagement. In addition, an exercise had to be completed and submitted by each pair during these labs. The marks achieved on this exercise contributed only a small percentage to the final grade. The course also had a mid-term exam which provided a measure of student's programming ability prior to the test itself.

The course had 176 students, including both CS and NCS students from a number of different degree programmes. Students were classified as CS or NCS on the basis of the undergraduate degree programme that they were taking. The students on programmes that involved at least two mandatory programming courses in the first two semesters of the programme and that subsequently had additional programming content were classified as CS students and the others were classified as NCS students.

The NCS students were split into two groups: the control group who adopted a traditional approach to learning programming during their lab sessions and the experimental group who adopted the PP approach to learning programming. The control group had 33 students and the experimental group had 28 students. Each student lab session was supported by five lab assistants. The lab assistants were advised of their role within both the PP and NPP lab sessions. The lab itself facilitated the pair programmers in viewing the workstation screen and passing the keyboard between the driver and navigator.

The experiment was conducted over a six week period towards the end of the first semester. This included a mid-term pre-test, 3 laboratory sessions, an end-of-term post-test and a questionnaire. During the first lab session for the PP group, the students were introduced to PP, the concepts of driver and navigator and the collaborative nature of the approach, where each pair works towards a joint solution. Students were asked to self-select pairs at the start of this first lab session. In the event that students didn't select a pair the coordinator assisted in selecting pairs.

As the PP portion of the study was shorter than a full term, there was no re-allocation of partners during the study, but students were asked to raise any issues they had with their partner. Finally, both the PP and NPP sessions were in closed module labs and all PP lab assignments resulted in both PP partners getting the same grade, reinforcing the notion that both were working towards a common goal. This experimental design incorporates many of the recommendations proposed in the literature for the adoption of PP in an educational context [4, 21].

3.2 Data Collection

Lab attendance data was collected for the 3 weeks prior to when students were introduced to PP. The pre-intervention attendance data is used as a baseline for attendance. Within the context of recording attendance data during the 3 weeks of the experimental labs, for both student cohorts, only those participants that attended their lab on the initial week of the study were to be included in the attendance data. This is to ensure that the attendance data recorded over the following 2 weeks of the experiment is tightly aligned with the subject's awareness of the continuance of PP past this initial lab, with the joint responsibility that each PP partner has towards assignments and with adherence to the structural aspects of PP. This resulted in 28 subjects in the PP cohort and 22 subjects in the NPP cohort with respect to attendance.

Students' mid-term exam and their final grade is used to examine the performance impact of PP for the NCS students. The performance data will be categorised as pass or fail, in line with previous research in this area [7, 16]. The mid-term exam was completed in advance of the introduction of PP and thus formed a baseline for performance measurement. The final grade used student performance data from a project (after PP), lab submissions, the mid-term and the final exam.

Finally, students were asked to fill out a questionnaire reporting on their perceptions of the PP approach and the impact that their pairing may have had on these perceptions.

4. RESULTS

All statistical quantitative analysis was carried out using the SPSS V20 package. The confidence limit was set to 0.05. The statistical significance of differences for attendance levels and performance levels was checked using the Chi square test and, where required, the Fisher Exact probability test as both tests allow for the comparison of categorical data.

4.1 Research Question 1

Do NCS students employing a PP approach have higher attendance rates than those not using a PP approach?

Table 1 presents the attendance data, where each participant was categorised as either Full (attendance at all three labs) or Non-Full attendance (attendance at 2 or less). This data shows that all NCS-PP students that attended the initial experiment lab, also continued to attend their two remaining labs during the experiment period. They also maintained the collaborative learning and working relationship with the same PP partner. On the other hand, almost 1 in 4 of the NCS-NPP who attended the initial experimental lab, failed to attend both of the two remaining experimental labs even though all lab assignments constituted part of their overall module grade.

A Chi Square test was applied to the attendance data (see Table 1) to test whether the difference between the attendance rates of the NCS-PP and NCS-NPP cohorts was statistically significant. Table 1 shows that the PP students showed a significantly higher level of attendance than their NPP peers with the Chi Square calculated as (χ^2 (1) = 7.071) and the Fishers exact probability test (as 2 of the expected frequencies are below 5) showing a highly significant value of $p < 0.012$.

To baseline the experimental attendance data, pre-experiment attendance data for the relevant subjects was analysed to assess whether, prior to the experiment, both cohorts (PP and NPP) showed similar levels of attendance (i.e. they were initially statistically similar in terms of their attendance when all were using the traditional solo method of lab learning). Hence, lab attendance figures for weeks 5, 6 and 7 of the semester for these students were categorised as full attendance or non-full attendance. These pre-experiment labs were similar in structure and requirements to the experiment labs (i.e. closed labs where assignments had to be completed and submitted for assessment by the end of the lab period).

Table 1. Experiment full and non-full lab attendance by learning method

Groups		Full Attendance	Non-Full Attendance	Total
NCS-PP	Count	28	0	28
	Expected Count	25.2	2.8	
NCS-NPP	Count	17	5	22
	Expected Count	19.8	2.2	
Total Count		45	5	50
Fisher's Exact Probability Test		$\chi^2 = 7.071$	$df = 1$	$p < 0.012$

The Chi square results suggest highly statistically independent lab attendance rates (χ^2 (1) = 0.014, $p < 0.907$) before exposure to PP. This supports the assertion that PP had an effect on NCS student attendance rates during the experiment. Specifically, NCS students attending the PP labs registered a 39.3% increase in their full lab attendance rates during the experiment (see Figure 1). The notable 18% increase in NCS-NPP full lab attendance may suggest a Hawthorne effect [1]. However, even taking the Hawthorne effect into account, there was a considerable increase during PP labs.

To assess whether this was true of weaker students (Hypothesis H1a), the students in the attendance analysis data set (PP=28, NPP=22) were split into academically-weaker or academically-stronger subgroups.

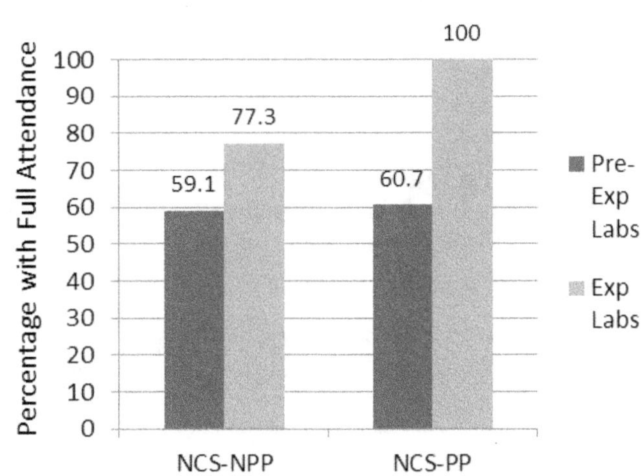

Figure 1. NCS attendance rates prior to and during the experiment by learning method

Within this research, academically weaker students are defined as those that achieved a grade C or less in the mid-term exam (13 NCS-PP and 9 NCS-NPP students) with academically stronger students being defined as those that achieved a grade B or higher in the mid-term exam (15 NCS-PP and 13 NCS-NPP). Analysis of these academic sub-groups allows us characterise the student sub-group that may be most impacted by PP [5, 7] in terms of attendance.

Table 2. Weaker Student Experiment full and non-full lab attendance by learning method

Groups		Full Attendance	Non-Full Attendance	Total
NCS-PP	Count	13	0	13
	Expected Count	10	3	
NCS-NPP	Count	4	5	9
	Expected Count	7	2	
Total Count		17	5	22
Fisher's Exact Probability Test		$\chi^2 = 9.346$	$df = 1$	$p < 0.005$

Table 2 shows that attendance by weaker-students participating in PP was significantly better than those weaker-students using the traditional solo form of lab learning ($p < 0.005$). This suggests that PP may particularly help to retain/engage weaker students. This is re-enforced by baseline analysis of these sub-groups using pre-experiment lab attendance data in weeks 5, 6 and 7: In this data, the attendance data of weaker student groups, prior to the experiment, are shown as statistically independent ($p > 0.05$).

Interestingly, the same trend is not evident for stronger students: all stronger-students both within the PP group (n=15) and the NPP group (n=13) that attended the initial experiment lab subsequently attended the remaining 2 labs during the experiment period. Thus, in this instance, the effects of PP on attendance only pertained to weaker students.

4.2 Research Question 2

Do NCS students employing a PP approach outperform NCS students not using a PP approach?

In line with the measurement method employed by [7, 14, 16], this study compared the final module passing-grade performance of the NCS-PP cohort with the NCS-NPP cohort. Within the context of module performance, a grade of C or higher in the final module grade constitutes success (a passing grade) as this is the grade which allows automatic progression onto subsequent stage modules.

All subjects were included regardless of their attendance levels within the experiment labs to align with the findings of Nagappan et al. [16] and Braught et al. [7], who used the same inclusion criteria. The total number of NCS subjects included in this analysis was 61, made up of 28 PP and 33 NPP students.

To baseline the experimental performance data, a Chi Square test was performed (using the mid-term grades of students) and confirmed that prior to the experimental intervention, both the PP and NPP cohorts were statistically independent ($p < 0.375$). A Chi Square test using the final grades of students to determine if there is a statistical difference in the performance of the two cohorts of students (H2) shows no statistically significant difference in student performance (χ^2 (1) = 1.624, $p < 0.202$). To address this hypothesis specifically for weaker students (H2a), the data set was again split into subgroups of academically weaker and stronger students, as per hypothesis H1a. An analysis of these sub-groups allows us to ascertain whether or not the weaker-student PP cohort performed better than the weaker-student NPP cohort. In total, 13 weaker students were designated to use the PP approach and 20 peers were designated to use NPP approach. A Chi square shows that there is no statistically significant difference between the performance of the weaker PP cohort and the weaker NPP cohort.

A detailed analysis of final grades showed that 15% more of the NCS-PP cohort achieved a "grade C or more" than their NPP peers (Figure 2). Likewise, the failure rates in the NPP cohort are nearly double those of the PP cohort. This approximates to a pass/fail ratio of nearly 4:1 (79% - 21%) for PP and 2:1 for NPP (64% - 36%).

It is notable that most difference can be seen in the lower grades (C, D and F), suggesting that a difference may be more apparent when focusing on weaker students. Further analysis of the weaker student subgroups shows that 22% more PP students achieved a grade C or higher than their weaker NPP peers (see Figure 3). Thus, the inability to show a statistically significant performance impact for PP within the academically weaker sub-group may be down to the relatively small number of subjects, suggesting that this hypothesis should also be evaluated on a larger cohort of students in the future.

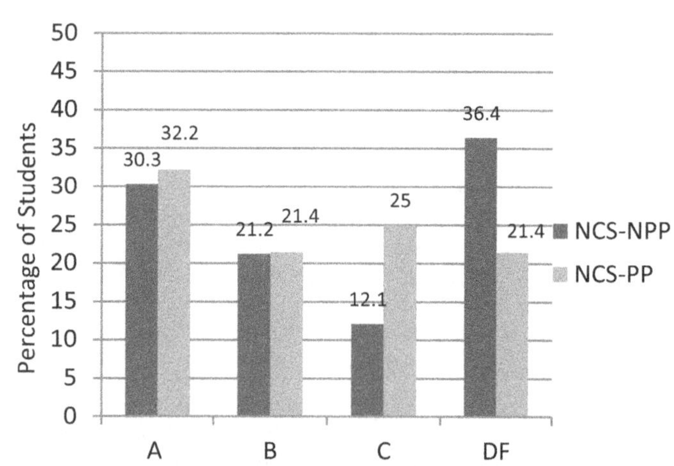

Figure 2. Final grades achieved by students across learning methods.

This data shows that of those 48.5% of NPP students that showed no attendance or did not fully attend the experiment labs, a significant 75% (n=16) of these failed to pass the module with a grade C or higher. While hypothesis 2 was not supported statistically, this data suggests that those lower achieving students that do engage using PP seem to have better performance in the programming module.

4.3 Qualitative Reflection on Students' Performance and Perspectives

On completion of the 3 weeks of lab assignments, all NCS-PP students were surveyed to gain feedback on their attitude towards PP and their perceptions of PP. The survey response rate for the NCS-PP cohort was 42.9% (n=28).

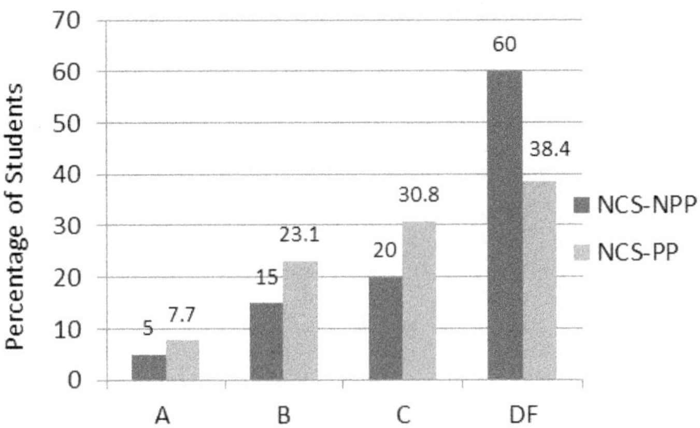

Figure 3. Final grades achieved by weaker students across learning methods.

4.3.1 Attitude to PP in the NCS Student Group

Over 58% of NCS-PP respondents suggested that they would want to continue to use PP in future programming labs, should it become an option. Of the five respondents that were negative towards the future use of PP, all achieved a final grade of A, and three of these had partnered with students that subsequently failed to achieve a passing grade of C in the module. This suggests that academic compatibility issues may have played a part in these negative responses, as suggested by Van Toll et al. [20]. It was also interesting to note that most of the positive responses came from lower achieving students with final grades of B, C or less. In fact, all students that received a B or C grade said they would continue to use PP in the future. For respondents in compatible pairs, as measured by similar resultant grades, double the number of positive to negative responses was reported. Seventy five per cent of NCS-PP respondents gave a neutral or positive rating (3-5) of their partner and 58% stated that they used the PP method outside of lab time to complete another assignment for this module. This feedback suggests that NCS students had an overall positive attitude towards PP in their labs but that compatibility issues need to be addressed in future studies and that high achieving students are less drawn to PP.

4.3.2 Effectiveness of PP – Emotional and Cognitive Engagement Feedback

All NCS-PP respondents thought that PP was highly effective for driving attendance and problem solving during the labs. Significantly, nearly 92% of the respondents found PP effective in labs for helping to focus on the task and to help them understand Java concepts, whilst 83% believed that it helped them to find and fix bugs in their code. Surprisingly, the lowest positive percentages registered for responses were with respect to enjoyment (66.7%) and productivity (75%), although these are still very high scores. An analysis relating students' final grade to negative comments reported here showed that all 5 negative respondents achieved a final grade of A. Three of these respondents were in incompatible pairs. As per the previous analysis, this suggests that these negative responses may have been partly caused by incompatible pairs or by the student feeling that they were being slowed down by their partner [4]. Hence, the findings indicate that incompatibility of pairs should be avoided for higher achieving students. Combining these results with the results presented in section 4.3.1, and the fact that just 2 students that received an A grade also provided positive feedback in relation to all of the categories, this research questions the suitability of PP as a learning method for high achieving students. Finally, it is also worth noting that the more abstract categories (focus on task and problem solving) received more positive feedback than the categories focused directly on coding (productivity and bug fixing). This may suggest that a collaborative approach (such as pairing students) may be even more beneficial for abstract tasks in computing such as software design, an issue highlighted by Salleh et al. [18].

5. CONCLUSIONS AND FUTURE WORK

Previous research by Nagappan et al. [16] and Braught et al. [5], [7] provisionally suggested that NCS students using PP in their module labs performed better than their NCS peers in the NPP cohort. However, neither of these research studies set out to investigate NCS students and thus their findings were of a post-hoc nature. This research sought to evaluate the efficacy of PP for NCS students by assessing both attendance and performance levels engendered by PP. It found that students that use PP within their labs do display significantly higher levels of attendance than their NCS peers using NPP. This was particularly true of weaker students. This research did not identify a statistically significant difference in the performance of students in the PP and NPP groups. However, the analysis suggests that PP may improve the performance of weaker students. Our results indicate that while the percentage of students in each group that achieve an A or B grade is similar, a much higher percentage of the PP group achieve a C grade while a much lower percentage (22% lower) of the PP group obtain a failing grade. Given that there was no difference in the performance of these groups prior to the experiment, the results suggest that the adoption of PP may have had an impact on weaker students. It may be the case that the higher attendance of the weaker PP students impacted on their performance in a positive way. However, further studies are required to investigate if this is the case. Our qualitative analysis of the attitudes and perceptions of PP further support the impression that PP may benefit weaker students more and have less impact for higher achievers. The weaker students provided positive feedback on the benefits of PP and are likely to utilise PP in future, whereas high achieving students were less inclined to recognise the benefits of PP and less likely to adopt this collaborative learning approach in the future. Validity issues such as limited number of students, self-selection of partners possibly not yielding the most compatible pairs and limited timescales will be addressed in a larger replication study to be carried out in the University over the next 2 years.

6. REFERENCES

[1] Adair, J.G., 1984. The Hawthorne effect: A reconsideration of the methodological artifact. *Journal of applied psychology 69*, 2, 334.

[2] Becerra-Fernandez, I., Elam, J., and Clemmons, S., 2010. Reversing the landslide in computer-related degree programs. *Communications of the ACM 53*, 2, 127-133.

[3] Bennedsen, J. and Caspersen, M.E., 2007. Failure rates in introductory programming. *ACM SIGCSE Bulletin 39*, 2, 32-36.

[4] Bevan, J., Werner, L., and Mcdowell, C., 2002. Guidelines for the use of pair programming in a freshman programming class. In *Proceedings of the Software Engineering Education and Training, 2002. (CSEE&T 2002). Proceedings. 15th Conference on* (2002 2002), 100-107. DOI= http://dx.doi.org/10.1109/csee.2002.995202.

[5] Braught, G., Eby, L.M., and Wahls, T., 2008. The effects of pair-programming on individual programming skill. In *Proceedings of the Proceedings of the 39th SIGCSE technical symposium on Computer science education* (Portland, OR, USA2008), ACM, 1352207, 200-204. DOI= http://dx.doi.org/10.1145/1352135.1352207.

[6] Braught, G., Maccormick, J., and Wahls, T., 2010. The Benefits of Pairing by Ability. In *Proceedings of the ACM Technical Symposium on Computer Science Education* (Milwaukee, WI, USA, 10-13 March 2010 2010), SIGSCSE.

[7] Braught, G., Wahls, T., and Eby, L.M., 2011. The Case for Pair Programming in the Computer Science Classroom. *Trans. Comput. Educ. 11*, 1, 1-21. DOI= http://dx.doi.org/1921607.1921609.

[8] Carver, J.C., Henderson, L., Lulu, H., Hodges, J., and Reese, D., 2007. Increased Retention of Early Computer Science and Software Engineering Students Using Pair Programming. In *Proceedings of the Software Engineering Education & Training, 2007. CSEET '07. 20th Conference on* (3-5 July 2007 2007), 115-122. DOI= http://dx.doi.org/10.1109/cseet.2007.29.

[9] Cliburn, D.C., 2003. Experiences with pair programming at a small college. *Journal of Computing Sciences in Colleges 19*, 1, 20-29.

[10] Hanks, B., Fitzgerald, S., Mccauley, R., Murphy, L., and Zander, C., 2011. Pair programming in education: a literature review. *Computer Science Education 21*, 2 (2011/06/01), 135-173. DOI= http://dx.doi.org/10.1080/08993408.2011.579808.

[11] Jacobson, N. and Schaefer, S.K., 2008. Pair Programming in CS1: Overcoming Objections To Its Adoption. *SIGSCE Bulletin 40*, 93-96.

[12] Katira, N., Williams, L., Wiebe, E., Miller, C., Balik, S., and Gehringer, E., 2004. On Understanding Compatibility of Student Pair Programmers. In *Proceedings of the 35th SIGSCE Technical Symposium on Computer Science Education* (USA, 3-7 March 2004 2004), ACM.

[13] Lenox, T.L., Woratschek, C.R., and Davis, G.A., 2008. Exploring declining cs/is/it enrollments. *Information Systems Education Journal 6*, 44, 1-11.

[14] Mcdowell, C., Werner, L., Bullock, H.E., and Fernald, J., 2003. The impact of pair programming on student performance, perception and persistence. In *Proceedings of the Proceedings of the 25th International Conference on Software Engineering* (Portland, Oregon2003), IEEE Computer Society, 776899, 602-607.

[15] Mendes, E., Al-Fakhri, L.B., and Luxton-Reilly, A., 2005. Investigating Pair-Programming in a 2nd Year Software Development & Design Computer Science Course. *SIGSCE Bulletin 37*, 296-300.

[16] Nagappan, N., Williams, L., Ferzli, M., Wiebe, E., Yang, K., Miller, C., and Balik, S., 2003. Improving the CS1 experience with pair programming. *SIGCSE Bull. 35*, 1, 359-362. DOI= http://dx.doi.org/10.1145/792548.612006.

[17] Reading, C., 2008. Recognising and measuring engagement in ICT-rich learning environments. In *Proceedings of the Australian Computers in Education Conference* (2008).

[18] Salleh, N., Mendes, E., and Grundy, J., 2011. Empirical studies of pair programming for CS/SE teaching in higher education: A systematic literature review. *Software Engineering, IEEE Transactions on 37*, 4, 509-525.

[19] Simon, B. and Hanks, B., 2008. First-year students' impressions of pair programming in CS1. *Journal on Educational Resources in Computing (JERIC) 7*, 4, 5.

[20] Van Toll, T., Lee, R., and Ahlswede, T., 2007. Evaluating the Usefulness of Pair Programming in a Classroom Setting. In *Proceedings of the Computer and Information Science, 2007. ICIS 2007. 6th IEEE/ACIS International Conference on* (11-13 July 2007 2007), 302-308. DOI= http://dx.doi.org/10.1109/icis.2007.96.

[21] Williams, L., Scott Mccrickard, D., Layman, L., and Hussein, K., 2008. Eleven Guidelines for Implementing Pair Programming in the Classroom. In *Proceedings of the Agile, 2008. AGILE '08. Conference* (4-8 Aug. 2008 2008), 445-452. DOI= http://dx.doi.org/10.1109/Agile.2008.12.

From 9 to 90: Engaging Learners of All Ages

Allison Sauppé, Daniel Szafir, Chien-Ming Huang, and Bilge Mutlu
Department of Computer Sciences, University of Wisconsin–Madison
1210 West Dayton Street, Madison, WI 53706, USA
{asauppe, dszafir, cmhuang, bilge}@cs.wisc.edu

ABSTRACT

This paper details the creation of a two-day computer science and robotics outreach course aimed at simultaneously engaging youth (children, ages 9–14) and senior (their grandparents, ages 55+) students. Our goal is to encourage enthusiasm for science and technology in students of all ages as well as provide practical instruction regarding common computer science concepts, including variables, loops, and boolean logic. To this end, we ground our course in the emerging field of social robotics, which enables the design of several multidisciplinary hands-on activities for students. We report on a four-year experience in the development of our course, which has been offered twelve times and involved over 210 youth and senior students. Our work presents a discussion regarding the challenges in designing a course for students from diverse ages, guidelines for creating similar courses, and a reflection on how we might improve our own class. The activities and project code developed for our course are available online as open-source resources.

Categories and Subject Descriptors

K.3 [**Computer and Information Science Education**]: Curriculum

Keywords

Outreach, Education, Curriculum, Social Robotics, Robots, Intergenerational Learning

1. INTRODUCTION

Computer science has emerged as a field with broad appeal and the potential for great impact across society. As such, there is an increasing interest on the development of tools that support computer science education and enthusiasm at younger ages, including software, such as Alice [7] and Scratch [11] that directly target youth, and hardware, such as Lego Mindstorms [2], Arduino [1], and Raspberry Pi [18], which encourage hands-on experimentation.

In addition to using such tools, youth computer science education might be further supplemented by engaging in simultaneous learning alongside their older familial mentors, such as siblings, parents, or grandparents. Programs with youth-mentor pairings in small, focused outreach courses are becoming increasingly popular and are now offered at several universities, including the University of Wisconsin, Michigan State University, Winona State University, University of North Texas, and Grand Valley State University. Such outreach courses represent a unique opportunity for encouraging computer science education in young and old alike, and thus offer a rich potential design space for the creation of new computer science curricula that inspire life-long learning. However, creating classroom experiences that tailor to a variety of age ranges simultaneously can also introduce new educational challenges due to discrepancies between young and old attention spans, prior technological familiarity, and topic interest.

Figure 1: A grandfather and two of his grandchildren work together to program a Lego Mindstorms robot.

In this paper, we share our experiences addressing such challenges during the creation and ongoing development of a two-day *Social Robotics* outreach course at a public university that offers instruction in computer science topics for children and their grandparents. The class has been offered twelve times over a four year time period and has instructed over 210 students regarding concepts integral to computing, artificial intelligence, robotics, and social interaction research. We report on the design of a variety of classroom activities and programming exercises (see Figure 1), which are available online for use in developing similar courses[1], our experience teaching the course, and conclude with an analysis regarding how our teaching approach might extend to include additional computer science topics, utilize additional platforms, and inform the development of similar courses in the future.

[1] http://hci.cs.wisc.edu/outreach/gpu

SIGCSE'15, March 4–7, 2015, Kansas City, MO, USA.

http://dx.doi.org/10.1145/2676723.267724

2. BACKGROUND

Although many students are introduced to computer science at the high school or college level, there is an increasing effort to adapt instruction to support learning in other age groups. Below, we discuss prior work that tailors computer science curricula, particularly those involving robots, to younger students. To situate our course, we also give background on the field of social robotics and describe our classroom environment, which is part of an initiative known as Grandparents University that caters to multiple age groups.

2.1 Teaching Diverse Age Ranges

In an effort to diversify the demographics of computer scientists, many programs have been created to foster an interest in computer science concepts in the K-12 age range. Tools and curricula have been made accessible for younger students in topics such as parallel programming [5], digital image processing [12], game development [15], and big data [4]. These courses aim to provide active engagement while adapting concepts for the less developed mathematical and cognitive skills of younger students [8].

To date, such adaptations in instruction have often been reserved for the K-12 demographic, while older generations have largely been ignored. Prior work has found that *computer shyness*—an aversion to learning about technology—is positively correlated with age [16], potentially increasing the difficulty of motivating senior students to invest in learning computer science and suggesting that engaging older generations might require modifying the tactics used with young children.

Prior work on *intergenerational learning* (IGL)—where participants from two or more generations work together in a learning environment—suggests that each generation has unique capabilities and perspectives to offer students in the other generation(s), enhancing the learning experience of each group [14]. IGL has additional social benefits by fostering the creation of meaningful intergenerational relationships, with each generation gaining an increased appreciation for other generations [14]. Given the unique challenges of teaching computer science to older and younger generations of students, IGL has the potential to leverage the strengths of each demographic to enhance the overall learning experience of the group, with each generation bolstering the weaknesses of the other.

2.2 Robotics in CS Education

Robots are increasingly being used as integral parts within computer science and engineering curricula. Educators and curriculum organizers cite that robots are beneficial to their programs by providing a hands-on approach to learning and tangible outcomes for students engaged in programming tasks [6, 9, 17]. Robotics curricula have been developed to augment introductory computer science courses to engage a more diverse audience [9, 17] and are also being created to attract younger students to the field [6].

While robots appear to be a promising tool in supporting the instruction of various computer science concepts, they are simultaneously becoming further integrated in applications throughout society, for instance acting as hospital aides, museum tour guides, and domestic assistants. As robots become increasingly prevalent, it is important to develop robots that behave and interact with humans in a socially acceptable manner [13]. While research fields such as human-robot interaction (HRI) and social robotics explore this issue, little work has been done examining how programming social robots might be used to convey traditional computer science topics to younger students. However, work in cognitive psychology suggests that the use of a robot contextualized amongst social cues might be a beneficial approach. *Embodied cognition* emphasizes the role of the body and its place in the environment in creating cognition, while *grounded cognition* emphasizes the role of external factors in shaping cognition [3, 10]. While differing they are viewpoints, both suggest that cognitive functions are inherently influenced by the body and connected to the world. Thus, the use of a robot contextualized in social behaviors, which has physical presence and familiar embodied action, might be a beneficial approach for learning computer science concepts.

2.3 Grandparents University

The curriculum we describe in this paper was developed for a two-day summer camp called Grandparents University (GPU) at the University of Wisconsin–Madison. GPU is sponsored by the university's alumni association, and is an opportunity for grandchildren and their grandparents to "major" together in a field of study. Each year, GPU offers several majors, ranging from *Textile & Design Studies* to *Limnology*. The concept of GPU has become popular in recent years, and multiple incarnations of the program now exist, both at other universities and through local clubs and societies. At our institution, grandchildren and grandparents spend a total of six hours in their major, three on each day of the camp.

In this work, we focus on the *Social Robotics* major, which the authors created and have offered twelve times since 2011. In our course, we teach children and their grandparents about how humans interact with each other and how we might imbue robots with similar behaviors to facilitate natural and intuitive interaction with users. For instance, we describe how humans use social cues, such as facial expressions and body language, to communicate, and how those same cues can be emulated on robots. We then instruct students regarding how to program several simple social behaviors on Lego Mindstorm robots. Our major targets children 9-14 years of age and their grandparents, with each course divided evenly between grandparents and grandchildren. We chose nine as our lower bound due to the math background needed to complete basic programming tasks. Our local GPU does not admit children older than 14, hence our upper bound. Although a *Computer Science* major concerning Scratch is also offered at GPU, it is not a prerequisite for our course and, thus far, it is rare for a student to have taken the Computer Science major prior to participating in our major.

While prior work has explored how computer science curricula and tools can be adapted for age ranges younger than the traditional college classroom, our work addresses designing curriculum for multiple age groups in a single class, such as in the GPU setting. Additionally, we provide the template for a social robotics outreach program, which offers a unique opportunity to engage students using a blend of computer science, robotics, and social sciences.

3. COURSE DESIGN

In this section, we describe the characteristics of our students and their associated challenges and opportunities, the objectives of the course, and our course design.

3.1 Challenges and Objectives

Our course targets students with two distinct age groups—grandchildren from 9-14 and grandparents from 55 and above. Grandchildren might be better with and willing to explore technology uses, however they may demonstrate shorter attention spans to focus on course materials and have more limited math and cognitive skills. On the other hand, grandparents have more life experience and cognitive capability to associate and process course materials, but may be less willing to experiment and try new technology. While these characteristics of our students introduce challenges in curriculum design and implementation, they present opportunities for intergenerational learning, allowing grandchildren and grandparents to complement one another.

In addition to creating opportunities for children and grandparents to learn together, we have the following objectives for our course.

1. Expose students to the emerging field of social robotics
2. Introduce students to basic computer science concepts
3. Encourage students to learn from doing, participating, and exploring

We developed a two-day course to address our curriculum objectives for both grandchildren and grandparents. In the first day, instructors provide students with background knowledge of robotics, direct activities that develop real-world research skills, and encourage students to think about and explore the design space of social robots. In the second day, students put their newfound knowledge into practice while programming robots during hands-on exercises that teach introductory computer science concepts.

3.2 Day 1: Introduction to Social Robotics

We created a series of lecture topics and group activities on the first day of the course to familiarize students with the emerging field of social robotics. Our goal was to engage students about the topic, as well as leverage the cognitive capabilities of grandparents in transmitting that understanding to grandchildren. Lecture topics are loosely grouped into four high-level categories, detailed below.

3.2.1 Cultural and societal background

The class starts with an overview of how social robots, such as Furby toys and Keepons, have emerged in popular culture and society. Students then offer other robots they have encountered, either in popular culture or their own experiences, and what might make them appear more or less social. Common answers include R2-D2 and C-3PO from *Star Wars*, Rosie the robot maid from *The Jetsons*, Roombas, and the AIBO robotic dog toy. This discussion encourages students to think about the applications of robots, the difference between robots and other mechanical tools, why it is important for robots to have social knowledge, and the potential impact robots can have on culture and society. While children are often more familiar with current robotic technologies, grandparents can help their grandchildren contextualize robots' roles in society.

3.2.2 Design space of social robots

The class is then exposed to the design space of social robots. We utilize two activities to highlight the importance of social cues and appearance design in this area.

Social Cues: To introduce the class to the concept of social cues, we ask for a single grandchild to volunteer to help us. With the grandchild and instructor at the front of the room, we ask the grandchild to tell the instructor about their favorite movie. As the volunteer starts discussing the movie, the instructor acts to give the impression of boredom, such as looking away from the volunteer, yawning, or even using their cell phone. After a few moments, the instructor stops the volunteer and asks them if they thought the instructor was paying attention. When the volunteer says no, the instructor asks both the volunteer and the class what gave the impression of boredom. The instructor then asks the volunteer to resume discussing their favorite movie. This time, the instructor appears engaged by making eye contact, facing toward the volunteer, nodding and using appropriate backchannels (e.g., "uh-huh"), and asking questions to the volunteer about the movie. Again, the volunteer and class then discuss what impression the instructor gave and what social cues the instructor used to convey that impression. This activity introduces the class how we humans are wired to produce and interpret social cues and highlights implications of designing social cues for robots.

Appearance Design: The class is introduced to the importance of robot appearance and design in communicating functionality and completing tasks. Grandchildren work together with their grandparents to design a robot for a particular task of their choice, such as playing baseball, helping with homework, or doing the dishes. Grandchildren frequently choose their robot's task focus, helping to engage them. Grandparents then help their grandchildren focus on creating a design that addresses the robot's communication with humans when completing the task.

3.2.3 Design methods

After exploring the design space of social robots, we conduct three activities that engage the class while exposing them to real-world design methods used when developing social robots.

Ethnography: One of the foremost challenges in social robotics is understanding and defining the variant social behavior of the human population. For example, some people are more prone than others to nodding during a conversation. Observing human-human interaction using *ethnographic* data collection, where researchers study interactions *in situ*, is a typical approach to capture the variability in human behavior and interpersonal interaction (e.g., [13]). To let the class experience this research method, the instructor separates the class into groups of three to five people, with four people being ideal. Each group chooses a *speaker* and a *listener*, and the remaining group members are assigned the role of *observers*. All observers receive a slip of paper with their instruction: count the number of times the listener nods. The speakers then give a brief narration to the listeners on a topic of their choice for approximately three minutes (e.g., recalling a memory spent with their grandchild/grandparent). At the end of the allotted time, the instructor asks observers to share how many nods they counted. Usually, the number of nods varies from near zero to the teens, and the count often varies between observers in the same group, showcasing not only the variety of human behavior but also the difficulty translating it into objective phenomena. If the point has not already been raised, the instructor can ask observers what behaviors they considered to be a nod. Some participants will suggest that multiple up and down head movements in short succession constitute a single nod, while others will count each oscillation individually. This discussion helps the class understand the challenges involved in defining human social behavior, which can be difficult for multiple people to agree on, even with a single data point.

Affinity Diagramming: Affinity diagramming is a common design practice that aims to categorize data by forming logical groups. As a followup activity to the initial discussion of social cues, we conduct an affinity diagramming activity that allows the class to better understand the variety of social cues used by humans in day-to-day interactions. Groups have 5-10 minutes to brainstorm as many social cues as possible, writing each social cue on a separate sticky note. Grandparents help grandchildren expand their initial set of social cues (e.g., gazing) to more nuanced social cues (e.g., winking). When the groups are finished brainstorming, the instructor asks grandchildren to bring up sticky notes for each of the following categories in order: "face" (e.g., smiling, gaze, winking), "gestures" (e.g., "posture" (e.g., facing toward/away, slouching) and "vocal" (e.g., "uh-huh," "um"). As grandchildren categorize their social cues, the instructor can read aloud what cues are being posted, discussing the variety present. Once all the cues are posted, it becomes apparent that many of the social cues are placed under the "face" category. The relative distribution of cues amongst these four categories creates an opportunity for discussion about how humans direct the majority of their focus to others' faces during interactions.

Storyboarding: We teach the class how to use storyboards to design scenarios that integrate desired social cues, learned from previous activities, into human-robot interactions. Storyboards are an important tool that allows researchers and designers to prototype how cues might shape interactions at a high level. First, storyboarding is taught by examining a number of comic strips that have a range of social cues in them. Each group is then given five pieces of paper, allowed to choose their storyboarding scenario from a variety of options, and instructed to create their scenario visually using one frame on each piece of paper. For example, scenarios might describe a favorite memory the grandparent and grandchild share (potentially one described in the ethnography activity), or might involve further developing a particular use case for the robot they designed in the appearance design activity. Students are told to pay particular attention to how social cues are exhibited in the resulting interaction. Grandchildren and grandparents are then invited to share their storyboard with the rest of the class, pointing out why those chose particular social cues and how they might support the interaction in the scenario.

3.2.4 Robots in the wild

After gaining background knowledge about robotics, the rich design space of social robots, and research methods used in developing social robots, the class is provided opportunities to see social robots in action during a series of interactive demos. This in-person experience with social robots help students contextualize the concepts they learned from the lectures and activities into concrete outcomes.

Robot Demonstration: Each year, the class spends about an hour in our robotics lab, where the instructor and other affiliated graduate students demonstrate various robots, including humanoid robots, telepresence robots, and flying robots. Students are encouraged to think back to previous class discussions regarding potential use cases and how and why such robots may or may not appear social. The instructor discusses how each robot is being used in the lab's research, the studies each robot has been used in, and the central research questions of each study, which often directly pertain to concepts covered earlier in the day, such as modeling human behaviors, implementing them on the robot platform, and testing their effects in small interaction scenarios. The session includes a demo using a small humanoid robot that dances and plays a guessing game with students, foreshadowing the coding activities they will complete in the second day. Following the demonstration period, we offer an impromptu question-and-answer session between grandchildren and grandparents and lab members, allowing students to get a behind-the-scenes look at research activities.

3.3 Day 2: Programming a Social Robot

In the second day of class, we guide students through a series of five programming exercises that teach students basic concepts in computer science and how they can use these concepts to develop social robots. In the first three years of the class, all programming exercises were conducted in the Lego Mindstorms NXT 2.0 development environment. The fourth year used the newer, but similar, Lego Mindstorms EV3 environment. Both Mindstorms software use a visual programming paradigm similar to Scratch[2], allowing users to arrange programming blocks in a sequential or parallel fashion in their workspace. Students are provided a workstation and Lego Mindstorms NXT 2.0 robot, configured as the humanoid robot "Alpha Rex" (Figure 2), for these programming exercises. Grandparents and grandchildren work together on a single platform, allowing grandchildren to illuminate their grandparents understanding of programming. Grandparents also help to keep their grandchildren focused and augment the grandchild's problem solving capabilities.

[2]http://scratch.mit.edu/

Figure 2: The Lego Mindstorms NXT 2.0 robot configured as "Alpha Rex." The eyes are an ultrasonic sensor and the robot's right hand is equipped with a color sensor. Behind the robot is the Mindstorms programming environment.

The computer science concepts we teach include conditional statements, loops, data storage and retrieval (i.e., variables), random number generation, iterative development, and debugging. In addition, we also highlight building blocks for social robots involving input sensing and output generation, such as sound and robot motions. In the following paragraphs, we describe our designed programming exercises and how concepts in computer science and social robots were integrated into the exercises (Figure 3).

3.3.1 Program 1: Robot Voice

The first programming exercise teaches students the basics of the programming environment through the use of a sound block, which emits a chosen sound or phrase from the robot. The class first learns how to place a sound block in the environment, choose a pre-recorded sound for the block, and then execute the program. The class also learns sequential programming by arranging multiple sound blocks in a row, enabling the robot to speak a phrase.

3.3.2 Program 2: Motion Sensing

In social robotics, the ability to sense and respond to the environment is fundamental to interaction. We teach the class about making decisions based on sensor input through the use of an ultrasonic sensor, which is located in the eyes of the robot. We also introduce conditional statements. This exercise involves using the ultrasonic sensor to detect nearby movement. The goal is to produce a simple social interaction in which the robot says "hello" when a waving motion is detected. Building on the first program, if movement is detected, then a sound block that says "hello" is executed.

While such a program enables students to produce their first "interactive" robot, the algorithm only allows a single use. To enable the robot to repeatedly engage in the greeting interaction, a while loop is needed. To teach the concept of loops, we first create a new program with a single while loop that updates the display on the robot to show the number of iterations the loop has completed. When the class executes the program, the instructors ask them what number they see on the display and how that number is changing, eventually leading to the concept of a while loop and how quickly the program executes. We then extend the program from the previous exercise with a while loop, and have students wave multiple times to trigger the robot's greeting.

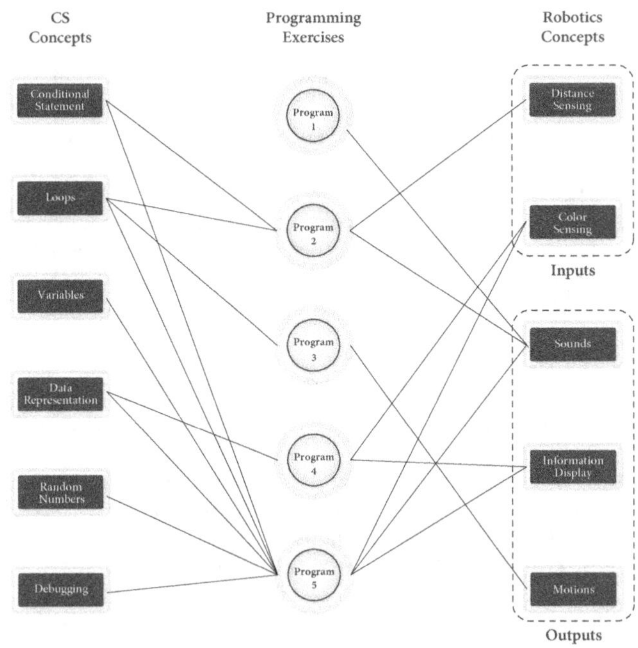

Figure 3: Programming exercises introduced students to concepts in computer science and social robotics.

3.3.3 Program 3: Robot Motion

Movements and gestures make a social robot more engaging and lively while enabling non-stationary tasks. In this exercise, we teach the class how to make the robot walk. The Mindstorms programming environment provides a walking block to allow programmers to achieve a fluid walking motion without the need to program parallel move actions. We also cover how to move individual motors, allowing students to move the arms to create simple gestures. Students thus gain mastery of the concepts of input and output, and how to use inputs to drive outputs.

3.3.4 Program 4: Data Representation

The Mindstorms programming environment creates abstractions for many of the data representations necessary in programming. For example, the Mindstorms robots have a color sensor that can detect six colors, which are stored as integers ranging from 1 to 6. We show students how to create a program that detects a color and displays the internal representation on the robot's screen. We then give students four colored balls each and let students experiment with the color sensor on their robot. Students can use the colored balls or often have colored pieces of paper, their name tags, mouse pads, dollar bills, and even their own shirts to try under the color sensor. Eventually, the class reaches the conclusion that each number represents a color, that colors are "rounded" to the nearest recognized color, and as a class creates the decoding map that translates each displayed number into a color. We then guide students in extending their color-recognition program to translate the numbers for each color such that, instead of numbers, a string representation of the color (the color name) appears on the display. This exercise further exposes students to conditional logic and environmental sensing while developing the notion of different types of data.

3.3.5 Program 5: Interactive Guessing Game

In the last exercise, we develop an interactive guessing game, similar to the demo students saw during the robotics lab tour in the previous day, which integrates the skills developed in previous programs and adds the concepts of variables and random numbers. In this game, the robot uses a random number generator to select one of the four available ball colors—red, yellow, green, and blue—and stores it in a variable. The human player makes guesses by placing one of the colored balls underneath the robot's color sensor, while the robot compares the data from the color sensor to the randomly chosen color stored in memory. If the player is correct, the robot says "good job." An incorrect guess elicits a "try again." Students usually encounter "bugs" in this exercise, such as the robot repeatedly saying "try again" while no guesses are being made, because it involves multiple components and coordination between them. Therefore, as part of this exercise, we teach the class basic debugging strategies and highlight the importance of developing small pieces of working, modular code before adding extensions.

After working through the above exercises, the class has been exposed to the core concepts of programming and how to implement these concepts in the Mindstorms programming environment. With the remaining time left in the class (between 45 and 60 minutes), grandparents and grandchildren have the opportunity to design and implement their own robot routine. The instructor is available for help with more advanced concepts the students would like to implement but were not covered in class, such as parallel programming. During the last 10 minutes of the class, each grandchild has the opportunity to show and explain their program to the rest of the class. Examples of past programs include a robot that uses the colored balls to make decisions about what to say to humans, dance routines, variations on the interactive guessing game, and even a robot "duel" that formed as a collaboration between two student groups.

4. LESSONS LEARNED

Over the course of teaching this program, we have found some approaches that work well, and others that could be improved. Additionally, there are some aspects of the program we would like to change, but cannot due to the limitations of our particular program. Below, we highlight and reflect on some of these issues.

4.1 Reflection

Reorganization of Activities: Currently, the course is structured to complete all the programming activities on the second day. However, experience and student feedback has shown that students enjoy working with the robots and would prefer to do some programming on both days. Ideally, the programming would be interspersed throughout the course to better engage students and to allow tighter loops between knowledge acquisition and implementation.

Movement is Engaging: While grandparents report being engaged with all the programming activities outlined in the prior section, those activities involving movement, in the form of walking, appear particularly popular with grandchildren. Additionally, nearly all student-designed robot routines end up incorporating movement in some way, highlighting the desire of students to physically "see something happen" as the result of successfully implementing an algorithm. The Mindstorms NXT 2.0 kits only have three motors, limiting the diversity of movement available to the robot. To enable a greater range of motions, the Mindstorms could be augmented with additional motors, or a different robot platform (alternatives discussed below) could be used.

4.2 Adoption for Other Programs

While our program is tailored to teach diverse age ranges about social robotics, the lessons presented can be adapted for other audiences. Below, we highlight ways our approach might be tailored for the needs of a particular program.

Targeting Other CS Topics: At a high level, we have designed our curriculum to engage a diverse age range by developing hands-on activities, tying activities to shared student experiences, and creating a framework where information is presented in an iterative fashion, where concepts are first introduced and then explored in greater depth. Many of these strategies might be adapted or extended for use in teaching other computer science topics. For example, to provide instruction on sorting algorithms, grandparents and grandchildren could order their shared relatives according to birthday, a hands-on activity tied to shared experiences. To teach parallel programming, a grandchild volunteer could come to the front of the class while a team of students each "manage" a "thread" controlling the volunteer (e.g., one student tells the volunteer what to do with their legs, another student controls the volunteer's arms, etc.).

Alternative Robot Platforms: The Mindstorms platform used in our course is commonly used in outreach. However, other robotics platforms are available with varying degrees of capabilities. Some examples include TinkerBots,[3] Cubelets,[4] and BetterBots.[5] Other commercially available platforms, such as Keepon, can be altered for more in-depth use by participants at a low cost.[6] For older or more experienced students, the Arduino robot platform may offer more creative freedom and advanced capabilities.[7]

5. CONCLUSION

We present the design of an outreach course aimed at simultaneously engaging young and senior students while encouraging enthusiasm for science and technology by providing instruction in computer science and social robotics. We highlight the challenges and opportunities involved in developing an intergenerational computer science course and present our curriculum developed over the past four years. In our experience, robots are an effective means of generating interest in all ages, provide a platform for hands-on instruction, and can generate a fruitful environment for discussion of technological progress between generations. Our experience has indicated that providing the lens of social robotics is both novel and timely. While developing material for both young and old students is a challenging endeavor, we have found it to be a tremendous opportunity to generate excitement and diversity in the field.

6. ACKNOWLEDGMENTS

We would like to thank the National Science Foundation award 1149970, the University of Wisconsin Alumni Association for their administration of GPU, and Shiyu Luo, who helped develop and teach our program.

7. REFERENCES

[1] R. Balasubramanian, Z. York, M. Doran, A. Biswas, T. Girgin, and K. Sankaralingam. Hands-on introduction to computer science at the freshman level. In *SIGCSE '14*.

[2] B. S. Barker and J. Ansorge. Robotics as means to increase achievement scores in an informal learning environment. *Journal of Research on Technology in Education*, 39(3):229–243, 2007.

[3] L. W. Barsalou. Grounded cognition. *Annu. Rev. Psychol.*, 59:617–645, 2008.

[3] http://tinkerbots.net/

[4] https://www.modrobotics.com/cubelets/cubelets-kt06/

[5] http://www.betterbots.com/

[6] http://probo.vub.ac.be/HackingKeepon/

[7] http://arduino.cc/en/Main/Robot

[4] P. S. Buffum, A. G. Martinez-Arocho, M. H. Frankosky, F. J. Rodriguez, E. N. Wiebe, and K. E. Boyer. CS principles goes to middle school: learning how to teach "big data.". In *SIGCSE '14*.

[5] C. Gregg, L. Tychonievich, J. Cohoon, and K. Hazelwood. EcoSim: a language and experience teaching parallel programming in elementary school. In *SIGCSE '12*.

[6] T. Karp, R. Gale, L. A. Lowe, V. Medina, and E. Beutlich. Generation NXT: Building young engineers with Legos. *IEEE Transactions on Education*, 53(1), 2010.

[7] C. Kelleher, R. Pausch, and S. Kiesler. Storytelling Alice motivates middle school girls to learn computer programming. In *CHI '07*.

[8] M. Knobelsdorf and J. Vahrenhold. Addressing the full range of students: Challenges in k-12 computer science education. 2013.

[9] T. Lauwers, I. Nourbakhsh, and E. Hamner. CSbots: design and deployment of a robot designed for the CS1 classroom. In *ACM SIGCSE Bulletin*, volume 41, 2009.

[10] B. Z. Mahon and A. Caramazza. A critical look at the embodied cognition hypothesis and a new proposal for grounding conceptual content. *Journal of physiology-Paris*, 102(1):59–70, 2008.

[11] J. H. Maloney, K. Peppler, Y. Kafai, M. Resnick, and N. Rusk. Programming by choice: urban youth learning programming with Scratch. In *ACM SIGCSE Bulletin*, volume 40, 2008.

[12] A. McAndrew and A. Venables. A secondary look at digital image processing. In *ACM SIGCSE Bulletin*, volume 37, 2005.

[13] B. Mutlu and J. Forlizzi. Robots in organizations: the role of workflow, social, and environmental factors in human-robot interaction. In *HRI '08*.

[14] S. Newman and A. Hatton-Yeo. Intergenerational learning and the contributions of older people. *Ageing horizons*, 8:31–39, 2008.

[15] A. Repenning and A. Ioannidou. Broadening participation through scalable game design. In *ACM SIGCSE Bulletin*, volume 40, 2008.

[16] N. Selwyn. Teaching information technology to the 'computer shy': a theoretical perspective on a practical problem. *Journal of Vocational Education & Training*, 49(3):395–408, 1997.

[17] J. Summet, D. Kumar, K. O'Hara, D. Walker, L. Ni, D. Blank, and T. Balch. Personalizing CS1 with robots. *ACM SIGCSE Bulletin*, 41(1), 2009.

[18] D. Wing and E. Meyers. Easy as Pi: Designing a library program to support computational thinking in preteens. *BCLA Browser: Linking the Library Landscape*, 6(3), 2014.

A Socio-Cognitive Analysis of Summer Camp Outcomes and Experiences

Chulakorn Aritajati[1], Mary Beth Rosson[1], Joslenne Pena[1], Dana Cinque[1], Ana Segura[2]

[1]The Pennsylvania State University
16802 U.S.A
{cya5092,mrosson,jop5190}@ist.psu.edu,
dcinque@psu.edu

[2]University of Houston-Downtown
77002 U.S.A
segura.ana0104@gmail.com

ABSTRACT

In this paper, we describe the first phase of a longitudinal study focusing on young people's attitudes towards computing careers and their computational self-efficacy. Using summer camps as a springboard to pique their interests, we are interested in enhancing their knowledge in computing topics and assessing their views through surveys. Working from the findings of this first phase in the project, we discuss our future plans for an online community learning system that is grounded in a socio-cognitive learning process, and intended to engage young people in continuous engagement with and exposure to computing concepts and skills.

Categories and Subject Descriptors

K.3.0 [**Computers and Education**]: General Education

General Terms

Design, Human Factors

Keywords

Summer camps, introductory programming, self-efficacy, career orientation, intrinsic motivation, social-cognitive factors.

1. INTRODUCTION

Many students hold negative attitudes toward computer-related education and careers [5]. This is particularly prevalent among female students, for example researchers have found that senior high school girls think that information and communications technology subjects are not interesting and not related to their future careers [1]. Both males and females worry that they cannot learn programming because they are not smart enough, or they may prefer to avoid it because they believe that programmers have poor social skills or are simply odd [5].

One of the measures often used to assess people's inclination to carry out or learn about programming tasks is computer self-efficacy [3, 11, 14]; it is common for young people – especially young women – to report low self-efficacy for computer-related tasks like writing code or debugging [3]. Believing that one simply cannot learn computational tasks reinforces the lack of interest in computing careers, such that young people will not event "try out" programming activities to see if it might be a good fit to their inclinations and abilities. However, researchers have also found that well-designed learning activities can change learners' perspective on computing subjects and increase their computer self-efficacy [4, 5, 8]. In this paper, we describe the first phase of a long-term project that is using the learning activities provided through summer camps on a range of topics to enhance young people's computer self-efficacy and their attitudes toward computing careers.

A well-designed summer camp can increase the self-efficacy that learners report concerning computational thinking tasks [14]. Efficacy affects students' engagement with and learning about learn computer-related subjects [3, 5, 15].When camps are designed and delivered by experienced teachers, they can be customized for the needs of the specific groups of learners. For example, a storytelling teaching technique has been shown to motivate high school girls to spend more time to do programming in Alice [9]. Moreover, an effective summer camp can also motivate students to be interested in software development and to continue such activities in the future, even as a potential career path [4, 6].

It is clear that summer camps can introduce computer programming concepts, provide engaging and enriching experiences, and have measureable effects on self-efficacy and career interests. However, little is known about the longer-term impacts of summer camp experiences, for instance whether students who participate in such a camp are more likely to pursue further education and eventually careers that benefit from that early exposure. It is difficult to conduct the longitudinal studies that would allow researchers to track these sorts of enrichment effects over time.

The work reported here is a first step toward a longitudinal study of the impacts of a regular summer camp outreach program. The project was conceived under the lens of socio-cognitive theories of learning and development [2, 13]. Such views see learning as driven by personal cognitive and motivational factors that are in constant interaction with social context in which the learning occurs. The learning that is possible for an individual (or even simply believed to be possible, e.g., as reflected in self-efficacy measures) is quite dependent on the social structures and supports that are available (for a student these might come from the home, from friends, or from peers and teachers at school). In this framework, students' ultimate decisions about whether to pursue or persist in computing-related education and careers is influenced by a complex mix of socio-cognitive variables, including intrinsic interest in computer-based activities, computer self-efficacy, and social support for addressing computer-based problems [11].

To inject the summer camps experiences into a persistent and dynamic socio-cognitive learning process, we are constructing an online learning community system [12] that can operate in parallel with the summer camps as well as other enrichment programs we may offer in the future (e.g., after-school or weekend workshops

SIGCSE'14, March 4–7, 2015, Kansas City, MO, USA.

http://dx.doi.org/10.1145/2676723.2677292

scheduled during the school year). The online community design concept is to support and foster students' natural interactions and collaborative learning activities [10]. For example, they might share tips with their friends about how to use Scratch or Alice to create a music video, or they might post a pointer to an interesting new computing device or technique. The online community can also provide continuous access to instructors or learning assistants, as well as carefully crafted example-based learning activities [15], offering additional scaffolding for learners to attempt activities they might otherwise believe unattainable.

The over-arching project of the summer camps and other outreach activities that will be carried out in parallel with the online learning community is called iTechAcademy. It is aimed at different target groups, from middle school to high school, sometimes girls or boys only and at other times for mixed gender groups. It will also offer different camp topics in the hopes of attracting different people or even attracting the same people to different experiences.

In the current paper we report the initial phase of the iTechAcademy project, namely student experiences, outcomes and reflections from a first set of summer camps. As part of the camp process, we have gathered survey data related to the socio-cognitive variables shown to influence students' attitudes about computing education and careers, in an effort to position the camps as a first step within a longer process of student engagement and learning over time. The results reported here arise from analyses of these survey data. In collecting and analyzing the survey data, we were guided by two general research questions:

How does the camp experience influence participants' self-efficacy with respect to computational thinking? What about their identification with computing education and careers?

How do the socio-cognitive factors of computational self-efficacy, intrinsic interest in computing, and social support affect students' experiences and attitudes about computing?

2. METHODS

2.1 The Camps

As part of its ongoing outreach mission, the College of Information Sciences & Technology (IST) at Penn State conducted four summer day camps during Summer 2014. The summer program goals were two-fold: a) to provide introductory and enrichment experiences related to computing to area students; b) to raise awareness and develop specific relationships with students and their families that might attract them to IST's education programs in the future. As a result, the camps were varied in both topics and participant ages (Table 1). Except for the Mindstorms programming in Camp 3, all of the other camps covered concepts and skills often taught in our undergraduate courses, and were taught by experienced instructors. Only students whose parents and themselves agreed to be research participants are included in the analyses reported here (a total of 59 students).

Three of the camps were aimed at high school students of any age and gender; our participants tended to be those from the younger grades, ranging in age from 13 to 17 with a mean of 14.6. The high school participants were mostly males (35/41). Camp 3 was designed for girls only and the average age was 11.6.

2.2 Surveys

To investigate our research questions we designed background and feedback surveys that included a mix of questions probing the starting beliefs and attitudes of students as well as their reactions after the camp. In some cases, high school students participated in more than one camp; in such situations a single background survey was collected and the analyses here focus on the feedback we gathered from their first camp.

Table 1. Summaries of four summer camps

Camp	Ages	Topics Covered
Camp 1	13-18	Programming with Scratch and Arduino (breadboard, wires, microcontrollers)
Camp 2	13-18	Cyber-security concepts and programming with Terminal, Linux, Python
Camp 3	10-13	Programming with Lego Mindstorms, building and working with robots
Camp 4	13-18	Concepts and programming of websites with HTML5, CSS3, JavaScript, Design

The background survey included general demographic information (gender, age, grade) as well as a number of 7-point (from 1 = very strongly disagree to 7 = very strongly agree) Likert scales adapted from prior research [11, 14]: *computer playfulness* (6 items assessing people's feelings of enjoyment when using computers); *computational self-efficacy* (5 items assessing capacity for problem solving, a computational analysis, planning, and programming); *technology social support* (4 items assessing help available from other people to solve computational problems); and *career identification* (5 items assessing knowledge of and personal expectations about careers in computer-related fields). After first confirming each scale's internal reliability, we averaged the scale items to create composite constructs as shown in Table 2. The background survey also collected open-ended questions asking what students hoped to get out of the camp experience.

Table 2. Constructs measured in background survey

Construct	N	Cronbach's α	Mean	SD
Playfulness	53	0.714	4.85	0.69
Self-efficacy	52	0.805	4.58	0.74
Support	53	0.847	4.65	1.13
Career ID	53	0.877	4.80	1.02

Note that the sample size varies across constructs because not all students completed all ratings for all scales.

As the table conveys, average ratings tended to be just above the neutral point of 4; this is not surprising given that these students (or their parents) chose to participate in the summer program. Not surprisingly, the Career ID values for the middle school camp was somewhat lower than the average (4.33); but because the number of participants varied significantly across the camps, and because the overall number was relatively small, we have combined the data across all camps in our subsequent analysis and discuss camp differences using student comment data only.

The feedback survey repeated the scales for self-efficacy and career identity, and added a third scale probing general positivity about the camp experience (4 items assessing how well they thought they had done, whether they had fun and would like to do more things like this in the future). Again after confirming internal reliability, we created composite values as summarized in Table 3. The feedback survey also collected open-ended comments about aspects of the camps that participants particularly enjoyed or did not like, what they learned, and suggestions for improving the camp program in the future.

Table 3. Constructs measured in feedback survey

Construct	N	Cronbach's α	Mean	SD
Positivity	59	0.900	5.57	1.04
Self-efficacy	52	0.805	4.79	0.82
Career ID	59	0.846	5.13	1.18

Note that the sample size varies across constructs because not all students completed all ratings for all scales.

3. RESULTS

3.1 Changes in self-efficacy and career ID

Our first set of analyses addressed the first and very basic research question, namely whether the camp activities had an immediate (though perhaps short-term) impact on how participants felt about their own capacity for computer-related activities and their identification with computer-related education and careers. Similar findings have been reported in the past [14], so we expected to see the increases in these two constructs.

A quick review of the means for self-efficacy and career identification in Tables 2 and 3 suggests that there was a modest increase in mean value for both constructs; while these differences were small, they were consistent enough across participants to be statistically significant (mean differences of 0.23 for self-efficacy and 0.31 for career identify with $t(50) = 2.34$, $p<.05$ and $t(51) = 1.17$, $p<.01$ respectively).

Looking across the different camps, the increase in computational self-efficacy was most pronounced for Camp 1, a high school camp that covered basic programming techniques. Interestingly, the increase in career identification was greatest for Camp 3, a camp for middle school girls that also focused on basic programming skills. The smallest increases for both constructs were for Camp 2, which had the most specialized topic (cyber-security). We had included the cyber-security topic because it is part of our undergraduate education, so we had experienced faculty members teach the material; we also believe that it added variety to the more traditional summer camp topics that emphasize programming. It may be however that the camp should be refined with these younger learners in mind, for instance to include a greater number of hands on "security building and breaking" activities.

In a few cases, students told us that they came to camp explicitly as a way to "try out" the College, because they were considering attending in the near future. For instance when asked what he hoped to gain from the camp, P48 said "*More knowledge of the IST field so I can better prepare myself for College next year.*" More generally, some students were curious about IST as a topic and saw this as a way to see what it was about, for example as expressed by P36, "*I hope to gain knowledge of what it is like to work in the IST field, and I want to know if it could possibly be a career choice in the future.*" Even though only a handful of students expressed these types of goals, we were happy to see that the camp program is serving this outreach function.

More commonly, the students approached the camp with goals related to programming skills or "making stuff", for example "*I hope to learn more ways to do computer programming and different software that will help me to do more things*" (P66) or "*Learn more stuff about programs and computers, see if it is interesting*" (P22). One girl even mentioned the broader topic of "STEM" education, "*I hope to learn a lot more about STEM and to learn to understand more complex things*". These sorts of goals mapped particularly well to the camps that focused on creation of something – robots, websites, Scratch games – and may help to explain the somewhat more positive reaction from those camps.

We found very little content in students' comments that gave insight into feelings of computational self-efficacy. However, in answers to a question about things they liked best, a few students did stress learning to do things on their own, for instance "*Creating my own webpage with my new knowledge*" (P82); " and "*being able to decide a bit about what your robot could do*" (P53). Such comments are consistent with a learner who is feeling more able to take on and achieve his or her own computational goals.

3.2 Socio-cognitive variables and processes

Prior research on undergraduates in computing and information sciences has proposed a socio-cognitive model of student development, suggesting that students' self-efficacy with respect to computing and the social support they have for solving computer problems are separate contributors in the evolving process of personal identification with computer-related careers [11]. The socio-cognitive argument in that work considers learners to be embedded within a social context as they encounter new material, using interaction with others to co-construct new knowledge.

In this view, people's beliefs about social support for problem solving should impact their formal education (e.g., as an undergraduate) as well as their subsequent career activities. That is, if students feel that they have ready access to a social network of individuals who help them while being trained (e.g., as undergraduates in computer courses), they might anticipate analogous experiences if and when they join the computing workforce. This social-cognitive framework also helps to explain the important role played by family and friends in shaping children's attitudes toward computing careers – namely, if a youngster sees someone she knows and likes participating in computing education or careers, it may be easy to imagine herself in that same situation in the future, getting help from peers who are similar in some way to her current acquaintance.

To investigate the usefulness of this general framework as a guiding model for our summer camp program, we gathered data on several of the constructs studied in the earlier work, which included computer self-efficacy, computer playfulness (a surrogate for intrinsic motivation [15]), social support for solving computer-related problems, and career identification. Some of these were gathered in the background survey and were considered starting characteristics of the learners that might predict aspects of their camp experiences (self-efficacy, playfulness, social support, career identification). As explained earlier, self-efficacy and career identification were also gathered after the camp was over, as was the scale assessing the general positivity of the camp experience.

We were particularly interested in career identification as an outcome variable, because this construct is most clearly related to our long-term goal of attracting these students into computing education programs and careers; it was also the main outcome variable in the earlier work that produced the social-cognitive model [11] However, we were also interested in the positivity construct, because students' general feelings of enjoyment and success should also play an important role in their decisions whether to return for another camp in the future, and perhaps eventually to enroll in one of our College undergraduate programs.

A preliminary review of bivariate correlations among the predictor variables revealed considerable co-linearity; thus we used stepwise multiple regression to determine which constructs had most predictive power for a given outcome variable. The resulting regression of positivity on self-efficacy, career identification, playfulness and social support produced a two-variable model, with the linear combination of playfulness and social support accounting for 36% of the variance in positivity (F(2,48)=10.60, p<.001). Figure 1 depicts these regression results, with standardized ß values shown for each of the predictor variables.

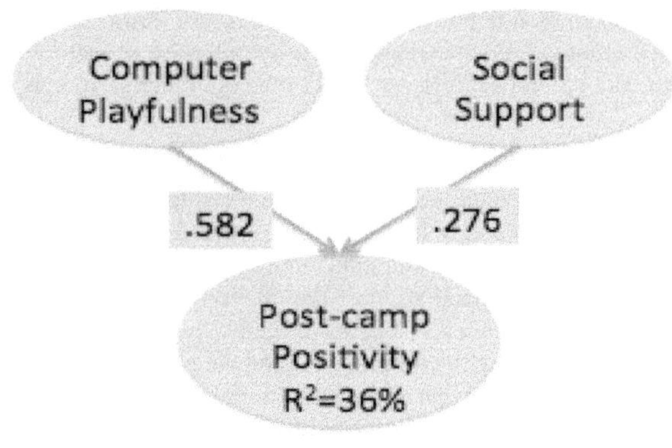

Figure 1. Stepwise linear regression model for positivity

The relationship of playfulness on positivity is easy to interpret, as one would naturally expect that students who are likely to say that they have fun doing computer-related projects will in fact be most likely to enjoy the activities of a computer-related summer camp. The impact of social support is less clear, but can be understood within the socio-cognitive framework introduced earlier: children who regularly receive support when they encounter computer-related problems may become more confident and willing to "just try it" when they are presented new kinds of activities, fully expecting that someone (a peer or the instructor) will be there to help them if and when they struggle. In fact, a few students commented on just this feeling, for instance P68 liked "*being able to program things on your own but get help when you needed it*".

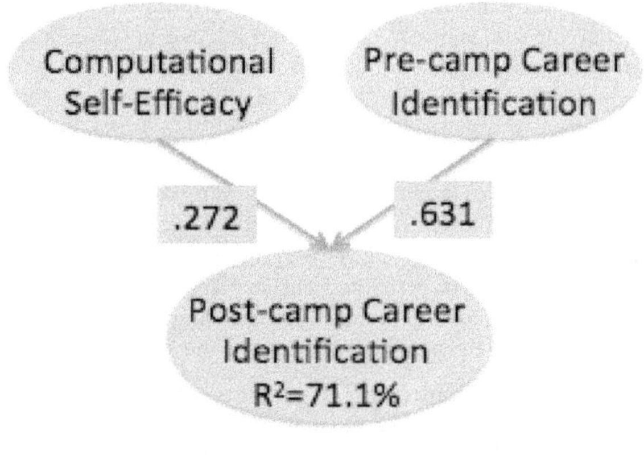

Figure 2. Stepwise linear regression model for career ID.

The stepwise regression on career identification revealed a different pattern. In this model, we found that only the pre-camp values for career identification and self-efficacy were significant predictors, accounting for 71.1% of the variance in post-camp career identification (F(2,48)=58.95, p<.001). The strong relationship of the pre-camp career identification measure is natural, simply indicating that students who were more or less oriented toward computing careers finished the week in the same relative position. The relationship of self-efficacy also makes sense, as students with higher efficacy should be more likely to attempt and succeed in camp activities, which in turn should reinforce their pre-existing beliefs about how well they are suited to computing careers.

Initially, these two regression models suggested to us that the camp experiences might be influencing students through two separate processes. In one, characteristics like playfulness and expectations of social support contribute to general enjoyment. In the other, beliefs about one's capacities for accomplishing computer-related tasks contribute to enhanced levels of identification with computer-related careers. However we also discovered that students' general positivity had a strong relationship with the *size of the increase* in career identification. That is, the students who had most fun also showed the most upward movement on that particular scale (r(52)=0.47, p<.001). When we used a median split on positivity to create two ad-hoc groups (students who had more or less positive experiences at camp), we observed virtually no movement on the career identification scale for the low-positivity group (mean=0.03), while the high-positivity group increased their ratings on this scale by more than have a point (mean=0.55; t(57)=3.8, p<.001). This suggests an interpretation that ties the two socio-cognitive processes together: playfulness and social support enhance enjoyment of the camp, and this positivity in turn leads to larger gains in career identification.

3.3 Student comments and suggestions

We collected open-ended comments in both the background survey (asking students about what they hoped to get from the camps) and in the feedback survey (asking them what they liked best and least about the camps, what they learned, and suggestions for improving the camps in the future. We have already reported a few of these comments, but now turn to a more general summary of what the students told us.

3.3.1 We like programming!

The most common comment from students regarded reactions to programming: Students in all camps said they liked the programming projects the best, whether using Scratch, Lego Mindstorms, Python, JavaScript or CSS. Only two students from the first camp reported *not* liking the programming activities. We were not surprised that students enjoyed these activities, as many have been specifically designed for novices who are first being exposed to programming (e.g., Scratch, Lego Mindstorms):

"*Making games and learning about Scratch*" (P65)

"*Building robots / Programming robots / Learning about terraforming.*" (P70)

"*Making Web pages with HTML and CSS / Learning Python / Arts Fest*" (P45)

However, we noted that even the students from the cyber-security camp (mostly high school males) liked the programming they did, even though the activities in this camp were drawn from a college course in network security (they wrote a chat client using Python). However the activity was popular because Python has many features that assist students in learning to program [7], such that progress is possible without a tool specifically designed for novices [8]. We concluded that an undergraduate programming class based in Python may be suitable for a future camp:

"Programming with Python on Ubuntu / Presentation by real cyber security employee / Learning how the internet works" (P36)

"*Learning Python / learning about how servers work and function / and the fun activities*" (P40)

In contrast to other comments about programming, half of the students in the first camp said they did *not* enjoy building electronic circuits and writing the codes to control them. Students felt that the instructions regarding the Arduino boards were complex, making it hard to know how to set up this tool. In the future, more attention needs to be spent on instructions for these activities:

"Setting up Arduino hardware and some of the activities we did outside." (P25)

"I just thought the Arduino wasn't very engaging and was sort of confusing, so if I had to change something it would be that." (P19)

"Maybe work on the instructions with Arduino." (P31)

3.3.2 More flexibility in pacing and support

Not surprisingly, some students arrived with more background than others, but the instructors tended to convey the material in a way that even the least prepared students could make progress. As a result, students noticed that they had different levels of expertise and this caused problems at times, for both the more and the less advanced students:

"I didn't like the slow pace, ..." (P38)

"*Spending an immense amount of time on things we already learned*" (P48)

"*Go slower when explaining something complicated like packets.*" (P42)

Other students complained that instructors tended to be busy, so they had to wait to ask questions or gain assistance. Some suggested that the camps should have more staff:

"*There needed to be more instructors to walk around and help out students, because there were lots of times when people needed help but there were no free instructors to help out.*" (P75)

"*I would suggest having more people in the room for when people are having problems with their programs or don't know what to do. I would also suggest having a few more things that can be accomplished so that people do not get bored.*" (P68)

3.3.3 More opportunities to explore and share

The camp activities were designed in advance and for the most part students were engaged and having fun. But at times students mentioned a desire for more freedom, for example one student did not like:

"*Not being able to take the robot home, having to create our own programs with harder features, and making the same type of robots as everybody else"* (P50)

A related proposal was to provide some way for sharing, because even though students were able to exhibit some of their work at the end of camp, they did not get a full sense of what their peers had done over the entire week:

"*Maybe set up a website where we can all post them to there so we can see what others have done*" (P72)

This second comment of course is exactly the sort of function we are hoping to support in the online learning community. Although the community will offer new learning activities and related conversations, it can also serve as a repository of ongoing or past work, including artifacts produced during camps or workshops.

4. DISCUSSION AND FUTURE WORK

Our first series of summer camps were a success: they were well attended (most were at or near capacity), the students were engaged and active throughout the week, and their comments in the feedback survey suggested that they had learned a lot and had a great time. The small but consistent increases in computational self-efficacy and in attitudes regarding careers in computing both reinforce similar findings from other camp programs and assure us that we have found effective topics, activities and instructors for our own offerings.

From the perspective of our longer-term goals of raising awareness and recruiting more young people into computer-related education and careers, we propose that by enhancing middle and high school students' identification with computing careers, our camp program makes it more likely that these students will be attracted to and engage in other computer-related activities. Furthermore, the increases in computational self-efficacy should increase their confidence that they can perform well in new computer tasks, making it more likely that they will experiment and try new things. In this sense the camps appear to be positioning these young people to take advantage of additional education opportunities provided by our own or some other institution.

With respect to our second research question, we did confirm the impact of variables such as computer playfulness (a surrogate for intrinsic motivation [15]) and social support for solving computer-related problems. Students who were high in social support and playfulness seemed to enjoy themselves more and were more positive about pursuing future activities similar to what they had done in camp. At the same time students who began with higher values of computational self-efficacy finished with higher scores on the career identification scale, even after controlling for their starting career attitudes. This combination of findings underscore the importance of providing experiences early in childhood that lead to feelings of playfulness about computer tasks and to feelings of competency when attempting such tasks.

The impact of social support networks is quite interesting, in that we asked about social support in advance, not *during* the camp. Nonetheless, those who began with a sense of good support seemed to enjoy themselves more. One possibility is that a child who has always had good support for computer-based problem solving is practiced at working with others on such problems, recognizing when they need help and comfortable making requests for support. Such students are well prepared to meet new people in a camp, whether it is other students or instructors, and to incorporate these new acquaintances into their support network. Indeed a few students specifically mentioned the opportunity to meet new people as a major positive about the camp experience.

Going forward, one way to think about the summer camps and other outreach activities – especially when construed as part of an ongoing academy concept – is that they give children the opportunity to expand the social networks available to them for solving computer-related problem. Many students arrived with friends, but just as many reported that meeting new people and friends was a favorite part of camp. Some even called out the importance of "meeting fellow computer nerds" to collaborate on shared computer-based interests.

Our findings also have implications for the design of the online learning community system that we are creating as part of the iTechAcademy project. For example,

- The important role of playfulness in predicting students' positivity emphasizes the important role of intrinsic motivation. The website should offer online learning activities that are designed to evoke a range of different forms of intrinsic motivation, perhaps emphasizing artistic, logical, social, or competitive rubrics.

- The influence of perceived social support suggests that the online community should include mechanisms for expressing and reinforcing the social support that is inherent in an online community. That is, there should be easy and comfortable Q&A opportunities with peers, as well as low-cost access to more expert perspectives and advice. The community should also leverage the social networks that emerge from the camps themselves, perhaps by offering camp-specific "exhibits" and conversation areas.
- Some students wished that the camp could be more flexible with respect to support from instructors or the pace of the instruction. In an online environment, many help interactions will take place asynchronously (e.g. via Q&A), decreasing the contention for instructor attention. Because the online members will be engaging with the system from their own context at whatever time they choose use the system, their activities can be much more self-directed and custom.
- More generally, because we gather data about students' attitudes and self-efficacy during the camp, we will be able to create custom profiles for each member. We can use this information to help them locate partners for activities (e.g., pairing more advanced students with each other), to suggest new and appropriately challenging learning activities, and to help with sense-making about requests that are submitted.

Returning to the socio-cognitive framework we used to motivate the iTechAcademy project, the results from this first phase of the project are quite promising. We have confirmed the role of personal motivation, the social supports related to computing, and the self-efficacy of individuals encountering new computer tasks. Although we cannot yet describe the detailed interactions of these variables, it is clear that they are all important in guiding learners' trajectories toward computing education and careers. In our future work we will follow students who join the online community and engage in additional learning activities, all the while seeking to meet their needs for personal engagement and social interaction.

5. REFERENCES

[1] Anderson, N. et al. 2008. "Because it"s boring, irrelevant and I don't like computers': Why high school girls avoid professionally-oriented ICT subjects. *Computers & Education*. 50, 4 (May 2008), 1304–1318.

[2] Bandura, A. et al. 1999. Self-efficacy: The exercise of control. *Journal of Cognitive Psychotherapy*. 13, 2 (1999), 158–166.

[3] Beckwith, L. et al. 2007. On to the Real World: Gender and Self-Efficacy in Excel. *Visual Languages and Human-Centric Computing, 2007. VL/HCC 2007. IEEE Symposium on* (Sep. 2007), 119–126.

[4] Bell, S. et al. 2014. Spreading the Word: Introducing Pre-service Teachers to Programming in the K12 Classroom. *Proceedings of the 45th ACM Technical Symposium on Computer Science Education* (New York, NY, USA, 2014), 187–192.

[5] Charters, P. et al. 2014. Challenging Stereotypes and Changing Attitudes: The Effect of a Brief Programming Encounter on Adults' Attitudes Toward Programming. *Proceedings of the 45th ACM Technical Symposium on Computer Science Education* (New York, NY, USA, 2014), 653–658.

[6] Dabney, M.H. et al. 2013. No Sensor Left Behind: Enriching Computing Education with Mobile Devices. *Proceeding of the 44th ACM Technical Symposium on Computer Science Education* (New York, NY, USA, 2013), 627–632.

[7] Grandell, L. et al. 2006. Why Complicate Things?: Introducing Programming in High School Using Python. *Proceedings of the 8th Australasian Conference on Computing Education - Volume 52* (Darlinghurst, Australia, Australia, 2006), 71–80.

[8] Hulsey, C. et al. 2014. Camp CyberGirls: Using a Virtual World to Introduce Computing Concepts to Middle School Girls. *Proceedings of the 45th ACM Technical Symposium on Computer Science Education* (New York, NY, USA, 2014), 331–336.

[9] Kelleher, C. et al. 2007. Storytelling Alice Motivates Middle School Girls to Learn Computer Programming. *Proceedings of the SIGCHI Conference on Human Factors in Computing Systems* (New York, NY, USA, 2007), 1455–1464.

[10] Liccardi, I. et al. 2007. The Role of Social Networks in Students' Learning Experiences. *Working Group Reports on ITiCSE on Innovation and Technology in Computer Science Education* (New York, NY, USA, 2007), 224–237.

[11] Rosson, M.B. et al. 2011. Orientation of Undergraduates Toward Careers in the Computer and Information Sciences: Gender, Self-Efficacy and Social Support. *Trans. Comput. Educ.* 11, 3 (Oct. 2011), 14:1–14:23.

[12] Rosson, M.B. et al. 2009. wConnect: A Facebook-based Developmental Learning Community to Support Women in Information Technology. *Proceedings of the Fourth International Conference on Communities and Technologies* (New York, NY, USA, 2009), 125–134.

[13] Vygotsky, L.S. 1980. *Mind in society: The development of higher psychological processes*. Harvard university press.

[14] Webb, H. and Rosson, M.B. 2013. Using Scaffolded Examples to Teach Computational Thinking Concepts. *Proceeding of the 44th ACM Technical Symposium on Computer Science Education* (New York, NY, USA, 2013), 95–100.

[15] Wiedenbeck, S. 2005. Factors affecting the success of non-majors in learning to program. *Proceedings of the 2005 international workshop on Computing education research - ICER '05*. (2005), 13–24.

Computational Bead Design: A Pilot Summer Camp in Computer Aided Design and 3D Printing for Middle School Girls

Courtney Starrett
Winthrop University
701 Oakland Ave.
Rock Hill, South Carolina 29733
starrettc@winthrop.edu

Marguerite Doman
Winthrop University
701 Oakland Ave.
Rock Hill, South Carolina 29733
domanm@winthrop.edu

Chlotia Garrison
Winthrop University
701 Oakland Ave.
Rock Hill, South Carolina 29733
garrisonc@winthrop.edu

Merry Sleigh
Winthrop University
701 Oakland Ave.
Rock Hill, South Carolina 29733
sleighm@winthrop.edu

ABSTRACT

Computing, together with jewelry design and 3D printing offers an innovative introduction to the possibilities of technology and programming. This combination was presented to participants of a weeklong summer technology day camp focusing on computer-aided design (CAD) using jewelry design and modeling. The participants then saw their design creations built through 3D printing. In this paper we present the design of a weeklong day camp called "Computing and Jewelry Design". Initial findings are positive and suggest opportunities for improvement.

Categories and Subject Descriptors

J.5 [**Arts and Humanities**]: Arts, fine and performing; Fine arts. K.3.2 [**Computer and Information Science Education**] Literacy Computer science education.

General Terms

Design, Experimentation, Human Factors.

Keywords

Broadening Participation; Multi-disciplinary STEM-to-STEAM program; Outreach and Education, Promoting Computer Science, Girls and Computers.

1. INTRODUCTION

There continues to be a shortage of STEM (Science, Technology, Engineering and Math) professionals. Attracting student interest into the STEM field has been the focus of many summer camps for K-12 students [1, 2, and 3]. Camps programming in Scratch or Alice often are expanded to include tangible tools such as robots [6, 7] or microcontrollers, such as Arduino [5], and Androids [4] have been researched.

Blending Art with Science and technology began early in computing history with artists experimenting with the computer as a visual arts medium [8]. Technology provided a medium for creative work in graphics and animation. Recently interactive art, a medium of installation-based art, puts the computer inside the art [9]. The arts and technology are intersecting at the local level, where artists and hobbyists are meeting with computer scientists. 'Hacker-Spaces' are expanding to 'Maker-spaces' [10, 11] where programmers can create art and artists can design technology. Adding art to STEM, yielding STEAM, provides another avenue to introduce computing to students during summer camps.

Women are one of the multiple under-represented groups in computing. Research has shown that girls lose interest in computing early in the educational pipeline. Computing, together with jewelry design and 3D printing, offers an innovative introduction to the possibilities of technology and programming.

This summer we held a week long technology day camp focusing on computer aided design (CAD) and 3D printing using jewelry design and modeling. Our computing and jewelry making camp was designed as part of a project that incorporates fine art and technology. The 'Computational Bead Design' is an interdisciplinary project started by the authors that is designed to introduce students (K-20) to computing (beginning programming), digital modeling and additive manufacturing techniques. Throughout history beads have been considered to hold symbolic and sacred knowledge. They can communicate social standing, political history, and religious beliefs. Beads have been a representation of a civilizations' technological advancement. The technical sophistication of bead manufacturing often mirrors the general technological level of the society. This project highlights the bead, once again, as a marker of our current technological advancements. Through the process of bead generation, this project introduces the participant to design principles, computational thinking and computer science concepts.

In this paper, we report on our computing and jewelry design camp and its impact on the attitudes of the participants toward computing. The rest of the paper is presented as follows: Section 2 describes the design of the camp week. Section 3 describes our

SIGCSE '15, March 4 –7, 2015, Kansas City, MO, USA.

http://dx.doi.org/10.1145/2676723.2677303

findings and a discussion of what we learned. Section 4 describes our future goals and continued work.

2. CAMP DESIGN/PROGRAM

The primary focus of the camp was to introduce the participants to computing through the ubiquitous and accessible subject matter of jewelry, or human adornment. Through lecture, slides, film and discussions the history of the bead as a form of human adornment, was introduced and paralleled with the evolution of industrial technology and computing. The camp consisted of five six-hour days. Activities included free-form digital modeling, focused digital modeling using a CAD tool, 3D printing, graphical algorithmic editing of digital models, programming, installation and gallery display, and an industry tour.

2.1 Participants

The camp was limited to middle school girls. A maximum of twenty slots were available. Participants paid a fee to attend the camp.

2.2 Camp Instruction

The camp combined experiences in free form and directed creative exploration through a modeling program called Rhinoceros® (Rhino) [12]. Rhino is a 3D modeling application based on a mathematical model called NURBS (non-uniform rational B-spline). At the start of the modeling sections, an introduction and demonstration of modeling and manipulation of primitive geometry was presented. Strategic design and computational thinking were introduced through the exploration of the graphical algorithmic modeling editor Grasshopper® (a plug-in for Rhino) [13]. Grasshopper is tightly integrated with Rhino and provides an interface to build form generators of the 3D modeling tool. The physical design constraints and tolerances of digital output were presented through 3D printing. Computational thinking was reinforced and computer science concepts were introduced through Blocky and Python.

2.2.1 Free-form modeling

Free-form modeling is designing without restriction by conventional ideas or patterns. Within minutes the participants were modeling without reservation. This section was the most technically comfortable for the participants. They worked intuitively and quickly to manipulate forms to create unique and exciting designs. The facilitators felt that these abstract forms were the most successful and unique of all designs created throughout the week. Principles introduced in this exercise included: concept, composition, form, content, unity, scale and balance.

2.2.2 Directed modeling

The participants used geometric shapes to create common or trendy symbolic forms (hearts, dancers, animals, crosses, etc.). Most designs were not technically challenging but were the most interesting to the participants. Principles introduced in this exercise included: representation, units of measure, analysis, feasibility, and quality assurance.

2.2.3 Algorithmic modeling

Participants used graphical algorithms through Grasshopper to create bead forms. The participants found this area most challenging. Instructors also considered this area the most challenging to instruct. Instruction connected NURBS modeling, graphical algorithmic modeling and programming. Principles introduced and reiterated in this lesson were: troubleshooting, strategy, units of measure and measurements, tolerance, feasibility, and user interface.

2.2.4 Programming and modeling

Participants used Code.org to solve puzzles and write Python code. They also created drawings using Blocky. The established options worked well, and minimal instruction was needed to guide the participants. These forms were then repeated in both Rhino and Grasshopper to further explain the functionality of the design software. Principles introduced or reiterated in this lesson: strategy, critical thinking, problem solving, persistence, programming languages, and generalizing and transferring knowledge.

2.3 Schedule

The camp day was 9:00am to 3:00pm with lunch at 11:30am. The day began with an icebreaker following the pre-camp surveys on day 1. The day alternated between instruction and hands on activities. For example, the instructor presented the concept of computer-aided design prior to the students performing 3D modeling using Rhino. The participants learned about 3D printing prior to seeing a bead printed on a 3D printer.

2.4 Camp Exhibition

Participants displayed their 3D printed jewelry in a gallery on the final day of the camp. Examples of the pieces completed by the students include a geometric bead design (Figure 1) and a bead related to the student's interest, field hockey (Figure 2)

Figure 1: Example of student work

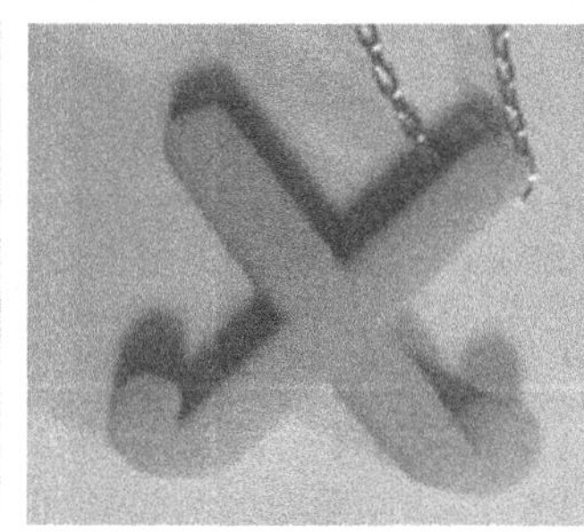

Figure 2: Bead as field hockey sticks

3. PRELIMINARY FINDINGS

3.1 Demographics

The camp was limited to middle school age girls. Seventeen girls attended the weeklong camp. Their ages ranged from 11years to 13 years with the school grades ranging from 6th to 8th grade; 7% in the 6th grade, 33% in the 7th grade and 60% in the 8th grade. The ethnicities of the participants were as follows: 5% Native American, 5% Hispanic, 24% Black, and 65% White.

3.2 Survey Results

To evaluate the impact of the camp, we administered pre- and post-camp surveys. The surveys were used to identify and assess participant attitudes. Participants were asked to rate each attitude statement on a Likert scale (1 – strongly disagree, 3-neutral, 5-strongly agree). Here we present our preliminary findings.

While we cannot draw statistical conclusion on the limited population of camp attendance, we analyzed the survey data to determine if it demonstrated the possibility of a change in attitudes and warrant further investigation. We performed a paired t-test (n=17) on the individual responses and found a statistically significant positive effect ($p<.05$) on attitudes on 2 questions. Figure 3(a) and Figure 3(b) present the pre- and post-camp results of these two questions:

1. Programming is hard.
2. I am interested in studying art, but I don't think there are jobs for artists.

The X axis labels represent: SD: Strongly Disagree, D: Disagree, N: Neutral, A: Agree, SA: Strongly Agree.

Figure 2(a): Programming is hard.

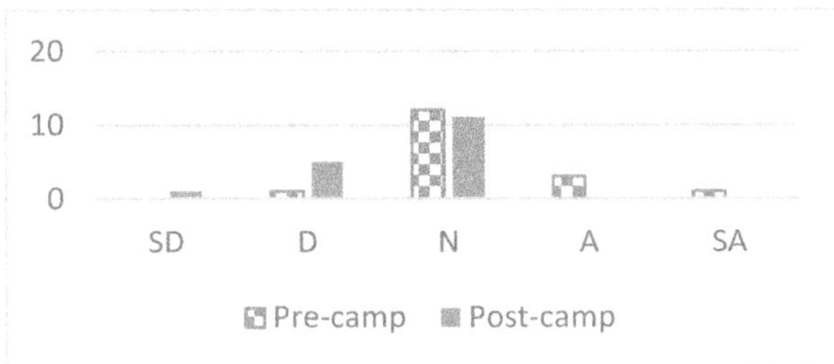

Figure 1(b): I am interested in studying art, but I don't think there are jobs for artists.

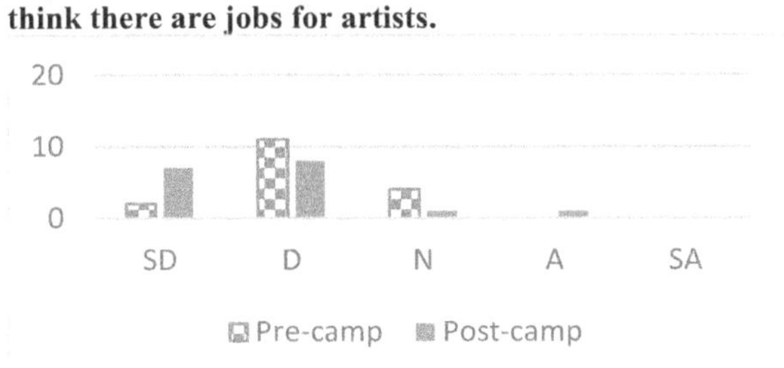

We found a positive effect approaching significance ($p<.069$) on 1 question:

1. Artists are generally not good with computers.

In addition, we found a slight positive effect, though not statistically significant, in the responses for the following questions:

1. I am not the type to do well in computing classes.
2. I will be able to get a good job if I learn how to use a computer.
3. I can see myself working in a computing field.
4. I enjoy solving problems in computing.
5. Using computing to help people is very important to me.
6. How much would you like doing computer programming for things other than making jewelry?
7. Math, Art, Design and Science have very little in common.

3.3 Participant Comments

During the week, the participants were asked to give anonymous comments about the camp. Following are comments from the campers (only 16 comments were submitted):

- Awesome teachers and friends and getting to do this on the computer
- Graphing does not have to be involving graphs or charts. It can be anything
- That each of us can create anything we can think of /set our mind to
- The fact we can print things in 3D
- Making our own jewelry on the computer
- I liked making the bracelets
- The design around the making of jewelry
- I liked making bracelets ☺
- What I like is how we create things in Rhino and how
- We make beads that's cool to very cool
- The entire process is just super cool ~ I love making the beads
- How to make one of a kind things
- Learning to design the beads
- I enjoyed watching the videos
- How many things have codes that we didn't even know they did
- Interesting thing I found: You can take something from our mind and put it on the computer. Then you can make that thing come to life

4. DISCUSSION AND FUTURE WORK

The participants for our camp were self-selected (parent selected) and the number of participants was small. Therefore we do not extend our findings to a general population. However, as a pilot program, these results give a positive indication and agree with the positive impact of other camp research.

We plan to conduct additional summer camp research combining art and technology. In future camps, we plan to increase the programming components of the camp. Directly connecting programming output performed by the participants with jewelry modeling may increase the impact on participant attitudes. We also plan to revisit the presentation of modeling using graphical algorithms. A more focused interaction with these tools could increase the participants' confidence related to computers and problem solving, and reinforce the relationship between Math, Art, Design and Science.

5. CONCLUSION

Computational Bead Design is a relevant K-20 activity with interdisciplinary STEAM learning objectives. The project addresses a missing component to many STEM projects, design and aesthetics. Through the context of the bead these topics are addressed as the participant is introduced to computing.

6. ACKNOWLEDGMENTS

Our thanks to Winthrop University Research Council, Georgia Tech Institute for Computing Education, and National Center for Women in IT – AspireIT program for their funding.

7. REFERENCES

[1] Janet E. Burge, Gerald C. Gannod, Maureen Doyle, and Karen C. Davis. 2013. Girls on the go: a CS summer camp to attract and inspire female high school students. In *Proceeding of the 44th ACM technical symposium on Computer science education* (SIGCSE '13). ACM, New York, NY, USA, 615-620. DOI=10.1145/2445196.2445376 http://doi.acm.org/10.1145/2445196.2445376

[2] Amber Wagner, Jeff Gray, Jonathan Corley, and David Wolber. 2013. Using app inventor in a K-12 summer camp. In *Proceeding of the 44th ACM technical symposium on Computer science education* (SIGCSE '13). ACM, New York, NY, USA, 621-626. DOI=10.1145/2445196.2445377 http://doi.acm.org/10.1145/2445196.2445377

[3] Barbara Ericson and Tom McKlin. 2012. Effective and sustainable computing summer camps. In*Proceedings of the 43rd ACM technical symposium on Computer Science Education* (SIGCSE '12). ACM, New York, NY, USA, 289-294. DOI=10.1145/2157136.2157223 http://doi.acm.org/10.1145/2157136.2157223

[4] Timothy Urness and Eric D. Manley. 2013. Generating interest in computer science through middle-school Android summer camps. *J. Comput. Sci. Coll.* 28, 5 (May 2013), 211-217.

[5] Winnie W.Y. Lau, Grace Ngai, Stephen C.F. Chan, and Joey C.Y. Cheung. 2009. Learning programming through fashion and design: a pilot summer course in wearable computing for middle school students. *SIGCSE Bull.* 41, 1 (March 2009), 504-508. DOI=10.1145/1539024.1509041 http://doi.acm.org/10.1145/1539024.1509041

[6] D. Brian Larkins, J. Christopher Moore, Louis J. Rubbo, and Laura R. Covington. 2013. Application of the cognitive apprenticeship framework to a middle school robotics camp. In*Proceeding of the 44th ACM technical symposium on Computer science education* (SIGCSE '13). ACM, New York, NY, USA, 89-94. DOI=10.1145/2445196.2445226 http://doi.acm.org/10.1145/2445196.2445226

[7] Sebastian van Delden and Kuo-Pao Yang. 2014. Robotics summer camps as a recruiting tool: a case study. *J. Comput. Sci. Coll.* 29, 5 (May 2014), 14-22.

[8] Jean Ippolito. 2005. Dare to be digital: Japan's pioneering contributions to today's international art and technology movement. In *ACM SIGGRAPH 2005 Electronic Art and Animation Catalog*(SIGGRAPH '05). ACM, New York, NY, USA, 177-180. DOI=10.1145/1086057.1086143 http://doi.acm.org/10.1145/1086057.1086143

[9] Martin Fischbach, Marc E. Latoschik, Gerd Bruder, and Frank Steinicke. 2012. smARTbox: out-of-the-box technologies for interactive art and exhibition. In *Proceedings of the 2012 Virtual Reality International Conference* (VRIC '12). ACM, New York, NY, USA, , Article 19 , 7 pages. DOI=10.1145/2331714.2331737 http://doi.acm.org/10.1145/2331714.2331737

[10] Emily Smith. 2014. An inside look at Vancouver's vibrant maker community. In *ACM SIGGRAPH 2014 Studio* (SIGGRAPH '14). ACM, New York, NY, USA, , Article 12 , 1 pages. DOI=10.1145/2619195.2656296 http://doi.acm.org/10.1145/2619195.2656296

[11] Kim Chestney-Harvey. 2011. Art + technology: the new frontier of creativity and innovation.*SIGGRAPH Comput. Graph.* 45, 1, Article 2 (February 2011), 6 pages. DOI=10.1145/1982562.1982566 http://doi.acm.org/10.1145/1982562.1982566

[12] Rhinoceros® 3D, Robert McNeel & Associates, http://rhino3d.com

[13] Grasshopper® 3D, Robert McNeel & Associates, http://grasshopper3d.com

Big Data in Computer Science Education Research

Orit Hazzan
Department of Education in Science and Technology
Technion – Israel Institute of Technology
Haifa 3200003
oritha@technion.ac.il

Clifford A. Shaffer
Department of Computer Science
Virginia Tech
Blacksburg, VA 24061
shaffer@cs.vt.edu

SUMMARY
Recent years have seen the emergence of applications and concepts that rely on the involvement of the general public (the "crowd") and, consequently, create big data (e.g., MOOCs, search engines, crowdsourcing, crowdfunding, citizen/crowd science, and more). Education in particular is changing dramatically with the use of online resources and courses that generate large streams of data. In this special session, we ask: What research questions in computer science education can be explored using big data? And how can computer science education researchers apply big data analysis to support education in other disciplines? To answer these and related questions, we focus in this special interactive session on how computer science education research can be promoted by integrating big data into the research process.

Categories and Subject Descriptors
K.3.2 [**Computers and Education**]: Computer and Information Science Education - *Computer science education*

General Terms
Measurement, Documentation, Design, Experimentation, Human Factors, Legal Aspects.

Keywords
Big data, computer science education, research in computer science education, citizen science.

1. INTRODUCTION
Computer science, like other disciplines, keeps on changing. While its core ideas remain (more or less) constant, its relevance to society increases; one illustrative example of this relevance is big data. Of all the wide variety of possible uses society makes of big data (e.g., Surowiecki, 2005), this special session focuses on the applications of big data in *computer science education research*.

Figure 1 illustrates the position of the special session within the larger picture of big data. The external circle refers to big data usages in general (e.g., Google and Google Trends, Waze: https://www.waze.com/); the next circle focuses on big data uses in the sciences in general (e.g., citizen science - http://en.wikipedia.org/wiki/Citizen_science); the next circle focuses on big data in the discipline of computer science (e.g., https://www.cs.washington.edu/research/bigdata/); the next is about big data in computer science education, and finally, the innermost circle—the focus of the special session—is about big data in computer science education *research*.

Figure 1: Big data (BD) in science, computer science, computer science education, and computer science education *research*

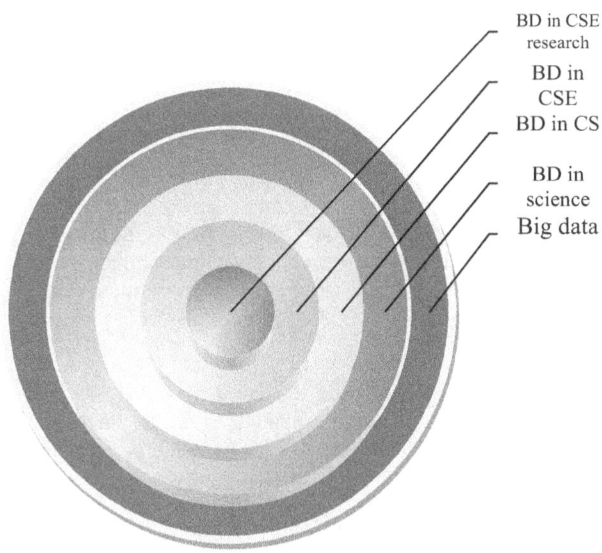

2. BIG DATA IN COMPUTER SCIENCE EDUCATION
In parallel to the increased use of big data, its application is receiving special attention in the educational scene in general, and in computer science education in particular. For example, Mayer-Schönberger and Cukier (2014) describe tomorrow's education landscape thanks to the power of big data; Columbia University offers a course entitled Big Data in Education on its Coursera platform - https://www.coursera.org/course/bigdata-edu.

In the context of computer science education, more and more courses on big data are being introduced into in the study programs offered by computer science departments (see, for example, Anderson et al., 2014). In this special session we

SIGCSE'15, March 4–7, 2015, Kansas City, MO, USA.
ACM 978-1-4503-2966-8/15/03.
http://dx.doi.org/10.1145/2676723.2677318

explore the opportunities that big data offers for *researchers* in computer science education.

3. SPECIAL SESSION STRUCTURE (75 minutes)

15 minutes	Introduction and organizers' statements
15 minutes	Interactive activity: Big data – exploring central themes and questions
20 minutes	Group work on central themes and questions
20 minutes	Reports from group work
5 minutes	Conclusion and future work

4. ORGANIZERS' STATEMENTS

Cliff Shaffer, Virginia Tech

CS education is seeing major innovations due to use of computer-based courseware including

- introductory programming environments with automated assessment of exercises.
- eTextbooks with interactive exercises.
- MOOCs and related distance learning efforts.

All of these courseware artifacts generate large amounts of clickstream and grading data, sometimes referred to as student analytics. This information can and should be mined for important reasons.

- Formative evaluation of the courseware can be greatly improved through the student analytics data. For example, we can do simple analysis to determine whether or not various exercises are at the right level of difficulty.
- We can try to determine student behavior to better engineer the courseware, such as to make sure that students do not solve problems by guessing, or skip key material in an eTextbook.
- Intelligent tutoring systems can be built on the behavior of the individual student.
- Instructors can be given better feedback on student performance.

For all of these reasons, student analytics and techniques for analyzing the data are poised to become a major focus of CS education research (and more generally, CS contribution to education research in all disciplines).

Orit Hazzan, Technion – Israel Institute of technology

In order to approach the issue of big data research in computer science education, questions, such as the following ones, can be asked:

- What research opportunities do big data offer to computer science educators? Specifically, what research questions in computer science education are especially suitable to be answered using big data?
- How do computer science education researchers view research processes that are based on big data?
- What research design is appropriate for this kind of research, in terms of:
    - o participants – number and ways of approaching them,
    - o data-gathering tools
    - o data-analysis processes?
- What are the expected research results?
- How may such research contribute to the community of computer science educators?
- What are the benefits and pitfalls of big data in computer science education research compared with traditional research in computer science education?

My belief is that as researchers in computer science education, we cannot proceed to explore our research themes solely using traditional data-collection tools and data-analysis processes. I hope that as a community, this special session will open a new research thread in computer science education whose applications will be used in other domains as well.

5. LITERATURE

[1] Anderson, P., Bowring, J., McCauley, R., Pothering, G. and Starr, C. (2014). An undergraduate degree in data science: Curriculum and a decade of implementation experience. *Proceedings of SIGCSE 2014 - The 45th ACM Technical Sym on Comp Science Edu*, Atlanta, GA, USA: 145-150.

[2] Mayer-Schönberger, V. and Cukier, K. (2014). *Learning with Big Data - The Future of Education*, Houghton Mifflin Harcourt.

[3] Surowiecki J. (2005). *The Wisdom of Crowds,* Anchor.

Scaling High School Computer Science: Exploring Computer Science and Computer Science Principles

Owen Astrachan
Duke University
ola@cs.duke.edu

Ralph Morelli
Trinity College
ralph.morelli@trincoll.edu

Gail Chapman
UCLA
chapgail@gmail.com

Jeff Gray
University of Alabama
gray@cs.ua.edu

Categories and Subject Descriptors: K.3.2 [**Computers and Education**]: Computer and Information Science Education – *computer science education*

General Terms: Measurement, Experimentation, Standardization

Keywords: Computer Science Education; K-12 Curriculum; CS Principles; Exploring Computer Science; Professional Development

1. SUMMARY

Changing the landscape of computer science education at the high school level is a key component of several initiatives of (1) the National Science Foundation (NSF), e.g., as the cornerstone of the CE21 program partnered with academic institutions and (2) the private sector with both non-profits such as Code.org, CodeVA, and MassCan; and for-profits such as Tynker, CodeHS, and Trinket. This collaboration between privately and publicly funded initiatives is designed to reach every student; and to achieve this at scale.

This special session brings together leaders from four groups working specifically on reaching teachers at *very-large-scale*, a necessary first step in reaching every student. These groups have worked to scale both Exploring Computer Science [1-3](ECS) and Computer Science Principles [4, 5] (CSP) on a national scale --- having already implemented very different approaches to reaching a large number of teachers. Two presenters talk about their initiatives to expand Computer Science Principles/NSF projects on a national scale using MOOCs funded under the new Google CS4HS program. One presenter, who oversees outreach efforts for Exploring Computer Science, discusses a different, more hands-on and personal approach, to expanding via partnerships that include NSF-sponsored projects at local and state levels and Code.org partnerships with large school districts. These leaders report on work completed and the lessons learned that will impact ongoing and future work to help the community broaden participation in computer science while scaling and facilitating communities teachers and students.

SIGCSE'15, March 5–8, 2014, Kansas City, MO, USA.
ACM978-1-4503-2605-6/14/03.
http://dx.doi.org/10.1145/2676723.2677322

In the past, several special sessions, panels, and papers have presented the work of ECS and CSP [6, 7]. This session highlights new approaches that have already been implemented, and that will continue in the next years to reach communities of teachers at scale.

We will discuss the synergies and benefits enabled by these different approaches, the limits of each, and the lessons that can be used by others contemplating similar approaches. The sessions will provide an opportunity for input from the educational community, and how the community can actively contribute to these efforts.

2. The Big Picture (Owen Astrachan)

CSP and ECS are the two successful cornerstones of the CS10K initiative, working to scale nationally. Both projects were built on community input and provide integrated curriculum and professional development. They differ in several important ways that will be highlighted during the session. As an example, the CSP curriculum framework is designed to foster different approaches to realizing the learning objectives. The ECS curriculum allows local tuning, but is a day-to-day curriculum rather than a framework for developing curricula. During the special session we will discuss the different partnerships in play in advocating for and providing support for adoption of ECS, CSP, and other programs that seek to broaden participation in computer science teaching and learning.

Owen Astrachan is the PI of the CS Principles project, he works to help the community of educators working on this and related projects achieve their goals. He helps coordinate CSP initiatives for the CS10K Community of Practice and is a co-PI in a new grant to scale cooperative learning for CSP in 2015-2017.

3. Expanding CS Principles (Jeff Gray)

CS Principles (CSP) is a new Advanced Placement course designed and constructed by a community of educators. It is far more than an a traditional introduction to programming and the fundamental concepts of computing --- it is a rigorous, engaging, and approachable course designed so that each student will understand how these concepts are transforming the world we live in and how each student can use the concepts in their own lives, studies, and in collaborating to participate in that transformation [6]. This course is intended to broaden participation with the goal of a massive increase in both the number and diversity of students taking computer science courses at many levels. Reaching this goal requires an expansion in the type, number, and reach of schools and teachers involved in teaching computer science. Jeff Gray has led a statewide initiative to expand CSP in Alabama while serving as a pilot instructor for the College Board/NSF CSP project. The project he leads, CS4Alabama, develops master teachers to help expand the reach of the project within Alabama. Prof. Gray led a CS4HS-funded MOOC in the summer of 2014 using the same master teacher model. He will report on the challenges of delivering the MOOC, the differences between statewide and national scale, and plans for ongoing work with scaling cooperative learning to every CSP teacher.

Jeff Gray is the PI on the NSF CS4Alabama project, the designer, developer, and implementer of a CS4HS/CSP MOOC, and the PI on a new NSF grant to scale cooperative learning to CSP teachers from 2015-2017 .

4. ECS: Regional and National Expansion (Gail Chapman)

Exploring Computer Science (ECS) is an NSF-sponsored program deigned to address the historical lack of computer science curriculum, engaging pedagogy, and institutional support available for schools serving high numbers of students of color [refs].The daily lessons in the ECS curriculum are designed to promote an inquiry-based approach to teaching and learning foundational concepts in computer science. The core of the ECS curriculum highlights the computational practices and problem solving associated with doing computer science, rather than narrowly focusing only on particular syntax or tools. A key component of the Exploring Computer Science program is the extensive and ongoing professional development support, which helps foster a teacher learning community that focuses on issues of effective pedagogy and inclusive practices. In the six years since this course was first offered in LAUSD, enrollment statistics point to consistent success in reaching a highly diverse student population. The success of this course and the instructional design of the program for broadening participation in computing can serve as a model for other districts and local regions looking to expand computer science education. Since 2011, the Exploring Computer Science program has been implemented in multiple areas of the US. Initially these partners were funded via NSF projects. In 2013-14, ECS began partnering with Code.org to implement the ECS program within Code.org partner districts. Currently, ECS programs exist in 13 different regions, including the three largest school districts in the country: New York, Los Angeles, and Chicago. With expansion comes challenges. We will discuss lessons learned about how programs can scale effectively while maintaining program integrity and building a sustainable foundation. Gail Chapman is the director of outreach for ECS. She is one of the designers of the ECS curriculum and the ECS Professional Development model that includes developing facilitators who can expand the reach of ECS PD.

Gail Chapman is one of the designers of the ECS curriculum and leads the ECS Professional Development. She helps develop facilitators who can expand the reach of ECS PD.

5. Expanding CS Principles (Ralph Morelli)

The CS Principles course has been designed to broaden participation in computer science education with an accessible, engaging curriculum and an assessment designed to encourage and facilitate an equitable and student-centered approach. Ralph Morelli designed and implemented an expansive CSP course in Connecticut, with expansion to Massachusetts. This project is grounded in a blended PD model, but with extensive face-to-face contact. In 2014 he developed a CS4HS-funded MOOC to expand the reach of the MobileCSP project he oversees.

Ralph Morelli is the PI on the NSF/MobileCSP project, designer, developer, and implementer of a CS4HS/CSP MOOC, and a key contributor to the most recent version of AppInventor, an online,drag-and-drop programming environment for creating Android apps.

6. Intended Audience

This special session is designed for all educators interested in broadening participation in computer science teaching, particularly in high school, but the lessons of the projects here extend beyond high school to post-secondary institutions. The methods and lessons from scaling both ECS and CSP have included best practices in educational research, in using established pedagogical approaches designed to change how students learn, and in providing professional development opportunities for teachers will be discussion topics that transcend their particulars in the case of Computer Science Principles and Exploring Computer Science. The partnerships represented in this special session continue a community-driven collaboration to support adoption by many different groups at scale.

7. REFERENCES

[1] J. Goode and G. Chapman. (2013). *Exploring Computer Science.*

[2] J. Margolis, R. Estrella, J. Goode, J. J. Holme, and K. Nao, *Stuck in the shallow end: Education, race, and computing*: MIT Press, 2008.

[3] J. Goode and J. Margolis, "Exploring Computer Science: A Case Study of School Reform," *ACM Transactions on Computing Education,* vol. 11, 2011.

[4] O. Astrachan and R. B. Osborne. (2012) Computer Science Principles: portfolio-based assessment. *ACM SIGCSE Bulletin*. 4.

[5] A. Arpaci-Dusseau, O. Astrachan, D. Barnette, M. Bauer, M. Carrell, R. Dovi, B. Franke, C. Gardner, J. Gray, J. Griffin, R. Kick, A. Kuemmel, R. Morelli, D. Muralidhar, R. B. Osborne, and C. Uche, "Computer Science Principles: Analysis of a Propsed Advanced Placement Course," in *SIGCSE Technical Symposium on Computer Science Education*, Denver, CO, 2013.

[6] B. Franke, J. Century, M. Lach, C. Wilson, M. Guzdial, G. Chapman, and O. Astrachan, "Expanding Access to K-12 Computer Science Education: Research on the Landscape of Computer Science Professional Development," in *SIGCSE Technical Symposium on Computer Science Education*, Denver, CO, 2013.

SPOCs: What, Why, and How

Janet Burge
Wesleyan University
Dept. of Mathematics and Computer Science
jburge@wesleyan.edu

Armando Fox (moderator)
UC Berkeley
Dept. of Electrical Engineering and Computer Science
Faculty Advisor, UC Berkeley MOOCLab
fox@cs.berkeley.edu

Dan Grossman
University of Washington
Dept. of Computer Science and Engineering
djg@cs.washington.edu

Gerald Roth (organizer)
Vanderbilt University
Dept. of Electrical Engineering and Computer Science
j.roth@vanderbilt.edu

Joe Warren
Rice University
Dept. of Computer Science
jwarren@rice.edu

Categories and Subject Descriptors
K.3.2 [**Computer and Education**]: Computers and Information Science Education.

General Terms
Human factors, Design.

Keywords
Online lectures, MOOCs, blended courses, SPOCs, flipped classroom.

1. SUMMARY
Many CS instructors are embracing MOOCs by creating their own course offering on one of the major MOOC platforms. Along with MOOCs has come a debate about their effect on academia. But rather than discussing MOOCs as a stand-alone entity, we want to discuss the usage of MOOCs to augment normal lecture classes. In such cases, instructors are supplementing their live lectures with on-line lectures which are often produced by leading experts of the field. Fox refers to these as SPOCs: *small private online courses* [1].

The marriage of live lectures and MOOC materials has the potential of maximizing both their strengths while minimizing some of their perceived weaknesses. On the one hand you have a live instructor who has a vested interest in conveying course material in the best way possible. An instructor who lectures to the students on a regular basis and keeps them on task. An instructor who holds office hours where students can get face-to-face help when needed. And on the other hand you have high quality lectures available 24 hours a day that students can watch as many times as desired. You have well vetted homework assignments that have powerful auto-graders to grade them.

This panel is made up of CS faculty members who have used MOOC materials to augment their courses, not replace them. In some cases the MOOC material constitutes the bulk of the course, while in other cases it may just be a small portion of the class. In some cases the MOOC materials were created by the instructors themselves, while in other cases the instructors are using MOOCs produced by others.

The panel will address the logistics of such a course, and will share experiences, both good and bad, about running such a course. In the end, we hope to encourage more to consider leveraging the power of MOOC platforms to augment their own courses.

SIGCSE '15, Mar 04-07 2015, Kansas City, MO, USA
ACM 978-1-4503-2966-8/15/03.
http://dx.doi.org/10.1145/2676723.2677331

2. JANET BURGE
I have not produced a MOOC myself but I have used MOOCs produced by others in my teaching. Most recently, I am using Armando Fox and David Patterson's Software Engineering as a Service SPOC in my Fall 2014 software engineering course. The SPOC allows the students to access lecture videos, quizzes, and homework assignments. I am not using the SPOC to completely flip my course—a prior experience using Coursera videos to teach Machine Learning left me feeling somewhat disconnected from the course material. Instead, I'm doing most of the lectures myself, while making the SPOC lectures available to either reinforce topics already covered in class or to cover material that I did not have time to go over in class. I also hope that this approach keeps the workload within reason for the students—a danger with the flipped classroom is that the outside of class work can become burdensome if lectures are watched outside of class in addition to projects and homework. Faculty who enjoy and are effective at using lecture in their courses can still benefit from MOOC activities by choosing which aspects they want to use to supplement their own materials.

3. ARMANDO FOX (moderator)
Armando, as the faculty advisor of the UC Berkeley MOOCLab, has a unique vantage point from which to view the usage and

effects of MOOCs on college classes. He will strictly be acting as the moderator for this panel discussion.

4. DAN GROSSMAN

As the instructor for a popular MOOC on Programming Languages (https://www.coursera.org/course/proglang) that has now been offered three times, my primary focus and motivation has been creating and maintaining a high-quality learning experience for MOOC participants. However, the experience has also been enriched by many side benefits of creating public online course materials, notably the ability for others -- and myself -- to use the materials in delivering their own on-campus courses.

For myself, I have moved quite conservatively with regard to ideas like "flipping the classroom" --- my in-classroom activities, while encouraging student interaction, still closely mirror the lecture videos and reading notes provided in the MOOC. But having the materials still adds new flexibility that may seem minor to an outsider but makes a real difference for the students and myself. Just the 7-12 minute videos covering the course content allows for:

- Students who miss class, are confused, or struggle with English can re-watch the videos. Pause, rewind, and change speed are three features my in-classroom teaching will never have for individuals.
- Providing optional more challenging material for higher-performing students (or additional examples for struggling students, though I have done less of that).
- Not having to rush at the end of class. I have said a couple times with 10 minutes to go on Friday, "That's a great question. I'm going to answer it but that means we won't get through what you need for the last problem for the homework due on Tuesday. We'll do that material on Monday but for those of you who need to finish the homework this weekend, see the relevant video."
- The auto-grader makes valuable TA time more efficient, though TAs still look at each assignment and grade by hand, just using the auto-grader results as a guide for what to look for.

I view my materials as a community resource to be leveraged where convenient. I have hewn to an extreme position of making my materials freely available to any instructor to modify in any way he/she desires (I have ignored any licensing/legal issues and gotten away with it so far). In this way, I hold myself to two standards: (1) that the goal should be to help improve computing education by complementing other materials and approaches, and (2) that as much as I prefer all the exact details of my presentation, others who modify or subset my materials need the space to experiment with their own potential improvements.

The two downsides I see to leveraging MOOC materials are: (1) It provides a disincentive to evolve a course: The materials are time-consuming to create and modify, so I and others may be less inclined to improve something or add something new that "isn't in the videos and auto-grader". (2) Once thousands of MOOC participants have completed a programming assignment, it is likely infeasible to keep good solutions hard to find via web search, yet creating SPOC variants that are harder to cheat on is additional work and benefits less from the robustness of the MOOC variants.

5. GERALD ROTH

This past fall semester I taught a junior-level class (Programming Languages) that utilized a closed course on Coursera to deliver some lectures and assignments to my students. Only the students enrolled in my on-campus class had access to this private class on Coursera. The material itself was Dan Grossman's Programming Languages course that is offered on Coursera, but we went through the material on a schedule that I established for my course. It was an interesting exercise just to get all the approvals to allow this to happen.

This online portion of the course constituted about half of the entire course. While the students were utilizing these materials, we met as a class once a week for open discussion and live demonstrations that supplemented the online material. For the other half of the semester, I lectured as I normally would on topics not covered by the Coursera class, such as the history of programming languages, defining language structure & context free grammars, logic programming & Prolog, memory management issues, runtime systems, etc.

6. JOE WARREN

In my opinion, the potential impact of MOOCs on on-campus education is tremendous. The Department of Computer Science at Rice University offers a sequence of three coordinated MOOCs on first-year CS that cover the "Fundamentals of Computing". This sequence of MOOCs is roughly based on the same material covered by freshman CS majors at Rice.

Our on-campus classes have been improved in several ways by the availability of these MOOCs. First, we have used the online content (video, machine-graded quizzes, etc.) to flip the classroom and focus in-class time on problem-solving session in small groups. Second, we have developed several innovation tools, such as CodeSkulptor (http://www.codeskulptor.org/), that are now being used extensively in our on-campus versions of these classes. Finally, these on-campus classes have access to a collection of highly-polished materials that have been used by tens of thousands of students.

Incorporating portions on the content, tools, and methodology used in these MOOCs has allowed our on-campus classes to cope with an explosion in class size (200-300%) while maintaining the high-quality education that Rice prides itself on.

7. REFERENCES

[1] Fox, A. From MOOCs to SPOCs. *Commun. ACM* 56, 12 (Dec. 2013)

Technology We Can't Live Without!

Daniel D. Garcia (moderator)
University of California, Berkeley
777 Soda Hall
Berkeley, CA 94720
+1 (510) 517-4041
ddgarcia@cs.berkeley.edu

Eric Allatta
Academy for Software Engineering
40 Irving Pl
New York, NY 10003
+1 (212) 253-3299
eallatta@afsenyc.org

Manuel Pérez-Quiñones
Virginia Tech
2202 Kraft Drive
Blackburg, VA 24060
+1 (540) 231-2646
perez@cs.vt.edu

Jeff Solin
Lane Tech College Prep High School
2501 W. Addison St.
Chicago, IL 60618
+1 (773) 592-3477
jeff@solinsystems.com

Categories and Subject Descriptors
K.3.2 [**Computer and Information Science Education**]: Computer science education

General Terms
Experimentation

Keywords
Computer science education, technology and teaching

1. SUMMARY

The pace of technology for use in computing education is staggering. In the last five years, the following technologies have completely transformed our teaching: *Piazza*, *Google Docs*, *PandaGrader* (now *GradeScope*), *YouTube*, *Doodle*, *Skype*, *Google Hangout*, *Khan Academy,* etc. Hardware has also played a part; we love our *Zoom H2 digital voice recorder* (for CD-quality lecture audio), *Blue Yeti USB mike* (for audio / videoconferences), and *iClickers* (for engaging students in class).

This panel is an outgrowth of the *Technology that Educators of Computing Hail (TECH)* Birds-Of-a-Feather session that we've held at SIGCSE for seven years. It will provide a chance for seasoned high school and university educators to show you the technologies that have "bubbled to the top", what problems they solve, and why they are so valuable. Like concert musicians, presenters will give live demonstrations and reveal the particular configuration options required to make their technology "sing". We hope this forum will allow the chance to dive deeply into the common use cases of these technologies, and explain how others can adopt them at their institutions.

SIGCSE'15, March 4–7, 2015, Kansas City, MO, USA.
ACM 978-1-4503-2966-8/15/03.
http://dx.doi.org/10.1145/2676723.2677336

2. DANIEL D. GARCIA

Piazza is an incredibly useful and powerful Question-and-Answer website for outside-of-class discussions among students and instructors [1]. Whenever a question is posted, there is a "student answer" area and an "instruction answer" area. Each behaves like a wiki, allowing a team of instructors (or TAs) to refine the official instructor answer, and all the students to contribute to the student response. If the student answer is perfect, instructors can "bless" the answer with a simple click, saving the need to answer the question themselves. It keeps track of contributions (posts read, notes and questions asked, and answers provided) so instructors can give credit at the close of the term for participation and altruism. It allows students and instructors to control how often they receive updates, but also allows the instructor to overwrite those settings to broadcast important announcements to students' email. Instructors have full control, can edit and delete anyone's posts, and upload assignments and resources so the class' Piazza page can serve as a one-stop-shop. It supports LaTeX for typesetting expressions in math-heavy classes. It remembers what questions you've answered and highlights the ones you haven't yet. It also sports a mobile app, which allows you to ask and answer questions on the go. It replaced *four* different LMS tools/websites, simplifying my life incredibly.

GradeScope (formerly Pandagrader) is a website for grading exams and homework that has fundamentally changed how we grade student exams [2]. After a template is set up to indicate where on each page to find responses, all student exams have their staples cut off, scanned into PDFs, and imported into the system. An army of graders can collaboratively and iteratively build a grading rubric of checkboxes (that either count up or down), and assign points and commentary (explanations, mini-tutorials, etc.) to each feature. You can grade a hundred exams, then decide to change the point value of a particular answer, and the system remembers what students got it wrong (or right) and updates their grades instantly. The moment grading is done, all students can be immediately notified via email. All questions that were missed are indicated, with the commentary. Requesting a re-grade for a problem is as easy as following a link in their email. Statistics are automatically generated about who missed what question to investigate misconceptions and correlations. Finally, exporting grades is as simple as a click of a button. In summary, the system has fundamentally changed how I approach exam grading; love it!

3. ERIC ALLATTA

Many teachers are aware of the power of the Google Apps For Education (GAFE) platform [3]. It provides a suite of powerful organizational and collaborative tools that can facilitate many functions of an organization. Secondary schools are extremely complex environments that need to be run on thin technological resources and a minimal staff. What's less-known is that GAFE also offers an extremely powerful software-as-a-service platform that allows for the automation of a myriad of app functions. A community of developers has taken on the GAFE scripting space to develop a layer of nimble programs that can be added on to regular Google Apps. Emails can be automatically generated from spreadsheets, documents can be shared with a roster of individuals, calendar events can be automated to respond to form submissions. Essentially, all of the organization work of school-wide systems and in-classroom assignment management can be accomplished through a combination of these scripts.

Google Apps Scripts have evolved a more formal interface called *add-ons* that lower the entry point for installing and getting automations up and running in a school. A whole new population of teachers that was intimidated by the original script gallery interface now have a familiar "store" view with persistent data storage and memory of previous settings. Some of the scripts that have emerged as add-ons have names that make us grin and remember them: Doctopus, Autocrat, Flubaroo, g(Math), gClassFolders and siteMaestro. Many more are still available in the old Google Sheets product and installable scripts, accessible through the Scripts Gallery. Together, the Doctopus add-on and Goobric Chrome extension create a comprehensive assignment distribution and grading system. Teachers can create, distribute and grade an assignment, automated templated emails, and produce redundant populations of rubric-based scoring data.

Schools are building out entire management systems using these tools, and teachers are bringing them into the classroom and innovating in a thousand ways. With the creation of the CS Principles course we need systems that are flexible enough to respond to the unique needs of individual schools and classrooms through a system of user-friendly automations built on a ubiquitous and powerful enterprise productivity suite.

4. MANUEL PÉREZ-QUIÑONES

Prototype On Paper (POP) is a mobile app that allows users to take pictures of sketches of user interface prototypes and build navigation on top of them [4]. The navigation is very simple, consisting mostly of identifying regions on one screen that when tapped will transition to another screen. The result is that it is very easy to create "live" prototypes, all the skills needed are literally drawing an interface, taking a picture and doing a simple point and click to connect these pictures. The result is an animated application with navigation. The beauty of POP for education is that students can draw the interface on the board, in their notebooks and even in a drawing program on their laptop. In some activities, we can do simple sketches on the board, drawing several steps in an interaction. Then we can take pictures, connect them, and quickly get a sense of the interactivity of the proposed idea. Group work in class is easily supported as students can work on the board or on paper, draw many different mockups and then connect them with POP. I have used POP in undergraduate, graduate courses and in outreach seminars about computing for middle school girls [5]. A similar application with slightly different functionality is the Marvel app [6].

Most of us these days use a laptop in the classroom to project slides to the class. *Reflector* allows you to stream any iOS device or MacOSX computer in class to that laptop [7]. I use it to mirror my tablet's display when I walk around, and to allow a student's computer or smart device to drive the screen. It also supports multiple "senders", so two students can present their work at the same time, side by side, to compare alternative designs.

These two technologies, when used together, produce wonderful results. They allow design discussions in classrooms to become dynamic, interactive and collaborative. Add screen-recording software and you have an automatic capture of all of the interaction in the classroom, including student presentations, without changing cables for projections or playing musical chairs.

5. JEFF SOLIN

Prototype's *Cloud9* combines a powerful online code editor with a full Ubuntu workspace in the cloud [8]. In the K-12 environment, teachers are often locked out of having administrator privileges on their classroom computers and work computers. Sometimes updating their IDE is not an option, or the OS is old enough that it doesn't support the current IDE. There have been a few online web-based IDEs showing up, but none have worked better for me than Cloud9. With the free account you are given one private workspace and unlimited public workspaces. The workspaces can be shared between students and with teachers and allow for real-time collaboration similar to how concurrent editing in Google Docs works.

The IDE handles HTML5, CSS, Python, Node.js, Django, C++, Rails, PHP, Meteor, and more. It even allows you to use familiar key mappings like Vi. When working on HMTL and CSS content, you have a live preview window built right into the IDE. All of these features allow for an always-up-to-date IDE that is as full-featured as most desktop applications, and has the added bonus of allowing students to login to their account from any computer to pick up right back up where they left off. In my classes, each student has a Cloud9 account, shares edit permissions with me (so I can help them when needed), and then submits a Google Form to me with a link to their profile.

6. REFERENCES

[1] NY Times. *Homework Help Site Has a Social Networking Twist.* July, 2011. `www.nytimes.com/2011/07/04/technology/04piazza.html`

[2] Gradescope. *Gradescope (formerly PandaGrader).* September, 2014. `www.pandagrader.com`

[3] GAFE. `www.google.com/enterprise/apps/education`

[4] Prototype On Paper. Website. `http://popapp.in`

[5] Robison, A.; Perez-Quinones, M. A. (2014) Underrepresented middle school girls: on the path to computer science through paper prototyping. In Proceedings of SIGCSE '14 Proceedings of the 45th ACM technical symposium on Computer science education, pp. 97-102. ACM New York, NY, USA

[6] Marvel App. Website. `https://marvelapp.com/`

[7] Air Squirrels. *Reflector*, `www.airsquirrels.com/reflector`

[8] Cloud9. Website. `http://c9.io`

DEMONSTRATION SESSION

JavaTutor: An Intelligent Tutoring System that Adapts to Cognitive and Affective States during Computer Programming

Joseph B. Wiggins, *North Carolina State University*
Kristy Elizabeth Boyer, *North Carolina State University*
Alok Baikadi, *North Carolina State University*
Aysu Ezen-Can, *North Carolina State University*
Joseph F. Grafsgaard, *North Carolina State University*
Eun Young Ha, *North Carolina State University*
James C. Lester, *North Carolina State University*
Christopher M. Mitchell, *North Carolina State University*
Eric N. Wiebe, *North Carolina State University*
Contact: jbwiggi3@ncsu.edu

Introductory computer science courses cultivate the next generation of computer scientists. The impressions students take away from these courses are crucial, setting the tone for the rest of the students' computer science education. It is known that students struggle with many concepts central to computer science, struggles that could be alleviated in part through hands-on practice and individualized instruction. However, even the best existing instructional practices do not facilitate individualized hands-on support for students at large. We have built JavaTutor, an intelligent tutoring system for introductory computer science, which works alongside students to support them through both cognitive (skills and knowledge) and affective (emotion-based) feedback. JavaTutor aims to make advances in interactive, scalable student support. JavaTutor's behaviors were developed within a novel framework that leverages machine learning to acquire tutorial strategies from data collected within tutorial sessions between novice students and experienced human tutors. This demo presents an overview of the data-driven development of JavaTutor and shows how JavaTutor assesses and responds to students' contextualized needs. It is hoped that JavaTutor will help to usher in a new generation of tutorial systems for computer science education that adapt to individual students based not only on incoming student knowledge, but on a broad range of other student characteristics.

ACM Categories & Descriptors: K.3.2 [**Computers & Education**]: Computer and Information Sciences Education - *Computer Science Education*

Keywords: Intelligent Tutoring Systems; CS1; Individualized Instruction

Acknowledgments: This work is supported in part by NSF (DRL-1007962).

DOI: http://dx.doi.org/10.1145/2676723.2691877

SIGCSE'15, March 4–7, 2015, Kansas City, MO, USA.
ACM 978-1-4503-2966-8/15/03.

MIST, The Mathematical Image Synthesis Toolkit

Eileen Fordham, *Grinnell College*
Halley Freger, *Grinnell College*
Amanda Hinchman-Dominguez, *Grinnell College*
Alexander Mitchell, *Grinnell College*
Daniel Rebelsky, *Grinnell College*
Victoria Tsou, *Grinnell College*
Earnest Wheeler, *Grinnell College*
Zoe Wolter, *Grinnell College*
Samuel A. Rebelsky, *Grinnell College*
Contact: rebelsky@grinnell.edu

MIST, the Mathematical Image Synthesis Toolkit, is an open-source, Web-based graphics application in which students develop skills in computational thinking and deepen their understanding of mathematical functions through creative play in making images. Using a drag-and-drop interface, students build functions that describe animated abstract images. These functions combine a few basic images (e.g., a horizontal blend, a vertical blend, and a time-based blend) using mathematical operators whose semantics are based on corresponding points in each image (e.g., MIST includes models for adding and multiplying colors). Students develop a variety of skills in computational thinking by using the small set of images and operations to develop complex images, not only images that the system challenges them to make but also images that they find themselves inspired to create and even images that their peers challenge them to build. MIST also incorporates a community of artists/learners. Images created in MIST are available to other MIST users to comment on and remix (provided the designer permits reuse). MIST community members may also create challenges for other community members and can curate "galleries" of images they find particularly engaging, interesting, or even useful as challenges for others. Users can also share their images via Facebook or "tweet" their recent creations. We find that this additional community further encourages students to develop new and interesting images.

ACM Categories & Descriptors: D.1.7 [Programming Techniques]: Visual Programming; J.5 [Arts and Humanities]; K.3.2 [Computers and Education]: Computer and Information Science Education–*Literacy*; K.8.1 [Personal Computing]: Application Packages–*Freeware/shareware, Graphics*

Keywords: Computational thinking; Social media; Animation; Functional programming; Web software; Open source

DOI: http://dx.doi.org/10.1145/2676723.2691878

Insights into Teaching and Learning: Reflections on MOOC Experiences

Janet Burge
Mathematics and Computer Science
Wesleyan University
Middletown, CT 06459
+1 860-685-2413
jburge@wesleyan.edu

ABSTRACT

There has been significant interest in MOOCs, both inside and outside the educational community. Some of this interest focuses on how they could be used to replace traditional brick-and-mortar education while others are interested in using them to supplement more traditional courses. Instructors can also use MOOCs to gain new insight into teaching and learning by taking on a student perspective. This paper describes how taking several MOOCs has given me a better understanding of student motivation, time commitment issues, and student perception of grading and describes how I am feeding this knowledge back into my own courses.

Categories and Subject Descriptors

K.3.2 [**Computers and Education**]: Computer science education

General Terms

Experimentation

Keywords

MOOCs; Flipped Classroom

1. INTRODUCTION

The educational community, as well as the popular press, has been abuzz about MOOCs (Massive Open On-line Courses) for several years now. They're commonly viewed as a "disruptive technology" whose predicted impact on education varies from competing with traditional university education [6][7][9][9], complementing it [2][13], or as being simply over-hyped [11][5]. There are a number of different MOOC providers and platforms out there but what they have in common is that they are designed to be taken entirely on-line by thousands of students at a time. This means that all assessment is either graded automatically (usually auto-graded programs and multiple-choice quizzes) or peer graded (where students are required to grade other students in order to receive credit). Some courses have a class instructor and/or TAs available in a discussion forum to answer questions while others appear to be running largely on auto-pilot. Some MOOCs are electronic versions of in-person college courses while others were developed specifically as MOOCs without a direct university counterpart. Those adapted from in-person courses usually have at least some of the assignments either removed or simplified so they can be scaled to potentially thousands of students.

SIGCSE '15, March 4–7, 2015, Kansas City, MO, USA

http://dx.doi.org/10.1145/2676723.2677243

Studies on who participates in MOOCs show that the majority of those enrolled are already fairly well-educated [1] and that students take courses for various reasons being nearly evenly split between taking the courses for fun (about half) to taking courses to enhance job skills (around 44%) [1]. The completion rates are typically low with a study of 29 MOOCs showing an average of 6.8 percent [10].

MOOCs can be a valuable resource to instructors. Some instructors have used them as part of a blended/hybrid classroom approach where material from the MOOCs is used to replace standard classroom lectures so that in-class time can be spent doing other things [3][4][8]. In addition to direct use of the material, MOOCs can also serve instructors in two very valuable ways. First, there's the direct use of gaining or refreshing knowledge on a new course topic. Computer science is a rapidly changing field and at some point all faculty are going to need to pick up new technologies to use in their courses. MOOCs are not the only resource available but unlike other on-line tutorials they have deadlines. Second, there's the insight gained into teaching and learning by participating in a course taught by others.

This paper will be discussing the second use—insight gained into teaching and learning based on my personal experiences participating in several MOOCs and dropping out of several more. The MOOCs will not be named (although some could probably be guessed fairly easily) because the intent is not to review or criticize specific instructors or instructional designs. All the courses were high quality products taught by experts in the subject area although they varied in how closely they managed to duplicate the rigor of an in-person college course (and some did not have that goal to start with).

The paper is organized as follows: Section 2 discusses some factors in what may motivate someone to complete a MOOC, Section 3 describes how taking a MOOC can help instructors view the material from a student's perspective, Section 4 provides some insights into grading, Section 5 summarizes what I feel were the important lessons learned from my MOOC experiences and Section 6 gives my conclusions.

2. MOTIVATION

One major requirement to succeed when taking a MOOC is the same as in taking any course—motivation. As mentioned earlier, MOOC drop-out rates are quite high [10]. I signed up for far many more MOOCs than I ended up completing. For the five MOOCs I did complete, there were a number of factors contributing to that success:

- Immediate need for the material. Three classes were on topics that I was planning on teaching within six months of completing the course. That was enough of an incentive to stick with the material even when there were time conflicts making it challenging. Courses on topics where I knew I would need to know the material but not quite yet were not completed.
- Engaging material and low time commitment. One MOOC had the winning combination of engaging lectures and very little work to do in order to earn the certificate. This MOOC was on social psychology not computer science so the only thing needed for a passing grade was to do well on some very easy quizzes. I do not feel I got as much out of this course as I did for courses where I had to spend more time mastering the material.
- Novelty of the medium and interest in the subject. The first MOOC I took was a literature course. In this case, I completed the course assignments but did not actually manage to watch all the lectures (so does that count as success?) although I did do all the readings. It also helped that I was on an academic sabbatical at the time.

For the MOOCS that I did not complete, there are some common reasons there as well:

- Over-commitment in signing up for too many courses. At one point I was signed up for three different courses. Only one was completed (the one started first).
- Lack of time. It is easy to sign up for a course that will be offered at some future (or unknown) time but then discover when the course actually starts that the timing just does not work. This is particularly a problem when a course is offered at the same time as the course professor's in-person courses and has the same semester start time as our own courses.
- Fear of failure. As professors we should be immune to the extrinsic motivation of certificates and test scores but I am not, and I suspect I am not alone in that. One course that I had stopped participating in fairly early had issues with the mid-term where they had to change the grading structure because many students had low scores and were threatening to drop out when it was clear they could not possibly get the certificate at the end.
- Boredom with watching videos. I made two unsuccessful attempts to take classes on a programming language that I knew I would need to teach in the future (but not immediate future). Watching videos explaining how a for loop worked and other concepts I already knew was painful (although there were some nuances I did not know so I did not want to just skip the videos and jump into the assignments). Obviously this is not the fault of the instructor – these details are critical to the intended audience for a CS0 class.

Motivation is a combination of value and expectancy [12] and this was born out in my experience. The courses I stuck with were ones where I was learning something that was useful in the near-term and those where I had a high confidence that I could successfully complete the class in the time I had available. High valued classes were stuck with even when time pressure was an issue but those that could be postponed to a later time were.

3. PERSPECTIVE

Taking on a student perspective is a valuable exercise. Certainly all of us have spent a lot of time as students but our student experiences, especially those of being undergraduates, recede into the distance more and more with each passing year. Taking an on-line course is a fairly low-risk way to experience being a student again and is certainly easier to fit into our schedules than registering for a real course at our own institution. Several things stood out to me during my student experience.

The discussion boards on Coursera were helpful in showing how students responded to the material and to how it was graded. This was particularly useful when looking at courses aimed at first-time programmers—I have never taught students at that level so it was valuable to see what the sticking points were for the assignments. Most MOOC platforms allow users to up or down-vote questions so it was easy to see what parts of an assignment were the most challenging or what kinds of answers and support were the most helpful.

It was also interesting to see student feedback on course workload and grading. The courses being free and not counting towards anyone's GPA did not keep participants from expressing their displeasure when they did not agree with a grade or the way quiz questions were worded. Peer grading feedback varied quite a bit in quality since participants varied in their backgrounds. Students were not supposed to post feedback received during the course but some did anyway and it was interesting to see feedback presented as an example of someone being "harsh" or "mean" that actually seemed quite fair and reasonable. Multiple choice quiz questions were also challenging – as a student I often was not sure what the goals of the question were (is it to test the topic in general or looking for nuances in definitions?) and lost more than a few points for not choosing the right question goal in providing my answer. This gave me a new sympathy with students who complained about questions being "tricky."

All the MOOCs I participated in used video lectures as a primary means of providing course lectures. Shorter segments worked considerably better – I was less likely to postpone (procrastinate) watching an 8 minute video than I was one that would take 25 minutes (or more). It still felt like the videos took more time to watch than their actual length. I hope that it's more engaging to attend a 60-80 minute long class than it was to watch the equivalent in video! Some classes sprinkled in mini-quizzes inside the video segments – those were very helpful in maintaining interest.

Time investment was a large concern when I was taking MOOCs. As with our students, I had to balance how much time I had available for the MOOC classes in competition with other classes (those I was teaching) as well as other things I needed to do. Class descriptions would state how much time they anticipated students would need to devote to the MOOC but those times were often very inaccurate. One MOOC estimated it would involve 3-5 hours of work a week. It turned out that the MOOC had 3-5 hours of video to watch every week, plus readings, plus an essay due that needed to link the video and readings (with citations), plus peer grading multiple essays from classmates. Even though the class was free and I could drop out without penalty, it was still annoying; if this was a class that I absolutely had to take, along with taking other courses, the miscalculated time estimate would have been a disaster.

Another area where time investment came into play was in trying to complete assignments with minimal guidance. Generally it's considered to be good for students to have to struggle to figure things out on their own and to have to work through difficulties but I have a new understanding of how frustrating this can really be when a couple of hints or clarifications in the instructions could have saved me hours and hours of time. Being able to ask for help on the forums was critical – in one case I found guidance on something that put me on the right course, in another I came to the answer on my own in the process of formulating the question. Seeing questions from other students was very encouraging as well—it felt good to be able to point someone in the right direction when they hit a strange problem that I had already fixed.

A third aspect of time investment was in how the readings, lectures, and assignments connected with how grades were assigned. One of the courses was a literature class where students read books, wrote essays, and then, after the essays were due, the video lectures were released where the professor interpreted the texts. Grading for the course was entirely based on the essays. This meant that there was no direct grade reward for watching the videos. Towards the end of the class, when I had to do some traveling and had some other commitments, I stopped watching the videos completely. Maybe watching the videos would have helped me with essays for other (unrelated) readings? I think that was how it was supposed to work but I was able to get by without it. I remember wishing that there were at least some simple quizzes on the readings as an incentive and reward for watching all of them and also remember wondering how many other students were just skipping them entirely.

4. GRADING

One of the biggest challenges for a MOOC is grading strategies that scale to thousands of students. In the courses I took, this is handled in several ways: multiple choice quizzes and exams, auto-graded programming assignments, and peer grading. While "live" classes have many more options, we still rely at least occasionally on some of these techniques and it was interesting to see how they worked as a student.

Multiple choice exams are always challenging to put together with a big concern being that we do not want the answers to seem too obvious. In a MOOC, students generally have access to the entire internet while taking their quizzes so this is even more of a challenge. As a result, quizzes can end up being fiendishly tricky. Many of the questions would involve choosing multiple answers ("which of these…"). When quizzes gave partial credit for catching some of the answers (and not giving wrong ones) it felt a lot more fair than quizzes where if one element was missed the entire answer was wrong. The frustrating thing about multiple choice questions was that the penalties for missing (or misinterpreting) some nuance of a topic were high yet there was no way to give credit for mostly understanding something.

The auto-graded programming assignments were great from both the student and teacher perspective. In the two courses I took that utilized these, the students were allowed multiple submissions so they could correct problems and get a higher score. This was very helpful, especially in cases where there were minor misinterpretations of the instructions that became instantly clear based on grader feedback. There is a small risk that in lower-level assignments it might be possible to hack your way to a correct answer using multiple submissions but this seemed to be out weighed by the value in being able to correct problems and misunderstandings.

The peer grading was one of the more frustrating parts of being a MOOC student. The quality of feedback varied widely and, more importantly, it felt like it was not really possible to learn what the course expectations were since every reader could potentially be looking for different things. I noticed that scores tended to just average to the middle. There is some value in getting feedback from different perspectives, and it was very interesting to read work by other students and compare it to my own, but I did not like having feedback from randomly assigned peers be the only source of evaluation. The discussion boards had many students expressing a desire to give feedback on the quality of the peer grading. While grading someone who is grading you has problems (is the feedback evaluation low because the feedback is poor or because the grade given is lower than desired?) there were issues with meaningless feedback. I did not experience this myself but some students had feedback that read "one two three four" etc. where it was obvious that the grader wanted credit for having done the peer evaluation without actually doing any work.

5. TAKE-AWAYS

I started taking MOOC courses for fun and for a way to refresh my knowledge in areas I wanted to teach in or planned to each in. I ended up coming away with several things to keep in mind in future courses (and some I have already applied):

1. **Multiple choice tests do not need to be that (deliberately) difficult to test student knowledge.** I taught a course in requirements engineering with a quiz for every class and got a surprisingly wide grade distribution even when I gave quite a few questions where I thought the answers would be obvious or guessable. I also changed how I graded them to give partial credit if answers were partially correct. Unlike in a MOOC, students taking exams in class do not usually have "open internet."

2. **Be careful with the time commitment expected from students.** This can be tricky with programming courses where the time required can be somewhat non-deterministic (one odd bug can turn a four hour assignment into a fourteen hour one). It is important to provide stronger encouragement for students to ask for help if things seem to be getting out of hand. The value of struggling to find an answer looks very different when you are the one struggling than when you are the one praising the results at the end.

3. **Visibility into struggles of others is also useful, as is having to clearly ask for help.** I had observed the phenomenon for years where a student would write me an e-mail explaining a problem they were having with their code only to see them follow it half an hour later with an e-mail saying they had just figured out the problem and have considered deliberately not responding right away to encourage these "ah hah" moments that often come after having to explain the problem to someone else. Using forums to pose questions to the instructor and classmates is another

excellent strategy for this. While there is the risk that someone posts too much of their own code (which did happen in some of the MOOCs) the value outweighs the risk. I plan to offer instruction on using forums and posing questions.

4. **If we want (expect) the students to do something outside of class then we should incorporate it into assessment.** On the surface this is pretty obvious. What I gained from experiencing this myself is that if a student does not do the reading because they can get away without doing the reading it does not necessarily mean they do not see the value in doing it, they may simply be having to trade off doing that versus something else that will impact their grade.

5. **Offering multiple submissions on programming projects is very useful.** The down-side to this approach is that students could use it as a way to "code to the grader" but the advantage is that it gives them incentive to fix mistakes rather than just submitting something they "think" is right and find out later it is not. Immediate grading and feedback can help point out incorrect assumptions with either the task or the instructions and give the students more opportunity for learning. Limiting the number of submissions or time between submissions might make students less likely to try to hack their way to creating code that provides the right answers.

6. **Peer grading can be useful and save instructor time but it should not be a major means of assessment or the only feedback given.** The courses that used peer grading had assessment done by multiple peers and usually dropped the lowest scores but it still did not seem as useful as receiving more consistent feedback from a single instructor. It is also important to consider the time required to do peer grading when assessing the workload required for the course. Providing useful feedback is not easy.

7. **Grading harshness is subjective.** Students may take grades more personally than instructors realize. Using a rubric may make it less personal but even then the students often need some explanation of why their work fit into the grading scale where it did.

8. **Even great lecturers have trouble keeping student attention.** It was very difficult to maintain concentration for some of the longer videos. Most courses had broken the lectures into smaller pieces but some still had segments more than 20 minutes in length and it was very hard to stay focused and engaged. Embedded questions and quizzes helped some and would probably be even more effective in a live lecture setting.

Another thing worth noting is that these observations did not all come solely from taking technical courses—some were from non-technical ones taken just out of curiosity.

6. CONCLUSIONS

Some faculty view MOOCs as competitors, others as instructional aids, some dismiss them as having little value. Many of the MOOCs I participated in would need supplemental assignments or exams before I would consider them to be complete college courses. The courses I took that were based on in-person college classes had all been modified to reduce the number of, or length of, assignments. Still, the experience of taking them was quite valuable. In addition to the reasons listed earlier, I also appreciated the opportunity to observe other instructors "in action." As a general rule, those offering MOOCs are considered experts in the subject matter taught and it was a treat to see material so well presented. It was also comforting to see the occasional slip-up where a typo made it onto a slide or someone stumbled over their words when presenting. It is hard to find the time to commit to a class but it is certainly a worthwhile experience for both professional and personal reasons and I, for one, am happy that we have the opportunity to do so.

7. ACKNOWLEDGMENTS

Many thanks to the faculty members and institutions that are willing to put themselves out there and offer MOOCs.

8. REFERENCES

[1] Christensen, G., Steinmetz, A., Alcorn, B., Bennett, A., Woods, D., and Emanuel, E.J. 2013. The MOOC Phenomenon: Who Takes Massive Open Online Courses and Why? (November 6).

[2] Connolly, R. 2013. There's a MOOC For That: How My Grad Students Complement Our Curriculum with MOOCs, MOOC News and Reviews, May 6

[3] Fisher, D. 2012. Warming up to MOOCs, Chronicle of Higher Education, November 6.

[4] Fox, A. 2013. From MOOCs to SPOCs: How MOOCs Can Strengthen Academia, Communications of the ACM, 56(12), 38-40.

[5] Greenstein, D. Innovation Exhaustion and a Path to Moving Forward, Inside Higher Ed, July 1, 2013

[6] Lenox, M. 2013. The Imminent Shakeout? Disruptive Innovation and Higher Education, Forbes, March 29.

[7] Lewin, T. 2013. California Bill Would Force Colleges to Honor Online Classes, New York Times, March 13.

[8] Martin, F.. 2012. Will massive open online courses change how we teach?. *Commun. ACM* 55, 8 (August 2012), 26-28

[9] Newsome, J. 2012. MOOCs: Online courses might change face of higher education, News and Record, 13 October.

[10] Parr, C. 2013. Not Staying the Course, Inside Higher Ed, May 10.

[11] Rivard, R. Beyond MOOC Hype, Inside Higher Ed, July 9, 2013

[12] Wigfield, A., Eccles, J. 2000. Expectancy—Value Theory of Achievement Motivation. Conteporary Educational Psychology, 25(1) (January 2000), 68-81

[13] Young, J. 2013. Will MOOCs Change the Way Professors Handle the Classroom?, Chronicle of Higher Education, November 7.

What Influences CS Faculty to Adopt Teaching Practices?

Lecia Barker
University of Texas at Austin
School of Information
1616 Guadalupe Suite #5.202
Austin, TX USA
lecia@ischool.utexas.edu

Christopher Lynnly Hovey
Northeastern University
500 Holmes Hall
360 Huntington Ave
Boston, MA USA
hovey.c@northeastern.edu

Jane Gruning
University of Texas at Austin
School of Information
1616 Guadalupe Suite #5.202
Austin, TX USA
jane.gru@gmail.com

ABSTRACT
Despite widespread development, research, and dissemination of teaching and curricular practices that improve student retention and learning, faculty often do not adopt them. This paper describes the first findings of a two-part study to improve understanding of adoption of teaching practices and curriculum by computer science faculty. The paper closes with recommendations for designers and developers of teaching innovations hoping to increase their chance of adoption.

Categories and Subject Descriptors
K.3.2 [**Computer and Information Science Education**]

General Terms
Human Factors

Keywords
Adoption of teaching innovations; Retention; Dissemination

1. INTRODUCTION
Retaining students in computer science (CS) is important, not only because of the lifelong benefits to students and the added boon to the U.S. economy, but also because each admitted student represents a substantial investment of time and resources from their departments. Since admissions criteria only rate entry characteristics and not the in-major academic and social experiences shown to better predict retention [3,21,35], a student who leaves is a wasted opportunity for another, potential student.

Women's participation in CS remains a serious problem. In public and not-for-profit private institutions, women were awarded only 13 percent of all CS bachelor's degrees in the U.S. in 2013 [25]. Underrepresentation in computing is a public concern, affecting the availability of an adequate, stable computing workforce, global competitiveness, defense, health, national security, and social justice. Women in CS leave the major more frequently than men despite their high performance [6,19,31,33].

CS educational research shows that teaching and curricular changes could eliminate much attrition, while improving outcomes for all students [1,2,7,15,22]. Despite the wealth of innovative teaching practices that have been demonstrated to retain students, many of those practices are still not known, adopted, or adapted by computer science faculty broadly. We report here on the first phase of a triangulated study of factors that encourage and discourage the adoption of teaching and curricular practices among undergraduate faculty in CS. First, we briefly review literature on adoption, our research methods, and sample profile. We then present results and conclude with recommendations for improving adoption.

SIGCSE '15, March 4–7, 2015, Kansas City, MO, USA

http://dx.doi.org/10.1145/2676723.2677282

2. SCHOLARSHIP ON ADOPTION
We build on findings from empirical studies and theories of innovation adoption. By *innovation*, we mean a practice or process new to the adopter [32]. In this section, we briefly review literature on the influences on change in teaching practices.

2.1 Organization-Level Research
An organizational context surrounds and influences the individuals who adopt innovative teaching practices. Organizational influences on faculty include organization structure, culture, climate, and reward system [17,34]. Research often faults the higher education reward system as the main barrier to teaching reform [10,24]. In research universities, faculty members who develop and implement teaching innovations do so "at their own risk, [since] these time-consuming projects take faculty members away from ... research and publication" [30]. Departmental and institutional cultures and policies may encourage adoption by making risk acceptable. For example, in many institutions, developing excellence in teaching is at least espoused, and sometimes promoted (e.g., [5]). However, a departmental constraint on adoption is the degree to which course content is controlled at the department or higher level [27].

2.2 Individual-Level Characteristics
Individual-level characteristics that influence innovation adoption include awareness of and receptiveness to new ideas; values and attitudes toward certain types of innovations and toward students; pedagogical content knowledge; and perceptions of costs and benefits relative to existing practices [9,18,20,29,36,37]. While CS faculty do not dismiss research evidence about teaching practices, it may not influence their decisions to adopt, as is conventionally assumed [27]. Many faculty members use traditional (i.e., lecture-based) teaching methods because they are familiar, even when they have the opportunity to make changes [37]. Faculty who wish to try out new methods may lack materials for guiding them through successful implementation. Awareness and support alone are not enough to motivate adoption. When considering teaching innovations, most faculty members want to know the benefits for themselves and their students. Another powerful influence on adoption is how faculty conceive of their role as teachers (for a comprehensive review of this literature, see [18]). An assumption often made in education literature is that accomplishing change requires first understanding and changing

existing conceptions about one's role as a teacher, though the assumption that conceptual change precedes, rather than follows, adoption of innovative practices has been challenged [8].

2.3 External Social Networks and Movements

A social discourse [13] comprises all the discussion that goes on in society, including those at conferences, workshops, and in journal articles, letters to the editor, and editorial statements concerning such a theme. In computer science, for example, a 2012 SIGCSE keynote included the example of the "flipped" classroom [4], familiarizing hundreds of CS faculty with the concept. Similarly, pair programming caught on in many departments nationally after the publication of articles in popular venues and "how-to" guides on the subject [23,26,38,39,40]. While not all CS faculty attend educational conferences, those who do may return home with stories to tell about teaching approaches. Few studies have assessed awareness and change caused by trends or communication from social networks [14], yet social discourse about teaching practices may have influence, at least on those predisposed to adopt.

2.4 Framework for the Study of Adoption

We combined the influences of local organizational structure, individual beliefs and characteristics, and the influence of networks into a stage model of adoption, borrowing from Rogers and others [12,32,41]. The adoption process begins with awareness, then implementing, testing, and modifying an innovation. Deciding to make an innovation part of everyday practice is routinization or adoption. Our interview questions focused on awareness, trying practices out, and adopting.

3. RESEARCH METHODS AND SAMPLE

The results presented below are based on interviews and observation conducted with 66 CS faculty members teaching early courses in 36 postsecondary institutions across the U.S. Qualitative methods provide an in-depth understanding of human behavior and the influences of contexts in which it is embedded. The institutions were chosen to represent a diverse set of geographic locations, rankings, and viewpoints, including research universities, all-women, minority-serving, public, private, elite, two-year, four-year liberal arts, and technical institutes. Faculty rank varied from Ph.D. student instructors, part- and full-time teaching faculty to tenure-track faculty and chairs.

Interviews were semi-structured, prompting informants to talk about topics relevant to the framework described in 2.4, but also to express and expand upon what was most salient to them. Interview questions asked faculty to describe their teaching experience and background, number of students in classes, their role as teachers, and motivations for past and present teaching practices. All but eight interviews included a classroom observation. Observations helped interviewers visualize the contexts and practices interviewees described, including student behavior, technology available or used in classrooms, and physical spaces that enable or constrain teaching practices. Moreover, observation illuminated faculty reports of what they do in the classroom, since people do not always remember what they do or why. Also, the words faculty use are often ambiguous. For example, at an engineering school, when asked to reflect on what he had done that day in class, a professor said, "When it's a new concept, like today's, I am just like a traditional teacher. I explain what this concept is. How you can use it." In contrast, the observer noted that the professor began by addressing common misconceptions; related the concept to previous and future course themes; wrote and drew on the board while talking (which gave students time to write it, too); asked students questions, and commented on why an answer was or was not correct; and previewed the courses in which students could learn more about the concept, implying that he believed students were interested, not just that they should know the material. As noted in [18], linking observations to interviews is critical for interpretation. All interviews were recorded and transcribed. Detailed notes of interviews and observations were appended to the transcripts. The authors listened to and read the transcripts multiple times and coded them to identify answers to the questions addressed here.

4. RESULTS

4.1 How do Faculty Hear About Practices?

Motivated to solve a problem. Faculty often intentionally sought out teaching practices because they wanted to solve problems regarding student learning, student engagement, or to increase diversity. An assistant professor in an eastern Hispanic-serving institution sought ideas from her colleagues to improve her students' performance. She said, "For us it's very frustrating to have 50 percent failure rate or passing rate in a core course. We want to make sure that our students are well prepared and succeed in our program." A senior lecturer at a large, private, research school used robots as a "hook" for students with low programming experience, saying that it would "encourage them to spend the time that they need and get the most bang for the buck." On the other hand, a professor at a private liberal arts college who also wanted students to be able to see the results of their programming switched to an all-software environment using Processing, because of unpredictable battery problems of robots.

Many faculty members talked about the desire to increase student engagement, because they felt students were bored or inattentive in class. One adjunct described using jokes and connections to real-world issues for entertainment value. Similarly, a professor at an all-women's college described using examples that were more relevant to students' life experiences, saying, "Everybody has all these Instagrams and things like that, so in that course they actually learn how to manipulate images." In other cases, faculty responded directly to students' explicit comments and suggestions in teaching evaluations and in two cases, students asked professors outright to change the way they taught the course. Both professors subsequently switched from lecture-based teaching to interactive classrooms. Several interviewees identified problems with broader impact on the future of computing, suggesting that lecture-based teaching methods may deter certain groups of students from completing a CS degree.

Awareness through Funded and Institutional Initiatives. Many faculty found out about new teaching practices by participating in initiatives funded by the National Science Foundation, non-governmental foundations, and corporations. For example, an assistant professor at a Hispanic-serving institution went to "CAHSI conferences," funded by the NSF Broadening Participation in Computing program. Integrating a graphics approach into several courses was institutionalized at a southeastern university because of a funded project. At several institutions, funding from both corporations and the NSF led to the integration of robots into introductory courses. In a few cases, faculty mentioned administrative support for special initiatives at their institutions for the purposes of creating awareness and action. For example, a teaching center at one Midwestern university held a small conference with talks about improving teaching, exposing one professor to new ways of using teamwork in his class. A lecturer at a state teaching institution described hearing about innovative teaching methods while participating in a project funded by her university's teaching center. A new assistant professor in a small college described monthly participation in a sponsored reading group that met over lunch for a "free-for-all discussion" about best teaching practices. However, while all but one of our 66 interviewees said their institutions had centralized teaching support, very few had ever used them.

Expected and Unexpected Awareness from Conferences. Faculty talked about learning about teaching practices at conferences such as SIGCSE, ASEE, FIE, and the NCWIT Summit. In many cases, information that faculty encountered at conferences suggested a solution to a problem they were experiencing. For example, one professor said she found out "about pair programming when I was at the ACM conference… I had given a test and I was just destroyed over the grades I had got, so I said, 'Ok I'm going to try this idea that I heard about.'" Another inverted his course based on a presentation at ASEE, saying, "I was reacting to what had happened to me in my first semester here, when I felt I was not able to keep the attention of the students." One professor said, "I really think about things like SIGCSE as making the difference in how we do big changes." While these comments are unsurprising for educational conferences, faculty spoke less often about discussing teaching at technical conferences. A full professor in the Rocky Mountain region described teaching conversations as "not completely unusual," implying they are at least somewhat uncommon.

Learning from Colleagues. Many faculty reported discussing teaching issues and borrowing ideas and syllabi with colleagues. A professor at a small private college said, "I learned most of what I know about this from my colleagues. I learned a lot about curriculum from <colleague>, who's sort of the national expert on this." In some cases, departments are laid out physically in ways that allow "water cooler talk" about teaching: unplanned, casual conversations. For example, a focus group interviewee said "We chat in the hallway [laughs]" and his colleague explained, "The printer is at one end and the restrooms are at the other." It might be possible to attribute these interchanges to local culture: most of our interviewees in teaching colleges expressed a strong commitment to teaching and collegiality around teaching. In contrast, a professor at a large, public research university said she rarely spoke to her colleagues about teaching: "It's an enormous building…for me to go from my office, which is way up in the tower, to the most distant office is probably something like a 15 minute walk." Research faculty seemed more likely to mention seeking syllabi and ideas from colleagues they knew from research conferences than from their local colleagues.

Some Faculty Don't Find Out. Awareness of the possibilities for changing teaching practices is required in order to make a change. Some professors simply are not on the lookout for and never hear about teaching innovations. For instance, a lecturer at a small technical school in the southeast seemed to assume that the interviewer was asking about research journals and conferences (not educational conferences) when he was asked about whether he used those as sources for teaching innovations, saying "I haven't been to many conferences. I'm a lecturer so I have a teaching load…There's no time for research…" When asked if he had heard of SIGCSE or read any articles about teaching in journals, he said, "Not much. No." Similarly, when a doctoral instructor was asked if there were teaching approaches he would like to use if he had time, he was unable to provide any examples.

4.2 Why do Faculty Try Out Practices?

Institutional Influences on Exploration. Some faculty had both the freedom and encouragement to explore teaching innovations and take risks. Asked, "How big of a factor is teaching on tenure and promotion around here?" a department chair at a state teaching university responded, "Very important. You have to be an above-average teacher to get tenure. You can be slacking in publications, but you have to be above average in teaching." But this did not imply that exploration was not encouraged. When asked, "When people decide they're gonna try something new around here, how critical are those student evaluations?" the same chair replied, "People like to see people trying new things. I've been on personnel committees and we tend to look favorably on people who tried and failed rather than not try anything at all."

At research institutions, however, faculty described a tension between teaching and research. Even where there is public rhetoric to the contrary, faculty disbelieve it because of the pressure to produce research and because of tacit beliefs that you can't be a good researcher if you're a good teacher (e.g., "the provost said our top priority is undergraduate education and … [laugh] on whose planet?"). Describing her tenure case, a professor at a large, state university described her involvement in a textbook project and the development of lab materials. She was ranked as excellent for both teaching and research, but that was perceived as a problem: "When I came up for tenure I got kind of smacked around at the college level because I had this big education credential. And they were just like, 'she shouldn't have this education work if she's serious about being a researcher'."

Cost-Benefit Analysis. Faculty implicitly or explicitly weigh the costs and benefits of adopting new practices relative to existing practices. Without any real evidence in favor of a practice, faculty may decide not to take the risk of experimenting because of the possibility that it will be counterproductive or make problems worse. For example, a few interviewees felt that their students would not be receptive to change. Discussing the potential of in-class group work, a department chair said, "Wonder if students would react well to that though…I'm thinking that some of the very shy students wouldn't really participate. There's always one or two who you never really hear from during class. I wonder how to get everyone involved."

Weighing time for preparation against time saved from other teaching work was also common. In describing what a colleague had told her that convinced her to experiment, a full professor at a research university said, "And he decided to teach it in a conversational style where he came into the classroom and they just had conversations about the material they were supposed to have read. And he somehow minimized the homework so he wouldn't have as much grading." Yet the time needed for modifying a course is a nontrivial consideration. An assistant professor in an engineering college said, "So the first semester I spent a lot of time, maybe the equivalent of six or eight hours a week extra over my normal preparation, to build all of the online slides and quizzes to make this all work. And now it's more of just the management process where I make a few updates and changes but it's pretty smooth." But this professor's addition of preparation time is not possible for everyone. Another professor's dream was echoed by many: "I'd love to be able to take a semester off and just rethink all the examples in my course."

Power of Role Models. The professors that faculty themselves had learned from can be powerful influences on teaching approaches and attitudes toward students. For example, a professor at a private liberal arts college in the northeast spoke with reverence about his role model, a "very famous computer scientist" who "had a class of typically 40-45 students, and by the second week had all of our names down." The interviewee went on to say that his professor had genuinely cared about students. The class this interviewee taught that day, the first week of the semester, had 36 students, yet he took the time to call out students' first names and look them in the eye. It was clear that he was carrying forward the commitment to students that he perceived from his former professor. Another professor chose not to use slides because he felt he had learned more effectively from a favorite professor who did not use them. The deep socialization from experiencing school in a certain way can be tacitly normative. Another said, "I bought the idea because that was how I used to study when I was a student." In describing the decision to change to a peer instruction approach, a lecturer from a large public research university said, "Frankly it just seemed kind of crazy until I tried it myself. You know, like one of these fad diets. I think it's unfortunate that for almost all of us, our experience of education has been just the straight lecture and so everything else does feel really out there."

Trusting Sources and Shared Values. Participants often mentioned colleagues (local or distant) as having influenced the use of specific teaching practices by describing ways in which they were similar. Faculty trust colleagues who have similar teaching and research contexts, share attitudes toward students and teaching, or teach similar subjects. In describing what conference speakers he finds credible at SIGCSE, a professor at a private liberal arts university acknowledged, "I do have the anti-'Research One' bias. Like if the speaker is somebody who teaches at <prestigious public research university>, the mental clout that I give them as a teacher—unless they're a lecturer—I drop them a notch. When someone stands up to speak and they're from a really successful teaching college <names several> or universities that have a real reputation of being great undergraduate teaching institutions, I give them a lot of merit." He said that he has to try to consciously correct for that bias. Similarly, but more subtly, a professor at a private religious school accounted for trusting someone from an R1 university because "When she was a grad student, she taught classes and took education classes, and she really had a big focus on self-improvement and being an excellent teacher, saying, "And she is." Similarly, a professor at a research university referred to a colleague at another university as a "research superstar" with whom she had discussed a teaching strategy at a research conference, because he teaches the same subject area. The assumption that he could be a good teacher was not automatic–"He turns out to be a spectacular teacher and he's won teaching awards at <his university>"–and yet she sought advice from him rather than approaching colleagues in her own department who had published a series of articles on the approach.

Senior faculty or faculty with high student evaluations can also be credible influencers. In response to a question about where he had learned of a new technique, an interviewee from an engineering school said, "Yeah, there is a senior faculty and after my first semester, he asked me how am I doing and he told me I could bring the [student] evaluations and he could try to give me advice on how to improve them…He's very tough but still he gets chosen as the best professor by students."

Competing with "Covering." There is also a tension between adopting new practices and "covering" content. If a professor adopts a new teaching method, it may take more time, so some content may not get "covered." In that case, a professor may annoy a colleague or slow down students' progress in a subsequent course, as described by the following professor. Asked, "So, there is an expectation that you will cover certain things, but it's not a mandate?" she replied, "Oh, it's a mandate. I mean, if I send students up and they feel none of the students from my course knew how to iterate, that's gonna be a big problem…There is a document that says 'This is what this course teaches.'" This was the case both in teaching-focused and research-focused institutions, but it was not universal. Although there can be heavy constraints on what material is covered, professors have the freedom to change the emphasis or order within the syllabus. For example, an assistant professor said, "So when I introduce concepts at the beginning, those concepts get practiced more because they use them more through time, than [topics covered] at the end." Covering a certain set of material did not necessarily translate to ensuring that students know it, but is often critical for retaining accreditation.

Classroom Layouts. We heard from multiple faculty about how the physical space and affordances of the classrooms either supported or hindered implementation of particular practices. For example, when desks or chairs are bolted to classroom floors, it is physically difficult for students to face each other and work in groups. A professor at a large public research university said, "This class is really kind of traditional in its structure partly because of the classroom." In other words, she chose a lecture-style approach because she taught in a stadium-style lecture hall, where long tables and chairs were bolted to risers.

Equipment, too, can enable or impede practices. For example, a lecturer at a public teaching university said, "It would be very easy for me to implement [a collaborative learning approach], because lecture and lab are in the same room. So it would be very easy to stop for 15 or 20 minutes and you know, work on a small problem." In several classrooms, large, flat-screen monitors in front of students made even 'making eye contact' with students difficult, though some faculty managed the issue. For example, although an imperfect solution, one professor had students turn their chairs perpendicular to the tables and face the side of the room for lecture, because he couldn't see students behind the monitors. Although faculty often cannot control the physical space, they can change what the students do in it.

Research Evidence? Despite being researchers themselves, the CS faculty we spoke to for the most part did not believe that results from educational studies were credible reasons to try out teaching practices. One professor heard a keynote talk at SIGCSE about flipping the classroom and decided to try it. He said he thought there were also a couple of "presentations with data," but did not attend them. When asked whether educational studies are convincing, he said, "No, there's a big push to do those kinds of studies, but I don't buy the significance of the studies. It sounds good, it sounds like it's worth trying, but the data that's presented is often not very convincing."

4.3 Why do Faculty Keep Using Practices?

Student Feedback is Critical. Perhaps the single strongest kind of evidence that supports a decision to routinize practices was student feedback. Faculty are concerned with student learning, student engagement (often as the opposite of "bored"), students "liking" their classes, and students being able to gauge their own learning. Faculty use comments in office hours, class, and student evaluations, assessments of performance, attendance in class, and inferences drawn from nonverbal behavior to make judgments about effectiveness. At an engineering school where graphics had been heavily integrated into early courses, the professor said that students were so pleased with their work that they "showed it to their mom and dad." In a similar example, students displaying their robot programming prowess in dormitory halls created huge demand for the introductory course. Student attendance was also perceived as a sign of excitement; for example, a professor at a Midwestern state teaching university trying out a more interactive teaching style said, "This semester, I was amazed that the first month in discrete mathematics almost had perfect attendance." Student excitement about what they are doing in class, even if unrelated to evidence of learning, was considered very important.

On the other hand, if students don't "like it," faculty are unlikely to continue using a new practice. At a public research university, a professor said, "You can do something that you think, 'Wow! If the learning experience was way better this term, the experiment really worked.' And then you read your teaching reviews, and it's like the students are pissed off because you did not do what they expected." Even when students "like" it, however, faculty may not commit to a practice if they believe students are not learning as much—even when the evidence is based on inference rather than performance. A lecturer at a four-year public school felt that lecturing in class gave him more feedback on whether students were understanding the material, as well as more opportunities to use alternative examples and explanations, than a flipped classroom approach, saying, "The students do really like it. But I'm worried that they're not learning as much so far. I worry about the discipline and concentration that they put into watching the videos as opposed to in a classroom and I'm lecturing. I can gauge whether or not they're getting something, whether they are paying attention, and then hammer the points that maybe they are not catching as clearly."

If faculty have self-assessed evidence, such as "I started to do this and grades improved," they are more likely to retain the practice. Similarly, if faculty believe that students are more engaged, they may routinize practices even if it competes with covering concepts. Describing the integration of an interactive teaching approach, a professor at a teaching college said, "There is material that I would cover that I don't now because of things getting slowed down for the interactive stuff. But I felt like when I have lectured and just blasted through things on overheads, my course evaluations have a definite percentage of students that said, 'He's pretty boring.'"

Requirements from Funders and Faculty Buy-In. In some cases, practices became routinized because of the desires of granting agencies for pilot project outcomes to be sustained or institutionalized. For example, at an engineering school in the southeast, grant-funded revised curriculum was integrated into several courses. And as described above, in departments where curriculum is fixed (and enforced) by departments or committees, it cannot be changed later without a lot of wrangling. One of the professors (not a principal investigator of the grant), said "No one can prove that this technique is better than another. But our choice was to experiment. Overall it's been positive." When there is buy-in from other faculty in the department or even outside the department, curriculum is more likely to be routinized. In another grant-funded initiative, a professor at a private liberal arts college worked with faculty in other disciplines to create theme-based courses. She also helped faculty in "15 different disciplines [to] infuse a computational component into their courses."

5. DISCUSSION AND CONCLUSION

Adoption of teaching practices follows the stages of awareness, experimentation, and routinization. Adoption is not a "rational action," however, but an iterative series of decisions made in a social context, relying on normative traditions, social cueing, and emotional or intuitive processes. Consistent with other studies on CS faculty, [11,27,28] faculty are not likely to use educational research findings as the basis for adoption decisions. Faculty become aware of innovative practices either because a problem leads them to intentionally seek them out, or they hear about them through funded initiatives, conferences and journals, or from colleagues. They experiment (or not) for several reasons, depending on institutional expectations and policies, perceived costs and benefits for themselves and students, and the influence of role models. Faculty tend to trust other faculty whose work and institutional context is more like their own. The choice to try out practices competes with the need to "cover" material, as well as with classroom layouts. Positive student feedback is taken as strong evidence by faculty that they should continue a practice. Funded initiatives that are designed to get buy-in within the department are more likely to become routine.

Designers and developers of educational innovations might use the information presented here to improve adoption. Getting the word out about innovations is a critical part of dissemination. Presenting and demo-ing at educational and technical conferences can help to reach potential adopters. However, finding a way to get those who attend conferences to communicate to colleagues on behalf of developers can reach much further. For example, providing information cards or other materials to take home can be an effective way to start conversations, provided that the messaging is relevant to faculty concerns.

Developers might increase the chance that faculty try out innovative practices by using messages that address faculty concerns. For example, highlighting a problem to be solved, the time needed for implementation, the outcomes to be expected, how to evaluate outcomes, and perhaps pointing to textual or multimedia information online could be useful. In their communications, developers can demonstrate understanding of institutional constraints, classroom spaces, and how teaching practices or curricular material fit in with the need to cover existing material. By acknowledging the tension between "covering" content and ensuring that students have a robust understanding of a topic, developers may have more success in convincing potential adopters. Faculty may decide that a new approach is too risky if the preparation time outweighs the time saved in other teaching work (such as grading), especially if the expected gains are minimal. By explicitly addressing how long it takes to implement a teaching practice, and outlining the benefits and costs to themselves and to students, developers can help faculty make informed decisions both when they try out innovative practices and for continued use. Although CS faculty do not use educational research evidence as their first selection criterion, research evidence doesn't hurt, as long as the context in which the research was conducted seems analogous to their own.

Faculty are more likely to innovate—even if they think the idea "sounds crazy"—when they are promoted by people whom they believe understand their teaching and research context. Role models, whether their reputation is that of a great teacher, research collaborator, or preeminent researcher in the field, offer developers a useful hook. While faculty get ideas to try something innovative from conference presentations or journal articles, they might filter the information through biases about the author's (or presenter's) research and teaching background, the (dis)similarities of the course material, and the characteristics of the institutions from which they come. Developers might circumvent biases by marshaling trusted sources and demonstrating shared values when approaching potential adopters. Funding is a substantial lever for potential innovation adopters. Developers with funds can influence adoption by providing grants, provided they encourage faculty to gain buy-in and integrate curriculum and practices beyond the single course.

ACKNOWLEDGMENTS

This research was sponsored by the National Science Foundation under Division of Undergraduate Education #1123332. We thank Rick Barker, Jesus Contreras, Jonatan Contreras, Evan Hofmockel, Russell Mehring, and Kamar Nassor for their interview, logistics, and transcription support. Finally, we especially thank the computer science faculty members who committed to be interviewed and allow us in their classes.

REFERENCES

1. Barker, L.J., Hovey, C.L., & Thompson, L.D. Results of a large-scale, multi-institutional study of undergraduate retention in computing. *The 44th Annual Frontiers in Education Conference*, (2014).
2. Barker, McDowell, C., & Kalahar, K. Exploring factors that influence computer science introductory course students to persist in the major. *Proceedings of the 40th ACM Technical Symposium on Computer Science Education*, (2009), 153-157.
3. Braxton, J.M. *Rethinking college student retention.* Jossey-Bass, 2014.
4. Brooks, F.P., Jr. The teacher's job is to design learning experiences; Not primarily to impart information. *Proceedings of the 43rd ACM Technical Symposium on Computer Science Education*, ACM (2012), 1-2.
5. Carroll, J., M. *Innovative practices in teaching information sciences and technology: Experience reports and reflections.* Springer International Publishing, Switzerland, 2014.
6. Cohoon and Aspray, W. A critical review of the research on women's participation in postsecondary computing education. In *Women and information technology: Research on underrepresentation*. MIT Press, Cambridge, MA, 2006, 137-180.
7. DeClue, D.T.H. Pair programming and pair trading: Effects on learning and motivation in a CS2 course. *Pair Programming, Learning Theory, and Qualitative*, (2003), 1-8.
8. Devlin, M. Challenging accepted wisdom about the place of conceptions of teaching in university teaching improvement. *International Journal of Teaching and Learning in Higher Education 18*, 2 (2006), 112-119.
9. Van Driel, J.H., Beijaard, D., & Verloop, N. Professional development and reform in science education: The role of teachers' practical knowledge. *Journal of Research in Science Teaching 38*, 2 (2001), 137-158.
10. Fairweather, J.S. The mythologies of faculty productivity: Implications for institutional policy and decision making. *The Journal of Higher Education 73*, 1 (2002), 26-48.
11. Fossati, D. and Guzdial, M. The use of evidence in the change making process of computer science educators. *Proceedings of the 42nd ACM technical symposium on Computer science education*, ACM (2011), 685-690.
12. Gallivan, M.J. Organizational adoption and assimilation of complex technological innovations: Development and application of a new framework. *SIGMIS Database 32*, 3 (2001), 51-85.
13. Gee, J.P. *An Introduction to Discourse Analysis.* Routledge, London, 1999.
14. Grey, S. Can we measure the influence of social movements? (2004).
15. Guzdial, M. Exploring hypotheses about media computation. *Proceedings of the 9th Annual International ACM Conference on International Computing Education Research*, ACM (2013), 19-26.
16. Habermas, J. *Jürgen Habermas on society and politics: A reader.* Beacon Press, Boston, 1989. [[DELETED]]
17. Hogg, M.A. and Terry, D.J. Social identity and self-categorization processes in organizational contexts. *The Academy of Management Review 25*, 1 (2000), 121–140.
18. Kane, R., Sandretto, S., & Heath, C. Telling half the story: A critical review of research on the teaching beliefs and practices of university academics. *Review of Educational Research 72*, 2 (2002), 177-228.
19. Katz, S., Allbritton, D., Aronis, J., Wilson, C., & Soffa, M.L. Gender, achievement, and persistence in an undergraduate computer science program. *ACM SIGMIS Database 37*, 4 (2006), 42-57.
20. Klein, K.J. and Sorra, J.S. The challenge of innovation implementation. *The Academy of Management Review, 21*, 4 (1996), 1055-1080.
21. Kuh, G.D., Kinzie, J., Buckley, J.A., Bridges, B.K., & Hayek, J.C. *what matters to student success: A review of the literature.* National Postsecondary Education Cooperative, 2006.
22. Margolis, J. and Fisher, A. *Unlocking the clubhouse: Women in computing.* MIT Press, Cambridge, MA, 2002.
23. McDowell, C., Werner, L., Bullock, H.E., & Fernald, J. Pair programming improves student retention, confidence, and program quality. *Communications of the ACM 49*, 8 (2006), 90-95.
24. McMillan, L.A. and Berberet, W.G. *A new academic compact: Revisioning the relationship between faculty and their institutions.* Anker Publishing Company, Boston, 2001.
25. National Center for Education Statistics. The Integrated Postsecondary Education Data System. 2014.
26. NCWIT. Pair Programming-in-a-box.
27. Ni, L. What makes CS teachers change? Factors influencing CS teachers' adoption of curriculum innovations. *SIGCSE Bull. 41*, 1 (2009), 544-548.
28. Ni, L., McKlin, T., & Guzdial, M. How do computing faculty adopt curriculum innovations? The story from instructors. *Proceedings of the 41st ACM Technical Symposium on Computer Science Education*, ACM (2010), 544-548.
29. Putnam, R.T. and Borko, H. What do new views of knowledge and thinking have to say about research on teacher learning? *Educational Researcher 29*, 1 (2000), 4-15.
30. Reis, R. Designing and assessing course curricula, Msg. #442. *Tomorrow's Professor*. Stanford Center for Teaching and Learning.
31. Roberts, M.R.H., McGill, T., & Koppi, T. What students are telling us about why they left their ICT course. *Innovation in Teaching and Learning in Information and Computer Sciences 10*, 3 (2011), 68-83.
32. Rogers, E.M. *Diffusion of innovations.* Free press, 1995.
33. Strenta, A.C., Elliott, R., Adair, R., Matier, M., & Scott, J. Choosing and leaving science in highly selective institutions. *Res. High. Educ. 35*, 5 (1994), 513–547.
34. Taylor Huber, M. and Hutchings, P. Building the teaching commons. *Change 38*, 3 (2006).
35. Tinto, V. *Completing college: Rethinking institutional action.* The University of Chicago Press, Chicago, IL, 2012.
36. Tornatzky, L.G., Eveland, J.D., Boylan, M.G., et al. *The process of technological innovation: Reviewing the literature.* National Science Foundation, Washington, D.C., 1983.
37. Wankat, P.C., Felder, R.M., Smith, K.A., & Oreovicz, F.S. The scholarship of teaching and learning in engineering. In *Disciplinary styles in the scholarship of teaching and learning: Exploring common ground.* American Association for Higher Education and The Carnegie Foundation, Washington, DC, 2002.
38. Werner, L.L., Hanks, B., McDowell, C., Bullock, H., & Fernald, J. Want to increase retention of your female students? *Computing Research News 17*, 2 (2005).
39. Williams, L.A. Strengthening the case for pair programming. *IEEE Software 17*, 4 (2000), 17–25.
40. Williams, L.A. and Kessler, R.R. All I really need to know about programming I learned in kindergarten. *Communications of the ACM 43*, 5 (2000), 108–114.
41. Yin, R.K. Life histories of innovations: How new practices become routinized. *Public Administration Review 41*, 1 (1981), 21-28.

Personalized Attention @ Scale

Talk Isn't Cheap, But It's Effective

Dirk Grunwald, Elizabeth Boese, Rhonda Hoenigman, Andy Sayler and Judith Stafford
University of Colorado
Boulder, CO, USA
<first>.<last>@colorado.edu

ABSTRACT

Fostering an effective learning environment in large classes is a challenge: instructors and teaching assistants are stretched thin across many students, students often lack opportunities for personal interaction with course staff, and the size of the classes makes them seem impersonal. Furthermore, students in large classes can often find solutions to their labs and assignments online or copy them from other students, diminishing their impetus to learn and raising plagiarism concerns.

This paper describes our experience and evaluation of an assessment method that resolves many of these problems and appears to scale to large classes of 600+ students. Using this method, students are evaluated via a combination of automatic grading mechanisms (or clear objective rubrics) *and* a 1-on-1 "grading interview". The grading interview serves to ensure the provenance of the student's work product and their depth of understanding. This change allows us to make more effective use of peer-instruction and pair-programming in our courses. It also provides the ability to re-use assignments, the insurance of timely feedback to students, and the opportunity for individualized staff attention.

This paper describes variations on this method across numerous classes over the past seven years, some of the goals of this method, modifications and adaptations of the method over time, and the student experience of using this method based on survey feedback.

Categories and Subject Descriptors

K.3.2 [**Computer and Information Science Education**]: Curriculum; Computer science education

General Terms

Management

Keywords

Education; Best Practices; Grading; Interviews; Face to Face

SIGCSE'15, March 4–7, 2015, Kansas City, MO, USA.

ACM 978-1-4503-2966-8/15/03 $15.00
http://dx.doi.org/10.1145/2676723.2677283.

1. INTRODUCTION

The practice of Computer Science and software development has undergone a revolution in the last decade: programmers are now expected to be well versed in Agile programming techniques including pair programming and related collaborative development methods. Computer Science education is reflecting that change – early studies in the effectiveness of pair programming for introductory classes demonstrated improved student enjoyment and attainment of programming proficiency [10] and more recent studies [1, 2, 4, 5, 13] have further demonstrated that collaborative methods of learning are effective. Other studies [11, 12] have shown that these methods, coupled with peer instruction, can improve retention, similar to the impact that peer instruction has had in other STEM disciplines [7].

At the same time, the practice of teaching and evaluating student work in Computer Science classes appears to be increasingly automated. That automation has led to mechanisms to identify "cheating" in programming courses. Such "cheating" is reported as epidemic in top institutions such as Stanford [3, 8] where 23% of the honor code violations involve Computer Science students, even though those students only make up 6.5% of the school's enrollment. The University of Washington [9] finds that 1-2% of assignments involve "academic dishonesty". In part, this occurs because technology makes it easier to evaluate code and introductory Computer Science courses are undergoing incredible enrollment growth.

There is a tension in these two trends (collaboration & cheating) – what instructor has not uttered the mentally dissonant phrase "*You may work together, but you are each responsible for your own work*"? How are instructors and students to make effective use of peer instruction, pair programming, and collaboration while demonstrating their own competence?

This paper describes and quantifies our multi-year experience with one solution to this tension: interview-based grading. A core observation of our instruction method is that much "cheating" occurs because faculty evaluate ***products*** and not ***people***.

We use direct oral examination of students to evaluate understanding of the "product" of assignments. Students may work in pairs, but they are individually evaluated. These grading interviews occur weekly in our CS1 classes and transition to every 2-3 weeks for later courses. We first designed and deployed our method in a CS1 class in 2006; over time, it has been adopted by an increasing number of courses in our department and more recently has been standardized for our lower-division curriculum, including

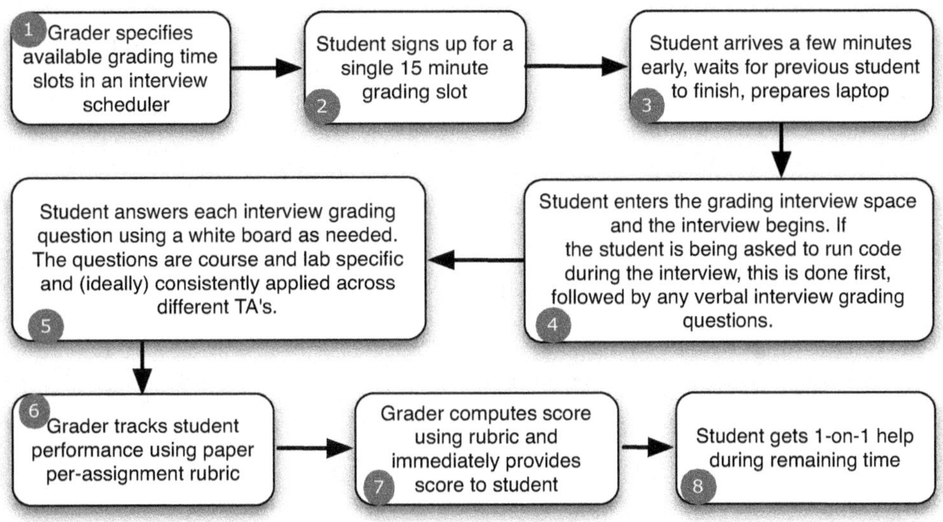

Figure 1: Grading Process

classes of 600+ students. Our initial goals were to enable the use of pair programming in introductory classes, allow other forms of collaboration such as peer instruction, ensure more timely evaluation and feedback to students, and, ideally, to improve the educational experience in an effort to increase retention.

In §2 we describe the implementation of interview grading. In §3 we review related work. In §4 we describe a survey instrument we designed to evaluate the effectiveness of this method. We analyze the results from this survey (using 600+ respondents) in §5. We describe future plans in §6 and conclude in §7.

2. INTERVIEW IMPLEMENTATION

Our interview grading process varies in detail from course to course, but the basic mechanics are standardized across all courses. Via trail and error, we have settled on 15 minute grading sessions. This means that the entire process must fit into a single 15 minute window, from the student's arrival to their exit. During this time, we generally try to ask two to four primary questions, with a variety of follow up questions to further probe a student's response when necessary. The structure of questions, and the order they are offered, is guided by an assignment-specific rubric. Although developing a rubric is time consuming, we have found that that effort can at least be amortized over several semesters since interview grading permits us to reuse material across multiple semesters.

If the student is able to answer all the questions in under 15 minutes, we use the remaining time to allow the student to ask questions regarding the topics covered in the interview and ensure they understand the material: after all, they will be seeing the same material again on the midterm or final, even if they didn't get the correct answer during the interview. Ideally, we complete all grading interviews within one week of the assignment due date. This ensures that the material is still fresh in the student's mind and helps keep the course on track and moving forward.

We have endeavored to separate *correctness* from *authenticity*. Most labs and assignments have a mechanism to report the success or failure of the assignment to the student; this is done either by a centralized auto-grading system or per-lab evaluation harnesses. Students receive a smaller percentage of their final grade for "correctness" (*e.g.* up to 40% of the total points for an assignment can be awarded for having a correctly functioning assignment) and a larger percentage (*e.g.* 60%) for the ability to explain and attest to the functioning of the program during an interview. This split of both evaluation and "points" insures that students have a mechanism for self-checking their work and also must be able to properly explain the functioning of their code to achieve a passing grade.

The 15 minute grading interview and the goal of completing all grading interviews for a given assignment within a one week window defines the lower bound on the number of interview graders (i.e. teaching assistants) per course. Our TAs are paid for 20 hours per week, but must split their time between grading, leading recitations, and other support duties. Most TAs thus have $\approx$ 15 hours per week that can be devoted to interview grading, requiring 1 TA per $\approx$ 60 students. These numbers vary a bit by course: some courses have dedicated interview grading staff that can devote a full 20 hours per week to interview grading and thus accommodate $\approx$ 80 students per grader, and some courses do not use interview grading at all, but have TAs who must spend comparable amounts of time performing non-interview grading methods (e.g. manually reviewing code submissions, etc). Most graders break up their interview grading hours into two to three hour segments spread throughout the week: *e.g.* a single three hour grading segment each day, Monday through Friday.

Figure 1 shows the steps involved conducting a standard grading interview for a given assignment.

3. RELATED WORK

There is considerable work on the efficacy of pair-programming, peer-learning and collaborative work, but there is significantly less analysis of the impact of direct oral interviews on class performance and student affect.

The most relevant study is by East & Schafer [6], who analyzed the impact of three different evaluation methods (student-initiated discussion, instructor-led discussion and in-person grading) on performance and affect in a ≈60-person CS1 class. In general, the study found no statistical difference in student grades or outcomes between the three evaluation methods, but did find that students preferred the in-person grading.

The in-person grading used in that study had a different structure and purpose from that examined in this paper. Students were evaluated in 20-minute sessions over all aspects of their work, including style, structure and correctness. By comparison, our structure uses other methods to evaluate correctness of the resulting programs and grading interviews focus on demonstrated understanding and explication of the program. Moreover, [6] did not promote pair-programming or the use of other student assistants such focusing just on the evaluation.

Surprisingly, we found it difficult to find extensive experience reports with in-person or interview grading; [6] had a similar experience. We have informally described our structure to faculty and instructors at other universities (and our own), and there was general surprise that such a method would be scalable to large 600+ person classes.

4. STUDY METHODOLOGY

We conducted a study to gain a better understanding of whether students viewed interview grading as beneficial, a hassle, or somewhere in between. We also wanted to know if we were accomplishing our goals for instituting interview grading. Namely, did students feel that they were receiving more timely feedback on assignments than they would through traditional grading?; did student feel they had permission to collaborate and research solutions to problems using outside resources?; and did students develop a deeper connection with their TAs through 1-on-1 meetings? We asked 15 questions about developing connections with course instructors, the feedback students received on interview graded assignments, and collaboration with peers and the ability to consult outside resources. For each of the 15 questions, we asked students if they strongly agreed, agreed, neither agreed nor disagreed, disagreed, or strongly disagreed with the statement presented (Figure 2).

There were additional questions on the survey asking for comments. We asked students what they liked most and least about interview grading. We also collected information on gender, year in school, previous experience with interview grading, and in which class they were currently enrolled.

4.1 Data Collection

We posted the survey on our department Learning Management System (we use Moodle) used for course management for several classes, including all lower division classes. Students were asked in the last two weeks of the semester to complete the survey. In the introductory classes, students were asked to complete the survey during their weekly recitation. They were not graded on whether or not they completed the survey, and the survey responses were anonymous. None of the questions were mandatory; students were able to answer some questions and not others. The survey was administered through the campus Qualtrics online survey system, where any student who had the link to the survey could complete it.

The survey was administered for Fall, Spring, and Summer semesters during the 2013-2014 school year to the freshman-level introductory computing classes (CS1) and data structures classes (CS2), the sophomore-level computer systems classes, and the junior-level software engineering classes. These were the classes where interview grading was being used consistently and where we believed the interview-grading process would have the most benefit for students.

5. ANALYSIS

There were 667 students who responded to the survey; their responses are shown in Figure 3. The results from the survey show that students' response to interview grading has been overwhelmingly positive. Many students agreed that being able to consult outside resources and collaborate with their peers not only increased their ability to complete their assignments, but also gave them confidence in their ability to learn new material. Many students went so far as to support the statement that the 1-on-1 connection they developed with their TA helped them to not drop the class. Comments about the feedback they received were also present in survey results.

5.1 Consulting outside resources

The strongest responses in the survey were to questions about consulting outside resources and the positive effect this had on students' ability to complete assignments, collaborate with peers, and confidently learn new material without outside assistance. In response to the statement,

> "*Having permission to consult outside people and references improved my ability to complete my assignments.*"

78% (521 out of 666) of respondents said they strongly agreed or agreed.

The positive effect of consulting outside resources was not limited to completing assignments. In another question, we asked students to respond to the statement,

> "*Permission to collaborate and consult outside resources has improved my confidence in learning new material.*"

70% (461 out of 663) strongly agreed or agreed with the statement. There was also a strong link between positive responses on the question about completing assignments and the question about learning new material. Of 521 students who answered positively to the first statement about collaboration, 82% also answered positively about their improved confidence to learn new material. While we believe it is important for students to be able to complete assignments, we find the improved confidence to be the larger gain, particularly for introductory courses.

In our questions about consulting outside resources and collaboration, we didn't explicitly draw the connection between interview grading and our comfort with letting students consult outside resources and collaborate. We use interview grading as a guard against cheating, and we feel confident letting students work together on assignments knowing that they will need to explain their solutions to a trained grader. Based on students' responses on the positive effects of collaboration, we feel that we have achieved our goal of encouraging student collaboration.

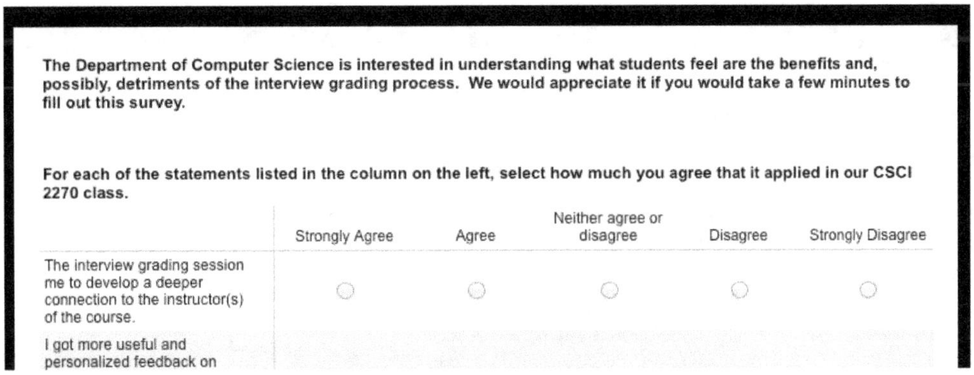

The Department of Computer Science is interested in understanding what students feel are the benefits and, possibly, detriments of the interview grading process. We would appreciate it if you would take a few minutes to fill out this survey.

For each of the statements listed in the column on the left, select how much you agree that it applied in our CSCI 2270 class.

	Strongly Agree	Agree	Neither agree or disagree	Disagree	Strongly Disagree
The interview grading session me to develop a deeper connection to the instructor(s) of the course.	○	○	○	○	○
I got more useful and personalized feedback on					

Figure 2: Survey Format

#	Question	Strongly Agree	Agree	Neither agree or disagree	Disagree	Strongly Disagree	Total Responses	Mean
1	The interview grading session helped me to develop a deeper connection to the instructor(s) of the course.	118	280	143	92	32	665	2.46
2	I got more useful and personalized feedback on interviewed graded assignments than I did on other assignments.	215	289	91	53	19	667	2.06
3	Having permission to collaborate in this class helped increase my connection to my peers.	196	207	170	62	29	664	2.28
4	Having permission to consult outside people and references improved my ability to complete assignments.	273	248	104	29	12	666	1.89
5	I think the interview grading process gave the instructor(s) a better understanding of my gaps in understanding of the material than more traditional assessment would.	180	265	122	63	33	663	2.25
6	Interview grading gave me an opportunity to discuss things with the instructor(s) that were important to me.	186	241	140	66	31	664	2.27
7	When I left interview grading sessions, I felt that I had improved my understanding of course concepts.	172	232	135	92	33	664	2.37
8	The interview grading process resulted in me getting more timely feedback on assignment submissions than I usually get in paper graded courses.	187	254	140	49	31	661	2.22
9	The interview grading session provided an opportunity for me to give feedback about the course.	97	188	205	125	46	661	2.75
10	The increased 1-on-1 contact with instructor(s) that is a part of the interview grading process reduced my intentions to drop the course.	87	130	291	94	60	662	2.86
11	The timely feedback I received on my assignments helped me stay on track with the course material.	113	241	184	95	30	663	2.53
12	The feedback I received in interview grading helped me learn the course material.	139	275	131	84	33	662	2.39
13	The interview grading process helped me understand course expectations.	135	302	139	63	22	661	2.30
14	The interview grading process has increased my confidence for doing job interviews.	85	182	231	117	46	661	2.78
15	15. Permission to collaborate and consult resources for this course has improved my confidence in learning new material on my own.	183	278	150	34	18	663	2.13

Figure 3: Survey Results for All Respondents

5.2 Student retention

We asked other questions directly related to developing a stronger connection with course instructors and in one question, asked if the one-on-one contact with course instructors reduced their intention to drop the class. Over all classes, there were 217/662 (33%) students who agreed or strongly agreed that the one-on-one interviews helped them stay in the class. There was no statistical difference in the answers in the lower division classes – of those 217 students, 74% were from the introductory course, and the other 26% were from five other courses. This matches the distribution for the students who took the survey.

For the remaining two thirds of students who did not agreed with the statement, it is possible that many of them were not at risk of dropping the class. The interview grading process resonated with some students. Of the 154 students who disagreed or strongly disagreed with the statement about dropping the class, many of them still responded favorably to statements about collaboration with peers and to statements about interview grading providing more useful feedback than traditional grading methods. For many students (291), they neither agreed nor disagreed that interview grading helped them stay in the class. These students also demonstrated a favorable response to statements about feedback and collaboration.

The answers to the question about dropping the class shows a potential limitation in our survey. Without background on the student answering the question, we don't know if they were ever at risk of dropping. They may have been at risk, and interview grading did not play a role in keeping them in the class. Or, they may have had no intention of ever dropping the class, and therefore, interview grading had a neutral effect on them in terms of staying in the class.

5.3 Timely feedback

Our questions about assignment feedback asked students if they felt they received more timely feedback, more useful feedback, and if the feedback they received helped them learn the course material. Just as with questions about student retention and collaboration, questions about feedback also received mostly positive responses. In response to the statement,

> "*I got more useful and personal feedback on interview graded assignments than I did on other assignments.*"

76% (504 out of 667) of students either agreed or strongly agreed. Students also responded favorably about how the

#	Question	Strongly Agree	Agree	Neither agree or disagree	Disagree	Strongly Disagree	Total Responses	Mean
1	The interview grading session helped me to develop a deeper connection to the instructor(s) of the course.	81	113	20	2	1	217	1.75
2	I got more useful and personalized feedback on interviewed graded assignments than I did on other assignments.	113	89	14	1	0	217	1.55
3	Having permission to collaborate in this class helped increase my connection to my peers.	100	75	33	6	3	217	1.79
4	Having permission to consult outside people and references improved my ability to complete assignments.	120	79	13	4	0	216	1.54
5	I think the interview grading process gave the instructor(s) a better understanding of my gaps in understanding of the material than more traditional assessment would.	96	100	16	3	1	216	1.67
6	Interview grading gave me an opportunity to discuss things with the instructor(s) that were important to me.	97	95	20	3	1	216	1.69
7	When I left interview grading sessions, I felt that I had improved my understanding of course concepts.	97	99	16	4	0	216	1.66
8	The interview grading process resulted in me getting more timely feedback on assignment submissions than I usually get in paper graded courses.	99	97	19	1	1	217	1.65
9	The interview grading session provided an opportunity for me to give feedback about the course.	72	88	43	13	0	216	1.99
10	The increased 1-on-1 contact with instructor(s) that is a part of the interview grading process reduced my intentions to drop the course.	87	130	0	0	0	217	1.60
11	The timely feedback I received on my assignments helped me stay on track with the course material.	78	103	26	7	3	217	1.87
12	The feedback I received in interview grading helped me learn the course material.	92	105	14	4	1	216	1.69
13	The interview grading process helped me understand course expectations.	76	116	18	7	0	217	1.80
14	The interview grading process has increased my confidence for doing job interviews.	63	84	45	24	1	217	2.15
15	15. Permission to collaborate and consult resources for this course has improved my confidence in learning new material on my own.	91	96	25	2	3	217	1.76

Figure 4: Survey Results for Respondents Who Agreed or Strongly Agreed that Interview Grading Helped Them Not Drop

feedback helped them learn the course material. In response to the statement,

> "*The feedback I received in interview grading helped me learn the course material.*"

63% (414 out of 662) of students either agreed or strongly agreed.

5.4 Difficulties encountered

The most common complaints about interview grading from students were logistical in nature. Students commented that they had difficulty finding the grading rooms, or finding a meeting time that fit into their schedule. Students who did not schedule a time as soon as they were able to would find that the only remaining times conflicted with their class schedule. For the graders/TAs, this meant they had to open up more time slots or arrange a time individually with the student. With each grader responsible for 60-80 students, these scheduling issues could waste considerable time.

There was also a scheduling problem of gaps in the schedule created when students don't sign up for a time slot that is sandwiched between other selected time slots. There is not much for a grader to do with an extra 15 minutes while waiting for their next meeting, which also results in lost time in their schedule. Scheduling is not as simple as setting up time slots and having all students fit into them. There will be gaps and missed meetings that ultimately require more time from the graders.

Related to the scheduling difficulty was another issue we encountered with students not showing up for grading meeting, or showing up late. The TA still "lost" that time, and depending on the make-up policy for the class, may have to make more time for the student to make up the meeting. In some classes, the policy was for students to receive a 0 or a maximum of 40% (reflecting the "correctness" portion of the grade) for an assignment with a missed grading meeting. Unfortunately, students would still miss meeting in the first few weeks of class and then request a second chance. For introductory classes with 300+ students, these frequent emails from students asking for a makeup meeting presented a burden for course instructors.

There were also comments about TA inconsistency. Students commented that some TAs were interested in teaching, while others just wanted to get it over with and didn't take the time to explain concepts. One student commented that his least favorite thing about interview grading was *"Very inconsistent TAs. Some were very helpful, while others seemed a bit condescending."* Another student commented that their favorite thing about interview grading was, *"1 on 1 feedback and being able to discuss the material"*.

Some students, and TAs, expressed anxiety about the discourse arising from grading meetings – the social engagement exacerbated language differences or comfort levels of social interaction. We did not quantify or measure these concerns in this study, but we believe that students and TAs will encounter similar experiences in interviews, job talks, and group projects; it is unclear if interview grading presents a unique barrier for these students, and it may even help better prepare them for similar real-world social experiences.

6. FUTURE PLANS

We are working on improving our interview grading process on several levels. The first is the number of TAs required per course. Our goal is to reduce time spent on other TA duties to enable more time for grading interviews. One such method is to hire peer-teachers (termed *Learning Assistants* or LAs at our university); these are drawn from undergraduate students who have recently taken the class in question. The LAs provide direct peer instruction to the students, supplanting the traditional role of "office hours" for the graduate TA. While we are making progress by hiring extra LAs for helping students and minimizing TA prep time by having pre-made recitation/lab exercises available, our TAs still must dedicate time to a number of non-grading duties: *e.g.* handling grading issues, responding to student and staff emails, weekly meetings, and managing missed appointments. Many of these duties are communication related, and we are working to increase TA communication efficiency (e.g. using real-time communication systems like Google Hangouts instead of emails, relying on FAQs and forums to address common student questions, etc).

Another area for improvement is to find a way to make it a fulfilling and beneficial experience for the TAs. Interview grading tends to rank last amongst desired TA tasks. This is partly due to the amount of energy it takes a TA to create an effective interview, jumping from one student's submission to the next and actively analyzing their code for specific questions related to their submission. While TAs could do this prep work ahead of time, that does add extra time to their already cramped schedule, and since students often switch their scheduled grading times up until the last minute, even knowing which students to prep for can be difficult. Furthermore, the introduction of grading interviews requires our graduate TAs to consistently work the full 20 hours per week for which they are paid, something TAs often could get away without doing in less time structured, non-interview graded courses. It is also harder for TAs to defer the evaluation work when conducting interview grading (because their schedules are publicly visible), but, conversely, the instructor is more aware of any delay in providing feedback to students.

In response to the students' comments about TA inconsistency, we have added training sessions on how to effectively run interview grading meetings. We cover the logistics of setting up the interviews, what type of questions are appropriate, how to look at a student's code and question specific aspects of it, and personal hygiene (similar to rules for pair programming). This is now a required seminar at the beginning of the semester. Equally important, we have focused on more precise grading rubrics for each class so that instructors, students and TAs have a clear and consistent understanding of how students should be evaluated.

While we have dabbled in exploring interview grading for quizzes and exams, more experience and evaluation still needs to be done to draw similar conclusions in those contexts.

Overall, we have had tremendous success for students experiencing interview grading. Our department is including interview grading in more and more courses. We plan to continue using interview grading in many of our courses going forward.

7. CONCLUSION

Using interview grading as a part of our effort to foster a more effective learning environment for large classes appears to be working very well. As we have shown through our surveys, students are positive about interview grading for many different reasons including the fact that it supports an environment in which they can collaborate and use other external resources freely. They also enjoy the one-on-one time with the instructional staff. Faculty involved in with interview grading are very positive about it and find, among other things, that it increases their connection to their classes, allows them to reuse assignments from one semester to another, and find the feedback useful in gauging student progress in the class. These early results from our experience with and evaluation of interview grading lead us to conclude that interview grading is both beneficial and scalable. We will continue to refine the interview grading process and are expanding its use across a wider range of courses.

8. REFERENCES

[1] V. Balijepally, R. Mahapatra, S. Nerur, and K. H. Price. Are two heads better than one for software development? the productivity paradox of pair programming. *MIS Q.*, 33(1):91–118, Mar. 2009.

[2] L. L. Beck and A. W. Chizhik. An experimental study of cooperative learning in cs1. In *Proceedings of the 39th SIGCSE Technical Symposium on Computer Science Education*, SIGCSE '08, pages 205–209, New York, NY, USA, 2008. ACM.

[3] N. Y. T. B. Blog. Stanford finds computer science students cheat more than others. `http://bits.blogs.nytimes.com/2010/02/11/stanford-finds-computer-science-students-cheat-more-than-others/?_php=true&_type=blogs&_r=0`, Feb 2010.

[4] G. Braught, T. Wahls, and L. M. Eby. The case for pair programming in the computer science classroom. *Trans. Comput. Educ.*, 11(1):2:1–2:21, Feb. 2011.

[5] J. C. Carver, L. Henderson, L. He, J. Hodges, and D. Reese. Increased retention of early computer science and software engineering students using pair programming. In *Proceedings of the 20th Conference on Software Engineering Education & Training*, CSEET '07, pages 115–122, Washington, DC, USA, 2007. IEEE Computer Society.

[6] J. P. East and J. B. Schafer. In-person grading: an evaluative experiment. In *Proceedings of the 36th SIGCSE technical symposium on Computer science education - SIGCSE '05*, page 378, New York, New York, USA, 2005. ACM Press.

[7] A. P. Fagen, C. H. Crouch, and E. Mazur. Peer instruction: Results from a range of classrooms. *The Physics Teacher*, 40(4):206–209, 2002.

[8] R. Mac. The temptation to cheat in computer science classes at stanford. `http://bayarea.blogs.nytimes.com/2010/02/11/heading-off-the-temptation-to-cheat-in-computer-science-classes-at-stanford/`, Feb 2010.

[9] C. D. Marsan. Why computer science students cheat. Network World: `http://www.pcworld.com/article/194486/Computer_Science_Students_Cheating.html`, April 2010.

[10] C. McDowell, L. Werner, H. Bullock, and J. Fernald. The effects of pair-programming on performance in an introductory programming course. In *Proceedings of the 33rd SIGCSE Technical Symposium on Computer Science Education*, SIGCSE '02, pages 38–42, New York, NY, USA, 2002. ACM.

[11] L. Porter, C. Bailey Lee, and B. Simon. Halving fail rates using peer instruction: A study of four computer science courses. In *Proceeding of the 44th ACM Technical Symposium on Computer Science Education*, SIGCSE '13, pages 177–182, New York, NY, USA, 2013. ACM.

[12] L. Porter, M. Guzdial, C. McDowell, and B. Simon. Success in introductory programming: What works? *Commun. ACM*, 56(8):34–36, Aug. 2013.

[13] H. M. Walker. A lab-based approach for introductory computing that emphasizes collaboration. In *Computer Science Education Research Conference*, CSERC '11, pages 21–31, Open Univ., Heerlen, The Netherlands, The Netherlands, 2011. Open Universiteit, Heerlen.

Transferring Skills at Solving Word Problems from Computing to Algebra Through Bootstrap

Emmanuel Schanzer, Kathi Fisler, Shriram Krishnamurthi, Matthias Felleisen
Harvard Graduate School of Education, WPI Computer Science, Brown University Computer Science,
Northeastern University College of Computing and Information Science
schanzer@bootstrapworld.org

ABSTRACT

Many educators have tried to leverage computing or programming to help improve students' achievement in mathematics. However, several hopes of performance gains—particularly in algebra—have come up short. In part, these efforts fail to align the computing and mathematical concepts at the level of detail typically required to achieve transfer of learning. This paper describes Bootstrap, an early-programming curriculum that is designed to teach key algebra topics as students build their own videogames. We discuss the curriculum, explain how it aligns with algebra, and present initial data showing student performance gains on standard algebra problems after completing Bootstrap.

Categories and Subject Descriptors: K.3.2 [Computers & Education]: Computer & Information Science Education

Keywords: algebra; skills transfer; game programming

1. INTRODUCTION

Computing educators have long argued that learning to program improves mathematics and problem-solving skills [8]. Research-based evidence for this claim has, however, been slim. While there are notable exceptions [7], a majority of projects that seek to improve problem-solving ability through programming have failed to produce measured results. Indeed, researchers versed in the computing-education literature frequently warn that programming is not known to transfer problem-solving skills to mathematics.

Transfer of learning between domains typically requires both deep structural connections between the domains and explicit instruction in how to apply concepts from one discipline in the other [1, 10, 12]. Many computing projects that target transfer to mathematical problem-solving fail to handle one of these two requirements. This raises two challenges: can we identify specific problem-solving practices in computing that have direct analogs to processes in mathematics, and can we teach them in such a way that students realize performance gains in mathematics?

SIGCSE'15, March 4–7, 2015, Kansas City, MO, USA.

http://dx.doi.org/10.1145/2676723.2677238.

This paper describes an approach to teaching program design that measurably improves student performance on algebra word problems from standardized mathematics exams (in the USA). Our approach is embodied in a curriculum, Bootstrap, that is used in both middle- and high-school math and computing classes across the USA. This paper describes Bootstrap and how it simultaneously teaches students how to design programs and solve algebra word problems. We also present preliminary data from a pre/post-test evaluation showing student gains on algebra problems after completing Bootstrap. Our data come from students at multiple schools in multiple states in the USA; the student population includes mainstream students, not only elite ones. These data suggest that Bootstrap is achieving transfer from programming to specific topics in mathematics.

2. THE CURRICULUM: BRIDGING COMPUTING AND ALGEBRA

Bootstrap teaches students to program a videogame of their own design using algebraic and geometric concepts. Each game features a user-controlled avatar called the *player*, a *target* that the player is trying to catch, a *danger* that the player is trying to avoid, and a *background* setting in which the game takes place. In the first lesson, students "design" their games by choosing values for these elements. This customization gives students ownership and investment in the game they are trying to produce. Recent student designs vary widely: catching candy, avoiding the lunch lady, meeting aliens, collecting butterflies, etc.

Students build up their games by incrementally adding features involving their players, dangers, and targets: dangers and targets wrap-around (in side-scrolling behavior), scores rise as the player collides with the target, and the game ends when the player collides with the danger. The project is carefully designed so that each game feature teaches a particular mathematical concept. Each unit in the curriculum has three integrated components: a new feature for students to add to their games, a new programming construct or concept needed to implement the feature, and an underlying mathematics concept that relates to the programming concept. Figure 1 summarizes the curricular structure, showing the game features, programming concepts, and mathematical concepts addressed in each unit.

Bootstrap's alignment with algebra is further embodied in three aspects of our curriculum: our tools for migrating from computations to code, the shape of code that comprises a game program, and the process used to determine the required computations. We discuss each in turn.

Unit	Game Feature	Programming Concept	Math Concept
1	locating elements on screen	expressions, Circles of Evaluation	coordinates
2	creating text and images	string and image operations	domain, range, kinds of data
3–5	making moving images	defining functions, examples	multiple function representations: as formulas and as tables
6	determine when game elements are off-screen	Booleans and Boolean operators	inequalities
7	responding to key-presses	conditional	piecewise function
8	collision detection	(nothing new)	Pythagorean Theorem
9	polishing games for presentation	code reviews	explaining math concepts to others

Figure 1: Curriculum structure: each unit introduces game, programming, and math concepts in parallel.

2.1 Diagramming Expressions: Circles of Evaluation

Algebra teachers often struggle to help students learn order of operations. Most teach monikers such as PEMDAS to summarize the order in which operations apply in an expression, along with phrases such as "please excuse my dear aunt sally" to help students decode the moniker. Mastering order of operations actually requires two distinct skills: understanding the structure of expressions (parsing), and applying operations in order within that structure (evaluation). Both are articulated in many state mathematics standards, but PEMDAS focuses only on the latter.

Bootstrap begins by teaching students to diagram expressions with a notation that we call "Circles of Evaluation". Assume a student is working with the expression $6 * (4 + 5)$. Bootstrap diagrams this expression as shown on the right. Each circle names a function above the line and lists arguments to the function (in left-to-right order) below the line. Nested circles correspond to nested expressions. Students learn how to evaluate a circle by reducing the innermost circle to an answer, then replacing the circle with its answer and repeating. Circles of evaluation naturally extend beyond arithmetic to other expressions that arise in programming (e.g., nested boolean expressions and computations that compose images).

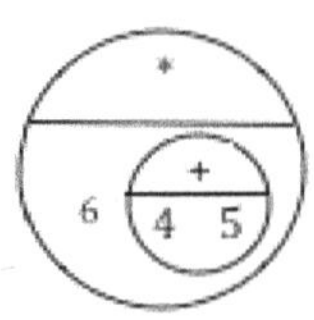

From Circles to Code.

Bootstrap teaches a simple process for turning circles into syntactically-valid textual code (in a language called BSL, a pedagogically-oriented subset of Racket). We represent a circle in code by splitting it open (into a pair of parentheses) and writing its content linearly inside. The function name goes after the opening parenthesis, and the arguments follow the function name in left-to-right order. Our arithmetic circle yields the following code:

```
(* 6 (+ 4 5))
```

Circles of evaluation gently introduce students to formal notation (as many blocks-based languages do), while also drilling a challenging algebra topic. The same steps to translate circles to code apply whether the circle is for an arithmetic function, a built-in function on another datatype, or a user-defined function. This regularity, which infix syntax lacks, eases the transition from visual to textual code. Other common representations of expressions, such as abstract syntax trees, lack the visual metaphor of "opening the circle," which eases this transition.

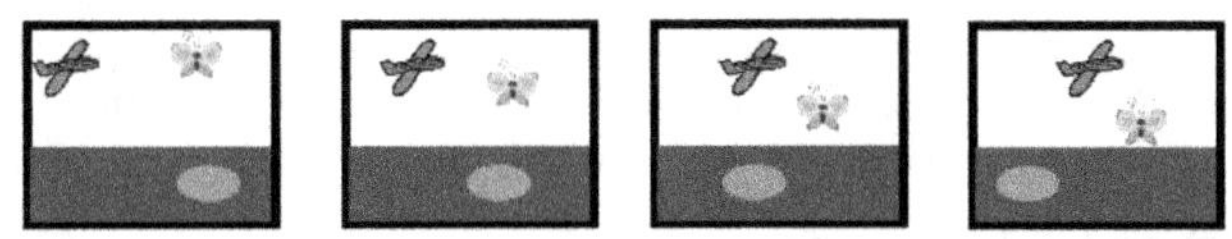

Figure 2: A videogame as a sequence of frames.

2.2 Programming Algebra: The Shape of a Game Program

Bootstrap's next connection to algebra comes from the programming model in which students develop their games. Understanding this model requires a particular perspective on how games are constructed. Figure 2 shows a game decomposed into a sequence of frames; the decomposition resembles the filmstrips that yield movies. In this game, the player uses arrow keys to move the butterfly up and down, aiming to land on the lily pad while avoiding the airplane.

In each frame of the game, each of the airplane, butterfly, and lilypad is located at a specific coordinate. The coordinates suffice to create the picture that corresponds to that frame; thus, they form the underlying *model* that characterizes individual frames (in the software engineering sense of the term, e.g., as in model-view-controller architectures). In a simple game in which each element moves in only one dimension, the model simply contains three numbers.

Between frames, the coordinates of each game element (can) change: in our example, the lilypad drifts left, the airplane flies right, and the butterfly moves according to the keys (if any) pressed by the human user. The amount by which each element's position changes between frames can be captured in a function. For example, to move the airplane rightwards across the sky, a simple linear function such as

$$f(x) = x + 5$$

computes a new x-coordinate for one frame from the x-coordinate in the previous frame.

In Bootstrap, students provide images for each of their danger, target, and player, as well as a background image (here, the blue pond); for each game element that moves, they also define a function (in code) that computes its new single-dimension coordinate from its coordinate in the previous frame. The platform iteratively produces a screenshot with the given images, updates the positions based on the functions and any key presses, then repeats, displaying the sequence of screenshots as the game. The platform also consults student-supplied functions to detect when elements have gone off screen (after which it wraps positions to the opposite edge) and to detect when game elements have collided (to raise scores or end the game).

The following examples illustrate the code that students write. The function (previously called f) that calculates the new position of the airplane is called *update-danger*:

```
(define (update-danger x)
  (+ x 5))
```

(BSL allows hyphens in function and identifier names). The *update-player* function takes an additional argument: a key-press that is used to make the player move in response to user input. The following function moves the player 3 pixels up when the up-arrow key is pressed, and 3 pixels down when down-arrow is pressed. This is an example of a *piece-wise* function in mathematics. User-interactivity provides a concrete motivation for this otherwise abstract concept:

```
(define (update-player y key)
  (cond [(key=? key "up") (- y 3)]
        [(key=? key "down") (+ y 3)]
        [else y]))
```

An element has gone offscreen when its x-coordinate falls outside of the screen boundaries. Bootstrap uses this function as an opportunity to practice function composition, by having students write separate functions to check each of the left and right edges of the screen.

```
(define (onscreen? x)
  (and (onscreen-left? x) (onscreen-right? x)))
(define (onscreen-left? x)
  (> x 0))
```

Contrast to Other Early Programming Models.
These code samples illustrate how Bootstrap's underlying programming model keeps students focused on algebraic concepts. Functions are a natural and essential part of the model, not an advanced concept. The model is also interesting for what it omits relative to other early-programming platforms. Students do not use looping constructs (such as Scratch's "forever" block), mutable variables, or assignment statements. Instead, students simply write side-effect-free functions that describe how positions (and potentially other game attributes) change from one frame to the next. The lack of side effects is particularly important because it reflects the nature of functions and variables in mathematics (see Section 4). The platform, called the World framework [4], takes care of the rest.

2.3 Solving Word Problems: The Design Recipe

Bootstrap's third connection to algebra arises from the process that we teach students to use when designing functions. Consider the *update-danger* function that moves the danger 5 pixels to the right. The student is taught to follow the following steps:

1. *Write a contract, specifying the domain and range for the function.* In this case, the contract is

   update-danger : number → number

2. *Write examples that illustrate the expected behavior of the function.* Examples contain actual calls to the function in BSL. Examples for *update-danger* include:

```
(EXAMPLE (update-danger 0) (+ 0 5))
(EXAMPLE (update-danger 5) (+ 5 5))
(EXAMPLE (update-danger 100) (+ 100 5))
```

3. *Circle changes across the examples, give a descriptive name to each independent change, then write a function whose parameters are the descriptive names and whose body is the unchanging part of the example output, substituting parameters for changes.* This case has one change: the function input and first operand to +:

```
(define (update-danger xcoord)
  (+ xcoord 5))
```

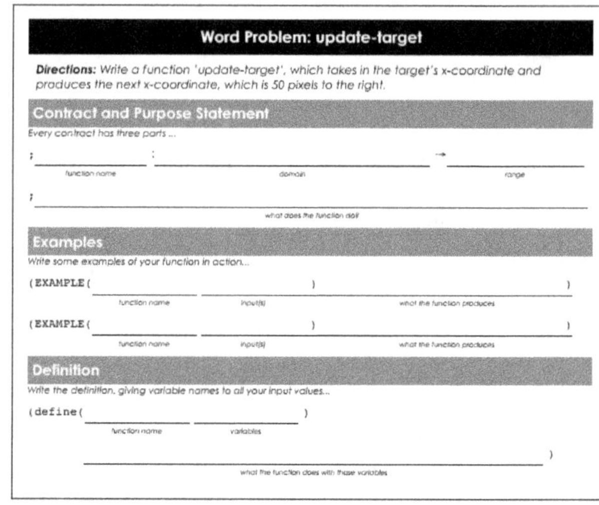
Word Problem: update-target

Directions: Write a function 'update-target', which takes in the target's x-coordinate and produces the next x-coordinate, which is 50 pixels to the right.

Contract and Purpose Statement

Every contract has three parts ...

; ______ (function name) : ______ (domain) → ______ (range)

; ______ (what does the function do?)

Examples

Write some examples of your function in action...

(EXAMPLE(______ (function name) ______ (input(s))) ______ (what the function produces))

(EXAMPLE(______ (function name) ______ (input(s))) ______ (what the function produces))

Definition

Write the definition, giving variable names to all your input values...

(define(______ (function name) ______ (variables))

______ (what the function does with those variables))

Figure 3: A design-recipe worksheet, showing the process for solving word problems.

This sequence of steps, inspired by Pólya's work [11], is called the Design Recipe [3]. It helps Bootstrap students think through a function definition problem step-by-step. If they can't articulate the domain and range or write examples, they usually don't understand the problem well enough to write a correct function either. The steps thus provide teachers a valuable diagnostic when students are stuck. We use a paper-and-pencil worksheet (Figure 3) to reinforce the steps: students complete these worksheets for a variety of practice functions (including some typical mathematics word problems) as well as for every function needed for their games. Students type in and run each function that they develop through the worksheet before moving on to the next problem: this both tests their code against examples and lets them see new functionality in their games.

The design recipe is much more than a guide to writing code; it also embodies a key concept in algebra standards. Learning standards for algebra expect students to be able to work with different representations of functions. Three common representations (domain/range, input-output tables, and symbolic form) have corresponding constructs in programming (type specification or contract, test cases, and function definition, respectively). Bootstrap helps students work with all three of these representations, using the concrete context of programming to motivate when and how each representation can be helpful in problem solving. The fourth common representation, graphs, could also be supported in Bootstrap with more instructional time.

2.4 Deployment Status

Interest from teachers has been strong and growing rapidly. To date, we have offered training workshops to hundreds of teachers, most of whom are math teachers looking for ways to help students master and appreciate mathematics. Many work with students who typically struggle with math; many provide anecdotal comments about student enthusiasm and engagement in math following Bootstrap. Several thousand students have completed the curriculum, some in formal classrooms and some in after-school settings.

3. EVALUATION

Our assessment finds that Bootstrap helps students gain proficiency in certain topics in algebra. Bootstrap also helps mathematics teachers see potential connections between algebra and (some approaches to) computer science.

3.1 Teacher Perceptions

We gather feedback from teachers just after they complete one of our professional development workshops, then again after they have taught the curriculum with students at least once. Teachers' perceptions of the connections to mathematics is covered in both surveys. Many of the teachers who attend our workshops are primarily math teachers, looking to use Bootstrap to help with challenges they face in teaching Algebra I. This population does not teach Bootstrap simply for the sake of teaching computing.

In end-of-workshop surveys of 143 teachers (collected from June 2013 through August 2014), 101 indicated that they taught math. 95% of these 101 teachers strongly agreed (72%) or agreed (23%) that Bootstrap was relevant to algebra. 93% strongly agreed (74%) or agreed (19%) that Bootstrap was relevant to their own teaching. A separate survey (of in-school teachers who had used Bootstrap) confirmed that teachers see Bootstrap's relevance to math after using it: 84% (out of 32) agreed or (more often) strongly agreed with the statement "Bootstrap is an effective curriculum for teaching students math skills".

3.2 Student Performance in Algebra

Our algebra-performance assessment focuses on (1) word problems that ask students to identify domain and range, produce input/output tables, and produce symbolic representations, and (2) problems about function composition. Concretely, we are testing the following hypotheses:

HYPOTHESIS 1. *Students who complete Bootstrap will improve in their performance on algebra word problems and function composition problems.*

HYPOTHESIS 2. *Students who complete Bootstrap will show more improvement in performance on algebra word problems and function composition problems than students who did not take Bootstrap.*

3.2.1 The Assessment Exam

We use a standard pre-post design to test these hypotheses. Students take a pre-test as they begin the Bootstrap module, and a post-test of similar but different questions after completing Bootstrap. Both tests are done on paper. All questions are taken from standardized algebra tests in the US state of Massachusetts (students take these tests in their 8th grade year, roughly age 13). We extend the state-exam questions on word problems (which ask only for symbolic representations) to ask about domain, range, and input/output examples, as those are included in state math standards (albeit emphasized less on the exams). Figure 4 shows sample questions. There are 8 word problems and 9 function-composition questions on each of the pre- and post-tests, with the latter appearing first.

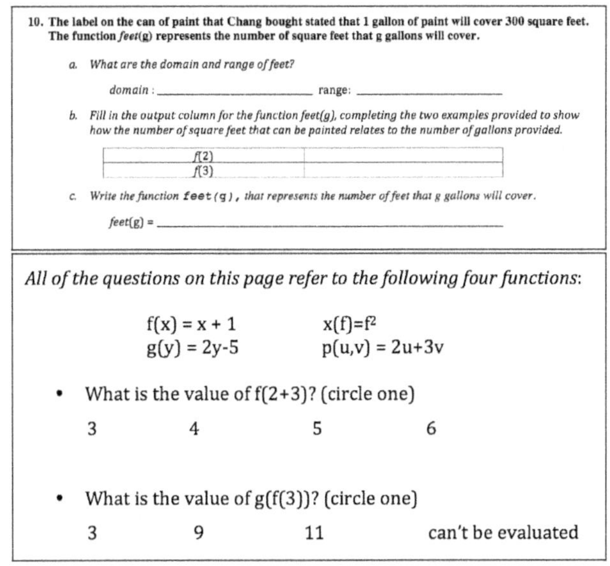

10. The label on the can of paint that Chang bought stated that 1 gallon of paint will cover 300 square feet. The function *feet*(g) represents the number of square feet that g gallons will cover.

a. *What are the domain and range of feet?*

domain : ______ range: ______

b. *Fill in the output column for the function feet(g), completing the two examples provided to show how the number of square feet that can be painted relates to the number of gallons provided.*

f(2)	
f(3)	

c. *Write the function* `feet(g)`, *that represents the number of feet that g gallons will cover.*

feet(g) = ______

All of the questions on this page refer to the following four functions:

f(x) = x + 1   x(f)=f²
g(y) = 2y-5   p(u,v) = 2u+3v

- What is the value of f(2+3)? (circle one)

  3   4   5   6

- What is the value of g(f(3))? (circle one)

  3   9   11   can't be evaluated

Figure 4: Sample questions from Bootstrap's assessment of algebra performance. The top box shows a word problem. The bottom box shows two problems on function evaluation and composition.

3.2.2 Student Population and Study Logistics

The evaluation data reported here comes from computing classes at three schools: 8th grade classes at a public middle school in Massachusetts, 8th grade classes at a private school in Florida, and 9th grade classes at a private school (religiously-affiliated) in Illinois. While we have data from other schools (that show similar trends), we do not report them here: each has either too few matched pre- and post-tests, too few students for significant comparison, or insufficient IRB approval for publishing results.

Each of the teachers had completed a professional development workshop on Bootstrap. Some gathered data the first time they taught the module, while others had taught it once or twice before gathering data. Students in all classes had 30 minutes to work on each of the pre- and post tests. The same tests were used across all of the classes.

3.2.3 Data Analysis

We present data from a total of six classes: two from the school in Massachusetts, three from the school in Florida (one a control group that had not taken Bootstrap, labeled "Cntrl" in the tables), and one from the school in Illinois. All classes from the same state were taught by the same teacher to students at the same grade level. We present one table on each of function composition and word problems. In each table, the reported pre- and post-test score are averages across all students. In computing significance, however, pre- and post-test scores were matched for each student (rather than

Class	# Students	Pre-test	Post-test	Change
MA-fall	26	2.31	6.85	197%
MA-spring	32	2.56	5.53	116 %
FL-1	25	2.00	3.12	56%
FL-2	25	1.80	3.72	106%
FL-Cntrl	26	2.62	3.12	19%
IL	15	4.33	6.53	51%

Table 1: Pre/post-test scores on problems about function application and function composition.

Class	# Students	Pre-test	Post-test	Change
MA-fall	26	0.62	4.00	550%
MA-spring	32	1.28	3.00	134%
FL-1	25	0.80	1.72	115%
FL-2	25	0.92	1.96	133%
FL-Cntrl	26	1.54	0.81	-47%
IL	15	2.00	5.53	177%

Table 2: Pre/post-test scores on word problems.

averaged across the class), allowing us to use a two-tailed t-test to compare outcomes at the student level. Significant ($p<0.02$) gains in both function composition and word problems were found for all classes that used Bootstrap with the exception of the IL class, whose small sample size prevents us from making significance claims for the reported gains.

Table 1 reports on student performance on questions related to function application and function composition; samples of these questions appear in the lower half of Figure 4. Students earned 1 point for each problem that they answered correctly. On the per-student two-tailed t-tests, gains were significant at ranges from .003 for the Florida-1 class to 2.84e11 for the spring Massachusetts class.

Table 2 reports student performance on word problems; a sample question appears in the top half of Figure 4. Students earned 1 point for each problem on which they provided a correct function in symbolic form (part c in the sample question). On the per-student two-tailed t-tests, gains were significant at ranges from .01 for the Florida-2 class to 8.84e8 for the fall Massachusetts class.

The word-problem data reported in this paper omits student performance on the domain/range and input/output parts of the questions. State assessment exams do not include these parts, and algebra teachers often de-emphasize these representations (despite their inclusion in state standards). Reporting on only the symbolic form therefore gives us a more realistic comparison to control-group students who have not had Bootstrap. When including the results for other representations, Bootstrap students displayed far higher gains than their control group counterparts. This may speak more to the results of de-emphasizing those representations in traditional math instruction than it does to strengths of Bootstrap, but the fact that Bootstrap students were able to identify these representations on an algebra task after seeing them solely in the programming domain may strengthen the case for evidence of transfer.

The control group did not see significant gains in either function composition or word problems (word-problem scores actually dropped noticeably for this group; the teacher hypothesized that the students were less motivated for the test). We found no significant differences in pre-test scores between the control and experimental classes in Florida, and students in both conditions were taking the same mathematics class (concurrent with Bootstrap for the experimental group). This suggests that Bootstrap is having an impact beyond what students are learning in math class (perhaps affecting engagement as well as skills).

At first glance, the average scores on these tests seem rather low; on word problems, for example, some classes correctly answered fewer than 2 problems on average. For word problems, this is partly an artifact of our scoring: students answered 3 subquestions per problem (as shown in Figure 4), but we scored only one of these for this paper. Students thus answered more questions than the scores reflect. This partly explains why scores are generally higher on the function application and composition questions.

Time constraints are likely a significant factor. Word problem questions follow those for function composition, and students have only 30 minutes to complete both sections (though they may answer questions in any order). Students typically attempt no more than 5 of the 8-9 problems, yet make few errors on problems for which they write an answer. This time constraint—dictated by the participating teachers—thus appears significant in these marks being low.

The performance gains from pre-test to post-test were lower in the MA-spring courses (in both tables) than in the MA-fall courses, despite having the same teacher leading both classes. This is partly explained by higher pre-test scores in the spring class. The teacher in that course hypothesizes that the spring students had simply had more coverage of mathematics in their other classes, which could have led to higher pre-test scores.

Threats to Generalizability.

Our brief discussion of the two Massachusetts classes offers a glimpse of the many variables that differ across offerings of Bootstrap. Students could be taking Bootstrap within their math class, alongside a math class (taught by the same or a different teacher), or out of sequence with a math class. Students vary in grade levels, prior preparation in math, and confidence. Due to these (and other) variables, we cannot generalize too much from these findings. Accordingly, we do not report effect sizes and other statistical parameters.

The extra questions (on domain/range and examples) that we add to the word problems from the state exams provide a form of scaffolding that students would have to do on their own on the state exams. Additional studies must explore whether students internalize the design recipe well enough to produce correct symbolic representations in isolation.

4. RELATED WORK

While programming has had some success at developing other mathematical competencies [7], transfer to algebra has been difficult to establish. Logo was designed explicitly to teach mathematics, and many researchers have studied it as a vehicle for algebra (e.g., [5, 6]). Pea and Kurland [9] found no evidence of improved mathematical reasoning among students who had been exposed to more than 30 hours of instruction in Logo, and later questioned the entire expectation of transfer into algebra. Clements [2] found that students who mastered the concept of variables in Logo were unable to apply that understanding to algebra tasks.

Recent research suggests that deep structural similarities between thought processes in different disciplines, along with explicit instruction in those similarities, are key components to transfer [1, 10, 12]. Early-programming curricula typically lack clearly-articulated processes for problem solving (such as Bootstrap's Design Recipe), much less ones that also apply to solving problems in algebra.

In imperative programming, the terms "variable" and "function" have different meaning than in algebra. Algebra functions always return the same output for a given input (students even use the "vertical line test" to confirm this); imperative functions fail this test. Similarly, an algebra variable (called a "parameter" in programming) varies *across* function invocations, but is *constant within a given invocation*. An imperative programming variable changes its value within a function. In contrast, BSL functions and variables behave exactly like those of mathematics. Because of this relationship, students can trace function behavior in Bootstrap using *substitution* (just as they do in algebra, thereby reinforcing the idea), but this would produce the wrong answer for many Logo or SNAP functions. Wright, Rich, and Lee [14] independently deployed and assessed Bootstrap with their own instrument. Their study, which included middle- and high-school students, some experimental and some control, found significant improvements in students' understanding of variables after Bootstrap. Thomas [13] used simple BASIC programs to convey general concepts of algebraic variables, but not in the context of functions.

Bootstrap's pedagogic goals differ from those of Scratch. Scratch is designed to get students writing animation code in a matter of minutes: it focuses on rapid engagement and encouraging exploration. Bootstrap was designed to reinforce algebra: students write their first animation later than with Scratch, but having already covered key topics in mathematics standards. Its engagement is achieved differently: by having students *design* their games at the very beginning (giving them something to look forward to and repeatedly draw upon) and by using images (rather than arithmetic) to practice function composition and expression structure.

Bootstrap's Circles of Evaluation resemble the blocks that have become ubiquitous in early programming. Clearly, however, by the end of the curriculum students need to be familiar with textual notations. When to make the transition from visual to textual syntax remains open. In Bootstrap, students make the transition early (all their programming is done in text), and this has worked smoothly across several thousand middle-school students. Teachers still return to Circles periodically to emphasize expression structure (e.g., when introducing Boolean operators, or when students are confused). How these notations impact transfer to algebra remains an open research problem.

5. CONCLUSION AND ONGOING WORK

Bootstrap is a computing curriculum designed to reinforce specific learning objectives in algebra. This paper describes three key features of the curriculum and the algebraic concepts that they reinforce. Bootstrap's programming model and choice of programming language allow students to directly apply problem-solving processes for programming to standard problems in algebra. We hypothesize that these enable transfer. Preliminary data showing student performance gains in algebra after Bootstrap is encouraging. We continue to expand our data to include more teachers and more control groups.

In focusing on computing concepts that tie directly and deeply to algebra, Bootstrap also creates a gentle entry ramp for math teachers to begin teaching computing. Many countries have efforts to vastly increase the pool of qualified computing teachers, such as the CS10K project in the USA. Bootstrap appeals to content that math teachers accept as important, while simultaneously staying close enough to teachers' comfort zones that they are willing to bring it into the classroom. Several hundred math teachers completed Bootstrap professional development workshops this summer, with post-workshop surveys showing high participant confidence in their ability to begin teaching computing. This is an exciting result in and of itself as we look to expand educational opportunities in computer science.

Acknowledgements.

The NSF, Google, and Microsoft funded initial development of Bootstrap. Emma Youndtsmith and Rosanna Sobata energetically train and support teachers; Danny Yoo built the programming environment. Rachel Mark and Chris Burns helped create our earliest student workshops. Helpful reviewer comments prompted clarifications in the paper.

6. REFERENCES

[1] J. Bransford and D. Schwartz. Rethinking transfer: A simple proposal with multiple implications. In *Review of Research in Education*, volume 24, pages 61–100. American Educational Research Association, 1999.

[2] D. Clements. The future of educational computing research: The case of computer programming. *Information Technology in Childhood Education*, pages 147–179, 1999.

[3] M. Felleisen, R. B. Findler, M. Flatt, and S. Krishnamurthi. *How to Design Programs*. MIT Press, 2001.

[4] M. Felleisen, R. B. Findler, M. Flatt, and S. Krishnamurthi. A functional I/O system or, fun for freshman kids. In *ACM SIGPLAN International Conference on Functional Programming*, 2009.

[5] W. Feurzeig, S. Papert, M. Bloom, R. Grant, and C. Solomon. Programming-languages as a conceptual framework for teaching mathematics. *SIGCUE Outlook*, 4(2):13–17, Apr. 1970.

[6] R. Noss. Constructing a conceptual framework for elementary algebra through Logo programming. *Educational Studies in Mathematics*, 7:335–357, 1986.

[7] R. Noss. Children's learning of geometrical concepts through Logo. *Journal for Research in Mathematics Education*, 18(5):343–362, 1987.

[8] S. Papert. Teaching children to be mathematicians versus teaching about mathematics. *International Journal of Mathematical Education in Science and Technology*, 3(3):249–262, 1972.

[9] R. Pea and D. Kurland. On the cognitive effects of learning computer programming. *New Ideas in Psychology*, 2:137–168, 1984.

[10] D. Perkins. *Making Learning Whole*. Jossey-Bass, San Francisco, 2009.

[11] G. Pólya. *How to Solve It: A New Aspect of Mathematical Method*. Doubleday, 1957.

[12] P. J. Rich, K. R. Leatham, and G. A. Wright. Convergent cognition. *Instructional Science*, 41(2):431–453, Mar. 2013.

[13] M. O. J. Thomas. *A conceptual approach to the early learning of algebra using a computer*. PhD thesis, University of Warwick, 1988.

[14] G. Wright, P. Rich, and R. Lee. The influence of teaching programming on learning mathematics. In *Society for Information Technology & Teacher Education International Conference*, 2013.

A Practical Guide to Developing and Validating Computer Science Knowledge Assessments with Application to Middle School

Philip Sheridan Buffum
Computer Science

Eleni V. Lobene
Computer Science

Megan Hardy Frankosky
Psychology

Kristy Elizabeth Boyer
Computer Science

Eric N. Wiebe
STEM Education

James C. Lester
Computer Science

North Carolina State University
Raleigh, NC, USA
{psbuffum, eleni.lobene, rmhardy, keboyer, wiebe, lester}@ncsu.edu

ABSTRACT
Knowledge assessment instruments, or tests, are commonly created by faculty in classroom settings to measure student knowledge and skill. Another crucial role for assessment instruments is in gauging student learning in response to a computer science education research project, or intervention. In an increasingly interdisciplinary landscape, it is crucial to validate knowledge assessment instruments, yet developing and validating these tests for computer science poses substantial challenges. This paper presents a seven-step approach to designing, iteratively refining, and validating knowledge assessment instruments designed not to assign grades but to measure the efficacy or promise of novel interventions. We also detail how this seven-step process is being instantiated within a three-year project to implement a game-based learning environment for middle school computer science. This paper serves as a practical guide for adapting widely accepted psychometric practices to the development and validation of computer science knowledge assessments to support research.

Categories and Subject Descriptors
K.3.2 [**Computers & Education**]: Computer and Information Sciences Education --- *Computer Science Education*

General Terms: Human Factors.

Keywords: Computer science education, assessment, middle school.

1. INTRODUCTION
Assessing student knowledge is a crucial task across many levels of computer science education, as in any discipline. College and university faculty are most familiar with tests that they themselves author in order to measure their students' understanding and skill in course-related topics. These *assessment instruments* constitute an active area of investigation within the SIGCSE community [16, 17], and their role is often prominent in assigning student grades. Another crucial role for assessment instruments of computer science skills and knowledge is within research projects that aim to measure the promise or efficacy of interventions [7, 15]. While computer science educators and computer science education researchers have the expertise to craft assessment items for computing skills and concepts, these same educators and researchers often do not have formal training in establishing the *validity* (the extent to which a test measures what it is intended to measure) and *reliability* (the consistency of an instrument across administrations of that test) of the assessments they create. Only a small number of computer science education research projects have emphasized these steps [15, 17], and creating assessments is challenging for computer science due to the complexity and dynamic nature of the content [12]. Yet, in an increasingly interdisciplinary research landscape, it is becoming crucial to validate assessment instruments on which research findings rely [13, 14]. Moreover, developing assessments of student learning is an urgent area of need for the relatively young computer science education community as it advances toward the ranks of more mature disciplines such as physics that have established standardized assessments over time.

SIGCSE '15, March 04 – 07, 2015, Kansas City, MO, USA.
Copyright 2015 ACM 978-1-4503-2966-8/15/03…$15.00.
http://dx.doi.org/10.1145/2676723.2677295

The wealth of literature on instrument validation within education, psychometrics, and other disciplines is vast. The approaches in much of this literature rely upon administering instruments repeatedly to the same students, or administering them to many hundreds or even thousands of students. These techniques are impractical for the vast majority of computer science education research projects. This paper presents a **practical approach to validating knowledge assessment instruments** that has been developed over several years of collaboration between computer scientists, computer science education researchers, educational psychologists, and an industrial/organizational psychologist. First, we present widely accepted practices for establishing validity and reliability of knowledge assessment instruments. Second, we describe the application of this approach to the ENGAGE project, a computer science education research project focused on developing a game-based learning environment for middle school computer science. This case study illustrates how, within the constraints of a typical research project, and with the availability of only a handful of classrooms in which to operate, widely accepted practices can be adapted to validate and iteratively refine computer science knowledge assessment instruments.

2. BACKGROUND

In psychometrics, to be effective a test must be both *valid* and *reliable* [2]. Validity refers to the extent to which a test, referred to as an instrument, measures what it was intended to measure. Validity is of crucial concern when constructing knowledge assessment instruments because authors of test items hold extensive expertise in the target domain, and the test items that these experts write intending to discriminate students' knowledge of a particular concept may, in practice, be testing a different skill. There are three primary types of validity: construct, criterion-related, and content [3]. Establishing *construct validity* is a process of testing and confirming inferences in measurement and prediction. This complex form of validation involves investigating the relationships between the theoretical variable and the measure for both the test and relevant outcomes. This type of validity can include a number of advanced statistical techniques to investigate each relationship. Alternatively, *criterion-related validity* is the extent to which the test scores correlate with other variables, or other related tests, as one would expect. Finally, *content validity* is how well the items, or questions, match the desired variable definition based on the opinion of subject matter experts.

Of the three types of validity, establishing content validity is an important step for assessments of educational interventions, and it is the most accessible type of validity study to perform in computer science education research. While there is no uniformly accepted process for establishing content validity, generally the steps include creating a panel of experts in the domain of interest and providing a structured framework for collecting and analyzing the panel's feedback on the items. Sections 3 and 4 will describe this process in more detail.

Reliability is the consistency of a test's measurement or the extent to which an instrument is free of error [2]. In other words, if an individual were given the same test multiple times, assuming there was no learning effect between administrations (and no testing effect from the instrument itself [11]), that individual would score nearly the same every time. However, it is often not practical to give the same test multiple times to the same individual; doing so requires securing an "empty treatment" control group that does not participate in the intervention. Additionally, for K-12 learners whose understanding of target computer science concepts could be affected by their learning in related subject areas such as mathematics, science, and technology, the "no learning effect" assumption is called into question.

There are a number of types of reliability estimates. For example, *inter-rater reliability* is used when two or more trained raters independently score a test [8]. This is an appropriate method for qualitative items, such as free responses, where scoring the responses may be subjective. Another kind of reliability estimate is *internal consistency*, which is based upon the extent to which items are correlated within a test itself [5]. If the test being developed is multiple-choice, typically a statistical measure called Cronbach's alpha is utilized to establish internal consistency. Cronbach's alpha can be computed using many off-the-shelf statistical packages (e.g., SPSS or SAS). In general, a score of 0.7 and above is desirable to indicate a "sound" test.

3. PRACTICAL GUIDELINES FOR TEST CONSTRUCTION

The process of constructing an assessment instrument, much like the process of building software artifacts, can proceed in many different ways depending upon the goals of the project and the expertise of the team members. This section presents a seven-phase process for developing an assessment instrument that can be used as both a pre- and post-test, addressing the open need in computer science education research for evaluating the strength of a given intervention. This process has been created and honed within a multi-year collaboration between the authors, a team including computer scientists and psychologists.

1. **Identify the purpose of the test.** It is important to articulate the purpose of the test, whether it is intended to assess conceptual knowledge, problem solving, other skills such as, for example, computational thinking or collaboration. This purpose guides the remaining phases of test development.

2. **Define the construct of interest.** Based upon the determined purpose of the test, defining the construct of interest typically involves a content analysis of the domain guided by literature and observations. For computer science projects that involve pre-defined curricula, guidance for the constructs of interest is often found within the curriculum and learning objectives.

3. **Prepare the test specifications.** There are numerous **test formats** ranging from multiple-choice to open-ended essay questions, with many in between. The choice of which type of test to use often comes with tradeoffs: open-ended questions can provide rich insight into student learning, but these items can be labor-intensive to grade and reliability of the grading must be established to ensure consistency and objectivity. On the other hand, multiple-choice questions are straightforward to grade but can be labor-intensive to construct and do not provide the same variety and richness of student responses as open-ended questions. Nonetheless, multiple-choice tests are scalable to many students, and many validation techniques including those detailed in this paper are aimed at multiple-choice tests.

   If a multiple-choice test format is selected, the literature provides guidance on the **number of responses per question**, which should never exceed five to nine for simple items [6]. For computer science knowledge assessments, four response options may be appropriate in order to minimize extraneous cognitive load, since the items are often not simple. Additionally, four choices strikes a balance with the likelihood of false positives from guessing, with an expected 25% rate of correct responses attributed to random chance alone.

   Another important specification is **test length**, which in classroom settings and many computer science education research projects is constrained by the available contact hours for administering the tests. For example, if a middle school class period is 45 minutes long then a test duration of 30 minutes may be an appropriate target to allow for classroom management activities that typically surround the beginning and ending of a class period. While there are no hard and fast rules for how many items should be included on an instrument [9], in our experience of developing learning assessments, adequate reliability is typically observed with tests that include at least 20 items. More items provides a more substantial basis for establishing validity, but "testing fatigue" can cause the quality of student responses to degrade as tests become lengthier, which is of particular concern for younger students.

4. **Generate the test items.** With the question format and desired length selected, the question writers are trained (if necessary), possible questions are generated, and the quality of the questions is checked. It is recommended that test developers write twice as many questions at this stage as are

needed on the final test, because many candidate test items will be eliminated during the next phases.

5. **Conduct a formal review for validity of the candidate test items.** While there are many forms of establishing validity, a highly recommended approach is to obtain the independent feedback of three to five subject matter experts. Depending upon the specific test purpose, these experts may all share the same general background (e.g., computer science faculty at postsecondary institutions) or may comprise a set of complementary expertise (e.g., one computer science faculty member, one middle school mathematics teacher, one middle school science teacher, and one educational psychology faculty member). Each expert will rate the question according to a pre-determined rubric that could be as simple as a binary "include/exclude" recommendation to, for example, a five-point Likert rating. Additionally, each expert may provide specific feedback for refining and improving test items. Following this process, the strongest set of refined items is retained, and the rest excluded. It is recommended that this set of items still be larger than the ultimately desired test length since some items are likely to be eliminated after piloting.

6. **Pilot the test items with a representative sample from the population of interest.** The closer that these students are to the target population being studied, the better. For K-12 research studies, for example, this means choosing students ideally in the same grade as the target population of study, and when possible, students who are at a similar point of maturity within the grade (for example, students who have just entered seventh grade are different from students who are in the final week of seventh grade). Additionally, a number of considerations typically contribute to determining the required number of respondents needed to adequately assess the quality of an instrument [9]. The type of analysis the test developer is planning to use, and the number of items on the test, typically drive recommendations ranging from 80-200 participants. In the experience of our interdisciplinary project team, adequate statistical power and reliability is achieved with a sample of approximately 100 students.

   Once pilot data are collected, a number of statistical analysis techniques can be used to investigate the quality of the items on a test and then refine accordingly. *Item analysis* describes a set of simple statistics, based on Classical Test Theory [2], which can help differentiate good and bad test questions and improve overall test quality. Usually item analysis includes procedures to determine "difficulty" and "discrimination" as well as looking at item-total correlations. *Difficulty* refers to the percent of students who correctly respond to an item. It is preferable to have a range of difficulty scores (excluding those that are excessively difficult or easy) on a test so that some items are harder than others, and thereby the test will have the ability to differentiate performance levels. *Discrimination* is the percentage of students who got the item correct in the group of highest performers, minus the percentage of students who got the item correct in the lowest group of performers. This index indicates how well an item distinguishes among high and low performers. Generally discrimination values of less than 0.2 are considered poor and suggest dropping an item. Values between 0.2 and 0.3 are marginal and may call for revision. Values between 0.3 and 0.4 are acceptable and values above 0.4 are considered good. Finally, item-total correlations (ITCs) are the correlation between the total test and each individual item. Typically, it is recommended that items with ITCs less than 0.3 be dropped because such a low score indicates a lack of consistency with the rest of the test.

7. **Iteratively refine and re-test.** Using the data collected when piloting, the final stage of test development involves refinement and re-testing. The reliability and item analyses, described previously, guide this process. Regardless of test format, most assessment instruments are iteratively refined from year to year or data collection to data collection, as test "development clearly involves a bit of art as well as a lot of science" [9].

4. DRAFTING AN ASSESMENT FOR MIDDLE SCHOOL COMPUTER SCIENCE

Informed by the psychometrics and psychology literatures described in Section 2 and following the test development processes described in Section 3, we are drafting an assessment for middle school computer science knowledge. This assessment is being created as part of the ENGAGE project, a three-year project to build and investigate the promise of an immersive game-based learning environment (Figure 1) that teaches a subset of the CS Principles course to middle school learners [4]. The focus is on grade seven but the learning environment is intended to be accessible to grades six through eight.

Because ENGAGE's three-year project timeline necessitates developing the intervention (the game-based learning environment and the accompanying lesson plans and in-class learning materials) concurrently with the assessment items, test questions were developed by a subset of the project team while the learning environment and curricular content were developed by another subset of the team. Designing such assessments for computer science knowledge is difficult. They are however crucial for evaluating the strength of interventions, such as ENGAGE's game-based learning environment. Even at the relatively young stage of middle school, students enter interventions with widely varying degrees of prior computer science knowledge. In order to understand how effective the game is at teaching students computer science, the students' *learning gains* need to be assessed, rather than merely their success in the game. This section describes the seven steps of the test development process as they were instantiated.

4.1 Identifying the Purpose of the Test

Step 1 of the test creation process is to identify the purpose of the test. For many computer science education research projects, the purpose of a test is to determine whether the novel intervention was effective in supporting learning for students. This is the case for this project, whose knowledge assessment has a purpose of, "Measure students' computer science learning from interacting with the ENGAGE game-based learning environment."

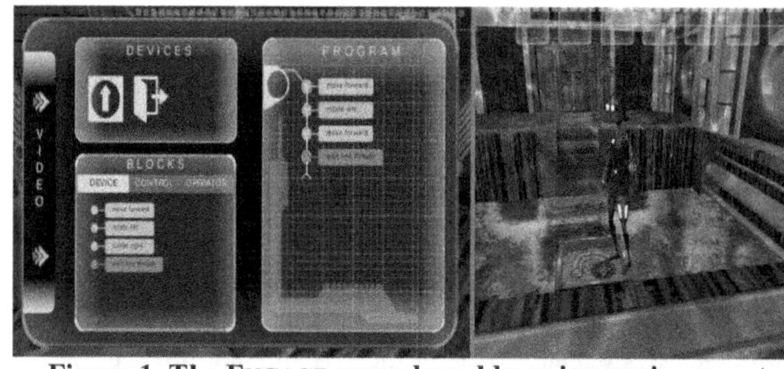

Figure 1. The ENGAGE game-based learning environment

4.2 Defining the Construct of Interest

Step 2, which is to define the construct of interest, was informed by the CS Principles curriculum [1] learning objectives and evidence statements, taken in concert with the US Common Core standards [10]. Crucially, expert input from middle school teachers within a summer workshop in 2013 guided the team in specifying the constructs of interest [4]. Through this process, some CS Principles evidence statements were designated as *overarching*, intended to permeate many if not all the learning challenges in the game. An example of one such overarching evidence statement is 5.1.3.B: *Collaboration facilitates multiple perspectives in developing ideas for solving problems by programming*. Other evidence statements are more *focused*, in that a specific portion of the game-based learning environment will address this concept. Determining which evidence statements to designate as focused, as well as the order they would appear, helped guide the design of ENGAGE's game-based learning environment and its accompanying assessment instruments.

With this correspondence between the intervention and the knowledge assessments, we have a clear understanding of where in the game a student should be expected to master the content needed to correctly answer a given assessment item. This crucially allows the team to use the knowledge assessment as a way to improve the game-based learning environment. For example, if students exhibit low learning gain on a particular assessment item, and the item itself is determined to be sound, this can point to an area of improvement for the intervention itself. An example of this is given in section 4.7.

4.3 Preparing the Test Specifications

In developing the knowledge assessment items, we decided to use a consistent multiple-choice format with four options per item. As described in the previous section, multiple-choice allows for objective, automatic grading, and reduces the subjectivity and manual labor that can be seen with open-ended questions. Moreover, students at the middle school level are known to sometimes contribute as little as possible to open-ended assessment items, and multiple-choice items mitigate this risk.

The target test length was selected as 20 questions, the minimum that has been observed in the team's research experience to provide sufficient reliability coefficients. The smallest plausible number of questions is desirable because the amount of classroom time available for assessments is limited. Only a small fraction of class days can be devoted to assessment, and moreover, in addition to the CS knowledge assessments, the research project requires administering numerous other instruments as well. Class time and testing fatigue are important considerations for the overall length of all instruments combined.

4.4 Generating the Test Items

With the goal test length of 20 questions, the research team set out to author 40 candidate items. Importantly, because the test items are tied closely to the learning objectives that were ultimately decided upon for inclusion in the game-based learning environment, the test was authored in several stages corresponding to the three "levels" of the game. In each phase a computer science education researcher generated the assessment items based upon the focused evidence statements [1] for each game level.

4.5 Conducting a Formal Review

The items underwent expert review in two formats. At first, the computer science education researcher who was new to writing test items held collaborative feedback sessions with an expert panel consisting of at least one other computer science education researcher, two computer science professors, an educational psychologist, and a human factors psychologist. During these face-to-face meetings recommendations for inclusion/exclusion of items were made verbally and discussed, and feedback for improving items was given. In later phases of test item authoring, the same experts provided feedback one at a time in series with refinements between. After several iterations of refinement based upon this expert panel content validation, it was determined that the assessment instrument was ready for piloting.

4.6 Piloting the Test Items

Two pilot studies were conducted in Spring 2014 at an urban middle school in the southeastern United States. Four teachers at this school agreed to have their classes participate in the studies.

For the first pilot, 103 sixth to eighth grade students played the entire first level of the game, which took approximately an hour for most students. ENGAGE emphasizes collaborative problem solving, so most students played the game in pairs on the same computer. In order to assess individual knowledge, however, each student completed assessments individually (taking them concurrently on separate computers). Of the 103 students, 43 were female and 60 were male. Race/ethnicity demographics were not collected from all students, but for those who responded, 32 identified as African-American, 4 Asian, 14 Hispanic, 31 White, and 6 Other. The version of the knowledge assessment in this first pilot consisted of six items taken both before and after interacting with the game-based learning environment. These six items represented the first set of knowledge assessment items (out of a total target of 20), covering the first of three levels of gameplay. Although more test items had been drafted, a small set was given in this round of piloting for two reasons: first, these six items corresponded to the only level of gameplay being piloted in this study, and second, other cognitive and affective survey instruments were being piloted in the same study, constraining the time available for piloting the knowledge assessment test items.

For the second pilot, 42 sixth and seventh graders returned to play a segment of the second level of the game, which took approximately half an hour for most students. The same protocol of paired gameplay and individual assessment was followed as in the first pilot. Of the 42 students, 17 were female and 25 were male. Of those who supplied race/ethnicity demographics, 10 identified as African-American, 3 Asian, 6 Hispanic, 13 White, and 3 Other. This pilot focused on ten questions: five were directly relevant to the gameplay segment from this pilot and were administered both pre and post. The other five items corresponded to future gameplay segments that had not yet been developed, and were only given pre. The reason for administering these items sooner than their corresponding gameplay segments were fully developed is because, as will be discussed in the next section, a ceiling effect (too many students answering items correctly even before being exposed to the learning content) was noted on several of the test items from the first pilot, and it was desirable to allow more time to revise and address any ceiling effects or other issues with the newest items.

4.7 Iteratively Refining and Re-Testing

Table 1 summarizes the fifteen items that were piloted within these first two studies, including the percent of students who answered each item correctly on the pre- and post-test. Based upon these statistics as well as finer grained response choice breakdowns, the items were refined.

Table 1. Evaluation of 15 knowledge assessment items piloted in Spring 2014

Item	Concept	Pre-test %	Post-test %	Notes
Pilot 1 (ENGAGE Tutorial Level)				
000	Sequencing	54	77	***Dropped***
001	Sequencing	56	61	One option too obviously wrong, so that option replaced with more plausible option
002	Iteration	37	38	Fine as written. During gameplay, a popular misconception was observed, so we replaced the least popular option with a distractor for this potential mistake
003	Domain Vocab: "run"	53	65	Ceiling effect suggests that some students enter with higher domain knowledge
004	Security	72	67	***Dropped***
005	Broadcast	35	49	Substantial revisions needed on the options (but not question itself)
Pilot 2 (ENGAGE Digital World Level)				
002	Iteration	36	---	Fine as written
100	Selection	16	---	One option too obviously wrong
101	Selection & Sequencing	63	---	One option too obviously wrong
102	Variables	74	---	Revision needed on the question itself (too easy)
103	Variables & Selection	37	---	One option too obviously wrong
104	Vocab: "binary"	42	27	***Dropped***
105	Vocab: "binary number"	26	32	Fine as written
106	Domain Vocab: "bit"	37	21	Fine as written. Results suggest revising game.
107	Interpret Binary: one bit "on"	10	47	Fine as written
108	Interpret Binary: multiple bits "on"	26	37	Fine as written

A particularly important consideration for determining the suitability of individual test items involves ceiling and floor effects. Ceiling effects occur when test items are "too easy," meaning that students tend to get the item correct more frequently than expected. Floor effects, in contrast, occur when test items are "too hard," and fewer students than expected answer the item correctly. On a pre-test, it is expected for most students to randomly guess the answers to questions since they have not encountered the learning material yet. With four response options in multiple-choice format, the random chance correctness rate would be 25%. As Table 1 shows, many of the test items display a substantially higher correctness rate on the pre-test. There are several possible reasons for this, one of which is that one of the response items was too clearly incorrect (it was not a viable distractor). This was found to be the case for some items. For others, the team hypothesizes that the instructions to each test item may have been too extensive, "teaching" prior to the pre-test. A floor effect is generally not problematic on a pre-test, but for items where a floor effect was observed on the post-test, reasons for this effect included that ENGAGE's game-based learning environment was not teaching that concept as well as intended, and in some cases as shown in Table 1 this feedback shaped the next steps of the development team to improve the game.

5. Example Test Items and Discussion

This section provides examples of three test items that were refined in different ways based upon pilot testing.

Example 1: Iteration. Item 002 was authored to assess student's understanding of iteration with an item in which they need to use a REPEAT block to navigate a moving platform to a specific location. Each of the four response options contains a sequence of program blocks in the same style as the ones used in the gameplay. The correct option is a sequence that starts with REPEAT 2, with a sequence of four various movement blocks nested underneath the REPEAT block. There was an acceptable distribution of responses on the pre-test for this item, with 37% answering correctly. However, during pilot gameplay observation the research team noted a common misconception: putting the REPEAT at the *end* of a sequence of blocks, rather than at the beginning. None of the original distractor options reflected this misconception, so accordingly the option that had received the lowest number of responses on the pre-test was replaced with this variation (Figure 2). In the second pilot, the new option received the largest number of incorrect responses (32%). This is a desirable outcome, because students will be exposed to the correct construct while interacting with ENGAGE, and this learning can now be captured at a fine-grained level from pre-test to post-test.

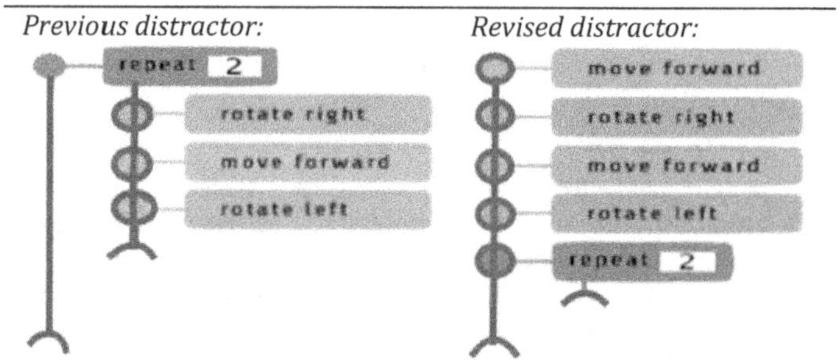

Figure 2. Original and revised distractor for *iteration* item

Example 2: Variables. Variables were not covered in the gameplay levels that students completed for these pilot studies, but the test items for variables were piloted within the pre-test. They were excluded from the post-test since there would be no expectation of students learning the concept during the gameplay.

<table>
<tr><td colspan="4">102.What will "number" equal at the end of this program?</td></tr>
<tr><td>Version1:
set number to 0
add 1 to number
add 2 to number
add 4 to number</td><td>a) 0
b) 1
c) 4
d) 7</td><td>Version 2:
set number to 0
add 1 to number
set number to 0
add 2 to number
add 4 to number</td><td>a) 0
b) 4
c) 6
d) 7</td></tr>
</table>

Figure 3. Items on assessing understanding of *variables*

Figure 3 shows two version of Item 102. Version 1 appeared on the pre-test, and students overwhelmingly answered this item correctly by selecting option D, with 74%. All other students except one selected the distractor option C. The ceiling effect on pre-test indicated that it was too easy to get this question correct by chance, so the revised Version 2 requires thinking more deeply about the behavior of a variable.

Example 3: Domain Vocabulary. Item 106 reads, "How many bits does the binary number 100 have?" with four number choices (3, 4, 50, 100). This question had a slightly high but acceptable distribution of responses on the pre-test, with 37% of students selecting the correct option, 3. However, that percent dropped to 21% correct on the post-test, with more students selecting incorrect choices of 4 and 50. In this case, after careful consideration and observation of gameplay, the research team concluded that the game levels were not using this vocabulary word prominently enough, which led to revision of the game itself rather than the assessment item.

6. CONCLUSION AND FUTURE WORK

This paper has presented an approach to developing computer science knowledge assessment instruments, based upon literature from psychometrics and psychology. Creating these assessments for computer science education research projects is vital for two key reasons. Firstly, the ability to assess an intervention's strength is an essential component to empirical research. Assessments are extensively validated in sister fields such as physics education; the time is ripe for emulating this practice in the comparatively young field of computer science education. Secondly, these assessments can provide invaluable insight into how to make targeted refinements to the given intervention. As shown here, a process of iterative refinement is essential to formulating effective test items, and this process can often take the same length of time (and run concurrently with) the research project that develops the intervention itself.

There are many promising avenues for future work, chief among these being the expanded development of validated knowledge assessment instruments at all levels of computer science. ENGAGE's knowledge assessment, described in this paper, stands as an exemplar of an assessment for seventh grade students, and the process described in the paper provides guidance for how to design analogous knowledge assessments at other levels of K-12 education. The more of these instruments that are created, validated, and shared across research projects and interventions, the greater common foundation can be built for measuring and supporting student learning. These knowledge assessment instruments play a central role in the give-and-take of research for developing effective interventions that support rigorous computer science education.

7. ACKNOWLEDGEMENTS

This work is supported in part by the National Science Foundation through Grants CNS-113897 and CNS-1042468. Any opinions, findings, conclusions, or recommendations expressed in this report are those of the participants, and do not necessarily represent the official views, opinions, or policy of the National Science Foundation.

8. REFERENCES

[1] AP® Computer Science Principles Draft Curriculum Framework: 2014. *http://www.csprinciples.org/*. Accessed: 2014-09-05.

[2] Ayala, R.J. De 2008. *The Theory and Practice of Item Response Theory*.

[3] Binning, J.F. and Gerald V. Barrett 1989. Validity of Personal Decisions: A Conceptual Analysis of the Inferential and Evidential Bases. *Journal of Applied Psychology*. 74, 3 (1989), 478–494.

[4] Buffum, P.S. et al. 2014. CS Principles Goes to Middle School: Learning How to Teach "Big Data". *SIGCSE '14* (2014), 151–156.

[5] Cronbach, L.J. 1951. Coefficient Alpha and the Internal Structure of Tests. *Psychometrika*. 16, (1951), 297–334.

[6] Eli P. Cox III 1980. The Optimal Number of Response Alternatives for a Scale: A Review. *Journal of Marketing Research*. 17, (1980), 407–422.

[7] Franklin, D. et al. 2013. Assessment of Computer Science Learning in a Scratch-Based Outreach Program. *SIGCSE '13* (2013), 371-376.

[8] Gwet, K.L. 2012. *Handbook of Inter-Rater Reliability*. Advanced Analytics, LLC.

[9] Hinkin, T.R. 1998. A Brief Tutorial on the Development of Measures for Use in Survey Questionnaires. *Organizational Research Methods*.

[10] National Governors Association Center for Best Practices 2010. *Common Core State Standards*.

[11] Roediger, H.L. and Karpicke, J.D. 2006. The Power of Testing Memory Basic Research and Implications for Educational Practice. *Perspectives on Psychological Science*. 1, (2006), 181–210.

[12] Shuhidan, S. et al. 2010. Instructor Perspectives of Multiple-Choice Questions in Summative Sssessment for Novice Programmers. *Computer Science Education*. 20, 3 (2010), 229–259.

[13] Sudol, L.A. and Studer, C. 2010. Analyzing Test Items: Using Item Response Theory to Validate Assessments. *SIGCSE '10* (2010), 436–440.

[14] Tew, A.E. and Guzdial, M. 2010. Developing a Validated Assessment of Fundamental CS1 Concepts. *SIGCSE '10* (2010), 97–101.

[15] Tew, A.E. and Guzdial, M. 2011. The FCS1: A Language Independent Assessment of CS1 Knowledge. *SIGCSE '11 (2011)*, 111–116.

[16] Vasilevskaya, M. et al. 2014. An Assessment Model for Large Project Courses. *SIGCSE '14 (2014)*, 253–258.

[17] Werner, L. et al. 2012. The Fairy Performance Assessment : Measuring Computational Thinking in Middle School. *SIGCSE '12* (2012), 7–12.

Reactive Game Engine Programming for STEM Outreach

Alan Cleary
Montana State University
Computer Science
PO Box 173880
Bozeman, MT 59717
alan.cleary@cs.montana.edu

Lucas Vandenbergh
Western State Colorado University
600 South Adams St
Gunnison, CO 81231
lucas.vandenbergh@western.edu

John Peterson
Western State Colorado University
600 South Adams St
Gunnison, CO 81231
jpeterson@western.edu

ABSTRACT

In this paper we present our experiences using a novel programming style, reactive programming, to deliver a summer camp for students in grades 8 through 12. This software uses a declarative programming approach to allow students without a background in computing to explore a wide variety of subject material within a 3D virtual environment, including computer science, mathematics, physics, and art. This work is based on PyFRP, a reactive programming library written in Python. We describe our camp experience and provide examples of how this style of programming supports a wide variety of educational activities.

Categories and Subject Descriptors

K.3.2 [**Computers and Education**]: Computer and Information Science Education—*computer science education, curriculum*

General Terms

Design, Documentation, Human Factors

Keywords

STEM; K-12 Instruction; Functional Reactive Programming; Virtual Worlds; Python; Game Development

1. INTRODUCTION

Summer camps provide an excellent opportunity to introduce computing to new audiences. Since 2006, Western State Colorado University (WSCU) has hosted a computer science summer camp for students in grades 8 through 12. Each session lasts one week, during which time the students build 3D virtual worlds as a means of interdisciplinary learning. The worlds are created using the *Panda3D* game engine and a *Functional Reactive Programming* (FRP) Python library. The goal of this camp is not to teach solely computing but rather to use computing as a vehicle for the exploration of a wide range of topics. Campers use our library to create a variety of compact interactive animations and games without requiring in-depth knowledge of computing. We will demonstrate how the addition of FRP to the Python environment significantly increases the ease of programming in an interactive 3D environment without overly constraining the set of programs supported by our system. In particular, we are able to use continuous mathamatical operators such as integral and derivative to simplify movement within the 3D environment.

Our system currently uses Panda3D[10], a cross-platform open source game engine with extensive Python support. However, our reactive programming library, PyFRP, is independent of the details of this engine and is currently being ported to other similar systems. We believe that Python provides an excellent introduction to computing and many students come to our camp wanting to learn a "real" programming language. In fact, some parents make a point to mention they want their student to learn Python. Our camp also uses the *Blender*[7] modeling system to create new 3D models beyond those that are packaged with our library. Blender is a cross-platform open source project as well.

Some of the topics covered include 3D geometry, coordinate systems, vectors, trigonometry, calculus, projectile motion, object collision, control systems, functions, loops, reactive programming, and 3D modeling. We strive to bring mathematics to the foreground in hopes that the students will develop a deeper understanding of the content. The use of FRP allows the mathematics to closely integrate with the graphical environment.

Students work on a variety of projects during the course of the camp. We try to provide them with an open, creative, and collaborative environment with all the resources they need to succeed and have fun.

Our paper is structured as follows: In Section 2 we give a brief description of FRP and our implementation, in Section 3 we discuss the goals of the camp, in Section 4 we outline the design of the camp, in Section 5 we provide examples to demonstrate our programming style and the curriculum of the camp, in Section 6 we reflect on the experience of the camp from both our perspective and that of the students, in Section 7 we survey related work, and in Section 8 we explore future directions of PyFRP and the camp.

SIGCSE '15, March 4–7 2015, Kansas City, MO, USA.

http://dx.doi.org/10.1145/2676723.2677312.

2. REACTIVE GAME ENGINE PROGRAMMING

FRP is a general framework for programming hybrid systems in a high-level, declarative manner. It integrates the idea of time flow into the purely functional programming style. By handling time flow in a uniform and pervasive manner an application gains clarity and reliability.

FRP is composed of two key ideas: *behaviors* and *events*. Behaviors are time-varying reactive values, though some are constant, such as numbers and colors. Events are time-ordered sequences of discrete-time event occurrences. Basic events include mouse button and keyboard presses. There is a rich set of operators the user can use to compose new behaviors and events from existing ones. In essence, a FRP program is just a set of mutually-recursive behaviors and events.

A major design goal for FRP is to free the programmer from presentation details by providing the ability to think in terms of modeling. FRP achieves this by making a clear distinction between the *what* of a presentation and the *how*. It attempts to automate the how by providing the user high-level abstractions, which prevent them from having to explicitly manage common implementation chores that have nothing to do with the content of an animation.

We found that due to its dynamic typing, semantic overloading, and non-strict semantics, Python[15] lends itself to the data-types and functions of FRP. An added benefit of this approach is that students are learning a full featured language, regardless of the fact that they have no background in computing. While Python is not a purely functional language like Haskell, we use only the functional core of Python.

Our library augments the original FRP library with a notion of objects. A *reactive object* is one in which the attributes of the object are described using reactive equations. For example, the following program serves as a kind of "hello world" in our system:

```
panda(hpr = hpr(time,0,0))
```

The `panda` function creates a new model, a panda, whose hpr (heading, pitch, and roll) are defined by the given reactive equation. Here, the heading is the elapsed time, causing the panda to rotate. Every 3D model has a set of reactive attributes, including position, orientation (hpr), size, color, and texture.

A more complex example of the reactive style is as follows:

```
panda(position = integral(hold(p3(0,0,0),
              key("upArrow",p3(0,0,1)) +
              key("downArrow",p3(0,0,-1)))
```

This creates a panda which moves up and down using the arrow keys. This is an example of a velocity controller: the `hold` function (a primitive in FRP) is used to remember the current velocity. The `key` functions create events which carry new velocities to the `hold` function; the + operator merges the event streams. Finally, the `integral` function converts the velocity to a position.

This style of programming avoids the complexity of event handlers and explicit time flow. The primitives in FRP allow the programmer to work with continuous equations in a very natural manner. As our work is concerned with presenting PyFRP from a user's perspective, we refer the reader to [16] for an exploration of the formal semantics of FRP and to [6] for a useful collection of data types and functions, as-well-as FRP implementation details. The examples provided in Section 5 will demonstrate our programming style and the curriculum of our camp.

3. CAMP GOALS

The camp is built around STEM (Science, Technology, Engineering, and Mathematics) topics. Specifically, we focus on teaching fundamental mathematics and programming constructs that are important for game programming and animations, as well as the basic physics that allows games to mimic or bend the rules of reality. We also focus on the artistic side of programming, showing the students how to create animations and pieces of art programatically and with Blender. In essence, we are trying to put computer science into context by showing students how it is connected to other disciplines.

We want the students to confront the mathematics required for game programming and animations, rather than hiding it behind a GUI. This is why we have taken a purely text-based approach. By leveraging FRP, it allows students to more easily work at the level of equations and models.

We also want to provide the students with quality mentoring. Mathematics and programming does not come naturally to all students. By providing the students with mentors, we are accommodating a variety of learning styles and speeds.

4. CAMP DESIGN

The camp is designed to accommodate a wide variety of abilities, from complete novices to camp regulars. This is done by having the students learn by experimentation and giving them creative freedom in their work.

Throughout the day the students are given lectures on various topics, each supplemented by a concise code example. The students are walked through the code and periodically given time to experiment with the parameter values. We believe this allows them to develop their own intuitive understanding of the lecture material while becoming more comfortable with the code. In this way, the students are gradually introduced to more complex topics and features of the library. During this time, advanced students are encouraged to extend the code to do something more interesting within the realm of the lecture topic.

Students are also given individual projects that require them to draw on material from the lectures. Some scaffold code is provided as a starting point for each project. The projects are designed to make the students solve a particular problem, such as describing the behavior of an object mathematically or using logic to constrain where an object can move on the screen. Beyond this, the projects are open-ended. This allows the students to put their own creative spin on the projects and pursue what interests them. We find that some students focus on the physics of the projects while others prefer to make their own 3D models for everything, and some just want to make games that the other students can compete for high scores on.

Mentors (student assistants) are an essential part of our camp. We use one mentor for every three participants, giving us a lot of opportunity for one on one interaction with the campers. As we have a wide range of age and ability in our camp, having mentors allows each camper to work at the level of their abilities. It also allows more advanced students to work with features of the game engine that are not covered in lecture, enabling them to pursue projects that are much more open ended. Because we are working directly in the Python environment, these mentors are necessary to assist the students with debugging and errors as well as offer further insight and encouragement with the material.

The mentors receive a couple of days of training prior to the camp to ensure that they are familiar with the curriculum and the software. Many of them are WSCU mathematics and computer science undergraduates who helped write the FRP library. On multiple occasions mentors had attended the camp themselves prior to enrolling at WSCU. One such mentor is an author of this paper.

On some days professors from other departments give guest lectures in topics such as physics, mathematics, or programming. These lectures bring an essential variety to the camp, helping to engage campers in multiple ways. We have been able to build software for these lectures on the fly without having to teach our guests how to program in our system.

While learning programming, mathematics, and physics, the students also get to experience great outdoor activities such as rock climbing, mountain biking, kayaking, and rafting. Apparently students get restless if they have to sit in front of a computer for hours on end. These activities allow them to get a break from learning, enjoy the outdoors, and let off some steam.

At the end of the camp the students showcase their work to their parents. This gives the parents an opportunity to evaluate for themselves what their students have learned and discuss their students experiences with the mentors.

5. EXAMPLES

The following examples demonstrate our programming style and the curriculum of our camp. Specifically, they demonstrate that FRP's declarative nature makes creating interactions and animations quick and painless and that FRP can be used to teach a variety of subjects.

5.1 Computer Science

Example Dodge:

```
1  # Spawning dodgeballs
2  def generate(m,v):
3      for i in range(amount.value):
4          h = randomRange(-pi/2,pi/2)
5          p = -acos(0.5)/h
6          s = sphere(size = 0.0005*time+0.05, color =
               color(0.7,0.02,0.02))
7          launch(s, neck, hprToP3(hpr(h,p,0)))
8          hit(b,s,death)
9
10 # Getting user input
11 v = hold(p3(0,-.5,0),
12               key("leftArrow",p3(-1.5,0,0))
13             + key("rightArrow",p3(1.5,0,0))
14             + happen(getX(b.position)<-2,p3(0.25,0,0))
15             + happen(getX(b.position)>2,p3(-0.25,0,0)))
16
17 # Get input to move player model
18 b.position = p3(0,0,-2.5)+integral(v)
19
20 # Making it run
21 react(clock(10),lambda m,v:amount.add(1))
22 react(clock(0.5),generate)
```

The dodge game example teaches the students how to create interactions between game objects as well as getting user input. The dodge game works well for this because the two main components to the game are moving the player model around the screen and checking if they hit any of the dodgeballs.

The collision detection is handled on line 8 by creating a hit reaction between the player character and each dodgeball as they are created. User input is done on line 11 which maps the input directly to the position of the player model. This line also handles keeping the player in bounds. Note the use of an anonymous function on line 21.

5.2 Mathematics

Example Tornado:

```
# Aeroplane path
def path(t):
    return p3c(t/10,t-time*time,(t-25)/10)

# Make an aeroplane
def plane(m,v):
    boeing707(position = path(localTime*2.7), color =
         black, size = .4)

# Making it run
react(clock(.1),plane)
```

The tornado example shows how the students can manipulate the objects on screen using time and mathematical functions to create interesting patterns and shapes. The models spawned in the example get their position adjusted each time-step based on the time of their spawn relative to global time. The image below shows the product of the code in its entirety.

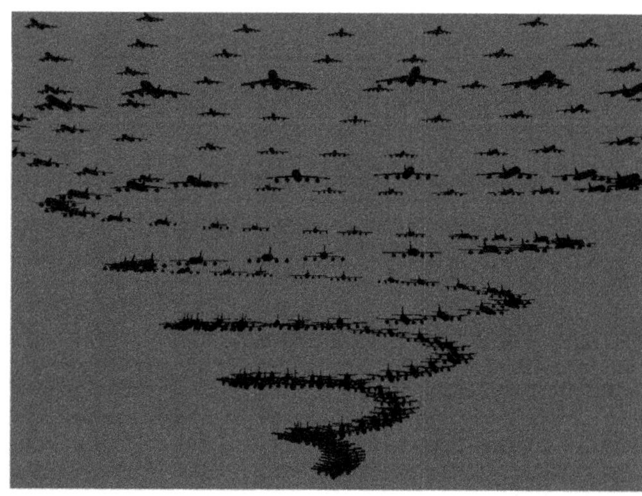

5.3 Physics

Example Driving:

```
# Setting up the camera
flatRod(camera, car, distance = 2)

# Steering
def driving(model, p0, h0, speed0):
    model.angle = integral(delta + decay)
    # Force on vehicle
    forward = (speed0 * 4) + engineForce *
         integral(dspeed)
    # Vehicle velocity
```

```
10     fvelocity = abs(model.velocity)
11     # Friction on vehicle
12     pushBack = track.friction(model.position)
13     friction = pushBack * frictionForce * fvelocity
14     speed = integral(forward - friction)
15     speed1 = choose(speed < -.4, -.4, speed)
16     # Vehicle heading
17     h = h0 + integral(speed1 * model.angle)
18     model.hpr = hpr(h,0,0)
19     model.velocity = p3c(speed1,h-pi/2,0)
20     model.position = p0 + integral(model.velocity)
21
22 # Making it run
23 driving(car, p3(4,4,0), pi/2, 0)
24 start()
```

The driving game teaches students about basic physics principles such as friction, velocity, and acceleration, all of which are important in game development. It also strongly reinforces the declarative nature of FRP by allowing us to ignore loops, which can be confusing to novice programmers. The `driving` function is a perfect example of this. Students can declare how the car will move in a way that makes sense to them without having to fiddle with loops.

Notice the use of the `integral` function in this example. On line 17 it is used to determine the car's heading from its speed and angle, and on line 20 it is used to determine the car's position from its velocity.

5.4 Art

Example Volcano

```
1  # Make the scene
2  ambientLight(color = color(.5,.5,.5))
3  directionalLight(color = orange, hpr = hpr(0,3,0))
4  world.color = lightBlue
5  pandaModel("volcanoModel", texture =
       "volcanoModelTexture.png", size = .9, position =
       p3(0,0,-2.8))
6  rectangle(p3(-25,-25,d), p3(-25,25,d), p3(25,-25,d),
       texture = "grass")
7
8  # How to erupt
9  def erupt(m,v):
10     h = randomRange(0,2*pi)
11     p = randomRange(degrees(35),degrees(50))
12     s = sphere(color = orange, size =
           randomRange(.07,.3))
13     launch(s, neck, hprToP3(hpr(h,p,0))*3)
14     when(s, getZ(s.position) <= -2, flower)
15
16 # Create flowers at landing point
17 def flower(m,v):
18     exit(m)
19     pandaModel("flower#3", texture =
           "flowerPurple.png", position = now(m.position),
           size = randomRange(.3,.9))
20
21 # Rotate camera around center
22 camera.position = p3c(25,time/4, 1)
23 camera.hpr = hpr(h + pi/2,0,0)
```

The camp teaches the students to create their own models using Blender. We facilitate this by making it very easy to import your own models and textures into the software. Lines 4 and 17 in this example demonstrate how this is done. The first defines a volcano, and the second defines a flower, complete with both a model file and a texture image. The image below was produced by this example.

6. EXPERIENCES

The camp started in 2006 and has seen growing attendance since. Typically one third the students are girls and a quarter of the students have attended the camp in the past. Occasionally a veteran student will make the transition to mentor.

As our intention is to help students explore a variety of subject material while fostering creativity, we do not utilize testing as a measure of the camp's effectiveness. Instead, we rely on feedback from the students and that of their parents. For example, when a student was asked why they preferred our camp over another they attended that same summer, they responded, "It's just funner... I can do a lot more here". Recently, a parent stated that, "While the camp is only a week long, the quality of knowledge gained has been substantial... Having the opportunity to study under and work with college professors and students has been monumental for [my students]".

We rely on the feedback of the mentors as well, since they work closely with the students throughout the duration of the camp. One mentor that was studying computer science at WSCU said, "The students had a lot of fun, and it was a good experience for them to use a full programming language". A mentor that had just graduated with a degree in computer science said, "I've had a lot of experience teaching college students, but not that age group... It solidified the fact that teaching has always been an option for me, even grade school". Obviously the mentors benefit from the camp as well.

7. RELATED WORK

There are many programming languages that specifically target novice programmers. For example, Alice[3] was designed to teach event driven object oriented programming to children by creating interactive stories. And Scratch[13] is a blocks-based graphical programming language used to create animated stories and games. These projects hide the underlying mathematics from the users and do not provide the full set of features that a more advanced programming language offers. In contrast, our method emphasizes mathematics within a full featured language.

A system intended for both novices and experts is Game Maker[9]. It accommodates the creation of cross-platform video games using drag and drop and/or a scripting language known as Game Maker Language, which can be used to develop more advanced games. Game Maker was designed to allow novice programmers to be able to make computer games without much programming knowledge via a GUI. Though more feature rich than Alice and Scratch, Game Maker is still domain specific and relies heavily on a GUI to accommodate novice users. Conversely, our method is purely text based.

Unreal[8] is a game engine that features an advanced suite of tools for creating 3D models, textures, and other game assets. It supports C++ for UI elements and classes, and a graphic scripting language called Blueprints. It is intended for beginner and advanced programmers. A project that is more similar to ours is PyGame[14]. PyGame is a set of modules for Python specifically designed for writing games. It is a full featured game engine designed for users that have more programming experience than our target demographic. The PyFRP software simplifies the game engine by using continuous time where Unreal and PyGame use explicit time and event handlers to run the game, something that may be unintuitive for novices.

Lastly there is Elm[4]. Elm is a standalone FRP language designed to make interactive web programming easier. Elm, like Game Maker, is more robust than Alice and Scratch but lacks the features a "real" language provides.

There is a variety of math and computer science summer camps for K-12 students, such as those offered by Digital Media Academy[1], iD Tech[12], Classroom Antics[2], and ProjectFun[5]. These camps provide a serious programming experience but lack the interdisciplinary aspect of our camp. While we agree that immersing students in an instructed environment is more engaging and productive than simply giving them the material, we believe the high-level, declarative syntax of FRP allows students to learn a wider variety of material in a shorter period of time.

A drawback of our method is that it was designed for and tested in a classroom environment. Though our code is publicly available online for anyone to download, it is intended to be used in an instructed environment.

8. FUTURE WORK

As mentioned in Section 1, we are currently porting our library to systems similar to Panda3D, namely, Unity-3D[11]. As development and support of Panda3D seems to be in decline, Unity-3D is an appealing alternative. It offers much of the same functionality as Panda3D and more. As mentioned in Section 4, some advanced students and mentors work directly with the game engine. By moving to Unity-3D, they will be learning to use a tool that has a strong presence in industry.

The modularity of our library allows it to interact with systems other than game engines. For example, we have coupled it with micro-controllers and various IO devices. This was done in a collaborative effort between the computer science and art departments at WSCU for a course on interactive art, an emerging genre. This work is ongoing.

Our system currently targets the PC, Mac, and Linux operating systems. We would like to further extend it to support Windows Mobile, iOS, and Android as well.

As touched on in Section 7, our method was designed for a classroom environment. To make it accessible outside the classroom, we would like to create videos to supplement the existing documentation and tutorials.

9. CONCLUSIONS

In this paper we discussed our use of FRP to deliver a summer camp for students in grades 8 through 12. Our method was used to cover a variety of topics, many of which relied heavily on math. We demonstrated how FRP in the Python environment significantly increases the ease of programming interactive 3D environments, abstracting away the non-trivial boiler plate code without overly constraining the capabilities of the system. In particular, we showed the ease of use of continuous mathematical operators in our system. We also emphasized the use of mentors in our camp, which allows us to accommodate a variety of learning styles, speeds, and interests. Based on our experiences and the feedback we have received, we believe our method is a fun and effective means of interdisciplinary study.

The source code, documentation, and camp material are available at our website, `www.reactive-engine.org`.

This work is supported by NSF Grant 1302327.

10. REFERENCES

[1] D. M. Academy. Digital media academy, 2002.

[2] C. Antics. Tech camps, 2007.

[3] S. Cooper, W. Dann, and R. Pausch. Alice: a 3-d tool for introductory programming concepts. In *Journal of Computing Sciences in Colleges*, volume 15, pages 107–116. Consortium for Computing Sciences in Colleges, 2000.

[4] E. Czaplicki and S. Chong. Asynchronous functional reactive programming for guis. In *ACM SIGPLAN Notices*, volume 48, pages 411–422. ACM, 2013.

[5] DigiPen. Project fun, 1988.

[6] C. Elliott and P. Hudak. Functional reactive animation. In *ACM SIGPLAN Notices*, volume 32, pages 263–273. ACM, 1997.

[7] B. Foundation. Blender, 2002.

[8] E. Games. Unreal engine 3. *URL: http://www. unrealtechnology. com/html/technology/ue30. shtml*, 2006.

[9] Y. Games. Gamemaker, 2007.

[10] M. Goslin and M. R. Mine. The panda3d graphics engine. *Computer*, 37(10):112–114, 2004.

[11] T. Higgins. Unity-3d game engine, 2010.

[12] iD Tech. id tech camps, 1999.

[13] J. Maloney, M. Resnick, N. Rusk, B. Silverman, and E. Eastmond. The scratch programming language and environment. *ACM Transactions on Computing Education (TOCE)*, 10(4):16, 2010.

[14] P. Shinners et al. Pygame–python game development, 2011.

[15] G. van Rossum et al. The python language. *See http://www. python. org*, 1990.

[16] Z. Wan and P. Hudak. Functional reactive programming from first principles. In *ACM SIGPLAN Notices*, volume 35, pages 242–252. ACM, 2000.

Building CS Research Capacity in sub-Saharan Africa by Implementing a Doctoral Training Program

Mikko Apiola
University of Eastern Finland
School of Computing, and
College of Business Education
Dar es Salaam, Tanzania
first.last@ieee.org

Jarkko Suhonen
University of Eastern Finland
School of Computing
Joensuu, Finland
first.last@uef.fi

Abbi Nangawe
College of Business Education
Dar es Salaam, Tanzania
first.last@cbe.ac.tz

Erkki Sutinen
University of Eastern Finland
School of Computing
Joensuu, Finland
first.last@uef.fi

ABSTRACT

Sub-Saharan Africa (SSA) needs to transform from an information society that consumes information technologies into a knowledge economy that creates technologies. Key domains for transformation include computer science education, research and development. The lack of research culture and support for research activities often results in low research outcomes, and slows down the development of innovative and independent thinkers and problem solvers. To increase research capacities, we have launched a doctoral level computer science research training program between the College of Business Education (CBE), Dar es Salaam, Tanzania, and the University of Eastern Finland (UEF), School of Computing. This paper discusses the preliminary experiences of planning and setting up that program.

Categories and Subject Descriptors

K.3.2 [**Computer and Information Science Education**]: Computer science education, Curriculum

General Terms

Management, Design, Human Factors

Keywords

Sub-Saharan Africa, R&D, Research capacity building

1. INTRODUCTION

This paper explains a research capacity building program that has been launched at the College of Business Education (CBE), Dar es Salaam, Tanzania, in collaboration with the University of Eastern Finland (UEF), School of Computing. The idea is that a number of faculty members from CBE are given doctoral training on-site at CBE by researchers from UEF. The PhD studies of the faculty members follow the UEF's IMPDET (International Multidisciplinary PhD Studies in Educational Technology)[1] curriculum for doctoral studies, and at the end of their doctoral study careers, the PhD degrees (in computer science) are awarded by UEF.

Launching of the program was motivated by the identification of two things. First, there is a need to improve computing curricula both at undergraduate level as well as at doctoral level in sub-Saharan Africa (SSA). While there exists a small but growing number of projects to improve undergraduate computing education in SSA, projects that focus on doctoral level education are more scarce. Second, a generally low level of research culture complicates the development of independent thinkers and innovators. This often stems from faculty members lacking research experience and research skills. Faculty members are often also heavily loaded with teaching and administrative duties, leaving limited opportunities for research activities.

The need to increase innovation and research and design (R&D) activities in SSA has become well recognised (see for example [5, 18]). In recent years, Africa has seen a rapid increase in information and communication technologies (ICT), especially mobile technologies (MT). ICT is often argued to hold high potential for development and economic growth [21, 17]. However, ICT may also strengthen existing power relations, reinforce technological dependence and underdevelopment, and in some cases increase poverty instead of decreasing it [5]. ICT is not an automatic silver bullet for success, but improving research, education, and innovation activities is essential in order to match the potential of technology with sustainable development.

2. BACKGROUND

In recent decades, a number of efforts to setup computing education have been undertaken in SSA. Higher education institutions (HEI) in Europe and USA have formed collaborations with HEIs in SSA, set up educational programs, and

[1] http://www.impdet.org

SIGCSE'15, March 4–7, 2015, Kansas City, MO, USA.

http://dx.doi.org/10.1145/2676723.2677242.

arranged teacher and student exchange programs between their HEIs. Many of those efforts have targeted at undergraduate level computing education, while doctoral education, and especially doctoral training given on-site in SSA is more rare. This section describes known challenges of implementing computing education in SSA, and the IMPDET PhD training program upon which this project is built.

2.1 Traditions of computing

It is important to ask *What kind of computing professionals are needed in SSA?* Computer science consists of three traditions: *mathematical tradition* that deals with theoretical structures such as algorithms and data structures, *scientific tradition* that aims at finding causalities and generalisations based on models and theories (that derive from empirical observations), and *engineering tradition* that aims at practical implementations and inventions [7].

Of these computing traditions, the engineering tradition has close connection points with for example the design research track of ICT4D (ICT for development) research, including research on software development in common development domains of education, health, governance, livelihoods, small-scale farming, banking, commerce, rural supply chain management, agriculture, and fight against HIV and AIDS (for many references, see [9]), and digital finance (see [18]). Thus, the engineering tradition is an active computing tradition in SSA, while the mathematical and scientific traditions are probably less active at the moment.

2.2 Undergraduate level education in SSA

In recent years, a number of computing education programs have been launched in SSA. The weaknesses of direct copying of curriculum from outside have been well known already for some time [15, 22], because local aspects of education as well as the social, cultural, and physical factors that are affecting the educational situation must be understood well in order to succeed [22]. Common challenges include lack of relevant jobs for graduating students, lack in literacy, poor background in science, lack of industry-academia interaction, and lack of internship training in industry [22]. Other important factors may include educational infrastructure, facilities, university organization, competence of staff, and challenges in pedagogy [13, 20, 2].

2.3 Doctoral level education in SSA

Implementing doctoral level computing education in SSA is currently not a well studied area. Our own experiences tell that HEIs in some parts of SSA are often not supportive of research activities. The reasons for this are that faculty members are often Masters degree holders and they lack skills in conducting research. In addition, research activities are often not supported by the universities, but faculty members have a high workload with other duties, often related to teaching and administration. Generally speaking, the lack of research culture slows down the development of independent, original thinkers, and problem solvers.

A typical way of *research capacity building* between African and western universities is to send African doctoral students abroad for research training. This approach has positive sides, but limitations also apply. For example, research skills learned abroad may become underused if the university of origin is not supportive of research activities. Also, the research competencies obtained abroad may not be fully applicable or relevant for research in an African context.

3. IMPDET@CBE INITIATIVE

To increase the research capacities, we have initiated a research capacity building program between the College of Business Education (CBE), Dar es Salaam, Tanzania, and the University of Eastern Finland (UEF), School of Computing. The aims of our project are to build research culture and to increase research capacities at CBE. At the beginning, five faculty members from CBE have been selected to work four years full-time in the training program. All five PhD candidates' research proposals have been accepted by UEF, and they have been accepted as PhD students into the IMPDET online doctoral training program. In addition we have few external PhD candidates.

3.1 Online Doctoral Training: IMPDET

IMPDET is an online doctoral program where students study to attain a doctoral degree in computer science, education or special education. The program was launched in 2004, and the first PhD degree was awarded in October 2007. The first student who did majority of his studies remotely received his doctoral degree in 2008, and in 2013 the first African based student completed his studies in the program. In November 2014, 41 doctoral students from 20 different countries were enrolled in the program. In 2003-2014, 14 doctoral students have graduated from IMPDET.

The program follows a blended learning mode, where most of the required courses are completed online. The candidates enrolled in the program are required to visit the UEF campus a couple of times during the course of their studies: (1) to participate in a one week preparatory workshop before applying, (2) to receive intensive supervision during the studies, (3) to establish contact with the local research community at the host university and (4) to defend their dissertation publicly at the end of the studies. The focus areas of the IMPDET program are educational technology, ICT4D, and computer science education with an emphasis on digital storytelling, natural language processing, and design science research.

3.2 Aims of the project

The main aim of the project is to build research culture and increase research capacities inside CBE. As means to do this, the project aims to increase the number of PhD holders among the faculty members of CBE, and to conduct a number of contextually relevant research projects. Hence, the project is a pioneer in designing, and implementing researcher training in higher education institutions of SSA.

All research initiatives undertaken within the project aim to connect with international and national research projects. The research projects will work on contextually relevant research topics in the intersections between computing, computing education, business informatics, social science, design research, and educational action research.

3.3 Degree Structure

The doctoral degrees in the IMPDET program consist of two main components, (1) coursework of 30-50 ECTS points (European Credit Transfer System), where one ECTS credit equals approximately 26 hours of work, and (2) a dissertation that is defended in public. The coursework is combined from three different types of study modules: 1) transferable skills studies, 2) online courses and seminars, and 3) individual scholarly learning tasks.

The doctoral dissertation in the IMPDET program can be either a compilation dissertation or a monograph. The compilation thesis starts with an introduction to the research topic. After the introduction, a doctoral candidate usually attaches 5 to 7 of his or her research papers published in peer-reviewed international scientific forums, mainly scholarly journals and research conferences. At the end of the studies two external experts pre-examine and approve or disapprove the printing of the doctoral dissertation. After the thesis is approved a doctoral students defends his or her work in a public defence. All doctoral defences in the IMPDET program are broadcasted online.

3.4 Research Methods and Topics

First, this program trains researchers to work with a combination of social science research methods (see for example [6, 8]) for increasing understanding about contextually relevant challenges and obstacles. Second, this program trains researchers to study the design and implementation of computer science, and education based solutions to the identified obstacles by using design research [12], software engineering, and educational action research [16].

3.5 Current and Future Activities

The planning of the research capacity building program started in 2013. The first students completed their research proposals in the beginning of 2014, after which the admission procedure to University of Eastern Finland was completed by May 2014. The program was launched in June 2014. The future plans include expanding the activities by taking more PhD candidates, with more supervisors.

4. RESEARCH TOPICS AND AREAS

The research topics stem from previous research in computing education, educational technology research, curriculum development, and from common development research, and ICT4D domains. The topics are divided between three research contexts; *the business context*, *the infra context*, and *the academic context* (see Table 1), which together form the R&D ecology, where each of the research projects contributes to building a research culture within the IMPDET hub. Of the current research projects, the projects in the business context and the infra context are conducted by PhD candidates that are among CBE staff members. Projects that operate in the academic context are currently conducted by researchers that are not CBE staff members.

Table 1: Three Contexts of Research Projects

Context	Projects
Business Context	Street Business School Women Entrepreneurship Small Scale Farming, m-Agriculture
Infra Context	MFI and SME interaction Mobile Business Innovations
Academic Context	Pedagogy of HPC Methods for CS1 Computing Curriculum Design Educational Technology in Schools

4.1 Business Context

Projects in the business context study grassroots-level information technology solutions for businesses.

Street Business School

Informal employment is more common than formal employment in developing countries. The most common form of informal retail business activity in developing countries is street vending. Street vending has been studied from many different perspectives in a number of different parts of the world. However, a low number of studies have addressed street vending in Dar es Salaam, Tanzania, and from the viewpoint of skill development. This research project studies street vending skills and skill development in Dar es Salaam, Tanzania. As a part of the study, educational and ICT-based solutions are developed and researched in collaboration with street vendors. The final aim of the research project is to setup a street business school at CBE.

Women Entrepreneurs and Mobile Learning

Women entrepreneurs (WE) have a significant contribution to the economies in sub-Saharan Africa. However, WEs in sub-Saharan Africa are facing a shocking array of challenges that arise from the economic, socio-cultural, legal, political, and technological aspects of their business environment. A number of studies have approached women entrepreneurship from many different perspectives. This research project is being conducted in Dar es Salaam, Tanzania, and studies women entrepreneurship from the perspective of education and ICT.

Small-Scale Farming and Mobile Learning

Small Scale Farmers (SSF) need to make a number of crucial decisions in their agricultural business activities. However, SSFs in SSA rely on a number of information sources ranging from traditional norms and old-fashioned means to more modern information channels. The conditions of SSFs vary between contexts, making a one-size-fits-all ICT-solution impossible, and making it a necessity for ICT-projects to be geared with social science research. In this research project SSF communities' information needs and related educational ICT solutions are studied in the Chamwino District, Tanzania.

4.2 Infra Context

Projects in the infra context conduct R&D about the business infrastructure related to information technology businesses.

Micro Finance (MFI) and SME interaction

Small and medium sized enterprises (SME) form the backbone of modern economies. Also in developing economies, the contribution of SMEs is remarkable. In sub-Saharan Africa, SMEs are facing many financial challenges including rough regulatory climates, and weak access to capital. The interplay between MFIs and SMEs has gained increased attention recently and attracted a number of research studies. This research project studies the MFI-SME interactions in Dar es Salaam, Tanzania. The research aims to increase the understanding about the current technological challenges between MFI and SME interactions, and to design and research ICT, mobile, and education based solutions to address those challenges.

Business Innovation and Mobile Learning

While the number of R&D activities and mobile services has seen a rapid increase in the past five years in sub-Saharan Africa, those activities are still in their infancies. It has been argued that in SSA there is a serious need to transform from an information society of passive ICT use, into a knowledge economy where new knowledge is created. One important factor of this transformation is innovation. This research project studies the factors affecting the management of innovation and incubation services, and design of mobile learning based incubation and innovation services in Dar es Salaam, Tanzania. The study uses educational action research and design research approaches.

4.3 Academic Context

Projects in the academic context operate on both primary education and HEI level to research and develop improvements for computing and science education.

Integrating HPC into an IT Engineering Curriculum

Integrating high performance computing (HPC) into a Tanzanian computer engineering curriculum poses a number of challenges. Those challenges arise partly from the students' educational background, and the country's educational history. In this research project, the challenges of integrating HPC into one specific Tanzanian technology university is studied from an educational point of view. A mixed-methods approach has been used to collect both qualitative and quantitative data about students' perceptions of the biggest challenges in learning HPC, and about the students' improvement suggestions. The current results have pinpointed a number of improvement needs in the teaching and learning environment. The most acute improvement needs include increasing the amount of teaching that is based on project-based and problem-based approaches, and developing teaching of the prerequisite topics required to learn HPC. This project plans to study the impact of a number of practical activities that aim at enhancing the integration of HPC into a Tanzanian engineering curriculum.

New methods for CS1 in Tanzanian HEIs

Previous studies have identified programming as a challenging topic both for students and teachers in Tanzanian HEIs [2]. Studies have also identified a number of challenge factors of teaching and learning programming, which include students' educational background, learning strategies, motivational orientations, groupwork tendencies, study environment and habits [2]. This study aims to design and develop new interventions for CS1 courses in Tanzanian HEIs. Those interventions include small group coaching, automatic assessment and electronic learning environments. Also measurement practices for understanding the relationships between students' background skills and their skill development in CS1 courses are researched.

Educational Technology in Schools

This research project targets primary and secondary level education, and includes research about new pedagogical methods that use technology. For example, OLPC (One Laptop Per Child) computers are studied in a primary school to bring student-centered learning and to teach IT-skills to pupils (see for example [1]). Technology-related methods for improving science education are studied.

Table 2: LBDR Coaching Matrix

Component	One-on-one coaching				
Achievement	RP1	RP2	RP3	RP4	RP5
Skill					
RP Management	max	high	avg	low	min
Researcher subskills	high	high	avg	low	low
Effort					
Mindset	*High support for growth mindset*				
Willpower	*Optimize control of choices*				
Expertise	*Maximize time spent on practice*				

5. SMALL GROUP COACHING

Our supervision guidelines follow a small group coaching approach, where a group of one to seven PhD candidates work together with one group leader (who is typically a PhD holder), and a number of other supervisors. The learning approach is *learning-by-doing-research (LBDR)*, which is based on *learning-by-doing*. This means that as a general guideline, all learning activities are based on conducting real research cases, first under extensive guidance, and later as skills develop, more independently. The research activities are connected to the edTechΔ-research group at the University of Eastern Finland's School of Computing via online seminars and online courses. The working approach is a combination of local coaching and online study opportunities.

5.1 Coaching Psychology

A theory of achievement, based on wide range of research on *positive psychology*[2], defines achievement in the following way: $Achievement = Skill + Effort$ [19, pp. 114]. The skill-component of the equation is built up from a combination of cognitive components *Speed*, *Slowness*, and *Rate-of-learning* [19, pp. 114]. *Speed* refers to cognitive material "on automatic", how much knowledge relevant to the task a person has. *Slowness* relates to heavyweight processes of planning, refining, error-checking, and creativity. *Rate-of-learning* refers to the knowledge that one can accumulate for each unit of time one works on a task [19].

Extensive studies about *expertise* in domains such as chess, art, and science, show that time and energy one spends in deliberate practice is the cornerstone of all expertise [11]. The component of *effort*, based on extensive research, equals no more or no less to how much time one spends on practicing a task [19, pp. 115]. Spending more time on a task will build achievement. Self-discipline, and *willpower* play a very important role in building *effort* [3].

[2]http://www.ppc.sas.upenn.edu

5.2 Building Research Skills

Conducting research requires a range of skills, which include academic reading and writing, research design, identifying relevant research gaps, selecting the proper research method, using a research method, collecting data, analysing data, and communicating the results. Each of the subtask included in a research project requires certain skills. In addition to mastering the skills required in the subtasks, a researcher needs the skill to manage all the subtasks of the project, and is responsible for making choices, all of which have an impact to the research outcomes.

A novice researcher needs to be provided with a learning environment for building the required research skills. In the case of a novice researcher, one of the supervisors' responsibilities is to cut down a research project into manageable subtasks, so that the researcher can concentrate on learning the skills required in the subtasks of a research project, without having to take full responsibility of managing a research project. As specific skills develop, the responsibilities in conducting a research project may be rethinked.

5.3 Building Effort

Decades of research on achievement and success have revealed a mechanism of *mindset*, a simple but extremely powerful mechanism, which has profound impact to *effort* [10]. Basic beliefs that one's qualities are carved in stone (*the fixed mindset*), or that one's qualities are things that can be cultivated through effort (*the growth mindset*), are proven to have serious effects in practically all life domains [10]. The growth mindset can be built by repeatedly teaching to attribute success and failure in different tasks to the amount of effort, not to personal characteristics [10].

Another extensively studied mechanism that has a profound impact to effort is *willpower* [3]. *Willpower* is affected by a number of factors including the glucose levels in a persons blood [3]. A well known mechanism to cut down willpower is to increase amount of *choices* a person has to make [4, 3]. The willpower of a novice researcher can be maintained by restricting required decision making by cutting down amount of choices the researcher has to make. This can be approached by adjusting amount of guidance and research project management provided by a supervisor.

5.4 Nature of Guidance

A minimally guided environment is not appropriate for novice learners, because novices require direct instructional guidance [14]. Our main coaching approach is to build research competence iteratively by adjusting the level and type of guidance. The research projects will be combined together from a number of smaller research studies, which are published in research journals and conference proceedings. When the researchers work on their first research cases, the supervisors take more responsibility of managing the research projects, and provide a lot of guidance in the required research subtasks.

A main general guideline is that the nature of guidance changes towards the final research cases, which will increase the responsibility granted to the researcher. Table 2 gives an overview of the estimated amount of one-on-one guidance provided by supervisors in the approximated five research projects to be included in a doctoral thesis.

Table 3: Research perspectives of the program

	1. Human Perspective
1.1	What are the expectations of different stakeholders towards the program?
1.2	What are the best measures for skill development?
1.3	What are the best recruitment practices for getting the most motivated new candidates?
1.4	What are the experiences of doctoral candidates and supervisors?
1.5	What needs to be taken into consideration when building up the research community in SSA context?
1.6	What are the good practices in getting candidates' to support each other and also receive guidance from experts?
	2. Societal Relevance Perspective
2.1	What are the factors that affect running a program like this?
2.2	What are the practical implications of the research results?
2.3	What are the expectations of different stakeholders towards the program?
	3. Pedagogical Perspective
3.1	What are good practices of coaching and supervision: candidates' and coaches' viewpoints.
3.2	What are the most useful learning assignments: candidates' and coaches' perspectives.
	4. Practical Arrangement Perspective
4.1	What are the requirements of setting up similar doctoral training hubs?

6. RESEARCH PERSPECTIVES

Implementing doctoral level computing researcher training and developing research culture in HEIs of SSA is not a well studied area. This emphasises the importance of research and monitoring. Table 3 provides perspectives of the project activities that need to be studied.

To address these questions, small to larger scale studies need to be activated during the running of the program. Ethnographic diary writing is an important tool for data collection, as well as continuous feedback from candidates as well as other stakeholders by interviews and questionnaires. Well done monitoring and research practices will, first, inform the future development of the program, and second, disseminate good practices and lessons to CSE research community. The best research and monitoring practices are under constant development within the program.

7. DISCUSSION AND CONCLUSIONS

This project aims to have multiple implications. First, the project aims to increase the research capacities in CBE by increasing the number of PhD holders, the number of research publications, and the number of active research projects. Second, the research projects aim to have multiple impacts into undergraduate computing education in Tanzanian HEIs, and to many other development domains such as small-scale farming, street vending business, business incubation, and the use of educational technology in varying projects.

7.1 Conclusions

Sub-Saharan Africa and its relationship with technology is under a constant change. The rapid expansion of ICT and mobile technologies has resulted in many change processes, and new opportunities for development and economic growth. How to best take grasp of those opportunities and avoid remaining a passive recipient of technology is an important question for the future of SSA. Improving computing research, development, and education initiatives is of high priority. With our project, described in this paper, we have opened an avenue for research about the functional practices for building computing research capacities in SSA.

8. REFERENCES

[1] M. Apiola, S. Pakarinen, and M. Tedre. Pedagogical outlines for OLPC initiatives: A case of Ukombozi school in Tanzania. In *Proceedings of IEEE Africon 2011 Conference*, Livingstone, Zambia, 13th–15th September 2011.

[2] M. Apiola and M. Tedre. New Perspectives on the Pedagogy of Programming in a Developing Country Context. *Computer Science Education*, 22(03):285–313, 2012.

[3] R. F. Baumeister and J. Tierney. *Willpower: Rediscovering the Greatest Human Strength*. Penguin Press, 2012.

[4] R. F. Baumeister, K. D. Vohs, and D. M. Tice. The strength model of self-control. *Current Directions in Psychological Science*, 16(6):351–355, 2007.

[5] P. Carmody. A knowledge economy or an information society in Africa? Thintegration and the mobile phone revolution. *Information Technology for Development*, 19(1):24–39, 2013.

[6] J. W. Creswell. *Research Design: Qualitative, Quantitative, and Mixed Methods Approaches*. Sage Publications, California, USA, 4th edition, 2014.

[7] P. J. Denning, D. E. Comer, D. Gries, M. C. Mulder, A. Tucker, A. J. Turner, and P. R. Young. Computing as a Discipline. *Communications of the ACM*, 32(1):9–23, 1989.

[8] M. Denscombe. *The Good Research Guide for Small-Scale Social Research Projects*. Open University Press, 2010.

[9] J. Donner. Research approaches to mobile use in the developing world: A review of the literature. *The Information Society*, 24(3):140–159, 2008.

[10] C. S. Dweck. *Mindset: How You Can Fulfill Your Potential*. Random House, New York, NY, USA, 2006.

[11] K. A. Ericsson and P. Ward. Capturing the Naturally Occurring Superior Performance of Experts in the Laboratory: Toward a Science of Expert and Exceptional Performance. *Current Directions in Psychological Science*, 16(6):346–350, 2007.

[12] A. Hevner, M. Salvatore, P. Jinsoo, and R. Sudha. Design science in information systems research. *MIS Quarterly*, 28(1):75–105, 2004.

[13] J. Kemppainen. *Appropriating IT Service Management Education in a Tanzanian University: Global and Local Perspectives*. PhD thesis, University of Eastern Finland, Joensuu, Finland, November 2014.

[14] P. A. Kirschner, J. Sweller, and R. E. Clark. Why Minimal Guidance During Instruction Does Not Work: An Analysis of the Failure of Constructivist, Discovery, Problem-Based, Experiential, and Inquiry-Based Teaching. *Educational Psychologist*, 41(2):75–86, 2006.

[15] K. Mgaya. Development of information technology in Tanzania. In E. P. Drew and F. G. Foster, editors, *Information Technology in Selected Countries*. United Nations University, Tokyo, Japan, 1994.

[16] S. E. Noffke and B. Somekh. Introduction. In S. E. Noffke and B. Somekh, editors, *The Handbook of Educational Action Research*. SAGE Publications, 2009.

[17] A. Ojo, T. Janowsky, and J. Awotwi. Enabling development through governance and mobile technology. *Government Information Quarterly*, 30(Supplement 1):S32–S45, 2013.

[18] M. Parada and G. Bull. In the fast lane: Innovations in digital finance. Technical report, The MasterCard Foundation and International Finance Corporation (IFC), Johannesburg, South Africa, 2014.

[19] M. E. P. Seligman. *Flourish: A Visionary New Understanding of Happiness and Well-being*. ATRIA Paperback, New York, NY, USA, 2011.

[20] M. Tedre, F. D. Ngumbuke, N. Bangu, and E. Sutinen. Implementing a Contextualized IT Curriculum: Ambitions and Ambiguities. In *Proceedings of the 8th Koli Calling International Conference on Computing Education Research*, Lieksa, Finland, 2009.

[21] T. Unwin, editor. *ICT4D: Information and Communication Technology for Development*. Cambridge University Press, Cambridge, UK, 2009.

[22] A. A. Zaky. Developing engineers: Some reflections on university education in developing countries. *IEE Review*, 35(6):229–232, June 1989.

Engaging Non-Traditional Students in Computer Science through Socially-Inspired Learning and Sustained Mentoring

Jennifer Burg
Dept. of Computer Science
Wake Forest University
(336) 758-4465
burg@wfu.edu

V. Paúl Pauca
Dept. of Computer Science
Wake Forest University
(336) 758-5454
paucavp@wfu.edu

William Turkett
Dept. of Computer Science
Wake Forest University
(336) 758-4427
turketwh@wfu.edu

Errin Fulp
Dept. of Computer Science
Wake Forest University
(336) 758-3752
fulp@wfu.edu

Samuel S. Cho
Depts. of Comp. Sci. & Physics
Wake Forest University
(336) 758-3922
choss@wfu.edu

Peter Santago
Dept. of Computer Science
Wake Forest University
(336) 758-4190
ps@wfu.edu

Daniel Cañas
Dept. of Computer Science
Wake Forest University
(336) 758-5355
canas@wfu.edu

H. Donald Gage
Dept. of Computer Science
Wake Forest University
(336) 758-4982
gagehd@wfu.edu

ABSTRACT

This paper describes a new program for attracting non-traditional students into computer science and retaining them through sustained peer and faculty mentoring. The program is centered on socially-inspired learning, -- learning *in* and *for* a community. It consists of a STEM Incubator course, hands-on projects with real-world applications, a sandbox lab, and a mentoring system that begins in the STEM Incubator course and continues with students who choose to remain involved in projects and courses. Our program is in its second year. Data collected on enrollment and retention and results of student questionnaires show promise for the success and sustainability of the program.

Categories and Subject Descriptors

K.3.2 Computer and Information Science Education

General Terms

experimentation

Keywords

computer science education; socially-inspired learning; mentoring; non-traditional students; active learning

SIGCSE '15, March 4 - 7, 2015, Kansas City, MO, USA
Copyright 2015 ACM 978-1-4503-2966-8/15/03…$15.00
http://dx.doi.org/10.1145/2676723.2677266

1. BACKGROUND

1.1 Motivation: To Attract and Retain Non-Traditional Students

Our overall motivation for the STEM Incubator Program is to attract and retain non-traditional students into computer science and other STEM disciplines. We define "non-traditional students" as women, ethnic minorities, and students who describe themselves as not being inclined toward STEM subjects. These groups historically have been under-represented in STEM disciplines. Nationally, while about 50% of college students are female, only about 14% major in computer science. About 30% of college students are African-American and about 15% are Hispanic [22], but they make up approximately 3.8% and 6% of the computer science majors, respectively [28]. At our university, 52.3% of the students are female, 7.6% are African-American, and 5.6% are Hispanic [14], but these under-represented groups account for only 19%, 1% and 2% of our computer science majors, respectively.

Like many universities, we are trying to be pro-active to address this imbalance, recognizing that diversity enriches both our learning environment and the nation's pool of scientists and problem-solvers. Our means of attracting and retaining non-traditional students is through *socially-inspired learning* – learning *in* and *for* a community, motivated by collaboration, caring, creativity, and competition. The practical realization of these ideas is our STEM Incubator Program, which consists of four components:

- A one-hour STEM course offered on a variety of topics, all requiring computational problem-solving.
- Team work on hands-on projects centered on specific real-world applications introducing students to STEM knowledge and skills.
- A sandbox-like STEM Incubator Lab offering a collaborative environment with experimental equipment free for use.
- A sustained mentoring program with both faculty and peer mentors.

1.2 Our Program Compared to Related Work

1.2.1 *Incubator Programs*

The concept of incubator programs, even in computer science, is not new. We aim to distinguish our STEM Incubator by combining inspiration and pedagogy in a well-focused, vibrant, and sustainable program. As part of this effort, we are conducting a long-term study of student learning, changes in student perception of the computer science discipline, and effects of sustained mentoring.

Incubator programs have been around for a long time. Business incubators, which began in the 1950s and burgeoned through the 1980s and beyond, are targeted toward helping early-stage companies get started. There is even a national organization for business incubators [13]. Technology business incubators are also common, often emerging as university/business collaborations [12,19].

Our STEM Incubator Program combines a for-credit introductory-level course with involvement in undergraduate research by means of experimental projects. We have established a relationship with our university's Innovation, Creativity, and Entrepreneurship program, enabling subsequent opportunities for entrepreneurship development [1]. Another participating program providing socially-inspired learning opportunities for our STEM teams is the Center for Energy, Environment and Sustainability.

1.2.2 *Mentoring Programs*

A proliferation of mentoring programs can be found in STEM education, many of them industry-affiliated or grant-funded [7,18,21,23,24,26].

Our mentoring program is distinguished by providing the means for both *peer (horizontal) and faculty (vertical) mentor* relationships that are *sustained* over the students' computer science education. We also have a trained mentor coordinator to help develop peer mentoring skills among the students.

1.2.3 *Socially-Relevant Vs. Socially-Inspired Computing*

Socially-relevant applications of computer science have been extensively explored as learning motivators in recent years [3,4,16,17]. Our concept of *socially-inspired* learning extends the idea of relevance to *context* and *environment.* Our intent is to make learning interesting and relevant by giving students a sense that they are working *in* a *community* of learners and *for* the benefit of the broader community in which they live. Elements of community are *collaboration* (working in groups), *caring* (working for the benefit of others or the environment), *creativity* (curiosity in the exploration of the interplay among computation, STEM disciplines, and the arts), and *competition* (a natural motivator).

Collaboration takes place primarily within small teams of apprentices along with student and faculty mentors. Collaboration is also often interdisciplinary, as exemplified in STEM Incubator courses that have focused on applications related to remote sensing and conservation, bioinformatics and computational physics, digital music, digital image processing, and network security. Caring refers to the relevance of STEM team work in addressing problems of society [5,15], including the immediate campus community in which the students live. Creativity is emphasized in projects of all types, but most obviously in the arts-related ones. Teams are encouraged to explore their general topic freely, formulating both the problem and solutions in the process. Healthy competition is motivated by public oral and poster presentations, demos, etc. We see the socially-inspired work taking shape within our STEM Incubator program as a catalyst for subsequent scientific, artistic, business, and entrepreneurship student ventures.

1.2.4 *Undergraduate Research and Vertically-Integrated Programs*

Closely related to science incubator programs in academia are programs that involve undergraduates in research. Two examples of such programs are the Freshman Research Initiative at the University of Texas [6] and Georgia Tech's Vertically-Integrated Projects (VIP) Program [2,8]. In the program at Texas, freshmen become part of 30-student cohorts working on research projects in a wide variety of science applications. This program also provides peer mentoring. The Georgia Tech VIP Program is vertically-integrated in that it involves students from the sophomore to the PhD levels. Projects are multidisciplinary.

Our STEM Incubator Program is similar to the Texas initiative in that it engages freshman in research and experimental projects within small teams. It is similar to Georgia Tech's vertically-integrated concept in that we encourage students to remain involved in projects that they first encounter in their STEM Incubator course (or migrate to projects on related topics), maintaining their peer and faculty mentors. Also, in addition to upperclassmen, a few MS-level graduate students have helped out in our STEM courses as mentors.

Like the Georgia Tech program, our program encourages students to remain involved in projects after the completion of their course. We think that a result of our socially-inspired learning approach, students will feel *invested* in their work and will *want* to continue to be involved. In the 2013-2014 academic year, several of our STEM Incubator students have leveraged their STEM Incubator work to propose and apply for summer research, funded by our university's undergraduate research fellowship program or faculty grant funding. Summer 2014 projects included algorithms for creative 2D image manipulation, 3D bio-printing, and wearable sensors and algorithms for stress detection.

1.2.5 *Computational Problem-Solving*

A distinguishing feature of our STEM Incubator Program is not only the relevance but also the intentionality we give to computational problem-solving. Although our sections of the STEM Incubator course vary by topic, they share learning outcomes, listed below (and condensed for space).

At the end of the STEM Incubator Course, students will be able to

- ***describe*** and ***apply*** strategies for ***identifying and refining*** a computational or technology-based problem.
- ***describe*** and ***apply*** strategies for ***solving*** a computational or technology-based problem.
- ***describe*** and ***apply*** strategies for ***troubleshooting or debugging*** when roadblocks are encountered in a computational or technology-based problem.

Some of these concepts and skills are expected to be learned spontaneously as students are guided through real-world problem solving. Group meetings, short presentations with required key points to cover, and retrospection on their projects help students to become aware of what they have learned and how they have applied it. Templates of student slide presentations are available at http://csweb.cs.wfu.edu/~burg/STEMIncubator/CSC192Fall2014.

2. IMPLEMENTATION

2.1 The STEM Incubator Course

Our practical means of attracting non-traditional students is a one-hour course called the STEM Incubator. Each section of the course has a focus application area in which students develop a hands-on project. The course is being offered for the third time in fall 2014. Interest areas have included mobile apps for campus life; wearable sensors development for health applications; quadcopter/drone development for conservation; digital sound and music for the arts; the art and science of 2D imaging; bioinformatics for genetics; and network hacking and security.

The course is offered at two-levels: the apprentice level and the mentor level. Mentors must have taken at least one computer science course. Some mentors have experience in the application area, and/or are already working on an on-going project with a STEM professor. There are no pre-requisites for apprentices.

Although all sections share the learning outcomes described above, the manner in which individual instructors handle their courses can vary greatly. Some sections are open-ended in problem definition, while others begin with a fairly well-defined problem. Students from all sections meet together as a group four times during the semester, sharing their problems and results in lightening talks that focus on approach and problem solving skills. Brainstorming among groups is particularly encouraged. The semester finishes with oral presentations illustrated with posters. In addition, this Fall 2014, teams will be required to submit general-audience three minute videos to be shared online.

Enrollment in sections of the course is limited to about ten students, and usually the sections are closer to six. A ratio of one peer mentor to about three apprentices works well. Although enrollment for apprentices is not limited to freshmen, we give freshmen priority. Apprentices are being recruited during the summer before their freshman year by our University's Office of Academic Advising and through word of mouth during the Fall for the Spring semester. Academic advising reports a high rate of students in the waiting list for the STEM Incubator course.

2.2 The STEM Incubator Lab

In conjunction with the STEM Incubator course, we have a STEM Lab that serves as a sandbox for students and an environment to foster a community of learners. Students in the Incubator Program (those in a course or involved in on-going projects) have access to the STEM Lab 24/7. The Lab is equipped with computers and "toys" for experimenting – Makey-Makeys, Raspberry Pis, Kinect cameras, a 3D printer, a digital audio workstation for music production, GPU computers, hackable computer networks, quadcopters, simple electronic tools, and so forth. Students work and interact in the lab, seeing each other's projects and exchanging knowledge and ideas.

2.3 Motivation for Faculty Participation

Faculty have been willing to teach STEM courses in spite of the fact that the course becomes a one-hour overload from the usual teaching load. The courses are attractive to some faculty because they offer an opportunity to experiment and explore special interests in a way that may not be practical with their normal research students. Faculty from departments other than computer science are also directly or indirectly involved as mentors.

Having peer mentors in each team lessens the burden on the faculty. The mentor/apprentice design of the program encourages the creation of sustained experimentation-and-research teams that can benefit a faculty member's own research program. Apprentices are introduced to on-going projects by mentors and they may become mentors themselves, leading to natural evolution and development of projects. In principle, the mentors can become more effective researchers for the faculty.

2.4 Example Projects and Outcomes

2.4.1 *Projects and Other Material Shared*

The STEM Incubator Program reflects the strong interest among our faculty in computer science education. Supported in part by curriculum-development grants that correlate with the STEM Incubator Program, curriculum material has been developed (and is continuing to be developed) to be used in STEM Incubator courses.

Our STEM Incubator program is structured in a way that can be replicated at other universities, and our material is freely shared for others who wish to implement a similar program of their own.

Example projects are illustrated at our website, some by means of short videos, to offer ideas for faculty at other institutions [26]. Among these projects are those outlined below.

2.4.2 *Curriculum Material for Digital Media*

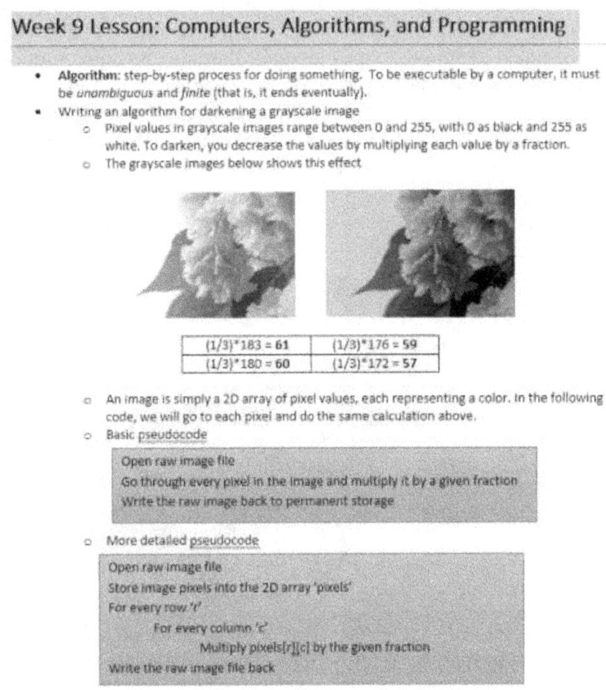
Week 9 Lesson: Computers, Algorithms, and Programming

- **Algorithm:** step-by-step process for doing something. To be executable by a computer, it must be *unambiguous* and *finite* (that is, it ends eventually).
- Writing an algorithm for darkening a grayscale image
  - Pixel values in grayscale images range between 0 and 255, with 0 as black and 255 as white. To darken, you decrease the values by multiplying each value by a fraction.
  - The grayscale images below shows this effect

(1/3)*183 = 61	(1/3)*176 = 59
(1/3)*180 = 60	(1/3)*172 = 57

  - An image is simply a 2D array of pixel values, each representing a color. In the following code, we will go to each pixel and do the same calculation above.
  - Basic pseudocode

```
Open raw image file
Go through every pixel in the image and multiply it by a given fraction
Write the raw image back to permanent storage
```

  - More detailed pseudocode

```
Open raw image file
Store image pixels into the 2D array 'pixels'
For every row 'r'
        For every column 'c'
                Multiply pixels[r][c] by the given fraction
Write the raw image file back
```

Figure 1 Excerpt from 2D imaging exercise

In summer 2014, curriculum material for the "Science and Art of 2D Imaging" STEM course was created in a collaboration between the faculty instructor and one of the student mentors. This material consists of ten lessons and related assignments that move students from high to low levels of abstraction in creative manipulation of digital images. Using a digital image processing tool at a high level of abstraction, students learn concepts of pixels, resolution, image size, file types and compression, histograms, transform functions for contrast or brightness, convolutions, and blending modes. With the help of the mentors, the apprentices are introduced to the mathematics and algorithms underlying these concepts, and they begin to see how a computer program could be written to accomplish the functions provided by GIMP. By this means, the apprentices are also exposed to basic programming logic and constructs. Simple exercises guide them through the material, and the learning is motivated by a creative final project that they work on incrementally throughout the semester. A lesson and related exercise are illustrated in Figure 1 to give the flavor of the curriculum material [9].

In the area of digital sound and music, a similar learning module has been created to move students from high to low levels of abstraction in audio processing. In this module, students learn about digitization, sampling, quantization, the representation of sound through sinusoidal functions, frequency related to pitch, amplitude related to loudness, time domain vs. frequency domain representations, musical frequencies and harmonics, modulation, LFOs, and amplitude envelopes. With a base set of MATLAB or Octave functions, the students are challenged to "hand-craft" their own musical piece by summing frequencies; experimenting with square, sawtooth, triangle, and sine waves; applying amplitude envelopes and LFOs for tremolo or vibrato, and so forth. (See http://csweb.cs.wfu.edu/~burg/MATLAB&OctavePrograms/).

2.4.2.1 Drones, Health, and Art: An Exploration of Sensor Applications
Data-collecting sensors are becoming ubiquitous across all aspects of society. Optical sensors collect image data remotely, GPS sensors track geographic location, accelerometers track motion, and others can track heart rate and physiological data. One of our STEM Incubator courses explores the use of these types of sensors for conservation, health, and alternative human-computer interaction purposes. Current and past projects include quadcopter development, heart rate monitors for stress awareness, translation of American sign language to voice [10], Arduino based bat sonar systems, and alternative mouse design for disabilities.

Figure 2 Working on novel input devices

2.4.2.2 Remote Sensing for Music Education and Exercise Therapy through Music
One STEM course gave students an opportunity to experiment with remote sensing (Kinect cameras) in applications related to music. The first experiment (done as a prototype for the following semester's STEM course) used remote sensing coupled with MAX/MSP programming to create systems for ear-training in perfect or relative pitch [11,20]. The following semester, students did a variation of this application, creating a system to encourage exercise and motion by sensing user movement and "measuring out" musical strains accordingly [27].

2.4.2.3 Bioinformatics
The Bioinformatics STEM course provided students the opportunity to explore the role that computers and algorithms play in modern biology and to experience interdisciplinary interactions between computer scientists and biologists. The first focus of the course was for students to investigate mechanisms for determining how to define and efficiently compute DNA and protein sequence similarity, within the real-world context of needing to be able to rapidly identify a new virus. The second focus was to process, with statistical filtering, clustering, and machine learning algorithms, microarray datasets in order to determine subsets of genes with interesting behaviors. The course ended with a tour of the lab of a collaborator from the Department of Biology that allowed the STEM students to see the source of the microarray data they analyzed and to see and hear why such analyses were important to be undertaken in the context of modern agriculture.

2.4.2.4 The Internet of all Things
As the Internet continues to evolve to interconnect a larger and more diverse set of devices, maintaining cyber security has become more important. This STEM course sought to introduce students to offense and defense approaches by tracing the general steps of a cyberattack (reconnaissance, access, privilege, foothold, and cover). At each step, students were introduced to basic security concepts and current tools, and given a challenge for that week. For example, for the access step, a web server was created and students used hydra (a web-form password cracker) to gain access to a protected page. For the defensive counter measure, students learned about secure passwords and well-established web access policies. As a final project, students were challenged to practice all steps of a standard attack against set of servers, which is considered a stepping-stone attack (with movement through a series of servers required). The course relied heavily on Virtual Machines (VMs), Virtual Local Area Networks (VLANs), and firewalls to ensure the students stayed within designated areas of the campus network. Virtualization also greatly reduced the administration of the course since any damaged systems could quickly be reestablished.

3. RESULTS

3.1 Demographics
Our STEM Incubator courses thus far have had good success attracting underrepresented minorities and women. Demographics for all apprentices are shown in Table 1, while Table 2 shows the demographics for freshmen only.

Table 1 Demographics of STEM Incubator Courses

Semester	Total # students	African-American	Hispanic	Male	Female
Fall 2013	30	3 10%	3 10%	18 60%	12 40%
Spr 2014	46	1 2%	4 9%	27 59%	19 41%
Fall 2014	47	2 4%	3 6%	30 64%	17 36%

Table 2 Demographics of STEM Incubator courses, freshmen only

Semester	Total # freshmen	African-American	Hispanic	Male	Female
Fall 2013	24	2 1%	2 1%	14 58%	10 42%
Spr 2014	20	1 5%	3 15%	11 55%	9 45%
Fall 2014	23	2 9%	1 4%	14 61%	9 39%

Table 3 Demographics of computer science majors at WFU

	Total # CS Majors	African-American	Hispanic	Male	Female
CS Majors	84	2 2%	2 2%	68 81%	16 19%
CS Minors	25	0 0%	0 0%	13 52%	12 48%

In light of the fact that less than 20% of our majors are currently female, having more than 40% women in our STEM courses is a good initial showing. We achieved this result even without the more targeted recruiting that we are now putting into place. We observed almost no difference between the African-American and Hispanic demographics of computer science majors and the STEM Incubator courses, but this is likely the result of our campus-wide demographics.

3.2 Survey Results

Apprentice students were requested to complete a pre-course and a post-course survey relating to the students' interest in and self-perception of skills related to STEM, computer science, and problem solving. Questions were either free-response (for example: *Likely Major?*) or on a 5-point Likert scale. A total of 29 and 22 students enrolled in the STEM courses completed the pre- and post-course surveys respectively during the spring 2014 semester, with 16 of those students completing both surveys. A little more than half of the students submitting surveys were freshmen.

At our university, students cannot select their major until the end of their sophomore year, so analysis was done for three groups: all apprentices, freshman and sophomore apprentices, and freshman-only apprentices.

Even with the small sample size, there are encouraging initial results indicated by the survey. Responses were averaged across the pre- survey respondents and the post-survey respondents. The largest positive change observed was for the question *How would you rate your logical problem solving skills at this time* (1- *Quite Weak to 5 – Very Strong)*? for which increases on the Likert scale of 0.28, 0.41, and 0.48 were observed when breaking the surveys out by all apprentices, freshman and sophomore apprentices, and freshman-only apprentices respectively. When only students who responded to both surveys were analyzed, even greater increases were seen in response to this question. Pre- to post-course increases of 0.32 and 0.34 were observed for freshman and sophomore and freshman-only students respectively in responses to the question of *What is the likelihood you will minor in a STEM subject at WFU?* Other smaller increases were observed that warrant following up on in future semesters - primarily in the responses from first-year students, the primary target population of the STEM program.

3.3 Retention

The STEM Incubator Program has had good initial success in retaining freshmen in STEM courses after they take the first STEM Incubator course. Of 33 freshmen who took the STEM course in Fall 2013, 17 of whom were from under-represented groups, a significant number took subsequent science, computer science, or mathematics courses, as shown in the table below.

One of the most encouraging results of the STEM Program is manifested in the continued involvement of students in research and experimental projects with faculty beyond the initial STEM Incubator course. The program is showing success in engaging students in the discipline with interest and enthusiasm. Five students have repeated as mentors in Incubator courses. One former STEM student is now working on 3D bio-printing with the Wake Forest Institute for Regenerative Medicine.

Table 4 Retention in STEM, after STEM Incubator course

freshmen who took STEM Incubator course, Fall 2013	# who took a subsequent natural science course	# who took a subsequent computer science course	# who took a subsequent mathematics course
33	12	4	15

4. DISCUSSION

In this paper, we presented our approach for attracting and retaining non-traditional students through a socially-inspired learning process. Creating small teams of apprentices, student mentors, and faculty mentors under an STEM Incubator umbrella is a key component of this process. A one-hour credit course implemented through a number of specialized sections is used to elicit student work. Through our STEM Incubator Lab, students are also provided a sandbox environment for collaboration, exploration, and creativity.

Early results from our STEM Incubator program are very encouraging. Our University's Office of Academic Advising reports a high number of incoming students interested in the program. Information about the program is disseminated through the computer science department website. Because the program is still in its early stages, STEM retention rates past major/minor area declaration and after graduation are not yet determined. However, we believe retention will occur as a result of our sustained apprentice/mentorship approach and student investment in being a part of a community working on real-world projects.

5. CHALLENGES AND FUTURE WORK

A fundamental challenge in this program is finding and attracting the right students – non-traditional STEM students who have *unrealized aptitude* for computational science. We are getting help from educational specialists in refining our pre- and post-course surveys, with the intention of including a small questions that measure problem-solving ability before and after the STEM Incubator course. We are also beginning collaborations with K-12 educators and educators who have been active in women-in-science initiatives. These collaborations may help us establish coherent paths for non-traditional students from K-12 to STEM education in college.

Our plans for continued development of the STEM Incubator program include:

- more targeted recruiting, including outreach to high schools
- refinement of the mentoring program in collaboration with our mentor coordinator
- increased data gathering to assess the program's success in attracting and retaining non-traditional students
- continued development of curriculum material, including a refinement of our learning objectives geared toward computational problem-solving
- dissemination of the program's methods and results

6. REFERENCES

[1] "2014 Excellence in Entrepreneurship Award Winners WFU." 2014. Accessed July 9. http://entrepreneurship.wfu.edu/events/annual-excellence in-entrepreneurship-awards-banquet-/2014-excellence-in-entrepreneurship-award-winners.

[2] Abler, R., E. Coyle, A Kiopa, and J. Melkers. 2011. "Team-Based Software/system Development in Vertically Integrated Project-Based Course." In Frontiers in Education Conference (FIE), 2011, T3F–1–T3F–7. doi:10.1109/FIE.2011.6142974.

[3] Buckley, Michael, Helene Kershner, Kris Schindler, Carl Alphonce, and Jennifer Braswell. 2004. "Benefits of Using Socially-Relevant Projects in Computer Science and Engineering Education." In Proceedings of the 35th SIGCSE Technical Symposium on Computer Science Education, 482–86. SIGCSE '04. New York, NY, USA: ACM. doi:10.1145/971300.971463.

[4] Buckley, Michael, John Nordlinger, and Devika Subramanian. 2008. "Socially Relevant Computing." In Proceedings of the 39th SIGCSE Technical Symposium on Computer Science Education, 347–51. SIGCSE '08. New York, NY, USA: ACM. doi:10.1145/1352135.1352255.

[5] Ferguson, Will. 2013. "Empowering the Voiceless | News Center | Wake Forest University." http://news.wfu.edu/2013/10/17/empowering-the-voiceless/.

[6] "Freshman Research Initiative." 2014. Accessed July 9. http://cns.utexas.edu/fri.

[7] Georgia Tech. 2014a. "VentureLab." Accessed July 9. http://venturelab.gatech.edu/.

[8] ———. 2014b. "The Vertically-Integrated Projects (VIP) Program." Accessed July 9. http://vip.gatech.edu/.

[9] Hack, Becky, and Jennifer Burg. 2014. "CSC192 Course Material, Burg/Hack." Accessed July 16. http://csweb.cs.wfu.edu/~burg/STEMIncubator/CSC192Fall2014/.

[10] Lewis, Marsha. 2014a. "Giving A Voice To The Voiceless | Inside Science." Accessed July 10. http://www.insidescience.org/content/giving-voice-voiceless/1654.

[11] ———. 2014b. "Raise Your Hand For Perfect Pitch | Inside Science." Accessed July 9. http://www.insidescience.org/content/raise-your-hand-perfect-pitch/1661.

[12] Mac, Ryan. 2012. "Top Startup Incubators And Accelerators: Y Combinator Tops With $7.8 Billion In Value." http://www.forbes.com/sites/tomiogeron/2012/04/30/top-tech-incubators-as-ranked-by-forbes-y-combinator-tops-with-7-billion-in-value/.

[13] "National Business Incubation Association." 2014. Accessed July 9. http://www.nbia.org/.

[14] Office of Institutional Research Wake Forest University. 2013. "Wake Forest University Fact Book 2012-2013." http://www.wfu.edu/ir/factbook-2012-2013/index.html.

[15] Pauca, Paul. 2013. "▸ How to Use Verbal Victor 2.0 – YouTube." www.youtube.com/ watch?v=9DxtFT5doZc.

[16] Pauca, Victor Paul, and Richard T. Guy. 2012. "Mobile Apps for the Greater Good: A Socially Relevant Approach to Software Engineering." In Proceedings of the 43rd ACM Technical Symposium on Computer Science Education, 535–40. SIGCSE '12. New York, NY, USA: ACM. doi:10.1145/2157136.2157291.

[17] Rader, Cyndi, Doug Hakkarinen, Barbara M. Moskal, and Keith Hellman. 2011. "Exploring the Appeal of Socially Relevant Computing: Are Students Interested in Socially Relevant Problems?" In Proceedings of the 42Nd ACM Technical Symposium on Computer Science Education, 423–28. SIGCSE '11. New York, NY, USA: ACM. doi:10.1145/1953163.1953288.

[18] St. Francis University. 2014. "STEPping Up: An Interdisciplinary Mentoring Network to Recruit and Retain STEM Majors." Accessed July 9. http://stepcentral.net/projects/245#.U71c8D-TGlv.

[19] State of New Jersey Commission on Science & Technology. 2014. "Technology Incubators." Accessed July 9. http://www.state.nj.us/scitech/techinc/.

[20] "STEM Dr Burg - YouTube." 2014. Accessed July 10. https://www.youtube.com/watch?v=tD8Ps9pqMaw.

[21] Texas A & M University Kingsville. 2014. "CASCaded Mentoring and Design Experiences." Accessed July 9.

[22] Trotta, Daniel. 2013. "Hispanic College Enrollment In U.S. Rose 15 Percent Despite Overall Student Population Decline."http://www.huffingtonpost.com/2013/09/04/hispanic-college-enrollment-_n_3861789.html.

[23] University of Houston. 2014. "STEP Forward: STEM Talent Expansion Program for Women and Under Represented Group Recruitment and Retention Development at the University of Houston." Accessed July 9. http://stepcentral.net/posters/969/#.U71dqD-TGls.

[24] University of New Mexico. 2014. "STEPs in the Right Direction: Transforming Engineering/Computer Science Education at the University of New Mexico." Accessed July 9. http://stepcentral.net/projects/222#.U71dWz-TGls.

[25] Wake Forest University. 2014. "Innovation, Creativity, and Entrepreneurship." Accessed July 9. http://entrepreneurship.wfu.edu/.

[26] Wake Forest University Computer Science. 2014. "STEM Incubator | Cs | Wake Forest University." Accessed July 16. http://college.wfu.edu/cs/undergraduate-program/stem-incubator.

[27] Zhao, Edward, and Garrett Johns. 2014. "WFU Computer Science STEM Lab Project- Remote Sensing - YouTube." Accessed July 16. https://www.youtube.com/watch?v=WTgzZftDjs0.

[28] Zweben, Stuart. 2014. "Computing Degree and Enrollment Trends (from the 2012-2013 Taulbee Survey)." Computing Degree and Enrollment Trends (from the 2012-2013 Taulbee Survey). Accessed July 9. http://www.cra.org/uploads/documents/resources/taulbee/CRA_Taulbee_CS_Degrees_and_Enrollment_2012-13.pdf.

How Much Impact Can Be Made in a Week? Designing Effective International Service Learning Projects for Computing

Grace Ngai[1] Stephen C.F. Chan[1,2]

[1]Department of Computing [2]Office of Service Learning
Hong Kong Polytechnic University
Kowloon, Hong Kong
{grace.ngai, stephen.c.chan}@polyu.edu.hk

ABSTRACT

Service learning has been gaining attention in recent years. It has been established as an effective method to teach students a variety of concepts that are not easily taught in the classroom, and much effort has gone into making service learning accessible and relevant to computer science students. This paper investigates a popular mode of computing-related service learning – offshore projects that seek to introduce information and computing technologies (ICTs) into a beneficiary population. Based on multiple years of experience working with ICTs in service learning, the authors examine the impact on students and beneficiaries through several critical questions, and draw conclusions and recommendations on good practices for designing offshore service learning projects for computing students.

Categories and Subject Descriptors

K.3.2. [**Computers and Education**]: Computer and Information Sciences Education; K.4. [**Computers and Society**]: General

General Terms

Design, Human Factors.

Keywords

service-learning; international projects

1. INTRODUCTION

Service learning has been gaining much attention as an effective way to teach students about concepts, such as social responsibility and empathy, which are not easily covered in the classroom. In addition, offshore service learning projects, which are defined as projects that require the students to leave their home communities and be immersed into a different environment for an extended length of time, are also gaining in popularity. Similar to exchange studies or semester abroad, they offer very rich learning opportunities that tie together service to the community with a cross-cultural experience of new languages, culture, food and people. Many of these activities have resulted in much benefit to the local communities as well as substantive learning gains from the participants.

Benefits aside, however, the increase in such activities has inevitably led to some backlash and soul-searching about their impact upon the local community, or the non-profit organizations (NGOs) that usually are involved with sponsoring or organizing these projects. In a general service-learning context, Blouin and Perry [3] examined the impact of service learning on the community partners. Grusky [10] and Crabtree [5] present in-depth analyses of the impact and consequences of international service learning. From the Computing front, Connolly [6] argues that many computing-related service learning activities often over-focus on the students' discipline learning gains at the expense of addressing real needs and facilitating real understanding of the target community. This topic surfaces regularly in popular literature as well, with many such reports pointing to physical as well as emotional disruption that such activities inflict upon the local community.

Given such disparate opinions, and the resources that inevitably need to be invested into offshore projects, this paper seeks to investigate the issue of how such projects could best be designed to maximize the potential of (1) producing the biggest positive impact on the target community, and (2) eliciting the maximum learning outcomes from the students.

2. BACKGROUND

At the Hong Kong Polytechnic University and the Department of Computing, there is a long tradition of organizing ICT-related service learning projects that bring students to serve underprivileged communities. The majority of students serve the local community, but a growing number are involved in offshore projects. Since 2005, our students have contributed over 13,000 man-hours of service in 14 ICT-related offshore service learning projects in China, Cambodia, Rwanda and Myanmar.

There are two main "models" when it comes to offshore service projects. The first model involves small teams of experienced, or highly trained, individuals, often for longer periods of time, such as several weeks or even months. A second model brings larger teams of relatively inexperienced members, often for shorter periods of time, such as a week or two weeks.

The model discussed in this paper is the latter. Many of our students are first-generation college students from working class backgrounds, and a good number have never travelled away from home on vacation or study abroad prior to arriving at university. In order to not disadvantage these students relative to their more affluent peers, our philosophy is "attitude before ability" – meaning

SIGCSE '15, March 4–7, 2015, Kansas City, MO, USA.
Copyright 2014 ACM 978-1-4503-2966-8/15/03…$15.00
http://dx.doi.org/10.1145/2676723.2677267

that any student with a proper attitude (willingness to learn, willingness to be a team player, willingness to "pull their own weight") would be accepted. (The college generously sponsors a significant part of their expenses.) Our teams almost wholly comprise of undergraduate students in their first and second years. This oftentimes means inexperienced students who have not yet acquired much expertise, and most of their knowledge is confined to in-class theoretical concepts, untested by real-world constraints. Since Hong Kong is relatively ethnically homogeneous, this also means that most of our students have no prior experience interacting on a peer level with people of a different ethnicity.

3. Computing in Service Learning

Computers, in various shapes and forms, have become almost indispensible for many types of services. For many young people in first world countries, it is difficult to imagine life without the computers or the Internet. Computing devices govern and manage almost all facets and transactions in daily life, including social communication and networking, which have taken on dramatically different formats. Even in developing countries, commerce and communications are slowly becoming more and more dependent on ICT, and computing is a popular discipline of study in many such countries. Since computing devices are low in both size and cost, transportation and installation is convenient and feasible. Therefore, it is not surprising that computing-related service learning has become quite popular. As an example, there are many projects, such as computing outreach efforts, which aim to bridge the digital divide or to facilitate digital inclusion.

From the learning standpoint, when students go on projects in developing communities, there is a wide gap between the level of availability of ICT in the resource-rich society where they come from, and the community that they are serving. Concepts such as the digital divide and the inconveniences, or even inequities, that arise as a result, are obvious to even the casual observer. At a deeper level, issues such as information ethics, education and privacy have to be addressed and examined. The impact of ICT upon daily life leads to differences in expectations, working style and even culture and self-expression between the service team and their beneficiaries. For example, the convenience brought about by ICT services and the greater (and faster) availability of information usually results in a faster pace of life, and hence a different sense of time and punctuality, which pervades into other aspects such as individuality and even commitment. All of these are issues that need to be addressed during the planning and execution of the service project. At the same time, they afford many valuable opportunities for learning and reflection.

4. Critical Questions in Designing an Computing-Related Service Project

Computing-related service projects usually fall into one of two broad types. Design-based projects have the objective of providing technology-based solutions for needy communities. Examples are designing and installing computer labs; constructing websites; or developing content management systems. Instructional-nature projects aim to provide training in various ICT-related topics. These include "computing outreach" workshops that teach innovative technology or computer literacy. (A third type of ICT-related project – the "ICT for development" (ICT4D) project – is not covered in this paper.)

Similarly, all projects can be divided into three phases. The participants usually need to spend time and effort in preparation.

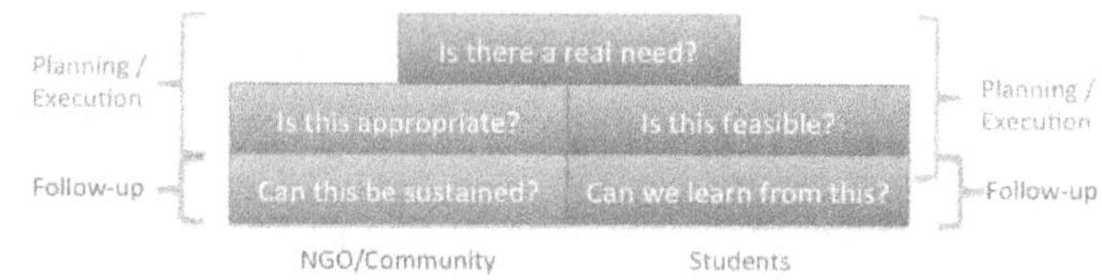

Figure 1: Critical Questions for Designing Computing-related Service Learning Projects

For example, projects that involve development, such as design and development of webpages and content management systems, obviously will require much effort before the product can be deployed, and infrastructure installation projects often require substantive research into the local context before decisions on hardware can be made. Even instructional-nature projects require participants to design lesson plans and teaching content, and often, also assembling supporting software.

The execution phase starts once the team gets onto the ground and the designed plans are put into motion. Depending on the complexity of the project and the conditions at the site, this phase often involves adaptations and modifications of the original plan

The follow up phase begins after the team leaves the site and can last for an extended period of time. This phase mainly involves the local communities who have to take charge of the project deliverables and continue with the services. Many ICT-related projects also require support from the team after their departure.

Finally, all projects involve at least two or three parties. The students travel to the site as service providers. The local community receives the service or the deliverables. The project is oftentimes facilitated by a non-government organization (NGO).

Based on our own experiences and studies of literature, we formulated a sequence of four critical questions to be addressed in the design of international ICT-related service learning projects.

1. To start with, is there really a need for an overseas team, travelling to the site, to address the problem identified?
2. Assuming that the need for the trip is real, is the proposed method sound – in terms of addressing the need? That is: is it appropriate for the community? And is it really feasible, given that it is students who will be carrying this out?
3. Assuming that the method is sound, is the solution sustainable? Or it is only a short-term or a once-off solution?
4. For true service-learning, there must be balance between the community service and the educational objectives. Are there real benefits to the students participating in the project?

Figure 1 shows the relationship between the project phases, the parties, and the critical questions. The following sub-sections will discuss each question in more detail, illustrating with real cases.

Finally, the ethical aspects of the project must be addressed. We are putting them into a separate section to ensure that they receive the attention deserved.

4.1 Do they actually need a visiting team for this service?

A critical question to ask of any project – ICT or not – is whether the nature of the project really requires an overseas team. Much has been made about the "contributions" of overseas teams who arrive with little or no preparation and undertake tasks that could easily have been performed by local residents. Is it really a learning experience, or worse, a tour, disguised as service-learning? Each of these activities can be legitimate in their own right, but they should be identified as such properly.

This applies to computing-related projects as well. It is common to see teams going to offshore locations to teach classes on Office software or email. These types of services are very popular mainly because they make use of skill-sets that the participants already possess, and thus do not require much preparation. However, people possessing the same types of skills (basic computer operations, email, Office software) are often easily found in the target population. Given the amount of funds that are involved in bringing the service teams to the offshore location, it would seem to make sense to "set the bar higher", as it were, and bring in new concepts/skills that are not commonly available in the local population. This is also congruent with the philosophy of reciprocity [12], with a mutually and *equally* beneficial relationship to both sides.

In our experience, some of the most effective services of an instructional nature involve the use of educational technology in creative hands-on learning. These projects serve as an interesting and exciting introduction to many concepts in digital literacy, and they also have the side effect of arousing the beneficiaries' interest in technology and studying. The latter is not to be overlooked, for in many poor communities, staying in school does have a real opportunity cost in terms of lost income.

There is much literature documenting successful cases of teaching technology to underrepresented groups, such as multimedia computing to disabled children [9], robotics for blind children [14] and wearable computing for low-income children [13], among others. Obviously, there is a resource gap and some of the more expensive equipment (such as Lego robots) would not be appropriate in developing countries. However, many applications of creative technology do not require expensive equipment.

We describe one example for illustration. A primary school in rural China had received a donation of computers. Since they wanted to introduce computer classes, they asked for training in Office software for their teachers, who would in turn teach it to the children. After discussion with the school authorities, the authors made a counterproposal – the service team would teach the children directly, with the teachers present to assist in classroom management, and digital storytelling would be used as a vehicle for teaching computer literacy.

In preparation for the service, the students researched the concepts and methods behind digital storytelling. Micro-movie production was finally chosen, as it requires a diversity of computer operations (e.g. basic operations, file manipulation, etc). It also encourages artistic creativity and self-expression. To familiarize themselves with the software and to help with time allocation and planning, the students produced several movies and drew from the experience to design a comprehensive lesson plan that covered topics from storyboarding to shooting to subtitling and rendering.

The project was executed over one workweek (5 full days). Some adaptations were made on site to accommodate the interests of the children – for example, some wanted to incorporate scenes from movies or TV shows or famous artworks into their own micro-movies, and so the lesson plan was modified to introduce information search and downloading images from the Internet. Some of the processes (such as movie rendering) were deemed to be too boring, so they were removed from the schedule.

The workshop familiarized the children and their teachers with certain aspects of multimedia production, which were worked into their regular classes after the team left. For example, some of the teachers incorporated multimedia content and project work into their teaching, which had previously relied mainly on rote learning and memorization. In addition, after the short introduction to the Internet and information searching, the children and teachers started exploring the Internet on their own. One year after the workshop, observers on a followup visit reported the use of Google Maps in General Studies lessons!

In general, for instructional-based projects, we have found that project-based learning usually produces better results than teaching specific skills or concepts. First, it is easier to motivate a project within a short period of time than a particular topic or concept. In addition, projects often involve a diversity of skills and topics, each of which would be difficult and tedious to teach and motivate on their own. Project-based learning has also been shown to promote self-learning and life-long learning in engineering and computing [11][17], which is appropriate for short workshops that serve as an introduction into a broader field that the recipients will have to learn to explore on their own.

4.2 Is the service appropriate? Can it be feasibly carried out?

ICT-related projects have to adapt to the available resources and constraints of the service environment, which are beyond the control of the service team. Some constraints are infrastructural, such as the availability of electricity, Internet, or spare parts. More often, however, the constraints relate to human and societal factors, such as the readiness of the target beneficiaries for the deliverables. Put together, these constraints often make conventional ICT solutions inappropriate and require creative thinking to come up with a workable solution.

We illustrate with an example from our experience. An NGO in Cambodia wanted to expand their services. Their vision was to bring computing literacy to children living in rural communities just outside the city. The challenge was that the communities did not have electricity supply, and while they could have constructed a computer lab in the community center, they were not confident about ensuring the security of the equipment.

Given the constraints, it was quickly determined that a conventional computer laboratory would not be a feasible solution. After a lot of discussion, an alternate solution was devised. The final solution drew inspiration from the "bookmobile libraries" that serve underprivileged communities in the US. A Raspberry Pi single-board computer was used as a server hosting e-Learning resources such as electronic books, with the operating system and data on an SD card. A mobile router created a local area network, and the computing devices were smartphones and tablets. The setup fits into a suitcase and was outfitted with enough batteries to run for up to 6 hours on one overnight charge. The idea is that the "lab" would be charged up in the city, and transported into the rural community for regular sessions.

During the execution phase, the project team conducted intensive training for the NGO staff, and also organized workshops in computer literacy for rural schoolchildren, using digital storytelling as an illustration, in collaboration and with the assistance of the local NGO staff. While the most obvious objective of the workshops was to teach the children computer literacy, they also served as demonstration classes to familiarize the NGO staff with the new equipment, and to give them an idea of how this equipment could be used in their services. The NGO staff continued with the services after the team departed. A follow-up visit a year later found that inevitably, the nature of the services had undergone some evolution as the mission of the NGO adapted to the changing needs of the community. The lab was still in regular use, but the target had shifted from rural children to urban street children, so arguably the portability was not needed, but the comments from the NGO were that the reliability of the devices made them easy and convenient to use, and therefore allowed them to run sessions more regularly.

In a similar manner, many service proposals, if scrutinized carefully, may turn out to be too risky, or even infeasible. As engineers or computer scientists, practitioners of ICT-related projects tend to look towards the technical aspects when considering feasibility challenges. However, many challenges come from the human or societal aspect, which (in a way) are harder to address than technical challenges.

4.3 Can the deliverables be sustained/maintained?

Sustainability is a key concern in all service projects. Due to the (usually) short duration and the gap (both in distance as well as cultural habits) between the service team and the target beneficiaries, offshore service learning projects are often criticized as being unsustainable.

ICT-related projects face an especial challenge in this aspect. Most technology solutions need to be maintained, and the maintenance process usually requires a minimum of technological know-how. For example, a software package or a web page that was developed for an NGO will often need debugging, or updating, which is often extremely difficult, if not impossible, for local individuals. The short-term nature of service learning projects worsens the situation, as it is often difficult to find volunteers who are willing to continue to help after the project.

Even hardware and infrastructure installations require maintenance and upkeep. For example, any computer that is connected to the Internet or has the capability to accept a USB flash drive will require periodic anti-virus scans. Since many anti-virus software packages are configured to run the scanning process at start-up or when a new USB drive is inserted, this may seem like an automatic, pain-free process. However, anti-virus software needs to be updated regularly, and many such software packages need user confirmation before the new signatures are incorporated into the package. Adding to the problem is that when a virus is discovered, the software usually gives the user a list of options, which is often couched in technical jargon and almost unintelligible to non-computer-literate people.

An example can be found from the authors' own experiences in a rural school in China. The project involved installing a network of computers for students and staff at the school. The project also included training in computer literacy and maintenance for the staff at the school, including anti-virus scanning and removal. About a month after the project, however, the computers started to malfunction. Frequent crashes and application lock-ups were experienced, and some computers had trouble accessing the Internet. It was determined that the computers had become infected with a variety of viruses and Trojans, and despite several video-conferencing sessions that attempted to troubleshoot and solve the problem online, the situation deteriorated and the machines soon became unusable.

A follow-up project was organized at short notice to fix the problems. After much discussion and debate, it was decided to take a draconian approach to the problem. "Reborn cards" were installed into the computers, which essentially restored the computers to the same starting state upon each reboot. The training was then modified to incorporate the use of USB flash drives for file storage and frequent reboots of the computer (especially before/after any insertion of USB drives.) The result of the changes was that computer-related problems dropped dramatically: over the 12 months after the follow-on project, only one support request was made when a new piece of software had to be installed into the machine.

This solution, which would probably *not* be acceptable in most contexts in first-world countries, illustrates one of the biggest challenges for ICT-related projects – that of follow-up and maintainability, and the trade-off between flexibility and predictability. Such a solution would be seen (and was seen at the time) as being a waste of computing resources, (since the hard drive becomes unavailable for long-term storage), and adding unnecessary steps to what would normally be a simple process of opening a file stored on a flash drive. For our particular context, however, it made the computers more predictable, more reliable, and therefore, *more* user-friendly. We suspect that a similar situation exists for many other contexts in developing countries.

The problem of maintenance and upkeep poses an especially big challenge when older models of computing equipment are involved, for example, when used computers are donated to developing countries. In general, older equipment requires more maintenance, and the rapid pace of change in technology also makes it difficult to find spare parts for replacement or to identify people with the needed know-how. Indeed, with the introduction of the tablet computer and the rapidly declining prices, even for new units, we feel that it is worth considering using these new technologies for computing setups in service contexts.

4.4 Does this provide learning opportunities for our students?

Service learning puts equal focus on both service to the community and learning gains by the students [8]. It has often been argued that just simply placing students in the community or putting them to work on real projects already affords learning gains. However, in the continuum of service-based activities, such statements are probably more appropriately applied to volunteerism, community service or service-based internships, than to service learning, which should include directed learning of societal issues in addition to service to the community.

In this sense, it can be argued that many developmental or infrastructural installation projects are lacking in the learning aspect. Putting it another way, the tasks that are carried out in these projects are oftentimes very similar in nature to tasks that would be carried out in a corporate setting in the developed world, the only differences coming from infrastructural factors such as electricity supply or fast broadband access. These are illustrations of the digital divide, and students may well have to adjust their plans or design their solutions around these constraints, but they do not afford students the opportunity to observe the impact upon the users, or the underprivileged that they have come to serve.

We illustrate with an example from our own experience. An NGO in China accepts donations of used computers, which are then donated to poor children living in rural regions. Since many of the computers that they receive are not working properly, they proposed a service project to take place at their headquarters in Beijing (the capital of China), where students would fix up the old computers, which would then be delivered to the beneficiaries.

This project, if carried out (we did not accept the proposal) would have provided a useful service, but at the cost of very little learning gain for our students. Ensconced in an office setting in a world-class city and fixing up old computers would not have offered them any insights into the impact of ICT upon the underprivileged (beyond an abstract grasp of the concept of the digital divide by realising that children in rural areas use computers that would be considered trash by urbanites). Indeed, this project arguably provides little in the way of *discipline-specific* gains. Given the rate of change of technology, many of the techniques that apply to fixing up old computers are not applicable in the newer generation of machines. Unless the students intend to take a job in a low-resource setting, they would likely never need to use those sorts of skills again.

Another example is a software development project that was carried out for an NGO in Cambodia. The NGO shelters abused children, and they wanted a database system to keep track of the children's medical records, such as doctors' visits, diagnoses, etc.

A team of students took on this project, with supervision and guidance from faculty members experienced in software management and development. The bulk of the development took place in Hong Kong, and the team travelled to Cambodia for deployment and training of the local NGO staff. It was expected that the system would be deployed without much problems. Upon reaching the site, however, a myriad of challenges such as differences between the stated user requirements and the expectations, inconsistencies between the existing data that had to be imported into the system, etc, caused so many problems that the team was forced to spend the entire time in Cambodia debugging the system. In essence, their project had turned into what could have been amounted to a term project in a database class, albeit with a real user and in an exotic location!

While one could say that the aforementioned problems could have been prevented with enough foresight and user testing, it is a fact that ICT system development is complex and difficult, even in professional settings, where a large majority of IT projects either fail, or go over-budget and fall behind schedule [4]. It is therefore debatable whether projects of this nature are truly feasible, especially given that most students on service learning projects are likely to be inexperienced.

This is not to say that all developmental projects should be avoided in service learning. Indeed, projects of a design nature do provide a much-needed service to many NGOs that provide valuable service to needy communities. However, the risks and feasibility must be thoroughly analysed before taking on the project. It would also certainly not be desirable for the *entire* project to be of this nature. For example, an installation of a computer laboratory could very feasibly be combined with workshops in computer maintenance and information literacy, either for the NGO staff or even for members of the community that they are serving. Such a combination would highlight examples of the realities and impact of the digital divide, together with potential solutions, that could be elaborated on later in reflection and discussion sessions.

5. Do Some Good — and Minimize the Harm

The focus of this paper is on the design of ICT-related service projects, but no such paper would be complete without a discussion of at least some of the associated ethical issues. On one hand, carrying out service projects without due consideration of the ethical implications is simply irresponsible. On the other hand, tackling ethical issues encountered in the middle of service makes the issues come alive and relevant to the students. It is much more effective compared to a discussion in the calm of the classroom.

There is a lot of debate in the developed world about the benefits and harms brought about by ICT, especially where young people are concerned. There has been much study into the problems that are brought about by the pervasiveness of the Internet. Its affordability and its "always-on" nature has been blamed for a myriad of social ills, including loneliness and depression [7], a decreased ability to focus and commit [16], increased stress [15], increased social friction and polarization [2], and even addiction and other mental disorders [18].

In addition, many of the offshore sites involved in these ICT-related projects are situated in poor communities, many of which do not yet have access to the prerequisite infrastructural support (such as electricity), or even basic life necessities such as clean water and medical care.

Given these issues, one often cannot help but feel ambivalent about ICT-related service projects. Should we, from developed countries, introduce ICTs into developing communities where the medical and social infrastructure may not be in a state to deal with the associated ills that will invariably arrive? Similarly, would the resources invested into ICT projects be better spent on projects that bring life necessities to the community?

It is the authors' opinion that even with all the potential problems, well-thought-out ICT projects do more good than harm. Simply put, ICTs and the Internet *will* arrive at these communities, with or without our help. In all of the communities that we have worked with, people have *some* form of access to the Internet and communications, usually through mobile phones. Left to their own devices, these resources stay in the hands of the well-off in the communities. The service then is not necessarily introducing new resources, but perhaps simply "leveling the playing field".

This being said, the potential problems associated with computers and the Internet also suggests that whenever a service team introduces ICTs into a community, there is also a moral imperative to conduct training, not just in technical know-how, but also in the human, organisational and ethical issues associated with technology. This is even more critical if Internet access is included, as it introduces concerns with information privacy, security and ethics. These are complex issues to address and they usually do not surface until the technology has been in use for some time. We therefore believe that it is critical for project teams introducing new technology to build up a reciprocal relationship [1] or even a partnership with the beneficiary community. This provides additional support and training when the need arises, and sustainability in the project.

With respect to differing service natures, even though ICT is not traditionally considered a necessity of life, there is increasing awareness of the role that ICT plays in poverty alleviation, community empowerment and child development. Many of these efforts are classified as ICT4D (ICT for development), which is a huge topic that is outside the scope of this paper.

We believe that introducing ICTs brings benefits to education, even when the children/students are not the ones that have direct access to the computing devices. An example can be found from a recent experience installing the "Lab in a Suitcase" at a rural school in Rwanda. The lab server was equipped with, among other things, an off-line copy of the Khan Academy[1], which contained videos illustrating teaching of different concepts in Mathematics.

Since the content was in English, the children were not able to understand the videos, and showed very little interest in the material. (They were more excited about photo-taking and video-making.) However, the local teachers were very appreciative. Even though the same language barrier existed for them (though to a lesser degree), they were extremely interested in the videos, spending a lot of time watching and rewatching certain sequences, and even comparing the content to their own textbooks. Follow-up studies will be made to ascertain the longitudinal impact of project, but it is clear that in this particular case, the introduction of ICTs has enabled access to new ways of teaching, and even new educational content, that was not previously available.

In other words, the consequences of ICT-based service learning projects must be carefully ascertained before embarking on the project. The reader may wonder why we state "minimize the harm" instead of the commonly-used "do no harm". The reason is that practically *all* efforts that have *any* impact on the community will have *some* negative consequences. The responsibility of the service provider is then to minimise this harm and provide support and follow-up to the community to address issues as they arise.

6. Conclusion

It is our belief that ICT facilitates service learning in a unique way. The low cost and small footprint of ICT equipment means that there is no need for much infrastructural support and heavy investment, as is the case for many engineering and construction-type projects. The pervasiveness of ICTs in daily life in the developed world means that the skill-sets required are possessed by a wide range of people — and these same skill-sets would also be useful to a wide diversity of people in the target population. Few other service types combine accessibility to the service provider and impact to the target population in the same manner.

Given this accessibility, it is therefore important to carefully consider all aspects of an ICT-based service learning project, in order to maximize the benefit to the target community while protecting them from potential harm, and to ensure opportunities for student learning. This paper has presented an investigation of the use of ICT in service learning, and analysed the impact of such services through four critical questions.

7. REFERENCES

[1] Bailis, Lawrence N. (2000). "Taking service-learning to the next level: Emerging lessons form the national community development program". Springfield, VA: *National Society for Experiential Education.*

[2] Bennett, W. Lance, Shanto Iyengar. 2008. "A new era of minimal effects? The changing foundations of political communication". *Journal of Communication* 58: 707–31

[3] Blouin, David D. and Evelyn M. Parry, 2009. "Whom Does Service Learning Really Serve? Community Based Organizations' Perspectives on Service Learning." *Teaching Sociology* 37:120-35

[4] Cerpa, Narciso and June M. Verner. 2009. Why did your project fail?. *Communications of the ACM 52*, 12 (December 2009), 130-134.

[5] Crabtree, Robbin D.. "The Intended and Unintended Consequences of International Service-Learning." *Journal of Higher Education Outreach and Engagement*, North America, 17, May. 2013.

[6] Connolly, Randy W.. 2012. "Is there service in computing service learning?". In *Proceedings of the 43rd ACM technical symposium on Computer Science Education* (SIGCSE '12). ACM, New York, NY, USA, 337-342.

[7] van den Eijnden, R.J., G.J. Meerkerk, A.A. Vermulst, R. Spijkerman, R.C. Engels. "Online communication, compulsive Internet use, and psychosocial well-being among adolescents: a longitudinal study." 2008. *Development Psychology*. 44(3):655-65.

[8] Furco, Andrew. 1996. "Service-learning: a balanced approach to experiential education." *Expanding Boundaries: Serving and Learning*. Washington, DC: Corporation for National Service, 2-6.

[9] Garzotto, Franca and Manuel Bordogna. 2010. "Paper-based multimedia interaction as learning tool for disabled children". In P*roceedings of the 9th International Conference on Interaction Design and Children* (IDC '10). ACM, New York, NY, USA, 79-88.

[10] Grusky, Sara. 2000. "International Service Learning: A Critical Guide from an Impassioned Advocate". *American Behavioral Scientist.* February 2000 43: 858-867

[11] Hadim, H.A; Esche, S.K.. 2002. "Enhancing the engineering curriculum through project-based learning," *32nd Annual Frontiers in Education. FIE 2002.* Vol.2, pp.F3F-1,F3F-6

[12] Jacoby, Barbara. (2003). *Building partnerships for service-learning*. San Francisco: Jossey-Bass

[13] Kuznetsov, Stacey, Laura C. Trutoiu, Casey Kute, Iris Howley, Eric Paulos, and Dan Siewiorek. 2011. "Breaking boundaries: strategies for mentoring through textile computing workshops". In *Proceedings of the SIGCHI Conference on Human Factors in Computing Systems* (CHI '11). ACM, New York, NY, USA, 2957-2966.

[14] Ludi, Stephanie and Tom Reichlmayr. 2011. "The Use of Robotics to Promote Computing to Pre-College Students with Visual Impairments". *Transactions in Computing Education* 11, 3, Article 20 (October 2011), 20 pages

[15] Mark, Gloria, Yiran Wang, and Melissa Niiya. 2014. "Stress and multitasking in everyday college life: an empirical study of online activity". In *Proceedings of the SIGCHI Conference on Human Factors in Computing Systems* (CHI '14). ACM, New York, NY, USA, 41-50.

[16] Ophir, Eyal, Clifford Nass, Anthony D. Wagner. 2009. "Cognitive control in media multitaskers." *Proceedings of the National Academy of Sciences.* 106 (37), 15583-15587

[17] Terenzini, Patrick T., Alberto F. Cabrera, Carol L. Colbeck, John M. Parente & Stefani A. Bjorkland. 2001. "Collaborative learning vs. lecture/discussion: Students' reported learning gains". *Journal of Engineering Education*, 90(1), 123-130.

[18] Young, K.S.. 1998. "Internet addiction: the emergence of a new clinical disorder." *CyberPsychology Behavior,* 1:237-244

[1] https://www.khanacademy.org/

Lowering the Barrier to Systems-level Networking Projects

Joel Sommers
Colgate University
jsommers@colgate.edu

ABSTRACT

Developing systems-level networking software to implement switches, routers, and middleboxes is challenging, rewarding, and arguably an essential component for developing a deep understanding of modern computer networks. Unfortunately, existing techniques for building networked system software use low-level and error-prone tools and languages, making this task inaccessible for many undergraduates. Moreover, working at such a low-level of abstraction complicates debugging and testing and can make assessment difficult for instructors and TAs.

We describe a Python-based environment called Switchyard that is designed to facilitate student projects for building and testing software-based network devices like switches, routers, and middleboxes. Switchyard exposes a networking abstraction similar to a *raw socket*, which allows a developer to receive and send Ethernet frames on specific network ports, and provides a set of classes to simplify parsing and construction of packets and packet headers. Systems-level software created using Switchyard can be deployed on a standard Linux host or in an emulated environment like Mininet. Perhaps most importantly, Switchyard provides facilities for test-driven development by transparently allowing the underlying network to be replaced with a test harness that is specifically designed to help students through the development and debugging process. We describe experiences with using Switchyard in an undergraduate networking course in which students created an Ethernet learning switch, a fully functional IPv4 router, a firewall with rate limiter, and a deep-packet inspection middlebox device.

Categories and Subject Descriptors

K.3.2 [**Computer and Information Science Education**]: Computer science education; C.2.5 [**Local and Wide-Area Networks**]: Internet (*e.g.*, TCP/IP); C.2.6 [**Internetworking**]: Routers

General Terms

Design, Experimentation

SIGCSE'15, March 4–7, 2015, Kansas City, MO, USA.

http://dx.doi.org/10.1145/2676723.2677211.

Keywords

Routing, switching, middleboxes, test-driven development

1. INTRODUCTION

One of the most effective ways to *learn* is to *do*. In computer science, the process of building software and "getting their hands dirty" [7] often leads students to develop deeper understanding. Creating significant software artifacts—especially programs perceived as *real*—can be hugely motivating, engaging, and rewarding, and can spur new ways of thinking about what may otherwise be abstract or complex concepts.

Particularly in computer networking, there have been many systems and tools developed over the past decade to facilitate hands-on activities in order to bring concepts to life. For example, publicly accessible large-scale emulation platforms [10] can be used to experiment with networking protocols and programs, virtualization tools are available for creating and working with complete "networks-in-a-box" [9, 16], and recent generations of simulation tools can seamlessly incorporate "real" network components [3]. Moreover, advanced courses have been created with the explicit goal of building significant systems such as a complete IPv4 router [5]. Each of these platforms represent significant advances to teaching and learning in computer networking.

Unfortunately, many of the most compelling and realistic hands-on environments for building networked systems have a very steep learning curve and present a high barrier to entry for many undergraduates. One reason is that the more realistic systems tend to be implemented using low-level languages and tools, *e.g.*, C/C++. As a consequence, it can be extremely challenging for students to test and debug their programs since the underlying tools are implemented at a rather low level of abstraction. For networked systems, testing often involves the need to create carefully crafted packets in order to verify an intended behavior or feature. As a result, creating and executing tests often involves low-level and error-prone tools, too. Any error or erroneous assumption can be difficult to detect, and can lead to frustration and discouragement for students.

In this paper, we describe a new framework for building real networked system software called *Switchyard*[1]. Switchyard provides a Python API, and helps students avoid pitfalls associated with low-level implementation languages by providing higher-level abstractions with which to work. Our motivation for providing carefully designed abstractions for students to work with is to enable them to focus on the key problems and concepts of building a router, switch, middlebox, or other device, as opposed to struggling with an arcane low-level language environment. Perhaps most importantly, Switchyard provides facilities for *test-driven development*,

[1] `https://github.com/jsommers/switchyard`

so that students can create or be provided with a suite of tests for testing, debugging, and verifying intended behavior. The Switchyard framework enables seamless execution of student programs in either the test harness environment, on a bare Linux host, or in a Linux-based virtual machine environment such as Mininet [9]. In short, Switchyard *lowers the barrier* to system-level networking projects by *raising the level of abstraction* of the tools used to construct networked systems, and by including *purpose-built debugging and testing capabilities* to help students with what are often the most challenging aspects of systems software development.

We describe our initial experiences with using Switchyard in an introductory undergraduate course in computer networking. In this course, students were able to build a variety of systems, including an Ethernet learning switch, a fully-functional IPv4 router, a firewall with rate-limiting capabilities, and a deep-packet inspection middlebox device. Nearly all students completed the various milestones for these projects, which is significant considering the technical and conceptual complexity involved with each system. We discuss observations from student evaluations, and describe our ongoing efforts to expand and improve Switchyard.

2. RELATED WORK

Over the last decade, a number of hands-on educational environments that use either real or emulated network components have been developed. At one end of the spectrum are platforms employing real networking hardware and components. For example, the NetFPGA platform is a compelling platform for developing both software and hardware components of networked systems such as switches and routers [12], and entire courses have been developed with the goal of building a complete IPv4 router [2]. Similarly, the Open Networking Laboratory [20, 21] enables students to remotely access and control real networking hardware in a laboratory setting. Likewise, Yuan *et al.* [6] describe a set of hands-on experiences for students using commodity PCs running Linux, and other free and open source software such as Wireshark, Snort, and the Zebra router. Yoo *et al.* [17] also describe an environment that relies on the Zebra router and a set of scripts to configure hosts in particular logical topologies for use in experiments. Similar to these approaches is the one described by Pan [15] that centers on using the Linksys WRT54GL and the OpenWRT firmware to provide students with a realistic platform for experiments. Lastly, the Wisconsin Advanced Internet Laboratory [4] employs a variety of networking components such as switches and routers, and uses configuration and experiment management software based on Emulab [10].

Hands-on settings that make use of the Emulab software have seen fairly wide use in networking education. These environments allow students to create virtual topologies using a set of commodity hosts, and to emulate different link characteristics such as delay and loss. They enable a fair amount of realism, while allowing lab resources to be multiplexed among students. Laverell *et al.* [11] describe their experiences setting up and using the Emulab software in networking courses. The Tinkernet system described in [13] contains functionality similar to that in Emulab. The authors of that paper describe a set of laboratory experiences that focus on building a networking protocol stack.

While Emulab-type systems virtualize links, other systems present entire virtual network topologies to students, enabling different levels of interaction with the virtual network. For example, the GINI system [14] creates virtual networks using tunnels and Linux virtual machines, enabling students to use standard tools and APIs to interact with the virtual network. Similarly, the Virtual Distributed Ethernet system [8] emulates an Ethernet switch and allows virtual and real machines to be stitched together into topologies that students can interact with using standard tools.

In a similar vein, the Virtual Network System (VNS) [5] allows students to construct virtual network topologies and to safely interact with their virtual network, as well as the rest of the Internet, to send and receive raw packets. As a result, students can design and develop a simplified Internet router that runs in user space. VNS has been decommissioned in favor of the lightweight virtual machine-based Mininet system [9] that provides a Python-based API for creating virtual topologies within a single host. Although Mininet is largely designed for use with Openflow and software-defined networking, it is more generally useful for student experimentation, and projects created originally for VNS have been adapted for use with Mininet [3]. The Netkit system [16] is also based on using Linux virtual machines for building virtual topologies and running networking experiments. A fairly large number of ready-made laboratory exercises have been developed for use with Netkit. It is important to note that for each of these Linux VM-based systems, the programming API is C-based, and there are only limited capabilities provided for testing and debugging (*e.g.*, to help with `printf`-style debugging), unlike Switchyard.

3. SWITCHYARD GOALS AND DESIGN

In this section we discuss the goals and motivation behind Switchyard, and describe its design, implementation, and how it is used in student projects.

3.1 Goals

As discussed above, many of the educational platforms and tools developed over the past several years to enable students to gain hands-on experience with networking protocols and systems software development require use of low-level tools and language environments. Although low-level implementation languages such as C are important for undergraduates to be exposed to, they can make it difficult for students to focus on and grapple with the underlying systems concepts that they *should* be learning. A key motivation for developing Switchyard was to address the limited availability of systems-building environments that leverage higher-level abstractions and tools. Below, we describe the main pedagogical goals of Switchyard.

1. Engage students in building networked systems and protocols, such as Ethernet learning switches, IPv4 routers, and implementations of TCP. As mentioned previously, this is one of the key motivations for Switchyard. We strongly believe that "hands-on" projects are the best ways to develop a deep understanding of networks and other computer systems.

2. Construct the framework such that, as far as possible, students are able to focus on networking and systems concepts rather than on arcane language or API details. Simply put, use of low-level languages can pose a significant barrier for students with limited experience (*i.e.*, many undergraduates) to engage in systems-level projects. Our experience is that raising the level of abstraction through use of a higher-level language can help significantly. Moreover, careful design of the API that students use can help to focus student efforts on core concepts rather than extraneous details.

3. Provide debugging and testing facilities to assist students with development of complex systems software. When facing

[2] `http://www.cl.cam.ac.uk/teaching/1415/P33/`

[3] `https://github.com/mininet/mininet/wiki/Teaching-and-Learning-with-Mininet`

challenging programming assignments, students often do not know where to start. Encouraging a *test-driven development* cycle can help to funnel students through specific functionality milestones toward completing an assignment. Moreover, we believe that in an educational context, it is important to integrate testing facilities with capabilities to assist with debugging and inspection of program state so that when tests fail students have enough context to understand *why* a test fails.

4. Ease the burden of assessing technically complex student projects. As many faculty can attest, examining complex software systems created by students ~~can be~~ is extremely time consuming. Especially for faculty who do not have graduate student TAs to assist with grading, the difficulty posed by assessing such projects creates a disincentive to assigning challenging projects such as construction of an IPv4 router.

3.2 Framework design and API

Switchyard is designed as a Python program and module that exposes a fairly minimal and simple API to a programmer. The conceptual structure of Switchyard is depicted in Figure 1. The API is designed to provide the most basic and essential functions for implementing the core logic of a network device, including sending a packet, receiving a packet, and obtaining a list of ports (interfaces) and their configurations on the device. Switchyard also includes a library to simplify packet parsing and construction.

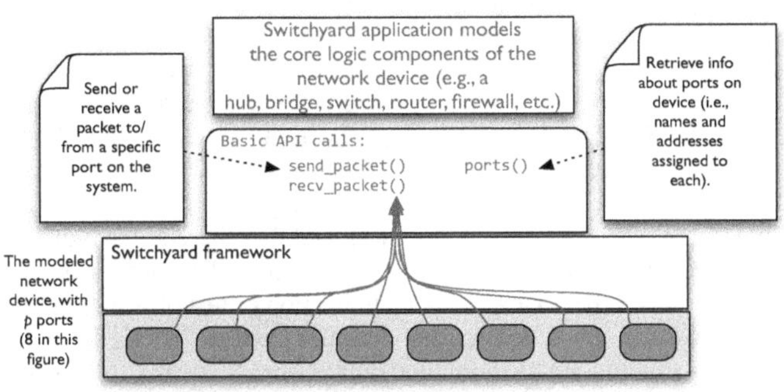

Figure 1: Switchyard design

A program designed to work within Switchyard is written as a Python program that includes one required function: `srpy_main` [4], as shown in Listing 1. This required function must take one parameter, which is an object on which a student can call the core Switchyard API functions `send_packet`, `recv_packet`, and `ports`. As Listing 1 shows, a conventional structure to a Switchyard program is to have an infinite `while` loop within the main entrypoint function. Inside that loop packets are received and handled in some way, *e.g.*, to forward them out one or more ports. The `recv_packet` function returns a tuple containing a reference to a packet and the name of the port on which the packet arrived (*e.g.*, `eth0`). The `recv_packet` can optionally take a timeout value. If no packets arrive before the timeout value, a `Timeout` exception is raised. When the underlying framework shuts down, it raises an exception that can be handled in the device implementation code in order to perform a graceful shutdown.

3.3 Framework implementation

Switchyard is implemented as a Python module that consists of classes to enable interaction with *real* network interfaces on the

[4]The name `srpy` is a reference to the venerable `sr` (software router) projects developed as part of the VNS project [5].

```
def srpy_main(net):
    while True:
        try:
            packet, port_name = net.recv_packet()
        except Shutdown:
            # we got shutdown signal
            break
        # handle an incoming packet
```

Listing 1: Basic structure of a Switchyard program.

host system or to enable interaction with a test harness that involves no actual network I/O. Invoking the framework is accomplished through a command-line interface. The main Switchyard program (`srpy`) requires at least one argument, which is the name of a file containing an entrypoint to the student's network device implementation. The `srpy` program loads the student's file and locates the `srpy_main` function to be executed. Additional command line options determine whether Switchyard starts up in *real* mode or in *test* mode. Each of these modes are described below.

Students can build and parse packets using a library built into Switchyard. In the version of Switchyard that we initially used in the classroom, we delegated calls to the packet parsing libraries in the POX Openflow controller [2]. There were various pitfalls we encountered with that approach, and we developed a new set of packet parsing libraries from scratch (though based on the POX libraries) which we describe in Section 4.2.

3.3.1 Real network mode

By default, `srpy` attempts to use all network interfaces on the host system (except for the loopback interface) for sending and receiving packets. It uses a Python wrapper around `libpcap` for sending and receiving packets, which enables some degree of portability for Switchyard.

Upon framework startup, a thread is started to handle I/O for each separate network interface used. If the underlying libpcap implementation supports it, the threads open pcap devices for each interface in a non-blocking manner. Packets that arrive on any network device are converted to a packet object representation (rather than as a raw sequence of bytes) and added to the tail of a shared queue along with the name of the device on which the packet was received, and a timestamp. When user-level code calls `recv_packet`, the packet at the head of the queue is removed and returned.

When user code calls `send_packet`, it supplies a packet object and the name of the device on which to send the packet as parameters. The Switchyard framework serializes the packet and delivers it to the thread that handles I/O for the given device via another queue. If there are errors associated with the packet object given to `send_packet` or if there is an invalid device name specified (*e.g.*, no device exists for the given name), an error is returned.

One key implication of using libpcap as the low-level network access mechanism is that it is often necessary to install packet filters to prevent host processing of incoming packets. For example, if a Switchyard user program should be responsible for ARP requests and responses, the host system must be prevented from responding. The way this situation is currently handled is that students are given a wrapper script to start Switchyard that installs `iptables` and/or `ebtables` rules. This same pattern of providing custom handling for packets and preventing host processing for the same packets by installing firewall rules is a common approach taken with some network measurement tools, *e.g.*, [18, 19].

3.3.2 Test harness mode

When started in *testing* mode, Switchyard requires at least one *test scenario* to be supplied as a command-line argument. The scenario specification defines some set of physical or logical ports that are configured on an imaginary network device, as well as any addressing information associated with each port, *i.e.*, an Ethernet address and (optionally) an IPv4 address and subnet mask. The scenario also defines a series of test *expectations*. In particular, an expectation may be that a specific packet arrives on a given interface of the device or that the Switchyard user program sends a packet out a particular interface.

An (incomplete) example of a program for creating a test scenario is shown in Listing 2. The `TestScenario` class in Switchyard encapsulates various details associated with a set of tests. After constructing the scenario object, three network interfaces with specific Ethernet addresses are added to an imaginary device. Following that, a `PacketInputEvent` expectation is created to indicate that a packet should arrive on a particular interface. The meaning of this statement is that the creator of the test expects the Switchyard user program to call `recv_packet`, and that the packet object `testpkt` will be returned in response to that call. Lastly, a `PacketOutputEvent` expectation is created to indicate that the packet `testpkt` should be sent out two interfaces. The meaning of this expection is that the Switchyard test framework will require the user program to send a packet that *exactly matches* `testpkt` out the two interfaces `eth1` and `eth2`.

```
scenario = TestScenario('hub tests')
scenario.add_interface('eth0', '10:00:00:00:00:01')
scenario.add_interface('eth1', '10:00:00:00:00:02')
scenario.add_interface('eth2', '10:00:00:00:00:03')
testpkt = ... # code to create testpkt packet object
scenario.expect(
  PacketInputEvent('eth1', testpkt),
  '''An Ethernet frame with a broadcast
  destination address should arrive on eth1''')
scenario.expect(
  PacketOutputEvent('eth0', testpkt,
                    'eth2', testpkt),
  '''The Ethernet frame with a broadcast destination
  address should be forwarded out eth0 and eth2''')
```

Listing 2: Test scenario example.

Expectations created for a `PacketInputEvent` are straightforward: the test creator must construct a packet object that will be delivered to the user program under test. While this portion of the example is incomplete, the steps used to create the test packets are identical to the steps required in a standard user program.

Expectations created for a `PacketOutputEvent` are somewhat more complex, because they require *matching* a packet sent by a user program against a reference packet. Currently, Switchyard accommodates exact match testing as well as matching on selected header fields (including support for "wildcards"). The header fields used for this latter type of match are currently the same fields allowed for matching packet header fields in the Openflow 1.0 specification [1]. In addition, arbitrary predicate functions may be supplied, *e.g.*, to test that an IP TTL is decremented by 1 when forwarding an IP packet. Finally, test expectations can be created to handle the situation in which a test creator expects the user program to call `recv_packet`, but the test creator wants the call to `recv_packet` to *time out* and not return anything. This expectation is useful for testing situations in which a protocol implementation must handle the lack of response to a request, such as a failed ARP query.

The test scenario API is designed to be used either by an instructor or TA or by students. In the case of instructor-created test scenarios, it would clearly be inappropriate to distribute the test scenario construction code itself, since that code would naturally contain expressions for creating the same packets that students must construct as part of a given assignment. Switchyard contains facilities to ***serialize*** a test scenario for public distribution to students. The serialization procedure first uses Python facilities for serializing the `TestScenario` object created in a given test scenario file. The result of this step is a string that contains representations of each of the expectations in a given scenario, including string representations of each of the packets used. Importantly, the program code that created the packet objects is no longer present. Next, the serialization procedure compresses the serialized test scenario, converts it to a base-64 string, and writes that string to a file. This file can be posted as part of an assignment for students to then use while developing their code.

3.4 Example: a simple hub

We now show through an example how a test scenario can be used, and how it can facilitate test-driven development by students. The example user application we use is a network hub—an extremely simple network device that floods any packet received on an interface out all interfaces except the input interface. The test scenario example above (Listing 2) shows the beginning of the testing code used for this example, which consists of 8 total expectations (4 packet input event expectations, and 4 corresponding packet output expectations).

We first show in Listing 3 a *broken* implementation of a hub. Instead of flooding a packet out all ports except the input, this program incorrectly sends each packet received back out the *same* port on which it arrived. When applying the test scenario to this program, the Switchyard framework gives output similar to that shown in Figure 2. We see in the figure that Switchyard reports that one test passed (the first packet input event expectation), 1 failed (the first output expectation was not met), and that there are 6 tests that could not be evaluated due to a test failure. The output is normally color-coded to give a visual indication of test passage (green) and/or failure (red). When a test does not pass, Switchyard can optionally execute the Python debugger in such a way as to start the debugger as close to the part of the user program that failed as possible. This capability is enabled with a command-line switch.

We also see in the test output quite a bit of detail related to different expectation events and individual packets that were either received or sent. Switchyard can optionally show *full* packet dumps instead of abbreviated contents (which is the default) when tests pass or fail. Any explanatory text for a given test is created as part of a test scenario and supplied verbatim from the original scenario so the writer of a test can supply as much or as little context as he or she wishes, in order to help students to understand why a test may pass or fail.

When the broken hub program in Listing 3 is fixed to correctly flood a packet out all interfaces except the input, the output of Switchyard becomes green to reflect the fact that all the tests now pass. The partial test output for a correct hub implementation is shown in Figure 3. Once all tests pass successfully, the code can be refactored to improve its design and structure while preserving the correct functionality in a cycle commonly known as "red-green-refactor".

4. SWITCHYARD IN ACTION

In this section, we describe the set of assignments that we have used thus far with Switchyard, and discuss student experiences with using Switchyard in an introductory undergraduate networking course.

```
def srpy_main(net):
    while True:
        try:
            dev,packet = net.recv_packet()
        except Shutdown:
            return
        net.send_packet(dev, packet)
    net.shutdown()
```

Listing 3: Switchyard program for implementing a hub device (broken).

```
Results for test scenario hub tests: 1 passed, 1 failed,
6 pending

Passed:
1   An Ethernet frame with a broadcast destination address
    should arrive on eth1
        Expected event: recv_packet
        [30:00:00:00:00:02>ff:ff:ff:ff:ff:ff IP] on eth1

Failed:
    The Ethernet frame with a broadcast destination address
    should be forwarded out ports eth0 and eth2
        Expected event: send_packet(s)
        [30:00:00:00:00:02>ff:ff:ff:ff:ff:ff IP] out eth2 and
        [30:00:00:00:00:02>ff:ff:ff:ff:ff:ff IP] out eth0

Pending (couldn't test because of prior failure):
1   An Ethernet frame from 20:00:00:00:00:01 to
    30:00:00:00:00:02 should arrive on eth0
        Expected event: recv_packet
        [20:00:00:00:00:01>30:00:00:00:00:02 IP] on eth0
2   Ethernet frame destined for 30:00:00:00:00:02 should be
    flooded out eth1 and eth2
        Expected event: send_packet(s)
        [20:00:00:00:00:01>30:00:00:00:00:02 IP] out eth2 and
        [20:00:00:00:00:01>30:00:00:00:00:02 IP] out eth1
```

Figure 2: Code and output snippet for failed test

4.1 Assignments

We have used Switchyard as a basis for four projects of varying scope and difficulty in an undergraduate networking course, and have plans for additional projects and activities.

Learning Switch. Developing an Ethernet learning switch is quite simple using Switchyard (about 40 lines of code). This exercise was used as an introduction to Switchyard and its APIs, to executing and understanding test output, and to running Switchyard code on a Linux (virtual machine) host in Mininet. Students were supplied with a comprehensive set of tests for this project since they were unfamiliar with the APIs.

```
Results for test scenario hub tests: 8 passed, 0 failed,
0 pending

Passed:
1   An Ethernet frame with a broadcast destination address
    should arrive on eth1
        Expected event: recv_packet
        [30:00:00:00:00:02>ff:ff:ff:ff:ff:ff IP] on eth1
2   The Ethernet frame with a broadcast destination address
    should be forwarded out ports eth0 and eth2
        Expected event: send_packet(s)
        [30:00:00:00:00:02>ff:ff:ff:ff:ff:ff IP] out eth2 and
        [30:00:00:00:00:02>ff:ff:ff:ff:ff:ff IP] out eth0
```

Figure 3: Output snippet for two passed tests

IP Router. Students developed a full IPv4 router over three progressive stages. The first stage required students to develop code for responding to ARP requests, and also served as an introduction to the router projects. The second stage required students to generate ARP requests and handle ARP responses, and to implement IP routing (longest prefix match) using a statically configured forwarding table. The third stage required students to respond to ICMP echo requests ("pings") as well as generate ICMP errors such as time exceeded messages and network/host/port unreachable messages. Creating a fully functional IPv4 router involves quite a bit of technical complexity, and students were provided with several tests for each stage to help guide them through the development process. Students were also provided with scripts for running their router in a Mininet environment in order to observe its behavior (*e.g.*, using `traceroute` and other "real" tools).

Firewall. This project was designed as an add-on to the IPv4 router project, but could easily be designed differently. Students developed firewall functionality for their router based on a simple rule syntax. In addition to accept/deny firewall processing, students also implemented a token bucket rate limitation feature for rules that had specified rate limits. Students were given guidance for writing tests, but were not provided with any automated Switchyard tests.

Deep-packet Inspection Middlebox. For this project, students developed two network components: a Openflow-based switching element that would forward packets from pre-specified flows to a "deep-packet inspection" (DPI) device and forward other flows normally, and a DPI middlebox that inspected and optionally rewrote application-layer content if certain "suspicious" strings were found. When application content was modified, fields in lower-layer packet headers also needed to be amended (*i.e.*, length fields). This project gave students some exposure to SDN protocols and non-standard packet forwarding, and also provided the basis for discussing current news events related to government spying.

Additionally, we intend to create a new introductory-level exercise oriented around understanding packet headers by having students build a Wireshark-like tool, and we have plans to create several more projects including adding a dynamic routing stage to the IP router, a network/port address translator, and an IPv4–IPv6 gateway. Currently, all the exercises are oriented around networking functionality at intermediate devices such as switches, routers, and middleboxes, but we are planning to expand Switchyard to accommodate projects oriented around end-host functionality such as transport and application layer capabilities.

4.2 Classroom experiences

Thus far, qualitative and some quantitative feedback have been collected from students through surveys. Responses to these surveys have been overwhelmingly positive. Students reported that the system-building activities were very beneficial to their learning and developing a better understanding of networking concepts. Student evaluations also indicated very low-levels of frustration, which we attribute to the test-driven nature of development and the potential for students to focus efforts on passing one test at a time. Indeed, several students expressed that they wished they had been able to tackle additional system-building projects.

Two specific quantitative questions we asked were: (Q1) *To what degree did the router and switch projects help your understanding of course concepts* (e.g., *link-layer and network addressing, packet headers and encapsulation, IP forwarding, routing, etc.)?*, and (Q2) *To what degree did the test-driven nature of SRPY projects help with the projects?* For each of these questions, students responses were based on a 1–5 scale (1=not helpful, 3=moderately helpful, 5=extremely helpful). We received 23 responses to these questions. For Q1, the student response average was 4.38 ($\sigma = 0.96$) and for Q2, the student response average was 4.69 ($\sigma = 0.48$).

Common themes that emerged from other (qualitative feedback) questions were that students felt that the router-building projects were "cool" and that the testing and debugging facilities in Switchyard were "essential" to them being able to accomplish the various tasks to build the router. One student noted that "the router projects were hard due to the inherent complexity, not because of [Switchyard] or [Python]", and another student captured the feeling of several students, that "the projects were not easy, and when we struggled it was mostly with conceptual topics". Similarly, another student wrote that "[Switchyard] was easy to learn and struggling with the concepts a little was actually helpful."We view the fact that students reported that when they struggled it was with networking concepts rather than the Switchyard API or language details as particularly encouraging.

Lastly, the responses suggested some areas for improving the APIs and pedagogical approach with Switchyard. First, although Python is taught in our CS1 course, a couple students did remark that they felt their biggest problem was Python syntax. Also, although the automated tests were generally viewed positively, one student noted that they felt like the tests made the projects feel too easy. There is certainly a balance to be struck between providing too few and too many tests, and having students write more or less tests. Most students felt that the projects still contained substantial difficulty, but the number of tests given to students may need to be modified semester-to-semester, depending on the group of students in a course. Finally, three students noted that the packet construction and parsing libraries were sometimes difficult to work with. The version of Switchyard used by the students leveraged the packet library from the POX Openflow controller, which does not prevent a variety of common error patterns. One particular problem is that new attributes (instance variables) can be added to objects dynamically. As a result, a misspelled attribute (*e.g.*, using `source` instead of `src` as the attribute for assigning an Ethernet source address) becomes a difficult-to-detect *logic* error. We completely revised the packet parsing and creation library in Switchyard to prevent many of the problems we observed students to have, using Python language features and implementation patterns. Among other improvements, misspelled attributes now result in an obvious runtime exception.

5. CONCLUSIONS AND FUTURE WORK

In this paper, we describe a new Python-based framework called Switchyard for building networked systems such as switches, routers, and middleboxes. By virtue of using a higher-level language (Python) and through careful design of its APIs and libraries, Switchyard helps undergraduate students avoid pitfalls associated with low-level implementation languages, while still enabling them to build *real* systems. Switchyard supports test-driven development so that students can be given a set of tests or tasked to create them, and the framework seamlessly supports execution of student programs within the test harness or in a Linux environment. We describe our initial experiences with using Switchyard in an undergraduate networking course, and discuss how these experiences have shaped our ongoing efforts to improve the framework and libraries.

Our plans for future development of Switchyard include further simplifying and error-proofing its APIs and libraries and significantly expanding the set of exercises and materials available. We also plan to simplify execution of Switchyard in various environments (*e.g.*, by automating installation of `iptables`/`ebtables` rules as appropriate). Lastly, we plan to improve forwarding performance so that Switchyard can effectively be used in Gigabit-speed environments.

Acknowledgments

This material is based upon work supported by the National Science Foundation under grant CNS-1054985. Any opinions, findings, and conclusions or recommendations expressed in this material are those of the author and do not necessarily reflect the views of the National Science Foundation.

6. REFERENCES

[1] Openflow switch specification, version 1.0.0. `http://archive.openflow.org/documents/openflow-spec-v1.0.0.pdf`, 2009.

[2] About POX. `http://www.noxrepo.org/pox/about-pox/`, 2014.

[3] Network Simulator ns-3. `http://www.nsnam.org`, 2014.

[4] Wisconsin Advanced Internet Laboratory. `http://wail.cs.wisc.edu`, 2014.

[5] M. Casado and N. McKeown. The virtual network system. *ACM SIGCSE Bulletin*, 37(1), 2005.

[6] D. Yuan *et al.* An instructional design of open source networking laboratory and curriculum. In *Proceedings of the 10th ACM SIGITE*, 2009.

[7] N. Feamster and J. Rexford. Getting students' hands dirty with clean-slate networking. In *ACM SIGCOMM Education Workshop*, 2011.

[8] M. Goldweber and R. Davoli. VDE: an emulation environment for supporting computer networking courses. *ACM SIGCSE Bulletin*, 40(3), 2008.

[9] N. Handigol, B. Heller, V. Jeyakumar, B. Lantz, and N. McKeown. Reproducible network experiments using container-based emulation. In *Proceedings of CoNEXT '12*, 2012.

[10] M. Hibler, R. Ricci, L. Stoller, J. Duerig, S. Guruprasad, T. Stack, K. Webb, and J. Lepreau. Large-scale Virtualization in the Emulab Network Testbed. In *USENIX Annual Technical Conference*, 2008.

[11] W. D. Laverell, Z. Fei, and J. N. Griffioen. Isn't it time you had an Emulab? *SIGCSE Bull.*, 40, March 2008.

[12] J. Lockwood, N. McKeown, G. Watson, G. Gibb, P. Hartke, J. Naous, R. Raghuraman, and J. Luo. NetFPGA—An Open Platform for Gigabit-Rate Network Switching and Routing. In *IEEE International Conference on Microelectronic Systems Education*, pages 160–161, 2007.

[13] M. Erlinger *et al.* Tinkernet: a low-cost networking laboratory. In *Proceedings of the sixth ACE*, 2004.

[14] M. Maheswaran, *et al.* GINI: a user-level toolkit for creating micro internets for teaching & learning computer networking. In *Proceedings of the 40th ACM SIGCSE*, 2009.

[15] J. Pan. Teaching computer networks in a real network: the technical perspectives. In *Proceedings of the 41st ACM SIGCSE*. ACM, 2010.

[16] M. Pizzonia and M. Rimondini. Netkit: easy emulation of complex networks on inexpensive hardware. In *Proceedings of the 4th International Conference on Testbeds and research infrastructures for the development of networks & communities*, 2008.

[17] S. Yoo *et al.* Remote access internetworking laboratory. In *Proceedings of the 35th ACM SIGCSE*, 2004.

[18] S. Savage. Sting: A TCP-based Network Measurement Tool. In *USENIX Symposium on Internet Technologies and Systems*, volume 2, 1999.

[19] J. Sommers, P. Barford, and W. Willinger. A Proposed Framework for Calibration of Available Bandwidth Estimation Tools. In *Proceedings of IEEE Symposium on Computers and Communication*, June 2006.

[20] C. Wiseman, K. Wong, T. Wolf, and S. Gorinsky. Operational experience with a virtual networking laboratory. *SIGCSE Bull.*, 40, March 2008.

[21] K. Wong, T. Wolf, S. Gorinsky, and J. Turner. Teaching experiences with a virtual network laboratory. *SIGCSE Bull.*, 39, March 2007.

A Simple Laboratory Environment for Real-World Offensive Security Education

Maxim Timchenko and David Starobinski
Electrical and Computer Engineering Department, Boston University
8 Saint Mary's Street, Boston, MA 02215, USA
maxvt@bu.edu, staro@bu.edu

ABSTRACT

In recent years cybersecurity has gained prominence as a field of expertise and the relevant practical skills are in high demand. To reduce the cost and amount of dedicated hardware required to set up a cybersecurity lab to teach those skills, several virtualization and outsourcing approaches were developed but the resulting setup has often increased in total complexity, hampering adoption. In this paper we present a very simple (and therefore highly scalable) setup that incorporates state-of-the-art industry tools. We also describe a structured set of lab assignments developed for this setup that build one on top of the other to cover the material of a semester-long *Cybersecurity* course taught at Boston University. We explore alternative lab architectures, discuss other existing sets of lab assignments and present some ideas for further improvement.

Categories and Subject Descriptors

K.3.2 [**Computer and Information Science Education**]: Curriculum, Information systems education

General Terms

Security, Design, Experimentation

Keywords

Cybersecurity; Course design; Education; Virtualization

1. INTRODUCTION

The importance of practical, and not only theoretical, education in cybersecurity has long been recognized but has been brought in focus due to events of recent years. Traditionally, the practical skills were developed in expensive hardware-based security labs that allowed experimentation without causing damage beyond the lab limits, but the costs of building and maintainining those laboratories are high.

SIGCSE'15, March 4–7, 2015, Kansas City, MO, USA.

http://dx.doi.org/10.1145/2676723.2677225.

Recognizing that cost, the academic community has proposed several education-focused solutions that offer hands-on training in virtualized environments, but many of them have drawbacks: some require elaborate setup and centralized server resources [10], or do not provide hands-on experience on offensive tools common in the industry, or have teaching material focusing on advanced, programmer friendly topics that is less suitable for an introductory course [2].

From the industry side, a virtualized environment with a variety of known weaknesses [4] and a full collection of commonly used offensive and defensive tools [3] can be freely downloaded, but the available didactic material using this environment is rather limited to a motley collection of Internet tutorials on specific exploits and does not present a systematic, gradual approach to the field.

In Fall 2013, a semester-length *Cybersecurity* course has been taught at Boston University using a virtualised environment based on freely available and minimally modified virtual machine images. The contributions in this paper, as detailed in the following sections, are: first, a blueprint that allows quick and easy deployment of a simple, secure and isolated environment for a cybersecurity class on commodity workstations or even on students' personal laptops; and second, a coherent collection of lab assignments (topics, text, and full solutions are available) that use standard industry tools and actual known vulnerabilities to offer students an introductory exposure to practice of offensive cybersecurity.

2. COURSE STRUCTURE

The *Cybersecurity* course (EC 521) is taught over one semester (typically 15 weeks) with two scheduled weekly meetings of two hours each, about 60 hours of instruction in total. The goal of the course is to provide a holistic yet technically in-depth examination of security of computers and computer networks, exposing students to adversarial thinking and placing an emphasis on offensive techniques used for penetration testing. The course describes the underlying foundations of popular penetration tools, practical use of these tools, and mitigating solutions against attacks launched with these tools.

About ten distinct topics are covered during the course, with most topics following a three-step teaching pattern:

1. A lecture in a classroom setting introduces the topic and discusses the general methods associated with it. For example, general network structure, desired information, and associated protocols may be covered while discussing the information gathering stage of network security testing.

2. A lecture in a lab setting presents specific cybersecurity tools associated with the topic, with students following along, trying the provided commands and parameters and observing the responses from the tools. For example, `nmap` would be one of the tools presented for performing information gathering.

3. Finally, a lab assignment is given to students to reinforce the material provided in the lectures, to promote further exploration of the topic and the tools with guided questions, and to apply the resulting knowledge to a typical scenario. For example, a lab may ask students to use `nmap` to answer specific questions about a particular host of interest, request them to use a parameter or feature not covered in class, and ask to explain why and how the specific method used achieves its goals.

Students usually have one to two weeks to complete a given lab and work in pairs, promoting discussion and teamwork and reducing the lab grading workload.

The course is intended for first-year graduate and advanced undergraduate students. Its prerequisite is EC 327 (*Introduction to Software Engineering*) and familiarity with at least one programming language and the Linux operating system. Course co-requisites include EC 441 (a first course in computer networking) and familiarity with TCP/IP.

The second and third steps utilise the virtual course environment as presented in the following section.

3. LAB ENVIRONMENT

The laboratory setup used by EC 521 was constructed with the following objectives in mind:

Isolation: the actions of one student should not impact another student's environment.

Persistence: allow the state of a student's environment to be saved between sessions, even if the same lab workstation is used by other students / other courses in the meanwhile.

Hardware independence: it should not matter which lab workstation a given student is using; if a workstation fails, the student's environment should be minimally impacted.

Resource efficiency: minimize resource use (beyond lab workstations themselves).

Security: keep the target (vulnerable) machine off the public Internet; minimize possible effects of student actions on the university intranet.

Reuse: reuse existing components / software / standard industry tools as much as possible.

Simplicity: an introductory course in cybersecurity should not need a complicated environment to achieve its objectives.

The networking laboratory is equipped with approximately 50 workstations with 4 Gb RAM running BU Linux [1], a customized version of CentOS 6. Each machine runs VMWare Workstation 9. Figure 1 shows the connections for a single workstation, which has three virtual machines:

1. The attacker is represented by a *Kali Linux* [3] virtual machine. This distribution is based on Debian Linux, includes a multitude of security audit and penetration tools (including all the tools introduced in the course), and is officially available for download as a VMWare image that boots into a desktop environment. *Kali* also includes a range of GUI tools that make some exploration possible even by users who may not be comfortable with the underlying command line tools.

2. The target is represented by a *Metasploitable 2* [4] virtual machine. This image contains a number of services with known exploits (ftp, http, and so on), insecure settings, and three vulnerable web applications. This VM is also officially available as a VMWare image, and has low memory requirements since it does not offer a graphical user interface.

3. One of the assignments requires a third "zombie" machine. Almost any OS that has networking support would do; we have chosen FreeBSD 6.0 for its low system requirements and for some diversity in the virtual environment (i.e. not 100% Linux). An unofficial VMWare image for this OS is publicly available [7].

Each student was provisioned a copy of the attacker and the target VM on a shared file server. The permissions were set so that a student could access only their own copy of these VMs. These VMs were persistent–changes made by students would be retained throughout the course.

A copy of both attacker and target VMs was also deployed locally on each workstation. These VMs were not persistent and would revert to their original contents whenever

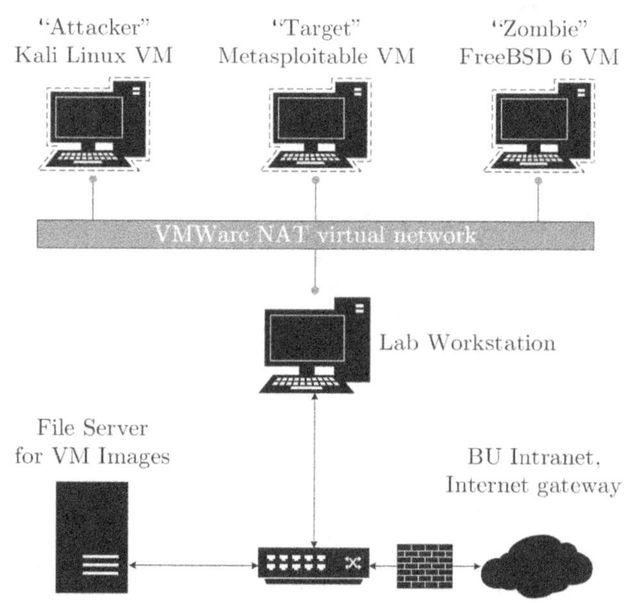

Figure 1: Diagram of the lab environment

[1] `http://www.bu.edu/tech/support/desktop/distribution/bulinux`

they were shut down. The purpose of these VMs was to reduce the load on the network when working with the persistent image was not required, and to let students experiment freely without the risk of damaging their persistent VM. Students were instructed to use either their personal/persistent or the local/temporary VMs as they saw fit.

For the lab requiring a "zombie" VM, the lab instructions provide a sequence of steps to download and run the additional VM on the workstation, offering a hands-on experience of obtaining and exploring a new OS.

The virtual network was configured to use network address translation (NAT), therefore all VMs could access the Internet but external access to VMs was limited (no port forwarding was configured). This was done to let students practice installing additional packages onto VMs and to allow Internet searches, etc. from the attacker VM itself. An even more locked-down approach (that would also reduce the risk of students inadvertently launching an attack on the lab network instead of the virtual LAN) would be to use the host-only networking mode.

4. LAB ASSIGNMENTS

A set of eight lab assignments has been developed for the course [9]. Each lab is accompanied by a comprehensive solution including relevant screenshots and further discussion.

Law and Ethics
This assignment is closer to a homework than a lab assignment, and asks students to evaluate various actions in context of applicable law and ethics standards of relevant bodies (professional groups, Boston University, etc.)

Introduction
The first hands-on assignment introduces VMWare (the virtual environment) and the virtual machines used in the course and guides a student through the installation and configuration process, as well as tests understanding of some standard Linux tools and basic networking concepts.

Search Engine Hacking and Social Engineering
Students are asked to investigate an organization and discover relevant organizational and personal information using a search engine, illustrating the amount of publicly available sensitive information that can routinely be found on the Internet. Another part of the assignment poses several search questions that can be answered using search engine queries with appropriate options, allowing search of historical website content (information that is no longer publicly available but still present in Internet archives) and quick identification of instances of a vulnerable system.

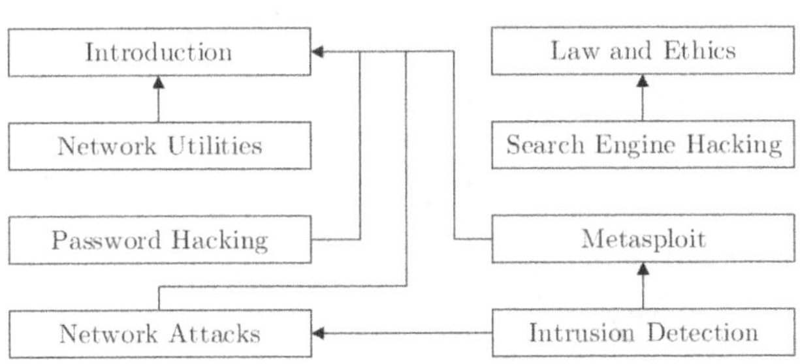

Figure 2: Dependencies between lab assignments

Network Utilities and Scripting
Students explore various uses of common versatile network utilities (such as `netcat` and `wget`) and do some scripting: in a shell script (utilizing the learned network utilities) and, on a lower level, by interacting with TCP/IP sockets directly from the Python scripting language.

Network Attacks
This lab focuses on network attack tools included with Kali Linux. Specifically, ways to mount ARP and DNS spoofing attacks on a network are demonstrated. The lab also asks students to do an `nmap` scan uzing the "zombie" technique.

Metasploit
Using the *Metasploit* framework, students are asked to perform several exploits on Metasploitable's services that are known to be vulnerable, mount different denial-of-service attacks on a web server running on the target VM, and explain why only some of the attacks are successful.

Password Cracking
The assignment introduces students to an off-line password cracking tool (*John the Ripper*) and an on-line tool (*Hydra*) that can be used to guess passwords to a website requiring authentication. Students are asked to use the on-line tool to find valid credentials to a different web application supplied with Metasploitable, and to crack Metasploitable's password database that they would download after compromising the target machine.

Intrusion Detection
A popular intrusion detection tool `snort` is introduced, students investigate varous modes of its operation and develop a custom filter that detects a previously studied Metasploit exploit attempt on a specific service.

Whenever possible, the assignments reference topics that were covered by earlier labs. For example, the Network Attacks lab walks students through using `ettercap` to perform ARP poisoning and tests their understanding of the attack. A few weeks later, the Intrusion Detection lab asks students to "perform ARP poisoning" with the expectation they already learned how to do it (or remember the previous lab and go to it for instructions). Figure 2 shows the dependencies among the lab assignments.

5. DISCUSSION AND RELATED WORK

We start the discussion with a brief overview of architectures for cybersecurity lab environments. For a longer survey, see Stewart et al [8].

Originally, cybersecurity labs started from mini-networks containing actual hardware. While offering the most realism, such labs are expensive to acquire and maintain, and tend to fall behind state-of-the-art as new hardware is introduced. The choice of hardware limits the range of possible configurations and caps the number of students that can share a lab without interfering with each other.

The other option is a virtualized environment. Three classes of virtualized environments exist:

- Centralized virtualization: a single server or a group of servers maintain virtual lab environments for all students, who access their environments remotely; one comprehensive centralized virtualization-based system is Tele-Lab [10].
- Cloud virtualization: similar to centralized virtualization, substituting the underlying server resources with data centers of the cloud services provider, and hosted hypervisors with the cloud provider's tools for spinning up, managing, and monitoring virtual server instances. Salah [6] described an instance of this architecture on the Amazon Web Services platform.
- Local virtualization (leveraging the resources of student workstations to maintain their virtual environments; students have local access to their virtualized networks). This is the approach we have adopted.

Both centralized and cloud approaches carry some complexity and cost involved in setting up and maintaining the environment. For organizations already having a server virtualization infrastructure, the former choice could be an attractive one; for organizations with limited on-site resources or technical personnel, the promise of "infrastructure offloading" to a cloud service may appear attractive but it comes with a bill for the resources consumed and does not really alleviate the demand for qualified technical staff to manage the environment.

The method of providing the entire virtual network on a single workstation benefits greatly from advances in capabilities of modern hardware. For example, Stewart et al mentioned being able to run at most three virtual machines using 256 MB each on a host with 1GB RAM in 2009 [8]. At the time this lab was run, the three guest operating systems used 1.5 GB of RAM on a host equipped with 4 GB, using less than 50% of the workstation's capacity.

As RAM and core count of typical lab machines go up while the system requirements of virtualizing a small number of operating systems and network devices remain roughly constant (since the relevant concepts can be demonstrated effectively on older versions of operating systems), hosting such a selection of 10-20 devices (counting user machines and servers, network hardware and filters/firewalls, and peripheral emulators) should be within capacity of a single modern workstation equipped with 16 GB RAM.

As a side effect of using commonly available software in a simple configuration, students could (and some of them did) use their personal laptops running Windows, Linux or OS X (with VMWare Fusion) to run the entire lab environment, including performing most of the lab assignments. There are several benefits to this flexibility: students can experiment with the setup anywhere, not only at the lab; students are working with the host OS that is most familiar to them; and it might well be that their personal laptop is more powerful and therefore runs the lab more smoothly than a lab workstation. If this configuration is allowed, students should be instructed to use host-only networking mode: otherwise, they could inadvertently use dangerous tools on any network they happen to be connected to.

Since we hosted persistent per-student virtual machine images on network storage, we were concerned with the possibility of "long delays in copying large virtual machine images across the network for each student's work" [8]. We did not find this to be a problem in practice. This might be attributable to some students choosing to use local non-persistent VM images in the lab (or their own computers with local images), or to modern virtualization software being able to access only the data it needs from a network hosted disk image, instead of copying the entire image to local storage.

5.1 Scalability

We would like to examine the scalability of each virtualization option (and of the set of labs) in the context of scaling up to a large student audience, such as a MOOC (massive open online course) environment.

Out of the three virtualized approaches, centralized virtualization is the one most likely to run into scaling issues as number of students grows and resource use approaches hardware capacity. Network use between virtual machines can also become a bottleneck, particularly in scenarios that involve large amounts of traffic (DoS exercises, for example). It appears unlikely that most institutions would provision enough spare on-site capacity to deploy the environment for thousands of students.

Cloud virtualization enjoys a flexible and deep pool of resources, but the cost of maintaining the environment scales linearly with the number of students. Particularly in the context of the "open" (free) online course, the cost for the hosting institution can escalate quickly. The complexity of managing a large number of students, particularly when not using any dedicated tools beyond the standard cloud provider's provisioning user interfaces, can also explode in a non-linear fashion. However, it would be possible to develop a specialized interface to handle specific user interface issues and enable both a broad overview and a quick drill-down to a specific student's environment.

In contrast to the above approaches, scaling to a large number of local virtualized environments is fairly easy as each student utilizes one standard computer (either university's or their own) to deploy the full environment. The remaining services (a learning management system hosting the assignments, a file server hosting the VM images) are readily available at MOOC scales. There are examples of MOOCs that have chosen this approach and have run successfully with thousands of students.[2]

One potential issue with a locally hosted virtual environment is that the student's computer must be powerful enough to support it. This will inevitably not be the case for some students, who would have to seek alternative options. An interesting possibility could be to deploy cloud instances only for those students, and have the students cover the costs of running those instances. [3]

5.2 Didactic Materials

There are several documented sets of lab assignments for cybersecurity courses. The set produced by the SEED project [2] is perhaps the largest collection available that is designed

[2]For example, the *Software Defined Networking* MOOC on Coursera has provided a VirtualBox VM containing all the necessary tools for the course.
`https://class.coursera.org/sdn-002`.

[3]A relevant survey from the SDN MOOC:
`https://piazza.com/class/hvjn9udjegm75q?cid=426`

specifically for instruction and uses a unified virtual environment (a version of Ubuntu) for most of the labs. It might be surprising, then, that there is not much overlap between labs developed for this course and SEED labs; only the *Network Attacks* lab corresponds to a SEED *TCP/IP Attack Lab.* Compared to SEED labs, which are often exploratory in nature, our labs offer more guidance on the steps to perform and pose specific questions for students to answer, making them easier to grade and reducing the overall time required to complete a lab.

Another set of labs is the *OWASP Hackademic* [5]. Its original focus is web applications security, and it uses a more involved setup to administer specific challenges. The authors do intend[4] to expand the system to cover virtual machine-based security challenges, but at the time our course was offered the functionality was not available.

There are many papers presenting one or more lab assignments that can be used in a cybersecurity course. For example, Yuan et al [11] introduced two such labs: a wireless network attacks lab and a stack overflow lab. However, with each such work offering only partial coverage of the course's intended topics, it would be a significant effort to reconcile labs from disparate sources (having different setup requirements, writing style, level of difficulty and so on) into a harmonious set for the complete course.

It is worthwhile to note that our course plan includes an *Laws and Ethics* lab early on, before any tools and methods are introduced. Information security skills in general, and offensive security skills in particular, can be used for both good and nefarious purposes, and covering the relevant laws, ethical principles, and guidelines at the outset helps students evaluate their actions. While explicitly not technical, the importance of having an ethics lesson or lab early in a course plan has been pointed out in previous work [1], but such a lesson is absent from both SEED and OWASP lab sets at this time.

5.3 Choice of Virtual Machines

We have chosen to use *Kali Linux* and *Metasploitable* because these readily available images represent and teach the set of tools commonly used in the security industry and typical weaknesses that can be attacked using those tools respectively. Since both VMs were designed from the outset to be usable by individuals learning at their own pace and on their own equipment, the recommended environment already had to exclude anything that requires elaborate configuration or a complicated process.

Choosing a stable and popular environment that had all the necessary tools and required minimal modification enabled us to focus on creating content for the course instead of dealing with setting up a more elaborate system.

5.4 Choice of Virtualization Software

We used VMWare Workstation because the virtual machine images for both *Kali Linux* and *Metasploitable* were only "officially" available in VMWare format. VMWare Player can be used for free by students to run the images on their computers, and a compatible Mac version (VMWare Fusion) exists. Furthermore, the university already had a license for VMWare software, so licensing cost was not a concern.

Image compatibility of virtualization software is constantly improving. We successfully converted the VM images into VirtualBox `.ovf` format and verified several lab questions to work. The instructions to do so, and the results of our testing in Parallels on a Mac, will be posted to GitHub [9].

6. STUDENT FEEDBACK

Towards the end of the semester, students were asked to fill an anonymous survey evaluating several teaching-related and course-related questions. Each question uses a scale from 1 (poor) to 5 (excellent). Out of 38 students, 27 have chosen to fill the survey; of those, 18% identified as undergraduate and 67% as graduate (15% did not answer the question). Figure 3 shows the responses to several of the questions asked on the survey.

The survey also allows students to write a freeform feedback about the course. The following are a few chosen responses:

> "The course was fun. I enjoyed the labs a lot. I definitely learned quite a bit about cybersecurity from these labs alone."
>
> "Strengths: in-class exercises and labs. Practical applications of the course tools helped to clarify somewhat semantic [sic] lecture material..."
>
> "Strong: good organization and explanation. Fun labs. Weak: even more hands-on would be great."

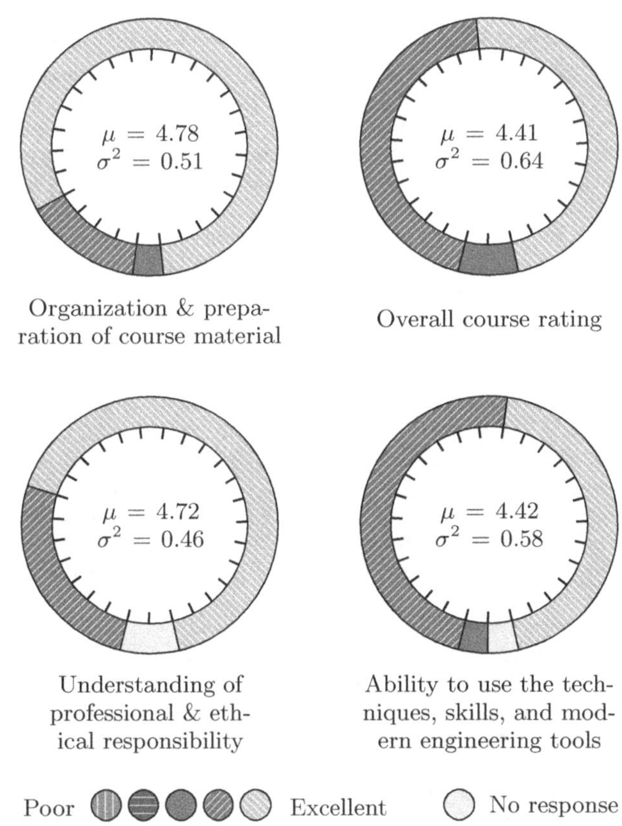

Figure 3: Student survey results (27 respondents)

[4]"We intend to expand the available challenges with additional scenarios that involve cryptography, and even vulnerable systems implemented in download-able virtual machines." - `https://www.owasp.org/index.php/OWASP_Hackademic_Challenges_Project` as of March 10, 2014

A few students mentioned that the labs were too easy. Due to diverse background of students, we consciously chose exercises and provided guidance such that our labs would be accessible to most students, accepting the fact that advanced students would find some of the labs too easy. A related survey question shows that a larger number of students do find the labs challenging and, on average, the difficulty is reasonable: 14 students (52% of respondents) rated the level of difficulty as "average", 8 students (30%) rated it "too difficult" and only one student rated the course "easy".

7. CHALLENGES AND FUTURE WORK

While Kali Linux (the attacker VM) has been updated every few months so far, the Metasploitable VM has been released in mid-2012 and saw no updates since. It remains usable as a snapshot, but if any changes have to be made to the image (for example, adding a package that was not installed by default) some workarounds and configuration changes are already needed, as the base OS used for Metasploitable has transitioned from supported to archived status in 2013. As such, and without explicit commitment to supporting Metasploitable going forward, its future and expansion are uncertain.

We have spent some effort modifying a Metasploitable image in an attempt to create a different environment for the course's final exam (different available services, exploits, passwords and so on), but adding new exploits was not possible due to limited time. The task would have been easier if the VM was designed in a modular, customizable manner–for example, if it was possible to install vulnerable services from a pre-built package repository.

A single Linux VM is enough for a first cybersecurity course since it can demonstrate the relevant concepts. However, the current computing environment is characterized by a multitude of popular architectures and operating systems. A more realistic environment would include other vulnerable virtual machines based, for example, on Microsoft Windows XP and Mac OS X; and different architectures, for example Android on ARM providing an example of a smartphone platform or Linux-based OpenWRT on MIPS32 for an example of a home router platform. We are not aware of an effort to provide such images specifically for cybersecurity training (with known security holes and supporting didactic material), even as vulnerabilities in smartphone operating systems and embedded devices are making news throughout the tech industry.

Specifically for Windows XP, Metasploit exploits are available for the operating system itself (unpatched or on earlier service pack level), but obtaining known vulnerable (old) versions of third-party software has proven more difficult than authors expected. Using a proprietary OS also carries licensing issues, but many institutions would have Windows XP licenses available from previous deployments.

From the scalability perspective, the biggest challenge in scaling a cybersecurity course to a massively online audience is likely to be in grading. MOOC classes typically use automated grading; developing a method to collect relevant output from different machines of the local virtualized environment, automatically grading, and providing meaningful feedback for each of the proposed subject areas would be a big step forward towards enabling a MOOC instance of the course.

Acknowledgements

The authors would like to acknowledge the contributions of James K. Goebel, including the initial idea of switching to the virtual machine-based environment and technical aspects of the implementation, which are not described in this paper since they are likely to be specific to Boston University's IT services configuration and therefore are of less general interest.

Yuguang Li and James Christianson wrote the initial versions of some of the lab assignments mentioned in this paper and helped in testing the virtual course environment.

This research was supported in part by NSF under grants CNS-1012910 and CNS-1409053.

References

[1] Thomas Cook, Gregory Conti, and David Raymond. "When good Ninjas turn bad: Preventing your students from becoming the threat". In: *Proc. 16th Colloquium for Information System Security Education.* 2012, pp. 61–67.

[2] Wenliang Du. "SEED: hands-on lab exercises for computer security education". In: *Security & Privacy, IEEE* 9.5 (2011), pp. 70–73.

[3] Offensive Security Ltd. *Kali Linux.* 2014. URL: `http://www.kali.org` (visited on 03/05/2014).

[4] HD Moore. *Metasploitable 2 Exploitability Guide.* 2012. URL: `https://community.rapid7.com/docs/DOC-1875` (visited on 03/05/2014).

[5] Alexandros Papanikolaou et al. "A Hacker's Perspective on Educating Future Security Experts". In: *Informatics (PCI), 2011 15th Panhellenic Conference on.* IEEE. 2011, pp. 68–72.

[6] Khaled Salah. "Harnessing the cloud for teaching cybersecurity". In: *Proceedings of the 45th ACM technical symposium on Computer science education.* ACM. 2014, pp. 529–534.

[7] *Some VMWare Images.* 2013. URL: `http://www.thoughtpolice.co.uk/vmware/` (visited on 03/05/2014).

[8] Kyle E. Stewart, Jeffrey W. Humphries, and Todd R. Andel. "Developing a virtualization platform for courses in networking, systems administration and cyber security education". In: *SpringSim '09: Proceedings of the 2009 Spring Simulation Multiconference.* San Diego, California: Society for Computer Simulation International, 2009, pp. 1–7.

[9] Maxim Timchenko and David Starobinski. *EC 521 Cybersecurity Lab Assignments.* 2014. URL: `http://github.com/maxvt/cyberlabs` (visited on 11/20/2014).

[10] Christian Willems and Christoph Meinel. "Tele-Lab IT-Security: An Architecture for an Online Virtual IT Security Lab". In: *International Journal of Online Engineering* 4.2 (2008).

[11] Xiaohong Yuan et al. "Developing Faculty Expertise in Information Assurance through Case Studies and Hands-On Experiences". In: *System Sciences (HICSS), 2014 47th Hawaii International Conference on.* IEEE. 2014, pp. 4938–4945.

An Educational Networking Framework for Full Layer Implementation and Testing

Keunhong Lee, Joongi Kim, Sue Moon
Department of Computer Science, KAIST
{khlee, joongi}@an.kaist.ac.kr, sbmoon@kaist.edu

ABSTRACT

We present the KENSv2 (KAIST Educational Network System) framework for network protocol implementation. The framework is event-driven to guarantee deterministic behaviour and reproducibility, which in turn delivers ease of debugging and evaluation. Our framework consists of four components: the event generator, the virtual host, the TCP driver and the IP driver. The two drivers are what students have to implement, and we offer to the students the drivers in the binary format for paired testing and debugging. We have developed a test suite that covers three categories of test cases: specification, paired, and logic tests. The framework logs packet transmissions in the PCAP format to allow use of widely available packet analysis tools. Those tools help inspecting logical behaviour of student solutions, such as congestion control. We have designed five step-by-step assignments and evaluated student submissions. With our automated test suite, we have cut down the number of TAs by half for the doubled class size from the previous semester, in total of 3 TAs and 49 students. We plan to continue using KENSv2 in our undergraduate networking course and expand the test suite.

Categories and Subject Descriptors

C.2.2 [**Computer-Communication Networks**]: Network Protocols—*Protocol verification*; D.2.5 [**Software Engineering**]: Testing and Debugging—*Testing tools*; K.3.2 [**Computers and Education**]: Computer and Information Science Education—*Computer science education, self-assessment*

General Terms

Design; Verification

Keywords

Educational Networking Framework; Full Layer Implementation; Automated Test Suite; Network protocols; TCP; IP

SIGCSE'15, March 4–7, 2015, Kansas City, MO, USA.

http://dx.doi.org/10.1145/2676723.2677304.

1 Introduction

In our computer science discipline, hands-on projects challenge students to build systems they learn in class. These projects have always been an integral part of our curricula. Kurose and Ross supplement their textbook on computer networking with Wireshark[1] labs and programming assignments for network applications [1]. Wireshark labs help students to grasp quickly the workings of today's Internet via packet trace analysis without writing code. MYSOCK/STCP[2] have been used in undergraduate networking courses for students to implement the socket API and a simplified TCP connection mechanism to work over simulated packet losses and reordering. Clack [2] provides modular network stack implementations including TCP, and students observe TCP congestions in a graphical way. The popular network simulation tool, `ns2`[3], has accumulated an extensive set of protocol implementations in the past two decades, but its primary goal is to examine the protocol performance against other competing traffic rather than to provide abstractions for learning and implementation. While `ns2` operates strictly in a simulated environment, emulab[4] and ONL (Open Network Laboratory) [3] offer an emulated networking environment with ease of access and configurability. VNS [4] and its successor Mininet [5, 6] have empowered researchers with a container-based emulation environment that closely matches the performance of a real testbed with high fidelity.

For a complete learning experience, students should be able to implement and test the full protocol stack in realistic settings but focus on core networking features only. The assignment should avoid including extra burdens such as kernel programming or concurrency management. It is a common method to punch-hole a set of functions in educational frameworks for systems and let the students fill them as assignments. While it gives the instructor the power to choose at will features for programming assignments, it burdens the students with understanding of the entire framework and interaction of their own code with the rest of the framework. However, this punch-hole approach alone is not suitable for network protocols because of their *paired* and *asynchronous* nature—an implementation of a network protocol cannot operate and be tested without a counterpart. Thus an educational framework for network protocols should be able

[1]`http://www.wireshark.org/`
[2]`http://www.stanford.edu/class/cs244a/hw3/hw3.html`
[3]`http://www.isi.edu/nsnam/ns/`
[4]`http://www.emulab.net`

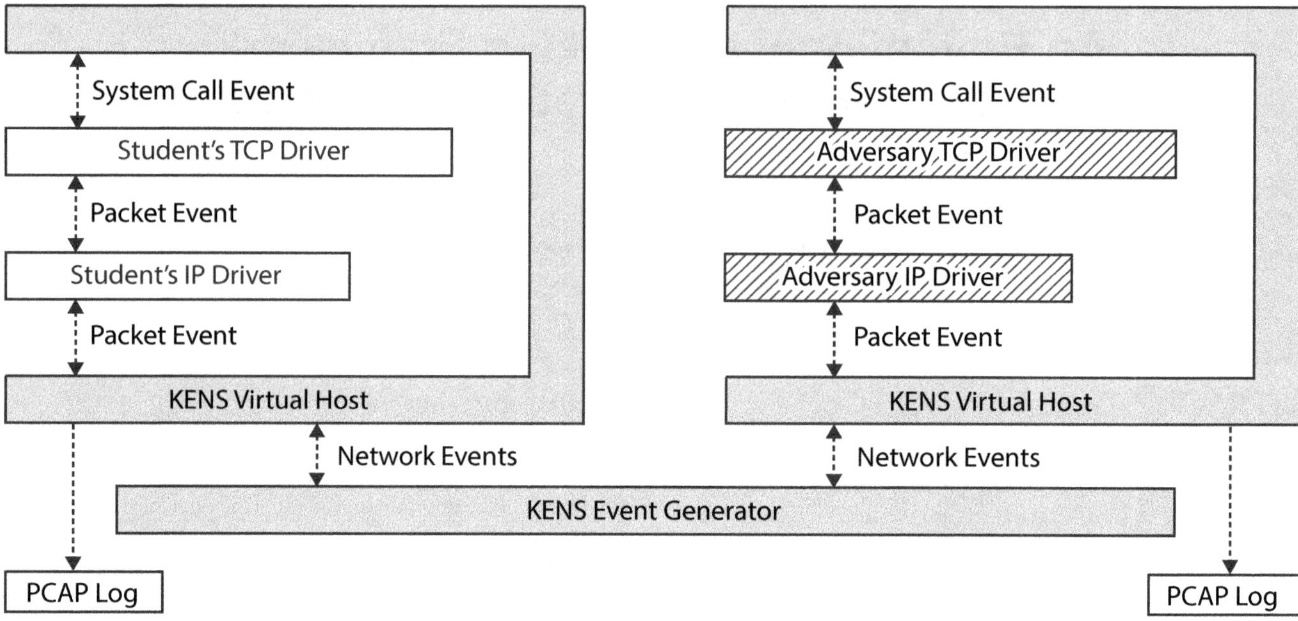

Figure 1: Overview structure of KENSv2 framework

to launch multiple instances of different protocol implementations for paired testing, in addition to punch-holed functions for individual implementations. The framework needs to work as a demonstration of protocol abstractions instead of a simple code template. Moreover, asynchronous executions over multiple hosts make the system unpredictable. The framework should be deterministic to ease tracking, debugging, and evaluation of students' solutions.

In this work we present KENSv2 (KAIST Educational Network System), a framework for students to implement TCP, IP, and routing protocols, and test against adversary implementations. Our framework is event-driven for deterministic behaviour and reproducibility. We have designed KENSv2, implemented it and have used it in an undergraduate computer networking course. In Section 2 we elaborate on our design decisions and in Section 3 present the framework overview. In Section 4 we describe our assignments, and in Section 5 evaluation results. We summarize our experience and lay out future work in Section 6.

2 Design Decisions

KENSv2 is an educational framework, and our design decisions are differ from that of general-purpose frameworks.

2.1 Adversary Implementation

A unique requirement of an educational framework for network programming is the need for adversary implementation. Most functionalities in network protocols are not one-sided but require a responding counterpart. For a student to have a working implementation of `connect()`, s/he must have a matching implementation of `accept()`. We provide these counterparts to allow students to use them for running their code under development. Since this is an educational framework, we should not expose the reference solution. Thus, the counterparts are in the binary format to hide the source code, while providing the required functionality.

Another motivation for adversary implementation is decoupling of the test code and implementation code for Test-driven development (TDD).

For example in Pintos [7], testing thread functionalities, running threads and checking the execution order are all independent from context switching and scheduling and can be performed in separate units. The source code of the testing suite is available with the framework and is independent of the source code being tested. On the contrary, the testing suite of network protocols follows the protocol logic and are not independent from the target implementation. The source code for the network logic should not be exposed to the students, but testing logic itself should be available to students.

2.2 Event-Driven Framework

Reproducibility is critical for an educational framework since students should have a consistent view on how things work [6]. Like other network simulation tools such as ns2, our framework offers a deterministic, reproducible environment that make evaluation straightforward.

To achieve this goal KENSv2 provides an event-driven programming model for layers and a discrete virtual clock. The event-driven model simplifies execution of multiple layers and multiple instances of layer implementation by multiplexing them in a single process. To avoid function calls that cross multiple layers from indefinitely blocking other events, we split a blocking call into two parts, raise and completion, to simulate asynchronous function calls. The virtual clock allows insertion of arbitrary network delay and losses while we run the simulation. We constrain all layer modules to register callback functions for network events. The event generator provides inputs from their upper/lower layers and and the timing information through the registered callback functions.

To deploy KENSv2 on real netweorks, it needs to adapt with existing userspace packet IO schemes such as `netmap`

```
struct kens_tcp_driver_t
{
   //system call mapping
   void (*startup)(kens_system_lib*);
   void (*shutdown)(kens_tcp_driver*);

   my_context (*open)(kens_tcp_driver*, int*);
   void (*close)(kens_tcp_driver*, my_context,int*);
   bool (*bind)(kens_tcp_driver*, my_context,
        const struct sockaddr *, socklen_t, int*);
   bool (*listen)(kens_tcp_driver*, my_context, int, int*);
   bool (*connect)(kens_tcp_driver*, my_context,
        const struct sockaddr *, socklen_t, int*);
   bool (*accept)(kens_tcp_driver*, my_context, int*);
   bool (*getsockname)(kens_tcp_driver*, my_context,
        struct sockaddr *, socklen_t *, int*);
   bool (*getpeername)(kens_tcp_driver*, my_context,
        struct sockaddr *, socklen_t *, int*);

   void (*timer)(kens_tcp_driver*, my_context, int);

   //automatically called by ip layer
   void (*ip_dispatch_tcp)(kens_tcp_driver*,
        struct in_addr, struct in_addr, const void *, size_t);

   //application link
   int (*app_dispatch_tcp)(kens_tcp_driver*, my_context,
        const void*, size_t);
};
```

Figure 2: Function prototypes of the KENSv2 TCP driver

[8], psio [9], and Intel DPDK (Data-plane Development Kit) [10]. The challenge here is to combine our event-driven scheduler with the polling loops used in modern userspace packet IO libraries for high-performance. We plane to add an adaptor that runs in polling mode and translates input packets to packet events.

3 KENSv2 Framework

3.1 Framework Overview

Our KENSv2 framework consists of the following four components: an event generator, virtual hosts, IP drivers, and TCP drivers. Figure 1 show the overall architecture of KENSv2. We have implemented our framework in C.

KENSv2 Virtual Host acts as an application layer to TCP and as the combined data link and physical layer to IP. The virtual host encapsulates all the interfaces that the student's code has with the framework. It is also capable of logging all network events in the PCAP[5] format. Students can easily visualize and evaluate the log by using Wireshark[6] or other packet analysis tools. This approach is also used in [11]. Like Web100[12], the virtual host pumps system call events to its TCP driver.

KENSv2 Event Generator feeds events to the virtual hosts. It functions both as a virtual application and the underlying network. It keeps track of a virtual clock and drives the simulation according to it. As the underlying network, it introduces network latency and packet drops. As a virtual application, it initiates system call events towards the TCP layer and they propagate through the TCP and IP layers back to the event generator. By running multiple virtual hosts on top of a single event generator, the framework can simulate a network of multiple hosts running a set of applications.

[5]MIME type vnd.tcpdump.pcap. See http://www.iana.org/assignments/media-types/application/vnd.tcpdump.pcap

[6]https://www.wireshark.org/

```
typedef struct
{
   //access the local routing table
   uint32_t (*ip_host_address)(struct in_addr target);

   //send packet to lower layer
   int (*tcp_dispatch_ip)(struct in_addr src_addr,
        struct in_addr dest_addr, void * data, size_t data_size);
   //send packet to upper layer
   int (*tcp_dispatch_app)(my_context handle,
        const void* data, size_t data_size);

   //wake up sleeping 'accept' system call
   bool (*tcp_passive_open)(my_context server_handle,
        my_context new_handle);
   //wake up sleeping 'connect' system call
   bool (*tcp_active_open)(my_context handle);

   //current time in milliseconds
   int (*tcp_get_mtime)();

   bool (*tcp_register_timer)(my_context context, int mtime);
   void (*tcp_unregister_timer)(my_context context);
   //disconnect tcp-app linkage for a socket hanle
   void (*tcp_shutdown_app)(my_context handle);

}kens_system_lib;
```

Figure 3: System APIs. It shows the case for TCP drivers, but the IP drivers share the similar interface prefixed with "ip_" instead.

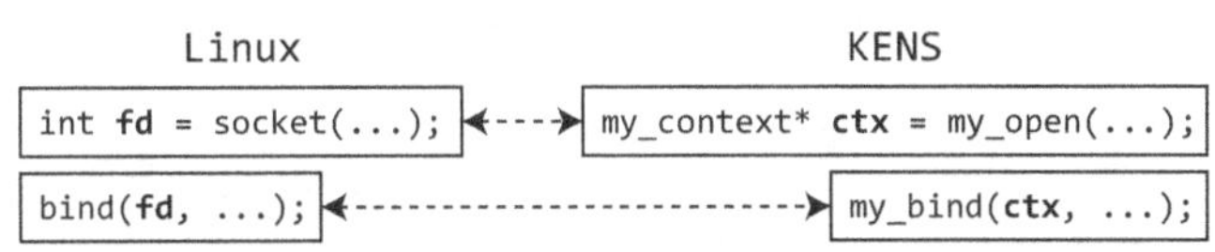

Figure 4: Context mapping between file descriptors and KENSv2 TCP contexts

Students' TCP and IP Drivers are the part that students should actually implement. The structure of driver is shown in Figure 2.

Adversary Drivers are binary counterparts for debugging and testing.

3.2 Network Driver Abstraction

Our driver abstraction provides a unified interface for network layer implementations. Drivers cannot access the system or other drivers directly but only through a set of API and utility functions. The API hides environment-specific details from the drivers; students can run their implementations on both real and testing environments seamlessly without modifying their codes. The TCP and IP drivers share the similar abstraction with minor differences depending on what their lower/upper layers are.

System API. Drivers have access to the system resources via the following functions. Figure 3 illustrates them:

- retrieve system clock
- register/unregister timer
- wake up blocked applications
- send data to lower/upper network layer

Network/System Event Callbacks. To interact with other layers and run timed operations, each driver registers a few callback functions:

- initialization/destruction event of the driver
- system call requests

- timer events
- data arrival from lower/upper network layer

Students receive a skeleton of a driver (either TCP or IP) and are assigned to fill the above callback functions. They can use the system API as they need.

To reduce the burden of managing unique numbering for process IDs and file descriptors, we also offer a context mapping scheme as shown in Figure 4, which internally maps each context data to individual TCP socket. The framework translates each file descriptor into the pointer of its context data. Drivers use this information to distinguish each socket from the attached context data.

3.3 Test Suite

At the moment we have implemented only the TCP test suite and are working on the IP test suite. The test suite consists of three parts: specification tests, pairing tests, and logic tests.

Specification test validates the input parameters and return values of the standard system calls. We check the return value and the content of the buffer. For example, the test checks if the TCP driver detects a collision with an existing port number when calling a **bind()** system call. The specification test also needs to repeat with different orders of system call events and packet events as the execution result depends on their execution order. To achieve that, our test suite enumerates every possible ordering. For example, Figure 5 illustrates two different cases for **accept()**: "returning already established connection" and "blocking until new connection has arrived".

Pairing test ensures that the code behaves in a matching manner with its counterpart because the communication may fail regardless of the specification test result. It tests if the data transmitted from one side is received correctly at the other side. For example, even though **write()** system call reports back the success of a transmission, packets may have been dropped or unrecognized in the lower layers or in **read()** implementation running at the destination virtual host due to bugs.

Logic test validates if the implementation conforms with the runtime requirements such as congestion control. Neither specification nor pairing tests covers correctness of context-dependent runtime behaviour because they are black-box approaches confirming the execution results statically. For example, unsolicited or duplicate ACKs are dependent to the TCP protocol states and not straightforward to validate. We leverage the existing analysis tools for the logic test, which has reduced our development effort greatly at the same time making our framework easy to maintain. The framework generates the packet traces in the widely-used PCAP format. We use Wireshark since it provides context-dependent protocol checks such as advanced TCP filters verifying SEQ/ACK numbers. For simpler tests, more options are available—such as Packetdrill [13] providing packet-level assertions to verify constant fields and checksums.

4 KENSv2 Assignments

We are currently using the prototype of KENSv2 framework in a computer networks course for undergraduate students as a programming assignment. The goal of the assignment is to help the students to understand how actual network layers operate by requiring them to participate in TCP implementation.

```
------------------------------------------------------------
Starting testListen


     CUnit - A unit testing framework for C - Version 2.1-2
     http://cunit.sourceforge.net/


Suite: testListen
  Test: _testListen_Accept_Before_Connect ...passed
  Test: _testListen_Accept_After_Connect ...passed
  Test: _testListen_Accept_Multiple ...passed
  Test: _testListen_Multiple_Interfaces ...passed

Run Summary:    Type  Total    Ran Passed Failed Inactive
              suites      1      1    n/a      0        0
               tests      4      4      4      0        0
             asserts    145    145    145      0      n/a

Elapsed time =    0.000 seconds
testListen: progress = 4/4
------------------------------------------------------------
```

Figure 5: Example result of a successful test result

What we expect the students to do are as follows:

- Manipulating protocol headers properly
- Demultiplexing flows from the lower layer
- Multiplexing flows from the upper layer
- Context management for demultiplexed flows
- Implementing functions in protocol specification

What we do *NOT* want the students to deal with are as follows:

- Hassles of managing multiple threads and protecting critical regions
- Issues on connecting their network stacks with other pre-built network stacks
- Reinventing the wheel such as commonly used data structures (e.g. lists, maps)
- Platform compatibility issues

In the assignment we split the TCP layer implementation into a series of small tasks (sub-assignment) as shown in the following class schedule:

- (Week 1) Assigning own TCP context for each socket creation request
- (Week 2) Implementing basic accept/connect protocol
- (Week 3,4) Data transfer on reliable network connection
- (Week 5) Data transfer and connection establishment on unreliable network connection
- (Week 6) Implementing basic AIMD congestion algorithm

We gave students two weeks to submit each sub-assignment, and they had a week off between each assignment. As we did not provide any skeleton codes except the abstract function interfaces, students had to design their own TCP context data structure, demultiplexer, reorder window, etc. We left the implementation details to the students' discretion.

In spring 2014, 49 students participated in the project, supervised by 3 TAs. Students worked in pairs as a team to work on the assignments together. This was an incremental assignment and the final submissions consist of hundreds to 2K lines of code.

```
----------------------------------------------------------
Starting testBind


     CUnit - A unit testing framework for C - Version 2.1-2
     http://cunit.sourceforge.net/


Suite: testBind
  Test: __testBind_Simple ...passed
  Test: __testBind_GetSockName ...passed
  Test: __testBind_DoubleBind ...passed
  Test: __testBind_OverlapPort ...passed
  Test: __testBind_OverlapClosed ...passed
  Test: __testBind_DifferentIP_SamePort ...FAILED
    1. testbind.c:244  - CU_ASSERT_EQUAL(err,0)
    2. testbind.c:245  - CU_ASSERT_TRUE(ret)
  Test: __testBind_SameIP_DifferentPort ...passed

Run Summary:    Type  Total    Ran Passed Failed Inactive
              suites      1      1    n/a      0        0
               tests      7      7      6      1        0
             asserts     60     60     58      2      n/a

Elapsed time =    0.000 seconds
testBind: progress = 6/7
----------------------------------------------------------
```

Figure 6: Example result of a failed test result

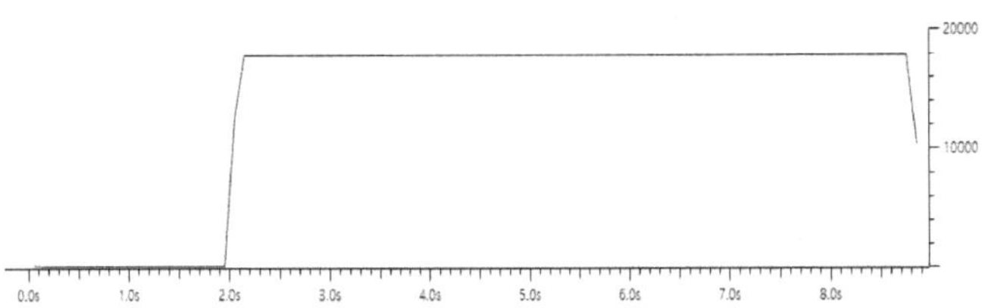

Figure 7: Transmission rate over reliable network

5 Evaluation of Students' Submissions

We had 49 students working in pair and collected 23 submissions for each assignment. In this section, we introduce how we evaluate the assignments using our framework.

5.1 Correctness of system call functionality

Each system call implementation is required to satisfy some functionalities. Some examples of functionalities we want to verify include:

- Finding existing TCP context with port number/IP address
- Checking port number collision while binding address to socket
- Returning correct socket address on getsockname
- Backlog management

Our test suite contains assert statements for system calls on various execution environment. We have placed virtual system events to cover every TCP state transitions. Also, we have tests that covers some complicated situations. Figure 6 contains corner cases of **bind()** system call. We verify the functionalities by checking whether the students' implementation passes all asserts.

5.2 Correctness of Data Transfer

The core function of TCP is to send data from one to the other. We verify it by comparing the sent data and the received data byte-by-byte. This transmission request is handled by a virtual user application that generates proper system call requests (socket-connect-write-close).

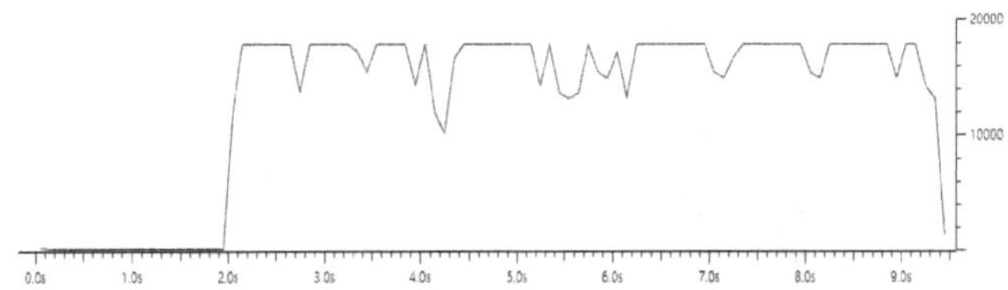

Figure 8: Transmission rate over reliable network (0.1% drop rate)

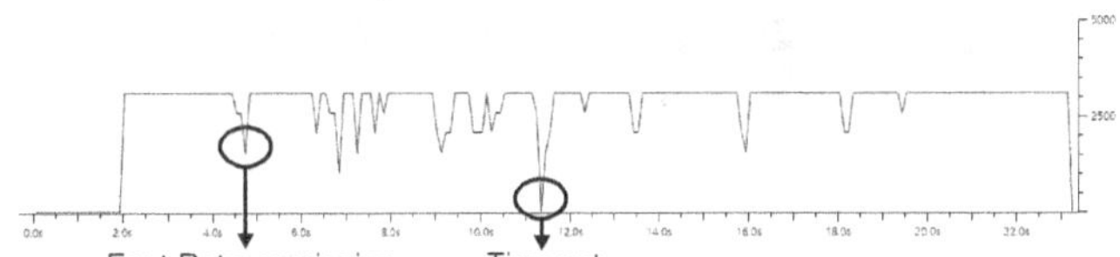

Figure 9: Bytes on flight over unreliable network (0.1% drop rate)

5.3 Correctness of Header Manipulation

We want to check the correctness of TCP checksum, whether a user has sent unseen ACK number, etc. Wireshark provides most verification algorithms we want. After the test application is finished, we analyze the generated PCAP log via Wireshark and check whether an implementation violates the TCP protocol compatibility.

5.4 Reliable Transfer over Unreliable Network

KENSv2 physical layer supports artificial drop/reorder/corruption of packets. The framework allows the verification of TCP behaviours on unreliable connections by simply turning on the unreliable transfer mode. Our Week 5 assignment is simply announced as passing same test suite while unreliable transfer mode is turned on. Students can observe the realistic dynamics of Bytes Per Second under these conditions.

5.5 Implementing congestion control and its verification

Students can implement any TCP congestion control algorithms as KENSv2 provides the virtual system clock and registration of timers. We offered students to implement TCP Reno algorithm[7]. Without any packet drops, the network I/O throughput looks flat like Figure 7. If there are some packet drops, the network throughput looks like Figure 8. However, this does not imply that AIMD congestion control is working. To distinguish AIMD congestion control from multiple retransmissions (though both supports reliable transfers over unreliable network), we have applied advanced TCP filters from Wireshark. These filters compute and compare SEQ/ACK numbers and allows us to determine how many bytes are on flight and not ACKed. Figure 9 illustrates the halved window size on fast-retransmission and the slow start phase on timeout. Wireshark filters also detect fast-retransmissions and timeouts. Currently we have manually observe the macroscopic behaviour of congestion control because the desired windows size is implementation-specific, for example, depends on the initial window size and round-up/round-down choices. However, we plan to adopt TShark (Terminal version of Wireshark) to automate parsing the filter results and evaluation of the logic test.

[7]`http://tools.ietf.org/html/rfc6582`

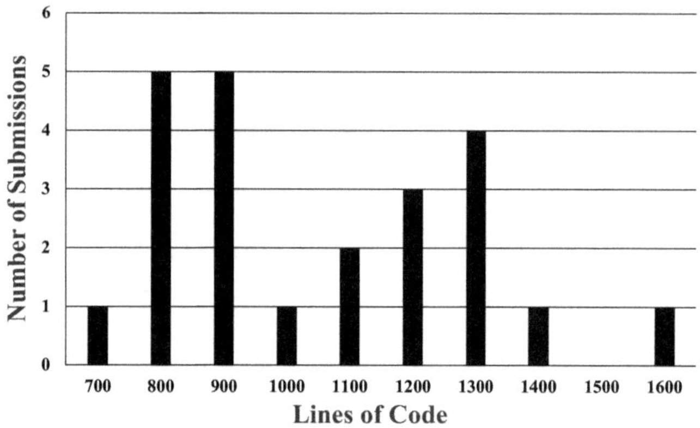

Figure 10: LoC distribution for the final project

5.6 Diversity of Submissions

Until the end of the semester, we had 23 submissions on total. Figure 10 shows the distribution of LoC[8] of all submissions. The shortest solution had 692 LoC and the longest had 1588 LoC. This high variation of LoC shows that our abstraction is general and embraces diverse solutions by students, *i.e.*, freedom of design. Also, the amount of assignment is about a thousand LoC, which is suitable for a single semester assignment.

6 Summary and Future Work

KENSv2 is an educational framework for transport and network layer implementation that supports:

- Realistic Protocol Implementation
- Incremental Development
- Automated Test Suite
- Packet Level Inspection

Our improvements are based on eight years of accumulated lab experiences. In Spring 2014 we are already experiencing benefits from the improvements. We could run TCP implementing assignments over 49 students having 3 TAs for management, which is halved from the previous semester. We plan to release the refactored framework as an open-source software and encourage other universities to try KENSv2 by this year.

We have the following extension ideas for KENSv2. The first is to extend our automated test suite to cover the IP layer. The current version has a functional interference and a reference implementation of the IP layer including packet fragmentation and reassembly, but lacks automated test suites. The second is to redesign KENSv2's data link layer as a generalized adaptor that can receive/transmit packets from/to various underlying packet IO schemes, such as userspace packet IO libraries or the native Linux kernel. The third is to add an IPv6 layer. We expect that IPv6 will become a standard suite for educational frameworks as its adoption is going to accelerate in the near future and the IPv4 address space is being exhausted. Finally, though our system call abstraction for blocking calls can represent the blocking behaviour of both **connect()** and **accept()**, the test code itself does not look like real-world TCP applications. We have a plan to extend our system call abstraction layer to cover every system call with a unified interface.

[8]The number of lines are measured with CLOC. See `http://cloc.sourceforge.net/`

7 Acknowledgements

KENSv2 is based on KENS (KAIST Educational Network System) developed by Junehwa Song and his students (`http://nclab.kaist.ac.kr/kens`). The original motivation and design of KENS has been a great inspiration. We are grateful to Yejin Park and Junhyun Shim for their help with writing. This work was supported by the Basic Science Research Program by the National Research Foundation of Korea (NRF) of MSIP (2014R1A2A1A01007580).

8 References

[1] James F Kurose and Keith W Ross. *Computer networking: a top-down approach featuring the Internet*. Pearson Education India, 2005.

[2] Dan Wendlandt, Martin Casado, Paul Tarjan, and Nick McKeown. The clack graphical router: visualizing network software. In *Proceedings of the 2006 ACM symposium on Software visualization*, pages 7–15. ACM, 2006.

[3] John DeHart, Fred Kuhns, Jyoti Parwatikar, Jonathan Turner, Charlie Wiseman, and Ken Wong. The open network laboratory. In *ACM SIGCSE Bulletin*. ACM, 2006.

[4] Martin Casado and Nick McKeown. The virtual network system. In *ACM SIGCSE Bulletin*. ACM, 2005.

[5] Bob Lantz, Brandon Heller, and Nick McKeown. A network in a laptop: rapid prototyping for software-defined networks. In *ACM SIGCOMM HotNets*. ACM, 2010.

[6] Nikhil Handigol, Brandon Heller, Vimalkumar Jeyakumar, Bob Lantz, and Nick McKeown. Reproducible network experiments using container-based emulation. In *Proceedings of the 8th international conference on Emerging networking experiments and technologies*, pages 253–264. ACM, 2012.

[7] Ben Pfaff, Anthony Romano, and Godmar Back. The pintos instructional operating system kernel. In *ACM SIGCSE Bulletin*, volume 41, pages 453–457. ACM, 2009.

[8] Luigi Rizzo. netmap: A Novel Framework for Fast Packet I/O. In *USENIX ATC*, 2012.

[9] PacketShader I/O Engine. `github.com/PacketShader/Packet-IO-Engine`.

[10] Intel DPDK (Data Plane Development Kit). `https://dpdk.org`.

[11] Marko Lackovic, Robert Inkret, and Miljenko Mikuc. An approach to education oriented tcp simulation. In *SoftCOM 2002: international conference on software, telecommunications and computer networks*, pages 181–185, 2002.

[12] Matt Mathis, John Heffner, and Raghu Reddy. Web100: extended tcp instrumentation for research, education and diagnosis. *ACM SIGCOMM Computer Communication Review*, 33(3):69–79, 2003.

[13] Neal Cardwell, Yuchung Cheng, Lawrence Brakmo, Matt Mathis, Barath Raghavan, Nandita Dukkipati, Hsiao-keng Jerry Chu, Andreas Terzis, and Tom Herbert. packetdrill: Scriptable network stack testing, from sockets to packets. In *USENIX Annual Technical Conference*, pages 213–218, 2013.

The CS Concept Inventory Quiz Show

Nafeesa Dewji
Dept. of CS
U. British Columbia
201-2366 Main Mall
Vancouver, BC, Canada
nafeesa.dewji@gmail.com

Steven A. Wolfman
Dept. of CS
U. British Columbia
201-2366 Main Mall
Vancouver, BC, Canada
wolf@cs.ubc.ca

Geoffrey L. Herman, PhD
U. Illinois, Urbana-Champaign
Curriculum & Instruction
Illinois Foundry for Innovation
in Engineering Education
glherman@illinois.edu

Leo Porter
CS and Eng. Dept.
U. California, San Diego
La Jolla, CA 92093
leporter@cs.ucsd.edu

Cynthia Taylor
CS Dept.
Oberlin College
ctaylor@oberlin.edu

Jan Vahrenhold
Dept. of CS, Westfälische
Wilhelms-Universität Münster
48149 Münster, Germany
jan.vahrenhold@uni-muenster.de

Categories and Subject Descriptors

K.3.2 [**Computers and Education**]: Computer Science Education

General Terms

Human Factors

Keywords

misconceptions, concept inventory

1. SUMMARY

This session is a chance for researchers studying concept inventories (CIs)—low-cost assessments highlighting student misconceptions in a field [2]—and CS education practitioners to communicate about advances in concept inventories in an engaging and utterly ridiculous way.

We use a "quiz show" format to present CI items from various authors' work across the computing curriculum. On each question, audience members and volunteer contestants consider their own response and guess students' common responses. Then, they see how authentic student data illustrate the misconceptions these items probe.

The session's goal is three-fold: educate practitioners about recent results in concept inventory research that may suggest surprising trends in student learning, popularize concept inventories as a tool in research and practice, and collect the audience's expert responses to concept inventory items.

Along with making the session fun, the quiz show format gives audience members a stake in their own responses and in predicting students' responses to the CI items. Our challenges for contestants—which are not simply to answer the items but rather to guess aspects of students' response to the items—focus attention on key misconceptions exposed by these items. As a side benefit, this avoids requiring anyone to **publicly** answer the questions, which could be professionally embarrassing.[1]

Below, we briefly recount background on concept inventories, give an outline of the session's activities, illustrate how a sample question might be used for the show, explain our expectations of the audience, and explain why this session's plan is well-suited to the SIGCSE special session format.

SIGCSE'15, March 4–7, 2015, Kansas City, MO, USA.
ACM 978-1-4503-2966-8/15/03.
http://dx.doi.org/10.1145/2676723.2677315.

2. CONCEPT INVENTORIES

Concept inventories are inexpensive but powerful tools for probing student misconceptions and the longitudinal impact of pedagogical changes [2]. A typical CI is a multiple choice assessment of about 20–30 minutes' length. Researchers design each question and its responses to capture observed student misconceptions around key ideas in the target discipline. CIs have highlighted surprising student difficulties in grasping core concepts across a variety of disciplines [3, pp. 20–43]. Recent work has introduced CIs or CI-like instruments for various subjects in computing, including digital logic [3], introductory programming [6], data structures and algorithms [1, 4, 5], and architecture [7]. However, it remains quite difficult—in computing and other fields—to communicate the results of concept inventory research to practitioners and to collect their crucial, expert feedback on CI items under development.

3. SESSION OUTLINE

We break the session down into parts below. Both session organizers are involved in almost all parts of the planned session. However, where we use other researchers' CI items, we will solicit those researchers' help with planning, presentation, and discusion of their own items.

Intro (7 mins) Introduce the idea of a Concept Inventory, the quiz show format, and audience participation op-

[1]Instead, we only ask people to *personally* embarrass themselves by participating in a quiz show with the moral equivalent of chicken hats as prizes.

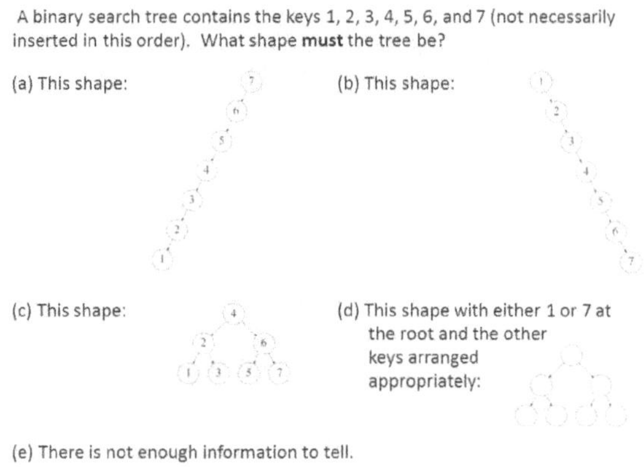

Figure 1: Sample concept inventory question for the quiz show, adapted from Karpierz and Wolfman [4].

tions (e.g., provided clickers). Collect consent from audience members to use data in future research.

Contestants (3 mins) Solicit volunteer contestants for the quiz show. (Prearranging interesting SIGCSE regulars as "plants" in case few people volunteer.)

Quiz Rounds (2 × 25 mins each)

- **Questions (3–5 × 4 mins each)**
  - **Context** Course and background information.
  - **Display Question & Audience Response**
  - **Challenge Contestants** E.g., "Predict the most popular distractor for students."
  - **Reveal Responses** of audience, students, and contestants.
  - **Reflection** on how the question, data, and responses will impact the audience's teaching.
- **Discussion (10 mins)** about the full round.

Conclusion (5 mins) Tie discussion back to what a concept inventory is and what role CIs can play in practitioners' courses. Hand out summary of questions, references, concept inventories, and next steps.

(We leave 10 minutes for scheduling flexibility.)

4. SAMPLE QUESTION

As an example of a CI item we might use, Figure 1 shows a question adapted from Karpierz and Wolfman [4], which exposes interesting student misconceptions surrounding binary search trees, balance, and heaps.

For this question, we might: (1) skip contextual information since the area of CS is well known, (2) show the question and ask everyone to respond to it on their clickers, (3) challenge the contestants to predict the most popular answer besides (e)[2], (4) reveal in succession the audience's response, the responses from student data, and then the contestants' answers, (5) award a point to successful contestants, and (6) give audience members time to reflect on the question.

[2]In our experience, experts often suspect a different "most popular distractor" from the one students chose.

5. EXPECTATIONS

Our primary audience is computing educators, particularly those who teach first- and second-year university-level CS courses, as most CI work focuses on these courses. We do **not** aim to give a complete overview of CI work; instead, we want to show high-impact examples that may make a difference in audience members' teaching approach directly and also encourage them to look further into the available research.

At the start of the session, we will distribute a handout to facilitate audience members' note-taking and reflection about the CI items we discuss. At the end of the session, we will distribute a handout with all the CI items and data presented in the session and literature references to the CI development work. Together, these handouts will make excellent starting points for audience members' further exploration.

6. SUITABILITY

A session like this would be difficult or impossible to accomplish in the other available formats. In particular, a paper or panel could summarize results on concept inventory work at this time but would not dramatize the misalignment of expert and novice perspectives as well as our direct, live format. (And would be rather dull in comparison.)

Conversely, getting substantial feedback from an audience of experts is a persistent problem in concept inventory development, and this session offers a mutually beneficial format giving researchers access to experts.

If successful, this format will also lend itself well to future presentations as concept inventory work in CS matures.

7. REFERENCES

[1] H. Danielsiek, W. Paul, and J. Vahrenhold. Detecting and understanding students' misconceptions related to algorithms and data structures. In *Proc. of the Tech. Symp. on CS Ed.*, pages 21–26, 2012.

[2] R. R. Hake. Interactive-engagement versus traditional methods: A six-thousand-student survey of mechanics test data for introductory physics courses. *American Journal of Physics*, 66(1):64–74, 1998.

[3] G. L. Herman. *The development of a digital logic concept inventory.* PhD thesis, UIUC, 2011.

[4] K. Karpierz and S. A. Wolfman. Misconceptions and concept inventory questions for binary search trees and hash tables. In *Proc. of the Tech. Symp. on CS Ed.*, pages 109–114, 2014.

[5] W. Paul and J. Vahrenhold. Hunting high and low: instruments to detect misconceptions related to algorithms and data structures. In *Proc. of the Tech. Symp. on CS Ed.*, pages 29–34, 2013.

[6] A. E. Tew and M. Guzdial. Developing a validated assessment of fundamental CS1 concepts. In *Proc. of the Tech. Symp. on CS Ed.*, pages 97–101, 2010.

[7] K. C. Webb and C. Taylor. Developing a pre- and post-course concept inventory to gauge operating systems learning. In *Proc. of the Tech. Symp. on CS Ed.*, pages 103–108, 2014.

Bringing Grades K-5 to the Mainstream of Computer Science Education

Katie Apone
Code.org
katie@code.org

Marina Bers
Tufts University
marina.bers@tufts.edu

Karen Brennan
Harvard University
karen_brennan@gse.harvard.edu

Diana Franklin
UC Santa Barbara
franklin@cs.ucsb.edu

Maya Israel
University of Illinois
misrael@illinois.edu

Pat Yongpradit
Code.org
pat@code.org

Categories and Subject Descriptors

K.3.2 [**Computers and Education**]: Computer and Information Science Education – *computer science education*

General Terms

Design, Experimentation, Human Factors

Keywords

Computer Science Education, K-5 Curriculum, Elementary School, Code.org, Scratch, ScratchJr, Outreach, Professional Development

1. SUMMARY

As awareness of computer science education grows in the general public, it is important to showcase computer science education as accessible for all grades K-12 and beyond. As panelists present the projects and research they've been conducting, we will highlight three overarching topics:

- The importance of K-5 computer science education to educators of all grade levels,
- Thoughts on why K-5 has traditionally been less prominent in the computer science education landscape, and
- Strategies on how we, the computer science education community, can promote K-5 computer science education as worthwhile as 6-12+ computer science education.

Barriers to why K-5 computer science education is not as prominent as that in grades 6-12, such as scarcity of wide-spread curriculum or scarcity of research, will lead to panelists presenting how their work is rectifying this imbalance. This session's panelists are pioneers and important thought leaders in the K-5 computer science education field. Panelists in this session are either producing research in the K-5 computer science education field or working at a large scale to promote or increase participation of K-5 students in computer science.

SIGCSE '15, Mar 04-07 2015, Kansas City, MO, USA.
ACM 978-1-4503-2966-8/15/03.
http://dx.doi.org/10.1145/2676723.2677332

2. Code.org's commitment to K-5 (Katie Apone)

On September 5, 2014, Code.org launched three new computer science courses for K-5 students. Code.org's vision is that every student in every K-12 public school have the opportunity to learn computer science. Part of Code.org's mission is to broaden participation of women and underrepresented students of color, and early exposure to computer science education has been identified as an important factor for female students who go on to choose computer science as a career [1]. Not only does Code.org create curriculum for grades K-5, but it actively promotes and encourages the integration of computer science in elementary school by offering free professional development opportunities around the nation.

Katie Apone is the K-8 Program Manager at Code.org.

3. Tufts University (Marina Bers)

Marina Bers heads the interdisciplinary Developmental Technologies research group. Her research involves the design and study of innovative learning technologies to promote children's positive development. She co-developed the ScratchJr programming language in collaboration with Mitch Resnick from the MIT Media Lab and Paula Bonta, from the PICO company. ScratchJr is a free app funded by the National Science Foundation, the Code to Learn Foundation and a very successful Kickstarter campaign.

Marina Umaschi Bers is a professor at the Eliot-Pearson Department of Child Development and an adjunct professor in the Computer Science Department at Tufts University.

4. Harvard Graduate School of Education (Karen Brennan)

Given the centrality of computing in modern life, everyone should have access to computer science education—and that learning should not be delayed to high school or college. Computer programming can serve as a compelling introduction, enabling the exploration of computer science concepts in a grounded, personally meaningful context. To support this exploration in the K-5 classroom (and beyond), the ScratchEd Team at Harvard has been developing a model of professional learning for teachers working with the Scratch programming environment. The model—which includes an online community, face-to-face gatherings, and curriculum—has enabled tens of thousands of teachers to work with Scratch [2]. Karen Brennan will share some of the challenges unique to bringing programming to the K-5 classroom.

Karen Brennan is an Assistant Professor of Education at Harvard University. She directs the ScratchEd project.

5. University of California, Santa Barbara (Diana Franklin)

Computing is becoming ubiquitous, and the next generation needs to have a new level of fluency with computational thinking in order to become innovators. Elementary school is a critical time to expose, engage, and excite all students about computing. To support this, our team is investigating two important questions. First, how do elementary school students with a variety of backgrounds learn computing concepts? Second, what environment (language, curriculum, tools) are needed to make computing successful for a broad cross-section of classrooms. Diana Franklin will share some of the successes and challenges in bringing block-based visual language curricula to 4th-6th grade classrooms.

Diana Franklin is teaching faculty at the University of California at Santa Barbara. She and Danielle Harlow co-developed LaPlaya and KELP CS, a new tool and curriculum tailored to 4th-6th grade students.

6. University of Illinois at Urbana Champaign (Maya Israel)

There is a growing movement to integrate computing and computational thinking in K-5 instruction with an emphasis on including students with diverse learning needs including English language learners, students with disabilities, and students living in poverty. Despite this momentum, many teachers have either naïve or incorrect conceptions about how to teach computing, especially to students with limited computing experience or with academic challenges. Maya Israel will share findings from a year-long mixed methods study investigating how elementary school teachers with limited computer science experience in a high-need school integrated computational thinking into their instruction, with a focus on engaging with diverse learners. Data related to implementation structures, overcoming instructional barriers, and strategies for including diverse learners will be presented.

Maya Israel is an Assistant Professor of Special Education at the University of Illinois, Urbana Champaign. She heads the computing research initiative within the Office of Mathematics, Science, and Technology Education (MSTE).

7. Code.org (Pat Yongpradit, Moderator)

As a national voice on K-12 computer science education, Pat Yongpradit's knowledge of the landscape allows him to facilitate a meaningful discussion among panelists. Throughout his career as a high school computer science teacher, he inspired students through authentic, project-based learning experiences, and implemented initiatives to broaden participation in computer science among underrepresented groups.

Pat Yongpradit is Director of Education at Code.org.

8. Intended Audience

This special session is designed for all educators interested in broadening participation in computer science teaching, including elementary school educators. Educators of all grade levels can benefit from promoting K-5 computer science education, as it builds a pathway of students to continue learning computer science throughout their educational careers.

9. REFERENCES

[1] "Women Who Choose Computer Science—What Really Matters," Google Corp. May 26, 2014, http://static.googleusercontent.com/media/www.google.com/en/us/edu/pdf/women-who-choose-what-really.pdf

[2] Brennan, K. (2013). Learning computing through creating and connecting. *IEEE Computer, Special Issue: Computing in Education.* doi:10.1109/MC.2013.229

Nifty Assignments

Nick Parlante, Julie Zelenski
(moderators)
Stanford University
nick.parlante@cs.stanford.edu
zelenski@cs.stanford.edu

Peter-Michael Osera
University of Pennsylvania
posera@cis.upenn.edu

Marty Stepp
Stanford University
stepp@cs.stanford.edu

Mark Sherriff
Luther Tychonievich
Ryan Layer
University of Virginia
(mark) sherriff@virginia.edu
(luther) lat7h@virginia.edu
(ryan) rl6sf@virginia.edu

Suzanne J. Matthews
United States Military Academy
suzanne.matthews@usma.edu

Allison Obourn
University of Washington
aeobourn@cs.washington.edu

David R Raymond
United States Military Academy
david.raymond@usma.edu

Josh Hug
University of California, Berkeley
hug@cs.berkeley.edu

Stuart Reges
University of Washington
reges@uw.edu

Categories and Subject Descriptors
K.3.0 [**Computers and Education**]: General

General Terms
Algorithms, Design, Languages

Keywords
Education; assignments; homeworks; examples; repository; library; nifty; pedagogy

Abstract
A great CS assignment is a delight to all, but the path to one can be most roundabout. Many CS students have had their characters built up on assignments that worked better as an idea than as an actual assignment. Assignments are hard to come up with, yet they are the key to student learning. The Nifty Assignments special session is all about promoting and sharing the ideas and ready-to-use materials of successful assignments.

Each presenter will introduce their assignment, give a quick demo, and describe its niche in the curriculum and its strengths and weaknesses. The presentations (and the descriptions below) merely introduce each assignment. A key part of Nifty Assignments is the mundane but vital role of distributing the materials – handouts, data files, starter code – that make each assignment ready to adopt. The Nifty Assignments home page, **http://nifty.stanford.edu**, gathers all the assignments and makes them and their support materials freely available.

If you have an assignment that works well and would be of interest to the CSE community, please consider applying to present at Nifty Assignments. See the nifty.stanford.edu home page for more information.

SIGCSE '15, March 4-7, 2015, Kansas City, MO, USA.
ACM 978-1-4503-2966-8/15/03.
http://dx.doi.org/10.1145/2676723.2677327

Counting Squares (CS0/CS1) - Mark Sherriff, Luther Tychonievich, and Ryan Layer

This intro assignment is used to help introductory students think about the process of creating a basic algorithm, with a particular emphasis on generality and efficiency. Students try to think of different ways for a robot to count all the squares on a grid using a very basic set of commands. Code is provided in both Python and Java to allow them to test out their solutions; we have also had success using it "unplugged" on paper. We have found that this assignment is a great introduction to computer science and programming in general. It's a relatively easy problem to start with if you consider a square grid, but the complexity can quickly escalate as the students compete for the fastest solution (efficiency) while considering grids with missing squares or irregular shapes (generality). This assignment can be used as a quick glimpse into AI for early classes as well. Counting Squares has been used with great success with both our introductory course as a lab session and as a group activity in lecture. We have also used it with middle school students in a camp setting.

Speed Reader (CS1) - Peter-Michael Osera

Many people, students especially, wish they could read faster. In addition to the various speed reading courses out there today, we can employ software to help us learn to read faster. Most of these programs employ Rapid Serial Visual Presentation (RSVP) to help you focus your eyes and eliminate sub-vocalization, allowing you to read at more than twice the rate of the average person. However, are these programs truly effective? Are we able to read at this rate and still comprehend what we are reading?

Luckily, speed readers are simple programs that we can have our students implement in a CS1 course and run experiments over to see for themselves! In this assignment, students build a prototype speed reader that reads in plain text files and displays them in the RSVP style. They are then charged to run small usability studies on their friends and families to determine if RSVP is effective.

The speed reader program has highly flexible requirements. At its core, students practice the basics of file IO, string tokenization, and animation. Depending on the instructor's preference, students can implement a curses-style console-based speed reader or a fancier speed reader in a GUI. The assignment is also extensible in many ways to give it as much depth as the instructor desires.

Geo Location (CS1) - Stuart Reges

This assignment involves writing a simple class that is a variation of another class. The CS education community has struggled to find simple class examples that don't seem contrived or confusing. The most successful examples involve some form of scaffolding where the instructor provides a lot of supporting code. This assignment also involves scaffolding, but the interface is very simple. The code calls a method that accesses the Google Maps API to get information about a location given its coordinates (latitude and longitude).

Students are shown the implementation of a GeoLocation class that keeps track of information about a location. Students intuitively understand that a location involves two pieces of information: a latitude and a longitude. It also has the nice property that these values are often expressed in two different ways: as three integers (hours, minutes, seconds) and as a single real number, which means that it makes sense to have two different constructors. It also has a nontrivial bit of behavior that you would not want to make others implement. Instead of something like the boring but classic Fahrenheit to Centigrade conversion, this class includes a method that finds the distance between two locations on Earth, which is not a simple calculation.

In the assignment, students first practice being a client of the GeoLocation class and then they write a variation of the class that keeps track of additional information about the location (it's name, address, and associated tags). Our observation is that students make many classic mistakes as they learn about objects in this assignment. For example, instead of storing their own GeoLocation object that computes the distance between two locations, they often copy the code from the GeoLocation class. That kind of confusion is useful to clear up early so that we can point out that one object often delgates some task to another object to complete.

The nifty part is the ability to access the Google Maps API. This makes the assignment more compelling. It also allows for many extensions to the basic assignment. For example, we wanted to have a large amount of data of places of interest near the University of Washington. This wasn't easy to get directly from Google, so we created our own through crowdsourcing. Each student submitted entries for a massive data file that we compiled.

Packet Sniffing in Python (CS1) – Suzanne J. Matthews and David R. Raymond

This lab highlights the real-world dangers of packet-sniffing by enabling students to analyze a packet capture (PCAP) file using the Scapy package in Python. After a quick overview on how information is transferred on wired and wireless networks, we discuss the ethics and legality of packet sniffing unsecured wireless networks (like those at coffee shops, airports, and hotels). During the main portion of the lab, students write Python code to extract and inspect packets contained in a PCAP file purportedly collected from four individuals surfing the web using a coffee shop's unsecured wireless network. The PCAP file is in fact artificial; it was created on our sandboxed networks. The end goal is for students to collect as much information as possible (e.g. names, e-mail addresses, passwords, occupations, e-mail contents) about the individuals at the coffee shop. Most students are shocked that they can read other people's e-mails and learn what websites they visited. The exercise quickly underscores the need for packet encryption, and promotes discussion on how students can best protect themselves. The lab can easily be tailored as a homework assignment or project. We assume students have covered the basics of sequence, selection and iteration in the Python language, and are knowledgeable about Python lists and dictionaries.

Melody Player (CS1/CS2) - Allison Obourn and Marty Stepp

This assignment involves writing a class to play music. Students are given files containing the notes of songs in a simple text format. Part of what makes the data interesting is that most songs have repeated sections commonly called a refrain or chorus. Students implement a class to store notes and rests in a song. Repeated sections must be represented without duplication. They write methods to perform various operations such as playing the song, changing its octave/pitch or tempo, reversing it, etc. Students are given a library for playing individual tones. They can be provided a UI or can write it themselves.

We have given this assignment using arrays/lists and using stacks/queues, so it can fit in mid/late CS1 or early CS2. The assignment is extensible and makes it simple to adjust the list of operations that the students will implement; for example, advanced students may implement playback from a given time index.

The data is interesting without being "big" data, so it is simple to visualize and debug. Students understand the data and understand what they are expected to do, while getting good practice of linear data structures. Also, students often like multimedia content, but many of such assignments focus on graphics. It's fun to hear the songs play and to perform manipulations on familiar melodies. Students also enjoy writing their own custom songs.

Seam Carving: A Content Aware Image Resizing Algorithm (CS2) - Josh Hug

Given an image, it is sometimes desirable to scale that image in only one dimension, for example when moving from a 16:9 aspect ratio to a 4:3 aspect ratio. The easiest approach is to simply crop the image, or with a bit more work, to rescale the image. However these approaches either remove image content or make everything in the image look skinnier or fatter than it should.

Seam carving is a simple and elegant image resizing technique published in 2007 by Shai Avidan and Ariel Shamir that avoids these flaws by rescaling in a content-aware manner. Specifically, seam carving reduces the size of an image by one pixel of height (or with) at a time by removing 'seams', which are contiguous paths of pixels with minimum total energy.

Despite being a relatively new published result, the algorithm is simple to explain and implement, and the quality of the results can be quite impressive for the right kinds of images. Furthermore, when applied to the wrong sorts of images (like the student's own faces), the results can be both horrifying and hilarious.

The assignment can be cast as a difficult challenge involving nested for loops over a two dimensional array, as an example of dynamic programming, or as a graph traversal problem on a directed acyclic graph. There are also opportunities for exploration, including finding ways to expand the size of images, remove specific regions of images, and more.

POSTER SESSION I

Factors Affecting High School Student Engagement in Introductory Computer Science Classes

Sarah J. Wille, *University of Chicago*
Dae Kim, *University of Chicago*
Contact: swille@uchicago.edu

Little research exists on factors that affect high school computer science student engagement. The BASICS Study (Barriers and Supports to Implementing Computer Science) brings rigor to this issue by building on instruments developed to measure implementation and factors affecting implementation of math and science programs, and customizing them for use with Exploring Computer Science (ECS). One goal of the 2-½ year BASICS Study is to provide the computer science education community with tools to systematically and rigorously measure computer science program implementation components, like student engagement. Aligning efforts in computer science around data collection and description can support the collective effort to grow and sustain computing education.

This poster reports on BASICS Study Year 1 findings about factors related to student engagement in ECS classes. The sample includes 232 students from eight public high schools in Chicago and Washington, DC. Student questionnaire data collected focused on: 1) Student engagement, 2) Teacher instruction, 3) Student attitudes, and 4) Other student characteristics, such as grade, gender, race/ethnicity, and previous computing experience. Analyses included multi-factor confirmatory factor analysis to examine the validity of the measures, and multiple linear regression analysis to estimate the effects of teacher instruction and student attitudes on engagement. Results indicate teacher instruction significantly positively affects student engagement in ECS classes. Some student attitude variables are also significantly related to student engagement, but there was no significant variation in engagement across gender or race/ethnicity categories.

ACM Categories & Descriptors: K.3 Computers and Education; K3.2 Computer and Information Science Education

Keywords: K-12 Education; Student Engagement; Implementation; Supports and Barriers; Exploring Computer Science

DOI: http://dx.doi.org/10.1145/2676723.2691891

SIGCSE'15, March 4–7, 2015, Kansas City, MO, USA.
ACM 978-1-4503-2966-8/15/03.

Exploring Computer Science Course and Math Achievement

Daniel W. Lewis, *Santa Clara University*
Lisa Kohne, *SmartStart Evaluation & Research*
Timothy Mechlinski, *SmartStart Evaluation & Research*
Mariana Schmalstig, *SmartStart Evaluation & Research*
Contact: dlewis@scu.edu

This poster presents preliminary data in the field of computing education research, focusing on the relationship between high school student participation in Exploring Computer Science (ECS) and their achievement on the math portion of the California Standard Test (CST). The course uses an inquiry-based approach that is expected to improve students' problem solving skills. Students who enrolled in ECS at ten high schools in San Jose, California were monitored over a three-year period to investigate possible relationships between participation in ECS and scores on standardized math tests. Results show a statistically significant difference between ECS participants and their peers for two of three project years.

ACM Categories & Descriptors: K.3.2 [Computer and Information Science Education]: Computer Science Education

Keywords: Pre-college; high school; pre-AP; curricula; math

DOI: http://dx.doi.org/10.1145/2676723.2691895

Just Enough Programming for Eight-years Olds

Karen H. Jin, *University of New Hampshire*
Gavin Kearns, *Paul Elementary School*
Contact: jin@cs.unh.edu

Programmable robots have become a very popular tool to introduce children to technology. However, most curricula that emphasize on actual programming typically target kids10 years and older. This summer, the University of New Hampshire organized an Elementary Program Introducing Computing (EPIC) camp. Children 7-9 years old, with no prior programming experience, were introduced to problem solving and creative program design using Lego EV3 Mind-storms robotics. The program followed a just enough principle, such that just barely enough contents were presented to the children in spite of a wider range of available materials. For example, a simple robot model was prebuilt to help children focus on programming rather than construction; program control flow and sensor data processing were introduced early on, but only using a very limited set of visual programming blocks and sensors. These basic structure blocks provide enough functionality to construct a moderately complex program, and help students stay focused on problem solving in a non-overwhelming setting. In order to gauge the learning outcome, a test was given before and after the camp. The comparison of the results showed that our method helped the children retain the programming skills and knowledge of general concepts of computing.

ACM Categories & Descriptors: **K.3.2** Computer and Information Science Education

Keywords: Early Programming Instruction; Lego Mindstorms Robotics; K-12

DOI: http://dx.doi.org/10.1145/2676723.2691899

Moving Ahead with Computational Science Programs

Lori Carter, *Point Loma Nazarene University*
Tim Little, *Point Loma Nazarene University*
Claire Mathews, *Point Loma Nazarene University*
Contact: lcarter@pointloma.edu

The use of computation alongside the natural sciences is moving research forward at unprecedented rates. Computational scientists are in high demand, and the undergraduate level is a great place to begin training students for work in this area. Furthermore, studies have shown that applied programs such as computational science are attractive to students and aid in retention. Yet, the number of undergraduate computational science programs remains very limited. Throughout informal conversations with colleagues who were interested in combining computing and science, we repeatedly heard 2 reasons why a computational science program was missing from their institution: 1) they lacked counterparts in the natural sciences who were interested in working with them and 2) their department couldn't support the change in personnel or curriculum that they thought was required to introduce and maintain a computational science program. Addressing the first concern, this poster displays some of what was learned from interviews with 20 natural scientists regarding how they currently or might work with a computational counterpart. Our hope is that this information might be used in conversations with reluctant natural scientists. Addressing the second concern, this poster summarizes the content of computational science programs that currently exist for undergraduates, including majors, minors, computational tracks in science majors or science tracks in computational majors, and science or computational courses with complementary material. Our hope is that this summary will encourage colleagues that, given such variety, there is a place for some form of computational science at their institution.

ACM Categories & Descriptors: J.2 [Computer Applications]: Physical Sciences J.3 [Computer Applications]: Life and Medical Sciences. K.4.3 [Computing Mileux]: Computers and Society - Computer-supported collaborative work

Keywords: Computational Science; Computational Biology; Bioinformatics; Computational Chemistry; Computational Physics; Interdisciplinary Computing; Multidisciplinary Computing

DOI: http://dx.doi.org/10.1145/2676723.2691950

SIGCSE'15, March 4–7, 2015, Kansas City, MO, USA.
ACM 978-1-4503-2966-8/15/03.

Computing in the Classroom: A Workshop for Teachers to Infuse Computational Thinking into K-12 Classrooms

Yeşem Kurt-Peker, *Columbus State University*
Lydia Ray, *Columbus State University*
Rania Hodhod, *Columbus State University*
Shamim Khan, *Columbus State University*
Contact: peker_yesem@columbusstate.edu

Computational thinking is an essential skill for everyone in today's world. It is a problem solving skill that incorporates problem decomposition, patter recognition, abstraction, logical and algorithmic thinking. Yet the exposure of students in K-12 curriculum to computational thinking is minimal in most schools. There are various opportunities for computational thinking to be included in almost all content areas in the curriculum. In order for this to be realized, teachers need introduction to the concept of computational thinking and they need to be equipped with tools to provide practices in this concept in the classrooms. Inspired by this idea, we organized a workshop in June 2014 to involve all teachers from all grade levels and all disciplines where we introduced them to the concept of computational thinking and taught them tools such as Scratch, Google Sites, HTML, and AppInventor. The workshop attracted 34 teachers mostly from the Muscogee County School District in Georgia. In this poster we present our recruitment strategy, methodology of our workshop, and results from our pre and post surveys. In particular, we present the influence of our workshop on teachers' views of computational thinking. We also share highlights from the projects that the teachers worked on during the workshop and presented at the end.

ACM Categories & Descriptors: K.3.2 [Computer and Information Science Education], Curriculum

Keywords: Computational thinking; computing in K-12; computing workshop for teachers

DOI: http://dx.doi.org/10.1145/2676723.2691906

Using POGIL Activities to Teach CS Principles to Diverse Students

Helen H. Hu, *Westminster College*
Contact: hhu@westminstercollege.edu

As part of the new AAC&U TIDES initiative (TIDES: Teaching to Increase Diversity and Equity in STEM), Westminster College has created a new computer science course for non-majors and paired it with a biology course as a first-year Learning Community. The new CS0 course relies heavily on culturally sensitive POGIL activities to be welcoming of all students, shifting to a more equitable, multicultural approach to CS curriculum and instruction. Process Oriented Guided Inquiry Learning (POGIL) is a student-centered learning approach that 1) assigns students to work in self-managed *learning teams*, 2) on specially designed *guided inquiry* materials, 3) while the instructor facilitates the development of *process skills* [1]. By requiring students to derive CS concepts for themselves while working together in learning teams, POGIL activities allow diverse student voices to be heard. They also provide a framework for instructors to act as "guides on the side" rather than "sage on the stage" for a large portion of class time. These CS Principles POGIL activities are among the first POGIL activities in any discipline to be deliberately designed to be culturally sensitive. In Fall 2015, CS instructors at four partner institutions will adopt these POGIL activities in their CS0 courses.

ACM Categories & Descriptors: K.3.2 [Computers and Education] - Computer and Information Science Education - Computer science education, information systems education,

Keywords: Active Learning; Cooperative Learning; POGIL; Teams

DOI: http://dx.doi.org/10.1145/2676723.2691909

A Case Study on Adding Computer Science as a Math Graduation Elective: A Report from the Alabama CS/Mathematics Crosswalk Committee

Jeff Gray, *University of Alabama*
Mary Boehm, *A+ College Ready*
Carol Crawford, *A+ College Ready*
Jeff Baker, *Huntsville High School*
Gina McCarley, *Lawrence County High School*
Kitty Morgan, *A+ College Ready*
Kelley Rouze, *Montgomery County Schools*
Jill Westerlund, *Hoover High School*
Carol Yarbrough, *Alabama School of Fine Arts*
Contact: gray@cs.ua.edu

This poster describes our experience with the convening of a statewide committee of Mathematics and Computer Science teachers and content specialists to compare the content of the AP Computer Science A Course (AP CS A) and the Computer Science Principles (CSP) course with the Alabama Course of Study-Mathematics. The purpose of the comparison was to identify overlaps in content and to make recommendations to the State Department of Education and the State Board of Education regarding the option of awarding mathematics credit for completion of the Computer Science courses. This crosswalk activity led to the December 2013 decision by the Alabama State Department of Education (ALSDE) to count both CS Principles and CS A as courses satisfying the four-course requirement for high school graduation in Alabama. The poster will describe the crosswalk activity, the results, and the specific strategic approach to involve the ALSDE as collaborators in the activity.

ACM Categories & Descriptors: K.3.2 [**Computer and Information Science Education**]: Computer science education

Keywords: K-12 Graduation Elective; CS Principles; AP CS A

DOI: http://dx.doi.org/10.1145/2676723.2691915

SIGCSE'15, March 4–7, 2015, Kansas City, MO, USA.
ACM 978-1-4503-2966-8/15/03.

Creating New Languages in Blockly: Two Case Studies in Media Computation and Robotics

Jake Trower, *University of Alabama*
Jeff Gray, *University of Alabama*
Contact: gray@cs.ua.edu

Introducing programming concepts to children early in their education can be beneficial because the type of problem solving that encompasses computational thinking is becoming increasingly relevant in our daily lives. A relatively new breed of programming environments has emerged to address this need. Visual programming languages (VPLs) allow programming logic to be represented with diagrams that illustrate its execution flow. Popular VPLs (e.g., Scratch, Snap, Alice, App Inventor) exist as full-featured, stand-alone programming environments with diagrammatic representations of the program instructions. This representation removes the syntactical barrier to entry that may exist with textual languages.
Blockly, developed by Google, is a type of block language development kit that allows the rapid construction of new block-based visual programming languages to address a specific pedagogical or content focus. This poster provides a brief tutorial on the steps used to create a new Blockly environment, along with two case studies demonstrating the power of Blockly. The two environments introduced are focused on the manipulation of images via operations on pixels (Pixly), and programmatic control of a Sphero robot (Spherly). The construction and specific details of these two environments are described and illustrated with html, xml, and Javascript code examples and some of their potential applications. This project was supported in part by an NSF CE21 grant and a Google CS4HS award. More information about Pixly and Spherly can be found at: http://outreach.cs.ua.edu/pixly and http://outreach.cs.ua.edu/spherly

ACM Categories & Descriptors: D.3.2 [**Language Classifications**]: Very high-level languages

Keywords: Blockly; Media Computation; Robotics Programming

DOI: http://dx.doi.org/10.1145/2676723.2691871

Automating Software Engineering Best Practices Using an Open Source Continuous Integration Framework

Sarah Heckman, *North Carolina State University*
Jason King, *North Carolina State University*
Michael Winters, *North Carolina State University*
Contact: sarah_heckman@ncsu.edu

Ideally, software engineering courses should adequately reflect real-world software development so that students obtain a better understanding and experience with practices and techniques used in industry. *Our objective is to improve software engineering courses by incorporating best practices for automated software engineering and facilitating rapid feedback for students using an open source continuous integration framework for evaluating student software development.* The open source Jenkins Continuous Integration Server is the core of our framework, which provides a consistent environment for building student projects, executing automated test cases, calculating code coverage, executing static analysis, and generating reports for students. By using continuous integration, a common tool in real-world software development, we can incorporate software engineering best practices, introduce students to continuous integration in practice, and provide formative feedback to students throughout the software development lifecycle. We found that 76% or more of students in each of the classes that deploy our framework reported that using Jenkins increased their productivity, and that 84% or more of students in each of the classes reported that using Jenkins increased their code quality.

ACM Categories & Descriptors: K.3.1 [Computers and Education] Computer-assisted instruction (CAI)

Keywords: software engineering skills; continuous integration; automated evaluation and feedback

DOI: http://dx.doi.org/10.1145/2676723.2691921

A Bottom-Up Approach to Teaching Server-Side Web Development Skills

Ariel Ortiz, *Tecnológico de Monterrey, Campus Estado de México*
Contact: ariel.ortiz@itesm.mx

When dealing with the topic of back-end programming many CS web development courses typically focus on how to use a popular web framework, for example Spring MVC or Ruby on Rails. The problem with this approach is that students will most likely end up using some other different framework or technology if ever they decide to become professional web developers. Our students need to learn concepts and skills that serve as a foundation to learn whatever different technologies are used now or happen to appear in the future. This poster presents the author's experience on using a bottom-up approach to teach the fundamental aspects of how the HTTP protocol works, and how this knowledge can be used to get a deep understanding of the inner workings of the web by building a simple yet complete server-side web framework. Using Node.js as the development platform, students are able to take TCP sockets as the building blocks for higher-level web abstractions. This approach allows covering a variety of specific topics that are essential for a professional web developer: request and response structure and headers, HTTP methods, form processing, cookies and sessions, text encodings, MVC software architectural pattern, database integration using ORM (Object-Relational Mapping), REST (Representational State Transfer) architecture, security issues (HTTPS protocol, common web vulnerabilities), and client-side integration using AJAX (Asynchronous JavaScript and XML). Anecdotal evidence shows that students with this knowledge repertoire are better suited for learning, using and debugging new and existing web technologies.

ACM Categories & Descriptors: K.3.2 Computer and Information Science Education; C.2.4 Distributed Systems

Keywords: Web development; Server-side programming; JavaScript; Node.js

DOI: http://dx.doi.org/10.1145/2676723.2691922

SIGCSE'15, March 4–7, 2015, Kansas City, MO, USA.
ACM 978-1-4503-2966-8/15/03.

Teaching Text-based Programming in a Blocks-based World

David Weintrop, *Northwestern University*
Uri Wilensky, *Northwestern University*
Jennifer Rosceo, *Lane Tech College Prep*
Daniel Law, *Lane Tech College Prep*
Contact: dweintrop@u.northwestern.edu

This poster presents an environment and set of pedagogical strategies designed to explore how best to use blocks-based programming tools to prepare learners for future, text-based programming languages. Starting with the snap! programming environment, we added the capability to view the JavaScript equivalent of any blocks-based script authored inside the environment. Additionally, when students define behaviors for new blocks, they do so in JavaScript. This makes it possible to compose blocks-based scripts alongside text-based JavaScript programs and have the two run side-by-side. This environment was used during the first 5-weeks of an introductory programming class at the high school level as part of a quasi-experimental study investigating the relationship between programming modality and emerging student understanding. Teachers of the course used the blocks/text hybrid features in various ways to support learners developing an understanding of programming concepts and laying the foundation for future text-based instruction. These strategies included having students compose programs with graphical blocks then view the equivalent JavaScript, prompting class discussion on similarities and differences between the two modalities; having students write pseudocode for their blocks-based programs before comparing the pseudocode to the JavaScript; and finally, having students implement their algorithm directly in JavaScript, using blocks as a resource to reference proper syntax.

ACM Categories & Descriptors: D.1.7 Visual Programming. K.3.2 Computer and Information Science Education

Keywords: Introductory Programming Environments; Blocks-based Programming; High School Computer Science

DOI: http://dx.doi.org/10.1145/2676723.2691923

Summer Programming Boot Camp: A Strategy For Retaining Women In IT

Sonal Dekhane, *Georgia Gwinnett College*
Kristine Nagel, *Georgia Gwinnett College*
Nannette Napier, *Georgia Gwinnett College*
Contact: sdekhane@ggc.edu

This project addresses the issue of retaining women in Information Technology (IT) at an open access institution. To meet the goal of retention, we focused on supporting students' learning and mentoring needs. Female IT majors and minors were recruited and participated in a weeklong summer boot camp. At the boot camp they participated in Java programming sessions, various professional development and peer mentoring sessions and a field trip. These activities were aimed to increase not only the participants' knowledge of programming, but they were also designed to increase the participants' confidence, their knowledge of IT careers and fields of research and most importantly to form a community of support. Initial data collection shows that 61% of participants enrolled in a programming course following the boot camp, which is a crucial step in retention of majors and minors. Authors have also experienced an increase in the participants' engagement in an on-campus community building effort. Formal data analysis of pre and post surveys for evaluating changes in computing attitudes and engagement is currently being performed.

ACM Categories & Descriptors: K.3.0 [Computer and Education]: General

Keywords: summer boot camp; women in IT; retention

DOI: http://dx.doi.org/10.1145/2676723.2691924

Evaluating Scratch Programs to Assess Computational Thinking in a Science Lesson

Jennifer Albert, *North Carolina State University*
Barry Peddycord III, *North Carolina State University*
Tiffany Barnes, *North Carolina State University*
Contact: jennifer_albert@ncsu.edu

In this poster, we describe efforts to assess computational thinking activities that can be easily implemented in any science classroom. Studies have shown that a set of conditions must be met for computational thinking tools to be used in K-12 education and that when they are used, there is a wide spectrum in the level of computational thinking that the tool enables. This study extends this work by examining how middle school students translated their science fair projects into Scratch and what evidence of computational thinking is present. Scrape, a tool designed to analyze Scratch projects was used. Overall, it was found that most students simply created a presentation of their project without much complexity. Eight students created interactive projects that required user participation and used more advanced computational concepts. Finally, recommendations are given for next steps in the creation of a series of activities that would scaffold student learning as they apply to computational thinking concepts of a science concept.

ACM Categories & Descriptors: K.3.2 [**Computing Milieux**]: Computers and Education – *Computer Use in Education*

Keywords: Computational Thinking; Computational Science; Next Generation Science Standards; Middle School Computer Education

DOI: http://dx.doi.org/10.1145/2676723.2691928

Integrating Cutting Edge Devices to Increase Student Retention in Programming

Evelyn Brannock, *Georgia Gwinnett College*
Robert Lutz, *Georgia Gwinnett College*
Mai Yin Tsoi, *Georgia Gwinnett College*
Contact: mtsoi@ggc.edu

Literature has estimated that about 33% of students who start a computer science degree program eventually drop or fail their first programming course. With the decreasing number of college graduates entering the computing industry, the workforce is missing out on the wealth and breadth of innate student ability and skills that are switching to non-STEM fields. This project developed, implemented and researched the effects of an innovative instructional strategy that integrated cutting-edge devices into an intermediate programming curriculum. Assignments were designed with the Java Software Ddevelopment Kkit for Java to strengthen student motivation and engagement by tapping into their creativity, collaborative skills, and critical thinking by using the InterAxon Muse, Oculus Rift, and the LeapMotion devices. Preliminary data indicates that although students may have enough motivation and interest in programming to persevere through the course, the implementation of this teaching methodology positively impacted their views and beliefs about programming skills and their relevance to their education. As well, survey data shows that student self-efficacy increased immediately after this educational intervention. Finally, instructor reflections point to a general shift in class morale and engagement with the inclusion of the assignments where students were required to solve problems without documentation. Future implications are also presented in this poster.

SIGCSE'15, March 4–7, 2015, Kansas City, MO, USA.
ACM 978-1-4503-2966-8/15/03.

ACM Categories & Descriptors: K.3.2 [Computer and Information Science Education]: Computer Science Education; B.4.2 Input/Output Devices

Keywords: Active Learning Model; Programming Instruction; Cutting Edge Devices; Retention; Motivation; Self-Efficacy; College Instruction

DOI: http://dx.doi.org/10.1145/2676723.2691929

E-Assess: A Web-Based Tool for Coordinating and Managing Program Assesment

Jean H. French, *Coastal Carolina University*
D. Brian Larkins, *Coastal Carolina University*
Contact: jennis@coastal.edu

This poster describes the operation and implementation of the E-Assess web-based program assessment tool. The E-Assess tool provides a centralized management system for generalized program assessment and has been used to support ABET program assessment within the CS/IS department at Coastal Carolina University for the past two years. This system defines multiple roles for several different assessment activities -- allowing individual faculty to operate independently, yet still providing an always up-to-date view of the process to assessment coordinators. Coordinators provide mappings between overall program objectives and specific measurement points across the curriculum. At the conclusion of a class, the instructor enters the assessment measures specific to the course. When all course data has been added, the E-Assess system automatically compiles the overall assessment data into summary reports that are used to evaluate program progress and to inform the continuous improvement process.

ACM Categories & Descriptors: K.3.2 Computer and Information Science Education

Keywords: assessment; web-based tools; ABET; accreditation management

DOI : http://dx.doi.org10.1145/2676723.2691930

CS2013 Assessment Exam

E. Kent Palmer, *MacMurray College*
Terry Linkletter, *Central Washington University*
Paulette Alexander, *University of North Alabama*
Patricia L. Roden, *University of North Alabama*
Kewal Dhariwal, *Institute for Certification of Computing Professionals*
Indira R. Guzman, *Trident University International*
James McGuffee, *Northern Kentucky University*
Contact: kent.palmer@mac.edu

In the Fall of 2013, the Institute for Certification of Computing Professionals (ICCP) appointed the authors of this paper to the CS2013 Assessment Council. This council created a standardized exam to assess computer programs and identify areas of the curriculum that a school needed to strengthen to meet *CS2013: Curriculum Guidelines for Undergraduate Degree Programs in Computer Science.* The existing Major Field Test for Computer Science from Educational Testing Service does not provide schools with sufficient guidance to determine what aspects of their computer programs are strong and what aspects need to be strengthened to meet the CS 2013 guidelines. The ICCP exam covers the Core Tier 1 Knowledge Units (KU). CS 2013 indicates that all computer programs should teach these KUs. The ICCP exam selects questions in proportion to the number of hours the CS2013 guidelines indicate are necessary to teach the Core Tier 1 learning objectives for a KU. Choices for multiple choice questions were limited to three per question, since research indicated that student mastery of topics could be assessed more rapidly with fewer distractors without reducing reliability. The exam was alpha tested in 2014 and beta tested in January and February 2015. The exam will be available in Spring of 2015.

ACM Categories & Descriptors: K.3.2 [Computer and Information Science Education]: Curriculum

Keywords: CS2013; assessment; standardized exam; computer science curriculum

DOI: http://dx.doi.org/10.1145/2676723.2691931

Case Studies of Use: Creating Counselor Champions for Change in K12 Computing Education

Sarah Hug, *University of Colorado,Boulder*
Jane Krauss, *NCWIT*
Catherine Ashcraft, *NCWIT*
Contact: hug@colorado.edu

Counselors for Computing leverages the National Center for Women & Information Technology (NCWIT)'s organizational membership, applies evidence-based approaches for professional development, and monitors and adjusts practices to make inroads into CS education through K12 counselor engagement. This engagement is needed to assure more girls and other underrepresented people are prepared for careers in computing. Colleges and universities, businesses, youth-serving organizations, computer science educators, professional counselor associations and others work to bring C4C to places where reform is underway (e.g., CS Principles, CS10K, Exploring Computer Science initiatives). These new education and teaching initiatives have implications for K12 student computer science guidance, and C4C materials can provide the knowledge necessary to promote counselor and educator engagement with computing. In this poster presentation, the authors: a) illustrate how computer science educators have partnered with NCWIT and incorporated counselor education into multiple elements of their own work, b) direct K12 computer science educators and stakeholders to free resources developed for C4C, c) provide initial evidence of the program's effectiveness, and d) develop future partnerships with poster viewers at SIGCSE 2015 to educate K12 counselors about the opportunities available for their students in the computing fields.

ACM Categories & Descriptors: K.3.2 Computer and Information Science Education

Keywords: computer science education policy, K12 counselors

DOI: http://dx.doi.org/10.1145/2676723.2691932

A Qualitative Analysis of Students' Difficulties with the Quicksort Algorithm Using Arrays

Amit Maor, *Harvey Mudd College & Claremont McKenna College*
Contact: amaor16@cmc.edu

Undergraduate computer science students can have difficulty understanding quicksort and other divide-and-conquer sorting algorithms. It is important to understand how students think about quicksort in order to find out how to better teach the students, and also for those students to be able to write and analyze these algorithms for their own use. Data was collected from two interviews, each about an hour long, with undergraduate computer science students. The data was then qualitatively analyzed in order to draw conclusions on how the students approached the coding of the quicksort algorithm. Both interview participants were able to quickly and efficiently write quicksort using linked lists. However, both students struggled when asked to rewrite their algorithms using static arrays. From the transcripts and hand-written notes taken from the two interviews, it seems plausible that their issues stem from challenges with their treatment of the pivot in the array implementation. Additionally, the array implementation may have caused the participants to change the visualization of the algorithm to which they had grown accustomed, further accentuating their difficulties. While both students showed obvious proficiency with the linked-list algorithm, they failed to realize key intuitions when attempting to make their algorithms space-efficient by using a single array. Future work may include analysis of other divide-and-conquer algorithms, as well as a closer look into how visualizations of sorting algorithms affect student understanding.

ACM Categories & Descriptors: K.3.2 [Computers and Education]: Computer and Information Science Education – computer science education

SIGCSE'15, March 4–7, 2015, Kansas City, MO, USA.
ACM 978-1-4503-2966-8/15/03.

Keywords: Divide-and-conquer algorithms; Quicksort; Arrays; Linked Lists

DOI: http://dx.doi.org/10.1145/2676723.2691933

STEM Careers Infographic Project (SCIP): Teaching Media-Based Computational Thinking Practices

Brittany Ann Kos, *University of Colorado Boulder*
Elizabeth Sims, *St. Vrain Valley School District*
Contact: brittany.kos@colorado.edu

The STEM Career Infographic Project (SCIP) was a 4-week exploratory project deployed in an 8th grade classroom at Mountain Vista Middle School (MVMS). SCIP was poised to address the growing focus on STEM fields at MVMS and within the school district. We piloted SCIP in Spring 2014 with six science classes or about 180 students. SCIP allowed for students to explore their own STEM interests, while simultaneously engaging in the 6 Computational Thinking Practices (CTP) outlined by the College Board.

Students were required to research a STEM career in-depth, then report on their careers using infographics (CTP #2: Creating Computational Artifacts and CTP #3: Abstracting). We used free and online programs to create the infographics; this provided the students the opportunity to learn software they were not previously exposed to and to explore new communication tools (CTP #1: Connecting Computing and CTP #2: Analyzing Problems and Artifacts). SCIP also provided many occasions for the students to work together by sharing career information or helping each other with the software (CTP #6: Collaborating). At the end of the project the students presented their infographics in front of the class and taught their classmates about their career (CTP #5: Communicating).

The project was incredibly successful. The students had a positive affect through the duration of the project and many also expressed an extreme level of interest in doing similar projects in the future. We will be repeating this project in Spring 2015, with a few adaptations and formal evaluation scheme.

ACM Categories & Descriptors: K.3.2 [Computer and Information Science Education]: Computer Science Education

Keywords: infographics; computational thinking; media-based computing; middle school education; STEM education; computing education

DOI: http://dx.doi.org/10.1145/2676723.2691934

Algorithmic Thinking: Program that Solve Well-defined Visual Problems

Elodie Fourquet, *Colgate University*
Contact: efourquet@colgate.edu

In early 2014 I created and taught an introductory CS course for non-CS students at Mount Holyoke College. I chose to emphasize algorithmic thinking as a way of solving problems on and off the computer, so I needed concrete and appealing problems for the students to solve. Having the students create their own problems was my way of doing so.

Based on a one week introduction to visual design, each student designed the image or animation that they would later program. As they did so outside class, the students and I collaborated in class solving the problems of implementing a design I had chosen: solving design problems of their own overlapped with algorithmic solution of implementation problems in class. Subsequently, they applied the classroom lessons to their own designs. The result was a collection of programmed images and animations the students were eager to show their families and friends.

The dual nature of their practice appealed to the students: they were motivated to do the course-work; they took ownership of their work and of skills they acquired; they formed a cohesive community working together in the lab. Modeling on the classroom work in which they participated was effective in building programming skills. Most important several students expressed unprompted interest in taking a follow-on course.

ACM Categories & Descriptors: K.3.2 [Computers and Education]: Computer and Information Science Education-computer science education.

Keywords: CS0; computer science; education; pedagogy; problem solving; algorithmic thinking; visual art; Processing

DOI: http://dx.doi.org/10.1145/2676723.2691935

Culturally Responsive Computing: An In-depth Examination of Outcomes in COMPUGIRLS

Catherine Ashcraft, *National Center for Women & IT*
Contact: catherine.ashcraft@ncwit.org

Girls and women continue to be underrepresented in computing, and this results in costly consequences for U.S. innovation and productivity; it also reproduces existing socioeconomic inequities, especially for women of color. This poster session will provide an in-depth look into Compugirls, a culturally responsive technology enrichment program for girls in under-resourced districts. The program ultimately enables girls to design technologies to address social inequities and foster social justice. Girls participate in three courses over the course of a year: 1) learning to use technologies such as iMovie, GarageBand, and iPhoto, 2) designing games with SCRATCH, and 3) programming "builds" in a virtual world environment. Throughout all three courses, the girls engage in a research project that connects the technologies they are learning to social justice issues they choose to address in their communities. The poster will also present findings from our three-year, NSF supported mixed-method study of the program. In particular, the session will illustrate how the girls developed their identities and abilities as technosocial change agents. The session also identifies conditions that, at times, limited the power of these possibilities and will report on key "lessons learned" in developing large-scale, sustainable computing programs.

ACM Categories & Descriptors: K.3.2 Computer and Information Science Education --- curriculum

Keywords: Gender and Computing; Broadening Participation in

Computing; Diversity; K-12 Education

DOI: http://dx.doi.org/10.1145/2676723.2691936

Students' (Mis)Understanding of Dictionaries

Emily Stansbury, *Harvey Mudd College*
Contact: estansbury@hmc.edu

This research found that some students conflate Python lists and dictionaries. This confusion could result from the visual similarity between the data-structures in Python print output. The goal of this research was to identify student's misconceptions about Python dictionaries. The data was collected in one-on-one, think-aloud interviews with two participants. When coding, one student treated her dictionary as if it were a literal list of two-element lists and could be accessed as such. Additionally, when asked to draw a visualization of dictionaries, she drew a representation that was identical to Python print output. It is likely that the output she is used to dealing with has shaped this visualization. This may be an example of negative transfer, where people transfer knowledge to a new setting and form an incorrect model. Based upon this research, educators should consider how print output can shape incorrect mental models, as well as emphasize the differences between lists and dictionaries.

ACM Categories & Descriptors: K.3.2 [Computers and Education]: Computer and Information Science Education – *computer science education.*

Keywords: mental models; misconceptions; Python; list; dictionary; hash tables

DOI: http://dx.doi.org/10.1145/2676723.2691937

It's Not Just About Functionality Anymore: Expanding Student Projects with Web Ecosystems

Samuel A. Rebelsky, *Grinnell College*
Contact: rebelsky@grinnell.edu

Student projects play a central role in the CS curriculum and are can be used everywhere, from low-level courses to upper-level capstones. Projects help students tie together ideas from their courses and put them in a "tangible" form for which they can feel a sense of pride. Projects also provide a clear way for students to show off their work to others. When we talk about student projects, we often focus on the functionality of the project: "Build something that does *this*."

The modern Web suggests that software (or at least Web-based software) is often defined by more than a core computational task; in addition to the core functionality, modern Web software situates that core functionality in a broader "ecosystem" that often includes a community of users that share ideas and comment on each other's work; ways to link the software to and from social media sites, such as Facebook and Twitter; analytic tools to understand how people use the software; and more.

I report on an experiment in which I asked students to expand their Web software project (an online drawing application) into a broader ecosystem. The extension from core functionality to broader ecosystem helped students think about different issues in computing, encouraged students to find aspects that most interested them (e.g., some liked analytics, some liked building the functionality, some liked thinking about how to create communities, and some liked designing and testing the interface), and made students think more carefully about their responsibilities as software builders.

ACM Categories & Descriptors: K.3.2 [Computers and Education]: Computer and Information Science Education– *Computer Science Education*

Keywords: Web ecosystems; Social media; Project-based courses; Web communities

DOI: http://dx.doi.org/10.1145/2676723.2691942

"Maker Innovators": A Workshop for Youth Creating Responsive and Wearable Game Interfaces with Tangible and Digital Construction Toolkits

Gabriela T. Richard, *University of Pennsylvania*
Yasmin B. Kafai, *University of Pennsylvania*
Contact: gric@upenn.edu, kafai@upenn.edu

We describe a workshop for high school youth to create interactive responsive and wearable interfaces for computing and gaming. The tools used in the workshop included tangible construction toolkits (the *Lilypad Arduino* and the *MaKeyMaKey*) and visual programming languages (*Scratch*, a coding and game design environment, and *ModKit*, a visual programming kit for Arduino devices and similar tangible kits) in addition to various conductive materials such as special fabric and aluminum foil. Past efforts with each of these toolkits have focused on interaction in one direction. This workshop focused on creating bidirectional tangible interfaces for gaming, meaning that interaction would happen on the screen and in the physical artifact or controller simultaneously. A further feature was the focus on creating wearable games. Thirteen student's ages 13-15 years participated in the eight-session workshop. After learning the tools during the first four sessions, they started designing their own projects. Student teams created one bidirectional game with a textile interface, three inventive uni-directional wearable games and interfaces, and one half-completed design. Students felt that the workshop provided them with multiple entry points to computing, by capitalizing on different skill sets, and many expressed understanding bidirectional design, though they felt they needed more time. This poster will discuss the affordances and constraints of the workshop activities and toolkits, and how projects created relate to the students' understanding of tangible computing with different kinds of responsiveness. Finally, we offer recommendations for future workshops based on our own redesign of activities. ***Handouts will be given.***

Categories and Subject Descriptors
H.5.2 User Interfaces; K.3.2. Computer and Information Science Education – *computer science education, curriculum, information systems education, literacy*

SIGCSE'15, March 4–7, 2015, Kansas City, MO, USA.
ACM 978-1-4503-2966-8/15/03.

Keywords: wearable computing; tangible computing; game design; collaborative learning; youth informal learning

DOI: http://dx.doi.org/10.1145/2676723.2691943

Using Big Data and BKT to Evaluate Course Resources

Zachary MacHardy, *University of California Berkeley*
Daniel D. Garcia, *University of California Berkeley*
Contact: zmmzchar@cs.berkeley.edu

Now finding footing in objective research methodology, MOOCs have made significant strides toward developing into mature platforms for not only offering educational materials but also performing exploratory analysis of educational methods. Bayesian Knowledge Tracing (BKT) has been repeatedly shown to be successful at providing an accurate model of student knowledge in more traditional classroom settings, and recent research has explored the application of BKT to MOOCs with promising results. Using data from several MOOCs run by Stanford university, we propose to extend earlier research into the application of BKT to MOOCS by developing a framework within which the use of course resources and student performance can be leveraged both to increase the predictive accuracy of BKT modeling and to provide an evaluative metric for the utility of those resources. We hope that such a framework can contribute not only to MOOC courses, but traditional classrooms as well.

ACM Categories & Descriptors: K.3.1 Computer-assisted instruction (CAI)

Keywords: BKT; Course Resources; MOOCs; Student Modeling; Prediction; Machine learning, BKT; Course Resources; MOOCs

DOI: http://dx.doi.org/10.1145/2676723.2691948

SIGCSE'15, March 4–7, 2015, Kansas City, MO, USA.
ACM 978-1-4503-2966-8/15/03.

POSTER SESSION II

Student Board-Writing to Integrate Communication Skills and Content to Enhance Student Learning

Mark E Hoffman, *Quinnipiac University*
Contact: mark.hoffman@quinnipiac.edu

Students frequently use a whiteboard to individually demonstrate understanding or interactively develop understanding in groups. The practice is employed to develop content knowledge; however, an opportunity to intentionally develop communication skills is overlooked. On the other hand, instructors carefully integrate instructional organization and communication to maximize student content learning. Taken together, this presents an opportunity for students to intentionally improve their communication skills in the service of content learning. This poster details a "work in progress" project where students follow organizational guidelines for written homework and board-writing to facilitate in-class, problem solution presentation. Problem solution presentations occur during one class period each week. Students are given colored pencils for written homework and colored markers for board-writing. Student work including written homework and board-writing was gathered from the 2013 and 2014 iterations of a sophomore-level computer architecture course. Preliminary analysis of student work shows that students either adopt the guidelines from the start or learn to use them through feedback and practice. On the semester-end survey, students report that adopting guidelines for written homework, board-writing, and color scheme improve presentation, and board-writing improves student learning. Future work includes gathering data from more students including recorded student presentations, developing quantitative scores to analyze student work, and developing measures of student learning.

ACM Categories & Descriptors: K.3.2 [**Computer and Education**]: Computer and Information Science Education - *Computer Science education*

Keywords: student board-writing; communication skills; content learning

DOI: http://dx.doi.org/10.1145/2676723.2691890

Correlating ACM Core IT Learning Outcomes with Associate Degree and Certificate Programs

Cara Tang, *Portland Community College*
Cindy S. Tucker, *Bluegrass Community and Technical College*
Elizabeth K. Hawthorne, *Union County College*
Contact: hawthorne@ucc.edu

As directed by the ACM Education Board, the ACM Committee for Computing Education in Community Colleges (CCECC) delivered the final version of its curricular guidance for associate-degree Information Technology (IT) programs. The guidance, An ACM Competency Model of Core Learning Outcomes and Assessment for Associate-Degree Curriculum in Information Technology, includes core IT learning outcomes with associated assessment metrics. Examples of degree and certificate programs that align with the ACM core IT learning outcomes are part of a growing repository at CAPspace.org. These correlations demonstrate the adaptability of this competency-based curriculum approach to a variety of computing courses, certificates, and degree programs. The CCECC invites institutions to highlight their IT degree and certificate programs by submitting correlations at capspace.org/correlation/ using an easy-to-use web form.

ACM Categories & Descriptors: K.3.2 [Computers and Education]: Computer and Information Science Education - Curriculum, Self-assessment

Keywords: Two-Year College; Community College; Education; Information Technology

DOI: http://dx.doi.org/10.1145/2676723.2691892

Madeup: A Language for Making Things Up

Chris Johnson, *University of Wisconsin, Eau Claire*
Peter Bui, *University of Wisconsin, Eau Claire*
Contact: johnch@uwec.edu

Madeup is a programming language for making things up. Its speakers walk paths through space to generate printable 3D models. The language is designed to teach computation from a tangible, first-person perspective and help students integrate computation back into the physical world. Madeup is inspired largely by Seymour Papert, whose goal was to provide learners objects to think with. Madeup joins a significant crowd of existing introductory teaching tools. What sets Madeup apart from many of these other projects is its physical product. The model that a programmer creates does not remain virtual. It can be printed, felt, carried in a pocket, and handed to a parent or friend—all of which may make computation more real and relevant in the eyes of the programmer. In this poster we demonstrate the language and how we have used it in outreach with local schools and libraries.

ACM Categories & Descriptors: K.3.2 [Computer and Information Science Education]: Computer science education

Keywords: 3D modeling; 3D printers; educational programming languages

DOI: http://dx.doi.org/10.1145/2676723.2691893

SIGCSE'15, March 4–7, 2015, Kansas City, MO, USA.
ACM 978-1-4503-2966-8/15/03.

Student Discovery of Network Security Ethics

Alisa Neeman, *University of Rio Grande & Rio Grande Community College*
Michael Snider, *University of Rio Grande & Rio Grande Community College*
Allen Hudson, *University of Rio Grande & Rio Grande Community College*
Contact: aneeman@rio.edu

In this poster we present a new approach to teaching ethics in a Network Security Programming course. Ethics is a crucial component of any network security course. As students learn to protect network services, they necessarily learn to attack network services, disguise their identities, et cetera. While a few colleges have gone as far as giving students background checks before teaching hacking skills, some simple new tactics can motivate students to employ their skills legally and ethically. These tactics lead students to discover what is ethical for themselves, rather than being told what is or is not ethical.

ACM Categories & Descriptors: K.7.4 [The Computing Profession]: Professional Ethics - *Codes of ethics;* C.2.0 [Computer-Communication Networks]: General—Security and Protection; K.3.2 [Computers and Education]: Computer and Information Science Education

Keywords: Ethics; Network Security; Education

DOI: http://dx.doi.org/10.1145/2676723.2691894

Extending SQL Auto-Grading to DML and DDL Statements

Carsten Kleiner, *University of Applied Sciences & Arts Hannover*
Felix Heine, *University of Applied Sciences & Arts Hannover*
Bastian Fischer, *University of Applied Sciences & Arts Hannover*
Contact: carsten.kleiner@hs-hannover.de

Automated assessment of computer programs submitted by students serves two main purposes: it may be used to increase grading efficiency and process optimization in large courses on one hand. On the other hand, if integrated properly into a suitable learning context, it may also improve student learning by supporting tutoring capabilities. Both aspects have been important in developing aSQLg, an automated grader for SQL statements ([1]). Unfortunately aSQLg so far only supports SQL queries. In order to provide a comprehensive efficiency and tutoring tool for SQL an extension to statements of the data manipulation (DML) and data definition language (DDL) is required. On this poster we present concepts for auto-grading of the most important DML and DDL statements as well as ideas on how to integrate those into the existing aSQLg grader.

SIGCSE'15, March 4–7, 2015, Kansas City, MO, USA.
ACM 978-1-4503-2966-8/15/03.

ACM Categories & Descriptors: K.3.2 Computer and Information Science Education: Information Systems Education; H.2.3 Languages: Data description languages (DDL); Data manipulation languages (DML); Query languages

Keywords: Automated grading; SQL; Tutoring software; database systems; relational database systems

DOI: http://dx.doi.org/10.1145/2676723.2691896

Conflict-Driven Cooperative-Learning in Computing Courses

Swaroop Joshi, *The Ohio State University*
Neelam Soundarajan, *The Ohio State University*
Rajiv Ramnath, *The Ohio State University*
Contact: joshis@cse.ohio-state.edu

Conflict and cooperation would seem to be ideas that are diametrically opposed to each other. But, in fact, classic work by Piaget on how children and adults learn shows that when learners engage with peers in critical discussion of ideas concerning which they have different understandings, that contributes very effectively to learners developing deep understanding of the concepts involved. At the same time, getting students in undergraduate computing (or other technical/engineering) courses to engage with other students in thoughtful discussion of important concepts is very challenging. It can be especially difficult to get women students and students from other underrepresented groups to participate effectively in such discussions. In our work, we exploit the affordances of mobile and web technologies to address these challenges. Our approach not only helps address these challenges, it has a number of other important advantages over face-to-face discussions. We present the theoretical underpinnings of the approach, some details of our prototype implementation, preliminary results from the use of the prototype in a junior/senior level class on Software Engineering, and the design for the next version of our tool. We also discuss the possibilities and usefulness of applying this approach in a range of computing courses from traditional classrooms to MOOCs.

ACM Categories & Descriptors: K.3.1 [Computer Uses in Education]: Collaborative Learning

Keywords: Cooperative learning; Cognitive conflict

DOI: http://dx.doi.org/10.1145/2676723.2691897

A Nearest Neighbors Analysis of Student Academic Performance in Computer Science

R. Mitchell Parry, *Appalachian State University*
Contact: parryrm@appstate.edu

Students increasingly decide to go to college in order to get better jobs and make more money. However, these advantages are typically thwarted if a student fails to graduate. Although much research has been aimed at predicting college performance using data collected before entering college, this preliminary work focuses on how college-level data could be used to inform student decision making. This work acquired historical class grades, test scores, and degree information for all students who have taken any computer science classes at Appalachian State University. This poster presents a web application that allows users to explore these data by selecting a target activity such as a class, and filtering students based on test scores, degrees, or how they have performed in other classes. The application displays overlaid histograms comparing how students in the subset perform relative to the class as a whole. For example, when a student considers retaking a course they may find it useful to know how other students with similar grades have performed in the major. For example, among the 29 attempts by 22 students with a 'C' in discrete math and CS 1, only 10 earned the required 'C' in CS 2 (35%) and 12 failed the course (41%). Three of these students went on to graduate with a degree in computer science (14%) and six in computer information systems (27%) while five did not graduate from Appalachian (23%).

ACM Categories & Descriptors: K.3.2 [Computers and Education]: Computer and Information Science Education - Computer Science Education; H.4.3 [Information Systems Applications]: Communications Applications - Information browsers; H.2.8 [Database Management]: Database Applications - Data mining

Keywords: Advising; Interactive visualization; Retention

DOI: http://dx.doi.org/10.1145/2676723.2691898

Integrating Mobile Computing and Security into a Computer Science Curriculum

Xiaohong Yuan, *North Carolina A&T State University*
Kelvin S. Bryant, *North Carolina A&T State University*
Kenneth Williams, *North Carolina A&T State University*
Jinsheng Xu, *North Carolina A&T State University*
Contact: xhyuan@ncat.edu

The poster describes our project of integrating mobile computing and security into the Computer Science program at North Carolina A&T State University. Twelve (12) course modules in mobile computing and security are being developed and integrated into existing Computer Science courses such as computer programming, software development, operating systems, and information assurance courses. Each course module includes learning objectives, a tutorial, presentation slides, hands-on labs and/or case studies, test questions, etc. The course module material we develop and our teaching experiences will be beneficial to computer science educators who are considering including mobile computing and mobile security into their curricula.

ACM Categories & Descriptors: K.3.2 [Computers and Education]: Computer and Information Science Education - *computer science education, curriculum;* K.6.5 [Management of Computing and Information Systems]: Security and Protection - *invasive software, unauthorized access*

Keywords: Graduate Degree Aspirations; Underrepresented Students; Undergraduate Research; Computing Research Pipeline

SIGCSE'15, March 4–7, 2015, Kansas City, MO, USA.
ACM 978-1-4503-2966-8/15/03.

The Effects of Formal Undergraduate Research Experiences on Student Aspirations for Graduate Study in Computer Science: Explaining the Relative Influence of Racial Identity Status

Ama Nyame-Mensah, *Computing Research Association*
Contact: ama@cra.org

This poster explores the differential effects of formal undergraduate research experiences on the graduate degree intentions of underrepresented racial-ethnic minority and racial majority computing majors. Across two studies, it was found that formal undergraduate research experiences in computing have a greater and more positive effect on the educational aspirations of underrepresented racial-ethnic minorities as compared to racial majorities. For underrepresented racial-ethnic minorities, this effect is manifested in the gains in academic and career self-efficacy and gains in knowledge about the graduate admission process they develop as a result of their formal research experience. Together, these findings suggest that psychosocial skills that are strengthened during formal undergraduate research experiences play an important role in influencing the educational intentions of underrepresented racial-ethnic minorities in the field of computer science.

ACM Categories & Descriptors: K.3.2 [Computer and Information Science Education]: Computer Science Education

Keywords: Graduate Degree Aspirations; Underrepresented Students; Undergraduate Research; Computing Research Pipeline

DOI: http://dx.doi.org/10.1145/2676723.2691903

CSteach: Engaging Latino/a Youth in Computer Science with Social Justice and Near Peers

Louise Ann Lyon, *ETR*
Jill Denner, *ETR*
Jacob Martinez, *DigitalNEST*
Contact: louann.lyon@etr.org

Latinos are the fastest growing ethnic minority group in the US but are underrepresented in computer science. To increase the numbers of Latinos, we need learning environments that excite them about becoming a computer scientist starting in elementary school. This poster describes CSteach, an afterschool program that aims to move Latino/a students along the path to becoming a computer scientist by fostering capacities, identities, and relationships starting in 5th grade. It is the first known effort to integrate CS and social justice in elementary schools, and it builds off examples of "computing for the social good" in college (Goldweber et al., 2011).

The poster includes a description of the curriculum, and research findings from over 200 5th graders and 13 high school "near peer" educators. It includes a list of tested strategies for how to introduce CS and social justice concepts in a developmentally appropriate way to 5th graders, and how to integrate those concepts to increase motivation and understanding. The poster also describes how to establish an effective "near peer" component in a K-12 CS program by selecting high school students who are from the community, excited about computers and want to teach, and also providing them with ongoing training and support. Screenshots of the students' Scratch projects show how they used CS to address a social justice issue at their school. And graphs provide a visual description of the pre-post survey data that were collected. This includes changes in students' knowledge of CS, attitudes toward CS, interest in pursuing CS, and their understanding of how computing can be used to address needs in their community.

ACM Categories & Descriptors: K.3.m [Computers and Education]: Miscellaneous; K.4.m [Computers and Society]: Miscellaneous

Keywords: K-12; Latino/as; broadening participation; social justice

DOI: http://dx.doi.org/10.1145/2676723.2691904

Security Injections 2.0: Using Segmentation, Instant-feedback, and Auto-grading to Enhance Secure Coding Modules for Lower-level Programming Courses

Sagar Raina, *Towson University*
Blair Taylor, *Towson University*
Siddharth Kaza, *Towson University*
Contact: sraina1@students.towson.edu

Learning interventions based on modules are common in computer science education. Traditional learning modules that present a large amount of content in a linear format can induce cognitive overload in learners. We present theoretical support for increasing the effectiveness of learning modules, describe a system that implements these principles, and discuss the results of a pilot study across two sections of CS0. Using the Security Injections @Towson cybersecurity modules that target key secure coding concepts including integer error, buffer overflow, input validation, for CS0, CS1, and CS2, we enhanced select modules by incorporating the e-learning design principles of segmentation and interactivity. The pilot study compares student engagement and knowledge of software security and secure coding between the current (1.0) modules and the enhanced (2.0) modules. The use of the enhanced 2.0 modules significantly increased both secure coding and software security knowledge. In addition, student engagement increased and feedback from instructors indicates higher student and instructor interest. This project is partially supported by NSF through grant DUE-1241738.

ACM Categories & Descriptors: K.3.2 Computers and Education

Keywords: CS0; CS1; CS2; Secure Coding; Security Injections; Learning Sciences; Interactive Learning; Instant-feedback; Auto-grading

DOI: http://dx.doi.org/10.1145/2676723.2691905

SIGCSE'15, March 4–7, 2015, Kansas City, MO, USA.
ACM 978-1-4503-2966-8/15/03.

Conceptum: An Online Infrastructure for Concept Inventories

Gautam Mohan, *Swarthmore College*
Benjamin Rempel, *Oberlin College*
Eli Rosenberg, *Oberlin College*
David Wurtele, *Swarthmore College*
Cynthia Taylor, *Oberlin College*
Kevin Webb, *Swarthmore CollegeG*
Contact: ctaylor@oberlin.edu

Concept Inventories (CIs) are short, multiple-choice exams that evaluate a student's understanding of core concepts of a particular course. CIs are especially useful for evaluating the effects of pedagogical techniques and interventions on student learning, as their focus on core concepts means any student should be able to answer the questions, and their use as a pre- and post-test allows them to measure student learning gains. However, CI development requires significant overhead: the current state of the art calls for an intensive, six step process. As a result, there are few CIs available for Computer Science, despite their effectiveness.
Our research is devoted to solving this problem by implementing an online platform for developing, deploying, and evaluating concept inventories. This open-source software will support any number of collaborators in following the process to develop a CI, including identifying concepts, interviewing both domain experts and students, developing and deploying surveys on concepts, and developing multiple-choice CI questions. Additionally, the tool will be able to manage, administer, and iteratively improve CIs after they are created, including allowing instructors to deploy the CI to their classes, and to compare their results with others who have used the CI. This work is part of a larger project, in which it will be used to develop a CI for CS2.

ACM Categories & Descriptors: K.3.2 [Computer and Information Science Education]: Computer Science Education

Keywords: Concept Inventory; Misconceptions; Assessment

DOI: http://dx.doi.org/10.1145/2676723.2691907

Raspberry HadooPI: A Low-Cost, Hands-On Laboratory in Big Data and Analytics

Kenneth Fox, Drexel University
William Mongan, Drexel University
Jeffrey Popyack, Drexel University
Contact: kwf26@drexel.edu

Educating STEM students in the techniques of massively parallel computing anticipates a growing current and future need for scientists, engineers, and analysts who are facile with Big Data. Using very low cost hardware (Raspberry Pi) and free software (Hadoop) we are exposing students to distributed computing while limiting expense. We anticipate that micro-cluster labs and projects will give students hands on experience necessary so they can be prepared to use these methods in real world applications. A series of lessons and projects were developed to teach Hadoop and MapReduce, and were extended into STAR (Students Tackling Advanced Research) summer competitive research projects.

ACM Categories & Descriptors: C.1.4 Parallel Architectures - Distributed architectures; D.1.3 Concurrent Programming -

Distributed programming; K.3.2 Computer and Information Science Education - Computer science education

Keywords: Hadoop; RaspberryPi; MapReduce; Big Data; micro-cluster; inexpensive; education

DOI: http://dx.doi.org/10.1145/2676723.2691908

The State of CS Circles: Open Source and Outreach with an Introductory Python Website

David Pritchard, *University of Southern California*
Sandy Graham, *University of Waterloo*
Troy Vasiga, *University of Waterloo*
Contact: david.pritchard@usc.edu

Computer Science Circles is a website (http://cscircles.cemc.uwaterloo.ca) that teaches Python for beginners, presented at SIGCSE 2013. It includes lessons, automatically-graded exercises, examples and visualizations. One purpose of the website is outreach with real human interaction: anyone who is stuck solving an exercise can privately send a question to the "CS Circles Assistant" (the author and two colleagues). As part of this poster, we will show some information about the 2500 student questions we have answered through this system, e.g. the questions where students most often reach out for help. We will also provide feedback from teachers using the site with their own classes.

The website was open-sourced in August 2013 thanks to a SIGCSE Special Projects grant, bringing it in line with the great open-source components used to create it. One unique outcome of this open licensing is installing a site mirror in a correctional institute.

The website was originally launched in English and French. Since then, we have worked with CS institutes from other countries: versions in German and Dutch have been released, with other translations under way. The poster will highlight some tools and caveats involved in this process.

Users of the site submit their solutions for online auto-grading, with about 500000 exercises now completed. This has yielded a large amount of data about the frequency of different error messages. We will include a chart of the most common errors, and an illustration of how we used this to generate clickable hints to give better beginner-level explanations for the most common errors.

ACM Categories & Descriptors: K.3.2 Computer and Information Science Education (Computer science education)

Keywords: Open Source; Online Education; Browser-Based Tools

DOI: http://dx.doi.org/10.1145/2676723.2691910

Building the Pascaline: Digital Computing Like It's 1642

David S. Touretzky, Carnegie Mellon University
Contact: dst@cs.cmu.edu

SIGCSE'15, March 4–7, 2015, Kansas City, MO, USA.
ACM 978-1-4503-2966-8/15/03.

The Pascaline was the first working mechanical calculator, created in 1642 by the French polymath Blaise Pascal. Over the next two decades Pascal built 40 of these machines, of which nine survive today. Several good web resources describe the Pascaline, but to properly appreciate the sautoir, Pascal's kinetic energy solution to jam-free ripple carry, building a working replica is invaluable.

Thanks to the growing availability of rapid prototyping tools, it has become relatively easy for CS educators to fabricate physical artifacts to help students explore computational ideas. I've created a Pascaline kit using laser-cut acrylic and standard fasteners that can be assembled with just a screwdriver, pliers, and Loctite. High school or college students with minimal skills can put it together in a few hours and have a functioning calculator. Exploring the Pascaline's design is an engaging way to connect a milestone in the early history of computing with more modern theoretical concepts. Students can investigate questions such as: What makes a device "digital"? (Slide rules have numeric scales but are analog devices.) How does nonlinearity produce discrete states in a continuous world? How are nonlinearities induced in the Pascaline vs. in digital electronics? How do the logic design concepts "half adder" and "full adder" map onto the components of the Pascaline? Is the Pascaline really adding, or merely counting? How does the Pascaline use nines complement arithmetic to perform subtraction, and why isn't it tens complement?

The Pascaline kit, designed in SolidWorks, is open source and available at http://www.cs.cmu.edu/~dst/Pascaline.

ACM Categories & Descriptors: K.2 History of Computing; K.3.2 Computer and Information Science Education

Keywords: Pascaline; Mechanical computing; Laser cutter

DOI: http://dx.doi.org/10.1145/2676723.2691911

Using Workflow Technology to Create Scenario-based Workflows for Information Security Education

Wu He, Ashish Kshirsagar, Alexander Nwala, Yaohang Li, *Old Dominion University*
Contact: whe@odu.edu

Teaching information security courses is technically challenging. In an information security course, students and instructors often end up struggling in low-level and complicated software installation, system setup, service configuration, command operations, and data manipulation while losing concentration in learning the important information security principles. To help students in information security courses learn information security principles more effectively and efficiently, we used the workflow technology to create scenario-based workflows in order to improve the effectiveness of teaching and learning of several key information security principles and techniques. Two case studies simulating real-life scenarios, including one for an online banking system and one for an online grading system, are recreated within a laboratory setting using workflow technology and are then presented in information security classes. Our educational practice shows that the benefits of using workflow technology in information security education have been well received by students.

ACM Categories & Descriptors: K.3.2 Computer and Information Science Education

Keywords: Workflow Technology; Case-based Learning; Case-based Instruction; Case study; Information Security; Cyber security

DOI: http://dx.doi.org/10.1145/2676723.2691951

Gender Differences in High School Students' Decisions to Study Computer Science and Related Fields

Hai Hong, *Google Inc.*
Jennifer Wang, *Google Inc.*
Jason Ravitz, *Google Inc.*
Mo-Yun Lei Fong, *Google Inc.*
Contact: jennifertwang@google.com

Increasing women's participation in Computer Science (CS) is a critical workforce and equity concern. The technology industry has committed to reversing negative trends for women in CS, engineering, and related fields. Building on previous research, we surveyed 1,739 high school students and recent college graduates to understand factors influencing decisions to pursue CS-related college degrees. Results indicate social encouragement, career perception, academic exposure, and self-perception are the leading factors for women, while the influence of these factors is different for men. These factors are actionable, and understanding differences in their influence on men and women will inform our approaches to achieving gender parity in tech.

ACM Categories & Descriptors: K.3.2 [**Computers and Education**]: Computer and Information Science Education - *computer science education.*

Keywords: Gender differences; factors; high school; college; encouragement, perceptions; self-confidence; K-12 education.

DOI: http://dx.doi.org/10.1145/2676723.2691920

Learning from What Works: Improving an Introductory Computing Course for Architects with Teaching Methods from Media Computation

Nicholas Senske, *University of North Carolina at Charlotte*
Contact: nsenske@uncc.edu

This poster describes an ongoing five-year assessment of a new introductory programming course for architecture students at the University of North Carolina at Charlotte. The goal of this course is to teach the fundamentals of computing with an emphasis on their relation to design and aesthetics. Many of the students struggle with the material, as they typically come into the course with no prior programming experience. To improve class performance, the author turned to instructional methods developed for Media Computation, which have been successfully used to teach introductory programming to non-major students for more than a decade. Our data suggest that the same methods – media-based contextual content, pair programming, and peer instruction – can have positive effects for students taking an introductory programming course taught by and for disciplines other than computer science. Compared to the first version of the course, which used traditional labs and lectures, the second iteration of the course, updated with the three instructional methods from Media Computation, resulted in higher student retention and an increase in student interest in computing topics. These improvements have remained consistent over the past three years. The data implies that research-based practices from computer science education can be used to improve computing education in other domains.

SIGCSE'15, March 4–7, 2015, Kansas City, MO, USA.
ACM 978-1-4503-2966-8/15/03.

ACM Categories & Descriptors: K.3.2 [Computers and Education]: Computer and Information Science Education – computer science education

Keywords: Education research; Non-Majors; Architecture; Media Computation; Pair Programming; Peer Instruction

DOI: http://dx.doi.org/10.1145/2676723.2691925

MIPSUnit: A Unit Testing Framework for MIPS Assembly

Zachary Kurmas, *Grand Valley State University*
Jack Rosenhauer, Grand Valley State University
Contact: kurmasz@gvsu.edu

We present `MIPSUnit`, a unit test framework for MIPS assembly. `MIPSUnit`'s primary benefit is that it reduces the time needed to grade assembly language assignments. It also provides a time-efficient means for providing students additional testing experience. (We believe that students should be exposed to testing throughout the curriculum — including their Computer Organization and/or Assembly Language courses.) `MIPSUnit` is a suite of two tools: `MUnit`, which allows users to test their assembly code with `JUnit` tests, and `MSpec`, which uses `RSpec`-style unit tests

ACM Categories & Descriptors: B.8.1 [Performance and Reliability]: Reliability, Testing, and Fault-Tolerance

Keywords: Digital logic; Assembly language; Testing; MARS; MIPS; JUnit

DOI: http://dx.doi.org/10.1145/2676723.2691926

A Web-based Simulator for Learning Multiprocessor Real-time Scheduling

Yuting Zhang, *Boston University Metropolitan College*
Xin Shan, *Boston University Metropolitan College*
Yingyuan Zhang, *Boston University Metropolitan College*
Juejie Wang, *Boston University Metropolitan College*
Contact: danazh@bu.edu

CPU scheduling is one of the most important topics discussed in Operating Systems (OS) courses. In recent years, CPU scheduling for multiprocessor and real-time systems has become more and more essential as those systems can be found everywhere. While these topics should be introduced in OS courses, they are much harder to understand than simple uniprocessor scheduling algorithms due to the complexity involved. Particularly in introductory OS courses, only a couple of lectures can be used to cover these topics. To help students understand these complex topics more easily, we introduce a web-based simulator for learning multiprocessor real-time scheduling that is easy-to-use and self-explanatory. With this simulator, students can get visualized step-by-step instructions of how the algorithms work. They can also run the simulators interactively, and explore the algorithms in an empirical setting. The initial feedback from our students indicates that the tool is very useful in learning these complex algorithms. A demo will be shown in the poster session.

ACM Categories & Descriptors: D.4.1 [Operating Systems]: Process Management Scheduling; D.4.8 [Operating Systems]: Performance Simulator; K.3.2 [COMPUTERS AND EDUCATION]: Computer and Information Science Education Computer science education

Keywords: Simulator, Multiprocessor real-time scheduling

DOI: http://dx.doi.org/10.1145/2676723.2691938

Teaching Debugging Skills in Shader-Based Computer Graphics Programming

Ying Zhu, *Georgia State University*
G. Scott Owen, *Georgia State University*
Contact: yzhu@gsu.edu

We present a set of online materials that teach debugging skills in college level computer graphics courses. Almost all the computer graphics textbooks use OpenGL and OpenGL Shading Language (GLSL). Most of the college level computer graphics courses are also taught using OpenGL/GLSL. Most students find OpenGL/GLSL programming very challenging. One of the reasons is that debugging is particularly difficult for computer graphics programming because many traditional debugging techniques can no longer be used. Debugging graphics programs requires a good understanding of OpenGL's error reporting mechanisms and different debugging techniques. Students also need to learn special GPU debugging tools.
However, debugging is rarely covered in computer graphics textbooks and courses. Online resources on debugging OpenGL/GLSL programs are also scarce. To address this issue, we have developed online materials that teach students how to systematically debug shader-based OpenGL programs. This web site [1] provides error classification, debugging techniques, a list of common bugs, description of the OpenGL error reporting mechanisms, description of GPU debugging tools, symptom checker, code samples, and tutorials. This online resource fills an important gap in the current computer graphics curriculum. Students can use it to learn OpenGL/GLSL debugging skills. Instructors can use it as a supplement to their existing teaching materials.

ACM Categories & Descriptors: D.2.5 [**Testing and Debugging**]: Code inspections and walk-throughs, debugging aids, diagnostics.

Keywords: Computer Graphics; Debugging; Shader; OpenGL; Education Materials

DOI: http://dx.doi.org/10.1145/2676723.2691939

Developing Computational Thinking through Image Making and Constructionist Learning

Eileen Fordham, Halley Freger, Amanda Hinchman-Dominguez, Alexander Mitchell, Daniel Rebelsky, Victoria Tsou, Earnest Wheeler, Zoe Wolter, and Samuel A. Rebelsky, *Grinnell College*
Contact: rebelsky@grinnell.edu

Consider the following scenario: A student is browsing Facebook and sees a strangely compelling image on her friend's page. She follows the "how I made this link" to learn more. She finds herself on a page with a gallery of animations that she browses. Then she sees a "Create" button and clicks it. She skims the instructions and decides that this is not a "standard" graphics program - rather than using a timeline and "tools", it has just a few basic images (e.g., a horizontal blend, a vertical blend, some-time-blends) and a few operations that you use to build new images from existing images. She plays a bit. And she finds that she can create some strange and interesting images, but not necessarily the ones she wants to make, and certainly not anything like her friend made. So she looks further. She learns that there are "challenges" that help you learn the system (and, as importantly, that help you consider and master different aspects of computational thinking), and tries to figure out how to make images as seemingly simple as a triangle or a circle using the limited selection of basic images and operations. It's not easy, but she finds it fun to try (and sometimes more fun to fail – failures also create interesting images).
You've just read a sample encounter with the Mathematical Image Synthesis Toolkit, or MIST. MIST is an open-source, Web-based graphics application that takes a constructionist approach in which open experimentation in image making helps students develop skills in computational thinking and deepen their understanding of mathematical functions. MIST is available at http://glimmer.grinnell.edu.

ACM Categories & Descriptors: D.1.7 [Programming Techniques]: Visual Programming; J.5 [Arts and Humanities]; K.3.2 [Computers and Education]: Computer and Information Science Education - *Literacy*; K.8.1 [Personal Computing]: Application Packages - *Freeware/shareware, Graphics*

Keywords: Computational thinking; Social media; Animation; Functional programming; Web software; Open source; Constructionism

DOI: http://dx.doi.org/10.1145/2676723.2691940

SIGCSE'15, March 4–7, 2015, Kansas City, MO, USA.
ACM 978-1-4503-2966-8/15/03.

Smartwatches for Junior/Senior Level CS Education

Andrey Esakia, *Virginia Tech*
Contact: esakia@vt.edu

Incorporating smartwatch app development into mobile app development classes has educational benefits. However, choice of a smartwatch platform imposes constraints on eligibility of students that can take the class because some of the platforms (ex. Pebble, Samsung Gear2, AGENTWATCH) use proprietary SDKs with programing environment very different from the smartphone's. This makes such classes too difficult for CS1/CS2 level students.

This poster shows how newer smartwatches (Android Wear OS and Watch OS based) can make such classes accessible to CS1/CS2 students and how these newer smartwatches can broaden the CS topics that can be learned. For example, the hardware of Android Wear devices coupled with similar programing approach with Android OS, make a friendly platform for integrating smartwatch development into an Android app development class. These smartwatches offer new levels of information affordance with instantly obtainable interactive information on the wrist. It is possible to use such smartwatches as a tool for exploration of the fundamentals of Human Computer Interaction. Students can identify problems in existing interactive systems and design solutions with smartwatch capabilities in mind. Problems can be identified through exploratory studies of existing systems. Prototypes can be designed and implemented followed by evaluations. Students can also exercise concepts of Usability Engineering as there is need to address the ergonomic constraints of smartwatches, such as, small screen, poor visibility and fixed position on the body. In addition, Designing Android apps with Android Wear extensibility in mind can reinforce fundamental modularity concepts from Software Engineering in a natural setting.

ACM Categories & Descriptors: K.3.2 Computer and Information Science Education

Keywords: Smartwatch, Android Wear, Apple Watch, Mobile, Android, HCI, Usability Engineering, Software Engineering

DOI: http://dx.doi.org/10.1145/2676723.2691941

A Gateway Game to Make Computational Problem Solving Accessible and Engaging

Emmett Tomai, *University of Texas-Pan American*
Roberto Flores, *University of Texas-Pan American*
Casey Richardson, *University of Texas-Pan American*
Jose Rojas, *University of Texas-Pan American*
Julio Oliva, *University of Texas-Pan American*
German Zuniga, *University of Texas-Pan American*
Contact: tomaie@utpa.edu

SIGCSE'15, March 4–7, 2015, Kansas City, MO, USA.
ACM 978-1-4503-2966-8/15/03.

In this work, we seek to better understand how game design principles impact the effectiveness of a video game learning environment for computational problem solving. Video games naturally encourage problem solving and incremental learning of their game play systems, but it remains unclear how well that transfers to learning the structures and processes of computing. We are building a *gateway game* that establishes familiar problem solving game play, then expands player affordances to include the use of automation and abstraction. Programming in-game entities is presented to players as a constrained selection and refinement process, which they explore and master in order to achieve in-game goals. We are exploring whether computational problem solving can be cast as accessible, intrinsically engaging game play, by following principles of good game design: exploratory player-controlled pace and direction, encouraging trial and low-cost failure, immediate formative feedback, level-appropriate challenge, non-intrusive assessment and expanding affordances. The game we are building to evaluate these factors will be positioned as a bridge for middle- and early high-school students to engage with computational problem solving.

ACM Categories & Descriptors: D.3.3 Language Constructs and Features; K.3.2 Computer and Information Sciences Education;

Keywords: Computational Thinking; Computational Problem Solving; Educational Games; Game Design; Introduction to Programming;

DOI: http://dx.doi.org/10.1145/2676723.2691949

Oh, Snap! Enabling and Encouraging Success in CS1

Michael Ball, *UC Berkeley*
Lauren Mock, *UC Berkeley*
Jonathan McKinsey, *UC Berkeley*
Zack Machardy, *UC Berkeley*
Omoju Miller, *UC Berkeley*
Dan Garcia, *UC Berkeley*
Nate Titterton, *UC Berkeley*
Brian Harvey, *UC Berkeley*
Contact: conferences@cs10.org

CS10, is UC Berkeley's CS0 course. Each semester we have between 40% and 50% of our students continue on to CS61A, our CS1 course. Meanwhile, an average of 25% more students express interest in continuing learning computer science through other means. CS10 is taught in a visual language called Snap*!* and CS61A in Python. This poster explores some of the trends we have seen between CS10 and CS61A enrollment, and our new "Besides Blocks" curriculum which helps transition students from a visual to text based language. Besides Block is approximately one fourth of the CS10 curriculum which introduces Python in the context of the Turtle Graphics system, and a tool called *Codification* which is a way of translating Snap*!* blocks to Python.

ACM Categories & Descriptors: K.3.2 [COMPUTERS AND EDUCATION]: Computer and Information Science Education - *Curriculum; Computer science education*

Keywords: CS0; CS1; curriculum; visual programming;

DOI: http://dx.doi.org/10.1145/2676723.2691947

Birds of a Feather
FLOCK I

Universal Access to Computing Education

Richard E. Ladner, *University of Washington*
Brianna Blaser, *University of Washington*
Daniela Maghitu, *Auburn University*
Contact: blaser@uw.edu

Approximately 10% of computer science and engineering majors have a disability of some kind. Students with disabilities are more likely to drop out of the major than those without disabilities. This BOF will bring together individuals who are interested in increasing the representation of students with disabilities in computing and improving their success. Participants will share strategies and promising practices to help each other do a better job of including these students in our classes and research projects. Resources, including those produced by AccessComputing (uw.edu/accesscomputing), will be shared.

ACM Categories & Descriptors: Computer and Information Science Education

Keywords: disability; broadening participation; universal design

DOI: http://dx.doi.org/10.1145/2676723.2691834

Birds of a Feather: Mapping Alice Curriculum to Standards

Donald Slater, *Carnegie Mellon University*
Wanda Dann, *Carnegie Mellon University*
Stephen Cooper, *Stanford University*
Contact: dslater@cmu.edu

This session is for anyone currently using Alice 2 and / or Alice 3, or those exploring the possibility of using Alice in their curriculum. The session will focus on a mapping of an Alice curriculum and instructional materials to CSTA, code.org and ACM curriculum standards and guidelines for a wide range of age/grade levels. The discussion leaders and attendees will share teaching strategies, tips, and techniques for implementing these standards. This is an opportunity to share assignments and pointers to web sites to access instructional materials, such as syllabi, student projects, exams, and other resources with experienced Alice instructors and those new to Alice.

Goals for this session include:

- Review a course mapping of the Alice curriculum to well-known introductory curricula and pedagogy learning standards.
- Discuss learning standards and objectives encountered in the use of Alice in different environments and educational contexts.
- Allow educators using Alice to share exemplary assignments and teaching strategies.
- Provide an opportunity for those thinking about using Alice to ask questions as they determine how it may be most useful in their particular situation.
- Foster the development of community by allowing Alice teachers to connect and become resources for each other throughout the year.
- Allow educators to interact with Alice team members to learn more about the latest features of Alice 3 and Alice 2.

ACM Categories & Descriptors: K.3.2 [COMPUTERS AND EDUCATION]: Computer and Information Science Education - *Curriculum; Computer science education*

Keywords: Alice; Curriculum Standards; Instructional Materials; Pedagogy

DOI: http://dx.doi.org/10.1145/2676723.2691838

Brainstorming How to Use Lego Mindstorms EV3 in the Classroom

Greg Kawell, *Samford University*
Ben Schafer, *University of Northern Iowa*
Contact: gakawell@samford.edu

Many people know that Lego Mindstorms are great for teaching a wide range of different computer concepts to students. Some use them to teach programming, engineering, and of course robotics. In September of 2013, Lego released the latest generation of Mindstorms called EV3. This workshop focused on introducing participants on how to use Mindstorms EV3 and what many of the new features of the system are. At the workshop it was mentioned how some people are using this generation of Mindstorms for architecture classes, assembler coding projects, CS0 or CS1 courses, and conducting kids camps for k-12 students. This BOF is designed for people currently using any generation of Mindstorms and for those who are interested in finding out how they might start using Mindstorms in the classroom. The focus of this session will be to encourage people to use Mindstorms EV3 in a variety of different settings. During the BOF, people will have an opportunity to brainstorm new ways to use these tools to help students learn important CS concepts.

ACM Categories & Descriptors: K.3.2 [Computer and Information Science Education]: Computer Science Education

Keywords: educational robotics; ev3; Lego; Mindstorms; CS0; CS1

DOI: http://dx.doi.org/10.1145/2676723.2691840

SIGCSE'15, March 4–7, 2015, Kansas City, MO, USA.
ACM 978-1-4503-2966-8/15/03.

What Math is the Right Math for Computing?

Doug Baldwin, *SUNY Geneseo*
John P. Dougherty, *Haverford College*
Contact: baldwin@geneseo.edu

"... we note that undergraduate CS students need enough mathematical maturity to have the basis on which to then build CS-specific mathematics (for example, as specified in the Discrete Structures Knowledge Area), which, importantly, does not explicitly require any significant college-level coursework in calculus, differential equations, or linear algebra."

[Computer Science Curricula 2013]

Is this true? Perhaps we are finally acknowledging what critics have claimed for many years; namely, that the math traditionally studied by other engineers is the wrong math for computer science. But perhaps the even longer history of organizing college-level math curricula around continuous mathematics recognizes some important source of "mathematical maturity." This session will debate Curricula 2013's claim in order to explore what topics in mathematics, and perhaps logic, statistics, and other related disciplines, a computer science program should include in order to develop appropriate "mathematical maturity" in its students.

ACM Categories & Descriptors: K.3.2 [Computer and Information Science Education]: Computer Science Education

Keywords: mathematics to support computing; curriculum

DOI: http://dx.doi.org/10.1145/2676723.2691841

K12 CS Teaching Methods Courses

Shuchi Grover, *SRI International*
R. Benjamin Shapiro, *Tufts University*
Brian Dorn, *University of Nebraska Omaha*
Contact: ben@cs.tufts.edu

CS teacher development has become a major effort for the SIGCSE community in part due to NSF's CS10K efforts and expanding CSTA involvement. However there are few examples of university courses explicitly designed to train CS teachers. We do not yet have complete clarity on the topics CS education methods courses should cover and how best to prepare teachers to teach learners new to computational problem solving and programming. As an interdisciplinary field of study, CS education must necessarily draw on domain knowledge in CS, research in computing education, as well as research in education and the learning sciences about how students learn, both generally and in computing. At the same time, a methods course must provide prospective teachers with practical, hands-on experiences wherein they integrate research-based best practices with age-appropriate content for their target student population.

BOF attendees are asked to bring materials from their classes and be ready to discuss multiple viewpoints about topics, pedagogical strategies and readings from a rich history of research in computing education and the learning sciences. Such a session will also afford attendees an opportunity to start an important conversation, connect with others who are currently developing and/or teaching CS methods courses, and form a community to share ideas, literature, and syllabi on an ongoing basis. Materials will be shared with the SIGCSE community.

ACM Categories & Descriptors: K.3.2 [Computer and Information Science Education]: Computer science education

Keywords: K12; teacher training

DOI: http://dx.doi.org/10.1145/2676723.2691842

Process Oriented Guided Inquiry Learning (POGIL) in Computer Science

Clif Kussmaul, *Muhlenberg College*
Helen H. Hu, *Westminster College*
Chris Mayfield, *James Madison University*
Contact: kussmaul@muhlenberg.edu

Process-Oriented Guided Inquiry Learning (POGIL) is a research-based instructional strategy with a proven history across STEM disciplines. In a POGIL classroom, teams of students work on activities that are specifically designed to guide them to construct their own understanding of key concepts. At the same time, students develop key process skills such as communication, teamwork, problem solving, and critical thinking. For example, an activity might start with a simple game, and questions would guide teams to identify, analyze, and compare algorithms to play the game, leading them to develop techniques and identify issues and tradeoffs. POGIL incorporates practices shown to be particularly helpful for students from underrepresented populations. In a POGIL classroom, teachers are facilitators, not lecturers. Multiple studies have shown the students in POGIL classes do better on common exams and in subsequent courses.

This BOF will enable people unfamiliar with POGIL to ask questions and learn more, and enable experienced POGIL practitioners to share experiences, concerns, ideas, and insights. As in a POGIL classroom, we will discuss topics in small teams and report out to the larger group. The CS-POGIL community has grown rapidly in the last few years. Our discuss forum has over 40 members, and http://cspogil.org has over 100 activities shared publicly or within the community. For more information, see http://cspogil.org and http://pogil.org.

ACM Categories & Descriptors: K.3.2 [Computers and Education]: Computer and Information Science Education

Keywords: POGIL; active learning; communication; inquiry learning; teamwork

DOI: http://dx.doi.org/10.1145/2676723.2691846

A Town Meeting: SIGCSE Committee on Expanding the Women-in-Computing Community

Gloria Childress Townsend, *DePauw University*
Contact: gct@depauw.edu

In January 2004, we organized the second SIGCSE Committee ("Expanding the Women-in-Computing Community"). Our annual Town Meeting provides dissemination of information concerning successful gender issues projects, along with group discussion and brainstorming, in order to create committee goals

SIGCSE'15, March 4–7, 2015, Kansas City, MO, USA.
ACM 978-1-4503-2966-8/15/03.

for the coming year. We select projects to highlight through listserv communication and through our connections with NCWIT, ABI, ACM-W, CRA-W, etc. This year we will highlight ACM-W Chapters and ACM-W Regional Celebrations.

ACM Categories & Descriptors: K.4.2 Social Issues; K.4 Computers and Society; K. Computing Milieu

Keywords: Gender Issues; Underrepresentation

DOI: http://dx.doi.org/10.1145/2676723.2691847

Resources and Strategies for Flipped Classrooms

Edward F. Gehringer, *North Carolina State University*
Mark S. Hall, *University of Wisconsin-Marathon Co.*
Contact: efg@ncsu.edu

With interest in "flipped classrooms" rapidly growing, CS faculty are looking for ways to "flip" with a reasonable amount of effort and good results, There is no lack of resources or advice; videos and video-recording apps are proliferating, as are articles and web sites devoted to flipping. Only a small fraction of this is specifically targeted at CS, so it is a daunting task to sort through the available material to find what works well in computing. This BoF will bring together educators who have used, and can recommend, resources for flipping to their colleagues.

ACM Categories & Descriptors: K.3.2 Computer and Information Science Education - *computer science education*

Keywords: "flipped" classroom; inverted lecture model

DOI: http://dx.doi.org/10.1145/2676723.2691848

Sharing Best Practices for Alumni Engagement

Meghan Allen, *University of British Columbia*
Ben Coleman, *Moravian College*
Diane Horton, *University of Toronto*
Lynn Lambert, *Christopher Newport University*
Michele Ng, *University of British Columbia*
Contact: meghana@cs.ubc.ca

Alumni make contributions to a Computer Science program in three interconnected ways, all of which relate to the interplay between the academic environment and the "real world." For students who aim to enter the job market upon graduation, alumni provide a friendly way to receive mentoring and advice and develop a professional network. When faculty are looking for real-world projects and experiences for students, alumni provide an avenue for entrance into industry. Finally, alumni can provide assessment data about the performance of students in the workplace after graduation.

In this BoF session, we will consider how individual faculty members or a department can engage alumni in meaningful ways. Small groups will consider each of the three ways to partner with alumni, with particular emphasis on sharing past experiences. Participants will be encouraged to consider ways to collaborate with their alumni office, development office, career center and student groups to leverage the potential of their alumni.

ACM Categories & Descriptors: K.3.2 [Computer and Information Science Education]: Computer Science Education

Keywords: computer science education; alumni engagement

DOI: http://dx.doi.org/10.1145/2676723.2691839

Teaching Track Faculty in CS

Mark Sherriff, *University of Virginia*
Daniel Garcia, *University of California, Berkeley*
Contact: sherriff@virginia.edu

Many computer science departments have chosen to hire faculty to teach in a teaching-track position that parallels the standard tenure-track position. These teaching-track positions include the possibility for promotion, longer-term contracts and greater pay as demonstrated by excellence in teaching, educational material development, and service. Since this type of position is relatively new in CS departments, the expectations and responsibilities for such faculty vary from one university to another, but they certainly differ from the traditional tenure-track positions. This birds-of-a-feather is designed to gather educators who are currently in such a position to share their experiences as members of the faculty of their departments and schools, and to provide opportunities for schools considering such positions to gather information. In past sessions, we have laid the groundwork for keeping this community together through online discussions and consolidating information about teaching-track positions at various universities together into an online database.

ACM Categories & Descriptors: K.3.2 Computer and Information Science Education: Computer Science Education

Keywords: Non-tenure track faculty, teaching faculty

DOI: http://dx.doi.org/10.1145/2676723.2691852

Juggling the Jigsaw: Enabling CS1 Growing Enrollment and Diversity at Undergraduate Institutions

Farzana Rahman, *James Madison University*
Dee Weikle, Eastern Mennonite University
Contact: rahma2fx@jmu.edu

The enrollment in introductory computer science courses has been growing steadily for the last couple of years. Interest in the field is exploding across the nation. Colleges and universities of all shapes and sizes have seen enrollment in introductory computer science courses and to some extent in upper-division electives explode as well. Most R1 institutions handle such growth through the use of graduate TAs to teach CS1 courses. Many primarily undergraduate and/or liberal arts institutions don't have these resources, however. Complicating the scenario further, students coming to these non-research institutions expect personal interaction, are from a growingly diverse set of high-school graduates and seem to be less prepared for college than ever. Given the current funding climate for higher education, it is difficult to imagine how most universities and colleges will be able to negotiate this scenario. This BOF will provide a platform to discuss how to handle the growing, diverse, and uninitiated CS1 enrollment from many perspectives - individual, departmental, and institutional. What creative solutions can be brought to improve institutional motivation and how do we

SIGCSE'15, March 4–7, 2015, Kansas City, MO, USA.
ACM 978-1-4503-2966-8/15/03.

ensure that traditionally under-represented groups don't get left behind in the onslaught?

ACM Categories & Descriptors: K.3 COMPUTERS AND EDUCATION

Keywords: CS1; Enrollment Growth; Institutional readiness; Diversity

DOI: http://dx.doi.org/10.1145/2676723.2691855

Interactive Ebooks and Course Materials - A BOF for Authors and Instructors

Cay Horstmann, San José State University
Smita Bakshi, *Zyante Inc.*
Amruth Kumar, *Ramapo College of New Jersey*
Frank Vahid, *University of California, Riverside*
Contact: Cay.Horstmann@sjsu.edu

Interactive activities in textbooks and online courses are no longer just decorative, but have become compelling tools for engaging students. This BOF, led by professors and authors with experience in designing complex interactive tutoring materials, invites interested instructors and authors to discuss best practices in designing activities, integrating them into courses, and measuring outcomes.

ACM Categories & Descriptors: K.3.1 Computer Uses in Education: Computer-assisted instruction (CAI); K.3.2 Computer and Information Science Education: Computer science education

Keywords: Interactive activities; ebooks

DOI: http://dx.doi.org/10.1145/2676723.2691856

Updating the ACM/IEEE 2008 Curriculum in Information Technology

Mihaela Sabin, *University of New Hampshire*
Svetlana Peltsverger, *Southern Polytechnic State University*
Cara Tang, *Portland Community College*
Contact: mihaela.sabin@unh.edu

At the direction of the ACM Education Board, the IT2017 Task Group was formed with the charge of updating the joint ACM and IEEE Computer Society Curriculum Guidelines for Undergraduate Degree Programs in Information Technology, known as IT2008. The revised document, called IT2017, should be appropriately forward looking given the significant advances in information technology that have occurred since 2008. Participants attending the BOF will contribute their insights and assist with the revision process to update IT2008. Discussions will center on delineating knowledge areas and learning outcomes specific to IT; exploring the current and future roles of IT in computing disciplines; recommending changes to improve the usefulness of the report; and planning further communications to fully engage the academic and professional community in the revision process. The objective is to ensure that the updated document is a forward-looking curriculum framework of the disciplinary content and practices in the field of information technology and remains relevant into 2020 and beyond for incoming students, computing departments with IT programs, accreditation bodies, and employers in the U.S. and anywhere else in the world.

SIGCSE'15, March 4–7, 2015, Kansas City, MO, USA.
ACM 978-1-4503-2966-8/15/03.

ACM Categories & Descriptors: K.3.2 [Computer and Information Science Education]: Curriculum

Keywords: Information Technology; Curriculum Guidelines; IT2017; IT2008

DOI: http://dx.doi.org/10.1145/2676723.2691857

Teaching Algebra and Computing through Bootstrap and Program by Design

Emmanuel Schanzer, *Harvard Graduate School of Education*
Kathi Fisler, *WPI*
Contact: schanzer@bootstrapworld.org

Bootstrap teaches students to create their own videogames using a programming approach that directly reinforces state and national algebra standards. Used in classrooms across the country, Bootstrap is proving successful at transferring skills from programming to algebra word problems in 8th and 9th grade students. Due to the algebraic foundation for both content and pedagogy, math teachers with limited programming experience find the curriculum highly approachable; many offer it as a module within an algebra course. Bootstrap is a prefix to a higher-level computer science curriculum called Program by Design that emphasizes data-driven design and testing (with or without the videogame focus). In this BOF, current and potential users of these curricula will discuss the connections between introductory computing education and algebra education, share best practices for teaching and moving beyond these curricula, and generate ideas for future evolution of both curricula. The two facilitators will adapt the format as needed to support the interests of the participants.

ACM Categories & Descriptors: K.3.2 [Computers and Education]: Computer and Information Science Education

Keywords: integrating math and computing; K-12 instruction; game programming; skill transfer

DOI: http://dx.doi.org/10.1145/2676723.2691860

Teaching Security Using Hands-on Exercises in 2015

Richard Weiss, *The Evergreen State College*
Michael Locasto, *The University of Calgary*
Jens Mache, *Lewis & Clark College*
Blair Taylor, *Towson University*
Elizabeth Hawthorne, *Union County College*
Justin Cappos, *New York University*
Ambereen Siraj, *Tennessee Tech University*
Contact: weissr@evergreen.edu

We see teaching cybersecurity through hands-on, interactive exercises as a way to engage students. Some of the exercises that we have seen require significant preparation on the part of the instructor. Having a community makes it easier to share exercises, knowing what works and what problems students and instructors have encountered. The purpose of this BOF is to bring together instructors who have developed hands-on exercises, those who have used them and those who would like to. We recognize that few CS programs can afford new required courses, so we will discuss ways to integrate security-related exercises into existing ones. This could include networking, OS, computer architecture, programming languages, software engineering, algorithms and programming. The questions we will ask are, "What exercises have you tried? What are your experiences? What are you looking for?"

Recent hiring forecasts indicate that there is still a tremendous need for skilled information security experts. Security is one of the core areas in the ACM/IEEE COMPUTER SCIENCE 2013 Curricula. It is particularly important to share stories from the classroom (what worked and what didn't), discuss ethical hacking, and discuss how to teach analytical skills. We plan to share experiences, practices and ongoing efforts, including our own (e.g., our teaching experiences, the SISMAT program, Security Injections, the Seattle Platform, the Security Knitting Kit project, EDURange and the dissemination of infosec interactive exercises).

ACM Categories & Descriptors: K.3.2 Computer and Information Science Education; K.6.5 Security and Protection

Keywords: security; laboratory exercises; hacker curriculum; secure coding

DOI: http://dx.doi.org/10.1145/2676723.2691862

Creating Assessment Tools for Cybersecurity Education

Geoffrey L Herman, *University of Illinois at Urbana-Champaign*
Ronald Dodge, *United States Military Academy*
Contact: glherman@illinois.edu

Recent large-scale data breaches such as the credit card scandals of Target and Home Depot have significantly raised the public awareness of the importance of the security of their data and personal information. These incidents highlight a growing need and urgency to develop the cybersecurity infrastructure of our country and in the world. The development of ACM's Computer Science Curriculum 2013 and the National Initiative for Cybersecurity Education framework further highlight the growing importance of cybersecurity in computing education. Critically, recent studies predict that there will be a significant demand for cybersecurity professionals in the coming years, yet there is a lack of rigorous evidence-based infrastructure to advise educators on how best to engage, inform, educate, nurture, and retain cybersecurity students and how best to structure cybersecurity curricula to prepare new professionals for careers in this field. The development of validated assessment tools of student learning provide one means for increasing the rigor with which we make pedagogical and curricular decisions. During this Birds of a Feather session, participants will engage in a structured dialogue to identify what assessment tools are needed to improve cybersecurity education. Further, participants will provide feedback on initial efforts to identify a core set of concepts and skills that will be essential for students' success in cybersecurity fields.

SIGCSE'15, March 4–7, 2015, Kansas City, MO, USA.
ACM 978-1-4503-2966-8/15/03.

ACM Categories & Descriptors: K.3.2 [Computers and Education]: Computer and Information Science Education—Computer science education, K6.5 [Management of Computing and Information Systems] Security and Protection

Keywords: cybersecurity; concept inventories; assessment; computer science education

DOI: http://dx.doi.org/10.1145/2676723.2691863

Automatically Generated Feedback for CS Student Work: Best Practices

Bruce Char, *Drexel University*
Jeremy Johnson, *Drexel University*
Jeffrey Popyack, *Drexel University*
William Mongan, *Drexel University*
Contact: charbw@drexel.edu

This session invites educators interested in sharing and/or learning about experiences with tools for automatic feedback on technical work: the "if", "why" and "how". This includes experiences with program testing, problem-solving exercises, or quizzes, generated or checked with engines with expert-level technical capabilities, to scale up feedback to cope with burgeoning enrollment in CS courses while maintaining or improving student learning outcomes. Commercial, free and open-source tools now exist to assist in this endeavor.

The benefits of providing timely, detailed, and insightful feedback for student effort are well known. Yet as enrollment in CS courses increases, many are hard pressed to find the human resources to scale up their feedback efforts. TAs and instructors may struggle to deal with the increased evaluation load, resulting in inconsistent, untimely, or lessened insight in feedback.

Automatic grading and feedback offer a way to scale detailed and individualized feedback and for instructors to write materials with enhanced shelf-life, but with additional courseware engineering and administrative cost. It raises pedagogical questions about good ways for machine-based feedback to be blended with other types of learning activities, both conventional and novel. It has significance and relevance to departments facing the "scaling up" situation when it is understood if, how and why it can help address the problem.

ACM Categories & Descriptors: K.3.1 Computer Uses in Education – Computer-assisted instruction, Computer managed instruction, K.3.2 Computer and Information Science Education – Computer Science Education, Self-assessment.

Keywords: autograding; automatic feedback; scaling instruction

DOI: http://dx.doi.org/10.1145/2676723.2691865

New Concepts in Database System Education – Experiences and Ideas

Carsten Kleiner, *University of Applied Scienes&Arts Hannover*
Contact: carsten.kleiner@hs-hannover.de

Compared to their fundamental part of computer science curricula the small number of papers on database system education comes as a surprise. The apparent draught in new ideas in database system education is even more surprising given the fact that this area of computer science has arguably undergone its most significant changes for more than 30 years within the last 5 to 10 years. Many new database system paradigms (most of them appearing under the NoSQL label) have been introduced for various reasons. Some of these massively distributed database systems facilitate unprecedented data processing capabilities often labeled as BigData. In order to offer a sustainable and practical CS education, at least some of those new paradigms and methodologies should be included into database education. The BoF is meant to continue the discussion from the 2014 BoF about which of those deserve inclusion into a typical CS curriculum and (even more interestingly) at what time in the curriculum and by replacing what other topics. It shall offer participants a forum to share their opinions and ideas on recent and future changes in database system education as well as to present practical experiences with new concepts picked up at last year's BoF or elsewhere.

ACM Categories & Descriptors: H.2.0 General; K.3.2 Computer and Information Science Education; Information Systems Education

Keywords: database systems; Big Data; NoSQL; database paradigms; curriculum; database courses

DOI: http://dx.doi.org/10.1145/2676723.2691835

Computer Science Principles: Expanding the Community

Owen Astrachan, *Duke University*
Lien Diaz, *College Board*
Amy Briggs, *Middlebury College*
Fran Trees, *Rutgers University*
Rich Kick, *Newbury Park High School*
Contact: ola@duke.edu

Computer Science Principles will become an Advanced Placement course in AY 2016-2017, with the launch of the first APCSP exam in May of 2017, with through-course assessments/performance tasks being completed by students starting at the beginning of that academic year. In this BOF we will hear from participants about their questions and concerns in anticipation of the launch of the course and exam. The BOF will be part of launching a community of practice for teachers and educators who are not part of a formal NSF project, Project Lead the Way, or Code.org whose participants may have a community of practice.

ACM Categories & Descriptors: K.3 Computers and Education

Keywords: Computer Science Principles, K-12 Education, Broadening Participation

DOI: http://dx.doi.org/10.1145/2676723.2691868

SIGCSE'15, March 4–7, 2015, Kansas City, MO, USA.
ACM 978-1-4503-2966-8/15/03.

Birds of a Feather FLOCK II

Proposed ABET Computer Science Criteria and the CS2013 Curriculum

Michael Oudshoorn, *Wentworth Institute of Technology*
Stan Thomas, *Wake Forest University*
Barbara Boucher Owens, *Southwestern University*
Deborah Trytten, *University of Oklaholma*
Mary-Jane Willshire, *Capella University*
Contact: oudshoornm@wit.edu

The ACM/IEEE CS2013 Curriculum provides a somewhat rigid identification of topics to be covered by a model computer science curriculum. It was developed with significant input from industry, educators and other stakeholders and represents best practices in terms of Computer Science education. ABET is the accreditation body accrediting computer science programs in the US, and it also accredits a number of international programs. ABET's goal is to allow programs to identify their own outcomes and measure their success in delivering programs that achieve this, while also ensuring that all students receive a solid core education including key areas of the discipline without being excessively prescriptive. Both documents address excellence in computer science education. Changes to the Computer Science program criteria are being recommended which will more closely align the two documents in terms of identifying key areas to be covered by programs. This session provides participants with the opportunity to hear about the proposed changes and the rationale behind them and to offer feedback and input into the process.

ACM Categories & Descriptors: K.3.2 [Computers and Education]: Computer and Information Science Education - *Accreditation, Curriculum*

Keywords: Accreditation; Curriculum

DOI: http://dx.doi.org/10.1145/2676723.2691831

AP CS A – Sharing Teching Strategies and Curricular Ideas

Paul Tymann, *Rochester Institute of Technology*
Lester Wainright, *Charlottesville High School*
Sandy Czajka, *Riverside Brookfield High School*
Contact: paul.tymann@rit.edu

This BOF will provide an opportunity for high school and college faculty to discuss the AP CS A curriculum and to explore possibilities for collaborations and outreach activities between high schools and colleges.

ACM Categories & Descriptors: K.3.2 [Computer and Information Science Education]: *Computer Science Education*

SIGCSE'15, March 4–7, 2015, Kansas City, MO, USA.
ACM 978-1-4503-2966-8/15/03.

Keywords: **AP CS A; Teaching Strategies; Curricular Ideas**

DOI: http://dx.doi.org/10.1145/2676723.2691832

Perspectives on How Computer Science Curricula 2013 Influences Two-Year College Programs

Cindy S. Tucker, *Bluegrass Community and Technical College*
Cara Tang, *Portland Community College*
Elizabeth K. Hawthorne, *Union County College*
Contact: cindy.tucker@kctcs.edu

The *ACM Computer Science Curricula 2013* (CS2013) guidance for undergraduate degrees was released in December 2013. This BOF will provide a platform for two-year and four-year computer science faculty and academic administrators to discuss CS2013 and its influence on associate-degree computer science curricula. The session will include a brief overview of the Core Tier-1 and Core Tier-2 CS2013 topics and attendees will primarily engage in an open dialog about which CS2013 topics and learning outcomes are most relevant to be included in a transfer curriculum. This CS2013 discussion will help inform the forthcoming update to *Computing Curricular 2009: Guidelines for Associate-Degree Transfer Curriculum in Computer Science* (www.capspace.org).

ACM Categories & Descriptors: K.3.2 [Computers and Education]: Computer and Information Science Education - *Curriculum, Computer Science Education*

Keywords: Two-Year College; Community College; Education; Computer Science

DOI: http://dx.doi.org/10.1145/2676723.2691833

Handling Very Large Lecture Courses: Keeping the Wheels on the Bus

Josh Hug, *UC Berkeley*
Daniel D. Garcia, *UC Berkeley*
Contact: hug@cs.berkeley.edu

As classes grow beyond hundreds or even a thousand students, instructors must come to grapple with handling course logistics at scale. Otherwise mundane tasks can no longer be handled in an ad hoc way, and standard course design challenges become more acute. Just to name a few issues, the instructor might have to contend with: Exam scheduling, recruiting and managing a teaching staff that consists of dozens of people, ensuring consistency of grading, identifying and providing interventions for struggling students, providing a consistent policy for makeup work, and creating diverse course content (e.g. lab, HW, discussion section) that allows for an efficient path to mastery for each student regardless of diverse backgrounds and ability. If you have good ideas for handling these issues you'd like to share, or just want to learn what others are doing, come join us! Discussion will ideally include staffing techniques, technologies (including automated assessments), and ways of developing course content.

ACM Categories & Descriptors: K.3.2 Computer and Information Science Education

Keywords: large lecture courses; course logistics; instructional technologies; automated assessments

DOI: http://dx.doi.org/10.1145/2676723.2691867

Addressing Professional Development Needs for K-12 CS – Working with Your Local CSTA Chapter

David Reed, *Creighton University*
Frances P. Trees, *Rutgers University*
Contact: davereed@creighton.edu

One of the greatest challenges for K-12 computer science educators is finding the opportunities and resources to stay up-to-date with the field and its pedagogical practices. Teachers often lack CS colleagues at their school, which makes the lack of professional development opportunities even more significant. As part of its commitment to developing a strong community of computer science educators, the Computer Science Teachers Association (CSTA) supports the development of regional CSTA chapters. A CSTA chapter is a local branch of CSTA designed to facilitate discussion of local issues and to help connect teachers with professional development resources. This BOF will discuss existing professional development resources available to K-12 teachers, as well as providing a community building forum between high school teachers and college faculty. Attendees will be asked to share their professional development needs and desires, which will then guide the CSTA Professional Development committee in future efforts.

ACM Categories & Descriptors: K.3.2 [COMPUTERS AND EDUCATION]: Computer and Information Science Education—Computer Science Education; K.7.1 [THE COMPUTING PROFESSION]: Occupations.

Keywords: K-12 Computer Science Education; Professional Development; Computer Science Teachers Association; CSTA.

DOI: http://dx.doi.org/10.1145/2676723.2691836

Study Abroad Experiences in Computer Science

Michael Goldweber, *Xavier University*
mikeyg@xavier.edu

This BoF is to gather computer science educators interested in helping to create successful study abroad experiences for computer science students. While study abroad consistency places number one as the most impactful experience an undergraduate can have, computer science students have some of the lowest study abroad participation rates. While some of the reasons for this are financial, it is believed that the primary reason is the lack of meaningful study abroad opportunities.

In the world of study abroad programs, it is a basic axiom that a study abroad program, to be successful, has to have a reason for being in its chosen location. Simply transplanting a course to an exotic location is considered educational tourism. The most successful study abroad programs leverage being present in a foreign location to provide some value added to the course over its back home-based counterpart. We define meaningful study abroad opportunities as ones where students can make forward progress in their major, but avoid becoming exercises in educational tourism. Furthermore, at all but the largest of institutions, discipline-specific study abroad programs, due to enrollment sizes need to be inter-institutional.

How to create a meaningful study abroad experience in computer science is a difficult open question. The purpose of this BoF is to gather interested colleagues to brainstorm ideas and to begin a community-wide dialog on developing successful and meaningful study abroad programs for computer science students.

ACM Categories & Descriptors: K.3.2{Computer and Information Science Education}[Computer Science Education]

Keywords: Study Abroad

DOI: http://dx.doi.org/10.1145/2676723.2691837

The Great Objective-C Swift Migration of 2015

Michael P. Rogers, *Northwest Missouri State University*
William Siever, *Western Illinois University*
Contact: mprogers@mac.com

Apple recently announced Swift, a new development language for iOS and OSX. While designed with developers in mind, it is also a boon to those who teach programming topics. Its relatively simple and familiar syntax; its integration in a scripting environment, Playgrounds, complete with built-in visualization tools; and the ability to incorporate live code in textbook form means that Swift is far better suited for teaching mobile app development than Objective-C. Indeed, the tools are so learner-friendly and the language so inviting that Swift might even find a place in a CS1 course. The language itself and the migration from Objective-C raise both logistical and pedagogical issues that will be addressed in this Birds of a Feather session.

ACM Categories & Descriptors: D.3.3 [PROGRAMMING LANGUAGES] Language Constructs and Features---Swift; K.3.2 [COMPUTING MILIEUX] Computer and Information Science Education - Swift

Keywords: iOS Development

DOI: http://dx.doi.org/10.1145/2676723.2691849

SIGCSE'15, March 4–7, 2015, Kansas City, MO, USA.
ACM 978-1-4503-2966-8/15/03.

Assessments for Computational Thinking in K-12

Shuchi Grover, *SRI International*
Marie Bienkowski, *SRI International*
Eric Snow, *SRI International*
Contact: shuchi.grover@sri.com

As computer science (CS) and computational thinking (CT) make their way into all levels of K-12 education, valid assessments aligned with new curricula can assist in measuring student learning, easing the way for adoption of new computing courses, and evaluation of pedagogical approaches for teaching computing ideas and concepts. Without attention to rigorous assessment, CT can have little hope of making its way successfully into K–12 school education settings at scale. This BoF session will involve discussion around ongoing work at SRI International (under several NSF-funded projects) on the design and development of formative and summative assessments for the ECS curriculum. Additionally, various forms of assessment (including free response and multiple-choice questions, and computational artifacts), and insights from past research on their use will be discussed. BOF attendees will be able to discuss multiple viewpoints, connect with others who care about assessment of CT, and share resources and ideas.

ACM Categories & Descriptors: K.3 Computers and Education; K.3.0 General

Keywords: Computational thinking; assessment; evidence-centered design

DOI: http://dx.doi.org/10.1145/2676723.2691843

Student Contributions to Humanitarian Free and Open Source Software (HFOSS)

Lori Postner, *Nassau Community College*
Stoney Jackson, *Western New England University*
Ben Coleman, *Moravian College*
Suzanne Mello-Stark, *Univ. of Rhode Island*
Samuel Rebelsky, *Grinnell College*
Contact: Lori.Postner@ncc.edu

Can students contribute to HFOSS projects as part of their computing curriculum? How and at what level can HFOSS be integrated? What are the success stories and challenges? This BOF will be led by a diverse group of faculty who have incorporated HFOSS into their classes. They will lead a discussion on the various approaches, successes and challenges they have encountered. Their experiences will provide a backdrop for this BOF session, which should lead to a lively discussion of how and why to use HFOSS in computing courses. Faculty who are interested in HFOSS, but who are novices, will learn about potential projects and classroom materials as well as make connections with more experienced faculty in this area.

ACM Categories & Descriptors: K.3.2 [Computers and Education]: Computer and Information Science Education

Keywords: Humanitarian Free and Open Source Software

DOI: http://dx.doi.org/10.1145/2676723.2691844

Partnering to Promote State-by-State Computing Education Reform

W. Richards Adrion, *University of Massachusetts Amherst*
Mark Guzdial, *Georgia Institute of Technology*
Barbara Ericson, *Georgia Institute of Technology*
Contact: adrion@cs.umass.edu

We are all excited to see an increasing number of national efforts to reform computing education. Persistent and sustainable change in a state, its higher education institutions, and its K12 districts requires the active participation of individuals and local organizations to engage policy makers, higher education, school districts and communities. U.S. education is highly distributed, with critical decisions pushed more to the community level and less at the national (or even state) level. The system is organized along K20 pathways and a reform process to improve these pathways will take place at multiple levels and state by state.

This BOF will bring together emerging leaders at the state level with representatives from national initiatives to share best practices for implementing change. The NSF BPC Expanding Computing Education Pathways (ECEP) Alliance will present its 4-step model for state change: identify leaders, assess the CS education landscape, organize the statewide stakeholders, and find resources to enable change. We will moderate a discussion of how the ECEP model, its services and federal/foundation resources might be adapted to enhance state-based initiatives and partnerships. ECEP provides experts for state policy events, teacher professional development, and 2-4-year transfer summits. It provides training and funding to help start computing summer camps. ECEP trial interventions are helping more African American students pass the AP-CS-A exam.

ACM Categories & Descriptors: K.3.2 Computer and Information Science Education; K.4.1 Public Policy Issues; K.7.1 Occupations; K.7.2 Organizations

Keywords: Computing Education Reform; Advocacy, Outreach; Diversity and Inclusion

DOI: http://dx.doi.org/10.1145/2676723.2691845

SIGCSE'15, March 4–7, 2015, Kansas City, MO, USA.
ACM 978-1-4503-2966-8/15/03.

Open Educational Resources: What Next?

Lillian (Boots) Cassel, *Villanova University*
Cynthia Lee, *Stanford University*
Cliff Shaffer, Virginia Tech
Darina Dicheva, *Winston-Salem State University*
David Hovemeyer, *York College of Pennsylvania*
Contact: dhovemey@ycp.edu

Open educational resources—assignments, labs, course notes, and other types of materials made available for anyone interested in using them—have the potential to have a significant positive impact on courses and students at many institutions. Distribution and use of course materials is also an important factor in encouraging the adoption and use of innovative teaching practices. However, the use of open resources is still somewhat uncommon, with most instructors preferring to use their own materials.

This BoF will bring together providers and users of open educational resources to pose the following questions: Who is using open resources? Who *isn't* using open resources? How could open resources, and the repositories where they are made available, better meet the needs of potential users? What is necessary to make sharing of educational resources easier and more effective? Are there inherent barriers to sharing and reuse, and how can they be overcome?

ACM Categories & Descriptors: K.3.2 [Computer and Information Science Education]: *Computer science education*

Keywords: open educational resources

DOI: http://dx.doi.org/10.1145/2676723.2691850

Computer Science: Small Department Initiative

Catherine Bareiss, *Olivet Nazarene University*
Contact: cbareiss@olivet.edu

Faculty members in a small department (5 FTE or less) face special challenges and strengths because of their size. This BOF is a time for faculty to meet and discuss ways to meet the shared challenges and take advantage of their strengths. The actual topics covered will be based on those attending. Possible topics might include: sharing classes, increasing enrollment, general education, and specialized courses.

ACM Categories & Descriptors: K.3.0 [Computing Milieux]: Computer and Education - *General*

Keywords: small department

DOI: http://dx.doi.org/10.1145/2676723.2691851

SIGCSE'15, March 4–7, 2015, Kansas City, MO, USA.
ACM 978-1-4503-2966-8/15/03.

Empirical Research in CS Education

Mark Sherriff, *University of Virginia*
Sarah Heckman, *North Carolina State University*
Contact: sherriff@virginia.edu

Over the past several years, there has been a marked increase in empirical validation in research papers presented at the SIGCSE Symposium. This birds-of-a-feather session intends to bring together faculty interested in empirical research in computer science education to share methodologies and techniques, while also continuing the conversation about how to move empirical computer science education research forward. The computer science education (CSEd) research community consists of a large group of passionate CS educators who often contribute to other disciplines of CS research. There has been a trend in other disciplines toward more rigorous and empirical evaluation of various hypotheses. Prior meta-analyses of the then-current state of CSEd research showed a distinct lack of rigor in the top CSEd publication venues, with most papers falling in the general category of experience reports. Our goal is to engage the SIGCSE community in a discussion as to how we can move empirical research in CSEd forward. We hope to help researchers establish connections that will allow them to share research methodologies and challenges.

ACM Categories & Descriptors: K.3.2 [Computer and Information Science Education]: *Computer Science Education*

Keywords: Empirical research, Scholarship of Teaching and Learning

DOI: http://dx.doi.org/10.1145/2676723.2691853

CS 4 Everyone: Diversifying the K-12 Pipeline for CS at College and High School Level

Farzana Rahman, *James Madison University*
Jennifer Stevens, *Virginia Advanced Study Strategies*
Sharon Simmons, *James Madison University*
Contact: rahma2fx@jmu.edu

It is widely known that computer science students do not reflect the diversity of the population at large. Studies have shown that effective outreach programs can educate the public, increase student interest, help recruit and retain majors in computing disciplines. Traditionally the outreach events are organized by higher education institutions or nonprofit organizations. It will be highly effective if high school teachers are provided with the right tools so they can organize outreach events in their school or local community. Outreach programs can vary widely in terms of target audience, duration and objective. And it might seem daunting to design and deploy outreach events to make it sustainable. Our goal in this BOF is to discuss effective outreach activities to recruit and retain diverse students in CS K-12 pipeline. In particular, each facilitator will address the objective of the activity, the target audience, a description of the activity, and key aspects for successful deployment. This BOF will also provide an effective model for high school teachers to design and implement computing outreach activities in their schools. We will share techniques to increase students and parents interest in computer related discipline and provide them with appropriate tools to pursue their interest more. Facilitators will also share information about various funding agencies that can sponsor CS outreach programs. It will provide an opportunity for high school and college faculty to explore possibilities for collaborations and outreach between high schools and colleges.

ACM Categories & Descriptors: K.3 Computers & Education

Keywords: Outreach; Diversity; K-12 Pipeline; Recruitment and Retention in CS

DOI: http://dx.doi.org/10.1145/2676723.2691913

Preparing Undergraduates to Make the Most of Attending CS Conferences

Janet Davis, *Grinnell College*
Christine Alvarado, *UC San Diego*
Miranda Parker, *Georgia Tech*
Jennelle Nystrom, *Yahoo!*
Contact: davisjan@cs.grinnell.edu

Students who attend academic conferences can broaden their horizons, increase their commitment to the discipline, find role models and mentors, and gain concrete opportunities for work and study. However, attending one's first conference can be an overwhelming experience. We often focus on the procurement of funding to send students to conferences, and do not spend as much time considering what will happen once they get there. In this BoF, we will share strategies for guiding and supporting undergraduates to take full advantage of attending a CS conference.

This session will be led by two faculty members and two young alumni. We will draw on our collective experience helping our students/classmates make the most of attending the Grace Hopper Celebration of Women in Computing, SIGCSE, and other CS research conferences. We invite discussion of any and all conferences participants have experience with, as similar strategies may apply. Specifically, we may consider how to help students: act with confidence in a professional setting; rehearse an "elevator pitch"; navigate career fairs and exhibit halls; choose wisely among parallel sessions and the "hallway track"; network effectively with potential mentors, advisers, and employers; present their own work in talks or poster sessions; reflect on their experiences; and share what they learn at their home institution.

ACM Categories & Descriptors: K.3.2 [Computers and Education]: *Computer and Information Science Education*; K.7.0 [The Computing Profession]: *General*

Keywords: Careers; communication; conferences; undergraduate.

DOI: http://dx.doi.org/10.1145/2676723.2691858

SIGCSE'15, March 4–7, 2015, Kansas City, MO, USA.
ACM 978-1-4503-2966-8/15/03.

Can Programming Boot Camp Help Under-represented College Students Succeed in Computing Degrees?

Kristine Nagel, *Georgia Gwinnett College*
Sonal Dekhane, *Georgia Gwinnett College*
Nannette Napier, *Georgia Gwinnett College*
Contact: {knagel, sdekhane, nnapier} @ggc.edu

Programming Boot Camp is one strategy to overcome the perceived and actual difficulties undergraduate students encounter in an introductory programming course. It is estimated that of the over two million students starting computer science studies in universities and colleges all over the world in 1999, 33% dropped or failed their first programming course. Consequently, undergraduate students delay enrolling in programming courses, which interrupts progress toward their degree and decreases confidence in their ability to succeed in college and computing careers. Programming Boot Camp provides a combination of intense programming labs with professional development and community building activities to help increase confidence, create awareness of opportunities, and build a supporting peer network. How does this strategy work on different campuses with different demographics? Attendees will be able to connect with people who have implemented boot camp, are interested in sharing resources, and discussing how appropriate a boot camp would be for their students. Those who have already implemented a boot camp will be encouraged to share their curriculum, workshop strategies, and how effective they were in goals like: increasing the programming skills of the participants and their confidence in it, inspiring participants to persist in computing, and building a network of mentors and peers to support persistence in computing. Participants who seek to increase success in programming courses will be encouraged to discuss campus specific needs to gather input from those who have implemented boot camps and how they adapted the concept to their population and institutional culture.

ACM Categories & Descriptors: K.3.2 [COMPUTERS AND EDUCATION]: *Computer and Information Science Education, Computer science education*

Keywords: summer boot camp; women in IT; retention

DOI: http://dx.doi.org/10.1145/2676723.2691859

SIGCSE Reads: Time for Book Discussion

Rebecca Bates, *Minnesota State University, Mankato*
Judy Goldsmith, *University of Kentucky*
Valerie Summet, *Emory University*
Contact: bates@mnsu.edu

Did you read any of the common reads for SIGCSE 2015? Now's your chance to talk about them! Three books: *I, Robot* by Isaac Asimov (Bantam Spectra, 1950), *Bellwether* by Connie Willis (Bantam Spectra, 1997) and *Ready Player One* by Ernest Cline (Broadway Books, 2012) were proposed at the end of the 2014 conference. If you're interested in science fiction, whether on a personal, academic, or pedagogical level, come join us in this BoF and discuss one or more of the three suggested books. We'll provide potential topics and discussion questions targeting how to incorporate these books into a CS course, but the discussion will be open. The BoF will close with a discussion of potential books for the 2016 conference.

ACM Categories & Descriptors: K.3.2 [Computer and Information Science Education]: Computer science education

Keywords: Science fiction; computer science; computer science education.

DOI: http://dx.doi.org/10.1145/2676723.2691861

Working with Undergraduate Teaching Assistants: Best Practices and Lessons Learned

Chris Gregg, *Tufts University*
Colleen M. Lewis, *Harvey Mudd College*
Contact: cgregg@cs.tufts.edu

Instructors struggling to support their ever-growing undergraduate population may be interested in starting, expanding, or improving an undergraduate teaching assistant (TA) program. This session seeks to connect individuals interested brainstorming and sharing strategies for improving the impact of undergraduate TAs. We will break into small groups to discuss tips for (0) structuring *funded* and *unfunded* undergraduate TA programs, (1) training undergraduate TAs, and (2) recruiting and selecting undergraduate TAs. All tips will be posted on http://CSTeachingTips.org for dissemination to other CS educators. This BoF welcomes instructors already supporting undergraduate TAs and instructors who are interested in build an undergraduate TA program.

ACM Categories & Descriptors: K. Computing Milieux, K.3 COMPUTERS AND EDUCATION, K.3.0 General

Keywords: undergraduate; teaching assistants; instruction; pedagogy; classroom management

DOI: http://dx.doi.org/10.1145/2676723.2691864

SIGCSE'15, March 4–7, 2015, Kansas City, MO, USA.
ACM 978-1-4503-2966-8/15/03.

Blended CS Courses using Massive, Open, Online Courses (and other Online Resources)

Douglas H. Fisher, *Vanderbilt University*
Janet Burge, *Wesleyan University*
Mary Lou Maher, *Univ of North Carolina, Charlotte*
Jerry Roth, Vanderbilt University
Contact: douglas.h.fisher@vanderbilt.edu

Computer science instructors are incorporating Massive Open Online Courses (MOOCs), and MOOC material, into their campus courses. The closed instance is the dominant model being followed, in which MOOC material (e.g., in AI, in Programming Languages, in Software Engineering) is ported to a protected LMS so that campus students can use the MOOC video and other material (e.g., assessments) and infrastructure (e.g., autograders) in a "private" manner. In an embedded instance, campus students take a live MOOC as one component of their on-campus course. Another model, albeit nascent, is to exploit self-paced open online courses so that campus cohorts can move through a course when a campus instructor wants, and at a pace the instructor wants, but still availing campus students to the advantages of interacting with global students (and vice versa). The BoF session will allow participants to talk about MOOC-based blended models, form a group interested to archiving experience, synthesizing best practices, creating shared learning-object repositories (e.g., of active learning, in-class activities), and to discuss issues of policy (e.g., FERPA).

ACM Categories & Descriptors: K.3.1 [Computer Uses in Education]: *Collaborative learning, Computer-assisted instruction, Distance learning*; K.3.2 [Computer and Information Science Education]: *Computer science education*

Keywords: massive open online courses; blended learning; small private online courses; closed courses; embedded courses; MOOCs; SPOCs; classroom management; active learning; self-paced courses

DOI: http://dx.doi.org/10.1145/2676723.2691866

Wednesday Workshops

Teaching Computing Foundations to Non-Majors

Catherine Bareiss, *Olivet Nazarene University*
Larry Vail, *Olivet Nazarene University*
Contact: cbareiss@olivet.edu

This workshop shows participants about a new way to teach non-computing majors about computing fundamentals. This involves teaching computing concepts (such as sources of error, algorithm analysis, data storage, and simulations) that students encounter when they use computers to do work in their own disciplines. While this new way of teaching can use any discipline, the workshop will use the sciences as the working example. It will focus on how scientists use computers in their work but will also introduce ways to expand this to other disciplines. The course that will be presented presents different modules of computer science interspersed with different science modules that apply the computing knowledge. More details can be found at http://cf4s.olivet.edu. Participants are highly encouraged to bring a laptop. Handouts associated with the entire course will be provided.

This material is based on work supported by the National Science Foundation under grant DUE-0942362. Any opinions, findings, and conclusions or recommendations expressed in this material are those of the authors and do not necessarily reflect those of the National Science Foundation.

ACM Categories & Descriptors: K.3.2 [Computing Milieux]: Computer and Education---Computer and Information Science Education

Keywords: Non-majors; Computational Science

DOI: http://dx.doi.org/10.1145/2676723.2678283

Teaching Parallel & Distributed Computing with MPI

Joel C. Adams, *Calvin College*
Richard A. Brown, *St. Olaf College*
Elizabeth Shoop, *Macalester College*
Contact: adams@calvin.edu

CS2013 brings parallel and distributed computing (PDC) into the CS curricular mainstream. The Message Passing Interface (MPI) is a platform independent, industry-standard PDC library that includes support for C, C++, and Fortran; third parties have created implementations for Python and Java. This hands-on workshop introduces MPI basics using parallel patterns, including the *single program multiple data* (SPMD), *send-receive* message passing, *master-worker*, *parallel loop*, *broadcast*, *reduction*, *scatter*, *gather*, and *barrier* patterns. Participants will explore 12 short programs designed to help students understand MPI and PDC basics, plus longer programs that use MPI to solve significant problems. The intended audience is CS educators who want to learn about how message passing can be used to teach PDC. No prior experience with PDC or MPI is required; familiarity with a C-family language and the command-line are helpful but not required. The workshop includes: (i) self-paced hands-on experimentation with the working MPI programs, and (ii) a discussion of how these may be used to achieve the goals of CS2013. Participants will work on a remote Beowulf cluster accessed via SSH, and will need a laptop or a tablet with an SSH client (e.g., BitVise, iSSH), or a laptop with both a recent C/C++ compiler and MPI (e.g., OpenMPI or MPICH) installed. See *http://csinparallel.org*.

ACM Categories & Descriptors: D.1.3 [Programming Techniques]: Concurrent Programming – *Distributed programming, Parallel programming*; K.3.2 [Computers and Education]: Computer and Information Science Education – *Curriculum*

Keywords: Computer science; curriculum; design; distributed; memory; message passing; MPI; parallel; patterns; software

DOI: http://dx.doi.org/10.1145/2676723.2678285

Teaching Computer Science Soft Skills

Orit Hazzan, *Technion – Israel Institute of Technoogy*
Gadi Har-shai, *Technion – Israel Institute of Technoogy*
Contact: oritha@technion.ac.il

This workshop addresses the teaching of computer science soft skills, such as teamwork, diversity, presentation and communication skills, and ethical behaviors. It is based on the assumption that the people involved in software development processes deserve more attention, and therefore, their soft skills should also be addressed, beyond their scientific and engineering skills. In the workshop, we will highlight such soft skills using activities that aim to analyze them from a social and cognitive perspective. We will also present and discuss a course outline dealing with soft skills of computer science, including suggestions for specific activities and tasks.

ACM Categories & Descriptors: K.6.3 Software Management

Keywords: soft skills; teamwork; diversity; presentation and communication skills; ethics; social perspective; cognitive perspective; short presentation styles; reflection

DOI: http://dx.doi.org/10.1145/2676723.2678289

SEED Labs: Using Hands-on Lab Exercises for Computer Security Education

Wenliang Du, *Syracuse University*
Contact: wedu@syr.edu

Security courses have been integrated into many mainstream undergraduate and graduate computer science curricula. To achieve effective education, learning security principles must be grounded in experience. Over the last 12 years, we have developed 30 hands-on lab exercises for computer security education. These labs, called SEED labs (SEcurity EDucation),

SIGCSE'15, March 4–7, 2015, Kansas City, MO, USA.
ACM 978-1-4503-2966-8/15/03.

cover a variety of security topics, including vulnerabilities, attacks, software security, system security, network security, web security, access control, authentication, cryptography, etc. These labs are built upon a Linux virtual machine, the image of which can be downloaded from our web site. Students just need to use a single computer (can be their own laptop) to work on these labs, so there is no need for a dedicated physical laboratory. All software used in the labs is open-source and free. The SEED project has been funded by 3 NSF grants with a total budget of 1.3 million dollars. So far, SEED labs have been used by over 250 institutes in 30 countries. In this workshop, we will select some of the most popular SEED labs, demonstrate how they work. We will then select three labs, and guide the participants to work on these labs in the workshop. Participants are expected to bring their own laptops. Participants who want to gain experiences with more SEED labs can apply to attend our free 3-day workshop in June.

ACM Categories & Descriptors: K.3.2 [Computer & Information Science Education]: Computer Science Education

Keywords: Computer security education; Hands-on exercises

DOI: http://dx.doi.org/10.1145/2676723.2678290

Teaching Introductory Computer Science for a Diverse Student Body: Girls Who Code Style

Jeff Stern, *University of Michigan*
Ashley Gavin, *Girls Who Code*
Kari Bancroft, *Girls Who Code*
Contact: jeffster@umich.edu

At a time when less than twenty percent of AP Computer Science test-takers are female, Girls Who Code [GWC] has developed a unique teaching philosophy and effective curriculum to engage young women in CS early in their careers. This curriculum is built around cultivating exposure, interest, community and support, and technical skills. More than 500 young women have participated in GWC's Summer Immersion Programs, a seven-week, full-time computer science program for high school students. Ninety-five percent of participants said they are definitely or more likely to consider a major / minor in computer science after participation.
This workshop shares GWC's best practices with educators looking for new ways to effectively teach computer science. At the end of this workshop, participants will have concrete examples of how to effectively teach students who are underrepresented in computer science. Participants will also have the opportunity to practice teaching in the style and spirit of the GWC Summer Immersion Program, with the goal of engaging young women, and expanding this knowledge to reach minorities and other diverse populations.

ACM Categories & Descriptors: K.3.2. Computer and Information Science Education

Keywords: underrepresented groups; broadening participation; CS education; women in computing; computing principles

DOI: http://dx.doi.org/10.1145/2676723.2678291

SIGCSE'15, March 4–7, 2015, Kansas City, MO, USA.
ACM 978-1-4503-2966-8/15/03.

Making Music with Computers: Creative Programming in Python

Bill Manaris, *College of Charleston, USA*
Andrew R. Brown, *Griffith University, Australia*
Tobias Kohn, *ETH Zürich, Switzerland*
Contact: manarisb@cofc.edu

This is an introduction to creative software development and music making in Python. This material is intended for CS0/CS1 courses and for courses at the intersection of computing and the arts. The workshop will introduce music making activities for teaching traditional CS1 topics, GUIs, event-driven programming, and connecting to external devices (e.g., smartphones, digital pianos) via MIDI and OSC (Open Sound Control). Participants will be introduced to Jython Music (**http://jythonMusic.org**), a library of Python modules for creative programming and music making, and will be making their own music artifacts a few minutes later. Intended audience: Computer science educators interested in teaching creative programming and computational thinking for CS0, CS1, introductory courses in the intersection of computing and the arts, and courses intended to attract and retain new CS majors. Each participant will receive a copy of (1) handouts to be used during the workshop, (2) sample student assignments and projects, (3) API documentation, (4) all required software, and (5) numerous sample programs. **Laptop required (with Java JDK 7 or higher)**. All other software will be provided. Headphones are recommended.

ACM Categories & Descriptors: I.m. Miscellaneous; J.5 [Computer Applications]: Arts and Humanities - *Music*

Keywords: music; creative programming; Python; CS0/CS1; MIDI; audio; OSC (open sound control); image manipulation; graphical user interfaces; event-driven programming; computing and the arts

DOI: http://dx.doi.org/10.1145/2676723.2678295

Intellectual Property Law Basics for Computer Science Instructors

David G. Kay, *University of California, Irvine*
Contact: kay@uci.edu

Increasingly the practice of computing involves legal issues. Patenting algorithms, domain name poaching, downloading music, and "re-using" HTML and graphics from web sites all raise questions of intellectual property (IP) law (which includes patents, copyrights, trade secrets, and trademarks). In the classroom, computer science educators often confront questions that have legal ramifications. The presenter, who is both a computer scientist and a lawyer, will introduce the basics of intellectual property law to give instructors a framework for recognizing the issues, answering students' questions, debunking the most egregious misconceptions about IP, and understanding generally how the law and computing interact. All CS educators are welcome; no computer is required.

ACM Categories & Descriptors: K.5.1 [Hardware/Software Protection]: Copyrights; Patents; Trade secrets

Keywords: law; legal system; intellectual property; teaching professionalism and ethics

DOI: http://dx.doi.org/10.1145/2676723. 2678298

Friday Workshops

A Swift Introduction to Swift App Development

Michael P. Rogers, *Northwest Missouri State University*
Bill Siever, *Western Illinois University*
Contact: mprogers@mac.com

Swift is a new programming language recently introduced by Apple as a replacement for Objective-C. Considering that Objective-C ranks third on the Tiobe Index and is the progenitor of virtually all the 1.2 million apps in the App Store, Swift is likely to become the dominant language for creating both iOS and OS X apps. While Swift is aimed at application developers, the language and the tools that accompany it are also a boon for CS educators. Many of the features in Swift that aid commercial development, such as type-safety, clean syntax, closures, and named parameters, are also beneficial when learning programming. In addition to the language itself, Apple has introduced a remarkable feature called Playgrounds. As the name suggests, Playgrounds allow students to "play", that is, to interactively experiment, with code. They also provide a convenient visualization tool to graphically depict the impact of iteration, providing crucial insights for novice programmers. It is also possible to use Playgrounds to write tutorials or even entire textbooks with embedded, live code for students to experiment with. The workshop will introduce Swift through the use of Playgrounds. Participants will work through a variety of hands-on, active learning exercises to learn Swift's syntax and semantics. More importantly, they will experience a sample of active learning exercises that can be used in to introduce students to programming with Swift. ***Participants will need a MacBook with Xcode 6.1.1 or later installed***.

ACM Categories & Descriptors: K.3.2 [Computer and Information Science Education]: Computer Science Education

Keywords: Swift; Objective-C; Introductory Programming Languages

DOI: http://dx.doi.org/10.1145/2676723.2678281

Conducting Educational Research in the Computer Science Classroom: Choosing the Appropriate Research Design to Address your Research Questions

Aman Yadav, *Michigan State University*
Contact: *ayadav@msu.edu*

This workshop will provide CS educators with tools to conduct educational research. Primary objectives of this workshop are: (1) learn basic principles of research design; (2) learn about various types of research designs: qualitative vs. quantitative; experimental vs. quasi-experimental; case studies, survey; and (3) to practice designing research. This workshop will help participants make informed decisions when faced with limitations of educational research and collect empirical evidence about what works in the classroom. In addition, we will also discuss how to develop robust student outcome measures, such as surveys and tests. The workshop will be beneficial to participants who have not yet done all of these activities as well as those who have some background in educational research. Participants will be provided with material on research designs.

ACM Categories & Descriptors: K.3.2 [Computers and Education]: Computer and Information Science Education

Keywords: Educational Research; Research Design

DOI: http://dx.doi.org/10.1145/2676723.2678284

Using Pencil Code to Bridge the Gap between Visual and Text-Based Coding

David Bau, *Google*
Matthew Dawson, *Google CS First*
Anthony Bau, *Phillips Exeter Academy*
Contact: davidbau@google.com

This workshop introduces a new educational programming environment Pencil Code, which helps bridge the learning gap between visual programming and text-based coding. The free open-source online tool allows students to work with programs using either blocks or Coffeescript or Javascript text code. Students can switch between visual and text modes at any time.

The workshop will begin with a collaborative discussion of the opportunities, challenges, and differences presented when learning with block code and moving to text code. Then we will give a short presentation of how Pencil Code is used in classrooms, with some preliminary findings.

The main part of the workshop is a hands-on activity where participants gain experience with Pencil Code. Participants will use the tool with lessons in a curriculum framework, for teaching functions and interactivity using both text code and block code. Finally, there will be a discussion of best practices for teaching students in the transition, and an opportunity to create your own lessons using Pencil Code or other tools.

Attendees will come away with an understanding the issues faced by students transitioning to text code for the first time, and they will gain practical experience with teaching lessons with Pencil Code. Participants will receive curriculum material appropriate for middle-school and high-school classrooms. The tool is open-source and free to use at http://pencilcode.net/. ***Participants should each bring their own laptop. To simplify use of drag-and-drop, we also recommend that participants bring a mouse or a touchscreen-enabled laptop.***

ACM Categories & Descriptors: K.3.2 Computers and Education - *Computer science education*

Keywords: Computer Science Education; Visual Programming; Pencil Code; K-12; Curriculum; Javascript; Coffeescript

DOI: http://dx.doi.org/10.1145/2676723.2678293

SIGCSE'15, March 4–7, 2015, Kansas City, MO, USA.
ACM 978-1-4503-2966-8/15/03.

Teaching Cryptography and Access Control Hands-On

Steve Carr, *Western Michigan University*
Melissa Keranen, *Michigan Technological University*
Jean Mayo, *Michigan Technological University*
Contact: jmayo@mtu.edu

Cryptography and access control are perhaps the two most fundamental mechanisms for data protection. This workshop presents hands-on methods for teaching cryptography and access control that leverage software tools developed with funding from the NSF. The workshop will proceed in two sessions. The first session will address teaching well-known ciphers (including Vigenère, DES, AES, RSA, and SHA) and elliptic-curve cryptography using tools from the ***cryptoVisual*** software suite. These tools step students through an algorithm with either the system or the student computing the result of each step. The second session will address access control and the Multilevel Security, Role Based Access Control, and Domain Type Enforcement models using tools from the ***acVisual*** software suite. These tools support graphical policy development and analysis. The presenters have used this material in undergraduate courses in Cryptography and Computer Security. The tools have been used and evaluated favorably at multiple institutions. Participants will install and use the software on their own laptops running Linux, Windows, or MacOS. The ***acVisual*** software runs natively on Linux and MacOS and through a Linux virtual machine under Windows. The ***cryptoVisual*** software suite is available at http://www.cs.mtu.edu/~shene/NSF-4/. The ***acVisual*** software suite is available at http://acv.cs.mtu.edu. Development of these tools was supported by the National Science Foundation under grants DUE-1140512, DUE-1245310 and IIS-1319363.

ACM Categories & Descriptors: K3.2 [**Computers and Education**]: Computer and Information Science Education – *computer science education, information systems education*

Keywords: cryptography; access control; security education

DOI: http://dx.doi.org/10.1145/2676723.2678296

Bridging the Divide: Developing Culturally-Responsive Curriculum for K-12 Computer Science Education

A. Nicki Washington, *Howard University*
Legand Burge, *Howard University*
Marlon Mejias, *Howard University*
Ketly Jean-Pierre, *Howard University*
Qi'Anne Knox, *Howard University*
Contact: awashington@scs.howard.edu

In order to increase the computer science pipeline, emphasis must be placed on not only who is taught, but also how they are taught. Traditional computer science pedagogy has been unsuccessful in attracting, engaging, instructing, and retaining underrepresented students. Culturally-responsive pedagogy must be leveraged to successfully instruct a diverse range of computer science students. With the onset of technologies such as Facebook, iPods, Xbox, smart phones, mobile applications, and more, underrepresented students are already actively engaged in utilizing computer technology. However, in order to transition them from consumers to creators of this technology, culturally-responsive curriculum must teach fundamental concepts such as algorithms, problem solving, and abstraction in the context of issues that affect their daily lives. This workshop is designed to help K-16 computer science educators, professionals, and others understand and identify activities and assignments that infuse culturally-responsive content throughout. By the end of the workshop, participants will have a clear understanding of culturally-responsive pedagogy, its importance in computer science, and how to begin infusing more of it into lessons and activities. **Laptops are recommended.**

ACM Categories & Descriptors: K.3.2 [Computer and Information Science Education]: Computer Science Education

Keywords: Culturally-responsive teaching; Cultural relevance; Computer science education

DOI: http://dx.doi.org/10.1145/2676723.2678297

On Beyond Sudoku: Pencil Puzzles for Introductory Computer Science

Zack Butler, *Rochester Institute of Technology*
Ivona Bezakova, *Rochester Institute of Technology*
Contact: zjb@cs.rit.edu

Problem solving is a powerful teaching methodology for computer science — giving students a real problem to solve instead of simply discussing abstract concepts can motivate them and give them a path to better understanding. However, it is challenging to create novel example problems that are meaningful and engaging yet can be easily understood by all students. In this workshop, we will introduce participants to the vibrant world of pencil puzzles and show how many different types of puzzles can be used for a variety of topics throughout the introductory CS curriculum. Pencil puzzles are those designed to be solved by hand with pencil and paper (such as Sudoku, but including dozens of new types!) that have clear rules and are made to be solved deductively. As such, they are explicitly designed to be easy to understand and intriguing and naturally inspire algorithmic thought. We will explore a variety of on-line resources, including our own curated repository, to see how assignments throughout the introductory CS curriculum can be easily kept fresh. Participants will also experience a sample problem-solving session and collaboratively develop a new assignment for a topic of the group's choice. This workshop is intended for all teachers (late secondary and post-secondary) of introductory programming courses. Laptops are recommended.

ACM Categories & Descriptors: K.3.2 Computer and Information Science Education – Computer Science Education

Keywords: Problem solving; Introductory computing; Puzzles

DOI: http://dx.doi.org/10.1145/2676723.2678299

SIGCSE'15, March 4–7, 2015, Kansas City, MO, USA.
ACM 978-1-4503-2966-8/15/03.

How to Plan and Run Summer Computing Camps - Logistics

Marguerite A. Doman, *Winthrop University*
Barbara J. Ericson, *Georgia Institute of Technology*
Kristine S. Nagel, *Georgia Gwinnett College*
Nannette P. Napier, *Georgia Gwinnett College*
Krishnendu Roy, *Valdosta State University*
Contact: ericson@cc.gatech.edu

This workshop will provide details on how to plan and run non-residential computing summer camps for 4th – 12th grade students. Georgia Tech has been offering computing summer camps since 2004. These camps are financially self-sustaining and effective. Items used in past camps include: CS Unplugged, LightBot, Scratch, Alice, LEGO robots (WeDo, NXT, EV3, and Tetrix), EarSketch, and App Inventor. Georgia Tech helped start or expand other computing camps at eleven other colleges and universities in Georgia from 2007 to 2010 as part of Georgia Computes!. This last year as part of the Expanding Computing Education Pathways (ECEP) NSF grant we have also helped institutions start or expand summer computing camps in South Carolina, Massachusetts, and California.

The workshop will distribute a link to forms, a timeline, sample agendas, sample flyers, budget plans, a planning checklist, suggested projects, surveys, pre and post-tests, evaluation results, lessons learned, and more. ***Laptops Recommended***

ACM Categories: K.3.2 [Computers and Education] Computer science education

Keywords: summer camps; diversity; K-12; underrepresented minorities

DOI: http://dx.doi.org/10.1145/2676723.2678302

Small or Liberal Arts Colleges Adapting to CS2013: Making It Work

Andrea Danyluk, *Williams College*
Michael Jipping, *Hope College*
Rhys Price Jones, *Wellesley College*
David Reed, *Creighton University*
Brad Richards, *University of Puget Sound*
Richard Wicentowski, *Swarthmore College*
Contact: andrea@cs.williams.edu

Roughly once per decade, the ACM and IEEE-Computer Society form a joint task force to produce curricular guidelines for undergraduate computer science programs. The latest guidelines document, Computer Science Curricula 2013 (CS2013), was released in December 2013. CS faculty, at many institutions, are interested in understanding CS2013, evaluating their curricula against it, and adopting some or all of the recommendations. This task is non-trivial at any institution, but it can be particularly challenging at small or liberal arts institutions. For instance, small schools with few faculty are limited in the number of courses they can offer, and many liberal arts colleges place limits on the number of courses that can be required for a major. How might a department with limited resources trade off covering the core while still providing electives to students? A meta-issue involves mapping CS2013 at all: Given the demands on a small department, are there ways to improve and update a curriculum without having to go through a complete CS2013 mapping? In this workshop we will: (1) give a brief overview of CS2013, (2) describe experiences mapping individual courses or an entire curriculum to CS2013, (4) split participants into working groups for course or curricular mapping based on starting points and goals, (4) re-group to share lessons learned from the mapping experience. Laptop Strongly Recommended.

ACM Categories & Descriptors: K.3.2 [Computer and Information Science Education]: Curriculum

Keywords: Curriculum review; Curriculum planning; CS2013

DOI: http://dx.doi.org/10.1145/2676723.2678303

Steal This Courseware: FOSS, Github, Python, and OpenShift

Remy DeCausemaker, *Rochester Institute of Technology*
Stephen Jacobs, *Rochester Institute of Technology*
Contact: remydcsi@rit.edu

This workshop introduces participants to the pedagogy and practice of using Free/Open Source Software development practices into their curriculum, and then guides them through deployment of a turnkey courseware framework to be used for their own courses. The framework supports automatic blog checking, automatically generated student profile pages, Gravatar integration for profile pictures, Travis-CI continuous Integration tests, and repository changes reported via Github webhooks to IRC. Participants will learn how to use Github in the Classroom, the basics of Flask, a python web framework, and how to deploy their courseware to Red Hat's OpenShift Cloud, a free Platform-as-a-Service to host courseware and/or other web sites. ***A laptop is needed, a USB will be provided with electronic copy of (1) the courseware itself (2) creative commons licensed content used within the Humanitarian Free/Open Source Software Development Course at RIT.***

ACM Categories & Descriptors: K.3.2 [Computer and Information Science Education] - *Curriculum*; K.4.1 [Public Policy Issues] - *Intellectual property rights*; K.5.1 [Hardware software protection] - *Proprietary rights*; K.7 [The Computing Profession]

Keywords: Free Software, Open Source Software, Free Content, Python, GitHub, Web Blocks, Flask, OpenSHift

DOI: http://dx.doi.org/10.1145/2676723.2678305

SIGCSE'15, March 4–7, 2015, Kansas City, MO, USA.
ACM 978-1-4503-2966-8/15/03.

The Internet, Creativity and Global Impact: Curriculum Modules for the New AP Computer Science Principles Course

Lien Diaz, *College Board*
Richard Kick, *Newbury Park High School*
Andrew Kuemmel, *Madison West High School*
Contact: ldiaz@collegeboard.org

This workshop focuses on content in two curriculum modules for AP Computer Science Principles (CSP) developed by the College Board. They highlight instructional approaches for teaching concepts about 1) the Internet and 2) the interplay between creative aspects of computing and impact of computing on society. The Internet module activities allow students to construct their own solutions to problems similar to some that the builders of the Internet faced. The topics in the Creativity and Global Impact module were chosen because they have rich potential for increasing interest with students, especially those from underrepresented demographics, and because they present instructional challenges for instructors new to AP CSP. Participants will learn detailed concepts addressed in the AP CSP course and will receive classroom materials from in each of the curriculum modules. These modules serve as exemplary resources for teachers.

Intended audience: High school computer science teachers and AP CS teachers who are interested in learning more about how to teach some of the major concepts in the new AP Computer Science Principles course.
Materials provided: Each participant will receive paper copies and electronic files of (1) handouts to be used during the workshop, and (2) the complete curriculum modules in PDF format.

ACM Categories & Descriptors: A.1. Introductory and Survey

Keywords: active learning; computing applications; teaching and learning; broadening participation; high school computer science instruction

DOI: http://dx.doi.org/10.1145/2676723.2678306

Augmenting Introductory Computer Science Classes with GameMaker and Mobile Apps

Veronica Catete, *NC State University*
Barry Peddycord III, *NC State University*
Tiffany Barnes, *NC State University*

Students often take computing classes because they are eager to create games, to learn to create meaningful and useful software, or both. Connecting computing to real, cutting-edge applications has been shown to increase engagement of women and minorities. The new CS Principles curriculum, a pilot Advanced Placement course, seeks to broaden the participation in computing to a larger and more diverse audience. This curriculum emphasizes that computing is a creative activity where people work together to solve relevant problems. In this workshop, we introduce free software and curricula to enable novice high school and college students in a first computing course to learn basic game and mobile phone development. We discuss how these activities facilitate teaching high school and non-major (CS0) course topics, but they can also be used to illustrate more advanced topics. Participants will learn GameMaker and mobile phone programming using AppInventor, and/or Touch Develop. These tools allow students to create and have fun with computing while teaching object-oriented and event-driven programming and game architectures. We will provide links to curricular modules for the CS Principles: Beauty and Joy of Computing course, as well as links to the GameMaker, AppInventor, and Touch Develop platforms and tutorials. Participants must bring a network-connected laptop with a modern browser, and the latest version of Java, and may optionally bring an Android, Windows, or iPhone. ***Note: a laptop is recommened.***

SIGCSE'15, March 4–7, 2015, Kansas City, MO, USA.
ACM 978-1-4503-2966-8/15/03.

ACM Categories & Descriptors: K.3.2 Computer and Information Science Education; Computer Science Education

Keywords: introductory course, game development, mobile applications, broadening participation

DOI: http://dx.doi.org/10.1145/2676723.2678307

Infusing Cooperative Learning into Early Computer Science Courses to Support Improved Engagement

Jeff Gray, *University of Alabama*
Fran Trees, *Rutgers University*
Owen Astrachan, *Duke University*
Contact: gray@cs.ua.edu

Many new curricula and tools have been developed recently to promote the exciting opportunities available in computer science. However, curriculum and supporting tools alone do not drive engagement – the most interesting and innovative curriculum can still be taught in a disengaged manner, leading to lost opportunities for broadening the appeal and interest in computing across a diverse student population. The learning science literature on Cooperative Learning (CL) has been shown to increase class participation and student learning, while also promoting diversity in a manner that supports the differentiated instruction needed to engage students who have mixed abilities. This workshop will demonstrate how the best practices of CL can be applied in early CS courses (e.g., CS Principles, AP CS A, or CS1). Workshop participants will first be introduced to the CL structures that have been used in many different disciplines across multiple age/grade levels. These structures will then be used to demonstrate specific application toward computer science concepts. The workshop itself will be taught in a cooperative learning style so that participants can understand the dynamics and structure of a CL classroom. This workshop is for two categories of educations: 1) K-12 teachers who have experience with either AP CS A or CS Principles, or 2) university faculty who teach CS1 or other early courses.

ACM Categories & Descriptors: K.3.1 Computer Uses in Education: Collaborative learning

Keywords: cooperative learning; broadening participation; student engagement

DOI: http://dx.doi.org/10.1145/2676723.2678310

Saturday Workshops

Computer Science Principles with EarSketch

Jason Freeman, *Georgia Institute of Technology*
Brian Magerko, *Georgia Institute of Technology*
Regis Verdin, *Georgia Institute of Technology*
Contact: jason.freeman@gatech.edu

EarSketch (http://earsketch.gatech.edu) is an integrated curriculum, software toolset, audio loop library, and social sharing site that teaches computing principles through digital music composition and remixing. Attendees will learn to code in Python and/or JavaScript to place audio clips, create rhythms, and add and control effects within a multi-track digital audio workstation (DAW) environment while learning computing concepts such as variables, iteration, conditionals, strings, lists, functions, and recursion. Participants write code to make music, with a focus on popular genres such as hip hop. The agenda outlines the pedagogy of connecting musical expression to computation to broaden participation and engagement in computing; the underlying concept of thickly authentic STEAM that drives this approach; the alignment of the curriculum and learning environment with CS Principles; and basic musical concepts underlying EarSketch. The intended audience for this workshop is secondary and early post-secondary CS educators. The course is of particular relevance to CS Principles teachers but also applicable to any introductory programming or computing course. No prior musical knowledge or experience is expected and no prior programming experience with Python or JavaScript is required.

ACM Categories & Descriptors: J.5 [Arts and Humanities], K.3.2 [Computer Education]: Computers and Information Science Education – *computer science education, curriculum.*

Keywords: Remixing; music composition; broadening participation; education; computer science principles; music production; STEAM.

DOI: http://dx.doi.org/10.1145/2676723.2678282

Teaching Computing with Processing, the Bridge Between High School and College

Aaron Cadle, *James Martin High School*
Ira Greenberg, *Southern Methodist University*
Deepak Kumar, *Bryn Mawr College*
Darby Thompson, *Sidwell Friends School*
Ursula Wolz, *RiverSound Solutions*
Dianna Xu, *Bryn Mawr College*
Contact: acadle@asid.net

This workshop showcases an engaging way to attract students who typically avoid a traditional introductory Computer Science course (CS1), with fully developed, classroom-tested course materials. This workshop has been successful at SIGCSE and other venues in the past. This year we highlight our successful approach in pre-AP courses, as well as continued refinement of curriculum for college-level CS1. Our courses focus on essential CS1 principles, but show applications of these principles with contemporary, diverse examples of computing in a modern context, including advanced areas typically not accessible in CS1 such as: physics-based simulations, fractals and L-systems, image processing, emergent systems, cellular automata and data visualization. Students produce dynamic visual work using the programming language Processing, which is fully compatible with Java. We aim to inspire the Computer Science community to use innovative and creative approaches to attract a broader audience to their classes.

Participants will be introduced to the Processing language as well as its lightweight IDE through a series of on-the-fly coding examples. Additionally, course materials and handouts detailing the software, curricula and teaching resources will be given to the participants. Instructors of all levels are welcome; high school computer science teachers are particularly encouraged to attend. All participants will need to bring their own laptops.

Supported by NSF Awards DUE-1323463 and DUE-1323305.

ACM Categories & Descriptors: K.3.2 Computer and Information Science Education

Keywords: High School, AP, CS1, Curriculum, Graphics

DOI: http://dx.doi.org/10.1145/2676723.2678286

Supporting New Adopters to Peer Instruction in Computing

Daniel Zingaro, *University of Toronto, Mississauga*
Leo Porter, *University of California, San Diego*
Quintin Cutts, *University of Glasgow*
John Glick, *University of San Diego*
Joe Hummel, *University of Illinois at Chicago*
Cynthia Lee, *Stanford University*
Jaime Spacco, *Knox College*
Contact: daniel.zingaro@utoronto.ca

Recent work in computing has converged on a collection of complementary findings suggesting the value of the Peer Instruction (PI) pedagogy. Compared to lecture, PI has been shown to decrease fail rates, increase final exam grades, and increase engagement and enjoyment. In PI, students work together to exchange perspectives and use clickers to answer challenging conceptual questions in the presence of a knowledgeable instructor.

In our efforts to mentor potential PI adopters, we note difficulties bootstrapping PI uptake at new institutions and new departments. In this workshop, our main goal is to support potential adopters in the process of shifting from lectures to PI. In recent months, we have contributed materials for many freely-available PI courses, and led a successful 3-day NSF-funded PI workshop. We will work with participants and their existing lecture-based resources to begin considering the ways that PI might be effective in new contexts.

Instructors interested in increasing engagement in any CS course may attend. Participants are encouraged to bring current lecture materials. Laptop optional.

SIGCSE'15, March 4–7, 2015, Kansas City, MO, USA.
ACM 978-1-4503-2966-8/15/03.

ACM Categories & Subject Descriptors: K.3.2 [Computer Science Education]: Computer and Information Science Education

Keywords: Peer instruction; clickers; adoption

DOI: http://dx.doi.org/10.1145/2676723.2678287

Reviewing NSF Proposals: Learn about Effective Proposal Writing via the Review Process

Michael Erlinger, National Science Foundation
Paul Tymann, National Science Foundations
Contact: ptymann@nsf.gov

This workshop focuses on the NSF proposal review process. Via close examination of the review process, participants gain an understanding of how to write good reviews and how to improve their own proposal writing. The workshop covers the following topic areas: the proposal review process from submission of a proposal to award or decline; elements of a good review; NSF merit criteria (intellectual merit and broader impacts); elements of a good proposal; and how to volunteer to review proposals.
The workshop uses a structured guided-interactive methodology to lead participants through each topic by introducing related issues, engaging participants in group exercises designed to explore and share their understanding of the issues, and then providing some "expert" opinion on these issues. Good and bad examples and a Top Ten List of Do's and Don'ts will be provided.

ACM Categories & Descriptors: A.m [General Literature]: Miscellaneous

Keywords: grant writing; proposal review

DOI: http://dx.doi.org/10.1145/2676723.2678288

Creating Stimulating, Relevant, and Manageable Introductory Computer Science Projects that Utilize Real-Time, Large, Web-Based Datasets

Eli Tilevich, *Virginia Tech*
Clifford A. Shaffer, *Virginia Tech*
Austin Cory Bart, *Virginia Tech*
Contact: tilevich@cs.vt.edu

This workshop introduces participants to CORGIS, a technology developed under the auspices of an NSF-funded project at Virginia Tech. The CORGIS Datasets Project comprises a software architecture framework and carefully engineered client libraries through which students can access either large datasets or those generated by real-time web services from domains, including weather reports, stocks, earthquakes, and news updates. The CORGIS technical scaffolding gradually introduces students to some of the most vexing complexities of distributed computing. To support the diverse needs of computing educators when teaching introductory CS classes, each CORGIS dataset is available in Python, Java, and Racket, with compatibility on key platforms. The dataset libraries are available through an online curated gallery, designed to be easily adapted to instructors' specific academic needs, including the ability to rapidly prototype new CORGIS libraries. With CORGIS, computing educators can introduce important big data or real-time distributed computing concepts without overwhelming students with the low-level details that working with such data typically requires.
This workshop introduces CORGIS via a hands-on approach, familiarizing participants with the core functionality of our architectural framework and client libraries. We will proceed in three parts: (1) present CORGIS by working through a case study of creating a programming project in a typical CS 2 course; (2) demonstrate how the framework can be used to rapidly prototype a new library of the participants' choice; and (3) critically discuss the technology in small and large groups. This presentation improves on our offering from SIGCSE 2014. Further information is at: http://think.cs.vt.edu/corgis.

SIGCSE'15, March 4–7, 2015, Kansas City, MO, USA.
ACM 978-1-4503-2966-8/15/03.

ACM Categories & Descriptors: K.3.2 Computer and Information Science Education

Keywords: distributed computing; projects; introductory courses

DOI: http://dx.doi.org/10.1145/2676723.2678292

Building Code Magnet Labs for Tablets and Other Devices

Barry L Kurtz, *Appalachian State University*
Rahman Tashakkori, *Appalachian State University*
Ahmad Esmaili, *Stony Brook University*
Contact: blk@cs.appstate.edu

Code magnet labs are 5-10 minute activities where students are asked to construct a method, function or rule to complete a specific task. The programming languages Java, C/C++, Python and Prolog are supported. In a code magnet lab the student is presented with a sequence of possible code magnets that can be arranged using drag-and-drop to create the desired method. Magnets for control statements can nest other magnets, including nested control statements. The completed method is compiled and subject to unit testing. Test results guide students towards a correct solution; multiple submissions are allowed. Since there is no keyboard entry when using code magnet labs, the labs can be completed using laptops, desktops, tablets and other mobile devices. This workshop is a shorter version of the half-day workshop presented with support from three NSF grants. Participants will experience using existing labs and learn to build their own code magnet lab for Java, Python, C or Prolog (participant's choice). Significant stipends averaging about $1000 will be available for after-workshop activities where the participant develops and tests multiple code magnet labs for his/her own courses in the 2014-2015 academic year. All participants will need a laptop to complete lab activities; teams will only require one laptop per team.

ACM Categories & Descriptors: K.3.2 Computer and Information Science Education

Keywords: Active Learning; Tablets; Code Magnets

DOI: http://dx.doi.org/10.1145/2676723.2678294

Introducing Secure Coding in CS0, CS1, and CS2

Blair Taylor, *Towson University*
Siddharth Kaza, *Towson University*
Elizabeth K. Hawthorne, *Union County College*

The CS 2013 curriculum includes Information Assurance and Security as a pervasive knowledge area. However, introducing security in lower level courses is challenging because of lack of appropriate teaching resources and training. This workshop will provide a well-tested strategy for introducing secure coding concepts in CS0, CS1, and CS2. We will introduce attendees to secure coding through hands-on exercises, and provide self-contained, lab-based modules designed to be injected into CS0-CS2 with minimal impact on the course (www.towson.edu/securityinjections). Participants will be encouraged to bring in their own syllabus and labs to modify to include secure coding concepts. The first 15 participants will be reimbursed for the workshop cost on attendance. *Laptop recommended.*

ACM Categories & Descriptors: K.3.2 Computers and Education

Keywords: CS0; CS1; CS2; Secure Coding; Security Injections

DOI: http://dx.doi.org/10.1145/2676723.2678300

Puzzle-Based Learning: Introducing Creative Thinking and Problem Solving for Computer Science and Engineering

Raja Sooriamurthi, *Carnegie Mellon University*
Nickolas Falkner, *University of Adelaide*
Ed Meyer, *Baldwin Wallace University*
Zbigniew Michalewicz, *University of Adelaide*
Contact: raja@cmu.edu

Puzzle-based learning (PBL) is an emerging model of teaching critical thinking and problem solving used in Universities and schools. Today's market place needs skilled graduates capable of solving real problems of innovation in a changing environment. A learning goal of PBL is to distill domain independent transferable heuristics for tackling problems. While solving puzzles is innately fun, companies also use puzzles to assess the creative problem solving skills of potential employees. In this interactive workshop we will examine a range of puzzles and games. What general problem solving strategies can we learn from the way we solve these examples? Participants will emerge with the needed pedagogical foundation to offer a full course on PBL or to include it as part of another course.

ACM Categories & Descriptors: K.3.2 [COMPUTERS AND EDUCATION]: Computer and Information Science Education - *Computer science education*

SIGCSE'15, March 4–7, 2015, Kansas City, MO, USA.
ACM 978-1-4503-2966-8/15/03.

Keywords: Puzzle-based Learning; Critical Thinking; Problem Solving

DOI: http://dx.doi.org/10.1145/2676723.2678301

KELP CS and LaPlaya: A Computational Thinking Curriculum and Development Environment for 4th – 6th Grade

Diana Franklin, *UC Santa Barbara*
Hilary A. Dwyer, *UC Santa Barbara*
Contact: franklin@cs.ucsb.edu

This workshop introduces our elementary school programming curriculum, KELP-CS, and the corresponding programming environment LaPlaya. KELP-CS (Kids Engaged in Learning Programming) is an innovative, modular computational thinking curriculum for 4th-6th grade students. Off-computer activities connect computer science concepts to students' every day experiences. On-computer activities in LaPlaya develop students' computational thinking and programming skills. Finally, an engineering design project allows students to apply these new skills through an open-ended, creative project (e.g. digital storytelling in Module 1, and virtual game in Module 2). LaPlaya is a modified Scratch programming environment tailored to the developmental needs of 4th-6th grade students. In this workshop, we begin by introducing the KELP-CS curriculum; LaPlaya, the development environment used in the on-computer activities; and the resources for teachers embedded in both. Workshop participants will do sample on- and off- computer activities from Module 1 (4th grade) and discuss tips and strategies for teaching computational thinking with this age group. For the second part of the workshop, we provide additional background for participants interested in creating their own curriculum with LaPlaya. This includes how to create projects and their analysis.. ***A laptop is strongly recommended. Handouts of sample teaching materials will be provided.***

ACM Categories & Descriptors: D.1.7 [Programming Techniques]: Visual Programming; K.3.2 [Computer and Information Science Education]: Computer Science Education

Keywords: computer science education; elementary school; novice programming environments

DOI: http://dx.doi.org/10.1145/2676723.2677288

Teaching Privacy: What Every Student Needs to Know

Gerald Friedland, *International Computer Science Institute*
Serge Egelman, *International Computer Science Institute*
Daniel D. Garcia, *University of California–Berkeley*
Contact: fractor@icsi.berkeley.edu

Although frequent stories in the popular media have raised awareness about online privacy, most young people do not have a very good handle on what the specific issues are, nor the practical steps they can take to manage them. Teachers recognize that all their students—from future engineers to those totally bored by science—need a realistic understanding of how online privacy works, so they can protect themselves online. In fact, the latest CS curricular recommendations include privacy—but there is no comprehensive set of field-tested teaching materials. To address this, we are developing TROPE (Teachers' Resources for Online Privacy Education), a set of classroom-ready teaching materials (teachingprivacy.org). TROPE will provide educators with lesson modules, interactive demonstrations, and a teachers' guide, so they can readily integrate privacy into high school and college classes. Our goal for this workshop is twofold. First, we will introduce educators to TROPE and provide guidance on how they can cover privacy-related topics in their classrooms without being subject-matter experts. Second, we will solicit feedback and on-the-ground stories; by gaining a better understanding of specific problems faced by educators and students, we can increase TROPE's utility to teachers. We will provide teachers with up-to-date technical information about online privacy, including relevant highlights from our research; hands-on activities illustrating principles of online privacy; and an overview of the materials we are creating for TROPE. This will be an interactive workshop, driven by participants' questions, experiences, and interests. For CS educators at all levels; laptop or tablet recommended.

ACM Categories & Descriptors: K.3.2 [Computer and Information Science Education]: Curriculum; K.4.1 [Public Policy Issues]: Privacy

Keywords: privacy education; computer science; high school; undergraduate; teachers

DOI: http://dx.doi.org/10.1145/2676723.2678308

SIGCSE'15, March 4–7, 2015, Kansas City, MO, USA.
ACM 978-1-4503-2966-8/15/03.

Decoding CS Principles – A Curriculum from Code.org

Baker Franke, *Code.org*
Brook Osborne, *Code.org*
Contact: baker@code.org

Code.org is developing a complete curriculum and professional development program for the new (AP) Computer Science Principles course. In this hands-on workshop, modeled after the professional development program, participants will get access to, and interact with the new curricular materials for this course: daily lesson plans, instructional guides, assessments, and custom-built software tools woven throughout. Code.org's CS Principles curriculum engages students by having them invent and create their own solutions to some of the great problems in computing upon which many CS principles are based. For example, the course begins by asking students to invent their own bit-sending device to send a single bit of information from one place to another. The curriculum employs a variety of instructional strategies, plugged and unplugged, to build a classroom experience that is engaging and emphasizes accessibility for both the students and instructors. The curriculum also emphasizes student preparation for the AP Performance Tasks by including model tasks at the conclusion of each unit of study. Participants will experience a snapshot of the professional development program, engaging with lessons from the curriculum as they would in a realistic classroom context (i.e. diving into the materials and planning to teach the lesson rather than just talking about it). Participants will hear from high school teachers who have taught the lessons in their classrooms during the 2014-15 field-testing year. Code.org's partner schools will pilot the course in the 2015-16 school year, but the course and its materials will be open and free for all to use. ***A laptop is strongly recommednded. Participants will also receive hard copies of curricular and promotional materials.***

ACM Categories & Descriptors: K.3.2 [Computer and Information Science Education]: Curriculum; Computer Science Education

Keywords: AP; CS Principles; Curriculum; K-12

DOI: http://dx.doi.org/10.1145/2676723.2678309

Undergraduate Abstracts

Improvement of Robot Mapping and Localization Using Combined Sensory Data

Deanna Biesan, *Baldwin Wallace University*
Contact: dbiesan11@mail.bw.edu

Robotic mapping and localization are two large areas in robotics research that focus on how robots know and navigate within an environment. The current methods used to complete these tasks are not extremely accurate due to errors that are compounded as the robot moves. Since robots are often used in situations where precise navigation is a necessity, there is a strong motivation for the mapping and localization processes to be as accurate as possible.

This project reduces the accumulated error which occurs during the mapping and localization processes through the integration of a Kinect sensor, which provides both visual and depth data about objects in front of a mobile robot and a sonar sensor which provides depth information about objects on the sides of the robot. The Kinect's images and depth information will be used to form an occupancy grid map of the environment, while the sonar data will track the walls as the robot moves throughout the environment in order to assist in keeping track of both position and orientation of the robot. These two sensors will allow the robot to reduce the errors accumulated during localization and navigation within the map being created and in navigating the subsequently completed map.

When the occupancy grid map is completed, the cells in it will be combined into a topological map, which will hold information about the rooms such as doorway locations. The topological map will then be used as the robot plans a path to its goal.

ACM Categories & Descriptors: I.2.9 Robotics

Keywords: robotics; mapping; localization

DOI: http://dx.doi.org/10.1145/2676723.2693623

Speed Estimation Using Computer Vision

Matt Bowen, *University of Alabama*
Contact: mdbowen1@crimson.ua.edu

With recent advancements in smartphone digital camera technology, the opportunity to integrate computer vision into daily activities has become possible. A unique application of computer vision is ESPN's use of K-Zone during Major League Baseball broadcasts, which uses a combination of three cameras and multiple computers running sophisticated algorithms, to track a thrown baseball to within $2/5^{ths}$ of an inch. While the sophistication of the K-Zone hardware and software allows for a high degree of accuracy, there is the potential for obtaining similar results using only a smartphone. The Mobile Video Velocity Estimation (MoVVE) project investigated the application of computer vision in the development of a speed-tracking app on a smartphone. This presentation will describe the design of the MoVVE software which uses OpenCV computer vision library functions to track the velocity and location of objects such as a thrown baseball using video obtained from a mobile digital camera. MoVVE was shown to successfully detect and track the baseball with a success rate greater than 90%. Baseball velocity estimates obtained with MoVVE were compared to those measured using a professional grade radar gun. For a test population of 112 pitches, 84% of the program's estimated velocities agreed to within 10% of the radar gun measurement, and 43% agreed to within 5%. Test pitch velocities varied from 30 mph to 60 mph with the program showing equal accuracy throughout the full range.

ACM Categories & Descriptors: I.4.8 [Image Processing and Computer Vision]: Scene Analysis - - - Depth Cues, Object Recognition, Tracking

Keywords: Computer vision; Speed estimation; Object tracking; Object recognition

DOI: http://dx.doi.org/10.1145/2676723.2693624

Developing a Robotics Education Platform using Android Based Cellbots

Donald Buhl-Brown, Austin Peay State University
Contact: dbuhlbrown@my.apsu.edu

Robotics education is one of the most important subjects now and for the foreseeable future. Our project focuses on designing a robotics education platform, which includes extensive libraries of code that allows any student from high school to college level to study robotics. We also have significantly addressed two of the major problems in robotics, usability and affordability. Using a Cellbot, a robot that uses an Arduino microcontroller and an Android smartphone, enables us to quickly and affordably add new sensors or features to the entire robotics system. By combining a Cellbot with the advance software we developed, we have designed a system, which is easy to learn and allows the robot to perform numerous high performance tasks. As students advance in their programming abilities more complex algorithms and sensors can be easily added to the system. Effectively making the robot "grow" with the students.

ACM Categories & Descriptors: I.1.2.9 Robotics

Keywords: Robotics; Mobile Development; Education; Android; Arduino; Computer Vision

DOI: http://dx.doi.org/10.1145/2676723.2693625

SIGCSE'15, March 4–7, 2015, Kansas City, MO, USA.
ACM 978-1-4503-2966-8/15/03.

ACEit!
(Assist Children in English-language)

Jae Hyun Choe, *Kalamazoo College*
Contact: jaehyun.choe11@kzoo.edu

Reading is an integral part of our lives. Most of us learned to read while we were young and never thought about how we learned to read. "ACEit!" (Assist Children in English-language) is an Android app developed to facilitate children in learning to read English. The app consists of a subset of the Dolch words (a set of 220 sight words that are proven to improve reading skill when they are learned) and uses a fading image strategy to support children in the early stages of learning to read and/or in special education. It gradually transitions the user from depending on pictures clues to recognize words, to recognizing words by themselves. This app is geared towards visual learners and provides them a more succinct yet entertaining way to learn using mobile devices.

ACM Categories & Descriptors: K.3.1 [Computers and Education]: Computer Uses in Education – Computer Assisted Instruction (CAI); K.4.2 [Computers and Society]: Social Issues - *Assistive technologies for persons with disabilities*

Keywords: Sight words, Dolch list, Fading, Mobile application, Game

DOI: http://dx.doi.org/10.1145/2676723.2693626

Computational Creativity in the Culinary Arts

Erol Cromwell, *Davidson College*
Contact: ercromwell@davidson.edu

The goal of our research project was to create an artificial chef program that produces novel salad recipes with limited human assistance. Our program was designed in two steps: first, we constructed a statistical model to rank recipes. Then, we experimented with various search algorithms to explore the salad recipe space for novel ingredient combinations. Surprisingly, we discovered that the top ranked recipes from a randomly generated population, as determined by our model, were already of high quality. To validate the quality of our automatically generated salads, we conducted a blind taste test with three computer designed and three human designed salads. The best performing computer salad was competitive with the human salads, but received a lower rating.

ACM Categories & Descriptors: I.5.1 [Models]: Statistical; I.2.m Miscellaneous

Keywords: Artificial chef; Artificial intelligence; Computational creativity; Search algorithm; Salad recipes

DOI: http://dx.doi.org/10.1145/2676723.2693627

SIGCSE'15, March 4–7, 2015, Kansas City, MO, USA.
ACM 978-1-4503-2966-8/15/03.

Data Mining: Building Better Bug Messages

Mindy DeWaal, *Southern Utah University*
Contact: dewaal.mindy@gmail.com

An important and challenging part of the computer science curriculum is learning to program. A source of aggravation when learning this skill is finding syntactic mistakes in the code commonly referred to as bugs. This learning process is frustrating for new programmers because bug messages given by the compiler are incomprehensible and dominantly occupied by jargon. A group in the UK has started a data logging project called Blackbox to record novice programmers' source code and the related bug messages. In this project, we intend to build better bug messages through the utilization of Blackbox's logged data to anticipate student errors. In the second part of the project, we will test these improved bug messages in a plugin for BlueJ, a popular IDE for instructors to use in CS1 classes.

ACM Categories & Descriptors: K.3.2 [Computer and Information Science Education]: Computer science education

Keywords: Data mining; bug messages; Blackbox; BlueJ

DOI: http://dx.doi.org/10.1145/2676723.2693628

Using CABECTPortal as a Case Study to Extend the Capabilities of Penetration Testing Tools

Derek Duchesne, *The College of New Jersey*
Contact: duchesd1@tcnj.edu

This project presents an approach to web application security that modifies general penetration testing tools to test for advanced vulnerabilities. As a proof of concept, the ZAP (Zed Attack Proxy) security tool was extended with functionality to find vulnerabilities such as server-side security misconfiguration, to test CABECTPortal (a website housing collaborations between multiple disciplines). By combining the general vulnerability checks built into tools like ZAP and the server-side maintenance checks that are normally conducted manually by system administrators and programmers, this project provides a more tailored approach to security testing that can be applied to any web application, making testing easier and more precise.

ACM Categories & Descriptors: K.6.5 Security and Protection

Keywords: Penetration testing; Fuzzing; Vulnerabilities; Web application security

DOI: http://dx.doi.org/10.1145/2676723.2693629

Focused Mining of University Course Descriptions from Highly Variable Sources

Thomas Effland, SUNY University at Buffalo
Contact: tom.effland@gmail.com

Finding topically relevant content from disparate sources on the Web requires robust techniques due to the variability of sites. A focused web crawler is a type of crawler that attempts to make predictions about page relevance and traverse the web efficiently. In this work, we attempt to design a novel system of focused crawling tailored to identifying and extracting semantically similar topical information from disparate but known seed domains with highly variable structure that do not reference each other. We first extract rich predictive features from web pages. We then utilize Weakly-Supervised Machine Learning techniques to predict the link distance of current pages to target pages by employing two separate Random Forest classifiers that rank the current page and potential relevance gain of hyper-links. We use these page representations and rankings to efficiently tunnel through irrelevant pages and reach target pages with more optimal path traversals.

ACM Categories & Descriptors: H.3.3[Information Storage and Retrieval]: Information Search and Retrieval; I.2.7[Artificial Intelligence]: Natural Language Processing - Text Analysis; I.2.8[Artificial Intelligence]: Problem Solving, Control Methods, and Search - Graph and tree search strategies

Keywords: Focused Web Traversal; Relevance Prediction; Information Extraction; Hyper-Text Classification; Weakly-Supervised Learning

DOI: http://dx.doi.org/10.1145/2676723.2693630

Real Time Occupancy Notification: A Comparison Between Passive Infrared and iBeacon Implementations

Brandon Gottlob, *The College of New Jersey*
Contact: gottlob1@tcnj.edu

iBeacon technology has the potential to evolve occupancy detection over the traditional passive infrared motion sensor approach due to portability, relatively low cost, and capabilities beyond motion detection alone. This project implements study room occupancy detection in the TCNJ Library using a Raspberry Pi with a PIR sensor and an Estimote Beacon. The scalability of each approach is directly compared by cost, ease of setup and maintenance, and accuracy. Prototype occupancy detection systems that are set up in study room environments provide end-users with a listing of available rooms in real-time through new functionality in the TCNJ Library iOS app. Using iBeacon sensors can bring extra functionality to existing systems and new environments where portability is essential.

SIGCSE'15, March 4–7, 2015, Kansas City, MO, USA.
ACM 978-1-4503-2966-8/15/03.

ACM Categories & Descriptors: J Computer Applications, J.7 Computers in Other Systems, *Real Time*

Keywords: iBeacon; Occupancy Detection; Passive Infrared; Sensors

DOI: http://dx.doi.org/10.1145/2676723.2693631

Automation of Layer 7 DDoS Attacks and Post Forensic Analysis of Server Logs

Barry Hamilton, *Jacksonville University*
Contact: bhamilt4@jacksonville.edu

Application layer (L7) Distributed Denial of Service attacks are becoming more common and an emerging threat to legitimate sites. The goal of these attacks is to prevent legitimate users from accessing a website. Due to the nature of the attacks, the low rate, and the sophisticated imitation of user behavior from automated bots, it is difficult to diagnose these on time. There is an evolving 'industry' of blackmailing and using these attacks for illegal profit [1]. Even though L7 DDoS attacks are a serious threat, studying and experimenting with them is challenging. Organizations do not share server logs because of privacy concerns. Furthermore, implementing these attacks requires instrumentation and real testbeds in order to produce realistic attacks for analysis. Therefore, it is difficult to evaluate mitigation and detection techniques. Our contribution is twofold. First, we have developed a set of testbeds on the GENI (Global Environment for Network Infrastructure) cloud infrastructure [2] to facilitate research and development of detection and mitigation techniques of L7 DDoS attacks. Second, we have used a library of attacks to perform post forensic analysis and classify L7 DDoS attacks based on their individual characteristics. Our work automates and simplifies log generation of L7 DDoS attacks for research and experimentation, as well as provides criteria to detect abnormal requests using a library of attacks.

Categories and Subject Descriptors: K.6 [Management of Computing and Information Systems]: Miscellaneous

Keywords: Layer 7 Denial of Service, Application Layer DDoS, DDoS

DOI: http://dx.doi.org/10.1145/2676723.2693632

NeuroSoccer: Neural Network Q-Learning

Andrew Keenan, *Villanova University*
Contact: akeena03@villanova.edu

Q-Learning is a type of reinforcement learning which learns how to optimize an agent's choice of actions in a given environment based on experience. Typically, Q-Learning is implemented using a lookup table indexed by state/action tuples. For many applications, this approach can be difficult or impossible, as their state space is too large or cannot accurately be captured in a table. A neural network can act as a function approximator for the Q-Learning Table. This reduces learning time and allows for generalization on unvisited states The neural network can be trained using the Back propagation algorithm with the state/action tuple as input and the output of the update rule as the new target value. The weights of the network are updated to produce the correct output value for inputs in the training set. We have implemented this technique in a 2-D simulation of soccer, where agents learn how to maneuver the ball in order to score a goal.

ACM Categories & Descriptors: Connectionism and neural nets

Keywords: Machine Learning, Neural Net, Q-Learning

DOI: http://dx.doi.org/10.1145/2676723.2693633

Parallel Author Verfication of Email

Andreas Kellas, *United States Military Academy*
Alexander Molnar, *United States Military Academy*
Leo St. Amour, *United States Military Academy*
Frederick Ulrich, *United States Military Academy*
Suzanne J. Matthews, *United States Military Academy*
Contact: suzanne.matthews@usma.edu

Cyber-crime is becoming alarmingly common through the use of anonymous e-mails. Author attribution helps digital forensics investigators filter through a large set of possible authors and focus traditional investigative techniques on the most probable culprits. A recent promising technique is to construct a write-print for each known author, and compare it to the write-print extracted from the anonymous message(s). A write-print is a unique digital fingerprint created by mining frequent patterns from a particular author's writing style. However, the process for generating a write-print is very slow, making it a poor choice for author attribution situations of a time-sensitive nature such as anonymous threats of attack, exposure, or ongoing harassment.

We develop the Parallel Author Verification of E-mail (PAVE) algorithm for determining author write-prints. Our goal is to create a parallel approach that enables the analysis of large collections of e-mail. PAVE employs the Phoenix++ MapReduce framework hybridized with MPI, allowing us to exploit multiple nodes and cores. Our approach is significant because it drastically reduces the run-time complexity required to produce write-prints, and may expedite the process of author identification in time-sensitive situations. Our preliminary results suggest that our algorithm will enable the fast analysis of larger e-mail datasets and may be a potential asset to future investigations.

ACM Categories & Descriptors: I.2.7 Natural Language Processing [Text Analysis]; D.1.3 Concurrent Programming [Parallel Programming]

Keywords: Author attribution, write-print, MapReduce, PAVE

DOI: http://dx.doi.org/10.1145/2676723.2693634

Development of an Offset Detection Task for MIREX 2015

Darrion Long, *Lincoln University*
Contact: Darrion.long687@my.lincolnu.edu

Analysis of musical audio is of interest for a variety of tasks within the field of music information retrieval (MIR). One component of MIR is audio event detection, of which onset detection is one component. Audio offset detection is a complementary task to audio onset detection, but this task has received scant attention in the literature. This research will develop an offset detection task that can be included in the Music Information Retrieval Evaluation Exchange (MIREX) 2015 suite of evaluation tasks. The development of this task will provide a tool for researchers to evaluate performance of offset detection algorithms while establishing a baseline of performance for the current state-of-the-art. An existing offset detection algorithm will be utilized for testing prior to public release of the task in Summer 2015. Results of the public evaluation will be presented during the MIREX session at the 2015 International Society for Music Information Retrieval (ISMIR) conference, to be held 26-30 October 2015 in Malaga, Spain.

ACM Categories & Descriptors: H.5.5 [Information Interfaces and Presentation]:Sound and Music Computing - *Modeling, Signal analysis, synthesis and processing, Systems*

Keywords: Audio onset detection; Audio offset detection; Sound event detection; MIREX; Music Information Retrieval

DOI: http://dx.doi.org/10.1145/2676723.2693635

Automatic Fall Detection Using Mobile Devices

Melissa Mulcahy, *Central Connecticut State University*
Contact: mel.mulcahy@my.ccsu.edu

Mobile devices are becoming an integrated part of every person's life regardless of age. Several studies have shown that falls account for over sixty percent of injuries in adults older than 65. These falls can leave permanent scars and limit the everyday lives of those people. Since people that fall are instructed not to move, it is crucial to provide them with a means to call for help. Systems like LifeAlert© have provided means for their clients to call for assistance by pressing a button they wear around their neck. However, if a person who has fallen is rendered unconscious, they are unable to do anything to obtain the assistance they need. This project focuses on developing a mobile application and related algorithms to allow mobile devices to determine if a person has fallen. The algorithms developed in this project takes in real-time data from a smartphone's accelerometer and determine whether the sequential readings satisfy the three stages of falling (the free fall stage, collision with the floor stage, and remaining at rest stage). The results of the experiments demonstrate promising hands-free responses to the smartphone user falling. By using a smartphone or similar device, it is possible to autonomously call for assistance without the user having to manually press a button.

ACM Categories & Descriptors: J.7. [COMPUTERS IN OTHER SYSTEMS]: Real time.

Keywords: Fall detection, mobile devices, accelerometer, Android.

DOI: http://dx.doi.org/10.1145/2676723.2693636

SIGCSE'15, March 4–7, 2015, Kansas City, MO, USA.
ACM 978-1-4503-2966-8/15/03.

Web-based Application for Virtual Exercise Regimen

Christina Noe, *University of Alabama*
Contact: cpnoe@crimson.ua.edu

The WAVER (Web-based Application for Virtual Exercise Regimen) project takes advantage of available 3D motion technology to provide stroke patients with an inexpensive and more accessible alternative to conventional rehabilitation. Specifically, WAVER uses the LEAP device to assist patients who have mobility and dexterity limitations due to a stroke, disability, or even sports-related injury. Patients may face physical adversity in pursuing rehabilitation. Not all patients are conveniently distanced from a medical facility and may find that commuting daily worsens their pain, lightens their wallets, and forces them from the comfort of their homes as they deal with pain and circumstances affected by their disability. The WAVER solution to these problems is a web-based application that utilizes the 3D LEAP Motion sensory controller, which is an affordable and compact device that can be used by any home computer or laptop. WAVER presents exercises to a patient that can be performed by the patient in their own 3D space, which is then tracked by WAVER for on-screen feedback to the patient, as well as the potential to share the results remotely with a therapist.

ACM Categories & Descriptors: J.3 [Computer Applications]: Life and Medical Sciences - *Health, Medical Information Systems*

Keywords: Home-based rehabilitation; Web-based rehabilitation; Motion tracking; Medical applications of software

DOI: http://dx.doi.org/10.1145/2676723.2693637

Selection in 3D Graphics Enviornments

Lindsey Press, *Villanova University*
Contact: lindseypress@gmail.com

The level of detail portrayed in graphics environments is steadily increasing, and so does the challenge to enable users to accurately select 3D objects from a graphics scene in real time[2]. From a gaming perspective, complexity in computer graphics has increased drastically because thousands of users can now participate together in games that involve a high frequency of selecting objects. This poses a challenge because each three-dimensional object exists in a native, local coordinate system which will eventually be realistically displayed on a two-dimensional screen and then selected by users. Our project is broken down into two phases – phase one will focus on the theory and mathematics behind these operations and phase two will evaluate the more efficient picking algorithm, ray casting[3] or color picking[4]. Our criteria for determining the better algorithm is to discover which algorithm is faster and more accurate in complex graphics scenes, with the ultimate goal of minimizing delay responses associated with selection.

ACM Categories & Descriptors: I.3.7 - *Three-Dimensional Graphics and Realism*; I.3.1 - *Three Dimensional Displays[**]*

SIGCSE'15, March 4–7, 2015, Kansas City, MO, USA.
ACM 978-1-4503-2966-8/15/03.

Keywords: Picking Algorithms; Graphics Scenes; Ray Casting

DOI: http://dx.doi.org/10.1145/2676723.2693638

Jumping Implementation in Video Games

Joseph Rioux, *Benedictine College*
James Vanderhyde, *Benedictine College*
Contact: riou1233@ravens.benedictine.edu

Jumping has been a prevalent and versatile game mechanic from the early days of games like *Donkey Kong* to our own sophisticated era of smartphone games like *Temple Run* and entertainment industry giants like the *Call of Duty* series. While the physical activity of jumping itself seems simple, a lot can change in the translation of this action to its game counterpart. Jumping must serve to make the game playable and enjoyable, and so realism is sacrificed in order to facilitate the particular "feel" that the game developers desire for the physics of their game. This project is a study of jumping as a game mechanic and its implementation in video games, and includes a playable simulation program that allows for hands-on experience of different jump implementations that were studied.

ACM Categories & Descriptors: K.8.0 [Computing Milieux]

Keywords: video games; platformer; jumping; game mechanics

DOI: http://dx.doi.org/10.1145/2676723.2693639

The Backbone Project

Dharmin Shah, *Rose-Hulman Institute of Technology*
Contact: shahdk@rose-hulman.edu

It is well-known that software maintenance is an arduous task. It is particularly so because of poor design decisions made by software engineers during the development phase. Past research has shown that there are smells in the code that can be used to gauge the quality of the project. Nevertheless, code maintenance due to these research tools is still costly because they are focused on curative solutions rather than preventive measures.

Majority of the past research techniques detect code smells after the fact; and the classification of code changes rely on the commit messages written by the developers. However, developers do not always mention the necessary meta-data to determine the changes. The goal of my research is to find a set of design and implementation change categories using abstract syntax trees from the code rather than the commit messages. The categories will help classify the common changes in software projects and identify the resulting unstable regions. A rule-based system will be developed using these regions to recommend the potential improvements required to stabilize the code-base.

The result of my research will contribute a toolset that will be used from the start of the development phase to evaluate the stability of the system using software metrics and recommend improvements. This will help project managers mitigate the design and implementation flaws early on during the product life-cycle and reduce the cost during the maintenance phase. Hence, the toolset will have the potential to change the software maintenance paradigm from corrective to preventative measures.

ACM Categories & Descriptors: K.6.3 [Software Management]: Software Maintenance; D.2.7 [Distribution, Maintenance, and Enhancement]: Version Control; D.2.8 [Metrics]: Complexity Measures

Keywords: software maintenance; software metrics

DOI: http://dx.doi.org/10.1145/2676723.2693640

Graduate Abstracts

Situating Computational Thinking with Big Data: Pedagogy and Technology

Austin Cory Bart, *Virginia Tech*
Contact: acbart@vt.edu

As Computational Thinking becomes pervasive in undergraduate programs, new students must be educated in meaningful, authentic contexts that they find both motivating and relatable. I propose working with big data as a novel context for introductory programming, authentic given its importance in diverse fields such as agriculture, history, and more. Big data is considered difficult to use because of its inherent technical obstacles. To overcome these difficulties, I introduce a new project: CORGIS -- a "Collection of Real-time, Giant, Interesting, Situated Datasets". The CORGIS project comprises a collection of libraries that provide an interface to big data for students, architectures for rapidly enabling new datasets, and a web-based textbook platform for disseminating relevant course materials. This textbook features an online block-based programming environment, real-time collaborative text editing, and continuous server-side storage. In this poster, I describe the educational theory guiding this work, the novel technolgy created and deployed, and the initial, promising results.

ACM Categories & Descriptors: K.3.2 [Computer and Information Science Education]: Computer Science Education

Keywords: Computational Thinking; Motivation; Big data; CORGIS

DOI: http://dx.doi.org/10.1145/2676723.2693616

FrenchPress Gives Students Automated Feedback on Java Program Flaws

Hannah Blau, *University of Massachusetts Amherst*
Contact: blau@cs.umass.edu

FrenchPress is an Eclipse plug-in that partially automates the task of giving students feedback on their Java programs. It is designed not for novices but for students taking their second or third Java course: students who know enough Java to write a working program but lack the judgment to recognize bad code when they see it. FrenchPress does not diagnose compile-time or runtime errors, or logical errors that produce incorrect output. It targets silent flaws, flaws the student is unable to identify for herself because nothing in the programming environment alerts her.

FrenchPress diagnoses flaws characteristic of programmers who have not yet assimilated the object-oriented idiom. Such shortcomings include misuse of the **public** modifier and instance variables that function as local variables or class constants. Other rules address the all too common misunderstanding of the boolean datatype. Where it finds a problem, FrenchPress delivers an explanatory message in a vocabulary appropriate to the student's current level of understanding.

FrenchPress is easy to use for both students and instructors. The instructor does not have to write a model solution or customized diagnostics for each assignment. The analysis applies to any compilable Java program. The Eclipse plug-in integrates seamlessly into the student's development environment. The student can get feedback as she works, so she can iteratively improve the code before submitting her project.

ACM Categories & Descriptors: K.3.2 [Computers and Education]: Computer and Information Science Education-*Computer science education*; D.2.5 [Software Engineering]: Testing and Debugging-*Diagnostics*; D.3.2 [Programming Languages]: Language Classifications-*Java*

Keywords: educational technology; program analysis; static analysis; Eclipse plug-in

DOI: http://dx.doi.org/10.1145/2676723.2693617

Selecting the Optimal Hardware Prefetching Algorithm for Parallel Workloads

Saami Rahman, *Texas State University*
Contact: saami.rahman@txstate.com

Prefetching is a commonly used technique of improving low-level cache usage that predicts memory requests ahead of time and thus, improves performance by hiding memory latency. Several prefetching algorithms are implemented in hardware. For example, the Intel Core2 processor has 4 different prefetchers, each of which serves a different type of data access pattern. These prefetchers are enabled by default, based on the assumption that the prefetch unit will be triggered when it can successfully prefetch data. However, we have discovered that this assumption is incorrect and can at times hurt performance by up to 11%. We present a simple and easy-to-use framework that determines which hardware-prefetching configuration should be used for a specific workload. The guiding principle of this work that sets it apart from other similar ones is that it fits well within the development process of an average programmer possessing no detailed hardware specific knowledge. For two programs in the PARSEC benchmark, on an Intel Core2 machine, our framework results in an effective speedup of 19% compared to the baseline default setting of using all available prefetchers.

ACM Categories & Descriptors: B.3.2 [Memory Structures]: Design Styles—*Cache memories*

Keywords: Hardware prefetching

DOI: http://dx.doi.org/10.1145/2676723.2693618

SIGCSE'15, March 4–7, 2015, Kansas City, MO, USA.
ACM 978-1-4503-2966-8/15/03.

Using Active Learning Techniques in Mixed Undergraduate / Graduate Courses

Brian P. Railing, *Georgia Institute of Technology*
Contact: brian.railing@gatech.edu

Active learning techniques are increasingly used in lower-level Computer Science courses. This work explores the use of active learning techniques in a graduate Computer Science course on computer architecture, where the course enrollment is composed of both undergraduates and graduate students. Initial results are presented on how the two groups of students respond differently to the techniques. In particular, the study includes the effect of using POGIL in place of a subset of lectures, measured through both student responses and test scores.

ACM Categories & Descriptors: K.3.2 [Computer and Information Science Education]: Computer Science Education

Keywords: Active Learning; Computer Architecture Education; Computer Science Education; Experience Report; Graduate Course; POGIL

DOI: http://dx.doi.org/10.1145/2676723.2693619

User Interface Design and Agility: Practices for Integration in CS Classrooms

Mohammed Seyam, *Virginia Tech*
Contact: seyam@vt.edu

Today's Computer Science (CS) students may not give enough attention for the importance of the User Interfaces (UIs) they design for class projects, which becomes even more critical when they design for mobile applications. They also lack the required organization skills that help them manage how they work together. Although agile methods proponents and UI experts follow different guidelines for each to achieve their goals, integrating agile and UI design practices seems to be a promising combination that can help CS students (and developers in general) to better design for various mobile devices (smartphones, tablets, smart watches…etc.) as well as to follow a semi-structured development approach to help them manage their programming work. Our research is concerned with studying the various approaches that can be used to combine agile practices with UI design guidelines for designing mobile applications. We are designing a framework that uses Pair Programming (PP) – as an agile practice – to guide the mobile UI design and application development processes. Unlike the previous studies that applied agile methods in classrooms, we are concerned with the special requirements of mobile devices as well as the regular development tasks. Moreover, we are focusing on applying certain practices that we believe to be easier to follow than the broader agile guidelines. Our current work aims at providing CS educators with a new adaptive teaching approach that is more student-oriented instead of the traditional task assignment approaches. Our research will then be extended to include teams from software development companies that are working on mobile application development. We believe that our practice-oriented framework that integrates agile with mobile UI design and development practices has much to do with industry as well as classrooms.

ACM Categories & Descriptors: D.2.2 [Design Tools and Techniques]; User Interface; K.3.2 [Computer and Information Science Education]: Computer Science Education

Keywords: Agile methods; User Interface; Mobile development; Pair Programming

DOI: http://dx.doi.org/10.1145/2676723.2693621

Minding the Gap Between Blocks-Based and Text-Based Programming

David Weintrop, *Northwestern University*
Contact: dweintrop@u.northwestern.edu

Graphical blocks-based programming environments, such as Scratch and Snap!, are becoming increasingly popular tools for introducing learners to programming in formal educational settings. However, a growing body of research is finding that students struggle when transitioning from these tools to more conventional, text-based programming languages. To better understand students' difficulties and begin to explore potential solutions to facilitate this transition, a 10-week, quasi-experimental study was conducted with 80 students across three high-school introductory programming classes. Each class spent five weeks working with different version of a blocks-based programming tool, each of which integrated text-based programming in a different way. After working in the introductory environments, students transitioned to Java for the remainder of the study. The goal of this project is to understand the effects of blocks-based programming on students' emerging understandings, document challenges students face in transitioning from blocks-based to text-based programming, and investigate potential ways to bridge these two modalities. To answer these questions, a mixed-method approach was taken that included cognitive interviews with learners, automated collection of student authored programs, and pre/mid/post attitudinal and content assessments.

ACM Categories & Descriptors: D.1.7 Visual Programming. K.3.2 Computer and Information Science Education

Keywords: Introductory Programming Environments; Blocks-based Programming; High School Computer Science

DOI: http://dx.doi.org/10.1145/2676723.2693622

SIGCSE'15, March 4–7, 2015, Kansas City, MO, USA.
ACM 978-1-4503-2966-8/15/03.

Author Index

www.ingramcontent.com/pod-product-compliance
Lightning Source LLC
LaVergne TN
LVHW080107011026
849160LV00013B/1049